Scholarships

2007 Edition

**OTHER KAPLAN BOOKS FOR COLLEGE-BOUND STUDENTS**

Essay Writing for High School Students: A Step-by-Step Guide

SAT Comprehensive Program

SAT Premier Program

# Scholarships
## 2007 Edition

by Gail Schlachter, R. David Weber,
and the Staff of Reference Service Press

Introduction by Douglas Bucher

PUBLISHING

New York • Chicago

Editorial Director: Jennifer Farthing
Editor: Anne Kemper
Production Artist: Maria Warren
Cover Designer: Carly Schnur

© 2006 by Kaplan, Inc.

Published by Kaplan Publishing, a division of Kaplan, Inc.
888 Seventh Ave.
New York, NY 10106

Printed in the United States of America

August 2006
10 9 8 7 6 5 4 3

ISBN-13: 978-1-4195-4195-7
ISBN-10: 1-4195-4195-1

Kaplan Publishing books are available at special quantity discounts to use for sales promotions, employee premiums, or educational purposes. Please call our Special Sales Department to order or for more information at 800-621-9621, ext. 4444, email kaplanpubsales@kaplan.com, or write to Kaplan Publishing, 30 South Wacker Drive, Suite 2500, Chicago, IL 60606-7481.

# CONTENTS

About the Authors. . . . . . . . . . . . . . . . . . . . . . . . . . . . . . . . . . . . . . . . . . . . . . vii

Reference Service Press. . . . . . . . . . . . . . . . . . . . . . . . . . . . . . . . . . . . . . . . . viii

Preface . . . . . . . . . . . . . . . . . . . . . . . . . . . . . . . . . . . . . . . . . . . . . . . . . . . . . . . xi

## PART ONE: GETTING STARTED

Searching for Scholarships . . . . . . . . . . . . . . . . . . . . . . . . . . . . . . . . . . . . . . . 1

A Special Note for International Students . . . . . . . . . . . . . . . . . . . . . . . . . . . 13

## PART TWO: SCHOLARSHIP LISTINGS

Unrestricted by Subject Area . . . . . . . . . . . . . . . . . . . . . . . . . . . . . . . . . . . . . 15

Humanities. . . . . . . . . . . . . . . . . . . . . . . . . . . . . . . . . . . . . . . . . . . . . . . . . . . 219

Sciences. . . . . . . . . . . . . . . . . . . . . . . . . . . . . . . . . . . . . . . . . . . . . . . . . . . . . . 303

Social Sciences . . . . . . . . . . . . . . . . . . . . . . . . . . . . . . . . . . . . . . . . . . . . . . . . 477

## INDEXES

Subject Index. . . . . . . . . . . . . . . . . . . . . . . . . . . . . . . . . . . . . . . . . . . . . . . . . . 549

Residency Index. . . . . . . . . . . . . . . . . . . . . . . . . . . . . . . . . . . . . . . . . . . . . . . . 558

Tenability Index. . . . . . . . . . . . . . . . . . . . . . . . . . . . . . . . . . . . . . . . . . . . . . . . 562

Sponsoring Organization Index. . . . . . . . . . . . . . . . . . . . . . . . . . . . . . . . . . . . 567

Calendar Index . . . . . . . . . . . . . . . . . . . . . . . . . . . . . . . . . . . . . . . . . . . . . . . . 583

# Lots of books list scholarships. What makes this book different?

**1. The funding opportunities described here can be used at any number of schools.**
Look through other scholarship books and you'll see that most of them contain large numbers of scholarships that can be used only at a particular college or university. Even if you're lucky, only a handful of these school-specific scholarships will be for the schools you're considering. And even that handful of scholarship listings is of little value since the schools you apply to (or are considering applying to) will gladly send you information about their scholarship programs free of charge.

*Not one of the scholarships listed in this book is limited to only one particular school.* The result: more listings in this book have the potential to be of use to you.

**2. Only the biggest and the best funding programs are covered in this book.**
Most of the other scholarship books are bulked up with awards that may be worth only a few hundred dollars. While any free money you can get your hands on for college is good, you will have to be careful that you don't waste your time and money chasing scholarships that will hardly put a dent in your overall college cost burden.

*The scholarships in this book all offer at least $1,000 per year.* So, more of the scholarships in this book will really be worth the investment of your time.

**3. Not one dollar of the programs listed in this book needs to be repaid.**
Most scholarship books list awards that are really loans. We're not against loans, especially college loans with reduced interest rates or delayed repayment.

*Of the funding opportunities covered in this book, not one dollar has to be repaid, provided the stated requirements are met.* Accepting one of these need not add to the debt burden you'll face when you finish school.

In fact, we're so convinced this book contains the most helpful and most accurate scholarship information on the market that we offer satisfaction guaranteed or your money back (details on the inside front cover).

# About the Authors

## PART ONE

### Douglas Bucher

Douglas Bucher recently was Director of Financial Aid Operations at Drexel University in Philadelphia. He formerly served as President of the Eastern Association of Student Financial Aid Administrators and is a member of the New York Association of Student Financial Aid Administrators. He teaches seminars for the U.S. Department of Education, and acts as a consultant for public, private, and proprietary two- and four-year schools.

## PART TWO

### Gail Schlachter

Dr. Gail Schlachter is President of Reference Service Press, a publishing company specializing in the development of electronic and print directories of financial aid. Dr. Schlachter has taught library-related courses on the graduate school level and has presented dozens of workshops and lectures to the field. Since 1991, she has been a visiting professor at San Jose State University. Dr. Schlachter has served on the councils of the American Library Association and the California Library Association, is a past president of the ALA's Reference and User Services Association, and has served as editor-in-chief of *Reference and User Services Quarterly,* the official journal of ALA's Reference and User Services Association.

In recognition of her outstanding contributions to the field of reference librarianship, Dr. Schlachter has been a recipient of both the Isadore Gilbert Mudge Award and the Louis Shores-Oryx Press Award. In addition, her financial aid print resources have won numerous awards, including the *Choice* "Outstanding Reference Book Award," *Library Journal's* "Best Reference Book of the Year" award, the National Education and Information Center Advisory Committee "Best of the Best" award, and the Knowledge Industry Publications' "Award for Library Literature."

### R. David Weber

Dr. R. David Weber has served as Reference Service Press's chief editor since 1988. In that capacity, he has been involved in building, refining, and maintaining RSP's award-winning financial aid database. In addition, Dr. Weber has taught at both East Los Angeles and Harbor Colleges, where he was named "Teacher of the Year" on several occasions. Besides his work in the area of financial aid, Dr. Weber has written a number of critically acclaimed reference books, including *Dissertations in Urban History* and the three-volume *Energy Information Guide.*

# Reference Service Press

Reference Service Press (RSP) began in 1977 with a single financial aid publication, *Directory of Financial Aids for Women*, and now specializes in the development of financial aid resources in multiple formats, including books, large-print books, eBooks, CD-ROMs, print-on-demand reports, and online sources. RSP is committed to collecting, organizing, and disseminating—in both print and electronic format—the most current and accurate information available on scholarships, fellowships, loans, grants, awards, internships, and other types of funding opportunities. The company has compiled one of the largest financial aid databases currently available—with up-to-date information on more than 26,000 portable programs (not restricted to any one school) that are open to high school students, high school graduates, undergraduates, graduate students, professionals, and postdoctorates. The database identifies billions of dollars in funding opportunities that will be awarded to millions of recipients each year. RSP publishes a number of award-winning financial aid directories aimed at specific groups.

After you've mined the resources described in this book, you might be interested in continuing your funding search by looking through other RSP books. You may be able to find these titles in your local public or academic library, or contact RSP to order your own copy:

**Reference Service Press**
5000 Windplay Drive, Suite 4
El Dorado Hills, CA 95762
Phone: (916) 939-9620; Fax: (916) 939-9626
E-mail: info@rspfunding.com
Website: www.rspfunding.com

## Specialized Financial Aid Directories from Reference Service Press

### College Student's Guide to Merit and Other No-Need Funding, 2005–2007
Named "best of the best" by *Choice*. The focus here is on 1,300 merit scholarships and other no-need funding programs open specifically to students currently in or returning to college. 464 pages. ISBN 1-58841-102-8. $32, plus $6 shipping.

### Directory of Financial Aids for Women, 2005–2007
Published since 1977, this is the only comprehensive and current source of information on 1,500 scholarships, fellowships, loans, grants, internships, and awards designed primarily or exclusively for women. *School Library Journal* calls this "the cream of the crop." 528 pages. ISBN 1-58841-131-1. $45, plus $6 shipping.

### Financial Aid for African Americans, 2006–2008
Named "Editor's Choice" by *Reference Books Bulletin*, this directory describes 1,400 scholarships, fellowships, loans, grants, awards, and internships for African Americans. 522 pages. ISBN 1-58841-133-8. $40, plus $6 shipping.

### Financial Aid for Asian Americans, 2006–2008

Use this award-winning source to find funding for Americans of Chinese, Japanese, Korean, Vietnamese, Filipino, or other Asian origin. Nearly 1,000 opportunities described. 346 pages. ISBN 1-58841-134-6. $37.50, plus $6 shipping.

### Financial Aid for Hispanic Americans, 2006–2008

Called a "landmark resource" by *Reference Books Bulletin*, this directory describes more than 1,200 funding programs open to Americans of Mexican, Puerto Rican, Central American, or other Latin American heritage. 482 pages. ISBN 1-58841-135-4. $40, plus $6 shipping.

### Financial Aid for Native Americans, 2006–2008

Detailed information is provided in this award-winning directory on more than 1,300 funding opportunities open to American Indians, Native Alaskans, and Native Hawaiians. 554 pages. ISBN 1-58841-136-2. $42.50, plus $6 shipping.

### Financial Aid for Research and Creative Activities Abroad, 2006–2008

More than 1,000 funding programs (scholarships, fellowships, grants, etc.) available to support research, professional, or creative activities abroad are described here. 388 pages. ISBN 1-58841-107-9. $45, plus $6 shipping.

### Financial Aid for Study and Training Abroad, 2006–2008

This directory, which *Children's Bookwatch* calls "invaluable," covers more than 1,000 financial aid opportunities available to support structured or independent study abroad. 364 pages. ISBN 1-58841-094-3. $39.50, plus $6 shipping.

### Financial Aid for the Disabled and Their Families, 2006–2008

Named one of the "Best Reference Books of the Year" by *Library Journal*, this directory describes in detail more than 1,200 funding opportunities for these groups. 500 pages. ISBN 1-58841-148-6. $40, plus $6 shipping.

### Financial Aid for Veterans, Military Personnel, and Their Dependents, 2006–2008

According to *Reference Book Review*, this directory (with its 1,200 entries) is "the most comprehensive guide available on the subject." 432 pages. ISBN 1-58841-143-5. $40, plus $6 shipping.

### High School Senior's Guide to Merit and Other No-Need Funding, 2005–2007

Described here are 1,200 merit awards and other no-need funding programs that never look at income when awarding money to high school seniors for college. 412 pages. ISBN 1-58841-100-1. $29.95, plus $6 shipping.

### How to Pay for Your Degree in Education, 2004–2006

Use this directory to identify more than 600 scholarships, fellowships, loans, grants, and awards available to support undergraduate and graduate students working on a degree in education or related fields. 230 pages. ISBN 1-58841-146-X. $30, plus $6 shipping.

**Money for Christian College Students, 2005–2007**

This is the only directory to describe 800 funding opportunities available to support Christian students working on an undergraduate or graduate degree (secular or religious). 250 pages. ISBN 158841-118-4. $30, plus $6 shipping.

**Money for Graduate Students in the Arts & Humanities, 2005–2007**

This directory identifies nearly 1,100 funding opportunities available to support graduate study, training, research, and creative activities in the humanities. Identified as "highly recommended" by *Choice*. 312 pages. ISBN 1-58841-138-9. $40, plus $6 shipping.

**Money for Graduate Students in the Biological & Health Sciences, 2005–2007**

If you are looking for money to support graduate study or research in the biological or health sciences, use this directory (1,100 funding programs are described). 344 pages. ISBN 1-58841-139-7. $42.50, plus $6 shipping.

**Money for Graduate Students in the Physical & Earth Sciences, 2005–2007**

More than 900 funding opportunities for graduate study or research in the physical and earth sciences are described in detail and accessed through five indexes. 276 pages. ISBN 1-58841-140-0. $40, plus $6 shipping.

**Money for Graduate Students in the Social & Behavioral Sciences, 2005–2007**

1,100 funding opportunities for graduate study and research in the social sciences are covered in detail and indexed by title, sponsor, subject, geographic coverage, and deadline. 332 pages. ISBN 1-58841-141-9. $42.50, plus $6 shipping.

**RSP Funding for Nursing Students, 2006–2008**

More than 600 scholarships, fellowships, and loans that support study or research for nurses or nursing students (both undergraduate and graduate) are described in this directory—more than twice the number of programs listed in any other nursing-related directory. 230 pages. ISBN 1-58841-157-5. $30, plus $6 shipping.

# Preface

While getting a college degree may be the best investment you will ever make, paying for it is another matter. Going to college is expensive. It can cost $100,000 or more just to complete a bachelor's degree. That's more than most students can afford to pay on their own. So what can you do?

Fortunately, money is available. According to the College Board, there is more than $100 billion in financial aid available each year. Of this, at least $60 billion comes from federal loans and grants, $18 billion from the colleges, $8 billion from tuition tax credits, $9 billion from the states, $4 billion from employer-paid tuition plans, and $3 billion from private sources.

How can you find out about financial aid that might be available to you? For some sources of funding, it's not difficult at all. To learn about federal resources, call (800) 4-FEDAID or visit the U.S. Department of Education's website (studentaid.ed.gov). To find out what your state is offering, visit www.ed.gov/Programs/bastmp/SHEA.htm to link to your state higher education agency. Alternatively, you can write to the colleges of your choice or check with your employer to learn about funding from those sources.

Information on private sources of funding is more elusive. That's where this book can help. Here, in one place, you'll find detailed information on over 3,000 of the biggest and best scholarships available to fund education after high school. These programs are open to high school seniors, high school graduates, currently enrolled college students, and those returning to college after a break. They can be used to support study in any area, in junior and community colleges, vocational and technical institutes, four-year colleges, and universities. No other source can match the scope, currency, and detail provided in this book. That's why we have a satisfaction-guaranteed-or-your-money-back offer (see details on the inside front cover).

## What's Unique about This Book?

All scholarship directories identify funding opportunities. But this directory is unique in several ways:

- **The directory covers only programs open to support college studies.** Most other directories mix together programs for a number of groups—high school students, college students, and even graduate students or postdoctorates. Here, you won't spend your time sifting through programs that aren't aimed at you.
- **Only free money is identified.** If a program requires repayment or charges interest, it's not listed. Here's your chance to find out about billions of dollars in aid, knowing that not one dollar will ever need to be repaid, provided the stated requirements are met.
- **Not every funding opportunity is based on need or on academics.** Many sources award money based on career plans, writing ability, research skills, religious or ethnic background, military or organizational activities, athletic success, personal characteristics, and even pure luck in random drawings.
- **The money awarded by these scholarships can be taken to any number of schools.** Unlike other financial aid directories that often list large numbers of scholarships available only to students enrolled at one specific school, all of the entries in this book are "portable."
- **Only the biggest and best funding programs are covered.** To be listed here, a program has to offer at least $1,000 per year. Many go way beyond that, paying $20,000 or more

each year, or covering the full cost of college attendance. Other scholarship books are often bulked up with awards that may be worth only a few hundred dollars. While any free money you can get your hands on for college is good, you will have to be careful that you don't waste your time and energy chasing scholarships that will hardly put a dent in your overall college cost burden.

- **Searching for scholarships couldn't be easier.** You can identify funding programs by discipline, specific subject, sponsoring organization, where you live, where you want to go to school, and when you want to apply. Plus, you'll find all the information you need to decide if a program is right for you: eligibility requirements, financial data, duration, special features, limitations, number awarded, and application date.

## What's Not Covered?

While this book is intended to be the most current and comprehensive source of free money available to college students in the United States, there are some things we have specifically excluded:

- **Funding not aimed at incoming, currently enrolled, or returning college students.** If a program is open only to graduate school students, for instance, or to adults of any age interested in photography, it is not covered. If a scholarship is not specifically for college students, it has not been included.
- **Individual school-based programs.** Financial aid given by individual schools solely for the benefit of their own students is not covered. Instead, the directory identifies "portable" programs—ones that can be used at any number of schools.
- **Money for study outside the United States.** Only funding that supports study in the United States is covered. For information on sources of funding to go abroad, see the books listed in the Reference Service Press section in this directory.
- **Very restrictive programs.** In general, programs are excluded if they are open only to a very limited geographic area (students in specific cities or counties), are available to a very limited membership group (e.g., a local union or a tightly targeted organization), or offer very limited financial support.
- **Programs that did not respond to our research inquiries.** Despite our best efforts—up to four letters and three phone calls—some organizations did not supply information. Consequently, their programs have not been included.

## How to Use This Book

We've divided this book into three sections: introductory materials, scholarship listings organized by discipline, and a set of indexes to help you pinpoint appropriate funding programs.

### Getting Started
The first section of the directory, written by Douglas Bucher, offers tips on searching for scholarships, applying for aid, and avoiding scholarship search scams.

### Scholarship Listings
The main section of the directory, prepared by Gail Schlachter, R. David Weber, and the staff of Reference Service Press, describes more than 3,000 scholarships, grants, competitions, and awards that provide free money for college. The programs listed are sponsored by federal and state government agencies, professional organizations, foundations, educational associations, and military/veterans organizations. All areas of the sciences, social sciences, and humanities are covered.

To help you tailor your search, the entries in this section are grouped into four main categories:

**Unrestricted by Subject Area.** Described here are funding opportunities that can be used to support study in any subject area (though the programs may be restricted in other ways).

**Humanities.** Described here are programs that 1) reward outstanding artistic and creative work by students or 2) support college studies in the humanities, including architecture, art, creative writing, design, history, journalism, languages, literature, music, and religion.

**Sciences.** Described here are sources of free money that 1) reward student speeches, essays, inventions, organizational involvement, and other activities in the sciences or 2) support college studies in a number of scientific fields, including agricultural science, chemistry, computer science, engineering, environmental science, food science, horticulture, mathematics, marine science, nursing, nutrition, pharmacology, and technology.

**Social Sciences.** Described here are programs that 1) reward outstanding speeches, essays, organizational involvement, and other activities in the social sciences or 2) support college studies in various social science fields, including accounting, business administration, criminology, economics, education, geography, home economics, international relations, labor relations, political science, sales and marketing, sociology, social services, sports and recreation, and tourism.

Each program entry in Section Two has been prepared to give you a concise but clear picture of the available funding. Information, as available, is provided on organization contact information, eligibility, money awarded, duration, special features, limitations, number of awards, and application deadline.

## Indexes

To help you find the aid you need, we have included five indexes; these will let you access the listings by specific subject, residency, tenability (where you want to study), sponsoring organization, and deadline date. These indexes use a word-by-word alphabetical arrangement. Note: numbers in the index refer to *entry* numbers, not to page numbers.

**Subject Index.** Use this index when you want to identify funding programs by specific subject.

**Residency Index.** Some programs listed in this book are restricted to residents of a particular city, county, state, or region. Others are open to students wherever they live. This index helps you identify programs available only to residents in your area as well as programs that have no residency restrictions.

**Tenability Index.** Some programs described in this book are restricted to persons attending schools in specific cities, counties, states, or regions. This index will help you locate funding specifically for the geographic area where you attend or plan to attend school.

**Sponsoring Organization Index.** This index makes it easy to identify agencies that offer free money for college. Sponsoring organizations are listed alphabetically, word by word. In addition, we've used a code to help you identify which programs sponsored by these organizations fall within your general area of interest (unrestricted by subject area, humanities, sciences, or social sciences).

**Calendar Index.** Since most financial aid programs have specific deadline dates, some may have already closed by the time you begin to look for funding. You can use the Calendar Index to identify which programs are still open.

# How to Get the Most Out of This Book

**To Locate Financial Aid by Discipline.** If you want to get an overall picture of the funding available for any area of college study, turn to the first category, Unrestricted by Subject Area. You'll find more than 1,200 general programs that support study in any area (though they may be restricted in other ways). If you've decided on your area of specialization, turn next to the appropriate chapter (Humanities, Sciences, or Social Sciences) and browse through the listings there.

**To Find Information on a Particular Financial Aid Program.** If you know the name and disciplinary focus of a particular financial aid program, you can go directly to the appropriate category in part two, where you'll find program profiles grouped by discipline and arranged alphabetically by title.

**To Browse Quickly Through the Listings.** Turn to the section in part 2 that interests you (Unrestricted by Subject Area, Humanities, Sciences, Social Sciences) and read the "Summary" field in each entry. In seconds, you'll know if this is an opportunity that might apply to you. If it is, be sure to read the entire entry to make sure you meet all of the requirements. Don't apply if you don't qualify!

**To Locate Financial Aid for Studies in a Particular Subject Area.** Turn to the Subject Index first if you are interested in identifying funding by specific subject area. Be sure also to check the listings under the General Programs index; these programs support studies in any area (though they may be restricted in other ways).

**To Locate Financial Aid Based on Where You Live.** Use the Residency Index to identify funding that supports applicants in your area. The index is subdivided by broad subject area. When using this index, be sure also to check the listings under the term "United States," since the programs indexed there have no geographic restrictions and can be used in any area.

**To Locate Financial Aid Based on Where You Want to Study.** Use the Tenability Index to identify funding that supports study in a particular geographic location. The index is subdivided by broad subject area. When using this index, be sure also to check the listings under the term "United States," since the programs indexed there have no geographic restrictions and can be used in any area.

**To Locate Financial Aid Programs Sponsored by a Particular Organization.** The Sponsoring Organization Index makes it easy to determine which groups are providing free money for college and to identify specific financial aid programs offered by a particular sponsor. Each entry number in the index is coded to indicate broad subject coverage, to help you target appropriate entries.

## Let Us Hear from You

We'd like to hear from you. Send your comments, questions, or success stories to: Gail Schlachter, Kaplan Scholarships, 5000 Windplay Drive, Suite 4, El Dorado Hills, CA 95762, or email her at GailSchlachter@rspfunding.com.

# SAMPLE ENTRY

① **541** KAPLAN/NEWSWEEK "MY TURN" ESSAY COMPETITION
② Kaplan, Inc.
③ Attn: Pre-College
1440 Broadway, Ninth Floor
New York, NY 10018
Phone: (212) 997-5886; (800) KAP-TEST
Web: www.kaptest.com/oneoff/essay/index.jhtml
④ **Summary:** To recognize and reward, with college scholarships, high school students who write outstanding essays on topics related to their personal development and growth.
⑤ **Eligibility:** Open to U.S. high school students planning to attend college after graduation. Applicants must write an essay of 500 to 1,000 words on a topic of their choice that is similar in format to the weekly "My Turn" column in *Newsweek* magazine, in which a member of the public shares an opinion, experience, or personal feeling. Judges look for direct personal experiences and observations with a fresh, original, engaging, moving, and thought-provoking point of view that appeals to a national readership. Selection is based on 1) effectiveness, insightfulness, creativity, and completeness; 2) organization and development of the ideas expressed, with clear and appropriate examples to support them; and 3) consistency in the use of language, variety in sentence structure and range of vocabulary, and use of proper grammar, spelling, and punctuation.
⑥ **Financial data:** First prize is $5,000, second $2,000, and third $1,000. All funds are to be used for future educational needs.
⑦ **Duration:** The competition is held annually.
⑧ **Number awarded:** 10 each year: 1 first-prize winner, 1 second-prize winner, and 8 third-prize winners.
⑨ **Deadline:** February of each year.

## Definitions

① **Entry number:** Consecutive number assigned to the references and used to index the entry.

② **Program title:** Title of scholarship, competition, or award.

③ **Sponsoring organization:** Name, address, telephone number, toll-free number, fax number, e-mail address, and website location (when information was supplied) for organization.

④ **Summary:** Identifies the major program requirements; read the rest of the entry for additional detail.

⑤ **Eligibility:** Qualifications required of applicants.

⑥ **Financial data:** Financial details of the program, including fixed sum, average amount, or range of funds offered, expenses for which funds may and may not be applied, and cash-related benefits supplied (e.g., room and board).

⑦ **Duration:** Time period for which support is provided; renewal prospects.

⑧ **Number awarded:** Total number of recipients each year or other specified period.

⑨ **Deadline:** The month by which applications must be submitted.

## PART ONE

# GETTING STARTED

## by Douglas Bucher

# Searching for Scholarships

If you are reading this book, it's a good bet that you're looking for money to help you achieve your higher-education goals. As you will see, the key to success in this area is motivated, energetic research—a process that you have already started by reading these very words. There are numerous sources of aid available; many of these are listed in this volume. In addition, this book includes other strategies for finding resources, locally and globally, using both technology, such as computers and the Internet, and old-fashioned methods, such as talking to people who may be able to help.

All of the information we will discuss is available to you in books or other easily obtainable sources that will cost you little or nothing to use. Any company that says you have to pay them to research the same data you could research on your own is not worthy of your dollars. Ignore all of the promises. In most cases, the companies will provide no more information than you could have gleaned yourself.

## Scholarship Scams

For years, in fact, students' desire to finance their education has been fodder for those who would take advantage of people with trusting natures. Financial aid personnel at colleges and universities have been aware of such unethical approaches for some time now, and recently the Federal Trade Commission (FTC) issued a warning about these "scholarship scams." Among the telltale signs you should look for—and then stay far away from—are:

*"We guarantee you'll get a scholarship or your money back."* In reality, almost every financial aid applicant is eligible for something. A guarantee like this is, therefore, worth nothing.

*"You can't get this information anywhere else."* Nonsense. We live in an information-rich society. Any legitimate source of financial aid will make information widely available through a number of means and media. Don't pay a premium for what is free or readily available in an inexpensive format—like this one!

*"Credit card or bank account number required to hold scholarship."* Don't even think about it. Legitimate scholarship providers do not require this information as a condition for receiving funds.

*"We'll do all the work."* Okay, this one is tempting. We are all very busy people with a million things to do who feel that we can't possibly find the time to do this kind of research. But there is only one person who is going to benefit from the kind of work that this entails, and that is you. A pitch like this appeals to the lazy instincts in all of us, but there is no one you can expect to be more motivated to do the research than yourself.

*"The scholarship will cost you some money."* This one hardly deserves comment. There is a strong preconception in this country that, as a general rule, you need to spend money to make money. While this may be true on Wall Street, it doesn't apply here. The investment you are making is in your education, and the best resource you can invest is your time.

*"You are a finalist"* or *"You have been selected"* in a contest you never entered. The absurdity of this is clear once you think about it for a moment. It is very flattering to think that some organization pored through the records of every person in the country to find that you are the most qualified to receive its generous award—and you didn't even apply! Remember, if it seems too good to be true, it is.

In other words, *caveat emptor!*

## Setting a Timetable for Your Search

If there is one piece of advice that can be a key to a successful search for scholarship funding, it is to start early. In fact, keep in mind that each step described in this book requires a good deal of time. Furthermore, many small sources of funding have deadlines some nine to twelve months before the beginning of the term for which you will be applying.

When should you start? The answer depends on your personal pace. If you have the time and energy to research a subject extensively for a short period of time, you could start some 14 months before the beginning of school. If, on the other hand, you wish to make this a more leisurely process, give yourself a good 18 months. In any case, the bottom line is that you can never begin too early. When you are done reading this, sit down with a calendar and make a plan. When can you start? How much time can you devote each week?

Here is a summary timetable to help you plan:

- *24–18 months before money is needed:* Perform the extensive searches discussed in this chapter.

- *18–12 months before money is needed:* Write for applications; follow up if necessary.

- *12–9 months before money is needed:* Mail all applications with required documentation.

- *9–6 months before money is needed:* Follow up with any organization from which you have not heard a decision (if deadline has passed).

- *Summer before school:* Notify the financial aid office of any scholarships you have been awarded. Be sure to ask what effect this will have on earlier awards and your options.

- *Late summer right before school:* Write thank-you notes to organizations.

- *Fall:* Begin the process again for renewing scholarships and finding new sources of aid.

## Types of Scholarships

The types of scholarships you may receive for your education can be broken down into three general categories: individual scholarships, state scholarships, and loans.

### Individual Scholarships

While going through your college search, be sure to ask admissions officers about scholarships. Each school has different rules for scholarship consideration. Be sure to find out about all scholarships available, what must be done to be considered, and—very important—the deadline by which to apply. More and more schools are offering scholarships for reasons other than athletic or academic achievement. Some scholarships are reserved for very specific types of students. See if any of these exist at the colleges to which you are applying. Much of this information may be on their home page, so you can research on your own.

Become familiar with your college's financial aid office, which might be able to provide additional information on scholarship sources. At some schools, the financial aid officers are more familiar with scholarship sources than the admissions officers.

Another great source of scholarship information might be the academic departments with which you are affiliated. Many of the faculty members know about scholarships specifically for your major. Some departments have their own scholarships that other offices on campus may not even know about. Professors also have many contacts outside of the college that might be sources of scholarship information.

### State Scholarship Resources

Some state education authorities and other state agencies offer assistance above and beyond the usual tuition-assistance programs. Some states offer aid for particular fields of study to residents of the state who remain in-state to complete their studies. You should contact your state's higher-education agency to investigate opportunities.

### Loans and Forgivable Loans

There is another form of aid that predominates in certain fields, particularly those with a shortage of qualified professionals. Often called *forgivable loans,* these arrangements provide funding for school and a guaranteed job after graduation.

Sometimes offered by private employers, sometimes by government agencies, forgivable loans work in the following way. An organization provides funding for a student's academic expenses in the form of a loan. In return, the student agrees to work for the organization (under terms usually outlined in a contract) for a given period of time. If the student keeps up his or her part of the bargain, the loan will be forgiven or reduced. If the student chooses not to work for the organization, he or she is given a repayment schedule and must pay back the entire balance with interest. Depending on the field, the jobs provided are usually competitively paid, though, more often than not, located in areas that are underserved or understaffed.

Some organizations offer regular loans as well as scholarships. Some philanthropic agencies even offer interest-free loans to students. These can be very good opportunities to save money on interest you would otherwise pay on federal or private loans. Again, consider carefully the terms of any loan agreement you sign.

## Getting on with the Search

There are a number of sources of aid to consider, and several strategies for finding them. Some sources may be obscure, while others may be quite obvious to you. Who might have money to give? Unions, professional organizations, high schools, clubs, lodges, foundations, and local and state governments might have resources to share with you. At the very least, they are worth exploring.

A parent can easily check with his or her union or professional organization regarding available opportunities. A teacher, guidance counselor, or professor might know of opportunities with a variety of organizations. The key to finding aid in this way is networking. People you know are wonderful sources of information. If you are a bright, motivated person and let people know what you want out of life, many simply will inform you whenever a possible opportunity presents itself.

Many high school guidance offices have a list of scholarships that have been secured by former students. These scholarships are often provided by local agencies that lack the resources to publicize them in other ways. Contacting guidance offices at local high schools is an effective way to canvass the entire community. While the local scholarships might be small, they add up to larger sums of money.

You might even consider contacting civic, fraternal, religious, and business organizations in your community. Many of them have scholarships that are not well publicized. These awards are also usually small, but they add up quickly. These organizations enjoy supporting the future of their community through education, and make themselves visible in the yellow pages or on lists at local Chambers of Commerce. Even if you don't know anyone at a given organization, you should still contact it about the possibility of a scholarship.

I have met students in my career who actually talked some of these organizations into creating scholarships. A few hundred dollars may not be much to an organization, but it can really help an individual recipient. Soliciting these organizations may make you that lucky recipient. They may like your tenacity and award you a scholarship for this. Don't be pushy, but do be aggressive.

Employers represent another major local source of scholarships. You may be working part-time or full-time for a company that offers scholarships to its employees. If it is a national chain, your boss may not even know if a scholarship exists. Ask him or her to check with the central office. If you are planning to attend school locally and keep your job, you might want to check out tuition remission scholarships from your employer.

Many parents or relatives have employers that offer scholarships to dependents. Have your parents check with their benefits/personnel office to see if any programs exist. Don't assume you have to be a high school student or live at home to qualify; you'll find out if such restrictions exist when you ask. Many of these scholarships can be awarded to dependents other than just sons or daughters. Ask all your family members to check out the possibilities.

## Graduate Funding

A graduate student is one who is pursuing an advanced degree beyond the bachelor's. When an individual has not yet received a bachelor's degree, he or she is referred to as an undergraduate student. While some aid resources are specifically geared towards undergraduate students, others are earmarked solely for graduate students involved in advanced study of a given field. Knowing this will help you avoid wasting your time on resources for which you are not eligible. Concentrate only on scholarships available to you.

## Books

There are many places to search for scholarships. This book contains extensive lists of scholarships, but no book can be totally inclusive. Therefore, as with any research project, you should not depend on only one source. Multiple sources will yield the most extensive data and thus the most scholarship dollars.

There is usually a scholarship section in the reference room of any public library. Many of these books focus exclusively on particular types of scholarships for majors/grade levels, etc., saving you time you would otherwise spend reading fruitlessly. Of course, there is always the chance that human error may enter into the picture, and you may overlook a valuable source. Having family members look through the same books you're reading will allow you to compare lists and eliminate duplicates. Many people also do group searches with friends. The possibility of your friends applying for the same scholarships should not deter you, since most scholarships offer more than one award, and having more eyes search the same books will reduce the chance of overlooking resources.

## Electronic Resources

Students are increasingly turning to the Internet for scholarship searches, many of which allow you to access data free of charge. The great advantage of using the Internet is that it is less labor-intensive than using books; the computer can match details about yourself with criteria in the database faster than you can, saving valuable time. Another advantage is that most of these sites are up-to-date and have the most current information. Criteria for scholarships change, and using the Internet will allow you to search for the most current criteria. In addition, many schools list their own scholarships in these services, so you may discover special scholarships at schools you may attend. In some cases, you can apply online for scholarships.

There's a good deal of overlap among these databases, but you'll find exclusive listings in each one. Try, then, to search a number of databases; eliminate duplicates by checking the application information on the listings. If you get duplicates, use the application information from the most recently updated scholarship listing.

It's important to have a good basic knowledge about financial aid before searching for scholarships. The Kaplan website at kaptest.com is a good place to begin.

Another excellent reference is the *Parents and Students* page on the National Association of

Student Financial Aid Administrators (NASFAA) website: www.nasfaa.org. This organization is the professional association for financial aid administrators, and it has links to extensive resources for financial aid.

Many colleges now have websites that may have important information about aid. You may be able to get information about scholarships offered through the college, and how to apply. Many of these sites also have links to other financial aid information or scholarship search databases. Check the sites of all colleges you are considering.

Some other sites that may be of interest in your research are:

- U.S. Department of Education; www.ed.gov/students
- U.S. Department of Education: Federal Student Aid; studentaid.ed.gov
- FastWeb—Scholarship Search; fastweb.com
- Scholarship Resource Network Express; www.srnexpress.com
- Scholarships.com; www.scholarships.com
- Reference Service Press Funding; www.rspfunding.com
- Sallie Mae College Answer: www.collegeanswer.com

Many high schools, colleges, and libraries have purchased scholarship databases with which you can broaden your search. They may not be as up-to-date as the Internet sources, but they should not be overlooked.

## How to Apply

As previously mentioned, early planning is important to a successful scholarship search. Once you have your list of addresses of possible donors, you must contact them. Be sure to check the application deadlines for the scholarships you have discovered. Eliminate any for which the deadline has passed, or will soon pass (usually within six to eight weeks). This way you will not waste the donor's or your time. Scholarships that you eliminate now could be resources for the following years. Remember, the college experience lasts more than one year; your scholarship research should extend for the number of years you need to complete your degree.

### Writing the First Letter

Your first letter to a scholarship provider should be a very simple letter of introduction. Some providers may have you do initial processing online through a scholarship database. If you must write a letter, it probably will not be read by the actual committee that will choose the scholarship recipient, so there is no need to go into great detail about yourself or why you are applying. Keep it simple so the request moves quickly. Use a regular business letter format.

Today's Date

AAA Foundation
999 7th Avenue
New York, NY 10000

Attn.: Talent Scholarship Office

Dear AAA Foundation,

I am a high school student at ABC High School and am applying to attend XYZ College for fall 2007.

I would like to receive application forms for the Talent Scholarship that I read about in Kaplan's *Scholarships 2007*.

Also, I would like to receive any other scholarship or fellowship program information that is available through your organization. Enclosed is a self-addressed, stamped envelope for your convenience. I have also provided a phone number and email address if you would like to contact me.

Thank you in advance for your assistance and information.

Sincerely,


Suzy Student
123 High Street
Philadelphia, PA 19100
(555) 444-4444
suzys@xxx.com

## Sample Letter of Introduction

Try to address the letter to a specific individual. If you have a phone number, call to make sure the letter is going directly to the right office. If there is no phone number or specific office, send your letter to the attention of the scholarship's name. Someone in the organization will know which office should receive your request.

Be sure to date your letter so you remember when it was sent. Include your return address so that the organization can easily send you the application. Keep your letter brief; its purpose is simply to request an application. It will not be used to make any recipient decisions; that is the purpose of the application.

The text should mention the specific scholarships for which you are applying. Some agencies administer more than one scholarship, so you must help ensure that they send you the correct application. If an organization administers more than one scholarship and you are applying for more than one of them, you should use a separate letter for each scholarship. Mail these letters in separate envelopes.

The letter should briefly describe how you will use the scholarship money (i.e., to attend a certain college, to conduct research, etc.) and also mention how you found out about the scholarship. Many agencies like to know how their information is disseminated. They want to make sure it is going to the correct "market" and to a diverse population. They will appreciate this data as they plan future cycles. You should also tell them when you intend to use the money so that they send you information for the right year, and ask them to send any other scholarship applications that they administer that may be appropriate for you. Include a phone number and/or an e-mail address in case the organization wants to contact you.

There is no need to send the letter by certified mail, but be sure to include a self-addressed, stamped envelope with the letter. Many of these organizations are nonprofit and will appreciate the help to reduce postage costs. A self-addressed envelope will also get you an earlier response, since the organization won't have to type an envelope. Remember, time is critical!

## The Follow-Up Letter

Once the initial letters have been mailed, you must carefully keep track of responses. Be sure to note the application deadline (if known) of each scholarship for your records. Obviously, those due the soonest should be watched very carefully.

If you still have not received anything after six to eight weeks, it is appropriate to send a second letter. You should send your original letter (with a new date) again as if it had never been sent to the organization. It is not wise to send a different letter that says something about the organization's not getting or answering your first request. That could be perceived as being too pushy. You don't want to turn off any possible donors.

If you send a second letter and still receive no response, you might not want to send another letter. Even if the organization's listing contains the most up-to-date information, there's a chance the organization may no longer be offering scholarships. You might want to call to see if it has your application and will mail it soon, or if it is no longer offering the scholarship. If you don't have a contact number, use directory assistance.

When you do call, remember to be very polite. You might want to begin your conversation by asking general questions about the scholarship. This way you can discreetly find out if it is still being offered. If it isn't being offered, ask if the organization has any new scholarship programs for which you qualify. If so, have them send you an application. If the scholarship is still being offered, tell them you have sent a request and want to make sure they have received it (remember, don't be too aggressive). You may find that it is not easy to confirm that they have the request. If this is the case, ask if you can fax a copy of the letter. Some agencies will be able to tell you if they have the letter, in which case you should ask when you can expect to receive the application. Be sure to confirm the deadline for submission.

Be sure to keep good records on the progress of each individual search. Record notes and conversations on the file copy of the letter so you can easily check the status of the search. Organizations that drop out along the way should be considered when you begin your search again the following year.

## The Application

Once you have secured the applications, it's time to begin the process of completing them. You should approach this step as if you are applying for a job. Initial impressions on paper are very important, so you want your application to stand out from all the others. Neatness is very important. You should type your application and make several photocopies so you can go through some drafts before the final edition. Use all personal resources to review your various drafts. The application should be your own, but seeking input from others can improve it.

Be sure to read the entire application and any accompanying instructions before completing it, because failing to answer as instructed might eliminate you from consideration. For most scholarships, there are many more applicants than recipients. It is easy to eliminate the applicants who did not provide all requested information. Don't lose out because of a mistake that could have been avoided with proper planning.

Many applications may require supplemental information from other sources. If such information is needed, be sure to plan your time to secure what is requested. Some items, such as academic transcripts and letters of reference, may take some time to obtain. Don't wait until the last minute; it may be too late to send in a complete application. The importance of planning cannot be overemphasized.

If letters of recommendations are needed, seek people who will provide the most positive influence on your application. You might need recommendations for many of the applications. If this is the case, it is best to have these recommendations tailored to the specific application, because general recommendations do not make as much of an impact. Find out if the recommendations are to be sealed and included with the application or to be sent in separately by the recommendation writers. If the recommendations must be separate, tell the writers not to send them until the day you expect your application to reach the organization, as it is easier for the scholarship provider to match up documents if the application arrives first. If any of the documents are misplaced, you could be eliminated from consideration.

If the instructions say nothing about enclosing other documents, you might consider including a cover letter with your application. This letter should be short and precise, highlighting the reasons why you would make an excellent recipient of the scholarship. A letter with bullet points might be most effective. You might also want to include a statement of your academic and career objectives and how the donor's scholarship may influence these. A cover letter might help differentiate your application from the others, but don't overdo it. A quick summary is all that is needed.

In mailing your application, there are different techniques that can be used to ensure that it is received. A simple approach is to send the application via certified mail, so that you can be sure the envelope gets to the organization. Another approach is to send a response form for the organization with a self-addressed, stamped envelope. This could be a check-off letter to acknowledge that all necessary documents have been received. This approach may be particularly helpful if documents are being sent under separate cover. If you send the application via first-class mail, you might want to call the scholarship office (if you have the phone number) a few weeks later to make sure it was received.

## When You Get Your Scholarship(s)

Congratulations! You've done the hard work, and are now receiving aid from one or a number of organizations. What should you do next?

### Thank-You Letters

If you are awarded a scholarship by an organization, foundation, or individual, an important final step is the thank-you letter. After all, many of these organizations award scholarships for purely philanthropic reasons, and the only immediate reward they can expect is sincere thanks. Thank you letters are an effective method to communicate gratitude, lay groundwork for future renewal, and encourage the continuation of these programs for future recipients.

The letter itself need not be a terribly complicated affair. Short, simple, sincere, and to the point will do just fine (see the sample letter on the next page). You do not need to, nor should you, copy this version verbatim. Your thank-you letter should, like your initial letters and application, let your own personality shine through. If you have nice penmanship, a handwritten version may help achieve the desired personal effect. Remember, you are receiving an award because you deserve it and because someone is willing to grant it. Don't be afraid to let your happiness show!

---

Today's Date

AAA Foundation
999 7th Avenue
New York, NY 10000

To Whom It May Concern (or, if you have a contact name, by all means use it!),

I am taking this occasion to express my deep appreciation for the opportunity that your generous (grant, loan, etc.) has given me. I know that it will allow me to achieve my goals, and I hope that the results will justify your faith in me.

Thank you for your time and attention.

Sincerely,

Your name

---

### Sample Thank-You Letter

## Notifying the School

You must tell your school about any outside scholarships you receive. Most financial aid packages need to be adjusted in order to "make room" for outside sources of aid. This is because most packages contain federal aid, and therefore have to follow federal guidelines as to how much aid a student who receives other forms of aid can receive. The internal policies of various schools might also require changes to your package. Most financial aid offices will reduce the least desirable forms of aid first (loans with higher interest rates, work-study).

If your school guarantees its own scholarship over your academic period and the outside award does not, or is explicitly one-time-only, it may make more financial sense to turn down the outside offer in order to keep the money your school is offering.

Depending on the kind of outside aid you are receiving, you might also have to make arrangements with the business, or bursar's, office of your college. Depending on the documentation you have, your school might extend credit to you based upon a certain expectation of funds.

Finally, remember that the aid you are receiving may be contingent on certain aspects of your enrollment; you may have to register for a certain number of credits or a certain major, for example. Keep any requirements for the award in mind as you enroll in school.

## Renewing Scholarships for Subsequent Years

Renewal procedures vary depending on the kind of award you receive. Some groups offer one-time-only forms of aid, while others automatically renew previous recipients as long as they are enrolled in an eligible program. More commonly, scholarship programs require new applications each year from all interested parties. Remember that you've done it before; use your knowledge of the process to your advantage. Start early in gathering applications, recommendations, and other supporting materials to reapply for your hard-won award. At this time, you should also consider using the research you have already done to reapply for aid for which you may not have been eligible the previous year. There is no reason to limit your options and waste your hard work from the year before.

Once you are in school, there are usually many announcements of large-scale scholarship competitions. Most schools have specific offices that coordinate these prestigious awards. Sometimes this coordination is done at the financial aid office, but not always. Begin at the aid office; if they don't coordinate or know about these awards, check with the academic dean. Academic deans administer applications for the many awards that are associated with strong academic performance.

## Summary

If you remember nothing else from this chapter, be sure to recall the following key points:

### Start Early

Give yourself plenty of time to find what you are looking for and apply for it. Missed deadlines are nobody's fault but your own, and even the most benevolent organization will usually not make exceptions to its deadline rules.

### Use All Resources and Strategies Available to You

Don't hobble your search by ignoring possibilities you don't know much about. Investigate everything, because you never know when an unlikely source of funding may decide to grant you a scholarship. Look everywhere you can, using every tool available to you. Be sure to use the power of the Internet. Anything else would be cheating yourself.

### Know What You Are Looking For

On the other hand, when it becomes clear that a particular source is not appropriate for you, move on. If you are going to be an undergraduate student and you find a listing of graduate aid, it is probably pointless to follow that path any farther.

### Follow All Steps and Instructions

You would be surprised at how many people ignore this simple advice. Remember, you are asking for assistance with your education. The least you can do is precisely follow the instructions given to you. One of the qualities these organizations might be looking for is an ability to read and understand instructions and deadlines.

### Be Confident and Self-Assured but Polite and Respectful

You need to have a good self-image, a high level of confidence in your abilities, and pride in your past achievements. But remember, nobody owes you anything, and if you treat people with anything less than polite respect, you almost are automatically proving yourself to be unworthy of their assistance. Just show folks the same respect and courtesy that you expect to be shown yourself.

## Remember to Thank Those Who Have Helped

Remember, the most that many of these organizations and individuals receive in return for their generosity is the occasional thank you (and maybe a tax deduction!). An expression of gratitude will confirm that they have made the right choice, and will lay the groundwork for possible renewals.

## Don't Pay Anyone to Do This Work for You

No need to dwell on this any further. You have been warned, but if you want to learn more about this subject, the FTC in 1996 inaugurated "Project $cholar$cam," an educational campaign to alert students and parents about fraudulent scholarship companies. These warnings can be found on its website (www.ftc.gov/bcp/conline/edcams/scholarship).

With that, good luck in your search for financial aid and, more importantly, best wishes on all of your academic endeavors.

# A Special Note for International Students

In our quickly shrinking world, cross-border education has become an ever more important feature of American colleges. Large and small schools alike are sending students abroad in increasing numbers and have opened at least part of their U.S. enrollment to students from around the world.

If you are a non-U.S. student who is considering coming here to study, you probably already know that while American colleges and universities are highly regarded around the world, the American custom of actually paying for an education truly is a foreign notion. Many countries provide free or heavily subsidized higher education for their citizens. Study in the United States, in contrast, requires careful financial planning—especially for international students, who are cut off from most need-based U.S. government aid programs.

While some students who come here receive funding from their college or university—or from the U.S. government—and others are supported by their home government, the vast majority are here without support other than their savings and family back home. The rules governing those residing in the United States on a student visa largely prohibit or limit the ability to work. The result is that for all but the wealthiest families, study in the United States requires a great deal of sacrifice, and for many is not even in the realm of possibility.

Fortunately, many of the resources discussed in this book are not necessarily limited to U.S. students. Most of the advice within these pages applies to the international student just as much as to the domestic. In fact, the one piece of advice that this book hopes to drive home more than any other—start early!—applies to international students even more. Despite the Internet revolution (a technology which you should certainly take advantage of), much business continues to be transacted through the mail. As you may know, international post brings a whole new meaning to the term *snail mail*.

Of course, a key part of your research should be to look for financial assistance at the school you plan to attend. The admissions and financial aid offices may have information on both institutional and external sources of assistance. Many schools also have offices that specialize in assisting international students in all facets of the enrollment process, including finding or facilitating sources of funding. Check your college's website for a guide to services it offers. There are other sources of information particularly designed for international students, as well:

In addition to administering the Fulbright program, the Institute of International Education (IIE) is a particularly rich source of information on all aspects of international education in the United States.

Institute of International Education
809 United Nations Plaza
New York, NY 10017-3580 USA
Phone: (212) 984-5400
Fax: (212) 984-5452
Website: www.iie.org

Another source of information for international students is NAFSA: Association of International Educators. This is the professional association of those who administer the college international student offices mentioned above.

NAFSA: Association of International Educators
1307 New York Avenue, NW, 8th Floor
Washington, DC 20005-4701 USA
Phone: (202) 737-3699
Fax: (202) 737-3657
Website: www.nafsa.org

You may also visit the Financial Aid Information Page (FinAid) at www.edupass.org for more general information about financing a U.S. education.

Every year Kaplan helps students from over 60 countries navigate the U.S. higher education system. Find out more about Kaplan's programs for international students:

Kaplan International Programs
700 South Flower, Suite 2900
Los Angeles, CA 90017 USA
Phone (if calling from within the United States): (800) 818-9128
Phone (if calling from outside the United States): (213) 452-5800
Fax: (213) 892-1364
Website: www.Kaplan.com/Kaplaninternational.htm
Email: world@kaplan.com

While financial resources for international students are by no means plentiful, opportunities do exist. As international education becomes an ever more important feature of American higher education, you can be sure that more sources of funding will become available. Some schools have begun to work with banks to develop financing tools for this key population. More developments are sure to follow.

# Unrestricted by Subject Area

## 1 A. PATRICK CHARNON SCHOLARSHIP

Center for Education Solutions
P.O. Box 208
San Francisco, CA 94104-0208
Phone: (925) 934-7304; Email: scholarship@cesresources.org
Web: www.cesresources.org/charnon.html
**Summary:** To provide financial assistance to undergraduate students who demonstrate a commitment to their community.
**Eligibility:** Open to applicants admitted or enrolled in a full-time undergraduate program of study at an accredited 4-year college or university. They must demonstrate dedication and commitment to their communities. Along with their application, they must submit a 2- to 4-page essay on how community service experiences have shaped their lives and how they will use their college education to build communities in a manner consistent with values of compassion, tolerance, generosity, and respect. The selection committee looks for candidates whose values reflect the goals of the program and who have demonstrated their commitments to those values by their actions.
**Financial data:** The stipend is $1,500 per year.
**Duration:** 1 year; may be renewed up to 3 additional years.
**Number awarded:** 1 each year.
**Deadline:** March of each year.

## 2 A-OK STUDENT REWARD PROGRAM

U.S. Navy, Attn: Navy Exchange Service Command
3280 Virginia Beach Boulevard
Virginia Beach, VA 23452-5724
Phone: (800) NAV-EXCH
Web: www.navy nex.com/command/about_us/a.ok.program.html
**Summary:** To provide financial assistance for college to children of active and retired military personnel who shop at Navy Exchange (NEX) stores.
**Eligibility:** Open to dependent children of active-duty military members, Reservists, and military retirees who are enrolled in grades 1-12 and have a GPA of 3.0 or higher. Applicants submit an entry at the service desk of their NEX store. Winners are selected in a drawing.
**Financial data:** Winners receive savings bonds for $5,000, $3,000, $2,000, or $1,000. Funds are intended to help pay expenses of college.
**Duration:** Drawings are held 4 times a year (in February, May, August, and November).
**Number awarded:** 16 each year: at each drawing, 1 savings bond for each of the 4 denominations is awarded.

## 3 A.B. "HAPPY" CHANDLER FOUNDATION SCHOLARSHIPS

A.B. "Happy" Chandler Foundation, Attn: Executive Director
1718 Alexandria Drive, Suite 203
Lexington, KY 40504
Phone: (859) 278-5550; Fax: (859) 276-2090; Email: ChandlerFdn@aol.com
**Summary:** To provide financial assistance to Kentucky high school seniors who are interested in attending college in the state.
**Eligibility:** Open to seniors graduating from high schools in Kentucky who have a GPA of 3.0 or higher or an ACT score of 25 or higher. Applicants must be planning to attend a college or university in Kentucky. Selection is based on academic achievement, participation in community and/or school activities, 2 letters of recommendation, and a 500-word essay.
**Financial data:** The stipend is $4,000 per year.
**Duration:** 1 year.
**Number awarded:** 1 or more each year.
**Deadline:** March of each year.

## 4 ACCEL PROGRAM

Georgia Student Finance Commission, Attn: Scholarships and Grants Division
2082 East Exchange Place, Suite 200
Tucker, GA 30084-5305
Phone: (770) 724-9000; (800) 505-GSFC; Fax: (770) 724-9089;
Email: info@mail.gsfc.state.ga.us
Web: www.gsfc.org
**Summary:** To provide financial assistance to high school students in Georgia who are enrolled concurrently in college-level courses.
**Eligibility:** Open to Georgia residents who are enrolled simultaneously as a junior or senior at an eligible public or private high school in the state and at an eligible Georgia public or private postsecondary institution. Applicants must be taking college degree-level courses in English language arts, mathematics, social studies, science, or foreign language. U.S. citizenship or permanent resident status is required.
**Financial data:** Accel Scholars who attend public colleges or universities receive full tuition and mandatory fees plus a book allowance of $300 per academic year. The stipend for Accel Scholarships at private colleges and universities is $125 per semester hour, or up to $3,000 per year; funds may be used only for tuition and mandatory fees.
**Duration:** 1 year; may be renewed for 1 additional year.
**Number awarded:** Varies each year.

## 5 ADA MUCKLESTONE MEMORIAL SCHOLARSHIPS

American Legion Auxiliary, Attn: Department of Illinois
2720 East Lincoln Street
P.O. Box 1426
Bloomington, IL 61702-1426
Phone: (309) 663-9366; Fax: (309) 663-5827; Email: ilala@ilala.org
Web: illegion.org/auxiliary/scholar.html
**Summary:** To provide financial assistance for college to the children of Illinois veterans.
**Eligibility:** Open to Illinois residents. Applicants must be the children or grandchildren of veterans who served during eligibility dates for membership in the American Legion. They must be high school seniors or high school graduates who have not yet attended an institution of higher learning. They must be sponsored by their local American Legion Auxiliary unit. Winners are selected on the basis of character, Americanism, leadership, scholarship, and need.
**Financial data:** The first winner receives a scholarship of $1,200, the second winner a scholarship of $1,000, and several other winners each receive $800.
**Duration:** 1 year.
**Number awarded:** Varies each year.
**Deadline:** March of each year.

## 6 ADELANTE! FUND SCHOLARSHIP PROGRAM

Adelante! U.S. Education Leadership Fund
8415 Datapoint Drive, Suite 400
San Antonio, TX 78229
Phone: (210) 692-1971; Fax: (210) 692-1951; (877) 692-1971;
Email: info@adelantefund.org
Web: www.adelantefund.org
**Summary:** To provide financial aid, internships, and leadership training to upper-division Hispanic students enrolled in Hispanic Serving Institutions (HSIs).
**Eligibility:** Open to Hispanic students currently enrolled in HSIs. Applicants must have a GPA of 3.0 or higher, be eligible to receive financial aid, be juniors or seniors in college, agree to attend the Adelante Leadership Institute, be eligible to participate in a summer internship, exhibit leadership, and provide 2 letters of recommendation. Most recipients are the first in their families to complete a college education.
**Financial data:** The maximum stipend is $3,000 per year.
**Duration:** 1 year.
**Number awarded:** Varies each year; recently, 22 students received scholarships.

## 7 AEF AIR FORCE SPOUSE SCHOLARSHIPS

Aerospace Education Foundation, Attn: Manager of Foundation Programs
1501 Lee Highway
Arlington, VA 22209-1198
Phone: (703) 247-5839; (800) 291-8480, ext 4877; Fax: (703) 247-5853;
Email: AEFStaff@aef.org
Web: www.aef.org/aid/spouse.asp
**Summary:** To provide financial assistance for undergraduate or graduate study to spouses of Air Force members.
**Eligibility:** Open to spouses of Air Force active duty, Air National Guard, or Air Force Reserve members. Spouses who are themselves military members or in ROTC are not eligible. Applicants must have a GPA of 3.5 or higher in college (or high school if entering college for the first time) and be able to provide proof of acceptance into an accredited undergraduate or graduate degree program. They must submit a 2-page essay on their academic and career goals, the motivation that led them to that decision, and how Air Force and other local community activities in which they are involved will enhance their goals. Selection is based on the essay and 2 letters of recommendation.

**Financial data:** The stipend is $3,000 per year; funds are sent to the recipients' schools to be used for any reasonable cost related to working towards a degree.

**Duration:** 1 year; nonrenewable.

**Number awarded:** 10 each year: 1 for each Air Force Major Air Command (MAJCOM).

**Deadline:** January of each year.

## 8 AFL-CIO SKILLED TRADES EXPLORING SCHOLARSHIPS

Boy Scouts of America, Attn: Learning for Life Division, S210
1325 West Walnut Hill Lane
P.O. Box 152079
Irving, TX 75015-2079
Phone: (972) 580-2418; Fax: (972) 580-2137
Web: www.learning-for-life.org/exploring/scholarships/index.html

**Summary:** To provide financial assistance for trade school to graduating high school seniors who are Explorer Scouts.

**Eligibility:** Open to graduating high school seniors who are Explorers and interested in attending a public or proprietary institution or union apprentice program. Their achievements must "reflect the high degree of motivation, commitment, and skills that epitomize the skilled trades." Selection is based on academic record, recommendations, and a 500-word essay on why the applicant should be selected for the scholarship. All completed applications must be approved by the local council scout executive.

**Financial data:** The stipend is $1,000.

**Duration:** 1 year.

**Number awarded:** 2 each year.

**Deadline:** April of each year.

## 9 AGENDA FOR DELAWARE WOMEN TRAILBLAZER SCHOLARSHIPS

Delaware Higher Education Commission
Carvel State Office Building
820 North French Street
Wilmington, DE 19801
Phone: (302) 577-3240; (800) 292-7935; Fax: (302) 577-6765;
Email: dhec@doe.k12.de.us
Web: www.doe.state.de.us/high-ed/agenda.htm

**Summary:** To provide financial assistance for undergraduate education to women in Delaware.

**Eligibility:** Open to women who are Delaware residents planning to enroll in a public or private nonprofit college in Delaware as an undergraduate student in the coming year. Applicants must have a cumulative GPA of 2.5 or higher. Selection is based on financial need (50%) and community and school activities, vision, participation, and leadership (50%).

**Financial data:** The stipend is $2,500 per year.

**Duration:** 1 year; may be renewed.

**Number awarded:** 1 or more each year.

**Deadline:** April of each year.

## 10 AGNES JONES JACKSON SCHOLARSHIPS

National Association for the Advancement of Colored People
Attn: Education Department
4805 Mt. Hope Drive
Baltimore, MD 21215-3297
Phone: (410) 580-5760; (877) NAACP-98; Email: youth@naacpnet.org
Web: www.naacp.org/work/education/eduscholarship.shtml

**Summary:** To provide financial assistance to members of the National Association for the Advancement of Colored People (NAACP) who are attending or planning to attend college or graduate school.

**Eligibility:** Open to members of the NAACP who are younger than 25 years of age and full-time undergraduates or full- or part-time graduate students. The minimum GPA is 2.5 for graduating high school seniors and undergraduate students, or 3.0 for graduate students. All applicants must be able to demonstrate financial need (family income must be less than $13,470 for a family of 1, ranging up to $46,440 for a family of 8) and U.S. citizens. Along with their application, they must submit a 1-page essay on their interest in their major and a career, their life's ambition, what they hope to accomplish in their lifetime, and what they consider their most significant contribution to their community.

**Financial data:** The stipend is $1,500 per year for undergraduate students or $2,500 per year for graduate students.

**Duration:** 1 year; recipients may apply for renewal.

**Number awarded:** Varies each year; recently, 17 of these scholarships were awarded.

**Deadline:** April of each year.

## 11 AGNES M. LINDSAY SCHOLARSHIP PROGRAM

Massachusetts Office of Student Financial Assistance
454 Broadway, Suite 200
Revere, MA 02151
Phone: (617) 727-9420; Fax: (617) 727-0667; Email: osfa@osfa.mass.edu
Web: www.osfa.mass.edu

**Summary:** To provide financial assistance for college to residents of rural areas of Massachusetts.

**Eligibility:** Open to permanent Massachusetts residents who are U.S. citizens or permanent residents. Applicants must come from areas designated as "rural." They must be enrolled as a full-time undergraduate at a public college or university in Massachusetts. Financial need is considered in the selection process.

**Financial data:** A stipend is awarded (amount not specified).

**Duration:** 1 year; may be renewed if the recipient maintains satisfactory progress.

**Number awarded:** Varies each year.

## 12 AGRON SEAL SCHOLARSHIP

Naval Special Warfare Foundation, Attn: Scholarship Committee
P.O. Box 5965
Virginia Beach, VA 23471
Phone: (757) 363-7490; Fax: (757) 363-7491; Email: info@nswfoundation.org
Web: www.nswfoundation.org

**Summary:** To provide financial assistance for college to Navy personnel serving on active duty in the SEALs and their families.

**Eligibility:** Open to active-duty SEALs, their current spouses, and immediate children. Applicants must be high school seniors or current college students working towards or planning to work towards an associate's or bachelor's degree. Selection is based on academic merit, extracurricular and community activities, and contributions made within the SEAL community.

**Financial data:** The stipend is $1,000 per year.

**Duration:** Up to 4 years, provided the recipient maintains a GPA of 3.2 or higher.

**Number awarded:** 1 each year.

**Deadline:** March of each year.

## 13 AIMMS EXCELLENCE SCHOLARSHIPS

Maryland State Department of Education
Attn: Achievement Initiative for Maryland's Minority Students Council
200 West Baltimore Street
Baltimore, MD 21201
Phone: (410) 887-2446
Web: www.msde.state.md.us/minority/WhatsNew/WHATSNEW.html

**Summary:** To provide financial assistance for college to Maryland high school seniors who have demonstrated leadership in addressing diversity.

**Eligibility:** Open to seniors in high schools in Maryland who plan to attend a community college, university, college, or technical/vocational school. Applicants must have a GPA of 3.0 or higher. They must submit an essay about their leadership in 1 or more of the following areas: 1) academic, school, or community support for diverse students; 2) promotion of positive intergroup relations and understanding; or 3) performance of services to increase success among diverse groups of students. Diverse groups include race/ethnicity, gender, age, disability, or poverty. Selection is based on academic success and contributions to better understanding and appreciation among diverse groups.

**Financial data:** Stipends are $1,000 or $500.

**Duration:** 1 year.

**Number awarded:** 11 each year: 1 at $1,000 and 10 at $500.

**Deadline:** July of each year.

## 14 AIR FORCE REGULAR ROTC HISPANIC SERVING INSTITUTION SCHOLARSHIP PROGRAM

U.S. Air Force, Attn: Headquarters AFROTC/RRUC
551 East Maxwell Boulevard
Maxwell AFB, AL 36112-5917
Phone: (334) 953-2091; (866) 423-7682; Fax: (334) 953-6167
Web: www.afrotc.com/scholarships/incolschol/minority/hsi.php

**Summary:** To provide financial assistance to students at Hispanic Serving Institutions (HSIs) who are willing to join Air Force ROTC in college and serve as Air Force officers following completion of their bachelor's degree.

**Eligibility:** Open to U.S. citizens at least 17 years of age who are currently enrolled at 1 of the 42 HSIs that has an Air Force ROTC unit on campus or that has a cross-enrollment agreement with another school that hosts a unit. Applicants do not need to be Hispanic as long as they are attending an HSI and have a cumulative GPA of 2.5 or higher. At the time of commissioning, they may be no more than 31 years of age. They must be able to pass the Air Force Officer Qualifying Test (AFOQT) and the Air Force ROTC Physical Fitness Test.

**Financial data:** Awards are type 2 AFROTC scholarships that provide for payment of tuition and fees, to a maximum of $15,000 per year, plus an annual book allowance of $600. Recipients are also awarded a tax-free subsistence allowance for 10 months of each year that is $300 per month during the sophomore year, $350 during the junior year, and $400 during the senior year.

**Duration:** 2 to 3 years, beginning during the current term.

**Number awarded:** Varies each year. AFROTC units at every HSI may nominate an unlimited number of cadets to receive these scholarships.

**Deadline:** Applications may be submitted at any time.

---

## 15 AIR FORCE REGULAR ROTC HISTORICALLY BLACK COLLEGES AND UNIVERSITIES SCHOLARSHIP PROGRAM

U.S. Air Force, Attn: Headquarters AFROTC/RRUC
551 East Maxwell Boulevard
Maxwell AFB, AL 36112-5917
Phone: (334) 953-2091; (866) 423-7682; Fax: (334) 953-6167
Web: www.afrotc.com/scholarships/incolschol/minority/hbcu.php

**Summary:** To provide financial assistance to students at Historically Black Colleges and Universities (HBCUs) who are willing to serve as Air Force officers following completion of their bachelor's degree.

**Eligibility:** Open to U.S. citizens at least 17 years of age who are currently enrolled at 1 of the 48 HBCUs that has an Air Force ROTC unit on campus or that has a cross-enrollment agreement with another school that hosts a unit. Applicants do not need to be African American as long as they are attending an HBCU and have a cumulative GPA of 2.5 or higher. At the time of commissioning, they may be no more than 31 years of age. They must be able to pass the Air Force Officer Qualifying Test (AFOQT) and the Air Force ROTC Physical Fitness Test.

**Financial data:** Awards are type 2 AFROTC scholarships that provide for payment of tuition and fees, to a maximum of $15,000 per year, plus an annual book allowance of $600. Recipients are also awarded a tax-free subsistence allowance for 10 months of each year that is $300 per month during the sophomore year, $350 during the junior year, and $400 during the senior year.

**Duration:** 2 to 3 years, beginning during the current term.

**Number awarded:** Varies each year. AFROTC units at every HBCU may nominate an unlimited number of cadets to receive these scholarships.

**Deadline:** Applications may be submitted at any time.

---

## 16 AIR FORCE ROTC GENERAL MILITARY COURSE INCENTIVE

U.S. Air Force, Attn: Headquarters AFROTC/RRUC
551 East Maxwell Boulevard
Maxwell AFB, AL 36112-5917
Phone: (334) 953-2091; (866) 423-7682; Fax: (334) 953-6167
Web: www.afrotc.com/overview/programs.php

**Summary:** To provide financial assistance to college sophomores interested in joining Air Force ROTC and serving as Air Force officers following completion of requirements towards their bachelor's degree.

**Eligibility:** Open to U.S. citizens who are entering the spring semester of their sophomore year in the general military course at a college or university with an Air Force ROTC unit on campus or a college with a cross-enrollment agreement with such a school. Applicants must be full-time students, have a GPA of 2.0 or higher both cumulatively and during the prior term, be enrolled in both the Aerospace Studies 200 class and the Leadership Laboratory, pass the Air Force Officer Qualifying Test, meet Air Force physical fitness and weight requirements, and be able to be commissioned before they become 31 years of age. They must agree to serve for at least 4 years as active-duty Air Force officers following graduation from college.

**Financial data:** Selected cadets receive up to $1,500 for tuition and a stipend of $250 per month.

**Duration:** 1 semester (the spring semester of junior year); nonrenewable.

---

## 17 AIR FORCE ROTC HIGH SCHOOL SCHOLARSHIPS

U.S. Air Force, Attn: Headquarters AFROTC/RRUC
551 East Maxwell Boulevard
Maxwell AFB, AL 36112-5917
Phone: (334) 953-2091; (866) 423-7682; Fax: (334) 953-6167
Web: www.afrotc.com/scholarships/hsschol/types.php

**Summary:** To provide financial assistance to high school seniors or graduates

who are interested in joining Air Force ROTC in college and are willing to serve as Air Force officers following completion of their bachelor's degree.

**Eligibility:** Open to high school seniors who are U.S. citizens at least 17 of age and have been accepted at a college or university with an Air Force ROTC unit on campus, or a college with a cross-enrollment agreement with such a college. Applicants must have a cumulative GPA of 3.0 or higher, an ACT composite score of 24 or higher, or an SAT score of 1100 (mathematics and verbal portion only) or higher. At the time of their commissioning in the Air Force, they must be no more than 31 years of age. They must agree to serve for at least 4 years as active-duty Air Force officers following graduation from college.

**Financial data:** Type 1 scholarships provide payment of full tuition and most laboratory fees, as well as $600 for books. Type 2 scholarships pay the same benefits except tuition is capped at $15,000 per year; students who attend an institution where tuition exceeds $15,000 must pay the difference. Type 7 scholarships pay full tuition and most laboratory fees, but students must attend a college or university where the tuition is less than $9,000 per year, or a public college or university where they qualify for the in-state tuition rate; they may not attend an institution with higher tuition and pay the difference. Approximately 5% of scholarship offers are for Type 1, approximately 20% are for Type 2, and approximately 75% are for type 7. All recipients are also awarded a tax-free subsistence allowance for 10 months of each year that is $250 per month as a freshman, $300 per month as a sophomore, $350 per month as a junior, and $400 per month as a senior.

**Duration:** 4 years.

**Number awarded:** Approximately 2,000 each year.

**Deadline:** November of each year.

---

## 18 AIR FORCE ROTC IN-COLLEGE SCHOLARSHIP PROGRAM

U.S. Air Force, Attn: Headquarters AFROTC/RRUC
551 East Maxwell Boulevard
Maxwell AFB, AL 36112-5917
Phone: (334) 953-2091; (866) 423-7682; Fax: (334) 953-6167
Web: www.afrotc.com/scholarships/incolschol/incolProgram.php

**Summary:** To provide financial assistance to undergraduate students who are willing to join Air Force ROTC in college and serve as Air Force officers following completion of their bachelor's degree.

**Eligibility:** Open to U.S. citizens enrolled as freshmen or sophomores at 1 of the 144 colleges and universities that have an Air Force ROTC unit on campus. Applicants must have a cumulative GPA of 2.5 or higher and be able to pass the Air Force Officer Qualifying Test and the Air Force ROTC Physical Fitness Test. At the time of commissioning, they may be no more than 31 years of age. They must agree to serve for at least 4 years as active-duty Air Force officers following graduation from college. Phase 1 is open to students enrolled in the Air Force ROTC program who do not currently have a scholarship but now wish to apply. Phase 2 is open to Phase 1 nonselects and students not enrolled in Air Force ROTC. Phase 3 is open only to Phase 2 nonselects.

**Financial data:** Cadets selected in Phase 1 are awarded type 2 AFROTC scholarships that provide for payment of tuition and fees, to a maximum of $15,000 per year. A limited number of cadets selected in Phase 2 are also awarded type 2 AFROTC scholarships, but most are awarded type 3 AFROTC scholarships with tuition capped at $9,000 per year. Cadets selected in Phase 3 are awarded type 6 AFROTC scholarships with tuition capped at $3,000 per year. All recipients are also awarded a book allowance of $600 and a tax-free subsistence allowance for 10 months of each year that is $300 per month during the sophomore year, $350 during the junior year, and $400 during the senior year.

**Duration:** 3 years for students selected as freshmen or 2 years for students selected as sophomores.

**Number awarded:** Varies each year.

**Deadline:** January of each year.

---

## 19 AIR FORCE ROTC PROFESSIONAL OFFICER CORPS INCENTIVE

U.S. Air Force, Attn: Headquarters AFROTC/RRUC
551 East Maxwell Boulevard
Maxwell AFB, AL 36112-5917
Phone: (334) 953-2091; (866) 423-7682; Fax: (334) 953-6167
Web: www.afrotc.com/overview/programs.php

**Summary:** To provide financial assistance for undergraduate and graduate education to individuals who have completed 2 years of college and who are willing to join Air Force ROTC and serve as Air Force officers following completion of their degree.

**Eligibility:** Open to U.S. citizens who have completed 2 years of the general military course at a college or university with an Air Force ROTC unit on campus or a college with a cross-enrollment agreement with such a college. They must be full-time students, have a GPA of 2.0 or higher both cumulatively and for the prior term, be enrolled in both Aerospace Studies class and Leadership Laboratory, pass the Air Force Officer Qualifying Test, meet Air Force physical fitness and weight requirements, and be able to be commissioned before they become 31 years of age. They must agree to serve for at least 4 years as active-duty Air Force officers following graduation from college with either a bachelor's or graduate degree.

**Financial data:** This scholarship provides $3,000 per year for tuition and a monthly subsistence allowance of $350 as a junior or $400 as a senior.

**Duration:** Until completion of a graduate degree.

**Number awarded:** Varies each year.

## 20 AIR FORCE SERGEANTS ASSOCIATION AUXILIARY EDUCATION GRANTS

Air Force Sergeants Association, Attn: Scholarship Coordinator
P.O. Box 50
Temple Hills, MD 20757
Phone: (301) 899-3500, ext. 237; (800) 638-0594; Fax: (301) 899-8136;
Email: staff@amf.org
Web: www.afsahq.org/body_education06.htm

**Summary:** To provide financial assistance to members of the Air Force Sergeants Association (AFSA) Auxiliary who wish to gain further training.

**Eligibility:** Open to individuals who have been AFSA Auxiliary members for at least 1 year and who will remain members for 2 additional years. They must be 21 years of age or older, able to demonstrate financial need, and accepted at an accredited institution. At the conclusion of the course, class, or program for which they are applying, they must receive a certificate, diploma, or degree. They must show that they are acquiring or enhancing marketable skills that will increase their economic security, and at the end of their studies they must enter or rejoin the work force. Along with their application, they must include a description of their career goals and how the training will help them accomplish those goals.

**Financial data:** Stipends up to $2,000 per year are available. Funds are sent directly to the recipient's school to be used for tuition, room and board, fees, books, supplies, child care, meals, and transportation.

**Duration:** 1 year; may be renewed if the student maintains full-time enrollment.

**Number awarded:** Varies each year. Since the program began, it has awarded grants for more than $75,000.

**Deadline:** Applications may be submitted at any time.

## 21 AIRMEN MEMORIAL FOUNDATION SCHOLARSHIP PROGRAM

Air Force Sergeants Association, Attn: Scholarship Coordinator
P.O. Box 50
Temple Hills, MD 20757
Phone: (301) 899-3500, ext. 237; (800) 638-0594; Fax: (301) 899-8136;
Email: staff@amf.org
Web: www.afsahq.org/body_education01.htm

**Summary:** To provide financial assistance for college to the dependent children of enlisted Air Force personnel.

**Eligibility:** Open to the unmarried children (including stepchildren and legally adopted children) of active-duty, retired, or veteran members of the U.S. Air Force, Air National Guard, or Air Force Reserves. Applicants must be younger than 23 years of age and dependent upon the parent or guardian for more than half of their support. Selection is based on academic ability (ACT score of 24 or higher or the equivalent on the SAT and GPA of 3.5 or higher), character, leadership, writing ability, and potential for success. Financial need is not a consideration.

**Financial data:** The stipend is $1,500 or $1,000; funds may be used for tuition, room and board, fees, books, supplies, and transportation.

**Duration:** 1 year; may be renewed if the recipient maintains full-time enrollment.

**Number awarded:** 20 each year: the Sharon L. Piccoli Memorial Scholarship at $1,500 and 19 others at $1,000 each.

**Deadline:** March of each year.

## 22 AK-SAR-BEN COMMUNITY COLLEGE SCHOLARSHIP

Knights of Ak-Sar-Ben, Attn: Ak-Sar-Ben Scholarship Program
302 South 36th Street, Suite 800
Omaha, NE 68131
Phone: (402) 554-9600; Fax: (402) 554-9609; Email: greiner@aksarben.org
Web: www.aksarben.org/programs/scholarship.htm

**Summary:** To provide financial assistance to students from Nebraska and western Iowa who plan to attend a community college within the Ak-Sar-Ben region.

**Eligibility:** Open to high school seniors, high school graduates, and currently-enrolled community college students in Nebraska and western Iowa who are interested in attending college in the Ak-Sar-Ben region. For the purposes of this program, western Iowa is defined as the following counties: Adair, Adams, Audubon, Buena Vista, Calhoun, Carroll, Cass, Cherokee, Clay, Crawford, Dickinson, Fremont, Greene, Guthrie, Harrison, Ida, Lyon, Mills, Monona, Montgomery, O'Brien, Osceola, Page, Pottawattamie, Plymouth, Ringgold, Sac, Shelby, Sioux, Taylor, Union, and Woodbury. Applicants must be U.S. citizens. They must submit their application to the financial aid office at the community college they are attending or planning to attend; the college nominates 3 incoming freshmen and 3 currently-enrolled students from this group. As part of the application process, students must include a completed application form, a 250-word personal essay, 2 letters of reference, a transcript, and their federal student aid report. Selection is based on leadership potential, academic achievement, desire to earn a degree, and financial need.

**Financial data:** The stipend is $1,000, paid in 2 equal installments. To receive the second installment, recipients must have maintained full-time enrollment and a GPA of 2.5 or higher the previous semester. Funds must be used for tuition, fees, and books.

**Duration:** 1 year.

**Number awarded:** Up to 12 each year.

**Deadline:** March of each year.

## 23 AK-SAR-BEN LEADERSHIP COLLEGE SCHOLARSHIP

Knights of Ak-Sar-Ben, Attn: Ak-Sar-Ben Scholarship Program
302 South 36th Street, Suite 800
Omaha, NE 68131
Phone: (402) 554-9600; Fax: (402) 554-9609; Email: greiner@aksarben.org
Web: www.aksarben.org/programs/scholarship.htm

**Summary:** To provide financial assistance to high school seniors from Nebraska and western Iowa who plan to attend a 4-year college or university within the Ak-Sar-Ben region.

**Eligibility:** Open to high school seniors in Nebraska and western Iowa who are interested in attending college in the Ak-Sar-Ben region. Applicants must be U.S. citizens and rank in the top 50% of their graduating class. As part of the application process, students must submit a completed application form, a 300-word personal essay, 2 letters of reference, a transcript, and the original college funding estimator form and report from the EducationQuest Foundation. Selection is based on leadership potential, academic achievement, desire to earn a college degree, and financial need.

**Financial data:** The stipend totals $10,000 ($2,500 per year). Funds must be used for tuition, fees, books, room, and board (at university-owned housing only).

**Duration:** 4 years, provided the recipient maintains a GPA of 3.0 or higher in college.

**Number awarded:** 20 each year.

**Deadline:** February of each year.

## 24 ALABAMA FIRST IN FAMILY SCHOLARSHIPS

J. Craig and Page T. Smith Scholarship Foundation
505 20th Street North, Suite 1800
Birmingham, AL 35203
Phone: (205) 250-6669; Email: scholarships@jcraigsmithfoundation.org
Web: www.jcraigsmithfoundation.org

**Summary:** To provide financial assistance to high school seniors in Alabama, especially those who are the first in their family to attend college.

**Eligibility:** Open to seniors graduating from high schools in Alabama who have a GPA of 2.0 or higher. Applicants must be planning to attend a 4-year college or university in the state as a full-time student. They must submit an essay on their future plans or goals of accomplishment for themselves, an essay documenting community and civic-oriented activities or assistance to family members, an official transcript, ACT or SAT scores (no minimum is required), and documentation of financial need. Special consideration is given to applicants who will be the first in either their mother's or father's (or both parents') families to attend college.

**Financial data:** Funding covers full payment of tuition, campus room, board, and books.

**Duration:** 4 years, provided the recipient remains enrolled full time, makes significant progress toward completion of an undergraduate degree, verifies community service during the school year, and maintains a GPA of at least "C+."

**Number awarded:** Approximately 10 each year.

**Deadline:** January of each year.

## 25 ALABAMA G.I. DEPENDENTS' SCHOLARSHIP PROGRAM

Alabama Department of Veterans Affairs
770 Washington Avenue, Suite 530
P.O. Box 1509
Montgomery, AL 36102-1509
Phone: (334) 242-5077; Fax: (334) 242-5102; Email: willie.moore@va.state.al.us
Web: www.va.state.al.us/scholarship.htm

**Summary:** To provide educational benefits to the dependents of disabled, deceased, and other Alabama veterans.

**Eligibility:** Open to spouses, children, stepchildren, and unremarried widow(er)s of veterans who served honorably for 90 days or more and 1) are currently rated as 20% or more service-connected disabled or were so rated at time of death; 2) were a former prisoner of war; 3) have been declared missing in action; 4) died as the result of a service-connected disability; or 5) died while on active military duty in the line of duty. The veteran must have been a permanent civilian resident of Alabama for at least 1 year prior to entering active military service; veterans who were not Alabama residents at the time of entering active military service may also qualify if they have a 100% disability and were permanent residents of Alabama for at least 5 years prior to filing the application for this program or prior to death, if deceased. Children and stepchildren must be under the age of 26, but spouses and unremarried widow(er)s may be of any age.

**Financial data:** Eligible dependents may attend any state-supported Alabama institution of higher learning or enroll in a prescribed course of study at any Alabama state-supported trade school without payment of any tuition, book fees, or laboratory charges.

**Duration:** This is an entitlement program for 4 years of full-time undergraduate or graduate study or part-time equivalent. Spouses and unremarried widow(er)s whose veteran spouse is rated between 20 and 90% disabled, or 100% disabled but not permanently so, may attend only 2 standard academic years.

**Number awarded:** Varies each year.

**Deadline:** Applications may be submitted at any time.

## 26 ALABAMA JUNIOR AND COMMUNITY COLLEGE ATHLETIC SCHOLARSHIPS

Alabama Commission on Higher Education
Attn: Grants and Scholarships Department
100 North Union Street
P.O. Box 302000
Montgomery, AL 36130-2000
Phone: (334) 242-2274; Fax: (334) 242-0268; Email: wwall@ache.state.al.us
Web: www.ache.state.al.us/StudentAsst/Programs.htm

**Summary:** To provide financial assistance to athletes in Alabama interested in attending a junior or community college.

**Eligibility:** Open to full-time students enrolled in public junior and community colleges in Alabama. Selection is based on athletic ability as determined through try-outs.

**Financial data:** Awards cover the cost of tuition and books.

**Duration:** Scholarships are available as long as the recipient continues to participate in the designated sport or activity

**Number awarded:** Varies each year.

## 27 ALABAMA POLICE OFFICERS' AND FIRE FIGHTERS' SURVIVORS' EDUCATIONAL ASSISTANCE PROGRAM

Alabama Commission on Higher Education
Attn: Grants and Scholarships Department
100 North Union Street
P.O. Box 302000
Montgomery, AL 36130-2000
Phone: (334) 242-2274; Fax: (334) 242-0268; Email: wwall@ache.state.al.us
Web: www.ache.state.al.us/StudentAsst/Programs.htm

**Summary:** To provide financial assistance for college to the spouses and dependents of police officers and fire fighters killed in Alabama.

**Eligibility:** Open to the unremarried spouses and children of police officers and fire fighters killed in the line of duty in Alabama. Applicants may be high school seniors or currently-enrolled undergraduates in Alabama.

**Financial data:** Grants are offered to cover tuition, fees, books, and supplies. There is no limit on the amount awarded to recipients.

**Duration:** 1 year; may be renewed.

**Number awarded:** Varies each year.

## 28 ALABAMA STUDENT ASSISTANCE PROGRAM

Alabama Commission on Higher Education
Attn: Grants and Scholarships Department
100 North Union Street
P.O. Box 302000
Montgomery, AL 36130-2000
Phone: (334) 242-2274; Fax: (334) 242-0268; Email: wwall@ache.state.al.us
Web: www.ache.state.al.us/StudentAsst/Programs.htm

**Summary:** To provide financial assistance to undergraduate students who are residents of Alabama.

**Eligibility:** Open to residents of Alabama who are attending or planning to attend eligible Alabama institutions (nearly 80 schools participate in this program). Applicants must be able to demonstrate financial need. Eligible students are required to submit the Free Application for Federal Student Aid (FAFSA).

**Financial data:** Stipends range from $300 to $2,500 per academic year.

**Duration:** 1 year; may be renewed.

## 29 ALABAMA STUDENT GRANT PROGRAM

Alabama Commission on Higher Education
Attn: Grants and Scholarships Department
100 North Union Street
P.O. Box 302000
Montgomery, AL 36130-2000
Phone: (334) 242-2274; Fax: (334) 242-0268; Email: wwall@ache.state.al.us
Web: www.ache.state.al.us/StudentAsst/Programs.htm

**Summary:** To provide financial assistance to undergraduates at private colleges or universities in Alabama.

**Eligibility:** Open to undergraduate students who are attending 1 of 14 designated private colleges or universities in Alabama on at least a half-time basis. Alabama residency is required, but financial need is not considered.

**Financial data:** Stipends up to $1,200 per year are available.

**Number awarded:** Varies each year.

**Deadline:** Each participating institution sets its own deadline date.

## 30 ALABAMA 2-YEAR COLLEGE ACADEMIC SCHOLARSHIPS

Alabama Commission on Higher Education
Attn: Grants and Scholarships Department
100 North Union Street
P.O. Box 302000
Montgomery, AL 36130-2000
Phone: (334) 242-2274; Fax: (334) 242-0268; Email: wwall@ache.state.al.us
Web: www.ache.state.al.us/StudentAsst/Programs.htm

**Summary:** To provide financial assistance to entering junior college students in Alabama.

**Eligibility:** Open to students who have been accepted for enrollment at any Alabama public 2-year postsecondary educational institution. Selection is based on academic merit. Preference is given to Alabama residents.

**Financial data:** Scholarships are available to cover the cost of in-state tuition and books.

**Duration:** 1 year; may be renewed if the recipient maintains a high level of academic achievement.

**Number awarded:** Varies each year.

## 31 ALASKA FREE TUITION FOR SPOUSES AND DEPENDENTS OF ARMED SERVICES MEMBERS

Department of Military and Veterans Affairs, Attn: Office of Veterans Affairs
P.O. Box 5800
Fort Richardson, AK 99505-5800
Phone: (907) 428-6016; Fax: (907) 428-6019;
Email: jerry_beale@ak-prepared.com
Web: www.ak-prepared.com/vetaffairs/state_benefits.htm

**Summary:** To provide financial assistance for college to dependents and spouses in Alaska of service members who died, were declared prisoners of war, or were declared missing in action.

**Eligibility:** Open to spouses and dependent children of Alaska residents who died in the line of duty, died of injuries sustained in the line of duty, or were listed by the Department of Defense as a prisoner of war or missing in action. Applicants must be in good standing at a state-supported educational institution in Alaska.

**Financial data:** Those eligible may attend any state-supported educational institution in Alaska without payment of tuition or fees.

**Duration:** 1 year; may be renewed.

**Number awarded:** Varies each year.

## 32 ALASKA LEGION AUXILIARY SCHOLARSHIP

American Legion Auxiliary, Attn: Department of Alaska
Secretary/Treasurer
1392 Sixth Avenue
Fairbanks, AK 99701
Phone: (907) 455-4420; Fax: (907) 474-3040; Email: akaladep@ptialaska.net
Web: www.alada.net
**Summary:** To provide financial assistance for college to veterans' children in Alaska.
**Eligibility:** Open to the children of veterans who served during eligibility dates for membership in the American Legion. Applicants must be between 17 and 24 years of age, high school seniors or graduates who have not yet attended an institution of higher learning, and residents of Alaska.
**Financial data:** The stipend is $1,000, half of which is payable each semester toward tuition, matriculation, laboratory, or similar fees.
**Duration:** 1 year.
**Number awarded:** 1 each year.
**Deadline:** March of each year.

## 33 ALASKA SEA SERVICES SCHOLARSHIPS

Navy League of the United States, Attn: Scholarships
2300 Wilson Boulevard
Arlington, VA 22201-3308
Phone: (703) 528-1775; (800) 356-5760; Fax: (703) 528-2333;
Email: cjarvis@navyleague.org
Web: www.navyleague.org/scholarship
**Summary:** To provide financial assistance for college to spouses and dependent children of naval personnel in Alaska.
**Eligibility:** Open to the spouses and dependent children of active duty, inactive duty, and retired (with or without pay) members of the regular and Reserve Navy, Marine Corps, or Coast Guard who are residents of Alaska. Applicants must be enrolled or planning to enroll full time at an accredited 4-year college or university to work on an undergraduate degree. Selection is based on academic proficiency, character, leadership ability, community involvement, and financial need.
**Financial data:** The stipend is $1,000 per year; funds are paid directly to the academic institution for tuition, books, and fees.
**Duration:** 1 year; may be renewed 1 additional year.
**Number awarded:** Up to 4 each year.
**Deadline:** February of each year.

## 34 ALBERTA E. CROWE STAR OF TOMORROW AWARD

United States Bowling Congress, Attn: SMART Program
5301 South 76th Street
Greendale, WI 53129-1192
Phone: (414) 423-3343; (800) 514-BOWL, ext. 3343; Fax: (414) 421-3014;
Email: smart@bowl.com
Web: www.bowl.com/scholarships/main.aspx
**Summary:** To provide financial assistance for college to outstanding women bowlers.
**Eligibility:** Open to women amateur bowlers who are current members in good standing of the United States Bowling Congress (USBC) or USBC Youth and competitors in events sanctioned by those organizations. Applicants must be high school or college students younger than 22 years of age, have a GPA of 2.5 or higher, and have a bowling average of 175 or greater. They may not have competed in a professional bowling tournament. Along with their application, they must submit an essay, up to 500 words, on how this scholarship will influence their bowling, academic, and personal goals. Selection is based on bowling performances on local, regional, state, and national levels; academic achievement; and extracurricular involvement.
**Financial data:** The stipend is $1,500 per year.
**Duration:** 1 year; may be renewed for 3 additional years.
**Number awarded:** 1 each year.
**Deadline:** September of each year.

## 35 ALFRED H. NOLLE SCHOLARSHIPS

Alpha Chi, Attn: Executive Director
900 East Center
Box 12249 Harding University
Searcy, AR 72149-0001
Phone: (501) 279-4443; (800) 477-4225; Fax: (501) 279-4589;
Email: dorgan@harding.edu
Web: www.harding.edu/alphachi/nolle.htm
**Summary:** To provide financial assistance for college to members of Alpha Chi, a national honor scholarship society.
**Eligibility:** Open to full-time college juniors who have been initiated into Alpha Chi; they must have 1 full year of college left before graduation. Only 1 nomination may be submitted by each chapter. Included in the nomination package must be a sample of the nominee's school work: a paper, painting, music score, film, slides, video, cassette tape recording, or other medium.
**Financial data:** The stipend is $1,500.
**Duration:** 1 year.
**Number awarded:** 10 each year.
**Deadline:** February of each year.

## 36 ALL "A" CLASSIC SCHOLARSHIPS

Touchstone Energy All "A" Classic
c/o Dave Cowden, Chair
Hancock County High School
80 State Route 271 South
Lewisport, KY 42351
Phone: (270) 927-6953; Fax: (270) 927-8677;
Email: dcowden@hancock.k12.ky.us
Web: www.allaclassic.org
**Summary:** To provide financial assistance for college to seniors at small high schools in Kentucky.
**Eligibility:** Open to seniors graduating from high schools in Kentucky that are members or eligible to be a member of the All "A" Classic. Applicants must be planning to attend a public or private college or university, community college, or vocation and technical school in Kentucky. Along with their application, they must submit family financial information, transcripts, SAT and/or ACT scores, and a list of extracurricular activities, honors, awards, and community activities. They must be U.S. citizens or in the process of obtaining citizenship.
**Financial data:** The stipend is $1,000.
**Duration:** 1 year; nonrenewable.
**Number awarded:** Varies each year; recently, 55 of these scholarships were awarded.
**Deadline:** December of each year.

## 37 ALL-INK COLLEGE SCHOLARSHIPS

All-Ink.com
P.O. Box 50868
Provo, UT 84605-0868
Phone: (801) 794-0123; (888) 567-6511; Fax: (801) 794-0124;
Email: scholarship@all-ink.com
Web: www.all-ink.com/scholarship.html
**Summary:** To provide financial assistance for college or graduate school to students who submit a scholarship application online.
**Eligibility:** Open to U.S. citizens and permanent residents who are enrolled or planning to enroll at an accredited college or university at any academic level from freshman through graduate student. Applicants must have a GPA of 2.5 or higher. They must submit, through an online process, an essay of 50 to 200 words on a person who has had a great impact on their life, and another essay of the same length on what they hope to accomplish in their personal and professional life after graduation. Applications are not accepted through the mail.
**Financial data:** Stipends range from $1,000 to $2,000.
**Duration:** 1 year.
**Number awarded:** Varies each year; a total of $10,000 is available for this program each year.
**Deadline:** December of each year.

## 38 ALL-USA ACADEMIC TEAM FOR COMMUNITY COLLEGES

Phi Theta Kappa, Attn: Scholarship Programs Director
1625 Eastover Drive
P.O. Box 13729
Jackson, MS 39236-3729
Phone: (601) 984-3504, ext. 560; (800) 946-9995, ext. 560; Fax: (601) 984-3550;
Email: clancy.mitchell@ptk.org
Web: www.ptk.org
**Summary:** To recognize and reward the outstanding achievements of community college students.
**Eligibility:** Open to students at community, technical, and junior colleges in the United States. They must be nominated by their school, which must be a member of the American Association of Community Colleges (membership

in Phi Theta Kappa is not required). Nominees must have completed at least 12 semester hours in pursuit of an associate's degree and have achieved a cumulative GPA of at least 3.25. Selection is based on awards, honors, and recognition for academic achievement; GPA; participation in honors programs; and service to the college and the community.

**Financial data:** The award is $2,500.

**Duration:** The competition is held annually.

**Number awarded:** 20 each year.

**Deadline:** December of each year.

## 39 ALL-USA COLLEGE ACADEMIC TEAM

USA Today
c/o Carol Skalski
7950 Jones Branch Drive
McLean, VA 22108-9995
Phone: (703) 854-5890; Email: allstars@usatoday.com
Web: allstars.usatoday.com

**Summary:** To recognize and reward outstanding college students in the United States.

**Eligibility:** Open to full-time college or university students at accredited 4-year institutions in the United States. U.S. citizenship is not required. Students must be nominated. Nominees must submit a 500-word essay describing their most outstanding original academic or intellectual product. Selection is based primarily on the students' ability to describe their endeavor in their own words.

**Financial data:** Winners receive $2,500 cash prizes and are guests of *USA Today* at a special awards luncheon.

**Duration:** This competition is held annually.

**Number awarded:** 60 students are chosen for the All-USA Academic Team and receive recognition in *USA Today;* of those, 20 are named to the first team and receive cash prizes.

**Deadline:** November of each year.

## 40 ALL-USA HIGH SCHOOL ACADEMIC TEAM

USA Today
c/o Carol Skalski
7950 Jones Branch Drive
McLean, VA 22108-9995
Phone: (703) 854-5890; Email: allstars@usatoday.com
Web: allstars.usatoday.com

**Summary:** To recognize and reward outstanding high school students in the United States.

**Eligibility:** Open to students graduating from high schools in the United States or its territories, Department of Defense schools overseas, or home-schooled students in the United States. Candidates must be nominated by a teacher or other school official. Nominees must write a 500-word essay describing their most outstanding academic, artistic, or leadership endeavor. Selection is based primarily on the students' ability to describe their outstanding endeavor in their own words.

**Financial data:** Winners receive $2,500 cash prizes and are guests of *USA Today* at a special awards luncheon.

**Duration:** This competition is held annually.

**Number awarded:** 20 students are chosen for the All-USA High School Academic Team and receive recognition in *USA Today.*

**Deadline:** February of each year.

## 41 ALLAN JEROME BURRY SCHOLARSHIP

United Methodist Church
Attn: General Board of Higher Education and Ministry
Office of Loans and Scholarships
1001 19th Avenue South
P.O. Box 340007
Nashville, TN 37203-0007
Phone: (615) 340-7344; Fax: (615) 340-7367; Email: umscholar@gbhem.org
Web: www.gbhem.org

**Summary:** To provide financial assistance to undergraduate students attending schools affiliated with the United Methodist Church.

**Eligibility:** Open to U.S. citizens and permanent residents who have been active, full members of a United Methodist Church for at least 3 years prior to applying. Applicants must be attending a college or university related to the United Methodist Church and be nominated by their campus ministry unit or college chaplain. They must have a GPA of 3.5 or higher and be able to document financial need. Selection is based on academic performance, leadership

skills, and participation in the activities of the Methodist campus ministry or chaplaincy program at their institution.

**Financial data:** The stipend ranges from $500 to $1,200.

**Duration:** 1 year.

**Number awarded:** 1 each year.

**Deadline:** January of each year.

## 42 ALLIANZ SOUTH DAKOTA SCHOLARSHIP PROGRAM

Allianz Global Investors Distributors LLC, Attn: CollegeAccess 529
2187 Atlantic Street
Stamford, CT 06902
Phone: (866) 529-7462
Web: www.collegeaccess529.com/benefits.html

**Summary:** To provide financial assistance to high school seniors in South Dakota who plan to attend a college or university in the state.

**Eligibility:** Open to seniors graduating from high schools in South Dakota who plan to attend a 2-year or 4-year college or university in the state. Applicants must have an ACT score of at least 27 and be on track to complete the Regent Scholar curriculum. Financial need is not considered in the selection process.

**Financial data:** The stipend is $2,000 per year.

**Duration:** 1 year; may be renewed up to 3 additional years, provided the recipient maintains a GPA of 3.0 or higher.

**Number awarded:** 70 each year.

**Deadline:** March of each year.

## 43 ALLIE RANEY HUNT SCHOLARSHIP

Alexander Graham Bell Association for the Deaf
Attn: Financial Aid Coordinator
3417 Volta Place, N.W.
Washington, DC 20007-2778
Phone: (202) 337-5220; Fax: (202) 337-8314; TTY: (202) 337-5221; Email: financialaid@agbell.org
Web: www.agbell.org

**Summary:** To provide financial assistance to undergraduate and graduate students with moderate to profound hearing loss.

**Eligibility:** Open to undergraduate and graduate students who have been diagnosed with a moderate to profound hearing loss prior to acquiring spoken language (hearing loss averages 60dB or greater in the better ear in the speech frequencies of 500, 1000, and 2000 Hz). Applicants must be committed to using spoken language as their primary mode of communication. They must be accepted or enrolled at a mainstream college or university as a full-time student. Along with their application, they must submit a 1-page essay discussing their career goals and how spoken communication is helping them to reach those goals as a person with a hearing loss. Financial need is considered in the selection process. This scholarship is reserved for students who are oral deaf.

**Financial data:** The stipend is $2,000 per year.

**Duration:** 1 year; may be renewed 1 additional year.

**Number awarded:** 1 each year.

**Deadline:** April of each year.

## 44 ALLOGAN SLAGLE MEMORIAL SCHOLARSHIP

Association on American Indian Affairs, Inc., Attn: Scholarship Coordinator
966 Hungerford Drive, Suite 12-B
Rockville, MD 20850
Phone: (240) 314-7155; Fax: (240) 314-7159; Email: lw.aaia@verizon.net
Web: www.indian-affairs.org/alloganslagle.htm

**Summary:** To provide financial assistance for college to Native American students whose tribe is not federally-recognized.

**Eligibility:** Open to American Indian and Native Alaskan full-time undergraduate students. Applicants must be members of tribes that are either state-recognized or that are not federally-recognized but are seeking federal recognition. Along with their application, they must submit documentation of financial need, a Certificate of Indian Blood showing at least one-quarter Indian blood, proof of tribal enrollment, an essay on their educational goals, 2 letters of recommendation, and their most recent transcript. Selection is based on need.

**Financial data:** The stipend is $1,000 per year. Funds are paid directly to accredited educational institutions to be used for tuition, books, and other academic-related expenses.

**Duration:** 1 year; renewable if academic progress is satisfactory.

**Number awarded:** 1 or more each year.

**Deadline:** July of each year.

## 45 ALOHA CHAPTER SCHOLARSHIPS

Military Officers Association of America-Aloha Chapter
Attn: Tak Yoshihara, Scholarship Committee Chair
P.O. Box 19267
Honolulu, HI 96817-8267
Phone: (808) 488-7013; Email: Takyosh@aol.com
Web: www.aloha-moaa.org
**Summary:** To provide financial assistance for college to residents of Hawaii who have a connection to the military.
**Eligibility:** Open to residents of Hawaii who are members of the uniformed services, their spouses and children, members of Military Officers Association of America (MOAA), or their spouses, children, and grandchildren. Applicants must be attending or planning to attend a college or university. Selection is based on scholastic ability, personal qualities, and financial need.
**Financial data:** The stipend is $1,000.
**Duration:** 1 year.
**Number awarded:** 4 each year.
**Deadline:** March of each year.

## 46 AMARANTH FUND AWARDS

California Masonic Foundation, Attn: Scholarship Coordinator
1111 California Street
San Francisco, CA 94108-2284
Phone: (415) 776-7000; (800) 900-2727; Fax: (415) 776-7170;
Email: gloffice@freemason.org
Web: www.freemason.org/programs_scholarship.php
**Summary:** To provide financial assistance to female high school seniors in California who are interested in attending college.
**Eligibility:** Open to graduating female high school seniors who have been residents of California for at least 1 year and have a GPA of 3.0 or higher. Applicants must be planning to attend a 2-year or 4-year institution of higher education in California as a full-time freshman in the following fall. They must be U.S. citizens or permanent residents and able to show evidence of financial need. Along with their application, they must submit a personal essay outlining their background, goals, and scholastic achievements; a copy of their latest high school transcript; 2 letters of recommendation; documentation of financial need; SAT or ACT scores; and a copy of their college acceptance letter. Selection is based on academic achievement, applicant essay, and financial need. Preference is given to women who have a Masonic relationship or are members of Masonic youth groups.
**Financial data:** The amount of the stipend varies, depending on the availability of funds.
**Duration:** 1 year; may be renewed for up to 3 additional years.
**Number awarded:** Varies each year.
**Deadline:** February of each year for new applicants; April of each year for renewal applicants.

## 47 AMELIA KEMP MEMORIAL SCHOLARSHIP

Women of the Evangelical Lutheran Church in America, Attn: Scholarships
8765 West Higgins Road
Chicago, IL 60631-4189
Phone: (773) 380-2730; (800) 638-3522, ext. 2730; Fax: (773) 380-2419;
Email: womenelca@elca.org
Web: www.womenoftheelca.org/whatwedo/scholarships.html
**Summary:** To provide financial assistance to lay women of color who are members of Evangelical Lutheran Church of America (ELCA) congregations and who wish to study on the undergraduate, graduate, professional, or vocational school level.
**Eligibility:** Open to ELCA lay women of color who are at least 21 years of age and have experienced an interruption of at least 2 years in their education since high school. Applicants must have been admitted to an educational institution to prepare for a career in other than a church-certified profession. U.S. citizenship is required.
**Financial data:** The amount of the award varies, depending on the availability of funds.
**Duration:** Up to 2 years.
**Number awarded:** Varies each year, depending upon the funds available.
**Deadline:** February of each year.

## 48 AMERICAN ASSOCIATION OF JAPANESE UNIVERSITY WOMEN SCHOLARSHIP PROGRAM

American Association of Japanese University Women
c/o Ms. Reiko Yamashita, Scholarship Committee Co-Chair
15325 South Menlo Avenue
Gardena, CA 90247-4240
**Summary:** To provide financial assistance to female students currently enrolled in upper-division or graduate classes in California.
**Eligibility:** Open to female students enrolled in accredited colleges or universities in California. They must have junior, senior, or graduate standing. Applicants must be a contributor to U.S.-Japan relations, cultural exchanges, and leadership development in the areas of their designated field of study. To apply, they must submit a current resume, an official transcript of the past 2 years of college work, 2 letters of recommendation, and an essay (up to 2 pages in English or 1,200 characters in Japanese) on 1 of the following topics: 1) what I hope to accomplish in my field of study to develop leadership and role model qualities; or 2) thoughts on how my field of study can contribute to U.S.-Japan relations and benefit international relations.
**Financial data:** The stipend is $1,000.
**Duration:** 1 year.
**Number awarded:** 1 or more each year.
**Deadline:** September of each year.

## 49 AMERICAN BAPTIST UNDERGRADUATE SCHOLARSHIPS

American Baptist Churches USA, Attn: National Ministries
P.O. Box 851
Valley Forge, PA 19482-0851
Phone: (610) 768-2067; (800) ABC-3USA, ext. 2067; Fax: (610) 768-2453;
Email: karen.drummond@abc-usa.org
Web: www.nationalministries.org/financial-aid/student_info.cfm
**Summary:** To provide financial assistance to undergraduate students who are members of American Baptist-related churches.
**Eligibility:** Open to undergraduate students who are full-time students at a college or university in the United States or Puerto Rico. Applicants must be U.S. citizens who have been a member of a church affiliated with American Baptist Churches USA for at least 1 year. Preference is given to students attending a college or university affiliated with American Baptist Churches USA. Students receiving assistance from other American Baptist scholarship programs are not eligible.
**Financial data:** The stipend is $2,000 per year for students at American Baptist colleges and universities or $1,000 per year for students at colleges and universities that are not American Baptist-related. Funds are paid directly to the recipient's school and credited towards tuition.
**Duration:** 1 year; may be renewed if the recipient maintains a GPA of 2.75 or higher.
**Number awarded:** Varies each year.
**Deadline:** May of each year.

## 50 AMERICAN DARTS ORGANIZATION MEMORIAL SCHOLARSHIPS

American Darts Organization
230 North Crescent Way, #K
Anaheim, CA 92801
Phone: (714) 254-0212; Fax: (714) 254-0214
**Summary:** To provide financial aid for college to players in the American Darts Organization (ADO) Youth Playoff Program.
**Eligibility:** Open to ADO members who are U.S. citizens, have lived in the United States for at least 2 years, are area or national winners in the ADO Youth Playoff Program, are under 21 years of age, are enrolled in (or accepted at) an accredited American college on a full-time basis, and have at least a 2.0 GPA.
**Financial data:** Stipends are: $500 for quarter finalists in the National Championship; $750 for each semifinalist; $1,000 for each runner-up; and $1,500 for each National Champion. Any participant/winner who is eligible to compete in more than 1 area/national championship may repeat as a scholarship winner, up to $8,000 in prizes. Funds may be used for any legitimate college expense, including fees for parking stickers, library fees, student union fees, tuition, and books.
**Duration:** The funds are awarded annually.
**Number awarded:** 8 each year: 4 quarter finalists, 2 semifinalists, 1 runner-up, and 1 National Champion.

## 51 AMERICAN FAMILY INSURANCE COMMUNITY INVOLVEMENT SCHOLARSHIP

Wisconsin Foundation for Independent Colleges, Inc., Attn: Program Manager
735 North Water Street, Suite 600
Milwaukee, WI 53202-4100
Phone: (414) 273-5980; Fax: (414) 273-5995; Email: wfic@wficweb.org

Web: www.wficweb.org/documents/schinfo.htm

**Summary:** To provide financial assistance to students from selected states who are enrolled or planning to enroll at member institutions of the Wisconsin Foundation for Independent Colleges (WFIC).

**Eligibility:** Open to students enrolled or planning to enroll at a WFIC member college or university on a full-time basis. Applicants must be residents of Arizona, Colorado, Idaho, Illinois, Indiana, Iowa, Kansas, Minnesota, Missouri, Nebraska, Nevada, North Dakota, Ohio, Oregon, South Dakota, Utah, or Wisconsin. Along with their application, they must submit a 1-page autobiography that includes their future plans, a listing of their campus and community involvement, including time committed to each, a listing of their academic honors and achievements, and a letter of recommendation. Selection is based on academic achievement (GPA of 3.0 or higher or ranking in the top 25% of high school class for entering freshmen), involvement in campus and community, and financial need.

**Financial data:** The stipend is $1,000.

**Duration:** 1 year.

**Number awarded:** 1 or more each year.

**Deadline:** Each participating college sets its own deadline.

## 52 AMERICAN FOREIGN SERVICE ASSOCIATION FINANCIAL AID SCHOLARSHIPS

American Foreign Service Association, Attn: Scholarship Director
2101 E Street, N.W.
Washington, DC 20037
Phone: (202) 944-5504; (800) 704-AFSA; Fax: (202) 338-6820;
Email: dec@afsa.org
Web: www.afsa.org/scholar/index.cfm

**Summary:** To provide financial assistance to undergraduate students who are dependents of U.S. government employees involved in foreign service activities.

**Eligibility:** Open to applicants who are or plan to be full-time undergraduates at an accredited college, postsecondary art school, conservatory, community college, or university in the United States; and tax or legally dependent children of foreign service employees in the Department of State, USIA, Commerce Service, IBB, Foreign Agriculture Service, or Agency for International Development. The parent may be active, retired with pension, or deceased but must have served at least 1 year abroad. Scholarships are established by private donors, as a group or individually; each has its own particular eligibility rules but most require financial need. Some scholarships are limited to students majoring in international affairs.

**Financial data:** Awards range from $1,000 to $3,000 annually.

**Duration:** 1 year; may be renewed if the recipient maintains satisfactory progress.

**Number awarded:** Varies each year; recently, 63 students received scholarships worth $129,500.

**Deadline:** February of each year.

## 53 AMERICAN INDIAN EDUCATION FOUNDATION SCHOLARSHIP PROGRAM

American Indian Education Foundation
10029 S.W. Nimbus Avenue, Suite 200
Beaverton, OR 97008
Phone: (866) 866-8642; Fax: (503) 641-0495; Email: scholarships@nrc1.org
Web: www.aiefprograms.org/scholars/index.html

**Summary:** To provide financial assistance for college to American Indian and Alaskan Native students.

**Eligibility:** Open to full-time students of Native American or Alaskan Native descent who are currently residing on a federally-recognized reservation and attending or planning to attend a 2-year college, a 4-year college or university, or a vocational/technical school. Applicants may be either graduating high school seniors or undergraduates who are entering, continuing, or returning to school and are not high school seniors. They must submit an essay in which they describe themselves as a student, their ultimate career goals, their plans for working in or with the Indian community, and their participation in leadership and/or community service activities. An ACT score of 14 or higher is desirable. Financial need is considered in the selection process. All finalists are considered for the Paul Francis Memorial Scholarship and the Josephine Nipper Memorial Scholarship. Priority for those awards is given to applicants who demonstrate true commitment to bettering their community.

**Financial data:** Freshman scholarships are $3,000 per school year. Undergraduate scholarships are $1,500 per school year. The amounts of the 2 memorial scholarships vary each year.

**Duration:** 1 year; undergraduate scholarships may be renewed.

**Number awarded:** More than 200 each year.

**Deadline:** April of each year.

## 54 AMERICAN INDIAN SERVICES SCHOLARSHIP PROGRAM

American Indian Services
1902 North Canyon Road, Suite 100
Provo, UT 84604
Phone: (801) 375-1777; (888) 227-4120; Fax: (801) 375-1643
Web: www.americanindianservices.org/students.html

**Summary:** To provide financial assistance for college to needy Native Americans.

**Eligibility:** Open to undergraduate students who have completed no more than 150 semester credits at a university, college, junior college, or technical school with a GPA of 2.25 or higher. Applicants must be of at least one-quarter northern Native American Indian blood. Along with their application, they must submit a 1-page letter about themselves, including their tribe and home area, the school they are attending, their area of study, their educational goals and future plans, and why they need this scholarship.

**Financial data:** Students are expected to arrange for payment of half their tuition, and this program pays the other half.

**Duration:** 1 semester; may be renewed if the recipient maintains a GPA of 2.25 or higher.

**Number awarded:** Recently, more than 1,500 of these scholarships were awarded.

**Deadline:** February of each year for classes starting in April or May; January of each year for classes starting in June; August of each year for classes starting in August or September; November of each year for classes starting in January.

## 55 AMERICAN JUNIOR BRAHMAN ASSOCIATION SCHOLARSHIPS

American Brahman Breeders Association, Attn: Youth Activities Director
3003 South Loop West, Suite 140
Houston, TX 77054
Phone: (713) 349-0854; Fax: (713) 349-9795; Email: abba@brahman.org
Web: www.brahman.org

**Summary:** To provide financial assistance for college to members of the American Junior Brahman Association (AJBA).

**Eligibility:** Open to applicants who are active members of AJBA (the youth division of the American Brahman Breeders Association) who are graduating high school seniors. Selection is based on involvement and contribution in AJBA (20 points); involvement and contribution in other agricultural organizations (5 points); involvement in school, civic, and church groups (5 points); experience and knowledge of the livestock industry (5 points); industry leadership potential and goals (20 points); academic achievements (40 points); and general effect (5 points).

**Financial data:** Stipends are $1,000, $500, or $250 per year.

**Duration:** 1 year.

**Number awarded:** Varies each year. Recently, 9 of these scholarships were awarded: 4 at $1,000, 3 at $500, and 2 at $250.

**Deadline:** May of each year.

## 56 AMERICAN LEGACY SCHOLARSHIPS

American Legion, Attn: Americanism and Children & Youth Division
P.O. Box 1055
Indianapolis, IN 46206-1055
Phone: (317) 630-1249; Fax: (317) 630-1223; Email: acy@legion.org
Web: www.legion.org

**Summary:** To provide financial assistance for college to children of U.S. military personnel killed on active duty on or after September 11, 2001.

**Eligibility:** Open to the children (including adopted children and stepchildren) of active-duty U.S. military personnel (including federalized National Guard and Reserve members) who died on active duty on or after September 11, 2001. Applicants must be high school seniors or graduates planning to enroll full time at an accredited institution of higher education in the United States. Selection is based on academic achievement, school and community activities, leadership skills, and financial need.

**Financial data:** The stipend depends on the availability of funds.

**Duration:** 1 year; may be renewed.

**Number awarded:** Varies each year.

**Deadline:** April of each year.

## 57 AMERICAN LEGION AUXILIARY DEPARTMENT OF ARKANSAS ACADEMIC SCHOLARSHIP

American Legion Auxiliary
Department of Arkansas, Attn: Department Secretary
1415 West Seventh Street

Little Rock, AR 72201-2903
Phone: (501) 374-5836; Email: arkaux@juno.com
**Summary:** To provide financial assistance for college to children of veterans who are residents of Arkansas.
**Eligibility:** Open to the children of veterans in Arkansas who served during eligibility dates for membership in the American Legion. Both the student and the parent must be residents of Arkansas. The student must be a high school senior or graduate who has not yet attended an institution of higher learning. Selection is based on character (15%), Americanism (15%), leadership (15%), financial need (15%), and scholarship (40%).
**Financial data:** The stipend is $1,000; funds are paid in 2 equal installments.
**Duration:** 1 year.
**Number awarded:** 1 each year.
**Deadline:** February of each year.

## 58 AMERICAN LEGION AUXILIARY NATIONAL PRESIDENT'S SCHOLARSHIP

American Legion Auxiliary
777 North Meridian Street, Third Floor
Indianapolis, IN 46204-1189
Phone: (317) 955-3845; Fax: (317) 955-3884; Email: alahq@legion-aux.org
Web: www.legion-aux.org/scholarships/docs/natlpressch.htm
**Summary:** To provide financial assistance for college to the children of war veterans.
**Eligibility:** Open to children of veterans who served in World War I, World War II, Korea, Vietnam, Grenada, Lebanon, Panama, or the Persian Gulf. Applicants must be high school seniors who have completed at least 50 hours of volunteer service within the community. Each Department (state) organization of the American Legion Auxiliary nominates 1 candidate for the National President's Scholarship annually. Nominees must submit a 1,000-word essay on a topic that changes annually; recently, students were asked to write on "My Role in Sustaining Our Freedoms." Selection is based on the essay (20%), character and leadership (20%), scholarship, (40%), and financial need (20%).
**Financial data:** Stipends are $2,500, $2,000, or $1,000. Funds are paid directly to the recipient's school.
**Duration:** 1 year; recipients may not reapply.
**Number awarded:** 15 each year: in each of the 5 divisions of the Auxiliary, 1 scholarship at $2,500, 1 at $2,000, and 1 at $1,000 are awarded.
**Deadline:** March of each year.

## 59 AMERICAN LEGION AUXILIARY NON-TRADITIONAL STUDENT SCHOLARSHIPS

American Legion Auxiliary
777 North Meridian Street, Third Floor
Indianapolis, IN 46204-1189
Phone: (317) 955-3845; Fax: (317) 955-3884; Email: alahq@legion-aux.org
Web: www.legion-aux.org/scholarships/docs/nontradsch.htm
**Summary:** To provide financial assistance for college to nontraditional students affiliated with the American Legion.
**Eligibility:** Open to members of the American Legion, American Legion Auxiliary, or Sons of the American Legion who have paid dues for the 2 preceding years and the calendar year in which application is being made. Applicants must be 1) nontraditional students returning to school after some period of time during which their formal education was interrupted or 2) students who have had at least 1 year of college and are working on an undergraduate degree. Along with their application, they must submit a statement explaining why they are entering college at this time, why their education was interrupted, and why they feel they should be selected for this scholarship. Selection is based on scholastic standing and academic achievement (25%), character and leadership (25%), initiative and goals (25%), and financial need (25%).
**Financial data:** The scholarship is $1,000 per year, paid directly to the school.
**Duration:** 1 year.
**Number awarded:** 5 each year: 1 in each division of the American Legion Auxiliary.
**Deadline:** Applications must be submitted to the unit president by March.

## 60 AMERICAN LEGION BASEBALL SCHOLARSHIP

American Legion Baseball
700 North Pennsylvania Street
Indianapolis, IN 46204
Phone: (317) 630-1249; Fax: (317) 630-1223; Email: acy@legion.org
Web: www.baseball.legion.org/awards.htm

**Summary:** To recognize and reward outstanding participants in the American Legion baseball program.
**Eligibility:** Open to participants in the American Legion baseball program who are high school graduates or college freshmen; students still in high school are not eligible. In each of the 50 states and Puerto Rico, candidates may be nominated by a team manager or head coach. The department baseball committee selects a player who demonstrates outstanding leadership, citizenship, character, scholarship, and financial need.
**Financial data:** The award is a $1,000 scholarship. Funds are disbursed jointly to the winner and the school.
**Duration:** Students have 8 years to utilize the scholarship funds from the date of the award, excluding any time spent on active military duty.
**Number awarded:** 51 each year: 1 in each state and Puerto Rico.
**Deadline:** July of each year.

## 61 AMERICAN LEGION JUNIOR AIR RIFLE NATIONAL CHAMPIONSHIP SCHOLARSHIPS

American Legion, Attn: Americanism and Children & Youth Division
P.O. Box 1055
Indianapolis, IN 46206-1055
Phone: (317) 630-1249; Fax: (317) 630-1223; Email: acy@legion.org
Web: www.legion.org
**Summary:** To provide college scholarships to the top competitors in the American Legion Junior Position Air Rifle Tournament.
**Eligibility:** Open to students between the ages of 14 and 20 who compete in air rifle tournaments sponsored by local posts of the American Legion. Based on posted scores in the precision and sporter categories, the top 30 competitors and state and regional champions compete in a qualification round, also a postal tournament. The top 15 shooters then participate in a shoulder-to-shoulder match in August at the Olympic Training Center, Colorado Springs, Colorado.
**Financial data:** The awards are $1,000 college scholarships.
**Duration:** The awards are presented annually.
**Number awarded:** 2 each year: 1 in the precision category and 1 in the sporter category.

## 62 AMERICAN MILITARY SPOUSE EDUCATION FOUNDATION SCHOLARSHIPS

American Military Spouse Education Foundation
9912 Great Oaks Way
Fairfax, VA 22030
Phone: (703) 591-8444; Fax: (703) 591-8333; Email: garybottorff@aol.com
Web: www.americanmilitaryspouse.org/scholarship/scholarship.asp
**Summary:** To provide financial assistance for undergraduate study to spouses of military personnel.
**Eligibility:** Open to spouses of U.S. uniformed military service members (active-duty, Reserve, National Guard, and retired). Applicants must be enrolled in an undergraduate degree program. Spouses who are also uniformed military service members are ineligible. Within each category of military service (active-duty, Reserve, National Guard, retired), applicants with the lowest rank receive the highest priority. Ties are broken by date of rank. Special consideration is given to spouses whose military member was 1) killed while serving on active duty, or 2) wounded while serving on active duty and has received a disability rating of 50% or higher.
**Financial data:** Stipends range up to $3,000 per year.
**Duration:** 1 year; may be renewed.
**Number awarded:** Varies each year.
**Deadline:** Applications may be submitted at any time.

## 63 AMERICAN PATRIOT SCHOLARSHIPS

Military Officers Association of America
Attn: Educational Assistance Program
201 North Washington Street
Alexandria, VA 22314-2539
Phone: (703) 549-2311; (800) 234-MOAA; Email: edassist@moaa.org
Web: www.moaa.org
**Summary:** To provide financial assistance for undergraduate education to children of members of the uniformed services who have died.
**Eligibility:** Open to children under 24 years of age of active, Reserve, and National Guard uniformed service personnel (Army, Navy, Air Force, Marines, Coast Guard, Public Health Service, or National Oceanographic

and Atmospheric Administration) whose parent has died on active service. Applicants must be working on an undergraduate degree.

**Financial data:** The stipend is $2,500 per year.

**Duration:** 1 year.

**Number awarded:** Varies each year, depending on the availability of funds.

**Deadline:** February of each year.

## 64 AMERICAN QUARTER HORSE FOUNDATION YOUTH SCHOLARSHIPS

American Quarter Horse Foundation, Attn: Scholarship Coordinator
2601 I-40 East
Amarillo, TX 79104
Phone: (806) 376-5181; (888) 209-8322; Fax: (806) 376-1005;
Email: lowens@aqha.org
Web: www.aqha.com/foundation/scholarships/index.html

**Summary:** To provide financial assistance for college to members of the American Quarter Horse Youth Association (AQHYA).

**Eligibility:** Open to members in good standing for at least 3 years who are high school seniors or entering college freshmen. They must have ranked in the upper 25% of their high school graduating class and be able to demonstrate financial need. All majors in college are eligible.

**Financial data:** The stipend is $2,000 per year.

**Duration:** Up to 4 years.

**Number awarded:** Varies each year; recently, 30 of these scholarships were awarded.

**Deadline:** January of each year.

## 65 AMERICAN RADIO RELAY LEAGUE GENERAL FUND SCHOLARSHIPS

American Radio Relay League, Attn: ARRL Foundation
225 Main Street
Newington, CT 06111
Phone: (860) 594-0397; Fax: (860) 594-0259; Email: foundation@arrl.org
Web: www.arrl.org/arrlf

**Summary:** To provide financial assistance to licensed radio amateurs who are interested in working on an undergraduate or graduate degree.

**Eligibility:** Open to undergraduate or graduate students at accredited institutions in any subject area who are licensed radio amateurs (any class). Applicants must submit an essay on the role amateur radio has played in their lives and provide documentation of financial need.

**Financial data:** The stipend is $1,000.

**Duration:** 1 year.

**Number awarded:** Varies each year; recently, 4 of these scholarships were awarded.

**Deadline:** January of each year.

## 66 AMERICAN WATER SKI EDUCATIONAL FOUNDATION SCHOLARSHIPS

American Water Ski Educational Foundation, Attn: Director
1251 Holy Cow Road
Polk City, FL 33868-8200
Phone: (863) 324-2472; Fax: (863) 324-3996; Email: awsefhalloffame@cs.com
Web: www.waterskihalloffame.com

**Summary:** To provide financial assistance to currently-enrolled college students who participate in water skiing.

**Eligibility:** Open to full-time students at 2-year or 4-year accredited colleges. Applicants must have completed at least their freshmen year and be active members of a sport division within USA Water Ski (AWSA, ABC, AKA, WSDA, NSSA, NCWSA, NWSRA, and AWA). U.S. citizenship is required. Along with their application, they must submit a 500-word essay on a topic that changes annually but relates to water skiing; recently, the topic was, "How can USA Water Ski create tournaments so that the competing is more enjoyable and more fun for the athletes participating?" Selection is based on the essay, academic record, leadership, extracurricular involvement, letters of recommendation, AWSA membership activities, and financial need.

**Financial data:** The stipend is $1,500 per year.

**Duration:** 1 year; may be renewed for up to 2 additional years.

**Number awarded:** 6 each year.

**Deadline:** March of each year.

## 67 AMVETS NATIONAL SCHOLARSHIPS FOR ENTERING COLLEGE FRESHMEN

AMVETS National Headquarters, Attn: Scholarships
4647 Forbes Boulevard
Lanham, MD 20706-3807
Phone: (301) 459-9600; (877) 7-AMVETS, ext. 3043; Fax: (301) 459-7924;
Email: amvets@amvets.org
Web: www.amvets.org

**Summary:** To provide financial assistance to the children and grandchildren of members of AMVETS who are entering college.

**Eligibility:** Open to graduating high school seniors who are the children or grandchildren of an AMVETS member or of a deceased veteran who would have been eligible to be an AMVETS member. U.S. citizenship is required. Selection is based on financial need, academic promise (GPA of 3.0 or higher), involvement in extracurricular activities, and an essay of 50 to 100 words on "What a Higher Education Means to Me."

**Financial data:** The stipend is $1,000 per year.

**Duration:** 4 years (provided the recipient maintains a GPA of 2.0 or higher).

**Number awarded:** 6 each year (1 in each AMVETS national district).

**Deadline:** April of each year.

## 68 AMVETS NATIONAL SCHOLARSHIPS FOR VETERANS

AMVETS National Headquarters, Attn: Scholarships
4647 Forbes Boulevard
Lanham, MD 20706-3807
Phone: (301) 459-9600; (877) 7-AMVETS, ext. 3043; Fax: (301) 459-7924;
Email: amvets@amvets.org
Web: www.amvets.org

**Summary:** To provide financial assistance for college or graduate school to certain veterans who are members of AMVETS.

**Eligibility:** Open to AMVETS members who are veterans and U.S. citizens. Applicants must be interested in working full time on an undergraduate degree, graduate degree, or certification from an accredited technical/trade school. Selection is based on financial need, academic promise, military duty and awards, volunteer activities, community services, jobs held during the past 4 years, and an essay of 50 to 100 words on "What a Higher Education Means to Me."

**Financial data:** The stipend is $1,000 per year.

**Duration:** Up to 4 years.

**Number awarded:** 3 each year.

**Deadline:** April of each year.

## 69 ANCHOR SCHOLARSHIP FOUNDATION AWARD

Anchor Scholarship Foundation
P.O. Box 9535
Norfolk, VA 23505
Phone: (757) 374-3769; Email: cnslschf@erols.com
Web: www.anchorscholarship.com

**Summary:** To provide financial assistance for college to dependents of active-duty or retired personnel serving in the Naval Surface Forces.

**Eligibility:** Open to dependents of active-duty or retired personnel who have served at least 6 years (need not be consecutive) in a unit under the administrative control of Commanders, Naval Surface Forces, U.S. Atlantic Fleet, or U.S. Pacific Fleet. Applicants must be attending or planning to attend an accredited 4-year college or university to work on a bachelor's degree as a full-time student. Selection is based on academic proficiency, extracurricular activities, character, all-around ability, and financial need.

**Financial data:** Stipends range up to $2,000.

**Duration:** 1 year; may be renewed.

**Number awarded:** Varies each year; recently, 35 of these scholarships, worth $60,000, were awarded.

**Deadline:** March of each year.

## 70 ANDRE SOBEL AWARD

Andre Sobel River of Life Foundation, Attn: Awards
8899 Beverly Boulevard, Suite 111
Los Angeles, CA 90048
Phone: (310) 276-7111; Fax: (310) 276-0244; Email: info@andreriveroflife.org
Web: www.andreriveroflife.org

**Summary:** To recognize and reward young cancer survivors who submit outstanding essays on their illness.

**Eligibility:** Open to cancer survivors under 21 years of age. Applicants are allowed to define themselves as a survivor; no medical definition or certain amount of time is required. They must submit an essay, up to 1,500 words in length, on a topic that changes annually but relates to their illness. Recently, applicants were invited to write on "The Letter I Would Like to Have Received From My Best Friend During My Illness."

**Financial data:** First prize is $5,000. Other cash prizes are awarded to second-through fifth-place winners.

**Duration:** The competition is held annually.

**Number awarded:** 5 cash prizes are awarded each year.

**Deadline:** June of each year.

---

## 71 ANGELFIRE SCHOLARSHIP

Datatel Scholars Foundation
4375 Fair Lakes Court
Fairfax, VA 22033
Phone: (703) 968-9000, ext. 4549; (800) 486-4332; Fax: (703) 968-4573;
Email: scholars@datatel.com
Web: www.datatel.com

**Summary:** To provide financial assistance to graduating high school seniors, continuing college students, and graduate students who will be studying at a Datatel client school and are veterans, veterans' dependents, or refugees from southeast Asia.

**Eligibility:** Open to 1) veterans who served in the Asian theater (Vietnam, Cambodia, or Laos) between 1964 and 1975; 2) their spouses and children; 3) refugees from Vietnam, Cambodia, or Laos; and 4) veterans who served in Operation Desert Storm, Operation Enduring Freedom, and/or Operation Iraqi Freedom. Applicants must attend a Datatel client college or university during the upcoming school year. They must first apply to their institution, which selects 2 semifinalists and forwards their applications to the sponsor. Along with the application, they must include a 1,000-word personal statement that discusses how the conflict has affected them and their educational goals, and describes how this scholarship will help them achieve their goals. Selection is based on the quality of the personal statement (40%), academic merit (30%), achievements and civic involvement (20%), and 2 letters of recommendation (10%).

**Financial data:** Stipends are $2,400, $1,600, or $1,000, depending upon the cost of undergraduate tuition at the participating institution. Funds are paid directly to the institution.

**Duration:** 1 year.

**Number awarded:** Varies each year. Recently, 10 of these scholarships were awarded: 7 at $2,400, 2 at $1,600, and 1 at $1,000.

**Deadline:** Students must submit online applications to their institution or organization by January of each year.

---

## 72 ANGUS FOUNDATION SCHOLARSHIPS

National Junior Angus Association, Attn: Director Junior Activities
3201 Frederick Boulevard
St. Joseph, MO 64506
Phone: (816) 383-5100; Fax: (816) 233-9703; Email: jfisher@angus.org
Web: www.njaa.info/awards.html

**Summary:** To provide financial assistance to students who have been members of the National Junior Angus Association (NJAA) and are enrolled or planning to enroll in any field in college.

**Eligibility:** Open to applicants who 1) are and have been a member of the NJAA and 2) are currently a junior, regular, or life member of the American Angus Association. They must be either a high school senior or already enrolled in college working full time on an undergraduate degree and younger than 25 years of age. All fields of study are eligible. Selection is based on involvement in Angus associations, other agriculture-related associations, school organizations, and church, civic, and community groups.

**Financial data:** The stipends are $3,500 or $1,000.

**Duration:** 1 year. Recipients of the $1,000 awards may reapply for 1 additional year; recipients of the $3,500 awards may not reapply.

**Number awarded:** 20 each year: 2 at $3,500 and 18 at $1,000.

**Deadline:** May of each year.

---

## 73 ANNE AND MATT HARBISON SCHOLARSHIP

P. Buckley Moss Society
20 Stoneridge Drive, Suite 102
Waynesboro, VA 22980
Phone: (540) 943-5678; Fax: (540) 949-8408; Email: society@mosssociety.org
Web: www.mosssociety.org

**Summary:** To provide financial assistance for college to high school seniors with language-related learning disabilities.

**Eligibility:** Open to high school seniors with language-related learning disabilities. Nominations may be submitted by society members only. The nomination packet must include verification of a language-related learning disability from a counselor or case manager, a high school transcript, 2 letters of recommendation, and 4 essays by the nominees (on themselves; their learning disability and its effect on their lives; their extracurricular, community, work, and church accomplishments; and their plans for next year).

**Financial data:** The stipend is $1,000. Funds are paid to the recipient's college or university.

**Duration:** 1 year; may be renewed for up to 3 additional years.

**Number awarded:** 1 each year.

**Deadline:** March of each year.

---

## 74 ANNE FORD SCHOLARSHIP

National Center for Learning Disabilities, Attn: Scholarship
381 Park Avenue South, Suite 1401
New York, NY 10016-8806
Phone: (212) 545-7510; Fax: (212) 545-9665; Email: AFScholarship@ncld.org
Web: www.ld.org/awards/afscholarinfo.cfm

**Summary:** To provide financial assistance for college to high school seniors with learning disabilities.

**Eligibility:** Open to high school seniors with learning disabilities who plan to work on a university degree. Applicants must have a GPA of 3.0 or higher and be able to demonstrate financial need. Along with their application, they must submit an essay (750 to 1,000 words in length) describing their frustrations and triumphs in dealing with their specific learning disability. Their essay should also include the characteristics they possess that make them an ideal candidate for this scholarship and should make specific mention of how they believe a college education will enhance their lives. If they prefer, they may submit a video or audiotape (up to 15 minutes in length) with accompanying script or outline that presents the same information as the essay. Other required submissions include high school transcripts, 3 letters of recommendation, a financial statement, standardized test (SAT, ACT) scores, and current documentation of a learning disability that includes evaluation reports, I.E.P., and/or 504 plan. U.S. citizenship is required.

**Financial data:** The stipend is $2,500 per year.

**Duration:** 4 years, provided the recipients submit annual reports (written or in video format) detailing their progress in school and describing their insights about their personal growth.

**Number awarded:** 1 each year.

**Deadline:** December of each year.

---

## 75 ANNUAL ZEB SCHOLARSHIP

United States Bowling Congress, Attn: SMART Program
5301 South 76th Street
Greendale, WI 53129-1192
Phone: (414) 423-3223; (800) 514-BOWL, ext. 3223; Fax: (414) 421-3014;
Email: smart@bowl.com
Web: www.bowl.com/scholarships/main.aspx

**Summary:** To recognize and reward, with college scholarships, young bowlers who demonstrate outstanding community service.

**Eligibility:** Open to United States Bowling Congress (USBC) Youth members in their junior or senior year of high school. Applicants must have a GPA of 2.0 or higher and not have competed in a professional bowling tournament. Along with their application, they must submit an essay of 500 words on a topic of their choosing. Selection is based on the essay, grades, letters of reference, and academic and community involvement.

**Financial data:** The award consists of a $2,500 college scholarship.

**Duration:** The award is presented annually.

**Number awarded:** 1 each year.

**Deadline:** March of each year.

---

## 76 APHA YOUTH DEVELOPMENT FOUNDATION SCHOLARSHIPS

American Paint Horse Association, Attn: Director of Youth Activities
2800 Meacham Boulevard
P.O. Box 961023
Fort Worth, TX 76161-0023
Phone: (817) 834-APHA, ext. 248; Fax: (817) 834-3152;
Email: rstotler@apha.com
Web: www.apha.com/ydf/index.html

**Summary:** To provide financial assistance for college to members of the American Paint Horse Association (APHA).

**Eligibility:** Open to members in good standing (regular or junior) of the association involved in horse activity using a paint horse or contributing actively to a regional club for at least a year prior to and at the time of application. They must be high school graduates who have never been married and are applying within 1 year of the date of high school graduation. A 3.0 minimum GPA is required. Selection is based on 1) scholastic record, including a 500-word essay on educational plans and goals (15%); 2) APHA club activities (25%); 3) APHA horse activities (25%); 4) extracurricular activities (20%); and 5) 3 letters of recommendation (15%).

**Financial data:** The stipend is $1,000 per year. Funds are paid directly to the recipient's school.

**Duration:** 1 year; may be renewed for up to 4 additional years if the recipient maintains full-time enrollment and a GPA of 3.0 or higher.

**Number awarded:** Varies each year; recently, 32 of these scholarships (7 new and 25 renewal) were awarded.

**Deadline:** February of each year.

## 77 AQHF WORKING STUDENT SCHOLARSHIP

American Quarter Horse Foundation, Attn: Scholarship Coordinator
2601 I-40 East
Amarillo, TX 79104
Phone: (806) 376-5181; (888) 209-8322; Fax: (806) 376-1005;
Email: lowens@aqha.org
Web: www.aqha.com/foundation/scholarships/index.html

**Summary:** To provide financial assistance for college to members of the American Quarter Horse Association (AQHA) or the American Quarter Horse Youth Association (AQHYA) who are working while they attend college.

**Eligibility:** Open to applicants who have been members of either organization for at least 1 year and are graduating high school seniors or already enrolled in college. They must have a GPA of 2.5 or higher and be working or planning to work at least 200 hours per school year. Financial need is considered in the selection process.

**Financial data:** The maximum stipend is $3,125 per year.

**Duration:** Up to 4 years, provided the recipient maintains a GPA of 3.0 or higher and full-time enrollment.

**Number awarded:** 1 each year.

**Deadline:** January of each year.

## 78 AQUATROLS ESSAY CONTEST

Aquatrols Corporation
1273 Imperial Way
Paulsboro, NJ 08066
Phone: (856) 537-6003; (800) 257-7797; Fax: (856) 537-6018;
Email: essay.contest@aquatrols.com
Web: www.aquatrols.com

**Summary:** To recognize and reward, with college scholarships, students whose parents are employed in a turf or landscape management capacity and who submit outstanding essays on a related subject.

**Eligibility:** Open to children of employees in a turf or landscape management capacity. Applicants must be enrolled or planning to enroll in an undergraduate program. They must submit an original essay of 1,500 to 2,000 words on a topic that changes annually. Recently, students were invited to write on "The role of surfactants in enhancing water use and/or irrigation efficiency." Essays should be original, compelling, well-organized, readable, persuasive, and creative. Technical accuracy, composition skills, and adherence to contest rules are also considered.

**Financial data:** First prize is a $2,000 scholarship and second prize is a $1,000 scholarship.

**Duration:** The contest is held annually.

**Number awarded:** 2 each year.

**Deadline:** February of each year.

## 79 ARABIAN HORSE FOUNDATION REGIONAL SCHOLARSHIPS

Arabian Horse Foundation, Attn: Scholarship Office
Ten Farnham Park Drive
Houston, TX 77024-7501
Phone: (713) 952-7081; Fax: (713) 977-9883;
Email: jean@parkwaychevrolet.com
Web: pages.sbcglobal.net/jvenhaus/horse/Scholar/scholar.html

**Summary:** To provide financial assistance to undergraduate and graduate students who have a record of equine involvement.

**Eligibility:** Open to students who have a record of involvement with horses. Applicants must be enrolled or planning to enroll as a full-time undergraduate or graduate student at an accredited college or university. High school seniors must have a GPA of B average or higher; college students must have at least a 3.5 GPA. Along with their application, they must submit information on their financial need, honors or academic awards, extracurricular activities and offices, leadership role, career goal, and equine involvement for the past 2 years.

**Financial data:** A stipend is awarded (amount not specified).

**Duration:** 1 year; may be renewed if the recipient maintains of GPA of 2.5 or higher with no grade below a D.

**Number awarded:** 18 each year: 1 in each region of the Arabian Horse Association.

**Deadline:** January of each year.

## 80 ARBY'S BIG BROTHERS BIG SISTERS SCHOLARSHIP AWARD

Big Brothers Big Sisters of America, Attn: Scholarship
230 North 13th Street
Philadelphia, PA 19107-1538
Phone: (215) 567-7000; Fax: (215) 567-0394
Web: www.bbbsa.org

**Summary:** To provide financial assistance for college to students who have participated in the Big Brothers Big Sisters program as matched Little Brothers or Little Sisters.

**Eligibility:** Open to participants who have been Little Brothers or Little Sisters in an affiliated Big Brothers Big Sisters program for at least 1 year. The match need not be current. Nominees may be presently enrolled or accepted at an accredited college or university. They must submit an essay on their past experiences, present efforts, and future dreams as related to their life experiences and association with Big Brothers Big Sisters. Selection is based on the applicant's vision for the future as revealed in the essay, academic achievement, volunteer work, community involvement, extracurricular activities, and financial need.

**Financial data:** The stipends are $5,000 or $1,000 per year.

**Duration:** 1 year; the $1,000 scholarships are nonrenewable; the $5,000 scholarships may be renewed for up to 3 additional years.

**Number awarded:** 12 each year: 2 at $5,000 and 10 at $1,000.

**Deadline:** March of each year.

## 81 ARIZONA CHAPTER MOAA EDUCATIONAL SCHOLARSHIPS

Military Officers Association of America-Arizona Chapter
Attn: Daniel Conway, President
14435 North 66th Place
Scottsdale, AZ 85254
Phone: (480) 368-1427; Email: arizconway@msn.com
Web: www.azchaptermoaa.org/awards_scholarship/awards_&_scholarships.htm

**Summary:** To provide financial assistance for college to high school seniors in Arizona who have participated in the Junior ROTC program.

**Eligibility:** Open to seniors at high schools in Arizona who have participated in the JROTC program. Applicants must rank in the upper half of their class and be able to demonstrate qualities of leadership, moral character, and concern for their fellow man through service to others.

**Financial data:** The stipend is $1,000.

**Duration:** 1 year.

**Number awarded:** Varies each year; recently, 5 of these scholarships were awarded.

## 82 ARIZONA KIDS' CHANCE SCHOLARSHIPS

Kids' Chance of Arizona
P.O. Box 36753
Phoenix, AZ 85067-6753
Phone: (602) 253-4360
Web: www.kidschance.org/Arizona/arizona.html

**Summary:** To provide financial assistance for college to Arizona residents whose parent was killed or permanently disabled in an employment-related accident.

**Eligibility:** Open to Arizona residents between 16 and 25 years of age whose parent was killed or disabled in an employment-related accident. Applicants must be attending or planning to attend a college, university, or trade school.

They must submit high school transcripts, letters of recommendation, verification of school attendance, and a 1-page letter explaining their educational goals and need for financial assistance.

**Financial data:** A stipend is awarded (amount not specified).

**Duration:** 1 year; may be renewed.

**Number awarded:** Varies each year; since the program was established, it has awarded 54 scholarships worth $104,545.

---

### 83 ARIZONA LEVERAGING EDUCATIONAL ASSISTANCE PARTNERSHIP GRANTS

Arizona Commission for Postsecondary Education
2020 North Central Avenue, Suite 550
Phoenix, AZ 85004-4503
Phone: (602) 258-2435; Fax: (602) 258-2483; Email: toni@azhighered.org
Web: www.azhighered.org

**Summary:** To provide financial assistance to undergraduate and graduate students in Arizona who can demonstrate financial need.

**Eligibility:** Open to Arizona residents who are attending or planning to attend a participating Arizona postsecondary educational institution as either a full-time or part-time undergraduate or graduate student. Applicants must be able to demonstrate financial need.

**Financial data:** Awards range from $100 to $2,500 per year.

**Duration:** 1 year; may be renewed.

**Number awarded:** Varies each year.

**Deadline:** Each participating institution in Arizona sets its own deadline.

---

### 84 ARIZONA PRIVATE POSTSECONDARY EDUCATION STUDENT FINANCIAL ASSISTANCE PROGRAM

Arizona Commission for Postsecondary Education
2020 North Central Avenue, Suite 550
Phoenix, AZ 85004-4503
Phone: (602) 258-2435; Fax: (602) 258-2483; Email: toni@azhighered.org
Web: www.azhighered.org

**Summary:** To provide financial assistance to graduates of Arizona community colleges who wish to attend a private postsecondary institution in the state.

**Eligibility:** Open to students who have graduated or are about to graduate from a public community college in Arizona with an associate's degree. Applicants must be planning to attend a private baccalaureate degree-granting institution in Arizona and be enrolled in a bachelor's degree program on a full-time basis. They must be able to demonstrate financial need.

**Financial data:** The award is $1,500 per year. Participants must agree when they accept the award to repay the full amount if they do not graduate with their bachelor's degree within 3 years of the initial receipt of the award.

**Duration:** 2 years.

**Number awarded:** Varies; grants are awarded on a priority of receipt basis.

**Deadline:** Applications are accepted throughout the year to accommodate the various enrollment periods for the different private postsecondary institutions.

---

### 85 ARKANSAS ACADEMIC CHALLENGE SCHOLARSHIP

Arkansas Department of Higher Education, Attn: Financial Aid Division
114 East Capitol Avenue
Little Rock, AR 72201-3818
Phone: (501) 371-2050; (800) 54-STUDY; Fax: (501) 371-2001;
Email: finaid@adhe.arknet.edu
Web: www.arkansashighered.com/challenge.html

**Summary:** To provide financial assistance to undergraduate students in Arkansas.

**Eligibility:** Open to Arkansas residents who are graduating high school seniors, are planning to attend an approved Arkansas 2- or 4-year public or private college or university, and can demonstrate financial need. The maximum family income is $60,000 for a family with 1 dependent child; it increases $5,000 for each additional dependent child and another $10,000 for each additional dependent child in college full time. Eligibility depends on a correlation between ACT scores, GPA, and whether the applicant wishes to attend a 2-year or a 4-year institution. Students with an ACT score of 15 to 18 must have a GPA of 3.25 or higher if they wish to attend a 4-year school or 3.0 for a 2-year school. Students with an ACT score of 19 must have a GPA of 3.0 or higher if they wish to attend a 4-year school or 2.75 for a 2-year school. Students with an ACT score of 20 to 24 must have a GPA of 2.75 or higher if they wish to attend a 4-year school or 2.5 for a 2-year school. Students with an ACT score of 25 to 36 must have a GPA of 2.5 or higher if they wish to attend a 4-year school or 2.25 for a 2-year school.

**Financial data:** The maximum stipend is $3,500 per year.

**Duration:** 1 year; may be renewed up to 3 additional years if the recipient maintains full-time enrollment and a GPA of 2.75 or higher.

**Number awarded:** Varies each year; recently, 8,728 of these scholarships were awarded.

**Deadline:** May of each year.

---

### 86 ARKANSAS GOVERNOR'S DISTINGUISHED SCHOLARS PROGRAM

Arkansas Department of Higher Education, Attn: Financial Aid Division
114 East Capitol Avenue
Little Rock, AR 72201-3818
Phone: (501) 371-2050; (800) 54-STUDY; Fax: (501) 371-2001;
Email: finaid@adhe.arknet.edu
Web: www.arkansashighered.com/governorscholars.html

**Summary:** To provide financial assistance to exceptional high school seniors in Arkansas.

**Eligibility:** Open to high school seniors who are U.S. citizens or permanent residents, are residents of Arkansas, can demonstrate leadership, and are planning to enroll in a college or university in Arkansas. Applicants must have an ACT score of 32 or higher (or the equivalent on the SAT), be a National Merit Finalist or a National Achievement Scholar, or have a GPA of 3.5 or higher. Selection is based on high school GPA, class rank, ACT or SAT score, school leadership, and community leadership.

**Financial data:** Stipends up to $10,000 per year are provided.

**Duration:** 1 year; may be renewed for up to 3 additional years provided the recipient maintains a cumulative GPA of 3.25 or higher and completes at least 30 semester hours each year.

**Number awarded:** Up to 250 each year.

**Deadline:** January of each year.

---

### 87 ARKANSAS GOVERNOR'S SCHOLARS PROGRAM

Arkansas Department of Higher Education, Attn: Financial Aid Division
114 East Capitol Avenue
Little Rock, AR 72201-3818
Phone: (501) 371-2050; (800) 54-STUDY; Fax: (501) 371-2001;
Email: finaid@adhe.arknet.edu
Web: www.arkansashighered.com/governorscholars.html

**Summary:** To provide financial assistance to outstanding high school seniors in Arkansas.

**Eligibility:** Open to high school seniors who are U.S. citizens or permanent residents, are residents of Arkansas, can demonstrate leadership, and are planning to enroll in a college or university in the state. Applicants must have an ACT score of 27 or higher (or the equivalent on the SAT), or a GPA of 3.5 or higher in academic courses. Selection is based on high school GPA, class rank, ACT or SAT score, school leadership, and community leadership.

**Financial data:** The stipend is $4,000 per year.

**Duration:** 1 year; may be renewed for up to 3 additional years provided the recipient maintains a 3.0 cumulative GPA and completes at least 30 semester hours each year.

**Number awarded:** Up to 75 each year.

**Deadline:** January of each year.

---

### 88 ARKANSAS KIDS' CHANCE SCHOLARSHIPS

Kids' Chance of Arkansas, Inc.
501 Woodlane, Suite 101
Little Rock, AR 72201-1024
Phone: (866) 880-8444; Email: KidsChance@awcc.state.ar.us
Web: www.awcc.state.ar.us/kids_chance/kchance1.html

**Summary:** To provide financial assistance for college to Arkansas residents whose parent was killed or permanently disabled in an employment-related accident.

**Eligibility:** Open to children of workers who have been killed or become permanently and totally disabled from a compensable Arkansas Workers' Compensation injury or accident. Applicants must be between 16 and 22 years of age; be able to demonstrate academic achievement and aptitude; and be attending or planning to attend an accredited vocational/technical school, college, or university. The injury or death of their parent must have resulted in a decrease in family earnings that creates an obstacle to the continuation of their education.

**Financial data:** The stipend depends on the financial need of the recipient.

**Duration:** 1 year.

**Number awarded:** Varies each year. Recently, 22 of these scholarships were awarded.

**Deadline:** May of each year.

## 89 ARKANSAS LAW ENFORCEMENT OFFICERS' DEPENDENTS' SCHOLARSHIPS

Arkansas Department of Higher Education, Attn: Financial Aid Division
114 East Capitol Avenue
Little Rock, AR 72201-3818
Phone: (501) 371-2050; (800) 54-STUDY; Fax: (501) 371-2001;
Email: finaid@adhe.arknet.edu
Web: www.arkansashighered.com/lawenforcement.html

**Summary:** To provide financial assistance for undergraduate education to the dependents of deceased or disabled Arkansas law enforcement officers, fire fighters, or other designated public employees.

**Eligibility:** Open to the spouses and/or children (natural, adopted, or step) of Arkansas residents who were killed or permanently disabled in the line of duty as law enforcement officers, municipal police officers, sheriffs and deputy sheriffs, constables, state correction employees, game wardens, state park employees who are commissioned law enforcement officers or emergency response employees, full-time or volunteer fire fighters, state forestry employees engaged in fighting forest fires, certain Arkansas Highway and Transportation Department employees, and public school teachers. Children must be less than 23 years of age. Spouses may not have remarried. All applicants must have been Arkansas residents for at least 6 months.

**Financial data:** The scholarship covers tuition, on-campus room charges, and fees (but not books, school supplies, food, materials, or dues for extracurricular activities) at any state-supported college or university in Arkansas.

**Duration:** Up to 8 semesters, as long as the student is working on a baccalaureate or associate's degree.

**Number awarded:** Varies each year.

**Deadline:** July of each year for fall term, November of each year for spring or winter term, April of each year for first summer session, or June of each year for second summer session.

## 90 ARKANSAS MISSING IN ACTION/KILLED IN ACTION DEPENDENTS' SCHOLARSHIP PROGRAM

Arkansas Department of Higher Education, Attn: Financial Aid Division
114 East Capitol Avenue
Little Rock, AR 72201-3818
Phone: (501) 371-2050; (800) 54-STUDY; Fax: (501) 371-2001;
Email: finaid@adhe.arknet.edu
Web: www.arkansashighered.com/miakia.html

**Summary:** To provide financial assistance for educational purposes to dependents of Arkansas veterans who were killed in action or became POWs or MIAs after January 1, 1960.

**Eligibility:** Open to the natural children, adopted children, stepchildren, and spouses of Arkansas residents who became a prisoner of war, killed in action, missing in action, or killed on ordnance delivery after January 1, 1960. Applicants may be working or planning to work 1) on an undergraduate degree in Arkansas or 2) on a graduate or professional degree in Arkansas if their undergraduate degree was not received in Arkansas. Applicants need not be current Arkansas residents, but their parents or spouses must have been an Arkansas resident at the time of entering military service or at the time they were declared a prisoner of war, killed in action, or missing in action.

**Financial data:** The program pays for tuition, general registration fees, special course fees, activity fees, room and board (if provided in campus facilities), and other charges associated with earning a degree or certificate.

**Duration:** 1 year; undergraduates may obtain renewal as long as they make satisfactory progress toward a baccalaureate degree; graduate students may obtain renewal as long as they maintain a minimum GPA of 2.5 and make satisfactory progress toward a degree.

**Number awarded:** Varies each year; recently, 4 of these scholarships were awarded.

**Deadline:** July of each year for the fall term; November of each year for the spring term; April of each year for summer term I; June of each year for summer term II.

## 91 ARKANSAS SECOND EFFORT SCHOLARSHIP

Arkansas Department of Higher Education, Attn: Financial Aid Division
114 East Capitol Avenue
Little Rock, AR 72201-3818
Phone: (501) 371-2050; (800) 54-STUDY; Fax: (501) 371-2001;
Email: finaid@adhe.arknet.edu
Web: www.arkansashighered.com/secondeffort.html

**Summary:** To provide financial assistance for undergraduate study to students in Arkansas who have earned a General Educational Development (GED) certificate.

**Eligibility:** Open to Arkansas residents who did not graduate from high school but completed their GED certificate in the previous year. Applicants must be attending or planning to attend an approved Arkansas 2- or 4-year public or private postsecondary institution. They must be at least 18 years of age or a former member of a high school class that has graduated. The students who received the highest GED scores are awarded this scholarship. Financial need is not considered. Students do not apply for this award; eligible candidates are contacted directly by the Arkansas Department of Higher Education if they achieve the highest scores.

**Financial data:** The stipend is $1,000 per year or the cost of tuition, whichever is less.

**Duration:** 1 year; may be renewed for an additional 3 years (or equivalent for part-time students) or until completion of a baccalaureate degree, provided the recipient maintains a GPA of 2.5 or higher.

**Number awarded:** 10 each year.

## 92 ARKANSAS SERVICE MEMORIAL FUND

Arkansas Community Foundation
700 South Rock Street
Little Rock, AR 72202
Phone: (501) 372-1116; (800) 220-ARCF; Fax: (501) 372-1166;
Email: acf@arcf.org
Web: www.arcf.org

**Summary:** To provide financial assistance for college to children of deceased veterans or other government officials in Arkansas.

**Eligibility:** Open to seniors graduating from high schools in Arkansas whose parent died in service to the community, state, or nation. Applicants must be planning to attend an accredited 2- or 4-year college in Arkansas on a full-time basis. Selection is based on such factors as academics, school activities, community service, future goals, faculty and advisor recommendations, and financial need.

**Financial data:** Stipends range from $500 to $5,000 per year.

**Duration:** 1 year; may be renewed as long as the recipient is making satisfactory progress toward a degree.

**Number awarded:** Varies each year; since this program was established, it has awarded 115 scholarships worth $125,000.

**Deadline:** April of each year.

## 93 ARMED SERVICES YMCA ANNUAL ESSAY CONTEST

Armed Services YMCA
6359 Walker Lane, Suite 200
Alexandria, VA 22310
Phone: (703) 313-9600; (800) 597-1260; Fax: (703) 313-9668;
Email: essaycontest@asymca.org
Web: www.asymca.org

**Summary:** To recognize and reward outstanding essays by children of armed service personnel.

**Eligibility:** Open to children of active-duty and retired military personnel in the Army, Navy, Marines, Air Force, Coast Guard, and National Guard. Applicants must submit an essay on why they like to read. Essays by students in grades 1-8 may not exceed 300 words and essays by students in grades 9-12 may not exceed 500 words. Department of Defense civilian dependents are eligible to enter an honorary category.

**Financial data:** For grades preschool through 8, first prize is a $500 savings bond and second prize is a $100 savings bond. For grades 9-12, first prize is a $1,000 savings bond, second prize is a $200 savings bond, and honorable mention is a $100 savings bond.

**Duration:** The contest is held annually.

**Number awarded:** A total of 14 prizes are awarded each year. A first prize and a second prize are awarded for 6 categories: first and second grade, third and fourth grade, fifth and sixth grade, seventh and eighth grade, ninth and tenth grade, and eleventh and twelfth grade. An additional 2 honorable mentions are awarded at the high school level.

**Deadline:** March of each year.

## 94 ARMY COLLEGE FUND

U.S. Army
Human Resources Command
AHRC-PDE-EI, Attn: Education Incentives and Counseling Branch

200 Stovall Street, Suite 3N17
Alexandria, VA 22332-0472
Phone: (703) 325-0285; (800) 872-8272; Fax: (703) 325-6599;
Email: pdeei@hoffman.army.mil
Web: www.hrc.army.mil/site/education/Text/ACF.html
**Summary:** To provide financial assistance for college to Army enlistees after they have completed their service obligation.
**Eligibility:** Open to high school seniors or graduates who enlist in an approved military occupational specialty (MOS) for at least 2 years, score 50 or above on the Armed Forces Qualification Test (AFQT), enroll in the Montgomery GI Bill, and attend a Department of Veterans Affairs-approved postsecondary educational institution on a full-time basis after completion of their service obligation.
**Financial data:** The Army College Fund (ACF) provides money for college in addition to that which the enlistee receives under the Montgomery GI Bill. The maximum benefit is $26,500 for a 2-year enlistment, $33,000 for a 3-year enlistment, or $40,000 for a 4-year enlistment. For specified MOSs, the maximum benefit (including payments under the Montgomery GI Bill) is $50,000.
**Duration:** 36 months; funds must be utilized within 10 years of leaving the Army.
**Number awarded:** Varies each year.
**Deadline:** Applications may be submitted at any time.

## 95 ARMY ROTC ADVANCED COURSE

U.S. Army
ROTC Cadet Command, Attn: ATCC-OP-I-S
55 Patch Road, Building 56
Fort Monroe, VA 23651-1052
Phone: (757) 727-4558; (800) USA-ROTC; Email: atccps@usaac.army.mil
Web: www.rotc.usaac.army.mil/scholarship_HPD2/index.asp
**Summary:** To provide financial assistance to non-scholarship participants in the Army ROTC Program who have qualified for the Advanced Course.
**Eligibility:** Open to non-scholarship cadets in the ROTC Program, if they have qualified for the ROTC Advanced Course. The Advanced Course is usually taken during the final 2 years of college.
**Financial data:** Participants receive a stipend of $350 per month during their junior year and $400 per month during their senior year, as well as pay for attending the 6-week advanced camp during the summer between the junior and senior years of college.
**Duration:** 2 years.
**Number awarded:** Varies each year.

## 96 ARMY ROTC COLLEGE SCHOLARSHIP PROGRAM

U.S. Army
ROTC Cadet Command, Attn: ATCC-OP-I-S
55 Patch Road, Building 56
Fort Monroe, VA 23651-1052
Phone: (757) 727-4558; (800) USA-ROTC; Email: atccps@usaac.army.mil
Web: www.rotc.usaac.army.mil/scholarship_HPD2/index.asp
**Summary:** To provide financial assistance to students who are or will be enrolled in Army ROTC.
**Eligibility:** Open to U.S. citizens at least 17 years of age who have already completed 1 or 2 years in a college or university with an Army ROTC unit on campus or in a college with a cross-enrollment agreement with a college with an Army ROTC unit on campus. Applicants must have 2 or 3 years remaining for their bachelor's degree (or 4 years of a 5-year bachelor's program) and must be able to complete that degree before their 31st birthday. They must have a GPA of 2.5 or higher in their previous college study and scores of at least 19 on the ACT or the equivalent on the SAT.
**Financial data:** These scholarships provide financial assistance for college tuition and educational fees, up to an annual amount of $16,000. In addition, a flat rate of $510 is provided for the purchase of textbooks, classroom supplies, and equipment. Recipients are also awarded a stipend for up to 10 months of each year that is $300 per month during their sophomore year, $350 per month during their junior year, and $400 per month during their senior year.
**Duration:** 2 or 3 years, until the recipient completes the bachelor's degree.
**Number awarded:** Varies each year; a recent allocation provided for 700 4-year scholarships, 1,800 3-year scholarships, and 2,800 2-year scholarships.
**Deadline:** December of each year.

## 97 ARMY ROTC 4-YEAR SCHOLARSHIPS

U.S. Army
ROTC Cadet Command, Attn: ATCC-OP-I-S
55 Patch Road, Building 56

Fort Monroe, VA 23651-1052
Phone: (757) 727-4558; (800) USA-ROTC; Email: atccps@usaac.army.mil
Web: www.rotc.usaac.army.mil/scholarship_HPD2/fouryear/program.htm
**Summary:** To provide financial assistance to high school seniors or graduates who are interested in enrolling in Army ROTC in college.
**Eligibility:** Open to applicants who 1) are U.S. citizens; 2) are at least 17 years of age by October of the year in which they are seeking a scholarship; 3) are able to complete a college degree and receive their commission before their 31st birthday; 4) score at least 19 on the ACT (or the equivalent on the SAT; 5) have a high school GPA of 2.5 or higher; and 6) meet medical and other regulatory requirements. Current college or university students may apply if their school considers them beginning freshmen with 4 academic years remaining for a bachelor's degree.
**Financial data:** This scholarship provides financial assistance of up to $20,000 per year for college tuition and educational fees or for room and board, whichever the student selects. In addition, a flat rate of $600 per year is provided for the purchase of textbooks, classroom supplies and equipment. Recipients are also awarded a stipend for up to 10 months of each year that is $250 per month during their freshman year; $300 per month during their sophomore year; $350 per month during their junior year; and $400 per month during their senior year.
**Duration:** 4 years, until completion of a baccalaureate degree.
**Number awarded:** Approximately 1,500 each year.
**Deadline:** November of each year.

## 98 ARNITA YOUNG BOSWELL SCHOLARSHIP

National Hook-Up of Black Women, Inc., Attn: Scholarship Committee
1809 East 71st Street, Suite 205
Chicago, IL 60649
Phone: (773) 667-7061; Fax: (773) 667-7064; Email: nhbwdir@aol.com
Web: www.nhbwinc.com
**Summary:** To provide financial assistance to African American high school and college students who are interested in earning an undergraduate degree.
**Eligibility:** Open to African American high school seniors or currently-enrolled college students. They must be attending or preparing to attend an accredited school and have a GPA of 2.75 or higher. They must demonstrate written communication skills by preparing an essay of 300 to 500 words on a topic that changes annually; recently, the topic was "Electing a U.S. President: Should the Electoral College Process Remain a Component of the Election Procedure?" Selection is based on academic record, financial need, community service, concern for the African American family, and a desire to complete a college degree.
**Financial data:** The stipend is $1,000. Funds are paid directly to the college or university of the recipient's choice.
**Duration:** 1 year.
**Number awarded:** 5 each year.
**Deadline:** February of each year.

## 99 ARNOLD SOBEL ENDOWMENT FUND SCHOLARSHIPS

Coast Guard Foundation
Commandant (G-WKW-2), Attn: Foundation Scholarships
2100 Second Street, S.W., Room 6320
Washington, DC 20593-0001
Phone: (202) 267-6728; (800) 872-4957; Email: ywright@comdt.uscg.mil
Web: www.uscg.mil
**Summary:** To provide financial assistance for college to the dependent children of Coast Guard enlisted personnel.
**Eligibility:** Open to the dependent children of enlisted members of the U.S. Coast Guard on active duty, retired, or deceased; and of enlisted personnel in the Coast Guard Reserve currently on extended active duty 180 days or more. Applicants must be attending or planning to attend a college, university, or vocational school as a full-time undergraduate student. Along with their application, they must submit their SAT or ACT scores, a letter of recommendation, transcripts, and a financial information statement.
**Financial data:** The stipend is $5,000 per year.
**Duration:** 1 year; may be renewed up to 3 additional years.
**Number awarded:** 4 each year.
**Deadline:** March of each year.

## 100 ARRID TOTAL WOMEN OF TOMORROW SCHOLARSHIPS

Church & Dwight Company, Inc.
Attn: Total Women of Tomorrow Scholarship Contest
469 North Harrison Street

Princeton, NJ 08543

Phone: (609) 683-5900

Web: www.totalwomen.org

**Summary:** To provide financial assistance for college to female high school students who demonstrate strength of character, clear vision, pioneering spirit, and community stewardship.

**Eligibility:** Open to women currently enrolled in high schools in the United States as a junior or senior. They must be nominated by a resident of the United States who is 18 years of age or older; self-nominations are not accepted. Nominators must submit an original essay, up to 500 words, describing the young woman. The nomination essay must include 1) the nominee's strength of character, including the depth of her convictions and her unwavering commitment to integrity; 2) her clear vision of her future goals and the relentless pursuit of those goals; 3) ways in which she has demonstrated a pioneering spirit, with the courage to transcend barriers and exceed expectations; and 4) her community stewardship as evidenced through participation in meaningful community activities and her ability to motivate others to become involved. Selection is based on how well the nominee exemplifies the 4 qualities of this program.

**Financial data:** The woman with the highest score receives a $10,000 scholarship, second highest a $5,000 scholarship, and third highest a $3,000 scholarship. Nominators of the winners receive prizes of $1,000, $500, and $300, respectively.

**Duration:** The scholarships are awarded annually.

**Number awarded:** 3 scholarships are awarded each year.

**Deadline:** Letters of nomination must be received (either online or by mail) by April of each year.

## 101 ASIAN AMERICAN SCHOLARSHIP

US Pan Asian American Chamber of Commerce

Attn: Scholarship Coordinator

1329 18th Street, N.W.

Washington, DC 20036

Phone: (202) 296-5221; Fax: (202) 296-5225;

Email: administrator@uspaacc.com

Web: www.uspaacc.com/web/programs/aa_supplier_council.htm

**Summary:** To provide financial assistance for college to Asian American high school seniors who demonstrate financial need.

**Eligibility:** Open to high school seniors of Asian heritage who are U.S. citizens or permanent residents. Applicants must be planning to begin full-time study at an accredited postsecondary educational institution in the United States. Along with their application, they must submit a 500-word essay on "Why I need this scholarship." Selection is based on academic excellence (GPA of 3.3 or higher), leadership in extracurricular activities, community service involvement, and financial need.

**Financial data:** The maximum stipend is $5,000. Funds are paid directly to the recipient's college or university.

**Duration:** 1 year.

**Number awarded:** 1 each year.

**Deadline:** February of each year.

## 102 ASIAN & PACIFIC ISLANDER AMERICAN SCHOLARSHIPS

Asian & Pacific Islander American Scholarship Fund

1628 16th Street, N.W., Suite 400

Washington, DC 20009

Phone: (202) 986-6892; (877) 808-7032; Fax: (202) 667-6449;

Email: scholarshipquestions@apiasf.org

Web: www.apiasf.org

**Summary:** To provide financial assistance to Asian and Pacific Islander Americans who are entering college for the first time.

**Eligibility:** Open to U.S. citizens, nationals, permanent residents, and citizens of the Freely Associated States who are first-time incoming college students and of Asian or Pacific Islander heritage. Applicants must be enrolling full time in an accredited 2-year or 4-year college or university in the United States, Guam, American Samoa, or the Commonwealth of the Northern Mariana Islands. They must have a GPA of 2.7 or higher or the GED equivalent. Along with their application, they must submit an essay of 275 words or less that describes an experience in their life that either demonstrates their character or helped to shape it. Selection is based on the essay, academic record, academic plans and career goals, community service, a letter of recommendation, and financial need.

**Financial data:** The stipend is $2,000.

**Duration:** 1 year.

**Number awarded:** Varies each year; recently, 165 of these scholarships were awarded.

**Deadline:** February of each year.

## 103 ASSISTANCE FOR SURVIVING CHILDREN OF NAVAL PERSONNEL DECEASED AFTER RETIREMENT (CDR)

Navy-Marine Corps Relief Society, Attn: Education Division

875 North Randolph Street, Suite 225

Arlington, VA 22203-1977

Phone: (703) 696-4960; Fax: (703) 696-0144; Email: education@hq.nmcrs.org

Web: www.nmcrs.org/child-dec.html

**Summary:** To provide financial assistance for college to the children of Navy or Marine Corps personnel who died as a result of disabilities or length of service.

**Eligibility:** Open to the unmarried, dependent children, stepchildren, or legally adopted children (under the age of 23) of members of the Navy or Marine Corps who died after retirement.

**Financial data:** Grants up to $4,000 per year are available.

**Number awarded:** Varies each year.

**Deadline:** February of each year.

## 104 ASSISTANCE FOR SURVIVING CHILDREN OF NAVAL PERSONNEL DECEASED WHILE ON ACTIVE DUTY (CDAD)

Navy-Marine Corps Relief Society, Attn: Education Division

875 North Randolph Street, Suite 225

Arlington, VA 22203-1977

Phone: (703) 696-4960; Fax: (703) 696-0144; Email: education@hq.nmcrs.org

Web: www.nmcrs.org/child-dec.html

**Summary:** To provide financial assistance for college to the children of deceased Navy or Marine Corps personnel.

**Eligibility:** Open to the unmarried, dependent children, stepchildren, or legally adopted children (under the age of 23) of members of the Navy or Marine Corps who died while on active duty. Applicants must possess a current valid dependents' Uniformed Services Identification and Privilege Card.

**Financial data:** Grants up to $4,000 per year are available.

**Number awarded:** Varies each year.

**Deadline:** February of each year.

## 105 ASSOCIATED COLLEGES OF ILLINOIS SCHOLARSHIP PROGRAM

Associated Colleges of Illinois, Attn: Executive Director

20 North Wacker Drive, Suite 1456

Chicago, IL 60606

Phone: (312) 263-2391, ext. 23; Fax: (312) 263-3424; Email: aci@acifund.org

Web: www.acifund.org/pages/programs/scholarships_app.htm

**Summary:** To provide financial assistance to students attending or planning to attend an academic institution affiliated with the Associated Colleges of Illinois (ACI).

**Eligibility:** Open to students entering or currently enrolled at the 24 private colleges and universities that are members of ACI. The program includes 5 categories of awards: 1) first-generation and minority scholarships, to support students who are the first in their family to attend college and encourage minority achievement and graduation; 2) college-to-work scholarships, to attract more students to specific fields of study and career paths; 3) basic needs scholarships, to address students' unmet financial needs; 4) emergency assistance scholarships, to direct critical financial support to students experiencing personal or family emergencies; and 5) academic merit scholarships, to reward the best and the brightest students.

**Financial data:** Awards depend on the availability of funds and the need of the recipient.

**Duration:** 1 year; may be renewed.

**Number awarded:** Varies each year; since 1990, this program has awarded more than $2 million in financial aid to 1,600 students.

## 106 ASSOCIATION OF BLIND CITIZENS SCHOLARSHIPS

Association of Blind Citizens

P.O. Box 246

Holbrook, MA 02343

Phone: (781) 961-1023; Fax: (781) 961-0004;

Email: scholarship@blindcitizens.org

Web: www.blindcitizens.org/abc_scholarship.html

**Summary:** To provide financial assistance for college to individuals who are blind or visually impaired.

**Eligibility:** Open to high school seniors, high school graduates, and currently-enrolled college students who are blind or visually impaired. They must be interested in working on a college degree. To apply, students must submit an autobiography, indicating how the scholarship award would help them achieve their goal of attending college or a recognized vocational program; a high school or college transcript; a certificate of legal blindness or a letter from their ophthalmologist; and 2 letters of reference. The highest ranked applicant receives the Reggie Johnson Memorial Scholarship.

**Financial data:** Stipends are $3,000, $2,000, or $1,000. Funds may be used to pay for tuition, living expenses, or related expenses resulting from vision impairment.

**Duration:** 1 year.

**Number awarded:** 15 each year: 1 at $3,000 (the Reggie Johnson Memorial Scholarship), 3 at $2,000, and 11 at $1,000.

**Deadline:** April of each year.

### 107 AUDRE LORDE SCHOLARSHIP FUND

ZAMI, Inc.
P.O. Box 2502
Decatur, GA 30031
Phone: (404) 370-0920; Email: zami@zami.org
Web: www.zami.org/scholarship.htm

**Summary:** To provide financial assistance to lesbians and gay men of African descent who are entering or attending a college or university as a graduate or undergraduate student.

**Eligibility:** Open to "out" lesbians and gay men of African descent who are graduating high school seniors or enrolled in a technical, undergraduate, or graduate program located in the United States. Applicants must have a GPA of 2.5 or higher. They must submit 2 essays of 300 words or less on from a list of 5 topics that relate to their experiences being "out," their dreams for the future, how their friends would characterize them as a lesbian or gay person, their favorite books or other works of art, or the most difficult time in their life. Lesbians and gay men who are over 40 years of age are especially encouraged to apply.

**Financial data:** The stipend is $1,000. Funds are paid directly to the student's academic institution.

**Duration:** 1 year.

**Number awarded:** Varies each year; recently, 21 of these scholarships were awarded.

**Deadline:** May of each year.

### 108 AUTOMOTIVE EDUCATIONAL FUND SCHOLARSHIP PROGRAM

Automotive Hall of Fame, Attn: Scholarship Programs
21400 Oakwood Boulevard
Dearborn, MI 48124
Phone: (313) 240-4000; Fax: (313) 240-8641
Web: www.automotivehalloffame.org

**Summary:** To provide funding to undergraduate and graduate students who are majoring in any subject area but are interested in an automotive career after graduation.

**Eligibility:** Open to 1) high school seniors who have been accepted to an 18-month or 2-year program, and 2) current undergraduate or graduate students who have completed at least 1 year at a 4-year institution. Applicants must have a sincere interest in pursuing an automotive career upon graduation, regardless of their major (except divinity and pre-med). Financial need is not a requirement.

**Financial data:** Stipends range from $250 to $2,000. Funds are sent to the recipient's institution.

**Duration:** 1 year; may be renewed.

**Number awarded:** Varies; generally, 26 to 30 each year.

**Deadline:** May of each year.

### 109 A.W. BODINE-SUNKIST MEMORIAL SCHOLARSHIP

Sunkist Growers, Attn: Administrator
P.O. Box 7888
Van Nuys, CA 91409-7888
Phone: (818) 986-4800
Web: www.sunkist.com/about/bodine_scholarship.asp

**Summary:** To provide financial assistance to undergraduate students in California and Arizona who have an agricultural background and need financial assistance to further their education.

**Eligibility:** Open to students entering an undergraduate program at any level. Applicants must have a background in California or Arizona agriculture (i.e., the student or someone in the student's immediate family must derive the majority of income from agriculture). They must have earned a 3.0 GPA and be able to demonstrate financial need. Along with their application, they must submit a 500-word essay on their background and goals. Selection is based on the essay, financial need, college board test scores, GPA, and recommendations.

**Financial data:** Stipends average $2,000 per year.

**Duration:** 1 year; may be renewed for up to 3 additional years provided the recipients carry at least 12 units per term and earn a minimum GPA of 2.7.

**Number awarded:** Varies each year; recently, 16 of these scholarships were awarded. Since the establishment of the program, more than 275 scholarships have been awarded.

**Deadline:** April of each year.

### 110 AWARD OF EXCELLENCE ASTHMA SCHOLARSHIPS

American Academy of Allergy, Asthma & Immunology
555 East Wells Street, Suite 1100
Milwaukee, WI 53202-3823
Phone: (414) 272-6071; (800) 822-2762; Fax: (414) 272-6070;
Email: info@aaaai.org
Web: www.aaaai.org/members/associates/asthmascholarship

**Summary:** To provide financial assistance for college to high school seniors who have asthma.

**Eligibility:** Open to U.S. citizens who are graduating high school seniors with asthma. Applicants must submit a high school transcript, a letter of recommendation from a principal or guidance counselor, and a 1-page essay on how they have achieved their educational goals while coping with asthma. Selection is based on academic achievement, extracurricular activities, and community service.

**Financial data:** The scholarship stipend is $1,000 per year. Merit awards are $100.

**Duration:** 1 year; nonrenewable.

**Number awarded:** At least 30 scholarships and 30 merit awards are presented each year.

**Deadline:** December of each year.

### 111 AXA ACHIEVEMENT SCHOLARSHIPS

Scholarship America, Attn: Scholarship Management Services
One Scholarship Way
P.O. Box 297
St. Peter, MN 56082
Phone: (507) 931-1682; (800) 537-4180; Fax: (507) 931-9168;
Email: axaachievement@scholarshipamerica.org
Web: www.axa-achievement.com

**Summary:** To provide financial assistance for college to high school seniors who demonstrate outstanding achievement.

**Eligibility:** Open to graduating high school seniors who plan to enroll full time in an accredited 2-year or 4-year college or university in the United States. Applicants must demonstrate ambition and achievement in school and community activities or work experience. In the selection process, primary consideration is given to the demonstrated achievement as reported by the applicant and supported by an appraisal completed by an adult professional who is not a relative. Other factors considered include extracurricular activities in school and community, work experience, and academic record. From among the recipients, students whose achievements are especially noteworthy are designated as national AXA Achievers.

**Financial data:** The stipend is $10,000. Funds may be used only for undergraduate educational expenses. Students selected as national AXA Achievers receive an additional stipend of $15,000, a computer, and the offer of an internship.

**Duration:** 1 year. Awards are not renewable, but recipients may arrange to receive payment in installments over multiple years as long as they continue to meet eligibility requirements.

**Number awarded:** 52 each year: 1 from each state, the District of Columbia, and Puerto Rico. Of those 52, 10 are designated as national AXA Achievers.

**Deadline:** December of each year.

### 112 BAKER FAMILY FOUNDATION SCHOLARSHIP

Baker Family Foundation
17 Gelnnon Farm Lane
Lebanon, NJ 08833
Email: info@bakerfamilyfoundation.org
Web: www.baakerfamilyfoundation.org/program_summary.htm

**Summary:** To provide financial assistance to high school students facing obstacles when trying to attend college.

**Eligibility:** Open to high school seniors interested in attending college. While the foundation does not target any specific ethnic group, the majority of the recipients come from urban minority groups. The first step in the application process is to find a sponsor, who will then submit part 1 of the preliminary application. If selected for the next stage, students submit part 2 of the application, as well as financial, academic, and any other necessary documentation. References are contacted and the candidates are interviewed. From this group, finalists are selected. Selection is based on financial need, desire to achieve, and academic performance (generally a GPA of 3.0 or higher).

**Financial data:** The amount awarded varies, depending upon several factors: personal and family resources, the applicant's financial aid package, other outside scholarships, and any unusual circumstances that might have financial impact. The foundation attempts to "fill the gap" between the true costs of attending school and all other sources of financial aid. Funds may be used for tuition, room and board, transportation, day care expenses, family assistance, computer training, and college prep classes.

**Duration:** 1 year; may be renewed if the recipient maintains at least a "B" average, continues to demonstrate financial need, and remains a student in good standing.

**Number awarded:** Varies each year.

**Deadline:** While applications may be submitted at any time, students are encouraged to submit their applications as soon after the first of the new year as possible.

## 113 BANK OF NEW HAMPSHIRE LEAP SCHOLARSHIPS

New Hampshire Charitable Foundation
37 Pleasant Street
Concord, NH 03301-4005
Phone: (603) 225-6641; (800) 464-6641; Fax: (603) 225-1700;
Email: info@nhcf.org
Web: www.nhcf.org

**Summary:** To provide financial assistance for college to graduating high school seniors in New Hampshire.

**Eligibility:** Open to seniors at high schools in New Hampshire who will be enrolling full time in a postsecondary institution. Selection is based on financial need, academic achievement, involvement in school activities, community volunteer activity, and work experience.

**Financial data:** The stipend is $2,500 per year.

**Duration:** 1 year.

**Number awarded:** 9 each year.

**Deadline:** March of each year.

## 114 BARBARA JEAN BARKER MEMORIAL SCHOLARSHIP FOR A DISPLACED HOMEMAKER

General Federation of Women's Clubs of Vermont
c/o Kathy Moaratty, Scholarship Chair
183 Power House Road
Canaan, VT 05903
Phone: (802) 266-3031; Email: kathmoaratty@aol.com

**Summary:** To provide financial assistance for college to displaced homemakers in Vermont.

**Eligibility:** Open to Vermont residents who have been homemakers (primarily) for at least 15 years and have lost their main means of support through death, divorce, separation, spouse's long-time illness, or spouse's long-time unemployment. Applicants must be interested in upgrading their skills so they can work outside the home. As part of the application process, they must submit a completed application form and a letter of recommendation (from a personal friend or their postsecondary school). Selection is based on the information provided in the application form and a personal interview (finalists only).

**Financial data:** The stipend ranges from $500 to $1,500.

**Duration:** 1 year.

**Number awarded:** 1 to 3 each year.

**Deadline:** March of each year.

## 115 BARKING FOUNDATION SCHOLARSHIPS

Barking Foundation, Attn: Executive Director
49 Florida Avenue
P.O. Box 855
Bangor, ME 04402-0885
Phone: (207) 990-2910; Fax: (207) 990-2975;
Email: info@barkingfoundation.org
Web: www.barkingfoundation.org

**Summary:** To provide financial assistance to residents of Maine for education at the undergraduate, graduate, and postgraduate level.

**Eligibility:** Open to students who have been residents of Maine for at least 4 years and are interested in pursuing higher education anywhere in the United States. Applicants may be entering college, already enrolled in college, working on a graduate degree, or studying at the postgraduate level. They must submit an essay, up to 750 words, describing a challenge or adventure in their life. Selection is based on financial need; academic, community, organizational, and cocurricular accomplishments; character; demonstrated values; potential and aspirations; and references.

**Financial data:** The stipend is $3,000.

**Duration:** 1 year; may be renewed for 1 additional year.

**Number awarded:** Approximately 30 each year.

**Deadline:** February of each year.

## 116 BEN SELLING SCHOLARSHIP

Oregon Student Assistance Commission
Attn: Grants and Scholarships Division
1500 Valley River Drive, Suite 100
Eugene, OR 97401-2146
Phone: (541) 687-7395; (800) 452-8807, ext. 7395; Fax: (541) 687-7419;
Email: awardinfo@mercury.osac.state.or.us
Web: www.osac.state.or.us

**Summary:** To provide financial assistance for college to residents of Oregon.

**Eligibility:** Open to residents of Oregon who are entering their sophomore or higher years in college. Applicants must have a cumulative GPA of 3.5 or higher.

**Financial data:** Stipends are least $1,000.

**Duration:** 1 year.

**Number awarded:** Varies each year; recently, 25 of these scholarships were awarded.

**Deadline:** February of each year.

## 117 BENJAMIN FRANKLIN/EDITH GREEN SCHOLARSHIP

Oregon Student Assistance Commission
Attn: Grants and Scholarships Division
1500 Valley River Drive, Suite 100
Eugene, OR 97401-2146
Phone: (541) 687-7395; (800) 452-8807, ext. 7395; Fax: (541) 687-7419;
Email: awardinfo@mercury.osac.state.or.us
Web: www.osac.state.or.us

**Summary:** To provide financial assistance for college to graduating high school seniors in Oregon.

**Eligibility:** Open to seniors graduating from high schools in Oregon. Applicants must be planning to attend a 4 year college or university in the state.

**Financial data:** Stipends are at least $1,000.

**Duration:** 1 year; nonrenewable.

**Number awarded:** Varies each year; recently, 14 of these scholarships were awarded.

**Deadline:** February of each year.

## 118 BENNION FAMILY SCHOLARSHIP

Alexander Graham Bell Association for the Deaf
Attn: Financial Aid Coordinator
3417 Volta Place, N.W.
Washington, DC 20007-2778
Phone: (202) 337-5220; Fax: (202) 337-8314; TTY: (202) 337-5221;
Email: financialaid@agbell.org
Web: www.agbell.org

**Summary:** To provide financial assistance to undergraduate students with moderate to profound hearing loss.

**Eligibility:** Open to undergraduate students who have been diagnosed with a moderate to profound hearing loss prior to acquiring spoken language (hearing loss averages 60dB or greater in the better ear in the speech frequencies of 500, 1000, and 2000 Hz). Applicants must be committed to using spoken language as their primary mode of communication. They must be accepted or enrolled at a mainstream college or university as a full-time student. Along with their application, they must submit a 1-page essay discussing their career goals and how spoken communication is helping them to reach those goals as a person with a hearing loss. Financial need is considered in the selection process.

**Financial data:** The stipend is $2,000 per year.

**Duration:** 1 year; may be renewed 1 additional year.

**Number awarded:** 1 each year.

**Deadline:** April of each year.

**119 BEST BUY SCHOLARSHIPS**

Scholarship America, Attn: Scholarship Management Services
One Scholarship Way
P.O. Box 297
St. Peter, MN 56082
Phone: (507) 931-1682; (800) 537-4180; Fax: (507) 931-9168;
Email: bestbuy@scholarshipamerica.org
Web: bestbuy.scholarshipamerica.org/index.php
**Summary:** To provide financial assistance for college to high school seniors who demonstrate outstanding volunteer community service.
**Eligibility:** Open to graduating high school seniors who plan to enroll full time at an accredited 2-year or 4-year college or university or vocational/technical school in the United States. Applicants must be able to demonstrate "solid academic performance and exemplary community service." Consideration may also be given to participation in school activities and work experience, but financial need is not considered.
**Financial data:** The stipend is $2,000 or $1,000.
**Duration:** 1 year; nonrenewable.
**Number awarded:** Up to 1,308 each year. In each of the 435 Congressional districts in the United States plus the District of Columbia, up to 3 scholarships are awarded: 2 at $2,000 to the top qualifying students and 1 at $1,000 to the next qualifying applicant.
**Deadline:** February of each year.

**120 BETH CAREW MEMORIAL SCHOLARSHIPS**

AHF, Inc.
31 Moody Road
P.O. Box 985
Enfield, CT 06083-0985
Phone: (800) 243-4621; Fax: (860) 763-7022; Email: info@ahfinfo.com
Web: www.ahfinfo.com/ahfinfo/bc_mem_scholarship.html
**Summary:** To provide financial assistance for college to students who have a bleeding disorder.
**Eligibility:** Open to high school seniors and college freshmen, sophomores, and juniors who have hemophilia, von Willebrand Disease, or another related inherited bleeding disorder. Applicants must be attending or planning to attend an accredited college or university in the United States as a full-time student. As part of their application, they must submit essays on their academic goals, why they would be a good choice for this scholarship, their participation in volunteer community activities, their greatest challenge as a person living with a bleeding disorder, examples of choices they have made that demonstrate good and bad judgment on their part, and other financial assistance they are or may be receiving.
**Financial data:** The stipend is $2,000.
**Duration:** 1 year.
**Number awarded:** 5 each year.
**Deadline:** April of each year.

**121 BETTE MATKOWSKI SCHOLARSHIP**

Vermont Student Assistance Corporation
Champlain Mill, Attn: Scholarship Programs
P.O. Box 2000
Winooski, VT 05404-2601
Phone: (802) 654-3798; (888) 253-4819; Fax: (802) 654-3765; TDD: (802) 654-3766; TDD: (800) 281-3341 (within VT); Email: info@vsac.org
Web: www.vsac.org
**Summary:** To provide financial assistance to adults in Vermont who are interested in attending college to upgrade their employment skills.
**Eligibility:** Open to adults in Vermont who wish to attend an accredited college or university in order to upgrade their employment skills. Selection is based on financial need and required essays.
**Financial data:** The stipend is $1,000.
**Duration:** 1 year.
**Number awarded:** 2 each year.
**Deadline:** July of each year.

**122 BETTER CHANCE SCHOLARSHIP**

Associates of Vietnam Veterans of America, Attn: Scholarship Program
8605 Cameron Street, Suite 400
Silver Spring, MD 20910
Phone: (800) VVA-1316

Web: www.avva.org/scholarship.htm
**Summary:** To provide financial assistance for college to members of Vietnam Veterans of American (VVA) and Associates of Vietnam Veterans of America (AVVA), their families, and the families of Vietnam veterans killed or missing in action.
**Eligibility:** Open to members of VVA and AVVA; their spouses, children, and grandchildren; and the spouses, children, and grandchildren of a Vietnam veteran killed in action (KIA) or missing in action (MIA). Especially encouraged to apply are average students who are not eligible for academic scholarships but who can demonstrate financial need. Applicants must submit essays on their long-term goals, work experience, organizations or activities, and community service.
**Financial data:** Stipends are $1,000 or $500.
**Duration:** 1 year.
**Number awarded:** 3 each year: 1 at $1,000 and 2 at $500.
**Deadline:** May of each year.

**123 BEVERAGE INDUSTRY SCHOLARSHIP PROGRAM**

Christermon Foundation, Attn: Beverage Industry Scholarship Program
9 Orchard Road, Suite 100
Lake Forest, CA 92630
Phone: (949) 837-5291; Fax: (949) 837-9481;
Email: information@cfsc.occoxmail.com
Web: www.christermon.com/scholarship
**Summary:** To provide financial assistance to students transferring from a California community college to a 4-year institution who have a parent or grandparent working in the California beverage industry.
**Eligibility:** Open to residents of California who may be either high school seniors or community college students as long as they are planning to attend an accredited 4-year college or university in the United States in the following fall term. Students currently enrolled in a 4-year institution or just entering a 2-year college are ineligible. Applicants must be the children, grandchildren, or legal guardians of persons who hold full-time employment with, or who are the proprietor of, a company holding a valid California liquor, beer, or wine license (including restaurants, hotels, retail and wholesale grocery establishments, airlines, breweries, wineries, and distributors). Student employment with an establishment holding a California liquor license and/or eligibility established through a family relationship other than parent, grandparent, or legal guardian does not qualify. Applicants must be planning to enroll full time and have a GPA of 3.0 or higher.
**Financial data:** Stipends range from $1,500 to $5,000.
**Duration:** 1 year; nonrenewable.
**Number awarded:** Varies each year; recently, 47 of these scholarships were awarded.
**Deadline:** January of each year.

**124 BIG 33 ACADEMIC SCHOLARSHIPS**

Big 33 Scholarship Foundation, Attn: Scholarship Committee
511 Bridge Street
P.O. Box 213
New Cumberland, PA 17070
Phone: (717) 774-3303; (877) PABIG-33; Fax: (717) 774-1749;
Email: info@big33.org
Web: www.big33.org/scholarships/default.ashx
**Summary:** To provide financial assistance for college to graduating high school seniors in Ohio and Pennsylvania.
**Eligibility:** Open to seniors graduating from public and accredited private high schools in Ohio and Pennsylvania. Applications are available from high school guidance counselors. Selection is based on special talents, leadership, obstacles overcome, academic achievement (at least a 2.0 GPA), community service, unique endeavors, financial need, and a 1-page essay on why the applicant deserves the scholarship.
**Financial data:** Stipends range up to $4,000, but most are $1,000.
**Duration:** 1 year; nonrenewable.
**Number awarded:** Varies each year; recently, 111 of these scholarships were awarded: 3 at $4,000, 1 at $1,500, 60 at $1,000, 3 at $600, 42 at $500, and 2 at $250
**Deadline:** February of each year.

**125 BILL MCADAM SCHOLARSHIP FUND**

Hemophilia Foundation of Michigan
c/o Cathy McAdam
22226 Doxtator

Dearborn, MI 48128

Phone: (313) 563-0515; Fax: (313) 563-1412; Email: mcmcadam@comcast.net

**Summary:** To provide financial assistance for college to students with a bleeding disorder or members of their families.

**Eligibility:** Open to 1) students with a hereditary bleeding disorder (hemophilia, von Willebrand, etc.) or 2) members of their families (spouse, partner, child, sibling). Applicants must be U.S. citizens and enrolled or planning to enroll at an accredited 2- or 4-year college, trade or technical school, or other certification program. Along with their application, they must submit 2 letters of recommendation and 3 essays: 1) their short- and long-term goals and who or what influenced the shaping of their goals; 2) why they should receive this scholarship; and 3) if they had 3 wishes, what those would be.

**Financial data:** The stipend is $2,000.

**Duration:** 1 year.

**Number awarded:** 1 each year.

**Deadline:** May of each year.

## 126 BILLY WELU SCHOLARSHIP

Professional Bowlers Association, Attn: Billy Welu Bowling Scholarship
719 Second Avenue, Suite 701
Seattle, WA 98104

Phone: (206) 332-9688; Fax: (206) 654-6030

Web: www.pba.com/corporate/scholarships.asp

**Summary:** To provide financial assistance to college students who are active bowlers.

**Eligibility:** Open to currently-enrolled college students who compete in the sport of bowling. Applicants must submit a 500-word essay describing how the scholarship will positively affect their bowling, academic, and personal goals. They must have a GPA of 2.5 or higher. Financial need is not considered in the selection process.

**Financial data:** The stipend is $1,000.

**Duration:** 1 year.

**Number awarded:** 1 each year.

**Deadline:** May of each year.

## 127 BISA SCHOLARSHIP ASSISTANCE PROGRAM

Black Women in Sisterhood for Action, Attn: Chair of Scholarship Committee
P.O. Box 1592
Washington, DC 20013

Phone: (202) 543-6013; Fax: (202) 543-5719; Email: info@bisa-hq.org

Web: www.bisa-hq.org/scholarships.index.htm

**Summary:** To provide financial assistance for college to disadvantaged Black women.

**Eligibility:** Open to Black women graduating from inner-city high schools and planning to attend a college or university, especially a designated Historically Black College or University (HBCU). Applicants must submit a transcript, SAT or ACT scores, documentation of financial need, and a 1-page self-portrait highlighting where they expect to be in their career development in 10 years. Selection is based on academic achievement, leadership potential, financial need, honors, and potential for academic growth and leadership development.

**Financial data:** The stipend is $1,000 per year. Support is also provided for books and transportation.

**Duration:** 4 years.

**Number awarded:** 40 to 50 each year.

**Deadline:** February of each year.

## 128 BISHOP JOSEPH B. BETHEA SCHOLARSHIPS

United Methodist Church
Attn: General Board of Higher Education and Ministry
Office of Loans and Scholarships
1001 19th Avenue South
P.O. Box 340007
Nashville, TN 37203-0007

Phone: (615) 340-7344; Fax: (615) 340-7367; Email: umscholar@gbhem.org

Web: www.gbhem.org

**Summary:** To provide financial assistance for college to African American Methodist students from the southeastern states.

**Eligibility:** Open to full-time undergraduate students at accredited colleges and universities who have been active, full members of a United Methodist Church for at least 1 year prior to applying. Applicants must be African Americans and members of Black Methodists for Church Renewal in the Southeastern Jurisdiction (which covers Alabama, Florida, Georgia, Kentucky, Mississippi,

North Carolina, South Carolina, Tennessee, and Virginia). They must have a GPA of 2.8 or higher and be able to demonstrate financial need. U.S. citizenship or permanent resident status is required.

**Financial data:** A stipend is awarded (amount not specified).

**Duration:** 1 year; recipients may reapply.

**Number awarded:** 1 or more each year.

**Deadline:** April of each year.

## 129 BLANCHE NAUGHER FOWLER CHARITABLE SCHOLARSHIP

Blanche Naugher Fowler Charitable Scholarship Trust
c/o AmSouth Bank, Attn: Scholarship Trust
2330 University Boulevard
P.O. Box 2028
Tuscaloosa, AL 35403

Phone: (205) 391-5720; Fax: (205) 391-5598

**Summary:** To provide financial assistance to undergraduate or graduate students attending colleges or universities in Alabama.

**Eligibility:** Open to students attending or accepted at a public or private non-profit college or university (at least a 4-year baccalaureate-level institution) located in Alabama. Applicants must submit an application form, a transcript, a letter of admission or other evidence of acceptance to or enrollment in a school located in Alabama, SAT or ACT test scores, 2 letters of recommendation, a 1-page statement of educational and career goals and aspirations, and a list of all honors, activities, interests, and employment experiences. Financial need is not required, but applicants who wish to be considered on the basis of financial need must also submit a completed College Scholarship Service Financial Aid Form (FAF) and current tax return.

**Financial data:** A stipend is awarded (amount not specified).

**Duration:** 1 year; may be renewed until completion of an undergraduate, graduate, or professional degree.

**Deadline:** March of each year.

## 130 BOB GAINEY HONORARY SCHOLARSHIP

Dallas Stars Foundation
2601 Avenue of the Stars
Frisco, TX 75034

Phone: (214) 387-5526; Fax: (214) 387-5610;
Email: starscommunity@dallasstars.com

Web: www.dallasstars.com/community/education-scholarship.jsp

**Summary:** To provide financial assistance for college to high school seniors in Texas who have been active in athletics.

**Eligibility:** Open to seniors graduating from high schools in Texas who have been an active member of 1 or more of their school's athletic teams. Applicants must be planning to attend an accredited U.S. 2- or 4-year college or university as a full-time student. They must have a GPA of 3.0 or higher and an ACT score of 24 or higher (or the equivalent on the SAT). Along with their application, they must submit an essay, up to 500 words in length, on the qualities that distinguish them from other applicants and explaining their career plans and goals. Selection is based on academic achievement, community and extracurricular involvement, and financial need. U.S. citizenship is required.

**Financial data:** The stipend is $1,250 per year. Funds are paid directly to the recipient's institution.

**Duration:** 4 years, provided the recipient maintains full-time enrollment and a GPA of 3.0 or higher.

**Number awarded:** 1 each year.

**Deadline:** March of each year.

## 131 BOB MCGUIRE MEMORIAL SCHOLARSHIP

North Carolina Child Support Council, Attn: Scholarships
P.O. Box 20421
Raleigh, NC 27619-0421

Web: www.nccscouncil.org/scholarship.htm

**Summary:** To provide financial assistance for college to high school seniors who have a connection to the North Carolina Child Support Council (NCCSC).

**Eligibility:** Open to graduating high school seniors who are residents of North Carolina planning to attend a college, university, or technical institute in the state. At least 1 parent must be a member of the NCCSC or a client of the child support program (either through IVD services or AOC Clerk of Court services). Applicants must have maintained an overall "C" average or above during their high school career. Financial need is not considered in the selection process.

**Financial data:** The stipend is $1,000. Funds are paid directly to the recipient's school.

**Duration:** 1 year; nonrenewable.

**Number awarded:** 3 each year: 1 in each of 3 regions in the state.

**Deadline:** April of each year.

## 132 BOETTCHER FOUNDATION SCHOLARSHIPS

Boettcher Foundation, Attn: Directory, Scholars Program
600 17th Street, Suite 2210 South
Denver, CO 80202-5422
Phone: (303) 534-1937; (800) 323-9640;
Email: scholarships@boettcherfoundation.org
Web: www.boettcherfoundation.org

**Summary:** To provide merit scholarships to Colorado high school seniors who are interested in attending a college or university in the state.

**Eligibility:** Open to seniors who have attended high school in Colorado for at least the last 2 years and are in the upper 5% of their graduating class with scores of at least 27 on the ACT or the equivalent on the SAT. U.S. citizenship is required. Selection is based on scholastic record, leadership potential, service to community and school, and character. Financial need is not considered.

**Financial data:** These scholarships provide full tuition and fees at a participating accredited 4-year undergraduate institution in Colorado, a stipend of $2,800 per year to help cover living expenses, and a book allowance. Funds are paid directly to the recipient's institution. Each college or university receives $1,000 per scholar per year attending that school to fund special opportunities and programs for the scholars. In addition, all scholars nominate 1 teacher who has had a special influence on their lives; nominees each receive $1,000 to be used at their home schools. Scholars may choose to exchange half of 1 year's scholarship for a $5,500 international education grant to be used for a study abroad program arranged through their college or university.

**Duration:** These are 4-year scholarships, but they are not renewed annually if the recipient fails to maintain a GPA of 3.0 or higher.

**Number awarded:** 40 each year.

**Deadline:** October of each year.

## 133 BONNER SCHOLARS PROGRAM

Corella and Bertram F. Bonner Foundation
10 Mercer Street
Princeton, NJ 08540
Phone: (609) 924-6663; Fax: (609) 683-4626; Email: info@bonner.org
Web: www.bonner.org/campus/bsp/home.htm

**Summary:** To provide scholarships to high school seniors who need help paying for college and who have a commitment to strengthening their communities through service.

**Eligibility:** Open to graduating high school seniors planning to attend a participating college throughout the southeastern and midwestern United States. Applicants must have significant financial need, a solid academic performance in high school (graduating in the top 40% of their class), acceptance at a participating college, and demonstrated responsibility and good citizenship at home, school, church/synagogue, or in the community. Interested students must contact the admissions office at the participating Bonner college they wish to attend.

**Financial data:** Participating schools provide a financial aid package that meets the total documented need for the cost of education. Only subsidized Stafford, Perkins, or equivalent loans may be used in meeting a scholar's documented need; those are limited to a total of $17,350 over 4 years. The sponsor provides (directly to scholars) $2,100 per year to assist them in meeting the cost of their education. It also provides a stipend of up to $1,500 as summer earnings to scholars who complete their summer service project for each of their first 2 summers, a summer living expense account of $2,000 that scholars can draw upon for 2 summers, an additional $500 to support summer service activities, up to $250 per trip for up to 2 trips to cover travel expenses to Bonner Congress meetings, up to $250 per first-year Bonner Scholar to cover expenses related to the required first-year service trip, and a grant of up to $1,600 for reducing their total educational loan indebtedness at the time of graduation.

**Duration:** 1 year; may be renewed up to 3 additional years.

**Number awarded:** Approximately 1,500 each year.

## 134 BOOMER ESIASON FOUNDATION SCHOLARSHIP PROGRAM

Boomer Esiason Foundation
c/o Jerry Cahill
417 Fifth Avenue, Second Floor
New York, NY 10016
Phone: (646) 344-3765; Fax: (646) 344-3757; Email: jcahill@esiason.org
Web: www.esiason.org

**Summary:** To provide financial assistance to undergraduate and graduate students who have cystic fibrosis (CF).

**Eligibility:** Open to CF patients who are working on an undergraduate or graduate degree. Applicants must submit a letter from a social worker describing their needs, a detailed breakdown of tuition costs from their academic institution, transcripts, and a 1-page essay on their post-graduation goals. Selection is based on academic ability, character, leadership potential, service to the community, and financial need. Finalists are interviewed by telephone.

**Financial data:** Stipends range from $500 to $2,000. Funds are paid directly to the academic institution to assist in covering the cost of tuition and fees.

**Duration:** 1 year; nonrenewable.

**Number awarded:** 10 to 15 each year.

## 135 BOSTON ALUMNAE CHAPTER SCHOLARSHIPS

Delta Sigma Theta Sorority, Inc.-Boston Alumnae Chapter
Attn: Scholarship Committee
P.O. Box 51424
Boston, MA 02205
Web: www.geocities.com/bostonalumnaechapter/index.html

**Summary:** To provide financial assistance to high school seniors in Massachusetts interested in attending a 4-year college or university.

**Eligibility:** Open to seniors graduating from high schools in Massachusetts. Applicants must be planning to attend a 4-year college or university. They must be able to demonstrate academic achievement and commitment to community service. Along with their application, they must submit a 500-word essay on the following topic: "What skills do you think you will need to be competitive in the 21st century and why? What are you doing now to prepare yourself?" Financial need is not considered in the selection process.

**Financial data:** A stipend is awarded (amount not specified).

**Duration:** 1 year.

**Number awarded:** 1 or more each year.

**Deadline:** April of each year.

## 136 BOWFIN MEMORIAL ACADEMIC SCHOLARSHIPS

Pacific Fleet Submarine Memorial Association
c/o USS Bowfin Submarine Museum and Park
11 Arizona Memorial Drive
Honolulu, HI 96818
Phone: (808) 423-1341; Fax: (808) 422-5201; Email: info@bowfin.org
Web: www.bowfin.org

**Summary:** To provide financial assistance for college to the children of submarine force personnel who live in Hawaii.

**Eligibility:** Open to the children of submarine force personnel (active duty, retired, or deceased) who are under 23 years of age. Applicants may attend school anywhere in the United States, but their submarine sponsor or surviving parent must live in Hawaii. Selection is based on scholastic proficiency, financial need, extracurricular activities, and demonstrated potential.

**Financial data:** Stipends range from $500 to $2,500 per year.

**Duration:** 1 year; may be renewed upon annual reapplication.

**Number awarded:** Varies each year; recently, 11 of these scholarships were awarded.

**Deadline:** February of each year.

## 137 BOWFIN MEMORIAL CONTINUING EDUCATION SCHOLARSHIPS

Pacific Fleet Submarine Memorial Association
c/o USS Bowfin Submarine Museum and Park
11 Arizona Memorial Drive
Honolulu, HI 96818
Phone: (808) 423-1341; Fax: (808) 422-5201; Email: info@bowfin.org
Web: www.bowfin.org

**Summary:** To provide financial assistance for continuing education to former or current Submarine Force personnel or their spouses, living in Hawaii.

**Eligibility:** Open to active-duty and retired submarine force personnel, their spouses, and the spouses of deceased submarine force personnel. Applicants must be entering college, returning to college, or training for entry into the work force. They must live and attend school in Hawaii. Selection is based on academic performance, community involvement, motivation, goals, and financial need.

**Financial data:** Stipends range from $500 to $2,500 per year.

**Duration:** 1 year; may be renewed upon annual reapplication.

**Number awarded:** Varies each year; recently, 14 of these scholarships were awarded.

**Deadline:** February of each year.

## 138 BOYS & GIRLS CLUBS OF AMERICA NATIONAL YOUTH OF THE YEAR PROGRAM

Boys & Girls Clubs of America
c/o National Headquarters
1230 West Peachtree Street
Atlanta, GA 30309
Phone: (404) 487-5700; Email: Info@bgca.org
Web: www.bgca.org/members/youth_of_year.asp

**Summary:** To recognize and reward outstanding leadership and service by participants in the Boys & Girls Clubs.

**Eligibility:** Open to members of these clubs. Each local club selects a Youth of the Year; selection may be based on academic performance, contributions to family and spiritual life, or service to the club. Recipients must be between the ages of 14 and 18 and have a record of active and continuing service to their club for at least 1 year. Each club Youth of the Year is nominated to be the state Youth of the Year, and those state-level winners enter regional competitions. The 5 regional winners are then invited to Washington, D.C. for interviews and selection of the National Youth of the Year.

**Financial data:** The regional winners receive $5,000 scholarships and the National Youth of the Year receives an additional scholarship of $10,000; funds are held in trust and then made available to the recipients as needed for tuition, books, school fees, and transportation.

**Duration:** The competition is held annually.

**Number awarded:** 5 regional scholarships are awarded each year and 1 of the recipients receives the national scholarship.

**Deadline:** Local clubs must submit their nominations by May of each year.

## 139 BP COMMUNITY SCHOLARSHIP PROGRAM

BP Products North America
c/o Charitable Management Systems, Inc.
700 West Fifth Avenue
Mail Code: 1003
Naperville, IL 60563

**Summary:** To provide financial assistance for college to high school seniors, in the Washington, D.C., metropolitan area.

**Eligibility:** Open to seniors graduating from high schools in Washington, D.C., Montgomery and Prince George's counties, Maryland; and Fairfax and Prince William counties, Virginia. Applicants must have a GPA of 2.0 or higher and be able to demonstrate financial need. They must be planning to enroll full time in an accredited college or university in the United States. Along with their application, they must submit an essay on a topic that changes annually. Recently, applicants were invited to write on the importance of education in a free society. Selection is based on the essay, academic performance, extracurricular activities, work experience, individual goals, and financial need.

**Financial data:** The stipend is $1,000.

**Duration:** 1 year; nonrenewable.

**Number awarded:** 1 or more each year.

**Deadline:** April of each year.

## 140 BPW/KY FOUNDATION GRANTS

Kentucky Federation of Business and Professional Women
Attn: BPW/KY Foundation
c/o Zayda Hurd Flanery, Chair
563 Red Lick Road
Berea, KY 40403
Phone: (606) 287-4964; Fax: (606) 287-4710; Email: zayda25@yahoo.com
Web: www.bpw-ky.org/ky_foundation.html

**Summary:** To provide funding to Kentucky residents interested in pursuing educational and personal development activities.

**Eligibility:** Open to residents of Kentucky (male and female) over 18 years of age. Applicants must be interested in pursuing 1 of the following activities: 1) job-related seminars, workshops, and other continuing education programs (not degree programs); 2) training programs that increase the number of public leadership positions; 3) research, as it applies to labor market trends or issues facing Kentucky business and industry; 4) retraining for reentering the workforce, upgrading skills, or changing careers; 5) degree programs for nontraditional students (those not straight out of high school); or 6) literacy or GED

programs. They must be currently in or planning a career in the Kentucky workforce. Selection is based on the availability of funds, the need of the applicant, and compliance with deadline, eligibility, and funding requirements.

**Financial data:** The amount of the grant depends on the nature of the activity to be funded.

**Duration:** An individual may receive a grant only once every 24 months.

**Number awarded:** Varies each year.

**Deadline:** April or October of each year.

## 141 BRUCE LEE SCHOLARSHIP

US Pan Asian American Chamber of Commerce
Attn: Scholarship Coordinator
1329 18th Street, N.W.
Washington, DC 20036
Phone: (202) 296-5221; Fax: (202) 296-5225;
Email: administrator@uspaacc.com
Web: www.uspaacc.com/web/programs/bruce_lee.htm

**Summary:** To provide financial assistance for college to high school seniors who have persevered over adversity.

**Eligibility:** Open to high school seniors who are U.S. citizens or permanent residents. Applicants must be planning to begin full-time study at an accredited postsecondary educational institution in the United States. Along with their application, they must submit a 500-word essay on "What adversities have you overcome?" Selection is based on academic excellence (GPA of 3.0 or higher), character, ability to persevere and prevail over adversity, community service involvement, and financial need.

**Financial data:** The maximum stipend is $5,000. Funds are paid directly to the recipient's college or university.

**Duration:** 1 year.

**Number awarded:** 1 each year.

**Deadline:** February of each year.

## 142 BUCKINGHAM MEMORIAL SCHOLARSHIPS

Air Traffic Control Association, Attn: Scholarship Fund
1101 King Street, Suite 300
Alexandria, VA 22314
Phone: (703) 299-2430; Fax: (703) 299-2437; Email: info@atca.org
Web: www.atca.org/activities/scholarships.asp

**Summary:** To provide financial assistance for college or graduate school to children of current or former air traffic control specialists.

**Eligibility:** Open to U.S. citizens who are the children, natural or adopted, of a person currently or formerly serving as an air traffic control specialist with the U.S. government, with the U.S. military, or in a private facility in the United States. Applicants must be enrolled or planning to enroll at least half time in a baccalaureate or graduate program at an accredited college or university, and have at least 30 semester hours to be completed before graduation. Along with their application, they must submit an essay on "How My Educational Efforts Will Enhance My Potential Contribution in My Chosen Career Field." The essay should address the applicant's financial need.

**Financial data:** The amounts of the awards depend on the availability of funds and the number, qualifications, and need of the applicants.

**Duration:** 1 year; may be renewed.

**Number awarded:** Varies each year.

**Deadline:** April of each year.

## 143 BUENA M. CHESSHIR MEMORIAL WOMEN'S EDUCATIONAL SCHOLARSHIP

Business and Professional Women of Virginia, Attn: Virginia BPW Foundation
P.O. Box 4842
McLean, VA 22103-4842
Web: www.bpwva.org/Foundation.shtml

**Summary:** To provide financial assistance to mature women in Virginia who are interested in upgrading their skills or education at a college, law school, or medical school in the state.

**Eligibility:** Open to women who are residents of Virginia, U.S. citizens, and at least 25 years of age. Applicants must have been accepted into an accredited program or course of study at a Virginia institution, have a definite plan to use their training to improve their chances for upward mobility in the work force, and be graduating within 2 years. Undergraduate applicants may by majoring in any field, but graduate student applicants must be working on a degree in law or medicine. Selection is based on demonstrated financial need and defined career goals.

**Financial data:** Stipends range from $100 to $1,000 per year; funds may be used for tuition, fees, books, transportation, living expenses, and dependent care.
**Duration:** Recipients must complete their course of study within 2 years.
**Number awarded:** 1 or more each year.
**Deadline:** March of each year.

## 144 BUREAU OF INDIAN AFFAIRS HIGHER EDUCATION GRANT PROGRAM

Bureau of Indian Affairs, Attn: Office of Indian Education Programs
1849 C Street, N.W.
MS 3512-MIB
Washington, DC 20240-0001
Phone: (202) 208-6123; Fax: (202) 208-3312
Web: www.oiep.bia.edu
**Summary:** To provide financial assistance to undergraduate students who belong to or are affiliated with federally-recognized Indian tribes.
**Eligibility:** Open to 1) members of American Indian tribes who are eligible for the special programs and services provided through the Bureau of Indian Affairs (BIA) because of their status as Indians, and 2) individuals who are at least one-quarter degree Indian blood descendants of those members. Applicants must be 1) enrolled or planning to enroll at an accredited college or university in a course of study leading to an associate of arts or bachelor's degree and 2) able to demonstrate financial need. Most tribes administer the grant program directly for their members, but other tribal members may contact the BIA Office of Indian Education Programs to learn the name and address of the nearest Education Line Officer who can provide an application and assistance in completing it.
**Financial data:** Individual awards depend on the financial need of the recipient. They range from $300 to $5,000 and average $2,800 per year. Recently, a total of $20,290,000 was available for this program.
**Duration:** 1 year; may be renewed for up to 4 additional years.
**Number awarded:** Approximately 9,500 students receive assistance through this program annually.
**Deadline:** June of each year for fall term; October of each year for spring term; April of each year for summer school.

## 145 BUSINESS AND PROFESSIONAL WOMEN'S FOUNDATION OF MARYLAND SCHOLARSHIP

Maryland Federation of Business and Professional Women's Clubs, Inc.
c/o Pat Schroeder, Chair
354 Driftwood Lane
Solomons, MD 20688
Phone: (410) 326-0167; (877) INFO-BPW; Email: patsc@csmd.edu
Web: www.bpwmaryland.org/HTML/scholarships.html
**Summary:** To provide financial assistance for college to mature women in Maryland.
**Eligibility:** Open to women who are at least 25 years of age and who are interested in working on undergraduate studies to upgrade their skills for career advancement, to train for a new career field, or to reenter the job market. Applicants must be residents of Maryland or, if a resident of another state, a member of the Maryland Federation of Business and Professional Women's Clubs. They must have been accepted into an accredited program or course of study at a Maryland academic institution and be able to demonstrate critical financial need.
**Financial data:** The stipend is $1,000 per year.
**Duration:** 1 year.
**Number awarded:** 1 or more each year.
**Deadline:** May of each year.

## 146 CAA YOUTH SCHOLARSHIP

California Alarm Association
3401 Pacific Avenue, Suite 1C
Marina del Rey, CA 90401
Phone: (310) 305-1277; (800) 437-7658; Fax: (310) 305-2077;
Email: info@CAAonline.org
Web: www.CAAonline.org
**Summary:** To provide financial assistance for college to the children of active-duty law enforcement and fire service personnel in California.
**Eligibility:** Open to applicants who are between the ages of 15 and 20; are a graduating high school senior in California; are accepted at an accredited college or university; and have a father, mother, or legal guardian who is a full-time active employee (not on disability) of the police or sheriff's department or a paid employee or volunteer of a fire department in California. Applicants must submit a high school transcript, proof of acceptance to a college or university, and proof of parent's occupation. Selection is based on class rank (25 points), class average (25 points), SAT scores (20 points), essay on "How Your Father, Mother, or Guardian Helps Us Secure Our Community" (15 points), and extracurricular activities (15 points). Financial need is not considered in the selection process. First, regional winners (northern and southern California) are selected. From them, a state winner is selected and that winner is entered in the national competition of the National Burglar & Fire Alarm Association.
**Financial data:** The stipend is $1,500.
**Duration:** 1 year; nonrenewable.
**Number awarded:** 1 each year.
**Deadline:** March of each year.

## 147 CAL GRANT A

California Student Aid Commission, Attn: Customer Service Branch
10811 International Drive
P.O. Box 419027
Rancho Cordova, CA 95741-9027
Phone: (916) 526-7590; (888) CA-GRANT; Fax: (916) 526-8002;
Email: custsvcs@csac.ca.gov
Web: www.csac.ca.gov
**Summary:** To provide financial assistance to low- and middle-income students in California who need help to pay tuition/fee costs.
**Eligibility:** Open to California residents who are U.S. citizens or eligible non-citizens, have financial need, are attending a qualifying college in California at least half time, are in a program of study leading directly to an undergraduate degree or certificate, do not possess a bachelor's degree prior to receiving a Cal Grant award, and do not owe a refund on any state or federal educational grant or have not defaulted on a student loan. They must complete and file both the Free Application for Federal Student Aid and GPA verification forms. Selection is based on financial need and GPA. The income ceiling for dependent students and independent students with dependents other than a spouse is $70,290 with 6 or more family members, $65,160 with 5 family members, $60,840 with 4 family members, $55,980 with 3 family members, or $54,630 with 2 family members. For independent students, the income ceiling is $25,470 for married students with no dependents other than a spouse or $22,320 for single students. The asset ceiling is $52,300 for dependent students or $24,900 for independent students. All graduating high school seniors in California who have a GPA of 3.0 or higher, meet the Cal Grant financial and academic requirements, and apply on time receive a Cal Grant A Entitlement Award. Other eligible students who have a GPA of 3.0 or higher may apply for a Cal Grant A Competitive Award; selection of those is based on family income, parents' educational level, GPA, time out of high school, and whether or not the applicant comes from a single-parent household. The performance standards and resources available to the applicant's high school may also be taken into account.
**Financial data:** Grants depend on financial need and academic qualifications, ranging from $1,500 (for students in the California State University system) to $9,708 (for students at independent colleges and universities in California). Students who qualify for a Cal Grant A and want to attend a California community college may reserve a tuition/fee award for up to 3 years, until they transfer to a tuition/fee charging college.
**Duration:** 1 year; may be renewed up to 3 additional years. Students in a teaching credential or mandatory 5-year program may apply for a fifth year of support.
**Number awarded:** Varies each year; recently, 27,358 entitlement (18,373 new and 8,985 renewal) and 29,917 competitive (1,053 new and 28,864 renewal) grants were awarded. Up to half of the competitive grants are reserved for students transferring from community colleges.
**Deadline:** High school seniors must apply for an entitlement grant by February of each year. Students entering a community college and applying for a competitive grant must do so by the end of August of each year.

## 148 CAL GRANT B

California Student Aid Commission, Attn: Customer Service Branch
10811 International Drive
P.O. Box 419027
Rancho Cordova, CA 95741-9027
Phone: (916) 526-7590; (888) CA-GRANT; Fax: (916) 526-8002;
Email: custsvcs@csac.ca.gov
Web: www.csac.ca.gov
**Summary:** To provide financial assistance to disadvantaged and low-income students in California who need help to pay tuition/fee costs.
**Eligibility:** Open to California residents who are U.S. citizens or eligible non-citizens, have financial need, are attending a qualifying college in California at least half time, are in a program of study leading directly to an undergraduate

degree or certificate, do not possess a bachelor's degree prior to receiving a Cal Grant award, and do not owe a refund on any state or federal educational grant or have not defaulted on a student loan. They must complete and file both the Free Application for Federal Student Aid and GPA verification forms. Selection is based on financial need and GPA. The income ceiling for dependent students and independent students with dependents other than a spouse is $38,610 with 6 or more family members, $35,730 with 5 family members, $31,950 with 4 family members, $28,710 with 3 family members, or $25,470 with 2 family members. For independent students, the income ceiling is $25,470 for married students with no dependents other than a spouse, or $22,320 for single students. The asset ceiling is $52,300 for dependent students or $24,900 for independent students. All graduating high school seniors in California who have a GPA of 2.0 or higher, meet the Cal Grant financial and academic requirements, and apply on time receive a Cal Grant B Entitlement Award. Other eligible students who have a GPA of 2.0 or higher may apply for a Cal Grant B Competitive Award; selection of those is based on family income, parents' educational level, GPA, time out of high school, whether or not the applicant comes from a single-parent household, and the performance standards and resources available to the applicant's high school.

**Financial data:** In the first year of college, these grants provide only an allowance of $1,551 for books and living expenses. When renewed or applied for after the freshman year, grants provide that living allowance plus a tuition and fee allowance that depends on financial need and academic qualifications, ranging from $1,500 for students in the California State University system to $9,708 for students at independent colleges and universities in California.

**Duration:** 1 year; may be renewed up to 3 additional years. Students in a teaching credential or mandatory 5-year program may apply for a fifth year of support.

**Number awarded:** Varies each year; recently, 63,702 entitlement (42,933 new and 20,769 renewal) and 55,817 competitive (21,447 new and 34,370 renewal) grants were awarded. Up to half of the competitive grants are reserved for students transferring from community colleges.

**Deadline:** High school seniors must apply for an entitlement grant by February of each year. Students entering a community college and applying for a competitive grant must do so by the end of August of each year.

## 149 CAL GRANT C

California Student Aid Commission, Attn: Customer Service Branch
10811 International Drive
P.O. Box 419027
Rancho Cordova, CA 95741-9027
Phone: (916) 526-7590; (888) CA-GRANT; Fax: (916) 526-8002;
Email: custsvcs@csac.ca.gov
Web: www.csac.ca.gov

**Summary:** To provide financial assistance to vocational school students in California who need help with tuition and training costs.

**Eligibility:** Open to California residents who are U.S. citizens or eligible noncitizens, have financial need, have a high school GPA of 2.0 or higher, are attending a qualifying occupational or vocational training program in California at least half time, are in a program of study that is at least 4 months in length, do not possess a bachelor's degree prior to receiving a Cal Grant award, and do not owe a refund on any state or federal educational grant or have not defaulted on a student loan. They must complete and file both the Free Application for Federal Student Aid and GPA verification forms. The income ceiling for dependent students and independent students with dependents other than a spouse is $70,290 with 6 or more family members, $65,160 with 5 family members, $60,840 with 4 family members, $55,980 with 3 family members, or $54,630 with 2 family members. For independent students, the income ceiling is $25,470 for married students with no dependents other than a spouse or $22,320 for single students. The asset ceiling is $52,300 for dependent students or $24,900 for independent students.

**Financial data:** Grants provide $576 for books, tools, and equipment. Students who attend a school other than a California community college may also receive up to $2,592 in assistance.

**Duration:** 1 year; may be renewed.

**Number awarded:** Varies each year; recently, 7,761 new and 2,848 renewal grants were awarded.

**Deadline:** February of each year.

## 150 CALGON TAKE ME AWAY TO COLLEGE SCHOLARSHIPS

Coty US LLC
1325 Avenue of the Americas
New York, NY 10019
Phone: (212) 479-4300; Fax: (212) 479-4399
Web: www.takemeaway.com

**Summary:** To recognize and reward, with college scholarships, women who are graduating high school seniors or already enrolled in college and provide excellent answers to online essay questions.

**Eligibility:** Open to women residents of the United States who are 18 years of age or older. Applicants must be enrolled or planning to enroll as a full-time undergraduate student at a 4-year U.S. college or university and have a GPA of 3.0 or higher. They must submit online answers (up to 900 characters) to questions about luxuries in life they most enjoy and where they would go (and why) if they could go anywhere. Those short answers are judged on the basis of originality, quality of expression, and accordance with standard rules of English grammar, mechanics, and spelling. Financial need is not considered. The 25 finalists are then invited to submit a short essay on a specified topic, transcripts, a list of extracurricular activities, and other documents as part of an application packet to be provided. Scholarship America ranks the finalists on the basis of merit, exclusive of the essays. Maddenmedia selects the winner on the basis of that ranking and the essays.

**Financial data:** First place is a $5,000 scholarship, second a $2,000 scholarship, third a $1,000 scholarship.

**Duration:** The competition is held annually.

**Number awarded:** 3 each year: 1 first place, 1 second, 1 third.

**Deadline:** February of each year.

## 151 CALIFORNIA CHAFEE GRANT PROGRAM

California Student Aid Commission, Attn: Specialized Programs
10811 International Drive
P.O. Box 419029
Rancho Cordova, CA 95741-9029
Phone: (916) 526-8276; (888) CA-GRANT; Fax: (916) 526-7977;
Email: specialized@csac.ca.gov
Web: www.chaffee.csac.ca.gov

**Summary:** To provide financial assistance for college to residents of California who have been in foster care.

**Eligibility:** Open to residents of California who have been in foster care between their sixteenth and eighteenth birthday and are currently younger than 22 years of age. Applicants must be enrolled at least half time in a college or vocational school in any state. They must be able to demonstrate financial need.

**Financial data:** The stipend depends on the need of the recipient, to a maximum of $5,000 per year.

**Duration:** 1 year; may be renewed if the recipient maintains at least half-time enrollment and satisfactory academic progress.

**Number awarded:** Varies each year.

## 152 CALIFORNIA FEE WAIVER PROGRAM FOR CHILDREN OF VETERANS

California Department of Veterans Affairs, Attn: Division of Veterans Services
1227 O Street, Room 101
Sacramento, CA 95814
Phone: (916) 503-8397; (800) 952-LOAN (within CA); Fax: (916) 653-2563;
TDD: (800) 324-5966; Email: ruckergl@cdva.ca.gov
Web: www.cdva.ca.gov/service/feewaiver.asp

**Summary:** To provide financial assistance for college to the children of disabled or deceased veterans in California.

**Eligibility:** Open to the children of veterans who 1) died of a service-connected disability; 2) had a service-connected disability at the time of death; or 3) currently have a service-connected disability of any level of severity. Applicants must plan to attend a community college in California, a branch of the California State University system, or a campus of the University of California. Their income, including the value of support received from parents, cannot exceed the national poverty level. California veteran status is not required for this program. Dependents in college who are eligible to receive federal education benefits from the U.S. Department of Veterans Affairs are not eligible for these fee waivers.

**Financial data:** This program provides for the waiver of registration fees to students attending any publicly-supported community or state college or university in California.

**Duration:** 1 year; may be renewed.

**Number awarded:** Varies each year.

## 153 CALIFORNIA FEE WAIVER PROGRAM FOR DEPENDENTS OF DECEASED OR DISABLED NATIONAL GUARD MEMBERS

California Department of Veterans Affairs, Attn: Division of Veterans Services
1227 O Street, Room 101
Sacramento, CA 95814
Phone: (916) 503-8397; (800) 952-LOAN (within CA); Fax: (916) 653-2563;
TDD: (800) 324-5966; Email: ruckergl@cdva.ca.gov

Web: www.cdva.ca.gov/service/feewaiver.asp

**Summary:** To provide financial assistance for college to dependents of disabled and deceased members of the California National Guard.

**Eligibility:** Open to the spouses, children, and unremarried widow(er)s of members of the California National Guard who, in the line of duty and in the active service of the state, were killed, died of a disability, or became permanently disabled. Applicants must be attending or planning to attend a community college, a branch of the California State University system, or a campus of the University of California.

**Financial data:** Full-time college students receive a waiver of tuition and registration fees at any publicly-supported community or state college or university in California.

**Duration:** 1 year; may be renewed.

**Number awarded:** Varies each year.

### 154 CALIFORNIA FEE WAIVER PROGRAM FOR DEPENDENTS OF TOTALLY DISABLED VETERANS

California Department of Veterans Affairs, Attn: Division of Veterans Services
1227 O Street, Room 101
Sacramento, CA 95814
Phone: (916) 503-8397; (800) 952-LOAN (within CA); Fax: (916) 653-2563; TDD: (800) 324-5966; Email: ruckergl@cdva.ca.gov
Web: www.cdva.ca.gov/service/feewaiver.asp

**Summary:** To provide financial assistance for college to dependents of disabled and other California veterans.

**Eligibility:** Open to the spouses (including registered domestic partners), children, and unremarried widow(er)s of veterans who are currently totally service-connected disabled (or are being compensated for a service-connected disability at a rate of 100%) or who died of a service-connected cause or disability. The veteran parent must have served during a qualifying war period and must have been discharged or released from military service under honorable conditions. The child cannot be over 27 years of age (extended to 30 if the student was in the military); there are no age limitations for spouses or surviving spouses. This program does not have an income limit. Dependents in college are not eligible if they are qualified to receive educational benefits from the U.S. Department of Veterans Affairs. Applicants must be attending or planning to attend a community college, branch of the California State University system, or campus of the University of California.

**Financial data:** Full-time college students receive a waiver of tuition and registration fees at any publicly-supported community or state college or university in California.

**Duration:** Children of eligible veterans may receive postsecondary benefits until the needed training is completed or until the dependent reaches 27 years of age (extended to 30 if the dependent serves in the armed forces). Widow(er)s and spouses are limited to a maximum of 48 months' full-time training or the equivalent in part-time training.

**Number awarded:** Varies each year.

### 155 CALIFORNIA FEE WAIVER PROGRAM FOR RECIPIENTS OF THE MEDAL OF HONOR AND THEIR CHILDREN

California Department of Veterans Affairs, Attn: Division of Veterans Services
1227 O Street, Room 101
Sacramento, CA 95814
Phone: (916) 503-8397; (800) 952-LOAN (within CA); Fax: (916) 653-2563; TDD: (800) 324-5966; Email: ruckergl@cdva.ca.gov
Web: www.cdva.ca.gov/service/feewaiver.asp

**Summary:** To provide financial assistance for college to California veterans, or the children of veterans, who received the Medal of Honor and their children.

**Eligibility:** Open to recipients of the Medal of Honor and their children who are residents of California. Applicants must be attending or planning to attend a community college, a branch of the California State University system, or a campus of the University of California.

**Financial data:** Full-time college students receive a waiver of tuition and registration fees at any publicly-supported community or state college or university in California.

**Duration:** 1 year; may be renewed.

**Number awarded:** Varies each year.

### 156 CALIFORNIA HIGHER EDUCATION SCHOLARSHIPS

Chela Financial USA, Inc.
388 Market Street, 12th Floor
San Francisco, CA 94111

Phone: (415) 283-2800; (866) 34-CHELA; Fax: (415) 283-2888;
Email: scholarships@chelafin.org
Web: www.chelastudentloans.org/helpcal

**Summary:** To provide financial assistance for college to high school seniors and college students in California.

**Eligibility:** Open to high school seniors and current college students who are residents of California and/or enrolled in a college or university in the state. Applicants must have a GPA of 2.0 or higher and a valid email address. They must be enrolled at least half time.

**Financial data:** The stipend is $5,000.

**Duration:** 1 year.

**Number awarded:** 10 each year.

**Deadline:** June of each year.

### 157 CALIFORNIA LAW ENFORCEMENT PERSONNEL DEPENDENTS GRANT PROGRAM

California Student Aid Commission, Attn: Specialized Programs
10811 International Drive
P.O. Box 419029
Rancho Cordova, CA 95741-9029
Phone: (916) 526-8276; (888) CA-GRANT; Fax: (916) 526-7977;
Email: specialized@csac.ca.gov
Web: www.csac.ca.gov

**Summary:** To provide financial assistance for college to the dependents of California law enforcement officers who have been totally disabled or killed in the line of duty.

**Eligibility:** Open to the natural children, adopted children, and spouses of a California peace officer (Highway Patrol, marshal, sheriff, police officer), employee of the Department of Corrections or Youth Authority, or fire fighter. The parent or spouse must have died or become totally disabled as the result of an accident or injury caused by external violence or physical force incurred in the performance of duty. Applicants must be enrolled for at least 6 units at an accredited California postsecondary institution and able to demonstrate financial need.

**Financial data:** Stipends range from $100 to $11,259 per year, depending on the need of the recipient.

**Duration:** 1 academic year; may be renewed for up to 5 additional years at 4-year colleges and universities or up to 3 additional years at community colleges.

**Number awarded:** Varies each year; recently, 14 students received $86,670 in assistance from this program.

**Deadline:** Applications may be submitted at any time.

### 158 CALIFORNIA LEGION AUXILIARY EDUCATIONAL ASSISTANCE

American Legion Auxiliary, Attn: Department of California
Veterans War Memorial Building
401 Van Ness Avenue, Room 113
San Francisco, CA 94102-4586
Phone: (415) 861-5092; Fax: (415) 861-8365; Email: calegionaux@calegionaux.org
Web: www.calegionaux.org/scholarships.html

**Summary:** To provide financial assistance to California residents who are the children of veterans and require assistance to continue their education.

**Eligibility:** Open to California residents who are the children of veterans of World War I, World War II, Korea, Vietnam, Grenada/Lebanon, Panama, or Desert Shield/Desert Storm. Applicants must be high school seniors or graduates planning to continue their education at a college, university, or business/trade school in California. Financial need is considered in the selection process. Each high school in California may nominate only 1 student for these scholarships; the faculty selects the nominee if more than 1 student wishes to apply. Selection is based on financial need (30%), character (20%), scholastic merit (20%), Americanism (20%), and leadership (10%).

**Financial data:** Stipends are $1,000 or $500 per year.

**Duration:** 1 year; 1 of the scholarships may be renewed 1 additional year.

**Number awarded:** 11 each year: 1 at $1,000 that may be renewed, 5 at $1,000 that are nonrenewable, and 5 at $500 that are nonrenewable.

**Deadline:** March of each year.

### 159 CALIFORNIA LEGION AUXILIARY PAST DEPARTMENT PRESIDENT'S JUNIOR SCHOLARSHIP

American Legion Auxiliary, Attn: Department of California
Veterans War Memorial Building
401 Van Ness Avenue, Room 113

San Francisco, CA 94102-4586
Phone: (415) 861-5092; Fax: (415) 861-8365; Email: calegionaux@calegionaux.org
Web: www.calegionaux.org/scholarships.html

**Summary:** To provide financial assistance for college to the daughters of California veterans active in the American Legion Junior Auxiliary.

**Eligibility:** Open to the daughters, granddaughters, and great-granddaughters of veterans who served in World War I, World War II, Korea, Vietnam, Grenada/Lebanon, Panama, or Desert Shield/Desert Storm. Applicants must be in their senior year at an accredited high school, must have been members of the Junior Auxiliary for at least 3 consecutive years, and must be residents of California (if eligibility for Junior Auxiliary membership is by a current member of the American Legion or Auxiliary in California, the applicant may reside elsewhere). Selection is based on scholastic merit (20%); active participation in Junior Auxiliary (15%); record of service or volunteerism within the applicant's community, school, and/or unit (35%); a brief description of the applicant's desire to pursue a higher education (15%); and 3 letters of reference (15%).

**Financial data:** The stipend depends on the availability of funds but ranges from $300 to $1,000.

**Duration:** 1 year.

**Number awarded:** 1 each year.

**Deadline:** April of each year.

---

## 160 CALIFORNIA LEGION AUXILIARY SCHOLARSHIPS FOR CONTINUING AND/OR REENTRY STUDENTS

American Legion Auxiliary, Attn: Department of California
Veterans War Memorial Building
401 Van Ness Avenue, Room 113
San Francisco, CA 94102-4586
Phone: (415) 861-5092; Fax: (415) 861-8365; Email: calegionaux@calegionaux.org
Web: www.calegionaux.org/scholarships.html

**Summary:** To provide financial assistance to California residents who are the children of veterans and require assistance to continue their education.

**Eligibility:** Open to California residents who are the children of veterans of World War I, World War II, Korea, Vietnam, Grenada/Lebanon, Panama, or Desert Shield/Desert Storm. Applicants must be continuing or reentry students at a college, university, or business/trade school in California. Financial need is considered in the selection process.

**Financial data:** The stipend is $1,000.

**Duration:** 1 year.

**Number awarded:** 2 each year.

**Deadline:** March of each year.

---

## 161 CALIFORNIA MASONIC FOUNDATION EDUCATIONAL SCHOLARSHIPS

California Masonic Foundation, Attn: Scholarship Coordinator
1111 California Street
San Francisco, CA 94108-2284
Phone: (415) 776-7000; (800) 900-2727; Fax: (415) 776-7170;
Email: gloffice@freemason.org
Web: www.freemason.org/programs_scholarship.php

**Summary:** To provide financial assistance to California high school seniors who are interested in attending college.

**Eligibility:** Open to graduating high school seniors who have been residents of California for at least 1 year and have a GPA of 3.0 or higher. Applicants must be planning to attend a 2-year or 4-year institution of higher education as a full-time freshman in the following fall. They must be U.S. citizens or permanent residents and able to show evidence of financial need. Along with their application, they must submit a personal essay outlining their background, goals, and scholastic achievements; a copy of their latest high school transcript; 2 letters of recommendation; documentation of financial need; SAT or ACT scores; and a copy of their college acceptance letter. Selection is based on academic achievement, applicant essay, and financial need. Preference is given to applicants who have a Masonic relationship or are members of Masonic youth groups.

**Financial data:** Stipends range from $500 to $2,500 per year.

**Duration:** 1 year; may be renewed for up to 3 additional years.

**Number awarded:** Varies each year; recently, 80 of these scholarships were awarded.

**Deadline:** February of each year for new applicants; April of each year for renewal applicants.

---

## 162 CALIFORNIA SCOTTISH RITE FOUNDATION MEMORIAL SCHOLARSHIP FUND

California Scottish Rite Foundation, Attn: Secretary

---

855 Elm Avenue
Long Beach, CA 90813-4491
Phone: (562) 435-6061
Web: www.scottishritecalifornia.org/california_foundation.htm

**Summary:** To provide financial assistance for college to California residents.

**Eligibility:** Open to California residents between 17 and 25 years of age who are attending or planning to attend an accredited college or university as a full-time student. Applicants must be able to demonstrate high ideals and ability, strong grades in school (GPA of 3.0 or higher), financial need, and part-time employment. No affiliation with a Masonic-related organization is required.

**Financial data:** The stipend is $1,500 per year.

**Duration:** 1 year; may be renewed until graduation if funds permit and the recipient maintains acceptable progress.

**Number awarded:** Varies each year, depending on the availability of funds.

**Deadline:** March of each year.

---

## 163 CALIFORNIA STATE FAIR ACADEMIC ACHIEVERS SCHOLARSHIPS

California State Fair, Attn: Friends of the Fair Scholarship Program
1600 Exposition Boulevard
P.O. Box 15649
Sacramento, CA 95852
Phone: (916) 274-5969; Email: wross@calexpo.com
Web: www.bigfun.org

**Summary:** To provide financial assistance for college to high school seniors in California who rank in the top 10% of their class.

**Eligibility:** Open to seniors graduating from high schools in California who rank in the top 10% of their class for academic performance. Applicants must be planning to attend an accredited college or university in the state. Along with their application, they must submit a 500-word essay on why it is important to know where our food comes from. Selection is based on personal commitment, goals established for their chosen field, leadership potential, and civic accomplishments.

**Financial data:** Stipends are $2,500 or $1,000.

**Duration:** 1 year.

**Number awarded:** 2 each year: 1 at $2,500 and 1 at $1,000.

**Deadline:** March of each year.

---

## 164 CALIFORNIA TABLE GRAPE WORKERS' SCHOLARSHIP PROGRAM

California Table Grape Commission, Attn: Scholarship Committee
392 West Fallbrook, Suite 101
Fresno, CA 93711-6150
Phone: (559) 447-8350; (800) 813-8478; Fax: (559) 447-9184;
Email: info@freshcaliforniagrapes.com
Web: www.tablegrape.com

**Summary:** To provide financial assistance to the children of California table grape field workers who are interested in attending a branch of the California State University system.

**Eligibility:** Open to high school graduates or seniors graduating in June. They or their parents must have worked in either of the 2 previous California table grape harvests. Farmers and their families, raisin and wine grape workers, students currently enrolled in college, permanent staff and members of the California Table Grape Commission and their families, and commission suppliers are not eligible. All applicants must intend to attend a 4-year college or university in California. Selection is based on academic performance, financial need, obstacles overcome, leadership ability and/or community service, and ability to succeed.

**Financial data:** The stipend is $4,000 per year.

**Duration:** 4 years, provided the recipient maintains a GPA of 2.0 or higher.

**Number awarded:** 3 each year.

**Deadline:** March of each year.

---

## 165 CALIFORNIA WINE GRAPE GROWERS FOUNDATION SCHOLARSHIPS

California Association of Winegrape Growers
Attn: California Wine Grape Growers Foundation
601 University Avenue, Suite 135
Sacramento, CA 95825
Phone: (916) 924-5370; (800) 241-1800; Fax: (916) 924-5374;
Email: info@cawg.org
Web: www.cawg.org/cwggf/scholar.htm

**Summary:** To provide financial assistance for college to high school seniors in California whose parent(s) work in the grape wine vineyards.

**Eligibility:** Open to high school seniors in California who plan to attend a branch of the University of California, a branch of the California State University system, or a community college in the state. Applicants must have a parent or legal guardian who was employed as a vineyard worker by a wine-grape grower during either or both of the 2 preceding seasons. Applications are available in either English or Spanish. Along with their application, they must submit a high school transcript, a copy of their SAT or ACT scores (if they are planning to attend a 4-year university), a letter of recommendation from a school official, an endorsement from a member of the California Association of Winegrape Growers (CAWG), and a 2-page essay on themselves and their career goals. Selection is based on financial need, demonstrated academic ability, community involvement and leadership and/or work history, and determination to succeed.

**Financial data:** The stipend is $1,000 per year at a 4-year university or $500 per year at a community college.

**Duration:** 4 years at branches of the University of California or California State University system; 2 years at community colleges.

**Number awarded:** 6 each year: 2 at 4-year universities and 4 at community colleges.

**Deadline:** March of each year.

---

### 166 CALIFORNIA-HAWAII ELKS ASSOCIATION VOCATIONAL GRANTS

California-Hawaii Elks Association, Attn: Scholarship Committee
5450 East Lamona Avenue
Fresno, CA 93727-2224
Phone: (559) 255-4531; Fax: (559) 456-2659
Web: www.chea-elks.org/vocationalgrant.html

**Summary:** To provide financial assistance for vocational school to residents of California and Hawaii.

**Eligibility:** Open to residents of California or Hawaii who are high school seniors or older. Applicants must be enrolled or planning to enroll in a vocational/technical program of 2 years or less that leads to a terminal associate degree, diploma, or certificate, but less than a bachelor's degree. Students planning to transfer to a 4-year school to work on a bachelor's degree are not eligible. Selection is based on motivation, financial need, aptitude toward chosen vocation, grades, and completeness and neatness of the application brochure. Applications are available from an Elks Lodge in California or Hawaii; they must be endorsed by the lodge. U.S. citizenship is required.

**Financial data:** The stipend is $1,000 per year. Funds may be used for tuition and fees, room and board (if living on campus), and books and supplies. They may not be used for general living expenses or child care costs.

**Duration:** 1 year; may be renewed for 1 additional year.

**Number awarded:** 58 each year: 55 to residents of California and 3 to residents of Hawaii.

**Deadline:** Applications may be submitted at any time.

---

### 167 CALIFORNIA-HAWAII ELKS MAJOR PROJECT UNDERGRADUATE SCHOLARSHIP PROGRAM FOR STUDENTS WITH DISABILITIES

California-Hawaii Elks Association, Attn: Scholarship Committee
5450 East Lamona Avenue
Fresno, CA 93727-2224
Phone: (559) 255-4531; Fax: (559) 456-2659
Web: www.chea-elks.org/uspsd.html

**Summary:** To provide financial assistance for college to residents of California and Hawaii with disabilities.

**Eligibility:** Open to residents of California or Hawaii who have a physical impairment, neurological impairment, visual impairment, hearing impairment, and/or speech/language disorder. Applicants must be a senior in high school, be a high school graduate, or have passed the GED test. U.S. citizenship is required. Selection is based on financial need, GPA, severity of disability, seriousness of purpose, and depth of character. Applications are available from an Elks Lodge in California or Hawaii; students must first request an interview with the lodge's scholarship chairman or Exalted Ruler.

**Financial data:** The annual stipend is $1,000 for community colleges and vocational schools or $2,000 per year for 4-year colleges or universities.

**Duration:** 1 year; may be renewed for up to 3 additional years.

**Number awarded:** 20 to 30 each year.

**Deadline:** March of each year.

---

### 168 CALIFORNIANS FOR DISABILITY RIGHTS SCHOLARSHIP

Californians for Disability Rights, Attn: CDR Foundation
909 12th Street, Suite 200
Sacramento, CA 95814
Phone: (916) 447-2237; (800) 838-9237; Email: cdr@disabilityrights-cdr.org
Web: www.disabilityrights-cdr.org

**Summary:** To provide financial assistance for college to students with disabilities in California.

**Eligibility:** Open to persons with a verified physical, mental, or learning disability that substantially limits 1 or more major life activities. Applicants must be admitted to or enrolled at an accredited state university, community college, private college, or university in California. Along with their application, they must submit a 3-page essay of their disability advocacy and leadership skills, including how their student advocacy will improve the awareness and participation of Californians with disabilities in society.

**Financial data:** The stipend is $1,000 for first place, $700 for second place, and $300 for third place.

**Duration:** 1 year.

**Number awarded:** 3 each year.

**Deadline:** January of each year.

---

### 169 CAMP SCHOLARSHIPS

College Assistance Migrant Program, Attn: Alumni Association
202 Sixth Avenue
Lewiston, ID 83501
Phone: (208) 792-2101; Fax: (208) 792-2550; Email: ggalindo@campaa.org
Web: campaa.org/Scholarships.html

**Summary:** To provide financial assistance for college to high school seniors from migrant or seasonal farmworker families.

**Eligibility:** Open to migrant and seasonal farmworkers and their families working in agricultural activities directly related to the production of crops, dairy products, poultry, or livestock; the cultivation or harvesting of trees; or fish farms. Applicants may verify eligibility in 1 of 3 ways: 1) participation during high school or eligibility to participate in a Title 1 Migrant Education Program; 2) participation or eligibility to participate in the Workforce Investment Act (WIA); or 3) verification that they or their parents have spent at least 75 days during the past 24 months as a migrant and/or seasonal (not year-round) farmworker as their primary employment. They must also plan to enroll as a freshman at a 4-year college or university that participates in the College Assistance Migrant Program (Camp) of the U.S. Department of Education to complete a bachelor's degree, be a U.S. citizen or permanent resident, and be able to document financial need.

**Financial data:** The stipends depend on the need of the recipients and the school they attend.

**Duration:** 1 year.

**Number awarded:** Approximately 2,400 each year.

**Deadline:** February of each year.

---

### 170 CANCER TEACHES US SURVIVORSHIP AWARD

Ulman Cancer Fund for Young Adults, Attn: Scholarship Committee
4725 Dorsey Hall Drive, Suite A
PMB 505
Ellicott City, MD 21042
Phone: (410) 964-0202; (888) 393-FUND;
Email: scholarship@ulmanfund.org
Web: www.ulmanfund.org/Services/Scholarship/scholarship_main.htm

**Summary:** To provide financial assistance for college to cancer survivors, patients, and caregivers.

**Eligibility:** Open to young adults who are cancer survivors, patients, or caregivers and survivors of childhood cancer. Applicants must be able to demonstrate financial need. They must be between 15 and 40 years of age and working on, or planning to work on, an academic or professional degree. Along with their application, they must submit a 500-word essay on 1 of 4 assigned topics that relate to cancer. Selection is based on the quality of the essay, recommendations, their overall story of cancer survivorship, and financial need.

**Financial data:** The stipend is $1,000.

**Duration:** 1 year.

**Number awarded:** 1 or more each year.

**Deadline:** March of each year.

---

### 171 CAPED GENERAL EXCELLENCE SCHOLARSHIP

California Association for Postsecondary Education and Disability
Attn: Executive Assistant

71423 Biskra Road
Rancho Mirage, CA 92270
Phone: (760) 346-8206; Fax: (760) 340-5275; TTY: (760) 341-4084;
Email: caped2000@aol.com
Web: www.caped.net/scholarship.html

**Summary:** To provide financial assistance to undergraduate and graduate students in California who have a disability and can demonstrate academic achievement and involvement in community and campus activities.

**Eligibility:** Open to students at public and private colleges and universities in California who have a disability. Undergraduates must have completed at least 6 semester credits and have a GPA of 2.5 or higher. Graduate students must have completed at least 3 semester units and have a GPA of 3.0 or higher. Applicants must submit a 1-page personal letter that demonstrates writing skills; progress toward meeting educational and vocational goals; how they accommodate their disability; involvement in community activities; and any other personal factor that might strengthen their application. They must also submit a letter of recommendation from a faculty member, verification of disability, official transcripts, proof of current enrollment, and documentation of financial need. This award is presented to the applicant who demonstrates the highest level of academic achievement and involvement in community and campus life.

**Financial data:** The stipend is $1,500.

**Duration:** 1 year.

**Number awarded:** 1 each year.

**Deadline:** August of each year.

## 172 CAPITOL SCHOLARSHIP PROGRAM

Connecticut Department of Higher Education
Attn: Office of Student Financial Aid
61 Woodland Street
Hartford, CT 06105-2326
Phone: (860) 947-1855; Fax: (860) 947-1313; Email: csp@ctdhe.org
Web: www.ctdhe.org/SFA/sfa.htm

**Summary:** To provide financial assistance for undergraduate education to high school seniors or graduates in Connecticut.

**Eligibility:** Open to residents of Connecticut who are U.S. citizens or nationals and high school seniors or graduates. They must be in the top 20% of their graduating class or have above-average SAT scores, and they must be planning to attend a college in Connecticut or in a state that has a reciprocity agreement with Connecticut. Financial need must be demonstrated.

**Financial data:** Stipends range from $1,500 to $2,000 at Connecticut 4-year degree and 2-year proprietary colleges or from $500 to $700 at Connecticut 2-year public colleges. Students attending out-of-state colleges receive grants of $500 per year.

**Duration:** 1 year.

**Number awarded:** Varies each year.

**Deadline:** February of each year.

## 173 CAPSTONE CORPORATION SCHOLARSHIP AWARD

National Naval Officers Association-Washington, D.C. Chapter
Attn: Scholarship Program
2701 Park Center Drive, B704
Alexandria, VA 22302
Email: williams.stephen@hq.navy.mil
Web: www.dcnnoa.org

**Summary:** To provide financial assistance to minority high school seniors from the Washington, D.C., area.

**Eligibility:** Open to minority seniors at high schools in the Washington, D.C., metropolitan area who plan to enroll full time at an accredited 2-year or 4-year college or university. Applicants must have a GPA of 3.0 or higher. U.S. citizenship or permanent resident status is required. Selection is based on academic achievement, community involvement, and financial need.

**Financial data:** The stipend is $1,000 per year.

**Duration:** 1 year.

**Number awarded:** 1 each year.

**Deadline:** April of each year.

## 174 CAPTAIN CALIENDO COLLEGE ASSISTANCE FUND SCHOLARSHIP

U.S. Coast Guard Chief Petty Officers Association
Attn: CCCAF Scholarship Committee
5520-G Hempstead Way
Springfield, VA 22151-4009

Phone: (703) 941-0395; Fax: (703) 941-0397; Email: cgcpoa@aol.com
Web: www.uscgcpoa.org/0-main/scholarships/scholarships.htm

**Summary:** To recognize and reward, with college scholarships, children of members or deceased members of the U.S. Coast Guard Chief Petty Officers Association (CPOA) or the Coast Guard Enlisted Association (CGEA) who submit outstanding essays.

**Eligibility:** Open to children of members or deceased members of the CPOA or CGEA who are attending or planning to attend a college, university, or vocational school. Applicants may not be older than 24 years of age (the age limit does not apply to disabled children). They must submit an essay, up to 500 words, on a topic that changes annually. A recent topic was "What impact does the Patriot Act make on you and your community?" The author of the essay judged most outstanding receives this scholarship.

**Financial data:** The award is a $3,500 scholarship.

**Duration:** The competition is held annually.

**Number awarded:** 1 each year.

**Deadline:** February of each year.

## 175 CAREER AID FOR TECHNICAL STUDENTS PROGRAM

New Hampshire Charitable Foundation
37 Pleasant Street
Concord, NH 03301-4005
Phone: (603) 225-6641; (800) 464-6641; Fax: (603) 225-1700;
Email: info@nhcf.org
Web: www.nhcf.org

**Summary:** To provide financial assistance to New Hampshire residents preparing for a vocational or technical career.

**Eligibility:** Open to residents of New Hampshire entering a 2-year or 3-year degree program or a shorter-term technical degree training program that leads to an associate's degree, a trade license, or certification. Applicants must be dependent students younger than 24 years of age and planning to enroll at least half time at a community college, vocational school, trade school, or other short-term training program. They must be able to demonstrate financial need. Although academic excellence is not considered in the selection process, applicants should be able to demonstrate reasonable achievement and a commitment to their chosen field of study.

**Financial data:** Stipends range from $100 to $2,500, depending on the need of the recipient. A total of $200,000 is distributed annually.

**Duration:** 1 year.

**Number awarded:** Varies each year.

**Deadline:** June of each year.

## 176 CAREER COLLEGES & SCHOOLS OF TEXAS SCHOLARSHIP

Career Colleges & Schools of Texas
P.O. Box 140647
Austin, TX 78714-0647
Phone: (512) 454-8626; Fax: (512) 454-3036; Email: ccst@assnmgmt.com
Web: www.colleges-schools.org/scholarships.html

**Summary:** To provide financial assistance to high school seniors in Texas who are interested in attending a career college and majoring in selected fields.

**Eligibility:** Open to high school seniors in Texas who are interested in attending a career college in the state, to prepare for a career in such fields as computer or information technology, health care, cosmetology, massage, business, criminal justice, welding, or health occupations. The sponsor provides 4 scholarships to each of the 1,500 high schools in the state. Recipients are then selected by the scholarship directors or counselors at their high school. Selection criteria vary by school but usually include academic excellence, financial need, and/or student leadership.

**Financial data:** The stipend is a $1,000 award certificate to be used to pay for tuition at any of the 44 career colleges in Texas.

**Duration:** 1 year.

**Number awarded:** 6,000 each year (4 at each of the 1,500 high schools in the state).

## 177 CARGILL COMMUNITY SCHOLARSHIP PROGRAM

National FFA Organization, Attn: Scholarship Office
6060 FFA Drive
P.O. Box 68960
Indianapolis, IN 46268-0960
Phone: (317) 802-4321; Fax: (317) 802-5321; Email: scholarships@ffa.org
Web: www.ffa.org

**Summary:** To provide financial assistance for college to high school seniors who live near a facility of Cargill, Inc.

**Eligibility:** Open to graduating high school seniors who live near a Cargill facility and have their application signed by a local Cargill manager. Applicants must be planning to work full time on a 2-year or 4-year degree in any major at an accredited college or university in the United States. They must submit information on their work experience with an explanation of how it relates to their future goals; FFA members must include their Supervised Agricultural Experience (SAE) activities and 4-H members must include their projects. Other selection criteria include leadership activities and academic achievement.

**Financial data:** The stipend is $1,000. Funds are paid directly to the recipient. Each recipient's high school is eligible for a $200 library grant.

**Duration:** 1 year; nonrenewable.

**Number awarded:** 350 each year.

**Deadline:** February of each year.

## 178 CAROL NIGUS LEADERSHIP SCHOLARSHIP

Kansas Federation of Business & Professional Women's Clubs, Inc.
Attn: Kansas BPW Educational Foundation
c/o Diane Smith, Executive Secretary
10418 Haskins
Lenexa, KS 66215-2162
Email: desmith@fcbankonline.com
Web: www.bpwkansas.org/bpw_foundation.htm

**Summary:** To provide financial assistance for college to residents of Kansas who can demonstrate a record of public and community service.

**Eligibility:** Open to Kansas residents (men and women) who are enrolled in a school of higher education in the state and have demonstrated an extensive record of public service and outstanding leadership potential. Applicants must submit 1) a written summary of their involvement in community affairs, and 2) a 3-page personal biography in which they express their career goals, the direction they want to take in the future, their proposed field of study, their reason for selecting that field, the institutions they plan to attend and why, their circumstances for reentering school (if a factor), and what makes them uniquely qualified for this scholarship. They must also be able to document financial need. Applications must be submitted through a local organization of the sponsor.

**Financial data:** A stipend is awarded (amount not specified).

**Duration:** 1 year.

**Number awarded:** 1 or more each year.

**Deadline:** December of each year.

## 179 CAROLINE H. NEWHOUSE SCHOLARSHIP FUND

Career Transition for Dancers
c/o The Caroline & Theodore Newhouse Center for Dancers
165 West 46th Street, Suite 701
New York, NY 10036-2501
Phone: (212) 764-0172; Fax: (212) 764-0343; Email: info@careertransition.org
Web: www.careertransition.org/progsscholarmain.html

**Summary:** To provide financial assistance to current and former professional dancers interested in acquiring an academic degree or a new skill.

**Eligibility:** Open to current and former professional dancers who can demonstrate paid employment as a dancer under union jurisdiction for at least 100 weeks over a period of 7 years or more and earnings of at least $8,000 per year from dance employment in the 7 best years of their performing career; the performing years need not be consecutive. Applicants must be at least 27 years of age, although that age requirement may be lowered depending on their age at the start of a professional performing dance career or because of a debilitating injury or illness. They must be interested in obtaining funding for 1) tuition for an academic degree; 2) retraining for the acquisition of a new skill; or 3) seed money to begin a business enterprise.

**Financial data:** Recipients are entitled to grants totaling $2,500 over their lifetime. Funds may be used for tuition, fees, books, and materials at schools, institutes, and specialized certificate programs.

**Duration:** Funding may extend over a period of years, as long as the total awarded does not exceed $2,000.

**Number awarded:** Varies each year; recently, a total of $300,000 was available for this program.

**Deadline:** January, March, May, July, September, or November of each year.

## 180 CARVER SCHOLARS PROGRAM

Roy J. Carver Charitable Trust
202 Iowa Avenue
Muscatine, IA 52761-3733
Phone: (563) 263-4010; Fax: (563) 263-1547; Email: info@carvertrust.org
Web: www.carvertrust.org

**Summary:** To provide financial assistance for college to students in Iowa who have overcome significant obstacles to attend college.

**Eligibility:** Open to students attending the 3 public universities in Iowa, the 24 participating private 4-year colleges and universities in the state, or a community college in Iowa, and planning to transfer to 1 of those 4-year institutions. Applicants must be sophomores seeking support for their junior year. They must present evidence of unusual social and/or other barriers to attending college full time; examples include, but are not limited to, students who 1) are from 1-parent families; 2) are attending college while working full time; 3) have social, mental, or physical disabilities; and 4) have families to support. They must have graduated from a high school in Iowa or have been residents of the state for at least 5 consecutive years immediately prior to applying, be full-time students, have at least a 2.8 GPA, be U.S. citizens, and submit a financial profile indicating insufficient personal, family, and institutional resources to pay full-time college tuition. A particular goal of the program is to assist students "who fall between the cracks of other financial aid programs." Applications must be submitted to the financial aid office at the Iowa college or university the applicant attends.

**Financial data:** Stipends generally average $5,200 at public universities or $7,600 at private colleges in Iowa.

**Duration:** 1 year; may be renewed 1 additional year.

**Number awarded:** Varies each year; since the program's establishment, it has awarded more than 1,300 scholarships worth more than $10 million.

**Deadline:** March of each year.

## 181 CASEY FAMILY SCHOLARSHIPS FOR MALE STUDENTS OF COLOR

Orphan Foundation of America, Attn: Director of Student Services
Tall Oaks Village Center
12020-D North Shore Drive
Reston, VA 20190-4977
Phone: (571) 203-0270; (800) 950-4673; Fax: (571) 203-0273;
Email: scholarships@orphan.org
Web: www.orphan.org/scholarships.html

**Summary:** To recognize and reward minority male students who have been in foster care and are completing a vocational or undergraduate degree.

**Eligibility:** Open to male minority students enrolled in their final year of a vocational program or their senior year of an undergraduate program. Applicants must have aged out of the U.S. foster care system. Along with their application, they must submit 1) verification of their foster care status; 2) documentation of their total outstanding federal loan amount; 3) documentation from their school regarding any outstanding tuition balance they currently owe; and 4) a 5-paragraph essay explaining the single most important thing their postsecondary education has taught them and how they will take that lesson and apply it to their professional and personal life to help ensure their future success. Selection is based on financial need and merit, as commendation for ambition and tenacity in pursuing a higher education.

**Financial data:** Awards range up to $5,000.

**Duration:** These are onetime awards.

**Number awarded:** Awards are presented until funds are exhausted.

## 182 CAYETANO FOUNDATION SCHOLARSHIPS

Hawai'i Community Foundation, Attn: Scholarship Department
1164 Bishop Street, Suite 800
Honolulu, HI 96813
Phone: (808) 566-5570; (888) 731-3863; Fax: (808) 521-6286;
Email: scholarships@hcf-hawaii.org
Web: www.hawaiicommunityfoundation.org/scholar/scholar.php

**Summary:** To provide financial assistance for college to high school seniors in Hawaii.

**Eligibility:** Open to seniors at public and private high schools in Hawaii who plan to attend an accredited college or university as a full-time student. Applicants must be able to demonstrate academic achievement (GPA of 3.5 or higher), good moral character, and financial need. In addition to filling out the standard application form, they must write a short statement describing their participation in community service projects or activities and an essay where they imagine they are in their late 50s, reflecting on the major accomplishments of their adult life. Preference is given to applicants with the greatest financial need.

**Financial data:** The amounts of the awards depend on the availability of funds and the need of the recipient; recently, stipends averaged $2,000.

**Duration:** 1 year.

**Number awarded:** Varies each year; recently, 10 of these scholarships were awarded.

**Deadline:** February of each year.

## 183 CELEBRATION OF EXCELLENCE SCHOLARSHIP

Georgia Association of Homes and Services for Children
Attn: Celebration of Excellence
34 Peachtree Street, N.W., Suite 1710
Atlanta, GA 30303
Phone: (404) 572-6170; Fax: (404) 572-6171; Email: cara@gahsc.org
Web: www.celebrationofexcellence.org

**Summary:** To provide financial assistance for college or graduate school to residents of Georgia who have been in foster care.

**Eligibility:** Open to Georgia residents who were in the custody of the Georgia Department of Family and Children Services or placed at a licensed private residential program at the time of their 18th birthday. Applicants must be attending or planning to attend an approved college, university, vocational program, or graduate school. They must submit an essay of 3 to 5 pages that describes their educational and career goals, their extracurricular activities and community involvement, and why they think this scholarship will help them reach their goals. Selection is based on that essay, transcripts, SAT/ACT scores, 2 letters of reference, and financial need.

**Financial data:** The stipend is $1,000 per year.

**Duration:** 1 year; may be renewed for a total of 4 years of undergraduate and/or graduate study.

**Number awarded:** 1 or more each year.

**Deadline:** April of each year.

## 184 CHAFEE EDUCATION AND TRAINING VOUCHERS PROGRAM

Orphan Foundation of America, Attn: Executive Director
Tall Oaks Village Center
12020-D North Shore Drive
Reston, VA 20190-4977
Phone: (571) 203-0270; (800) 950-4673; Fax: (571) 203-0273,
Email: eileenm@orphan.org
Web: www.orphan.org/etv.html

**Summary:** To provide financial assistance for college to students who have been in foster care.

**Eligibility:** Open to U.S. citizens and permanent residents who are in foster care or were in foster care as a teenager. Applicants must have aged out of the foster care system at age 18 or were adopted from foster care with adoption finalization after their 16th birthday. They must have been accepted to or be enrolled in a degree, certificate, or other program at a college, university, technical school, or vocational school, and be able to show progress toward that degree or certificate. Other eligibility requirements vary from state to state.

**Financial data:** Stipends range up to $5,000.

**Duration:** 1 year; may be renewed up to 3 additional years.

**Number awarded:** Varies; approximately $42 million is available nationwide to this program each year.

## 185 CHAIRSCHOLARS FOUNDATION NATIONAL SCHOLARSHIPS

ChairScholars Foundation, Inc.
16101 Carencia Lane
Odessa, FL 33556-3278
Phone: (813) 920-2737; Email: info@chairscholars.org
Web: www.chairscholars.org

**Summary:** To provide financial assistance for college to physically challenged students.

**Eligibility:** Open to high school seniors and college freshmen who are physically challenged, although they are not required to be in a wheelchair. Applicants should be able to demonstrate financial need, have a record of satisfactory academic performance (at least a B+ average), and show some form of community service or social contribution in the past. Along with their application, they must submit an essay of 300 to 500 words on how they became physically challenged, how their situation has affected them and their family, and their goals and aspirations for the future. Graduate students and all students over 21 years of age are not eligible.

**Financial data:** Stipends are $5,000 or $3,000 per year. Funds are to be used for tuition and school expenses.

**Duration:** Up to 4 years for high school seniors; up to 3 years for college freshmen.

**Number awarded:** 10 each year.

**Deadline:** February of each year.

## 186 CHAPEL OF FOUR CHAPLAINS ANNUAL ESSAY CONTEST

Chapel of Four Chaplains
Naval Business Center, Building 649
1201 Constitution Avenue
Philadelphia, PA 19112
Phone: (215) 218-1943; Fax: (215) 218-1949; Email: chapel@fourchaplains.org
Web: www.fourchaplains.org

**Summary:** To recognize and reward outstanding high school senior essays on a topic related to public service.

**Eligibility:** Open to seniors at public and private high schools. The children of members of the Chapel of Four Chaplains, youth committee, board of directors, or trustees are ineligible. The topic of the essay changes annually. Recently, the topic was "How can we build bridges of understanding through commitment and service to humanity?" Essays must be typed, double-spaced, and no more than 450 words. Selection is based on exploration of the essay topic, incorporation of the Four Chaplains story within the essay, personal commitment, proper grammar and spelling, and clear and logical order.

**Financial data:** First prize is $1,000, second $750, third $500, fourth $400, and fifth $300.

**Duration:** The competition is held annually.

**Number awarded:** 5 each year.

**Deadline:** November of each year.

## 187 CHAPEL OF FOUR CHAPLAINS "PROJECT LIFESAVER"

Chapel of Four Chaplains
Naval Business Center, Building 649
1201 Constitution Avenue
Philadelphia, PA 19112
Phone: (215) 218-1943; Fax: (215) 218-1949; Email: chapel@fourchaplains.org
Web: www.fourchaplains.org

**Summary:** To recognize and reward outstanding high school senior teams that develop projects related to the work of the sponsoring organization.

**Eligibility:** Open to seniors in public and private high schools. They are invited to form teams to participate in this program. A team consists of a team leader, 5 team members, and a teacher (with faculty approval) who acts as team advisor. The team creates a plan to initiate the sponsor's Save-A-Life program within their school. Selection is based on originality and creativity of the project; community involvement in developing the project; impact of the project on the community; organizational skills of the students; selfless service, compassion, and humanity demonstrated by the students in conducting their project; proper grammar and punctuation in the project paper; and incorporation of the Four Chaplains story within the project.

**Financial data:** The prizes for the winning project include $1,000 to the team leader, $1,000 to the team advisor, and $750 to each of the 5 team members.

**Duration:** The competition is held annually.

**Number awarded:** 1 project is awarded each year.

**Deadline:** December of each year.

## 188 CHARLES AND MELVA T. OWEN MEMORIAL SCHOLARSHIPS

National Federation of the Blind
c/o Peggy Elliott, Scholarship Committee Chair
805 Fifth Avenue
Grinnell, IA 50112
Phone: (641) 236-3366
Web: www.nfb.org/sch_intro.htm

**Summary:** To provide financial assistance to blind undergraduate or graduate students.

**Eligibility:** Open to legally blind students who are working on or planning to work full time on an undergraduate or graduate degree. Scholarships, however, will not be awarded for the study of religion or solely to further general or cultural education; the academic program should be directed towards attaining financial independence. Selection is based on academic excellence, service to the community, and financial need.

**Financial data:** Stipends are $10,000 or $3,000.

**Duration:** 1 year; recipients may resubmit applications up to 2 additional years.

**Number awarded:** 2 each year: 1 at $10,000 and 1 at $3,000.

**Deadline:** March of each year.

## 189 CHARLES B. WASHINGTON SCHOLARSHIP

Urban League of Nebraska, Inc., Attn: Scholarships
3022 North 24th Street
Omaha, NE 68110
Phone: (402) 453-9730; Fax: (402) 453-9676
Web: www.urbanleagueneb.org
**Summary:** To provide financial assistance for college to residents of Nebraska.
**Eligibility:** Open to Nebraska residents who are seniors in high school or students currently enrolled in college. Applicants must have a GPA of 2.5 or higher and be able to demonstrate financial need. They must be able to demonstrate at least 5 to 10 hours of community involvement. Along with their application, they must submit a 500-word essay on their goals and ambitions and the reasons they should receive this scholarship.
**Financial data:** A stipend is awarded (amount not specified).
**Duration:** 1 year.
**Number awarded:** 1 or more each year.
**Deadline:** March of each year.

## 190 CHARLES GALLAGHER STUDENT FINANCIAL ASSISTANCE PROGRAM

Missouri Department of Higher Education, Attn: Student Financial Assistance
3515 Amazonas Drive
Jefferson City, MO 65109-5717
Phone: (573) 526-7958; (800) 473-6757; Fax: (573) 751-6635;
Email: info@dhe.mo.gov
Web: www.dhe.mo.gov/hsstudentscharlesgallagher.shtml
**Summary:** To provide financial assistance to college students in Missouri who demonstrate financial need.
**Eligibility:** Open to residents of Missouri who are full-time students working on their first baccalaureate degree at a participating postsecondary school in the state. Applicants must be able to demonstrate financial need. Students working on a degree or certificate in theology or divinity are not eligible. U.S. citizenship or permanent resident status is required.
**Financial data:** The annual award is the lesser of 1) the unmet financial need (after counting any federal Pell Grant the student receives); 2) half of the school's prior year tuition and fees; or 3) $1,500.
**Duration:** 1 year; may be renewed.
**Number awarded:** Varies each year; recently, 12,704 students received support through this program.
**Deadline:** March of each year.

## 191 CHARLES H. GRANT SCHOLARSHIP

Academy of Model Aeronautics, Attn: Education Coordinator
5161 East Memorial Drive
Muncie, IN 47302-9252
Phone: (765) 287-1256; Fax: (765) 289-4248
Web: www.buildandfly.com/AMAchgrantscholarship.asp
**Summary:** To provide financial assistance for college to members of the Academy of Model Aeronautics (AMA).
**Eligibility:** Open to graduating high school seniors who have been AMA members for the last full 36 months prior to applying. They must have been accepted by a college or university offering a certificate or degree program. Along with their application, they must submit a 1-page statement on why they are applying for this scholarship. Selection is based on that statement, academic achievement (class rank, GPA, test scores), school and community activities, work experience, and modeling experience. Financial need is not considered.
**Financial data:** The stipend depends on the number of recipients.
**Duration:** 1 year; nonrenewable.
**Number awarded:** Varies each year; a total of $20,000 is available for this program annually.
**Deadline:** April of each year.

## 192 CHARLES, LELA AND MARY SLOUGH FOUNDATION ONE-TIME SCHOLARSHIP

Charles, Lela and Mary Slough Foundation, Attn: Scholarship Administrator
3600 North Garfield
Midland, TX 79705
Phone: (432) 685-6493; Fax: (432) 685-6451; Email: jriggs@midland.edu
Web: www.midland.edu/admissions/aid/slough.html
**Summary:** To provide onetime financial assistance for college to needy students from Texas.

**Eligibility:** Open to U.S. citizens who are Texas residents entering or currently enrolled in a college or university anywhere in the United States. Applicants must have at least a 3.0 GPA and be able to demonstrate financial need. Home-school students may apply, but they must submit an official high school transcript showing their GPA and courses completed. Selection is based on need and academic achievement.
**Financial data:** A stipend is awarded (amount not specified).
**Duration:** 1 year; recipients may reapply.
**Number awarded:** Varies each year.
**Deadline:** March of each year.

## 193 CHARLES, LELA AND MARY SLOUGH FOUNDATION RECURRING SCHOLARSHIP

Charles, Lela and Mary Slough Foundation, Attn: Scholarship Administrator
3600 North Garfield
Midland, TX 79705
Phone: (432) 685-6493; Fax: (432) 685-6451; Email: jriggs@midland.edu
Web: www.midland.edu/admissions/aid/slough.html
**Summary:** To provide recurring financial assistance for college to needy students from Texas.
**Eligibility:** Open to U.S. citizens who are Texas residents entering or currently enrolled in a college or university anywhere in the United States. Applicants must have at least a 3.0 GPA and be able to demonstrate financial need. Home-school students may apply, but they must submit an official high school transcript showing their GPA and courses completed. Selection is based on need and academic achievement.
**Financial data:** The maximum stipend is $5,000 per year.
**Duration:** Up to 5 years or completion of a bachelor's degree, whichever occurs first. To receive the recurring funding, recipients must complete at least 12 credit hours with a 3.0 GPA every semester and submit the Free Application for Federal Aid each year.
**Number awarded:** 10 new scholarships are awarded each year.
**Deadline:** March of each year.

## 194 THE CHARTER FUND SCHOLARSHIPS

The Charter Fund, Attn: Jeanette Montoya
370 17th Street, Suite 5300
Denver, CO 80202
Phone: (303) 572-1727; Fax: (303) 628-3839
**Summary:** To provide financial assistance for college to financially needy high school seniors in Colorado.
**Eligibility:** Open to seniors graduating from high schools in Colorado who have worked during summer breaks. Applicants must be U.S. citizens or permanent residents planning to enter an accredited institution in the following fall. Selection is based on academic performance, aptitude, potential for achievement, and financial need.
**Financial data:** Stipends range from $100 to $2,500.
**Duration:** 1 year; nonrenewable.
**Number awarded:** Approximately 90 each year.
**Deadline:** May of each year.

## 195 CHESTER M. VERNON MEMORIAL EAGLE SCOUT SCHOLARSHIP

Boy Scouts of America, Attn: National Jewish Committee on Scouting, S226
1325 West Walnut Hill Lane
P.O. Box 152079
Irving, TX 75015-2079
Phone: (972) 580-2000
Web: www.jewishscouting.org/njcs/awards/eagle.html
**Summary:** To provide financial assistance for college to Jewish Boy Scouts, Varsity Scouts, and Venturers.
**Eligibility:** Open to registered, active members of a Boy Scout troop, Varsity Scout team, or Venturing crew who have received the Eagle Scout Award and have also earned the Ner Tamid or Etz Chaim emblem. Applicants must be enrolled in an accredited high school in their final year and must be an active member of a synagogue. They must have demonstrated practical citizenship in their synagogue, school, Scouting unit, and community. Selection is based on financial need; high school record, including school activities, awards, honors, and GPA; participation in community organizations; participation in religious youth organizations, clubs, or groups, including honors earned and offices held; involvement in Scouting; career goals; and 4 letters of recommendation, from leaders of their religious institution, school, community, and Scouting unit.

**Financial data:** The stipend is $1,000 per year.
**Duration:** 4 years.
**Number awarded:** 1 every other year.
**Deadline:** December of the year in which the scholarship is awarded.

## 196 CHEVROLET EXCELLENCE IN EDUCATION AWARD FOR AFRICAN AMERICAN STUDENTS

General Motors Corporation
Chevrolet Motor Division, Attn: GM Scholarship Administration Center
700 West Fifth Avenue
Mail Code 2001
Naperville, IL 60563
Phone: (888) 377-5233; Email: scholarshipinfo@gmsac.com
**Summary:** To provide financial assistance for college to African American high school seniors.
**Eligibility:** Open to African American students currently completing the senior year of high school with sufficient credits to graduate in the spring term with a GPA of 3.2 or higher. Applicants must be planning to enroll in an accredited 2-year or 4-year college or university in the following fall. They must be able to demonstrate both academic excellence and community service (e.g., activities, volunteerism, work experience) and be a U.S. citizen or have eligibility to work in the United States. Along with their application, they must include a letter of recommendation from a high school teacher or administrator, official transcripts from their high school, and a personal statement (500 to 750 words) about how their high school experiences (academics, extracurricular activities, outside activities, work experience) have prepared them for college and why they should be considered for this scholarship. Selection is based on that statement, academic performance, leadership and participation in school and community activities, work experience, and career and educational aspirations. Financial need is not considered.
**Financial data:** The stipend is $1,000 per year.
**Duration:** 1 year.
**Number awarded:** Varies each year.
**Deadline:** April of each year.

## 197 CHEVROLET EXCELLENCE IN EDUCATION AWARD FOR HISPANIC STUDENTS

General Motors Corporation
Chevrolet Motor Division, Attn: GM Scholarship Administration Center
700 West Fifth Avenue
Mail Code 2001
Naperville, IL 60563
Phone: (888) 377-5233; Email: scholarshipinfo@gmsac.com
**Summary:** To provide financial assistance for college to Hispanic American high school seniors.
**Eligibility:** Open to Hispanic students currently completing the senior year of high school with sufficient credits to graduate in the spring term with a GPA of 3.2 or higher. Applicants must be planning to enroll in an accredited 2-year or 4-year college or university in the following fall. They must be able to demonstrate both academic excellence and community service (e.g., activities, volunteerism, work experience) and be a U.S. citizen or have eligibility to work in the United States. Along with their application, they must include a letter of recommendation from a high school teacher or administrator, official transcripts from their high school, and a personal statement (500 to 750 words) about how their high school experiences (academics, extracurricular activities, outside activities, work experience) have prepared them for college and why they should be considered for this scholarship. Selection is based on that statement, academic performance, leadership and participation in school and community activities, work experience, and career and educational aspirations. Financial need is not considered.
**Financial data:** The stipend is $1,000 per year.
**Duration:** 1 year.
**Number awarded:** Varies each year.
**Deadline:** April of each year.

## 198 CHEVROLET SCHOLARSHIPS

National FFA Organization, Attn: Scholarship Office
6060 FFA Drive
P.O. Box 68960
Indianapolis, IN 46268-0960
Phone: (317) 802-4321; Fax: (317) 802-5321; Email: scholarships@ffa.org
Web: www.ffa.org
**Summary:** To provide financial assistance for college to current FFA members.
**Eligibility:** Open to members who are graduating high school seniors planning to enroll full time in college. Applicants must 1) have recruitment and leadership skills that have contributed to their local FFA chapter; 2) show participation in a Supervised Agricultural Experience (SAE) program; and 3) be recommended by their local FFA advisor. They may be working on a 2- or 4-year degree in any major. Selection is based on academic achievement (10 points for GPA, 10 points for SAT or ACT score, 10 points for class rank), leadership in FFA activities (30 points), leadership in community activities (10 points), and participation in the SAE program (30 points). U.S. citizenship is required.
**Financial data:** The stipend is $2,500. Funds are paid directly to the recipient.
**Duration:** 1 year; nonrenewable.
**Number awarded:** 40 each year.
**Deadline:** February of each year.

## 199 CHEVROLET/MICHELLE KWAN R.E.W.A.R.D.S. SCHOLARSHIPS

General Motors Corporation
Chevrolet Motor Division, Attn: GM Scholarship Administration Center
702 West Fifth Avenue
Naperville, IL 60563-2948
Phone: (888) 377-5233; Fax: (630) 428-2695;
Email: scholarshipinfo@gmsac.com
Web: www.chevrolet.com/rewards/main.htm
**Summary:** To provide financial assistance for college to women athletes graduating from high school.
**Eligibility:** Open to female high school seniors who have been active in athletics (including school teams, intramural athletics, organized athletic clubs, or other community-based sports organizations) and plan to remain involved in athletics in college. Applicants must be U.S. citizens or permanent residents and have a GPA of 3.2 or higher. They must be able to demonstrate financial need, leadership, community involvement, and volunteerism. As part of the application process, they must submit an essay of 500 to 750 words on how their high school experiences (athletics, academics, extracurricular activities, outside activities, and work experiences) have prepared them for college, the impact of athletics during their high school years, and why they should be considered for scholarship support.
**Financial data:** The stipend is $2,000 for the first year and $1,000 for each of the next 3 years.
**Duration:** 4 years, provided the recipient maintains a GPA of 3.0 or higher, normal progress towards a degree, and active participation in athletics.
**Number awarded:** 10 each year.
**Deadline:** March of each year.

## 200 CHICK AND SOPHIE MAJOR MEMORIAL DUCK CALLING CONTEST

Stuttgart Chamber of Commerce
507 South Main Street
P.O. Box 932
Stuttgart, AR 72160
Phone: (870) 673-1602; Fax: (870) 673-1604;
Email: chamber@stuttgartarkansas.com
Web: www.stuttgartarkansas.com/contest/future.shtml
**Summary:** To recognize and reward, with college scholarships, high school students who are outstanding duck callers.
**Eligibility:** Open to high school seniors interested in entering a duck calling contest. Contestants are allowed 90 seconds in which to present a 1) hail or long distance call, 2) mating or lonesome duck call, 3) feed or clatter call, and 4) comeback call.
**Financial data:** The prizes are a $1,500 scholarship for the winner, a $500 scholarship for the first runner-up, a $300 scholarship for the second runner-up, and a $200 scholarship for the third runner-up. Funds must be applied toward higher education.
**Duration:** The competition is held annually.
**Number awarded:** 4 prizes are presented each year.
**Deadline:** The competition is held annually on the Friday and Saturday following Thanksgiving.

## 201 CHICK EVANS CADDIE SCHOLARSHIPS

Western Golf Association, Attn: Evans Scholars Foundation
1 Briar Road
Golf, IL 60029-0301

Phone: (847) 724-4600; Fax: (847) 724-7133;
Email: evansscholars@wgaesf.com
Web: www.evansscholarsfoundation.com

**Summary:** To provide financial assistance for college to students who have worked as golf caddies.

**Eligibility:** Open to students who have completed their junior year in high school, rank in the upper quarter of their graduating class, have a GPA of 3.0 or higher, have taken the SAT or ACT test, are able to demonstrate financial need, and have been a full-time caddie on a regular basis for at least 2 years. Applicants from 12 states (Colorado, Illinois, Indiana, Michigan, Minnesota, Missouri, Ohio, Oregon, Pennsylvania, Virginia, Washington, and Wisconsin) must attend designated universities; applicants from other states must attend their state university, as approved by the scholarship committee. Selection is based on character, integrity, leadership, and financial need.

**Financial data:** The awards cover tuition and housing at universities approved by the scholarship committee.

**Duration:** 1 year; may be renewed for up to 3 additional years.

**Number awarded:** Varies each year; recently, 820 caddies were receiving support from this program.

**Deadline:** September of each year.

## 202 CHIEF MASTER SERGEANTS OF THE AIR FORCE SCHOLARSHIPS

Air Force Sergeants Association, Attn: Scholarship Coordinator
P.O. Box 50
Temple Hills, MD 20757
Phone: (301) 899-3500, ext. 237; (800) 638-0594; Fax: (301) 899-8136;
Email: staff@amf.org
Web: www.afsahq.org/body_education01.htm

**Summary:** To provide financial assistance for college to the dependent children of enlisted Air Force personnel.

**Eligibility:** Open to the unmarried children (including stepchildren and legally adopted children) of active-duty, retired, or veteran members of the U.S. Air Force, Air National Guard, or Air Force Reserves. Applicants must be younger than 23 years of age and dependent upon the parent or guardian for more than half of their support. Selection is based on academic ability (ACT score of 24 or higher or the equivalent on the SAT and GPA of 3.5 or higher), character, leadership, writing ability, and potential for success. Financial need is not a consideration. A unique aspect of these scholarships is that applicants may supply additional information regarding circumstances that entitle them to special consideration. Examples of such circumstances include student disabilities, financial hardships, parent disabled and unable to work, parent missing in action/killed in action/prisoner of war, or other unusual extenuating circumstances.

**Financial data:** Stipends are $3,000, $2,000, or $1,000; funds may be used for tuition, room and board, fees, books, supplies, and transportation.

**Duration:** 1 year; may be renewed if the recipient maintains full-time enrollment.

**Number awarded:** 11 each year: 1 at $3,000, 2 at $2,000, and 8 at $1,000. Since this program began it has awarded more than $200,000 in scholarships.

**Deadline:** March of each year.

## 203 CHIEF OF SUPPLY CORPS OFFICER DEVELOPMENT SCHOLARSHIPS

Navy Supply Corps Foundation
c/o Jack Evans
1425 Prince Avenue
Athens, GA 30606-2205
Phone: (706) 354-4111; Fax: (706) 354-0334; Email: foundation@usnscf.com
Web: www.usnscf.com/scholarship.php

**Summary:** To provide financial assistance for college to high school seniors willing to serve in the Navy Supply Corps.

**Eligibility:** Open to high school seniors who agree to serve on active duty as a Navy Supply Corps officer upon graduation from college. Applicants must be have a high school GPA of 3.0 or higher and be physically able to serve in the Supply Corps. They must be planning to attend a 2-year or 4-year college or university as a full-time student. Selection is based on the applicant's willingness and suitability to serve as an officer in the Supply Corps.

**Financial data:** The stipend is $10,000 per year.

**Duration:** 4 years, provided the recipient maintains a GPA of 3.0 or higher.

**Number awarded:** 2 each year.

**Deadline:** April of each year.

## 204 CHILDREN, ADULT, AND FAMILY SERVICES SCHOLARSHIP

Oregon Student Assistance Commission
Attn: Grants and Scholarships Division
1500 Valley River Drive, Suite 100
Eugene, OR 97401-2146
Phone: (541) 687-7395; (800) 452-8807, ext. 7395; Fax: (541) 687-7419;
Email: awardinfo@mercury.osac.state.or.us
Web: www.osac.state.or.us

**Summary:** To provide financial assistance for college to residents of Oregon who are or were in foster care or related programs.

**Eligibility:** Open to residents of Oregon who are either 1) graduating high school seniors currently in foster care or participating in the Independent Living Program (ILP); and 2) GED recipients and continuing college students formerly in foster care. Applicants must be attending or planning to attend a public college or university in Oregon.

**Financial data:** Stipends range from $500 to $5,000.

**Duration:** 1 year.

**Number awarded:** Varies each year.

**Deadline:** February of each year.

## 205 CHILDREN OF BREAST CANCER SCHOLARSHIPS

Children of Breast Cancer Foundation
P.O. Box 4032
Chattanooga, TN 37405
Web: www.childrenofbreastcancer.org/scholarships.html

**Summary:** To provide financial assistance for college to children of mothers who have had breast cancer.

**Eligibility:** Open to students who have lost a mother either to breast cancer or to complications resulting from breast cancer, or who have a mother who has survived breast cancer. Applicants must have been accepted as a full-time student an accredited 2- or 4-year college or university. Along with their application, they must submit 3 essays on their choice of selected topics. Selection is based on those essays, grades, and financial need.

**Financial data:** Stipends are either $3,000 or $1,500.

**Duration:** 1 year; may be renewed up to 3 additional years.

**Number awarded:** Varies each year. Recently, 22 of these scholarships were awarded: 18 at $3,000 and 4 at $1,500.

**Deadline:** February of each year.

## 206 CHILDREN OF INJURED WORKERS SCHOLARSHIPS

Children of Injured Workers, Inc.
4983 Brittonfield Parkway
East Syracuse, NY 13057
Phone: (315) 449-4306; Fax: (315) 449-4358; Email: info@kidschanceny.org
Web: www.kidschanceny.org

**Summary:** To provide financial assistance for college to residents of New York whose parent was seriously injured or killed in a workplace accident.

**Eligibility:** Open to New York residents attending or planning to attend a college or technical school. Applicants must be the child of a worker who suffered injury or death in an accident that is either established or accepted under the Workers' Compensation Law of the state of New York. The injury or death must have had a demonstrable impact on the financial ability of the child to attend college.

**Financial data:** A stipend is awarded (amount not specified).

**Duration:** 1 year; recipients may reapply.

**Number awarded:** Varies each year.

## 207 CHILDREN OF MISSIONARIES SCHOLARSHIPS

Presbyterian Church (USA), Attn: Office of Financial Aid for Studies
100 Witherspoon Street, Room M-052
Louisville, KY 40202-1396
Phone: (502) 569-5776; (888) 728-7228, ext. 5776; Fax: (502) 569-8766;
Email: fcook@ctr.pcusa.org
Web: www.pcusa.org/financialaid/programfinder/missionkids.htm

**Summary:** To provide financial assistance for college or graduate school to children of Presbyterian missionaries.

**Eligibility:** Open to students whose parents are engaged in active service as foreign missionaries for the Presbyterian Church (USA). Applicants must be enrolled full time at an accredited institution in the United States, making satisfactory progress toward an undergraduate or graduate degree, able to demonstrate financial need, U.S. citizens or permanent residents, and members of the PC(USA).

**Financial data:** Stipends range from $200 to $1,400 per year, depending upon the financial need of the recipient.

**Duration:** 1 year; may be renewed up to 3 additional years.

**Number awarded:** Varies each year.

**Deadline:** June of each year.

## 208 "CHILI" CURRIER SCHOLARSHIP FUND

New Mexico Land Title Association
500 Marquette, N.W., Suite 1480
Albuquerque, NM 88240
Phone: (505) 883-2683; (888) 65-NMLTA; Fax: (505) 872-3759;
Email: director@nmlta.org
Web: www.nmlta.org

**Summary:** To provide financial assistance for college to students in New Mexico.

**Eligibility:** Open to U.S. citizens who are current New Mexico residents, have graduated from a New Mexico high school (or received a GED through a New Mexico Department of Education approved program), and are attending a postsecondary institution of higher education in the state. Applicants must be enrolled for a minimum of 6 hours if they have a full-time job, for a minimum of 9 hours if they have a part-time job, or for a minimum of 12 hours (full-time student) if they are not employed. Financial need and academic achievement must be demonstrated. All applicants must be recommended by an individual within the title industry and an individual from their own community.

**Financial data:** Initially, each scholarship is $200 per semester for part-time students and $500 for full-time students. Recipients who reapply and have maintained at least a 3.0 GPA are awarded an additional $100 per semester after completion of every third semester, up to a maximum of $700 per semester. Funds must be used for tuition and/or books.

**Duration:** 1 semester; may be renewed.

**Number awarded:** Varies each year.

## 209 CHITTENDEN BANK SCHOLARSHIP

Vermont Student Assistance Corporation
Champlain Mill, Attn: Scholarship Programs
P.O. Box 2000
Winooski, VT 05404-2601
Phone: (802) 654-3798; (888) 253-4819; Fax: (802) 654-3765;
TDD: (802) 654-3766; TDD: (800) 281-3341 (within VT); Email: info@vsac.org
Web: www.vsac.org

**Summary:** To provide financial assistance for college to high school seniors in Vermont.

**Eligibility:** Open to U.S. citizens who are residents of Vermont and graduating from a high school in the state. Applicants must be planning to attend an accredited 2-year or 4-year college or university. Selection is based on letters of recommendation, required essays, academic achievement, and financial need.

**Financial data:** The stipend is $2,500 per year.

**Duration:** 1 year; may be renewed up to 3 additional years.

**Number awarded:** 2 each year.

**Deadline:** April of each year.

## 210 CHRISTIAN CONNECTOR UNDERGRADUATE SCHOLARSHIP

Christian Connector, Inc., Attn: Thom Seagren
518 28 Road, Suite B102
Grand Junction, CO 81501
Phone: (970) 256-1610; (800) 667-0600
Web: www.christianconnector.com

**Summary:** To provide financial assistance to high school seniors and transfer students interested in attending a Christ-centered Christian college or bible college.

**Eligibility:** Open to students planning to enroll for the first time at a Christ-centered Christian college or bible college. Schools that are members of the CCCU, NACCAP, or AABC automatically qualify. Students currently enrolled at a Christian college or bible college are not eligible. Applicants enter the competition by registering online with the sponsoring organization, indicating if they wish to receive information from Christian colleges and universities, bible colleges, short-term missions opportunities, Christian music/concerts/festivals, Christian teen publications, or Christian teen events and conferences. The recipient of the scholarship is selected in a random drawing.

**Financial data:** The award is $1,000. Funds are sent directly to the winner's school.

**Duration:** The competition is held annually.

**Number awarded:** 1 each year.

**Deadline:** May of each year.

## 211 CHRISTIAN SCIENCE MONITOR FRESHMAN COLLEGE AWARD

National Foundation for Women Legislators, Inc.
910 16th Street, N.W., Suite 100
Washington, DC 20006
Phone: (202) 293-3040; Fax: (202) 293-5430; Email: nfwl@erols.com
Web: www.womenlegistors.org

**Summary:** To recognize and reward college-bound young women who have made significant contributions to the well-being of young people in their communities.

**Eligibility:** Open to high school senior women who are invited to write a 1-page essay about their contribution to the well-being of young people in their community. The essay should tell why they were motivated to do this work, how this work is important in improving the well-being of young people, what they believe it has accomplished, and what they learned from this experience. Applicants should also submit 2 personal letters of reference.

**Financial data:** The award is $2,500. The winner's essay may be published in the *Christian Science Monitor*.

**Duration:** The award is granted annually.

**Number awarded:** 1 each year.

**Deadline:** June of each year.

## 212 CHUCK HALL STAR OF TOMORROW AWARD

United States Bowling Congress, Attn: SMART Program
5301 South 76th Street
Greendale, WI 53129-1192
Phone: (414) 423-3343; (800) 514-BOWL, ext. 3343; Fax: (414) 421-3014;
Email: smart@bowl.com
Web: www.bowl.com/scholarships/main.aspx

**Summary:** To provide financial assistance for college to outstanding male bowlers.

**Eligibility:** Open to men amateur bowlers who are current members in good standing of the United States Bowling Congress (USBC) or USBC Youth and competitors in events sanctioned by those organizations. Applicants must be high school or college students younger than 22 years of age, have a GPA of 2.5 or higher, and have a bowling average of 175 or greater. They may not have competed in a professional bowling tournament. Along with their application, they must submit an essay, up to 500 words, on how bowling has influenced their life, academic, and personal goals. Selection is based on bowling performances on local, state, and national levels; academic achievement; and community involvement.

**Financial data:** The stipend is $1,250 per year.

**Duration:** 1 year; may be renewed up to 3 additional years.

**Number awarded:** 1 each year.

**Deadline:** November of each year.

## 213 CIF SCHOLAR-ATHLETE OF THE YEAR

California Interscholastic Federation, Attn: State Office
333 Hegenberger Road, Suite 511
Oakland, CA 94621
Phone: (510) 639-4445; Fax: (510) 639-4449; Email: info@cifstate.org
Web: www.cifstate.org

**Summary:** To provide financial assistance to college-bound high school seniors in California who have participated in athletics.

**Eligibility:** Open to high school seniors in California who have an unweighted cumulative GPA of 3.7 or higher and have demonstrated superior athletic ability in at least 2 years of varsity play within California. Students must submit an application to their principal or counselor and an essay, up to 500 words, on how they display character in their athletic and academic efforts. They may include examples of meaningful behavior in their high school experience, lessons learned about the importance of character in their life, and opportunities that coaches, cheerleaders, athletes, and fans have to promote character in interscholastic athletics. Based on those essays, school officials nominate students for these scholarships. Males and females are judged separately.

**Financial data:** The stipend is $2,000.

**Duration:** 1 year; nonrenewable.

**Number awarded:** 2 each year: 1 for a female and 1 for a male.

**Deadline:** Students must submit their application and essay to their counselor or principal by mid-February of each year. School officials forward the packets to the state office by the end of March.

## 214 CINDY KOLB MEMORIAL SCHOLARSHIP

California Association for Postsecondary Education and Disability
Attn: Executive Assistant
71423 Biskra Road
Rancho Mirage, CA 92270
Phone: (760) 346-8206; Fax: (760) 340-5275; TTY: (760) 341-4084;
Email: caped2000@aol.com
Web: www.caped.net/scholarship.html
**Summary:** To provide financial assistance to 4-year college and university students in California who have a disability.
**Eligibility:** Open to students at 4-year colleges and universities in California who have a disability. Applicants must have completed at least 6 semester credits with a GPA of 2.5 or higher. They must submit a 1-page personal letter that demonstrates writing skills; progress toward meeting educational and vocational goals; how they accommodate their disability; involvement in community activities; and any other personal factor that might strengthen their application. They must also submit a letter of recommendation from a faculty member, verification of disability, official transcripts, proof of current enrollment, and documentation of financial need.
**Financial data:** The stipend is $1,000.
**Duration:** 1 year.
**Number awarded:** 1 each year.
**Deadline:** August of each year.

## 215 CIT IS PRO EDUCATION ACADEMIC SCHOLARSHIPS

CIT Group Inc.
1 CIT Drive
Livingston, NJ 07039
Phone: (973) 740-5000
Web: www.cit.com
**Summary:** To provide financial assistance for college to high school seniors in New Jersey.
**Eligibility:** Open to seniors graduating from high schools in New Jersey who are nominated by their guidance counselors. Selection is based on academic achievement and financial need.
**Financial data:** The stipend is $2,500 per year. Runners-up receive $500 U.S. savings bonds.
**Duration:** 4 years.
**Number awarded:** Varies each year. Recently, 6 of these scholarships were awarded. In addition, 7 students received $500 savings bonds and another 5 students at designated high schools and Rutgers University received scholarships.

## 216 CITE SCHOLARSHIPS

Consortium of Information and Telecommunications Executives, Inc.
c/o Diane C. Lewis, Scholarship Committee Chair
6000 Hadley Road
South Plainfield, NJ 07080
Phone: (908) 412-6421
Web: www.forcite.org
**Summary:** To provide financial assistance for college to African American high school seniors in selected states.
**Eligibility:** Open to African American high school seniors who have been accepted by an accredited college or university. Applicants must have a GPA of 3.0 or higher and be able to document financial need. They must submit their application to a chapter of the Consortium of Information and Telecommunications Executives (CITE), currently located in California, Florida, Indiana, Maryland, Metropolitan Washington, New England, New Jersey, New York, Pennsylvania and Delaware, Texas, Virginia, and West Virginia. Employees of Verizon Communications or an affiliated subsidiary and their family members are ineligible.
**Financial data:** The stipend is $2,000.
**Duration:** 1 year; nonrenewable.
**Number awarded:** 12 each year: 1 to a student in each of the chapter areas.
**Deadline:** May of each year.

## 217 CLAIRE OLIPHANT MEMORIAL SCHOLARSHIPS

American Legion Auxiliary, Attn: Department of New Jersey
c/o Lucille M. Miller, Secretary, Treasurer
1540 Kuser Road, Suite A-8
Hamilton, NJ 08619
Phone: (609) 581-9580; Fax: (609) 581-8429
**Summary:** To provide financial assistance for college to New Jersey residents who are the children or grandchildren of veterans.
**Eligibility:** Open to the children and grandchildren of living, deceased, or divorced honorably-discharged veterans of the U.S. armed forces. Applicants must have been residents of New Jersey for at least 2 years and be members of the current graduating class of a senior high school or equivalent.
**Financial data:** The stipend is $1,800.
**Duration:** 1 year.
**Number awarded:** 1 each year.
**Deadline:** March of each year.

## 218 CLYDE RUSSELL SCHOLARSHIP

Clyde Russell Scholarship Fund
P.O. Box 2457
Augusta, ME 04338
**Summary:** To provide financial assistance to Maine residents interested in pursuing additional educational activities.
**Eligibility:** Open to applicants in 3 categories: high school seniors, full-time and part-time college and graduate students, and Maine residents interested in pursuing further educational/cultural opportunities. For high school and college students, selection is based on personal traits and qualities, extracurricular activities, community activities, academic ability and motivation, financial need, and personal goals and objectives. For other Maine residents, selection is based on the nature of the project, projected costs, personal traits and qualities, community activities, and professional/educational characteristics.
**Financial data:** Up to $10,000.
**Duration:** 1 year; nonrenewable.
**Number awarded:** 3 each year: 1 to a high school senior; 1 to a college student; and 1 to a citizen of Maine who is interested in pursuing further educational/cultural opportunities.
**Deadline:** January of each year.

## 219 CLYDE W. MORRIS MEMORIAL SCHOLARSHIP

Virginia Association for Pupil Transportation
c/o David L. Pace, Scholarship Chair
2650 Leroy Road, Building 1
Virginia Beach, VA 23456
Phone: (757) 263-1569; Email: dpace@vbcps.k12.va.us
Web: www.pen.k12.va.us/VDOE/Finance/VAPT/scholarship.htm
**Summary:** To provide financial assistance for college to high school seniors in Virginia who have a parent or grandparent employed in a public school pupil transportation field in the state.
**Eligibility:** Open to seniors at public high schools in Virginia who have a parent or grandparent employed in a public school pupil transportation field in the state. Applicants should have a GPA of 3.0 or higher. As part of the application process, they must write a 500-word essay on why they applied for the scholarship and how the funds will be used. Selection is based on academic record, leadership, citizenship, service, and the essay.
**Financial data:** The stipend is $1,000.
**Duration:** 1 year.
**Number awarded:** 1 or more each year.
**Deadline:** April of each year.

## 220 COAGULIFE NATIONAL EDUCATION SCHOLARSHIP

CoaguLife, Attn: Scholarship Selection Committee
10800 Lyndale Avenue, Suite 112
Bloomington, MN 55420
Phone: (952) 886-9200; (866) 858-9200; Fax: (800) 867-7145;
Email: info@coagulife.com
Web: coagulife.com/4a-scholarships.html
**Summary:** To provide financial assistance for college to students who have an inherited bleeding disorder.
**Eligibility:** Open to college-bound graduating high school seniors or students already enrolled full time at an accredited college, university, or trade school. Applicants must have hemophilia, von Willebrand disease, or a similar inherited bleeding disorder. Along with their application, they must submit an essay

on 1 of 3 assigned topics. Selection is based on the essay, GPA, difficulty of course work, letters of recommendation, community service, and a statement regarding personal, academic, and career goals.

**Financial data:** The maximum stipend is $2,500 per year. Awards may not exceed the total yearly cost of tuition, books, fees, room, and board. Funds are paid directly to the institution.

**Duration:** 1 year; may be renewed as long as the recipient maintains a GPA of 3.0 or higher.

**Number awarded:** 2 each year.

**Deadline:** July of each year for spring semester; December of each year for fall semester.

## 221 COAST GUARD FOUNDATION SCHOLARSHIP FUND

Coast Guard Foundation
Commandant (G-WKW-2), Attn: Foundation Scholarships
2100 Second Street, S.W., Room 6320
Washington, DC 20593-0001
Phone: (202) 267-6728; (800) 872-4957; Email: ywright@comdt.uscg.mil
Web: www.uscg.mil

**Summary:** To provide financial assistance for college to the dependent children of Coast Guard enlisted personnel.

**Eligibility:** Open to the dependent children of enlisted members of the U.S. Coast Guard on active duty, retired, or deceased and of enlisted personnel in the Coast Guard Reserve currently on extended active duty 180 days or more. Applicants must be attending or planning to attend a college, university, or vocational school as a full-time undergraduate student. Along with their application, they must submit their SAT or ACT scores, a letter of recommendation, transcripts, and a financial information statement.

**Financial data:** Stipends range from $2,500 to $5,000 per year.

**Duration:** 1 year; may be renewed up to 3 additional years.

**Number awarded:** 10 each year.

**Deadline:** March of each year.

## 222 COCA-COLA SCHOLARSHIPS

Coca-Cola Scholars Foundation, Inc.
P.O. Box 442
Atlanta, GA 30301-0442
Phone: (800) 306-COKE; Fax: (404) 733-5439;
Email: questions@coca-colascholars.org
Web: www.coca-colascholars.org

**Summary:** To provide financial assistance for college to meritorious students.

**Eligibility:** Open to high school and home-school seniors who are planning to attend an accredited U.S. college or university. Applicants must have a GPA of 3.0 or higher at the end of their junior year in high school. They must be a U.S. citizen, national, permanent resident, refugee, asylee, Cuban-Haitian entrant, or humanitarian parolee. The program selects students who are leaders involved in school and the community; have special talents, skills, and interests; are socially aware; take advantage of opportunities; are persistent and overcome barriers; show character and commitment to high ideals; excel academically; express their thoughts clearly, originally, and creatively; and volunteer their time.

**Financial data:** The stipend is $5,000 per year (for National Scholars) or $1,000 per year (for Regional Scholars).

**Duration:** All scholarships are for 4 years.

**Number awarded:** 250 each year: 50 National Scholars and 200 Regional Scholars.

**Deadline:** October of each year; between 1,500 and 2,000 semifinalists are chosen and they submit an additional application, including detailed biographical data, an essay, secondary school report, and recommendations, by the end of January.

## 223 COCA-COLA TWO-YEAR COLLEGE SCHOLARSHIPS

Coca-Cola Scholars Foundation, Inc.
P.O. Box 1615
Atlanta, GA 30301-1615
Phone: (800) 306-COKE; Fax: (404) 733-5439;
Email: questions@coca-colascholars.org
Web: www.coca-colascholars.org

**Summary:** To provide financial assistance to students at 2-year colleges.

**Eligibility:** Open to U.S. citizens and permanent residents who are nominated by the 2-year degree-granting institution they are attending. Applicants must have a GPA of 2.5 or higher and be able to document at least 100 hours of community service they have performed in the past 12 months. They must be planning to enroll in at least 2 courses during the next term. Selection is based on merit.

**Financial data:** The stipend is $1,000.

**Duration:** 1 year; nonrenewable.

**Number awarded:** 400 each year.

**Deadline:** May of each year.

## 224 COHEAO SCHOLARSHIPS

Coalition of Higher Education Assistance Organizations
c/o Dean, Blakey, and Moskowitz
1101 Vermont Avenue, N.W., Suite 400
Washington, DC 20005-3586
Phone: (202) 289-3910; Fax: (202) 371-0197
Web: www.coheao.org/scholarship/scholarship.asp

**Summary:** To provide financial assistance to students at colleges and universities that are members of the Coalition of Higher Education Assistance Organizations (COHEAO).

**Eligibility:** Open to students entering their sophomore, junior, or senior year at a member institution. Applicants must have a GPA of 3.75 or higher and be a U.S. citizen. Along with their application, they must submit a 300-word essay on their future plans and goals, and how this scholarship will benefit them. Financial need is not considered in the selection process.

**Financial data:** The stipend is $1,000.

**Duration:** 1 year.

**Number awarded:** Up to 8 each year.

**Deadline:** March of each year.

## 225 COLIN HIGGINS FOUNDATION YOUTH COURAGE AWARDS

Colin Higgins Foundation, Attn: Youth Courage Awards
P.O. Box 29903
San Francisco, CA 94129-0903
Phone: (415) 561-6323; Fax: (415) 561-6401; Email: info@colinhiggins.org
Web: www.colinhiggins.org/courageawards/index/html

**Summary:** To recognize and reward young people who have shown courage in the face of adversity related to discrimination against members of the lesbian, gay, bisexual, transgender, and questioning (LGBTQ) communities.

**Eligibility:** Open to young people (under 24 years of age) who are 1) LGBTQ youth who have "bravely stood up to hostility and intolerance based on their sexual orientation and triumphed over bigotry"; or 2) allies who are working to end homophobia and discrimination against LGBTQ communities. Letters of nomination must include 350-word essays describing why the nominee represents the ideals of this award. Self-nominations are not accepted.

**Financial data:** The award is a $10,000 grant.

**Duration:** The awards are presented annually.

**Number awarded:** 2 or 3 each year.

**Deadline:** March of each year.

## 226 COLLEGE FINANCIAL NEWSLETTER SCHOLARSHIP

Earl G. Graves Ltd., Attn: College Financial Newsletter
130 Fifth Avenue, Tenth Floor
New York, NY 10011-4399
Phone: (212) 242-8000
Web: www.blackenterprise.com

**Summary:** To provide financial assistance to college students who utilize the College Financial Newsletter of BlackEnterprise.com.

**Eligibility:** Open to U.S. citizens and permanent residents who are enrolled full time in a recognized college or university within the United States. Applicants must register online to utilize the College Financial e-Newsletter. Selection is based on a random drawing.

**Financial data:** The stipend is $1,000.

**Duration:** 1 year.

**Number awarded:** 3 each year.

## 227 COLLEGE SCHOLARSHIP PROGRAM OF THE HISPANIC SCHOLARSHIP FUND

Hispanic Scholarship Fund, Attn: Selection Committee
55 Second Street, Suite 1500
San Francisco, CA 94105

Phone: (415) 808-2350; (877) HSF-INFO; Fax: (415) 808-2302; Email: college1@hsf.net

Web: www.hsf.net/scholarship/programs/college.php

**Summary:** To provide financial assistance for college or graduate school to Hispanic American students.

**Eligibility:** Open to U.S. citizens, permanent residents, and visitors with a passport stamped I-551. Applicants must be of Hispanic heritage and enrolled full time in a degree-seeking program at an accredited community college, 4-year university, or graduate school in the United States, Puerto Rico, or the U.S. Virgin Islands. They must have completed at least 12 undergraduate units with a GPA of 3.0 or higher and have applied for federal financial aid. Along with their application, they must submit 600-word essays on 1) how their Hispanic heritage, family upbringing, and/or role models have influenced their personal long-term goals; 2) how they contribute to their community and what they have learned from their experiences; and 3) an academic challenge they have faced and how they have overcome it. Selection is based on academic achievement, personal strengths, leadership, and financial need.

**Financial data:** Stipends normally range from $1,000 to $3,000 per year.

**Duration:** 1 year; recipients may reapply.

**Number awarded:** More than 4,000 each year.

**Deadline:** October of each year.

### 228 COLLEGE STUDENT PRE-COMMISSIONING INITIATIVE

U.S. Coast Guard, Attn: Coast Guard Recruiting

4200 Wilson Boulevard, Suite 450

Arlington, VA 22203

Phone: (877) NOW-USCG, ext. 2115

Web: www.gocoastguard.com/scholarships.html

**Summary:** To provide financial assistance to college students at minority institutions willing to serve in the Coast Guard following graduation.

**Eligibility:** Open to students enrolled as sophomores or juniors at approved 4-year Historically Black Colleges and Universities (HBCUs), Hispanic Serving Institutions (HSIs), and other approved minority institutions of higher learning. Applicants must be U.S. citizens; have a GPA of 2.5 or higher; have scores of 1000 or higher on the SAT, 1100 or higher on the SAT I, 23 or higher on the ACT, or 110 or higher on the ASVAB GT; be between 21 and 26 years of age at the time of college graduation; and meet all physical requirements for a Coast Guard commission. They must agree to attend the Coast Guard Officer Candidate School following graduation and serve on active duty as an officer for at least 3 years.

**Financial data:** Those selected to participate receive full payment of tuition, books, and fees; monthly housing and food allowances; medical and life insurance; special training in leadership, management, law enforcement, navigation, and marine science; 30 days paid vacation per year; and a monthly salary of up to $2,200.

**Duration:** 2 years.

**Number awarded:** Varies each year.

**Deadline:** February of each year.

### 229 COLLEGEBOUND STUDENT OF THE YEAR SCHOLARSHIPS

CollegeBound Network, Attn: Student of the Year Contest

1200 South Avenue, Suite 202

Staten Island, NY 10314

Phone: (718) 761-4800; Fax: (718) 761-3300; Email: information@collegebound.net

Web: www.collegebound.net/nycolor/index.html

**Summary:** To recognize and reward, with college scholarships, high school students who submit essays on a topic related to college.

**Eligibility:** Open to juniors and seniors at high schools in the United States. Applicants must submit an essay of 300 to 500 words on a topic that changes annually but relates to their anticipated college experiences. Recently, they were invited to write the chapter on "My College Years" for their autobiography. Finalists are interviewed by telephone.

**Financial data:** The prize includes a $5,000 scholarship and other gifts.

**Duration:** This competition is held annually.

**Number awarded:** 2 each year.

**Deadline:** May of each year.

### 230 COLLEGEBOUNDFUND ACADEMIC PROMISE SCHOLARSHIP

Rhode Island Higher Education Assistance Authority

Attn: Scholarship and Grant Division

560 Jefferson Boulevard

Warwick, RI 02886

Phone: (401) 736-1170; (800) 922-9855; Fax: (401) 732-3541; TDD: (401) 734-9481; Email: scholarships@riheaa.org

Web: www.riheaa.org/borrowers/scholarships

**Summary:** To provide financial assistance for college to high school seniors in Rhode Island who can demonstrate academic promise.

**Eligibility:** Open to U.S. citizens and permanent residents who have been residents of Rhode Island since the beginning of the year prior to the academic year in which they enroll in college. Applicants must be high school seniors accepted for full-time enrollment in a program that leads to a certificate or degree, not owe a refund on a federal Title IV grant, not be in default on a Title IV loan, and not already possess a bachelor's degree. They must file a Free Application for Federal Student Aid (FAFSA) and take the SAT or ACT test. Selection is based on those test scores and high school GPA.

**Financial data:** The stipend is $2,500.

**Duration:** 1 year; may be renewed for up to 3 additional years provided the recipient maintains a cumulative GPA of 3.0 or minimum GPAs of 2.50 for the first year, 2.75 for the second year, or 3.0 for the third year.

**Number awarded:** Varies each year.

**Deadline:** February of each year.

### 231 COLLEGENET SCHOLARSHIP

CollegeNET, Attn: Heidi Peterson

805 S.W. Broadway, Suite 1600

Portland, OR 97205-3356

Phone: (503) 973-5253; Fax: (503) 973-5252; Email: heidip@collegenet.com

Web: www.collegenet.com

**Summary:** To provide financial assistance to students using the CollegeNET service to apply to college.

**Eligibility:** Open to students who apply to college via CollegeNET's Applyweb system, are accepted by the school or schools to which they apply electronically, enroll in a CollegeNET school to which they apply, and are nominated by that college. If they are nominated by their institution, they must submit an essay on a topic that changes annually; recently, the topic was "Next Steps for the U.S. in Iraq." Final selection of the scholarship winners is based on the essay.

**Financial data:** The stipend is $10,000.

**Duration:** 1 year.

**Number awarded:** 1 each year.

**Deadline:** Students must submit their college application by the end of August of each year. Each participating college then nominates its students in January and those nominees have 3 weeks to prepare their essays and submit them online.

### 232 COLLEGESTEPS PROGRAM SCHOLARSHIPS

Wells Fargo Education Financial Services

301 East 58th Street North

Sioux Falls, SD 57104

Phone: (800) 658-3567; Fax: (800) 456-0561;

Email: studentloans@wellsfargoefs.com

Web: www.wellsfargo.com/collegesteps

**Summary:** To provide financial assistance for college to high school seniors who enroll in the CollegeSTEPS program sponsored by Wells Fargo Bank.

**Eligibility:** Open to residents of the United States (except New York and Florida) who are seniors in high school. Applicants must be actively enrolled in the CollegeSTEPS program. They must have access to the Internet and an active E-mail account. Selection is based on random drawings, held monthly from October through May in 6 regions of the country.

**Financial data:** Each prize is a $1,000 tuition scholarship. Funds are paid jointly to the winner and the U.S. institution of higher learning.

**Duration:** Scholarships are for 1 year.

**Number awarded:** 100 each year.

**Deadline:** Entries may be submitted any month between October and May of each year.

### 233 COLORADO BPW EDUCATION FOUNDATION SCHOLARSHIPS

Colorado Federation of Business and Professional Women

Attn: Colorado BPW Education Foundation

P.O. Box 1189

Boulder, CO 80306

Phone: (303) 443-2573; Fax: (303) 564-0397; Email: cbpwf@earthnet.net

Web: www.cbpwef.org

**Summary:** To provide financial assistance for college to mature women residing in Colorado.

**Eligibility:** Open to women 25 years of age and older who are enrolled in an accredited Colorado college or university. Applicants must be U.S. citizens who have resided in Colorado for at least 12 months. Along with their application, they must submit a copy of their most recent high school or college transcript, proof of Colorado residency and U.S. citizenship, a statement of their educational and career goals, 2 letters of recommendation, and documentation of financial need.

**Financial data:** Stipends range from $250 to $1,000. Funds are to be used for tuition, fees, or books.

**Duration:** 1 semester; recipients may reapply.

**Number awarded:** Varies each year; recently, 30 of these scholarships, worth $18,050, were awarded.

**Deadline:** March or September of each year.

## 234 COLORADO COLLEGE OPPORTUNITY FUND

Colorado Commission on Higher Education
1380 Lawrence Street, Suite 1200
Denver, CO 80204
Phone: (303) 866-2723; Fax: (303) 866-4266; Email: cche@state.co.us
Web: www.state.co.us/cche/finaid/gos/index.html

**Summary:** To provide financial assistance to Colorado residents who have significant financial need and are planning to enter a college or university in the state as a first-time freshman.

**Eligibility:** Open to residents of Colorado who are enrolled or planning to enroll at an eligible college or university in the state. Applicants must be able to demonstrate financial need.

**Financial data:** The stipend varies annually, but does not exceed the student's total in-state tuition. At private colleges and universities in the state, the stipend is 50% of the annually set amount. Funds are paid directly to the recipient's institution.

**Duration:** 1 year; may be renewed for a total of 145 undergraduate credit hours.

**Number awarded:** Varies each year.

## 235 COLORADO COUNCIL VOLUNTEERISM/COMMUNITY SERVICE SCHOLARSHIPS

Colorado Council on High School/College Relations
Attn: Scholarship Committee
600 17th Street, Suite 2210 South
Denver, CO 80202
Phone: (970) 264-2231, ext. 226; Email: mthompson@pagosa.k12.co.us
Web: www.coloradocouncil.org

**Summary:** To provide financial assistance for college to high school seniors in Colorado who have been involved in community service activities.

**Eligibility:** Open to high school seniors who have been Colorado residents for at least their final 2 years of high school. Applicants must have a GPA of 2.5 or higher and acceptance at a college or university that is a member of the Colorado Council on High School/College Relations as a full-time student. They must submit a 500-word essay on a significant experience or achievement that has special meaning to them in their involvement in a volunteer role. Selection is based on volunteerism and community service, extracurricular activities, and dedication to serving others. U.S. citizenship or permanent resident status is required.

**Financial data:** The stipend is $1,000.

**Duration:** 1 year.

**Number awarded:** 8 each year: 1 in each of the sponsor's districts.

**Deadline:** February of each year.

## 236 COLORADO DEPENDENTS TUITION ASSISTANCE PROGRAM

Colorado Commission on Higher Education
1380 Lawrence Street, Suite 1200
Denver, CO 80204
Phone: (303) 866-2723; Fax: (303) 866-4266; Email: cche@state.co.us
Web: www.state.co.us/cche/finaid/students/stateaid/types.html

**Summary:** To provide financial assistance for college to the dependents of disabled or deceased Colorado National Guardsmen, law enforcement officers, and fire fighters.

**Eligibility:** Open to the dependents of Colorado law enforcement officers, fire fighters, and National Guardsmen disabled or killed in the line of duty, as well as dependents of prisoners of war or service personnel listed as missing in action. Students must be Colorado residents enrolled at a school participating in the program. Only dependents of disabled personnel must demonstrate financial need.

**Financial data:** Eligible students receive free tuition at Colorado public institutions of higher education. If the recipient wishes to attend a private college, university, or proprietary school, the award is limited to the amount of tuition at a comparable state-supported institution. Students who do not live at home also receive the actual cost of room and board charged for on-campus housing or, if no space is available at on-campus dormitories, a supplemental grant of $1,000 per semester to assist with living expenses.

**Duration:** Up to 8 academic semesters or 12 academic quarters, provided the recipient maintains a GPA of 2.5 or higher.

**Number awarded:** Varies each year.

## 237 COLORADO GOVERNOR'S OPPORTUNITY SCHOLARSHIP

Colorado Commission on Higher Education
1380 Lawrence Street, Suite 1200
Denver, CO 80204
Phone: (303) 866-2723; Fax: (303) 866-4266; Email: cche@state.co.us
Web: www.state.co.us/cche/finaid/gos/index.html

**Summary:** To provide financial assistance to Colorado residents who have significant financial need and are planning to enter a college or university in the state as a first-time freshman.

**Eligibility:** Open to residents of Colorado who are entering an eligible college or university in the state as a full-time freshman with no previous postsecondary experience after high school graduation. Applicants must come from a family with an adjusted gross income less than $29,767 (plus $6,031 for each family member in excess of 3) and an estimated family contribution (EFC) of zero. Students may nominate themselves or they may be nominated by a teacher, counselor, parent, or someone else who knows them well. U.S. citizenship or permanent resident status is required.

**Financial data:** The amount of assistance varies, to a maximum of $10,700 per year.

**Duration:** 1 year; may be renewed up to 4 additional years if the recipient continues to meet financial need requirements, remains enrolled full time, and demonstrates satisfactory academic progress.

**Number awarded:** More than 250 each year.

**Deadline:** Each participating institution sets its own deadlines.

## 238 COLORADO LEVERAGING EDUCATIONAL ASSISTANCE PARTNERSHIP (CLEAP)

Colorado Commission on Higher Education
1380 Lawrence Street, Suite 1200
Denver, CO 80204
Phone: (303) 866-2723; Fax: (303) 866-4266; Email: cche@state.co.us
Web: www.state.co.us/cche/finaid/students/stateaid/types.html

**Summary:** To provide financial assistance for undergraduate education to residents of Colorado who can demonstrate financial need.

**Eligibility:** Open to residents of Colorado who are enrolled or accepted for enrollment in eligible postsecondary institutions in the state. Selection is based on financial need.

**Financial data:** The amount of assistance varies, to a maximum of $5,000 per year.

**Duration:** 1 year; renewable.

**Number awarded:** Varies each year.

**Deadline:** Each participating institution sets its own deadlines.

## 239 COLORADO STUDENT GRANTS

Colorado Commission on Higher Education
1380 Lawrence Street, Suite 1200
Denver, CO 80204
Phone: (303) 866-2723; Fax: (303) 866-4266; Email: cche@state.co.us
Web: www.state.co.us/cche/finaid/students/stateaid/types.html

**Summary:** To provide financial assistance for undergraduate education to residents of Colorado who can demonstrate financial need.

**Eligibility:** Open to residents of Colorado who are enrolled or accepted for enrollment in participating postsecondary institutions in the state. Selection is based on financial need, as indicated by the student's expected family contribution (EFC) and the amount required for a federal Pell Grant. Students whose EFC is between zero and 150% of that required for a Pell Grant are in level 1, students whose EFC is between 150 and 200% of that required for the minimum Pell Grant are in level 2, and all other students who demonstrate financial need are in level 3.

**Financial data:** The amount of assistance varies. Students in level 1 receive from $1,500 to the maximum amount of unmet need, up to $5,000; students in level 2 receive up to $2,500 or the maximum amount of unmet need, whichever is less; students in level 3 receive up to $500.

**Duration:** 1 year; renewable.

**Number awarded:** Varies each year.

**Deadline:** Each participating institution sets its own deadlines.

## 240 COLORADO UNDERGRADUATE MERIT SCHOLARSHIP PROGRAM

Colorado Commission on Higher Education
1380 Lawrence Street, Suite 1200
Denver, CO 80204
Phone: (303) 866-2723; Fax: (303) 866-4266; Email: cche@state.co.us
Web: www.state.co.us/cche/finaid/students/stateaid/types.html

**Summary:** To provide financial assistance for college to residents of Colorado with special skills.

**Eligibility:** Open to residents of Colorado (as well as a limited number of non-residents) who are enrolled or accepted for enrollment at public, private, and proprietary schools of higher education in Colorado. High school seniors must demonstrate academic achievement on the basis of GPA or class rank, standardized test scores, or a competitive process or portfolio review. Transfer students must demonstrate academic excellence by transferring into the institution with a cumulative college GPA of 3.0 or higher.

**Financial data:** The amount of assistance varies, up to the actual cost of tuition and fees.

**Duration:** 1 year; renewable if the recipient maintains a GPA of 3.0 or higher.

**Number awarded:** Varies each year.

**Deadline:** Each participating institution sets its own deadlines.

## 241 COMMANDER WILLIAM S. STUHR SCHOLARSHIPS

Commander William S. Stuhr Scholarship Fund
c/o Joseph A. LaRivere, Executive Director
1200 Fifth Avenue, Suite 9-D
New York, NY 10029
Email: stuhrstudents@earthlink.net

**Summary:** To provide financial assistance for college to the dependent children of retired or active-duty military personnel.

**Eligibility:** Open to the dependent children of military personnel who are serving on active duty or retired with pay after 20 years' service (not merely separated from service). Applicants must be high school seniors who rank in the top 10% of their class for their junior year and the first half of their senior year. They must plan to attend a 4-year accredited college. Selection is based on academic performance, extracurricular activities, demonstrated leadership potential, and financial need.

**Financial data:** The stipend is $1,125 per year.

**Duration:** 4 years, provided the recipient makes the dean's list at their college at least once during their first 2 years.

**Number awarded:** 5 each year: 1 for a child of a military servicemember from each of the 5 branches (Air Force, Army, Coast Guard, Marine Corps, and Navy).

**Deadline:** February of each year.

## 242 COMMONWEALTH "GOOD CITIZEN" SCHOLARSHIPS

Association of Independent Colleges and Universities of Pennsylvania
101 North Front Street
Harrisburg, PA 17101-1405
Phone: (717) 232-8649; Fax: (717) 233-8574; Email: info@aicup.org
Web: www.aicup.org

**Summary:** To provide financial assistance to students at member institutions of the Association of Independent Colleges and Universities of Pennsylvania (AICUP) who have demonstrated outstanding commitment to community service.

**Eligibility:** Open to full-time undergraduate students at AICUP colleges and universities. Applicants must have shown an extraordinary commitment to community service and have demonstrated creativity in shaping their volunteer activities. As part of their application, they must submit a 2-page essay on their volunteer/extracurricular activities on and off campus, how those activities relate to their major, their career and academic goals after graduation, and how they will remain involved in their community after graduation. Selection is

based on the extent of their volunteer and community service activities (30%), leadership activities and taking initiative (30%), evidence of commitment to community service (30%), and additional material, such as reference letters (10%). There is no minimum GPA requirement; grades are considered only in the event of a tie. Applications must be submitted to the financial aid office at the AICUP college or university that the student attends.

**Financial data:** The stipend is $1,000.

**Duration:** 1 year.

**Number awarded:** Varies each year; recently, 6 of these scholarships were awarded.

**Deadline:** April of each year.

## 243 COMMONWEALTH SCHOLARSHIPS

Kentucky Community and Technical College System, Attn: Financial Aid
300 North Main Street
Versailles, KY 40383
Phone: (859) 256-3100; (877) 528-2748 (within KY)
Web: www.kctcs.edu/student/financialaidscholarships/index.htm

**Summary:** To provide financial assistance to outstanding students at participating institutions within the Kentucky Community and Technical College System (KCTCS).

**Eligibility:** Open to Kentucky residents who are 1) current-year valedictorians in their high school class, 2) valedictorians who graduated from high school during the previous academic year, and 3) salutatorian or the top 10% of the current high school graduating class. Applicants must be attending or planning to attend a participating KCTCS institution. They must be able to demonstrate unmet financial need. Most colleges require full-time enrollment.

**Financial data:** Stipends vary at each participating college, but are intended to provide full payment of tuition and required fees.

**Duration:** 1 year; may be renewed 1 additional year.

**Number awarded:** Varies each year.

**Deadline:** Each college sets its own deadline.

## 244 COMMONWEALTH SEPTEMBER 11, 2001 TRAGEDY TUITION WAIVER PROGRAM

Massachusetts Office of Student Financial Assistance
454 Broadway, Suite 200
Revere, MA 02151
Phone: (617) 727-9420; Fax: (617) 727-0667; Email: osfa@osfa.mass.edu
Web: www.osfa.mass.edu

**Summary:** To provide financial assistance for college to Massachusetts residents who are the spouse or child of a victim of the terrorism that occurred on September 11, 2001.

**Eligibility:** Open to the spouses and children of residents of Massachusetts who died or are missing and presumed dead as a result of the acts of terrorism that occurred on September 11, 2001. Applicants must be enrolled or planning to enroll at a public higher education institution in Massachusetts.

**Financial data:** Eligible students are exempt from any tuition payments for an undergraduate degree or certificate program at public colleges or universities in Massachusetts.

**Duration:** Up to 4 academic years, for a total of 130 semester hours.

**Number awarded:** Varies each year.

## 245 CONGRESSIONAL HISPANIC CAUCUS INSTITUTE SCHOLARSHIP AWARDS

Congressional Hispanic Caucus Institute, Inc.
911 Second Street, N.E.
Washington, DC 20002
Phone: (202) 543-1771; (800) EXCEL-DC; Fax: (202) 546-2143;
Email: chci@chci.org
Web: www.chciyouth.org

**Summary:** To provide financial assistance for college or graduate school to students of Hispanic descent.

**Eligibility:** Open to U.S. citizens and permanent residents who are Hispanic as defined by the U.S. Census Bureau (individuals of Mexican, Puerto Rican, Cuban, Central and South American, and other Spanish and Latin American descent). Applicants must be attending or planning to attend an accredited community college, 4-year university, or professional or graduate program as a full-time student. They must submit evidence of financial need, consistent active participation in public and/or community service activities, good writing skills, and 1-page essays on 1) how effective the public education system has been in addressing the needs of the Latino community and what policy recommendations they suggest to improve the system; and 2) the field of study they plan to pursue and how the Latino community will benefit.

**Financial data:** The stipend is $2,500 at 4-year and graduate institutions or $1,000 at 2-year community colleges.

**Duration:** 1 year.

**Number awarded:** Varies each year. Recently, 63 of these scholarships were awarded: 5 to community college students, 40 to undergraduates, and 18 to graduate students.

**Deadline:** April of each year.

## 246 CONGRESSIONAL MEDAL OF HONOR SOCIETY SCHOLARSHIPS

Congressional Medal of Honor Society
40 Patriots Point Road
Mt. Pleasant, SC 29464
Phone: (843) 884-8862; Fax: (843) 884-1471; Email: medalhq@earthlink.net
Web: www.cmohs.org

**Summary:** To provide financial assistance to dependents of Congressional Medal of Honor winners who are interested in pursuing postsecondary education.

**Eligibility:** Open to sons and daughters of Congressional Medal of Honor recipients. they must be high school seniors or graduates and have been accepted by an accredited college or university.

**Financial data:** The stipend is $2,000 per year.

**Duration:** 1 year; may be renewed for up to 3 additional years.

**Number awarded:** Varies; approximately 15 each year.

**Deadline:** August or December of each year.

## 247 CONNECTICUT AID FOR PUBLIC COLLEGE STUDENTS

Connecticut Department of Higher Education
Attn: Office of Student Financial Aid
61 Woodland Street
Hartford, CT 06105-2326
Phone: (860) 947-1855; Fax: (860) 947-1311; Email: sfa@ctdhe.org
Web: www.ctdhe.org/SFA/sfa.htm

**Summary:** To provide financial assistance to Connecticut residents attending public colleges in the state.

**Eligibility:** Open to residents of Connecticut who are attending a public college in the state. Selection is based on financial need.

**Financial data:** Awards up to the amount of unmet financial need are provided.

**Duration:** 1 year.

**Number awarded:** Varies each year.

## 248 CONNECTICUT DUNKIN' DONUTS FRANCHISEE SCHOLARSHIP PROGRAM

Connecticut Association of Schools, Attn: Executive Director
30 Realty Drive
Cheshire, CT 06410
Phone: (203) 250-1111; Fax: (203) 250-1345; Email: msavage@casciac.org
Web: www.casciac.org

**Summary:** To provide financial assistance for college to "well-rounded" high school seniors in Connecticut.

**Eligibility:** Open to seniors graduating from high schools in Connecticut who plan to enroll at least half time in a baccalaureate degree program at an accredited college or university, an associate's degree program at an accredited junior or community college, or a certificate program at an approved vocational or technical institute. Applicants must be able to demonstrate qualities of a "well-rounded" student: academic excellence (GPA of 3.0 or higher), leadership, and involvement in school and community activities.

**Financial data:** The stipend is $1,000.

**Duration:** 1 year.

**Number awarded:** 100 each year.

**Deadline:** April of each year.

## 249 CONNECTICUT INDEPENDENT COLLEGE STUDENT GRANTS

Connecticut Department of Higher Education
Attn: Office of Student Financial Aid
61 Woodland Street
Hartford, CT 06105-2326

Phone: (860) 947-1855; Fax: (860) 947-1311; Email: sfa@ctdhe.org
Web: www.ctdhe.org/SFA/sfa.htm

**Summary:** To provide financial assistance for undergraduate education to students attending independent colleges in Connecticut.

**Eligibility:** Open to residents of Connecticut who are attending an independent college in the state. Selection is based on financial need.

**Financial data:** Grants up to $8,500 per year are provided.

**Duration:** 1 year.

**Number awarded:** Varies each year.

## 250 CONNECTICUT NATIONAL GUARD FOUNDATION SCHOLARSHIPS

Connecticut National Guard Foundation, Inc., Attn: Scholarship Committee
360 Broad Street
Hartford, CT 06015
Phone: (860) 241-1550; Fax: (860) 293-2929;
Email: scholarship.committee@ctngfoundation.org
Web: www.ctngfoundation.org/Scholarship.asp

**Summary:** To provide financial assistance for college to members of the Connecticut National Guard and their families.

**Eligibility:** Open to members of the Connecticut Army National Guard and Organized Militia, their children, and their spouses. Applicants must be enrolled or planning to enroll in an accredited college degree or technical program. Along with their application, they must submit a letter of recommendation, list of extracurricular activities, high school or college transcripts, and a 200-word statement on their educational and future goals. Selection is based on achievement and citizenship.

**Financial data:** The stipend is $1,500.

**Duration:** 1 year.

**Number awarded:** 3 each year.

**Deadline:** April of each year.

## 251 CONNECTICUT STATE DAR SCHOLARSHIPS

Connecticut Daughters of the American Revolution
c/o Lynn Stewart, State Scholarship Chair
215 Loomis Street
North Granby, CT 06060
Fax: (860) 653-4203
Web: www.ctdar.org.htm

**Summary:** To provide financial assistance for college to high school seniors in Connecticut.

**Eligibility:** Open to seniors graduating from high schools in Connecticut in the top 25% of their class. They must be sponsored by their local chapter of the Daughters of the American Revolution. Selection is based on scholastic achievement, leadership, and financial need.

**Financial data:** The stipend is $1,000.

**Duration:** 1 year; nonrenewable.

**Number awarded:** 4 each year.

**Deadline:** January of each year.

## 252 CONNECTICUT TUITION SET ASIDE AID

Connecticut Department of Higher Education
Attn: Office of Student Financial Aid
61 Woodland Street
Hartford, CT 06105-2326
Phone: (860) 947-1855; Fax: (860) 947-1311; Email: sfa@ctdhe.org
Web: www.ctdhe.org/SFA/sfa.htm

**Summary:** To provide financial assistance for undergraduate education to students from any state attending public colleges in Connecticut.

**Eligibility:** Open to residents of any state who are attending a public college in Connecticut. Selection is based on financial need.

**Financial data:** Awards up to the amount of unmet financial need.

**Duration:** 1 year.

**Number awarded:** Varies each year.

## 253 CONNECTICUT TUITION WAIVER FOR VETERANS

Connecticut Department of Higher Education
Attn: Education and Employment Information Center
61 Woodland Street
Hartford, CT 06105-2326

Phone: (860) 947-1816; (800) 842-0229 (within CT); Fax: (860) 947-1310; Email: veterans@ctdhe.org

Web: www.ctdhe.org/vet/default.htm

**Summary:** To provide financial assistance for college to certain Connecticut veterans.

**Eligibility:** Open to honorably-discharged Connecticut veterans who served at least 90 days in World War II, the Korean hostilities, Vietnam, Operations Desert Shield and Desert Storm, Somalia, or Bosnia, or who served in a combat or combat-support role in the peace-keeping mission in Lebanon, the Grenada invasion, Operation Earnest Will, or the Panama invasion.

**Financial data:** The program provides a waiver of 100% of tuition for general fund courses at a Connecticut public college or university, 50% of tuition for extension and summer courses at Connecticut State University, and 50% of part-time fees at *OnlineCSU.*

**Duration:** Up to 4 years.

**Number awarded:** Varies each year.

### 254 COURAGE CENTER SCHOLARSHIP FOR PEOPLE WITH DISABILITIES

Courage Center, Attn: Vocational Services

3915 Golden Valley Road

Minneapolis, MN 55422

Phone: (763) 520-0553; (888) 8-INTAKE; Fax: (763) 520-0392; TTY: (763) 520-0245; Email: suep@courage.org

Web: www.courage.org

**Summary:** To provide financial assistance for college to Minnesota residents who have a disability.

**Eligibility:** Open to U.S. citizens who are residents of Minnesota or have received Courage Center services. Applicants must have a sensory impairment or physical disability and a desire to gain technical expertise beyond high school. Along with their application, they must submit a concise essay that reflects their educational aspirations, career goals, and how a scholarship will help meet their needs. Selection is based on that essay, employment history, honors and awards, leadership experience, and financial need. Graduation ranking is not considered.

**Financial data:** The stipend is $1,000.

**Duration:** 1 year.

**Number awarded:** 1 or more each year.

**Deadline:** May of each year.

### 255 CPO SCHOLARSHIP FUND

Senior Enlisted Academy Alumni Association, Attn: CPO Scholarship Fund

1269 Elliot Avenue

Newport, RI 02841-1525

Email: john@seaaa.org

Web: www.cposf.org

**Summary:** To provide financial assistance for college to the dependents of Navy Chief Petty Officers (CPOs).

**Eligibility:** Open to the spouses and children (natural born, adopted, or step) of active, Reserve, retired, and deceased Navy CPOs. Applicants must be high school graduates or seniors planning to graduate and must intend to enter their first year of college or university with the goal of obtaining an associate, bachelor's, or graduate degree. Members of the armed services are not eligible. Scholarships are awarded in 5 categories: 1) active duty east coast (stationed east of or at Great Lakes, Illinois); 2) active duty west coast (stationed west of Great Lakes, Illinois); 3) active duty stationed outside the continental United States; 4) Reserve; and 5) retired and deceased. Applicants must submit an essay of 250 to 300 words on "How My Education Will Help Society." Selection is based on the essay, honors and awards received during high school, extracurricular activities, community activities, and employment experience.

**Financial data:** The amount of the stipend depends on the availability of funds; awards are sent directly to the recipient's school.

**Duration:** 1 year.

**Number awarded:** 10 each year: 2 in each of the categories.

**Deadline:** March of each year.

### 256 CREON FAMILY SCHOLARSHIP PROGRAM

Solvay Pharmaceuticals, Inc., Attn: Creon Family Scholarship Program

901 Sawyer Road

Marietta, GA 30062

Phone: (770) 578-5898; (800) 354-0026, ext. 5898; Fax: (770) 578-5586

Web: www.solvaypharmaceuticals-us.com

**Summary:** To provide financial assistance for college to students with Cystic Fibrosis (CF).

**Eligibility:** Open to high school seniors, vocational school students, and college students with CF. U.S. citizenship is required. Applicants must submit an academic transcript, documentation of financial need, a photograph, 2 letters of recommendation, and a creative representation (essay, poem, photograph, painting, sculpture, video, cassette tape, etc.) on what they have learned from living with CF. Selection is based on academic excellence, extracurricular activities, the creative representation, the ability to serve as a role model to others with CF, and financial need.

**Financial data:** The stipend is $2,000 per year.

**Duration:** 2 years.

**Number awarded:** 30 each year.

**Deadline:** June of each year.

### 257 CUNAT INTERNATIONAL SCHOLARSHIP

Key Club International, Attn: Manager of Youth Funds

3636 Woodview Trace

Indianapolis, IN 46268-3196

Phone: (317) 875-8755, ext. 244; (800) KIWANIS, ext. 244; Fax: (317) 879-0204; Email: youthfunds@kiwanis.org

Web: www.keyclub.org

**Summary:** To provide financial assistance for college to high school seniors who are Key Club International members.

**Eligibility:** Open to college-bound graduating high school members who have completed at least 100 service hours during their Key Club career and have held an elected officer position on the club, district, or international level. Applicants must have a GPA of 3.5 or higher. Along with their application, they must submit a 200-word essay describing how their studies will help them achieve their goals while benefiting the lives of others. Financial need is not considered in the selection process.

**Financial data:** The stipend is $2,500.

**Duration:** 1 year.

**Number awarded:** 1 each year.

**Deadline:** April of each year.

### 258 CURT GREENE MEMORIAL SCHOLARSHIP

Harness Horse Youth Foundation, Attn: Executive Director

16575 Carey Road

Westfield, IN 46074

Phone: (317) 867-5877; Fax: (317) 867-5896; Email: hhyfetaylor@iquest.net

Web: www.hhyf.org/scholarships.htm

**Summary:** To provide financial assistance to undergraduate students in any major who have an interest in harness-horse racing.

**Eligibility:** Open to students who are at least high school seniors and preferably younger than 25 years of age. Applicants may be pursuing any course of study, but they must have "a passion for harness racing." Selection is based on academic achievement, completeness of the application, the quality of an essay, and financial need.

**Financial data:** A stipend is awarded (amount not specified).

**Duration:** 1 year.

**Number awarded:** 1 or more each year.

**Deadline:** April of each year.

### 259 CYNTHIA RUTH RUSSELL MEMORIAL GRANTS

Kansas Masonic Foundation, Inc.

320 S.W. Eighth Avenue

P.O. Box 1217

Topeka, KS 66601-1217

Phone: (785) 357-7646; Fax: (785) 357-7406; Email: info@kmfonline.org

Web: www.kmfonline.org/education.html

**Summary:** To provide financial assistance to physically challenged Kansas residents attending a college or university in the state.

**Eligibility:** Open to residents of Kansas who are physically challenged. Applicants must be planning to attend an institution of higher education in the state as a full-time undergraduate or graduate student. Along with their application, they must submit a cover letter on their educational and career plans, a recent official transcript, a photograph, and at least 1 letter of recommendation.

**Financial data:** A stipend is awarded (amount not specified).

**Duration:** 1 year; recipients may reapply.

**Number awarded:** 2 each year.

**Deadline:** March of each year.

**260 CYSTIC FIBROSIS SCHOLARSHIPS**

Cystic Fibrosis Scholarship Foundation
2814 Grant Street
Evanston, IL 60201
Phone: (847) 328-0127; Fax: (847) 328-0127; Email: MKBCFSF@aol.com
Web: www.cfscholarship.org

**Summary:** To provide financial assistance to undergraduate students who have cystic fibrosis.

**Eligibility:** Open to students enrolled or planning to enroll in college (either a 2-year or a 4-year program) or vocational school. Applicants must have cystic fibrosis. Selection is based on academic achievement, leadership, and financial need.

**Financial data:** The stipend is $1,000. Funds are sent directly to the student's institution to be used for tuition, books, room, and board.

**Duration:** 1 year; recipients may reapply.

**Number awarded:** Varies each year; recently, 49 of these scholarships were awarded.

**Deadline:** March of each year.

**261 DANA CHRISTMAS SCHOLARSHIP FOR HEROISM**

New Jersey Higher Education Student Assistance Authority
Attn: Financial Aid Services
4 Quakerbridge Plaza
P.O. Box 540
Trenton, NJ 08625-0540
Phone: (609) 588-2349; (800) 792-8670; Fax: (609) 588-2390;
Email: gjoachim@hesaa.org
Web: www.hesaa.org

**Summary:** To provide financial assistance for college or graduate school to residents of New Jersey who have performed an act of heroism.

**Eligibility:** Open to U.S. citizens and eligible noncitizens who are New Jersey residents and have performed an act of heroism when they were 21 years of age or younger. Both applications and nominations from others are required. Letters of nomination must be accompanied by a description of the act of heroism, including such additional documentation as newspaper articles. Nominees must be enrolled or planning to enroll as an undergraduate or graduate student at an institution eligible to participate in the federal Title IV student aid programs.

**Financial data:** The stipend is $10,000.

**Duration:** 1 year; nonrenewable.

**Number awarded:** 5 each year.

**Deadline:** October of each year.

**262 DANIEL L. PEDUZZI MEMORIAL SCHOLARSHIP**

Vertical Flight Foundation, Attn: Scholarship Coordinator
217 North Washington Street
Alexandria, VA 22314-2538
Phone: (703) 684-6777; Fax: (703) 739-9279; Email: Staff@vtol.org
Web: www.vtol.org/vff.html

**Summary:** To provide financial assistance for college to high school seniors in the area of the Federal City chapter of the American Helicopter Society (AHS).

**Eligibility:** Open to seniors graduating from high schools in the Federal City chapter area, which covers Washington, D.C., Maryland (except zip codes 20600-20699), and Virginia (except zip codes 22000-22499). Applicants must have been accepted as a freshman at an accredited college or university. They must submit a narrative covering their future academic interest, their future career interest, and other reasons why they should be considered for this scholarship. Selection is based only on merit.

**Financial data:** The stipend is $2,000.

**Duration:** 1 year.

**Number awarded:** 1 each year.

**Deadline:** May of each year.

**263 DATATEL SCHOLARS FOUNDATION RETURNING STUDENT SCHOLARSHIPS**

Datatel Scholars Foundation
4375 Fair Lakes Court
Fairfax, VA 22033
Phone: (703) 968-9000, ext. 4549; (800) 486-4332; Fax: (703) 968-4573;
Email: scholars@datatel.com
Web: www.datatel.com

**Summary:** To provide financial assistance to undergraduate and graduate students returning to school who will be studying at a Datatel client institution.

**Eligibility:** Open to undergraduate and graduate students who are returning to school after an absence of 5 years or longer. Applicants must attend a Datatel client college or university during the upcoming school year. They must first apply to their institution, which selects 1 semifinalist and forwards the application to the sponsor. Along with their application, they must include a 1,000-word personal statement that discusses the impact of being a returning student, the challenges of combining life interests (such as work and family) along with school, and the importance of receiving this scholarship to help achieve a dream. Selection is based on the quality of the personal statement (40%), academic merit (30%), achievements and civic involvement (20%), and 2 letters of recommendation (10%).

**Financial data:** The stipend is $1,500. Funds are paid directly to the institution.

**Duration:** 1 year.

**Number awarded:** 50 each year.

**Deadline:** Students must submit online applications to their institution or organization by January of each year.

**264 DATATEL SCHOLARS FOUNDATION SCHOLARSHIPS**

Datatel Scholars Foundation
4375 Fair Lakes Court
Fairfax, VA 22033
Phone: (703) 968-9000, ext. 4549; (800) 486-4332; Fax: (703) 968-4573;
Email: scholars@datatel.com
Web: www.datatel.com

**Summary:** To provide financial assistance to graduating high school seniors, continuing college students, or graduate students who will be studying at a Datatel client school.

**Eligibility:** Open to undergraduate and graduate students who will attend a Datatel client college or university during the upcoming school year. Applicants must first apply to their institution, which selects 2 semifinalists and forwards their application to the sponsor. Along with their application, they must include a 1,000-word personal statement that summarizes their educational goals and objectives, where they have been as an individual, and where they hope their education will take them. Selection is based on the quality of the personal statement (40%), academic merit (30%), achievements and civic involvement (20%), and 2 letters of recommendation (10%).

**Financial data:** Stipends are $2,400, $1,600, or $1,000, depending upon the cost of undergraduate tuition at the participating institution. Funds are paid directly to the institution.

**Duration:** 1 year.

**Number awarded:** Varies each year; recently, 225 of these scholarships (totaling $375,000) were awarded.

**Deadline:** Students must submit online applications to their institution or organization by January of each year.

**265 DAUGHTERS OF THE CINCINNATI SCHOLARSHIP PROGRAM**

Daughters of the Cincinnati, Attn: Scholarship Administrator
122 East 58th Street
New York, NY 10022
Phone: (212) 319-6915
Web: fdncenter.org/grantmaker/cincinnati

**Summary:** To provide financial assistance for college to high school seniors who are the daughters of active-duty, deceased, or retired military officers.

**Eligibility:** Open to high school seniors who are the daughters of career commissioned officers of the regular Army, Navy, Air Force, Coast Guard, or Marine Corps on active duty, deceased, or retired. Applicants must submit an official school transcript, SAT or ACT scores, a letter of recommendation, and documentation of financial need.

**Financial data:** Scholarship amounts vary but generally range from $1,000 to $3,000 per year. Funds are paid directly to the college of the student's choice.

**Duration:** Scholarships are awarded annually and may be renewed up to 3 additional years while recipients are studying at an accredited college and are in good standing.

**Number awarded:** Approximately 12 each year.

**Deadline:** March of each year.

**266 DAVE WARD MEMORIAL SCHOLARSHIP**

Monumental Rifle and Pistol Club, Inc.
c/o Joe Schwartz, Scholarship Committee Chair
P.O. Box 494
New Windsor, MD 21776
Phone: (410) 465-6360; Email: joe@qis.net

Web: www.monumental.org/Scholarshippressrelease.htm

**Summary:** To provide financial assistance for college to high school juniors and seniors in Maryland who submit an outstanding essay on citizenship.

**Eligibility:** Open to juniors and seniors at high schools in Maryland who plan to attend college. Selection is based primarily on an essay on "What Citizenship Means to Me." Finalists are invited to attend a meeting of the sponsoring organization to present their essay to its members.

**Financial data:** The stipend is $1,000.

**Duration:** 1 year.

**Number awarded:** 1 each year.

**Deadline:** June of each year.

## 267 DAVID HANCOCK MEMORIAL SCHOLARSHIP

Key Club International, Attn: Manager of Youth Funds
3636 Woodview Trace
Indianapolis, IN 46268-3196
Phone: (317) 875-8755, ext. 244; (800) KIWANIS, ext. 244;
Fax: (317) 879-0204; Email: youthfunds@kiwanis.org
Web: www.keyclub.org

**Summary:** To provide financial assistance for college to high school seniors who are Key Club International members.

**Eligibility:** Open to college-bound graduating high school members who have completed at least 100 service hours during their Key Club career and have held an elected officer position on the club, district, or international level. Applicants must have a GPA of 3.5 or higher. Along with their application, they must submit 1) a 500-word essay describing the Key Club service project on which they have participated and that has had the greatest impact on them; and 2) up to 10 pages of additional leadership and academic achievement documentation. Financial need is not considered in the selection process.

**Financial data:** The stipend is $1,000 per year.

**Duration:** 4 years.

**Number awarded:** 1 each year.

**Deadline:** February of each year.

## 268 DAVID M. IRWIN FRIEND OF HIGHER EDUCATION AWARD

Independent Colleges of Washington
600 Stewart Street, Suite 600
Seattle, WA 98101
Phone: (206) 623-4494; Fax: (206) 625-9621; Email: info@icwashington.org
Web: www.icwashington.org/parents_students/financial_aid/index.htm

**Summary:** To provide financial assistance to upper-division students enrolled at colleges and universities that are members of Independent Colleges of Washington (ICW).

**Eligibility:** Open to students completing their sophomore or junior year at ICW-member colleges and universities. Applicants must submit a 1-page essay on "Why an independent college suits my needs for a college education." Selection is based on leadership qualities. Students with a cumulative GPA between 2.5 and 3.0 are encouraged to apply.

**Financial data:** The stipend is $1,000.

**Duration:** 1 year; nonrenewable.

**Number awarded:** 1 each year.

**Deadline:** April of each year.

## 269 DAVIS-PUTTER SCHOLARSHIPS

Davis-Putter Scholarship Fund
P.O. Box 7307
New York, NY 10116-7307
Email: information@davisputter.org
Web: www.davisputter.org

**Summary:** To provide financial assistance to undergraduate and graduate student activists.

**Eligibility:** Open to undergraduate and graduate students who are involved in "the fight to preserve and expand civil rights, economic justice, international solidarity, as well as other struggles that will lead to an equitable, just, and peaceful society." While U.S. citizenship is not required, applicants must be living in the United States and planning to enroll in school here. They must submit a completed application, a personal statement, financial need reports, recommendation letters, transcripts, and a photograph.

**Financial data:** Grants range up to $6,000, depending upon need.

**Duration:** 1 year.

**Number awarded:** Varies each year; recently, a total of 32 of these scholarships were awarded.

**Deadline:** March of each year.

## 270 DEGREE OF HONOR HIGHER EDUCATION SCHOLARSHIPS

Degree of Honor Foundation
400 Robert Street North, Suite 1600
St. Paul, MN 55101-2029
Phone: (651) 228-7600; (800) 947-5812; Fax: (651) 224-7446
Web: www.degreeofhonor.com/pages/Scholar.html

**Summary:** To provide financial assistance to high school senior members of Degree of Honor who wish to attend college.

**Eligibility:** Open to graduating high school seniors who have been insured with Degree of Honor for at least 2 years and have a GPA of 2.75 or higher. Additional funding is provided to students who have also completed the Fraternal Heart (or "Teens With a Heart") Program. Applicants must submit an affirmation of their acceptance of Christian beliefs and other Degree of Honor principles; information on their Degree of Honor and other community service activities; a statement of what they enjoy most about their volunteer involvement; a list of hobbies, talents, or interests; an essay on their anticipated areas of study and career goals; and a description of their leadership qualities and positions held.

**Financial data:** The stipend is $1,000. Recipients of Teens With a Heart Scholarships are awarded an additional $500 scholarship.

**Number awarded:** Varies each year; recently, 13 students received these scholarships, including 3 who received Teens with a Heart Scholarships.

**Deadline:** March of each year.

## 271 DELAWARE EDUCATIONAL BENEFITS FOR CHILDREN OF DECEASED VETERANS AND OTHERS

Delaware Higher Education Commission
Carvel State Office Building
820 North French Street
Wilmington, DE 19801
Phone: (302) 577-3240; (800) 292-7935; Fax: (302) 577-6765;
Email: dhec@doe.k12.de.us
Web: www.doe.state.de.us/high-ed/vets.htm

**Summary:** To provide financial assistance for undergraduate education to dependents of deceased Delaware veterans and state police officers and members of the armed forces declared prisoners of war or missing in action.

**Eligibility:** Open to applicants who have been Delaware residents for at least 3 years and are the children, between 16 and 24 years of age, of members of the armed forces who were Delaware residents when they entered the services and who 1) were killed while on active duty; 2) died from disease, wounds, injuries, or disabilities suffered as a result of active service; or 3) have been declared prisoners of war or missing in action. Also eligible are children of Delaware State Police Officers who were killed in the line of duty or died as a result of disease, wounds, or disabilities incurred in the pursuit of official duties. Financial need must be demonstrated. U.S. citizenship or permanent resident status is required.

**Financial data:** Eligible students receive full tuition at any state-supported institution in Delaware or, if the desired educational program is not available at a state-supported school, at any private institution in Delaware. If the desired educational program is not offered at either a public or private institution in Delaware, this program pays the full cost of tuition at the out-of-state school the recipient attends. Students who wish to attend a private or out-of-state school, even though their program is offered at a Delaware public institution, receive the equivalent of the average tuition and fees at the state school, currently set at $525 per year.

**Duration:** 1 year; may be renewed for 3 additional years.

**Number awarded:** Varies each year.

**Deadline:** Applications may be submitted at any time but at least 4 weeks before the beginning of classes.

## 272 DELAWARE GOVERNOR'S WORKFORCE DEVELOPMENT GRANTS

Delaware Higher Education Commission
Carvel State Office Building
820 North French Street
Wilmington, DE 19801
Phone: (302) 577-3240; (800) 292-7935; Fax: (302) 577-6765;
Email: dhec@doe.k12.de.us
Web: www.doe.state.de.us/high-ed/workforce.htm

**Summary:** To provide financial assistance for part-time education to Delaware working adults with financial need.

**Eligibility:** Open to residents of Delaware and individuals employed in Delaware who are 18 years of age and older. Applicants must be 1) employed on a part-time basis only by 1 or more employers; 2) employed by a small business (with 100 or fewer employees); 3) employed temporarily or by a temporary staffing agency; or 4) self-employed. Employers must contribute to the Blue Collar Training Fund Program. Applicants must be able to demonstrate financial need and part-time enrollment in a participating Delaware college or training program. Full-time students and students who receive any other federal or state educational grants are not eligible.

**Financial data:** Awards up to $2,000 per year are available.

**Duration:** 1 year; renewable.

**Number awarded:** Varies each year.

**Deadline:** Applications may be submitted at any time, but they must be received by the end of the drop/add date at the participating college.

## 273 DELAWARE SCHOLARSHIP INCENTIVE PROGRAM

Delaware Higher Education Commission
Carvel State Office Building
820 North French Street
Wilmington, DE 19801
Phone: (302) 577-3240; (800) 292-7935; Fax: (302) 577-6765;
Email: dhec@doe.k12.de.us
Web: www.doe.state.de.us/high-ed/scip.htm

**Summary:** To provide financial assistance for undergraduate or graduate study to Delaware residents with financial need.

**Eligibility:** Open to Delaware residents who are 1) enrolled full time in an undergraduate degree program at a Delaware or Pennsylvania college or university, or 2) enrolled full time in a graduate degree program at an accredited out-of-state institution or at a private institution in Delaware if their major is not offered at the University of Delaware or Delaware State University. All applicants must be able to demonstrate financial need and have a GPA of 2.5 or higher. U.S. citizenship or permanent resident status is required.

**Financial data:** The amount awarded depends on the need of the recipient but does not exceed the cost of tuition, fees, and books. Currently, the maximum for undergraduates ranges from $700 to $2,200 per year, depending on GPA; the maximum for graduate students is $1,000 per year.

**Duration:** 1 year; renewable.

**Number awarded:** Approximately 1,500 each year.

**Deadline:** April of each year.

## 274 DELAWARE STATE FEDERATION OF WOMEN'S CLUBS SCHOLARSHIP

Delaware State Federation of Women's Clubs
9 East Loockerman, Suite 314
Dover, DE 19901
Email: sharronshulder@dsfwc.org
Web: www.dsfwc.org

**Summary:** To provide financial assistance for college to high school seniors in Delaware.

**Eligibility:** Open to high school seniors in Delaware. Applicants must submit a 150-word statement on what they intend to study in college and why, an official high school transcript, recommendations from their school counselor and clergyman, and a letter of sponsorship from the Delaware State Federation of Women's Clubs (local president). Selection is based on career interests, extracurricular activities, work experience, academic record, and financial need.

**Financial data:** The maximum stipend is $1,500.

**Duration:** 1 year.

**Number awarded:** 1 or more each year.

**Deadline:** March of each year.

## 275 DELL SCHOLARS PROGRAM

Michael & Susan Dell Foundation, Attn: Scholarships
c/o Weber Shandwick
6555 Sierra Drive
Irving, TX 75039
Phone: (972) 830-2526; Email: tdonalson@webershandwick.com
Web: www.dellscholars.org

**Summary:** To provide financial assistance for college to high school seniors who have participated in a college readiness program sponsored by the Michael & Susan Dell Foundation (MSDF).

**Eligibility:** Open to graduating high school seniors who have participated in an MSDF approved college readiness program for at least 2 years. Applicants must have a GPA of 2.4 or higher and be able to demonstrate financial need. They must be planning to enroll at an accredited 2-year or 4-year college or university in the following fall to work on a bachelor's degree. Selection is based on individual determination to succeed, future goals and plans to achieve them, ability to communicate the hardships they have overcome or currently face, self-motivation in completing challenging course work, and financial need. U.S. citizenship or permanent resident status is required.

**Financial data:** The stipend is $5,000 per year. Funds may be used for tuition, fees, books, and on-campus room and board. With approval of the sponsor, they may also be used for approved internships and study abroad programs.

**Duration:** 4 years.

**Number awarded:** 160 each year.

**Deadline:** January of each year.

## 276 DENISE BERTUCCI MEMORIAL SCHOLARSHIP

Jaycees of Wisconsin Foundation, Inc., Attn: Scholarship Committee
P.O. Box 1547
Appleton, WI 54912
Phone: (920) 386-2393
Web: www.jcwf.org/BertucciScholarship.htm

**Summary:** To provide financial assistance to students at Wisconsin postsecondary institutions who are working on a college degree after having been out of school for at least 2 years.

**Eligibility:** Open to full-time students attending a Wisconsin postsecondary institution pursuing at least a 2-year undergraduate program. Applicants must be at least 21 years of age and have completed at least 2 semesters of school since returning after an absence of at least 2 years. They must have a GPA of 3.0 or higher. Along with their application, they must submit brief essays describing the activities in which they have participated within their community, identifying honors and other recognitions they have received, explaining why they decided to return to work on a degree after taking a break in their education, explaining how this education will help to prepare them to be a leader in their community, and describing any obstacles (financial or otherwise) that will affect their working on a degree.

**Financial data:** A stipend is awarded (amount not specified).

**Duration:** 1 year.

**Number awarded:** 1 or more each year.

**Deadline:** May of each year.

## 277 DEPARTMENT OF CHILDREN AND FAMILY SERVICES SCHOLARSHIP PROGRAM

Illinois Department of Children and Family Services
Attn: Scholarship Coordinator
406 East Monroe Street
Springfield, IL 62701-1498
Phone: (217) 785-2509; Fax: (217) 524-3715; TDD: (217) 785-6605;
Email: JHamm@idcfs.state.il.us
Web: www.state.il.us/dcfs

**Summary:** To provide financial support for college to children under the care of the Illinois Department of Children and Family Services (DCFS).

**Eligibility:** Open to high school seniors and students currently enrolled in college who are under guardianship of the Illinois DCFS or have left guardianship through adoption or private guardianship arrangements. Applicants must be attending or planning to attend a public institution in Illinois. Along with their application, they must submit a transcript of high school grades or a copy of their GED certificate, ACT or SAT test scores, and 3 letters of recommendation. Selection is based on scholastic record and aptitude, community and extracurricular activities, and interest in higher education. Some scholarships are reserved for the children of veterans.

**Financial data:** Scholarships provide waiver of all tuition and fees at designated universities plus a stipend equal to the standard board rate for youth of that age (recently, $444.85 per month). Funding is not provided for room, board, or dormitory fees. Children of veterans receive an additional stipend of $500.

**Duration:** Up to 4 years or until students reach 21 years of age, provided they maintain full-time enrollment and a GPA of 2.0 or higher.

**Number awarded:** 48 each year; of those, 4 are awarded to children of veterans.

**Deadline:** March of each year.

## 278 DEPARTMENT OF HOMELAND SECURITY UNDERGRADUATE SCHOLARSHIPS

Oak Ridge Institute for Science and Education
Attn: Science and Engineering Education
P.O. Box 117
Oak Ridge, TN 37831-0117
Phone: (865) 576-8239; Fax: (865) 241-5219; Email: igrid.gregory@orau.gov

Web: www.orau.gov/orise.htm

**Summary:** To provide financial assistance and summer research experience to undergraduate students who are working on a degree in a field of interest to the Department of Homeland Security (DHS).

**Eligibility:** Open to 1) full-time students who are in their second year of college attendance as of the application deadline; and 2) part-time students who have completed at least 45 but no more than 60 semester hours as of the application deadline. Applicants must be majoring in the agricultural sciences, biological and life sciences, computer and information sciences, engineering, mathematics, physical sciences, psychology, social sciences, or selected humanities (religious studies, cultural studies, public policy, advocacy, communications, or science writing). They must have a GPA of 3.3 or higher. Along with their application, they must submit 2 statements on 1) their educational and professional goals, the kinds of research they are interested in conducting, specific questions that interest them, and how they became interested in them; and 2) how they think their interests, talents, and initiative would contribute to make the homeland safer and secure. Selection is based on those statements, academic record, references, and SAT or ACT scores. As part of their program, they must be interested in participating in summer research and development activities at a DHS-designated facility. U.S. citizenship is required.

**Financial data:** This program provides a stipend of $1,000 per month during the academic year and $5,000 for the internship plus full payment of tuition and mandatory fees.

**Duration:** 2 academic years plus 10 weeks during the intervening summer.

**Number awarded:** Approximately 50 each year.

**Deadline:** January of each year.

## 279 DHHS SCHOLARSHIP FUND

Alexander Graham Bell Association for the Deaf
Attn: Financial Aid Coordinator
3417 Volta Place, N.W.
Washington, DC 20007-2778
Phone: (202) 337-5220; Fax: (202) 337-8314; TTY: (202) 337-5221;
Email: financialaid@agbell.org
Web: www.agbell.org

**Summary:** To provide financial assistance to undergraduate and graduate students who are members of the Alexander Graham Bell Association for the Deaf (AG Bell).

**Eligibility:** Open to undergraduate and graduate students who have been diagnosed with a moderate to profound hearing loss prior to acquiring spoken language (hearing loss averages 60dB or greater in the better ear in the speech frequencies of 500, 1000, and 2000 Hz). Applicants must be committed to using spoken language as their primary mode of communication. They must be accepted or enrolled at a mainstream college or university as a full-time student. Along with their application, they must submit a 1-page essay discussing their career goals and how spoken communication is helping them to reach those goals as a person with a hearing loss. Financial need is considered in the selection process. This scholarship is reserved for students who are members of AG Bell and its Deaf and Hard of Hearing Section (DHHS).

**Financial data:** The stipend is $1,000 per year.

**Duration:** 1 year; may be renewed 1 additional year.

**Number awarded:** 2 each year.

**Deadline:** April of each year.

## 280 DIAMOND STATE SCHOLARSHIPS

Delaware Higher Education Commission
Carvel State Office Building
820 North French Street
Wilmington, DE 19801
Phone: (302) 577-3240; (800) 292-7935; Fax: (302) 577-6765;
Email: dhec@doe.k12.de.us
Web: www.doe.state.de.us/high-ed/diamond.htm

**Summary:** To provide financial assistance for college to Delaware high school seniors with outstanding academic records.

**Eligibility:** Open to graduating high school seniors who are Delaware residents with a combined score of 1800 on the SAT and who rank in the upper quarter of their class. Applicants must be planning to enroll in an accredited college or university on a full-time basis. U.S. citizenship or permanent resident status is required.

**Financial data:** Awards up to $1,250 per year are available.

**Duration:** 1 year; may be renewed up to 3 additional years.

**Number awarded:** Approximately 50 each year.

**Deadline:** March of each year.

## 281 DISCOVER CARD TRIBUTE AWARDS

American Association of School Administrators
Attn: Awards and Scholarships
801 North Quincy Street, Suite 700
Arlington, VA 22203-1730
Phone: (703) 528-0700; Fax: (703) 841-1543; Email: tributeaward@aasa.org
Web: www.aasa.org/Discover.htm

**Summary:** To provide financial assistance for college to high school juniors who have demonstrated excellence in many areas of their lives, in addition to academics.

**Eligibility:** Open to high school juniors who are enrolled in public or accredited private schools in the 50 United States and the District of Columbia. Both U.S. citizens and noncitizens are eligible if they plan to graduate from their U.S. high school and continue their education or training at a U.S. postsecondary institution (including certification or license, trade or technical school, 2- or 4-year college, or university). Applicants must have earned a cumulative GPA of 2.75 or higher. They must describe their future career plans; demonstrate outstanding accomplishments in special talents, leadership, and community service; and have faced a significant roadblock or challenge. Selection is based on those accomplishments in addition to academic achievement.

**Financial data:** State scholarships are $2,500 each. National scholarships are $25,000 each.

**Duration:** 1 year.

**Number awarded:** 468 each year: 9 scholarships in each of the 50 states and the District of Columbia and 9 national scholarships.

**Deadline:** January of each year.

## 282 DISTRICT OF COLUMBIA TUITION ASSISTANCE GRANT PROGRAM

Government of the District of Columbia, Attn: Tuition Assistance Grant Office
One Judiciary Square
441 Fourth Street, N.W., Suite 350 North
Washington, DC 20001
Phone: (202) 727-2824; (877) 485-6751; TTY: (202) 727-1675
Web: www.tuitiongrant.washingtondc.gov

**Summary:** To provide financial assistance to residents of the District of Columbia who are interested in attending a study abroad program, a public college or university anywhere in the United States, or a private institution in the Washington metropolitan area.

**Eligibility:** Open to all residents of the District of Columbia who are high school seniors or recent graduates, regardless of where they attended high school. Applicants must be interested in attending 1) a public college or university anywhere in the United States (except in the District of Columbia); 2) a private nonprofit college or university in the Washington metropolitan area (defined as the District of Columbia, the cities of Alexandria, Falls Church, and Fairfax, and the counties of Arlington, Fairfax, Montgomery, and Prince George's); or 3) a private Historically Black College or University (HBCU). Students attending proprietary institutions are not eligible. Study abroad programs do qualify if they are approved for credit by the institution attended. Financial need is not required.

**Financial data:** Awards at public institutions are equal to the difference between the in-state and out-of-state tuition, to an annual maximum of $10,000 or lifetime maximum of $50,000. At private institutions, the maximum award is $2,500 per year or $12,500 over a lifetime. Funds are sent directly to the eligible school and may be used for tuition and fees only.

**Duration:** 1 year; may be renewed up to 4 additional years or until completion of a bachelor's degree provided the recipient maintains at least half-time enrollment.

**Number awarded:** Varies each year.

**Deadline:** June of each year.

## 283 DIVISION I DEGREE-COMPLETION AWARD PROGRAM

National Collegiate Athletic Association, Attn: Leadership Advisory Board
700 West Washington Avenue
P.O. Box 6222
Indianapolis, IN 46206-6222
Phone: (317) 917-6307; Fax: (317) 917-6364; Email: kcooper@ncaa.org
Web: www.ncaa.org/membership/scholarships/degree-completion/d1/index.html

**Summary:** To provide financial assistance to student-athletes at Division I colleges and universities who have exhausted their eligibility for aid from the institutions they attend.

**Eligibility:** Open to student-athletes who have exhausted their 5 years of eligibility for institutional aid at a Division I member institution of the National

Collegiate Athletic Association (NCAA). Applicants must be entering at least their sixth year of college and be within 30 semester hours of their degree requirements. They must submit documentation of financial need,

**Financial data:** Full-time students receive grants equal to a full athletics grant at their institution; part-time students receive tuition and an allowance for books. The NCAA foundation contributes $950,000 to this program each year.

**Duration:** Up to 5 semesters of part-time study or 2 semesters of full-time work.

**Number awarded:** Varies each year.

**Deadline:** May of each year.

## 284 DIVISION II DEGREE-COMPLETION AWARD PROGRAM

National Collegiate Athletic Association, Attn: Leadership Advisory Board
700 West Washington Avenue
P.O. Box 6222
Indianapolis, IN 46206-6222
Phone: (317) 917-6307; Fax: (317) 917-6364; Email: dstephens@ncaa.org
Web: www.ncaa.org/membership/scholarships/degree-completion/d2/index.html

**Summary:** To provide financial assistance to student-athletes at Division II colleges and universities who have exhausted their eligibility for aid from the institutions they attend.

**Eligibility:** Open to student-athletes who have exhausted their eligibility for institutional aid at a Division II member institution of the National Collegiate Athletic Association (NCAA). Applicants must be within their first 10 semesters or 15 quarters of full-time college attendance. They must have a GPA of 2.5 or higher and be within 30 semester hours of their first undergraduate degree. Selection is based on financial circumstances, athletic achievement, and involvement in campus and community activities.

**Financial data:** The award is the lesser of 1) the recipient's athletics aid for the final year of eligibility; 2) tuition for the remaining credits toward completing an undergraduate degree; or 3) $5,000.

**Duration:** Until completion of an undergraduate degree.

**Number awarded:** Varies each year; 98 of these awards were granted.

**Deadline:** April of each year.

## 285 DIXIE BOYS BASEBALL SCHOLARSHIPS

Dixie Boys Baseball, Inc.
P.O. Box 1778
Marshall, TX 75671
Phone: (903) 927-1845; Fax: (903) 927-1846; Email: boys@dixie.org
Web: www.dixie.org

**Summary:** To provide financial assistance for college to high school senior males who have participated in a Dixie Boys or Dixie Majors franchised baseball program.

**Eligibility:** Open to high school senior males who played baseball in a Dixie Boys (for boys 13 and 14 years of age) or Dixie Majors (for boys from 15 through 18 years of age) franchised program. Applicants must submit a 150-word essay on their career objectives, how college relates to those, and how they expect to contribute to society. While it is a basic requirement that the applicants have participated in the baseball program, ability is not a factor. Selection is based on high school grades and testing, school and community leadership, and financial need.

**Financial data:** The stipend is $1,500.

**Duration:** 1 year.

**Number awarded:** 11 each year.

**Deadline:** March of each year.

## 286 DIXIE SOFTBALL SCHOLARSHIPS

Dixie Softball, Inc., Attn: President
1101 Skelton Drive
Birmingham, AL 35224
Phone: (205) 785-2255; Fax: (205) 785-2258; Email: softball@dixie.org
Web: www.dixie.org

**Summary:** To provide financial assistance for college to high school senior women who have participated in the Dixie Softball program.

**Eligibility:** Open to high school senior women who played in the Dixie Softball program for at least 2 seasons. Applicants must submit a transcript of grades, letter of recommendation from a high school principal or other school official, statement from a Dixie Softball local official verifying the number of years the applicant participated in the program, and documentation of financial need. Ability as an athlete is not considered in the selection process.

**Financial data:** The stipend is $1,500.

**Duration:** 1 year.

**Number awarded:** 4 each year.

**Deadline:** February of each year.

## 287 DIXIE YOUTH BASEBALL SCHOLARSHIPS

Dixie Youth Baseball, Inc., Attn: Scholarship Committee
P.O. Box 877
Marshall, TX 75671-0877
Phone: (903) 927-2255; Fax: (903) 927-1846; Email: dyb@dixie.org
Web: www.dixie.org

**Summary:** To provide financial assistance for college to high school senior males who have participated in a Dixie Youth Baseball franchised league.

**Eligibility:** Open to high school senior males who played in a Dixie Youth Baseball franchised league when they were 12 years of age or younger. Applicants must submit a transcript of grades, letter of recommendation from high school principal or other school official, verification from a Dixie Youth local official of participation in a franchised league, and documentation of financial need. Ability as an athlete is not considered in the selection process.

**Financial data:** The stipend is $2,000.

**Duration:** 1 year.

**Number awarded:** Varies each year; recently, 50 of these scholarships were awarded.

**Deadline:** February of each year.

## 288 DOLPHIN SCHOLARSHIP

Dolphin Scholarship Foundation
5040 Virginia Beach Boulevard, Suite 104-A
Virginia Beach, VA 23462
Phone: (757) 671-3200; Fax: (757) 671-3330; Email: dsf@exis.net
Web: www.dolphinscholarship.org

**Summary:** To provide financial assistance for college to the children of members or former members of the Submarine Service.

**Eligibility:** Open to the unmarried children and stepchildren (under 24 years of age) who were members or former members of the Submarine Service and who 1) qualified in submarines and served in the submarine force for at least 8 years, 2) served in submarine support activities for at least 10 years, or 3) died on active duty in the submarine force regardless of time served. Applicants must be working or intending to work toward a bachelor's degree at an accredited 4-year college or university. Awards are based on scholastic proficiency, non-scholastic activities, character, all-around ability, and financial need.

**Financial data:** The stipend is $3,000 per year.

**Duration:** 1 year; may be renewed for 3 additional years.

**Number awarded:** Approximately 30 each year.

**Deadline:** March of each year.

## 289 DON THOMPSON MEMORIAL SCHOLARSHIP

Arabian Horse Foundation, Attn: Scholarship Office
Ten Farnham Park Drive
Houston, TX 77024-7501
Phone: (713) 952-7081; Fax: (713) 977-9883;
Email: jean@parkwaychevrolet.com
Web: pages.sbcglobal.net/jvenhaus/horse/Scholar/scholar.html

**Summary:** To provide financial assistance to undergraduate and graduate students who have a record of equine involvement.

**Eligibility:** Open to students who have a record of involvement with horses. Applicants must be enrolled or planning to enroll as a full-time undergraduate or graduate student at an accredited college or university. Preference is given to students who have a GPA between 2.8 and 3.25, whose financial resources are modest, and who are attending a school with relatively low tuition. Along with their application, they must submit information on their financial need, honors or academic awards, extracurricular activities and offices, leadership role, career goal, and equine involvement for the past 2 years.

**Financial data:** A stipend is awarded (amount not specified).

**Duration:** 1 year; may be renewed if the recipient maintains a GPA of 2.5 or higher with no grade below a D.

**Number awarded:** 1 or more each year.

**Deadline:** January of each year.

## 290 DONALD AND ITASKER THORNTON MEMORIAL SCHOLARSHIP

Thornton Sisters Foundation

P.O. Box 21
Atlantic Highlands, NJ 07716
Phone: (732) 872-1353; Email: tsfoundation2001@yahoo.com
Web: www.thorntonsisters.com/ttsf.htm

**Summary:** To provide financial assistance for college to women of color in New Jersey.

**Eligibility:** Open to women of color (defined as African Americans, Latino Americans, Caribbean Americans, and Native Americans) who are graduating from high schools in New Jersey. Applicants must have a GPA of C+ or higher and be able to document financial need. They must be planning to attend an accredited 4-year college or university. Along with their application, they must submit a 500-word essay describing their family background, personal and/or economic disadvantages, honors or academic distinctions, and community involvement and activities.

**Financial data:** A stipend is awarded (amount not specified). Funds are to be used for tuition and/or books.

**Duration:** 1 year; nonrenewable.

**Number awarded:** 1 or more each year.

**Deadline:** May of each year.

### 291 DONNA JAMISON LAGO MEMORIAL SCHOLARSHIP

NextGen Network, Inc.
c/o Urbanomics Consulting Group
1010 Wisconsin Avenue, Suite 430
Washington, DC 20007
Phone: (202) 298-8226; Fax: (202) 298-8074;
Email: info@nextgennetwork.com
Web: www.nextgennetwork.com

**Summary:** To recognize and reward outstanding essays written by minority high school seniors who will be going on to college.

**Eligibility:** Open to ethnic minority high school seniors in good academic standing. Entrants must be U.S. citizens and intending to attend a college or university after graduation. They must submit an essay, from 500 to 1,000 words, on a topic that changes annually; recently, students were invited to write on the following topic: "You have been elected President of the United States. What three initiatives would you want to introduce? Be specific rather than general and give arguments to support your choice." The essay should demonstrate critical thinking, creativity, and strong communication skills.

**Financial data:** Finalists receive $1,500 each; semifinalists receive $1,000 each.

**Duration:** The competition is held annually.

**Number awarded:** 6 each year: 3 finalists and 3 semifinalists.

**Deadline:** March of each year.

### 292 DON'T MESS WITH TEXAS SCHOLARSHIP

Don't Mess with Texas Scholarship Program
c/o EnviroMedia
1717 West Sixth Street, Suite 400
Austin, TX 78703
Email: info@dontmesswithtexas.org
Web: www.dontmesswithtexas.org

**Summary:** To provide financial assistance to high school seniors in Texas who have taken leadership roles in preventing litter in their schools or communities.

**Eligibility:** Open to U.S. citizens who are Texas residents and high school seniors. Applicants must be planning to attend college in the state. They must have been involved in projects that prevent litter in their schools or communities. Along with their application, they must submit an essay (300 words) identifying their project and the action they took to correct the litter program; 2 letters of recommendation; a transcript. Selection is based on the applicants' participation and creativity in litter prevention efforts. Financial need is not considered.

**Financial data:** Stipends are either $3,000 or $1,000. Funds must be used for tuition, fees, or books.

**Duration:** 1 year.

**Number awarded:** 3 each year: 1 at $3,000 and 2 at $1,000.

**Deadline:** April of each year.

### 293 DOUBLE YOUR DOLLARS FOR SCHOLARS PROGRAM

United Methodist Higher Education Foundation
1001 19th Avenue South
P.O. Box 340005
Nashville, TN 37203-0005

Phone: (615) 340-7385; (800) 811-8110; Fax: (615) 340-7330;
Email: umhef@gbhem.org
Web: www.umhef.org/double.html

**Summary:** To provide financial assistance to students at Methodist colleges, universities, and seminaries whose home churches agree to contribute to their support.

**Eligibility:** Open to students attending or planning to attend a United Methodist-related college, university, or seminary as a full-time student. Applicants must have been an active, full member of a United Methodist church for at least 1 year prior to applying. Their home church must nominate them and agree to contribute to their support. Awards are granted on a first-come, first-served basis.

**Financial data:** The sponsoring church contributes $1,000 and the United Methodist Higher Education Foundation contributes a matching $1,000. A check for $2,000 is sent to the institution.

**Duration:** 1 year; may be renewed as long as the recipients maintain satisfactory academic progress as defined by their institution.

**Number awarded:** 275 each year.

**Deadline:** Local churches must submit applications in February of each year.

### 294 DR. DONALD L. MOAK SCHOLARSHIP

Alabama Bankers Association, Attn: Scholarship Applications
534 Adams Avenue
Montgomery, AL 36104
Phone: (334) 834-1890; (800) 239-5521; Fax: (334) 834-4443;
Email: info@alabamabankers.org
Web: www.alabamabankers.org

**Summary:** To provide financial assistance for college to high school seniors in Alabama whose parents are employed in a bank.

**Eligibility:** Open to seniors graduating from high schools in Alabama whose parents are employed full time at a bank in the state. Applicants must be planning to enroll in a college or university as a full-time student. Along with their application, they must submit a statement about themselves and their college plans, transcripts, and their ACT or SAT scores. Selection is based on academic record, character, leadership, potential for development, and financial need.

**Financial data:** The stipend is $1,000.

**Duration:** 1 year.

**Number awarded:** 1 or more each year.

**Deadline:** February of each year.

### 295 DR. MAE DAVIDOW MEMORIAL SCHOLARSHIP

American Council of the Blind, Attn: Coordinator, Scholarship Program
1155 15th Street, N.W., Suite 1004
Washington, DC 20005
Phone: (202) 467-5081; (800) 424-8666; Fax: (202) 467-5085;
Email: info@acb.org
Web: www.acb.org

**Summary:** To provide financial assistance to blind students entering their freshman year of college.

**Eligibility:** Open to freshmen who are legally blind and entering academic programs. They must be U.S. citizens. In addition to letters of recommendation and copies of academic transcripts, applications must include an autobiographical sketch. A cumulative GPA of 3.3 or higher is generally required. Selection is based on demonstrated academic record, involvement in extracurricular and civic activities, and academic objectives. The severity of the applicant's visual impairment and his/her study methods are also taken into account.

**Financial data:** The stipend is $1,500. In addition, the winner receives a Kurzweil-1000 Reading System.

**Duration:** 1 year.

**Number awarded:** 1 each year.

**Deadline:** February of each year.

### 296 DR. NICHOLAS S. DICAPRIO SCHOLARSHIP

American Council of the Blind, Attn: Coordinator, Scholarship Program
1155 15th Street, N.W., Suite 1004
Washington, DC 20005
Phone: (202) 467-5081; (800) 424-8666; Fax: (202) 467-5085;
Email: info@acb.org
Web: www.acb.org

**Summary:** To provide financial assistance to outstanding blind undergraduates.

**Eligibility:** Open to legally blind U.S. citizens or resident aliens who are undergraduate students. In addition to letters of recommendation and copies of academic transcripts, applications must include an autobiographical sketch. A cumulative GPA of 3.3 or higher is generally required. Selection is based on demonstrated academic record, involvement in extracurricular and civic activities, and academic objectives. The severity of the applicant's visual impairment and his/her study methods are also taken into account.

**Financial data:** The stipend is $2,500. In addition, the winner receives a Kurzweil-1000 Reading System.

**Duration:** 1 year.

**Number awarded:** 1 each year.

**Deadline:** February of each year.

## 297 DR. RICHARD CHINN SCHOLARSHIP

American Atheists
P.O. Box 5733
Parsippany, NJ 07054-6733
Phone: (908) 276-7300; Fax: (908) 276-7402; Email: info@atheists.org
Web: www.atheists.org/family/temp/scholarship

**Summary:** To provide financial assistance for college to gay and lesbian students who identify themselves as atheists.

**Eligibility:** Open to college-bound high school seniors and current college students. Applicants must be lesbian or gay, be atheists, and have a cumulative GPA of 2.5 or higher. Selection is based on activism, with special attention given to students who show activism in their schools (e.g., starting atheist/freethinker groups, fighting against violations of the separation of church and state in the school).

**Financial data:** The stipend is $1,000.

**Duration:** 1 year.

**Number awarded:** 1 each year.

**Deadline:** January of each year.

## 298 DRS. POH SHIEN AND JUDY YOUNG SCHOLARSHIP

US Pan Asian American Chamber of Commerce
Attn: Scholarship Coordinator
1329 18th Street, N.W.
Washington, DC 20036
Phone: (202) 296-5221; Fax: (202) 296-5225;
Email: administrator@uspaacc.com
Web: www.uspaacc.net/drs_poh_shien_and_judy_young.htm

**Summary:** To provide financial assistance for college to Asian American high school seniors who demonstrate financial need.

**Eligibility:** Open to high school seniors of Asian heritage who are U.S. citizens or permanent residents. Applicants must be planning to begin full-time study at an accredited postsecondary educational institution in the United States. Along with their application, they must submit a 500-word essay on "Why I need this scholarship." Selection is based on academic excellence (GPA of 3.5 or higher), leadership in extracurricular activities, community service involvement, and financial need.

**Financial data:** The maximum stipend is $4,000. Funds are paid directly to the recipient's college or university.

**Duration:** 1 year.

**Number awarded:** 1 each year.

**Deadline:** February of each year.

## 299 DUANE BUCKLEY MEMORIAL SCHOLARSHIP

American Council of the Blind, Attn: Coordinator, Scholarship Program
1155 15th Street, N.W., Suite 1004
Washington, DC 20005
Phone: (202) 467-5081; (800) 424-8666; Fax: (202) 467-5085;
Email: info@acb.org
Web: www.acb.org

**Summary:** To provide financial assistance for college to blind high school seniors.

**Eligibility:** Open to legally blind U.S. citizens or resident aliens who are college-bound high school seniors. Applicants must be able to demonstrate that they strive to overcome extraordinary challenges. In addition to letters of recommendation and copies of academic transcripts, they must submit an autobiographical sketch. A cumulative GPA of 3.3 or higher is generally required. Selection is based on demonstrated academic record, involvement in extracurricular and civic activities, and academic objectives. The severity of the applicant's visual impairment and his/her study methods are also taken into account.

**Financial data:** The stipend is $1,000. In addition, the winner receives a Kurzweil-1000 Reading System.

**Duration:** 1 year.

**Number awarded:** 1 each year.

**Deadline:** February of each year.

## 300 DUNKIN' DONUTS SCHOLARSHIPS

Scholarship America, Attn: Scholarship Management Services
One Scholarship Way
P.O. Box 297
St. Peter, MN 56082
Phone: (507) 931-1682; (800) 537-4180; Fax: (507) 931-9168

**Summary:** To provide financial assistance for college to high school seniors in Rhode Island and southeastern Massachusetts.

**Eligibility:** Open to 1) seniors graduating from high schools in Rhode Island and Bristol County, Massachusetts, and 2) recent graduates of those high schools already enrolled in college. Applicants must be able to demonstrate academic excellence, leadership qualities, community involvement, and a clear goal for their future.

**Financial data:** The stipend is $1,000.

**Duration:** 1 year.

**Number awarded:** 100 each year.

**Deadline:** April of each year.

## 301 E. WAYNE COOLEY SCHOLARSHIP AWARD

Iowa Girls' High School Athletic Union, Attn: Scholarships
2900 Grand Avenue
P.O. Box 10348
Des Moines, IA 50306-0348
Phone: (515) 288-9741; Fax: (515) 284-1969; Email: lisa@ighsau.org
Web: www.ighsau.org

**Summary:** To provide financial assistance to female high school seniors in Iowa who have participated in athletics and plan to attend college in the state.

**Eligibility:** Open to females graduating from high schools in Iowa who have a GPA of 3.75 or higher. Applicants must 1) have earned a varsity letter in at least 2 different sports, 2) be a first team all-conference selection, and/or 3) have participated in a state tournament in at least 1 sport. They must be planning to attend a college or university in Iowa. Each high school in the state may nominate 1 student. Selection is based on academic achievements, athletic accomplishments, non-sports extracurricular activities, and community involvement.

**Financial data:** The stipend is $3,750 per year.

**Duration:** 4 years, provided the recipient maintains at least a 2.5 GPA while enrolled in college.

**Number awarded:** 1 each year.

**Deadline:** December of each year.

## 302 EARL ANTHONY MEMORIAL SCHOLARSHIPS

United States Bowling Congress, Attn: SMART Program
5301 South 76th Street
Greendale, WI 53129-1192
Phone: (414) 423-3223; (800) 514-BOWL, ext. 3223; Fax: (414) 421-3014;
Email: smart@bowl.com
Web: www.bowl.com/scholarships/main.aspx

**Summary:** To provide financial assistance for college to members of the United States Bowling Congress (USBC) Youth who demonstrate outstanding community service and financial need.

**Eligibility:** Open to USBC Youth members who are seniors in high school or current college students. Applicants must have a GPA of 2.5 or higher and not have competed in a professional bowling tournament. Along with their application, they must submit an essay of 500 words on how their bowling, community service, and educational achievements have influenced their life and their goals for the future. Financial need is also considered in the selection process.

**Financial data:** The stipend is $5,000.

**Duration:** 1 year; nonrenewable.

**Number awarded:** 5 each year.

**Deadline:** April of each year.

## 303 EASTERN REGION KOREAN AMERICAN SCHOLARSHIPS

Korean American Scholarship Foundation
Eastern Region
c/o William S. Lee, Scholarship Committee Chair

10301 Georgia Avenue, Suite 303
Silver Spring, MD 20902
Phone: (703) 748-5935; Fax: (703) 748-1874; Email: kasfdc@hotmail.com
Web: www.kasf.org/home/regional/eastern/eastern.html
**Summary:** To provide financial assistance to Korean American undergraduate and graduate students who attend school in the eastern states.
**Eligibility:** Open to Korean American students who are currently enrolled in a college or university in an eastern state as a full-time undergraduate or graduate student. Applicants may reside anywhere in the United States as long as they attend school in the eastern region: Delaware, District of Columbia, Kentucky, Maryland, North Carolina, Pennsylvania, Virginia, and West Virginia. Selection is based on academic achievement, school activities, community service, and financial need.
**Financial data:** Stipends range from $350 to $5,000.
**Duration:** 1 year; renewable.
**Number awarded:** Varies each year. Recently, 65 of these scholarships were awarded: 1 at $5,000, 20 at $2,000, 3 at $1,500, 33 at $1,000, 2 at $500, and 6 at $350.
**Deadline:** May of each year.

## 304 EASTERN STAR ACADEMIC SCHOLARSHIPS

Eastern Star-Grand Chapter of California
16960 Bastanchury Road, Suite E
Yorba Linda, CA 92886-1711
Phone: (714) 986-2380
Web: www.oescal.org/scholarship/Scholarships.htm
**Summary:** To provide financial assistance for college to students in California.
**Eligibility:** Open to California residents who are members of the Order of the Eastern Star or others who are graduating high school seniors entering their first year of college or university; students who have begun their higher education but need financial aid to continue; and those who have not been able to go directly from high school to college. U.S. citizenship is required. Applicants must have a GPA of 3.0 or higher. They may be attending or planning to attend a college, university, community college, or trade school in California, although consideration is given to students applying for out-of-state schools. Along with their application, they must submit brief essays on their educational goals, reasons for choice of schools, reasons for applying for financial aid, and what they understand the order of Eastern Star to be. Selection is based on scholastic record, financial need, the need for higher education, and character of the applicant.
**Financial data:** Annual stipends vary but range from $500 to $1,000 for students in 4-year colleges and universities and from $250 to $500 for students in community colleges and trade schools.
**Duration:** 1 year; may be renewed.
**Number awarded:** Varies each year.
**Deadline:** March of each year.

## 305 ECI SCHOLARSHIP FOUNDATION SCHOLARSHIP FOR THE TECHNOLOGY STUDENT ASSOCIATION

Technology Student Association
1914 Association Drive
Reston, VA 20191-1540
Phone: (703) 860-9000; Fax: (703) 758-4852; Email: general@tsaweb.org
Web: www.tsaweb.org
**Summary:** To provide financial support for college to members of the Technology Student Association (TSA).
**Eligibility:** Open to TSA members who are rising high school seniors and have taken the SAT or ACT examination. Selection is based on those aptitude test scores, cumulative GPA, community involvement, demonstrated leadership, and financial need.
**Financial data:** The stipend is $1,000.
**Duration:** 1 year.
**Number awarded:** 1 each year.
**Deadline:** May of each year.

## 306 ECI SCHOLARSHIPS

American Legion Baseball
700 North Pennsylvania Street
Indianapolis, IN 46204
Phone: (317) 630-1249; Fax: (317) 630-1223; Email: acy@legion.org
Web: www.baseball.legion.org/awards.htm
**Summary:** To recognize and reward, with college scholarships, participants in the American Legion baseball program who demonstrate outstanding academic achievement.
**Eligibility:** Open to participants in the American Legion baseball regional tournaments and the American Legion World Series. Candidates must be high school seniors or graduates who will be entering college as a freshman in the fall; students still in high school are not eligible. Selection is based on academic achievement.
**Financial data:** The awards are $1,000 scholarships.
**Duration:** The awards are presented annually.
**Number awarded:** 9 each year.

## 307 EDEN SERVICES CHARLES H. HOENS, JR. SCHOLARS PROGRAM

Autism Society of America, Attn: Awards and Scholarships
7910 Woodmont Avenue, Suite 300
Bethesda, MD 20814-3015
Phone: (301) 657-0881; (800) 3-AUTISM; Fax: (301) 657-0869;
Email: info@autism-society.org
Web: www.autism-society.org
**Summary:** To provide financial assistance for college to high school seniors, high school graduates, and college students with autism.
**Eligibility:** Open to high school seniors or graduates who have been accepted to or are already enrolled in an accredited postsecondary school (college, trade school, etc.) and who have autism. Applicants must submit 3 copies of 1) documentation of their status as an individual with autism; 2) secondary school transcripts; 3) documentation of acceptance into an accredited postsecondary educational or vocational program of study; 4) 2 letters of recommendation; and 5) a 500-word statement outlining their qualifications and proposed plan of study. A telephone interview may be required.
**Financial data:** The stipend is $1,000.
**Duration:** 1 year.
**Number awarded:** 1 each year.
**Deadline:** February of each year.

## 308 EDUCATION EXCHANGE COLLEGE GRANT PROGRAM

ACCEL/Exchange Network
c/o Fiserv
255 Fiserv Drive
P.O. Box 979
Brookfield, WI 53008-0979
Phone: (262) 879-5966; (800) 872-7882; Fax: (262) 879-5013;
Email: general_info@fiserv.com
Web: www.fiserv.com
**Summary:** To provide financial assistance for college to needy high school seniors.
**Eligibility:** Open to seniors graduating from high school who have been accepted at an accredited 4-year college or university. Students must pick up an application at a participating Exchange member institution (primarily banks and credit unions). For a list of financial institutions that will have applications, write to the sponsor or visit their web site. U.S. citizenship is required. Selection is based on extracurricular activities, character, leadership, financial need, and a required essay.
**Financial data:** Stipends are either $5,000 or $1,000. A total of $100,000 is distributed annually.
**Duration:** 1 year.
**Number awarded:** 34 each year: 4 at $5,000 and 30 at $1,000.
**Deadline:** March of each year.

## 309 EDUCATION IS FREEDOM NATIONAL SCHOLARSHIP PROGRAM

Education is Freedom Foundation
c/o 7-Eleven, Inc.
2711 North Haskell Avenue
Dallas, TX 75204
Phone: (866) EIF-EDUC
Web: www.educationisfreedom.com/Scholarships/scholarships.asp
**Summary:** To provide financial assistance to high school seniors who have financial need and would be unable to attend college without assistance.
**Eligibility:** Open to high school seniors and graduates under 24 years of age who have resided in the United States for at least 1 year. Applicants must be planning to enroll for the first time in a full-time undergraduate course of study

at an accredited 2- or 4-year college or university. They must be able to demonstrate a GPA of 3.0 to 3.5, activities and leadership, work history, and unmet financial need.

**Financial data:** The stipend is $2,000. Funds are paid to the student and institution for payment of tuition, fees, and books.

**Duration:** 1 year; may be renewed up to 3 years as long as the recipient remains enrolled full time with a GPA of 3.0 or higher.

**Number awarded:** Approximately 250 each year.

**Deadline:** January of each year.

## 310 EDWARD J. BLOUSTEIN DISTINGUISHED SCHOLARS PROGRAM

New Jersey Higher Education Student Assistance Authority
Attn: Financial Aid Services
4 Quakerbridge Plaza
P.O. Box 540
Trenton, NJ 08625-0540
Phone: (609) 588-2349; (800) 792-8670; Fax: (609) 588-2390;
Email: gjoachim@hesaa.org
Web: www.hesaa.org

**Summary:** To provide financial assistance to outstanding high school seniors in New Jersey who are interested in attending college.

**Eligibility:** Open to seniors at New Jersey high schools who rank in the top 10% of their class and have above average SAT scores. They must be planning to attend a college or university in New Jersey as a full-time undergraduate. Students may not apply directly for this program; they must be nominated by their high school.

**Financial data:** Scholars receive $950 per year, regardless of financial need.

**Duration:** Up to 5 semesters at a 2-year institution; up to 8 semesters at a 4-year institution; up to 10 semesters if enrolled in a bona fide 5-year program.

**Number awarded:** Varies each year.

**Deadline:** Participating secondary schools must submit nominations by the end of September of each year.

## 311 EDWARD T. CONROY MEMORIAL SCHOLARSHIP PROGRAM

Maryland Higher Education Commission
Attn: Office of Student Financial Assistance
839 Bestgate Road, Suite 400
Annapolis, MD 21401-3013
Phone: (410) 260-4563; (800) 974-1024, ext. 4563; Fax: (410) 974-5376;
TTY: (800) 735-2258; Email: osfamail@mhec.state.md.us
Web: www.mhec.state.md.us/financialAid/Program/Descriptions/prog_conroy.asp

**Summary:** To provide financial assistance for college or graduate school to specified categories of veterans, public safety employees, and their children in Maryland.

**Eligibility:** Open to undergraduate and graduate students in the following categories: 1) children and unremarried surviving spouses of state or local public safety employees or volunteers who died in the line of duty; 2) children of armed forces members whose death or 100% disability was directly caused by military service; 3) POW/MIA veterans of the Vietnam Conflict and their children; 4) children and surviving spouses of victims of the September 11, 2001, terrorist attacks who died in the World Trade Center in New York City, the Pentagon in Virginia, or United Airlines Flight 93 in Pennsylvania; 5) veterans who have, as a direct result of military service, a disability of 25% or greater and have exhausted or are no longer eligible for federal veterans' educational benefits; and 6) state or local public safety officers or volunteers who were 100% disabled in the line of duty. The parent, veteran, POW, or public safety officer or volunteer must have been a resident of Maryland at the time of death or when declared disabled. Financial need is not considered.

**Financial data:** The amount of the award is equal to tuition and fees at a Maryland postsecondary institution, to a maximum of $17,800 for children and spouses of the September 11 terrorist attacks or $8,550 for all other recipients.

**Duration:** Up to 5 years of full-time study or 8 years of part-time study.

**Number awarded:** Varies each year.

**Deadline:** July of each year.

## 312 ELIZABETH AND WALLACE KINGSBURY SCHOLARSHIP

United Daughters of the Confederacy, Attn: Education Director
328 North Boulevard
Richmond, VA 23220-4057

Phone: (804) 355-1636; Fax: (804) 353-1396; Email: hqudc@rcn.com
Web: www.hqudc.org/scholarships/scholarships.html

**Summary:** To provide financial assistance for college to lineal descendants of Confederate veterans who have been members of the Children of the Confederacy for at least 3 years.

**Eligibility:** Open to lineal descendants of worthy Confederates or collateral descendants who have been members of the Children of the Confederacy for at least 3 years. Applicants must submit a family financial report and certified proof of the Confederate record of 1 ancestor, with the company and regiment in which he served. They must have at least a 3.0 GPA in high school.

**Financial data:** The amount of the scholarship depends on the availability of funds.

**Duration:** 1 year; may be renewed for up to 3 additional years.

**Number awarded:** 1 each year.

**Deadline:** March of each year.

## 313 ELIZABETH NASH FOUNDATION SCHOLARSHIP PROGRAM

Elizabeth Nash Foundation
P.O. Box 1260
Los Gatos, CA 95031-1260
Email: scholarships@elizabethnashfoundation.org
Web: www.elizabethnashfoundation.org/scholarshipprogram.html

**Summary:** To provide financial assistance for college or graduate school to individuals with cystic fibrosis (CF).

**Eligibility:** Open to undergraduate and graduate students who have CF. Applicants must be able to demonstrate clear academic goals and a commitment to participate in activities outside the classroom. Selection is based on academic record, character, demonstrated leadership, service to the community, and financial need.

**Financial data:** Stipends range from $500 to $2,000. Funds are paid directly to the academic institution to be applied to tuition and fees.

**Duration:** 1 year; recipients may reapply.

**Number awarded:** 1 or more each year.

**Deadline:** September of each year.

## 314 ELKS GOLD AWARD SCHOLARSHIPS

Girl Scouts of the USA, Attn: Program, Membership, and Research
420 Fifth Avenue
New York, NY 10018-2798
Phone: (212) 852-8000; (800) GSUSA-4U
Web: www.girlscouts.org/program/gs_central/scholarships

**Summary:** To provide financial assistance for college to members of the Girl Scouts of America who have achieved its Gold Award.

**Eligibility:** Open to Gold Award winners who are graduating high school seniors. Applicants must be planning to attend an accredited college or university. Selection is based on academics, activities, community involvement, leadership, and pursuit of individual interests.

**Financial data:** The stipend is $1,500 per year.

**Duration:** 4 years.

**Number awarded:** 8 each year: 1 in each Girl Scout Service Area.

**Deadline:** Each Girl Scout Council sets its own deadline, but each council must submit its top application to headquarters by the end of April of each year.

## 315 ELKS NATIONAL FOUNDATION "MOST VALUABLE STUDENT" SCHOLARSHIP AWARD

Elks National Foundation, Attn: Scholarship Department
2750 North Lake View Avenue
Chicago, IL 60614-1889
Phone: (773) 755-4732; Fax: (773) 755-4729; Email: scholarship@elks.org
Web: www.elks.org/enf/scholars/mvs.cfm

**Summary:** To provide financial assistance to outstanding high school seniors who can demonstrate financial need and are interested in attending college.

**Eligibility:** Open to graduating high school students (or the equivalent) who are U.S. citizens and residents within the jurisdiction of the B.P.O. Elks of the U.S.A. Applicants must be planning to work on a 4-year degree on a full-time basis at a college or university within the United States. They must submit an official form furnished by the Elks National Foundation (no photocopies); these are available at local Elks Lodges. Applications must be filed with the scholarship chair, Exalted Ruler, or secretary of the Elks Lodge in whose jurisdiction the applicant resides. Applications are reviewed by Lodge and District scholarship committees and then judged by the scholarship committee of the State Elks Association for inclusion in the state's quota of entries in the national competition. On the national level, selection is based on financial need (200 points), leadership (350 points), and scholarship (450 points). Male and female students compete separately.

**Financial data:** First place is $15,000 per year; second place is $10,000 per year; third place is $5,000 per year; fourth place is $1,000 per year. More than $2.2 million is distributed through this program each year.

**Duration:** 4 years.

**Number awarded:** 500 each year: 2 first awards (1 male and 1 female), 2 second awards (1 male and 1 female), 2 third awards (1 male and 1 female), and 494 fourth awards (247 males and 247 females).

**Deadline:** January of each year.

## 316 ELSIE M. BELL GROSVENOR SCHOLARSHIP AWARDS

Alexander Graham Bell Association for the Deaf
Attn: Financial Aid Coordinator
3417 Volta Place, N.W.
Washington, DC 20007-2778
Phone: (202) 337-5220; Fax: (202) 337-8314; TTY: (202) 337-5221;
Email: financialaid@agbell.org
Web: www.agbell.org

**Summary:** To provide financial assistance to undergraduate and graduate students who have moderate to profound hearing loss and attend school in the Washington, D.C. area.

**Eligibility:** Open to undergraduate and graduate students who have been diagnosed with a moderate to profound hearing loss prior to acquiring spoken language (hearing loss averages 60dB or greater in the better ear in the speech frequencies of 500, 1000, and 2000 Hz). Applicants must be committed to using spoken language as their primary mode of communication. They must be accepted or enrolled at a mainstream college or university in the Washington, D.C., area as a full-time student. Along with their application, they must submit a 1-page essay discussing their career goals and how spoken communication is helping them to reach those goals as a person with a hearing loss. Financial need is considered in the selection process.

**Financial data:** The stipend is $2,000 per year.

**Duration:** 1 year; may be renewed 1 additional year.

**Number awarded:** 1 each year.

**Deadline:** April of each year.

## 317 EMILIE HESEMEYER MEMORIAL SCHOLARSHIP

Association on American Indian Affairs, Inc., Attn: Scholarship Coordinator
966 Hungerford Drive, Suite 12-B
Rockville, MD 20850
Phone: (240) 314-7155; Fax: (240) 314-7159; Email: lw.aaia@verizon.net
Web: www.indian-affairs.org/alloganslagle.htm

**Summary:** To provide financial assistance for college to Native American students, especially those interested in majoring in education.

**Eligibility:** Open to American Indian and Native Alaskan full-time undergraduate students. Preference is given to students working on a degree in education. Applicants must submit documentation of financial need, a Certificate of Indian Blood showing at least one-quarter Indian blood, proof of tribal enrollment, an essay on their educational goals, 2 letters of recommendation, and their most recent transcript.

**Financial data:** The stipend is $1,500 per year. Funds are paid directly to accredited educational institutions to be used for tuition, books, and other academic-related expenses.

**Duration:** 1 year; may be renewed up to 3 additional years or until completion of a degree, provided the recipient maintains satisfactory progress.

**Number awarded:** 1 or more each year.

**Deadline:** July of each year.

## 318 ERCA COMMUNITY CONTRIBUTION SCHOLARSHIP

Educational Research Center of America, Inc., Attn: Scholarship Committee
2020 Pennsylvania Avenue, N.W., Room 7799
Washington, DC 20006
Phone: (202) 393-7799; Email: info@studentresearch.org
Web: www.studentresearch.org/public/application.html

**Summary:** To provide financial assistance for college to high school seniors who have provided outstanding service to their community

**Eligibility:** Open to college-bound high school seniors. Applicants must submit a description of an activity in which they have participated that demonstrates their commitment to their community. Selection is based on that description, honors or awards received, GPA, and a letter of reference.

**Financial data:** The stipend is $1,000.

**Duration:** 1 year.

**Number awarded:** Between 25 and 100 each year.

**Deadline:** June of each year.

## 319 ERIC DELSON MEMORIAL SCHOLARSHIP

Caremark Rx, Inc., Attn: Heather Post
211 Commerce Street. Suite 800
Nashville, TN 37201
Phone: (866) 792-2731
Web: www.caremark.com

**Summary:** To provide financial assistance for college or graduate school to students with clinical hemophilia.

**Eligibility:** Open to students diagnosed with clinical hemophilia. They must be 1) high school seniors, high school graduates, college students, or graduate students currently enrolled or planning to enroll in an accredited 2-year or 4-year college, university, vocational/technical school, or graduate school; or 2) students entering grades 7-12 at a private secondary school in the United States. This program is not open to students with related blood disorders (e.g., von Willebrand Disease). Selection is based on academic record, potential to succeed, leadership, participation in school and community activities, honors, work experience, statement of educational and career goals, recommendations, and unusual personal or family circumstances.

**Financial data:** The stipend is $2,500 or $1,500. Funds are paid in 2 equal installments directly to the recipient.

**Duration:** 1 year; may be renewed for up to 3 additional years, provided the recipient maintains a 3.0 GPA.

**Number awarded:** 4 each year: 3 at $2,500 per year and 1 at $1,500 per year.

**Deadline:** June of each year.

## 320 ERIC DOSTIE MEMORIAL COLLEGE SCHOLARSHIP

NuFACTOR, Attn: Scholarship Administrator
41093 Country Center Drive, Suite B
Temecula, CA 92591
Phone: (951) 296-2516; (800) 323-6832, ext. 1300; Fax: (951) 296-2565;
Email: info@kelleycom.com
Web: www.nufactor.com/web_pages/edostie_scholarship.html

**Summary:** To provide financial assistance for college to students with hemophilia or members of their families.

**Eligibility:** Open to 1) students with hemophilia or a related bleeding disorder or 2) members of their families. Applicants must be U.S. citizens and enrolled or planning to enroll full time in an accredited 2- or 4-year college program. They must have a GPA of 2.5 or higher. Along with their application, they must submit a 400-word essay that explains what motivates them to pursue a higher education, what subjects they plan to study, what major forces or obstacles in their life has led to that path of study, what they plan to do with their education after school, and how that may be of benefit to humankind. Financial need is also considered in the selection process.

**Financial data:** The stipend is $1,000.

**Duration:** 1 year.

**Number awarded:** 10 each year.

**Deadline:** February of each year.

## 321 ESERA TUALOLO SCHOLARSHIP FOR ATHLETIC ACHIEVEMENT

Parents, Families and Friends of Lesbians and Gays
Attn: National Scholarships Program
1726 M Street, N.W., Suite 400
Washington, DC 20036
Phone: (202) 467-8180, ext. 219; Fax: (202) 467-8194;
Email: schools@pflag.org
Web: www.pflag.org

**Summary:** To provide financial assistance for college to high school seniors and recent graduates who have a connection to Parents, Families and Friends of Lesbians and Gays (PFLAG).

**Eligibility:** Open to high school seniors and prior-year graduates who have not attended college. Applicants must have applied to an accredited high education institution to work on 1) an associate's degree leading to transfer to complete a bachelor's degree, or 2) a bachelor's degree at a 4-year college or university. They must self-identify either as a gay, lesbian, bisexual, or transgender (GLBT) person or as a supporter of GLBT people. Along with their application, they must submit a high school transcript showing a GPA of 3.0 or higher, 2 letters of recommendation, and a 2-page essay discussing either their life as an LGBT student or how they have been involved with and supported the LGBT community. Financial need is also considered in the selection process. This scholarship is presented to the applicant who demonstrates outstanding athletic achievement.

**Financial data:** The stipend is $2,500.
**Duration:** 1 year; nonrenewable.
**Number awarded:** 1 each year.
**Deadline:** February of each year.

## 322 ESTER BOONE MEMORIAL SCHOLARSHIPS

National Naval Officers Association-Washington, D.C. Chapter
Attn: Scholarship Program
2701 Park Center Drive, B704
Alexandria, VA 22302
Email: williams.stephen@hq.navy.mil
Web: www.dcnnoa.org
**Summary:** To provide financial assistance to minority high school seniors from the Washington, D.C., area.
**Eligibility:** Open to minority seniors at high schools in the Washington, D.C., metropolitan area who plan to enroll full time at an accredited 2-year or 4-year college or university. Applicants must have a GPA of 2.5 or higher. Selection is based on academic achievement, community involvement, and financial need.
**Financial data:** The stipend is $1,000 per year.
**Duration:** 1 year.
**Number awarded:** 4 each year.
**Deadline:** April of each year.

## 323 ETHEL AND EMERY FAST SCHOLARSHIP

Ethel and Emery Fast Scholarship Foundation, Inc.
12620 Rolling Road
Potomac, MD 20854
Phone: (301) 762-1102
**Summary:** To provide financial assistance to qualified Native Americans enrolled as undergraduates or graduate students.
**Eligibility:** Open to Native Americans enrolled in a federally-recognized tribe who have successfully completed 1 year of their undergraduate or graduate school program. They must be enrolled in school full time and be able to demonstrate financial need. To apply, students must submit a completed application, documentation of Native American eligibility, an original transcript, a letter confirming enrollment, a federal income tax return, a statement of financial need, and a personal statement (up to 2 pages) describing educational and career goals.
**Financial data:** A stipend is awarded (amount not specified). Funds are paid directly to the recipient's college or university and can only be used to pay for tuition, room, board, and fees.
**Duration:** 1 year.
**Number awarded:** Varies each year.
**Deadline:** August of each year for the fall semester; December of each year for the spring semester.

## 324 ETHNIC AWARENESS COMMITTEE SCHOLARSHIP

Washington Financial Aid Association
c/o James D. Flowers, Scholarship Committee
University of Washington
105 Schmitz, Box 355880
Seattle, WA 98195-5880
Phone: (206) 616-2309; Email: jflowers@washington.edu
Web: www.wfaa.org/ethnicawareness.html
**Summary:** To provide financial assistance for college to high school seniors or currently-enrolled college students of color in Washington.
**Eligibility:** Open to graduating high school seniors or currently-enrolled college students of color who are or will be attending a college or university belonging to the Washington Financial Aid Association. Applicants must be able to demonstrate leadership abilities, have at least a 3.0 GPA, have financial need, and enroll or plan to enroll at least half time at an eligible private or public community college, technical school, college, or university. To apply, they must submit a typed personal statement, 2 letters of recommendation, and an official college and/or high school transcript.
**Financial data:** Stipends range up to $1,000.
**Duration:** 1 year.
**Number awarded:** 1 or more each year.
**Deadline:** June of each year.

## 325 E.U. PARKER SCHOLARSHIP

National Federation of the Blind
c/o Peggy Elliott, Scholarship Committee Chair
805 Fifth Avenue
Grinnell, IA 50112
Phone: (641) 236-3366
Web: www.nfb.org/sch_intro.htm
**Summary:** To provide financial assistance to blind undergraduate and graduate students.
**Eligibility:** Open to legally blind students who are working on or planning to work full time on an undergraduate or graduate degree. Selection is based on academic excellence, service to the community, and financial need.
**Financial data:** The stipend is $3,000.
**Duration:** 1 year; recipients may resubmit applications up to 2 additional years.
**Number awarded:** 1 each year.
**Deadline:** March of each year.

## 326 EUNICE FIORITO MEMORIAL SCHOLARSHIP

American Council of the Blind, Attn: Coordinator, Scholarship Program
1155 15th Street, N.W., Suite 1004
Washington, DC 20005
Phone: (202) 467-5081; (800) 424-8666; Fax: (202) 467-5085;
Email: info@acb.org
Web: www.acb.org
**Summary:** To provide financial assistance to outstanding blind undergraduates.
**Eligibility:** Open to legally blind U.S. citizens or resident aliens who are undergraduate students. Applicants must be planning to enter the advocacy/disability field. In addition to letters of recommendation and copies of academic transcripts, they must include an autobiographical sketch. A cumulative GPA of 3.3 or higher is generally required. Preference is given to students with little or no vision. Selection is based on demonstrated academic record, involvement in extracurricular and civic activities, and academic objectives. The severity of the applicant's visual impairment and his/her study methods are also taken into account.
**Financial data:** The stipend is $2,000. In addition, the winner receives a Kurzweil-1000 Reading System.
**Duration:** 1 year.
**Number awarded:** 1 each year.
**Deadline:** February of each year.

## 327 EVELYN BARTY SCHOLARSHIP AWARDS PROGRAM

Billy Barty Foundation
10222 Crosby Road
Harrison, OH 45030
Phone: (513) 738-4428; Fax: (513) 738-4428
**Summary:** To provide financial assistance for college to people of short stature and members of their families.
**Eligibility:** Open to high school seniors, high school graduates, and students currently enrolled in a 4-year college or university who are less than 4 feet 10 inches tall. Their parents and siblings are also eligible. Selection is based on scholarship, leadership, and financial need.
**Financial data:** The amount of the scholarship varies.
**Duration:** 1 year; recipients may reapply.
**Number awarded:** Up to 5 each year.
**Deadline:** October of each year.

## 328 EVERLY SCHOLARSHIP

Everly Scholarship Fund, Inc., Attn: John R. Lolio, Jr.
Fairway Corporate Center
4300 Haddonfield Road, Suite 311
Pennsauken, NJ 08109
Phone: (856) 661-2094; Fax: (856) 662-0165
**Summary:** To provide financial assistance for college to high school seniors in New Jersey.
**Eligibility:** Open to residents of New Jersey who are graduating from high school in the top 20% of their class. Applicants must have a GPA of 3.0 or higher and an above average SAT score. Along with their application, they must submit 2 essays: 1) the events or people that have shaped their thinking and why; and 2) the career they will be pursuing and how it will contribute to society. Semifinalists are interviewed. Financial need is not considered in the selection process.

**Financial data:** Stipends range up to $2,500 per year. Funds are paid to the student in equal installments each semester upon receipt of the term bill and verification of payment (cancelled check or receipt).

**Duration:** 1 year; may be renewed until graduation as long as the recipient maintains full-time enrollment and a GPA of 2.75 or higher the first year and 3.0 or higher in subsequent years.

**Deadline:** April of each year.

## 329 EXCEPTIONAL CIRCUMSTANCES SCHOLARSHIPS

Workforce Safety & Insurance
1600 East Century Avenue, Suite 1
P.O. Box 5585
Bismarck, ND 58506-5585
Phone: (701) 328-3828; (800) 440-3796; Fax: (701) 328-3820;
TDD: (701) 328-3786
Web: www.workforcesafety.com/workers/typesofbenefits.asp

**Summary:** To provide financial assistance for college to injured workers in North Dakota.

**Eligibility:** Open to injured workers in North Dakota who can demonstrate that a program of higher or technical education would be beneficial and appropriate because of exceptional circumstances. Applicants must have completed a rehabilitation process with Workforce Safety & Insurance (WSI) and have not outstanding litigation on any rehabilitation plan.

**Financial data:** The maximum stipend is $10,000 per year.

**Duration:** 1 year; may be renewed up to 4 additional years provided the recipient reapplies and maintains a satisfactory GPA.

**Number awarded:** Varies each year.

## 330 EXEMPTION FROM TUITION FEES FOR DEPENDENTS OF KENTUCKY VETERANS

Kentucky Department of Veterans Affairs, Attn: Division of Field Operations
545 South Third Street, Room 123
Louisville, KY 40202
Phone: (502) 595-4447; (800) 928-4012 (within KY); Fax: (502) 595-4448
Web: www.kdva.net/tuitionwaiver.htm

**Summary:** To provide financial assistance for undergraduate or graduate education to the children or unmarried widow(er)s of deceased Kentucky veterans.

**Eligibility:** Open to the children, stepchildren, adopted children, and unremarried widow(er)s of veterans who were residents of Kentucky when they entered military service or joined the Kentucky National Guard. The qualifying veteran must have been killed in action during a wartime period or died as a result of a service-connected disability incurred during a wartime period. Applicants must be attending or planning to attend a state-supported college or university in Kentucky to work on an undergraduate or graduate degree.

**Financial data:** Eligible dependents and survivors are exempt from tuition and matriculation fees at any state-supported institution of higher education in Kentucky.

**Duration:** There are no age or time limits on the waiver.

**Number awarded:** Varies each year.

## 331 EXPLOSIVE ORDNANCE DISPOSAL (EOD) MEMORIAL SCHOLARSHIPS

Explosive Ordnance Disposal Memorial, Attn: EOD Administrator
P.O. Box 594
Niceville, FL 32588
Phone: (850) 729-2401; Fax: (850) 729-2401; Email: eod@cox.net
Web: www.eodmemorial.org/scholarship.html

**Summary:** To provide financial assistance for college to family members of technicians or military officers who have worked in explosive ordnance disposal.

**Eligibility:** Open to the family members of explosive ordnance disposal (EOD) technicians or officers in the Army, Navy, Air Force, or Marine Corps who are currently on active duty (includes activated Reserves), retired, or deceased. Awards are presented in the following priority: 1) family members of those whose names are on the EOD Memorial; 2) applicants who have never received an EOD scholarship; and 3) prior EOD scholarship recipients. Selection is based on academic merit, community involvement, and financial need.

**Financial data:** The stipend is currently $1,800 per year. Funds are paid directly to the academic institution for the student's tuition, books, fees, and on-campus housing.

**Duration:** 1 year; may be renewed up to 3 additional years.

**Number awarded:** Varies each year; recently, 45 of these scholarships were awarded.

**Deadline:** February of each year.

## 332 FAMILIES OF FREEDOM SCHOLARSHIP FUND

Scholarship America, Attn: Scholarship Management Services
One Scholarship Way
P.O. Box 297
St. Peter, MN 56082
Phone: (507) 931-1682; (877) 862-0136; Fax: (507) 931-9168;
Email: familiesoffreedom@csfa.org
Web: www.familiesoffreedom.org

**Summary:** To provide college scholarships to financially-needy individuals and the families of individuals who were victims of the terrorist attacks on September 11, 2001.

**Eligibility:** Open to the individuals who were disabled as a result of the terrorist attacks on September 11, 2001, and to the relatives of those individuals who were killed or permanently disabled during the attacks. Primarily, the fund will benefit dependents (including spouses and children) of the following groups: airplane crew and passengers; World Trade Center workers and visitors; Pentagon workers and visitors; and rescue workers, including fire fighters, emergency medical personnel, and law enforcement personnel. Applicants must be enrolled or planning to enroll in an accredited 2- or 4-year college, university, or vocational/technical school in the United States. They must be able to demonstrate financial need.

**Financial data:** Stipends range from $1,000 to $28,000 per year, depending upon the need of the recipient. Recently, awards averaged $13,100 per academic year. Funds are distributed annually, in 2 equal installments. Checks are made payable jointly to the student and the student's school.

**Duration:** 1 year; may be renewed.

**Number awarded:** This is an entitlement program; all eligible students will receive funding. Recently 180 students received nearly $1.6 million in scholarship funds.

**Deadline:** Applications may be submitted at any time.

## 333 FAMILY DISTRICT 1 SCHOLARSHIPS

American Hellenic Educational Progressive Association-District 1
Attn: Family District 1 Educational Fund, Inc.
c/o Melva Zinaich, Co-Chair
P.O. Box 1011
Charleston, SC 29402
Web: www.ahepa1.org

**Summary:** To provide financial assistance for college or graduate school to residents of designated southeastern states.

**Eligibility:** Open to residents of Alabama, Florida, Georgia, Mississippi, South Carolina, and Tennessee who are high school seniors or graduates or current undergraduate or graduate students. Applicants must be attending or planning to attend an accredited college or university as a full-time student. They must submit a 500-word essay on the topic, "How has your family history, culture, or environment influenced who you are?" High school seniors must also submit an official transcript and SAT or ACT scores. College freshmen and sophomores must submit an official high school transcript, SAT and ACT scores, and their most recent college transcript. College juniors and seniors must submit their most recent college transcript. Graduate students must submit undergraduate and graduate transcripts and GRE scores. Consideration is also given to extracurricular activities, athletic achievements, work, and community service. Students who also demonstrate financial need are considered in a separate selection process.

**Financial data:** Stipends range from $500 to $1,500.

**Duration:** 1 year.

**Number awarded:** Varies each year.

**Deadline:** December of each year.

## 334 FARM AND RANCH HERITAGE SCHOLARSHIPS

American Quarter Horse Foundation, Attn: Scholarship Coordinator
2601 I-40 East
Amarillo, TX 79104
Phone: (806) 376-5181; (888) 209-8322; Fax: (806) 376-1005;
Email: lowens@aqha.org
Web: www.aqha.com/foundation/scholarships/index.html

**Summary:** To provide financial assistance for college to members of the American Quarter Horse Association (AQHA) or the American Quarter Horse Youth Association (AQHYA) who come from a farming and/or ranching background.

**Eligibility:** Open to the members of either organization (for at least 1 year) who are graduating high school seniors or already enrolled in college. They must have a GPA of 3.0 or higher and come from a farming and/or ranching background. Financial need is considered in the selection process.

**Financial data:** The maximum stipend is $3,125 per year.

**Duration:** Up to 4 years, provided the recipient maintains a GPA of 3.0 or higher and full-time enrollment.

**Number awarded:** Varies each year; recently, 4 of these scholarships were awarded.

**Deadline:** January of each year.

## 335 FARM BUREAU INSURANCE-VHSL ACHIEVEMENT AWARDS

Virginia High School League
1642 State Farm Boulevard
Charlottesville, VA 22911
Phone: (434) 977-8475; Fax: (434) 977-5943
Web: www.wvbinsurance.com/VHSL/VHSLAbout.asp

**Summary:** To provide financial assistance for college to high school seniors who have participated in activities of the Virginia High School League (VHSL).

**Eligibility:** Open to college-bound seniors graduating from high schools that are members of the VHSL. Applicants must have participated in 1 or more VHSL athletic activities (baseball, basketball, cheer, cross country, field hockey, football, golf, gymnastics, soccer, softball, swimming, tennis, indoor and outdoor track, volleyball; wrestling) and/or academic activities (student publications, creative writing, theater, forensics, debate, scholastic bowl). They must have a GPA of 3.0 or higher. Each school may nominate up to 4 students: 1 female athlete, 1 male athlete, 1 academic participant, and 1 courageous achievement candidate. The courageous achievement category is reserved for students who have overcome serious obstacles to make significant contributions to athletic and/or academic activities. The obstacles may include a serious illness, injury, or disability; a challenging social or home situation; or another extraordinary situation where the student has displayed tremendous courage against overwhelming odds. Along with their application, students must submit a 500-word essay describing how extracurricular activities have enhanced their educational experience. Candidates are judged separately in the 3 VHSL groups (A, AA, and AAA). Selection is based on the essay; involvement in other school-sponsored activities; involvement in activities outside of school; and 2 letters of support.

**Financial data:** The stipend is $1,000.

**Duration:** 1 year.

**Number awarded:** 10 each year. For each of the 3 groups (A, AA, and AAA), 1 female athlete, 1 male athlete, and 1 academic participant are selected. In addition, 1 courageous achievement candidate is selected statewide.

**Deadline:** March of each year.

## 336 FEDERAL EMPLOYEE EDUCATION AND ASSISTANCE FUND SCHOLARSHIPS

Federal Employee Education and Assistance Fund, Attn: Scholarship Program
8441 West Bowles Avenue, Suite 200
Littleton, CO 80123-3245
Phone: (303) 933-7580; (800) 323-4140; Fax: (303) 933-7587;
Email: feeahq@aol.com
Web: www.feea.org/scholarships.shtml

**Summary:** To provide financial assistance for college or graduate school to civilian federal and postal employees and their families.

**Eligibility:** Open to civilian federal and postal employees with at least 3 years of federal service and their dependent spouses and children; military retirees and active-duty personnel are not eligible. All applicants must have at least a 3.0 GPA and high school seniors must provide copies of their SAT or ACT scores, although those scores for students already in college are optional. Applicants must be working or planning to work toward a degree at an accredited 2- or 4-year postsecondary, graduate, or postgraduate program; employees may be part-time students, but dependents must be full time. Selection is based on academic achievement, community service, a recommendation, and an essay on a topic selected annually.

**Financial data:** Stipends range from $300 to $1,500.

**Duration:** 1 year; recipients may reapply.

**Number awarded:** Approximately 500 each year.

**Deadline:** March of each year.

## 337 FEDERAL PELL GRANTS

Department of Education, Attn: Federal Student Aid Information Center
P.O. Box 84
Washington, DC 20044-0084
Phone: (317) 337-5665; (800) 4-FED-AID; TTY: (800) 730-8913

Web: www.studentaid.ed.gov

**Summary:** To provide financial assistance for undergraduate education to students with financial need.

**Eligibility:** Open to students who have not earned a bachelor's or professional degree. They must meet specified financial need qualifications and be U.S. citizens or eligible noncitizens working toward a degree in an eligible program. They must have a valid Social Security number and have completed registration with the Selective Service if required.

**Financial data:** The amount of the award is based on the cost of attendance at the recipient's college or university, minus the expected family contribution, up to a specified maximum, which depends on annual program funding. Recently, awards ranged from $400 to $4,050 per year and averaged $2,404.

**Duration:** Up to 5 years of undergraduate study.

**Number awarded:** Varies each year; under this program, the federal government guarantees that each participating school will receive enough money to pay the Pell grants of its eligible students. Recently, 4,844,000 new grants, worth more than $11.3 billion, were anticipated for this program.

**Deadline:** Students may submit applications between January of the current year through June of the following year.

## 338 FEDERAL SUPPLEMENTAL EDUCATIONAL OPPORTUNITY GRANTS

Department of Education, Attn: Federal Student Aid Information Center
P.O. Box 84
Washington, DC 20044-0084
Phone: (317) 337-5665; (800) 4-FED-AID; TTY: (800) 730-8913
Web: www.studentaid.ed.gov

**Summary:** To provide financial assistance for undergraduate education to students with exceptional financial need.

**Eligibility:** Open to students who have not earned a bachelor's or professional degree. They must meet specified financial need qualifications and be U.S. citizens or eligible noncitizens working toward a degree in an eligible program. They must have a valid Social Security number and have completed registration with the Selective Service if required. Applicants for federal Pell Grants who demonstrate the greatest financial need qualify for these grants.

**Financial data:** The amount of the award is based on the cost of attendance at the recipient's college or university, minus the expected family contribution. Grants range between $100 and $4,000 per year and recently averaged $772.

**Duration:** Up to 5 years of undergraduate study.

**Number awarded:** Varies each year, depending on the availability of funds; under this program, the federal government does not guarantee that each participating school will receive enough money to pay the FSEOG grants of all of its eligible students. Recently, 1,246,000 new awards, worth $962 million, were anticipated for this program.

**Deadline:** Each participating school sets its own deadline.

## 339 FEDERATION OF JEWISH WOMEN'S ORGANIZATION SCHOLARSHIP

Alexander Graham Bell Association for the Deaf
Attn: Financial Aid Coordinator
3417 Volta Place, N.W.
Washington, DC 20007-2778
Phone: (202) 337-5220; Fax: (202) 337-8314; TTY: (202) 337-5221;
Email: financialaid@agbell.org
Web: www.agbell.org

**Summary:** To provide financial assistance to undergraduate and graduate students with moderate to profound hearing loss.

**Eligibility:** Open to undergraduate and graduate students who have been diagnosed with a moderate to profound hearing loss prior to acquiring spoken language (hearing loss averages 60dB or greater in the better ear in the speech frequencies of 500, 1000, and 2000 Hz). Applicants must be committed to using spoken language as their primary mode of communication. They must be accepted or enrolled at a mainstream college or university as a full-time student. Along with their application, they must submit a 1-page essay discussing their career goals and how spoken communication is helping them to reach those goals as a person with a hearing loss. Financial need is considered in the selection process. This scholarship is reserved for students who are hearing impaired.

**Financial data:** The stipend is $2,000 per year.

**Duration:** 1 year; may be renewed 1 additional year.

**Number awarded:** 1 each year.

**Deadline:** April of each year.

### 340 FEEA/WORLD TRADE CENTER/PENTAGON FUND SCHOLARSHIPS

Federal Employee Education and Assistance Fund, Attn: Scholarship Program
8441 West Bowles Avenue, Suite 200
Littleton, CO 80123-3245
Phone: (303) 933-7580; (800) 323-4140; Fax: (303) 933-7587;
Email: feeahq@aol.com
Web: www.feea.org/wtc_pentagon/wtc_pentagon.shtml

**Summary:** To provide financial assistance for college or graduate school to children and spouses of civilian federal employees killed or injured in the Pentagon on September 11, 2001.

**Eligibility:** Open to children who lost a civilian federal employee parent in the attack on the Pentagon on September 11, 2001. Children whose parent was critically injured are also eligible, as are victims' spouses who were already attending college on September 11. Spouses wishing to return to college are considered on a case-by-case basis.

**Financial data:** Full college scholarships are available.

**Number awarded:** All affected family members will be supported.

### 341 FHSAA ACADEMIC ALL-STATE AWARDS

Florida High School Athletic Association
1801 N.W. 80th Boulevard
Gainesville, FL 32606
Phone: (352) 372-9551; Fax: (352) 373-1528
Web: www.fhsaa.org

**Summary:** To provide financial assistance for college to student-athletes in Florida who have excelled in academics and athletics.

**Eligibility:** Open to college-bound seniors graduating from high schools in Florida. Candidates must have a cumulative unweighted GPA of 3.5 or higher and have earned a varsity letter in at least 2 different sports during each of their junior and senior years. Boys and girls are judged separately.

**Financial data:** Each honoree receives a $500 award. From among those honorees, the Scholar-Athletes of the Year receive an additional $2,500 scholarship.

**Duration:** The awards are presented annually.

**Number awarded:** 24 honorees (12 boys and 12 girls) are selected each year. From among those, 2 Scholar-Athletes of the Year (1 boy and 1 girl) are selected each year.

### 342 FINANCIAL SERVICE CENTERS OF FLORIDA DISADVANTAGED SCHOLARSHIP

Financial Service Centers of Florida
P.O. Box 14629
Tallahassee, FL 32317
Phone: (850) 222-6000; Fax: (850) 222-6002; Email: Corey@fscfl.com
Web: www.fscfl.com

**Summary:** To provide financial assistance for college to disadvantaged high school seniors in Florida.

**Eligibility:** Open to seniors graduating from high schools in Florida who qualify as disadvantaged. Applicants must have been admitted to a Florida college or university as a full-time student. They must have a GPA of 2.5 or higher.

**Financial data:** The stipend is $1,000.

**Duration:** 1 year.

**Number awarded:** 10 each year.

**Deadline:** June of each year.

### 343 FIRST COMMAND EDUCATIONAL FOUNDATION SCHOLARSHIPS

First Command Financial Planning
Attn: First Command Educational Foundation
1 FirstComm Plaza
P.O. Box 901091
Fort Worth, TX 76109-1091
Phone: (817) 731-8621; (877) 872-8289; Fax: (817) 569-2970;
Email: edufoundation@firstcommand.org
Web: www.firstcommand.org/fcef/scholarship/index.htm

**Summary:** To provide financial assistance for college to the children of active, retired, or deceased military personnel.

**Eligibility:** Open to all undergraduate students, although it was originally established to serve the sons and daughters of active, retired, or deceased military personnel (officer or enlisted) and to deserving ROTC cadets. Students must be nominated by an officers' spouses' club or a noncommissioned officers' spouses' club at participating U.S. military installations worldwide. They must apply through their local First Command representative or spouses' club at their installation. The foundation does not accept applications directly. Selection is based primarily on academic achievement and financial need.

**Financial data:** Scholarships are available in the amounts of $3,000, $2,000, or $1,000.

**Duration:** 1 year.

**Number awarded:** Varies each year; recently, 146 were awarded.

### 344 FIRST DATA WESTERN UNION FOUNDATION SCHOLARSHIP

First Data Western Union Foundation, Attn: Scholarship Program
6200 South Quebec Street, Suite 370 AU
Greenwood Village, CO 80111
Phone: (303) 967-6606; Fax: (303) 967-6492
Web: www.firstdatawesternunion.org/scholarships

**Summary:** To provide financial assistance to nontraditional students so they can realize their educational dreams.

**Eligibility:** Open to nontraditional students, from high school seniors to currently-enrolled college students. Applicants must have a high school diploma or GED and have been accepted at an accredited postsecondary educational institution in the United States or Puerto Rico. They must have a GPA of 2.0 or higher. Selection is based on ability to accept and deal with personal challenges, commitment to learning and working hard, and financial need. Special consideration is given to applicants from Colorado, Florida, Maryland, New Jersey, New York, and Texas (where a majority of First Data employees live and work).

**Financial data:** Stipends range from $500 to $3,000. Funds must be used for tuition, fees, or books and must be used within 1 year of the award date.

**Duration:** Both 1-time and renewable scholarships (up to 4 years) are offered.

**Deadline:** March of each year.

### 345 FIRST LIEUTENANT MICHAEL L. LEWIS, JR. MEMORIAL FUND SCHOLARSHIP

American Legion Auxiliary, Attn: Department of New York
112 State Street, Suite 1310
Albany, NY 12207
Phone: (518) 463-1162; (800) 421-6348; Fax: (518) 449-5406;
Email: alanyhdqtrs@worldnet.att.net
Web: www.deptny.org/scholarships.htm

**Summary:** To provide financial assistance for college to members of the American Legion Auxiliary in New York.

**Eligibility:** Open to 1) junior members of the New York Department of the American Legion Auxiliary who are high school seniors or graduates younger than 20 years of age; and 2) senior members who are continuing their education to further their studies or update their job skills. Applicants must submit a 200-word essay on "Why a college education is important to me," or "Why I want to continue my post high school education in a business or trade school." Selection is based on character (25%), Americanism (25%), leadership (25%), and scholarship (25%).

**Financial data:** The stipend is $1,000.

**Duration:** 1 year.

**Number awarded:** 2 each year: 1 to a junior member and 1 to a senior member. If no senior members apply, both scholarships are awarded to junior members.

**Deadline:** March of each year.

### 346 FIRST MARINE DIVISION ASSOCIATION SCHOLARSHIPS

First Marine Division Association
410 Pier View Way
Oceanside, CA 92054
Phone: (760) 967-8561; (877) 967-8561; Fax: (760) 967-8567;
Email: oldbreed@sbcglobal.net
Web: www.1stmarinedivisionassociation.org/scholarship-fund-page.html

**Summary:** To provide financial assistance for college to dependents of deceased or disabled veterans of the First Marine Division.

**Eligibility:** Open to dependents of veterans who served in the First Marine Division or in a unit attached to that Division who are honorably discharged and are now either totally and permanently disabled or deceased from any cause. Applicants must be attending or planning to attend an accredited college, university, or trade school as a full-time undergraduate student. Graduate students and students still in high school or prep school are not eligible.

**Financial data:** The stipend is $1,500 per year.

**Duration:** 1 year; may be renewed up to 3 additional years.

**Number awarded:** Varies each year.

## 347 FIRST STATE MANUFACTURED HOUSING ASSOCIATION SCHOLARSHIP

Delaware Higher Education Commission
Carvel State Office Building
820 North French Street
Wilmington, DE 19801
Phone: (302) 577-3240; (800) 292-7935; Fax: (302) 577-6765;
Email: dhec@doe.k12.de.us
Web: www.doe.state.de.us/high-ed/firststatemanufactured.htm
**Summary:** To provide financial assistance for college to Delaware residents who live in a manufactured home.
**Eligibility:** Open to Delaware residents who have lived in a manufactured home for at least 1 year. Applicants may be planning to pursue any type of accredited training, licensing, or certification program or any accredited degree program. Selection is based on academic record, an essay, recommendations, and financial need.
**Financial data:** The maximum stipend is $4,000 per year.
**Duration:** 1 year.
**Number awarded:** 1 or more each year.
**Deadline:** March of each year.

## 348 FISCA SCHOLARSHIPS

Financial Service Centers of America, Inc.
25 Main Street
P.O. Box 647
Hackensack, NJ 07602
Phone: (201) 487-0412; Fax: (201) 487-3954; Email: mailbox@fisca.org
Web: www.fisca.org/scholar.htm
**Summary:** To provide financial assistance to high school seniors from families in areas served by members of Financial Service Centers of America (FISCA).
**Eligibility:** Open to high school seniors who are family members of check cashing customers at FISCA-member locations throughout the country. Students already enrolled in college are not eligible. Applications must be validated by the customer's local check cashing outlet. Along with their application, they must submit a 100-word essay in which they profile a person who has influenced them and explain how that person has made an impact on their life. Selection is based on academic achievement, financial need, leadership skills in school and the community, and the essay.
**Financial data:** The stipend is $2,000.
**Duration:** 1 year.
**Number awarded:** At least 10 each year (at least 2 from each of the 5 geographic regions across the nation).
**Deadline:** May of each year.

## 349 FLEETWOOD MEMORIAL FOUNDATION GRANTS

Fleetwood Memorial Foundation
501 South Fielder Road
Arlington, TX 76013
Phone: (817) 261-8954; Fax: (817) 261-2368;
Email: fleetwood@fleetwoodmemorial.org
Web: www.fleetwoodmemorial.org/middle.html
**Summary:** To provide no-strings-attached grants to injured law enforcement or fire protection personnel in Texas or to the families of deceased personnel.
**Eligibility:** Open to certified Texas law enforcement or fire protection personnel who have been injured in the performance of their duties or to the families of personnel who were killed in the performance of their duties. For the purposes of this program, "line of duty" does not automatically mean "on duty;" for example, no injuries considered Section V or strains during normal exercise, automobile accidents while going to lunch, etc. are viewed as "line of duty" by this program.
**Financial data:** These grants, up to $10,000, are designed to provide immediate financial relief to meet unexpected expenses until insurance or more permanent sources of funds can be arranged. Grants may be used to re-educate qualified personnel if they are unable to return to their normal duties after an accident. Educational funds are also available to the dependent children of deceased peace and fire personnel as long as they attend a public educational institution.
**Duration:** These are 1-time grants.
**Number awarded:** Since its inception in 1974, the foundation has provided more than 400 grants to qualified recipients, totaling nearly $1.5 million.
**Deadline:** Applications may be submitted at any time.

## 350 FLICKER OF HOPE SCHOLARSHIPS

Flicker of Hope Foundation, Attn: Scholarship Committee
8624 Janet Lane
Vienna, VA 22180
Phone: (703) 698-1626; Fax: (703) 573-8161; Email: info@flickerofhope.org
Web: www.flickerofhope.org/FOHScholarship.html
**Summary:** To provide financial assistance for college to burn survivors.
**Eligibility:** Open to high school seniors and graduates who are burn survivors and enrolled or planning to enroll in college. Applicants must submit a 500-word essay describing the circumstances of how they were burned, how that injury has affected their life, and the benefits to be derived from their planned course of study. Financial need is also considered in the selection process.
**Financial data:** A stipend is awarded (amount not specified). Funds are paid directly to the postsecondary institution.
**Duration:** 1 year.
**Number awarded:** Varies each year; recently, 6 of these scholarships were awarded.

## 351 FLORENCE AND MARVIN ARKANS EAGLE SCOUT SCHOLARSHIP

Boy Scouts of America, Attn: National Jewish Committee on Scouting, S226
1325 West Walnut Hill Lane
P.O. Box 152079
Irving, TX 75015-2079
Phone: (972) 580-2000
Web: www.jewishscouting.org/njcs/awards/eagle.html
**Summary:** To provide financial assistance for college to Jewish Boy Scouts, Varsity Scouts, and Venturers.
**Eligibility:** Open to registered, active members of a Boy Scout troop, Varsity Scout team, or Venturing crew who have received the Eagle Scout Award and have also earned the Ner Tamid or Etz Chaim emblem. Applicants must be enrolled in an accredited high school in their final year and must be an active member of a synagogue. They must have demonstrated practical citizenship in their synagogue, school, Scouting unit, and community. Selection is based on financial need; high school record, including school activities, awards, honors, and GPA; participation in community organizations; participation in religious youth organizations, clubs, or groups, including honors earned and offices held; involvement in Scouting; career goals; and 4 letters of recommendation, from leaders of their religious institution, school, community, and Scouting unit.
**Financial data:** The stipend is $1,000.
**Duration:** 1 year; nonrenewable.
**Number awarded:** 1 each year.
**Deadline:** December of each year.

## 352 FLORIDA ACADEMIC SCHOLARS AWARD PROGRAM

Florida Department of Education, Attn: Office of Student Financial Assistance
1940 North Monroe Street, Suite 70
Tallahassee, FL 32303-4759
Phone: (850) 410-5200; (888) 827-2004; Fax: (850) 487-1809;
Email: osfa@fldoe.org
Web: www.myfloridaeducation.com/brfuture
**Summary:** To provide financial assistance for college to outstanding high school seniors in Florida.
**Eligibility:** Open to seniors in Florida public and private high schools who have been Florida residents for at least 1 year and will attend eligible Florida institutions of higher education. Applicants must have 1) earned a GPA of 3.5 or higher in a specified high school academic curriculum, 2) achieved scores of at least 28 on the ACT (or the equivalent on the SAT), and 3) completed at least 75 hours of community service. Also eligible are National Merit and Achievement scholars and finalists, National Hispanic Scholars, IB Diploma recipients, and home-schooled students and GED recipients who achieve the same minimum SAT or ACT scores. U.S. citizenship or permanent resident status is required.
**Financial data:** The scholarships provide 100% of tuition and fees (including lab fees up to $300 per semester) at Florida public colleges and universities or an equivalent amount at private institutions. Students also receive a stipend of $300 for college-related expenses.
**Duration:** Recipients may use this award 1) for up to 132 credit hours required to complete a standard undergraduate degree at their institution; 2) for up to 7 years from high school graduation (if initially funded within 3 years after high school graduation); or 3) until completion of their first baccalaureate degree program, whichever comes first. Renewal requires a GPA of 3.0 or higher.
**Number awarded:** Varies each year.
**Deadline:** March of each year.

## 353 FLORIDA ACADEMIC TOP SCHOLARS AWARD PROGRAM

Florida Department of Education, Attn: Office of Student Financial Assistance

1940 North Monroe Street, Suite 70

Tallahassee, FL 32303-4759

Phone: (850) 410-5200; (888) 827-2004; Fax: (850) 487-1809;

Email: osfa@fldoe.org

Web: www.myfloridaeducation.com/brfuture

**Summary:** To provide financial assistance for college to the top high school seniors in Florida.

**Eligibility:** Open to seniors in Florida public and private high schools who have been Florida residents for at least 1 year and will attend eligible Florida institutions of higher education. They must have completed a specified curriculum while in high school. U.S. citizenship or permanent resident status is required. The Academic Top Scholars Award is presented to the student with the highest academic ranking in each county, based on GPA and SAT/ACT test scores.

**Financial data:** The Academic Top Scholars awardees receive an annual stipend of $1,500 in addition to their Academic Scholars Award.

**Duration:** Recipients may use this award 1) for up to 132 credit hours required to complete a standard undergraduate degree at their institution; 2) for up to 7 years from high school graduation (if initially funded within 3 years after high school graduation); or 3) until completion of their first baccalaureate degree program, whichever comes first. Renewal requires a GPA of 3.0 or higher.

**Number awarded:** 67 each year: 1 in each Florida county.

**Deadline:** March of each year.

## 354 FLORIDA ACCESS TO BETTER LEARNING AND EDUCATION GRANT PROGRAM

Florida Department of Education, Attn: Office of Student Financial Assistance

1940 North Monroe Street, Suite 70

Tallahassee, FL 32303-4759

Phone: (850) 410-5200; (888) 827-2004; Fax: (850) 487-1809;

Email: osfa@fldoe.org

Web: www.FloridaStudentFinancialAid.org

**Summary:** To provide financial assistance to Florida residents enrolled at private colleges and universities in the state.

**Eligibility:** Open to students enrolled full time at eligible private Florida colleges and universities who have been residents of the state for at least 1 year. Applicants may not have previously received a bachelor's degree and may not be enrolled in a program of study leading to a degree in theology or divinity.

**Financial data:** The stipend is specified each year by the Florida legislation, but it may not exceed the total charged for tuition and fees by the institution.

**Duration:** Funds may be received for up to 9 semesters or 14 quarters or until receipt of a bachelor's degree, whichever comes first. Renewal requires that the student earn a GPA of 2.0 or higher each semester.

**Number awarded:** Varies each year.

**Deadline:** Each participating institution sets its own deadline.

## 355 FLORIDA AMERICAN LEGION SCHOLARSHIPS

American Legion, Attn: Department of Florida

1912 Lee Road

P.O. Box 547859

Orlando, FL 32854-7859

Phone: (407) 295-2631; Fax: (407) 299-0901; Email: fal@fllegion.newsouth.net

Web: www.floridalegion.org/programs/scholarships/scholarship.html

**Summary:** To provide financial assistance for college to the descendants of American Legion members in Florida.

**Eligibility:** Open to the direct descendants (children, grandchildren, great-grandchildren, and legally adopted children) of a member of the American Legion's Department of Florida or of a deceased U.S. veteran who would have been eligible for membership in the American Legion. Applicants must be seniors attending a Florida high school and planning to attend an accredited U.S. college or university.

**Financial data:** Stipends are $2,500, $1,500, or $1,000.

**Duration:** 1 year; nonrenewable.

**Number awarded:** 3 each year.

**Deadline:** February of each year.

## 356 FLORIDA COLLEGE STUDENT OF THE YEAR AWARD

College Student of the Year, Inc.

412 N.W. 16th Avenue

P.O. Box 14081

Gainesville, FL 32604-2081

Phone: (352) 373-6907; (888) 547-6310; Fax: (352) 373-8120;

Email: info@studentleader.com

Web: www.floridaleader.com/soty

**Summary:** To recognize and reward outstanding Florida college or graduate students who are involved in campus and community activities, excel academically, and exhibit financial self-reliance by working and earning scholarships to pay their way through school.

**Eligibility:** Open to students (need not be Florida residents) who are currently enrolled at least half time at a Florida-based community college, private university, state university, or accredited vocational, technical, or business school. Undergraduate and graduate students, non-American citizens, nontraditional students, and distance-learning students are all eligible. Applicants must have completed at least 30 credit hours with a GPA of 3.25 or higher. They must submit an essay (from 500 to 600 words) that addresses this topic: "What I have accomplished that makes a difference at my college and in my community." Students do not have to be nominated by their colleges to be eligible; they are permitted and encouraged to apply on their own. There is no limit to the number of applicants who can apply from a particular institution. Open to current employees or relatives of employees of *Florida Leader* magazine, Oxendine Publishing, Inc., College Student of the Year, Inc., or any cosponsor. Winners are selected on the basis of 3 main criteria: academic excellence, financial self-reliance, and community and campus service. Financial need is not a requirement.

**Financial data:** Nearly $65,000 in scholarships and prizes is available each year. The actual distribution of those funds among the various recipients depends on the support provided by the sponsors. Recently, the winner received a $3,500 scholarship from SunTrust Education Loans, a $1,000 gift certificate from Office Depot, and many other gifts and prizes. The first runner-up received a $2,500 scholarship from SunTrust, a $500 gift certificate from Office Depot, and other gifts and prizes. The other finalists each received a $2,000 scholarship from SunTrust, a $500 gift certificate from Office Depot, and other gifts and prizes. The honorable mention winners each received a $1,000 scholarship from SunTrust, a $250 gift certificate from Office Depot, and other gifts and prizes.

**Duration:** The prizes are awarded annually.

**Number awarded:** 20 each year: 1 winner, 1 first runner-up, 5 other finalists, and 13 honorable mentions.

**Deadline:** January of each year.

## 357 FLORIDA GOLD SEAL VOCATIONAL SCHOLARS AWARDS

Florida Department of Education, Attn: Office of Student Financial Assistance

1940 North Monroe Street, Suite 70

Tallahassee, FL 32303-4759

Phone: (850) 410-5200; (888) 827-2004; Fax: (850) 487-1809;

Email: osfa@fldoe.org

Web: www.myfloridaeducation.com/brfuture

**Summary:** To provide financial assistance for vocational education to outstanding high school seniors in Florida.

**Eligibility:** Open to graduating high school seniors in Florida who plan to attend a vocational, technical, trade, or business school in the state. Applicants must have earned a GPA of 3.0 or higher in their required academic program and 3.5 or higher in their vocational classes in high school. They must also have achieved the following minimum scores: 1) on the CPT, 83 in reading, 83 in sentence skills, and 72 in algebra; or 2) on the ACT, 17 in English, 18 in reading, and 19 in mathematics (or an equivalent score on the SAT). U.S. citizenship or permanent resident status is required.

**Financial data:** The scholarships cover 75% of tuition and mandatory fees (including lab fees up to $300 per semester) at public vocational/technical institutions in Florida, or an equivalent amount at private schools.

**Duration:** Recipients may use this award 1) for up to 90 semester hours; 2) for up to 7 years from high school graduation (if initially funded within 3 years after high school graduation); or 3) until completion of their first baccalaureate degree program, whichever comes first. Renewal requires a GPA of 2.75 or higher.

**Number awarded:** Varies each year.

**Deadline:** March of each year.

## 358 FLORIDA LEGION AUXILIARY DEPARTMENT SCHOLARSHIP

American Legion Auxiliary, Attn: Department of Florida

1912 Lee Road

P.O. Box 547917

Orlando, FL 32854-7917

Phone: (407) 293-7411; Fax: (407) 299-6522; Email: alaflorida@aol.com

**Summary:** To provide financial assistance for college to the children of Florida veterans.

**Eligibility:** Open to children of honorably-discharged veterans who are Florida residents. Applicants must be attending a postsecondary school in the state on a full-time basis.

**Financial data:** The stipends are up to $1,000 for a 4-year university or up to $500 for a junior college or technical-vocational school. All funds are paid directly to the institution.

**Duration:** 1 year; may be renewed if the recipient needs further financial assistance and has maintained a GPA of 2.5 or higher.

**Number awarded:** Varies each year, depending on the availability of funds.

**Deadline:** December of each year.

## 359 FLORIDA MEDALLION SCHOLARS AWARDS

Florida Department of Education, Attn: Office of Student Financial Assistance
1940 North Monroe Street, Suite 70
Tallahassee, FL 32303-4759
Phone: (850) 410-5200; (888) 827-2004; Fax: (850) 487-1809;
Email: osfa@fldoe.org
Web: www.myfloridaeducation.com/brfuture

**Summary:** To provide financial assistance for college to outstanding high school seniors in Florida.

**Eligibility:** Open to seniors in Florida public and private high schools who have been Florida residents for at least 1 year and who plan to attend eligible Florida institutions of higher education. Applicants must have 1) earned a GPA of 3.0 or higher in a specified high school academic curriculum, and 2) achieved scores of at least 20 on the ACT (or the equivalent on the SAT). Also eligible are National Medallion and Achievement scholars and finalists who complete 75 hours of community service, National Hispanic Scholars who complete 75 hours of community service, home-schooled students who achieve scores of at least 23 on the ACT (or the equivalent on the SAT), and GED recipients who achieve test scores of at least 20 on the ACT (or the equivalent on the SAT) and a GPA of 3.0 or higher.

**Financial data:** The scholarships cover 75% of tuition and mandatory fees (including lab fees up to $300 per semester) at public colleges and universities in Florida, or an equivalent amount at private schools.

**Duration:** Recipients may use this award 1) for up to 132 semester hours; 2) for up to 7 years from high school graduation (if initially funded within 3 years after high school graduation); or 3) until completion of their first baccalaureate degree program, whichever comes first. Renewal requires a GPA of 2.75 or higher.

**Number awarded:** Varies each year.

**Deadline:** March of each year.

## 360 FLORIDA PTA SCHOLARSHIP PROGRAMS

Florida PTA
1747 Orlando Central Parkway
Orlando, FL 32809
Phone: (407) 855-7604; (800) 373-5782; Fax: (407) 240-9577;
Email: info@floridapta.org
Web: www.floridapta.org/involved-scholarships.htm

**Summary:** To provide financial assistance for college to high school seniors in Florida.

**Eligibility:** Open to seniors graduating from high schools in Florida. Applicants must have attended a Florida PTA/PTSA high school for at least 2 years and have a GPA of 2.5 or higher. They must be planning to enroll as a full-time undergraduate student at a Florida postsecondary institution. U.S. citizenship is required. Financial need is considered in the selection process. The program includes 4 types of scholarships: academic, vocational/technical, community/junior college, and fine arts.

**Financial data:** The stipend is $1,000 per year.

**Duration:** 1 year. Academic scholarships may be renewed if the recipient maintains a GPA of 2.5 or higher. The other 3 types are nonrenewable.

**Number awarded:** Varies each year; recently, the program awarded 2 academic scholarships, 2 vocational/technical scholarships, 4 community/junior college scholarships, and 4 fine arts scholarships.

**Deadline:** February of each year.

## 361 FLORIDA SCHOLARSHIPS FOR CHILDREN OF DECEASED OR DISABLED VETERANS

Florida Department of Education, Attn: Office of Student Financial Assistance
1940 North Monroe Street, Suite 70
Tallahassee, FL 32303-4759
Phone: (850) 410-5200; (888) 827-2004; Fax: (850) 487-1809;
Email: osfa@fldoe.org
Web: www.FloridaStudentFinancialAid.org

**Summary:** To provide financial assistance for college to the children of Florida veterans who are disabled, deceased, or officially classified as prisoners of war (POW) or missing in action (MIA).

**Eligibility:** Open to residents of Florida between 16 and 22 years of age who are the dependent children of veterans or servicemen who 1) died as a result of service-connected injuries, diseases, or disabilities sustained while on active duty during a period of war; 2) have a service-connected 100% total and permanent disability; or 3) was classified as POW or MIA during the Korean War or Vietnam era and has not returned alive or remains have not been found. The official military and residency status of the veteran parent must be verified by the Florida Department of Veterans' Affairs.

**Financial data:** Qualified students who attend a Florida public institution of higher education receive payment of tuition and fees. Students who attend an eligible nonpublic Florida institution of higher education receive an award equal to the amount they would be required to pay for the average tuition and fees at a public institution at the comparable level.

**Duration:** 1 quarter or semester; may be renewed for up to 11 additional quarters or 7 additional semesters as long as the student maintains a GPA of 2.0 or higher and full-time enrollment.

**Number awarded:** Varies each year; recently, this program provided 215 awards.

**Deadline:** March of each year.

## 362 FLORIDA STUDENT ASSISTANCE GRANTS

Florida Department of Education, Attn: Office of Student Financial Assistance
1940 North Monroe Street, Suite 70
Tallahassee, FL 32303-4759
Phone: (850) 410-5200; (888) 827-2004; Fax: (850) 487-1809;
Email: osfa@fldoe.org
Web: www.FloridaStudentFinancialAid.org

**Summary:** To provide financial assistance for undergraduate studies to needy Florida residents.

**Eligibility:** Open to 1) full-time undergraduate students who are attending an eligible public or private Florida institution, and 2) part-time undergraduate students at Florida public institutions. Applicants must be U.S. citizens or eligible noncitizens. A minimum of 1 year of Florida residency is required. Financial need must be documented; applicants must submit the Free Application for Federal Student Aid (FAFSA) and demonstrate substantial financial need. Priority is given to students who rank in the top 20% of their high school class and plan to attend 1 of the 11 state universities.

**Financial data:** Stipends range from $200 to a maximum that varies each year but recently was $1,592 per year.

**Duration:** Grants may be received for up to 9 semesters or 14 quarters or until receipt of a bachelor's degree, whichever comes first. Renewal requires that the student earn a GPA of 2.0 or higher each semester.

**Number awarded:** Varies each year; recently, this program provided 40,040 awards.

**Deadline:** Each participating institution sets its own deadline.

## 363 FLOYD QUALLS MEMORIAL SCHOLARSHIPS

American Council of the Blind, Attn: Coordinator, Scholarship Program
1155 15th Street, N.W., Suite 1004
Washington, DC 20005
Phone: (202) 467-5081; (800) 424-8666; Fax: (202) 467-5085;
Email: info@acb.org
Web: www.acb.org

**Summary:** To provide financial assistance to undergraduate and graduate students who are blind.

**Eligibility:** Open to students who are legally blind. Recipients are selected in each of 4 categories: entering freshmen in academic programs, undergraduates (sophomores, juniors, and seniors) in academic programs, graduate students in academic programs, and vocational school students or students working on an associate's degree from a community college. In addition to letters of recommendation and copies of academic transcripts, applications must include an autobiographical sketch. A cumulative GPA of 3.3 or higher is generally required. Selection is based on demonstrated academic record, involvement in extracurricular and civic activities, and academic objectives. The severity of the applicant's visual impairment and his/her study methods are also taken into account.

**Financial data:** The stipend is $2,500. In addition, the winners receive a Kurzweil-1000 Reading System.

**Duration:** 1 year.

**Number awarded:** Up to 8 each year: 2 in each of the 4 categories.

**Deadline:** February of each year.

### 364 FOLSOM SCHOLARSHIPS

Datatrac Information Systems, Inc., Attn: Scholarship Committee
14120 Newbrook Drive, Suite 200
Chantilly, VA 20151
Phone: (703) 817-9700, ext. 4208; Fax: (703) 817-9791;
Email: b.blakney@datatrac-dc.com
Web: www.datatrac-dc.com
**Summary:** To provide financial assistance for college to high school seniors in the Washington, D.C., metropolitan area who plan to attend a 2-year college or trade school.
**Eligibility:** Open to seniors graduating from high schools in the Washington, D.C., metropolitan area. Residents of Maryland and Virginia must be planning to attend a 2-year accredited institution, certification or licensure program, or trade school in their state of residency; residents of Washington, D.C., may attend a similar institution in the area. Students planning to attend a 4-year college or university are not eligible. Applicants must submit brief essays on their financial need and their personal goals.
**Financial data:** The stipend is $5,000.
**Duration:** 1 year.
**Number awarded:** 2 each year.
**Deadline:** April of each year.

### 365 FORD OPPORTUNITY PROGRAM SCHOLARSHIP

Oregon Student Assistance Commission
Attn: Ford Family Foundation Scholarship Office
1700 Valley River Drive, Suite 400
Eugene, OR 97401
Phone: (541) 485-6211; (877) 864-2872; Email: fordscholarships@tfff.org
Web: www.osac.state.or.us/ford_opportunity.html
**Summary:** To provide financial assistance to Oregon residents who are single parents working on a college degree.
**Eligibility:** Open to residents of Oregon who are U.S. citizens or permanent residents. Applicants must be single heads of household with custody of a dependent child or children. They must have a cumulative high school or college GPA of 3.0 or higher or a GED score of 2650 or higher, and they must be planning to earn a 4-year degree at an Oregon college. Selection is based on community service, work ethic, personal initiative, and financial need.
**Financial data:** This program provides up to 90% of a recipient's unmet financial need; recently, stipends averaged $11,261.
**Duration:** 1 year; may be renewed for up to 3 additional years.
**Number awarded:** 50 each year.
**Deadline:** February of each year.

### 366 FORD SCHOLARS PROGRAM

Oregon Student Assistance Commission
Attn: Ford Family Foundation Scholarship Office
1700 Valley River Drive, Suite 400
Eugene, OR 97401
Phone: (541) 485-6211; (877) 864-2872; Email: fordscholarships@tfff.org
Web: www.osac.state.or.us/ford_scholars.html
**Summary:** To provide financial assistance to residents of Oregon and Siskiyou County, California who are seeking a college degree.
**Eligibility:** Open to U.S. citizens and permanent residents who are residents of Oregon or of Siskiyou County, California. Applicants must be 1) graduating high school seniors; 2) high school graduates who have not yet been full-time undergraduates; or 3) students who have completed 2 years at a community college and are entering their junior year at a 4-year college. They must have a cumulative high school or college GPA of 3.0 or higher or a GED score of 2650 or higher, and they must be planning to complete a 4-year degree. Students from Oregon must attend a college or university in the state; students from Siskiyou County, California must attend a college or university in California. Selection is based on community service, work ethic, personal initiative, and financial need.
**Financial data:** This program provides up to 90% of a recipient's unmet financial need; recently, stipends averaged $5,836.
**Duration:** 1 year; may be renewed for up to 3 additional years.
**Number awarded:** 100 each year from Oregon plus others from Siskiyou County, California.
**Deadline:** February of each year.

### 367 FORD TRUCK SCHOLARSHIP PROGRAM

National FFA Organization, Attn: Scholarship Office
6060 FFA Drive
P.O. Box 68960
Indianapolis, IN 46268-0960
Phone: (317) 802-4321; Fax: (317) 802-5321; Email: scholarships@ffa.org
Web: www.ffa.org
**Summary:** To provide financial assistance to FFA members who are interested in working on a 2-year or 4-year college degree in any field.
**Eligibility:** Open to members who are graduating high school seniors planning to enroll or students currently enrolled full time at an accredited 2- or 4-year college, university, or vocational/technical school. Applicants may be majoring in any field. They must visit a Ford Truck dealership and obtain a signature on the scholarship application. Selection is based on academic achievement (10 points for GPA, 10 points for SAT or ACT score, 10 points for class rank), leadership in FFA activities (30 points), leadership in community activities (10 points), and participation in the Supervised Agricultural Experience (SAE) program (30 points). U.S. citizenship is required.
**Financial data:** The stipend is $1,000. Funds are paid directly to the recipient.
**Duration:** 1 year; nonrenewable.
**Number awarded:** Approximately 705 each year: approximately 700 on behalf of participating Ford Truck dealerships and 5 on a nationwide basis.
**Deadline:** February of each year.

### 368 FOSTERING HOPE SCHOLARSHIP FUND

Parkersburg Area Community Foundation
501 Avery Street, Lobby
P.O. Box 1762
Parkersburg, WV 26102-1762
Phone: (304) 428-GIFT; Fax: (304) 428-1200; Email: info@pacfwv.com
Web: www.pacfwv.com
**Summary:** To provide financial assistance for college to high school seniors in West Virginia who have been enrolled in the foster care system.
**Eligibility:** Open to seniors graduating from high schools in West Virginia who are actively enrolled, or have been enrolled, in the foster care system. Preference is given to residents of Wood County. Applicants must have been accepted to a postsecondary educational institution. Selection is based on academic promise, character, citizenship, and financial need.
**Financial data:** A stipend is awarded (amount not specified).
**Duration:** 1 year; recipients may reapply.
**Deadline:** March of each year.

### 369 FOUNDATION FOR RURAL SERVICE COLLEGE SCHOLARSHIP PROGRAM

Foundation for Rural Service, Attn: Selection Committee
4121 Wilson Boulevard, Tenth Floor
Arlington, VA 22203
Phone: (703) 351-2026; Fax: (703) 351-2027
Web: www.frs.org
**Summary:** To provide financial assistance for college to high school seniors who live in rural areas of the United States.
**Eligibility:** Open to graduating high school seniors who receive local telecommunications service from a current member of the National Telecommunications Cooperative Association (NTCA) that serves as a sponsor; associate NTCA members (businesses that provide goods and services to the telecommunications industry) may also sponsor a student. Applicants must live in a rural area, as defined by the Office of Rural Health Policy of the U.S. Department of Health and Human Services. They must have a GPA of 2.0 or higher and have been accepted by an accredited 2-year or 4-year college, university, or vocational/technical school. Along with their application, they must submit transcripts and information on their work experience, school activities, community and volunteer activities, awards and honors, and special circumstances such as family financial need. The must also submit a 300-word essay on 1 of 3 assigned topics. Preference is given to applicants who express an interest in returning to a rural community after graduation.
**Financial data:** The stipend is $2,500 (of which $500 is provided by the sponsoring NTCA member cooperative).
**Duration:** 1 year; nonrenewable.
**Number awarded:** 25 each year: 1 per geographic region of NTCA membership, 1 to a student sponsored by an NTCA associate member, and 14 distributed proportionately to the number of applications received per region.
**Deadline:** February of each year.

### 370 FOUR-YEAR SBAA EDUCATIONAL SCHOLARSHIP FUND

Spina Bifida Association of America, Attn: Scholarship Committee
4590 MacArthur Boulevard, N.W., Suite 250

Washington, DC 20007-4226
Phone: (202) 944-3285, ext. 19; (800) 621-3141; Fax: (202) 944-3295;
Email: sbaa@sbaa.org
Web: www.sbaa.org
**Summary:** To provide financial assistance to members of the Spina Bifida Association of America (SBAA) who are planning to attend a 4-year college or university.
**Eligibility:** Open to persons born with spina bifida who are current members of the association. Applicants must be high school juniors or seniors planning to attend a 4-year college or university. Selection is based on academic record, other efforts shown in school, financial need, work history, community service, leadership, and commitment to personal goals.
**Financial data:** The stipend is $5,000 per year. Funds may be used for tuition, room, and board.
**Duration:** 4 years.
**Number awarded:** 1 each year.
**Deadline:** February of each year.

### 371 FRANCIS OUIMET SCHOLARSHIPS

Francis Ouimet Scholarship Fund
c/o William F. Connell Golf House and Museum
300 Arnold Palmer Boulevard
Norton, MA 02766
Phone: (774) 430-9090; Fax: (774) 430-9091; Email: bobd@ouimet.org
Web: www.ouimet.org
**Summary:** To provide financial assistance for college to young people in Massachusetts who have worked at a golf course.
**Eligibility:** Open to students entering or attending college or technical school in Massachusetts. They must have worked for at least 2 years at a public, private, semi-private, resort, or municipal golf club in Massachusetts as caddies, helpers in pro shop operations (including bag room, range, cart storage, and starter's area), or course superintendent operations. Ineligible students include those who have worked at a golf course but in a position not in direct service to golf (e.g., workers in the dining room, office, kitchen, banquet area), and those who have worked in a job related to golf but not actually at a golf course (e.g., driving range, off-course golf stores, miniature golf course). Selection is based on academic achievement and potential, leadership (including school and community activities), interviews, essays, motivation, character, integrity, service to golf, and recommendations. In addition, awards may be either financial need-based or "Honorary," with need not considered.
**Financial data:** Stipends range from $1,500 to $6,500 per year.
**Duration:** 1 year; may be renewed for 3 additional years.
**Number awarded:** Approximately 350 each year.
**Deadline:** November of each year.

### 372 FRANK L. WEIL MEMORIAL EAGLE SCOUT SCHOLARSHIP

Boy Scouts of America, Attn: National Jewish Committee on Scouting, S226
1325 West Walnut Hill Lane
P.O. Box 152079
Irving, TX 75015-2079
Phone: (972) 580-2000
Web: www.jewishscouting.org/njcs/awards/eagle.html
**Summary:** To provide financial assistance for college to Jewish Boy Scouts, Varsity Scouts, and Venturers.
**Eligibility:** Open to registered, active members of a Boy Scout troop, Varsity Scout team, or Venturing crew who have received the Eagle Scout Award and have also earned the Ner Tamid or Etz Chaim emblem. Applicants must be enrolled in an accredited high school in their final year and must be an active member of a synagogue. They must have demonstrated practical citizenship in their synagogue, school, Scouting unit, and community. Selection is based on high school record, including school activities, awards, honors, and GPA; participation in community organizations; participation in religious youth organizations, clubs, or groups, including honors earned and offices held; involvement in Scouting; career goals; and 4 letters of recommendation, from leaders of their religious institution, school, community, and Scouting unit.
**Financial data:** First place is $1,000 and second place is $500.
**Duration:** 1 year; not renewable.
**Number awarded:** 3 each year: 1 first place and 2 second place awards.
**Deadline:** December of each year.

### 373 FRANK O'BANNON GRANT PROGRAM

State Student Assistance Commission of Indiana, Attn: Grant Division
150 West Market Street, Suite 500

Indianapolis, IN 46204-2811
Phone: (317) 232-2350; (888) 528-4719 (within IN); Fax: (317) 232-3260;
Email: grants@ssaci.state.in.us
Web: www.in.gov/ssaci/programs/hea.html
**Summary:** To provide financial assistance to Indiana residents who are working full time on an undergraduate degree.
**Eligibility:** Open to Indiana residents who are high school seniors, high school graduates, or GED certificate recipients. Applicants must be attending or planning to attend an eligible Indiana postsecondary institution as a full-time undergraduate student working on an associate or first bachelor's degree. They must be able to demonstrate financial need for tuition assistance. U.S. citizenship or permanent resident status is required.
**Financial data:** This program offers tuition assistance from $200 to several thousand dollars per year, depending on the level of appropriations, the number of eligible students making application, the calculation of student's financial need, and the cost of tuition and fees at the schools of choice.
**Duration:** 1 year.
**Number awarded:** Varies each year.
**Deadline:** March of each year.

### 374 FRED AND MARIE CHRISTOPHERSON SCHOLARSHIP

Sioux Falls Area Community Foundation, Attn: Scholarship Coordinator
300 North Phillips Avenue, Suite 120
Sioux Falls, SD 57104-6006
Phone: (605) 336-7055; Fax: (605) 336-0038; Email: sbrown@sfacf.org
Web: www.sfacf.org
**Summary:** To provide financial assistance for college to high school seniors in South Dakota.
**Eligibility:** Open to seniors graduating from a high school in South Dakota. Applicants must be interested in attending a 4-year college or university in the state. They must have a GPA of 3.9 or higher and an ACT score of at least 28. Along with their application, they must submit an essay on their educational and career goals, 2 letters of recommendation, and an official transcript.
**Financial data:** The stipend is $2,500 the first year and $1,000 in subsequent years. Funds are paid annually in 2 equal installments and are to be used for tuition, fees, and/or books.
**Duration:** 1 year; may be renewed for 3 additional years if the recipient maintains a GPA of 3.0 or higher and full-time enrollment.
**Number awarded:** Varies each year; recently, 3 of these scholarships were awarded.
**Deadline:** March of each year.

### 375 FRED SCHEIGERT SCHOLARSHIPS

Council of Citizens with Low Vision International
c/o Pat Beattie, President
906 North Chambliss Street
Alexandria, VA 22312-3005
Phone: (703) 570-6513; (800) 733-2258; Fax: (703) 671-9053;
Email: pbeattie@nib.org
Web: www.cclvi.org/scholarship.html
**Summary:** To provide financial assistance to undergraduate and graduate students with low vision.
**Eligibility:** Open to students who are certified by an ophthalmologist as having low vision (acuity of 20/70 or worse in the better seeing eye with best correction or side vision with a maximum diameter of no greater than 30 degrees). They may be part-time or full-time entering freshmen, undergraduates, or graduate students. A cumulative GPA of at least 3.0 is required.
**Financial data:** The stipend is $1,000.
**Duration:** 1 year.
**Number awarded:** 2 each year.
**Deadline:** April of each year.

### 376 FREE TUITION FOR DEPENDENTS OF DISABLED OR DECEASED SOUTH DAKOTA NATIONAL GUARD MEMBERS

South Dakota Board of Regents, Attn: Scholarship Committee
306 East Capitol Avenue, Suite 200
Pierre, SD 57501-2545
Phone: (605) 773-3455; Fax: (605) 773-2422; Email: info@ris.sdbor.edu
Web: www.sdbor.edu
**Summary:** To provide financial assistance for college to the dependents of disabled and deceased members of the South Dakota National Guard.
**Eligibility:** Open to the spouses and children of members of the South Dakota

Army or Air National Guard who died or sustained a total and permanent disability while on state active duty or any authorized duty training. Applicants must be younger than 25 years of age and proposing to work on an undergraduate degree at a public institution of higher education in South Dakota.

**Financial data:** Qualifying applicants are eligible to attend a state-supported postsecondary institution in South Dakota without payment of tuition.

**Duration:** 8 semesters or 12 quarters of either full- or part-time study.

**Number awarded:** Varies each year.

### 377 FREEDOM ALLIANCE SCHOLARSHIPS

Freedom Alliance, Attn: Scholarship Fund
22570 Markey Court, Suite 240
Dulles, VA 20166-6915
Phone: (703) 444-7940; (800) 475-6620; Fax: (703) 444-9893
Web: www.freedomalliance.org/scholarship.htm

**Summary:** To provide financial assistance for college to the children of deceased and disabled military personnel.

**Eligibility:** Open to high school seniors, high school graduates, and undergraduate students who are dependent children of military personnel (soldier, sailor, airman, Marine, or Guardsman). The military parent must have been killed or permanently disabled in the line of duty or be currently classified as a POW or MIA. For disabled parents, the disability must be permanent, service-connected, and rated at 100% by the U.S. Department of Veterans Affairs. Family income must be less than $75,000. Along with their application, they must submit a 500-word essay on what their parent's service means to them.

**Financial data:** A stipend is awarded (amount not specified).

**Duration:** 1 year; may be renewed up to 3 additional years provided the recipient remains enrolled full time with a GPA of 2.0 or higher.

**Number awarded:** Varies each year; recently, 70 of these scholarships were awarded.

**Deadline:** June of each year.

### 378 FRESH START SCHOLARSHIP

Wilmington Women in Business
Attn: Fresh Start Scholarship Foundation, Inc.
P.O. Box 7784
Wilmington, DE 19803
Phone: (302) 656-4411
Web: www.wwb.org/fresh.htm

**Summary:** To provide financial assistance for college to women in Delaware who have experienced an interruption in their education.

**Eligibility:** Open to women who are at least 20 years of age, have a high school diploma or GED, and have been admitted to an accredited Delaware college in a 2- or 4-year undergraduate degree program. Applicants must have had at least a 2-year break in education either after completing high school or during college studies. They must have at least a C average if currently enrolled in college and be recommended by a social service agency (or a college representative if a social service agency is not available). U.S. citizenship or permanent resident status is required. Financial need is considered in the selection process.

**Financial data:** The stipend varies annually, depending on the availability of funds. Awards are paid to the college at the beginning of each semester.

**Duration:** 1 year.

**Number awarded:** Varies each year.

**Deadline:** May of each year.

### 379 FUTURAMA FOUNDATION CAREER ADVANCEMENT SCHOLARSHIP

Maine Federation of Business and Professional Women
Attn: Futurama Foundation
c/o Jeanne L. Hammond, President
RR 1, Box 1610
Albion, ME 04910-9719
Phone: (207) 437-2325; Email: jlhammon@colby.edu
Web: www.bpwmaine.org/Scholarship.htm

**Summary:** To provide financial assistance to Maine women over 30 years of age who are continuing a program of higher education.

**Eligibility:** Open to women who are older than 30 years of age and residents of Maine. Applicants must be continuing in, or returning to, an accredited program of higher education or job-related training, either full or part time. They must be able to demonstrate financial need.

**Financial data:** The stipend is $1,200.

**Duration:** 1 year.

**Number awarded:** 1 or more each year.

**Deadline:** March of each year.

### 380 FUZZY BROWN MEMORIAL SCHOLARSHIPS

Louisiana High School Athletic Association, Attn: Commissioner
8075 Jefferson Highway
Baton Rouge, LA 70809-7675
Phone: (225) 925-0100; Fax: (225) 925-5901; Email: lhsaa@lhsaa.org
Web: www.lhsaa.org/scholarships.htm

**Summary:** To provide financial assistance to student-athletes in Louisiana who plan to attend college in the state.

**Eligibility:** Open to student-athletes who are seniors graduating from high schools in Louisiana. Applicants must be planning to attend a college or university in the state. They must be nominated by their principal.

**Financial data:** The stipend is $1,000.

**Duration:** 1 year.

**Number awarded:** 2 each year.

**Deadline:** April of each year.

### 381 GALLAGHER'S ARMY EDUCATIONAL ASSISTANCE FUND

Mike Gallagher Show Charitable Foundation
Attn: Educational Assistance Fund
350 Fifth Avenue, Suite 1818
New York, NY 10118
Phone: (212) 244-5311; Email: jhudson@gallaghersarmy.com
Web: www.gallaghersarmy.com

**Summary:** To provide financial assistance for college to the children of armed forces personnel killed in action while fighting the war on terror.

**Eligibility:** Open to the children of members of the U.S. armed forces who were killed in action while fighting the war on terror. Applicants must be U.S. citizens who are graduating from high school and entering an accredited college or university as a full-time student. They must submit a statement describing their educational goals and why they need assistance.

**Financial data:** A stipend is awarded (amount not specified).

**Duration:** 1 year; may be renewed.

**Number awarded:** 1 or more each year.

### 382 GARY B. MULTANEN APPLIED RESEARCH SCHOLARSHIP

American Composites Manufacturers Association, Attn: Scholarship Office
1010 North Glebe Road, Suite 450
Arlington, VA 22201
Phone: (703) 525-0511; Fax: (703) 525-0743; Email: info@acmanet.org
Web: www.acmanet.org/scholarships/index.cfm

**Summary:** To recognize and reward, with college scholarships, students who submit outstanding reports on research related to composites.

**Eligibility:** Open to students who submit reports of research they have conducted in the field of composites, including industrial technology and plastics engineering.

**Financial data:** Winners receive a $1,000 scholarship and a trip to the Composites conference where they present their research.

**Duration:** The competition is held annually.

**Number awarded:** 1 each year.

### 383 GATES MILLENNIUM UNDERGRADUATE SCHOLARS PROGRAM

Bill and Melinda Gates Foundation
P.O. Box 10500
Fairfax, VA 22031-8044
Phone: (877) 690-GMSP
Web: www.gmsp.org

**Summary:** To provide financial assistance to outstanding low-income minority students, particularly those interested in majoring in specific fields in college.

**Eligibility:** Open to African Americans, Alaska Natives, American Indians, Hispanic Americans, and Asian Pacific Islander Americans who are graduating high school seniors with a GPA of 3.3 or higher. Principals, teachers, guidance counselors, tribal higher education representatives, and other professional educators are invited to nominate students with outstanding academic qualifications, especially those likely to succeed in the fields of mathematics, science, engineering, education, or library science. Nominees should have significant financial need and demonstrated leadership abilities through participation in community service, extracurricular, or other activities. U.S. citizenship or permanent resident status is required. Nominees must be planning to enter an accredited college or university as a full-time, degree-seeking freshman in the following fall.

**Financial data:** The program covers the cost of tuition, fees, books, and living expenses not paid for by grants and scholarships already committed as part of the recipient's financial aid package.

**Duration:** 4 years or the completion of the undergraduate degree, if the recipient maintains at least a 3.0 GPA.

**Number awarded:** Under the Gates Millennium Scholars Program, a total of 4,000 students receive support each year.

**Deadline:** January of each year.

## 384 GATEWAY TO SUCCESS SCHOLARSHIPS

Chela Financial USA, Inc.
388 Market Street, 12th Floor
San Francisco, CA 94111
Phone: (415) 283-2800; (866) 34-CHELA; Fax: (415) 283-2888;
Email: scholarships@chelafin.org
Web: www.chelastudentloans.org/Scholarships/GatewayToSuccess.asp

**Summary:** To recognize and reward (with scholarships) college-bound high school seniors who submit outstanding essays on borrowing and money management.

**Eligibility:** Open to high school seniors who have a GPA of 2.0 or higher and are planning to attend an accredited U.S. 2-year or 4-year at least half time. Applicants must complete an essay, up to 300 words, on "How I am Financing My College Education." They do not need to have a student loan to qualify, but their essays should focus on how responsible borrowing and money management are helping them pay for college and meet their life goals. Other requirements include U.S. citizenship or permanent resident status and possession of a valid email address. Essays are evaluated on the basis of appropriateness to overall theme (30%), persuasiveness (30%), quality of writing (20%), and creativity (20%).

**Financial data:** The award is a $5,000 scholarship.

**Duration:** Awards are presented annually.

**Number awarded:** 10 each year.

**Deadline:** April of each year.

## 385 GATORADE LEADERSHIP AWARDS

American Legion Baseball
700 North Pennsylvania Street
Indianapolis, IN 46204
Phone: (317) 630-1249; Fax: (317) 630-1223; Email: acy@legion.org
Web: www.baseball.legion.org/awards.htm

**Summary:** To recognize and reward, with college scholarships, participants in the American Legion baseball program who demonstrate outstanding leadership.

**Eligibility:** Open to participants in the American Legion baseball regional tournaments and the American Legion World Series. Candidates must be high school seniors or graduates who will be entering college as a freshman in the fall; students still in high school are not eligible. Selection is based on integrity, mental attitude, cooperation, citizenship, sportsmanship, scholastic aptitude, and general good conduct.

**Financial data:** The outstanding participants in the regional tournaments receive $1,000 scholarships; the outstanding participant in the American Legion World Series receives an additional $2,000 scholarship.

**Duration:** The awards are presented annually.

**Number awarded:** 8 winners in regional tournaments receive $1,000 scholarships; 1 of those receives an additional scholarship as the George W. Rulon American Legion Player of the Year.

## 386 GEAR UP ALASKA SCHOLARSHIP PROGRAM

Alaska Commission on Postsecondary Education
Attn: AlaskAdvantage Programs
3030 Vintage Boulevard
Juneau, AK 99801-7109
Phone: (907) 465-2962; (800) 441-2962; Fax: (907) 465-5316;
TTY: (907) 465-3143; Email: customer_service@acpe.ak.us
Web: www.eed.state.ak.us/gearup/scholarship.html

**Summary:** To provide financial assistance for college to Alaska residents who participated in federal GEAR UP programs while in middle school.

**Eligibility:** Open to residents of Alaska who are high school seniors or graduates or recipients of a GED. Applicants must be younger than 22 years of age and able to demonstrate financial need. They must have participated in a federal GEAR UP program during grades 6-8 and met other academic milestones. They must be planning to attend an approved postsecondary institution.

**Financial data:** The maximum stipend is $7,000 per year for full-time study or $3,500 per year for half-time study.

**Duration:** 1 year; may be renewed up to 3 additional years.

**Number awarded:** Varies each year.

**Deadline:** May of each year.

## 387 GENERAL HENRY H. ARNOLD EDUCATION GRANT PROGRAM

Air Force Aid Society, Attn: Education Assistance Department
241 18th Street South, Suite 202
Arlington, VA 22202-3409
Phone: (703) 607-3072, ext. 51; (800) 429-9475
Web: www.afas.org

**Summary:** To provide financial assistance for college to dependents of active-duty, retired, or deceased Air Force personnel.

**Eligibility:** Open to 1) dependent children of Air Force personnel who are either active duty, Reservists on extended active duty, retired due to length of active-duty service or disability, or deceased while on active duty or in retired status; 2) spouses of active-duty Air Force members and Reservists on extended active duty; and 3) surviving spouses of Air Force members who died while on active duty or in retired status. Applicants must be enrolled or planning to enroll as full-time undergraduate students in an accredited college, university, or vocational/trade school. Spouses must be attending school within the 48 contiguous states. Selection is based on family income and education costs.

**Financial data:** The stipend is $1,500.

**Duration:** 1 year; may be renewed if the recipient maintains a GPA of 2.0 or higher.

**Number awarded:** Varies each year.

**Deadline:** April of each year.

## 388 GENERAL MILLS TRIBAL COLLEGE SCHOLARSHIP PROGRAM

American Indian College Fund, Attn: Scholarship Department
8333 Greenwood Boulevard
Denver, CO 80221
Phone: (303) 426-8900; (800) 776-FUND; Fax: (303) 426-1200;
Email: info@collegefund.org
Web: www.collegefund.org/scholarships/generalmills.html

**Summary:** To provide financial assistance to American Indian students who are attending tribal colleges in California, Minnesota, and New Mexico.

**Eligibility:** Open to American Indians or Alaska Natives working full time on an associate's or bachelor's degree at an accredited tribal college or university in California, Minnesota, or New Mexico. Applicants must be able to demonstrate exceptional academic achievement (GPA of 3.0 or higher), as well as leadership, service, and commitment to the American Indian community. Along with their application, they must submit official college transcripts; a personal essay (500 words or less) on their personal and academic background, career goals, and how this scholarship will help them achieve those goals; a statement regarding any financial hardship they have; 2 letters of recommendation; tribal enrollment information; and a color photograph.

**Financial data:** The stipend is $2,000.

**Duration:** 1 year.

**Number awarded:** 25 each year.

**Deadline:** April of each year.

## 389 GENERAL MOTORS MINORITY DEALERS ASSOCIATION MINORITY SCHOLARSHIP PROGRAM

General Motors Minority Dealers Association
29433 Southfield Road, Suite 210
Southfield, MI 48076
Phone: (248) 552-9040; (888) 377-5233; Fax: (248) 552 9022;
Email: scholarshipinfo@gmsac.com
Web: www.gmmda.org

**Summary:** To provide financial assistance for college to ethnic minority high school seniors and college students.

**Eligibility:** Open to ethnic minority graduating high school seniors and current college students who are enrolled or planning to enroll full time at an accredited 2-year or 4-year college or university in the United States. Applicants must be U.S. citizens with a GPA of 3.0 or higher. Along with their application, they must submit a personal statement of 500 to 750 words explaining 1) how their school experiences, including academics, extracurricular activities, outside activities, and work experiences, are shaping their educational and career goals, and 2) why they should be considered for this scholarship. Selection is based on that statement, academic excellence, leadership and participation in school and community activities, work experience, education, and career aspirations.

**Financial data:** The stipend is $2,500.

**Duration:** 1 year.

**Number awarded:** Varies each year; recently, 18 of these scholarships were awarded.

**Deadline:** November of each year.

### 390 GEOFFREY FOUNDATION SCHOLARSHIPS

Geoffrey Foundation
Ocean Avenue
P.O. Box 1112
Kennebunkport, ME 04046
Phone: (207) 967-5798

**Summary:** To provide financial assistance to deaf students who attend school with hearing students and communicate using spoken language.

**Eligibility:** Open to U.S. citizens who are hearing impaired (severe to profound hearing loss greater than 80 dB) and are utilizing an auditory-verbal approach to communication. Applicant must be currently enrolled or planning to attend a preschool, elementary school, junior high or high school, or college for hearing students on a full-time basis in the forthcoming year. They must submit a current audiogram plus 3 letters of recommendation.

**Financial data:** The amount awarded varies, depending upon the needs of the recipient.

**Duration:** 1 year or longer.

**Number awarded:** Varies each year. The foundation awards grants in excess of $30,000 each year to children and college students.

**Deadline:** March of each year.

### 391 GEORGE BARTOL MEMORIAL SCHOLARSHIPS

George Bartol Memorial Scholarship Fund
c/o Heather M. Bartol
4863 Riverton Drive
Orlando, FL 32817
Phone: (407) 382-5982; Email: livebait3@aol.com

**Summary:** To provide financial assistance for college to children of brain cancer patients.

**Eligibility:** Open to full-time students at accredited 2-year and 4-year colleges and universities who have a GPA of 2.5 or higher. Applicants must have lost a biological mother or father to a form of brain cancer or have a biological mother or father who has been diagnosed with brain cancer. They must be between 18 and 23 years of age. Along with their application, they must submit 5 essays on the following topics: 1) their parent who has lost their battle to brain cancer or who is currently battling brain cancer; 2) how the scholarship will affect them and their family; 3) how cancer has impacted their life; 4) their biggest adjustment since their parent's battle with brain cancer began; and 5) what they have learned from this experience and how they might help others as a result. Selection is based on the essays, grades, letters of recommendation, and financial need. Children of Vietnam veterans who have not been awarded VA Chapter 35 benefits are strongly encouraged to apply.

**Financial data:** The stipend is $1,000 per semester ($3,000 per year, including summer semester). Students at schools on the quarter system may receive $750 per quarter ($3,000 per year, including summer quarter). Funds are paid directly to the financial aid office at the school the recipient is attending.

**Duration:** 1 semester or quarter; may be renewed if the recipient maintains a GPA of 2.5 or higher.

**Number awarded:** 1 or more each year.

**Deadline:** September of each year.

### 392 GEORGIA GOVERNOR'S SCHOLARSHIP

Georgia Student Finance Commission, Attn: Scholarships and Grants Division
2082 East Exchange Place, Suite 200
Tucker, GA 30084-5305
Phone: (770) 724-9000; (800) 505-GSFC; Fax: (770) 724-9089;
Email: info@mail.gsfc.state.ga.us
Web: www.gsfc.org/gsfc/grants/dsp_ggov.cfm

**Summary:** To provide financial assistance for college to outstanding high school seniors in Georgia.

**Eligibility:** Open to Georgia residents planning to attend accredited institutions of higher education in the state as full-time entering freshmen. They must be graduating from a Georgia high school as a STAR Student or valedictorian

and be in compliance with the Georgia Drug-Free Postsecondary Education Act. U.S. citizenship or permanent resident status is required.

**Financial data:** The stipend is currently $804 per year.

**Duration:** 1 year; may be renewed for up to 3 additional years if the recipient maintains a cumulative GPA of 3.0 or higher and full-time enrollment.

**Number awarded:** Varies each year; recently, 2,828 of these scholarships were awarded.

### 393 GEORGIA LAW ENFORCEMENT PERSONNEL DEPENDENTS GRANT

Georgia Student Finance Commission, Attn: Scholarships and Grants Division
2082 East Exchange Place, Suite 200
Tucker, GA 30084-5305
Phone: (770) 724-9000; (800) 505-GSFC; Fax: (770) 724-9089;
Email: info@mail.gsfc.state.ga.us
Web: www.gsfc.org/gsfc/grants/dsp_glepd.cfm

**Summary:** To provide financial assistance for college to children of disabled or deceased Georgia law enforcement officers, fire fighters, and prison guards.

**Eligibility:** Open to dependent children of law enforcement officers, fire fighters, and prison guards in Georgia who have been permanently disabled or killed in the line of duty. Applicants must be enrolled as full-time undergraduate students in a Georgia private or public college, university, or technical institution. U.S. citizenship or permanent resident status and compliance with the Georgia Drug-Free Postsecondary Education Act are required.

**Financial data:** The grant is $2,000 per academic year, not to exceed $8,000 during an entire program of study.

**Duration:** 1 year; may be renewed (if satisfactory progress is maintained) for up to 3 additional years.

**Number awarded:** Varies each year; recently, 20 of these grants were awarded.

**Deadline:** July of each year.

### 394 GEORGIA LEAP GRANT PROGRAM

Georgia Student Finance Commission, Attn: Scholarships and Grants Division
2082 East Exchange Place, Suite 200
Tucker, GA 30084-5305
Phone: (770) 724-9000; (800) 505-GSFC; Fax: (770) 724-9089;
Email: info@mail.gsfc.state.ga.us
Web: www.gsfc.org/gsfc/grants/dsp_leap.cfm

**Summary:** To provide financial assistance for college to residents of Georgia who demonstrate financial need.

**Eligibility:** Open to Georgia residents who are enrolled as regular undergraduate students in an eligible Georgia public or private college, university, or technical college. Applicants must be able to demonstrate substantial financial need and must be eligible for a federal Pell Grant. They must be at least a half-time student maintaining satisfactory academic progress. U.S. citizenship or permanent resident status and compliance with the Georgia Drug-Free Postsecondary Education Act are required.

**Financial data:** The maximum grant is $2,000 per academic year.

**Duration:** 1 year; may be renewed (if satisfactory progress is maintained) for up to 3 additional years.

**Number awarded:** Varies each year; recently, 3,008 of these grants were awarded.

### 395 GEORGIA LEGION AUXILIARY PAST DEPARTMENT PRESIDENTS SCHOLARSHIP

American Legion Auxiliary, Attn: Department of Georgia
3035 Mt. Zion Road
Stockbridge, GA 30281-4101
Phone: (678) 289-8446; Email: amlegaux@bellsouth.net

**Summary:** To provide financial assistance for college to the children of Georgia veterans.

**Eligibility:** Open to residents of Georgia who are high school seniors and children of veterans. Preference is given to children of deceased veterans. Applicants must be sponsored by a local unit of the American Legion Auxiliary in Georgia. Selection is based on a statement explaining why they want to further their education and their need for a scholarship.

**Financial data:** The stipend is $1,000.

**Duration:** 1 year.

**Number awarded:** 2 each year.

**Deadline:** May of each year.

## 396 GEORGIA PUBLIC SAFETY MEMORIAL GRANT

Georgia Student Finance Commission, Attn: Scholarships and Grants Division
2082 East Exchange Place, Suite 200
Tucker, GA 30084-5305
Phone: (770) 724-9000; (800) 505-GSFC; Fax: (770) 724-9089;
Email: info@mail.gsfc.state.ga.us
Web: www.gsfc.org/gsfc/grants/dsp_gps.cfm

**Summary:** To provide financial assistance for college to the children of Georgia public safety officers who have been permanently disabled or killed in the line of duty.

**Eligibility:** Open to dependent children of Georgia law enforcement officers, fire fighters, EMT, correction officers, or prison guards who have been permanently disabled or killed in the line of duty. Applicants must be enrolled or accepted as full-time undergraduate students in a Georgia public college, university, or technical institution and be in compliance with the Georgia Drug-Free Postsecondary Education Act. U.S. citizenship or permanent resident status is required.

**Financial data:** The award covers the cost of attendance at a public postsecondary school in Georgia, minus any other aid received.

**Duration:** 1 year; may be renewed (if satisfactory progress is maintained) for up to 3 additional years.

**Number awarded:** Varies each year; recently, 18 of these grants were awarded.

**Deadline:** July of each year.

## 397 GERTRUDE BOTTS SAUCIER SCHOLARSHIP

United Daughters of the Confederacy, Attn: Education Director
328 North Boulevard
Richmond, VA 23220-4057
Phone: (804) 355-1636; Fax: (804) 353-1396; Email: hqudc@rcn.com
Web: www.hqudc.org/scholarships/scholarships.html

**Summary:** To provide financial assistance for college to lineal descendants of Confederate veterans who are residents of Texas, Mississippi, or Louisiana.

**Eligibility:** Open to lineal descendants of worthy Confederates or collateral descendants who are members of the Children of the Confederacy or the United Daughters of the Confederacy. Applicants must reside in Texas, Mississippi, or Louisiana and must submit a family financial report and certified proof of the Confederate record of 1 ancestor, with the company and regiment in which he served. They must have at least a 3.0 GPA in high school.

**Financial data:** The amount of the scholarship depends on the availability of funds.

**Duration:** 1 year; may be renewed for up to 3 additional years.

**Number awarded:** 1 each year.

**Deadline:** March of each year.

## 398 GIDEON ELAD SCHOLARSHIP

Boy Scouts of America, Attn: National Jewish Committee on Scouting, S226
1325 West Walnut Hill Lane
P.O. Box 152079
Irving, TX 75015-2079
Phone: (972) 580-2000
Web: www.jewishscouting.org/njcs/awards/eagle.html

**Summary:** To provide financial assistance for college to Jewish Boy Scouts and Varsity Scouts.

**Eligibility:** Open to registered, active members of a Boy Scout troop or Varsity Scout team who have received the Eagle Scout Award and have also earned the Ner Tamid or Etz Chaim emblem. Applicants must be enrolled in an accredited high school in their final year and must be an active member of a synagogue. They must have demonstrated practical citizenship in their synagogue, school, Scouting unit, and community. Selection is based on high school record, including school activities, awards, honors, and GPA; participation in community organizations; participation in religious youth organizations, clubs, or groups, including honors earned and offices held; involvement in Scouting; career goals; and 4 letters of recommendation, from leaders of their religious institution, school, community, and Scouting unit.

**Financial data:** The stipend is $1,000.

**Duration:** 1 year; nonrenewable.

**Number awarded:** 3 each year: 1 first place and 2 second place awards.

**Deadline:** December of each year.

## 399 GIFT FOR LIFE SCHOLARSHIPS

United States Bowling Congress, Attn: SMART Program
5301 South 76th Street
Greendale, WI 53129-1192
Phone: (414) 423-3343; (800) 514-BOWL, ext. 3343; Fax: (414) 421-3014;
Email: smart@bowl.com
Web: www.bowl.com/scholarships/main.aspx

**Summary:** To provide financial assistance for college to members of the United State Bowling Congress (USBC) who demonstrate a financial hardship.

**Eligibility:** Open to USBC members who are high school students (grades 9-12) and who have not yet competed in a professional bowling tournament. Applicants must be able to demonstrate a financial hardship, defined as residing in a household where the number of children, the income level of their parents, and possible extenuating circumstances make obtaining a college education financially unlikely. They must submit an essay, up to 500 words, explaining how their financial situation could hinder or stop them from achieving their educational goals. Other factors considered in the selection process include GPA (2.0 or higher required), scholastic honors, extracurricular activities, and bowling activities. Applications from males and females are evaluated separately. In honor of the heroes of September 11, 2001, 2 scholarships are reserved for a son and a daughter of fire/police/emergency rescue personnel.

**Financial data:** The stipend is $1,000.

**Duration:** Scholarships are presented annually. Students may apply each year they are eligible and may win 1 scholarship each year before their high school graduation.

**Number awarded:** 12 each year: 6 specifically for females and 6 for males. That includes 2 awards reserved for children (1 daughter and 1 son) of fire/police/emergency rescue department employees.

**Deadline:** March of each year.

## 400 GIFT OF HOPE: 21ST CENTURY SCHOLARS PROGRAM

United Methodist Church
Attn: General Board of Higher Education and Ministry
Office of Loans and Scholarships
1001 19th Avenue South
P.O. Box 340007
Nashville, TN 37203-0007
Phone: (615) 340-7344; Fax: (615) 340-7367; Email: umscholar@gbhem.org
Web: www.gbhem.org

**Summary:** To provide financial assistance to undergraduate and graduate Methodist students who can demonstrate leadership in the church.

**Eligibility:** Open to full-time undergraduate and graduate students at United Methodist institutions who have been active, full members of a United Methodist Church for at least 3 years prior to applying. Undergraduates must have a GPA of 3.0 or higher; graduate students must have a GPA of 3.5 or higher. Applicants must show evidence of leadership and participation in religious activities during college either through their campus ministry or through local United Methodist churches in the city where their college is located. They must also show how their education will provide leadership for the church and society and improve the quality of life for others. U.S. citizenship, permanent resident status, or membership in the Central Conferences of the United Methodist Church is required. Financial need is considered in the selection process.

**Financial data:** The stipend is $1,000.

**Duration:** 1 year; recipients may reapply.

**Number awarded:** Varies each year; recently, 950 of these scholarships were awarded.

**Deadline:** April of each year.

## 401 GILBERT MARTINEZ DIVERSITY SCHOLARSHIPS

Colorado Educational Services and Development Association
P.O. Box 40214
Denver, CO 80204
Web: www.cesda.org

**Summary:** To provide financial assistance for college to high school seniors in Colorado who are first-generation college students and/or members of underrepresented ethnic or racial minorities.

**Eligibility:** Open to seniors graduating from high schools in Colorado who are 1) the first member of their family to attend college; 2) members of an underrepresented ethnic or racial minority (African American, Asian-Pacific Islander, American Indian, Hispanic/Chicano/Latino); and/or 1) able to demonstrate financial need. Applicants must have a GPA of 2.8 or higher and be planning to enroll at a 2- or 4-year college or university in Colorado. U.S. citizenship or permanent resident status is required. Selection is based on leadership and community service (particularly within minority communities), past academic performance, personal and professional accomplishments, personal attributes, special abilities, academic goals, and financial need.

**Financial data:** The stipend is $1,000.

**Duration:** 1 year; nonrenewable.
**Number awarded:** 6 each year.
**Deadline:** February of each year.

---

### 402 GILBERT MATCHING STUDENT GRANT PROGRAM

Massachusetts Office of Student Financial Assistance
454 Broadway, Suite 200
Revere, MA 02151
Phone: (617) 727-9420; Fax: (617) 727-0667; Email: osfa@osfa.mass.edu
Web: www.osfa.mass.edu
**Summary:** To provide financial assistance for college to Massachusetts residents who are attending accredited independent institutions.
**Eligibility:** Open to permanent legal residents of Massachusetts (for at least 1 year) who are working full time on an associate's or bachelor's degree at an independent, regionally accredited college or university in the state. U.S. citizenship or permanent resident status is required. Selection is based on financial need.
**Financial data:** Awards range from $200 to $2,500 per year, depending on the need of the recipient.
**Duration:** 1 year; may be renewed.
**Number awarded:** Varies each year.
**Deadline:** Deadlines are established by the school the student attends.

---

### 403 GIRL SCOUT ACHIEVEMENT AWARD

American Legion Auxiliary
777 North Meridian Street, Third Floor
Indianapolis, IN 46204-1189
Phone: (317) 955-3845; Fax: (317) 955-3884; Email: alahq@legion-aux.org
Web: www.legion-aux.org/scholarships/docs/girlscoutsch.htm
**Summary:** To provide financial assistance for college to members of the Girl Scouts who have received the Gold Award.
**Eligibility:** Open to applicants who belong to the Girl Scouts; have received the Gold Award; are an active member of a religious institution (and have received the appropriate religious emblem); have demonstrated practical citizenship in their religious institution, school, Scouting, and community; and submit at least 4 letters of recommendation, with 1 letter required from each of the following group leaders: religious institution, school, community, and Scouting. Candidates must be nominated at the local level; those selected at the state level compete at the national level.
**Financial data:** The stipend is $1,000.
**Duration:** 1 year; the award must be utilized within 1 year of high school graduation.
**Number awarded:** 1 each year.
**Deadline:** Local nominations must be submitted no later than February of each year.

---

### 404 GIRLS INCORPORATED NATIONAL SCHOLARS PROGRAM

Girls Incorporated, Attn: Scholarships and Awards
120 Wall Street, Third Floor
New York, NY 10005-3902
Phone: (212) 509-2000; (800) 374-4475; Fax: (212) 509-8708;
Email: girlsincorporated@girls-inc.org
Web: www.girls-inc.org
**Summary:** To provide financial assistance for college to Girls Incorporated members.
**Eligibility:** Open to members of Girls Incorporated affiliates who are currently in high school (in grades 11 or 12) and have been members of the association for at least 2 years. They must have a GPA of 2.8 or higher. Selection is based on extracurricular activities, goals and objectives, soundness of ideas, motivation, communication skills, and presentation. Financial need is not considered. Academic record is of secondary importance.
**Financial data:** The scholarships are either $15,000 or $2,500. Funds are held in escrow and paid directly to the recipient's college, professional school, or technical institute.
**Duration:** Up to 5 years.
**Number awarded:** Up to 20 each year: 7 to 10 at $15,000 and 10 at $2,500.

---

### 405 GLADYS A. AND RUSSELL M. BIRTWISTLE AWARD

Vasa Order of America, Attn: Vice Grand Master
3236 Berkeley Avenue
Cleveland Heights, OH 44118-2055

Phone: (216) 371-5141; Email: rolf.bergman@sbcglobal.net
Web: www.vasaorder.com
**Summary:** To provide financial assistance for college to members of the Vasa Order of America from designated states.
**Eligibility:** Open to members of the organization (for at least 1 year) who live in districts 1 (Connecticut), 2 (Massachusetts), or 3 (Rhode Island). They must be high school seniors or college undergraduates who plan to continue their education on a full-time basis at an accredited institution. Selection is based on a grade transcript, letters of recommendation from school and local Vasa lodge officials, and an essay of up to 1,000 words on a topic related to Vasa.
**Financial data:** The stipend is $1,500.
**Duration:** 1 year.
**Number awarded:** 1 each year.
**Deadline:** February of each year.

---

### 406 GLORIA BARRON PRIZE FOR YOUNG HEROES

The Barron Prize
P.O. Box 17
Boulder, CO 80306-0017
Phone: (970) 875-1448; Email: ba_richman@barronprize.org
Web: www.barronprize.org
**Summary:** To recognize and reward young people from diverse backgrounds who have "shown extraordinary leadership in making our world better."
**Eligibility:** Open to students between the ages of 8 and 18 who have shown leadership in making the world a better place: by helping people, protecting the environment, halting violence, or leading other important service work. They must be residents of the United States or Canada. They must be nominated. In all cases, nominees must have been the prime mover of the service activity; the service activity cannot have been done solely to complete an assignment for school or work. They must be nominated by an adult who is familiar with their service activity. Selection is based on the nominees' positive spirit, courage, intelligence, generosity, and high moral purpose.
**Financial data:** Winners receive $2,000. Funds may be used for higher education or completion of the service project.
**Duration:** The competition is held annually.
**Number awarded:** 10 or more each year.
**Deadline:** Nominations must be submitted by the end of May of each year.

---

### 407 GO THE DISTANCE SCHOLARSHIPS

Chela Financial USA, Inc.
388 Market Street, 12th Floor
San Francisco, CA 94111
Phone: (415) 283-2800; (866) 34-CHELA; Fax: (415) 283-2888;
Email: info@deresource.org
Web: www.deresource.org/financing/gothedistance/gtdeligibility.asp
**Summary:** To recognize and reward (with scholarships) undergraduate and graduate students enrolled in a distance education program.
**Eligibility:** Open to undergraduate and graduate students enrolled in a distance education program. Applicants must complete an essay, up to 300 words, on "My Challenges in Financing a Distance Degree." The essay should focus on challenges they have faced in covering the cost of their distance education responsibly and how they will do that while achieving their goals. They do not need to have a student loan to qualify. Essays are evaluated on the basis of appropriateness to overall theme (30%), persuasiveness (30%), quality of writing (20%), and creativity (20%).
**Financial data:** The award is a $5,000 scholarship.
**Duration:** Awards are presented annually.
**Number awarded:** 30 each year: 15 undergraduates (3 each for freshmen, sophomores, juniors, seniors, and fifth-year students) and 15 graduate students (3 in each year of graduate school).
**Deadline:** April of each year.

---

### 408 GO-GETTER SCHOLARSHIP

Incight Company, Attn: Executive Director
733 S.W. Oak Street, Suite 200
Portland, OR 97205
Phone: (971) 244-0305; Fax: (503) 223-9488; Email: scholarship@incight.org
Web: www.incight.com/incight/edu1.html
**Summary:** To provide financial assistance for college to students who have a physical disability or impairment.
**Eligibility:** Open to students who have a physical disability or impairment, including a learning disability or sight or hearing impairment. Applicants must

have a GPA of 2.5 or higher and be entering or attending college as a full-time student. Along with their application, they must submit a 250-word essay on what they think of the word "handicrap," a term that the sponsoring organization feels is prevalent in the disabled and non-disabled communities and that it is trying to change. They must also submit another 250-word essay, either on the topic, "If you were a tree, how would you describe yourself," or on their choice of a quotation from Franklin D. Roosevelt or from Christopher Reeve.

**Financial data:** A stipend is awarded (amount not specified).

**Duration:** 1 year

**Number awarded:** 1 or more each year.

**Deadline:** April of each year.

### 409 GOLDEN KEY SPEECH AND DEBATE AWARDS

Golden Key International Honour Society
621 North Avenue N.E., Suite C-100
Atlanta, GA 30308
Phone: (404) 377-2400; (800) 377-2401; Fax: (678) 420-6757;
Email: scholarships@goldenkey.org
Web: www.goldenkey.org/GKweb/ScholarshipsandAwards

**Summary:** To recognize and reward members of the Golden Key International Honour Society who demonstrate excellence in a public speaking competition.

**Eligibility:** Open to undergraduate, graduate, and postgraduate members of the society who submit a videotaped monologue up to 5 minutes in length on a topic that changes annually. Recently, the topic was "What will bring planet Earth's climate back into balance?" Based on those tapes, finalists are invited to attend the society's international conference for a public competition. Winners are selected on the basis of demonstrated public speaking skills.

**Financial data:** The winner receives a $1,000 award and the runner-up receives $500.

**Duration:** These awards are presented annually.

**Number awarded:** 1 winner and 1 runner-up are selected each year.

**Deadline:** March of each year.

### 410 GOOD SAMARITAN FOUNDATION HIGH SCHOOL ESSAY CONTEST

Good Samaritan Foundation, Inc., Attn: Essay Contest
270 South Limestone Street
Lexington, KY 40508
Phone: (859) 255-1691; Fax: (859) 254-7337; Email: info@gsfky.org
Web: www.gsfky.org

**Summary:** To recognize and reward high school students in Kentucky who write outstanding essays on smoking.

**Eligibility:** Open to Kentucky high school students who submit essays on the topic "Why Do Teens Smoke?" Papers, up to 4 pages in length, may cover such issues as the effects of the price of tobacco products on teen smoking, the role of advertising tobacco products, whether smoke-free laws affect teen smoking, and how interested teen smokers are in quitting. Selection is based on compliance with instructions and general scholarship.

**Financial data:** First place is $5,000, second $1,000, and third $500.

**Duration:** The competition is held annually.

**Number awarded:** 31 prizes are awarded each year: 1 first, 10 seconds, and 20 thirds.

**Deadline:** October of each year.

### 411 GOVERNOR'S COALITION FOR YOUTH WITH DISABILITIES SCHOLARSHIPS

Governor's Coalition for Youth with Disabilities, Attn: Karen Burgess
P.O. Box 2485
Hartford, CT 06146-2485
Phone: (860) 263-6018; Email: karen.burgess@gcyd.org
Web: www.gcyd.org

**Summary:** To provide financial assistance for college to Connecticut residents who have a disability.

**Eligibility:** Open to Connecticut residents with a disability who are graduating high school seniors. Applicants must be planning to attend 1) a college or university in Connecticut or any other state; 2) any of the 4 campuses of the Connecticut State University System; or 3) any of the 12 Connecticut community colleges. Applicants must submit letters of recommendation, transcripts, information on their high school activities and work experience, a statement on how they feel this scholarship will assist them in their career, and an essay of 1 to 2 pages describing their disability and how they have overcome the challenges it has presented. Applications must be submitted to high school counselors.

**Financial data:** For students at colleges and universities nationwide, the stipend is $3,000. For students at Connecticut State Universities, the stipend is $500 per semester. For students at Connecticut community colleges, the stipend is up to $2,672 per year.

**Duration:** 1 year. National scholarships are nonrenewable, Connecticut State University scholarships may be renewed for a total of 8 semesters, and Connecticut community college scholarships may be renewed for a total of 3 years.

**Number awarded:** The number of national scholarships varies each year; 4 Connecticut State University scholarships (1 at each campus) and 12 community college scholarships (1 at each college) are awarded each year. Since the program began, 174 students with disabilities from 82 Connecticut towns have received support from this program.

**Deadline:** January of each year.

### 412 GOVERNOR'S KENTUCKY TECHNICAL COLLEGE SCHOLARSHIPS

Kentucky Community and Technical College System, Attn: Financial Aid
300 North Main Street
Versailles, KY 40383
Phone: (859) 256-3100; (877) 528-2748 (within KY)
Web: www.kctcs.edu/student/financialaidscholarships/index.htm

**Summary:** To provide financial assistance to high school seniors in Kentucky who are interested in working on a technical diploma or degree at a participating institution within the Kentucky Community and Technical College System (KCTCS).

**Eligibility:** Open to Kentucky high school seniors and GED recipients who plan to work on a diploma or degree at a KCTCS technical college. Selection is based on academic achievement, character excellence, and career potential.

**Financial data:** Stipends vary at each participating college, but are intended to provide full payment of tuition and required fees, books, supplies, tools, personal safety equipment, and uniforms.

**Duration:** 1 year; may be renewed 1 additional year.

**Number awarded:** Varies each year; participating colleges generally award new scholarships to 2 high school seniors and 1 GED recipient each year.

**Deadline:** Each college sets its own deadline.

### 413 GRAEME CLARK SCHOLARSHIP

Cochlear Americas, Attn: Scholarships
400 Inverness Parkway, Suite 400
Englewood, CO 80112
Phone: (303) 790-9010; (800) 458-4999; TTY: (800) 483-3123;
Email: Recipients@Cochlear.com
Web: www.cochlearamericas.com

**Summary:** To provide financial assistance for college to students who have received a cochlear implant.

**Eligibility:** Open to graduating high school seniors, current university students, and mature aged students who have been accepted into a university course. Applicants must have received a Cochlear Nucleus implant. Along with their application, they must submit a 1,000-word personal statement on their academic aspiration and other interests, including why they chose their proposed area of study, their post-graduation aspirations, their definition of success, and why they wish to receive this scholarship. Selection is based on academic achievement and demonstrated commitment to the ideals of leadership and humanity.

**Financial data:** The stipend is $3,000 per year.

**Duration:** 1 year; may be renewed up to 3 additional years.

**Number awarded:** Varies each year; recently, 3 of these scholarships were awarded.

**Deadline:** June

### 414 GRAND LODGE OF IOWA MASONIC SCHOLARSHIP

Grand Lodge of Iowa, A.F. & A.M., Attn: Scholarship Selection Committee
P.O. Box 279
Cedar Rapids, IA 52406-0279
Phone: (319) 365-1438; Fax: (319) 365-1439; Email: Scholarships@gl-iowa.org
Web: showcase.netins.net/web/iowamasons/Scholarship.html

**Summary:** To provide financial assistance for college to high school seniors in Iowa.

**Eligibility:** Open to high school seniors who are graduating from a public high school within the state of Iowa. Applicants need not have a Masonic connection. Finalists are interviewed. Selection is based on service to school and community (with special emphasis on leadership roles in those areas), academic record, communication skills, and financial need.

**Financial data:** The stipend is $2,000. Funds may be used for tuition, fees, and books.

**Duration:** 1 year.

**Number awarded:** Varies each year; recently, 60 of these scholarships were awarded.

**Deadline:** January of each year.

## 415 GREATER NEW JERSEY CONFERENCE TRUST FUND SCHOLARSHIPS

United Methodist Church-Greater New Jersey Conference
Board of Higher Education and Campus Ministry
Attn: Rev. Kathleen A. Stolz, Scholarship Committee
1001 Wickapecko Drive
Ocean, NJ 07712-4733
Phone: (732) 359-1042; (877) 677-2594; Fax: (732) 359-1019;
Email: office@gnjumc.org
Web: www.gnjumc.org/conferenceloans.html

**Summary:** To provide financial assistance to Methodist undergraduate students from New Jersey.

**Eligibility:** Open to undergraduate students who are members of congregations affiliated with the Greater New Jersey Conference of the United Methodist Church. Along with their application, they must submit a statement on why they should be considered for this scholarship, including information on their financial need and Christian commitment. Selection is based on academic achievement, financial need, and participation in church activities.

**Financial data:** A stipend is awarded.

**Duration:** 1 year.

**Number awarded:** Varies each year.

**Deadline:** March of each year.

## 416 GUARDIAN SCHOLARSHIPS

Workforce Safety & Insurance
1600 East Century Avenue, Suite 1
P.O. Box 5585
Bismarck, ND 58506-5585
Phone: (701) 328-3828; (800) 440-3796; Fax: (701) 328-3820;
TDD: (701) 328-3786
Web: www.workforcesafety.com/workers/typesofbenefits.asp

**Summary:** To provide financial assistance for college to children and spouses of workers who died in work-related accidents in North Dakota.

**Eligibility:** Open to spouses and dependent children of workers who lost their lives in work-related accidents in North Dakota. Applicants must be attending or planning to attend an accredited college, university, or technical school.

**Financial data:** The maximum stipend is $4,000 per year.

**Duration:** 1 year; may be renewed up to 4 additional years.

**Number awarded:** Varies each year; recently, 32 of these were awarded.

## 417 GUILDSCHOLAR PROGRAM

Jewish Guild for the Blind, Attn: GuildScholar Program
15 West 65th Street
New York, NY 10023
Phone: (212) 769-7801; (800) 284-4422; Fax: (212) 769-6266;
Email: guildscholar@jgb.org
Web: www.jgb.org

**Summary:** To provide financial assistance for college to blind high school seniors.

**Eligibility:** Open to college-bound high school seniors who can document legal blindness. Applicants must submit copies of school transcripts and SAT/ACT scores, proof of U.S. citizenship, 3 letters of recommendation, a 500-word personal statement describing their educational and personal goals, and documentation of financial need (if they wish that to be considered).

**Financial data:** The stipend is approximately $15,000.

**Duration:** 1 year.

**Number awarded:** Up to 15 each year.

## 418 GUISTWHITE SCHOLAR PROGRAM

Phi Theta Kappa
Scholarship Programs Director

1625 Eastover Drive
P.O. Box 13729
Jackson, MS 39236-3729
Phone: (601) 984-3504, ext. 560; (800) 946-9995, ext. 560; Fax: (601) 984-3550;
Email: clancy.mitchell@ptk.org
Web: www.ptk.org

**Summary:** To provide financial assistance to members of Phi Theta Kappa, the international honor society for 2-year colleges, who plan to transfer to a 4-year institution.

**Eligibility:** Open to members of the society. Applicants must be completing an associate degree at a community, technical, or junior college in the United States or Canada, be planning to transfer to an accredited senior institution, and have a cumulative GPA of 3.5 or higher. Along with their application, they must submit a 500-word essay on their most significant community college endeavor in which they applied their academic, intellectual, or leadership skills to benefit their school, community, or society. Selection is based on that essay, academic achievement, participation in Phi Theta Kappa programs, and service to their colleges and communities.

**Financial data:** The stipend is $2,500 per year for Scholars or $500 per year for Finalists.

**Duration:** 2 years for full-time students; part-time students receive pro-rated amounts until the disbursement of the total award ($5,000 for Scholars or $1,000 for Finalists).

**Number awarded:** 20 each year: 10 Scholars and 10 Finalists.

**Deadline:** December of each year.

## 419 GUY AND GLORIA MUTO MEMORIAL SCHOLARSHIP

Guy and Gloria Muto Memorial Scholarship Foundation, Inc.
P.O. Box 60159
Sacramento, CA 95860
Email: ggmuto@aol.com
Web: www.ggmuto.org

**Summary:** To provide financial assistance for college to individuals (or their immediate families) who are working in the swimming pool and spa industry.

**Eligibility:** Open to applicants engaged in any way in the swimming pool and spa industry (or their immediate family members). Immediate family is defined as husband, wife, or children under the age of 30. Applicants must be enrolled or planning to enroll in an academic course, certification program, trade or technical course, or other educational program. Along with their application, they must submit a statement on why they want to take this program or course of study and how they think it will help them in their business or professional life. Financial need is not considered in the selection process.

**Financial data:** Stipends up to $1,000 are available. Award checks are made out jointly to the recipient and the recipient's school or agency and may only be used for the course of study, not travel, lodging, food, etc.

**Duration:** 1 year.

**Number awarded:** Varies each year; recently, 6 of these were awarded.

**Deadline:** March of each year.

## 420 HACE SCHOLARSHIPS

Hispanic Alliance for Career Enhancement, Attn: College Programs
25 East Washington Street, Suite 1500
Chicago, IL 60602
Phone: (312) 435-0498; Fax: (312) 435-1494; Email: haceorg@hace-usa.org
Web: www.hace-usa.org/collegepage.htm

**Summary:** To provide financial assistance to Hispanic students working on an undergraduate degree.

**Eligibility:** Open to U.S. citizens and permanent residents who are enrolled or planning to enroll in a college or university in the United States (other than a partner institution of the sponsoring organization). Applicants must have a GPA of 2.5 or higher and at least 1 parent of Hispanic or Latino heritage. Along with their application, they must submit 300-word essays on 1) their autobiography, including their Hispanic background, where they grew up, and their immediate family; and 2) their career plans for the next 5 to 10 years.

**Financial data:** The stipend is $1,000.

**Duration:** 1 year; nonrenewable.

**Number awarded:** Varies each year; recently, 9 of these were awarded.

**Deadline:** February of each year.

## 421 HAL CONNOLLY SCHOLAR-ATHLETE AWARD

California Governor's Committee on Employment of People with Disabilities
Employment Development Department

Attn: Scholar-Athlete Awards Program
800 Capitol Mall, MIC 41
Sacramento, CA 95814
Phone: (916) 654-8055; (800) 695-0350; Fax: (916) 654-9821;
TTY: (916) 654-9820; Email: rnagle@edd.ca.gov
Web: www.disabilityemployment.org/yp_hal_con.htm
**Summary:** To provide financial assistance to disabled high school seniors in California who have participated in athletics.
**Eligibility:** Open to high school seniors with disabilities, no more than 19 years of age on January 1 of the year of application, who have competed in California high school athletics at a varsity or equivalent level and possess academic and athletic records that demonstrate qualities of leadership and accomplishment. They must have completed high school with a GPA of 2.8 or better and plan to attend an accredited college or university in California, but they do not have to intend to participate formally in collegiate athletic activities. Selection is based on cumulative GPA (15%), cumulative GPA as it relates to the nature of the student's disability (15%), athletic accomplishments as they relate to the student's disability (30%), an essay on "How Sports Participation Has Affected My Life at School and in the Community As a Person with a Disability" (25%), and overall personal achievement (15%). The top finalists may be interviewed before selections are made. Male and female students compete separately.
**Financial data:** The stipend is $1,000, contingent upon the winners' acceptance at an accredited California college or university. Funds may be used for tuition, books, supplies, and other educational expenses. Exceptions are granted to students who choose to attend schools out of state primarily to accommodate their disability.
**Duration:** Awards are granted annually.
**Number awarded:** Up to 6 each year: 3 are set aside for females and 3 for males.
**Deadline:** January of each year.

## 422 HALLIE Q. BROWN SCHOLARSHIP FUND

National Association of Colored Women's Clubs
5808 16th Street, N.W.
Washington, DC 20011-2898
Phone: (202) 726-2044; Fax: (202) 726-0023
**Summary:** To provide financial assistance to Black American college students who are interested in pursuing postsecondary education.
**Eligibility:** Open to Black students who are U.S. citizens and can demonstrate financial need. They must have completed at least 1 semester of postsecondary education with a minimum GPA of 2.0. Candidates must be nominated by a member of the National Association of Colored Women's Clubs; students may not apply directly.
**Financial data:** The amount awarded varies, according to financial need, but does not exceed $1,000 per year.
**Duration:** The award is presented biennially, in even-numbered years.
**Number awarded:** Approximately 20 every other year.
**Deadline:** April of even-numbered years.

## 423 HANA SCHOLARSHIPS

United Methodist Church
Attn: General Board of Higher Education and Ministry
Office of Loans and Scholarships
1001 19th Avenue South
P.O. Box 340007
Nashville, TN 37203-0007
Phone: (615) 340-7344; Fax: (615) 340-7367; Email: umscholar@gbhem.org
Web: www.gbhem.org
**Summary:** To provide financial assistance to upper-division and graduate Methodist students who are of Hispanic, Asian, Native American, Alaska Native, or Pacific Islander ancestry.
**Eligibility:** Open to full-time juniors, seniors, and graduate students at accredited colleges and universities in the United States who have been active, full members of a United Methodist Church for at least 1 year prior to applying. Applicants must have at least 1 parent who is Hispanic, Asian, Native American, Alaska Native, or Pacific Islander. They must be able to demonstrate involvement in their Hispanic, Asian, or Native American (HANA) community. Selection is based on that involvement, academic ability, and financial need. U.S. citizenship or permanent resident status is required.
**Financial data:** The stipend is $1,000 for undergraduates or $3,000 for graduate students.
**Duration:** 1 year; recipients may reapply.
**Number awarded:** 50 each year.
**Deadline:** March of each year.

## 424 HANK LEBONNE SCHOLARSHIP

National Federation of the Blind
c/o Peggy Elliott, Scholarship Committee Chair
805 Fifth Avenue
Grinnell, IA 50112
Phone: (641) 236-3366
Web: www.nfb.org/sch_intro.htm
**Summary:** To provide financial assistance to legally blind students working on an undergraduate or graduate degree.
**Eligibility:** Open to legally blind students who are working on or planning to work full time on an undergraduate or graduate degree. Selection is based on academic excellence, service to the community, and financial need.
**Financial data:** The stipend is $5,000.
**Duration:** 1 year; recipients may resubmit applications up to 2 additional years.
**Number awarded:** 1 each year.
**Deadline:** March of each year.

## 425 HANSCOM OFFICERS' WIVES' CLUB SCHOLARSHIPS

Hanscom Officers' Wives' Club, Attn: Scholarship Chair
P.O. Box 557
Bedford, MA 01730
Phone: (781) 275-1251; Email: scholarship@hanscomowd.org
Web: www.hanscomowc.org
**Summary:** To provide financial assistance for college to spouses and children of military personnel and veterans in New England.
**Eligibility:** Open to high school seniors and spouses living in New England who are dependents of active-duty, retired, or deceased military members of any branch of service. Also eligible are dependents of military recruiters working in the New York area and students living elsewhere but whose military sponsor is stationed at Hanscom Air Force Base. Applicants must demonstrate qualities of responsibility, leadership, scholastics, citizenship, and diversity of interest. They must have a valid military identification card and be working on or planning to work on a bachelor's or associate's degree. Along with their application, they must submit a 2-page essay on their educational goals, how their educational experience will help prepare them to pursue future goals, and how they intend to apply their education to better their community. The Chief of Staff Award is presented to the highest-ranked high school applicant. The Carmen Schipper Memorial Award is presented to the highest-ranked spouse applicant. The Scott Corey Scholarship is awarded to another spouse applicant.
**Financial data:** Stipends range from $1,200 to $4,000.
**Duration:** 1 year; nonrenewable.
**Number awarded:** Varies each year; recently, 17 of these scholarships were awarded.
**Deadline:** March of each year.

## 426 HARNESS TRACKS OF AMERICA SCHOLARSHIP PROGRAM

Harness Tracks of America, Attn: Sable Downs
4640 East Sunrise, Suite 200
Tucson, AZ 85718
Phone: (520) 529-2525; Fax: (520) 529-3235; Email: info@harnesstracks.com
Web: www.harnesstracks.com/scholarships.htm
**Summary:** To provide financial assistance for college or graduate school to people engaged in the harness racing industry and their children.
**Eligibility:** Open to 1) children of licensed drivers, trainers, caretakers, or harness racing management, and 2) young people actively engaged in the harness racing industry themselves. Applicants must submit essays on their present and future educational goals, the extent to which they and/or other members of their family are involved in the harness racing industry, and why they believe they are deserving of scholarship support. Selection is based on academic merit, financial need, and active harness racing involvement.
**Financial data:** The stipend is $7,500 per year.
**Duration:** 1 year.
**Number awarded:** 6 each year.
**Deadline:** June of each year.

## 427 HARRY ALAN GREGG FOUNDATION GRANTS

Harry Alan Gregg Foundation
One Verney Drive
Greenfield, NH 03047
Phone: (603) 547-3311, ext. 401; (800) 394-3311, ext. 401; Fax: (603) 547-6212;
Email: hag@cmf.org

Web: www.crotchedmountain.org

**Summary:** To provide financial assistance to children and adults in New Hampshire who have physical, emotional, or intellectual disabilities.

**Eligibility:** Open to New Hampshire residents of all ages who have physical, intellectual, or emotional disabilities. Funds may be requested for broad purposes but must specifically benefit the applicant. Examples of acceptable purposes include, but are not limited to: the costs of nonreimbursed medical, dental, vision, hearing, or therapy treatments; special equipment, services, or supplies; modifications to living area, workplace, or vehicle; respite services for the recipient or care givers; recreational functions, such as camperships or other activities; and vocational, educational, or driver training tuition assistance. Selection is based on demonstrated need for a product of service, the applicant's financial circumstances, and the ability of the foundation to help improve the quality of life of a grant recipient.

**Financial data:** Most grants range from $100 to $1,000, but they may be larger.

**Duration:** Recipients may receive a maximum of 4 grants (no more than 2 in any year).

**Number awarded:** More than 300 each year.

**Deadline:** Applications may be submitted at any time.

## 428 HATTIE TEDROW MEMORIAL FUND SCHOLARSHIP

American Legion, Attn: Department of North Dakota
722 First Avenue North
Fargo, ND 58102
Phone: (701) 293-3120; Fax: (701) 293-9951; Email: adjutant@ndlegion.org
Web: www.ndlegion.org

**Summary:** To provide financial assistance for college to high school seniors in North Dakota who are direct descendants of veterans.

**Eligibility:** Open to college bound seniors graduating from high schools in North Dakota. Applicants must be the children, grandchildren, or great-grandchildren of veterans who served honorably in the U.S. armed forces.

**Financial data:** The stipend is $2,000.

**Duration:** 1 year; nonrenewable.

**Number awarded:** 1 each year.

## 429 HAWAIIAN CIVIC CLUB OF HONOLULU SCHOLARSHIP

Hawaiian Civic Club of Honolulu, Attn: Scholarship Committee
P.O. Box 1513
Honolulu, HI 96806
Email: newmail@hotbot.com
Web: hcchscholarship.tripod.com/scholarship/index.html

**Summary:** To provide financial assistance for undergraduate or graduate studies to persons of Hawaiian descent.

**Eligibility:** Open to Hawaiian residents of Hawaiian descent (descendants of the aboriginal inhabitants of the Hawaiian Islands prior to 1778) who are able to demonstrate academic achievement and are enrolled or planning to enroll full time in an accredited 2-year college, 4-year college, or graduate school. Graduating seniors and current undergraduate students must have a GPA of 2.5 or higher; graduate students must have at least a 3.0 GPA. As part of the selection process, applicants must submit a 2-page essay on a topic that changes annually but relates to issues of concern to the Hawaiian community; a recent topic related to the leadership, cultural and governmental, of the Hawaiian community. Selection is based on the quality of the essay, academic standing, financial need, and the completeness of the application package.

**Financial data:** The amount of the stipend varies. Scholarship checks are made payable to the recipient and the institution and are mailed to the college or university financial aid office. Funds may be used for tuition, fees, books, and other educational expenses.

**Duration:** 1 year.

**Number awarded:** Varies each year; recently, 54 of these scholarships, worth $34,800, were awarded.

**Deadline:** May of each year.

## 430 HAZLEWOOD EXEMPTION FOR DEPENDENTS OF TEXAS VETERANS

Texas Higher Education Coordinating Board
Attn: Grants and Special Programs
1200 East Anderson Lane
P.O. Box 12788, Capitol Station
Austin, TX 78711-2788
Phone: (512) 427-6101; (800) 242-3062; Fax: (512) 427-6127;
Email: grantinfo@thecb.state.tx.us

Web: www.collegefortexans.com

**Summary:** To exempt children of deceased veterans from payment of tuition at public universities in Texas.

**Eligibility:** Open to the children of Texas servicemen who died in the line of duty or as a result of injury or illness directly related to service in the U.S. military or the National Guard. Applicants must have used up all federal educational benefits for which they are eligible. They must have resided in Texas for at least 12 months and be attending or planning to attend a public college or university in the state.

**Financial data:** Eligible students are exempt from payment of tuition, dues, fees, and charges at state-supported colleges and universities in Texas.

**Duration:** 1 year; may be renewed for a cumulative total of 150 credit hours.

**Number awarded:** Varies each year; recently, 8 of these awards were granted.

## 431 HAZLEWOOD EXEMPTION FOR TEXAS VETERANS

Texas Higher Education Coordinating Board
Attn: Grants and Special Programs
1200 East Anderson Lane
P.O. Box 12788, Capitol Station
Austin, TX 78711-2788
Phone: (512) 427-6101; (800) 242-3062; Fax: (512) 427-6127;
Email: grantinfo@thecb.state.tx.us
Web: www.collegefortexans.com

**Summary:** To exempt Texas veterans from payment of tuition for undergraduate or graduate study at public universities in the state.

**Eligibility:** Open to veterans who were legal residents of Texas at the time they entered the U.S. armed forces and served for at least 181 days of active military duty, excluding basic training. Applicants must have received an honorable discharge or separation or a general discharge under honorable conditions. They must be enrolled at a public college or university in Texas but have used up all other federal education benefits (e.g., Montgomery Bill, Pell grants, federal SEOG grants).

**Financial data:** Veterans who are eligible for this benefit are entitled to free tuition and fees at state-supported colleges and universities in Texas.

**Duration:** Exemptions may be claimed up to a cumulative total of 150 credit hours, including undergraduate and graduate study.

**Number awarded:** Varies each year; recently, 8.858 of these awards were granted.

## 432 HELEN ABBOTT INDIVIDUAL COMMUNITY SERVICE AWARDS

Arab American Institute Foundation, Attn: Executive Director
1600 K Street, N.W., Suite 601
Washington, DC 20006
Phone: (202) 429-9210; Fax: (202) 429-9214; Email: aaif@aaiusa.org
Web: www.aaiusa.org/for_students.htm

**Summary:** To recognize and reward Arab American undergraduate students who can demonstrate a strong record of community service.

**Eligibility:** Open to U.S. citizens and permanent residents of Arab descent who are currently enrolled as an undergraduate or about to enter such a program. Applicants must have a GPA of 3.0 or higher. Along with their application, they must submit 1) a resume that indicates a strong interest and commitment to community service; and 2) a 500-word essay on how their field of study is a springboard for a life of community service.

**Financial data:** The award is $1,000.

**Duration:** The awards are granted annually.

**Number awarded:** 2 each year.

**Deadline:** March of each year.

## 433 HELEN KLIMEK STUDENT SCHOLARSHIP

American Legion Auxiliary, Attn: Department of New York
112 State Street, Suite 1310
Albany, NY 12207
Phone: (518) 463-1162; (800) 421-6348; Fax: (518) 449-5406;
Email: alanyhdqtrs@worldnet.att.net
Web: www.deptny.org/scholarships.htm

**Summary:** To provide financial assistance for college to New York residents who are the children or grandchildren of veterans.

**Eligibility:** Open to residents of New York who are the children grandchildren, or great grandchildren of veterans of World War II, the Korean Conflict, the Vietnam War, Grenada/Lebanon, Panama, or the Persian Gulf. Applicants must be high school seniors or graduates younger than 20 years of age. They must be interested in attending an accredited college or university. Along with their application they must submit a 700-word statement on the significance or value of volunteerism as a resource towards the positive development of the applicant's personal and professional future. Selection is based on character (20%), Americanism (15%), volunteer involvement (20%), leadership (15%), scholarship (15%), and financial need (15%).

**Financial data:** The stipend is $1,000.

**Duration:** 1 year.

**Number awarded:** 1 each year.

**Deadline:** February of each year.

## 434 HELEN L. AND DOUGLAS ELIASON SCHOLARSHIPS

Delaware Community Foundation, Attn: Executive Vice President
100 West 10th Street, Suite 115
P.O. Box 1636
Wilmington, DE 19899
Phone: (302) 504-5222; Fax: (302) 571-1553; Email: rgentsch@delcf.org
Web: www.delcf.org

**Summary:** To provide financial assistance to working adults and low-income high school seniors in Delaware interested in pursuing additional education.

**Eligibility:** Open to residents of Delaware whose total family income is limited. Preference is given to working adults who want to improve their employment potential through continuing education, although low- and moderate-income high school students are also eligible. Applicants must be able to demonstrate that they possess the ability and motivation to achieve their academic goal. Along with their applications, they must include brief essays on their immediate educational goals, how achieving those goals will improve their lives, their need for assistance (including any special circumstances or expenses), and the least amount of assistance enabling them to start their educational plans. Aid is available for credit courses or, in special circumstances, non-credit courses.

**Financial data:** Stipends depend on the need of the recipient

**Duration:** 1 year; may be renewed if the recipient continues to make good academic progress toward their goal.

**Number awarded:** Varies each year.

**Deadline:** July of each year for fall semester; October of each year for winter semester; December of each year for spring semester; April of each year for summer semester.

## 435 HELLENIC TIMES SCHOLARSHIPS

Hellenic Times Scholarship Fund, Attn: Nick Katsoris
823 Eleventh Avenue, Fifth Floor
New York, NY 10019-3535
Phone: (212) 986-6881; Fax: (212) 977-3662; Email: HTSFund@aol.com
Web: www.HTSFund.org

**Summary:** To provide financial assistance to undergraduate or graduate students of Greek descent.

**Eligibility:** Open to undergraduate and graduate students of Greek descent who are between 17 and 25 years of age and enrolled in an accredited college or university. Students who are receiving other financial aid that exceeds 50% of their annual tuition are ineligible. Selection is based on need and merit.

**Financial data:** The amount of the awards depends on the availability of funds and the number of recipients.

**Number awarded:** Varies; approximately $100,000 is available for this program each year.

**Deadline:** January of each year.

## 436 HELM LEADERSHIP FELLOWS

Christian Church (Disciples of Christ)
Attn: Higher Education and Leadership Ministries
11477 Olde Cabin Road, Suite 310
St. Louis, MO 6314-7130
Phone: (314) 991-3000; Fax: (314) 991-2957; Email: helm@helmdisciples.org
Web: www.helmdisciples.org/aid/fellows.htm

**Summary:** To provide financial assistance for college to members of the Christian Church (Disciples of Christ) who are interested in taking a leadership role in the church.

**Eligibility:** Open to high school seniors and transfers from community college who plan to be a full-time student at a 4-year college or university in the United States or Canada. Applicants must be a participating member of a congregation of the Christian Church (Disciples of Christ) who express a commitment to serve the church as a clergy or lay leader. Some preference is given to students attending colleges and universities related to the Christian Church.

**Financial data:** The stipend is $2,000 per year.

**Duration:** 1 year; may be renewed up to 3 additional years provided the recipient has a GPA of 2.5 or higher after the first semester of undergraduate work, 2.8 or higher after 3 semesters, and 3.0 or higher after 5 semesters.

**Number awarded:** Approximately 6 each year.

**Deadline:** March of each year.

## 437 HEMASPHERES UNIVERSITY SCHOLARSHIP FUND

American Red Cross
c/o Scholarship America, Attn: Scholarship Management Services
One Scholarship Way
P.O. Box 297
St. Peter, MN 56082
Phone: (507) 931-1682; (800) 537-4180; Fax: (507) 931-9168;
Email: smsinfo@csfa.org

**Summary:** To provide financial assistance for college to persons with hemophilia and their children.

**Eligibility:** Open to high school seniors, high school graduates, or college students already enrolled in full-time study. Applicants must either be receiving treatment for hemophilia or have a parent receiving treatment for hemophilia. They must be planning to enroll full time at an accredited 2- or 4-year college, university, or vocational/technical school. Selection is based on academic performance, leadership ability, school and community activities, work experience, educational and career goals, and personal or family financial circumstances.

**Financial data:** The stipend is $5,000 per year. Funds may be used for tuition, fees, books, and room and board.

**Duration:** 1 year; may be renewed 1 additional year.

**Number awarded:** 3 each year: 2 to students with hemophilia and 1 to the child of a parent with hemophilia.

**Deadline:** February of each year.

## 438 HEMOPHILIA FEDERATION OF AMERICA EDUCATIONAL SCHOLARSHIPS

Hemophilia Federation of America, Attn: Scholarship Committee
1405 West Pinhook Road, Suite 101
Lafayette, LA 70503
Phone: (337) 261-9787; (800) 230-9797; Fax: (337) 261-1787;
Email: info@hemophiliafed.org
Web: www.hemophiliafed.org/scholarships.php

**Summary:** To provide financial assistance for college to students who have a blood clotting disorder.

**Eligibility:** Open to high school seniors and current college students who have a blood clotting disorder. Applicants must be attending or planning to attend an accredited 2-year or 4-year college, university, or trade school in the United States. Along with their application, they must submit a 1-page essay on their goals and aspirations and how the blood clotting community has played a part in their lives. Financial need is also considered in the selection process.

**Financial data:** The stipend is $1,500 per year.

**Duration:** 1 year; may be renewed.

**Number awarded:** 4 each year.

**Deadline:** March of each year.

## 439 HEMOPHILIA HEALTH SERVICES MEMORIAL SCHOLARSHIPS

Hemophilia Health Services, Attn: Scholarship Committee
6820 Charlotte Pike, Suite 100
Nashville, TN 37209-4234
Phone: (615) 850-5175; (800) 800-6606, ext. 5175; Fax: (615) 352-2588;
Email: scholarship@HemophiliaHealth.com
Web: www.HemophiliaHealth.com/consumers/products_services/scholarship.htm

**Summary:** To provide financial assistance for college or graduate school to people with hemophilia or other bleeding disorders.

**Eligibility:** Open to individuals with hemophilia (factor VIII or IX), von Willebrand Disease (type 1, 2, 2A, 2B, 2M, 2N, or 3), or other bleeding disorders. Applicants must be 1) high school seniors; 2) college freshmen, sophomores, or juniors; or 3) college seniors planning to attend graduate school or students already enrolled in graduate school. They must be attending or planning to attend an accredited nonprofit college, university, or vocational/technical school in the United States or Puerto Rico as a full-time student. Along with their application, they must submit an essay, up to 250 words, on the following topic: "What has been your own personal challenge in living with a bleeding disorder?" U.S. citizenship is required. Selection is based on academic achievement in relation to tested ability, involvement in extracurricular and community activities, and financial need.

**Financial data:** The stipend is $1,500. Funds are issued payable to the recipient's school.

**Duration:** 1 year; recipients may reapply.

**Number awarded:** Several each year.

**Deadline:** April of each year.

## 440 HERBERT FULLAM SCHOLARSHIP

Vermont Student Assistance Corporation
Champlain Mill, Attn: Scholarship Programs
P.O. Box 2000
Winooski, VT 05404-2601
Phone: (802) 654-3798; (888) 253-4819; Fax: (802) 654-3765;
TDD: (802) 654-3766; TDD: (800) 281-3341 (within VT); Email: info@vsac.org
Web: www.vsac.org

**Summary:** To provide financial assistance for college to high school seniors in Vermont whose parent is a police officer in the state.

**Eligibility:** Open to high school seniors in Vermont who are planning to enroll in a degree program at a 2-year or 4-year college. Applicants must be the child of a Vermont police officer. Selection is based on required essays and financial need.

**Financial data:** The stipend is $1,000.

**Duration:** 1 year.

**Number awarded:** 1 each year.

**Deadline:** April of each year.

## 441 HERMIONE GRANT CALHOUN SCHOLARSHIPS

National Federation of the Blind
c/o Peggy Elliott, Scholarship Committee Chair
805 Fifth Avenue
Grinnell, IA 50112
Phone: (641) 236-3366
Web: www.nfb.org/sch_intro.htm

**Summary:** To provide financial assistance to female blind students interested in working on an undergraduate or graduate degree.

**Eligibility:** Open to legally blind women students who are working on or planning to work full time on an undergraduate or graduate degree. Selection is based on academic excellence, service to the community, and financial need.

**Financial data:** The stipend is $3,000.

**Duration:** 1 year; recipients may resubmit applications up to 2 additional years.

**Number awarded:** 1 each year.

**Deadline:** March of each year.

## 442 HIGH SCHOOL SCHOLARSHIP PROGRAM OF THE HISPANIC SCHOLARSHIP FUND

Hispanic Scholarship Fund, Attn: Selection Committee
55 Second Street, Suite 1500
San Francisco, CA 94105
Phone: (415) 808-2350; (877) HSF-INFO; Fax: (415) 808-2302;
Email: highschool@hsf.net
Web: www.hsf.net/scholarship/programs/hs.php

**Summary:** To provide financial assistance to Hispanic American high school seniors who are interested in attending college.

**Eligibility:** Open to U.S. citizens, permanent residents, and visitors with a passport stamped I-551. Applicants must be high school seniors of Hispanic heritage and have applied for federal financial aid. They must have a GPA of 3.0 or higher and concrete plans to enroll full time at an accredited 2-year or 4-year college or university in the United States, Puerto Rico, or the U.S. Virgin Islands for the following fall. Along with their application, they must submit 600-word essays on 1) how their Hispanic heritage, family upbringing, and/or role models have influenced their personal long-term goals; 2) how they contribute to their community and what they have learned from their experiences; and 3) an academic challenge they have faced and how they have overcome it. Selection is based on academic achievement, personal strengths, leadership, and financial need.

**Financial data:** Stipends range from $1,000 to $2,500 per year.

**Duration:** 1 year.

**Number awarded:** Varies each year.

**Deadline:** December of each year.

## 443 HIGHWAY WORKER MEMORIAL SCHOLARSHIP PROGRAM

American Road and Transportation Builders Association
Attn: Transportation Development Foundation
1219 28th Street, N.W.
Washington, DC 20007-3389
Phone: (202) 289-4434; Email: rbritton@artba.org
Web: www.artba.org/foundation/hwy_worker_scholarship.htm

**Summary:** To provide financial assistance for college to children of highway workers killed or disabled on the job.

**Eligibility:** Open to the sons, daughters, and legally adopted children of highway workers who die or have become permanently disabled in roadway construction zone accidents. Applicants must be attending or planning to attend an accredited 4-year college or university, 2-year college, or vocational/technical school. Their parent must have been employed by a transportation construction firm or a transportation public agency at the time of death or disabling injury. Selection is based on academic performance (GPA of 2.5 or higher), a 200-word statement from the applicant on reasons for wanting to continue education, letters of recommendation, and financial need.

**Financial data:** The stipend is $2,000. Funds are paid directly to the recipient's institution to be used for tuition, books, or required fees, but not for room and board.

**Duration:** 1 year.

**Number awarded:** Varies each year; recently, 12 of these scholarships were awarded.

**Deadline:** March of each year.

## 444 HILDEGARD LASH MERIT SCHOLARSHIP

Orphan Foundation of America, Attn: Director of Student Services
Tall Oaks Village Center
12020-D North Shore Drive
Reston, VA 20190-4977
Phone: (571) 203-0270; (800) 950-4673; Fax: (571) 203-0273;
Email: scholarships@orphan.org
Web: www.orphan.org

**Summary:** To provide financial assistance for college to students currently or previously in foster care.

**Eligibility:** Open to students who are entering their sophomore, junior, or senior year as a full-time student at a 4-year college or university. Applicants must have been in foster care or a ward of the court for at least 1 year at the time of their 18th birthday and currently be under 25 years of age. They must submit a 2- to 3-page essay on their goals for school, career, and personal fulfillment. Selection is based on the essay, 2 letters of recommendation, academic record, extracurricular involvement, and other personal achievements. Finalists are interviewed by telephone.

**Financial data:** The stipend is $5,000. Half the funds are paid at the beginning of the first semester and the other half at the beginning of the second semester if the recipient maintains a full-time course load and a GPA of 3.2 or higher.

**Duration:** 1 year; nonrenewable.

**Number awarded:** 1 each year.

**Deadline:** Applicants must first register online by the end of March of each year.

## 445 HISPANIC COLLEGE FUND SCHOLARSHIPS

Hispanic College Fund, Attn: National Director
1717 Pennsylvania Avenue, N.W., Suite 460
Washington, D.C., 20006
Phone: (202) 296-5400; (800) 644-4223; Fax: (202) 296-3774;
Email: hispaniccollegefund@earthlink.net
Web: www.hispanicfund.org

**Summary:** To provide financial assistance to Hispanic American undergraduate students.

**Eligibility:** Open to U.S. citizens of Hispanic background (at least 1 grandparent must be 100% Hispanic) who are entering their freshman, sophomore, junior, or senior year of college. Applicants must be working on a bachelor's or associate degree and have a cumulative GPA of 3.0 or higher. They must be applying to or enrolled in a college or university in the 50 states or Puerto Rico as a full-time student. Financial need is considered in the selection process.

**Financial data:** Stipends range from $500 to $5,000, depending on the need of the recipient, and average approximately $3,000. Funds are paid directly to the recipient's college or university to help cover tuition and fees.

**Duration:** 1 year; recipients may reapply.

**Number awarded:** Varies each year; recently, 208 students were supported by this program, including 70 freshmen, 57 sophomores, 47 juniors, and 34 seniors.

**Deadline:** April of each year.

## 446 HISTORICALLY BLACK COLLEGES/UNIVERSITIES SCHOLARSHIP PROGRAM

U.S. Army
ROTC Cadet Command, Attn: ATCC-OP-I-S
55 Patch Road, Building 56
Fort Monroe, VA 23651-1052
Phone: (757) 727-4558; (800) USA-ROTC; Email: atccps@usaac.army.mil
Web: www.rotc.usaac.army.mil/scholarship_HPD2/fouryear/hbcu.htm

**Summary:** To provide financial assistance to high school seniors or graduates who are interested in enrolling in Army ROTC at an Historically Black College or University (HBCU).

**Eligibility:** Open to applicants who 1) are U.S. citizens; 2) are at least 17 years of age by October of the year in which they are seeking a scholarship; 3) are able to complete a college degree and receive their commission before their 31st birthday; 4) score at least 19 on the ACT or the equivalent on the SAT; 5) have a high school GPA of 2.5 or higher; 6) meet medical and other regulatory requirements; and 7) are planning to attend 1 of 73 designated HBCUs that have an ROTC detachment or a cross-town agreement with a college or university that does. Current college or university students may apply if their school considers them beginning freshmen with 4 academic years remaining for a bachelor's degree.

**Financial data:** This scholarship provides financial assistance of up to $20,000 per year for college tuition and educational fees or for room and board, whichever the student selects. In addition, a flat rate of $600 per year is provided for the purchase of textbooks, classroom supplies and equipment. Recipients are also awarded a stipend for up to 10 months of each year that is $250 per month during their freshman year; $300 per month during their sophomore year $350 per month during their junior year, and $400 per month during their senior year.

**Duration:** 4 years.

**Number awarded:** A limited number of these scholarships is offered each year.

**Deadline:** November of each year.

## 447 HO'OMAKA HOU SCHOLARSHIP

Hawai'i Community Foundation, Attn: Scholarship Department
1164 Bishop Street, Suite 800
Honolulu, HI 96813
Phone: (808) 566-5570; (888) 731-3863; Fax: (808) 521-6286;
Email: scholarships@hcf-hawaii.org
Web: www.hawaiicommunityfoundation.org/scholar/scholar.php

**Summary:** To provide financial assistance to Hawaii residents who are interested in attending college or graduate school and have turned their lives around after facing social problems.

**Eligibility:** Open to Hawaii residents who have turned their lives around after facing social problems (e.g., substance abuse, domestic violence). Applicants must be or planning to become full-time students at the undergraduate or graduate school level. They must be able to demonstrate academic achievement (GPA of 2.7 or higher), good moral character, and financial need.

**Financial data:** The amounts of the awards depend on the availability of funds and the need of the recipient.

**Duration:** 1 year.

**Number awarded:** Varies each year.

**Deadline:** February of each year.

## 448 HOPE GRANTS FOR CERTIFICATE AND DIPLOMA PROGRAMS

Georgia Student Finance Commission, Attn: Scholarships and Grants Division
2082 East Exchange Place, Suite 200
Tucker, GA 30084-5305
Phone: (770) 724-9000; (800) 505-GSFC; Fax: (770) 724-9089;
Email: hope@mail.gsfc.state.ga.us
Web: www.gsfc.org/HOPE/index.cfm

**Summary:** To help outstanding students who are interested in earning a certificate or diploma at a public technical institute in Georgia.

**Eligibility:** Open to Georgia residents who are working on a certificate or diploma in a non-degree program of study at a public institution in the state. The certificate or degree program must be approved by the Georgia Department of Technical and Adult education or be a comparable program approved by the Board of Regents. Continuing education programs are not eligible.

**Financial data:** These grants pay tuition and mandatory fees at public technical institutes in Georgia, along with a book allowance of up to $300 per year.

**Duration:** This assistance may be used for a total of 2 technical programs of study leading to a certificate or diploma.

**Number awarded:** Varies each year.

## 449 HOPE SCHOLARSHIPS FOR DEGREE-SEEKING STUDENTS

Georgia Student Finance Commission, Attn: Scholarships and Grants Division
2082 East Exchange Place, Suite 200
Tucker, GA 30084-5305
Phone: (770) 724-9000; (800) 505-GSFC; Fax: (770) 724-9089;
Email: hope@mail.gsfc.state.ga.us
Web: www.gsfc.org/HOPE/index.cfm

**Summary:** To provide financial assistance to outstanding students who are attending or planning to attend a college or university in Georgia.

**Eligibility:** Open to Georgia residents who are attending or planning to attend a college or university within the state. Students who are applying as high school seniors must have earned at least a 3.0 cumulative GPA if they followed the college preparatory track in high school or a 3.2 cumulative GPA if they followed a technical/career track. The college preparatory diploma requires completion of 4 units of English, 4 units of mathematics, 3 units of social studies, 3 units of science, and 2 units of a foreign language. The technical/career diploma requires completion of 4 units of English, 3 units of mathematics, 3 units of social studies, and 3 units of science. Students who are applying for the first time as college students must have earned a GPA of 3.0 or higher in college regardless of their high school GPA. Students who complete home study requirements may receive a scholarship retroactively if they earn a GPA of 3.0 or higher in their first year of college. U.S. citizenship or permanent resident status is required.

**Financial data:** HOPE Scholars who attend public colleges or universities receive full tuition and mandatory fees plus a book allowance of $300 per academic year. The stipend for HOPE Scholarships at private colleges and universities is up to $3,000 per year; funds may be used only for tuition and mandatory fees.

**Duration:** 1 year; may be renewed for up to 3 additional years if the recipient maintains a cumulative GPA of 3.0 or higher in college.

**Number awarded:** Varies each year.

## 450 HORACE MANN STUDENT SCHOLARSHIPS

Horace Mann Companies, Attn: Scholarship Program
1 Horace Mann Plaza
P.O. Box 20490
Springfield, IL 62708
Phone: (217) 788-5343
Web: www.horacemann.com/html/edprograms/scholarships.html

**Summary:** To provide financial assistance for college to children of teachers.

**Eligibility:** Open to college-bound high school seniors whose parent or legal guardian is employed by a U.S. public school district or public college/university. The student must have a GPA of 3.0 or higher and a score of at least 23 on the ACT or the equivalent on the SAT. Selection is based on an essay, grades, 2 letters of recommendation, school and community activities, and academic honors. Financial need is not considered.

**Financial data:** Stipends are either $5,000 or $1,000 per year. Funds are paid directly to the student's college or university for tuition, fees, and other educational expenses.

**Duration:** 4 years or 1 year.

**Number awarded:** 26 each year: 1 at $5,000 per year for 4 years, 5 at $1,000 per year for 4 years, and 20 at $1,000 for 1 year.

**Deadline:** February of each year.

## 451 HORATIO ALGER MILITARY VETERANS SCHOLARSHIP

Horatio Alger Association of Distinguished Americans, Inc.
99 Canal Center Plaza
Alexandria, VA 22314
Phone: (703) 684-9444; Fax: (703) 684-9445; Email: horatioaa@aol.com
Web: www.horatioalger.com/scholarships_military

**Summary:** To provide financial assistance for college to veterans who served in the Iraq/Afghanistan theater.

**Eligibility:** Open to veterans who served in the U.S. military in the Iraq/Afghanistan theater beginning in 2001 or later. Applicants must be planning to enter college to work on a bachelor's degree at an accredited institution (they may begin at a 2-year college and then transfer to a 4-year college or university). They must be U.S. citizens or in the process of becoming a citizen, demonstrate critical financial need ($50,000 or less adjusted gross income per family is preferred), have a GPA of 2.0 or higher, and evidence integrity and perseverance in the face of adversity. Along with their application, they must submit 3 essays: 1) explaining how their current financial situation qualifies them for financial assistance to attend college (50 to 100 words); 2) describing the adversities they have faced in detail and what they have done to overcome and cope with those obstacles (250 to 350 words); and 3) a personal statement (150 to 200 words). Selection is based on integrity, perseverance in overcoming adversity, strength of character, academic record, commitment to pursue a college education, desire to contribute to society, and financial need.

**Financial data:** A stipend is awarded (amount not specified).

**Duration:** Up to 4 years.

**Number awarded:** 1 or more each year.

**Deadline:** August of each year.

### 452 HORATIO ALGER NATIONAL SCHOLARSHIP FINALIST PROGRAM

Horatio Alger Association of Distinguished Americans, Inc.

99 Canal Center Plaza

Alexandria, VA 22314

Phone: (703) 684-9444; Fax: (703) 684-9445; Email: horatioaa@aol.com

Web: www.horatioalger.com/scholarships/program_national_finalist.cfm

**Summary:** To provide financial assistance for college to students who have demonstrated academic achievement as well as tenacity and courage in overcoming obstacles.

**Eligibility:** Open to seniors at high schools in states that do not currently have a state scholarship program of the Horatio Alger Association of Distinguished Americans. Applicants must be planning to enter college in the fall following graduation and work on a bachelor's degree at an accredited institution (they may begin at a 2-year college and then transfer to a 4-year college or university). They must be U.S. citizens or in the process of becoming a citizen, demonstrate critical financial need ($50,000 or less adjusted gross income per family is preferred), have a GPA of 2.0 or higher, and evidence perseverance in the face of adversity. Examples of adversity include having been in foster care or a ward of the state; having been homeless; experiencing the death, incarceration, or abandonment of a parent or guardian; living in a household where alcohol or drugs are or were abused; having a physical or mental disability or serious illness; or suffering from physical or mental abuse. Along with their application, they must submit 3 essays: 1) explaining how their current financial situation qualifies them for financial assistance to attend college (50 to 100 words); 2) describing the adversities they have faced in detail and what they have done to overcome and cope with those obstacles (250 to 350 words); and 3) selecting a member of the Horatio Alger Association and explaining how and why they intend to apply the virtues and principles exemplified in the life of that member to reach their personal goals (150 to 200 words).

**Financial data:** The stipend is $1,000.

**Duration:** 1 year.

**Number awarded:** 200 each year.

**Deadline:** The end of September for applications submitted on paper; mid-October for applications submitted online.

### 453 HORATIO ALGER NATIONAL SCHOLARSHIP PROGRAM

Horatio Alger Association of Distinguished Americans, Inc.

99 Canal Center Plaza

Alexandria, VA 22314

Phone: (703) 684-9444; Fax: (703) 684-9445; Email: horatioaa@aol.com

Web: www.horatioalger.com/scholarships/program_national.cfm

**Summary:** To provide financial assistance for college to students who have demonstrated academic achievement as well as tenacity and courage in overcoming obstacles.

**Eligibility:** Open to seniors at high schools in all 50 states, the District of Columbia, and Puerto Rico. Applicants must be planning to enter college in the fall following graduation and work on a bachelor's degree at an accredited institution (they may begin at a 2-year college and then transfer to a 4-year college or university). They must be U.S. citizens or in the process of becoming a citizen, demonstrate critical financial need ($50,000 or less adjusted gross income per family is preferred), have a GPA of 2.0 or higher, and evidence perseverance in the face of adversity. Examples of adversity include having been in foster care or a ward of the state; having been homeless; experiencing the death, incarceration, or abandonment of a parent or guardian; living in a household where alcohol or drugs are or were abused; having a physical or mental disability or serious illness; or suffering from physical or mental abuse. Along with their application, they must submit 3 essays: 1) explaining how their current financial situation qualifies them for financial assistance to attend college (50 to 100 words); 2) describing the adversities they have faced in detail and what they have done to overcome and cope with those obstacles (250 to 350 words); and 3) selecting a member of the Horatio Alger Association and explaining how and why they intend to apply the virtues and principles exemplified in the life of that member to reach their personal goals (150 to 200 words).

**Financial data:** The stipend is $10,000, distributed over 4 years.

**Duration:** 4 years.

**Number awarded:** 100 each year.

**Deadline:** The end of September for applications submitted on paper; mid-October for applications submitted online.

### 454 HORIZON SCHOLARSHIPS

Maine Employers' Mutual Insurance Company, Attn: MEMIC Education Fund

261 Commercial Street

P.O. Box 11409

Portland, ME 04104

Phone: (207) 791-3300; (800) 660-1306; Fax: (207) 791-3335;

Email: mbourque@memic.com

Web: www.memic.com

**Summary:** To provide financial assistance for college or graduate school to Maine residents whose parent or spouse was killed or permanently disabled in a work-related accident.

**Eligibility:** Open to Maine residents who are the child or spouse of a worker killed or permanently disabled as the result of a work-related injury. The worker must have been insured through the sponsor at the time of the workplace injury. Applicants must be attending or planning to attend an accredited college or university as an undergraduate or graduate student. They must submit a personal statement of 500 words or less on their aspirations and how their educational plans relate to them. Selection is based on financial need, academic performance, community involvement, and other life experiences.

**Financial data:** Stipends range up to $5,000, depending on the need of the recipient. Funds are paid directly to the recipient's institution.

**Duration:** 1 year; may be renewed.

**Number awarded:** Varies each year; recently, 2 of these scholarships were awarded.

**Deadline:** April of each year.

### 455 HOWARD STILES NUCHOLS SCHOLARSHIP

United Daughters of the Confederacy-Virginia Division

c/o Suzie Snyder, Education Committee Chair

8440 Bradshaw Road

Salem, VA 24153-2246

Phone: (540) 384-6884; Email: Suzienotes@aol.com

Web: users.erols.com/va-udc/scholarships.html

**Summary:** To provide financial assistance for college to Confederate descendants from Virginia.

**Eligibility:** Open to residents of Virginia who are 1) lineal descendants of Confederates, or 2) collateral descendants and also members of the Children of the Confederacy or the United Daughters of the Confederacy (UDC). Applicants must submit proof of the Confederate military record of at least 1 ancestor, with the company and regiment in which he served. They must also submit a personal letter pledging to make the best possible use of the scholarship; describing their health, social, family, religious, and fraternal connections within the community; and reflecting on what a Southern heritage means to them (using the term "War Between the States" in lieu of "Civil War"). They must have a GPA of 3.0 or higher and be able to demonstrate financial need. Preference is given to applicants who are current or former members of the Virginia division of the Children of the Confederacy.

**Financial data:** The amount of the stipend depends on the availability of funds. Payment is made directly to the college or university the recipient attends.

**Duration:** 1 year; may be renewed up to 3 additional years if the recipient maintains a GPA of 3.0 or higher.

**Number awarded:** This scholarship is offered whenever a prior recipient graduates or is no longer eligible.

**Deadline:** May of years in which the scholarship is available.

### 456 H.S. AND ANGELINE LEWIS SCHOLARSHIPS

American Legion Auxiliary

Department of Wisconsin, Attn: Department Secretary/Treasurer

2930 American Legion Drive

P.O. Box 140

Portage, WI 53901-0140

Phone: (608) 745-0124; (866) 664-3863; Fax: (608) 745-1947;

Email: alawi@amlegionauxwi.org

Web: www.amlegionauxwi.org

**Summary:** To provide financial assistance for undergraduate or graduate study to Wisconsin residents who are related to veterans or members of the American Legion Auxiliary.

**Eligibility:** Open to the children, wives, and widows of veterans who are high school seniors or graduates with a GPA of 3.2 or higher. Granddaughters as well as great-granddaughters of veterans are eligible if they are members of the American Legion Auxiliary. Applicants must be able to demonstrate financial need, be interested in working on an undergraduate or graduate degree, and be residents of Wisconsin. They do not need to attend a college in the state. Along with their application, they must submit a 300-word essay on "Education-An Investment in the Future."

**Financial data:** The stipend is $1,000.

**Duration:** 1 year; nonrenewable.

**Number awarded:** 6 each year: 1 to a graduate student and 5 to undergraduates.

**Deadline:** March of each year.

## 457 HUBERT K. SEYMOUR SCHOLARSHIP

National Farmers Union, Attn: Director of Education
11900 East Cornell Avenue
Aurora, CO 80014
Phone: (303) 337-5500; (800) 347-1961, ext. 2529; Fax: (303) 368-1390;
Email: jennifer.luitjens@nfu.org
Web: www.nfu.org

**Summary:** To provide financial assistance for college to high school seniors who are members of the National Farmers Union.

**Eligibility:** Open to graduating high school seniors who are planning to continue their education in a 2-year or 4-year accredited college or university. Applicants must be members of the National Farmers Union. They may be planning to major in any field. Along with their application, they must submit an essay on the significance of rural values in America on their life. Selection is based on the essay, academic record, and school and community activities. A telephone interview is also required.

**Financial data:** The stipend is $2,000. Funds may be used for tuition and books.

**Duration:** 1 year.

**Number awarded:** 1 each year.

**Deadline:** February of each year.

## 458 HUEBNER/ZIMMERMAN SCHOLARSHIPS

Society of the First Infantry Division, Attn: 1st Infantry Division Foundation
1933 Morris Road
Blue Bell, PA 19422-1422
Phone: (888) 324-4733; Fax: (215) 661-1934; Email: soc1ID@aol.com
Web: www.bigredone.org/foundation/scholarships.cfm

**Summary:** To provide financial support for college to the children or grandchildren of members of the First Infantry Division.

**Eligibility:** Open to high school seniors who are the children or grandchildren of soldiers who served in the First Infantry Division of the U.S. Army. Applicants must submit academic transcripts, letters of recommendation, and a 200-word essay on a major problem facing the country today and their recommendations for the solution of the problem. Selection is based on the applicant's scholastic accomplishments and career objectives, along with insight gained from the essay and letters of recommendation.

**Financial data:** The stipend is $1,000 per year, payable to the recipient's school annually.

**Duration:** 4 years.

**Number awarded:** Varies each year; recently, 4 of these scholarships were awarded.

**Deadline:** May of each year.

## 459 IDAHO FREEDOM SCHOLARSHIPS

Idaho State Board of Education
Len B. Jordan Office Building
650 West State Street, Room 307
P.O. Box 83720
Boise, ID 83720-0037
Phone: (208) 332-1574; Fax: (208) 334-2632; Email: board@osbe.state.id.us
Web: www.idahoboardofed.org/scholarships/freedom.asp

**Summary:** To provide financial assistance for college to dependent children of Idaho veterans who are listed as prisoners of war or missing in action.

**Eligibility:** Open to the dependent children of Idaho veterans who are listed as prisoners of war (POW) or missing in action (MIA) in southeast Asia (including Korea) or who become listed as POW or MIA in any area of armed conflict in which the United States is a party.

**Financial data:** Each scholarship provides a full waiver of tuition and fees at public institutions of higher education or public vocational schools within Idaho, an allowance of $500 per semester for books, and on-campus housing and subsistence.

**Duration:** Benefits are available for a maximum of 36 months.

**Number awarded:** Varies each year.

## 460 IDAHO GOVERNOR'S CHALLENGE ACADEMIC SCHOLARSHIP

Idaho State Board of Education
Len B. Jordan Office Building
650 West State Street, Room 307
P.O. Box 83720
Boise, ID 83720-0037
Phone: (208) 332-1574; Fax: (208) 334-2632; Email: board@osbe.state.id.us
Web: www.idahoboardofed.org/scholarships/challenge.asp

**Summary:** To provide financial assistance to outstanding high school seniors in Idaho who wish to attend a postsecondary institution in the state.

**Eligibility:** Open to graduating high school seniors who are U.S. citizens, Idaho residents, and planning to enroll full time at an eligible postsecondary educational institution in the state. Applicants must have maintained a GPA of 2.8 or better, must take the ACT or SAT examinations, and must have demonstrated a commitment to public service.

**Financial data:** The stipend is $3,000 per year.

**Duration:** 1 year; may be renewed for up to 3 additional years.

**Number awarded:** 6 each year.

**Deadline:** December of each year.

## 461 IDAHO GOVERNOR'S CHALLENGE PROFESSIONAL-TECHNICAL SCHOLARSHIP

Idaho State Board of Education
Len B. Jordan Office Building
650 West State Street, Room 307
P.O. Box 83720
Boise, ID 83720-0037
Phone: (208) 332-1574; Fax: (208) 334-2632; Email: board@osbe.state.id.us
Web: www.idahoboardofed.org/scholarships/challenge.asp

**Summary:** To provide financial assistance to outstanding high school seniors in Idaho who wish to attend a professional/technical school in the state.

**Eligibility:** Open to graduating high school seniors who are U.S. citizens, Idaho residents, and planning to enroll full time in a professional/technical program in the state. Applicants must have maintained a GPA of 2.8 or better and have demonstrated a commitment to public service. They must identify their proposed program; selection is based in part on their identified professional-technical program.

**Financial data:** The stipend is $3,000 per year.

**Duration:** 1 year; may be renewed for up to 2 additional years.

**Number awarded:** 6 each year.

**Deadline:** December of each year.

## 462 IDAHO LEVERAGING EDUCATIONAL ASSISTANCE STATE PARTNERSHIP PROGRAM

Idaho State Board of Education
Len B. Jordan Office Building
650 West State Street, Room 307
P.O. Box 83720
Boise, ID 83720-0037
Phone: (208) 332-1574; Fax: (208) 334-2632; Email: board@osbe.state.id.us
Web: www.idahoboardofed.org/scholarships/leap.asp

**Summary:** To provide financial assistance to students from any state attending a college or university in Idaho.

**Eligibility:** Open to students from any state attending a designated public or private college or university within Idaho. Applicants must have financial need; they may be enrolled part time.

**Financial data:** Awards range up to $5,000 per year for full-time students.

**Number awarded:** Varies each year; recently, approximately 1,800 students received these grants.

## 463 IDAHO MINORITY AND "AT RISK" STUDENT SCHOLARSHIP

Idaho State Board of Education
Len B. Jordan Office Building
650 West State Street, Room 307
P.O. Box 83720
Boise, ID 83720-0037
Phone: (208) 332-1574; Fax: (208) 334-2632; Email: board@osbe.state.id.us
Web: www.idahoboardofed.org/scholarships/minority.asp

**Summary:** To provide financial assistance for college to disabled and other "at risk" high school seniors in Idaho.

**Eligibility:** Open to talented students who may be at risk of failing to meet their goals because of physical, economic, or cultural limitations. Applicants must be high school graduates, be Idaho residents, and meet at least 3 of the following 5 requirements: 1) have a disability; 2) be a member of an ethnic minority group historically underrepresented in higher education in Idaho; 3) have substantial financial need; 4) be a first-generation college student; 5) be a migrant farm worker or a dependent of a farm worker.

**Financial data:** The maximum stipend is $3,000 per year.

**Duration:** 1 year; may be renewed for up to 3 additional years.

**Number awarded:** Approximately 40 each year.

## 464 IDAHO PUBLIC SAFETY OFFICER DEPENDENT SCHOLARSHIP

Idaho State Board of Education
Len B. Jordan Office Building
650 West State Street, Room 307
P.O. Box 83720
Boise, ID 83720-0037
Phone: (208) 332-1574; Fax: (208) 334-2632; Email: board@osbe.state.id.us
Web: www.idahoboardofed.org/scholarships/freedom.asp

**Summary:** To provide financial assistance for college to dependents of disabled or deceased Idaho public safety officers.

**Eligibility:** Open to the dependents of full-time Idaho public safety officers employed in the state who were killed or disabled in the line of duty.

**Financial data:** Each scholarship provides a full waiver of tuition and fees at public institutions of higher education or public vocational schools within Idaho, an allowance of $500 per semester for books, and on-campus housing and a campus meal plan.

**Duration:** Benefits are available for a maximum of 36 months.

**Number awarded:** Varies each year; recently, 4 of these scholarships were awarded.

## 465 ILLINOIS AMVETS JUNIOR ROTC SCHOLARSHIPS

AMVETS-Department of Illinois
2200 South Sixth Street
Springfield, IL 62703
Phone: (217) 528-4713; (800) 638-VETS (within IL); Fax: (217) 528-9896
Web: www.amvets.com/scholarship.htm

**Summary:** To provide financial assistance for college to high school seniors in Illinois who have participated in Junior ROTC (JROTC), especially children and grandchildren of veterans.

**Eligibility:** Open to seniors graduating from high schools in Illinois who have taken the ACT or SAT and have participated in the JROTC program. Financial need is considered in the selection process. Priority is given to children and grandchildren of veterans.

**Financial data:** The stipend is $1,000 per year.

**Duration:** 4 years.

**Number awarded:** 1 or more each year.

**Deadline:** February of each year.

## 466 ILLINOIS AMVETS SERVICE FOUNDATION SCHOLARSHIPS

AMVETS-Department of Illinois
2200 South Sixth Street
Springfield, IL 62703
Phone: (217) 528-4713; (800) 638-VETS (within IL); Fax: (217) 528-9896
Web: www.amvets.com/scholarship.htm

**Summary:** To provide financial assistance for college to high school seniors in Illinois, especially children and grandchildren of veterans.

**Eligibility:** Open to seniors graduating from high schools in Illinois who have taken the ACT or SAT. Financial need is considered in the selection process. Priority is given to children and grandchildren of veterans.

**Financial data:** The stipend is $1,000 per year.

**Duration:** 4 years.

**Number awarded:** Up to 30 each year.

**Deadline:** February of each year.

## 467 ILLINOIS AMVETS TRADE SCHOOL SCHOLARSHIPS

AMVETS-Department of Illinois
2200 South Sixth Street
Springfield, IL 62703
Phone: (217) 528-4713; (800) 638-VETS (within IL); Fax: (217) 528-9896
Web: www.amvets.com/scholarship.htm

**Summary:** To provide financial assistance to high school seniors in Illinois, especially children and grandchildren of veterans, who are interested in attending trade school.

**Eligibility:** Open to seniors graduating from high schools in Illinois who have been accepted at an approved trade school. Financial need is considered in the selection process. Priority is given to children and grandchildren of veterans.

**Financial data:** The stipend is $1,000 per year.

**Duration:** 2 years.

**Number awarded:** 1 or more each year.

**Deadline:** February of each year.

## 468 ILLINOIS GENERAL ASSEMBLY SCHOLARSHIPS

Illinois State Board of Education
100 North First Street
Springfield, IL 62777-0001
Phone: (217) 782-4321; (866) 262-6663; Fax: (217) 524-4928; TTY: (217) 782-1900
Web: www.isbe.state.il.us/gov-relations/html/scholarships.htm

**Summary:** To provide financial assistance for college to high school seniors in Illinois who are sponsored by members of the state legislature.

**Eligibility:** Open to high school seniors in Illinois. Illinois law provides for each state legislator, each year, to award a 4-year scholarship to the University of Illinois and a 4-year scholarship or 4 1-year scholarships to any other state-supported university. High school seniors in Illinois applying for these scholarships must be a resident within the legislative district of the awarding legislator and contact their state senator or state representative for information on the application process.

**Financial data:** A stipend is awarded (amount not specified).

**Duration:** Either 1 year or 4 years.

**Number awarded:** Each state legislator awards two 4-year scholarships or one 4-year scholarship and four 1-year scholarships.

## 469 ILLINOIS GRANT PROGRAM FOR DEPENDENTS OF CORRECTIONAL OFFICERS

Illinois Student Assistance Commission, Attn: Scholarship and Grant Services
1755 Lake Cook Road
Deerfield, IL 60015-5209
Phone: (847) 948-8550; (800) 899-ISAC; Fax: (847) 831-8549;
TDD: (847) 831-8326, ext. 2822; Email: collegezone@isac.org
Web: www.collegezone.com

**Summary:** To provide financial assistance for college to the children or spouses of disabled or deceased Illinois correctional workers.

**Eligibility:** Open to the spouses and children of Illinois correctional officers who were at least 90% disabled or killed in the line of duty. Applicants must be enrolled on at least a half-time basis as an undergraduate at an approved Illinois public or private 2-year or 4-year college, university, or hospital school. They need not be Illinois residents at the time of application.

**Financial data:** The grants provide full payment of tuition and mandatory fees at approved public colleges in Illinois or an equivalent amount at private colleges.

**Duration:** Up to 8 academic semesters or 12 academic quarters of study.

**Number awarded:** Varies each year.

## 470 ILLINOIS GRANT PROGRAM FOR DEPENDENTS OF POLICE OR FIRE OFFICERS

Illinois Student Assistance Commission, Attn: Scholarship and Grant Services
1755 Lake Cook Road
Deerfield, IL 60015-5209
Phone: (847) 948-8550; (800) 899-ISAC; Fax: (847) 831-8549;
TDD: (847) 831-8326, ext. 2822; Email: collegezone@isac.org
Web: www.collegezone.com

**Summary:** To provide financial assistance for college or graduate school to the children or spouses of disabled or deceased Illinois police or fire officers.

**Eligibility:** Open to the spouses and children of Illinois police and fire officers who were at least 90% disabled or killed in the line of duty. Applicants must be enrolled on at least a half-time basis in either undergraduate or graduate study at an approved Illinois public or private 2-year or 4-year college, university, or hospital school. They need not be Illinois residents at the time of application.

**Financial data:** The grants provide full payment of tuition and mandatory fees at approved public colleges in Illinois or an equivalent amount at private colleges.

**Duration:** Up to 8 academic semesters or 12 academic quarters of study.

**Number awarded:** Varies each year.

## 471 ILLINOIS LEGION BOY SCOUT SCHOLARSHIPS

American Legion, Attn: Department of Illinois
2720 East Lincoln Street
P.O. Box 2910
Bloomington, IL 61702-2910
Phone: (309) 663-0361; Fax: (309) 663-5783; Email: hdqs@illegion.org
Web: www.illegion.org/scholarship.html

**Summary:** To provide financial assistance for college to Scouts in Illinois.

**Eligibility:** Open to residents of Illinois who are high school seniors and qualified Scouts or Venturers. Both males and females are eligible. Selection is based on a 500-word essay on the American Legion, Americanism, and Scouting.

**Financial data:** Awards are $1,000 or $200.

**Duration:** 1 year.

**Number awarded:** 5 each year: 1 at $1,000 and 4 runners-up at $200 each.

**Deadline:** April of each year.

## 472 ILLINOIS MERIT RECOGNITION SCHOLARSHIPS

Illinois Student Assistance Commission
Attn: Scholarship and Grant Services
1755 Lake Cook Road
Deerfield, IL 60015-5209
Phone: (847) 948-8550; (800) 899-ISAC; Fax: (847) 831-8549;
TDD: (847) 831-8326, ext. 2822; Email: collegezone@isac.org
Web: www.collegezone.com

**Summary:** To provide financial assistance for college to outstanding students in Illinois.

**Eligibility:** Open to Illinois high school seniors who either 1) rank in the top 5% of their class through the end of the sixth semester of high school, or 2) received a score in the top 5% of Illinois students on the ACT, SAT, or Prairie State Achievement Examination. U.S. citizenship or permanent resident status is required. Recipients must use the award within 1 year of high school graduation as at least a half-time student at an approved Illinois postsecondary institution or at 1 of the nation's 4 military service academies. Financial need is not considered in the selection process.

**Financial data:** The stipend is $1,000. Funds may be used for payment of tuition, fees, and other educational expenses.

**Duration:** 1 year; nonrenewable.

**Number awarded:** Varies each year.

**Deadline:** June of the year following high school graduation.

## 473 ILLINOIS MIA/POW SCHOLARSHIP

Illinois Department of Veterans' Affairs
833 South Spring Street
P.O. Box 19432
Springfield, IL 62794-9432
Phone: (217) 782-6641; (800) 437-9824 (within IL); Fax: (217) 524-0344;
TDD: (217) 524-4645; Email: webmail@dva.state.il.us
Web: www.state.il.us/agency/dva

**Summary:** To provide financial assistance for 1) the undergraduate education of Illinois dependents of disabled or deceased veterans or those listed as prisoners of war or missing in action, and 2) the rehabilitation or education of disabled dependents of those veterans.

**Eligibility:** Open to the spouses, natural children, legally adopted children, or stepchildren of a veteran or service member who 1) has been declared by the U.S. Department of Defense or the U.S. Department of Veterans Affairs to be permanently disabled from service-connected causes with 100% disability, deceased as the result of a service-connected disability, a prisoner of war, or missing in action, and 2) at the time of entering service was an Illinois resident or was an Illinois resident within 6 months of entering such service. Special support is available for dependents who are disabled.

**Financial data:** An eligible dependent is entitled to full payment of tuition and certain fees at any Illinois state-supported college, university, or community college. In lieu of that benefit, an eligible dependent who has a physical, mental, or developmental disability is entitled to receive a grant to be used to cover the cost of treating the disability at 1 or more appropriate therapeutic, rehabilitative, or educational facilities. For disabled dependents, the total benefit cannot exceed the cost equivalent of 4 calendar years of full-time enrollment, including summer terms, at the University of Illinois.

**Duration:** This scholarship may be used for a period equivalent to 4 calendar years, including summer terms. Dependents have 12 years from the initial term of study to complete the equivalent of 4 calendar years. Disabled dependents who elect to use the grant for rehabilitative purposes may do so as long as the total benefit does not exceed the cost equivalent of 4 calendar years of full-time enrollment at the University of Illinois.

**Number awarded:** Varies each year.

## 474 ILLINOIS MONETARY AWARD PROGRAM

Illinois Student Assistance Commission, Attn: Scholarship and Grant Services
1755 Lake Cook Road
Deerfield, IL 60015-5209
Phone: (847) 948-8550; (800) 899-ISAC; Fax: (847) 831-8549;
TDD: (847) 831 8326, ext. 2822; Email: collegezone@isac.org
Web: www.collegezone.com

**Summary:** To provide financial assistance to undergraduate students in Illinois.

**Eligibility:** Open to Illinois residents who are U.S. citizens or eligible noncitizens. They must be able to demonstrate financial need, be enrolled at least half time as an undergraduate student at an approved Illinois institution of higher education, and not be in default on any student loan. High school grades and test scores are not considered in the selection process.

**Financial data:** The actual dollar amount of the award depends on financial need and the cost of the recipient's schooling; in no case does the award exceed the actual cost of tuition and fees or $4,968 per year, whichever is less. The funds may be used only for tuition and mandatory fees; funds cannot be spent on books, travel, or housing. All awards are paid directly to the recipient's school.

**Duration:** 1 year; may be renewed up to 4 additional years.

**Number awarded:** Varies each year.

**Deadline:** Funding for this program is limited. To increase your chances of receiving funding, apply as soon after the beginning of January as possible.

## 475 ILLINOIS ODD FELLOWS-REBEKAH SCHOLARSHIP PROGRAM

Independent Order of Odd Fellows-Grand Lodge of Illinois
Attn: Grand Secretary
305 North Kickapoo Street
P.O. Box 248
Lincoln, IL 62656-0248
Phone: (217) 772-3469; Fax: (217) 735-2562; Email: glioof@ccaonline.com
Web: www.ioof-il.org/Scholarship.htm

**Summary:** To provide financial assistance to residents of Illinois who are interested in attending college, vocational school, or technical training school.

**Eligibility:** Open to U.S. citizens who are residents of Illinois, can show financial need, and wish to attend a postsecondary school or accredited vocational or technical training school. Applicants must have a GPA of 2.0 or higher. They must submit their application through the Grand Lodge Office. Selection is based on scholastic standing, academic ability, and financial need.

**Financial data:** Stipends are $1,000 or $500 per year.

**Duration:** 1 year.

**Number awarded:** Varies each year. Recently, 23 of these scholarships were awarded: 3 at $1,000 and 20 at $500.

**Deadline:** Applications must be requested by November of each year.

## 476 ILLINOIS VETERAN GRANT PROGRAM

Illinois Student Assistance Commission, Attn: Scholarship and Grant Services
1755 Lake Cook Road
Deerfield, IL 60015-5209
Phone: (847) 948-8550; (800) 899-ISAC; Fax: (847) 831-8549;
TDD: (847) 831-8326, ext. 2822; Email: collegezone@isac.org
Web: www.collegezone.com

**Summary:** To provide financial assistance for undergraduate and graduate education to Illinois veterans.

**Eligibility:** Open to Illinois residents who served in the U.S. armed forces (including members of the Reserves and the Illinois National Guard) for at least 1 year on active duty and have been honorably discharged. The 1-year service requirement does not apply to veterans who 1) served in a foreign country in a time of hostilities in that country, 2) were medically discharged for service-related reasons, or 3) were discharged prior to August 11, 1967. Applicants must have been Illinois residents for at least 6 months before entering service and they must have returned to Illinois within 6 months after separation from service. Current members of the Reserve Officer Training Corps are not eligible.

**Financial data:** This program pays all tuition and certain fees at all Illinois public colleges, universities, and community colleges.

**Duration:** This scholarship may be used for the equivalent of up to 4 years of full-time enrollment, provided the recipient maintains the minimum GPA required by their college or university.

**Number awarded:** Varies each year.

**Deadline:** Applications may be submitted at any time.

## 477 IMMUNE DEFICIENCY FOUNDATION SCHOLARSHIP

Immune Deficiency Foundation, Attn: Scholarship/Medical Programs
40 West Chesapeake Avenue, Suite 308
Towson, MD 21204-4803
Phone: (410) 321-6647; (800) 296-4433, ext. 211; Fax: (410) 321-9165;
Email: tb@primaryimmune.org
Web: www.primaryimmune.org/services/scholarship.htm

**Summary:** To provide financial assistance to undergraduates with a primary immune deficiency disease.

**Eligibility:** Open to students entering or attending colleges, universities, and community colleges who have a primary immune deficiency disease. Applicants must submit an autobiographical statement, 2 letters of recommendation, a family financial statement, and a letter of verification from their immunologist. Financial need is the main factor considered in selecting the recipients and the size of the award.

**Financial data:** Stipends range from $750 to $2,000, depending on the recipient's financial need.

**Duration:** 1 year; may be renewed.

**Number awarded:** Varies each year. Recently, 43 of these scholarships were awarded.

**Deadline:** March of each year.

## 478 INA BRUDNICK SCHOLARSHIP AWARD

Great Comebacks Award Program
c/o ConvaTec Customer Interaction Center
P.O. Box 5254
Princeton, NJ 08543-5254
Phone: (800) 422-8811; Email: info@greatcomebacks.com
Web: www.greatcomebacks.com/us/awardprogram/index.html

**Summary:** To provide financial assistance to college students with an inflammatory bowel disease (IBD) or other related physical conditions.

**Eligibility:** Open to people under 24 years of age who have undergone an ostomy and/or have an IBD (Crohn's disease or ulcerative colitis). Applicants must be able to demonstrate financial need. Along with their application, they must submit statements on how their life has been changed or affected by IBD or their ostomy, who or what helped them most in getting through their physical and emotional struggle, what advice they would give to someone struggling with IBD and/or facing ostomy surgery, and their dreams of what they want to accomplish in the future.

**Financial data:** The stipend is $2,500.

**Duration:** 1 year.

**Number awarded:** 1 each year.

**Deadline:** September of each year.

## 479 INDIANA BPW WOMEN IN TRANSITION SCHOLARSHIP

Indiana Business and Professional Women's Foundation, Inc.
P.O. Box 33
Knightstown, IN 46148-0033
Email: bpwin@msn.com
Web: www.indianabpwfoundation.org

**Summary:** To provide financial assistance for college to mature women in Indiana.

**Eligibility:** Open to women who are 30 years of age or older and have been an Indiana resident for at least 1 year. Applicants must be reentering the workforce, be changing careers, or be a displaced worker. They must have applied to a postsecondary institution for at least part-time attendance. Along with their application, they must submit 1) a statement (up to 200 words) on their career goals and how their education relates to those goals, and 2) documentation of financial need.

**Financial data:** A stipend is awarded (amount not specified). Funds are paid directly to the recipient's school.

**Duration:** 1 year; recipients may reapply.

**Number awarded:** 2 each year.

**Deadline:** February of each year.

## 480 INDIANA BPW WORKING WOMAN SCHOLARSHIP

Indiana Business and Professional Women's Foundation, Inc.
P.O. Box 33
Knightstown, IN 46148-0033
Email: bpwin@msn.com
Web: www.indianabpwfoundation.org

**Summary:** To provide financial assistance for college to women in Indiana who are also working at least part time.

**Eligibility:** Open to women who are 25 years of age or older and have been an Indiana resident for at least 1 year. Applicants must be employed at least 20 hours per week and must have applied to or be attending a postsecondary institution on at least a part-time basis. Along with their application, they must submit 1) a statement (up to 200 words) on their career goals and how their education relates to those goals, and 2) documentation of financial need.

**Financial data:** A stipend is awarded (amount not specified). Funds are paid directly to the recipient's school.

**Duration:** 1 year; recipients may reapply.

**Number awarded:** 2 each year.

**Deadline:** February of each year.

## 481 INDIANA CHILD OF VETERAN AND PUBLIC SAFETY OFFICER SUPPLEMENTAL GRANT PROGRAM

State Student Assistance Commission of Indiana, Attn: Grant Division
150 West Market Street, Suite 500
Indianapolis, IN 46204-2811
Phone: (317) 232-2350; (888) 528-4719 (within IN); Fax: (317) 232-3260;
Email: grants@ssaci.state.in.us
Web: www.in.gov/ssaci/programs/cvo.html

**Summary:** To provide financial assistance for undergraduate or graduate education to students in Indiana who are 1) the children of disabled or other veterans, and 2) the children and spouses of certain deceased or disabled public safety officers.

**Eligibility:** Open to Indiana residents who are the natural or adopted children of veterans who served in the active-duty U.S. armed forces during a period of wartime. Applicants may be of any age; parents must have lived in Indiana for at least 3 years during their lifetime. The veteran parent must also 1) have a service-connected disability as determined by the U.S. Department of Veterans Affairs or the Department of Defense; 2) have received a Purple Heart Medal; or 3) have been a resident of Indiana at the time of entry into the service and declared a POW or MIA after January 1, 1960. Students at the Indiana Soldiers' and Sailors' Children's Home are also eligible. In addition to the veteran part of the program, there is a public safety officer portion, which is open to 1) the children and spouses of regular law enforcement officers, regular fire fighters, volunteer fire fighters, county police reserve officers, city police reserve officers, paramedics, emergency medical technicians, and advanced emergency medical technicians killed in the line of duty, and 2) the children and spouses of Indiana state police troopers permanently and totally disabled in the line of duty. Children must be younger than 23 years of age and enrolled full time in an undergraduate or graduate degree program. Spouses must be enrolled in an undergraduate program and must have been married to the covered public safety officer at the time of death or disability.

**Financial data:** Qualified applicants receive a 100% remission of tuition and all mandatory fees for undergraduate or graduate work at state-supported postsecondary schools and universities in Indiana. It does not cover such fees as room and board.

**Duration:** Up to 124 semester hours of study.

**Number awarded:** Varies each year.

**Deadline:** Applications must be submitted at least 30 days before the start of the college term.

## 482 INDIANA KIDS' CHANCE SCHOLARSHIP PROGRAM

Kids' Chance of Indiana, Inc., Attn: Scholarship Committee
721 East Broadway
Fortville, IN 46040
Phone: (317) 485-0043, ext. 123; Fax: (317) 485-4299;
Email: office@kidschancein.org
Web: www.kidschancein.org

**Summary:** To provide financial assistance for college or graduate school to Indiana residents whose parent was killed or permanently disabled in a work-related accident.

**Eligibility:** Open to Indiana residents between 16 and 25 years of age who are the children of workers fatally or catastrophically injured as a result of a work-related accident or occupational disease. The death or injury must be compensable by the Workers' Compensation Board of the state of Indiana and must have resulted in a substantial decline in the family's income that is likely to impede the student's pursuit of his or her educational objectives. Applicants must be attending or planning to attend a trade/vocational school, junior/community college, 4-year college or university, or graduate school. Financial need is considered in the selection process.

**Financial data:** Stipends range up to $6,000 per year. Funds may be used for tuition and fees, books, room and board, and utilities.

**Duration:** 1 year; may be renewed.

**Number awarded:** Varies each year.

## 483 INDIANA PART-TIME GRANT PROGRAM

State Student Assistance Commission of Indiana, Attn: Grant Division
150 West Market Street, Suite 500
Indianapolis, IN 46204-2811
Phone: (317) 232-2350; (888) 528-4719 (within IN); Fax: (317) 232-3260;
Email: grants@ssaci.state.in.us
Web: www.in.gov/ssaci/programs/parttime.html

**Summary:** To provide financial assistance to Indiana residents who are working part time on an undergraduate degree.

**Eligibility:** Open to Indiana residents who are high school seniors, high school graduates, or GED certificate recipients. Applicants must be attending or planning to attend an eligible Indiana postsecondary institution as a part-time undergraduate student working on an associate's or first bachelor's degree. They must be able to demonstrate financial need for tuition assistance.

**Financial data:** The amount of the award depends on the availability of funds and the number of credit hours taken.

**Duration:** 1 term (quarter or semester); may be renewed.

**Number awarded:** Varies each year.

## 484 INDIANHEAD DIVISION SCHOLARSHIPS

Second (Indianhead) Division Association, Attn: Scholarship Foundation
c/o Ed Mize
4848 Highland Drive, Number 613
Salt Lake City, UT 84117-6007
Phone: (801) 277-7901; Email: mizedjean@hotmail.com
Web: www.swiftsite.com/2IDA

**Summary:** To provide financial assistance for college to children and grand-children of members of the Second (Indianhead) Division Association.

**Eligibility:** Open to 1) children and grandchildren of veterans who have been members of the association for the past 3 years and have a current membership, and 2) children and grandchildren of men or women killed in action while serving with the Second Division. Applicants may be high school seniors or currently-enrolled college students. They must submit a personal letter giving reasons for the request and plans for the future; a high school and, if appropriate, college transcript; ACT or SAT test scores; a statement from their school principal attesting to their character and involvement in extracurricular activities; 2 letters of recommendation from current teachers or professors; a 200- to 300-word essay on such subjects as "What Being an American Means to Me," "Why I Should Receive This Scholarship," or "What Significant Part of U.S. Army History Has the Second Infantry Division Contributed;" and a statement from their parents or guardians on the financial support they will be able to provide the applicant.

**Financial data:** The stipend is usually $1,000 per year.

**Duration:** 1 year; may be renewed.

**Number awarded:** 1 or more each year.

**Deadline:** May of each year.

## 485 INTERNATIONAL ARABIAN BREEDERS SWEEPSTAKES SCHOLARSHIPS

Arabian Horse Association, Attn: Sweepstakes Scholarships
10805 East Bethany Drive
Aurora, CO 80014
Phone: (303) 696-4500; Fax: (303) 696-4599
Web: www.arabianhorses.org/education/education_scholarships_foundation.asp

**Summary:** To provide financial assistance for college to high school seniors who are members of the Arabian Horse Association (AHA).

**Eligibility:** Open to AHA members who are graduating from high school and planning to attend an accredited college or university as a full-time student. Applicants must have competed at the regional or national level on a sweepstakes nominated horse. Along with their application, they must submit their most recent high school transcript, a list of sweepstakes horses and the regional or national competitions where they have shown, a description of their extracurricular activities and leadership roles, a list of any honors or academic distinctions they have received, a description of their specific equine involvement over the past 2 years, and a brief essay on their future career goals. Selection is based on merit.

**Financial data:** The stipend is $2,500.

**Duration:** 1 year.

**Number awarded:** 40 each year.

**Deadline:** June of each year.

## 486 IOWA DIVISION SCHOLARSHIPS

Midwest Dairy Association-Iowa Division, Attn: Industry Relations Manager
101 N.E. Trilein Drive
Ankeny, IA 50021
Phone: (515) 964-0696, ext. 14; Fax: (515) 964-5498;
Email: info@midwestdairy.com
Web: www.midwestdairy.com

**Summary:** To provide financial assistance for college to family members of dairy farmers in Iowa.

**Eligibility:** Open to producers who fund Midwest Dairy Association, their spouses, and their children. The producer must have an active dairy operation and must reside in Iowa. Applicants must be attending or planning to attend an accredited college or university as a full-time student, but there are no restrictions on the length of the program or major. Along with their application, they must submit an essay that includes their career aspirations, special dairy projects or other accomplishments, involvement in the dairy industry and/or participation in their family farm, and any special circumstances related to financial need. Selection is based on that essay (25 points), school leadership activities and events (20 points), other leadership activities and work experience (20 points), academic performance (20 points), and 2 to 3 references (15 points).

**Financial data:** Stipends are $1,000 or $500.

**Duration:** 1 year; recipients may reapply.

**Number awarded:** 11 each year: 3 at $1,000 and 8 at $500.

**Deadline:** February of each year.

## 487 IOWA GRANTS

Iowa College Student Aid Commission
200 Tenth Street, Fourth Floor
Des Moines, IA 50309-3609
Phone: (515) 242-3344; (800) 383-4222; Fax: (515) 242-3388;
Email: info@iowacollegeaid.org
Web: www.iowacollegeaid.org/scholarshipsandgrants/grantlist.html

**Summary:** To provide financial assistance for undergraduate study to needy Iowa residents.

**Eligibility:** Open to residents of Iowa who are enrolled or planning to enroll at least part time in an undergraduate degree program at an eligible state university, independent college or university, or area community college in the state. Selection is based on financial need, with priority given to the neediest applicants. U.S. citizenship or permanent resident status is required.

**Financial data:** The maximum grant is $1,000 per year (may be adjusted for less than full-time study).

**Duration:** Up to 4 years of undergraduate study.

**Number awarded:** More than 1,600 each year.

**Deadline:** Applicants must submit a FAFSA form as early as possible after January 1. For priority consideration, the form must be completed and mailed in time to reach the processing center by the third week in April.

## 488 IOWA KIDS' SCHOLARSHIPS

Kids' Chance of Iowa
c/o Vern Vogel
P.O. Box 7673
Des Moines, IA 50322
Phone: (515) 267-2848; Email: vvogel@hy-vee.com
Web: www.kidschanceiowa.org

**Summary:** To provide financial assistance for college to Iowa residents whose parent was killed or permanently disabled in an employment-related accident.

**Eligibility:** Open to Iowa residents between 17 and 25 years of age who have had a parent permanently or catastrophically injured or killed in an employment-related accident. Applicants must be attending or planning to attend an accredited college or technical school. The parent's death or injury must have resulted in a substantial decline in the family income.

**Financial data:** The stipend depends on the financial need of the recipient. Funding is intended to cover tuition and books, but it may also include housing and meals.

**Duration:** 1 year; may be renewed if the recipient maintains acceptable grades.

**Number awarded:** Varies each year.

## 489 IOWA MOTOR CARRIERS FOUNDATION SCHOLARSHIPS

Iowa Motor Truck Association, Attn: Iowa Motor Carriers Foundation
717 East Court Avenue
Des Moines, IA 50309
Phone: (515) 244-5193; Fax: (515) 244-2204;
Email: imta@iowamotortruck.com
Web: www.iowamotortruck.com/Scholarships/Foundation.asp

**Summary:** To provide financial assistance for college or the study of diesel technology to residents of Iowa.

**Eligibility:** Open to Iowa residents attending or planning to attend a college, university, trade school, or community college in the state. Applicants must submit a brief letter describing why they are applying for this scholarship, their intended career goal, its estimated cost, and their choices of educational institutions. Some scholarships are reserved for students in diesel technology. Selection is based on academic record, outside activities that pertain to school and community citizenship, and financial need.

**Financial data:** The stipend is $1,000.

**Duration:** 1 year.

**Number awarded:** 6 each year.

**Deadline:** March of each year.

## 490 IOWA TUITION GRANTS

Iowa College Student Aid Commission
200 Tenth Street, Fourth Floor
Des Moines, IA 50309-3609
Phone: (515) 242-3344; (800) 383-4222; Fax: (515) 242-3388;
Email: info@iowacollegeaid.org
Web: www.iowacollegeaid.org/scholarshipsandgrants/grantlist.html

**Summary:** To provide financial assistance to Iowa residents who are interested in attending a private college or university.

**Eligibility:** Open to residents of Iowa who are enrolled or planning to enroll at least part time in an undergraduate degree program at an eligible independent college or university in the state. Selection is based on financial need, with priority given to the neediest applicants. U.S. citizenship or permanent resident status is required.

**Financial data:** The maximum grant is $4,000 per year (may be adjusted for less than full-time study).

**Duration:** Up to 4 years of full-time undergraduate study.

**Number awarded:** More than 14,000 each year.

**Deadline:** Applicants must submit a FAFSA form as early as possible after January 1. For priority consideration, the form must be completed and mailed in time to reach the processing center by the end of June.

## 491 IOWA VOCATIONAL/TECHNICAL TUITION GRANTS

Iowa College Student Aid Commission
200 Tenth Street, Fourth Floor
Des Moines, IA 50309-3609
Phone: (515) 242-3344; (800) 383-4222; Fax: (515) 242-3388;
Email: info@iowacollegeaid.org
Web: www.iowacollegeaid.org/scholarshipsandgrants/grantlist.html

**Summary:** To provide financial assistance for study at vocational/technical schools to needy Iowa residents.

**Eligibility:** Open to residents of Iowa who are enrolled or planning to enroll at least part time in an Iowa career education or career option course lasting at least 12 weeks. Students enrolled in college parallel programs offered by area community colleges are not eligible. Financial need must be demonstrated. U.S. citizenship or permanent resident status is required.

**Financial data:** The maximum grant is $1,200 per year (may be adjusted for less than full-time study).

**Duration:** Up to 2 years of full-time undergraduate study.

**Number awarded:** Varies each year.

**Deadline:** Applicants must submit a FAFSA form as early as possible after January 1. For priority consideration, the form must be completed and mailed in time to reach the processing center by the end of June.

## 492 IRENE CORREIA RAMOS SCHOLARSHIP

Portuguese Heritage Scholarship Foundation, Attn: Academic Secretary
P.O. Box 30246
Bethesda, MD 20824-0246
Phone: (301) 652-2775; Email: phsf@vivaportugal.com
Web: www.vivaportugal.com/phsf/apply.htm

**Summary:** To provide financial assistance for college to students of Portuguese American heritage.

**Eligibility:** Open to high school seniors or currently-enrolled college students who are of Portuguese American ancestry. Applicants must be U.S. residents and attending or planning to attend an accredited 4-year college or university. Selection is based on academic achievement and financial need.

**Financial data:** The stipend is $2,000 per year.

**Duration:** 4 years, provided the recipient maintains a GPA of 3.0 or higher.

**Number awarded:** 1 each year.

**Deadline:** January of each year.

## 493 IRIS SCHOLARSHIP FUND

Finance Authority of Maine, Attn: Education Finance Programs
5 Community Drive
P.O. Box 949
Augusta, ME 04332-0949
Phone: (207) 623-3263; (800) 228-3734; Fax: (207) 623-0095;
TTY: (207) 626-2717; Email: info@famemaine.com
Web: www.famemaine.com

**Summary:** To provide financial assistance to Maine residents who are the first member of their family to attend college.

**Eligibility:** Open to residents of Maine who are high school seniors or full- or part-time college students. Applicants must be first generation college-bound students (neither parent holds an associate degree or higher). They must submit 2 letters of recommendation, a 250-word essay on why they need the scholarship and how they plan to use their education, and documentation of financial need.

**Financial data:** The stipend is $1,500 per year.

**Duration:** 1 year; may be renewed.

**Number awarded:** 1 or more each year.

**Deadline:** April of each year.

## 494 IRMA AND KNUTE CARLSON AWARD

Vasa Order of America, Attn: Vice Grand Master
3236 Berkeley Avenue
Cleveland Heights, OH 44118-2055
Phone: (216) 371-5141; Email: rolf.bergman@sbcglobal.net
Web: www.vasaorder.com

**Summary:** To provide financial assistance for undergraduate or graduate study to members of the Vasa Order of America.

**Eligibility:** Open to members of the organization (for at least 1 year) who are college juniors, seniors, or graduate students. Selection is based on a transcript, letters of recommendation from school and local Vasa lodge officials, and an essay of up to 1,000 words on a topic related to Vasa.

**Financial data:** The stipend is $1,000.

**Duration:** 1 year.

**Number awarded:** 1 each year.

**Deadline:** February of each year.

## 495 IRMA GESCHE SCHOLARSHIP

Rebekah Assembly of Texas, Attn: Scholarship Committee
16400 KC Road 4060
Scurry, TX 75158

**Summary:** To provide financial assistance for college to high school seniors in Texas.

**Eligibility:** Open to Texas high school seniors who are interested in attending a 2-year or 4-year college or university in the state. Selection is based on academic ability, community service, personal development, and financial need.

Applicants must submit a completed application along with a high school transcript, a typed letter describing their educational goals, and 3 letters of recommendation.

**Financial data:** The stipend is $1,000.

**Duration:** 1 year.

**Number awarded:** 1 each year.

**Deadline:** December of each year.

## 496 ISIA EDUCATION FOUNDATION SCHOLARSHIP

Ice Skating Institute of America, Attn: ISIA Education Foundation
17120 North Dallas Parkway, Suite 140
Dallas, TX 75248-1187
Phone: (972) 735-8800; Fax: (972) 735-8815; Email: kchase@skateisi.com
Web: www.skateisi.com

**Summary:** To provide financial assistance to high school seniors and currently-enrolled undergraduates who are members of the Ice Skating Institute of America (ISI).

**Eligibility:** Open to graduating high school seniors or currently-enrolled college students. They must have completed at least 3 years of high school with a GPA of 3.0 or higher, have been an individual member of ISI for at least 4 years, have participated in ISI group classes or ISI endorsed competitions within the last 2 years, and have completed 240 hours of verified service (of which 120 must be volunteered) with an ISI administrative member rink or skating school. Along with their application process, they must submit an official transcript, SAT/ACT scores, 2 evaluation forms, and a statement (up to 500 words) on "Why I should receive an ISIA Education Foundation Scholarship." Selection is based on community service, education awards and recognition, educational goals, and competitive ice skating experience.

**Financial data:** The stipend is at least $4,000 per year.

**Duration:** 1 year.

**Number awarded:** Varies each year; recently, 4 of these scholarships were awarded.

**Deadline:** February of each year.

## 497 IVYANE D.F. DAVIS MEMORIAL SCHOLARSHIP

Delaware Child Placement Review Board
Attn: Ivyane D.F. Davis Memorial Scholarship
820 North French Street
Wilmington, DE 19801
Phone: (302) 577-8750; Fax: (302) 577-2605
Web: www.state.de.us/cprb/scholarship.htm

**Summary:** To provide financial assistance for college to students who have been in the foster care system in Delaware.

**Eligibility:** Open to residents of Delaware (for at least 1 year prior to the application) who have been in foster care in the state. Selection is based on academic achievement, community service, participation in extracurricular activities, promise of success, and financial need.

**Financial data:** A stipend is awarded (amount not specified).

**Duration:** 1 year; may be renewed.

**Number awarded:** Varies each year.

**Deadline:** March of each year.

## 498 JACK KENT COOKE FOUNDATION SEPTEMBER 11 SCHOLARSHIPS

Jack Kent Cooke Foundation
44115 Woodridge Parkway, Suite 200
Lansdowne, VA 20176-5199
Phone: (703) 723-8000; (800) 846-9025; Fax: (703) 723-8030;
Email: jkc@jackkentcookefoundation.org
Web: www.jackkentcookefoundation.org

**Summary:** To provide financial assistance for college to family members of those directly affected by the events of September 11, 2001.

**Eligibility:** Open to 1) dependents and spouses of people killed aboard United Airlines Flight 93, American Airlines Flight 77, American Airlines Flight 11, or United Airlines Flight 175; 2) dependents or spouses of people killed, missing, or permanently disabled at the Pentagon or World Trade Center on September 11, 2001; and 3) dependents and spouses of persons killed in the anthrax attacks of September and October of 2001. Applicants must be working on an undergraduate degree at a 2-year, 4-year, technical, or trade school in the United States. Along with their application, they must submit documentation of financial need and (if appropriate) verification of the disability of a parent or spouse.

**Financial data:** Grants up to $15,000 per semester are available to help cover tuition, required fees, books, room, board, and other educational costs.

**Duration:** 1 semester. Recipients must reapply each school term.

**Number awarded:** A total of $1 million was set aside for this program. Grants are awarded on a first-come, first-served basis until all funds have been disbursed.

**Deadline:** June of each year.

## 499 JACK KENT COOKE UNDERGRADUATE TRANSFER SCHOLARSHIPS

Jack Kent Cooke Foundation
44115 Woodridge Parkway, Suite 200
Lansdowne, VA 20176-5199
Phone: (703) 723-8000; (800) 498-6478; Fax: (703) 723-8030;
Email: jkc@jackkentcookefoundation.org
Web: www.jackkentcookefoundation.org

**Summary:** To provide financial assistance to students at 2-year colleges planning to transfer to a 4-year college or university in the United States or abroad.

**Eligibility:** Open to students who are currently enrolled as sophomores at accredited U.S. community or 2-year colleges (or who graduated from such a college within the past 5 years). Candidates must be interested in transferring to a full-time baccalaureate program at an accredited college or university in the United States or abroad. They must be nominated by their college and have a GPA of 3.5 or higher. Selection is based on academic ability and achievement, critical thinking ability, financial need, will to succeed, leadership and public service, and appreciation for and participation in the arts and humanities. appreciation for and participation in the arts and humanities.

**Financial data:** Stipends up to $30,000 per year are provided. Funds are paid directly to the institution.

**Duration:** 1 year; may be renewed until completion of an undergraduate degree, as long as the fellow continues to meet the eligibility requirements.

**Number awarded:** Approximately 25 each year.

**Deadline:** Campus faculty representatives must submit applications by January of each year.

## 500 JACKIE CHAN SCHOLARSHIPS

US Pan Asian American Chamber of Commerce
Attn: Scholarship Coordinator
1329 18th Street, N.W.
Washington, DC 20036
Phone: (202) 296-5221; Fax: (202) 296-5225;
Email: administrator@uspaacc.com
Web: www.uspaacc.com/web/programs/jackie_chan.htm

**Summary:** To provide financial assistance for college to Asian American high school seniors who demonstrate special talents.

**Eligibility:** Open to high school seniors of Asian heritage who are U.S. citizens or permanent residents. Applicants must be planning to begin full-time study at an accredited postsecondary educational institution in the United States. Along with their application, they must submit a 500-word essay on "How do you plan to use your special talents to achieve your professional goals?" Selection is based on academic excellence (GPA of 3.3 or higher), leadership in extracurricular activities, community service involvement, and financial need.

**Financial data:** The maximum stipend is $8,000. Funds are paid directly to the recipient's college or university.

**Duration:** 1 year.

**Number awarded:** 2 each year.

**Deadline:** February of each year.

## 501 JACKIE ROBINSON SCHOLARSHIPS

Jackie Robinson Foundation
Attn: Education and Leadership Development Program
3 West 35th Street, 11th Floor
New York, NY 10001-2204
Phone: (212) 290-8600; Fax: (212) 290-8081;
Email: general@jackierobinson.org
Web: www.jackierobinson.org

**Summary:** To provide financial assistance for college to minority high school seniors.

**Eligibility:** Open to members of an ethnic minority group who are high school seniors accepted at a 4-year college or university. Applicants must be able to demonstrate high academic achievement (ACT score of 21 or higher or equivalent SAT scores), financial need, and leadership potential. U.S. citizenship is required.

**Financial data:** The stipend is $6,000 per year.
**Duration:** 4 years.
**Number awarded:** 100 or more each year.
**Deadline:** March of each year.

## 502 JAGANNATHAN SCHOLARSHIPS

North Carolina State Education Assistance Authority
Attn: Scholarship and Grant Services
10 T.W. Alexander Drive
P.O. Box 14103
Research Triangle Park, NC 27709-4103
Phone: (919) 549-8614; (800) 700-1775; Fax: (919) 549-8481;
Email: information@ncseaa.edu
Web: www.ncseaa.edu
**Summary:** To provide financial assistance to high school seniors planning to attend 1 of the branches of the University of North Carolina.
**Eligibility:** Open to high school seniors in North Carolina who are planning to attend any of the constituent institutions of the University of North Carolina as a full-time student. Special consideration is given to applicants whose parents are employees of TIEPET, Universal Fibers, and related companies. Selection is based on academic achievement (as measured by class rank, cumulative GPA, and SAT scores), leadership, and financial need.
**Financial data:** Awards cannot exceed demonstrated financial need, to a maximum of $3,500 per year.
**Duration:** 1 year; may be renewed up to 3 additional years if the recipient continues to demonstrate financial need and maintains satisfactory academic progress.
**Number awarded:** Varies each year; recently, a total of 14 students received $46,077 in scholarships through this program.
**Deadline:** February of each year.

## 503 JAMES LEE LOVE SCHOLARSHIPS

North Carolina State Education Assistance Authority
Attn: Scholarship and Grant Services
10 Alexander Drive
P.O. Box 14103
Research Triangle Park, NC 27709-4103
Phone: (919) 549-8614; (800) 700-1775; Fax: (919) 549-8481;
Email: information@ncseaa.edu
Web: www.ncseaa.edu
**Summary:** To provide financial assistance to residents of North Carolina who are attending or planning to attend a public university in the state.
**Eligibility:** Open to residents of North Carolina who are entering or attending a public university in the state. Applicants must be enrolled or planning to enroll full time and able to demonstrate financial need. Current high school seniors must rank in the top 25% of their graduating class; current university students must have a GPA of 3.0 or higher.
**Financial data:** The stipend depends on the availability of funds; recently, a total of $41,600 was awarded through this program.
**Duration:** 1 year; nonrenewable.
**Number awarded:** 16 each year: 1 at each constituent institution of the University of North Carolina system.
**Deadline:** February of each year.

## 504 JANICE RICHARDSON TECHNICAL SCHOLARSHIPS

Georgia PTA, Attn: Scholarship Committee
114 Baker Street, N.E.
Atlanta, GA 30308-3366
Phone: (404) 659-0214; Fax: (404) 525-0210; Email: gapta@bellsouth.net
Web: www.georgiapta.org
**Summary:** To provide financial assistance to residents of Georgia who are interested in attending a technical school in the state.
**Eligibility:** Open to seniors graduating from Georgia high school with a PTA/PTSA chapter that is in good standing with the Georgia PTA. Applicants must be interested in attending a technical school or other non-college postsecondary institution in the state to develop specific career skills. Selection is based on character, academic record, and financial need.
**Financial data:** Stipends range from $1,000 to $1,500.
**Duration:** 1 year; nonrenewable.
**Number awarded:** Varies each year.
**Deadline:** January of each year.

## 505 JAY RAMSDELL SCHOLARSHIPS

Jay Ramsdell Foundation, Attn: Daniel Lay
First National Bank
Trust Department
P.O. Box 258
Bar Harbor, ME 04609
Email: oct60@acadia.net
Web: www.jramsdellfoundation.org
**Summary:** To provide financial assistance for college to high school seniors in Maine who have been active in athletics.
**Eligibility:** Open to residents of Maine who are seniors graduating from a high school in the state. Students must be nominated by the athletic director at their high school; each director may nominate 1 student. Nominees must have been active in athletics; special attention is paid to team managers and statisticians. Financial need must be demonstrated, although need is not the primary consideration in making the award.
**Financial data:** The stipend is $5,000. Funds are paid to the college or university after the recipient has successfully completed the first semester and is enrolled for the second semester.
**Duration:** 1 year; recipients may reapply.
**Number awarded:** 1 each year.

## 506 JEANNE MANNFORD SCHOLARSHIP FOR LGBT LEADERSHIP

Parents, Families and Friends of Lesbians and Gays
Attn: National Scholarships Program
1726 M Street, N.W., Suite 400
Washington, DC 20036
Phone: (202) 467-8180, ext. 219; Fax: (202) 467-8194;
Email: schools@pflag.org
Web: www.pflag.org
**Summary:** To provide financial assistance for college to high school seniors and recent graduates who have a connection to Parents, Families and Friends of Lesbians and Gays (PFLAG).
**Eligibility:** Open to high school seniors and prior-year graduates who have not attended college. Applicants must have applied to an accredited high education institution to work on 1) an associate degree leading to transfer to complete a bachelor's degree, or 2) a bachelor's degree at a 4-year college or university. They must self-identify either as a gay, lesbian, bisexual, or transgender (GLBT) person or as a supporter of GLBT people. Along with their application, they must submit a high school transcript showing a GPA of 3.0 or higher, 2 letters of recommendation, and a 2-page essay discussing either their life as an LGBT student or how they have been involved with and supported the LGBT community. Financial need is also considered in the selection process. This scholarship is presented to the applicant who demonstrates outstanding leadership in the LGBT community.
**Financial data:** The stipend is $2,500.
**Duration:** 1 year; nonrenewable.
**Number awarded:** 1 each year.
**Deadline:** February of each year.

## 507 JEANNETTE RANKIN AWARD

Jeannette Rankin Foundation, Inc.
P.O. Box 6653
Athens, GA 30604-6653
Phone: (706) 208-1211; Fax: (706) 548-0202;
Email: info@rankinfoundation.org
Web: www.rankinfoundation.org
**Summary:** To provide financial assistance for college to women who are 35 years or older.
**Eligibility:** Open to women who are 35 years of age or older. if they are in financial need and have clear educational goals. They must be U.S. citizens and enrolled in a certified program of technical/vocational training or undergraduate education.
**Financial data:** The stipend is $2,000.
**Duration:** 1 year; nonrenewable.
**Number awarded:** Varies each year; recently, 45 of these scholarships were awarded.
**Deadline:** February of each year.

## 508 JEFF KROSNOFF SCHOLARSHIP

Jeff Krosnoff Scholarship Fund
P.O. Box 8585

La Crescenta, CA 91224-0585
Email: badjefft@charter.net
Web: www.krosnoffscholarship.com/Scholarship.htm
**Summary:** To provide financial assistance for college to high school seniors in California who submit outstanding essays.
**Eligibility:** Open to seniors graduating from high schools in California who plan to attend a 4-year college or university. Applicants must be able to demonstrate excellent academic credentials, a breadth of interests, a driving desire to succeed in their chosen endeavors, outstanding community citizenship, and the ability to share their experiences through the written word. They must have a GPA of 3.0 or higher. Selection is based on an essay on a topic that changes annually; recently, applicants were asked to select a song or poem that inspires them and to explain why.
**Financial data:** The stipend is $10,000.
**Duration:** 1 year.
**Number awarded:** 1 each year.
**Deadline:** January of each year.

## 509 JENNICA FERGUSON MEMORIAL SCHOLARSHIP
National Federation of the Blind
c/o Peggy Elliott, Scholarship Committee Chair
805 Fifth Avenue
Grinnell, IA 50112
Phone: (641) 236-3366
Web: www.nfb.org/sch_intro.htm
**Summary:** To provide financial assistance to undergraduate and graduate blind students.
**Eligibility:** Open to legally blind students who are working on or planning to work full time on an undergraduate or graduate degree. Selection is based on academic excellence, service to the community, and financial need.
**Financial data:** The stipend is $5,000.
**Duration:** 1 year; recipients may resubmit applications up to 2 additional years.
**Number awarded:** 1 each year.
**Deadline:** March of each year.

## 510 JENNINGS AND BEULAH HAGGERTY SCHOLARSHIP
Lincoln Community Foundation
215 Centennial Mall South, Suite 200
Lincoln, NE 68508
Phone: (402) 474-2345; Fax: (402) 476-8532; Email: lcf@lcf.org
Web: www.lcf.org
**Summary:** To provide financial assistance for college to high school seniors in Nebraska who can demonstrate financial need.
**Eligibility:** Open to seniors graduating from high schools in Nebraska who are interested in attending a 2-year or 4-year college or university in the state. Applicants must be in the upper one third of their graduating class and must apply for financial aid at the institution they plan to attend before approaching this sponsor for assistance. Along with their application, they must submit an essay on the topic: "If you could change one thing about your hometown, what would it be and why?"
**Financial data:** A stipend is awarded (amount not specified).
**Duration:** 1 year.
**Number awarded:** Varies each year; recently, 14 of these scholarships were awarded.
**Deadline:** June of each year.

## 511 JESSE BROWN MEMORIAL YOUTH SCHOLARSHIP PROGRAM
Disabled American Veterans
Attn: National Service and Legislative Headquarters
807 Maine Avenue, S.W.
Washington, DC 20024
Phone: (202) 554-3501
Web: www.dav.org/volunteers/jesse_brown_scholarship.html
**Summary:** To provide financial assistance to college students who demonstrate outstanding volunteer service to hospitalized disabled veterans.
**Eligibility:** Open to students who are 21 years of age or younger and have volunteered at least 100 hours for the Department of Veterans Affairs Voluntary Service (VAVS) programs to assist disabled veterans. They may be attending an accredited college, university, community college, or vocational school. Nominations must be submitted by Chiefs of Voluntary Services at VA medical centers. Self-nominations are also accepted if the student includes a 750-word essay on what volunteering at a VA medical center means to them.

**Financial data:** Stipends range up to $15,000.
**Duration:** Funds must be used before the recipient's 25th birthday.
**Number awarded:** Varies each year; since the establishment of the program, 63 scholarships worth $413,000 have been awarded.
**Deadline:** February of each year.

## 512 JESSICA POWELL LOFTIS SCHOLARSHIP FOR ACTEENS
Woman's Missionary Union, Attn: WMU Foundation
P.O. Box 11346
Birmingham, AL 35202-1346
Phone: (205) 408-5525; (877) 482-4483; Fax: (205) 408-5508;
Email: wmufoundation@wmu.org
Web: www.wmufoundation.com
**Summary:** To provide financial assistance for college or other activities to female high school seniors who have been active in the Southern Baptist Convention's Acteens (Academic/Events/Training).
**Eligibility:** Open to female high school seniors who are members of a Baptist church and active in Acteens. Applicants must 1) be planning to attend college and have completed *Quest for Vision* in the MissionsQuest program or StudiAct; 2) have been an Acteen for at least 1 year and be planning to attend an Acteens event; or 3) be an Acteens leader who is pursuing academic or leadership training to lead an Acteens group. Along with their application, they must submit an essay listing their major accomplishments and missions activities.
**Financial data:** A stipend is awarded (amount not specified).
**Duration:** 1 year.
**Number awarded:** 1 or more each year.
**Deadline:** September of each year.

## 513 IFWFLL HILTON BONNER SCHOLARSHIP
Navy League of the United States, Attn: Scholarships
2300 Wilson Boulevard
Arlington, VA 22201-3308
Phone: (703) 528-1775; (800) 356-5760; Fax: (703) 528-2333;
Email: cjarvis@navyleague.org
Web: www.navyleague.org/scholarship
**Summary:** To provide financial assistance for college to dependent children of sea service personnel, especially Native Americans.
**Eligibility:** Open to U.S. citizens who are 1) dependents or direct descendants of an active, Reserve, retired, or honorably discharged member of the U.S. sea service (including the Navy, Marine Corps, Coast Guard, or Merchant Marines), or 2) currently an active member of the Naval Sea Cadet Corps. Applicants must be entering their freshman year of college. Along with their application, they must submit transcripts, 2 letters of recommendation, SAT/ACT scores, documentation of financial need, proof of qualifying sea service duty, and a 1-page personal statement on why they should be considered for this scholarship. Preference is given to applicants of Native American heritage.
**Financial data:** The stipend is $2,500 per year.
**Duration:** 4 years, provided the recipient maintains a GPA of 3.0 or higher.
**Number awarded:** 1 each year.
**Deadline:** February of each year.

## 514 J.F. SCHIRMER SCHOLARSHIP
American Mensa Education and Research Foundation
1229 Corporate Drive West
Arlington, TX 76006-6103
Phone: (817) 607-0060; (800) 66-MENSA; Fax: (817) 649-5232;
Email: Scholarships@merf.us.mensa.org
Web: merf.us.mensa.org/scholarships/index.php
**Summary:** To provide financial assistance for undergraduate or graduate study to qualified students.
**Eligibility:** Open to any student who is enrolled or will enroll in a degree program at an accredited American institution of postsecondary education in the fall following the application deadline. Membership in Mensa is not required, but applicants must be U.S. citizens or permanent residents. There are no restrictions as to age, race, gender, level of postsecondary education, GPA, or financial need. Selection is based on a 550-word essay that describes the applicant's career, vocational, or academic goals.
**Financial data:** The stipend is $1,000.
**Duration:** 1 year; may be renewed for up to 3 additional years if the recipient remains in school and achieves satisfactory grades.
**Number awarded:** 1 each year.
**Deadline:** January of each year.

### 515 JIM AND MARY PEARCE SCHOLARSHIPS

Easter Seals South Carolina, Attn: Scholarship Program
3020 Farrow Road
Columbia, SC 29203
Phone: (803) 256-0735, ext. 27; TDD: (800) 951-4090, ext. 27;
Fax: (803) 765-9765
Web: sc.easterseals.com
**Summary:** To provide financial assistance for college or graduate school to South Carolina students who have a disability.
**Eligibility:** Open to South Carolina residents and students attending a college or university in the state who have a significant and medically certified mobility impairment. Applicants must be enrolled or planning to enroll in an undergraduate or graduate program. They must be able to demonstrate financial need. Preference is given to students carrying at least 9 credit hours and making satisfactory academic progress toward graduation.
**Financial data:** The maximum stipend is $1,000.
**Duration:** 1 year; may be renewed.
**Number awarded:** 1 or more each year.
**Deadline:** June of each year.

### 516 JIM KINNEY SCHOLARSHIP

Illinois Association of Realtors
Attn: Illinois Real Estate Educational Foundation
3180 Adloff Lane, Suite 400
P.O. Box 19451
Springfield, IL 62794-9451
Phone: (217) 529-2600; Email: IARaccess@iar.org
Web: www.illinoisrealtor.org/iar/about/scholarships.htm
**Summary:** To provide financial assistance for college to children and grandchildren of Illinois realtors.
**Eligibility:** Open to the children and grandchildren of 1) members of the Illinois Association of Realtors, and 2) employees of a local, state or national association of realtors in Illinois. Applicants must be attending or planning to attend a college or university. Along with their application, they must submit a 1,000-word statement that covers their general activities and intellectual interests, employment, planned line of study, and career they expect to follow; a description of their proposed program of study; transcripts; and 2 letters of recommendation. Selection is based on academic achievement, economic need, and letters of recommendation.
**Financial data:** A stipend is awarded (amount not specified).
**Duration:** 1 year.
**Number awarded:** 1 or more each year.
**Deadline:** March of each year.

### 517 JIMMY RANE FOUNDATION SCHOLARSHIPS

Jimmy Rane Foundation
1100 Highway 431 North
P.O. Box 40
Abbeville, AL 36310
Phone: (334) 585-9505; (866) 606-2470;
Email: info@jimmyranefoundation.org
Web: www.jimmyranefoundation.org
**Summary:** To provide financial assistance for college to students who can demonstrate financial need.
**Eligibility:** Open to high school seniors and students enrolled in college or vocational institutions; preference is given to high school seniors. Applicants must submit a biography that includes school and unpaid community activities, special awards, honors, and offices held; an essay on why they feel they should be awarded this scholarship, including their plans as they relate to their education, career, and long-term goals; 3 letters of recommendation; and documentation of financial need.
**Financial data:** 1 year; may be renewed up to 3 additional years.
**Duration:** The stipend depends on the need of the recipient.
**Number awarded:** Varies each year; recently, 17 of these were awarded.
**Deadline:** February of each year.

### 518 JOANNE HOLBROOK PATTON MILITARY SPOUSE SCHOLARSHIP PROGRAM

National Military Family Association, Inc., Attn: Spouse Scholarship Program
2500 North Van Dorn Street, Suite 102
Alexandria, VA 22302-1601
Phone: (703) 931-NMFA; (800) 260-0218; Fax: (703) 931-4600;
Email: families@nmfa.org
Web: www.nmfa.org
**Summary:** To provide financial assistance for college or graduate school to spouses of active and retired uniformed services personnel.
**Eligibility:** Open to the spouses of uniformed services personnel (active, retired, Reserve, Guard, or survivor). Applicants must be attending or planning to attend an accredited postsecondary institution to work on a professional certificate or undergraduate or graduate degree. Selection is based on an essay question, community involvement, and academic achievement.
**Financial data:** The stipend is $1,000. Funds are paid directly to the educational institution to be used for tuition, fees, books, and school room and board.
**Duration:** 1 year; recipients may reapply.
**Number awarded:** Varies each year; recently, 25 of these were awarded.
**Deadline:** March of each year.

### 519 JOE FOSS, AN AMERICAN HERO SCHOLARSHIP

Sioux Falls Area Community Foundation, Attn: Scholarship Coordinator
300 North Phillips Avenue, Suite 120
Sioux Falls, SD 57104-6006
Phone: (605) 336-7055; Fax: (605) 336-0038; Email: sbrown@sfacf.org
Web: www.sfacf.org
**Summary:** To provide financial assistance for college to high school seniors in South Dakota.
**Eligibility:** Open to seniors graduating from high schools in South Dakota. Applicants must have a GPA of 3.5 or higher and an ACT score of at least 21. They must be able to demonstrate the characteristics of an American patriot. Along with their application, they must submit an essay either on "What is an American Patriot?" or an event or individual that was helpful to them in forming their value system.
**Financial data:** The stipend is $1,000. Funds are paid in 2 equal installments and are to be used for tuition, fees, and/or books.
**Duration:** 1 year.
**Number awarded:** Varies each year; recently, 6 of these were awarded.
**Deadline:** March of each year.

### 520 JOEL ABROMSON MEMORIAL SCHOLARSHIP

EqualityMaine
1 Pleasant Street, Fourth Floor
P.O. Box 1951
Portland, ME 04104
Phone: (207) 761-3732; Fax: (207) 828-8620; Email: info@equalitymaine.org
Web: www.equalitymaine.org
**Summary:** To provide financial assistance for college to high school seniors in Maine who submit an essay on preventing discrimination based on sexual orientation.
**Eligibility:** Open to seniors graduating from high schools in Maine who are planning to attend a college or university. Applicants must submit an essay on "How can schools become safer for all students regardless of their sexual orientation and gender expression?"
**Financial data:** The stipend is $1,000.
**Duration:** 1 year; nonrenewable.
**Number awarded:** 2 each year.
**Deadline:** April of each year.

### 521 JOHN AND ABIGAIL ADAMS SCHOLARSHIP PROGRAM

Massachusetts Office of Student Financial Assistance
454 Broadway, Suite 200
Revere, MA 02151
Phone: (617) 727-9420; Fax: (617) 727-0667; Email: osfa@osfa.mass.edu
Web: www.osfa.mass.edu
**Summary:** To provide financial assistance for college to Massachusetts residents who earn high scores on the MCAS tests.
**Eligibility:** Open to permanent Massachusetts residents who are U.S. citizens or permanent residents. Applicants must score "Advanced" in either the mathematics or the English language section of the grade 10 MCAS and score either "Advanced" or "Proficient" in the other of those 2 sections. They must also have a combined MCAS score on those assessments that ranks in the top 25% in their school district and be planning to enroll full time at a Massachusetts public college or university.
**Financial data:** Recipients of these scholarships are eligible for an award of a

non-need-based tuition waiver for state-supported undergraduate courses in Massachusetts.

**Duration:** Up to 4 academic years, provided the student maintains a college GPA of 3.0 or higher.

**Number awarded:** Varies each year.

### 522 JOHN B. LYNCH SCHOLARSHIP

John B. Lynch Scholarship Foundation
P.O. Box 4248
Wilmington, DE 19807-0248
Phone: (302) 654-3444; Email: info@johnblynchfoundation.com
Web: www.johnblynchfoundation.com

**Summary:** To provide financial assistance for college to students who reside or attend school in Delaware or nearby areas.

**Eligibility:** Open to 1) seniors graduating from high schools in Delaware and planning to attend college in any state; 2) students currently attending college in Delaware (regardless of place of permanent residence); and 3) students who live in an adjoining state (Pennsylvania, New Jersey, or Maryland) within 20 miles of Delaware and attending college in any state. Graduating high school seniors must have a GPA of 3.0 or higher and a recent SAT score that's above average. Current undergraduate students must have a GPA of 2.75 or higher. Priority is given to students already enrolled in college. Students working on a second bachelor's degree are eligible if they received no support from this foundation for their first undergraduate degree. Applicants must be younger than 30 years of age and attending or planning to attend college on a full-time basis. Selection is based on academic achievement and financial need.

**Financial data:** The stipend is normally $2,500 per year.

**Duration:** Up to 4 years.

**Number awarded:** Varies each year.

**Deadline:** March of each year.

### 523 JOHN C. ROUILLARD AND ALICE TONEMAH MEMORIAL SCHOLARSHIPS

National Indian Education Association, Attn: Awards Committee
700 North Fairfax Street, Suite 210
Alexandria, VA 22314
Phone: (703) 838-2870; Fax: (703) 838-1620; Email: niea@niea.org
Web: www.niea.org

**Summary:** To provide financial assistance for college or graduate school to members of the National Indian Education Association (NIEA).

**Eligibility:** Open to American Indians, Native Hawaiians, and Alaska Natives working full time on an associate's, bachelor's, master's, or doctoral degree. Applicants must be members of NIEA and be nominated by a member. They must have demonstrated leadership qualities, maintained high academic achievement, served as a role model for other students, and shown creativity or commitment in the following areas: 1) promoted an understanding and an appreciation of Native American culture in an educational setting; 2) demonstrated positive, active leadership in student affairs; 3) demonstrated and/or encouraged student involvement in educational or community activities; and/or 4) achieved their educational goals and objectives.

**Financial data:** Stipends range from $1,500 to $2,500. Funds may be used for educational expenses not covered by other sources.

**Duration:** 1 year.

**Number awarded:** 1 or more each year.

**Deadline:** September of each year.

### 524 JOHN D. O'BRYANT NATIONAL THINK TANK FOR BLACK PROFESSIONALS IN HIGHER EDUCATION ON PREDOMINANTLY WHITE CAMPUSES MERIT SCHOLARSHIPS

John D. O'Bryant National Think Tank for Black Professionals in Higher Education on Predominantly White Campuses
c/o Jonathan Hopkins, Director, Alana Services
Loyola College
Student Center, Room 313
4501 North Charles Street
Baltimore, MD 21220
Phone: (410) 617-2310; Email: jhopkins@loyola.edu
Web: www.jdott.org/scholarship.html

**Summary:** To provide financial assistance to Black undergraduate students attending predominantly white colleges and universities.

**Eligibility:** Open to Black students who are enrolled full time at a predominantly white 2-year or 4-year college or university in the United States.

Applicants must be undergraduates who have completed at least 30 credit hours with a GPA of 3.0 or higher. Along with their application, they must submit a 2-page statement explaining why they deserve and/or need the scholarship, transcripts, letters of recommendation, and a 500-word essay; recently, the essay topic related to the impact of the civil rights movement on Black Americans.

**Financial data:** Regional winners receive $1,000 scholarships; the national winner receives an additional $1,000.

**Duration:** 1 year.

**Number awarded:** 6 regional scholarships are awarded each year; 1 of those recipients is selected as the national winner.

**Deadline:** March of each year.

### 525 JOHN GYLES EDUCATION AWARDS

John Gyles Education Fund, Attn: Secretary
165 Riverside Drive
P.O. Box 4808, Station A
Fredericton, New Brunswick E3B 5G4
Canada
Phone: (506) 459-7460
Web: www.johngyleseducationcenter.com

**Summary:** To provide financial assistance for college to American and Canadian residents.

**Eligibility:** Open to full-time students who are citizens of the United States or Canada. Applicants must have a GPA of 2.7 or higher. Along with their application, they must submit an essay on their career plans, goals, and personal ambitions. Selection is based on academic ability, financial need, and other criteria.

**Financial data:** Stipends up to $3,000 are provided.

**Duration:** 1 year.

**Number awarded:** Varies each year.

**Deadline:** May or November of each year.

### 526 JOLLY GREEN MEMORIAL SCHOLARSHIP

Jolly Green Association, Attn: Secretary
P.O. Box 965
O'Fallon, IL 62269
Email: bill6100@aol.com
Web: www.jollygreen.org/jolly_green_memorial_scholarship.htm

**Summary:** To provide financial assistance for college to dependents of current and former members of the Air Force Combat Rescue or Support Forces.

**Eligibility:** Open to high school seniors who are dependents of current or former uniformed members of the USAF Combat Rescue or Support Forces. Applicants must have taken the ACT or SAT examinations and be eligible for admission to the college or university of their choice. Selection is based on academic achievement (40%), scholastic or public service achievements (10%), and financial need (50%).

**Financial data:** A stipend is awarded (amount not specified).

**Duration:** 1 year.

**Number awarded:** 1 or more each year.

**Deadline:** April of each year.

### 527 JON C. LADDA MEMORIAL FOUNDATION SCHOLARSHIP

Jon C. Ladda Memorial Foundation
P.O. Box 55
Unionville, CT 06085
Email: info@jonladda.org
Web: www.jonladda.org

**Summary:** To provide financial assistance for college to children of deceased and disabled U.S. Naval Academy graduates and members of the Navy submarine service.

**Eligibility:** Open to children of U.S. Naval Academy graduates and members of the U.S. Navy submarine service. The parent must have died on active duty or been medically retired with a 100% disability. Applicants must be enrolled or accepted at a 4-year college or university, including any of the service academies. Along with their application, they must submit an essay on the topic, "When choosing a leader, what quality is most important to you and how does that reflect your values?" Selection is based on academic achievement, financial need, and merit.

**Financial data:** A stipend is awarded (amount not specified). Funds are disbursed directly to the recipient's institution.

**Duration:** 1 year; may be renewed.

**Number awarded:** 1 or more each year.

**Deadline:** March of each year.

## 528 JON OOSTERMEYER MEMORIAL SCHOLARSHIP

Arabian Horse Foundation, Attn: Scholarship Office
Ten Farnham Park Drive
Houston, TX 77024-7501
Phone: (713) 952-7081; Fax: (713) 977-9883;
Email: jean@parkwaychevrolet.com
Web: pages.sbcglobal.net/jvenhaus/horse/Scholar/scholar.html
**Summary:** To provide financial assistance to undergraduate and graduate students who have a record of equine involvement.
**Eligibility:** Open to students who have a record of involvement with horses. Applicants must be enrolled or planning to enroll as a full-time undergraduate or graduate student at an accredited college or university. High school seniors must have a GPA of B or higher; college students must have at least a 3.5 GPA. Along with their application, they must submit information on their financial need, honors or academic awards, extracurricular activities and offices, leadership role, career goal, and equine involvement for the past 2 years.
**Financial data:** A stipend is awarded (amount not specified).
**Duration:** 1 year; may be renewed if the recipient maintains a GPA of 2.5 or higher with no grade below a D.
**Number awarded:** 1 or more each year.
**Deadline:** January of each year.

## 529 JOSEPH AND MARION GREENBAUM SCHOLARSHIP FUND

Jewish Federation of Delaware, Attn: Jewish Fund for the Future
100 West Tenth Street, Suite 301
Wilmington, DE 19801-1628
Phone: (302) 427-2100, ext. 20; Fax: (302) 427-2438;
Email: gina.kozicki@shalomdelaware.org
Web: www.shalomdelaware.org
**Summary:** To provide financial assistance to Jewish undergraduates from Delaware studying in Israel or Jewish studies in the United States and to Jewish students from outside the United States studying in Delaware.
**Eligibility:** Open to (in order of priority) 1) Jewish residents of Delaware who wish to attend a college in Israel as an undergraduate; 2) Jewish residents of Delaware who wish to major or minor in Jewish studies at a college or university in the United States; 3) graduates of Delaware Gratz Hebrew High School or other full-day Jewish high school in Delaware who are enrolled or planning to enroll in an undergraduate college program in the United States; and 4) Jewish students from Israel or other foreign country who wish to work on an undergraduate degree at a college or university in Delaware. Residents of adjacent communities (Elkton, Maryland or the Pennsylvania towns of Avondale, Chadds Ford, Kennett Square, Landenberg, Lincoln University, or Westchester) are also eligible. Applicants must submit a brief essay on what they have learned or hope to learn during the proposed course of study and what they hope to be able to carry with them throughout their lifetime as a result of the courses. Selection is based on the essay, GPA, references, volunteer and community activity, and information about the study program abroad or the courses the applicant plans to take. Financial need is considered only if there are more applicants than available funds or if the applicant is seeking funds beyond the amount of the current guideline award; lack of financial need does not disqualify any applicant.
**Financial data:** The stipend is normally $2,500 per year for study in Israel; $625 per year for graduates of Gratz Hebrew High School; or $83 per credit for Jewish studies or for foreign students in Delaware.
**Duration:** 1 year.
**Number awarded:** Varies each year.
**Deadline:** July of each year for study during the fall semester or winter session; November of each year for spring semester or summer session.

## 530 JOSEPH B. FERNANDES SCHOLARSHIP

Portuguese Heritage Scholarship Foundation, Attn: Academic Secretary
P.O. Box 30246
Bethesda, MD 20824-0246
Phone: (301) 652-2775; Email: phsf@vivaportugal.com
Web: www.vivaportugal.com/phsf/apply.htm
**Summary:** To provide financial assistance for college to students of Portuguese American heritage.
**Eligibility:** Open to high school seniors or currently-enrolled college students who are of Portuguese American ancestry. Applicants must be U.S. residents and attending or planning to attend an accredited 4-year college or university. Selection is based on academic achievement and financial need.
**Financial data:** The stipend is $2,000 per year.
**Duration:** 4 years, provided the recipient maintains a GPA of 3.0 or higher.
**Number awarded:** 1 each year.
**Deadline:** January of each year.

## 531 JOSEPHINE DE KARMAN FELLOWSHIPS

Josephine de Karman Fellowship Trust, Attn: Judy McClain, Secretary
P.O. Box 3389
San Dimas, CA 91773
Phone: (909) 592-0607
Web: www.dekarman.org
**Summary:** To provide financial assistance to outstanding college seniors or students in their last year of a Ph.D. program.
**Eligibility:** Open to students in any discipline who will be entering their senior undergraduate year or their terminal year of a Ph.D. program in the fall of the next academic year. Postdoctoral students are not eligible. Foreign students may apply if they are already enrolled in a university in the United States. Applicants must be able to demonstrate exceptional ability and seriousness of purpose. Special consideration is given to applicants in the humanities and to those who have completed their qualifying examinations for the doctoral degree.
**Financial data:** The stipend is $16,000 per year. Funds are paid in 2 installments to the recipient's school. No funds may be used for travel.
**Duration:** 1 year; may not be renewed or postponed.
**Number awarded:** Approximately 10 each year.
**Deadline:** January of each year.

## 532 KANSAS BPW EDUCATIONAL FOUNDATION CAREER DEVELOPMENT SCHOLARSHIP

Kansas Federation of Business & Professional Women's Clubs, Inc.
Attn: Kansas BPW Educational Foundation
c/o Diane Smith, Executive Secretary
10418 Haskins
Lenexa, KS 66215-2162
Email: desmith@fcbankonline.com
Web: www.bpwkansas.org/bpw_foundation.htm
**Summary:** To provide financial assistance to residents of Kansas who are interested in broadening their education and/or increasing their earning abilities.
**Eligibility:** Open to Kansas residents (men and women) who have a career and want to broaden their education and/or increase their earning abilities. Applicants must submit a 3-page personal biography in which they express their career goals, the direction they want to take in the future, their proposed field of study, their reason for selecting that field, the institutions they plan to attend and why, their circumstances for reentering school (if a factor), and what makes them uniquely qualified for this scholarship. They must also be able to document financial need. Applications must be submitted through a local unit of the sponsor.
**Financial data:** A stipend is awarded (amount not specified).
**Duration:** 1 year.
**Number awarded:** 1 or more each year.
**Deadline:** December of each year.

## 533 KANSAS BPW EDUCATIONAL FOUNDATION CAREER PREPARATORY SCHOLARSHIP

Kansas Federation of Business & Professional Women's Clubs, Inc.
c/o Diane Smith, Executive Secretary
10418 Haskins
Lenexa, KS 66215-2162
Email: desmith@fcbankonline.com
Web: www.bpwkansas.org/bpw_foundation.htm
Attn: Kansas BPW Educational Foundation
**Summary:** To provide financial assistance to residents of Kansas who are interested in working on a 1- or 2-year college degree or certificate.
**Eligibility:** Open to Kansas residents (men and women) who are enrolled in either a 1- or 2-year academic, career, vocational, or technical program that will qualify them for immediate employment or transfer to a 4-year undergraduate program. Applicants must submit a 3-page personal biography in which they express their career goals, the direction they want to take in the future, their proposed field of study, their reason for selecting that field, the institutions they plan to attend and why, their circumstances for reentering school (if a factor), and what makes them uniquely qualified for this scholarship. They must also be able to document financial need. Applications must be submitted through a local unit of the sponsor.
**Financial data:** A stipend is awarded (amount not specified).
**Duration:** 1 year.
**Number awarded:** 1 or more each year.
**Deadline:** December of each year.

## 534 KANSAS BPW EDUCATIONAL FOUNDATION UNDERGRADUATE SCHOLARSHIP

Kansas Federation of Business & Professional Women's Clubs, Inc.
Attn: Kansas BPW Educational Foundation
c/o Diane Smith, Executive Secretary
10418 Haskins
Lenexa, KS 66215-2162
Email: desmith@fcbankonline.com
Web: www.bpwkansas.org/bpw_foundation.htm

**Summary:** To provide financial assistance for college to residents of Kansas.
**Eligibility:** Open to Kansas residents (men and women) who are college sophomores, juniors, or seniors enrolled in a 4-year academic program at an accredited college or university. Applicants must submit a 3-page personal biography in which they express their career goals, the direction they want to take in the future, their proposed field of study, their reason for selecting that field, the institutions they plan to attend and why, their circumstances for reentering school (if a factor), and what makes them uniquely qualified for this scholarship. They must also be able to document financial need. Applications must be submitted through a local unit of the sponsor.
**Financial data:** A stipend is awarded (amount not specified).
**Duration:** 1 year.
**Number awarded:** 1 or more each year.
**Deadline:** December of each year.

## 535 KANSAS COMPREHENSIVE GRANTS

Kansas Board of Regents, Attn: Student Financial Aid
1000 S.W. Jackson Street, Suite 520
Topeka, KS 66612-1368
Phone: (785) 296-3518; Fax: (785) 296-0983; Email: dlindeman@ksbor.org
Web: www.kansasregents.com/financial_aid/awards.html

**Summary:** To provide need-based grants to Kansas residents who are attending college in the state.
**Eligibility:** Open to residents of Kansas who are enrolled full time at 1) 18 private colleges and universities located in the state, 2) the 6 public universities, or 3) Washburn University. Financial need must be demonstrated.
**Financial data:** Stipends range from $200 to $3,000 per year at the private institutions and from $100 to $1,100 at the public institutions.
**Duration:** 1 year; may be renewed as long as the recipient remains in academic "good standing" and is able to demonstrate financial need.
**Number awarded:** Varies; generally, 7,000 or more each year. The funding level allows about 1 in 3 eligible students to be assisted.
**Deadline:** March of each year.

## 536 KANSAS EDUCATIONAL BENEFITS FOR DEPENDENTS OF POWS/KIAS/MIAS OF THE VIETNAM WAR

Kansas Commission on Veterans' Affairs
Jayhawk Towers
700 S.W. Jackson Street, Suite 701
Topeka, KS 66603-3150
Phone: (785) 296-3976; Fax: (785) 296-1462; Email: KVH007@ink.org
Web: www.kcva.org

**Summary:** To provide financial assistance for college to children of Kansas veterans who were prisoners of war or killed in Vietnam.
**Eligibility:** Open to residents of any state, as long as their veteran parent was a legal resident of Kansas upon entering military service and, while serving in Vietnam after January 1, 1960, either died of service-connected causes or was declared by the Secretary of Defense to be a prisoner of war or missing in action.
**Financial data:** Eligible dependents receive free tuition and fees at any Kansas state-supported college, university, community college, or area vocational school.
**Duration:** Up to 12 semesters.
**Number awarded:** Varies each year.

## 537 KANSAS ENROLLMENT WITHOUT CHARGE FOR DEPENDENTS OF DECEASED PUBLIC SAFETY OFFICERS.

Kansas Board of Regents, Attn: Student Financial Aid
1000 S.W. Jackson Street, Suite 520
Topeka, KS 66612-1368
Phone: (785) 296-3518; Fax: (785) 296-0983; Email: dlindeman@ksbor.org
Web: www.kansasregents.com/financial_aid/awards.html

**Summary:** To provide financial assistance for college to residents of Kansas whose parent died in the line of duty as a public safety officer.
**Eligibility:** Open to residents of Kansas who are the dependent children of public safety officers (law enforcement officers, fire fighters, and emergency medical services attendants) who died as the result of injuries sustained in the line of duty. Applicants must be enrolled or planning to enroll full time at educational institutions in Kansas, including area vocational/technical schools and colleges, community colleges, regents universities, and Washburn University.
**Financial data:** Qualifying students are permitted to enroll at an approved Kansas institution without payment of tuition or fees. They are responsible for other costs, such as books, and room and board.
**Duration:** 1 year; may be renewed up to 8 semesters of full-time enrollment.
**Number awarded:** Varies each year.

## 538 KANSAS ENROLLMENT WITHOUT CHARGE FOR FOSTER CHILDREN PROGRAM

Kansas Board of Regents, Attn: Student Financial Aid
1000 S.W. Jackson Street, Suite 520
Topeka, KS 66612-1368
Phone: (785) 296-3518; Fax: (785) 296-0983; Email: dlindeman@ksbor.org
Web: www.kansasregents.com/financial_aid/awards.html

**Summary:** To provide financial assistance for college to residents of Kansas who have been in foster care.
**Eligibility:** Open to residents of Kansas who were 1) foster care children in the custody of the Department of Social and Rehabilitation Services at age 18; 2) in foster care placement while graduating from high school or completing their GED requirements prior to their 18th birthday; or 3) adopted from foster care after 16 years of age. Applicants must be enrolled or planning to enroll full time at educational institutions in Kansas, including area vocational/technical schools and colleges, community colleges, regents universities, and Washburn University. Enrollment must begin within 2 years following graduation from high school or completion of GED requirements.
**Financial data:** Qualifying students are permitted to enroll at an approved Kansas institution without payment of tuition or fees. They are responsible for other costs, such as books, room, and board.
**Duration:** 1 year; may be renewed as long as the recipient remains enrolled as a full-time undergraduate and employed an average of at least 10 hours per week.
**Number awarded:** Varies each year. No institution is required to honor more than 5 waivers in any academic year.

## 539 KANSAS ETHNIC MINORITY SCHOLARSHIP PROGRAM

Kansas Board of Regents, Attn: Student Financial Aid
1000 S.W. Jackson Street, Suite 520
Topeka, KS 66612-1368
Phone: (785) 296-3518; Fax: (785) 296-0983; Email: dlindeman@ksbor.org
Web: www.kansasregents.com/financial_aid/minority.html

**Summary:** To provide financial assistance to minority students who are interested in attending college in Kansas.
**Eligibility:** Open to Kansas residents who fall into 1 of these minority groups: American Indian, Alaskan Native, African American, Asian, Pacific Islander, or Hispanic. Applicants may be current college students (enrolled in community colleges, colleges, or universities in Kansas), but high school seniors graduating in the current year receive priority consideration. Minimum academic requirements include 1 of the following: 1) ACT score of 21 or higher or the equivalent on the SAT; 2) cumulative GPA of 3.0 or higher; 3) high school rank in upper 33%; 4) completion of the Kansas Scholars Curriculum (4 years of English, 3 years of mathematics, 3 years of science, 3 years of social studies, and 2 years of foreign language); 5) selection by the National Merit Corporation in any category; or 6) selection by the College Board as a Hispanic Scholar.
**Financial data:** A stipend of up to $1,850 is provided, depending on financial need and availability of state funds.
**Duration:** 1 year; may be renewed for up to 3 additional years (4 additional years for designated 5-year programs) if the recipient maintains a 2.0 cumulative GPA and has financial need.
**Number awarded:** Approximately 200 each year.
**Deadline:** April of each year.

## 540 KANSAS STATE SCHOLARSHIPS

Kansas Board of Regents, Attn: Student Financial Aid
1000 S.W. Jackson Street, Suite 520
Topeka, KS 66612-1368
Phone: (785) 296-3518; Fax: (785) 296-0983; Email: dlindeman@ksbor.org
Web: www.kansasregents.com/financial_aid/state.html

**Summary:** To provide need-based assistance to students who are in the top of their high school class in Kansas and planning to attend college.

**Eligibility:** Open to high school seniors in Kansas who are designated as State Scholars. Selection for this program is based on ACT Assessment scores (recently, the average score of designees was 29), completion of the Kansas Scholars Curriculum (4 years of English, 4 years of mathematics, 3 years of science, 3 years of social studies, 2 years of foreign language, and 1 year of computer technology), and academic record (recently, the average GPA of designees was 3.90). State Scholars who demonstrate financial need are eligible for these scholarships.

**Financial data:** The stipend ranges up to $1,000 per year, depending upon the recipient's financial need.

**Duration:** Up to 4 academic years (unless enrolled in a designated 5-year program) as long as the recipient maintains a 3.0 GPA and financial need.

**Number awarded:** Varies; generally, at least 1,200 each year. Generally, between 20 and 40% of high school seniors who complete the Kansas Scholars Curriculum are designated as Kansas State Scholars.

**Deadline:** April of each year.

## 541 KAPLAN/NEWSWEEK "MY TURN" ESSAY COMPETITION

Kaplan, Inc., Attn: Pre-College
1440 Broadway, Ninth Floor
New York, NY 10018
Phone: (212) 997-5886; (800) KAP-TEST
Web: www.kaptest.com/oneoff/essay/index.jhtml

**Summary:** To recognize and reward, with college scholarships, high school students who write outstanding essays on topics related to their personal development and growth.

**Eligibility:** Open to U.S. high school students planning to attend college after graduation. Applicants must write an essay of 500 to 1,000 words on a topic of their choice that is similar in format to the weekly "My Turn" column in *Newsweek* magazine, in which a member of the public shares an opinion, experience, or personal feeling. Judges look for direct personal experiences and observations with a fresh, original, engaging, moving, and thought-provoking point of view that appeals to a national readership. Selection is based on 1) effectiveness, insightfulness, creativity, and completeness; 2) organization and development of the ideas expressed, with clear and appropriate examples to support them; and 3) consistency in the use of language, variety in sentence structure and range of vocabulary, and use of proper grammar, spelling, and punctuation.

**Financial data:** First prize is $5,000, second $2,000, and third $1,000. All funds are to be used for future educational needs.

**Duration:** The competition is held annually.

**Number awarded:** 10 each year: 1 first-prize winner, 1 second-prize winner, and 8 third-prize winners.

**Deadline:** February of each year.

## 542 KAREN B. LEWIS CAREER EDUCATION SCHOLARSHIP

Business and Professional Women of Virginia, Attn: Virginia BPW Foundation
P.O. Box 4842
McLean, VA 22103-4842
Web: www.bpwva.org/Foundation.shtml

**Summary:** To provide financial assistance to girls and women pursuing post-secondary job-oriented career education (in business, trade, or industrial occupations) in Virginia.

**Eligibility:** Open to women who are at least 18 years of age; are U.S. citizens and Virginia residents; have been accepted into an accredited training program in Virginia; have a definite plan to use their education in a business, trade, or industrial occupation; and are able to demonstrate financial need. They may not be pursuing education leading to a bachelor's or higher degree.

**Financial data:** Stipends range from $100 to $1,000 per year; funds may be used for tuition, fees, books, transportation, living expenses, and dependent care.

**Duration:** Funds must be used within 12 months. Prior recipients may reapply, but they are not given priority.

**Number awarded:** At least 1 is awarded each year.

**Deadline:** March of each year.

## 543 KATHERN F. GRUBER SCHOLARSHIPS

Blinded Veterans Association
477 H Street, N.W.
Washington, DC 20001-2694
Phone: (202) 371-8880; (800) 669-7079; Fax: (202) 371-8258;
Email: bva@bva.org

Web: www.bva.org/services.html

**Summary:** To provide financial assistance for undergraduate or graduate study to spouses and children of blinded veterans.

**Eligibility:** Open to dependent children and spouses of blinded veterans of the U.S. armed forces. The veteran need not be a member of the Blinded Veterans Association. The veteran's blindness may be either service connected or nonservice connected, but it must meet the following definition: central visual acuity of 20/200 or less in the better eye with corrective glasses, or central visual acuity of more than 20/200 if there is a field defect in which the peripheral field has contracted to such an extent that the widest diameter of visual field subtends an angular distance no greater than 20 degrees in the better eye. The applicant must have been accepted or be currently enrolled as a full-time student in an undergraduate or graduate program at an accredited institution of higher learning. Selection is based on high school and/or college transcripts, 3 letters of recommendation, and a 300-word essay on the applicant's career goals and aspirations.

**Financial data:** The stipends are $2,000 or $1,000 and are intended to be used to cover the student's expenses, including tuition, other academic fees, books, dormitory fees, and cafeteria fees. Funds are paid directly to the recipient's school.

**Duration:** 1 year; recipients may reapply.

**Number awarded:** 6 each year: 3 at $2,000 and 3 at $1,000.

**Deadline:** April of each year.

## 544 KCTCS PRESIDENTIAL SCHOLARSHIPS

Kentucky Community and Technical College System, Attn: Financial Aid
300 North Main Street
Versailles, KY 40383
Phone: (859) 256-3100; (877) 528-2748 (within KY)
Web: www.kctcs.edu/student/financialaidscholarships/index.htm

**Summary:** To provide financial assistance to students at participating institutions within the Kentucky Community and Technical College System (KCTCS).

**Eligibility:** Open to students entering or attending participating KCTCS institutions. Each college establishes its own selection criteria, but most are based on academic excellence and financial need.

**Financial data:** Stipends vary at each participating college, but are intended to provide full payment of tuition and required fees.

**Duration:** 1 year; may be renewed 1 additional year.

**Number awarded:** Varies each year.

**Deadline:** Each college sets its own deadline.

## 545 KENJI KASAI MEMORIAL SCHOLARSHIP

Japanese American Citizens League, Attn: National Scholarship Awards
1765 Sutter Street
San Francisco, CA 94115
Phone: (415) 921-5225; Fax: (415) 931-4671; Email: jacl@jacl.org
Web: www.jacl.org/scholarships.html

**Summary:** To provide financial assistance for college to student members of the Japanese American Citizens League (JACL) who are high school seniors.

**Eligibility:** Open to JACL members who are high school seniors interested in attending a college, university, trade school, business college, or other institution of higher learning. Applicants must submit a statement describing their current level of involvement in the Japanese American community or Asian Pacific community and how they will continue their involvement in future years. Selection is based on academic record, extracurricular activities, and community involvement.

**Financial data:** The stipend depends on the availability of funds but usually ranges from $1,000 to $5,000.

**Duration:** 1 year; nonrenewable.

**Number awarded:** At least 1 each year.

**Deadline:** February of each year.

## 546 KENNETH JERNIGAN SCHOLARSHIP

National Federation of the Blind
c/o Peggy Elliott, Scholarship Committee Chair
805 Fifth Avenue
Grinnell, IA 50112
Phone: (641) 236-3366
Web: www.nfb.org/sch_intro.htm

**Summary:** To provide financial assistance to undergraduate and graduate blind students.

**Eligibility:** Open to legally blind students who are working on or planning to work full time on an undergraduate or graduate degree. Selection is based on academic excellence, service to the community, and financial need.

**Financial data:** The stipend is $12,000.

**Duration:** 1 year; recipients may resubmit applications up to 2 additional years.

**Number awarded:** 1 each year.

**Deadline:** March of each year.

## 547 KENTUCKY COLLEGE ACCESS PROGRAM GRANTS

Kentucky Higher Education Assistance Authority, Attn: Student Aid Branch
100 Airport Road
P.O. Box 798
Frankfort, KY 40602-0798
Phone: (502) 696-7397; (800) 928-8926, ext. 7397; Fax: (502) 696-7373;
TTY: (800) 855-2880; Email: tphelps@kheaa.com
Web: www.kheaa.com/prog_cap.html

**Summary:** To provide financial assistance to college students in Kentucky who have financial need.

**Eligibility:** Open to Kentucky residents enrolled in 2-year or 4-year public or private nonprofit colleges, proprietary schools, or vocational/technical schools for a minimum of 6 semester hours in an academic program that takes at least 2 years to complete. Applicants must be able to demonstrate financial need (the total expected family contribution toward educational expenses cannot exceed $3,850). Students majoring in divinity, theology, or religious education are not eligible.

**Financial data:** The maximum stipend is $1,400 per year. Eligible part-time college students receive an award calculated at the rate of $58 per credit hour.

**Duration:** Students at 2-year schools may receive the equivalent of 5 semesters of grants; students at 4-year schools may receive the equivalent of 9 semesters of grants.

**Number awarded:** Varies each year; awards are made to eligible students until funds are depleted. Recently, approximately 35,550 students received these grants.

**Deadline:** Applications may be submitted at any time, but students who file by March of each year have the best chance of receiving funds.

## 548 KENTUCKY COLONELS BETTER LIFE SCHOLARSHIPS

Kentucky Community and Technical College System, Attn: Financial Aid
300 North Main Street
Versailles, KY 40383
Phone: (859) 256-3100; (877) 528-2748 (within KY)
Web: www.kctcs.edu/student/financialaidscholarships/index.htm

**Summary:** To provide financial assistance to single parents attending or planning to attend 1 of the schools within the Kentucky Community and Technical College System (KCTCS).

**Eligibility:** Open to Kentucky residents who are single working parents with at least 1 child under 12 years of age. Applicants must be attending or planning to attend a KCTCS institution and able to demonstrate unmet financial need. Selection is based on demonstrated enthusiasm for learning and potential for academic success.

**Financial data:** The stipend is $2,500 per year.

**Duration:** 1 year; may be renewed 1 additional year if the recipient maintains full-time enrollment and satisfactory academic progress.

**Number awarded:** 16 each year: 1 in each of the KCTCS districts.

## 549 KENTUCKY DECEASED OR DISABLED LAW ENFORCEMENT OFFICER AND FIRE FIGHTER DEPENDENT TUITION WAIVER

Kentucky Fire Commission, Attn: Executive Director
300 North Main Street
Versailles, KY 40383
Phone: (859) 256-3478; (800) 782-6823; Fax: (859) 256-3125;
Email: ronnie.day@kctcs.net
Web: www.kctcs.net/kyfirecommission

**Summary:** To provide financial assistance for college to the children and spouses of Kentucky police officers or fire fighters deceased or disabled in the line of duty.

**Eligibility:** Open to spouses, widow(er)s, and children of Kentucky residents who became a law enforcement officer, fire fighter, or volunteer fire fighter and who 1) was killed while in active service or training for active service; 2) died as a result of a service-connected disability; or 3) became permanently and totally disabled as a result of active service or training for active service. Children must be younger than 23 years of age; spouses and widow(er)s may be of any age.

**Financial data:** Recipients are entitled to a waiver of tuition at state-supported universities, community colleges, and technical training institutions in Kentucky.

**Duration:** 1 year; may be renewed up to a maximum total of 36 months.

**Number awarded:** Varies each year; all qualified applicants are entitled to this aid.

## 550 KENTUCKY EDUCATIONAL EXCELLENCE SCHOLARSHIPS

Kentucky Higher Education Assistance Authority, Attn: Student Aid Branch
100 Airport Road
P.O. Box 798
Frankfort, KY 40602-0798
Phone: (502) 696-7397; (800) 928-8926, ext. 7397; Fax: (502) 696-7373;
TTY: (800) 855-2880; Email: kees@kheaa.com
Web: www.khcaa.com/kceshome.html

**Summary:** To provide financial assistance for college to Kentucky residents who achieve high GPAs and ACT scores in high school.

**Eligibility:** Open to Kentucky high school students who achieve at least a 2.5 GPA each year in high school and a score of at least 15 on the ACT (or SAT equivalent). Students must graduate from a high school in Kentucky and fulfill the state's core curriculum requirements. They must attend an accredited public or private institution in Kentucky, including community and technical colleges.

**Financial data:** For each year in high school that students achieve at least a 2.5 GPA, they receive at least $125 per year for college. Higher GPAs mean larger scholarships, rising to $500 per year for a 4.0 GPA. In addition, students receive a bonus award based on their best ACT score, starting at $36 for 15 and rising to $500 for a score of 28 or higher. The maximum potential award is $2,500 per year of college for a student who achieves a 4.0 GPA for each of 4 years of high school (thus earning an annual college scholarship of $2,000—$500 for each of the years with a 4.0 GPA) plus a bonus of $500 for an ACT score of 28 or higher.

**Duration:** Up to 4 years, provided the recipient earns a GPA of 2.5 or higher during the first year of college and 3.0 or higher during each succeeding year. In those last 3 years, a student whose GPA falls below 3.0 but remains 2.5 or higher will receive only 50% of their scholarship award for the next academic year; a student whose GPA falls below 2.5 will lose the scholarship for the next award period. Eligibility is restored if the student reestablishes a GPA of 2.5 or higher. Students in designated programs that require 5 years for a bachelor's degree (architecture, landscape architecture, and engineering) are entitled to 5 years of support from this program.

**Number awarded:** Varies each year; recently, 55,990 students received awards.

## 551 KENTUCKY HOUSING ASSOCIATION SCHOLARSHIPS

Kentucky Housing Association
c/o Gerald Board
Lyon County Housing Authority
P.O. Box 190
Eddyville, KY 42038-0190
Phone: (270) 388-7108; Email: lyoncoun@bellsouth.net
Web: www.kyhousingassn.com

**Summary:** To provide financial assistance for college to high school seniors and graduates in Kentucky who live in public housing.

**Eligibility:** Open to Kentucky residents who live in low-rent public housing programs managed by the public housing authority or Section 8 program. Applicants must be in their senior year of high school, have graduate from high school, have received a GED, or be attending college. They must be sponsored by their housing authority, which must agree to support their travel expenses to an interview and the award ceremony. Along with their application, they must submit essays on their extracurricular, school, and community activities; objective in continuing education beyond high school; and financial need.

**Financial data:** Annual stipends are $5,000, $2,500, or $750.

**Duration:** The scholarships for $5,000 per year and $750 per year may be renewed for up to 4 years. The scholarship for $2,500 is for 1 year.

**Number awarded:** 5 each year: 1 at $5,000 per year for 4 years, 1 at $2,500 for 1 year only, and 3 at $750 per year for 4 years.

**Deadline:** April of each year.

## 552 KENTUCKY KIDS' CHANCE SCHOLARSHIPS

Kids' Chance of Kentucky, Attn: Gary Davis, President
P.O. Box 910234
Lexington, KY 40591
Phone: (502) 564-5550, ext. 4526; Fax: (502) 564-0916;
Email: garyw.davis@ky.gov
Web: www.kidschance.org/kentucky.htm

**Summary:** To provide financial assistance for college to Kentucky residents whose parent was killed or seriously injured in an employment-related accident.

**Eligibility:** Open to residents of Kentucky between 16 and 25 years of age. Applicants must be the natural child, adopted child, step-child, or full dependent of a worker killed or permanent injured in a compensable work-related accident during the course of employment with a Kentucky employer and entitled to receive benefits under the Kentucky Workers' Compensation Act. The parent's death or injury must have resulted in a substantial decline in the family income. Selection is based primarily on financial need, although academic achievement, aptitude, and community service are also considered.

**Financial data:** The stipend depends on the need of the recipient. Funds may be used to cover tuition, books, housing, and meals.

**Duration:** 1 year; may be renewed.

**Number awarded:** Varies each year.

**Deadline:** April of each year for fall and spring semester; October of each year for spring semester.

## 553 KENTUCKY TUITION GRANTS

Kentucky Higher Education Assistance Authority, Attn: Student Aid Branch
100 Airport Road
P.O. Box 798
Frankfort, KY 40602-0798
Phone: (502) 696-7397; (800) 928-8926, ext. 7397; Fax: (502) 696-7373;
TTY: (800) 855-2880; Email: tphelps@kheaa.com
Web: www.kheaa.com/prog_ktg.html

**Summary:** To provide financial assistance to Kentucky residents who are attending independent colleges in the state.

**Eligibility:** Open to Kentucky residents enrolled in eligible Kentucky independent nonprofit institutions as full-time undergraduate students in eligible courses of study. They must be able to demonstrate financial need. Programs in divinity, theology, or religious education are not eligible.

**Financial data:** Awards range from $200 to $2,400 per academic year.

**Duration:** Students at 2-year schools may receive the equivalent of 5 semesters of grants; students at 4-year schools may receive the equivalent of 9 semesters of grants.

**Number awarded:** Varies each year; awards are made to eligible students until funds are depleted. Recently, approximately 10,230 students received grants.

**Deadline:** Applications may be submitted at any time, but students who file by March of each year have the best chance of receiving funds.

## 554 KENTUCKY VETERANS TUITION WAIVER PROGRAM

Kentucky Department of Veterans Affairs, Attn: Division of Field Operations
545 South Third Street, Room 123
Louisville, KY 40202
Phone: (502) 595-4447; (800) 928-4012 (within KY); Fax: (502) 595-4448
Web: www.kdva.net/tuitionwaiver.htm

**Summary:** To provide financial assistance for college to the children, spouses, or unremarried widow(er)s of disabled or deceased Kentucky veterans.

**Eligibility:** Open to the children, stepchildren, spouses, and unremarried widow(er)s of veterans who are residents of Kentucky (or were residents at the time of their death). The qualifying veteran must meet 1 of the following conditions: 1) died on active duty (regardless of wartime service); 2) died as a result of a service-connected disability (regardless of wartime service); 3) has a 100% service-connected disability; or 4) was a prisoner of war or declared missing in action. The military service may have been as a member of the U.S. armed forces, the Kentucky National Guard, or a Reserve component; service in the Guard or Reserves must have been on state active duty, active duty for training, inactive duty training, or active duty with the U.S. armed forces. Children of veterans must be under 23 years of age; no age limit applies to spouses or unremarried widow(er)s. All applicants must be attending or planning to attend a 2-year, 4-year, or vocational technical school operated and funded by the Kentucky Department of Education.

**Financial data:** Eligible dependents and survivors are exempt from tuition and matriculation fees at any state-supported institution of higher education in Kentucky.

**Duration:** Tuition is waived until the recipient completes 36 months of training, receives a college degree, or (in the case of children of veterans) reaches 23 years of age, whichever comes first. Spouses and unremarried widow(er)s are not subject to the age limitation.

**Number awarded:** Varies each year.

## 555 KERMIT B. NASH ACADEMIC SCHOLARSHIP

Sickle Cell Disease Association of America, Attn: Scholarship Committee
16 South Calvert Street, Suite 600
Baltimore, MD 21202-1314

Phone: (410) 528-1555; (800) 421-8453; Fax: (410) 528-1495;
Email: scdaa@sicklecelldisease.org
Web: www.sicklecelldisease.org/programs/nash_scholarship.phtml

**Summary:** To provide financial assistance for college to graduating high school seniors who have sickle cell disease.

**Eligibility:** Open to graduating high school seniors who have sickle cell disease (not the trait). Applicants must have a GPA of 3.0 or higher and be U.S. citizens or permanent residents planning to attend an accredited 4-year college or university as a full-time student. They must submit a personal essay, up to 1,000 words, on an aspect of the impact of the disease on their lives or on society. Selection is based on GPA, general academic achievement and promise, SAT scores, leadership and community service, severity of academic challenges and obstacles posed by sickle cell disease, and the quality of their essay.

**Financial data:** The stipend is $5,000 per year.

**Duration:** Up to 4 years.

**Number awarded:** 1 each year.

**Deadline:** June of each year.

## 556 KEVIN CHILD SCHOLARSHIP

National Hemophilia Foundation
Attn: Department of Finance, Administration & MIS
116 West 32nd Street, 11th Floor
New York, NY 10001-3212
Phone: (212) 328-3700; (800) 42-HANDI, ext. 3700; Fax: (212) 328-3777;
Email: info@hemophilia.org
Web: www.hemophilia.org

**Summary:** To provide financial assistance for college to students with hemophilia.

**Eligibility:** Open to high school seniors entering their first year of undergraduate study as well as those currently enrolled in college. Applicants must have hemophilia or another bleeding disorder. Selection is based on academic performance, participation in school and community activities, and an essay on their occupational objectives and goals in life.

**Financial data:** The stipend is $1,000.

**Duration:** 1 year.

**Number awarded:** 1 each year.

**Deadline:** June of each year.

## 557 KFC COLONEL'S SCHOLARS

KFC Corporation, Attn: KFC Colonel's Kids
P.O. Box 725489
Atlanta, GA 31139
Phone: (866) KFC-7240; Email: kfcscholars@act.org
Web: www.kfcscholars.org

**Summary:** To provide financial assistance to high school seniors who agree to work while attending college.

**Eligibility:** Open to graduating high school seniors planning to at public college or university in their home state to work on a bachelor's degree. They must have a GPA of 2.75 or higher and be able to demonstrate financial need. U.S. citizenship is required.

**Financial data:** The stipend is $5,000 per year.

**Duration:** 1 year; may be renewed up to 3 additional years provided the recipients remain enrolled full time with a GPA of 2.75 or higher. Beginning in the second year of the scholarship, they must also work an average of 10 hours per week in an approved position.

**Number awarded:** 50 each year.

**Deadline:** March of each year.

## 558 KIDS' CHANCE SCHOLARSHIPS

Kids' Chance, Inc.
P.O. Box 623
Valdosta, GA 31603
Phone: (229) 244-0153; Fax: (229) 245-0413; Email: kids300@bellsouth.net
Web: kidschance.org

**Summary:** To provide financial assistance for college to Georgia residents whose parent was killed or permanently disabled in an employment-related accident.

**Eligibility:** Open to Georgia residents between 16 and 25 years of age whose parent's on-the-job death or injury resulted in a substantial decline in family income. Applicants must be attending or planning to attend college or technical school.

**Financial data:** The stipend depends on the financial need of the recipient, to a maximum of $5,333. Funds may be used for tuition, books, housing, meals, transportation, and/or as a supplement to the income of the family to compensate for money the student would earn by dropping out of school.

**Duration:** 1 year; may be renewed if the recipient maintains satisfactory academic progress.

**Number awarded:** Varies each year; recently, 60 students were receiving $176,076 in support through this program.

---

### 559 KIWANIS INTERNATIONAL FOUNDATION/DISTRICT MATCHING SCHOLARSHIP PROGRAM

Key Club International, Attn: Manager of Youth Funds
3636 Woodview Trace
Indianapolis, IN 46268-3196
Phone: (317) 875-8755, ext. 244; (800) KIWANIS, ext. 244;
Fax: (317) 879-0204; Email: youthfunds@kiwanis.org
Web: www.keyclub.org

**Summary:** To provide financial assistance for college to high school seniors who are Key Club International members.

**Eligibility:** Open to graduating high school seniors who have been active members of the club for at least 2 years and have a GPA of 3.0 or higher. Applicants must be planning to attend a college, university, technical school, or vocational school. They must have excelled in leadership and provided service to others. Key Club International board members and district governors are not eligible. Financial need is not considered in the selection process.

**Financial data:** The award is $1,000.

**Duration:** 1 year; nonrenewable.

**Number awarded:** 1 to 5 per year in each participating district.

**Deadline:** Each participating district sets its own deadline.

---

### 560 KNIGHTS OF LITHUANIA SCHOLARSHIP PROGRAM

Knights of Lithuania
c/o John P. Baltrus, Scholarship Committee Chair
118 Vine Street
Jefferson Hills, PA 15025
Web: www.knightsoflithuania.com/scholarships.html

**Summary:** To provide financial assistance to undergraduate or graduate students of Lithuanian ancestry.

**Eligibility:** Open to members of the Knights of Lithuania (for at least 2 years) who are of Lithuanian ancestry and in financial need. There is no age limitation. Selection is based on recommendations, scholastic record, financial need, a personal interview, and organizational activity within the Knights of Lithuania.

**Financial data:** Stipends range up to $1,000 per year. Funds are generally paid in 2 equal installments.

**Duration:** 1 year; nonrenewable.

**Number awarded:** Varies each year.

**Deadline:** June of each year.

---

### 561 KPAAPA SCHOLARSHIPS

Kaiser Permanente African American Professional Association
c/o Kaiser Permanente
Waterpark One
2500 Havana Street
Aurora, CO 80014
Email: P.J.Ballard@kp.org

**Summary:** To provide financial assistance to undergraduate and graduate students who identify with an ethnic minority group.

**Eligibility:** Open to new and continuing undergraduate and graduate students enrolled or planning to enroll full time at an accredited college or university. Applicants must have a GPA of 3.0 or higher, although students who have strong leadership skills and community service but a lower GPA are encouraged to apply. Along with their application, they must submit a 1-page essay on their personal philosophy how obtaining a college degree could benefit this country in building a stronger foundation in areas of youth issues, educational opportunities, and career potential. On their application, they must also indicate the ethnic minority group with which they identify and include a photograph.

**Financial data:** The stipend is $1,000 per year.

**Duration:** 1 year.

**Number awarded:** 5 each year.

**Deadline:** December of each year.

---

### 562 KUCHLER-KILLIAN MEMORIAL SCHOLARSHIP

National Federation of the Blind
c/o Peggy Elliott, Scholarship Committee Chair
805 Fifth Avenue
Grinnell, IA 50112
Phone: (641) 236-3366
Web: www.nfb.org/sch_intro.htm

**Summary:** To provide financial assistance to undergraduate and graduate blind students.

**Eligibility:** Open to legally blind students who are working on or planning to work full time on an undergraduate or graduate degree. Selection is based on academic excellence, service to the community, and financial need.

**Financial data:** The stipend is $3,000.

**Duration:** 1 year; recipients may resubmit applications up to 2 additional years.

**Number awarded:** 1 each year.

**Deadline:** March of each year.

---

### 563 KYLE LEE FOUNDATION SCHOLARSHIP

Kyle Lee Foundation, Inc.
c/o Arnold C. Uy
Comerica Bank
611 Anton Boulevard, Fourth Floor
Costa Mesa, CA 92926
Phone: (714) 433-3204; Email: foundation@kylelee28.com
Web: www.kylelee28.com

**Summary:** To provide financial assistance for college to cancer survivors.

**Eligibility:** Open to high school seniors and current college students who have had cancer, especially Ewing's sarcoma. Applicants must submit a letter from their doctor confirming their cancer diagnosis, copies of academic transcripts, 2 letters of recommendation, and a 700-word essay outlining their goals in college and how their fight with cancer has affected their life and goals.

**Financial data:** Stipends are $1,000 or $500.

**Duration:** 1 year.

**Number awarded:** Varies each year. Recently, 3 of these scholarships were awarded: 2 at $1,000 and 1 at $500.

**Deadline:** February of each year.

---

### 564 K2TEO MARTIN J. GREEN, SR. MEMORIAL SCHOLARSHIP

American Radio Relay League, Attn: ARRL Foundation
225 Main Street
Newington, CT 06111
Phone: (860) 594-0397; Fax: (860) 594-0259; Email: foundation@arrl.org
Web: www.arrl.org/arrlf

**Summary:** To provide financial assistance to licensed radio amateurs who are interested in working on an undergraduate or graduate degree.

**Eligibility:** Open to undergraduate or graduate students in any field who are enrolled at accredited institutions and are licensed radio amateurs of general class. Applicants must submit an essay on the role amateur radio has played in their lives and provide documentation of financial need. Preference is given to students whose parents, grandparents, siblings, or other relatives are also ham radio operators.

**Financial data:** The stipend is $1,000.

**Duration:** 1 year.

**Number awarded:** 1 each year.

**Deadline:** January of each year.

---

### 565 LA ESTRELLA LATINA DE CARL'S JR. SCHOLARSHIP PROGRAM

Carl's Jr., Attn: Cheryl Beamer
6307 Carpinteria Avenue, Suite A
Carpinteria, CA 93013
Phone: (805) 745-7663; (800) 422-4141; Email: cbeamer@ckr.com
Web: www.carlsjr.com

**Summary:** To provide financial assistance to students in designated states who can demonstrate that they have been "A Star" in their community.

**Eligibility:** Open to seniors graduating from high schools in Arizona, California, Nevada, New Mexico, and Texas. Applicants must be high school seniors or graduates younger than 21 years of age and planning to enroll for the first time as a full-time undergraduate student at an accredited 2-year or 4-year college, university, or vocational school. Along with their application, they must submit an essay describing how they have been "A Star" in their community. Selection is based on academic record, school and community leadership and participation, work experience, future goals, financial need, and other family circumstances.

**Financial data:** The stipend is $1,000.

**Duration:** 1 year; nonrenewable.

**Number awarded:** 60 each year.

**Deadline:** January of each year.

## 566 LA FRA NATIONAL PRESIDENT'S SCHOLARSHIP

Ladies Auxiliary of the Fleet Reserve Association
Attn: Scholarship Administrator
125 North West Street
Alexandria, VA 22314-2754
Phone: (703) 683-1400; (800) 372-1924; Fax: (703) 549-6610;
Email: fra@fra.org
Web: www.fra.org/Content/fra/MyFRA/Scholarships/Scholarships.htm

**Summary:** To provide financial assistance for college to the children and grandchildren of naval personnel.

**Eligibility:** Open to the children and grandchildren of Navy, Marine, Coast Guard, active Fleet Reserve, Fleet Marine Corps Reserve, and Coast Guard Reserve personnel on active duty, retired with pay, or deceased while on active duty or retired with pay. Selection is based on financial need, academic proficiency, and character. Preference is given to dependents of members of the Fleet Reserve Association and the Ladies Auxiliary of the Fleet Reserve Association, if other factors are equal.

**Financial data:** The stipend is $2,500.

**Duration:** 1 year; may be renewed.

**Number awarded:** 1 each year.

**Deadline:** April of each year.

## 567 LA FRA SCHOLARSHIP

Ladies Auxiliary of the Fleet Reserve Association
Attn: Scholarship Administrator
125 North West Street
Alexandria, VA 22314-2754
Phone: (703) 683-1400; (800) 372-1924; Fax: (703) 549-6610;
Email: fra@fra.org
Web: www.fra.org/Content/fra/MyFRA/Scholarships/Scholarships.htm

**Summary:** To provide financial assistance for college to the daughters and granddaughters of naval personnel.

**Eligibility:** Open to the daughters and granddaughters of Navy, Marine, Coast Guard, active Fleet Reserve, Fleet Marine Corps Reserve, and Coast Guard Reserve personnel on active duty, retired with pay, or deceased while on active duty or retired with pay. Selection is based on financial need, academic proficiency, and character. Preference is given to dependents of members of the Fleet Reserve Association and the Ladies Auxiliary of the Fleet Reserve Association, if other factors are equal.

**Financial data:** The stipend is $2,500.

**Duration:** 1 year; may be renewed.

**Number awarded:** 1 each year.

**Deadline:** April of each year.

## 568 LA UNIDAD LATINA SCHOLARSHIPS

La Unidad Latina Foundation, Inc.
359 Prospect Avenue
Brooklyn, NY 11215
Email: foundation@launidadlatina.org
Web: foundation.launidadlatina.org

**Summary:** To provide financial assistance to Hispanic students who are working on a bachelor's or master's degree.

**Eligibility:** Open to students of Hispanic background who have completed at least 1 semester of higher education. Applicants must be enrolled full time at an accredited 4-year college or university in the United States. Along with their application, they must submit brief essays on the courses in which they are enrolled in the current semester, their financial need, their academic plans and career goals, an instance in which someone has left an indelible mark in their life and why, their extracurricular activities, any honors or awards they have received, and their special interests or hobbies.

**Financial data:** Stipends range from $250 to $1,000.

**Duration:** 1 year.

**Number awarded:** Varies each year; recently, 24 of these scholarships (18 in fall, 6 in spring) were awarded.

**Deadline:** February of each year for spring semester; October of each year for fall semester.

## 569 LADIES' AUXILIARY NATIONAL RURAL LETTER CARRIERS SCHOLARSHIP

Alexander Graham Bell Association for the Deaf
Attn: Financial Aid Coordinator
3417 Volta Place, N.W.
Washington, DC 20007-2778
Phone: (202) 337-5220; Fax: (202) 337-8314; TTY: (202) 337-5221;
Email: financialaid@agbell.org
Web: www.agbell.org

**Summary:** To provide financial assistance to undergraduate and graduate students with moderate to profound hearing loss.

**Eligibility:** Open to undergraduate and graduate students who have been diagnosed with a moderate to profound hearing loss prior to acquiring spoken language (hearing loss averages 60dB or greater in the better ear in the speech frequencies of 500, 1000, and 2000 Hz). Applicants must be committed to using spoken language as their primary mode of communication. They must be accepted or enrolled at a mainstream college or university as a full-time student. Along with their application, they must submit a 1-page essay discussing their career goals and how spoken communication is helping them to reach those goals as a person with a hearing loss. Financial need is considered in the selection process. This scholarship is reserved for students who are deaf.

**Financial data:** The stipend is $2,000 per year.

**Duration:** 1 year; may be renewed 1 additional year.

**Number awarded:** 1 each year.

**Deadline:** April of each year.

## 570 LAURA BLACKBURN MEMORIAL SCHOLARSHIP

American Legion Auxiliary, Attn: Department of Kentucky
105 North Public Square
P.O. Box 189
Greensburg, KY 42743-1530
Phone: (270) 932-7533; Fax: (270) 932-7672; Email: secretarykyala@aol.com

**Summary:** To provide financial assistance for college to descendants of veterans in Kentucky.

**Eligibility:** Open to the children, grandchildren, and great-grandchildren of veterans who served in the armed forces during eligibility dates for membership in the American Legion. Applicants must be Kentucky residents enrolled in their senior year at an accredited high school.

**Financial data:** The stipend is $1,000.

**Duration:** 1 year.

**Number awarded:** 1 each year.

**Deadline:** March of each year.

## 571 LAWRENCE MADEIROS SCHOLARSHIP

Adirondack Spintacular, Attn: Scholarship Panel
485 Bunker Hill Road
Mayfield, NY 12117
Phone: (518) 863-2668; Email: lamspintacular@aol.com
Web: www.adirondackspintacular.com/pages/scholarship.html

**Summary:** To provide financial assistance for college to high school seniors who have a bleeding disorder or other chronic disorder.

**Eligibility:** Open to seniors graduating from high school who have been accepted at an accredited college or university. Applicants must be diagnosed with a bleeding disorder or other chronic disorder. Along with their application, they must submit brief essays on 1) how living with or around a chronic disorder has impacted their life; 2) their goals and aspirations in life; and 3) their passion. Financial need may also be considered.

**Financial data:** The stipend is $1,000.

**Duration:** 1 year.

**Number awarded:** Varies each year; recently, 5 of these scholarships were awarded.

**Deadline:** June of each year.

## 572 LAZOF FAMILY FOUNDATION SCHOLARSHIPS

Spina Bifida Association of America, Attn: Scholarship Committee
4590 MacArthur Boulevard, N.W., Suite 250
Washington, DC 20007-4226
Phone: (202) 944-3285, ext. 19; (800) 621-3141; Fax: (202) 944-3295;
Email: sbaa@sbaa.org
Web: www.sbaa.org

**Summary:** To provide financial assistance to members of the Spina Bifida

Association of America (SBAA) who are planning to attend a 4-year college or university.

**Eligibility:** Open to persons born with spina bifida who are current members of the association. Applicants must be high school juniors or seniors planning to attend a 4-year college or university. Selection is based on academic record, other efforts shown in school, financial need, work history, community service, leadership, and commitment to personal goals.

**Financial data:** The stipend is $2,500 per year. Funds may be used for tuition.

**Duration:** 4 years, provided the recipient maintains a GPA of 3.0 or higher.

**Number awarded:** 4 each year.

**Deadline:** February of each year.

---

## 573 LEADERS OF PROMISE SCHOLARSHIP PROGRAM

Phi Theta Kappa
Scholarship Programs Director
1625 Eastover Drive
P.O. Box 13729
Jackson, MS 39236-3729
Phone: (601) 984-3504, ext. 560; (800) 946-9995, ext. 560; Fax: (601) 984-3550;
Email: clancy.mitchell@ptk.org
Web: www.ptk.org

**Summary:** To provide financial assistance to members of Phi Theta Kappa, the international honor society for 2-year colleges, who plan to continue work on an associate degree.

**Eligibility:** Open to members of the society. Applicants must have completed 36 semester hours or less of course work for an associate degree at a community, technical, or junior college in the United States or Canada. Applicants must have a cumulative GPA of 3.5 or higher. Selection is based on a 500-word essay, college transcripts, and a letter of recommendation from a community college faculty member.

**Financial data:** The stipend is $1,000. The first $500 is disbursed upon documentation of enrollment at the community college and the second $500 upon documentation of continued participation in Phi Theta Kappa activities and a GPA of 3.25 or higher.

**Duration:** 1 year.

**Number awarded:** 30 each year.

**Deadline:** April of each year.

---

## 574 LEAGUE AT AT&T FOUNDATION ACADEMIC SCHOLARSHIPS

Lesbian, Bisexual, Gay and Transgendered United Employees (LEAGUE) at AT&T Foundation
c/o Charles Eader, President
One AT&T Way, Room 4B214J
Bedminster, NJ 07921-2694
Phone: (703) 713-7820; TDD: (800) 855-2880; Email: attleague@aol.com
Web: www.league-att.org/foundation/fscholarships.html

**Summary:** To provide financial assistance for college to high school seniors who identify with the gay, lesbian, bisexual, or transgender communities.

**Eligibility:** Open to applicants who meet the following requirements: be high school seniors and accepted for full-time study at an accredited 2- or 4-year college or university; have at least a 3.0 GPA; be actively involved in community service; identify as a gay, lesbian, bisexual, or transgendered person; send 3 sealed letters of recommendation from adults who know their abilities and skills; provide a copy of their high school transcripts and college or university acceptance letter; and write 250-word essays on 1) their academic, career, and personal goals and plans for service to the community, especially on how they plan to increase respect for the individual and aid inclusion of human differences; and 2) how being a lesbian, gay, bisexual, or transgendered person has affected their personal life. Selection is based on academic record, personal plans, community service, leadership, and concern for others.

**Financial data:** Stipends are $2,500 (for the Matthew Shepard Memorial Scholarship) or $1,500.

**Duration:** 1 year.

**Number awarded:** Varies each year. Recently, 5 of these scholarships were awarded: the Matthew Shepard Memorial Scholarship plus 4 others.

**Deadline:** April of each year.

---

## 575 LEBANESE AMERICAN HERITAGE CLUB SCHOLARSHIPS

Lebanese American Heritage Club
Attn: Arab American Scholarship Foundation
4337 Maple Road

Dearborn, MI 48126
Phone: (313) 846-8480; Fax: (313) 846-2710; Email: lahc@lahc.org
Web: www.lahc.org/scholarship/scholarship.htm

**Summary:** To provide financial assistance for college or graduate school to Americans of Arab descent who reside in Michigan.

**Eligibility:** Open to students who are already in college or graduate school. Only full-time students may apply. Applicants must be of Arab descent, be U.S. citizens or permanent residents, reside in the state of Michigan, and be able to demonstrate financial need. Undergraduate students must have at least a 3.0 GPA; graduate students must have at least a 3.5. Applicants must submit a completed application form, official copies of academic transcripts, 2 letters of recommendation, financial aid transcripts, copies of their current Student Aid Report, and a 500-word essay on their educational background, field of study, future goals, and contributions to their community. Preference is given to students who are working on a degree in mass communications.

**Financial data:** The stipend is $1,000. Funds are paid directly to the recipient's institution.

**Duration:** 1 year; recipients may reapply.

**Number awarded:** 1 or more each year.

**Deadline:** April of each year.

---

## 576 LEE DUBIN SCHOLARSHIP FUND

Children of Lesbians and Gays Everywhere, Attn: Scholarship Committee
3543 18th Street, #1
San Francisco, CA 94110
Phone: (415) 861-KIDS; Email: colage@colage.org
Web: www.colage.org/scholarship.html

**Summary:** To provide financial assistance for college to children of lesbian, gay, bisexual, and transgender (LGBT) parents.

**Eligibility:** Open to undergraduate students who have a GPA of 2.0 or higher and 1 or more LGBT parent. Applicants must be able to demonstrate ability in and commitment to affecting change in the LGBT community. As part of the application process, they must submit a 500- to 1,000-word essay on why support from this fund is important and meaningful to them; their community service, extracurricular activities, honors, or other special events that will help the committee see their strengths; how their experience as a child of LGBT parents has impacted their sense of civic responsibility; an event that dealt with social and/or political differences and their response to that situation; and how they think their reaction was impacted by their experience with their parents. Special consideration is given to applicants with demonstrated financial need.

**Financial data:** The stipend is $1,000 per year.

**Duration:** 1 year; may be renewed.

**Number awarded:** 3 to 5 each year.

**Deadline:** April of each year.

---

## 577 LEGACY OF LEARNING SCHOLARSHIPS

Workers Compensation Fund
392 East 6400 South
P.O. Box 57929
Salt Lake City, UT 84157-0929
Phone: (801) 288-8000; (800) 446-2667; Email: cmorris@wcfgroup.com
Web: www.wcfgroup.com

**Summary:** To provide financial assistance for college to children and spouses of workers who died in work-related accidents in Utah.

**Eligibility:** Open to Utah residents who are the children and spouses of workers who died in accidents that occurred on job sites covered by the sponsoring company. Applicants must be attending or planning to attend an accredited college or university. Selection is based on GPA, standard test scores, general character, community involvement, and financial need.

**Financial data:** The stipend is $1,500 per year.

**Duration:** 1 year; may be renewed as long as the recipient remains in college.

**Number awarded:** Varies each year; recently, 52 students received these scholarships.

---

## 578 LEGISLATIVE INCENTIVE FOR FUTURE EXCELLENCE (LIFE) SCHOLARSHIP PROGRAM

South Carolina Commission on Higher Education
Attn: Director of Student Services
1333 Main Street, Suite 200
Columbia, SC 29201
Phone: (803) 737-2280; (877) 349-7183; Fax: (803) 737-2297;
Email: srhyne@che.sc.gov

Web: www.che.sc.gov

**Summary:** To provide financial assistance for college to residents of South Carolina.

**Eligibility:** Open to residents of South Carolina who graduate from high school or complete a home-school program and attend an eligible South Carolina public or private college or university. As an entering freshman at a 4-year college or university, they must meet any 2 of the following requirements: 1) have earned a GPA of 3.0 or higher in high school; 2) score at least 1100 on both the mathematics and critical reading sections of the SAT or 24 on the ACT; and/or 3) graduate in the top 30% of their high school class. Students entering a 2-year or technical institution must have a high school GPA of 3.0 or higher. Continuing college students must have completed an average of 30 credit hours for each academic year and maintained a GPA of 3.0 or higher. Students transferring must have completed 30 credit hours for a second-year transfer, 60 for a third-year transfer, or 90 for a fourth-year transfer; their cumulative GPA must be 3.0 or higher. U.S. citizenship or permanent resident status is required. Applicants may not have been convicted of any felonies or alcohol- or drug-related charges.

**Financial data:** The stipend is $4,700 per year, plus a $300 book allowance, at 4-year colleges or universities. Students at public and private 2-year colleges receive a stipend of the cost of tuition at a regional campus of the University of South Carolina plus a $300 book allowance. Technical school students receive the cost of tuition plus a $300 book allowance. Funds may be applied only toward the cost of attendance at an eligible South Carolina institution.

**Duration:** 1 year; may be renewed up to a total of 10 semesters for a 5-year program, 8 semesters for a 4-year program, 4 semesters for a 2-year program, or 2 semesters for a 1-year certificate or diploma program.

**Number awarded:** Varies each year; recently, 28,390 of these scholarships, worth more than $127 million, were awarded.

## 579 LEONETTE LEAL FELICIANO MEMORIAL AWARD

Portuguese Heritage Scholarship Foundation, Attn: Academic Secretary
P.O. Box 30246
Bethesda, MD 20824-0246
Phone: (301) 652-2775; Email: phsf@vivaportugal.com
Web: www.vivaportugal.com/phsf/apply.htm

**Summary:** To provide financial assistance for college to students of Portuguese American heritage.

**Eligibility:** Open to high school seniors or currently-enrolled college students who are of Portuguese American ancestry. Applicants must be U.S. residents and attending or planning to attend an accredited 4-year college or university. Selection is based on community involvement and academic achievement.

**Financial data:** The stipend is $1,000 per year.

**Duration:** 1 year; nonrenewable.

**Number awarded:** 1 each year.

**Deadline:** January of each year.

## 580 LEOPOLD SCHEPP FOUNDATION SCHOLARSHIPS

Leopold Schepp Foundation
551 Fifth Avenue, Suite 3000
New York, NY 10176-2597
Phone: (212) 692-0191

**Summary:** To provide financial assistance to undergraduate and graduate students.

**Eligibility:** Open to undergraduates under 30 years of age and graduate students under 40 years of age. Applicants must either be currently enrolled full time or have completed 1 year of undergraduate work at an accredited college or university. They must have a GPA of 3.0 or higher. High school seniors, graduate students completing a dissertation and not enrolled in class, and students working on a second degree at the same level, are not eligible. U.S. citizenship or permanent resident status is required. Selection is based on character, ability, and financial need.

**Financial data:** The maximum stipend is $8,000 per year.

**Duration:** 1 year; may be renewed.

**Number awarded:** Approximately 200 each year.

**Deadline:** The foundation stops accepting applications when a sufficient number has been received, usually in January.

## 581 LEST WE FORGET POW/MIA/KIA SCHOLARSHIP FUND

Maine Community Foundation, Attn: Program Director
245 Main Street
Ellsworth, ME 04605
Phone: (207) 667-9735; (877) 700-6800; Fax: (207) 667-0447;
Email: info@mainecf.org

Web: www.mainecf.org/html/scholarships/index.html

**Summary:** To provide financial assistance for undergraduate or graduate study to Vietnam veterans or the dependents of Vietnam or other veterans in Maine.

**Eligibility:** Open to residents of Maine who are Vietnam veterans or the descendants of veterans who served in the Vietnam Theater. As a second priority, children of veterans from other time periods are also considered. Graduating high school seniors, nontraditional students, undergraduates, and graduate students are eligible to apply. Selection is based on financial need, extracurricular activities, work experience, academic achievement, and a personal statement of career goals and how the applicant's educational plans relate to them.

**Financial data:** The stipend is $1,000 per year.

**Duration:** 1 year.

**Number awarded:** 3 to 6 each year.

**Deadline:** April of each year.

## 582 LETENDRE EDUCATION FUND SCHOLARSHIPS

National Association for the Education of Homeless Children and Youth
Attn: LeTendre Education Fund
4701 Connecticut Avenue, N.W., Suite 402
Washington, DC 20008
Phone: (202) 364-7392; Fax: (763) 545-9499; Email: bduffield@naehcy.org
Web: www.naehcy.org/about_letendre.html

**Summary:** To provide financial assistance for college to high school students and recent graduates who are currently or formerly homeless.

**Eligibility:** Open to high school juniors, seniors, and recent graduates/GED recipients (under 20 years of age) who are homeless or who have been homeless during their school attendance. This includes students who live in shelters, cars, campgrounds, or other places "not meant for human habitation." Also eligible are students who are living with friends or relatives temporarily because they lack permanent housing. Applicants must be high school seniors, students enrolled in GED or other alternative education programs, or students who recently obtained their diploma or GED certificate. They must submit an essay of at least 500 words about the impact of homelessness on their lives and their desire to attend college. Selection is based on demonstrated commitment to education during the experience of homelessness, academic achievement, discussion of how the scholarship would be used to help advance the desire to attend college, statement of goals, use of language, and organization of essay.

**Financial data:** The stipend is $1,000. Funds must be used for tuition, application fees, books, preparation courses, visits to prospective colleges, or other educationally-related expenses.

**Duration:** 1 year; nonrenewable.

**Number awarded:** At least 2 each year.

**Deadline:** September of each year.

## 583 LEWIS A. KINGSLEY FOUNDATION SCHOLARSHIP FUND

Naval Sea Cadet Corps, Attn: Executive Director
2300 Wilson Boulevard
Arlington, VA 22201-3308
Phone: (703) 243-6910; Fax: (703) 243-3985
Web: www.seacadets.org

**Summary:** To provide financial assistance to Naval Sea Cadet Corps cadets and former cadets who are interested in continuing their education at an accredited 4-year college/university.

**Eligibility:** Open to cadets and former cadets who are interested in continuing their education at an accredited 4-year college or university. They must have been a member of the corps for at least 2 years, have attained a minimum rating of NSCC E-3, be recommended by their commanding officer or other official, have earned at least a 3.0 GPA, and have been accepted by an accredited college or university. Applicants may submit financial need statements. All other factors being equal, these statements may be considered in determining award recipients. Applicants who have received full scholarships from other sources (e.g., ROTC) will be considered for this award only if there are no other qualified applicants.

**Financial data:** The stipend is $1,000.

**Duration:** 1 year.

**Number awarded:** 5 each year.

**Deadline:** May of each year.

## 584 LIFE MEMBERS' SCHOLARSHIP

American Atheists
P.O. Box 5733
Parsippany, NJ 07054-6733
Phone: (908) 276-7300; Fax: (908) 276-7402; Email: info@atheists.org

**Summary:** To provide financial assistance for college to students who identify themselves as atheists.

**Eligibility:** Open to college-bound high school seniors and current college students. Applicants must be atheists and have a cumulative GPA of 2.5 or higher. Selection is based on activism, with special attention given to students who show activism in their schools (e.g., starting atheist/freethinker groups, fighting against violations of the separation of church and state in the school).

**Financial data:** The stipend is $2,000

**Duration:** 1 year.

**Number awarded:** 1 each year.

**Deadline:** January of each year.

## 585 LILLY MOVING LIVES FORWARD REINTEGRATION SCHOLARSHIPS

The Center for Reintegration, Inc., Attn: Lilly Secretariat
310 Busse Highway
PMB 327
Park Ridge, IL 60068-3251
Phone: (800) 809-8202; Email: lillyscholarships@reintegration.com
Web: www.reintegration.com/resources/scholarships/scholarships.asp

**Summary:** To provide financial assistance to undergraduate and graduate students diagnosed with schizophrenia.

**Eligibility:** Open to U.S. citizens diagnosed with bipolar disorder, schizophrenia, schizophreniform disorder, or schizoaffective disorder. Applicants must be receiving medical treatment for the disease and be actively involved in rehabilitative or reintegrative efforts. They must be interested in pursuing postsecondary education, including trade or vocational school programs, high school equivalency programs, associate degrees, bachelor's degrees, and graduate programs. Along with their application, they must submit an essay on their career goal and their rationale for choosing that goal, how this course of study will help them achieve their career goal, obstacles they have faced in life and how they have overcome them, steps they have taken to prepare for pursuit of this education, rationale for the specific school chosen, and their plans to continue treatment while pursuing an education. Selection is based on the quality of the essay, academic success, 3 references, thoughtfulness and appropriateness of academic and vocational/career goals, rehabilitation involvement, success in dealing with the disease, recent volunteer and/or vocational experience, and completion of application requirements.

**Financial data:** The amount awarded varies, depending upon the specific needs of the recipient. Funds may be used to pay for tuition and related expenses, such as textbooks and laboratory fees.

**Duration:** 1 year; may be renewed.

**Number awarded:** Varies each year; recently, 50 of these scholarships (including renewals) were awarded.

**Deadline:** January of each year.

## 586 LINLY HEFLIN SCHOLARSHIP

Linly Heflin Unit
c/o Mrs. Beff King, Scholarship Committee Co-Chair
13 Office Park Circle, Suite 8
Birmingham, AL 35223
Phone: (205) 870-4192

**Summary:** To provide financial assistance to women attending colleges and universities in Alabama.

**Eligibility:** Open to female residents of Alabama attending accredited 4-year colleges in the state. Applicants must have an ACT score of 22 or higher. U.S. citizenship is required. Selection is based on academic proficiency and financial need.

**Financial data:** The stipend is $2,500 per year.

**Duration:** 1 year; may be renewed until completion of an undergraduate degree, provided the recipient continues to demonstrate financial need and maintains a GPA of 2.5 or higher.

**Number awarded:** A limited number of these scholarships are awarded each year.

**Deadline:** January of each year.

## 587 LISA SECHRIST MEMORIAL FOUNDATION SCHOLARSHIP

Lisa Sechrist Memorial Foundation
Attn: Kim Mackmin, Scholarship Selection Committee
Brookfield Homes
8500 Executive Park Avenue, Suite 300

Fairfax, VA 22031
Web: www.lisasechrist.com/scholarship.html

**Summary:** To provide financial assistance for college to female high school seniors from Virginia who come from disadvantaged backgrounds.

**Eligibility:** Open to women graduating from high schools in Virginia who come from a disadvantaged background. Applicants should be able to demonstrate membership in honor societies, participation in sports or other extracurricular activities, citizenship and service within the community, and/or leadership skills within the school or community. Selection is based on merit, integrity, academic potential, and financial need.

**Financial data:** The stipend is $2,500 per year.

**Duration:** 4 years, provided the recipient maintains a GPA of 2.5 or higher.

**Number awarded:** 1 each year.

**Deadline:** March of each year.

## 588 LOIS COCHRAN FINCH YOUTH EXCELLENCE AWARDS

LCF Memorial Foundation, Inc., Attn: Foundation Manager
2615 S.E. McCorkle
Olympia, WA 98501
Phone: (360) 786-9650; Email: robhesspho@aol.com
Web: www.lois4kids.com

**Summary:** To recognize and reward, with college scholarships, young people who submit outstanding essays on their community service, including involvement in Arabian horse activities.

**Eligibility:** Open to youth in Canada and the United States who are 18 years of age or younger. Applicants must submit 3 essays, each illustrating their community service in the following areas: 1) family and/or friends; 2) school, community, and/or church/synagogue; and 3) Arabian, half-Arabian, and/or Anglo-Arabian horses. Selection is based entirely on the essays. No consideration is given to the applicants' financial need or horse show record.

**Financial data:** Stipends are $2,000, $1,000, or $500.

**Duration:** The awards are presented annually.

**Number awarded:** 10 each year: 1 at $2,000, 4 at $1,000, and 5 at $500.

**Deadline:** April of each year.

## 589 LOLA B. CURRY SCHOLARSHIP

United Daughters of the Confederacy, Attn: Education Director
328 North Boulevard
Richmond, VA 23220-4057
Phone: (804) 355-1636; Fax: (804) 353-1396; Email: hqudc@rcn.com
Web: www.hqudc.org/scholarships/scholarships.html

**Summary:** To provide financial assistance for college to lineal descendants of Confederate veterans in Alabama.

**Eligibility:** Open to Alabama residents who are lineal descendants of worthy Confederates or collateral descendants who are members of the Children of the Confederacy or the United Daughters of the Confederacy. Applicants must submit a family financial report and certified proof of the Confederate record of 1 ancestor, with the company and regiment in which he served. They must have a GPA of 3.0 or higher in high school.

**Financial data:** The amount of the scholarship depends on the availability of funds.

**Duration:** 1 year; may be renewed.

**Number awarded:** 1 each year.

**Deadline:** March of each year.

## 590 L'OREAL/FAMILY CIRCLE CUP "PERSONAL BEST" SCHOLARSHIP

Family Circle Cup
c/o Family Circle Tennis Center
161 Seven Farms Drive
Charleston, SC 29492
Phone: (843) 856-7900; (800) 677-2293
Web: www.familycirclecup.com

**Summary:** To provide financial assistance for college to female high school seniors in North Carolina, South Carolina, and Georgia.

**Eligibility:** Open to women graduating from high schools in North Carolina, South Carolina, and Georgia. Applicants must be planning to enroll full time at an accredited 2-year or 4-year college or university. They must have a GPA of 2.0 or higher and be able to demonstrate that they have made a difference in the lives of others through role modeling, community involvement and services, volunteer experiences, athletics, and extracurricular activities.

**Financial data:** The stipend is $2,500.

**Duration:** 1 year.
**Number awarded:** 3 each year: 1 from each of the eligible states.
**Deadline:** February of each year.

### 591 LOUIS B. RUSSELL, JR. MEMORIAL SCHOLARSHIP

Indiana State Teachers Association, Attn: Scholarships
150 West Market Street, Suite 900
Indianapolis, IN 46204
Phone: (317) 263-3400; (800) 382-4037; Fax: (317) 655-3700;
Email: kmcallen@ista-in.org
Web: www.ista-in.org

**Summary:** To provide financial assistance to ethnic minority high school seniors in Indiana who are interested in pursuing vocational education.
**Eligibility:** Open to ethnic minority high school seniors in Indiana who are interested in continuing their education in the area of industrial arts, vocational education, or technical preparation at an accredited postsecondary institution. Selection is based on academic achievement, leadership ability as expressed through co-curricular activities and community involvement, recommendations, and a 300-word essay on their educational goals and how they plan to use this scholarship.
**Financial data:** The stipend is $1,000.
**Duration:** 1 year; may be renewed for 1 additional year.
**Number awarded:** 1 each year.
**Deadline:** February of each year.

### 592 LOUISIANA KIDS' CHANCE SCHOLARSHIPS

Kids' Chance of Louisiana
c/o The Louisiana Bar Foundation
601 St. Charles Avenue, Third Floor
New Orleans, LA 70130
Phone: (504) 561-1046; Fax: (504) 566-1926;
Email: kidschance@raisingthebar.org
Web: www.raisingthebar.org

**Summary:** To provide financial assistance for college to Louisiana residents whose parent was killed or permanently disabled in an employment-related accident.
**Eligibility:** Open to Louisiana residents between 16 and 25 years of age who are the dependent of a worker killed or permanently and totally disabled in an accident that is compensable under a state or federal Workers' Compensation Act or law. Applicants must be attending or planning to attend an accredited Louisiana university; community, technical, or vocational college; or state-approved proprietary school. Financial need is considered in the selection process.
**Financial data:** Stipends range from $500 to $3,000. Funds, paid directly to the school where the child is enrolled, may be used for tuition, books, fees, room, and general living expenses.
**Duration:** 1 year; recipients may reapply as long as they maintain a "C" average or higher.
**Number awarded:** Varies each year.
**Deadline:** February of each year.

### 593 LOUISIANA LEVERAGING EDUCATIONAL ASSISTANCE PARTNERSHIP

Louisiana Office of Student Financial Assistance
1885 Wooddale Boulevard
P.O. Box 91202
Baton Rouge, LA 70821-9202
Phone: (225) 922-1012; (800) 259-LOAN, ext. 1012; Fax: (225) 922-0790;
Email: custserv@osfa.state.la.us
Web: www.osfa.state.la.us

**Summary:** To provide need-based funds to academically qualified high school seniors and graduates in Louisiana who are planning to attend college.
**Eligibility:** Open to Louisiana residents (for at least 1 year) who have substantial financial need, are enrolled as a full-time undergraduate student, are a U.S. citizen or eligible noncitizen, have earned at least a 2.0 GPA in high school (or a minimum average score of 45 on the GED), have achieved a composite score of at least 20 on the ACT, have applied for federal aid, do not owe a refund on federal aid, and are not in default on federal aid. The Louisiana Office of Student Financial Assistance allocates award funds to Louisiana postsecondary schools based on prior fall enrollment. Students are selected for the award by the financial aid officers at their participating schools.
**Financial data:** Individual grants range from $200 to $2,000 per year; the average award is $600; a total of approximately $2.0 million is distributed each year.

Funds may be used for educational expenses, including tuition, fees, supplies, and living expenses (e.g., room and board, transportation).
**Duration:** 1 year; may be renewed if the recipient continues to meet all eligibility requirements and maintains a GPA of 2.0 or higher.
**Number awarded:** Approximately 3,000 each year.

### 594 LOUISIANA TOPS–HONORS AWARD

Louisiana Office of Student Financial Assistance
1885 Wooddale Boulevard
P.O. Box 91202
Baton Rouge, LA 70821-9202
Phone: (225) 922-1012; (800) 259-LOAN, ext. 1012; Fax: (225) 922-0790;
Email: custserv@osfa.state.la.us
Web: www.osfa.state.la.us

**Summary:** To provide financial assistance for college to graduating high school seniors in Louisiana who have outstanding academic records.
**Eligibility:** Open to graduating seniors at high schools in Louisiana who have completed a core curriculum of 16.5 units and have filed a Free Application for Federal Student Aid (FAFSA). Applicants must be registered with Selective Service (if required), may have no criminal convictions, and must enter an eligible postsecondary institution as a first-time freshman by the first semester following the first anniversary of their high school graduation (unless entering into military service). Independent students or at least 1 parent or legal guardian of dependent students must have been a Louisiana resident for at least 24 months prior to the date of high school graduation. For the Honors component, students must have at least a 3.5 GPA and a minimum score of 27 on the ACT.
**Financial data:** This program provides tuition reimbursement plus $800 per year to students who attend public colleges or universities in Louisiana or provides the equivalent of the average public tuition charged in Louisiana plus $800 per year to students attending independent colleges or universities in the state.
**Duration:** 1 year; may be renewed for up to 3 additional years if the recipient continues to attend a Louisiana public or independent college or university as a full-time undergraduate student and maintains at least a 3.0 GPA.
**Number awarded:** Varies each year.
**Deadline:** April of each year for priority consideration; June of each year for final consideration.

### 595 LOUISIANA TOPS–OPPORTUNITY AWARD

Louisiana Office of Student Financial Assistance
1885 Wooddale Boulevard
P.O. Box 91202
Baton Rouge, LA 70821-9202
Phone: (225) 922-1012; (800) 259-LOAN, ext. 1012; Fax: (225) 922-0790;
Email: custserv@osfa.state.la.us
Web: www.osfa.state.la.us

**Summary:** To provide financial assistance for college to graduating high school seniors in Louisiana.
**Eligibility:** Open to graduating seniors at high schools in Louisiana who have completed a core curriculum of 16.5 units and have filed a Free Application for Federal Student Aid (FAFSA). Applicants must be registered with Selective Service (if required), may have no criminal convictions, and must enter an eligible postsecondary institution as a first-time freshman by the first semester following the first anniversary of their high school graduation (unless entering into military service). Independent students or at least 1 parent or legal guardian of dependent students must have been a Louisiana resident for at least 24 months prior to the date of high school graduation. For the Opportunity component, students must have at least a 2.5 GPA and a minimum score of 20 on the ACT.
**Financial data:** This program provides tuition reimbursement to students who attend public colleges or universities in Louisiana or provides the equivalent of the average public tuition charged in Louisiana to students attending independent colleges or universities in the state.
**Duration:** 1 year; may be renewed for up to 3 additional years if the recipient continues to attend a Louisiana public or independent college or university as a full-time undergraduate student and maintains at least a 2.3 GPA at the end of the first academic year and 2.5 at the end of all other academic years.
**Number awarded:** Varies each year.
**Deadline:** April of each year for priority consideration; June of each year for final consideration.

### 596 LOUISIANA TOPS–PERFORMANCE AWARD

Louisiana Office of Student Financial Assistance
1885 Wooddale Boulevard
P.O. Box 91202

Baton Rouge, LA 70821-9202

Phone: (225) 922-1012; (800) 259-LOAN, ext. 1012; Fax: (225) 922-0790;
Email: custserv@osfa.state.la.us

Web: www.osfa.state.la.us

**Summary:** To provide financial assistance for college to graduating high school seniors in Louisiana with outstanding academic records.

**Eligibility:** Open to graduating seniors at high schools in Louisiana who have completed a core curriculum of 16.5 units and have filed a Free Application for Federal Student Aid (FAFSA). Applicants must be registered with Selective Service (if required), may have no criminal convictions, and must enter an eligible postsecondary institution as a first-time freshman by the first semester following the first anniversary of their high school graduation (unless entering into military service). Independent students or at least 1 parent or legal guardian of dependent students must have been a Louisiana resident for at least 24 months prior to the date of high school graduation. For the Performance component, students must have either 1) a GPA of 3.5 or higher and a score of at least 23 on the ACT, or 2) a GPA of 3.0 or higher and a score of at least 24 on the ACT.

**Financial data:** This program provides tuition reimbursement plus $400 per year to students who attend public colleges or universities in Louisiana or provides the equivalent of the average public tuition charged in Louisiana plus $400 per year to students attending independent colleges or universities in the state.

**Duration:** 1 year; may be renewed for up to 3 additional years if the recipient continues to attend a Louisiana public or independent college or university as a full-time undergraduate student and maintains at least a 3.0 GPA.

**Number awarded:** Varies each year.

**Deadline:** April of each year for priority consideration; June of each year for final consideration.

## 597 LOUISIANA TOPS–TECH AWARD

Louisiana Office of Student Financial Assistance

1885 Wooddale Boulevard

P.O. Box 91202

Baton Rouge, LA 70821-9202

Phone: (225) 922-1012; (800) 259-LOAN, ext. 1012; Fax: (225) 922-0790;

Email: custserv@osfa.state.la.us

Web: www.osfa.state.la.us

**Summary:** To provide financial assistance to graduating high school seniors in Louisiana who are interested in pursuing a technical or vocational education.

**Eligibility:** Open to graduating seniors at high schools in Louisiana who have completed a core curriculum of 16.5 units and have filed a Free Application for Federal Student Aid (FAFSA). Applicants must be registered with Selective Service (if required), may have no criminal convictions, and must enter an eligible postsecondary institution as a first-time freshman by the first semester following the first anniversary of their high school graduation (unless entering into military service). Independent students or at least 1 parent or legal guardian of dependent students must have been a Louisiana resident for at least 24 months prior to the date of high school graduation. For the Tech component, students must have a GPA of 2.5 or higher and an ACT score of at least 17. Applicants must plan to attend 1) a public postsecondary school that does not offer a baccalaureate degree; 2) a public postsecondary school that does offer a baccalaureate degree; or 3) a private institution that is a member of the Louisiana Association of Independent Colleges and Universities (LAICA).

**Financial data:** At public postsecondary institutions that do not offer baccalaureate degrees, this program provides full payment of tuition and certain fees. At public postsecondary institutions that do offer baccalaureate degrees and at private institutions, the program provides payment of the average of awards paid to students at public schools that do not offer baccalaureate degrees.

**Duration:** 1 year; may be renewed for 1 additional year if the recipient earns at least 24 credits per academic year and maintains a GPA of 2.5 or higher.

**Number awarded:** Varies each year.

**Deadline:** April of each year for priority consideration; June of each year for final consideration.

## 598 LOUISIANA VETERANS STATE AID PROGRAM

Louisiana Department of Veterans Affairs

1885 Wooddale Boulevard, Room 1013

P.O. Box 94095, Capitol Station

Baton Rouge, LA 70804-9095

Phone: (225) 922-0500; Fax: (225) 922-0511; Email: dperkins@vetaffairs.com

Web: www.vetaffairs.com

**Summary:** To provide financial assistance for college to children and surviving spouses of certain disabled or deceased Louisiana veterans.

**Eligibility:** Open to children (between 16 and 25 years of age) of veterans who served during World War I, World War II, the Korean war, or the Vietnam conflict and either died or sustained a disability rated as 90% or more by the U.S. Department of Veterans Affairs. Deceased veterans must have resided in Louisiana for at least 12 months prior to entry into service. Living disabled veterans must have resided in Louisiana for at least 24 months prior to the child's admission into the program. Also eligible are surviving spouses (of any age) of veterans who had been residents of Louisiana for at least 1 year preceding entry into service and who died in war service in the line of duty or from an established wartime service-connected disability subsequently.

**Financial data:** Eligible persons accepted as full-time students at Louisiana state-supported colleges, universities, trade schools, or vocational/technical schools will be admitted free and are exempt from payment of all tuition, laboratory, athletic, medical, and other special fees. Free registration does not cover books, supplies, room and board, or fees assessed by the student body on themselves (such as yearbooks and weekly papers).

**Duration:** Tuition, fee exemption, and possible payment of cash subsistence allowance are provided for a maximum of 4 school years to be completed in not more than 5 years from date of original entry.

**Number awarded:** Varies each year.

**Deadline:** Applications must be received no later than 3 months prior to the beginning of a semester.

## 599 LOWRIDER MAGAZINE SCHOLARSHIP FUND

Lowrider Magazine, Attn: Scholarship Fund

2400 East Katella Avenue, 11th Floor

Anaheim, CA 92806

Phone: (714) 939-2400; Fax: (714) 978-6390

Web: www.lowridermagazine.com

**Summary:** To provide financial assistance for college to Chicano/Latino students.

**Eligibility:** Open to applicants who are of Latino descent, have a GPA of 3.0 or higher, and are currently enrolled as college sophomores, juniors, or seniors. They must submit an official transcript, 2 letters of recommendation, a 1-page essay outlining their financial situation, and a 2-page essay on 1 of 3 topics that change annually. Recently, the topics were 1) "What does calling yourself Chicano or Chicana mean to you?" 2) "How can you use your education/degree to help the Chicano community?" or 3) "Has Affirmative Action served a good purpose and should institutes of higher learning continue to use this policy?"

**Financial data:** Stipends range from $100 to $1,000.

**Duration:** 1 year.

**Number awarded:** Varies each year.

**Deadline:** May of each year.

## 600 LTG AND MRS. JOSEPH M. HEISER SCHOLARSHIP

U.S. Army Ordnance Corps Association, Attn: Heiser Scholarship

P.O. Box 377

Aberdeen Proving Ground, MD 21005-0377

Phone: (410) 272-8540; Fax: (410) 272-8425

Web: www.usaoca.org/heiser.html

**Summary:** To provide financial assistance for college to students who submit, along with their application, an essay on the U.S. Army.

**Eligibility:** Open to high school seniors and students already enrolled in college. Applicants must submit an essay of 1,000 to 1,500 words on a topic related to the history or heritage of the U.S. Army, a statement describing any circumstances that would impact their attending college, letters of recommendation, transcripts, and an essay of 300 to 500 words on their educational and career goals.

**Financial data:** The stipend is $1,000.

**Duration:** 1 year.

**Number awarded:** Varies each year; recently, 4 of these scholarships were awarded.

**Deadline:** June of each year.

## 601 LUCILLE B. ABT SCHOLARSHIPS

Alexander Graham Bell Association for the Deaf

Attn: Financial Aid Coordinator

3417 Volta Place, N.W.

Washington, DC 20007-2778

Phone: (202) 337-5220; Fax: (202) 337-8314; TTY: (202) 337-5221;

Email: financialaid@agbell.org

Web: www.agbell.org

**Summary:** To provide financial assistance to undergraduate and graduate students with moderate to profound hearing loss.

**Eligibility:** Open to undergraduate and graduate students who have been diagnosed with a moderate to profound hearing loss prior to acquiring spoken language (hearing loss averages 60dB or greater in the better ear in the speech frequencies of 500, 1000, and 2000 Hz). Applicants must be committed to using spoken language and lipreading as their preferred mode of communication. They must be accepted or enrolled at a mainstream college or university as a full-time student. Along with their application, they must submit a 1-page essay discussing their career goals and how spoken communication is helping them to reach those goals as a person with a hearing loss. Financial need is considered in the selection process.
**Financial data:** The stipend is $5,000 per year.
**Duration:** 1 year; may be renewed 1 additional year.
**Number awarded:** 10 each year.
**Deadline:** April of each year.

## 602 LYNN M. SMITH MEMORIAL SCHOLARSHIP

California Association for Postsecondary Education and Disability
Attn: Executive Assistant
71423 Biskra Road
Rancho Mirage, CA 92270
Phone: (760) 346-8206; Fax: (760) 340-5275; TTY: (760) 341-4084;
Email: caped2000@aol.com
Web: www.caped.net/scholarship.html
**Summary:** To provide financial assistance to community college students in California who have a disability.
**Eligibility:** Open to students at community colleges in California who have a disability. Applicants must be preparing for a vocational career and have completed at least 6 semester credits with a GPA of 2.5 or higher. They must submit a 1-page personal letter that demonstrates writing skills; progress toward meeting educational and vocational goals; how they accommodate their disability; involvement in community activities; and any other personal factor that might strengthen their application. They must also submit a letter of recommendation from a faculty member, verification of disability, official transcripts, proof of current enrollment, and documentation of financial need.
**Financial data:** The stipend is $1,000.
**Duration:** 1 year.
**Number awarded:** 1 each year.
**Deadline:** August of each year.

## 603 MADISON/DAVIS SCHOLARSHIP AWARD

National Naval Officers Association-Washington, D.C., Chapter
Attn: Scholarship Program
2701 Park Center Drive, B704
Alexandria, VA 22302
Email: williams.stephen@hq.navy.mil
Web: www.dcnnoa.org
**Summary:** To provide financial assistance to minority high school seniors from the Washington, D.C., area.
**Eligibility:** Open to minority seniors at high schools in the Washington, D.C., metropolitan area who plan to enroll full time at an accredited 2-year or 4-year college or university. Applicants must have a GPA of 3.0 or higher. Selection is based on academic achievement, community involvement, and financial need.
**Financial data:** The stipend is $1,000 per year.
**Duration:** 1 year.
**Number awarded:** 1 each year.
**Deadline:** April of each year.

## 604 MAIDS OF ATHENA SCHOLARSHIPS

Maids of Athena
1909 Q Street, N.W., Suite 500
Washington, DC 20009-1007
Phone: (202) 232-6300; Fax: (202) 232-2140
Web: www.ahepa.org/maids/index.html
**Summary:** To provide financial assistance for undergraduate and graduate education to women of Greek descent.
**Eligibility:** Open to women who are members of the Maids of Athena. Applicants may be a graduating high school senior, an undergraduate student, or a graduate student. Selection is based on academic merit, financial need, and participation in the organization.
**Financial data:** The stipend is $1,000.
**Duration:** 1 year.
**Number awarded:** 3 each year: 1 each to a graduating high school senior, undergraduate student, and graduate student.

## 605 MAINE BPW CONTINUING EDUCATION SCHOLARSHIP

Maine Federation of Business and Professional Women
Attn: Futurama Foundation
c/o Jeanne L. Hammond, President
RR 1, Box 1610
Albion, ME 04910-9719
Phone: (207) 437-2325; Email: jlhammon@colby.edu
Web: www.bpwmaine.org/Scholarship.htm
**Summary:** To provide financial assistance for college to women in Maine.
**Eligibility:** Open to women who are residents of Maine. Applicants must be continuing in an accredited program of higher education or job-related training, either full or part time. They must be able to demonstrate financial need.
**Financial data:** The stipend is $1,200.
**Duration:** 1 year.
**Number awarded:** 1 or more each year.
**Deadline:** March of each year.

## 606 MAINE DEMOLAY AND PINE TREE YOUTH FOUNDATION SCHOLARSHIPS

Maine DeMolay and Pine Tree Youth Foundation
c/o Anah Shriners
The Oasis of Bangor Maine
586 Main Street
P.O. Box 735
Bangor, ME 04402-0735
Phone: (207) 942-2254; (888) 225-2624; Fax: (207) 942-1994;
Email: pinetree@bangordemolay.org
Web: www.bangordemolay.org/pinetree.htm
**Summary:** To provide financial assistance for college to high school seniors in Maine.
**Eligibility:** Open to high school seniors in Maine. Certain scholarships are limited to graduates of particular schools, but most are given based on an open competition. Scholarships are awarded without regard to race, religion, age, gender, national origin, or "Masonic Family" relationships. Applicants should submit their high school transcript, a summary of their honors and extracurricular activities, and a narrative describing themselves, their background, and their future plans. Financial need is considered in the selection process.
**Financial data:** Stipends are $1,500 or $1,000.
**Duration:** 1 year.
**Number awarded:** Varies each year. Recently, 13 of these scholarships were awarded: 2 at $1,500 and 11 at $1,000.
**Deadline:** March of each year.

## 607 MAINE LEGISLATURE MEMORIAL SCHOLARSHIP FUND

Maine Education Services, Attn: MES Foundation
One City Center, 11th Floor
Portland, ME 04101
Phone: (207) 791-3600; (800) 922-6352; Fax: (207) 791-3616;
Email: info@mesfoundation.com
Web: www.mesfoundation.com/college/scholarships_mes.asp
**Summary:** To provide financial assistance to residents of Maine planning to attend or currently attending a college or university in the state.
**Eligibility:** Open to residents of Maine who are either seniors graduating from high schools in the state or already in college. Applicants must be planning to enroll or currently enrolled in an accredited 2- or 4-year degree-granting Maine college, university, or technical school as an undergraduate or graduate student. Selection is based on academic excellence as demonstrated by transcripts and GPA, contributions to community and employment, letters of recommendation, a 300-word essay on educational goals and intentions, and financial need.
**Financial data:** The stipend is $1,000.
**Duration:** 1 year.
**Number awarded:** 16 each year: 1 from each county in Maine.
**Deadline:** April of each year.

## 608 MAINE MASONIC AID FOR CONTINUING EDUCATION

Maine Education Services, Attn: MES Foundation
One City Center, 11th Floor
Portland, ME 04101
Phone: (207) 791-3600; (800) 922-6352; Fax: (207) 791-3616;
Email: info@mesfoundation.com
Web: www.mesfoundation.com/college/scholarships_mes_masonic.asp

**Summary:** To provide financial assistance for college or graduate school to students in Maine who meet the federal definition of an independent student.
**Eligibility:** Open to residents of Maine who meet at least 1 of the following criteria: 1) are at least 24 years of age; 2) are married; 3) are enrolled in a graduate level or professional education program; 4) have legal dependents other than a spouse; 5) are an orphan or ward of the court (or were a ward of the court until age 18); or 6) are a veteran of the U.S. armed forces. Selection is based on work experience, educational history, school and community activities, an essay on career goals, a community reference, and financial need.
**Financial data:** The stipend is $1,000 per year.
**Duration:** 1 year.
**Number awarded:** 12 each year.
**Deadline:** April of each year.

### 609 MAINE SENTINEL SCHOLARSHIP FUND

Maine Community Foundation, Attn: Program Director
245 Main Street
Ellsworth, ME 04605
Phone: (207) 667-9735; (877) 700-6800; Fax: (207) 667-0447;
Email: info@mainecf.org
Web: www.mainecf.org/html/scholarships/index.html
**Summary:** To provide financial assistance for college to children of members of the Maine National Guard who have been called to active duty.
**Eligibility:** Open to children of members of the Maine National Guard who have been called to active duty after September 11, 2001. Applicants must be attending or planning to attend a 2-year or 4-year college or university. Preference is given to students who can demonstrate financial need.
**Financial data:** A stipend is awarded (amount not specified).
**Duration:** 1 year.
**Number awarded:** Varies each year.
**Deadline:** April of each year.

### 610 MAINE STATE CHAMBER OF COMMERCE SCHOLARSHIPS

Maine Education Services, Attn: MES Foundation
One City Center, 11th Floor
Portland, ME 04101
Phone: (207) 791-3600; (800) 922-6352; Fax: (207) 791-3616;
Email: info@mesfoundation.com
Web: www.mesfoundation.com/college/scholarships_mes_chamber.asp
**Summary:** To provide financial assistance for a college-level technical, education, or business program to residents of Maine.
**Eligibility:** Open to residents of Maine who are 1) high school seniors planning to work on a technical associate degree at a 2-year college; 2) high school seniors planning to work on a business-related bachelor's degree at a 4-year college or university; and 3) adult learners planning to attend a 2-year college to work on a degree in a business- or education-related field (those applicants must meet federal financial aid criteria for independent student status, i.e., be 24 years of age or older, or be married, or have legal dependents other than a spouse, or be an orphan or ward of the court, or be a veteran of the U.S. armed forces). Preference is given to applicants planning to attend college in Maine. Selection is based on academic achievement, employment and community activities, a letter of recommendation from a high school or community official, an essay describing challenges that businesses face in Maine, and financial need.
**Financial data:** The stipend is $1,500.
**Duration:** 1 year.
**Number awarded:** 3 each year: 1 to a high school senior pursuing a technical degree at a 2-year college, 1 to a high school senior pursuing a business degree at a 4-year institution, and 1 to an adult learner working on a 2-year degree in business or education.
**Deadline:** April of each year.

### 611 MAINE STATE GRANT PROGRAM

Finance Authority of Maine, Attn: Education Finance Programs
5 Community Drive
P.O. Box 949
Augusta, ME 04332-0949
Phone: (207) 623-3263; (800) 228-3734; Fax: (207) 623-0095;
TTY: (207) 626-2717; Email: info@famemaine.com
Web: www.famemaine.com/html/education/fameprogs.html
**Summary:** To provide financial assistance to Maine residents interested in working on a college degree.
**Eligibility:** Open to residents of Maine who have lived in the state for at least 1 year, have graduated from an approved secondary school, can demonstrate financial need, and are enrolled as full-time or part-time students in an approved institution for their first undergraduate degree. Approved schools include all accredited 2- and 4-year colleges, universities, and nursing programs in Maine, as well as regionally accredited 2- and 4-year colleges in states that have a reciprocity agreement with Maine (Connecticut, Massachusetts, New Hampshire, Pennsylvania, Rhode Island, Vermont, and Washington, D.C.).
**Financial data:** The maximum annual stipend is $1,250 at private schools in Maine, $1,000 at public schools in Maine, $500 at public schools outside of Maine, or $1,000 at private schools outside of Maine.
**Duration:** 1 year; may be renewed up to 4 additional years if the recipient remains a Maine resident and maintains satisfactory academic progress.
**Number awarded:** Scholarships are presented to students who demonstrate the greatest financial need. The award process continues until all available funds have been exhausted.
**Deadline:** April of each year.

### 612 MAINE STATE SOCIETY OF WASHINGTON, D.C., FOUNDATION SCHOLARSHIP PROGRAM

Maine State Society of Washington, D.C.,
c/o Hugh L. Dwelley
3508 Wilson Street
Fairfax, VA 22030
Web: www.mainestatesociety.org/MSSFoundation.htm
**Summary:** To provide financial assistance to students who are currently enrolled full time at a university or 4-year degree-granting, nonprofit institution of higher learning within Maine.
**Eligibility:** Open to full-time students enrolled at a 4-year degree-granting, nonprofit institution of higher learning in Maine. High school seniors are not eligible to apply. Applicants must have been legal residents of Maine for at least 4 years (or have at least 1 parent who has been a resident of Maine for at least 4 years). They must be under 25 years of age, be enrolled in at least 14 semester hours or the equivalent, have at least a 3.0 GPA, be working on a baccalaureate degree, and write an essay (up to 500 words) with background information on their qualifications for this scholarship.
**Financial data:** The stipend is at least $1,000.
**Duration:** 1 year; nonrenewable.
**Number awarded:** 3 each year.
**Deadline:** March of each year.

### 613 MAINE TUITION WAIVER PROGRAM FOR CHILDREN AND SPOUSES OF FIRE FIGHTERS, LAW ENFORCEMENT OFFICERS, AND EMERGENCY MEDICAL SERVICES PERSONNEL KILLED IN THE LINE OF DUTY

Finance Authority of Maine, Attn: Education Finance Programs
5 Community Drive
P.O. Box 949
Augusta, ME 04332-0949
Phone: (207) 623-3263; (800) 228-3734; Fax: (207) 623-0095;
TTY: (207) 626-2717; Email: info@famemaine.com
Web: www.famemaine.com/html/education/fameprogs.html
**Summary:** To provide financial assistance for college to children and spouses of deceased law enforcement officers, fire fighters, and emergency medical services personnel in Maine.
**Eligibility:** Open to children and spouses of fire fighters, law enforcement officers, and emergency medical services personnel who have been killed in the line of duty or died as a result of injuries received during the performance of their duties. Applicants must be enrolled in or accepted for enrollment in a branch of the University of Maine system, the Maine Community College System, or the Maine Maritime Academy.
**Financial data:** Eligible students receive waivers of tuition and fees.
**Duration:** 1 year; may be renewed up to 3 additional years.

### 614 MAINE TUITION WAIVER PROGRAM FOR FOSTER CHILDREN UNDER THE CUSTODY OF THE DEPARTMENT OF HUMAN SERVICES

Finance Authority of Maine, Attn: Education Finance Programs
5 Community Drive
P.O. Box 949
Augusta, ME 04332-0949
Phone: (207) 623-3263; (800) 228-3734; Fax: (207) 623-0095;
TTY: (207) 626-2717; Email: info@famemaine.com

Web: www.famemaine.com/html/education/fameprogs.html

**Summary:** To provide financial assistance for college to foster children in Maine.

**Eligibility:** Open to applicants who were foster children under the custody of the Maine Department of Human Services when they graduated from high school. They must be enrolled in or accepted for enrollment in a branch of the University of Maine system, the Maine Community College System, or the Maine Maritime Academy.

**Financial data:** Eligible students receive waivers of tuition and fees.

**Duration:** 1 year; may be renewed up to 3 additional years.

## 615 MAINE VETERANS DEPENDENTS EDUCATIONAL BENEFITS

Bureau of Maine Veterans' Services
117 State House Station
Augusta, ME 04333-0117
Phone: (207) 626-4464; (800) 345-0116 (within ME); Fax: (207) 626-4471;
Email: mvs@me.ngb.army.mil
Web: www.state.me.us/va/defense/vb.htm

**Summary:** To provide financial assistance for undergraduate or graduate education to dependents of disabled and other Maine veterans.

**Eligibility:** Open to children (high school seniors or graduates under 25 years of age), non-divorced spouses, or unremarried widow(er)s of veterans who meet 1 or more of the following requirements: 1) living and determined to have a total permanent disability resulting from a service-connected cause; 2) killed in action; 3) died from a service-connected disability; 4) died while totally and permanently disabled due to a service-connected disability but whose death was not related to the service-connected disability; or 5) a member of the armed forces on active duty who has been listed for more than 90 days as missing in action, captured, forcibly detained, or interned in the line of duty by a foreign government or power. The veteran parent must have been a resident of Maine at the time of entry into service or a resident of Maine for 5 years preceding application for these benefits. Children may be seeking no higher than a bachelor's degree. Spouses, widows, and widowers may work on an advanced degree if they already have a bachelor's degree at the time of enrollment into this program.

**Financial data:** Recipients are entitled to free tuition at institutions of higher education supported by the state of Maine.

**Duration:** Benefits extend for a maximum of 8 semesters. Recipients have 6 consecutive academic years to complete their education.

**Number awarded:** Varies each year.

## 616 MAINE VIETNAM VETERANS SCHOLARSHIP FUND

Maine Community Foundation, Attn: Program Director
245 Main Street
Ellsworth, ME 04605
Phone: (207) 667-9735; (877) 700-6800; Fax: (207) 667-0447;
Email: info@mainecf.org
Web: www.mainecf.org/html/scholarships/index.html

**Summary:** To provide financial assistance for college or graduate school to Vietnam veterans or the dependents of Vietnam or other veterans in Maine.

**Eligibility:** Open to residents of Maine who are Vietnam veterans or the descendants of veterans who served in the Vietnam Theater. As a second priority, children of veterans from other time periods are also considered. Graduating high school seniors, nontraditional students, undergraduates, and graduate students are eligible to apply. Selection is based on financial need, extracurricular activities, work experience, academic achievement, and a personal statement of career goals and how the applicant's educational plans relate to them.

**Financial data:** The stipend is $1,000 per year.

**Duration:** 1 year.

**Number awarded:** 3 to 6 each year.

**Deadline:** April of each year.

## 617 MAINELY CHARACTER SCHOLARSHIP

Mainely Character
P.O. Box 11131
Portland, ME 04104
Email: info@mainelycharacter.org
Web: www.mainelycharacter.org

**Summary:** To provide financial assistance for college to Maine residents who demonstrate principles of character.

**Eligibility:** Open to residents of Maine who are high school seniors or have received a high school diploma and are entering the first year of postsecondary education. Selection is based on character, determined by an assessment process that includes a written essay demonstrating the principles of courage, integrity, responsibility, and concern. A personal interview is also required.

**Financial data:** The stipend is $5,000.

**Duration:** 1 year; nonrenewable.

**Number awarded:** 1 or more each year.

**Deadline:** February of each year.

## 618 MAMORU AND AIKO TAKITANI FOUNDATION SCHOLARSHIPS

Mamoru and Aiko Takitani Foundation
P.O. Box 10687
Honolulu, HI 98616-0687
Email: info@takitani.org
Web: www.takitani.org

**Summary:** To provide financial assistance for college to needy high school seniors in Hawaii.

**Eligibility:** Open to college-bound seniors graduating from high schools in Hawaii. Applicants must prepare a 1-page essay describing their personal goals and how this scholarship would help them attain those, their plans for serving the community after graduation, and any financial or unique circumstances that the sponsor should consider. They must submit those essays and other application materials to their college counselor or senior advisor. Selection is based on academic and extracurricular achievement, the personal essay, the applicant's unique circumstances, and financial need. Each school selects its winner. From those, 6 semifinalists are selected from each school district, 1 from the Hawaii Catholic Schools, and 2 from the Hawaii Association of Independent Schools. From among those semifinalists, the sponsor's board of directors selects finalists.

**Financial data:** The stipend for each high school winner is $1,000. Semifinalists receive an additional $1,000 scholarship. Finalists receive stipends of $10,000 or $5,000.

**Duration:** 1 year.

**Number awarded:** Each qualifying high school in the state (approximately 60) awards 1 of these scholarships. Semifinalist awards are presented to 10 students. The finalist awards include 2 at $10,000 and 1 at $5,000.

**Deadline:** February of each year.

## 619 MANCHESTER REGIONAL COMMUNITY FOUNDATION MEDALLION FUND

New Hampshire Charitable Foundation
37 Pleasant Street
Concord, NH 03301-4005
Phone: (603) 225-6641; (800) 464-6641; Fax: (603) 225-1700;
Email: info@nhcf.org
Web: www.nhcf.org

**Summary:** To provide financial assistance to New Hampshire residents preparing for a vocational or technical career.

**Eligibility:** Open to residents of New Hampshire of any age who are enrolling in an accredited vocational or technical program that does not lead to a 4-year baccalaureate degree. Applicants must be planning to attend a community college, vocational school, trade school, apprenticeship, or other short-term training program. They must be able to demonstrate financial need. Applicants should be able to demonstrate competence and a commitment to their chosen field of study. Preference is given to applicants 1) whose fields are in the traditional manufacturing trade sector (e.g., plumbing, electrical, constructing, machining); 2) who have a clear vision for how their education will help them achieve or improve their employment goals; 3) who have had little or no other educational or training opportunities; and 4) who have made a commitment to their educational program both financially and otherwise.

**Financial data:** Stipends are provided (amount not specified).

**Duration:** 1 year.

**Number awarded:** Varies each year.

**Deadline:** Applications may be submitted at any time.

## 620 MANNE FAMILY FOUNDATION SCHOLARSHIPS

SuperSibs!, Attn: Scholarship Committee
4300 Lincoln Avenue, Suite I
Rolling Meadows, IL 60008
Phone: (847) 705-SIBS; (866) 444-SIBS; Fax: (847) 776-7084;
Email: info@supersibs.org

Web: www.supersibs.org

**Summary:** To provide financial assistance for college to high school seniors who are siblings of children with cancer and can demonstrate financial need.
**Eligibility:** Open to seniors graduating from high schools in the United States, Puerto Rico, or the Virgin Islands with a GPA of 3.2 or higher. Applicants must be the siblings of children who have or have had cancer. They must be planning to attend an accredited college, university, or vocational institution in the following fall. Half-siblings and stepsiblings who reside in the same home as the cancer patient are also eligible. Along with their application, they must submit an essay, up to 1,000 words, on what they learned from their experience as the sibling of a brother or sister with cancer, how they will apply those learnings in their life and the lives of others, the advice they can share with other siblings to help them manage through this challenging time, how this scholarship will make a difference in their life, and anything else they would like the sponsor to know about them. Selection is based on the essay, a high school transcript, a letter of recommendation, and financial need.

**Financial data:** The stipend is $5,000.

**Duration:** 1 year.

**Number awarded:** Up to 5 each year.

**Deadline:** March of each year.

## 621 MARA CRAWFORD HALL OF FAME SCHOLARSHIP

Kansas Federation of Business & Professional Women's Clubs, Inc.
Attn: Kansas BPW Educational Foundation
c/o Diane Smith, Executive Secretary
10418 Haskins
Lenexa, KS 66215-2162
Email: desmith@fcbankonline.com
Web: www.bpwkansas.org/bpw_foundation.htm

**Summary:** To provide financial assistance to women in Kansas who are already in the workforce but are interested in pursuing additional education.
**Eligibility:** Open to women residents of Kansas who graduated from high school more than 5 years previously and are already in the workforce. Applicants may be seeking a degree in any field of study and may be attending a 2-year, 4-year, vocational, or technological program. They must submit 1) documentation of financial need, and 2) a 3-page personal biography in which they express their career goals, the direction they want to take in the future, their proposed field of study, their reason for selecting that field, the institutions they plan to attend and why, their circumstances for reentering school (if a factor), and what makes them uniquely qualified for this scholarship. Applications must be submitted through a local unit of the sponsor.

**Financial data:** A stipend is awarded (amount not specified).

**Duration:** 1 year.

**Number awarded:** 1 or more each year.

**Deadline:** December of each year.

## 622 MARGUERITE ROSS BARNETT MEMORIAL SCHOLARSHIP

Missouri Department of Higher Education, Attn: Student Financial Assistance
3515 Amazonas Drive
Jefferson City, MO 65109-5717
Phone: (573) 526-7958; (800) 473-6757; Fax: (573) 751-6635;
Email: info@dhe.mo.gov
Web: www.dhe.mo.gov/hsstudentsrossbarnett.shtml

**Summary:** To provide financial assistance for college to students in Missouri who are employed while attending school part time.
**Eligibility:** Open to residents of Missouri who are enrolled at least half time but less than full time at participating Missouri postsecondary institutions. Applicants must be able to demonstrate financial need and must be employed at least 20 hours per week. Students working on a degree or certificate in theology or divinity are not eligible. U.S. citizenship or permanent resident status is required.

**Financial data:** The maximum annual award is the least of 1) the actual tuition charged at the school the recipient is attending part time; 2) the amount of tuition charged to a Missouri undergraduate resident enrolled part time in the same class level at the University of Missouri; or 3) the recipient's demonstrated financial need.

**Duration:** 1 semester; may be renewed until the recipient has obtained a baccalaureate degree or has completed 150 semester credit hours, whichever comes first.

**Number awarded:** Varies each year; recently, 239 of these scholarships were awarded.

**Deadline:** March of each year.

## 623 MARI AND JAMES MICHENER SCHOLARSHIP

Japanese American Citizens League, Attn: National Scholarship Awards
1765 Sutter Street
San Francisco, CA 94115
Phone: (415) 921-5225; Fax: (415) 931-4671; Email: jacl@jacl.org
Web: www.jacl.org/scholarships.html

**Summary:** To provide financial assistance for college to student members of the Japanese American Citizens League (JACL).
**Eligibility:** Open to JACL members who are currently enrolled or planning to reenter a college, university, trade school, business college, or other institution of higher learning. Applicants must submit a statement describing their current level of involvement in the Japanese American community or Asian Pacific community and how they will continue their involvement in future years. Selection is based on academic record, extracurricular activities, financial need, and community involvement.

**Financial data:** The stipend depends on the availability of funds but usually ranges from $1,000 to $5,000.

**Duration:** 1 year; nonrenewable.

**Number awarded:** 1 each year.

**Deadline:** March of each year.

## 624 MARIA & ANTONIO PEREIRA SCHOLARSHIP

Portuguese Heritage Scholarship Foundation, Attn: Academic Secretary
P.O. Box 30246
Bethesda, MD 20824-0246
Phone: (301) 652-2775; Email: phsf@vivaportugal.com
Web: www.vivaportugal.com/phsf/apply.htm

**Summary:** To provide financial assistance for college to students of Portuguese American heritage.
**Eligibility:** Open to high school seniors or currently-enrolled college students who are of Portuguese American ancestry. Applicants must be U.S. residents and attending or planning to attend an accredited 4-year college or university. Selection is based on academic achievement and financial need.

**Financial data:** The stipend is $2,000 per year.

**Duration:** 4 years, provided the recipient maintains a GPA of 3.0 or higher.

**Number awarded:** 1 each year.

**Deadline:** January of each year.

## 625 MARIE L. ROSE HUGUENOT SCHOLARSHIPS

Huguenot Society of America, Attn: Office of the Scholarship Committee
122 East 58th Street
New York, NY 10022
Phone: (212) 755-0592
Web: www.huguenotsocietyofamerica.org/scholarships.html

**Summary:** To provide financial assistance for undergraduate education to the descendants of Huguenots.
**Eligibility:** Open to applicants able to submit proof of descent from a Huguenot who emigrated from France and either settled in what is now the United States or left France for other countries before 1787. The scholarships are available to students at 1 of 50 participating universities; for a list, contact the Huguenot Society.

**Financial data:** The award is $3,000 per year.

**Duration:** 1 year.

**Number awarded:** Varies each year.

## 626 MARILYN YETSO MEMORIAL SCHOLARSHIP

Ulman Cancer Fund for Young Adults, Attn: Scholarship Committee
4725 Dorsey Hall Drive, Suite A
PMB 505
Ellicott City, MD 21042
Phone: (410) 964-0202; (888) 393-FUND;
Email: scholarship@ulmanfund.org
Web: www.ulmanfund.org/Services/Scholarship/scholarship_main.htm

**Summary:** To provide financial assistance to college students who have a parent with cancer.
**Eligibility:** Open to students who have or have lost a parent to cancer. Applicants must be able to demonstrate financial need. They must be between 15 and 40 years of age and working on, or planning to work on, an academic or professional degree. Along with their application, they must submit a 500-word essay on 1 of 4 assigned topics that relate to cancer. Selection is based on

the quality of the essay, recommendations, their overall story of cancer survivorship, and financial need.

**Financial data:** The stipend is $1,000.

**Duration:** 1 year.

**Number awarded:** Varies each year; recently, 10 of these scholarships were awarded.

**Deadline:** March of each year.

---

### 627 MARINE CORPS LEAGUE SCHOLARSHIPS

Marine Corps League, Attn: National Executive Director
P.O. Box 3070
Merrifield, VA 22116-3070
Phone: (703) 207-9588; (800) MCL-1775; Fax: (703) 207-0047;
Email: mcl@mcleague.org
Web: www.mcleague.org

**Summary:** To provide college aid to students whose parents served in the Marines and to members of the Marine Corps League or Marine Corps League Auxiliary.

**Eligibility:** Open to qualified applicants in the following order of preference: 1) sons and daughters of Marines who lost their lives in the line of duty; 2) children and grandchildren of active Marine Corps Leaguers and/or Auxiliary members; and 3) members of the Marine Corps League and/or Marine Corps League Auxiliary who are honorably discharged and in need of rehabilitation training not provided by government programs. Applicants must be seeking further education and training as a full-time student and be recommended by the commandant of an active chartered detachment of the Marine Corps League or the president of an active chartered unit of the Auxiliary. Financial need is not considered in the selection process.

**Financial data:** The stipend varies. Funds are paid directly to the recipient.

**Duration:** 1 year; may be renewed up to 3 additional years (all renewals must complete an application and attach a transcript from the college or university).

**Number awarded:** Varies, depending upon the amount of funds available each year.

**Deadline:** June of each year.

---

### 628 MARINE CORPS SCHOLARSHIPS

Marine Corps Scholarship Foundation, Inc.
P.O. Box 3008
Princeton, NJ 08543-3008
Phone: (609) 921-3534; (800) 292-7777; Fax: (609) 452-2259;
Email: mcsfnj@marine-scholars.org
Web: www.marine-scholars.org

**Summary:** To provide financial assistance for college to the children of present or former members of the U.S. Marine Corps.

**Eligibility:** Open to the children of 1) Marines on active duty or in the Reserves; 2) former Marines and Marine Reservists who have received an honorable discharge, received a medical discharge, or were killed while serving in the U.S. Marines; 3) active duty, Reserve, and former U.S. Navy Corpsmen who are serving or have served with the U.S. Marine Corps; and 4) U.S. Navy Corpsmen who have served with the U.S. Marine Corps and have received an honorable discharge, medical discharge, or who were killed while serving in the U.S. Navy. Applicants must be high school seniors, high school graduates, or current undergraduates in an accredited college, university, or postsecondary vocational/technical school. They must submit academic transcripts; a written statement of service from their parent's commanding officer or a copy of their parent's honorable discharge; and a 300-word essay on topics that change periodically. Recently, they were invited to write on the topic, "What is the most valuable lesson you have learned and who was responsible for teaching it?" The family income of applicants must be less than $63,000 per year.

**Financial data:** The stipends of most scholarships range from $500 to $2,500 per year, depending upon the recipient's financial needs and educational requirements. The Toyota Scholars Program, established in 2004 by Toyota Motor Sales, U.S.A., Inc., provides stipends of $5,000 per year. Certain named scholarships (including the Dr. Jack C. Berger and Virginia Butts Berger Memorial Cornerstone Scholarship, the General and Mrs. Graves B. Erskine Memorial Cornerstone Scholarship, the Frederick L. Swindal Cornerstone Scholarship, the Davenport Family Foundation Cornerstone Scholarship, and the Ralph M. Parsons Foundation Cornerstone Scholarship) are for $10,000 per year.

**Duration:** 1 year; may be renewed upon reapplication.

**Number awarded:** Varies each year; recently, 967 of these scholarships, with a total value of more than $1,750,000, were awarded.

**Deadline:** April of each year.

---

### 629 MARION HUBER LEARNING THROUGH LISTENING AWARDS

Recording for the Blind and Dyslexic
Attn: Strategic Communications Department
Anne T. Macdonald Center
20 Roszel Road
Princeton, NJ 08540
Phone: (609) 520-8044; (866) RFBD-585; Email: jhaggith@rfbd.org
Web: www.rfbd.org/applications_awards.htm

**Summary:** To provide financial assistance to outstanding high school students with learning disabilities who plan to continue their education.

**Eligibility:** Open to seniors graduating from public or private high schools in the United States or its territories who have a specific learning disability (visual impairment alone does not satisfy this requirement). Applicants must be planning to continue their education at a 2-year or 4-year college or vocational school. They must be registered Recording for the Blind and Dyslexic borrowers and have earned a GPA of 3.0 or higher in grades 10-12. Selection is based on outstanding scholastic achievement, leadership, enterprise, and service to others.

**Financial data:** Stipends are $6,000 or $2,000.

**Duration:** 1 year.

**Number awarded:** 6 each year: 3 at $6,000 and 3 at $2,000.

**Deadline:** February of each year.

---

### 630 MARION J. BAGLEY SCHOLARSHIP

American Legion Auxiliary, Attn: Department of New Hampshire
State House Annex
25 Capitol Street, Room 432
Concord, NH 03301-6312
Phone: (603) 271-2212; Fax: (603) 271-5352; Email: sankenj@comcast.net

**Summary:** To provide financial assistance for college to New Hampshire residents.

**Eligibility:** Open to New Hampshire residents who are high school seniors, high school graduates or equivalent, or attending a school of higher learning. Applicants must submit 3 letters of recommendation; a list of school, church, and community activities or organizations in which they have participated; transcripts; and a 1,000-word essay on "My obligations as an American." Financial need is considered in the selection process.

**Financial data:** The stipend is $1,000.

**Duration:** 1 year.

**Number awarded:** 1 each year.

**Deadline:** April of each year.

---

### 631 MARLIN R. SCARBOROUGH MEMORIAL SCHOLARSHIP

South Dakota Board of Regents, Attn: Scholarship Committee
306 East Capitol Avenue, Suite 200
Pierre, SD 57501-2545
Phone: (605) 773-3455; Fax: (605) 773-2422; Email: info@ris.sdbor.edu
Web: www.sdbor.edu/administration/academics/Scholarships.htm

**Summary:** To provide financial assistance to students at public universities in South Dakota who are entering their junior year.

**Eligibility:** Open to students entering their junior year at public universities in South Dakota. Applicants must have a GPA of 3.5 or higher. They must be nominated by their university. Along with their application, they must submit an essay explaining their leadership and academic qualities, career plans, and educational interests.

**Financial data:** The stipend is $1,500; funds are allocated to the institution for distribution to the student.

**Duration:** 1 year; nonrenewable.

**Number awarded:** 1 each year.

---

### 632 MARTHA C. JOHNSON TUITION SCHOLARSHIPS

Kentucky Community and Technical College System, Attn: Financial Aid
300 North Main Street
Versailles, KY 40383
Phone: (859) 256-3100; (877) 528-2748 (within KY)
Web: www.kctcs.edu/student/financialaidscholarships/index.htm

**Summary:** To provide financial assistance to sophomores attending a school within the Kentucky Community and Technical College System (KCTCS).

**Eligibility:** Open to KCTCS students entering their sophomore year with a GPA of 3.0 or higher. Applicants must have completed at least 30 hours of a pre-baccalaureate program for transfer to a 4-year college or university. They must be able to demonstrate financial need and outside community service and involvement. Along with their application, they must submit a 1-page essay on their career choice, personal values, and community service. Preference is given to women.

**Financial data:** Stipends vary at each participating college but are intended to provide full payment of tuition and required fees.

**Duration:** 1 year.

**Number awarded:** Varies each year.

### 633 MARTIN LUTHER KING, JR. SCHOLARSHIP

North Carolina Association of Educators, Inc.
Attn: Minority Affairs Commission
700 South Salisbury Street
P.O. Box 27347
Raleigh, NC 27611-7347
Phone: (919) 832-3000, ext. 211; (800) 662-7924, ext. 211; Fax: (919) 839-8229
Web: www.ncae.org

**Summary:** To provide financial assistance for college to minority and other high school seniors in North Carolina.

**Eligibility:** Open to North Carolina residents enrolled as seniors in high school. They must be planning to continue their education upon graduation. Applications are considered and judged by members of the association's Minority Affairs Commission. Selection is based on character, personality, and scholastic achievement.

**Financial data:** The amount of the stipend depends on the availability of funding.

**Duration:** 1 year.

**Number awarded:** 1 each year.

**Deadline:** January of each year.

### 634 MARY KARELE MILLIGAN SCHOLARSHIP

Czech Cultural Center, Attn: Scholarship Coordinator
4920 San Jacinto Street
Houston, TX 77004
Phone: (713) 528-2060; Fax: (713) 528-2017; Email: czech@czechcenter.org
Web: www.czechcenter.org

**Summary:** To provide financial assistance for college to students of Czech descent.

**Eligibility:** Open to full-time undergraduate students currently enrolled at a 4-year college or university. Applicants must be born of Czech parentage (at least 1 parent), be able to identify and communicate with the Czech community, be U.S. citizens, and be able to demonstrate financial need.

**Financial data:** The stipend is $1,000.

**Duration:** 1 year.

**Number awarded:** 3 each year.

**Deadline:** February of each year.

### 635 MARY P. OENSLAGER SCHOLASTIC ACHIEVEMENT AWARDS

Recording for the Blind and Dyslexic
Attn: Strategic Communications Department
Anne T. Macdonald Center
20 Roszel Road
Princeton, NJ 08540
Phone: (609) 520-8044; (866) RFBD-585; Email: jhaggith@rfbd.org
Web: www.rfbd.org/applications_awards.htm

**Summary:** To recognize and reward the outstanding academic achievements of blind college seniors.

**Eligibility:** Open to applicants who 1) are legally blind; 2) have received, or will receive, a bachelor's degree from a 4-year accredited college or university in the United States or its territories during the year the award is given; 3) have an overall academic average of 3.0 or higher; and 4) have been registered borrowers from Recording for the Blind and Dyslexic for at least 1 year and have borrowed at least 1 of its audiobooks during that time. Selection is based on evidence of leadership, enterprise, and service to others.

**Financial data:** Top winners receive $6,000 each, Special Honors winners $3,000 each, and Honors winners $1,000 each.

**Duration:** The awards are presented annually.

**Number awarded:** 9 each year: 3 Top winners, 3 Special Honors winners, and 3 Honors winners.

**Deadline:** February of each year.

### 636 MARY PAOLOZZI MEMBER'S SCHOLARSHIP

Navy Wives Club of America
P.O. Box 54022
Millington, TN 39053-6022
Phone: (866) 511-NWCA; Email: nwca@navywivesclubofamerica.org
Web: www.navywivesclubofamerica.org/nwc/scholarships.htm

**Summary:** To provide financial assistance for undergraduate or graduate study to members of the Navy Wives' Club of America (NWCA).

**Eligibility:** Open to NWCA members who can demonstrate financial need. Applicants must be 1) a high school graduate or senior planning to attend college full time next year; 2) currently enrolled in an undergraduate program and planning to continue as a full-time undergraduate; 3) a college graduate or senior planning to be a full-time graduate student next year; and 4) a high school graduate or GED recipient planning to attend vocational or business school next year.

**Financial data:** Stipends range from $500 to $1,000 each year (depending upon the donations from the NWCA chapters).

**Duration:** 1 year.

**Number awarded:** 1 or more each year.

**Deadline:** May of each year.

### 637 MARYANN K. MURTHA MEMORIAL SCHOLARSHIP

American Legion Auxiliary, Attn: Department of New York
112 State Street, Suite 1310
Albany, NY 12207
Phone: (518) 463-1162; (800) 421-6348; Fax: (518) 449-5406;
Email: alanyhdqtrs@worldnet.att.net
Web: www.deptny.org/scholarships.htm

**Summary:** To provide financial assistance for college to New York residents who are the descendants of veterans.

**Eligibility:** Open to residents of New York who are the children, grandchildren, or great grandchildren of veterans of World War II, the Korean Conflict, the Vietnam War, Grenada/Lebanon, Panama, or the Persian Gulf. Applicants must be high school seniors or graduates younger than 20 years of age. They must be interested in attending an accredited college or university. Along with their application, they must submit a 700-word article describing their plans and goals for the future and how they hope to use their talent and education to help others. Selection is based on character (20%), Americanism (15%), community involvement (15%), leadership (15%), scholarship (20%), and financial need (15%).

**Financial data:** The stipend is $1,000.

**Duration:** 1 year.

**Number awarded:** 1 each year.

**Deadline:** March of each year.

### 638 MARYLAND ASSOCIATION OF PRIVATE COLLEGES AND CAREER SCHOOLS SCHOLARSHIPS

Maryland Association of Private Colleges and Career Schools
Attn: Scholarship Committee
3100 Dunglow Road
Baltimore, MD 21222
Phone: (410) 282-4012; Fax: (410) 282-4133; Email: mdapcs@yahoo.com
Web: www.mapccs.org/scholarships-c.html

**Summary:** To provide financial assistance to students interested in attending selected private career schools in Maryland.

**Eligibility:** Open to high school seniors and graduates who are interested in attending a participating private career school in Maryland. Applicants should be interested in working on a degree in such business or technical areas as cosmetology, barbering, diesel mechanics, automotive technology, massage therapy, allied health, secretarial sciences, or drafting. The H.R. Leslie Scholarship is open to any student who applies to a member school. Selection is based on GPA, involvement in school and community activities, recommendations from school officials, desire, and potential to succeed in their career field. Financial need is not considered in the selection process.

**Financial data:** Individual awards range from $500 to more than $5,000. The H.R. Leslie Scholarship is $1,000. Funds must be applied for full or partial payment of tuition. Recently, a total of $164,000 was awarded.

**Duration:** 1 year.

**Number awarded:** Varies each year; since the program was established in 1983, more than $3 million in scholarships have been awarded.

**Deadline:** March of each year.

## 639 MARYLAND DELEGATE SCHOLARSHIP PROGRAM

Maryland Higher Education Commission
Attn: Office of Student Financial Assistance
839 Bestgate Road, Suite 400
Annapolis, MD 21401-3013
Phone: (410) 260-4565; (800) 974-1024; Fax: (410) 974-5376;
TTY: (800) 735-2258; Email: osfamail@mhec.state.md.us
Web: www.mhec.state.md.us/financialAid/ProgramDescriptions/prog_delegate.asp

**Summary:** To provide financial assistance to vocational, undergraduate, and graduate students in Maryland.

**Eligibility:** Open to students enrolled or planning to enroll either part time or full time in a vocational, undergraduate, or graduate program in Maryland. Applicants and their parents must be Maryland residents. Awards are made by state delegates to students in their district. Financial need must be demonstrated if the Office of Student Financial Assistance makes the award for the delegate.

**Financial data:** The minimum annual award is $200. The total amount of all state awards may not exceed the cost of attendance as determined by the school's financial aid office or $17,800, whichever is less.

**Duration:** 1 year; may be renewed for up to 3 additional years if the recipient maintains satisfactory academic progress.

**Number awarded:** Varies each year.

**Deadline:** February of each year.

## 640 MARYLAND DISTINGUISHED SCHOLAR AWARDS

Maryland Higher Education Commission
Attn: Office of Student Financial Assistance
839 Bestgate Road, Suite 400
Annapolis, MD 21401-3013
Phone: (410) 260-4569; (800) 974-1024, ext. 4569; Fax: (410) 974-5376;
TTY: (800) 735-2258; Email: osfamail@mhec.state.md.us
Web: www.mhec.state.md.us/financialAid/ProgramDescriptions/prog_ds.asp

**Summary:** To provide financial assistance for college to outstanding high school juniors in Maryland.

**Eligibility:** Open to outstanding high school juniors in Maryland who intend to work on an undergraduate degree on a full-time basis at an accredited college, university, or private career school in the state. Students may qualify in 1 of 3 ways: 1) superior academic achievement, in which finalists are selected on the basis of GPA (minimum 3.7) and scores on PSAT, SAT, or ACT exams; 2) National Achievement Scholarship and National Merit Scholarship programs, in which finalists automatically receive these scholarships if they enroll in eligible Maryland institutions; and 3) superior talent in the arts, in which finalists are selected in statewide auditions or portfolio evaluations in visual art, instrumental music, vocal music, dance, or drama. Financial need is not considered.

**Financial data:** The stipend is $3,000 per year. The total amount of all state awards may not exceed the cost of attendance as determined by the school's financial aid office or $17,800, whichever is less.

**Duration:** 1 year; may be renewed up to 3 additional years if the recipient maintains at least a 3.0 GPA and remains enrolled full time at an eligible Maryland institution.

**Number awarded:** 350 each year.

**Deadline:** Applications in the academic achievement category must be submitted in February of each year; nominations in the talent category must be submitted in April of each year.

## 641 MARYLAND EDUCATIONAL ASSISTANCE GRANTS

Maryland Higher Education Commission
Attn: Office of Student Financial Assistance
839 Bestgate Road, Suite 400
Annapolis, MD 21401-3013
Phone: (410) 260-4565; (800) 974-1024; Fax: (410) 974-5376;
TTY: (800) 735-2258; Email: osfamail@mhec.state.md.us
Web: www.mhec.state.md.us/financialAid/ProgramDescriptions/prog_ea.asp

**Summary:** To provide financial assistance to undergraduate students in Maryland.

**Eligibility:** Open to Maryland residents who are enrolled or planning to enroll full time as an undergraduate student at a Maryland 2- or 4-year college or university. Financial need must be documented.

**Financial data:** The amount of the grant equals 35% of the financial need, ranging from $400 to $2,700 per year. The total amount of all state awards may not exceed the cost of attendance as determined by the school's financial aid office or $17,800, whichever is less.

**Duration:** 1 year; recipients may reapply for up to 3 additional years if they maintain satisfactory academic progress and continue to demonstrate financial need.

**Number awarded:** Varies each year.

**Deadline:** February of each year.

## 642 MARYLAND GUARANTEED ACCESS GRANTS

Maryland Higher Education Commission
Attn: Office of Student Financial Assistance
839 Bestgate Road, Suite 400
Annapolis, MD 21401-3013
Phone: (410) 260-4555; (800) 974-1024, ext. 4555; Fax: (410) 974-5376;
TTY: (800) 735-2258; Email: osfamail@mhec.state.md.us
Web: www.mhec.state.md.us/financialAid/ProgramDescriptions/prog_ga.asp

**Summary:** To provide financial assistance to needy undergraduate students in Maryland.

**Eligibility:** Open to seniors graduating from high schools in Maryland and planning to enroll as full-time undergraduate students in a program leading to a degree, diploma, or certificate at a 2- or 4-year college or university in the state. Applicants must have a high school GPA of 2.5 or higher and be able to demonstrate financial need. Currently, the maximum allowable total income is $12,103 for a family of 1, rising to $41,041 for a family of 8 plus $4,134 for each additional family member.

**Financial data:** Awards equal 100% of financial need, ranging from $400 to $13,800 per year. The total amount of all state awards may not exceed the cost of attendance as determined by the school's financial aid office or $17,800, whichever is less.

**Duration:** 1 year; recipients may reapply for up to 3 additional years if they maintain satisfactory academic progress and continue to demonstrate financial need.

**Number awarded:** Varies each year.

**Deadline:** February of each year.

## 643 MARYLAND KIDS' CHANCE SCHOLARSHIPS

Kids' Chance of Maryland, Inc.
P.O. Box 20262
Baltimore, MD 21284
Phone: (410) 832-4702; Fax: (410) 832-4726; Email: info@kidschance-md.org
Web: www.kidschance-md.org

**Summary:** To provide financial assistance for college to Maryland residents whose parent was killed or permanently disabled in an employment-related accident.

**Eligibility:** Open to Maryland residents between 16 and 25 years of age who had a parent permanently or catastrophically injured or killed in an employment-related accident compensable under the Maryland Workers' Compensation Act. Applicants must be attending or planning to attend college or technical school. Financial need is considered in the selection process.

**Financial data:** Stipends depend on the need of the students. Funds are intended to cover tuition and books but may also including housing and meals.

**Duration:** 1 year; recipients may reapply.

**Number awarded:** Varies each year.

## 644 MARYLAND PART-TIME GRANTS

Maryland Higher Education Commission
Attn: Office of Student Financial Assistance
839 Bestgate Road, Suite 400
Annapolis, MD 21401-3013
Phone: (410) 260-4565; (800) 974-1024; Fax: (410) 974-5376;
TTY: (800) 735-2258; Email: osfamail@mhec.state.md.us
Web: www.mhec.state.md.us/financialAid/ProgramDescriptions/prog_ptgrant.asp

**Summary:** To provide financial assistance to students in Maryland who are attending college on a part-time basis.

**Eligibility:** Open to students at Maryland colleges who are enrolled for at least 6 but no more than 11 credits each semester. Applicants must be able to demonstrate financial need. Both they and their parents must be Maryland residents.

**Financial data:** Grants range from $200 to $1,000 per year.

**Duration:** 1 year; may be renewed for up to 7 additional years.

**Number awarded:** Varies each year.

**Deadline:** February of each year.

## 645 MARYLAND SENATORIAL SCHOLARSHIPS

Maryland Higher Education Commission
Attn: Office of Student Financial Assistance
839 Bestgate Road, Suite 400
Annapolis, MD 21401-3013
Phone: (410) 260-4565; (800) 974-1024; Fax: (410) 974-5376;
TTY: (800) 735-2258; Email: osfamail@mhec.state.md.us
Web: www.mhec.state.md.us/financialAid/ProgramDescriptions/prog_senatorial.asp

**Summary:** To provide financial assistance to vocational, undergraduate, and graduate students in Maryland.

**Eligibility:** Open to students enrolled either part time or full time in a vocational, undergraduate, or graduate program in Maryland. Applicants and their parents must be Maryland residents and able to demonstrate financial need. Awards are made by state senators to students in their districts. Some senators ask the Office of Student Financial Assistance to make awards for them; those awards are made on the basis of financial need.

**Financial data:** Stipends range from $200 to $2,000 per year, depending on the need of the recipient. The total amount of all state awards may not exceed the cost of attendance as determined by the school's financial aid office or $17,800, whichever is less.

**Duration:** 1 year; may be renewed for up to 3 additional years of full-time study or 7 additional years of part-time study, provided the recipient maintains satisfactory academic progress.

**Number awarded:** Varies each year.

**Deadline:** February of each year.

## 646 MARYLAND STATE GRANGE DEAF SCHOLARSHIP

Maryland State Grange, Attn: Master
8743 Old Kiln Road
Thurmont, MD 21788-1219
Phone: (301) 447-2075; Fax: (301) 447-2019; Email: rlt-rox@juno.com

**Summary:** To provide financial assistance for college or graduate school to Maryland residents who are either deaf or preparing to work with hearing-impaired people.

**Eligibility:** Open to residents of Maryland who graduated from a high school in the state and are attending college or graduate school in the state. Applicants must be 1) deaf or hearing impaired, or 2) preparing for a career working with deaf or hearing-impaired people.

**Financial data:** A stipend is awarded (amount not specified).

**Duration:** 1 year; may be renewed if the recipient maintains a GPA of 3.0 or higher.

**Number awarded:** 1 or more each year.

**Deadline:** May of each year.

## 647 MARYLAND TUITION WAIVER FOR FOSTER CARE RECIPIENTS

Maryland Higher Education Commission
Attn: Office of Student Financial Assistance
839 Bestgate Road, Suite 400
Annapolis, MD 21401-3013
Phone: (410) 260-4565; (800) 974-1024; Fax: (410) 974-5376;
TTY: (800) 735-2258; Email: osfamail@mhec.state.md.us
Web: www.mhec.state.md.us/financialAid/ProgramDescriptions/prog_fostercare.asp

**Summary:** To provide financial assistance for college to residents of Maryland who have lived in foster care.

**Eligibility:** Open to Maryland residents under 21 years of age who either 1) resided in a foster care home in the state at the time they graduated from high school or completed a GED examination, or 2) resided in a foster care home in the state on their 14th birthday and were then adopted. Applicants must be planning to enroll as a degree candidate at a public 2-year or 4-year higher educational institution in Maryland.

**Financial data:** Recipients are exempt from paying tuition and mandatory fees at public colleges and universities in Maryland.

**Duration:** 1 year; may be renewed for an additional 4 years or until completion of a bachelor's degree, whichever comes first, provided the recipient maintains satisfactory academic progress.

**Number awarded:** Varies each year.

**Deadline:** February of each year.

## 648 MAS AND MAJIU UYESUGI MEMORIAL SCHOLARSHIP

Japanese American Citizens League, Attn: National Scholarship Awards
1765 Sutter Street
San Francisco, CA 94115
Phone: (415) 921-5225; Fax: (415) 931-4671; Email: jacl@jacl.org
Web: www.jacl.org/scholarships.html

**Summary:** To provide financial assistance for college to student members of the Japanese American Citizens League (JACL) who are high school seniors.

**Eligibility:** Open to JACL members who are high school seniors interested in attending a college, university, trade school, business college, or other institution of higher learning. Applicants must submit a statement describing their current level of involvement in the Japanese American community or Asian Pacific community and how they will continue their involvement in future years. Selection is based on academic record, extracurricular activities, and community involvement.

**Financial data:** The stipend depends on the availability of funds but usually ranges from $1,000 to $5,000.

**Duration:** 1 year; nonrenewable.

**Number awarded:** At least 1 each year.

**Deadline:** February of each year.

## 649 MASAO AND SUMAKO ITANO MEMORIAL SCHOLARSHIP

Japanese American Citizens League, Attn: National Scholarship Awards
1765 Sutter Street
San Francisco, CA 94115
Phone: (415) 921-5225; Fax: (415) 931-4671; Email: jacl@jacl.org
Web: www.jacl.org/scholarships.html

**Summary:** To provide financial assistance for college to student members of the Japanese American Citizens League (JACL) who are high school seniors.

**Eligibility:** Open to JACL members who are high school seniors interested in attending a college, university, trade school, business college, or other institution of higher learning. Applicants must submit a statement describing their current level of involvement in the Japanese American community or Asian Pacific community and how they will continue their involvement in future years. Selection is based on academic record, extracurricular activities, and community involvement.

**Financial data:** The stipend depends on the availability of funds but usually ranges from $1,000 to $5,000.

**Duration:** 1 year; nonrenewable.

**Number awarded:** At least 1 each year.

**Deadline:** February of each year.

## 650 MASONIC FOUNDATION OF UTAH SCHOLARSHIPS

Masonic Foundation of Utah, Attn: Grand Secretary
650 East South Temple
Salt Lake City, UT 84102
Phone: (801) 363-2936
Web: www.utahgrandlodge.org

**Summary:** To provide financial assistance for college to students in Utah.

**Eligibility:** Open to Utah residents who are attending or planning to attend an accredited college or university. No relationship or connection to Masonry or Masonic organizations is required. Applicants must submit transcripts from the previous year and 2 letters of recommendation.

**Financial data:** The stipend is $1,600.

**Duration:** 1 year.

**Number awarded:** Varies each year; recently, 33 of these scholarships were awarded.

**Deadline:** June of each year.

## 651 MASSACHUSETTS CASH GRANT PROGRAM

Massachusetts Office of Student Financial Assistance
454 Broadway, Suite 200
Revere, MA 02151
Phone: (617) 727-9420; Fax: (617) 727-0667; Email: osfa@osfa.mass.edu
Web: www.osfa.mass.edu

**Summary:** To provide financial assistance to Massachusetts residents who are attending state-supported colleges and universities.

**Eligibility:** Open to permanent legal residents of Massachusetts (for at least 1 year) who are enrolled as an undergraduate student at a state-supported college or university. U.S. citizenship or permanent resident status is required. Financial need must be demonstrated.

**Financial data:** These awards provide assistance in meeting institutionally-held charges, such as mandatory fees and non-state-supported tuition. The amount of the award depends on the need of the recipient.

**Duration:** 1 year; may be renewed.

**Number awarded:** Varies each year.

**Deadline:** Deadlines are established by the financial aid office of each participating Massachusetts institution.

### 652 MASSACHUSETTS COMMUNITY COLLEGES ACCESS GRANT PROGRAM

Massachusetts Community Colleges, Attn: Executive Office
Old South Building
294 Washington Street, Suite 301
Boston, MA 02108
Phone: (617) 542-2911; Email: mherbert@mcceo.mass.edu
Web: www.masscc.org/student_tuition.asp

**Summary:** To provide reduced tuition at community colleges in Massachusetts to students who meet financial need requirements.

**Eligibility:** Open to students at community colleges in Massachusetts who are working on an associate degree. Applicants must have a household income of $36,000 or less to qualify for full assistance. Students with a household income greater than $36,000 may also qualify for partial assistance.

**Financial data:** Students who qualify for full assistance receive payment of the full cost of tuition and fees.

**Duration:** 1 year; may be renewed.

**Number awarded:** Varies each year.

### 653 MASSACHUSETTS DSS ADOPTED CHILDREN TUITION WAIVER

Massachusetts Office of Student Financial Assistance
454 Broadway, Suite 200
Revere, MA 02151
Phone: (617) 727-9420; Fax: (617) 727-0667; Email: osfa@osfa.mass.edu
Web: www.osfa.mass.edu

**Summary:** To provide financial assistance for college to students adopted through the Massachusetts Department of Social Services (DSS).

**Eligibility:** Open to students 24 years of age or younger who were adopted through DSS by state employees or eligible Massachusetts residents, regardless of the date of adoption. Applicants must be U.S. citizens or permanent residents attending or planning to attend a Massachusetts public institution of higher education as an undergraduate student.

**Financial data:** All tuition for state-supported courses is waived.

**Duration:** Up to 4 academic years.

**Number awarded:** Varies each year.

### 654 MASSACHUSETTS DSS TUITION WAIVER FOR FOSTER CARE CHILDREN

Massachusetts Office of Student Financial Assistance
454 Broadway, Suite 200
Revere, MA 02151
Phone: (617) 727-9420; Fax: (617) 727-0667; Email: osfa@osfa.mass.edu
Web: www.osfa.mass.edu

**Summary:** To provide financial assistance for college to foster children in the custody of the Massachusetts Department of Social Services (DSS).

**Eligibility:** Open to students 24 years of age or younger who have been in the custody of the DSS for at least 12 consecutive months. Applicants may not have been adopted or returned home. They must be U.S. citizens or permanent residents attending or planning to attend a college or university in Massachusetts as a full-time undergraduate student.

**Financial data:** All tuition for state-supported courses is waived.

**Duration:** Up to 4 academic years.

**Number awarded:** Varies each year.

### 655 MASSACHUSETTS FOSTER CHILD GRANT PROGRAM

Massachusetts Office of Student Financial Assistance
454 Broadway, Suite 200
Revere, MA 02151
Phone: (617) 727-9420; Fax: (617) 727-0667; Email: osfa@osfa.mass.edu
Web: www.osfa.mass.edu

**Summary:** To provide financial assistance for college to foster children in the custody of the Massachusetts Department of Social Services (DSS).

**Eligibility:** Open to students 24 years of age or younger who are current or former foster children placed in the custody of the DSS through a care and protection petition. Applicants must have signed a voluntary agreement with DSS establishing terms and conditions for receiving this aid. They must be U.S. citizens or permanent residents attending or planning to attend a college or university in the continental United States as a full-time undergraduate student.

**Financial data:** The stipend is $6,000 per year.

**Duration:** Up to 5 academic years.

**Number awarded:** Varies each year.

### 656 MASSACHUSETTS JOINT ADMISSIONS TUITION ADVANTAGE PROGRAM

Massachusetts Office of Student Financial Assistance
454 Broadway, Suite 200
Revere, MA 02151
Phone: (617) 727-9420; Fax: (617) 727-0667; Email: osfa@osfa.mass.edu
Web: www.osfa.mass.edu

**Summary:** To provide financial assistance to Massachusetts students who transfer from a community college to a public 4-year institution in the state.

**Eligibility:** Open to students who completed an associate degree at a public community college in Massachusetts within the prior calendar year as a participant in a Joint Admissions Program. Applicants must have earned a GPA of 3.0 or higher and be transferring to a state college or participating university.

**Financial data:** Eligible students receive a waiver of tuition equal to 33% of the resident tuition rate at the college or university they attend.

**Duration:** Up to 2 academic years, if the recipient maintains a cumulative GPA of 3.0 or higher.

**Number awarded:** Varies each year.

### 657 MASSACHUSETTS NEED BASED TUITION WAIVER PROGRAM

Massachusetts Office of Student Financial Assistance
454 Broadway, Suite 200
Revere, MA 02151
Phone: (617) 727-9420; Fax: (617) 727-0667; Email: osfa@osfa.mass.edu
Web: www.osfa.mass.edu

**Summary:** To provide financial assistance for college to Massachusetts residents who demonstrate financial need.

**Eligibility:** Open to permanent legal residents of Massachusetts (for at least 1 year) who are U.S. citizens or permanent residents, are in compliance with Selective Service registration, are not in default on any federal student loan, are enrolled in at least 3 undergraduate units in an eligible program at a Massachusetts institution of higher learning, and are able to document financial need.

**Financial data:** Eligible students are exempt from any tuition payments for an undergraduate degree or certificate program at public colleges or universities in Massachusetts. These awards, in combination with other resources in the student's financial aid package, may not exceed the student's demonstrated financial need.

**Duration:** Up to 4 academic years, for a total of 130 semester hours.

**Number awarded:** Varies each year.

### 658 MASSACHUSETTS PART-TIME GRANT PROGRAM

Massachusetts Office of Student Financial Assistance
454 Broadway, Suite 200
Revere, MA 02151
Phone: (617) 727-9420; Fax: (617) 727-0667; Email: osfa@osfa.mass.edu
Web: www.osfa.mass.edu

**Summary:** To provide financial assistance to Massachusetts residents who are attending colleges and universities on a part-time basis.

**Eligibility:** Open to permanent legal residents of Massachusetts (for at least 1 year) who are part-time undergraduates at a public, private, independent, for profit, or nonprofit institution in Massachusetts. U.S. citizenship or permanent resident status is required. Financial need must be demonstrated.

**Financial data:** Awards range from $200 to a maximum that depends on the type of institution the student attends.

**Duration:** 1 year; may be renewed.

**Number awarded:** Varies each year.

**Deadline:** Deadlines are established by the financial aid office of each participating Massachusetts institution.

## 659 MASSACHUSETTS PUBLIC SERVICE GRANT PROGRAM

Massachusetts Office of Student Financial Assistance
454 Broadway, Suite 200
Revere, MA 02151
Phone: (617) 727-9420; Fax: (617) 727-0667; Email: osfa@osfa.mass.edu
Web: www.osfa.mass.edu

**Summary:** To provide financial assistance for college to children or widow(er)s of deceased public service officers and others in Massachusetts.

**Eligibility:** Open to Massachusetts residents. They must be 1) the children or spouses of fire fighters, police officers, or corrections officers who were killed or died from injuries incurred in the line of duty; 2) children of prisoners of war or military service personnel missing in action in southeast Asia whose wartime service was credited to Massachusetts and whose service was between February 1, 1955 and the termination of the Vietnam campaign; or 3) children of veterans whose service was credited to Massachusetts and who were killed in action or died as a result of their service.

**Financial data:** Scholarships provide up to the cost of tuition at a state-supported college or university in Massachusetts; if the recipient attends a private Massachusetts college or university, the scholarship is equivalent to tuition at a public institution, up to $2,500.

**Duration:** 1 year; renewable.

**Number awarded:** Varies each year.

**Deadline:** April of each year.

## 660 MASSACHUSETTS VALEDICTORIAN TUITION WAIVER PROGRAM

Massachusetts Office of Student Financial Assistance
454 Broadway, Suite 200
Revere, MA 02151
Phone: (617) 727-9420; Fax: (617) 727-0667; Email: osfa@osfa.mass.edu
Web: www.osfa.mass.edu

**Summary:** To provide financial assistance for college to Massachusetts residents who have been designated as valedictorians at their high school.

**Eligibility:** Open to seniors designated by a public or private high school in Massachusetts as a valedictorian. Applicants must have been permanent legal residents of Massachusetts for at least 1 year and be planning to enroll at a public higher education institution in the state. They must be in compliance with Selective Service registration and may not be in default on any federal student loan.

**Financial data:** Eligible students are exempt from any tuition payments for an undergraduate degree or certificate program at public colleges or universities in Massachusetts.

**Duration:** Up to 4 academic years, for a total of 130 semester hours.

**Number awarded:** Varies each year.

## 661 MASSACHUSETTS VETERANS TUITION WAIVER PROGRAM

Massachusetts Office of Student Financial Assistance
454 Broadway, Suite 200
Revere, MA 02151
Phone: (617) 727-9420; Fax: (617) 727-0667; Email: osfa@osfa.mass.edu
Web: www.osfa.mass.edu

**Summary:** To provide financial assistance for college to Massachusetts residents who are veterans.

**Eligibility:** Open to permanent legal residents of Massachusetts (for at least 1 year) who served actively during the Spanish-American War, World War I, World War II, Korea, Vietnam, the Lebanese peace keeping force, the Grenada rescue mission, the Panamanian intervention force, the Persian Gulf, or Operation Restore Hope in Somalia. They may not be in default on any federal student loan.

**Financial data:** Eligible veterans are exempt from any tuition payments for an undergraduate degree or certificate program at public colleges or universities in Massachusetts.

**Duration:** Up to 4 academic years, for a total of 130 semester hours.

**Number awarded:** Varies each year.

## 662 MASSGRANT PROGRAM

Massachusetts Office of Student Financial Assistance
454 Broadway, Suite 200
Revere, MA 02151
Phone: (617) 727-9420; Fax: (617) 727-0667; Email: osfa@osfa.mass.edu
Web: www.osfa.mass.edu

**Summary:** To provide financial assistance for college to Massachusetts residents who are attending approved schools in designated states.

**Eligibility:** Open to students enrolled in a certificate, associate, or bachelor's degree program. Applicants must have been permanent legal residents of Massachusetts for at least 1 year and attending state-approved postsecondary schools (public, private, independent, for profit, or nonprofit) as full-time undergraduate students in Connecticut, Maine, Massachusetts, New Hampshire, Pennsylvania, Rhode Island, Vermont, or Washington, D.C. U.S. citizenship or permanent resident status is required. Selection is based on financial need, with an expected family contribution between zero and $3,850.

**Financial data:** Awards range from $300 to $2,300 per year.

**Duration:** 1 year; may be renewed for up to 4 additional years.

**Number awarded:** Varies each year.

**Deadline:** April of each year.

## 663 MASTERGUARD FALLEN HEROES SCHOLARSHIP FUND

MasterGuard Corporation, Attn: Scholarship Committee
801 Hammond Street, Suite 200
Coppell, TX 75019-4471
Phone: (972) 393-1700; Fax: (972) 393-1701
Web: www.fallenheroes.org/masterguard-eligibility.html

**Summary:** To provide financial assistance for undergraduate or graduate study to dependents of deceased fire fighters.

**Eligibility:** Open to the spouses, sons, daughters, legally adopted children, and stepchildren of deceased fire fighters who met the criteria for inclusion on the National Fallen Firefighters Memorial in Emmitsburg, Maryland. Applicants must have a high school diploma or equivalent or be within the final year of high school and be working on or planning to work on undergraduate or graduate study or job skills training at an accredited university, college, community college, or technical school. Both full- and part-time students are eligible. Children of fallen fire fighters must be under 30 years of age. Along with their application, they must submit a 200-word personal letter on why they want their scholarship, what they intend to do upon completion of their education, and any special circumstances (such as financial hardship or family responsibilities) they want the selection committee to know. Selection is based on the essay, academic standing (GPA of 2.0 or higher), involvement in extracurricular (including community and volunteer) activities, and 2 letters of recommendation (at least 1 of which should be from a member of the fire service).

**Financial data:** A stipend is awarded (amount not specified).

**Duration:** 1 year.

**Number awarded:** Varies each year; recently, 18 of these scholarships were awarded.

**Deadline:** March of each year.

## 664 MATT STAUFFER MEMORIAL SCHOLARSHIPS

Ulman Cancer Fund for Young Adults
Attn: Scholarship Committee, 4725 Dorsey Hall Drive, Suite A
PMB 505
Ellicott City, MD 21042
Phone: (410) 964-0202; (888) 393-FUND;
Email: scholarship@ulmanfund.org
Web: www.ulmanfund.org/Services/Scholarship/scholarship_main.htm

**Summary:** To provide financial assistance for college to undergraduates who have had cancer.

**Eligibility:** Open to students who are battling, or have overcome, cancer. Applicants must be able to demonstrate financial need. They must be between 15 and 40 years of age and working on, or planning to work on, an academic or professional degree. Along with their application, they must submit a 500-word essay on 1 of 4 assigned topics that relate to cancer. Selection is based on the quality of the essay, recommendations, their overall story of cancer survivorship, and financial need.

**Financial data:** The stipend is $1,000.

**Duration:** 1 year.

**Number awarded:** Varies each year; recently, 12 of these scholarships were awarded.

**Deadline:** March of each year.

## 665 MBNA DELAWARE SCHOLARS PROGRAM

MBNA Education Foundation
c/o MBNA Corporation, National Headquarters
1100 North King Street
Wilmington, DE 19884-0722

Phone: (302) 432-4800; (800) 205-8877
Web: www.mbna.com/about/foundation/scholarsde2.html
**Summary:** To provide financial assistance for college to graduating high school seniors in Delaware.
**Eligibility:** Open to seniors graduating from high schools in Delaware. Applicants must be interested in attending a 4-year college or university in the state as a full-time student. They must be U.S. citizens or legal residents, be able to demonstrate financial need, have at least a 2.5 GPA, and be actively applying for other sources of financial aid (such as federal and state grants). Selection is based on academic record, standardized test scores, financial need, recommendations, extracurricular activities, leadership qualities, work records, and an interview.
**Financial data:** Stipends range up to $7,500 per year, depending on the financial need of the recipient. Funds are paid to the financial aid office of the student's chosen college or university.
**Duration:** 1 year; may be renewed for up to 3 additional years provided the recipient remains enrolled full time, maintains a GPA of 2.5 or higher at the end of the freshman year and 3.0 for the following years; and makes satisfactory progress toward a degree.
**Number awarded:** Varies each year.
**Deadline:** December of each year.

### 666 MEDAL OF HONOR AFCEA ROTC SCHOLARSHIPS

Armed Forces Communications and Electronics Association
Attn: AFCEA Educational Foundation
4400 Fair Lakes Court
Fairfax, VA 22033-3899
Phone: (703) 631-6149; (800) 336-4583, ext. 6149; Fax: (703) 631-4693;
Email: scholarship@afcea.org
Web: www.afcea.org/education/scholarships/rotc/MedalofHonor.asp
**Summary:** To provide financial assistance to ROTC cadets who demonstrate outstanding leadership performance and potential.
**Eligibility:** Open to ROTC cadets enrolled full time at an accredited degree-granting 4-year college or university in the United States. Applicants must be sophomores or juniors at the time of application and have a GPA of 3.0 or higher with a major in an academic discipline. Selection is based on demonstrated leadership performance and potential and strong commitment to serve in the U.S. armed forces.
**Financial data:** The stipend is $3,000.
**Duration:** 1 year.
**Number awarded:** 4 each year: 1 each for Army, Navy, Marine Corps, and Air Force ROTC students.
**Deadline:** March of each year.

### 667 METHODIST SEPTEMBER 11 MEMORIAL SCHOLARSHIPS

United Methodist Higher Education Foundation
1001 19th Avenue South
P.O. Box 340005
Nashville, TN 37203-0005
Phone: (615) 340-7385; (800) 811-8110; Fax: (615) 340-7330;
Email: umhef@gbhem.org
Web: www.umhef.org/sept11fund.html
**Summary:** To provide financial assistance to students at Methodist institutions and Methodist students whose parent or guardian was disabled or killed in the terrorist attacks on September 11, 2001.
**Eligibility:** Open to 1) students attending a United Methodist-related college or university in the United States, and 2) United Methodist students attending a higher education institution in the United States. Applicants must have lost a parent or guardian or had a parent or guardian disabled as a result of the September 11, 2001 terrorist attacks. They must be enrolled full time.
**Financial data:** The stipend depends on the number of applicants.
**Duration:** 1 year; may be renewed as long as the recipients maintain satisfactory academic progress as defined by their institution.
**Number awarded:** Varies each year; a total of $30,000 is available for this program.
**Deadline:** Applications may be submitted at any time.

### 668 MG JAMES URSANO SCHOLARSHIP FUND

Army Emergency Relief
200 Stovall Street
Alexandria, VA 22332-0600
Phone: (703) 428-0000; (866) 878-0000; Fax: (703) 325-7183;
Email: Education@aerhq.org

Web: www.aerhq.org/education_dependentchildren_MGJames.asp
**Summary:** To provide financial assistance for college to the dependent children of Army personnel.
**Eligibility:** Open to dependent children under 22 years of age (including stepchildren and legally adopted children) of soldiers on active duty, retired, or deceased while on active duty or after retirement. Applicants must be unmarried and enrolled, accepted, or pending acceptance as full-time students in accredited postsecondary educational institutions. Selection is based primarily on financial need, but academic achievements and individual accomplishments are also considered.
**Financial data:** The amount varies, depending on the needs of the recipient, but ranges from $900 to $1,900 per academic year.
**Duration:** 1 year; may be renewed for up to 3 additional years if the recipient maintains a GPA of 2.0 or higher.
**Number awarded:** Varies each year; recently, 2,165 of these scholarships, with a value of $3,923,000 were awarded.
**Deadline:** February of each year.

### 669 MG WILLIAM E. DEPUY MEMORIAL SCHOLARSHIP PROGRAM

Society of the First Infantry Division, Attn: 1st Infantry Division Foundation
1933 Morris Road
Blue Bell, PA 19422-1422
Phone: (888) 324-4733; Fax: (215) 661-1934; Email: soc1ID@aol.com
Web: www.bigredone.org/foundation/scholarships.cfm
**Summary:** To provide financial assistance for college to the children of certain deceased members of the First Infantry Division.
**Eligibility:** Open to the children of soldiers who served in the First Infantry Division and were killed while serving in combat with the Division and in peacetime training accidents. This is an entitlement program. All eligible applicants receive an award.
**Financial data:** The stipend is $2,500.
**Duration:** 1 year; may be renewed.
**Number awarded:** Varies each year.

### 670 MICHAEL A. HUNTER MEMORIAL SCHOLARSHIP

Orange County Community Foundation, Attn: Administrative Assistant
30 Corporate Park, Suite 410
Irvine, CA 92606
Phone: (949) 553-4202, ext. 42; Fax: (949) 553-4211; Email: rho@oc-cf.org
Web: www.oc-cf.org
**Summary:** To provide financial assistance for college to leukemia patients and the children of non-surviving leukemia patients.
**Eligibility:** Open to graduating high school seniors, community college students, and 4-year university students nationwide. Applicants must be leukemia patients and/or the children of non-surviving leukemia patients who are enrolled or planning to enroll full time. They must have a GPA of 3.0 or higher and be able to document financial need. Along with their application, they must submit an essay (up to 600 words) on how leukemia has affected their life, including the type of leukemia, date of diagnosis, and current status.
**Financial data:** The stipend is $5,000.
**Duration:** 1 year.
**Number awarded:** 2 each year.
**Deadline:** March of each year.

### 671 MICHIGAN COMPETITIVE SCHOLARSHIP PROGRAM

Michigan Department of Treasury
Bureau of Student Financial Assistance
Attn: Office of Scholarships and Grants
P.O. Box 30462
Lansing, MI 48909-7962
Phone: (517) 373-3394; (888) 4-GRANTS; Fax: (517) 335-5984;
Email: treasscholgrant@michigan.gov
Web: www.michigan.gov/mistudentaid
**Summary:** To provide financial assistance for college to residents of Michigan.
**Eligibility:** Open to Michigan residents who are attending or planning to attend an eligible Michigan college at least half time. Applicants must demonstrate financial need, achieve a qualifying score on the ACT test (recently, the qualifying score was 23 or higher), and be a U.S. citizen, permanent resident, or approved refugee. Students working on a degree in theology, divinity, or religious education are ineligible.
**Financial data:** Awards are restricted to tuition and fees, recently to a maximum of $1,300 per academic year.

**Duration:** 1 year; the award may be renewed until 1 of the following circumstances is reached: 1) 10 years following high school graduation; 2) completion of an undergraduate degree; or 3) receipt of 10 semesters or 15 quarters of undergraduate aid. Renewals are granted only if the student maintains a GPA of 2.0 or higher and meets the institution's satisfactory academic progress policy.

**Number awarded:** Varies each year; recently, 28,463 students received these scholarships.

**Deadline:** Priority is given to students who apply by February of each year.

## 672 MICHIGAN EDUCATIONAL OPPORTUNITY GRANTS

Michigan Department of Treasury
Bureau of Student Financial Assistance
Attn: Office of Information and Resources
P.O. Box 30466
Lansing, MI 48909-7966
Phone: (517) 373-0457; (877) FA-FACTS; Fax: (517) 335-6851;
Email: oir@michigan.gov
Web: www.michigan.gov/mistudentaid

**Summary:** To provide financial assistance to students at Michigan public community colleges and universities.

**Eligibility:** Open to Michigan residents who are enrolled at least half time at a public community college or university in the state. U.S. citizenship or permanent residence is required. Financial need must be demonstrated; if funds are insufficient to meet the needs of all eligible applicants, preference is given to students with the greatest financial need.

**Financial data:** The maximum award is $1,000 per academic year.

**Duration:** 1 year.

**Number awarded:** Varies each year; recently, 5,564 of these grants were awarded.

## 673 MICHIGAN ELKS ASSOCIATION GOLD KEY SCHOLARSHIP PROGRAM

Michigan Elks Association
c/o Dale O. Orchard, Chair, Charitable Grant Fund Scholarship Commission
2699 Mohawk Lane
Rochester Hills, MI 48306
Phone: (248) 652-0116; Fax: (248) 650-5749; Email: dorchard@msn.com
Web: www.mielks.org

**Summary:** To provide financial assistance for college to "special needs" students in Michigan.

**Eligibility:** Open to "special needs" students who are Michigan residents. For the purposes of this program, "special needs" students are defined as those who are physically or mentally challenged. Applicants must be high school seniors and planning to attend an accredited college, university, trade school, or vocational school. They must submit a statement on the nature and degree of their "special needs;" the school they have chosen to attend and why; their educational and career goals; how they anticipate financing school; the special equipment, devices, and/or supportive services they require; and their extracurricular activities, interests, and/or hobbies. Other required submissions include high school transcripts, a letter from their parent describing the family financial situation and the student's need for assistance, 3 letters of recommendation, and verification of "special needs" from a doctor. Men and women students are judged separately. Sponsorship by a local Elks lodge is required.

**Financial data:** The stipend is $2,000 per year.

**Duration:** 1 year; may be renewed up to 3 additional years.

**Number awarded:** 2 each year: 1 woman and 1 man.

**Deadline:** The sponsoring lodge must forward the application to the district commissioner by January of each year.

## 674 MICHIGAN LEGION AUXILIARY NATIONAL PRESIDENT'S SCHOLARSHIP

American Legion Auxiliary, Attn: Department of Michigan
212 North Verlinden Street
Lansing, MI 48915
Phone: (517) 371-4720; Fax: (517) 371-2401; Email: michalaux@voyager.net
Web: www.michalaux.org/scholarship.htm

**Summary:** To provide financial assistance for college to children of veterans in Michigan.

**Eligibility:** Open to Michigan residents who are the children of veterans who served in World War I, World War II, Korea, Vietnam, Grenada/Lebanon, Panama, or Desert Shield/Desert Storm. Applicants must be in their senior year or graduates of an accredited high school and may not yet have attended an institution of higher learning. Selection is based on scholarship, character, leadership, Americanism, and financial need. The winner competes for the American Legion National President's Scholarship. If the Michigan winners are not awarded the national scholarship, then they receive this departmental scholarship.

**Financial data:** The stipend ranges from $1,000 to $2,500.

**Duration:** 1 year.

**Number awarded:** 1 each year.

**Deadline:** March of each year.

## 675 MICHIGAN MERIT AWARD

Michigan Department of Treasury, Attn: Michigan Merit Award
P.O. Box 30719
Lansing, MI 48909-8219
Phone: (517) 241-4430; (888) 95-MERIT; Fax: (517) 241-4638;
Email: MeritAward@state.mi.us
Web: www.meritaward.state.mi.us

**Summary:** To recognize and reward high school seniors in Michigan who achieve high scores on the Michigan Educational Assessment Program (MEAP) High School Tests (HST).

**Eligibility:** Open to high school seniors who take all 4 MEAP tests (mathematics, science, reading, and writing) and 1) score at level 1 ("exceeds State standards") or level 2 ("meets State standards") on all 4 tests, or 2) score at level 1 or level 2 on 2 of the 4 MEAP tests and pass an alternate test (SAT, ACT, or Work Keys Skills Test) with a qualifying score. Students who were juniors in high school in 1999 or later and subsequently complete a GED are also eligible if they achieve the required scores. Additional funding is available to students who had achieved a level 1 or 2 on their MEAP reading and writing scores in grade 7 and their MEAP mathematics and science scores in grade 8.

**Financial data:** Students who attend an approved institution in Michigan receive $2,500, paid in 2 installments of $1,250 each for the freshman and sophomore years. Students who attend an approved institution outside Michigan receive $1,000. Students who had achieved level 1 or 2 scores on their grade 7 and 8 MEAP tests receive an additional $250 if they achieved those scores on 2 of the tests, an additional $375 for 3 of the tests, or an additional $500 for all 4 of the tests. All funds are paid directly to the institution.

**Duration:** These are 1-time awards. Recipients may utilize the awards up to 4 years after they graduate from high school or complete a GED.

**Number awarded:** Varies each year; recently, 51,331 students qualified for these awards.

## 676 MICHIGAN POLICE OFFICER AND FIRE FIGHTERS SURVIVOR TUITION

Michigan Commission on Law Enforcement Standards
Attn: Michigan Department of State Police
7426 North Canal Road
Lansing, MI 48913
Phone: (517) 322-6627; Email: email@mcoles.org
Web: www.michigan.gov/msp

**Summary:** To provide financial assistance for college to children and spouses of deceased Michigan police officers and fire fighters.

**Eligibility:** Open to children and spouses of Michigan police officers (including sheriffs, deputy sheriffs, village or township marshals, police officers of any city or other local jurisdiction, or officer of the state police) or fire fighter (including a member, volunteer or paid, of a fire department or other organization who was directly involved in fire suppression) killed in the line of duty. Children must have younger than 21 at the time of death of the police officer or fire fighter and must apply for this assistance before the age of 21. Applicants must have been residents of Michigan for 12 consecutive months prior to applying. Their family income must be less than 400% of the federal poverty level.

**Financial data:** This program provides waiver of tuition at Michigan public colleges, universities, and community colleges.

**Duration:** Until completion of 124 credit hours or 9 semesters of study.

**Number awarded:** Varies each year.

**Deadline:** April of each year.

## 677 MICHIGAN STATE TROOPERS ASSISTANCE FUND SCHOLARSHIP PROGRAM

Michigan State Troopers Assistance Fund
c/o Scholarship Committee
1715 Abbey Road, Suite B
East Lansing, MI 48823

**Summary:** To provide financial assistance for college to high school seniors in Michigan.
**Eligibility:** Open to seniors graduating from high schools in Michigan to plan to attend an accredited college or vocational school. Applicants must submit an essay describing the community events in which they have participated and how the experience has affected them. Selection is based on GPA, extracurricular and leadership service activities, and financial need.
**Financial data:** The stipend is $1,000.
**Duration:** 1 year.
**Number awarded:** 20 each year.
**Deadline:** March of each year.

### 678 MICHIGAN TUITION GRANT PROGRAM

Michigan Department of Treasury
Bureau of Student Financial Assistance
Attn: Office of Scholarships and Grants
P.O. Box 30462
Lansing, MI 48909-7962
Phone: (517) 373-3394; (888) 4-GRANTS; Fax: (517) 335-5984;
Email: treasscholgrant@michigan.gov
Web: www.michigan.gov/mistudentaid
**Summary:** To provide financial assistance for undergraduate or graduate education to residents of Michigan.
**Eligibility:** Open to Michigan residents who are attending or planning to attend an independent, private, nonprofit degree-granting Michigan college or university at least half time as an undergraduate or graduate student. Applicants must demonstrate financial need and be a U.S. citizen, permanent resident, or approved refugee. Students working on a degree in theology, divinity, or religious education are ineligible.
**Financial data:** Awards are limited to tuition and fees, recently to a maximum of $2,000 per academic year.
**Duration:** 1 year; the award may be renewed for a total of 10 semesters or 15 quarters of undergraduate aid, 6 semesters or 9 quarters of graduate aid, or 8 semesters or 12 quarters of graduate dental student aid.
**Number awarded:** Varies each year; recently, 28,441 of these grants were awarded.
**Deadline:** Priority is given to students who apply by mid-July of each year.

### 679 MICHIGAN TUITION INCENTIVE PROGRAM

Michigan Department of Treasury
Bureau of Student Financial Assistance
Attn: Office of Information and Resources
P.O. Box 30466
Lansing, MI 48909-7966
Phone: (517) 373-0457; (877) FA-FACTS; Fax: (517) 335-6851;
Email: oir@michigan.gov
Web: www.michigan.gov/mistudentaid
**Summary:** To provide financial assistance for college to high school seniors in Michigan.
**Eligibility:** Open to Michigan residents who have (or have had) Medicaid coverage for 24 months within a 36 consecutive month period as identified by the Family Independence Agency (FIA). That financial eligibility can be established as early as sixth grade. Students who meet the financial eligibility guidelines are then eligible for this assistance if they graduate from high school or complete a GED prior to becoming 20 years of age. All applicants must be U.S. citizens or eligible noncitizens (including those designated as refugee; asylum granted, humanitarian parole, indefinite parole, or Cuban-Haitian entrant). Phase I is for students who enroll in a program leading to an associate degree or certificate. Phase II is for students who enroll at least half time at a Michigan degree-granting college or university in a 4-year program other than theology or divinity. Participants must have earned at least 56 transferable semester credits or an associate degree or certificate in Phase I before admission to Phase II.
**Financial data:** Phase I provides payment of tuition and mandatory fees. Phase II pays tuition and mandatory fees up to $500 per semester to a lifetime maximum of $2,000.
**Duration:** Students may participate in Phase I for up to 80 semester credits. Course work for Phase II must be completed within 30 months of completion of Phase I requirements.
**Number awarded:** Varies each year.

### 680 MICHIGAN VETERANS TRUST FUND TUITION GRANTS

Department of Military and Veterans Affairs
Attn: Michigan Veterans Trust Fund

2500 South Washington Avenue
Lansing, MI 48913-5101
Phone: (517) 483-5469; Email: paocmn@michigan.gov
Web: www.michigan.gov/dmva
**Summary:** To provide financial assistance for college to the children of Michigan veterans who are totally disabled or deceased as a result of service-connected causes.
**Eligibility:** Open to children of Michigan veterans who are totally disabled as a result of wartime service, or died from service-connected conditions, or were killed in action, or are listed as missing in action. Applicants must be between 16 and 26 years of age and must have lived in Michigan at least 12 months prior to the date of application. They must be or plan to become a full-time undergraduate student at a public institution of higher education in Michigan.
**Financial data:** Recipients are exempt from payment of the first $2,800 per year of tuition or any other fee that takes the place of tuition.
**Duration:** 1 year; may be renewed for up to 36 months if the recipient maintains full-time enrollment and a GPA of 2.25 or higher.
**Number awarded:** Varies each year.

### 681 MIDEASTERN REGION KOREAN AMERICAN SCHOLARSHIPS

Korean American Scholarship Foundation
Mideastern Region
c/o Chang S. Choi, Scholarship Committee Chair
6410 Lahser Road
Bloomfield Hills, MI 48301
Phone: (248) 752-3180; Fax: (248) 644-0507; Email: cschoi@comcast.net
Web: www.kasf.org/home/regional/mideastern/mideastern.html
**Summary:** To provide financial assistance to Korean American undergraduate and graduate students who attend school in Indiana, Michigan, or Ohio.
**Eligibility:** Open to Korean American students who are currently enrolled in a college or university as full-time undergraduate or graduate students. Applicants may reside anywhere in the United States as long as they attend school in Indiana, Michigan, or Ohio. Selection is based on academic achievement, school activities, community service, and financial need.
**Financial data:** Stipends range from $1,000 to $2,000.
**Duration:** 1 year; renewable.
**Number awarded:** Varies each year. Recently, the midwestern regional chapter (which then included the current mideastern regional chapter) awarded 69 of these scholarships.
**Deadline:** March of each year.

### 682 MIDWEST STUDENT EXCHANGE PROGRAM

Midwestern Higher Education Commission
Attn: Midwest Student Exchange Program
1300 South Second Street, Suite 130
Minneapolis, MN 55454-1079
Phone: (612) 626-8288; Fax: (612) 626-8290; Email: mhec@mhec.org
Web: www.mhec.org/msep/index.htm
**Summary:** To provide a tuition discount to undergraduate and graduate students from selected midwestern states who are attending schools affiliated with the Midwest Student Exchange Program.
**Eligibility:** Open to students at academic institutions affiliated with the Midwest Student Exchange Program. That program is an interstate initiative established to increase interstate educational opportunities for students in the member states. The Tuition Discount Program includes the 6 participating states of Kansas, Michigan, Minnesota, Missouri, Nebraska and North Dakota. Residents of these states may enroll in programs in the other participating states, but only at the level at which their home state admits students. All of the enrollment and eligibility decisions for the program are made by the institution.
**Financial data:** Participants in this program pay no more than 150% of the regular resident tuition, plus any required fees, at public colleges and universities in the state where are enrolled. Students attending designated independent colleges and universities participating in the program receive at least a 10% reduction in their tuition. Savings typically range from $500 to $3,000.
**Duration:** Students receive these benefits as long as they are enrolled in the program to which they were originally admitted and are making satisfactory progress towards a degree.
**Number awarded:** Varies each year.

### 683 MIDWESTERN REGION KOREAN AMERICAN SCHOLARSHIPS

Korean American Scholarship Foundation
Midwestern Region
c/o Tony S. Hahm, Scholarship Committee Chair
P.O. Box 0416
Northbrook, IL 60065-0416
Phone: (847) 797-1291; Fax: (847) 797-1304; Email: tonyhahm@yahoo.com
Web: www.kasf.org/home/regional/midwestern/midwestern.html
**Summary:** To provide financial assistance to Korean American undergraduate and graduate students who attend school in the Midwest.
**Eligibility:** Open to Korean American students who are currently enrolled in a college or university in the midwestern states as full-time undergraduate or graduate students. Applicants may reside anywhere in the United States as long as they attend school in the midwest region: Illinois, Iowa, Kansas, Minnesota, Missouri, Nebraska, North Dakota, South Dakota, and Wisconsin. Selection is based on academic achievement, school activities, community service, and financial need.
**Financial data:** Stipends range from $1,000 to $2,000.
**Duration:** 1 year; renewable.
**Number awarded:** Varies each year. Recently, the midwestern regional chapter (which then included the current mideastern regional chapter) awarded 69 of these scholarships.
**Deadline:** June of each year.

### 684 MIGRANT FARMWORKER BACCALAUREATE SCHOLARSHIP

Geneseo Migrant Center
27 Lackawanna Avenue
Mount Morris, NY 14510-1096
Phone: (585) 658-7960; (800) 245-5681; Fax: (585) 658-7969;
Email: info@migrant.net
Web: www.migrant.net/sch_mfb.htm
**Summary:** To provide financial assistance to migrant farmworkers who are currently enrolled in college.
**Eligibility:** Open to migrant farmworker students with a history of migrating for employment in agriculture. Applicants must have completed at least 1 year of college. Along with their application, they must submit a personal essay of at least 500 words on their background, career and personal goals, and why they should receive this assistance; 3 letters of recommendation; a college transcript; and documentation of financial need.
**Financial data:** The stipend is $2,000 per year. These funds are intended to be in addition to any that the student receives through federal, state, or other scholarship assistance as an undergraduate. The same annual amount is available for graduate study or loan repayment.
**Duration:** 1 year; may be renewed for an additional 2 years of undergraduate study. Recipients also have the option of an additional 2 years of graduate support or 3 years of loan repayment.
**Number awarded:** 1 each year.
**Deadline:** June of each year.

### 685 MIKE HYLTON AND RON NIEDERMAN SCHOLARSHIPS

Factor Support Network Pharmacy, Attn: Scholarship Committee
900 Avenida Acaso, Suite A
Camarillo, CA 93012-8749
Phone: (805) 388-9336; (877) FSN-4-YOU; Fax: (805) 482-6324;
Email: Scholarships@FactorSupport.com
Web: www.factorsupport.com/scholarships.htm
**Summary:** To provide financial assistance for college to men with hemophilia and their immediate families.
**Eligibility:** Open to men with bleeding disorders and their immediate family members. Applicants must be entering or attending a college, university, juniors college, or vocational school. They must submit 3 short essays: 1) their career goals; 2) how hemophilia or von Willebrand disease has affected their life; and 3) how they are educating themselves, their family, and their community about hemophilia and/or von Willebrand disease. Selection is based on academic goals, volunteer work, school activities, other pertinent experience and achievements, and financial need.
**Financial data:** The stipend is $1,000. Funds are paid directly to the recipient.
**Duration:** 1 year.
**Number awarded:** 10 each year.
**Deadline:** April of each year.

### 686 MIKE NASH MEMORIAL SCHOLARSHIP FUND

Vietnam Veterans of America, Attn: Mike Nash Scholarship Program
8605 Cameron Street, Suite 400
Silver Spring, MD 20910-3710
Phone: (301) 585-4000; (800) VVA-1316; Email: finance@vva.org
Web: www.vva.org/Scholarshp/index.htm
**Summary:** To provide financial assistance for college to members of Vietnam Veterans of America (VVA), their families, and the families of other Vietnam veterans.
**Eligibility:** Open to 1) members of VVA; 2) the spouses, children, stepchildren, and grandchildren of VVA members; and 3) the spouses, children, stepchildren, and grandchildren of MIA, KIA, or deceased Vietnam veterans. Applicants must be enrolled or planning to enroll at least half time at an accredited college, university, or technical institution. Along with their application, they must submit high school or college transcripts; SAT, ACT, or other recognized test scores; a letter of recommendation from a VVA state council, chapter, or national; 2 letters of recommendation; a letter describing their current educational goals and objectives, individual accomplishments, and any other personal information that may assist in the selection process; and documentation of financial need.
**Financial data:** The stipend is $1,000 per year.
**Duration:** 1 year; may be renewed for up to 3 additional years.
**Number awarded:** Varies each year; recently, 9 of these scholarships were awarded.
**Deadline:** June of each year.

### 687 MILDRED R. KNOLES OPPORTUNITY SCHOLARSHIPS

American Legion Auxiliary, Attn: Department of Illinois
2720 East Lincoln Street
P.O. Box 1426
Bloomington, IL 61702-1426
Phone: (309) 663-9366; Fax: (309) 663-5827; Email: ilala@ilala.org
Web: illegion.org/auxiliary/scholar.html
**Summary:** To provide financial assistance for college or graduate school to Illinois veterans and their children.
**Eligibility:** Open to veterans or children and grandchildren of veterans of World War I, World War II, Korea, Vietnam, Grenada/Lebanon, Panama, or Desert Storm who have begun college but need financial assistance to complete their college or graduate education. Applicants must have resided in Illinois for at least 3 years prior to application. Selection is based on character, Americanism, leadership, financial need, and academic record.
**Financial data:** Stipends are $1,200 or $800.
**Duration:** 1 year.
**Number awarded:** Varies; each year 1 scholarship at $1,200 and several at $800 are awarded.
**Deadline:** March of each year.

### 688 MILITARY OFFICERS' BENEVOLENT CORPORATION SCHOLARSHIPS

Military Officers' Benevolent Corporation
1010 American Eagle Boulevard
P.O. Box 301
Sun City Center, FL 33573
Phone: (813) 634-4675; Fax: (813) 633-2412; Email: office@mobc-online.org
Web: www.mobc-online.org
**Summary:** To provide financial assistance for college to children and grandchildren of retired and deceased officers who served in the military or designated public service agencies.
**Eligibility:** Open to graduating high school seniors who have a GPA of 3.0 and a minimum score of 21 on the ACT or equivalent score on the SAT. Applicants must have a parent, guardian, or grandparent who is 1) a retired active-duty, National Guard, or Reserve officer or former officer of the U.S. Army, Navy, Marine Corps, Air Force, Coast Guard, Public Health Service, or National Oceanic and Atmospheric Administration, at the rank of O-1 through O-10, WO-1 through WO-5, or E-7 through E-9; 2) an officer who died while on active duty in service to the country; 3) a recipient of the Purple Heart, regardless of pay grade or length of service; 4) a World War II combat veteran of the Merchant Marine; 5) a federal employee at the grade of GS-7 or higher; 6) a Foreign Service Officer at the grade of FSO-8 or lower; or 7) an honorably discharged or retired foreign military officer of an allied nation meeting the service and disability retirement criteria of the respective country and living in the United States. Applicants must have been accepted to an accredited program at a college or university. Selection is based on leadership (40%), scholarship (30%), and financial need (30%).
**Financial data:** Stipends are $2,000, $1,500, or $500 per year.

**Duration:** 4 years, provided the recipient maintains a GPA of 3.0 or higher.
**Number awarded:** 9 each year: 2 at $2,000 per year, 4 at $1,500 per year, and 3 at $500 per year.
**Deadline:** February of each year.

## 689 MILITARY ORDER OF THE PURPLE HEART SCHOLARSHIP PROGRAM

Military Order of the Purple Heart, Attn: Scholarships
5413-B Backlick Road
Springfield, VA 22151-3960
Phone: (703) 642-5360; Fax: (703) 642-2054; Email: info@purpleheart.org
Web: www.purpleheart.org/scholar.html
**Summary:** To provide financial assistance for college or graduate school to spouses and children of members of the Military Order of the Purple Heart.
**Eligibility:** Open to children (natural, step-, and adopted), grandchildren, great-grandchildren and spouses of veterans who are members in good standing of the order or who received the Purple Heart. Applicants must be U.S. citizens, graduating seniors or graduates of an accredited high school, enrolled or accepted for enrollment in a full-time program of study in a college, trade school, or graduate school with a GPA of 3.5 or higher. Selection is based on merit; financial need is not considered in the selection process.
**Financial data:** The stipend is $1,750 per year.
**Duration:** 1 year; may be renewed up to 3 additional years.
**Number awarded:** Varies each year; recently, 28 of these scholarships were awarded.
**Deadline:** March of each year.

## 690 MILITARY TUITION WAIVER DURING ASSIGNMENT AFTER TEXAS

Texas Higher Education Coordinating Board
Attn: Grants and Special Programs
1200 East Anderson Lane
P.O. Box 12788, Capitol Station
Austin, TX 78711-2788
Phone: (512) 427-6101; (800) 242-3062; Fax: (512) 427-6127;
Email: grantinfo@thecb.state.tx.us
Web: www.collegefortexans.com
**Summary:** To provide educational assistance to the spouses and children of Texas military personnel assigned elsewhere.
**Eligibility:** Open to the spouses and dependent children of members of the U.S. armed forces or commissioned officers of the Public Health Service who remain in Texas when the member is reassigned to duty outside of the state. The spouse or dependent child must reside continuously in Texas. Applicants must be attending or planning to attend a Texas public college or university.
**Financial data:** Eligible students are entitled to pay tuition and fees at the resident rate at publicly-supported colleges and universities in Texas.
**Duration:** The waiver remains in effect for the duration of the member's first assignment outside of Texas.
**Number awarded:** Varies each year.

## 691 MILLIE BROTHER SCHOLARSHIP

CODA International
P.O. Box 30715
Santa Barbara, CA 93130-0715
Email: coda@coda-international.org
Web: coda-international.org/scholar.html
**Summary:** To provide financial assistance for college to the children of deaf parents.
**Eligibility:** Open to the hearing children of deaf parents who are high school seniors or graduates. Applicants must submit a 2-page essay on their experience as the child of deaf parents, how it has shaped them as individuals, and their future career aspirations; essays are judged on organization, content, creativity, and sense of purpose. In addition to the essay, selection is based on a high school transcript and 2 letters of recommendation.
**Financial data:** The stipend is $3,000.
**Duration:** 1 year.
**Number awarded:** 2 each year.
**Deadline:** May of each year.

## 692 MILLIE GONZALEZ MEMORIAL SCHOLARSHIPS

Factor Support Network Pharmacy, Attn: Scholarship Committee
900 Avenida Acaso, Suite A
Camarillo, CA 93012-8749
Phone: (805) 388-9336; (877) FSN-4-YOU; Fax: (805) 482-6324;
Email: Scholarships@FactorSupport.com
Web: www.factorsupport.com/scholarships.htm
**Summary:** To provide financial assistance to women with hemophilia.
**Eligibility:** Open to women with bleeding disorders who are entering or attending a college, university, juniors college, or vocational school. Applicants must submit 3 short essays: 1) their career goals; 2) how hemophilia or von Willebrand disease has affected their life; and 3) how they are educating themselves, their family, and their community about hemophilia and/or von Willebrand disease. Selection is based on academic goals, volunteer work, school activities, other pertinent experience and achievements, and financial need.
**Financial data:** The stipend is $1,000. Funds are paid directly to the recipient.
**Duration:** 1 year.
**Number awarded:** 5 each year.
**Deadline:** April of each year.

## 693 MILTON FISHER SCHOLARSHIP FOR INNOVATION AND CREATIVITY

Community Foundation for Greater New Haven
70 Audubon Street
New Haven, CT 06510-9755
Phone: (203) 777-2386; Fax: (203) 777-6584; Email: contactus@cfgnh.org
Web: www.cfgnh.org
**Summary:** To provide financial assistance for college to residents of Connecticut who demonstrate outstanding innovation and creativity.
**Eligibility:** Open to Connecticut residents who are high school juniors or seniors, recent high school graduates entering college for the first time, or first-year college students. Students attending or planning to attend a Connecticut college, university, vocational school, or technical school are also eligible. Applicants must submit a 400-word essay on their plans and goals, including what they hope to accomplish, how their goals build on what they have already accomplished, and special circumstances or obstacles in their lives. They must also submit a transcript, although academic achievement is not a major consideration. Selection is based primarily on innovation and creativity, as illustrated by another essay, up to 800 words in length, on whether they have solved a scientific, artistic, or technical problem in a new and unusual way; whether they have come up with a distinctive solution to a problem faced by their school, community, or family; and if they have created a group or organization that serves an important need. Financial need is not considered in the selection process, but it is used to determine the amount of the stipend.
**Financial data:** Stipends range from $1,000 to $5,000, depending on the need of the recipient.
**Duration:** 1 year; nonrenewable.
**Number awarded:** 4 to 6 each year.
**Deadline:** April of each year.

## 694 MINNESOTA ACADEMIC EXCELLENCE SCHOLARSHIP

Minnesota Higher Education Services Office
1450 Energy Park Drive, Suite 350
St. Paul, MN 55108-5227
Phone: (651) 642-0567; (800) 657-3866; Fax: (651) 642-0675;
TTY: (800) 627-3529; Email: info@heso.state.mn.us
Web: www.mheso.state.mn.us
**Summary:** To provide financial assistance for college to outstanding high school seniors or graduates in Minnesota.
**Eligibility:** Open to Minnesota residents who have demonstrated outstanding ability, achievement, and potential in English, creative writing, fine arts, foreign language, mathematics, science, or social science. Applicants must have been admitted as full-time students at a branch of the University of Minnesota, a Minnesota state university, or a private, baccalaureate degree-granting college or university in Minnesota.
**Financial data:** Scholarships at public institutions cover the cost of full-time attendance; scholarships at private institutions cover an amount equal to the lesser of the actual tuition and fees charged by the institution or the tuition and fees in comparable public institutions.
**Duration:** 1 year; may be renewed up to 3 additional years.
**Number awarded:** Varies each year.

## 695 MINNESOTA ASSOCIATION OF TOWNSHIPS SCHOLARSHIP PROGRAM

Minnesota Association of Townships
Attn: Scholarship Program
P.O. Box 267
St. Michael, MN 55376
Phone: (763) 497-2330; Fax: (763) 497-3361; (800) 228-0296;
Email: info@mntownships.org
Web: www.mntownships.org

**Summary:** To provide financial assistance to college-bound high school juniors in Minnesota.

**Eligibility:** Open to students currently enrolled as juniors at public, private, and parochial high schools and home study programs in Minnesota. Applicants must be planning to attend a college, university, or vocational school following graduation from high school. They must submit an essay, from 450 to 500 words, on a topic that changes annually but relates to the township form of government in Minnesota, its place and purpose in local government, and the involvement of citizens in grassroots government. Along with their application and essay, they must submit a current high school transcript and a letter of recommendation from a high school teacher or counselor.

**Financial data:** The stipend is $1,000.

**Duration:** 1 year.

**Number awarded:** 2 each year.

**Deadline:** April of each year.

## 696 MINNESOTA BENEFIT ASSOCIATION SCHOLARSHIPS

Minnesota Benefit Association, Attn: Scholarship Committee
6701 Upper Afton Road
Woodbury, MN 55125
Phone: (651) 735-9874; (800) 360-6117; Fax: (651) 739-3260;
Email: mail@minnesotabenefitassociation.com
Web: www.minnesotabenefitassociation.com/scholarship.htm

**Summary:** To provide financial assistance for college to public employees and elected officials in Minnesota and their family members.

**Eligibility:** Open to high school seniors and current college students who are Minnesota public employees, elected officials, or members of their families. Applicants must submit an essay, of 300 to 500 words, on a topic that changes annually but relates to matters of interest to public employees in Minnesota. Selection is based on that essay, academic achievement, vocational goals, employment history, community involvement, and financial need.

**Financial data:** The stipend is $1,000.

**Duration:** 1 year.

**Number awarded:** 4 each year.

**Deadline:** January of each year.

## 697 MINNESOTA CHILD CARE GRANT PROGRAM

Minnesota Higher Education Services Office
1450 Energy Park Drive, Suite 350
St. Paul, MN 55108-5227
Phone: (651) 642-0567; (800) 657-3866; Fax: (651) 642-0675;
TTY: (800) 627-3529; Email: info@heso.state.mn.us
Web: www.mheso.state.mn.us

**Summary:** To provide financial assistance for child care to students in Minnesota who are not receiving Minnesota Family Investment Program (MFIP) benefits.

**Eligibility:** Open to Minnesota residents who are working on an undergraduate degree or vocational certificate in the state, have children age 12 and under (14 and under if disabled), and need help to pay their child care expenses. Recipients must demonstrate financial need but must not be receiving MFIP benefits. U.S. citizenship or permanent resident status is required.

**Financial data:** The amount of the assistance depends on the income of applicant and spouse, number of day care hours necessary to cover education and work obligations, the student's enrollment status, and number of eligible children in applicant's family. The maximum available is $2,200 per eligible child per academic year.

**Duration:** 1 year; may be renewed as long as the recipient remains enrolled on at least a half-time basis in an undergraduate program.

**Number awarded:** Varies each year. Recently, a total of $1.1 million was provided for this program.

## 698 MINNESOTA EDUCATION AND TRAINING VOUCHERS FOR FORMER YOUTH IN CARE

Minnesota Department of Human Services
Attn: Social Services Program Consultant
444 Lafayette Road, Third Floor South
St. Paul, MN 55155-3832
Phone: (651) 296-4471; Email: claire.d.hill@state.mn.us
Web: www.dhs.state.mn.us

**Summary:** To provide financial assistance for college to Minnesota residents who have been foster children.

**Eligibility:** Open to Minnesota residents who experienced a county approved out-of-home placement after the age of 14, are currently under state guardianship, or were adopted at age 16 or older. Applicants must have been accepted into an accredited postsecondary program that they began or will begin when they are between 18 and 21 years of age. They must attach a copy of their Free Application for Federal Student Aid (FAFSA), apply for other sources of financial aid, and submit 2 letters of recommendation.

**Financial data:** Stipends depend on the need of the recipient, to a maximum of $5,000 per year.

**Duration:** 1 year; may be renewed provided the recipient maintains a GPA of 2.0 or higher.

**Number awarded:** Varies each year; recently, a total of 42 students had received support through this program.

**Deadline:** May of each year.

## 699 MINNESOTA EDUCATIONAL ASSISTANCE FOR WAR ORPHANS

Minnesota Department of Veterans Affairs
Veterans Service Building
20 West 12th Street, Room 206C
St. Paul, MN 55155-2006
Phone: (651) 297-4141; Fax: (651) 296-3954;
Email: paula.plum@mdva.state.mn.us
Web: www.mdva.state.mn.us

**Summary:** To provide financial assistance for college to the dependents of deceased Minnesota veterans.

**Eligibility:** Open to students who have been residents of Minnesota for 2 years prior to application. They must be the children of veterans who were Minnesota residents prior to entry on active duty and who died on active duty or as a result of service-connected injuries or diseases.

**Financial data:** Students who attend technical and community colleges and state universities are granted free tuition until they have earned a bachelor's or equivalent degree (this does not apply to private institutions or the University of Minnesota). All eligible students may also receive up to $750 in any 1 calendar year to be used for tuition, fees, board, room, books, and supplies at the University of Minnesota, state universities, community colleges, vocational/technical institutions, or any other accredited college of higher learning, nursing school, trade school, or business school within Minnesota.

**Duration:** 1 year; may be renewed.

**Number awarded:** Varies each year.

## 700 MINNESOTA PUBLIC SAFETY OFFICERS' SURVIVOR GRANT

Minnesota Higher Education Services Office
1450 Energy Park Drive, Suite 350
St. Paul, MN 55108-5227
Phone: (651) 642-0567; (800) 657-3866; Fax: (651) 642-0675;
TTY: (800) 627-3529; Email: info@heso.state.mn.us
Web: www.mheso.state.mn.us

**Summary:** To provide financial assistance for college to survivors of deceased Minnesota public safety officers.

**Eligibility:** Open to dependent children (under 23 years of age) and surviving spouses of public safety officers killed in the line of duty on or after January 1, 1973. Applicants must be Minnesota residents who are enrolled at least half time in an undergraduate degree or certificate program at a Minnesota public postsecondary institution or at a private, residential, 2- or 4-year, liberal arts, degree-granting college or university in Minnesota.

**Financial data:** Scholarships cover tuition and fees at state-supported institutions or provide an equivalent amount at private colleges and universities. Recently, awards averaged $3,230.

**Duration:** 1 year; may be renewed for a maximum of 8 semesters or 12 quarters.

**Number awarded:** Varies each year; recently, a total of $40,000 was available for this program.

## 701 MINNESOTA STATE GRANT PROGRAM

Minnesota Higher Education Services Office
1450 Energy Park Drive, Suite 350
St. Paul, MN 55108-5227
Phone: (651) 642-0567; (800) 657-3866; Fax: (651) 642-0675;
TTY: (800) 627-3529; Email: info@heso.state.mn.us
Web: www.mheso.state.mn.us

**Summary:** To provide financial assistance to undergraduate students in Minnesota who demonstrate financial need.

**Eligibility:** Open to Minnesota residents who are enrolled for at least 3 credits as undergraduate students at 1 of 128 eligible schools in Minnesota. They must be 1) an independent student who has resided in Minnesota for purposes other than postsecondary education for at least 12 months; 2) a dependent student whose parent or legal guardian resides in Minnesota; 3) a student who graduated from a Minnesota high school, if the student was a resident of Minnesota during high school; or 4) a student who, after residing in Minnesota for a minimum of 1 year, earned a high school equivalency certificate in Minnesota. Students in default on a student loan or more than 30 days behind for child support owed to a public agency are not eligible.

**Financial data:** Applicants are required to contribute at least 46% of their cost of attendance (tuition and fees plus allowances for room and board, books and supplies, and miscellaneous expenses) from savings, earnings, loans, or other assistance from school or private sources. The other 54% is to be contributed by parents (for dependent students) or by independent students, along with a federal Pell Grant and these State Grants. The average State Grant is approximately $1,860; the minimum award is $100 per year and the maximum ranges from $4,802 at a public technical college to $7,662 at a private 4-year college.

**Duration:** Assistance continues until the student has completed a baccalaureate degree or full-time enrollment of 8 semesters or 12 quarters, whichever comes first.

**Number awarded:** Varies each year; recently, approximately 72,000 undergraduate students received $133.6 million in support through this program.

**Deadline:** June of each year.

## 702 MINNESOTA STATE HIGH SCHOOL LEAGUE TRIPLE "A" AWARDS

Minnesota State High School League
2100 Freeway Boulevard
Brooklyn Center, MN 55430-1735
Phone: (763) 560-2262
Web: www.mshsl.org

**Summary:** To provide financial assistance for college to high school seniors in Minnesota who excel in the Triple "A" activities: academics, arts, and athletics.

**Eligibility:** Open to college-bound seniors graduating from high schools in Minnesota. Each school may nominate 2 students, a female and a male. Selection of state winners is based on academic performance; involvement in athletic programs sponsored by the Minnesota State High School League (badminton, baseball, basketball, cross country running, football, golf, gymnastics, hockey, lacrosse, skiing, soccer, softball, swimming and diving, synchronized swimming, tennis, track, volleyball, wrestling, and adapted soccer, bowling, floor hockey, and softball); involvement in League-sponsored fine arts activities (state, section, sub-section, school, or community-sponsored activities in instrumental or vocal music, drama, debate, or speech); and involvement in other school and community activities. Nominees must have a GPA of 3.0 or higher and be in compliance with the League's Student Code of Conduct. Students from Class A and Class AA schools are judged separately, as are females and males.

**Financial data:** The stipend is $1,000 per year.

**Duration:** 4 years.

**Number awarded:** 4 each year: a female and a male from each of the 2 classes of schools.

**Deadline:** January of each year.

## 703 MINNESOTA VETERANS' DEPENDENTS ASSISTANCE PROGRAM

Minnesota Higher Education Services Office
1450 Energy Park Drive, Suite 350
St. Paul, MN 55108-5227
Phone: (651) 642-0567; (800) 657-3866; Fax: (651) 642-0675;
TTY: (800) 627-3529; Email: info@heso.state.mn.us
Web: www.mheso.state.mn.us

**Summary:** To provide financial assistance for college to the dependents of Minnesota veterans and military personnel listed as POWs or MIAs.

**Eligibility:** Open to 1) spouses of a prisoner of war or person missing in action,

or 2) children born before or during the period of time the parent served as a POW or was declared MIA, or 3) children legally adopted or in the legal custody of a parent prior to and during the time the parent served as a POW or was declared to be MIA. Veteran parents must have been residents of Minnesota at the time of entry into service or at the time declared to be a POW or MIA, which must have occurred after August 1, 1958.

**Financial data:** Students who attend private postsecondary institutions receive up to $250 per year for tuition and fees. Students who attend a Minnesota public postsecondary institution are exempt from tuition charges.

**Duration:** Assistance continues until the student completes a bachelor's degree or receives a certificate of completion.

**Number awarded:** Varies each year.

## 704 MINNIE PEARL SCHOLARSHIP PROGRAM

EAR Foundation, Attn: Minnie Pearl Scholarship Program
1817 Patterson Street
P.O. Box 330867
Nashville, TN 37203
Phone: (615) 627-2724; (800) 545-HEAR; Fax: (615) 627-2728;
TDD: (800) 545-HEAR; Fax: info@earfoundation.org
Web: www.earfoundation.org

**Summary:** To provide financial assistance to hearing impaired students who want to attend college.

**Eligibility:** Open to mainstreamed high school seniors with severe to profound bilateral hearing loss. Their primary means of communication may be manual or oral. They must have a GPA of 3.0 or higher; plan to attend a junior college, university, or technical school on a full-time basis; and be U.S. citizens. Along with their application, they must submit brief essays on how they feel about mainstreaming, their goals after graduating from college, and why they are a good candidate for this scholarship.

**Financial data:** The stipend is $2,500 per year.

**Duration:** 1 year; may be renewed up to 3 additional years if the recipient maintains a GPA of 3.0 or higher.

**Number awarded:** Varies each year; recently, 6 of these scholarships were awarded.

**Deadline:** February of each year.

## 705 MISS AMERICA COMPETITION AWARDS

Miss America Pageant, Attn: Scholarship Department
Two Miss America Way, Suite 1000
Atlantic City, NJ 08401
Phone: (609) 345-7571, ext. 27; (800) 282-MISS; Fax: (609) 347-6079;
Email: info@missamerica.org
Web: www.missamerica.org/scholarships/competitionawards.asp

**Summary:** To provide educational scholarships to participants in the Miss America Pageant on local, state, and national levels.

**Eligibility:** Open to women who meet certain basic requirements and agree to abide by all the rules of the local, state, and national Miss America Pageants. Among the qualifications required are that the applicant be between the ages of 17 and 24, a resident of the town or state in which they first compete, in good health, of good moral character, and a citizen of the United States. A complete list of all eligibility requirements is available from each local and state pageant. In addition to the general scholarship awards, participants are also considered for a number of special awards: the Active International Scholarship for Business and Marketing is presented to the highest scoring contestant who lists business, marketing, or a related business career as a stated ambition; the Bernie Wayne Performing Arts Award is presented to the contestant with the highest talent score among those women with performing arts as a stated ambition; the Eleanor (Big Mama) Andrews Scholarship is presented to the non-finalist contestant with the highest talent score among those women with performing arts as a stated ambition; the Charles and Theresa Brown Scholarships are presented to Miss America, the 4 runners-up, Miss Alaska, Miss Hawaii, Miss Illinois, and Miss Ohio; and the Quality of Life Awards are presented to the 3 contestants who demonstrate the most outstanding commitment to enhancing the quality of life for others through volunteerism and community service.

**Financial data:** More than $45 million in cash and tuition assistance is awarded annually at the local, state, and national Miss America Pageants. At the national level, a total of $455,000 is awarded: Miss America receives $50,000 in scholarship money, the first runner-up $40,000, second runner-up $30,000, third runner-up $25,000, fourth runner-up $20,000, semifinalists $10,000 each, finalists $6,000 each, and national contestants $5,000 each. Among the preliminary winners, those for community achievement in interview receive $5,000, those for artistic expression in talent receive $4,000, those for on-stage knowledge and awareness receive $3,000, those for presence and poise in evening wear receive $2,000, and those for lifestyle and fitness in swimsuit receive $2,000. In addition, the overall knowledge and community achievement in interview winner receives $5,000, the overall artistic expression in talent winner receives $4,000, and the overall elegance and lifestyle winner (including both evening wear and swimsuit) receives $3,000. Of the special awards presented to national contestants, the Active International Scholarship for Business and Marketing is $3,000; the Bernie Wayne Performing Arts Award is $2,500; the Charles and Theresa Brown Scholarships are $2,500 each; and the Quality of Life Awards are $6,000 for first place, $4,000 for second, and $3,000 for third.

**Duration:** The pageants are held every year.

**Number awarded:** At the national level, 52 contestants (1 from each state, the District of Columbia, and the Virgin Islands) share the awards.

**Deadline:** Varies, depending upon the date of local pageants leading to the state and national finals.

---

## 706 MISS AMERICA HOSTESS COMMITTEE SCHOLARSHIPS

Miss America Pageant, Attn: Scholarship Department
Two Miss America Way, Suite 1000
Atlantic City, NJ 08401
Phone: (609) 345-7571, ext. 27; (800) 282-MISS; Fax: (609) 347-6079;
Email: info@missamerica.org
Web: www.missamerica.org/scholarships/hostesscommittee.asp

**Summary:** To provide financial assistance for undergraduate or graduate study to women who served as volunteer hostesses for the Miss America Pageant.

**Eligibility:** Open to women who have fulfilled the necessary time commitment to be considered an "Active Hostess" or "Active VIH Hostess" for the Miss America Pageant. Applicants must be interested in furthering their education on an undergraduate or graduate level, certification program, or with courses leading to improvement of career skills. Selection is based on career goals, course selection, and anticipated expenses.

**Financial data:** The stipend is $2,000.

**Duration:** 1 year.

**Number awarded:** Varies each year.

**Deadline:** September of each year.

---

## 707 MISS AMERICAN COED PAGEANT

American Coed Pageants
4120 Piedmont Road
Pensacola, FL 32503
Phone: (850) 438-2078; Email: nationals@americancoedpageants.com
Web: www.americancoed.com

**Summary:** To recognize and reward girls who could become "tomorrow's leaders."

**Eligibility:** Open to girls in 5 age divisions: princess for girls from 3 to 6 years of age, sweetheart for girls from 7 to 9, pre-teen for girls from 10 to 12, junior teen for girls from 13 to 15, and teen for girls from 16 to 18. Selection is based on poise and appearance in formal wear, personality during an interview, and presentation and appearance in the interview outfit. Girls may also enter several additional optional contests: talent, photogenic, Miss Model, and sportswear. Other optional contests (speech, academic achievement, and volunteer service) are only open to girls in the junior teen and teen divisions.

**Financial data:** In each division, state winners receive up to $300 in travel expenses to compete in the national competition; a $1,000 cash award; a $200 VIP Day in Walt Disney World for 2; the official state crown, banner, and trophy; and a free weekend at next year's pageant to crown their successor. Prizes in the optional contests include $250 for talent, $250 for photogenic, $100 for Miss Model, $250 for sportswear, $150 for speech, $150 for academic achievement, and $150 for volunteer service. In the national competition, more than $20,000 in cash, trophies, and prizes are awarded each year.

**Duration:** The competition is held annually.

**Number awarded:** Varies on the state and national level.

**Deadline:** State deadlines vary; check with your state pageant director to determine the deadline in your area.

---

## 708 MISS CHEERLEADER OF AMERICA SCHOLARSHIPS

Miss Cheerleader of America, Attn: Program Director
P.O. Box 667
Taylor, MI 48180
Phone: (734) 946-1200; Fax: (734) 946-1204;
Email: misscheerleaderofamerica@yahoo.com
Web: www.misscheerleaderofamerica.com

**Summary:** To recognize and reward, with college scholarships, women who are high school cheerleaders.

**Eligibility:** Open to female high school cheerleaders in grades 9 through 12. Girls who are interested apply to participate in a pageant in their home state.

Based on their applications, finalists are invited to their state pageant where they participate in an evening gown demonstration and an interview. The program is not a beauty, bathing suit, cheer skill, or talent competition. Judges attempt to select "the all-American girl, who normally would not even think about being in a pageant."

**Financial data:** Prizes are generally scholarships of $1,000 for first place, $750 for second, and $500 for third.

**Duration:** The competition is held annually.

**Number awarded:** Varies each year; normally, 3 prizes are awarded in each state in which a pageant is held.

---

## 709 MISS NEW JERSEY EDUCATIONAL SCHOLARSHIP PROGRAM

New Jersey Higher Education Student Assistance Authority
Attn: Financial Aid Services
4 Quakerbridge Plaza
P.O. Box 540
Trenton, NJ 08625-0540
Phone: (609) 588-2349; (800) 792-8670; Fax: (609) 588-2390;
Email: gjoachim@hesaa.org
Web: www.hesaa.org

**Summary:** To provide financial assistance to undergraduate and graduate students in New Jersey who can demonstrate community involvement.

**Eligibility:** Open to residents of New Jersey who have demonstrated involvement in civic, cultural, or charitable affairs for at least 3 years prior to applying for the scholarship. Applicants must be enrolled in or accepted to a full-time initial bachelor's or graduate degree program at an approved public institution of higher education in New Jersey. They must submit 2 letters of recommendation and a statement on their leadership in civic, cultural, or charitable endeavors. Male students must submit proof of registration with Selective Service.

**Financial data:** The award covers the annual cost of tuition at the public institution in New Jersey that the recipient attends.

**Duration:** 1 year; may be renewed until completion of an initial bachelor's or graduate/professional degree, provided the recipient remains a full-time student in good standing with a GPA of 3.0 or higher.

**Number awarded:** 1 each year.

**Deadline:** July of each year.

---

## 710 MISS TEEN USA

Miss Universe Organization
1370 Avenue of the Americas, 16th Floor
New York, NY 10019
Phone: (212) 373-4999; Fax: (212) 315-5378;
Email: MissUPR@missuniverse.com
Web: www.missteenusa.com

**Summary:** To recognize and reward beautiful and talented women between 15 and 19 years of age in the United States.

**Eligibility:** Open to teenage girls (15 years and above) who are interested in participating in a beauty contest. Some cities and all states have preliminary pageants. The winner of the city pageant goes on to compete in the state pageant for her home city. A delegate may also enter a state pageant without having won a city title. One delegate from each of the 50 states and the District of Columbia is selected to compete in the pageant. Participants must be between 15 and 19 years of age. They must never have been married or pregnant. Selection is based on beauty, intelligence, and ability to handle an interview.

**Financial data:** Miss Teen USA receives cash and prizes worth more than $150,000. Recently, that included a $45,000 scholarship to the School for Film and Television, a Preciosa trophy worth $3,500, a crystal chandelier from Preciosa worth $5,000, a $2,500 pre-paid VISA BUXX card, a $2,000 cash prize and complimentary UV-Free Tanning for the year of her reign from Mystic Tan, a pearl tiara worth $12,000 from Mikimoto, a fashion footwear wardrobe from Nina Footwear, a swimwear wardrobe from Pink Sands Swim, a 5-day/4 night trip for 2 anywhere American Airlines flies in the continental United States or Caribbean, a pajama wardrobe by Jamatex worth $500, a 1-year salary, a luxury apartment while in New York City, a personal appearance wardrobe, a modeling portfolio, and other services and training. Other prizes included $3,000 for first runner-up, $2,000 for second runner-up, $1,000 for third and fourth runners-up, and $500 for semifinalists. In addition, the delegate selected by the television audience as Miss Photogenic and the delegate selected by her peers as Miss Congeniality each received $1,000 cash prizes and a commemorative Preciosa crystal trophy worth $3,500.

**Duration:** The national pageant is held annually, usually at the end of the summer.

**Number awarded:** 1 national winner each year.

**Deadline:** June of each year.

## 711 MISS USA

Miss Universe Organization
1370 Avenue of the Americas, 16th Floor
New York, NY 10019
Phone: (212) 373-4999; Fax: (212) 315-5378;
Email: MissUPR@missuniverse.com
Web: www.missusa.com

**Summary:** To identify and reward the most beautiful women selected in a competition among women from each state.

**Eligibility:** Open to women between 18 and 27 years of age who have never been married or pregnant. Entrants are first selected in state competitions, and then 51 women (1 from each state and the District of Columbia) compete in the Miss USA Pageant. Selection of the winner is based on interviews by pageant judges (on successes, talents, goals, and ambitions), a swimsuit competition (with swimsuit styles provided by the pageant), and an evening gown competition (with gowns chosen by the competitors). The Photogenic Award is presented to the delegate voted on and selected by the television audience, and the Congeniality Award is presented to the delegate selected by her sister delegates as the most charismatic and inspirational.

**Financial data:** Miss USA receives cash and prizes worth more than $225,000. Recently, that included a scholarship valued $45,000 from The School for Film and Television, a Preciosa trophy worth $3,500, a crystal chandelier from Preciosa worth $5,000, a pearl tiara worth $12,000 from Mikimoto, a fashion footwear wardrobe from Steve Madden, a swimwear wardrobe from Endless Sun Apparel, a 5-day/4 night trip for 2 anywhere American Airlines flies in the continental United States or Caribbean, a 1-year salary, a luxury apartment while in New York City, a personal appearance wardrobe from Tadashi Fashions, a modeling portfolio, and other services and training. Other prizes included $3,000 for first runner-up, $2,000 for second runner-up, $1,000 for third and fourth runners-up, and $500 for semifinalists. In addition, the delegate selected by the television audience as Miss Photogenic and the delegate selected by her peers as Miss Congeniality each received $1,000 cash prizes and a commemorative Preciosa crystal trophy worth $3,500.

**Duration:** The national pageant is held annually, in February or March.

**Number awarded:** 1 each year.

**Deadline:** January of each year.

## 712 MISSISSIPPI EDUCATIONAL ASSISTANCE FOR MIA/POW DEPENDENTS

Mississippi State Veterans Affairs Board
3460 Highway 80 East
P.O. Box 5947
Pearl, MS 39288-5947
Phone: (601) 576-4850; Fax: (601) 576-4868; Email: grice@vab.state.ms.us
Web: www.vab.state.ms.us

**Summary:** To provide financial assistance for college to the children of Mississippi residents who are POWs or MIAs.

**Eligibility:** Open to the children of members of the armed services whose official home of record and residence is in Mississippi and who are officially reported as being either a prisoner of a foreign government or missing in action. Applicants must be attending or planning to attend a state-supported college or university in Mississippi.

**Financial data:** This assistance covers all costs of college attendance.

**Duration:** Up to 8 semesters.

**Number awarded:** Varies each year.

## 713 MISSISSIPPI EMINENT SCHOLARS GRANTS

Mississippi Office of Student Financial Aid
3825 Ridgewood Road
Jackson, MS 39211-6453
Phone: (601) 432-6997; (800) 327-2980 (within MS); Fax: (601) 432-6527;
Email: sfa@ihl.state.ms.us
Web: www.ihl.state.ms.us/financialaid/mesg.html

**Summary:** To provide financial assistance for college to residents of Mississippi who have exceptional academic records.

**Eligibility:** Open to seniors graduating from high schools in Mississippi, home-schooled students in the state with less than 12 college hours, and college students who graduated from high school or completed a home school program within the past 3 years and have completed 12 or more college hours. Applicants must have been residents of Mississippi for at least 1 year prior to enrolling in college and have a high school GPA of 3.5 or higher and a score of 29 or higher on the ACT or 1280 or an equivalent score on the SAT; if they qualified as a semifinalist or finalist in the National Merit Scholarship Competition or the National Achievement Scholarship Competition, they are not required to have

the minimum ACT score. They must be enrolled or planning to enroll as a full-time student at an approved college or university in the state.

**Financial data:** The stipend is $2,500 per year, not to exceed tuition and required fees.

**Duration:** 1 year; may be renewed for up to 4 additional years or completion of an undergraduate degree, as long as the recipient maintains continuous full-time enrollment and a cumulative GPA of 3.5 or higher.

**Number awarded:** Varies each year.

**Deadline:** September of each year.

## 714 MISSISSIPPI HIGHER EDUCATION LEGISLATIVE PLAN FOR NEEDY STUDENTS

Mississippi Office of Student Financial Aid
3825 Ridgewood Road
Jackson, MS 39211-6453
Phone: (601) 432-6997; (800) 327-2980 (within MS); Fax: (601) 432-6527;
Email: sfa@ihl.state.ms.us
Web: www.ihl.state.ms.us/financialaid/help.html

**Summary:** To provide financial assistance for college to residents of Mississippi who demonstrate financial need.

**Eligibility:** Open to residents of Mississippi (for at least 2 years) who have graduated from high school within the immediate past 2 years. They must be enrolled or planning to enroll full time at a college or university in the state. High school seniors entering their freshman year in college must have a cumulative high school GPA of 2.5 or higher and have completed specific high school core curriculum requirements. College freshmen entering their sophomore year must have achieved a cumulative GPA of 2.5 or higher on all college course work previously completed. All applicants must have scored 20 or higher on the ACT and be able to demonstrate financial need with an average family adjusted gross income of $36,500 or less over the prior 2 years (rising by $5,000 for each sibling in the family under 21 years of age).

**Financial data:** Students in this program receive a full waiver of tuition at eligible Mississippi public institutions of higher learning or eligible Mississippi public community/junior colleges. Students attending private institutions receive an award amount equal to the award of a student attending the nearest comparable public institution.

**Duration:** 1 year; may be renewed up to 4 additional years provided the recipient continues to meet all program requirement and maintains a GPA of 2.5 or higher.

**Number awarded:** Varies each year, depending on the availability of funds; awards are granted on a first-come, first-served basis.

**Deadline:** March of each year.

## 715 MISSISSIPPI LAW ENFORCEMENT OFFICERS AND FIREMEN SCHOLARSHIP PROGRAM

Mississippi Office of Student Financial Aid
3825 Ridgewood Road
Jackson, MS 39211-6453
Phone: (601) 432-6997; (800) 327-2980 (within MS); Fax: (601) 432-6527;
Email: sfa@ihl.state.ms.us
Web: www.ihl.state.ms.us/financialaid/law.html

**Summary:** To provide financial assistance for college to the spouses and children of disabled or deceased Mississippi law enforcement officers and fire fighters.

**Eligibility:** Open to children and spouses of full-time law enforcement officers and fire fighters who became permanently and totally disabled or who died in the line of duty and were Mississippi residents at the time of death or injury. Applicants must be high school seniors or graduates interested in attending a state-supported postsecondary institution in Mississippi on a full-time basis. Children may be natural, adopted, or stepchildren up to 23 years of age; spouses may be of any age.

**Financial data:** Students in this program receive full payment of tuition fees, the average cost of campus housing, required fees, and applicable course fees at state-supported colleges and universities in Mississippi. Funds may not be used to pay for books, food, school supplies, materials, dues, or fees for extra-curricular activities.

**Duration:** Up to 8 semesters.

**Number awarded:** Varies each year.

**Deadline:** Applications may be submitted at any time.

## 716 MISSISSIPPI LEVERAGING EDUCATIONAL ASSISTANCE PARTNERSHIP PROGRAM

Mississippi Office of Student Financial Aid

3825 Ridgewood Road
Jackson, MS 39211-6453
Phone: (601) 432-6997; (800) 327-2980 (within MS); Fax: (601) 432-6527;
Email: sfa@ihl.state.ms.us
Web: www.ihl.state.ms.us/financialaid/leap.html
**Summary:** To provide financial assistance for college to Mississippi residents who demonstrate significant financial need.
**Eligibility:** Open to current legal Mississippi residents who are enrolled or accepted for enrollment as full-time undergraduate students at a nonprofit college or university in Mississippi and who demonstrate substantial financial need. U.S. citizenship or permanent resident status is required.
**Financial data:** The amount of assistance varies.
**Duration:** 1 year; may be renewed for up to 3 additional years.
**Number awarded:** Varies each year.
**Deadline:** Each participating college and university establishes its own deadline date for applications.

## 717 MISSISSIPPI RESIDENT TUITION ASSISTANCE GRANTS

Mississippi Office of Student Financial Aid
3825 Ridgewood Road
Jackson, MS 39211-6453
Phone: (601) 432-6997; (800) 327-2980 (within MS); Fax: (601) 432-6527;
Email: sfa@ihl.state.ms.us
Web: www.ihl.state.ms.us/financialaid/mtag.html
**Summary:** To provide financial assistance for college to Mississippi residents who demonstrate significant financial need.
**Eligibility:** Open to legal Mississippi residents (for at least 1 year) who are receiving less than the full federal Pell Grant for college. High school seniors must have a GPA of 2.5 or higher and either an ACT score of 15 or higher or an equivalent score on the SAT. Home-schooled students must submit a transcript showing the course work corresponding to that of a high school graduate for grades 9-12 and either an ACT score of 15 or higher or an equivalent score on the SAT. Students already enrolled in college must have a cumulative GPA of 2.5 or higher. All applicants must be attending or planning to attend a 2-year or 4-year public or private accredited college or university in Mississippi.
**Financial data:** Awards depend on the availability of funds and the need of the recipient; the maximum award for a freshman or sophomore is $500 per year; the maximum award for a junior or senior is $1,000 per year.
**Duration:** 1 year; may be renewed for up to 4 additional years or completion of an undergraduate degree, as long as the recipient maintains continuous full-time enrollment and a GPA of 2.5 or higher.
**Number awarded:** Varies each year.
**Deadline:** September of each year.

## 718 MISSOURI COLLEGE GUARANTEE PLUS PROGRAM

Missouri Department of Higher Education, Attn: Student Financial Assistance
3515 Amazonas Drive
Jefferson City, MO 65109-5717
Phone: (573) 526-7958; (800) 473-6757; Fax: (573) 751-6635;
Email: info@dhe.mo.gov
Web: www.dhe.mo.gov/hsstudentscollegeguaranteeplus.shtml
**Summary:** To provide financial assistance for college to full-time students in Missouri who have financial need and who participate in a federal TRIO program or who graduated from a high school GEAR UP program.
**Eligibility:** Open to residents of Missouri who are attending or planning to attend participating Missouri postsecondary institutions as full-time undergraduate students. Applicants must have a high school GPA of 2.5 or higher and a score of 20 or higher on the ACT (or the equivalent on the SAT). They must be able to demonstrate financial need and participation in high school extracurricular activities. This program is limited to students who 1) participate in a federal TRIO program (e.g., Upward Bound), or 2) graduated from a high school GEAR UP (Gaining Early Awareness and Readiness for Undergraduate Programs) activity. Students working on a degree or certificate in theology or divinity are not eligible. U.S. citizenship or permanent resident status is required.
**Financial data:** The maximum annual award is based on the tuition cost at the University of Missouri.
**Duration:** 1 year; may be renewed.
**Number awarded:** Varies each year.
**Deadline:** March of each year.

## 719 MISSOURI COLLEGE GUARANTEE PROGRAM

Missouri Department of Higher Education, Attn: Student Financial Assistance
3515 Amazonas Drive

Jefferson City, MO 65109-5717
Phone: (573) 526-7958; (800) 473-6757; Fax: (573) 751-6635;
Email: info@dhe.mo.gov
Web: www.dhe.mo.gov/hsstudentscollegeguarantee.shtml
**Summary:** To provide financial assistance for college to full-time students in Missouri who have financial need.
**Eligibility:** Open to residents of Missouri who are attending or planning to attend participating Missouri postsecondary institutions as full-time undergraduate students. Applicants must have a high school GPA of 2.5 or higher and a score of 20 or higher on the ACT (or 950 or the equivalent on the SAT). They must be able to demonstrate financial need. Students working on a degree or certificate in theology or divinity are not eligible. U.S. citizenship or permanent resident status is required.
**Financial data:** The maximum annual award is based on the tuition cost at the University of Missouri.
**Duration:** 1 year; may be renewed.
**Number awarded:** Varies each year; recently, 4,006 students received support through this program.
**Deadline:** March of each year.

## 720 MISSOURI GENERAL BPW SCHOLARSHIPS

Missouri Business and Professional Women's Foundation, Inc.
P.O. Box 338
Carthage, MO 64836-0338
Web: www.bpwmo.org/scholarship.htm
**Summary:** To provide financial assistance for college to women in Missouri.
**Eligibility:** Open to women in Missouri who have been accepted into an accredited program or course of study to upgrade their skills and/or complete education for career advancement. Along with their application, they must submit brief statements on the following: their achievements and/or specific recognitions in their field of endeavor; professional and/or civic affiliations; present and long-range career goals; how they plan to participate in and contribute to their community upon completion of their program of study; why they feel they would make a good recipient; and any special circumstances that may have influenced their ability to continue or complete their education. They must also demonstrate financial need and U.S. citizenship.
**Financial data:** A stipend is awarded (amount not specified).
**Duration:** 1 year.
**Number awarded:** Varies each year; recently, 3 of these scholarships were awarded.
**Deadline:** January of each year.

## 721 MISSOURI HIGHER EDUCATION ACADEMIC "BRIGHT FLIGHT" SCHOLARSHIP PROGRAM

Missouri Department of Higher Education, Attn: Student Financial Assistance
3515 Amazonas Drive
Jefferson City, MO 65109-5717
Phone: (573) 526-7958; (800) 473-6757; Fax: (573) 751-6635;
Email: info@dhe.mo.gov
Web: www.dhe.mo.gov/hsstudentsbrightflight.shtml
**Summary:** To provide financial assistance for college to outstanding high school seniors in Missouri.
**Eligibility:** Open to high school seniors in Missouri who score in the top 3% of all Missouri students taking the SAT or ACT. Applicants must be planning to attend a participating college or university in Missouri full time. Students working on a degree or certificate in theology or divinity are not eligible. U.S. citizenship or permanent resident status is required.
**Financial data:** The stipend is $2,000 per year.
**Duration:** 1 year; may be renewed for up to 4 additional years or until completion of a baccalaureate degree, if the recipient maintains full-time status and satisfactory academic progress.
**Number awarded:** Varies each year; recently, 8,262 of these scholarships were awarded.
**Deadline:** July of each year.

## 722 MISSOURI KIDS' CHANCE SCHOLARSHIPS

Kids' Chance Inc. of Missouri, Attn: Scholarship Committee
P.O. Box 410384
St. Louis, MO 63141
Phone: (314) 997-3390; (800) 484-5733, ext. 5437; Fax: (314) 432-5894;
Email: susgrp@charter.net
Web: www.mokidschance.org

**Summary:** To provide financial assistance for college to Missouri residents whose parent was killed or permanently disabled in a work-related accident.

**Eligibility:** Open to Missouri residents whose parent sustained a serious injury or fatality in a Missouri work-related accident covered by workers' compensation. Applicants must be attending or planning to attend an accredited vocational school or college within the United States. They must be able to demonstrate financial need.

**Financial data:** Stipends depend on the need of the recipient. Funds may be used to cover tuition, books, supplies, housing, meals, and other expenses not covered by other grants and/or scholarships.

**Duration:** 1 year; may be renewed.

**Number awarded:** Varies each year.

**Deadline:** April or October of each year.

### 723 MISSOURI PUBLIC OFFICER OR EMPLOYEE'S CHILD SURVIVOR GRANT PROGRAM

Missouri Department of Higher Education, Attn: Student Financial Assistance
3515 Amazonas Drive
Jefferson City, MO 65109-5717
Phone: (573) 526-7958; (800) 473-6757; Fax: (573) 751-6635;
Email: info@dhe.mo.gov
Web: www.dhe.mo.gov/hsstudentspublicservice.shtml

**Summary:** To provide financial assistance for college to spouses and children of disabled and deceased Missouri public employees and public safety officers.

**Eligibility:** Open to dependent children and spouses of 1) Missouri Department of Transportation employees who were killed or permanently disabled while engaged in the construction or maintenance of highways, roads, and bridges; and 2) Missouri public safety officers who were killed or permanently disabled in the line of duty. Applicants must be Missouri residents enrolled or accepted for enrollment as a full-time undergraduate student at a participating Missouri college or university; children must be younger than 24 years of age. Students working on a degree or certificate in theology or divinity are not eligible. U.S. citizenship or permanent resident status is required.

**Financial data:** The maximum annual grant is the lesser of 1) the actual tuition charged at the school where the recipient is enrolled, or 2) the amount of tuition charged to a Missouri undergraduate resident enrolled full time in the same class level and in the same academic major as an applicant at the University of Missouri at Columbia.

**Duration:** 1 year; may be renewed.

**Number awarded:** Varies each year.

**Deadline:** There is no application deadline, but early submission of the completed application is encouraged.

### 724 MISSOURI STAATS COMPANY SCHOLARSHIP

Missouri Association of Fairs & Festivals, Attn: Executive Director
941 East Rodney
Cape Girardeau, MO 63701
Phone: (573) 334-9250; Fax: (573) 270-0898
Web: www.mofairsfest.org/scholarships.htm

**Summary:** To provide financial assistance for college to high school seniors in Missouri who have participated in county fairs or festivals.

**Eligibility:** Open to seniors graduating from high schools in Missouri with a GPA of 2.5 or higher. Applicants must be planning to enroll full time at a 2- or 4-year college or university. They must be able to demonstrate past support of school, community, and the fair and festival environment. Along with their application, they must submit a letter of recommendation from their high school guidance counselor and the sponsoring Missouri Association of Fairs & Festivals (MAFF) member fair board. Financial need is also considered in the selection process.

**Financial data:** The stipend is $1,000.

**Duration:** 1 year.

**Number awarded:** 1 each year.

**Deadline:** December of each year.

### 725 MISSOURI VIETNAM VETERANS SURVIVOR GRANT PROGRAM

Missouri Department of Higher Education, Attn: Student Financial Assistance
3515 Amazonas Drive
Jefferson City, MO 65109-5717
Phone: (573) 526-7958; (800) 473-6757; Fax: (573) 751-6635;
Email: info@dhe.mo.gov
Web: www.dhe.mo.gov/hsstudentsvietnamvet.shtml

**Summary:** To provide financial assistance for college to survivors of certain deceased Missouri Vietnam veterans.

**Eligibility:** Open to surviving spouses and children of veterans who served in the military in Vietnam or the war zone in southeast Asia, who were residents of Missouri when first entering military service and at the time of death, whose death was attributed to or caused by exposure to toxic chemicals during the Vietnam conflict, and who served in the Vietnam theater between 1961 and 1972. Applicants must be Missouri residents enrolled in a program leading to a certificate, associate degree, or baccalaureate degree at an approved postsecondary institution in the state. Students working on a degree or certificate in theology or divinity are not eligible. U.S. citizenship or permanent resident status is required.

**Financial data:** The maximum annual grant is the lesser of 1) the actual tuition charged at the school where the recipient is enrolled, or 2) the amount of tuition charged to a Missouri undergraduate resident enrolled full time in the same class level and in the same academic major as an applicant at the Missouri public 4-year regional institutions.

**Duration:** 1 semester; may be renewed until the recipient has obtained a baccalaureate degree or has completed 150 semester credit hours, whichever comes first.

**Number awarded:** Varies each year.

### 726 MISSOURI'S A+ SCHOOLS FINANCIAL INCENTIVE PROGRAM

Missouri Department of Elementary and Secondary Education
Attn: Division of School Improvement
205 Jefferson Street
P.O. Box 480
Jefferson City, MO 65102-0480
Phone: (573) 751-1394; Fax: (573) 751-4261;
Email: wworts@mail.dese.state.mo.us
Web: www.dese.state.mo.us/divimprove/aplus/index.html

**Summary:** To provide financial assistance to high school seniors who graduate from a designated "A+ School" in Missouri and are interested in attending a community college or vocational institute in the state.

**Eligibility:** Open to students who graduate from a designated "A+ School" in Missouri. Applicants must meet the following requirements: have attended a designated A+ School for 3 consecutive years prior to graduation, have a GPA of at least 2.5, have at least a 95% attendance record, perform at least 50 hours of unpaid tutoring or mentoring, maintain a record of good citizenship and avoid the unlawful use of drugs or alcohol, and be planning to attend a community college or postsecondary vocational/technical school on a full-time basis in Missouri.

**Financial data:** Recipients are offered state-paid assistance (full tuition and books) to attend any public community college or technical school in the state.

**Duration:** 1 year; may be renewed if the recipient maintains a GPA of 2.5 or higher.

**Number awarded:** Since the tuition program began in 1997, more than 33,000 students have qualified for assistance.

### 727 MITSUYUKI YONEMURA MEMORIAL SCHOLARSHIP

Japanese American Citizens League, Attn: National Scholarship Awards
1765 Sutter Street
San Francisco, CA 94115
Phone: (415) 921-5225; Fax: (415) 931-4671; Email: jacl@jacl.org
Web: www.jacl.org/scholarships.html

**Summary:** To provide financial assistance for college to student members of the Japanese American Citizens League (JACL) who are high school seniors.

**Eligibility:** Open to JACL members who are high school seniors interested in attending a college, university, trade school, business college, or other institution of higher learning. Applicants must submit a statement describing their current level of involvement in the Japanese American community or Asian Pacific community and how they will continue their involvement in future years. Selection is based on academic record, extracurricular activities, and community involvement.

**Financial data:** The stipend depends on the availability of funds but usually ranges from $1,000 to $5,000.

**Duration:** 1 year; nonrenewable.

**Number awarded:** At least 1 each year.

**Deadline:** February of each year.

### 728 MOAA BASE/POST SCHOLARSHIPS

Military Officers Association of America
Attn: Educational Assistance Program

201 North Washington Street
Alexandria, VA 22314-2539
Phone: (703) 549-2311; (800) 234-MOAA; Email: edassist@moaa.org
Web: www.moaa.org

**Summary:** To provide financial assistance for undergraduate education to dependents of active-duty military officers and enlisted personnel.

**Eligibility:** Open to dependent children under 24 years of age of active-duty (including drilling Reserves and National Guard) officers and enlisted military personnel. Applicants are not required to be related to a member of the Military Officers Association of America (MOAA) and do not need to meet a minimum GPA requirement. Selection is based on a random drawing.

**Financial data:** The stipend is $1,000 per year.

**Duration:** 1 year.

**Number awarded:** 50 each year.

**Deadline:** February of each year.

---

**729 MOAA SPECIAL GRANTS**

Military Officers Association of America
Attn: Educational Assistance Program
201 North Washington Street
Alexandria, VA 22314-2539
Phone: (703) 549-2311; (800) 234-MOAA; Email: edassist@moaa.org
Web: www.moaa.org

**Summary:** To provide financial assistance to dependent children of members of Military Officers Association of America (MOAA) who are rising seniors in college.

**Eligibility:** Open to never married dependent children under 24 years of age of active, Reserve, National Guard, and retired uniformed service personnel (Army, Navy, Air Force, Marines, Coast Guard, Public Health Service, or National Oceanographic and Atmospheric Administration). Parents who are officers eligible for membership in the association must be members. Applicants must be entering their senior year of college. Unmarried dependent children of enlisted personnel are also eligible to apply. Applicants for the MOAA Educational Assistance Program loans are automatically considered for these scholarships; no separate application is necessary. Selection is based on scholastic ability (GPA of 3.0 or higher), participation, character, leadership, and financial need.

**Financial data:** The stipend is $5,000 per year.

**Duration:** 1 year.

**Number awarded:** Varies each year.

**Deadline:** February of each year.

---

**730 MONTANA COMMUNITY COLLEGE HONOR SCHOLARSHIPS**

Montana Guaranteed Student Loan Program
2500 Broadway
P.O. Box 203101
Helena, MT 59620-3101
Phone: (406) 444-0638; (800) 537-7508; Fax: (406) 444-1869;
Email: scholar@mgslp.state.mt.us
Web: www.mgslp.state.mt.us

**Summary:** To provide financial assistance to outstanding community college students in Montana planning to transfer to a university in the state.

**Eligibility:** Open to residents of Montana who are graduating from a community college in the state and planning to transfer to a branch of the Montana University System. Their college must verify that they are the highest ranking member of their class desiring to attend a Montana University System unit.

**Financial data:** Students eligible for this benefit are entitled to attend any unit of the Montana University System without payment of undergraduate registration or incidental fees.

**Duration:** The waiver is valid through the completion of the first academic year of enrollment.

**Number awarded:** 1 scholarship is awarded to a member of each community college graduating class.

---

**731 MONTANA CUSTODIAL STUDENT FEE WAIVER**

Montana Guaranteed Student Loan Program
2500 Broadway
P.O. Box 203101
Helena, MT 59620-3101
Phone: (406) 444-0638; (800) 537-7508; Fax: (406) 444-1869;
Email: scholar@mgslp.state.mt.us

Web: www.mgslp.state.mt.us

**Summary:** To provide financial assistance for undergraduate education to residents of custodial facilities in Montana.

**Eligibility:** Open to residents of Montana who attend the Riverside Correctional Facility at Boulder, the Pine Hills Youth Correctional Facility at Miles City, or similar facilities or private charitable institutions. Applicants must be recommended by the Department of Corrections or the administration of the private institutions. Financial need is considered.

**Financial data:** Students eligible for this benefit are entitled to attend any unit of the Montana University System without payment of undergraduate registration or incidental fees.

**Duration:** Undergraduate students are eligible for continued fee waiver as long as they maintain reasonable academic progress as full-time students.

**Number awarded:** Varies each year.

---

**732 MONTANA DEPENDENTS OF PRISONERS OF WAR FEE WAIVER**

Montana Guaranteed Student Loan Program
2500 Broadway
P.O. Box 203101
Helena, MT 59620-3101
Phone: (406) 444-0638; (800) 537-7508; Fax: (406) 444-1869;
Email: scholar@mgslp.state.mt.us
Web: www.mgslp.state.mt.us

**Summary:** To provide financial assistance for college to dependents of veterans and military personnel declared missing in action or prisoners of war in southeast Asia.

**Eligibility:** Open to the spouses or children of residents of Montana who, while serving in southeast Asia after January 1, 1961 either in the armed forces or as a civilian, have been declared missing in action or prisoner of war. Financial need is considered.

**Financial data:** Students eligible for this benefit are entitled to attend any unit of the Montana University System without payment of undergraduate registration or incidental fees.

**Duration:** Undergraduate students are eligible for continued fee waivers as long as they maintain reasonable academic progress as full-time students.

**Number awarded:** Varies each year.

---

**733 MONTANA GEAR UP ACHIEVEMENT GRANTS**

Montana Guaranteed Student Loan Program
2500 Broadway
P.O. Box 203101
Helena, MT 59620-3101
Phone: (406) 444-0638; (800) 537-7508; Fax: (406) 444-1869;
Email: scholar@mgslp.state.mt.us
Web: www.mgslp.state.mt.us

**Summary:** To provide financial assistance for college to juniors at high schools in Montana that are participating in the Gaining Early Awareness and Readiness for Undergraduate Programs (GEAR UP) federal program.

**Eligibility:** Open to high school juniors who have been enrolled in the college preparatory curriculum for at least 2 years at a Montana high school that is participating in the GEAR UP program. Applicants must have a cumulative GPA of 2.0 or higher at the end of the fourth semester of high school and upon high school graduation. They must enroll in a Montana postsecondary institution within 18 months of high school graduation.

**Financial data:** The stipend is $1,000.

**Duration:** 1 year.

**Number awarded:** Varies each year; recently, 77 students received these grants.

---

**734 MONTANA HONOR SCHOLARSHIPS FOR NATIONAL MERIT SCHOLARSHIP SEMIFINALISTS**

Montana Guaranteed Student Loan Program
2500 Broadway
P.O. Box 203101
Helena, MT 59620-3101
Phone: (406) 444-0638; (800) 537-7508; Fax: (406) 444-1869;
Email: scholar@mgslp.state.mt.us
Web: www.mgslp.state.mt.us

**Summary:** To provide financial assistance for undergraduate education to National Merit Scholarship semifinalists in Montana.

**Eligibility:** Open to residents of Montana who are National Merit Scholarship semifinalists. Students must enroll at a campus of the Montana University System or community college in the state within 9 months of high school graduation.

**Financial data:** Students eligible for this benefit are entitled to attend any unit of the Montana University System without payment of undergraduate registration or incidental fees.

**Duration:** The waiver is valid through the completion of the first academic year of enrollment.

**Number awarded:** Varies each year.

### 735 MONTANA HONORABLY DISCHARGED VETERAN FEE WAIVER

Montana Guaranteed Student Loan Program
2500 Broadway
P.O. Box 203101
Helena, MT 59620-3101
Phone: (406) 444-0638; (800) 537-7508; Fax: (406) 444-1869;
Email: scholar@mgslp.state.mt.us
Web: www.mgslp.state.mt.us

**Summary:** To provide financial assistance for undergraduate education to selected Montana veterans.

**Eligibility:** Open to honorably-discharged veterans who served with the U.S. armed forces in any war and who are residents of Montana. Only veterans who at some time qualified for U.S. Department of Veterans Affairs (VA) educational benefits, but who are no longer eligible, are entitled to this waiver. Veterans who served in the armed forces subsequent to the conflict in Vietnam and are working on their initial undergraduate degree are also eligible if they received an Armed Forces Expeditionary Medal for service in Lebanon, Grenada, or Panama; or served in a combat theater in the Persian Gulf between August 2, 1990 and April 11, 1991 and received the Southwest Asia Service Medal; or were awarded the Kosovo Campaign Medal. Veterans who served in World War II, Korea, or Vietnam are eligible to work on undergraduate or graduate degrees; other veterans are eligible only to work on their first undergraduate degree. Financial need is considered in the selection process.

**Financial data:** Students eligible for this benefit are entitled to attend any unit of the Montana University System without payment of undergraduate registration or incidental fees.

**Duration:** Undergraduate students are eligible for continued fee waiver as long as they maintain reasonable academic progress as full-time students.

**Number awarded:** Varies each year.

### 736 MONTANA SEPTEMBER 11, 2001 VICTIMS FEE WAIVER

Montana Guaranteed Student Loan Program
2500 Broadway
P.O. Box 203101
Helena, MT 59620-3101
Phone: (406) 444-0638; (800) 537-7508; Fax: (406) 444-1869;
Email: scholar@mgslp.state.mt.us
Web: www.mgslp.state.mt.us

**Summary:** To provide financial assistance for undergraduate education in Montana to dependents of victims of the September 11, 2001 terrorist action.

**Eligibility:** Open to persons whose spouse, parent, or legal guardian was a victim of the September 11, 2001 terrorist actions at the New York World Trade Center, the Pentagon, or the Pennsylvania airplane crash. The term "victim" includes a person killed as a direct result of physical injuries suffered on or about September 11 directly related to the terrorist actions and includes rescuers, relief workers, or fire and policy personnel. It does not include any individuals identified by federal law enforcement personnel as likely perpetrators of the terrorist activities. Applicants must be enrolled in a program leading to their initial associate or baccalaureate degree at a unit of the Montana University System.

**Financial data:** Students eligible for this benefit are entitled to attend any unit of the Montana University System without payment of undergraduate registration, incidental fees, or out-of-state fees.

**Duration:** Undergraduate students are eligible for continued fee waiver as long as they maintain reasonable academic progress as full-time students.

**Number awarded:** Varies each year.

### 737 MONTANA TUITION ASSISTANCE PROGRAM BAKER GRANTS

Montana Guaranteed Student Loan Program
2500 Broadway
P.O. Box 203101
Helena, MT 59620-3101

Phone: (406) 444-0638; (800) 537-7508; Fax: (406) 444-1869;
Email: scholar@mgslp.state.mt.us
Web: www.mgslp.state.mt.us

**Summary:** To provide financial assistance to Montana residents who are attending college in the state and are working to support themselves.

**Eligibility:** Open to residents of Montana who are attending units of the Montana University System, community colleges, Indian colleges, or designated private institutions in the state full time. Applicants must be working and have at least $2,575 in earned income during the prior calendar year. (That amount is based on the minimum wage multiplied by 500 hours; if the minimum wage is increased, the amount a student must earn is increased accordingly.) They must be making satisfactory academic progress toward their first undergraduate degree and have an expected family contribution from the results of their Free Application for Federal Student Aid (FAFSA) of $6,500 or less.

**Financial data:** The grant is intended to offset any federal Pell Grant dollars the student may have lost due to earned wages. Recently, grants ranged from $100 to $1,000.

**Duration:** 1 year.

**Number awarded:** Varies each year. Recently, a total of $1.5 million was available for this program.

### 738 MONTANA UNIVERSITY SYSTEM HONOR SCHOLARSHIPS

Montana Guaranteed Student Loan Program
2500 Broadway
P.O. Box 203101
Helena, MT 59620-3101
Phone: (406) 444-0638; (800) 537-7508; Fax: (406) 444-1869;
Email: scholar@mgslp.state.mt.us
Web: www.mgslp.state.mt.us

**Summary:** To provide financial assistance for undergraduate education to outstanding high school students in Montana.

**Eligibility:** Open to residents of Montana who are graduating from high school and planning to attend a branch of the Montana University System or a community college in the state. Applicants must have been enrolled in an accredited high school for at least 2 of the 3 years prior to graduation, meet the college preparatory requirements, rank in the top quarter of their class, and have a GPA of 3.5 or higher.

**Financial data:** Students eligible for this benefit are entitled to attend any unit of the Montana University System or any community college in the state without payment of tuition or registration fees.

**Duration:** 1 year; may be renewed for up to 3 additional years if the recipient maintains full-time enrollment and a GPA of 3.4 or higher.

**Number awarded:** Varies each year.

### 739 MONTANA WAR ORPHANS FEE WAIVER

Montana Guaranteed Student Loan Program
2500 Broadway
P.O. Box 203101
Helena, MT 59620-3101
Phone: (406) 444-0638; (800) 537-7508; Fax: (406) 444-1869;
Email: scholar@mgslp.state.mt.us
Web: www.mgslp.state.mt.us

**Summary:** To provide financial assistance for undergraduate education to the children of Montana veterans who died in the line of duty or as a result of service-connected disabilities.

**Eligibility:** Open to children of members of the U.S. armed forces who served on active duty during World War II, the Korean Conflict, or the Vietnam Conflict; were legal residents of Montana at the time of entry into service; and were killed in action or died as a result of injury, disease, or other disability while in the service. Applicants must be no older than 25 years of age. Financial need is considered in the selection process.

**Financial data:** Students eligible for this benefit are entitled to attend any unit of the Montana University System without payment of undergraduate registration or incidental fees.

**Duration:** Undergraduate students are eligible for continued fee waiver as long as they maintain reasonable academic progress as full-time students.

**Number awarded:** Varies each year.

### 740 MONTGOMERY GI BILL (ACTIVE DUTY)

Department of Veterans Affairs
810 Vermont Avenue, N.W.
Washington, DC 20420

Phone: (202) 418-4343; (888) GI-BILL1
Web: www.gibill.va.gov

**Summary:** To provide financial assistance for college, graduate school, and other types of postsecondary schools to new enlistees in any of the armed forces after they have completed their service obligation.

**Eligibility:** Open to veterans who received an honorable discharge and have a high school diploma, a GED, or, in some cases, up to 12 hours of college credit. Applicants must also meet the requirements of 1 of the following categories: 1) entered active duty for the first time after June 30, 1985, had military pay reduced by $100 per month for the first 12 months, and continuously served for 3 years, or 2 years if that was original enlistment, or 2 years if they entered Selected Reserve within a year of leaving active duty and served 4 years (the 2 by 4 program); 2) entered active duty before January 1, 1977, had remaining entitlement under the Vietnam Era GI Bill on December 31, 1989, served at least 1 day between October 19, 1984 and June 30, 1985, and stayed on active duty through June 30, 1988 (or June 30, 1987 if they entered Selected Reserve within 1 year of leaving active duty and served 4 years; 3) on active duty on September 30, 1990 and separated involuntarily after February 2, 1991, involuntarily separated on or after November 30, 1993, or voluntarily separated under either the Voluntary Separation Incentive (VSI) or Special Separation Benefit (SSB) program, and before separation had military pay reduced by $1,200; or 4) on active duty on October 9, 1996, had money remaining in an account from the Veterans Educational Assistance Program (VEAP), elected MGIB by October 9, 1997, and paid $1,200. Certain National Guard servicemembers may also qualify under category 4 if they served on full-time active duty between July 1, 1985 and November 28, elected MGIB between October 9, 1996 and July 8, 1997, and paid $1,200. Following completion of their service obligation, participants may enroll in colleges or universities for associate, bachelor, or graduate degrees; in courses leading to a certificate or diploma from business, technical, or vocational schools; for apprenticeships or on-job training programs; in correspondence courses; in flight training; for preparatory courses necessary for admission to a college or graduate school; for licensing and certification tests approved for veterans; or in state-approved teacher certification programs. Veterans who wish to enroll in certain high-cost technology programs (life science, physical science, engineering, mathematics, engineering and science technology, computer specialties, and engineering, science, and computer management) may be eligible for an accelerated payment

**Financial data:** For veterans in categories 1, 3, and 4 who served on active duty for 3 years or more, the current monthly stipend for college or university work is $1,034 for full-time study, $775.50 for three-quarter time study, or $517 for half-time study, or $258.50 for quarter-time study or less; for apprenticeship and on-the-job training, the monthly stipend is $878.90 for the first 6 months, $672.10 for the second 6 months, and $465.30 for the remainder of the program. For enlistees whose initial active-duty obligation was less than 3 years, the current monthly stipend for college or university work is $840 for full-time study, $630 for three-quarter time study, $420 for half-time study, or $210 for quarter-time study or less; for apprenticeship and on-the-job training, the monthly stipend is $714 for the first 6 months, $546 for the second 6 months, and $378 for the remainder of the program. For veterans in category 2 with remaining eligibility, the current monthly stipend for institutional study full time is $1,222 for no dependents, $1,258 with 1 dependent, $1,289 with 2 dependents, and $16 for each additional dependent; for three-quarter time study, the monthly stipend is $917 for no dependents, $943.50 with 1 dependent, $967 with 2 dependents, and $12 for each additional dependent; for half-time study, the monthly stipend is $611 for no dependents, $629 with 1 dependent, $644.50 with 2 dependents and $8.50 for each additional dependent. For those veterans pursuing an apprenticeship or on-the-job training, the current monthly stipend for the first 6 months is $995.35 for no dependents, $1,009.38 with 1 dependent, $1,021.70 with 2 dependents, and $5.95 for each additional dependent; for the second 6 months, the current monthly stipend is $738.73 for no dependents, $749.78 with 1 dependent, $758.88 with 2 dependents, and $4.55 for each additional dependent; for the third 6 months, the current monthly stipend is $495.90 for no dependents, $503.78 with 1 dependent, $509.85 with 2 dependents, and $3.15 for each additional dependent; for the remainder of the training period, the current monthly stipend is $480.60 for no dependents, $488.03 with 1 dependent, $494.78 with 2 dependents, and $3.15 for each additional dependent. Other rates apply for less than half-time study, cooperative education, correspondence courses, and flight training. Veterans who qualify for the accelerated payment and whose entitlement does not cover 60% of tuition and fees receive an additional lump sum payment to make up the different between their entitlement and 60% of tuition and fees.

**Duration:** 36 months; active-duty servicemembers must utilize the funds within 10 years of leaving the armed services; Reservists may draw on their funds while still serving.

**Number awarded:** Varies each year.

---

## 741 MONTGOMERY GI BILL (SELECTED RESERVE)

Department of Veterans Affairs
810 Vermont Avenue, N.W.
Washington, DC 20420
Phone: (202) 418-4343; (888) GI-BILL1
Web: www.gibill.va.gov

**Summary:** To provide financial assistance for college or graduate school to members of the Reserves or National Guard.

**Eligibility:** Open to members of the Reserve elements of the Army, Navy, Air Force, Marine Corps, and Coast Guard, as well as the Army National Guard and the Air National Guard. To be eligible, a Reservist must 1) have a 6-year obligation to serve in the Selected Reserves signed after June 30, 1985 (or, if an officer, to agree to serve 6 years in addition to the original obligation); 2) complete Initial Active Duty for Training (IADT); 3) meet the requirements for a high school diploma or equivalent certificate before completing IADT; and 4) remain in good standing in a drilling Selected Reserve unit. Reservists who enlisted after June 30, 1985 can receive benefits for undergraduate degrees, graduate training, or technical courses leading to certificates at colleges and universities. Reservists whose 6-year commitment began after September 30, 1990 may also use these benefits for a certificate or diploma from business, technical, or vocational schools; cooperative training; apprenticeship or on-the-job training; correspondence courses; independent study programs; tutorial assistance; remedial, deficiency, or refresher training; flight training; or state-approved alternative teacher certification programs.

**Financial data:** The current monthly rate is $297 for full-time study, $222.75 for three-quarter time study, $148.50 for half-time study, or $74.25 for less than half-time study. For apprenticeship and on-the-job training, the monthly stipend is $252.45 for the first 6 months, $193.05 for the second 6 months, and $133.65 for the remainder of the program. Other rates apply for cooperative education, correspondence courses, and flight training.

**Duration:** Up to 36 months for full-time study, 48 months for three-quarter study, 72 months for half-time study, or 144 months for less than half-time study.

**Number awarded:** Varies each year.

**Deadline:** Applications may be submitted at any time.

---

## 742 MONTGOMERY GI BILL TUITION ASSISTANCE TOP-UP

Department of Veterans Affairs
810 Vermont Avenue, N.W.
Washington, DC 20420
Phone: (202) 418-4343; (888) GI-BILL1
Web: www.gibill.va.gov

**Summary:** To supplement the tuition assistance provided by the military services to their members.

**Eligibility:** Open to military personnel who have served at least 2 full years on active duty and are approved for tuition assistance by their military service. Applicants must be participating in the Montgomery GI Bill (MGIB) Active Duty program and be eligible for MGIB benefits. This assistance is available to service members whose military service does not pay 100% of tuition and fees.

**Financial data:** This program pays the difference between what the military services pay for tuition assistance and the full amount of tuition and fees.

**Duration:** Up to 36 months of payments are available.

**Number awarded:** Varies each year.

---

## 743 MORRIS SCHOLARSHIP

Morris Scholarship Fund, Attn: Scholarship Selection Committee
525 S.W. Fifth Street, Suite A
Des Moines, IA 50309-4501
Phone: (515) 282-8192; Fax: (515) 282-9117; Email: morris@assoc-mgmt.com
Web: www.morrisscholarship.org

**Summary:** To provide financial assistance to minority undergraduate, graduate, and law students in Iowa.

**Eligibility:** Open to minority students (African Americans, Asian/Pacific Islanders, Hispanics, or Native Americans) who are interested in studying at a college (any field), graduate school, or law school. Applicants must be either Iowa residents and high school graduates who are attending a college or university anywhere in the United States or non-Iowa residents who are attending a college or university in Iowa; preference is given to native Iowans who are attending an Iowa college or university. Along with their application, they must submit an essay of 250 to 500 words on why they are applying for this scholarship, activities or organizations in which they are involved, and their future plans. Selection is based on the essay, academic achievement (GPA of 2.5 or higher), community service, and financial need.

**Financial data:** The stipend is $1,500 per year.

**Duration:** 1 year; may be renewed.

**Number awarded:** Varies each year; recently, 11 of these scholarships were awarded.

**Deadline:** January of each year.

## 744 MR. AND MRS. MOICHI OKAZAKI SCHOLARSHIP

100th Infantry Battalion Veterans Club, Attn: Scholarship Committee
520 Kamoku Street
Honolulu, HI 96826
Phone: (808) 732-5216; Email: daisyy@hgea.net
Web: emedia.leeward.hawaii.edu/mnakano

**Summary:** To provide financial assistance to high school seniors and college students from Hawaii who attend mainland institutions and exemplify the sponsor's motto of "Continuing Service."

**Eligibility:** Open to high school seniors planning to attend an institution of higher learning on the mainland and full-time undergraduate students at mainland community colleges, vocational/trade schools, 4-year colleges, and universities. Applicants must have a GPA of 2.5 or higher and be able to demonstrate civic responsibility and community service. Along with their application, they must submit a 4-page essay on how their postsecondary education at an out-of-state school will benefit them, their community, and their state. Selection is based on that essay and the applicant's demonstration that he or she can effectively promote the legacy of the 100th Infantry Battalion and its motto of "Continuing Service." Financial need is not considered.

**Financial data:** The stipend is $1,000.
**Duration:** 1 year; nonrenewable.
**Number awarded:** 1 each year.
**Deadline:** April of each year.

## 745 MR. AND MRS. TAKASHI MORIUCHI SCHOLARSHIP

Japanese American Citizens League, Attn: National Scholarship Awards
1765 Sutter Street
San Francisco, CA 94115
Phone: (415) 921-5225; Fax: (415) 931-4671; Email: jacl@jacl.org
Web: www.jacl.org/scholarships.html

**Summary:** To provide financial assistance for college to student members of the Japanese American Citizens League (JACL) who are high school seniors.

**Eligibility:** Open to JACL members who are high school seniors interested in attending a college, university, trade school, business college, or other institution of higher learning. Applicants must submit a statement describing their current level of involvement in the Japanese American community or Asian Pacific community and how they will continue their involvement in future years. Selection is based on academic record, extracurricular activities, and community involvement.

**Financial data:** The stipend depends on the availability of funds but usually ranges from $1,000 to $5,000.
**Duration:** 1 year; nonrenewable.
**Number awarded:** At least 1 each year.
**Deadline:** February of each year.

## 746 MS. LATINA USA

Dawn Ramos Productions
607 South Loving Avenue
Sherman, TX 75090-6743
Phone: (903) 891-9761; Email: info@misslatina.com
Web: www.misslatina.com

**Summary:** To recognize and reward young Latina women who compete in a national beauty pageant.

**Eligibility:** Open to women between 18 and 29 years of age who are at least 25% Hispanic. Applicants may be single, married, or divorced, and they may have children. They appear in a nationally-televised pageant where selection is based one third on an interview, one third on swimsuit appearances, and one third on evening gown appearances. Height and weight are not factors, but contestants should be proportionate. Pageant experience and fluency in Spanish are not required.

**Financial data:** Each year, prizes include scholarships, gifts, a cruise to the Bahamas, a trip to Las Vegas, a modeling contract, and use of an apartment in Miami. The total value is more than $100,000.
**Duration:** The pageant is held annually
**Number awarded:** 1 winner and 4 runners-up are selected each year.

## 747 MULTICULTURAL ASSOCIATION SCHOLARSHIP

Urban League of Nebraska, Inc., Attn: Scholarships
3022 North 24th Street
Omaha, NE 68110
Phone: (402) 453-9730; Fax: (402) 453-9676
Web: www.urbanleagueneb.org

**Summary:** To provide financial assistance for college to residents of Nebraska, especially minority students.

**Eligibility:** Open to Nebraska residents who are seniors in high school or students currently enrolled in college. Applicants must have a GPA of 2.5 or higher. Preference is given to students from a multicultural (American Indian, African American, Asian American, Hispanic American) background.

**Financial data:** A stipend is awarded (amount not specified).
**Duration:** 1 year.
**Number awarded:** 1 or more each year.
**Deadline:** March of each year.

## 748 MVSNA STUDENT SCHOLARSHIP

Missouri Vocational Special Need Association
c/o Shawn Brice
Missouri Department of Elementary and Secondary Education
Division of Career Education–Special Needs
205 Jefferson Street
P.O. Box 480
Jefferson City, MO 65102-0480
Phone: (573) 522-1775; Fax: (573) 526-4261; Email: Shawn.Brice@dese.mo.us
Web: dese.mo.gov/divcareered/sn_mvsna_scholarship.htm

**Summary:** To provide financial assistance to vocational/technical students in Missouri who are members of designated special populations.

**Eligibility:** Open to Missouri vocational/technical students who are members of special populations, defined as individuals who are academically or economically disadvantaged, have limited English proficiency, or are nontraditional, disabled, pregnant teenagers, single/teen parents, or foster children. Applicants must submit brief essays on their professional or career goals; the challenges they have had to overcome to reach their educational goals; how they have received help from their school, teachers, or community; and how the award will help them in pursuing continued education. Selection is based on realism of career goal, financial need, unusual circumstances, and personal references.

**Financial data:** A stipend is awarded (amount not specified).
**Duration:** 1 year.
**Number awarded:** 1 each year.
**Deadline:** April of each year.

## 749 NAAPAE SCHOLARSHIPS

National Association for Asian and Pacific American Education
P.O. Box 3366
Daley City, CA 94015-3366
Email: jlu69@jps.net

**Summary:** To provide financial assistance for college to high school seniors and college students of Asian or Pacific Islander descent.

**Eligibility:** Open to high school seniors and college juniors and seniors who 1) are of Asian or Pacific Islander descent; 2) are actively involved in extracurricular activities; 3) have outstanding academic records; and 4) are young leaders who show concern and commitment to Asian and Pacific communities. Applicants must submit high school and/or college transcripts, 2 letters of recommendation, a 50-word statement of career goals, a 300-word essay on how to end hate crime or how they can best serve the Asian Pacific community, and a list of their most important school and/or community activities and services over the past 2 years. Financial need is not considered in the selection process.

**Financial data:** For high school seniors, the stipend is $500; for college juniors and seniors, the stipend is $1,000.
**Duration:** 1 year.
**Number awarded:** 4 of these scholarships are awarded each year: 2 to high school seniors and 2 to college juniors and seniors.
**Deadline:** January of each year.

## 750 NAAS-II NATIONAL AWARDS

National Academy of American Scholars, Attn: Merit Committee
5196 Benito Street, Suite 15, Room A
Montclair, CA 91763-2891
Phone: (909) 621-6856; Email: staff@naas.org
Web: www.naas.org/college.htm

**Summary:** To recognize and reward college freshmen and sophomores who have exhibited outstanding character and scholastic excellence.

**Eligibility:** Open to U.S. citizens or permanent residents who are enrolled full time in an accredited 2- or 4-year institution as college freshmen or sophomores, are older than 18 years of age, and are working on a bachelor's degree with a cumulative GPA of 2.0 or higher. Selection is made without regard to financial need, affiliation status, or study area.

**Financial data:** The stipend ranges from $1,000 to $3,000 per year. The scholarships are paid to the recipient's institution.

**Duration:** 1 year; renewable.

**Number awarded:** 1 each year.

**Deadline:** April of each year.

## [751] NAAS-USA AWARDS

National Academy of American Scholars, Attn: Merit Committee
5196 Benito Street, Suite 15, Room A
Montclair, CA 91763-2891
Phone: (909) 621-6856; Email: staff@naas.org
Web: www.naas.org/senior.htm

**Summary:** To recognize and reward high school seniors who have exhibited outstanding academic excellence and personal integrity.

**Eligibility:** Open to U.S. citizens or permanent residents who are enrolled in a public, private, Department of Defense, Bureau of Indian Affairs, charter, or parochial high school as a senior or who are home-schooled seniors. Applicants must have been (or will be) accepted at an accredited 4-year institution, be planning to work on a bachelor's degree, and express an intent to benefit humanity. They must have earned at least a 2.0 GPA and completed either the SAT or ACT. Selection is made without regard to financial need, affiliation status, or study area.

**Financial data:** Scholarship levels are $2,000, $3,000, $4,000, or $5,000 per year. Finalists receive $200 plus a merit certificate. The scholarships are paid to the recipient's institution of choice.

**Duration:** 4 years.

**Number awarded:** 4 scholarships plus 10 finalists each year.

**Deadline:** April of each year.

## [752] NACA REGIONAL COUNCIL STUDENT LEADER SCHOLARSHIPS

National Association for Campus Activities, Attn: Educational Foundation
13 Harbison Way
Columbia, SC 29212-3401
Phone: (803) 732-6222; Fax: (803) 749-1047; Email: scholarships@naca.org
Web: www.naca.org

**Summary:** To provide financial assistance to outstanding college student leaders.

**Eligibility:** Open to full-time undergraduate students who have made significant contributions to their campus communities, have played leadership roles in campus activities, and have demonstrated leadership skills and abilities. Financial need is not considered in the selection process.

**Financial data:** The amounts of the awards vary each year; scholarships are to be used for educational expenses, including tuition, books, fees, or other related expenses.

**Number awarded:** Up to 14 each year: 2 in each of the association's 7 regions.

**Deadline:** April of each year.

## [753] NANBPWC SCHOLARSHIPS

National Association of Negro Business and Professional Women's Clubs
Attn: Scholarship Committee
1806 New Hampshire Avenue, N.W.
Washington, DC 20009-3208
Phone: (202) 483-4206; Fax: (202) 462-7253; Email: nanbpwc@aol.com
Web: www.nanbpwc.org/Education/shtml

**Summary:** To provide financial assistance to high school seniors interested in working on a college education.

**Eligibility:** Open to graduating high school seniors planning to enroll in an accredited college or university. Applicants must have a GPA of 3.0 or higher, be full-time students, and be U.S. citizens or enrolled in a college in the United States. They may be of any race or gender, but they must be referred by a member of the National Association of Negro Business and Professional Women's Clubs (NANBPWC). Along with their application, they must submit an essay (at least 300 words) on "Why is education important to me?" Financial need is not considered in the selection process.

**Financial data:** The stipend is $1,000.

**Duration:** 1 year.

**Number awarded:** 10 each year.

**Deadline:** February of each year.

## [754] NANCIE RIDEOUT-ROBERTSON BONUS INTERNSHIP SCHOLARSHIP

American Water Ski Educational Foundation, Attn: Director
1251 Holy Cow Road
Polk City, FL 33868-8200
Phone: (863) 324-2472; Fax: (863) 324-3996; Email: awsefhalloffame@cs.com
Web: www.waterskihalloffame.com

**Summary:** To provide financial assistance and work experience to upper-division and graduate students who are interested in water skiing.

**Eligibility:** Open to upper-division and graduate students who are members of the United States Water Ski Association (USWSA) and the American Water Ski Educational Foundation (AWSEF). Applicants must have participated in the sport of water skiing as a skier, official, and/or volunteer worker and be able to demonstrate leadership potential. They must have a GPA of at least "B+" overall and an "A" average in their major field of study. Along with their application, they must submit 1) a 500-word personal statement on why they wish to be awarded this scholarship and serve as an intern at AWSEF; and 2) an internship proposal, covering their learning goals and how they want to apply the skills and knowledge related to their program of study in college or graduate school to their internship, the kinds of contributions they think they can make toward the goals of AWSEF, how they would allocate their time toward their internship activities, when they could complete their "onsite" requirement, and the kinds of skills and knowledge of people with whom they might like to work during their internship.

**Financial data:** The stipend is $2,500.

**Duration:** 1 year, including at least 4 weeks (during semester breaks, spring break, summer) at AWSEF headquarters in Polk City, Florida.

**Number awarded:** 1 each year.

**Deadline:** January of each year.

## [755] NANCY PENN LYONS SCHOLARSHIP FUND

Community Foundation for Greater Atlanta, Inc.
50 Hurt Plaza, Suite 449
Atlanta, GA 30303
Phone: (404) 688-5525; Fax: (404) 688-3060; Email: vweekes@atlcf.org
Web: www.atlcf.org/GrantsScholarships/Scholarships/NancyPennLyons.aspx

**Summary:** To provide financial assistance to seniors at high schools in Georgia planning to attend a "prestigious" or out-of-state university.

**Eligibility:** Open to seniors graduating from high schools in Georgia who have been residents of the state for at least 1 year. Applicants must have a cumulative high school GPA of 3.0 or higher and an ACT composite score of 22 or higher (or the equivalent on the SAT). They must be able to demonstrate financial need and commitment to community service. The program is limited to students attending selective private and/or out-of-state universities.

**Financial data:** Stipends range up to $5,000 per year.

**Duration:** 1 year; recipients may reapply.

**Number awarded:** Varies each year; recently, 5 of these scholarships were awarded.

**Deadline:** April of each year.

## [756] NASCAR/WENDELL SCOTT AWARD

Hispanic Association of Colleges and Universities
Attn: National Scholarship Program
One Dupont Circle, N.W. Suite 605
Washington, DC 20036
Phone: (202) 467-0893; Fax: (202) 496-9177; TTY: (800) 855-2880;
Email: scholarships@hacu.net
Web: scholarships.hacu.net/applications/applicants

**Summary:** To provide financial assistance to undergraduate and graduate students majoring in any field at member institutions of the Hispanic Association of Colleges and Universities (HACU) who are interested in the motorsports industry.

**Eligibility:** Open to undergraduate and graduate students at HACU member and partner colleges and universities. Applicants may be majoring in any field, but they must be able to demonstrate a recreational or professional interest in the motorsports industry. Undergraduates must be enrolled full time, have a GPA of 3.0 or higher, and be able to use the scholarship during their junior or senior year. Graduate students must be enrolled at least part time and have a GPA of 3.2 or higher. Applicants must submit an essay of 200 to 250 words that describes their academic and/or career goals, where they expect to be and what they expect to be doing 10 years from now, and what skills they can bring to an employer. Financial need is considered in the selection process.

**Financial data:** The stipend is $1,500 for undergraduates or $2,000 for graduate students.

Duration: 1 year.
Number awarded: 1 or more each year.
Deadline: May of each year.

## 757 NATIONAL ALLIANCE FOR SCHOLASTIC ACHIEVEMENT SCHOLARSHIPS

National Alliance for Scholastic Achievement, Attn: Selection Committee
10820 Beverly Boulevard A5
PMB 600
Whittier, CA 90601-2576
Web: www.eee.org/bus/nasa
Summary: To provide financial assistance for college to high school seniors who demonstrate outstanding academic achievement.
Eligibility: Open to high school seniors who have been accepted or anticipate being accepted at a 4-year academic institution. Applicants must have a GPA of 2.75 or higher and have taken the SAT or ACT test. Along with their application, they must submit a 500-word essay on an experience during their high school career that taught them something of great importance and how that will impact or shape their future learning. Financial need, race, and gender are not considered in the selection process. Generally, GPAs are 3.9 to 4.0 for the top award, 3.7 to 4.0 for the second award, 3.5 to 3.9 for third, 2.8 to 3.7 for fourth, and 2.75 to 3.5 for fifth. U.S. citizenship or permanent resident status is required.
Financial data: The top award is $3,750 per year, second award is $2,500 per year, third award is $1,250 per year, fourth award is $750 per year, and fifth award is $500 per year. Funds are paid directly to the recipient's institution of choice.
Duration: 1 year; may be renewed up to 3 additional years.
Number awarded: 5 each year.
Deadline: March of each year.

## 758 NATIONAL BETA CLUB SCHOLARSHIP PROGRAM

National Beta Clubs
151 Beta Club Way
Spartanburg, SC 29306-3012
Phone: (864) 583-4554; (800) 845-8281; Fax: (864) 542-9300;
Email: betaclub@betaclub.org
Web: www.betaclub.org/scholarship/scholarship.html
Summary: To recognize and reward outstanding senior Beta Club members.
Eligibility: Open to Beta Club members who best exemplify the club's goals of academic excellence, leadership, and school/community service. Each Beta Club may nominate 2 high school senior members to compete. Nominees will be required to complete application and nomination forms and return them to their Beta Club sponsor. Nominees must also take the ACT or SAT. Advancement to the semifinalist stage is contingent upon the submission of test scores and class rank. Selection is based on academic excellence, demonstrated leadership, character, and school and community service.
Financial data: Stipends range from $1,000 to $15,000 per year.
Duration: The competition is held annually.
Number awarded: 208 each year: 1 at $15,000, 1 at $10,000, 1 at $8,000, 1 at $6,000, 1 at $4,000, and 203 at $1,000.
Deadline: December of each year.

## 759 NATIONAL CAUCUS OF HISPANIC SCHOOL BOARD MEMBERS SCHOLARSHIPS

National School Boards Association
Attn: National Caucus of Hispanic School Board Members
1680 Duke Street
Alexandria, VA 22314-3493
Phone: (703) 838-6157; Fax: (703) 683-7590; Email: info@nsba.org
Web: www.nsba.org/caucus
Summary: To provide financial assistance for college to Hispanic high school seniors.
Eligibility: Open to high school seniors of Hispanic origin who have been accepted to an accredited 4-year college or university. Applicants must have a GPA of 3.0 or higher and be able to demonstrate financial need. Along with their application, they must submit an autobiographical statement that includes a paragraph about their financial need.
Financial data: The stipend is $1,000.
Duration: 1 year.
Number awarded: 5 each year.
Deadline: March of each year.

## 760 NATIONAL CITY/KHSAA SWEET 16 SCHOLARSHIPS

Kentucky High School Athletic Association
2280 Executive Drive
Lexington, KY 40505
Phone: (859) 299-5472; Fax: (859) 293-5999
Web: www.khsaa.org
Summary: To provide financial assistance for college to student-athletes in Kentucky high schools.
Eligibility: Open to high school seniors in Kentucky who have participated in athletics or cheerleading. The awards are presented in conjunction with the state basketball tournament, but all student-athletes, not just basketball players, are eligible. Students must be nominated by a school representative. Letters of nomination must explain why the student is an exemplary leader and should receive the scholarship. Selection is based on academic achievement, leadership, citizenship, and sportsmanship. Men and women are judged separately.
Financial data: The stipend is $1,000.
Duration: 1 year; nonrenewable.
Number awarded: 32 each year: 1 female and 1 male in each of 16 regions in Kentucky.
Deadline: February of each year.

## 761 NATIONAL DEAN'S LIST SCHOLARSHIPS

ECI Scholarship Foundation
1701 Directors Boulevard, Suite 920
P.O. Box 149319
Austin, TX 78714-9319
Phone: (512) 440-2300; Fax: (512) 447-1687
Web: www.thenationaldeanslist.com/3scholarshipsgrants/scholarshipprogram.aspx
Summary: To provide financial assistance to college students who are listed in The National Dean's List.
Eligibility: Open to college students who are U.S. citizens and 1) have a GPA of "B+" or better or 2) rank in the upper 10% of their class. Candidates must first be nominated by their dean, honor society advisor, or other college official to have their name appear in The National Dean's List. All students listed in that publication automatically receive an application for these scholarships in the mail. Selection is based on GPA, achievement test scores, leadership qualifications, work experience, evaluation of an essay, and some consideration for financial need.
Financial data: Scholarships are $1,000; payments are issued directly to the financial aid office at the institution the student attends.
Duration: 1 year.
Number awarded: 50 each year.
Deadline: May of each year.

## 762 NATIONAL FEDERATION OF THE BLIND SCHOLARSHIPS

National Federation of the Blind
c/o Peggy Elliott, Scholarship Committee Chair
805 Fifth Avenue
Grinnell, IA 50112
Phone: (641) 236-3366
Web: www.nfb.org/sch_intro.htm
Summary: To provide financial assistance for college or graduate school to blind students.
Eligibility: Open to legally blind students who are working on or planning to work on an undergraduate or graduate degree. In general, full-time enrollment is required, although 1 scholarship may be awarded to a part-time student who is working full time. Selection is based on academic excellence, service to the community, and financial need.
Financial data: Stipends are $7,000 or $3,000.
Duration: 1 year; recipients may resubmit applications up to 2 additional years.
Number awarded: 17 each year: 2 at $7,000 and 15 at $3,000.
Deadline: March of each year.

## 763 NATIONAL FRATERNAL SOCIETY OF THE DEAF SCHOLARSHIPS

National Fraternal Society of the Deaf
1118 South Sixth Street
Springfield, IL 62703
Phone: (217) 789-7429; Fax: (217) 789-7489; TTY: (217) 789-7438;
Email: thefrat@nfsd.com

Web: www.nfsd.com/scholarships.htm

**Summary:** To provide financial assistance for college to members of the National Fraternal Society of the Deaf.

**Eligibility:** Open to deaf, hard of hearing, or hearing persons who are enrolled in or accepted as a full-time student at a postsecondary educational institution. Applicants must have been members of the society for at least 1 year prior to application.

**Financial data:** The stipend is $1,000.

**Duration:** 1 year; may be renewed 1 additional year.

**Number awarded:** 10 each year.

**Deadline:** June of each year.

---

**764 NATIONAL GUARD ASSOCIATION OF MICHIGAN EDUCATION GRANTS**

National Guard Association of Michigan, Attn: Scholarships
300 Elvin Court
Lansing, MI 48913-5103
Phone: (517) 484-1644; (800) 477-1644; Fax: (517) 484-1680;
Email: ngam@voyager.net
Web: www.ngam.org/edgrant.htm

**Summary:** To provide financial assistance for college to members of the National Guard Association of Michigan.

**Eligibility:** Open to members of the association who are also current members of the Michigan National Guard. Applicants may be enlisted members of any rank, warrant officers through CW3, or commissioned officers through the rank of captain.

**Financial data:** The stipend is $500 per semester.

**Duration:** 1 semester; may be renewed.

**Number awarded:** Varies each year.

**Deadline:** June of each year for the fall term/semester; November of each year for the winter term/semester.

---

**765 NATIONAL HONOR SOCIETY SCHOLARSHIPS**

National Association of Secondary School Principals
Attn: Department of Student Activities
1904 Association Drive
Reston, VA 20191-1537
Phone: (703) 860-0200; (800) 253-7746, ext. 252; Fax: (703) 476-5432;
Email: carrollw@principals.org
Web: www.nhs.us/schlr_awards/nhs_schlrgen.cfm

**Summary:** To recognize and reward, with college scholarships, outstanding high school seniors who are members of the National Honor Society.

**Eligibility:** Open to seniors who are members of their National Honor Society chapter. Each public, private, and parochial high school in the United States may nominate 2 qualified students. Selection is based on academic achievement, leadership, service, and character. Financial need is not considered.

**Financial data:** The award is $1,000.

**Duration:** The awards are presented annually.

**Number awarded:** 200 each year.

**Deadline:** Nominations must be submitted by January of each year.

---

**766 NATIONAL HUGUENOT SOCIETY SCHOLARSHIPS**

National Huguenot Society, Attn: Executive Director
9033 Lyndale Avenue South, Suite 108
Bloomington, MN 55420-3535
Phone: (952) 885-9776; Email: scholarship@huguenot.netnation.com
Web: huguenot.netnation.com/general/scholarship.htm

**Summary:** To provide financial assistance for college or graduate school to members of the National Huguenot Society.

**Eligibility:** Open to students at accredited colleges, universities, and graduate schools who have completed at least 2 years of college with a GPA of 3.0 or higher. Applicants must be a regular member of the National Huguenot Society which requires that they 1) be at least 18 years of age; 2) adhere to the Huguenot principles of faith and liberty; 3) be a member of the Protestant faith; and 4) be lineally descended from a Huguenot who either emigrated from France to North America or another country between 1520 and 1787 or remained in France. Their program of study must have included at least 2 semesters of history, including a history of religion. Along with their application, they may submit a short statement on their scholastic achievements and goals and how a scholarship would be advantageous to them. Financial need is not considered in the selection process.

**Financial data:** The stipend is $5,000.

**Duration:** 1 year; nonrenewable.

**Number awarded:** 1 each year.

---

**767 NATIONAL LATINA ALLIANCE SCHOLARSHIPS**

National Latina Alliance
633 West Fifth Street, Suite 1150
Los Angeles, CA 90071
Phone: (323) 980-7992; Email: info@nationallatinaalliance.org
Web: www.nationallatinaalliance.org/ScholProg.htm

**Summary:** To provide financial assistance for college or other career education to Latinas.

**Eligibility:** Open to Latinas who are 1) graduating high school seniors; 2) currently enrolled in a college or university; 3) returning to school after an absence of at least 2 years; or 4) preparing for a non-traditional career (e.g., chef, artist, entrepreneur, nurse). Applicants must have a GPA of 2.5 or higher and be able to document financial need. They must submit a 1-page essay on the question, "As a Latina, what do you think is important for the success of the community?" Reentry applicants must also provide a 1-page essay discussing their reason for withdrawing from school. Non-traditional career students must provide documentation regarding their career.

**Financial data:** Stipends range from $500 to $1,000, depending on the need of the recipient.

**Duration:** 1 year.

**Number awarded:** Varies each year; recently, 17 of these scholarships were awarded.

**Deadline:** March of each year.

---

**768 NATIONAL MS SOCIETY SCHOLARSHIP PROGRAM**

National Multiple Sclerosis Society, Attn: Scholarship Fund
700 Broadway, Suite 810
Denver, CO 80203
Phone: (303) 813-6664; (800) FIGHT-MS; Fax: (212) 986-7981;
Email: Katherine.Swank@nmss.org
Web: www.nationalmssociety.org/Research-otherawards.asp

**Summary:** To provide financial assistance for college to students who have Multiple Sclerosis (MS) or are the children of people with MS.

**Eligibility:** Open to 1) high school seniors who have MS and will be attending an accredited postsecondary school for the first time; 2) high school seniors who are the children of people with MS and will be attending an accredited postsecondary school for the first time; and 3) high school (or GED) graduates of any age who have MS and will be attending an accredited postsecondary school for the first time. Applicants must be U.S. citizens or permanent residents who plan to enroll in an undergraduate course of study at an accredited 2- or 4-year college, university, or vocational/technical school in the United States to work on a degree, license, or certificate. Selection is based on academic record, leadership and participation in school or community activities; work experience, a statement of educational and career goals, an outside appraisal, unusual personal or family circumstances, an essay on the impact of MS on their life, and financial need.

**Financial data:** Stipends range from $1,000 to $3,000.

**Duration:** 1 year; nonrenewable.

**Number awarded:** Varies each year; recently, 88 of these scholarships, worth $207,000, were awarded.

**Deadline:** February of each year.

---

**769 NATIONAL PRESBYTERIAN COLLEGE SCHOLARSHIP**

Presbyterian Church (USA), Attn: Office of Financial Aid for Studies
100 Witherspoon Street, Room M-052
Louisville, KY 40202-1396
Phone: (502) 569-8235; (888) 728-7228, ext. 8235; Fax: (502) 569-8766;
Email: mwillman@yahoo.com
Web: www.pcusa.org/financialaid/programfinder/npcs.htm

**Summary:** To provide financial assistance to high school seniors planning to attend a Presbyterian college.

**Eligibility:** Open to be high school seniors preparing to enter as full-time incoming freshmen at a participating college related to the Presbyterian Church (USA). Applicants must be members of the PC(USA), have a GPA of 3.0 or higher, be U.S. citizens or permanent residents, and be able to demonstrate financial need. They must submit an essay (up to 500 words) on either 1) what they think is 1 of the greatest opportunities facing youth or society today or what they think is 1 of the most urgent problems facing youth or society today, or 2) the career path they wish to take, the reasons why they have selected that particular career, what it means to them, what they hope to accomplish, and their dreams and aspirations. Selection is based on that essay; personal qualities of character and leadership as reflected in contributions to church, school, and community; academic achievements; and recommendations from school and church officials.

**Financial data:** Stipends range from $200 to $1,400 per year, depending upon the financial need of the recipient.

**Duration:** 1 year; may be renewed up to 3 additional years.

**Number awarded:** Approximately 100 each year.

**Deadline:** January of each year.

## 770 NATIONAL TECHNICAL HONOR SOCIETY SCHOLARSHIPS

DECA
1908 Association Drive
Reston, VA 20191-1594
Phone: (703) 860-5000; Fax: (703) 860-4013; Email: decainc@aol.com
Web: www.deca.org/scholarships/index.html

**Summary:** To provide financial assistance for college to DECA members who are also members of the National Technical Honors Society (NTHS) and interested in attending a career or technical school.

**Eligibility:** Open to high school seniors who are members of both DECA and NTHS. Applicants must be interested in continuing with career and technical education after graduating from high school. Along with their application, they must submit a 1-page essay on what technical education means to them and how being a member of DECA and NTHS has contributed to their school performance and future career plans. Selection is based on academic achievement, skill development, leadership, honesty, responsibility, good character, and involvement in DECA.

**Financial data:** The stipend is $1,000.

**Duration:** 1 year.

**Number awarded:** 2 each year.

**Deadline:** March of each year.

## 771 NATIVE AMERICAN EDUCATION GRANTS

Presbyterian Church (USA), Attn: Office of Financial Aid for Studies
100 Witherspoon Street, Room M-052
Louisville, KY 40202-1396
Phone: (502) 569-5776; (888) 728-7228, ext. 5776; Fax: (502) 569-8766;
Email: fcook@ctr.pcusa.org
Web: www.pcusa.org/financialaid/programfinder/natameredgrnt.htm

**Summary:** To provide financial assistance to needy Native American student members of the Presbyterian Church (USA) interested in continuing their college education.

**Eligibility:** Open to Alaska Native and Native American students enrolled full time at an accredited institution in the United States. Applicants must be making satisfactory progress toward a degree, able to provide proof of tribal membership, U.S. citizens or permanent residents, and able to demonstrate financial need. Preference is given to members of the PC(USA) and to students who have completed at least 1 semester of work at an accredited institution of higher education.

**Financial data:** Stipends range from $200 to $2,500 per year, depending upon the recipient's financial need.

**Duration:** 1 year; may be renewed.

**Number awarded:** Varies each year.

**Deadline:** May of each year.

## 772 NAVAL ENLISTED RESERVE ASSOCIATION SCHOLARSHIPS

Naval Enlisted Reserve Association, Attn: National Headquarters
6703 Farragut Avenue
Falls Church, VA 22042-2189
Phone: (703) 534-1329; (800) 776-9020; Fax: (703) 534-3617;
Email: members@nera.org
Web: www.nera.org

**Summary:** To provide financial assistance for college to enlisted members of the sea service Reserves and their families.

**Eligibility:** Open to drilling Reservists of the Navy, Marines, and Coast Guard who are in a satisfactory participation status, including Training and Administration of Reserves (TAR) personnel, Canvasser Recruiters (CANREC), and U.S. Navy personnel assigned to a Naval Reserve Activity (NRA). Their dependents and grandchildren are also eligible. Applicants must be enrolled in an accredited college or university. They must submit proof of

enrollment, a copy of their military identification card, and a 1-page essay on "What a strong Naval Reserve means to me."

**Financial data:** The stipend is $2,500.

**Duration:** 1 year.

**Number awarded:** 4 each year.

**Deadline:** April of each year.

## 773 NAVAL HELICOPTER ASSOCIATION UNDERGRADUATE SCHOLARSHIPS

Naval Helicopter Association, Attn: Scholarship Fund
P.O. Box 180578
Coronado, CA 92178-0578
Phone: (619) 435-7139; Fax: (619) 435-7354;
Email: nhascholars@hotmail.com
Web: www.navalhelicopterassn.org/scholar/scholar.htm

**Summary:** To provide financial assistance for full-time undergraduate study to students in the United States.

**Eligibility:** Open to U.S. citizens, regardless of race, religion, age, or gender, who are seniors in high school or currently enrolled in or accepted at an accredited college or university in the United States in an undergraduate program. Selection is based on academic proficiency, scholastic achievements and awards, extracurricular activities, employment history, letters of recommendation, and a personal statement on educational plans and future goals.

**Financial data:** Stipends are $3,000 or $1,500 per year.

**Duration:** 1 year; may be renewed if the recipient maintains at least a 2.75 GPA.

**Number awarded:** 7 each year: 2 at $3,000 (the named scholarships) and 5 at $1,500.

**Deadline:** November of each year.

## 774 NAVAL SPECIAL WARFARE SCHOLARSHIPS FOR SPOUSES AND CHILDREN

Naval Special Warfare Foundation, Attn: Scholarship Committee
P.O. Box 5965
Virginia Beach, VA 23471
Phone: (757) 363-7490; Fax: (757) 363-7491;
Email: info@nswfoundation.org
Web: www.nswfoundation.org

**Summary:** To provide financial assistance for college to dependents of military personnel serving on active duty in Naval Special Warfare (NSW) commands.

**Eligibility:** Open to the dependent spouses and children of active-duty SEALs or Special Warfare Combatant crewmen (SWCC) and other active-duty military personnel serving in NSW commands. Family members of a SEAL or SWCC who died in service to the country are also eligible. Applicants must be entering or continuing in college with the goal of working on an associate or bachelor's degree. Selection is based on merit and academic potential, judged by scholastic achievement and a written essay.

**Financial data:** A stipend is awarded (amount not specified).

**Duration:** 1 year; may be renewed.

**Number awarded:** 1 or more each year.

**Deadline:** March of each year.

## 775 NAVESNP/PINEY MOUNTAIN PRESS STUDENT AWARD

National Association of Vocational Education Special Needs Personnel
c/o Marjorie Eckman, Awards Chair
719 Gulf Lab Road
Cheswick, PA 15024
Phone: (412) 323-3970; Email: ME50@aol.com
Web: www.specialpopulations.org/award_student.htm

**Summary:** To provide financial assistance to vocational/technical students who are members of a special population.

**Eligibility:** Open to vocational/technical students who are members of a special population, defined to include those who are academically or economically disadvantaged, limited English proficient, nontraditional, disabled, pregnant teenagers, single/teen parents, or foster children. Applicants must submit brief essays on the vocational program they plan to study or are currently studying, why they chose that vocational program, their professional and career goals, the challenges they have had to overcome to reach their educational goal, what they did to overcome those challenges successfully, how any special services they have received helped them, and how this award will help them in their vocational program. Selection is based on their choice of a realistic career goal, financial need, unusual circumstances, and letters of reference.

**Financial data:** The stipend is $1,000.

**Duration:** 1 year.

**Number awarded:** 1 each year.

**Deadline:** October of each year.

## 776 NAVY ADVANCED EDUCATION VOUCHER PROGRAM

U.S. Navy

Naval Education and Training Professional Development and Technology Center

Attn: AEV Program Office

6490 Saufley Field Road

Pensacola, FL 32509-5204

Phone: (850) 452-1001, ext. 2076; Fax: (850) 452-1357;

Email: rick.cusimano@navy.mil

Web: www.navycollege.navy.mil/aev

**Summary:** To provide financial assistance to Navy enlisted personnel who are interested in earning an undergraduate or graduate degree during off-duty hours.

**Eligibility:** Open to senior enlisted Navy personnel in ranks E-7 through E-9. Applicants should be transferring to, or currently on, shore duty with sufficient time ashore to complete a bachelor's or master's degree. Personnel at rank E-7 may have no more than 17 years time in service, E-8 no more than 20 years, or E-9 no more than 22 years. The area of study must be certified by the Naval Postgraduate School as Navy-relevant.

**Financial data:** This program covers 100% of graduate education costs (tuition, books, and fees), up to a maximum of $6,700 per year for a bachelor's degree or $20,000 per year for a master's degree.

**Duration:** Up to 36 months from the time of enrollment for a bachelor's degree; up to 24 months from the time of enrollment for a master's degree.

**Number awarded:** Varies each year. Recently, 30 of these positions were available: 25 for bachelor's degrees and 5 for master's degrees.

**Deadline:** March of each year.

## 777 NAVY COLLEGE FUND

U.S. Navy, Attn: Navy Personnel Command (PERS-675)

5720 Integrity Drive

Millington, TN 38055-6040

Phone: (901) 874-4258; (866) U ASK-NPC; Fax: (901) 874-2052;

Email: MILL_MGIB@navy.mil

Web: www.npc.navy.mil/CareerInfor/Education/GIBill/
NavyCollegeFundProgram.htm

**Summary:** To provide financial assistance for college to Navy enlistees during and after they have completed their service obligation.

**Eligibility:** Open to high school seniors and graduates between 17 and 35 years of age who enlist in the Navy for 3 to 4 years of active duty. They must score 50 or above on the AFQT and also enroll in the Montgomery GI Bill. Sailors currently on active duty in selected Navy ratings with critical personnel shortages are also eligible. Applicants must be interested in attending a Department of Veterans Affairs-approved postsecondary educational institution on a full-time basis after completion of their service obligation.

**Financial data:** The Navy College Fund provides, in addition to the Montgomery GI Bill, up to $15,000 for college tuition and expenses.

**Duration:** Enlistees may begin using this educational benefit on a part-time basis after 2 years of continuous active duty. Funds must be utilized within 10 years of leaving the Navy.

**Number awarded:** Varies each year.

**Deadline:** Applications may be submitted at any time.

## 778 NAVY LEAGUE FOUNDATION SCHOLARSHIPS

Navy League of the United States, Attn: Scholarships

2300 Wilson Boulevard

Arlington, VA 22201-3308

Phone: (703) 528-1775; (800) 356-5760; Fax: (703) 528-2333;

Email: cjarvis@navyleague.org

Web: www.navyleague.org/scholarship

**Summary:** To provide financial assistance for college to dependent children of sea service personnel.

**Eligibility:** Open to U.S. citizens who are 1) dependents or direct descendants of an active, Reserve, retired, or honorably discharged member of the U.S. sea service (including the Navy, Marine Corps, Coast Guard, or Merchant Marines), or 2) currently an active member of the Naval Sea Cadet Corps. Applicants must be entering their freshman year of college. Along with their application, they must submit transcripts, 2 letters of recommendation, SAT/

ACT scores, documentation of financial need, proof of qualifying sea service duty, and a 1-page personal statement on why they should be considered for this scholarship.

**Financial data:** The stipend is $2,500 per year.

**Duration:** 4 years, provided the recipient maintains a GPA of 3.0 or higher.

**Number awarded:** Approximately 5 each year.

**Deadline:** February of each year.

## 779 NAVY SUPPLY CORPS FOUNDATION NIB/NISH SCHOLARSHIPS

Navy Supply Corps Foundation

c/o Jack Evans

1425 Prince Avenue

Athens, GA 30606-2205

Phone: (706) 354-4111; Fax: (706) 354-0334; Email: foundation@usnscf.com

Web: www.usnscf.com/scholarship.php

**Summary:** To provide financial assistance for college to the dependents of Navy Supply Corps personnel who are blind or disabled.

**Eligibility:** Open to dependents of a Navy Supply Corps officer, warrant officer, or enlisted personnel on active duty, with prior service in the Supply Corps, in Reserve status, retired with pay, or deceased. Enlisted ratings that apply are AK (Aviation Storekeeper), SK (Storekeeper), MS (Mess Specialist), DK (Disbursing Clerk), SH (Ship Serviceman), LI (Lithographer), and PC (Postal Clerk). Applicants must be attending or planning to attend a 2-year or 4-year accredited college on a full-time basis and have a GPA of 2.5 or higher in high school and/or college. They must be able to document blindness or severe disability. Selection is based on character, leadership, academic performance, and financial need.

**Financial data:** A stipend is awarded (amount not specified).

**Duration:** 1 year; may be renewed if the recipient maintains a GPA of 2.5 or higher.

**Number awarded:** 1 or more each year.

**Deadline:** April of each year.

## 780 NAVY SUPPLY CORPS FOUNDATION SCHOLARSHIPS

Navy Supply Corps Foundation

c/o Jack Evans

1425 Prince Avenue

Athens, GA 30606-2205

Phone: (706) 354-4111; Fax: (706) 354-0334; Email: foundation@usnscf.com

Web: www.usnscf.com/scholarship.php

**Summary:** To provide financial assistance for college to the dependents of Navy Supply Corps personnel.

**Eligibility:** Open to dependents of a Navy Supply Corps officer, warrant officer, or enlisted personnel on active duty, with prior service in the Supply Corps, in Reserve status, retired with pay, or deceased. Enlisted ratings that apply are AK (Aviation Storekeeper), SK (Storekeeper), MS (Mess Specialist), DK (Disbursing Clerk), SH (Ship Serviceman), LI (Lithographer), and PC (Postal Clerk). Applicants must be attending or planning to attend a 2-year or 4-year accredited college on a full-time basis and have a GPA of 2.5 or higher in high school and/or college. Selection is based on character, leadership, academic performance, and financial need.

**Financial data:** A stipend is awarded (amount not specified).

**Duration:** 1 year; may be renewed if the recipient maintains a GPA of 2.5 or higher.

**Number awarded:** Varies each year; recently, the foundation awarded 78 scholarships with a value of $190,000.

**Deadline:** April of each year.

## 781 NAVY WIVES CLUB OF AMERICA NATIONAL SCHOLARSHIPS

Navy Wives Club of America

P.O. Box 54022

Millington, TN 39053-6022

Phone: (866) 511-NWCA; Email: nwca@navywivesclubsofamerica.org

Web: www.navywivesclubsofamerica.org/nwc/scholarships.htm

**Summary:** To provide financial assistance for college or medical school to the children of naval personnel.

**Eligibility:** Open to the children (natural born, legally adopted, or stepchildren) of enlisted members of the Navy, Marine Corps, or Coast Guard on active duty, retired with pay, or deceased. Applicants must be attending or planning to attend an accredited college or university. Along with their application, they must submit an essay on their career objectives and the reasons they chose those objectives. Selection is based on academic standing, moral character, and financial need. Some scholarships are reserved for students majoring in special education, medical students, and children of members of Navy Wives Club of American (NWCA).

**Financial data:** The stipend is $1,500.

**Duration:** 1 year; may be renewed up to 3 additional years.

**Number awarded:** 41 each year: 6 to freshmen, 18 for renewals, 4 to current undergraduates applying for the first time, 2 to medical students, 2 to students majoring in special education, and 9 to children of NWCA members.

**Deadline:** May of each year.

## 782 NAVY-MARINE CORPS ROTC COLLEGE PROGRAM

U.S. Navy, Attn: Chief of Naval Education and Training
Code N79A2
250 Dallas Street
Pensacola, FL 32508-5220
Phone: (850) 452-4941, ext. 29381; (800) NAV-ROTC, ext. 29381;
Fax: (850) 452-2486; Email: PNSC_NROTC.scholarship@navy.mil
Web: www.nrotc.navy.mil

**Summary:** To provide financial assistance to lower-division students who are interested in joining Navy ROTC in college.

**Eligibility:** Open to U.S. citizens between the ages of 17 and 21 who are already enrolled as non-scholarship students in naval science courses at a college or university with a Navy ROTC program on campus. They must apply before the spring of their sophomore year. All applications must be submitted through the professors of naval science at the college or university attended.

**Financial data:** Participants in this program receive free naval science textbooks, all required uniforms, and a stipend for 10 months of the year that is $250 per month as a freshman, $300 per month as a sophomore, $350 per month as a junior and $400 per month as a senior.

**Duration:** 2 or 4 years.

**Deadline:** March of each year.

## 783 NAVY-MARINE CORPS ROTC 2-YEAR SCHOLARSHIPS

U.S. Navy, Attn: Chief of Naval Education and Training
Code N79A2
250 Dallas Street
Pensacola, FL 32508-5220
Phone: (850) 452-4941, ext. 29381; (800) NAV-ROTC, ext. 29381;
Fax: (850) 452-2486; Email: PNSC_NROTC.scholarship@navy.mil
Web: www.nrotc.navy.mil

**Summary:** To provide financial assistance to upper-division students who are interested in joining Navy ROTC in college.

**Eligibility:** Open to students who have completed at least 2 years of college (or 3 years if enrolled in a 5-year program) with a GPA of 2.5 or higher overall and 2.0 or higher in calculus and physics. Preference is given to students at colleges with a Navy ROTC unit on campus or at colleges with a cross-enrollment agreement with a college with an NROTC unit. Applicants must be U.S. citizens between the ages of 17 and 21 who plan to pursue an approved course of study in college and complete their degree before they reach the age of 27. Former and current enlisted military personnel are also eligible if they will complete the program by the age of 30.

**Financial data:** These scholarships provide payment of full tuition and required educational fees, as well as a specified amount for textbooks, supplies, and equipment. The program also provides a stipend for 10 months of the year that is $350 per month as a junior and $400 per month as a senior.

**Duration:** 2 years, until the recipient completes the bachelor's degree.

**Number awarded:** Approximately 800 each year.

**Deadline:** March of each year.

## 784 NAVY-MARINE CORPS ROTC 4-YEAR SCHOLARSHIPS

U.S. Navy, Attn: Chief of Naval Education and Training
Code N79A2
250 Dallas Street
Pensacola, FL 32508-5220
Phone: (850) 452-4941, ext. 29381; (800) NAV-ROTC, ext. 29381;
Fax: (850) 452-2486; Email: PNSC_NROTC.scholarship@navy.mil
Web: www.nrotc.navy.mil

**Summary:** To provide financial assistance to graduating high school seniors who are interested in joining Navy ROTC in college.

**Eligibility:** Open to graduating high school seniors who have been accepted at a college with a Navy ROTC unit on campus or a college with a cross-enroll-

ment agreement with such a college. Applicants must be U.S. citizens between 17 and 23 years of age who are willing to serve for 4 years as active-duty Navy officers following graduation from college. They must not have reached their 27th birthday by the time of college graduation and commissioning; applicants who have prior active-duty military service may be eligible for age adjustments for the amount of time equal to their prior service, up to a maximum of 36 months. Current enlisted and former military personnel are also eligible if they will complete the program by the age of 30.

**Financial data:** These scholarships provide payment of full tuition and required educational fees, as well as a specified amount for textbooks, supplies, and equipment. The program also provides a stipend for 10 months of the year that is $250 per month as a freshman, $300 per month as a sophomore, $350 per month as a junior, and $400 per month as a senior.

**Duration:** 4 years.

**Number awarded:** Approximately 2,200 each year.

**Deadline:** January of each year;

## 785 NAVY/MARINE CORPS JROTC SCHOLARSHIP

National Naval Officers Association-Washington, D.C. Chapter
Attn: Scholarship Program
2701 Park Center Drive, B704
Alexandria, VA 22302
Email: williams.stephen@hq.navy.mil
Web: www.dcnnoa.org

**Summary:** To provide financial assistance for college to minority high school seniors from the Washington, D.C. area who have participated in Navy or Marine Corps Junior ROTC.

**Eligibility:** Open to minority seniors at high schools in the Washington, D.C. metropolitan area who have participated in Navy or Marine Corps JROTC. Applicants must be planning to enroll full time at an accredited 2-year or 4-year college or university. They must have a GPA of 2.5 or higher and be U.S. citizens or permanent residents. Selection is based on academic achievement, community involvement, and financial need.

**Financial data:** The stipend is $1,000 per year.

**Duration:** 1 year; nonrenewable.

**Number awarded:** 1 each year.

**Deadline:** April of each year.

## 786 NAVY/MARINE CORPS/COAST GUARD ENLISTED DEPENDENT SPOUSE SCHOLARSHIP

Navy Wives Club of America
P.O. Box 54022
Millington, TN 39053-6022
Phone: (866) 511-NWCA; Email: nwca@navywivesclubsofamerica.org
Web: www.navywivesclubsofamerica.org/nwc/scholarships.htm

**Summary:** To provide financial assistance for undergraduate or graduate study to spouses of naval personnel.

**Eligibility:** Open to the spouses of active-duty Navy, Marine Corps, or Coast Guard members who can demonstrate financial need. Applicants must be 1) a high school graduate or senior planning to attend college full time next year; 2) currently enrolled in an undergraduate program and planning to continue as a full-time undergraduate; 3) a college graduate or senior planning to be a full-time graduate student next year; and 4) a high school graduate or GED recipient planning to attend vocational or business school next year.

**Financial data:** The stipends range from $500 to $1,000 each year (depending upon the donations from chapters of the Navy Wives Club of America).

**Duration:** 1 year.

**Number awarded:** 1 or more each year.

**Deadline:** May of each year.

## 787 NCAIAW SCHOLARSHIP

North Carolina Alliance for Athletics, Health, Physical Education, Recreation and Dance, Attn: Executive Director
P.O. Box 27751
Raleigh, NC 27611
Phone: (888) 840-6500; Fax: (919) 463-8393;
Email: ncaahperd@ncaahperd.org
Web: www.ncaahperd.org/awards/index.htm

**Summary:** To provide financial assistance to women who are college seniors involved in sports at an institution that is a member of the former North Carolina Association of Intercollegiate Athletics for Women (NCAIAW).

**Eligibility:** Open to women who have been a participant on 1 or more varsity athletic teams either as a player or in the support role of manager, trainer, etc.

Applicants must be attending 1 of the following former NCAIAW colleges or universities in North Carolina: Appalachian State, Belmont Abbey, Bennett, Campbell, Davidson, Duke, East Carolina, Gardner-Webb, High Point, Mars Hill, Meredith, North Carolina A&T, North Carolina State, Pembroke State, Salem, St. Mary's, University of North Carolina at Ashville, University of North Carolina at Chapel Hill, University of North Carolina at Charlotte, University of North Carolina at Wilmington, Wake Forest, or Western Carolina. They must be college seniors at the time of application, be able to demonstrate high standards of scholarship, and show evidence of leadership potential (as indicated by participation in school and community activities).

**Financial data:** The stipend is $1,000. Funds are sent to the recipient's school.

**Duration:** 1 year.

**Number awarded:** 1 each year.

**Deadline:** June of each year.

## 788 NCFOP FOUNDATION SCHOLARSHIPS

North Carolina Fraternal Order of Police, Attn: NCFOB Foundation, Inc.
1500 Walnut Street
Cary, NC 27511-5927
Phone: (919) 461-4939; Email: ncfop@aol.com
Web: www.ncfop.com/foundation.htm

**Summary:** To provide financial assistance for college to families of disabled or deceased law enforcement officers in North Carolina.

**Eligibility:** Open to North Carolina residents who are enrolled in an appropriate postsecondary institution, including colleges and vocational schools. Applicants must be the child or spouse of a North Carolina law enforcement officer killed or disabled in the line of duty.

**Financial data:** A stipend is awarded (amount not specified).

**Duration:** 1 year.

**Number awarded:** Varies each year; recently, 3 of these scholarships were awarded.

## 789 NEBRASKA CATTLEMEN FOUNDATION SCHOLARSHIPS

Nebraska Cattlemen Association
Attn: Nebraska Cattlemen Research and Education Foundation
134 South 13th Street, Suite 900
Lincoln, NE 68508-1901
Phone: (402) 475-2333; Fax: (402) 475-0822; Email: nc@necattlemen.org
Web: www.nebraskacattlemen.org

**Summary:** To provide financial assistance to residents of Nebraska who have been involved in the beef industry and are interested in majoring in any field in college.

**Eligibility:** Open to Nebraska residents who are high school seniors or college undergraduates currently enrolled or planning to enroll in a 2-year or 4-year college or university. There are no restrictions on institution or field of study. Selection is based on academic achievement, quality of the application, and involvement in the beef industry.

**Financial data:** The stipend is $1,000.

**Duration:** 1 year.

**Number awarded:** 6 each year.

**Deadline:** March of each year.

## 790 NEBRASKA ELKS ASSOCIATION VOCATIONAL SCHOLARSHIP GRANTS

Nebraska Elks Association
c/o Melvin Nespor, Scholarship Committee
P.O. Box 14
Endicott, NE 68350
Email: mnespor@beatricene.com

**Summary:** To provide financial assistance to high school seniors in Nebraska who plan to attend a vocational school in the state.

**Eligibility:** Open to seniors graduating from high schools in Nebraska. Applicants must be planning to attend a 2-year or less vocational/technical program for an associate degree, diploma, or certificate. Selection is based on motivation (general worthiness, desire); aptitude toward chosen vocation; grades and test scores; completeness, neatness, and accuracy in following instructions when filling out the application; and financial need. Each Nebraska Elks Lodge can submit 1 application.

**Financial data:** Stipends depend on the need of the recipient, to a maximum of $1,000.

**Duration:** 1 year.

**Number awarded:** 6 each year.

**Deadline:** January of each year.

## 791 NEBRASKA POSTSECONDARY EDUCATION AWARD PROGRAM

Coordinating Commission for Postsecondary Education
140 North Eighth Street, Suite 300
P.O. Box 95005
Lincoln, NE 68509-5005
Phone: (402) 471-2847; Fax: (402) 471-2886; Email: ccpe01@nol.org
Web: www.ccpe.state.ne.us

**Summary:** To provide financial assistance for college to residents of Nebraska who demonstrate financial need.

**Eligibility:** Open to residents of Nebraska who demonstrate financial need. Applicants must be attending or planning to attend a private institution of higher education in Nebraska. Full-time students receive priority.

**Financial data:** The amount of the award depends on the needs of the recipient.

**Duration:** 1 year.

**Number awarded:** Varies each year.

**Deadline:** Each participating institution establishes its own deadline.

## 792 NEBRASKA RURAL SCHOOLS SCHOLARSHIPS

Lincoln Community Foundation
215 Centennial Mall South, Suite 200
Lincoln, NE 68508
Phone: (402) 474-2345; Fax: (402) 476-8532; Email: lcf@lcf.org
Web: www.lcf.org

**Summary:** To provide financial assistance for college to residents of rural Nebraska.

**Eligibility:** Open to graduating seniors or former graduates of a high school in rural Nebraska (for this program, defined as a community with a population of less than 10,000). Applicants must either attend or plan to attend a 2-year or 4-year college or university in the state. They should apply through that school. Financial need must be demonstrated. High school applicants must be graduating in the top 10% of their class; college applicants must have earned at least a 3.5 GPA. Along with their application, they must submit an essay on the topic: "If you could change one thing about your hometown, what would it be and why?"

**Financial data:** A stipend is awarded (amount not specified).

**Duration:** 1 year; may be renewed.

**Number awarded:** Varies each year; recently, 4 of these scholarships were awarded.

**Deadline:** July of each year.

## 793 NEBRASKA SCHOLARSHIP ASSISTANCE PROGRAM

Coordinating Commission for Postsecondary Education
140 North Eighth Street, Suite 300
P.O. Box 95005
Lincoln, NE 68509-5005
Phone: (402) 471-2847; Fax: (402) 471-2886; Email: ccpe01@nol.org
Web: www.ccpe.state.nc.us

**Summary:** To provide financial assistance for college to residents of Nebraska who demonstrate financial need.

**Eligibility:** Open to residents of Nebraska who demonstrate financial need. Applicants must be attending or planning to attend a public or private institution of higher education in the state.

**Financial data:** The amount of the award depends on the needs of the recipient.

**Duration:** 1 year.

**Number awarded:** Varies each year.

**Deadline:** Each participating institution establishes its own deadline.

## 794 NEBRASKA STATE SCHOLARSHIP AWARD PROGRAM

Coordinating Commission for Postsecondary Education
140 North Eighth Street, Suite 300
P.O. Box 95005
Lincoln, NE 68509-5005
Phone: (402) 471-2847; Fax: (402) 471-2886; Email: ccpe01@nol.org
Web: www.ccpe.state.ne.us

**Summary:** To provide financial assistance to residents of Nebraska who plan to attend college on a full-time basis and can demonstrate financial need.

**Eligibility:** Open to residents of Nebraska who demonstrate financial need. Applicants must be attending or planning to attend a public or private institution of higher education in Nebraska on a full-time basis.

**Financial data:** The amount of the award depends on the needs of the recipient.

**Duration:** 1 year.

**Number awarded:** Varies each year.

**Deadline:** Each participating institution establishes its own deadline.

## 795 NEBRASKA WAIVER OF TUITION FOR VETERANS' DEPENDENTS

Department of Veterans' Affairs

State Office Building

301 Centennial Mall South, Sixth Floor

P.O. Box 95083

Lincoln, NE 68509-5083

Phone: (402) 471-2458; Fax: (402) 471-2491; Email: dparker@notes.state.ne.us

Web: www.vets.state.ne.us

**Summary:** To provide financial assistance for college to dependents of deceased and disabled veterans and military personnel in Nebraska.

**Eligibility:** Open to spouses, widow(er)s, and children who are residents of Nebraska and whose parent, stepparent, or spouse was a member of the U.S. armed forces and 1) died of a service-connected disability; 2) died subsequent to discharge as a result of injury or illness sustained while in service; 3) is permanently and totally disabled as a result of military service; or 4) is classified as missing in action or as a prisoner of war during armed hostilities after August 4, 1964. Applicants must be attending or planning to attend a branch of the University of Nebraska, a state college, or a community college in Nebraska.

**Financial data:** Tuition is waived at public institutions in Nebraska.

**Duration:** The waiver is valid for 1 degree, diploma, or certificate from a community college and 1 baccalaureate degree.

**Number awarded:** Varies each year; recently, 302 of these grants were awarded.

## 796 NEBRASKANS OF WORLD WAR II SCHOLARSHIPS

Nebraska State Historical Society Foundation, Attn: Executive Director

Kinman-Oldfield Suite 1010

128 North 13th Street

Lincoln, NE 68508-1565

Phone: (402) 435-3535; (888) 515-3535; Fax: (402) 435-3986;

Email: nshsf@alltel.net

Web: www.nebraskahistory.org/foundatn/index.htm

**Summary:** To provide financial assistance for college to high school seniors in Nebraska.

**Eligibility:** Open to seniors graduating from high schools in Nebraska with a GPA of 3.5 or higher. Applicants must be planning to attend a 4-year college or university as a full-time student. Along with their application, they must submit a 1- to 2-page essay on the significance of the history of World War II to them and their community.

**Financial data:** The stipend is $1,000.

**Duration:** 1 year; nonrenewable.

**Number awarded:** 5 each year.

**Deadline:** January of each year.

## 797 NED MCWHERTER SCHOLARS PROGRAM

Tennessee Student Assistance Corporation

Parkway Towers

404 James Robertson Parkway, Suite 1950

Nashville, TN 37243-0820

Phone: (615) 741-1346; (800) 342-1663; Fax: (615) 741-6101;

Email: tsac@mail.state.tn.us

Web: www.tnscholardollars.com/mon_college/ned_mc_shcolar.htm

**Summary:** To provide financial assistance to outstanding Tennessee high school seniors and recent graduates who plan to attend college in the state.

**Eligibility:** Open to recent high school graduates and high school seniors in Tennessee who are residents of the state, whose parents are residents of the state, who ranked in the top 5% on the ACT or SAT tests, and who earned a GPA of 3.5 or higher in high school. Selection is based on academic record, test scores, and demonstrated leadership.

**Financial data:** Stipends up to $6,000 per year are provided.

**Duration:** 1 year; may be renewed for up to 3 additional years if the recipient remains a full-time student and maintains a minimum GPA of 3.0 per term and 3.2 per year.

**Number awarded:** Approximately 50 each year.

**Deadline:** February of each year.

## 798 NEW ENGLAND REGIONAL STUDENT PROGRAM

New England Board of Higher Education

45 Temple Place

Boston, MA 02111

Phone: (617) 357-9620; Fax: (617) 338-1577; Email: tuitionbreak@nebhe.org

Web: www.nebhe.org

**Summary:** To enable students in New England to attend a college or graduate school within the region at reduced tuition when their area of study is not offered at their own state's public institutions.

**Eligibility:** Open to residents of the 6 New England states: Connecticut, Maine, Massachusetts, New Hampshire, Rhode Island, and Vermont. Students may apply for this support when their chosen field of study is not offered at any of the public institutions within their own state. Contact the New England Board of Higher Education for a catalog of degree programs and states that qualify for this program. Undergraduate program eligibility is based on entire degree programs only, not on concentrations or options within degree programs. Some highly specialized graduate programs might be available even if they are not listed in the catalog. Eligibility is not based on financial need.

**Financial data:** With this program, students accepted at a public college or university in New England (but outside their own state) generally pay 150% of the in-state tuition for residents of the state. The average tuition saving is approximately $5,000.

**Duration:** Up to 4 years.

**Number awarded:** Varies each year; recently, more than 8,050 New England students took advantage of this program.

## 799 NEW HAMPSHIRE CHARITABLE FOUNDATION ADULT STUDENT AID PROGRAM

New Hampshire Charitable Foundation

37 Pleasant Street

Concord, NH 03301-4005

Phone: (603) 225-6641; (800) 464-6641; Fax: (603) 225-1700;

Email: info@nhcf.org

Web: www.nhcf.org

**Summary:** To provide funding for undergraduate study to adults in New Hampshire who are returning to school.

**Eligibility:** Open to New Hampshire residents who are 24 years of age or older. Applicants should 1) have had little or no education beyond high school, and 2) be now returning to school to upgrade skills for employment or career advancement, to qualify for a degree program, or to make a career change. They must demonstrate that they have secured all available financial aid and still have a remaining unmet need. Preference for funding is given in the following order: 1) students who have previously received funding through this program and have successfully completed prior work; 2) students with the least amount of higher education or training; and 3) single parents. Only undergraduate students are eligible.

**Financial data:** The maximum award is $500 each term ($1,000 per year). Most awards are in the form of grants, although no-interest or low-interest loans are also available.

**Duration:** 1 academic term; may be renewed up to 2 additional terms.

**Number awarded:** Varies each year.

**Deadline:** May, August, or December of each year.

## 800 NEW HAMPSHIRE CHARITABLE FOUNDATION STATEWIDE STUDENT AID PROGRAM

New Hampshire Charitable Foundation

37 Pleasant Street

Concord, NH 03301-4005

Phone: (603) 225-6641; (800) 464-6641; Fax: (603) 225-1700;

Email: info@nhcf.org

Web: www.nhcf.org

**Summary:** To provide scholarships or loans for undergraduate or graduate study to New Hampshire residents.

**Eligibility:** Open to New Hampshire residents who are graduating high school seniors or undergraduate students between 17 and 23 years of age or graduate students of any age. Applicants must be enrolled in or planning to enroll in an accredited 2- or 4-year college, university, or vocational school on at least a half-time basis. The school may be in New Hampshire or another state. Selection is based on financial need, academic merit, community service, school activities, and work experience. Priority is given to students with the fewest financial resources and to vocational/technical school students.

**Financial data:** Awards range from $500 to $2,500 and average $1,800. Most are made in the form of grants (recently, 82% of all awards) or no-interest or low-interest loans (recently 18% of all awards).

**Duration:** 1 year; approximately one third of the awards are renewable.

**Number awarded:** Varies each year; recently, a total of $3 million was awarded.

**Deadline:** April of each year.

---

### 801 NEW HAMPSHIRE INCENTIVE PROGRAM

New Hampshire Postsecondary Education Commission
3 Barrell Court, Suite 300
Concord, NH 03301-8543
Phone: (603) 271-2555, ext. 355; Fax: (603) 271-2696; TDD: (800) 735-2964;
Email: pedes@pec.state.nh.us
Web: www.state.nh.us/postsecondary/finnhip.html

**Summary:** To provide financial assistance to New Hampshire residents who are interested in attending college.

**Eligibility:** Open to residents of New Hampshire, if they are U.S. citizens or permanent residents, are accepted at or enrolled part or full time in an eligible postsecondary institution in 1 of the 6 New England states, and can demonstrate both academic ability and financial need. Upperclassmen must have a GPA of 2.0 or higher.

**Financial data:** The stipends range from $125 to $1,000 per year.

**Duration:** 1 year.

**Number awarded:** Varies each year; recently, 2,586 of these awards were granted.

**Deadline:** April of each year.

---

### 802 NEW HAMPSHIRE LEGION DEPARTMENT SCHOLARSHIP

American Legion, Attn: Department of New Hampshire
State House Annex
25 Capitol Street, Room 431
Concord, NH 03301-6312
Phone: (603) 271-2211; Fax: (603) 271-5352

**Summary:** To provide financial assistance for college to students in New Hampshire.

**Eligibility:** Open to students who are or will be graduates of a New Hampshire high school and have been New Hampshire residents for at least 3 years. Applicants must be entering their first year of college.

**Financial data:** The stipend is $1,000.

**Duration:** 1 year.

**Number awarded:** 2 each year.

**Deadline:** April of each year.

---

### 803 NEW HAMPSHIRE LEGION DEPARTMENT VOCATIONAL SCHOLARSHIP

American Legion, Attn: Department of New Hampshire
State House Annex
25 Capitol Street, Room 431
Concord, NH 03301-6312
Phone: (603) 271-2211; Fax: (603) 271-5352

**Summary:** To provide financial assistance for vocational education to students in New Hampshire.

**Eligibility:** Open to students who are or will be graduates of a New Hampshire high school and have been New Hampshire residents for at least 3 years. Applicants must be entering their first year of higher education in a vocational field.

**Financial data:** The stipend is $1,000.

**Duration:** 1 year.

**Number awarded:** 1 each year.

**Deadline:** April of each year.

---

### 804 NEW HAMPSHIRE LEVERAGED INCENTIVE GRANT PROGRAM

New Hampshire Postsecondary Education Commission
3 Barrell Court, Suite 300
Concord, NH 03301-8543
Phone: (603) 271-2555; Fax: (603) 271-2696; TDD: (800) 735-2964;
Email: pedes@pec.state.nh.us
Web: www.state.nh.us/postsecondary/finligp.html

**Summary:** To provide financial assistance to New Hampshire residents who are attending college in the state and can demonstrate financial need.

**Eligibility:** Open to residents of New Hampshire who are currently enrolled as sophomores, juniors, or seniors at accredited colleges and universities in the state. Selection is based on financial need (as determined by federal formulas) and academic merit (as determined by the institution.

**Financial data:** The stipend depends on the need of the recipient, as determined by the institution.

**Duration:** 1 year; may be renewed.

**Number awarded:** Varies each year.

---

### 805 NEW HAMPSHIRE SCHOLARSHIPS FOR ORPHANS OF VETERANS

New Hampshire Postsecondary Education Commission
3 Barrell Court, Suite 300
Concord, NH 03301-8543
Phone: (603) 271-2555, ext. 352; Fax: (603) 271-2696; TDD: (800) 735-2964;
Email: pedes@pec.state.nh.us
Web: www.state.nh.us/postsecondary/finsfoov.html

**Summary:** To provide financial assistance for college to the children of New Hampshire veterans who died of service-connected disabilities.

**Eligibility:** Open to New Hampshire residents between 16 and 25 years of age whose parent(s) died as a result of a service-related disability incurred during World War I, World War II, the Korean Conflict, or the southeast Asian Conflict. These parents must have been residents of New Hampshire at the time of death. Applicants must be enrolled as full-time undergraduate students at a public college or university in New Hampshire.

**Financial data:** The stipend is $1,000 per year, to be used for the payment of room, board, books, and supplies.

**Duration:** 1 year; may be renewed for up to 3 additional years.

**Number awarded:** Varies each year.

---

### 806 NEW JERSEY EDUCATIONAL OPPORTUNITY FUND GRANTS

New Jersey Commission on Higher Education
Attn: Educational Opportunity Fund
20 West State Street, Seventh Floor
P.O. Box 542
Trenton, NJ 08625-0542
Phone: (609) 984-2709; Fax: (609) 292-7225; Email: nj_che@che.state.nj.us
Web: www.nj.gov/highereducation/eligible.htm

**Summary:** To provide financial assistance for undergraduate or graduate study in New Jersey to students from disadvantaged backgrounds.

**Eligibility:** Open to students from economically and educationally disadvantaged backgrounds who have been legal residents of New Jersey for at least 12 consecutive months. Applicants must be from families with annual incomes below specified limits, ranging from $18,620 for a household size of 1 to $63,140 for a household size of 8. They must be attending or accepted for attendance as full-time undergraduate or graduate students at institutions of higher education in New Jersey. To apply, students must fill out the Free Application for Federal Student Aid. Some colleges may also require students to complete the College Scholarship Service's (CSS) Financial Aid Form to apply for institutional aid.

**Financial data:** Undergraduate grants range from $200 to $2,400 and graduate grants from $200 to $4,250, depending on college costs and financial need.

**Duration:** 1 year; renewable annually (based on satisfactory academic progress and continued eligibility).

**Deadline:** September of each year.

---

### 807 NEW JERSEY LEGION AUXILIARY DEPARTMENT SCHOLARSHIPS

American Legion Auxiliary, Attn: Department of New Jersey
c/o Lucille M. Miller, Secretary, Treasurer
1540 Kuser Road, Suite A-8
Hamilton, NJ 08619
Phone: (609) 581-9580; Fax: (609) 581-8429

**Summary:** To provide financial assistance for college to the children or grandchildren of veterans in New Jersey.

**Eligibility:** Open to the children or grandchildren of honorably discharged veterans of the U.S. armed forces. Applicants must have resided in New Jersey for at least 2 years and be members of a New Jersey senior high school graduating class.

**Financial data:** The amount awarded varies, depending upon the needs of the recipient and the money available.

**Duration:** 1 year.

**Number awarded:** Several each year.

**Deadline:** March of each year.

## 808 NEW JERSEY OUTSTANDING SCHOLAR RECRUITMENT PROGRAM

New Jersey Higher Education Student Assistance Authority
Attn: Financial Aid Services
4 Quakerbridge Plaza
P.O. Box 540
Trenton, NJ 08625-0540
Phone: (609) 588-2349; (800) 792-8670; Fax: (609) 588-2390;
Email: gjoachim@hesaa.org
Web: www.hesaa.org

**Summary:** To provide financial assistance for college to residents of New Jersey who have outstanding high school records.

**Eligibility:** Open to graduating high school seniors in New Jersey who plan to attend a selected university in the state. Applicants must have outstanding academic records, including class rank and SAT scores. They must apply directly to the university in New Jersey that participates in this program.

**Financial data:** Stipends depend on class rank and SAT scores, ranging from $2,500 to $7,500 per year.

**Duration:** 1 year; may be renewed as along as the recipient maintains full-time enrollment and a GPA of 3.0 or higher.

**Number awarded:** Varies each year.

## 809 NEW JERSEY POW/MIA TUITION BENEFIT PROGRAM

New Jersey Department of Military and Veterans Affairs
Attn: Division of Veterans Programs
101 Eggert Crossing Road
P.O. Box 340
Trenton, NJ 08625-0340
Phone: (609) 530-7045; (800) 624-0508 (within NJ); Fax: (609) 530-7075
Web: www.state.nj.us/military/veterans/programs.html

**Summary:** To provide financial assistance for college to the children of New Jersey military personnel reported as missing in action or prisoners of war during the southeast Asian conflict.

**Eligibility:** Open to New Jersey residents attending or accepted at a New Jersey public or independent postsecondary institution whose parents were military service personnel officially declared prisoners of war or missing in action after January 1, 1960.

**Financial data:** This program entitles recipients to full undergraduate tuition at any public or independent postsecondary educational institution in New Jersey.

**Duration:** Assistance continues until completion of a bachelor's degree.

**Number awarded:** Varies each year.

**Deadline:** February of each year for the spring term and September for the fall and spring terms.

## 810 NEW JERSEY SCHOOL COUNSELOR ASSOCIATION SCHOLARSHIPS

New Jersey School Counselor Association, Inc.
c/o Marcy Rosner, Scholarship Chair
Elizabeth Haddon Elementary School
501 Redman Avenue
Haddonfield, NJ 08033
Phone: (856) 234-8884; Email: trosner1@comcast.net
Web: www.njsca.org

**Summary:** To provide financial assistance for college to high school seniors in New Jersey who submit outstanding essays on their school counselor.

**Eligibility:** Open to college-bound seniors graduating from high schools in New Jersey. Applicants must submit an essay of 300 to 500 words on how a school counselor has influenced their life in a positive way. The counselor must be a member of the New Jersey School Counselor Association. Along with the essay and the application, students must submit, through their counselor, copies of their high school transcript, high school profile, and letter of acceptance to a postsecondary institution. Financial need is not considered in the selection process.

**Financial data:** The stipend is $1,000.

**Duration:** 1 year.

**Number awarded:** 3 each year.

**Deadline:** April of each year.

## 811 NEW JERSEY STATE ELKS HANDICAPPED CHILDREN'S SCHOLARSHIP

New Jersey State Elks, Attn: Handicapped Children's Committee
665 Rahway Avenue
P.O. Box 1596
Woodbridge, NJ 07095-1596
Phone: (732) 326-1300; Email: info@njelks.org
Web: www.njelks.org

**Summary:** To provide financial assistance for college to high school seniors in New Jersey who have a disability.

**Eligibility:** Open to seniors graduating from high schools in New Jersey who have a disability. Selection is based on academic standing, general worthiness, and financial need. Boys and girls are judged separately.

**Financial data:** The stipend is $2,500 per year. Funds are paid directly to the recipient's college or university.

**Duration:** 4 years.

**Number awarded:** 2 each year: 1 to a boy and 1 to a girl.

**Deadline:** April of each year.

## 812 NEW JERSEY SURVIVOR TUITION BENEFITS PROGRAM

New Jersey Higher Education Student Assistance Authority
Attn: Financial Aid Services
4 Quakerbridge Plaza
P.O. Box 540
Trenton, NJ 08625-0540
Phone: (609) 588-2349; (800) 792-8670; Fax: (609) 588-2390;
Email: gjoachim@hesaa.org
Web: www.hesaa.org

**Summary:** To provide financial assistance to the spouses and children of New Jersey emergency service personnel or law enforcement officers killed in the performance of their duties.

**Eligibility:** Open to surviving spouses, daughters, and sons of law enforcement officials and emergency service personnel killed on the job. Applicants must be residents of New Jersey attending or planning to attend a private or public undergraduate institution in the state. Surviving spouses must apply within 8 years of the date of death; children must apply within 8 years following high school graduation.

**Financial data:** Grants pay the actual cost of tuition up to the highest tuition charged at a New Jersey public institution of higher education.

**Duration:** 1 year; may be renewed for up to 7 additional years as long as the recipient attends a New Jersey institution of higher education as an undergraduate student on at least a half-time basis.

**Number awarded:** Varies each year.

**Deadline:** September of each year for fall and spring term; February of each year for spring term only.

## 813 NEW JERSEY TUITION AID GRANTS

New Jersey Higher Education Student Assistance Authority
Attn: Financial Aid Services
4 Quakerbridge Plaza
P.O. Box 540
Trenton, NJ 08625-0540
Phone: (609) 588-2349; (800) 792-8670; Fax: (609) 588-2390;
Email: gjoachim@hesaa.org
Web: www.hesaa.org

**Summary:** To provide financial assistance for college to students in New Jersey.

**Eligibility:** Open to U.S. citizens and eligible noncitizens who have been residents of New Jersey for at least 12 consecutive months before receiving the grant. Applicants must be, or planning to be, full-time undergraduates at approved New Jersey colleges, universities, and degree-granting proprietary schools. They must demonstrate financial need by completing the Free Application for Federal Student Aid (FAFSA).

**Financial data:** Stipends depend on the financial need of the recipient, to a maximum of $1,868 at New Jersey county colleges, $4,092 at New Jersey state colleges and universities, $7,272 at New Jersey independent colleges and universities, $5,250 at Rutgers/University of Medicine and Dentistry of New Jersey, or $6,158 at New Jersey Institute of Technology.

**Duration:** 1 year; may be renewed if the recipient maintains satisfactory academic progress and continued eligibility.

**Number awarded:** Varies each year.

**Deadline:** May of each year for renewal students; September of each year for new applicants for fall term; February of each year for new applicants for spring term only.

### 814 NEW JERSEY VIETNAM VETERANS' MEMORIAL SCHOLARSHIPS

New Jersey Vietnam Veterans' Memorial, Attn: Scholarship Committee
1 Memorial Lane
P.O. Box 648
Holmdel, NJ 07733
Phone: (732) 335-0033; Fax: (732) 335-1107
Web: www.njvvmf.org

**Summary:** To recognize and reward, with college scholarships, New Jersey high school seniors who have visited the New Jersey Vietnam Veterans' Memorial and written an essay about the experience.

**Eligibility:** Open to seniors graduating from high schools in New Jersey who have visited the New Jersey Vietnam Veterans' Memorial. Applicants must submit an essay of 250 to 300 words in which they reflect upon their visit. They must submit proof of acceptance to a college or trade school, but letters of recommendation and transcripts are not required.

**Financial data:** The award is a $2,500 scholarship.

**Duration:** The awards are granted annually.

**Number awarded:** 2 each year.

**Deadline:** April of each year.

### 815 NEW JERSEY WORLD TRADE CENTER SCHOLARSHIP FUND

New Jersey Higher Education Student Assistance Authority
Attn: Financial Aid Services
4 Quakerbridge Plaza
P.O. Box 540
Trenton, NJ 08625-0540
Phone: (609) 588-2349; (800) 792-8670; Fax: (609) 588-2390;
Email: gjoachim@hesaa.org
Web: www.hesaa.org

**Summary:** To provide financial assistance for college to residents of New Jersey whose parent or spouse was killed in the terrorist attacks of September 11, 2001.

**Eligibility:** Open to the dependent children and surviving spouses of New Jersey residents who were killed in the terrorist attacks against the United States on September 11, 2001, or who died as the result of injuries received in the attacks, or who are missing and officially presumed dead as a direct result of the attacks. Applicants must be attending or planning to attend a college or university (may be in any state) as a full-time undergraduate. They are considered to have financial need. Surviving spouses must apply within 8 years of the date of death; children must apply within 8 years following high school graduation.

**Financial data:** The maximum stipend is $6,500 per year. Funds must be used for tuition, fees, room, and board.

**Duration:** 1 year; may be renewed.

**Number awarded:** Varies each year.

**Deadline:** May of each year for renewal students; September of each year for new applicants for fall term; February of each year for new applicants for spring term only.

### 816 NEW MEXICO ATHLETIC SCHOLARSHIPS

New Mexico Commission on Higher Education
Attn: Financial Aid and Student Services
1068 Cerrillos Road
P.O. Box 15910
Santa Fe, NM 87506-5910
Phone: (505) 827-1217; (800) 279-9777; Fax: (505) 827-7392;
Email: highered@che.state.nm.us
Web: www.nmche.org/collegefinance/athlete.asp

**Summary:** To provide financial assistance to student-athletes in New Mexico.

**Eligibility:** Open to both residents and nonresidents of New Mexico who are accepted by the athletic department of a public postsecondary institution in New Mexico.

**Financial data:** Awards vary but are applied to tuition and fees.

**Duration:** 1 year; may be renewed.

**Number awarded:** Varies each year.

**Deadline:** Deadlines are established by the participating institutions.

### 817 NEW MEXICO CHILDREN OF DECEASED MILITARY AND STATE POLICE PERSONNEL SCHOLARSHIPS

New Mexico Department of Veterans' Services

P.O. Box 2324
Santa Fe, NM 87504-2324
Phone: (505) 827-6300; (866) 433-VETS; Fax: (505) 827-6372;
Email: nmdvs@state.nm.us
Web: www.state.nm.us/veterans/scholarship.html

**Summary:** To provide financial assistance for college or graduate school to the children of deceased military and state police personnel in New Mexico.

**Eligibility:** Open to the children of 1) military personnel killed in action or as a result of such action during a period of armed conflict; 2) members of the New Mexico National Guard killed while on active duty; and 3) New Mexico State Police killed on active duty. Applicants must be between the ages of 16 and 26 and enrolled in a state-supported school in New Mexico. Children of deceased veterans must be nominated by the New Mexico Veterans' Service Commission; children of National Guard members must be nominated by the adjutant general of the state; children of state police must be nominated by the New Mexico State Police Board. Selection is based on merit and financial need.

**Financial data:** The scholarships provide payment of matriculation fees, board, room, books, and supplies at state-supported institutions of higher education in New Mexico.

**Duration:** 1 year; may be renewed.

### 818 NEW MEXICO COMPETITIVE SCHOLARSHIPS

New Mexico Commission on Higher Education
Attn: Financial Aid and Student Services
1068 Cerrillos Road
P.O. Box 15910
Santa Fe, NM 87506-5910
Phone: (505) 827-1217; (800) 279-9777; Fax: (505) 827-7392;
Email: highered@che.state.nm.us
Web: www.nmche.org/collegefinance/competitive.asp

**Summary:** To provide financial assistance to residents of other states who wish to attend a college or university in New Mexico.

**Eligibility:** Open to students who are not residents of New Mexico but who wish to attend public institutions of higher education in the state. Selection is based on high school GPA and ACT scores.

**Financial data:** For recipients, the out-of-state portion of tuition is waived and a stipend of at least $100 is paid.

**Number awarded:** Varies each year, depending on the availability of funds.

**Deadline:** Deadlines are established by the participating institutions.

### 819 NEW MEXICO ELKS ASSOCIATION CHARITABLE AND BENEVOLENT TRUST SCHOLARSHIPS

New Mexico Elks Association
Attn: Charitable and Benevolent Trust Commission
c/o Jim Larrabbee, Scholarship Committee
302 Ciniza Court
Gallup, NM 87301
Fax: (505) 863-3821; Email: JimLarrabee@cnetco.com
Web: www.nmelks.org

**Summary:** To provide financial assistance for college to high school seniors in New Mexico.

**Eligibility:** Open to seniors graduating from a high school in New Mexico. They must have exhibited outstanding scholastic and leadership ability, including extracurricular and civic activities. High school class rank, GPA, and standardized test scores must be validated by a school official. An endorsement from the local Elks Lodge is required. Financial need is also considered in the selection process. Some awards are designated for females and some for males.

**Financial data:** Stipends are either $2,000 or $1,000 per year.

**Duration:** 1 or 4 years.

**Number awarded:** 14 each year: 1 at $2,000 per year for 4 years to the top female applicant, 1 at $2,000 per year for 4 years to the top male applicant, 6 at $2,000 for 1 year, and 6 at $1,000 for 1 year.

**Deadline:** March of each year.

### 820 NEW MEXICO LEGISLATIVE ENDOWMENT SCHOLARSHIPS

New Mexico Commission on Higher Education
Attn: Financial Aid and Student Services
1068 Cerrillos Road
P.O. Box 15910
Santa Fe, NM 87506-5910
Phone: (505) 827-1217; (800) 279-9777; Fax: (505) 827-7392;
Email: highered@che.state.nm.us

Web: www.nmche.org/collegefinance/legislative.asp

**Summary:** To provide financial assistance for college to needy residents of New Mexico.

**Eligibility:** Open to residents of New Mexico enrolled or planning to enroll at a public institution of higher education in the state. Applicants must be able to demonstrate substantial financial need. Preference is given to 1) students transferring from New Mexico 2-year public postsecondary institutions to 4-year institutions and 2) returning adult students at 2-year and 4-year public institutions. Recipients must be enrolled at least half time.

**Financial data:** Full-time students receive up to $2,500 per year at 4-year institutions or up to $1,000 per year at 2-year institutions. Part-time students are eligible for prorated awards.

**Duration:** 1 year; may be renewed.

**Number awarded:** Varies each year.

**Deadline:** Deadlines are established by the participating institutions.

---

### 821 NEW MEXICO LOTTERY SUCCESS SCHOLARSHIPS

New Mexico Commission on Higher Education
Attn: Financial Aid and Student Services
1068 Cerrillos Road
P.O. Box 15910
Santa Fe, NM 87506-5910
Phone: (505) 827-1217; (800) 279-9777; Fax: (505) 827-7392;
Email: highered@che.state.nm.us
Web: www.nmche.org/collegefinance/lotto.asp

**Summary:** To provide financial assistance to college students in New Mexico with good academic records.

**Eligibility:** Open to full-time students at New Mexico public colleges and universities who graduated from a public or private high school in New Mexico or obtained a New Mexico GED. Applicants who earn at least a 2.5 GPA during their first college semester are eligible to begin receiving the award for their second semester of full-time enrollment.

**Financial data:** Scholarships are equal to 100% of tuition at the New Mexico public postsecondary institution where the student is enrolled.

**Duration:** Up to 8 consecutive semesters.

**Number awarded:** Varies each year, depending on the availability of funds.

**Deadline:** Deadlines are established by the participating institutions.

---

### 822 NEW MEXICO MANUFACTURED HOUSING SCHOLARSHIP FUND

Albuquerque Community Foundation, Attn: Scholarship Program
3301 Menaul N.E., Suite 2
P.O. Box 36960
Albuquerque, NM 87176-6960
Phone: (505) 883-6240; Email: acf@albuquerquefoundation.org
Web: www.albuquerquefoundation.org/scholar/scholar.htm

**Summary:** To provide financial assistance for college to residents of New Mexico who live in mobile homes.

**Eligibility:** Open to graduating seniors who reside in mobile/manufactured housing in New Mexico. Applicants must be able to demonstrate financial need and have a high school GPA of 3.0 or higher.

**Financial data:** The stipend is $1,000.

**Duration:** 1 year.

**Number awarded:** 1 or more each year.

**Deadline:** March of each year.

---

### 823 NEW MEXICO SCHOLARS PROGRAM

New Mexico Commission on Higher Education
Attn: Financial Aid and Student Services
1068 Cerrillos Road
P.O. Box 15910
Santa Fe, NM 87506-5910
Phone: (505) 827-1217; (800) 279-9777; Fax: (505) 827-7392;
Email: highered@che.state.nm.us
Web: www.nmche.org/collegefinance/scholars.asp

**Summary:** To provide financial assistance for college to graduating high school seniors in New Mexico.

**Eligibility:** Open to graduating high school seniors in New Mexico who plan to attend a public institution of higher education or selected private college in the state. Applicants must be in the top 5% of their high school graduating class and have an ACT score of at least 25 (or the equivalent on the SAT). If 1 member of a family is enrolled in college, the family income may be no greater than

$30,000 a year; if 2 or more members of the family are enrolled in college, the family income may be no greater than $40,000.

**Financial data:** This program provides recipients with tuition, fees, and books at a participating college or university in New Mexico.

**Duration:** 1 year; may be renewed.

**Number awarded:** Varies each year, depending on the availability of funds.

**Deadline:** Deadlines are established by the participating institutions.

---

### 824 NEW MEXICO STUDENT INCENTIVE GRANTS

New Mexico Commission on Higher Education
Attn: Financial Aid and Student Services
1068 Cerrillos Road
P.O. Box 15910
Santa Fe, NM 87506-5910
Phone: (505) 827-1217; (800) 279-9777; Fax: (505) 827-7392;
Email: highered@che.state.nm.us
Web: www.nmche.org/collegefinance/incentive.asp

**Summary:** To provide financial assistance to needy residents of New Mexico attending public or private nonprofit colleges in the state.

**Eligibility:** Open to full-time and half-time undergraduate students at public or private nonprofit colleges and universities in New Mexico who can demonstrate substantial financial need. Applicants must be U.S. citizens and New Mexico residents.

**Financial data:** The amount of the award is set by the participating college or university; generally, the awards range from $200 to $2,500 per year.

**Duration:** 1 year; may be renewed.

**Number awarded:** Varies each year, depending on the availability of funds.

**Deadline:** Deadlines are established by the participating institutions.

---

### 825 NEW MEXICO VIETNAM VETERANS SCHOLARSHIPS

New Mexico Department of Veterans' Services
P.O. Box 2324
Santa Fe, NM 87504-2324
Phone: (505) 827-6300; (866) 433-VETS; Fax: (505) 827-6372;
Email: nmdvs@state.nm.us
Web: www.state.nm.us/veterans/scholarship.html

**Summary:** To provide financial assistance for undergraduate and graduate education to Vietnam veterans in New Mexico.

**Eligibility:** Open to Vietnam veterans who have been residents of New Mexico for at least 10 years. Applicants must have been honorably discharged and have been awarded the Vietnam Service Medal or the Vietnam Campaign Medal. They must be planning to attend a state-supported college, university, or community college in New Mexico to work on an undergraduate or graduate degree.

**Financial data:** The scholarships pay tuition, fees, and books at any postsecondary institution in New Mexico, up to $1,520 for tuition and fees and $500 for books.

**Duration:** 1 year.

---

### 826 NEW MEXICO 3 PERCENT SCHOLARSHIP PROGRAM

New Mexico Commission on Higher Education
Attn: Financial Aid and Student Services
1068 Cerrillos Road
P.O. Box 15910
Santa Fe, NM 87506-5910
Phone: (505) 827-1217; (800) 279-9777; Fax: (505) 827-7392;
Email: highered@che.state.nm.us
Web: www.nmche.org/collegefinance/three.asp

**Summary:** To provide financial assistance for college or graduate school to residents of New Mexico.

**Eligibility:** Open to residents of New Mexico enrolled or planning to enroll at a public institution of higher education in the state as an undergraduate or graduate student. Selection is based on moral character, satisfactory initiative, scholastic standing, personality, and additional criteria established by each participating college or university. At least a third of the scholarships are based on financial need.

**Financial data:** The amount of assistance varies but covers at least tuition and some fees.

**Duration:** 1 year; may be renewed.

**Number awarded:** Varies each year.

**Deadline:** Deadlines are established by the participating institutions.

## 827 NEW YORK AID FOR PART-TIME STUDY (APTS) PROGRAM

New York State Higher Education Services Corporation
Attn: Student Information
99 Washington Avenue
Albany, NY 12255
Phone: (518) 473-1574; (888) NYS-HESC; Fax: (518) 473-3749;
TDD: (800) 445-5234; Email: webmail@hesc.com
Web: www.hesc.com

**Summary:** To provide money for students who are attending college on a part-time basis in New York.

**Eligibility:** Open to students who are enrolled part time (at least 3 but less than 12 hours per semester) in an undergraduate degree program in New York; meet the income limits established for this program (students whose parents could not claim them as dependents may earn no more than $34,250 per year; the total family income if parents do claim the student as a dependent may not exceed $50,550 per year); are a New York resident and a U.S. citizen or permanent resident or refugee; have a tuition bill of at least $100 per year; have not used up their Tuition Assistance Program (TAP) eligibility; and are not in default on a student loan. Interested students must get an application from the college they are attending, complete the application, and return it to their college for processing as early as possible. Funds are distributed by the New York State Higher Education Services Corporation (NYSHESC) to participating colleges in New York. College financial aid administrators select recipients from eligible students.

**Financial data:** Up to $2,000 per year; awards may not exceed actual tuition charges.

**Duration:** 1 year; recipients may reapply for up to 8 years of part-time study if they maintain a GPA of at least 2.0.

**Number awarded:** Varies each year; recently, more than 20,000 students received more than $12 million in assistance through this program.

## 828 NEW YORK LEGION AUXILIARY DEPARTMENT SCHOLARSHIP

American Legion Auxiliary, Attn: Department of New York
112 State Street, Suite 1310
Albany, NY 12207
Phone: (518) 463-1162; (800) 421-6348; Fax: (518) 449-5406;
Email: alanyhdqtrs@worldnet.att.net
Web: www.deptny.org/scholarships.htm

**Summary:** To provide financial assistance for college to New York residents who are the descendants of deceased veterans.

**Eligibility:** Open to residents of New York who are the children, grandchildren, or great grandchildren of deceased veterans of World War I, World War II, the Korean Conflict, the Vietnam War, Grenada/Lebanon, Panama, or the Persian Gulf. Applicants must be high school seniors or graduates younger than 20 years of age. They must be interested in attending an accredited college or university. Along with their application, they must submit a 500-word essay on a subject of their choice. Selection is based on character (20%), Americanism (20%), leadership (20%), scholarship (15%), and financial need (25%).

**Financial data:** The stipend is $1,000.

**Duration:** 1 year.

**Number awarded:** 1 each year.

**Deadline:** February of each year.

## 829 NEW YORK LEGION AUXILIARY DISTRICT SCHOLARSHIPS

American Legion Auxiliary, Attn: Department of New York
112 State Street, Suite 1310
Albany, NY 12207
Phone: (518) 463-1162; (800) 421-6348; Fax: (518) 449-5406;
Email: alanyhdqtrs@worldnet.att.net
Web: www.deptny.org/scholarships.htm

**Summary:** To provide financial assistance to descendants of veterans in New York who are interested in attending college.

**Eligibility:** Open to residents of New York who are the children, grandchildren, or great grandchildren of veterans (living or deceased) of World War I, World War II, the Korean Conflict, the Vietnam War, Grenada/Lebanon, Panama, or the Persian Gulf. Applicants must be high school seniors or graduates younger than 20 years of age. They must be interested in attending an accredited college or university. Along with their application they must submit a 500-word essay on "Why I choose to further my education." Selection is based on character (30%), Americanism (20%), leadership (10%), scholarship (20%), and financial need (20%).

**Financial data:** The stipend is $1,000.

**Duration:** 1 year.

**Number awarded:** 10 each year: 1 in each of the 10 judicial districts in New York state.

**Deadline:** March of each year.

## 830 NEW YORK MEMORIAL SCHOLARSHIPS

New York State Higher Education Services Corporation
Attn: Student Information
99 Washington Avenue
Albany, NY 12255
Phone: (518) 473-1574; (888) NYS-HESC; Fax: (518) 473-3749;
TDD: (800) 445-5234; Email: webmail@hesc.com
Web: www.hesc.com

**Summary:** To provide financial aid for college to the children or spouses of police officers, peace officers, fire fighters, and volunteer fire fighters in New York State who died as the result of injuries sustained in the line of duty.

**Eligibility:** Open to New York State residents who are attending or accepted at an approved program of study in the state and whose parent or spouse was a police officer, peace officer (including corrections officer), fire fighter, or volunteer fire fighter in New York and died as the result of injuries sustained in the line of duty. Applicants must be full-time undergraduates at a public college or university or private institution in New York.

**Financial data:** At public colleges and universities, this program provides payment of actual tuition and mandatory educational fees; actual room and board charged to students living on campus or an allowance for room and board for commuter students; and allowances for books, supplies, and transportation. At private institutions, the award is equal to the amount charged at the State University of New York (SUNY) for 4-year tuition and average mandatory fees (or the student's actual tuition and fees, whichever is less) plus allowances for room, board, books, supplies, and transportation.

**Duration:** This program is available for 4 years of full-time undergraduate study (or 5 years in an approved 5-year bachelor's degree program).

**Number awarded:** Varies each year; recently, more than 60 students received $558,000 in assistance through this program.

**Deadline:** April of each year.

## 831 NEW YORK STATE LEADERS OF TOMORROW SCHOLARSHIPS

New York Lottery, Attn: LOT Scholarship
One Broadway Center
P.O. Box 7540
Schenectady, NY 12301-7540
Phone: (518) 388-3415; Fax: (518) 366-3423;
Email: lotscholar@lottery.state.ny.us
Web: www.nylottery.org/lot

**Summary:** To provide financial assistance for college to seniors graduating from high schools in New York State.

**Eligibility:** Open to high school seniors in New York. The principal of every public and non-public high school in the state is entitled to nominate 2 graduating seniors for this program. For each high school, 1 nominee is selected. Nominees must have at least a 3.0 GPA, leadership skills, U.S. citizenship, and experience in extracurricular and community activities. They must plan to attend a New York State accredited college, university, trade school, or community college as a full-time student.

**Financial data:** The stipend is $1,000 per year.

**Duration:** Up to 4 years, provided the recipient remains enrolled full time at an accredited New York State institution with a GPA of 3.0 or higher. The college program must be completed within 5 years of high school graduation.

**Number awarded:** 1 from each high school in New York State.

**Deadline:** March of each year.

## 832 NEW YORK STATE MILITARY SERVICE RECOGNITION SCHOLARSHIPS

New York State Higher Education Services Corporation
Attn: Student Information
99 Washington Avenue
Albany, NY 12255
Phone: (518) 473-1574; (888) NYS-HESC; Fax: (518) 473-3749;
TDD: (800) 445-5234; Email: webmail@hesc.com
Web: www.hesc.com

**Summary:** To provide financial assistance for college in New York to disabled veterans and the family members of deceased or disabled veterans.

**Eligibility:** Open to New York residents who served in the armed forces of the United States or state organized militia at any time on or after August 2, 1990 and became severely and permanently disabled as a result of injury or illness suffered or incurred in a combat theater or combat zone or during military training operations in preparation for duty in a combat theater or combat zone of operations. Also eligible are the children, spouses, or financial dependents of members of the armed forces of the United States or state organized militia who at any time after August 2, 1990 1) died, became severely and permanently disabled as a result of injury or illness suffered or incurred, or are classified as missing in action in a combat theater or combat zone of operations, 2) died as a result of injuries incurred in those designated areas, or 3) died or became severely and permanently disabled as a result of injury or illness suffered or incurred during military training operations in preparation for duty in a combat theater or combat zone of operations. Applicants must be attending or accepted at an approved program of study as full-time undergraduates at a public college or university or private institution in New York. Residents of the state who were enrolled as an undergraduate at a college or university outside the state as of September 11, 2001 are eligible for scholarship payment at that school.

**Financial data:** At public colleges and universities, this program provides payment of actual tuition and mandatory educational fees; actual room and board charged to students living on campus or an allowance for room and board for commuter students; and allowances for books, supplies, and transportation. At private institutions, the award is equal to the amount charged at the State University of New York (SUNY) for 4-year tuition and average mandatory fees (or the student's actual tuition and fees, whichever is less) plus allowances for room, board, books, supplies, and transportation.

**Duration:** This program is available for 4 years of full-time undergraduate study (or 5 years in an approved 5-year bachelor's degree program).

**Number awarded:** Varies each year.

**Deadline:** April of each year.

### 833 NEW YORK STATE SCHOLARSHIPS FOR ACADEMIC EXCELLENCE

New York State Education Department
Office of K-16 Initiatives and Access Programs
Attn: Scholarships and Grants Administration Unit
Education Building Addition, Room 1078
Albany, NY 12234
Phone: (518) 486-1319; Email: kiap@mail.nysed.gov
Web: www.highered.nysed.gov/kiap/scholarships/sae.htm

**Summary:** To provide financial assistance to graduating high school seniors in New York State who achieve high grades on the Regents exams.

**Eligibility:** Open to seniors at high schools in New York who have been accepted as a full-time student in an approved undergraduate program of study at a postsecondary institution in the state. Applicants must be U.S. citizens or qualifying noncitizens and New York State residents. Awards are based on student grades in certain Regents exams. The top graduating scholar at each registered high school in the state automatically receives 1 of these scholarships. The remaining scholarships are awarded to other outstanding high school graduates in the same ratio of total students graduating from each high school in the state as compared to the total number of students who graduated during the prior school year.

**Financial data:** The annual stipends are either $1,500 or $500. Awards cannot exceed the actual cost of attendance.

**Duration:** Up to 4 years (or 5 years in approved 5-year baccalaureate programs). Recipients must remain enrolled full time, in good academic standing, and not in default on any guaranteed loan administered by the New York State Higher Education Services Corporation (HESC).

**Number awarded:** 8,000 each year: 2,000 at $1,500 and 6,000 at $500.

**Deadline:** December of each year.

### 834 NEW YORK STATE SCHOLARSHIPS FOR ACADEMIC EXCELLENCE

**Summary:** To provide financial assistance to high school seniors in New York who have a record of academic excellence and plan to attend a college or university in the state.
*See Listing #833.*

### 835 NEW YORK STATE VOLUNTEER RECRUITMENT SCHOLARSHIPS

New York State Higher Education Services Corporation
Attn: Student Information
99 Washington Avenue

Albany, NY 12255
Phone: (518) 473-1574; (888) NYS-HESC; Fax: (518) 473-3749;
TDD: (800) 445-5234; Email: webmail@hesc.com
Web: www.hesc.com

**Summary:** To provide financial assistance for college to New York residents who have recently volunteered to serve in a fire fighter or ambulance unit.

**Eligibility:** Open to volunteer fire fighters and ambulance personnel who have been New York residents for at least 1 year, are enrolled in an undergraduate degree program in the state for at least 6 credits per term, and have applied for state and federal financial aid. Applicants must be attending a school within 50 miles of their volunteer organization or, if no college is available within the 50-mile limit, the nearest institution. If they are 23 years of age or older, they must have less than 6 months of volunteer service; no minimum or maximum time of volunteer service is required for applicants under 23 years of age. Each volunteer organization in the state may nominate 1 candidate. If the number of nominees exceeds available funding, selection is based on a random drawing.

**Financial data:** The program provides payment of full tuition, less any other assistance received, up to the amount charged at the State University of New York (SUNY) for 4-year tuition.

**Duration:** 1 year; may be renewed as long as the recipient maintains good academic standing, a GPA of 2.0 or higher, and status as an active volunteer fire fighter or ambulance person.

**Number awarded:** Varies each year.

**Deadline:** Nominations must be submitted by July of each year.

### 836 NEW YORK STATE WORLD TRADE CENTER MEMORIAL SCHOLARSHIPS

New York State Higher Education Services Corporation
Attn: Student Information
99 Washington Avenue
Albany, NY 12255
Phone: (518) 473-1574; (888) NYS-HESC; Fax: (518) 473-3749;
TDD: (800) 445-5234; Email: webmail@hesc.com
Web: www.hesc.com

**Summary:** To provide financial assistance to undergraduates in New York who are relatives of people killed or severely and permanently disabled as a result of the terrorist attacks on September 11, 2001.

**Eligibility:** Open to the children, spouses, and financial dependents of deceased or severely and permanently disabled victims of the September 11, 2001 terrorist attacks or the subsequent rescue and recovery operations. Applicants must be attending or accepted at an approved program of study as full-time undergraduates at a public college or university or private institution in New York. They are not required to be New York residents or U.S. citizens. New York residents who were enrolled as an undergraduate at a college or university outside the state as of September 11, 2001 are eligible for scholarship payment at that school.

**Financial data:** At public colleges and universities, this program provides payment of actual tuition and mandatory educational fees; actual room and board charged to students living on campus or an allowance for room and board for commuter students; and allowances for books, supplies, and transportation. At private institutions, the award is equal to the amount charged at the State University of New York (SUNY) for 4-year tuition and average mandatory fees (or the student's actual tuition and fees, whichever is less) plus allowances for room, board, books, supplies, and transportation.

**Duration:** This program is available for 4 years of full-time undergraduate study (or 5 years in an approved 5-year bachelor's degree program).

**Number awarded:** Varies each year.

**Deadline:** April of each year.

### 837 NEW YORK TUITION ASSISTANCE PROGRAM (TAP)

New York State Higher Education Services Corporation
Attn: Student Information
99 Washington Avenue
Albany, NY 12255
Phone: (518) 473-1574; (888) NYS-HESC; Fax: (518) 473-3749;
TDD: (800) 445-5234; Email: webmail@hesc.com
Web: www.hesc.com

**Summary:** To help New York State residents pay undergraduate or graduate tuition at postsecondary institutions in the state.

**Eligibility:** Open to residents of New York who 1) are a U.S. citizen, permanent resident, conditional entrant, or refugee; and 2) do not exceed the income limitations for this program: for undergraduate students who are dependents or are married or have tax dependents, the limit is $80,000 net taxable family income; for graduate students who are dependents or are married or have tax dependents, the limit is $20,000 net taxable family income; for single independent undergraduate students with no dependents, the limit is $10,000 net taxable income; for single independent graduate students with no dependents, the limit is $5,666 net taxable income. Applicants must be enrolled in school full time in New York (at least 12 credits per semester); have tuition charges of at least $200 per year; and not be in default on a federal or state loan.

**Financial data:** TAP awards are based on net taxable income, tuition charges, and type of institution attended. For undergraduate students at degree-granting and not-for-profit institutions, the award range is $500 to $5,000 for dependent students or independent students who are married or have tax dependents, or $500 to $3,025 for independent students who are single with no dependents. For students at proprietary registered non-degree private business schools, the award range is $100 to $800 for dependent students or independent students who are married or have tax dependents, or $100 to $640 for independent students who are single with no dependents. For all graduate students, awards range from $75 to $550.

**Duration:** Up to 4 years for undergraduate students (or 5 years in approved 5-year baccalaureate programs); up to 4 years for graduate or professional students. The combined undergraduate-graduate total cannot exceed 8 years.

**Number awarded:** Varies each year; recently, nearly 342,000 students received approximately $636 million in assistance through this program.

**Deadline:** April of each year.

---

### 838 NEW YORK VIETNAM TUITION AWARD (VTA) PROGRAM

New York State Higher Education Services Corporation
Attn: Student Information
99 Washington Avenue
Albany, NY 12255
Phone: (518) 473-1574; (888) NYS-HESC; Fax: (518) 473-3749;
TDD: (800) 445-5234; Email: webmail@hesc.com
Web: www.hesc.com

**Summary:** To provide tuition assistance to eligible veterans enrolled in an undergraduate or graduate program in New York.

**Eligibility:** Open to veterans who served in the U.S. armed forces in 1) Indochina between December 22, 1961 and May 7, 1975; 2) in the Persian Gulf on or after August 2, 1990; or 3) in Afghanistan on or after September 11, 2001. Applicants must have been discharged from the service under other than dishonorable conditions, must be a New York resident, must be enrolled full or part time at an undergraduate or graduate degree-granting institution in New York State or in an approved vocational training program in the state, and must apply for a New York Tuition Assistance Program (TAP) award if a full-time student (12 or more credits) or a Pell Grant if a part-time student (at least 3 but less than 12 credits).

**Financial data:** Awards are $1,000 per semester for full-time study or $500 for part-time study, but in no case can the award exceed the amount charged for tuition. Total lifetime awards for undergraduate and graduate study under this program cannot exceed $10,000.

**Duration:** For full-time undergraduate study, up to 8 semesters, or up to 10 semesters for a program requiring 5 years for completion; for full-time graduate study, up to 6 semesters; for full-time vocational programs, up to 4 semesters; for part-time undergraduate study, up to 16 semesters, or up to 20 semesters for a 5-year program; for part-time graduate study, up to 12 semesters; for part-time vocational programs, up to 8 semesters.

**Number awarded:** Varies each year.

**Deadline:** April of each year.

---

### 839 NEXTGEN ACCESS SCHOLARSHIP PROGRAM

Finance Authority of Maine, Attn: Education Finance Programs
5 Community Drive
P.O. Box 949
Augusta, ME 04332-0949
Phone: (207) 623-3263; (800) 228-3734; Fax: (207) 623-0095;
TTY: (207) 626-2717; Email: info@famemaine.com
Web: www.famemaine.com/html/education/fameprogs.html

**Summary:** To provide financial assistance to Maine residents who are interested in working on a college degree but do not qualify for a Maine State Grant.

**Eligibility:** Open to residents of Maine who are enrolled in the first year of college or university. Applicants may not be eligible for a Maine State Grant and must have an estimated family contribution of $1,500 or less. They must be enrolled at an institution in Maine or in a state that has a reciprocity agreement with Maine (Connecticut, Massachusetts, New Hampshire, Pennsylvania, Rhode Island, Vermont, or Washington, D.C.).

**Financial data:** The maximum annual stipend is $1,000 at institutions in Maine or $500 at institutions outside of Maine.

**Duration:** 1 year; may be renewed up to 4 additional years if the recipient remains a Maine resident and maintains satisfactory academic progress.

**Deadline:** April of each year.

---

### 840 NEXTGEN STUDENT GRANT PROGRAM

Finance Authority of Maine, Attn: Education Finance Programs
5 Community Drive
P.O. Box 949
Augusta, ME 04332-0949
Phone: (207) 623-3263; (800) 228-3734; Fax: (207) 623-0095;
TTY: (207) 626-2717; Email: info@famemaine.com
Web: www.famemaine.com/html/education/fameprogs.html

**Summary:** To provide financial assistance for college to Maine residents who can demonstrate financial need.

**Eligibility:** Open to residents of Maine who are enrolled full time at a college or university in Maine, Connecticut, Massachusetts, New Hampshire, Pennsylvania, Vermont, or Washington, D.C. Selection is based primarily on financial need.

**Financial data:** Stipends range from $400 to $1,000 per year, depending on the need of the recipient.

**Duration:** 1 year; may be renewed up to 4 additional years if the recipient remains a Maine resident and maintains satisfactory academic progress.

**Deadline:** April of each year.

---

### 841 NICHOLAS C. VRATARIC SCHOLARSHIP AWARDS PROGRAM

Paper, Allied-Industrial, Chemical and Energy Workers International Union
Attn: Scholarship Coordinator
3340 Perimeter Hill Drive
P.O. Box 1475
Nashville, TN 37202
Phone: (615) 834-8590; Fax: (615) 834-7741; Email: debitay@isdn.net
Web: www.paceunion.org

**Summary:** To provide financial assistance for college to members of the Paper, Allied-Industrial, Chemical and Energy Workers (PACE) International Union.

**Eligibility:** Open to members of the union who are currently enrolled in a program to further their education. Applicants must submit a 500-word essay on the history of their local. Selection is based on a random drawing.

**Financial data:** The stipend is $1,000.

**Duration:** 1 year.

**Number awarded:** 2 each year.

**Deadline:** March of each year.

---

### 842 NICHOLAS GREEN HIGH SCHOOL SENIOR AWARD PROGRAM

National Association for Gifted Children, Attn: Chair, Awards Committee
1707 L Street, N.W., Suite 550
Washington, DC 20036
Phone: (202) 785-4268; Fax: (202) 785-4248; Email: nagc@nagc.org
Web: www.nagc.org

**Summary:** To recognize and reward high school seniors who demonstrate excellence in academics, leadership, community service, or the arts.

**Eligibility:** Open to seniors in their last year of high school who are nominated by an interested party. Nominees must have distinguished themselves in academics, leadership, community service, or the arts. They must submit a personal statement of 250 to 600 words on how their abilities have made a difference in their lives and in the lives of others, what they hope to do with their abilities in the future, and how they would spend the award money.

**Financial data:** The winner receives $1,500 and the runners-up receive $1,000.

**Duration:** The awards are presented annually.

**Number awarded:** 3 each year: 1 winner and 2 runners-up.

**Deadline:** February of each year.

---

### 843 NISSAN MISSISSIPPI SCHOLARSHIPS

Mississippi Office of Student Financial Aid
3825 Ridgewood Road
Jackson, MS 39211-6453
Phone: (601) 432-6997; (800) 327-2980 (within MS);
Fax: (601) 432-6527; Email: sfa@ihl.state.ms.us

Web: www.ihl.state.ms.us/financialaid/nissan.html

**Summary:** To provide financial assistance for college to high school seniors in Mississippi who plan to attend a public college in the state.

**Eligibility:** Open to residents of Mississippi who are graduating seniors at high schools in the state. Applicants must have been accepted for enrollment at a public 2-year or 4-year college or university in the state. They must have a GPA of 2.0 or higher after 7 semesters of high school and minimum scores of 20 on the ACT or the equivalent on the SAT. Along with their application, they must submit a 200-word essay on the topic, "How do my plans for the future and my college major support the automotive industry in Mississippi?" Selection is based on the essay (5%); academic achievement (50%); 2 letters of nomination (5%); extracurricular activities, work, leadership, and community involvement (20%); and demonstrated financial need (20%).

**Financial data:** Students in this program receive full payment of tuition and required fees plus an allowance for books.

**Duration:** 1 year; may be renewed 1 additional year for students at 2-year public colleges (followed by up to 3 years of support if the recipient transfers to a 4-year college or university) or up to 4 additional years for students at 4-year public colleges and universities. Renewal requires that the recipient reapplies each year; maintains a GPA of 2.5 or higher; displays leadership skills through participation in community service, extracurricular, or other activities; demonstrates full-time enrollment and satisfactory academic progress toward completion of a degree; maintains Mississippi residency; and maintains good standing at the college or university.

**Number awarded:** 1 or more each year.

**Deadline:** February of each year.

## 844 NISSAN NORTH AMERICA, INC. TRIBAL COLLEGE TRANSFER PROGRAM

American Indian College Fund, Attn: Scholarship Department
8333 Greenwood Boulevard
Denver, CO 80221
Phone: (303) 426-8900; (800) 776-FUND; Fax: (303) 426-1200;
Email: info@collegefund.org
Web: www.collegefund.org/scholarships/nissan.html

**Summary:** To provide financial assistance to American Indian students in an associate degree program at a tribal college who will be transferring to a bachelor's degree program at a tribal or mainstream college.

**Eligibility:** Open to American Indians or Alaska Natives enrolled full time in an associate degree program at a tribal college or university (juniors and seniors are ineligible to apply) who are planning to transfer to a bachelor's degree program at a tribal college or a mainstream institution. Applicants must be able to demonstrate exceptional academic achievement, as well as leadership, service, and commitment to the American Indian community. Along with their application, they must submit official college transcripts; a personal essay (500 words or less) on their personal and academic background, career goals, and how this scholarship will help them achieve those goals; a statement regarding any financial hardship they have; 2 letters of recommendation; tribal enrollment information; and a color photograph.

**Financial data:** The stipend is $2,000 per year, starting in the recipient's sophomore year.

**Duration:** 1 year; may be renewed up to 2 additional years.

**Number awarded:** 20 each year.

**Deadline:** April of each year.

## 845 NLUS STOCKHOLM SCHOLARSHIP FUND

Naval Sea Cadet Corps, Attn: Executive Director
2300 Wilson Boulevard
Arlington, VA 22201-3308
Phone: (703) 243-6910; Fax: (703) 243-3985
Web: www.seacadets.org

**Summary:** To provide financial assistance to Naval Sea Cadet Corps cadets and former cadets who are interested in continuing their education at an accredited 4-year college/university.

**Eligibility:** Open to cadets and former cadets who are interested in continuing their education at an accredited 4-year college or university. They must have been a member of the corps for at least 2 years, have a minimum rating of NSCC E-3, be recommended by their commanding officer or other official, have earned at least a 3.0 GPA, and have been accepted by an accredited college or university. Applicants may submit financial need statements. All other factors being equal, these statements may be considered in determining award recipients. Applicants who have received full scholarships from other sources (e.g., ROTC) will be considered for this award only if there are no other qualified applicants.

**Financial data:** The stipend is $2,000 per year.

**Duration:** Up to 4 years.

**Number awarded:** 1 every 4 years.

**Deadline:** May of the competition year.

## 846 NMJGSA SCHOLARSHIPS

National Minority Junior Golf Scholarship Association
Attn: Scholarship Committee
4950 East Thomas Road
Phoenix, AZ 85018
Phone: (602) 258-7851; Fax: (602) 258-3412; Email: sdean@nmjgsa.org
Web: www.nmjgsa.org/scholarships.html

**Summary:** To provide financial assistance to minority high school seniors and undergraduate students who excel at golf.

**Eligibility:** Open to minority high school seniors and undergraduate students already enrolled in college. Applicants are asked to write a 500-word essay on this question: "One of the principal goals of education and golf is fostering ways for people to respect and get along with individuals who think, dress, look, and act differently. How might you make this goal a reality?" Selection is based on academic achievement; personal recommendations; participation in golf, school, and community activities; and financial need.

**Financial data:** Stipends range from 1-time awards of $1,000 to 4-year awards of $6,000 per year. Funds are paid directly to the recipient's college.

**Duration:** 1 year or longer.

**Number awarded:** Varies; generally 80 or more each year.

**Deadline:** April of each year.

## 847 NOBUKO R. KODAMA FONG MEMORIAL SCHOLARSHIP

Japanese American Citizens League, Attn: National Scholarship Awards
1765 Sutter Street
San Francisco, CA 94115
Phone: (415) 921-5225; Fax: (415) 931-4671; Email: jacl@jacl.org
Web: www.jacl.org/scholarships.html

**Summary:** To provide financial assistance for college to student members of the Japanese American Citizens League (JACL), particularly those in the Pacific Northwest.

**Eligibility:** Open to JACL members who are currently enrolled or planning to reenter a college, university, trade school, business college, or other institution of higher learning. Applicants must submit a statement describing their current level of involvement in the Japanese American community or Asian Pacific community and how they will continue their involvement in future years. Selection is based on academic record, extracurricular activities, financial need, and community involvement. Preference is given to residents of the Pacific Northwest District.

**Financial data:** The stipend depends on the availability of funds but usually ranges from $1,000 to $5,000.

**Duration:** 1 year; nonrenewable.

**Number awarded:** 1 each year.

**Deadline:** March of each year.

## 848 NORMAN AND RUTH GOOD EDUCATIONAL ENDOWMENT AWARDS

Lincoln Community Foundation
215 Centennial Mall South, Suite 200
Lincoln, NE 68508
Phone: (402) 474-2345; Fax: (402) 476-8532; Email: lcf@lcf.org
Web: www.lcf.org

**Summary:** To provide financial assistance to upper-division students attending private colleges in Nebraska.

**Eligibility:** Open to juniors or seniors attending a private college in Nebraska. Applicants must have at least a 3.5 GPA and be working on a degree program, not special studies. Selection is based on academic achievement; financial need is not considered.

**Financial data:** The amount awarded varies, up to one half of the recipient's educational expenses.

**Duration:** 1 year; recipients may reapply.

**Number awarded:** Varies each year; recently, 14 of these awards were presented.

**Deadline:** April of each year.

## 849 NORTH CAROLINA BAR ASSOCIATION SCHOLARSHIPS

North Carolina Bar Association
Attn: Young Lawyers Division Scholarship Committee
8000 Weston Parkway
P.O. Box 3688
Cary, NC 27519-3688
Phone: (919) 677-0561; (800) 662-7407; Fax: (919) 677-0761;
Email: jtfount@mail.ncbar.org
Web: www.ncbar.org

**Summary:** To provide financial assistance for college or graduate school to the children of disabled or deceased law enforcement officers in North Carolina.

**Eligibility:** Open to the natural or adopted children of North Carolina law enforcement officers who were permanently disabled or killed in the line of duty. Applicants must be younger than 27 years of age and enrolled in or accepted at an accredited institution of higher learning (including community colleges, trade schools, colleges, universities, and graduate programs) in North Carolina. Selection is based on academic performance and financial need.

**Financial data:** The stipend is $2,000 per academic year.

**Duration:** Up to 4 years.

**Number awarded:** Varies each year; recently, 4 new and 14 renewal scholarships were awarded.

**Deadline:** March of each year.

## 850 NORTH CAROLINA COMMUNITY COLLEGE GRANT PROGRAM

North Carolina Community College System
Attn: Student Development Services
200 West Jones Street
5016 Mail Service Center
Raleigh, NC 27699-5016
Phone: (919) 807-7104; Fax: (919) 807-7164;
Email: whitehurstk@ncccs.cc.nc.us
Web: www.ncccs.cc.nc.us

**Summary:** To provide financial assistance to students attending community colleges in North Carolina.

**Eligibility:** Open to North Carolina residents enrolled at least half time at 1 of the 58 institutions in North Carolina's community college system. Applicants must be able to demonstrate financial need. Students who already have a bachelor's degree are ineligible.

**Financial data:** Stipends depend on the recipient's enrollment status and financial need. Stipends range from $250 to $1,900 per year for full-time students, from $188 to $1,425 per year for three-quarter-time students, or from $125 to $950 per year for half-time students.

**Duration:** 1 year; may be renewed.

**Number awarded:** Approximately 10,000 each year.

## 851 NORTH CAROLINA COMMUNITY COLLEGE TARGETED FINANCIAL ASSISTANCE PROGRAM

North Carolina Community College System
Attn: Student Development Services
200 West Jones Street
5016 Mail Service Center
Raleigh, NC 27699-5016
Phone: (919) 807-7104; Fax: (919) 807-7164;
Email: whitehurstk@ncccs.cc.nc.us
Web: www.ncccs.cc.nc.us

**Summary:** To provide financial assistance to students attending community colleges in North Carolina and majoring in selected fields.

**Eligibility:** Open to North Carolina residents enrolled at least half time at 1 of the 58 institutions in North Carolina's community college system. Applicants must be able to demonstrate financial need. They must be majoring in a low-enrollment program that prepares students for high demand occupations. Students who already have a bachelor's degree are ineligible.

**Financial data:** Stipends depend on the recipient's enrollment status and financial need.

**Duration:** 1 year; may be renewed.

**Number awarded:** Varies each year; recently, $500,000 was available for this program.

## 852 NORTH CAROLINA KIDS' CHANCE SCHOLARSHIPS

Kids' Chance of North Carolina, Inc.
c/o Martha Dealy, President
P.O. Box 470426
Charlotte, NC 28247-0426
Phone: (704) 264-9111; Fax: (704) 553-0241; Email: mdealy@cesinet.com
Web: www.kidschancenc.org

**Summary:** To provide financial assistance for college to North Carolina residents who parent was seriously injured or killed in a workplace accident.

**Eligibility:** Open to residents of North Carolina between 16 and 25 years of age who are attending or planning to attend college or vocational school. Applicants must be children of employees who have been seriously injured or killed as a result of a workplace accident that is covered under the North Carolina Workers' Compensation Act. They must be able to demonstrate financial hardship caused by the death or serious injury of their parent.

**Financial data:** A stipend is awarded (amount not specified). Funds may be used for tuition, books, and meals.

**Duration:** 1 year; may be renewed if the recipient maintains an acceptable academic level.

**Number awarded:** Varies each year.

## 853 NORTH CAROLINA LEGISLATIVE TUITION GRANTS

North Carolina State Education Assistance Authority
Attn: Scholarship and Grant Services
10 T.W. Alexander Drive
P.O. Box 14103
Research Triangle Park, NC 27709-4103
Phone: (919) 549-8614; (800) 700-1775; Fax: (919) 549-8481;
Email: information@ncseaa.edu
Web: www.ncseaa.edu

**Summary:** To provide financial assistance to students enrolled in private colleges in North Carolina.

**Eligibility:** Open to North Carolina residents attending a legislatively-designated private college in the state on a full-time basis. Financial need is not considered in the selection process. Students of theology, divinity, religious education, or any other course of study designed primarily for career preparation in a religious vocation are not eligible.

**Financial data:** The stipend is $1,800 per year. Funds are paid to the institution on behalf of the recipient.

**Duration:** 1 year; may be renewed.

**Number awarded:** Varies each year; recently, a total of 30,732 students were receiving $47,980,273 through this program.

## 854 NORTH CAROLINA PTA STUDENT SCHOLARSHIPS

North Carolina PTA
3501 Glenwood Avenue
Raleigh, NC 27612-4934
Phone: (919) 787-0534; (800) 255-0417 (within NC);
Fax: (919) 787-0569; Email: office@ncpta.org
Web: www.ncpta.org/student_scholarship.html

**Summary:** To provide financial assistance for college to high school seniors who are members of the North Carolina PTA/PTSA.

**Eligibility:** Open to graduating seniors in North Carolina who are members of their high school PTA/PTSA. Applicants must submit a copy of their most recent high school transcript, 2 letters of recommendation from high school faculty, a copy of their PTA/PTSA membership card, and essays on 5 topics that change annually. Financial need is considered in the selection process.

**Financial data:** The stipend is $1,000.

**Duration:** 1 year.

**Number awarded:** 1 or more each year.

**Deadline:** January of each year.

## 855 NORTH CAROLINA SCHOLARSHIPS FOR CHILDREN OF WAR VETERANS

Division of Veterans Affairs
Albemarle Building
325 North Salisbury Street, Suite 1065
Raleigh, NC 27603-5941
Phone: (919) 733-3851; Fax: (919) 733-2834; Email: Charlie.Smith@ncmail.net
Web: www.doa.state.nc.us/vets/va.htm

**Summary:** To provide financial assistance for college to the children of disabled and other classes of North Carolina veterans.

**Eligibility:** Open to applicants in 5 categories: Class I-A: the veteran parent died in wartime service or as a result of a service-connected condition incurred in wartime service; Class I-B: the veteran parent is rated by the U.S. Department of Veterans Affairs (VA) as 100% disabled as a result of wartime service and currently or at the time of death drawing compensation for such disability; Class II: the veteran parent is rated by the VA as much as 20 but less than 100% disabled due to wartime service, or was awarded a Purple Heart medal for wounds received, and currently or at the time of death drawing compensation for such disability; Class III: the veteran parent is currently or was at the time of death receiving a VA pension for total and permanent disability, or the veteran parent is deceased but does not qualify under any other provisions, or the veteran parent served in a combat zone or waters adjacent to a combat zone and received a campaign badge or medal but does not qualify under any other provisions; Class IV: the veteran parent was a prisoner of war or missing in action. For all classes, the veteran parent must have been a legal resident of North Carolina at the time of entrance into the armed forces or the child must have been born in North Carolina and lived in the state continuously since birth.

**Financial data:** Students in Classes I-A, II, III, and IV receive $4,500 per academic year if they attend a private college or junior college; if attending a public postsecondary institution, they receive free tuition, a room allowance, a board allowance, and exemption from certain mandatory fees. Students in Class I-B receive $1,500 per academic year if they attend a private college or junior college; if attending a public postsecondary institution, they receive free tuition and exemption from certain mandatory fees.

**Duration:** 4 academic years.

**Number awarded:** An unlimited number of awards are made under Classes I-A, I-B, and IV. Classes II and III are limited to 100 awards each year in each class.

**Deadline:** April of each year.

---

### 856 NORTH CAROLINA STATE CONTRACTUAL SCHOLARSHIP FUND PROGRAM

North Carolina State Education Assistance Authority
Attn: Scholarship and Grant Services
10 T.W. Alexander Drive
P.O. Box 14103
Research Triangle Park, NC 27709-4103
Phone: (919) 549-8614; (800) 700-1775; Fax: (919) 549-8481;
Email: information@ncseaa.edu
Web: www.ncseaa.edu

**Summary:** To provide financial assistance for education at private colleges and universities to students in North Carolina with financial need.

**Eligibility:** Open to North Carolina residents who are enrolled as full-time or part-time undergraduate students at approved North Carolina private colleges and universities. Students enrolled in a program of study in theology, divinity, religious education, or any other program of study designed primarily for career preparation in a religious vocation are not eligible.

**Financial data:** Stipends range up to $1,100 per year, depending on the need of the recipient and the availability of funds.

**Duration:** 1 year.

**Number awarded:** Varies each year; recently, a total of 13,415 students were receiving $33,793,025 through this program.

---

### 857 NORTH DAKOTA EDUCATIONAL ASSISTANCE FOR DEPENDENTS OF VETERANS

Department of Veterans Affairs
1411 32nd Street South
P.O. Box 9003
Fargo, ND 58106-9003
Phone: (701) 239-7165; (866) 634-8387; Fax: (701) 239-7166
Web: www.state.nd.us/veterans/benefits/waiver.html

**Summary:** To provide financial assistance for college to the spouses, widow(er)s, and children of disabled and other North Dakota veterans and military personnel.

**Eligibility:** Open to the spouses, widow(er)s, and dependent children of veterans who are totally disabled as a result of service-connected causes, or who were killed in action, or who have died as a result of wounds or service-connected disabilities, or who were identified as prisoners of war or missing in action. Veteran parents must have been born in and lived in North Dakota until entrance into the armed forces (or must have resided in the state for at least 6 months prior to entrance into military service) and must have served during wartime.

**Financial data:** Eligible dependents receive free tuition and are exempt from fees at any state-supported institution of higher education, technical school, or vocational school in North Dakota.

**Duration:** Up to 36 months or 8 academic semesters.

**Number awarded:** Varies each year.

---

### 858 NORTH DAKOTA FEE WAIVER FOR SURVIVORS OF DECEASED FIRE FIGHTERS AND PEACE OFFICERS

North Dakota University System, Attn: Director of Financial Aid
State Capitol, Tenth Floor
600 East Boulevard Avenue, Department 215
Bismarck, ND 58505-0230
Phone: (701) 328-4114; Fax: (701) 328-2961;
Email: peggy_wipf@ndus.nodak.edu
Web: www.ndus.nodak.edu

**Summary:** To waive tuition and fees for survivors of deceased fire fighters and peace officers at public institutions in North Dakota.

**Eligibility:** Open to residents of North Dakota who are the survivors of fire fighters and peace officers who died as a direct result of injuries received in the performance of official duties. Applicants must be attending or planning to attend a public college or university in North Dakota.

**Financial data:** Qualified students are entitled to a waiver of all tuition and fees (except fees charged to retire outstanding bonds).

**Duration:** 1 academic year; renewable.

**Number awarded:** Varies each year.

---

### 859 NORTH DAKOTA SCHOLARS PROGRAM

North Dakota University System, Attn: Director of Financial Aid
State Capitol, Tenth Floor
600 East Boulevard Avenue, Department 215
Bismarck, ND 58505-0230
Phone: (701) 328-4114; Fax: (701) 328-2961;
Email: peggy_wipf@ndus.nodak.edu
Web: www.ndus.nodak.edu

**Summary:** To provide financial assistance to outstanding high school seniors in North Dakota who are interested in attending college in the state.

**Eligibility:** Open to seniors at high schools in North Dakota who took the ACT test in their junior year and scored in the upper 5th percentile of all North Dakota ACT test takers. Applicants must be interested in attending a college or university in North Dakota.

**Financial data:** Students who attend a public or tribal college receive full payment of tuition. Students who attend a private institution in North Dakota receive a stipend equivalent to tuition at North Dakota State University or the University of North Dakota.

**Duration:** 1 academic year; renewable up to 3 additional years, if the recipient maintains a cumulative GPA of 3.5 or higher.

**Number awarded:** 25 to 30 each year.

---

### 860 NORTH DAKOTA VETERANS DEPENDENTS FEE WAIVER

North Dakota University System, Attn: Director of Financial Aid
State Capitol, Tenth Floor
600 East Boulevard Avenue, Department 215
Bismarck, ND 58505-0230
Phone: (701) 328-4114; Fax: (701) 328-2961;
Email: peggy_wipf@ndus.nodak.edu
Web: www.ndus.nodak.edu

**Summary:** To waive tuition and fees for dependents of deceased or other veterans at public institutions in North Dakota.

**Eligibility:** Open to dependents of veterans who were North Dakota residents when they entered the armed forces and died of service-related causes, were killed in action, were prisoners of war, or were declared missing in action. Applicants must be attending or planning to attend a public college or university in North Dakota.

**Financial data:** Qualified students are entitled to a waiver of all tuition and fees (except fees charged to retire outstanding bonds) at public institutions in North Dakota.

**Duration:** 1 academic year; renewable.

**Number awarded:** Varies each year.

---

### 861 NORTH DAKOTA WOMEN'S OPPORTUNITY SCHOLARSHIP FUND

North Dakota Council on Abused Women's Services
418 East Rosser, Suite 320
Bismarck, ND 58501-4046
Phone: (701) 255-6240; (888) 255-6240; Fax: (701) 255-1904
Web: www.ndcaws.org/projects/scholarship/scholarship.asp

**Summary:** To provide financial assistance to women in North Dakota who are interested in attending a college or university in the state.

**Eligibility:** Open to women residents of North Dakota who plan to enroll as a full-time student at a college, university, or certification program in the state. Applicants must be able to demonstrate income lower than established financial guidelines (currently less than $11,638 for a single person, rising to $39,463 for a family of 8). Along with their application, they must submit an essay of 500 to 1,000 words on their motivation for attending college and their plans for the future. Priority is given to 1) first-time students and current students in special circumstances that may prevent them from completing a pending degree or program; and 2) applicants who may not be eligible for sources of funding normally available to low-income applicants.

**Financial data:** A stipend is awarded (amount not specified).
**Duration:** 1 year; may be renewed.
**Number awarded:** Varies each year.
**Deadline:** June of each year.

## 862 NORTHEASTERN REGION KOREAN AMERICAN SCHOLARSHIPS

Korean American Scholarship Foundation
NorthEastern Region
c/o William Kim, Scholarship Committee Chair
51 West Overlook
Port Washington, NY 11050
Phone: (516) 883-1142; Fax: (516) 883-1964; Email: wkim@alson.com
Web: www.kasf.org/home/regional/northeastern/northeastern.html
**Summary:** To provide financial assistance to Korean American undergraduate and graduate students who attend school in the northeastern states.
**Eligibility:** Open to Korean American students who are currently enrolled in a college or university in a northeastern state as a full-time undergraduate or graduate student. Applicants may reside anywhere in the United States as long as they attend school in the northeastern region: Connecticut, Maine, Massachusetts, New Hampshire, New Jersey, New York, Rhode Island, and Vermont. Selection is based on academic achievement, school activities, community service, and financial need.
**Financial data:** Stipends range from $1,000 to $2,000.
**Duration:** 1 year; renewable.
**Number awarded:** Varies each year; recently, 60 of these scholarships were awarded
**Deadline:** June of each year.

## 863 NOVO NORDISK DONNELLY AWARDS

World Team Tennis, Inc., Attn: Billie Jean King WTT Charities
1776 Broadway, Suite 600
New York, NY 10019
Phone: (212) 586-3444; Fax: (212) 586-6277
Web: www.wtt.com/charities/donnelly.asp
**Summary:** To recognize and reward young tennis players who have diabetes.
**Eligibility:** Open to scholar/athletes between 14 and 21 years of age who play tennis competitively either on a school team or as a ranked tournament player and have type I diabetes. Applicants must submit a 500-word essay on the significance of diabetes in their lives. Selection is based on values, commitment, sportsmanship, community involvement, and financial need.
**Financial data:** The award is $5,000; funds may be used for education, tennis development, and/or medical care.
**Duration:** The nonrenewable awards are presented annually.
**Number awarded:** 2 each year.
**Deadline:** April of each year.

## 864 NPC FOUNDATION REGIONAL SCHOLARSHIPS

National Panhellenic Conference, Attn: NPC Foundation
8777 Purdue Road, Suite 117
Indianapolis, IN 46268
Phone: (317) 872-3185; Fax: (317) 872-3192;
Email: npccentral@npcwomen.org
Web: www.npcwomen.org/foundation/f_scholarships.php
**Summary:** To provide financial assistance to undergraduate women who are members of Greek-letter societies.
**Eligibility:** Open to Greek-affiliated women at colleges and universities in the United States. Applicants must provide information on their university committees, activities, and honors received; Panhellenic offices, committees, and honors received; chapter offices, committees, and honors received; and financial need. Scholarships are presented to students in each of 4 regions of the country.
**Financial data:** The stipend is $1,000.
**Duration:** 1 year.
**Number awarded:** 5 each year.
**Deadline:** January of each year.

## 865 NSCC BOARD OF DIRECTORS SCHOLARSHIP FUND

Naval Sea Cadet Corps, Attn: Executive Director
2300 Wilson Boulevard
Arlington, VA 22201-3308
Phone: (703) 243-6910; Fax: (703) 243-3985
Web: www.seacadets.org
**Summary:** To provide financial assistance to Naval Sea Cadet Corps cadets and former cadets who are interested in continuing their education at an accredited 4-year college/university.
**Eligibility:** Open to cadets and former cadets who are interested in continuing their education at an accredited 4-year college or university. They must have been a member of the corps for at least 2 years, have a minimum rating of NSCC E-3, be recommended by their commanding officer or other official, have earned at least a 3.0 GPA, and have been accepted by an accredited college or university. Applicants may submit financial need statements. All other factors being equal, these statements may be considered in determining award recipients. Applicants who have received full scholarships from other sources (e.g., ROTC) will be considered for this award only if there are no other qualified applicants.
**Financial data:** The stipend is $1,500.
**Duration:** 1 year.
**Number awarded:** 1 each year.
**Deadline:** May of each year.

## 866 NSCC NAMED SCHOLARSHIP PROGRAM

Naval Sea Cadet Corps, Attn: Executive Director
2300 Wilson Boulevard
Arlington, VA 22201-3308
Phone: (703) 243-6910; Fax: (703) 243-3985
Web: www.seacadets.org
**Summary:** To provide financial assistance to Naval Sea Cadet Corps cadets and former cadets who are interested in continuing their education at an accredited 4-year college/university.
**Eligibility:** Open to cadets and former cadets who are interested in continuing their education at an accredited 4-year college or university. They must have been a member of the corps for at least 2 years, have a minimum rating of NSCC E-3, be recommended by their commanding officer or other official, have earned at least a 3.0 GPA, and have been accepted by an accredited college or university. Applicants may submit financial need statements. All other factors being equal, these statements may be considered in determining award recipients. Applicants who have received full scholarships from other sources (e.g., ROTC) will be considered for this award only if there are no other qualified applicants.
**Financial data:** Stipends depend on the availability of funds; recently, they ranged up to $2,000.
**Duration:** 1 year.
**Number awarded:** Varies each year.
**Deadline:** May of each year.

## 867 NSCC SCHOLARSHIP FUND

Naval Sea Cadet Corps, Attn: Executive Director
2300 Wilson Boulevard
Arlington, VA 22201-3308
Phone: (703) 243-6910; Fax: (703) 243-3985
Web: www.seacadets.org
**Summary:** To provide financial assistance to Naval Sea Cadet Corps cadets and former cadets who are interested in continuing their education at an accredited 4-year college/university.
**Eligibility:** Open to cadets and former cadets who are interested in continuing their education at an accredited 4-year college or university. They must have been a member of the corps for at least 2 years, have a minimum rating of NSCC E-3, be recommended by their commanding officer or other official, have earned at least a 3.0 GPA, and have been accepted by an accredited college or university. Applicants may submit financial need statements. All other factors being equal, these statements may be considered in determining award recipients. Applicants who have received full scholarships from other sources (e.g., ROTC) will be considered for this award only if there are no other qualified applicants.
**Financial data:** The stipend is $1,000.
**Duration:** 1 year.
**Number awarded:** 2 each year.
**Deadline:** May of each year.

### 868 OCA/AVON SCHOLARSHIPS

Organization of Chinese Americans, Inc.
1001 Connecticut Avenue, N.W., Suite 601
Washington, DC 20036
Phone: (202) 223-5500; Fax: (202) 296-0540; Email: oca@ocanatl.org
Web: www.ocanatl.org
**Summary:** To provide financial assistance to Asian Pacific American women entering their first year at a 2-year or 4-year college.
**Eligibility:** Open to Asian Pacific American women (including east Asian Americans, Filipino Americans, Pacific Islander Americans, south Asian Americans, and southeast Asian Americans) who are entering their first year of college. Applicants must be U.S. citizens or permanent residents who have earned a GPA of 3.0 or higher in high school. Selection is based on academic achievement, community service, and financial need.
**Financial data:** The stipend is $2,000.
**Duration:** 1 year.
**Number awarded:** 15 each year.
**Deadline:** April of each year.

### 869 OCA/AXA ACHIEVEMENT SCHOLARSHIPS

Organization of Chinese Americans, Inc.
1001 Connecticut Avenue, N.W., Suite 601
Washington, DC 20036
Phone: (202) 223-5500; Fax: (202) 296-0540; Email: oca@ocanatl.org
Web: www.ocanatl.org
**Summary:** To provide financial assistance for college to Asian Pacific Americans who are entering their first year of college and can demonstrate academic merit.
**Eligibility:** Open to Asian Pacific American students entering their first year of college, university, or community college in the following fall. Applicants must be able to demonstrate academic achievement, leadership ability, and community service. They must have a cumulative GPA of 3.0 or higher and be a U.S. citizen or permanent resident.
**Financial data:** The stipend is $2,000.
**Duration:** 1 year.
**Number awarded:** 6 each year.
**Deadline:** April of each year.

### 870 OCA/KFC BRANDS NATIONAL ESSAY CONTEST

Organization of Chinese Americans, Inc.
1001 Connecticut Avenue, N.W., Suite 601
Washington, DC 20036
Phone: (202) 223-5500; Fax: (202) 296-0540; Email: oca@ocanatl.org
Web: www.ocanatl.org
**Summary:** To recognize and reward Asian Pacific American high school students who participate in an essay contest.
**Eligibility:** Open to Asian Pacific American students in grades 9 through 12. Applicants must submit an essay, from 800 to 1,000 words, on a topic that changes annually; recently, the topic was "As a leader, what is your vision for building unity within the Asian Pacific American community and how will you play a role?" Selection is based on theme and content (50%), organization and development (20%), grammar and mechanics (20%), and style (10%).
**Financial data:** First prize is $1,000, second prize is $500, and third prize is $300.
**Duration:** The contest is held annually.
**Number awarded:** 3 each year.
**Deadline:** May of each year.

### 871 OCA/SYSCO SCHOLARSHIPS

Organization of Chinese Americans, Inc.
1001 Connecticut Avenue, N.W., Suite 601
Washington, DC 20036
Phone: (202) 223-5500; Fax: (202) 296-0540; Email: oca@ocanatl.org
Web: www.ocanatl.org
**Summary:** To provide financial assistance for college to Asian Pacific Americans who are entering their first year of college and can demonstrate financial need.
**Eligibility:** Open to Asian Pacific American students entering their first year of college, university, or community college in the following fall. Applicants must be able to demonstrate financial need, have a cumulative GPA of 3.0 or higher, and be a U.S. citizen or permanent resident.
**Financial data:** The stipend is $2,000.
**Duration:** 1 year.
**Number awarded:** 6 each year.
**Deadline:** April of each year.

### 872 OCA/VERIZON SCHOLARSHIPS

Organization of Chinese Americans, Inc.
1001 Connecticut Avenue, N.W., Suite 601
Washington, DC 20036
Phone: (202) 223-5500; Fax: (202) 296-0540; Email: oca@ocanatl.org
Web: www.ocanatl.org
**Summary:** To provide financial assistance for college to Asian Pacific Americans who are entering their first year of college and have significant financial need.
**Eligibility:** Open to Asian Pacific American students entering their first year of college, university, or community college in the following fall. Applicants must be able to demonstrate significant financial need, have a cumulative GPA of 3.0 or higher, and be a U.S. citizen or permanent resident.
**Financial data:** The stipend is $2,000.
**Duration:** 1 year.
**Number awarded:** 25 each year.
**Deadline:** April of each year.

### 873 OHIO ACADEMIC SCHOLARSHIP PROGRAM

Ohio Board of Regents, Attn: State Grants and Scholarships
57 East Main Street, Fourth Floor
P.O. Box 182452
Columbus, OH 43218-2452
Phone: (614) 466-7420; (888) 833-1133; Fax: (614) 752-5903;
Email: bmetheney@regents.state.oh.us
Web: www.regents.state.oh.us/sgs/OAS.htm
**Summary:** To provide financial assistance for college to outstanding high school seniors in Ohio.
**Eligibility:** Open to seniors graduating from high schools in Ohio. Applicants must be planning to enroll for full-time undergraduate study at a college or university in Ohio. Selection is based on ACT scores and high school grades. Each high school in the state identifies the top 5 applicants and submits those 5 applications to the Ohio Board of Regents. The top candidate receives an award and the remaining applicants are placed in a statewide pool and chosen on a competitive basis until all the awards have been presented.
**Financial data:** The stipend is $2,205 per year.
**Duration:** Up to 8 semesters or 12 quarters.
**Number awarded:** 1 for each public, private, or vocational high school in Ohio; additional awards are then granted until a total of 1,000 have been presented.
**Deadline:** February of each year.

### 874 OHIO INSTRUCTIONAL GRANT PROGRAM

Ohio Board of Regents, Attn: State Grants and Scholarships
57 East Main Street, Fourth Floor
P.O. Box 182452
Columbus, OH 43218-2452
Phone: (614) 466-7420; (888) 833-1133; Fax: (614) 752-5903;
Email: bmetheney@regents.state.oh.us
Web: www.regents.state.oh.us/sgs/oig.htm
**Summary:** To provide financial assistance for college to students from Ohio.
**Eligibility:** Open to Ohio residents and U.S. citizens who are attending or planning to attend eligible colleges and universities in Ohio or Pennsylvania as full-time undergraduate students. Financial need (family income of $39,000 per year or less) must be demonstrated.
**Financial data:** Awards are based on the need of the recipient and range from $174 to $5,466 per year. They may not exceed tuition costs.
**Duration:** 1 year; may be renewed up to 3 additional years.
**Number awarded:** Varies, depending upon the funds available. Recently, approximately 83,000 students received these grants.
**Deadline:** September of each year.

### 875 OHIO LEGION AUXILIARY DEPARTMENT SCHOLARSHIP

American Legion Auxiliary, Attn: Department of Ohio
1100 Brandywine Boulevard, Building D
P.O. Box 2760
Zanesville, OH 43702-2760
Phone: (740) 452-8245; Fax: (740) 452-2620; Email: ala_pam@rrohio.com
**Summary:** To provide financial assistance for college to the descendants of veterans in Ohio.
**Eligibility:** Open to the children, grandchildren, and great-grandchildren of living or deceased veterans of World War I, World War II, Korea, Vietnam, Lebanon/Grenada, Panama, or Desert Storm. Applicants must be residents of Ohio, seniors at an accredited high school, and sponsored by an American

Legion Auxiliary Unit. Applications must include an original article (up to 500 words) written by the applicant on "What the American Flag Represents to Me." The winner is selected on the basis of character, Americanism, leadership, scholarship, and financial need.

**Financial data:** Awards are $2,000 or $1,500. Funds are paid to the recipient's school.

**Duration:** 1 year.

**Number awarded:** 2 each year: 1 at $2,000 and 1 at $1,500.

**Deadline:** February of each year.

### 876 OHIO PART-TIME STUDENT INSTRUCTIONAL GRANT PROGRAM

Ohio Board of Regents, Attn: State Grants and Scholarships
57 East Main Street, Fourth Floor
P.O. Box 182452
Columbus, OH 43218-2452
Phone: (614) 466-7420; (888) 833-1133; Fax: (614) 752-5903;
Email: bmetheney@regents.state.oh.us
Web: www.regents.state.oh.us/sgs/parttimegrant.htm

**Summary:** To provide financial assistance for part-time undergraduate education to students in Ohio.

**Eligibility:** Open to Ohio residents who are attending or planning to attend public, private, and proprietary colleges and universities in Ohio and take fewer than 12 credit hours per term. Financial need must be demonstrated. Special consideration is given to single heads of household and displaced homemakers. Participating schools select the recipients.

**Financial data:** Participating schools determine the amount of each award, based on guidelines set by the Board of Regents and the need of the recipient. Grants may not exceed the actual cost of attendance.

**Duration:** 1 year; may be renewed up to 3 additional years.

**Number awarded:** Varies each year; recently, 28,349 students received these grants.

**Deadline:** Each participating college or university sets its own deadline.

### 877 OHIO SAFETY OFFICERS COLLEGE MEMORIAL FUND

Ohio Board of Regents, Attn: State Grants and Scholarships
57 East Main Street, Fourth Floor
P.O. Box 182452
Columbus, OH 43218-2452
Phone: (614) 466-7420; (888) 833-1133; Fax: (614) 752-5903;
Email: bmetheney@regents.state.oh.us
Web: www.regents.state.oh.us/sgs/ohiosafetyofficers.htm

**Summary:** To provide financial assistance for the undergraduate education of children of Ohio peace officers and fire fighters killed in the line of duty.

**Eligibility:** Open to Ohio residents whose parent or spouse was a peace officer, fire fighter, or other safety officer killed in the line of duty anywhere in the United States. Applicants must be interested in attending a participating Ohio college or university.

**Financial data:** At Ohio public colleges and universities, the program provides full payment of tuition. At Ohio private colleges and universities, the stipend is equivalent to the average amounts paid to students attending public institutions, currently $3,990 per year.

**Duration:** 1 year; may be renewed up to 3 additional years.

**Number awarded:** Varies each year; recently, 54 students received benefits from this program.

**Deadline:** Application deadlines are established by each participating college and university.

### 878 OHIO WAR ORPHANS SCHOLARSHIP

Ohio Board of Regents, Attn: State Grants and Scholarships
57 East Main Street, Fourth Floor
P.O. Box 182452
Columbus, OH 43218-2452
Phone: (614) 466-7420; (888) 833-1133; Fax: (614) 752-5903;
Email: bmetheney@regents.state.oh.us
Web: www.regents.state.oh.us/sgs/warorphans.htm

**Summary:** To provide financial assistance for college to the children of deceased or disabled Ohio veterans.

**Eligibility:** Open to students between 16 and 21 years of age at the time of application who 1) have been residents of Ohio for the past year or, if the parent was not a resident of Ohio at the time of enlistment, for the year immediately preceding application and any other 4 of the last 10 years; and 2) are enrolled for full-time undergraduate study at an eligible Ohio college or university. At least 1 parent must have been a member of the U.S. armed forces, including the organized Reserves and Ohio National Guard, for a period of 90 days or more (or discharged because of a disability incurred after less than 90 days of service) who served during World War I, World War II, the Korean Conflict, the Vietnam era, or the Persian Gulf War, and who, as a result of that service, either was killed or became at least 60% service-connected disabled. Also eligible are children of veterans who have a permanent and total non-service-connected disability and are receiving disability benefits from the U.S. Department of Veterans Affairs. Children of veteran parents who served in the organized Reserves or Ohio National Guard are also eligible if the parent was killed or became permanently and totally disabled while at a scheduled training assembly (of any duration or length) or active duty for training, pursuant to bona fide orders issued by a competent authority.

**Financial data:** At Ohio public colleges and universities, the program provides full payment of tuition. At Ohio private colleges and universities, the stipend is equivalent to the average amount paid to students attending public institutions, currently $4,710 per year.

**Duration:** 1 year; may be renewed up to 4 additional years.

**Number awarded:** Varies, depending upon the funds available. If sufficient funds are available, all eligible applicants are given a scholarship. Recently, 861 students received benefits from this program.

**Deadline:** June of each year.

### 879 OKLAHOMA BPW FOUNDATION SCHOLARSHIPS

Oklahoma Business and Professional Women
Attn: OK/BPW State Foundation
P.O. Box 160
Maud, OK 74854-0160
Phone: (405) 374-2866; Fax: (405) 374-2316; Email: askkathy@okbpw.org
Web: www.okbpw.org/found.htm

**Summary:** To provide financial assistance for college to women, especially nontraditional students, in Oklahoma.

**Eligibility:** Open to women who are attending a college, university, or technical school in Oklahoma. Special consideration is given to nontraditional students. Selection is based on financial need, a description of career plans and goals, academics, and employment and volunteer record.

**Financial data:** Stipends are $1,000, $750, or $500.

**Duration:** 1 year.

**Number awarded:** Varies each year. Recently, 8 of these scholarships were awarded: 3 at $1,000, 3 at $750, and 2 at $500.

### 880 OKLAHOMA HIGHER LEARNING ACCESS PROGRAM

Oklahoma State Regents for Higher Education
Attn: Director of Scholarship and Grant Programs
655 Research Parkway, Suite 200
P.O. Box 108850
Oklahoma City, OK 73101-8850
Phone: (405) 225-9239; (800) 858-1840; Fax: (405) 225-9230;
Email: ohlapinfo@osrhe.edu
Web: www.okpromise.org

**Summary:** To provide financial assistance to Oklahoma residents who complete a specified high school curriculum.

**Eligibility:** Open to students who sign up during their 8th, 9th, or 10th grade year at an Oklahoma high school. If they complete a specified high school curriculum and demonstrate a commitment to academic success, they receive assistance when they attend college. Applicants must 1) demonstrate financial need (currently defined as a family income less than $50,000); 2) achieve a GPA of 2.5 or higher both cumulatively and in the required curriculum; 3) fulfill an agreement to attend school, do homework regularly, refrain from substance abuse and criminal or delinquent acts, and have school work and records reviewed by mentors; and 4) be admitted as a regular entering freshman at an Oklahoma college, university, or area vocational technical school.

**Financial data:** Students enrolled at an institution in the Oklahoma State System of Higher Education receive resident tuition, paid to the institution on their behalf. Students enrolled at an accredited private institution have tuition paid at an amount equivalent to the resident tuition at a comparable institution of the state system. Students enrolled in eligible vocational/technical programs have their tuition paid. No provision is made for other educational expenses, such as books, supplies, room, board, or other special fees.

**Duration:** Up to 5 years or until completion of a bachelor's degree, whichever occurs first. The award must be taken up within 3 years of high school graduation.

**Number awarded:** Varies each year.

**Deadline:** Applications must be submitted by June following completion of the student's 8th, 9th, or 10th grade year.

## 881 OKLAHOMA INDEPENDENT LIVING ACT TUITION WAIVERS

Oklahoma State Regents for Higher Education
Attn: Director of Scholarship and Grant Programs
655 Research Parkway, Suite 200
P.O. Box 108850
Oklahoma City, OK 73101-8850
Phone: (405) 225-9239; (800) 858-1840; Fax: (405) 225-9230;
Email: studentinfo@osrhe.edu
Web: www.okhighered.org/student-center/financial-aid/dhs.shtml

**Summary:** To provide financial assistance for college to residents in Oklahoma who have been in a foster care program of the Department of Human Services (DHS).

**Eligibility:** Open to residents of Oklahoma who graduated within the previous 3 years from an accredited high school in the state or from a high school bordering Oklahoma as approved by the State Board of Education, or who have completed the GED requirements. Applicants must be younger than 21 years of age and have been in DHS custody for at least 9 months between 16 and 18 years of age. They must currently be enrolled at an Oklahoma public college or university or in certain programs at technology centers.

**Financial data:** Under this program, all resident tuition fees are waived.

**Duration:** 1 year; may be renewed until the student reaches 26 years of age or completes a baccalaureate degree or program certificate, whichever comes first.

**Number awarded:** Varies each year.

## 882 OKLAHOMA STATE REGENTS ACADEMIC SCHOLARS PROGRAM

Oklahoma State Regents for Higher Education
Attn: Director of Scholarship and Grant Programs
655 Research Parkway, Suite 200
P.O. Box 108850
Oklahoma City, OK 73101-8850
Phone: (405) 225-9239; (800) 858-1840; Fax: (405) 225-9230;
Email: aharris@osrhe.edu
Web: www.okhighered.org/academic-scholars

**Summary:** To provide financial assistance to outstanding high school seniors and recent graduates who wish to attend a college or university in Oklahoma.

**Eligibility:** Open to high school seniors who have 5 ways to qualify: 1) residents of Oklahoma whose ACT or SAT score is at least at the 99.5 percentile level and whose GPA and/or class rank are considered exceptional; 2) residents of any state designated as a National Merit Scholar; 3) residents of any state designated as a National Merit Scholar Finalist; 4) residents of any state designated as a Presidential Scholar; or 5) institutional nominees, from Oklahoma's comprehensive universities (University of Oklahoma, University of Tulsa, Oklahoma State University) who have either an ACT of at least 32 (or SAT equivalent) or a GPA of 3.9 or higher and a ranking in the top 2% of their class, from Oklahoma's regional universities who have either an ACT of at least 30 (or SAT equivalent) or a GPA of 3.8 or higher and a ranking in the top 4% of their class, or from Oklahoma's 2-year colleges who have either an ACT of at least 29 (or SAT equivalent) or a GPA of 3.7 or higher and a ranking in the top 5% of their class.

**Financial data:** The program provides funding for tuition, fees, room and board, and textbooks. The exact amount of funding awarded varies each year; for "automatic qualifiers" (the first 4 ways to qualify), it is currently $5,500 per year for students at the 3 comprehensive universities, $4,000 per year for students at other 4-year public or private colleges or universities in Oklahoma, or $3,500 per year for students at Oklahoma 2-year colleges. For institutional nominees, the current rate is $2,800 per year at the 3 comprehensive universities, $2,000 per year at other 4-year institutions, or $1,800 at 2-year colleges. Students who enroll at public universities and colleges are also eligible for a tuition waiver.

**Duration:** Up to 4 years of undergraduate study, as long as the recipient remains a full-time student with a GPA of 3.25 or higher.

**Number awarded:** Varies each year; recently, 620 entering freshmen received this support (including 382 "automatic qualifiers" and 238 institutional nominees. A total of 2,078 students were enrolled in the program.

**Deadline:** September of each year.

## 883 OKLAHOMA TUITION AID GRANT PROGRAM

Oklahoma State Regents for Higher Education
655 Research Parkway, Suite 200
P.O. Box 108850
Oklahoma City, OK 73101-8850
Phone: (405) 225-9456; (877) 662-6231; Fax: (405) 225-9476;
Email: otaginfo@otag.org
Web: www.okhighered.org/student-center/financial-aid/otag.shtml

**Summary:** To provide financial assistance for college to Oklahoma residents who demonstrate financial need.

**Eligibility:** Open to residents of Oklahoma who are attending or planning to attend public or private institutions in Oklahoma. To apply, they must complete the Free Application for Federal Student Aid and demonstrate financial need.

**Financial data:** At public colleges, universities, and technology centers, the annual stipend is $1,000 or 75% of enrollment costs, whichever is less. At private colleges and universities, the annual stipend is $1,300 or 75% of enrollment costs, whichever is less.

**Duration:** 1 year; renewable.

**Number awarded:** Varies each year.

**Deadline:** Applications are accepted through June of each year, but students should apply as early after the beginning of January as possible and by the end of April for best consideration.

## 884 OKLAHOMA TUITION EQUALIZATION GRANT PROGRAM

Oklahoma State Regents for Higher Education
Attn: Director of Scholarship and Grant Programs
655 Research Parkway, Suite 200
P.O. Box 108850
Oklahoma City, OK 73101-8850
Phone: (405) 225-9456; (877) 662-6231; Fax: (405) 225-9230;
Email: studentinfo@osrhe.edu
Web: www.okhighered.org/student-center/financial-aid/oteg.shtml

**Summary:** To provide financial assistance to Oklahoma residents who meet financial need requirements and are entering college as first-time freshmen.

**Eligibility:** Open to residents of Oklahoma entering a nonprofit private or independent institution of higher education in the state as a full-time undergraduate for the first time. Applicants must have a family income of $50,000 or less.

**Financial data:** The stipend is $2,000 per year.

**Duration:** 1 year.

**Number awarded:** Varies each year.

## 885 OKLAHOMA TUITION WAIVER FOR DEPENDENTS OF PEACE OFFICERS AND FIRE FIGHTERS

Oklahoma State Regents for Higher Education
Attn: Director of Scholarship and Grant Programs
655 Research Parkway, Suite 200
P.O. Box 108850
Oklahoma City, OK 73101-8850
Phone: (405) 225-9239; (800) 858-1840; Fax: (405) 225-9230;
Email: studentinfo@osrhe.edu
Web: www.okhighered.org

**Summary:** To provide financial assistance for college to the children of deceased Oklahoma peace officers and fire fighters.

**Eligibility:** Open to the children of Oklahoma peace officers or fire fighters who lost their lives in the line of duty. Selection is based on financial need, academic aptitude and achievement, student activity participation, academic level, and academic discipline or field of study.

**Financial data:** Eligible applicants are entitled to receive free tuition at any Oklahoma state-supported postsecondary educational, technical, or vocational school.

**Duration:** Assistance continues for 5 years or until receipt of a bachelor's degree, whichever occurs first.

**Number awarded:** Varies each year.

## 886 OKLAHOMA TUITION WAIVER FOR PRISONERS OF WAR, PERSONS MISSING IN ACTION, AND DEPENDENTS

Oklahoma State Regents for Higher Education
Attn: Director of Scholarship and Grant Programs
655 Research Parkway, Suite 200
P.O. Box 108850
Oklahoma City, OK 73101-8850
Phone: (405) 225-9239; (800) 858-1840; Fax: (405) 225-9230;
Email: studentinfo@osrhe.edu
Web: www.okhighered.org

**Summary:** To provide financial assistance for college to Oklahoma residents (or their dependents) who were declared prisoners of war or missing in action.

**Eligibility:** Open to veterans who were declared prisoners of war or missing in action after January 1, 1960 and were residents of Oklahoma at the time of entrance into the armed forces or when declared POW/MIA. Dependent children of those veterans are also eligible as long as they are under 24 years of age. Selection is based on financial need, academic aptitude and achievement, student activity participation, academic level, and academic discipline or field of study

**Financial data:** Eligible applicants are entitled to receive free tuition at any Oklahoma state-supported postsecondary educational, technical, or vocational school.

**Duration:** Assistance continues for 5 years or until receipt of a bachelor's degree, whichever occurs first.

**Number awarded:** Varies each year.

## 887 OMAHA VOLUNTEERS FOR HANDICAPPED CHILDREN SCHOLARSHIPS

Omaha Volunteers for Handicapped Children
c/o Lois Carlson
2010 Country Club Avenue
Omaha, NE 68104
Phone: (402) 553-0378

**Summary:** To provide financial assistance for college to Nebraska residents who have a physical disability or are preparing for a career related to people with orthopedic impairments or physical disabilities.

**Eligibility:** Open to residents of Nebraska who are U.S. citizens. First priority applicants must have an orthopedic impairment or physical disability and be 1) high school seniors with a GPA of 2.25 or higher and accepted into the school of their choice or 2) college students making satisfactory progress toward graduation. Second priority applicants must be enrolled in the college of their choice and preparing for a teaching or health-related career of service to people with orthopedic impairments or physical disabilities. All applicants must submit a 250-word essay on their future goals and need for the scholarship.

**Financial data:** The stipend is $1,000 per year.

**Duration:** 1 year; may be renewed.

**Number awarded:** 5 to 10 each year.

**Deadline:** July of each year.

## 888 ONE PUKA PUKA SCHOLARSHIP

100th Infantry Battalion Veterans Club, Attn: Scholarship Committee
520 Kamoku Street
Honolulu, HI 96826
Phone: (808) 732-5216; Email: daisyy@hgca.net
Web: emedia.leeward.hawaii.edu/mnakano

**Summary:** To provide financial assistance for college to family members of veterans who served in the 100th Infantry Battalion of World War II.

**Eligibility:** Open to direct family members and descendants of 100th Infantry Battalion World War II veterans. Applicants must be high school seniors planning to attend an institution of higher learning or full-time undergraduate students at community colleges, vocational/trade schools, 4-year colleges, and universities. Along with their application, they must submit a 4-page essay that reviews the experience of Nisei men who fought in the racially-segregated 100th Infantry Battalion during World War II and asks, in the light of that experience and the meaning of democracy, if American troops should continue fighting in Iraq. Selection is based on that essay, academic achievement, extracurricular activities, and community service. Financial need is not considered.

**Financial data:** The stipend is $2,000.

**Duration:** 1 year; nonrenewable.

**Number awarded:** 1 each year.

**Deadline:** April of each year.

## 889 ONE-YEAR SBAA EDUCATIONAL SCHOLARSHIP FUND

Spina Bifida Association of America, Attn: Scholarship Committee
4590 MacArthur Boulevard, N.W., Suite 250
Washington, DC 20007-4226
Phone: (202) 944-3285, ext. 19; (800) 621-3141; Fax: (202) 944-3295;
Email: sbaa@sbaa.org
Web: www.sbaa.org

**Summary:** To provide financial assistance for college or graduate school to members of the Spina Bifida Association of America (SBAA).

**Eligibility:** Open to persons of any age born with spina bifida who are current members of the association. Applicants must 1) be a high school graduate or possess a GED, and 2) be enrolled in or accepted by a junior college, 4-year college, graduate school, or approved trade, vocational, or business school. Selection is based on academic record, other efforts shown in school, financial need, work history, community service, leadership, and commitment to personal goals.

**Financial data:** The stipend is $2,000.

**Duration:** 1 year.

**Number awarded:** Up to 5 each year.

**Deadline:** February of each year.

## 890 OPPORTUNITIES FOR THE BLIND GRANTS

Opportunities for the Blind, Inc., Attn: Grant Committee
P.O. Box 98
Fairplay, MD 21733
Phone: (240) 420-6500; Email: OppBlind@yahoo.com
Web: www.opportunitiesfortheblind.org

**Summary:** To provide funding to blind people interested in improving their employment situation.

**Eligibility:** Open to legally blind U.S. citizens. Applicants must be seeking funding for the following categories: scholarships and training, job-related service, special equipment, or self-employment projects. Preference is given to applicants who are preparing for careers in fields where the blind are not typically found.

**Financial data:** Grants normally range from $3,000 to $5,000, and may go as high as $10,000.

**Duration:** This is a 1-time award.

**Number awarded:** Varies each year.

**Deadline:** February, May, August, or October of each year.

## 891 OPTIMIST INTERNATIONAL COMMUNICATION CONTEST FOR THE DEAF AND HARD OF HEARING

Optimist International, Attn: Programs Department
4494 Lindell Boulevard
St. Louis, MO 63108
Phone: (314) 371-6000; (800) 500-8130, ext. 224; Fax: (314) 371-6006;
Email: programs@optimist.org
Web: www.optimist.org

**Summary:** To recognize and reward outstanding presentations made by hearing impaired high school students.

**Eligibility:** Open to young people up to and including grade 12 in the United States and Canada, to CEGEP in Quebec, and to grade 13 in the Caribbean. Applicants must be identified by a qualified audiologist as deaf or hard of hearing with a hearing loss of 40 decibels or more. They are invited to make a presentation (using oral communication, sign language, or a combination of both) from 4 to 5 minutes on a topic that changes annually; a recent topic was "My Future is Bright because..." Competition is first conducted at the level of individual clubs, with winners advancing to zone and then district competitions. Selection is based on material organization (40 points), delivery and presentation (30 points), and overall effectiveness (30 points).

**Financial data:** Each district winner receives a $1,500 college scholarship, payable to an educational institution of the recipient's choice, subject to the approval of Optimist International.

**Duration:** The competition is held annually.

**Number awarded:** Nearly 300 Optimist International clubs participate in this program each year. Each participating district offers 1 scholarship; some districts may offer a second award with separate competitions for signing and oral competitors, or for male and female entrants.

**Deadline:** Each club sets its own deadline. The district deadline is the end of September of each year.

## 892 OPTIMIST INTERNATIONAL ESSAY CONTEST

Optimist International, Attn: Programs Department
4494 Lindell Boulevard
St. Louis, MO 63108
Phone: (314) 371-6000; (800) 500-8130, ext. 235; Fax: (314) 371-6009;
Email: programs@optimist.org
Web: www.optimist.org

**Summary:** To recognize and reward, with college scholarships, outstanding essays by high school students on a topic that changes annually.

**Eligibility:** Open to high school students in the United States, the Caribbean, or Canada who are younger than 19 years of age. Applicants are invited to write an essay of 400 to 500 words on a topic that changes each year; a recent topic was

"I'm Unique because..." They compete on the local club, district, and national/international levels. Essays may be written in the official language of the area where the club is located (English, Spanish, or French). Selection is based on material organization (40 points); vocabulary and style (30 points); grammar, punctuation, and spelling (20 points); neatness (5 points); and adherence to contest rules (5 points).

**Financial data:** The international first-place winner receives $5,000, second $3,000, and third $2,000. Funds are to be used to pay college costs. District winners are awarded a $650 college scholarship.

**Duration:** The competition is held annually.

**Number awarded:** 3 international winners are selected each year. A total of $44,000 in scholarships is awarded annually.

**Deadline:** Essays must be submitted to local clubs by the end of February of each year. The district deadline is in April.

### 893 OPTIMIST INTERNATIONAL ORATORICAL CONTEST

Optimist International, Attn: Programs Department
4494 Lindell Boulevard
St. Louis, MO 63108
Phone: (314) 371-6000; (800) 500-8130, ext. 235; Fax: (314) 371-6009;
Email: programs@optimist.org
Web: www.optimist.org

**Summary:** To recognize and reward outstanding orators at the high school or younger level.

**Eligibility:** Open to all students in public, private, or parochial elementary, junior high, and senior high schools in the United States, Canada, or the Caribbean who are under 16 years of age. All contestants must prepare their own orations of 4 to 5 minutes, but they may receive advice and make minor changes or improvements in the oration at any time. Each year a different subject is selected for the orations; a recent topic was "My Future in Bright because..." The orations may be delivered in a language other than English if that language is an official language of the country in which the sponsoring club is located. Selection is based on poise (20 points), content of speech (35 points), delivery and presentation (35 points), and overall effectiveness (10 points). Competition is first conducted at the level of individual clubs, with winners advancing to zone and then district competitions. At the discretion of the district, boys may compete against boys and girls against girls in separate contests.

**Financial data:** Each district awards either 2 scholarships of $1,500 (1 for a boy and 1 for a girl) or (if the district chooses to have a combined gender contest) a first-place scholarship of $1,500, a second-place scholarship of $1,000, and a third-place scholarship of $500.

**Duration:** The competition is held annually.

**Number awarded:** Each year, more than $150,000 is awarded in scholarships.

**Deadline:** Each local club sets its own deadline. The district deadline is the end of June.

### 894 OREGON CHAFEE EDUCATION AND TRAINING SCHOLARSHIPS

Oregon Student Assistance Commission
Attn: Grants and Scholarships Division
1500 Valley River Drive, Suite 100
Eugene, OR 97401-2146
Phone: (541) 687-7394; (800) 452-8807, ext. 7394; Fax: (541) 687-7414;
Email: awardinfo@mercury.osac.state.or.us
Web: www.osac.state.or.us/chafeeetv.html

**Summary:** To provide financial assistance for college to Oregon residents who are or have been in foster care.

**Eligibility:** Open to residents of Oregon who either currently are in foster care or have been in foster care for at least 180 days after their 14th birthday. Foster care placement must have been with Oregon's Department of Human Services or 1 of the 9 federally-recognized tribes in the state. Applicants must be younger than 21 years of age. Along with their application, they must submit essays of 250 to 350 words on 1) their most significant challenge or accomplishment and its value to their life, and 2) their long-range goals and why they need to achieve them.

**Financial data:** The stipend is $5,000.

**Duration:** 1 year; may be renewed until recipient reaches 23 years of age.

**Number awarded:** 1 or more each year.

**Deadline:** February of each year.

### 895 OREGON DECEASED OR DISABLED PUBLIC SAFETY OFFICER GRANT PROGRAM

Oregon Student Assistance Commission

Attn: Grants and Scholarships Division
1500 Valley River Drive, Suite 100
Eugene, OR 97401-2130
Phone: (541) 687-7466; (800) 452-8807, ext. 7466; Fax: (541) 687-7419;
Email: awardinfo@mercury.osac.state.or.us
Web: www.ossc.state.or.us/disabled_officers.html

**Summary:** To provide financial assistance for college to the children of disabled or deceased Oregon peace officers.

**Eligibility:** Open to the natural, adopted, or stepchildren of Oregon public safety officers (fire fighters, state fire marshal, chief deputy fire marshal, deputy state fire marshals, police chiefs, police officers, sheriffs, deputy sheriffs, county adult parole and probation officers, correction officers, and investigators of the Criminal Justice Division of the Department of Justice) who, in the line of duty, were killed or disabled. Applicants must be enrolled or planning to enroll as a full-time undergraduate student at a public or private college or university in Oregon. Children of deceased officers are also eligible for graduate study. Financial need must be demonstrated.

**Financial data:** At a public 2- or 4-year college or university, the amount of the award is equal to the cost of tuition and fees. At an eligible private college, the award amount is equal to the cost of tuition and fees at the University of Oregon.

**Duration:** 1 year; may be renewed for up to 3 additional years of undergraduate study, if the student maintains satisfactory academic progress and demonstrates continued financial need. Children of deceased public safety officers may receive support for 12 quarters of graduate study.

**Number awarded:** Varies each year.

### 896 OREGON LEGION AUXILIARY DEPARTMENT SCHOLARSHIPS

American Legion Auxiliary, Attn: Department of Oregon
30450 S.W. Parkway Avenue
P.O. Box 1730
Wilsonville, OR 97070-1730
Phone: (503) 682-3162; Fax: (503) 685-5008; Email: pcalhoun@pcez.com

**Summary:** To provide financial assistance for college to the dependents of Oregon veterans.

**Eligibility:** Open to Oregon residents who are children or wives of disabled veterans or widows of veterans. Applicants must be interested in obtaining education beyond the high school level. Selection is based on ability, aptitude, character, seriousness of purpose, and financial need.

**Financial data:** The stipend is $1,000. It must be used for college, university, business school, vocational school, or any other accredited postsecondary school in the state of Oregon.

**Duration:** The awards are offered each year. They are nonrenewable.

**Number awarded:** 3 each year; 1 of these is to be used for vocational or business school.

**Deadline:** March of each year.

### 897 OREGON LEGION AUXILIARY NATIONAL PRESIDENT'S SCHOLARSHIP

American Legion Auxiliary
Attn: Department of Oregon
30450 S.W. Parkway Avenue
P.O. Box 1730
Wilsonville, OR 97070-1730
Phone: (503) 682-3162; Fax: (503) 685-5008; Email: pcalhoun@pcez.com

**Summary:** To provide financial assistance for college to the children of war veterans in Oregon.

**Eligibility:** Open to Oregon residents who are the children of veterans who served in World War I, World War II, Korea, Vietnam, Grenada, Lebanon, Panama, or the Persian Gulf. They must be high school seniors or graduates who have not yet attended an institution of higher learning. Selection is based on character, Americanism, leadership, scholarship, and financial need. The winner then competes for the American Legion Auxiliary National President's Scholarship. If the Oregon winner is not awarded a national scholarship, then he or she receives the first-place award and the second winner receives the second-place award; if the Oregon winner is also a national winner, then the second-place winner in Oregon receives the first-place award and the alternate receives the second-place award.

**Financial data:** The first-place award is $2,000 and the second-place award is $1,500.

**Duration:** The awards are offered each year. They are nonrenewable.

**Number awarded:** 2 each year.

**Deadline:** March of each year.

## 898 OREGON OCCUPATIONAL SAFETY AND HEALTH DIVISION WORKERS MEMORIAL SCHOLARSHIPS

Oregon Student Assistance Commission
Attn: Grants and Scholarships Division
1500 Valley River Drive, Suite 100
Eugene, OR 97401-2146
Phone: (541) 687-7395; (800) 452-8807, ext. 7395; Fax: (541) 687-7419;
Email: awardinfo@mercury.osac.state.or.us
Web: www.osac.state.or.us

**Summary:** To provide financial assistance for undergraduate or graduate education to the children and spouses of disabled or deceased workers in Oregon.
**Eligibility:** Open to residents of Oregon who are U.S. citizens or permanent residents. Applicants must be high school seniors or graduates who 1) are dependents or spouses of an Oregon worker who has suffered permanent total disability on the job; or 2) are receiving, or have received, fatality benefits as dependents or spouses of a worker fatally injured in Oregon. Selection is based on financial need and an essay of up to 500 words on "How has the injury or death of your parent or spouse affected or influenced your decision to further your education?"
**Financial data:** Stipend amounts vary; recently, they were at least $4,786.
**Duration:** 1 year.
**Number awarded:** 1 or more each year.
**Deadline:** February of each year.

## 899 OREGON OPPORTUNITY GRANTS

Oregon Student Assistance Commission
1500 Valley River Drive, Suite 100
Eugene, OR 97401-2130
Phone: (541) 687-7400; (800) 452-8807; Fax: (541) 687-7419;
Email: awardinfo@mercury.osac.state.or.us
Web: www.ossc.state.or.us/ong.html

**Summary:** To provide financial assistance for college to residents of Oregon who have financial need.
**Eligibility:** Open to residents of Oregon who are attending or planning to attend a nonprofit college or university in Oregon as a full-time student. Applicants must have an annual family income below specified levels; for dependent students, the maximum family income ranges from $20,960 for a household size of 2 to $43,460 for a household size of 9; for independent students, the maximum family income ranges from $8,740 for a household size of 1 to $38,660 for a household size of 8. Students who are working on a degree in theology, divinity, or religious education are not eligible.
**Financial data:** Awards depend on the need of the recipient. At public schools, the maximum annual award is $1,323 at a community college, $1,587 at an institution within the Oregon University system, or $2,121 at Oregon Health and Sciences University. Specific award amounts are established for each eligible private college or university within Oregon, ranging from $2,410 at Mount Angel Seminary to $4,432 at Reed College. Contact the sponsor for the amount of the supplemental awards available at other private institutions.
**Duration:** 1 year; may be renewed for up to 3 additional years, if the student maintains satisfactory academic progress and demonstrates continued financial need.
**Number awarded:** Varies each year; recently, more than 30,000 of these grants were awarded.

## 900 ORPHAN FOUNDATION OF AMERICA SCHOLARSHIPS

Orphan Foundation of America, Attn: Director of Student Services
Tall Oaks Village Center
12020-D North Shore Drive
Reston, VA 20190-4977
Phone: (571) 203-0270; (800) 950-4673; Fax: (571) 203-0273;
Email: scholarships@orphan.org
Web: www.orphan.org/scholarships.html

**Summary:** To provide financial assistance for college to students currently or previously in foster care.
**Eligibility:** Open to students who are currently enrolled in or have applied to college or a postsecondary training program. Applicants must have been in foster care or a ward of the court for at least 1 year at the time of their 18th birthday and currently be under 25 years of age. They must submit a 2- to 3-page essay on their goals for school, career, and personal fulfillment. Selection is based on the essay, 2 letters of recommendation, transcripts, and financial need.
**Financial data:** Stipends range up to $10,000 per year. Recently, the average was more than $4,000.
**Duration:** 1 year; may be renewed if the recipient maintains a GPA of 2.0 or higher and financial need.

**Number awarded:** Varies each year. Recently, Casey Family Programs alone supported 122 new and 150 renewal scholarships.
**Deadline:** Applicants must first register online by the end of March of each year.

## 901 OSBORNE SCHOLARSHIP

Urban League of Nebraska, Inc., Attn: Scholarships
3022 North 24th Street
Omaha, NE 68110
Phone: (402) 453-9730; Fax: (402) 453-9676
Web: www.urbanleagueneb.org

**Summary:** To provide financial assistance for college to residents of Nebraska.
**Eligibility:** Open to Nebraska residents who are seniors in high school or students currently enrolled in college. Applicants must have a GPA of 2.5 or higher and be able to demonstrate financial need. They must be able to demonstrate at least 5 to 10 hours of community involvement. Along with their application, they must submit a 500-word essay on their goals and ambitions and the reasons they should receive this scholarship.
**Financial data:** A stipend is awarded (amount not specified).
**Duration:** 1 year.
**Number awarded:** 1 or more each year.
**Deadline:** March of each year.

## 902 OSCAR AND MILDRED LARSON AWARD

Vasa Order of America, Attn: Vice Grand Master
3236 Berkeley Avenue
Cleveland Heights, OH 44118-2055
Phone: (216) 371-5141; Email: rolf.bergman@sbcglobal.net
Web: www.vasaorder.com

**Summary:** To provide financial assistance for college or graduate school to students of Swedish heritage.
**Eligibility:** Open to applicants who are Swedish born or of Swedish ancestry; residents of the United States, Canada, or Sweden; and enrolled or accepted as full-time undergraduate or graduate students in an accredited 4-year college or university in the United States. Membership in Vasa Order of America is not required. Selection is based on a grade transcript, letters of recommendation from school and local Vasa lodge officials, and an essay of up to 1,000 words on a topic related to Vasa.
**Financial data:** The stipend is $3,000 per year.
**Duration:** 1 year; may be renewed up to 3 additional years for a total award of $16,000.
**Number awarded:** 1 each year.
**Deadline:** February of each year.

## 903 OUTSTANDING SECONDARY CAREER AND TECHNICAL EDUCATION STUDENT AWARD

Vocational Foundation of Nebraska
P.O. Box 22607
Lincoln, NE 68542-2607
Phone: (402) 423-6786

**Summary:** To provide financial assistance to career and technical students in Nebraska.
**Eligibility:** Open to students who are currently enrolled in career and technical education in Nebraska or have been enrolled within the past 12 months. Students must be nominated by a teacher who 1) describes how they have demonstrated a high level of competence in the program through classroom, work experience, laboratory training, related projects, or extracurricular activities, and 2) explains what distinguishes them from others in terms of capability, motivation, achievements, performances, and contributions. Nominees must also complete an application in which they describe how they will apply their career and technical education to their future plans and list projects or experiences that have seemed most interesting or important to them, school and community activities, and honors or awards.
**Financial data:** The award is a $1,000 scholarship. Funds must be used for attendance at a Nebraska postsecondary institution.
**Duration:** The award is presented annually.
**Number awarded:** 1 each year.
**Deadline:** Nominations must be submitted by March of each year.

## 904 OUTSTANDING SECONDARY SPECIAL POPULATIONS CAREER AND TECHNICAL EDUCATION STUDENT AWARD

Vocational Foundation of Nebraska

P.O. Box 22607
Lincoln, NE 68542-2607
Phone: (402) 423-6786

**Summary:** To provide financial assistance to career and technical students in Nebraska who are members of groups defined as "special populations."

**Eligibility:** Open to students who are currently enrolled in career and technical education in Nebraska or have been enrolled within the past 12 months. Students must be members of a "special populations" group, including individuals with disabilities and economically and academically disadvantaged individuals. They must be nominated by a teacher who 1) describes how they have demonstrated a high level of competence in the program through classroom, work experience, laboratory training, related projects, or extracurricular activities, and 2) explains what distinguishes them from others in terms of capability, motivation, achievements, performances, and contributions. Nominees must also complete an application in which they describe how they will apply their career and technical education to their future plans and list projects or experiences that have seemed most interesting or important to them and school and community activities.

**Financial data:** The award is a $1,000 scholarship. Funds must be used for attendance at a Nebraska postsecondary institution.

**Duration:** The award is presented annually.

**Number awarded:** 1 each year.

**Deadline:** Nominations must be submitted by March of each year.

---

## 905 P.A. MARGARONIS SCHOLARSHIPS

American Hellenic Educational Progressive Association
Attn: AHEPA Educational Foundation
1909 Q Street, N.W., Suite 500
Washington, DC 20009
Phone: (202) 232-6300; Fax: (202) 232-2140
Web: www.ahepa.org/educ_foundation/index.html

**Summary:** To provide financial assistance to undergraduate and graduate students of Hellenic heritage.

**Eligibility:** Open to applicants who are of Hellenic heritage (although their ancestry does not need to be 100% Greek) and currently enrolled or planning to enroll as undergraduate or graduate students. High school seniors must submit their most recent official transcript as well as SAT or ACT scores; college freshmen and sophomores must submit high school transcripts, SAT or ACT scores, and their most recent college transcript; college juniors and seniors must submit their most recent college transcript; graduate students must submit college transcripts, GRE or MCAT scores (if available), and their most recent graduate school transcript. Selection is based on academic achievement, extracurricular activities, athletic achievements, work experience, community service, and financial need.

**Financial data:** Stipends range from $500 to $2,000 per year.

**Duration:** 1 year.

**Number awarded:** Varies each year. Recently, 14 of these scholarships were awarded: 6 to graduate students and 8 to undergraduates.

**Deadline:** March of each year.

---

## 906 PACERS TEAMUP SCHOLARSHIPS

Pacers Foundation, Inc., Attn: Foundation Coordinator
125 South Pennsylvania Street
Indianapolis, IN 46204
Phone: (317) 917-2500; Fax: (317) 917-2599; Email: Foundation@pacers.com
Web: www.pacersfoundation.org

**Summary:** To provide financial assistance for college to high school seniors in Indiana who have made significant contributions to their community.

**Eligibility:** Open to high school seniors in Indiana who will be attending college and have proven records of community service. Interested students must write a 500-word essay on the importance of their community service activity to themselves and others, the societal need that it addresses, how their neighborhood or community has benefited, what they have learned from their community service experience, and how it will impact their future. Along with the essay, they must submit their high school transcript, their class rank and GPA, and a letter of recommendation from a community leader with whom they have done service. Selection is based on record of service to the community, letter of recommendation, and the essay.

**Financial data:** The stipend is $2,000. Funds are paid directly to the recipient's school.

**Duration:** 1 year; nonrenewable.

**Number awarded:** 5 each year.

**Deadline:** February of each year.

---

## 907 PADGETT BUSINESS SERVICES SCHOLARSHIP PROGRAM

Padgett Business Services Foundation, Attn: Scholarship Program
160 Hawthorne Park
Athens, GA 30606
Phone: (706) 548-1040; (800) 723-4388; Fax: (800) 548-1040;
Email: scholarship@smallbizpros.com
Web: www.smallbizpros.com/spb/founda.htm

**Summary:** To provide financial assistance for college to high school seniors whose parents own and operate a small business.

**Eligibility:** Open to 1) dependents of small business owners who employ fewer than 20 individuals, own at least 10% of the stock or capital in the business, and are active in the day-to-day operations; and 2) graduating high school seniors planning to attend an accredited postsecondary institution. They may reside in the United States or Canada. Applications must be obtained from a local Padgett Business Service office (the phone number and address will be in the local telephone directory). Applicants must submit a completed questionnaire and write a 100-word essay describing their education and career plans. Students first compete for regional scholarships. Each regional winner in Canada is eligible for the Canada National Scholarship and each regional winner in the United States is eligible for the U.S. National Scholarship. The national scholarship winners are eligible for the international scholarship.

**Financial data:** Regional scholarships are $500; the national scholarships are an additional $1,000; the international scholarship is an additional $2,000.

**Duration:** 1 year.

**Number awarded:** The number of regional scholarships varies; 2 national scholarships and 1 international scholarship are awarded each year. Approximately $50,000 is awarded by this program each year.

**Deadline:** February of each year.

---

## 908 PAGE EDUCATION FOUNDATION GRANTS

Page Education Foundation
P.O. Box 581254
Minneapolis, MN 55458-1254
Phone: (612) 332-0406; Email: info@page-ed.org
Web: www.page-ed.org

**Summary:** To provide funding for college to students of color in Minnesota.

**Eligibility:** Open to students of color who are graduating from high school in Minnesota and planning to attend a postsecondary school in the state. Applicants must submit an essay of 400 to 500 words that deals with why they believe education is important, their plans for the future, and the service-to-children project they would like to complete in the coming school year. Selection is based on the essay, 3 letters of recommendation, and financial need.

**Financial data:** Stipends range from $900 to $2,500 per year.

**Duration:** 1 year; may be renewed up to 3 additional years.

**Number awarded:** Varies each year; recently, 570 Page Scholars were enrolled, of whom 61% were African American, 27% Asian American, 11% Chicano/Latino, and 1% American Indian.

**Deadline:** April of each year.

---

## 909 PALMER B. CARSON-PFLAG GENERAL SCHOLARSHIPS

Parents, Families and Friends of Lesbians and Gays
Attn: National Scholarships Program
1726 M Street, N.W., Suite 400
Washington, DC 20036
Phone: (202) 467-8180, ext. 219; Fax: (202) 467-8194;
Email: schools@pflag.org
Web: www.pflag.org

**Summary:** To provide financial assistance for college to high school seniors and recent graduates who have a connection to Parents, Families and Friends of Lesbians and Gays (PFLAG).

**Eligibility:** Open to high school seniors and prior-year graduates who have not attended college. Applicants must have applied to an accredited high education institution to work on 1) an associate degree leading to transfer to complete a bachelor's degree, or 2) a bachelor's degree at a 4-year college or university. They must self-identify either as a gay, lesbian, bisexual, or transgender (GLBT) person or as a supporter of GLBT people. Along with their application, they must submit a high school transcript showing a GPA of 3.0 or higher, 2 letters of recommendation, and a 2-page essay discussing either their life as an LGBT student or how they have been involved with and supported the LGBT community. Financial need is also considered in the selection process.

**Financial data:** The stipend is $1,000.

**Duration:** 1 year; nonrenewable.

**Number awarded:** 13 each year.

**Deadline:** February of each year.

## 910 PALMER B. CARSON-PFLAG SCHOLARSHIP FOR LGBT ADVOCACY

Parents, Families and Friends of Lesbians and Gays
Attn: National Scholarships Program
1726 M Street, N.W., Suite 400
Washington, DC 20036
Phone: (202) 467-8180, ext. 219; Fax: (202) 467-8194;
Email: schools@pflag.org
Web: www.pflag.org

**Summary:** To provide financial assistance for college to high school seniors and recent graduates who have a connection to Parents, Families and Friends of Lesbians and Gays (PFLAG).

**Eligibility:** Open to high school seniors and prior-year graduates who have not attended college. Applicants must have applied to an accredited high education institution to work on 1) an associate degree leading to transfer to complete a bachelor's degree, or 2) a bachelor's degree at a 4-year college or university. They must self-identify either as a gay, lesbian, bisexual, or transgender (GLBT) person or as a supporter of GLBT people. Along with their application, they must submit a high school transcript showing a GPA of 3.0 or higher, 2 letters of recommendation, and a 2-page essay discussing either their life as an LGBT student or how they have been involved with and supported the LGBT community. Financial need is also considered in the selection process. This scholarship is presented to the applicant who demonstrates outstanding LGBT advocacy.

**Financial data:** The stipend is $2,500.
**Duration:** 1 year; nonrenewable.
**Number awarded:** 1 each year.
**Deadline:** February of each year.

## 911 PALMETTO FELLOWS SCHOLARSHIPS

South Carolina Commission on Higher Education
Attn: Director of Student Services
1333 Main Street, Suite 200
Columbia, SC 29201
Phone: (803) 737-2262; (877) 349-7183; Fax: (803) 737-2297;
Email: shubbard@che.sc.gov
Web: www.che.sc.gov

**Summary:** To provide financial assistance for college to high school students in South Carolina who have achieved a high score on a college entrance examination.

**Eligibility:** Open to residents of South Carolina who are enrolled in a public or private high school or an approved home-school program. Applicants must be planning to attend a 4-year public or private college or university in South Carolina during the fall immediately following graduation. They must either 1) score at least 27 on the ACT (or the equivalent on the SAT), have a GPA of 3.5 or higher, and rank in the top 6% of their class; or 2) score at least 32 on the ACT (or SAT equivalent) and have a GPA of 4.0. Early awards are based on test scores, GPA, and class rank at the end of the junior year; final awards are based on test scores, GPA, and class rank at the end of the senior year. U.S. citizenship or permanent resident status is required.

**Financial data:** Grants up to $6,700 per year are available, half provided by the South Carolina Commission on Higher Education and half by the institution the student attends.

**Duration:** 1 year; may be renewed for 3 additional years provided the recipient maintains full-time enrollment and a GPA of 3.0 or higher.

**Number awarded:** Varies each year; recently, 3,727 of these scholarships, worth more than $24 million, were awarded.

**Deadline:** December of each year for early awards; June of each year for final awards.

## 912 PALOMINO HORSE BREEDERS OF AMERICA YOUTH SCHOLARSHIP AND EDUCATIONAL FUND

Palomino Horse Breeders of America
Attn: Youth Scholarship and Educational Fund
15253 East Skelly Drive
Tulsa, OK 74116-2637
Phone: (918) 438-1234; Fax: (918) 438-1232; Email: yellahrses@aol.com
Web: www.palominohba.com/scholarship.htm

**Summary:** To provide financial assistance for college to youth members of the Palomino Horse Breeders of America (PHBA-Y).

**Eligibility:** Open to 1) high school seniors who have been a member in good standing of the PHBA-Y during the previous 2 years and either rank in the upper 20% of their high school graduating class or achieved a rank above the 80th percentile on a national college entrance examination; and 2) full-time students who have completed at least 1 semester of college and are younger than 21 years of age. Applicants must provide information on their career goals, academic achievements, extracurricular activities, hobbies, PHBA-Y activities and experiences, awards and honors, and 4-H or FFA projects and achievements. They must also submit a letter on why they desire to continue their education and their personal qualities that qualify them to receive a scholarship. Financial need is not considered in the selection process.

**Financial data:** The amount of the stipend varies each year.
**Duration:** 1 year; may be renewed if the recipient maintains a GPA of 2.5 or higher.
**Number awarded:** Varies each year.
**Deadline:** January of each year.

## 913 PAPA JOHN'S SCHOLARSHIPS

Papa John's International, Inc., Attn: Scholarship Program
2002 Papa John's Boulevard
Louisville, KY 40299
Phone: (502) 261-7272; (800) 865-9373; Email: info@papajohnsscholars.com
Web: www.papajohnsscholars.com

**Summary:** To provide financial assistance for college to high school seniors at selected U.S. high schools.

**Eligibility:** Open to graduating high school seniors who have a GPA of 2.5 or higher. Applicants must attend a high school located near a participating Papa John's restaurant. Selection is based on creative ability, community involvement, academic achievement, quality of character, demonstrated leadership, obstacles overcome, life goals and interests, athletic achievement, and meaningful obstacles overcome.

**Financial data:** The stipend is $1,000.
**Duration:** 1 year.
**Number awarded:** Varies each year; recently, 1,185 of these scholarships were awarded.

## 914 PARENT CONTINUING EDUCATION SCHOLARSHIPS

Hemophilia Federation of America, Attn: Scholarship Committee
1405 West Pinhook Road, Suite 101
Lafayette, LA 70503
Phone: (337) 261-9787; (800) 230-9797; Fax: (337) 261-1787;
Email: info@hemophiliafed.org
Web: www.hemophiliafed.org/scholarships.php

**Summary:** To provide financial assistance for college to parents of children with a blood clotting disorder.

**Eligibility:** Open to parents of children who have a blood clotting disorder. Applicants must be attending or planning to attend an accredited 2-year or 4-year college, university, or trade school in the United States. Along with their application, they must submit a 1-page essay on their goals and aspirations and how the blood clotting community has played a part in their lives. Financial need is also considered in the selection process.

**Financial data:** The stipend is $1,500 per year.
**Duration:** 1 year; may be renewed.
**Number awarded:** 2 each year.
**Deadline:** March of each year.

## 915 PATRICIA AND GAIL ISHIMOTO MEMORIAL SCHOLARSHIP

Japanese American Citizens League, Attn: National Scholarship Awards
1765 Sutter Street
San Francisco, CA 94115
Phone: (415) 921-5225; Fax: (415) 931-4671; Email: jacl@jacl.org
Web: www.jacl.org/scholarships.html

**Summary:** To provide financial assistance for college to student members of the Japanese American Citizens League (JACL) who are high school seniors.

**Eligibility:** Open to JACL members who are high school seniors interested in attending a college, university, trade school, business college, or other institution of higher learning. Applicants must submit a statement describing their current level of involvement in the Japanese American community or Asian Pacific community and how they will continue their involvement in future years. Selection is based on academic record, extracurricular activities, and community involvement.

**Financial data:** The stipend depends on the availability of funds but usually ranges from $1,000 to $5,000.

**Duration:** 1 year; nonrenewable.
**Number awarded:** At least 1 each year.
**Deadline:** February of each year.

### 916 PATRICIA CREED SCHOLARSHIP

Connecticut Women's Golf Association
c/o Deborah Boynton, Scholarship Committee
52 Mountain Spring Road
Farmington, CT 06032
Email: juniors@cwga.org
Web: www.cwga.org/JrScholarships.htm
**Summary:** To provide financial assistance for college to women high school seniors from Connecticut who are golfers.
**Eligibility:** Open to female high school seniors who are residents of Connecticut planning to attend a college or university in the state. Applicants must be active golfers with a handicap. Along with their application, they must submit a statement on why they want to go to college and why they should receive this scholarship. Selection is based on character, academic achievement and financial need.
**Financial data:** A stipend is awarded (amount not specified).
**Duration:** 1 year.
**Number awarded:** 1 each year.
**Deadline:** April of each year.

### 917 PATRICIA M. MCNAMARA MEMORIAL SCHOLARSHIP

Ropage Group LLC
8877 North 107th Avenue, Suite 302
P.O. Box 287
Peoria, AZ 85345
Email: questions@patricias-scholarship.org
Web: www.patricias-scholarship.org
**Summary:** To provide financial assistance for college to students who have overcome great obstacles.
**Eligibility:** Open to students who are attending or planning to attend an institution of higher education. Applicants must submit a short essay about 1 of the greatest obstacles they have had to overcome.
**Financial data:** The stipend is $1,000.
**Duration:** 1 year.
**Number awarded:** 1 each year.
**Deadline:** December of each year.

### 918 PATRICK KERR SKATEBOARD SCHOLARSHIP

Patrick Kerr Skateboard Scholarship Fund
P.O. Box 2054
Jenkintown, PA 19046
Fax: (215) 663-5897; Email: info@skateboardscholarship.org
Web: www.skateboardscholarship.org
**Summary:** To provide financial assistance for college to high school seniors who are skateboarders.
**Eligibility:** Open to graduating high school seniors who are skateboarders planning to enroll full time at an accredited 2-year or 4-year college or university. Applicants must have a GPA of 2.5 or higher and be able to demonstrate financial need. Along with their application, they must submit a 300-word essay on how skateboarding has been a positive influence in their life. Special consideration is given to applicants who have been actively promoting skateboarding in their community, but skateboarding skill is not considered in the selection process. U.S. citizenship is required.
**Financial data:** Stipends are $5,000 or $1,000.
**Duration:** 1 year.
**Number awarded:** 4 each year: 1 at $5,000 and 3 at $1,000.
**Deadline:** April.

### 919 PATSY TAKEMOTO MINK EDUCATION FOUNDATION EDUCATION SUPPORT AWARD

Patsy Takemoto Mink Education Foundation for Low-Income Women and Children, Attn: Gwendolyn Mink
P.O. Box 1599
Northampton, MA 01061-1599
Email: admin@ptmfoundation.net
Web: www.ptmfoundation.net

**Summary:** To provide financial assistance for college or graduate school to low-income women.
**Eligibility:** Open to women who are at least 18 years of age and are from a low-income family (less than $14,000 annually for a family of 1, rising to $30,000 annually for a family of 4). Applicants must be 1) enrolled in a skills training, ESL, or GED program; or 2) working on an associate, bachelor's, master's, professional, or doctoral degree. Along with their application, they must submit brief essays on what this award will help them accomplish, the program in which they are or will be enrolled, how they decided on that educational pursuit, their educational goals, their educational experience, and their personal and educational history.
**Financial data:** The stipend is $2,000.
**Duration:** 1 year.
**Number awarded:** 7 each year.
**Deadline:** June of each year.

### 920 PATTY & MELVIN ALPERIN FIRST GENERATION SCHOLARSHIP

Rhode Island Foundation, Attn: Scholarship Coordinator
One Union Station
Providence, RI 02903
Phone: (401) 274-4564; Fax: (401) 751-7983; Email: libbym@rifoundation.org
Web: www.rifoundation.org
**Summary:** To provide financial assistance for college to students in Rhode Island whose parents did not attend college.
**Eligibility:** Open to college-bound Rhode Island high school seniors and graduates whose parents did not have the benefit of attending college. Applicants must intend to work on either a 2-year degree at an accredited nonprofit postsecondary institution or a 4-year college degree. Along with their application, they must submit an essay (up to 300 words) on what it means to them to be of the first generation in their family to work on a college degree. Selection is based on academic excellence, character, and financial need.
**Financial data:** The stipend is $1,000.
**Duration:** 1 year; may be renewed for up to 3 additional years if the recipient maintains good academic standing.
**Number awarded:** 2 or 3 each year.
**Deadline:** May of each year.

### 921 PAUL F. RONCI MEMORIAL SCHOLARSHIPS

Paul F. Ronci Memorial Trust
c/o Mary Lou Fonseca
P.O. Box 515
Harmony, RI 02829-0515
Phone: (401) 349-4404; Fax: (401) 349-4404
Web: www.paulfroncischolarship.org
**Summary:** To provide financial assistance to undergraduate and graduate students from Rhode Island.
**Eligibility:** Open to full-time undergraduate and graduate students who have been residents of Rhode Island for at least 10 of the last 12 years. Applicants must rank in the top 10% of their class. Along with their application, they must submit documentation of financial need and an essay on their goals, ambitions, and desires, with specific reference to what they intend to accomplish for the good of humanity.
**Financial data:** Stipends range from $500 up to full payment of tuition.
**Duration:** 1 year; recipients may reapply.
**Number awarded:** 1 each year.
**Deadline:** March of each year.

### 922 PAUL R. KACH, 33 DEMOLAY ESSAY COMPETITION

Ancient and Accepted Scottish Rite of Freemasonry, Southern Jurisdiction
Supreme Council, 33, Attn: Director of Education
1733 16th Street, N.W.
Washington, DC 20009-2103
Phone: (202) 232-3579; Fax: (202) 464-0487; Email: grndexec@srmason-sj.org
Web: www.srmason-sj.org
**Summary:** To recognize and reward members of the Order of DeMolay who submit outstanding essays in a competition.
**Eligibility:** Open to active DeMolays in 2 categories: grades 11 and above and grades 10 and below. Entrants must submit an essay of 1,000 to 1,500 words on a topic that changes annually; a recent topic was "The Value of DeMolay's 7 Basic Principles." Essays are first submitted to a regional competition and

regional winners are entered in the national competition. The content of the essay is the primary concern in the judging, but grammar and spelling are also considered.

**Financial data:** National winners receive $1,500; regional winners receive $300.

**Duration:** The competition is held annually.

**Number awarded:** In each of the 2 categories, 1 national winner and 8 regional winners are selected.

**Deadline:** January of each year.

## 923 PAUL TSONGAS SCHOLARSHIP PROGRAM

Massachusetts Office of Student Financial Assistance
454 Broadway, Suite 200
Revere, MA 02151
Phone: (617) 727-9420; Fax: (617) 727-0667; Email: osfa@osfa.mass.edu
Web: www.osfa.mass.edu

**Summary:** To provide financial assistance to Massachusetts students who attend 1 of the state colleges in Massachusetts.

**Eligibility:** Open to residents of Massachusetts who have graduated from high school within 3 years and are attending or planning to attend a state college in Massachusetts. Applicants must be U.S. citizens or permanent residents and have a GPA of 3.75 or higher and above average SAT scores.

**Financial data:** Eligible students receive a waiver of tuition and mandatory fees.

**Duration:** Up to 4 academic years, if the recipient maintains a GPA of 3.3 or higher in college.

**Number awarded:** 45 each year: 5 at each state college in Massachusetts.

## 924 PELLEGRINI SCHOLARSHIP FUND

Swiss Benevolent Society of New York
Attn: Scholarship Committee
608 Fifth Avenue, Suite 309
New York, NY 10020-2303
Phone: (212) 246-0655; Fax: (212) 246-1366;
Email: info@swissbenevolentny.com
Web: www.swissbenevolentny.com/scholarships.htm

**Summary:** To provide financial assistance to undergraduate and graduate students of Swiss descent in the Northeast.

**Eligibility:** Open to undergraduate and graduate students who are residents of Connecticut, New Jersey, Pennsylvania, Delaware, or New York. Applicants must demonstrate a strong academic record (GPA of 3.0 or higher), aptitude in their chosen field of study, and financial need. Either the applicant or at least 1 parent must be a Swiss citizen.

**Financial data:** The stipend ranges from $500 to $4,000 per year. Funds are paid directly to the recipient's school in 2 installments (beginning of fall semester and beginning of spring semester).

**Duration:** 1 year; recipients may reapply.

**Number awarded:** Approximately 55 each year.

**Deadline:** March of each year.

## 925 PENNSYLVANIA CHAFEE EDUCATION AND TRAINING GRANT PROGRAM

Pennsylvania Higher Education Assistance Agency
Attn: Development and Regional Services
1200 North Seventh Street
P.O. Box 2455
Harrisburg, PA 17105-2455
Phone: (717) 720-2800; (800) 831-0797; TDD: (717) 720-2366;
Email: paetg@pheaa.org
Web: www.pheaa.org/specialprograms/index.shtml

**Summary:** To provide financial assistance for college to residents of Pennsylvania who have been in foster care.

**Eligibility:** Open to residents of Pennsylvania who are eligible for services under the state's Chafee Foster Care Independence Program, were adopted from foster care after their 16th birthday, or were participating in this program on their 21st birthday (until they turn 23 years of age). Applicants must be enrolled in an approved college or career school on at least a half time basis.

**Financial data:** The maximum stipend is $5,000 per year. Awards may not exceed the actual cost of attendance, minus other financial aid the student receives.

**Duration:** 1 year; may be renewed if the recipient remains enrolled at least half time and makes satisfactory academic progress.

**Number awarded:** Varies each year.

**Deadline:** April of each year.

## 926 PENNSYLVANIA EDUCATIONAL GRATUITY FOR VETERANS' DEPENDENTS

Bureau for Veterans Affairs
Fort Indiantown Gap
Annville, PA 17003-5002
Phone: (717) 865-8910; (800) 54 PA VET (within PA);
Fax: (717) 865-8589; Email: jdavison@state.pa.us
Web: sites.state.pa.us/PA_Exec/Military_Affairs/va/benefits.htm

**Summary:** To provide financial assistance for college to the children of disabled or deceased Pennsylvania veterans.

**Eligibility:** Open to children of honorably-discharged veterans who are rated totally and permanently disabled as a result of wartime service or who have died of such a disability. Applicants must be between 16 and 23 years of age, have lived in Pennsylvania for at least 5 years immediately preceding the date of application, be able to demonstrate financial need, and have been accepted or are currently enrolled in a Pennsylvania state or state-aided secondary or postsecondary educational institution.

**Financial data:** The stipend is $500 per semester ($1,000 per year). The money is paid directly to the recipient's school and is to be applied to the costs of tuition, board, room, books, supplies, and/or matriculation fees.

**Duration:** The allowance is paid for up to 4 academic years or for the duration of the course of study, whichever is less.

**Number awarded:** Varies each year.

## 927 PENNSYLVANIA GRANTS FOR CHILDREN OF SOLDIERS DECLARED POW/MIA

Pennsylvania Higher Education Assistance Agency
Attn: State Grant and Special Programs Division
1200 North Seventh Street
Harrisburg, PA 17102-1444
Phone: (717) 720-2800; (800) 692-7392; TDD: (717) 720-2366;
Email: info@pheaa.org
Web: www.pheaa.org/specialprograms/index.shtml

**Summary:** To provide financial assistance for college to the children of POWs/MIAs from Pennsylvania.

**Eligibility:** Open to dependent children of members or former members of the U.S. armed services who served on active duty after January 31, 1955, who are or have been prisoners of war or are or have been listed as missing in action, and who were residents of Pennsylvania for at least 12 months preceding service on active duty. Eligible children must be enrolled in a program of at least 1 year in duration on at least a half-time basis at an approved school and must demonstrate financial need.

**Financial data:** The amount of the award depends on the financial need of the recipient, up to a maximum of $3,500 at a Pennsylvania school or $800 at a school outside of Pennsylvania that is approved for participation in the program.

**Duration:** 1 year; may be renewed for 3 additional years.

**Number awarded:** Varies each year.

**Deadline:** March of each year.

## 928 PENNSYLVANIA GRANTS FOR VETERANS

Pennsylvania Higher Education Assistance Agency
Attn: State Grant and Special Programs Division
1200 North Seventh Street
Harrisburg, PA 17102-1444
Phone: (717) 720-2800; (800) 692-7392; TDD: (717) 720-2366;
Email: info@pheaa.org
Web: www.pheaa.org/specialprograms/index.shtml

**Summary:** To provide financial assistance for college to Pennsylvania veterans.

**Eligibility:** Open to veterans who served on active duty with the U.S. armed services (or were a cadet or midshipman at a service academy); were released or discharged under conditions other than dishonorable, bad conduct, uncharacterized, or other than honorable; have resided in Pennsylvania for at least 12 months immediately preceding the date of application; graduated from high school; and are enrolled on at least a half-time basis in an approved program of study that is at least 2 academic years in length. First priority is given to veterans who have separated from active duty after January 1 of the current year. All veterans are considered without regard to the financial status of their parents.

**Financial data:** The amount of the award depends on the financial need of the recipient, up to a maximum of $3,300 at a Pennsylvania school or $800 at a school outside of Pennsylvania that is approved for participation in the program.

**Duration:** 1 year; may be renewed for 3 additional years.

**Number awarded:** Varies each year.

**Deadline:** April of each year for renewal applicants and any nonrenewals who will enroll in a baccalaureate degree program; July of each year for nonrenewals who will enroll in a 2-year or 3-year terminal program.

### 929 PENNSYLVANIA KIDS' CHANCE SCHOLARSHIPS

Kids' Chance of Pennsylvania
P.O. Box 543
Pottstown, PA 19464
Phone: (484) 945-2104; Fax: (610) 970-7520; Email: info@kidschanceofpa.org
Web: www.kidschanceofpa.org

**Summary:** To provide financial assistance for college to Pennsylvania residents whose parent was killed or permanently disabled in a work-related accident.

**Eligibility:** Open to Pennsylvania residents between 16 and 25 years of age who have been accepted by an accredited postsecondary educational institution anywhere in the United States. At least 1 parent must have been killed or seriously injured as a result of a work-related accident covered under the Pennsylvania Workers' Compensation Act. Financial need is considered in the selection process.

**Financial data:** Regardless of the state where the recipient attends school, the stipend may not exceed the annual cost of tuition and books at the most expensive public postsecondary educational institution in Pennsylvania.

**Duration:** 1 year; may be renewed.

**Number awarded:** Varies each year; recently, 35 students were receiving support through this program.

**Deadline:** April of each year.

### 930 PENNSYLVANIA KNIGHTS TEMPLAR EDUCATIONAL FOUNDATION SCHOLARSHIPS

Pennsylvania Youth Foundation, Attn: Educational Endowment Fund
1244 Bainbridge Road
Elizabethtown, PA 17022-9423
Phone: (717) 367-1536; (800) 266-8424 (within PA);
Fax: (717) 367-0616; Email: pyf@pagrandlodge.org
Web: www.pagrandlodge.org/pyf/scholar/index.html

**Summary:** To provide financial assistance for college or graduate school to residents of Pennsylvania.

**Eligibility:** Open to residents of Pennsylvania who are working on a 2-year college, trade school, 4-year college, or graduate degree. Applicants are considered without regard to age, race, religion, national origin, sex, or Masonic ties or affiliations.

**Financial data:** The stipend varies.

**Duration:** 1 year.

**Number awarded:** 1 or more each year.

**Deadline:** March of each year.

### 931 PENNSYLVANIA POSTSECONDARY EDUCATIONAL GRATUITY PROGRAM

Pennsylvania Higher Education Assistance Agency
Attn: State Grant and Special Programs Division
1200 North Seventh Street
Harrisburg, PA 17102-1444
Phone: (717) 720-2800; (800) 692-7392; TDD: (717) 720-2366;
Email: info@pheaa.org
Web: www.pheaa.org/specialprograms/index.shtml

**Summary:** To provide financial assistance for college to the children of Pennsylvania public service personnel who died in the line of service.

**Eligibility:** Open to residents of Pennsylvania who are the children of 1) Pennsylvania police officers, fire fighters, rescue and ambulance squad members, corrections facility employees, or National Guard members who died in the line of duty after January 1, 1976; or 2) Pennsylvania sheriffs, deputy sheriffs, National Guard members, and certain other individuals on federal or state active military duty who died after September 11, 2001 as a direct result of performing their official duties. Applicants must be 25 years of age or younger and enrolled or accepted at a Pennsylvania community college, state-owned institution, or state-related institution as a full-time student working on an associate or baccalaureate degree. They must have already applied for other scholarships, including state and federal grants and financial aid from the postsecondary institution to which they are applying.

**Financial data:** Grants cover tuition, fees, room, and board charged by the institution, less awarded scholarships and federal and state grants.

**Duration:** Up to 5 years.

**Number awarded:** Varies each year.

**Deadline:** March of each year.

### 932 PENNSYLVANIA STATE GRANTS

Pennsylvania Higher Education Assistance Agency
Attn: State Grant and Special Programs Division
1200 North Seventh Street
Harrisburg, PA 17102-1444
Phone: (717) 720-2800; (800) 692-7392; TDD: (717) 720-2366;
Email: info@pheaa.org
Web: www.pheaa.org/stategrants/index.shtml

**Summary:** To provide financial assistance for college to students in Pennsylvania who have financial need.

**Eligibility:** Open to seniors graduating from high schools in Pennsylvania who plan to attend a postsecondary school in Pennsylvania on at least a half-time basis. Applicants may also attend accredited colleges in other states, except those states that border Pennsylvania and do not allow their grant recipients to attend Pennsylvania schools (i.e., Maryland, New Jersey, and New York). Their family income may not exceed $69,000.

**Financial data:** Grants depend on financial need and the type of school attended. Recently, annual grants ranged from $2,750 to $3,300 at 4-year private schools, from $1,000 to $3,250 at state system schools, from $1,700 to $3,300 at state-related schools, from $1,650 to $3,300 at junior colleges, from $300 to $1,050 at community colleges, from $1,150 to $3,200 at nursing school, and from $1,600 to $3,300 at business, trade, and technical schools.

**Duration:** 1 year; may be renewed for 3 additional years.

**Number awarded:** Varies each year.

**Deadline:** April of each year for renewal applicants, new applicants who plan to enroll in a baccalaureate degree program, and students in college transfer programs at 2-year public or junior colleges; July of each year for first-time applicants for business, trade, or technical schools, hospital schools of nursing, or 2-year terminal programs at community, junior, or 4-year colleges.

### 933 PENTAGON ASSISTANCE FUND

Navy-Marine Corps Relief Society, Attn: Education Division
875 North Randolph Street, Suite 225
Arlington, VA 22203-1977
Phone: (703) 696-4960; Fax: (703) 696-0144; Email: education@hq.nmcrs.org
Web: www.nmcrs.org/child-dec.html

**Summary:** To provide financial assistance for college to the children and spouses of deceased military personnel who died at the Pentagon on September 11, 2001.

**Eligibility:** Open to the children and spouses of deceased military personnel who died at the Pentagon as a result of the terrorist attack of September 11, 2001. The families of Marines whose aircraft crashed in Pakistan and Afghanistan in mid-January 2002 are also eligible.

**Financial data:** The amount of assistance varies; funds may be used for any purpose, including tuition, fees, books, room, or board at a college or university offering a 2-year or 4-year course of study or at a vocational training school.

**Duration:** Up to 4 years.

**Number awarded:** Varies each year.

**Deadline:** Applications may be submitted at any time.

### 934 P.E.O. PROGRAM FOR CONTINUING EDUCATION

P.E.O. Sisterhood, Attn: Executive Office
3700 Grand Avenue
Des Moines, IA 50312-2899
Phone: (515) 255-3153; Fax: (515) 255-3820
Web: www.peointernational.org

**Summary:** To provide financial assistance to mature women interested in resuming or continuing their education.

**Eligibility:** Open to mature women who are citizens of the United States or Canada and have experienced an interruption in their education that has lasted at least 24 consecutive months during their adult life. Applicants are frequently single parents who must acquire marketable skills to support their families. They must be within 2 years of completing an academic or technical course of study. Applicants must be sponsored by a local P.E.O. chapter. Students enrolled in a doctoral degree program are not eligible.

**Financial data:** The maximum award is $1,500.

**Duration:** 1 year; nonrenewable.

**Number awarded:** Varies each year; recently, 1,467 of these grants were awarded, including 365 for the full amount of $1,500.

**Deadline:** Applications may be submitted at any time.

### 935 PEOPLES PROMISE SCHOLARSHIP PROGRAM

Maine Education Services, Attn: MES Foundation
One City Center, 11th Floor
Portland, ME 04101

Phone: (207) 791-3600; (800) 922-6352; Fax: (207) 791-3616;
Email: info@mesfoundation.com
Web: www.mesfoundation.com/college/scholarships_mes.asp
**Summary:** To provide financial assistance for college and work experience to high school seniors in Maine.
**Eligibility:** Open to seniors at high schools in Maine who plan to attend a postsecondary institution. Preference is given to students from low-to-moderate income households. Selection is based on academic achievement, involvement in school activities, community volunteer activity, work experience, and financial need.
**Financial data:** The stipend is $2,500.
**Duration:** 1 year.
**Number awarded:** 10 each year.
**Deadline:** April of each year.

### 936 PEPSI USBC YOUTH BOWLING CHAMPIONSHIPS

United States Bowling Congress
Attn: Pepsi-Cola Youth Bowling Event Manager
5301 South 76th Street
Greendale, WI 53129-1192
Phone: (414) 423-3442; (800) 514-BOWL, ext. 3442;
Fax: (414) 421-3014; Email: maureen.vicena@bowl.com
Web: www.bowl.com/tournaments/youth/pepsi/main.aspx
**Summary:** To recognize and reward (with college scholarships) members of the United States Bowling Congress (USBC) who achieve high scores in an international competition.
**Eligibility:** Open to USBC members in the United States, Puerto Rico, U.S. military zones, and Canada. Applicants enter in 1 of 6 categories: 11 and under boys' handicap, 12 and above boys' handicap, 12 and above boys' scratch, 11 and under girls' handicap, 12 and above girls' handicap, and 12 and above girls' scratch. Based on their bowling scores in state and zone competitions, the top bowlers in the 12 and above boys' and girls' handicap categories advance to the international finals. Also advancing to the international finals are the state and zone winners in the 12 and above boys' and girls' scratch categories who are also USBC Junior Gold members (boys must have an average of 175 or above, girls must have an average of 165 or above). All selected finalists (more than 200 qualify each year), are then assigned to Division I or Division II for the international competition, held annually at a site in the United States; assignment is based on their adjusted score from year-end averages and state and zone competitions. Bowlers whose scores are in the top half are assigned to Division I and bowlers whose scores are in the bottom half are assigned to Division II. Scholarships are awarded solely on the basis of bowling performance in the international finals.
**Financial data:** At the international finals, the top finishers in each division receive scholarships of $2,000, $1,500, $1,000, and $500, respectively.
**Duration:** The competition is held annually.
**Number awarded:** Each year, 16 scholarships are awarded: 8 are set aside for girls (4 in each division) and 8 for boys (4 in each division).
**Deadline:** Qualifying tournaments are held in bowling centers from October through February of each year. Center and section qualifying takes place in March and April. State and zone competitions take place through the end of May. The national finals are held in July.

### 937 PETER CONNACHER MEMORIAL TRUST FUND

Oregon Student Assistance Commission
Attn: Grants and Scholarships Division
1500 Valley River Drive, Suite 100
Eugene, OR 97401-2146
Phone: (541) 687-7395; (800) 452-8807, ext. 7395; Fax: (541) 687-7419;
Email: awardinfo@mercury.osac.state.or.us
Web: www.osac.state.or.us
**Summary:** To provide financial assistance for college or graduate school to ex-prisoners of war and their descendants.
**Eligibility:** Open to American citizens who 1) were military or civilian prisoners of war or 2) are the descendants of ex-prisoners of war. They may be undergraduate or graduate students. A copy of the ex-prisoner of war's discharge papers from the U.S. armed forces must accompany the application. In addition, written proof of POW status must be submitted, along with a statement of the relationship between the applicant and the ex-prisoner of war (father, grandfather, etc.). Selection is based on academic record and financial need. Preference is given to Oregon residents or their dependents.
**Financial data:** The stipend amount varies; recently, it was at least $1,150.
**Duration:** 1 year; may be renewed for up to 3 additional years for undergraduate students or 2 additional years for graduate students. Renewal is dependent on evidence of continued financial need and satisfactory academic progress.

**Number awarded:** Varies each year; recently, 4 of these scholarships were awarded.
**Deadline:** February of each year.

### 938 PETER KIEWIT FOUNDATION LEGACY SCHOLARSHIP PROGRAM

Peter Kiewit Foundation, Attn: Legacy Scholarship Program
8805 Indian Hills Drive, Suite 225
Omaha, NE 68114
Phone: (402) 344-7890
**Summary:** To provide financial assistance for college to high school seniors in Nebraska.
**Eligibility:** Open to seniors graduating from high schools in Nebraska who rank in the top 20% of their class. Applicants must be planning to attend a 4-year college or university in Nebraska. Along with their application, they must submit a 1-page essay on the single extracurricular activity that has meant the most to them and why. Selection is based on academic achievement and financial need.
**Financial data:** The stipend is $7,500 per year.
**Duration:** 1 year; may be renewed up to 3 additional years.
**Number awarded:** 50 each year.
**Deadline:** January of each year.

### 939 PFIZER EPILEPSY SCHOLARSHIP AWARD

Pfizer Inc.
c/o Eden Communications Group
515 Valley Street, Suite 200
Maplewood, NJ 07040
Phone: (973) 275-6518; (800) AWARD-PF; Fax: (973) 275-9792;
Email: info@epilepsy-scholarship.com
Web: www.epilepsy-scholarship.com
**Summary:** To provide financial assistance for undergraduate or graduate study to individuals with epilepsy.
**Eligibility:** Open to applicants who are under a physician's care for epilepsy (and taking prescribed medication). They must submit an application with 2 letters of recommendation (1 from the physician) and verification of academic status. They must also be high school seniors entering college in the fall; college freshmen, sophomores, or juniors continuing in the fall; or college seniors planning to enter graduate school in the fall. Along with their application, they must submit a 250-word essay on something of direct personal importance to them as a person with epilepsy. Selection is based on demonstrated achievement in academic and extracurricular activities; financial need is not considered.
**Financial data:** The stipend is $3,000.
**Duration:** 1 year; nonrenewable.
**Number awarded:** 25 each year.
**Deadline:** February of each year.

### 940 PFLAG NATIONAL DONOR SCHOLARSHIPS

Parents, Families and Friends of Lesbians and Gays
Attn: National Scholarships Program
1726 M Street, N.W., Suite 400
Washington, DC 20036
Phone: (202) 467-8180, ext. 219; Fax: (202) 467-8194;
Email: schools@pflag.org
Web: www.pflag.org
**Summary:** To provide financial assistance for college to high school seniors and recent graduates who have a connection to Parents, Families and Friends of Lesbians and Gays (PFLAG).
**Eligibility:** Open to high school seniors and prior-year graduates who have not attended college. Applicants must have applied to an accredited high education institution to work on 1) an associate degree leading to transfer to complete a bachelor's degree, or 2) a bachelor's degree at a 4-year college or university. They must self-identify either as a gay, lesbian, bisexual, or transgender (GLBT) person or as a supporter of GLBT people. Along with their application, they must submit a high school transcript showing a GPA of 3.0 or higher, 2 letters of recommendation, and a 2-page essay discussing either their life as an LGBT student or how they have been involved with and supported the LGBT community. Financial need is also considered in the selection process.
**Financial data:** Stipends are $2,500 or $1,000.
**Duration:** 1 year; nonrenewable.
**Number awarded:** 2 each year: 1 at 2,500 and 1 at $1,000.
**Deadline:** February of each year.

## 941 PHEAA ACADEMIC EXCELLENCE SCHOLARSHIP AWARD PROGRAM

Pennsylvania Higher Education Assistance Agency
Attn: State Grant and Special Programs Division
1200 North Seventh Street
Harrisburg, PA 17102-1444
Phone: (717) 720-2800; (800) 692-7392; TDD: (717) 720-2366;
Email: info@pheaa.org
Web: www.pheaa.org/specialprograms/index.shtml

**Summary:** To provide financial assistance for college to students in Pennsylvania who qualify for a federal Robert C. Byrd Honors Scholarship but did not receive that scholarship.

**Eligibility:** Open to seniors graduating from high schools in Pennsylvania who plan to attend a postsecondary school in Pennsylvania on a full-time basis. Applicants must have applied and qualified for a Robert C. Byrd Honors Scholarship and also be a Pennsylvania State Grant recipient for at least 1 term during their freshman year. Eligibility for the Byrd Scholarship requires that applicants be U.S. citizens, nationals, or permanent residents; rank in the top 5% of their graduating class (or in the top 3 if their class has 60 students or less); have a GPA of 3.5 or higher; and have a combined mathematics and critical reading SAT score of 1150 or higher, an ACT score of 25 or higher, or a GED score of 3550 or above. If they qualify for the Byrd Scholarship but fail to receive it, they are automatically eligible for this scholarship from the Pennsylvania Higher Education Assistance Agency (PHEAA).

**Financial data:** The stipend is $1,500 per year.

**Duration:** 1 year; may be renewed if the recipient remains enrolled full time and makes satisfactory academic progress.

**Number awarded:** Varies each year.

**Deadline:** April of each year.

## 942 PHI ETA SIGMA HONOR SOCIETY DISTINGUISHED MEMBER UNDERGRADUATE SCHOLARSHIPS

Phi Eta Sigma
c/o John F. Sagabiel
Western Kentucky University
525 Grise Hall
1 Big Red Way
Bowling Green, KY 42101
Phone: (270) 745-6540; Fax: (270) 745-3893;
Email: Phi.Eta.Sigma@WKU.edu
Web: www.phietasigma.org/scholarships.htm

**Summary:** To provide financial assistance for college to members of Phi Eta Sigma Honor Society.

**Eligibility:** Open to members of the honor society who are enrolled full time in a college or university. Membership in the society requires a GPA of 3.5 or higher. Selection is based on academic record, participation in Phi Eta Sigma chapter activities, creative ability, potential for success in their chosen field, and 3 letters of recommendation.

**Financial data:** The stipend is $2,000.

**Duration:** 1 year.

**Number awarded:** Varies each year; recently, 31 of these scholarships were awarded.

**Deadline:** February of each year.

## 943 PHI ETA SIGMA HONOR SOCIETY UNDERGRADUATE SCHOLARSHIPS

Phi Eta Sigma
c/o John F. Sagabiel
Western Kentucky University
525 Grise Hall
1 Big Red Way
Bowling Green, KY 42101
Phone: (270) 745-6540; Fax: (270) 745-3893;
Email: Phi.Eta.Sigma@WKU.edu
Web: www.phietasigma.org/scholarships.htm

**Summary:** To provide financial assistance for college to members of Phi Eta Sigma Honor Society.

**Eligibility:** Open to members of the honor society who are enrolled full time in a college or university. Membership in the society requires a GPA of 3.5 or higher. Selection is based on academic record, participation in Phi Eta Sigma chapter activities, creative ability, potential for success in their chosen field, and 3 letters of recommendation.

**Financial data:** The stipend is $1,000.

**Duration:** 1 year.

**Number awarded:** Varies each year; recently, 72 of these scholarships were awarded.

**Deadline:** February of each year.

## 944 PHI THETA KAPPA SCHOLARSHIP PROGRAM

Phi Theta Kappa
Scholarship Programs Director
1625 Eastover Drive
P.O. Box 13729
Jackson, MS 39236-3729
Phone: (601) 984-3504, ext. 560; (800) 946-9995, ext. 560;
Fax: (601) 984-3550; Email: clancy.mitchell@ptk.org
Web: www.ptk.org

**Summary:** To provide financial assistance for college to members of Phi Theta Kappa, the international honor society of 2-year colleges.

**Eligibility:** Open to members of Phi Theta Kappa, if they wish to transfer to 4-year or senior-level institutions. Scholarships are funded by participating universities, which also establish the specific requirements for their institutions.

**Financial data:** The amounts and terms of the awards are established by the senior institutions; more than $34 million in awards are available each year.

**Duration:** Varies at each institution.

**Number awarded:** More than 550 institutions in 49 states, the District of Columbia, and Canada offer scholarships to Phi Theta Kappa members.

**Deadline:** Deadlines are established by participating institutions.

## 945 PINNACOL FOUNDATION SCHOLARSHIP PROGRAM

Pinnacol Foundation, Attn: Elizabeth Starkey
7501 East Lowry Boulevard
Denver, CO 80230
Phone: (303) 361-4775; (800) 873-7248, ext. 4775; Fax: (303) 361-5775
Web: www.pinnacol.com/foundation

**Summary:** To provide financial assistance for college to Colorado residents whose parent was killed or permanently disabled in a work-related accident.

**Eligibility:** Open to the natural, adopted, step, or fully dependent children of workers killed or permanently injured in a compensable work-related accident during the course and scope of employment with a Colorado-based employer and entitled to receive benefits under the Colorado Workers' Compensation Act. Applicants must be between 16 and 24 years of age and attending or planning to attend a college or technical school. Selection is based on academic achievement and aptitude, community service, and financial need.

**Financial data:** The stipend depends on the need of the recipient.

**Duration:** 1 year; may be renewed.

**Number awarded:** Varies each year; recently, 31 of these scholarships were awarded.

**Deadline:** March of each year.

## 946 POINT FOUNDATION SCHOLARSHIPS

Point Foundation
P.O. Box 11210
Chicago, IL 60611
Phone: (866) 33-POINT; Fax: (866) 39-POINT;
Email: info@thepointfoundation.org
Web: www.thepointfoundation.org

**Summary:** To provide financial assistance for college or graduate school to students who have been involved in the lesbian, gay, bisexual, or transgender (LGBT) community.

**Eligibility:** Open to citizens of any country who are attending or planning to attend a college or university in the United States to work on an undergraduate or graduate degree. Applicants are not required to be LGBT, but they should have a history of leadership in the LGBT community and plan to be a LGBT leader in the future. Selection is based on academic accomplishment; financial, emotional, and social need; extracurricular activities; personal circumstances; and goals.

**Financial data:** Stipends range from $5,000 to $28,000 per year.

**Duration:** 1 year; may be renewed if the recipient maintains a GPA of 3.5 or higher.

**Number awarded:** Varies each year; recently, 20 of these scholarships were awarded.

**Deadline:** February of each year.

### 947 POLISH WOMEN'S CIVIC CLUB FINANCIAL SCHOLARSHIPS

Polish Women's Civic Club, Attn: Education Committee Chair
P.O. Box 684
Lake Villa, IL 60046

**Summary:** To provide financial assistance for college or graduate school to Illinois residents of Polish heritage.

**Eligibility:** Open to U.S. citizens who have at least 1 parent of Polish heritage. Applicants must reside in Illinois area and be full-time students at the undergraduate, graduate, or postgraduate level in at least their second year of study. Selection is based on academic achievement, student activities, community involvement (including Polish activities), and financial need.

**Financial data:** The stipend depends on the need of the recipient and the availability of funds.

**Number awarded:** Varies each year.

**Deadline:** June of each year.

### 948 PORTLAND WOMEN'S CLUB SCHOLARSHIP

Oregon Student Assistance Commission
Attn: Grants and Scholarships Division
1500 Valley River Drive, Suite 100
Eugene, OR 97401-2146
Phone: (541) 687-7395; (800) 452-8807, ext. 7395; Fax: (541) 687-7419;
Email: awardinfo@mercury.osac.state.or.us
Web: www.osac.state.or.us

**Summary:** To provide financial assistance to college students who graduated from a high school in Oregon.

**Eligibility:** Open to graduates of high schools in Oregon who had a cumulative high school GPA of 3.0 or higher. Preference is given to women.

**Financial data:** The stipend is at least $1,500 per year.

**Duration:** 1 year; may be renewed if the recipient shows satisfactory academic progress and continued financial need.

**Number awarded:** Varies each year; recently, 5 of these scholarships were awarded.

**Deadline:** February of each year.

### 949 PORTUGUESE FOUNDATION SCHOLARSHIPS

Portuguese Foundation of Connecticut, Attn: Gabriel R. Serrano, President
86 New Park Avenue
Hartford, CT 06106-2127
Phone: (860) 236-5514; Fax: (860) 236-5514; Email: info@pfict.org
Web: www.pfict.org/scholar.html

**Summary:** To provide financial assistance for college or graduate school to students of Portuguese ancestry in Connecticut.

**Eligibility:** Open to residents of Connecticut who are U.S. citizens or permanent residents. At least 1 great-grandparent must be of Portuguese ancestry. Applicants must be attending, or planning to attend, a college or university as a full-time undergraduate or full- or part-time graduate student. Along with their application, they must submit an essay describing financial need, an essay detailing proof of Portuguese ancestry and interest in the Portuguese language and culture, 2 letters of recommendation, their high school or college transcripts, a copy of the FAFSA form or their most recent federal income tax return, and their SAT report. Selection is based on financial need and academic record.

**Financial data:** Stipends are at least $1,000 each; a total of $12,000 is distributed annually.

**Duration:** 1 year; recipients may reapply.

**Number awarded:** Approximately 9 each year.

**Deadline:** March of each year.

### 950 PORTUGUESE HERITAGE SCHOLARSHIP FOUNDATION GENERAL SCHOLARSHIPS

Portuguese Heritage Scholarship Foundation, Attn: Academic Secretary
P.O. Box 30246
Bethesda, MD 20824-0246
Phone: (301) 652-2775; Email: phsf@vivaportugal.com
Web: www.vivaportugal.com/phsf/apply.htm

**Summary:** To provide financial assistance for college to students of Portuguese American heritage.

**Eligibility:** Open to high school seniors or currently-enrolled college students who are of Portuguese American ancestry. Applicants must be U.S. residents and attending or planning to attend an accredited 4-year college or university. Selection is based on academic achievement and financial need.

**Financial data:** The stipend is $2,000 per year.

**Duration:** 4 years, provided the recipient maintains a GPA of 3.0 or higher.

**Number awarded:** 1 or more each year.

**Deadline:** January of each year.

### 951 POSSIBLE WOMAN FOUNDATION INTERNATIONAL SCHOLARSHIP

Possible Woman Enterprises, Attn: Possible Woman Foundation International
2968 Four Oaks Drive
Atlanta, GA 30360
Phone: (770) 863-1515; (888) 663-4767; Fax: (770) 863-1090;
Email: denise@possiblewomanfoundation.org
Web: www.possiblewoman.com/newwebsite/scholarships.htm

**Summary:** To provide financial assistance for college or graduate school to women of all ages.

**Eligibility:** Open to women who are changing careers and/or seeking advancement in their current career or worklife; stay at home mothers looking to enhance their skills; volunteers supporting society through giving to organizations in the community; and young women in the early stages of achieving their educational aspirations. Applicants may be of any age and at any level of education (high school graduate, some college, 4-year college graduate, graduate school, doctoral). Along with their application, they must submit a 2-page essay on the topic, "How Having the Opportunity for Beginning or Continuing My Academic Education Will Positively Impact My Life." Selection is based on the essay, career and life goals, leadership and participation in community activities, honors and awards received, and financial need.

**Financial data:** The stipend ranges from $3,000 to $3,500.

**Duration:** 1 year; nonrenewable.

**Number awarded:** 1 each year.

**Deadline:** March of each year.

### 952 POWDER RIVER BASIN SECTION ANNUAL SCHOLARSHIP AWARDS

Society of Petroleum Engineers-Powder River Basin Section
P.O. Box 3977
Gillette, WY 82717-3977

**Summary:** To provide financial assistance to Wyoming students interested in preparing for a career in the oil and gas industry.

**Eligibility:** Open to Wyoming students preparing for a career in the oil and gas industry. Applicants should be majoring in engineering (especially petroleum engineering and petroleum technology, although some of the scholarships may go to non-engineering students. They must be enrolled full time as entering freshmen, sophomores, juniors, or seniors in a 4-year program or freshmen or sophomores in a 2-year program and have a GPA of 2.75 or higher. Along with their application, they must submit a letter that covers their academic qualifications, primary career interests, extracurricular activities, and names of 2 references. Financial need is not considered in the selection process.

**Financial data:** Stipends range from $250 to $1,000.

**Duration:** 1 year.

**Number awarded:** 5 to 15 each year.

**Deadline:** March of each year.

### 953 PRINCIPAL'S LEADERSHIP AWARDS

National Association of Secondary School Principals
Attn: Department of Student Activities
1904 Association Drive
Reston, VA 20191-1537
Phone: (703) 860-0200; (800) 253-7746, ext. 252; Fax: (703) 476-5432;
Email: carrollw@principals.org
Web: www.principals.org/awards/pla.cfm

**Summary:** To recognize and reward, with college scholarships, outstanding high school seniors.

**Eligibility:** Open to high school student leaders. Each principal of a public, private, or parochial high school in the United States may nominate 1 qualified student. Nominees must be in the top 20% of their class and demonstrate leadership. Financial need is not considered.

**Financial data:** The award is $1,000.

**Duration:** The awards are presented annually.

**Additional information:** Funding for this program is provided by Herff Jones, Inc.

**Number awarded:** 150 each year.

**Deadline:** Principals must submit their nomination by December of each year.

## 954 PRISCILLA MAXWELL ENDICOTT SCHOLARSHIPS

Connecticut Women's Golf Association
c/o Deborah Boynton, Scholarship Committee
52 Mountain Spring Road
Farmington, CT 06032
Email: juniors@cwga.org
Web: www.cwga.org/JrScholarships.htm

**Summary:** To provide financial assistance for college to women golfers from Connecticut.

**Eligibility:** Open to high school seniors and college students who are residents of Connecticut attending or planning to attend a 4-year college or university. Applicants must be active women golfers with a handicap. Along with their application, they must submit a statement on why they want to go to college and why they should receive this scholarship. Selection is based on participation in golf programs, academic achievement and financial need.

**Financial data:** The maximum stipend is $1,000 per year.

**Duration:** Up to 4 years.

**Number awarded:** 4 each year.

**Deadline:** April of each year.

## 955 PRISCILLA R. MORTON SCHOLARSHIP

United Methodist Church
Attn: General Board of Higher Education and Ministry
Office of Loans and Scholarships
1001 19th Avenue South
P.O. Box 340007
Nashville, TN 37203-0007
Phone: (615) 340-7344; Fax: (615) 340-7367; Email: umscholar@gbhem.org
Web: www.gbhem.org

**Summary:** To provide financial assistance to undergraduate students attending schools affiliated with the United Methodist Church.

**Eligibility:** Open to U.S. citizens and permanent residents who have been active, full members of a United Methodist Church for at least 1 year prior to applying. Applicants must be attending a college or university related to the United Methodist Church as a full-time student. Preference is given to students who have a GPA of 3.5 or higher.

**Financial data:** A stipend is awarded (amount not specified).

**Duration:** 1 year; recipients may reapply.

**Number awarded:** 1 or more each year.

**Deadline:** May of each year.

## 956 PRIVATE COLLEGES & UNIVERSITIES MAGAZINE MULTICULTURAL SCHOLARSHIP

Private Colleges & Universities, Inc.
Attn: *PC&U* Multicultural Edition Scholarship Program
2 LAN Drive, Suite 100
P.O. Box 349
Westford, MA 01886
Phone: (978) 692-5092; Email: mc.scholar@privatecolleges.com
Web: www.privatecolleges.com

**Summary:** To provide financial assistance to high school seniors and graduates of color who are planning to enroll as a freshman in a private college or university.

**Eligibility:** Open to all students of color who are currently residents of the United States or its territories and planning to enroll in a baccalaureate degree program at a participating private college or university (for a list, write to the sponsor). Applicants must submit a 1,000-word statement about their community service activities, a high school transcript, and a recommendation by someone in their community (not a family member). Selection is based on academic merit (transcripts, class rank, and GPA) and on service to the community.

**Financial data:** The stipend is $2,000.

**Duration:** 1 year; nonrenewable.

**Number awarded:** 5 each year.

**Deadline:** December of each year.

## 957 PROJECT RED FLAG ACADEMIC SCHOLARSHIP FOR WOMEN WITH BLEEDING DISORDERS

National Hemophilia Foundation
Attn: Department of Finance, Administration & MIS
116 West 32nd Street, 11th Floor
New York, NY 10001-3212
Phone: (212) 328-3700; (800) 42-HANDI, ext. 3700;
Fax: (212) 328-3777; Email: info@hemophilia.org
Web: www.hemophilia.org

**Summary:** To provide financial assistance for college or graduate school to women who have a bleeding disorder.

**Eligibility:** Open to women who are entering or already enrolled in an undergraduate or graduate program at a university, college, or accredited vocational school. Applicants must have von Willebrand disease, hemophilia or other clotting factor deficiency, or carrier status. Along with their application, they must submit a 250-word essay that describes their educational and future career plans, including how they intend to use their education to enhance the bleeding disorders community. Financial need is not considered in the selection process.

**Financial data:** The stipend is $2,500.

**Duration:** 1 year.

**Number awarded:** 2 each year.

**Deadline:** May of each year.

## 958 PRUDENTIAL SPIRIT OF COMMUNITY AWARDS

National Association of Secondary School Principals
Attn: Department of Student Activities
1904 Association Drive
Reston, VA 20191-1537
Phone: (703) 860-0200; (800) 253-7746, ext. 324; Fax: (703) 476-5432;
Email: spirit@principals.org
Web: www.principals.org/awards/prudential.cfm

**Summary:** To recognize and reward middle level and high school students who demonstrate exemplary community service.

**Eligibility:** Open to students in grades 5 through 12 at public and private schools in the United States (including the District of Columbia and Puerto Rico). Each school may select 1 honoree for every 1,000 students. At the local level, honorees are chosen on the basis of their individual community service activity or significant leadership in a group activity that has taken place during the previous year. Local honorees are then certified by their school principal, Girl Scout council executive director, county 4-H agent, Campfire USA council director, American Red Cross chapter official, YMCA representative, or member Volunteer Center of the Points of Light Foundation and Volunteer Center National Network to compete at the state level. As a result of that judging, 1 high school and 1 middle level student in each state, the District of Columbia, and Puerto Rico are named state honorees. The state honorees then compete for national awards.

**Financial data:** Each state honoree receives $1,000, a silver medallion, and an all-expense paid trip to Washington, D.C. to compete at the national level. National honorees receive an additional $5,000, a gold medallion, and a crystal trophy for their school.

**Duration:** The competition is held annually.

**Number awarded:** 104 state honorees are chosen each year: 1 middle level student and 1 high school student from each state, the District of Columbia, and Puerto Rico; 10 of those (5 middle level students and 5 high school students) are named national honorees.

**Deadline:** Students must submit applications to their principal, Girl Scout council, county 4-H agent, Campfire USA council, American Red Cross chapter, YMCA, or Volunteer Center by October of each year.

## 959 PUBLIC EDUCATION AND CITIZENSHIP STATEWIDE ESSAY CONTEST

Grand Lodge of Florida Masons
Attn: Public Education and Citizenship Committee
220 Ocean Street
P.O. Box 1020
Jacksonville, FL 32201-1020
Phone: (800) 375-2339; Email: scholarship@glflamason.org
Web: www.glflamason.org

**Summary:** To recognize and reward, with college scholarships, outstanding essays written by high school seniors in Florida on the importance of education.

**Eligibility:** Open to all graduating high school seniors in Florida who will be attending a state-supported school in Florida during the following semester/quarter. State-supported schools include any community college, university, or division of higher learning governed by the State Board of Regents. Students are invited to submit a 1,000-word essay on "Why Education Is Important." All work must be original. Essays are judged on merit, without regard to sex, race, creed, or religion.

**Financial data:** The award is $1,000. Funds are paid to the recipient's school.

**Duration:** The competition is held annually.

**Number awarded:** 10 each year.

**Deadline:** February of each year.

## 960 PUERTO RICO NATIONAL GUARD TUITION ASSISTANCE FUND

Puerto Rico National Guard, Attn: Education Services Officer

P.O. Box 9023786

San Juan, PR 00902-3786

Phone: (787) 721-3131; Fax: (787) 723-6360; Email: ortegaj@pr.ngb.army.mil

**Summary:** To provide financial assistance for college or graduate school to National Guard members in Puerto Rico and their families.

**Eligibility:** Open to 1) active members of the Puerto Rico National Guard who are interested in preparing for a career on the undergraduate or graduate level (up to the Ph.D. degree); 2) spouses of members interested in working on an undergraduate or graduate degree (up to a master's degree); and 3) children of members interested in undergraduate or vocational study. Guard members may not receive support at the same time as a spouse and/or child.

**Financial data:** For Guard members, the program pays $50 per credit to a maximum of $900 per year for undergraduate or vocational study, $75 per credit to a maximum of $1,350 per year for graduate study, or a maximum of $1,000 per year for study for an M.D. degree. For spouses, the program pays $75 per credit to a maximum of $1,350 per semester for graduate study. For spouses and children, the program pays $50 per credit to a maximum of $900 per semester for undergraduate or vocational study ($1,800 per year).

**Duration:** 1 year; may be renewed. Guard members are limited to 18 credits of study per year; spouses and children are limited to 18 credits per semester.

**Number awarded:** Varies each year.

## 961 R. PRESTON WOODRUFF, JR. SCHOLARSHIPS

Arkansas Student Loan Authority

101 East Capitol Avenue, Suite 401

Little Rock, AR 72201

Phone: (800) 443-6030

Web: www.asla.info/collegeplanning/woodruffscholarship.aspx

**Summary:** To provide financial assistance for college to residents of Arkansas or students attending a postsecondary institution in the state.

**Eligibility:** Open to 1) residents of Arkansas, who may be attending a postsecondary institution in or out of the state, and 2) residents of other states attending a postsecondary institution in Arkansas. Postsecondary educational institutions include 2-year colleges, 4-year colleges and universities, and technical and trade schools. Applicants may enter online or by submitting a postcard with their name, address, telephone number, and name of their educational institution. Winners are selected at random.

**Financial data:** The stipend is $1,000. Funds are mailed to the financial aid office at the designated school.

**Duration:** 1 year; of the scholarships awarded each year, 1 may be renewed up to 3 additional years but the others are nonrenewable.

**Number awarded:** 20 each year.

**Deadline:** March of each year.

## 962 RACHEL E. LEMIEUX YOUTH SCHOLARSHIP

Maine Federation of Business and Professional Women

Attn: Futurama Foundation

c/o Jeanne L. Hammond, President

RR 1, Box 1610

Albion, ME 04910-9719

Phone: (207) 437-2325; Email: jlhammon@colby.edu

Web: www.bpwmaine.org/Scholarship.htm

**Summary:** To provide financial assistance for college to female high school seniors in Maine.

**Eligibility:** Open to women who are seniors graduating from high schools in Maine. Applicants must be planning to attend an accredited college or university. They must be able to demonstrate financial need.

**Financial data:** The stipend is $1,200.

**Duration:** 1 year.

**Number awarded:** 1 or more each year.

**Deadline:** March of each year.

## 963 RACIAL ETHNIC EDUCATIONAL SCHOLARSHIPS

Synod of the Trinity, Attn: Scholarships

3040 Market Street

Camp Hill, PA 17011-4599

Phone: (717) 737-0421, ext. 232; (800) 242-0534, ext. 232; Fax: (717) 737-8211; Email: Pnash@syntrinity.org

Web: www.syntrinity.org/Programs/ScholarshipsGrantsLoan.htm

**Summary:** To provide financial assistance for college to ethnic minority students in Pennsylvania, West Virginia, and designated counties in Ohio.

**Eligibility:** Open to members of a racial minority group (African American, Asian, Hispanic, Latino, Middle Eastern, or Native American) who are attending or planning to attend an accredited college or vocational school as a full-time student. Applicants may be of any religious denomination, but they must be residents of the Presbyterian Church (USA) Synod of the Trinity, which covers all of Pennsylvania; West Virginia except for the counties of Berkeley, Grant, Hampshire, Hardy, Jefferson, Mineral, Morgan, and Pendleton; and the Ohio counties of Belmont, Harrison, Jefferson, Monroe, and the southern sector of Columbiana. They must be able to demonstrate financial need and U.S. citizenship or permanent resident status.

**Financial data:** Awards range from $100 to $1,000 per year, depending on the need of the recipient.

**Duration:** 1 year; may be renewed up to 3 additional years, provided that the recipient maintains a GPA of 1.75 or higher for the second year and 2.0 or higher for the third and fourth years.

**Number awarded:** Varies each year.

**Deadline:** April of each year.

## 964 RATH DISTINGUISHED SCHOLARSHIPS

Wisconsin Foundation for Independent Colleges, Inc., Attn: Program Manager

735 North Water Street, Suite 600

Milwaukee, WI 53202-4100

Phone: (414) 273-5980; Fax: (414) 273-5995; Email: wfic@wficweb.org

Web: www.wficweb.org/documents/schinfo.htm

**Summary:** To provide financial assistance to students attending or planning to attend a member institution of the Wisconsin Foundation for Independent Colleges (WFIC).

**Eligibility:** Open to students enrolled or planning to enroll at a WFIC member college or university on a full-time basis. Applicants must have a GPA of 3.0 or higher; entering freshmen must rank in the top 25% of their high school class. They must be able to demonstrate financial need and campus and community leadership. Preference is given to students from Wisconsin, but residency is not required.

**Financial data:** The stipend is $10,000.

**Duration:** 1 year.

**Number awarded:** 1 or more each year.

**Deadline:** Each participating college sets its own deadline.

## 965 RAYMOND T. WELLINGTON, JR. MEMORIAL SCHOLARSHIP

American Legion Auxiliary, Attn: Department of New York

112 State Street, Suite 1310

Albany, NY 12207

Phone: (518) 463-1162; (800) 421-6348; Fax: (518) 449-5406; Email: alanyhdqtrs@worldnet.att.net

Web: www.deptny.org/scholarships.htm

**Summary:** To provide financial assistance for college to New York residents who are the descendants of veterans.

**Eligibility:** Open to residents of New York who are the children, grandchildren, or great grandchildren of veterans of World War II, the Korean Conflict, the Vietnam War, Grenada/Lebanon, Panama, or the Persian Gulf. Applicants must be high school seniors or graduates younger than 20 years of age. They must be interested in attending an accredited college or university. Along with their application, they must submit a 700-word autobiography that includes their interests, experiences, long-range plans, and goals. Selection is based on character (15%), Americanism (15%), community involvement (15%), leadership (15%), scholarship (20%), and financial need (20%).

**Financial data:** The stipend is $1,000.

**Duration:** 1 year.

**Number awarded:** 1 each year.

**Deadline:** March of each year.

**966 RBC DAIN RAUSCHER COLORADO SCHOLARSHIPS**

Denver Foundation, Attn: Scholarships and Special Projects
950 South Cherry Street, Suite 200
Denver, CO 80246
Phone: (303) 300-1790, ext. 141; Fax: (303) 300-6547;
Email: kbellina@denverfoundation.org
Web: www.denverfoundation.org

**Summary:** To provide financial assistance for college to high school seniors from Colorado who can demonstrate exceptional levels of achievement.

**Eligibility:** Open to seniors graduating from high schools in Colorado who can demonstrate exceptional levels of achievement in such areas as arts, athletics, community service, leadership, or academics. Applicants must have a GPA of 3.75 or higher, a rank in the top 5% of their class, or an ACT score of 26 (or the equivalent on the SAT). They must have received an acceptance letter from an accredited college, university, or technical school. Selection is based on academic excellence, leadership in school and community, personal achievements, significant challenges that have been overcome, and financial need. A personal interview may be required.

**Financial data:** Stipends are at least $3,000.

**Duration:** 1 year.

**Number awarded:** 10 or more each year.

**Deadline:** March of each year.

**967 REAM'S FOOD STORES SCHOLARSHIPS**

Utah Sports Hall of Fame Foundation, Attn: Scholarship Chair
2248 Texas Street
Salt Lake City, UT 84109
Phone: (801) 484-0666

**Summary:** To recognize and reward outstanding high school seniors in Utah who have been involved in athletics and are interested in attending college in the state.

**Eligibility:** Open to high school seniors in Utah. Each high school may nominate 1 boy and 1 girl who are graduating this year. Nominees must be planning to attend college in the state. Selection is based on academic record, personal character, financial need, leadership qualities, and involvement in athletic activities, including football, basketball, cross country, volleyball, tennis, track and field, soccer, rodeo, baseball, swimming, wrestling, officiating, or community recreation.

**Financial data:** The stipend is $2,000. Funds are paid to the recipient's institution.

**Duration:** 1 year; nonrenewable.

**Number awarded:** 6 each year: 3 boys and 3 girls.

**Deadline:** March of each year.

**968 RED RIVER VALLEY FIGHTER PILOTS ASSOCIATION SCHOLARSHIP GRANT PROGRAM**

Red River Valley Association Foundation
P.O. Box 1916
Harrisonburg, VA 22801
Phone: (540) 442-7782; Fax: (540) 443-3105; Email: afbridger@aol.com
Web: www.river-rats.org

**Summary:** To provide financial assistance for college or graduate school to the spouses and children of selected service personnel and members of the Red River Valley Fighter Pilots Association.

**Eligibility:** Open to the spouses and children of 1) service members missing in action (MIA) or killed in action (KIA) in armed conflicts by U.S. forces since August 1964, including those lost in the World Trade Center or Pentagon on September 11, 2001; 2) surviving dependents of U.S. military aircrew members killed in a non-combat aircraft accident in which they were performing aircrew duties; and 3) current members of the association and deceased members who were in good standing at the time of their death. Applicants must be interested in attending an accredited college or university to work on an undergraduate or graduate degree. Selection is based on demonstrated academic achievement, college entrance examination scores, financial need, and accomplishments in school, church, civic, and social activities.

**Financial data:** The amount awarded varies, depending upon the need of the recipient. Recently, undergraduate stipends have ranged from $500 to $3,500 and averaged $1,725; graduate stipends have ranged from $500 to $2,000 and averaged $1,670. Funds are paid directly to the recipient's institution and are to be used for tuition, fees, books, and room and board for full-time students.

**Duration:** 1 year.

**Number awarded:** Varies each year; since this program was established, it has awarded more than 900 scholarships worth nearly $1,500,000.

**Deadline:** May of each year.

**969 REGIONAL UNIVERSITY BACCALAUREATE SCHOLARSHIP PROGRAM**

Oklahoma State Regents for Higher Education
Attn: Director of Scholarship and Grant Programs
655 Research Parkway, Suite 200
P.O. Box 108850
Oklahoma City, OK 73101-8850
Phone: (405) 225-9239; (800) 858-1840; Fax: (405) 225-9230;
Email: studentinfo@osrhe.edu
Web: www.okhighered.org/student-center/financial-aid/rubs.shtml

**Summary:** To provide financial assistance to Oklahoma residents who are attending designated publicly-supported regional universities in the state.

**Eligibility:** Open to residents of Oklahoma who are attending 1 of 11 designated regional public institutions in the state and working on an undergraduate degree. Applicants must 1) be designated a National Merit Semifinalist or Commended Student, or 2) have an ACT score of at least 30 and have an exceptional GPA and class ranking as determined by the collegiate institution. Selection is based on academic promise.

**Financial data:** The stipend is $3,000 per year. Awardees also receive a resident tuition waiver from the institution.

**Duration:** Up to 4 years if the recipient maintains a cumulative GPA of 3.25 or higher and full-time enrollment.

**Number awarded:** Up to 165 each year: 15 at each of the 11 participating regional universities.

**970 RHODE ISLAND ASSOCIATION OF FORMER LEGISLATORS SCHOLARSHIP**

Rhode Island Foundation, Attn: Scholarship Coordinator
One Union Station
Providence, RI 02903
Phone: (401) 274-4564; Fax: (401) 751-7983; Email: libbym@rifoundation.org
Web: www.rifoundation.org

**Summary:** To provide financial assistance for college to graduating high school seniors in Rhode Island who have been involved in public service activities.

**Eligibility:** Open to graduating high school seniors who are Rhode Island residents. Applicants must have distinguished themselves by their outstanding involvement in public service, have been accepted into an accredited postsecondary institution, and be able to demonstrate financial need. Along with their application, they must submit an essay (up to 300 words), explaining the nature of their community service participation, the work's influence on them, and how they plan to continue their public service work into the future.

**Financial data:** The stipend is $1,500 per year.

**Duration:** 1 year; nonrenewable.

**Number awarded:** 5 each year.

**Deadline:** May of each year.

**971 RHODE ISLAND EDUCATIONAL BENEFITS FOR DISABLED AMERICAN VETERANS**

Division of Veterans' Affairs
480 Metacom Avenue
Bristol, RI 02809-0689
Phone: (401) 462-0324; Fax: (401) 254-2320; TDD: (401) 254-1345;
Email: devangelista@dhs.ri.gov
Web: www.dhs.state.ri.us

**Summary:** To provide assistance to disabled veterans in Rhode Island who wish to pursue higher education at a public institution in the state.

**Eligibility:** Open to permanent residents of Rhode Island who have been verified by the Department of Veterans Affairs (DVA) as having a disability of at least 10% resulting from military service.

**Financial data:** Eligible veterans are entitled to take courses at any public institution of higher education in Rhode Island without the payment of tuition, exclusive of other fees and charges.

**Number awarded:** Varies each year.

**972 RHODE ISLAND STATE GRANT PROGRAM**

Rhode Island Higher Education Assistance Authority
Attn: Scholarship and Grant Division
560 Jefferson Boulevard
Warwick, RI 02886
Phone: (401) 736-1170; (800) 922-9855; Fax: (401) 732-3541;

TDD: (401) 734-9481; Email: grants@riheaa.org

Web: www.riheaa.org/borrowers/grants

**Summary:** To provide financial assistance for college to residents of Rhode Island who can demonstrate financial need.

**Eligibility:** Open to U.S. citizens and permanent residents who have been residents of Rhode Island since the beginning of the year prior to the academic year in which they enroll in college. Applicants must be enrolled or accepted for enrollment in a program that leads to a certificate or degree, not owe a refund on a federal Title IV grant, not be in default on a Title IV loan, and not already possess a bachelor's degree. If they are already enrolled in college, they must be making satisfactory academic progress as defined by their school's academic progress policy. The only application procedure is filing a Free Application for Federal Student Aid (FAFSA); all Rhode Island residents who submit that form are automatically considered for these grants. Applicants must be interested in attending an eligible school in the United States, Canada, or Mexico on at least a half-time basis.

**Financial data:** Stipends range from $300 to $1,400 per year, depending on the recipient's financial need.

**Duration:** 1 year; may be renewed for up to 3 additional years (or 4 years for a bona fide 5-year program of study) as long as the recipient files a new FAFSA, continues to meet all eligibility requirements, and maintains satisfactory progress as defined by the institution.

**Number awarded:** Varies each year.

**Deadline:** February of each year.

## 973 RMHC NATIONAL SCHOLARSHIP PROGRAM

Ronald McDonald House Charities, Attn: National Scholarship Program

One Kroc Drive

Oak Brook, IL 60523

Phone: (630) 623-7048; Fax: (630) 623-7488

Web: www.rmhc.org/rmhc/index/programs/rmhc_scholarship_program.html

**Summary:** To provide financial assistance for college to high school seniors in specified geographic areas.

**Eligibility:** Open to high school seniors in designated McDonald's market areas. Applicants must be planning to attend a 2-year or 4-year college or university on a full-time basis. Along with their application, they must submit a personal statement, up to 2 pages in length, on their community involvement, career goals, and desire to contribute to their community; information about unique, personal, or financial circumstances may be added. Selection is based on that statement, high school transcripts, a letter of recommendation, and financial need.

**Financial data:** Most awards are $1,000 per year. Funds are paid directly to the recipient's school.

**Duration:** 1 year; nonrenewable.

**Number awarded:** Varies each year; since the program began, it has awarded more than $19 million in scholarships.

**Deadline:** January of each year.

## 974 ROADWAY WORKER MEMORIAL SCHOLARSHIPS

American Traffic Safety Services Foundation, Attn: Foundation Director

15 Riverside Parkway, Suite 100

Fredericksburg, VA 22406-1022

Phone: (540) 368-1701; (800) 272-8772; Fax: (540) 368-1717;

Email: foundation@atssa.com

Web: www.atssa.com/found/roadway.htm

**Summary:** To provide financial assistance for college to children of roadway workers killed or permanently disabled in work zones.

**Eligibility:** Open to students enrolled or planning to enroll at a 4-year college or university, 2-year accredited college, or vocational/technical school or training institution. Applicants must be children of roadway workers killed or permanently disabled in work zones, including mobile operations and the installation of roadway safety features. They must submit a statement, up to 200 words, explaining their reasons for wanting to continue their education and listing any volunteer activities or accomplishments. Selection is based on that statement, academic performance, 2 letters of recommendation, and financial need.

**Financial data:** The stipend is $2,000. An additional $1,000 may be awarded to recipients who demonstrate a strong commitment to volunteerism.

**Duration:** 1 year.

**Number awarded:** Varies each year.

**Deadline:** January of each year.

## 975 ROBERT C. BYRD HONORS SCHOLARSHIP PROGRAM

Department of Education

Office of Postsecondary Education

Attn: Institutional Development and Undergraduate Education Service

1990 K Street, N.W., Sixth Floor

Washington, DC 20006-8500

Phone: (202) 502-7582; Fax: (202) 502-7861;

Email: argelia.velez-rodriguez@ed.gov

Web: www.ed.gov/programs/iduesbyrd/index.html

**Summary:** To provide financial assistance for college to outstanding high school seniors.

**Eligibility:** Open to U.S. citizens or eligible noncitizens who are graduating from a public or private high school (home-schooled students are not eligible) and planning to attend an accredited college, university, postsecondary vocational school, or proprietary institution of higher education as a full-time student. These awards are administered by an officially designated state educational agency (SEA) in each state that establishes the exact requirements for that state; typically, states require students to rank in the upper quarter of their high school class and have minimum scores of 27 on the ACT (or the equivalent on the SAT).

**Financial data:** The stipend is $1,500 per year.

**Duration:** 1 year; may be renewed up to 3 additional years as long as recipients maintain full-time enrollment and meets the satisfactory academic progress requirements of their school.

**Number awarded:** Varies each year; each state is allocated a number of these scholarships proportional to its population. Recently, 6,370 new scholarships were granted.

**Deadline:** March of each year.

## 976 ROBERT GUTHRIE PKU SCHOLARSHIP

National PKU News

6869 Woodlawn Avenue, N.E., Suite 116

Seattle, WA 98115-5469

Phone: (206) 525-8140; Fax: (206) 525-5023; Email: schuett@pkunews.org

Web: www.pkunews.org

**Summary:** To provide financial assistance for college to students with phenylketonuria (PKU).

**Eligibility:** Open to college-age people with PKU who are on the required diet. Applicants must be accepted to an accredited college or technical school before the scholarship is awarded, but they may apply before acceptance is confirmed. Residents of all countries are eligible to apply. Selection is based on academic achievement and financial need.

**Financial data:** Stipends vary but recently have been $2,000.

**Duration:** 1 year.

**Number awarded:** Varies each year; recently, 2 of these scholarships were awarded.

**Deadline:** October of each year.

## 977 ROBERT R. LEE CATEGORY A PROMISE SCHOLARSHIP

Idaho State Board of Education

Len B. Jordan Office Building

650 West State Street, Room 307

P.O. Box 83720

Boise, ID 83720-0037

Phone: (208) 332-1574; Fax: (208) 334-2632; Email: board@osbe.state.id.us

Web: www.idahoboardofed.org/scholarships/promisea.asp

**Summary:** To provide financial assistance for college or professional/technical school to outstanding high school seniors in Idaho.

**Eligibility:** Open to graduating high school seniors who are Idaho residents planning to enroll full time in academic or professional/technical programs in public or private institutions in the state. Academic applicants must also be in the top 10% of their class and have a cumulative GPA of 3.5 or higher and an ACT score of 28 or higher. Professional/technical applicants must have a cumulative GPA of 2.8 or higher and must take the COMPASS test (reading, writing, and algebra scores are required). U.S. citizenship is also required.

**Financial data:** The stipend is $3,000 per year.

**Duration:** 1 year. Academic scholarships may be renewed for up to 3 additional years and professional/technical scholarships may be renewed for up to 2 additional years; renewal is granted only if the recipient remains enrolled full time with a rank in the top 50% of the students in the class and a GPA of 3.0 or higher.

**Number awarded:** Approximately 30 each year. Academic students receive 75% of the awards and professional/technical students receive 25%.

**Deadline:** December of each year.

## 978 ROBERT SMILEY SCHOLARSHIP

Iowa Girls' High School Athletic Union, Attn: Scholarships
2900 Grand Avenue
P.O. Box 10348
Des Moines, IA 50306-0348
Phone: (515) 288-9741; Fax: (515) 284-1969; Email: lisa@ighsau.org
Web: www.ighsau.org

**Summary:** To provide financial assistance to female high school seniors in Iowa who have participated in athletics and plan to attend college in the state.

**Eligibility:** Open to females graduating from high schools in Iowa who have lettered in 1 varsity sport sponsored by the Iowa Girls' High School Athletic Union (IGHSAU) each year of high school and have a GPA of 2.5 or higher. Applicants must be planning to attend a college or university in Iowa. Each high school in the state may nominate 1 student. Selection is based on academic achievements, athletic accomplishments, non-sports extracurricular activities, and community involvement.

**Financial data:** The stipend is $1,000.

**Duration:** 1 year.

**Number awarded:** 1 each year.

**Deadline:** January of each year.

## 979 ROBERT THAL SCHOLARSHIP

Key Club International, Attn: Manager of Youth Funds
3636 Woodview Trace
Indianapolis, IN 46268-3196
Phone: (317) 875-8755, ext. 244; (800) KIWANIS, ext. 244;
Fax: (317) 879-0204; Email: youthfunds@kiwanis.org
Web: www.keyclub.org

**Summary:** To provide financial assistance for college to high school seniors who are Key Club International members.

**Eligibility:** Open to college-bound graduating high school members who have completed at least 100 service hours during their Key Club career and have held an elected officer position on the club, district, or international level. Applicants must have a GPA of 3.5 or higher. Along with their application, they must submit 1) a 500-word essay describing the Key Club service project on which they have participated and that has had the greatest impact on them; 2) a list of high school organizations and activities; 3) a list of religious and community activities; 4) a list of honors, awards, and special recognitions; and 5) 2 letters of recommendation. Financial need is not considered in the selection process.

**Financial data:** The stipend is $1,000.

**Duration:** 1 year.

**Number awarded:** 1 each year.

**Deadline:** February of each year.

## 980 ROBIN ROMANO MEMORIAL SCHOLARSHIP

Robin Romano Memorial Fund
c/o Ken Fratus
Boston Globe Sports
135 Morrissey Boulevard
P.O. Box 55819
Boston, MA 02105-5819
Phone: (617) 929-7949; (800) 628-6214

**Summary:** To provide financial assistance for college to high school seniors and graduates who are cancer survivors.

**Eligibility:** Open to high school seniors, high school graduates, and currently-enrolled college students who are cancer survivors.

**Financial data:** The stipend is $7,500.

**Duration:** Up to 4 years.

**Number awarded:** 1 or more each year.

## 981 RON BROWN SCHOLAR PROGRAM

CAP Charitable Foundation, Attn: Ron Brown Scholar Program
1160 Pepsi Place, Suite 206
Charlottesville, VA 22901
Phone: (434) 964-1588; Fax: (434) 964-1589; Email: franh@ronbrown.org
Web: www.ronbrown.org

**Summary:** To provide financial assistance for college to African American high school seniors.

**Eligibility:** Open to academically-talented African American high school seniors who have demonstrated social commitment and leadership potential. They must be interested in working on a college degree on a full-time basis. U.S. citizenship or permanent resident status is required. Finalists are invited to participate in a weekend selection process in Washington, D.C.; their expenses are reimbursed. Final selection is based on academic promise, leadership ability, communication skills, school and community involvement, and financial need.

**Financial data:** The stipend is $10,000 per year. Funds may be used to cover tuition, fees, books, room, board, and other college-related expenses. Payment is made directly to the recipient's school.

**Duration:** 4 years.

**Number awarded:** At least 10 each year.

**Deadline:** January of each year.

## 982 RONALD REAGAN FUTURE LEADERS SCHOLARSHIP PROGRAM

Phillips Foundation
7811 Montrose Road, Suite 100
Potomac, MD 20854
Phone: (301) 340-7788, ext. 6028; Fax: (301) 424-0245;
Email: jhollingsworth@phillips.com
Web: www.thephillipsfoundation.org/futureleaders.htm

**Summary:** To provide financial assistance to college students who "demonstrate leadership on behalf of the cause of freedom, American values, and constitutional principles."

**Eligibility:** Open to U.S. citizens enrolled as full-time students in accredited 4-year degree-granting institutions in the United States or its possessions who are applying during their sophomore or junior year. Applicants must submit an essay of 500 to 750 words describing their background, educational and career objectives, and scope of participation in activities that promote the cause of freedom, American values, and constitutional principles (such as leadership and achievements in responsible political organizations or clubs, community activities, newspaper columns, speeches, or debates). The award is merit-based, but evidence of financial need is welcome and will be taken into consideration.

**Financial data:** Stipends currently are $10,000, $7,500, $5,000, or $2,500 per year.

**Duration:** 1 year. Recipients who apply as sophomores use the scholarship during their junior year and may apply for renewal for their senior year. Recipients who apply as juniors use the scholarship during their senior year.

**Number awarded:** Varies each year; recently, this program awarded 36 new scholarships (5 at $10,000, 2 at $7,500, 13 at $5,000, and 16 at $2,500) and 17 renewal scholarships (1 at $10,000, 7 at $5,000, 7 at $2,500, and 2 at $1,000).

**Deadline:** January of each year.

## 983 ROOTHBERT FUND SCHOLARSHIPS AND GRANTS

Roothbert Fund, Inc.
475 Riverside Drive, Room 252
New York, NY 10115
Phone: (212) 870-3116; Email: mail@roothbertfund.org
Web: www.roothbertfund.org/scholarships.php

**Summary:** To help undergraduate and graduate students who are in financial need and primarily motivated by spiritual values.

**Eligibility:** Open to undergraduate and graduate students at accredited colleges or universities (or, on occasion, at a secondary school). The competition is open to all qualified applicants in the United States, regardless of sex, age, ethnicity, nationality, or religion. Financial need and a motivation by "spiritual values" must be demonstrated. Preference is given to applicants with outstanding academic records who are considering teaching as a vocation. Finalists are invited to New York, New Haven, Philadelphia, or Washington, D.C. for an interview; applicants must affirm their willingness to attend the interview if invited. The fund does not pay transportation expenses for those asked to interview. Being invited for an interview does not guarantee a scholarship, but no grants are awarded without an interview.

**Financial data:** Grants average from $2,000 to $3,000 per year.

**Duration:** 1 year; may be renewed.

**Number awarded:** Approximately 20 each year.

**Deadline:** January of each year.

## 984 ROSS N. AND PATRICIA PANGERE FOUNDATION SCHOLARSHIPS

American Council of the Blind, Attn: Coordinator, Scholarship Program
1155 15th Street, N.W., Suite 1004
Washington, DC 20005
Phone: (202) 467-5081; (800) 424-8666; Fax: (202) 467-5085;
Email: info@acb.org
Web: www.acb.org

**Summary:** To provide financial assistance for undergraduate or graduate study to outstanding blind students.

**Eligibility:** Open to legally blind U.S. citizens or resident aliens who are undergraduate or graduate students. In addition to letters of recommendation and copies of academic transcripts, applications must include an autobiographical sketch. A cumulative GPA of 3.3 or higher is generally required. Selection is based on demonstrated academic record, involvement in extracurricular and civic activities, and academic objectives. The severity of the applicant's visual impairment and his/her study methods are also taken into account.

**Financial data:** A stipend is awarded (amount not specified). In addition, the winner receives a Kurzweil-1000 Reading System.

**Duration:** 1 year.

**Number awarded:** 1 each year.

**Deadline:** February of each year.

## 985 ROY WILKINS SCHOLARSHIP PROGRAM

National Association for the Advancement of Colored People
Attn: Education Department
4805 Mt. Hope Drive
Baltimore, MD 21215-3297
Phone: (410) 580-5760; (877) NAACP-98; Email: youth@naacpnet.org
Web: www.naacp.org/work/education/eduscholarship.shtml

**Summary:** To provide financial assistance for college to student members of the National Association for the Advancement of Colored People (NAACP).

**Eligibility:** Open to graduating high school seniors who have a GPA of 2.5 or higher and intend to be full-time students at an accredited college in the United States. Along with their application, they must submit a 1-page essay on their interest in their major and a career, their life's ambition, what they hope to accomplish in their lifetime, and what they consider their most significant contribution to their community. Membership and participation in the association are highly desirable. U.S. citizenship and financial need are required.

**Financial data:** The stipend is $1,000 per year.

**Duration:** 1 year; nonrenewable.

**Number awarded:** Varies each year; recently, 6 of these scholarships were awarded.

**Deadline:** April of each year.

## 986 ROYAL NEIGHBORS OF AMERICA NONTRADITIONAL SCHOLARSHIPS

Royal Neighbors of America
Attn: Fraternal Services
230 16th Street
Rock Island, IL 61201-8645
Phone: (309) 788-4561; (800) 627-4762; Email: contact@royalneighbors.org
Web: www.royalneighbors.org/MemberBenefits/scholarships.cfm

**Summary:** To provide financial assistance for college to members of the Royal Neighbors of America who are nontraditional students.

**Eligibility:** Open to members of the society (for at least 2 years immediately prior to the application deadline) who are 23 years of age or older and have been admitted to an accredited college, university, community college, or vocational school. Selection is based on character and personal goals, participation in school and community activities, ability to meet the specific entrance requirements of the accredited college or university or of the vocational school selected, and financial need.

**Financial data:** The stipend is $1,000 per year for full-time students or $500 per year for part-time students.

**Duration:** 1 year; nonrenewable.

**Number awarded:** 15 each year.

**Deadline:** December of each year.

## 987 ROYAL NEIGHBORS OF AMERICA STATE/TERRITORIAL SCHOLARSHIPS

Royal Neighbors of America
Attn: Fraternal Services
230 16th Street
Rock Island, IL 61201-8645
Phone: (309) 788-4561; (800) 627-4762; Email: contact@royalneighbors.org
Web: www.royalneighbors.org/MemberBenefits/scholarships.cfm

**Summary:** To provide financial assistance for college to members of the Royal Neighbors of America in designated states.

**Eligibility:** Open to members of the society (for at least 2 years immediately prior to the application deadline) who are high school seniors recommended by their local lodge and field representative, are in the top third of their graduating class, and have been admitted to an accredited college, university, community college, or vocational school as a full-time student. Selection is based on character and personal goals, school and community activities, ability to meet the specific entrance requirements of the accredited college or university or of the vocational school selected, and general aptitude for college work as indicated by aptitude tests or scholastic records.

**Financial data:** Stipends are $1,000 or $500 per year.

**Duration:** 1 year; nonrenewable.

**Number awarded:** More than 20 each year.

**Deadline:** December of each year.

## 988 ROYAL NEIGHBORS OF AMERICA TRADITIONAL SCHOLARSHIPS

Royal Neighbors of America,
Attn: Fraternal Services
230 16th Street
Rock Island, IL 61201-8645
Phone: (309) 788-4561; (800) 627-4762; Email: contact@royalneighbors.org
Web: www.royalneighbors.org/MemberBenefits/scholarships.cfm

**Summary:** To provide financial assistance for college to members of the Royal Neighbors of America (RNA).

**Eligibility:** Open to high school seniors who have a qualifying RNA benefit certificate. Applicants must be recommended by their local lodge and field representative, be in the top quarter of their graduating class, and have been admitted to an accredited 4-year college or university as a full-time student. Selection is based on character and personal goals, school and community activities, ability to meet the specific entrance requirements of the accredited college or university selected, and general aptitude for college work as indicated by aptitude tests or scholastic records.

**Financial data:** The stipend is $2,000 per year.

**Duration:** 4 years.

**Number awarded:** 10 each year.

**Deadline:** December of each year.

## 989 RUTH ANN JOHNSON FUND SCHOLARSHIPS

Greater Kanawha Valley Foundation,
Attn: Scholarship Coordinator
1600 Huntington Square
900 Lee Street, East
P.O. Box 3041
Charleston, WV 25331-3041
Phone: (304) 346-3620; Fax: (304) 346-3640; Email: tgkvf@tgkvf.com
Web: www.tgkvf.com/scholar.html

**Summary:** To provide financial assistance for college to residents of West Virginia.

**Eligibility:** Open to residents of West Virginia who are attending or planning to attend a college or university anywhere in the country. Applicants must have an ACT score of 20 or higher; be able to demonstrate good moral character, academic excellence, and extreme financial need; and have a GPA of 2.5 or higher.

**Financial data:** The stipend is $1,000 per year.

**Duration:** 1 year; may be renewed.

**Number awarded:** Varies each year; recently, 39 of these scholarships were awarded.

**Deadline:** February of each year.

## 990 RUTH E. BLACK SCHOLARSHIP FUND

American Association of University Women-Honolulu Branch
Attn: Scholarship Committee
1802 Keeaumoku Street
Honolulu, HI 96822
Phone: (808) 537-4702; Fax: (808) 537-4702*51; Email: aauwhnb@att.net

**Summary:** To provide financial assistance to undergraduate women in Hawaii.

**Eligibility:** Open to women who are residents of Hawaii and are currently enrolled in an accredited college, university, or vocational/technical institute in the state. Selection is based on academic record after at least 2 semesters of college or university study, career plans, personal involvement in school and community activities, and financial need. First-time applicants receive priority. U.S. citizenship is required.

**Financial data:** The amount awarded varies, depending upon the needs of the recipient. Generally, individual awards range from $500 to $1,000.

**Duration:** 1 year.

**Number awarded:** Varies; at least 1 each year.

**Deadline:** February of each year.

## 991 RUTH M. BATSON SCHOLARSHIPS

Ruth M. Batson Educational Foundation

250 Cambridge Street, Suite 701

Boston, MA 02114

Phone: (617) 742-1070; Email: dao5753@aol.com

**Summary:** To provide financial assistance to African American college students who face serious financial need.

**Eligibility:** Open to African American college students who need aid as a supplement to other financial assistance. Emergency grants are also available to students who need assistance to remain in school. Selection is based on academic achievement, character, extracurricular activities, and financial need.

**Financial data:** Assistance ranges from $500 to $1,500.

**Duration:** 1 year.

**Number awarded:** Varies each year.

**Deadline:** June of each year.

## 992 RUTH MU-LAN CHU AND JAMES S.C. CHAO SCHOLARSHIP

US Pan Asian American Chamber of Commerce

Attn: Scholarship Coordinator

1329 18th Street, N.W.

Washington, DC 20036

Phone: (202) 296-5221; Fax: (202) 296-5225;

Email: administrator@uspaacc.com

Web: www.uspaacc.com/web/programs/ruth_mu_lan.htm

**Summary:** To provide financial assistance for college to female Asian American high school seniors who demonstrate financial need.

**Eligibility:** Open to female high school seniors of Asian heritage who are U.S. citizens or permanent residents. Applicants must be planning to begin full-time study at an accredited postsecondary educational institution in the United States. Along with their application, they must submit a 500-word essay on "Why I need this scholarship." Selection is based on academic excellence (GPA of 3.5 or higher), community service involvement, and financial need.

**Financial data:** The maximum stipend is $5,000. Funds are paid directly to the recipient's college or university.

**Duration:** 1 year.

**Number awarded:** 1 each year.

**Deadline:** February of each year.

## 993 SABURO KIDO MEMORIAL SCHOLARSHIP

Japanese American Citizens League

Attn: National Scholarship Awards

1765 Sutter Street

San Francisco, CA 94115

Phone: (415) 921-5225; Fax: (415) 931-4671; Email: jacl@jacl.org

Web: www.jacl.org/scholarships.html

**Summary:** To provide financial assistance for college to student members of the Japanese American Citizens League (JACL).

**Eligibility:** Open to JACL members who are currently enrolled or planning to reenter a college, university, trade school, business college, or other institution of higher learning. Applicants must submit a statement describing their current level of involvement in the Japanese American community or Asian Pacific community and how they will continue their involvement in future years. Selection is based on academic record, extracurricular activities, financial need, and community involvement.

**Financial data:** The stipend depends on the availability of funds but usually ranges from $1,000 to $5,000.

**Duration:** 1 year; nonrenewable.

**Number awarded:** At least 1 each year.

**Deadline:** March of each year.

## 994 SAKIA GUNN SCHOLARSHIP FOR LGBT COMMUNITY INVOLVEMENT

Parents, Families and Friends of Lesbians and Gays

Attn: National Scholarships Program

1726 M Street, N.W., Suite 400

Washington, DC 20036

Phone: (202) 467-8180, ext. 219; Fax: (202) 467-8194;

Email: schools@pflag.org

Web: www.pflag.org

**Summary:** To provide financial assistance for college to high school seniors and recent graduates who have a connection to Parents, Families and Friends of Lesbians and Gays (PFLAG).

**Eligibility:** Open to high school seniors and prior-year graduates who have not attended college. Applicants must have applied to an accredited high education institution to work on 1) an associate degree leading to transfer to complete a bachelor's degree, or 2) a bachelor's degree at a 4-year college or university. They must self-identify either as a gay, lesbian, bisexual, or transgender (GLBT) person or as a supporter of GLBT people. Along with their application, they must submit a high school transcript showing a GPA of 3.0 or higher, 2 letters of recommendation, and a 2-page essay discussing either their life as an LGBT student or how they have been involved with and supported the LGBT community. Financial need is also considered in the selection process. This scholarship is presented to the applicant who demonstrates outstanding LGBT involvement.

**Financial data:** The stipend is $2,500.

**Duration:** 1 year; nonrenewable.

**Number awarded:** 1 each year.

**Deadline:** February of each year.

## 995 SALLIE MAE 911 EDUCATION FUND SCHOLARSHIP PROGRAM

Sallie Mae 911 Education Fund

c/o The Community Foundation for the National Capital Region

1201 15th Street, N.W., Suite 420

Washington, DC 20005-2842

Phone: (202) 955-5890; (800) 441-4043; Fax: (202) 955-8084

Web: www.thesalliemaefund.org

**Summary:** To provide financial assistance for college to children of those killed or disabled in the terrorist attacks of September 11, 2001.

**Eligibility:** Open to the children of the victims of the September 11, 2001 terrorist attacks, including children of people killed in airplanes or buildings as well as police, fire safety, or medical personnel killed or disabled as a result of the attacks. Applicants must be enrolled or planning to enroll full time as an undergraduate student at a public or private 2-year or 4-year college or university.

**Financial data:** The stipend is $2,500 per year.

**Duration:** 1 year; may be renewed up to 3 additional years.

**Number awarded:** Varies each year.

**Deadline:** May of each year.

## 996 SAM LEVY SCHOLARSHIP FUND

Alexander Graham Bell Association for the Deaf

Attn: Financial Aid Coordinator

3417 Volta Place, N.W.

Washington, DC 20007-2778

Phone: (202) 337-5220; Fax: (202) 337-8314; TTY: (202) 337-5221;

Email: financialaid@agbell.org

Web: www.agbell.org

**Summary:** To provide financial assistance to undergraduate students with moderate to profound hearing loss.

**Eligibility:** Open to undergraduate students who have been diagnosed with a moderate to profound hearing loss prior to acquiring spoken language (hearing loss averages 60dB or greater in the better ear in the speech frequencies of 500, 1000, and 2000 Hz). Applicants must be committed to using spoken language as their primary mode of communication. They must be accepted or enrolled at a mainstream college or university as a full-time student. Along with their application, they must submit a 1-page essay discussing their career goals and how spoken communication is helping them to reach those goals as a person with a hearing loss. Financial need is considered in the selection process. This scholarship is reserved for students who are oral deaf.

**Financial data:** The stipend is $2,000 per year.

**Duration:** 1 year; may be renewed 1 additional year.

**Number awarded:** 1 each year.

**Deadline:** April of each year.

## 997 SAM ROSE MEMORIAL SCHOLARSHIP

Ladies Auxiliary of the Fleet Reserve Association
Attn: Scholarship Administrator
125 North West Street
Alexandria, VA 22314-2754
Phone: (703) 683-1400; (800) 372-1924; Fax: (703) 549-6610;
Email: fra@fra.org
Web: www.fra.org/Content/fra/MyFRA/Scholarships/Scholarships.htm
**Summary:** To provide financial assistance for college to the children and grandchildren of naval personnel or deceased members of the Fleet Reserve Association (FRA).
**Eligibility:** Open to children and grandchildren of deceased members of the association or those who were eligible to be members at the time of death. While they are given preference for this scholarship, the children and grandchildren of active-duty and retired Navy, Marine, and Coast Guard personnel are also considered. Selection is based on financial need, academic proficiency, and character.
**Financial data:** The stipend is $2,500.
**Duration:** 1 year.
**Number awarded:** 1 each year.
**Deadline:** April of each year.

## 998 SAM WALTON COMMUNITY SCHOLARSHIPS

Wal-Mart Foundation
Scholarship Programs Director
702 S.W. Eighth Street
Bentonville, AR 72716-8071
Phone: (501) 277-1905; (800) 530-9925; Fax: (501) 273-6850
Web: www.walmartfoundation.org
**Summary:** To provide financial assistance to high school seniors who live in communities served by Wal-Mart stores.
**Eligibility:** Open to graduating seniors at high schools designated by each Wal-Mart store and SAM'S CLUB in the community where it operates. Students interested in applying must contact their high school counselor or local Wal-Mart store or SAM'S CLUB; applications are not available from the foundation or the Internet. Wal-Mart associates and their children are not eligible. Selection is based on academic record ACT and/or SAT scores, work experience, community and extracurricular involvement, and financial need. Local winners are automatically entered into a state competition for a chance to win an additional scholarship. State winners are then automatically entered into a national competition for a chance to win an additional scholarship.
**Financial data:** The stipend for local winners is $1,000. State winners receive an additional $4,000 for a total award of $5,000. The national winner receives an additional $20,000 for a total award of $25,000. All funds must be used during the recipient's first year in college for tuition, books, fees, and on-campus room and board.
**Duration:** 1 year; nonrenewable.
**Number awarded:** More than 6,000 each year; 2 at each participating Wal-Mart store and SAM'S CLUB.
**Deadline:** January of each year.

## 999 SAMMY AWARDS

National Fluid Milk Processor Promotion Board
Attn: Scholar Athlete Milk Mustache of the Year (SAMMY)
1250 H Street, N.W., Suite 950
Washington, DC 20005
Phone: (202) 737-0153; (800) WHY-MILK
Web: www.whymilk.com
**Summary:** To provide financial assistance for college to outstanding high school scholar-athletes.
**Eligibility:** Open to residents of the 48 contiguous United States and the District of Columbia who are currently high school seniors and who participate in a high school or club sport. The country is divided into 25 geographic regions, and 3 finalists are selected from each region. From those, 1 winner from each region is chosen. Selection is based on academic achievement (35%), athletic excellence (35%), leadership (15%), citizenship/community service (10%), and a 75-word essay on how drinking milk is part of their life and training regimen (5%).
**Financial data:** College scholarships of $7,500 each are awarded. In addition, each winner plus 2 guests are invited to attend the winners' ceremony at Disney World in Orlando, Florida.
**Duration:** The awards are presented annually.
**Number awarded:** 25 each year (1 from each of 25 geographic districts).
**Deadline:** March of each year.

## 1000 SAMSUNG AMERICAN LEGION SCHOLARSHIPS

American Legion, Attn: Americanism and Children & Youth Division
P.O. Box 1055
Indianapolis, IN 46206-1055
Phone: (317) 630-1249; Fax: (317) 630-1223; Email: acy@legion.org
Web: www.legion.org
**Summary:** To provide financial assistance for college to children and grandchildren of veterans who participate in Girls State or Boys State.
**Eligibility:** Open to students entering their senior year of high school who are selected to participate in Girls State or Boys State, sponsored by the American Legion Auxiliary or American Legion in their state. If they are also the child, grandchild, or great-grandchild of a veteran who saw active-duty service during World War I, World War II, Korea, Vietnam, Lebanon/Grenada, Panama, or the Persian Gulf War, they are eligible for these scholarships. Finalists are chosen at each participating Girls and Boys State, and they are then nominated for the national awards. Selection is based on academic record, community service, involvement in school and community activities, and financial need. Special consideration is given to descendants of U.S. veterans of the Korean War.
**Financial data:** Stipends are $20,000 or $1,000.
**Duration:** 4 years.
**Number awarded:** Varies each year; recently, 7 scholarships at $20,000 and 91 at $1,000 were awarded.

## 1001 SARA E. JENNE SCHOLARSHIP

Montana State Elks Association
c/o Ted Byers
P.O. Box 1018
Great Falls, MT 59401
Phone: (406) 727-1288
Web: www.elksmt.com
**Summary:** To provide financial assistance to second-year students at Montana colleges and universities.
**Eligibility:** Open to students who have completed their first year of education at a Montana university, college, vocational school, or community college with at least a 2.0 GPA. Selection is based primarily on financial need, effort, activities, and community involvement (and less on academic achievement).
**Financial data:** A stipend is awarded (amount not specified).
**Duration:** 1 year.
**Number awarded:** 1 or more each year.

## 1002 SBC L.C. AND DAISY BATES MEMORIAL SCHOLARSHIP

Arkansas Community Foundation
700 South Rock Street
Little Rock, AR 72202
Phone: (501) 372-1116; (800) 220-ARCF; Fax: (501) 372-1166;
Email: acf@arcf.org
Web: www.arcf.org
**Summary:** To provide financial assistance for college to minorities graduating from high schools in Arkansas.
**Eligibility:** Open to minority high school seniors who are U.S. citizens and residents of Arkansas. They must be planning to attend an accredited 4-year college in Arkansas on a full-time basis. Along with their application, they must submit an essay, up to 500 words, on their plans as they relate to their educational and career objectives and long-term goals. Selection is based on such factors as academics, school activities, community service, future goals, faculty and advisor recommendations, and financial need.
**Financial data:** The stipend is $2,500 per year. Funds are paid directly to the recipient's school and may be used for any legitimate educational expense, such as tuition, fees, books, room, and board.
**Duration:** 1 year.
**Number awarded:** Varies each year; since this program was established, it has awarded more than $875,000 to more than 100 Arkansas high school students.
**Deadline:** March of each year.

## 1003 SCHERING/KEY "WILL TO WIN" ASTHMA ATHLETE SCHOLARSHIP

Schering/Key Asthma Athlete Scholarship Program
2000 Galloping Hill Road
Kenilworth, NJ 07033
Phone: (800) 558-7305
**Summary:** To provide financial assistance for college to outstanding high school athletes who have asthma.

**Eligibility:** Open to high school seniors with asthma who have achieved both excellence in competitive sports and a superior high school academic record. Applications must be accompanied by an official high school academic transcript, a letter of support from a physical education director or coach, a statement from a physician describing the type of asthma and the treatment for it, and a letter from the applicant describing educational and career goals. Leadership qualities and notable extracurricular activities and accomplishments are also considered in the selection process.

**Financial data:** The Gold Award is $20,000, Silver Awards are $12,500, and Bronze Awards are $5,000.

**Duration:** 1 year; nonrenewable.

**Number awarded:** 11 each year: 1 Gold Award, 4 Silver Awards, and 6 Bronze Awards.

**Deadline:** April of each year.

## 1004 SCHOLARSHIP HONORING SENATOR BARRY GOLDWATER, K7UGA

American Radio Relay League, Attn: ARRL Foundation
225 Main Street
Newington, CT 06111
Phone: (860) 594-0397; Fax: (860) 594-0259; Email: foundation@arrl.org
Web: www.arrl.org/arrlf

**Summary:** To provide financial assistance to licensed radio amateurs who are interested in working on an undergraduate or graduate degree.

**Eligibility:** Open to undergraduate or graduate students at accredited institutions who are licensed radio amateurs at the novice level or higher. Applicants must submit an essay on the role amateur radio has played in their lives and provide documentation of financial need.

**Financial data:** The stipend is $5,000.

**Duration:** 1 year.

**Number awarded:** 1 each year.

**Deadline:** January of each year.

## 1005 SCHOLARSHIP PROGRAM FOR YOUNG WOMEN AND TRANSGENDER ACTIVISTS

Third Wave Foundation
511 West 25th Street, Suite 301
New York, NY 10002
Phone: (212) 675-0700; Fax: (212) 255-6653;
Email: info@thirdwavefoundation.org
Web: www.thirdwavefoundation.org/programs/scholarships.html

**Summary:** To provide educational assistance to undergraduate and graduate women who have been involved as social change activists.

**Eligibility:** Open to full-time and part-time students under 30 years of age who are enrolled in, or have been accepted to, an accredited university, college, vocational/technical school, community college, or graduate school. Women and transgender students of all races and ethnicities are eligible. Applicants should have been involved as activists, artists, or cultural workers on such issues as racism, homophobia, sexism, or other forms of inequality. They must submit 500-word essays on 1) their current social change involvement and how it relates to their educational and life goals; and 2) if they would describe themselves as a feminist and why. Graduate students and students planning to study abroad through a U.S. university program are also eligible. Selection is based on financial need and commitment to social justice work.

**Financial data:** Stipends range from $500 to $5,000 per year.

**Duration:** 1 year.

**Number awarded:** Varies each year; recently, 4 undergraduates and 3 graduate students received a total of $12,000 in support through this program.

**Deadline:** March or September of each year.

## 1006 SCHOLARSHIPS FOR MILITARY CHILDREN

Defense Commissary Agency, Attn: SSP
1300 E Avenue
Fort Lee, VA 23801-1800
Phone: (804) 734-8134; Fax: (804) 734-8248; Email: info@militaryscholar.org
Web: www.militaryscholar.org

**Summary:** To provide financial assistance for college to the children of veterans and military personnel.

**Eligibility:** Open to sons and daughters of U.S. military ID card holders, including active duty, retirees, Guard/Reserves and survivors of deceased members, who are enrolled or accepted for enrollment at a college or university. The eligibility of applicants, including survivors of deceased members, is based on the DoD ID Card Directive, which provides for eligibility up to 21 years of age

or 23 if still enrolled as a full-time student. Applicants must have a GPA of 3.0 or higher and write a short essay on "What Being a Military Dependent Means to Me." Selection is based on merit.

**Financial data:** The stipend is $1,500.

**Duration:** 1 year; recipients may reapply.

**Number awarded:** 1 scholarship is allocated for each of the commissaries worldwide operated by the Defense Commissary Agency (DeCA).

**Deadline:** February of each year.

## 1007 SCIRUS SCHOLARSHIP ESSAY AWARD

Elsevier Science Ltd.
84 Theobald's Road
London WC1X 8RR
England
Phone: 44 20 7611 4451; Fax: 44 20 7611 4463
Web: www.info.scirus.com/scholarship_info.html

**Summary:** To recognize and reward undergraduate and graduate students in the United States and United Kingdom who submit outstanding essays on their use of the SCIRUS web site to conduct research projects.

**Eligibility:** Open to full-time undergraduates and part- or full-time graduate students who are citizens of the United States or United Kingdom. Applicants must review and use the SCIRUS web site and then write an essay of 1,000 to 1,500 words on either 1) the ways in which they would inform other college students about its attributes and ease of use, or 2) how search engines have changed the way you locate and gather research information. Majors in any field of study may apply. Selection is based on clear, concise writing that is original, articulate, logically organized, and well-supported.

**Financial data:** The award is $1,000. Funds are transferred directly to the college or university that the winner is attending.

**Duration:** The competition is held annually.

**Number awarded:** 2 each year: 1 to an undergraduate and 1 to a graduate student.

**Deadline:** December of each year.

## 1008 SDATAT SCHOLARSHIP

South Dakota Association of Towns and Townships
351 Wisconsin, S.W., Suite 101
P.O. Box 903
Huron, SD 57350-0903
Phone: (605) 353-1439; Fax: (605) 352-5322; Email: sdatat@basec.net

**Summary:** To provide financial assistance for college to high school seniors in South Dakota.

**Eligibility:** Open to seniors graduating from high schools in South Dakota or who are home-schooled. Applicants must be planning to attend a university, college, or technical school in South Dakota. Along with their application, they must submit a 500-word essay on "Local Government Consolidation: What Happens to Local Control?"

**Financial data:** The stipend is $1,000.

**Duration:** 1 year.

**Number awarded:** 1 each year.

**Deadline:** March of each year.

## 1009 SEABEE MEMORIAL SCHOLARSHIP ASSOCIATION PROGRAM

Seabee Memorial Scholarship Association
P.O. Box 6574
Silver Spring, MD 20916
Phone: (301) 570-2850; Fax: (301) 570-2873; Email: smsa@erols.com
Web: www.seabee.org

**Summary:** To provide financial assistance for college to the children or grandchildren of active or deceased members of the Naval Construction Battalion (Seabees) or Navy Civil Engineering Corps.

**Eligibility:** Open to the children, stepchildren, and grandchildren of regular, Reserve, retired, or deceased officers and enlisted members who are now serving in or have been honorably discharged from the Naval Construction Force (Seabees) or Navy Civil Engineering Corps. Applicants may be high school seniors, high school graduates, or students currently enrolled in a 4-year college or university. Full-time college enrollment is required. Selection is based on financial need, character, good citizenship, leadership, and scholastic record.

**Financial data:** The stipend is $2,200 per year.

**Duration:** 1 year; may be renewed for 3 additional years.

**Number awarded:** Varies each year; recently, 18 new scholarships were awarded through this program.

**Deadline:** April of each year.

## 1010 SEAFARERS SCHOLARSHIP PROGRAM FOR SEAFARERS

Seafarers International Union, Attn: Scholarship Program
5201 Auth Way
Camp Springs, MD 20746
Phone: (301) 899-0675; Fax: (301) 899-7355
Web: www.seafarers.org

**Summary:** To provide financial assistance for college to members of the Seafarers International Union.

**Eligibility:** Open to high school graduates who have credit for a total of 730 days of employment with an employer who is obligated to make contributions to the Seafarers' Welfare Plan. They must be active seamen and members of the union planning to attend an accredited college or trade school in the United States. Selection is based on high school equivalency scores or secondary school records, SAT or ACT scores, college transcripts (if any), references on character or personality, and an autobiographical essay.

**Financial data:** The stipend is either $20,000 (paid at the rate of $5,000 per year) or $6,000 (paid at the rate of $3,000 per year). The $20,000 scholarships are intended to cover a 4-year college-level course of study and the $6,000 scholarships are designed for 2-year courses of study at a postsecondary vocational school or community college.

**Duration:** The $20,000 scholarships are for 4 years and the $6,000 scholarships are for 2 years.

**Number awarded:** Two $6,000 scholarships and one $20,000 scholarship are awarded each year; a second $20,000 scholarship may be awarded to a qualified applicant.

**Deadline:** April of each year.

## 1011 SECOND MARINE DIVISION ASSOCIATION MEMORIAL SCHOLARSHIP

Second Marine Division Association, Attn: Memorial Scholarship Fund
P.O. Box 8180
Camp Lejeune, NC 28547-8180
Phone: (910) 451-3167

**Summary:** To provide financial assistance for college to the children and grandchildren of veterans or members of the Second Marine Division.

**Eligibility:** Open to unmarried dependent children and grandchildren of individuals who are serving or have served in the Second Marine Division or in a unit attached to it. Applicants must be high school seniors, high school graduates, or full-time undergraduate students in accredited colleges or vocational/technical schools. They must have a family income of less than $50,000 and a GPA of 2.5 or higher.

**Financial data:** The award is $1,000 per year.

**Duration:** 1 year; may be renewed.

**Number awarded:** Varies each year.

**Deadline:** March of each year.

## 1012 SENATOR GEORGE J. MITCHELL SCHOLARSHIPS

The Mitchell Institute
22 Monument Square, Suite 200
Portland, ME 04101
Phone: (207) 773-7700; (888) 220-7209; Fax: (207) 773-1133;
Email: info@mitchellinstitute.org
Web: www.mitchellinstitute.org/scholarship/body.html

**Summary:** To provide financial assistance for college to graduating high school seniors in Maine.

**Eligibility:** Open to high school seniors in Maine who plan to attend a 2-year or 4-year college or university in the state. Some scholarships are available to students planning to attend college out of state. Nontraditional students and students who earned their high school diplomas through GED or Job Corps programs are eligible. Students who attend high school in Maine but are not legal residents of Maine are not eligible. Selection is based on academic achievement and potential, financial need, and community service.

**Financial data:** The stipend is $1,000 per year.

**Duration:** 2 years or 4 years (depending on whether the recipient attends a 2-year or 4-year institution.

**Number awarded:** 160 each year: 1 to a graduating senior from each public high school in Maine, along with 30 additional awards available to students from other backgrounds (gradating from private or parochial schools, home-schooled students, Maine residents attending high school out of state, nontraditional students).

**Deadline:** March of each year.

## 1013 SERTEENS SCHOLARSHIPS

Sertoma International
Attn: Director of Finance and Administration
1912 East Meyer Boulevard
Kansas City, MO 64132-1174
Phone: (816) 333-8300, ext. 214; Fax: (816) 333-4320; TTY: (816) 333-8300;
Email: aellington@sertoma.org
Web: www.sertoma.org

**Summary:** To provide financial assistance for college to members of Serteens.

**Eligibility:** Open to members of the organization in the United States who are graduating from high school and planning to attend college in the following fall. Applicants must have maintained a GPA of 3.0 or higher during their sophomore, junior, and senior years of high school. Along with their application, they must submit a 1-page statement explaining how this scholarship will help them achieve their goals. U.S. citizenship is required. Selection is based on academic achievement, participation in Serteen Club activities, and participation in non-Serteen service activities.

**Financial data:** The stipend is $1,000 per year.

**Duration:** 1 year.

**Number awarded:** 4 each year.

**Deadline:** March of each year.

## 1014 SERTOMA COLLEGIATE CLUB SCHOLARSHIPS

Sertoma International, Attn: Director of Finance and Administration
1912 East Meyer Boulevard
Kansas City, MO 64132-1174
Phone: (816) 333-8300, ext. 214; Fax: (816) 333-4320; TTY: (816) 333-8300;
Email: aellington@sertoma.org
Web: www.sertoma.org

**Summary:** To provide financial assistance for college to members of the Sertoma Collegiate Club.

**Eligibility:** Open to U.S. citizens who are active members of the organization. Applicants must be working full time on a bachelor's degree with a cumulative GPA of 3.2 or higher. Associate degrees, community colleges, and vocational programs do not qualify. Along with their application, they must submit a 1-page statement of purpose describing how this scholarship will help them achieve their goals. Selection is based on academic achievement and participation in both Sertoma Collegiate Club programs and non-Sertoma service activities.

**Financial data:** The stipend is $1,000 per year.

**Duration:** 1 year.

**Number awarded:** 4 each year.

**Deadline:** March of each year.

## 1015 SERTOMA SCHOLARSHIPS FOR HEARING-IMPAIRED STUDENTS

Sertoma International, Attn: Director of Finance and Administration
1912 East Meyer Boulevard
Kansas City, MO 64132-1174
Phone: (816) 333-8300, ext. 214; Fax: (816) 333-4320; TTY: (816) 333-8300;
Email: aellington@sertoma.org
Web: www.sertoma.org

**Summary:** To provide financial assistance for college to hearing impaired students.

**Eligibility:** Open to students who have a minimum 40dB bilateral hearing loss and are interested in working full time on a bachelor's degree at a 4-year college or university. Students working on a community college degree, associate degree, or vocational program degree are ineligible. Applicants must be able to document their hearing loss. They must be entering or continuing undergraduate studies in the United States. A GPA of at least 3.2 and U.S. citizenship are required. Selection is based on past academic performance, goals, a statement of purpose, and overall merit. Financial need is not considered.

**Financial data:** The stipend is $1,000 per year.

**Duration:** 1 year; may be renewed up to 4 times.

**Number awarded:** 20 each year.

**Deadline:** April of each year.

## 1016 SEYMOUR MEMORIAL AWARDS

California Scholarship Federation
16458 Bolsa Chica
PMB 421

Huntington Beach, CA 92649
Phone: (800) 437-3347; Fax: (714) 373-4749;
Email: lraabe@csf-cjsfstateboard.org
Web: www/csf-cjsfstateboard.org/CSF.php
**Summary:** To recognize and reward outstanding members of the California Scholarship Federation (CSF), an honorary association of academically talented students in California high schools.
**Eligibility:** Open to seniors at high schools that are CSF members. Each school may nominate 2 candidates. All nominees must be CSF Sealbearers. Selection is based on participation in school and community activities, academic transcripts, hobbies or interests, and 3 letters of recommendation.
**Financial data:** Finalists in each region receive $1,000. The winner in each region receives an additional $500.
**Duration:** The awards are granted annually.
**Number awarded:** 50 finalists (10 in each of the 5 regions) receive awards. In each region, 1 of those finalists receives an additional award of $500.
**Deadline:** February of each year.

## 1017 SGT FELIX DELGRECO JR. SCHOLARSHIP

Connecticut National Guard Foundation, Inc., Attn: Scholarship Committee
360 Broad Street
Hartford, CT 06015
Phone: (860) 241-1550; Fax: (860) 293-2929;
Email: scholarship.committee@ctngfoundation.org
Web: www.ctngfoundation.org/Scholarship.asp
**Summary:** To provide financial assistance for college to children of members of the Connecticut Army National Guard.
**Eligibility:** Open to children of members of the Connecticut Army National Guard who are enrolled or planning to enroll in an accredited college degree or technical program. Applicants must submit a letter of recommendation, list of extracurricular activities, high school or college transcripts, and a 200-word statement on their educational and future goals. Selection is based on achievement and citizenship.
**Financial data:** The stipend is $2,500.
**Duration:** 1 year.
**Number awarded:** 1 each year.
**Deadline:** April of each year.

## 1018 SHEPHERD SCHOLARSHIP

Ancient and Accepted Scottish Rite of Freemasonry, Southern Jurisdiction
Supreme Council, 33
Attn: Director of Education
1733 16th Street, N.W.
Washington, DC 20009-2103
Phone: (202) 232-3579; Fax: (202) 464-0487; Email: grndexec@srmason-sj.org
Web: www.srmason-sj.org
**Summary:** To provide financial assistance to undergraduate and graduate students who are working on degrees in areas associated with public service.
**Eligibility:** Open to undergraduate and graduate students who have taken part in social, civic, religious, or fraternal activities in their communities. Applicants must be working on a baccalaureate or graduate degree in a field "associated with service to country and generally perceived as benefiting the human race." U.S. citizenship is required. Selection is based on dedication, ambition, academic record, financial need, and promise of outstanding performance at the advanced level.
**Financial data:** The stipend is $1,500 per year.
**Duration:** 4 years.
**Number awarded:** 1 or more each year.
**Deadline:** March of each year.

## 1019 SHIRLEY U. GRABER SCHOLARSHIP

National Organization for Women-New York State, Inc.
Attn: NOW-NYS Foundation, Inc.
800 Main Street, Suite 3B
Niagara Falls, NY 14301
Phone: (716) 285-5598; Fax: (716) 285-5602; Email: nownys@nownys.com
Web: www.nownys.org/sgs.html
**Summary:** To provide financial assistance to undergraduate and graduate students in New York.
**Eligibility:** Open to students in New York enrolled at a 2-year or 4-year college or university, graduate school, law school, or other professional graduate program. Applicants must have completed at least 1 course in women's studies.

At least 1 award is reserved for a student attending Brooklyn College. Financial need is considered in the selection process.
**Financial data:** Stipends range from $200 to $2,000.
**Duration:** 1 year.
**Number awarded:** Varies each year.
**Deadline:** Applications are accepted on a rolling basis, but they should be submitted from 8 months to 1 year in advance of the semester for which funding is requested.

## 1020 SHOPKO SCHOLARSHIPS

ShopKo Stores Inc.
700 Pilgrim Way
P.O. Box 19060
Green Bay, WI 54307-9060
Phone: (920) 497-2211
Web: www.shopko.com
**Summary:** To provide financial assistance for college to residents of states where ShopKo stores operate.
**Eligibility:** Open to residents of California, Colorado, Idaho, Illinois, Iowa, Michigan, Minnesota, Montana, Nebraska, Nevada, Oregon, South Dakota, Utah, Washington, and Wisconsin. Applicants must be high school seniors or graduates who plan to enroll or students who are already enrolled in a full-time undergraduate course of study at an accredited 2-year or 4-year college, university, or vocational/technical school. Selection is based on academic record, potential to succeed, leadership and participation in school and community activities, honors, work experience, a statement of educational and career goals, and an outside appraisal. Financial need is not considered.
**Financial data:** The stipend is $1,000 per year.
**Duration:** 1 year; nonrenewable.
**Number awarded:** 100 each year.
**Deadline:** November of each year.

## 1021 SIBLING CONTINUING EDUCATION SCHOLARSHIPS

Hemophilia Federation of America, Attn: Scholarship Committee
1405 West Pinhook Road, Suite 101
Lafayette, LA 70503
Phone: (337) 261-9787; (800) 230-9797; Fax: (337) 261-1787;
Email: info@hemophiliafed.org
Web: www.hemophiliafed.org/scholarships.php
**Summary:** To provide financial assistance for college to siblings of people with a blood clotting disorder.
**Eligibility:** Open to siblings of people who have a blood clotting disorder. Applicants must be attending or planning to attend an accredited 2-year or 4-year college, university, or trade school in the United States. Along with their application, they must submit a 1-page essay on their goals and aspirations and how the blood clotting community has played a part in their lives. Financial need is also considered in the selection process.
**Financial data:** The stipend is $1,500 per year.
**Duration:** 1 year; may be renewed.
**Number awarded:** 3 each year.
**Deadline:** March of each year.

## 1022 SIG MEMORIAL SCHOLARSHIP

Academy of Model Aeronautics, Attn: Education Coordinator
5161 East Memorial Drive
Muncie, IN 47302-9252
Phone: (765) 287-1256; Fax: (765) 289-4248
Web: www.buildandfly.com/AMAchgrantscholarship.asp
**Summary:** To provide financial assistance for college to members of the Academy of Model Aeronautics (AMA).
**Eligibility:** Open to graduating high school seniors who have been AMA members for the last full 36 months prior to applying. They must have been accepted by a college or university offering a certificate or degree program. Along with their application, they must submit a 1-page statement on why they are applying for this scholarship. Selection is based on that statement, financial need, school and community activities, work experience, and modeling experience. Academic achievement is not considered.
**Financial data:** The stipend depends on the number of recipients.
**Duration:** 1 year; nonrenewable.
**Number awarded:** Varies each year.
**Deadline:** April of each year.

## 1023 SISTER ELIZABETH CANDON SCHOLARSHIP

Vermont Student Assistance Corporation
Champlain Mill, Attn: Scholarship Programs
P.O. Box 2000
Winooski, VT 05404-2601
Phone: (802) 654-3798; (888) 253-4819; Fax: (802) 654-3765;
TDD: (802) 654-3766; TDD: (800) 281-3341 (within VT); Email: info@vsac.org
Web: www.vsac.org

**Summary:** To provide financial assistance for college to single parent mothers in Vermont.

**Eligibility:** Open to women residents of Vermont who are single parents with primary custody of at least 1 child 12 years of age or younger. Applicants must be enrolled at least half time in an accredited undergraduate degree program. Selection is based on financial need, a letter of recommendation, and required essays.

**Financial data:** The stipend is $1,000 per year.

**Duration:** 1 year; may be renewed up to 3 additional years.

**Number awarded:** 1 each year.

**Deadline:** June of each year.

## 1024 THE SISTERS' ECONOMIC AND SOCIAL JUSTICE SCHOLARSHIP FUND

The Sisters of Perpetual Indulgence, Inc.
Attn: Scholarship Fund Committee Chair
584 Castro Street
PMB 392
San Francisco, CA 94114
Web: www.SisterFund.com

**Summary:** To provide financial assistance for college or graduate school to students who are committed to working for social and economic justice.

**Eligibility:** Open to students enrolled in an accredited college or university and working on a bachelor's, master's, M.D., J.D., or Ph.D. degree. Applicants must be able to demonstrate a history of working for social and economic justice in their local or national community and be able to describe their plans to use their education to further economic and social justice. Ineligible students include those who are attending 1) military schools, law enforcement academies, or related preparatory programs; 2) institutions associated with religious groups known for discrimination or intolerance; or 3) institutions that, either through intentional or unintentional action or inaction, promote, encourage, or foster social or economic injustice. Selection is based on financial need, prior community involvement, future community involvement, and commitment to economic and social justice issues. Age, ethnicity, race or national origin, gender, and sexual orientation are not considered.

**Financial data:** Stipends are either $1,000 or $500.

**Duration:** 1 year.

**Number awarded:** Varies each year; recently, 23 of these scholarships were awarded.

**Deadline:** November of each year.

## 1025 SKANDALARIS FAMILY FOUNDATION SCHOLARSHIPS

Skandalaris Family Foundation
P.O. Box 2061
Venica, FL 34284
Phone: (941) 544-8659; Fax: (941) 408-9526; Email: info@skandalaris.com
Web: www.skandalaris.com

**Summary:** To provide financial assistance for college to high school seniors and current college students, especially those from Michigan.

**Eligibility:** Open to graduating high school seniors and students already enrolled in college. The majority of the scholarships are awarded to residents of Michigan. High school seniors must have a GPA of 3.5 or higher, minimum scores of 24 on the ACT (or the SAT equivalent), and a record of involvement in school, athletic, and community activities. College students must have a cumulative GPA of 3.4 or higher and a record of active involvement in university, athletic, or community services. All applicants must be U.S. citizens and able to demonstrate financial need.

**Financial data:** The stipend is at least $2,000.

**Duration:** 1 year; may be renewed.

**Number awarded:** Varies each year; recently, 115 of these scholarships were awarded.

**Deadline:** April of each year.

## 1026 SMART PROGRAM SCHOLARSHIPS

United States Bowling Congress, Attn: SMART Program
5301 South 76th Street
Greendale, WI 53129-1192
Phone: (414) 423-3343; (800) 514-BOWL, ext. 3343; Fax: (414) 421-3014;
Email: smart@bowl.com
Web: www.bowl.com/scholarships/main.aspx

**Summary:** To provide financial assistance for college and other educational activities to young bowlers.

**Eligibility:** Open to bowlers throughout the United States and Canada. Some scholarships are presented to winners of bowling tournaments, but others require written applications. Some require demonstrations of financial need, but others are based on bowling and/or academic accomplishments. Some are limited to students, but others are open to bowlers at other levels. All scholarships must conform to standards of the Scholarship Management and Accounting Reports for Tenpins (SMART) program of the United States Bowling Congress (USBC).

**Financial data:** The awards vary; recently, a total of $2,914,100 was awarded through this program. Some scholarships must be used at accredited colleges and universities for tuition, housing, and books. Other uses that are specified include: bowling camps and lessons; bowling coaching seminars; business, technical, or trade schools; continuing education classes; and educational camps in mathematics, science, art, or computers.

**Number awarded:** Varies each year; recently, more than 35,000 bowlers received scholarships.

## 1027 SOCIETY OF DAUGHTERS OF THE UNITED STATES ARMY SCHOLARSHIPS

Society of Daughters of the United States Army
c/o Mary P. Maroney,
Chair, Memorial and Scholarship Funds
11804 Grey Birch Place
Reston, VA 20191-4223

**Summary:** To provide financial assistance for college to daughters and granddaughters of active, retired, or deceased career Army warrant and commissioned officers.

**Eligibility:** Open to the daughters, adopted daughters, stepdaughters, or granddaughters of career commissioned officers or warrant officers of the U.S. Army (active, regular, or Reserve) who 1) are currently on active duty, 2) retired after 20 years of active duty or were medically retired, or 3) died while on active duty or after retiring from active duty with 20 or more years of service. Applicants must have at least a 3.0 GPA and be studying or planning to study at the undergraduate level. Selection is based on depth of character, leadership, seriousness of purpose, academic achievement, and financial need.

**Financial data:** Scholarships, to a maximum of $1,000, are paid directly to the college or school for tuition, laboratory fees, books, or other expenses.

**Duration:** 1 year; may be renewed up to 4 additional years if the recipient maintains at least a 3.0 GPA.

**Number awarded:** Varies each year.

**Deadline:** February of each year.

## 1028 SODEXHO PAN ASIAN NETWORK GROUP SCHOLARSHIP

US Pan Asian American Chamber of Commerce
Attn: Scholarship Coordinator
1329 18th Street, N.W.
Washington, DC 20036
Phone: (202) 296-5221; Fax: (202) 296-5225;
Email: administrator@uspaacc.com
Web: www.uspaacc.com/sodexho

**Summary:** To provide financial assistance and work experience to Asian American college students.

**Eligibility:** Open to college sophomores and juniors of Asian heritage who are U.S. citizens or permanent residents. Applicants must be enrolled in full-time study at an accredited 4-year college or university in the United States and working on a degree in business management, preferably food service management, hotel restaurant institution management, facilities management, or similar program leading to a bachelor's degree. They must be willing to commit to a paid internship with Sodexho during the summer. Along with their application, they must submit a 500-word essay on how they plan to use their special talents to achieve their professional goals. Selection is based on academic excellence (GPA of 3.0 or higher), leadership in extracurricular activities, community service involvement.

**Financial data:** The stipend is $5,000. Funds are paid directly to the recipient's college or university. An additional stipend is paid for the internship.
**Duration:** 1 academic year for the scholarship; 8 weeks for the internship.
**Number awarded:** 1 each year.
**Deadline:** February of each year.

### [1029] SONIA STREULI MAGUIRE OUTSTANDING SCHOLASTIC ACHIEVEMENT AWARD

Swiss Benevolent Society of New York, Attn: Scholarship Committee
608 Fifth Avenue, Suite 309
New York, NY 10020-2303
Phone: (212) 246-0655; Fax: (212) 246-1366;
Email: info@swissbenevolentny.com
Web: www.swissbenevolentny.com/scholarships.htm
**Summary:** To provide financial assistance to college seniors and graduate students of Swiss descent in the Northeast.
**Eligibility:** Open to college seniors and graduate students who are residents of Connecticut, New Jersey, Pennsylvania, Delaware, or New York. Applicants must be able to demonstrate sustained academic excellence (at least a 3.8 GPA) in a demanding course of study. Either the applicant or at least 1 parent must be a Swiss citizen. Financial need is not considered in the selection process.
**Financial data:** The stipend ranges from $4,000 to $6,000 per year. Funds are paid directly to the recipient's school in 2 installments (beginning of fall semester and beginning of spring semester).
**Duration:** 1 year; nonrenewable.
**Number awarded:** 1 or 2 each year.
**Deadline:** March of each year.

### [1030] SONLIGHT SCHOLARSHIPS

Sonlight Curriculum, Ltd., Attn: Scholarship Committee
8042 South Grant Way
Littleton, CO 80122
Phone: (303) 730-6292; Fax: (303) 795-8668;
Email: scholarship@sonlight.com
Web: www.sonlight.com/scholarships.html
**Summary:** To provide financial assistance for college to home-schooled students who have utilized Sonlight Core programs.
**Eligibility:** Open to high school seniors and current college students who have been home-schooled and used at least 3 Sonlight Core programs. Preference is given to students who have used the curriculum most recently and at the higher levels. Applicants must demonstrate a heart for learning, mission mindedness, spiritual mindedness, balance in their activities and interests, and leadership. They must submit a 2-page personal essay on how their future plans and aspirations fit in with the purposes of God (including references to seeking God's Kingdom, asserting the crown rights of King Jesus, and how their future plans or purposes will help extend His Kingdom) and a 3-page argumentative essay that they have written. Selection is based on those essays, academic achievement, extracurricular activities, and 3 reference letters.
**Financial data:** Stipends are $20,000 ($5,000 per year), $10,000 ($2,500 per year), or $4,000 ($1,000 per year).
**Duration:** 4 years, provided the recipients maintain a GPA of 3.5 or higher and provide the sponsor with a copy of their college transcript.
**Number awarded:** 8 each year: 1 at $5,000 per year, 2 at $2,500 per year, and 5 at $1,000 per year.
**Deadline:** December of each year.

### [1031] SONS OF ITALY NATIONAL LEADERSHIP GRANT COMPETITION

Order Sons of Italy in America, Attn: Sons of Italy Foundation
219 E Street, N.E.
Washington, DC 20002
Phone: (202) 547-5106; Fax: (202) 546-8168; Email: scholarships@osia.org
Web: www.osia.org/public/scholarships/grants.asp
**Summary:** To provide financial assistance to undergraduate and graduate students of Italian descent.
**Eligibility:** Open to U.S. citizens of Italian descent who are enrolled as full-time students in an undergraduate or graduate program at an accredited 4-year college or university. Both high school seniors and students already enrolled in college are eligible for the undergraduate awards. Applications must be accompanied by essays, from 500 to 750 words in length, on the principal contribution of Italian Americans to the development of U.S. culture and society. These merit-based awards are presented to students who have demonstrated exceptional leadership qualities and distinguished scholastic abilities.

**Financial data:** Stipends range from $4,000 to $25,000.
**Duration:** 1 year; nonrenewable.
**Number awarded:** Varies each year; recently, 14 of these awards were presented.
**Deadline:** February of each year.

### [1032] SONS OF PERICLES UNDERGRADUATE SCHOLARSHIPS

American Hellenic Educational Progressive Association
Attn: AHEPA Educational Foundation
1909 Q Street, N.W., Suite 500
Washington, DC 20009
Phone: (202) 232-6300; Fax: (202) 232-2140
Web: www.ahepa.org/educ_foundation/index.html
**Summary:** To provide financial assistance to undergraduate students who are members of the Sons of Pericles.
**Eligibility:** Open to current undergraduates who are members of the Sons of Pericles. Freshmen and sophomores must submit a complete high school transcript, SAT or ACT scores, and their most recent college transcript. Juniors and seniors must submit their most recent college transcript. In addition to the transcripts and test scores, selection is based on extracurricular activities, athletic achievements, work and community service, and a 500-word essay on past achievements and future goals.
**Financial data:** Stipends range from $500 to $2,000 per year.
**Duration:** 1 year.
**Number awarded:** 1 each year.
**Deadline:** March of each year.

### [1033] SONS OF UNION VETERANS OF THE CIVIL WAR SCHOLARSHIPS

Sons of Union Veterans of the Civil War
P.O. Box 1865
Harrisburg, PA 17105
Phone: (717) 232-7000; Email: suvcinc@aol.com
Web: www.suvcw.org/scholar.htm
**Summary:** To provide financial assistance for college to descendants of Union Civil War veterans.
**Eligibility:** Open to both high school seniors and currently-enrolled 4-year college students. Applicants should 1) be a descendant of a Union Civil War veteran who was honorably discharged or who died while in service; 2) rank in the upper quarter of their high school graduating class (preferably in the upper tenth); 3) have a record of performance in school and community activities; 4) have an interest in and positive attitude toward college; 5) provide 3 letters of recommendation; and 6) submit an official grade transcript. Financial need is not considered in the selection process.
**Financial data:** The stipend is $1,000. Funds are to be used for tuition and books. Checks are mailed directly to the recipient's school.
**Duration:** 1 year.
**Number awarded:** 2 each year.
**Deadline:** March of each year.

### [1034] SOOZIE COURTER SHARING A BRIGHTER TOMORROW HEMOPHILIA SCHOLARSHIP

Wyeth Pharmaceuticals, Attn: Wyeth Hemophilia Hotline
5 Giralda Farms
Madison, NJ 07940
Phone: (888) 999-2349
Web: www.hemophiliavillage.com/programs_scholar.asp
**Summary:** To provide financial assistance for college or graduate school to persons with hemophilia.
**Eligibility:** Open to persons with hemophilia (A or B) who are high school seniors, have a GED, or are currently attending an accredited college, university, junior college, vocational school, or graduate school. They must need financial assistance to work on an undergraduate degree.
**Financial data:** The stipends are $5,000 for undergraduate students, $7,500 for graduate students, or $2,500 for recipients at a vocational school.
**Duration:** 1 year.
**Number awarded:** 19 each year: 16 to undergraduates, 2 to graduate students, and 1 to a vocational student.
**Deadline:** April of each year.

### [1035] SOUTH CAROLINA ACCESS AND EQUITY UNDERGRADUATE SCHOLARS PROGRAM

South Carolina Commission on Higher Education

Attn: Director of Student Services

1333 Main Street, Suite 200

Columbia, SC 29201

Phone: (803) 737-2280; (877) 349-7183; Fax: (803) 737-2297;

Email: srhyne@che.sc.gov

Web: www.che.sc.gov

**Summary:** To provide financial assistance to underrepresented students at public colleges or universities in South Carolina.

**Eligibility:** Open to residents of South Carolina who are members of a traditionally underrepresented group at the senior institution, regional campus of the University of South Carolina, or South Carolina technical college they are or will be attending. Full-time entering freshmen must have a high school GPA of at least 3.0; continuing full-time college students must have a cumulative GPA of at least 2.0; part-time students must have completed at least 12 hours of college work with a GPA of at least 2.0 and be at least 21 years old or have been out of school at least 2 years prior to reenrolling. Priority is given to full-time students. U.S. citizenship is required.

**Financial data:** Stipends of up to $1,000 per year are provided, funding permitting.

**Duration:** 1 year; may be renewed.

**Number awarded:** Varies each year, but no more than 20% of the grant funds at each institution may be used for entering freshmen.

## 1036 SOUTH CAROLINA HOPE SCHOLARSHIPS

South Carolina Commission on Higher Education

Attn: Director of Student Services

1333 Main Street, Suite 200

Columbia, SC 29201

Phone: (803) 737-4544; (877) 349-7183; Fax: (803) 737-2297;

Email: kwham@che.sc.gov

Web: www.che.sc.gov

**Summary:** To provide financial assistance to high school seniors in South Carolina who plan to attend a 4-year institution in the state.

**Eligibility:** Open to seniors graduating from high schools or completing a home-school program in South Carolina. Applicants must be planning to attend a 4-year public or private college or university in the state and have a GPA of 3.0 or higher. They may not have been convicted of any felony or drug- or alcohol-related misdemeanor during the past academic year and may not be eligible for the Palmetto Fellows or LIFE Scholarship Programs. U.S. citizenship or permanent resident status is required. Selection is based on merit.

**Financial data:** The maximum stipend is $2,650, including a $150 book allowance.

**Duration:** 1 year; nonrenewable.

**Number awarded:** Varies each year; recently, 2,521 students received more than $6 million in support from this program.

## 1037 SOUTH CAROLINA JUNIOR GOLF FOUNDATION SCHOLARSHIP PROGRAM

Center for Scholarship Administration, Inc.

Attn: South Carolina Junior Golf Foundation Scholarship Program

P.O. Box 1465

Taylors, SC 29687-1465

Phone: (864) 268-3363; Fax: (864) 268-7160; Email: cfsainc@bellsouth.net

Web: www.scholarshipprograms.org/cscholarships.php

**Summary:** To provide financial assistance for college to residents of South Carolina who have a competitive or recreational interest in golf.

**Eligibility:** Open to residents of South Carolina who are seniors in high school or already attending college in the state. Applicants must have a GPA of 2.75 or higher and a competitive or recreational interest in golf. Along with their application, they must submit a 1-page essay describing themselves, including their strengths and their most important achievements in school and community. Selection is based on academic merit (SAT/ACT scores, rank in class, and GPA), potential to succeed in their chosen education field, and financial need.

**Financial data:** The stipend is $2,500 per year. Funds are sent directly to the college, university, or technical college to be used for educational expenses, including tuition, fees, books, room, and board.

**Duration:** 1 year; may be renewed up to 3 additional years or until completion of a bachelor's degree, whichever is earlier, provided the recipient maintains a GPA of 2.75 or higher and enrolled at a college or university in South Carolina.

**Number awarded:** 1 or more each year.

**Deadline:** February of each year.

## 1038 SOUTH CAROLINA LOTTERY TUITION ASSISTANCE PROGRAM

South Carolina Commission on Higher Education

Attn: Director of Student Services

1333 Main Street, Suite 200

Columbia, SC 29201

Phone: (803) 737-4544; (877) 349-7183; Fax: (803) 737-2297;

Email: kwham@che.sc.gov

Web: www.che.sc.gov

**Summary:** To provide financial assistance to needy students at 2-year colleges in South Carolina.

**Eligibility:** Open to students at 2-year public and private colleges and technical schools in South Carolina who meet the qualifications of financial need as established by the financial aid office at the institution they are attending. Applicants must be U.S. citizens or permanent residents and residents of South Carolina. They may not be receiving other scholarship assistance from the South Carolina Commission on Higher Education.

**Financial data:** The amount of the assistance varies each year. Recently, full-time students were eligible for up to $924 per semester and part-time students were eligible for up to $77 per credit hour.

**Duration:** 1 semester; may be renewed.

**Number awarded:** Varies each year; recently, 33,219 students received more than $33.2 million in support from this program.

## 1039 SOUTH CAROLINA NEED-BASED GRANTS PROGRAM

South Carolina Commission on Higher Education

Attn: Director of Student Services

1333 Main Street, Suite 200

Columbia, SC 29201

Phone: (803) 737-2280; (877) 349-7183; Fax: (803) 737-2297;

Email: srhyne@che.sc.gov

Web: www.che.sc.gov

**Summary:** To provide financial assistance for college to South Carolina residents with financial need.

**Eligibility:** Open to residents of South Carolina who meet the qualifications of financial need as established by the financial aid office at the college or university in South Carolina that they are attending or planning to attend. Assistance is provided at participating South Carolina public or private 2- or 4-year colleges and universities. Applicants must be enrolled for their first 1-year program, first associate degree, first 2-year program leading to a bachelor's degree, first bachelor's degree, or first professional degree.

**Financial data:** Grants up to $2,500 per academic year are available to full-time students and up to $1,250 per academic year to part-time students.

**Duration:** 1 year; may be renewed for up to 8 full-time equivalent terms.

**Number awarded:** Varies each year; recently, 26,936 students received more than $18.5 million in support from this program.

## 1040 SOUTH CAROLINA SHERIFFS' ASSOCIATION SCHOLARSHIPS

South Carolina Sheriffs' Association, Attn: Executive Director

112 West Park Boulevard

Columbia, SC 29210

Phone: (803) 772-1101; Fax: (803) 772-1197; Email: sheriffsc@aol.com

Web: www.sheriffssc.com

**Summary:** To provide financial assistance to seniors graduating from South Carolina high schools who are interested in attending college in the state.

**Eligibility:** Open to graduating high school seniors from South Carolina who are interested in attending a college within the state. Applicants must submit an essay on a topic that changes annually; recently, they were invited to write on "The Sheriff's Office and Domestic Violence." Financial need is not considered in the selection process.

**Financial data:** The stipend is $1,000.

**Duration:** 1 year.

**Number awarded:** 4 each year.

**Deadline:** February of each year.

## 1041 SOUTH CAROLINA STATE FAIR ACADEMIC SCHOLARSHIPS

South Carolina State Fair, Attn: Director of Entertainment and Exhibits

1200 Rosewood Drive

P.O. Box 393

Columbia, SC 29202

Phone: (803) 799-3387; Fax: (803) 799-1760; Email: nancys@scstatefair.org
Web: www.scstatefair.org

**Summary:** To provide financial assistance to high school seniors in South Carolina who will be attending a college or university in the state.

**Eligibility:** Open to seniors at public and private high schools in South Carolina. Applicants must fill out an application form, attach a current photograph, provide a copy of their transcript, and intend to attend a public or private college, technical college, or university in the state. Selection is based on financial need, academic and extracurricular achievement, and communication skills.

**Financial data:** The stipend is $2,000. Funds are paid directly to the recipient's college or university.

**Duration:** 1 year; nonrenewable.

**Number awarded:** 30 each year.

**Deadline:** March of each year.

## 1042 SOUTH CAROLINA TUITION GRANTS PROGRAM

South Carolina Higher Education Tuition Grants Commission
Attn: Executive Director
101 Business Park Boulevard, Suite 2100
Columbia, SC 29203-9498
Phone: (803) 896-1120; Fax: (803) 896-1126; Email: info@sctuitiongrants.org
Web: www.sctuitiongrants.com

**Summary:** To provide financial assistance to students at independent colleges and universities in South Carolina.

**Eligibility:** Open to residents of South Carolina who are attending or accepted for enrollment as full-time students at eligible private institutions in the state. Applicants must 1) graduate in the upper 75% of their high school class, 2) score 19 or above on the ACT (or the equivalent on the SAT, or 3) graduate with a high school GPA of 2.0 or higher. Selection is based on financial need.

**Financial data:** The amounts of the awards depend on the need of the recipient and the tuition and fees at the institution to be attended. Recently, the average grant was approximately $2,300. Funds may not be used for part-time enrollment, room and board charges, summer school enrollment, or graduate school enrollment.

**Duration:** 1 year; may be renewed.

**Number awarded:** Varies each year; recently, 3,154 new scholarships were awarded through this program.

**Deadline:** June of each year.

## 1043 SOUTH CAROLINA TUITION PROGRAM FOR CHILDREN OF CERTAIN WAR VETERANS

South Carolina Office of Veterans Affairs
1205 Pendleton Street, Suite 369
Columbia, SC 29201-3789
Phone: (803) 734-0200; Fax: (803) 734-0197; Email: va@oepp.sc.gov
Web: www.govoepp.state.sc.us/vetaff.htm

**Summary:** To provide free college tuition to the children of disabled and other South Carolina veterans.

**Eligibility:** Open to the children of wartime veterans who were legal residents of South Carolina both at the time of entry into military or naval service and during service, or who have been residents of South Carolina for at least 1 year. Veteran parents must 1) be permanently and totally disabled as determined by the U.S. Department of Veterans Affairs; 2) have been a prisoner of war; 3) have been killed in action; 4) have died from other causes while in service; 5) have died of a disease or disability resulting from service; 6) be currently missing in action; 7) have received the Congressional Medal of Honor; 8) have received the Purple Heart Medal from wounds received in combat; or 9) be now deceased but qualified under categories 1 or 2 above. The veteran's child must be 26 years of age or younger and working on an undergraduate degree.

**Financial data:** Children who qualify are eligible for free tuition at any South Carolina state-supported college, university, or postsecondary technical education institution. The waiver applies to tuition only. The costs of room and board, certain fees, and books are not covered.

**Duration:** Students are eligible to receive this support as long as they are younger than 26 years of age and working on an undergraduate degree.

**Number awarded:** Varies each year.

## 1044 SOUTH DAKOTA FREE TUITION FOR CHILDREN OF RESIDENTS WHO DIED DURING SERVICE IN THE ARMED FORCES

South Dakota Board of Regents

Attn: Scholarship Committee
306 East Capitol Avenue, Suite 200
Pierre, SD 57501-2545
Phone: (605) 773-3455; Fax: (605) 773-2422; Email: info@ris.sdbor.edu
Web: www.sdbor.edu

**Summary:** To provide free tuition at South Dakota public colleges and universities to children of military personnel who died while in service.

**Eligibility:** Open to residents of South Dakota younger than 25 years of age. The applicant's parent must have been killed in action or died of other causes while on active duty and must have been a resident of South Dakota for at least 6 months immediately preceding entry into active service.

**Financial data:** Eligible children are entitled to attend any South Dakota state-supported institution of higher education or state-supported technical or vocational school free of tuition and mandatory fees.

**Duration:** 8 semesters or 12 quarters of either full- or part-time study.

**Number awarded:** Varies each year.

## 1045 SOUTH DAKOTA FREE TUITION FOR DEPENDENTS OF PRISONERS OR MISSING IN ACTION

South Dakota Board of Regents, Attn: Scholarship Committee
306 East Capitol Avenue, Suite 200
Pierre, SD 57501-2545
Phone: (605) 773-3455; Fax: (605) 773-2422; Email: info@ris.sdbor.edu
Web: www.sdbor.edu

**Summary:** To provide free tuition at South Dakota public colleges and universities to dependents of prisoners of war (POWs) and persons missing in action (MIAs).

**Eligibility:** Open to residents of South Dakota who are the spouses or children of POWs or of MIAs. Applicants may not be eligible for equal or greater benefits from any federal financial assistance program.

**Financial data:** Eligible dependents are entitled to attend any South Dakota state-supported institution of higher education or state-supported technical or vocational school free of tuition and mandatory fees.

**Duration:** 8 semesters or 12 quarters of either full- or part-time study.

**Number awarded:** Varies each year.

## 1046 SOUTH DAKOTA FREE TUITION FOR SURVIVORS OF DECEASED FIRE FIGHTERS, CERTIFIED LAW ENFORCEMENT OFFICERS, AND EMERGENCY MEDICAL TECHNICIANS

South Dakota Board of Regents, Attn: Scholarship Committee
306 East Capitol Avenue, Suite 200
Pierre, SD 57501-2545
Phone: (605) 773-3455; Fax: (605) 773-2422; Email: info@ris.sdbor.edu
Web: www.sdbor.edu

**Summary:** To provide free tuition at South Dakota public colleges and universities to children of deceased fire fighters, law enforcement officers, and emergency medical technicians.

**Eligibility:** Open to residents of South Dakota who are the survivor of a fire fighter, certified law enforcement officer, or emergency medical technician who died as a direct result of injuries received in performance of official duties. Applicants must have been accepted for enrollment at a state-supported institution of higher education or technical or vocational school.

**Financial data:** Eligible survivors are entitled to attend any South Dakota state-supported institution of higher education or state-supported technical or vocational school free of tuition.

**Duration:** Until completion of a bachelor's or vocational degree; the degree must be earned within 36 months or 8 semesters.

**Number awarded:** Varies each year.

## 1047 SOUTH DAKOTA FREE TUITION FOR VETERANS AND OTHERS WHO PERFORMED WAR SERVICE

South Dakota Board of Regents, Attn: Scholarship Committee
306 East Capitol Avenue, Suite 200
Pierre, SD 57501-2545
Phone: (605) 773-3455; Fax: (605) 773-2422; Email: info@ris.sdbor.edu
Web: www.sdbor.edu

**Summary:** To provide free tuition at South Dakota public colleges and universities to certain veterans.

**Eligibility:** Open to current residents of South Dakota who have been discharged from the military forces of the United States under honorable conditions. Applicants must meet 1 of the following criteria: 1) served on active duty at any time between August 2, 1990 and March 3, 1991; 2) received an Armed

Forces Expeditionary Medal, Southwest Asia Service Medal, or other U.S. campaign or service medal for participation in combat operations against hostile forces outside the boundaries of the United States: or 3) have a service-connected disability rating of at least 10%. They may not be eligible for any other educational assistance from the U.S. government. Qualifying veterans must apply for this benefit within 20 years after the date proclaimed for the cassation of hostilities or within 6 years from and after the date of their discharge from military service, whichever is later.

**Financial data:** Eligible veterans are entitled to attend any South Dakota state-supported institution of higher education or state-supported technical or vocational school free of tuition and mandatory fees.

**Duration:** Eligible veterans are entitled to receive 1 month of free tuition for each month of qualifying service, from a minimum of 1 year to a maximum of 4 years.

**Number awarded:** Varies each year.

## 1048 SOUTH DAKOTA OPPORTUNITY SCHOLARSHIP

South Dakota Board of Regents, Attn: Scholarship Committee
306 East Capitol Avenue, Suite 200
Pierre, SD 57501-2545
Phone: (605) 773-3455; Fax: (605) 773-2422; Email: info@ris.sdbor.edu
Web: www.sdbor.edu/SDOpportunityScholarship.htm

**Summary:** To provide financial assistance to South Dakota high school seniors who plan to attend college in the state.

**Eligibility:** Open to seniors who are graduating from high schools South Dakota and have completed the Regents Scholar curriculum. Applicants may have received no grade below a "C" and must have a cumulative high school GPA of 3.0 or higher as well as a score of at least 24 on the ACT or the equivalent on the SAT.

**Financial data:** The stipend is $1,000 per year for the first 3 years and $2,000 for the fourth year.

**Duration:** 4 years, provided they maintain a GPA of 3.0 or higher and full-time enrollment.

**Number awarded:** Varies each year.

**Deadline:** August of each year.

## 1049 SOUTH FLORIDA SWEA SCHOLARSHIP

Swedish Women's Education Association International-South Florida Chapter
c/o Yerti Nelson, Scholarship Committee
3759 Mykonos Court
Boca Raton, FL 33486
Phone: (561) 997-2050; Fax: (561) 997-8010; Email: florida@swea.org
Web: www.chapters-swea.org/florida

**Summary:** To provide financial assistance to Florida residents interested in studying in Sweden or an area related to Swedish studies.

**Eligibility:** Open to all residents of Florida interested in participating in an exchange program in Sweden. Applicants may also propose to study in the United States, if the studies specifically emphasize Sweden and Swedish aspects, including 1) Swedish language; 2) Swedish culture or traditions; 3) environmental science; 4) a health care program promoting better health for women and children; or 5) handicraft, art, glass art, music, literature, or design. Study proposals must be well-defined in time and content. Along with their application, they must submit a transcript from college, university, or vocational school; curriculum vitae; project proposal, describing the planned studies, length of studies, and goals; financial statement; and letter of recommendation from an instructor.

**Financial data:** The stipend is $3,000.

**Number awarded:** 1 each year.

**Deadline:** January of each year.

## 1050 SOUTH PARK JAPANESE COMMUNITY SCHOLARSHIP

Japanese American Citizens League, Attn: National Scholarship Awards
1765 Sutter Street
San Francisco, CA 94115
Phone: (415) 921-5225; Fax: (415) 931-4671; Email: jacl@jacl.org
Web: www.jacl.org/scholarships.html

**Summary:** To provide financial assistance for college to student members of the Japanese American Citizens League (JACL) who are high school seniors.

**Eligibility:** Open to JACL members who are high school seniors interested in attending a college, university, trade school, business college, or other institution of higher learning. Applicants must submit a statement describing their current level of involvement in the Japanese American community or Asian Pacific community and how they will continue their involvement in future

years. Selection is based on academic record, extracurricular activities, and community involvement.

**Financial data:** The stipend depends on the availability of funds but usually ranges from $1,000 to $5,000.

**Duration:** 1 year; nonrenewable.

**Number awarded:** At least 1 each year.

**Deadline:** February of each year.

## 1051 SOUTHERN REGION KOREAN AMERICAN SCHOLARSHIPS

Korean American Scholarship Foundation
Southern Region
c/o Dr. Sam Sook Chung, Scholarship Committee Chair
2989 Preston Drive
Rex, GA 30273
Phone: (770) 968-6768; Email: southern@kasf.org
Web: www.kasf.org/home/regional/southern/southern.html

**Summary:** To provide financial assistance to Korean American undergraduate and graduate students who attend school in the southern states.

**Eligibility:** Open to Korean American students who are currently enrolled in a college or university in the southern states as full-time undergraduate or graduate students. Applicants may reside anywhere in the United States as long as they attend school in the southern region: Alabama, Arkansas, Florida, Georgia, Louisiana, Mississippi, Oklahoma, South Carolina, Tennessee, and Texas. Selection is based on academic achievement, school activities, community service, and financial need.

**Financial data:** Stipends range from $1,000 to $2,000.

**Duration:** 1 year; renewable.

**Number awarded:** Varies each year. Recently, 39 of these scholarships, worth $42,700, were awarded.

**Deadline:** June of each year.

## 1052 SPIRIT OF A WINNER SCHOLARSHIP

Arabian Horse Foundation, Attn: Scholarship Office
Ten Farnham Park Drive
Houston, TX 77024-7501
Phone: (713) 952-7081; Fax: (713) 977-9883;
Email: jean@parkwaychevrolet.com
Web: pages.sbcglobal.net/jvenhaus/horse/Scholar/scholar.html

**Summary:** To provide financial assistance for college to high school students who have a record of equine involvement.

**Eligibility:** Open to students who have a record of involvement with horses. Applicants must be juniors or seniors in high school who have shown at the Youth Nationals of the Arabian Horse Association. They must have a GPA of "B" or higher. Along with their application, they must submit information on their financial need, honors or academic awards, extracurricular activities and offices, leadership role, career goal, and equine involvement for the past 2 years.

**Financial data:** The stipend is $2,000 per year.

**Duration:** 1 year

**Number awarded:** 7 each year.

**Deadline:** January of each year.

## 1053 SPIRIT OF YOUTH SCHOLARSHIP FOR JUNIOR MEMBERS

American Legion Auxiliary
777 North Meridian Street, Third Floor
Indianapolis, IN 46204-1189
Phone: (317) 955-3845; Fax: (317) 955-3884; Email: alahq@legion-aux.org
Web: www.legion-aux.org/scholarships/docs/soysch.htm

**Summary:** To provide financial assistance for college to junior members of the American Legion Auxiliary.

**Eligibility:** Open to applicants who have been junior members of the Auxiliary for at least the past 3 years. They must be seniors at an accredited high school in the United States and have earned a GPA of 3.0 or higher. Each unit of the Auxiliary may select a candidate for application to the department level, and each department submits a candidate for the national award. Nominees must submit a 1,000-word essay on a topic that changes annually; a recent topic was "My Vision of Freedom." Selection is based on character and leadership (30%), the essay (30%) and academic record (40%).

**Financial data:** The scholarship is $1,000 per year, to be used at an accredited institution of higher learning or a professional or technical school that awards a certificate upon completion of an accredited course.

**Duration:** 4 years.

**Number awarded:** 5 each year: 1 in each division of the American Legion Auxiliary.

**Deadline:** Applications must be submitted to the unit president by March of each year.

## 1054 SPORTQUEST ALL-AMERICAN SCHOLARSHIPS FOR FEMALES

Athletes of Good News, Attn: SportQuest All-American Program
6425 N.W. Cache Road, Suites 217 and 218
P.O. Box 6272
Lawton, OK 73506
Phone: (580) 536-9524; Fax: (580) 536-7495; Email: allamerican@aogn.org
Web: www.aogn.org

**Summary:** To provide financial assistance for college to outstanding female Christian high school athletes.

**Eligibility:** Open to female high school sophomores, juniors, and seniors who believe in the Lord Jesus Christ as their personal Lord and Savior and attend a church regularly. Nominees must be 1 of the top 3 Christian athletes in their school and have an overall GPA of 3.0 or higher. They must be able to demonstrate an active Christian influence in school and community. Selection is based on athletics, academics, and Christian influence.

**Financial data:** The award is a $1,000 scholarship for the winner and a $500 scholarships for the runner-up.

**Duration:** 1 year.

**Number awarded:** 2 each year: 1 winner and 1 runner-up.

**Deadline:** November of each year.

## 1055 SPORTQUEST ALL-AMERICAN SCHOLARSHIPS FOR MALES

Athletes of Good News, Attn: SportQuest All-American Program
6425 N.W. Cache Road, Suites 217 and 218
P.O. Box 6272
Lawton, OK 73506
Phone: (580) 536-9524; Fax: (580) 536-7495; Email: allamerican@aogn.org
Web: www.aogn.org

**Summary:** To provide financial assistance for college to outstanding male Christian high school athletes.

**Eligibility:** Open to male high school sophomores, juniors, and seniors who believe in the Lord Jesus Christ as their personal Lord and Savior and attend a church regularly. Nominees must be 1 of the top 3 Christian athletes in their school and have an overall GPA of 3.0 or higher. They must be able to demonstrate an active Christian influence in school and community. Selection is based on athletics, academics, and Christian influence.

**Financial data:** The award is a $1,000 scholarship for the winner and a $500 scholarships for the runner-up.

**Duration:** 1 year.

**Number awarded:** 2 each year: 1 winner and 1 runner-up.

**Deadline:** November of each year.

## 1056 SPORTSMANSHIP RECOGNITION PROGRAM SCHOLARSHIP

Kentucky High School Athletic Association
2280 Executive Drive
Lexington, KY 40505
Phone: (859) 299-5472; Fax: (859) 293-5999
Web: www.khsaa.org

**Summary:** To recognize and reward, with college scholarships, outstanding student-athletes (including cheerleaders) in Kentucky high schools.

**Eligibility:** Open to high school seniors in Kentucky who have participated in athletics or cheerleading. Applicants must have at least a 2.5 GPA, 3 letters of recommendation from coaches and administrators illustrating the student's traits of good sportsmanship, demonstrated leadership within the school and the community, and a 2-page response to a case study developed for each competition. They must be planning to attend a college or university in Kentucky. A male and a female are recognized from each school in the state. They are chosen on the basis of these traits: playing the game by the rules; treating game officials and others with due respect, shaking hands with opponents, taking victory and defeat without undue emotionalism, controlling their tempers, being positive with officials and others who criticize them, cooperating with officials and others, being positive with opponents, letting student and adult audiences know that inappropriate behavior reflects poorly on the team, and serving as a role model for future student-athletes. These students are awarded a certificate and

are entered into a regional competition. Males and females continue to compete separately. The regional winners are given a plaque and are considered for the Sportsmanship Recognition Program Scholarship. Selection is based on GPA, recommendations, leadership roles and honors, and the case study essay.

**Financial data:** The stipend is $2,500.

**Duration:** 1 year.

**Number awarded:** 2 each year: 1 for a female and 1 for a male.

**Deadline:** Applications must be submitted to the school's athletic director in March.

## 1057 SPORTSTOSCHOOL COLLEGE SCHOLARSHIP

SportsToSchool
P.O. Box 6071
Middletown, RI 02842
Phone: (401) 849-2639; Fax: (401) 679-0308; Email: info@sportstoschool.com
Web: www.sportstoschool.com/scholarship.html

**Summary:** To provide financial assistance for college to high school students who participate in athletics.

**Eligibility:** Open to students who are currently enrolled as a freshman, sophomore, junior, or senior in high school. Applicants must participate in athletics and be interested in continuing their sports activity in college. Along with their application, they must submit a 150-word essay on how sports play a positive role in their lives. Financial need is not considered in the selection process.

**Financial data:** The stipend is $1,000. Funds are sent directly to the recipient.

**Duration:** 1 year.

**Number awarded:** 1 each year.

**Deadline:** February of each year.

## 1058 SREB ACADEMIC COMMON MARKET

Southern Regional Education Board
592 10th Street N.W.
Atlanta, GA 30318-5790
Phone: (404) 875-9211, ext. 261; Fax: (404) 872-1477;
Email: acm-rcp@sreb.org
Web: www.sreb.org/programs/acm/acmindex.asp

**Summary:** To enable students from southern states to attend a public college or university in another southern state at reduced tuition.

**Eligibility:** Open to residents of 16 southern states (Alabama, Arkansas, Delaware, Florida, Georgia, Kentucky, Louisiana, Maryland, Mississippi, North Carolina, Oklahoma, South Carolina, Tennessee, Texas, Virginia, and West Virginia) who wish to study in a program not available at any public institution of higher education in their home state. If their state has made arrangements to send students to another state, they may participate in this program.

**Financial data:** Participants pay only the in-state tuition at the institution outside their home state while they are studying in a program not available in their home state.

**Duration:** 1 year; may be renewed.

**Number awarded:** Varies each year; recently, more than 2,200 students participated in this program.

## 1059 STANLEY O. MCNAUGHTON COMMUNITY SERVICE AWARD

Independent Colleges of Washington
600 Stewart Street, Suite 600
Seattle, WA 98101
Phone: (206) 623-4494; Fax: (206) 625-9621; Email: info@icwashington.org
Web: www.icwashington.org/parents_students/financial_aid/index.htm

**Summary:** To provide financial assistance to upper-division students enrolled at colleges and universities that are members of Independent Colleges of Washington (ICW).

**Eligibility:** Open to students completing their sophomore or junior year at ICW-member colleges and universities. Applicants must submit a 1-page essay on their experience and views on volunteerism and community service. Selection is based on demonstrated commitment to volunteer community service both in high school and in college.

**Financial data:** The stipend is $2,500.

**Duration:** 1 year; nonrenewable.

**Number awarded:** 1 each year.

**Deadline:** April of each year.

## 1060 STANLEY W. MARION FUND

Polish Roman Catholic Union of America
Attn: Education Fund Scholarship Program
984 North Milwaukee Avenue
Chicago, IL 60622-4101
Phone: (773) 782-2600; (800) 772-8632; Fax: (773) 278-4595;
Email: info@prcua.org
Web: www.prcua.org/benefits/educationfundscholarship.htm

**Summary:** To provide financial assistance to undergraduate and graduate students of Polish heritage.

**Eligibility:** Open to students enrolled full time as sophomores, juniors, and seniors in an undergraduate program or full or part time as a graduate or professional school students. Selection is based on academic achievement, Polonia involvement, and community service.

**Financial data:** A stipend is awarded (amount not specified). Funds are paid directly to the institution.

**Duration:** 1 year.

**Number awarded:** 1 or more each year.

**Deadline:** May of each year.

## 1061 STANLEY Z. KOPLIK CERTIFICATE OF MASTERY TUITION WAIVER PROGRAM

Massachusetts Office of Student Financial Assistance
454 Broadway, Suite 200
Revere, MA 02151
Phone: (617) 727-9420; Fax: (617) 727-0667; Email: osfa@osfa.mass.edu
Web: www.osfa.mass.edu

**Summary:** To provide financial assistance for college to Massachusetts residents who earn a Stanley Z. Koplik Certificate of Mastery while in high school.

**Eligibility:** Open to permanent Massachusetts residents who are U.S. citizens or permanent residents. In order to become a candidate for the Stanley Z. Koplik Certificate of Mastery, students must score "Advanced" on at least 1 grade 10 MCAS test subject and score "Proficient" on the remaining sections of the grade 10 MCAS. Once they become candidates, they must then fulfill additional requirements through 1 of the following combinations covering both arts/humanities and mathematics/science: 2 AP exams; 2 SAT II exams; 1 SAT II exam and 1 AP exam; 1 SAT II exam and 1 other achievement; or 1 AP exam and 1 other achievement. They must score at least 3 on any AP exam; if there are SAT II and AP exams in the same subject area, they must receive a score on the SAT II exam determined by the Department of Education to be comparable to a score of 3 on the AP exam. In subject areas where they are no corresponding AP exams, a student must achieve an SAT II score designated by the Department of Education.

**Financial data:** Recipients of Koplik Certificates are eligible for an award of a non-need-based tuition waiver for state-supported undergraduate courses in Massachusetts.

**Duration:** Up to 4 academic years, provided the student maintains a college GPA of 3.3 or higher.

**Number awarded:** Varies each year.

## 1062 STATE VOCATIONAL REHABILITATION SERVICES PROGRAM

Department of Education
Office of Special Education and Rehabilitative Services
Attn: Rehabilitation Services Administration
400 Maryland Avenue, S.W.,
Washington, DC 20202-2800
Phone: (202) 245-7488
Web: www.ed.gov/about/offices/list/osers/rsa/index.html

**Summary:** To provide financial assistance to individuals with disabilities for undergraduate or graduate study pursued as part of their program of vocational rehabilitation.

**Eligibility:** Open to individuals who 1) have a physical or mental impairment that is a substantial impediment to employment; 2) are able to benefit in terms of employment from vocational rehabilitation services; and 3) require vocational rehabilitation services to prepare for, enter, engage in, or retain gainful employment. Priority is given to applicants with the most significant disabilities. Persons accepted for vocational rehabilitation develop an Individualized Written Rehabilitation Program (IWRP) in consultation with a counselor for the vocational rehabilitation agency in the state in which they live. The IWRP may include a program of postsecondary education if the disabled person and counselor agree that such a program will fulfill the goals of vocational rehabilitation. In most cases, the IWRP will provide for postsecondary education only to a level at which the disabled person will become employable, but that may include graduate education if the approved occupation requires an advanced degree as a minimum condition of entry. Students accepted to a program of postsecondary education as part of their IWRP must apply for all available federal, state, and private financial aid.

**Financial data:** Funding for this program is provided by the federal government through grants to state vocational rehabilitation agencies. Grants under the basic support program currently total nearly $2.7 billion per year. States must supplement federal funding with matching funds of 21.3%. Persons who are accepted for vocational rehabilitation by the appropriate state agency receive financial assistance based on the cost of their education and other funds available to them, including their own or family contribution and other sources of financial aid. Allowable costs in most states include tuition, fees, books, supplies, room, board, transportation, personal expenses, child care, and expenses related to disability (special equipment, readers, attendants, interpreters, or notetakers).

**Duration:** Assistance is provided until the disabled person achieves an educational level necessary for employment as provided in the IWRP.

**Number awarded:** Varies each year. Recently, more than 1.2 million people (of whom more than 80% have significant disabilities) were participating in this program.

## 1063 STEPHEN PHILLIPS MEMORIAL SCHOLARSHIP

Stephen Phillips Memorial Scholarship Fund
34 Chestnut Street
Salem, MA 01970
Phone: (978) 744-2111; Fax: (978) 744-0456; Email: info@spscholars.org
Web: www.Phillips-scholarship.org

**Summary:** To provide financial assistance for college to residents of the New England and mid-Atlantic states.

**Eligibility:** Open to residents of the New England and mid-Atlantic states (Connecticut, Delaware, District of Columbia, Maine, Maryland, Massachusetts, New Hampshire, New Jersey, New York, Pennsylvania, Rhode Island, Vermont, Virginia, or West Virginia) who are entering or returning college students. Preference is given to graduating high school seniors. Applicants must have a GPA of 3.0 or higher, be enrolled in a demanding course of study, demonstrate skilled writing ability, have at least 22 on their ACTs (or the equivalent on the SAT), and rank in the top 20% of their graduating high school class. In addition, they should demonstrate a desire to make a meaningful contribution to society; be involved in a balance of community, school, and work activities; be able to demonstrate integrity, resolution, self-discipline, and judgment; and have substantial unmet financial need.

**Financial data:** Stipends generally range from $3,000 to $10,000 per year. Funds are paid in 2 equal installments to the recipient's school and must be used to pay for tuition and fees.

**Duration:** 1 year; may be renewed for up to 3 additional years, provided the recipient maintains a GPA of 2.5 or higher.

**Number awarded:** Varies each year; recently, 175 new and 416 renewal scholarships were awarded.

**Deadline:** April of each year.

## 1064 STEPHEN SAPAUGH MEMORIAL SCHOLARSHIP

Key Club International, Attn: Manager of Youth Funds
3636 Woodview Trace
Indianapolis, IN 46268-3196
Phone: (317) 875-8755, ext. 244; (800) KIWANIS, ext. 244;
Fax: (317) 879-0204; Email: youthfunds@kiwanis.org
Web: www.keyclub.org

**Summary:** To provide financial assistance for college to high school seniors who are Key Club International members.

**Eligibility:** Open to college-bound graduating high school members who have completed at least 100 service hours during their Key Club career and have held an elected officer position on the club, district, or international level. Applicants must have a GPA of 3.5 or higher. Along with their application, they must submit 1) a 500-word essay describing the Key Club service project on which they have participated and that has had the greatest impact on them; 2) a list of high school organizations and activities; 3) a list of religious and community activities; 4) a list of honors, awards, and special recognitions; and 5) 2 letters of recommendation. Financial need is not considered in the selection process.

**Financial data:** The stipend is $1,000 per year.

**Duration:** 4 years.

**Number awarded:** 1 each year.

**Deadline:** February of each year.

## 1065 STERGIOS B. MILONAS SCHOLARSHIP

American Hellenic Educational Progressive Association
Attn: AHEPA Educational Foundation

1909 Q Street, N.W., Suite 500
Washington, DC 20009
Phone: (202) 232-6300; Fax: (202) 232-2140
Web: www.ahepa.org/educ_foundation/index.html
**Summary:** To provide financial assistance to incoming college freshmen who are members of the Sons of Pericles.
**Eligibility:** Open to incoming college freshmen who are members of the Sons of Pericles. Applicants must submit their most recent high school transcript as well as SAT or ACT scores. In addition to the transcripts and test scores, selection is based on extracurricular activities, athletic achievements, work and community service, and a 500-word essay on past achievements and future goals.
**Financial data:** Stipends range from $500 to $2,000 per year.
**Duration:** 1 year.
**Number awarded:** 1 each year.
**Deadline:** March of each year.

## 1066 STERLING SCHOLAR AWARDS OF UTAH

Deseret News, Attn: Marketing/Promotions/Special Events Department
30 East 100 South, Suite 400
Salt Lake City, UT 84111
Phone: (801) 237-2900
Web: deseretnews.com/scholars
**Summary:** To provide financial assistance for college to outstanding high school seniors in Utah.
**Eligibility:** Open to graduating seniors at high schools in Utah. Candidates must be nominated by their principals in 1 of the following categories: English, mathematics, social science, science, foreign language, computer technology, trade and technical education, family and consumer sciences, business and marketing, speech and drama, visual arts, music, and dance. Nominees submit portfolios demonstrating their work; the contents of the portfolio depend on the category for which they have been nominated. Selection is based on scholarship (50 points), leadership (25 points), and community service and citizenship (25 points). The program is conducted in 5 regions throughout Utah: Wasatch Front (Box Elder, Cache, Weber, Davis, Salt Lake, Tooele, and Utah counties), Northeast (Rich, Morgan, Summit, Wasatch, Duchesne, Dagget, and Uintah counties), Central (Juab, Sanpete, Millard, Sevier, Piute, and Wayne counties), Southwest (Beaver, Iron, Garfield, Washington, and Kane counties), and Southeast (Carbon, Emery, Grand, and San Juan counties).
**Financial data:** In the Wasatch Front region, a total of $21,000 is awarded, including a general scholarship award of $1,500 and category awards of $1,000 for first place and $250 for each runner-up. In the Northeast region, each category winner receives $500 plus a scholarship to a Utah college and each category runner-up receives $300 plus a scholarship to a Utah college. For information on the awards in the other regions, contact your high school principal or counselor. Many Utah colleges and universities also designate special awards exclusively for Sterling Scholars.
**Duration:** 1 year.
**Number awarded:** In the Wasatch Front region, 39 awards are presented (a winner and 2 runners-up in each category); 1 of those recipients is selected to receive the additional general scholarship award, 1 to be designated the Douglas Bates Awardee, and 1 to be designated the Philo T. Farnsworth Awardee.
**Deadline:** In the Wasatch Front region, schools must submit nominations by January of each year and nominees must complete their portfolios by February.

## 1067 STEVE FASTEAU PAST PRESIDENTS' SCHOLARSHIP

California Association for Postsecondary Education and Disability
Attn: Executive Assistant
71423 Biskra Road
Rancho Mirage, CA 92270
Phone: (760) 346-8206; Fax: (760) 340-5275; TTY: (760) 341-4084;
Email: caped2000@aol.com
Web: www.caped.net/scholarship.html
**Summary:** To provide financial assistance to undergraduate and graduate students in California who have a disability.
**Eligibility:** Open to students at public and private colleges and universities in California who have a disability. Undergraduates must have completed at least 6 semester credits and have a GPA of 2.5 or higher. Graduate students must have completed at least 3 semester units and have a GPA of 3.0 or higher. Applicants must submit a 1-page personal letter that demonstrates writing skills; progress toward meeting educational and vocational goals; how they accommodate their disability; involvement in community activities; and any other personal factor that might strengthen their application. They must also submit a letter of recommendation from a faculty person, verification of disability, official transcripts, proof of current enrollment, and documentation of financial need.

**Financial data:** The stipend is $1,000.
**Duration:** 1 year.
**Number awarded:** 1 each year.
**Deadline:** August of each year.

## 1068 STUDENT AID FUND FOR NONREGISTRANTS

Mennonite Church USA
Executive Board, Attn: Student Aid Fund for Nonregistrants
P.O. Box 1245
Elkhart, IN 46515-1245
Phone: (574) 523-3041; Email: KathrynR@MennoniteUSA.org
Web: peace.mennolink.org/safnr.html
**Summary:** To provide financial assistance for college or graduate school to men who are ineligible to receive government grants and loans because they have declined to register with the U.S. Selective Service System for reasons of Christian conscience.
**Eligibility:** Open to students who have declined to register with the U.S. Selective Service because of their Christian conscience. They must be either 1) attending a Mennonite Church USA college or seminary or 2) attending a congregation of Mennonite Church USA and enrolled in undergraduate or graduate studies in other-than-Mennonite institutions.
**Financial data:** Aid is available in the form of both grants and loans. The amount of assistance is based on formulas that would have been used if the student were eligible for government aid. For loans, no interest is charged until 6 months following completion of undergraduate study; at that time (even if the recipient continues on to graduate school), the loan must be repaid with a fixed interest rate based upon the long-term 120% AFR monthly rate, set 90 days after the student graduates or discontinues school; the minimum payment is $50 per month and the total repayment period cannot exceed 10 years.
**Number awarded:** Varies each year. Recently, 4 students received grants worth $9,000 and 4 students received loans worth $17,250.
**Deadline:** August of each year.

## 1069 STUDENT OPPORTUNITY SCHOLARSHIPS FOR ETHNIC MINORITY GROUPS

Presbyterian Church (USA), Attn: Office of Financial Aid for Studies
100 Witherspoon Street, Room M-052
Louisville, KY 40202-1396
Phone: (502) 569-5745; (888) 728-7228, ext. 5745; Fax: (502) 569-8766;
Email: KSmith@ctr.pcusa.org
Web: www.pcusa.org/financialaid/programfinder/sos.htm
**Summary:** To provide financial assistance for college to high school seniors of racial/ethnic minority heritage who are Presbyterians.
**Eligibility:** Open to members of the Presbyterian Church (USA) who are from racial/ethnic minority groups (Asian American, African American, Hispanic American, Native American, Alaska Native). Applicants must be able to demonstrate financial need, be high school seniors entering college as full-time students, and be U.S. citizens or permanent residents. They must submit a recommendation from their high school guidance counselor, a high school transcript, and an essay (up to 500 words in length) on their career goals and how they plan to achieve them.
**Financial data:** Stipends range from $100 to $1,000 per year, depending upon the financial need of the recipient.
**Duration:** 1 year; may be renewed for up to 3 additional years if the recipient continues to need financial assistance and demonstrates satisfactory academic progress.
**Number awarded:** Varies each year.
**Deadline:** April of each year.

## 1070 STUDENT-VIEW SCHOLARSHIP

Student Insights
136 Justice Drive
Valencia, PA 16059
Phone: (724) 612-3685; Email: contact@studentinsights.com
Web: www.student-view.com
**Summary:** To provide financial assistance for college to high school seniors in selected states who complete an online questionnaire about schools in their area.
**Eligibility:** Open to college-bound high school seniors in Connecticut, Delaware, the District of Columbia, Illinois, Indiana, Kentucky, Maryland, Michigan, New York, New Jersey, North Carolina, Ohio, Pennsylvania, Tennessee, Virginia, West Virginia, and Wisconsin. Applicants must complete

an online questionnaire in which they rate their awareness of a number of colleges in their region, including their academic strength, tuition cost, etc. They must also submit an essay, up to 250 words, on their own college search experience.

**Financial data:** The stipend is $3,000, $1,000, or $500.

**Duration:** 1 year.

**Number awarded:** 9 each year: 1 at $3,000; 2 at $1,000; and 6 at $500.

### 1071 SUBIC BAY-CUBI POINT SCHOLARSHIP

Navy League of the United States, Attn: Scholarships
2300 Wilson Boulevard
Arlington, VA 22201-3308
Phone: (703) 528-1775; (800) 356-5760; Fax: (703) 528-2333;
Email: cjarvis@navyleague.org
Web: www.navyleague.org/scholarship

**Summary:** To provide financial assistance for college to dependent children of sea service personnel or veterans who were attached to U.S. Naval Facility commands in the Philippines during specified times.

**Eligibility:** Open to U.S. citizens who are 1) dependents or direct descendants of an active, Reserve, retired, or honorably discharged member of the U.S. sea service (including the Navy, Marine Corps, Coast Guard, or Merchant Marines), or 2) currently an active member of the Naval Sea Cadet Corps. Applicants must be entering their freshman year of college. Along with their application, they must submit transcripts, 2 letters of recommendation, SAT/ACT scores, documentation of financial need, proof of qualifying sea service duty, and a 1-page personal statement on why they should be considered for this scholarship. Preference is given to dependents of sea service personnel who were permanently attached to the U.S. Naval Facility commands at Subic Bay, Cubi Point, or San Miguel in the Philippines between January 1980 and December 1992. There is no citizenship restriction for this scholarship.

**Financial data:** The stipend is $2,500 per year.

**Duration:** 4 years, provided the recipient maintains a GPA of 3.0 or higher.

**Number awarded:** 1 each year.

**Deadline:** February of each year.

### 1072 SUNSTUDENTS SCHOLARSHIP PROGRAM

Phoenix Suns Charities
201 East Jefferson Street
P.O. Box 1369
Phoenix, AZ 85001-1369
Phone: (602) 379-7969; Fax: (602) 379-7922
Web: www.suns.com

**Summary:** To provide financial assistance for college to high school seniors in Arizona.

**Eligibility:** Open to high school seniors in Arizona who have a cumulative GPA of 2.5 or higher and a record of involvement in charitable activities or volunteer service (in school, church, or community). Applicants must submit a 1-page essay on a topic that changes annually (recently, "Who has taught you about the importance of community involvement, and how are you putting this person's lessons into practice in your own life?"). Selection is based on community service (50 points), content and overall presentation of the essay (30 points), grades (15 points), and letters of recommendation (5 points). The applicant judged most outstanding is awarded the Kevin Johnson Scholarship.

**Financial data:** Stipends are $5,000 or $1,000.

**Duration:** The scholarship is offered annually.

**Number awarded:** 11 each year: 1 at $5,000 (the Kevin Johnson Scholarship) and 10 at $1,000.

**Deadline:** February of each year.

### 1073 SUPERSIBS! SCHOLARSHIPS

SuperSibs!, Attn: Scholarship Committee
4300 Lincoln Avenue, Suite I
Rolling Meadows, IL 60008
Phone: (847) 705-SIBS; (866) 444-SIBS; Fax: (847) 776-7084;
Email: info@supersibs.org
Web: www.supersibs.org

**Summary:** To provide financial assistance for college to siblings of children with cancer.

**Eligibility:** Open to seniors graduating from high schools in the United States, Puerto Rico, or the Virgin Islands with a GPA of 2.0 or higher. Applicants must be the siblings of children who have or have had cancer. They must be planning to attend an accredited college, university, or vocational institution in the fol-

lowing fall. Half-siblings and stepsiblings who reside in the same home as the cancer patient are also eligible. Along with their application, they must submit an essay, up to 1,000 words, on what they learned from their experience as the sibling of a brother or sister with cancer, how they will apply those learnings in their life and the lives of others, the advice they can share with other siblings to help them manage through this challenging time, how this scholarship will make a difference in their life, and anything else they would like the sponsor to know about them. Selection is based on the essay (60 points), a high school transcript (10 points), and a letter of recommendation (30 points).

**Financial data:** The stipend is $5,000.

**Duration:** 1 year.

**Number awarded:** Up to 5 each year.

**Deadline:** March of each year.

### 1074 SURVIVING DEPENDENTS OF MONTANA FIRE FIGHTERS/PEACE OFFICERS WAIVER

Montana Guaranteed Student Loan Program
2500 Broadway
P.O. Box 203101
Helena, MT 59620-3101
Phone: (406) 444-0638; (800) 537-7508; Fax: (406) 444-1869;
Email: scholar@mgslp.state.mt.us
Web: www.mgslp.state.mt.us

**Summary:** To provide financial assistance for college to dependents of deceased fire fighters or peace officers in Montana.

**Eligibility:** Open to residents of Montana who are surviving spouses or children of Montana fire fighters or peace officers killed in the course and scope of employment. Financial need is considered.

**Financial data:** Students eligible for this benefit are entitled to attend any unit of the Montana University System without payment of undergraduate registration or incidental fees.

**Duration:** Undergraduate students are eligible for continued fee waiver as long as they maintain reasonable academic progress as full-time students.

**Number awarded:** Varies each year.

### 1075 SURVIVING DEPENDENTS OF MONTANA NATIONAL GUARD MEMBER WAIVER

Montana Guaranteed Student Loan Program
2500 Broadway
P.O. Box 203101
Helena, MT 59620-3101
Phone: (406) 444-0638; (800) 537-7508; Fax: (406) 444-1869;
Email: scholar@mgslp.state.mt.us
Web: www.mgslp.state.mt.us

**Summary:** To provide financial assistance for undergraduate study to dependents of deceased National Guard members in Montana.

**Eligibility:** Open to residents of Montana who are surviving spouses or children of Montana National Guard members killed as a result of injury, disease, or other disability incurred in the line of duty while serving on state active duty. Financial need is considered.

**Financial data:** Students eligible for this benefit are entitled to attend any unit of the Montana University System without payment of undergraduate registration or incidental fees.

**Duration:** Undergraduate students are eligible for continued fee waiver as long as they maintain reasonable academic progress as full-time students.

**Number awarded:** Varies each year.

### 1076 SURVIVORS' AND DEPENDENTS' EDUCATIONAL ASSISTANCE PROGRAM

Department of Veterans Affairs
810 Vermont Avenue, N.W.
Washington, DC 20420
Phone: (202) 418-4343; (888) GI-BILL1
Web: www.gibill.va.gov

**Summary:** To provide financial assistance for undergraduate or graduate study to children and spouses of deceased and disabled veterans, MIAs, and POWs.

**Eligibility:** Open to spouses and children of 1) veterans who died or are permanently and totally disabled as the result of active service in the armed forces; 2) veterans who died from any cause while rated permanently and totally disabled from a service-connected disability; 3) servicemembers listed for more than 90 days as currently missing in action or captured in the line of duty by a hostile force; and 4) servicemembers listed for more than 90 days as presently detained or interned by a foreign government or power. Children must be between 18 and 26 years of age, although extensions may be granted. Spouses and children over 14 years of age with physical or mental disabilities are also eligible.

**Financial data:** Monthly stipends from this program for study at an academic institution are $827 for full time, $621 for three-quarter time, or $413 for half-time. For farm cooperative work, the monthly stipends are $667 for full-time, $500 for three-quarter time, or $334 for half-time. For an apprenticeship or on-the-job training, the monthly stipend is $650 for the first 6 months, $507 for the second 6 months, $366 for the third 6 months, and $151 for the remainder of the program.

**Duration:** Up to 45 months (or the equivalent in part-time training). Spouses must complete their training within 10 years of the date they are first found eligible.

**Number awarded:** Varies each year.

**Deadline:** Applications may be submitted at any time.

## 1077 SUSAN G. KOMEN BREAST CANCER FOUNDATION COLLEGE SCHOLARSHIP AWARDS

Susan G. Komen Breast Cancer Foundation, Attn: Grants Department
5005 LBJ Freeway, Suite 250
Dallas, TX 75244
Phone: (972) 855-1616; (888) 300-5582; Fax: (972) 855-1605;
Email: ccombs@komen.org
Web: www.komen.org

**Summary:** To provide financial assistance for college to high school seniors who lost a parent to breast cancer.

**Eligibility:** Open to students who lost a parent to breast cancer and would otherwise find attending college to be a significant financial burden or impossible. Applicants must be sponsored by a local affiliate of the foundation in the area where they live. They must be high school seniors or young adults under 25 years of age, be U.S. citizens or permanent residents, have a college GPA of 2.8 or higher (if already attending college), and be attending or planning to attend a state-supported college or university in the state where they permanently reside. Along with their application, they must submit 2 essays of 500 words each on 1) how breast cancer has changed them, and 2) how their education will help them achieve their career objectives and personal goals. Financial need is also considered in the selection process. All eligible applicants are interviewed at the local level and finalists are invited to the foundation's headquarters in Dallas for final interviews.

**Financial data:** Stipends up to $10,000 per year are available. Funds may be used for tuition, books, fees, and on-campus room and board.

**Duration:** 4 years, provided the recipient remains enrolled full time and makes reasonable progress toward completion of a baccalaureate degree.

**Number awarded:** 5 each year.

**Deadline:** November of each year.

## 1078 SUSAN THOMPSON BUFFETT FOUNDATION SCHOLARSHIP PROGRAM

Susan Thompson Buffett Foundation, Attn: Scholarship Office
222 Kiewit Plaza
Omaha, NE 68131
Phone: (402) 943-1383; Fax: (402) 943-1380;
Email: scholarships@stbfoundation.org
Web: www.BuffettScholarships.org

**Summary:** To provide financial assistance to entering or currently-enrolled students at public colleges and universities in Nebraska.

**Eligibility:** Open to U.S. citizens who are Nebraska residents. Applicants must be entering or currently enrolled in a state public college, university, community college, or trade school in Nebraska. They must be in financial need, be the only family member presently receiving a grant from the foundation, have at least a 2.5 GPA, and have applied for federal financial aid. Selection is based on academic performance and financial need. Preference is given to minority students, students with special needs, and married or nonmarried students with dependents.

**Financial data:** The maximum stipend is $2,800 per semester. Funds are sent directly to the recipient's school and must be used to pay tuition and fees; they may not be used to pay for books or other expenses.

**Duration:** Up to 5 years for a 4-year college, or up to 3 years for a 2-year school. Students on scholarship may not drop out for a period of time and be reinstated as a scholarship recipient; they must reapply along with first-time students.

**Deadline:** April of each year.

## 1079 SUSIE HOLMES MEMORIAL SCHOLARSHIP

International Order of Job's Daughters
Supreme Guardian Council Headquarters, Attn: Executive Manager
233 West Sixth Street
Papillion, NE 68046-2177
Phone: (402) 592-7987; Fax: (402) 592-2177; Email: sgc@iojd.org
Web: www.iojd.org

**Summary:** To provide financial assistance for college to members of Job's Daughters.

**Eligibility:** Open to high school graduates who are members of Job's Daughters. Applicants must be able to demonstrate dedicated, continuous, and joyful service to Job's Daughters; regular attendance at Supreme and/or Grand Sessions; participation in competitions at Supreme and/or Grand Sessions; friendship and impartiality in their Bethel; good character and integrity; and a GPA of 2.5 or higher.

**Financial data:** The stipend is $1,000.

**Duration:** 1 year.

**Number awarded:** 1 or more each year.

**Deadline:** April of each year.

## 1080 SUSSMAN-MILLER EDUCATIONAL ASSISTANCE FUND

Albuquerque Community Foundation, Attn: Scholarship Program
3301 Menaul N.E., Suite 2
P.O. Box 36960
Albuquerque, NM 87176-6960
Phone: (505) 883-6240; Email: acf@albuquerquefoundation.org
Web: www.albuquerquefoundation.org/scholar/scholar.htm

**Summary:** To provide financial assistance to undergraduate students from New Mexico.

**Eligibility:** Open to residents of New Mexico (for at least 1 year) who are able to demonstrate financial need. They may be either graduating high school seniors (who apply during the spring semester of their senior year) or current undergraduate students (who apply after completing 1 semester of undergraduate study). U.S. citizenship or permanent resident status is required. High school applicants must have a GPA of 3.0 or higher in academic subjects; current college students must have a GPA of 2.5 or higher. Selection is based primarily on financial need.

**Financial data:** The minimum stipend is $500 per year. The maximum stipend is 20% of the student's total budget or $2,500, whichever is less.

**Duration:** 1 year; may be renewed up to 3 additional years.

**Number awarded:** Varies each year.

**Deadline:** April of each year for high school seniors planning to attend college outside New Mexico or in-state private schools; June of each year for current undergraduate students and high school seniors planning to attend public schools in New Mexico.

## 1081 SWISS BENEVOLENT SOCIETY OF CHICAGO SCHOLARSHIPS

Swiss Benevolent Society of Chicago, Attn: Education Committee
P.O. Box 2137
Chicago, IL 60690-2137
Email: education@sbschicago.org
Web: www.sbschicago.org

**Summary:** To provide financial aid for college to Swiss students in Illinois or southern Wisconsin.

**Eligibility:** Open to 1) Swiss nationals with permanent U.S. residency status, and 2) people of documented Swiss descent; Swiss students studying in the United States on a student or visitor's visa are not eligible. Applicants must reside in Illinois or southern Wisconsin (Dane, Grant, Green, Iowa, Jefferson, Kenosha, Lafayette, Milwaukee, Ozaukee, Racine, Rock, Walworth, Washington, and Waukesha counties) and intend to attend college on a full-time basis during the following school year. High school seniors must have test scores of at least 26 on the ACT or equivalent on the SAT; current college freshmen must have the same minimum test scores and at least a 3.3 GPA in college work completed through the current semester; current college sophomores and juniors must have a minimum cumulative GPA of 3.3 in all college work completed through the current semester. Selection is based on academic merit only; financial need is not considered.

**Financial data:** Stipends are $1,500, $1,000, or $500.

**Duration:** 1 year; may be renewed for up to 3 additional years of full-time undergraduate study.

**Number awarded:** Varies each year; recently, scholarships were awarded to 11 high school seniors (4 at $1,500, 4 at $1,000, and 3 at $500); 8 college freshmen

(3 at $1,500, 3 at $1,000, and 2 at $500); and 14 college sophomores or juniors (6 at $1,500, 4 at $1,000, and 4 at $500).

**Deadline:** March of each year.

### 1082 TAILHOOK EDUCATIONAL FOUNDATION SCHOLARSHIPS

Tailhook Educational Foundation
9696 Businesspark Avenue
P.O. Box 26626
San Diego, CA 92196-0626
Phone: (858) 689-9223; (800) 269-8267; Email: thookassn@aol.com
Web: www.tailhook.org/foundation.html

**Summary:** To provide financial assistance for college to personnel associated with naval aviation and their children.

**Eligibility:** Open to 1) the children (natural, step, and adopted) of current or former U.S. Navy personnel who served as a naval aviator, naval flight officer, or designated naval air crewman, or 2) personnel and children of personnel who are serving or have served on board a U.S. Navy aircraft carrier as a member of the ship's company or assigned airwing. Applicants must be enrolled or accepted for enrollment at an accredited college or university. Selection is based on educational and extracurricular achievements, merit, and citizenship.

**Financial data:** The stipend ranges from $2,000 to $3,000.

**Duration:** 1 year.

**Number awarded:** Varies each year; recently, 43 of these scholarships were awarded.

**Deadline:** March of each year.

### 1083 TAKE AIM TRANSFER SCHOLARSHIPS

Washington Education Foundation
1605 N.W. Sammamish Road, Suite 100
Issaquah, WA 98027
Phone: (425) 416-2000; (877) 655-4097; Fax: (425) 416-2001;
Email: info@waedfoundation.org
Web: www.waedfoundation.org/nela_takeaim/index.htm

**Summary:** To provide financial assistance to students at community and technical colleges in Washington who plan to transfer to a 4-year institution in the state.

**Eligibility:** Open to students currently enrolled at community and technical colleges in Washington. Applicants must be planning to complete their associate degree in the year they apply and then transfer to a 4-year college or university in the state to complete their bachelor's degree. They must be able to demonstrate financial need. Each college in Washington may nominate 3 to 5 students.

**Financial data:** The stipend is $2,000.

**Duration:** 1 year.

**Number awarded:** Varies each year.

### 1084 TALBOTS WOMEN'S SCHOLARSHIP FUND

Talbots Charitable Foundation
c/o Scholarship America
Scholarship Management Services
One Scholarship Way
P.O. Box 297
St. Peter, MN 56082
Phone: (507) 931-1682; (800) 537-4180; Fax: (507) 931-9168;
Email: smsinfo@csfa.org
Web: www.talbots.com/about/scholar/scholar.asp

**Summary:** To provide financial assistance to women returning to college after an absence of at least 10 years.

**Eligibility:** Open to women who earned their high school diploma or GED at least 10 years ago and are now seeking a degree from an accredited 2- or 4-year college, university, or vocational/technical school. Applicants must have at least 2 full-time semesters remaining to complete their undergraduate degree. As part of the selection process, they must submit an essay on their plans as they relate to their educational and career objectives and long-term goals. In addition to that essay, selection is based on academic record, leadership and participation in community activities, honors, work experience, an outside appraisal, and financial need.

**Financial data:** Stipends are either $10,000 or $1,000. Checks are mailed to the recipient's home address and are made payable jointly to the student and the school.

**Duration:** 1 year; nonrenewable.

**Number awarded:** 55 each year: 5 at $10,000 and 50 at $1,000.

**Deadline:** January of each year.

### 1085 TARGET ALL-AROUND SCHOLARSHIPS

Target Stores, Attn: Community Relations
1000 Nicollet Mall
Minneapolis, MN 55403
Phone: (612) 696-6098; (800) 537-4180
Web: www.target.com/target_group/community_giving/scholarships.jhtml

**Summary:** To provide financial assistance for college to students committed to helping their communities.

**Eligibility:** Open to high school seniors, high school graduates, and current college students who are younger than 24 years of age and making contributions to their community through volunteer service, education, and family involvement. Applicants must have a GPA of 2.0 or higher and be enrolled or planning to enroll full time at an accredited 2- or 4-year college, university, or vocational/technical school in the continental United States. Selection is based on number of community volunteer service hours, the applicant's list of volunteer leadership awards and honors, an appraisal form completed by a volunteer supervisor or leader, and the applicant's short essay on volunteer service. Applications are available at any Target store.

**Financial data:** Most stipends are $1,000, but the highest-ranked applicant receives an award of $25,000.

**Duration:** 1 year.

**Number awarded:** More than 600 each year.

**Deadline:** October of each year.

### 1086 TAYLOR J. ERTEL SCHOLARSHIPS

Taylor J. Ertel Foster Children Foundation
2245 Heim Hill Road
Montoursville, PA 17754-9699
Phone: (570) 433-3494; Fax: (570) 326-1050; Email: aertel@regscan.com
Web: www.tjefoundation.org

**Summary:** To provide financial assistance for college or graduate school to residents of Pennsylvania who have been in foster care.

**Eligibility:** Open to Pennsylvania residents who have been placed in foster care by a child welfare agency. Applicants must be attending or planning to attend a vocational school, college, university, or graduate school in the state. Along with their application, they must submit information on their school activities, educational record, school awards and honors, community activities, employment record, and a budget.

**Financial data:** The stipend is $2,000 per year.

**Duration:** 1 year.

**Number awarded:** 1 or more each year.

### 1087 TEEN LATINA USA

Dawn Ramos Productions
607 South Loving Avenue
Sherman, TX 75090-6743
Phone: (903) 891-9761; Email: info@misslatina.com
Web: www.misslatina.com

**Summary:** To recognize and reward teen-aged Latina women who compete in a national beauty pageant.

**Eligibility:** Open to women between 13 and 17 years of age who are at least 25% Hispanic. Applicants must be single and they may not have children. They appear in a nationally-televised pageant where selection is based one third on an interview, one third on swimsuit appearances, and one third on evening gown appearances. Height and weight are not factors, but contestants should be proportionate. Pageant experience and fluency in Spanish are not required.

**Financial data:** Each year, prizes include scholarships, gifts, a cruise to the Bahamas, a trip to Las Vegas, a modeling contract, and use of an apartment in Miami. The total value is more than $25,000.

**Duration:** The pageant is held annually

**Number awarded:** 1 winner and 4 runners-up are selected each year.

### 1088 TELAMON SCHOLARSHIP

US Pan Asian American Chamber of Commerce
Attn: Scholarship Coordinator
1329 18th Street, N.W.
Washington, DC 20036
Phone: (202) 296-5221; Fax: (202) 296-5225;
Email: administrator@uspaacc.com
Web: www.uspaacc.com/web/programs/telamon.htm

**Summary:** To provide financial assistance for college to Asian American high school seniors.

**Eligibility:** Open to high school seniors of Asian heritage who are U.S. citizens or permanent residents. Applicants must be planning to begin full-time study at an accredited postsecondary educational institution in the United States. Along with their application, they must submit a 500-word essay on "What are the characteristics or qualities needed in order to achieve success?" Selection is based on academic excellence (GPA of 3.5 or higher), leadership in extracurricular activities, community service involvement, and financial need.

**Financial data:** The maximum stipend is $3,500. Funds are paid directly to the recipient's college or university.

**Duration:** 1 year.

**Number awarded:** 1 each year.

**Deadline:** February of each year.

---

**1089 TENNESSEE DEPENDENT CHILDREN SCHOLARSHIP**

Tennessee Student Assistance Corporation
Parkway Towers
404 James Robertson Parkway, Suite 1950
Nashville, TN 37243-0820
Phone: (615) 741-1346; (800) 342-1663; Fax: (615) 741-6101;
Email: tsac@mail.state.tn.us
Web: www.tnscholardollars.com/mon_college/depend_child-scholar.htm

**Summary:** To provide financial assistance for college to the dependent children of disabled or deceased Tennessee law enforcement officers, fire fighters, or emergency medical service technicians.

**Eligibility:** Open to Tennessee residents who are the dependent children of a Tennessee law enforcement officer, fire fighter, or emergency medical service technician who was killed or totally and permanently disabled in the line of duty. Applicants must be enrolled or accepted for enrollment as a full-time undergraduate student at a college or university in Tennessee.

**Financial data:** The award covers tuition and fees, books, supplies, and room and board, minus any other financial aid for which the student is eligible.

**Duration:** 1 year; may be renewed for up to 3 additional years or until completion of a program of study.

**Number awarded:** Varies each year; recently, 19 students received $77,786 in support from this program

**Deadline:** July of each year.

---

**1090 TENNESSEE GENERAL ASSEMBLY MERIT SCHOLARSHIPS**

Tennessee Student Assistance Corporation
Parkway Towers
404 James Robertson Parkway, Suite 1950
Nashville, TN 37243-0820
Phone: (615) 741-1346; (800) 342-1663; Fax: (615) 741-6101;
Email: tsac@mail.state.tn.us
Web: www.tnscholardollars.com/mon_college/gams.htm

**Summary:** To provide supplemental financial assistance for college to high school seniors in Tennessee who meet academic requirements in excess of those for the Tennessee HOPE Scholarships.

**Eligibility:** Open to seniors graduating from public and private high schools in Tennessee and other residents of the state who qualify for a Tennessee HOPE Scholarship. Applicants for this supplemental funding must have higher levels of academic achievement: 1) ACT scores of at least 29 (instead of 21) or the equivalent on the SAT and 2) GPA of 3.75 or higher (instead of 3.0). The GPA may be weighted to include extra credit for AP or other advanced courses. They must be planning to attend an accredited public or private college or university in Tennessee.

**Financial data:** The stipend is an additional $1,000, so the total award is $4,000 per year for students at 4-year colleges and universities or $2,500 per year for students at 2-year schools.

**Duration:** 1 year; students may receive this supplemental funding only once.

**Number awarded:** Varies each year.

**Deadline:** April of each year.

---

**1091 TENNESSEE HOPE ACCESS GRANTS**

Tennessee Student Assistance Corporation
Parkway Towers
404 James Robertson Parkway, Suite 1950
Nashville, TN 37243-0820
Phone: (615) 741-1346; (800) 342-1663; Fax: (615) 741-6101;
Email: tsac@mail.state.tn.us
Web: www.tnscholardollars.com/mon_college/hope_grant.htm

**Summary:** To provide financial assistance for college to high school seniors in Tennessee who do not qualify for the Tennessee HOPE Scholarships but meet other academic and income requirements.

**Eligibility:** Open to seniors graduating from public and private high schools in Tennessee who have an unweighted GPA of 2.75 or higher and an ACT score of at least 18 or the equivalent on the SAT. Applicants must have an annual family income of $36,000 or less. They must be planning to attend an accredited public or private college or university in Tennessee.

**Financial data:** The stipend is $2,000 per year for students at 4-year colleges and universities or $1,250 per year for students at 2-year schools.

**Duration:** 1 year; this grant is nonrenewable but recipients may apply for a Tennessee HOPE Scholarship after 1 year of college if they have a cumulative GPA of 2.75 or higher.

**Number awarded:** Varies each year.

**Deadline:** April of each year.

---

**1092 TENNESSEE HOPE SCHOLARSHIPS**

Tennessee Student Assistance Corporation
Parkway Towers
404 James Robertson Parkway, Suite 1950
Nashville, TN 37243-0820
Phone: (615) 741-1346; (800) 342-1663; Fax: (615) 741-6101;
Email: tsac@mail.state.tn.us
Web: www.tnscholardollars.com/mon_college/hope_scholar.htm

**Summary:** To provide financial assistance for college to high school seniors in Tennessee.

**Eligibility:** Open to seniors graduating from public and private high schools in Tennessee, students in Tennessee who have completed a home-school program, and residents of Tennessee who have attained a GED. High school seniors must have an ACT score of at least 21 (or the equivalent on the SAT) or an unweighted GPA of 3.0 or higher; home-school students must have an ACT score of at least 21 (or the equivalent on the SAT); and GED recipients must have a GED score of at least 525 and an ACT score of at least 21 (or an equivalent SAT score). Applicants must be planning to attend an accredited public or private college or university in Tennessee.

**Financial data:** The stipend is $3,000 per year for students at 4-year colleges and universities or $1,500 per year for students at 2-year schools.

**Duration:** 1 year; may be renewed up to 4 additional years if the recipient maintains a cumulative GPA of 2.75 or higher.

**Number awarded:** Varies each year.

**Deadline:** April of each year.

---

**1093 TENNESSEE NEED-BASED SUPPLEMENTAL AWARDS**

Tennessee Student Assistance Corporation
Parkway Towers
404 James Robertson Parkway, Suite 1950
Nashville, TN 37243-0820
Phone: (615) 741-1346; (800) 342-1663; Fax: (615) 741-6101;
Email: tsac@mail.state.tn.us
Web: www.tnscholardollars.com/mon_college/need_based_award.htm

**Summary:** To provide supplemental financial assistance for college to high school seniors in Tennessee who qualify for the Tennessee HOPE Scholarships and also demonstrate financial need.

**Eligibility:** Open to seniors graduating from public and private high schools in Tennessee and other residents of the state who qualify for a Tennessee HOPE Scholarship. Applicants must have an annual family income of $36,000 or less. They must be planning to attend an accredited public or private college or university in Tennessee.

**Financial data:** The stipend is an additional $1,000, so the total award is $4,000 per year for students at 4-year colleges and universities or $2,500 per year for students at 2-year schools.

**Duration:** 1 year; students may receive this supplemental funding only once.

**Number awarded:** Varies each year.

**Deadline:** April of each year.

---

**1094 TENNESSEE STUDENT ASSISTANCE AWARDS**

Tennessee Student Assistance Corporation
Parkway Towers
404 James Robertson Parkway, Suite 1950
Nashville, TN 37243-0820
Phone: (615) 741-1346; (800) 342-1663; Fax: (615) 741-6101;
Email: tsac@mail.state.tn.us
Web: www.tnscholardollars.com/mon_college/tsa_award.htm

**Summary:** To provide financial assistance to students in Tennessee who have financial need.

**Eligibility:** Open to students in Tennessee who are U.S. citizens, are Tennessee residents, are enrolled at least half time as undergraduate students, and can demonstrate financial need (expected family contribution of $2,100 or less).

**Financial data:** Recently, the maximum award was $2,322 at eligible Tennessee public postsecondary institutions or $5,538 at eligible Tennessee independent postsecondary institutions.

**Duration:** 1 year; nonrenewable.

**Number awarded:** Varies each year.

**Deadline:** April of each year.

---

## 1095 TEXAS CHILDREN OF DISABLED OR DECEASED FIREMEN, PEACE OFFICERS, GAME WARDENS, AND EMPLOYEES OF CORRECTIONAL INSTITUTIONS EXEMPTION PROGRAM

Texas Higher Education Coordinating Board
Attn: Grants and Special Programs
1200 East Anderson Lane
P.O. Box 12788, Capitol Station
Austin, TX 78711-2788
Phone: (512) 427-6101; (800) 242-3062; Fax: (512) 427-6127;
Email: grantinfo@thecb.state.tx.us
Web: www.collegefortexans.com

**Summary:** To provide educational assistance to the children of disabled or deceased Texas fire fighters, peace officers, game wardens, and employees of correctional institutions.

**Eligibility:** Open to children of Texas paid or volunteer fire fighters; paid municipal, county, or state peace officers; custodial employees of the Department of Corrections; or game wardens. The parent must have suffered an injury in the line of duty, resulting in disability or death. Applicants must be under 21 years of age.

**Financial data:** Eligible students are exempted from the payment of all dues, fees, and tuition charges at publicly-supported colleges and universities in Texas.

**Duration:** Support is provided for up to 120 semester credit hours of undergraduate study or until the recipient reaches 26 years of age, whichever comes first.

**Number awarded:** Varies each year; recently, 116 students received support through this program.

---

## 1096 TEXAS CHILDREN OF U.S. MILITARY WHO ARE MISSING IN ACTION OR PRISONERS OF WAR EXEMPTION PROGRAM

Texas Higher Education Coordinating Board
Attn: Grants and Special Programs
1200 East Anderson Lane
P.O. Box 12788, Capitol Station
Austin, TX 78711-2788
Phone: (512) 427-6101; (800) 242-3062; Fax: (512) 427-6127;
Email: grantinfo@thecb.state.tx.us
Web: www.collegefortexans.com

**Summary:** To provide educational assistance to the children of Texas military personnel declared prisoners of war or missing in action.

**Eligibility:** Open to dependent children of Texas residents who are either prisoners of war or missing in action. Applicants must be under 21 years of age, or under 25 if they receive the majority of support from their parent(s).

**Financial data:** Eligible students are exempted from the payment of all dues, fees, and tuition charges at publicly-supported colleges and universities in Texas.

**Duration:** Up to 8 semesters.

**Number awarded:** Varies each year; recently, 2 of these exemptions were granted.

---

## 1097 TEXAS DIVISION SCHOLARSHIPS

United Daughters of the Confederacy-Texas Division
c/o Sally E. Peterson, Education Committee Chair
11830 Spruce Hill
Houston, TX 77077-4927
Phone: (281) 556-1451; Email: sepfromlsu@houston.rr.com
Web: txudc.org/education.htm

**Summary:** To provide financial assistance to the descendants of Confederate veterans who are interested in attending college in Texas.

**Eligibility:** Open to high school seniors and current college students who are lineal or collateral descendants of men who served in the Confederate military. Collateral descendants must be members of the United Daughters of the Confederacy (UDC) or Children of the Confederacy (CofC). Applicants must be endorsed by officials of their local UDC Chapter in Texas. They must be attending or planning to attend an accredited college or university in Texas. Along with their application, they must submit a 300-word letter pledging to make the best possible use of the opportunity offered through the scholarship and outlining goals and plans for obtaining them; the letter should evaluate the significance of a Southern heritage in today's world. Financial need is also considered in the selection process.

**Financial data:** Stipends range up to $1,000. Funds are paid directly to the recipient's university.

**Duration:** Up to 4 years, as long as the recipient remains enrolled full time with a GPA of 3.0 or higher.

**Number awarded:** Varies each year.

**Deadline:** February of each year.

---

## 1098 TEXAS EARLY HIGH SCHOOL GRADUATION SCHOLARSHIPS

Texas Higher Education Coordinating Board
Attn: Grants and Special Programs
1200 East Anderson Lane
P.O. Box 12788, Capitol Station
Austin, TX 78711-2788
Phone: (512) 427-6387; (800) 242-3062, ext. 6387; Fax: (512) 427-6127;
Email: grantinfo@thecb.state.tx.us
Web: www.collegefortexans.com

**Summary:** To provide financial assistance to students in Texas who are planning to attend college after completing high school in less than specified times.

**Eligibility:** Open to residents of Texas who have attended high school in the state and plan to attend a Texas public or private college or university. Applicants must have completed either the recommended high school curriculum or the distinguished achievement high school curriculum in no more than 36 consecutive months. Smaller awards are available to applicants who 1) complete the requirements for grades 9-12 within 41 months, or 2) complete the requirements within 46 months and also earn at least 30 hours of college credit.

**Financial data:** Stipends are 1) $2,000 for students who complete the requirements within 36 months (an additional $1,000 is awarded if the student also graduates with at least 15 hours of college credit); 2) $500 for students who complete the requirements in more than 36 but less than 41 months (an additional $1,000 is awarded if the student also graduates with at least 30 hours of college credit); or 3) $1,000 for students who complete the requirements in more than 41 but less than 46 months and also have at least 30 hours of college credit. If the award is used at a private college or university, the school must provide a matching scholarship.

**Duration:** 1 year; nonrenewable.

**Number awarded:** Varies each year; recently, 232 of these scholarships were awarded.

---

## 1099 TEXAS EDUCATION AND TRAINING VOUCHERS FOR YOUTHS AGING OUT OF FOSTER CARE

Texas Higher Education Coordinating Board
Attn: Grants and Special Programs
1200 East Anderson Lane
P.O. Box 12788, Capitol Station
Austin, TX 78711-2788
Phone: (512) 427-6101; (800) 242-3062; Fax: (512) 427-6127;
Email: grantinfo@thecb.state.tx.us
Web: www.collegefortexans.com

**Summary:** To provide financial assistance for college to students in Texas who have been in foster care.

**Eligibility:** Open to residents of Texas who 1) are between 16 and 21 years of age, have a high school diploma or equivalent, and are attending a Texas public or private college that provides a bachelor's degree or not less than a 2-year program that provides credit towards an associate degree or certificate; 2) are beyond the age of compulsory school attendance (age 18) and are attending an accredited or preaccredited program that provides not less than 1 year of training toward gainful employment; 3) are in foster care of the Texas Department of Family and Protective Services (TDFPS), are at least 16 years of age, and are likely to remain in foster care until turning 18; 4) have aged out of TDFPS foster care but have not yet turned 21; or 5) are adopted from TDFPS foster care after turning 16 years of age but are not yet 21. Applicants must be attending or planning to attend a Texas public or private educational institution that is accredited or granted preaccredited status.

**Financial data:** Vouchers can be used to cover the cost of attendance (tuition and fees, books and supplies, room and board, transportation, child care, and some personal expenses) or $5,000 per year, whichever amount is less.

**Duration:** 1 year. Participants in the program remain eligible until age 23 ad long as they are enrolled and making satisfactory progress toward completing their postsecondary education or training program.

**Number awarded:** Varies each year.

---

## 1100 TEXAS EDUCATIONAL OPPORTUNITY GRANT PROGRAM

Texas Higher Education Coordinating Board
Attn: Grants and Special Programs
1200 East Anderson Lane
P.O. Box 12788, Capitol Station
Austin, TX 78711-2788
Phone: (512) 427-6101; (800) 242-3062; Fax: (512) 427-6127;
Email: grantinfo@thecb.state.tx.us
Web: www.collegefortexans.com

**Summary:** To provide financial assistance to students entering a public 2-year college in Texas.

**Eligibility:** Open to residents of Texas enrolled at least half time in the first 30 credit hours at a public community college, public technical college, or public state college in the state. Applicants must have an expected family contribution of no more than $2,000.

**Financial data:** Full-time stipends are approximately $1,795 per semester for public state college students, $635 per semester for community college students, or $990 per semester for technical college students.

**Duration:** 1 year. Students can receive awards for up to 75 semester credit hours, for 4 years, or until they receive an associate degree, whichever occurs first. Renewal requires completion of at least 75% of the hours taken in the prior year plus a cumulative college GPA of 2.5 or higher.

**Number awarded:** Varies each year; recently, 4,512 of these grants were awarded.

---

## 1101 TEXAS EXEMPTION FOR HIGHEST RANKING HIGH SCHOOL GRADUATE PROGRAM

Texas Higher Education Coordinating Board
Attn: Grants and Special Programs
1200 East Anderson Lane
P.O. Box 12788, Capitol Station
Austin, TX 78711-2788
Phone: (512) 427-6101; (800) 242-3062; Fax: (512) 427-6127;
Email: grantinfo@thecb.state.tx.us
Web: www.collegefortexans.com

**Summary:** To recognize and reward the top students in Texas high schools.

**Eligibility:** Open to the highest ranking graduates (i.e., valedictorians) of accredited high schools in Texas. Applicants may be Texas residents, nonresidents, or foreign students.

**Financial data:** Tuition is waived for award winners at any public college or university in Texas.

**Duration:** 1 year; nonrenewable.

**Number awarded:** Varies each year; recently, 1,102 of these exemptions were granted.

---

## 1102 TEXAS EXEMPTION FOR SURVIVING SPOUSES AND DEPENDENT CHILDREN OF CERTAIN DECEASED PUBLIC SERVANTS

Texas Higher Education Coordinating Board
Attn: Grants and Special Programs
1200 East Anderson Lane
P.O. Box 12788, Capitol Station
Austin, TX 78711-2788
Phone: (512) 427-6101; (800) 242-3062; Fax: (512) 427-6127;
Email: grantinfo@thecb.state.tx.us
Web: www.collegefortexans.com

**Summary:** To provide educational assistance to the children and spouses of certain deceased Texas public employees.

**Eligibility:** Open to residents of Texas whose parent or spouse was killed in the line of duty in certain public service positions after September 1, 2000. Eligible public service positions include peace officers, probation officers, parole officers, jailers, members of organized police reserve and auxiliary units, juvenile correctional employees, paid and volunteer fire fighters, and emergency medi-

cal service volunteers and paid personnel. Applicants must be enrolled or planning to enroll full time at a Texas public college or university.

**Financial data:** Eligible students are exempted from the payment of all dues, fees, and tuition charges at publicly-supported colleges and universities in Texas. In addition, the institution provides them with an allowance for textbooks. If the student qualifies to live in the institution's housing, the institution must provide either free room and board or an equivalent room and board stipend.

**Duration:** 1 year; may be renewed.

**Number awarded:** Varies each year; recently, 65 students received support through this program.

---

## 1103 TEXAS EXEMPTION PROGRAM FOR ADOPTED STUDENTS FORMERLY IN FOSTER OR OTHER RESIDENTIAL CARE

Texas Higher Education Coordinating Board
Attn: Grants and Special Programs
1200 East Anderson Lane
P.O. Box 12788, Capitol Station
Austin, TX 78711-2788
Phone: (512) 427-6101; (800) 242-3062; Fax: (512) 427-6127;
Email: grantinfo@thecb.state.tx.us
Web: www.collegefortexans.com

**Summary:** To provide educational assistance to students in Texas who once were in foster or other residential care and have been adopted.

**Eligibility:** Open to students who have been in foster care or other residential care, under the conservatorship of the Texas Department of Family and Protective Services and have been adopted. Applicants must be attending or planning to attend a public college or university in Texas.

**Financial data:** Eligible students are exempted from the payment of all dues, fees, and tuition charges at publicly-supported colleges and universities in Texas.

**Duration:** 1 year; may be renewed.

**Number awarded:** Varies each year; recently, 11 students received support through this program.

---

## 1104 TEXAS FOSTER CARE EXEMPTION PROGRAM

Texas Higher Education Coordinating Board
Attn: Grants and Special Programs
1200 East Anderson Lane
P.O. Box 12788, Capitol Station
Austin, TX 78711-2788
Phone: (512) 427-6101; (800) 242-3062; Fax: (512) 427-6127;
Email: grantinfo@thecb.state.tx.us
Web: www.collegefortexans.com

**Summary:** To exempt students in Texas who were in foster care when they became 18 years of age from payment of tuition at public colleges and universities in the state.

**Eligibility:** Open to students who have been in the care or conservatorship of the Texas Department of Family and Protective Services 1) on the day before their 18th birthday, the day they graduated from high school, or the day they received a GED certificate; or 2) through their 14th birthday and were then adopted. Applicants must enroll as an undergraduate at a public college or university in Texas within 3 years of that relevant date, but no later than their 21st birthday.

**Financial data:** Eligible students are exempted from the payment of all dues, fees, and tuition charges at publicly-supported colleges and universities in Texas.

**Duration:** 1 year.

**Number awarded:** Varies each year; recently, 950 students received support through this program.

---

## 1105 TEXAS GRANT

Texas Higher Education Coordinating Board
Attn: Grants and Special Programs
1200 East Anderson Lane
P.O. Box 12788, Capitol Station
Austin, TX 78711-2788
Phone: (512) 427-6101; (800) 242-3062; Fax: (512) 427-6127;
Email: grantinfo@thecb.state.tx.us
Web: www.collegefortexans.com

**Summary:** To provide financial assistance to undergraduate students entering college in Texas from high school or a community college.

**Eligibility:** Open to residents of Texas enrolled at a college or university in the state who have applied for other financial assistance and have an expected family contribution of no more than $4,000. Applicants may be 1) enrolled in the first 30 credit hours, having graduated from high school no earlier than the 1998-99 school year, where they completed the recommended or distinguished achievement high school curriculum or its equivalent, and having enrolled at an eligible Texas college or university within 16 months of high school graduation; or 2) transferring from a community college from which they received their first associate degree in May 2001 or later and enrolling in a higher level undergraduate program within 12 months of receiving their associate degree. At least three-quarter time enrollment is required.

**Financial data:** Full-time stipends are approximately $1,795 per semester for public university students, $635 per semester for community college students, or $990 per semester for technical college students. Stipends at private institutions are based on the public university amount.

**Duration:** 1 year. Students who qualify on the basis of their high school curriculum can receive awards for up to 150 semester credit hours, for 6 years, or until their receive their bachelor's degree, whichever occurs first. Students who qualify on the basis of an associate degree can receive awards for up to 90 semester credit hours, for 4 years, or until they complete a baccalaureate degree, whichever occurs first. Renewal requires completion of at least 75% of the hours taken in the prior year plus a cumulative college GPA of 2.5 or higher.

**Number awarded:** Varies each year.

## 1106 TEXAS LEVERAGING EDUCATIONAL ASSISTANCE PARTNERSHIP PROGRAM

Texas Higher Education Coordinating Board
Attn: Grants and Special Programs
1200 East Anderson Lane
P.O. Box 12788, Capitol Station
Austin, TX 78711-2788
Phone: (512) 427-6101; (800) 242-3062; Fax: (512) 427-6127;
Email: grantinfo@thecb.state.tx.us
Web: www.collegefortexans.com

**Summary:** To provide financial assistance to undergraduate and graduate students at colleges and universities in Texas who are also receiving other state funds.

**Eligibility:** Open to Texas residents who are enrolled or accepted for enrollment at least half time at a college or university in Texas on the undergraduate or graduate level. Financial need must be demonstrated. Applicants must also be receiving funding from another state program (either the Texas Student Incentive Grant Program for students at public colleges and universities or the Texas Tuition Equalization Grant Program for students at private colleges and universities).

**Financial data:** The stipend depends on the need of the recipient, to a maximum of $1,250.

**Duration:** 1 year; may be renewed.

**Number awarded:** Varies each year.

## 1107 TEXAS MUTUAL SCHOLARSHIP PROGRAM

Texas Mutual Insurance Company, Attn: Office of the President
6210 East Highway 290
Austin, TX 78723-1098
Phone: (512) 224-3820; (800) 859-5995, ext. 3820; Fax: (512) 224-3889;
Email: information@texasmutual.com
Web: www.texasmutual.com/workers/scholarship.shtm

**Summary:** To provide financial assistance for college to workers and their families covered by workers' compensation insurance in Texas.

**Eligibility:** Open to 1) employees who qualify for lifetime income benefits as a result of injuries suffered on the job as covered by the Texas Workers' Compensation Act; 2) children and spouses of injured workers; and 3) children and unmarried spouses of employees who died as a result of a work-related injury. Workers must be covered by the Texas Mutual Insurance Company, formerly the Texas Workers' Compensation Insurance Fund. Children must be between 16 and 25 years of age. Surviving spouses must still be eligible for workers' compensation benefits. Financial need is considered in the selection process.

**Financial data:** Scholarships are intended to cover normal undergraduate, technical, or vocational school tuition and fees, to a maximum of $4,000 per semester. Those funds are paid directly to the college or vocational school. The cost of course-related books and fees are also reimbursed, up to a maximum of $500 per semester. Those funds are paid directly to the student.

**Duration:** 1 year; may be renewed if the recipient maintains a GPA of 2.5 or higher.

**Number awarded:** Varies each year.

**Deadline:** Applications may be submitted at any time.

## 1108 TEXAS PUBLIC EDUCATIONAL GRANT PROGRAM

Texas Higher Education Coordinating Board
Attn: Grants and Special Programs
1200 East Anderson Lane
P.O. Box 12788, Capitol Station
Austin, TX 78711-2788
Phone: (512) 427-6101; (800) 242-3062; Fax: (512) 427-6127;
Email: grantinfo@thecb.state.tx.us
Web: www.collegefortexans.com

**Summary:** To provide financial assistance to undergraduate and graduate students in Texas.

**Eligibility:** Open to residents of Texas, nonresidents, and foreign students. Applicants may be undergraduate or graduate students. They must be attending a public college or university in Texas. Financial need is considered as part of the selection process.

**Financial data:** The amount awarded varies, depending upon the financial need of the recipient. No award may exceed the student's unmet financial need. Each institution sets its own maximum award amounts.

**Duration:** 1 year; may be renewed.

**Number awarded:** Varies each year; recently, 102,696 of these grants were awarded.

## 1109 TEXAS TANF EXEMPTION PROGRAM

Texas Higher Education Coordinating Board
Attn: Grants and Special Programs
1200 East Anderson Lane
P.O. Box 12788, Capitol Station
Austin, TX 78711-2788
Phone: (512) 427-6101; (800) 242-3062; Fax: (512) 427-6127;
Email: grantinfo@thecb.state.tx.us
Web: www.collegefortexans.com

**Summary:** To provide educational assistance to students in Texas whose families are receiving Temporary Assistance to Needy Families (TANF).

**Eligibility:** Open to students who graduated from a public high school in Texas and are dependent children whose parents received, during the year of their high school graduation, TANF for at least 6 months. Applicants must be younger than 22 years of age at the time of enrollment in college and must enroll in college within 24 months of high school graduation.

**Financial data:** Eligible students are exempt from the payment of all fees (other than building use fees) and tuition charges at publicly-supported colleges and universities in Texas.

**Duration:** 1 year; nonrenewable.

**Number awarded:** Varies each year; recently, 106 students received this assistance.

## 1110 TEXAS TUITION EQUALIZATION GRANT PROGRAM

Texas Higher Education Coordinating Board
Attn: Grants and Special Programs
1200 East Anderson Lane
P.O. Box 12788, Capitol Station
Austin, TX 78711-2788
Phone: (512) 427-6101; (800) 242-3062; Fax: (512) 427-6127;
Email: grantinfo@thecb.state.tx.us
Web: www.collegefortexans.com

**Summary:** To provide financial assistance to undergraduate and graduate students attending private postsecondary schools in Texas.

**Eligibility:** Open to 1) residents of Texas, and 2) residents of other states who are National Merit Scholarship finalists. Applicants must be enrolled at least half time as an undergraduate or graduate student at an eligible nonprofit independent college in the state. They may not be receiving an athletic scholarship. Financial need is considered in the selection process.

**Financial data:** The maximum awarded is the lesser of the student's unmet need or the amount they would pay at a public institution (currently, $3,653).

**Duration:** 1 year; may be renewed.

**Number awarded:** Varies each year; recently, 27,994 of these grants were awarded.

## 1111 TEXAS WAIVERS OF NONRESIDENT TUITION FOR MILITARY PERSONNEL AND THEIR DEPENDENTS

Texas Higher Education Coordinating Board
Attn: Grants and Special Programs

1200 East Anderson Lane
P.O. Box 12788, Capitol Station
Austin, TX 78711-2788
Phone: (512) 427-6101; (800) 242-3062; Fax: (512) 427-6127;
Email: grantinfo@thecb.state.tx.us
Web: www.collegefortexans.com

**Summary:** To exempt military personnel stationed in Texas and their dependents from the payment of nonresident tuition at public institutions of higher education in the state.

**Eligibility:** Open to members of the U.S. armed forces and commissioned officers of the Public Health Service from states other than Texas, their spouses, and dependent children. Applicants must be assigned to Texas and attending or planning to attend a public college or university in the state.

**Financial data:** Although persons eligible under this program are classified as nonresidents, they are entitled to pay the resident tuition at Texas institutions of higher education, regardless of their length of residence in Texas.

**Duration:** 1 year; may be renewed.

**Number awarded:** Varies each year; recently, 10,333 students received these waivers.

## 1112 TEXAS WAIVERS OF NONRESIDENT TUITION FOR VETERANS AND THEIR DEPENDENTS

Texas Higher Education Coordinating Board
Attn: Grants and Special Programs
1200 East Anderson Lane
P.O. Box 12788, Capitol Station
Austin, TX 78711-2788
Phone: (512) 427-6101; (800) 242-3062; Fax: (512) 427-6127;
Email: grantinfo@thecb.state.tx.us
Web: www.collegefortexans.com

**Summary:** To exempt veterans who move to Texas and their dependents from the payment of nonresident tuition at public institutions of higher education in the state.

**Eligibility:** Open to former members of the U.S. armed forces and commissioned officers of the Public Health Service who are retired or have been honorably discharged, their spouses, and dependent children. Applicants must have moved to Texas upon separation from the service and be attending or planning to attend a public college or university in the state. They must have indicated an intent to become a Texas resident by registering to vote and doing 1 of the following: owning real property in Texas, registering an automobile in Texas, or executing a will indicating that they are a resident of the state.

**Financial data:** Although persons eligible under this program are still classified as nonresidents, they are entitled to pay the resident tuition at Texas institutions of higher education on an immediate basis.

**Duration:** 1 year.

**Number awarded:** Varies each year.

## 1113 TEXTBOOKX.COM SCHOLARSHIP PROGRAM

Akademos, Inc., Attn: TextbookX.com
25 Van Zant Street, Suite 1A-2
Norwalk, CT 06855-1727
Phone: (203) 866-0190; Fax: (203) 866-0199
Web: www.textbookx.com/scholarship

**Summary:** To recognize and reward undergraduate and graduate students who submit outstanding essays on a topic that changes annually.

**Eligibility:** Open to undergraduate and graduate students enrolled at an accredited college or university in the United States. Applicants must be legal residents of the United States or international students with valid visas. They must submit an essay, from 250 to 750 words in length, on a topic that changes each semester. Recently, the topic was "How, if at all, would American society change if the current legal right to abortion is either severely restricted or eliminated?" Essays must be the original work of the applicant and must reference a book that has influenced the response to the essay.

**Financial data:** The grand prize is $2,000 and runner-up prizes are $250 gift certificates for the sponsor. Prizes are paid directly to the winners.

**Duration:** The competition is held annually.

**Number awarded:** 3 each semester: 1 grand prize and 2 runners-up.

**Deadline:** April of each year for spring; October of each year for fall.

## 1114 THEODORE R. AND VIVIAN M. JOHNSON SCHOLARSHIP PROGRAM

State University System of Florida

Attn: Office of Academic and Student Affairs
325 West Gaines Street, Suite 1501
Tallahassee, FL 32399-1950
Phone: (850) 245-0467; Fax: (850) 245-9667; Email: we're.listening@fldoe.org
Web: www.fldoe.org

**Summary:** To provide financial assistance to Florida undergraduate students with disabilities.

**Eligibility:** Open to students with disabilities enrolled at a State University System of Florida institution. Applicants must submit an official transcript (with GPA of 2.0 or higher); documentation of the nature and/or extent of their disability, which may be in 1 or more of the following classifications: hearing impairment, physical impairment, specific learning disability, speech/language impairment, visual impairment, or other impairment; and documentation of financial need.

**Financial data:** The stipend depends on the availability of funds.

**Duration:** 1 year; may be renewed if recipient maintains a GPA of 2.0 or higher and enrolls in at least 18 credits each academic year.

**Number awarded:** Several each year.

**Deadline:** May of each year.

## 1115 THIRD WAVE FOUNDATION WOODLAKE SCHOLARSHIPS

Third Wave Foundation
511 West 25th Street, Suite 301
New York, NY 10002
Phone: (212) 675-0700; Fax: (212) 255-6653;
Email: info@thirdwavefoundation.org
Web: www.thirdwavefoundation.org/programs/scholarships.html

**Summary:** To provide educational assistance to undergraduate and graduate women of color who have been involved as social change activists.

**Eligibility:** Open to full-time and part-time students under 30 years of age who are enrolled in, or have been accepted to, an accredited university, college, vocational/technical school, community college, or graduate school. Applicants must be women of color who place greater emphasis on social justice and the struggle for justice and equality over academic performance and who integrate social justice into all areas of their lives. They must submit 500-word essays on 1) their current social change involvement and how it relates to their educational and life goals; and 2) if they would describe themselves as a feminist and why. Graduate students and students planning to study abroad through a U.S. university program are also eligible. Selection is based on financial need and commitment to social justice work.

**Financial data:** Stipends are $3,000 or $1,000 per year.

**Duration:** 1 year.

**Number awarded:** Varies each year. Recently, 8 of these scholarships were awarded: 6 at $3,000 and 2 at $1,000.

**Deadline:** March or September of each year.

## 1116 THURGOOD MARSHALL SCHOLARSHIPS

Thurgood Marshall Scholarship Fund
90 William Street, Suite 1203
New York, NY 10038
Phone: (212) 573-8888; Fax: (212) 573-8497; Email: bcolbert@tmsf.org
Web: www.thurgoodmarshallfund.org

**Summary:** To provide financial assistance to African American high school seniors or graduates who are interested in working on a degree at colleges and universities that are members of the Thurgood Marshall Scholarship Fund (TMSF).

**Eligibility:** Open to full-time students enrolled or accepted at 1 of 47 designated TMSF institutions, most of which are Historically Black Colleges and Universities or other schools with large African American enrollments. Applicants must be African Americans who are U.S. citizens, have a high school GPA of 3.0 or higher, have scored at least 25 on the ACT (or the equivalent on the SAT), are recommended by their high school as academically exceptional or outstanding in the creative and performing arts, and can demonstrate financial need. They must apply through the TMSF school they attend, and the institutions select the recipients.

**Financial data:** Stipends range up to $2,200 per semester, depending on the need of the recipient. Funds are awarded through the institution to be used for tuition, room, board, books, and fees.

**Duration:** 1 year; may be renewed for up to 3 additional years if the recipient maintains a GPA of 3.0 or higher in college.

**Number awarded:** Varies each year; recently, nearly 1,000 students were receiving support from this program.

**Deadline:** Deadline dates vary by school; check with the institution you plan to attend.

## 1117 TILF SCHOLARSHIPS

University Interscholastic League
Attn: Texas Interscholastic League Foundation
1701 Manor Road
P.O. Box 8028
Austin, TX 78713
Phone: (512) 232-4938; Fax: (512) 471-5908;
Email: carolyn.scott@mail.utexas.edu
Web: www.uil.texas.edu/tilf/scholar.html

**Summary:** To provide financial assistance to students who participate in programs of the Texas Interscholastic League Foundation (TILF) and plan to attend college or university in Texas.

**Eligibility:** Open to students who meet the 5 basic requirements of the TILF: 1) graduate from high school during the current year and begin college or university in Texas by the following fall; 2) enroll full time and maintain a GPA of 2.5 or higher during the first semester; 3) compete in a University Interscholastic League (UIL) academic state meet contest in accounting, calculator applications, computer applications, computer science, current issues and events, debate (cross-examination and Lincoln-Douglas), journalism (editorial writing, feature writing, headline writing, and news writing), literary criticism, mathematics, number sense, 1-act play, ready writing, science, social studies, speech (prose interpretation, poetry interpretation, informative speaking, and persuasive speaking), or spelling and vocabulary; 4) submit high school transcripts that include SAT and/or ACT scores; and 5) submit parents' latest income tax returns.

**Financial data:** Stipends range from $3,500 to $500 per year.
**Duration:** 1 year; some programs may be renewed up to 4 additional years.
**Number awarded:** Varies each year; recently, 262 new scholarships (worth $1,171,000) and 271 renewal scholarships were awarded.
**Deadline:** May of each year.

## 1118 TIM & TOM GULLIKSON FOUNDATION COLLEGE SCHOLARSHIPS

Tim & Tom Gullikson Foundation, Attn: Executive Director
175 North Main Street
Branford, CT 06405
Phone: (888) GULLIKSON
Web: www.gullikson.com

**Summary:** To provide financial assistance for college to patients or survivors and/or children of patients or survivors of brain tumors.

**Eligibility:** Open to high school seniors, high school graduates, and currently-enrolled or returning college students. Applicants must be brain tumor patients/survivors and/or children of brain tumor patients or survivors. Special consideration is given to applicants who have a connection to the tennis community. Financial need is considered in the selection process.

**Financial data:** The maximum stipend is $5,000 per year. Funds are paid directly to the recipient's school and may be used for tuition, fees, books, room, and board.

**Duration:** 1 year. Recipients may reapply up to 3 additional years; however, the total money awarded to each recipient cannot exceed $20,000.

**Number awarded:** Varies each year; a maximum of $25,000 is available for these scholarships each year.
**Deadline:** March of each year.

## 1119 TIMBERWOLVES AND LYNX/AMERICAN FAMILY INSURANCE SCHOLARSHIPS

Minnesota Timberwolves, Attn: FastBreak Foundation
600 First Avenue North
Minneapolis, MN 55403-1416
Phone: (612) 673-1200
Web: www.nba.com/timberwolves/community/education.html

**Summary:** To provide financial assistance for college to high school seniors in Minnesota, North Dakota, and South Dakota.

**Eligibility:** Open to seniors graduating from high schools in Minnesota, North Dakota, and South Dakota who plan to attend a college or university in the following fall. Applicants must 1) have a GPA of 3.0 or higher; 2) have an ACT of 19 or higher or an equivalent on the SAT; 3) participate in extracurricular activities; and 4) complete 45 hours of community service, outside of school, during the course of a school year. Along with their application, they must submit an essay of 500 words or less that describes who they are, how they view themselves, and any other information they want the selection committee to consider. Financial need is not required.

**Financial data:** The stipend is $2,000.
**Duration:** 1 year.
**Number awarded:** 5 each year.
**Deadline:** February of each year.

## 1120 TOBY WRIGHT SCHOLARSHIP FUND

Worker's Compensation Association of New Mexico, Attn: Brock Carter
P.O. Box 35757, Station D
Albuquerque, NM 87176
Phone: (505) 881-1112; (800) 640-0724; Email: batcbear@aol.com
Web: www.wcaofnm.com

**Summary:** To provide financial assistance for college to residents of New Mexico whose parent was permanently disabled or killed in an employment-related accident.

**Eligibility:** Open to residents of New Mexico between 16 and 25 years of age who attending or planning to attend a college, university, or trade school in the state. Applicants must have a parent who was permanently or catastrophically injured or killed in an employment-related accident that resulted in a New Mexico workers' compensation claim. The parent's death or injury must have resulted in a substantial decline in the family income.

**Financial data:** A stipend is awarded (amount not specified). Funds may be used for tuition, books, housing, meals, and course fees.

**Duration:** 1 semester or quarter; may be renewed if the recipient maintains a GPA of 2.5 or higher and full-time enrollment.
**Number awarded:** Varies each year.

## 1121 TOM STEELE MEMORIAL SCHOLARSHIPS

Student Loan Finance Corporation
105 First Avenue S.W.
Aberdeen, SD 57401-4173
Phone: (605) 622-4400; (800) 592-1270; Fax: (605) 622-4547;
TDD: (800) 645-1606; Email: service@slfc.com
Web: www.slfc.com

**Summary:** To provide financial assistance for college to high school seniors in South Dakota.

**Eligibility:** Open to seniors graduating from high schools in South Dakota who plan to enroll full time at an accredited 2-year or 4-year college, university, or technical/vocational school. Selection is based on academic achievement (GPA of 3.25 or higher); work experience; activities, awards, and honors; a brief statement of educational and career objectives and long-term goals; and a statement of unusual family or personal circumstances that have affected achievement in school, work experience, or participation in school and community activities. Financial need is not considered.

**Financial data:** The stipend is $1,000.
**Duration:** 1 year.
**Number awarded:** Up to 220 each year: 1 to a senior at each high school in South Dakota.
**Deadline:** January of each year.

## 1122 TORAJI AND TOKI YOSHINAGA SCHOLARSHIP

Hawai'i Community Foundation, Attn: Scholarship Department
1164 Bishop Street, Suite 800
Honolulu, HI 96813
Phone: (808) 566-5570; (888) 731-3863; Fax: (808) 521-6286;
Email: scholarships@hcf-hawaii.org
Web: www.hawaiicommunityfoundation.org/scholar/scholar.php

**Summary:** To provide financial assistance to Hawaii residents who are attending college in the state at schools other than the University of Hawai'i.

**Eligibility:** Open to Hawaii residents who are sophomores attending college at a school in the state that is not part of the University of Hawai'i system. Applicants must meet at least 3 of the following criteria: 1) born in Hawaii; 2) graduate of a Hawaii high school; 3) registered to vote in Hawaii; and 4) lived in Hawaii for 4 years. They must be able to demonstrate academic achievement (GPA of 2.7 or higher), good moral character, and financial need. In addition to filling out the standard application form, applicants must write a short statement indicating their reasons for attending college, their planned course of study, and their career goals.

**Financial data:** The amounts of the awards depend on the availability of funds and the need of the recipient; recently, stipends averaged $1,250.
**Duration:** 1 year.
**Number awarded:** Varies each year; recently, 2 of these scholarships were awarded.
**Deadline:** February of each year.

## 1123 TOYOTA COMMUNITY SCHOLARS PROGRAM

Toyota USA Foundation, Attn: Toyota Community Scholars Program
9 West 57th Street, Suite 4900
New York, NY 10019

Phone: (212) 715-7486
Web: www.toyota.com/about/community/education/scholars_index.html

**Summary:** To provide financial assistance to high school seniors who have outstanding records of academic performance and volunteerism.

**Eligibility:** Open to high school seniors. Each high school in the United States may nominate 1 graduating senior for these scholarships; schools with more than 600 graduating seniors may nominate 2 of them. Nominees must be U.S. citizens, nationals, or permanent residents who plan to work on an undergraduate degree at an accredited 4-year college or university in the United States. Selection is based on academic record (GPA of 3.0 or higher) and involvement in a service organization or project that has a positive impact on the school and/or community.

**Financial data:** The stipend is $5,000 or $2,500 per year. Winners also receive an all-expense paid trip to Louisville, Kentucky where they meet fellow awardees and are recognized for their achievements.

**Duration:** 4 years.

**Number awarded:** 100 each year: 12 national winners at $5,000 per year and 88 regional winners at $2,500 per year.

**Deadline:** December of each year.

## 1124 TROY BARBOZA EDUCATION FUND

Hawai'i Community Foundation, Attn: Scholarship Department
1164 Bishop Street, Suite 800
Honolulu, HI 96813
Phone: (808) 566-5570; (888) 731-3863; Fax: (808) 521-6286;
Email: scholarships@hcf-hawaii.org
Web: www.hawaiicommunityfoundation.org/scholar/scholar.php

**Summary:** To provide financial assistance for college to disabled public employees in Hawaii or their dependents.

**Eligibility:** Open to 1) disabled public employees in Hawaii who were injured in the line of duty or 2) dependents or other immediate family members of public employees in Hawaii who were disabled or killed in the line of duty. The public employee must work or have worked in a job where lives are risked for the protection and safety of others. The injury must have left the employee incapacitated or incapable or continuing in his or her profession and must have occurred after October 22, 1977. Also eligible are private citizens who have performed a heroic act for the protection and welfare of others.

**Financial data:** The amount awarded varies, depending upon the needs of the recipient and the funds available.

**Duration:** 1 year.

**Number awarded:** 1 or more each year.

**Deadline:** February of each year.

## 1125 TU'IPELEHAKE LEADERSHIP SCHOLARSHIP

National Tongan American Society
2480 South Main Street, Suite 108
Salt Lake City, UT 84115
Phone: (801) 467-8712; Email: ntas@planet-tonga.com
Web: www.planet-tonga.com/NTAS/scholarship.htm

**Summary:** To provide financial assistance to undergraduate students of Tongan background who live in Utah.

**Eligibility:** Open to residents of Utah who are of Tongan background and enrolled or planning to enroll as a full-time undergraduate or graduate student. Applicants must have a cumulative GPA of 3.0 or higher. They must be able to demonstrate financial need, leadership abilities, community service, extracurricular activities, and motivation to succeed in school.

**Financial data:** The stipend is $1,000.

**Duration:** 1 year.

**Number awarded:** 1 or more each year.

**Deadline:** January of each year.

## 1126 TUITION WAIVER FOR DISABLED CHILDREN OF KENTUCKY VETERANS

Kentucky Department of Veterans Affairs, Attn: Division of Field Operations
545 South Third Street, Room 123
Louisville, KY 40202
Phone: (502) 595-4447; (800) 928-4012 (within KY); Fax: (502) 595-4448
Web: www.kdva.net/tuitionwaiver.htm

**Summary:** To provide financial assistance for college to the children of Kentucky veterans who have a disability related to their parent's military service.

**Eligibility:** Open to the children of veterans who have acquired a disability as a direct result of their parent's military service. The disability must have been designated by the U.S. Department of Veterans Affairs as compensable (currently defined as spina bifida). The veteran parent must 1) have served on active duty with the U.S. armed forces or in the National Guard or Reserve component on state active duty, active duty for training, or inactive duty training; and 2) be (or if deceased have been) a resident of Kentucky. Applicants must have been admitted to a state-supported university, college, or vocational training institute in Kentucky.

**Financial data:** Eligible children are exempt from payment of tuition at state-supported institutions of higher education in Kentucky.

**Duration:** There are no age or time limits on the waiver.

**Number awarded:** Varies each year.

## 1127 TWO/TEN INTERNATIONAL FOOTWEAR FOUNDATION COLLEGE SCHOLARSHIP PROGRAM

Two/Ten International Footwear Foundation, Attn: Scholarship Director
1466 Main Street
Waltham, MA 02451
Phone: (781) 736-1500; (800) FIND-210; Fax: (781) 736-1555;
Email: scholarship@twoten.org
Web: www.twoten.org/ClassicScholarships.aspx

**Summary:** To provide financial assistance to full-time undergraduate students who work, or whose parent works, in the footwear, leather, or allied industries.

**Eligibility:** Open to students attending or planning to attend a college, university, nursing school, or vocational/technical school to work on a 2-year or 4-year undergraduate degree. Either their parent (natural, step, or adopted) must be employed (for at least 2 years) in the footwear, leather, or allied industries or the applicants must be employed for at least 500 hours in 1 of those industries. The employer must do 50% of its business in footwear, or the applicant or parent must work in a specific footwear division. U.S. citizenship or permanent resident status is required. Selection is based on academic record, personal promise, character, and financial need.

**Financial data:** Classic scholarships range up to $3,000 per year, depending on the need of the recipient. For students who demonstrate exceptional financial need, stipends up to $15,000 per year are available. Funds are sent directly to the recipient's school.

**Duration:** 1 year; may be renewed up to 3 additional years.

**Number awarded:** Varies; generally, more than 200 new awards and 300 renewals each year.

**Deadline:** January of each year.

## 1128 UNITED DAUGHTERS OF THE CONFEDERACY SCHOLARSHIPS

United Daughters of the Confederacy, Attn: Education Director
328 North Boulevard
Richmond, VA 23220-4057
Phone: (804) 355-1636; Fax: (804) 353-1396; Email: hqudc@rcn.com
Web: www.hqudc.org/scholarships/scholarships.html

**Summary:** To provide financial assistance for college to lineal descendants of Confederate veterans.

**Eligibility:** Open to lineal descendants of worthy Confederates or collateral descendants who are members of the Children of the Confederacy or the United Daughters of the Confederacy. Applicants must be high school seniors or college students and submit a family financial report and certified proof of the Confederate record of 1 ancestor, with the company and regiment in which he served. They must have a high school GPA of 3.0 or higher.

**Financial data:** The amount of the scholarships depends on the availability of funds.

**Duration:** 1 year; may be renewed up to 3 additional years.

**Number awarded:** 17 unrestricted scholarships are available; another 11 scholarships with varying restrictions are also offered.

**Deadline:** March of each year.

## 1129 UNITED METHODIST ETHNIC MINORITY SCHOLARSHIPS

United Methodist Church
Attn: General Board of Higher Education and Ministry
Office of Loans and Scholarships
1001 19th Avenue South
P.O. Box 340007
Nashville, TN 37203-0007
Phone: (615) 340-7344; Fax: (615) 340-7367; Email: umscholar@gbhem.org
Web: www.gbhem.org

**Summary:** To provide financial assistance to undergraduate Methodist students who are of ethnic minority ancestry.

**Eligibility:** Open to full-time undergraduate students at accredited colleges and universities in the United States who have been active, full members of a United Methodist Church for at least 1 year prior to applying. Applicants must have at least 1 parent who is African American, Hispanic, Asian, Native American, Alaska Native, or Pacific Islander. They must have a GPA of 2.5 or higher and be able to demonstrate financial need. U.S. citizenship, permanent resident status, or membership in a central conference of the United Methodist Church is required.

**Financial data:** A stipend is awarded (amount not specified).

**Duration:** 1 year; recipients may reapply.

**Number awarded:** Varies each year.

**Deadline:** April of each year.

## 1130 UNITED METHODIST FOUNDATION ANNUAL CONFERENCE SCHOLARS PROGRAM

United Methodist Higher Education Foundation
1001 19th Avenue South
P.O. Box 340005
Nashville, TN 37203-0005
Phone: (615) 340-7385; (800) 811-8110; Fax: (615) 340-7330;
Email: umhef@gbhem.org
Web: www.umhef.org/annual.html

**Summary:** To provide financial assistance to undergraduate and seminary students attending schools affiliated with the United Methodist Church.

**Eligibility:** Open to entering freshmen at United Methodist-related colleges or universities and first-year students at United Methodist-related seminaries or theological schools. Applicants must be U.S. citizens and have been active members of the United Methodist Church for at least 1 year prior to applying. They must be planning to enroll full time. Along with their application, they must submit a statement covering their philosophy of life, religious development, and career goal. Financial need is also considered in the selection process.

**Financial data:** The stipend is $1,000.

**Duration:** 1 year; nonrenewable.

**Number awarded:** 63 each year: 1 for each of the annual conferences of the United Methodist Church.

**Deadline:** Nominations from the annual conference must be received in the scholarship office of the General Board of Higher Education and Ministry by April of each year.

## 1131 UNITED METHODIST FOUNDATION UNDERGRADUATE/PREPARATORY SCHOLARS PROGRAM

United Methodist Higher Education Foundation
1001 19th Avenue South
P.O. Box 340005
Nashville, TN 37203-0005
Phone: (615) 340-7385; (800) 811-8110; Fax: (615) 340-7330;
Email: umhef@gbhem.org
Web: www.umhef.org/found.html

**Summary:** To provide financial assistance to college and preparatory school students attending schools affiliated with the United Methodist Church.

**Eligibility:** Open to freshmen, sophomores, juniors, and seniors at United Methodist-related preparatory schools, colleges, and universities. Applicants must have been active members of the United Methodist Church for at least 1 year prior to application. They must be planning to enroll full time.

**Financial data:** The stipend is $1,000.

**Duration:** 1 year; nonrenewable.

**Number awarded:** 420 each year: 1 to a member of each class at each school.

**Deadline:** Nominations from schools must be received by August of each year.

## 1132 UNITED METHODIST SCHOLARSHIP PROGRAM

United Methodist Church
Attn: General Board of Higher Education and Ministry
Office of Loans and Scholarships
1001 19th Avenue South
P.O. Box 340007
Nashville, TN 37203-0007
Phone: (615) 340-7344; Fax: (615) 340-7367; Email: umscholar@gbhem.org
Web: www.gbhem.org

**Summary:** To provide financial assistance to undergraduate and graduate students attending schools affiliated with the United Methodist Church.

**Eligibility:** Open to U.S. citizens and permanent residents who have been active, full members of a United Methodist Church for at least 1 year prior to applying; members of the A.M.E., A.M.E. Zion, and other "Methodist" denominations are not eligible. Undergraduates must have been admitted to a full-time degree program at a United Methodist-related college or university and have a GPA of 2.5 or above. Most graduate scholarships are designated for persons working on a degree in theological studies (M.Div., D.Min., Ph.D.) or higher education administration, or for older adults changing their careers. Some scholarships are designated for racial ethnic undergraduate or graduate students. Applications are available from the financial aid office of the United Methodist school the applicant attends or from the chair of their annual conference Board of Higher Education and Campus Ministry.

**Financial data:** The funding is intended to supplement the students' own resources.

**Duration:** 1 year; renewal policies are set by participating universities.

**Number awarded:** Varies each year.

## 1133 UNITED PARCEL SERVICE SCHOLARSHIP PROGRAM FOR FLORIDA STUDENTS

Florida Independent College Fund
929 North Spring Garden Avenue, Suite 165
DeLand, FL 32720-0981
Phone: (386) 734-2745; Fax: (386) 734-0839; Email: Scholarships@ficf.org
Web: www.ficf.org

**Summary:** To provide financial assistance to students at designated private colleges and universities in Florida.

**Eligibility:** Open to students enrolled at 23 designated independent colleges or universities in Florida. Applicants must be nominated by their institution. They may be residents of any state. Selection is based on academic achievement and financial need.

**Financial data:** The stipend is $2,500.

**Duration:** 1 year.

**Number awarded:** 23 each year: 1 at each of the participating institutions.

**Deadline:** December of each year.

## 1134 UNITED PARCEL SERVICE SCHOLARSHIPS

Wisconsin Foundation for Independent Colleges, Inc., Attn: Program Manager
735 North Water Street, Suite 600
Milwaukee, WI 53202-4100
Phone: (414) 273-5980; Fax: (414) 273-5995; Email: wfic@wficweb.org
Web: www.wficweb.org/documents/schinfo.htm

**Summary:** To provide financial assistance to students attending or planning to attend member institutions of the Wisconsin Foundation for Independent Colleges (WFIC).

**Eligibility:** Open to students enrolled or planning to enroll at WFIC member colleges and universities on a full-time basis. Applicants may be majoring in any field, but they must have a GPA of 3.0 or higher; entering freshmen must rank in the top 25% of their high school class. Recipients are selected by the participating schools. Financial need is considered in the selection process.

**Financial data:** Stipends are $2,500 or $1,250.

**Duration:** 1 year.

**Number awarded:** Each WFIC institution may award 1 scholarship at $2,500 or 2 at $1,250.

**Deadline:** Each participating college sets its own deadline.

## 1135 UNITED STATES SENATE YOUTH PROGRAM SCHOLARSHIPS

William Randolph Hearst Foundation
90 New Montgomery Street, Suite 1212
San Francisco, CA 94105-4504
Phone: (415) 543-4057; (800) 841-7048; Fax: (415) 243-0760;
Email: ussyp@hcarstfdn.org
Web: www.ussenateyouth.org

**Summary:** To recognize and reward, with a trip to Washington, D.C. and college scholarships, outstanding high school student leaders.

**Eligibility:** Open to high school juniors and seniors who are currently serving in 1 of the following student government offices: student body president, vice president, secretary, or treasurer; class president, vice president, secretary, or treasurer; student council representative; or student representative to a district, regional, or state-level civic or educational organization. Applications are available only through high school principals and state education administrators. Selection is based on ability and demonstrated qualities of leadership. Recipients must, within 2 years after high school graduation, enroll at an accredited U.S. college or university, pledging to include courses in government or related subjects in their undergraduate program.

**Financial data:** Winners receive an all-expense paid trip to Washington, D.C. for 1 week (to be introduced to the operation of the federal government and Congress) and are presented with a $5,000 college scholarship.

**Duration:** The awards are presented annually.

**Number awarded:** 104 each year: 2 from each state, Washington, D.C., and the Department of Defense Education Activity.

**Deadline:** September of each year.

## 1136 UNIVERSITY OF NORTH CAROLINA CAMPUS SCHOLARSHIPS-PART I

North Carolina State Education Assistance Authority
Attn: Scholarship and Grant Services
10 Alexander Drive
P.O. Box 14103
Research Triangle Park, NC 27709-4103
Phone: (919) 549-8614; (800) 700-1775; Fax: (919) 549-8481;
Email: information@ncseaa.edu
Web: www.ncseaa.edu

**Summary:** To provide financial assistance to students at University of North Carolina (UNC) constituent institutions whose enrollment contributes to the diversity of the undergraduate population.

**Eligibility:** Open to undergraduate students who are enrolled or planning to enroll full time at 1 of the 16 UNC institutions. Applicants must have graduated in the top 40% of their high school class, have a weighted GPA of 3.0 or higher, have an SAT score higher than the SAT score of the previous freshman class, and have a record of positive involvement in extracurricular activities. They must be able to demonstrate "exceptional financial need." Their enrollment must "contribute to the intellectual experiences and diversity of the undergraduate population."

**Financial data:** The amount of the award depends upon the financial need of the recipient and the availability of funds.

**Duration:** 1 year; may be renewed.

**Number awarded:** Varies each year; recently, a total of 3,076 UNC Campus Scholarships, with a total value of $5,648,874, were awarded.

**Deadline:** Deadline dates vary; check with the appropriate constituent institution.

## 1137 UNIVERSITY OF NORTH CAROLINA SYSTEM NEED-BASED GRANTS

North Carolina State Education Assistance Authority
Attn: Scholarship and Grant Services
10 T.W. Alexander Drive
P.O. Box 14103
Research Triangle Park, NC 27709-4103
Phone: (919) 549-8614; (800) 700-1775; Fax: (919) 549-8481;
Email: information@ncseaa.edu
Web: www.ncseaa.edu

**Summary:** To provide financial assistance to students enrolled at 1 of the branches of the University of North Carolina.

**Eligibility:** Open to residents of North Carolina enrolled for at least 6 credit hours at any of the constituent institutions of the University of North Carolina. Applicants must be able to demonstrate financial need, based on data from the Free Application for Federal Student Aid (FAFSA).

**Financial data:** Stipends depend on the need of the recipient and the availability of funds, to a maximum of $3,000 per year.

**Duration:** 1 year.

**Number awarded:** Varies each year. Recently, 26,630 students were receiving $28,785,533 in support through this program

## 1138 UPS GOLD MOUNTAIN SCHOLARSHIP

Organization of Chinese Americans, Inc.
1001 Connecticut Avenue, N.W., Suite 601
Washington, DC 20036
Phone: (202) 223-5500; Fax: (202) 296-0540; Email: oca@ocanatl.org
Web: www.ocanatl.org

**Summary:** To provide financial assistance for college to Asian Pacific Americans who are the first person in their family to attend an institution of higher education.

**Eligibility:** Open to Asian Pacific American students entering their first year of

college in the following fall. Applicants must be the first person in their immediate family to attend college, have a cumulative GPA of 3.0 or higher, be in financial need, and be a U.S. citizen or permanent resident.

**Financial data:** The stipend is $2,000.

**Duration:** 1 year.

**Number awarded:** 12 each year.

**Deadline:** April of each year.

## 1139 U.S. BANK INTERNET SCHOLARSHIP PROGRAM

U.S. Bancorp
U.S. Bancorp Center
800 Nicollet Mall
Minneapolis, MN 55402
Phone: (612) US-BANKS; (800) US-BANKS
Web: www.usbank.com/cgi_w/cfm/studentloans/marketing.cfm

**Summary:** To provide financial assistance for college to high school seniors who apply through an online procedure.

**Eligibility:** Open to high school seniors planning to enroll full time at a 2-year or 4-year accredited college or university that participates in the Federal Family Education Loan Program (FFELP). U.S. citizenship or permanent resident status is required. Applications are available only through an online procedure. Selection is based on a random drawing.

**Financial data:** The stipend is $1,000.

**Duration:** 1 year; nonrenewable.

**Number awarded:** Up to 30 each year.

**Deadline:** February of each year.

## 1140 USA FUNDS ACCESS TO EDUCATION SCHOLARSHIPS

Scholarship America, Attn: Scholarship Management Services
One Scholarship Way
P.O. Box 297
St. Peter, MN 56082
Phone: (507) 931-1682; (800) 537-4180; Fax: (507) 931-9168;
Email: scholarship@usafunds.org
Web: www.usafunds.org/planning/access_to_education_scholarship/index.html

**Summary:** To provide financial assistance to undergraduate and graduate students, especially those who are members of ethnic minority groups or have physical disabilities.

**Eligibility:** Open to high school seniors and graduates who plan to enroll or are already enrolled in full-time undergraduate or graduate course work at an accredited 2- or 4-year college, university, or vocational/technical school. Half-time undergraduate students are also eligible. Up to 50% of the awards are targeted at students who have a documented physical disability or are a member of an ethnic minority group, including but not limited to Native Hawaiian, Alaskan Native, Black/African American, Asian, Pacific Islander, American Indian, or Hispanic/Latino. Residents of all 50 states, the District of Columbia, Puerto Rico, Guam, the U.S. Virgin Islands, and all U.S. territories and commonwealths are eligible. Applicants must also be U.S. citizens or eligible noncitizens and come from a family with an annual adjusted gross income of $35,000 or less. In addition to financial need, selection is based on past academic performance and future potential, leadership and participation in school and community activities, work experience, career and educational aspirations, and goals.

**Financial data:** The stipend is $1,500 per year for full-time undergraduate or graduate students or $750 per year for half-time undergraduate students. Funds are paid jointly to the student and the school.

**Duration:** 1 year; may be renewed until the student receives a final degree or certificate or until the total award to a student reaches $6,000, whichever comes first. Renewal requires the recipient to maintain a GPA of 2.5 or higher.

**Number awarded:** Varies each year; recently, a total of $3 million was available for this program.

**Deadline:** February of each year.

## 1141 USBC JUNIOR GOLD CHAMPIONSHIPS

United States Bowling Congress, Attn: Junior Gold Program
5301 South 76th Street
Greendale, WI 53129-1192
Phone: (414) 423-3171; (800) 514-BOWL, ext. 3171; Fax: (414) 421-3014;
Email: USBCjuniorgold@bowl.com
Web: www.bowl.com/bowl/yaba

**Summary:** To recognize and reward, with college scholarships, United States

Bowling Congress (USBC) Junior Gold program members who achieve high scores in a national competition.

**Eligibility:** Open to USBC members who qualify for the Junior Gold program by maintaining a bowling average score of 165 for girls or 175 for boys, based on at least 21 games. Competitions for Junior Gold members are held throughout the season at bowling centers and in bowling leagues in the United States. Each approved competition may enter its top 10% of scorers in the Junior Gold Championships, held annually at a site in the United States. In addition, USBC Junior Gold members who participate in the Pepsi USBC Youth Bowling Championship in the girls' and boys' 12 and over scratch categories and achieve high scores in state and zone competitions are eligible to advance to the national tournament of this program. They compete in separate divisions for boys and girls. Scholarships are awarded solely on the basis of bowling performance in the national tournament.

**Financial data:** Scholarships depend on the availability of funding provided by sponsors. Recently, more than $50,000 in scholarships was awarded. Another $15,000 in scholarships was awarded to Junior Gold participants who qualified for the national tournament through the Pepsi competition. That includes $3,000 for first, $2,000 for second, $1,500 for third, and $1,000 for fourth for boys and girls.

**Duration:** The competition is held annually.

**Number awarded:** Varies each year. Recently, a total of 1,458 spots were available at the national tournament and scholarships were provided to approximately 10% of the competitors. For bowlers from the Pepsi competition, 4 girls and 4 boys win scholarships.

**Deadline:** Applications must by submitted by May of each year. The national finals are held in July.

## [1142] USBC YOUTH LEADERS OF THE YEAR AWARDS

United States Bowling Congress, Attn: SMART Program
5301 South 76th Street
Greendale, WI 53129-1192
Phone: (414) 423-3223; (800) 514-BOWL, ext. 3223; Fax: (414) 421-3014;
Email: smart@bowl.com
Web: www.bowl.com/scholarships/main.aspx

**Summary:** To recognize and reward, with college scholarships, outstanding young bowlers.

**Eligibility:** Open to participants in the Youth Leader program of the United States Bowling Congress (USBC) who are 18 years of age or older. Males and females are considered in separate competitions. Selection is based on exemplary Youth Leader activities and contributions to the sport of bowling.

**Financial data:** The awards consist of $1,500 college scholarships.

**Duration:** The awards are presented annually.

**Number awarded:** 2 each year: 1 for a female and 1 for a male.

**Deadline:** Nominations must be submitted by January of each year.

## [1143] USCF SCHOLAR-CHESSPLAYER OUTSTANDING ACHIEVEMENT AWARDS

United States Chess Federation
Attn: Scholastic Department
3054 U.S. Route 9W
New Windsor, NY 12553
Phone: (845) 562-8350, ext. 128; (800) 388-KING; Fax: (845) 561-CHES;
Email: clubs@uschess.org
Web: www.uschess.org

**Summary:** To recognize and reward, with college scholarships, high school students who excel in academics, chess play, and sportsmanship.

**Eligibility:** Open to high school juniors and seniors who are members of the United States Chess Federation (USCF) and have shown outstanding merit in academics, sportsmanship, and chess. Applicants must submit a high school transcript, a letter of recommendation from a chess coach, a letter of recommendation from a teacher, a recent photograph, and an essay (up to 500 words) describing the positive influence that chess has had on their life. Financial need is not considered in the selection process.

**Financial data:** First place is $2,000, second $1,000, third $700, fourth $500, fifth $400, and sixth and seventh $200 each.

**Duration:** 1 year.

**Number awarded:** 7 each year.

**Deadline:** February of each year.

## [1144] USS LITTLE ROCK ASSOCIATION NROTC SCHOLARSHIP PROGRAM

USS Little Rock Association
P.O. Box 16846

Stamford, CT 06905-8846
Email: littlerocksol@acsworld.com
Web: www.usslittlerock.org/scholarship.html

**Summary:** To provide financial assistance to Naval ROTC midshipmen who have a personal or family connection to the sea services or are members of the USS Little Rock Association.

**Eligibility:** Open to students entering their third academic year of an NROTC program (scholarship, college program, Enlisted Commissioning Program, or Seaman to Admiral). Applicants must 1) be children or direct descendants of active, retired, or honorably discharged members of the sea services (U.S. Navy, U.S. Marine Corps, or U.S. Coast Guard) or their Reserve components; 2) themselves be serving or have served in any of the regular or Reserve sea services; or 3) have been Junior Associate members of the USS Little Rock Association for at least 2 years. They must have a GPA of 3.0 or higher and have demonstrated superior leadership qualities and aptitude for service in all of their NROTC activities. Along with their application, they must submit a 500-word letter describing why they consider themselves worthy of the award.

**Financial data:** The stipend is $1,000 per year.

**Duration:** 1 year; may be renewed 1 additional year.

**Number awarded:** 1 or 2 each year.

**Deadline:** May of each year.

## [1145] UTAH CENTENNIAL OPPORTUNITY PROGRAM FOR EDUCATION

Utah Higher Education Assistance Authority
Board of Regents Building, The Gateway
60 South 400 West
Salt Lake City, UT 84101-1284
Phone: (801) 321-7294; (877) 336-7378; Fax: (801) 321-7299;
TDD: (801) 321-7130; Email: uheaa@utahsbr.edu
Web: www.uheaa.org/grants.htm

**Summary:** To provide financial assistance and work-study to students at designated Utah institutions.

**Eligibility:** Open to students at participating colleges in Utah. They may request an application directly from their college's financial aid office. The participating institutions in Utah are: Brigham Young University, College of Eastern Utah, Dixie State College, LDS Business College, Salt Lake Community College, Snow College, Southern Utah University, University of Utah, Utah State University, Utah Valley State College, Weber State University, and Westminster College. Applicants must meet the federal guidelines for financial need. They must also be willing to accept a work-study assignment in 1) an institutional job on campus; 2) school assistant jobs, as tutors, mentors, or teacher assistants, to work with educationally disadvantaged and high risk school pupils, by contract, at individual schools or school districts; 3) community service jobs, with volunteer community service organizations; or 4) matching jobs, by contract with government agencies, private businesses, or nonprofit corporations.

**Financial data:** The maximum award to each eligible student is $5,000, of which no more than $2,500 may be a grant and the remainder provided in the form of a work study award. For the work-study portion, students receive the current federal minimum wage.

**Duration:** 1 year; may be renewed.

**Number awarded:** Varies each year.

## [1146] UTAH CENTENNIAL SCHOLARSHIP FOR EARLY GRADUATION

Utah Higher Education Assistance Authority
Board of Regents Building, The Gateway
60 South 400 West
Salt Lake City, UT 84101-1284
Phone: (801) 321-7294; (877) 336-7378; Fax: (801) 321-7299;
TDD: (801) 321-7130; Email: uheaa@utahsbr.edu
Web: www.uheaa.org/scholarships.htm

**Summary:** To provide financial assistance for college to Utah residents who graduate from high school early.

**Eligibility:** Open to public high school students in Utah who complete early graduation having completed all required courses and demonstrated mastery of required skills and competencies. Applicants must enroll full time in an accredited Utah college or university within 1 calendar year of high school graduation.

**Financial data:** Stipends are $1,000 for students who graduate after their junior year, $750 after the first quarter of their senior year, $500 after the second quarter of their senior year, or $250 after the third quarter of their senior year. Funds are sent directly to the student's postsecondary institution.

**Duration:** These are 1-time awards.

**Number awarded:** Varies each year.

## 1147 UTAH ELKS ASSOCIATION SCHOLARSHIP PROGRAM

Utah Elks Association
c/o Jim Fugua, Scholarship Chair
Provo Lodge 849
1000 South University Avenue
P.O. Box 83
Provo, UT 84603
Phone: (801) 373-0849
Web: www.utahelks.org

**Summary:** To provide financial assistance for college to high school seniors in Utah.

**Eligibility:** Open to seniors graduating from high schools in Utah. Applicants must submit a 500-word essay on their career and life goals and their plan to achieve those. Selection is based on that essay, academic achievement, community service, honors and awards, leadership, and financial need. U.S. citizenship is required.

**Financial data:** Stipends are $4,000, $800, or $700.

**Duration:** 1 year.

**Number awarded:** Varies each year, recently, the program awarded 4 scholarships (2 to males and 2 to females) at $4,000, 16 (8 to males and 8 to females) at $800, and 16 (8 to males and 8 to females) at $700.

**Deadline:** January of each year.

## 1148 UTAH ELKS ASSOCIATION SPECIAL NEEDS STUDENT SCHOLARSHIP AWARD

Utah Elks Association
c/o Jim Fugua, Scholarship Chair
Provo Lodge 849
1000 South University Avenue
P.O. Box 83
Provo, UT 84603
Phone: (801) 373-0849
Web: www.utahelks.org

**Summary:** To provide financial assistance for college to high school seniors in Utah who have a disability or other special need.

**Eligibility:** Open to seniors graduating from high schools in Utah who have a special need, such as a disability. Applicants must submit 1) a supporting letter from a doctor or professional person stating the nature of the special need, and 2) a 500-word essay on their career and life goals and their plan to achieve those. Selection is based on that essay, academic achievement, community service, honors and awards, leadership, and financial need. U.S. citizenship is required.

**Financial data:** A stipend is awarded (amount not specified).

**Duration:** 1 year.

**Number awarded:** Varies each year, depending upon the funds available.

**Deadline:** January of each year.

## 1149 UTAH LEGION AUXILIARY NATIONAL PRESIDENT'S SCHOLARSHIP

American Legion Auxiliary, Attn: Department of Utah
B-61 State Capitol Building
Salt Lake City, UT 84114
Phone: (801) 538-1014; Fax: (801) 537-9191; Email: utaux@aol.com

**Summary:** To provide financial assistance for college to children of veterans in Utah.

**Eligibility:** Open to Utah residents who are the children of veterans who served in World War I, World War II, Korea, Vietnam, Grenada, Lebanon, Panama, or the Persian Gulf. They must be high school seniors or graduates who have not yet attended an institution of higher learning. Selection is based on character, Americanism, leadership, scholarship, and financial need. The winners then compete for the American Legion Auxiliary National President's Scholarship. If the Utah winners are not awarded a national scholarship, then they receive these departmental scholarships.

**Financial data:** Stipends are $2,000 or $1,500.

**Duration:** 1 year.

**Number awarded:** 2 each year: 1 at $2,000 and 1 at $1,500.

**Deadline:** February of each year.

## 1150 UTAH LEVERAGING EDUCATIONAL ASSISTANCE PARTNERSHIP PROGRAM

Utah Higher Education Assistance Authority

Board of Regents Building, The Gateway
60 South 400 West
Salt Lake City, UT 84101-1284
Phone: (801) 321-7294; (877) 336-7378; Fax: (801) 321-7299;
TDD: (801) 321-7130; Email: uheaa@utahsbr.edu
Web: www.uheaa.org/grants.htm

**Summary:** To provide financial assistance for college to students in Utah with financial need.

**Eligibility:** Open to students at participating colleges in Utah. They may request an application directly from their college's financial aid office. The participating colleges in Utah are: College of Eastern Utah, Dixie State College, Salt Lake Community College, Snow College, Southern Utah University, University of Utah, Utah State University, Utah Valley State College, Weber State University, and Westminster College. Applicants must have substantial financial need. Students taking correspondence courses are not eligible.

**Financial data:** The maximum stipend is $2,500.

**Duration:** 1 year; may be renewed.

**Number awarded:** Varies each year.

## 1151 UTAH NEW CENTURY SCHOLARSHIP PROGRAM

Utah Higher Education Assistance Authority
Board of Regents Building, The Gateway
60 South 400 West
Salt Lake City, UT 84101-1284
Phone: (801) 321-7107; (877) 336-7378; Fax: (801) 321-7299;
TDD: (801) 321-7130; Email: uheaa@utahsbr.edu
Web: www.uheaa.org/scholarships.htm

**Summary:** To provide financial assistance for college to Utah residents who complete an associate degree at a community college while still enrolled in high school.

**Eligibility:** Open to high school students in Utah who take classes at a local community college and complete an associate degree by September of the year their class graduates from high school. Applicants must be planning to attend an accredited college or university in the states.

**Financial data:** Stipends equal 75% of an eligible student's tuition cost at a Utah public institution of higher education that offers a bachelor's degree, or an equivalent amount at designated private institutions.

**Duration:** Up to 2 years, provided the student maintains at least a 3.0 GPA.

**Number awarded:** Varies each year.

## 1152 VASA ORDER OF AMERICA COLLEGE OR VOCATIONAL SCHOOL SCHOLARSHIPS

Vasa Order of America, Attn: Vice Grand Master
3236 Berkeley Avenue
Cleveland Heights, OH 44118-2055
Phone: (216) 371-5141; Email: rolf.bergman@sbcglobal.net
Web: www.vasaorder.com

**Summary:** To provide financial assistance for college or vocational education to members of the Vasa Order of America.

**Eligibility:** Open to members of the organization (for at least 1 year). They must be planning to continue their academic or vocational education on a full-time basis. Selection is based on a grade transcript, letters of recommendation from school and local Vasa lodge officials, and an essay of up to 1,000 words on a topic related to Vasa.

**Financial data:** Stipends are $1,000.

**Duration:** 1 year.

**Number awarded:** 10 each year.

**Deadline:** February of each year.

## 1153 VCOPS COLLEGE SCHOLARSHIP PROGRAM

Virginia Coalition of Policy and Deputy Sheriffs
Attn: Scholarship Competition
10500 Sager Avenue, Suite C
Fairfax, VA 22030
Web: www.virginiacops.org/programs/Scholar/Scholarship.htm

**Summary:** To recognize and reward, with college scholarships, high school seniors in Virginia who submit outstanding essays on law enforcement.

**Eligibility:** Open to college-bound seniors graduating from high schools in Virginia. Applicants must submit an essay, up to 1,500 words in length, on Virginia law enforcement and the general theme, "Virginia Law Enforcement: A Commitment to Community." They must also include a 150-word statement on their plans for college.

**Financial data:** The award is a $1,000 scholarship. Funds are paid directly to the winners' college or university account.
**Duration:** The competition is held annually.
**Number awarded:** 3 winners are selected each year.
**Deadline:** April of each year.

## 1154 VENIZELION SCHOLARSHIP PROGRAM

Pancretan Association of America, Attn: General Secretary
8530 Sharon Drive
White Lake, MI 48386-3472
Fax: (248) 698-8573; Email: erasmia@aol.com
Web: www.pancretan.org
**Summary:** To provide financial assistance for college or graduate school to members of the Pancretan Association of America (PAA) or affiliated organizations.
**Eligibility:** Open to members in good standing, for at least 2 years, of a duly recognized chapter of PAA or a chapter of Pancretan Youth of America (PYA) (or they may be a PAA member at large). They must have a GPA of 3.0 or higher and be attending, or planning to attend, a college or university as a full-time undergraduate or graduate student.
**Financial data:** A stipend is awarded (amount not specified).
**Duration:** 1 year.
**Number awarded:** 1 or more each year.
**Deadline:** December of each year.

## 1155 VERMONT INCENTIVE GRANTS

Vermont Student Assistance Corporation
Champlain Mill, Attn: Scholarship Programs
P.O. Box 2000
Winooski, VT 05404-2601
Phone: (802) 654-3798; (888) 253-4819; Fax: (802) 654-3765; TDD: (802) 654-3766;
TDD: (800) 281-3341 (within VT); Email: info@vsac.org
Web: www.vsac.org
**Summary:** To provide financial assistance for college to needy residents of Vermont.
**Eligibility:** Open to residents of Vermont who wish to attend college, either within or outside Vermont, as a full-time undergraduate student. U.S. citizenship or permanent resident status is required. Selection is based on financial need.
**Financial data:** Stipends range from $500 to $9,100 per year.
**Duration:** 1 year; may be renewed.
**Number awarded:** Varies each year.

## 1156 VERMONT PART-TIME GRANTS

Vermont Student Assistance Corporation
Champlain Mill, Attn: Scholarship Programs
P.O. Box 2000
Winooski, VT 05404-2601
Phone: (802) 654-3798; (888) 253-4819; Fax: (802) 654-3765;
TDD: (802) 654-3766; TDD: (800) 281-3341 (within VT); Email: info@vsac.org
Web: www.vsac.org
**Summary:** To provide financial assistance to needy residents of Vermont who wish to attend college on a part-time basis.
**Eligibility:** Open to residents of Vermont who are enrolled or accepted for enrollment in an undergraduate degree, diploma, or certificate program. Applicants must be taking fewer than 12 credits per semester and not have received a baccalaureate degree. Financial need is considered in the selection process.
**Financial data:** The amounts of the awards depend on the number of credit hours and the need of the recipient.
**Duration:** 1 year; may be renewed.
**Number awarded:** Varies each year.

## 1157 VETERANS EDUCATIONAL ASSISTANCE PROGRAM (VEAP)

Department of Veterans Affairs
810 Vermont Avenue, N.W.
Washington, DC 20420
Phone: (202) 418-4343; (888) GI-BILL1
Web: www.gibill.va.gov
**Summary:** To provide funding to veterans who, while on active duty, partici-

pate voluntarily in a plan for future education in which their savings are administered and augmented by the government.
**Eligibility:** Open to veterans and current military service members who 1) entered active duty between January 1, 1977 and June 30, 1985; 2) were released under conditions other than dishonorable or continue on active duty; 3) served for a continuous period of 181 days or more (or were discharged earlier for a service-connected disability); and 4) have satisfactorily contributed to the program. No individuals on active duty could enroll in this program after March 31, 1987. Veterans who enlisted for the first time after September 7, 1980 or entered active duty as an office or enlistee after October 16, 1981 must have completed 24 continuous months of active duty.
**Financial data:** Participants contribute to the program, through monthly deductions from their military pay, from $25 to $100 monthly, up to a maximum of $2,700. They may also, while on active duty, make a lump sum contribution to the training fund. At the time the eligible participant elects to use the benefits to pursue an approved course of education or training, the Department of Veterans Affairs (VA) will match the contribution at the rate of $2 for every $1 made by the participant.
**Duration:** Participants receive monthly payments for the number of months they contributed, or for 36 months, whichever is less. The amount of the payments is determined by dividing the number of months benefits will be paid into the participant's training fund total. Participants have 10 years from the date of last discharge or release from active duty within which to use these benefits.
**Number awarded:** Varies each year.
**Deadline:** Applications may be submitted at any time.

## 1158 VETERANS TRIBUTE SCHOLARSHIPS

Veterans of Foreign Wars of the United States
VFW Building
406 West 34th Street
Kansas City, MO 64111
Phone: (816) 968-1117; Fax: (816) 968-1149; Email: SWilson@vfw.org
Web: www.vfw.org
**Summary:** To provide financial assistance for college to children and grandchildren of veterans and military personnel who have been active in programs of the Veterans of Foreign Wars (VFW).
**Eligibility:** Open to students between 15 and 18 years of age who are children or grandchildren of living U.S. military veterans, as well as those currently serving (active duty, Reserves, or National Guard). Selection is based on the number of points that applicants achieve out of a possible total of 1,500. Points are awarded for GPA (50 for 2.0 to 2.4, 75 for 2.5 to 2.9, 100 for 3.0 to 3.4, 125 for 3.5 to 3.9, or 150 for 4.0+); 100 for participation in the VFW's Voice of Democracy Scholarship Program; 100 for participation in the VFW's Patriot's Pen Youth Essay Contest; 100 for participation in the VFW Auxiliary's Outstanding Young Volunteer of the Year Program; 100 for participation in the VFW Auxiliary's Young American Creative Patriotic Art program; up to 100 for documented community service (at least 50 hours); 50 if the parent served in the U.S. military overseas; 10 to 100 if the veteran has a service-connected disability (based on the degree of disability); 300 if the veteran is a VFW member; 200 if the veteran is a VFW life member; 100 if the veteran's spouse is a member of the Ladies or Men's Auxiliary to the VFW; and 100 if the veteran has held or holds a VFW office.
**Financial data:** The highest ranked applicant receives a $10,000 scholarship, second a $5,000 scholarship, and third a $3,000 scholarship.
**Duration:** 1 year.
**Number awarded:** 3 each year.
**Deadline:** December of each year.

## 1159 VICE ADMIRAL E.P. TRAVERS SCHOLARSHIP

Navy-Marine Corps Relief Society, Attn: Education Division
875 North Randolph Street, Suite 225
Arlington, VA 22203-1977
Phone: (703) 696-4960; Fax: (703) 696-0144; Email: education@hq.nmcrs.org
Web: www.nmcrs.org/travers.html
**Summary:** To provide financial assistance for college to the dependents of Navy and Marine Corps personnel.
**Eligibility:** Open to the dependent children of active-duty and retired Navy and Marine Corps personnel and the spouses of active-duty Navy and Marine Corps personnel. Applicants must have a cumulative GPA of 2.0 or higher and must demonstrate financial need. They must be enrolled or planning to enroll as a full-time undergraduate student at an accredited college, university, or vocational/technical school.
**Financial data:** The stipend is $2,000 per year.
**Duration:** 1 year; may be renewed up to 3 additional years as long as the recipi-

ent maintains a GPA of 2.0 or higher and the parent remains on active duty in the Navy or Marines.

**Number awarded:** Up to 500 each year.

**Deadline:** February of each year.

## 1160 VICTORIA S. AND BRADLEY L. GEIST FOUNDATION SCHOLARSHIP

Hawai'i Community Foundation, Attn: Scholarship Department
1164 Bishop Street, Suite 800
Honolulu, HI 96813
Phone: (808) 566-5570; (888) 731-3863; Fax: (808) 521-6286;
Email: scholarships@hcf-hawaii.org
Web: www.hawaiicommunityfoundation.org/scholar/scholar.php

**Summary:** To provide financial assistance to Hawaii residents who are interested in attending college or graduate school and have been in the foster care (or similar) system.

**Eligibility:** Open to Hawaii residents who are permanently separated from their parents and currently in (or formerly in) the foster care system. Applicants must be or planning to become full-time students at the undergraduate or graduate school level. They must be able to demonstrate academic achievement, good moral character, and financial need. In addition to filling out the standard application form, applicants must 1) write a short statement indicating their reasons for attending college, their planned course of study, and their career goals, and 2) supply a confirmation letter from their social worker, foster parent, hanai parent, or other appropriate individual.

**Financial data:** The amounts of the awards depend on the availability of funds and the need of the recipient; recently, stipends averaged $2,400.

**Duration:** 1 year.

**Number awarded:** Varies each year; recently, 54 of these scholarships were awarded.

**Deadline:** February of each year.

## 1161 VIETNOW SCHOLARSHIPS

VietNow National Headquarters
1835 Broadway
Rockford, IL 61104-5409
Phone: (815) 227-5100; (800) 837-VNOW; Fax: (815) 227-5127;
Email: vnnatl@inwave.com
Web: www.vietnow.com

**Summary:** To provide financial assistance for college to dependents of certain veterans.

**Eligibility:** Open to 1) a dependent (biological child, stepchild, adopted child, or foster child) under the age of 35 of a VietNow member in good standing, or 2) a dependent of a veteran listed as missing in action, prisoner of war, or killed in action. Selection is based on academic achievement, ability, and extracurricular activities; financial need is a minor consideration.

**Financial data:** The stipend is $1,000 per year.

**Duration:** 1 year.

**Number awarded:** Varies each year; recently, 9 of these scholarships were awarded.

**Deadline:** March of each year.

## 1162 VINCENT L. HAWKINSON FOUNDATION FOR PEACE & JUSTICE SCHOLARSHIP

Vincent L. Hawkinson Foundation for Peace & Justice
c/o Grace University Lutheran Church
324 Harvard Street, S.E.
Minneapolis, MN 55414
Phone: (612) 331-8125

**Summary:** To provide financial assistance for college to students in selected midwestern states who are committed to peace and justice.

**Eligibility:** Open to currently-enrolled college students who reside in or attend school in 1 of the following midwestern states: Iowa, Minnesota, North Dakota, South Dakota, or Wisconsin. Students must be nominated. Nominees must submit a copy of their current academic transcript, a nomination form, and a 2-page essay either on 1) their commitment to peace and justice, or 2) how the use of the award money for special study, an internship, or a special project will deepen their personal commitment to peace and justice and will promote peace and justice for others. Finalists are interviewed in Minneapolis.

**Financial data:** Stipends range from $500 to $1,500.

**Duration:** 1 year.

**Number awarded:** Varies each year. Recently, 5 of these scholarships were awarded: 1 at $1,500, 1 at $1,000, and 3 at $500.

**Deadline:** March of each year.

## 1163 VIRGINIA COLLEGE SCHOLARSHIP ASSISTANCE PROGRAM

State Council of Higher Education for Virginia, Attn: Financial Aid Office
James Monroe Building
101 North 14th Street, Ninth Floor
Richmond, VA 23219-3659
Phone: (804) 225-2600; (877) 515-0138; Fax: (804) 225-2604;
TDD: (804) 371-8017; Email: fainfo@schev.edu
Web: www.schev.edu

**Summary:** To provide financial assistance for college to residents of Virginia who demonstrate extreme financial need.

**Eligibility:** Open to residents of Virginia who have been admitted into a Virginia public 2- or 4-year college or university or a participating Virginia private nonprofit 4-year college or university. Applicants must be enrolled or planning to enroll at least half time, be a U.S. citizen or eligible noncitizen, and have a computed expected family contribution that is less than half the total cost of attendance.

**Financial data:** The amount awarded ranges from $400 to $5,000 per year, depending on the need of the recipient.

**Duration:** 1 year; may be renewed for up to 3 additional years if the recipient maintains at least half-time status and satisfactory academic progress.

**Number awarded:** Varies each year.

## 1164 VIRGINIA COMMONWEALTH AWARDS

State Council of Higher Education for Virginia, Attn: Financial Aid Office
James Monroe Building
101 North 14th Street, Ninth Floor
Richmond, VA 23219-3659
Phone: (804) 225-2600; (877) 515-0138; Fax: (804) 225-2604;
TDD: (804) 371-8017; Email: fainfo@schev.edu
Web: www.schev.edu

**Summary:** To provide financial assistance to needy undergraduate students and some graduate students enrolled in Virginia colleges or universities.

**Eligibility:** Open to residents of Virginia who are undergraduate students enrolled at least half time in Virginia's public colleges and universities. Applicants must be U.S. citizens or eligible noncitizens and able to demonstrate financial need. Some full-time graduate students, regardless of need or residency, are also eligible.

**Financial data:** Awards may be as much as full tuition and required fees.

**Duration:** 1 year.

**Number awarded:** Varies each year.

**Deadline:** Deadline dates vary by school.

## 1165 VIRGINIA DIVISION GIFT SCHOLARSHIPS

United Daughters of the Confederacy-Virginia Division
c/o Suzie Snyder, Education Committee Chair
8440 Bradshaw Road
Salem, VA 24153-2246
Phone: (540) 384-6884; Email: Suzienotes@aol.com
Web: users.erols.com/va-udc/scholarships.html

**Summary:** To provide financial assistance for college to Confederate descendants from Virginia.

**Eligibility:** Open to residents of Virginia who are 1) lineal descendants of Confederates, or 2) collateral descendants and also members of the Children of the Confederacy or the United Daughters of the Confederacy. Applicants must submit proof of the Confederate military record of at least 1 ancestor, with the company and regiment in which he served. They must also submit a personal letter pledging to make the best possible use of the scholarship; describing their health, social, family, religious, and fraternal connections within the community; and reflecting on what a Southern heritage means to them (using the term "War Between the States" in lieu of "Civil War"). They must have a GPA of 3.0 or higher and be able to demonstrate financial need.

**Financial data:** The amount of the stipend depends on the availability of funds. Payment is made directly to the college or university the recipient attends.

**Duration:** 1 year; may be renewed up to 3 additional years if the recipient maintains a GPA of 3.0 or higher.

**Number awarded:** These scholarships are offered whenever a prior recipient graduates or is no longer eligible.

**Deadline:** May of years in which any of the scholarships is available.

## 1166 VIRGINIA FOSTER CHILDREN GRANTS

State Council of Higher Education for Virginia, Attn: Financial Aid Office
James Monroe Building

101 North 14th Street, Ninth Floor
Richmond, VA 23219-3659
Phone: (804) 225-2600; (877) 515-0138; Fax: (804) 225-2604;
TDD: (804) 371-8017; Email: fainfo@schev.edu
Web: www.schev.edu

**Summary:** To provide financial assistance to community college students in Virginia who were in foster care.

**Eligibility:** Open to residents of Virginia who were in foster care, in the custody of the Department of Social Services, or considered a special needs adoption when their high school diploma or GED was awarded. Applicants may not have been previously enrolled in a postsecondary institution as a full-time student for more than 5 years, but they must be attending a community college in Virginia full time in an eligible academic program of at least 1 academic year in length. Colleges rank eligible first-year applicants on the basis of when the college received the application for admission, federal financial aid data, and appropriate supporting documentation. Renewal applicants are given priority for selection.

**Financial data:** Awards up to full tuition and fees are provided to students who are not receiving other assistance.

**Duration:** 1 year; may be renewed.

**Number awarded:** Varies each year.

### 1167 VIRGINIA GUARANTEED ASSISTANCE PROGRAM

State Council of Higher Education for Virginia, Attn: Financial Aid Office
James Monroe Building
101 North 14th Street, Ninth Floor
Richmond, VA 23219-3659
Phone: (804) 225-2600; (877) 515-0138; Fax: (804) 225-2604;
TDD: (804) 371-8017; Email: fainfo@schev.edu
Web: www.schev.edu

**Summary:** To provide financial assistance to exceptionally needy students who plan to attend a public college or university in Virginia.

**Eligibility:** Open to residents of Virginia who are currently attending an elementary or secondary school in the state. Students are eligible to receive these awards if they graduate from a Virginia high school with a cumulative GPA of 2.5 or higher, are classified as a dependent, are a U.S. citizen or eligible noncitizen, are able to demonstrate financial need, and are admitted to a Virginia public 2- or 4-year college or university as a full-time student.

**Financial data:** Awards vary by institution but range up to the full cost of tuition, required fees, and an allowance for books. Students with the greatest need receive the largest awards.

**Duration:** 1 year; may be renewed as long as the recipient maintains full-time enrollment with at least a 2.0 GPA, demonstrated financial need, residency in Virginia, and satisfactory academic progress.

**Number awarded:** Varies each year.

### 1168 VIRGINIA PART-TIME ASSISTANCE PROGRAM

State Council of Higher Education for Virginia, Attn: Financial Aid Office
James Monroe Building
101 North 14th Street, Ninth Floor
Richmond, VA 23219-3659
Phone: (804) 225-2600; (877) 515-0138; Fax: (804) 225-2604;
TDD: (804) 371-8017; Email: fainfo@schev.edu
Web: www.schev.edu

**Summary:** To provide financial assistance to community college students in Virginia who are attending part time.

**Eligibility:** Open to residents of Virginia who are attending a community college in the state on a part-time basis. Applicants must be able to demonstrate financial need.

**Financial data:** Awards up to full tuition and fees are available.

**Duration:** 1 year; may be renewed.

**Number awarded:** Varies each year.

### 1169 VIRGINIA PUBLIC SAFETY FOUNDATION SCHOLARSHIPS

Virginia Public Safety Foundation, Inc.
P.O. Box 1355
Richmond, VA 23218
Phone: (804) 282-0148; Fax: (804) 282-2127; Email: vpsf@globalweb.net
Web: www.vpsf.org/what.htm

**Summary:** To provide financial assistance for college to the children of current and selected former Virginia public safety officers.

**Eligibility:** Open to the children of all active-duty Virginia public safety officers and those officers forced to retire because of an injury incurred in the line of duty. "Public safety" officers are defined as state and local police, sheriffs, their deputies, corrections and jail officers, fire fighters, agents of the Alcoholic Beverage Control Department, and volunteer members of a fire company or rescue squad. Applicants may be high school seniors or currently enrolled in college. Selection is based on merit (academic record, character, personal and career goals, extracurricular activities, and school service). Financial need is not considered in the selection process.

**Financial data:** Stipends range up to $3,000 per year.

**Duration:** 1 year; nonrenewable.

**Number awarded:** Varies each year; recently 29 were awarded.

**Deadline:** February of each year.

### 1170 VIRGINIA TUITION ASSISTANCE GRANT PROGRAM

State Council of Higher Education for Virginia, Attn: Financial Aid Office
James Monroe Building
101 North 14th Street, Ninth Floor
Richmond, VA 23219-3659
Phone: (804) 225-2600; (877) 515-0138; Fax: (804) 225-2604;
TDD: (804) 371-8017; Email: fainfo@schev.edu
Web: www.schev.edu

**Summary:** To provide financial assistance to undergraduate and graduate students attending private colleges or universities in Virginia.

**Eligibility:** Open to undergraduate and graduate or professional students who are Virginia residents attending private colleges or universities in the state on a full-time basis in a degree program. There is no financial need requirement. Students pursuing religious training or theological education are not eligible.

**Financial data:** The amount awarded varies, depending on annual appropriations and number of applicants; recently, the maximum award was $2,210 for undergraduates or $1,700 for graduate students.

**Duration:** 1 year; may be renewed.

**Number awarded:** Varies each year.

**Deadline:** The deadline for priority consideration for fall semester is July of each year. Applicants submitted through the end of November are considered only if funds are available.

### 1171 VIRGINIA WAR ORPHANS EDUCATION PROGRAM

Virginia Department of Veterans' Affairs
270 Franklin Road, S.W., Room 503
Roanoke, VA 24011-2215
Phone: (540) 857-7104; Fax: (540) 857-7573
Web: www.dvs.virginia.gov/education_benefits.htm

**Summary:** To provide educational assistance to the children of disabled and other Virginia veterans or service personnel.

**Eligibility:** Open to residents of Virginia who have at least 1 parent who served in the U.S. armed forces and is permanently and totally disabled due to an injury or disease incurred in a time of war or other period of armed conflict, has died as a result of war or other armed conflict, or is listed as a prisoner of war or missing in action. Applicants must be between 16 and 25 years of age and be accepted at a public secondary or postsecondary educational institution in Virginia. The veteran parent must have been a resident of Virginia at the time of entry into active military service or for at least 5 consecutive years immediately prior to the date of application or death. The surviving parent must have been a resident of Virginia for at least 5 years prior to marrying the deceased parent or for at least 5 years immediately prior to the date on which the application was submitted.

**Financial data:** Eligible individuals receive free tuition and are exempted from any fees charged by state-supported schools in Virginia.

**Duration:** Entitlement extends to a maximum of 48 months.

**Number awarded:** Varies; generally more than 150 each year.

### 1172 VOCATIONAL REHABILITATION FOR DISABLED VETERANS

Department of Veterans Affairs
810 Vermont Avenue, N.W.
Washington, DC 20420
Phone: (202) 418-4343; (800) 827-1000
Web: www.va.gov

**Summary:** To provide vocational rehabilitation to certain categories of veterans with disabilities.

**Eligibility:** Open to veterans who have a service-connected disability of at least

10% and a serious employment handicap or 20% and an employment handicap. They must have been discharged or released from military service under other than dishonorable conditions. The Department of Veterans Affairs (VA) must determine that they would benefit from a training program that would help them prepare for, find, and keep suitable employment. The program may be 1) institutional training at a certificate, 2-year college, 4-year college or university, or technical program; 2) unpaid on-the-job training in a federal, state, or local agency or a federally-recognized Indian tribal agency, training in a home, vocational course in a rehabilitation facility or sheltered workshop, independent instruction, or institutional non-farm cooperative; or 3) paid training through a farm cooperative, apprenticeship, on-the-job training, or on-the-job non-farm cooperative.

**Financial data:** While in training and for 2 months after, eligible disabled veterans may receive subsistence allowances in addition to their disability compensation or retirement pay. For training at an institution of higher education or in an unpaid work experience program, the full-time monthly rate is $474.27 with no dependents, $588.30 with 1 dependent, $693.25 with 2 dependents, and $50.54 for each additional dependent; the three-quarter time monthly rate is $356.36 for no dependents, $441.86 with 1 dependent, $518.31 with 2 dependents, and $38.86 for each additional dependent; the half-time monthly rate is $238.45 for no dependents, $295.44 with 1 dependent, $347.27 with 2 dependents, and $25.93 for each additional dependent. For unpaid on-the-job training, the monthly rate is $474.27 for no dependents, $588.30 with 1 dependent, $693.25 with 2 dependents, and $50.54 for each additional dependent. For paid training, the monthly rate is based on the wage received, to a maximum of $414.67 for no dependents, $501.46 with 1 dependent, $577.92 with 2 dependents, and $37.59 for each additional dependent. The VA also pays the costs of tuition, books, fees, supplies, and equipment; it may also pay for special supportive services, such as tutorial assistance, prosthetic devices, lipreading training, and signing for the deaf. If during training or employment services the veteran's disabilities cause transportation expenses that would not be incurred by nondisabled persons, the VA will pay for at least a portion of those expenses. If the veteran encounters financial difficulty during training, the VA may provide an advance against future benefit payments.

**Duration:** Up to 48 months of full-time training or its equivalent in part-time training. If a veteran with a serious disability receives services under an extended evaluation to improve training potential, the total of the extended evaluation and the training phases of the rehabilitation program may exceed 48 months. Usually, the veteran must complete a rehabilitation program within 12 years from the date of notification of entitlement to compensation by the VA. Following completion of the training portion of a rehabilitation program, a veteran may receive counseling and job search and adjustment services for 18 months.

**Number awarded:** Varies each year.

**Deadline:** Applications are accepted at any time.

---

## 1173 VOLTA SCHOLARSHIP FUND

Alexander Graham Bell Association for the Deaf
Attn: Financial Aid Coordinator
3417 Volta Place, N.W.
Washington, DC 20007-2778
Phone: (202) 337-5220; Fax: (202) 337-8314; TTY: (202) 337-5221;
Email: financialaid@agbell.org
Web: www.agbell.org

**Summary:** To provide financial assistance to undergraduate and graduate students with moderate to profound hearing loss.

**Eligibility:** Open to undergraduate and graduate students who have been diagnosed with a moderate to profound hearing loss prior to acquiring spoken language (hearing loss averages 60dB or greater in the better ear in the speech frequencies of 500, 1000, and 2000 Hz). Applicants must be committed to using spoken language as their primary mode of communication. They must be accepted or enrolled at a mainstream college or university as a full-time student. Along with their application, they must submit a 1-page essay discussing their career goals and how spoken communication is helping them to reach those goals as a person with a hearing loss. Financial need is considered in the selection process. This scholarship is reserved for students who are oral deaf.

**Financial data:** The stipend is $2,000 per year.

**Duration:** 1 year; may be renewed 1 additional year.

**Number awarded:** 1 each year.

**Deadline:** April of each year.

---

## 1174 VOLUNTEER REGIONAL SCHOLARSHIPS

Royal Neighbors of America, Attn: Fraternal Services
230 16th Street
Rock Island, IL 61201-8645

Phone: (309) 788-4561; (800) 627-4762; Email: contact@royalneighbors.org
Web: www.royalneighbors.org/MemberBenefits/scholarships.cfm

**Summary:** To provide financial assistance for college to members of the Royal Neighbors of America who have been involved in volunteer activities.

**Eligibility:** Open to members of the society who are graduating high school seniors. Applicants must demonstrate outstanding and significant volunteer qualities.

**Financial data:** The stipend is $1,000 per year.

**Duration:** 4 years.

**Number awarded:** 8 each year: 1 in each of the society's regions.

**Deadline:** December of each year.

---

## 1175 WACHOVIA CITIZENSHIP AWARDS

Virginia High School League
1642 State Farm Boulevard
Charlottesville, VA 22911
Phone: (434) 977-8475; Fax: (434) 977-5943
Web: www.whsl.org

**Summary:** To provide financial assistance for college to high school seniors who have participated in activities of the Virginia High School League (VHSL).

**Eligibility:** Open to college-bound seniors graduating from high schools that are members of the VHSL. Applicants must have participated in 1 or more of the following VHSL activities: baseball, basketball, cheer, creative writing, cross country, debate, drama, field hockey, football, forensics, golf, gymnastics, lacrosse, leaders conference, magazines, newspapers/newsmagazines, scholastic bowl, soccer, softball, sportsmanship summit/committee, swimming and diving, tennis, track (indoor and outdoor), volleyball, wrestling, and yearbook. They must submit an essay (from 500 to 1,000 words) on what they have done that meets a definition of citizenship and how others have benefited. Each school may nominate 1 female and 1 male. Candidates are judged separately in the 3 VHSL groups (A, AA, and AAA). Selection is based on the essay; contributions to family, school, and community; promotion of good citizenship and sportsmanship; and 2 letters of support.

**Financial data:** The stipend is $1,000.

**Duration:** 1 year.

**Number awarded:** 6 each year: a female and a male in each of the 3 VHSL groups.

**Deadline:** March of each year.

---

## 1176 WAIVERS OF NONRESIDENT TUITION FOR DEPENDENTS OF MILITARY PERSONNEL MOVING TO TEXAS

Texas Higher Education Coordinating Board
Attn: Grants and Special Programs
1200 East Anderson Lane
P.O. Box 12788, Capitol Station
Austin, TX 78711-2788
Phone: (512) 427-6101; (800) 242-3062; Fax: (512) 427-6127;
Email: grantinfo@thecb.state.tx.us
Web: www.collegefortexans.com

**Summary:** To exempt dependents of military personnel who move to Texas from the payment of nonresident tuition at public institutions of higher education in the state.

**Eligibility:** Open to the spouses and dependent children of members of the U.S. armed forces and commissioned officers of the Public Health Service who move to Texas while the service member remains assigned to another state. Applicants must be attending or planning to attend a public college or university in the state. They must indicate their intent to become a Texas resident. For dependent children to qualify, the spouse must also move to Texas.

**Financial data:** Although persons eligible under this program are still classified as nonresidents, they are entitled to pay the resident tuition at Texas institutions of higher education on an immediate basis.

**Duration:** 1 year.

**Number awarded:** Varies each year.

---

## 1177 WAIVERS OF NONRESIDENT TUITION FOR DEPENDENTS OF MILITARY PERSONNEL WHO PREVIOUSLY LIVED IN TEXAS

Texas Higher Education Coordinating Board
Attn: Grants and Special Programs
1200 East Anderson Lane
P.O. Box 12788, Capitol Station
Austin, TX 78711-2788

Phone: (512) 427-6101; (800) 242-3062; Fax: (512) 427-6127; Email: grantinfo@thecb.state.tx.us
Web: www.collegefortexans.com

**Summary:** To provide a partial tuition exemption to the spouses and dependent children of military personnel who are Texas residents but are not assigned to duty in the state.

**Eligibility:** Open to the spouses and dependent children of members of the U.S. armed forces who are not assigned to duty in Texas but have previously resided in the state for at least 6 months. Service members must verify that they remain Texas residents by designating Texas as their place of legal residence for income tax purposes, registering to vote in the state, and doing 1 of the following: owning real property in Texas, registering an automobile in Texas, or executing a will indicating that they are a resident of the state. The spouse or dependent child must be attending or planning to attend a Texas public college or university.

**Financial data:** Although persons eligible under this program are classified as nonresidents, they are entitled to pay the resident tuition at Texas institutions of higher education, regardless of their length of residence in Texas.

**Duration:** 1 year.

**Number awarded:** Varies each year.

---

## 1178 WALTER H. MEYER–GARRY L. WHITE MEMORIAL EDUCATIONAL FUND

College Planning Network, Attn: Vicki Breithaupt
171 East Uncas Road North
Port Townsend, WA 98368
Phone: (206) 323-0624; Email: seacpn@collegeplan.org
Web: www.collegeplan.org

**Summary:** To provide financial assistance for undergraduate or graduate study in the United States or other countries to mature residents of Washington state

**Eligibility:** Open to residents of Washington who are attending or planning to attend a college or university in the United States, Canada, or Europe. Undergraduates must be older than 24 years of age; graduate students must be older than 30. Applicants must submit a 1-page personal essay explaining where they see their career and life-style in 10 years. Selection is based on the essay, 2 letters of recommendation, academic transcripts, and financial need.

**Financial data:** The stipend depends on the need of the recipient but is at least $5,000 per year.

**Duration:** 1 year.

**Number awarded:** 15 each year.

**Deadline:** February of each year.

---

## 1179 WALTER W. AND THELMA C. HISSEY COLLEGE SCHOLARSHIPS

Alexander Graham Bell Association for the Deaf
Attn: Financial Aid Coordinator
3417 Volta Place, N.W.
Washington, DC 20007-2778
Phone: (202) 337-5220; Fax: (202) 337-8314; TTY: (202) 337-5221;
Email: financialaid@agbell.org
Web: www.agbell.org

**Summary:** To provide financial assistance to undergraduate and graduate students with moderate to profound hearing loss.

**Eligibility:** Open to undergraduate and graduate students who have been diagnosed with a moderate to profound hearing loss prior to acquiring spoken language (hearing loss averages 60dB or greater in the better ear in the speech frequencies of 500, 1000, and 2000 Hz). Applicants must be committed to using spoken language as their primary mode of communication. They must be accepted or enrolled at a mainstream college or university as a full-time student. Along with their application, they must submit a 1-page essay discussing their career goals and how spoken communication is helping them to reach those goals as a person with a hearing loss. Financial need is considered in the selection process.

**Financial data:** The stipend is $5,000 per year.

**Duration:** 1 year; may be renewed 1 additional year.

**Number awarded:** 2 each year.

**Deadline:** April of each year.

---

## 1180 WARREN FENCL SCHOLARSHIPS

100th Infantry Battalion Veterans Club, Attn: Scholarship Committee
520 Kamoku Street

Honolulu, HI 96826
Phone: (808) 732-5216; Email: daisyy@hgea.net
Web: emedia.leeward.hawaii.edu/mnakano

**Summary:** To provide financial assistance to high school seniors and college students who exemplify the sponsor's motto of "Continuing Service."

**Eligibility:** Open to high school seniors planning to attend an institution of higher learning and full-time undergraduate students at community colleges, vocational/trade schools, 4-year colleges, and universities. Applicants must have a GPA of 2.5 or higher and be able to demonstrate civic responsibility and community service. Along with their application, they must submit a 4-page essay that explains how valuing a diversity of different opinions, cultures, and lifestyles affects a nation that is challenged with resolving complex issues. Selection is based on that essay and the applicant's demonstration that he or she can effectively promote the legacy of the 100th Infantry Battalion and its motto of "Continuing Service." Financial need is not considered.

**Financial data:** The stipend is $1,000.

**Duration:** 1 year; nonrenewable.

**Number awarded:** 2 each year.

**Deadline:** April of each year.

---

## 1181 WASHINGTON ALUMNAE CHAPTER SCHOLARSHIPS

Delta Sigma Theta Sorority, Inc.-Washington DC Alumnae Chapter
Attn: Scholarship Committee
P.O. Box 90202
Washington, DC 20090-0202
Web: www.wdcac.org

**Summary:** To provide financial assistance for college to high school seniors in Washington, D.C.

**Eligibility:** Open to seniors graduating from public and private high schools in Washington, D.C. Applicants must submit an official high school transcript, a copy of their SAT or ACT scores, documentation of financial need, 2 letters of recommendation, and a 1-page autobiographical essay including their academic and career goals, public service involvement, why the scholarship is important, and its expected benefit.

**Financial data:** A stipend is awarded (amount not specified)

**Duration:** 1 year.

**Number awarded:** 1 or more each year.

**Deadline:** March of each year.

---

## 1182 WASHINGTON KIDS' CHANCE SCHOLARSHIPS

Kids' Chance of Washington
P.O. Box 185
Olympia, WA 98507-0185
Phone: (800) 572-5762; Fax: (360) 943-2333; Email: debbie@wscff.org
Web: www.kidschancewa.com

**Summary:** To provide financial assistance for college to residents of Washington whose parent or spouse was killed or seriously disabled in a workplace accident.

**Eligibility:** Open to Washington residents attending or planning to attend an accredited community college, university, college, or technical/vocational school. Applicants must be the child or spouse of a Washington worker permanently or catastrophically injured or deceased while on the job. Selection is based primarily on financial need.

**Financial data:** A stipend is awarded (amount not specified). Funds are paid directly to the student's school to be used for tuition, books, fees, room, and general living expenses.

**Duration:** 1 year; may be renewed.

**Number awarded:** Varies each year.

---

## 1183 WASHINGTON SCHOLARS PROGRAM

Washington Higher Education Coordinating Board
917 Lakeridge Way
P.O. Box 43430
Olympia, WA 98504-3430
Phone: (360) 753-7851; Fax: (360) 753-7808; TDD: (360) 753-7809;
Email: info@hecb.wa.gov
Web: www.hecb.wa.gov/financialaid/wsp/wspindex.asp

**Summary:** To provide financial assistance for education at colleges and universities in Washington to the top 1% of students who graduate from high schools in the state.

**Eligibility:** Open to high school seniors in Washington. High school principals may nominate graduating seniors in the top 1% of their class. Students are selected to receive awards based on academic accomplishments, leadership, and community service.

**Financial data:** Awards provide payment of full-time undergraduate resident tuition and fees, or approximately $3,700 per year.

**Duration:** Aid is provided for 12 quarters or 8 semesters of undergraduate study.

**Number awarded:** Up to 147 each year: 3 in each state legislative district.

## 1184 WASHINGTON STATE NEED GRANT

Washington Higher Education Coordinating Board
917 Lakeridge Way
P.O. Box 43430
Olympia, WA 98504-3430
Phone: (360) 753-7851; Fax: (360) 753-7808; TDD: (360) 753-7809;
Email: info@hecb.wa.gov
Web: www.hecb.wa.gov/financialaid/sng/sngindex.asp

**Summary:** To provide financial assistance for undergraduate study to Washington residents who come from a low-income or disadvantaged family.

**Eligibility:** Open to residents of Washington whose family income is equal to or less than 55% of the state median (currently defined as $18,000 for a family of 1 ranging to $48,000 for a family of 8) or who are disadvantaged (defined to mean a student who by reasons of adverse cultural, educational, environmental, experiential, or familial circumstance is unlikely to aspire to, or enroll in, higher education. Applicants must be enrolled or planning to enroll at least half time in an eligible certificate, bachelor's degree, or first associate degree program. They may not be working on a degree in theology.

**Financial data:** The stipend depends on the type of institution the recipient attends. Recently, it was $1,908 per year at community, technical, and private career colleges; $3,026 at public comprehensive universities (Central Washington University, Eastern Washington University, The Evergreen State College, and Western Washington University); $3,798 at public research universities (University of Washington and Washington State University); or $4,032 at independent universities.

**Duration:** 1 academic year; renewal is possible for up to 3 additional years.

**Number awarded:** Varies each year; recently, more than 49,000 students received about $106 million in benefits from this program.

**Deadline:** Varies according to the participating institution; generally in October of each year.

## 1185 WASHINGTON STATE PTA SCHOLARSHIPS

Washington State PTA, Attn: WSPTA Scholarship Foundation
2003 65th Avenue West
Tacoma, WA 98466-6215
Phone: (253) 565-2153; (800) 562-3804; Fax: (253) 565-7753;
Email: wapta@wastatepta.org
Web: www.wastatepta.org/sf/scholar_foundation.htm

**Summary:** To provide financial assistance for college to graduates of Washington public high schools.

**Eligibility:** Open to graduates of public high schools in Washington State who are entering postsecondary institutions; applicants may be current graduating seniors or graduates from prior years entering their freshman year as a full-time student. Selection is based primarily on financial need; academic criteria are not considered as long as the candidates are able to meet the admission requirements of the school they wish to attend.

**Financial data:** Stipends are $2,000 at 4-year colleges or universities or $1,000 at community colleges, vocational/technical schools, or other accredited institutions.

**Duration:** 1 year; nonrenewable.

**Number awarded:** Varies each year. Recently, 37 of these scholarships were awarded: 29 at $2,000 to 4-year college students and 8 at $1,000 to community college and vocational/technical school students.

**Deadline:** February of each year.

## 1186 WASIE FOUNDATION SCHOLARSHIP PROGRAM

Wasie Foundation, Attn: Program Officer
4999 France Avenue South, Suite 250
Minneapolis, MN 55410-1711
Phone: (612) 455-6880; Fax: (612) 455-6888

**Summary:** To provide financial assistance to undergraduates who are attending selected academic institutions in Minnesota.

**Eligibility:** Open to U.S. citizens who have been accepted as full-time students at 1 of the participating schools in Minnesota: College of St. Benedict, College of St. Catherine, College of St. Scholastica, Dunwoody College of Technology, Hamline University, Mayo Medical School, St. John's University, St. Mary's University of Minnesota, University of Minnesota, University of St. Thomas, and William Mitchell College of Law. A personal statement, academic transcripts, and a photograph must be submitted with the complete application. Preference is given to individuals of Polish ancestry who are members of the Christian faith. Preference is also given to individuals from north and northeast Minneapolis and surrounding communities. Selection is based on financial need, academic ability, education and career goals, leadership qualities, and involvement in volunteer and extracurricular activities.

**Financial data:** A stipend is awarded (amount not specified).

**Duration:** 1 year; recipients may reapply.

**Number awarded:** Generally, 9 each year.

**Deadline:** March of each year.

## 1187 WEST VIRGINIA HIGHER EDUCATION ADULT PART-TIME STUDENT GRANT PROGRAM

West Virginia Higher Education Policy Commission
Attn: Office of Financial Aid and Outreach Services
1018 Kanawha Boulevard, East, Suite 700
Charleston, WV 25301-2827
Phone: (304) 558-4614; (888) 825-5707; Fax: (304) 558-4622;
Email: kee@hepc.wvnet.edu
Web: www.hepc.wvnet.edu/students/heaps.html

**Summary:** To provide financial assistance to West Virginia residents who are working on a college degree or certificate in the state on a part-time basis.

**Eligibility:** Open to West Virginia residents who are U.S. citizens or permanent residents. Applicants must be enrolled or accepted for enrollment in a certificate, associate, or bachelor's degree program on a part-time basis at an eligible West Virginia institution, including a community college, a technical college, an adult technical preparatory education program or training, a state college or university, an independent college or university, or an approved distance education program (including web-based courses). Students who are financially dependent upon parents or a spouse may qualify if they demonstrate financial need and are otherwise eligible. Traditional college age students are also eligible. Applicants must be eligible to participate in the federal Pell Grant program, demonstrate financial need, not be in default on a higher education loan, and demonstrate that they have applied for or accepted other student financial assistance in compliance with federal financial aid rules.

**Financial data:** For students enrolled at a public college or university, the stipend is based on the actual per credit tuition and fees. For students at other eligible institutions, the award is based on the average per credit tuition and fees charged by all of the public undergraduate institutions of higher education during the previous year. The maximum award recently was $2,770 per year.

**Duration:** 1 year; may be renewed until the program of study is completed, up to a maximum of 9 additional years.

**Number awarded:** Varies each year; recently, more than 3,000 students received more than $3 million in aid through this program.

**Deadline:** Applications may be submitted at any time.

## 1188 WEST VIRGINIA HIGHER EDUCATION GRANT PROGRAM

West Virginia Higher Education Policy Commission
Attn: Office of Financial Aid and Outreach Services
1018 Kanawha Boulevard, East, Suite 700
Charleston, WV 25301-2827
Phone: (304) 558-4614; (888) 825-5707; Fax: (304) 558-4622;
Email: wicks@hepc.wvnet.edu
Web: www.hepc.wvnet.edu/students/wvgrant.html

**Summary:** To provide financial assistance to West Virginia residents who wish to attend an approved institution of higher education in West Virginia or Pennsylvania.

**Eligibility:** Open to U.S. citizens who have been residents of West Virginia for at least 1 year prior to applying. Applicants must plan to enroll as full-time undergraduate students at an approved college or university in West Virginia or Pennsylvania. Selection is based on financial need and academic performance.

**Financial data:** Awards are limited to payment of tuition and fees, from $350 to $2,718 per year. Funds are sent directly to the institution.

**Duration:** 1 year; may be renewed for up to 3 additional years.

**Number awarded:** Varies each year; recently, approximately 11,000 students received assistance worth $20.7 million.

**Deadline:** February of each year.

### 1189 WEST VIRGINIA KIDS' CHANCE SCHOLARSHIPS

Greater Kanawha Valley Foundation, Attn: Scholarship Coordinator
1600 Huntington Square
900 Lee Street, East
P.O. Box 3041
Charleston, WV 25331-3041
Phone: (304) 346-3620; Fax: (304) 346-3640; Email: tgkvf@tgkvf.com
Web: www.tgkvf.com/scholar.html

**Summary:** To provide financial assistance for college to students whose parents were injured in a West Virginia work-related accident.

**Eligibility:** Open to children between the ages of 16 and 25 whose parents were seriously injured in a West Virginia work-related accident. Applicants may reside in any state and be pursuing any field of study at an accredited trade or vocational school, college, or university. They must have at least a 2.5 GPA and demonstrate good moral character. Preference is given to applicants who can demonstrate financial need, academic excellence, leadership abilities, and contributions to school and community.

**Financial data:** The stipend is $1,000 per year.

**Duration:** 1 year; may be renewed.

**Number awarded:** Varies each year; recently, 11 of these scholarships were awarded.

**Deadline:** February of each year.

### 1190 WEST VIRGINIA PROMISE SCHOLARSHIPS

West Virginia Higher Education Policy Commission
Attn: PROMISE Scholarship Program
1018 Kanawha Boulevard, East, Suite 700
Charleston, WV 25301-2827
Phone: (304) 558-4417; (877) WV-PROMISE; Fax: (304) 558-3264;
Email: morgenstern@hepc.wvnet.edu
Web: www.promisescholarships.org

**Summary:** To provide financial assistance for college to high school seniors in West Virginia who have complied with core academic requirements.

**Eligibility:** Open to high school seniors in West Virginia who have earned a GPA of 3.0 or higher in core courses (4 credits of English/language arts, 3 credits of mathematics, 3 credits of social sciences, and 3 credits of natural sciences) and overall. All applicants (including those who earn a GED or who are home-schooled) must attain a composite score of 21 or higher on the ACT or an equivalent score on the SAT. High school graduates must apply for this program within 2 years of high school graduation if they still qualify as an entering college freshman. GED recipients must have earned the GED within 2 years of the date their high school class would normally have graduated and must apply for this program within 2 years after attaining the GED; they must have earned a score of 250 or higher on the GED examination. Home-schooled students must have attained a score of 250 or higher on the GED examination and must have earned the GED within 1 year of the time of completion of instruction, but not later than 20 years of age. All applicants must have lived in West Virginia for at least 12 months immediately preceding application for this program. Half of the credits required for high school graduation must have been completed in a public or private high school in West Virginia. Home-schooled students must have been provided instruction in West Virginia for 2 years immediately preceding application. Selection is based on merit; financial need is not considered. Additional funding, in the form of grants, is available to scholars whose family EFC is $4,000 or less.

**Financial data:** Students who attend a West Virginia state college or university receive a full tuition scholarship. Students who attend a West Virginia private college receive an equivalent dollar scholarship, recently for $2,800. Grant recipients receive funding for other education expenses.

**Duration:** 1 year; may be renewed for 1 additional year in an associate degree program, for 3 additional years in a baccalaureate degree program, or for 4 additional years in an approved 5-year undergraduate degree program. Recipients must maintain a GPA of 2.75 or higher during the first year of college and at least 3.0 cumulatively in successive years.

**Number awarded:** Varies each year; recently, a total of $17 million was appropriated for this program. A total of 4,300 students were eligible for these scholarships, of whom 1,200 were eligible for supplemental grant funding.

**Deadline:** January of each year.

### 1191 WEST VIRGINIA STATE WAR ORPHANS EDUCATIONAL PROGRAM

West Virginia Division of Veterans' Affairs
Charleston Human Resource Center
1321 Plaza East, Suite 101
Charleston, WV 25301-1400
Phone: (304) 558-3661; (888) 838-2332 (within WV); Fax: (304) 558-3662;
Email: wvdva@state.wv.us
Web: www.wvs.state.wv.us/va/state_fed.htm

**Summary:** To provide financial assistance for college to the children of deceased West Virginia veterans.

**Eligibility:** Open to residents of West Virginia (for at least 1 year) who are between the ages of 16 and 23 and have a veteran parent who entered service as a resident of West Virginia, served during World War I, World War II, the Korean Conflict, the Vietnam Era from August 5, 1964 to May 7, 1975, or any other time of conflict declared by Congress, and died of injuries or disease as a result of that service.

**Financial data:** High school students are eligible for a grant of $110 to $250 per semester. Students attending a state-supported college, university, or vocational school in West Virginia who are not receiving any aid from the U.S. Department of Veterans Affairs (VA) are entitled to a waiver of tuition and also to receive up to $500 per year for fees, board, room, books, supplies, and other expenses. Students attending a state-supported postsecondary institution who are getting VA assistance receive waiver of tuition and registration fees only. Students attending a private postsecondary school in West Virginia are only eligible for the monetary grant of $500 per year if they are not receiving any VA assistance.

**Duration:** 1 year; may be renewed upon reapplication if the student maintains a cumulative GPA of at least 2.0.

**Number awarded:** Varies each year.

**Deadline:** July for the fall semester; November for the spring semester.

### 1192 WESTERN REGION KOREAN AMERICAN SCHOLARSHIPS

Korean American Scholarship Foundation
Western Region, Attn: Scholarship Committee
3435 Wilshire Boulevard, Suite 2450B
Los Angeles, CA 90010
Phone: (213) 380-KASF; Fax: (213) 380-KASF; Email: western@kasf.org
Web: www.kasf.org/home/regional/western/western.html

**Summary:** To provide financial assistance to Korean American undergraduate and graduate students attending college in the western states.

**Eligibility:** Open to full-time Korean American students who have completed at least 1 year of study at a 4-year college, graduate school, or professional school. Applicants may be residents of any state as long as they attend school in the western region (Alaska, Arizona, California, Colorado, Hawaii, Idaho, Montana, Nevada, New Mexico, Oregon, Utah, Washington, or Wyoming). Selection is based on academic achievement, community service, school activities, and financial need.

**Financial data:** Stipends range from $1,000 to $2,000.

**Duration:** 1 year; renewable.

**Number awarded:** Varies each year. Recently, 60 of these scholarships were awarded.

**Deadline:** February of each year.

### 1193 WESTERN UNDERGRADUATE EXCHANGE

Western Interstate Commission for Higher Education
Attn: Student Exchange Programs
3035 Center Green Drive
P.O. Box 9752
Boulder, CO 80301-9752
Phone: (303) 541-0214; Fax: (303) 541-0291; Email: info-sep@wiche.edu
Web: www.wiche.edu/sep/wue

**Summary:** To underwrite some of the cost of out-of-state undergraduate schooling for students in selected western states.

**Eligibility:** Open to residents of states that participate in the Western Undergraduate Exchange (WUE): Alaska, Arizona, California, Colorado, Hawaii, Idaho, Montana, Nevada, New Mexico, North Dakota, Oregon, South Dakota, Utah, Washington, and Wyoming. To be eligible, students should be resident in 1 of these states for at least 1 year before applying and be interested in enrolling in a participating 2-year or 4-year college or university in 1 of the other states. The financial status of the applicants is not considered. Interested students apply for admission and for WUE assistance directly from the institution of their choice.

**Financial data:** Participants in this program attend out-of-state institutions but pay only 150% of resident tuition instead of the regular full nonresident tuition.

**Duration:** 1 year; may be renewed.

**Number awarded:** Varies each year; recently, more than 20,000 students (approximately 3,400 at 2-year colleges and 16,600 at 4-year universities) were enrolled at 127 campuses in the 15 states.

**Deadline:** Deadline dates vary; check with the institution you wish to attend.

## 1194 WHO'S WHO AMONG AMERICAN HIGH SCHOOL STUDENTS SCHOLARSHIPS

ECI Scholarship Foundation
1701 Directors Boulevard, Suite 920
P.O. Box 149319
Austin, TX 78714-9319
Phone: (512) 440-2300; Fax: (512) 447-1687
Web: www.ecisf.org/hs_main.aspx

**Summary:** To provide financial assistance to high school honor students who are listed in *Who's Who Among American High School Students*.

**Eligibility:** Open to high school students with a GPA of 3.0 or higher who are U.S. citizens and have been involved in school or community activities. Candidates must first be nominated by a school official, youth activity sponsor, or educational organization to have their name appear in *Who's Who Among American High School Students*. All students listed in that publication automatically receive an application for these scholarships in the mail. Selection is based on GPA, achievement test scores, leadership qualifications, work experience, evaluation of an essay, and some consideration for financial need.

**Financial data:** Stipends are $6,000, $5,000, $2,500, or $1,000; payments are issued directly to the financial aid office at the institution the student attends.

**Duration:** 1 year.

**Number awarded:** 127 each year: 1 at $6,000, 10 at $5,000, 20 at $2,500, and 96 at $1,000.

**Deadline:** May of each year.

## 1195 WHO'S WHO SPORTS EDITION ALL-ACADEMIC BOWLING TEAM SCHOLARSHIPS

United States Bowling Congress, Attn: SMART Program
5301 South 76th Street
Greendale, WI 53129-1192
Phone: (414) 423-3223; (800) 514-BOWL, ext. 3223; Fax: (414) 421-3014;
Email: smart@bowl.com
Web: www.bowl.com/scholarships/main.aspx

**Summary:** To provide financial assistance for college to members of the United States Bowling Congress (USBC) Youth who are also recognized in *Who's Who Among American High School Students-Sports Edition*.

**Eligibility:** Open to USBC Youth members who are juniors or seniors in high school. Applicants must have a GPA of 2.5 or higher and not have competed in a professional bowling tournament. They must be listed in the current edition of *Who's Who Among American High School Students-Sports Edition*. Along with their application, they must submit an essay of 500 words on how their involvement in bowling has influenced their life, academic, and personal goals. Financial need is not considered in the selection process.

**Financial data:** The stipend is $1,000.

**Duration:** 1 year; nonrenewable.

**Number awarded:** Up to 20 each year.

**Deadline:** March of each year.

## 1196 WILDER-NAIFEH TECHNICAL SKILLS GRANTS

Tennessee Student Assistance Corporation
Parkway Towers
404 James Robertson Parkway, Suite 1950
Nashville, TN 37243-0820
Phone: (615) 741-1346; (800) 342-1663; Fax: (615) 741-6101;
Email: tsac@mail.state.tn.us
Web: www.tnscholardollars.com/mon_college/wilder_naifeh.htm

**Summary:** To provide financial assistance to students enrolled at Tennessee Technology Centers.

**Eligibility:** Open to students working on a certificate or diploma at a Tennessee Technology Center. Applicants must be enrolled full time, but they are not required to meet any GPA or ACT minimum scores.

**Financial data:** The stipend is $1,250 per year.

**Duration:** 1 year.

**Number awarded:** Varies each year.

**Deadline:** April of each year.

## 1197 WILLIAM D. SQUIRES SCHOLARSHIP

William D. Squires Educational Foundation, Inc., Attn: Scholarship Director
P.O. Box 2940
Jupiter, FL 33468-2940
Phone: (561) 741-7751; Email: wmdsef@msn.com

Web: www.mwmd-squires-foundatin.org

**Summary:** To provide financial assistance for college to financially-needy high school seniors in Ohio.

**Eligibility:** Open to graduating high school seniors in Ohio. Applicants must have clear career goals and "a burning desire to reach that goal." In addition to completing an extensive application, students must submit a personally-written essay, 2 sealed letters of recommendation, a current official high school transcript, and a complete and final copy of their SAR. All applicants must be able to demonstrate substantial financial need (at least $3,000 of need for their freshman year). Also considered in the selection process are academic potential (must have at least a 3.2 GPA), character, and motivation.

**Financial data:** The stipend is $3,000 per year.

**Duration:** 1 year; renewable for up to 3 additional years.

**Number awarded:** At least 10 each year.

**Deadline:** April of each year.

## 1198 WILLIAM L. BOYD, IV, FLORIDA RESIDENT ACCESS GRANTS

Florida Department of Education, Attn: Office of Student Financial Assistance
1940 North Monroe Street, Suite 70
Tallahassee, FL 32303-4759
Phone: (850) 410-5200; (888) 827-2004; Fax: (850) 487-1809;
Email: osfa@fldoe.org
Web: www.FloridaStudentFinancialAid.org

**Summary:** To provide financial assistance to students at private colleges and universities in Florida.

**Eligibility:** Open to full-time undergraduate students who are attending an eligible private nonprofit college or university in Florida and have been Florida residents for at least 1 year. Financial need is not considered in the selection process.

**Financial data:** The amount of the award is specified by the state legislature annually; actual amounts depend on the number of applicants and availability of funds.

**Duration:** Up to 9 semesters or 14 quarters, provided the student maintains full-time enrollment and a GPA of 2.0 or higher.

**Number awarded:** Varies each year; recently, this program provided 23,425 awards.

## 1199 WILLIAM MAY MEMORIAL SCHOLARSHIP

California Association for Postsecondary Education and Disability
Attn: Executive Assistant
71423 Biskra Road
Rancho Mirage, CA 92270
Phone: (760) 346-8206; Fax: (760) 340-5275; TTY: (760) 341-4084;
Email: caped2000@aol.com
Web: www.caped.net/scholarship.html

**Summary:** To provide financial assistance to undergraduate and graduate students in California who have a disability.

**Eligibility:** Open to students at public and private colleges and universities in California who have a disability. Undergraduates must have completed at least 6 semester credits and have a GPA of 2.5 or higher. Graduate students must have completed at least 3 semester units and have a GPA of 3.0 or higher. Applicants must submit a 1-page personal letter that demonstrates writing skills; progress toward meeting educational and vocational goals; how they accommodate their disability; involvement in community activities; and any other personal factor that might strengthen their application. They must also submit a letter of recommendation from a faculty person, verification of disability, official transcripts, proof of current enrollment, and documentation of financial need.

**Financial data:** The stipend is $1,000.

**Duration:** 1 year.

**Number awarded:** 1 each year.

**Deadline:** August of each year.

## 1200 WILLIAM R. GOLDFARB MEMORIAL SCHOLARSHIP

American Radio Relay League, Attn: ARRL Foundation
225 Main Street
Newington, CT 06111
Phone: (860) 594-0397; Fax: (860) 594-0259; Email: foundation@arrl.org
Web: www.arrl.org/arrlf

**Summary:** To provide financial assistance to licensed radio amateurs who are interested in working on an undergraduate degree.

**Eligibility:** Open to licensed radio amateurs of any class who have applied or been accepted for enrollment at an accredited institution of higher education.

Preference is given to students planning to major in computers, medicine, nursing, engineering, science, or a business-related field. Applicants must submit an essay on the role amateur radio has played in their lives and provide documentation of financial need.

**Financial data:** The stipend is at least $10,000.
**Duration:** 1 year.
**Number awarded:** 1 each year.
**Deadline:** January of each year.

### 1201 WILLIAM ZEKAN MEMORIAL SCHOLARSHIP

Arabian Horse Trust
12000 Zuni Street
Westminster, CO 80234-2300
Phone: (303) 450-4710; Fax: (303) 450-4707
Web: www.imh.org/imh/bw/arabian.html
**Summary:** To provide financial assistance to high school seniors who have been involved with horses and are interested in attending college.
**Eligibility:** Open to high school seniors who are able to demonstrate financial need and have an ongoing interest in and commitment to Arabian horses. Selection is based on both need and achievement.
**Financial data:** The stipend is $2,500.
**Duration:** 1 year; nonrenewable.
**Number awarded:** At least 1 each year.
**Deadline:** January of each year.

### 1202 WILSON WADE MEMORIAL SCHOLARSHIPS

California Masonic Foundation, Attn: Scholarship Coordinator
1111 California Street
San Francisco, CA 94108-2284
Phone: (415) 776-7000; (800) 900-2727; Fax: (415) 776-7170;
Email: gloffice@freemason.org
Web: www.freemason.org/programs_scholarship.php
**Summary:** To provide financial assistance to female high school seniors in California who are interested in attending a college in the state.
**Eligibility:** Open to graduating female high school seniors who have been residents of California for at least 1 year and have a GPA of 3.0 or higher. Applicants must be planning to attend a 4-year institution of higher education in California as a full-time freshman in the following fall. They must be U.S. citizens or permanent residents and able to show evidence of financial need. Along with their application, they must submit a personal essay outlining their background, goals, and scholastic achievements; a copy of their latest high school transcript; 2 letters of recommendation; documentation of financial need; SAT or ACT scores; and a copy of their college acceptance letter. Selection is based on academic achievement, applicant essay, and financial need. Preference is given to women who have a Masonic relationship or are members of Masonic youth groups.
**Financial data:** The amount of the stipend varies, depending on the availability of funds.
**Duration:** 1 year; may be renewed for up to 3 additional years.
**Number awarded:** Varies each year.
**Deadline:** February of each year for new applicants; April of each year for renewal applicants.

### 1203 WINGS OVER AMERICA SCHOLARSHIPS

Wings Over America Scholarship Foundation
1551 Dillingham Boulevard
Norfolk, VA 23511
Email: info@wingsoveramerica.us
Web: www.wingsoveramerica.us
**Summary:** To provide financial assistance for college to dependents of naval aviators.
**Eligibility:** Open to dependent children and spouses of naval air command personnel. Applicants must be planning to continue their education. Selection is based on academic merit, community service, and financial need.
**Financial data:** A stipend is awarded (amount not specified).
**Duration:** 1 year.
**Number awarded:** Varies each year; recently, 31 of these scholarships were awarded.

### 1204 WINNIE C. DAVIS CHILDREN OF THE CONFEDERACY SCHOLARSHIP

United Daughters of the Confederacy, Attn: Education Director

328 North Boulevard
Richmond, VA 23220-4057
Phone: (804) 355-1636; Fax: (804) 353-1396; Email: hqudc@rcn.com
Web: www.hqudc.org/scholarships/scholarships.html
**Summary:** To provide financial assistance for college to lineal descendants of Confederate veterans who are members of the Children of the Confederacy.
**Eligibility:** Open to lineal descendants of worthy Confederates or collateral descendants. Applicants must submit a family financial report and certified proof of the Confederate record of 1 ancestor, with the company and regiment in which he served. In addition, applicants themselves must be, or have been until age 18, participating members of the Children of the Confederacy. They must have at least a 3.0 GPA in high school.
**Financial data:** The amount of this scholarship depends on the availability of funds.
**Duration:** 1 year; may be renewed for up to 3 additional years.
**Number awarded:** 1 each year.
**Deadline:** March of each year.

### 1205 WISCONSIN ACADEMIC EXCELLENCE SCHOLARSHIP PROGRAM

Wisconsin Higher Educational Aids Board
131 West Wilson Street, Room 902
P.O. Box 7885
Madison, WI 53707-7885
Phone: (608) 267-2213; Fax: (608) 267-2808;
Email: nancy.wilkison@heab.state.wi.us
Web: heab.state.wi.us/programs.html
**Summary:** To provide financial assistance for college to Wisconsin high school seniors with the highest GPAs in their schools.
**Eligibility:** Open to seniors at each public and private high school throughout Wisconsin who have the highest GPAs. Applicants must plan to attend a branch of the University of Wisconsin, a Wisconsin technical college, or an independent institution in the state as a full-time student in the following fall.
**Financial data:** The awards provide full tuition, up to $2,250 per year, during the first 3 years of undergraduate study; for subsequent years, the maximum award is equal to full tuition and fees at a campus of the University of Wisconsin.
**Duration:** Up to 10 semesters.
**Number awarded:** The number of scholarships allotted to each high school is based on total student enrollment, ranging from 1 scholarship for schools with enrollment of 80 to 499 up to 6 scholarships for schools with enrollment greater than 2,500. Students at schools with enrollment less than 80 compete statewide for an additional 10 scholarships.

### 1206 WISCONSIN G.I. BILL

Wisconsin Department of Veterans Affairs
30 West Mifflin Street
P.O. Box 7843
Madison, WI 53707-7843
Phone: (608) 266-1311; (800) WIS-VETS; Fax: (608) 267-0403;
Email: wdvaweb@dva.state.wi.us
Web: dva.state.wi.us/Ben_education.asp
**Summary:** To provide financial assistance for college or graduate school to Wisconsin veterans and their dependents.
**Eligibility:** Open to current residents of Wisconsin who 1) were residents of the state when they entered or reentered active duty in the U.S. armed forces, or 2) have moved to the state and have been residents for any consecutive 12-month period after entry or reentry into service. Applicants must have served on active duty for at least 2 continuous years or for at least 90 days during specified wartime periods. Also eligible are 1) qualifying children and unremarried surviving spouses of Wisconsin veterans who died in the line of duty; and 2) children and spouses of Wisconsin veterans who have a service-connected disability rated by the U.S. Department of Veterans Affairs as 30% or greater. Children must be between 18 and 26 years of age (regardless of the date of the veteran's death or initial disability rating), be a Wisconsin resident for tuition purposes, and register as a full-time student. Spouses remain eligible for 10 years following the date of the veteran's death or initial disability rating; they must be Wisconsin residents for tuition purposes but they may enroll full or part time. Students may attend any institution, center, or school within the University of Wisconsin (UW) System or the Wisconsin Technical College System (WCTS). There are no income limits, delimiting periods following military service during which the benefit must be used, or limits on the level of study (e.g., vocational, undergraduate, professional, or graduate).
**Financial data:** Veterans who qualify as a Wisconsin resident for tuition pur-

poses are eligible for a remission of 50% of tuition and fees at a UW or WCTS institution. Veterans who qualify as a Wisconsin veteran for purposes of this program but for other reasons fail to meet the definition of a Wisconsin resident for tuition purposes at the UW system are eligible for a remission of 100% of non-resident fees. Spouses and children of deceased or disabled veterans are entitled to a remission of 100% of tuition and fees at a UW or WCTS institution.

**Duration:** Up to 8 semesters or 128 credits, whichever is greater.

**Number awarded:** Varies each year.

**Deadline:** Applications may be submitted at any time, but they should be received as early as possible prior to the intended date of enrollment.

## 1207 WISCONSIN HIGHER EDUCATION GRANT

Wisconsin Higher Educational Aids Board
131 West Wilson Street, Room 902
P.O. Box 7885
Madison, WI 53707-7885
Phone: (608) 266-0888; Fax: (608) 267-2808;
Email: sandy.thomas@heab.state.wi.us
Web: heab.state.wi.us/programs.html

**Summary:** To provide financial assistance to financially needy undergraduate students attending public institutions of higher education in Wisconsin.

**Eligibility:** Open to Wisconsin residents enrolled at least half time at any branch of the University of Wisconsin, at any vocational/technical institution in the state, or at any Tribal College in the state. Selection is based on financial need.

**Financial data:** Awards range from $250 to $1,800 per year.

**Duration:** Up to 10 semesters.

**Number awarded:** Varies each year.

## 1208 WISCONSIN JOB RETRAINING GRANTS

Wisconsin Department of Veterans Affairs
30 West Mifflin Street
P.O. Box 7843
Madison, WI 53707-7843
Phone: (608) 266-1311; (800) WIS-VETS; Fax: (608) 267-0403;
Email: wdvaweb@dva.state.wi.us
Web: dva.state.wi.us/Ben_retraininggrants.asp

**Summary:** To provide funds to recently unemployed Wisconsin veterans or their families who need financial assistance while being retrained for employment.

**Eligibility:** Open to current residents of Wisconsin who 1) were residents of the state when they entered or reentered active duty in the U.S. armed forces, or 2) have moved to the state and have been residents for any consecutive 12-month period after entry or reentry into service. Applicants must have served on active duty for at least 2 continuous years or for at least 90 days during specified wartime periods. Unremarried spouses and minor or dependent children of deceased veterans who would have been eligible for the grant if they were living today may also be eligible. The applicant must, within the year prior to the date of application, have become unemployed (involuntarily laid off or discharged, not due to willful misconduct) or underemployed (experienced an involuntary reduction of income). Underemployed applicants must have current annual income from employment that does not exceed federal poverty guidelines. All applicants must be retraining at accredited schools in Wisconsin or in a structured on-the-job program. Course work toward a college degree does not qualify. Training does not have to be full time, but the program must be completed within 2 years and must reasonably be expected to lead to employment.

**Financial data:** The maximum grant is $3,000 per year; the actual amount varies, depending upon the amount of the applicant's unmet need. In addition to books, fees, and tuition, the funds may be used for living expenses.

**Duration:** 1 year; may be renewed 1 additional year.

**Number awarded:** Varies each year.

**Deadline:** Applications may be submitted at any time.

## 1209 WISCONSIN LEGION AUXILIARY MERIT AND MEMORIAL SCHOLARSHIPS

American Legion Auxiliary
Department of Wisconsin, Attn: Department Secretary/Treasurer
2930 American Legion Drive
P.O. Box 140
Portage, WI 53901-0140
Phone: (608) 745-0124; (866) 664-3863; Fax: (608) 745-1947;
Email: alawi@amlegionauxwi.org
Web: www.amlegionauxwi.org

**Summary:** To provide financial assistance for college to Wisconsin residents who are the children or spouses of veterans.

**Eligibility:** Open to the children, wives, and widows of veterans who are high school seniors or graduates with a GPA of 3.2 or higher. Grandchildren and great-grandchildren of veterans are eligible if they are members of the American Legion Auxiliary. Applicants must be able to demonstrate financial need and be residents of Wisconsin, although they do not need to attend college in the state. Along with their application, they must submit a 300-word essay on "Education-An Investment in the Future."

**Financial data:** The stipend is $1,000.

**Duration:** 1 year; nonrenewable.

**Number awarded:** 6 each year.

**Deadline:** March of each year.

## 1210 WISCONSIN MINORITY UNDERGRADUATE RETENTION GRANTS

Wisconsin Higher Educational Aids Board
131 West Wilson Street, Room 902
P.O. Box 7885
Madison, WI 53707-7885
Phone: (608) 267-2212; Fax: (608) 267-2808;
Email: mary.kuzdas@heab.state.wi.us
Web: heab.state.wi.us/programs.html

**Summary:** To provide financial assistance to minorities in Wisconsin who are currently enrolled in college.

**Eligibility:** Open to African Americans, Hispanic Americans, and American Indians in Wisconsin who are enrolled as sophomores, juniors, seniors, or fifth-year undergraduates in a 4-year nonprofit institution or as second-year students in a 2-year program at a public vocational institution in the state. Grants are also available to students who were admitted to the United States after December 31, 1975 and who are a former citizen of Laos, Vietnam, or Cambodia or whose ancestor was a citizen of 1 of those countries. They must be nominated by their institution and be able to demonstrate financial need.

**Financial data:** Stipends range from $250 to $2,500 per year, depending on the need of the recipient.

**Duration:** Up to 4 years.

**Number awarded:** Varies each year.

**Deadline:** Deadline dates vary by institution; check with your school's financial aid office.

## 1211 WISCONSIN TALENT INCENTIVE PROGRAM (TIP) GRANTS

Wisconsin Higher Educational Aids Board
131 West Wilson Street, Room 902
P.O. Box 7885
Madison, WI 53707-7885
Phone: (608) 266-1665; Fax: (608) 267-2808;
Email: john.whitt@heab.state.wi.us
Web: heab.state.wi.us/programs.html

**Summary:** To provide financial assistance for college to needy and educationally disadvantaged students in Wisconsin.

**Eligibility:** Open to residents of Wisconsin entering a college or university in the state who meet requirements of both financial need and educational disadvantage. Financial need qualifications include 1) family contribution (a dependent student whose expected parent contribution is $200 or less, an independent student with dependents whose academic year contribution is $200 or less, or an independent student with no dependents whose maximum contribution is $200 or less); 2) TANF or W2 benefits (a dependent student whose family is receiving TANF or W2 benefits or an independent student who is receiving TANF or W2 benefits); or 3) unemployment (a dependent student whose parents are ineligible for unemployment compensation and have no current income from employment, or an independent student and spouse, if married, who are ineligible for unemployment compensation and have no current income from employment). Educational disadvantage qualifications include students who are 1) minorities (African American, Native American, Hispanic, or southeast Asian); 2) enrolled in a special academic support program due to insufficient academic preparation; 3) a first-generation college student (neither parent graduated from a 4-year college or university); 4) disabled according to the Department of Workforce Development, Division of Vocational Rehabilitation or according to a Wisconsin college or university that uses the Americans with Disabilities Act definition; 5) currently or formerly incarcerated in a correctional institution; or 6) from an environmental and academic background that deters the pursuit of educational plans. Students already in college are not eligible.

**Financial data:** Grants range up to $1,800 per year.

**Duration:** 1 year; may be renewed up to 4 additional years provided the recipient continues to be a Wisconsin resident enrolled at least half time in a degree or certificate program, makes satisfactory academic progress, demonstrates financial need, and remains enrolled continuously from semester to semester and from year to year. If recipients withdraw from school or cease to attend classes for any reason (other than medical necessity), they may not reapply.

**Number awarded:** Varies each year.

### 1212 WISCONSIN TUITION GRANT

Wisconsin Higher Educational Aids Board
131 West Wilson Street, Room 902
P.O. Box 7885
Madison, WI 53707-7885
Phone: (608) 267-2212; Fax: (608) 267-2808;
Email: mary.kuzdas@heab.state.wi.us
Web: heab.state.wi.us/programs.html

**Summary:** To provide assistance to financially needy undergraduate students attending private institutions of higher education in Wisconsin.

**Eligibility:** Open to Wisconsin residents enrolled in independent nonprofit colleges and universities in Wisconsin. Selection is based on financial need.

**Financial data:** Awards are based on financial need, but may not exceed tuition charged at the University of Wisconsin at Madison.

**Duration:** Up to 10 semesters.

**Number awarded:** Varies each year.

### 1213 WISCONSIN VETERANS EDUCATION (VETED) REIMBURSEMENT GRANTS

Wisconsin Department of Veterans Affairs
30 West Mifflin Street
P.O. Box 7843
Madison, WI 53707-7843
Phone: (608) 266-1311; (800) WIS-VETS; Fax: (608) 267-0403;
Email: wdvaweb@dva.state.wi.us
Web: dva.state.wi.us/Ben_VetEd.asp

**Summary:** To provide financial assistance for undergraduate education to Wisconsin veterans.

**Eligibility:** Open to current residents of Wisconsin who 1) were residents of the state when they entered or reentered active duty in the U.S. armed forces, or 2) have moved to the state and have been residents for any consecutive 12-month period after entry or reentry into service. Applicants must have served on active duty for at least 2 continuous years or for at least 90 days during specified wartime periods. They must be working full or part time on a degree, certificate of graduation, or course completion at an eligible campus of the University of Wisconsin, technical college, or approved private institution of higher education in Wisconsin or Minnesota. Their household income must be below $50,000 plus $1,000 for each dependent in excess of 2 dependents. Veterans seeking reimbursement through this program must first apply for Wisconsin G.I. Bill benefits. To qualify for reimbursement, they must achieve at least a 2.0 GPA or an average grade of "C" in the semester for which reimbursement is requested. Veterans may use this program up to 10 years after leaving active duty. Once a veteran reaches the 10-year delimiting date, he or she may "bank" up to 60 unused credits for part-time study.

**Financial data:** Eligible veterans are entitled to reimbursement of 100% of the costs of tuition and fees not covered by other grants, scholarships, or remissions, to a maximum of the UW-Madison rate for the same number of credits.

**Duration:** The amount of reimbursement depends on the time the veteran served on active duty: 30 credits or 2 semesters for 90 to 180 days of active service, 60 credits or 4 semesters for 181 to 730 days of active service, or 120 credits or 8 semesters for 731 days or more of active service.

**Number awarded:** Varies each year.

**Deadline:** Veterans must make a pre-application within 30 days of the start of the semester or term to be eligible for reimbursement. End of semester applications must be received within 60 days of the end of the semester or term.

### 1214 WOMEN MARINES ASSOCIATION SCHOLARSHIP PROGRAM

Women Marines Association
P.O. Box 8405
Falls Church, VA 22041-8405
Email: wma@womenmarines.org
Web: www.womenmarines.org/scholarships.php

**Summary:** To provide financial assistance for college or graduate school to students sponsored by members of the Women Marines Association (WMA).

**Eligibility:** Open to applicants sponsored by a WMA member who fall into 1 of the following categories: 1) have served or are serving in the U.S. Marine Corps, regular or Reserve; 2) are a direct descendant by blood, legal adoption, or stepchild of a Marine on active duty or who has served honorably in the U.S. Marine Corps, regular or Reserve; 3) are a sibling or a descendant of a sibling by blood, legal adoption, or stepchild of a Marine on active duty or who has served honorably in the U.S. Marine Corps, regular or Reserve; or 4) have completed 2 years in a Marine Corps JROTC program. No WMA member is allowed to sponsor more than 1 applicant per year. High school applicants must have maintained at least a "B+" average for their sophomore, junior, and first semester of their senior year of high school and must have a combined mathematics and verbal ACT score of at least 25 or an equivalent score on the SAT. Graduate students are also eligible.

**Financial data:** The stipend is $1,500.

**Duration:** 1 year.

**Number awarded:** Varies each year.

**Deadline:** March of each year.

### 1215 WOMEN OF THE ELCA SCHOLARSHIP PROGRAM

Women of the Evangelical Lutheran Church in America, Attn: Scholarships
8765 West Higgins Road
Chicago, IL 60631-4189
Phone: (773) 380-2730; (800) 638-3522, ext. 2730; Fax: (773) 380-2419;
Email: womenelca@elca.org
Web: www.womenoftheelca.org/whatwedo/scholarships.html

**Summary:** To provide financial assistance to lay women who are members of Evangelical Lutheran Church of America (ELCA) congregations and who wish to take classes on the undergraduate, graduate, professional, or vocational school level.

**Eligibility:** Open to ELCA lay women who are at least 21 years of age and have experienced an interruption of at least 2 years in their education since high school. Applicants must have been admitted to an educational institution to prepare for a career in other than a church-certified profession. They may be working on an undergraduate, graduate, professional, or vocational school degree. U.S. citizenship is required.

**Financial data:** The amounts of the awards depend on the availability of funds.

**Duration:** Up to 2 years.

**Number awarded:** Varies each year, depending upon the funds available.

**Deadline:** February of each year.

### 1216 WOMEN'S ARMY CORPS VETERANS' ASSOCIATION SCHOLARSHIP

Women's Army Corps Veterans' Association
P.O. Box 5577
Fort McClellan, AL 36205-5577
Email: info@armywomen.org
Web: www.armywomen.org

**Summary:** To provide financial assistance for college to the relatives of Army military women.

**Eligibility:** Open to high school seniors who are the children, grandchildren, nieces, or nephews of Army service women. Applicants must have a cumulative GPA of 3.5 or higher and be planning to enroll as a full-time student at an accredited college or university in the United States. They must submit a 500-word biographical sketch that includes their future goals and how the scholarship would be used. Selection is based on academic achievement, leadership ability as expressed through cocurricular activities and community involvement, the biographical sketch, and recommendations. Financial need is not considered in the selection process.

**Financial data:** The stipend is $1,500.

**Duration:** 1 year.

**Number awarded:** 1 or more each year.

**Deadline:** April of each year.

### 1217 WOMEN'S BASKETBALL COACHES ASSOCIATION SCHOLARSHIP AWARDS

Women's Basketball Coaches Association
Attn: Manager of Office Administration and Awards
4646 Lawrenceville Highway
Lilburn, GA 30247-3620
Phone: (770) 279-8027, ext. 102; Fax: (770) 279-8473;
Email: wwade@wbca.org
Web: www.wbca.org/WBCAScholarAward.asp

**Summary:** To provide financial assistance for undergraduate or graduate study to women's basketball players.

**Eligibility:** Open to women's basketball players who are competing in any of the 4 intercollegiate divisions (NCAA Divisions I, II, and III, and NAIA). Applicants must be interested in completing an undergraduate degree or beginning work on an advanced degree. They must be nominated by a member of the Women's Basketball Coaches Association (WBCA). Selection is based on sportsmanship, commitment to excellence as a student-athlete, honesty, ethical behavior, courage, and dedication to purpose.

**Financial data:** The stipend is $1,000 per year.

**Duration:** 1 year.

**Number awarded:** 2 each year.

## 1218 WOMEN'S INDEPENDENCE SCHOLARSHIP PROGRAM

Sunshine Lady Foundation, Inc., Attn: WISP Program
4900 Randall Parkway, Suite H
Wilmington, NC 28403
Phone: (910) 397-7742; (866) 255-7742; Fax: (910) 397-0023;
Email: nancy@sunshineladyfdn.org
Web: www.sunshineladyfdn.org/wisp.htm

**Summary:** To provide financial assistance for college or graduate school to women who are victims of partner abuse.

**Eligibility:** Open to women who are victims of partner abuse and have worked for at least 1 month with a nonprofit domestic violence victim services provider that is willing to sponsor them. Applicants must be interested in attending a vocational school, community college, 4-year college or university, or (in exceptional circumstances) graduate school as a full or part time student. They should have left an abusive partner within the past 2 years; women who have been parted from their batterer for more than 2 years are also eligible but funding for such applicants may be limited. Preference is given to single mothers with young children. Special consideration is given to applicants who plan to use their education to further the rights of, and options for, women and girls. Selection is based primarily on financial need.

**Financial data:** Stipends depend on the need of the recipient, but they are at least $250 and average $2,500. First priority is given to funding for direct educational expenses (tuition, books, and fees), which is paid directly to the educational institution. Second priority is for assistance in reducing indirect financial barriers to education (e.g., child care, transportation), which is paid directly to the sponsoring agency.

**Duration:** 1 year; may be renewed if the recipient maintains a GPA of 3.0 or higher.

**Number awarded:** Varies each year.

**Deadline:** Applications may be submitted at any time, but they must be received at least 3 months before the start of the intended program.

## 1219 WOMEN'S OPPORTUNITY AWARDS PROGRAM

Soroptimist International of the Americas, Attn: Program Department
1709 Spruce Street
Philadelphia, PA 19103-6103
Phone: (215) 893-9000; Fax: (215) 893-5200; Email: siahq@soroptimist.org
Web: www.soroptimist.org

**Summary:** To help women reentering the job market upgrade their employment status through education.

**Eligibility:** Open to mature women who are the heads of their households with financial responsibility for their family. They may be interested in vocational or technical training or completing an undergraduate degree. Applicants must describe their career goals, how those relate to their educational or training goals, the economic and social barriers and personal hardships they have faced, and their financial need.

**Financial data:** Awards are $10,000, $5,000, or $3,000.

**Duration:** The awards are issued each year and are nonrenewable.

**Number awarded:** In each of the 28 regions, the winner receives an award of $5,000; most regions grant additional $3,000 awards. From among the regional winners, 3 receive an additional award of $10,000 from Soroptimist International of the Americas. Since the program was established, about 1,640 women have been assisted.

**Deadline:** Applications must be submitted to local clubs by December of each year.

## 1220 WOMEN'S OVERSEAS SERVICE LEAGUE SCHOLARSHIPS FOR WOMEN

Women's Overseas Service League
P.O. Box 7124
Washington, DC 20044-7124

**Summary:** To provide financial assistance for college to women who are committed to a military or other public service career.

**Eligibility:** Open to women who are committed to a military or other public service career. Applicants must have completed at least 12 semester or 18 quarter hours of postsecondary study with at a GPA of 2.5 or higher. They must be working on an academic degree (the program may be professional or technical in nature) and must agree to enroll for at least 6 semester or 9 quarter hours of study each academic period. Along with their application, they must submit an official transcript, a 1-page description of career goals, 3 current letters of reference, and a brief statement describing sources of financial support and the need for scholarship assistance. They must also provide information on their educational background, employment experience, civic and volunteer activities, and expected degree completion date.

**Financial data:** Stipends range from $500 to $1,000 per year.

**Duration:** 1 year; may be renewed 1 additional year.

**Deadline:** February of each year.

## 1221 W.P. BLACK FUND SCHOLARSHIPS

Greater Kanawha Valley Foundation, Attn: Scholarship Coordinator
1600 Huntington Square
900 Lee Street, East
P.O. Box 3041
Charleston, WV 25331-3041
Phone: (304) 346-3620; Fax: (304) 346-3640; Email: tgkvf@tgkvf.com
Web: www.tgkvf.com/scholar.html

**Summary:** To provide financial assistance for college to residents of West Virginia.

**Eligibility:** Open to residents of West Virginia who are attending or planning to attend a college or university anywhere in the country. Applicants must have an ACT score of 20 or higher, be able to demonstrate good moral character and extreme financial need, and have a GPA of 2.5 or higher.

**Financial data:** The stipend is $1,000 per year.

**Duration:** 1 year; may be renewed.

**Number awarded:** Varies each year; recently, 114 of these scholarships were awarded.

**Deadline:** February of each year.

## 1222 WSCA/TCF BANK SCHOLARSHIP

Wisconsin School Counselor Association
c/o Elizabeth Disch, Scholarship Chair
300 12th Avenue
P.O. Box 252
New Glarus, WI 53574
Phone: (608) 967-2372
Web: www.wscaweb.com

**Summary:** To provide financial assistance for college to high school seniors in Wisconsin.

**Eligibility:** Open to graduating seniors at public and private high schools in Wisconsin. Applicants must be planning to attend a 2-year or 4-year college or university. Along with their application, they must submit a 1-page essay describing how a school counselor or school counseling program has helped them plan, decide, resolve, or grow in some area of their life.

**Financial data:** The stipend is $1,000.

**Duration:** 1 year.

**Number awarded:** 4 each year.

**Deadline:** November of each year.

## 1223 WYOMING GRAND LODGE SCHOLARSHIPS

Grand Lodge A.F. & A.M. of Wyoming, Attn: Grand Secretary
P.O. Box 459
Casper, WY 82602
Phone: (307) 234-2692; Fax: (307) 234-7922;
Email: grandsecretary@wyomingmasons.com
Web: wy-srmason.org/scholarships.htm

**Summary:** To provide financial assistance for college to residents of Wyoming.

**Eligibility:** Open to Wyoming residents who are enrolled or planning to enroll in a college or university. Applicants must submit a 1-paragraph statement on their occupational and life goals. Selection is based on that statement, academic achievement, extracurricular activities, civic and community activities, outstanding achievements, work experience, and financial need.

**Financial data:** The stipend is $1,000. Funds are paid to the financial office the recipient attends.

**Duration:** 1 year.

**Number awarded:** Approximately 30 each year.

**Deadline:** April of each year.

## 1224 WYOMING SCOTTISH RITE FOUNDATION SCHOLARSHIPS

Scottish Rite Foundation of Wyoming
1820 Capitol Avenue
Cheyenne, WY 82001

**Summary:** To provide financial assistance to students currently enrolled in their second year in a Wyoming community college.

**Eligibility:** Open to community college students in Wyoming. Each community college may recommend 6 applicants or more. Nominees must be graduates of a Wyoming high school or hold a Wyoming GED. They must have sophomore standing at a Wyoming community college and be enrolled full time. Selection is based on leadership potential activities, GPA, and financial need.

**Financial data:** The stipend is $1,000.

**Duration:** 1 year.

**Number awarded:** 7 each year.

**Deadline:** May of each year.

## 1225 WYOMING VIETNAM VETERANS' AWARDS

University of Wyoming, Attn: Office of Student Financial Aid
Department 3335
1000 East University Avenue
Laramie, WY 82071
Phone: (307) 766-3016; Fax: (307) 766-3800; Email: finaid@uwyo.edu
Web: uwadmnweb.uwyo.edu/sfa/Vet/vietnam.asp

**Summary:** To provide financial assistance for college to Wyoming veterans who served during the Vietnam era.

**Eligibility:** Open to Wyoming veterans who 1) served on active duty with the U.S. armed forces between August 5, 1964 and May 7, 1975; 2) received a Vietnam service medal between those dates; 3) received an honorable discharge; 4) have lived in Wyoming for at least 1 year; and 5) have exhausted their veterans' benefits entitlement or for some other reason are no longer eligible for U.S. Department of Veterans Affairs benefits.

**Financial data:** Qualifying veterans may be eligible for free resident tuition at the University of Wyoming or at any of the state's community colleges.

**Duration:** Up to 10 semesters.

**Number awarded:** Varies each year.

**Deadline:** Applications may be submitted at any time, but they should be received 2 or 3 weeks before the beginning of the semester.

## 1226 WYOMING WAR ORPHANS SCHOLARSHIPS

University of Wyoming, Attn: Office of Student Financial Aid
Department 3335
1000 East University Avenue
Laramie, WY 82071
Phone: (307) 766-3016; Fax: (307) 766-3800; Email: finaid@uwyo.edu
Web: uwadmnweb.uwyo.edu/sfa

**Summary:** To provide financial assistance for college to children of deceased, POW, or MIA Wyoming veterans.

**Eligibility:** Open to children of veterans whose parent was a resident of Wyoming at the time of entering service and 1) died while in service during a period of war defined by law; 2) is listed officially as being a POW or MIA in the Korean or Vietnam conflicts; or 3) was honorably discharged from the military and subsequently died of an injury or disease incurred while in service and was a Wyoming resident at the time of death. Applicants must be attending or planning to attend the University of Wyoming or a community college in the state.

**Financial data:** Qualifying veterans' children may be eligible for free resident tuition at the University of Wyoming or at any of the state's community colleges.

**Duration:** Up to 10 semesters.

**Number awarded:** Varies each year.

**Deadline:** Applications may be submitted at any time, but they should be received 2 or 3 weeks before the beginning of the semester.

## 1227 YOSHIYAMA AWARD FOR EXEMPLARY SERVICE TO THE COMMUNITY

Hitachi Foundation

1509 22nd Street, N.W.
Washington, DC 20037-1073
Phone: (202) 457-0588, ext. 598; Fax: (202) 296-1098
Web: www.hitachifoundation.org/yoshiyama/index.html

**Summary:** To recognize and reward high school seniors for outstanding community service.

**Eligibility:** Open to graduating high school seniors. Anyone other than a family member or relative may nominate a student. Nominees must have provided community service activities that have impacted a socially, economically, or culturally isolated area. Their activities must have 1) created longer-term, sustainable social change; 2) surpassed what is ordinarily expected of a socially responsible citizen; 3) demonstrated self-motivation, leadership, creativity, dedication, and commitment to pursuing service; and 4) made a conscious effort to involve and inspire others to participate in community action. Selection is based on the significance and extent of the candidate's community service and the relevance of those activities to solving serious community and societal problems; GPA, SAT scores, and school club memberships are not considered.

**Financial data:** The award is $2,500 per year.

**Duration:** Funds are dispersed over a 2-year period.

**Number awarded:** 10 each year.

**Deadline:** March of each year.

## 1228 YOUNG AMERICAN AWARDS

Boy Scouts of America, Attn: Learning for Life Division, S210
1325 West Walnut Hill Lane
P.O. Box 152079
Irving, TX 75015-2079
Phone: (972) 580-2418; Fax: (972) 580-2137
Web: www.learning-for-life.org/exploring/scholarships/index.html

**Summary:** To recognize and reward young adults who demonstrate exceptional achievement and service.

**Eligibility:** Open to students between 15 and 25 years of age who are currently enrolled in high school, college, or graduate school. Candidates must be nominated by a Boy Scout troop, Explorer post, Venturing crew, Learning for Life group, individual, or other community youth-serving organization that shares the same program objectives. Nominees must have 1) achieved exceptional excellence in 1 or more fields, such as art, athletics, business, community service, education, government, humanities, literature, music, religion, or science; 2) be involved in service in their community, state, or country that adds to the quality of life; and 3) have maintained an above-average GPA. They must submit high school and college transcripts (graduate students need to submit only college transcripts) and at least 3 letters of recommendation. Nominations must be submitted to a local Boy Scout council, but nominees are not required to be a participant in a council unit or program.

**Financial data:** The award is $5,000. Local councils may also provide awards to their nominees.

**Duration:** The awards are presented annually.

**Number awarded:** 5 each year.

**Deadline:** Nominations must be submitted by December of each year.

## 1229 YOUNG SCHOLARS PROGRAM

Pauline S. Young Scholarship Foundation
115 West Short Street
Lexington, KY 40507
Email: Info@KyScholarships.org
Web: www.KyScholarships.org

**Summary:** To provide financial assistance to Kentucky high school seniors who plan to attend a college or university in the state.

**Eligibility:** Open to seniors graduating from high schools in Kentucky. Applicants must be planning to attend a college or university in the state. Selection is based primarily on financial need.

**Financial data:** The stipend is equivalent to the cost of attending the University of Kentucky (although recipients are not required to attend that university).

**Duration:** 1 year.

**Number awarded:** Varies each year; recently, 6 of these scholarships were awarded.

**Deadline:** April of each year.

## 1230 YOUTH EXCEL AWARD PROGRAM

Amateur Athletic Union, Attn: National Headquarters
Hotel Plaza Boulevard
P.O. Box 22409

Lake Buena Vista, FL 32830
Phone: (407) 934-7200; (800) AAU-4USA; Fax: (407) 934-7242;
Email: melissa@aausports.org
Web: www.aausports.org
**Summary:** To provide financial assistance for college to high school senior student-athletes who have achieved "excellence in athletics and academics, despite adversity."
**Eligibility:** Open to high school seniors who are student-athletes and can demonstrate excellence in athletics and academics, despite adversity. Applicants must have at least a 2.5 GPA, have participated in at least 1 sanctioned high school sport, and have been active in their community. Interested students must submit a completed application form and an essay describing their life experiences, focusing on the goals they have achieved and the obstacles they have overcome to reach those goals. Financial need is not considered in the selection process.
**Financial data:** Stipends are $3,500, $1,000, and $500.
**Duration:** 1 year.
**Number awarded:** 3 each year.
**Deadline:** December of each year.

---

## 1231 YOUTH OPPORTUNITIES FUND SCHOLARSHIPS

Key Club International, Attn: Manager of Youth Funds
3636 Woodview Trace
Indianapolis, IN 46268-3196
Phone: (317) 875-8755, ext. 244; (800) KIWANIS, ext. 244;
Fax: (317) 879-0204; Email: youthfunds@kiwanis.org
Web: www.keyclub.org
**Summary:** To provide financial assistance for college to high school seniors who are Key Club International members.
**Eligibility:** Open to college-bound graduating high school members who have completed at least 100 service hours during their Key Club career and have held an elected officer position on the club, district, or international level. Applicants must have a GPA of 3.5 or higher. Along with their application, they must submit 1) a 500-word essay describing the Key Club service project on which they have participated and that has had the greatest impact on them; 2) a list of high school organizations and activities; 3) a list of religious and community activities; 4) a list of honors, awards, and special recognitions; and 5) 2 letters of recommendation. Financial need is not considered in the selection process.
**Financial data:** The stipend is $1,000 per year.
**Duration:** 4 years.
**Number awarded:** 1 each year.
**Deadline:** February of each year.

---

## 1232 YUTAKA NAKAZAWA MEMORIAL SCHOLARSHIP

Japanese American Citizens League, Attn: National Scholarship Awards
1765 Sutter Street
San Francisco, CA 94115
Phone: (415) 921-5225; Fax: (415) 931-4671; Email: jacl@jacl.org
Web: www.jacl.org/scholarships.html
**Summary:** To provide financial assistance for college to student members of the Japanese American Citizens League (JACL) who are high school seniors.
**Eligibility:** Open to JACL members who are high school seniors interested in attending a college, university, trade school, business college, or other institution of higher learning. Applicants must submit a statement describing their current level of involvement in the Japanese American community or Asian Pacific community and how they will continue their involvement in future years. Selection is based on academic record, extracurricular activities, and community involvement.
**Financial data:** The stipend depends on the availability of funds but usually ranges from $1,000 to $5,000.
**Duration:** 1 year; nonrenewable.
**Number awarded:** 1 each year.
**Deadline:** February of each year.

---

## 1233 10TH MOUNTAIN DIVISION DESCENDANT MERIT SCHOLARSHIP

10th Mountain Division Descendants, Inc.
c/o Val Rios
6816 South Maple
Fresno, CA 93725
Phone: (559) 834-6230; Email: vrios913@aol.com

Web: www.10thmtndivdesc.org/scholarship.htm
**Summary:** To provide financial assistance for college to descendants of former members of the 10th Mountain Division.
**Eligibility:** Open to the descendants of veterans who served in the 10th Mountain Division during World War II. Applicants must be entering their first year of college. Selection is based on service to the World War II 10th Mountain Division (e.g., assisting at local chapter functions, involved in activities that support the legacy of the division, assisting at memorial services to the division, visiting veterans and/or wives or widows in nursing or private homes). Financial need is not considered. Membership in 10th Mountain Division Descendants, Inc. is not required, but it is recommended that the applicant or a parent be a member.
**Financial data:** The stipend is $1,000.
**Duration:** 1 year.
**Number awarded:** 1 each year.
**Deadline:** May of each year.

---

## 1234 100 BLACK MEN OF AMERICA NATIONAL SCHOLARSHIP PROGRAM

100 Black Men of America, Inc., Attn: Scholarship Administrator
141 Auburn Avenue
Atlanta, GA 30303
Phone: (404) 688-5100; (800) 598-3411; Fax: (404) 688-1028
Web: www.100blackmen.org
**Summary:** To provide financial assistance for college to high school seniors and current undergraduates who submit essays on topics related to African Americans, particularly African American males.
**Eligibility:** Open to high school seniors and undergraduates who are attending or planning to attend an accredited postsecondary institution as a full-time student. Applicants must submit a 600-word essay on 1 of the following topics: 1) what is the state of the African American male; 2) why are the academic results of African American youth in grades K-12 in the areas of reading and mathematics below the national average and what strategies do they believe school systems should implement to improve those statistics; 3) how should the African American community address the nation's current economic slow down; or 4) how would they define and address the current problem of race relations in America. They must have a GPA of 2.5 or higher and have completed at least 50 hours of active community service within the past 12 months. Financial need is not considered in the selection process.
**Financial data:** Stipends range from $1,000 to $3,000 and are paid directly to the institution.
**Duration:** 1 year.
**Number awarded:** Varies each year.
**Deadline:** February of each year.

---

## 1235 11TH ARMORED CAVALRY VETERANS OF VIETNAM AND CAMBODIA SCHOLARSHIP

11th Armored Cavalry Veterans of Vietnam and Cambodia
c/o Gene Johnson, Scholarship Committee Chair
3335 Casey Drive, Number 6-101
Las Vegas, NV 89120-1183
Phone: (702) 456-3218; Email: gene677@aol.com
Web: www.11thcavnam.com/scholar.html
**Summary:** To provide financial assistance to members of the 11th Armored Cavalry Veterans of Vietnam and Cambodia (ACVVC) and to their dependents.
**Eligibility:** Open to 11th ACVVC members and to their dependents. In addition, dependents of deceased troopers who served with the 11th Armored Cavalry in Vietnam or Cambodia may apply (a copy of the father's obituary must be supplied). Affiliation with the cavalry must be documented. Applicants must submit brief essays on 1) the field of study they plan to enter and why; and 2) why they would be a worthy recipient of this scholarship. Selection is based on the essays and grades; financial need is no longer considered. Priority is given to children of members who were killed in action or died of wounds.
**Financial data:** The stipend is $3,000; funds are paid directly to the recipient's school, in 2 equal installments.
**Duration:** 1 year; nonrenewable.
**Number awarded:** Varies each year; recently, 25 of these scholarships were awarded.
**Deadline:** May of each year.

## 1236 7TH GENERATION COMMUNITY SERVICE CORPORATION SCHOLARSHIP PROGRAM

7th Generation Community Service Corporation, Attn: Scholarship Program
4495 South Hopkins Avenue, Suite A
Titusville, FL 32780
Phone: (321) 385-0207; (888) 385-0207; Fax: (321) 385-1586;
Email: Info@7thGeneration.org
Web: www.7thgeneration.org/Scholarships.asp

**Summary:** To provide financial assistance to Native American students entering college for the first time.

**Eligibility:** Open to Native Americans who are under 21 years of age and graduating high school seniors or entering a 2-year or 4-year college or university as a full time student for the first time. Applicants must be tribally enrolled or have a Certificate of Degree of Indian Blood (CDIB) card. They must rank in the top quarter of their high school class and have a GPA of 3.25 or higher. Selection is based primarily on financial need. Applications are accepted beginning in mid-October of each year. Only the first 350 that are received are considered.

**Financial data:** Stipends depend on the need of the recipient, to a maximum of $20,000.

**Duration:** 1 year; may be renewed up to 3 additional years if the recipient maintains a GPA of 2.5 or higher.

**Number awarded:** 1 each year.

**Deadline:** January of each year.

# Humanities

## 1237 ABC HISPANIC SCHOLARSHIP FUNDS

American Baptist Churches USA, Attn: National Ministries
P.O. Box 851
Valley Forge, PA 19482-0851
Phone: (610) 768-2067; (800) ABC-3USA, ext. 2067; Fax: (610) 768-2453;
Email: karen.drummond@abc-usa.org
Web: www.nationalministries.org/financial-aid/student_info.cfm

**Summary:** To provide financial assistance to Hispanic Americans who are interested in preparing for or furthering a church career in the American Baptist Church (ABC).

**Eligibility:** Open to Hispanic American members of the church or its recognized institutions who demonstrate financial need. They must be enrolled on at least a two-thirds basis in an accredited institution, working on an undergraduate degree or first professional degree in a seminary. Applicants must be currently serving or planning to serve in a vocation with the church or with its recognized institutions. They must be U.S. citizens who have been a member of an American Baptist Church for at least 1 year.

**Financial data:** The stipends range from $500 to $3,000 per year.

**Duration:** 1 year; may be renewed.

**Deadline:** May of each year.

## 1238 ABE VORON SCHOLARSHIP

Broadcast Education Association, Attn: Scholarships
1771 N Street, N.W.
Washington, DC 20036-2891
Phone: (202) 429-5354; (888) 380-7222; Email: beainfo@beaweb.org
Web: www.beaweb.org/scholarships.html

**Summary:** To provide financial assistance to upper-division and graduate students who are interested in preparing for a career in radio broadcasting.

**Eligibility:** Open to juniors, seniors, and graduate students enrolled full time at a college or university where at least 1 department is an institutional member of the Broadcast Education Association. Applicants must be studying for a career in radio. Selection is based on evidence that the applicant possesses integrity, superior academic ability, potential to be an outstanding electronic media professional, and a sense of personal and professional responsibility.

**Financial data:** The stipend is $5,000.

**Duration:** 1 year; may not be renewed.

**Number awarded:** 1 each year.

**Deadline:** September of each year.

## 1239 ACADEMY OF TELEVISION ARTS & SCIENCES COLLEGE TELEVISION AWARDS

Academy of Television Arts & Sciences Foundation
Attn: Education Department
5220 Lankershim Boulevard
North Hollywood, CA 91601-3109
Phone: (818) 754-2830; Fax: (818) 761-ATAS;
Email: collegeawards@emmys.org
Web: www.emmys.tv/foundation/collegetvawards.php

**Summary:** To recognize and reward outstanding college student videos.

**Eligibility:** Open to full-time undergraduate and graduate students who have produced videos for course credit during the preceding 15 months. U.S. citizenship is not required, but all applicants must be enrolled at colleges and universities in the United States. All entries must be submitted on Beta, Beta SP, VHS, or DVD. Competitions are held in the following categories: 1) comedy; 2) drama; 3) music programs; 4) documentary; 5) newscasts; 6) magazine shows; 7) traditional animation; 8) nontraditional or computer-generated animation; and 9) children's programs. The maximum length is 1 hour (30 minutes for newscasts, magazine shows, comedy, and children's programs entries).

**Financial data:** The awards per category are: first place, $2,000; second place, $1,000; and third place, $500. In addition, each of the first- and second-place winners receive Eastman Product Grants ($2,000 of Kodak film stock for the first-place winner and $1,000 of film stock for the second-place winner). The Seymour Bricker College Award of $4,000 is also presented to the first-place College Award winner from any category whose work best represents a humanitarian concern.

**Duration:** The competition is held annually.

**Number awarded:** 23 each year: 1 first-place winner, 1 second-place winner, and 1 third-place winner in each category except music programs and children's programs (1 award only in each of those 2 categories).

**Deadline:** December of each year.

## 1240 ACL/NJCL NATIONAL GREEK EXAMINATION SCHOLARSHIP

American Classical League, Attn: National Greek Examination
Miami University
422 Wells Mill Drive
Oxford, OH 45056
Phone: (513) 529-7741; Fax: (513) 529-7742; Email: info@aclclassics.org
Web: www.aclclassics.org

**Summary:** To recognize and reward students who achieve high scores on the National Greek Examination.

**Eligibility:** Open to high school and college students studying Greek. High school teachers and college instructors may order copies of the National Greek Examination for their students who are enrolled in first year (elementary), second year (intermediate), or third year (advanced) Attic or Homeric Greek. The examinations consist of 40 multiple choice questions at 5 levels: beginning Attic (high school seniors only), intermediate Attic (first-year college and advanced high school students), Attic prose, Attic tragedy, and Homeric (*Odyssey*). The top scorers on each examination receive purple ribbons, followed by blue, red, and green ribbons. High school seniors who earn purple or blue ribbons are eligible to apply for this scholarship.

**Financial data:** The stipend is $1,000.

**Duration:** 1 year.

**Number awarded:** Varies each year.

**Deadline:** The examinations must be ordered by January of each year.

## 1241 ACSA/AISC STUDENT DESIGN COMPETITION

Association of Collegiate Schools of Architecture
Attn: Project Manager
1735 New York Avenue, N.W.
Washington, DC 20006
Phone: (202) 785-2324, ext. 2; Fax: (202) 628-0448;
Email: cparikh@acsa-arch.org
Web: www.acsa-arch.org/competitions

**Summary:** To recognize and reward architecture and design students who submit outstanding entries in a design competition that utilizes steel as a building material.

**Eligibility:** Open to architecture students in their third year or higher, including graduate students, at colleges and universities in the United States, Canada, and Mexico that are members of the Association of Collegiate Schools of Architecture (ACSA). Participants are invited to submit a design that addresses the specific criteria outlined in the competition program. Specifications change each year but involve the use of steel in design and construction. Presentations must include a site plan showing the relationship of surrounding development, landscaping, and circulation patterns; floor plans; elevations and sections sufficient to show site context and major program elements; large-scale drawings, either orthographic or 3-dimensional, illustrating the use of structural steel; and a 3-dimensional representation in the form of an axonometric, perspective, or model photographs. Submissions must be sponsored by a faculty member and are to be principally the product of design studio work. Both individual and team entries are eligible. Selection is based on creative use of structural steel in the design solution; successful response of the design to its surrounding context; and successful response to such basic architectural concepts as human activity needs, structural integrity, and coherence of architectural vocabulary.

**Financial data:** First prize is $3,000 for the student and $1,500 for the faculty sponsor, second prize is $2,000 for the student and $1,000 for the faculty sponsor, and third prize is $1,000 for the student and $500 for the faculty sponsor.

**Duration:** The competition is held annually.

**Number awarded:** 3 student prizes are awarded each year.

**Deadline:** Faculty who wish to enroll their studio classes must register by February of each year. Entries must be submitted by May.

## 1242 AFRO-ACADEMIC, CULTURAL, TECHNOLOGICAL AND SCIENTIFIC OLYMPICS (ACT-SO)

National Association for the Advancement of Colored People
Attn: ACT-SO Director
4805 Mt. Hope Drive
Baltimore, MD 21215
Phone: (410) 580-5650; Email: ACTSO@naacpnet.org
Web: www.naacp.org/programs/actso/actso_index.html

**Summary:** To recognize and reward outstanding African American high school students who distinguish themselves in the Afro-Academic, Cultural, Technological and Scientific Olympics (ACT-SO) program.

**Eligibility:** Open to high school students (grades 9-12) of African descent who are U.S. citizens and amateurs in the category in which they wish to participate.

Competitions are held in 25 categories in 5 general areas: humanities (music composition, original essay, playwriting, and poetry), sciences (architecture, biology, chemistry, computer science, mathematics, physics/electronics, physics/energy, and physics/general), performing arts (dance, dramatics, music instrumental/classical, music instrumental/contemporary, music vocal/classical, music vocal/contemporary, and oratory), visual arts (drawing, painting, photography, sculpture, and filmmaking/video), and business (entrepreneurship). Competition is first conducted by local chapters of the NAACP; winners in each event at the local level then compete at the national level.

**Financial data:** In each category, the first-prize winner receives a gold medal and a $2,000 scholarship, the second-prize winner receives a silver medal and a $1,500 scholarship, and the third-prize winner receives a bronze medal and a $1,000 scholarship.

**Duration:** The competition has been held annually since 1977.

**Number awarded:** 75 each year: 3 in each of 25 categories.

**Deadline:** Local competitions usually take place between March and May. The national finals are held each year in July.

## 1243 AGNES MCINTOSH GARDEN CLUB OBJECTIVES SCHOLARSHIP

Florida Federation of Garden Clubs, Inc., Attn: Office Manager
1400 South Denning Drive
Winter Park, FL 32789-5662
Phone: (407) 647-7016; Fax: (407) 647-5479; Email: ffgc@earthlink.net
Web: www.ffgc.org/scholarships/index.html

**Summary:** To provide financial aid to Florida undergraduates and graduate students majoring in designated areas related to gardening.

**Eligibility:** Open to Florida residents who are enrolled as full-time juniors, seniors, or graduate students in a Florida college. They must have a GPA of 3.0 or higher, be in financial need, and be majoring in ecology, horticulture, landscape design, conservation, botany, forestry, marine biology, city planning, or allied subjects. U.S. citizenship is required. Selection is based on academic record, commitment to career, character, and financial need.

**Financial data:** The stipend is $2,500. The funds are sent directly to the recipient's school and distributed semiannually.

**Duration:** 1 year.

**Number awarded:** 1 each year.

**Deadline:** April of each year.

## 1244 AIA/AAF MINORITY/DISADVANTAGED SCHOLARSHIP PROGRAM

American Institute of Architects
Attn: American Architectural Foundation
1735 New York Avenue, N.W.
Washington, DC 20006-5292
Phone: (202) 626-7511; Fax: (202) 626-7420; Email: info@archfoundation.org
Web: www.archfoundation.org/scholarships/index.htm

**Summary:** To provide financial assistance to high school and college students from minority and/or disadvantaged backgrounds who are interested in studying architecture in college.

**Eligibility:** Open to students from minority and/or disadvantaged backgrounds who are high school seniors, students in a community college or technical school transferring to an accredited architectural program, or college freshmen entering a professional degree program at an accredited program of architecture. Students who have completed 1 or more years of a 4-year college curriculum are not eligible. Initially, candidates must be nominated by 1 of the following organizations or persons: an individual architect or firm, a chapter of the American Institute of Architects (AIA), a community design center, a guidance counselor or teacher, the dean or professor at an accredited school of architecture, or the director of a community or civic organization. Nominees are reviewed and eligible candidates are invited to complete an application form in which they write an essay describing the reasons they are interested in becoming an architect and provide documentation of academic excellence and financial need. Selection is based primarily on financial need.

**Financial data:** Awards range from $500 to $2,500 per year, depending upon individual need. Students must apply for supplementary funds from other sources.

**Duration:** 9 months; may be renewed for up to 2 additional years.

**Number awarded:** Up to 20 each year.

**Deadline:** Nominations are due by December of each year; final applications must be submitted in January.

## 1245 AIA/AAF SCHOLARSHIP FOR FIRST PROFESSIONAL DEGREE CANDIDATES

American Institute of Architects, Attn: American Architectural Foundation
1735 New York Avenue, N.W.
Washington, DC 20006-5292
Phone: (202) 626-7318; Fax: (202) 626-7420; Email: info@archfoundation.org
Web: www.archfoundation.org/scholarships/index.htm

**Summary:** To provide financial assistance to students in professional degree programs in architecture.

**Eligibility:** Open to students who are in the final 2 years of a first professional degree: 1) the third or fourth year of a 5-year program for a bachelor of architecture or equivalent degree; 2) the fourth or fifth year of a 6-year program (4 + 2 or other combination) that results in a master of architecture or equivalent degree; or 3) the second or third year of a 3- to 4-year program that results in a master of architecture and whose undergraduate degree is in a discipline other than architecture. All programs must be accredited by the National Architectural Accrediting Board (NAAB) or recognized by the Royal Architectural Institute of Canada (RAIC). Selection is based on a statement of goals, academic performance, letters of recommendation, a drawing, and financial need.

**Financial data:** Awards range from $750 to $2,500 per year, depending upon individual need.

**Number awarded:** Varies each year.

**Deadline:** January of each year.

## 1246 AIKO SUSANNA TASHIRO HIRATSUKA MEMORIAL SCHOLARSHIP

Japanese American Citizens League, Attn: National Scholarship Awards
1765 Sutter Street
San Francisco, CA 94115
Phone: (415) 921-5225; Fax: (415) 931-4671; Email: jacl@jacl.org
Web: www.jacl.org/scholarships.html

**Summary:** To provide financial assistance for undergraduate education in the performing arts to student members of the Japanese American Citizens League (JACL).

**Eligibility:** Open to JACL members who are working on undergraduate study in the performing arts. Applicants should provide published performance reviews and/or evaluations by their instructor. They must also submit a statement describing their current level of involvement in the Japanese American community or Asian Pacific community and how they will continue their involvement in future years. Selection is based on academic record, extracurricular activities, and community involvement. Professional artists are not eligible.

**Financial data:** The stipend depends on the availability of funds but usually ranges from $1,000 to $5,000.

**Duration:** 1 year; nonrenewable.

**Number awarded:** 1 each year.

**Deadline:** March of each year.

## 1247 AIR FORCE BAND OF LIBERTY MUSICAL EXCELLENCE SCHOLARSHIP

Hanscom Officers' Wives' Club, Attn: Scholarship Chair
P.O. Box 557
Bedford, MA 01730
Phone: (781) 275-1251; Email: scholarship@hanscomowd.org
Web: www.hanscomowc.org

**Summary:** To provide financial assistance to children of military personnel and veterans in New England who are interested in studying music in college.

**Eligibility:** Open to college-bound high school seniors living in New England who are dependents of active-duty, retired, or deceased military members of any branch of service. Also eligible are dependents of military recruiters working in the New York area and students living elsewhere but whose military sponsor is stationed at Hanscom Air Force Base. Applicants must be able to demonstrate musical accomplishment. although they do not necessarily have to major in music in college. Musical categories include brass, woodwind, mallet percussion, voice, jazz or classical guitar, or piano. Along with their application, they must submit a 2-page essay on their educational goals, how their educational experience will help prepare them to pursue future goals, and how they intend to apply their education to better their community. On the basis of application material, 3 finalists are selected and asked to submit a recent solo recording of their playing or singing.

**Financial data:** A stipend is awarded (amount not specified).

**Duration:** 1 year; nonrenewable.

**Number awarded:** 1 each year.

**Deadline:** March of each year.

## 1248 AL MUAMMAR SCHOLARSHIPS FOR JOURNALISM

Arab American Institute Foundation, Attn: Scholarship Administrator
1600 K Street, N.W., Suite 601
Washington, DC 20006
Phone: (202) 429-9210; Fax: (202) 429-9214; Email: aaif@aaiusa.org
Web: www.aaiusa.org/for_students.htm
**Summary:** To provide financial assistance to Arab American students interested in working on an undergraduate or graduate degree in journalism.
**Eligibility:** Open to U.S. citizens and permanent residents of Arab descent who are enrolled full time at an accredited college or university in the United States. Applicants must be undergraduates or college seniors admitted to a graduate program. They must have a GPA of 3.3 or higher and a demonstrated commitment to the field of print or broadcast journalism. Selection is based on sensitivity to Arab American issues, demonstrated community involvement, initiative in social advocacy and civic empowerment, journalistic ability, academic ability, commitment to the field of journalism, and financial need.
**Financial data:** The stipend is $5,000.
**Duration:** 1 year.
**Number awarded:** Up to 4 each year.
**Deadline:** February of each year.

## 1249 AL SHACKLEFORD AND DAN MARTIN UNDERGRADUATE SCHOLARSHIP

Baptist Communicators Association, Attn: Scholarship Committee
1715-K South Rutherford Boulevard, Suite 295
Murfreesboro, TN 37130
Phone: (615) 904-0152; Email: bca.office@comcast.net
Web: www.baptistcommunicators.org/scholar.htm
**Summary:** To provide financial assistance to undergraduate students who are working on a college degree to prepare for a career in Baptist communications.
**Eligibility:** Open to undergraduate students who are majoring in communications, English, journalism, or public relations and have a GPA of 2.5 or higher. Their vocational objective must be in Baptist communications. Along with their application, they must submit a statement explaining why they desire to receive this scholarship.
**Financial data:** The stipend is $1,000.
**Duration:** 1 year; recipients may reapply.
**Number awarded:** 1 each year.
**Deadline:** January of each year.

## 1250 ALABAMA CONCRETE INDUSTRIES ASSOCIATION SCHOLARSHIPS

Alabama Concrete Industries Association
Attn: President
660 Adams Avenue, Suite 188
Montgomery, AL 36104
Phone: (334) 265-0501; (800) 732-9118; Fax: (334) 265-2250;
Email: jsorrell@alconcrete.org
Web: www.alconcrete.org/scholarships
**Summary:** To provide financial assistance to students majoring in architecture, building sciences, or engineering in Alabama.
**Eligibility:** Open to students completing their junior year at colleges and universities in Alabama. Applicants must be enrolled in an accredited program in architecture, engineering, or building sciences. Selection is based on academic and extracurricular activity record.
**Financial data:** A stipend is awarded (amount not specified).
**Duration:** 1 year.
**Number awarded:** 2 each year.

## 1251 ALABAMA JUNIOR AND COMMUNITY COLLEGE PERFORMING ARTS SCHOLARSHIPS

Alabama Commission on Higher Education
Attn: Grants and Scholarships Department
100 North Union Street
P.O. Box 302000
Montgomery, AL 36130-2000
Phone: (334) 242-2274; Email: wwall@ache.state.al.us
Web: www.ache.state.al.us/StudentAsst/Programs.htm
**Summary:** To provide financial assistance to performing artists interested in attending a junior or community college in Alabama.
**Eligibility:** Open to full-time students enrolled in public junior and community colleges in Alabama. Selection is based on artistic talent as determined through competitive auditions.
**Financial data:** Awards cover up to the cost of in-state tuition.
**Number awarded:** Varies each year.

## 1252 ALABAMA MEDIA PROFESSIONALS AWARD

Alabama Media Professionals
c/o Dianne Casolaro
7501 Roper Tunnel Road
Trussville, AL 35173
Phone: (205) 879-9218; Email: dcasolaro@charter.net
Web: www.alabamawriters.com/scholarship.html
**Summary:** To provide financial assistance to Alabama students interested in preparing for a career in journalism or a related field.
**Eligibility:** Open to seniors graduating from high schools in Alabama, students enrolled in a college or university in Alabama, and residents of Alabama attending college in other states. Applicants must be preparing for a career in journalism, communications, broadcasting, or other media fields. Along with their application, they must submit samples of their work, 2 letters of recommendation, and a brief statement telling why they are studying communications and describing their career plans.
**Financial data:** The stipend is $1,000.
**Duration:** 1 year.
**Number awarded:** 1 each year.
**Deadline:** March of each year.

## 1253 ALASKA PRESS WOMEN MEMORIAL SCHOLARSHIP

Alaska Press Women
c/o Connie Graffis
644 East 79th Avenue
Anchorage, AK 99518
Phone: (907) 273-9414; Email: connie@kska.org
Web: www.akpresswomen.com/pages/memorialscholar.htm
**Summary:** To provide financial assistance to undergraduate students at colleges and universities in Alaska who are majoring in journalism or public communications fields.
**Eligibility:** Open to students enrolled at colleges and universities in Alaska, especially those beyond the freshman year. Applicants must be majoring in a phase of public communications, including advertising, public relations, print, radio-television, or video. Students with other majors may be eligible if they have a definite commitment to enter the media profession. Along with their application, they must submit a resume, a transcript covering all college work in Alaska or elsewhere, a statement of their career goals and why they desire the scholarship, at least 3 letters of recommendation, and up to 3 samples of their work. Selection is based on promise in the journalism or public communications fields and the likelihood that the applicant will enter those fields, financial need, and academic progress.
**Financial data:** Stipends are $1,000 or $500.
**Duration:** 1 year.
**Number awarded:** 2 each year: 1 at $1,000 and 1 at $500.
**Deadline:** March of each year.

## 1254 ALCA EDUCATIONAL FOUNDATION SCHOLARSHIPS

Professional Landcare Network, Attn: ALCA Educational Foundation
950 Herndon Parkway, Suite 450
Herndon, VA 20170
Phone: (703) 736-9666; (800) 395-ALCA; Fax: (703) 736-9668;
Email: scholarship@landcarenetwork.org
Web: www.landcarenetwork.org/cms/programs/foundation.html
**Summary:** To provide financial assistance to students at colleges and universities that have a connection to the Professional Landcare Network (PLANET).
**Eligibility:** Open to students at colleges and universities that 1) have an accredited PLANET landscape contracting curriculum, 2) have a PLANET student chapter, and/or 3) participate in PLANET student career days activities. Applicants must provide information on awards, honors, and scholarships received in high school or college; high school, college, and community activities related to horticulture; PLANET events attended; work experience; and brief essays on what they have learned about financial management as part of their education that will help them in their career, how their landscape industry related curriculum has helped them in achieving their career goals, the kind of training and work experience they will complete to attain their goals, their plan to attain more leadership and human relations skills, their reasons for desiring the scholarship, their career objectives as they relate to

the field of landscape contracting and horticulture, and where they see their career 5 years after graduation.

**Financial data:** Stipends range from $500 to $2,500.

**Duration:** 1 year.

**Number awarded:** Varies each year. Recently, 37 of these scholarships were awarded: 1 at $2,500, 1 at $1,500, 34 at $1,000, and 1 at $500.

**Deadline:** January of each year.

## 1255 ALEXANDER M. TANGER SCHOLARSHIP

Broadcast Education Association, Attn: Scholarships
1771 N Street, N.W.
Washington, DC 20036-2891
Phone: (202) 429-5354; (888) 380-7222; Email: beainfo@beaweb.org
Web: www.beaweb.org/scholarships.html

**Summary:** To provide financial assistance to upper-division and graduate students who are interested in preparing for a career in broadcasting.

**Eligibility:** Open to juniors, seniors, and graduate students enrolled full time at a college or university where at least 1 department is an institutional member of the Broadcast Education Association. Applicants may be studying any area of broadcasting. Selection is based on evidence that the applicant possesses high integrity, superior academic ability, potential to be an outstanding electronic media professional, and a sense of personal and professional responsibility.

**Financial data:** The stipend is $5,000.

**Duration:** 1 year; may not be renewed.

**Number awarded:** 1 each year.

**Deadline:** September of each year.

## 1256 ALFRED T. GRANGER STUDENT ART FUND

Vermont Student Assistance Corporation
Champlain Mill, Attn: Scholarship Programs
P.O. Box 2000
Winooski, VT 05404-2601
Phone: (802) 654-3798; (888) 253-4819; Fax: (802) 654-3765; TDD: (802) 654-3766; TDD: (800) 281-3341 (within VT); Email: info@vsac.org
Web: www.vsac.org

**Summary:** To provide financial assistance to residents of Vermont who are interested in working on an undergraduate or graduate degree in a field related to design.

**Eligibility:** Open to residents of Vermont who are graduating high school seniors, high school graduates, or GED recipients. Applicants must be interested in attending an accredited postsecondary institution to work on a degree in architecture, interior design, fine arts, architectural engineering, mechanical drawing, or lighting design. Selection is based on academic achievement, a portfolio, letters of recommendation, required essays, and financial need.

**Financial data:** The stipend is $5,000 per year for graduate students or $2,500 per year for undergraduates.

**Duration:** 1 year; recipients may reapply.

**Number awarded:** 2 graduate scholarships and 4 undergraduate scholarships are awarded each year.

**Deadline:** May of each year.

## 1257 ALLISON FISHER SCHOLARSHIP

National Association of Black Journalists
Attn: Student Education Enrichment and Development Program
8701-A Adelphi Road
Adelphi, MD 20783-1716
Phone: (301) 445-7100, ext. 108; Fax: (301) 445-7101; Email: nabj@nabj.org
Web: www.nabj.org/scholarships.html

**Summary:** To provide financial assistance to undergraduate or graduate student members of the National Association of Black Journalists (NABJ) who are majoring in broadcast journalism.

**Eligibility:** Open to African American undergraduate or graduate students who are currently attending an accredited 4-year college or university. Applicants must be majoring in broadcast journalism, have a GPA of 3.0 or higher, and be able to demonstrate community service. They must submit samples of their work, an official college transcript, 2 letters of recommendation, a resume, and a 500- to 800-word essay describing their accomplishments as a student journalist, their career goals, and their financial need.

**Financial data:** The stipend is $2,500. Funds are paid directly to the recipient's college or university.

**Duration:** 1 year; nonrenewable.

**Number awarded:** 1 each year.

**Deadline:** April of each year.

## 1258 AMERICAN ACADEMY OF CHEFS BALESTRERI/CUTINO SCHOLARSHIPS

American Culinary Federation, Inc., Attn: American Academy of Chefs
10 San Bartola Drive
P.O. Box 3466
St. Augustine, FL 32085-3466
Phone: (904) 824-4468; (800) 624-9458; Fax: (904) 825-4758;
Email: acf@acfchefs.net
Web: www.acfchefs.org/educate/eduschlr.html

**Summary:** To provide financial assistance to students enrolled in culinary programs.

**Eligibility:** Open to students who are currently enrolled in an accredited post-secondary culinary program. Applicants must have completed at least one grading or marking period and have a career goal of becoming (or already be) a chef or pastry chef. Along with their application, they must submit 2 essays of 250 words each: 1) why they want to become a chef/pastry chef or continue their education in the field, and 2) what they hope to contribute to the culinary industry. Selection is based on the essays, 2 letters of recommendation, transcripts, and financial need.

**Financial data:** The stipend is $1,000.

**Duration:** 1 year.

**Number awarded:** 3 each year.

**Deadline:** March of each year.

## 1259 AMERICAN ACADEMY OF CHEFS CHAINE DES ROTISSEURS SCHOLARSHIPS

American Culinary Federation, Inc., Attn: American Academy of Chefs
10 San Bartola Drive
P.O. Box 3466
St. Augustine, FL 32085-3466
Phone: (904) 824-4468; (800) 624-9458; Fax: (904) 825-4758;
Email: acf@acfchefs.net
Web: www.acfchefs.org/educate/eduschlr.html

**Summary:** To provide financial assistance to students enrolled full time in a 2-year culinary program.

**Eligibility:** Open to students who are currently enrolled full time in a 2-year culinary program. Applicants must have completed at least one grading or marking period. Along with their application, they must submit brief essays on their career goals and what they hope to contribute to the culinary industry. Selection is based on 2 letters of recommendation, the essays, transcripts, and financial need.

**Financial data:** The stipend is $1,000.

**Duration:** 1 year.

**Number awarded:** 20 each year.

**Deadline:** November of each year.

## 1260 AMERICAN ACADEMY OF CHEFS CHAIR'S SCHOLARSHIPS

American Culinary Federation, Inc.
Attn: American Academy of Chefs
10 San Bartola Drive
P.O. Box 3466
St. Augustine, FL 32085-3466
Phone: (904) 824-4468; (800) 624-9458; Fax: (904) 825-4758;
Email: acf@acfchefs.net
Web: www.acfchefs.org/educate/eduschlr.html

**Summary:** To provide financial assistance to students enrolled in 2- or 4-year culinary programs.

**Eligibility:** Open to students who are currently enrolled full time in a 2- or 4-year culinary program. Applicants must have completed at least 1 grading or marking period and have a career goal of becoming a chef or pastry chef. Along with their application, they must submit 2 essays of 250 words each: 1) why they want to become a chef/pastry chef, and 2) what they hope to contribute to the culinary industry. Selection is based on the essays, 2 letters of recommendation, transcripts, and financial need.

**Financial data:** The stipend is $1,000.

**Duration:** 1 year.

**Number awarded:** 10 each year.

**Deadline:** June of each year.

## 1261 AMERICAN ADVERTISING FEDERATION FOURTH DISTRICT SCHOLARSHIP

American Advertising Federation-Fourth District

c/o Ginger Reichl, Academic Chair
1728 46 Avenue North
St. Petersburg, FL 33714
Phone: (727) 576-7073; Email: greichl@pinstripemarketing.com
Web: www.4aaf.com

**Summary:** To provide financial assistance to upper-division students at colleges and universities in Florida who are interested in entering the field of advertising.
**Eligibility:** Open to juniors and seniors at accredited colleges and universities in Florida. Applicants must be majoring in advertising or a related field and planning to enter the field of advertising. They must be a paid member of the American Advertising Federation, have a GPA of 3.0 or higher, and be able to demonstrate community service. Along with their application, they must submit a cover letter explaining how they plan to use the scholarship funds, a current transcript, and 2 letters of recommendation.
**Financial data:** The stipend is $1,000.
**Duration:** 1 year.
**Number awarded:** 5 each year.
**Deadline:** February of each year.

## 1262 AMERICAN INDIAN ARTS COUNCIL SCHOLARSHIP PROGRAM

American Indian Arts Council, Inc., Attn: Scholarship Committee
725 Preston Forest Shopping Center, Suite B
Dallas, TX 75230
Phone: (214) 891-9640; Fax: (214) 891-0221; Email: aiac@flash.net
Web: americanindianartfestival.org/scholarships.htm

**Summary:** To provide financial assistance to American Indian undergraduates or graduate students planning a career in the arts or arts administration.
**Eligibility:** Open to American Indian undergraduate and graduate students who are preparing for a career in fine arts, visual and performing arts, communication arts, creative writing, or arts administration or management. Applicants must be currently enrolled in and attending a fully-accredited college or university. They must provide official tribal documentation verifying American Indian heritage and have a GPA of 2.5 or higher. Applicants majoring in the visual or performing arts (including writing) must submit slides, photographs, videotapes, audio tapes, or other examples of their work. Letters of recommendation are required. Awards are based on either merit or merit and financial need. If the applicants wish to be considered for a need-based award, a letter from their financial aid office is required to verify financial need.
**Financial data:** Stipends range from $250 to $1,000 per semester.
**Duration:** 1 semester; may be renewed if the recipient maintains a GPA of 2.5 or higher.
**Number awarded:** Varies each year.
**Deadline:** September of each year for the fall semester; March of each year for the spring semester.

## 1263 AMERICAN INSTITUTE OF GRAPHIC ARTS (AIGA) HONOLULU CHAPTER SCHOLARSHIP FUND

Hawai'i Community Foundation, Attn: Scholarship Department
1164 Bishop Street, Suite 800
Honolulu, HI 96813
Phone: (808) 566-5570; (888) 731-3863; Fax: (808) 521-6286;
Email: scholarships@hcf-hawaii.org
Web: www.hawaiicommunityfoundation.org/scholar/scholar.php

**Summary:** To provide financial assistance to Hawaii residents who are interested in preparing for a career in the graphic arts.
**Eligibility:** Open to Hawaii residents who are interested in majoring in graphic design, visual communication, or commercial arts, including print production. Applicants must be able to demonstrate academic achievement (GPA of 2.7 or higher), good moral character, and financial need.
**Financial data:** A stipend is awarded (amount not specified).
**Duration:** 1 year.
**Number awarded:** Varies each year.
**Deadline:** February of each year.

## 1264 AMERICAN INSTITUTE OF WINE & FOOD CONNECTICUT CHAPTER SCHOLARSHIP

American Institute of Wine & Food-Connecticut Chapter
P.O. Box 1719
Darien, CT 06820
Phone: (203) 967-6238

**Summary:** To provide financial assistance to Connecticut residents interested in preparing for a career in the culinary arts or a related field.
**Eligibility:** Open to Connecticut residents studying full time in a recognized culinary program. Applicants must be working on a degree or certificate in culinary arts, baking and pastry arts, wine, hospitality, catering, hotel management, or a program related to the industry.
**Financial data:** The stipend is $2,500.
**Duration:** 1 year.
**Number awarded:** 1 each year.
**Deadline:** December of each year.

## 1265 AMERICANS FOR THE ARTS POSTER DESIGN COMPETITION

The Art Institutes International, Inc.
Free Markets Center
210 Sixth Avenue, 33rd Floor
Pittsburgh, PA 15222-2603
Phone: (800) 275-2440; Email: ai_sfs@aii.edu
Web: www.artinstitutes.edu/poster

**Summary:** To recognize and reward (with scholarships to participating Art Institutes) high school seniors who participate in a poster design competition.
**Eligibility:** Open to high school seniors who are planning to attend a participating Art Institute to study graphic design or other field. Applicants must submit an original poster that illustrates the concepts of a specified theme (recently, the theme was "Life is Better with Art in It"). The poster must include the logos of The Art Institutes and Americans for the Arts and must be appropriate for promotional and marketing purposes. Along with their entry, students must also submit a current high school transcript and a written statement describing their design concept and why they want to enter the graphic design field. Entries are first submitted to the Art Institute the applicant wishes to attend. Each institute then forwards its winning design to the national competition.
**Financial data:** Local prizes are $3,000 for first and $2,000 for second. At the national level, prizes are $25,000 for first place, $20,000 for second, $15,000 for third, $10,000 for fourth, $8,000 for fifth, $6,000 for sixth, $5,000 for seventh, $4,000 for eighth, $3,000 for ninth, and $2,000 for tenth. Awards may be used only for tuition at a participating Art Institute. Funds may not be applied to fees, living expenses, or supply costs.
**Duration:** The competition is held annually.
**Number awarded:** Each institute selects 2 winners, of whom 1 is entered in the national competition. At the national level, 10 winners are selected.
**Deadline:** Entries must be submitted for local competitions by February of each year.

## 1266 AMERICA'S FIRST FREEDOM STUDENT COMPETITION

Council for America's First Freedom
The Columbian Block Building
1301 East Cary Street, Suite C
Richmond, VA 23219-2111
Phone: (804) 643-1786; Fax: (804) 644-5024; Email: caff@firstfreedom.org
Web: www.firstfreedom.org

**Summary:** To recognize and reward outstanding essays, posters, and speeches on religious freedom by high school students in Virginia.
**Eligibility:** Open to students in grades 9-12 in Virginia public, private, and home schools. Applicants must be interested in interested in competing in poster, essay, or oratory contests on the theme: "Religious Freedom: An Inalienable Right." No more than 1 finalist per category can be chosen from any 1 school and no more than 1 finalist per category from any home-schooling region.
**Financial data:** First-place awards in each category are $1,000; second-place awards in each category are $500.
**Duration:** The competition is held annually.
**Number awarded:** 6 each year: 1 first-place winner and 1 second-place winner in each of the 3 categories (posters, essays, and oratory).
**Deadline:** October of each year.

## 1267 ANA MULTICULTURAL EXCELLENCE SCHOLARSHIP FUND

American Association of Advertising Agencies
Attn: Manager of Diversity Programs
405 Lexington Avenue, 18th Floor
New York, NY 10174-1801
Phone: (212) 682-2500; (800) 676-9333; Fax: (212) 682-8391;
Email: tiffany@aaaa.org

Web: www.aaaa.org/diversity/foundation/funds.htm

**Summary:** To provide financial assistance to multicultural students who are working on an undergraduate degree in advertising.

**Eligibility:** Open to undergraduate students who are U.S. citizens of proven multicultural heritage and have at least 1 grandparent of multicultural heritage. Final selection of recipients is made by advertising agencies that are chosen as winners of Multicultural Excellence Awards by the Association of National Advertisers (ANA). For that competition, advertising firms submit samples of their campaigns that ran for at least 3 months and were directed at multicultural markets. Entries are submitted in 5 categories: African American, Asian, Hispanic, General (e.g., Native American, Russian, Polish), or Campaign with Significant Results. Winners of those awards select recipients of these scholarships on the basis of demonstrated academic ability.

**Financial data:** A stipend is awarded (amount not specified).

**Duration:** 1 year.

**Number awarded:** 5 each year.

## 1268 ANCHORAGE PRESS THEATRE FOR YOUTH PLAYWRITING AWARD

John F. Kennedy Center for the Performing Arts
Education Department
Attn: Kennedy Center American College Theater Festival
2700 F Street, N.W.
Washington, DC 20566
Phone: (202) 416-8857; Fax: (202) 416-8802;
Email: skshaffer@kennedy-center.org
Web: kennedy-center.org/education/actf/actfancr.html

**Summary:** To recognize and reward the student authors of plays on themes that appeal to young people.

**Eligibility:** Open to students at an accredited junior or senior college in the United States or in countries contiguous to the continental United States, provided their college agrees to participate in the Kennedy Center American College Theater Festival (KCACTF). Undergraduate students must be carrying at least 6 semester hours, graduate students must be enrolled in at least 3 semester hours, and continuing part-time students must be enrolled in a regular degree or certificate program. These awards are presented to the best student-written plays based on a theme appealing to young people from kindergarten through grade 12. Special consideration is given to scripts that emphasize the growth of the central character.

**Financial data:** The prize is $1,000. The winner also receives a $1,250 fellowship to attend the Bonderman IUPUI National Youth Theatre Playwriting Development Workshop and Symposium in Indianapolis. In addition, Anchorage Press publishes the winning play.

**Duration:** The award is presented annually.

**Number awarded:** 1 each year.

**Deadline:** November of each year.

## 1269 ANDREW M. ECONOMOS SCHOLARSHIP

Broadcast Education Association, Attn: Scholarships
1771 N Street, N.W.
Washington, DC 20036-2891
Phone: (202) 429-5354; (888) 380-7222; Email: beainfo@beaweb.org
Web: www.beaweb.org/scholarships.html

**Summary:** To provide financial assistance to upper-division and graduate students who are interested in preparing for a career in radio broadcasting.

**Eligibility:** Open to juniors, seniors, and graduate students enrolled full time at a college or university where at least 1 department is an institutional member of the Broadcast Education Association (BEA). Applicants must be interested in preparing for a career in radio. Selection is based on evidence that the applicant possesses high integrity, superior academic ability, potential to be an outstanding electronic media professional, and a sense of personal and professional responsibility.

**Financial data:** The stipend is $5,000.

**Duration:** 1 year; may not be renewed.

**Number awarded:** 1 each year.

**Deadline:** September of each year.

## 1270 ANNE M. GANNETT AWARD FOR VETERANS

National Federation of Music Clubs
1336 North Delaware Street
Indianapolis, IN 46202-2481
Phone: (317) 638-4003; Fax: (317) 638-0503; Email: info@nfmc-music.org

Web: www.nfmc-music.org/Competitions/AnnualSeniorDiv/annual_senior_div.htm

**Summary:** To provide financial assistance for undergraduate education to members of the National Federation of Music Clubs (NFMC) whose careers have been delayed or interrupted as a result of their service in the U.S. armed forces.

**Eligibility:** Open to undergraduate students who are majoring in music and whose musical careers were interrupted by military service. Student membership in the federation and U.S. citizenship are required.

**Financial data:** The stipend is $1,250.

**Duration:** 1 year.

**Number awarded:** 1 each year.

**Deadline:** February of each year.

## 1271 ANNE SEAMAN MEMORIAL SCHOLARSHIP

Professional Grounds Management Society, Attn: Executive Director
720 Light Street
Baltimore, MD 21230-3816
Phone: (410) 752-3318; (800) 609-PGMS; Fax: (410) 752-8295;
Email: pgms@assnhqtrs.com
Web: www.pgms.org/seamanscholarship.htm

**Summary:** To provide financial assistance for college to students in fields related to grounds management.

**Eligibility:** Open to applicants studying landscape and grounds management, turf management, irrigation technology, or a closely-related field. They must submit a cover letter describing educational and professional goals and intended use of the scholarship funds; a resume listing past employment, awards, and certificates; college or school transcripts; and 2 letters of recommendation. A member of the Professional Grounds Management Society must sponsor each applicant. Financial need is considered in the selection process.

**Financial data:** A stipend is awarded (amount not specified).

**Number awarded:** Varies each year; recently, 3 of these scholarships were awarded.

**Deadline:** June of each year.

## 1272 ANNUAL MUSIC STUDENT SCHOLARSHIPS

School Band and Orchestra Magazine, Attn: Student Scholarships
21 Highland Circle, Suite 1
Needham, MA 02494
Phone: (781) 453-9310; (800) 964-5150; Fax: (781) 453-9389
Web: www.sbomagazine.com/Essay

**Summary:** To recognize and reward, with college scholarships, elementary and high school students who submit outstanding essays on playing a musical instrument.

**Eligibility:** Open to public and private school students in grades 4 through 12. Applicants must submit an essay of up to 250 words on "How Playing a Musical Instrument Made Me a Better Student."

**Financial data:** The award is a $1,000 college scholarship.

**Duration:** The competition is held annually.

**Number awarded:** 10 each year: 5 to students in grades 4-8 and 5 to students in grades 9-12.

**Deadline:** December of each year.

## 1273 APWA HORIZONS FRONT RANGE SCHOLARSHIP

American Public Works Association-Colorado Chapter
c/o Paul A. Hindman
Urban Drainage and Flood Control District
2480 West 26th Avenue, Suite 156-B
Denver, CO 80211
Phone: (303) 455-6277; Fax: (303) 455-7880; Email: coloapwa@eazy.net
Web: www.coloapwa.org/scholarships/scholar.html

**Summary:** To provide financial assistance to high school seniors in Colorado who plan to attend a college or university in the state to prepare for a career in public works.

**Eligibility:** Open to seniors graduating from high schools in Colorado who plan to attend a college, university, or junior college in the state. Applicants must be planning to major in accounting, architecture, biology, business, chemistry, construction management, engineering, finance, management, or other field associated with public works. They must have completed a course in trigonometry and have a GPA of 3.0 or higher. Preference is given to applicants preparing for a career that promotes the public sector. Financial need is not considered in the selection process.

**Financial data:** The stipend is $1,500.
**Duration:** 1 year.
**Number awarded:** 1 or more each year.
**Deadline:** March of each year.

## 1274 AQHF JOURNALISM OR COMMUNICATIONS SCHOLARSHIP

American Quarter Horse Foundation, Attn: Scholarship Coordinator
2601 I-40 East
Amarillo, TX 79104
Phone: (806) 376-5181; (888) 209-8322; Fax: (806) 376-1005;
Email: lowens@aqha.org
Web: www.aqha.com/foundation/scholarships/index.html
**Summary:** To provide financial assistance for college to members of the American Quarter Horse Association (AQHA) or the American Quarter Horse Youth Association (AQHYA) who are planning a career in journalism or communications.
**Eligibility:** Open to applicants who have been members of either organization for at least 1 year and are graduating high school seniors or already enrolled in college. They must have a GPA of 2.5 or higher and be planning to work on a degree in journalism, communications, or a related field. Along with their application, they must submit an essay on "How my experiences through equine-related activities have influenced my life." Financial need is considered in the selection process.
**Financial data:** The maximum stipend is $2,000 per year.
**Duration:** Up to 4 years, provided the recipient maintains a GPA of 2.5 or higher and full-time enrollment.
**Number awarded:** 1 each year.
**Deadline:** January of each year.

## 1275 ARCHIBALD RUTLEDGE SCHOLARSHIP PROGRAM

South Carolina State Department of Education
1429 Senate Street, Room 1010A
Columbia, SC 29201
Phone: (803) 734-8485; Email: sspade@sde.state.sc.us
Web: www.myscschools.com/offices/ombudsman/arscholarship
**Summary:** To recognize and reward high school seniors in South Carolina who participate in a competition in art, creative writing, drama, or music.
**Eligibility:** Open to U.S. citizens who have attended South Carolina public high schools for at least 2 years, are currently seniors, and are planning to attend a South Carolina college or university. Applicants compete by submitting samples of their work in 1 of 4 areas: 1) visual arts, limited to 2-dimensional work such as drawing and painting media, printmaking, and collage; no 3-dimensional works, photographs, or computer-generated images are accepted; 2) creative writing, as a sonnet, lyric, or narrative poem, up to 1 page; 3) drama, a 1-act play with a performing time of 20 to 45 minutes; or 4) music, a composition of 3 to 5 minutes for solo or small ensemble, vocal or instrumental, in any appropriate style. In addition to the work, they must submit a process folio that contains documentation of the planning and development of the project and a 1-page reflection statement addressing the intent of the work and comparing the final product with the original concept. A panel of professionals in the field selects up to 10 finalists, based on originality, creativity, and the correlation and implications of the process folio for the final composition. Finalists must attend the scholarship competition, where they present a portfolio of a number of selected works as specified by the judges.
**Financial data:** The award consists of a $4,000 scholarship, to be used for tuition, room, board, and instructional resource expenses.
**Duration:** 1 year.
**Number awarded:** 4 each year: 1 in each of the 4 categories.
**Deadline:** February of each year.

## 1276 ARKANSAS POST SCHOLARSHIPS

Society of American Military Engineers-Arkansas Post
P.O. Box 867
Little Rock, AR 72203-0867
Web: www.same.org/arkansas
**Summary:** To provide financial assistance to Arkansas high school seniors interested in studying architecture or engineering in college.
**Eligibility:** Open to seniors graduating from high schools in Arkansas. Applicants must be interested in studying architecture or engineering in college.
**Financial data:** Stipends are $1,000 or $500.
**Duration:** 1 year.
**Number awarded:** 4 each year: 2 at $1,000 and 2 at $500.

## 1277 ARTS COMPETITION SCHOLARSHIPS

National Foundation for Advancement in the Arts
444 Brickell Avenue, P-14
Miami, FL 33131
Phone: (305) 377-1140; (800) 970-ARTS; Fax: (305) 377-1149;
Email: info@NFAA.org
Web: www.ARTSawards.org
**Summary:** To recognize and reward outstanding high school students in the arts.
**Eligibility:** Open to U.S. citizens or permanent residents who are graduating high school seniors, or, if not enrolled in high school, are 17 or 18 years old. Applicants may enter competitions in dance, film and video, instrumental music, jazz, photography, theater, visual arts, voice, or writing by submitting samples of their work, as videotapes, audio tapes, or portfolios. On the basis of the tapes or portfolios, award winners are invited to Miami for the final competitions.
**Financial data:** Gold awards are $10,000, first-level $3,000 each, second level $1,500, third level $1,000, fourth level $500 (if any are awarded), and fifth level $100; honorable mention winners receive $100 awards but are not invited to Miami.
**Duration:** The competition is held annually.
**Number awarded:** Up to 125 award candidates compete in Miami (20 in dance, 5 in film and video, 20 in instrumental music, 5 in jazz, 5 in photography, 20 in theater, 20 in visual arts, 10 in voice, and 20 in writing); an unlimited number of honorable mention awards are made to candidates who are not invited to Miami. Recently, the 125 award candidates received 50 first-level awards, 51 second-level awards, and 24 third-level awards. In addition, 9 of them (1 in each category) were selected as gold award winners.
**Deadline:** Early applications must be submitted by May of each year; regular applications are due by September of each year.

## 1278 ASEI UNDERGRADUATE SCHOLARSHIPS

American Society of Engineers of Indian Origin
c/o Ramu Ramamurthy, Scholarship Committee Chair
47790 Pavillon Road
Canton, MI 48188
Phone: (248) 226-6895; Fax: (248) 226-7166; Email: awards@ascimichigan.org
Web: www.aseio.org
**Summary:** To provide financial assistance to undergraduate students of Indian origin (from India) who are majoring in architecture, engineering, or related areas.
**Eligibility:** Open to undergraduate students of Indian origin (by birth, ancestry, or relation). They must be enrolled full time at an accredited college or university in the United States and majoring in engineering, architecture, computer science, or allied science with a GPA of 3.2 or higher. Selection is based on demonstrated ability, academic achievement (including GPA, honors, and awards), career objectives, faculty recommendations, involvement in science fair and campus activities, and industrial exposure (including part-time work and internships).
**Financial data:** The stipend is $1,000.
**Duration:** 1 year.
**Number awarded:** Several each year.
**Deadline:** June of each year.

## 1279 ATLAS SHRUGGED ESSAY CONTEST

Ayn Rand Institute, Attn: Essay Contests
2121 Alton Parkway, Suite 250
P.O. Box 57044
Irvine, CA 92619-7044
Phone: (949) 222-6550; Fax: (949) 222-6558; Email: essay@aynrand.org
Web: www.aynrand.org/contests
**Summary:** To recognize and reward outstanding essays written by college students on Ayn Rand's novel, *Atlas Shrugged*.
**Eligibility:** Open to students enrolled full time in an undergraduate degree program. They must submit a typewritten essay on questions selected each year from Ayn Rand's novel, *Atlas Shrugged*. The essay must be between 1,000 and 1,200 words. Selection is based on style and content. Judges look for writing that is clear, articulate, and logically organized. To win, an essay must demonstrate an outstanding grasp of the philosophic meaning of the novel.
**Financial data:** First prize is $5,000; second prizes are $1,000; third prizes are $400, finalist prizes are $100, and semifinalist prizes are $50.
**Duration:** The competition is held annually.
**Number awarded:** 49 each year: 1 first prize, 3 second prizes, 5 third prizes, 20 finalist prizes, and 20 semifinalist prizes.
**Deadline:** September of each year.

## 1280 AWJ SCHOLARSHIP FOR WOMEN

Association for Women Journalists, Attn: AWJ Grant
P.O. Box 2199
Fort Worth, TX 76113
Phone: (817) 685-3876; Email: jessamybrown@star-telegram.com
Web: www.awjdfw.org/scholarships_awards.html

**Summary:** To provide financial assistance to women studying journalism at a college or university in Texas.

**Eligibility:** Open to full-time juniors and seniors at colleges and universities in Texas. Applicants must be majoring in print or broadcast journalism and have a GPA of 2.5 or higher in their major. They must submit 3 samples of their print or broadcast work or photographs, a letter of recommendation from an instructor or adviser, a statement of professional goals and how the scholarship will help, and a statement of financial need (if that is to be considered).

**Financial data:** A stipend is awarded (amount not specified). Funds are paid directly to the college or university to be applied to tuition.

**Duration:** 1 year.

**Number awarded:** 1 or more each year.

**Deadline:** March of each year.

## 1281 B. PHINIZY SPALDING AND HUBERT B. OWENS SCHOLARSHIPS

Georgia Trust
1516 Peachtree Street, N.W.
Atlanta, GA 30309
Phone: (404) 881-9980; Fax: (404) 875-2205; Email: info@georgiatrust.org
Web: www.georgiatrust.org/preservation_resources/spalding_owens.htm

**Summary:** To provide financial assistance to Georgia residents working on a degree in a field related to historical preservation at a college or university in the state.

**Eligibility:** Open to Georgia residents currently enrolled full time in their first year of college in the state. Applicants must be majoring in historic preservation or such related fields as archaeology, architecture, history, or planning. Selection is based on academic achievement and past and planned involvement with preservation-related fields.

**Financial data:** The stipend is $1,000.

**Duration:** 1 year.

**Number awarded:** 2 each year.

**Deadline:** February of each year.

## 1282 BACH ORGAN AND KEYBOARD MUSIC SCHOLARSHIP

Rhode Island Foundation, Attn: Scholarship Coordinator
One Union Station
Providence, RI 02903
Phone: (401) 274-4564; Fax: (401) 751-7983; Email: libbym@rifoundation.org
Web: www.rifoundation.org

**Summary:** To provide financial assistance to students in Rhode Island who demonstrate ability in playing the organ or other keyboard instrument and to church organists.

**Eligibility:** Open to music majors specializing in organ or piano in pursuit of a college degree. Applicants must be Rhode Island residents and church organists who are members of the American Guild of Organists (AGO). They must submit a letter of reference from their organ/keyboard teacher or church official and an essay (up to 300 words) on what they hope they will be doing in their professional life 10 years from now. Financial need is considered in the selection process.

**Financial data:** Stipends range from $300 to $1,000.

**Number awarded:** Up to 3 each year.

**Deadline:** June of each year.

## 1283 BANK OF AMERICA ACHIEVEMENT AWARDS

Bank of America Foundation, Attn: Achievement Awards Program
CA5-704-08-03
315 Montgomery Street, Eighth Floor
San Francisco, CA 94104-1866
Phone: (415) 953-0927; (888) 488-9802; Fax: (415) 622-3469
Web: www.bankofamerica.com/foundation

**Summary:** To recognize and reward high school seniors in California who excel in specific subject areas.

**Eligibility:** Open to high school seniors in California who are chosen by faculty committees in their schools. The committees select students to receive certificates in specific study areas (agriculture, art, business, communications, computer studies, drama, English, English as a Second Language, foreign language, history, home economics, mathematics, music, religious studies, science, social science, and trades and industrial studies). Small high schools (those with 199 or fewer students in grades 10-12) may award a total of 7 certificates and large high schools (those with 200 or more students) present a total of 14 certificates. In addition, the faculty committees select graduating seniors to receive plaques in 4 general study areas (applied arts, fine arts, liberal arts, and science and mathematics); certificate winners may not also receive plaques; the number of plaques awarded by each high school also depends on the size of the school (2 plaques with enrollment of 1 to 199 students in grades 10-12, 3 plaques with 200 to 599 students, and 4 plaques for schools with more than 600 students). Winners of plaques are then eligible to enter the Achievement Awards competition. Of all plaque winners statewide, 320 finalists (8 in each of 10 regions in each of the 4 general study areas) are selected to enter competitions involving 1) an essay judged on written expression, logical progression, ability to focus on topic, and creative interpretation, and 2) a group discussion judged on cooperation, sound and logical thinking, oral communication and command of English, and originality of thought.

**Financial data:** The cash awards are $2,000 for first-place winners, $1,500 for second-place winners, $1,000 for third-place winners, and $500 for other participating finalists.

**Duration:** Prizes are awarded annually.

**Number awarded:** All 320 finalists receive cash awards; the top 40 finalists (1 in each general study area in each region) receive first-place awards and other finalists receive awards depending on their scores in the competition.

**Deadline:** Schools must select their plaque recipients before the end of January of each year.

## 1284 BARBARA L. FRYE SCHOLARSHIP

Capital Press Club of Florida
336 East College Avenue, Room 303
Tallahassee, FL 32301
Phone: (850) 222-5564

**Summary:** To provide financial assistance to high school seniors and college students in Florida who are planning to prepare for a career in journalism.

**Eligibility:** Open to applicants who are 1) attending or expecting to attend a Florida college or university or 2) a graduate or prospective graduate of a Florida high school attending or expecting to attend a college inside or outside of the state. College seniors are not eligible to apply. As part of the application process, applicants must write an essay (of 300-500 words) describing their reason for choosing a career in journalism. Applicants should also send samples of their work (either clippings or tapes) and at least 1 letter of recommendation from either a teacher or professor or professional journalist. Selection is based on merit, dedication to journalism, and demonstrated aptitude for print or broadcast journalism. An applicant's racial minority status may be considered by the selection committee.

**Financial data:** The stipend is $2,000.

**Duration:** 1 year; recipients may reapply.

**Deadline:** June of each year.

## 1285 BAY AREA MEDIA NETWORK SCHOLARSHIPS

Bay Area Media Network, Attn: Bill Diaz, President
P.O. Box 20261
Tampa, FL 33622
Phone: (813) 354-2827; Fax: (813) 875-2828; Email: bdiaz@wfts.com
Web: www.bamnawrt.org/_ships.html

**Summary:** To provide financial assistance to high school seniors in Florida who are interested in studying a field related to media at a college or university in the state.

**Eligibility:** Open to high school seniors who plan to attend a college or university in Florida. Applicants must have an interest in entering the field of media.

**Financial data:** The stipend is $1,000.

**Duration:** 1 year.

**Number awarded:** 2 each year.

## 1286 BEA 2-YEAR/COMMUNITY COLLEGE AWARD

Broadcast Education Association, Attn: Scholarships
1771 N Street, N.W.
Washington, DC 20036-2891
Phone: (202) 429-5354; (888) 380-7222; Email: beainfo@beaweb.org
Web: www.beaweb.org/scholarships.html

**Summary:** To provide financial assistance to community college students who are interested in preparing for a career in broadcasting.

**Eligibility:** Open to students who are either 1) enrolled full time at a community college, or 2) graduates of a community college enrolled full time at a 4-year college or university. Their current or former community college must be an institutional member of the Broadcast Education Association. Applicants must be studying for a career in broadcasting. Selection is based on evidence that the applicant possesses high integrity, superior academic ability, potential to be an outstanding electronic media professional, and a sense of personal and professional responsibility.

**Financial data:** The stipend is $1,500.

**Duration:** 1 year; may not be renewed.

**Number awarded:** 1 each year.

**Deadline:** September of each year.

## 1287 BENJAMIN C. BLACKBURN SCHOLARSHIP

Friends of the Frelinghuysen Arboretum, Attn: Scholarship Committee
53 East Hanover Avenue
P.O. Box 1295
Morristown, NJ 07962-1295
Phone: (973) 326-7603; Fax: (973) 644-9627
Web: www.arboretumfriends.org/blackburn.html

**Summary:** To provide financial assistance to residents of New Jersey who are working on an undergraduate or graduate degree in horticulture, landscape architecture, or related fields.

**Eligibility:** Open to New Jersey residents who are working on an undergraduate or graduate degree in 1 of the following: horticulture, botany, landscape architecture, or a related field. Undergraduates must have completed at least 24 college credits. Applicants must submit brief essays on their short-term goals, work experience related to their career goals, involvement in community activities, and long-term career goals. Selection is based on those essays, college transcripts, 2 letters of recommendation from professors, and 2 letters of recommendation from people in their community. Financial need is not considered in the selection process.

**Financial data:** The stipend is $5,000. Funds are sent directly to the recipient's institution.

**Duration:** 1 year.

**Number awarded:** 1 each year.

**Deadline:** April of each year.

## 1288 BERKELEY PRIZE

University of California at Berkeley
Department of Architecture
Attn: Raymond Lifchez
474 Wurster Hall
Berkeley, CA 94720
Phone: (510) 642-7585; Fax: (510) 643-5607; Email: info@berkeleyprize.org
Web: www.berkeleyprize.org

**Summary:** To recognize and reward undergraduate students who submit outstanding essays on architecture as a social art.

**Eligibility:** Open to currently enrolled undergraduates majoring in architectural design in accredited schools of architecture worldwide. An architecture student may team up with another undergraduate in architecture, urban studies, or the social sciences. Applicants must submit a 500-word proposal for an essay on a question that relates to architecture as a social art. On the basis of those proposals, semifinalists are invited to submit 2,500-word essays.

**Financial data:** A total of $5,000 is available for prizes each year. Recently, that included $3,000 for first, $1,000 for second, and $500 for each third. If winning entries are submitted by teams of 2 students, the prize is divided equally between them.

**Duration:** The competition is held annually.

**Number awarded:** Recently, 4 of these prizes were awarded: 1 first, 1 second, and 2 thirds.

**Deadline:** Initial proposals must be submitted by December of each year.

## 1289 BERNADETTE WONG YU SCHOLARSHIP

US Pan Asian American Chamber of Commerce
Attn: Scholarship Coordinator
1329 18th Street, N.W.
Washington, DC 20036
Phone: (202) 296-5221; Fax: (202) 296-5225;
Email: administrator@uspaacc.com

Web: www.uspaacc.com/web/programs/bernadette_Wong_yu.htm

**Summary:** To provide financial assistance to high school seniors who are interested in studying Chinese language or Chinese studies at a college or university in the United States or China.

**Eligibility:** Open to high school seniors who are U.S. citizens or permanent residents. Applicants must be planning to begin full-time study of Chinese language or Chinese studies at an accredited postsecondary educational institution in the United States or China. Along with their application, they must submit a 500-word essay on "Why I am interested in the Chinese culture." Selection is based on academic excellence (GPA of 3.3 or higher), community service involvement, and financial need.

**Financial data:** The maximum stipend is $3,000. Funds are paid directly to the recipient's college or university.

**Duration:** 1 year.

**Number awarded:** 1 each year.

**Deadline:** February of each year.

## 1290 BERNESE B. DAVIS GARDEN CLUB OBJECTIVES SCHOLARSHIP

Florida Federation of Garden Clubs, Inc., Attn: Office Manager
1400 South Denning Drive
Winter Park, FL 32789-5662
Phone: (407) 647-7016; Fax: (407) 647-5479; Email: ffgc@earthlink.net
Web: www.ffgc.org/scholarships/index.html

**Summary:** To provide financial aid to Florida undergraduates and graduate students majoring in designated areas related to gardening.

**Eligibility:** Open to Florida residents who are enrolled as full-time juniors, seniors, or graduate students in a Florida college. They must have a GPA of 3.0 or higher, be in financial need, and be majoring in agriculture, agronomy, biology, botany, butterflies, city planning, conservation, ecology, forestry, horticulture, landscape design and architecture, marine biology, management of natural resources, native plants and wildlife, water management, xeriscaping, or a related subject. U.S. citizenship is required. Selection is based on academic record, commitment to career, character, and financial need.

**Financial data:** The stipend is $2,500. The funds are sent directly to the recipient's school and distributed semiannually.

**Duration:** 1 year.

**Number awarded:** 1 each year.

**Deadline:** April of each year.

## 1291 BEST TEEN CHEF CULINARY SCHOLARSHIP COMPETITION

The Art Institutes International, Inc.
Free Markets Center
210 Sixth Avenue, 33rd Floor
Pittsburgh, PA 15222-2603
Phone: (800) 275-2440; Email: ai_sfs@aii.edu
Web: www.artinstitutes.edu

**Summary:** To recognize and reward (with scholarships to participating Art Institutes) high school seniors who are winners in a culinary competition.

**Eligibility:** Open to graduating high school seniors who have a GPA of 2.0 or higher and are interested in attending an Art Institute that offers a culinary arts program. Applicants must submit 1) a menu with descriptions for a 2-course meal; 2) a detailed recipe with directions for each course; 3) a paragraph on why they would like to be a culinary professional and who inspires them and why; and 4) a current high school transcript. Based on those entries, semifinalists are selected at each Art Institute to compete in local cook-offs. First-place winners in each local competition advance to a national competition where they prepare a menu issued in advance by the sponsor.

**Financial data:** In the national competition, the first, second, and third-place winners receive scholarships of at least $30,000 for tuition at the Art Institute of their choice. The fourth, fifth, and sixth-place winners receive half-tuition scholarships of more than $15,000. The seventh, eighth, and ninth-place winners receive quarter-tuition scholarships worth more than $7,500. The remaining national competitors receive $2,000 tuition scholarships.

**Duration:** The competition is held annually.

**Number awarded:** 18 each year (1 from each of the participating Art Institutes).

**Deadline:** February of each year.

## 1292 BETSY PLANK/PRSSA SCHOLARSHIPS

Public Relations Student Society of America, Attn: Director of Education
33 Irving Place, Third Floor

New York, NY 10003-2376
Phone: (212) 460-1474; Fax: (212) 995-0757; Email: prssa@prsa.org
Web: www.prssa.org/resources/award-BetsyPlank.asp
**Summary:** To provide financial assistance for college to members of the Public Relations Student Society of America (PRSSA).
**Eligibility:** Open to members of the society who are currently enrolled as juniors or seniors in a program of public relations studies and preparing for a career in public relations. Applicants must be nominated by their PRSSA chapter. They must submit a statement (up to 300 words) expressing their commitment to public relations. Selection is based on academic achievement in public relations and overall studies, demonstrated leadership, practical experience (e.g., internships, other jobs, work with student firm), and commitment to public relations (particularly as expressed in their statement). Financial need is not considered.
**Financial data:** The highest-ranked applicant receives a scholarship of $2,000, second $1,500, and third $750. An additional scholarship may be awarded if there are qualifying applicants and sufficient funds.
**Duration:** 1 year.
**Number awarded:** 3 or 4 each year.
**Deadline:** June of each year.

## 1293 BMI STUDENT COMPOSER AWARDS

Broadcast Music Inc., Attn: BMI Foundation
320 West 57th Street
New York, NY 10019-3790
Phone: (212) 830-2537; Fax: (212) 246-2163; Email: classical@bmi.com
Web: www.bmifoundation.org/pages/SComposer.asp
**Summary:** To recognize and reward outstanding student composers from the Western Hemisphere.
**Eligibility:** Open to citizens of countries in North, Central, or South America, the Caribbean Island nations, or the Hawaiian Islands who are younger than 26 years of age. Applicants must be enrolled in accredited public, private, or parochial secondary schools, enrolled in accredited colleges or conservatories of music, or engaged in the private study of music with recognized and established teachers (other than a relative). Any composer having won the award 3 times previously is not eligible to enter the contest again. Compositions may be for vocal, instrumental, electronic, or any combination of those. There are no limitations on medium, instrumentation, or length of the work. Manuscripts may be submitted either on usual score paper or reproduced by a generally accepted reproduction process. Electronic music and recordings of graphic works that cannot adequately be presented in score may be submitted on cassette or CD. Selection is based on evidence of creative talent. Academic finesse is considered, but that is secondary to vital musicality and clarity of expression of the composer's work. Judges consider 1) formal content of the composition; 2) melodic, harmonic, and rhythmic idioms, but only in terms of their consistency and suitability for the intent of the particular composition; 3) instrumentation, orchestration, and vocal writing; and 4) age of the composer (if 2 compositions are of equal merit, preference is given to the younger contestant).
**Financial data:** Prizes range from $500 to $5,000.
**Duration:** The competition is held annually.
**Number awarded:** Varies each year; recently, 8 of these awards were presented. A total of $20,000 in prizes is awarded each year.
**Deadline:** February of each year.

## 1294 BOB EAST SCHOLARSHIP

National Press Photographers Foundation
3200 Croasdaile Drive, Suite 306
Durham, NC 27705-2586
Phone: (919) 383-7246; (800) 289-6772; Fax: (919) 383-7261;
Email: info@nppa.org
Web: www.nppa.org/professional_development/students/scholarships/east.html
**Summary:** To provide financial assistance to college photojournalists who are interested in continuing college or going to graduate school.
**Eligibility:** Open to full-time undergraduates in the first 3 and a half years of college or planning to work on a graduate degree. Eligible students must give evidence of photographic aptitude and academic ability, be able to demonstrate financial need, and submit at least 5 single images in addition to a picture story.
**Financial data:** The stipend is $1,000.
**Duration:** 1 year.
**Number awarded:** 1 each year.
**Deadline:** February of each year.

## 1295 BOB EDDY SCHOLARSHIP PROGRAM

Connecticut Society of Professional Journalists
Attn: Paul Gough, Awards Committee Chair
598 Route 148
Killingworth, CT 06419
Phone: (860) 663-3159; Email: ctspjcontest@ezmarelda.com
Web: www.ctspj.org
**Summary:** To provide financial assistance to upper-division students residing or studying in Connecticut who are interested in preparing for a career in journalism.
**Eligibility:** Open to juniors or seniors who are either Connecticut residents (may attend school in any state) or from other states enrolled in a 4-year college or university in Connecticut. All applicants must be preparing for a career in journalism, provide registrar-signed transcripts of all academic courses, fill out an application form, submit writing samples, tapes, or related work in any media that shows an interest and competency in journalism, and write a 500-word essay on why they want to become a journalist. Financial need must be demonstrated.
**Financial data:** Stipends are $2,500, $1,500, $1,000, or $500.
**Duration:** 1 year.
**Number awarded:** 4 each year: 1 at $2,500, 1 at $1,500, 1 at $1,000, and 1 at $500.
**Deadline:** April of each year.

## 1296 BOB STANLEY AND AL COMPTON MINORITY AND INTERNATIONAL SCHOLARSHIP

Baptist Communicators Association, Attn: Scholarship Committee
1715-K South Rutherford Boulevard, Suite 295
Murfreesboro, TN 37130
Phone: (615) 904-0152; Email: bca.office@comcast.net
Web: www.baptistcommunicators.org/scholar.htm
**Summary:** To provide financial assistance to minority and international students who are working on an undergraduate degree to prepare for a career in Baptist communications.
**Eligibility:** Open to undergraduate students of minority ethnic or international origin. Applicants must be majoring in communications, English, journalism, or public relations with a GPA of 2.5 or higher. Their vocational objective must be in Baptist communications. Along with their application, they must submit a statement explaining why they desire to receive this scholarship.
**Financial data:** The stipend is $1,000.
**Duration:** 1 year; recipients may reapply.
**Number awarded:** 1 each year.
**Deadline:** January of each year.

## 1297 BOB STEVENS MEMORIAL SCHOLARSHIP

Garden State Scholastic Press Association
c/o John Tagliareni, Scholarship Coordinator
Bergenfield High School
80 South Prospect Avenue
Bergenfield, NJ 07621
Phone: (201) 385-8898; Email: scholarship@gsspa.org
Web: www.gsspa.org/scholarships/stevens.html
**Summary:** To recognize and reward outstanding high school journalists in New Jersey.
**Eligibility:** Open to graduating high school seniors in New Jersey who have at least a 3.0 GPA, have served at least 2 years in some capacity in high school journalism, and are able to demonstrate their intent to study journalism in college and to prepare for a career in the field. Only 1 nomination per school may be submitted. The nominator must be a member of the Garden State Scholastic Press Association. Nominees must submit an official entry form, a self-analytical evaluation of their journalistic life, an official copy of their transcript, 3 to 4 letters of recommendation, and samples of their work, selected to show quality and diversity in reporting, writing, photography, design, etc. Selection is based on versatility (ability to handle a variety of subject areas with equal ability), responsibility (thorough research and ethical reporting), inquisitiveness (ability to seek out and investigate topics of importance to the high school audience and the community), and skill (quality work produced adeptly and creatively). Financial need is not considered in the selection process.
**Financial data:** The stipend is $1,000. Funds are to be used for college.
**Duration:** 1 year.
**Number awarded:** 1 each year.
**Deadline:** February of each year.

## 1298 BODIE MCDOWELL SCHOLARSHIP AWARDS

Outdoor Writers Association of America
121 Hickory Street, Suite 1
Missoula, MT 59801
Phone: (406) 728-7434; Fax: (406) 728-7445
Web: owaa.org/scholarship.htm

**Summary:** To provide financial assistance for college or graduate school to students interested in a career in outdoor writing.

**Eligibility:** Open to undergraduates entering their junior or senior year of study and graduate students at an accredited school of journalism or mass communications that has registered with the sponsoring organization. Each school may nominate 2 candidates. Nominees must be planning a career in outdoor communications, including writing, radio and television, wildlife photography, art, lecturing, or video and filmmaking. Selection is based on transcripts, examples of outdoor communication work, a 1- to 2-page statement of career goals, and optional letters of recommendation.

**Financial data:** Stipends range from $2,500 to $3,500 per year.

**Number awarded:** Varies each year. Recently, 5 of these scholarships were awarded: 2 to graduate students and 3 to undergraduates.

**Deadline:** February of each year.

## 1299 BOHDAN "BO" KOLINSKY MEMORIAL SCHOLARSHIP

Connecticut Sports Writers Alliance
c/o Manchester Journal Inquirer
P.O. Box 70
Unionville, CT 06085
Phone: (203) 789-5651; Email: mail@ctsportswriters.org
Web: www.ctsportswriters.org

**Summary:** To provide financial assistance to high school seniors in Connecticut who are interested in preparing for a career as a sports journalist.

**Eligibility:** Open to seniors graduating from high schools in Connecticut who are interested in attending a 4-year college or university to study sports journalism. Applicants must submit a resume showing good academic standing, involvement in journalism, extracurricular involvement, and awards; a 1-page essay on why they wish to prepare for a career in print journalism; a letter of recommendation; and 3 samples of their writing published in a daily or weekly newspaper, a magazine, or a school publication. Selection is based on promise as a journalist and ability to complete college-level academic work.

**Financial data:** The stipend is $1,000.

**Duration:** 1 year; may be renewed.

**Number awarded:** 1 each year.

**Deadline:** January of each year.

## 1300 BRASLER PRIZE

National Scholastic Press Association
2221 University Avenue, S.E., Suite 121
Minneapolis, MN 55414
Phone: (612) 625-8335; Fax: (612) 626-0720; Email: info@studentpress.org
Web: www.studentpress.org/nspa/contests.html

**Summary:** To recognize and reward outstanding high school journalists.

**Eligibility:** Open to high school journalists who submit samples of stories that they have written in 5 categories: news, diversity, features, sports, and editorials. In each category, 1 student is selected as the author of the Story of the Year. Selection of those stories is based on quality of writing, sensitivity, and fairness. The first-place winners in each category then compete for this prize.

**Financial data:** The prize is $1,000.

**Duration:** The competition is held annually.

**Number awarded:** 1 each year.

**Deadline:** August of each year.

## 1301 BROADCAST CABLE FINANCIAL MANAGEMENT ASSOCIATION SCHOLARSHIP

Broadcast Cable Financial Management Association
932 Lee Street, Suite 204
Des Plaines, Il 60016
Phone: (847) 296-0200; Fax: (847) 296-7510
Web: www.bcfm.com

**Summary:** To provide financial assistance to members of the Broadcast Cable Financial Management Association who are interested in working on an undergraduate or graduate degree.

**Eligibility:** Open to all fully-paid members in good standing. They must be interested in working on an undergraduate or graduate degree at an accredited college or university that has some relevance to their current job and/or to the broadcast or cable industries. To apply, individuals must submit an application, attach a current resume, include 2 letters of reference, and submit a 1-page essay that addresses the following: their current job responsibilities, the courses they intend to take, and a description of their career goals.

**Financial data:** The stipend is generally $1,000.

**Duration:** 1 year; recipients may reapply.

**Number awarded:** Varies each year; a total of $5,000 is distributed annually.

**Deadline:** March of each year.

## 1302 BRUCE EAGLESON MEMORIAL SCHOLARSHIP AWARDS

Connecticut Association of Schools, Attn: Executive Director
30 Realty Drive
Cheshire, CT 06410
Phone: (203) 250-1111; Fax: (203) 250-1345; Email: msavage@casciac.org
Web: www.casciac.org

**Summary:** To provide financial assistance to high school seniors in Connecticut who plan to study the arts in college.

**Eligibility:** Open to seniors graduating from high schools in Connecticut who plan to enroll in college to study the arts, including (but not limited to) visual arts, music, theater, dance, design, and architecture. Applicants must be able to demonstrate 1) considerable experience in the arts as evidenced by involvement in shows, exhibits, performances, video productions, or similar activities; 2) involvement in service to peers and/or community through artistic or other activities; and 3) financial need. Along with their application, they must submit a 250-word statement on what led them to their decision to prepare for a career in the arts.

**Financial data:** Stipends are $10,000 or $5,000.

**Duration:** 1 year.

**Number awarded:** 3 each year: 1 at $10,000 and 2 at $5,000.

**Deadline:** March of each year.

## 1303 BUFFALO CHAPTER NAWIC SCHOLARSHIP

National Association of Women in Construction-Buffalo Chapter 172
c/o Susan Zipp
Siemens Building Technologies
85 Northpointe Parkway, Suite 8
Amherst, NY 14228-1886
Phone: (716) 568-0983, ext. 2166
Web: buffalonawic.tripod.com/pr02.htm

**Summary:** To provide financial assistance to residents of New York attending college in the state to prepare for a career in construction.

**Eligibility:** Open to residents of New York entering the second, third, or fourth year at a 2- or 4-year college or university in the state. Applicants must be majoring in a construction-related program of study (e.g., architecture, construction technology, drafting and design, engineering, estimating). U.S. citizenship is required.

**Financial data:** The stipend is $1,000.

**Duration:** 1 year.

**Number awarded:** 1 each year.

**Deadline:** June of each year.

## 1304 BUILDING INDUSTRY SCHOLARSHIP PROGRAM

Builders Association of Minnesota
Attn: Minnesota Building Industry Foundation
570 Asbury Street, Suite 301
St. Paul, MN 55104
Phone: (651) 646-7959; (800) 654-7783; Fax: (651) 646-2860
Web: www.mbif.org/scholarships/cfm

**Summary:** To provide financial assistance to high school seniors in Minnesota who are interested in preparing for a career in a field related to construction.

**Eligibility:** Open to seniors graduating from high schools in Minnesota who are interested in continuing their education. Applicants must be interested in a program in carpentry, woodworking, residential design, architectural drafting, or residential construction management. Along with their application, they must include a list of classes they have already taken in the construction area where they are seeking further training, information on their work background, a current transcript, their attendance record, and a letter of recommendation from an instructor or counselor.

**Financial data:** The stipend is $1,000.

**Duration:** 1 year; nonrenewable.

**Number awarded:** 9 each year.

**Deadline:** April of each year.

## 1305 CABOT CREAMERY CULINARY SCHOLARSHIP

Vermont Student Assistance Corporation
Champlain Mill, Attn: Scholarship Programs
P.O. Box 2000
Winooski, VT 05404-2601
Phone: (802) 654-3798; (888) 253-4819; Fax: (802) 654-3765; TDD: (802) 654-3766; TDD: (800) 281-3341 (within VT); Email: info@vsac.org
Web: www.vsac.org

**Summary:** To provide financial assistance to Vermont residents who are interested in attending a culinary arts program.

**Eligibility:** Open to residents of Vermont who are high school seniors, high school graduates, or currently-enrolled college students. Applicants must be enrolled or planning to enroll in an academic, vocational, technical, or advanced training program related to the culinary arts. Selection is based on academic achievement, required essays, a letter of recommendation, and financial need.

**Financial data:** The stipend is either $1,000 or $500.

**Duration:** 1 year.

**Number awarded:** Either 1 at $1,000 or 2 at $500 each year.

**Deadline:** March of each year.

## 1306 CALIFORNIA RESTAURANT ASSOCIATION EDUCATIONAL FOUNDATION SCHOLARSHIPS FOR HIGH SCHOOL SENIORS

California Restaurant Association, Attn: Educational Foundation
1011 10th Street
Sacramento, CA 95814
Phone: (916) 431-2728; (800) 765-4842, ext. 2728; Fax: (916) 447-6182;
Email: warmour@calrest.org
Web: www.calrest.org/edfoundation/scholarships.asp

**Summary:** To provide financial assistance to California high school seniors planning to enroll in a postsecondary culinary program.

**Eligibility:** Open to high school seniors in California who have been accepted as a full-time student at a college or university (may be in any state) in a culinary program. Applicants must be U.S. citizens or permanent residents who have been employed at least 250 hours in a hospitality-related field. Selection is based on academic achievement, enthusiasm, creativity, and future promise in the food service/hospitality industry.

**Financial data:** Stipends range from $500 to $3,000.

**Duration:** 1 year; recipients may reapply.

**Number awarded:** Varies each year.

**Deadline:** April of each year.

## 1307 CALIFORNIA RESTAURANT ASSOCIATION EDUCATIONAL FOUNDATION SCHOLARSHIPS FOR UNDERGRADUATE STUDENTS

California Restaurant Association, Attn: Educational Foundation
1011 10th Street
Sacramento, CA 95814
Phone: (916) 431-2728; (800) 765-4842, ext. 2728; Fax: (916) 447-6182;
Email: warmour@calrest.org
Web: www.calrest.org/edfoundation/scholarships.asp

**Summary:** To provide financial assistance to California residents enrolled in a postsecondary culinary program.

**Eligibility:** Open to residents of California who are currently enrolled full time in a college or university (may be in any state) in a culinary program. Applicants must have completed at least 1 academic term with a GPA of 2.75 or higher. They must be U.S. citizens or permanent residents who have been employed at least 750 hours in a hospitality-related field. Selection is based on academic achievement, enthusiasm, creativity, and future promise in the food service/hospitality industry.

**Financial data:** Stipends range from $1,000 to $3,000.

**Duration:** 1 year; recipients may reapply.

**Number awarded:** Varies each year.

**Deadline:** April of each year.

## 1308 CALIFORNIA STATE FAIR ARTS SCHOLARSHIPS

California State Fair, Attn: Friends of the Fair Scholarship Program
1600 Exposition Boulevard
P.O. Box 15649
Sacramento, CA 95852
Phone: (916) 274-5969; Email: wross@calexpo.com
Web: www.bigfun.org

**Summary:** To provide financial assistance to residents of California who are studying the arts in college.

**Eligibility:** Open to residents of California currently working on an undergraduate degree at a college or university in the state. Applicants must be studying the arts, including visual arts, dance, music, film, etc. They must have a GPA of 3.0 or higher. Along with their application, they must submit a 2-page essay on why they are pursuing their desired career and life goals. Selection is based on personal commitment, goals established for their chosen field, leadership potential, and civic accomplishments.

**Financial data:** Stipends are $1,500 or $500.

**Duration:** 1 year.

**Number awarded:** 2 each year: 1 at $1,500 and 1 at $500.

**Deadline:** March of each year.

## 1309 CALIFORNIA STATE FAIR CULINARY COOKING AND HOSPITALITY MANAGEMENT SCHOLARSHIPS

California State Fair, Attn: Friends of the Fair Scholarship Program
1600 Exposition Boulevard
P.O. Box 15649
Sacramento, CA 95852
Phone: (916) 274-5969; Email: wross@calexpo.com
Web: www.bigfun.org

**Summary:** To provide financial assistance to residents of California who are studying culinary cooking or hospitality management.

**Eligibility:** Open to residents of California currently working on an associate degree at a culinary specialty school in the state. Applicants must be enrolled in a culinary cooking or hospitality management program. They must have a GPA of 3.0 or higher. Along with their application, they must submit a 2-page essay on why they are pursuing their desired career and life goals. Selection is based on personal commitment, goals established for their chosen field, leadership potential, and civic accomplishments. field, leadership potential, and civic accomplishments.

**Financial data:** Stipends are $1,500 or $500.

**Duration:** 1 year.

**Number awarded:** 2 each year: 1 at $1,500 and 1 at $500.

**Deadline:** March of each year.

## 1310 CALIFORNIA STATE FAIR CULINARY COOKING SCHOLARSHIPS

California State Fair, Attn: Friends of the Fair Scholarship Program
1600 Exposition Boulevard
P.O. Box 15649
Sacramento, CA 95852
Phone: (916) 274-5969; Email: wross@calexpo.com
Web: www.bigfun.org

**Summary:** To provide financial assistance to residents of California who are studying culinary cooking.

**Eligibility:** Open to residents of California currently enrolled at culinary arts vocational trade schools and community colleges in the state. Applicants must be enrolled in a culinary cooking program. They must have a GPA of 3.0 or higher. Along with their application, they must submit a 2-page essay on why they are pursuing their desired career and life goals. Selection is based on personal commitment, goals established for their chosen field, leadership potential, and civic accomplishments.

**Financial data:** Stipends are $1,000 or $500.

**Duration:** 1 year.

**Number awarded:** 2 each year: 1 at $1,000 and 1 at $500.

**Deadline:** March of each year.

## 1311 CAREER ADVANCEMENT SCHOLARSHIPS

Business and Professional Women's Foundation, Attn: Scholarships
1900 M Street, N.W., Suite 310
Washington, DC 20036
Phone: (202) 293-1100, ext. 173; Fax: (202) 861-0298; Email: dfrye@bpwusa.org
Web: www.bpwusa.org

**Summary:** To provide financial assistance for college or graduate school to mature women who are employed or seeking employment in selected fields.

**Eligibility:** Open to women who are at least 25 years of age, citizens of the United States, within 2 years of completing their course of study, officially accepted into an accredited program or course of study at an American institution (including those in Puerto Rico and the Virgin Islands), in financial need, and planning to use the desired training to improve their chances for advancement, train for a new career field, or enter/reenter the job market. They must be in a transitional period in their lives and be interested in studying 1 of the following fields: biological sciences, business studies, computer science, engineering, humanities, mathematics, paralegal studies, physical sciences, social science, teacher education certification, or for a professional degree (J.D., D.D.S., M.D.). Study at the Ph.D. level and for non-degree programs is not covered.

**Financial data:** The stipend is $1,000 per year.

**Duration:** 1 year; recipients may reapply.

**Number awarded:** Varies each year; recently, 120 of these scholarships were awarded.

**Deadline:** April of each year.

---

## 1312 CARL E. DARROW STUDENT DESIGN COMPETITION

Association of Collegiate Schools of Architecture, Attn: Project Manager
1735 New York Avenue, N.W.
Washington, DC 20006
Phone: (202) 785-2324, ext. 2; Fax: (202) 628-0448;
Email: cparikh@acsa-arch.org
Web: www.acsa-arch.org/competitions

**Summary:** To recognize and reward architecture and design students who submit outstanding entries in a design competition that utilizes wood as a building material.

**Eligibility:** Open to 1) architecture students in their third year or higher of a bachelor's degree program or any year of a master's degree program; and 2) students of interior design in their third year or higher of an undergraduate program or any year of a graduate program. Participants are invited to submit a design that addresses the specific criteria outlined in the competition program. Specifications change each year but require "the elegant, innovative, and creative use of wood as a material and determinant of form." Entries may be submitted in 3 categories: 1) requires a site plan, site and building sections, exterior perspectives, building plans for all levels, an interior perspective, and 2 large-scale detail drawings (1 illustrating the architectural and structural use of wood in the design solution and 1 describing a furnishing, fixture, or similar detail); 2) requires floor plans for all levels, color-rendered perspectives of 2 or more of the major spaces, elevations of descriptive walls, architectural woodwork details, and graphic or computer-generated reproductions of furnishings, finishes, and colors; 3) requires a rendered perspective of table and chair and 2 architectural woodwork details. Submissions must have a faculty sponsor and are to be principally the product of design studio work.

**Financial data:** In categories 1 and 2, first prize is $2,000 for the student and $800 for the faculty sponsor, second prize is $1,000 for the student and $400 for the faculty sponsor, and third prize is $500 for the student and $200 for the faculty sponsor. In category 3, first prize is $600 for the student and $250 for the faculty sponsor and second prize is $400 for the student and $150 for the faculty sponsor.

**Duration:** The competition is held annually.

**Number awarded:** 8 student prizes are awarded each year.

**Deadline:** Faculty who wish to enroll their studio classes must register by February of each year. Entries must be submitted by May.

---

## 1313 CARPE DIEM SCHOLARSHIPS

Carpe Diem Foundation of Illinois, Attn: Executive Director
P.O. Box 3194
Chicago, IL 60690-3194
Email: glevine@carpediemfoundation.org
Web: www.carpediemfoundation.org

**Summary:** To provide financial assistance to entering or continuing undergraduate students majoring or planning to major in specified fields.

**Eligibility:** Open to undergraduates majoring or planning to major in the following 6 areas: 1) political science; 2) pre-med, biomedical engineering, biology, and chemistry; 3) science and technology; 4) education; 5) art and architecture; and 6) music performance or composition. Applicants must be high school seniors or college freshmen, sophomores, or juniors. Along with their application, they must submit 1) a 200-word essay on their accomplishments during high school in which they take the greatest pride; 2) a 200-word essay on their family, especially with regard to service occupations and involvement in community organizations; and 3) a 500-word essay explaining why they have chosen their course of study. Music and art applicants must also submit samples of their work. Preference is given to students whose parents are or have been employed in education; local, state, or federal government; social service; public health (including medical providers); the administration of justice; and the fine arts. Selection is based on demonstrated leadership, community service, char-

---

acter, academics, and potential to improve the quality of human life. Applicants must be U.S. citizens, but they may be residents of any state.

**Financial data:** Stipends range from $2,500 to $5,000 per year.

**Duration:** 1 year; may be renewed for up to 3 additional years if the recipient maintains a GPA of "B+" or higher, full-time enrollment, and participation in activities that improve the quality of the academic and social life of their community.

**Number awarded:** Varies each year; recently, 17 of these scholarships were awarded.

**Deadline:** May of each year.

---

## 1314 CHALLENGERS NATIONAL MISSION SPEAK OUT CONTEST

Southern Baptist Convention
North American Mission Board, Attn: Youth Mission Education
4200 North Point Parkway
Alpharetta, GA 30022-4176
Phone: (770) 410-6489; Fax: (770) 410-6082; Email: ahuesing@namb.net
Web: www.studentz.com/challengers

**Summary:** To recognize and reward outstanding orators in the Southern Baptist Convention's Challengers Speak Out Contest.

**Eligibility:** Open to male members of Southern Baptist churches who are participating in a Challengers group as high school sophomores, juniors, or seniors. Challengers can represent their state in this national speech competition. They must prepare a speech, from 5 to 7 minutes in length, on 1 of the following topics: why I should be a mission volunteer; what mission involvement means to me; discovering my gifts for mission service; me, a missionary; the cooperative program: supporting missions around the world; encountering God through Bible study; or what Challengers means to me. Selection is based on content (50 points), composition (25 points), and delivery (25 points).

**Financial data:** At the national level, first place is a $1,000 scholarship plus $800 for a mission project/trip of the winner's choice. Second place is a $500 scholarship.

**Duration:** The competition is held annually.

**Number awarded:** 2 each year.

---

## 1315 CHAPEL OF FOUR CHAPLAINS NATIONAL ART CONTEST

Chapel of Four Chaplains
Naval Business Center, Building 649
1201 Constitution Avenue
Philadelphia, PA 19112
Phone: (215) 218-1943; Fax: (215) 218-1949; Email: chapel@fourchaplains.org
Web: www.fourchaplains.org

**Summary:** To recognize and reward outstanding high school student art on a topic related to public service.

**Eligibility:** Open to seniors at public and private high schools. Students are invited to submit any form of flat art (except photography) on a theme that changes annually; recently, the theme was "Making the World a Better Place Through Service and Sacrifice." They are encouraged to capture the spirit of the theme in whatever manner they wish, through representational, stylized, or abstract means of expression. The medium may be watercolor, crayons, tempera, collage, pen and ink, oil crayons, linoleum block or woodcut print, or any combination of those. The maximum size is 24"x30". The artwork should not contain any wording, including slogans, descriptions, narrative, or dialogue balloons.

**Financial data:** First prize is $1,000, second prize is $750, and third prize is $500.

**Duration:** The competition is held annually.

**Number awarded:** 3 each year.

**Deadline:** December of each year.

---

## 1316 CHARLES AND LUCILLE KING FAMILY FOUNDATION SCHOLARSHIPS

Charles and Lucille King Family Foundation, Inc., Attn: Educational Director
366 Madison Avenue, 10th Floor
New York, NY 10017
Phone: (212) 682-2913; Fax: (212) 949-0728; Email: info@kingfoundation.org
Web: www.kingfoundation.org

**Summary:** To provide financial assistance to undergraduate students who are majoring in television or film and to graduate students at selected universities.

**Eligibility:** Open to students who are entering their junior or senior year at a 4-year U.S. college or university and majoring in television or film. U.S. citizenship is not required. Selection is based on academic ability, professional potential, and financial need. In addition, special grants are available to undergraduate and graduate students at New York University, the University of California at Los Angeles, and the University of Southern California.

**Financial data:** Stipends range up to $2,500.

**Duration:** 1 year; students who receive an award as a junior may renew the award in their senior year if they earn at least a 3.0 GPA.

**Number awarded:** Varies; generally, up to 20 each year.

**Deadline:** April of each year.

### 1317 CHARLES D. MAYO STUDENT SCHOLARSHIP

International Furnishings and Design Association
Attn: IFDA Educational Foundation
330 Ferry Landing
Atlanta, GA 30328
Phone: (770) 612-0454; Fax: (770) 612-0445; Email: info@ifdaef.org
Web: www.ifdaef.org/scholarships.html

**Summary:** To provide financial assistance to undergraduate students working on a degree in interior design.

**Eligibility:** Open to full-time undergraduate students majoring in interior design or a related field. Applicants must submit a 300- to 500-word essay on their future plans, goals, and objectives and why they believe they deserve the scholarship. Selection is based on the essay; the applicant's achievements, awards, and accomplishments; and a letter of recommendation from a professor or instructor. Financial need is not considered.

**Financial data:** The stipend is $1,000.

**Duration:** 1 year.

**Number awarded:** At least 1 each year.

**Deadline:** March of each year.

### 1318 CHARLES DUBOSE SCHOLARSHIP

Connecticut Architecture Foundation, Attn: Executive Vice President
87 Willow Street
New Haven, CT 06511
Phone: (203) 865-2195; Fax: (203) 562-5378
Web: www.aiact.org

**Summary:** To provide financial assistance to Connecticut residents who are working on a bachelor's or master's degree in architecture.

**Eligibility:** Open to students who have completed at least 2 years of a bachelor of architecture program or have been accepted into an accredited graduate program. Connecticut residents are encouraged to apply. Applicants may be attending any college offering a 5-year accredited degree in architecture. Preference is given to students at the University of Pennsylvania, Georgia Institute of Technology, and the Fontainebleau summer program. Selection is based on academic record and financial need.

**Financial data:** Stipends range from $5,000 to $10,000.

**Duration:** 1 year; may be renewed.

**Number awarded:** 1 or 2 each year.

**Deadline:** April of each year.

### 1319 CHARLES E. PETERSON PRIZE

Athenaeum of Philadelphia, Attn: Assistant Director for Programs
219 South Sixth Street
Philadelphia, PA 19106-3794
Phone: (215) 925-2688; Fax: (215) 925-3755;
Email: magee@PhilaAthenaeum.org
Web: www.PhilaAthenaeum.org/grants.html

**Summary:** To recognize and reward sets of measured drawings prepared by students or teams of students that meet standards of the Historic American Buildings Survey (HABS) of the National Park Service.

**Eligibility:** Open to students or teams of students in architecture, architectural history, interior design, and American studies who have faculty sponsorship. There is no entrance fee. Participants are required to produce a set of measured drawings made to HABS standards. The drawings must be of a building that has not yet been recorded by HABS through measured drawings, or it must be an addendum to existing HABS drawings that makes a substantial contribution to the understanding of significant features of the building. Applicants should contact the HABS office to determine if a structure has already been recorded.

**Financial data:** First prize is $2,500, second prize is $2,000, third prize is $1,500, and fourth prize is $1,000.

**Duration:** The competition is held annually.

**Number awarded:** 4 prizes are awarded each year.

**Deadline:** Entry forms must be submitted by May of each year. Completed entries are due in June.

### 1320 CHARLES M. SCHULZ AWARD FOR COLLEGE CARTOONISTS

Scripps Howard Foundation, Attn: National Journalism Awards Administrator
312 Walnut Street, 28th Floor
P.O. Box 5380
Cincinnati, OH 45201
Phone: (513) 977-3035; (800) 888-3000; Fax: (513) 977-3800;
Email: cotting ham@scripps.com
Web: www.scripps.com/foundation

**Summary:** To recognize and reward outstanding college cartoonists.

**Eligibility:** Open to student cartoonists at a college newspaper or magazine in the United States or its territories. Work must have been completed during the calendar year of the contest. Cartoons may be panels, strips, and/or editorial cartoons. Entries must include a 250-word statement by the cartoonist outlining his or her goals in cartooning.

**Financial data:** The prize is $5,000 and a trophy.

**Duration:** The competition is held annually.

**Number awarded:** 1 each year.

**Deadline:** January of each year.

### 1321 CHARLOTTE HOYT BAGNALL SCHOLARSHIP FOR CHURCH MUSICIANS

First Church of Christ, Attn: Charlotte Hoyt Bagnall Scholarship Committee
689 Hopmeadow Street
Simsbury, CT 06070
Phone: (860) 651-3593; Fax: (860) 408-9229;
Email: CHBScholarship@1stchurchsimsbury.org
Web: www.1stchurchsimsbury.org

**Summary:** To provide financial assistance to high school and college students interested in studying religious music.

**Eligibility:** Open to musicians interested in improving their ability to support religious worship services by studying religious music and liturgy. Applicants must be interested in a program of music lessons; high school, college, or graduate level studies related to organ or religious music; or attendance at seminars. Competitions are limited to high school musicians in even-numbered years and post high school musicians in odd-numbered years. Along with their application, they must submit essays on their 1) goals and aspirations, including what they want to achieve in their ministry of music; and 2) course of study, including the course of study for which they want to use the scholarship and how it will help them achieve their goals and aspirations.

**Financial data:** Stipends up to $1,500 are available.

**Duration:** 1 year.

**Number awarded:** 1 or 2 each year.

**Deadline:** December of each year.

### 1322 CHARLOTTE M.F. BENTLEY/NEW YORK CHAPTER 103 SCHOLARSHIP

United Daughters of the Confederacy, Attn: Education Director
328 North Boulevard
Richmond, VA 23220-4057
Phone: (804) 355-1636; Fax: (804) 353-1396; Email: hqudc@rcn.com
Web: www.hqudc.org/scholarships/scholarships.html

**Summary:** To provide financial assistance for college to lineal descendants of Confederate veterans, especially those from New York.

**Eligibility:** Open to lineal descendants of worthy Confederates or collateral descendants who are current or former members of the Children of the Confederacy or current members of the United Daughters of the Confederacy. Preference is given to members from New York. Applicants must submit a family financial report and certified proof of the Confederate record of 1 ancestor, with the company and regiment in which he served. They must have at least a 3.0 GPA in high school.

**Financial data:** The amount of this scholarship depends on the availability of funds.

**Duration:** 1 year; may be renewed.

**Number awarded:** 1 each year.

**Deadline:** March of each year.

### 1323 CHOPIN PIANO COMPETITION

Kosciuszko Foundation, Attn: Director of Cultural Events
15 East 65th Street
New York, NY 10021-6595

Phone: (212) 734-2130, ext. 214; (800) 287-9956; Fax: (212) 628-4552; Email: culture@thekf.org

Web: www.thekf.org/MUChopin.html

**Summary:** To recognize and reward outstanding pianists.

**Eligibility:** Open to U.S. citizens, permanent residents of the United States, and international full-time students with valid student visas; all entrants must be between 16 and 22 years of age. Contestants prepare a program of 60 to 75 minutes encompassing a selection of works by Chopin, a mazurka by Szymanowski, a major work by J.S. Bach, a complete classical (Beethoven, Haydn, Mozart or Schubert) sonata, a major 19th-century work by a composer other than Chopin, and a substantial work by an American, Polish, or Polish American composer written after 1950; jurors choose works from the program for the auditions. Preliminary competitions take place in Chicago and New York; winners advance to the national competitions in New York.

**Financial data:** The preliminary competitions provide small cash prizes and round-trip airfare to the national finals. In the national competitions, first place is $5,000, second place $2,500, and third place $1,500.

**Duration:** The competition is held annually; the preliminaries are held in March and the national finals in April.

**Number awarded:** 3 national prizes are awarded each year.

**Deadline:** February of each year.

---

### 1324 CHRISTIAN FELLOWSHIP OF ART MUSIC COMPOSERS SCHOLARSHIP

Christian Fellowship of Art Music Composers

c/o Mark Hijleh

Houghton College

Greatbatch School of Music

Houghton, NY 14744

Phone: (585) 567-9424; Email: cfamc@cfamc.org

Web: www.cfamc.org

**Summary:** To provide financial assistance to Christian composers interested in studying art music composition.

**Eligibility:** Open to Christian student composers who enrolled in a program of art music composition study in a preparatory music program, a collegiate music program, or an approved summer music program. Applicants must submit 2 letters of recommendation, a brief Christian testimony, a brief essay on how their compositional activities and Christian life are related, a curriculum vitae, a detailed explanation of how the award will be used, and 1 or 2 scores of art music composed for voice, instruments, and/or electronic media.

**Financial data:** The stipend is $1,000; funds are sent directly to the educational institution or summer festival designated by the recipient.

**Duration:** 1 academic year or 1 summer; nonrenewable.

**Number awarded:** 1 each year.

**Deadline:** October of each year.

---

### 1325 CHRISTOPHERS POSTER CONTEST

The Christophers, Attn: Youth Department Coordinator

12 East 48th Street

New York, NY 10017

Phone: (212) 759-4050; Fax: (212) 838-5073;

Email: youth-coordinator@christophers.org

Web: www.christophers.org/contests.html

**Summary:** To recognize and reward posters drawn by high school students that best illustrate the motto of The Christophers, "It's better to light one candle than to curse the darkness."

**Eligibility:** Open to all students in grades 9-12 who prepare posters on the theme: "You Can Make a Difference." The posters must be 15"x20" and the original work of 1 student. Selection is based on overall impact, effectiveness in conveying the theme, originality, and artistic merit.

**Financial data:** First prize is $1,000, second prize is $500, third prize is $250, and honorable mentions are $100.

**Duration:** The competition is held annually.

**Number awarded:** 6 each year: 1 each for first, second, and third place plus 3 honorable mentions.

**Deadline:** January of each year.

---

### 1326 CHUCK FULGHAM SCHOLARSHIP

Dallas Foundation, Attn: Scholarship Administrator

900 Jackson Street, Suite 150

Dallas, TX 75202

Phone: (214) 741-9898; Fax: (214) 741-9848;

Email: cmcnally@dallasfoundation.org

Web: www.dallasfoundation.org/gs_schFundProfiles.cfm

**Summary:** To provide financial assistance to adult students and high school seniors in Texas interested in studying the humanities in college.

**Eligibility:** Open to 1) adult graduates of a literacy program who need financial assistance to attend a regionally-accredited college or university, and 2) high school seniors who have not been successful in high school by traditional academic standards (must have a GPA below 3.0) but who have a genuine interest in literature and humanities and show promise for achievement in college. Applicants must be Texas residents and able to demonstrate financial need; preference is given to applicants from the Dallas area and to applicants who have participated in sports activities.

**Financial data:** The maximum stipend is $2,500. Funds are paid directly to the recipient's school.

**Duration:** 1 year; nonrenewable.

**Number awarded:** 1 or more each year.

**Deadline:** March of each year.

---

### 1327 CLAN MACBEAN FOUNDATION GRANTS

Clan MacBean Foundation, Attn: Director

441 Wadsworth Boulevard, Suite 213

Lakewood, CO 80226-1545

Phone: (303) 233-6002; Email: macbean@ecentral.com

**Summary:** To provide financial assistance to college students interested in studying subjects or conducting research relating to 1) Scottish culture or 2) the "Human Family."

**Eligibility:** Open to students who have completed at least 2 years of college. Applicants may be either working on a degree or conducting a specific project. If they are working on a degree, their course of study must relate directly to Scottish culture or be in a field that leads directly to the improvement and benefit of the "Human Family." If they conducting a specific project, it must reflect direct involvement in the preservation or enhancement of Scottish culture or contribute directly to the improvement and benefit of the "Human Family."

**Financial data:** Grants up to $5,000 are available. Funds may be used for tuition, fees, books, room and board, printing and publishing costs, historical research fees, and/or initial costs in establishing a project.

**Duration:** 1 year.

**Number awarded:** 1 or more each year.

**Deadline:** April of each year.

---

### 1328 CLETE ROBERTS MEMORIAL JOURNALISM SCHOLARSHIP AWARD

Associated Press Television/Radio Association of California and Nevada

c/o Roberta Gonzales

CBS 5 TV

855 Battery Street

San Francisco, CA 94111

Phone: (415) 362-5550; Email: gonzales@kpix.cbs.com

Web: www.aptra.org

**Summary:** To provide financial assistance to students at colleges and universities in California and Nevada who are interested in broadcast journalism careers.

**Eligibility:** Open to students at colleges and universities in California and Nevada. Applicants must have a broadcast journalism career objective. Selection is based on a 500-word essay on why the students wish to pursue broadcast journalism; another 500-word essay on their honors, awards, and broadcast experience; 3 letters of recommendation; and a statement of how they are financing their education.

**Financial data:** The stipend is $1,500 per year.

**Duration:** 1 year.

**Number awarded:** 2 each year.

**Deadline:** December of each year.

---

### 1329 CLEVELAND ADVERTISING ASSOCIATION EDUCATION FOUNDATION SCHOLARSHIPS

Cleveland Advertising Association, Attn: Education Foundation

20325 Center Ridge Road, Suite 670

Cleveland, OH 44116

Phone: (440) 673-0020; Fax: (440) 673-0025; Email: adassoc@clevead.com

Web: www.clevead.com/education/scholarships.php

**Summary:** To provide financial assistance to undergraduate students who are residents of Ohio majoring in a field related to advertising at a college or university in the state.

**Eligibility:** Open to residents of Ohio who are full-time seniors, juniors, or second-semester sophomores at colleges and universities in the state. Applicants must be majoring in advertising or a related communications/marketing field and have a GPA of 3.0 or higher. They must submit transcripts, 2 letters of recommendation, and an essay describing their career goals. Financial need is not considered in the selection process. Some of the scholarships are set aside for U.S. citizens of African, Asian, Hispanic, Native American, or Pacific Island descent.

**Financial data:** Stipends range from $1,000 to $2,500.

**Duration:** 1 year.

**Number awarded:** Varies each year. Recently, this program awarded 11 scholarships: 2 at $2,500, 1 at $2,000, 3 at $1,500, and 5 at $1,000.

**Deadline:** October of each year.

---

## 1330 COATING AND GRAPHIC ARTS DIVISION SCHOLARSHIPS

Technical Association of the Pulp and Paper Industry
Attn: TAPPI Foundation
15 Technology Parkway South
Norcross, GA 30092
Phone: (770) 209-7536; (800) 332-8686; Fax: (770) 446-6947;
Email: vedmondson@tappi.org
Web: www.tappi.org

**Summary:** To provide financial assistance to student members of the Technical Association of the Pulp and Paper Industry (TAPPI) who are interested in preparing for a career in the paper industry, with a focus on coating and graphic arts.

**Eligibility:** Open to TAPPI student members who are enrolled full time in a program related to the coated paper and paperboard or the graphic arts industries. Applicants must be juniors or higher with a GPA of 3.0 or higher; graduate students are also eligible if they have not advanced to doctoral candidacy. Selection is based on demonstrated interest in a career in the coating and graphic arts industry; financial need is not considered.

**Financial data:** The stipend is $1,000.

**Duration:** 1 year.

**Number awarded:** Up to 4 each year.

**Deadline:** January of each year.

---

## 1331 COLBURN-PLEDGE MUSIC SCHOLARSHIP

Colburn-Pledge Music Scholarship Foundation, Attn: Secretary
6322 Cornplanter
San Antonio, TX 78209

**Summary:** To provide financial assistance to pre-college and college students who are Texas residents and interested in studying classical music.

**Eligibility:** Open to residents of Texas who are 1) studying a string instrument (violin, viola, cello, bass) in classical music with the intention of becoming a professional musician, and 2) less than high school age, currently in high school, or currently in college. Financial need must be demonstrated, but selection is based primarily on musical talent.

**Financial data:** Stipends range up to $2,000.

**Duration:** 1 year.

**Deadline:** April of each year.

---

## 1332 COLLEGE PHOTOGRAPHER OF THE YEAR

National Press Photographers Foundation
c/o University of Missouri at Columbia, Attn: CPOY Director
109 Lee Hills Hall
Columbia, MO 65211
Phone: (573) 882-4882; Fax: (573) 884-4999; Email: info@cpoy.org
Web: www.cpoy.org

**Summary:** To recognize and reward the outstanding photographic work of college students.

**Eligibility:** Open to students currently working on an undergraduate or graduate degree. They are eligible to submit work completed during the previous academic year. Single picture categories are: 1) spot news; 2) general news; 3) feature; 4) sports action; 5) sports feature; 6) portrait; 7) pictorial; 8) illustration; and 9) personal vision. Multiple picture categories are: 10) picture story; 11) sports portfolio; 12) documentary; 13) portfolio; and 14) online or multimedia photo story or essay. Professional photographers who have worked 2 years or more are not eligible.

**Financial data:** In the portfolio competition, the first-place winner receives an expenses-paid trip to receive the award, a summer internship at 1 of a consortium of newspapers, the Colonel William J. Lookadoo Award of $1,000, a Canon camera, and 100 rolls of Fuji film; second-place winner receives the Milton Freier Award of $500 and 60 rolls of Fuji film; third-place winner receives $250 and 40 rolls of Fuji film. For each of the other individual categories, first-place winners receive small cash awards.

**Duration:** The competition is held annually, in the fall.

**Deadline:** October of each year.

---

## 1333 COLORADO BROADCASTERS ASSOCIATION COLLEGE SCHOLARSHIPS

Colorado Broadcasters Association, Attn: Education Committee
2042 Boreas Pass Road
P.O. Box 2369
Breckenridge, CO 80424
Phone: (970) 547-1388; Fax: (970) 547-1384;
Email: cobroadcasters@earthlink.net
Web: www.e-cba.org/scholarships.htm

**Summary:** To provide financial assistance to Colorado residents who are working on an undergraduate degree related to broadcasting at a college or university in the state.

**Eligibility:** Open to residents of Colorado who are enrolled in an accredited college or university in the state that offers undergraduate degree programs in broadcast journalism, production or management, communications, speech, telecommunications, new media, or some other aspect of professional media education that explicitly prepares students for careers in broadcasting. Students must be nominated by their department, each of which may nominate up to 3 candidates but must identify a faculty or staff member who will be a liaison to the sponsoring organization. Applicants must submit a resume, their school transcript and any other relevant academic records, a statement of their educational and professional goals and their qualifications for the scholarship, a letter of recommendation from a faculty member, and an explanation of their financial need and other special circumstances that might bear on their application.

**Financial data:** The stipend is $2,000.

**Duration:** 1 year.

**Number awarded:** 3 each year.

**Deadline:** February of each year.

---

## 1334 COLORADO BROADCASTERS ASSOCIATION VOCATIONAL SCHOOL SCHOLARSHIP

Colorado Broadcasters Association, Attn: Education Committee
2042 Boreas Pass Road
P.O. Box 2369
Breckenridge, CO 80424
Phone: (970) 547-1388; Fax: (970) 547-1384;
Email: cobroadcasters@earthlink.net
Web: www.e-cba.org/scholarships.htm

**Summary:** To provide financial assistance to Colorado residents who are enrolled in a vocational broadcast program.

**Eligibility:** Open to residents of Colorado who are enrolled in an accredited professional training school offering programs in broadcasting or some other aspect of professional media education that explicitly prepares students for careers in broadcasting. Students must be nominated by their school, each of which may nominate up to 3 candidates but must identify a faculty or staff member who will be a liaison to the sponsoring organization. Applicants must submit a resume, their school transcript and any other relevant academic records, a statement of their educational and professional goals and their qualifications for the scholarship, a letter of recommendation from a faculty member, and an explanation of their financial need and other special circumstances that might bear on their application.

**Financial data:** The stipend is $1,000.

**Duration:** 1 year.

**Number awarded:** 1 each year.

**Deadline:** February of each year.

---

## 1335 COLVIN SCHOLARSHIP PROGRAM

Certified Angus Beef LLC, Attn: President
206 Riffel Road
Wooster, OH 44691-8588
Phone: (330) 345-2333; (800) 725-2333, ext. 279; Fax: (330) 345-0808;
Email: bbarner@certifiedangusbeef.com
Web: www.certifiedangusbeef.com

**Summary:** To provide financial assistance to upper-division students working on a degree related to the beef industry.

**Eligibility:** Open to students entering their junior or senior year of college. Applicants must have demonstrated a commitment to the beef industry through work on a degree in meat science, food science, animal science, marketing, business, communications, journalism, or other field related to the industry. Along with their application, they must submit a 1,000-word essay on the challenges facing the beef industry and their solutions. They may also submit a statement of financial need. Selection is based on, in this order of importance, activities and scholastic achievement, communication skills (both essay and verbal), and reference letters.

**Financial data:** The stipend is $2,500.

**Duration:** 1 year.

**Number awarded:** 1 each year.

**Deadline:** November of each year.

---

## 1336 COMPUTER GRAPHIC DESIGN SCHOLARSHIPS

Armed Forces Communications and Electronics Association
Attn: AFCEA Educational Foundation
4400 Fair Lakes Court
Fairfax, VA 22033-3899
Phone: (703) 631-6149; (800) 336-4583, ext. 6149; Fax: (703) 631-4693; Email: scholarship@afcea.org
Web: www.afcea.org/education/scholarships/undergraduate/graphicdes.asp

**Summary:** To provide financial assistance to students who are working on an undergraduate or graduate degree in computer graphic design.

**Eligibility:** Open to full-time students who are enrolled at an accredited college or university in the United States at least as a sophomore. Applicants must be U.S. citizens working on an undergraduate or graduate degree in computer graphic design or a related field. They must submit a sample of digital graphic artwork for intranets and internets, especially web-based graphics. Along with the artwork (in .JPEG, .GIF, or .TIF format on CD, zip disk, or diskette), they must include a textual statement of 100 to 200 words that describes the image submitted, how it was created, and what specific intent or purpose it represents. Selection is based on artistic creativity, mastery of web technology, a statement of career goals, school and community activities, and financial need.

**Financial data:** The stipend is $2,000.

**Duration:** 1 year; may be renewed.

**Number awarded:** 1 or more each year.

**Deadline:** October of each year.

---

## 1337 CONNECTICUT ARCHITECTURE FOUNDATION SCHOLARSHIPS

Connecticut Architecture Foundation, Attn: Executive Vice President
87 Willow Street
New Haven, CT 06511
Phone: (203) 865-2195; Fax: (203) 562-5378
Web: www.aiact.org

**Summary:** To provide financial assistance to Connecticut residents who are working on a bachelor's or master's degree in architecture.

**Eligibility:** Open to Connecticut residents who 1) have completed at least 2 years of an accredited bachelor of architecture program; 2) have been accepted to an accredited master's degree program in architecture (may be enrolled in a non-accredited undergraduate program; or 3) are enrolled in an accredited master's degree program in architecture. Applicants must be enrolled as full-time students. They must submit a 1-page letter describing their accomplishments and goals; a 1- to 2-page resume of education, experience, honors, activities, and interests; documentation of financial need; 2 faculty letters of reference; and a favorite project with their rationale for their design.

**Financial data:** Stipends range from $500 to $1,000.

**Duration:** 1 year.

**Number awarded:** Varies each year.

**Deadline:** April of each year.

---

## 1338 CONNECTICUT BROADCASTERS ASSOCIATION SCHOLARSHIPS

Connecticut Broadcasters Association
c/o Paul Taff, President
P.O. Box 678
Glastonbury, CT 06033
Phone: (860) 633-5031; (860) 657-2491; Email: pkt@ctba.org
Web: www.ctba.org

**Summary:** To provide financial assistance to Connecticut residents who are studying a field related to broadcasting in college.

**Eligibility:** Open to Connecticut residents who are entering their junior or senior year in college. Applicants must be majoring in communications, marketing, or other field related to broadcasting. Selection is based on academic achievement, community service, goals in the chosen field, and financial need.

**Financial data:** A stipend is awarded (amount not specified).

**Duration:** 1 year.

**Number awarded:** 1 or more each year.

---

## 1339 CONNECTICUT BUILDING CONGRESS SCHOLARSHIPS

Connecticut Building Congress, Attn: Scholarship Fund
2600 Dixwell Avenue, Suite 7
Hamden, CT 06514-1800
Phone: (203) 281-3183; Fax: (203) 281-8932; Email: info@cbc-ct.org
Web: www.cbc-ct.org/scholarship.html

**Summary:** To provide financial assistance to high school seniors in Connecticut who are interested in studying a field related to the construction industry in college.

**Eligibility:** Open to graduating seniors at high schools in Connecticut. Applicants must be interested in attending a 2- or 4-year college or university to major in a field related to construction (e.g., architecture, engineering, construction management, surveying, planning, drafting). They must submit an essay (up to 500 words) that explains how their planned studies will relate to a career in the construction industry. Selection is based on academic merit, extracurricular activities, potential, and financial need.

**Financial data:** Stipends range from $500 to $2,000 per year.

**Duration:** Up to 4 years.

**Number awarded:** Varies each year.

**Deadline:** February of each year.

---

## 1340 COPY EDITING SCHOLARSHIPS

American Copy Editors Society, Attn: Carol DeMasters, ACES Administrator
38309 Genesee Lake Road
Oconomowoc, WI 53066
Email: carolafi@execpc.com
Web: www.copydesk.org/scholarships.htm

**Summary:** To provide financial assistance to undergraduate and graduate students interested in becoming copy editors.

**Eligibility:** Open to college juniors, seniors, and graduate students who are interested in a career as a copy editor. Graduating students who will take full-time jobs or internships as copy editors are also eligible. Applicants must submit 1) a list of course work relevant to copy editing they have completed; 2) information on their copy editing experience, including work on student and professional newspapers; 3) an essay, up to 750 words, on what they think makes a good copy editor and why they want to prepare for that career; 4) 2 letters of recommendation; 5) 5 to 10 headlines they have written; and 6) a copy of a story they have edited, including an explanation of the changes they have made and the circumstances under which it was edited. Selection is based on commitment to copy editing as a career, work experience in copy editing, and abilities in copy editing. Financial need is not considered. The highest ranked applicant receives the Merv Aubespin Scholarship.

**Financial data:** Stipends are $2,500 (for the Merv Aubespin Scholarship) or $1,000.

**Duration:** 1 year.

**Number awarded:** 4 or 5 each year.

**Deadline:** October of each year.

---

## 1341 CORDIE HUGHES SCHOLARSHIP

National Association of Women in Construction-Nashville Chapter 16
Attn: Scholarship Fund
P.O. Box 22246
Nashville, TN 37202-2246
Email: info@nawicnashville.com
Web: www.nawicnashville.com

**Summary:** To provide financial assistance to residents of Tennessee working on an undergraduate degree in a construction-related field.

**Eligibility:** Open to residents of Tennessee attending a college or university in Alabama, Georgia, or Tennessee. Applicants must be working on a degree in a field related to construction (e.g., architecture, engineering, construction management). They must have a GPA of 2.8 or higher and be able to demonstrate financial need. Priority is given to applicants entering their junior or senior year at a 4-year institution. If no student at a 4-year school qualifies, students at 2-year colleges are considered.

**Financial data:** A stipend is awarded (amount not specified).

**Duration:** 1 year.

**Number awarded:** Varies each year; recently, a total of $2,000 was available for this program.

## 1342 COURAGE IN STUDENT JOURNALISM AWARDS

Student Press Law Center, Attn: Executive Director
1101 Wilson Boulevard, Suite 1100
Arlington, VA 22209-2211
Phone: (703) 807-1904; Email: splc@splc.org
Web: www.splc.org/csjaward.asp

**Summary:** To recognize and reward secondary school student journalists and school officials who have supported the First Amendment.

**Eligibility:** Open to deserving middle and high school student journalists and school officials who have stood up in support of the First Amendment. Student applicants must have shown determination, despite difficulty and resistance, in exercising their First Amendment press rights. School administrator applicants must have demonstrated support, under difficult circumstances, for the First Amendment press rights of their school's student media. Entrants should submit a written description (up to 600 words) of how their case meets the entry criteria, along with 2 letters of support and supporting materials or press clippings.

**Financial data:** The winners in each category (student and administrator) receive a $5,000 award.

**Duration:** The award is presented annually.

**Number awarded:** 2 each year: 1 student and 1 school official.

**Deadline:** June of each year.

## 1343 COX FOUNDATION SCHOLARSHIPS

Asian American Journalists Association, Attn: Student Programs Coordinator
1182 Market Street, Suite 320
San Francisco, CA 94102
Phone: (415) 346-2051, ext. 102; Fax: (415) 346-6343; Email: brandons@aaja.org
Web: www.aaja.org/programs/for_students/scholarships

**Summary:** To provide financial assistance to student members of the Asian American Journalists Association (AAJA) interested in careers in broadcast, photo, or print journalism.

**Eligibility:** Open to AAJA members who are high school seniors or college students (graduate or undergraduate) enrolled full time in accredited institutions. Applicants must submit a 500-word essay on their involvement or interest in the Asian American community and how, if they are awarded this scholarship, they would contribute to the field of journalism and/or media issues involving the Asian American and Pacific Islander community. Selection is based on scholastic ability, commitment to journalism, sensitivity to Asian American and Pacific Islander issues as demonstrated by community involvement, journalistic ability, and financial need.

**Financial data:** The stipend is $2,500.

**Duration:** 1 year; may be renewed.

**Number awarded:** Varies each year.

**Deadline:** April of each year.

## 1344 CRISTINA NAZARIO SCHOLARSHIP FOR THE FINE ARTS

Portuguese Heritage Scholarship Foundation, Attn: Academic Secretary
P.O. Box 30246
Bethesda, MD 20824-0246
Phone: (301) 652-2775; Email: phsf@vivaportugal.com
Web: www.vivaportugal.com/phsf/apply.htm

**Summary:** To provide financial assistance for college to students of Portuguese American heritage interested in studying fine arts or related fields.

**Eligibility:** Open to high school seniors or currently-enrolled college students who are of Portuguese American ancestry. Applicants must be U.S. residents and attending or planning to attend an accredited 4-year college or university. They must be interested in studying fine arts, architecture, or historic preservation. Selection is based on academic achievement and artistic accomplishments. Preference is given to students from the Washington, D.C. area, but all qualified applicants are considered.

**Financial data:** The stipend is $2,000 per year.

**Duration:** 4 years, provided the recipient maintains a GPA of 3.0 or higher.

**Number awarded:** 1 each year.

**Deadline:** January of each year.

## 1345 C.T. LANG JOURNALISM MINORITY SCHOLARSHIP AND INTERNSHIP

Albuquerque Journal, Attn: Scholarship Committee
7777 Jefferson Street, N.E.
P.O. Drawer J
Albuquerque, NM 87103
Phone: (505) 823-7777

**Summary:** To provide financial assistance and work experience to minority upper-division students in journalism programs at universities in New Mexico.

**Eligibility:** Open to minority students majoring or minoring in journalism at a New Mexico university in their junior year with a GPA of 2.5 or higher. Applicants must be enrolled full time. They must be planning a career in newswriting, photography, design, copy editing, or online. Selection is based on clips of published stories, a short autobiography that explains the applicant's interest in the field, a grade transcript, and a letter of recommendation.

**Financial data:** The scholarship is $1,000 per semester; the recipient also receives a paid internship and moving expenses.

**Duration:** The scholarship is for 2 semesters (fall and spring). The internship is for 1 semester.

**Number awarded:** 1 each year.

**Deadline:** December of each year.

## 1346 C.T. LANG JOURNALISM SCHOLARSHIP

Albuquerque Journal, Attn: Scholarship Committee
7777 Jefferson Street, N.E.
P.O. Drawer J
Albuquerque, NM 87103
Phone: (505) 823-7777

**Summary:** To provide financial assistance to students enrolled in journalism programs at designated universities in New Mexico and adjoining states.

**Eligibility:** Open to students majoring or minoring in journalism (including print, print-photo, computer aided design, or online) in their junior or senior year with a GPA of 3.0 or higher. Applicants must be enrolled full time at the University of New Mexico, Eastern New Mexico University, Western New Mexico University, Highlands University, New Mexico State University, College of Santa Fe, University of Texas at El Paso, University of Arizona, or Northern Arizona University. They must be planning a career in newswriting, photography, design, or copy editing. Selection is based on a letter of recommendation from a faculty member, a grade transcript, and 3 writing samples published commercially or in a school publication or (for photography students) 5 published pictures.

**Financial data:** A stipend is awarded (amount not specified).

**Duration:** 1 year.

**Number awarded:** 1 or more each year.

**Deadline:** February of each year.

## 1347 C.T. LANG JOURNALISM SCHOLARSHIPS FOR HIGH SCHOOL SENIORS

Albuquerque Journal, Attn: Scholarship Committee
7777 Jefferson Street, N.E.
P.O. Drawer J
Albuquerque, NM 87103
Phone: (505) 823-7777

**Summary:** To provide financial assistance to seniors graduating from high schools in New Mexico who are interested in studying journalism in college.

**Eligibility:** Open to graduating seniors at high schools in New Mexico who are planning to attend college full time and prepare for a career in print journalism. Applicants must write an essay (300 to 500 words) on questions that change annually; recently, the topics were 1) should the United States reinstate a draft for military service; 2) has the Albuquerque Police Department gone too far in trying to crack down on teen drinking; or 3) is there too much emphasis in our schools on athletics, to the detriment of academics. In addition to the essay, they must submit 2 letters of recommendation, 2 samples of their work (preferably articles or photos that have been published in a school newspaper or publication), and high school transcripts (with a GPA of 3.0 or higher).

**Financial data:** The stipend is $1,000 per year.

**Duration:** 1 year; may be renewed up to 3 additional years if the recipient continues to prepare for a career in print journalism and maintains a GPA of 3.0 or higher.

**Number awarded:** 1 or more each year.

**Deadline:** February of each year.

## 1348 CULINARY TRUST SCHOLARSHIPS

International Association of Culinary Professionals Foundation
Attn: Culinary Trust Scholarship Program
304 West Liberty Street, Suite 201
Louisville, KY 40202
Phone: (502) 581-9786, ext. 264; (800) 928-4227; Fax: (502) 589-3602;
Email: tgribbins@hqtrs.com
Web: www.iacpfoundation.org/scholarships.html
**Summary:** To provide financial assistance to culinary professionals and students interested in pursuing additional training in the United States or abroad in the culinary arts.
**Eligibility:** Open to 1) culinary professionals who have at least 2 years of food service experience (paid, volunteer, or a combination of both); and 2) students who have a GPA of 3.0 or higher. Applicants must submit 2 letters of recommendation and a 2-page essay on their educational and career goals and how they plan to achieve them. They may be from any country. Selection is based on merit, food service work experience, culinary goals and skills, and references.
**Financial data:** Stipends range from $1,500 to $5,000.
**Duration:** 1 year.
**Number awarded:** Varies each year.
**Deadline:** December of each year.

## 1349 DAMARIS SMITH DESIMONE SCHOLARSHIP

Daughters of the American Revolution-New York State Organization
c/o Layla Voll
311 West 21st Street
New York, NY 10011
Email: Layla_Voll@hotmail.com
Web: www.nydar.org/education/desimone.html
**Summary:** To provide financial assistance to high school seniors in New York who plan to study American history in college.
**Eligibility:** Open to seniors graduating from high schools in New York who plan to attend an accredited 4-year college or university in the state. Applicants must be intending to major in U.S. history. Selection is based on merit, including achievement in high school and the community and personal and academic interests.
**Financial data:** The stipend is $1,000.
**Duration:** 1 year; nonrenewable.
**Number awarded:** 1 each year.
**Deadline:** January of each year.

## 1350 DANIEL J. EDELMAN AWARD

Public Relations Student Society of America, Attn: Director of Education
33 Irving Place, Third Floor
New York, NY 10003-2376
Phone: (212) 460-1474; Fax: (212) 995-0757; Email: prssa@prsa.org
Web: www.prssa.org/resources/award-DanielEdelman.asp
**Summary:** To provide financial assistance for college to members of the Public Relations Student Society of America.
**Eligibility:** Open to members of the society who are currently enrolled in a full-time program of study at an accredited 4-year college or university. Applicants must submit 2 letters of recommendation and 10 samples of their individual public relations work. Selection is based on leadership, achievements and activities in public relations, and recommendations from faculty members and/or industry professionals. Financial need is not considered.
**Financial data:** The winner receives a cash award of $1,500, of which $1,000 is paid upon winning the award and $500 at the start of a 3-month paid internship at an Edelman Worldwide office in the United States. The runner-up receives $500 and an opportunity to interview at an Edelman U.S. office for a full-time position.
**Duration:** 1 year.
**Number awarded:** 1 winner and 1 runner-up are selected each year.
**Deadline:** December of each year.

## 1351 DAR AMERICAN HISTORY SCHOLARSHIP

National Society Daughters of the American Revolution
Attn: Scholarship Committee
1776 D Street, N.W.
Washington, DC 20006-5303
Phone: (202) 628-1776
Web: www.dar.org/natsociety/edout_scholar.cfm
**Summary:** To provide financial assistance to high school seniors planning to major in American history in college.

**Eligibility:** Open to graduating high school seniors who plan to major in American history. Applicants must be sponsored by a local chapter of the Daughters of the American Revolution (DAR). Judging first takes place at the state level; 2 state winners then enter the national competition. Selection is based on academic excellence, commitment to field of study, and financial need. U.S. citizenship is required.
**Financial data:** First-place stipends are $2,000 per year, second-place stipends are $1,000 per year, and third-place stipends are $1,000 per year.
**Duration:** 4 years.
**Number awarded:** Up to 3 each year.
**Deadline:** Applications must be submitted to the state chair by January of each year.

## 1352 DAVID S. BARR AWARDS

Newspaper Guild-CWA
501 Third Street, N.W., Suite 250
Washington, DC 20001-2797
Phone: (202) 434-7177; Fax: (202) 434-1472; Email: guild@cwa-union.org
Web: www.newsguild.org
**Summary:** To recognize and reward student journalists whose work has helped promote social justice.
**Eligibility:** Open to high school students (including those enrolled in vocational, technical, or special education programs) and college students (including those in community colleges and in graduate programs). Applicants must submit work published or broadcast during the preceding calendar year; entries should help to right a wrong, correct an injustice, or promote justice and fairness.
**Financial data:** The award is $1,500 for college students or $500 for high school students.
**Duration:** The awards are presented annually.
**Number awarded:** 2 each year.
**Deadline:** January of each year.

## 1353 DAVID W. MILLER AWARD FOR STUDENT JOURNALISTS

Chronicle of Higher Education, Attn: Deputy Managing Editor
1255 23rd Street, N.W.
Washington, DC 20037
Email: milleraward@chronicle.com; (202) 466-1000
Web: chronicle.com/help/milleraward.htm
**Summary:** To recognize and reward college journalists who submit outstanding samples of their published work.
**Eligibility:** Open to undergraduate students in any country. Applicants are invited to submit up to 3 samples of their published work (in English), accompanied by a 1-page letter describing the articles and why they were chosen for submission. Entries must have appeared in a campus publication during the previous academic year. Each piece should be journalistic, using expository, explanatory, narrative, or other techniques to report evenhandedly on a topic of intellectual interest. Opinion essays, personal columns, scholarly or research papers, and articles that present the author's own research findings are ineligible.
**Financial data:** The award is $2,000.
**Duration:** The award is presented annually.
**Number awarded:** 1 each year.
**Deadline:** June of each year.

## 1354 DAVID W. SELF SCHOLARSHIP

United Methodist Church, Attn: Division on Ministries with Young People
P.O. Box 340003
Nashville, TN 37203-0003
Phone: (615) 340-7184; (877) 899-2780, ext. 7184; Fax: (615) 340-1764;
Email: umyouthorg@gbod.org
Web: www.umyouth.org/scholarships.html
**Summary:** To provide financial assistance to Methodist high school seniors who wish to prepare for a church-related career.
**Eligibility:** Open to graduating high school seniors who have been active members of a United Methodist church for at least 1 year. Applicants must have been admitted to an accredited college or university to prepare for a church-related career. They must have maintained at least a "C" average throughout high school and be able to demonstrate financial need. Along with their application, they must submit brief essays on their participation in church projects and activities, a leadership experience, the role their faith plays in their life, the church-related vocation to which God is calling them, and their extracurricular interests and activities. U.S. citizenship or permanent resident status is required.

**Financial data:** The stipend is $1,000.
**Duration:** 1 year; nonrenewable.
**Number awarded:** 2 each year.
**Deadline:** May of each year.

### 1355 DELAWARE LEGISLATIVE ESSAY SCHOLARSHIPS

Delaware Higher Education Commission
Carvel State Office Building
820 North French Street
Wilmington, DE 19801
Phone: (302) 577-3240; (800) 292-7935; Fax: (302) 577-6765;
Email: dhec@doe.k12.de.us
Web: www.doe.state.de.us/high-ed/essay.htm
**Summary:** To recognize and reward, with college scholarships, Delaware high school seniors who submit outstanding essays on a topic of historical significance.
**Eligibility:** Open to seniors graduating from high schools in Delaware who plan to enroll full time in an accredited college or university. Applicants must submit an essay of 500 to 2,000 words on a topic that changes annually. U.S. citizenship or permanent resident status is required. Students first compete within their state senatorial and representative legislative district.
**Financial data:** Legislative district awards are $750. Statewide winners receive $7,500 for first, $3,750 for second, and $2,250 for third.
**Duration:** 1 year; nonrenewable.
**Number awarded:** 65 each year: 1 in each of the 21 senatorial districts and 41 representative districts plus 3 statewide winners.
**Deadline:** November of each year.

### 1356 DENDEL SCHOLARSHIPS

Handweavers Guild of America, Inc., Attn: Scholarship Chair
1255 Buford Highway, Suite 211
Suwanee, GA 30024
Phone: (678) 730-0010; Fax: (678) 730-0836; Email: hga@weavespindye.org
Web: www.weavespindye.org
**Summary:** To provide financial assistance to undergraduate and graduate students working on a degree in the field of fiber arts.
**Eligibility:** Open to undergraduate and graduate students enrolled in accredited colleges and universities in the United States, its possessions, and Canada. Applicants must be working on a degree in the field of fiber arts, including training for research, textile history, and conservation. Along with their application, they must submit 1) an essay on their study goals and how those fit into their future plans, and 2) 5 to 16 slides of their work. Selection is based on artistic and technical merit; financial need is not considered.
**Financial data:** The amount of the award depends on the availability of funds. Recipients may use the funds for tuition, materials (e.g., film for photographs), or travel.
**Duration:** 1 year.
**Number awarded:** Varies; more than $4,000 is available for this program each year.
**Deadline:** March of each year.

### 1357 DICK LARSEN SCHOLARSHIP

Washington News Council, Attn: Scholarship Committee
P.O. Box 3672
Seattle, WA 98124-3672
Phone: (206) 262-9793; Fax: (206) 464-7902; Email: info@wanewscouncil.org
Web: www.wanewscouncil.org
**Summary:** To provide financial assistance to Washington college students who are majoring in a communication-related field at an academic institution in the state.
**Eligibility:** Open to graduates of high schools in Washington who have a serious interest in communications, including journalism, politics, public relations, or related fields. Applicants must be enrolled at a 4-year public or private university in the state. They must be able to demonstrate financial need. Along with their application, they submit an essay of 500 to 1,000 words on themselves, why they want to prepare for a career in communications, and how they think they can contribute to their chosen profession.
**Financial data:** The stipend is $1,000.
**Duration:** 1 year.
**Number awarded:** 1 each year.
**Deadline:** May of each year.

### 1358 DIRECT MARKETING SCHOLARSHIP

New England Direct Marketing Association, Attn: NEDMA Foundation
193 Haverhill Street
North Reading, MA 01864
Phone: (978) 664-3877; Fax: (978) 664-2835; Email: mke@theworld.com
Web: www.nedma.com/foundation.html
**Summary:** To provide financial assistance and work experience to upper-division students in New England who are preparing for a career in direct marketing.
**Eligibility:** Open to students who have completed their sophomore or junior year at a college or university in New England. Applicants must be majoring in marketing, advertising, communications, or other field designed to prepare them for a career in direct marketing. Along with their application, they must submit an essay covering such topics as why they are applying for this scholarship, what courses in their major have interested them the most and why, the extracurricular activities in which they have participated, their employment or internship experiences (especially those related to marketing, advertising, or journalism), their special interest in the field, how they believe this scholarship will affect their short- and long-term goals, and what direct marketing means to them. Financial need is not considered in the selection process.
**Financial data:** The award includes a stipend of $3,000 to be applied to college tuition, attendance at a nationally sponsored seminar on the basics of direct marketing, a paid summer internship at a New England firm that represents a segment of the direct marketing industry, and attendance at the annual conference of the New England Direct Marketing Association (NEDMA).
**Duration:** 1 year.
**Number awarded:** 1 each year.
**Deadline:** February of each year.

### 1359 DIVISION OF ENGINEERING SERVICES ENGINEERING/ARCHITECTURAL SCHOLARSHIP

California Department of Transportation
Attn: Division of Engineering Services
MS 9 5/2J
P.O. Box 168041
Sacramento, CA 95816-8041
Phone: (916) 227-8126; Email: karen_bailey@dot.ca.gov
Web: www.dot.ca.gov/hq/esc/scholarships
**Summary:** To provide financial assistance to high school seniors in California who plan to study engineering or architecture at a college or university in the state.
**Eligibility:** Open to seniors graduating from high schools in California and planning to enroll in an engineering or architectural program at a community college, state college, or university in the state. Applicants must submit 1) a 100-word personal statement on their college and career plans and how they believe they can make a contribution to Caltrans; 2) a 500-word essay on how they would improve California's current transportation system; 3) a list of community and school activities; 4) information on work and/or volunteer experience; and 4) letters of recommendation.
**Financial data:** The stipend is $1,000.
**Duration:** 1 year.
**Number awarded:** At least 1 each year.
**Deadline:** March

### 1360 DONNA REED PERFORMING ARTS SCHOLARSHIPS

Donna Reed Foundation for the Performing Arts
1305 Broadway
Denison, IA 51442
Phone: (712) 263-3334; (800) 336-4692; Fax: (712) 263-8026;
Email: info@donnareed.org
Web: www.donnareed.org
**Summary:** To provide financial assistance to high school seniors interested in studying the performing arts in college.
**Eligibility:** Open to high school seniors who wish to pursue an education or a career in 1 of the following 3 performing arts: acting, vocal (classical, jazz, popular), or musical theater. Applicants must graduate or have graduated from high school during the period between September prior to applying and August after applying. They must submit audio or videotapes; based on those tapes, finalists are invited to a live competition in June at the Donna Reed Festival and Workshops for the Performing Arts in Denison, Iowa. Selection is based on talent. Grades and financial need are not considered. U.S. citizenship or permanent resident status is required. Separate award are presented to residents of Iowa and to residents of Crawford County, Iowa.
**Financial data:** National winners receive $1,000 per year and finalists receive $500. Funds may be used for an accredited postsecondary or approved program

of study of the recipient's choice. Iowa winners receive $1,000 scholarships and Crawford County winners receive $500 scholarships.

**Duration:** Scholarships for national winners are for 4 years. Scholarships for other winners are for 1 year.

**Number awarded:** 9 each year: in each of the 3 divisions, 1 national winner and 2 other finalists receive awards. In addition, each of the 9 national finalists receive free tuition and all expenses to participate in the Donna Reed Festival and Workshops for the Performing Arts. Another 3 scholarships (1 in each division) are awarded to Iowa residents, and another 3 scholarships (1 in each division) are awarded to residents of Crawford County, Iowa.

**Deadline:** February of each year.

## 1361 DORE SCHARY AWARDS

Anti-Defamation League, Attn: Dore Schary Awards
823 United Nations Plaza
New York, NY 10017
Phone: (212) 885-7949; Fax: (212) 867-0779; Email: hymac@adl.org
Web: www.adl.org

**Summary:** To recognize and reward outstanding film and video productions on human rights topics by students and young filmmakers.

**Eligibility:** Open to 1) university and graduate students majoring in film and/or television, and 2) amateur and professional filmmakers 25 years of age or younger. Applicants must submit productions that were completed during the 2 preceding calendar years and deal with such themes as prejudice and discrimination, hatred, bigotry, racism, anti-Semitism, or any theme that supports diversity. Entries may be submitted in either of 2 categories: narrative or documentary. Productions based on previously published works of fiction are not eligible. All entries should be submitted on videocassette format. Selection is based on subject matter, imagination and creativity, and technical excellence.

**Financial data:** The prizes are $2,000. Winners are flown to Los Angeles for the awards ceremony.

**Duration:** The competition is held annually.

**Number awarded:** 2 or 3 each year: 1 in each of the 2 categories plus a special jury award that may be presented.

**Deadline:** May of each year.

## 1362 DORIS AND CLARENCE GLICK CLASSICAL MUSIC SCHOLARSHIP FUND

Hawai'i Community Foundation, Attn: Scholarship Department
1164 Bishop Street, Suite 800
Honolulu, HI 96813
Phone: (808) 566-5570; (888) 731-3863; Fax: (808) 521-6286;
Email: scholarships@hcf-hawaii.org
Web: www.hawaiicommunityfoundation.org/scholar/scholar.php

**Summary:** To provide financial assistance to residents of Hawaii who are interested in preparing for a career in classical music.

**Eligibility:** Open to residents of Hawaii who are planning to study music (with an emphasis on classical music) as full-time students on the undergraduate or graduate level. Applicants must be able to demonstrate academic achievement (GPA of 2.7 or higher), good moral character, and financial need. In addition to filling out the standard application form, they must write a short statement indicating their reasons for attending college, their planned course of study, their career goals, and their program of study as it relates to classical music.

**Financial data:** The amount of the award depends on the availability of funds and the need of the recipient; recently, stipends averaged $1,000.

**Duration:** 1 year.

**Number awarded:** Varies each year; recently, 8 of these scholarships were awarded.

**Deadline:** February of each year.

## 1363 DOROTHY DANN BULLOCK MUSIC THERAPY AWARD

National Federation of Music Clubs
1336 North Delaware Street
Indianapolis, IN 46202-2481
Phone: (317) 638-4003; Fax: (317) 638-0503; Email: info@nfmc-music.org
Web: www.nfmc-music.org/Competitions/Annual_Student/annual_student.html

**Summary:** To provide financial assistance to members of the National Federation of Music Clubs (NFMC) who are majoring in music therapy.

**Eligibility:** Open to music therapy majors (college sophomores, juniors, and seniors) in accredited schools offering music therapy degrees approved by the National Association of Music Therapists. Student membership in the federa-

tion and U.S. citizenship are required. Applicants must demonstrate musical talent, skills, and training, especially pianistic ability in accompanying and sight reading; ability to direct; pleasant singing voice; emotional stability; self-reliance; patience; tact; leadership; intelligence; good health; ability to work with groups; and dedication to music therapy as a career.

**Financial data:** The award is $1,000; funds must be used for further study.

**Duration:** The award is presented annually.

**Number awarded:** 1 each year.

**Deadline:** February of each year.

## 1364 DOUGLAS HASKELL AWARDS FOR STUDENT JOURNALISM

American Institute of Architects-New York Chapter
Attn: New York Foundation for Architecture
200 Lexington Avenue, Sixth Floor
New York, NY 10016
Phone: (212) 683-0023, ext. 14; Email: pwest@aiany.org
Web: www.aiany.org/nyfoundation

**Summary:** To recognize and reward excellent college student writing on architecture and related design subjects.

**Eligibility:** Open to students enrolled in a professional architecture or related program (e.g., art history, interior design, urban studies, or landscape architecture). Submissions are limited to articles on architecture, urban design, or related topics published during the past 3 years, unpublished works scheduled for publication in the current year, and student-edited journals released this year or last. Entries must be accompanied by a concise statement describing the purpose of the piece, its intended audience, and the date and place of publication. Each entrant is limited to 2 submissions. Entrants must send 5 copies of each article and 3 copies of each journal.

**Financial data:** The prize is $2,000. The total amount may be awarded to a single student or divided among several.

**Duration:** The competition is held annually.

**Number awarded:** 1 or more each year.

**Deadline:** April of each year.

## 1365 DR. JULIANNE MALVEAUX SCHOLARSHIP

National Association of Negro Business and Professional Women's Clubs
Attn: Scholarship Committee
1806 New Hampshire Avenue, N.W.
Washington, DC 20009-3208
Phone: (202) 483-4206; Fax: (202) 462-7253; Email: nanbpwc@aol.com
Web: www.nanbpwc.org/Education/shtml

**Summary:** To provide financial assistance to African American women studying journalism, economics, or a related field in college.

**Eligibility:** Open to African American women enrolled in an accredited college or university as a sophomore or junior. Applicants must have a GPA of 3.0 or higher and be majoring in journalism, economics, or a related field.

**Financial data:** The stipend is $1,000.

**Duration:** 1 year.

**Number awarded:** 1 or more each year.

**Deadline:** February of each year.

## 1366 EASTERN STAR TRAINING AWARDS FOR RELIGIOUS LEADERSHIP

Order of the Eastern Star, Attn: Right Worthy Grand Secretary
1618 New Hampshire Avenue, N.W.
Washington, DC 20009-2549
Phone: (202) 667-4737; (800) 648-1182; Fax: (202) 462-5162;
Email: easternstar@erols.com
Web: www.easternstar.org

**Summary:** To provide financial assistance for college to individuals who are willing to dedicate their lives to full-time religious service.

**Eligibility:** Open to applicants preparing for leadership in various fields of religious service, such as ministers, missionaries, directors of church music, directors of religious education, and counselors of youth leadership. They need not be affiliated with the Masonic Fraternity or the Order of the Eastern Star. Specific eligibility is determined by each Grand Jurisdiction (state or province) and each chapter under jurisdiction of the General Grand Chapter.

**Financial data:** The amounts are determined by each jurisdiction or committee on the basis of funds available, number of applicants, and needs of the individual. Funds are paid directly to the recipient's school and may be used, as needed, for books, tuition, board, or medical aid.

**Duration:** 1 year; may be renewed.
**Number awarded:** Varies each year.
**Deadline:** Deadlines vary by jurisdiction or committee; check with the unit in your area for details.

## 1367 EASTMAN SCHOLARSHIP PROGRAM

University Film and Video Foundation
c/o Jennifer Arndt
Brian Johns
1428 Sixth Street, Suite 302
Santa Monica, CA 90401
Phone: (310) 319-2099; Fax: (310) 899-0876; Email: EastmanScholars@aol.com
Web: www.kodak.com/US/en/motion/students/program/scholarship.shtml
**Summary:** To provide funding for tuition scholarships or production grants to undergraduate and graduate film students.
**Eligibility:** Open to students working on a bachelor's or master's degree at U.S. and Canadian colleges and universities offering programs in film, cinematography, or film production. Each school may nominate up to 2 candidates. Nominees must submit samples of their work that communicate a story or theme in some fashion; clips or short vignettes are not acceptable. Selection is based on academic achievement, creative and technical ability, communications ability, and range of filmmaking experience.
**Financial data:** Up to $5,000 (or Canadian equivalent) is awarded to each recipient. Funds are paid directly to the recipient's school and may be used for tuition or as a production grant.
**Duration:** 1 year.
**Number awarded:** Varies each year.
**Deadline:** Nominations must be submitted by May of each year.

## 1368 EDITH H. HENDERSON SCHOLARSHIP

Landscape Architecture Foundation, Attn: Scholarship Program
818 18th Street, N.W., Suite 810
Washington, DC 20006-3520
Phone: (202) 331-7070; Fax: (202) 331-7079; Email: rfigura@lafoundation.org
Web: www.laprofession.org
**Summary:** To provide financial assistance to undergraduate or graduate students in landscape architecture.
**Eligibility:** Open to landscape architecture students in any year of graduate or undergraduate work. The prize is awarded to a student committed to the goal of developing practical communication skills as part of the role of a landscape architect. Applicants must submit a 200- to 400-word review of the book *Edith Henderson's Home Landscape Companion*. They must also participate in a class in public speaking or creative writing. Selection is based on the essay and class participation, professional experience, community involvement, extracurricular activities, and financial need.
**Financial data:** This scholarship is $1,000.
**Number awarded:** 1 each year.
**Deadline:** April of each year.

## 1369 EDWARD D. STONE, JR. AND ASSOCIATES MINORITY SCHOLARSHIP

Landscape Architecture Foundation, Attn: Scholarship Program
818 18th Street, N.W., Suite 810
Washington, DC 20006-3520
Phone: (202) 331-7070; Fax: (202) 331-7079; Email: rfigura@lafoundation.org
Web: www.laprofession.org
**Summary:** To provide financial assistance to minority college students who wish to study landscape architecture.
**Eligibility:** Open to African American, Hispanic, Native American, and minority college students of other cultural and ethnic backgrounds, if they are entering their final 2 years of undergraduate study in landscape architecture. Applicants must submit a 500-word essay on a design or research effort they wish to pursue (explaining how it will contribute to the advancement of the profession and to their ethnic heritage), 4 to 8 35mm color slides or black-and-white photographs of their best work, and 2 letters of recommendation. Selection is based on professional experience, community involvement, extracurricular activities, and financial need.
**Financial data:** The stipend is $1,000.
**Duration:** 1 year.
**Number awarded:** 2 each year.
**Deadline:** April of each year.

## 1370 EDWARD PAYSON AND BERNICE PI'ILANI IRWIN SCHOLARSHIP

Hawai'i Community Foundation, Attn: Scholarship Department
1164 Bishop Street, Suite 800
Honolulu, HI 96813
Phone: (808) 566-5570; (888) 731-3863; Fax: (808) 521-6286;
Email: scholar ships@hcf-hawaii.org
Web: www.hawaiicommunityfoundation.org/scholar/scholar.php
**Summary:** To provide financial assistance to Hawaii residents who are interested in preparing for a career in journalism.
**Eligibility:** Open to Hawaii residents who are studying journalism or communications as college juniors, seniors, or graduate students. They must be able to demonstrate academic achievement (GPA of 2.7 or higher), good moral character, and financial need. In addition to filling out the standard application form, applicants must write a short statement indicating their reasons for attending college, their planned course of study, their career goals, and why they have chosen to major in journalism.
**Financial data:** The amounts of the awards depend on the availability of funds and the need of the recipient; recently, stipends averaged $1,840.
**Duration:** 1 year.
**Number awarded:** Varies each year; recently, 24 of these scholarships were awarded.
**Deadline:** February of each year.

## 1371 EISENHOWER HISPANIC-SERVING INSTITUTIONS FELLOWSHIPS

Department of Transportation
Federal Highway Administration, Attn: National Highway Institute, HNHI-20
4600 North Fairfax Drive, Suite 800
Arlington, VA 22203-1553
Phone: (703) 235-0538; Fax: (703) 235-0593;
Email: transportationedu@fhwa.dot.gov
Web: www.nhi.fhwa.dot.gov/ddetfp.asp
**Summary:** To provide financial assistance for undergraduate study in transportation-related fields to students at Hispanic Serving Institutions.
**Eligibility:** Open to students who are enrolled at federally-designated 4-year Hispanic Serving Institutions (HSIs) and who are working on a degree in a transportation-related field (i.e., engineering, accounting, business, architecture, environmental sciences, etc.). Applicants must have entered their junior year, have at least a 3.0 GPA, and have a faculty sponsor.
**Financial data:** The stipend covers the fellow's full cost of education, including tuition and fees.
**Duration:** 1 year.
**Number awarded:** Varies each year; recently, 18 students received support from this program.
**Deadline:** February of each year.

## 1372 EISENHOWER HISTORICALLY BLACK COLLEGES AND UNIVERSITIES FELLOWSHIPS

Department of Transportation
Federal Highway Administration, Attn: National Highway Institute, HNHI-20
4600 North Fairfax Drive, Suite 800
Arlington, VA 22203-1553
Phone: (703) 235-0538; Fax: (703) 235-0593;
Email: transportationedu@fhwa.dot.gov
Web: www.nhi.fhwa.dot.gov/ddetfp.asp
**Summary:** To provide financial assistance for undergraduate study in transportation-related fields to students at Historically Black Colleges and Universities.
**Eligibility:** Open to students who are enrolled at federally-designated 4-year Historically Black Colleges and Universities (HBCUs) and working on a degree in a transportation-related field (i.e., engineering, accounting, business, architecture, environmental sciences, etc.). Applicants must have entered their junior year, have at least a 3.0 GPA, and have a faculty sponsor.
**Financial data:** The stipend covers the fellow's full cost of education, including tuition and fees.
**Duration:** 1 year.
**Number awarded:** Varies each year; recently, 48 students received support from this program.
**Deadline:** February of each year.

## 1373 ELEANOR ALLWORK SCHOLARSHIP GRANTS

American Institute of Architects-New York Chapter
Attn: New York Foundation for Architecture

200 Lexington Avenue, Sixth Floor
New York, NY 10016
Phone: (212) 683-0023, ext. 14; Email: pwest@aiany.org
Web: www.aiany.org/nyfoundation
**Summary:** To provide financial assistance to students in New York who are majoring in architecture.
**Eligibility:** Open to U.S. citizens and permanent residents of New York City who are majoring in architecture. They must be enrolled in an accredited program at a college or university in the state. Only nominations are accepted; nominations must be submitted by the dean of the student's architectural school. Selection is based on academic record and financial need.
**Financial data:** Stipends are either $7,500 (designated as Honor Grants), $5,000, or $2,500 (designated as Citation Grants).
**Duration:** 1 year.
**Number awarded:** 3 each year: 1 Honor Grant at $7,500, 1 Citation Grant at $5,000, and 1 Citation Grant at $2,500.
**Deadline:** April of each year.

### 1374 ELIE WIESEL PRIZE IN ETHICS

Elie Wiesel Foundation for Humanity, Attn: Program Coordinator
529 Fifth Avenue, Suite 1802
New York, NY 10017
Phone: (212) 490-7777; Fax: (212) 490-6006;
Email: info@eliewieselfoundation.org
Web: www.eliewieselfoundation.org
**Summary:** To recognize and reward outstanding student essays on a topic related to ethics.
**Eligibility:** Open to full-time juniors and seniors at accredited colleges and universities in the United States. Essays must be submitted by the college or university, each of which may submit only 3 student works. Essays must be between 3,000 and 4,000 words in length and on a theme of the student's choice that involves ethical choices. Readers look for adherence to design format, carefully proofread essays, well thought-out essays that do not stray from the topic, depth of feeling and genuine grappling with a moral dilemma, originality and imagination, eloquence of writing style, and intensity and unity in the essay.
**Financial data:** First prize is $5,000, second prize is $2,500, third prize is $1,500, and each honorable mention is $500.
**Duration:** The competition is held annually.
**Number awarded:** 5 prizes each year: a first, second, and third prize as well as 2 honorable mentions.
**Deadline:** December of each year.

### 1375 ELIZABETH MCCULLAGH SCHOLARSHIP

Florida Federation of Garden Clubs, Inc., Attn: Office Manager
1400 South Denning Drive
Winter Park, FL 32789-5662
Phone: (407) 647-7016; Fax: (407) 647-5479; Email: ffgc@earthlink.net
Web: www.ffgc.org/scholarships/index.html
**Summary:** To provide financial aid to Florida high school seniors who are interested in majoring in a field related to horticulture in college.
**Eligibility:** Open to Florida residents who are high school seniors and planning to attend a college or university in the state. They must have a GPA of 3.0 or higher, be in financial need, and be interested in majoring in agriculture, agronomy, biology, botany, butterflies, city planning, conservation, ecology, forestry, horticulture, landscape design and architecture, marine biology, management of natural resources, native plants and wildlife, water management, xeriscaping, or a related subject. U.S. citizenship is required. Selection is based on academic record, commitment to career, character, and financial need.
**Financial data:** The stipend is $2,500. The funds are sent directly to the recipient's school and distributed semiannually.
**Duration:** 1 year.
**Number awarded:** 1 each year.
**Deadline:** April of each year.

### 1376 ELLEN MASIN PERSINA SCHOLARSHIP

National Press Club, Attn: General Manager's Office
529 14th Street, N.W.
Washington, DC 20045
Phone: (202) 662-7532; Email: jbooze@press.org
Web: www.press.org/programs/aboutscholarship.cfm
**Summary:** To provide funding to minority high school seniors interested in preparing for a journalism career in college.
**Eligibility:** Open to minority high school seniors who have been accepted to

college and plan to prepare for a career in journalism. Applicants must 1) demonstrate an ongoing interest in journalism through work in high school and/or other media; 2) submit a 1-page essay on why they want to prepare for a career in journalism; and 3) have a GPA of 2.75 or higher in high school. Financial need is considered in the selection process.
**Financial data:** The stipend is $5,000 per year.
**Duration:** 4 years.
**Number awarded:** 1 or more each year.
**Deadline:** February of each year.

### 1377 ELLICE T. JOHNSTON SCHOLARSHIP FOR THE CERAMIC ARTS

Clayfolk, Attn: Scholarship Committee
P.O. Box 274
Talent, OR 97540
**Summary:** To provide financial assistance to ceramic art students in California and Oregon who are interested in pursuing upper-division college courses, workshops at accredited institutions, or study at foreign institutions.
**Eligibility:** Open to residents of Oregon or northern California who have completed 2 years of college or the equivalent level of art education; this may include sculpture, drawing, design, and the study of aesthetics or technical ceramics. They must be looking for funding to further their education in upper-division college or art school courses, workshops at accredited institutions, or study abroad at accredited institutions. Applications are considered only after the following supporting documents are received: a portfolio of work (8 to 12 slides and/or photographs), a brief statement about their work and how they plan to use the award, 2 letters of recommendation, a recent academic transcript, a copy of the College Scholarship Service Financial Aid Form (FAF) or a 1040 tax form from the previous year, and a self-addressed stamped envelope to use in returning the portfolio. Financial need is considered in the selection process.
**Financial data:** The stipend is $1,500. Funds are provided directly to the recipient.
**Duration:** 1 year; may be renewed.
**Deadline:** June of each year.

### 1378 EMERGING YOUNG ARTIST AWARDS

California Alliance for Arts Education
495 East Colorado Boulevard
Pasadena, CA 91101
Phone: (626) 578-9315; Fax: (626) 578-9894; Email: eyaa@artsed411.org
Web: www.artsed411.org/projects/eya.stm
**Summary:** To provide financial assistance to outstanding high school seniors in California who are interested in training to become professional performing artists.
**Eligibility:** Open to high school seniors in California; they are eligible to apply in 1 or more of the following categories: dance, music, theater, or visual arts (including painting, drawing, illustration, and sculpture). Applicants must be planning to enter a 4-year institution or accredited professional training program in 1 of those areas. They must be able to demonstrate financial need. Students who apply in the areas of dance, music, and theater must submit a performance work sample. If they advance to the semifinals and finals, they are requested to demonstrate ability with a live performance.
**Financial data:** The stipend is $5,000 per year for the winners (for a total of $20,000) and 1-time awards of $1,000 for the runners-up.
**Duration:** The winners receive a 4-year scholarship.
**Number awarded:** 12 each year: 4 winners (1 in each category) and 8 runners-up (2 in each category).
**Deadline:** January of each year.

### 1379 ERNEST HEMINGWAY WRITING AWARDS

Kansas City Star, Attn: Lisa Lopez
1729 Grand Boulevard
Kansas City, MO 64108
Phone: (816) 234-4907; Email: lopezl@kcstarnet.com
Web: www.kcstar.com/hemingway/hem2.htm
**Summary:** To recognize and reward outstanding newspaper articles written by high school students.
**Eligibility:** Open to high school students who submit articles written during the previous calendar year and published in a student news publication (newspapers, news magazines, and magazine supplements published by student newspapers). Entries must be submitted by high schools, which may nominate up to 2 students in each of 4 areas: feature writing, newswriting (emphasis on breaking news or the presentation of new information), sports writing, and

commentary (including editorials and signed columns). Each student must submit 2 examples of original work per category.

**Financial data:** The prize is a $2,500 college scholarship.

**Duration:** The competition is held annually.

**Number awarded:** 4 each year: 1 in each category.

**Deadline:** January of each year.

## 1380 ERNEST I. AND EURICE MILLER BASS SCHOLARSHIP

United Methodist Church

Attn: General Board of Higher Education and Ministry

Office of Loans and Scholarships

1001 19th Avenue South

P.O. Box 340007

Nashville, TN 37203-0007

Phone: (615) 340-7344; Fax: (615) 340-7367; Email: umscholar@gbhem.org

Web: www.gbhem.org

**Summary:** To provide financial assistance to undergraduate Methodist students who are preparing for a career in a religious or helping profession.

**Eligibility:** Open to undergraduate students who are preparing for a career as a deacon, elder, or in another helping profession. Applicants must have been active, full members of a United Methodist Church for at least 1 year prior to applying and have an above average grade point. Preference is given to students preparing for religious vocations. U.S. citizenship or permanent resident status is required.

**Financial data:** The stipend is $1,000.

**Duration:** 1 year; recipients may reapply.

**Number awarded:** Varies each year.

**Deadline:** May of each year.

## 1381 ESTHER KANAGAWA MEMORIAL ART SCHOLARSHIP

Hawai'i Community Foundation, Attn: Scholarship Department

1164 Bishop Street, Suite 800

Honolulu, HI 96813

Phone: (808) 566-5570; (888) 731-3863; Fax: (808) 521-6286;

Email: scholarships@hcf-hawaii.org

Web: www.hawaiicommunityfoundation.org/scholar/scholar.php

**Summary:** To provide financial assistance to residents of Hawaii who are interested in working on a degree in fine art.

**Eligibility:** Open to residents of Hawaii who are planning to study fine art (drawing, painting, sculpture, ceramics, or photography) as full-time students on the undergraduate or graduate level. Students majoring in video, film, performing arts, or the culinary arts are not eligible. Applicants must be able to demonstrate academic achievement (GPA of 2.7 or higher), good moral character, and financial need.

**Financial data:** The amount of the award depends on the availability of funds and the need of the recipient; recently, stipends averaged $1,000.

**Duration:** 1 year.

**Number awarded:** Varies each year; recently, 1 of these scholarships was awarded.

**Deadline:** February of each year.

## 1382 EVANGELICAL PRESS ASSOCIATION SCHOLARSHIPS

Evangelical Press Association, Attn: Scholarships

P.O. Box 28129

Crystal, MN 55428

Phone: (763) 535-4793; Fax: (763) 535-4794; Email: director@epassoc.org

Web: www.epassoc.org/scholarships.html

**Summary:** To provide financial assistance to upper-division and graduate students interested in preparing for a career in Christian journalism.

**Eligibility:** Open to entering juniors, seniors, and graduate students who have at least 1 years of full-time study remaining. Applicants must be majoring or minoring in journalism or communications, preferably with an interest in the field of Christian journalism. They must be enrolled at an accredited Christian or secular college or university in the United States or Canada with a GPA of 3.0 or higher. Along with their application, they must submit a biographical sketch that includes their birth date, hometown, family, and something about the factors that shaped their interest in Christian journalism; a copy of their academic record; references from their pastor and from an instructor; samples of published writing from church or school publications; and an original essay (from 500 to 700 words) on the state of journalism today.

**Financial data:** Stipends range from $500 to $2,000.

**Duration:** 1 year.

**Number awarded:** Several each year.

**Deadline:** March of each year.

## 1383 EVELYN KEEDY MEMORIAL SCHOLARSHIP

The Art Institutes International, Inc.

Free Markets Center

210 Sixth Avenue, 33rd Floor

Pittsburgh, PA 15222-2603

Phone: (800) 275-2440; Email: ai_sfs@aii.edu

Web: www.artinstitutes.edu

**Summary:** To provide financial assistance to high school seniors who are planning to enroll in a participating Art Institute.

**Eligibility:** Open to high school seniors planning to attend a participating Art Institute. Applicants must demonstrate "dedication to their education and a desire for a creative career."

**Financial data:** The stipend is $30,000. The recipient may use the funds for tuition at the Art Institute of his or her choice.

**Duration:** 1 year.

**Number awarded:** 1 each year.

**Deadline:** April of each year.

## 1384 FASHION GROUP INTERNATIONAL OF PORTLAND SCHOLARSHIP

Oregon Student Assistance Commission

Attn: Grants and Scholarships Division

1500 Valley River Drive, Suite 100

Eugene, OR 97401-2146

Phone: (541) 687-7395; (800) 452-8807, ext. 7395; Fax: (541) 687-7419;

Email: awardinfo@mercury.osac.state.or.us

Web: www.osac.state.or.us

**Summary:** To provide financial assistance to students in Oregon interested in preparing for a career in a fashion-related field.

**Eligibility:** Open to residents of Oregon preparing for a career in a fashion-related field. Applicants must be enrolled at a college or university in California, Idaho, Oregon, or Washington as a sophomore or higher with a cumulative GPA of 3.0 or higher. Semifinalists are interviewed by the sponsor.

**Financial data:** The stipend is at least $1,500.

**Duration:** 1 year.

**Number awarded:** Varies each year; recently, 5 of these scholarships were awarded.

**Deadline:** February of each year.

## 1385 FEDERAL JUNIOR DUCK STAMP PROGRAM AND SCHOLARSHIP COMPETITION

Fish and Wildlife Service, Attn: Federal Duck Stamp Office

4401 North Fairfax Drive

MBSP-4040

Arlington, VA 22203-1622

Phone: (703) 358-2000; Fax: (703) 358-2009; Email: duckstamps@fws.gov

Web: duckstamps.fws.gov/junior/junior.htm

**Summary:** To recognize and reward student artwork submitted to the Junior Duck Stamp Program.

**Eligibility:** Open to students in public or private kindergartens through high schools in the United States; home-schooled students are also eligible. U.S. citizenship or permanent resident status are required. Applicants submit paintings of ducks as part of the federal government's Junior Duck Stamp program that supports awards and scholarships for conservation education. They must submit their applications to a designated receiving site in their home state. Each state selects 12 first-place winners (3 in each of 4 grade level groups: K-3, 4-6, 7-9, and 10-12), and then designates 1 of those 12 as best of show to compete in the national competition.

**Financial data:** First prize at the national level is $4,000. The winner also receives a free trip to Washington, D.C. in the fall to attend the (adult) Federal Duck Stamp Contest, along with an art teacher, a parent, and a state coordinator. Second prize is $2,000 and third prize is $1,000.

**Duration:** The competition is held annually.

**Number awarded:** 3 national prizes are awarded each year.

**Deadline:** Applications must be submitted to the respective state receiving site by March of each year (or January for South Carolina, February for Ohio).

## 1386 FEDERATED GARDEN CLUBS OF CONNECTICUT SCHOLARSHIP

Federated Garden Clubs of Connecticut, Inc.
14 Business Park Drive
P.O. Box 854
Branford, CT 06405-0854
Phone: (203) 488-5528; Fax: (203) 488-5528;
Email: gardenclubs@ctgarden clubs.org
Web: www.ctgardenclubs.org/scholarship.html

**Summary:** To provide financial assistance to Connecticut residents who are interested in majoring in horticulture-related fields at a Connecticut college or university.

**Eligibility:** Open to legal residents of Connecticut who are studying at a college or university in the state in horticulture, floriculture, landscape design, conservation, forestry, botany, agronomy, plant pathology, environmental control, city planning, land management, or related subjects. They must be entering their junior or senior year of college or be a graduate student, have a GPA of 3.0 or higher, and be able to demonstrate financial need.

**Financial data:** Stipends are generally about $1,000 each. Funds are sent to the recipient's school in 2 equal installments.

**Duration:** 1 year.

**Number awarded:** Varies each year, depending upon the availability of funds.

**Deadline:** June of each year.

## 1387 FELIX MORLEY JOURNALISM COMPETITION

Institute for Humane Studies at George Mason University
3301 North Fairfax Drive, Suite 440
Arlington, VA 22201-4432
Phone: (703) 993-4880; (800) 697-8799; Fax: (703) 993-4890;
Email: ihs@gmu.edu
Web: www.TheIHS.org

**Summary:** To recognize and reward outstanding writing by student journalists whose work demonstrates an appreciation of classical liberal principles.

**Eligibility:** Open to writers who are either 1) 25 years of age or younger, or 2) full-time students at the high school, undergraduate, or graduate level. Applicants must submit 3 to 5 articles, editorials, opinion pieces, essays, or reviews published in student newspapers or other periodicals during the preceding year that reflect classical liberal principles (inalienable individual rights; their protection through the institutions of private property, contract, and the rule of law; voluntarism in all human relations; and the self-ordering market, free trade, free migration, and peace). Selection is based on writing ability, potential for development as a writer, and an appreciation of classical liberal principles.

**Financial data:** First prize is $2,500, second prize $1,000, third prize $750, and runners up $250.

**Duration:** The competition is held annually.

**Number awarded:** 3 prizes and several runners-up are awarded each year.

**Deadline:** November of each year.

## 1388 FELLOWSHIP OF UNITED METHODISTS IN MUSIC AND WORSHIP ARTS MEMORIAL SCHOLARSHIPS

The Fellowship of United Methodists in Music and Worship Arts
Attn: Administrator
P.O. Box 24787
Nashville, TN 37202-4787
Phone: (615) 749-6875; (800) 952-8977; Fax: (615) 749-6874;
Email: FUMMWA@aol.com
Web: www.fummwa.org

**Summary:** To provide financial assistance to students who are training for a music ministry in the United Methodist Church.

**Eligibility:** Open to full-time music degree candidates entering or enrolled in an accredited college, university, or school of theology. Applicants must have been members of the United Methodist Church for at least 1 year immediately before applying. They must be able to demonstrate exceptional musical talents, leadership abilities, and outstanding promise of future usefulness to the church in the areas of worship and/or music.

**Financial data:** The stipend is $1,000.

**Duration:** 1 year.

**Number awarded:** 4 each year.

**Deadline:** February of each year.

## 1389 FERNANDES TRUST SCHOLARSHIP

Portuguese Foundation of Connecticut, Attn: Gabriel R. Serrano, President
86 New Park Avenue
Hartford, CT 06106-2127
Phone: (860) 236-5514; Fax: (860) 236-5514; Email: info@pfict.org
Web: www.pfict.org/scholar.html

**Summary:** To provide financial assistance to students of Portuguese ancestry in Connecticut who are interested in studying Portuguese language or culture in college or graduate school.

**Eligibility:** Open to residents of Connecticut who are U.S. citizens or permanent residents. At least 1 great-grandparent must be of Portuguese ancestry. Applicants must be attending, or planning to attend, a college or university as a full-time undergraduate or full- or part-time graduate student to study the Portuguese language or disseminate Portuguese culture. Along with their application, they qualified students must supply an essay describing financial need, an essay detailing proof of Portuguese ancestry and interest in the Portuguese language and culture, 2 letters of recommendation, their high school or college transcripts, a copy of the FAFSA form or their most recent federal income tax return, and their SAT report. Selection is based on financial need and academic record.

**Financial data:** Stipends are at least $1,500 each.

**Duration:** 1 year; recipients may reapply.

**Number awarded:** 1 each year.

**Deadline:** March of each year.

## 1390 FFTA SCHOLARSHIP COMPETITION

Flexographic Technical Association
Attn: Foundation of Flexographic Technical Association, Inc.
900 Marconi Avenue
Ronkonkoma, NY 11779-7212
Phone: (631) 737-6020; Fax: (631) 737-6813; Email: education@flexography.org
Web: www.flexography.org/online/education/scholarship_info.cfm

**Summary:** To provide funding for undergraduate study to students interested in a career in flexography.

**Eligibility:** Open to 1) high school seniors enrolled in a Flexo in High School program and planning to attend a postsecondary school; and 2) students currently enrolled at a college offering a course of study in flexography. Applicants must demonstrate interest in a career in flexography, exhibit exemplary performance in their studies (particularly in the area of graphic arts), and have an overall GPA of 3.0 or higher. Along with their application, they must submit a 1-page essay providing personal information about themselves (including special circumstances, interests, and activities); career and/or educational goals and how those relate to the flexo industry; employment and internship experience; and reasons why they feel they should be selected for this scholarship. Financial need is not considered.

**Financial data:** Stipends are $2,000 per year.

**Duration:** 1 year; may be renewed.

**Number awarded:** Varies each year; recently, 14 of these scholarships were awarded.

**Deadline:** March of each year.

## 1391 FIRST PERSON JOURNALISM SCHOLARSHIP FUND

MIGIZI Communications, Inc.
3123 East Lake Street
Minneapolis, MN 55406
Phone: (612) 721-6631; Fax: (612) 721-3936
Web: migizi.org/mig/organizational/scholarships/default.html

**Summary:** To provide financial assistance to Native American students working on an undergraduate or graduate degree in journalism.

**Eligibility:** Open to Native American undergraduate and graduate students preparing for a career in journalism or mass communications. Applicants must have a GPA of 3.0 or higher. They must also have applied to the Minnesota Indian Scholarship Program sponsored by the Minnesota State Department of Education. Along with their application, they must submit proof of tribal enrollment and/or blood quantum, transcripts, 2 letters of reference, a 250-word essay describing their involvement in the Indian community, and documentation of financial need. Special consideration is given to applicants with prior work experience on a student newspaper, broadcast outlet, or web site.

**Financial data:** The stipend is $1,000.

**Duration:** 1 year; nonrenewable.

**Number awarded:** 1 each year.

**Deadline:** January of each year.

## 1392 FISHER BROADCASTING SCHOLARSHIPS FOR MINORITIES

Fisher Communications, Attn: Minority Scholarship
100 Fourth Avenue North, Suite 510
Seattle, WA 98109
Phone: (206) 404-7000; Fax: (206) 404-6037; Email: Info@fsci.com
Web: www.fsci.com/x100.xml

**Summary:** To provide financial assistance to minority college students in selected states who are interested in preparing for a career in broadcasting, marketing, or journalism.

**Eligibility:** Open to students of non-white origin who are U.S. citizens, have a GPA of 2.5 or higher, and are at least sophomores enrolled in 1) a broadcasting, marketing, or journalism curriculum leading to a bachelor's degree at an accredited 4-year college or university; 2) a broadcast curriculum at an accredited community college, transferable to a 4-year baccalaureate degree program; or 3) a broadcast curriculum at an accredited vocational/technical school. Applicants must be either 1) residents of Washington, Oregon, Idaho, or Montana; or 2) attending a school in those states. They must submit an essay that explains their financial need, education and career goals, and school activities; a copy of their college transcript; and 2 letters of recommendation. Selection is based on need, academic achievement, and personal qualities.

**Financial data:** A stipend is awarded (amount not specified).

**Duration:** 1 year; recipients may reapply.

**Number awarded:** Varies; a total of $10,000 is available for this program each year.

**Deadline:** April of each year.

## 1393 FLORIDA PTA SCHOLARSHIP PROGRAMS

**Summary:** To provide financial assistance for college to high school seniors in Florida.

*See Listing #360.*

## 1394 FLORIDA SOCIETY OF NEWSPAPER EDITORS MINORITY SCHOLARSHIP PROGRAM

Florida Society of Newspaper Editors
c/o Florida Press Association
2636 Mitcham Drive
Tallahassee, FL 32308
Phone: (850) 222-5790; Fax: (850) 224-6012; Email: info@fsne.org
Web: www.fsne.org/minorityscholar.html

**Summary:** To provide financial assistance and summer work experience to minority upper-division students majoring in journalism at a college or university in Florida.

**Eligibility:** Open to minority students in accredited journalism or mass communication programs at Florida 4-year colleges and universities. Applicants must be full-time students in their junior year, have at least a 3.0 GPA, and be willing to participate in a paid summer internship at a Florida newspaper. Along with their application, they must submit a 300-word autobiographical essay explaining why they want to prepare for a career in print journalism and provide a standard resume, references, and clips or examples of relevant classroom work.

**Financial data:** Winners are given a paid summer internship at a participating newspaper between their junior and senior year. Upon successfully completing the internship, the students are awarded a $3,000 scholarship (paid in 2 equal installments) to be used during their senior year.

**Duration:** 1 summer for the internship; 1 academic year for the scholarship.

**Number awarded:** 1 each year.

**Deadline:** March of each year.

## 1395 FORREST BASSFORD STUDENT AWARD

Livestock Publications Council
910 Currie Street
Fort Worth, TX 76107
Phone: (817) 336-1130; Fax: (817) 232-4820; Email: dianej@flash.net
Web: www.livestockpublications.com/awards.htm

**Summary:** To provide financial assistance to students majoring in agricultural communications or related fields.

**Eligibility:** Open to students majoring in agricultural journalism, agricultural communications, or agricultural public relations. They must have at least 1 semester of school remaining at the time they receive the award. Selection is based on a transcript of college work completed and a list of courses in progress, a list of scholarships and awards received, club and other organization memberships, extracurricular activities, employment record, a 200-word biographical sketch that includes livestock and communication background and career plans, 3 samples of communications work, and 2 letters of recommendation.

**Financial data:** The winner receives a $2,500 scholarship, plus a $750 travel scholarship (to attend the council's annual meeting). The runners-up receive $750 travel scholarships to attend the meeting.

**Duration:** 1 year.

**Number awarded:** 1 winner and 3 runners-up are selected each year.

**Deadline:** February of each year.

## 1396 FORT COLLINS SYMPHONY ORCHESTRA SENIOR CONCERTO COMPETITION

Fort Collins Symphony Orchestra, Attn: Young Artist Competition
214 South College Avenue
P.O. Box 1963
Fort Collins, CO 80522
Phone: (970) 482-4823; Fax: (970) 482-4858; Email: note@fcsymphony.org
Web: www.fcsymphony.org/yac.htm

**Summary:** To recognize and reward outstanding young pianists and instrumentalists.

**Eligibility:** Open to students, 25 years of age or younger, who submit cassette tapes of a standard, readily available solo concerto or similar work played from memory. Based on the tapes, semifinalists are invited to Fort Collins for a second round in March. From the semifinalists, finalists are chosen for the third round of performances in April.

**Financial data:** The first-place winner receives the Adeline Rosenberg Memorial Prize of $6,000. Second prize is $4,000. The awards are cash prizes only.

**Duration:** The competition is held annually.

**Number awarded:** 10 semifinalists and 3 finalists are chosen each year; all 3 finalists receive a prize.

**Deadline:** January of each year.

## 1397 THE FOUNTAINHEAD ESSAY CONTEST

Ayn Rand Institute, Attn: Essay Contests
2121 Alton Parkway, Suite 250
P.O. Box 57044
Irvine, CA 92619-7044
Phone: (949) 222-6550; Fax: (949) 222-6558; Email: essay@aynrand.org
Web: www.aynrand.org/contests

**Summary:** To recognize and reward outstanding essays written by high school students on Ayn Rand's novel, *The Fountainhead.*

**Eligibility:** Open to juniors or seniors in high school. They must submit a typewritten essay on questions selected each year from Ayn Rand's novel, *The Fountainhead.* The essay must be between 800 and 1,600 words. Selection is based on style and content. Judges look for writing that is clear, articulate, and logically organized. To win, an essay must demonstrate an outstanding grasp of the philosophical and psychological meaning of the novel.

**Financial data:** First prize is $10,000; second prizes are $2,000; third prizes are $1,000; finalist prizes are $100; and semifinalist prizes are $50.

**Duration:** The competition is held annually.

**Number awarded:** 251 each year: 1 first prize, 5 second prizes, 10 third prizes, 35 finalist prizes, and 200 semifinalist prizes.

**Deadline:** April of each year.

## 1398 FRANCES A. MAYS SCHOLARSHIP AWARD

Virginia Association for Health, Physical Education, Recreation, and Dance
c/o Jack Schiltz, Executive Director
817 West Franklin Street
P.O. Box 842037
Richmond, VA 23284-2037
Phone: (804) 828-1948; (800) 918-9899; Fax: (804) 828-1946;
Email: info@vahperd.org
Web: www.vahperd.org

**Summary:** To provide financial assistance to college seniors majoring in health, physical education, recreation, or dance in Virginia.

**Eligibility:** Open to students who have been working full time for 3 years on a degree in health, physical education, recreation, or dance at a college or university in Virginia. Candidates must be nominated by their school and be members of the Virginia Association of Health, Physical Education, Recreation, and Dance (VAHPERD) and the American Association for Health, Physical Education, Recreation, and Dance (AAHPERD). Selection is based on academic achievement, leadership in campus life activities, service to college or university, awards and honors, and service to community.

**Financial data:** A stipend is awarded (amount not specified).

**Duration:** 1 year.

**Number awarded:** 1 each year.

**Deadline:** September of each year.

## [1399] FRANK CHAPMAN SHARP MEMORIAL PRIZE

American Philosophical Association, Attn: Executive Director
c/o University of Delaware
31 Amstel Avenue
Newark, DE 19716-4797
Phone: (302) 831-1112; Fax: (302) 831-8690; Email: apaonline@udel.edu
Web: www.apa.udel.edu/apa/opportunities/prizes/sharp.html

**Summary:** To recognize and reward outstanding unpublished writings on the philosophy of war and peace submitted by members and student associates of the American Philosophical Association (APA).

**Eligibility:** Open to students writing unpublished essays or monographs between 7,500 and 75,000 words in length on the philosophy of war and peace. Undergraduate entrants must be majoring in philosophy or a closely-related field; graduate students must be enrolled in, or on leave from, a graduate program in philosophy. All authors must be current members of the APA in good standing.

**Financial data:** The prize is $1,500.

**Duration:** The prize is award biennially, in odd-numbered years.

**Number awarded:** 1 every odd-numbered year.

**Deadline:** March of even-numbered years.

## [1400] FRANK WATTS SCHOLARSHIP

Watts Charity Association, Inc.
6245 Bristol Parkway, Suite 224
Culver City, CA 90230
Phone: (323) 671-0394; Fax: (323) 778-2613; Email: wattscharity@yahoo.com
Web: www.wattscharity.org

**Summary:** To provide financial assistance to upper-division college students interested in preparing for a career as a minister.

**Eligibility:** Open to U.S. citizens of African American descent who are enrolled full time as a college or university junior. Applicants must be studying to become a minister. They must have a GPA of 3.0 or higher, be between 17 and 24 years of age, and be able to demonstrate that they intend to continue their education for at least 2 years. Along with their application, they must submit 1) a 1-paragraph statement on why they should be awarded a Watts Foundation scholarship, and 2) a 1- to 2-page essay on a specific type of cancer, based either on how it has impacted their life or on researched information.

**Financial data:** A stipend is awarded (amount not specified).

**Duration:** 1 year.

**Number awarded:** 1 each year.

**Deadline:** May of each year.

## [1401] FREE SPEECH AND DEMOCRACY FILM CONTEST

Youth Free Expression Network
c/o National Coalition Against Censorship
275 Seventh Avenue, Ninth Floor
New York, NY 10001
Phone: (212) 807-6222, ext. 17; Fax: (212) 807-6245; Email: sgriest@ncac.org
Web: www.yfen.org/pages/events/upcomingevents.htm

**Summary:** To recognize and reward young filmmakers who create films on a topic related to free speech and democracy.

**Eligibility:** Open to filmmakers who are younger than 19 years of age. Applicants are invited to create a film in any category (e.g., documentary, animation, experimental, music video, public service announcement) on the topic, "What do you think of the state of freedom and democracy in the United States?" The film should be up to 4 minutes in length and in VHS or DVD format. It must be accompanied by a narrative explaining the director's creative process and ideas behind the work.

**Financial data:** First prize is $1,000, second $500, and third $250. All winners are invited to an all-expense paid trip to New York City for the award ceremony.

**Duration:** The competition is held annually.

**Number awarded:** 3 each year.

**Deadline:** September of each year.

## [1402] FREEDOM FORUM–NCAA SPORTS JOURNALISM SCHOLARSHIPS

National Collegiate Athletic Association, Attn: Leadership Advisory Board
700 West Washington Avenue
P.O. Box 6222
Indianapolis, IN 46206-6222
Phone: (317) 917-6816; Fax: (317) 917-6888
Web: www.ncaa.org/leadership_advisory_board/programs.html

**Summary:** To provide financial assistance to upper-division students interested in preparing for a career in sports journalism.

**Eligibility:** Open to college juniors who are planning a career in sports journalism and are either majoring in journalism or have experience in campus sports journalism. Along with their application, they must submit their official college transcript, 3 examples of sports journalism work, a letter of recommendation from a journalism professor, and (if they have had a professional internship) a letter of recommendation from their employer. They must also include a statement, 200 to 500 words in length, on a topic that changes annually; recently, they were asked to give their opinion on violence associated with prominent athletics events. Financial need is not considered.

**Financial data:** The stipend is $3,000.

**Duration:** The award is to be used in the recipient's senior year of study.

**Number awarded:** 8 each year: 1 in each of the geographical districts of the NCAA.

**Deadline:** December of each year.

## [1403] FREEDOM FROM RELIGION FOUNDATION COLLEGE ESSAY CONTEST

Freedom from Religion Foundation
P.O. Box 750
Madison, WI 53701
Phone: (608) 256-8900; (608) 256-1116; Email: dbarker@ffrf.org
Web: www.ffrf.org/essay.php

**Summary:** To recognize and reward outstanding student essays on the separation of church and state.

**Eligibility:** Open to any currently-enrolled college student. Entrants must write an essay on topics that change annually but always involve rejecting religion; recent topics were "Growing Up a Freethinker" or "Rejecting Religion." Students may write about their own experiences in rejecting religion in a religious society or use a philosophical or historical approach. Essays should be 5 to 6 typed double-spaced pages, accompanied by a paragraph biography identifying the student's college or university, year in school, major, and interests.

**Financial data:** First prize is $1,000, second prize is $500, and third prize is $250.

**Duration:** The competition is held annually.

**Number awarded:** 3 each year.

**Deadline:** June of each year.

## [1404] FREEDOM FROM RELIGION FOUNDATION HIGH SCHOOL ESSAY CONTEST

Freedom from Religion Foundation
P.O. Box 750
Madison, WI 53701
Phone: (608) 256-8900; (608) 256-1116; Email: dbarker@ffrf.org
Web: www.ffrf.org/essay.php

**Summary:** To recognize and reward outstanding essays written by high school students on freethought or state/church separation themes.

**Eligibility:** Open only to college-bound high school seniors. They are invited to write an essay on a topic that changes annually but relates to freethinking and separation of church and state; recently, the topic was "Why Our U.S. Founders Got it Right When They Adopted a Godless Constitution." Essays should be 2 or 3 typewritten pages in length, double spaced, with standard margins. Contestants may present an anecdotal essay describing personal experiences in rejecting religion in a religious society or they may use an historical approach in dealing with the general theme. They should include a paragraph biography, their address and telephone number, the name of the college they will be attending, and their planned major.

**Financial data:** First prize is $1,000, second prize is $500, and third prize is $250.

**Duration:** The competition is held annually.

**Number awarded:** 3 each year.

**Deadline:** May of each year.

## 1405 FREEDOM OF THE PRESS HIGH SCHOOL ESSAY CONTEST

Society of Professional Journalists, Attn: Awards and Fellowships Coordinator
3909 North Meridian Street
Indianapolis, IN 46208
Phone: (317) 927-8000; Fax: (317) 920-4789; Email: awards@spj.org
Web: www.spj.org/awards_hs.asp

**Summary:** To recognize and reward, with college scholarships, high school students who write outstanding essays on the importance of a free press.

**Eligibility:** Open to students in grade 9-12 in the United States. Applicants must submit an essay (300 to 500 words) on "What a Free Media Means to America" to their local chapter of the Society of Professional Journalists.

**Financial data:** Winners receive scholarships of $1,000 for first place, $500 for second place, and $300 for third place.

**Duration:** The competition is held annually.

**Number awarded:** 3 each year.

**Deadline:** March of each year.

## 1406 GARDEN CLUB FEDERATION OF MAINE SCHOLARSHIP

Garden Club Federation of Maine
c/o Mark Ericson
515 Little River Road
Lebanon, ME 04027
Phone: (207) 457-2188
Web: www.mainegardenclubs.com

**Summary:** To provide financial assistance to Maine residents who are upper-division or graduate students working on a garden-related degree.

**Eligibility:** Open to college juniors, seniors, and graduate students who are residents of Maine. Applicants must be majoring in horticulture, floriculture, landscape design, conservation, forestry, botany, agronomy, plant pathology, environmental control, city planning, or another garden-related field. Selection is based on goals, activities, academic achievement, personal commitment, 3 letters of recommendation, and financial need.

**Financial data:** The stipend is $3,000.

**Duration:** 1 year.

**Number awarded:** 1 each year.

**Deadline:** February of each year.

## 1407 GARY YOSHIMURA SCHOLARSHIP

Public Relations Student Society of America, Attn: Director of Education
33 Irving Place, Third Floor
New York, NY 10003-2376
Phone: (212) 460-1474; Fax: (212) 995-0757; Email: prssa@prsa.org
Web: www.prssa.org/resources/award-GaryYoshimura.asp

**Summary:** To provide financial assistance for college to members of the Public Relations Student Society of America (PRSSA) who demonstrate financial need.

**Eligibility:** Open to members of the society who are currently enrolled in a program of public relations studies and preparing for a career in public relations. Applicants must be able to demonstrate financial need and have a GPA of 3.0 or higher. They must submit an essay, up to 1,000 words, on a challenge they have faced, either personally or professionally, and how they have overcome it.

**Financial data:** The stipend is $2,400.

**Duration:** 1 year.

**Number awarded:** 1 each year.

**Deadline:** January of each year.

## 1408 GEORGE E. HADDAWAY SCHOLARSHIP

Communities Foundation of Texas, Attn: Scholarship Department
5500 Caruth Haven Lane
Dallas, TX 75225-8146
Phone: (214) 750-4222; Fax: (214) 750-4210; Email: grants@cftexas.org
Web: www.cftexas.org

**Summary:** To provide financial assistance to upper-division and graduate students who are working on a degree in journalism and have an interest in aviation.

**Eligibility:** Open to college juniors, seniors, and graduate students who can demonstrate interest in aviation by such activities as 1) current or former membership in the aviation program of a college or university, the Boy or Girl Scouts of America, the Civil Air Patrol, or a similar organization; or 2) pursuit or completion of the requirements for an aircraft license. Applicants must be working on a baccalaureate or advanced degree in print or electronic journalism and have completed at least 52 hours of college course work with a GPA of

2.75 or higher. They must be able to demonstrate financial need. Along with their application, they must submit an essay (200 to 500 words) describing their interest in aviation and how they might combine that interest with a career in journalism. U.S. citizenship is required.

**Financial data:** The stipend is $2,500 per year.

**Duration:** 1 year; nonrenewable.

**Number awarded:** 1 each year.

**Deadline:** March of each year.

## 1409 GEORGE E. HOERTER SCHOLARSHIP AWARDS

Society for Technical Communication-Rocky Mountain Chapter
c/o Don Zimmerman
Colorado State University
Department of Journalism and Technical Communication
Room C-225 Clark Building
Fort Collins, CO 80523-1785
Phone: (970) 491-5674; Email: don.zimmerman@colostate.edu
Web: www.stcrmc.org/chapter/scholar.htm

**Summary:** To provide financial assistance to undergraduate and graduate students working on a degree in technical communication at a college or university in Colorado.

**Eligibility:** Open to sophomores, juniors, seniors, and graduate students at Colorado colleges and universities within the geographic area of the Rocky Mountain chapter of the Society for Technical Communication (STC). Applicants must submit a 1- to 3-page letter describing their academic and career goals, a resume, an official transcript, and 2 letters of recommendation.

**Financial data:** The stipend is $1,000.

**Duration:** 1 year.

**Number awarded:** 2 each year.

## 1410 GEORGE MORRISON LANDSCAPE ARCHITECTURE SCHOLARSHIP

Florida Federation of Garden Clubs, Inc., Attn: Office Manager
1400 South Denning Drive
Winter Park, FL 32789-5662
Phone: (407) 647-7016; Fax: (407) 647-5479; Email: ffgc@earthlink.net
Web: www.ffgc.org/scholarships/index.html

**Summary:** To provide financial aid to undergraduate or graduate students who are working on a degree in landscape architecture in Florida.

**Eligibility:** Open to Florida residents who are enrolled as full-time juniors, seniors, or graduate students in a Florida college. They must have a GPA of 3.0 or higher, be in financial need, and be majoring in landscape design architecture. U.S. citizenship is required. Selection is based on academic record, commitment to career, character, and financial need.

**Financial data:** The stipend is $2,500. The funds are sent directly to the recipient's school and distributed semiannually.

**Duration:** 1 year.

**Number awarded:** 1 each year.

**Deadline:** April of each year.

## 1411 GEORGIA BEEF INDUSTRY INTERNSHIP

Georgia Beef Board, Attn: Coordinator of Consumer Relations
P.O. Box 24570
Macon, GA 31212-4570
Phone: (478) 474-1815; Fax: (877) 444-BEEF; Email: nikki@gabeef.org
Web: www.gabeef.org/gbb/index.htm

**Summary:** To provide financial assistance and work experience to Georgia residents interested in the beef industry.

**Eligibility:** Open to residents of Georgia who have completed at least the sophomore year of college. Applicants must be majoring in animal science, meat science, agricultural communications, or family and consumer sciences. They must have strong verbal and written communication skills, be involved in extracurricular activity related to their major, be interested in working during the summer at the Macon offices of the Georgia Beef Board and the Georgia Cattlemen's Association (GCA), and be able to work in February at the GCA convention. An interview is required.

**Financial data:** Interns receive a stipend of $1,000 per month and reimbursement of travel expenses during the summer. Upon completion of the internship, they receive a $1,000 scholarship.

**Duration:** 3 months during the summer for the internship; 1 year for the scholarship.

**Number awarded:** 1 each year.

**Deadline:** March of each year.

## 1412 GEORGIA PRESS EDUCATIONAL FOUNDATION SCHOLARSHIPS

Georgia Press Educatioml Foundation, Inc., Attn: Member Services
3066 Mercer University Drive, Suite 200
Atlanta, GA 30341-4137
Phone: (770) 454-6776; Fax: (770) 454-6778; Email: mail@gapress.org
Web: www.gapress.org/scholar_intern.html
**Summary:** To provide financial assistance to high school seniors and college students in Georgia who are interested in preparing for a career in journalism.
**Eligibility:** Open to high school seniors and currently-enrolled college students in Georgia. They must be U.S. citizens or permanent residents, have been legal residents of Georgia for at least 3 years or be the children of parents who have been legal residents of Georgia for at least 2 years, have had prior newspaper experience, and be recommended by a high school counselor, college professor, or member of the Georgia Press Educational Foundation. Selection is based on academic record, standardized test scores, career plans, and financial need.
**Financial data:** Stipends range from $1,000 to $2,000.
**Duration:** 1 year.
**Number awarded:** Varies each year. Recently, 15 of these scholarships were awarded: 3 at $2,000, 1 at $1,500, and 11 at $1,000.
**Deadline:** January of each year.

## 1413 GERALD BOYD/ROBIN STONE SCHOLARSHIP

National Association of Black Journalists
Attn: Student Education Enrichment and Development Program
8701-A Adelphi Road
Adelphi, MD 20783-1716
Phone: (301) 445-7100, ext. 108; Fax: (301) 445-7101; Email: nabj@nabj.org
Web: www.nabj.org/scholarships.html
**Summary:** To provide financial assistance to undergraduate or graduate student members of the National Association of Black Journalists (NABJ) who are majoring in print journalism.
**Eligibility:** Open to African American undergraduate or graduate students who are currently attending an accredited 4-year college or university. Applicants must be majoring in print journalism and have a GPA of 2.5 or higher. They must submit samples of their work, an official college transcript, 2 letters of recommendation, a resume, and a 500- to 800-word essay describing their accomplishments as a student journalist, their career goals, and their financial need.
**Financial data:** The stipend is $2,500. Funds are paid directly to the recipient's college or university.
**Duration:** 1 year; nonrenewable.
**Number awarded:** 1 each year.
**Deadline:** April of each year.

## 1414 GIBSON–LAEMEL SCHOLARSHIP

Connecticut Association for Health, Physical Education, Recreation and Dance
c/o Jodie Hellman, Scholarship Chair
376 Old Woodbury Road
Southbury, CT 06488
Phone: (203) 264-7921; Email: jahellman@yahoo.com
Web: www.ctahperd.org/laemel.htm
**Summary:** To provide financial assistance to college juniors and seniors from Connecticut who are interested in preparing for a career in health, physical education, recreation, or dance.
**Eligibility:** Open to residents of Connecticut who are entering their junior or senior year of college and preparing for a career in the professional studies of health (defined as school health teaching, not nursing, public health, or psychology), physical education, recreation, or dance. Applicants must submit 1) a 350-word statement expressing their thoughts and feelings on why they are entering the field of health, physical education, recreation, or dance; 2) transcripts (with a GPA of 2.7 or higher); and 3) letters of recommendation from 2 professionally related sources.
**Financial data:** The stipend is $1,000 per year. Funds are paid to the recipient's college or university to be applied toward tuition, books, room, and board.
**Duration:** 1 year.
**Number awarded:** 1 each year.
**Deadline:** May of each year.

## 1415 GILDER LEHRMAN PRIZE IN AMERICAN HISTORY

Gilder Lehrman Institute of American History
Attn: Prize in American History
19 West 44th Street, Suite 500
New York, NY 10036
Phone: (646) 366-9666; Fax: (646) 366-9669; Email: info@gilderlehrman.org
Web: www.gilderlehrman.org
**Summary:** To recognize and reward high school students who write outstanding essays on topics related to U.S. history.
**Eligibility:** Open to students at high schools in the United States. Candidates submit essays on topics related to American history to the *Concord Review*. The editors of that journal then select 10 outstanding essays on U.S. history and refer them to the sponsors of this competition.
**Financial data:** First prize is $5,000, second $3,000, and third $1,000.
**Duration:** The competition is held annually.
**Number awarded:** 3 cash prizes are awarded each year.

## 1416 GLADYS C. ANDERSON MEMORIAL SCHOLARSHIP

American Foundation for the Blind, Attn: Scholarship Committee
11 Penn Plaza, Suite 300
New York, NY 10001
Phone: (212) 502-7661; (800) AFB-LINE; Fax: (212) 502-7771; TDD: (212) 502-7662; Email: afbinfo@afb.net
Web: www.afb.org/scholarships.asp
**Summary:** To provide financial assistance to legally blind undergraduate or graduate women who are studying religious or classical music.
**Eligibility:** Open to legally blind women who are U.S. citizens and have been accepted in an accredited undergraduate or graduate program in religious or classical music. Along with their application, they must submit an essay that includes the field of study they are pursuing and why they have chosen it; their educational and personal goals; their work experience; any extracurricular activities with which they have been involved, including those in school, religious organizations, and the community; and how they intend to use scholarship monies that may be awarded. They must also submit a sample performance tape (a voice or instrumental selection).
**Financial data:** The stipend is $1,000.
**Duration:** 1 academic year.
**Number awarded:** 1 each year.
**Deadline:** April of each year.

## 1417 GLENN MILLER SCHOLARSHIP COMPETITION

Glenn Miller Birthplace Society, Attn: Scholarship Program
107 East Main Street
P.O. Box 61
Clarinda, IA 51632
Phone: (712) 542-4439; Fax: (712) 542-2461; Email: gmbs@heartland.net
Web: www.glennmiller.org
**Summary:** To provide financial assistance to present and prospective college music majors.
**Eligibility:** Open to 1) graduating high school seniors planning to major in music in college and 2) freshmen music majors at an accredited college, university, or school of music. Both instrumentalists and vocalists may compete. Those who entered as high school seniors and did not win first place are eligible to enter again as college freshmen. Each entrant must submit an audition tape, from which finalists are selected. Finalists are auditioned in person. They must perform a composition of concert quality, up to 5 to 10 minutes in length. Selection is based on talent in any field of applied music; the competition is not intended to select Glenn Miller look-alikes or sound-alikes.
**Financial data:** The first-place instrumentalist receives $2,400; the second-place instrumentalist receives $1,200. The first-place vocalist receives $2,000; the second-place vocalist receives $1,000. The funds are to be used for any school-related expense.
**Duration:** The competition is held annually, in June.
**Number awarded:** 4 each year.
**Deadline:** March of each year.

## 1418 GOLDEN KEY ART INTERNATIONAL AWARDS

Golden Key International Honour Society
621 North Avenue N.E., Suite C-100
Atlanta, GA 30308
Phone: (404) 377-2400; (800) 377-2401; Fax: (678) 420-6757; Email: scholar ships@goldenkey.org
Web: www.goldenkey.org/GKweb/ScholarshipsandAwards
**Summary:** To recognize and reward members of the Golden Key International Honour Society who are studying art.
**Eligibility:** Open to undergraduate, graduate, and postgraduate members of the society who submit slides of their work in the following categories: 1) sculpture;

2) photography; 3) painting; 4) drawing; 5) computer-generated art, graphic design, and illustration; 6) printmaking; 7) applied art; and 8) mixed media. All entries must be original work, submitted on a slide or CD. Selection is based on the quality of the work submitted.

**Financial data:** The award is a $1,000 scholarship.

**Duration:** These awards are presented annually.

**Number awarded:** 8 each year: 1 in each category.

**Deadline:** March of each year.

## 1419 GOLDEN KEY LITERARY ACHIEVEMENT AWARDS

Golden Key International Honour Society
621 North Avenue N.E., Suite C-100
Atlanta, GA 30308
Phone: (404) 377-2400; (800) 377-2401; Fax: (678) 420-6757;
Email: scholar ships@goldenkey.org
Web: www.goldenkey.org/GKweb/ScholarshipsandAwards

**Summary:** To recognize and reward literary achievements by members of the Golden Key National Honor Society.

**Eligibility:** Open to undergraduate, graduate, and postgraduate members of the Golden Key International Honour Society. Applicants may compete in the following 4 categories: fiction, nonfiction, poetry, or news writing. All entries must be original and limited to 1,000 words. Only 1 composition per member is accepted. Selection is based on the quality of the submitted writing.

**Financial data:** The winners receive $1,000 awards and publication of their work in CONCEPTS.

**Duration:** The competition is held annually.

**Number awarded:** 4 each year: 1 in each category.

**Deadline:** March of each year.

## 1420 GOLDEN KEY PERFORMING ARTS SHOWCASE

Golden Key International Honour Society
621 North Avenue N.E., Suite C-100
Atlanta, GA 30308
Phone: (404) 377-2400; (800) 377-2401; Fax: (678) 420-6757;
Email: scholarships@goldenkey.org
Web: www.goldenkey.org/GKweb/ScholarshipsandAwards

**Summary:** To recognize and reward members of the Golden Key International Honour Society who are studying the performing arts.

**Eligibility:** Open to undergraduate, graduate, and postgraduate members of the society who are studying in the following 6 categories: vocal performance, dance, drama, musical composition, instrumental performance, or filmmaking. Applicants must submit videotaped performances, up to 10 minutes in length. Selection is based on the quality of the work submitted.

**Financial data:** Winners receive $1,000 awards and the chance to perform at the society's annual convention.

**Duration:** These awards are presented annually.

**Number awarded:** 6 each year: 1 in each of the 6 categories.

**Deadline:** February of each year.

## 1421 GORDON STAFFORD SCHOLARSHIP IN ARCHITECTURE

Stafford King Wiese Architects, Attn: Scholarship Selection Committee
622 20th Street
Sacramento, CA 95814
Phone: (916) 443-4829; Fax: (916) 443-0719;
Email: connie_van_berkel@skwaia.com
Web: www.skwaia.com

**Summary:** To provide financial assistance to members of minority groups interested in studying architecture in college.

**Eligibility:** Open to students accepted by an accredited school of architecture as first-year or transfer students. Applicants must be U.S. citizens or permanent residents who are ethnic persons of color (defined as Black, Hispanic, Native American, Pacific-Asian, or Asian-Indian). They must submit a 500-word statement expressing their desire to study architecture. Finalists are interviewed and must travel to Sacramento, California at their own expense.

**Financial data:** The stipend is $2,000 per year. That includes $1,000 deposited in the recipient's school account and $1,000 paid to them directly.

**Duration:** 1 year; may be renewed up to 4 additional years.

**Number awarded:** Up to 5 of these scholarships may be active at a time.

**Deadline:** June of each year.

## 1422 GRANDMA MOSES SCHOLARSHIP

Western Art Association, Attn: Foundation
13730 Loumont Street
Whittier, CA 90601

**Summary:** To provide financial assistance for art school to female high school seniors whose art demonstrates a "congruence with the art of Grandma Moses."

**Eligibility:** Open to female graduating high school seniors. Applicants must be planning to study art in a college, university, or specialized school of art. Preference is given to applicants from the western United States. Candidates must submit samples of their artwork; selection is based on the extent to which their work "manifests a congruence with the work of the famed folk artist, Grandma Moses." Financial need is not considered.

**Financial data:** The stipend is $3,000 per year.

**Duration:** 1 year; may be renewed up to 3 additional years.

**Number awarded:** 1 each year.

**Deadline:** March of each year.

## 1423 GRANT K. PULEN SCHOLARSHIP

The Fellowship of United Methodists in Music and Worship Arts-Florida Chapter
c/o Luke Nash
5836-4 Queen Elizabeth Way
Fort Myers, FL 33907
Email: bigluke@peganet.com
Web: www.gbgm-umc.org/thefellowship/scholarship.htm

**Summary:** To provide financial assistance to undergraduate students majoring in music who are members of a United Methodist Church in Florida.

**Eligibility:** Open to high school seniors and current undergraduate students who are majoring in music. Applicants must have been a member of a United Methodist church in the Florida Conference for at least 1 year prior to applying. Preference is given to applicants currently active in religious and music activities in churches, schools, or other organizations. Selection is based on health, emotional stability, Christian character, talent, leadership ability, promise of future usefulness to the Methodist church, transcripts, 3 letters of recommendation, and financial need.

**Financial data:** The stipend is $1,500 per year.

**Duration:** 1 year; may be renewed.

**Number awarded:** 1 each year.

**Deadline:** May of each year.

## 1424 GREAT FALLS ADVERTISING FEDERATION ART EDUCATION SCHOLARSHIP

Great Falls Advertising Federation, Attn: Advertising Scholarship Committee
P.O. Box 634
Great Falls, MT 59403
Phone: (406) 761-6454; (800) 803-3351; Fax: (406) 453-1128;
Email: gfaf@gfaf.com
Web: www.gfaf.com/scholarships_art.html

**Summary:** To provide financial assistance to high school seniors in Montana interested in studying art at the postsecondary level.

**Eligibility:** Open to seniors graduating from high schools in Montana. Applicants must be interested in preparing for a career in art or a related field by enrolling in a program of postsecondary training (approval by the sponsoring organization may be required). They must submit a letter describing how they will use the scholarship; a resume highlighting their work experience, extracurricular activities, honors, and awards; at least 2 letters of recommendation; and a portfolio of their artwork.

**Financial data:** The stipend is $2,000.

**Duration:** 1 year.

**Number awarded:** 1 each year.

**Deadline:** February of each year.

## 1425 GREAT FALLS ADVERTISING FEDERATION COMMUNICATION/MARKETING SCHOLARSHIP

Great Falls Advertising Federation, Attn: Advertising Scholarship Committee
P.O. Box 634
Great Falls, MT 59403
Phone: (406) 761-6454; (800) 803-3351; Fax: (406) 453-1128;
Email: gfaf@gfaf.com
Web: www.gfaf.com/scholarships_adv.html

**Summary:** To provide financial assistance to high school seniors in Montana interested in preparing for a career related to advertising.
**Eligibility:** Open to residents of Montana who are high school seniors planning to attend a college or university. Applicants must be interested in preparing for a career in advertising, communication, electronic media, graphic design, marketing, or a related field. They must submit a letter describing how they will use the scholarship; a resume highlighting their work experience, extracurricular activities, honors, and awards; at least 2 letters of recommendation; and a marketing plan based on either an existing business or product or an imaginary business or product.
**Financial data:** The stipend is $2,000.
**Duration:** 1 year.
**Number awarded:** 1 each year.
**Deadline:** February of each year.

## 1426 GREATER OMAHA CHAPTER NAWIC SCHOLARSHIP

National Association of Women in Construction-Greater Omaha Chapter 116
Attn: Scholarship Committee
8712 West Dodge Road, Suite 200
Omaha, NE 68114
Email: nawicomaha@yahoo.com
Web: www.geocities.com/nawicomaha
**Summary:** To provide financial assistance to students in Nebraska who are preparing for a career in construction.
**Eligibility:** Open to graduating high school seniors and current college students in Nebraska. Applicants must be preparing for a career in the construction industry (e.g., architecture, engineering, construction management). They must have a GPA of 2.75 or higher and be enrolled or planning to enroll full time.
**Financial data:** A stipend is awarded (amount not specified).
**Duration:** 1 year.
**Number awarded:** 1 or more each year.
**Deadline:** March of each year.

## 1427 GRETCHEN E. VAN ROY MUSIC EDUCATION SCHOLARSHIP

National Federation of Music Clubs
1336 North Delaware Street
Indianapolis, IN 46202-2481
Phone: (317) 638-4003; Fax: (317) 638-0503; Email: info@nfmc-music.org
Web: www.nfmc-music.org/Competitions/Annual_Student/annual_student.html
**Summary:** To provide financial assistance to college student members of the National Federation of Music Clubs (NFMC) who are majoring in music education.
**Eligibility:** Open to college juniors majoring in music education at a college or university. U.S. citizenship and membership in the student division of the federation are required.
**Financial data:** The stipend is $1,000.
**Duration:** 1 year.
**Number awarded:** 1 each year.
**Deadline:** February of each year.

## 1428 GUIDEPOSTS YOUNG WRITERS CONTEST

Guideposts
16 East 34th Street
New York, NY 10016
Phone: (212) 251-8100; (800) 932-2145; Fax: (212) 684-0679
Web: www.guideposts.com/young_writers_contest.asp
**Summary:** To recognize and reward outstanding true spiritual stories written by high school students.
**Eligibility:** Open to high school juniors or seniors. They must submit a true first-person story about a memorable or moving experience and how faith in God has made a difference in their lives. Manuscripts must be written in English and be no more than 1,200 words. Children of *Guideposts* employees and staff members are not eligible.
**Financial data:** Prizes, in the form of scholarships to accredited colleges or schools of the recipients' choice, are $10,000 for first, $8,000 for second, $6,000 for third, $4,000 for fourth, $3,000 for fifth, and $1,000 for sixth through tenth. The 11th through 20th prize winners receive $250 gift certificates for college supplies.
**Duration:** The competition is held annually. Scholarships must be used within 5 years of high school graduation.
**Number awarded:** 10 scholarships and 10 gift certificates are awarded each year.
**Deadline:** November of each year.

## 1429 GUY P. GANNETT SCHOLARSHIP FUND

Maine Community Foundation, Attn: Program Director
245 Main Street
Ellsworth, ME 04605
Phone: (207) 667-9735; (877) 700-6800; Fax: (207) 667-0447;
Email: info@mainecf.org
Web: www.mainecf.org/html/scholarships/index.html
**Summary:** To provide financial assistance to Maine residents who are interested in studying journalism in college.
**Eligibility:** Open to graduates of Maine high schools (public and private) and to Maine residents who were schooled at home during their last year of secondary education. Applicants must be attending either an undergraduate (including a trade school or a technical institute program) or a graduate program at an accredited postsecondary institution in the United States. They must be majoring in journalism or a related field, including all forms of print, broadcast, or electronic media. Selection is based on academic achievement, financial need, and a demonstrated interest in a career in a form of journalism. Preference is given to renewal applicants.
**Financial data:** A stipend is paid (amount not specified).
**Duration:** 1 year; may be renewed.
**Number awarded:** 1 or more each year.
**Deadline:** April of each year.

## 1430 HAROLD B. & DOROTHY A. SNYDER SCHOLARSHIPS

Harold B. & Dorothy A. Snyder Scholarship Fund
P.O. Box 671
Moorestown, NJ 08057-0671
Phone: (856) 273-9745
**Summary:** To provide financial assistance to undergraduate and graduate students preparing for a career in the areas of Presbyterian ministry, nursing, building construction, or engineering.
**Eligibility:** Open to U.S. citizens who are attending or planning to attend institutions of higher learning. They must be preparing for a career in the areas of Presbyterian ministry (M.Div. degree), nursing (B.S.N.), building construction, or engineering. Applicants are evaluated on the basis of achievement, need, demonstrated commitment to community service, and character. Preference is given to applicants who are full-time students and who are New Jersey residents. In some instances, preference is also given to full-time enrollees of specific institutions and to members of certain denominations and congregations or residents of certain towns. There are no other preferences as to age, sex, religion (except when applicable), race, or country of origin. Personal interviews are required.
**Financial data:** The amount awarded varies, depending upon the needs of the recipient. Funds are paid directly to the recipient's institution.
**Duration:** 1 year; generally renewable until completion of the recipient's degree program.
**Number awarded:** Varies each year.
**Deadline:** March of each year.

## 1431 HAROLD E. FELLOWS SCHOLARSHIPS

Broadcast Education Association, Attn: Scholarships
1771 N Street, N.W.
Washington, DC 20036-2891
Phone: (202) 429-5354; (888) 380-7222; Email: beainfo@beaweb.org
Web: www.beaweb.org/scholarships.html
**Summary:** To provide financial assistance to upper-division and graduate students who are interested in preparing for a career in broadcasting.
**Eligibility:** Open to juniors, seniors, and graduate students enrolled full time at a college or university where at least 1 department is an institutional member of the Broadcast Education Association (BEA). Applicants may be studying in any area of broadcasting. They must have worked (or their parent must have worked) as an employee or paid intern at a station that is a member of the National Association of Broadcasters (NAB). Selection is based on evidence that the applicant possesses high integrity, superior academic ability, potential to be an outstanding electronic media professional, and a sense of personal and professional responsibility.
**Financial data:** The stipend is $1,250.
**Duration:** 1 year; may not be renewed.
**Number awarded:** 4 each year.
**Deadline:** September of each year.

## 1432 HARRIET E. PRYOR SCHOLARSHIP

Arkansas Baptist State Convention, Attn: Ministry Planning Team
525 West Capitol Avenue, Room 210
P.O. Box 552
Little Rock, AR 72203
Phone: (501) 376-4791, ext. 5102; (800) 838-2272 (within AR); Fax: (501) 374-2754; Email: mdavis@absc.org
Web: www.absc.org
**Summary:** To provide financial assistance to Arkansas residents preparing for a career as a Baptist missionary.
**Eligibility:** Open to residents of Arkansas currently enrolled full time at a college, university, or seminary. Applicants must be planning to serve in the missions field with the International Mission Board or the North American Mission Board of the Southern Baptist Convention.
**Financial data:** A stipend is awarded (amount not specified).
**Duration:** 1 year.
**Number awarded:** 1 or more each year.

## 1433 HARRIET IRSAY SCHOLARSHIP GRANT

American Institute of Polish Culture, Inc., Attn: Director of Public Relations
1440 79th Street Causeway, Suite 117
Miami, FL 33141
Phone: (305) 864-2349; Fax: (305) 865-5150; Email: info@ampolinstitute.org
Web: www.ampolinstitute.org
**Summary:** To provide financial assistance to Polish American and other students interested in working on an undergraduate or graduate degree in journalism or related fields.
**Eligibility:** Open to students working on an undergraduate or graduate degree in the following fields: journalism, communications, and/or public relations. These are merit awards. Preference is given to American students of Polish heritage. Applicants must submit a completed application, transcripts, a resume, and 3 letters of recommendation.
**Financial data:** The stipend is $1,000.
**Duration:** 1 year.
**Number awarded:** 10 to 15 each year.
**Deadline:** March of each year.

## 1434 HARRIETT BARNHART WIMMER SCHOLARSHIP

Landscape Architecture Foundation, Attn: Scholarship Program
818 18th Street, N.W., Suite 810
Washington, DC 20006-3520
Phone: (202) 331-7070; Fax: (202) 331-7079; Email: rfigura@lafoundation.org
Web: www.laprofession.org
**Summary:** To recognize and reward the outstanding achievements of women undergraduates majoring in landscape architecture.
**Eligibility:** Open to undergraduate women in their senior year who are majoring in landscape architecture. They must be able to demonstrate excellence in design ability and sensitivity to the environment. They are required to submit a letter of recommendation from a design instructor, a 500-word autobiographical essay that addresses personal and professional goals, and a sample of design work. Selection is based on professional experience, community involvement, extracurricular activities, and financial need.
**Financial data:** The award is $1,000.
**Duration:** The award is granted annually.
**Number awarded:** 1 each year.
**Deadline:** April of each year.

## 1435 HARRY BARFIELD KBA SCHOLARSHIP PROGRAM

Kentucky Broadcasters Association
101 Enterprise Drive
Frankfort, KY 40601
Phone: (502) 848-0426; (888) THE-KBA1; Fax: (502) 848-5710
Web: www.kba.org/scholarship.htm
**Summary:** To provide financial assistance to currently-enrolled college students in Kentucky who are majoring in broadcasting.
**Eligibility:** Open to Kentucky residents who are currently enrolled in college in the state (preferably but not limited to second-semester sophomore status) and majoring in broadcasting or telecommunications. To apply, students must submit a completed application form, a college transcript, a 500-word autobiographical sketch including career goals, a list of extracurricular activities and scholarships, and 1 recommendation from a faculty member. Financial need is not required, but it is the deciding factor if merit qualifications are equal.

**Financial data:** The stipend is $1,000.
**Duration:** 1 year; may be renewed for 1 additional year if the recipient maintains a GPA of 3.0 or higher.
**Number awarded:** 1 or more each year.
**Deadline:** April of each year.

## 1436 HAWAII ADVERTISING FEDERATION SCHOLARSHIPS

Hawaii Advertising Federation, Attn: Scholarship Committee
P.O. Box 2181
Honolulu, HI 96805
Phone: (808) 532-0555; Fax: (808) 532-0560; Email: info@hafspot.com
Web: www.hafspot.com/topics/media_scholarship.html
**Summary:** To provide financial assistance to residents of Hawaii who are attending or planning to attend college to prepare for a career in the advertising industry in the state.
**Eligibility:** Open to Hawaii residents who are either college-bound high school seniors or already enrolled full time in an accredited 2-year or 4-year college or university. Applicants must have a GPA of 2.5 or higher and a desire to work in the advertising industry in Hawaii after graduation. Along with their application, they must submit an essay on their goals and aspirations, a letter of recommendation, and information on financial need.
**Financial data:** The stipend is $3,500.
**Duration:** 1 year.
**Number awarded:** 3 each year.
**Deadline:** July of each year.

## 1437 HAWAII ASSOCIATION OF BROADCASTERS SCHOLARSHIP

Hawaii Association of Broadcasters, Inc., Attn: Scholarship Committee
P.O. Box 221122
Honolulu, HI 96823-2112
Email: mailtohab@aol.com
Web: www.hawaiibroadcasters.com/scholar.html
**Summary:** To provide financial assistance to high school seniors and current college students interested in preparing for a career in the broadcast industry in Hawaii.
**Eligibility:** Open to college-bound high school seniors and current students at 2-year and 4-year colleges and universities and recognized broadcast schools in the United States. Applicants must have a GPA of 2.5 or higher and a stated intention to work in the broadcast industry in Hawaii upon completion of school. Financial need is considered in the selection process. Finalists are invited to an interview.
**Financial data:** The stipend is $3,500 per year.
**Duration:** 1 year.
**Number awarded:** 1 or more each year.
**Deadline:** April of each year.

## 1438 HAWAII CHAPTER/DAVID T. WOOLSEY SCHOLARSHIP

Landscape Architecture Foundation, Attn: Scholarship Program
818 18th Street, N.W., Suite 810
Washington, DC 20006-3520
Phone: (202) 331-7070; Fax: (202) 331-7079; Email: rfigura@lafoundation.org
Web: www.laprofession.org
**Summary:** To provide financial assistance to landscape architecture students from Hawaii.
**Eligibility:** Open to third-, fourth-, or fifth-year undergraduate students and graduate students in landscape architecture from Hawaii. Applicants are required to submit 2 letters of recommendation (1 from a design instructor), a 500-word autobiographical essay that addresses personal and professional goals, and a sample of design work. Selection is based on professional experience, community involvement, extracurricular activities, and financial need.
**Financial data:** This scholarship is $1,000.
**Number awarded:** 1 each year.
**Deadline:** April of each year.

## 1439 HAWAI'I COMMUNITY FOUNDATION COMMUNITY SCHOLARSHIP FUND

Hawai'i Community Foundation, Attn: Scholarship Department
1164 Bishop Street, Suite 800
Honolulu, HI 96813
Phone: (808) 566-5570; (888) 731-3863; Fax: (808) 521-6286;
Email: scholarships@hcf-hawaii.org

Web: www.hawaiicommunityfoundation.org/scholar/scholar.php

**Summary:** To provide financial assistance to Hawaii residents who are interested in preparing for a career that will fill gaps in the local job market.

**Eligibility:** Open to students in Hawaii who show potential for filling a community need; demonstrate accomplishment, motivation, initiative, and vision; are residents of the state of Hawaii; intend to return to, or stay in, Hawaii to work; are able to demonstrate financial need; are interested in attending an accredited 2- or 4-year college or university as a full-time student at either the undergraduate or graduate level; plan to major in the arts, architecture, education, humanities, or social science; and are able to demonstrate academic achievement (GPA of 3.0 or higher).

**Financial data:** The amount awarded varies; recently, stipends averaged $1,000.

**Duration:** 1 year.

**Number awarded:** Varies each year; recently, 97 of these scholarships were awarded.

**Deadline:** February of each year.

## 1440 HAZEL SIMMONS HODGES GARDEN CLUB OBJECTIVES SCHOLARSHIP

Florida Federation of Garden Clubs, Inc., Attn: Office Manager
1400 South Denning Drive
Winter Park, FL 32789-5662
Phone: (407) 647-7016; Fax: (407) 647-5479; Email: ffgc@earthlink.net
Web: www.ffgc.org/scholarships/index.html

**Summary:** To provide financial aid to Florida students majoring or planning to major in designated areas related to gardening.

**Eligibility:** Open to Florida residents who are either high school seniors planning to enroll in a Florida college or current Florida college students entering their sophomore year. They must have a GPA of 3.0 or higher, be in financial need, and be majoring in ecology, horticulture, landscape design, conservation, forestry, marine biology, city planning, botany, or allied subjects. U.S. citizenship is required. Preference is given to students who were members of a high school gardener club. Selection is based on academic record, commitment to career, character, and financial need.

**Financial data:** The stipend is $2,500. The funds are sent directly to the recipient's school and distributed semiannually.

**Duration:** 1 year.

**Number awarded:** 1 each year.

**Deadline:** April of each year.

## 1441 HAZEL STONE MEMORIAL SCHOLARSHIP

Jews for Jesus
60 Haight Street
San Francisco, CA 94102
Phone: (415) 864-2600; Email: jfj@jewsforjesus.org
Web: www.jewsforjesus.org

**Summary:** To provide financial assistance to "Jewish women proclaiming Jesus" who are interested in going to a bible college.

**Eligibility:** Open to Jewish women who have committed their life to Jesus, are committed to going to bible college or seminary, are going to be committed to an evangelistic ministry after graduation, and are having difficulty meeting the cost of their education.

**Financial data:** The amount awarded varies, depending upon the needs of the recipient.

**Duration:** 1 year.

**Number awarded:** 1 or more each year.

## 1442 HBCU MINORITY STUDENT SCHOLARSHIPS

HBCUConnect.com, LLC., Attn: Scholarship Administrator
5300 East Main Street
Columbus, OH 43213-2580
Phone: (614) 864-4446; Email: scholarship@hbcuconnect.com
Web: hbcuconnect.com/scholarships.shtml

**Summary:** To provide financial assistance to underrepresented minority students attending or planning to attend an Historically Black College or University (HBCU).

**Eligibility:** Open to high school seniors and current full-time college students who are members of an underrepresented minority group (African American, Hispanic American, Native American). Applicants must be attending or interested in attending an HBCU to work on a 4-year degree. Preference is given to students planning to major in actuarial science or African studies. Along with their application, they must submit 4 essays: why they decided to attend an HBCU, what they want to do once they receive their degree, a situation that demonstrates initiative and their willingness to go above and beyond, and how they are currently funding their college education.

**Financial data:** The stipend is $1,000.

**Duration:** 1 year.

**Number awarded:** Varies each year; recently, 4 of these scholarships were awarded.

**Deadline:** July or December of each year.

## 1443 HEARST JOURNALISM AWARDS PROGRAM BROADCAST NEWS COMPETITIONS

William Randolph Hearst Foundation
90 New Montgomery Street, Suite 1212
San Francisco, CA 94105-4504
Phone: (415) 543-6033, ext. 308; Fax: (415) 348-0887;
Email: journalism@hearstfdn.org
Web: www.hearstfdn.org

**Summary:** To recognize and reward outstanding college student broadcast news journalists.

**Eligibility:** Open to full-time undergraduate students majoring in journalism at one of the 105 accredited colleges and universities that are members of the Association of Schools of Journalism and Mass Communication (ASJMC). For each of the 2 semifinal competitions, each student submits either an audio tape or a videotape. Entries must have been "published" in the sense of having been made available to an anonymous audience of substantial size. The first competition of each year is for "features;" entries must be soft news: non-deadline reporting of personalities, events, or issues. The second competition of each year is for "news;" entries must be hard news, including enterprise reporting. All entries must have been produced since September of the previous year and must consist of at least 2 reports. Broadcast news tapes are judged on the basis of writing quality, understandability, clarity, depth, focus, editing, knowledge of subject, and broadcast skills. The 10 audiotapes and 10 videotapes selected by the judges as the best in the semifinals are then entered in the finals. The finalists submit new and different tapes, up to 10 minutes in length with a minimum of 3 reports, of which only one may have been submitted previously. The reports must include at least one news story and one feature. Judges select the top 5 audio tapes and the top 5 videotapes, and those 10 finalists go to San Francisco for an on the spot news assignment to rank the winners.

**Financial data:** In each of the 2 semifinal competitions, the first-place winner receives a $2,000 scholarship, second place $1,500, third place $1,000, fourth place $750, fifth place $600, and sixth through tenth places $500 each; identical grants are awarded to the journalism schools attended by the winning students. For the finals competition, additional scholarships are awarded of $5,000 to the first-place winner, $4,000 for second, $3,000 for third, and $1,000 for each of the other 7 finalists; in addition, the students who make the best use of radio for news coverage and the best use of television for news coverage each receive another scholarship of $1,000. Scholarship funds are paid to the school. Schools receive points for their students who place in the top 20 places in the semifinals and in the finals; the school with the most points receives an additional cash prize of $10,000, second wins $5,000, and third wins $2,500.

**Duration:** The competition is held annually.

**Number awarded:** 20 semifinal and 10 final winners are chosen each year, and 2 additional scholarships are awarded each year for best use of radio and best use of television.

**Deadline:** The deadline for the first competition is in November of each year and for the second competition in early February of each year. Additional entries by finalists must be submitted by the end of March of each year. The competition among the top 10 finalists takes place in San Francisco in June.

## 1444 HEARST JOURNALISM AWARDS PROGRAM PHOTOJOURNALISM COMPETITIONS

William Randolph Hearst Foundation
90 New Montgomery Street, Suite 1212
San Francisco, CA 94105-4504
Phone: (415) 543-6033, ext. 308; Fax: (415) 348-0887;
Email: journalism@hearstfdn.org
Web: www.hearstfdn.org

**Summary:** To recognize and reward outstanding college student photojournalists.

**Eligibility:** Open to full-time undergraduate students majoring in journalism at 1 of the 105 accredited colleges and universities that are members of the Association of Schools of Journalism and Mass Communication (ASJMC). For each of the 3 semifinal competitions, each student submits photographs in 35mm slide form. For the first competition of each year, the categories are portrait/personality and feature; entries consist of 2 photographs in each of those

2 categories. For the second competition of each year, the categories are sports and news; entries consist of 2 photographs in each of those 2 categories. For the third competition of each year, the category is picture story/series; each entry must include 1 picture story/series, with up to 15 images. All photographs must have been taken since September of the previous year and may be in color or black and white. Photography is judged on the basis of quality, versatility, consistency, human interest, news value, and originality. The judges select the top 10 entrants in each of the 3 competitions; of those 10, the 4 top scoring entrants qualify for the photojournalism finals. Those 12 finalists must submit a portfolio consisting of prints of the slides previously judged, plus 2 additional photographs (published or unpublished) from each of the other categories in the overall contest; complete portfolios must thus consist of 2 pictures each in news, features, sports, portrait/personality, plus a picture story/series. Based on those portfolios, judges select the top 6 finalists to go to San Francisco for on-the-spot assignments to rank the winners.

**Financial data:** In each of the 3 semifinal competitions, the first-place winner receives a $2,000 scholarship, second place $1,500, third place $1,000, fourth place $750, fifth place $600, and sixth through tenth places $500 each; identical grants are awarded to the journalism schools attended by the winning students. For the finals competition, additional scholarships are awarded of $5,000 to the first-place winner, $4,000 for second, $3,000 for third; and $1,000 for each of the other 3 finalists. In addition, the photographers who submit the best single photo and the best picture story each receive another scholarship of $1,000. Scholarship funds are paid to the school. Schools receive points for their students who place in the top 20 places in the semifinals and in the finals; the school with the most points receives an additional cash prize of $10,000, second wins $5,000, and third wins $2,500.

**Duration:** The competition is held annually.

**Number awarded:** 30 semifinal and 6 final winners are chosen each year, and 2 additional scholarships are awarded each year for the best single photo and best picture story.

**Deadline:** The deadline for the first competition is in early November of each year, for the second competition in late January of each year, and for the third competition in mid-March of each year. Additional entries by finalists must be submitted by late May of each year. The competition among the top 6 finalists takes place in San Francisco in June.

### 1445 HEARST JOURNALISM AWARDS PROGRAM WRITING COMPETITIONS

William Randolph Hearst Foundation
90 New Montgomery Street, Suite 1212
San Francisco, CA 94105-4504
Phone: (415) 543-6033, ext 308; Fax: (415) 348-0887;
Email: journalism@hearstfdn.org
Web: www.hearstfdn.org

**Summary:** To recognize and reward outstanding college student journalists.

**Eligibility:** Open to full-time undergraduate students majoring in journalism at 1 of the 105 accredited colleges or universities that are members of the Association of Schools of Journalism and Mass Communication (ASJMC). Each entry consists of a single article written by the student with primary responsibility for the work and published in a campus or professional publication. Each month, a separate competition is held; November: feature writing—a background, color, or mood article as opposed to a conventional news story or personality profile; December: editorials or signed columns of opinion—must be well researched and express a clear and cogent viewpoint; January: in-depth writing—must illustrate the student's ability to handle a complex subject clearly, precisely, and with sufficient background; February: sports writing—relevant to an event or issue, not to a sports personality; March: personality profile—a personality sketch of someone; April: spot news writing—articles written about a breaking news event and against a deadline. The 6 monthly winners and the 2 finalists who place highest in their top 2 scores in the monthly competitions qualify for the national writing championship held in San Francisco in June; at that time, competition assignments consist of an on-the-spot assignment and a news story and personality profile from a press interview of a prominent individual in the San Francisco area. Writing is judged on the basis of knowledge of subject, understandability, clarity, color, reporting in depth, and construction.

**Financial data:** In each of the 6 competitions, the first-place winner receives a $2,000 scholarship, second place $1,500, third place $1,000, fourth place $750, fifth place $600, and sixth through tenth places $500 each; identical grants are awarded to the journalism schools attended by the students. For the finalists whose articles are judged best in the national writing championship, additional scholarships of $5,000 are awarded to the first-place winner, $4,000 for second place, $3,000 for third place, and $1,000 each for the other 5 finalists. Scholarship awards are paid to the school. Schools receive points for each of their students who place in the top 20 places in each monthly competition; the school with the most points receives an additional cash prize of $10,000, second wins $5,000, and third wins $2,500.

**Duration:** The competition is held annually.

**Number awarded:** Each year, 60 scholarships are awarded to the monthly winners, and an additional 8 are presented to the national finalists.

**Deadline:** Articles for the monthly competitions must be submitted early in the respective month of each year. The championship is held in June of each year.

### 1446 HEATON-PERRY SCHOLARSHIP

Society of Professional Journalists-Kansas Professional Chapter
c/o Lori O'Toole Buselt, Scholarship Chair
The Wichita Eagle
P.O. Box 820
Wichita, KS 67201-0820
Phone: (316) 268-6327; Fax: (316) 268-6627; Email: kansas@spj.org
Web: www.spj.org/kansas/scholarship.htm

**Summary:** To provide financial assistance to students at colleges and universities in Kansas who are interested in a career in journalism.

**Eligibility:** Open to juniors and seniors at colleges and universities in Kansas. Sophomores may apply, designating the award for their junior year. Applicants do not have to be journalism or communication majors, but they must demonstrate a strong and sincere interest in print journalism, broadcast journalism, or photojournalism. They must have a GPA of 2.5 or higher and participate in outside journalism-related activities, as demonstrated by involvement in student or trade organizations and/or student or other news organizations or publications. Along with their application, they must submit 4 to 6 examples of their best work (clips or stories, copies of photographs, tapes or transcripts of broadcasts). Selection is based on the quality of work submitted, academic standing, references, and financial need.

**Financial data:** The stipend is $1,000.

**Duration:** 1 year.

**Number awarded:** 1 each year.

**Deadline:** March of each year.

### 1447 HEBREW LADIES SHELTERING HOME SCHOLARSHIPS

Jewish Federation of Greater Hartford, Inc., Attn: Endowment Foundation
333 Bloomfield Avenue
West Hartford, CT 06117
Phone: (860) 523-7460; Fax: (860) 231-0576; Email: grants@jcfhartford.org
Web: www.jcfhartford.org

**Summary:** To provide financial assistance for college to students in Connecticut interested in Jewish education.

**Eligibility:** Open to Jewish residents of Connecticut who are graduating high school seniors. Applicants must be interested in working on a degree in Jewish education. U.S. citizenship is required. Selection is based on academic record and financial need.

**Financial data:** The stipend is $1,000.

**Duration:** 1 year.

**Number awarded:** 2 to 3 each year.

**Deadline:** April of each year.

### 1448 HELEN J. SIOUSSAT/FAY WELLS SCHOLARSHIPS

Broadcast Education Association, Attn: Scholarships
1771 N Street, N.W.
Washington, DC 20036-2891
Phone: (202) 429-5354; (888) 380-7222; Email: beainfo@beaweb.org
Web: www.beaweb.org/scholarships.html

**Summary:** To provide financial assistance to upper-division and graduate students who are interested in preparing for a career in broadcasting.

**Eligibility:** Open to juniors, seniors, and graduate students enrolled full time at a college or university where at least 1 department is an institutional member of the Broadcast Education Association. Applicants may be studying in any area of broadcasting. Selection is based on evidence that the applicant possesses high integrity, superior academic ability, potential to be an outstanding electronic media professional, and a sense of personal and professional responsibility.

**Financial data:** The stipend is $1,250.

**Duration:** 1 year; may not be renewed.

**Number awarded:** 2 each year.

**Deadline:** September of each year.

### 1449 HELEN JAMES BREWER SCHOLARSHIP

United Daughters of the Confederacy, Attn: Education Director
328 North Boulevard
Richmond, VA 23220-4057

Phone: (804) 355-1636; Fax: (804) 353-1396; Email: hqudc@rcn.com

Web: www.hqudc.org/scholarships/scholarships.html

**Summary:** To provide financial assistance to lineal descendants of Confederate veterans in certain southern states who are interested in majoring in southern history or literature.

**Eligibility:** Open to lineal descendants of worthy Confederates or collateral descendants who are current or former members of the Children of the Confederacy or current members of the United Daughters of the Confederacy. Applicants must intend to study English or southern history and literature and must submit a family financial report and certified proof of the Confederate record of 1 ancestor, with the company and regiment in which he served. They must have at least a 3.0 GPA in high school. Residency in Alabama, Florida, Georgia, South Carolina, Tennessee, or Virginia is required.

**Financial data:** The amount of this scholarship depends on the availability of funds.

**Duration:** 1 year; may be renewed.

**Number awarded:** 1 each year.

**Deadline:** March of each year.

### 1450 HELEN VERBA SCHOLARSHIPS

Society of Professional Journalists-Colorado Professional Chapter

c/o Denver Press Club

1330 Glenarm Place

Denver, CO 80204

Phone: (303) 571-5250

Web: www.reporters.net/colospj

**Summary:** To provide financial assistance to juniors majoring in journalism at colleges and universities in Colorado.

**Eligibility:** Open to students entering their junior year at a college or university in Colorado. Applicants must be majoring in print or broadcast journalism. They must submit a resume, 2 references, at least 1 clip of a story or article published in a school or professional publication, and a 500-word essay illustrating their writing abilities and indicating their plans for a career in journalism.

**Financial data:** The stipend is $1,500.

**Duration:** 1 year.

**Number awarded:** 2 each year: 1 to a student in print journalism and 1 to a student in broadcast journalism.

**Deadline:** February of each year.

### 1451 HENRY AND CHIYO KUWAHARA CREATIVE ARTS AWARD

Japanese American Citizens League, Attn: National Scholarship Awards

1765 Sutter Street

San Francisco, CA 94115

Phone: (415) 921-5225; Fax: (415) 931-4671; Email: jacl@jacl.org

Web: www.jacl.org/scholarships.html

**Summary:** To provide financial assistance to student members of the Japanese American Citizens League (JACL) interested in working on an undergraduate or graduate degree in the creative arts.

**Eligibility:** Open to JACL members who are interested in working on an undergraduate or graduate degree in the creative arts. Professional artists are not eligible. Applicants must submit a detailed proposal on the nature of their project, including a time-plan, anticipated date of completion, and itemized budget. They must also submit a statement describing their current level of involvement in the Japanese American community or Asian Pacific community and how they will continue their involvement in future years. Selection is based on academic record, extracurricular activities, and community involvement. Preference is given to students who are interested in creative projects that reflect the Japanese American experience and culture.

**Financial data:** The stipend depends on the availability of funds but usually ranges from $1,000 to $5,000.

**Duration:** 1 year; nonrenewable.

**Number awarded:** At least 1 each year.

**Deadline:** March of each year.

### 1452 HERB ROBINSON SCHOLARSHIP

Washington News Council, Attn: Scholarship Committee

P.O. Box 3672

Seattle, WA 98124-3672

Phone: (206) 262-9793; Fax: (206) 464-7902; Email: info@wanewscouncil.org

Web: www.wanewscouncil.org

**Summary:** To provide financial assistance to Washington high school seniors who are interested in majoring in a communication-related field at an academic institution in the state.

**Eligibility:** Open to seniors graduating from high schools in Washington who have a serious interest in communications, including journalism, politics, public relations, or related fields. Applicants must be accepted at a 4-year public or private university in the state. They must be able to demonstrate financial need. Along with their application, they submit an essay of 500 to 1,000 words on themselves, why they want to prepare for a career in communications, and how they think they can contribute to their chosen profession.

**Financial data:** The stipend is $1,000.

**Duration:** 1 year.

**Number awarded:** 1 each year.

**Deadline:** May of each year.

### 1453 HERBERT FERNANDES SCHOLARSHIP

Luso-American Education Foundation, Attn: Administrative Director

7080 Donlon Way, Suite 202

P.O. Box 2967

Dublin, CA 94568

Phone: (925) 828-3883; Fax: (925) 828-3883

Web: www.luso-american.org/laef

**Summary:** To provide financial assistance for undergraduate study in Portuguese language to students in California.

**Eligibility:** Open to students of Portuguese descent who are sophomores, juniors, or seniors at 4-year colleges or universities with a GPA of 3.5 or higher. Applicants must be California residents who are interested or involved in the Luso-American community and have taken or will enroll in Portuguese language classes. Selection is based on promise of success in college, financial need, qualities of leadership, vocational promise, and sincerity of purpose.

**Financial data:** The stipend is $1,000.

**Duration:** 1 year; renewable.

**Number awarded:** 1 each year.

**Deadline:** February of each year.

### 1454 HERFF JONES SCHOLARSHIP

University Interscholastic League

Attn: Interscholastic League Press Conference

1701 Manor Road

P.O. Box 8028

Austin, TX 78713

Phone: (512) 471-5883; Fax: (512) 232-7311;

Email: rvonderheid@mail.utexas.edu

Web: www.uil.utexas.edu/aca/journ/ilpc

**Summary:** To provide financial assistance to high school seniors in Texas who plan to study communications in college.

**Eligibility:** Open to graduating seniors in Texas who have worked on their high school yearbook and plan to continue their education in a communications-related field (major or minor) in college. Applicants must have a GPA of "B" or higher. Along with their application, they must submit a statement on their involvement in journalism while in high school, a description of their college and future plans, a letter of recommendation, and 3 to 5 samples of their work as a journalism student.

**Financial data:** The stipend is $1,500.

**Duration:** 1 year.

**Number awarded:** 1 each year.

**Deadline:** March of each year.

### 1455 HERMINE DALKOWITZ TOBOLOWSKY SCHOLARSHIP

Texas Federation of Business and Professional Women's Foundation, Inc.

Attn: TFBPW Foundation

803 Forest Ridge Drive, Suite 207

Bedford, TX 76022

Phone: (817) 283-0862; Fax: (817) 283-0872; Email: bpwtx@swbell.net

Web: www.bpwtx.org/foundation.asp

**Summary:** To provide financial assistance to women in Texas who are preparing to enter selected professions.

**Eligibility:** Open to women in Texas who are interested in attending school to prepare for a career in law, public service, government, political science, or women's history. Applicants must have completed at least 2 semesters of study at an accredited college or university in Texas, have a GPA of 3.0 or higher, and be U.S. citizens. Selection is based on academic achievement and financial need.

**Financial data:** A stipend is awarded (amount not specified).

**Duration:** 1 year.
**Number awarded:** 1 or more each year.
**Deadline:** April of each year.

## 1456 HGA SCHOLARSHIPS

Handweavers Guild of America, Inc., Attn: Scholarship Chair
1255 Buford Highway, Suite 211
Suwanee, GA 30024
Phone: (678) 730-0010; Fax: (678) 730-0836; Email: hga@weavespindye.org
Web: www.weavespindye.org
**Summary:** To provide financial assistance to undergraduate and graduate students working on a degree in the field of fiber arts.
**Eligibility:** Open to undergraduate and graduate students enrolled in accredited colleges and universities in the United States, its possessions, and Canada. Applicants must be working on a degree in the field of fiber arts, including training for research, textile history, and conservation. Along with their application, they must submit 1) an essay on their study goals and how they fit into their future plans, and 2) 5 to 16 slides of their work. Selection is based on artistic and technical merit; financial need is not considered.
**Financial data:** The amount of the award depends on the availability of funds. Use of funds is restricted to tuition.
**Duration:** 1 year.
**Number awarded:** Varies; more than $4,000 is available for this program each year.
**Deadline:** March of each year.

## 1457 HOME BUILDERS ASSOCIATION OF ILLINOIS STUDENT OF THE YEAR SCHOLARSHIPS

Home Builders Association of Illinois
112 West Edwards Street
Springfield, IL 62704
Phone: (217) 753-3963; TDD: (800) 255-6047; Fax: (217) 753-3811
Web: www.hbai.org/Student/index.asp
**Summary:** To recognize and reward, with funds for continuing education, students in Illinois who are preparing for a career in the building industry.
**Eligibility:** Open to students enrolled in a building trades or architecture program at a high school, university, community college, or technical school in Illinois. Students must be nominated by a local affiliate of the Home Builders Association of Illinois. They must have a "C+" average or higher. Selection is based on academics, involvement with the building industry, leadership and extracurricular activities, community involvement, and awards and honor.
**Financial data:** Awards are $2,000 for first place, $1,500 for second place, and $1,000 for third place. Funds are paid to the student's school to be used for continuing education. If the recipients is not remaining in school, they may use the award for certified graduate builder or remodeler courses offered through the home builders association.
**Duration:** Awards are offered annually.
**Number awarded:** 3 each year.

## 1458 HONORARY STATE REGENTS' AMERICAN HISTORY SCHOLARSHIP

Daughters of the American Revolution-Colorado State Society
c/o Marilyn Fishburn, State Scholarship Chair
1546 West 28th Street
Loveland, CO 80538
Email: admin@coloradodar.org
Web: www.coloradodar.org/scholarships.htm
**Summary:** To provide financial assistance to high school seniors in Colorado who are interested in majoring in American history in college.
**Eligibility:** Open to graduating high school seniors in Colorado who are 1) American citizens; 2) in the upper third of their graduating class; 3) accepted at an accredited college or university (in any state); and 4) planning to major in American history. Interested students are invited to submit their complete application to the state scholarship chair (c/o the sponsor's address); they must include a statement of their career interest and goals (up to 500 words), 2 character references, their college transcripts, a letter of sponsorship from the Daughters of the American Revolution's Colorado chapter, and a list of their scholastic achievements, extracurricular activities, honors, and other significant accomplishments. Selection is based on academic record and financial need.
**Financial data:** The maximum stipend is $2,500. Funds are paid directly to the students' school.

**Duration:** 1 year; nonrenewable.
**Number awarded:** 1 each year.
**Deadline:** January of each year.

## 1459 HORACE AND SUSIE REVELS CAYTON SCHOLARSHIP

Public Relations Society of America-Puget Sound Chapter
c/o Diane Beins
1006 Industry Drive
Seattle, WA 98188-4801
Phone: (206) 623-8632; Email: prsascholarship@asi-seattle.net
Web: www.prsapugetsound.org/cayton
**Summary:** To provide financial assistance to minority upper-classmen from Washington who are interested in preparing for a career in public relations.
**Eligibility:** Open to U.S. citizens who are members of minority groups, defined as African Americans, Asian Americans, Hispanic/Latino Americans, Native Americans, and Pacific Islanders. Applicants must be juniors or seniors attending a college in Washington or Washington students (who graduated from a Washington high school or whose parents live in the state year-round) attending college elsewhere. They must be able to demonstrate aptitude in public relations and related courses, activities, and/or internships. Along with their application, they must submit a description of their career goals and the skills that are most important in general to a public relations career (15 points in the selection process); a description of their activities in communications in class, on campus, in the community, or during internships, including 3 samples of their work (15 points); a statement on the value of public relations to an organization (10 points); a description of any barriers, financial or otherwise, they have encountered in pursuing their academic or personal goals and how they have addressed them (15 points); a discussion of their heritage, and how their cultural background and/or the discrimination they may have experienced has impacted them (15 points); a certified transcript (15 points); and 2 or more letters of recommendation (15 points).
**Financial data:** The stipend is $2,500.
**Duration:** 1 year.
**Number awarded:** 1 each year.
**Deadline:** March of each year.

## 1460 HOWARD BROWN RICKARD SCHOLARSHIPS

National Federation of the Blind
c/o Peggy Elliott, Scholarship Committee Chair
805 Fifth Avenue
Grinnell, IA 50112
Phone: (641) 236-3366
Web: www.nfb.org/sch_intro.htm
**Summary:** To provide financial assistance for college or graduate school to blind students studying or planning to study law, medicine, engineering, architecture, or the natural sciences.
**Eligibility:** Open to legally blind students who are enrolled in or planning to enroll in a full-time undergraduate or graduate course of study. Applicants must be studying or planning to study law, medicine, engineering, architecture, or the natural sciences. Selection is based on academic excellence, service to the community, and financial need.
**Financial data:** The stipend is $3,000.
**Duration:** 1 year; recipients may resubmit applications up to 2 additional years.
**Number awarded:** 1 each year.
**Deadline:** March of each year.

## 1461 HUMANE STUDIES FELLOWSHIPS

Institute for Humane Studies at George Mason University
3301 North Fairfax Drive, Suite 440
Arlington, VA 22201-4432
Phone: (703) 993-4880; (800) 697-8799; Fax: (703) 993-4890;
Email: ihs@gmu.edu
Web: www.TheIHS.org
**Summary:** To provide financial assistance to undergraduate and graduate students in the United States or abroad who intend to pursue "intellectual careers" and have demonstrated an interest in classical liberal principles.
**Eligibility:** Open to students who will be full-time college juniors, seniors, or graduate students planning academic or other intellectual careers, including law, public policy, and journalism. Applicants must have a clearly demonstrated interest in the classical liberal/libertarian tradition of individual rights and market economics. Applications from students outside the United States or studying abroad receive equal consideration. Selection is based on academic or

professional performance, relevance of work to the advancement of a free society, and potential for success.

**Financial data:** The maximum stipend is $12,000.

**Duration:** 1 year; may be renewed upon reapplication.

**Number awarded:** Approximately 100 each year.

**Deadline:** December of each year.

## 1462 HURSTON/WRIGHT AWARD FOR COLLEGE WRITERS

Zora Neale Hurston/Richard Wright Foundation
Attn: Hurston/Wright Awards
6525 Belcrest Road, Suite 531
Hyattsville, MD 20782
Phone: (301) 683-2134; Email: info@hurstonwright.org
Web: www.hurston-wright.org/hw_award.html

**Summary:** To recognize and reward the best fiction written by college students of African descent.

**Eligibility:** Open to students of African descent who are enrolled full time as undergraduate or graduate students in a college or university in the United States. Applicants should submit a previously unpublished short story or novel excerpt (up to 25 pages). They should indicate whether it is a short story or novel excerpt. Only 1 entry may be submitted per applicant. Writers who have published a book in any genre are ineligible.

**Financial data:** The first-place award is $1,000; finalist awards are $500.

**Duration:** The prizes are awarded annually.

**Number awarded:** 3 awards are presented each year: 1 first-place award and 2 finalist awards.

**Deadline:** December of each year.

## 1463 IAHPERD SCHOLARSHIPS

Illinois Association for Health, Physical Education, Recreation and Dance
Attn: Executive Secretary
1713 South West Street
Jacksonville, IL 62650
Phone: (217) 245-6413; Fax: (217) 245-5261; Email: iahperd@iahperd.org
Web: www.iahperd.org/textpages/grants/scholarships.php

**Summary:** To provide financial assistance to upper-division students in Illinois who are majoring in health, physical education, recreation, or dance.

**Eligibility:** Open to juniors and seniors at colleges and universities in Illinois who are enrolled as a major in a professional program in health, physical education, recreation, or dance. Applicants must submit a personal letter explaining why they chose to go into their field and where they see themselves professionally in 5 years. Selection is based on that letter, involvement in professional organizations, involvement in extracurricular activities, involvement in community organizations, transcripts, and 2 letters of recommendation.

**Financial data:** Stipends are $1,000 or $750.

**Duration:** 1 year.

**Number awarded:** 6 each year: 1 at $1,000 and 5 at $750.

**Deadline:** May of each year.

## 1464 IDAHO STATE BROADCASTERS ASSOCIATION SCHOLARSHIPS

Idaho State Broadcasters Association
270 North 27th Street, Suite B
Boise, ID 83702-4741
Phone: (208) 345-3072; Fax: (208) 343-8946; Email: isba@rmci.net
Web: www.idahobroadcasters.org/scholarships.aspx

**Summary:** To provide financial assistance to students at Idaho colleges and universities who are preparing for a career in the broadcasting field.

**Eligibility:** Open to full-time students at Idaho schools who are preparing for a career in broadcasting, including business administration, sales, journalism, and engineering. Applicants must have a GPA of at least 2.0 for the first 2 years of school or 2.5 for the last 2 years. Along with their application, they must submit a letter of recommendation from the general manager of a broadcasting state that is a member of the Idaho State Broadcasters Association and a 1-page essay describing their career plans and why they want the scholarship. Applications are encouraged from a wide and diverse student population. The Wayne C. Cornils Scholarship is reserved for a less advantaged applicant.

**Financial data:** The stipend for the general scholarships is $1,000. The stipend of the Wayne C. Cornils Scholarship depends on the need of the recipient.

**Duration:** 1 year.

**Number awarded:** 3 each year: 2 general scholarships and the Cornils Scholarship.

**Deadline:** March of each year.

## 1465 IDSA UNDERGRADUATE SCHOLARSHIPS

Industrial Designers Society of America, Attn: Design Foundation
Dulles, VA 20166-6717
Phone: (703) 707-6000; Fax: (703) 787-8501; Email: celiaw@idsa.org
Web: www.idsa.org

**Summary:** To provide financial assistance to upper-division students working on an undergraduate degree in industrial design.

**Eligibility:** Open to full-time students in an industrial design program listed with the sponsor who are in their next-to-final year (juniors in a 4-year program, fourth-year students in a 5-year program), have earned at least a 3.0 GPA since entering the industrial design program, are a member of an Industrial Designers Society of America (IDSA) student chapter, and are a U.S. citizen or resident. Applicants are asked to send a letter of intent that indicates their goals, 3 letters of recommendation, 20 visual examples of their work (i.e., slides, photographs, laser printouts), a completed application form, and a current transcript. Financial need is not considered in the selection process.

**Financial data:** A stipend is awarded (amount not specified).

**Duration:** 1 year.

**Number awarded:** 2 each year.

**Deadline:** April of each year.

## 1466 IFDA EDUCATIONAL FOUNDATION STUDENT SCHOLARSHIP

International Furnishings and Design Association
Attn: IFDA Educational Foundation
330 Ferry Landing
Atlanta, GA 30328
Phone: (770) 612-0454; Fax: (770) 612-0445; Email: info@ifdaef.org
Web: www.ifdaef.org/scholarships.html

**Summary:** To provide financial assistance to undergraduate student members of the International Furnishings and Design Association (IFDA).

**Eligibility:** Open to association members who are full-time undergraduate students majoring in interior design or a related field. Applicants must submit a 300- to 500-word essay on why they joined IFDA; their future plans, goals, and objectives; and why they believe they deserve the scholarship. Selection is based on the essay; the applicant's achievements, awards, and accomplishments; and a letter of recommendation from a professor or instructor. Financial need is not considered.

**Financial data:** The stipend is $1,500.

**Duration:** 1 year.

**Number awarded:** At least 1 each year.

**Deadline:** March of each year.

## 1467 IFEC SCHOLARSHIPS

International Foodservice Editorial Council
P.O. Box 491
Hyde Park, NY 12538
Phone: (845) 229-6973; Fax: (845) 229-6993; Email: ifec@aol.com
Web: www.ifec-is-us.com

**Summary:** To provide financial assistance to undergraduate or graduate students who are interested in preparing for a career in communications in the food service industry.

**Eligibility:** Open to currently-enrolled college students who are working on an associate, bachelor's, or master's degree. They must be enrolled full time and planning on a career in editorial, public relations, photography, food styling, or a related aspect of communications in the food service industry. The following food service majors are considered appropriate for this program: culinary arts; hospitality management; hotel, restaurant, and institutional management; dietetics; food science and technology; and nutrition. Applicable communications areas include journalism, English, mass communications, public relations, marketing, broadcast journalism, creative writing, graphic arts, and photography. Selection is based on academic record, character references, and demonstrated financial need.

**Financial data:** The stipend is $3,000 per year.

**Duration:** 1 year.

**Number awarded:** Varies each year; recently, 5 of these scholarships were awarded.

**Deadline:** March of each year.

## 1468 ILLINOIS BROADCASTERS ASSOCIATION ENDOWED SCHOLARSHIPS

Illinois Broadcasters Association

300 North Pershing Street, Suite B
Energy, IL 62933
Phone: (618) 942-2139; Fax: (618) 988-9056; Email: ilbrdcst@neondsl.com
Web: www.ilba.org
**Summary:** To provide financial assistance to upper-division college students in Illinois who are majoring in broadcasting.
**Eligibility:** Open to currently-enrolled college students with junior status at the following institutions: Bradley University, Southern Illinois University, Western Illinois University, University of Illinois at Urbana-Champaign, and Eastern Illinois University. Students at other accredited 4-year colleges or universities in Illinois are also eligible to apply if the institution offers an undergraduate program or major concentration in broadcasting. Applicants must be full-time students majoring in broadcasting, have a record of superior academic performance, and (preferably) have work experience in broadcasting. All other qualifications being equal, students with financial need are given preference.
**Financial data:** The stipend is $1,000.
**Duration:** 1 year (recipient's senior year).
**Number awarded:** 5 or more each year.

## 1469 ILMDA ACADEMIC SCHOLARSHIPS

Illinois Lumber and Material Dealers Association
Attn: Educational Foundation
932 South Spring Street
Springfield, IL 62704
Phone: (217) 544-5405; (800) 252-8641; Fax: (217) 544-4206;
Email: ilmda@ilmda.com
Web: www.ilmda.com
**Summary:** To provide financial assistance to residents of Illinois who are preparing for a career in the lumber and building materials industry.
**Eligibility:** Open to residents of Illinois who are enrolled or planning to enroll full time at an accredited trade school, 2-year college, or 4-year college or university in the state. Applicants must be preparing for a career in lumber and building materials or an allied field (e.g., millwork, design). They must submit a statement of activities and interest, record of military service (if any), an outline of their proposed program of study, a statement from a high school instructor, transcripts, and 2 letters of recommendation. Selection is based on academic achievement and financial need.
**Financial data:** Stipends range from $500 to $2,000.
**Duration:** 1 year.
**Number awarded:** 1 or more each year.
**Deadline:** April of each year.

## 1470 ILPC JOURNALISM SCHOLARSHIP

University Interscholastic League
Attn: Interscholastic League Press Conference
1701 Manor Road
P.O. Box 8028
Austin, TX 78713
Phone: (512) 471-5883; Fax: (512) 232-7311;
Email: rvonderheid@mail.utexas.edu
Web: www.uil.utexas.edu/aca/journ/ilpc
**Summary:** To provide financial assistance to seniors at high schools in Texas belonging to the Interscholastic League Press Conference (ILPC) who wish to study journalism in college.
**Eligibility:** Open to seniors at ILPC-member schools in Texas who plan to major in journalism in college. Applicants must submit statements on how scholastic competition in ILPC activities has helped them to be successful in high school journalism, their career plans as they relate to journalism, their high school awards for journalism and other activities, their involvement in school and outside activities, and their involvement in journalism outside of school-sponsored activities. They must also write an editorial to convince the selection committee that they are the correct choice for this scholarship.
**Financial data:** The stipend is $1,000.
**Duration:** 1 year.
**Number awarded:** 1 each year.
**Deadline:** February of each year.

## 1471 IMATION COMPUTER ARTS SCHOLARSHIP PROGRAM

Imation Corporation, Attn: Community Relations
1 Imation Place
Oakdale, MN 55128-3414
Phone: (651) 704-3892; (888) 466-3456; Fax: (888) 704-4200;

Email: CAS@imation.com
Web: www.imation.com
**Summary:** To recognize and reward high school artists who create original works of art on the computer.
**Eligibility:** Open to students at any grade in public and private high schools in the United States. Home-schooled students and U.S. students at U.S. military base schools are also eligible. Applicants must create original, unique works of art on a computer. There are no restrictions on theme. All art must be the original creation of the student, less than 1 MB in size, saved in JPEG format, and submitted online. Students must be nominated by their schools; each high school in the United States may nominate one candidate per 1,000 students enrolled (up to 3 per school) to participate in the competition. Entries must be submitted by the student and a representative of the school together. Selection is based on the quality and creativity of the artwork.
**Financial data:** Winners receive a $1,000 scholarship and a trip with a parent, guardian, or school official to St. Paul, Minnesota in April.
**Duration:** Scholarships are awarded annually.
**Number awarded:** 25 each year.
**Deadline:** December of each year.

## 1472 INDIANA BROADCASTERS ASSOCIATION SCHOLARSHIPS

Indiana Broadcasters Association, Attn: Scholarship Administrator
3003 East 98th Street, Suite 161
Indianapolis, IN 46280
Phone: (317) 573-0119; (800) 342-6276 (within IN); Fax: (317) 573-0895;
Email: INDBA@aol.com
Web: www.indianabroadcasters.org/services/scholarship.php
**Summary:** To provide financial assistance to students in Indiana who are interested in preparing for a career in a field related to broadcasting.
**Eligibility:** Open to graduating high school seniors planning to attend colleges that are members of the Indiana Broadcasters Association and to undergraduate students currently enrolled at those schools. Applicants must be majoring or planning to major in broadcasting, electronic media, telecommunications, or broadcast journalism. Selection is based on an essay on why they have chosen broadcasting as a career, special recognitions they have received, extracurricular activities, and financial need.
**Financial data:** The stipends are $500 for high school seniors or $2,000 for students already in college.
**Duration:** 1 year.
**Number awarded:** Varies each year: recently, 6 high school seniors and 7 current undergraduate students received these awards.
**Deadline:** March of each year.

## 1473 INTERNATIONAL ASSOCIATION OF LIGHTING DESIGNERS SCHOLARSHIPS

International Association of Lighting Designers, Attn: Education Trust Fund
The Merchandise Mart, Suite 9-104
200 World Trade Center
Chicago, IL 60654
Phone: (312) 527-3677; Fax: (312) 527-3680
Web: www.iald.org
**Summary:** To provide financial assistance to students pursuing a program in architectural lighting design.
**Eligibility:** Open to students who are pursuing architectural lighting design as a course of study. Applicants must submit 1) a 2-page resume; 2) an official transcript; 3) 2 letters of reference; 4) up to 10 images of their artwork that show their design ability; and 5) a personal statement, up to 2 pages, on their experience with lighting, why they want to study lighting, or why they should receive this scholarship. Selection is based on those submissions; financial need is not considered.
**Financial data:** Stipends are $3,000, $2,000, or $500.
**Duration:** 1 year.
**Number awarded:** Varies each year. Recently, 5 of these scholarships were awarded: 1 at $3,000, 2 at $2,000, and 2 at $500.
**Deadline:** January of each year.

## 1474 INTERNATIONAL COMMUNICATIONS INDUSTRIES ASSOCIATION COLLEGE SCHOLARSHIPS

International Communications Industries Association, Inc.
Attn: Director of Strategic Initiatives
11242 Waples Mill Road, Suite 200

Fairfax, VA 22030
Phone: (703) 273-7200; (800) 659-7469; Fax: (703) 278-8082;
Email: dwilbert@infocomm.org
Web: www.infocomm.org/Foundation/Scholarships/College.cfm
**Summary:** To provide financial assistance to college students in their final year of study who are interested in preparing for a career in the audiovisual industry.
**Eligibility:** Open to 1) college juniors completing their bachelor's degree in the following year; 2) college seniors who plan to enter graduate school; and 3) students in their final year of study for an associate degree. Applicants must have a GPA of 2.75 or higher in a program of audio, visual, audiovisual, electronics, telecommunications, technical theater, data networking, software development, or information technology. Students in other programs, such as journalism, may be eligible if they can demonstrate a relationship to career goals in the audiovisual industry. Along with their application, they must submit essays on why they are applying for this scholarship, why they are interested in the audiovisual industry, and their professional plans following graduation. Minority and women candidates are especially encouraged to apply. Selection is based on the essays, presentation of the application, GPA, work experience, and letters of recommendation.
**Financial data:** The stipend is $2,500.
**Duration:** 1 year.
**Number awarded:** Varies each year; recently, 7 of these scholarships were awarded.
**Deadline:** April of each year.

## 1475 INTERNATIONAL SCHOLARSHIP PROGRAM FOR COMMUNITY SERVICE

Memorial Foundation for Jewish Culture
50 Broadway, 34th Floor
New York, NY 10004
Phone: (212) 425-6606; Fax: (212) 425-6602; Email: office@mfjc.org
Web: www.mfjc.org
**Summary:** To assist well-qualified individuals to train for careers in a field related to Jewish community service.
**Eligibility:** Open to any individual, regardless of country of origin, who is presently receiving or plans to undertake training in his/her chosen field at a recognized yeshiva, teacher training seminary, school of social work, university, or other educational institution. Applicants must be interested in pursuing professional training for careers in Jewish education, Jewish social service, the rabbinate, or as religious functionaries (e.g., shohatim, mohalim) in Diaspora Jewish communities in need of such personnel. Students planning to serve in the United States, Canada, or Israel are not eligible.
**Financial data:** The amount of the grant varies, depending on the country in which the student will be trained and other considerations.
**Duration:** 1 year; may be renewed.
**Deadline:** November of each year.

## 1476 IOWA SCHOLARSHIPS FOR THE ARTS

Iowa Arts Council, Attn: Iowa Scholarships for the Arts
600 East Locust
Des Moines, IA 50319-0290
Phone: (515) 281-4081; Fax: (515) 242-6498; TDD: (515) 242-5147;
Email: Sarah.Oltrogge@iowa.gov
Web: www.iowaartscouncil.org
**Summary:** To provide financial assistance to Iowa high school seniors who plan to study the arts at a college or university in the state.
**Eligibility:** Open to graduating seniors at high schools in Iowa who have been accepted as full-time undergraduate students at an accredited college or university in the state. Applicants must be planning to major in music, dance, visual arts, traditional arts, theater, or literature. Along with their application, they must submit a 1-page essay on what they perceive to be their future in the arts. Selection is based on 1) proven artistic and academic abilities in the chosen artistic area and 2) future goals and objectives relating to the intended field of study.
**Financial data:** The stipends range from $1,000 to $2,000. Funds must be used for tuition at the Iowa institution where the recipient is enrolled.
**Duration:** 1 year.
**Number awarded:** Up to 5 each year.
**Deadline:** November of each year.

## 1477 IRENE RYAN ACTING SCHOLARSHIPS

John F. Kennedy Center for the Performing Arts
Education Department
Attn: Kennedy Center American College Theater Festival

2700 F Street, N.W.
Washington, DC 20566
Phone: (202) 416-8857; Fax: (202) 416-8802;
Email: skshaffer@kennedy-cen ter.org
Web: kennedy-center.org/education/actf/actfira.html
**Summary:** To recognize and reward outstanding college actors.
**Eligibility:** Open to students enrolled in an accredited junior or senior college in the United States or in countries contiguous to the continental United States. Participants must appear as actors in plays produced by their college and entered in one of the 8 regional festivals of the Kennedy Center American College Theater Festival (KCACTF). Undergraduate students must be carrying at least 6 semester hours, graduate students must be enrolled in at least 3 semester hours, and continuing part-time students must be enrolled in a regular degree or certificate program. From each of the regional festivals, 2 winners and their acting partners are invited to the national festival at the John F. Kennedy Center for the Performing Arts in Washington, D.C. to participate in an "Evening of Scenes." Scholarships are awarded to outstanding student performers at each regional festival and from the "Evening of Scenes."
**Financial data:** Regional winners receive $500 scholarships and payment of expenses (transportation, lodging, and per diem) to attend the national festival. National winners receive $2,500 scholarships; the best partner receives the Kingsley Colton Award. All scholarship funds are paid directly to the institutions designated by the recipients and may be used for any field of study.
**Duration:** The competition is held annually.
**Number awarded:** The number of regional winners varies each year; at the national festival "Evening of Scenes," 2 performers receive scholarships. Several other awards are also presented.
**Deadline:** The regional festivals are held in January and February of each year; the national festival is held in April of each year. Application deadlines are set within each region.

## 1478 J. NEEL REID PRIZE

Georgia Trust
1516 Peachtree Street, N.W.
Atlanta, GA 30309
Phone: (404) 881-9980; Fax: (404) 875-2205; Email: info@georgiatrust.org
Web: www.georgiatrust.org/preservation_resources/neel_reid-prize.htm
**Summary:** To recognize and reward architecture students and architects, especially those with a connection to Georgia, who are interested in a study travel program in the United States or abroad.
**Eligibility:** Open to architecture students, architect interns, and recently registered architects who are interested in a study travel program. The focus of the study travel should involve historic architecture (built prior to Neel Reid's death in 1926), historic preservation of classic architecture, or new construction that is classic and context-related. Applicants are encouraged to propose an independent study, but participation in an existing program is acceptable. Priority is given to applicants with a connection to Georgia (a resident of the state, a student in a Georgia academic institution, or an employee of a Georgia firm). The travel may be to any location in the world.
**Financial data:** The prize is $3,500.
**Duration:** The study travel should be completed within a year and a half of the announcement of the winner.
**Number awarded:** 1 each year.
**Deadline:** February of each year.

## 1479 JACK J. ISGUR SCHOLARSHIPS

Jack J. Isgur Foundation
c/o Stinson Morrison Hecker L.L.P., Attn: Charles F. Jensen
1201 Walnut Street, Suite 2800
Kansas City, MO 64106-2150
Phone: (816) 842-8600; (816) 691-3495
**Summary:** To provide financial assistance to Missouri residents majoring in education and planning to teach humanities in elementary and middle schools in the state after graduation.
**Eligibility:** Open to residents of Missouri who are enrolled at a 4-year college or university. Applicants must be majoring in education with the goal of teaching the humanities (e.g., literature, dance, fine arts, music, art, and poetry) at the elementary or middle school level following graduation. Preference is given to students entering their junior year of college and planning to teach in rural school districts in Missouri, rather than metropolitan districts. The application process includes brief essays on the following topics: 1) work and life experiences indicating an interest in teaching subjects in the humanities to grade school and middle school students in Missouri upon graduation; 2) other activities (organizations to which they belong, hobbies, volunteer work) and their

interest in them; 3) the 3 books that have most influenced them and why; and 4) their employment experiences.

**Financial data:** A stipend is awarded (amount not specified).

**Duration:** 1 year; recipients may reapply.

**Number awarded:** Varies each year.

**Deadline:** April of each year.

---

### 1480 JACKSON FOUNDATION JOURNALISM SCHOLARSHIP

Oregon Student Assistance Commission
Attn: Grants and Scholarships Division
1500 Valley River Drive, Suite 100
Eugene, OR 97401-2146
Phone: (541) 687-7395; (800) 452-8807, ext. 7395; Fax: (541) 687-7419;
Email: awardinfo@mercury.osac.state.or.us
Web: www.osac.state.or.us

**Summary:** To provide financial assistance to students in Oregon interested in majoring in journalism.

**Eligibility:** Open to graduates of Oregon high schools who are studying or planning to study journalism at a college or university in the state.

**Financial data:** Stipend amounts vary; recently, they were at least $1,429.

**Duration:** 1 year; may be renewed.

**Number awarded:** Varies each year; recently, 7 of these scholarships were awarded.

**Deadline:** February of each year.

---

### 1481 JAMES J. WYCHOR SCHOLARSHIPS

Minnesota Broadcasters Association, Attn: Scholarship Program
3033 Excelsior Boulevard, Suite 301
Minneapolis, MN 55416
Phone: (612) 926-8123; (800) 245-5838; Fax: (612) 926-9761;
Email: meischen@minnesotabroadcasters.com
Web: www.minnesotabroadcasters.com

**Summary:** To provide financial assistance to Minnesota residents interested in studying broadcasting in college.

**Eligibility:** Open to residents of Minnesota who are accepted or enrolled at an accredited postsecondary institution offering a broadcast-related curriculum. Applicants must have a high school or college GPA of 2.5 or higher and must submit a 200-word essay on why they wish to prepare for a career in broadcasting or electronic media. Employment in the broadcasting industry is not required, but students who are employed must include a letter from their general manager describing the duties they have performed as a radio or television station employee and evaluating their potential for success in the industry. Financial need is not considered in the selection process. Some of the scholarships are awarded only to minority and women candidates.

**Financial data:** The stipend is $1,500.

**Duration:** 1 year; recipients who are college seniors may reapply for an additional 1-year renewal.

**Number awarded:** 10 each year, distributed as follows: 3 within the 7-county metro area, 5 allocated geographically throughout the state (northeast, northwest, central, southeast, southwest), and 2 reserved specifically for women and minority applicants.

**Deadline:** May of each year.

---

### 1482 JAMES JAMIESON MEMORIAL SCHOLARSHIP

Delaware Community Foundation, Attn: Executive Vice President
100 West 10th Street, Suite 115
P.O. Box 1636
Wilmington, DE 19899
Phone: (302) 504-5222; Fax: (302) 571-1553; Email: rgentsch@delcf.org
Web: www.delcf.org

**Summary:** To provide financial assistance to dance students who reside in or study dance in Delaware.

**Eligibility:** Open to dance students who reside in or study dance in Delaware. Applicants must be preparing for a professional career in ballet. They must submit a short essay on why they desire to undertake a career in ballet. Finalists must attend a personal interview and audition.

**Financial data:** A stipend is awarded (amount not specified).

**Duration:** 1 year.

**Number awarded:** 1 or more each year.

**Deadline:** October of each year.

---

### 1483 JAMES M. AND VIRGINIA M. SMYTH SCHOLARSHIP FUND

Community Foundation for Greater Atlanta, Inc.
50 Hurt Plaza, Suite 449
Atlanta, GA 30303
Phone: (404) 688-5525; Fax: (404) 688-3060; Email: vweekes@atlcf.org
Web: www.atlcf.org/GrantsScholarships/Scholarships/Smyth.aspx

**Summary:** To provide financial assistance for college to high school seniors, especially those from designated-states.

**Eligibility:** Open to graduating high school seniors, with special consideration given to residents of Georgia, Illinois, Mississippi, Missouri, Oklahoma, Tennessee, and Texas. Applicants must have a GPA of 3.0 or higher and be interested in attending a college, university, or community college to work on a degree in the arts and sciences, human services, music, or ministry. They must be able to demonstrate financial need and a commitment to community service through school, community, or religious organizations. Adults returning to school to increase employability are also eligible.

**Financial data:** Stipends range up to $2,500.

**Duration:** 1 year; recipients may reapply.

**Number awarded:** Varies each year.

**Deadline:** March of each year.

---

### 1484 JAZZ PERFORMANCE AWARDS

Sigma Alpha Iota Philanthropies, Inc.
One Tunnel Road
Asheville, NC 28805
Phone: (828) 251-0606; Fax: (828) 251-0644;
Email: philonline@sai-national.org
Web: www.sai-national/org/phil/philsch3.html

**Summary:** To provide financial assistance to members of Sigma Alpha Iota (an organization of women musicians) who are interested in working on an undergraduate or graduate degree in jazz performance.

**Eligibility:** Open to members of the organization who are enrolled in an undergraduate or graduate degree program in jazz performance or studies. Applicants must be younger than 32 years of age. Along with their application, they must submit a CD recording of a performance "set" of 30 to 45 minutes.

**Financial data:** Stipends are $2,000 for the winner or $1,500 for the runner-up.

**Duration:** 1 year.

**Number awarded:** 2 every 3 years.

**Deadline:** March of the year of the awards (2009, 2012, etc.).

---

### 1485 JAZZ STUDIES SCHOLARSHIP

Sigma Alpha Iota Philanthropies, Inc.
One Tunnel Road
Asheville, NC 28805
Phone: (828) 251-0606; Fax: (828) 251-0644;
Email: philonline@sai-national.org
Web: www.sai-national/org/phil/philsch1.html

**Summary:** To provide financial assistance to members of Sigma Alpha Iota (an organization of women musicians) who are interested in working on an undergraduate degree in jazz studies.

**Eligibility:** Open to members of the organization who are enrolled in a university jazz studies program. Applicants must submit a 500-word essay on their career plans and professional goals in jazz studies and why they feel they are deserving of this scholarship.

**Financial data:** The stipend is $1,500.

**Duration:** 1 year.

**Number awarded:** 1 each year.

**Deadline:** March of each year.

---

### 1486 JEAN KENNEDY SMITH PLAYWRITING AWARD

John F. Kennedy Center for the Performing Arts
Education Department
Attn: Kennedy Center American College Theater Festival
2700 F Street, N.W.
Washington, DC 20566
Phone: (202) 416-8857; Fax: (202) 416-8802;
Email: skshaffer@kennedy-center.org
Web: kennedy-center.org/education/actf/actfjks.html

**Summary:** To recognize and reward the student authors of plays on the theme of disability.

**Eligibility:** Open to students at any accredited junior or senior college in the United States or in countries contiguous to the continental United States, provided their college agrees to participate in the Kennedy Center American College Theater Festival (KCACTF). Undergraduate students must be carrying at least 6 semester hours, graduate students must be enrolled in at least 3 semester hours, and continuing part-time students must be enrolled in a regular degree or certificate program. This award is presented to the best student-written script that explores the human experience of living with a disability.

**Financial data:** The winning playwright receives a cash award of $2,500, active membership in the Dramatists Guild, Inc., and a fellowship providing transportation, housing, and per diem to attend a prestigious playwriting program.

**Duration:** The award is presented annually.

**Number awarded:** 1 each year.

**Deadline:** November of each year.

## 1487 JEAN LEE/JEFF MARVIN COLLEGIATE SCHOLARSHIPS

Indiana Association for Health, Physical Education, Recreation, and Dance
c/o Nikki Assmann, Executive Director
2301 Christy Lane
Muncie, IN 47304
Phone: (765) 289-8549; Email: IndianaAHPERD@aol.com
Web: www.indiana-ahperd.org

**Summary:** To provide financial assistance to upper-division students in Indiana who are majoring in health, physical education, recreation, or dance.

**Eligibility:** Open to juniors and seniors at colleges and universities in Indiana who are majoring in health education, physical education, recreation, dance education, or related areas (including sports administration). Applicants must submit a statement in which they describe their plans for after graduation, why they need this scholarship, their extracurricular activities, and their personal philosophy relating to their future profession. Selection is based on participation in collegiate activities; professional competencies; potential as a professional; GPA; 2 letters of recommendation from members of the Indiana Association for Health, Physical Education, Recreation, and Dance; and financial need.

**Financial data:** The stipend is $1,000.

**Duration:** 1 year.

**Number awarded:** 4 each year.

**Deadline:** January of each year.

## 1488 JIM DEVAN RADIO-TV SCHOLARSHIP

Georgia Association of Broadcasters, Inc., Attn: Georgia Radio-TV Foundation
8010 Roswell Road, Suite 260
Atlanta, GA 30350
Phone: (770) 395-7200; (877) 395-7200 (within GA); Fax: (770) 395-7235
Web: www.gab.org/Schol_Fund.html

**Summary:** To provide financial assistance to students in Georgia interested in preparing for a career in broadcasting.

**Eligibility:** Open to residents of Georgia who are rising juniors or seniors studying for a career in radio or television at a college, professional school, or university in Georgia. As part of their application, students must submit brief essays on 10 questions (e.g., what specific area of broadcasting most interests you and why, what national network do you admire most and why, what role should news play in radio and television programming, what is the single most important fact that the judges should know about you). Selection is based primarily on depth of thought, clarity of expression, and maturity. Extracurricular activities, community involvement, and leadership potential are secondary considerations. Neither scholastic record nor financial need are considered.

**Financial data:** The stipend is $1,000. Funds are paid directly to the recipient's institution.

**Duration:** 1 year.

**Number awarded:** 1 or more each year.

**Deadline:** January of each year.

## 1489 JOANNA BISTANY MEMORIAL SCHOLARSHIP PROGRAM

National Association of Hispanic Journalists, Attn: Scholarship Committee
1000 National Press Building
529 14th Street, N.W.
Washington, DC 20045-2001
Phone: (202) 662-7145; (888) 346-NAHJ; Fax: (202) 662-7144;
Email: nahj@nahj.org
Web: www.nahj.org/student/scholarshipinformation.html

**Summary:** To provide financial assistance to Hispanic American students interested in preparing for a career in English-language television news.

**Eligibility:** Open to college students who are interested in preparing for a career as a reporter or producer in the field of English-language television news. Selection is based on commitment to the field of journalism, academic achievement, awareness of the Latino community, and financial need.

**Financial data:** A stipend is awarded (amount not specified).

**Duration:** 1 year.

**Number awarded:** 1 each year.

**Deadline:** January of each year.

## 1490 JOHANSEN INTERNATIONAL COMPETITION FOR YOUNG STRING PLAYERS

Friday Morning Music Club, Inc., Attn: FMMC Foundation
2233 Wisconsin Avenue, N.W., Suite 326
Washington, DC 20007-4126
Phone: (202) 333-2075
Web: www.fmmc.org/johansen/johansen.html

**Summary:** To recognize and reward outstanding young string players.

**Eligibility:** Open to young string players (13 through 17 years of age). Applicants must submit an audiocassette or CD with 1) 5 minutes or less of an unaccompanied sonata, partita, or suite of J.S. Bach; 2) 12 minutes or less of a sonata from the classical, romantic, impressionist, or contemporary period; and 3) 13 minutes or less of a concerto or major work for soloist or orchestra by a composer other than Bach. Based on those recordings, semifinalists are invited to compete in Washington, D.C. They must be prepared to play any selection from their preliminary repertoire as well as a new work commissioned for this competition and sent to them prior to the semifinals. Finalists are selected from those auditions and compete the following day. All repertoire must be performed from memory. Separate awards are presented for violin, viola, and cello.

**Financial data:** First prize in each category is $10,000. Other prizes vary in each competition. Recently, violin players received second prizes of $7,000, third prizes of $5,000, honorable mention of $750, and best performance on the commissioned piece $500. No other awards were presented to viola players. Honorable mentioned for cello was $750.

**Duration:** The competition is held triennially (2006, 2009, etc.).

**Number awarded:** 3 first prizes (1 each for violin, viola, and cello) are awarded in each competition. The number of other prizes varies; recently, those included 2 second prizes, 2 third prizes, an honorable mention, and an award for best performance of the commissioned piece for violin players and 1 honorable mention for cello players.

**Deadline:** December of the year prior to the competition.

## 1491 JOHN BAYLISS BROADCAST FOUNDATION SCHOLARSHIPS

John Bayliss Broadcast Foundation, Attn: Executive Director
171 17th Street
P.O. Box 51126
Pacific Grove, CA 93950-6126
Phone: (831) 655-5229; Fax: (831) 655-5228; Email: info@baylissfoundation.org
Web: www.baylissfoundation.org/radio.html

**Summary:** To provide financial assistance to upper-division or graduate students who are preparing for a career in the radio industry.

**Eligibility:** Open to juniors, seniors, and graduate students who are studying for a career in the radio industry. They must have at least a 3.0 GPA. Although financial need is a consideration, students of merit with an extensive history of radio-related activities are given preference. Applicants must supply transcripts, 3 letters of recommendation, and a 2-page essay describing their broadcasting goals as they relate to radio.

**Financial data:** The stipend is $5,000.

**Duration:** 1 year.

**Number awarded:** Up to 15 each year.

**Deadline:** April of each year.

## 1492 JOHN CAUBLE SHORT PLAY AWARD

John F. Kennedy Center for the Performing Arts
Education Department
Attn: Kennedy Center American College Theater Festival
2700 F Street, N.W.
Washington, DC 20566
Phone: (202) 416-8857; Fax: (202) 416-8802;

Email: skshaffer@kennedy-center.org
Web: kennedy-center.org.education/actf/actfspa.html
**Summary:** To recognize and reward outstanding undergraduate and graduate student playwrights.
**Eligibility:** Open to students at any accredited junior or senior college in the United States or in countries contiguous to the continental United States, provided their college agrees to participate in the Kennedy Center American College Theater Festival (KCACTF). Undergraduate students must be carrying at least 6 semester hours, graduate students must be enrolled in at least 3 semester hours, and continuing part-time students must be enrolled in a regular degree or certificate program. For the Short Play Awards Program, students must submit a play of one act without intermission that, within itself, does not constitute a full evening of theater. The plays selected as the best by the judges are considered for presentation at the national festival and their playwrights receive these awards.
**Financial data:** The prize is $1,000. Other benefits for the recipients of these awards include appropriate membership in the Dramatists Guild and publication by Samuel French, Inc.
**Duration:** The competition is held annually.
**Number awarded:** 1 or more each year.
**Deadline:** The final script must be submitted by November of each year.

## [1493] JOHN F. KENNEDY SCHOLARSHIP

Massachusetts Democratic Party, Attn: Executive Director
56 Roland Street, North Lobby, Suite 203
Boston, MA 02169
Phone: (617) 776-2676; Fax: (617) 776-2579;
Email: Susan.Thompson@massdems.org
Web: www.massdems.org/involved/internship.htm
**Summary:** To provide financial assistance for college to Massachusetts residents, with preference given to registered Democrats.
**Eligibility:** Open to Massachusetts residents who are entering their third or fourth year of study at a college or university anywhere in the United States. Applicants must be majoring in political science, government, or history. They must be able to demonstrate a serious commitment to the study of American politics and be qualified to receive financial aid (as certified by their financial aid officer). Males and females compete separately. Preference is given to registered Democrats who have a GPA of 3.0 or higher. Finalists may be interviewed in Boston.
**Financial data:** The stipend is $1,500.
**Duration:** 1 year.
**Number awarded:** 2 each year: 1 is set aside specifically for a female and 1 for a male.
**Deadline:** April of each year.

## [1494] JOHN LENNON SCHOLARSHIP

Broadcast Music Inc., Attn: BMI Foundation
320 West 57th Street
New York, NY 10019-3790
Phone: (212) 830-2520; Fax: (212) 246-2163;
Email: LennonScholarship@bmifoundation.org
Web: www.bmifoundation.org/pages/JLennon.asp
**Summary:** To recognize and reward outstanding student composers.
**Eligibility:** Open to musicians between 15 and 24 years of age who are 1) current students or graduates of 50 selected colleges, universities, or schools of music, or 2) participating through a local collegiate chapter of the National Association for Music Education at their school. Applicants may not have had any musical work commercially recorded or distributed or have been a prior winner in this competition. They must submit (on audio cassette or CD with a typed copy of the lyrics) an original song with lyrics and accompanied by any instrumentation. Both lyrics and music must be original and not based on any prior work.
**Financial data:** Prizes are $10,000 or $5,000.
**Duration:** The competition is held annually.
**Number awarded:** 3 each year: 1 at $10,000 and 2 at $5,000.
**Deadline:** January of each year.

## [1495] JOHN SCHWARTZ SCHOLARSHIP

American Institute of Wine & Food-Pacific Northwest Chapter
c/o Ken Rudee, Scholarship Chair
Barnes & Watson Fine Teas
P.O. Box 24061

Seattle, WA 98124
Phone: (206) 625-9435; Email: Krudee@barnesandwatson.com
Web: www.aiwf.org/pnw
**Summary:** To provide financial assistance to students in Washington state working on a degree in the culinary arts.
**Eligibility:** Open to Washington residents who have been enrolled for at least 2 quarters in a culinary arts program in the state. Applicants must submit an essay that explains why they think they qualify for a scholarship, including their 2-year and 5-year professional goals. Selection is based on merit, including the essay, a resume, 2 letters of reference, and GPA (must be at least 3.0).
**Financial data:** The stipend is $1,000.
**Duration:** 1 year.
**Number awarded:** 1 each year.

## [1496] JOSEPH ADAMS SENIOR SCHOLARSHIPS

Sociedad Honoraria Hispanica, Attn: National Directors
P.O. Box 5318
Buffalo Grove, IL 60089-5318
Phone: (847) 550-0455; Email: sociedad@comcast.net
Web: www.sociedadhonorariahispanica.org
**Summary:** To provide financial assistance to members of the Sociedad Honoraria Hispanica for college education.
**Eligibility:** Open to high school seniors who are members of the Sociedad and studying Spanish and/or Portuguese at the time of application. Each chapter of the society recommends its best student. A national committee selects the winners.
**Financial data:** Stipends are either $2,000 or $1,000.
**Duration:** 1 year; nonrenewable.
**Number awarded:** 48 each year: 8 at $2,000 and 40 at $1,000.
**Deadline:** February of each year.

## [1497] JOSEPH AND MARION GREENBAUM SCHOLARSHIP FUND

**Summary:** To provide financial assistance to Jewish undergraduates from Delaware studying in Israel or Jewish studies in the United States and to Jewish students from outside the United States studying in Delaware.
*See Listing #529.*

## [1498] JOSEPH EHRENREICH SCHOLARSHIPS

National Press Photographers Foundation
3200 Croasdaile Drive, Suite 306
Durham, NC 27705-2586
Phone: (919) 383-7246; (800) 289-6772; Fax: (919) 383-7261;
Email: info@nppa.org
Web: www.nppa.org/professional_development/students/scholarships/ehrenreich.html
**Summary:** To provide financial assistance to college students interested in preparing for a career in photojournalism.
**Eligibility:** Open to students who have completed at least one year at a recognized 4-year college or university in the United States or Canada that offers courses in photojournalism, are working on a bachelor's degree, are intending to prepare for a career in journalism, and have at least half a year of undergraduate study remaining. These awards are aimed at those with journalism potential but with little opportunity and great need.
**Financial data:** The stipend is $1,000 per year.
**Duration:** 1 year; nonrenewable.
**Number awarded:** 5 each year.
**Deadline:** February of each year.

## [1499] JOSEPH THOMAS MEMORIAL SCHOLARSHIP

Portland Players, Attn: Vice President, Artistic Development
420 Cottage Road
South Portland, ME 04106
Phone: (207) 799-7337; Fax: (207) 767-6208;
Email: portlandplayers@portlandplayers.com
Web: www.portlandplayers.com
**Summary:** To provide financial assistance to Maine high school seniors interested in studying theater in college.
**Eligibility:** Open to graduating high school seniors and current college students who are residents of Maine and interested in studying performing or

technical aspects of drama in college. Singers must submit a sample tape; actors must submit a tape of a monologue; students interested in technical aspects are interviewed. All applicants should submit a 750-word essay describing their experiences with theater and their plans to include the theater in the future. Selection is based on merit.

**Financial data:** The stipend is at least $1,000.
**Duration:** 1 year.
**Number awarded:** 1 each year.
**Deadline:** May of each year.

## 1500 JOSEPHINE DE KARMAN FELLOWSHIPS

**Summary:** To provide financial assistance to outstanding college seniors or students in their last year of a Ph.D. program.
*See Listing #531.*

## 1501 JOSTENS SCHOLARSHIP

University Interscholastic League
Attn: Interscholastic League Press Conference
1701 Manor Road
P.O. Box 8028
Austin, TX 78713
Phone: (512) 471-5883; Fax: (512) 232-7311;
Email: rvonderhcid@mail.utexas.edu
Web: www.uil.utexas.edu/aca/journ/ilpc
**Summary:** To provide financial assistance to high school seniors in Texas who plan to study communications in college.
**Eligibility:** Open to seniors graduating from high schools in Texas who have been involved in journalism and plan to continue their education in a communications-related field (major or minor) in college. Applicants must have a GPA of B or higher. Along with their application, they must submit a statement on their involvement in journalism while in high school, a description of their college and future plans, a letter of recommendation, and 3 to 5 samples of their work as a journalism student.
**Financial data:** The stipend is $1,000.
**Duration:** 1 year.
**Number awarded:** 1 each year.
**Deadline:** March of each year.

## 1502 JOYCE WALSH JUNIOR DISABILITY AWARD

National Federation of Music Clubs
1336 North Delaware Street
Indianapolis, IN 46202-2481
Phone: (317) 638-4003; Fax: (317) 638-0503; Email: info@nfmc-music.org
Web: www.nfmc-music.org/Competitions/Annual_Junior/annual_junior.html
**Summary:** To provide financial assistance to young instrumentalists and vocalists with disabilities who are members of the National Federation of Music Clubs (NFMC).
**Eligibility:** Open to disabled musicians (instrumentalists or vocalists) who are between 12 and 19 years of age, U.S. citizens, and junior members of the federation. Applicants must submit a cassette tape, up to 10 minutes in length, of their performance of 2 selections from contrasting style periods.
**Financial data:** The awards are $2,000 for first place and $1,500 for second place. In addition, regional awards are $500. All awards must be used for musical study.
**Duration:** The awards are presented annually.
**Number awarded:** 14 each year: 1 first-place award, 1 second-place award, and 12 regional awards (3 in each of the 4 NFMC regions).
**Deadline:** January of each year.

## 1503 JTG SCHOLARSHIP IN SCIENTIFIC AND TECHNICAL TRANSLATION OR INTERPRETATION

American Foundation for Translation and Interpretation
Columbia Plaza, Suite 101
350 East Michigan Avenue
Kalamazoo, MI 49007
Phone: (269) 383-6893; Email: aftiorg@aol.com
Web: www.afti.org
**Summary:** To provide financial assistance to undergraduate and graduate students in translator or interpreter education programs.
**Eligibility:** Open to students enrolled or planning to enroll in graduate or undergraduate programs in scientific and technical translation on in interpretation at accredited U.S. colleges and universities. Applicants must be full-time students who have completed at least one year of postsecondary education and have at least one year of academic work remaining to complete their program of study. They must have a GPA of 3.0 or higher overall and 3.5 or higher in translation and interpretation related courses. U.S. citizenship is required. Along with their application, they must submit an essay of 300 to 500 words on their interests and goals as they relate to the field of translation or interpretation. Selection is based on the essay, demonstrated achievement in translation and interpretation, academic record, and 3 letters of recommendation.
**Financial data:** The stipend is $2,500.
**Duration:** 1 year; nonrenewable.
**Number awarded:** 1 each year.
**Deadline:** May of each year.

## 1504 KAB BROADCAST SCHOLARSHIP PROGRAM

Kansas Association of Broadcasters, Attn: Scholarship Committee
1916 S.W. Sieben Court
Topeka, KS 66611-1656
Phone: (785) 235-1307; Fax: (785) 233-3052; Email: info@kab.net
Web: www.kab.net/programs/student/brdcast_scholarship.html
**Summary:** To provide financial assistance for college to residents of Kansas who are interested in preparing for a career in broadcasting.
**Eligibility:** Open to residents of Kansas who are attending or planning to attend a 2-year or 4-year college or university or vocational/technical trade school in the state. Applicants must be enrolled or planning to enroll in a broadcast or related program as a full-time student. They must have a GPA of 2.5 or higher and submit a letter from the head of the college radio/TV department or high school counselor certifying their eligibility. Along with their application, they must submit a 3-page essay explaining why they selected broadcasting as a career, the specific area of broadcasting that most interests them and why, their first job preference after college, their career goal for 10 years after college, their eventual career goal, the broadcast activities in which they have participated, their feeling about broadcast advertising and its importance to a station, the role they think the government should play in a broadcast station's operations, how they think broadcasting could better serve society, the radio or television station they most admire, how their college career will improve their value as a broadcaster, and their most rewarding broadcast-related experience. Selection is based on the depth of thought, clarity of expression, and commitment to broadcasting as revealed in the essay; extracurricular activities; community involvement; and financial need.
**Financial data:** Stipends are awarded without regard to the type of school the recipient attends (2-year or 4-year college or university or technical/vocational trade school). A total of $20,000 is available for this program each year.
**Duration:** 1 year; may be renewed.
**Number awarded:** Varies each year.
**Deadline:** April of each year.

## 1505 KANSAS AMERICAN LEGION MUSIC SCHOLARSHIP

American Legion, Attn: Department of Kansas
1314 S.W. Topeka Boulevard
Topeka, KS 66612-1886
Phone: (785) 232-9315; Fax: (785) 232-1399
Web: www.ksamlegion.org/programs.htm
**Summary:** To provide financial assistance to students of music at institutions in Kansas.
**Eligibility:** Open to residents of Kansas who are high school seniors or college freshmen or sophomores. Applicants must be studying or planning to major or minor in music at an approved college, university, or community college in Kansas.
**Financial data:** The stipend is $1,000.
**Duration:** 1 year.
**Number awarded:** 1 each year.
**Deadline:** February of each year.

## 1506 KATHRYN DETTMAN MEMORIAL JOURNALISM SCHOLARSHIP AWARD

Associated Press Television/Radio Association of California and Nevada
c/o Roberta Gonzales
CBS 5 TV
855 Battery Street
San Francisco, CA 94111
Phone: (415) 362-5550; Email: gonzales@kpix.cbs.com

Web: www.aptra.org

**Summary:** To provide financial assistance to students at colleges and universities in California and Nevada who are interested in broadcast journalism careers.
**Eligibility:** Open to students at colleges and universities in California and Nevada. Applicants must have a broadcast journalism career objective. Selection is based on a 500-word essay on why the students wish to pursue broadcast journalism; another 500-word essay on their honors, awards, and broadcast experience; 3 letters of recommendation; and a statement of how they are financing their education.
**Financial data:** The stipend is $1,500 per year.
**Duration:** 1 year.
**Number awarded:** 1 each year.
**Deadline:** December of each year.

## 1507 KATU THOMAS R. DARGAN MINORITY SCHOLARSHIP

KATU-TV, Attn: Human Resources
2153 N.E. Sandy Boulevard
P.O. Box 2
Portland, OR 97207-0002
Phone: (503) 231-4222
Web: www.katu.com/insidekatu/scholarship.asp

**Summary:** To provide financial assistance and work experience to minority students from Oregon and Washington who are studying broadcasting or communications in college.
**Eligibility:** Open to Native Americans, African Americans, Hispanic Americans, or Asian Americans who are U.S. citizens, currently enrolled in the first, second, or third year at a 4-year college or university or an accredited community college in Oregon or Washington, or, if a resident of Oregon or Washington, at a school in any state. Applicants must be majoring in broadcasting or communications and have a GPA of 3.0 or higher. Community college students must be enrolled in a broadcast curriculum that is transferable to a 4-year accredited university. Finalists will be interviewed. Selection is based on financial need, academic achievement, and an essay on personal and professional goals.
**Financial data:** The stipend is $4,000. Funds are sent directly to the recipient's school.
**Duration:** 1 year; recipients may reapply if they have maintained a GPA of 3.0 or higher.
**Number awarded:** 1 each year.
**Deadline:** April of each year.

## 1508 KENNEDY CENTER AMERICAN COLLEGE THEATER FESTIVAL TEN-MINUTE PLAY FESTIVAL AWARD

John F. Kennedy Center for the Performing Arts
Education Department
Attn: Kennedy Center American College Theater Festival
2700 F Street, N.W.
Washington, DC 20566
Phone: (202) 416-8857; Fax: (202) 416-8802;
Email: skshaffer@kennedy-center.org
Web: kennedy-center.org/education/actf/actften.html

**Summary:** To recognize and reward outstanding 10-minute plays by student playwrights.
**Eligibility:** Open to students at any accredited junior or senior college in the United States or in a country contiguous to the continental United States. Undergraduate students must be carrying at least 6 semester hours, graduate students must be enrolled in at least 3 semester hours, and continuing part-time students must be enrolled in a regular degree or certificate program. The 8 regional winners are then entered in the national competition.
**Financial data:** The national prize is $1,000. Dramatic Publishing Company publishes each of the 8 regional winners' plays.
**Duration:** The competition is held annually.
**Number awarded:** 1 each year.
**Deadline:** November of each year.

## 1509 KING OLAV V NORWEGIAN-AMERICAN HERITAGE FUND

Sons of Norway Foundation
c/o Sons of Norway
1455 West Lake Street
Minneapolis, MN 55408-2666
Phone: (612) 827-3611; (800) 945-8851; Fax: (612) 827-0658;
Email: fraternal@sofn.com

Web: www.sofn.com/foundation/GrantsScholarships.html

**Summary:** To provide support to college students of Norwegian heritage who are interested in pursuing further study of that heritage in North America or Norway.
**Eligibility:** Open to North Americans of Norwegian heritage, 18 years of age or older, who have demonstrated an interest in their heritage and who desire to further the study of that heritage at a recognized educational institution in North America or Norway. The program of study may include arts, crafts, literature, history, music, or folklore. Applicants must submit a 500-word essay that describes their reasons for applying for the scholarship, the course of study to be pursued, the length of the course, the name of the institution which they plan to attend, the tuition and costs, the amount of financial aid desired, how their course of study will benefit their community, and how their study corresponds to the goals and objectives of the Sons of Norway Foundation. Selection is based on the essay, academic potential, benefit to Sons of Norway and the wider Norwegian community, involvement in school and community activities, work experience, and financial need.
**Financial data:** Stipends range from $250 to $3,000, depending upon the number of recipients in any given year.
**Duration:** 1 year; a student may be awarded 2 scholarships within a 5-year period.
**Number awarded:** Varies each year. Since 1984, 167 of these scholarships have been awarded.
**Deadline:** February of each year.

## 1510 KNIGHT RIDDER MINORITY SCHOLARS PROGRAM

Knight Ridder, Inc.
Attn: Office of Diversity
50 West San Fernando Street, Suite 1200
San Jose, CA 95113
Phone: (408) 938-7734; Fax: (408) 938-7755
Web: www.knightridderscholars.com/scholarships.html

**Summary:** To provide financial assistance and work experience to minority high school seniors who are interested in going to college to prepare for a career in journalism.
**Eligibility:** Open to minority seniors graduating from high schools in areas served by Knight Ridder. Applicants must be interested in attending college to prepare for a career in the newspaper industry. They first apply to their local Knight Ridder newspaper and compete for local scholarships; selected winners are then nominated for this award. Both "news" and "business" students are eligible.
**Financial data:** The stipend is $5,000 per year for the freshman and sophomore year and $15,000 per year for the junior and senior year.
**Duration:** 1 year; may be renewed for up to 3 additional years, if the recipient maintains a GPA of 3.0 or higher and satisfactory performance on internships.
**Number awarded:** Up to 5 each year: 2 for news, 2 for business, and 1 for either.

## 1511 KNIGHTS OF PYTHIAS POSTER CONTEST

Knights of Pythias
Office of Supreme Lodge
59 Coddington Street, Suite 202
Quincy, MA 02169-4150
Phone: (617) 472-8800; Fax: (617) 376-0363; Email: kop@earthlink.net
Web: www.pythias.org

**Summary:** To recognize and reward outstanding posters by high school students on topics that change periodically.
**Eligibility:** Open to any student enrolled in high school (grades 9 through 12) in the United States or Canada. Posters must be 14 by 22 inches. No collage, paste-on, or stencil lettering is allowed. Competitions are first held by each Knights of Pythias local lodge, with winners advancing to the Grand Domain (state or province) and from there to the national level. These winning entries are then submitted to the Supreme Lodge contest. Posters are evaluated on the basis of message, originality, effective display of message, and neatness. The topic changes periodically; recently, it was "Defensive Driving–Avoid Road Rage."
**Financial data:** Supreme Lodge prizes are $1,000 for first place, $500 for second place, $250 for third place, and $100 for fourth through eighth places. Grand Lodge prizes vary.
**Duration:** The contest is held annually.
**Number awarded:** 8 each year on the national level.
**Deadline:** Local lodges select their winners by the end of April of each year and submit them to the Grand Lodge in their Grand Domain (state or province) by the middle of May. Grand Domain winners must be submitted to the Supreme Lodge by the middle of June.

## 1512 KVA SCHOLARSHIP

Maine Media Women
P.O. Box 864
Rockport, ME 04856
Web: www.mainemediawomen.org/scholarships.html
**Summary:** To provide financial assistance to women who are interested in working on a degree in a media-related field at a college or university in Maine.
**Eligibility:** Open to women who are enrolled at a college, university, or other postsecondary school in Maine. Applicants must be preparing for a media-related career in such areas as art, photography, design and marketing, creative writing, desktop publishing, photojournalism, videography, or communications.
**Financial data:** The stipend is $1,500.
**Duration:** 1 year.
**Number awarded:** 1 each year.
**Deadline:** March of each year.

## 1513 KYUTARO AND YASUO ABIKO MEMORIAL SCHOLARSHIP

Japanese American Citizens League, Attn: National Scholarship Awards
1765 Sutter Street
San Francisco, CA 94115
Phone: (415) 921-5225; Fax: (415) 931-4671; Email: jacl@jacl.org
Web: www.jacl.org/scholarships.html
**Summary:** To provide financial assistance for college to student members of the Japanese American Citizens League (JACL), especially those majoring in journalism or agriculture.
**Eligibility:** Open to JACL members who are currently enrolled or planning to reenter a college, university, trade school, business college, or other institution of higher learning. Applicants must submit a statement describing their current level of involvement in the Japanese American community or Asian Pacific community and how they will continue their involvement in future years. Selection is based on academic record, extracurricular activities, financial need, and community involvement. Preference is given to students majoring in journalism or agriculture.
**Financial data:** The stipend depends on the availability of funds but usually ranges from $1,000 to $5,000.
**Duration:** 1 year; nonrenewable.
**Number awarded:** At least 1 each year.
**Deadline:** March of each year.

## 1514 L. PHIL WICKER SCHOLARSHIP

American Radio Relay League, Attn: ARRL Foundation
225 Main Street
Newington, CT 06111
Phone: (860) 594-0397; Fax: (860) 594-0259; Email: foundation@arrl.org
Web: www.arrl.org/arrlf
**Summary:** To provide financial assistance to licensed radio amateurs from designated states who are interested in working on an undergraduate or graduate degree, particularly in electronics or communications.
**Eligibility:** Open to undergraduate or graduate students at accredited institutions who are licensed radio amateurs of general class. Preference is given to students who are 1) residents of North Carolina, South Carolina, Virginia, or West Virginia and attending school in those states, and 2) majoring in electronics, communications, or related fields. Applicants must submit an essay on the role amateur radio has played in their lives and provide documentation of financial need.
**Financial data:** The stipend is $1,000.
**Duration:** 1 year.
**Number awarded:** 1 each year.
**Deadline:** January of each year.

## 1515 LAHEENAE REBECCA HART GAY SCHOLARSHIP

Hawai'i Community Foundation, Attn: Scholarship Department
1164 Bishop Street, Suite 800
Honolulu, HI 96813
Phone: (808) 566-5570; (888) 731-3863; Fax: (808) 521-6286;
Email: scholarships@hcf-hawaii.org
Web: www.hawaiicommunityfoundation.org/scholar/scholar.php
**Summary:** To provide financial assistance to residents of Hawaii who are interested in working on a degree in art.
**Eligibility:** Open to residents of Hawaii who are planning to study art (not video, film, performing arts, or the culinary arts) as full-time students on the undergraduate or graduate level. Applicants must be able to demonstrate academic achievement (GPA of 2.7 or higher), good moral character, and financial need.
**Financial data:** The amount of the award depends on the availability of funds and the need of the recipient; recently, stipends averaged $1,500.
**Duration:** 1 year.
**Number awarded:** Varies each year; recently, 1 of these scholarships was awarded.
**Deadline:** February of each year.

## 1516 LAMBDA IOTA TAU SCHOLARSHIPS

Lambda Iota Tau, College Literature Honor Society
c/o Bruce W. Hozeski, Executive Secretary/Treasurer
Ball State University
Department of English
2000 West University Avenue
Muncie, IN 47306-0460
Phone: (765) 285-8580
**Summary:** To provide financial assistance for college to members of Lambda Iota Tau, the College Literature Honor Society.
**Eligibility:** Open to initiated members of the society. Only society chapters may submit nominations. The nomination letter must include a sample of the student's essay/creative writing and an essay from the nominee on his/her career goals and objectives. Selection is based on the writing sample, academic record, leadership, character, and service. No consideration is given to age, race, creed, sex, or national citizenship of the nominee.
**Financial data:** The stipend is $1,000.
**Duration:** 1 year.
**Number awarded:** 3 each year.
**Deadline:** June of each year.

## 1517 LANDMARK SCHOLARS PROGRAM

Landmark Publishing Group
c/o Rich Martin, Managing Editor
The Roanoke Times
201 West Campbell Avenue
Roanoke, VA 24011
Phone: (540) 981-3211; (800) 346-1234; Email: rich.martin@roanoke.com
Web: www.landmarkcommunications.com/employment/scholarships.php
**Summary:** To provide work experience and financial aid to minority undergraduates who are interested in preparing for a career in journalism.
**Eligibility:** Open to minority college sophomores, preferably those with ties to the mid-Atlantic states (Delaware, Maryland, North Carolina, South Carolina, Virginia, and Washington, D.C.). Applicants must be full-time students with a GPA of 2.5 or higher. They must be interested in preparing for a career in print journalism and in an internship as a reporter, photographer, graphic artist, sports writer, copy editor, or page designer.
**Financial data:** The stipend is $5,000 per year. During the summers following their sophomore and junior years, recipients are provided with paid internships. Following graduation, they are offered a 1-year internship with full benefits and the possibility of continued employment.
**Duration:** 2 years (the junior and senior years of college).
**Number awarded:** 1 or more each year.
**Deadline:** November of each year.

## 1518 LAWRENCE ALAN SPIEGEL REMEMBRANCE SCHOLARSHIP

Holocaust Human Rights Center of Maine, Attn: Executive Director
P.O. Box 4645
Augusta, ME 04330-1644
Phone: (207) 933-2620; Email: hhrc@gwi.net
Web: www.hhrc.org
**Summary:** To recognize and reward high school seniors in Maine who write outstanding essays about the Holocaust.
**Eligibility:** Open to high school seniors and home-schooled students who are Maine residents and who have been accepted at an accredited college, university, or technical school. Applicants must write an essay, up to 4 pages in length, on "Why should students learn about Holocaust."
**Financial data:** The award is a $1,000 scholarship.
**Duration:** The competition is held annually.
**Number awarded:** 1 each year.
**Deadline:** March of each year.

## 1519 LAWRENCE G. FOSTER AWARD FOR EXCELLENCE IN PUBLIC RELATIONS

Public Relations Student Society of America, Attn: Director of Education
33 Irving Place, Third Floor
New York, NY 10003-2376
Phone: (212) 460-1474; Fax: (212) 995-0757; Email: prssa@prsa.org
Web: www.prssa.org/resources/award-LawrenceFoster.asp
**Summary:** To recognize and reward members of the Public Relations Student Society of America (PRSSA) who write outstanding essays on excellence in public relations.
**Eligibility:** Open to members of the society who are currently enrolled in an undergraduate program of study at an accredited college or university. Applicants must submit an essay of 1,000 to 1,200 words describing their conception of excellence in public relations and how they plan to achieve excellence in their own careers. They should address the ethical and work standards that they believe will be required of them as public relations professionals and describe how they personally will aspire to excellence in those areas. Students should also list those leadership qualities they believe are most important in public relations, and why.
**Financial data:** The prize is $1,500.
**Duration:** The competition is held annually.
**Number awarded:** 1 each year.
**Deadline:** June of each year.

## 1520 LEADING EDGE STUDENT DESIGN COMPETITION

New Buildings Institute, Attn: Program Manager
142 East Jewett Boulevard
P.O. Box 653
White Salmon, WA 98672
Phone: (509) 493-4468, ext. 10; Fax: (509) 493-4078;
Email: mjohnson@newbuildings.org
Web: www.leadingedgecompetition.org
**Summary:** To recognize and reward undergraduate and graduate students who submit outstanding energy-efficient entries in a design competition.
**Eligibility:** Open to students who are currently enrolled in architecture, engineering, drafting, or environmental design programs at 2-year colleges, 4- or 5-year colleges or programs, graduate programs, and technical schools. The first category is for students in their third, fourth, or fifth year of undergraduate study and all graduate and post-baccalaureate students; the second category is for students in the first or second year of their undergraduate design education. Entries may be submitted by individuals or teams. Participants are invited to submit designs for a problem at an actual site. Complete information is provided on site history, demographics, climate, utilities, site description, and special requirements. Each design must satisfy the sociological and environmental concerns of the community while also addressing advanced energy efficiency and sustainable building design issues.
**Financial data:** In each category, first prize is $3,000 and second prize is $2,000. If winning entries are submitted by teams of students, the prizes must be divided equally among them. The schools of the winning teams receive $1,500 for first prize and $1,000 for second prize.
**Duration:** The competition is held annually.
**Number awarded:** 4 cash prizes are awarded each year: 2 in each category.
**Deadline:** June of each year.

## 1521 LEBANESE AMERICAN HERITAGE CLUB SCHOLARSHIPS

**Summary:** To provide financial assistance for college or graduate school to Americans of Arab descent who reside in Michigan.
*See Listing #575.*

## 1522 LEE A. LYMAN MEMORIAL MUSIC SCHOLARSHIP

Vermont Student Assistance Corporation
Champlain Mill, Attn: Scholarship Programs
P.O. Box 2000
Winooski, VT 05404-2601
Phone: (802) 654-3798; (888) 253-4819; Fax: (802) 654-3765; TDD: (802) 654-3766; TDD: (800) 281-3341 (within VT); Email: info@vsac.org
Web: www.vsac.org
**Summary:** To provide financial assistance to residents of Vermont who are interested in working on a college degree in music.
**Eligibility:** Open to residents of Vermont who are seniors in high school, high school graduates, or currently enrolled in college. Applicants must be enrolled or planning to enroll in a postsecondary degree program in music. Selection is based on participation in music-related activities, performances, groups, etc.; academic achievement; required essays; letters of recommendation; and financial need.
**Financial data:** The stipend is $1,000.
**Duration:** 1 year; recipients may reapply.
**Number awarded:** 4 each year.
**Deadline:** May of each year.

## 1523 LEE-JACKSON FOUNDATION SCHOLARSHIP

Lee-Jackson Foundation
P.O. Box 8121
Charlottesville, VA 22906
Phone: (804) 977-1861; Fax: (804) 977-6083
Web: www.lee-jackson.org
**Summary:** To recognize and reward students in Virginia who enter an historical essay contest and plan to attend a college or university in the United States.
**Eligibility:** Open to high school juniors and seniors at any Virginia secondary school. They may compete for these scholarships by writing an essay that demonstrates an appreciation of the character and virtues of Generals Robert E. Lee and Thomas J. "Stonewall" Jackson. The length of the papers is not specified, but most are between 7 and 10 pages. Selection is based on historical accuracy, quality of research, and clarity of written expression. Students first compete in the 8 high school regions in the state; winners are selected by a screening committee in their localities. In each region, a bonus scholarship is awarded to the paper judged the best; a grand prize is awarded to the author of the essay judged best of all the essays submitted.
**Financial data:** Total prizes are $10,000, $2,000, or $1,000. Each winner receives $1,000. The winners of bonus scholarships receive an additional $1,000 and the grand prize winner receives an additional $8,000. A $1,000 award is given to schools or home-school regions that encourage the most participation. Funds are mailed to the financial aid director of the college the winner attends; they may be used only for payment of tuition and required fees.
**Duration:** The competition is held annually.
**Number awarded:** 27 each year: 3 winners in each of the 8 public high school regions of the state plus 3 to private and home-school students. Bonus scholarships are awarded to 8 public school students (1 in each region) and 1 private or home-schooled student. The grand prize is awarded to the public school, private school, or home-schooled student whose essay is judged to be the best in the state. In addition, 9 schools (1 in each public school region plus 1 private/home-school region) receive the awards for encouraging the most participation.
**Deadline:** December of each year.

## 1524 LEONARD M. PERRYMAN COMMUNICATIONS SCHOLARSHIP FOR ETHNIC MINORITY STUDENTS

United Methodist Communications, Attn: Communications Resourcing Team
810 12th Avenue South
P.O. Box 320
Nashville, TN 37202-0320
Phone: (615) 742-5481; (888) CRT-4UMC; Fax: (615) 742-5485;
Email: scholarships@umcom.org
Web: www.umcom.org
**Summary:** To provide financial assistance to minority United Methodist college students who are interested in careers in religious communications.
**Eligibility:** Open to United Methodist ethnic minority students enrolled in accredited institutions of higher education as juniors or seniors. Applicants must be interested in preparing for a career in religious communications. For the purposes of this program, "communications" is meant to cover audiovisual, electronic, and print journalism. Selection is based on Christian commitment and involvement in the life of the United Methodist church, academic achievement, journalistic experience, clarity of purpose, and professional potential as a religious journalist.
**Financial data:** The stipend is $2,500 per year.
**Duration:** 1 year.
**Number awarded:** 1 each year.
**Deadline:** March of each year.

## 1525 LEONARDO WATTS SCHOLARSHIP

Watts Charity Association, Inc.
6245 Bristol Parkway, Suite 224
Culver City, CA 90230
Phone: (323) 671-0394; Fax: (323) 778-2613; Email: wattscharity@yahoo.com
Web: www.wattscharity.org

**Summary:** To provide financial assistance to upper-division college students working on a degree in classical music.

**Eligibility:** Open to U.S. citizens of African American descent who are enrolled full time as a college or university junior. Applicants must be studying classical music, including voice and/or instrumental. They must have a GPA of 3.0 or higher, be between 17 and 24 years of age, and be able to demonstrate that they intend to continue their education for at least 2 years. Along with their application, they must submit 1) a 1-paragraph statement on why they should be awarded a Watts Foundation scholarship, and 2) a 1- to 2-page essay on a specific type of cancer, based either on how it has impacted their life or on researched information.

**Financial data:** A stipend is awarded (amount not specified).

**Duration:** 1 year.

**Number awarded:** 1 each year.

**Deadline:** May of each year.

## 1526 LEROY COLLINS MEMORIAL SCHOLARSHIP

Florida Independent College Fund
929 North Spring Garden Avenue, Suite 165
DeLand, FL 32720-0981
Phone: (386) 734-2745; Fax: (386) 734-0839; Email: Scholarships@ficf.org
Web: www.ficf.org

**Summary:** To provide financial assistance to students majoring in a broadcast-related field at designated colleges and universities in Florida.

**Eligibility:** Open to residents of Florida who are college seniors majoring in a field related to communications in preparation for a career in broadcasting. Applicants must be attending 1 of 20 designated colleges and universities (12 private and 8 public) in Florida. They must be nominated by their institution. Selection is based on financial need and a 1-page essay on why broadcasting is their chosen career.

**Financial data:** The stipend is $3,000.

**Duration:** 1 year.

**Number awarded:** 1 each year.

**Deadline:** September of each year.

## 1527 LIBERTY GRAPHICS OUTDOOR ACTIVITIES ART CONTEST

Liberty Graphics, Inc., Attn: Contest Coordinator
3 Main Street
Liberty, ME 04949
Phone: (207) 589-4596; (800) 338-0015; Fax: (207) 589-4415;
Email: jay@lgtees.com
Web: www.lgtees.com

**Summary:** To recognize and reward outstanding art related to outdoor activities created by high school students in Maine.

**Eligibility:** Open to high school seniors in Maine. Qualified students are invited to submit flat art using traditional media (maximum size: 20 by 24 inches). The art must portray human powered outdoor activities, not motor or wind powered.

**Financial data:** The award is $1,000 and must be used to further the recipient's art education.

**Duration:** The competition is held annually.

**Number awarded:** 1 each year.

**Deadline:** April of each year.

## 1528 LINCOLN FORUM SCHOLARSHIP PRIZE ESSAY CONTEST

Lincoln Forum
c/o Don McCue, Curator
Lincoln Memorial Shrine
125 West Vine Street
Redlands, CA 92373
Phone: (909) 798-7632; Email: archives@aksmiley.org
Web: www.thelincolnforum.org/pages/essaycontest.html

**Summary:** To recognize and reward college students who submit outstanding essays on topics related to Abraham Lincoln.

**Eligibility:** Open to all students, regardless of age or citizenship status, enrolled as a full-time undergraduate student at a U.S. college or university. Applicants must submit an essay, from 1,500 to 5,000 words, on a topic that changes annually but relates to Abraham Lincoln. Recently, the topic was "The Challenge of Holding an Election in the Midst of War," in which students were invited to compare and contrast Lincoln's re-election in 1864 with other wartime elections in U.S. history.

**Financial data:** Prizes are $1,000 for first, $500 for second, and $250 for third.

**Duration:** The competition is held annually.

**Number awarded:** 3 prizes are awarded each year.

**Deadline:** July of each year.

## 1529 LINDA SIMMONS EDUCATIONAL SCHOLARSHIP

Alaska Broadcasters Association
700 West 41st Street
P.O. Box 102424
Anchorage, AK 99510
Phone: (907) 258-2424; Fax: (907) 258-2414; Email: akba@gci.net
Web: www.akbroadcasters.org/scholarship/index.html

**Summary:** To provide financial assistance to residents of Alaska who are attending college to prepare for a career in broadcasting.

**Eligibility:** Open to Alaska residents who are working on an undergraduate degree or certified course of study at an accredited junior or community college, professional trade school, college, or university in any state. They must be majoring in public relations, journalism, advertising, radio, and/or television broadcasting; if there are no candidates with those majors, students whose main interest is in a communication profession but whose major is another field are considered. Applicants must submit a resume that covers employment, school and community extracurricular activities, awards, and honors; 3 letters of reference; and a short essay on personal goals. Financial need is not considered.

**Financial data:** The stipend is $2,000. Funds are paid directly to the student's institution.

**Duration:** 1 year.

**Number awarded:** 1 each year.

**Deadline:** March of each year.

## 1530 LONE STAR CHAPTER SCHOLARSHIPS

Society for Technical Communication-Lone Star Chapter
Attn: Scholarship Committee Manager
P.O. Box 515065
Dallas, TX 75251-5065
Phone: (972) 558-1622; Email: Scholarship@stc-dfw.org
Web: www.stc-dfw.org/pages/schol_main.htm

**Summary:** To provide financial assistance to undergraduate and graduate students in designated states working on a degree or certificate in the technical communication field.

**Eligibility:** Open to undergraduate and graduate students working on a degree or certificate in the technical communication field or preparing for a career in the field. Applicants must be members of the Lone Star Chapter of the Society for Technical Communication (STC) or living or attending school in STC region 5 (Arizona, Arkansas, Louisiana, New Mexico, Oklahoma, Texas, or Utah). Along with their application, they must submit a record of their technical communication experience and a description of their career goals, significant achievements, honors, and awards to date. Selection is based on academic record and potential for contributing to the technical communication profession. If applicants are judged comparable in those respects, financial need is considered.

**Financial data:** Stipends range up to $2,000 per year.

**Duration:** 1 year.

**Number awarded:** 1 or more each year.

**Deadline:** October of each year.

## 1531 LORD ACTON ESSAY COMPETITION

Acton Institute for the Study of Religion and Liberty
161 Ottawa N.W., Suite 301
Grand Rapids, MI 49503
Phone: (616) 454-3080; Fax: (616) 454-9454; Email: awards@acton.org
Web: www.acton.org/programs/students/essay

**Summary:** To recognize and reward seminarians and students at all levels who submit outstanding essays on the themes of religion and liberty.

**Eligibility:** Open to seminarians, undergraduates, graduate students, and postgraduates studying religion, theology, philosophy, or related fields, regardless of religious affiliation or denomination. Applicants must submit a 4- to 6-page essay focusing on a topic that changes annually but relates to themes of religion and freedom. Applications from those outside the United States and those studying abroad receive equal consideration. Selection is based on the integration of economic, theological, and political thought in response to the annual topic.

**Financial data:** First place is $2,000, second $1,000, and third $500.

**Duration:** The competition is held annually.

**Number awarded:** 3 cash prizes are awarded each year.

**Deadline:** November of each year.

## 1532 LORRAINE HANSBERRY PLAYWRITING AWARD

John F. Kennedy Center for the Performing Arts
Education Department
Attn: Kennedy Center American College Theater Festival
2700 F Street, N.W.
Washington, DC 20566
Phone: (202) 416-8857; Fax: (202) 416-8802;
Email: skshaffer@kennedy-center.org
Web: kennedy-center.org/education/actf/actflha.html

**Summary:** To recognize and reward student authors of plays on the African American experience in America.

**Eligibility:** Open to students at any accredited junior or senior college in the United States or in countries contiguous to the continental United States, provided their college agrees to participate in the Kennedy Center American College Theater Festival (KCACTF). Undergraduate students must be carrying at least 6 semester hours, graduate students must be enrolled in at least 3 semester hours, and continuing part-time students must be enrolled in a regular degree or certificate program. These awards are presented to the best student-written plays on the subject of the African American experience.

**Financial data:** The first-place award is $2,500 and the second-place award is $1,000. The first-place winner also receives an internship to the National Playwrights Conference at the O'Neill Theater Center and publication of the play by Dramatic Publishing Company. In addition to the student awards, grants of $750 and $500 are made to the theater departments of the colleges or universities producing the first- and second-place plays.

**Duration:** The awards are presented annually.

**Number awarded:** 2 students and 2 sponsoring institutions receive awards each year.

**Deadline:** November of each year.

## 1533 LOU WOLF MEMORIAL SCHOLARSHIP

Society of Motion Picture and Television Engineers
Attn: Secretary, Scholarship Committee
595 West Hartsdale Avenue
White Plains, NY 10607
Phone: (914) 761-1100; Fax: (914) 761-3115; Email: smpte@smpte.org
Web: www.smpte.org/students/awards.cfm

**Summary:** To provide financial assistance to undergraduate and graduate student members of the Society of Motion Picture and Television Engineers (SMPTE) interested in majoring in film or television.

**Eligibility:** Open to undergraduate and graduate student members of SMPTE who are currently enrolled full time in an accredited high school, 2-year or 4-year college, or university. Applicants must be majoring or planning to major in film or television, with an emphasis on technology. Along with their application, they must submit personal statements on their 1) work experience and/or interests that are relevant to the application; 2) goals and objectives of study, including the reasons why they wish to pursue studies in motion pictures and television; and 3) proposed use of the funds (tuition, books, supplies, and/or equipment that will further their studies).

**Financial data:** The maximum stipend is $2,000.

**Duration:** 1 year.

**Number awarded:** Varies each year; recently, 3 of these scholarships were awarded.

**Deadline:** May of each year.

## 1534 LUCI S. WILLIAMS HOUSTON PHOTOJOURNALISM AWARD

Bay Area Black Journalists Association, Attn: Scholarship Committee
484 Lake Park Avenue
P.O. Box 61
Oakland, CA 94610
Phone: (510) 986-9390; Email: info@babja.org
Web: www.babja.org/babja_programs.html

**Summary:** To provide financial assistance to African American students working on an undergraduate or graduate degree in photojournalism.

**Eligibility:** Open to African American undergraduate and graduate students enrolled in an program in photojournalism. Applicants must have a GPA of 2.5 or higher. They may be residents of any state attending school in any state. Along with their application, they must submit an essay of 500 to 1,000 words on their accomplishments in photojournalism, career goals, interest in the field of photojournalism, and how and why the scholarship can help them.

**Financial data:** The stipend is $2,000.

**Duration:** 1 year; nonrenewable.

**Number awarded:** 1 each year.

**Deadline:** March of each year.

## 1535 LUCILLE PARRISH WARD VETERAN'S AWARD

National Federation of Music Clubs
1336 North Delaware Street
Indianapolis, IN 46202-2481
Phone: (317) 638-4003; Fax: (317) 638-0503; Email: info@nfmc-music.org
Web: www.nfmc-music.org/Competitions/AnnualSeniorDiv/annual_senior_div.htm

**Summary:** To provide financial assistance for undergraduate education to members of the National Federation of Music Clubs (NFMC) whose careers have been delayed or interrupted as a result of their service in the U.S. armed forces.

**Eligibility:** Open to undergraduate students who are majoring in music and whose musical careers were interrupted by service in the armed forces. Veterans who served overseas receive preference. Student membership in the federation and U.S. citizenship are required.

**Financial data:** The award is $2,000.

**Duration:** 1 year; may be renewed if the recipient maintains a GPA of 3.0 or higher.

**Number awarded:** 1 each year.

**Deadline:** February of each year.

## 1536 LYNN FREEMAN OLSON COMPOSITION AWARD

National Federation of Music Clubs
1336 North Delaware Street
Indianapolis, IN 46202-2481
Phone: (317) 638-4003; Fax: (317) 638-0503; Email: info@nfmc-music.org
Web: www.nfmc-music.org/Competitions/BienStudentSpecial/BienStudentSpecial.htm

**Summary:** To recognize and reward outstanding young composers who are members of the National Federation of Music Clubs.

**Eligibility:** Open to keyboard composers in the advanced division (high school graduate through 25 years of age), the high school division (grades 10-12), or the intermediate division (grades 7 through 9). Applicants may be citizens of any country, but they must be members of either the junior or student division of the federation. They may not previously have published any works for the purpose of general public use or sales. Compositions must be written within the skill levels of early elementary through intermediate levels of piano study.

**Financial data:** The award is $1,500 for the advanced division, $1,000 for the high school division, or $500 for the intermediate division. Funds must be used for further music study.

**Number awarded:** 3 every other year: 1 in each of the divisions.

**Deadline:** February of odd-numbered years.

## 1537 M. LOUISE MILLER SCHOLARSHIP

American Guild of Organists-Greater Bridgeport Chapter
c/o K. Bryan Kirk
1700 Broadbridge Avenue, A32
Stratford, CT 06614
Phone: (203) 377-5240; Email: kbkirkorg@aol.com

**Summary:** To provide financial assistance to undergraduate students interested in preparing for a career in organ performance and church music.

**Eligibility:** Open to undergraduates enrolled or planning to enroll at a college, university, or conservatory in the United States. Applicants must be preparing for a career in organ performance and church music. They must submit a short essay and a recording of 2 standard organ pieces.

**Financial data:** The stipend is $1,000.

**Duration:** 1 year.

**Number awarded:** 1 each year.

**Deadline:** February of each year.

## 1538 MAB SCHOLARSHIP PROGRAM

Mississippi Association of Broadcasters, Attn: Scholarship Committee
855 South Pear Orchard Road, Suite 403
Ridgeland, MS 39157
Phone: (601) 957-9121; Fax: (601) 957-9175; Email: email@msbroadcasters.org
Web: www.msbroadcasters.org/scholarship.html
**Summary:** To provide financial assistance to students enrolled in broadcast programs at Mississippi colleges and universities.
**Eligibility:** Open to residents of Mississippi enrolled in accredited broadcast programs at 2-year and 4-year colleges and universities in the state. Applicants must submit a 3-page statement that covers why they selected broadcasting as their career choice, the specific area of broadcasting that most interests them and why, their first job preference after college, their career goal 10 years after graduation, their eventual career goal, the broadcast activities in which they have participated, how they feel about broadcast advertising and its importance to a station, how they feel about broadcast advertising and its obligation to consumers, how they think broadcasting could better serve society, the radio or television station they respect most, how their college career could improve their value as a broadcaster, and their most rewarding broadcast-related experience. Selection is based on the essay, extracurricular activities, community involvement, commitment to broadcasting, 3 letters of recommendation, and financial need.
**Financial data:** Up to $4,000 is available for this program each year.
**Duration:** 1 year.
**Number awarded:** 1 or more each year.
**Deadline:** April of each year.

## 1539 MAINE INNKEEPERS ASSOCIATION HOSPITALITY SCHOLARSHIPS

Maine Innkeepers Association, Attn: MEIA Education Foundation
304 US Route 1
Freeport, ME 04032
Phone: (207) 865-6100; Email: info@maineinns.com
Web: www.maineinns.com
**Summary:** To provide financial assistance to Maine residents who wish to prepare for a career in the hospitality industry.
**Eligibility:** Open to Maine residents who wish take courses related to the hospitality industry. Applicants must be interested in preparing for a career in the hotel and motel industry and accepted at an accredited school that specializes in hotel administration or culinary sciences. They may be graduating high school seniors, the children of members of the association, or employees of association properties; they must have a GPA of at least 2.5. Selection is based on academic record, employment history, extracurricular activities, desire for a career in the hospitality industry, and financial need.
**Financial data:** Stipends range from $500 to $1,500.
**Duration:** 1 year; recipients may reapply.
**Number awarded:** Varies each year. Recently, 8 of these scholarships were awarded: 1 at $1,500, 2 at $1,000, and 5 at $500.
**Deadline:** April of each year.

## 1540 MANAA MEDIA SCHOLARSHIPS

Media Action Network for Asian Americans
P.O. Box 11105
Burbank, CA 91510
Phone: (213) 486-4433; Email: manaaletters@yahoo.com
Web: www.manaa.org
**Summary:** To provide financial assistance to Asian Pacific Islander students interested in advancing a positive image of Asian Americans in the mainstream media.
**Eligibility:** Open to Asian Pacific Islander college students interested in preparing for careers in filmmaking and in television production (but not in broadcast journalism). Applicants must be interested in advancing a positive and enlightened understanding of the Asian American experience in the mainstream media. Along with their application, they must submit a 1,000-word essay that addresses the following questions: Where do you see yourself 10 years from now? What accomplishments and strides will you hope to have made in your career in the film and television industry? How will you have worked to advance more positive images of Asian Americans in the mainstream media? Selection is based on academic and personal merit, a desire to uplift the image of Asian Americans in film and television as demonstrated in the essay, potential as demonstrated in a work sample, and financial need.
**Financial data:** The stipend is $1,000.
**Duration:** 1 year.
**Number awarded:** 2 each year.
**Deadline:** May of each year.

## 1541 MANSON A. STEWART SCHOLARSHIPS

Classical Association of the Middle West and South
c/o Eleanor Winsor Leach
Indiana University
Department of Classical Studies
547 Ballantine Hall
1020 East Kirkwood
Bloomington, IN 47405
Phone: (812) 855-4129; Email: leach@indiana.edu
Web: www.camws.org/awards/MAScollege.html
**Summary:** To provide financial assistance to undergraduate students majoring in classics at a college or university in the area of the Classical Association of the Middle West and South (CAMWS).
**Eligibility:** Open to undergraduate students who are majoring in classics at the sophomore or junior level at a college or university in the geographic area served by the association. Candidates must be nominated by the chair of their department or program; students then fill out an application and send it along with transcripts and letters of recommendation from 2 members of the association. Nominees are expected to take at least 2 courses in Latin or Greek during the junior or senior year in which the scholarship is held.
**Financial data:** The award is $1,000.
**Duration:** 1 year.
**Number awarded:** Varies each year; recently, 6 of these scholarships were awarded.
**Deadline:** February of each year.

## 1542 MARCELLA SEMBRICH VOICE COMPETITION

Kosciuszko Foundation, Attn: Director of Cultural Events
15 East 65th Street
New York, NY 10021-6595
Phone: (212) 734-2130, ext. 214; (800) 287-9956; Fax: (212) 628-4552;
Email: culture@thekf.org
Web: www.thekf.org/MUvoice.html
**Summary:** To recognize and reward outstanding singers.
**Eligibility:** Open to U.S. citizens, permanent residents of the United States, and international full-time students with valid student visas; all entrants must be between 18 and 35 years of age and preparing for professional singing careers. They must submit an audio cassette recording of a proposed program if they are selected for the competition; the program must include a Baroque or Classical aria, an aria by Giuseppe Verdi, a Polish song, a 19th-century Romantic opera aria, a contemporary American aria or song, and an aria by Stanislaw Moniuszko.
**Financial data:** The first-prize winner receives a $1,000 cash scholarship; round-trip airfare from New York City to Warsaw, accommodations, and meals in Poland to perform in the International Moniuszko Competition; a recital at the Moniuszko Festival in Poland; and an invitation to perform at the Sembrich Memorial Association in Lake George, New York. Second and third prizes are $750 and $500, respectively.
**Duration:** The competition is held triennially, in March.
**Number awarded:** 3 prizes are awarded each year of the competition.
**Deadline:** December of the years prior to the competitions, which are held in 2007, 2010, etc.

## 1543 MARIA ELENA SALINAS SCHOLARSHIP PROGRAM

National Association of Hispanic Journalists, Attn: Scholarship Committee
1000 National Press Building
529 14th Street, N.W.
Washington, DC 20045-2001
Phone: (202) 662-7145; (888) 346-NAHJ; Fax: (202) 662-7144;
Email: nahj@nahj.org
Web: www.nahj.org/student/scholarshipinformation.html
**Summary:** To provide financial assistance and work experience to Hispanic American students interested in preparing for a career as a journalist in Spanish-language radio or television.
**Eligibility:** Open to high school seniors, undergraduates, and first-year graduate students. Applicants must demonstrate a sincere desire to prepare for a career as a journalist in Spanish-language television or radio. They must submit 1) an essay in Spanish that explains why they are interested in a career as a Spanish-language journalist, and 2) work samples that are in Spanish. Selection is based on commitment to the field of journalism, academic achievement, awareness of the Latino community, and financial need.
**Financial data:** The stipend is $5,000 per year; the program also provides funding for an internship during the summer
**Duration:** 2 years.
**Number awarded:** 2 each year.
**Deadline:** January of each year.

## 1544 MARION MACCARRELL SCOTT SCHOLARSHIP

Hawai'i Community Foundation, Attn: Scholarship Department
1164 Bishop Street, Suite 800
Honolulu, HI 96813
Phone: (808) 566-5570; (888) 731-3863; Fax: (808) 521-6286;
Email: scholarships@hcf-hawaii.org
Web: www.hawaiicommunityfoundation.org/scholar/scholar.php

**Summary:** To provide financial assistance to residents of Hawaii for under-graduate or graduate studies in fields related to achieving world cooperation and international understanding.

**Eligibility:** Open to graduates of public high schools in Hawaii. They must plan to attend school as full-time students (on the undergraduate or graduate level) on the mainland, majoring in history, government, political science, anthropology, economics, geography, international relations, law, psychology, philosophy, or sociology. They must be residents of the state of Hawaii, able to demonstrate financial need, interested in attending an accredited 2- or 4-year college or university, and able to demonstrate academic achievement (GPA of 2.8 or higher). Along with their application, they must submit an essay on their commitment to world peace that includes their learning experiences (courses, clubs, community activities, or travel) related to achieving world peace and international understanding and explaining how their experiences have enhanced their ability to achieve those goals.

**Financial data:** The amounts of the awards depend on the availability of funds and the need of the recipient; recently, stipends averaged $1,749.

**Duration:** 1 year.

**Number awarded:** Varies each year; recently, 258 of these scholarships were awarded.

**Deadline:** February of each year.

## 1545 MARION RICHTER AMERICAN MUSIC COMPOSITION AWARD

National Federation of Music Clubs
1336 North Delaware Street
Indianapolis, IN 46202-2481
Phone: (317) 638-4003; Fax: (317) 638-0503; Email: info@nfmc-music.org
Web: www.nfmc-music.org/Competitions/Annual_Student/annual_student.html

**Summary:** To recognize and reward outstanding young composers who are members of the National Federation of Music Clubs.

**Eligibility:** Open to members of the federation who are college juniors, seniors, or graduate students and U.S. citizens. Applicants must be between 18 and 26 years of age and majoring in composition. They must submit an original composition up to the equivalent of 4 engraved manuscript pages. Solo/ensemble arrangements and ensemble settings of standard works are not eligible.

**Financial data:** The stipend is $1,250.

**Duration:** The competition is held annually.

**Number awarded:** 1 each year.

**Deadline:** February of each year.

## 1546 MARK TWAIN COMEDY PLAYWRITING AWARD

John F. Kennedy Center for the Performing Arts
Education Department
Attn: Kennedy Center American College Theater Festival
2700 F Street, N.W.
Washington, DC 20566
Phone: (202) 416-8857; Fax: (202) 416-8802;
Email: skshaffer@kennedy-center.org
Web: kennedy-center.org/education/actf/actftwain.html

**Summary:** To recognize and reward the student authors of comedy plays.

**Eligibility:** Open to students at any accredited junior or senior college in the United States or in countries contiguous to the continental United States, provided their college agrees to participate in the Kennedy Center American College Theater Festival (KCACTF). Undergraduate students must be carrying at least 6 semester hours, graduate students must be enrolled in at least 3 semester hours, and continuing part-time students must be enrolled in a regular degree or certificate program. This award is presented to the best student-written full length comedy play.

**Financial data:** A first-place award of $2,500 and a second-place award of $1,500 are presented to student authors. Dramatic Publishing Company presents the winning playwright with an offer of a contract to publish, license, and market the winning play. The first-place winner also receives an all-expense paid fellowship to attend a 2-week residency at the Sundance Theatre Laboratory in Sundance, Utah. In addition to the student awards, grants of $750 and $500 are made to the theater departments of the colleges or universities producing the first- and second-place plays.

**Duration:** The award is presented annually.

**Number awarded:** 2 student winners and 2 sponsoring institutions each year.

**Deadline:** November of each year.

## 1547 MARY AND WALTER HEMPHILL SCHOLARSHIPS

Indianapolis Press Club Foundation Inc., Attn: Scholarship Committee
150 West Market Street
Indianapolis, IN 46204
Phone: (317) 237-6222
Web: www.indianapolispressclub.org/scholarships/hemphill.htm

**Summary:** To provide financial assistance to college students in Indiana who are interested in preparing for a career in journalism.

**Eligibility:** Open to students enrolled in an Indiana college or university who are interested in a career in the news business. Preference is given to students who are majoring in journalism or broadcast journalism. Along with their application, students must submit a 1-page essay in which they describe their career goals, how they plan to achieve those goals, why they are important to them, and how the scholarship will assist them in reaching their goal of a career in journalism. Financial need is considered, but career interest, writing ability, ethics, news judgment, and potential for success are the chief concerns in the selection process.

**Financial data:** Recently, stipends averaged $900 per year.

**Duration:** 1 year.

**Number awarded:** Varies each year.

**Deadline:** April of each year.

## 1548 MARY ANN TALLMAN SCHOLARSHIP ENDOWMENT

Arizona Society Daughters of the American Revolution
c/o Jean Oracheff, Scholarship Chair
5217 West Creedance Boulevard
Glendale, AZ 85310
Email: vglortho@aol.com
Web: arizonasociety.dat.homestead.com/Scholarships.html

**Summary:** To provide financial assistance to high school seniors in Arizona interested in studying U.S. history in college.

**Eligibility:** Open to seniors graduating from high schools in Arizona and preparing to enter an institution of higher learning. Applicants must be planning to major or minor in American history. They must submit a letter describing their leadership experiences, evidence of patriotism, and plans for the future.

**Financial data:** A stipend is awarded (amount not specified).

**Duration:** 1 year.

**Number awarded:** 1 each year.

**Deadline:** January of each year.

## 1549 MARY BENEVENTO SCHOLARSHIP

Connecticut Association for Health, Physical Education, Recreation and Dance
c/o Jodie Hellman, Scholarship Chair
376 Old Woodbury Road
Southbury, CT 06488
Phone: (203) 264-7921; Email: jahellman@yahoo.com
Web: www.ctahperd.org/mary_benevento.htm

**Summary:** To provide financial assistance to high school seniors in Connecticut who are interested in studying health, physical education, recreation, or dance in college.

**Eligibility:** Open to U.S. citizens who are graduating seniors at high schools in Connecticut. Applicants must be interested in attending a college or university that offers a bachelor's degree in order to prepare for a career in the professional studies of health (defined as school health teaching, not nursing, public health, or psychology), physical education, recreation, or dance. They must submit a 300-word statement describing the educational objectives that qualify them for the scholarship award and summarizing their school and out-of-school activities and accomplishments. Selection is based on that essay, academic achievement, honors and awards, school and community extracurricular activities, and financial need.

**Financial data:** The stipend is $1,000 per year. Funds are paid to the recipient's college or university to be applied toward tuition, books, room, and board.

**Duration:** 1 year.

**Number awarded:** 1 each year.

**Deadline:** March of each year.

### 1550 MARY MOY QUAN ING MEMORIAL SCHOLARSHIP

Asian American Journalists Association, Attn: Student Programs Coordinator
1182 Market Street, Suite 320
San Francisco, CA 94102
Phone: (415) 346-2051, ext. 102; Fax: (415) 346-6343; Email: brandons@aaja.org
Web: www.aaja.org/programs/for_students/scholarships

**Summary:** To provide financial assistance to graduating high school seniors who are members of the Asian American Journalists Association (AAJA) and interested in majoring in journalism in college.

**Eligibility:** Open to graduating high school seniors who are AAJA members enrolling in college to study journalism. Applicants must submit a 500-word essay on their involvement or interest in the Asian American community and how, if they are awarded this scholarship, they would contribute to the field of journalism and/or media issues involving the Asian Pacific American and Pacific Islander community. Selection is based on scholastic ability, commitment to journalism, sensitivity to Asian American and Pacific Islander issues as demonstrated by community involvement, journalistic ability, and financial need.

**Financial data:** The stipend is $2,000.

**Duration:** 1 year.

**Number awarded:** 1 each year.

**Deadline:** April of each year.

### 1551 MARYLAND DISTINGUISHED SCHOLAR AWARDS

**Summary:** To provide financial assistance for college to outstanding high school juniors in Maryland.

*See Listing #640.*

### 1552 MARYLAND LEGION AUXILIARY CHILDREN AND YOUTH FUND SCHOLARSHIP

American Legion Auxiliary, Attn: Department of Maryland
1589 Sulphur Spring Road, Suite 105
Baltimore, MD 21227
Phone: (410) 242-9519; Fax: (410) 242-9553; Email: anna@alamd.org

**Summary:** To provide financial assistance for college to the daughters of veterans who are Maryland residents and wish to study arts, sciences, business, public administration, education, or a medical field.

**Eligibility:** Open to Maryland senior high girls with veteran parents who wish to study arts, sciences, business, public administration, education, or a medical field other than nursing at a college or university in the state. Preference is given to children of members of the American Legion or American Legion Auxiliary. Selection is based on character (30%), Americanism (20%), leadership (10%), scholarship (20%), and financial need (20%).

**Financial data:** The stipend is $2,000.

**Duration:** 1 year; may be renewed up to 3 additional years.

**Number awarded:** 1 each year.

**Deadline:** April of each year.

### 1553 MARYLAND SPJ PRO CHAPTER COLLEGE SCHOLARSHIP

Society of Professional Journalists-Maryland Professional Chapter
c/o Sue Kopen Katcef
402 Fox Hollow Lane
Annapolis, MD 21403
Phone: (410) 269-5676; Email: susiekk@aol.com
Web: saber.towson.edu/~bhalle/scholarship.html

**Summary:** To provide financial assistance to undergraduate students from Maryland who are majoring in journalism.

**Eligibility:** Open to undergraduate students working on a bachelor's degree on a full- or part-time basis with an emphasis or major in journalism. Applicants must be residents of Maryland, although they may be attending a college or university outside the state in nearby Virginia, Pennsylvania, or the District of Columbia. This is no age restriction; adults beyond regular college age attending night school to earn an undergraduate degree are eligible. Selection is based on a brief essay on future plans for a career in journalism, transcripts for at least the 2 previous semesters in college, awards or honors received, letters of recommendation, and financial need.

**Financial data:** A stipend is awarded (amount not specified).

**Duration:** 1 year.

**Number awarded:** 1 or more each year.

**Deadline:** May of each year.

### 1554 MASSACHUSETTS AFL-CIO SCHOLARSHIP AWARDS

Massachusetts AFL-CIO
389 Main Street, Suite 101
Malden, MA 02148
Phone: (781) 324-8230; Fax: (781) 324-8225
Web: www.massaflcio.org

**Summary:** To recognize and reward the high school seniors in Massachusetts receiving the highest scores on a statewide labor history written examination.

**Eligibility:** Open to high school seniors in Massachusetts. They may submit an application to their guidance office, social studies teacher, or principal to take a competitive examination dealing with the history and structure of the labor movement in America, legislation affecting American workers, child labor laws, minimum wages, civil rights, safety in the workplace, old age and health insurance, unemployment compensation, workers' compensation, and current labor events. The students with the highest scores on the examination receive these scholarships.

**Financial data:** First prize is $3,000, second prize is $2,000, third through eighth prizes are $1,000, and ninth prize is $500. An additional prize of $1,000 is awarded to the vocational education student who achieves the highest score among all vocational education students. In addition, prizes are awarded to students who are children of members of many central labor councils or locals throughout the state and score highest from among the children of members of that council or local who take the examination; these additional awards range in value from $100 to $3,000; the total value of scholarships provided by the Massachusetts AFL-CIO, its locals, central labor councils, and other affiliates exceeds $847,000 each year.

**Duration:** Most scholarships are for 1 year.

**Number awarded:** More than 300 scholarships are awarded each year, of which 10 are awarded to the students with the highest scores in the state regardless of union affiliation and most of the others to children of various councils or locals.

**Deadline:** Applications to take the examination must be submitted by January of each year.

### 1555 MASSACHUSETTS STUDENT BROADCASTER SCHOLARSHIP

Massachusetts Broadcasters Association
43 Riverside Avenue
PMB 401
Medford, MA 02155
Phone: (800) 471-1875; Fax: (800) 471-1876
Web: www.massbroadcasters.org/students/index.cfm

**Summary:** To provide financial assistance for college to Massachusetts residents interested in preparing for a career in broadcasting.

**Eligibility:** Open to permanent residents of Massachusetts who are in the process of enrolling or are currently enrolled full time at an accredited institution of higher learning (in any state). Applicants must be preparing for a career in broadcasting. Selection is based on financial need, academic merit, community service, extracurricular activities, and work experience. Highest priority is given to students with the most limited financial resources.

**Financial data:** The stipend is $1,500. Checks are made payable to the recipient and the recipient's school.

**Duration:** 1 year.

**Number awarded:** 1 or more each year.

**Deadline:** April of each year.

### 1556 MESSENGER-ANDERSON JOURNALISM SCHOLARSHIP AND INTERNSHIP PROGRAM

National Gay and Lesbian Task Force
Attn: Messenger-Anderson Journalism Scholarship and Internship Program
5455 Wilshire Boulevard, Suite 1505
Los Angeles, CA 90036
Phone: (323) 954-9597; Fax: (323) 954-9454; Email: ngltf@ngltf.org
Web: www.thetaskforce.org/about/messenger.htm

**Summary:** To provide financial assistance and work experience to members of the National Gay and Lesbian Task Force (NGLTF) interested in studying journalism in college.

**Eligibility:** Open to high school seniors and undergraduate students who plan to work on a bachelor's degree in journalism at an accredited 4-year college or university. Applicants must be self-identified as lesbian, gay, bisexual, or transgender; have a GPA of 2.8 or higher; and be a member of NGLTF. They must also be interested in an 8-week summer internship at NGLTF's headquarters in Washington, D.C., or its field offices in New York City, Los Angeles, or Cambridge (Massachusetts). Along with their application, they must submit an essay of 500 to 1,000 words on media coverage of gay, lesbian, bisexual, and transgendered people in their community and the steps they would take as a working journalist to improve coverage of the GLBT movement. Financial need is considered in the selection process.

**Financial data:** The scholarship stipend is $5,000 per year for the first year and $2,500 per year for subsequent years. Intern stipends are $300 per week; round-trip transportation, a $50 ground transportation award, and a housing allowance of $1,000 are also provided.

**Duration:** 1 year; may be renewed for up to 2 additional years.

**Number awarded:** 4 each year.

**Deadline:** February of each year.

### 1557 MICHAEL BATES MEMORIAL SCHOLARSHIP

Society of Professional Journalists-Kansas Professional Chapter
c/o Lori O'Toole Buselt, Scholarship Chair
The Wichita Eagle
P.O. Box 820
Wichita, KS 67201-0820
Phone: (316) 268-6327; Fax: (316) 268-6627; Email: kansas@spj.org
Web: www.spj.org/kansas/scholarship.htm

**Summary:** To provide financial assistance to students at colleges and universities in Kansas who are interested in a career in journalism.

**Eligibility:** Open to juniors and seniors at colleges and universities in Kansas. Sophomores may apply, designating the award for their junior year. Applicants do not have to be journalism or communication majors, but they must demonstrate a strong and sincere interest in print journalism, broadcast journalism, or photojournalism. They must have a GPA of 3.0 or higher and participate in outside journalism-related activities (demonstrated by involvement in student or trade organizations and/or student or other news organizations or publications). Along with their application, they must submit 4 to 6 examples of their best work (clips or stories, copies of photographs, tapes or transcripts of broadcasts). Selection is based on the quality of work submitted, academic standing, references, and financial need.

**Financial data:** The stipend is $1,500.

**Duration:** 1 year.

**Number awarded:** 1 each year.

**Deadline:** March of each year.

### 1558 MICHIGAN PRESS ASSOCIATION FOUNDATION COLLEGE SCHOLARSHIPS

Michigan Press Association, Attn: MPA Foundation
827 North Washington Avenue
Lansing, MI 48906-5199
Phone: (517) 372-2424; Fax: (517) 372-2429; Email: mpa@michiganpress.org
Web: www.michiganpress.org/foundation.shtml

**Summary:** To provide financial assistance to students majoring in journalism at colleges and universities in Michigan.

**Eligibility:** Open to residents of Michigan majoring in journalism at colleges and universities in the state. Candidates must be nominated by faculty members at their schools. They must demonstrate interest in community journalism and have journalistic potential. Selection is based on scholastic achievement and financial need.

**Financial data:** The stipend is $1,000.

**Duration:** 1 year.

**Number awarded:** Varies each year; recently, 10 of these scholarships were awarded.

**Deadline:** December of each year.

### 1559 MINORU YASUI MEMORIAL SCHOLARSHIP AWARD

Asian American Journalists Association, Attn: Student Programs Coordinator
1182 Market Street, Suite 320
San Francisco, CA 94102
Phone: (415) 346-2051, ext. 102; Fax: (415) 346-6343; Email: brandons@aaja.org
Web: www.aaja.org/programs/for_students/scholarships

**Summary:** To provide financial assistance to male Asian American students who are members of the Asian American Journalists Association (AAJA) and interested in a career in broadcast journalism.

**Eligibility:** Open to Asian American male high school seniors, undergraduates, or graduate students enrolled full time at an accredited college or university in a broadcast journalism program. Applicants must be AAJA members. Along with their application, they must submit a 500-word essay on their involvement or interest in the Asian American community and how, if they are awarded this scholarship, they would contribute to the field of journalism and/or media issues involving the Asian American and Pacific Islander community. Selection

is based on scholastic ability, commitment to journalism, sensitivity to Asian American and Pacific Islander issues as demonstrated by community involvement, journalistic ability, and financial need.

**Financial data:** The stipend is $2,000.

**Duration:** 1 year.

**Number awarded:** 1 each year.

**Deadline:** April of each year.

### 1560 MIRIAM HOFFMAN SCHOLARSHIPS

United Methodist Church
Attn: General Board of Higher Education and Ministry
Office of Loans and Scholarships
1001 19th Avenue South
P.O. Box 340007
Nashville, TN 37203-0007
Phone: (615) 340-7344; Fax: (615) 340-7367; Email: umscholar@gbhem.org
Web: www.gbhem.org

**Summary:** To provide financial assistance to undergraduate and graduate Methodist students who are preparing for a career in music.

**Eligibility:** Open to undergraduate and graduate students who are enrolled full time and preparing for a career in music. Applicants must have been active, full members of a United Methodist Church for at least one year prior to applying and have a GPA of 2.5 or higher. Preference is given to students interested in music education or music ministry. U.S. citizenship or permanent resident status is required.

**Financial data:** The stipend is $1,000.

**Duration:** 1 year; recipients may reapply.

**Number awarded:** Varies each year; recently, 12 of these scholarships were awarded.

**Deadline:** May of each year.

### 1561 MISSISSIPPI BAPTIST CONVENTION BOARD MINISTERIAL SCHOLARSHIPS

Mississippi Baptist Convention Board, Attn: Board of Ministerial Education
515 Mississippi Street
P.O. Box 530
Jackson, MS 39205-0530
Phone: (601) 968-3800; (800) 748-1651 (within MS); Fax: (601) 968-3928
Web: www.mbcb.org/agencies/bme

**Summary:** To provide financial assistance to undergraduate ministerial students attending designated Baptist colleges in Mississippi.

**Eligibility:** Open to undergraduate ministerial students at Blue Mountain College, Mississippi College, and William Carey College (all affiliated with the Mississippi Baptist Convention Board). Applicants must have made a public commitment to Southern Baptist ministry through their local church, home, or foreign missions. They must be recommended by their pastors.

**Financial data:** Recently, assistance for the full enrollment period averaged $3,820.

**Duration:** The full enrollment period is 26 months.

**Number awarded:** Varies each year; recently, a total of 239 students were receiving support through this program.

### 1562 MISSOURI BROADCASTERS ASSOCIATION SCHOLARSHIPS

Missouri Broadcasters Association, Attn: Scholarship Committee
1808 Southwest Boulevard
P.O. Box 104445
Jefferson City, MO 65110-4445
Phone: (573) 636-6692; Fax: (573) 634-8258; Email: mba@mbaweb.org
Web: www.mbaweb.org/ScholarshipInternshipInformation.htm

**Summary:** To provide financial assistance to Missouri residents interested in studying broadcasting in college.

**Eligibility:** Open to Missouri residents who are currently attending a college, university, or accredited technical/trade school in the state or graduating high school seniors who have been admitted to a Missouri institution of higher education. Applicants must be enrolled or planning to enroll as a full-time student in a broadcast or related program that provides training and expertise applicable to broadcast operation. They must have a GPA of 3.0 or higher and submit their application to a radio or television station that is a member of the Missouri Broadcasters Association. Each station selects its top candidate to forward to the association for statewide consideration. Selection is based on curriculum and career goals, clarity of thought and expression, letters of recommendation, community involvement, extracurricular activities, and financial need. Finalists are invited for personal interviews.

**Financial data:** The stipend depends on the availability of funds.

**Duration:** 1 year; may be renewed if the recipient continues to meet eligibility requirements.

**Number awarded:** Several each year.

**Deadline:** March of each year.

## 1563 MJSA EDUCATION FOUNDATION JEWELRY SCHOLARSHIP

Rhode Island Foundation, Attn: Scholarship Coordinator
One Union Station
Providence, RI 02903
Phone: (401) 274-4564; Fax: (401) 751-7983; Email: libbym@rifoundation.org
Web: www.rifoundation.org

**Summary:** To provide financial assistance to college students studying a field related to jewelry.

**Eligibility:** Open to students in colleges, universities, and postsecondary non-profit technical schools in the United States. Applicants must be studying tool making, design, metals fabrication, or other field related to jewelry. Along with their application, they must submit an essay (up to 300 words), in which they describe their program of study, the length of the program, how far along they are towards completion, and their reason for choosing the program. Selection is based on course of study, career objectives, samples of work (if appropriate), jewelry industry experience, academic achievement, recommendations, and financial need.

**Financial data:** Stipends range from $500 to $2,000 per year.

**Duration:** 1 year; may be renewed for up to 3 additional years if the recipient maintains good academic standing.

**Number awarded:** Several each year.

**Deadline:** May of each year.

## 1564 MORRIS J. AND BETTY KAPLUN FOUNDATION ESSAY CONTEST

Morris J. and Betty Kaplun Foundation, Attn: Essay Contest Committee
P.O. Box 234428
Great Neck, NY 11023
Email: info@kaplun.org
Web: www.kaplun.org

**Summary:** To recognize and reward outstanding essays on topics related to being Jewish.

**Eligibility:** Open to students in grades 10-12 who write an essay of 250 to 1,500 words on a topic that changes annually but is related to being Jewish. A recent topic was "The Influence of the Hebrew Bible and Jewish Values on America's Founding Fathers, its Constitution and the American Way of Life." For students in junior high school (grades 7 through 9), the essay must be 250 to 1,000 words; a recent topic was "Honor Thy Father and Mother—Why and How, From My Personal Perspective."

**Financial data:** Prizes are $1,800, $750, or $18.

**Duration:** The competition is held annually.

**Number awarded:** Each year, 1 prize of $1,800 and 5 prizes of $750 are awarded at both the high school and junior high levels; the first 50 essays submitted for each level receive $18 each.

**Deadline:** March of each year.

## 1565 MORTON GOULD YOUNG COMPOSER AWARDS

American Society of Composers, Authors and Publishers
Attn: ASCAP Foundation
ASCAP Building
One Lincoln Plaza
New York, NY 10023
Phone: (212) 621-6320; Fax: (212) 621-6236;
Email: ascapfoundation@ascap.com
Web: www.ascapfoundation.org/gould-info.html

**Summary:** To recognize and reward outstanding young American composers.

**Eligibility:** Open to U.S. citizens, permanent residents, or enrolled students with proper visas who are younger than 30 years of age, including students in grades K-12, undergraduates, and graduate students. Original music of any style is considered. However, works that have earned awards or prizes in other national competitions are ineligible, as are arrangements. To compete, each applicant must submit a completed application form, one reproduction of a manuscript or score, biographical information, a list of compositions to date,

and 2 professional recommendations. Only one composition per composer may be submitted. A cassette tape or CD of the composition may be included. So that music materials may be returned, each entry must be accompanied by a self-addressed envelope with sufficient postage.

**Financial data:** The winners share cash awards of more than $30,000.

**Duration:** The award is presented annually.

**Number awarded:** Varies each year; recently, 21 students received these awards.

**Deadline:** February of each year.

## 1566 MOSMILLER SCHOLAR PROGRAM

American Floral Endowment
P.O. Box 945
Edwardsville, IL 62025
Phone: (618) 692-0045; Fax: (618) 692-4045; Email: afe@endowment.org
Web: www.endowment.org/mosmiller2.htm

**Summary:** To provide financial assistance and work experience to students working on an undergraduate degree in floriculture or business.

**Eligibility:** Open to U.S. citizens who are currently enrolled full time in a 2-year or 4-year college or university in the United States in a floriculture, environmental horticulture, or business program. Applicants must be maintaining satisfactory progress in a degree or certificate program and a GPA of C or better. They must be interested in interning at a wholesale, retail, or allied trade company located in the United States away from their home and school. Following completion of the internship, they receive a grant for continued study.

**Financial data:** Employers must agree to pay a fair market wage for the geographic area and position. In addition, students receive a grant of $2,000 following completion of the internship.

**Duration:** Internships are for 10 to 16 weeks. Preference is given to fall or spring internships, but summer internships are allowed if the location can provide valuable experience.

**Number awarded:** 1 or more each year.

**Deadline:** February or October of each year.

## 1567 MTNA SENIOR PERFORMANCE COMPETITIONS

Music Teachers National Association, Attn: MTNA Foundation
441 Vine Street, Suite 505
Cincinnati, OH 45202-2811
Phone: (513) 421-1420; (888) 512-5278; Fax: (513) 421-2503;
Email: mtnanet@mtna.org
Web: www.mtna.org/seniorpc.htm

**Summary:** To recognize and reward outstanding performances by high school-age musicians.

**Eligibility:** Open to musicians between 15 and 18 years of age who participate in a performance competition. Prizes are awarded in 6 categories: brass, strings, voice, woodwinds, piano, and percussion. Participants first compete in state and division levels and then in the national finals. The required repertoire includes works of different styles and periods. The entrants must be students of members of the Music Teachers National Association (MTNA).

**Financial data:** The national winners in the brass, strings, voice, and woodwinds categories each receive a cash prize of $1,000. The winners in the percussion and piano categories receive a cash prize of $1,500. The second-place winner in the piano category receives a cash prize of $500. The teachers of the brass, strings, voice, and woodwinds winners each receive $100. The teachers of the piano and percussion winners each receive $150. All national finalists receive a $100 merit award.

**Duration:** The competition is held annually.

**Number awarded:** 6 prizes are awarded each year: 1 in each category. The number of merit awards varies.

**Deadline:** September of each year.

## 1568 MTNA STUDENT COMPOSITION COMPETITIONS

Music Teachers National Association, Attn: MTNA Foundation
441 Vine Street, Suite 505
Cincinnati, OH 45202-2811
Phone: (513) 421-1420; (888) 512-5278; Fax: (513) 421-2503;
Email: mtnanet@mtna.org
Web: www.mtna.org/scc.htm

**Summary:** To recognize and reward outstanding musical compositions by students.

**Eligibility:** Open to students from elementary school through college level whose teachers are members of the Music Teachers National Association (MTNA). Applicants must submit original musical compositions in state competitions; winners advance to the national level. Performance times may not exceed 10 minutes. Compositions may be in any style for any medium. Competitions are held in 4 age-level divisions: elementary for 5 to 10 years of age. junior for 11 to 14 years of age, senior for 15 to 18 years of age, and young artist for 19 to 26 years of age.

**Financial data:** The national winners receive a certificate, plaque, and the following cash prizes: $300 for the elementary division, $400 for the junior division, $700 for the senior division, and $1,000 for the young artist division.

**Duration:** The competition is held annually.

**Number awarded:** 4 each year: 1 at each level.

**Deadline:** September of each year.

### 1569 MTNA YOUNG ARTIST PERFORMANCE COMPETITIONS

Music Teachers National Association, Attn: MTNA Foundation
441 Vine Street, Suite 505
Cincinnati, OH 45202-2811
Phone: (513) 421-1420; (888) 512-5278; Fax: (513) 421-2503;
Email: mtnanet@mtna.org
Web: www.mtnafoundation.org/youngartistpc.htm

**Summary:** To recognize and reward outstanding performances by college-age musicians.

**Eligibility:** Open to musicians between 19 and 26 years of age who participate in a performance competition. Prizes are awarded in 8 categories: brass, strings, organ, voice, woodwinds, piano, percussion, and guitar. Participants first compete in state and division levels and then in the national finals. The required repertoire includes works of different styles and periods. The entrants must be students of members of the Music Teachers National Association (MTNA).

**Financial data:** The national winners in the brass, strings, organ, voice, and woodwinds categories each receive a cash prize of $2,000 and their teachers receive $100. The winner in the piano category receives a Steinway grand piano and the teacher receives $300. The winners in the percussion and guitar categories each receive $3,000 and their teachers receive $300. All national finalists receive a $100 merit award.

**Duration:** The competition is held annually.

**Number awarded:** 8 prizes are awarded each year: 1 in each category. The number of merit awards varies.

**Deadline:** September of each year.

### 1570 MUSIC THERAPY SCHOLARSHIP

Sigma Alpha Iota Philanthropies, Inc.
One Tunnel Road
Asheville, NC 28805
Phone: (828) 251-0606; Fax: (828) 251-0644;
Email: philonline@sai-national.org
Web: www.sai-national/org/phil/philsch1.html

**Summary:** To provide financial assistance to members of Sigma Alpha Iota (an organization of women musicians) who are interested in working on an undergraduate or graduate degree in music therapy.

**Eligibility:** Open to members of the organization, if they wish to study music therapy at the undergraduate or graduate level. Applicants must submit an essay the includes their personal definition of music therapy, their career plans and professional goals as a music therapist, and why they feel they are deserving of this scholarship. Selection is based on music therapy skills, musicianship, fraternity service, community service, leadership, self-reliance, and dedication to the field of music therapy as a career.

**Financial data:** The stipend is $1,000.

**Duration:** 1 year.

**Number awarded:** 1 each year.

**Deadline:** March of each year.

### 1571 NABJ SCHOLARSHIPS

National Association of Black Journalists
Attn: Student Education Enrichment and Development Program
8701-A Adelphi Road
Adelphi, MD 20783-1716
Phone: (301) 445-7100, ext. 108; Fax: (301) 445-7101; Email: nabj@nabj.org
Web: www.nabj.org/scholarships.html

**Summary:** To provide financial assistance to undergraduate or graduate student members of the National Association of Black Journalists (NABJ) who are majoring in a field related to journalism.

**Eligibility:** Open to African American undergraduate or graduate students who are currently attending an accredited 4-year college or university. Applicants

must be majoring in broadcast (radio or television), print, or online journalism and have a GPA of 2.5 or higher. They must submit samples of their work, an official college transcript, 2 letters of recommendation, a resume, and a 500- to 800-word essay describing their accomplishments as a student journalist, their career goals, and their financial need.

**Financial data:** The stipend is $2,500. Funds are paid directly to the recipient's college or university.

**Duration:** 1 year; nonrenewable.

**Number awarded:** 2 each year.

**Deadline:** April of each year.

### 1572 NAHJ GENERAL SCHOLARSHIPS

National Association of Hispanic Journalists, Attn: Scholarship Committee
1000 National Press Building
529 14th Street, N.W.
Washington, DC 20045-2001
Phone: (202) 662-7145; (888) 346-NAHJ; Fax: (202) 662-7144;
Email: nahj@nahj.org
Web: www.nahj.org/student/scholarshipinformation.html

**Summary:** To provide financial assistance to Hispanic American undergraduate and graduate students interested in preparing for careers in the media.

**Eligibility:** Open to Hispanic American high school seniors, undergraduates, and graduate students who are interested in preparing for a career in English- or Spanish-language print, broadcast (radio or television), online. or photojournalism; students majoring in other fields must be able to demonstrate a strong interest in preparing for a career in journalism. Applicants must submit an official transcript; a 1-page resume with their educational background, work history, awards, internships, other scholarships, language proficiency, and any work done for their school newspaper, radio, and/or television station; samples of their work; 2 reference letters; a 500-word autobiography in the form of a news story; and documentation of financial need. Selection is based on commitment to the field of journalism, academic achievement, awareness of the Latino community, and financial need.

**Financial data:** Stipends range from $1,000 to $2,000.

**Duration:** 1 year.

**Number awarded:** Varies each year; recently 20 of these scholarships were awarded.

**Deadline:** January of each year.

### 1573 NATHAN TAYLOR DODSON SCHOLARSHIP

North Carolina Alliance for Athletics, Health, Physical Education, Recreation and Dance, Attn: Executive Director
P.O. Box 27751
Raleigh, NC 27611
Phone: (888) 840-6500; Fax: (919) 463-8393; Email: ncaahperd@ncaahperd.org
Web: www.ncaahperd.org/awards/index.htm

**Summary:** To provide financial assistance for college to members of the North Carolina Alliance for Athletics, Health, Physical Education, Recreation and Dance (NCAAHPERD).

**Eligibility:** Open to rising seniors majoring in health, physical education, recreation, and/or dance who are members of NCAAHPERD and have a GPA of 2.0 or higher for all college work and 3.0 or higher for their major. Selection is based two-thirds on academic achievement and one-third on leadership and contributions to the profession. Financial need is not considered.

**Financial data:** The stipend is $1,000 per year.

**Duration:** 1 year.

**Number awarded:** 1 each year.

**Deadline:** June of each year.

### 1574 NATIONAL AD 2 STUDENT CREATIVE COMPETITION

National Ad 2 c/o Tod Visdal, Williams-Helde Marketing Communications
711 Sixth Avenue North, Suite 200
Seattle, WA 98109
Phone: (206) 226-7367; Email: visdal@msn.com
Web: www.ad2.org/education/education.htm

**Summary:** To recognize and reward students who enter an advertising competition.

**Eligibility:** Open to students enrolled full or part time in an accredited U.S. college, university, or commercial art school. Applicants must have a C or better average overall and be majoring in advertising or a closely-related field (e.g., art, communication, journalism, marketing, or public relations). They must submit a complete advertisement in one of the following formats: print, outdoor, radio, television, or web. The work must be the student's own individual effort and developed specifically for this competition. Entries must be submitted through a local Ad 2 Club.

**Financial data:** The grand-prize winner receives $1,000 plus complimentary registration and travel vouchers for the sponsor's national conference.

**Duration:** The competition is held annually.

**Number awarded:** 1 each year.

**Deadline:** March of each year.

---

## 1575 NATIONAL ART HONOR SOCIETY SCHOLARSHIPS

The Art Institutes International, Inc.
Free Markets Center
210 Sixth Avenue, 33rd Floor
Pittsburgh, PA 15222-2603
Phone: (800) 275-2440; Email: ai_sfs@aii.edu
Web: www.artinstitutes.edu

**Summary:** To recognize and reward (with scholarships to participating Art Institutes) high school seniors who are members of the National Art Honor Society and enter an art competition.

**Eligibility:** Open to high school seniors who are members of the National Art Honor Society planning to attend a participating Art Institute. Applicants must submit 6 slides of 6 different original pieces of artwork representing their creative ability and interest. They must also submit a written statement describing their artistic career goals and why they want to be considered for a scholarship.

**Financial data:** Prizes are $25,000 for first place, $15,000 for second, $10,000 for third, $5,000 for fourth, and $2,500 for fifth. Awards may be used only for tuition at a participating Art Institute. Funds may not be applied to fees, living expenses, or supply costs.

**Duration:** The competition is held annually.

**Number awarded:** 5 each year.

**Deadline:** February of each year.

---

## 1576 NATIONAL ASSOCIATION OF PASTORAL MUSICIANS SCHOLARSHIPS

National Association of Pastoral Musicians, Attn: NPM Scholarships
962 Wayne Avenue, Suite 210
Silver Spring, MD 20910-4461
Phone: (240) 247-3000; Fax: (240) 247-3001; Email: npmsing@npm.org
Web: www.npm.org/Membership/scholarship.htm

**Summary:** To provide financial assistance to undergraduate or graduate student members of the National Association of Pastoral Musicians.

**Eligibility:** Open to members of the association who are enrolled part or full time in an undergraduate, graduate, or continuing education program. They must be studying in a field related to pastoral music, be able to demonstrate financial need, and be intending to work for at least 2 years in the field of pastoral music following graduation. Applicants must submit a 5-minute performance cassette tape of themselves or the choir-ensemble they direct.

**Financial data:** Stipends range from $1,000 to $5,000. Funds must be used to pay for registration, fees, or books.

**Duration:** 1 year; recipients may reapply.

**Number awarded:** 11 each year.

**Deadline:** February of each year.

---

## 1577 NATIONAL FFA SCHOLARSHIPS FOR UNDERGRADUATES IN THE HUMANITIES

National FFA Organization, Attn: Scholarship Office
6060 FFA Drive
P.O. Box 68960
Indianapolis, IN 46268-0960
Phone: (317) 802-4321; Fax: (317) 802-5321; Email: scholarships@ffa.org
Web: www.ffa.org

**Summary:** To provide financial assistance to FFA members who wish to study agricultural journalism and related fields in college.

**Eligibility:** Open to current and former members of the organization who are working or planning to work full time on a degree in fields related to agricultural journalism and communications, floriculture, and landscape design. For most of the scholarships, applicants must be high school seniors; others are open to students currently enrolled in college. The program includes a large number of designated scholarships that specify the locations where the members must live, the schools they must attend, the fields of study they must pursue, or other requirements. Some consider family income in the selection process, but most do not. Selection is based on academic achievement (10 points for GPA, 10 points for SAT or ACT score, 10 points for class rank), leadership in

FFA activities (30 points), leadership in community activities (10 points), and participation in the Supervised Agricultural Experience (SAE) program (30 points). U.S. citizenship is required.

**Financial data:** Stipends vary, but most are at least $1,000.

**Duration:** 1 year or more.

**Number awarded:** Varies; generally, a total of approximately 1,000 scholarships are awarded annually by the association.

**Deadline:** February of each year.

---

## 1578 NATIONAL HISTORY DAY AWARDS FOR STUDENTS

National History Day, Attn: Director
University of Maryland
0119 Cecil Hall
College Park, MD 20742
Phone: (301) 314-9739; Fax: (301) 314-9767;
Email: national.history.day@umail.umd.edu
Web: www.nationalhistoryday.org

**Summary:** To recognize and reward outstanding history papers, exhibits, performances, and media presentations prepared by middle and high school students around the country.

**Eligibility:** Open to middle and high school students in the United States. Contests are held in 2 divisions (junior, for grades 6 through 8, and senior, for grades 9-12) and, within each division, in 7 categories: paper, individual exhibit, group exhibit, individual performance, group performance, individual documentary, and group documentary. The 3 group categories may include 2 to 5 students. Papers must be standard research essays from 1,500 to 2,500 words in length. Individual and group exhibits must be visual representations of research and interpretation, much like a small museum exhibit. Individual and group performances must be dramatic portrayals of an historical topic; they may not exceed 10 minutes in length. Individual and group documentaries must utilize photographs, film, video, audiotapes, and graphic presentations to communicate a topic's historical significance. Following local school and district contests, winners compete in state contests, where 2 entries in each category are selected to compete at the national level. Special awards are presented to the best entries on various special topics, including African American history, the history of baseball, labor history, history of the American presidency, history of agriculture and rural life, colonial and revolutionary history, Irish or Irish American history, U.S. foreign relations history, Holocaust history, naval history, military history, Civil War history, history of religious freedom, innovation in American history, women's history, and history in the federal government. History Channel awards are presented to high school seniors who submit the best individual documentary, the best group documentary, the best project tied to an historic site, and the best project on an international theme.

**Financial data:** At the national level, winners in each category of the 2 divisions receive prizes of $1,000 for first place, $500 for second place, and $250 for third place. The amounts of the special awards vary. The History Channel awards are $5,000.

**Duration:** The competition is held annually.

**Number awarded:** At the local level, more than 500,000 students and 50,000 teachers participate in the competition. Nearly 2,000 students each year advance to the national competition where 3 prizes are presented in each of the 2 divisions and 7 categories. The number of special awards varies. There are 4 History Channel awards.

---

## 1579 NATIONAL JUNIOR CLASSICAL LEAGUE SCHOLARSHIPS

National Junior Classical League, Attn: Administrator
Miami University
422 Wells Mill Drive
Oxford, OH 45056-2118
Phone: (513) 529-7741; Fax: (513) 529-7742; Email: administrator@njcl.org
Web: www.njcl.org

**Summary:** To provide financial assistance to high school seniors who are members of the National Junior Classical League (NJCL).

**Eligibility:** Open to current members of the league who are high school seniors planning to enter college in the upcoming academic year to study the classics. Special consideration is given to those who intend to teach Latin, Greek, or the classical humanities. Applicants must submit a 500-word essay on the following: "How will you pass on the torch of classical civilization and convey your study of Latin/Greek into the modern world?" Selection is based on financial need, recommendations, academic record, and service to the league at local, state, and national levels.

**Financial data:** Stipends range from $1,000 to $2,000.

**Duration:** 1 year.

**Number awarded:** 8 each year: 1 at $2,000, 2 at $1,500, and 5 at $1,000.

**Deadline:** April of each year.

## 1580 NATIONAL LATIN EXAMINATION SCHOLARSHIPS

American Classical League c/o Mary Washington College
1301 College Avenue
Fredericksburg, VA 22401
Phone: (800) 459-9847; (888) 378-7721
Web: www.nle.org

**Summary:** To recognize and reward students who achieve high scores on the National Latin Examination.

**Eligibility:** Open to any high school student who is enrolled or has completed a Latin course during the current academic year. Applicants must take the National Latin Examination. The examinations consist of 40 multiple-choice questions on comprehension, grammar, historical background, classical literature, and literary devices. Different examinations are given for Introduction to Latin, Latin I, Latin II, Latin III-IV Prose, Latin III-IV Poetry, and Latin V-VI. The top scorers in each category receive gold medals; gold medal winners in Latin III-IV Prose, Latin III-IV Poetry, and Latin V-VI who are high school seniors are mailed applications for these scholarships.

**Financial data:** The stipend is $1,000.

**Duration:** 1 year; may be renewed if the recipient continues to study classical Greek or Latin in college.

**Number awarded:** Approximately 20 each year.

**Deadline:** The examinations must be ordered by January of each year.

## 1581 NATIONAL PROSTART SCHOLARSHIPS

The Art Institutes International, Inc.
Free Markets Center
210 Sixth Avenue, 33rd Floor
Pittsburgh, PA 15222-2603
Phone: (800) 275-2440; Email: ai_sfs@aii.edu
Web: www.artinstitutes.edu

**Summary:** To recognize and reward (with scholarships to participating Art Institutes) high school seniors who are winners in the National ProStart Student Invitational competition of the National Restaurant Association Educational Foundation (NRAEF).

**Eligibility:** Open to high school seniors who are winners of the National ProStart Student Invitational competition. That competition is open to students who participate in the ProStart School-to-Career Initiative while in high school. They enter a culinary contest in their state program (currently operating in Arizona, California, Colorado, Florida, Georgia, Illinois, Indiana, Iowa, Kansas, Louisiana, Michigan, Nebraska, Nevada, New Mexico, Ohio, Oklahoma, Oregon, Utah, Virginia, Washington, West Virginia, Wisconsin, and Wyoming). Teams of students demonstrate their creativity by preparing a meal consisting of a salad, choice of protein, starch, vegetable, and dessert. Members of winning teams who wish to attend an Art Institute that offers a culinary program are eligible to apply for these scholarships.

**Financial data:** The award is $10,000. Winners may apply the funds toward payment of tuition at the Art Institute of their choice.

**Duration:** The competition is held annually.

**Number awarded:** 1 or more each year.

## 1582 NATIONAL RELIGIOUS MUSIC WEEK ALLIANCE SCHOLARSHIPS

National Religious Music Week Alliance
201 Dayton Street
Hamilton, OH 45011
Phone: (513) 884-1500; Fax: (513) 884-1999; Email: musicweek@aol.com
Web: www.religiousmusicweek.com/scholar.html

**Summary:** To provide financial assistance to students enrolled in a college music program leading to a career in the ministry of music.

**Eligibility:** Open to students enrolled in a college or university and majoring in music. Applicants must be interested in preparing for a career in church music. Along with their application, they must submit a brief essay on their plans for continuing their education and their goals following graduation. Selection is based on the essay, grade transcripts, 2 letters of recommendation, scholastic distinctions and honors, and involvement in church, school, or community activities. Financial need is not considered.

**Financial data:** The stipend is $2,500.

**Duration:** 1 year.

**Number awarded:** 2 each year.

**Deadline:** March of each year.

## 1583 NATIONAL SCULPTURE COMPETITION PRIZES

National Sculpture Society, Attn: National Sculpture Competition
237 Park Avenue, Ground Floor
New York, NY 10017
Phone: (212) 764-5645; Fax: (212) 764-5651; Email: nss1893@aol.com
Web: www.nationalsculpture.org/nat_comp.asp

**Summary:** To recognize and reward outstanding creative work by young sculptors.

**Eligibility:** Open to student and other young sculptors. The competition is a 2-part event; entrants may participate in either or both parts. The young sculptor awards are presented to sculptors under 40 years of age who are citizens or residents of the United States. They must submit slides of up to 5 different works of sculpture in bas-relief. The use of figurative or realist sculpture is preferred. Artists who wish to be considered for this part of the competition do not need to be present. The Dexter Jones Award is presented for the best work of sculpture in bas-relief, the Roger T. Williams Prize is awarded to the sculptor "who reaches for excellence in representational sculpture," and the Edward Fenno Hoffman Prize is awarded to the sculptor "who strives to uplift the human spirit through the medium of his/her art." For the second part of the competition, the jury invites 18 entrants to participate in a 5-day figure modeling contest. Selection of winners is based on the following criteria: mastery of the figure in sculptural form; comprehension of the action, unity, and rhythm of the pose; and how well the artist gives evidence of understanding proportion, stance, solidity, and continuity of line.

**Financial data:** The Dexter Jones Award is $1,000, the Roger T. Williams Prize is $750, and the Edward Fenno Hoffman Prize is $350. For sculptors who choose to enter the figure modeling contest, the first-place winner receives the Walter and Michael Lantz Prize of $1,000, the second-place winner receives the Walker Hancock Prize of $500, and the third-place winner receives the Elizabeth Gordon Chandler Prize of $300.

**Duration:** The competition is held annually.

**Number awarded:** Each year, 3 prizes are awarded on the basis of slides and 3 prizes are awarded to winners of the figure modeling contest.

**Deadline:** April of each year.

## 1584 NATIONAL SCULPTURE SOCIETY SCHOLARSHIPS

National Sculpture Society, Attn: Scholarships
237 Park Avenue, Ground Floor
New York, NY 10017
Phone: (212) 764-5645; Fax: (212) 764-5651; Email: nss1893@aol.com
Web: www.nationalsculpture.org/scholarships.asp

**Summary:** To provide financial assistance for college to students of sculpture.

**Eligibility:** Open to students of figurative or representational sculpture. They must submit a letter of application that includes a brief biography and an explanation of their background in sculpture, 2 letters of recommendation, 8 to 10 photographs of at least 3 of their works (figurative, realist, or representational sculpture is preferred), and proof of financial need.

**Financial data:** The stipend is $1,000. Funds are paid directly to the academic institution through which the student applies, to be credited towards tuition.

**Duration:** 1 year.

**Number awarded:** At least 3 each year.

**Deadline:** April of each year.

## 1585 NATIONAL SPEAKERS ASSOCIATION SCHOLARSHIPS

National Speakers Association, Attn: NSA Foundation
1500 South Priest Drive
Tempe, AZ 85281
Phone: (480) 968-2552; Fax: (480) 968-0911; Email: information.nsaspeaker.org
Web: www.nsaspeaker.org/about/foundation.shtml

**Summary:** To provide financial assistance to students interested in focusing on speech communication in college.

**Eligibility:** Open to college juniors, seniors, and graduate students majoring or minoring in speech communications. Students majoring in speech pathology, television, radio, mass media, public relations, law, or human resources are not eligible. Applicants must intend to 1) become professional speakers, trainers, or speech educators; or 2) use their speaking talents for improving the lives of others. Along with their application, they must submit a 500-word essay on their career objectives and how they will use their skill in oral communication. Selection is based on that essay; a letter of recommendation from a speech teacher or the speech department head or dean; a list of awards, honors, extracurricular activities, and outside work interests; and an official transcript. Hardship and financial need may be considered, although the final decision is not based solely on financial need.

**Financial data:** The stipend is $4,000 per year.

**Duration:** 1 year.
**Number awarded:** 4 each year.
**Deadline:** May of each year.

## 1586 NATIONAL STUDENT ADVERTISING COMPETITION

American Advertising Federation, Attn: Education Services Program
1101 Vermont Avenue, Suite 500
Washington, DC 20005
Phone: (202) 898-0089; (800) 999-2231; Fax: (202) 898-0159;
Email: Education@aaf.org
Web: www.aaf.org/college/nsac_overview.html
**Summary:** To recognize and reward student members of the American Advertising Federation (AAF) who participate in an advertising competition.
**Eligibility:** Open to teams of undergraduate students who are members of their AAF college chapter. Each team may consist of up to 5 students. Teams develop advertising campaigns for actual nonprofit or for-profit organizations; recently, the client was the Florida Commission on Tourism. Competitions are first held in the 15 AAF districts. Winners of those competitions, along with a "wild card" team that is judged the best from the second-place winners, advance to the national competition.
**Financial data:** The first-place team wins a $3,500 prize, second $2,500, third $2,000, fourth $1,000, and other finalists $500.
**Duration:** The competition is held annually.
**Number awarded:** 16 teams win prizes each year.
**Deadline:** Teams must indicated their intent to enter the competition by March of each year.

## 1587 NATIONAL STUDENT PLAYWRITING AWARD

John F. Kennedy Center for the Performing Arts
Education Department
Attn: Kennedy Center American College Theater Festival
2700 F Street, N.W.
Washington, DC 20566
Phone: (202) 416-8857; Fax: (202) 416-8802;
Email: skshaffer@kennedy-center.org
Web: kennedy-center.org/education/actf/actfnsp.html
**Summary:** To recognize and reward outstanding undergraduate and graduate school playwrights.
**Eligibility:** Open to students at any accredited junior or senior college in the United States or in countries contiguous to the continental United States, provided their college agrees to participate in the Kennedy Center American College Theater Festival (KCACTF). Undergraduate students must be carrying at least 6 semester hours, graduate students must be enrolled in at least 3 semester hours, and continuing part-time students must be enrolled in a regular degree or certificate program. For the Michael Kanin Playwriting Awards Program, students must submit either 1 major work or 2 or more shorter works based on a single theme or encompassed within a unifying framework; all entries must provide a full evening of theater. The work must be written while the student was enrolled, and the production must be presented during that period or within 2 years after enrollment ends. The play selected as the best by the judges is presented at the national festival and its playwright receives this award.
**Financial data:** The winning playwright receives 1) production of the play at the Kennedy Center as part of the KCATF national festival, with expenses paid for the production and the playwright; 2) the William Morris Agency Award of $2,500; 3) the Dramatists Guild Award of active membership in the Guild; 4) the Samuel French Award of publication of the play by Samuel French, Inc.; and 5) an all-expense paid fellowship to participate in the Sundance Theater Laboratory in Sundance, Utah. The Association for Theatre in Higher Education (ATHE) presents a cash award of up to $1,000 to the theater department of the school producing the national wining script and $100 to the schools producing the winning plays at each of the 8 KCATF regional festivals.
**Duration:** The competition is held annually.
**Number awarded:** 1 each year.
**Deadline:** The final draft of the script must be submitted by November of each year.

## 1588 NATIONAL TRUMPET COMPETITION AWARDS

National Trumpet Competition
c/o Executive Director
3500 North Third Street
Arlington, VA 22201
Email: denny@nationaltrumpetcomp.org
Web: www.nationaltrumpetcomp.org
**Summary:** To recognize and reward outstanding student trumpet players.
**Eligibility:** Open to trumpet players who are interested in competing in the following divisions: the Stu's Music Shop Middle School Division (for students between 11 and 14 years of age); the Stephen & Bonnie Simon High School division (for students between 15 and 18 years of age); the Vincent Bach College Division (for full-time undergraduates up to 23 years of age); the Blackburn Trumpets Masters Division (for students up to 28 years of age); the Dillon Music Jazz Division (for students up to 28 years of age); the Southern Ohio Music Company Trumpet Ensemble Division (for ensembles of 4 to 8 students up to 28 years of age); the NTC Endowment Historical Trumpet Division (including the Shore Award for up to 18 years of age, the Fantini Award for students from 19 to 28 years of age, the Reiche Award for musicians 29 years of age and older, and the ensemble award for ensembles of 3 applicants of any age); or the NTC Endowment Pro-Am Division (for musicians 29 years of age and older). Entrants submit tapes of their performances; times and repertoire vary according to division. Based on those tapes, semifinalists are selected and invited to the competitions at George Mason University in March.
**Financial data:** A total of $30,000 in cash awards and prizes are presented each year.
**Duration:** The competition is held annually.
**Number awarded:** Varies each year.
**Deadline:** December of each year.

## 1589 NEBRASKA PRESS ASSOCIATION FOUNDATION SCHOLARSHIPS

Nebraska Press Association Foundation
845 S Street
Lincoln, NE 68508
Phone: (402) 476-2851; (800) 369-2850; Fax: (402) 476-2942;
Email: nebpress@nebpress.com
Web: www.nebpress.com
**Summary:** To provide financial assistance to high school seniors in Nebraska who are interested in preparing for a career in print journalism.
**Eligibility:** Open to high school seniors in Nebraska who are interested in attending a college or university in the state and majoring in print journalism. Preference is given to students with specific interests in news, editorial, photography, circulation, production, or advertising. Applicants must submit information on their academic accomplishments, reasons for applying for this scholarship (including their career plans), and family financial situation.
**Financial data:** The stipend is $1,250.
**Duration:** 1 year.
**Deadline:** February of each year.

## 1590 NEPEF JOURNALISM SCHOLARSHIPS

New England Press Association
Attn: New England Press Educational Foundation
360 Huntington Avenue, 428 CP
Boston, MA 02115
Phone: (617) 373-5610; Email: foundation@nepa.org
Web: www.nepa.org/scholarship.html
**Summary:** To provide financial assistance to students enrolled in a journalism program at a college or university in New England.
**Eligibility:** Open to students enrolled in an accredited journalism program at a New England college or university. Applicants must submit official transcripts, work that shows an interest in the newspaper field and competency in the skills required (e.g., clips of stories, photos, pages from internships, student papers), a current resume, and a 500-word essay on the reasons for wanting to work in the newspaper field and how the scholarship would help to fulfill that goal.
**Financial data:** A stipend is awarded (amount not specified).
**Duration:** 1 year.
**Number awarded:** 1 or more each year.

## 1591 NEW HAMPSHIRE ASSOCIATION OF BROADCASTERS SCHOLARSHIPS

New Hampshire Association of Broadcasters
707 Chestnut Street
Manchester, NH 03104
Phone: (603) 627-9600; Fax: (603) 627-9603; Email: info@nhab.org
Web: www.nhab.org/students/index.cfm
**Summary:** To provide financial assistance to New Hampshire residents interested in preparing for a career in broadcasting.
**Eligibility:** Open to residents of New Hampshire who are enrolled or planning

to enroll as a full-time student in a broadcast program at a 2-year or 4-year college or university in any state. Applicants must submit a 150-word statement on why they have chosen to prepare for a career in a broadcast-related field. Selection is based on financial need, academic merit, community service, extracurricular activities, and work experience. Highest priority is given to students with the most limited financial resources.

**Financial data:** The stipend is $2,250.
**Duration:** 1 year.
**Number awarded:** At least 6 each year.
**Deadline:** April of each year.

## 1592 NEW JERSEY POST SAME SCHOLARSHIP

Society of American Military Engineers-New Jersey Post c/o John Booth CTSC
P.O. Box 60
Fort Monmouth, NJ 07703
Phone: (732) 544-0995, ext. 102;
Email: john.booth@mail1.monmouth.army.mil
Web: www.same.org/newjersey
**Summary:** To provide financial assistance to students in New Jersey working on an undergraduate degree in architecture, engineering, or a related field.
**Eligibility:** Open to undergraduate students working on a degree in architecture, engineering, or a related field. Candidates must be nominated by a member of the New Jersey Post of the Society of American Military Engineers (SAME). Selection is based on school and community activities, educational goals, academics, recommendations, and employment.
**Financial data:** The stipend is $1,000.
**Duration:** 1 year.
**Number awarded:** 1 each year.
**Deadline:** March of each year.

## 1593 NEW MEXICO BROADCASTERS ASSOCIATION SCHOLARSHIPS

New Mexico Broadcasters Association
Attn: Scholarship Program
8014 Menaul, N.W.
Albuquerque, NM 87110
Phone: (505) 881-4444; (800) 622-2414; Fax: (505) 881-5353
Web: www.nmba.org
**Summary:** To provide financial assistance to undergraduate students in New Mexico who are preparing for a career in the broadcast industry.
**Eligibility:** Open to residents of New Mexico who are entering their sophomore, junior, or senior year at an accredited college, vocational institution, or university in the state. Applicants must be preparing for a career in the broadcast industry, including news, announcing, sales, accounting, management, engineering, traffic and billing, promotion, community affairs, programming, production, or other aspects of the industry. They must submit brief statements on their work experience at a broadcast facility and why they want to prepare for a career in the field. Race, gender, age, and financial need are not considered in the selection process. Nontraditional and reentry students are encouraged to apply.
**Financial data:** The maximum stipend is $2,500 per year. Funds are sent directly to the student to help pay the cost of tuition, books, supplies and fees.
**Duration:** 1 year.
**Number awarded:** Up to 10 each year.
**Deadline:** April of each year.

## 1594 NEW YORK BEEF PRODUCERS' ASSOCIATION SCHOLARSHIP

New York Beef Producers' Association
3 Second Street
Camden, NY 13316
Phone: (315) 245-3386
Web: www.tjbailey.com/nybpa
**Summary:** To provide financial assistance to college students from New York who are preparing for a career in the cattle industry.
**Eligibility:** Open to residents of New York who are currently enrolled in an accredited 2-year or 4-year agricultural college. Applicants must be majoring in a field of study related to agriculture (e.g., animal and/or crop science, business, economics, communications, agricultural engineering) and planning a career related to the beef industry. Along with their application, they must submit an essay that covers the following: 1) their experience and interest in the

beef industry; 2) their involvement in agricultural-related activities, including organizations (community, school, 4-H), events, awards, and leadership positions; 3) their future intentions and career plans as they relate to the beef industry; and 4) how they view the future of the beef industry. Selection is based primarily on involvement in the beef industry and future plans. Financial need is not considered.
**Financial data:** The stipend is $1,000.
**Duration:** 1 year.
**Number awarded:** 1 each year.
**Deadline:** December of each year.

## 1595 NEWHOUSE FOUNDATION SCHOLARSHIPS

National Association of Black Journalists
Attn: Student Education Enrichment and Development Program
8701-A Adelphi Road
Adelphi, MD 20783-1716
Phone: (301) 445-7100, ext. 108; Fax: (301) 445-7101; Email: nabj@nabj.org
Web: www.nabj.org/scholarships.html
**Summary:** To provide financial assistance and summer work experience to African American upper-division students majoring in print journalism.
**Eligibility:** Open to African American juniors or seniors who are currently attending an accredited 4-year college or university. Applicants must be majoring in print journalism, have a GPA of 3.0 or higher, and have experience working on their campus newspaper. They must submit samples of their work, an official college transcript, 2 letters of recommendation, a resume, and a 500- to 800-word essay describing their accomplishments as a student journalist, their career goals, and their financial need.
**Financial data:** The stipend is $5,000 per year.
**Duration:** 1 year; may be renewed for 1 additional year if the recipient maintains at least a 3.0 GPA, majors in print journalism, works with the campus newspaper, and works for 10 weeks as a paid intern (minimum salary of $325 per week) for 3 summers at a Newhouse Newspaper.
**Number awarded:** 2 each year.
**Deadline:** April of each year.

## 1596 NEWHOUSE SCHOLARSHIP PROGRAM

National Association of Hispanic Journalists
Attn: Scholarship Committee
1000 National Press Building
529 14th Street, N.W.
Washington, DC 20045-2001
Phone: (202) 662-7145; (888) 346-NAHJ; Fax: (202) 662-7144;
Email: nahj@nahj.org
Web: www.nahj.org/student/scholarshipinformation.html
**Summary:** To provide financial assistance and summer work experience to Hispanic American undergraduate students interested in preparing for careers in the media.
**Eligibility:** Open to college juniors and seniors who are of Hispanic descent and interested in preparing for a career in English-language journalism as a reporter, editor, photographer, or graphic artist. Applicants must submit an official transcript; a 1-page resume with their educational background, work history, awards, internships, other scholarships, language proficiency, and any work done for their school newspaper, radio, and/or television station; samples of their work; 2 reference letters; a 500-word autobiography written as a news story; and documentation of financial need. Selection is based on commitment to the field of journalism, academic achievement, awareness of the Latino community, and financial need.
**Financial data:** The stipend is $5,000 per year; the program also provides funding to attend the association's convention and an internship during the summer between the junior and senior year.
**Duration:** 2 years.
**Number awarded:** 2 each year.
**Deadline:** January of each year.

## 1597 NEWSROOM DIVERSITY SCHOLARSHIP

Society of Professional Journalists-Kansas Professional Chapter
c/o Lori O'Toole Buselt, Scholarship Chair
The Wichita Eagle
P.O. Box 820
Wichita, KS 67201-0820
Phone: (316) 268-6327; Fax: (316) 268-6627; Email: kansas@spj.org
Web: www.spj.org/kansas/scholarship.htm

**Summary:** To provide financial assistance to minority students at colleges and universities in Kansas who are interested in a career in journalism.

**Eligibility:** Open to members of racial minority groups who are juniors and seniors at colleges and universities in Kansas. Sophomores may apply, designating the award for their junior year. Applicants do not have to be journalism or communication majors, but they must demonstrate a strong and sincere interest in print journalism, broadcast journalism, or photojournalism. They must have a GPA of 2.5 or higher and participate in outside journalism-related activities demonstrated by involvement in student or trade organizations and/or student or other news organizations or publications. Along with their application, they must submit 4 to 6 examples of their best work (clips or stories, copies of photographs, tapes or transcripts of broadcasts). Selection is based on the quality of work submitted, academic standing, references, and financial need.

**Financial data:** The stipend is $1,000.

**Duration:** 1 year.

**Number awarded:** 1 each year.

**Deadline:** March of each year.

## 1598 NFMC BIENNIAL STUDENT AUDITION AWARDS

National Federation of Music Clubs
1336 North Delaware Street
Indianapolis, IN 46202-2481
Phone: (317) 638-4003; Fax: (317) 638-0503; Email: info@nfmc-music.org
Web: www.nfmc-music.org/Competitions/BienStudentAud/BienStudentAudi
tns.htm

**Summary:** To recognize and reward outstanding young musicians who are members of the National Federation of Music Clubs (NFMC).

**Eligibility:** Open to members of NFMC. Instrumentalists must be between 16 and 26 years of age; vocalists must be between 18 and 26. All applicants must be U.S. citizens and either student or junior division members of the federation. Competition categories include: women's voice, men's voice, piano, organ, harp, classical guitar, violin, viola, cello, double bass, orchestral woodwinds, orchestral brass, and percussion. Awards are presented at the national level after auditions at the state and district levels.

**Financial data:** The winner in each category is awarded $1,500.

**Duration:** The competition is held biennially, in odd-numbered years.

**Deadline:** January of odd-numbered years.

## 1599 NICK ADAMS SHORT STORY COMPETITION

Associated Colleges of the Midwest
Attn: Coordinator of Projects & Administration
205 West Wacker Drive, Suite 1300
Chicago, IL 60606
Phone: (312) 263-5000; Fax: (312) 263-5879; Email: acm@acm.edu
Web: www.acm.edu/nickadams/index.html

**Summary:** To recognize and reward outstanding short stories written by college students at schools belonging to the Associated Colleges of the Midwest (ACM).

**Eligibility:** Open to students at colleges that belong to ACM. They may submit up to 2 stories to their campus's English department. The story need not have been written especially for the competition, but it cannot have been previously published off-campus. Each department selects the 4 best stories submitted and sends them to ACM's national office. The finalist is selected from that group.

**Financial data:** The prize is $1,000.

**Duration:** The prize is awarded annually.

**Number awarded:** 1 each year.

**Deadline:** March of each year.

## 1600 NMAHPERD COLLEGE SCHOLARSHIP

New Mexico Association for Health, Physical Education, Recreation, and Dance
Attn: Scholarship Chair
P.O. Box 27040
Albuquerque, NM 87125-7040
Web: www.unm.edu/~nmahperd/Files/awards.html

**Summary:** To provide financial assistance to residents of New Mexico who are planning to work on an undergraduate degree in health, physical education, recreation, or dance at a college or university in the state.

**Eligibility:** Open to residents of New Mexico who are planning to enter a 4-year college or university in the state as a freshman. Applicants must have a GPA of 3.0 or higher for the first semester of their senior year in high school. They must have expressed an interest in studying in the health, physical education, recreation, or dance fields. Along with their application, they must submit 1) a 350-word narrative expressing their rationale for entering the field of health, physical education, recreation, or dance; 2) a brief narrative of their involvement in extracurricular and civic activities; 3) an explanation of how they have demonstrated their ability to work with a diverse population; and 4) 2 letters of recommendation.

**Financial data:** The stipend is $1,000.

**Duration:** 1 year.

**Number awarded:** 1 each year.

**Deadline:** April of each year.

## 1601 NORMA ROSS WALTER SCHOLARSHIP PROGRAM

Willa Cather Pioneer Memorial and Educational Foundation
Attn: Scholarship Program
413 North Webster
Red Cloud, NE 68970
Phone: (402) 746-2653; Fax: (402) 746-2652
Web: www.willacather.org/Scholarship.htm

**Summary:** To provide financial assistance to female graduates of Nebraska high schools who are or will be majoring in English at an accredited college or university.

**Eligibility:** Open to women who have graduated or plan to graduate from a Nebraska high school and enter a college or university as a first-year student. Applicants must plan to continue their education as English majors (journalism is not acceptable). Along with their application, they must submit a 1,500-word essay on several of the short stories or a novel written by Willa Cather. Selection is based on intellectual promise, creativity, and character.

**Financial data:** The stipend is $1,000.

**Duration:** 1 year; nonrenewable.

**Number awarded:** 1 each year.

**Deadline:** January of each year.

## 1602 NORTH AMERICAN SURVEYING HISTORY SCHOLARSHIP

Museum of Surveying
220 South Museum Drive
Lansing, MI 48933
Phone: (517) 484-6605; Email: museumofsurvey@acd.net
Web: www.surveyhistory.org

**Summary:** To provide financial assistance to upper-division surveying students in North America who have demonstrated an interest in history.

**Eligibility:** Open to juniors and seniors at accredited colleges and universities in North America who are majoring in surveying, geomatics, or a similar field. Applicants must have a GPA of 3.0 or higher. They must have demonstrated an interest in surveying history in ways that include, but are not limited to, the following: participating in a re-enactment group on a regular basis; participating in a significant historical survey retracement; preparing a paper (preferably published) about a historical surveying event, person, or technological development in equipment; or performing a service project related to surveying history for a museum.

**Financial data:** The stipend is $1,000.

**Duration:** 1 year.

**Number awarded:** 1 each year.

**Deadline:** October of each year.

## 1603 NORTHWEST JOURNALISTS OF COLOR SCHOLARSHIP AWARDS

Northwest Journalists of Color c/o Michael Ko
The Seattle Times
1120 John Street
Seattle, WA 98109
Phone: (206) 515-5653; Email: mko@aajaseattle.org
Web: www.aajaseattle.org

**Summary:** To provide financial assistance to minority students from Washington state who are interested in careers in journalism.

**Eligibility:** Open to minority (Asian American, African American, Native American, and Latino) students from Washington state who are planning a career in broadcast, photo, or print journalism. Applicants may be high school seniors or college undergraduates who are residents of Washington state, although they may attend college anywhere in the country. Along with their application, they must submit 1) a brief essay about themselves, including why they want to be a journalist, challenges they foresee, how they think they can contribute to the profession, and the influence their ethnic heritage might have on their perspective as a working journalist; 2) the kinds of experience they are seeking from this fellowship and why they are a good candidate for it; 3) up to 3 work samples; 4) reference letters; and 5) documentation of financial need.

**Financial data:** Stipends range up to $1,000.

**Duration:** 1 year; may be renewed.

**Number awarded:** Varies each year; recently, 11 of these scholarships were awarded.

**Deadline:** April of each year.

### 1604 NPPF STILL PHOTOGRAPHER SCHOLARSHIP

National Press Photographers Foundation
3200 Croasdaile Drive, Suite 306
Durham, NC 27705-2586
Phone: (919) 383-7246; (800) 289-6772; Fax: (919) 383-7261;
Email: info@nppa.org
Web: www.nppa.org/professional_development/students/scholarships/still.html

**Summary:** To provide financial assistance to outstanding photojournalism students.

**Eligibility:** Open to students who have completed at least one year at a recognized 4-year college or university in the United States or Canada that offers courses in photojournalism, are working on a bachelor's degree, are intending to prepare for a career in journalism, and have at least half a year of undergraduate study remaining. These awards are aimed at those with journalism potential but with little opportunity and great need.

**Financial data:** The stipend is $1,000.

**Duration:** 1 year.

**Number awarded:** 1 each year.

**Deadline:** February of each year.

### 1605 NPPF TELEVISION NEWS SCHOLARSHIP

National Press Photographers Foundation
3200 Croasdaile Drive, Suite 306
Durham, NC 27705-2586
Phone: (919) 383-7246; (800) 289-6772; Fax: (919) 383-7261;
Email: info@nppa.org
Web: www.nppa.org/professional_development/students/scholarships/tv.html

**Summary:** To provide financial assistance to photojournalism students interested in a career in television news.

**Eligibility:** Open to students enrolled at a recognized 4-year college or university in the United States or Canada that offers courses in television news photojournalism who are working on a bachelor's degree as a junior or senior and intending to prepare for a career in television news photojournalism. As part of the selection process, they must submit a videotape containing examples of their work (including up to 3 complete stories with voice narration from their professor or advisor) and a 1-page biographical sketch that includes a personal statement on professional goals. Financial need and academic achievement are also considered.

**Financial data:** The stipend is $1,000.

**Duration:** 1 year.

**Number awarded:** 1 each year.

**Deadline:** February of each year.

### 1606 NSPA JOURNALISM HONOR ROLL AWARD

National Scholastic Press Association
2221 University Avenue, S.E., Suite 121
Minneapolis, MN 55414
Phone: (612) 625-8335; Fax: (612) 626-0720; Email: info@studentpress.org
Web: www.studentpress.org/nspa/contests.html

**Summary:** To recognize and reward outstanding high school journalists.

**Eligibility:** Open to high school seniors who have earned a GPA of 3.75 or higher and have worked in student media for 1 or more years. The publication on which the student works must have a current membership in the National Scholastic Press Association (NSPA). Candidates must be nominated by their teacher. The nominee judged most outstanding receives this award. Selection is based on cumulative GPA, publication experience (including years on staff, positions held, and workshops/conventions attended), college plans, and an essay of 500 words or less that explains "Why I'm choosing a career in journalism."

**Financial data:** The award is a $1,000 scholarship.

**Duration:** The competition is held annually.

**Number awarded:** 1 each year.

**Deadline:** February of each year.

### 1607 NYWICI FOUNDATION SCHOLARSHIPS

New York Women in Communications, Inc., Attn: NYWICI Foundation
355 Lexington Avenue, 17th Floor
New York, NY 10017-6603
Phone: (212) 297-2133; Fax: (212) 370-9047; Email: nywicipr@nywici.org
Web: www.nywici.org/foundation.scholarships.html

**Summary:** To provide financial assistance for college or graduate school to residents of designated eastern states who are interested in preparing for a career in the communications profession.

**Eligibility:** Open to 1) seniors graduating from high schools in the state of New York; 2) undergraduate students who are permanent residents of New York, New Jersey, Connecticut, or Pennsylvania; 3) graduate students who are permanent residents of New York, New Jersey, Connecticut, or Pennsylvania; and 4) current members of New York Women in Communications, Inc. (NYWICI) who are returning to school. Applicants must be majoring in a communications-related field (advertising, broadcasting, communications, journalism, marketing, new media, or public relations) and have a GPA of 3.5 or higher in their major and 3.0 overall. Along with their application, they must submit a resume that includes school and extracurricular activities, significant achievements, academic honors and awards, and community service work; a statement of their future goals in the communications profession; a 300- to 500-word personal essay describing how events in their lives have inspired them to achieve success and overcome difficulty in the face of any financial and/or other obstacles; 2 letters of recommendation; and an official transcript.

**Financial data:** The maximum stipend is $10,000.

**Duration:** 1 year.

**Number awarded:** 1 or more each year.

**Deadline:** January of each year.

### 1608 OHIO CLASSICAL CONFERENCE SCHOLARSHIP FOR THE STUDY OF LATIN

Ohio Classical Conference
c/o Amy J. Sawan, Scholarship Committee
Medina Senior High School
777 East Union Street
Medina, OH 44256
Phone: (330) 636-3200, ext. 3380; Email: LIAMOT@aol.com
Web: dept.kent.edu/mcls/classics/occ/scholarships.htm

**Summary:** To provide financial assistance to Ohio high school seniors planning to study Latin in college.

**Eligibility:** Open to seniors graduating from high schools in Ohio and entering a college or university in the United States. Applicants must be planning to study Latin, although they do not need to major in Latin or classics. They must submit an official high school transcript, 2 letters of recommendation (including 1 from their high school Latin teacher), and a 1-page statement on their reasons for studying Latin or the classics.

**Financial data:** The stipend is $1,500.

**Duration:** 1 year; nonrenewable.

**Number awarded:** 1 each year.

**Deadline:** March of each year.

### 1609 OHIO NEWSPAPERS FOUNDATION MINORITY SCHOLARSHIPS

Ohio Newspapers Foundation
1335 Dublin Road, Suite 216-B
Columbus, OH 43215-7038
Phone: (614) 486-6677; Fax: (614) 486-4940; Email: kpouliot@ohionews.org
Web: www.ohionews.org/scholarships.html

**Summary:** To provide financial assistance for college to minority high school seniors in Ohio planning to prepare for a career in journalism.

**Eligibility:** Open to high school seniors in Ohio who are members of minority groups (African American, Hispanic, Asian American, or American Indian) and planning to prepare for a career in newspaper journalism. Applicants must have a high school GPA of 2.5 or higher and demonstrate writing ability in an autobiography of 750 to 1,000 words that describes their academic and career interests, awards, extracurricular activities, and journalism-related activities.

**Financial data:** The stipend is $1,500.

**Duration:** 1 year; nonrenewable.

**Number awarded:** 3 each year.

**Deadline:** March of each year.

## 1610 OHIO NEWSPAPERS FOUNDATION UNIVERSITY JOURNALISM SCHOLARSHIP

Ohio Newspapers Foundation
1335 Dublin Road, Suite 216-B
Columbus, OH 43215-7038
Phone: (614) 486-6677; Fax: (614) 486-4940; Email: kpouliot@ohionews.org
Web: www.ohionews.org/scholarships.html
**Summary:** To provide financial assistance to students majoring in journalism at a college or university in Ohio.
**Eligibility:** Open to sophomores, juniors, and seniors at Ohio colleges and universities who are majoring in journalism and have a GPA of 2.5 or higher. Applicants must demonstrate the ability to write clearly in an autobiography of 750 to 1,000 words that describes their academic and career interests, awards, extracurricular activities, and journalism-related activities. Priority is given to students planning careers in newspaper or print journalism.
**Financial data:** The stipend is $1,500.
**Duration:** 1 year.
**Number awarded:** 1 each year.
**Deadline:** March of each year.

## 1611 OKLAHOMA ASSOCIATION OF BROADCASTERS SCHOLARSHIP AWARDS

Oklahoma Association of Broadcasters, Attn: OAB Education Foundation
6520 North Western, Suite 104
Oklahoma City, OK 73116
Phone: (405) 848-0771; Fax: (405) 848-0772; Email: info@oabok.org
Web: www.oabok.org/Careers/scholarships.html
**Summary:** To provide financial assistance to upper-division students majoring in broadcasting in Oklahoma.
**Eligibility:** Open to students enrolled at an Oklahoma college or university and majoring in broadcasting. They must be entering their junior or senior year, have earned at least a 3.0 GPA, be taking a full course load (at least 12 credits), and be planning to enter the broadcast industry upon graduation. Selection is based on financial need, achievements, industry goals, and extracurricular activities.
**Financial data:** The stipend is $1,000.
**Duration:** 1 year.
**Number awarded:** 7 each year.
**Deadline:** December of each year.

## 1612 OKLAHOMA CITY CHAPTER SCHOLARSHIPS

Association for Women in Communications-Oklahoma City Chapter
c/o Erin Brewer, President
United Way of Central Oklahoma
1315 North Broadway Place
Oklahoma City, OK 73103
Phone: (405) 236-8441, ext. 281; Email: ebrewer@unitedwayokc.org
Web: www.okcawc.org/student.htm
**Summary:** To provide financial assistance to women studying journalism or a related field in Oklahoma.
**Eligibility:** Open to women who are residents of Oklahoma working on a degree in communications, journalism, or a related field at a 2-year or 4-year college or university in the state. Applicants must submit a statement of 300 to 500 words explaining why they are applying for the scholarship, their plan for completing their education, the number of hours they plan to take each semester, proposed date of graduation, the school they have chosen and why, long-term career goals, and how they learned about the scholarship. Selection is based on aptitude, interest in preparing for a career in journalism or communications, academic achievement, community service, extracurricular activities, and financial need. Preference is given to student or professional members of the Association of Women in Communications.
**Financial data:** Stipends range from $500 to $1,500.
**Duration:** 1 year.
**Number awarded:** Varies each year; the total amount awarded ranges from $5,000 to $8,000 each year.
**Deadline:** March of each year.

## 1613 OREGON ASSOCIATION OF BROADCASTERS SCHOLARSHIPS

Oregon Association of Broadcasters, Attn: Scholarship Committee
7150 S.W. Hampton Street, Suite 214
Portland, OR 97223-8366

Phone: (503) 443-2299; Fax: (503) 443-2488; Email: theoab@theoab.org
Web: www.theoab.org/eduopps_foundation.html
**Summary:** To provide financial assistance to students in Oregon who are interested in majoring in broadcast-related fields in college.
**Eligibility:** Open to Oregon residents who are either enrolled or accepted for enrollment at a 2- or 4-year public or private college or university in the state. Applicants must be planning to enroll or be currently enrolled in a full-time undergraduate course of study, majoring in broadcast journalism, production, management, or another broadcast-related field. They must be graduating high school seniors, first- or second-year students in a 2-year program, or sophomores, juniors, or seniors in a 4-year program. Preference is given to applicants with at least a 3.0 cumulative GPA and demonstrated academic and/or professional experience in broadcasting or other electronic-media fields. Along with their application, students must submit an essay that explains their reasons for choosing a broadcast major and includes any broadcast activities in which they have participated, their first job preference after college, their 10-year goals, any other scholarships they have received, and any academic honors they have received. Financial need is not considered in the selection process.
**Financial data:** The stipend is $1,000.
**Duration:** 1 year.
**Number awarded:** 6 each year: 2 to graduating high school seniors and 4 to students currently enrolled in 2- or 4-year college broadcast programs.
**Deadline:** February of each year.

## 1614 ORNELAS ASSOCIATES MINORITY SCHOLARSHIP FUND

American Association of Advertising Agencies
Attn: Manager of Diversity Programs
405 Lexington Avenue, 18th Floor
New York, NY 10174-1801
Phone: (212) 682-2500; (800) 676-9333; Fax: (212) 682-8391;
Email: tiffany@aaaa.org
Web: www.aaaa.org/diversity/foundation/funds.htm
**Summary:** To provide financial assistance to Latino students who are working on an undergraduate or graduate degree in advertising.
**Eligibility:** Open to undergraduate and graduate students who are U.S. citizens of proven Latino heritage or at least one parent of Latino heritage. Applicants must have participated in the Multicultural Advertising Intern Program of the American Association of Advertising Agencies. Along with their application, they must submit an essay of 250 to 500 words on the topic: "As a Latino, I value ganas (passion), adelante (progress), Latino pride, and diversity by..." Selection is based on the essay, academic ability, and community involvement.
**Financial data:** The stipend is $5,000.
**Duration:** 1 year.
**Number awarded:** 1 each year.
**Deadline:** June of each year.

## 1615 OVERSEAS PRESS CLUB FOUNDATION SCHOLARSHIPS

Overseas Press Club, Attn: Director, Overseas Press Club Foundation
40 West 45th Street
New York, NY 10036
Phone: (212) 626-9220; Fax: (212) 626-9210;
Email: foundation@opcofamerica.org
Web: www.opcofamerica.org
**Summary:** To provide financial assistance to undergraduate and graduate students who are preparing for a career as a foreign correspondent.
**Eligibility:** Open to undergraduate and graduate students who are studying in the United States and are interested in working as a foreign correspondent after graduation. Applicants are invited to submit an essay (up to 500 words) on an area of the world or an international topic that is in keeping with their interest. Also, they should attach a 1-page autobiographical letter that addresses such questions as how they developed their interest in that particular part of the world or issue, how they would use a scholarship to further their journalistic ambitions, and how they think journalists can deepen American interest in international affairs.
**Financial data:** The stipend is $2,000.
**Duration:** 1 year.
**Number awarded:** 11 each year.
**Deadline:** November of each year.

## 1616 PACIFIC ISLANDERS IN COMMUNICATIONS SCHOLARSHIPS

Pacific Islanders in Communications
Attn: Scholarship Committee

1221 Kapi'olani Boulevard, Suite 6A-4
Honolulu, HI 96814-3513
Phone: (808) 591-0059; Fax: (808) 591-1114; Email: info@piccom.org
Web: www.piccom.org
**Summary:** To provide financial assistance to undergraduate and graduate students, especially Pacific Islanders, who are working on a degree in media and/or communications.
**Eligibility:** Open to students who are working on a degree, certificate, and/or other certification in media and/or communications at the undergraduate, graduate, or unclassified level of study. Applicants must be 18 years of age or older and citizens, legal permanent residents, or nationals of the United States or its territories. All students are eligible, but the program especially encourages applications from Pacific Islanders, defined as descendants of the indigenous peoples of American Samoa, Guam, Hawai'i, the Northern Mariana Islands, and other Pacific Islands. Along with their application, they must submit a 500-word essay on why they feel Pacific Islander representation in media is important and their role in advancing equitable representation; their essay should include their reasons for attending school, their career goals and how this education will further those goals, prior and current service to school and community (in particular the Pacific Islander community), and a personal and professional history. Selection is based on the essay; academic proficiency; demonstrated experience in media, communications, and/or a related field; commitment to the Pacific Islander community; and financial need.
**Financial data:** The stipend is $5,000.
**Duration:** 1 year; nonrenewable.
**Number awarded:** Varies each year.
**Deadline:** March of each year.

### 1617 PARTNERSHIP FOR EXCELLENCE UNDERGRADUATE FELLOWS PROGRAM

The Fund for Theological Education, Inc., Attn: Partnership for Excellence
825 Houston Mill Road, Suite 250
Atlanta, GA 30329
Phone: (404) 727-1450; Fax: (404) 727-1490; Email: fte@thefund.org
Web: www.thefund.org/programs/fellowships/undergrad/index.html
**Summary:** To provide financial assistance to undergraduate students who are considering the ministry as a career.
**Eligibility:** Open to rising juniors and seniors in accredited undergraduate programs at North American colleges and universities. Applicants must be considering ministry as a career. They must demonstrate a GPA of 3.0 or higher, a love of God and church, imagination, creativity, compassion, a capacity for critical thinking, leadership skills, personal integrity, spiritual depth, dedication to a faith tradition, and an ability to understand and to serve the needs of others. U.S. or Canadian citizenship is required.
**Financial data:** The stipend is $1,500 per year; travel expenses for participation in the summer conference and a mentoring stipend of $500 are also provided.
**Duration:** 1 year.
**Number awarded:** Up to 70 each year.
**Deadline:** February of each year.

### 1618 PAS/REMO, INC. FRED HOEY MEMORIAL SCHOLARSHIP

Percussive Arts Society
701 N.W. Ferris Avenue
Lawton, OK 73507-5442
Phone: (580) 353-1455; Fax: (580) 353-1456; Email: percarts@pas.org
Web: www.pas.org
**Summary:** To provide financial assistance for college to student members of the Percussive Arts Society (PAS).
**Eligibility:** Open to PAS members entering their freshman year in the school of music at an accredited college or university. Selection is based on a videotape, up to 3 minutes in length, of a percussion performance. The videotape should demonstrate the student's ability to play at least 2 different percussion instruments.
**Financial data:** The stipend is $1,000.
**Duration:** 1 year.
**Number awarded:** 1 each year.
**Deadline:** March of each year.

### 1619 PAS/SABIAN, LTD. LARRIE LONDIN MEMORIAL SCHOLARSHIP

Percussive Arts Society
701 N.W. Ferris Avenue

Lawton, OK 73507-5442
Phone: (580) 353-1455; Fax: (580) 353-1456; Email: percarts@pas.org
Web: www.pas.org
**Summary:** To provide financial assistance to young drummers interested in furthering their drumset studies.
**Eligibility:** Open to drummers in 2 categories: those 17 years of age and under and those from 18 to 24 years of age. Applicants must submit 1) a videotape, up to 3 minutes in length, that demonstrates their ability to perform different drumming styles; 2) an essay (from 100 to 200 words in length) on why they feel they qualify for a scholarship and how the money would be used (e.g., college, summer camp, private teacher); and 3) a supporting letter of recommendation verifying their age and school attendance. Financial need is not considered in the selection process.
**Financial data:** The stipend is $2,000 for students in the 18-24 age category or $1,000 for students under 17.
**Duration:** 1 year.
**Number awarded:** 2 each year: 1 in each age category.
**Deadline:** March of each year.

### 1620 PAUL AND HELEN L. GRAUER SCHOLARSHIP

American Radio Relay League, Attn: ARRL Foundation
225 Main Street
Newington, CT 06111
Phone: (860) 594-0397; Fax: (860) 594-0259; Email: foundation@arrl.org
Web: www.arrl.org/arrlf
**Summary:** To provide financial assistance to licensed radio amateurs who are interested in working on an undergraduate or graduate degree, particularly in electronics or communications.
**Eligibility:** Open to undergraduate or graduate students at accredited institutions who are licensed radio amateurs of the novice class or higher. Preference is given to students who are 1) residents of Iowa, Kansas, Missouri, or Nebraska and attending schools in those states, and 2) majoring in electronics, communications, or related fields. Applicants must submit an essay on the role amateur radio has played in their lives and provide documentation of financial need.
**Financial data:** The stipend is $1,000.
**Duration:** 1 year.
**Number awarded:** 1 each year.
**Deadline:** January of each year.

### 1621 PAULA VOGEL AWARD IN PLAYWRITING

John F. Kennedy Center for the Performing Arts
Education Department
Attn: Kennedy Center American College Theater Festival
2700 F Street, N.W.
Washington, DC 20566
Phone: (202) 416-8857; Fax: (202) 416-8802;
Email: skshaffer@kennedy-cen ter.org
Web: kennedy-center.org/education/actf/actf_vogel.html
**Summary:** To recognize and reward the student authors of plays that relate to tolerance of diversity.
**Eligibility:** Open to students at any accredited junior or senior college in the United States or in countries contiguous to the continental United States, provided their college agrees to participate in the Kennedy Center American College Theater Festival (KCACTF). Undergraduate students must be carrying at least 6 semester hours, graduate students must be enrolled in at least 3 semester hours, and continuing part-time students must be enrolled in a regular degree or certificate program. This award is presented to the best student-written script that celebrates diversity and encourages tolerance while exploring issues of disempowered voices not traditionally considered mainstream.
**Financial data:** The winning playwright receives a cash award of $2,500 and an all-expense paid weeklong residency Manhattan Theatre Source where the work receives a staged reading; the producing department receives a grant of $500. The second-place playwright receives a cash award of $1,000 and the producing department receives a grant of $250.
**Duration:** The award is presented annually.
**Number awarded:** 1 each year.
**Deadline:** November of each year.

### 1622 PEERMUSIC LATIN SCHOLARSHIP

Broadcast Music Inc.
Attn: BMI Foundation
320 West 57th Street

New York, NY 10019-3790

Phone: (212) 830-2537; Fax: (212) 246-2163; Email: info@bmifoundation.org

Web: www.bmifoundation.org/pages/peermusic.asp

**Summary:** To recognize and reward students at colleges and universities in selected states who submit outstanding songs or instrumental works in a Latin genre.

**Eligibility:** Open to students between 16 and 24 years of age enrolled at colleges and universities in California, Florida, Illinois, Massachusetts, New York, Puerto Rico, or Texas. Applicants may not have had any musical work commercially recorded or distributed. They must submit an original song or instrumental work in a Latin genre. The entry must be submitted on audiocassette or CD, accompanied by 3 typed copies of the lyric.

**Financial data:** The award is $5,000.

**Duration:** The award is presented annually.

**Number awarded:** 1 each year.

**Deadline:** January of each year.

## 1623 PENNSYLVANIA WOMEN'S PRESS ASSOCIATION SCHOLARSHIP

Pennsylvania Women's Press Association

c/o Teresa Spatara

P.O. Box 152

Sharpsville, PA 16150

Phone: (724) 962-0990

Web: www.pa-newspaper.org/pwpa/newscholarship.htm

**Summary:** To provide financial assistance to Pennsylvania residents interested in majoring in journalism on the undergraduate or graduate school level in the state.

**Eligibility:** Open to Pennsylvania residents who are majoring in print journalism in a 4-year or graduate program at a Pennsylvania college or university. Both males and females are eligible. They must be classified as a junior, senior, or graduate student. Applications must be accompanied by a 500-word essay summarizing their interest in journalism, a copy of their current transcript, clippings of their published work, and a list of their brothers and sisters, along with their ages and educational status. Selection is based on proven journalistic ability, dedication to journalism, and general merit; financial need is not considered.

**Financial data:** The stipend is $1,000.

**Duration:** 1 year.

**Number awarded:** 1 each year.

**Deadline:** April of each year.

## 1624 PETER AGRIS MEMORIAL SCHOLARSHIP

Alpha Omega Council

c/o Nancy Agris Savage

9 Nonesuch Drive

Natick, MA 01760

Email: info@alphaomegacouncil.com

Web: www.alphaomegacouncil.com/Scholarship.htm

**Summary:** To provide financial assistance to Greek American undergraduate and graduate students majoring in journalism or communications.

**Eligibility:** Open to undergraduate and graduate students of Greek American descent. Applicants must be enrolled full time as a journalism or communications major at an accredited college or university in the United States. They must be able to demonstrate financial need, a GPA of 3.0 or higher, and active participation in school, community, and church organizations.

**Financial data:** The stipend is $5,000.

**Duration:** 1 year; nonrenewable.

**Number awarded:** 1 each year.

**Deadline:** February of each year.

## 1625 PETER ROGOT MEDIA SCHOLARSHIPS

KCNC-TV News 4, Attn: Media Scholarship

1044 Lincoln Street

Denver, CO 80203

Phone: (303) 861-4444; Fax: (303) 830-6537; Email: mailroom@kcncnews4.com

Web: www.kcncnews4.com

**Summary:** To provide financial assistance to high school seniors in Colorado who are interested in majoring in communications in college.

**Eligibility:** Open to seniors graduating from high schools in Colorado who plan to attend college to major in broadcasting; newspaper, radio, or magazine journalism; advertising; public relations; or production in video, film, or photography. Applicants must have a GPA of 2.5 or higher and be able to demonstrate financial need. They must submit a paragraph explaining their educational and career goals.

**Financial data:** The stipend is $5,000. Funds are paid directly to the recipient's school. The money must be used for tuition or fees; it cannot be used for personal expenses.

**Duration:** 1 year.

**Number awarded:** 1 each year.

**Deadline:** March of each year.

## 1626 PHG FOUNDATION SCHOLARSHIP

Hawai'i Community Foundation, Attn: Scholarship Department

1164 Bishop Street, Suite 800

Honolulu, HI 96813

Phone: (808) 566-5570; (888) 731-3863; Fax: (808) 521-6286;

Email: scholarships@hcf-hawaii.org

Web: www.hawaiicommunityfoundation.org/scholar/scholar.php

**Summary:** To provide financial assistance to Hawaii residents who are interested in preparing for a career in the arts.

**Eligibility:** Open to Hawaii residents who are interested in majoring in art or arts and crafts (not video, film, culinary arts, or the performing arts). They may be studying full or part time, on the undergraduate or graduate school level. They must be able to demonstrate academic achievement (GPA of 2.7 or higher), good moral character, and financial need. In addition to filling out the standard application form, applicants must write a short statement indicating their reasons for attending college, their planned course of study, and their career goals.

**Financial data:** The amounts of the awards depend on the availability of funds and the need of the recipient; recently, stipends averaged $1,000.

**Duration:** 1 year.

**Number awarded:** Varies each year; recently, 5 of these scholarships were awarded.

**Deadline:** February of each year.

## 1627 PHILO T. FARNSWORTH SCHOLARSHIP

Broadcast Education Association, Attn: Scholarships

1771 N Street, N.W.

Washington, DC 20036-2891

Phone: (202) 429-5354; (888) 380-7222; Email: beainfo@beaweb.org

Web: www.beaweb.org/scholarships.html

**Summary:** To provide financial assistance to upper-division and graduate students who are interested in preparing for a career in broadcasting.

**Eligibility:** Open to juniors, seniors, and graduate students enrolled full time at a college or university where at least one department is an institutional member of the Broadcast Education Association (BEA). Applicants may be studying in any area of broadcasting. Selection is based on evidence that the applicant possesses high integrity, superior academic ability, potential to be an outstanding electronic media professional, and a sense of personal and professional responsibility.

**Financial data:** The stipend is $1,500.

**Duration:** 1 year; may not be renewed.

**Number awarded:** 1 each year.

**Deadline:** September of each year.

## 1628 POLISH ARTS CLUB OF BUFFALO SCHOLARSHIP

Polish Arts Club of Buffalo Inc., Attn: Anne Flansburg, Scholarship Chair

P.O. Box 1362

Williamsville, NY 14231-1362

Phone: (716) 626-9083

**Summary:** To provide financial assistance to New York residents of Polish background who are majoring in the visual or performing arts.

**Eligibility:** Open to legal residents of the state of New York who are of Polish background, at the junior level or above in college, and majoring in visual or performing arts. Applicants must submit a 300-word essay on a Polish artist, composer, or musician who has contributed to their field of study. Letters of recommendation are also required. Finalists are interviewed. Financial need is not considered in the selection process.

**Financial data:** The stipend is $1,000.

**Duration:** 1 year.

**Deadline:** May of each year.

## 1629 PRESS CLUB OF NEW ORLEANS JOURNALISM SCHOLARSHIP PROGRAM

Press Club of New Orleans, Attn: Scholarship Committee
203 Carondelet Street, Suite 415
New Orleans, LA 70130
Phone: (504) 523-1010; Email: pressclubneworleans@cox.net
Web: www.pressclubneworleans.org
**Summary:** To provide financial assistance to students in Louisiana who will be majoring in journalism.
**Eligibility:** Open to Louisiana residents who will be enrolled in university-level print or broadcast journalism programs during the upcoming academic year. Applicants must submit 1) a brief (1 to 3 pages) written statement outlining their course of study, career goals, and financial need, and 2) examples of their published work, including newspaper stories, tapes, columns, and/or editorials.
**Financial data:** A total of $5,000 is awarded each year.
**Duration:** 1 year.
**Number awarded:** 1 or more each year.
**Deadline:** April of each year.

## 1630 PRINTING INDUSTRY OF MINNESOTA SCHOLARSHIPS

Printing Industry of Minnesota, Attn: Education Foundation
2829 University Avenue S.E., Suite 750
Minneapolis, MN 55414-3222
Phone: (612) 379-3360; Fax: (612) 379-6030; Email: lelfrink@pimn.org
Web: www.pimn.org/scholarships.htm
**Summary:** To provide financial assistance to high school seniors and graduates in Minnesota who are interested in attending college to prepare for a career in the print communications industry.
**Eligibility:** Open to residents of Minnesota and children of individuals employed by a Minnesota graphic arts firm. Applicants must be high school seniors or graduates (including GED recipients) who have a high school GPA of 3.0 or higher and scores of 23 or higher on the ACT (or the SAT equivalent). They must have been admitted to a technical school, college, or university to work on a full-time degree or certificate in graphic arts. Preference is given to children of employees of companies that are members of the Printing Industry of Minnesota. Selection is based on academic achievement, extracurricular activities, honors and awards, demonstrated leadership ability, commitment to a career in the print communication industry, a statement of personal aspirations, and the neatness and clarity of the application.
**Financial data:** The stipend is $1,000 per year.
**Duration:** 1 year; may be renewed.
**Number awarded:** Varies each year.
**Deadline:** February of each year.

## 1631 PROFESSOR SIDNEY GROSS MEMORIAL AWARD

Public Relations Student Society of America, Attn: Director of Education
33 Irving Place, Third Floor
New York, NY 10003-2376
Phone: (212) 460-1474; Fax: (212) 995-0757; Email: prssa@prsa.org
Web: www.prssa.org/resources/award-SidneyGross.asp
**Summary:** To recognize and reward members of the Public Relations Student Society of America (PRSSA) who write outstanding essays on ethical principles.
**Eligibility:** Open to members of the society who are currently enrolled in a full-time program of study at an accredited 4-year college or university. Applicants are presented with a hypothetical scenario of a situation they might encounter as a public relations professional. They must submit a 1-page essay on their response to the situation. Selection is based on their essay's demonstrated understanding of ethical principals in public relations.
**Financial data:** The prize is $1,000.
**Duration:** The competition is held annually.
**Number awarded:** 1 each year.
**Deadline:** April of each year.

## 1632 PROJECT 21 NEVADA SCHOLARSHIP PROGRAM

Nevada Council on Problem Gambling, Attn: Scholarship Program
4340 South Valley View Boulevard, Suite 220
Las Vegas, NV 89103
Phone: (702) 369-9740; Fax: (702) 369-9765; Email: NevCouncil@aol.com
Web: www.nevadacouncil.org/programs/project21.html
**Summary:** To recognize and reward, with college scholarships, high school and college students in Nevada who create original posters, essays, or public service announcements alerting their peers to the risks and consequences of underage gambling.
**Eligibility:** Open to Nevada students under 21 years of age who are enrolled in a high school, vocational or trade school, college, or university. Applicants must create an original work that educates their peers and discourages participation in gambling activities by persons under 21 years of age. They must disseminate their message to their peers prior to submitting it for the competition. Entries may be submitted in the following categories: 1) essays between 350 and 500 words and printed in the school newspaper or other authorized publication during the first 3 months of the year; 2) posters on standard-sized poster board (22"x28") and displayed in a public area of the student's school or other authorized public area for at least 1 week during the first 3 months of the year 3) video public service announcement 30 seconds long in VHS format and viewed by at least 50 students in a public showing at the applicant's school or other authorized public forum during the first 3 months of the year; or 4) audio public service announcement 30 seconds long on audio cassette and heard by at least 50 students at an open announcement at the applicant's school or other authorized public forum during the first 3 months of the year. Selection is based on originality, content, style, and educational value. The applicant's economic status and academic GPA are not considered.
**Financial data:** The awards consist of $1,000 college scholarships.
**Duration:** The competition is held annually.
**Number awarded:** Varies each year; recently, 11 students received these awards.
**Deadline:** March of each year.

## 1633 PUBLIC RELATIONS STUDENT SOCIETY OF AMERICA MULTICULTURAL AFFAIRS SCHOLARSHIPS

Public Relations Student Society of America, Attn: Director of Education
33 Irving Place, Third Floor
New York, NY 10003-2376
Phone: (212) 460-1474; Fax: (212) 995-0757; Email: prssa@prsa.org
Web: www.prssa.org/resources/award-MulticulturalAffairs.asp
**Summary:** To provide financial assistance to minority college students who are interested in preparing for a career in public relations.
**Eligibility:** Open to minority (African American/Black, Hispanic/Latino, Asian, Native American, Alaskan Native, or Pacific Islander) students who are at least juniors at an accredited 4-year college or university. Applicants must be attending full time, be able to demonstrate financial need, and have earned a GPA of 3.0 or higher. Membership in the Public Relations Student Society of America is preferred but not required. A major or minor in public relations is preferred; students who attend a school that does not offer a public relations degree or program must be enrolled in a communications degree program (e.g., journalism, mass communications).
**Financial data:** The stipend is $1,500.
**Duration:** 1 year.
**Number awarded:** 2 each year.
**Deadline:** April of each year.

## 1634 QUARTON-MCELROY/IOWA BROADCASTERS ASSOCIATION BROADCAST SCHOLARSHIPS

Iowa Broadcasters Association
P.O. Box 71186
Des Moines, IA 50325
Phone: (515) 224-7237; Fax: (515) 224-6560; Email: iowaiba@dwx.com
Web: www.iowabroadcasters.com
**Summary:** To provide financial assistance to high school seniors in Iowa who are interested in preparing for a career in broadcasting.
**Eligibility:** Open to students graduating from a high school in Iowa and planning to enroll full time in a 2- or 4-year college or university in the state. They must be planning to prepare for a career in the broadcasting field, including technical, telecommunicative arts broadcast production, or broadcast journalism. Along with their application, they must submit a 1- to 3-page letter on "Why I'm Interested in a Career in Broadcasting," including an analysis of their skills, interests, and work-related experience that would contribute to a career in broadcasting; their thoughts about the need for a college education to help them reach their career goals; and the importance of receiving this scholarship. Selection is based on the essay, academic record (as indicated by their high school transcripts and ACT or SAT scores), honors and/or awards, extracurricular activities, work experience and/or internships, and financial need.
**Financial data:** The stipend is $3,000 per year.
**Duration:** 4 years.
**Number awarded:** 5 each year.
**Deadline:** March of each year.

### 1635 R. QUINN PUGH EDUCATIONAL SCHOLARSHIP

Baptist Convention of New York, Attn: Church Growth Division
6538 Baptist Way
East Syracuse, NY 13057
Phone: (315) 433-1001; (800) 552-0004; Fax: (315) 433-1026;
Email: vmcquitty@bcnysbc.org
Web: www.bcnysbc.org/church_growth/scholarships.htm

**Summary:** To provide financial assistance to members of churches in the Baptist Convention of New York who are preparing for a vocation in full-time Christian service.

**Eligibility:** Open to high school seniors who are members in good standing of churches in the Baptist Convention of New York. Applicants must be interested in attending a postsecondary institution to prepare for a career in full-time Christian service. They must submit an essay in which they share their goals for the future and how a degree in higher education will help them achieve those goals. Financial need is also considered in the selection process.

**Financial data:** A stipend is awarded (amount not specified).

**Duration:** 1 year; may be renewed as long as the recipient maintains full-time enrollment and a GPA of 2.0 or higher.

**Number awarded:** 1 or more each year.

**Deadline:** February of each year.

### 1636 RADIO-TELEVISION JOURNALISM DIVISION PRIZES

Association for Education in Journalism and Mass Communication
Attn: Radio-Television Journalism Division
234 Outlet Pointe Boulevard, Suite A
Columbia, SC 29210-5667
Phone: (803) 798-0271; Fax: (803) 772-3509; Email: aejmc@aejmc.org
Web: www.aejmc.org

**Summary:** To recognize and reward outstanding student and faculty papers on broadcast journalism.

**Eligibility:** Open to faculty members and students who are interested in submitting research papers on an aspect of broadcast journalism or electronic communication with a journalism emphasis. A variety of methodological approaches are welcome. Papers are to be no more than 25 pages in length and must have been written during the past year.

**Financial data:** Cash prizes are awarded.

**Duration:** The competition is held annually.

**Number awarded:** 2 each year: 1 to a student and 1 to a faculty member.

**Deadline:** March of each year.

### 1637 RAIN BIRD SCHOLARSHIP

Landscape Architecture Foundation, Attn: Scholarship Program
818 18th Street, N.W., Suite 810
Washington, DC 20006-3520
Phone: (202) 331-7070; Fax: (202) 331-7079; Email: rfigura@lafoundation.org
Web: www.laprofession.org

**Summary:** To provide financial assistance to landscape architecture students who are in need of financial assistance.

**Eligibility:** Open to landscape architecture students in the final 2 years of undergraduate study and in need of financial assistance. Applicants must submit a 300-word essay describing their career goals and explaining how they will contribute to the advancement of the profession of landscape architecture. Selection is based on demonstrated commitment to the profession, extracurricular activities, and scholastic record.

**Financial data:** The award is $1,000.

**Number awarded:** 1 each year.

**Deadline:** April of each year.

### 1638 RALPH WALDO EMERSON PRIZES

Concord Review, Attn: Editor
730 Boston Post Road, Suite 24
Sudbury, MA 01776
Phone: (978) 443-0022; (800) 331-5007; Email: fitzhugh@tcr.org
Web: www.tcr.org/tcr/emerson.htm

**Summary:** To recognize and reward outstanding historical essays written by high school seniors in any country.

**Eligibility:** Open to high school students from any country. They are invited to submit historical essays to the *Concord Review,* the first and only quarterly journal in the world that publishes essays written by high school students from any country. Essays should be around 5,000 words, on any historical topic.

**Financial data:** The prize is $3,000.

**Duration:** The prizes are awarded annually.

**Number awarded:** 5 each year.

### 1639 RAYMOND E. PAGE SCHOLARSHIP

Landscape Architecture Foundation, Attn: Scholarship Program
818 18th Street, N.W., Suite 810
Washington, DC 20006-3520
Phone: (202) 331-7070; Fax: (202) 331-7079; Email: rfigura@lafoundation.org
Web: www.laprofession.org

**Summary:** To provide financial assistance to needy undergraduate landscape architecture students.

**Eligibility:** Open to undergraduate students in need of financial assistance who are majoring in landscape architecture. Applicants should submit a 2-page essay describing their need for financial assistance and a letter of recommendation from a current professor who is familiar with their character and goals in pursuing an education in landscape architecture.

**Financial data:** The stipend is $1,000.

**Duration:** 1 year.

**Number awarded:** 1 each year.

**Deadline:** April of each year.

### 1640 RAYMOND ROBERT WHITE MEMORIAL SCHOLARSHIP

Glenside/Abington United Methodist Church
Attn: Scholarship Selection Committee
137 North Easton Road
Glenside, PA 19038
Phone: (215) 884-5251; Fax: (215) 884-0402; Email: gaumc1@juno.com
Web: www.gbgm-umc.org/glenside-abington/index.htm

**Summary:** To provide financial assistance for college to members of the United Methodist Church who are interested in a church-related career.

**Eligibility:** Open to members of the United Methodist Church who are enrolled or planning to enroll in an accredited college or university. Preference is given to students at United Methodist controlled or oriented institutions. Applicants must be preparing for a career as a United Methodist minister, youth director, Christian education director, or missionary. They must be able to demonstrate evidence of leadership and Christian moral character. Beginning freshmen must be graduating in the top 50% of their high school class; current college students must have a GPA of 3.0 or higher.

**Financial data:** The stipend is $2,500 per year.

**Duration:** 1 year; may be renewed up to 2 additional years.

**Number awarded:** 1 or more each year.

**Deadline:** February of each year.

### 1641 R.C. WILLEY/PENTAX "SCHOLARSHIPS IN A SNAP" CONTEST

Utah Education Association, Attn: Director of Public Relations
875 East 5180 South
Murray, UT 84107
Phone: (801) 266-4461; (800) 594-8996; Fax: (801) 265-2249
Web: www.utea.org

**Summary:** To recognize and reward high school students in Utah who submit outstanding photographs.

**Eligibility:** Open to students at high schools in Utah who submit an example of their photographic work. Entries are accepted in 5 categories: landscapes, people, wildlife, sports, and general.

**Financial data:** The prize is $1,000. Funds are paid directly to the student's university or college of choice.

**Duration:** Prizes are presented annually.

**Number awarded:** 5 each year: 1 in each category.

**Deadline:** May of each year.

### 1642 RDW GROUP, INC. MINORITY SCHOLARSHIP FOR COMMUNICATIONS

Rhode Island Foundation, Attn: Scholarship Coordinator
One Union Station
Providence, RI 02903
Phone: (401) 274-4564; Fax: (401) 751-7983; Email: libbym@rifoundation.org
Web: www.rifoundation.org

**Summary:** To provide financial assistance to Rhode Island students of color interested in preparing for a career in communications.

**Eligibility:** Open to minority undergraduate and graduate students who are Rhode Island residents. Applicants must intend to major in communications (including computer graphics, art, cinematography, or other fields that would prepare them for a career in advertising). They must be able to demonstrate financial need and a commitment to a career in communications. Along with their application, they must submit an essay (up to 300 words) on the impact they would like to have on the communications field.

**Financial data:** The stipend is $2,000.

**Duration:** 1 year; nonrenewable.

**Number awarded:** 1 each year.

**Deadline:** April of each year.

## 1643 REACHING COMMON GROUND ESSAY CONTEST

Reaching Common Ground
c/o Institute for Christian and Jewish Studies
1316 Park Avenue
Baltimore, MD 21217
Phone: (410) 523-7227; Fax: (410) 523-0636;
Email: essay@reachingcommonground.com
Web: www.reachingcommonground.com

**Summary:** To recognize and reward students who submit outstanding essays on interfaith dialogue between Christians and Jews.

**Eligibility:** Open to all students between 16 and 22 years of age in the United States. Applicants must submit an essay, up to 2,500 words in length, on one of 3 assigned topics. The topics involve faith and the Bible, history, or current events and stress the common ground between Christians and Jews. Selection is based on ability to represent accurately multiple points of view (35%), range and depth of knowledge as demonstrated in the essay (30%), creativity (20%), and literary merit (15%).

**Financial data:** Prizes are $25,000 for first, $10,000 for second, $5,000 for third, and $1,000 for fourth.

**Duration:** The competition is held annually.

**Number awarded:** 27 each year: 1 first prize, 1 second prize, 10 third prizes, and 15 fourth prizes.

**Deadline:** July of each year.

## 1644 REID BLACKBURN SCHOLARSHIP

National Press Photographers Foundation
3200 Croasdaile Drive, Suite 306
Durham, NC 27705-2586
Phone: (919) 383-7246; (800) 289-6772; Fax: (919) 383-7261;
Email: info@nppa.org
Web: www.nppa.org/professional_development/students/scholarships/blackburn.html

**Summary:** To provide financial assistance to college students who are interested in preparing for a career in photojournalism.

**Eligibility:** Open to students who have completed at least one year at a recognized 4-year college or university in the United States or Canada that offers courses in photojournalism, are working on a bachelor's degree, are intending to prepare for a career in journalism, and have at least half a year of undergraduate study remaining. A statement of philosophy and goals is especially important in the selection process, although financial need and academic achievement are also considered.

**Financial data:** The stipend is $1,000 per year.

**Duration:** 1 year; nonrenewable.

**Number awarded:** 1 each year.

**Deadline:** February of each year.

## 1645 REV. BEVERLY E. BOND MEMORIAL SCHOLARSHIP

Jefferson United Methodist Church, Attn: Bond Memorial Scholarship
10328 Jefferson Highway
Baton Rouge, LA 70809
Phone: (225) 293-4440; Fax: (225) 293-6821; Email: staff@jeffersononline.org
Web: www.jeffersononline.org

**Summary:** To provide financial assistance to Methodists in Louisiana who are preparing for a career as a minister, Christian educator, missionary, or other Christian service professional.

**Eligibility:** Open to members of United Methodist churches in Louisiana who are enrolled or planning to enroll at an accredited college or university supported by the United Methodist Church. Applicants must be planning or currently studying to become a minister, Christian educator, missionary, or other Christian service professional.

**Financial data:** A stipend is awarded (amount not specified).

**Duration:** 1 year.

**Number awarded:** Varies each year.

**Deadline:** April of each year.

## 1646 RHODA D. HOOD MEMORIAL SCHOLARSHIP

Northwest Baptist Convention, Attn: Woman's Missionary Union
3200 N.E. 109th Avenue
Vancouver, WA 98682
Phone: (360) 882-2100; Fax: (360) 882-2295
Web: www.nwbaptist.org

**Summary:** To provide financial assistance for college or seminary to women from the Northwest who are preparing for a career in vocational ministry, preferably with a Southern Baptist Convention church.

**Eligibility:** Open to women who have been active members of a church affiliated with the Northwest Baptist Convention and a member of the Woman's Missionary Union within their church. Special consideration is given to children of ministers from the Northwest. Applicants must be attending or planning to attend an accredited college, university, or Southern Baptist seminary with the intention of serving in a vocational ministry position through a church or denomination; priority is given to applicants going into a mission vocation affiliated with the Southern Baptist Convention. Along with their application, they must submit 1) a written account of their conversion experience and their call to vocational ministry; and 2) a written endorsement from their church.

**Financial data:** A stipend is awarded (amount not specified).

**Duration:** 1 year; may be renewed if a 2.5 GPA or higher is maintained.

**Number awarded:** 1 or more each year.

**Deadline:** May of each year for fall term; October of each year for spring term.

## 1647 RIAHPERD SCHOLARSHIPS

Rhode Island Association for Health, Physical Education, Recreation and Dance c/o Gab Wynne
17 Blossom Court
Warwick, RI 02886
Web: www.riahperd.org/scholarshipapplication.html

**Summary:** To provide financial assistance for college to Rhode Island residents who are interested in preparing for a career in health education, physical education, recreation, or dance.

**Eligibility:** Open to residents of Rhode Island who are high school seniors or current undergraduate students. Applicants must be planning to enter the fields of health education, physical education, recreation, or dance; health-related programs such as nursing, pre-medicine, physical therapy, and occupational therapy do not qualify. Along with their application, they must submit 1) a personal letter on their philosophy of physical activity and wellness, awards and recognitions received, contributions to their community, and career goals; 2) high school or college transcripts; and 3) 3 letters of recommendation.

**Financial data:** The stipend is $2,000.

**Duration:** 1 year.

**Number awarded:** 1 or more each year.

**Deadline:** June of each year.

## 1648 RICHARD S. SMITH SCHOLARSHIP

United Methodist Church, Attn: Division on Ministries with Young People
P.O. Box 340003
Nashville, TN 37203-0003
Phone: (615) 340-7184; (877) 899-2780, ext. 7184; Fax: (615) 340-1764;
Email: umyouthorg@gbod.org
Web: www.umyouth.org/scholarships.html

**Summary:** To provide financial assistance to minority high school seniors who wish to prepare for a Methodist church-related career.

**Eligibility:** Open to graduating high school seniors who are members of racial/ethnic minority groups and have been active members of a United Methodist church for at least one year. Applicants must have been admitted to an accredited college or university to prepare for a church-related career. They must have maintained at least a C average throughout high school and be able to demonstrate financial need. Along with their application, they must submit brief essays on their participation in church projects and activities, a leadership experience, the role their faith plays in their life, the church-related vocation to which God is calling them, and their extracurricular interests and activities. U.S. citizenship or permanent resident status is required.

**Financial data:** The stipend is $1,000.

**Duration:** 1 year; nonrenewable.
**Number awarded:** 2 each year.
**Deadline:** May of each year.

## 1649 R.L. GILLETTE SCHOLARSHIPS

American Foundation for the Blind, Attn: Scholarship Committee
11 Penn Plaza, Suite 300
New York, NY 10001
Phone: (212) 502-7661; (800) AFB-LINE; Fax: (212) 502-7771; TDD: (212) 502-7662; Email: afbinfo@afb.net
Web: www.afb.org/scholarships.asp
**Summary:** To provide financial assistance to legally blind undergraduate women who are studying literature or music.
**Eligibility:** Open to women who are legally blind, U.S. citizens, and enrolled in a 4-year baccalaureate degree program in literature or music. Along with their application, they must submit an essay that includes the field of study they are pursuing and why they have chosen it; their educational and personal goals; their work experience; any extracurricular activities with which they have been involved, including those in school, religious organizations, and the community; and how they intend to use scholarship monies that may be awarded. They must also submit a sample performance tape (not to exceed 30 minutes) or a creative writing sample.
**Financial data:** The stipend is $1,000.
**Duration:** 1 academic year.
**Number awarded:** 2 each year.
**Deadline:** April of each year.

## 1650 ROLLING STONE COLLEGE JOURNALISM COMPETITION

Rolling Stone magazine, Attn: College Journalism Competition
1290 Avenue of the Americas, Second Floor
New York, NY 10104-0298
Phone: (212) 484-1636; Email: kerry.smith@rollingstone.com
Web: www.rollingstone.com
**Summary:** To recognize and reward outstanding articles published in college newspapers or magazines on popular entertainment or other subjects.
**Eligibility:** Open to students writers who submit entries in any of the following 3 categories: entertainment reporting (reporting on popular music, film, or television, including artist profiles and interviews), feature writing (stylishly-written narratives and profiles that illuminate issues and trends), or essays and criticism (commentary, including expressions of opinion and humor, on any subject). All entries must have been published in a student newspaper or magazine during the previous year; the author must have been a college student (full or part time) at the time the item was published. Students may enter in more than 1 category, but they are limited to one entry per category. Tear sheets (from the original newspaper or magazine) must be provided. The submissions are judged by the editors of *Rolling Stone*.
**Financial data:** The prize is $2,500.
**Duration:** The competition is held annually.
**Number awarded:** 3 each year: 1 in each of the categories.
**Deadline:** October of each year.

## 1651 RON AUTRY SCHOLARSHIP

Community Foundation for Greater Atlanta, Inc.
50 Hurt Plaza, Suite 449
Atlanta, GA 30303
Phone: (404) 688-5525; Fax: (404) 688-3060; Email: vweekes@atlcf.org
Web: www.atlcf.org/GrantsScholarships/Scholarships/RonAutry.aspx
**Summary:** To provide financial assistance to Georgia residents who are majoring in journalism at a 4-year college or university.
**Eligibility:** Open to legal residents of Georgia who are enrolled as a junior or senior at a college or university and preparing for a career in journalism or the newspaper industry (news, advertising, circulation, or human resources). Applicants must be enrolled full time, have a GPA of 2.0 or higher and be able to demonstrate financial need. Along with their application, they must submit a 500-word essay on a topic that changes annually; recently, applicants were invited to write on the topic: "What has been the impact of the Jayson Blair scandal on Black journalists and what should be done to avoid plagiarism?"
**Financial data:** The maximum stipend is $2,000 per year.
**Duration:** 1 year.
**Number awarded:** 1 each year.
**Deadline:** March of each year.

## 1652 ROY HOWARD NATIONAL REPORTING COMPETITION AND SEMINAR

Scripps Howard Foundation, Attn: Vickie Martin
312 Walnut Street, 28th Floor
P.O. Box 5380
Cincinnati, OH 45201
Phone: (513) 977-3034; Fax: (513) 977-3800; Email: vlmartin@scripps.com
Web: www.scripps.com/foundation
**Summary:** To recognize and reward outstanding college journalism students.
**Eligibility:** Open to undergraduate journalism students in their freshman, sophomore, or junior year. They must be nominated by their college, which must submit a story or series written by the nominee involving coverage of campus or community events, issues, trends, or personalities. Entries must have been published in a student newspaper between the first of March of the previous year and the end of February of the current year. They should reflect in-depth enterprise reporting in words or in photo essays that have an impact on the campus or community. Routine coverage of events and meetings, editorials, and commentaries are not eligible. Each college or university may nominate up to 3 students.
**Financial data:** First-place winners receive $3,000 scholarships, runners-up receive $2,000 scholarships, and honorable mentions receive $1,000 scholarships. All finalists also receive an all-expense paid trip to Indiana University for a seminar with journalism professionals and to attend the Roy W. Howard Lecture. Student newspapers of the winners each receive $1,000 grants, of the runners-up $750 grants, and of the honorable mentions $500 grants.
**Duration:** The competition is held annually.
**Number awarded:** 9 finalists are selected each year. Of those, 3 are designated as first-place winners, 3 as runners-up, and 3 as honorable mentions.
**Deadline:** April of each year.

## 1653 RUSSELL W. MYERS SCHOLARSHIP

Morris Land Conservancy, Attn: Scholarship Fund
19 Boonton Avenue
Boonton, NJ 07005
Phone: (973) 541-1010; Fax: (973) 541-1131;
Email: info@morrislandconservancy.org
Web: www.morrislandconservancy.org/Scholarship.html
**Summary:** To provide financial assistance to undergraduate and graduate students from New Jersey who are working on a degree in an environmental field.
**Eligibility:** Open to New Jersey residents who have completed at least 15 credits at a college or university offering a degree in environmental science, natural resource management, conservation, horticulture, park administration, or a related field. Applicants must have a cumulative GPA of 3.0 or higher. They must be considering a career in New Jersey in an environmental field. Along with their application, they must submit a 500-word essay on their career goals and how those will advance the effort of open space preservation, public education, or public recreation. Financial need is not considered in the selection process.
**Financial data:** The stipend is $5,000.
**Duration:** 1 year.
**Number awarded:** Several each year.
**Deadline:** March of each year.

## 1654 RUTH CLARK SCHOLARSHIP

International Furnishings and Design Association
Attn: IFDA Educational Foundation
330 Ferry Landing
Atlanta, GA 30328
Phone: (770) 612-0454; Fax: (770) 612-0445; Email: info@ifdaef.org
Web: www.ifdaef.org/scholarships.html
**Summary:** To provide financial assistance to undergraduate students pursuing degrees in residential furniture design.
**Eligibility:** Open to full-time undergraduate students enrolled in a design program at an accredited college or design school with a focus on residential furniture design. Applicants must have completed at least one year of postsecondary education with at least one semester of furniture design projects. They must submit 1) a 200-word essay on their future plans and goals and why they believe they deserve the scholarship; 2) at least 5 examples of their original designs; 3) a short description of each illustration; 4) an official college transcript; and 5) a letter of recommendation from a professor or instructor. Financial need is not considered.
**Financial data:** The stipend is $1,500.
**Duration:** 1 year.
**Number awarded:** 1 each year.
**Deadline:** March of each year.

## 1655 RUTH JACOBS MEMORIAL SCHOLARSHIP

Choristers Guild
Attn: Scholarship Fund
2834 West Kingsley Road
Garland, TX 75041-2498
Phone: (972) 271-1521, ext. 232; Fax: (972) 840-3113;
Email: Scholarships@choristersguild.org
Web: www.choristersguild.org
**Summary:** To provide financial assistance to upper-division and graduate students majoring in church music.
**Eligibility:** Open to juniors, seniors, and graduate students working full time on a degree in church music. Applicants must demonstrate an interest in working with children's and youth choir programs.
**Financial data:** The maximum stipend is $1,000.
**Duration:** 1 year.
**Number awarded:** 1 or more each year.

## 1656 RUTH LILLY POETRY FELLOWSHIPS

Poetry Magazine, Attn: Poetry Foundation
1030 North Clark Street
Chicago, IL 60610-5412
Phone: (312) 787-7070; Fax: (312) 787-6650; Email: mail@poetryfoundation.org
Web: www.poetryfoundation.org/prizes_fellowship.html
**Summary:** To provide financial assistance to undergraduate and graduate students who are studying poetry.
**Eligibility:** Open to undergraduate and graduate students in creative writing or English who have not yet received a master's or doctoral degree. Program directors and department chairs at colleges and universities in the United States are invited to nominate one student-poet from their program. Candidates must be younger than 31 years of age and may not have published a book of poems. Nominations must be accompanied by samples of the candidate's poetry.
**Financial data:** The stipend is $15,000 per year.
**Duration:** 1 year.
**Number awarded:** 2 each year.
**Deadline:** April of each year.

## 1657 R.V. "GADABOUT" GADDIS CHARITABLE FUND

Maine Community Foundation, Attn: Program Director
245 Main Street
Ellsworth, ME 04605
Phone: (207) 667-9735; (877) 700-6800; Fax: (207) 667-0447;
Email: info@mainecf.org
Web: www.mainecf.org/html/scholarships/index.html
**Summary:** To provide financial assistance to Maine students interested in the study of outdoor/nature writing.
**Eligibility:** Open to residents of Maine who are college juniors or seniors studying outdoor writing or a related environmental field. Applicants must include a writing sample, up to 10 pages in length, that demonstrates their skill at writing about the "outdoors," including outdoor sports, environmental concerns, and natural history topics.
**Financial data:** The stipend is $1,000 per year.
**Duration:** 1 year.
**Number awarded:** 2 each year.
**Deadline:** March of each year.

## 1658 SALLY HEET MEMORIAL SCHOLARSHIP

Public Relations Society of America-Puget Sound Chapter
c/o Diane Beins
1006 Industry Drive
Seattle, WA 98188-4801
Phone: (206) 623-8632; Email: prsascholarship@asi-seattle.net
Web: www.prsapugetsound.org/heet
**Summary:** To provide financial assistance to upper-classmen in Washington who are interested in preparing for a career in public relations.
**Eligibility:** Open to U.S. citizens who are enrolled as juniors or seniors at colleges and universities in Washington. Applicants must be preparing for a career in public relations. They must be able to demonstrate aptitude in public relations and related courses, activities, and/or internships. Along with their application, they must submit a description of their career goals and the skills that are most important in general to a public relations career (20 points in the selection process); a description of their activities in communications in class, on campus, in the community, or during internships, including 3 samples of their work (30 points); a statement on the value of public relations to an organization (10 points); a certified transcript (20 points); and 2 or more letters of recommendation (20 points).
**Financial data:** The stipend is $2,500.
**Duration:** 1 year.
**Number awarded:** 1 each year.
**Deadline:** March of each year.

## 1659 SAM PINE SCHOLARSHIP

Connecticut Chapter of the American Planning Association
c/o Alan L. Weiner, Member Services Committee
City Planner, City of Bristol
111 North Main Street
Bristol, CT 06010
Phone: (860) 584-6225; Fax: (860) 584-3838; Email: alanweiner@ci.bristol.ct.us
Web: www.ccapa.org
**Summary:** To provide financial assistance to undergraduate students in planning or architecture at schools in New England and New York.
**Eligibility:** Open to undergraduate students in planning, architecture or a related field. Applicants must be attending a college or university in New England or New York. Selection is based, first, on financial need and then on academic record.
**Financial data:** The stipend is $2,000.
**Duration:** 1 year.
**Number awarded:** 1 each year.

## 1660 SAMUEL ROBINSON AWARD

Presbyterian Church (USA), Attn: Office of Financial Aid for Studies
100 Witherspoon Street, Room M-052
Louisville, KY 40202-1396
Phone: (502) 569-5745; (888) 728-7228, ext. 5745; Fax: (502) 569-8766;
Email: KSmith@ctr.pcusa.org
Web: www.pcusa.org/financialaid/programfinder/sam.htm
**Summary:** To recognize and reward students in Presbyterian colleges who write essays on religious topics.
**Eligibility:** Open to juniors and seniors enrolled full time in one of the 68 colleges related to the Presbyterian Church (USA). Applicants must successfully recite the answers to the Westminster Shorter Catechism and write a 2,000-word original essay on an assigned topic related to the Shorter Catechism.
**Financial data:** Awards range from $200 to $1,000.
**Duration:** 1 year; nonrenewable.
**Number awarded:** 1 each year.
**Deadline:** March of each year.

## 1661 SAN ANTONIO CHAPTER NAWIC SCHOLARSHIP

National Association of Women in Construction-San Antonio Chapter 11
c/o Deborah L. Schievelbein, Scholarship Chair
405 North St. Mary's Street, Suite 150
San Antonio, TX 78205
Phone: (210) 476-0400; Email: dbdrumm@world-net.net
Web: www.nawicsat.org
**Summary:** To provide financial assistance to students in Texas working on an undergraduate degree in a construction-related field.
**Eligibility:** Open to full-time students who are residents of Texas and undergraduates attending a college or university in the state. Applicants must be majoring in a field related to construction (e.g., architecture, engineering, construction management). They must have a GPA of 3.0 or higher. Previous recipient are given priority in the selection process.
**Financial data:** A stipend is awarded (amount not specified). Funds are paid directly to the recipient's college or university.
**Duration:** 1 year; may be renewed.
**Number awarded:** 1 or more each year.
**Deadline:** January of each year.

## 1662 SARAH SOULE PATTON SCHOLARSHIP

Daughters of the American Revolution-Washington State Society
c/o Margaret Hamby, State Scholarship Chair
1307 144th Avenue, N.E.
Bellevue, WA 98007

Email: marghamby@msn.com

Web: www.rootsweb.com/~wassdar/scholars.html

**Summary:** To provide financial assistance to American history majors entering their senior year at designated universities in Washington.

**Eligibility:** Open to students entering their senior year at Washington State University, Whitman College, St. Martin University, Pacific Lutheran University, University of Puget Sound, Gonzaga University, Whitworth College, Eastern Washington University, Seattle Pacific University, University of Washington, Western Washington University, Central Washington University, and Seattle University. Applicants must be majoring in American history, U.S. citizens, able to demonstrate financial need and good character, and recommended by the financial aid office at their college or university.

**Financial data:** The stipend is $2,000.

**Duration:** 1 year.

**Number awarded:** 1 each year.

**Deadline:** January of each year.

## 1663 SCHOLARSHIPS IN TECHNICAL COMMUNICATION

Society for Technical Communication

901 North Stuart Street, Suite 904

Arlington, VA 22203-1822

Phone: (703) 522-4114; Fax: (703) 522-2075; Email: stc@stc.org

Web: www.stc.org/scholarshipInfo_national.asp

**Summary:** To provide financial assistance to undergraduate and graduate students who are preparing for a career in some area of technical communications.

**Eligibility:** Open to 1) full-time undergraduate students working on a bachelor's degree in technical communications who have completed at least 1 year of college and 2) full-time graduate students working on a master's or doctoral degree in technical communications. Applicants must be studying communication of information about technical subjects; other majors, such as general journalism, electronic communication engineering, computer programming, entertainment, and creative writing are not eligible. Selection is based on academic record, experience with technical communication, and potential for contributing to the profession; financial need is not considered unless applicants are judged to be equal in all other respects.

**Financial data:** The stipend is $1,000; funds are paid to the school for the benefit of the recipient.

**Duration:** 1 year.

**Number awarded:** 4 each year: 2 to undergraduate students and 2 to graduate students.

**Deadline:** February of each year.

## 1664 SCHOLASTIC ART AWARDS

Scholastic, Inc., Attn: Alliance for Young Artists & Writers, Inc.

557 Broadway

New York, NY 10012

Phone: (212) 343-6493; Fax: (212) 343-4885;

Email: A&WGeneralInfo@scho lastic.com

Web: www.scholastic.com

**Summary:** To recognize and reward outstanding middle school and high school artists and photographers.

**Eligibility:** Open to students in grades 7-12 who are currently enrolled in public and private schools in the United States, U.S. territories, or Canada or in U.S.-sponsored schools abroad. Categories include animation, ceramics and glass, computer art, design (apparel, graphics, installation/environmental, jewelry, plans/models/illustrations, and product), digital imagery, drawing, mixed media, painting, photography, printmaking, sculpture, and video and film. Participants who are graduating seniors planning to attend college may submit an art portfolio of 8 works, including at least 3 drawings, or a photography portfolio of 8 works.

**Financial data:** The Portfolio Gold Awards are $10,000 scholarships. In addition, teachers of the Portfolio Gold Award winners receive Portfolio Teacher Awards of $1,000. The teacher who submits the most outstanding group of entries in any category receives the Gold Apple Teacher Award of $500.

**Number awarded:** 4 Art Portfolio Gold Awards and 2 Photography Portfolio Gold Awards are presented each year. The teachers of those 6 winners receive Portfolio Teacher Awards. The Gold Apple Teacher Award is presented to one teacher.

**Deadline:** February of each year.

## 1665 SCHOLASTIC ART COMPETITION SCHOLARSHIPS

The Art Institutes International, Inc.

Free Markets Center

210 Sixth Avenue, 33rd Floor

Pittsburgh, PA 15222-2603

Phone: (800) 275-2440; Email: ai_sfs@aii.edu

Web: www.artinstitutes.edu

**Summary:** To recognize and reward (with scholarships to participating Art Institutes) high school seniors who win Silver Portfolio Awards in the Scholastic Art Awards competition.

**Eligibility:** Open to high school seniors who submit art portfolios in the Scholastic Art Awards competition. Applicants must submit a portfolio of 8 works, including at least 3 drawings. Winners of Silver Portfolio Awards are eligible to apply for these scholarships.

**Financial data:** The award is $15,000. Winners may apply the funds toward payment of tuition at the Art Institute of their choice.

**Duration:** The competition is held annually.

**Number awarded:** 4 each year.

**Deadline:** December of each year.

## 1666 SCHOLASTIC WRITING AWARDS

Scholastic, Inc., Attn: Alliance for Young Artists & Writers, Inc.

557 Broadway

New York, NY 10012

Phone: (212) 343-6493; Fax: (212) 343-4885;

Email: A&WGeneralInfo@scholastic.com

Web: www.scholastic.com

**Summary:** To recognize and reward outstanding middle school and high school writers.

**Eligibility:** Open to all students in grades 7-12 who are currently enrolled in public and private schools in the United States, U.S. territories, U.S.-sponsored schools abroad, and Canada. Competitions are held in Group 1 for grades 7 through 9 and Group 2 for grades 10 through 12 and in 9 categories: short story (1,300 to 3,000 words); short short story (600 to 1,300 words); personal essay/memoir (500 to 2,000 words for group 1, 750 to 3,000 words for group 2); journalism (400 to 2,000 words for Group 1, 500 to 3,000 words for Group 2); dramatic script (up to 50 pages); poetry (35 to 100 lines for Group 1, 50 to 200 lines for Group 2); humor (600 to 3,000 words); novel writing (3 to 5 chapters, or 15 to 50 pages, plus an outline for the entire book); and science fiction/fantasy (600 to 3,000 words). A separate general portfolio competition for graduating seniors only consists of a minimum of 3 and maximum of 8 narratives, individual poems, and/or dramatic scripts up to a total of 50 pages, and the James B. Reston Portfolio for graduating seniors only consists of a minimum of 3 and maximum of 8 essays, nonfiction, and/or opinion pieces up to a total of 50 pages. Works may not have been submitted previously in this or any other competition and must be original. Each student may enter only one category.

**Financial data:** The Portfolio Gold Awards, including the New York Times James B. Reston Portfolio Gold Award, are $10,000 scholarships. The Otto Friedrich Nonfiction Portfolio Silver Award is $1,000. In addition, teachers of the Portfolio Gold Award winners receive Portfolio Teacher Awards of $1,000. The teacher who submits the most outstanding group of entries receives the Gold Apple Teacher Award of $500.

**Number awarded:** Each year, this competition presents 5 portfolio awards (4 Writing Portfolio Gold Awards and 1 New York Times James B. Reston Portfolio Gold Award), 1 Otto Friedrich Nonfiction Portfolio Silver Award, 5 Portfolio Teacher Awards, and 1 Gold Apple Teacher Award.

**Deadline:** January of each year.

## 1667 SCUDDER ASSOCIATION EDUCATIONAL GRANTS

Scudder Association, Inc.

c/o Terry Sherman, Chair, Grant Committee

147 Forest Street

South Hamilton, MA 01982-2531

Phone: (978) 468-1348

Web: www.scudder.org

**Summary:** To assist undergraduate and graduate students preparing for "careers as servants of God in various forms of ministry to men and women around the world."

**Eligibility:** Open to undergraduate and graduate students who are preparing for careers in the ministry, medicine, nursing, teaching, or social service. Applicants must be a Scudder family member or recommended by a member of the Scudder Association. They are requested to submit an official transcript, 2 letters of recommendation from faculty members, a statement (up to 500 words) on their goals and objectives, and a verification of financial need from their school (financial need is considered in the selection process).

**Financial data:** Stipends range from $1,000 to $2,500. A total of $25,000 is distributed each year.

**Duration:** Up to 4 years of undergraduate studies, graduate studies, or a combination of the two.

**Number awarded:** Up to 25 each year.

## 1668 SEATTLE PROFESSIONAL CHAPTER SCHOLARSHIPS

Association for Women in Communications-Seattle Professional Chapter
Attn: Scholarship Chair
1319 Dexter Avenue North, Number 370
Seattle, WA 98109
Phone: (206) 654-2929; Fax: (206) 285-5220; Email: awcseattle@qwest.net
Web: www.seattleawc.org/scholarships.html

**Summary:** To provide financial assistance to upper-division and graduate students in Washington who are preparing for a career in the communications industry.

**Eligibility:** Open to Washington state residents who are enrolled at a 4-year college or university in the state as a junior, senior, or graduate student (sophomores at 2-year colleges applying to a 4-year institution are also eligible). Applicants must be majoring, or planning to major, in a communications program, including print and broadcast journalism, television and radio production, film, advertising, public relations, marketing, graphic design, multimedia design, photography, or technical communication. Selection is based on demonstrated excellence in communications; contributions made to communications on campus and in the community; scholastic achievement; financial need; and writing samples from journalism, advertising, public relations, or broadcasting.

**Financial data:** The stipend is $1,500. Funds are paid directly to the recipient's school and must be used for tuition and fees.

**Duration:** 1 year.

**Number awarded:** 2 each year.

**Deadline:** February of each year.

## 1669 SEJ AWARDS FOR REPORTING ON THE ENVIRONMENT

Society of Environmental Journalists
321 Old York Road, Suite 200
P.O. Box 2492
Jenkintown, PA 19046
Phone: (215) 884-8174; Fax: (215) 884-8175; Email: sej@sej.org
Web: www.sej.org/contest/index.htm

**Summary:** To recognize and reward journalists who provide outstanding coverage of environmental issues.

**Eligibility:** Open to journalists who submit stories about an environmental subject that was published or broadcast in a media outlet accessible to the general public during the preceding year. Candidates do not need to be environmental specialists to enter; reporters who cover health, politics, science, energy, local government, or any other beat are encouraged to enter their work on environmental subjects. Students may enter work that was published or broadcast in a media outlet accessible to the general public. Entries from outside the United States are welcome, but non-English entries must be accompanied by a complete and accurate English translation. The categories are: 1) outstanding in-depth reporting, print; 2) outstanding beat reporting, print; 3) outstanding in-depth reporting, television; 4) outstanding beat reporting, television; 5) outstanding in-depth reporting, radio; 6) outstanding beat reporting, radio; 7) outstanding small market reporting, print; 8) outstanding small market reporting, television and radio; and 9) outstanding online reporting.

**Financial data:** The award is $1,000.

**Duration:** Awards are presented annually.

**Number awarded:** 9 each year: 1 in each category.

**Deadline:** March of each year.

## 1670 SENIOR HIGH COMMUNICATION CONTEST

American Automobile Association, Attn: Poster Program Headquarters
1000 AAA Drive
Heathrow, FL 32746-5063
Phone: (407) 444-7916; Fax: (407) 444-7956
Web: www.aaa.com

**Summary:** To recognize and reward outstanding high school students who participate in a highway safety competition.

**Eligibility:** Open to 1) students enrolled in grades 9-12 in a public, parochial, private, or home school in the United States or Canada; and 2) senior high students affiliated with a national youth organization (such as the Boys and Girls Clubs of America). Entries are invited in 3 subject areas: DUI prevention, safe driving practices, and motor vehicle occupant protection. For each of those subject areas, students may enter in one of 3 formats: graphic arts (a poster, either hand-drawn or computer-generated, or a cartoon), written (either an editorial up to 500 words or the text of a brochure), or audiovisual (either a video cassette or audio recording, both from 30 seconds to 2 minutes in documentary, drama, music, or public service announcement format). All entries are judged on originality and the relationship of the message to traffic safety. In addition, art/design and its execution are considered for poster, brochure, and cartoon entries; visual impact is considered for poster designs and brochures; content, organization, persuasive effect, and grammar are considered for editorials and brochures; and content, organization, presentation, and use of technology are considered for video cassettes and audio recordings. All entries must be the student's exclusive work in idea, design, and execution, although they must be completed under supervision of an authorized instructor. Entries must be addressed to the local AAA club and then forwarded to the national office for the national judging.

**Financial data:** In each of the subject areas for each medium (graphic arts, written, and audiovisual), first-place awards are $150 U.S. savings bonds, second-place awards are $125 bonds, and third-place awards are $100 bonds. The grand award winner for each medium also receives a $5,000 scholarship or bond. In addition, each judge may award a $50 savings bond to any non-winning entry for outstanding work.

**Duration:** The competition is held annually.

**Number awarded:** Each year, 9 first-place awards, 9 second-place awards, and 9 third-place awards are presented (1 in each of the subject areas for each medium). In addition, 3 grand awards (1 for each medium) and up to 15 judge's awards are presented each year.

**Deadline:** January of each year.

## 1671 SENTRY INSURANCE FOUNDATION SCHOLARSHIPS

Wisconsin Foundation for Independent Colleges, Inc.
Attn: Program Manager
735 North Water Street, Suite 600
Milwaukee, WI 53202-4100
Phone: (414) 273-5980; Fax: (414) 273-5995; Email: wfic@wficweb.org
Web: www.wficweb.org/documents/schinfo.htm

**Summary:** To provide financial assistance to students majoring in selected fields at member institutions of the Wisconsin Foundation for Independent Colleges (WFIC).

**Eligibility:** Open to student enrolled or planning to enroll at WFIC member colleges and universities. Applicants must have a declared major in one of the following fields: business, economics, mathematics, management information systems, industrial design, communication design, or interior architecture and design. They must have a GPA of 3.3 or higher; entering freshmen must rank in the top 25% of their high school class. Financial need is considered in the selection process.

**Financial data:** The stipend is $1,000.

**Duration:** 1 year.

**Number awarded:** 20 each year: 1 at each of the participating schools.

**Deadline:** Each participating college sets its own deadline.

## 1672 SHIRLEY WILKINS VALENTIN VIOLIN AWARD

National Federation of Music Clubs
1336 North Delaware Street
Indianapolis, IN 46202-2481
Phone: (317) 638-4003; Fax: (317) 638-0503; Email: info@nfmc-music.org
Web: www.nfmc-music.org/Competitions/Annual_Student/annual_student.html

**Summary:** To recognize and reward outstanding young violinists who are members of the National Federation of Music Clubs.

**Eligibility:** Open to student members of the federation who are between 18 and 25 years of age. They must submit an audio or CD of a violin performance.

**Financial data:** The prize is $1,000.

**Duration:** The competition is held annually.

**Number awarded:** 1 each year.

**Deadline:** March of each year.

## 1673 SHORT FILM AND VIDEO COMPETITION

USA Film Festival
6116 North Central Expressway, Suite 105
Dallas, TX 75206
Phone: (214) 821-6300
Web: www.usafilmfestival.com

**Summary:** To recognize and reward outstanding short films and videos.

**Eligibility:** Open to professional, nonprofessional, or student film/videomakers who submit entries in 16mm film, 35mm film, 3/4-inch videocassettes, or conventional VHS videocassettes. The 4 categories are fiction (for narrative works, dramatized events, and adaptations of literary or dramatic works), nonfiction (for documentaries or portraits of actual persons or events), animation (of graphics or 3-dimensional objects), and experimental (for works that explore personal experience of film and video forms in innovative ways). The Charles Samu Family Award is presented to the work that best represents a standard of excellence for audiences of all ages. The G. William Jones Texas Award is presented to a work by a Texas resident. The Student Award is presented to the outstanding work by a student in any category. Special Jury Awards are presented to outstanding entries in any category.

**Financial data:** The first-prize winner in each category receives $1,000. In addition, the Charles Samu Family Award is $500, the G. William Jones Texas Award is $500, the Student Award is $500, and the Special Jury Awards are $250.

**Duration:** The competition is held annually, in April.

**Number awarded:** Each year, 4 first-place awards, 3 other awards, and 4 Special Jury Awards are presented.

**Deadline:** February of each year.

## 1674 S.I. NEWHOUSE FOUNDATION SCHOLARSHIPS

Asian American Journalists Association, Attn: Student Programs Coordinator
1182 Market Street, Suite 320
San Francisco, CA 94102
Phone: (415) 346-2051, ext. 102; Fax: (415) 346-6343; Email: brandons@aaja.org
Web: www.aaja.org/programs/for_students/scholarships

**Summary:** To provide financial assistance and summer work experience in print journalism to members of the Asian American Journalists Association (AAJA) who are undergraduate or graduate students.

**Eligibility:** Open to all students but especially welcomes applications from historically underrepresented Asian Pacific American groups, including southeast Asians (Vietnamese, Cambodians, and Hmong), south Asians, and Pacific Islanders. Applicants may be graduating high school seniors who declare journalism as a major or undergraduate or graduate students working on a degree in journalism and a career in print journalism. AAJA membership is required. Along with their application, they must submit a 500-word essay on their involvement or interest in the Asian American community and how, if they are awarded this scholarship, they would contribute to the field of journalism and/or media issues involving the Asian American and Pacific Islander community. Selection is based on scholastic ability, commitment to journalism, sensitivity to Asian American and Pacific Islander issues as demonstrated by community involvement, journalistic ability, and financial need.

**Financial data:** Stipends are $5,000, $3,000, or $1,000 per year.

**Duration:** 4 years for a graduating high school senior; 1 year for current undergraduate or graduate students.

**Number awarded:** Varies each year; recently, 7 of these scholarships (2 at $5,000, 3 at $4,000, 1 at $2,000, and 1 at $1,000) were awarded.

**Deadline:** April of each year.

## 1675 SI TV PLAYWRITING AWARD

John F. Kennedy Center for the Performing Arts
Education Department
Attn: Kennedy Center American College Theater Festival
2700 F Street, N.W.
Washington, DC 20566
Phone: (202) 416-8857; Fax: (202) 416-8802;
Email: skshaffer@kennedy-center.org
Web: kennedy-center.org/education/actf/actfsitv.html

**Summary:** To recognize and reward outstanding plays by Latino playwrights.

**Eligibility:** Open to Latino students at any accredited junior or senior college in the United States, provided their college agrees to participate in the Kennedy Center American College Theater Festival (KCACTF). Undergraduate students must be carrying at least 6 semester hours, graduate students must be enrolled in at least 3 semester hours, and continuing part-time students must be enrolled in a regular degree or certificate program. This award is presented to the best student-written play by a Latino.

**Financial data:** The prize is $2,500. The winner also receives an internship to a prestigious playwriting retreat program. Dramatic Publishing Company presents the winning playwright with an offer of a contract to publish, license, and market the winning play. A grant of $500 is made to the theater department of the college or university producing the award-winning play.

**Duration:** The award is presented annually.

**Number awarded:** 1 each year.

**Deadline:** November of each year.

## 1676 SIGMA ALPHA IOTA SCHOLARSHIPS FOR UNDERGRADUATE PERFORMANCE

Sigma Alpha Iota Philanthropies, Inc.
One Tunnel Road
Asheville, NC 28805
Phone: (828) 251-0606; Fax: (828) 251-0644;
Email: philonline@sai-national.org
Web: www.sai-national.org/phil/philsch3.html

**Summary:** To recognize and reward outstanding performances in vocal and instrumental categories by undergraduate members of Sigma Alpha Iota (an organization of women musicians).

**Eligibility:** Open to undergraduate student members of the organization who are vocalists or instrumentalists. Entrants must be younger than 25 years of age. Selection is based on taped auditions in 4 categories: voice, keyboard and percussion, strings, and winds and brass.

**Financial data:** The stipend is $1,500.

**Duration:** The competition is held triennially.

**Number awarded:** 4 every 3 years: 1 in each of the 4 categories.

**Deadline:** March of the year of the awards (2009, 2012, etc.).

## 1677 SIGMA ALPHA IOTA UNDERGRADUATE SCHOLARSHIPS

Sigma Alpha Iota Philanthropies, Inc.
One Tunnel Road
Asheville, NC 28805
Phone: (828) 251-0606; Fax: (828) 251-0644;
Email: philonline@sai-national.org
Web: www.sai-national.org/phil/philsch1.html

**Summary:** To provide financial assistance for college to members of Sigma Alpha Iota (an organization of women musicians).

**Eligibility:** Open to members of the organization in the first 3 years of undergraduate study. Candidates must be nominated by their chapter and their chapter adviser must submit a letter of recommendation. Selection is based on financial need, musical ability, scholarship, potential leadership, and contribution to campus and community life.

**Financial data:** Stipends are $2,000 or $1,500.

**Duration:** 1 year.

**Number awarded:** 15 each year: 3 at $2,000 and 12 at $1,500.

**Deadline:** March of each year.

## 1678 SIGNET CLASSIC STUDENT SCHOLARSHIP ESSAY CONTEST

Penguin Putnam Inc., Attn: Academic Marketing Department
375 Hudson Street
New York, NY 10014
Phone: (212) 366-2373; Fax: (212) 366-2385;
Email: online@penguinputnam.com
Web: www.penguinputnam.com/scessay

**Summary:** To recognize and reward the best essays written by high school students on topics that relate to the books in the Signet Classic series (published by Penguin Putnam, Inc.).

**Eligibility:** Open to high school juniors and seniors and to home-schooled students between 16 and 18 years of age. Applicants must submit essays, from 2 to 3 pages in length, on a topic that changes annually but relates to the books published in the Signet Classic series. Recently, the essay contest focused on *The Picture of Dorian Gray* by Oscar Wilde. Essays by high school students must be submitted by an English teacher. Essays by home-schooled students must be submitted by a parent or legal guardian. Submissions are judged on style, content, grammar, and originality. Judges look for clear, concise writing that is articulate, logically organized, and well supported.

**Financial data:** The grand-prize winners receive a $1,000 scholarship and a Signet Classic library for their school (valued at $1,700).

**Duration:** The competition is held annually.

**Number awarded:** 5 grand-prize winners each year.

**Deadline:** April of each year.

## 1679 SKILLSUSA CHAMPIONSHIP SCHOLARSHIPS

The Art Institutes International, Inc.
Free Markets Center
210 Sixth Avenue, 33rd Floor
Pittsburgh, PA 15222-2603
Phone: (800) 275-2440; Email: ai_sfs@aii.edu

Web: www.artinstitutes.edu

**Summary:** To recognize and reward (with scholarships to participating Art Institutes) high school seniors who are selected as National Gold Medalists in selected competitions conducted by SkillsUSA.

**Eligibility:** Open to high school seniors who participate in competitions conducted by SkillsUSA (former VICA). Scholarships are awarded to National Gold Medalists in the following categories: culinary, advertising design, photography, 3-D imaging and animation, and video production.

**Financial data:** Awards are $30,000 (for payment of full tuition) in the culinary, advertising design, and photography categories. Awards are $15,000 (for payment of half tuition) in the 3-D imaging and animation and video production categories. Recipients may use the funds for tuition at the Art Institute of their choice.

**Duration:** Competitions are held annually.

**Number awarded:** Varies each year. Each Art Institute location has a limited number of scholarships. Winners are permitted to choose their Art Institute location on a first-come, first-served basis.

## 1680 SOLO VIBRAPHONE CONTEST

Percussive Arts Society
701 N.W. Ferris Avenue
Lawton, OK 73507-5442
Phone: (580) 353-1455; Fax: (580) 353-1456; Email: percarts@pas.org
Web: www.pas.org

**Summary:** To recognize and reward student members of the Percussive Arts Society who perform in an outstanding manner in a solo vibraphone contest.

**Eligibility:** Open to college student members of the society who are between 18 and 25 years of age. Performers submit a CD, up to 15 minutes in length, of a performance on solo vibraphone of a work selected from a specified repertoire list. Based on those CDs, finalists are selected to compete at the Percussive Arts Society International Convention (PASIC).

**Financial data:** First prize is $1,000, second $750, third $500, and fourth $250. Matching grants are awarded to the winners' institutions to be used for scholarships, equipment needs or repairs, guest clinicians or performers, or other percussion area needs.

**Duration:** The competition is held annually.

**Number awarded:** 4 each year.

**Deadline:** April of each year.

## 1681 SONS OF ITALY ITALIAN LANGUAGE SCHOLARSHIP

Order Sons of Italy in America, Attn: Sons of Italy Foundation
219 E Street, N.E.
Washington, DC 20002
Phone: (202) 547-5106; Fax: (202) 546-8168; Email: scholarships@osia.org
Web: www.osia.org/public/scholarships/grants.asp

**Summary:** To provide financial assistance to upper-division students majoring in Italian.

**Eligibility:** Open to U.S. citizens of Italian descent who are enrolled as full-time undergraduate juniors or seniors at an accredited 4-year college or university. Applicants must be majoring in the Italian language. They must submit an essay of 750 to 1,000 words in Italian on how they plan to use their degree in Italian language in their career. Financial need is not considered in the selection process.

**Financial data:** Stipends range from $4,000 to $25,000.

**Duration:** 1 year; nonrenewable.

**Number awarded:** 1 or more each year.

**Deadline:** February of each year.

## 1682 SOUTH CAROLINA CHURCH RELATED VOCATIONAL SCHOLARSHIPS

South Carolina Baptist Convention, Attn: Collegiate Ministry Group
190 Stoneridge Drive
Columbia, SC 29210-8254
Phone: (803) 765-0030, ext. 4400; (800) 723-7242 (within SC); Fax: (803) 799-1044; Email: CRVS@scbaptist.org
Web: www.scbaptist.org

**Summary:** To provide financial assistance to South Carolina Baptists who are attending a college or university in the state to prepare for a church-related vocation.

**Eligibility:** Open to residents of South Carolina who have been active members of a Southern Baptist church for at least 9 months prior to the beginning of an academic year. Applicants must be 1) enrolled full time at an accredited

college or university in South Carolina; 2) recommended by their church; 3) able to demonstrate financial need; and 4) committed to a church-related vocation. They must agree to participate in a ministry-related practical experience approximately 2 to 6 hours per week under a designated supervisor. A personal interview is required.

**Financial data:** The stipend depends on the need of the recipient. Funds are sent directly to the school to be applied to tuition and academic fees.

**Duration:** 1 year; recipients may reapply if they maintain full-time enrollment and a GPA of 2.0 or higher.

**Number awarded:** 1 or more each year.

**Deadline:** March of each year.

## 1683 SOUTH CAROLINA VOCATIONAL REHABILITATION DEPARTMENT JOURNALISM CONTEST

South Carolina Vocational Rehabilitation Department
Attn: Lucerne Iseman, Assistant Commissioner
1410 Boston Avenue
P.O. Box 15
West Columbia, SC 29171-0015
Phone: (803) 896-6833; (866) 247-8354; TTY: (803) 896-6553;
Email: info@scvrd.state.sc.us
Web: www.svrd.net/g_journal_contest.html

**Summary:** To recognize and reward, with college scholarships, high school students in South Carolina who submit outstanding newspaper articles on topics related to employment of people with disabilities.

**Eligibility:** Open to South Carolina residents between 16 and 19 years of age enrolled as juniors or seniors in high school or otherwise qualified to begin postsecondary education no later than 2 years after the contest. Applicants are not required to have a disability, but they must submit a newspaper article, up to 3 pages in length, on a topic that changes annually but relates to employment of people with disabilities. A recent topic was "Workers with Disabilities: Ready for Tomorrow's Jobs Today." Articles should use correct grammar and sentence structure and follow standard journalistic practice of the 5 Ws (who, what, where, when, and why).

**Financial data:** The winner receives full payment of tuition and fees at a South Carolina state-supported institution. Some schools include room and board as part of tuition and fees.

**Duration:** 4 years, provided the recipient maintains general scholastic and conduct standards.

**Number awarded:** 1 each year.

**Deadline:** January of each year.

## 1684 STANFIELD AND D'ORLANDO ART SCHOLARSHIP

Unitarian Universalist Association
Attn: Unitarian Universalist Funding Program
25 Beacon Street
Boston, MA 02108-2800
Phone: (617) 971-9600; Fax: (617) 367-3237; Email: uufp@uua.org
Web: www.uua.org/awards/stanfield.html

**Summary:** To provide financial assistance for the study of art to Unitarian Universalists.

**Eligibility:** Open to Unitarian Universalist students entering or continuing undergraduate or graduate study. Applicants should be studying or planning to study painting, drawing, photography, and/or sculpture; art history, art therapy, film, and performing arts majors are not eligible. Candidates must submit 6 to 10 samples of their work on 35mm slides. Selection is based on financial need and academic performance.

**Financial data:** The amount of the award depends on the need of the recipient and the availability of funds.

**Duration:** 1 year; recipients may reapply.

**Number awarded:** 1 each year.

**Deadline:** February of each year.

## 1685 STEPHEN D. PISINSKI MEMORIAL SCHOLARSHIP

Public Relations Student Society of America, Attn: Director of Education
33 Irving Place, Third Floor
New York, NY 10003-2376
Phone: (212) 460-1474; Fax: (212) 995-0757; Email: prssa@prsa.org
Web: www.prssa.org/resources/award-PisinskiMemorial.asp

**Summary:** To provide financial assistance to upper-division members of the Public Relations Student Society of America (PRSSA).

**Eligibility:** Open to members of the society who are majoring in journalism, communications, or public relations. Applicants must be juniors or seniors with a GPA of 3.3 or higher. They must submit a resume that includes academic honors, special projects, activities, and/or work experience; an official transcript; an essay, up to 1,000 words, on their career goals; 2 or 3 writing samples; and 2 letters of recommendation. Financial need is not considered in the selection process.

**Financial data:** The stipend is $1,500.

**Duration:** 1 year.

**Number awarded:** 1 each year.

**Deadline:** June of each year.

### 1686 STEPHEN J. MANHARD SCHOLARSHIP-ESSAY COMPETITION FOR HIGH SCHOOL SENIORS

Society for the Preservation of English Language and Literature
Attn: Jim Wallace
P.O. Box 321
Braselton, GA 30517-0006
Phone: (770) 586-0184; Email: spellgang@juno.com
Web: www.spellorg.com

**Summary:** To recognize and reward high school seniors who demonstrate high standards in their writing.

**Eligibility:** Open to high school seniors in the United States and Canada. They are invited to submit an essay, which must be written solely by them and be previously unpublished. It should be at least 500 words (up to 3 typewritten, double-spaced pages). The subject must be related to some aspect of language and should support the society's primary objective of promoting high standards of English grammar, usage, spelling, punctuation, and syntax. Essays on other subjects will not be considered. Entries are judged on clarity of thought and expression, originality, technical correctness (i.e., grammar, diction), and suitability of the subject.

**Financial data:** First prize is $1,000, second $300, and third $200.

**Duration:** The competition is held annually.

**Number awarded:** 3 each year.

**Deadline:** February of each year.

### 1687 STEVE HARPER MEMORIAL SCHOLARSHIP

Kansas Wildscape Foundation, Inc.
1 Riverfront Plaza, Suite 311
Lawrence, KS 66044
Phone: (785) 843-9453; (866) 455-6377; Fax: (785) 843-6379;
Email: wild scape@sunflower.com
Web: www.kansaswildscape.org

**Summary:** To provide financial assistance to high school seniors in Kansas who plan to attend a college or university in the state to major in natural resources or photography.

**Eligibility:** Open to seniors graduating from high schools and planning to attend a 4-year college or university in the state. Applicants must be planning to study photography or natural resources. Selection is based on past or current involvement in the natural resources or photography area, strength of application, academic performance, and financial need.

**Financial data:** The stipend is $1,000.

**Duration:** 1 year.

**Number awarded:** 1 each year.

**Deadline:** April of each year.

### 1688 STILLMAN-KELLEY AWARDS

National Federation of Music Clubs
1336 North Delaware Street
Indianapolis, IN 46202-2481
Phone: (317) 638-4003; Fax: (317) 638-0503; Email: info@nfmc-music.org
Web: www.nfmc-music.org/Competitions/Annual_Junior/annual_junior.html

**Summary:** To recognize and reward outstanding young musicians who are members of the National Federation of Music Clubs (NFMC).

**Eligibility:** Open to instrumentalists who are younger than 17 years of age, U.S. citizens, and junior members of the federation. Applicants must present a program of 15 to 20 minutes, performed from memory, on their selected solo instrument. Awards are rotated by NFMC region, with northeastern and southeastern in even-numbered years and central and western in odd-numbered years.

**Financial data:** Awards, to be used for further study, are $1,000 for first place and $500 for second place.

**Number awarded:** 2 each year.

**Deadline:** January of each year.

### 1689 STUDENT ACADEMY AWARDS

Academy of Motion Picture Arts and Sciences, Attn: Academy Foundation
8949 Wilshire Boulevard
Beverly Hills, CA 90211-1972
Phone: (310) 247-3000, ext. 129; Fax: (310) 859-9619; Email: rmiller@oscars.org
Web: www.oscars.org/saa

**Summary:** To recognize and reward college filmmakers with no previous professional experience.

**Eligibility:** Open to student filmmakers who are enrolled in degree-granting programs at accredited colleges and universities as full-time students and have no previous professional experience. Applicants must submit films that they have completed within the past year as part of a teacher-student relationship within the curricular structure of their institution. There are 4 award categories: alternative, animation, narrative, and documentary. Entries must be submitted on videotape and be no longer than 60 minutes. Selection is based on resourcefulness, originality, entertainment, and production quality, without regard to cost of production or subject matter.

**Financial data:** Gold, silver, and bronze awards in each category are $5,000, $3,000, and $2,000, respectively.

**Duration:** The awards are presented annually.

**Number awarded:** Up to 12 awards may be presented each year: 3 in each of the 4 categories.

**Deadline:** March of each year.

### 1690 STUDENT COMPETITION IN LANDSCAPE ARCHITECTURE FOR AGGREGATE OPERATIONS

National Stone, Sand and Gravel Association
Attn: Director of Communications
1605 King Street
Arlington, VA 22314
Phone: (703) 525-8788; (800) 342-1415; Fax: (703) 525-7782;
Email: info@nssga.org
Web: www.nssga.org/careers/index.html

**Summary:** To recognize and reward students who submit outstanding designs for site beautification at quarry sites.

**Eligibility:** Open to students enrolled at universities in the United States and Canada with a degree program in landscape architecture. Entries may be submitted by individuals or teams of up to 3 students. Competitors must prepare plans for site beautification at quarry operations based on an active or proposed commercial aggregates operation. Sites that are abandoned or where operations have been completed are not eligible as the basis for entries. Selection is based on 1) a problem statement; 2) identification of siting and design factors; 3) methodology (including site and operations analysis, improvement and beautification plan, and final use and reclamation plan); 4) a narrative description of the project; and 5) cost analysis.

**Financial data:** Students receive prizes of $2,000 for first place, $1,000 for second place, and $600 for third place. In addition, the departments of landscape architecture at the schools in which the students are enrolled receive $1,400, $600, and $400 for the respective prize winners.

**Number awarded:** 3 each year.

**Deadline:** Preliminary entry forms must be submitted by April of each year; final entry forms are due in May.

### 1691 STUDENT DESIGN COMPETITION IN ACOUSTICS

Robert Bradford Newman Student Award Fund
c/o Acoustical Society of America
2 Huntington Quadrangle, Suite 1NO1
Melville, NY 11747-4502
Phone: (516) 576-2360; Fax: (516) 576-2377; Email: asa@aip.org
Web: www.newmanfund.org

**Summary:** To recognize and reward undergraduate and graduate students who submit outstanding entries in an acoustics design competition.

**Eligibility:** Open to undergraduate and graduate students who enter as individuals or as members of teams of up to 3 students. Applicants must submit an acoustics design for a problem given by the competition. Selection is based on technical merit, design vision, adherence to the design prompt and program requirements, and effectiveness of presentation.

**Financial data:** The prize for the winning individual or team is $1,250. Commendation awards are $700.

**Duration:** The competition is held annually.

**Number awarded:** 1 winner and 4 commendation awards are presented each year.

**Deadline:** March of each year.

### 1692 SUSAN G. MORAN SCHOLARSHIPS

Society for Technical Communication-Central Ohio Chapter
c/o Kathleen Stohrer, Education Chair
Battelle
505 King Avenue
Columbus, OH 43201
Email: stohrer@battelle.org
Web: www.centralohiostc.org/scholarship.html
**Summary:** To provide financial assistance to students from Ohio who are working on an undergraduate degree in technical communication.
**Eligibility:** Open to students working on a bachelor's or associate degree in a technical communication program, including (but not limited to) such courses as introductory and advanced technical communication, introductory and advanced technical editing, online documentation, technical presentations, document design and delivery methods, proofreading, style and mechanics for writers, desktop publishing, report writing, public relations writing, design, or engineering graphics. Applicants must be residents of Ohio or attending an Ohio institution. Along with their application, they must submit a 1- to 3-page description of their career goals and significant achievements to date, a transcript, 2 letters of recommendation, and a set of instructions on how to explain to space aliens how to brush their teeth. Financial need is not considered in the selection process.
**Financial data:** The stipend is $1,000.
**Duration:** 1 year.
**Number awarded:** 2 each year.
**Deadline:** April of each year.

### 1693 TADEUSZ SENDZIMIR FUND SCHOLARSHIPS

Connecticut Community Foundation
81 West Main Street, Fourth Floor
Waterbury, CT 06702-1216
Phone: (203) 753-1315; Fax: (203) 756-3054; Email: info@conncf.org
Web: www.conncf.org
**Summary:** To provide financial assistance to Connecticut residents who are interested in studying Polish language, history, or culture in the United States or in Poland.
**Eligibility:** Open to Connecticut residents currently enrolled or planning to enroll at a 4-year college or university. They must be planning to study Polish language, history, or culture on the undergraduate or graduate school level in the United States or Poland. Preference is given to applicants of Polish descent. Students may also apply to attend a summer school in Poland. Selection is based on academic record, extracurricular activities, work experience, financial need, and an essay.
**Financial data:** The stipend ranges from $3,000 to $5,000. Funds are paid directly to the recipient's school.
**Duration:** 1 year or 1 summer; recipients may reapply, provided they maintain a GPA of 2.5 or higher.
**Number awarded:** Varies each year.
**Deadline:** February of each year.

### 1694 TAYLOR MEMORIAL BAPTIST CHURCH SCHOLARSHIP

New Mexico Baptist Foundation
5325 Wyoming Boulevard, N.E.
P.O. Box 16560
Albuquerque, NM 87191-6560
Phone: (505) 332-3777; (877) 841-3777; Fax: (505) 332-2777
Web: www.bcnm.com/ministries/missions/school_house/scholarships.html
**Summary:** To provide financial assistance for college or seminary to members of Southern Baptist churches in New Mexico.
**Eligibility:** Open to members of Southern Baptist churches in New Mexico who are enrolled full time at an accredited college or seminary and preparing for full-time Christian service.
**Financial data:** A stipend is awarded (amount not specified).
**Duration:** 1 year.
**Number awarded:** 1 or more each year.
**Deadline:** April of each year.

### 1695 TECHNOLOGY STUDENT ASSOCIATION COMPETITION

The Art Institutes International, Inc.
Free Markets Center
210 Sixth Avenue, 33rd Floor
Pittsburgh, PA 15222-2603
Phone: (800) 275-2440; Email: ai_sfs@aii.edu
Web: www.artinstitutes.edu
**Summary:** To recognize and reward (with scholarships to participating Art Institutes) high school seniors who win first place in the Cyberspace Pursuit and Imaging Technology competition of the Technology Student Association.
**Eligibility:** Open to high school seniors who participate in competitions conducted by the Technology Student Association. The winner in the Cyberspace Pursuit and Imaging Technology category is eligible for this scholarship.
**Financial data:** The award is $5,000. The winner may apply the funds toward payment of tuition at the Art Institute of his or her choice.
**Duration:** The competition is held annually.
**Number awarded:** 1 each year.

### 1696 TERRY WALKER SCHOLARSHIP

Classical Association of the Empire State
P.O. Box 12722
Albany, NY 12212
Web: www.caesny.org/grants.asp
**Summary:** To provide financial assistance to students from New York who are preparing to teach Latin in school.
**Eligibility:** Open to students who are currently enrolled in college in at least the sophomore year and graduated from a high school in New York and/or are currently attending college in New York. Preference is given to students who are preparing to teach Latin on the elementary or secondary school level. Applicants must submit a self-evaluation essay in which they describe their competence in Latin, speaking skills, arguments for the retention and expansion of Latin in the schools, and ideas for the motivation and instruction of students. Selection is based on that essay, character, scholarship (especially in the field of classics), ability to work with young people, and intention to teach Latin on the elementary and/or secondary level.
**Financial data:** The stipend is $2,000.
**Duration:** 1 year; recipients may reapply.
**Number awarded:** 1 each year.
**Deadline:** March of each year.

### 1697 TEXAS BAPTIST MINISTERIAL TUITION ASSISTANCE

Baptist General Convention of Texas, Attn: Theological Education
333 North Washington
Dallas, TX 75246-1798
Phone: (214) 828-5254; Fax: (214) 828-5284; Email: rose@bgct.org
Web: www.bgct.org
**Summary:** To provide financial assistance to members of Baptist churches in Texas who are preparing for a career in ministry at a Texas Baptist institution.
**Eligibility:** Open to members of Baptist churches in Texas who can present a certificate of license or ordination, or letter of certification of call from a Baptist church. Applicants must demonstrate "a life style of commitment to the principles of the Christian life" and certification by their pastor that they are involved in, supportive of, and committed to the local cooperating church. They must be working on, or planning to work on, a certificate, undergraduate, graduate, or postgraduate program approved by the Theological Education Committee of the Baptist General Convention of Texas (BGCT) at a bible college, university, or seminary in Texas. Applications are submitted through the school.
**Financial data:** The amount of support is established by the school.
**Duration:** 1 year; may be renewed if the recipients reaffirm their sense of call to church-related ministry and furnish evidence of their continuing involvement and commitment to a local BGCT church.
**Number awarded:** Varies each year.
**Deadline:** Each school establishes its own deadline.

### 1698 TEXAS BROADCAST EDUCATION FOUNDATION SCHOLARSHIPS

Texas Association of Broadcasters
Attn: Texas Broadcast Education Foundation
502 East 11th Street, Suite 200
Austin, TX 78701-2619
Phone: (512) 322-9944; Fax: (512) 322-0522; Email: tab@tab.org
Web: www.tab.org/scholarships.php
**Summary:** To provide financial assistance to undergraduates in Texas who are interested in preparing for a career in broadcasting.
**Eligibility:** Open to students enrolled in a fully-accredited program of instruction that emphasizes radio or television broadcasting or communications. Either the student or their school must be a member of the Texas Association

of Broadcasters. Applicants must have a GPA of 3.0 or higher. Along with their application, they must submit a 3-page essay that covers why they selected broadcasting as their career choice, the specific area of broadcasting that most interests them and why, their first job preference after college, their career goal 10 years after graduation, their eventual career goal, the broadcast activities in which they have participated, how they feel about broadcast advertising and its importance to a station, how they feel about broadcast advertising and its obligation to consumers, how they think broadcasting could better serve society, the radio or television station they respect most, how their college career could improve their value as a broadcaster, and their most rewarding broadcast-related experience. Selection is based on the essay, commitment to broadcasting, extracurricular activities, community involvement, and financial need.

**Financial data:** The stipend is $2,000.
**Duration:** 1 year.
**Number awarded:** 8 each year.
**Deadline:** May of each year.

## 1699 TEXAS CHORAL DIRECTORS ASSOCIATION STUDENT SCHOLARSHIPS

Texas Choral Directors Association, Attn: Executive Director
7900 Centre Park Drive, Suite A
Austin, TX 78754
Phone: (512) 474-2801; Fax: (512) 474-7873; Email: tcda@ensemble.org
Web: www.ensemble.org/tcda/scholarship.htm

**Summary:** To provide financial assistance to upper-division and graduate students in Texas who are working on a degree in choral music or church music.
**Eligibility:** Open to undergraduates who have completed at least 60 hours and graduate students. Applicants must be enrolled at a Texas college or university, have at least a 3.0 GPA, and be enrolled in a program of study that will lead to a degree in elementary or secondary choral music or church music. Selection is based on musical contributions and accomplishments, potential for success in the choral music profession, and personal qualifications.
**Financial data:** The stipend is $1,000.
**Duration:** 1 year.
**Number awarded:** 3 each year.
**Deadline:** May of each year.

## 1700 THELMA A. ROBINSON AWARD IN BALLET

National Federation of Music Clubs
1336 North Delaware Street
Indianapolis, IN 46202-2481
Phone: (317) 638-4003; Fax: (317) 638-0503; Email: info@nfmc-music.org
Web: www.nfmc-music.org/Competitions/BiennialJuniorSpecial/BienJunior Special.htm

**Summary:** To recognize and reward outstanding young dancers who are members of the National Federation of Music Clubs.
**Eligibility:** Open to ballet dancers who are between 13 and 16 years of age, U.S. citizens, and members of the federation.
**Financial data:** The award is $2,000.
**Number awarded:** 1 every other year.
**Deadline:** September of even-numbered years for competition in the following year.

## 1701 THESPIAN SCHOLARSHIP PROGRAM

Educational Theatre Association, Attn: International Thespian Society
2343 Auburn Avenue
Cincinnati, OH 45219-2819
Phone: (513) 421-3900; Fax: (513) 421-7077
Web: www.edta.org/rehearsal_hall/thespian_scholarships.asp

**Summary:** To provide financial assistance for college to high school members of the International Thespian Society.
**Eligibility:** Open to graduating high school seniors who participate in the annual International Thespian Festival. Applicants must be members of the society, have a minimum GPA of 2.7, and intend to use the funds to further their education in the communicative arts (theater, film, speech, radio, television, broadcasting, music, or dance). They may participate in 1 of 4 categories: 1) performance, with a solo presentation of a 2-minute song or monologue; 2) technical theater, with a portfolio of renderings, sketches, models, or illustrations of scenic or costume designs; 3) theater educator, with an essay on why they want to be a theater teacher, their most inspirational teacher, or the most important issue facing high school theater today; or 4) playwriting, with a manuscript of a play. Only 2 students from each troupe may participate. Selection is

based on involvement with the thespian troupe at their school and their audition performance, portfolio, essay, or manuscript.
**Financial data:** The stipend is $1,500.
**Duration:** 1 year.
**Number awarded:** 8 each year.
**Deadline:** May of each year.

## 1702 THOM JONES SCHOLARSHIP

The Fellowship of United Methodists in Music and Worship Arts
Attn: Administrator
P.O. Box 24787
Nashville, TN 37202-4787
Phone: (615) 749-6875; (800) 952-8977; Fax: (615) 749-6874;
Email: FUMMWA@aol.com
Web: www.fummwa.org

**Summary:** To provide financial assistance to students who are training for a ministry in the United Methodist Church in an area of the arts other than music.
**Eligibility:** Open to full-time degree candidates entering or enrolled in an accredited college, university, or school of theology to prepare for a ministry in worship, drama, dance, visuals, or other liturgical art. Applicants must have been members of the United Methodist Church for at least one year immediately before applying. They must be able to demonstrate exceptional artistic talents, leadership abilities, and outstanding promise of future usefulness to the church in an area of worship.
**Financial data:** The stipend is $1,000.
**Duration:** 1 year.
**Number awarded:** 1 each year.
**Deadline:** February of each year.

## 1703 THRUST EQUINE INDUSTRY/JOURNALISM/ COMMUNICATIONS SCHOLARSHIP

Washington Thoroughbred Breeders Association
Attn: Thoroughbred Horse Racing's United Scholarship Trust
P.O. Box 1499
Auburn, WA 98071-1499
Phone: (253) 288-7878; Fax: (253) 288-7890;
Email: MainDesk@washington thoroughbred.com
Web: www.washingtonthoroughbred.com/crnrthrs/THRUST.htm

**Summary:** To provide financial assistance to residents of Washington who are studying a field related to the equine industry, journalism, or communications in college.
**Eligibility:** Open to full-time students who have declared or are intending to declare a major in a field of study related to the equine industry; journalism and communications majors are also eligible. Applicants (or an immediate family member) must be a resident of Washington at the time of application, although they may attend a college or university in any state. They must submit an essay on the thoroughbred horse racing industry and why and how they think their major will impact that industry. Selection is based on that essay, academic performance, and a personal interview.
**Financial data:** Stipends are $2,500, $2,000, or $1,000 per year.
**Duration:** The $2,500 scholarship may be renewed for a total of 4 years, provided the recipient maintains satisfactory progress toward a degree and a GPA of 3.0 or higher. The $2,000 and $1,000 awards are for one year.
**Number awarded:** 4 each year: 1 at $2,500, 1 at $2,000, and 2 at $1,000.
**Deadline:** January of each year.

## 1704 TIME WARNER SCHOLARSHIP AWARD

Hispanic Association of Colleges and Universities
Attn: National Scholarship Program
One Dupont Circle, N.W. Suite 605
Washington, DC 20036
Phone: (202) 467-0893; Fax: (202) 496-9177; TTY: (800) 855-2880;
Email: scholarships@hacu.net
Web: scholarships.hacu.net/applications/applicants

**Summary:** To provide financial assistance to undergraduate students at member institutions of the Hispanic Association of Colleges and Universities (HACU) who are majoring in fields related to the news industry.
**Eligibility:** Open to undergraduate students at 4-year HACU member and partner colleges and universities who have completed at least 12 units. Applicants may be majoring in any field, but they must have an interest in the entertainment, news, media, or telecommunications industries. They must have a GPA

of 3.0 or higher and be able to demonstrate financial need. Along with their application, they must submit an essay of 200 to 250 words that describes their academic and/or career goals, where they expect to be and what they expect to be doing 10 years from now, and what skills they can bring to an employer.

**Financial data:** The stipend is $2,000.

**Duration:** 1 year; may be renewed.

**Number awarded:** 1 or more each year.

**Deadline:** May of each year.

## 1705 TIMOTHY BIGELOW AND PALMER W. BIGELOW, JR. SCHOLARSHIPS

American Nursery and Landscape Association
Attn: Horticultural Research Institute
1000 Vermont Avenue N.W., Suite 300
Washington, DC 20005-4914
Phone: (202) 789-2900; Fax: (202) 789-1893; Email: hriresearch@anla.org
Web: www.anla.org/research/Scholarships/TandPBigelow.htm

**Summary:** To provide financial support to residents of New England interested in working on an undergraduate or graduate degree in landscape architecture or horticulture.

**Eligibility:** Open to full-time students enrolled in an accredited landscape or horticulture program in 1) the final year of a 2-year curriculum, 2) the third year of a 4-year curriculum, or 3) a graduate program. Applicants must have a minimum GPA of 2.25 as undergraduates or 3.0 as graduate students. They must be a resident of 1 of the 6 New England states, although attendance at an institution within those states is not required. Preference is given to applicants who plan to work in an aspect of the nursery industry, including a business of their own, and to applicants who demonstrate financial need.

**Financial data:** The stipend is $2,500.

**Duration:** 1 year; nonrenewable.

**Number awarded:** Up to 3 each year.

**Deadline:** March of each year.

## 1706 TOWN OF WILLISTON HISTORICAL SOCIETY SCHOLARSHIP

Vermont Student Assistance Corporation
Champlain Mill, Attn: Scholarship Programs
P.O. Box 2000
Winooski, VT 05404-2601
Phone: (802) 654-3798; (888) 253-4819; Fax: (802) 654-3765; TDD: (802) 654-3766; TDD: (800) 281-3341 (within VT); Email: info@vsac.org
Web: www.vsac.org

**Summary:** To provide financial assistance to upper-division students at colleges and universities in Vermont who are majoring in history.

**Eligibility:** Open to juniors and seniors at colleges and universities in Vermont working on a 4-year degree in history. Applicants must be residents of Vermont. Selection is based on required essays.

**Financial data:** The stipend is $1,000.

**Duration:** 1 year; nonrenewable.

**Number awarded:** 1 each year.

**Deadline:** May of each year.

## 1707 TRANSGENDER SCHOLARSHIP AND EDUCATION LEGACY FUND AWARDS

International Foundation for Gender Education
Attn: Transgender Scholarship and Education Legacy Fund
P.O. Box 540229
Waltham, MA 02454-0229
Phone: (781) 899-2212; Fax: (781) 899-5703; Email: carrie@tself.org
Web: www.tself.org

**Summary:** To provide financial assistance to transgender students who are working on an undergraduate or graduate degree in the caring professions.

**Eligibility:** Open to undergraduate and graduate students who are living full time in a gender or sex role that differs from that assigned to them at birth and who are "out and proud" about their transgender identity. Applicants must be working on a degree in the helping and caring professions, including, but not limited to, social services, health care, religious instruction, education, and the law. They must be enrolled or planning to enroll at a college, university, trade school, or technical college in the United States or Canada. Selection is based on affirmation of transgender identity; demonstration of integrity and honesty; participation and leadership in community activities; service as role model, mentor, colleague, or advisor for the transgender communities; and service as

transgender role model, mentor, colleague, or advisor to non-transpeople in the helping and caring professions.

**Financial data:** Stipends average $2,000. Funds are paid directly to the student.

**Duration:** 1 year; nonrenewable.

**Number awarded:** Varies each year; recently, 4 of these scholarships were awarded.

**Deadline:** January of each year.

## 1708 TSJCL GARETH MORGAN SCHOLARSHIP

Texas Classical Association
c/o Andrew Riggsby, Scholarship Committee Chair
University of Texas at Austin
Waggener 123
Austin, TX 78712-1181
Phone: (512) 471-5742; Email: ariggsby@utxvms.cc.utexas.edu
Web: www.txclassics.org/schol.htm

**Summary:** To provide financial assistance to high school seniors in Texas who plan to study Latin or Greek in college.

**Eligibility:** Open to residents of Texas who have been active members of the Texas Classical Association (TCA) for at least 2 years. Applicants must be graduating from high school and planning to continue their study of Latin and Greek during their freshman year in college. Enrollment in Latin cannot be at a beginning level. Courses in classical civilization are not accepted.

**Financial data:** The stipend is $1,000.

**Duration:** 1 year.

**Number awarded:** 1 each year.

**Deadline:** June of each year.

## 1709 TUSKEGEE AIRMEN SCHOLARSHIPS

Tuskegee Airmen, Inc.
1501 Lee Highway, Suite 130
Arlington, VA 22209-1109
Phone: (703) 522-8590; Fax: (703) 522-8542; Email: hqtai@tuskegeeairmen.org
Web: www.tuskegeeairmen.org/scholarships.htm

**Summary:** To provide financial assistance for college to high school seniors and graduates who submit an essay on the history of Tuskegee Airmen, a group of African Americans who served as pilots in World War II.

**Eligibility:** Open to students who have graduated or will graduate from high school in the current year with a GPA of 3.0 or higher. Applicants must submit a 1-page essay entitled "The Tuskegee Airmen" that reflects an overview of their history. They must also submit documentation of financial need and a 2-page essay that includes a brief autobiographical sketch, educational aspirations, career goals, and an explanation of why financial assistance is essential. Applications must be submitted to individual chapters of Tuskegee Airmen, Inc. which verify them as appropriate, evaluate them, and forward those considered worthy of further consideration to the national competition. Selection is based on academic achievement, extracurricular and community activities, financial need, recommendations, and both essays.

**Financial data:** The stipend is $1,500.

**Duration:** 1 year; nonrenewable.

**Number awarded:** Varies each year; recently, 41 of these scholarships were available.

**Deadline:** February of each year.

## 1710 UNITED METHODIST FOUNDATION ANNUAL CONFERENCE SCHOLARS PROGRAM

**Summary:** To provide financial assistance to undergraduate and seminary students attending schools affiliated with the United Methodist Church.
*See Listing #1130.*

## 1711 UNITED METHODIST SCHOLARSHIP PROGRAM

**Summary:** To provide financial assistance to undergraduate and graduate students attending schools affiliated with the United Methodist Church.
*See Listing #1132.*

## 1712 UPPER MIDWEST CHAPTER SCHOLARSHIPS

National Academy of Television Arts and Sciences-Upper Midwest Chapter
c/o Allen Costantini, Scholarship Committee Chair
KARE 11 TV

8811 Olson Memorial Highway
Minneapolis, MN 55427
Phone: (763) 797-7235; Fax: (763) 546-8606; Email: acostantini@kare11.com
Web: www.natas-mn.org/scholarship.htm
**Summary:** To provide financial assistance to high school seniors from upper midwestern states planning to major in journalism in college.
**Eligibility:** Open to seniors graduating from high schools in Minnesota, North Dakota, and South Dakota who have applied to or been accepted at a 4-year college or university. Applicants must have a GPA of 3.0 or higher and be planning to major in broadcasting, television, or electronic media. Along with their application, they must submit a personal statement about their goals and professional aspirations, how television has affected their life, and how television should affect society now and in years to come. Finalists may be invited to an interview.
**Financial data:** The stipend is $2,000.
**Duration:** 1 year.
**Number awarded:** 1 or more each year.
**Deadline:** February of each year.

## 1713 USA WEEKEND/JOHN LENNON SONGWRITING CONTEST FOR TEENS

USA Weekend, Attn: John Lennon Songwriting Contest
7950 Jones Branch Drive
McLean, VA 22108-0210
Phone: (800) 487-2956; Fax: (703) 854-2122
Web: www.usaweekend.com/classroom/song_entry.html
**Summary:** To recognize and reward outstanding songs written by high school students.
**Eligibility:** Open to full-time students in grades 7-12 in accredited public, private, parochial, or home schools. They are invited to submit the lyrics of an original song, up to 125 words in length, that relates to a theme that changes annually. Recently, the theme was "American Dreams." Selection is based on originality and creativity (30%); songwriting ability (30%); appropriateness of song lyrics for recording (20%), and appropriateness of song lyrics for the theme.
**Financial data:** The Grand Prize winner receives a $1,000 U.S. savings bond, a trip for 2 to Los Angeles, a walk-on role in an episode of the NBC series "American Dreams," publication of winning lyrics in *USA Weekend*, and other gifts.
**Duration:** The competition is held annually.
**Number awarded:** 1 each year.
**Deadline:** February of each year.

## 1714 USREY FAMILY SCHOLARSHIP

American Nursery and Landscape Association
Attn: Horticultural Research Institute
1000 Vermont Avenue N.W., Suite 300
Washington, DC 20005-4914
Phone: (202) 789-2900; Fax: (202) 789-1893; Email: hriresearch@anla.org
Web: www.anla.org/research/Scholarships/ANLANationalScholarship.htm
**Summary:** To provide financial support to residents of California interested in working on an undergraduate or graduate degree in landscape architecture or horticulture.
**Eligibility:** Open to California residents enrolled full time in a landscape or horticulture undergraduate or graduate program at an accredited 2-year or 4-year college or university in California. Students enrolled in a vocational agriculture program are also eligible. Applicants must have a minimum GPA of 2.25 overall and 2.7 in their major. Preference is given to applicants who plan to work within the nursery industry, including nursery operations; landscape architecture, design, construction, or maintenance; interiorscape; horticultural distribution; or retail garden center.
**Financial data:** The stipend is at least $1,000.
**Duration:** 1 year; may be renewed.
**Number awarded:** 1 each year.
**Deadline:** March of each year.

## 1715 VELMA BERNECKER GWINN GARDEN CLUB OBJECTIVES SCHOLARSHIP

Florida Federation of Garden Clubs, Inc., Attn: Office Manager
1400 South Denning Drive
Winter Park, FL 32789-5662
Phone: (407) 647-7016; Fax: (407) 647-5479; Email: ffgc@earthlink.net
Web: www.ffgc.org/scholarships/index.html
**Summary:** To provide financial aid to Florida undergraduates and graduate students majoring in designated areas related to gardening.

**Eligibility:** Open to Florida residents who are enrolled as full-time juniors, seniors, or graduate students in a Florida college. They must have a GPA of 3.0 or higher, be in financial need, and be majoring in agriculture, agronomy, biology, botany, butterflies, city planning, conservation, ecology, forestry, horticulture, landscape design and architecture, marine biology, management of natural resources, native plants and wildlife, water management, xeriscaping, or a related subject. U.S. citizenship is required. Selection is based on academic record, commitment to career, character, and financial need.
**Financial data:** The stipend is $2,500. The funds are sent directly to the recipient's school and distributed semiannually.
**Duration:** 1 year.
**Number awarded:** 1 each year.
**Deadline:** April of each year.

## 1716 VERMONT HAND CRAFTERS ARTISANSHIP SCHOLARSHIPS

Vermont Student Assistance Corporation
Champlain Mill, Attn: Scholarship Programs
P.O. Box 2000
Winooski, VT 05404-2601
Phone: (802) 654-3798; (888) 253-4819; Fax: (802) 654-3765; TDD: (802) 654-3766; TDD: (800) 281-3341 (within VT); Email: info@vsac.org
Web: www.vsac.org
**Summary:** To provide financial assistance to residents of Vermont who are interested in majoring in arts or crafts in college.
**Eligibility:** Open to high school seniors, high school graduates, and currently-enrolled college students in Vermont who are enrolled or planning to enroll at least half time in a postsecondary degree program in the visual arts (particularly arts and crafts). Applicants must have been residents of Vermont for at least 2 years. Selection is based on financial need, academic achievement, a portfolio, a letter of recommendation, required essays, and a personal interview (if necessary).
**Financial data:** Stipends range from $500 to $1,000.
**Duration:** 1 year.
**Number awarded:** Varies each year; recently, 5 of these scholarships were awarded.
**Deadline:** June of each year.

## 1717 VIC AND MARGARET BALL INTERNSHIP

American Floral Endowment
P.O. Box 945
Edwardsville, IL 62025
Phone: (618) 692-0045; Fax: (618) 692-4045; Email: afe@endowment.org
Web: www.endowment.org/ball3.htm
**Summary:** To provide financial assistance and work experience to students working on an undergraduate degree in floriculture.
**Eligibility:** Open to U.S. citizens who are currently enrolled full time in a 2-year or 4-year college or university in the United States in a floriculture or environmental horticulture program. Applicants must be maintaining satisfactory progress in a degree or certificate program and a GPA of C or better. They must be interested in gaining additional training by interning at a commercial production greenhouse or nursery of sufficient size to support a well-rounded internship program away from their home and school community.
**Financial data:** Employers must agree to pay a fair market wage for the geographic area and position. In addition, students receive a grant of $6,000 for a 6-month internship, $4,000 for a 4-month internship, or $1,500 for a 3-month summer internship.
**Duration:** 6 months, 4 months, or 3 summer months.
**Number awarded:** 1 or more each year.
**Deadline:** February or October of each year.

## 1718 VICTOR HERBERT ASCAP YOUNG COMPOSER AWARDS

National Federation of Music Clubs
1336 North Delaware Street
Indianapolis, IN 46202-2481
Phone: (317) 638-4003; Fax: (317) 638-0503; Email: info@nfmc-music.org
Web: www.nfmc-music.org/Competitions/Annual_Student/annual_student.html
**Summary:** To recognize and reward outstanding young composers who are members of the National Federation of Music Clubs.
**Eligibility:** Open to competitors who are between 18 and 26 years of age, U.S. citizens, and student members of the federation. Awards are presented in 4 categories of student compositions: 1) sonata or comparable work for solo wind

or string instrument with piano or for any combination of 3 to 5 instruments (including piano), at least 8 minutes in length; 2) choral work, either unaccompanied or with an accompaniment of piano, organ, or a group of up to 10 wind or string instruments, in English, at least 4 minutes in length; 3) piano solo, either a sonata or theme and variations, at least 5 minutes in length; and 4) vocal solo, with piano, organ, or orchestral accompaniment, text in English, at least 4 minutes in length.

**Financial data:** In each category, first prize is $1,000, second $500, and third $500. Special recognition awards of $50 are also presented.

**Duration:** The competition is held annually.

**Number awarded:** 12 prizes (3 in each category) and 2 special recognition awards each year.

**Deadline:** February of each year.

## 1719 VIDEO CONTEST FOR COLLEGE STUDENTS

The Christophers, Attn: Youth Department Coordinator
12 East 48th Street
New York, NY 10017
Phone: (212) 759-4050; Fax: (212) 838-5073;
Email: youth-coordinator@christophers.org
Web: www.christophers.org/contests.html

**Summary:** To recognize and reward videos produced by college students that best illustrate the motto of The Christophers, "It's better to light one candle than to curse the darkness."

**Eligibility:** Open to currently-enrolled college students who are interested in submitting films or videos on the theme: "One Person Can Make a Difference." They may use any style or format to express this theme in 5 minutes or less. Entries may be created using film or video, but they must be submitted on 3/4 inch or VHS cassette. Selection is based on content (the ability to capture the theme), artistic and technical proficiency, and adherence to all contest rules.

**Financial data:** First prize is $3,000, second prize is $2,000, third prize is $1,000, and honorable mention is $100.

**Number awarded:** 8 each year: 1 each for first, second, and third place plus 5 honorable mentions.

**Deadline:** June of each year.

## 1720 VIRGINIA ALLISON ACCOMPANYING AWARD

National Federation of Music Clubs
1336 North Delaware Street
Indianapolis, IN 46202-2481
Phone: (317) 638-4003; Fax: (317) 638-0503; Email: info@nfmc-music.org
Web: www.nfmc-music.org/Competitions/BienStudentSpecial/BienStudentSpecial.htm

**Summary:** To recognize and reward outstanding young musicians who are members of the National Federation of Music Clubs (NFMC).

**Eligibility:** Open to students majoring in vocal or instrumental accompanying. They must be between 18 and 25 years of age, U.S. citizens, and student members of the federation. Selection is based on a cassette tape, from 15 to 20 minutes in length. The tape must include, for vocal accompanying, some early Italian selections, German lied, French chanson, and at least one American composition, and, for instrumental accompanying, one selection for each period of music, including at least one American composition.

**Financial data:** The award is $2,000.

**Number awarded:** 1 every other year.

**Deadline:** February of odd-numbered years.

## 1721 VIRGINIA ASSOCIATION OF BROADCASTERS SCHOLARSHIP GRANT

Virginia Association of Broadcasters, Attn: Scholarship Committee
630 Country Green Lane
Charlottesville, VA 22902
Phone: (434) 977-3716; Fax: (434) 979-2439; Email: vab@easterassociates.com
Web: www.vabonline.com/education/scholarship.asp

**Summary:** To provide financial assistance to upper-division students (either residents of Virginia or attending school there) who are majoring in broadcasting.

**Eligibility:** Open to entering juniors and seniors at a college or university that offers undergraduate training in broadcasting-related fields, such as mass media, communications, journalism, and advertising. Applicants must be either 1) a Virginia resident attending a college or university anywhere in the United States or a professional broadcast school certified by the Virginia Department of Education; or 2) a nonresident student attending a Virginia college, university, or certified professional broadcast school. They must intend to prepare for a career in broadcasting. Along with their application, they must submit 1) a 250-word essay describing their reasons for choosing a broadcast-

ing career and their interest in radio or television broadcasting or engineering; 2) college transcript; and 3) documentation of financial need.

**Financial data:** The stipend is either $1,000 or $500.

**Duration:** 1 year.

**Number awarded:** 4 each year: 1 at $1,000 and 3 at $500.

**Deadline:** February of each year.

## 1722 VIRGINIA BAPTIST MISSION BOARD MINISTERIAL STUDENT AID

Virginia Baptist Mission Board, Attn: Assistant Executive Director
2828 Emerywood Parkway
P.O. Box 8568
Richmond, VA 23226-0568
Phone: (804) 915-5000; (800) 255-2428 (within VA); Fax: (804) 672-2051;
Email: help@vbmb.org
Web: www.vbmb.org/scholarships/default.htm

**Summary:** To provide financial assistance to members of Baptist churches in Virginia who are interested in working on an undergraduate degree in preparation for a ministerial career.

**Eligibility:** Open to students who have been members for at least one year of a church affiliated with the Baptist General Association of Virginia. Applicants must be working or planning to work full-time on a bachelor's or divinity degree or equivalent. They must intend to complete their education, after graduation, in a designated seminary or graduate school for special ministerial training. Along with their application, they must indicate their dedication to preaching or engaging in other full-time Christian work. Selection is based primarily on financial need.

**Financial data:** The stipend depends on the need of the recipient and the availability of funds.

**Duration:** 1 year; may be renewed up to 3 additional years.

**Number awarded:** 1 or more each year.

**Deadline:** May of each year for the school year; December of each year for the second semester.

## 1723 VIRGINIA DAR AMERICAN HISTORY SCHOLARSHIPS

Virginia Daughters of the American Revolution
c/o Catherine Rafferty, Scholarship Chair
10101 Sanders Court
Great Falls, VA 22066-2526
Web: www.vadar.org/history.html

**Summary:** To provide financial assistance to high school seniors in Virginia who wish to study American history in college.

**Eligibility:** Open to seniors graduating from high schools in Virginia in the top third of their class. Applicants must be planning to major in American history in college. Along with their application, they must submit a 1,000-word letter giving their reasons for desiring an education in American history, a transcript of grades, SAT or ACT scores, extracurricular activities, honors received, and documentation of financial need.

**Financial data:** Stipends are $1,000 or $500.

**Duration:** 1 year.

**Number awarded:** 2 each year: 1 at $1,000 and 1 at $500.

**Deadline:** January of each year.

## 1724 VIRGINIA DAR SCHOLARSHIPS

Virginia Daughters of the American Revolution
c/o Catherine Rafferty, Scholarship Chair
10101 Sanders Court
Great Falls, VA 22066-2526
Web: www.vadar.org/history.html

**Summary:** To provide financial assistance to high school seniors in Virginia who wish to study designated fields in college.

**Eligibility:** Open to seniors graduating from high schools in Virginia who plan to attend a Virginia college or university. Applicants must be planning to work on a degree in the field of science, medicine, conservation, ecology, forestry, home arts, genealogical research, or American history. Along with their application, they must submit a 1,000-word letter giving their reasons for interest in the scholarship, a transcript of grades, a letter of recommendation from a teacher in their chosen field, and documentation of financial need.

**Financial data:** Stipends are $1,000 or $500.

**Duration:** 1 year.

**Number awarded:** 2 each year: 1 at $1,000 and 1 at $500.

**Deadline:** January of each year.

## 1725 VISUAL TASK FORCE SCHOLARSHIPS

National Association of Black Journalists
Attn: Student Education Enrichment and Development Program
8701-A Adelphi Road
Adelphi, MD 20783-1716
Phone: (301) 445-7100, ext. 108; Fax: (301) 445-7101; Email: nabj@nabj.org
Web: www.nabj.org/scholarships.html

**Summary:** To provide financial assistance to undergraduate or graduate student members of the National Association of Black Journalists (NABJ) who are interested in a career in visual journalism.

**Eligibility:** Open to African American undergraduate or graduate students who are currently attending an accredited 4-year college or university. Applicants must be majoring in visual journalism, have a GPA of 2.75 or higher, have experience working on their campus newspaper or TV studio, and have had an internship. They must submit samples of their work, an official college transcript, 2 letters of recommendation, a resume, and a 500- to 800-word essay describing their accomplishments as a student journalist, their career goals, and their financial need.

**Financial data:** The stipend is $1,250. Funds are paid directly to the recipient's college or university.

**Duration:** 1 year; nonrenewable.

**Number awarded:** 2 each year.

**Deadline:** April of each year.

## 1726 VSA ARTS YOUNG SOLOISTS AWARD

VSA arts, Attn: Education Office
1300 Connecticut Avenue, N.W., Suite 700
Washington, DC 20036
Phone: (202) 628-2800; (800) 933-8721; Fax: (202) 737-0725; TTY: (202) 737-0645; Email: soloists@vsarts.org
Web: www.vsarts.org/x22.xml

**Summary:** To recognize and reward performing musicians who are physically or mentally challenged.

**Eligibility:** Open to vocalists or instrumentalists under 25 years of age who have a disability. Applicants may be performers in any type of music, including country, classical, jazz, rap, rock, bluegrass, or ethnic. They are required to submit an audition tape and a 1-page biography that describes why they should be selected to receive this award. Tapes are evaluated on the basis of technique, tone, intonation, rhythm, and interpretation.

**Financial data:** A monetary award is presented (amount not specified).

**Duration:** The competition is held annually.

**Number awarded:** 2 each year.

**Deadline:** October of each year.

## 1727 VSA ARTS/VOLKSWAGEN ART AWARDS

VSA arts, Attn: VOA Awards
P.O. Box 33699
Washington, DC 20033-3699
Phone: (202) 628-2800; (800) 933-8721, ext. 3877; Fax: (202) 737-0725; TTY: (202) 737-0645; Email: voa@vsarts.org
Web: www.vsarts.org/x267.xml

**Summary:** To recognize and reward young artists with disabilities.

**Eligibility:** Open to artists between 16 and 25 years of age who have a physical, cognitive, or mental disability. Applicants are invited to submit artwork that they have created in the last 3 years on a theme that changes annually. Recently, the theme was "Shifting Gears," in which artists were invited to reflect on a pivotal moment or event in their life that led them to a greater understanding of themselves in relation to their art and/or their disability. Both representational and abstract art may be submitted. Eligible media include paintings and drawings (oil, watercolor, acrylic, pencil, or charcoal), fine art prints (lithographs, etching, intaglio, or woodcuts), photography, computer generated prints, and 2-dimensional mixed media. Up to 5 slides may be submitted, along with a 400-word essay covering their artistic background and answers to questions on when they started creating artwork, what motivated them to begin, the techniques and media they use, the role their art plays in living with their disability, how their disability affects their artwork, a significant experience during their education where the arts played an important part, and when the arts were most effective in their education.

**Financial data:** The grand prize is $20,000, first prize is $10,000, second prize is $6,000, and awards of excellence are $2,000.

**Duration:** The competition is held annually.

**Number awarded:** A total of 15 cash prizes are awarded each year: 1 grand prize, 1 first prize, 1 second prize, and 12 awards of excellence.

**Deadline:** July of each year.

## 1728 WAHPERD STUDENT SCHOLARSHIP AWARDS

Wisconsin Association for Health, Physical Education, Recreation, and Dance
Attn: Executive Director
University of Wisconsin at La Crosse
24 Mitchell Hall
1725 State Street
La Crosse, WI 54601-3788
Phone: (608) 785-8175; (800) 441-4568; Email: wahperd@uwlax.edu
Web: www.uwlax.edu/eeshr/wahperd/scholarships.html

**Summary:** To provide financial assistance to members of the Wisconsin Association for Health, Physical Education, Recreation and Dance (WAHPERD) who are working on a college degree.

**Eligibility:** Open to WAHPERD members who have completed at least 2 years of study at a 4-year college or university with a major in physical education, health education, exercise fitness, recreation, athletic training, sports management, or dance. Applicants must have a GPA of 3.2 or higher, at least 2 years' WAHPERD membership, and a record of professional involvement and leadership responsibility. They must submit a resume and 2 letters of recommendation. Financial need is not considered in the selection process.

**Financial data:** The stipend is $4,000.

**Duration:** 1 year.

**Number awarded:** 4 each year.

**Deadline:** March of each year.

## 1729 WALLY WIKOFF SCHOLARSHIP FOR EDITORIAL LEADERSHIP

National Scholastic Press Association
2221 University Avenue, S.E., Suite 121
Minneapolis, MN 55414
Phone: (612) 625-8335; Fax: (612) 626-0720; Email: info@studentpress.org
Web: www.studentpress.org/nspa/contests.html

**Summary:** To provide financial assistance for college to high school journalists.

**Eligibility:** Open to high school seniors who have worked on the staff of a student newspaper that is a member of the National Scholastic Press Association (NSPA). Applicants must have a GPA of 3.5 or higher and must submit 3 published editorials and a brief recommendation from the program's adviser.

**Financial data:** The stipend is $1,000.

**Duration:** 1 year.

**Number awarded:** 1 each year.

**Deadline:** February of each year.

## 1730 WALSWORTH SCHOLARSHIP

University Interscholastic League
Attn: Interscholastic League Press Conference
1701 Manor Road
P.O. Box 8028
Austin, TX 78713
Phone: (512) 471-5883; Fax: (512) 232-7311;
Email: rvonderheid@mail.utexas.edu
Web: www.uil.utexas.edu/aca/journ/ilpc

**Summary:** To provide financial assistance to high school seniors in Texas who plan to study communications in college.

**Eligibility:** Open to seniors graduating from high schools in Texas who have been involved in journalism and plan to continue their education in a communications-related field (major or minor) in college. Applicants must have a GPA of B or higher. Along with their application, they must submit a statement on their involvement in journalism while in high school, a description of their college and future plans, a letter of recommendation, and 3 to 5 samples of their work as a journalism student.

**Financial data:** The stipend is $1,000.

**Duration:** 1 year.

**Number awarded:** 1 each year.

**Deadline:** March of each year.

## 1731 WALTER S. PATTERSON SCHOLARSHIPS

Broadcast Education Association, Attn: Scholarships
1771 N Street, N.W.
Washington, DC 20036-2891
Phone: (202) 429-5354; (888) 380-7222; Email: beainfo@beaweb.org
Web: www.beaweb.org/scholarships.html

**Summary:** To provide financial assistance to upper-division and graduate students who are interested in preparing for a career in radio.

**Eligibility:** Open to juniors, seniors, and graduate students enrolled full time at a college or university where at least 1 department is an institutional member of the Broadcast Education Association (BEA). Applicants must be studying for a career in radio. Selection is based on evidence that the applicant possesses high integrity, superior academic ability, potential to be an outstanding electronic media professional, and a sense of personal and professional responsibility.

**Financial data:** The stipend is $1,250.

**Duration:** 1 year; may not be renewed.

**Number awarded:** 2 each year.

**Deadline:** September of each year.

## [1732] WALTER W. RISTOW PRIZE

Washington Map Society
c/o John Docktor
33 East Philadelphia Street
York, PA 17401
Email: washmap@earthlink.net
Web: home.earthlink.net/~doctor/ristow.htm

**Summary:** To recognize and reward outstanding student papers on cartographic history and map librarianship.

**Eligibility:** Open to all full- and part-time upper-division undergraduate students, graduate students, and first-year postdoctorates. These students are eligible to submit research papers or bibliographic studies that relate to cartographic history and/or map librarianship. In the case of undergraduate and graduate students, the entries must have been completed in fulfillment of requirements for course work. A short edition of a longer paper is permitted, but the text may not exceed 7,500 words. All entries must be in English. Papers must be fully documented, in a style of the author's choice. Entries are judged on the importance of the research, the quality of the research, and the quality of writing.

**Financial data:** The prize is $1,000 and membership in the society.

**Duration:** The prize is offered annually.

**Number awarded:** 1 each year.

**Deadline:** May of each year.

## [1733] WASHINGTON FASHION GROUP INTERNATIONAL SCHOLARSHIP

Fashion Group International of Washington
Attn: Julie Caine Brooks, Scholarship Chair
P.O. Box 1288
Great Falls, VA 22066

**Summary:** To provide financial assistance for college or graduate school to residents of Maryland, Virginia, and Washington, D.C., interested in preparing for a career in fashion or a fashion-related field.

**Eligibility:** Open to residents of Washington, D.C., and all cities and counties in Maryland and Virginia. Applicants must be graduating high school seniors or current undergraduate or graduate students enrolled in a fashion or fashion-related degree program (commercial arts, textiles and clothing design, interior design, journalism, merchandising, or photography). They must submit a 200-word personal statement on their career goals and motivation for entering a fashion-related career. Selection is based on that statement, academic achievement, creative ability, related work activity (paid or unpaid), extracurricular activities and awards, and 3 letters of reference. Finalists are interviewed and asked to submit portfolio material of their work.

**Financial data:** The maximum stipend is $5,000.

**Duration:** 1 year; nonrenewable

**Number awarded:** 1 each year.

**Deadline:** April of each year.

## [1734] WAVELAND DIRECT PRINTING AND PUBLISHING SCHOLARSHIP

Big 33 Scholarship Foundation
Attn: Scholarship Committee
511 Bridge Street
P.O. Box 213
New Cumberland, PA 17070
Phone: (717) 774-3303; (877) PABIG-33; Fax: (717) 774-1749;
Email: info@big33.org
Web: www.big33.org/scholarships/default.ashx

**Summary:** To provide financial assistance and work experience to graduating high school seniors in Ohio and Pennsylvania who plan to study graphic arts in college.

**Eligibility:** Open to seniors graduating from public and accredited private high schools in Ohio and Pennsylvania who are planning to study graphic arts as related to printing and publishing technology in college. Applications are available from high school guidance counselors. Selection is based on special talents, leadership, obstacles overcome, academic achievement (at least a 2.0 GPA), community service, unique endeavors, financial need, and a 1-page essay on why the applicant deserves the scholarship.

**Financial data:** The stipend is $1,000.

**Duration:** 1 year; nonrenewable.

**Number awarded:** 1 each year.

**Deadline:** February of each year.

## [1735] WENDELL IRISH VIOLA AWARDS

National Federation of Music Clubs
1336 North Delaware Street
Indianapolis, IN 46202-2481
Phone: (317) 638-4003; Fax: (317) 638-0503; Email: info@nfmc-music.org
Web: www.nfmc-music.org/Competitions/Annual_Junior/annual_junior.html

**Summary:** To recognize and reward outstanding young violists who are members of the National Federation of Music Clubs (NFMC).

**Eligibility:** Open to violists between 12 and 19 years of age. Applicants must be members of the junior division of the federation and U.S. citizens. They must present at least 2 pieces selected from contrasting style periods.

**Financial data:** The award is $1,000.

**Number awarded:** 4 each year: 1 in each NFMC region.

**Deadline:** January of each year.

## [1736] WEST VIRGINIA BROADCASTERS FUND SCHOLARSHIPS

Greater Kanawha Valley Foundation, Attn: Scholarship Coordinator
1600 Huntington Square
900 Lee Street, East
P.O. Box 3041
Charleston, WV 25331-3041
Phone: (304) 346-3620; Fax: (304) 346-3640; Email: tgkvf@tgkvf.com
Web: www.tgkvf.com/scholar.html

**Summary:** To provide financial assistance to residents of West Virginia who are interested in majoring in a field related to broadcasting in college.

**Eligibility:** Open to residents of West Virginia who are students at a college or university anywhere in the country and majoring in communications, broadcasting, film, speech, broadcast journalism, advertising, broadcast electronics, or other arts and techniques of the communications field. Applicants must be recommended by a station that is a member of the West Virginia Broadcasters Association. They must have an ACT score of 20 or higher, be able to demonstrate good moral character, and have a GPA of 2.5 or higher.

**Financial data:** The stipend is $1,000 per year.

**Duration:** 1 year; may be renewed.

**Number awarded:** Varies each year; recently, 5 of these scholarships were awarded.

**Deadline:** February of each year.

## [1737] WESTERN WASHINGTON CHAPTER JOURNALISM SCHOLARSHIP

Society of Professional Journalists-Western Washington Chapter
Attn: Scholarship Competition
3838 Stone Way North
Seattle, WA 98103
Phone: (206) 545-7918; Email: president@spjwash.org
Web: www.spjwash.org

**Summary:** To provide financial assistance to undergraduate students in Washington state who are majoring in journalism.

**Eligibility:** Open to undergraduate students in Washington who are currently majoring in journalism or communications (including community college students planning to pursue journalism careers at a Washington college or university). As part of the application process, students must submit a letter of application, including an answer to the question "Why have you chosen a journalism career and what do you hope to accomplish" (500 words), a copy of their resume, a letter of recommendation, an official transcript of all college credits, and 3 work samples.

**Financial data:** The stipend is $1,000.

**Duration:** 1 year.

**Number awarded:** 5 each year.

**Deadline:** March of each year.

## 1738 WIENIAWSKI VIOLIN COMPETITION

Kosciuszko Foundation, Attn: Director of Cultural Events
15 East 65th Street
New York, NY 10021-6595
Phone: (212) 734-2130, ext. 214; (800) 287-9956; Fax: (212) 628-4552;
Email: culture@thekf.org
Web: www.thekf.org/MUViolin.html
**Summary:** To recognize and reward outstanding violinists.
**Eligibility:** Open to U.S. citizens, permanent residents of the United States, and international full-time students with valid student visas; all entrants must be between 16 and 22 years of age. Contestants prepare a program of 60 to 75 minutes encompassing a concerto by Wieniawski or Szymanowski, the first 2 movements of a Bach sonata, a sonata by Beethoven or Mozart, a virtuostic 19th-century work, a Paganini caprice, and a substantial work by an American, Polish, or Polish American composer written after 1950. They must submit an audition CD of approximately 15 minutes with selections from their program. Based on those CDs, finalists are invited to the competition in New York.
**Financial data:** First place is $5,000, second $2,500, and third $1,500.
**Duration:** The competition is held annually, in April.
**Number awarded:** 3 national prizes are awarded each year.
**Deadline:** March of each year.

## 1739 WILLIAM B. RUGGLES RIGHT TO WORK SCHOLARSHIP

National Institute for Labor Relations Research
Attn: Scholarship Selection Committee
5211 Port Royal Road, Suite 510
Springfield, VA 22151
Phone: (703) 321-9606; Fax: (703) 321-7342; Email: research@nilrr.org
Web: www.nilrr.org/ruggles.htm
**Summary:** To provide financial assistance for the undergraduate or graduate education of journalism students who are knowledgeable about the Right to Work principle.
**Eligibility:** Open to undergraduate or graduate students majoring in journalism at institutions of higher learning in the United States. Graduating high school seniors may also apply. Applicants must demonstrate potential for successful completion of educational requirements in an accredited journalism program and demonstrate an understanding of the principles voluntary unionism and the economic and social problems of compulsory unionism. Selection is based on scholastic ability and financial need.
**Financial data:** The stipend is $2,000.
**Duration:** 1 year.
**Number awarded:** 1 each year.
**Deadline:** December of each year.

## 1740 WILLIAM E. GREGORY SCHOLARSHIP

Imperial Polk Advertising Federation, Attn: Scholarship Program
P.O. Box 24201
Lakeland, FL 33802-4201
Phone: (863) 858-5736; Fax: (863) 858-3736
Web: www.polkadfed.com
**Summary:** To provide financial assistance to undergraduate students majoring in fields related to advertising at Florida colleges.
**Eligibility:** Open to full-time undergraduate students at universities, colleges, and technical schools in Florida. Applicants must be working on a degree in advertising, communications, graphic design, or marketing. They must have a GPA of 3.0 or higher. Along with their application, they must submit 1) a 500-word essay describing their future professional and educational goals; and 2) a project they have recently completed for a class or internship. Financial need is not considered in the selection process.
**Financial data:** A total of $2,000 is available for this program each year.
**Duration:** 1 year; nonrenewable.
**Number awarded:** 1 or more each year.
**Deadline:** November of each year.

## 1741 WILLIAM G. AND MARGARET B. FRASIER CHARITABLE FOUNDATION SCHOLARSHIP

Center for Scholarship Administration, Inc., Attn: Wachovia Accounts
4320-G Wade Hampton Boulevard
Taylors, SC 29687
Phone: (866) 608-0001; Email: wachoviascholars@bellsouth.net
Web: www.wachoviascholars.com/wscholarships.php

**Summary:** To provide financial assistance to undergraduate and graduate students from North Carolina who are preparing for a career in the Baptist ministry.
**Eligibility:** Open to residents of North Carolina who are studying for the Baptist ministry. Applicants must be full-time students working on a recognized undergraduate or graduate degree. Selection is based on academic merit, financial need, and potential to succeed in the student's chosen educational field.
**Financial data:** A stipend is awarded (amount not specified).
**Duration:** 1 year; recipients may reapply.
**Number awarded:** Several each year.
**Deadline:** May of each year.

## 1742 WILLIAM G. SALETIC SCHOLARSHIP

Independent Colleges of Washington
600 Stewart Street, Suite 600
Seattle, WA 98101
Phone: (206) 623-4494; Fax: (206) 625-9621; Email: info@icwashington.org
Web: www.icwashington.org/parents_students/financial_aid/index.htm
**Summary:** To provide financial assistance to upper-division students majoring in politics or history at colleges and universities that are members of Independent Colleges of Washington (ICW).
**Eligibility:** Open to students completing their sophomore or junior year at ICW-member colleges and universities. Applicants must be studying or majoring in politics or history. They must submit a 1-page essay on why their special interest is in politics and/or history. Students with a GPA of 2.5 or higher are especially encouraged to apply.
**Financial data:** The stipend is $1,000.
**Duration:** 1 year; nonrenewable.
**Number awarded:** 1 each year.
**Deadline:** April of each year.

## 1743 WILLIAM J. LOCKLIN SCHOLARSHIP

Landscape Architecture Foundation, Attn: Scholarship Program
818 18th Street, N.W., Suite 810
Washington, DC 20006-3520
Phone: (202) 331-7070; Fax: (202) 331-7079; Email: rfigura@lafoundation.org
Web: www.laprofession.org
**Summary:** To provide financial aid to landscape architecture students who plan to utilize lighting in their work.
**Eligibility:** Open to landscape architecture students pursuing a program in lighting design or focusing on lighting design in studio projects. Applications must be accompanied by a 300-word essay highlighting the design project, including the overall effect to be obtained, rationale for choice of lamp and placement of fixture, and anticipated results. Selection is based on professional experience, community involvement, extracurricular activities, and financial need.
**Financial data:** The stipend is $1,000.
**Duration:** 1 year.
**Number awarded:** 1 each year.
**Deadline:** April of each year.

## 1744 WILLIAM P. FRANK PRIZE FOR EXCELLENCE IN COMMUNICATIONS

Delaware Community Foundation, Attn: Executive Vice President
100 West 10th Street, Suite 115
P.O. Box 1636
Wilmington, DE 19899
Phone: (302) 504-5222; Fax: (302) 571-1553; Email: rgentsch@delcf.org
Web: www.delcf.org
**Summary:** To provide financial assistance for college to high school seniors in Delaware who have been active in journalism and/or communication activities.
**Eligibility:** Open to Delaware high school seniors who have been active in journalism and/or communication activities, including school newspapers and magazines and/or television and radio programs. Each school in the state may nominate one student.
**Financial data:** The stipend is $1,000 per year.
**Duration:** 1 year; nonrenewable.
**Number awarded:** 3 each year: 1 in each county of Delaware.
**Deadline:** February of each year.

**1745** WISCONSIN BROADCASTERS ASSOCIATION FOUNDATION COLLEGE/UNIVERSITY STUDENT SCHOLARSHIP PROGRAM

Wisconsin Broadcasters Association, Attn: WBA Foundation
44 East Mifflin Street, Suite 900
Madison, WI 53703
Phone: (608) 255-2600; Fax: (608) 256-3986; Email: torrie@wi-broadcasters.org
Web: www.wi-broadcasters.org/scholarships.htm
**Summary:** To provide financial assistance to students at Wisconsin colleges and universities who are preparing for a career in broadcasting.
**Eligibility:** Open to students majoring in broadcasting, communication, or a related field at a 4-year public or private college or university in Wisconsin. Applicants must be planning a career in radio or television broadcasting. Along with their application, they must submit an official transcript, 2 letters of recommendation, and an essay forecasting what the broadcasting industry will be like in 5 years and how they will contribute to radio or television during that time. Finalists may be asked to participate in a personal interview.
**Financial data:** The stipend is $2,000.
**Duration:** 1 year; nonrenewable.
**Number awarded:** 3 each year.
**Deadline:** October of each year.

**1746** WOMEN CHEFS & RESTAURATEURS SCHOLARSHIP PROGRAM

Women Chefs & Restaurateurs, Attn: Scholarship Department
304 West Liberty Street, Suite 201
Louisville, KY 40202
Phone: (502) 581-0300; (877) 927-7787; Fax: (502) 589-3602
Web: www.womenchefs.org
**Summary:** To provide financial assistance to members of Women Chefs & Restaurateurs (WCR) who are interested in preparing for a culinary or related career.
**Eligibility:** Open to women who are members of WCR, interested in attending a culinary or related school, and at least 18 years of age (21 for the wine scholarships). Applicants must submit a 1-page essay about their food service career, their culinary interests, what inspires them professionally, and how the scholarship will contribute to their career.
**Financial data:** In general, scholarships provide payment of full or partial tuition, or stipends of $5,000 or $7,500.
**Duration:** Program lengths vary; scholarships must be used during the calendar year in which they are awarded.
**Number awarded:** Varies each year; recently, 18 of these scholarships were awarded.
**Deadline:** March of each year.

**1747** WOMEN MARINES ASSOCIATION SCHOLARSHIP PROGRAM

**Summary:** To provide financial assistance for college or graduate school to students sponsored by members of the Women Marines Association (WMA).
*See Listing #1214.*

**1748** WOMEN'S JEWELRY ASSOCIATION SCHOLARSHIP

Women's Jewelry Association
Attn: Scholarship Committee
373 B Route 46 West, Building E, Suite 215
Fairfield, NJ 07004
Phone: (973) 575-7190; Fax: (973) 575-1445; Email: info@womensjewelry.org
Web: www.womensjewelry.org/scholarships.html
**Summary:** To provide financial assistance for college to women who are interested in careers in jewelry.
**Eligibility:** Open to women who are enrolled in a jewelry-related curriculum at an institution of higher learning located in the United States. Eligible fields of study range from design to gemological analysis and include metalsmithing, finance, business, and marketing. Applicants must submit 2 letters of recommendation, a short essay explaining why they wish to prepare for a career in jewelry/toolmaking and their aspirations for the future, 3 slides showing examples of their work, and a list of 3 courses related to jewelry that have been most important to them. Financial need is considered in the selection process.
**Financial data:** Stipends range from $500 to $5,000 per year.
**Duration:** 1 year.
**Number awarded:** Varies each year. Recently, 12 of these scholarships were awarded: 1 at $5,000, 2 at $3,000, 1 at $2,500, 1 at $1,500 and 7 at $1,000.
**Deadline:** April of each year.

**1749** WORLD POPULATION FILM/VIDEO FESTIVAL AWARDS

World Population Film/Video Festival
46 Fox Hill Road
Bernardston, MA 01337
Phone: (800) 638-9464; Fax: (413) 648-9204; Email: info@wpfvf.com
Web: www.wpfvf.com
**Summary:** To recognize and reward outstanding student films that deal with population issues.
**Eligibility:** Open to secondary and college students who produce films and videos that explore the connection between population growth, resource consumption, the environment, and the global future. Entries must be submitted in VHS (NTSC) format for preview judging, but they may be any length, originate in any format (film, video, or multimedia), and be any style (documentary, narrative, music video, animation, other). This is an international competition.
**Financial data:** A total of $10,000 in prizes is awarded.
**Duration:** The competition is held annually.
**Number awarded:** Varies each year; recently, 6 high school and 10 college films received awards.
**Deadline:** June of each year.

**1750** WORLD WIDE BARACA PHILATHEA UNION SCHOLARSHIP

World Wide Baraca Philathea Union
610 South Harlem Avenue
Freeport, IL 61032-4833
**Summary:** To provide financial assistance to students preparing for Christian ministry, Christian missionary work, or Christian education.
**Eligibility:** Open to students enrolled in an accredited college or seminary who are majoring in Christian ministry, Christian missionary work, or Christian education (e.g., church youth pastor, writer of Sunday school curriculum).
**Financial data:** Stipends are paid directly to the recipient's school upon receipt of the first semester transcript and a letter confirming attendance.
**Duration:** 1 year; may be renewed.
**Deadline:** March of each year.

**1751** WORLDSTUDIO FOUNDATION INDIGENOUS PEOPLES AWARD

Worldstudio Foundation
200 Varick Street, Suite 507
New York, NY 10014
Phone: (212) 366-1317, ext. 18; Fax: (212) 807-0024;
Email: scholarshipcoordinator@worldstudio.org
Web: www.worldstudio.org/schol/specawards.html
**Summary:** To provide financial support for college or graduate school to art students of Native American heritage.
**Eligibility:** Open to art students affiliated with Native American, Alaska Native/Inuit, or other indigenous tribes of the Americas. Applicants must be interested in maintaining traditional art, designs, or crafts. They must be undergraduate or graduate students at an accredited college or university in the United States with a GPA of 2.0 or higher. Selection is based on the quality of submitted work, a written statement of purpose, financial need, and academic record.
**Financial data:** The stipend ranges from $1,000 to $2,000.
**Duration:** 1 academic year. Recipients may reapply.
**Number awarded:** 1 or more each year.
**Deadline:** March of each year.

**1752** WORLDSTUDIO FOUNDATION SCHOLARSHIPS

Worldstudio Foundation
200 Varick Street, Suite 507
New York, NY 10014
Phone: (212) 366-1317, ext. 18; Fax: (212) 807-0024;
Email: scholarshipcoordinator@worldstudio.org
Web: www.worldstudio.org/schol/index.html
**Summary:** To provide financial assistance to undergraduate and graduate students who wish to study fine or commercial arts, design, or architecture.
**Eligibility:** Open to undergraduate and graduate students who are currently enrolled or planning to enroll at an accredited college or university and major in one of the following areas: advertising (art direction only), architecture, crafts, environmental graphics, fashion design, film/video (direction or cinematography only), film/theater design (including set, lighting, and costume design), fine arts, furniture design, graphic design, industrial/product design, interior

design, landscape architecture, new media, photography, surface/textile design, or urban planning. Although not required, minority status is a significant factor in the selection process. International students may apply if they are enrolled at a U.S. college or university. Applicants must have a GPA of 2.0 or higher. Along with their application, they must submit a 600-word statement of purpose that includes a brief autobiography, an explanation of how their experiences have influenced their creative work and/or their career plans, and how they see themselves contributing to the community at large in the future. Selection is based on that statement, the quality of submitted work, financial need, minority status, and academic record.

**Financial data:** Basic scholarships range from $1,000 to $2,000, but awards between $3,000 and $5,000 are also presented at the discretion of the jury. Honorable mentions are $100. Funds are paid directly to the recipient's school.

**Duration:** 1 academic year. Recipients may reapply.

**Number awarded:** Varies each year; recently, 24 scholarships and 7 honorable mentions were awarded.

**Deadline:** March of each year.

---

## 1753 WORLDSTUDIO FOUNDATION SPECIAL ANIMATION AND ILLUSTRATION SCHOLARSHIPS

Worldstudio Foundation
200 Varick Street, Suite 507
New York, NY 10014
Phone: (212) 366-1317, ext. 18; Fax: (212) 807-0024;
Email: scholarshipcoordinator@worldstudio.org
Web: www.worldstudio.org/schol/specawards.html

**Summary:** To provide financial assistance to members of disadvantaged and ethnic minority groups who wish to study illustration, animation, or cartooning in college.

**Eligibility:** Open to members of disadvantaged or minority groups who are currently enrolled or planning to enroll in an accredited college or university in the United States. Applicants must be majoring or planning to major in illustration, animation, or cartooning. They must submit their most recent college or high school transcripts, documentation of financial need, a portfolio of their work, and a 600-word statement of purpose that includes a brief autobiography and how they plan to contribute to the community. International students are also eligible. Selection is based on the quality of submitted work, the strength of the written statement of purpose, financial need, and academic record.

**Financial data:** The stipend is $1,500. Funds are paid directly to the recipient's school.

**Duration:** 1 academic year. Recipients may reapply.

**Number awarded:** 25 each year.

**Deadline:** March of each year.

---

## 1754 YOSHIKO TANAKA MEMORIAL SCHOLARSHIP

Japanese American Citizens League, Attn: National Scholarship Awards
1765 Sutter Street
San Francisco, CA 94115
Phone: (415) 921-5225; Fax: (415) 931-4671; Email: jacl@jacl.org
Web: www.jacl.org/scholarships.html

**Summary:** To provide financial assistance for college to student members of the Japanese American Citizens League (JACL), especially those studying Japanese language or U.S.-Japan relations.

**Eligibility:** Open to JACL members who are currently enrolled or planning to reenter a college, university, trade school, business college, or other institution of higher learning. Applicants must submit a statement describing their current level of involvement in the Japanese American community or Asian Pacific community and how they will continue their involvement in future years. Selection is based on academic record, extracurricular activities, financial need, and community involvement. Preference is given to applicants planning to study Japanese language, Japanese culture, and/or U.S.-Japan relations.

**Financial data:** The stipend depends on the availability of funds but usually ranges from $1,000 to $5,000.

**Duration:** 1 year; nonrenewable.

**Number awarded:** 1 each year.

**Deadline:** March of each year.

---

## 1755 YOUNG AMERICAN CREATIVE PATRIOTIC ART SCHOLARSHIPS

Ladies Auxiliary to the Veterans of Foreign Wars
c/o National Headquarters
406 West 34th Street
Kansas City, MO 64111

Phone: (816) 561-8655; Fax: (816) 931-4753; Email: info@ladiesauxvfg.com
Web: www.ladiesauxvfg.com

**Summary:** To recognize and reward high school students who submit outstanding works of art on patriotic themes.

**Eligibility:** Open to any student who is a U.S. citizen in grades 9-12. Home-schooled students are eligible; foreign exchange students are not. Entrants may submit art on paper or canvas using water color, pencil, pastel, charcoal, tempera, crayon, acrylic, pen-and-ink, or oil. Digital art may be submitted, but it must be on paper or canvas. Competitions are held in individual Veterans of Foreign Wars (VFW) Auxiliaries, then at department, and finally national levels. Students must be sponsored by an Auxiliary; they must attend school in the same state as the sponsoring Auxiliary. Entries are judged on the originality of concept, presentation, and patriotism expressed; content, how it relates to patriotism, and clarity of ideas; design technique; total impact of work; and uniqueness.

**Financial data:** National awards are $10,000 for first prize, $5,000 for second prize, and $2,500 for third prize. Funds must be used for continued art education or for art supplies.

**Number awarded:** 3 national winners are selected each year.

**Deadline:** March of each year.

---

## 1756 YOUNG COMPOSERS AWARDS

National Guild of Community Schools of the Arts, Attn: Executive Director
520 Eighth Avenue, Suite 302
New York, NY 10018
Phone: (212) 268-3337; Fax: (212) 268-3995; Email: info@nationalguild.org
Web: www.nationalguild.org

**Summary:** To recognize and reward outstanding high school composers.

**Eligibility:** Open to residents of the United States or Canada who are enrolled in a public or private secondary school, a recognized musical institution, or a private music studio with an established teacher. Students enrolled in an undergraduate program are not eligible. Competitions are held in 2 categories: senior for students 16 to 18 years of age and junior for students 13 to 15 years of age. Applicants must submit original compositions that may be in any category of music.

**Financial data:** Prizes in the senior category are $1,000 for first and $500 for second. Junior category prizes are $500 for first and $250 for second.

**Duration:** The competition is held annually.

**Number awarded:** 4 each year: 2 in the senior category and 2 in the junior category.

**Deadline:** April of each year.

---

## 1757 YOUNG FEMINIST SCHOLARSHIP

Spinsters Ink
191 University Boulevard, Suite 300
P.O. Box 22005
Denver, CO 80222
Phone: (303) 761-5552; Fax: (303) 761-5284; Email: spinster@spinsters-ink.com
Web: www.spinsters-ink.com

**Summary:** To recognize and reward feminists who are high school seniors and interested in writing on feminist issues.

**Eligibility:** Open to feminist students in their last year of high school. They are invited to submit an essay on feminism and what it means to them. Essays may be no longer than 1,200 words.

**Financial data:** The scholarship award is $1,000.

**Duration:** The competition is held annually.

**Number awarded:** 1 each year.

**Deadline:** December of each year.

---

## 1758 7 UP CHALLENGE

DECA
1908 Association Drive
Reston, VA 20191-1594
Phone: (703) 860-5000; Fax: (703) 860-4013; Email: decainc@aol.com
Web: www.deca.org/7UPChallenge/7up-open.htm

**Summary:** To recognize and reward (with college scholarships) DECA members who develop outstanding advertising campaigns for display on the Internet.

**Eligibility:** Open to high school DECA members who submit entries in either of 2 categories: 1) a web campaign of at least 400 x 400 pixels with up to 4 links and up to 500K in size; or 2) a banner ad of approximately 450 x 60 pixels, 72 dpi, and up to 20K. In either category, the campaign must promote brand awareness of lemon-lime and/or cherry-flavored soft drinks, involve the consumer, and utilize the themes of college basketball and/or music. Entries are received in 2 rounds, with finalists selected in each category in each round. Grand-prize winners are selected from among the finalists on the basis of how well and creatively the campaign or banner ad promotes the soft drinks, overall appearance, content of copy, ease of use, identification, layout, and impact.

**Financial data:** Each finalist receives a $500 award. The grand-prize winners receive $2,500 college scholarships.

**Duration:** The competition is held annually.

**Number awarded:** 4 finalists are selected in each category in each round (for a total of 16 finalists); from among those, 2 grand-prize winners (1 in each category) are selected.

**Deadline:** November of each year for the first round; February of each year for the second round.

# Sciences

## 1759 AAAE FOUNDATION SCHOLARSHIP

American Association of Airport Executives Foundation
Attn: AAAE Foundation Scholarship Program
601 Madison Street, Suite 400
Alexandria, VA 22314
Phone: (703) 824-0500; Fax: (703) 820-1395
Web: www.aaae.org
**Summary:** To provide financial assistance to upper-division college students who are majoring in aviation.
**Eligibility:** Open to full-time college juniors or seniors who are enrolled in an aviation program and have earned a GPA of 3.0 or higher. Selection is based on academic record, financial need, participation in school and community activities, work experience, and a personal statement.
**Financial data:** The stipend is $1,000.
**Duration:** 1 year.
**Number awarded:** 3 to 5 each year.
**Deadline:** May of each year.

## 1760 AAAE FOUNDATION SCHOLARSHIP FOR NATIVE AMERICANS

American Association of Airport Executives Foundation
Attn: AAAE Foundation Scholarship Program
601 Madison Street, Suite 400
Alexandria, VA 22314
Phone: (703) 824-0500; Fax: (703) 820-1395
Web: www.aaae.org
**Summary:** To provide financial assistance to Native American upper-division college students who are majoring in aviation.
**Eligibility:** Open to full-time Native American college juniors or seniors who are enrolled in an aviation program and have earned a GPA of 3.0 or higher. Each college or university may nominate only 1 student for this scholarship. Selection is based on academic record, financial need, participation in school and community activities, work experience, and a personal statement.
**Financial data:** The stipend is $1,000.
**Duration:** 1 year.
**Number awarded:** 1 or more each year.
**Deadline:** May of each year.

## 1761 AABB-BAXTER SBB SCHOLARSHIP AWARDS

AABB, Attn: Scholarship Award Program
8101 Glenbrook Road
Bethesda, MD 20814-2749
Phone: (301) 215-6482; Fax: (301) 907-6895; Email: education@aabb.org
Web: www.aabb.org/Professionals/Professional_Development/sbb.htm
**Summary:** To recognize and reward essays by students enrolled in programs accredited by AABB (formerly the American Association of Blood Banks).
**Eligibility:** Open to students enrolled in an accredited program for the education of Specialists in Blood Banking (SBB). Applicants must submit 1 of the following types of entries: 1) a scientific paper reporting experimental work (the work may be an original concept, extension of a major concept, or application of a new procedure in the basic sciences, clinical or laboratory medicine, or educational sciences); 2) an analytical or interpretational review suitable for publication in a professional journal; or 3) an innovative educational syllabus using traditional or advanced technology modalities. The essays or scientific papers must be less than 3,000 words on a subject pertaining to blood banking or a related field. Scientific papers should describe materials and methods used, including experimental design, in sufficient detail to enable other scientists to evaluate or duplicate the work. Reviews should analyze or interpret the subject and not just restate the literature. Educational entries should include a brief summary covering the need for the program, how the program is innovative, and a list of references. A student may submit more than one entry; however, no student may receive more than 1 award.
**Financial data:** The award is $1,500.
**Duration:** The competition is held annually.
**Number awarded:** Up to 5 each year.
**Deadline:** June of each year.

## 1762 AACC FOUNDATION UNDERGRADUATE SCHOLARSHIP PROGRAM

American Association of Cereal Chemists, Attn: Foundation
3340 Pilot Knob Road
St. Paul, MN 55121-2097
Phone: (651) 454-7250; Fax: (651) 454-0766; Email: aacc@scisoc.org
Web: www.aaccnet.org/foundation/undergraduate.asp
**Summary:** To provide financial assistance for college to members of the American Association of Cereal Chemists (AACC).
**Eligibility:** Open to AACC members who have completed at least 1 term of college with a GPA of 3.0 or higher both cumulatively and in science and mathematics courses. Applicants must demonstrate an interest in and intent to prepare for a career in grain-based food science and technology or in a related area in industry, academia, or government. They must be working on a degree from an institution that conducts fundamental investigations for the advancement of cereal science and technology, including oilseeds. Selection is based on scholarships previously or currently held; awards and honors received in high school and/or college; extracurricular activities and hobbies; work experience, internships, and related to projects; 3 letters of recommendation; transcripts of college or university undergraduate work; and a letter that describes career plans and their relationship to pertinent courses taken or planned, especially courses related to cereal science or technology, including oilseeds. Age, sex, race, financial need, and previous receipt or non-receipt of this scholarship are not considered.
**Financial data:** Stipends are $2,000, $1,500, or $1,000 per year.
**Duration:** 1 year; may be renewed.
**Number awarded:** Up to 15 each year.
**Deadline:** February of each year.

## 1763 AACE INTERNATIONAL COMPETITIVE SCHOLARSHIPS

Association for the Advancement of Cost Engineering
209 Prairie Avenue, Suite 100
Morgantown, WV 26505
Phone: (304) 296-8444; (800) 858-COST; Fax: (304) 291-5728;
Email: info@aacei.org
Web: www.aacei.org/education/scholarship.shtml
**Summary:** To provide financial assistance to undergraduate and graduate students in the United States or Canada working on a degree related to total cost management (the effective application of professional and technical expertise to plan and control resources, costs, profitability, and risk).
**Eligibility:** Open to undergraduate students (second year standing or higher) or graduate students. They must be enrolled full time in a degree program in the United States or Canada that is related to the field of cost management/cost engineering, including engineering, construction, manufacturing, technology, business, and computer science. Selection is based on academic record (35%), extracurricular activities (35%), and an essay (30%) on the value of study in cost engineering or total cost management and why it is important to their academic objectives and career goals.
**Financial data:** Stipends range from $750 to $3,000 per year.
**Duration:** 1 year.
**Number awarded:** Varies each year; recently, 28 of these scholarships were awarded.
**Deadline:** October of each year.

## 1764 AAHE UNDERGRADUATE SCHOLARSHIP

American Association for Health Education, Attn: Scholarship Committee
1900 Association Drive
Reston, VA 20191-1599
Phone: (703) 476-3437; (800) 213-7193, ext. 437; Fax: (703) 476-6638;
Email: aahe@aahperd.org
Web: www.aahperd.org/aahe/template.cfm?template=scholarships-main.html
**Summary:** To provide financial assistance to undergraduates who are currently enrolled in a health education program.
**Eligibility:** Open to undergraduate students who are enrolled full time in a health education program at a 4-year college or university. Applicants must a GPA of 3.25 or higher and be active in health education professional activities and organizations at their school and/or in their community. They must submit a list of extracurricular service activities; an official transcript; 3 letters of recommendation; and an essay that includes what they hope to accomplish as a health educator (during training and in the future) and attributes and aspirations brought to the field of health education. Financial need is not considered in the selection process.
**Financial data:** The stipend is $1,000 plus a 1-year complimentary student membership in the association.

**Duration:** 1 year; nonrenewable.
**Number awarded:** 1 each year.
**Deadline:** November of each year.

## 1765 AAIA SKILLSUSA-VICA NATIONAL CHAMPION PROGRAM

Automotive Aftermarket Industry Association
4600 East-West Highway, Suite 300
Bethesda, MD 20814-3415
Phone: (301) 654-6664; Fax: (301) 654-3299; Email: aaia@aftermarket.org
Web: www.aftermarket.org/Education/Scholarships/Scholarships.asp
**Summary:** To recognize and reward (with college scholarships) students participating in the automotive service technology or collision repair technology competitions conducted by SkillsUSA.
**Eligibility:** Open to high school seniors who participate in competitions conducted by SkillsUSA (formerly VICA). Scholarships are awarded to National Gold Medalists in the categories of automotive service technology or collision repair technology. No application is required. Students must be planning to attend a postsecondary school.
**Financial data:** The stipend is $1,500.
**Duration:** The competition is held annually.
**Number awarded:** 1 each year.

## 1766 AAMI YOUNG INVESTIGATOR COMPETITION

Association for the Advancement of Medical Instrumentation
Attn: Education Department
1110 North Glebe Road, Suite 220
Arlington, VA 22201-4795
Phone: (703) 525-4890, ext. 212; (800) 332-2264, ext. 212; Fax: (703) 276-0793; Email: ahaynes@aami.org
Web: www.aami.org/awards/yic.html
**Summary:** To recognize and reward student authors of outstanding research papers on medical instrumentation and technology.
**Eligibility:** Open to undergraduate, graduate, and medical students; interns; residents; postdoctoral fellows; and recent (within 6 months) graduates from accredited programs in the fields of engineering, computer science, medicine, physical and medical sciences, management, administration, or public health. Applicants must submit an abstract of a research paper for presentation at the annual meeting of the Association for the Advancement of Medical Instrumentation (AAMI). The abstract must relate to 1 or more of the following categories: 1) innovative medical instrumentation of medical devices having direct applications to patient care; 2) new applications of existing technology to improve patient management; or 3) clinical outcomes of patient safety studies directly related to the application of current or future medical technology.
**Financial data:** The first-prize winner receives $1,500 and a plaque.
**Duration:** The competition is held annually.
**Number awarded:** 1 each year.
**Deadline:** October of each year.

## 1767 AAPA VETERAN'S CAUCUS SCHOLARSHIPS

American Academy of Physician Assistants-Veterans Caucus
Attn: Veterans Caucus
950 North Washington Street
Alexandria, VA 22314-1552
Phone: (703) 836-2272; Fax: (703) 684-1924; Email: aapa@aapa.org
Web: www.veteranscaucus.org
**Summary:** To provide financial assistance to veterans and Reserve component personnel who are studying to become physician assistants.
**Eligibility:** Open to U.S. citizens who are currently enrolled in a physician assistant program. The program must be approved by the Commission on Accreditation of Allied Health Education. Applicants must be honorably discharged members of a uniformed service of the United States or an active member of the Guard or Reserve of a uniformed service of the United States. Selection is based on military honors and awards received, civic and college honors and awards received, professional memberships and activities, and GPA. An electronic copy of the applicant's DD Form 214 must accompany the application.
**Financial data:** Stipends are $2,000, $1,500, or $1,250.
**Duration:** 1 year.
**Number awarded:** Varies each year. Recently, 15 of these scholarships were awarded: 1 at $2,000, 2 at $1,500, and 12 at $1,250.
**Deadline:** February of each year.

## 1768 ABAK AGRICULTURE SCHOLARSHIP PROGRAM

AgriBusiness Association of Kentucky, Attn: Scholarship Program
512 Capitol Avenue
Frankfort, KY 40601
Phone: (502) 226-1122; Fax: (502) 875-1595
Web: www.kyagribusiness.org/education.htm
**Summary:** To provide financial assistance to Kentucky residents interested in working on an undergraduate degree in agriculture.
**Eligibility:** Open to residents of Kentucky enrolled or accepted for enrollment as an undergraduate at an institution of higher education. Applicants must have a declared major in an agricultural-related field of study or be accepted into an agricultural study program. They must submit 2 essays of 500 words each: 1) why they decided to major in agriculture and what they plan on doing after graduation; and 2) what they think the future holds for agriculture in the United States and the world. Selection is based on the essays, 2 letters of recommendation, activities and honors, and transcripts; financial need is not considered.
**Financial data:** The stipend is $1,000 per year.
**Duration:** 1 year.
**Number awarded:** 1 or more each year.
**Deadline:** May of each year.

## 1769 ABBIE SARGENT MEMORIAL SCHOLARSHIP PROGRAM

Abbie Sargent Memorial Scholarship
c/o New Hampshire Farm Bureau Federation
295 Sheep Davis Road
Concord, NH 03301
Phone: (603) 224-1934; Fax: (603) 228-8432; Email: nhfb@nhfarmbureau.org
Web: www.nhfarmbureau.org
**Summary:** To provide financial assistance to college students who graduated from a private or public high school in New Hampshire, particularly those interested in majoring in agriculture.
**Eligibility:** Open to residents of New Hampshire who have graduated from an approved public or private high school, have average or better grades, are able to demonstrate financial need, are dependable, and are able to show responsible behavior. Applicants must be currently enrolled (full or part time) at an institution of higher learning. Preference is given to students involved in agriculturally-related studies, including home economics.
**Financial data:** A stipend is awarded (amount not specified).
**Duration:** 1 year.
**Number awarded:** 1 or more each year.
**Deadline:** March of each year.

## 1770 ABELL-HANGER FOUNDATION NURSING AWARDS

University Interscholastic League
Attn: Texas Interscholastic League Foundation
1701 Manor Road
P.O. Box 8028
Austin, TX 78713
Phone: (512) 232-4938; Fax: (512) 471-5908;
Email: carolyn.scott@mail.utexas.edu
Web: www.uil.texas.edu/tilf/scholar.html
**Summary:** To provide financial assistance to students who participate in programs of the Texas Interscholastic League Foundation (TILF) and plan to study nursing.
**Eligibility:** Open to students who meet the 5 basic requirements of the TILF: 1) graduate from high school during the current year and begin college or university in Texas by the following fall; 2) enroll full time and maintain a GPA of 2.5 or higher during the first semester; 3) compete in a University Interscholastic League (UIL) academic state meet contest in accounting, calculator applications, computer applications, computer science, current issues and events, debate (cross-examination and Lincoln-Douglas), journalism (editorial writing, feature writing, headline writing, and news writing), literary criticism, mathematics, number sense, 1-act play, ready writing, science, social studies, speech (prose interpretation, poetry interpretation, informative speaking, and persuasive speaking), or spelling and vocabulary; 4) submit high school transcripts that include SAT and/or ACT scores; and 5) submit parents' latest income tax returns. Applicants for this scholarship must be planning to major in nursing.
**Financial data:** The stipend is $3,500 per year.
**Duration:** 2 years.
**Number awarded:** 1 each year.
**Deadline:** May of each year.

## 1771 ACEC OF MICHIGAN EDUCATION GRANT

American Council of Engineering Companies of Michigan, Inc.
215 North Walnut Street
P.O. Box 19189
Lansing, MI 48901-9189
Phone: (517) 332-2066; Fax: (517) 332-4333; Email: mail@acec-mi.org
Web: www.acec-mi.org

**Summary:** To provide financial assistance to undergraduate and graduate students majoring in engineering or surveying.

**Eligibility:** Open to applicants who are enrolled full or part time as a sophomore, junior, senior, or graduate student working on a degree in engineering or surveying in an ABET-accredited engineering or surveying program. They must have worked during the past 24 months for a consulting engineering, surveying, or architectural/engineering firm. Along with their application, they must submit an essay of 500 to 1,000 words on a topic that changes annually but relates to engineering and surveying; recently, the topic was "How have the events of September 11, 2001, affected your outlook on the engineering/surveying profession?" Selection is based on the essay, work experience, references, extracurricular and community activities, and GPA. Financial need is not considered in the selection process.

**Financial data:** A stipend is awarded (amount not specified); a total of $8,000 per year is awarded.

**Duration:** 1 year; recipients may reapply for 1 more award.

**Number awarded:** 1 or more each year.

**Deadline:** January of each year.

## 1772 ACI STUDENT FELLOWSHIP PROGRAM

American Concrete Institute
Attn: Concrete Research and Education Foundation
38800 Country Club Drive
P.O. Box 9094
Farmington Hills, MI 48333-9094
Phone: (248) 848-3700; Fax: (248) 848-3701; TDD: (248) 848-3823;
Email: scholarships@concrete.org
Web: www.concrete.org/STUDENTS/STU_SCHOLAR.HTM

**Summary:** To provide funding to undergraduate and graduate students preparing for a career in the field of concrete.

**Eligibility:** Open to full-time undergraduate and graduate students in engineering, construction management, and other appropriate fields. Applicants must first be nominated by a faculty member of the American Concrete Institute (ACI). They may be residing anywhere in the world, but graduate study must take place in the United States or Canada.

**Financial data:** The stipend is $10,000 per year; funds may be used for tuition, residence, books, and materials. Other financial benefits include reimbursement of expenses associated with attending the ACI convention and reimbursement of expenses associated with an internship.

**Duration:** 2 years; may be renewed, including through graduate school for students who first receive an award as an undergraduate.

**Number awarded:** Varies each year; recently, 3 of these fellowships were awarded.

**Deadline:** November of each year.

## 1773 ACIL ACADEMIC SCHOLARSHIPS

American Council of Independent Laboratories
Attn: ACIL Scholarship Alliance
1629 K Street, N.W., Suite 400
Washington, DC 20006-1633
Phone: (202) 887-5872; Fax: (202) 887-0021; Email: info@acil.org
Web: www.acil.org

**Summary:** To provide financial assistance to upper-division and graduate students working on a degree in the natural or physical sciences.

**Eligibility:** Open to college juniors, seniors, and graduate students majoring in physics, chemistry, engineering, geology, biology, or environmental sciences. Applicants must submit a brief resume or personal statement outlining their activities in college, including their field of study and future plans. Selection is based on academic achievement, career goals, leadership, and financial need. Children and grandchildren of the member employees of the American Council of Independent Laboratories (ACIL) are encouraged to apply.

**Financial data:** Stipends range from $1,000 to $2,000.

**Duration:** 1 year.

**Number awarded:** Varies each year.

**Deadline:** April of each year.

## 1774 ACMPE LEADERS SCHOLARSHIPS

American College of Medical Practice Executives
Attn: ACMPE Scholarship Fund Inc.
104 Inverness Terrace East
Englewood, CO 80112-5306
Phone: (303) 799-1111, ext. 232; (877) ASK-MGMA; Fax: (303) 643-4439;
Email: acmpe@mgma.com
Web: www.mgma.com/academics/scholar.cfm

**Summary:** To provide financial assistance to practitioners in medical practice management interested in pursuing professional development through undergraduate or graduate education.

**Eligibility:** Open to professionals working on an undergraduate or graduate degree in a program relevant to medical practice management, including public health, business administration, health care administration, or other related areas. Students working on a degree in medicine, physical therapy, nursing, or other clinically-related professions are not eligible. Applicants must submit a letter describing their career goals and objectives relevant to medical practice management; a resume; 2 reference letters commenting on their performance, character, potential to succeed, and need for scholarship support; and either documentation indicating acceptance into an undergraduate or graduate program or academic transcripts indicating undergraduate or graduate work completed to date.

**Financial data:** The stipend is $3,000. Funds are paid directly to the recipient's college or university.

**Duration:** 1 year.

**Number awarded:** 4 each year.

**Deadline:** April of each year.

## 1775 ACONE HONORED MEMBER SCHOLARSHIP

Aero Club of New England, Attn: Education Committee
Civil Air Terminal
200 Hanscom Drive, Suite 322
Bedford, MA 01730
Phone: (617) 277-0100; Fax: (617) 232-7571; Email: scholarships@acone.org
Web: www.acone.org/scholarship/overview.html

**Summary:** To provide financial assistance for flight school to New England residents who intend to prepare for a professional aviation career.

**Eligibility:** Open to residents of New England who are interested in attending a flight school in the region. Applicants must intend to prepare for a professional aviation career, have a current Airman Certificate, have a current Medical Certificate, have accumulated 160 hours total flight time, be at least 16 years of age, be a U.S. citizen, have a current Biennial Flight Review, and be able to demonstrate financial need. Along with their application, they must submit academic transcripts, a personal letter giving their reasons for selecting a professional aviation career path and describing their aviation-related activities, a financial statement, 2 letters of recommendation, and their flight time record. Selection is based on ability to meet the planned aviation goals (as shown by recommendations and academic records), participation in aviation activities (as described in the personal letter and recommendations), and financial need.

**Financial data:** The stipend is $2,000.

**Duration:** 1 year.

**Number awarded:** 1 each year.

**Deadline:** March of each year.

## 1776 ADA DENTAL ASSISTING SCHOLARSHIPS

American Dental Association, Attn: ADA Foundation
211 East Chicago Avenue
Chicago, IL 60611
Phone: (312) 440-2547; Fax: (312) 440-3526; Email: adaf@ada.org
Web: www.ada.org/ada/prod/adaf/prog_scholarship_prog.asp

**Summary:** To provide financial assistance to dental assisting students.

**Eligibility:** Open to U.S. citizens who are entering students accepted by a dental assisting program accredited by the Commission on Dental Accreditation. They must have a GPA of 3.0 or higher and be able to demonstrate financial need of at least $1,000. Selection is based on academic achievement, a written summary of personal and professional goals, letters of reference, and financial need.

**Financial data:** Stipends range up to $1,000 per year. Funds are to be used to cover school expenses (tuition, fees, books, supplies, living expenses) and are paid in 2 equal installments to the recipient's school.

**Duration:** 1 year.

**Number awarded:** 10 each year.

**Deadline:** September of each year.

## 1777 ADA DENTAL HYGIENE SCHOLARSHIPS

American Dental Association, Attn: ADA Foundation
211 East Chicago Avenue
Chicago, IL 60611
Phone: (312) 440-2547; Fax: (312) 440-3526; Email: adaf@ada.org
Web: www.ada.org/ada/prod/adaf/prog_scholarship_prog.asp
**Summary:** To provide financial assistance to dental hygiene students.
**Eligibility:** Open to U.S. citizens who are entering their final year of study at a dental hygiene program accredited by the Commission on Dental Accreditation. They must have a GPA of 3.0 or higher and be able to demonstrate financial need of at least $1,000. Selection is based on academic achievement, a written summary of personal and professional goals, letters of reference, and financial need.
**Financial data:** Stipends range up to $1,000 per year. Funds are to be used to cover school expenses (tuition, fees, books, supplies, living expenses) and are paid in 2 equal installments to the recipient's school.
**Duration:** 1 year.
**Number awarded:** 15 each year.
**Deadline:** August of each year.

## 1778 ADA DENTAL LABORATORY TECHNOLOGY SCHOLARSHIPS

American Dental Association, Attn: ADA Foundation
211 East Chicago Avenue
Chicago, IL 60611
Phone: (312) 440-2547; Fax: (312) 440-3526; Email: adaf@ada.org
Web: www.ada.org/ada/prod/adaf/prog_scholarship_prog.asp
**Summary:** To provide financial assistance to dental laboratory technology students.
**Eligibility:** Open to U.S. citizens who are entering their final year of study at a dental laboratory technology program accredited by the Commission on Dental Accreditation. They must have a GPA of 3.0 or higher and be able to demonstrate financial need of at least $1,000. Selection is based on academic achievement, a written summary of personal and professional goals, letters of reference, and financial need.
**Financial data:** Stipends range up to $1,000 per year. Funds are to be used to cover school expenses (tuition, fees, books, supplies, living expenses) and are paid in 2 equal installments to the recipient's school.
**Duration:** 1 year.
**Number awarded:** 5 each year.
**Deadline:** August of each year.

## 1779 ADHA INSTITUTE GENERAL SCHOLARSHIPS

American Dental Hygienists' Association, Attn: Institute for Oral Health
444 North Michigan Avenue, Suite 3400
Chicago, IL 60611
Phone: (312) 440-8918; (800) 735-4916; Fax: (312) 440-8929;
Email: institute@adha.net
Web: www.adha.org/institute/Scholarship/index.htm
**Summary:** To provide financial assistance to needy undergraduate students preparing for careers in dental hygiene.
**Eligibility:** Open to full-time undergraduate students who are active members of the Student American Dental Hygienists' Association (SADHA) or the American Dental Hygienists' Association (ADHA). Applicants must have a GPA of 3.0 or higher, be able to document financial need of at least $1,500, and have completed at least one year in an accredited dental hygiene program in the United States. Along with their application, they must submit a statement that covers their long-term career goals, their intended contribution to the dental hygiene profession, their professional interests, and the manner in which their degree will enhance their professional capacity.
**Financial data:** Stipends range from $1,000 to $2,000.
**Duration:** 1 year.
**Number awarded:** Varies each year; recently, 20 of these scholarships were awarded.
**Deadline:** April of each year.

## 1780 ADHA INSTITUTE MERIT SCHOLARSHIPS

American Dental Hygienists' Association, Attn: Institute for Oral Health
444 North Michigan Avenue, Suite 3400
Chicago, IL 60611
Phone: (312) 440-8918; (800) 735-4916; Fax: (312) 440-8929;
Email: institute@adha.net
Web: www.adha.org/institute/Scholarship/index.htm
**Summary:** To provide financial assistance to exceptional undergraduate students preparing for careers in dental hygiene.
**Eligibility:** Open to full-time undergraduate students who are active members of the Student American Dental Hygienists' Association (SADHA) or the American Dental Hygienists' Association (ADHA). Applicants must have a GPA of 3.0 or higher, be able to demonstrate exceptional academic merit, and have completed at least one year in an accredited dental hygiene program in the United States. Financial need is not considered in the selection process.
**Financial data:** Stipends range from $1,000 to $2,000.
**Duration:** 1 year.
**Number awarded:** Varies each year; the ADHA awards 10% of all general scholarship funds on the basis of academic merit.
**Deadline:** April of each year.

## 1781 ADHA INSTITUTE PART-TIME SCHOLARSHIP

American Dental Hygienists' Association, Attn: Institute for Oral Health
444 North Michigan Avenue, Suite 3400
Chicago, IL 60611
Phone: (312) 440-8918; (800) 735-4916; Fax: (312) 440-8929;
Email: institute@adha.net
Web: www.adha.org/institute/Scholarship/index.htm
**Summary:** To provide financial assistance to students enrolled part time in doctoral, master's, baccalaureate, or certificate/associate programs in dental hygiene.
**Eligibility:** Open to part-time undergraduate and graduate students who are active members of the Student American Dental Hygienists' Association (SADHA) or the American Dental Hygienists' Association (ADHA). Applicants must have a GPA of 3.0 or higher, be able to document financial need of at least $1,500, and have completed at least one year in an accredited dental hygiene program in the United States. Along with their application, they must submit a statement that covers their long-term career goals, their intended contribution to the dental hygiene profession, their professional interests, and the manner in which their degree will enhance their professional capacity.
**Financial data:** Stipends range from $1,000 to $2,000.
**Duration:** 1 year.
**Number awarded:** 1 each year.
**Deadline:** April of each year.

## 1782 ADMIRAL GRACE MURRAY HOPPER MEMORIAL SCHOLARSHIPS

Society of Women Engineers
230 East Ohio Street, Suite 400
Chicago, IL 60611-3265
Phone: (312) 596-5223; Fax: (312) 644-8557; Email: hq@swe.org
Web: www.societyofwomenengineers.org/scholarships
**Summary:** To provide financial assistance to women who will be entering college as freshmen and are interested in studying engineering or computer science.
**Eligibility:** Open to women who are entering college as freshmen with a GPA of 3.5 or higher. Applicants must be U.S. citizens planning to enroll full time at an ABET-accredited 4-year college or university and major in computer science or engineering. Along with their application, they must submit a 1-page essay on why they want to be an engineer or computer scientist, how they believe they will make a difference as an engineer or computer scientist, and what influenced them to study engineering or computer science. Selection is based on merit. Preference is given to students in computer-related engineering.
**Financial data:** The stipend is $1,000.
**Duration:** 1 year.
**Number awarded:** 5 each year.
**Deadline:** May of each year.

## 1783 ADOBE SYSTEMS COMPUTER SCIENCE SCHOLARSHIPS

Society of Women Engineers
230 East Ohio Street, Suite 400
Chicago, IL 60611-3265
Phone: (312) 596-5223; Fax: (312) 644-8557; Email: hq@swe.org
Web: www.societyofwomenengineers.org/scholarships
**Summary:** To provide financial assistance to upper-division women majoring in computer science.
**Eligibility:** Open to women entering their junior or senior year at an ABET-accredited college or university. Applicants must be majoring in computer sci-

ence and have a GPA of 3.0 or higher. Along with their application, they must submit a 1-page essay on why they want to be a computer scientist, how they believe they will make a difference as a computer scientist, and what influenced them to study computer science. Preference is given to students attending selected schools; for a list, contact the sponsor. Selection is based on merit.

**Financial data:** Stipends are $2,000 or $1,500.

**Duration:** 1 year.

**Number awarded:** 2 each year: 1 at $2,000 and 1 at $1,500.

**Deadline:** January of each year.

---

### 1784 ADOBE SYSTEMS/HENAAC SCHOLARS PROGRAM

Hispanic Engineer National Achievement Awards Conference
3900 Whiteside Street
Los Angeles, CA 90063
Phone: (323) 262-0997; Fax: (323) 262-0946; Email: info@henaac.org
Web: www.henaac.org/scholarships.htm

**Summary:** To provide financial assistance to Hispanic undergraduate students majoring in computer science.

**Eligibility:** Open to Hispanic undergraduate students who are enrolled full time in computer science. Applicants must be entering their junior or senior year and have a GPA of 3.0 or higher. Academic achievement and campus community activities are considered in the selection process.

**Financial data:** Stipends range from $1,000 to $5,000.

**Duration:** 1 year; recipients may reapply.

**Number awarded:** 1 or more each year.

**Deadline:** April of each year.

---

### 1785 ADVANCING HISPANIC EXCELLENCE IN TECHNOLOGY, ENGINEERING, MATH, AND SCIENCE (AHETEMS) SCHOLARSHIP PROGRAM

Society of Hispanic Professional Engineers
5400 East Olympic Boulevard, Suite 210
Los Angeles, CA 90022
Phone: (323) 725-3970; Fax: (323) 725-0316
Web: www.shpe.org

**Summary:** To provide financial assistance to Hispanic undergraduate and graduate students preparing for a career in science, technology, engineering, mathematics, or a related field.

**Eligibility:** Open to members of the Society of Hispanic Professional Engineers (SHPE) who are accepted into or attending an accredited 2-year or 4-year college or university in the United States or Puerto Rico. Applicants must be enrolled full time with a major in science, technology, engineering, mathematics, or a related field. High school seniors and undergraduates must have a GPA of 2.5 or higher; graduate students must have a GPA of 3.25 or higher. Along with their application, they must submit a 1-page personal statement covering their family background, community involvement, leadership roles, achievements, and short-term and long-term goals and aspirations. Both merit-based and need-based scholarships are available. U.S. citizenship or permanent resident status is required.

**Financial data:** Stipends range from $1,000 to $3,000.

**Duration:** 1 year.

**Number awarded:** 1 or more each year.

**Deadline:** March of each year.

---

### 1786 A.E. "ED" GRIFFIN MEMORIAL SCHOLARSHIP

California Land Surveyors Association, Attn: CLSA Education Foundation
P.O. Box 9098
Santa Rosa, CA 95405-9990
Phone: (707) 578-6016; Fax: (707) 578-4406;
Email: clsa@californiasurveyors.org
Web: californiasurveyors.org/files/scholarsh.html

**Summary:** To provide financial assistance to residents of California studying fields related to surveying in college.

**Eligibility:** Open to California residents currently enrolled in 1) an accredited baccalaureate program in surveying, or 2) an associate degree program in surveying or survey engineering with the intent to attend an accredited baccalaureate program in surveying or prepare for a career in the land surveying profession. Applicants must have a GPA of 2.5 or higher in college and 3.0 or higher in their major and must be able to demonstrate interest in studying boundary surveying and a record of activity in the profession. Along with their application, they must submit an essay on their educational objectives, future plans for study or research, professional activities, and need. Selection is based on the essay (30%), aca-

demic record (30%) letters of recommendation (20%), and professional activities (20%), Financial need may be considered if other criteria result in a tie.

**Financial data:** The stipend is $1,000.

**Duration:** 1 year.

**Number awarded:** 1 each year.

**Deadline:** December of each year.

---

### 1787 AEA TECHNOLOGY SCHOLARSHIP PROGRAM

Oregon University System
Attn: Chancellor's Office, Industry Affairs Division
Capital Center, Suite 1065
18640 N.W. Walker Road
Beaverton, OR 97006-8966
Phone: (503) 725-2918; Fax: (503) 775-2921; Email: aeaschol@ous.edu
Web: www.ous.edu/ecs/scholarships.html

**Summary:** To provide financial assistance to Oregon high school seniors interested in studying designated computer and engineering fields at selected public universities in the state.

**Eligibility:** Open to seniors graduating from high schools in Oregon who plan to attend Eastern Oregon University, Oregon Institute of Technology, Oregon State University, Portland State University, Southern Oregon University, Western Oregon University, or the University of Oregon. Applicants must be planning to major in biochemistry, chemical engineering, chemistry, computer engineering, computer science, electrical engineering, electronic engineering, engineering technology, industrial engineering, mathematics, mechanical engineering, or physics (not all majors are available at each institution). Women and ethnic minorities underrepresented in the technology industry (Black Americans, Hispanic Americans, and Native Americans) are strongly encouraged to apply. Selection is based on academic performance; college entrance examination scores; mathematics, science, and technology course work; achievements; leadership; civic participation; interests; employment; insight into and commitment to a career in technology; and communication skill.

**Financial data:** The stipend is $2,500 per year.

**Duration:** 1 year; may be renewed up to 3 additional years if the recipient maintains a GPA of 3.0 or higher.

**Number awarded:** Varies each year; recently, this program awarded 25 new scholarships.

**Deadline:** March of each year.

---

### 1788 AESF UNDERGRADUATE SCHOLARSHIP PROGRAM

American Electroplaters and Surface Finishers Society
Attn: AESF Scholarship Committee
Central Florida Research Park
12644 Research Parkway
Orlando, FL 32826-3298
Phone: (407) 281-6441; Fax: (407) 281-6446; Email: janice@aesf.org
Web: www.aesf.org/scholarship/scholar.html

**Summary:** To provide financial assistance to undergraduate students who are interested in majoring in subjects related to plating and surface finishing technologies.

**Eligibility:** Open to juniors and seniors in college who are majoring in chemistry, chemical engineering, environmental engineering, metallurgy, or materials science. Selection is based on career interest in surface finishing, scholarship, achievement, motivation, and potential. Financial need is not a factor.

**Financial data:** The stipend is at least $1,500 per year. Funds are sent directly to the recipient's college or university. Schools are requested not to reduce federal, state, or institutional support for students who receive this scholarship.

**Duration:** 1 year; recipients may reapply for one additional year.

**Number awarded:** At least 1 each year.

**Deadline:** April of each year.

---

### 1789 AETNA/NCEMNA SCHOLARS PROGRAM

National Coalition of Ethnic Minority Nurse Associations
c/o Dr. Betty Smith Williams, President
6101 West Centinela Avenue, Suite 378
Culver City, CA 90230
Phone: (310) 258-9515; Fax: (310) 258-9513; Email: bwilliams@ncemna.org
Web: www.ncemna.org/scholarships.html

**Summary:** To provide financial assistance to nursing students who are members of constituent organizations of the National Coalition of Ethnic Minority Nurse Associations (NCEMNA) working on a 4-year or master's degree.

**Eligibility:** Open to members of the 5 associations that comprise NCEMNA:

the Asian American/Pacific Islander Nurses Association, Inc. (AAPINA), the National Alaska Native American Indian Nurses Association, Inc. (NANAINA), the National Association of Hispanic Nurses, Inc. (NAHN), the National Black Nurses Association, Inc. (NBNA), and the Philippine Nurses Association of America, Inc. (PNAA). Applicants must be currently attending or making application to a 4-year or master's degree program in nursing. Along with their application, they must submit a letter of reference, demonstration of leadership and involvement in the ethnic community, and statement of career goals.

**Financial data:** The stipend is $2,000.

**Duration:** 1 year.

**Number awarded:** 5 each year: 1 nominee from each of the constituent associations.

---

### 1790 AFCEA DISTANCE-LEARNING/ON-LINE SCHOLARSHIPS

Armed Forces Communications and Electronics Association
Attn: AFCEA Educational Foundation
4400 Fair Lakes Court
Fairfax, VA 22033-3899
Phone: (703) 631-6149; (800) 336-4583, ext. 6149; Fax: (703) 631-4693;
Email: scholarship@afcea.org
Web: www.afcea.org/education/scholarships/undergraduate/pub1.asp

**Summary:** To provide financial assistance to undergraduate students who are working full time on a degree by means of a distance-learning or online program.

**Eligibility:** Open to U.S. citizens working full time on a bachelor's degree by means of a distance-learning or on-line program affiliated with a major, accredited 4-year college or university in the United States. Applicants must have completed at least one year of course work based on a 30-semester hour equivalent; classes in progress at the time of application cannot be used towards the 1-year minimum completion requirement. Completed courses must include at least 2 semesters of calculus (not pre-calculus). Majors are limited to the fields of engineering (chemical, computer, electrical, or systems), mathematics, physics, or computer science. Selection is based primarily on academic excellence.

**Financial data:** The stipend is $1,000.

**Duration:** 1 year.

**Number awarded:** 1 each year.

**Deadline:** July of each year.

---

### 1791 AFCEA ROTC SCHOLARSHIPS

Armed Forces Communications and Electronics Association
Attn: AFCEA Educational Foundation
4400 Fair Lakes Court
Fairfax, VA 22033-3899
Phone: (703) 631-6149; (800) 336-4583, ext. 6149; Fax: (703) 631-4693;
Email: scholarship@afcea.org
Web: www.afcea.org/education/scholarships/rotc/rotc1.asp

**Summary:** To provide financial assistance to ROTC cadets who are majoring in fields related to communications and electronics.

**Eligibility:** Open to ROTC cadets majoring in electronics, engineering (aerospace, chemical, computer, electrical, or systems), mathematics, physics, or computer science. Applicants must be nominated by their ROTC professor, be entering their junior or senior year, be U.S. citizens, be of good moral character, have demonstrated academic excellence, be motivated to complete a college education and serve as officers in the U.S. armed forces, and be able to demonstrate financial need.

**Financial data:** The stipend is $2,000.

**Duration:** 1 year; may be renewed.

**Number awarded:** 36 each year, divided equally among Army, Navy/Marine Corps, and Air Force ROTC programs; for each service, 6 are awarded to rising juniors, 6 to rising seniors.

**Deadline:** March of each year.

---

### 1792 AFCEA SCHOLARSHIP FOR WORKING PROFESSIONALS

Armed Forces Communications and Electronics Association
Attn: AFCEA Educational Foundation
4400 Fair Lakes Court
Fairfax, VA 22033-3899
Phone: (703) 631-6149; (800) 336-4583, ext. 6149; Fax: (703) 631-4693;
Email: scholarship@afcea.org
Web: www.afcea.org/education/scholarships/workingstudents/ws1.asp

**Summary:** To provide financial assistance to undergraduate students who

are working part time on a degree in engineering or the sciences while already employed.

**Eligibility:** Open to part-time students entering their sophomore, junior, or senior year at an accredited 2-year or 4-year college or university in the United States while already employed in a science or technology field. Applicants must be U.S. citizens working toward a degree in engineering (aerospace, chemical, electrical, or systems), mathematics, physics, or computer science with a GPA of 3.4 or higher. They must be able to demonstrate academic achievement, patriotism, and potential to contribute to the American work force.

**Financial data:** The stipend is $1,500.

**Duration:** 1 year; may be renewed.

**Number awarded:** 1 each year.

**Deadline:** September of each year.

---

### 1793 AFDO SCHOLARSHIP AWARDS

Association of Food and Drug Officials
2550 Kingston Road, Suite 311
York, PA 17402-3734
Phone: (717) 757-2888; Fax: (717) 755-8089; Email: afdo@afdo.org
Web: www.afdo.org/scholarship.asp

**Summary:** To provide financial assistance to currently-enrolled upper-division students who are preparing for a career in an aspect of food, drug, or consumer product safety.

**Eligibility:** Open to students entering their junior or senior year of college who have a GPA of 3.0 or higher for the first 2 years. Applicants should be interested in preparing to serve in a career of research, regulatory work, quality control, or teaching in an area related to some aspect of food, drug, or consumer product safety. Along with their application, they must submit transcripts, 2 letters of recommendation, and a 1-page biographical sketch that includes their choice of major and future career plans. Selection is based on those submissions and demonstrated leadership capabilities.

**Financial data:** The stipend is $1,500.

**Duration:** 1 year.

**Number awarded:** 2 each year.

**Deadline:** January of each year.

---

### 1794 AFRO-ACADEMIC, CULTURAL, TECHNOLOGICAL AND SCIENTIFIC OLYMPICS (ACT-SO)

**Summary:** To recognize and reward outstanding African American high school students who distinguish themselves in the Afro-Academic, Cultural, Technological and Scientific Olympics (ACT-SO) program.

*See Listing #1242.*

---

### 1795 AFSA ANNUAL ESSAY SCHOLARSHIP CONTEST

American Fire Sprinkler Association
9696 Skillman Street, Suite 300
Dallas, TX 75243-8264
Phone: (214) 349-5965; Fax: (214) 343-8898; Email: afsainfo@firesprinkler.org
Web: www.afsascholarship.org

**Summary:** To recognize and reward, with college scholarships, high school seniors who write outstanding essays on fire sprinklers.

**Eligibility:** Open to seniors at high schools in the United States. Home-schooled students are eligible if their course of study is equivalent to that of a senior in high school. Applicants must submit an essay of 700 to 1,000 words on a topic that varies annually but relates to fire sprinklers. Recently, students were invited to write about a successful fire sprinkler activation in their town, area, or state. Entries must be submitted through an online process. Selection is based on 1) content; 2) accuracy; 3) creativity and originality; and 4) spelling, grammar, and punctuation. Competitions are first held at the regional level.

**Financial data:** Each regional winner receives a $1,000 scholarship. From among those winners, the national first prize is an additional $3,000 scholarship, second prize an additional $2,000 scholarship, and third prize an additional $1,000 scholarship. Funds are paid directly to the recipients' educational institutions. The school of each winning student receives an additional $500 for its general fund.

**Duration:** The competition is held annually.

**Number awarded:** 7 regional winners are selected each year; from among those, 3 are selected as national winners

**Deadline:** January of each year.

## 1796 AGC UNDERGRADUATE SCHOLARSHIPS

Associated General Contractors of America
Attn: AGC Education and Research Foundation
333 John Carlyle Street, Suite 200
Alexandria, VA 22314
Phone: (703) 548-3118; Fax: (703) 548-3119; Email: agcf@agc.org
Web: www.agc.org/EducationTraining/undergraduate_scholarships.asp
**Summary:** To provide financial assistance for undergraduate studies in construction or civil engineering.
**Eligibility:** Open to college freshmen, sophomores, and juniors who are enrolled or planning to enroll in a 4- or 5-year program in construction or civil engineering. Beginning seniors in a 5-year program are also eligible. All applicants must be full-time students with at least one full academic year of course work remaining. They must be preparing for a career in construction. High school seniors are not eligible. Selection is based on academic performance, extracurricular activities, employment experience, financial status, and a demonstrated interest in a construction industry career. Finalists are interviewed.
**Financial data:** The stipend is $2,000 per year.
**Duration:** 1 year; may be renewed for up to 3 additional years.
**Number awarded:** More than 100 each year.
**Deadline:** October of each year.

## 1797 AGCO STUDENT DESIGN COMPETITION

American Society of Agricultural and Biological Engineers
Attn: Awards Coordinator
2950 Niles Road
St. Joseph, MI 49085-9659
Phone: (269) 429-0300; Fax: (269) 429-3852; Email: hq@asabe.org
Web: www.asabe.org/awards/competitions/National.html
**Summary:** To recognize and reward student members of the American Society of Agricultural and Biological Engineers (ASABE) who participate in the basic design of an engineering product useful to agriculture.
**Eligibility:** Open to biological and agricultural engineering students who are student members of the society. Applicants, operating as teams or individuals, submit an engineering design that involves devising a machine, component, system, or process to meet a desired need related to agricultural, food, or biological engineering. The project description they submit is judged on: establishment of need and benefit to agriculture (5 points); approach and originality (6 points); definition of design objectives and criteria (5 points); extent of analysis and synthesis of alternatives (10 points); evidence of sound evaluation and adherence to good engineering design and safety considerations (10 points); adequacy of drawings and specifications (7 points); appropriateness of tests and/or performance data (7 points); and achievement of objectives (10 points). They must also include a written report that is judged on: organization, clarity, and ease of reading (10 points); effective use of graphics, illustrations, video, etc. (5 points); and neatness, accuracy, and style (5 points). Based on the project description and written report, the top 3 entrants are invited to the society's annual meeting for an oral presentation; those are judged on: general effectiveness and audience appeal (8 points); organization and information flow (5 points); quality and adequacy of visuals (5 points); and compliance with 15-minute limit (2 points). The 3 finalists are then ranked on the basis of their total scores.
**Financial data:** First prize is $1,250, second $1,000, and third $750. Teams decide among themselves how to divide the money. The academic department of the first-place entry receives a $300 scholarship and a wall plaque.
**Duration:** The competition is held annually.
**Number awarded:** 3 each year.
**Deadline:** May of each year.

## 1798 AGILENT MENTORING SCHOLARSHIP

Society of Women Engineers
230 East Ohio Street, Suite 400
Chicago, IL 60611-3265
Phone: (312) 596-5223; Fax: (312) 644-8557; Email: hq@swe.org
Web: www.societyofwomenengineers.org/scholarships
**Summary:** To provide financial assistance to undergraduate women who are majoring in computer science or designated engineering specialties.
**Eligibility:** Open to women who are entering their sophomore or junior year at an ABET-accredited 4-year college or university. Applicants must be majoring in computer science or biomedical, computer, electrical, or mechanical engineering and have a GPA of 3.0 or higher. Along with their application, they must submit a 1-page essay on why they want to be an engineer or computer scientist, how they believe they will make a difference as an engineer or computer scientist, and what influenced them to study engineering or computer science. Selection is based on merit.

**Financial data:** The stipend is $1,000.
**Duration:** 1 year,
**Number awarded:** 1 each year.
**Deadline:** January of each year.

## 1799 AGNES MALAKATE KEZIOS SCHOLARSHIP

ASME International
Attn: American Society of Mechanical Engineers Auxiliary, Inc.
Three Park Avenue
New York, NY 10016-5990
Phone: (212) 591-7733; (800) THE-ASME; Fax: (212) 591-7674;
Email: horvathb@asme.org
Web: www.asme.org/auxiliary/scholarshiploans
**Summary:** To provide financial support for the study of mechanical engineering to students in their final year of undergraduate study.
**Eligibility:** Open to students completing the junior year of a 4-year program or the fourth year of a 5-year program in mechanical engineering. Applicants must be U.S. citizens enrolled in colleges and universities with accredited departments of mechanical engineering. If the school has a chapter of the Student Section of the American Society of Mechanical Engineers (ASME), the applicant must be a member. Selection is based on academic performance, financial need, character, and participation in ASME activities.
**Financial data:** The stipend is $2,000.
**Duration:** 1 year.
**Number awarded:** 1 or more each year.
**Deadline:** March of each year.

## 1800 AGNES MCINTOSH GARDEN CLUB OBJECTIVES SCHOLARSHIP

**Summary:** To provide financial aid to Florida undergraduates and graduate students majoring in designated areas related to gardening.
*See Listing #1243.*

## 1801 AGRICULTURAL YOUTH SCHOLARSHIP

New York Farm Bureau, Attn: Scholarship Committee
Route 9W
P.O. Box 992
Glenmont, NY 12077-0992
Phone: (518) 436-8495; (800) 342-4143, ext. 5633; Fax: (518) 431-5656
Web: www.nyfb.org/programs/ScholarshipInfo.htm
**Summary:** To recognize and reward high school students in New York who submit outstanding essays on their involvement in agriculture.
**Eligibility:** Open to high school juniors who live or work on a farm in New York or are involved with agriculture in some way. Farm Bureau membership is not required. Candidates must submit an essay, up to 2 pages in length, on "How Agriculture Affects My Life Now and Will Affect My Life in the Future." They must also provide information on the agricultural commodities on the farm where they live or work, their involvement in agricultural activities, their involvement in school and community activities, and their leadership roles and participation in any of those activities.
**Financial data:** First prize is $1,000, second $500, and third $250. All prizes must be used as college scholarships.
**Duration:** The competition is held annually.
**Number awarded:** 3 each year.
**Deadline:** November of each year.

## 1802 AIAA FOUNDATION UNDERGRADUATE DESIGN COMPETITIONS

American Institute of Aeronautics and Astronautics
Attn: Student Programs Director
1801 Alexander Bell Drive, Suite 500
Reston, VA 20191-4344
Phone: (703) 264-7536; (800) 639-AIAA, ext. 536; Fax: (703) 264-7551;
Email: stephenb@aiaa.org
Web: www.aiaa.org
**Summary:** To recognize and reward outstanding designs prepared by undergraduate student members of the American Institute of Aeronautics and Astronautics (AIAA).
**Eligibility:** Open to undergraduate students who are AIAA branch or at-large student members. Individuals may enter the aircraft design competition. Teams

of 3 to 10 students may enter in 4 competitions: the engine design competition, the aircraft design competition, the space design competition, and the space tourism vehicle design competition. Design projects that are used as part of an organized classroom requirement are eligible and encouraged. Designs that are submitted must be the work of the students, but a faculty advisor may provide guidance. Selection is based on technical content (35 points), organization and presentation (20 points), originality (20 points), and practical application and feasibility (25 points).

**Financial data:** For each of the 5 competitions, first place is $2,500, second place is $1,500, and third place is $1,000.

**Duration:** The competitions are held annually.

**Number awarded:** 3 cash awards are presented in each of the 5 competitions.

**Deadline:** Letters of intent must be submitted by March of each year; completed entries are due by the end of May.

---

## 1803 AIAA FOUNDATION UNDERGRADUATE SCHOLARSHIP PROGRAM

American Institute of Aeronautics and Astronautics
Attn: Student Programs Director
1801 Alexander Bell Drive, Suite 500
Reston, VA 20191-4344
Phone: (703) 264-7536; (800) 639-AIAA, ext. 536; Fax: (703) 264-7551;
Email: stephenb@aiaa.org
Web: www.aiaa.org

**Summary:** To provide financial assistance to undergraduate student members of the American Institute of Aeronautics and Astronautics (AIAA).

**Eligibility:** Open to college students who have completed at least 1 semester or quarter of full-time college work in engineering or science fields that relate to aerospace or aeronautics. Applicants must have a GPA of 3.0 or higher, be student members or willing to become student members of the sponsoring organization, and be interested in a career in the aerospace field. They may be of any nationality. Selection is based on GPA, career goals, letters of recommendation, and extracurricular activities.

**Financial data:** The stipend is $2,000.

**Duration:** 1 year; recipients may reapply if they have a GPA of 3.0 or higher

**Number awarded:** 30 each year.

**Deadline:** January of each year.

---

## 1804 AIR FORCE ROTC BIOMEDICAL SCIENCES CORPS

U.S. Air Force, Attn: Headquarters AFROTC/RRUC
551 East Maxwell Boulevard
Maxwell AFB, AL 36112-5917
Phone: (334) 953-2091; (866) 423-7682; Fax: (334) 953-6167
Web: www.afrotc.com/admissions/professional/biomed.php

**Summary:** To provide financial assistance to students who are interested in joining Air Force ROTC in college and preparing for a career as a physical therapist, optometrist, or pharmacist.

**Eligibility:** Open to U.S. citizens who are freshmen or sophomores in college and interested in a career as a physical therapist, optometrist, or pharmacist. Applicants must have a GPA of 2.0 or higher and meet all other academic and physical requirements for participation in AFROTC. At the time of their Air Force commissioning, they may be no more than 31 years of age. They must agree to serve for at least 4 years as nonline active-duty Air Force officers following graduation from college.

**Financial data:** Awards are type 2 AFROTC scholarships that provide for payment of tuition and fees, to a maximum of $15,000 per year, plus an annual book allowance of $600. All recipients are also awarded a tax-free subsistence allowance for 10 months of each year that is $300 per month during their sophomore year, $350 during their junior year, and $400 during their senior year.

**Duration:** 2 or 3 years, provided the recipient maintains a GPA of 2.0 or higher.

**Deadline:** June of each year.

---

## 1805 AIR FORCE ROTC EXPRESS SCHOLARSHIPS

U.S. Air Force, Attn: Headquarters AFROTC/RRUC
551 East Maxwell Boulevard
Maxwell AFB, AL 36112-5917
Phone: (334) 953-2091; (866) 423-7682; Fax: (334) 953-6167
Web: www.afrotc.com/scholarships/incolschol/expressSchol.php

**Summary:** To provide financial assistance to students who are interested in joining Air Force ROTC and majoring in critical Air Force officer fields in college.

**Eligibility:** Open to U.S. citizens who are completing at least their first year of college and are working on a degree in fields that may change annually but are

of critical interest to the Air Force. Applicants must have a GPA of 2.5 or higher and meet all other academic and physical requirements for participation in AFROTC. At the time of their Air Force commissioning, they may be no more than 31 years of age. They must be able to pass the Air Force Officer Qualifying Test (AFOQT) and the Air Force ROTC Physical Fitness Test. years as active-duty Air Force officers following graduation from college.

**Financial data:** Awards are type 2 AFROTC scholarships that provide for payment of tuition and fees, to a maximum of $15,000 per year, plus an annual book allowance of $600. All recipients are also awarded a tax-free monthly subsistence allowance that is $250 for freshmen, $300 for sophomores, $350 for juniors, and $400 for seniors.

**Duration:** 3 and a half years, until completion of a bachelor's degree.

---

## 1806 AIR FORCE ROTC NURSING SCHOLARSHIPS

U.S. Air Force, Attn: Headquarters AFROTC/RRUC
551 East Maxwell Boulevard
Maxwell AFB, AL 36112-5917
Phone: (334) 953-2091; (866) 423-7682; Fax: (334) 953-6167
Web: www.afrotc.com/admissions/professional/nursing.php

**Summary:** To provide financial assistance to college students who are interested in a career as a nurse, are interested in joining Air Force ROTC, and are willing to serve as Air Force officers following completion of their bachelor's degree.

**Eligibility:** Open to U.S. citizens who are freshmen or sophomores in college and interested in a career as a nurse. Applicants must have a cumulative GPA of 2.5 or higher at the end of their freshman year and meet all other academic and physical requirements for participation in AFROTC. They must be interested in working on a nursing degree from an accredited program. At the time of Air Force commissioning, they may be no more than 31 years of age. They must be able to pass the Air Force Officer Qualifying Test (AFOQT) and the Air Force ROTC Physical Fitness Test.

**Financial data:** Awards are type 2 AFROTC scholarships that provide for payment of tuition and fees, to a maximum of $15,000 per year, plus an annual book allowance of $600. All recipients are also awarded a tax-free subsistence allowance for 10 months of each year that is $300 per month during their sophomore year, $350 during their junior year, and $400 during their senior year.

**Duration:** 2 or 3 years, provided the recipient maintains a GPA of 2.5 or higher.

**Deadline:** June of each year.

---

## 1807 AIR PRODUCTS AND CHEMICALS SCHOLARSHIP FOR DIVERSITY IN ENGINEERING

Association of Independent Colleges and Universities of Pennsylvania
101 North Front Street
Harrisburg, PA 17101-1405
Phone: (717) 232-8649; Fax: (717) 233-8574; Email: info@aicup.org
Web: www.aicup.org

**Summary:** To provide financial assistance to women and minority students at member institutions of the Association of Independent Colleges and Universities of Pennsylvania (AICUP) who are majoring in designated fields of engineering.

**Eligibility:** Open to full-time undergraduate students at designated AICUP colleges and universities who are women and/or members of the following minority groups: American Indians, Alaska Natives, Asians, Blacks/African Americans, Hispanics/Latinos, Native Hawaiians, or Pacific Islanders. Applicants must be juniors majoring in chemical or mechanical engineering with a GPA of 2.7 or higher. Along with their application, they must submit an essay on their characteristics, accomplishments, primary interests, plans, and goals, and what sets them apart.

**Financial data:** The stipend is $7,500 per year.

**Duration:** 1 year; may be renewed 1 additional year if the recipient maintains appropriate academic standards.

**Number awarded:** 2 each year.

**Deadline:** April of each year.

---

## 1808 AIR TRAFFIC CONTROL ASSOCIATION STUDENT SCHOLARSHIP PROGRAM

Air Traffic Control Association, Attn: Scholarship Fund
1101 King Street, Suite 300
Alexandria, VA 22314
Phone: (703) 299-2430; Fax: (703) 299-2437; Email: info@atca.org
Web: www.atca.org/activities/scholarships.asp

**Summary:** To provide financial assistance to students working on a bachelor's degree or higher in aviation.

**Eligibility:** Open to half- or full-time students who are U.S. citizens, enrolled or accepted for enrollment in an accredited college or university, taking classes to prepare for an aviation-related career, working on a bachelor's or graduate degree, registered for at least 6 hours, and at least 30 semester or 45 quarter hours away from graduation. Applicants must submit an essay on "How My Educational Efforts Will Enhance My Potential Contribution to Aviation." The essay should address the applicant's financial need.

**Financial data:** Stipends range from $1,500 to $2,500.

**Duration:** 1 year; may be renewed.

**Number awarded:** Varies each year, depending on the number, qualifications, and need of the applicants.

**Deadline:** April of each year.

## 1809 AIRBUS LEADERSHIP GRANT

Women in Aviation, International, Attn: Scholarships
101 Corsair Drive, Suite 101
P.O. Box 11287
Daytona Beach, FL 32120-1287
Phone: (386) 226-7996; Fax: (386) 226-7998; Email: scholarships@wai.org
Web: www.wai.org/education/scholarships.cfm

**Summary:** To provide financial assistance for college to members of Women in Aviation, International (WAI).

**Eligibility:** Open to WAI members who are college sophomores or higher working on a degree in an aviation-related field. Applicants must have earned a GPA of 3.0 or higher and be able to demonstrate leadership potential. They must submit a 500-word essay addressing their career aspirations and how they have exhibited leadership skills, 3 letters of recommendation, a resume, copies of all aviation and medical certificates, and the last 3 pages of their pilot logbook, if applicable. Selection is based on achievements, attitude toward self and others, commitment to success, dedication to career, financial need, motivation, reliability, responsibility, and teamwork.

**Financial data:** The stipend is $2,000 per year.

**Duration:** 1 year.

**Number awarded:** Varies each year; recently, 2 of these scholarships were awarded.

**Deadline:** December of each year.

## 1810 AIRCRAFT ELECTRONICS ASSOCIATION AVIATION MAINTENANCE SCHOLARSHIP

Women in Aviation, International, Attn: Scholarships
101 Corsair Drive, Suite 101
P.O. Box 11287
Daytona Beach, FL 32120-1287
Phone: (386) 226-7996; Fax: (386) 226-7998; Email: scholarships@wai.org
Web: www.wai.org/education/scholarships.cfm

**Summary:** To provide financial assistance to members of Women in Aviation, International (WAI) who are studying aircraft maintenance.

**Eligibility:** Open to WAI members who are seeking a degree in the aviation maintenance field at an accredited college or technical school. Preference is given to avionics majors. Applicants must have a GPA of 2.75 or higher. Selection is based on achievements, attitude toward self and others, commitment to success, dedication to career, financial need, motivation, reliability, responsibility, and teamwork.

**Financial data:** The stipend is $1,000.

**Duration:** 1 year.

**Number awarded:** 1 each year.

**Deadline:** December of each year.

## 1811 AIRGAS SCHOLARSHIPS

American Welding Society, Attn: AWS Foundation, Inc.
550 N.W. LeJeune Road
Miami, FL 33126
Phone: (305) 445-6628; (800) 443-9353, ext. 461; Fax: (305) 443-7559; Email: found@aws.org
Web: www.aws.org/foundation/scholarships/airgas.html

**Summary:** To provide financial assistance to college students majoring in welding engineering.

**Eligibility:** Open to full-time undergraduate students who are working on a 4-year bachelor's degree in welding engineering or welding engineering technology; preference is given to welding engineering students interested in preparing for a career with an industrial gas or welding equipment distributor. Applicants must have a GPA of 2.8 or higher overall and 3.0 or higher in engineering courses. Along with their application, they must submit an essay

of 300 to 500 words on "Why I Want to Pursue a Career with an Industrial Gas or Welding Equipment Distributor." Financial need is not required, but priority is given to applicants who can demonstrate a financial need. Priority is given to applicants who reside or attend school in Alabama, Florida, or Georgia. U.S. or Canadian citizenship is required.

**Financial data:** The stipend is $2,500.

**Duration:** 1 year; recipients may reapply.

**Number awarded:** 2 each year.

**Deadline:** January of each year.

## 1812 A.L. BROWN SCHOLARSHIP FUND AWARDS

Society of Fire Protection Engineers-New England Chapter
c/o Engineering Center
One Walnut Street
Boston, MA 02108-3616
Email: scholarship@sfpe-newengland.org
Web: www.sfpe-newengland.org/scholarship.html

**Summary:** To provide financial assistance to engineering students in New England who are interested in preparing for a career in fire protection.

**Eligibility:** Open to students who are working full time on a bachelor's or graduate degree in engineering and have a desire to prepare for a career in fire protection. Applicants must have graduated from a high school or be attending a college or university in Connecticut, Maine, Massachusetts, New Hampshire, Rhode Island, or Vermont. Along with their application, they must submit a letter of introduction that addresses the following topics: 1) when they first became interested in preparing for a career in or related to fire protection engineering; 2) any past experiences and/or accomplishments that they feel will make them a more competent fire protection engineer; 3) their career goals, both short term and long term; 4) a demonstration of their financial need; and 5) how the receipt of this award will benefit their efforts to become a fire protection engineer.

**Financial data:** Stipends range from $1,000 to $5,000.

**Duration:** 1 year.

**Number awarded:** Varies each year.

**Deadline:** January of each year.

## 1813 ALABAMA CONCRETE INDUSTRIES ASSOCIATION SCHOLARSHIPS

**Summary:** To provide financial assistance to students majoring in architecture, building sciences, or engineering in Alabama.

*See Listing #1250.*

## 1814 ALABAMA COUNCIL OF TEACHERS OF MATHEMATICS SCHOLARSHIPS

Alabama Council of Teachers of Mathematics
c/o Lisa Miller, President
Hewitt-Trussville High School
5275 Trussville-Clay Road
Trussville, AL 35173
Phone: (205) 379-3950; Email: mathnbct@yahoo.com
Web: www.dpa.uab.edu/~tsmith/ACTM.htm

**Summary:** To provide financial assistance to students majoring in mathematics at Alabama colleges and universities.

**Eligibility:** Open to students enrolled as juniors or seniors at colleges and universities in Alabama. Applicants must be majoring in mathematics and have a GPA of 3.0 or higher.

**Financial data:** The stipend is $1,000.

**Duration:** 1 year.

**Number awarded:** 5 each year.

## 1815 ALABAMA HOME BUILDERS SCHOLARSHIPS

Home Builders Association of Alabama
Attn: Alabama Home Builders Foundation
P.O. Box 241305
Montgomery, AL 36124
Phone: (334) 834-3006; (800) 745-4222; Email: info@hbaa.org
Web: www.hbaa.org/consumers/scholarships.php

**Summary:** To provide financial assistance for college to Alabama residents interested in preparing for a career in the home building industry.

**Eligibility:** Open to residents of Alabama enrolled in, or attending, a junior college, technical school, or university in the state. Applicants must be working on a certificate or degree in a construction-related field. They must be able to demonstrate financial need.

**Financial data:** A stipend is awarded (amount not specified).

**Duration:** 1 year.

**Number awarded:** Varies each year.

**Deadline:** March of each year.

---

### 1816 ALASKA CHAPTER COLLEGE SCHOLARSHIP

Safari Club International-Alaska Chapter, Attn: Scholarship Committee
P.O. Box 558
Palmer, AK 99654-0558
Email: dau@mtaonline.net
Web: www.aksafariclub.org/hot_topics.htm

**Summary:** To provide financial assistance to high school seniors in Alaska who have participated in hunting activities and plan on majoring in a field related to wildlife management in college.

**Eligibility:** Open to graduating high school seniors in Alaska who have an excellent academic record, have participated in hunting activities, can demonstrate financial need, and plan to major in a field related to wildlife management, wildlife biology, or natural resource management in college. Applicants must be U.S. citizens and able to document participation in local or national conservation activities. Selection is based on academic achievement, leadership, financial need, planned major, and participation in conservation activities, shooting sports programs, and hunting sports.

**Financial data:** The stipend is $5,000. Funds, which are paid to the student's institution, must be used for tuition, fees, books, supplies, or required equipment.

**Duration:** 1 year.

**Number awarded:** 1 each year.

**Deadline:** March of each year.

---

### 1817 ALASKADVANTAGE EDUCATIONAL GRANTS

Alaska Commission on Postsecondary Education
Attn: AlaskAdvantage Programs
3030 Vintage Boulevard
Juneau, AK 99801-7109
Phone: (907) 465-6779; (866) 427-5683; Fax: (907) 465-5316; TTY: (907) 465-3143; Email: customer_service@acpe.ak.us
Web: alaskaadvantage.state.ak.us/page/225

**Summary:** To provide financial assistance to Alaska residents who attend college in the state to prepare for a career in designated fields with a workforce shortage.

**Eligibility:** Open to residents of Alaska who have been admitted to an undergraduate degree or vocational certificate program at a qualifying institution in the state. Applicants must be planning to work on a degree or certificate in a field that the state has designated as a workforce shortage area; currently, those are allied health sciences, community or social service, and teaching. They must be able to demonstrate financial need and SAT or ACT scores in the top quartile. U.S. citizenship or permanent resident status is required.

**Financial data:** Grants range from $500 to $2,000 per year, depending on the need of the recipient.

**Duration:** 1 year; may be renewed as long as the recipient remains enrolled at least half time, makes satisfactory academic progress, and continues to meet residency and financial need requirements.

**Number awarded:** Varies each year; students with the greatest financial need are awarded support until funds are exhausted.

**Deadline:** April of each year.

---

### 1818 ALBERT E. AND FLORENCE W. NEWTON NURSE SCHOLARSHIP

Rhode Island Foundation, Attn: Scholarship Coordinator
One Union Station
Providence, RI 02903
Phone: (401) 274-4564; Fax: (401) 751-7983; Email: libbym@rifoundation.org
Web: www.rifoundation.org

**Summary:** To provide financial assistance for further education to nurses in Rhode Island.

**Eligibility:** Open to 1) juniors and seniors enrolled in a baccalaureate nursing program; 2) second- or third-year students in a 3-year nursing program; 3) students in a 2-year associate degree nursing program; 4) active practicing R.N.s licensed in Rhode Island and working on a bachelor's degree in nursing; and 5) R.N.s licensed in Rhode Island working on a graduate degree in nurs-

ing. Applicants must be studying at a Rhode Island nursing school on a full- or part-time basis and able to demonstrate financial need. As part of the selection process, they must submit an essay, up to 300 words, on their career goals as they relate to patient care.

**Financial data:** Stipends range from $500 to $2,500 per year.

**Duration:** 1 year; may be renewed.

**Number awarded:** Numerous scholarships are awarded each year.

**Deadline:** March of each year.

---

### 1819 ALCA EDUCATIONAL FOUNDATION SCHOLARSHIPS

**Summary:** To provide financial assistance to students at colleges and universities that have a connection to the Professional Landcare Network (PLANET).
*See Listing #1254.*

---

### 1820 ALCOA FOUNDATION ACADEMIC SCHOLARSHIP

American Association of Occupational Health Nurses, Inc.
Attn: AAOHN Foundation
2920 Brandywine Road, Suite 100
Atlanta, GA 30341-4146
Phone: (770) 455-7757; Fax: (770) 455-7271; Email: foundation@aaohn.org
Web: www.aaohn.org/foundation/scholarships/academic_study.cfm

**Summary:** To provide financial assistance to registered nurses who are working on a bachelor's or graduate degree to prepare for a career in occupational and environmental health.

**Eligibility:** Open to registered nurses who are enrolled in a baccalaureate or graduate degree program. Applicants must demonstrate an interest in, and commitment to, occupational and environmental health. Selection is based on 2 letters of recommendation and a 500-word essay on the applicant's professional goals as they relate to the academic activity and the field of occupational and environmental health.

**Financial data:** The stipend is $1,500.

**Duration:** 1 year; may be renewed up to 2 additional years.

**Number awarded:** 1 each year.

**Deadline:** November of each year.

---

### 1821 ALFRED T. GRANGER STUDENT ART FUND

**Summary:** To provide financial assistance to residents of Vermont who are interested in working on an undergraduate or graduate degree in a field related to design.
*See Listing #1256.*

---

### 1822 ALICE GLAISYER WARFIELD MEMORIAL SCHOLARSHIP

Transportation Clubs International, Attn: Gay Fielding
7031 Manchester Street
New Orleans, LA 70126
Email: GayFielding@bellsouth.net
Web: www.transportationclubsinternational.com

**Summary:** To provide financial assistance to college students interested in preparing for a career in fields related to transportation.

**Eligibility:** Open to students enrolled in an academic institution that offers courses in transportation, logistics, traffic management, or related fields. Applicants must intend to prepare for a career in those fields. Selection is based on scholastic ability, character, potential, professional interest, and financial need.

**Financial data:** The stipend is $1,000.

**Duration:** 1 year.

**Number awarded:** 1 or more each year.

**Deadline:** April of each year.

---

### 1823 ALICE M. YARNOLD AND SAMUEL YARNOLD SCHOLARSHIP

Alice M. Yarnold and Samuel Yarnold Scholarship Trust
180 Locust Street
Dover, NH 03820-4033
Phone: (603) 749-5535

**Summary:** To provide financial assistance to currently-enrolled college students in New Hampshire who are majoring in nursing, medicine, social work, or other areas.

**Eligibility:** Open to residents of New Hampshire who are enrolled in college working on a degree in nursing, medicine, or social work. Applicants must be able to demonstrate financial need. Along with their application, they must submit their FAFSA, a copy of their latest transcript, and 2 letters of recommendation.

**Financial data:** Stipends range from $1,000 to $5,000 annually.

**Duration:** 1 year; may be renewed up to 3 additional years.

**Deadline:** April of each year.

## 1824 ALICE T. SCHAFER MATHEMATICS PRIZE

Association for Women in Mathematics

c/o University of Maryland

4114 Computer & Space Sciences Building

College Park, MD 20742-2461

Phone: (301) 405-7892; Email: awm@math.umd.edu

Web: www.awm-math.org/schaferprize.html

**Summary:** To recognize and reward undergraduate women who have demonstrated excellence in mathematics.

**Eligibility:** Open to college women; they must be nominated by a member of the mathematical community. The nominee may be at any level in her undergraduate career. Selection is based on the quality of the student's performance in advanced mathematics courses and special programs, evidence of a real interest in mathematics, an ability to work independently, and performance in local and national mathematics competitions.

**Financial data:** The prize is $1,000.

**Duration:** The competition is held annually.

**Number awarded:** 1 each year.

**Deadline:** Nominations must be submitted by September of each year.

## 1825 ALL OHIO CHAPTER SCHOLARSHIP

Soil and Water Conservation Society-All Ohio Chapter

c/o Doug Deardorff, Scholarship Committee

P.O. Box 436

Kenton, OH 43326-0436

Phone: (419) 673-7238, ext. 3; Email: doug.deardorff@oh.usda.gov

Web: www.ohiochapterswcs.org

**Summary:** To provide financial assistance to Ohio residents who are working on an undergraduate degree in a field related to natural resources conservation.

**Eligibility:** Open to residents of Ohio who are enrolled at a 2-year or 4-year college or university in the state. Applicants must be working on a degree in a natural resources conservation program, including agricultural engineering, agronomy, biology, environmental engineering, forestry, geology, land use planning, landscape architecture, plant science, resource management, soil science, or wildlife management. They must submit a 1-page statement describing their background, objectives of their educational goals, and career plans. Selection is based on that statement, transcript, 3 references, leadership and awards in college activities, and documentation of financial need.

**Financial data:** The stipend is $1,000.

**Duration:** 1 year.

**Number awarded:** 1 each year.

**Deadline:** May of each year.

## 1826 ALLEGHENY MOUNTAIN SECTION SCHOLARSHIPS

Air & Waste Management Association-Allegheny Mountain Section

Attn: Scholarship Committee Chair

700 North Bell Avenue, Suite 200

Carnegie, PA 15106

Email: LCHathaway@mactec.com

Web: www.ams-awma.org

**Summary:** To provide financial assistance to undergraduate students in West Virginia and western Pennsylvania who are interested in preparing for a career in an environmental field.

**Eligibility:** Open to students currently enrolled and high school seniors accepted full time in a 4- or 5-year college or university program that will lead to a career in the environmental field through environmental science, engineering, or law. Applicants must be 1) children or spouses of members of the Allegheny Mountain section of the Air & Waste Management Association (A&WMA); or 2) attending or planning to attend a college or university in western Pennsylvania or West Virginia. They must have a GPA of 3.0 or higher. Selection is based on academic record, plan of study, career goals, recommendations, and extracurricular activities; financial need is not considered.

**Financial data:** The stipend is $1,500.

**Duration:** 1 year.

**Number awarded:** Up to 3 each year.

**Deadline:** March of each year.

## 1827 ALLEN J. BALDWIN SCHOLARSHIP

ASME International

Attn: American Society of Mechanical Engineers Auxiliary, Inc.

Three Park Avenue

New York, NY 10016-5990

Phone: (212) 591-7733; (800) THE-ASME; Fax: (212) 591-7674;

Email: horvathb@asme.org

Web: www.asme.org/auxiliary/scholarshiploans

**Summary:** To provide financial support for the study of mechanical engineering to students in their final year of undergraduate study.

**Eligibility:** Open to students completing the junior year of a 4-year program or the fourth year of a 5-year program in mechanical engineering. Applicants must be U.S. citizens enrolled in colleges and universities with accredited departments of mechanical engineering. If the school has a chapter of the Student Section of the American Society of Mechanical Engineers (ASME), the applicant must be a member. Selection is based on academic performance, financial need, character, and participation in ASME activities.

**Financial data:** The stipend is $2,000.

**Duration:** 1 year.

**Number awarded:** 1 or more each year.

**Deadline:** March of each year.

## 1828 ALMA NEILSEN PERPETUAL SCHOLARSHIP

International Chiropractors Association

1110 North Glebe Road, Suite 1000

Arlington, VA 22201

Phone: (703) 528-5000; (800) 423-4690; Fax: (703) 528-5023;

Email: chiro@chiropractic.org

Web: www.chiropractic.org

**Summary:** To provide financial assistance to student members of the International Chiropractors Association (SICA).

**Eligibility:** Open to members of the SICA organization on the campus of a college approved by the International Chiropractors Association (ICA). Applicants must be sophomores, juniors, or seniors and able to demonstrate financial need. They must submit a short statement (100 to 120 words) on their commitment to chiropractic and why this scholarship should be awarded to them.

**Financial data:** A stipend is awarded (amount not specified).

**Duration:** 1 year.

**Number awarded:** Varies each year.

**Deadline:** April of each year.

## 1829 ALPHA MU TAU UNDERGRADUATE SCHOLARSHIPS

Alpha Mu Tau Fraternity

c/o American Society for Clinical Laboratory Science

6701 Democracy Boulevard, Suite 300

Bethesda, MD 20817

Phone: (301) 657-2768; Fax: (301) 657-2909; Email: ascls@ascls.org

Web: www.ascls.org/leadership/awards/amt.asp

**Summary:** To provide financial assistance for undergraduate studies to members of Alpha Mu Tau, a national fraternity for professionals in the clinical laboratory sciences.

**Eligibility:** Open to U.S. citizens or permanent residents who are members of Alpha Mu Tau and accepted into or currently enrolled in an undergraduate program in clinical laboratory science, including cytotechnology, histotechnology, clinical laboratory science/medical technology, and clinical laboratory technician/medical laboratory technician. Applicants must be entering their last year of study. Along with their application, they must submit a 500-word statement describing their interest and reasons for preparing for a career in clinical laboratory science. Financial need is also considered in the selection process.

**Financial data:** The stipend is $1,500.

**Duration:** 1 year.

**Number awarded:** Several each year.

**Deadline:** March of each year.

## 1830 AMBUCS SCHOLARSHIPS FOR THERAPISTS

National AMBUCS, Inc., Attn: Scholarship Coordinator

P.O. Box 5127

High Point, NC 27262

Phone: (336) 852-0052; Fax: (336) 852-6830; Email: ambucs@ambucs.org

Web: www.ambucs.org

**Summary:** To provide financial assistance to undergraduate and graduate students who are interested in preparing for a career serving disabled citizens in various fields of clinical therapy.

**Eligibility:** Open to U.S. citizens who have been accepted at the upper-division or graduate level in an accredited program that qualifies the students for clinical practice in occupational therapy, physical therapy, speech language pathology, or hearing audiology. Programs for therapy assistants are not included. Applicants must submit college transcripts for the last 3 semesters, a 500-word essay on their interest in therapy as a career, and a statement of family financial circumstances. Selection is based on financial need, commitment to local community, demonstrated academic accomplishment, character for compassion and integrity, and career objectives.

**Financial data:** Most of these awards range from $500 to $1,500 per year; one scholarship of $6,000 for 2 years is also awarded. Funds are paid directly to the recipient's school.

**Duration:** 1 year.

**Number awarded:** Approximately 400 each year, with a total value of $225,000.

**Deadline:** April of each year.

## 1831 AMD/HENAAC SCHOLARS PROGRAM

Hispanic Engineer National Achievement Awards Conference
3900 Whiteside Street
Los Angeles, CA 90063
Phone: (323) 262-0997; Fax: (323) 262-0946; Email: info@henaac.org
Web: www.henaac.org/scholarships.htm

**Summary:** To provide financial assistance to Hispanic undergraduate students majoring in computer and electrical engineering.

**Eligibility:** Open to Hispanic undergraduate students who are enrolled full time in computer or electrical engineering. Applicants must have a GPA of 3.5 or higher. Academic achievement and campus community activities are considered in the selection process.

**Financial data:** Stipends range from $1,000 to $5,000.

**Duration:** 1 year; recipients may reapply.

**Number awarded:** 1 or more each year.

**Deadline:** April of each year.

## 1832 AMERADA HESS/HENAAC SCHOLARS PROGRAM

Hispanic Engineer National Achievement Awards Conference
3900 Whiteside Street
Los Angeles, CA 90063
Phone: (323) 262-0997; Fax: (323) 262-0946; Email: info@henaac.org
Web: www.henaac.org/scholarships.htm

**Summary:** To provide financial assistance to Hispanic undergraduate students majoring in engineering and related fields.

**Eligibility:** Open to Hispanic undergraduate students who are enrolled full time in computer science, engineering, material science, mathematics, or applied science. Applicants must have a GPA of 3.0 or higher. There is no citizenship requirement. Academic achievement and campus community activities are considered in the selection process.

**Financial data:** Stipends range from $1,000 to $5,000.

**Duration:** 1 year; recipients may reapply.

**Number awarded:** 1 or more each year.

**Deadline:** April of each year.

## 1833 AMERICA RESPONDS MEMORIAL SCHOLARSHIP

American Society of Safety Engineers, Attn: ASSE Foundation
1800 East Oakton Street
Des Plaines, IL 60018
Phone: (847) 768-3441; Fax: (847) 296-9220; Email: mrosario@asse.org
Web: www.asse.org

**Summary:** To provide financial assistance to undergraduate student members of the American Society of Safety Engineers (ASSE).

**Eligibility:** Open to ASSE student members who are majoring in occupational safety and health or a closely-related field (e.g., safety engineering, safety management, systems safety, environmental science, industrial hygiene, ergonomics, fire science). Applicants must be full-time students who have completed at least 60 semester hours with a GPA of 3.0 or higher. As part of the selection process, they must submit 2 essays of 300 words or less: 1) why they are seeking a degree in safety, a brief description of their current activities, and how those relate to their career goals and objectives; and 2) why they should be awarded this scholarship (including career goals and financial need).

**Financial data:** The stipend is $1,000 per year.

**Duration:** 1 year; nonrenewable.

**Number awarded:** 1 each year.

**Deadline:** November of each year.

## 1834 AMERICAN ANGUS AUXILIARY SCHOLARSHIPS

National Junior Angus Association, Attn: Director Junior Activities
3201 Frederick Boulevard
St. Joseph, MO 64506
Phone: (816) 383-5100; Fax: (816) 233-9703; Email: jfisher@angus.org
Web: www.njaa.info/awards.html

**Summary:** To provide financial assistance for college to high school seniors who are members of the National Junior Angus Association (NJAA) and participate in state and regional activities related to Angus.

**Eligibility:** Open to members of the association who are nominated by state or regional scholarship chairs; each chair is entitled to nominate one boy and one girl. Boys and girls compete in separate divisions. Applicants must submit a 300-word essay that covers 1) Angus in their present farm operations, 2) what Angus cattle have meant to them, 3) their learning experiences, 4) their farm program, and 5) their ambitions and future plans. They must also document their Angus projects and activities; school activities; 4-H, FFA, and other agriculture-related activities; church, community, and other activities; owned junior Angus show record; bred and owned junior Angus show record; open show record; showmanship record; livestock judging contests; Angus herd improvement record; and sale consignments.

**Financial data:** For each division, first place is $1,100, second place is $950, third place is $900, fourth place is $800, and fifth place is $750. Funds are sent to the recipients' college or university upon proof of full-time enrollment.

**Duration:** 1 year.

**Number awarded:** 10 each year: 5 set aside for girls and 5 for boys.

**Deadline:** May of each year.

## 1835 AMERICAN ASSOCIATION OF BLACKS IN ENERGY SCHOLARSHIP

American Association of Blacks in Energy, Attn: Scholarship Committee
927 15th Street, N.W., Suite 200
Washington, DC 20005
Phone: (202) 371-9530; Fax: (202) 371-9218; Email: aabe@aabe.org
Web: www.aabe.org/mission/scholarships.html

**Summary:** To provide financial assistance to underrepresented minority high school seniors who are interested in majoring in engineering, mathematics, or physical science in college.

**Eligibility:** Open to members of minority groups underrepresented in the energy industry (African Americans, Hispanics, and Native Americans) who are graduating high school seniors. Applicants must have a B academic average overall and a B average in mathematics and science courses. They must be planning to attend an accredited college or university to major in engineering, mathematics, or the physical sciences. Along with their application, they must submit a 350-word essay covering why they should receive this scholarship, their professional career objectives, and any other pertinent information. Financial need is also considered in the selection process. The applicant who demonstrates the most outstanding achievement and promise is presented with the Premier Award. All applications must be submitted to the local office of the sponsoring organization in the student's state. For a list of local offices, contact the scholarship committee at the national office.

**Financial data:** The stipends are $1,500. The Premier Award is an additional $3,000. All funds are paid directly to the students upon proof of enrollment at an accredited college or university.

**Duration:** 1 year; nonrenewable.

**Number awarded:** 6 each year (1 in each of the organization's regions); of those 6 winners, 1 is chosen to receive the Premier Award.

**Deadline:** February of each year.

## 1836 AMERICAN ASSOCIATION OF OCCUPATIONAL HEALTH NURSES FOUNDATION ACADEMIC SCHOLARSHIP

American Association of Occupational Health Nurses, Inc.
Attn: AAOHN Foundation
2920 Brandywine Road, Suite 100
Atlanta, GA 30341-4146
Phone: (770) 455-7757; Fax: (770) 455-7271; Email: foundation@aaohn.org
Web: www.aaohn.org/foundation/scholarships/academic_study.cfm

**Summary:** To provide financial assistance to registered nurses who are working on a bachelor's or graduate degree to prepare for a career in occupational and environmental health.

**Eligibility:** Open to registered nurses who are enrolled in a baccalaureate or graduate degree program. Applicants must demonstrate an interest in, and commitment to, occupational and environmental health. Selection is based on 2 letters of recommendation and a 500-word essay on the applicant's professional goals as they relate to the academic activity and the field of occupational and environmental health.

**Financial data:** The stipend is $3,000.

**Duration:** 1 year; may be renewed up to 2 additional years.

**Number awarded:** 1 each year.

**Deadline:** November of each year.

## 1837 AMERICAN CHEMICAL SOCIETY SCHOLARS PROGRAM

American Chemical Society, Attn: Department of Diversity Programs
1155 16th Street, N.W.
Washington, DC 20036
Phone: (202) 872-6250; (800) 227-5558, ext. 6250; Fax: (202) 776-8003;
Email: scholars@acs.org
Web: www.chemistry.org/scholars

**Summary:** To provide financial assistance to underrepresented minority students with a strong interest in chemistry and a desire to prepare for a career in a chemically-related science.

**Eligibility:** Open to 1) college-bound high school seniors; 2) college freshmen, sophomores, and juniors enrolled full time at an accredited college or university; 3) community college graduates and transfer students who plan to study for a bachelor's degree; and 4) community college freshmen. Applicants must be African American, Hispanic/Latino, or American Indian. They must be majoring or planning to major in chemistry, biochemistry, chemical engineering, or other chemically-related fields, such as environmental science, materials science, or toxicology, and planning to prepare for a career in the chemical sciences or chemical technology. Students planning careers in medicine or pharmacy are not eligible. U.S. citizenship or permanent resident status is required. Selection is based on academic merit (GPA of 3.0 or higher) and financial need.

**Financial data:** The maximum stipend is $2,500 for the freshman year in college or $3,000 per year for sophomores, juniors, and seniors.

**Duration:** 1 year; may be renewed.

**Number awarded:** Approximately 100 new awards are granted each year.

**Deadline:** February of each year.

## 1838 AMERICAN COUNCIL OF ENGINEERING COMPANIES OF NEW JERSEY SCHOLARSHIP

American Council of Engineering Companies of New Jersey
Attn: Executive Director
66 Morris Avenue, Suite 1A
Springfield, NJ 07081-1409
Phone: (973) 564-5848; Fax: (973) 564-7480
Web: www.cecnj.org/Scholarships.htm

**Summary:** To provide financial assistance to engineering students in New Jersey.

**Eligibility:** Open to students in their third, fourth, or fifth year of undergraduate study at an ABET-approved engineering or land surveying program in New Jersey. U.S. citizenship is required. Awards are based on GPA (28 points), an essay (25 points), work experience (20 points), recommendations (17 points), and college activities (10 points).

**Financial data:** The award is $1,000, of which $500 is payable upon receipt of the award and $500 upon graduation.

**Duration:** 1 year.

**Number awarded:** Up to 5 each year.

**Deadline:** January of each year.

## 1839 AMERICAN COUNCIL OF ENGINEERING COMPANIES OF SOUTH DAKOTA SCHOLARSHIP

American Council of Engineering Companies of South Dakota
Attn: Executive Director
P.O. Box 398
Rapid City, SD 57709-0398
Email: contact@cecsd.org
Web: www.cecsd.org/scholar.html

**Summary:** To provide financial assistance to students in South Dakota currently working on a bachelor's degree in specified engineering fields.

**Eligibility:** Open to students working on a bachelor's degree in an Accreditation Board for Engineering and Technology (ABET)-approved engineering program in South Dakota. Applicants must be U.S. citizens entering their junior, senior, or fifth year with a major in civil, electrical, or mechanical engineering. They

must have expressed a desire to enter the field of consulting engineering after graduation. Along with their application, they must submit a 500-word essay on "What is the role or responsibility of the consulting engineer or land surveyor to shaping and protecting the natural environment?" Selection is based on the essay (25 points), cumulative GPA (28 points), work experience (20 points), a letter of recommendation (17 points), and college activities (10 points).

**Financial data:** The stipend is $1,000 per year.

**Duration:** 1 year; may be renewed.

**Number awarded:** 1 each year.

**Deadline:** December of each year.

## 1840 AMERICAN COUNCIL OF ENGINEERING COMPANIES SCHOLARSHIP PROGRAM

American Council of Engineering Companies
Attn: Awards Programs Director
1015 15th Street, N.W., Eighth Floor
Washington, DC 20005-2605
Phone: (202) 347-7474; Fax: (202) 898-0068, Email: acec@accc.org
Web: www.acec.org

**Summary:** To provide financial assistance to students currently working on a bachelor's degree in engineering.

**Eligibility:** Open to students working on a bachelor's degree in an ABET-approved engineering program. Applicants must be U.S. citizens entering their junior, senior, or fifth year. They must have received a scholarship from a participating state Member Organization (MO) of the American Council of Engineering Companies (ACEC). Along with their application, they must submit a 500-word essay on "What is the role or responsibility of the consulting engineer or land surveyor to shaping and protecting the natural environment?" Selection is based on the essay (25 points), cumulative GPA (28 points), work experience (20 points), a letter of recommendation (17 points), and college activities (10 points).

**Financial data:** Stipends are $5,000 or $3,000.

**Duration:** 1 year.

**Number awarded:** 2 each year: the Scholar of the Year at $5,000 and the College of Fellows award at $3,000.

**Deadline:** Participating MOs must forward applications by December of each year.

## 1841 AMERICAN DENTAL HYGIENISTS' ASSOCIATION INSTITUTE MINORITY SCHOLARSHIPS

American Dental Hygienists' Association, Attn: Institute for Oral Health
444 North Michigan Avenue, Suite 3400
Chicago, IL 60611
Phone: (312) 440-8918; (800) 735-4916; Fax: (312) 440-8929;
Email: institute@adha.net
Web: www.adha.org/institute/Scholarship/index.htm

**Summary:** To provide financial assistance to minority students and males of any race enrolled in undergraduate programs in dental hygiene.

**Eligibility:** Open to members of groups currently underrepresented in the dental hygiene profession (Native Americans, African Americans, Hispanics, Asians, and males) who are active members of the Student American Dental Hygienists' Association (SADHA) or the American Dental Hygienists' Association (ADHA). Applicants must have a GPA of 3.0 or higher, be able to document financial need of at least $1,500, and have completed at least 1 year of full-time enrollment in an accredited dental hygiene program in the United States. Along with their application, they must submit a statement that covers their long-term career goals, their intended contribution to the dental hygiene profession, their professional interests, and the manner in which their degree will enhance their professional capacity.

**Financial data:** Stipends range from $1,000 to $2,000.

**Duration:** 1 year; nonrenewable.

**Number awarded:** 2 each year.

**Deadline:** April of each year.

## 1842 AMERICAN ELECTRIC POWER SCHOLARSHIP

ASME International, Attn: Coordinator, Educational Operations
Three Park Avenue
New York, NY 10016-5990
Phone: (212) 591-8131; (800) THE ASME; Fax: (212) 591-7143;
Email: oluwanifiset@asme.org
Web: www.asme.org/education/enged/aid/scholar.htm

**Summary:** To provide financial assistance to undergraduate students, especially those from selected states, who are members of the American Society of Mechanical Engineers (ASME).

**Eligibility:** Open to student members in good standing who are enrolled in an ABET-accredited mechanical engineering baccalaureate program. They must be entering their junior or senior year when they apply. Preference is given to students who are interested in power engineering or who reside or attend school in Arkansas, Indiana, Kentucky, Louisiana, Michigan, Ohio, Oklahoma, Tennessee, Texas, Virginia, or West Virginia. Interested students should submit an application form, a nomination from the applicant's department head, a recommendation from a faculty member, and an official transcript. Only one nomination may be submitted per department. Selection is based on scholastic ability and potential contribution to the mechanical engineering profession.

**Financial data:** The stipend is $2,500.

**Duration:** 1 year.

**Number awarded:** 1 each year.

**Deadline:** March of each year.

---

**1843 AMERICAN HELICOPTER SOCIETY STUDENT DESIGN COMPETITION**

American Helicopter Society, Attn: Deputy Director
217 North Washington Street
Alexandria, VA 22314-2538
Phone: (703) 684-6777; Fax: (703) 739-9279; Email: Staff@vtol.org
Web: www.vtol.org/awards/sdcomp.html

**Summary:** To recognize and reward undergraduate and graduate students who submit outstanding designs for a helicopter.

**Eligibility:** Open to undergraduate and graduate students who may enter as individuals or as teams with no limit on the number of members. Undergraduates and graduate students compete in separate categories. Applicants must submit a completed design for a helicopter that meets annual competition specifications; recently, the program called for a mountain rescue helicopter. Selection is based on technical content (40 points), application and feasibility (25 points), originality (20 points), and organization and presentation (15 points).

**Financial data:** Awards in each category are $1,000 for first place and $500 for second. The best new entrant in each category receives $500.

**Duration:** The competition is held annually.

**Number awarded:** 5 awards are presented each year: 2 to undergraduates, 2 to graduate students, and 1 to a new entry.

**Deadline:** Letters of intent must be submitted by April of each year.

---

**1844 AMERICAN METEOROLOGICAL SOCIETY UNDERGRADUATE SCHOLARSHIPS**

American Meteorological Society, Attn: Fellowship/Scholarship Program
45 Beacon Street
Boston, MA 02108-3693
Phone: (617) 227-2426, ext. 246; Fax: (617) 742-8718;
Email: scholar@ametsoc.org
Web: www.ametsoc.org/amsstudentinfo/scholfeldocs/scholfel.html

**Summary:** To provide financial assistance to undergraduates majoring in meteorology or an aspect of atmospheric sciences.

**Eligibility:** Open to full-time students entering their final year of undergraduate study and majoring in meteorology or an aspect of the atmospheric or related oceanic and hydrologic sciences. Applicants must intend to make atmospheric or related sciences their career. They must be U.S. citizens or permanent residents enrolled at a U.S. institution and have a cumulative GPA of 3.25 or higher. Along with their application, they must submit 200-word essays on 1) their most important achievements that qualify them for this scholarship, and 2) their career goals in the atmospheric or related oceanic or hydrologic fields. Selection is based on academic excellence and achievement; financial need is not considered. The sponsor specifically encourages applications from women, minorities, and students with disabilities who are traditionally underrepresented in the atmospheric and related oceanic sciences.

**Financial data:** Stipends range from $700 to $5,000 per year.

**Duration:** 1 year.

**Number awarded:** 11 each year.

**Deadline:** February of each year.

---

**1845 AMERICAN PLASTICS COUNCIL (APC)/SPE PLASTICS ENVIRONMENTAL DIVISION SCHOLARSHIP**

Society of Plastics Engineers, Attn: SPE Foundation
14 Fairfield Drive
Brookfield, CT 06804-0403

Phone: (203) 740-5447; Fax: (203) 775-1157; Email: foundation@4spe.org
Web: www.4spe.org/foundation/scholarships.php

**Summary:** To provide financial assistance to undergraduate students who have a career interest in the plastics industry.

**Eligibility:** Open to full-time undergraduate students at 4-year colleges or in 2-year technical programs. Applicants must 1) have a demonstrated or expressed interest in the plastics industry; 2) be majoring in or taking courses that would be beneficial to a career in the plastics or polymer industry (e.g., plastics engineering, polymer sciences, chemistry, physics, chemical engineering, mechanical engineering, or industrial engineering); 3) be in good academic standing at their school; and 4) be able to document financial need. Along with their application, they must submit 3 letters of recommendation; a high school and/or college transcript; and a 1- to 2-page statement telling why they are interested in the scholarship, their qualifications, and their educational and career goals in the plastics industry.

**Financial data:** The stipend is $2,500 per year. Funds are paid directly to the recipient's school.

**Duration:** 1 year.

**Number awarded:** 1 each year.

**Deadline:** January of each year.

---

**1846 AMERICAN POLISH ENGINEERING SCHOLARSHIP**

American Polish Engineering Association c/o Dr. Barbara R. Koscierzynski
53657 Kristin Court
Shelby Township, Michigan 48316-2239
Web: www.apea.us

**Summary:** To provide financial assistance to high school seniors of Polish origin who plan to study engineering in college.

**Eligibility:** Open to high school seniors who are of Polish origin or descent. Applicants must have a GPA of 3.0 or higher and plans to attend a college or university with an accredited engineering-related program. They must be available for an interview with the sponsor's scholarship committee. Women and men applicants are judged separately.

**Financial data:** The stipend is $1,000.

**Duration:** 1 year.

**Number awarded:** 2 each year: 1 to a woman and 1 to a man.

**Deadline:** March of each year.

---

**1847 AMERICAN SOCIETY FOR ENOLOGY AND VITICULTURE SCHOLARSHIPS**

American Society for Enology and Viticulture
1784 Picasso Avenue, Suite D
P.O. Box 1855
Davis, CA 95617-1855
Phone: (530) 753-3142; Fax: (530) 753-3318; Email: society@asev.org
Web: www.asev.org/About/Scholarship.htm

**Summary:** To provide financial assistance to graduate and undergraduate students interested in working on a degree in enology, viticulture, or another area related to the wine and grape industry.

**Eligibility:** Open to both graduate and upper-division undergraduate students interested in working on a degree in enology, viticulture, or another field emphasizing a science basic to the wine and grade industry. Applicants must be enrolled or accepted full time at a 4-year accredited college or university. They must reside in North America (including Canada and Mexico), be in financial need, and have earned a GPA of 3.0 or higher for undergraduates or 3.2 for graduate students. Along with their application, students must supply a written statement of intent to prepare for a career in the wine or grape industry.

**Financial data:** The awards are not in predetermined amounts and may vary from year to year.

**Duration:** Students receive quarter or semester stipends. Recipients are eligible to reapply each year in open competition with new applicants.

**Number awarded:** Varies each year.

**Deadline:** February of each year.

---

**1848 AMERICAN SOCIETY OF NAVAL ENGINEERS SCHOLARSHIP PROGRAM**

American Society of Naval Engineers, Attn: Scholarship Committee
1452 Duke Street
Alexandria, VA 22314-3458
Phone: (703) 836-6727; Fax: (703) 836-7491;
Email: dpignotti@navalengineers.org
Web: www.navalengineers.org/Programs/Scholarships/sc_info.htm

**Summary:** To provide financial assistance to college and graduate students who are interested in the field of naval engineering.

**Eligibility:** Open to students entering the final year of a full-time or co-op undergraduate program or starting the first year of full-time graduate study leading to a designated engineering or physical science degree at an accredited college or university. Scholarships are not available to doctoral candidates or to persons who already have an advanced degree. Applicants must be U.S. citizens who have demonstrated an interest in a career in naval engineering; eligible programs of study include naval architecture; marine, mechanical, civil, aeronautical, ocean, electrical, and electronic engineering; and the physical sciences. Graduate student candidates must be members of the American Society of Naval Engineers (ASNE) or the Society of Naval Architects and Marine Engineers (SNAME). Selection is based on the candidate's academic record, work history, professional promise and interest in naval engineering, extracurricular activities, and recommendations. Financial need may also be considered.

**Financial data:** The stipends are $2,500 per year for undergraduates or $3,500 per year for graduate students. Funds may be used for the payment of tuition, fees, and school-related expenses.

**Duration:** 1 year.

**Number awarded:** Varies each year; recently, 12 undergraduate and 7 graduate students received scholarships.

**Deadline:** February of each year.

## 1849 AMOS AND MARILYN WINSAND–DETROIT SECTION NAMED SCHOLARSHIP

American Welding Society, Attn: AWS Foundation, Inc.
550 N.W. LeJeune Road
Miami, FL 33126
Phone: (305) 445-6628; (800) 443-9353, ext. 461; Fax: (305) 443-7559;
Email: found@aws.org
Web: www.aws.org/foundation/national_scholarships.html

**Summary:** To provide financial assistance to college students from Michigan majoring in welding engineering.

**Eligibility:** Open to undergraduate students working on a 2-year or 4-year degree in welding engineering, welding engineering technology, or a related field. Applicants must be residents of Michigan or attending a school in the state.

**Financial data:** A stipend is awarded (amount not specified). Funds must be used for tuition, books, and/or laboratory fees.

**Duration:** 1 year.

**Number awarded:** 1 each year.

**Deadline:** January of each year.

## 1850 AMSECT SCHOLARSHIP

American Society of Extra-Corporeal Technology, Inc.
Attn: AmSECT Foundation
2209 Dickens Road
P.O. Box 11086
Richmond, VA 23230-1086
Phone: (804) 565-6363; Fax: (804) 282-0090; Email: AmSECT@amsect.org
Web: www.amsect.org/scholarships/scholarships_grants.html

**Summary:** To provide financial assistance to student members of the American Society of Extra-Corporeal Technology (AmSECT) who are enrolled in a perfusion training program.

**Eligibility:** Open to student members of the society who are enrolled in (or accepted at) an accredited perfusion training program. Applicants must have completed at least one quarter of the required course work and have at least a 2.75 GPA. They must submit 250-word essays on how they would improve AmSECT and how they could improve the perfusion profession. Financial need is not considered in the selection process.

**Financial data:** The stipend is $1,000 per year.

**Duration:** 1 year.

**Number awarded:** 1 each year.

**Deadline:** November of each year.

## 1851 AMTROL INC. SCHOLARSHIP

American Ground Water Trust
16 Centre Street
P.O. Box 1796
Concord, NH 03302
Phone: (603) 228-5444; Fax: (603) 228-6557; Email: info@agwt.org
Web: www.agwt.org/amtrol.htm

**Summary:** To provide financial assistance to high school seniors who are interested in preparing for a career in a ground water-related field.

**Eligibility:** Open to high school seniors who have a GPA of 3.0 or higher and are entering a 4-year college or university as a full-time student. Applicants must be planning a career in a ground water-related field and must have completed a science/environmental project in high school that directly involved ground water resources or have had vacation/out-of-school work experience that is directly related to the environment and natural resources. They must submit a 500-word essay on "Ground Water—An Important Environmental and Economic Resource for America" and a 300-word description of their high school ground water project and/or practical environmental work experience. Selection is based on the above criteria, and on the applicant's references and academic record. Financial need is not considered. U.S. citizenship or permanent resident status is required.

**Financial data:** Stipends range from $1,000 to $2,000. Funds are paid directly to the recipient's college.

**Duration:** 1 year.

**Number awarded:** 2 each year.

**Deadline:** May of each year.

## 1852 ANITA BORG SCHOLARSHIPS

Google Inc., Attn: Scholarships
1600 Amphitheatre Parkway
Mountain View, CA 94043-8303
Phone: (650) 623-4000; Fax: (650) 618-1499;
Email: anitaborgscholars@google.com
Web: www.google.com/anitaborg

**Summary:** To provide financial assistance to women working on a bachelor's or graduate degree in a computer-related field.

**Eligibility:** Open to women who are entering their senior year of undergraduate study or are enrolled in a graduate program in computer science, computer engineering, or a related field. Applicants must be full-time students at a university in the United States with a GPA of 3.5 or higher. They must submit essays of 400 to 600 words on 1) a significant technical project on which they have worked; 2) examples of their leadership abilities; 3) what they would do if someone gave them the funding and resources for a 3- to 12-month project to investigate a technical topic of their choice; and 4) what they would do if someone gave them $1,000 to plan an event or project to benefit women in technical fields. Selection is based on academic background and demonstrated leadership.

**Financial data:** The stipend is $10,000.

**Duration:** 1 year.

**Number awarded:** Varies each year. Recently, 4 of these scholarships were awarded: 1 to an undergraduate, 2 to master's degree candidates, and 1 to a doctoral candidate.

**Deadline:** January of each year.

## 1853 ANN ARBOR AWC SCHOLARSHIP FOR WOMEN IN COMPUTING

Association for Women in Computing-Ann Arbor Chapter
Attn: Scholarship
P.O. Box 1864
Ann Arbor, MI 48106-1864
Email: awc@hvcn.org
Web: www.awc-aa.org/gala/scholarship.php

**Summary:** To provide financial assistance to women undergraduates working on a degree in a computer- or technology-related field at institutions in Michigan.

**Eligibility:** Open to undergraduate women enrolled at institutions of higher education in Michigan. Applicants must be U.S. citizens or permanent residents preparing for a career in a field related to computers or technology. They must have at least 2 semesters of course work remaining. As part of the application, they must answer the following 3 questions: 1) "Why are you excited about working with computers and information technology?" 2) "Describe your most fulfilling computer-related project or experience;" and 3) "Identify a current trend in technology and describe how it might evolve over the next ten years." Based on those essays, awards are presented to applicants who demonstrate motivation, passion, thoughtfulness, creativity, skillful communication, and participation in the computing community. Financial need is not considered.

**Financial data:** A stipend is awarded (amount not specified).

**Duration:** 1 year.

**Number awarded:** 1 or more each year.

**Deadline:** March of each year.

## 1854 ANNE MAUREEN WHITNEY BARROW MEMORIAL SCHOLARSHIP

Society of Women Engineers
230 East Ohio Street, Suite 400

Chicago, IL 60611-3265

Phone: (312) 596-5223; Fax: (312) 644-8557; Email: hq@swe.org

Web: www.societyofwomenengineers.org/scholarships

**Summary:** To provide financial assistance to women interested in studying engineering or computer science in college.

**Eligibility:** Open to women who are enrolled or planning to enroll full time at an ABET-accredited 4-year college or university. Applicants must have a GPA of 3.0 or higher and be planning to major in computer science or engineering. Along with their application, they must submit a 1-page essay on why they want to be an engineer or computer scientist, how they believe they will make a difference as an engineer or computer scientist, and what influenced them to study engineering or computer science. Selection is based on merit.

**Financial data:** The stipend is $5,000.

**Duration:** 1 year; may be renewed for 3 additional years.

**Number awarded:** 1 every 4 years.

**Deadline:** May of the years in which it is offered.

---

**1855 ANNE SEAMAN MEMORIAL SCHOLARSHIP**

**Summary:** To provide financial assistance for college to students in fields related to grounds management.

*See Listing #1271.*

---

**1856 ANS INCOMING FRESHMAN SCHOLARSHIPS**

American Nuclear Society, Attn: Scholarship Coordinator

555 North Kensington Avenue

La Grange Park, IL 60526-5592

Phone: (708) 352-6611; Fax: (708) 352-0499; Email: outreach@ans.org

Web: www.ans.org/honors/scholarships

**Summary:** To provide financial assistance to students entering their freshman year of college and planning to prepare for a career in nuclear science or nuclear engineering.

**Eligibility:** Open to graduating high school seniors who have enrolled as a full-time college student. Applicants must be taking science, mathematics, or technical courses with an interest in working in nuclear science and technology. They must be U.S. citizens or permanent residents. Selection is based on high school academic achievement, freshmen college courses enrolled in, an essay, and letters of recommendation.

**Financial data:** The stipend is $2,000.

**Duration:** 1 year; nonrenewable.

**Number awarded:** 5 each year.

**Deadline:** March of each year.

---

**1857 ANS UNDERGRADUATE SCHOLARSHIPS**

American Nuclear Society, Attn: Scholarship Coordinator

555 North Kensington Avenue

La Grange Park, IL 60526-5592

Phone: (708) 352-6611; Fax: (708) 352-0499; Email: outreach@ans.org

Web: www.ans.org/honors/scholarships

**Summary:** To provide financial assistance to undergraduate students who are interested in preparing for a career in nuclear science or nuclear engineering.

**Eligibility:** Open to undergraduate students enrolled in nuclear science, nuclear engineering, or a nuclear-related field at an accredited institution in the United States. There are separate competitions for 1) students who have completed at least one academic year and who will be sophomores, and 2) students who have completed 2 or more years and will be entering as juniors or seniors. All applicants must be U.S. citizens or permanent residents and be able to demonstrate academic achievement.

**Financial data:** The stipend is $2,000.

**Duration:** 1 year; nonrenewable.

**Number awarded:** 31 each year: 4 for students entering their sophomore year and 27 (including the 6 named scholarships plus 21 others) for students entering their junior or senior year.

**Deadline:** January of each year.

---

**1858 AOPA AIR SAFETY FOUNDATION/DONALD BURNSIDE MEMORIAL SCHOLARSHIPS**

Aircraft Owners and Pilots Association, Attn: AOPA Air Safety Foundation

421 Aviation Way

Frederick, MD 21701-4798

Phone: (301) 695-2000; (800) 638-3101; Fax: (301) 695-2375;

Email: asf@aopa.org

Web: www.aopa.org/asf/scholarship/burnside.html

**Summary:** To provide funding to upper-division students who need financial assistance to continue their studies in the field of aviation.

**Eligibility:** Open to U.S. citizens who are interested in working on a degree in the field of non-engineering aviation, are juniors or seniors in college, have earned at least a 3.25 GPA, and are able to demonstrate financial need. They must submit a 250-word essay on a topic that changes annually; recently, the topic was "Why do so many pilots continue VFR into IMC, and what can be done to convince them not to do so?" Previous recipients are not eligible to reapply.

**Financial data:** The stipend is $1,000.

**Duration:** 1 year; recipients may not reapply.

**Number awarded:** 1 each year.

**Deadline:** March of each year.

---

**1859 AOPA AIR SAFETY FOUNDATION/KOCH CORPORATION SCHOLARSHIP**

Aircraft Owners and Pilots Association, Attn: AOPA Air Safety Foundation

421 Aviation Way

Frederick, MD 21701-4798

Phone: (301) 695-2000; (800) 638-3101; Fax: (301) 695-2375;

Email: asf@aopa.org

Web: www.aopa.org/asf/scholarship/koch.html

**Summary:** To provide funding to undergraduate students interested in continuing their studies in the field of aviation.

**Eligibility:** Open to U.S. citizens who are working on a degree focusing on aviation. Applicants must have a GPA of 3.25 or higher. Selection is based on GPA and a 500-word essay on a topic that changes annually; recently, the topic was "How should pilot training be adapted to new technology aircraft?"

**Financial data:** The stipend is $1,500.

**Duration:** 1 year.

**Number awarded:** 1 each year.

**Deadline:** July of each year.

---

**1860 AOPA AIR SAFETY FOUNDATION/MCALLISTER MEMORIAL SCHOLARSHIPS**

Aircraft Owners and Pilots Association, Attn: AOPA Air Safety Foundation

421 Aviation Way

Frederick, MD 21701-4798

Phone: (301) 695-2000; (800) 638-3101; Fax: (301) 695-2375;

Email: asf@aopa.org

Web: www.aopa.org/asf/scholarship/mcallister.html

**Summary:** To provide funding to students who need financial assistance to continue their studies in the field of aviation.

**Eligibility:** Open to U.S. citizens who are interested in working on a degree in the field of non-engineering aviation, are juniors or seniors in college, have earned at least a 3.25 GPA, and are able to demonstrate financial need. They must submit a 250-word essay on a topic that changes annually; recently, the topic was "What is one safety issue not adequately taught to primary students, and how can that be changed?" Previous recipients are not eligible to reapply.

**Financial data:** The stipend is $1,000.

**Duration:** 1 year; recipients may not reapply.

**Number awarded:** 1 each year.

**Deadline:** March of each year.

---

**1861 AORN FOUNDATION BACCALAUREATE DEGREE IN NURSING SCHOLARSHIP**

Association of periOperative Registered Nurses, Attn: AORN Foundation

2170 South Parker Road, Suite 300

Denver, CO 80231-5711

Phone: (303) 755-6300, ext. 366; (800) 755-2676, ext. 366; Fax: (303) 755-4219;

Email: nharbin@aorn.org

Web: www.aorn.org/foundation/scholarship.htm

**Summary:** To provide financial assistance to members of the Association of periOperative Registered Nurses (AORN) who wish to work on a baccalaureate degree.

**Eligibility:** Open to registered nurses who are committed to perioperative nursing, have been members of the association for at least one year, and are currently enrolled in a baccalaureate degree program with a GPA of 3.0 or higher. Along with their application, they must submit a personal statement describing their role as a perioperative nurse; current and past contributions to AORN on a local, state, and national level; how they will apply their degree to perioperative nursing; their financial need; their professional goals; their commitment to

AORN and the AORN Foundation; and volunteer community activities related to perioperative nursing.

**Financial data:** A stipend is awarded (amount not specified). Funds are paid directly to the recipient.

**Duration:** 1 year; may be renewed if the recipient maintains a GPA of 3.0 or higher.

**Number awarded:** 1 or more each year.

**Deadline:** April of each year.

## 1862 APS SCHOLARSHIPS FOR MINORITY UNDERGRADUATE STUDENTS WHO MAJOR IN PHYSICS

American Physical Society, Attn: Committee on Minorities
One Physics Ellipse
College Park, MD 20740-3844
Phone: (301) 209-3232; Fax: (301) 209-0865
Web: www.aps.org/educ/com/scholars/index.cfm

**Summary:** To provide financial assistance to underrepresented minority students interested in studying physics on the undergraduate level.

**Eligibility:** Open to any African American, Hispanic American, or Native American who plans to major in physics and who is a high school senior or college freshman or sophomore. U.S. citizenship or permanent resident status is required. The selection committee especially encourages applications from students who are attending or planning to attend institutions with historically or predominantly Black, Hispanic, or Native American enrollment. Selection is based on commitment to the study of physics and plans to work on a physics baccalaureate degree.

**Financial data:** Stipends are $2,000 per year in the first year or $3,000 in the second year; funds must be used for tuition and room and board. In addition, $500 is awarded to the host department.

**Duration:** 1 year; renewable for 1 additional year with the approval of the APS selection committee.

**Number awarded:** Usually, 20 to 25 of these scholarships are awarded each year.

**Deadline:** January of each year.

## 1863 APWA HORIZONS FRONT RANGE SCHOLARSHIP

**Summary:** To provide financial assistance to high school seniors in Colorado who plan to attend a college or university in the state to prepare for a career in public works.

*See Listing #1273.*

## 1864 AQHF EDUCATION OR NURSING SCHOLARSHIP

American Quarter Horse Foundation, Attn: Scholarship Coordinator
2601 I-40 East
Amarillo, TX 79104
Phone: (806) 376-5181; (888) 209-8322; Fax: (806) 376-1005;
Email: lowens@aqha.org
Web: www.aqha.com/foundation/scholarships/index.html

**Summary:** To provide financial assistance for college to members of the American Quarter Horse Association (AQHA) or the American Quarter Horse Youth Association (AQHYA) who are planning a career in education or nursing.

**Eligibility:** Open to applicants who have been members of either organization for at least one year and are graduating high school seniors or already enrolled in college. They must have a GPA of 2.5 or higher and be planning to work on a degree in education or nursing. Financial need is considered in the selection process.

**Financial data:** The maximum stipend is $2,500 per year.

**Duration:** Up to 4 years, provided the recipient maintains a GPA of 2.5 or higher and full-time enrollment.

**Number awarded:** 1 each year.

**Deadline:** January of each year.

## 1865 AQHF ENGINEERING SCHOLARSHIP

American Quarter Horse Foundation, Attn: Scholarship Coordinator
2601 I-40 East
Amarillo, TX 79104
Phone: (806) 376-5181; (888) 209-8322; Fax: (806) 376-1005;
Email: lowens@aqha.org
Web: www.aqha.com/foundation/scholarships/index.html

**Summary:** To provide financial assistance for college to members of the American Quarter Horse Association (AQHA) or the American Quarter Horse Youth Association (AQHYA) who are planning a career in engineering.

**Eligibility:** Open to applicants who have been members of either organization for at least one year and are graduating high school seniors or already enrolled in college. They must have a GPA of 2.5 or higher and be planning to work on a degree in mechanical engineering or a related engineering field. Financial need is considered in the selection process.

**Financial data:** The maximum stipend is $4,000 per year.

**Duration:** Up to 5 years, provided the recipient maintains a GPA of 2.5 or higher and full-time enrollment.

**Number awarded:** 1 each year.

**Deadline:** January of each year.

## 1866 AQHF RACING SCHOLARSHIPS

American Quarter Horse Foundation, Attn: Scholarship Coordinator
2601 I-40 East
Amarillo, TX 79104
Phone: (806) 376-5181; (888) 209-8322; Fax: (806) 376-1005;
Email: lowens@aqha.org
Web: www.aqha.com/foundation/scholarships/index.html

**Summary:** To provide financial assistance for college or graduate school to members of the American Quarter Horse Association (AQHA) or the American Quarter Horse Youth Association (AQHYA) who are planning a career in the horse racing industry.

**Eligibility:** Open to members of either organization who are graduating high school seniors, already enrolled in college, or working on a graduate degree. Applicants must have a GPA of 2.5 or higher and be planning to prepare for a career in the racing industry or a related field. Along with their application, they must submit an essay on "How my experiences through equine-related activities have influenced my life." Financial need is considered in the selection process.

**Financial data:** The maximum stipend is $2,000 per year.

**Duration:** Up to 4 years, provided the recipient maintains a GPA of 2.5 or higher and full-time enrollment.

**Number awarded:** Varies each year; recently, 5 of these scholarships were awarded.

**Deadline:** January of each year.

## 1867 AREMA EDUCATIONAL FOUNDATION UNDERGRADUATE SCHOLARSHIPS

American Railway Engineering and Maintenance of Way Association
Attn: AREMA Educational Foundation Scholarship Committee
8201 Corporate Drive, Suite 1125
Landover, MD 20785
Phone: (301) 459-3200, ext. 705; Fax: (301) 459-8077; Email: sboyle@arema.org
Web: www.arema.org/foundation/foundation.htm

**Summary:** To provide financial assistance to undergraduate students who are interested in preparing for a career in railway engineering.

**Eligibility:** Open to undergraduate students at ABET-accredited 4-year or 5-year programs (or comparably accredited programs in Canada or Mexico) leading to a bachelor's degree in engineering or engineering technology. Applicants must be at least sophomores and have a GPA of 2.0 or higher. They must be interested in a career in railway engineering. Along with their application, they must submit a resume, official transcript, 2 letters of recommendation, and a 350-word cover letter explaining why they believe they are deserving of this scholarship. Financial need is not considered in the selection process.

**Financial data:** Stipends up to $1,000 are available.

**Duration:** 1 year.

**Number awarded:** Varies each year. Recently, 6 of these scholarships were awarded: 3 at $1,000 and 3 at $300.

**Deadline:** March of each year.

## 1868 ARIZONA NURSERY ASSOCIATION FOUNDATION SCHOLARSHIPS

Arizona Nursery Association
Attn: ANA Foundation Endowment for Research and Scholarship
1430 West Broadway, Suite A-180
Tempe, AZ 85282
Phone: (480) 966-1610; Fax: (480) 966-0923; Email: info@azna.org
Web: www.azna.org/scholarships/index.html

**Summary:** To provide financial assistance to students from Arizona who are enrolled or planning to enroll in a horticulture-related curriculum in college.

**Eligibility:** Open to Arizona residents who are currently enrolled, or planning to enroll, in a horticulture-related curriculum at a university, community college, or continuing education program. Applicants must be currently employed in or have an interest in the nursery industry as a career. They must have an above average GPA or at least 2 years of work experience in the nursery industry. Involvement in extracurricular activities related to the nursery industry must also be demonstrated. Financial need is not considered in the selection process.

**Financial data:** Stipends range from $500 to $3,000.

**Duration:** 1 year.

**Number awarded:** Varies each year.

**Deadline:** April of each year.

---

### 1869 ARIZONA NURSES FOUNDATION ACADEMIC SCHOLARSHIP PROGRAM

Arizona Nurses Association, Attn: Arizona Nurses Foundation
1850 East Southern Avenue, Suite 1
Tempe, AZ 85282-5832
Phone: (480) 831-0404; Fax: (480) 839-4780; Email: info@aznurse.org
Web: www.aznurse.org

**Summary:** To provide financial assistance to undergraduate and graduate students enrolled in or accepted to nursing programs in Arizona.

**Eligibility:** Open to undergraduate and graduate students enrolled in, or accepted for enrollment in, an academic nursing education program in Arizona. Selection is based on potential for leadership in nursing, commitment to professional nursing, and financial need.

**Financial data:** Stipends are $1,000 or $500.

**Duration:** 1 year.

**Number awarded:** 3 each year: 1 at $1,000 and 2 at $500.

**Deadline:** May of each year.

---

### 1870 ARIZONA PRIVATE SCHOOL ASSOCIATION SCHOLARSHIP

Arizona Private School Association
202 East McDowell Road, Suite 273
Phoenix, AZ 85004-4536
Phone: (602) 254-5199; Fax: (602) 254-5073; Email: apsa@eschelon.com
Web: www.arizonapsa.org/scholarships.html

**Summary:** To provide financial assistance to high school seniors in Arizona who are interested in attending a career college to prepare for jobs in selected fields.

**Eligibility:** Open to high school seniors in Arizona who are interested in attending a career college in the state, to prepare for a career in such fields as computer or information technology, health care, cosmetology, massage, business, criminal justice, or health occupations. The sponsor provides 2 scholarships to each high school in the state. Recipients are then selected by the scholarship directors or counselors at their high school.

**Financial data:** The stipend is a $1,000 award certificate to be used to pay for tuition at a career college in Arizona.

**Duration:** 1 year.

**Number awarded:** 2 each year at each high school in Arizona.

---

### 1871 ARKANSAS APWA SCHOLARSHIPS

American Public Works Association-Arkansas Chapter
c/o Walt Catlett, Scholarship Committee Chair
Hanson Pipe and Products
1300 Bond Avenue
Little Rock, AR 72202
Phone: (501) 376-3581; Email: walt.catlett@hansonamerica.com
Web: arkansas.apwa.net

**Summary:** To provide financial assistance to high school seniors in Arkansas who are interested in attending college to prepare for a career related to the public works profession.

**Eligibility:** Open to seniors graduating from high schools in Arkansas. Applicants must be planning to attend college to work on a degree related to the public works profession. Selection is based on academic record and participation in extracurricular activities.

**Financial data:** The stipend is $1,000.

**Duration:** 1 year.

**Number awarded:** 2 each year.

---

### 1872 ARKANSAS POST SCHOLARSHIPS

**Summary:** To provide financial assistance to Arkansas high school seniors interested in studying architecture or engineering in college.
*See Listing #1276.*

---

### 1873 ARN SCHOLARSHIP PROGRAM

Association of Rehabilitation Nurses, Attn: Scholarship Program
4700 West Lake Avenue
Glenview, IL 60025-1485
Phone: (847) 375-4710; (800) 229-7530; Fax: (888) 458-0456;
Email: info@rehabnurse.org
Web: www.rehabnurse.org/awards/index.htm

**Summary:** To provide financial assistance to members of the Association of Rehabilitation Nurses (ARN) who are working on a bachelor's degree in nursing.

**Eligibility:** Open to ARN members who are currently practicing rehabilitation nursing and have at least 2 years of experience in the field. Applicants must be enrolled in a B.S.N. degree program and have successfully completed at least one course. Along with their application, they must submit a 1- to 3-page summary of their professional and educational goals that includes 1) involvement in ARN at the national and local levels; 2) continuing education participation in the past 3 to 5 years; 3) professional publications or presentations; 4) community involvement, particularly relating to advocating for individuals with disabilities; and 5) efforts they have made to improve their rehabilitation nursing practice and the delivery of care in their work setting. Financial need is not considered in the selection process.

**Financial data:** The stipend is $1,000.

**Duration:** 1 year.

**Number awarded:** 2 each year.

**Deadline:** May of each year.

---

### 1874 ARNOLD SADLER MEMORIAL SCHOLARSHIP

American Council of the Blind, Attn: Coordinator, Scholarship Program
1155 15th Street, N.W., Suite 1004
Washington, DC 20005
Phone: (202) 467-5081; (800) 424-8666; Fax: (202) 467-5085;
Email: info@acb.org
Web: www.acb.org

**Summary:** To provide financial assistance to undergraduate or graduate students who are blind and are interested in studying in a field of service to persons with disabilities.

**Eligibility:** Open to students in rehabilitation, education, law, or other fields of service to persons with disabilities. Applicants must be legally blind and U.S. citizens. In addition to letters of recommendation and copies of academic transcripts, applications must include an autobiographical sketch. A cumulative GPA of 3.3 or higher is generally required. Selection is based on demonstrated academic record, involvement in extracurricular and civic activities, and academic objectives. The severity of the applicant's visual impairment and his/her study methods are also taken into account.

**Financial data:** The stipend is $2,000. In addition, the winner receives a Kurzweil-1000 Reading System.

**Duration:** 1 year.

**Number awarded:** 1 each year.

**Deadline:** February of each year.

---

### 1875 ARSHAM AMIRIKIAN ENGINEERING SCHOLARSHIP

American Welding Society, Attn: AWS Foundation, Inc.
550 N.W. LeJeune Road
Miami, FL 33126
Phone: (305) 445-6628; (800) 443-9353, ext. 461; Fax: (305) 443-7559;
Email: found@aws.org
Web: www.aws.org/foundation/scholarships/arsham.html

**Summary:** To provide financial assistance to college students working on a degree in civil engineering as it relates to welding.

**Eligibility:** Open to full-time undergraduate students who are working on a 4-year bachelor's degree in structural and civil engineering as related to welding at an accredited university. Applicants must have an overall GPA of 3.0 or higher and be able to demonstrate financial need. U.S. citizenship is required.

**Financial data:** The stipend is $2,500 per year.

**Duration:** 4 years, provided the recipient maintains a GPA of 3.0 or higher.

**Number awarded:** 1 each year.

**Deadline:** January of each year.

### 1876 ARTHUR AND GLADYS CERVENKA SCHOLARSHIP

Society of Manufacturing Engineers, Attn: SME Education Foundation
One SME Drive
P.O. Box 930
Dearborn, MI 48121-0930
Phone: (313) 425-3304; (800) 733-4763, ext. 3304; Fax: (313) 425-3411;
Email: foundation@sme.org
Web: www.sme.org
**Summary:** To provide financial assistance to students enrolled in a degree program in manufacturing engineering or manufacturing engineering technology in Florida.
**Eligibility:** Open to full-time undergraduate students enrolled in a manufacturing engineering or manufacturing engineering technology program. Applicants must have completed at least 30 units with a GPA of 3.0 or higher. Preference is given (but not limited) to students attending colleges or universities in Florida. Need is not considered in awarding scholarships (unless 2 or more applicants have equal qualifications).
**Financial data:** The stipend is $1,250.
**Duration:** 1 year; may be renewed.
**Number awarded:** 1 each year.
**Deadline:** January of each year.

### 1877 ARTHUR L. WILLISTON AWARD

ASME International, Attn: General Awards Committee
Three Park Avenue
New York, NY 10016-5990
Phone: (212) 591-7736; (800) THE-ASME; Fax: (212) 591-7674;
Email: infocentral@asme.org
Web: www.asme.org/students/Competitions/willistonaward.html
**Summary:** To recognize and reward student and junior members of ASME International (the professional society of mechanical engineers) who have written outstanding papers.
**Eligibility:** Open to undergraduate student members and associate members who received a bachelor's degree not more than 2 years earlier. Applicants must submit a paper on a subject that changes annually but that challenges the engineering abilities of participants; a recent topic was "Engineering and Public Disaster." Selection is based on originality (35 points), development (35 points), and presentation (30 points).
**Financial data:** First place consists of $1,000 and a bronze medal; second place is $500, and third place is $250.
**Duration:** The awards are presented annually.
**Number awarded:** 3 each year.
**Deadline:** February of each year.

### 1878 ARTHUR T. SCHRAMM MEMORIAL SCHOLARSHIP

Institute of Food Technologists, Attn: Scholarship Department
525 West Van Buren, Suite 1000
Chicago, IL 60607
Phone: (312) 782-8424; Fax: (312) 782-8348; Email: info@ift.org
Web: www.ift.org
**Summary:** To provide financial assistance to undergraduates interested in studying food science or food technology.
**Eligibility:** Open to sophomores, juniors, and seniors in a food science or food technology program at an educational institution in the United States or Canada. Applicants must have an outstanding scholastic record and a well-rounded personality. Along with their application, they must submit an essay on their career aspirations; a list of awards, honors, and scholarships they have received; a list of extracurricular activities and/or hobbies; and a summary of their work experience. Financial need is not considered in the selection process.
**Financial data:** The stipend is $2,250.
**Duration:** 1 year; recipients may reapply if they are members of the Institute of Food Technologists (IFT).
**Number awarded:** 1 each year.
**Deadline:** January of each year.

### 1879 ARTHUR W. PENSE SCHOLARSHIP

NYSARC, Inc.
393 Delaware Avenue
Delmar, NY 12054
Phone: (518) 439-8311; Fax: (518) 439-1893; Email: nysarc@nysarc.org
Web: www.nysarc.org/scholar.htm
**Summary:** To provide financial assistance to currently-enrolled college students in New York majoring in occupational or physical therapy.
**Eligibility:** Open to students working on a 4- or 5-year degree program leading to a career in physical or occupational therapy in New York. They must be at least at the sophomore level. Only nominations may be submitted.
**Financial data:** The stipend is $1,500 per year.
**Duration:** 2 years.
**Number awarded:** 1 each year.
**Deadline:** January of each year.

### 1880 ASABE FOUNDATION SCHOLARSHIP

American Society of Agricultural and Biological Engineers
Attn: ASABE Foundation
2950 Niles Road
St. Joseph, MI 49085-9659
Phone: (269) 429-0300; Fax: (269) 429-3852; Email: hq@asabe.org
Web: www.asabe.org/membership/students/foundation.html
**Summary:** To provide financial assistance to undergraduate student members of the American Society of Agricultural Engineers (ASAE).
**Eligibility:** Open to undergraduate students who have a declared major in biological or agricultural engineering (must be accredited by ABET or CEAB), are student members of the society, are in at least the second year of college, have at least one year of undergraduate student remaining, have a GPA of 2.5 or higher, can demonstrate financial need, and can verify that graduation from their degree program assures eligibility for the Professional Engineer (PE) licensing examination. Interested applicants should submit a personal letter (up to 2 pages long) stating how the money will be used and presenting proof that their degree program assures eligibility for the PE licensing examination.
**Financial data:** The stipend is $1,000. Funds must be used for tuition, fees, books, and on-campus room and board.
**Duration:** 1 year.
**Number awarded:** 1 each year.
**Deadline:** March of each year.

### 1881 ASABE STUDENT ENGINEER OF THE YEAR SCHOLARSHIP

American Society of Agricultural and Biological Engineers
Attn: ASABE Foundation
2950 Niles Road
St. Joseph, MI 49085-9659
Phone: (269) 429-0300; Fax: (269) 429-3852; Email: hq@asabe.org
Web: www.asabe.org/membership/students/engscholar.html
**Summary:** To recognize and reward student members of the American Society of Agricultural Engineers (ASAE) who participate in a competition to select the best student of the year.
**Eligibility:** Open to biological and agricultural engineering students at colleges and universities in Canada and the United States. Applicants must have completed at least one year of undergraduate study with a GPA of 3.0 or higher, have at least one year remaining, and be members of the society. Selection is based on: scholarship, with special consideration given to students who demonstrate improvement in academic work from freshman to sophomore to junior years (20 points); character and personal development, including participation in non-university activities and service to others (10 points); student membership in the society and active participation in a student branch organization (25 points); participation in other school activities (15 points); leadership qualities, creativity, initiative, and responsibility (25 points); and level of financial self-support provided by the student (5 points). In addition, the judges consider the candidate's paper, up to 500 words, on "My Goals in the Engineering Profession."
**Financial data:** The award is a $1,000 scholarship.
**Duration:** The competition is held annually.
**Number awarded:** 1 each year.
**Deadline:** March of each year.

### 1882 ASCE MAINE SECTION SCHOLARSHIP

American Society of Civil Engineers-Maine Section
c/o Leslie L. Corrow, Scholarship Chair
Kleinschmidt Associates
75 Main Street
P.O. Box 576
Pittsfield, ME 04967
Phone: (207) 487-3328
**Summary:** To provide financial assistance to high school seniors in Maine who are interested in studying civil engineering in college.

**Eligibility:** Open to graduating high school seniors who are Maine residents and who intend to study civil engineering in college. Women and minorities are especially encouraged to apply. Applicants must submit a 200-word statement describing why they have chosen civil engineering as a career and what they hope to accomplish by being a civil engineer. Selection is based on the statement, academic performance, extracurricular activities, and letters of recommendation.

**Financial data:** The stipend is $2,000.

**Duration:** 1 year; nonrenewable.

**Number awarded:** 1 each year.

**Deadline:** January of each year.

## 1883 ASCENT SCHOLARSHIPS

Space Foundation
310 South 14th Street
Colorado Springs, CO 80904
Phone: (719) 576-8000; (800) 691-4000; Fax: (719) 576-8801
Web: www.spacefoundation.org

**Summary:** To provide financial assistance to upper-division students interested in preparing for a high technology career in the aerospace industry.

**Eligibility:** Open to students who have completed at least 2 years of college with a major in mathematics, science, engineering, or computer sciences and a GPA of 3.0 or higher. Selection is based on stated interest and perspective about a career in the aerospace industry.

**Financial data:** Awards include a $5,000 stipend, sponsored attendance at space-related conferences, an internship with an industry sponsor, and the opportunity to visit a space-related site or event of the recipient's choice.

**Duration:** 1 year.

**Number awarded:** 4 each year.

## 1884 ASCLS EDUCATION AND RESEARCH FUND UNDERGRADUATE SCHOLARSHIPS

Alpha Mu Tau Fraternity
c/o American Society for Clinical Laboratory Science
6701 Democracy Boulevard, Suite 300
Bethesda, MD 20817
Phone: (301) 657-2768; Fax: (301) 657-2909; Email: ascls@ascls.org
Web: www.ascls.org/leadership/awards/e_and_r.asp

**Summary:** To provide financial assistance for undergraduate studies to members of Alpha Mu Tau, a national laboratory fraternity.

**Eligibility:** Open to applicants who are U.S. citizens or permanent residents, members of Alpha Mu Tau, and accepted into or currently enrolled in a program in clinical laboratory science, including clinical laboratory science/medical technology and clinical laboratory technician/medical laboratory technician for undergraduates. Applicants must be entering their last year of study.

**Financial data:** The stipend is $1,500.

**Duration:** 1 year.

**Number awarded:** 1 or more each year.

**Deadline:** March of each year.

## 1885 ASCP STUDENT SCHOLARSHIPS

American Society for Clinical Pathology, Attn: Associate Member Section
2100 West Harrison Street
Chicago, IL 60612-3798
Phone: (312) 738-1336; (800) 621-4142; Fax: (312) 738-1619;
Email: info@ascp.org
Web: www.ascp.org

**Summary:** To provide funding to students enrolled in programs related to clinical laboratory science.

**Eligibility:** Open to students enrolled in a NAACLS or CAAHEP accredited college/university program as a cytotechnologist (CT), histologic technician (HT), histotechnologist (HTL), medical laboratory technician (MLT), or medical technologist (MT). Applicants must be in the final clinical year of education and either U.S. citizens or permanent residents. HT applicants have no minimum GPA requirement, but other applicants must have a GPA of 3.0 or higher. Selection is based on academic achievement, leadership abilities, professional goals, and community activities.

**Financial data:** The stipend is $1,000.

**Duration:** 1 year.

**Number awarded:** Varies each year. Recently, 40 of these scholarships were awarded: 3 for CT students, 3 for HTL students, 10 for MLT students, and 24 for MT students.

**Deadline:** November of each year.

## 1886 ASEI UNDERGRADUATE SCHOLARSHIPS

**Summary:** To provide financial assistance to undergraduate students of Indian origin (from India) who are majoring in architecture, engineering, or related areas.

*See Listing #1278.*

## 1887 ASHP FOUNDATION STUDENT RESEARCH AWARD

American Society of Health-System Pharmacists
Attn: Research and Education Foundation
7272 Wisconsin Avenue
Bethesda, MD 20814-1439
Phone: (301) 657-3000, ext. 1447; Fax: (301) 664-8872;
Email: foundation@ashp.org
Web: www.ashpfoundation.org/Awards/litAwards.cfm

**Summary:** To recognize and reward outstanding papers or reports on pharmacy practice written by pharmacy students.

**Eligibility:** Open to student authors of unpublished papers or reports on a completed research project, prepared during the past year, that relates to pharmacy practice in hospitals or health systems. When a nomination is submitted (students may nominate themselves), it should be accompanied by a letter from a faculty member certifying that the nominated paper is the student's own work. At the time the nominated paper or report was written, the student author should have been a full-time student in an entry-level (B.S. or Pharm.D.) program at an accredited college of pharmacy. The nominated paper should be in publishable format. Selection is based on originality (20 points), significance (15 points), research methodology (25 points), data analysis (25 points), and validity of conclusions (15 points).

**Financial data:** The award consists of a plaque, a $1,500 honorarium, and a $1,000 travel allowance (to cover the costs of attending the society's mid-year meeting, where the award is presented).

**Duration:** The award is presented annually.

**Number awarded:** 1 each year.

**Deadline:** May of each year.

## 1888 ASHP STUDENT LEADERSHIP AWARDS

American Society of Health-System Pharmacists
Attn: Pharmacy Student Forum
7272 Wisconsin Avenue
Bethesda, MD 20814-1439
Phone: (301) 664-8862; Fax: (301) 657-8278; Email: students@ashp.org
Web: www.ashp.org

**Summary:** To recognize and reward outstanding pharmacy students who are members of the American Society of Health-System Pharmacists (ASHP).

**Eligibility:** Open to ASHP members who have completed at least the first year of full-time study in a professional baccalaureate or doctor of pharmacy program at an accredited college of pharmacy with a GPA of 2.5 or higher. Applicants must submit a resume or curriculum vitae, 3 letters of recommendation, and a 750-word essay on their perceptions of the qualities of a good leader, important outcomes resulting from their leadership, and how being named a recipient will help them to achieve their career goals. Selection is based on health-system pharmacy practice achievement, professional organization leadership, and personal leadership attributes.

**Financial data:** The award includes $2,500 in cash, a plaque, and a drug information reference library from AHSP.

**Duration:** The awards are presented annually.

**Number awarded:** 12 each year: 4 for students in each professional year of pharmacy school.

**Deadline:** November of each year.

## 1889 ASHS SCHOLARS AWARD

American Society for Horticultural Science
113 South West Street, Suite 200
Alexandria, VA 22314-2851
Phone: (703) 836-4606; Fax: (703) 836-2024; Email: ashs@ashs.org
Web: www.ashs.org/awards/student.html

**Summary:** To provide financial assistance to undergraduate students majoring in horticulture.

**Eligibility:** Open to full-time undergraduate students of any class standing who are actively working on a degree in horticulture at a 4-year college or university. Applicants must be nominated by the chair of the department in which they are majoring; each department may nominate only 1 student. They must submit transcripts, 3 letters of reference, a complete resume and/or vitae, and an essay of 250 to 500 words on their reasons for interest in horticulture and for selecting their intended field of work after graduation. Selection is based on academic excellence in the major and supporting areas of science; participation in extracurricular, leadership, and research activities relating to horticulture; participation in university and community service; demonstrated commitment to the horticultural science profession and related career fields; and related horticultural experiences. Financial need is not considered.

**Financial data:** The stipend is $1,500.

**Duration:** 1 year.

**Number awarded:** 2 each year.

**Deadline:** February of each year.

## 1890 ASM OUTSTANDING SCHOLAR AWARDS

ASM International, Attn: ASM Materials Education Foundation
Scholarship Program
9639 Kinsman Road
Materials Park, OH 44073-0002
Phone: (440) 338-5151; (800) 336-5152; Fax: (440) 338-4634;
Email: asmif@asminternational.org
Web: www.asminternational.org

**Summary:** To provide financial assistance to college sophomores and above who are members of ASM International.

**Eligibility:** Open to student members of the association who have an intended or declared major in metallurgy or materials science engineering. Applicants must have completed at least 1 year of college. Students majoring in related science or engineering disciplines are considered if they demonstrate a strong academic interest in materials science. International students are also eligible. Selection is based on academic achievement; interest in the field (including knowledge of metallurgy or materials engineering, activities, jobs, and potential for a related career); and personal qualities (such as motivation, social values, goals, and maturity). Financial need is not considered.

**Financial data:** The stipend is $2,000 per year.

**Duration:** 1 year; may be renewed for up to 1 additional year.

**Number awarded:** 3 each year.

**Deadline:** April of each year.

## 1891 ASME FOUNDATION SCHOLARSHIPS

ASME International, Attn: Coordinator, Educational Operations
Three Park Avenue
New York, NY 10016-5990
Phone: (212) 591-8131; (800) THE-ASME; Fax: (212) 591-7143;
Email: oluwanifiset@asme.org
Web: www.asme.org/education/enged/aid/scholar.htm

**Summary:** To provide financial assistance to undergraduate students who are members of the American Society of Mechanical Engineers (ASME).

**Eligibility:** Open to student members in good standing who are enrolled in an ABET-accredited mechanical engineering baccalaureate, mechanical engineering technology, or related program. They must be entering their sophomore, junior, or senior year of study. Interested students should submit an application form, a nomination from the applicant's department head, a recommendation from a faculty member, and an official transcript. Only one nomination may be submitted per department. There are no geographic or citizenship limitations. Selection is based on scholastic ability and potential contribution to the mechanical engineering profession.

**Financial data:** The stipend is $1,500.

**Duration:** 1 year.

**Number awarded:** 15 each year.

**Deadline:** March of each year.

## 1892 ASME STUDENT DESIGN CONTEST

ASME International, Attn: Student Center
Three Park Avenue
New York, NY 10016-5990
Phone: (212) 591-7722; (800) THE-ASME; Fax: (212) 591-7674;
Email: students@asme.org
Web: www.asme.org/students/Competitions/designcontest/index.html

**Summary:** To recognize and reward outstanding designs by student members of the American Society of Mechanical Engineers (ASME).

**Eligibility:** Open to student members of the society who have not yet received their first engineering degree. They may enter as individuals, but teams of 2 to 4 members are encouraged. Regional winners compete on the national level. Each year, a problem statement for a mechanical design is presented and students complete a design that meets the specifications of the problem. A recent problem involved a bulk material transporter that could be guided by a single person and could deliver moderate amounts of granular materials.

**Financial data:** Within each region, the first-place winner receives $200, a trophy, and up to $1,000 travel allowance to participate in the finals; the second-place winner receives $100 and a plaque; and the third-place winner receives $50 and a plaque. The national first-place winner receives $3,000 and $1,000 for the student section at their institution; the second-place winner receives $1,000 and $500 for the student section at their institution; the third-place winner receives $500 and $250 for the student section at their institution.

**Duration:** The competition is held annually.

**Number awarded:** 3 winners in the national finals and 3 in each regional student conference.

**Deadline:** Each region sets its own deadline; for Region XIII, the deadline is in June of each year.

## 1893 ASME-ASME AUXILIARY FIRST CLARKE SCHOLARSHIP

ASME International, Attn: ASME Foundation
Three Park Avenue
New York, NY 10016-5990
Phone: (212) 591-7397; (800) THE-ASME; Fax: (212) 591-7739;
Email: soukupd@asme.org
Web: www.asme.org/education/precollege/first/firstscholarship.htm

**Summary:** To provide financial assistance for college to high school seniors who have been active in the For Inspiration and Recognition of Science and Technology (FIRST) program.

**Eligibility:** Open to high school seniors who have been active with FIRST and are interested in studying mechanical engineering or mechanical engineering technology in college. Candidates must be nominated by a ASME member, ASME Auxiliary member, or student member active with FIRST. The letter of nomination must attest to the student's technical, creative, and leadership contributions to the FIRST team. Other selection criteria include academic performance and financial need.

**Financial data:** The stipend is $5,000.

**Duration:** 1 year; nonrenewable.

**Number awarded:** 1 each year.

**Deadline:** February of each year.

## 1894 ASNT ENGINEERING UNDERGRADUATE AWARDS

American Society for Nondestructive Testing, Inc., Attn: Executive Assistant
1711 Arlingate Lane
P.O. Box 28518
Columbus, OH 43228-0518
Phone: (614) 274-6003; (800) 222-2768, ext. 223; Fax: (614) 274-6899;
Email: sthomas@asnt.org
Web: www.asnt.org

**Summary:** To provide financial assistance to undergraduate engineering students who are interested in nondestructive testing and evaluation.

**Eligibility:** Open to undergraduate students enrolled in an engineering program at an ABET-accredited university who show an active interest in the field of nondestructive testing and evaluation. Students must be nominated. Nominations must include the official transcript of the student, 3 letters of recommendation from faculty members, and an essay by the student describing the role nondestructive testing and evaluation will play in their career.

**Financial data:** The stipend is $3,000.

**Duration:** 1 year.

**Number awarded:** Up to 3 each year.

**Deadline:** December of each year.

## 1895 ASSOCIATED GENERAL CONSTRUCTORS OF MAINE SCHOLARSHIPS

Associated General Constructors of Maine, Inc.
Attn: AGC of Maine Educational Foundation
188 Whitten Road
P.O. Box 5519
Augusta, ME 04332-5519
Phone: (207) 622-4741; Fax: (207) 622-1625
Web: www.acm-inc.org/Training_ScholarApps.aspx

**Summary:** To provide financial assistance to Maine residents interested in studying in a construction-related field.

**Eligibility:** Open to Maine residents who are entering their first, second, third, or fourth year at an accredited institution of higher education in Maine.

Applicants must be enrolled in a field of study related to construction. Selection is based on academic record and financial need.

**Financial data:** Stipends range from $500 to $2,000.

**Duration:** 1 year.

**Number awarded:** Varies each year. Recently, 10 of these scholarships were awarded: 2 at $2,000, 6 at $1,000, 1 at $600, and 1 at $500.

**Deadline:** March of each year.

## 1896 ASSOCIATED GENERAL CONTRACTORS OF CONNECTICUT SCHOLARSHIPS

Associated General Contractors of Connecticut, Inc.
912 Silas Deane Highway
Wethersfield, CT 06109-3433
Phone: (860) 529-6855; Fax: (860) 563-0616; Email: info@ctconstruction.org
Web: www.ctconstruction.org/agc/agc.asp

**Summary:** To provide financial assistance and work experience to high school seniors from Connecticut who are interested in entering a building technology, civil engineering, or construction course of study.

**Eligibility:** Open to graduating high school seniors in Connecticut who are interested in 1) entering a 4-year building technology or civil engineering program as a freshman or 2) entering a 2-year technical school with a construction course of study, with the intent of entering a 4-year college upon completion of the technical school. All applicants must be U.S. citizens or documented permanent residents. Semifinalists are interviewed. Final selection is based on interest in construction as a career, grades, extracurricular activities, employment experience, recommendations, and financial status.

**Financial data:** The stipend is $2,500 per year for both the freshman and sophomore years of college. In addition, recipients are awarded $2,500 each summer for student work experience with a qualified contractor.

**Duration:** 2 years of college and 2 summer internships.

**Deadline:** October of each year.

## 1897 ASSOCIATED GENERAL CONTRACTORS OF VERMONT SCHOLARSHIPS

Associated General Contractors of Vermont
Attn: Director of Workforce Development
148 State Street
P.O. Box 750
Montpelier, VT 05601
Phone: (802) 223-2374; Fax: (802) 223-1809; Email: info@agcvt.org
Web: www.agcvt.org/workforce/scholarships.cfm

**Summary:** To provide financial assistance to Vermont residents who are interested in studying a field related to construction.

**Eligibility:** Open to residents of Vermont who are high school seniors, high school graduates, or GED recipients and interested in pursuing an academic, vocational, technical, or advanced training program in a field related to construction. Applicants must be able to demonstrate financial need. Selection is based on a letter of recommendation, required essays, and financial need.

**Financial data:** The stipend is $1,000 and must be used within 1 year after being awarded.

**Duration:** 1 year.

**Number awarded:** 2 each year.

**Deadline:** April of each year.

## 1898 ASSOCIATED OREGON LOGGERS SCHOLARSHIPS

Associated Oregon Loggers, Inc.
P.O. Box 12339
Salem, OR 97309-0339
Phone: (503) 364-1330; (800) 452-6023; Fax: (503) 364-0836;
Email: aol@oregonloggers.org
Web: www.oregonloggers.org/non_member.htm

**Summary:** To provide financial assistance to high school seniors in Oregon who are planning to major in a forest resource production field of study.

**Eligibility:** Open to high school seniors in Oregon who will be attending a 4-year college or university accredited by the Society of American Foresters. Applicants must be planning to major in a forest resource production field of study, including forest management, forest engineering, and forest products. They must submit high school transcripts, SAT or ACT scores, verification of college acceptance, and an original essay (up to 3 pages) on "What challenges do you see in the field of forestry and what are your views on meeting these challenges?" Selection is based on academic record, SAT or ACT scores, rel-

evant experiences, and thought process, grammatical usage, and expression in the required essay. Financial need is not considered in the selection process. Finalists may be interviewed.

**Financial data:** The stipend is $1,500 per year.

**Duration:** 1 year; may be renewed for 3 additional years.

**Number awarded:** 1 or more each year.

**Deadline:** March of each year.

## 1899 ASSOCIATION FOR IRON & STEEL TECHNOLOGY SCHOLARSHIPS

Association for Iron & Steel Technology, Attn: AIST Foundation
186 Thorn Hill Road
Warrendale, PA 15086-7528
Phone: (724) 776-6040, ext. 621; Fax: (724) 776-1880;
Email: lwharrey@aist.org
Web: www.aistech.org/foundation/scholarships.htm

**Summary:** To provide financial assistance for college to students interested in preparing for a career in the iron and steel or steel-related industries.

**Eligibility:** Open to full-time students majoring in metallurgy, materials science, or metallurgical engineering as preparation for a career in the iron and steel or steel-related industries. Other majors are considered if the application is accompanied by a letter from an academic advisor, on official letterhead, regarding the program's preparation for advancement of steel product production, steel application, or the use of steel in material design. Interest in a career in ferrous-related industries should be demonstrated by internship, co-op, or related experiences and/or demonstrable plans to pursue such experience during college. Applicants must be a student member of the Association for Iron & Steel Technology (AIST). They may apply as early as their freshman year in college. Juniors and seniors should have a cumulative GPA of 3.0 or higher in their major; undeclared students should have a cumulative GPA of 3.25 or higher. Applicants must submit 1) a current resume; 2) a statement of their philosophy of their academic discipline and personal and professional goals; 3) a 300-word essay on why they are interested in working in the steel industry and what they will contribute to enhancing the well-being of the industry; and 4) letters of recommendation. Financial need is not considered in the selection process.

**Financial data:** The stipend is $2,000.

**Duration:** 1 year.

**Number awarded:** 5 each year, including 2 Willy Korf Memorial Fund Scholarships, 1 Ronald E. Lincoln Memorial Scholarship, and 2 Benjamin F. Fairless Scholarships.

**Deadline:** April of each year.

## 1900 ASSOCIATION FOR WOMEN GEOSCIENTISTS MINORITY SCHOLARSHIP

Association for Women Geoscientists, Attn: AWG Foundation
P.O. Box 30645
Lincoln, NE 68503-0645
Email: awgscholarship@yahoo.com
Web: www.awg.org/eas/minority.html

**Summary:** To provide financial assistance to minority women who are interested in working on an undergraduate degree in the geosciences.

**Eligibility:** Open to women who are African American, Hispanic, or Native American (including Eskimo, Hawaiian, Samoan, or American Indian). Applicants must be full-time students working on, or planning to work on, an undergraduate degree in the geosciences (including geology, geophysics, geochemistry, hydrology, meteorology, physical oceanography, planetary geology, or earth science education). They must submit a 500-word essay on why they have chosen to major in the geosciences and their career goals, 2 letters of recommendation, high school and/or college transcripts, and SAT or ACT scores. Financial need is not considered in the selection process.

**Financial data:** A total of $5,000 is available for this program each year.

**Duration:** 1 year; may be renewed.

**Number awarded:** 1 or more each year.

**Deadline:** May of each year.

## 1901 ASSOCIATION FOR WOMEN IN SCIENCE COLLEGE SCHOLARSHIPS

Association for Women in Science, Attn: AWIS Educational Foundation
1200 New York Avenue, N.W., Suite 650
Washington, DC 20005
Phone: (202) 326-8940; (866) 657-AWIS; Fax: (202) 326-8960;

Email: awisedfd@awis.org
Web: www.awis.org/resource/edfoundation.html

**Summary:** To provide financial assistance to female high school seniors interested in studying engineering or designated sciences in college.

**Eligibility:** Open to women who are high school seniors and U.S. citizens interested in a career in research and/or teaching. Applicants must have a GPA of 3.75 or higher and specified scores on the SAT or the ACT. They must plan to study astronomy, biology, chemistry, computer and information science, engineering, geoscience, mathematics, physics, or psychology in college. Along with their application, they must submit an essay on the following: 1) their scientific interests and career aspirations in research and/or teaching; 2) what led to their interest in science and the role of special mentors, if relevant; 3) key lessons they have learned during any research or teaching experiences they have had; 4) any social, economic, academic, or other barriers they have faced and how they overcame them; and 5) why they undertook community service or volunteer activities and key lessons they learned. Financial need is not considered.

**Financial data:** The stipend is $1,000. Citations of merit are $300 and recognition awards are $100.

**Duration:** 1 year.

**Number awarded:** 2 to 5 scholarships are awarded each year. The number of citations of merit and recognition awards varies.

**Deadline:** January of each year.

## 1902 ASSOCIATION OF CALIFORNIA WATER AGENCIES SCHOLARSHIPS

Association of California Water Agencies, Attn: Scholarship Program
910 K Street, Suite 100
Sacramento, CA 95814-3514
Phone: (916) 441-4545; Fax: (916) 325-4849; Email: lavonnew@acwa.com
Web: www.acwa.com/news_info/scholarships

**Summary:** To provide financial assistance to upper-division students in California who are majoring in water resources-related fields of study.

**Eligibility:** Open to California residents attending selected colleges and universities in the state. Applicants must be full-time students in their junior or senior year at the time of the award and majoring in a field related to or identified with water resources, including engineering, agricultural and/or urban water supply, environmental sciences, or public administration. Along with their application, they must submit 2-page essay on key water-related issues they would address if given the opportunity, why they have chosen a career in the water resources field, and how their educational and career goals relate to a future in California water resources. Selection is based on scholastic achievement, commitment to a career in the field of water resources, and financial need.

**Financial data:** The stipend is $1,500. Funds are paid directly to the recipient's school.

**Duration:** 1 year.

**Number awarded:** At least 6 each year.

**Deadline:** March of each year.

## 1903 ASSOCIATION OF CUBAN ENGINEERS SCHOLARSHIPS

Association of Cuban Engineers, Attn: Selection Committee
P.O. Box 557575
Miami, FL 33255-7575
Phone: (305) 649-7429
Web: www.a-i-c.org

**Summary:** To provide financial assistance to undergraduate and graduate students of Cuban American heritage who are interested in preparing for a career in engineering.

**Eligibility:** Open to U.S. citizens and legal residents who have completed at least 30 units of college work in the United States and are majoring or planning to major in some aspect of engineering. Applicants must be attending an ABET-accredited college or university within the United States or Puerto Rico as a full-time student with a GPA of 3.0 or higher. They must be of Cuban or other Hispanic heritage (at least one grandparent Cuban or other Hispanic nationality). Along with their application, they must submit brief essays on their family history, professional goals, extracurricular activities, work experience, and how they will help other Cuban and Hispanic engineering students in the future. Financial need is not considered in the selection process.

**Financial data:** Stipends range from $500 to $1,000.

**Duration:** 1 year.

**Number awarded:** Up to 20 each year.

**Deadline:** November of each year.

## 1904 ASSOCIATION OF ENERGY ENGINEERS SCHOLARSHIPS

Association of Energy Engineers, Attn: Foundation
4025 Pleasantdale Road, Suite 420
Atlanta, GA 30340
Phone: (770) 447-5083; Fax: (770) 446-3969; Email: info@aeecenter.org
Web: www.aeecenter.org

**Summary:** To provide financial assistance to undergraduate and graduate students interested in taking courses directly related to energy engineering or energy management.

**Eligibility:** Open to undergraduate and graduate students who are enrolled in engineering or management programs at accredited colleges and universities and who would be interested in taking courses directly related to energy engineering or energy management (preferably within a curriculum leading to a major or minor in energy engineering). Qualified students are invited to submit their applications to the association's local chapter, along with transcripts and letters of recommendation. Each chapter may then submit up to 6 nominees, no more than 2 of whom may be graduate students. Selection is based on scholarship, character, and need. In awarding scholarships, preference is given to candidates needing aid their final year; second, to candidates needing aid for the last 2 years; third, to candidates needing aid for 3 years; and finally, to first-year students.

**Financial data:** Stipends are $2,000, $1,000, or $500. In addition, the 2 most outstanding candidates receive the $1,000 Victor Ottaviano Scholarship and the $1,000 Al Thumann Scholarship.

**Duration:** 1 year.

**Number awarded:** Several each year, including 1 Victor Ottaviano Scholarship and 1 Al Thumann Scholarship.

**Deadline:** April of each year.

## 1905 ASSOCIATION OF PERIOPERATIVE REGISTERED NURSES (AORN) NURSING STUDENT SCHOLARSHIPS

Association of periOperative Registered Nurses, Attn: AORN Foundation
2170 South Parker Road, Suite 300
Denver, CO 80231-5711
Phone: (303) 755-6300, ext. 366; (800) 755-2676, ext. 366; Fax: (303) 755-4219; Email: nharbin@aorn.org
Web: www.aorn.org/foundation/scholarship.htm

**Summary:** To provide financial assistance to students interested in preparing for a career in nursing, especially perioperative nursing.

**Eligibility:** Open to students currently enrolled in an accredited nursing program leading to initial licensure as an R.N. The program may be for a diploma or an A.D.N., B.S.N., master's entry, or accelerated second B.S.N. degree. Applicants must have a GPA of 3.0 or higher. Along with their application, they must submit a personal statement describing why they have chosen to prepare for a career in nursing, their financial need, their career goals, their volunteer community activities, and what can be done to attract students to perioperative nursing.

**Financial data:** A stipend is awarded (amount not specified). Funds are paid directly to the recipient.

**Duration:** 1 year; may be renewed if the recipient maintains a GPA of 3.0 or higher.

**Number awarded:** 1 or more each year.

**Deadline:** April of each year.

## 1906 ASSOCIATION OF STATE DAM SAFETY OFFICIALS SCHOLARSHIPS

Association of State Dam Safety Officials, Attn: Scholarship Coordinator
450 Old Vine Street, Second Floor
Lexington, KY 40507
Phone: (859) 257-5140; Fax: (859) 323-1958; Email: info@damsafety.org
Web: www.damsafety.org

**Summary:** To provide financial assistance for undergraduate education to students interested in fields related to dam safety.

**Eligibility:** Open to college seniors with a GPA of 2.5 or higher studying civil engineering or a related field. They must have a demonstrated interest in preparing for a career in hydraulics, hydrology, or geotechnical disciplines related to the design, construction, and operation of dams. U.S. citizenship is required. Selection is based on academic achievement, financial need, work experience and activities, and a 2-page essay on their proposed course of study and why dam safety is important.

**Financial data:** The stipend is $5,000 per year.

**Duration:** 1 year; junior recipients may reapply for their senior year.

**Number awarded:** 2 or 3 each year.

**Deadline:** March of each year.

## 1907 ASTRONAUT SCHOLARSHIP FOUNDATION SCHOLARSHIPS

Astronaut Scholarship Foundation, Attn: Executive Director
6225 Vectorspace Boulevard
Titusville, FL 32780
Phone: (321) 269-6101, ext, 6176; Fax: (321) 264-9176;
Email: LinnLeBlanc@astronautscholarship.org
Web: www.astronautscholarship.org
**Summary:** To provide financial assistance to upper-division and graduate students in science and engineering.
**Eligibility:** Open to juniors, seniors, and graduate students working on degrees in the physical sciences (e.g., biology, chemistry, computer science, mathematics, physics) or engineering fields. Candidates must be nominated by faculty or staff at 1 of 17 participating universities; each may nominate 2 students. Students intending to practice professional medicine are not eligible, but those intending to do biomedical research are considered. No special consideration is given to aeronautical or astronautical engineering students or those intending to prepare for a career as astronauts. Special consideration is given to applicants who have shown initiative, creativity, excellence, and/or resourcefulness in their field. U.S. citizenship is required.
**Financial data:** The stipend is $10,000 per year.
**Duration:** 1 year; may be renewed for up to 2 additional years.
**Number awarded:** Normally 17 each year: 1 at each participating university.

## 1908 A.T. ANDERSON MEMORIAL SCHOLARSHIP PROGRAM

American Indian Science and Engineering Society
Attn: Scholarship Coordinator
2305 Renard, S.E., Suite 200
P.O. Box 9828
Albuquerque, NM 87119-9828
Phone: (505) 765-1052, ext. 106; Fax: (505) 765-5608; Email: shirley@aises.org
Web: www.aises.org/highered/scholarships
**Summary:** To provide financial assistance to members of the American Indian Science and Engineering Society who are majoring in designated fields as undergraduate or graduate students.
**Eligibility:** Open to members of the society who can furnish proof of tribal enrollment or Certificate of Degree of Indian Blood. Applicants must be full-time students at the undergraduate or graduate school level attending an accredited 4-year college or university or a 2-year college leading to an academic degree in engineering, mathematics, medicine, natural resources, physical science, or the sciences. They must submit a 500-word essay that demonstrates their interest in and motivation to continue higher education, an understanding of the importance of college and a commitment to completion, their educational and/or career goals, and a commitment to learning and giving back to the community. Selection is based on the essay, academic achievement (GPA of 2.0 or higher), leadership potential, and commitment to helping other American Indians. Financial need is not considered.
**Financial data:** The annual stipend is $1,000 for undergraduates or $2,000 for graduate students.
**Duration:** 1 year; nonrenewable.
**Number awarded:** Varies; generally, 200 or more each year, depending upon the availability of funds from corporate and other sponsors.
**Deadline:** June of each year.

## 1909 AUXILIARY SCHOLARSHIP

National Society of Professional Engineers, Attn: Education Services
1420 King Street
Alexandria, VA 22314-2794
Phone: (703) 684-2833; Fax: (703) 836-4875; Email: jiglesias@nspe.org
Web: www.nspe.org/scholarships/sc1-hs.asp
**Summary:** To provide financial assistance for college to women who are high school seniors and are interested in preparing for a career in engineering.
**Eligibility:** Open to women who are high school seniors planning to study engineering in an EAC-ABET accredited college program. Applicants must have a GPA of 3.5 or higher and above average scores on the SAT or ACT. They must submit an essay (up to 500 words) on their interest in engineering, their major area of study and area of specialization, and the occupation they propose to pursue after graduation. Selection is based on GPA (20 points), the essay (20 points), extracurricular activities, including work experience and volunteer activities (25 points), financial need (5 points), SAT/ACT scores (20 points), and the composite application (10 points). U.S. citizenship is required.
**Financial data:** The award is $1,000 per year; funds are paid directly to the recipient's institution.
**Duration:** 4 years.
**Number awarded:** 1 each year.
**Deadline:** November of each year.

## 1910 AVIATION COUNCIL OF PENNSYLVANIA SCHOLARSHIP

Aviation Council of Pennsylvania, Attn: Scholarship Program
3111 Arcadia Avenue
Allentown, PA 18103-6903
Phone: (610) 797-6911; Fax: (610) 797-8238
Web: www.acpfly.com
**Summary:** To provide financial assistance for college to students from Pennsylvania preparing for a career in aviation or aviation management.
**Eligibility:** Open to students who are interested in preparing for a career in aviation technology, aviation management, or the professional pilot field. Applicants must be residents of Pennsylvania. If they are applying for the aviation management scholarship, they may attend college in any state. Applicants for the aviation technology and professional pilot scholarships must attend school in Pennsylvania. Financial need is considered in the selection process.
**Financial data:** Typically, the stipend is $1,000 (although the amount may vary).
**Duration:** 1 year.
**Number awarded:** 4 each year: 1 for aviation technology, 1 for aviation management, and 2 for professional pilots.
**Deadline:** July of each year.

## 1911 AVIATION DISTRIBUTORS AND MANUFACTURERS ASSOCIATION SCHOLARSHIP PROGRAM

Aviation Distributors and Manufacturers Association
100 North 20th Street, Fourth Floor
Philadelphia, PA 19103-1443
Phone: (215) 564-3484; Fax: (215) 963-9784; Email: adma@fernley.com
Web: www.adma.org/aviation_scholarship.html
**Summary:** To provide financial assistance to students who are preparing for a career in the aviation field.
**Eligibility:** Open to college students who are either 1) a third- or fourth-year student enrolled at an accredited institution in a bachelor's degree program preparing for a career in aviation management or as a professional pilot; or 2) a second-year student in an aircraft and powerplant (A&P) mechanic program at a 2-year accredited institution. Applicants must submit 2 letters of recommendation, a 500-word essay describing their desire to prepare for a career in aviation, and verification of a GPA of 3.0 or higher. Selection is based on academic performance, recommendations, extracurricular activities, leadership contributions, and financial need.
**Financial data:** The stipend is $1,000.
**Duration:** 1 year.
**Number awarded:** Varies each year; recently, 4 of these scholarships were awarded.
**Deadline:** March of each year.

## 1912 AVIATION INSURANCE ASSOCIATION SCHOLARSHIP

Aviation Insurance Association
14 West Third Street, Suite 200
Kansas City, MO 64105
Phone: (816) 221-8488; Fax: (816) 472-7765; Email: info@aiaweb.org
Web: www.aiaweb.org
**Summary:** To provide financial assistance to college students preparing for a career in aviation.
**Eligibility:** Open to students enrolled in an undergraduate aviation degree program at a college or university that is a member of the University Aviation Association (UAA). Applicants must have completed at least 45 college credits, of which 15 must be in aviation, with a GPA of 2.5 or higher. Along with their application, they must submit 1) a letter describing their activities, leadership qualities, goals, and reasons for applying for these funds; 2) at least 1 letter of recommendation from an employer or instructor; 3) an official transcript; and 4) any FAA certificates.
**Financial data:** The stipend is $5,000.
**Duration:** 1 year.
**Number awarded:** 1 each year.
**Deadline:** February of each year.

## 1913 AWS DISTRICT SCHOLARSHIPS

American Welding Society, Attn: AWS Foundation, Inc.
550 N.W. LeJeune Road
Miami, FL 33126
Phone: (305) 445-6628; (800) 443-9353, ext. 461; Fax: (305) 443-7559;
Email: found@aws.org

Web: www.aws.org/foundation/district_scholarships.html

**Summary:** To provide financial assistance to students interested in studying in a vocational training, community college, or degree program in welding or a related field of study.

**Eligibility:** Open to students enrolled in a welding-related educational or training program. Applicants must be a high school graduate or possess a GED certificate. Selection is based on transcripts; a personal statement of ambitions, goals, background, and other factors that indicate a commitment to pursuing welding education; and financial need.

**Financial data:** Stipends average from $500 to $1,000. Funds, paid directly to the school, are applied to tuition, books, supplies, and related institutional charges.

**Duration:** 1 year; recipients may reapply.

**Number awarded:** Varies each year; recently, 131 of these scholarships were awarded.

**Deadline:** February of each year.

## 1914 B. CHARLES TINEY MEMORIAL STUDENT ASCE STUDENT CHAPTER SCHOLARSHIP

American Society of Civil Engineers, Attn: Student Services
1801 Alexander Bell Drive
Reston, VA 20191-4400
Phone: (703) 295-6120; (800) 548-ASCE; Fax: (703) 295-6132;
Email: student@asce.org
Web: www.asce.org

**Summary:** To provide financial assistance to student members of the American Society of Civil Engineers (ASCE) for undergraduate study in civil engineering.

**Eligibility:** Open to ASCE members who are freshmen, sophomores, juniors, or first-year seniors enrolled in a program of civil engineering. Applicants must submit an essay (up to 500 words) in which they discuss why they chose to become a civil engineer, their specific ASCE student chapter involvement, any special financial needs, and long-term goals and plans. Selection is based on their justification for the award, educational plan, academic performance and standing, potential for development, leadership capacity, ASCE activities, and demonstrated financial need.

**Financial data:** The stipend is $2,000 per year.

**Duration:** 1 year; may be renewed.

**Number awarded:** Approximately 4 each year.

**Deadline:** February of each year.

## 1915 BALL HORTICULTURAL COMPANY SCHOLARSHIP

Floriculture Industry Research and Scholarship Trust
Attn: Scholarship Program
P.O. Box 280
East Lansing, MI 48826-0280
Phone: (517) 333-4617; Fax: (517) 333-4494;
Email: scholarships@firstinfloriculture.org
Web: www.firstinfloriculture.org

**Summary:** To provide financial assistance to college students interested in a career in commercial floriculture.

**Eligibility:** Open to undergraduate students at 4-year colleges and universities who are entering their junior, senior, or fifth undergraduate year. Applicants must be horticulture majors who intend to prepare for a career in commercial floriculture. They must be U.S. or Canadian citizens or permanent residents with a GPA of 3.0 or higher. Selection is based on academic record, recommendations, career goals, extracurricular activities, and financial need.

**Financial data:** The stipend depends on the availability of funds. Recently, it was $1,000.

**Duration:** 1 year.

**Number awarded:** 1 each year.

**Deadline:** April of each year.

## 1916 BALTIMORE-WASHINGTON SECTION SCHOLARSHIPS

Society of Women Engineers-Baltimore-Washington Section
c/o Kathleen Hufnagel, Scholarship Chair
1601 Barnstead Drive
Reston, VA 20194
Email: Kphufnagel@cs.com
Web: www.swe-bws.org

**Summary:** To provide financial assistance to women who reside or attend school in the Washington, D.C. area and are interested in studying engineering in college or graduate school.

**Eligibility:** Open to women who reside in northern Virginia, Washington, D.C., or Maryland or who are or will be students at universities or colleges in that area. Student members of the Society of Women Engineers (SWE) are given preference. Applicants must be enrolled or accepted for enrollment in an ABET-accredited or SWE-approved engineering degree program. They may be entering freshmen, current college students, reentry women, or graduate students, but they must have a GPA of 3.0 or higher. U.S. citizenship is required. Students who receive tuition reimbursement from an employer are not eligible. Selection is based on merit and an essay on what influenced the applicant to select her current course of study, why she would like to be an engineer, and/or how she believes she will make a difference as an engineer.

**Financial data:** Stipends are $1,500 or $1,000.

**Duration:** 1 year.

**Number awarded:** Varies each year; recently, 4 of these scholarships (2 at $1,500 and 2 at $1,000) were awarded.

**Deadline:** February of each year.

## 1917 BANK OF AMERICA ACHIEVEMENT AWARDS

**Summary:** To recognize and reward high school seniors in California who excel in specific subject areas.
*See Listing #1283.*

## 1918 BARBARA MCBRIDE SCHOLARSHIP

Society of Exploration Geophysicists, Attn: SEG Foundation
8801 South Yale, Suite 500
P.O. Box 702740
Tulsa, OK 74170-2740
Phone: (918) 497-5513; Fax: (918) 497-5557; Email: scholarships@seg.org
Web: seg.org/business/foundation/scholarships/index.shtml

**Summary:** To provide financial assistance to women undergraduate and graduate students who are interested in the field of applied geophysics.

**Eligibility:** Open to women who are 1) high school students planning to enter college in the fall, or 2) undergraduate or graduate students whose grades are above average. Applicants must intend to work on a degree directed toward a career in applied geophysics or a closely-related field. Along with their application, they must submit a 150-word essay on how they plan to use geophysics in their future. Financial need is not considered in the selection process.

**Financial data:** The stipend ranges from $1,000 to $3,000 per year.

**Duration:** 1 academic year; may be renewable, based on scholastic standing, availability of funds, and continuance of a course of study leading to a career in applied geophysics.

**Number awarded:** 1 each year.

**Deadline:** January of each year.

## 1919 BARBARA PALO FOSTER MEMORIAL SCHOLARSHIP

Ulman Cancer Fund for Young Adults, Attn: Scholarship Committee
4725 Dorsey Hall Drive, Suite A
PMB 505
Ellicott City, MD 21042
Phone: (410) 964-0202; (888) 393-FUND;
Email: scholarship@ulmanfund.org
Web: www.ulmanfund.org/Services/Scholarship/scholarship_main.htm

**Summary:** To provide financial assistance to nursing students who have a parent with cancer.

**Eligibility:** Open to students who have or have lost a parent to cancer. Applicants must be able to demonstrate financial need. They must be between 15 and 40 years of age and enrolled in, or planning to enroll in, a postsecondary program in nursing. Along with their application, they must submit a 500-word essay on 1 of 4 assigned topics that relate to cancer. Selection is based on the quality of the essay, recommendations, their overall story of cancer survivorship, and financial need.

**Financial data:** The stipend is $1,000.

**Duration:** 1 year.

**Number awarded:** 1 each year.

**Deadline:** March of each year.

## 1920 BAROID SCHOLARSHIP

American Ground Water Trust
16 Centre Street
P.O. Box 1796
Concord, NH 03302

Phone: (603) 228-5444; Fax: (603) 228-6557; Email: info@agwt.org

Web: www.agwt.org/baroid.htm

**Summary:** To provide financial assistance to high school seniors who are interested in preparing for a career in a ground water-related field.

**Eligibility:** Open to high school seniors who have a GPA of 3.0 or higher and are entering a 4-year college or university as a full-time student. Applicants must be planning a career in a ground water-related field and must have completed a science/environmental project in high school that directly involved ground water resources or have had vacation/out-of-school work experience that is directly related to the environment and natural resources. They must submit a 500-word essay on "Ground Water—An Important Environmental and Economic Resource for America" and a 300-word description of their high school ground water project and/or practical environmental work experience. Selection is based on the above criteria, and on the applicant's references and academic record. Financial need is not considered. U.S. citizenship or permanent resident status is required.

**Financial data:** Stipends range from $1,000 to $2,000. Funds are paid directly to the recipient's college.

**Duration:** 1 year.

**Number awarded:** 1 each year.

**Deadline:** May of each year.

### 1921 BARRY AND JULIA SMITH FAMILY NURSE SCHOLARSHIP PROGRAM

Scholarship America, Attn: Scholarship Management Services

One Scholarship Way

P.O. Box 297

St. Peter, MN 56082

Phone: (507) 931-1682; (866) 243-4644; Fax: (507) 931-9168

Web: www.hospicenurse.scholarshipamerica.org

**Summary:** To provide financial assistance to nursing students interested in a career in hospice or end-of-life care nursing.

**Eligibility:** Open to college juniors enrolled in a full-time undergraduate course of study in nursing at an eligible 4-year college or university. Applicants must be at least 25 years of age and interested in a career in hospice or end-of-life care nursing. They must submit a personal essay describing their interest or plans to practice nursing involving hospice or end-of-life care. Selection is based on the essay, academic record, demonstrated leadership and participation in school and community activities, honors, work experience, a statement of goals and aspirations, unusual personal or family circumstances, and an outside appraisal. Financial need is not considered.

**Financial data:** The stipend is $1,000.

**Duration:** 1 year. Awards are not renewable, but recipients may reapply.

**Number awarded:** Varies each year; no more than 2 awards are granted to students attending the same school.

**Deadline:** April of each year.

### 1922 BARRY K. WENDT MEMORIAL SCHOLARSHIP

National Stone, Sand and Gravel Association

Attn: Human Resources Committee

1605 King Street

Arlington, VA 22314

Phone: (703) 525-8788; (800) 342-1415; Fax: (703) 525-7782;

Email: info@nssga.org

Web: www.nssga.org/careers/scholarships.htm

**Summary:** To provide financial assistance to engineering students intending to prepare for a career in the aggregates industry.

**Eligibility:** Open to engineering students who intend to prepare for a career in the crushed stone industry. Applications must be accompanied by a letter of recommendation and a 300- to 500-word statement describing those career plans. Financial need is not considered in the selection process.

**Financial data:** The award amount depends on the availability of funds.

**Duration:** 1 year.

**Number awarded:** 1 each year.

**Deadline:** April of each year.

### 1923 BECHTEL CORPORATION SCHOLARSHIP

Society of Women Engineers

230 East Ohio Street, Suite 400

Chicago, IL 60611-3265

Phone: (312) 596-5223; Fax: (312) 644-8557; Email: hq@swe.org

Web: www.societyofwomenengineers.org/scholarships

**Summary:** To provide financial assistance to undergraduate women who are members of the Society of Women Engineers and majoring in engineering.

**Eligibility:** Open to women who are entering their sophomore, junior, or senior year at an Accreditation Board for Engineering and Technology (ABET) accredited college or university. Applicants must be studying architectural, civil, electrical, environmental, or mechanical engineering with a GPA of 3.0 or higher. Applicants must also submit a 1-page essay on why they want to be an engineer, how they believe they will make a difference as an engineer, and what influenced them to study engineering. Only members of the society are considered for this award, selection merit-based.

**Financial data:** The stipend is $1,400.

**Duration:** 1 year.

**Number awarded:** 2 each year.

**Deadline:** January of each year.

### 1924 BECHTEL FOUNDATION SCHOLARSHIP FOR SAFETY AND HEALTH

American Society of Safety Engineers, Attn: ASSE Foundation

1800 East Oakton Street

Des Plaines, IL 60018

Phone: (847) 768-3441; Fax: (847) 296-9220; Email: mrosario@asse.org

Web: www.asse.org

**Summary:** To provide financial assistance to undergraduate student members of the American Society of Safety Engineers (ASSE), particularly those interested in construction safety.

**Eligibility:** Open to ASSE student members who are majoring in occupational safety and health or a closely-related field (e.g., safety engineering, safety management, systems safety, environmental science, industrial hygiene, ergonomics, fire science) with an emphasis on construction safety. Applicants must be full-time students who have completed at least 60 semester hours with a GPA of 3.0 or higher. As part of the selection process, they must submit 2 essays of 300 words or less: 1) why they are seeking a degree in safety, a brief description of their current activities, and how those relate to their career goals and objectives; and 2) why they should be awarded this scholarship (including career goals and financial need).

**Financial data:** The stipend is $3,000 per year.

**Duration:** 1 year; nonrenewable.

**Number awarded:** 1 each year.

**Deadline:** November of each year.

### 1925 BECKY COLE BOSWELL MEMORIAL SCHOLARSHIP

American Society of Extra-Corporeal Technology, Inc.

Attn: AmSECT Foundation

2209 Dickens Road

P.O. Box 11086

Richmond, VA 23230-1086

Phone: (804) 565-6363; Fax: (804) 282-0090; Email: AmSECT@amsect.org

Web: www.amsect.org/scholarships/scholarships_grants.html

**Summary:** To provide financial assistance to student members of the American Society of Extra-Corporeal Technology (AmSECT) who are enrolled in a perfusion training program.

**Eligibility:** Open to student members of the society who are enrolled in (or accepted at) an accredited perfusion training program. Applicants must have completed at least one quarter of the required course work and have at least a 2.75 GPA. They must submit 250-word essays on how they would improve AmSECT and how they could improve the perfusion profession. Financial need is not considered in the selection process.

**Financial data:** The stipend is $1,000 per year.

**Duration:** 1 year.

**Number awarded:** 1 each year.

**Deadline:** November of each year.

### 1926 BENJAMIN C. BLACKBURN SCHOLARSHIP

**Summary:** To provide financial assistance to residents of New Jersey who are working on an undergraduate or graduate degree in horticulture, landscape architecture, or related fields.

See Listing #1287.

### 1927 BERNA LOU CARTWRIGHT SCHOLARSHIPS

ASME International

Attn: American Society of Mechanical Engineers Auxiliary, Inc.

Three Park Avenue
New York, NY 10016-5990
Phone: (212) 591-7733; (800) THE-ASME; Fax: (212) 591-7674;
Email: horvathb@asme.org
Web: www.asme.org/auxiliary/scholarshiploans
**Summary:** To provide financial support for the study of mechanical engineering to students in their final year of undergraduate study.
**Eligibility:** Open to students completing the junior year of a 4-year program or the fourth year of a 5-year program in mechanical engineering. Applicants must be U.S. citizens enrolled in colleges and universities with accredited departments of mechanical engineering. If the school has a chapter of the Student Section of the American Society of Mechanical Engineers (ASME), the applicant must be a member. Selection is based on academic performance, financial need, character, and participation in ASME activities.
**Financial data:** The stipend is $2,000.
**Duration:** 1 year.
**Number awarded:** 6 to 12 each year.
**Deadline:** March of each year.

### 1928 BERNESE B. DAVIS GARDEN CLUB OBJECTIVES SCHOLARSHIP

**Summary:** To provide financial aid to Florida undergraduates and graduate students majoring in designated areas related to gardening.
*See Listing #1290.*

### 1929 BERTHA LAMME MEMORIAL SCHOLARSHIP

Society of Women Engineers
230 East Ohio Street, Suite 400
Chicago, IL 60611-3265
Phone: (312) 596-5223; Fax: (312) 644-8557; Email: hq@swe.org
Web: www.societyofwomenengineers.org/scholarships
**Summary:** To provide financial assistance to women who will be entering college as freshmen and are interested in studying electrical engineering.
**Eligibility:** Open to women who are entering college as freshmen with a GPA of 3.5 or higher. Applicants must be U.S. citizens planning to enroll full time at an ABET-accredited 4-year college or university and major in electrical engineering. Along with their application, they must submit a 1-page essay on why they want to be an engineer, how they believe they will make a difference as an engineer, and what influenced them to study engineering. Selection is based on merit.
**Financial data:** The stipend is $1,200.
**Duration:** 1 year.
**Number awarded:** 1 each year.
**Deadline:** May of each year.

### 1930 BERTHA P. SINGER SCHOLARSHIP

Oregon Student Assistance Commission
Attn: Grants and Scholarships Division
1500 Valley River Drive, Suite 100
Eugene, OR 97401-2146
Phone: (541) 687-7395; (800) 452-8807, ext. 7395; Fax: (541) 687-7419;
Email: awardinfo@mercury.osac.state.or.us
Web: www.osac.state.or.us
**Summary:** To provide financial assistance for the study of nursing to residents of Oregon.
**Eligibility:** Open to residents of Oregon who are studying nursing at a college in the state and have a cumulative GPA of 3.0 or higher. Applicants must provide documentation of enrollment in the third year of a 4-year nursing degree program or the second year of a 2-year associate degree nursing program.
**Financial data:** Stipend amounts vary; recently, they were at least $1,087.
**Duration:** 1 year.
**Number awarded:** Varies each year; recently, 23 of these scholarships were awarded.
**Deadline:** February of each year.

### 1931 BETTY BROEMMELSIEK MEMORIAL CONSERVATION SCHOLARSHIPS

Soil and Water Conservation Society-Missouri Show-Me Chapter
c/o Natural Resources Conservation Service
Parkade Center, Suite 250
601 Business Loop 70 West

Columbia, MO 65203-2546
Phone: (573) 876-0912
Web: swcs.missouri.edu
**Summary:** To provide financial assistance to undergraduate students at Missouri colleges and universities interested in preparing for a career in natural resources conservation.
**Eligibility:** Open to high school seniors and full-time undergraduate students who are attending or planning to attend a Missouri institution of higher education. Applicants must be majoring or planning to major in a natural resource conservation or resource-related field, including soil science, planned land use management, fisheries, forestry management, agricultural engineering, hydrology, rural sociology, agronomy, agricultural economics, education, water management, or a related environmental field. They must submit 2 letters of recommendation; an essay on a topic that changes annually; a list of positions of leadership in such organizations as the Soil and Water Conservation Society, 4-H, FFA, and student groups; publishing and speaking activities in which they participate; and their most recent high school, college, or university transcript. Financial need is not considered in the selection process.
**Financial data:** First place is $1,000 and second place is $500. Payment is made directly to the college or university.
**Duration:** 1 year.
**Number awarded:** 2 each year.
**Deadline:** November of each year.

### 1932 BG BENJAMIN B. TALLEY SCHOLARSHIP

Society of American Military Engineers-Anchorage Post
P.O. Box 6149
Elmendorf AFB, AK 99506-6149
Email: william_kontess@urscorp.com
Web: www.sameanchorage.org/scholarship.htm
**Summary:** To provide financial assistance to upper division students from Alaska who are majoring in engineering or the natural sciences.
**Eligibility:** Open to college juniors and seniors who are majoring in engineering or the natural sciences. Applicants must be U.S. citizens and either Alaska residents or attending school in Alaska. They must be 1) a member of the sponsoring organization, 2) the dependent of a member, 3) a member of the armed forces on active duty in Alaska, or 4) a dependent of a member of the armed forces on active duty in Alaska. Their GPA must be 2.5 or higher. Selection is based on academic achievement, participation in school and community activities, an essay on career goals (100 to 250 words), and work/family activities. Financial need is not considered in the selection process.
**Financial data:** Varies; generally, stipends are $3,000, $2,000, or $1,000.
**Duration:** 1 year.
**Number awarded:** Varies; recently, 6 were awarded.
**Deadline:** November of each year.

### 1933 BIG 33 NURSING SCHOLARSHIPS

Big 33 Scholarship Foundation, Attn: Scholarship Committee
511 Bridge Street
P.O. Box 213
New Cumberland, PA 17070
Phone: (717) 774-3303; (877) PABIG-33; Fax: (717) 774-1749;
Email: info@big33.org
Web: www.big33.org/scholarships/default.ashx
**Summary:** To provide financial assistance to graduating high school seniors in Ohio and Pennsylvania who plan to study nursing in college.
**Eligibility:** Open to seniors graduating from public and accredited private high schools in Ohio and Pennsylvania who are planning to attend nursing school. Applications are available from high school guidance counselors. Selection is based on special talents, leadership, obstacles overcome, academic achievement (at least a 2.0 GPA), community service, unique endeavors, financial need, and a 1-page essay on why the applicant wants to become a nurse and deserves the scholarship.
**Financial data:** Stipends range from $1,000 to $1,600.
**Duration:** 1 year; nonrenewable.
**Number awarded:** Varies each year; recently, 6 of these scholarships were awarded: 2 at $1,600, 2 at $1,500, and 2 at $1,000.
**Deadline:** February of each year.

### 1934 BILL MARTIN MEMORIAL SCHOLARSHIP

Rocky Mountain Water Environment Association
c/o Ray Kemp

City of Fort Collins Water Reclamation
3036 Environmental Drive
Fort Collins, CO 80525
Phone: (970) 221-6900; Fax: (970) 221-6970; Email: rkemp@fcgov.com
Web: www.rmwea.org

**Summary:** To provide financial assistance to students in Colorado, New Mexico, and Wyoming, including members of the Rocky Mountain Water Environment Association (RMWEA) and their dependents, who are interested in studying a water environment field in college.

**Eligibility:** Open to 1) members of the RMWEA and their dependents who are enrolled at a 2- or 4-year college or university and working on a degree related to the water environment profession (e.g., biology, environmental science, engineering with a strong emphasis in wastewater treatment, water pollution control, environmental protection); and 2) high school seniors planning to enroll at a 2- or 4-year college or university to prepare for a career in the water environmental field. Along with their application, they must submit an essay of 200 to 300 words on their interest in the environment and how this interest influences their career goals. Selection is based on that essay (25%), relevance of the course of study to the water environment profession (35%), letters of recommendation (20%), and GPA (20%).

**Financial data:** The stipend is $1,000. Recipients are also entitled to a 1-year complimentary student or associate membership in the RMWEA.

**Duration:** 1 year.

**Number awarded:** 2 each year: 1 from each category of applicant.

**Deadline:** April of each year.

## 1935 BILLY CONSALO MEMORIAL AGRICULTURAL SCHOLARSHIP

Billy Consalo Memorial Agricultural Scholarship Fund
c/o Dottie Kargman, Trustee
1485 Catawba Avenue
Newfield, NJ 08344
Phone: (856) 697-0581; Fax: (856) 697-1594

**Summary:** To provide financial assistance to high school seniors in New Jersey who are interested in studying agriculture in college.

**Eligibility:** Open to seniors graduating from high schools in New Jersey who have a C average or higher. Applicants must be planning to attend a college, university, technical school, or other institute of higher education to study agriculture or a related field. They must submit a letter explaining why they are interested in agriculture, a transcript, 3 letters of recommendation, and information on their financial need.

**Financial data:** The stipend is $2,500.

**Duration:** 1 year.

**Number awarded:** 1 each year.

**Deadline:** April of each year.

## 1936 BIOQUIP PRODUCTS SCHOLARSHIP

Entomological Society of America, Attn: Entomological Foundation
9332 Annapolis Road, Suite 210
Lanham, MD 20706-3150
Phone: (301) 459-9082; Fax: (301) 459-9084; Email: melodie@entfdn.org
Web: www.entfdn.org/Undergrad.html

**Summary:** To provide financial assistance to undergraduates interested in studying entomology.

**Eligibility:** Open to undergraduate students majoring in entomology, biology, zoology, or a related science at a recognized university or college in the United States, Canada, or Mexico. They must have accumulated a minimum of 30 semester hours at the time the award is presented. Selection is based on academic record, demonstrated enthusiasm, interest, and achievement in biology. Preference is given to students with demonstrated financial need.

**Financial data:** The stipend is $2,000.

**Duration:** 1 year.

**Number awarded:** 1 each year.

**Deadline:** May of each year.

## 1937 B.J. HARROD SCHOLARSHIPS

Society of Women Engineers
230 East Ohio Street, Suite 400
Chicago, IL 60611-3265
Phone: (312) 596-5223; Fax: (312) 644-8557; Email: hq@swe.org
Web: www.societyofwomenengineers.org/scholarships

**Summary:** To provide financial assistance to women who will be entering college as freshmen and are interested in studying engineering or computer science.

**Eligibility:** Open to women who are entering college as freshmen with a GPA of 3.5 or higher. Applicants must be planning to enroll full time at an ABET-accredited 4-year college or university and major in computer science or engineering. Along with their application, they must submit a 1-page essay on why they want to be an engineer or computer scientist, how they believe they will make a difference as an engineer or computer scientist, and what influenced them to study engineering or computer science. Selection is based on merit.

**Financial data:** The stipend is $1,500.

**Duration:** 1 year.

**Number awarded:** 2 each year.

**Deadline:** May of each year.

## 1938 B.K. KRENZER REENTRY SCHOLARSHIP

Society of Women Engineers
230 East Ohio Street, Suite 400
Chicago, IL 60611-3265
Phone: (312) 596-5223; Fax: (312) 644-8557; Email: hq@swe.org
Web: www.societyofwomenengineers.org/scholarships

**Summary:** To provide financial assistance to women interested in returning to college or graduate school to study engineering or computer science.

**Eligibility:** Open to women who are planning to enroll at an ABET-accredited 4-year college or university. Applicants must have been out of the engineering workforce and school for at least 2 years and must be planning to return as an undergraduate or graduate student to major in computer science or engineering. Along with their application, they must submit a 1-page essay on why they want to be an engineer or computer scientist, how they believe they will make a difference as an engineer or computer scientist, and what influenced them to study engineering or computer science. Selection is based on merit. Preference is given to engineers who already have a degree and are planning to reenter the engineering workforce after a period of temporary retirement.

**Financial data:** The stipend is $2,000.

**Duration:** 1 year.

**Number awarded:** 1 each year.

**Deadline:** May of each year.

## 1939 BLOW MOLDING DIVISION MEMORIAL SCHOLARSHIPS

Society of Plastics Engineers, Attn: SPE Foundation
14 Fairfield Drive
Brookfield, CT 06804-0403
Phone: (203) 740-5447; Fax: (203) 775-1157; Email: foundation@4spe.org
Web: www.4spe.org/foundation/scholarships.php

**Summary:** To provide financial assistance to undergraduate student members of the Society of Plastics Engineers (SPE) who have a career interest in the plastics industry.

**Eligibility:** Open to full-time students completing the second year of a 4-year undergraduate program in plastics engineering. Applicants must 1) have a demonstrated or expressed interest in the plastics industry; 2) be a member of an SPE student chapter; 3) be in good academic standing at their school; and 4) be able to document financial need. Along with their application, they must submit 3 letters of recommendation; a high school and/or college transcript; and a 1- to 2-page statement telling why they are interested in the scholarship, their qualifications, and their educational and career goals in the plastics industry.

**Financial data:** The annual stipend of $4,000 is paid directly to the school.

**Duration:** 2 years.

**Number awarded:** 2 each year.

**Deadline:** January of each year.

## 1940 BLUE CROSS BLUE SHIELD OF WISCONSIN NURSING SCHOLARSHIPS

Wisconsin League for Nursing
2121 East Newport Avenue
Milwaukee, WI 53211-2952
Phone: (414) 332-6271
Web: www.cuw.edu/wln/scholarship.htm

**Summary:** To provide financial assistance to residents of Wisconsin attending a school of nursing in the state.

**Eligibility:** Open to residents of Wisconsin who working on an undergraduate degree at an accredited school of nursing in the state. Applicants must have completed at least half the credits needed for graduation. They may obtain applications only from their school of nursing; no applications are sent from the sponsor's office. Ethnic minority students are especially encouraged to apply. Selection is based on scholastic ability, professional abilities and/or community service, understanding of the nursing profession, goals upon graduation, and financial need.

**Financial data:** Stipends range from $500 to $1,000.

**Duration:** 1 year.

**Number awarded:** Varies each year. Recently, 5 of these scholarships were awarded.

**Deadline:** July of each year.

## 1941 BNSF SCHOLARSHIP PROGRAM

Hispanic College Fund, Attn: National Director
1717 Pennsylvania Avenue, N.W., Suite 460
Washington, D.C. 20006
Phone: (202) 296-5400; (800) 644-4223; Fax: (202) 296-3774;
Email: hcf-info@hispanicfund.org
Web: www.hispanicfund.org

**Summary:** To provide financial assistance to Hispanic American undergraduate students from designated states who are interested in preparing for a career in a business-related field.

**Eligibility:** Open to U.S. citizens of Hispanic background (at least one grandparent must be 100% Hispanic) who are entering their freshman, sophomore, junior, or senior year of college. Applicants must be residents of Arizona, California, Colorado, Illinois, Kansas, Missouri, New Mexico, or Texas. They must be working on a bachelor's degree in accounting, economics, engineering, finance, information systems, marketing, or a related major and have a cumulative GPA of 3.0 or higher. They must be applying to or enrolled in a college or university in the 50 states or Puerto Rico as a full-time student. Financial need is considered in the selection process.

**Financial data:** Stipends range from $500 to $5,000, depending on the need of the recipient, and average approximately $3,000. Funds are paid directly to the recipient's college or university to help cover tuition and fees.

**Duration:** 1 year; recipients may reapply.

**Number awarded:** Varies each year.

**Deadline:** April of each year.

## 1942 BOB GLAHN SCHOLARSHIP IN STATISTICAL METEOROLOGY

American Meteorological Society, Attn: Fellowship/Scholarship Program
45 Beacon Street
Boston, MA 02108-3693
Phone: (617) 227-2426, ext. 246; Fax: (617) 742-8718;
Email: scholar@ametsoc.org
Web: www.ametsoc.org/amsstudentinfo/scholfeldocs/scholfel.html

**Summary:** To provide financial assistance to undergraduates majoring in meteorology or an aspect of atmospheric sciences with an interest in statistical meteorology.

**Eligibility:** Open to full-time students entering their final year of undergraduate study and majoring in meteorology or an aspect of the atmospheric or related oceanic and hydrologic sciences. Applicants must intend to make atmospheric or related sciences their career, with preference for students who have demonstrated a strong interest in statistical meteorology. They must be U.S. citizens or permanent residents enrolled at a U.S. institution and have a cumulative GPA of 3.25 or higher. Along with their application, they must submit 200-word essays on 1) their most important achievements that qualify them for this scholarship, and 2) their career goals in the atmospheric or related oceanic or hydrologic fields. Selection is based on academic excellence and achievement; financial need is not considered. The sponsor specifically encourages applications from women, minorities, and students with disabilities who are traditionally underrepresented in the atmospheric and related oceanic sciences.

**Financial data:** The stipend is $2,500 per year.

**Duration:** 1 year.

**Number awarded:** 1 each year.

**Deadline:** February of each year.

## 1943 BOEING CAREER ENHANCEMENT SCHOLARSHIP

Women in Aviation, International, Attn: Scholarships
101 Corsair Drive, Suite 101
P.O. Box 11287
Daytona Beach, FL 32120-1287
Phone: (386) 226-7996; Fax: (386) 226-7998; Email: scholarships@wai.org
Web: www.wai.org/education/scholarships.cfm

**Summary:** To provide financial assistance to members of Women in Aviation,

International (WAI) who are active in aerospace and need financial support to advance their career.

**Eligibility:** Open to WAI members who wish to advance their career in the aerospace industry in the fields of engineering, technology development, or management. Applicants may be 1) full-time or part-time employees working in the aerospace industry or a related field, or 2) students working on an aviation-related degree who are at least juniors and have a GPA of 2.5 or higher. They must submit an essay that addresses their career aspirations and goals, in addition to an application form, 3 letters of recommendation, a resume, copies of all aviation and medical certificates, and the last 3 pages of their pilot logbook, if applicable. Selection is based on achievements, attitude toward self and others, commitment to success, dedication to career, financial need, motivation, reliability, responsibility, and teamwork.

**Financial data:** A stipend is awarded (amount not specified).

**Duration:** 1 year.

**Number awarded:** 1 each year.

**Deadline:** December of each year.

## 1944 BRIAN SWEENEY MEMORIAL AWARD

Hanscom Officers' Wives' Club, Attn: Scholarship Chair
P.O. Box 557
Bedford, MA 01730
Phone: (781) 275-1251; Email: scholarship@hanscomwd.org
Web: www.hanscomwc.org

**Summary:** To provide financial assistance to children of military personnel and veterans in New England who are interested in studying aviation in college.

**Eligibility:** Open to college-bound high school seniors living in New England who are dependents of active-duty, retired, or deceased military members of any branch of service. Also eligible are dependents of military recruiters working in the New York area and students living elsewhere but whose military sponsor is stationed at Hanscom Air Force Base. Applicants must demonstrate qualities of responsibility, leadership, scholastics, citizenship, and diversity of interest. They must have a valid military identification card and be planning to work on a college degree in a field related to aviation (including civil, aeronautical, and environmental engineering; maintenance; management; aviation safety and security; and meteorology). Along with their application, they must submit a 2-page essay on their educational goals, how their educational experience will help prepare them to pursue future goals, and how they intend to apply their education to better their community.

**Financial data:** The stipend is $2,000.

**Duration:** 1 year; nonrenewable.

**Number awarded:** 1 each year.

**Deadline:** March of each year.

## 1945 BROWN AND CALDWELL MINORITY SCHOLARSHIP

Brown and Caldwell, Attn: Scholarship Program
201 North Civic Drive, Suite 115
P.O. Box 8045
Walnut Creek, CA 94596
Phone: (925) 937-9010; Fax: (925) 937-9026;
Email: scholarships@brwncald.com
Web: www.brownandcaldwell.com

**Summary:** To provide financial assistance to minority students working on an undergraduate degree in an environmental or engineering field.

**Eligibility:** Open to members of minority groups (African Americans, Hispanics, Asians, Pacific Islanders, Native Americans, and Alaska Natives) who are full-time students in their junior year at an accredited 4-year college or university. Applicants must have a GPA of 3.0 or higher with a declared major in civil, chemical, or environmental engineering or an environmental science (e.g., biology, ecology, geology, hydrogeology, industrial hygiene, toxicology). Along with their application, they must submit an essay (up to 250 words) on why they chose to major in an environmental discipline. They must be U.S. citizens or permanent resident and available to participate in a summer internship at a Brown and Caldwell office. Financial need is not considered in the selection process.

**Financial data:** The stipend is $3,000.

**Duration:** 1 year.

**Number awarded:** 1 each year.

**Deadline:** February of each year.

## 1946 BUD GLOVER MEMORIAL SCHOLARSHIP

Aircraft Electronics Association, Attn: AEA Educational Foundation
4217 South Hocker Drive

Independence, MO 64055-4723
Phone: (816) 373-6565; Fax: (816) 478-3100; Email: info@aea.net
Web: www.aea.net

**Summary:** To provide financial assistance to students preparing for a career in avionics or aircraft repair.

**Eligibility:** Open to high school seniors and currently-enrolled college students who are attending (or planning to attend) an accredited postsecondary institution in an avionics or aircraft repair program. Applicants must submit an official transcript (cumulative GPA of 2.5 or higher), a statement about their career plans, a description of their involvement in school and community activities, and a 300-word essay on how the job requirements of aviation technicians will change with advancements in technology. Selection is based on merit.

**Financial data:** The stipend is $1,000.

**Duration:** 1 year.

**Number awarded:** 1 each year.

**Deadline:** February of each year.

---

**1947 BUDWEISER CONSERVATION SCHOLARSHIP**

National Fish and Wildlife Foundation
1120 Connecticut Avenue, N.W., Suite 900
Washington, DC 20036
Phone: (202) 857-0166; Fax: (202) 857-0162; Email: tom.kelsch@nfwf.org
Web: www.nfwf.org/programs/budscholarship.htm

**Summary:** To provide financial assistance to undergraduate and graduate students who are interested in studying or conducting research related to the field of conservation.

**Eligibility:** Open to U.S. citizens enrolled in an accredited institution of higher education in the United States and working on a graduate or undergraduate degree (sophomores and juniors in the current academic year only) in environmental science, natural resource management, biology, public policy, geography, political science, or a related discipline. Applicants must submit transcripts, 3 letters of recommendation, and an essay (up to 1,500 words) describing their academic objectives and focusing on a specific issue affecting the conservation of fish, wildlife, or plant species in the United States and the research or study they propose to address the issue. Selection is based on the merits of the proposed research or study, its significance to the field of conservation, its feasibility and overall quality, the innovativeness of the proposed research or study, the student's academic achievements, and their commitment to leadership in the conservation field.

**Financial data:** Stipends range up to $10,000. Funds must be used to cover expenses related to the recipients' studies, including tuition, fees, books, room, and board. Payments may supplement but not duplicate benefits from their educational institution or from other foundations, institutions, or organizations. The combined benefits from all sources may not exceed the recipient's educational expenses.

**Duration:** 1 year.

**Number awarded:** At least 10 each year.

**Deadline:** January of each year.

---

**1948 BUENA M. CHESSHIR MEMORIAL WOMEN'S EDUCATIONAL SCHOLARSHIP**

**Summary:** To provide financial assistance to mature women in Virginia who are interested in upgrading their skills or education at a college, law school, or medical school in the state.
*See Listing #143.*

---

**1949 BUFFALO CHAPTER NAWIC SCHOLARSHIP**

**Summary:** To provide financial assistance to residents of New York attending college in the state to prepare for a career in construction.
*See Listing #1303.*

---

**1950 BUILDING INDUSTRY SCHOLARSHIP PROGRAM**

**Summary:** To provide financial assistance to high school seniors in Minnesota who are interested in preparing for a career in a field related to construction.
*See Listing #1304.*

---

**1951 BUREAU OF LAND MANAGEMENT AWARD**

Hispanic Association of Colleges and Universities
Attn: National Scholarship Program
One Dupont Circle, N.W. Suite 605

Washington, DC 20036
Phone: (202) 467-0893; Fax: (202) 496-9177; TTY: (800) 855-2880;
Email: scholarships@hacu.net
Web: scholarships.hacu.net/applications/applicants

**Summary:** To provide financial assistance to undergraduate students who are majoring in fields related to natural resources at institutions that are members of the Hispanic Association of Colleges and Universities (HACU).

**Eligibility:** Open to full-time undergraduate students at HACU member and partner colleges and universities who are majoring in natural resource management or a related field. Applicants must submit an essay of 200 to 250 words that describes their academic and/or career goals, where they expect to be and what they expect to be doing 10 years from now, and what skills they can bring to an employer. They must be able to demonstrate financial need and a GPA of 3.2 or higher.

**Financial data:** The stipend is $3,000 per year.

**Duration:** 1 year; nonrenewable.

**Number awarded:** 1 or more each year.

**Deadline:** May of each year.

---

**1952 BURLINGTON NORTHERN SANTA FE FOUNDATION SCHOLARSHIP**

American Indian Science and Engineering Society
Attn: Scholarship Coordinator
2305 Renard, S.E., Suite 200
P.O. Box 9828
Albuquerque, NM 87119-9828
Phone: (505) 765-1052, ext. 106; Fax: (505) 765-5608; Email: shirley@aises.org
Web: www.aises.org/highered/scholarships

**Summary:** To provide financial assistance for college to outstanding American Indian high school seniors from designated states who are members of American Indian Science and Engineering Society (AISES).

**Eligibility:** Open to AISES members who are high school seniors planning to attend an accredited 4-year college or university and major in business, engineering, mathematics, medicine, natural resources, physical science, science, or technology. Applicants must submit 1) proof of tribal enrollment or a Certificate of Degree of Indian Blood; 2) evidence of residence in the service area of the Burlington Northern and Santa Fe Corporation (Arizona, California, Colorado, Kansas, Minnesota, Montana, New Mexico, North Dakota, Oklahoma, Oregon, South Dakota, and Washington); 3) a statement of financial need; 4) a 500-word essay on why they chose their particular field of study, their career aspirations, an evaluation of past scholastic performance, obstacles faced as a student, and involvement in and commitment to tribal community life; and 5) high school transcripts showing a GPA of 2.0 or higher.

**Financial data:** The stipend is $2,500 per year.

**Duration:** 4 years or until completion of a baccalaureate degree, whichever occurs first.

**Number awarded:** 5 new awards are made each year.

**Deadline:** April of each year.

---

**1953 BURTON L. SPILLER CHAPTER SCHOLARSHIP**

Ruffed Grouse Society-Burton L. Spiller Chapter
c/o Carole Dyer
1058 River Road
Bowdoinham, ME 04008
Email: rcdyer@gwi.net

**Summary:** To provide financial assistance to high school seniors in Maine interested in continuing their education in the field of wildlife conservation.

**Eligibility:** Open to seniors graduating from high schools in Maine who are interested in attending college to prepare for a career in wildlife conservation. That includes wildlife law enforcement, forestry, or biology management. Applicants must submit a brief resume that includes their past experiences and plans for future endeavors.

**Financial data:** Stipends range from $1,000 to $2,000 per year.

**Duration:** 1 year.

**Number awarded:** 1 or 2 each year.

**Deadline:** March of each year.

---

**1954 C. BERTRAND AND MARIAN OTHMER SCULTZ COLLEGIATE SCHOLARSHIP**

Nebraska Academy of Sciences
c/o University of Nebraska

302 Morrill Hall
14th and U Streets
P.O. Box 880339
Lincoln, NE 68588-0339
Phone: (402) 472-2644; Email: nebacad@unl.edu
Web: www.neacadsci.org/Info/coll_scholarship.htm
**Summary:** To provide financial assistance to upper-division students majoring in science at colleges and universities in Nebraska.
**Eligibility:** Open to student entering their junior or senior year at 4-year colleges and universities in Nebraska. Applicants must have a declared major in a natural science discipline (chemistry, physics, biology, or geology). They must be preparing for a career in a science-related industry, science teaching, or scientific research. A member of the Nebraska Academy of Sciences must provide a letter of nomination.
**Financial data:** The stipend is $3,000 per year.
**Duration:** 1 year; may be renewed 1 additional year.
**Number awarded:** 1 each year.
**Deadline:** January of each year.

## 1955 C I HOST TECHNOLOGY SCHOLARSHIP

C I Host
1901 Central Drive
Bedford, TX 76021
Phone: (817) 868-9931; (888) 565-1115; Fax: (817) 868-7203;
Email: pr@cihost.com
Web: www.cihost.com
**Summary:** To provide financial assistance to high school students planning to attend college and study a technology-based field.
**Eligibility:** Open to students currently enrolled as juniors or seniors in high school. Applicants must be planning to attend an accredited 2-year or 4-year college or university to study technology or major in a technology-based field as a full-time student. Along with their application, they must submit a written proposal for a new and innovative online service or product; the proposal must include an outline of the idea, a complete technical description and/or drawing for execution of the idea, and a business to sell the idea.
**Financial data:** The stipend is $2,500.
**Duration:** 1 year; nonrenewable.
**Number awarded:** 1 each year.

## 1956 CA-ASA SCHOLARSHIPS

American Society of Agronomy-California Chapter
c/o Casey Walsh Cady, Scholarship Committee
California Department of Food and Agriculture
Office of Agriculture and Environmental Stewardship
1220 N Street, Room A-468
Sacramento, CA 95814
Phone: (916) 651-9447; Fax: (916) 657-5017; Email: ccady@cdfa.ca.gov
Web: calasa.ucdavis.edu/scholarship/scholarship.htm
**Summary:** To provide financial assistance to California residents enrolled in a program in plant or soil management at designated universities in the state.
**Eligibility:** Open to California residents enrolled full time as sophomores or higher at the following schools: California State University at Chico or Fresno, California State Polytechnic University at Pomona, California Polytechnic State University at San Luis Obispo, or the University of California at Berkeley, Davis, Riverside, or Santa Cruz. Applicants must be working on a degree in plant or soil management with a GPA of 2.5 or higher. Along with their application, they must submit a 300-word essay on the role of science in agricultural policy formation in California. Selection is based on the essay (50%), leadership and extracurricular activities (20%), letters of recommendation (20%), and work or business experience in agriculture (10%).
**Financial data:** The stipend is $1,000.
**Duration:** 1 year.
**Number awarded:** 1 or more each year.
**Deadline:** December of each year.

## 1957 CAB/NJAA SCHOLARSHIP

National Junior Angus Association, Attn: Director Junior Activities
3201 Frederick Boulevard
St. Joseph, MO 64506
Phone: (816) 383-5100; Fax: (816) 233-9703; Email: jfisher@angus.org
Web: www.njaa.info/awards.html

**Summary:** To provide financial assistance to students who have been members of the National Junior Angus Association (NJAA) and are interested in taking courses in selected beef-related subjects in college.
**Eligibility:** Open to applicants who have been a member of the NJAA in the past and who are presently a junior, regular, or life member of the American Angus Association. They must be entering their sophomore, junior, or senior year of college. The primary course work/declared major must be in animal science, meat science, food science, agricultural communications, or a related field. Selection is based on involvement in Angus associations, professional organizations, other agriculture-related groups, school organizations, and church and civic groups; experience in livestock production, marketing, and judging; experience in meats evaluation and processing; a statement of ambitions and goals; and transcripts.
**Financial data:** The stipend is $1,000.
**Duration:** 1 year; recipients may reapply.
**Number awarded:** 1 each year.
**Deadline:** May of each year.

## 1958 CADBURY ADAMS COMMUNITY OUTREACH SCHOLARSHIPS

American Dental Hygienists' Association, Attn: Institute for Oral Health
444 North Michigan Avenue, Suite 3400
Chicago, IL 60611
Phone: (312) 440-8918; (800) 735-4916; Fax: (312) 440-8929;
Email: institute@adha.net
Web: www.adha.org/institute/Scholarship/index.htm
**Summary:** To provide financial assistance to undergraduate students who are preparing for careers in dental hygiene and have been active in community service activities.
**Eligibility:** Open to full-time undergraduate students who are active members of the Student American Dental Hygienists' Association (SADHA) or the American Dental Hygienists' Association (ADHA). Applicants must have a GPA of 3.0 or higher, be able to document financial need of at least $1,500, and have completed at least 1 year in an accredited dental hygiene program in the United States. Along with their application, they must submit 2 essays: 1) a statement that covers their long-term career goals, their intended contribution to the dental hygiene profession, their professional interests, and the manner in which their degree will enhance their professional capacity; and 2) an essay on their commitment to improving oral health through community service and specific examples of community service projects in which they have participated.
**Financial data:** Stipends range from $1,000 to $2,000.
**Duration:** 1 year.
**Number awarded:** 10 each year.
**Deadline:** April of each year.

## 1959 CALCOT-SEITZ FOUNDATION SCHOLARSHIPS

Calcot-Seitz Foundation
1900 East Brundage Lane
P.O. Box 259
Bakersfield, CA 93302
Phone: (661) 327-5961; Fax: (661) 861-9870; Email: staff@calcot.com
Web: www.calcot.com
**Summary:** To provide financial assistance to students in Arizona and California who are interested in majoring in an agricultural-related field.
**Eligibility:** Open to students from cotton-growing areas of California and Arizona who are working on an agricultural-related degree at a 4-year college or university. Applicants may be high school seniors or currently-enrolled college students who are continuing their studies. Selection is based on scholastic aptitude and performance, leadership potential, demonstrated capability, financial need, and a personal interview.
**Financial data:** Stipends are generally $2,000 or $1,000 per year.
**Duration:** 3 years.
**Number awarded:** Varies each year. Recently, 19 of these scholarships were awarded: 17 at $2,000 and 2 at $1,000.

## 1960 CALIFORNIA ASSOCIATION OF PEST CONTROL ADVISERS SCHOLARSHIPS

California Association of Pest Control Advisers
Attn: Stanley W. Strew Educational Fund, Inc.
1143 North Market Boulevard, Suite 7
Sacramento, CA 95834

Phone: (916) 928-1625; Fax: (916) 928-0705; Email: capca@capca.com
Web: www.capca.com/scholarships.asp

**Summary:** To provide financial assistance to high school seniors, high school graduates, and currently-enrolled college students in California who are majoring in agriculture or horticulture and planning to prepare for a career in pest management.

**Eligibility:** Open to California students who are currently attending, entering, or returning to college. Applicants must be enrolled or planning to enroll in an agricultural or horticultural program and planning to prepare for a career in pest management. They must have a GPA of 2.5 or higher. Selection is based on academic record (25%), extracurricular activities (15%), pest management experience (20%), professional and career goals (20%), financial need (10%), and class standing (10%). Students working on a bachelor's degree are given priority.

**Financial data:** The stipend is $2,000.

**Duration:** 1 year.

**Number awarded:** 2 each year.

**Deadline:** May of each year.

### 1961 CALIFORNIA LEAGUE FOR NURSING SCHOLARSHIPS

California League for Nursing
Attn: Sheri Shields, Chair, Scholarship Committee
Santa Barbara City College
721 Cliff Drive
Santa Barbara, CA 93109-2394
Phone: (805) 965-0581, ext. 2373; Email: shiledss@sbcc.net
Web: www.californialeaguefornursing.com

**Summary:** To provide financial assistance to students in California who are working on an undergraduate or graduate degree in nursing.

**Eligibility:** Open to students enrolled in an associate's, bachelor's, master's, or doctoral degree nursing program in California. Applicants must have a GPA of 3.0 or higher and have completed at least 15 semester units or 23 quarter units of nursing courses. Along with their application, they must submit a 2-page essay documenting financial need, leadership activities, and other contributing personal qualities.

**Financial data:** The stipend is $1,000 for bachelor's, master's, and doctoral degree students or $500 for associate degree students.

**Duration:** 1 year.

**Number awarded:** Varies each year. Recently, 17 of these scholarships were available: 6 for associate degree students, 4 for bachelor's degree students, 5 for master's degree students, and 2 for doctoral degree students.

**Deadline:** April of each year.

### 1962 CALIFORNIA LEGION AUXILIARY PAST PRESIDENTS' PARLEY NURSING SCHOLARSHIPS

American Legion Auxiliary, Attn: Department of California
Veterans War Memorial Building
401 Van Ness Avenue, Room 113
San Francisco, CA 94102-4586
Phone: (415) 861-5092; Fax: (415) 861-8365;
Email: calegionaux@calegionaux.org
Web: www.calegionaux.org/scholarships.html

**Summary:** To provide financial assistance to California residents who are veterans or members of their families and interested in studying nursing.

**Eligibility:** Open to California residents who are 1) veterans of World War I, World War II, Korea, Vietnam, Grenada/Lebanon, Panama, or Desert Shield/Desert Storm, or 2) the spouse, widow(er), or child of such a veteran. Applicants must be entering or continuing students of nursing at an accredited institution of higher learning in California. Financial need is considered in the selection process.

**Financial data:** Stipends range from $500 to $1,500.

**Duration:** 1 year.

**Number awarded:** Varies each year.

**Deadline:** April of each year.

### 1963 CALIFORNIA STATE FAIR AGRICULTURAL COLLEGE SCHOLARSHIPS FOR HIGH SCHOOL STUDENTS

California State Fair, Attn: Friends of the Fair Scholarship Program
1600 Exposition Boulevard
P.O. Box 15649
Sacramento, CA 95852
Phone: (916) 274-5969; Email: wross@calexpo.com

Web: www.bigfun.org

**Summary:** To provide financial assistance to high school students in California who plan to attend a 4-year college or university in the state to study agriculture.

**Eligibility:** Open to juniors and seniors currently enrolled at high schools in California. Applicants must be planning to attend a 4-year college or university in the state to major in agriculture. They must have a GPA of 3.0 or higher. Along with their application, they must submit a 2-page essay on why they are pursuing their desired career and life goals. Selection is based on personal commitment, goals established for their chosen field, leadership potential, and civic accomplishments.

**Financial data:** Stipends are $1,500 or $500.

**Duration:** 1 year.

**Number awarded:** 2 each year: 1 at $1,500 and 1 at $500.

**Deadline:** March of each year.

### 1964 CALIFORNIA STATE FAIR AGRICULTURAL COMMUNITY COLLEGE SCHOLARSHIPS FOR HIGH SCHOOL STUDENTS

California State Fair, Attn: Friends of the Fair Scholarship Program
1600 Exposition Boulevard
P.O. Box 15649
Sacramento, CA 95852
Phone: (916) 274-5969; Email: wross@calexpo.com
Web: www.bigfun.org

**Summary:** To provide financial assistance to high school students in California who plan to attend a community college in the state to study agriculture.

**Eligibility:** Open to juniors and seniors currently enrolled at high schools in California. Applicants must be planning to attend a community college in the state to major in agriculture. They must have a GPA of 3.0 or higher. Along with their application, they must submit a 2-page essay on why they are pursuing their desired career and life goals. Selection is based on personal commitment, goals established for their chosen

**Financial data:** Stipends are $1,000 or $500.

**Duration:** 1 year.

**Number awarded:** 2 each year: 1 at $1,000 and 1 at $500.

**Deadline:** March of each year.

### 1965 CALIFORNIA STATE FAIR COMMUNITY COLLEGE SCHOLARSHIPS IN AGRICULTURE

California State Fair, Attn: Friends of the Fair Scholarship Program
1600 Exposition Boulevard
P.O. Box 15649
Sacramento, CA 95852
Phone: (916) 274-5969; Email: wross@calexpo.com
Web: www.bigfun.org

**Summary:** To provide financial assistance to community college students in California who are studying agriculture.

**Eligibility:** Open to students currently enrolled at community colleges in California. Applicants must have completed at least 12 units of undergraduate course work in agricultural classes. They must have a GPA of 3.0 or higher. Along with their application, they must submit a 2-page essay on why they are pursuing their desired career and life goals. Selection is based on personal commitment, goals established for their chosen field, leadership potential, and civic accomplishments.

**Financial data:** Stipends are $1,000 or $500.

**Duration:** 1 year.

**Number awarded:** 2 each year: 1 at $1,000 and 1 at $500.

**Deadline:** March of each year.

### 1966 CALIFORNIA STATE FAIR UNDERGRADUATE AND GRADUATE SCHOLARSHIPS IN AGRICULTURE

California State Fair, Attn: Friends of the Fair Scholarship Program
1600 Exposition Boulevard
P.O. Box 15649
Sacramento, CA 95852
Phone: (916) 274-5969; Email: wross@calexpo.com
Web: www.bigfun.org

**Summary:** To provide financial assistance to undergraduate and graduate students in California who are studying agriculture.

**Eligibility:** Open to undergraduate and graduate students currently enrolled at 4-year colleges and university in California. Applicants must have completed at least 12 units of course work in agricultural classes. They must have a GPA of 3.0 or higher. Along with their application, they must submit a 2-page essay on why they are pursuing their desired career and life goals. Selection is based on personal commitment, goals established for their chosen field, leadership potential, and civic accomplishments.

**Financial data:** Stipends are $1,500 or $500.

**Duration:** 1 year.

**Number awarded:** 2 each year: 1 at $1,500 and 1 at $500.

**Deadline:** March of each year.

### 1967 CALIFORNIA STATE FAIR VITICULTURE/ENOLOGY SCHOLARSHIPS

California State Fair, Attn: Friends of the Fair Scholarship Program

1600 Exposition Boulevard

P.O. Box 15649

Sacramento, CA 95852

Phone: (916) 274-5969; Email: wross@calexpo.com

Web: www.bigfun.org

**Summary:** To provide financial assistance to residents of California who are working on an undergraduate or graduate degree in viticulture or enology.

**Eligibility:** Open to residents of California currently working on an undergraduate or graduate degree at a college or university in the state. Applicants must be studying or majoring in viticulture or enology. They must have a GPA of 3.0 or higher. Along with their application, they must submit a 2-page essay on why they are pursuing their desired career and life goals. Selection is based on personal commitment, goals established for their chosen field, leadership potential, and civic accomplishments.

**Financial data:** Stipends are $1,500 or $500.

**Duration:** 1 year.

**Number awarded:** 2 each year: 1 at $1,500 and 1 at $500.

**Deadline:** March of each year.

### 1968 CAMPUSRN/AACN NURSING SCHOLARSHIP FUND

American Association of Colleges of Nursing

One Dupont Circle, N.W., Suite 530

Washington, DC 20036

Phone: (202) 463-6930; Fax: (202) 785-8320;

Email: scholarship@campuscareercenter.com

Web: aacn.campusrn.com/scholarships/scholarship_rn.asp

**Summary:** To provide financial assistance to students at institutions that are members of the American Association of Colleges of Nursing (AACN).

**Eligibility:** Open to students working on a baccalaureate, master's, or doctoral degree at an AACN member school. Preference is given to applicants who are 1) enrolled in a master's or doctoral program to prepare for a nursing faculty career; 2) completing an R.N. to baccalaureate (B.S.N.) program; or 3) enrolled in an accelerated baccalaureate or master's degree nursing program. Applicants must have a GPA of 3.25 or higher. Along with their application, they must submit an essay of 200 to 250 words on their goals and aspirations as related to their education, career, and future plans. They must also register and submit their resume to CampusRN.com.

**Financial data:** The stipend is $2,500.

**Duration:** 1 year.

**Number awarded:** 6 each year.

**Deadline:** February, April, June, August, October, or December of each year.

### 1969 CANERS COLLEGE SCHOLARSHIPS

California Association of Nurseries and Garden Center

Attn: California Association of Nurserymen Endowment for Research and Scholarship

3947 Lennane Drive, Suite 150

Sacramento, CA 95834

Phone: (916) 928-3900; (800) 748-6214; Fax: (916) 567-0505;

Email: association@cangc.org

Web: www.cangc.org/endowment/colegeScholarships.asp

**Summary:** To provide financial assistance to college students in California who are majoring in ornamental horticulture or related fields.

**Eligibility:** Open to students at 2-year and 4-year colleges and universities in California who are currently enrolled in at least 6 credits and are majoring or planning to major in a field related to horticulture. Applicants must submit essays on their educational objectives and their occupational goals as they relate to the nursery industry or horticulture. Selection is based on those essays, transcripts, high school and college activities related to horticulture, work experience, community activities related to horticulture, and 2 letters of reference. Financial need is not considered.

**Financial data:** Stipends range from $150 to $6,400.

**Duration:** 1 year.

**Number awarded:** The association awards more than 60 scholarships each year.

**Deadline:** March of each year.

### 1970 CANERS HIGH SCHOOL SCHOLARSHIPS

California Association of Nurseries and Garden Center

Attn: California Association of Nurserymen Endowment for Research and Scholarship

3947 Lennane Drive, Suite 150

Sacramento, CA 95834

Phone: (916) 928-3900; (800) 748-6214; Fax: (916) 567-0505;

Email: association@cangc.org

Web: www.cangc.org/endowment/HSScholarships.asp

**Summary:** To provide financial assistance to high school seniors in California who are planning to major in horticulture in college.

**Eligibility:** Open to graduating high school seniors in California who are planning to major in a field related to horticulture. Applicants must submit essays on their educational objectives and their occupational goals as they relate to the nursery industry or horticulture. Selection is based on those essays, transcripts, leadership activities and awards in FFA/ROP/4-H, high school supervised occupational experience or industry work experience, community activities related to horticulture, other activities and offices held in high school, and 2 letters of reference. Financial need is not considered.

**Financial data:** Stipends range from $150 to $6,400.

**Duration:** 1 year.

**Number awarded:** The association awards more than 60 scholarships each year.

**Deadline:** March of each year.

### 1971 CAREER ADVANCEMENT SCHOLARSHIPS

**Summary:** To provide financial assistance for college or graduate school to mature women who are employed or seeking employment in selected fields.

*See Listing #1311.*

### 1972 CAREERS IN AGRICULTURE SCHOLARSHIP PROGRAM

Agriliance, LLC, Attn: Careers in Agriculture, MS 408

P.O. Box 64089

St. Paul, MN 55164-0089

Phone: (651) 451-5126; (800) 232-3639, ext. 4584

Web: www.agriliance.com/4Careers/scholarships.asp

**Summary:** To provide financial assistance to high school seniors interested in studying agriculture in college.

**Eligibility:** Open to high school seniors planning to work on a 2-year or 4-year degree in livestock production, agronomy, or a closely-related field. Applicants must submit essays explaining why 1) they are interested in agriculture as a career, and 2) cooperatives are important to agriculture. Selection is based on academic achievement, leadership in agriculture, perceived ability to contribute to agriculture in the future, and financial need.

**Financial data:** The stipend is $1,000.

**Duration:** 1 year; nonrenewable.

**Number awarded:** 20 each year.

**Deadline:** February of each year.

### 1973 CAREERS THAT WORK! SCHOLARSHIP

Washington Federation of Private Career Schools & Colleges

10426 180th Court N.E.

Redmond, WA 87052

Phone: (425) 376-0369; Fax: (425) 881-1580;

Email: exec@washingtonschools.org

Web: www.washingtonschools.org

**Summary:** To provide financial assistance to high school seniors in Washington who are interested in attending a career college and majoring in selected fields.

**Eligibility:** Open to high school seniors in Washington who are interested in attending 1 of the 26 career colleges in the state, to prepare for a career in such fields as computer or information technology, health care, cosmetology, massage, business, criminal justice, or health occupations. The sponsor provides 3 scholarships to each high school in Washington. Recipients are then selected by the scholarship directors or counselors at their high school.

**Financial data:** The stipend is a $1,000 award certificate to be used to pay for tuition at a career college in Washington.

**Duration:** 1 year.

**Number awarded:** 3 each year at each high school in Washington.

## 1974 CAROL BAUHS BENSON MEMORIAL SCHOLARSHIP

American Dental Hygienists' Association, Attn: Institute for Oral Health
444 North Michigan Avenue, Suite 3400
Chicago, IL 60611
Phone: (312) 440-8918; (800) 735-4916; Fax: (312) 440-8929;
Email: institute@adha.net
Web: www.adha.org/institute/Scholarship/index.htm
**Summary:** To provide financial assistance to undergraduate students in selected states who are preparing for careers in dental hygiene.
**Eligibility:** Open to full-time undergraduate students who are active members of the Student American Dental Hygienists' Association (SADHA) or the American Dental Hygienists' Association (ADHA). Applicants must have a GPA of 3.0 or higher, be able to document financial need of at least $1,500, and have completed at least one year in an accredited dental hygiene program in Minnesota, North Dakota, South Dakota, or Wisconsin. Along with their application, they must submit a statement that covers their long-term career goals, their intended contribution to the dental hygiene profession, their professional interests, and the manner in which their degree will enhance their professional capacity.
**Financial data:** Stipends range from $1,000 to $2,000.
**Duration:** 1 year.
**Number awarded:** 1 each year.
**Deadline:** April of each year.

## 1975 CAROLINA STEEL SCHOLARSHIP

American Institute of Steel Construction
Attn: Director of University Relations
One East Wacker Drive, Suite 3100
Chicago, IL 60601-2001
Phone: (312) 670-5408; Fax: (312) 670-5403; Email: rosenberg@aisc.com
Web: www.aisc.org
**Summary:** To provide financial assistance to undergraduate engineering students from designated states who are interested in the structural field, especially structural steel.
**Eligibility:** Open to full-time civil or architectural engineering students entering their fourth year at universities in Alabama, North Carolina, South Carolina, and Virginia. Preference is given to students who have selected a concentration in the structural field, with particular emphasis on structural steel. Along with their application, they must submit a 2-page essay on their overall career objective and an original sample structural steel analysis/design solution, with calculations. Selection is based on those submissions, academic performance, and a faculty recommendation. U.S. citizenship is required.
**Financial data:** The stipend is $3,000.
**Duration:** 1 year.
**Number awarded:** 1 each year.
**Deadline:** April of each year.

## 1976 CAROLINA TRIANGLE SECTION SCHOLARSHIP

American Society of Highway Engineers-Carolina Triangle Section
Attn: Scholarship Committee
5800 Farington Place, Suite 105
Raleigh, NC 27609
Phone: (919) 878-9560; Email: gsboyles@stantec.com
Web: www.carolinatriangle.org/scholar.htm
**Summary:** To provide financial assistance to currently-enrolled college students from North Carolina who are majoring in a transportation-related field.
**Eligibility:** Open to residents of North Carolina who are U.S. citizens currently enrolled full time in a 4-year college or university in any state (must have completed at least one semester) working on a bachelor's degree in a transportation-related field, preferably civil engineering. A copy of the applicant's college transcript is required; high school transcripts, SAT scores, and resumes may also be submitted but are not required. Along with their application, students must submit a paragraph on their career goals, including a description of the value they place on civil engineering or other transportation-related field. Selection is based on that essay (25 points), academic performance (40 points), activities, honors, work experience, leadership, and distinguishing qualifications (25 points), and enrollment in a civil engineering curriculum (10 points). A personal interview may be requested. Financial need is not considered.
**Financial data:** The stipend is $1,000.
**Duration:** 1 year; nonrenewable.
**Number awarded:** 1 each year.
**Deadline:** March of each year.

## 1977 CAROLINAS AGC SCHOLARSHIPS

Carolinas AGC
Attn: Carolinas Construction Education and Research Foundation
1100 Euclid Avenue
P.O. Box 30277
Charlotte, NC 28230-0277
Phone: (704) 372-1450, ext. 5238; Fax: (704) 332-5032;
Email: sgennett@carolinasagc.org
Web: www.cagc.org/edu_training/careers_scholarships.cfm
**Summary:** To provide financial assistance to undergraduate students working on a degree in construction in North or South Carolina.
**Eligibility:** Open to students attending 1 of the 5 major universities in North or South Carolina with an accredited construction department.
**Financial data:** The stipend is $2,500.
**Duration:** 1 year.
**Number awarded:** 5 each year: 1 at each participating university.

## 1978 CARPE DIEM SCHOLARSHIPS

**Summary:** To provide financial assistance to entering or continuing undergraduate students majoring or planning to major in specified fields.
*See Listing #1313.*

## 1979 CATERPILLAR SCHOLARS AWARD

Society of Manufacturing Engineers, Attn: SME Education Foundation
One SME Drive
P.O. Box 930
Dearborn, MI 48121-0930
Phone: (313) 425-3304; (800) 733-4763, ext. 3304; Fax: (313) 425-3411;
Email: foundation@sme.org
Web: www.sme.org
**Summary:** To provide financial assistance to undergraduates enrolled in a degree program in manufacturing engineering or manufacturing engineering technology.
**Eligibility:** Open to full-time students attending a degree-granting institution in North America and preparing for a career in manufacturing engineering. They must have completed at least 30 units in a manufacturing engineering or manufacturing engineering technology curriculum with a minimum GPA of 3.0. Minority applicants may apply as incoming freshmen. Need is not considered in awarding scholarships (unless 2 or more applicants have equal qualifications).
**Financial data:** The stipend is $2,000.
**Duration:** 1 year; may be renewed.
**Number awarded:** 5 each year.
**Deadline:** January of each year.

## 1980 CATERPILLAR SCHOLARSHIPS

Society of Women Engineers
230 East Ohio Street, Suite 400
Chicago, IL 60611-3265
Phone: (312) 596-5223; Fax: (312) 644-8557; Email: hq@swe.org
Web: www.societyofwomenengineers.org/scholarships
**Summary:** To provide financial assistance to women from selected states interested in attending college or graduate school to study engineering or computer science.
**Eligibility:** Open to women who are enrolled or planning to enroll at an ABET-accredited 4-year college or university. Applicants must be U.S. citizens planning to major in computer science or engineering as an undergraduate or graduate student. They must have a GPA of 2.8 or higher and be residents of the sponsor's region C (Arkansas, Louisiana, Mississippi, and Texas); D (Alabama, Florida, Georgia, Puerto Rico, North Carolina, South Carolina, Tennessee, and the U.S. Virgin Islands); H (Illinois, Indiana, Iowa, Michigan, Minnesota, North Dakota, South Dakota, and Wisconsin); or I (Colorado, Kansas, Missouri, Nebraska, Oklahoma, and Wyoming). Along with their application, they must submit a 1-page essay on why they want to be an engineer or computer scientist, how they believe they will make a difference as an engineer or computer scientist, and what influenced them to study engineering or computer science. Selection is based on merit.
**Financial data:** The stipend is $2,400.
**Duration:** 1 year.
**Number awarded:** 3 each year.
**Deadline:** May of each year for entering freshmen; January of each for current undergraduates and graduate students.

## 1981 CDI AUXILIARY SCHOLARSHIPS

Conservation Districts of Iowa, Attn: Executive Director
1711 Osceola Avenue, Suite 251
P.O. Box 801
Chariton, IA 50049
Phone: (641) 774-4461; Fax: (641) 774-5319;
Email: latisha-cunningham@cdiowa.org
Web: www.cdiowa.org/education.htm

**Summary:** To provide financial assistance to high school seniors in Iowa interested in studying a field related to natural resources or agriculture in college.

**Eligibility:** Open to Iowa high school seniors entering their first year of college. Applicants must be interested in pursuing a program of study related to a field of agriculture or natural resources. Selection is based on financial need (45%), academic achievement (25%), service (10%), character (10%), and self-motivation (10%).

**Financial data:** Stipends are $1,500, $1,000, $800 (paid directly to the recipients' school) or $200 (paid directly to the student).

**Duration:** 1 year; nonrenewable.

**Number awarded:** 9 each year: 1 at $1,500, 1 at $1,000, 1 at $800, and 6 (1 in each of the conservation regions in Iowa) at $200.

**Deadline:** Applications must be submitted to the local Soil and Water Conservation District office by February of each year.

## 1982 CESSNA/ONR STUDENT DESIGN/BUILD/FLY COMPETITION

American Institute of Aeronautics and Astronautics
Attn: Student Programs Director
1801 Alexander Bell Drive, Suite 500
Reston, VA 20191-4344
Phone: (703) 264-7536; (800) 639-AIAA, ext. 536; Fax: (703) 264-7551;
Email: stephenb@aiaa.org
Web: www.aiaa.org

**Summary:** To recognize and reward outstanding aircraft that are designed, built, and flown by undergraduate and graduate student members of the American Institute of Aeronautics and Astronautics (AIAA)

**Eligibility:** Open to undergraduate and graduate students who are AIAA branch or at-large student members. Teams of 3 to 10 students (at least one third of whom must be freshmen, sophomores, or juniors) may enter this competition to design, build, and fly an unmanned, radio-controlled, propeller-driven, electric-powered aircraft. The design must comply with precise specifications; once those specifications are met, the aircraft must be able to take off, circle the field, and land within designated areas. Design projects that are used as part of an organized classroom requirement are eligible and encouraged. Designs that are submitted must be the work of the students, but a faculty advisor may provide guidance. Flight scores are based on the demonstrated mission performance in the best 3 flights obtained during the contest.

**Financial data:** First place is $2,500, second place is $1,500, and third place is $1,000.

**Duration:** The competition is held annually.

**Number awarded:** 3 cash awards are presented each year.

**Deadline:** Letters of intent must be submitted by October of each year; the competition takes place in April.

## 1983 CHAN-PADGETT SPECIAL FORCES MEMORIAL SCHOLARSHIP

American Academy of Physician Assistants-Veterans Caucus
Attn: Veterans Caucus
950 North Washington Street
Alexandria, VA 22314-1552
Phone: (703) 836-2272; Fax: (703) 684-1924; Email: aapa@aapa.org
Web: www.veteranscaucus.org

**Summary:** To provide financial assistance to children of veterans of the Army Special Forces who are studying to become physician assistants.

**Eligibility:** Open to U.S. citizens who are currently enrolled in a physician assistant program. The program must be approved by the Commission on Accreditation of Allied Health Education. Applicants must be children of honorably discharged members of the Army Special Forces. Selection is based on military honors and awards received, civic and college honors and awards received, professional memberships and activities, and GPA. An electronic copy of the sponsor's DD Form 214 must accompany the application.

**Financial data:** The stipend is $1,250.

**Duration:** 1 year.

**Number awarded:** 1 each year.

**Deadline:** February of each year.

## 1984 CHAPTER 4 LAWRENCE A. WACKER MEMORIAL AWARD

Society of Manufacturing Engineers, Attn: SME Education Foundation
One SME Drive
P.O. Box 930
Dearborn, MI 48121-0930
Phone: (313) 425-3304; (800) 733-4763, ext. 3304; Fax: (313) 425-3411;
Email: foundation@sme.org
Web: www.sme.org

**Summary:** To provide financial assistance to students enrolled or planning to enroll in a degree program in manufacturing, mechanical, or industrial engineering in Wisconsin.

**Eligibility:** Open to graduating high school seniors planning to enroll at a 4-year college or university in Wisconsin and current undergraduates already enrolled at such an institution. Applicants must be seeking a bachelor's degree in manufacturing, mechanical, or industrial engineering and have a GPA of 3.0 or higher. First preference is given to members of Chapter 4 (Milwaukee) of the Society of Manufacturing Engineers (SME), their spouses, children, and grandchildren. Second preference is given to residents of the following Wisconsin counties: Milwaukee, Ozaukee, Washington, and Waukesha. Third preference is given to residents of Wisconsin. Need is not considered in awarding scholarships (unless 2 or more applicants have equal qualifications).

**Financial data:** The stipend is $1,500.

**Duration:** 1 year; may be renewed.

**Number awarded:** 2 each year: 1 to a graduating high school senior and 1 to a student currently enrolled as an undergraduate.

**Deadline:** January of each year.

## 1985 CHARLES H. BENNETT MEMORIAL SCHOLARSHIP

Wisconsin Society of Professional Engineers
Attn: Engineers Foundation of Wisconsin
7044 South 13th Street
Oak Creek, WI 53154
Phone: (414) 768-8000, ext. 103; Fax: (414) 768-8001; Email: wspe@wspe.org
Web: www.wspe.org/efw.html

**Summary:** To provide financial assistance to high school seniors in Wisconsin who are interested in majoring in engineering in college.

**Eligibility:** Open to seniors graduating from high schools in Wisconsin who intend to enroll in an accredited engineering undergraduate program, earn a degree in engineering, and enter the practice of engineering after graduation. Applicants must have a GPA of 3.0 or higher and an ACT composite score of 24 or higher. As part of the selection process, they must submit a 250-word essay on how they became interested in engineering, the field of engineering that is most interesting to them and why, and why they want to become a practicing engineer. U.S. citizenship is required. Selection is based on academic achievement, community involvement, extracurricular activities, and need.

**Financial data:** Varies each year. The sponsor awards a total of $9,000 in scholarships each year.

**Duration:** 1 year.

**Number awarded:** 1 or more each year.

**Deadline:** December of each year.

## 1986 CHARLES KUNZ MEMORIAL UNDERGRADUATE SCHOLARSHIP

Emergency Nurses Association, Attn: ENA Foundation
915 Lee Street
Des Plaines, IL 60016-6569
Phone: (847) 460-4100; (800) 900-9659, ext. 4100; Fax: (847) 460-4004;
Email: foundation@ena.org
Web: www.ena.org/foundation/grants

**Summary:** To provide financial assistance for baccalaureate study to nurses who are members of the Emergency Nurses Association (ENA).

**Eligibility:** Open to nurses (R.N., L.P.N., L.V.N.) who are working on a bachelor's degree. Applicants must have been members of the association for at least 12 months. They must submit a 1-page statement on their professional and educational goals and how this scholarship will help them attain those goals. Selection is based on content and clarity of the goal statement (45%), professional association involvement (45%), and GPA (10%).

**Financial data:** The stipend is $4,000.

**Duration:** 1 year; nonrenewable.

**Number awarded:** 1 each year.

**Deadline:** May of each year.

## 1987 CHARLES MILLER MEMORIAL SCHOLARSHIP

American Mathematical Association of Two Year Colleges
c/o Southwest Tennessee Community College
5983 Macon Cove
Memphis, TN 38134
Phone: (901) 333-4643; Fax: (901) 333-4651; Email: amatyc@amatyc.org
Web: www.amatyc.org

**Summary:** To recognize and reward students at 2-year colleges who excel in a mathematics contest.

**Eligibility:** Open to teams of 5 or more students, or individual students if fewer than 5 students wish to compete, at any 2-year college in the United States or Canada. Students must have successfully completed at least 12 semester hours of community college course work but may not have earned a 2-year college or higher degree. Participants answer questions from a standard syllabus in college algebra and trigonometry that may involve precalculus algebra, trigonometry, synthetic and analytic geometry, and probability. All questions are short-answer or multiple choice. Students take 2 tests (in October/November and February/March) of one hour each. The prize is awarded to the individual with the highest total score on both examinations.

**Financial data:** The prize is $3,000. Recipients must use the prize as a scholarship to continue their education at an accredited 4-year institution.

**Duration:** The prize is awarded annually.

**Number awarded:** 1 each year.

**Deadline:** September of each year.

## 1988 CHARLES S. GARDNER MEMORIAL SCHOLARSHIP IN FOREST RESOURCES

Technical Association of the Pulp and Paper Industry
Attn: TAPPI Foundation
15 Technology Parkway South
Norcross, GA 30092
Phone: (770) 209-7536; (800) 332-8686; Fax: (770) 446-6947;
Email: vedmondson@tappi.org
Web: www.tappi.org

**Summary:** To provide financial assistance to college students enrolled in a school of forest resources in the South.

**Eligibility:** Open to rising sophomores who are enrolled in a school of forest resources located in one of the southern states. Applicants must summarize their goals after graduation. Financial need is considered in the selection process.

**Financial data:** The stipend is $2,000.

**Duration:** 1 year.

**Number awarded:** 1 each year.

**Deadline:** May of each year.

## 1989 CHARLES (TOMMY) THOMAS MEMORIAL SCHOLARSHIP

American Nuclear Society, Attn: Scholarship Coordinator
555 North Kensington Avenue
La Grange Park, IL 60526-5592
Phone: (708) 352-6611; Fax: (708) 352-0499; Email: outreach@ans.org
Web: www.ans.org/honors/scholarships

**Summary:** To provide financial assistance to upper-division students who are interested in preparing for a career dealing with the environmental aspects of nuclear science or nuclear engineering.

**Eligibility:** Open to students entering their junior or senior year in nuclear science, nuclear engineering, or a nuclear-related field at an accredited institution in the United States. Applicants must be interested in preparing for a career dealing with the environmental aspects of nuclear science or nuclear engineering. They must be U.S. citizens or permanent residents and able to demonstrate academic achievement.

**Financial data:** The stipend is $2,000.

**Duration:** 1 year; nonrenewable.

**Number awarded:** 1 each year.

**Deadline:** January of each year.

## 1990 CHARLIE WELLS MEMORIAL AVIATION SCHOLARSHIPS

Charlie Wells Memorial Scholarship Fund
P.O. Box 262
Springfield, IL 62705-0262
Email: Rog@wellsscholarship.com
Web: www.wellsscholarship.com

**Summary:** To provide financial assistance to students preparing for an aviation-related program in college.

**Eligibility:** Open to students who are currently majoring full time in an aviation-oriented curriculum at a college or university in the United States. Applicants must submit information on their career interests, 2 letters of reference, an essay on why they deserve the scholarship (including their past accomplishments, future goals, and financial need), and a list of their extracurricular activities.

**Financial data:** Stipends vary, depending on the availability of funds. Recently, they were $1,150. Funds are sent directly to the recipient's school to help pay the costs of tuition.

**Duration:** 1 year.

**Number awarded:** Varies each year; recently, 2 of these scholarships were awarded.

**Deadline:** March of each year.

## 1991 CHEM-E-CAR COMPETITION

American Institute of Chemical Engineers, Attn: Awards Administrator
Three Park Avenue
New York, NY 10016-5991
Phone: (212) 591-7107; Fax: (212) 591-8890; Email: awards@aiche.org
Web: www.aiche.org/awards

**Summary:** To recognize and reward student members of the American Institute of Chemical Engineers (AIChE) who design a chemically powered vehicle.

**Eligibility:** Open to AIChE student members who design and construct a chemically powered vehicle within certain size constraints that is designed to carry a specified cargo a given distance and stop. Entries must be submitted by teams of undergraduate students that have at least 5 participants, including students from at least 2 chemical engineering classes. The percentage of students from each class must not be greater than 80% of the total number of students on the team. Faculty and graduate students may only act as sounding boards for team members and may not be idea generators for the project. Teams are told at the time of the competition the distance that the car must travel and the cargo it will carry. Winners are determined by a combined score, for traveling the correct distance, and for creativity. Competitions are first held at the regional level, from which top entries proceed to the national competition.

**Financial data:** At the regional level, first prize is $200 and second prize is $100. At the national level, first prize is $2,000, second prize is $1,000, and third prize is $500.

**Duration:** The competition is held annually.

**Number awarded:** 3 national winners are selected each year.

**Deadline:** Regional competitions are held in spring of each year. Eligible winners must submit applications to participate in the national competition, held in November, by June of each year.

## 1992 CHEMICAL AND PETROLEUM INDUSTRIES DIVISION SCHOLARSHIP

Instrumentation, Systems, and Automation Society
Attn: ISA Educational Foundation
67 Alexander Drive
Research Triangle Park, NC 27709
Phone: (919) 549-8411; Fax: (919) 549-8288; Email: info@isa.org
Web: www.isa.org

**Summary:** To provide financial assistance to undergraduate and graduate students majoring in fields related to instrumentation, systems, and automation.

**Eligibility:** Open to full-time undergraduate and graduate students enrolled in a program in instrumentation, systems, automation, or a closely-related field. Applicants must have a GPA of 3.0 or higher. They may be from any country but must be attending an institution in their own country. Applicants in a 2-year program must have completed at least 1 academic semester of 12 hours or its equivalent. Applicants in a 4-year program must be in their sophomore year or higher. Along with their application, they must submit an essay (up to 400 words) on their ambitions and qualifications as an innovator or future leader in a career in instrumentation, systems, or automation; they should describe their career objectives, how the award of this scholarship will help them attain their objectives, why they want to enter this particular field of engineering, what they have achieved and learned through their studies and activities, and what this indicates about their character and determination. Preference is given to applicants studying technology related to chemical and petroleum industries. Financial need is not considered in the selection process.

**Financial data:** The stipend is $2,500.

**Duration:** 1 year; may be renewed.

**Number awarded:** 1 each year.

**Deadline:** February of each year.

## 1993 CHERYL TORRENCE-CAMPBELL SCHOLARSHIPS

National Institutes of Health Black Scientists Association
Attn: Scholarship Committee
P.O. Box 2262
Kensington, MD 20891-2262
Web: bsa.od.nih.gov

**Summary:** To provide financial assistance to underrepresented minority high school seniors from Washington, D.C. who plan to study science in college.
**Eligibility:** Open to seniors graduating from public and private high schools in the District of Columbia who are members of ethnic or racial groups underrepresented in the field of biomedical research. Applicants must have been accepted into an accredited college or university to major in the sciences. They must submit a 1-page essay on why they have chosen to major in science in college. Preference is given to students who are financially disadvantaged.
**Financial data:** The stipend is $1,000.
**Duration:** 1 year.
**Number awarded:** 2 each year.
**Deadline:** May of each year.

## 1994 CHEVRONTEXACO CORPORATION SCHOLARSHIPS

Society of Women Engineers
230 East Ohio Street, Suite 400
Chicago, IL 60611-3265
Phone: (312) 596-5223; Fax: (312) 644-8557; Email: hq@swe.org
Web: www.societyofwomenengineers.org/scholarships

**Summary:** To provide financial assistance to undergraduate women who are members of the Society of Women Engineers and majoring in designated engineering specialties.
**Eligibility:** Open to women who are entering their sophomore or junior year at an ABET-accredited 4-year college or university. Applicants must be majoring in chemical, civil, computer, mechanical, or petroleum engineering and have a GPA of 3.5 or higher. Along with their application, they must submit a 1-page essay on why they want to be an engineer, how they believe they will make a difference as an engineer, and what influenced them to study engineering. Only members of the society are considered for this award. Selection is based on merit.
**Financial data:** The stipend is $2,000.
**Duration:** 1 year.
**Number awarded:** 7 each year.
**Deadline:** January of each year.

## 1995 CHI EPSILON SCHOLARSHIP PROGRAM

Chi Epsilon
c/o Dr. Robert L. Henry
University of Texas at Arlington
Box 19316
Arlington, TX 76019-0316
Phone: (817) 272-2752; Fax: (817) 272-2826; Email: rhenry@uta.edu
Web: www.chi-epsilon.org

**Summary:** To provide financial assistance for college to members of Chi Epsilon, the national civil engineering honor society.
**Eligibility:** Open to members of Chi Epsilon (initiates are not eligible) who apply at the chapter level. The faculty advisor selects the chapter's nominee and forwards the nomination to the district councilor, who chooses the district winner. Applicants must submit a brief summary of their professional goals and objectives; a list of outside activities and hobbies; membership in organizations; offices they have held; honors, awards, and scholarships they have received; and 2 letters of recommendation.
**Financial data:** Stipends are $2,500, $1,250, $1,000, or $250.
**Duration:** 1 year.
**Number awarded:** 17 each year: 5 at $2,500 (including the John A. Focht National Chi Epsilon Scholarships and the Brother Austin Barry National Chi Epsilon Scholarships), 10 at $1,250 (the Chi Epsilon District Scholarships), 1 at $1,000 (the Dean's List Scholarship), and 1 at $250 (the Joseph L. Brandes National Chi Epsilon Scholarship).
**Deadline:** November of each year.

## 1996 CHOOSENURSING.COM SCHOLARSHIP PROGRAM

Coalition for Nursing Careers in California, Attn: chooseNursing.com
1800 Harrison Street, 17th Floor
Oakland, CA 94612
Phone: (510) 625-7109; Fax: (510) 987-1299
Web: www.choosenursing.com/paying/scholarships.html

**Summary:** To provide financial assistance to underrepresented and financially disadvantaged students at nursing schools in California.
**Eligibility:** Open to students enrolled in an accredited associate's or bachelor's nursing degree program in California. Applicants must come from an underrepresented and financially disadvantaged (family income may not exceed $50,000 per family member) group. They must have a GPA of 2.5 or higher and may not yet have a R.N. license. Along with their application, they must submit a 500-word essay on what led them to choose a career in nursing, the obstacles or challenges they have faced and overcome to get where they are today, and their professional goals or aspirations for their nursing career. Selection is based on financial need, academic achievement, health care involvement, and enthusiasm or passion for nursing.
**Financial data:** Stipends are $5,000, $2,500, or $2,000.
**Duration:** 1 year.
**Number awarded:** Varies each year. Recently, 28 of these scholarships were awarded: 11 for bachelor's degree students at $5,000, 2 for associate's degree students at $2,500, and 15 for associate degree students at $2,000.
**Deadline:** April of each year.

## 1997 CHUCK PEACOCK MEMORIAL SCHOLARSHIP

Aircraft Electronics Association, Attn: AEA Educational Foundation
4217 South Hocker Drive
Independence, MO 64055-4723
Phone: (816) 373-6565; Fax: (816) 478-3100; Email: info@aea.net
Web: www.aea.net

**Summary:** To provide financial assistance to students preparing for a career in aviation management.
**Eligibility:** Open to high school seniors and currently-enrolled college students who are attending (or planning to attend) an accredited postsecondary institution in an aviation management program. Applicants must submit an official transcript (cumulative GPA of 2.5 or higher), a statement about their career plans, a description of their involvement in school and community activities, and a 300-word essay on how the job requirements of aviation technicians will change with advancements in technology. Selection is based on merit.
**Financial data:** The stipend is $1,000.
**Duration:** 1 year.
**Number awarded:** 1 each year.
**Deadline:** February of each year.

## 1998 CHUNGHI HONG PARK SCHOLARSHIP

Korean-American Scientists and Engineers Association
1952 Gallows Drive, Suite 300
Vienna, VA 22182
Phone: (703) 748-1221; Fax: (703) 748-1331; Email: sejong@ksea.org
Web: www.ksea.org

**Summary:** To provide financial assistance to women who are undergraduate or graduate student members of the Korean-American Scientists and Engineers Association (KSEA).
**Eligibility:** Open to women who are Korean American undergraduate or graduate students, graduated from a high school in the United States, are KSEA members, and are majoring in science, engineering, or a related field. Along with their application, they must submit a 500-word essay on either of the following topics: 1) their career goals and intended contributions to society, or 2) the meaning of Korean heritage in their life. Selection is based on the essay (20%), work experience and extracurricular activities (20%), recommendation letters (30%), and academic performance (30%).
**Financial data:** The stipend is $1,000.
**Duration:** 1 year.
**Number awarded:** 2 each year.
**Deadline:** February of each year.

## 1999 CIND M. TRESER MEMORIAL SCHOLARSHIP

Washington State Environmental Health Association
Attn: Executive Secretary
103 Sea Pine Lane
Bellingham, WA 98226-9363
Phone: (360) 756-2040; Fax: (360) 756-2080; Email: kerri@wseha.org
Web: www.wseha.org

**Summary:** To provide financial assistance to undergraduate students who are majoring in environmental health or other life sciences and are interested in preparing for a career in environmental health in the state of Washington.

**Eligibility:** Open to undergraduates who 1) intend to become employed in the field of environmental health in Washington following graduation and 2) are enrolled in a program either accredited by the National Environmental Health Science and Protection Accreditation Council (EHAC) or with a curriculum comparable to the model curriculum recommended by the EHAC (i.e., the program must include substantial course work in biology and microbiology, organic and inorganic chemistry, epidemiology, biostatistics, and environmental health sciences). Applicants do not need to be members of the sponsoring organization, but they must become members if they receive the scholarship.

**Financial data:** A stipend is awarded (amount not specified).

**Duration:** 1 year.

**Number awarded:** 1 each year.

**Deadline:** March of each year.

## 2000 CLAIR A. HILL SCHOLARSHIP

Association of California Water Agencies, Attn: Scholarship Program
910 K Street, Suite 100
Sacramento, CA 95814-3514
Phone: (916) 441-4545; Fax: (916) 325-4849; Email: lavonnew@acwa.com
Web: www.acwa.com/news_info/scholarships

**Summary:** To provide financial assistance to upper-division students in California who are majoring in water resources-related fields of study.

**Eligibility:** Open to California residents attending a public college or university in the state. They should 1) have completed their sophomore work, 2) be full-time students in their junior or senior year at the time of the award, and 3) be majoring in a field related to or identified with water resources, including engineering, agricultural sciences, urban water supply, environmental sciences, and public administration. Selection is based on scholastic achievement, career plans, and financial need.

**Financial data:** The stipend is $3,000. Funds are paid directly to the recipient's school.

**Duration:** 1 year.

**Number awarded:** 1 each year.

**Deadline:** March of each year.

## 2001 CLAIR FANCY SCHOLARSHIP

Air & Waste Management Association-Florida Section
c/o C. David Cooper
University of Central Florida
Civil and Environmental Engineering Department
Orlando, FL 32816-2450
Email: cooper@mail.ucf.edu
Web: www.flawma.com/scholarship.html

**Summary:** To provide financial assistance to members of the Air & Waste Management Association (AWMA) enrolled at colleges and universities in Florida.

**Eligibility:** Open to juniors, seniors, and graduate students enrolled full time at 4-year colleges and universities in Florida. Applicants be student members of AWMA and have demonstrated service to AWMA in some capacity. They must submit a 1-page essay on their interest in the air environment or the waste management field. Selection is based on the essay, academic transcripts, and a letter of reference.

**Financial data:** The stipend is $1,000.

**Duration:** 1 year.

**Number awarded:** 1 each year.

**Deadline:** January of each year.

## 2002 CLARE BOOTHE LUCE SCHOLARSHIPS IN SCIENCE AND ENGINEERING

Clare Boothe Luce Fund
c/o Henry Luce Foundation, Inc.
111 West 50th Street, Suite 4601
New York, NY 10020
Phone: (212) 489-7700; Fax: (212) 581-9541; Email: jdaniels@hluce.org
Web: www.hluce.org

**Summary:** To provide funding to women interested in studying science or engineering at the undergraduate level at designated universities.

**Eligibility:** Open to female undergraduate students (particularly juniors and seniors) majoring in biology, chemistry, computer science, engineering (aeronautical, civil, electrical, mechanical, nuclear, and others), mathematics, meteorology, and physics. Applicants must be U.S. citizens attending 1 of the 12 designated colleges and universities affiliated with this program; periodically,

other institutions are invited to participate. Premedical science majors are ineligible for this competition. The participating institutions select the recipients without regard to race, age, religion, ethnic background, or need. All awards are made on the basis of merit.

**Financial data:** The amount awarded is established individually by each of the participating institutions. The stipends are intended to augment rather than replace any existing institutional support in these fields. Each stipend is calculated to include the cost of room and board as well as tuition and other fees or expenses.

**Duration:** 2 years; in certain special circumstances, awards for the full 4 years of undergraduate study may be offered.

**Number awarded:** Varies; since the program began, more than 800 of these scholarships have been awarded.

**Deadline:** Varies; check with the participating institutions for their current schedule.

## 2003 CLARENCE AND JOSEPHINE MYERS SCHOLARSHIP

Society of Manufacturing Engineers, Attn: SME Education Foundation
One SME Drive
P.O. Box 930
Dearborn, MI 48121-0930
Phone: (313) 425-3304; (800) 733-4763, ext. 3304; Fax: (313) 425-3411;
Email: foundation@sme.org
Web: www.sme.org

**Summary:** To provide financial assistance to students working on an undergraduate or graduate degree in engineering in Indiana.

**Eligibility:** Open to students working on an associate, bachelor's, or graduate degree in manufacturing, mechanical, or industrial engineering at a college or university in Indiana. Applicants must have a GPA of 3.0 or higher. Preference is given to applicants who attending Arsenal Technological High School in Indianapolis, student members of chapters sponsored by Chapter 37 of the Society of Manufacturing Engineers in Indianapolis, and children and grandchildren of current Chapter 37 members.

**Financial data:** The stipend is $1,200.

**Duration:** 1 year; may be renewed.

**Number awarded:** 1 each year.

**Deadline:** January of each year.

## 2004 CLIFFORD H. "TED" REES, JR. SCHOLARSHIP

Clifford H. "Ted" Rees, Jr. Scholarship Foundation
Attn: ARI Director of Education
4100 North Fairfax Drive, Suite 200
Arlington, VA 22203
Phone: (703) 524-8800; Fax: (703) 528-3816; Email: rmach@ari.org
Web: www.reesscholarship.org

**Summary:** To provide financial assistance to students preparing for a career as a heating, ventilation, air-conditioning, and refrigeration (HVACR) technician.

**Eligibility:** Open to U.S. citizens and permanent residents who are enrolled in a program for preparation for a career in residential air-conditioning and heating, light commercial air-conditioning and heating, or commercial refrigeration. They must be enrolled in a training program at an institutionally accredited school. Along with their application, they must submit an essay of 150 to 200 words on why this scholarship should be awarded to them.

**Financial data:** The stipend is $2,000.

**Duration:** 1 year; nonrenewable.

**Number awarded:** 2 each year.

**Deadline:** October of each year.

## 2005 CLIFFORD L. BEDFORD SCHOLARSHIP

Institute of Food Technologists-Great Lakes Section
c/o Janice Harte, Secretary
Michigan State University
Department of Food Science and Human Nutrition
114 Malcolm Trout Building
East Lansing, MI 48825
Phone: (517) 355-8474, ext. 105; Email: harteja@msu.edu
Web: www.ift.org/sections/greatlakes/scholarship.html

**Summary:** To provide financial assistance to undergraduate students in Michigan who are majoring in a field related to food science.

**Eligibility:** Open to students who are enrolled full time at a college or university in Michigan in food science, nutrition, food packaging, or food service courses leading to an associate's or bachelor's degree. Applicants must be preparing for a career in the food industry. Selection is based on both academic and non-academic performance.

**Financial data:** The stipend is $1,000 or $500.

**Duration:** 1 year; nonrenewable.

**Number awarded:** Either 1 scholarship at $1,000 or 2 at $500 are awarded each year.

**Deadline:** December of each year.

## 2006 COAL AND ENERGY DIVISION SCHOLARSHIPS

Society for Mining, Metallurgy, and Exploration, Inc., Attn: Student Center
8307 Shaffer Parkway
P.O. Box 277002
Littleton, CO 80127-7002
Phone: (303) 948-4203; (800) 763-3132; Fax: (303) 973-3845;
Email: sme@smenet.org
Web: www.smenet.org/education/students/sme_scholarships.crm

**Summary:** To provide financial assistance to student members of the Society for Mining, Metallurgy, and Exploration (SME) who are majoring in mining engineering with an emphasis on coal.

**Eligibility:** Open to student members who have completed their sophomore year in college and are majoring in mining or mineral engineering at an ABET-accredited college. Applicants must be U.S. citizens engaged in coal-related activities. Financial need is considered in the selection process.

**Financial data:** The stipends are approximately $1,500 per year.

**Duration:** 1 year.

**Number awarded:** Approximately 15 each year.

**Deadline:** October of each year.

## 2007 COATING AND GRAPHIC ARTS DIVISION SCHOLARSHIPS

**Summary:** To provide financial assistance to student members of the Technical Association of the Pulp and Paper Industry (TAPPI) who are interested in preparing for a career in the paper industry, with a focus on coating and graphic arts.
*See Listing #1330.*

## 2008 COL CHUCK JONES MEMORIAL AWARD

Hanscom Officers' Wives' Club, Attn: Scholarship Chair
P.O. Box 557
Bedford, MA 01730
Phone: (781) 275-1251; Email: scholarship@hanscomowd.org
Web: www.hanscomowc.org

**Summary:** To provide financial assistance to children of military personnel and veterans in New England who are interested in studying aeronautics and space in college.

**Eligibility:** Open to college-bound high school seniors living in New England who are dependents of active-duty, retired, or deceased military members of any branch of service. Also eligible are dependents of military recruiters working in the New York area and students living elsewhere but whose military sponsor is stationed at Hanscom Air Force Base. Applicants must demonstrate qualities of responsibility, leadership, scholastics, citizenship, and diversity of interest. They must have a valid military identification card and be planning to work on a college degree in a field related to aeronautics and space (including communications, meteorology, air/space maintenance, manufacturing processing, engineering, and the astronaut program). Along with their application, they must submit a 2-page essay on their educational goals, how their educational experience will help prepare them to pursue future goals, and how they intend to apply their education to better their community.

**Financial data:** The stipend is $2,000.

**Duration:** 1 year; nonrenewable.

**Number awarded:** 1 each year.

**Deadline:** March of each year.

## 2009 COLGATE "BRIGHT SMILES, BRIGHT FUTURES" MINORITY SCHOLARSHIPS

American Dental Hygienists' Association, Attn: Institute for Oral Health
444 North Michigan Avenue, Suite 3400
Chicago, IL 60611
Phone: (312) 440-8918; (800) 735-4916; Fax: (312) 440-8929;
Email: institute@adha.net
Web: www.adha.org/institute/Scholarship/index.htm

**Summary:** To provide financial assistance to minority students and males of any race enrolled in undergraduate programs in dental hygiene.

**Eligibility:** Open to members of groups currently underrepresented in the dental hygiene profession (Native Americans, African Americans, Hispanics, Asians, and males) who are active members of the Student American Dental Hygienists' Association (SADHA) or the American Dental Hygienists' Association (ADHA). Applicants must have a GPA of 3.0 or higher, be able to document financial need of at least $1,500, and have completed at least one year of full-time enrollment in an accredited dental hygiene program in the United States. Along with their application, they must submit a statement that covers their long-term career goals, their intended contribution to the dental hygiene profession, their professional interests, and the manner in which their degree will enhance their professional capacity.

**Financial data:** Stipends range from $1,000 to $2,000.

**Duration:** 1 year; nonrenewable.

**Number awarded:** 2 each year.

**Deadline:** April of each year.

## 2010 COLORADO LEGION AUXILIARY PAST PRESIDENT'S PARLEY NURSE'S SCHOLARSHIP

American Legion Auxiliary, Attn: Department of Colorado
7465 East First Avenue, Suite D
Denver, CO 80230
Phone: (303) 367-5388; Email: ala@coloradolegion.org

**Summary:** To provide financial assistance to wartime veterans and their descendants in Colorado who are interested in preparing for a career in nursing.

**Eligibility:** Open to 1) daughters, sons, spouses, granddaughters, and great-granddaughters of veterans, and 2) veterans who served in the armed forces during eligibility dates for membership in the American Legion. Applicants must be Colorado residents who have been accepted by an accredited school of nursing in the state. As part of the application process, they must submit a 500-word essay on the topic, "Americanism." Selection is based on scholastic ability (25%), financial need (25%), references (13%), a 500-word essay on Americanism (25%), and dedication to chosen field (12%).

**Financial data:** The amount of the award depends on the availability of funds.

**Duration:** 1 year; nonrenewable.

**Number awarded:** Varies each year, depending on the availability of funds.

**Deadline:** April of each year.

## 2011 COLORADO SCHOLARSHIP PROGRAM

American Council of Engineering Companies of Colorado
Attn: Scholarship Coordinator
899 Logan Street, Suite 109
Denver, CO 80203
Phone: (303) 832-2200; (303) 832-0400; Email: aced@acec-co.org
Web: www.accc-co.org/education/qualifications.html

**Summary:** To provide financial assistance to students in Colorado currently working on a bachelor's degree in engineering.

**Eligibility:** Open to students working on a bachelor's degree in an ABET-approved engineering program in Colorado. Applicants must be U.S. citizens entering their junior, senior, or fifth year. Along with their application, they must submit a 500-word essay on "What is the role or responsibility of the consulting engineer or land surveyor to shaping and protecting the natural environment." Selection is based on the essay (25 points), cumulative GPA (28 points), work experience (20 points), a letter of recommendation (17 points), and college activities (10 points).

**Financial data:** Stipends are $4,500, $3,000, or $2,000.

**Duration:** 1 year.

**Number awarded:** 5 each year: the William Russell Stoneman Scholarship at $4,500, the Fu Hua Chen Scholarship at $3,000, and 3 others at $2,000 each.

**Deadline:** January of each year.

## 2012 COLORADO SECTION SCHOLARSHIPS

American Congress on Surveying and Mapping-Colorado Section
Attn: Kurt Ernstberger
Flatirons Surveying
5717 Arapahoe
Boulder, CO 80303
Phone: (303) 443-7001; Fax: (303) 443-9830;
Email: kernstberger@flatsurv.com

**Summary:** To provide financial assistance to undergraduate and graduate students majoring in fields related to surveying and mapping at schools in Colorado.

**Eligibility:** Open to students enrolled in a Colorado university, college, community college, or technical school with a major in surveying, geography, remote sensing, geomatics, cartography, photogrammetry, geodesy, or GIS. Applicants must have a GPA of 2.5 or higher. Both undergraduate and graduate students are eligible, but preference is given to full-time students and members of the American Congress on Surveying and Mapping (ACSM). Applicants must submit an essay describing why they chose their field of study and their financial need, personal merit, career goals, academic honors, scholarships, community service, volunteer work, and awards.

**Financial data:** The stipend is $1,000.

**Duration:** 1 year.

**Number awarded:** 2 or more each year: 1 for each semester or term.

**Deadline:** May of each year for the fall semester or term; November of each year for the spring semester or term.

## [2013] COLORADO WEED MANAGEMENT ASSOCIATION SCHOLARSHIP

Colorado Weed Management Association, Attn: Scholarship Program
P.O. Box 1910
Granby, CO 80446-1910
Phone: (970) 887-1228; Fax: (970) 887-1229; Email: cwma@rkymtnhi.com
Web: www.cwma.org/scholarship.htm

**Summary:** To provide financial assistance to high school seniors and college students in Colorado who are interested in weed management.

**Eligibility:** Open to high school seniors and college students who have demonstrated an interest in weed management and are planning to major in agriculture, natural resource management, botany, range management, or a related field. Applicants must be attending or planning to attend a 2-year college or 4-year college or university in Colorado. Along with their application, they must submit an essay, up to 3 pages in length, on the topic, "The Threat of Noxious Weeds Is..." High school seniors must have a GPA of 2.5 or higher; college freshmen must have a cumulative GPA of 2.0 or higher; college sophomores, juniors, and seniors must have a GPA of 2.5 or higher. Financial need is also considered in the selection process.

**Financial data:** A stipend is awarded (amount not specified).

**Duration:** 1 year; nonrenewable.

**Number awarded:** 1 each year.

**Deadline:** March of each year.

## [2014] COLVIN SCHOLARSHIP PROGRAM

**Summary:** To provide financial assistance to upper-division students working on a degree related to the beef industry.

*See Listing #1335.*

## [2015] COMMITMENT TO AGRICULTURE SCHOLARSHIP PROGRAM

National FFA Organization, Attn: Scholarship Office
6060 FFA Drive
P.O. Box 68960
Indianapolis, IN 46268-0960
Phone: (317) 802-4321; Fax: (317) 802-5321; Email: scholarships@ffa.org
Web: www.ffa.org

**Summary:** To provide financial assistance to high school students from farm families who plan to study agriculture in college.

**Eligibility:** Open to high school seniors whose families are actively engaged in production agriculture. Applicants must be planning to study an agricultural field in college on a full-time basis and prepare for a career in agriculture. They must have an ACT composite score of 18 or higher or an SAT combined verbal and math score that s equivalent. As part of the application process, they must submit an essay on the importance of innovation to U.S. agriculture. If they are a member of FFA, they must also include a statement from their advisor evaluating their involvement in FFA activities and indicating special circumstances, such as financial need, that should be considered. If they are not FFA members, they must provide documentation of other school, community, leadership, and work activities.

**Financial data:** The stipend is $1,500.

**Duration:** 1 year; nonrenewable.

**Number awarded:** 100 each year.

**Deadline:** February of each year.

## [2016] COMM1 RADIO AVIATION SCHOLARSHIP

E-Publishing Group, LLC, Attn: COMM1 Radio Simulators
113A East Church Street
Frederick, MD 21701
Phone: (301) 620-9500; (888) 333-2855; Fax: (301) 620-9501;
Email: feedback@comm1radiosimulator.com
Web: www.comm1.com

**Summary:** To provide financial assistance to students attending college to prepare for a career in aviation.

**Eligibility:** Open to undergraduates working on a degree as preparation for a career in aviation. Applicants must complete the statement, "Proper pilot communications are essential to aviation safety because..." Selection is based on aviation career aspirations, academic and flight training records, recommendations from mentor, and financial need.

**Financial data:** The stipend is $1,000.

**Duration:** 1 year.

**Number awarded:** 1 each year.

**Deadline:** September of each year.

## [2017] COMPOSITES DIVISION/HAROLD GILES SCHOLARSHIP

Society of Plastics Engineers, Attn: SPE Foundation
14 Fairfield Drive
Brookfield, CT 06804-0403
Phone: (203) 740-5447; Fax: (203) 775-1157; Email: foundation@4spe.org
Web: www.4spe.org/foundation/scholarships.php

**Summary:** To provide financial assistance to undergraduate and graduate students who have a career interest in the plastics industry.

**Eligibility:** Open to full-time undergraduate and graduate students at 4-year colleges or in 2-year technical programs. Applicants must 1) have a demonstrated or expressed interest in the plastics industry; 2) be majoring in or taking courses that would be beneficial to a career in the plastics or polymer industry (e.g., plastics engineering, polymer sciences, chemistry, physics, chemical engineering, mechanical engineering, or industrial engineering); 3) be in good academic standing at their school; and 4) be able to document financial need. Along with their application, they must submit 3 letters of recommendation; a high school and/or college transcript; and a 1- to 2-page statement telling why they are interested in the scholarship, their qualifications, and their educational and career goals in the plastics industry.

**Financial data:** The stipend is $1,000 per year. Funds are paid directly to the recipient's school.

**Duration:** 1 year.

**Number awarded:** 1 each year.

**Deadline:** January of each year.

## [2018] COMPUTER SOCIETY INTERNATIONAL DESIGN COMPETITION

IEEE Computer Society, Attn: Student Awards
1730 Massachusetts Avenue, N.W.
Washington, DC 20036-1992
Phone: (202) 371-1013; Fax: (202) 778-0884; Email: csidc@computer.org
Web: www.computer.org/csidc

**Summary:** To recognize and reward undergraduate students who design and implement computer-based solutions to real-world problems

**Eligibility:** Open to teams of undergraduate students in computer science, computer engineering, and related fields. Each team consists of 4 undergraduates plus a faculty mentor. Teams must design and implement a computer-based project on a topic that changes annually. They must submit a report that includes an abstract, a system overview, a description of implementation and engineering considerations, and a summary. Based on those reports, finalists are chosen and invited to present their projects to the judging panel. Selection of winners is based on originality of the project, its relevance to the theme of being beneficial to society, the substance of the project, taking a systems approach, teamwork, quality and presentation of reports, creativity in design, plan for the project period, and practicality and feasibility of the project. The Microsoft Award for Software Engineering is awarded to the team that makes the best use of appropriate software engineering techniques. The Microsoft Multimedia Award is awarded to the team that makes best use of multimedia techniques in their formal presentation at the finals.

**Financial data:** Prizes are $20,000 for first, $12,000 for second, $8,000 for third, and $4,000 for honorable mentions. Students determine how the prize money is distributed among the team. The 2 special Microsoft Prizes are each $2,000.

**Duration:** The competition is held annually.

**Number awarded:** The competition is limited to 300 teams. If more teams apply, team selection is made at random. Of the entrants, 10 teams are selected as finalists and to receive prizes (including 7 honorable mentions).

**Deadline:** Applications must be submitted by November of each year. Project reports are due in April, and the world finals are held at the end of June.

### 2019 CONNECTICUT ASSOCIATION OF LAND SURVEYORS SCHOLARSHIPS

Connecticut Association of Land Surveyors, Inc.
78 Beaver Road
Wethersfield, CT 06109
Phone: (860) 563-1990; Fax: (860) 529-9700
Web: www.ctsurveyor.com/scholars.htm

**Summary:** To provide financial assistance to residents of Connecticut working on a degree in surveying.

**Eligibility:** Open to residents of Connecticut enrolled in a program leading to a degree in surveying. Applicants must have completed at least half of the degree program.

**Financial data:** A stipend is awarded (amount not specified).

**Duration:** 1 year.

**Number awarded:** Several each year.

**Deadline:** May of each year.

### 2020 CONNECTICUT BUILDING CONGRESS SCHOLARSHIPS

**Summary:** To provide financial assistance to high school seniors in Connecticut who are interested in studying a field related to the construction industry in college.

*See Listing #1339.*

### 2021 CONNECTICUT CHAPTER HFMA UNDERGRADUATE SCHOLARSHIP

Healthcare Financial Management Association-Connecticut Chapter
c/o Andy Czerniewski, Scholarship Committee Chair
VNA of Central Connecticut
One Long Wharf Drive
New Haven, CT 06511-5991
Phone: (203) 777-5521, ext. 1700; Fax: (203) 495-7483;
Email: aczerniewski@vnascc.org
Web: www.cthfma.org/Scholarship.asp

**Summary:** To recognize and reward, with college scholarships, undergraduate students in fields related to health care financial management at colleges and universities in Connecticut who submit outstanding related essays.

**Eligibility:** Open to undergraduate students at colleges and universities in Connecticut, children of members of the Connecticut chapter of Healthcare Financial Management Association (HFMA), and residents of Connecticut commuting to a college or university in a state that borders Connecticut. Applicants must be enrolled in a business, finance, accounting, or information systems program and have an interest in health care or be enrolled in a nursing or allied health program. They must submit an essay, up to 3 pages, on what they see as the most significant challenge facing the health care industry today and their proposal for a practical and feasible solution. Finalists may be interviewed.

**Financial data:** The winner receives a $1,000 scholarship, membership in the Connecticut chapter of HFMA and its scholarship committee, and waiver of chapter program fees for one year.

**Duration:** The competition is held annually.

**Number awarded:** 1 each year.

**Deadline:** March of each year.

### 2022 CONNECTICUT LEAGUE FOR NURSING SCHOLARSHIP

Connecticut League for Nursing, Attn: Executive Director
393 Center Street
P.O. Box 365
Wallingford, CT 06492-0365
Phone: (203) 265-4248; Fax: (203) 265-5311;
Email: education@ctleaguefornursing.org
Web: www.ctleaguefornursing.org/scholarships.html

**Summary:** To provide financial assistance to nursing students in Connecticut.

**Eligibility:** Open to Connecticut residents who are enrolled in an accredited school of nursing in the state. Baccalaureate applicants must have completed 3 years of a 4-year program; diploma applicants must have completed 1 year of a 2-year program; associate's degree applicants must have completed 1 year of a 2-year program; R.N. students in an upper-division B.S.N. program must be entering their senior year; graduate students must have completed 18 credits in an accredited nursing program. Selection is based on scholastic ability, professional potential, and financial need.

**Financial data:** The stipend depends on the recipient's qualifications and the availability of funds.

**Duration:** 1 year.

**Number awarded:** 1 or more each year.

**Deadline:** October of each year.

### 2023 CONNECTICUT SOCIETY OF PROFESSIONAL ENGINEERS SCHOLARSHIP

Connecticut Society of Professional Engineers, Attn: Scholarship Program
2600 Dixwell Avenue, Suite 7
Hamden, CT 06514-1833
Phone: (203) 281-4322; Fax: (203) 248-8932; Email: info@ctspe.org
Web: www.ctspe.net

**Summary:** To provide financial assistance to high school seniors in Connecticut who are interested in preparing for a career in engineering.

**Eligibility:** Open to Connecticut residents who are attending or planning to attend an ABET-accredited engineering program at a college or university anywhere in the United States. Applicants must submit a 500-word essay on their interest in engineering, their major area of study and area of specialization, and the occupation they plan to pursue after graduation. Selection is based on the essay, academic merit, extracurricular activities, potential, and financial need.

**Financial data:** A stipend is awarded (amount not specified).

**Duration:** 1 year.

**Number awarded:** Varies each year.

**Deadline:** October of each year.

### 2024 CONNECTICUT TREE PROTECTIVE ASSOCIATION ARBORIST SCHOLARSHIPS

Connecticut Tree Protective Association, Inc.
58 Old Post Road
P.O. Box 356
Northford, CT 06472-0356
Phone: (203) 484-2512; (888) 919-2872 (within CT); Fax: (203) 484-2512
Web: www.ctpa.org/scholarship.htm

**Summary:** To provide financial assistance to college students from Connecticut who are preparing for a career in tree care.

**Eligibility:** Open to Connecticut residents who are working full time on a bachelor's or associate degree in urban forestry or arboriculture. Applicants must be preparing for a career in tree care; preference is given to students who plan to practice arboriculture in Connecticut. A minimum GPA of 2.0 is required. Priority is given to applicants who demonstrate financial need.

**Financial data:** The stipend is $1,000 per year.

**Duration:** 1 year; may be renewed.

**Number awarded:** 2 each year.

**Deadline:** November of each year.

### 2025 CONSTANCE L. LLOYD SCHOLARSHIP

American College of Medical Practice Executives
Attn: ACMPE Scholarship Fund Inc.
104 Inverness Terrace East
Englewood, CO 80112-5306
Phone: (303) 799-1111, ext. 232; (877) ASK-MGMA; Fax: (303) 643-4439;
Email: acmpe@mgma.com
Web: www.mgma.com/academics/scholar.cfm

**Summary:** To provide financial assistance to undergraduate or graduate women in Georgia who are working on a degree in health care or health care administration.

**Eligibility:** Open to women enrolled at the undergraduate or graduate level at an accredited college or university in Georgia who are working on either an administrative or clinically-related degree in the health care field. Students working on a degree in medicine, physical therapy, nursing, or other clinically-related professions are not eligible. Applicants must submit a letter describing their career goals and objectives relevant to medical practice management; a resume; 3 reference letters commenting on their performance, character, potential to succeed, and need for scholarship support; and either documentation indicating acceptance into an undergraduate or graduate program or academic transcripts indicating undergraduate or graduate work completed to date.

**Financial data:** The stipend is $2,500. Funds are paid directly to the recipient's college or university.

**Duration:** 1 year.

**Number awarded:** 1 each year.

**Deadline:** April of each year.

---

### 2026 CONSTRUCTION ENGINEERING SCHOLARSHIPS

American Society of Civil Engineers, Attn: Construction Institute
1801 Alexander Bell Drive
Reston, VA 20191-4400
Phone: (703) 295-6390; (800) 548-ASCE; Fax: (703) 295-6391;
Email: ci@asce.org
Web: www.constructioninst.org/awards/cescholarship.cfm

**Summary:** To provide financial assistance to undergraduate student members of the American Society of Civil Engineers (ASCE) who are working on a degree in construction engineering.

**Eligibility:** Open to undergraduate students who are members of ASCE or its Construction Institute (CI). Applicants must be enrolled at a college or university with an engineering program that is accredited by ABET, ACCE, or similar agency. Along with their application, they must submit a statement on why they wish to enter the construction industry, special financial needs, and long-term goals and plans. Selection is based on their justification for the award, educational plan, academic performance and standing, potential for development, leadership capacity, and financial need.

**Financial data:** A stipend is awarded (amount not specified).

**Duration:** 1 year.

**Number awarded:** 1 or 2 each year.

**Deadline:** March of each year.

---

### 2027 CONSTRUCTION TRADES SCHOLARSHIP COMPETITION

National Association of Women in Construction
Attn: NAWIC Founders' Scholarship Foundation
327 South Adams
Fort Worth, TX 76104-1081
Phone: (817) 877-5551; (800) 552-3506; Fax: (817) 877-0324;
Email: nawic@nawic.org
Web: www.nawic.org/nfsf.htm

**Summary:** To provide financial assistance to students pursuing training in a construction-related crafts program.

**Eligibility:** Open to students who are currently enrolled or enrolling in a construction-related craft training program that is approved by the Bureau of Apprenticeship Training or their home state's postsecondary education commission. Applicants must be obtaining training in a construction-related craft or trade at an institution in the United States or Canada. Along with their application, they must submit brief essays on 1) their ultimate goal in the construction industry; 2) their most important extracurricular activity, their most important contribution to it, and what their participation has meant to them as an individual; and 3) why they are interested in a construction industry career and what event or series of events has led them to this decision. Selection is based on the applicant's interest in construction, extracurricular activities, employment experience, and financial need. Semifinalists may be interviewed.

**Financial data:** Stipends range from $1,000 to $2,000 per year.

**Duration:** 1 year; may be renewed if the recipient provide evidence of continued need, continued interest in construction, and continued enrollment and good standing in a construction-related field.

**Number awarded:** Varies; a total of $25,000 is available in scholarships each year.

**Deadline:** March of each year.

---

### 2028 CONSULTING ENGINEERS AND LAND SURVEYORS OF CALIFORNIA UNDERGRADUATE SCHOLARSHIPS

Consulting Engineers and Land Surveyors of California
Attn: Communications Director
1303 J Street, Suite 450
Sacramento, CA 95814
Phone: (916) 441-7991; Fax: (916) 441-6312; Email: staff@celsoc.org
Web: www.celsoc.org

**Summary:** To provide financial assistance to students working on a bachelor's degree at an approved engineering program or land surveying program in California.

**Eligibility:** Open to U.S. citizens who are working full time on a bachelor's degree in an ABET-approved engineering program or an accredited land surveying program in California. Applicants must be entering their junior, senior, or fifth year to qualify; students graduating this academic year are not eligible. They must have a GPA of 3.0 or higher; to be considered for some scholarships, they must have a GPA in engineering and land surveying courses of 3.5 or higher and an overall GPA of 3.2 or higher. Along with their application, they must submit an essay, approximately 500 words in length, on "What is a consulting engineer or land surveyor and why should you consider it as a career?" Selection is based on GPA (28 points); the essay (25 points); work experience (20 points); recommendations (17 points); and college activities (10 points). Financial need is not considered in the selection process.

**Financial data:** Stipends range up to $7,500.

**Duration:** 1 year; recipients may reapply for 1 additional year.

**Number awarded:** Varies each year. Recently, 4 of these scholarships were awarded: 1 at $7,500, 1 at $3,500, 1 at $2,000, and 1 at $1,000.

**Deadline:** January of each year.

---

### 2029 CORDIE HUGHES SCHOLARSHIP

**Summary:** To provide financial assistance to residents of Tennessee working on an undergraduate degree in a construction-related field.
*See Listing #1341.*

---

### 2030 CORRUGATED PACKAGING DIVISION SCHOLARSHIPS

Technical Association of the Pulp and Paper Industry, Attn: TAPPI Foundation
15 Technology Parkway South
Norcross, GA 30092
Phone: (770) 209-7536; (800) 332-8686; Fax: (770) 446-6947;
Email: vedmondson@tappi.org
Web: www.tappi.org

**Summary:** To provide financial assistance to students who are interested in preparing for a career in the paper industry, with a focus on the manufacture and use of corrugated, solid fiber, and associated packaging materials and products.

**Eligibility:** Open to 1) full- or part-time employees in the box business who are working on a graduate or undergraduate degree; and 2) students who are attending college full time, have a GPA of 3.0 or higher, are able to demonstrate an interest in the corrugated container industry, and are recommended and endorsed by an instructor or faculty member. Selection is based on financial need, overall scholarship, maturity, job potential, and current and future contribution to the corrugated container industry.

**Financial data:** The stipend is either $2,000 or $1,000.

**Duration:** 1 year.

**Number awarded:** Varies each year; recently, 8 of these scholarships, worth $10,000, were awarded.

**Deadline:** February or July of each year.

---

### 2031 CRMCA/CRPA SCHOLARSHIPS

Colorado Ready Mixed Concrete Association/Colorado Rock Products Association, Attn: Scholarship Fund
6855 South Havana Street, Suite 540
Centennial, CO 80112
Phone: (303) 290-0303; Fax: (303) 290-8008; Email: pschauer@crmca.org
Web: www.crmca.org/scholarships/default.php

**Summary:** To provide financial assistance to upper-division students from Colorado who are preparing for a career in areas of interest to the Colorado Ready Mixed Concrete Association (CRMCA) and the Colorado Rock Products Association (CRPA).

**Eligibility:** Open to full-time juniors and seniors at colleges and universities in Colorado who have a GPA of 3.0 or higher. Applicants must be preparing for a career in such fields as aggregate extraction, building construction, road building, municipal utility construction, building design, heavy equipment design, materials research or application, or other fields associated with the use of aggregates or concrete. Preference is given to students whose home residence is Colorado, have graduated from a high school in Colorado, and have a parent employed in concrete or aggregate production industries or associated or auxiliary industries. Along with their application, they must submit a brief resume of their current activities and work experience, 3 letters of character reference, and a 1-page statement on their plans for the future and career. Financial need is not considered in the selection process.

**Financial data:** The stipend is $1,000. Funds are paid directly to the student's institution.

**Duration:** 1 year.

**Number awarded:** 4 each year.

**Deadline:** July of each year.

## 2032 CRSI FOUNDATION UNDERGRADUATE SCHOLARSHIP PROGRAM

Concrete Reinforcing Steel Institute, Attn: CRSI Foundation
933 North Plum Grove Road
Schaumburg, IL 60173-4758
Phone: (847) 517-1200, ext. 14; Fax: (847) 517-1206; Email: lkelly@crsi.org
Web: www.crsi.org
**Summary:** To provide financial assistance to undergraduate students in civil or architectural engineering who are interested in preparing for a career in site-cast reinforced concrete construction.
**Eligibility:** Open to U.S. citizens who are entering their senior year as a full-time student in an ABET-accredited program in civil or architectural engineering. Applicants must demonstrate a career goal of employment in the site-cast reinforced concrete construction industry. Preference is given to students who have shown an interest, either through their educational program or by work experience, in a phase of that industry. Students having "hands-on" experience from full-time, part-time, or co-op work in the industry are especially encouraged to apply. Financial need is not considered in the selection process.
**Financial data:** A stipend is awarded (amount not specified).
**Duration:** 1 year.
**Number awarded:** 1 or more each year.
**Deadline:** June of each year.

## 2033 D. ANITA SMALL SCIENCE AND BUSINESS SCHOLARSHIP

Maryland Federation of Business and Professional Women's Clubs, Inc.
c/o Pat Schroeder, Chair
354 Driftwood Lane
Solomons, MD 20688
Phone: (410) 326-0167; (877) INFO BPW; Email: patsc@csmd.edu
Web: www.bpwmaryland.org/HTML/scholarships.html
**Summary:** To provide financial assistance to women in Maryland who are interested in working on an undergraduate or graduate degree in a science or business-related field
**Eligibility:** Open to women in Maryland who are at least 21 years of age and have been accepted to a bachelor's or advanced degree program at an accredited Maryland academic institution. Applicants must be preparing for a career in one of the following or a related field: accounting, aeronautics, business administration, computer sciences, engineering, finance, information technology, mathematics, medical sciences (including nursing, laboratory technology, therapy, etc.), oceanography, or physical sciences. They must have a GPA of 3.0 or higher and be able to demonstrate financial need.
**Financial data:** The stipend is $1,000 per year.
**Duration:** 1 year.
**Number awarded:** 1 or more each year.
**Deadline:** May of each year.

## 2034 DADE BEHRING MEDICAL TECHNICIAN SCHOLARSHIPS

American Society for Clinical Laboratory Science
Attn: Coordinating Council on the Clinical Laboratory Workforce
6701 Democracy Boulevard, Suite 300
Bethesda, MD 20817
Phone: (301) 657-2768; Fax: (301) 657-2909; Email: ascls@ascls.org
Web: www.ascls.org/education/index.asp
**Summary:** To provide financial assistance to students enrolled in an associate degree program in clinical laboratory technology.
**Eligibility:** Open to students entering the second year of an NAACLS accredited associate degree program in clinical laboratory technology or medical laboratory technology. Applicants must have a GPA of 2.5 or higher. Along with their application, they must submit a transcript of grades, 2 letters of recommendation, a statement explaining why they chose this field, and documentation of financial need.
**Financial data:** The stipend is $1,000.
**Duration:** 1 year.
**Number awarded:** 50 each year.
**Deadline:** July of each year.

## 2035 DAEDALIAN ACADEMIC MATCHING SCHOLARSHIP PROGRAM

Daedalian Foundation, Attn: Scholarship Committee
55 Main Circle (Building 676)
P.O. Box 249
Randolph AFB, TX 78148-0249
Phone: (210) 945-2113; Fax: (210) 945-2112; Email: daedalus@daedalians.org
Web: www.daedalians.org
**Summary:** To provide financial assistance to ROTC and other college students who wish to become military pilots.
**Eligibility:** Open to students who are attending or have been accepted at an accredited 4-year college or university and have demonstrated the desire and potential to become a commissioned military pilot. Usually, students in ROTC units of all services apply to local chapters (Flights) of Daedalian; if the Flight awards a scholarship, the application is forwarded to the Daedalian Foundation for 1 of these matching scholarships. College students not part of a ROTC program are eligible if their undergraduate goals and performance are consistent with Daedalian criteria. Selection is based on intention to pursue a career as a military pilot, demonstrated moral character and patriotism, scholastic and military standing and aptitude, and physical condition and aptitude for flight. Additional eligibility criteria may be set by a Flight Scholarship Selection Board.
**Financial data:** The amount awarded varies but is intended to serve as matching funds for the Flight scholarship. Generally, the maximum awarded is $2,000.
**Number awarded:** Up to 99 each year.
**Deadline:** Applications may be submitted at any time.

## 2036 DAIMLERCHRYSLER CORPORATION FUND SCHOLARSHIP

Society of Women Engineers
230 East Ohio Street, Suite 400
Chicago, IL 60611-3265
Phone: (312) 596-5223; Fax: (312) 644-8557; Email: hq@swe.org
Web: www.societyofwomenengineers.org/scholarships
**Summary:** To provide financial assistance to undergraduate women majoring in designated engineering specialties.
**Eligibility:** Open to women who are entering their sophomore year at an ABET accredited 4-year college or university. Applicants must be majoring in electrical or mechanical engineering and have a GPA of 3.0 or higher. Along with their application, they must submit a 1-page essay on why they want to be an engineer, how they believe they will make a difference as an engineer, and what influenced them to study engineering. Selection is based on merit.
**Financial data:** The stipend is $2,000.
**Duration:** 1 year; may be renewed for up to 2 additional years.
**Number awarded:** 1 each year.
**Deadline:** January of each year.

## 2037 DAIMLERCHRYSLER/HENAAC SCHOLARS PROGRAM

Hispanic Engineer National Achievement Awards Conference
3900 Whiteside Street
Los Angeles, CA 90063
Phone: (323) 262-0997; Fax: (323) 262-0946; Email: info@henaac.org
Web: www.henaac.org/scholarships.htm
**Summary:** To provide financial assistance to Hispanic undergraduate students majoring in electrical or mechanical engineering.
**Eligibility:** Open to Hispanic undergraduate students who are enrolled full time in electrical or mechanical engineering. Applicants must have a GPA of 3.0 or higher and be able to work in the United States. Academic achievement and campus community activities are considered in the selection process.
**Financial data:** Stipends range from $1,000 to $5,000.
**Duration:** 1 year; recipients may reapply.
**Number awarded:** 1 or more each year.
**Deadline:** April of each year.

## 2038 DANIEL B. FAMBRO STUDENT PAPER AWARD

Institute of Transportation Engineers
1099 14th Street, N.W., Suite 300 West
Washington, DC 20005-3438
Phone: (202) 289-0222; Fax: (202) 289-7722; Email: ite_staff@ite.org
Web: www.ite.org/awards/StudentPaper.asp
**Summary:** To recognize and reward student members of the Institute of Transportation Engineers (ITE) who submit outstanding papers on transportation engineering.
**Eligibility:** Open to ITE members who were student members sometime during the year prior to March of the current year. Applicants must have completed work on a paper while they were a student member. The paper must deal

with a topic in transportation engineering and be less than 15 pages in length. Selection is based on originality (20%), significance (20%), scope and format (20%), applicability (20%), and validity (20%).

**Financial data:** The award is $1,000.

**Duration:** The award is presented annually.

**Number awarded:** 1 each year.

**Deadline:** March of each year.

### 2039 DASSAULT FALCON JET CORPORATION SCHOLARSHIP

Women in Aviation, International, Attn: Scholarships
101 Corsair Drive, Suite 101
P.O. Box 11287
Daytona Beach, FL 32120-1287
Phone: (386) 226-7996; Fax: (386) 226-7998; Email: scholarships@wai.org
Web: www.wai.org/education/scholarships.cfm

**Summary:** To provide financial assistance to women who are working on an undergraduate or graduate degree in a field related to aviation.

**Eligibility:** Open to women who are working on an undergraduate or graduate degree in an aviation-related field. Applicants must be U.S. citizens, be U.S. citizens, and have a GPA of 3.0 or higher. They must submit a 1-page essay describing their current status, what they hope to achieve with a degree in aviation, and their aspirations in the field. Selection is based on the essay, achievements, attitude toward self and others, commitment to success, dedication to career, financial need, motivation, reliability, responsibility, and teamwork.

**Financial data:** The stipend is $1,000.

**Duration:** 1 year.

**Number awarded:** 1 each year.

**Deadline:** December of each year.

### 2040 DAVID A. LONG EDUCATIONAL SCHOLARSHIP

American Water Works Association-Pennsylvania Section
Attn: Educational Scholarship Committee
1309 Bridge Street
New Cumberland, PA 17070
Phone: (717) 774-8870; Fax: (717) 774-0288; Email: paawwa@pawwa.org
Web: www.paawwa.org

**Summary:** To provide financial assistance to upper-division and graduate students working on a degree in a water-related field at colleges and universities in Pennsylvania.

**Eligibility:** Open to juniors, seniors, and graduate students at colleges and universities in Pennsylvania. Applicants must be working on a degree in a field related to water quality and supply.

**Financial data:** The stipend is $1,500.

**Duration:** 1 year.

**Number awarded:** 1 each year.

**Deadline:** January of each year.

### 2041 DAVID ALAN QUICK SCHOLARSHIP

Experimental Aviation Association, Attn: Scholarship Office
EAA Aviation Center
P.O. Box 3086
Oshkosh, WI 54903-3086
Phone: (920) 426-6884; Fax: (920) 426-6865; Email: scholarships@eaa.org
Web: www.eaa.org/education/scholarships/index.html

**Summary:** To provide financial assistance to college juniors and seniors who are majoring in aerospace or aeronautical engineering.

**Eligibility:** Open to juniors and seniors enrolled at an accredited college or university and working on a degree in aerospace or aeronautical engineering. Applicants must submit a personal statement that covers their career aspirations, educational plan, why they want to receive this scholarship, what they learned from their work and volunteer experiences, how their education will be financed, and any unusual family circumstances.

**Financial data:** The stipend is $1,000.

**Duration:** 1 year; may be renewed.

**Number awarded:** 1 each year.

**Deadline:** March of each year.

### 2042 DAVID ARVER MEMORIAL SCHOLARSHIP

Aircraft Electronics Association, Attn: AEA Educational Foundation
4217 South Hocker Drive
Independence, MO 64055-4723
Phone: (816) 373-6565; Fax: (816) 478-3100; Email: info@aea.net
Web: www.aea.net

**Summary:** To provide financial assistance to students in selected states who are interested in studying avionics or aircraft repair in college.

**Eligibility:** Open to high school seniors and college students who plan to attend an accredited vocational or technical school in the Aircraft Electronics Association Region III; this includes the states of Illinois, Indiana, Iowa, Kansas, Michigan, Minnesota, Missouri, Nebraska, North Dakota, South Dakota, and Wisconsin. Applicants must be planning to enroll in an avionics or aircraft repair program. They must submit an official transcript (cumulative GPA of 2.5 or higher), a statement about their career plans, a description of their involvement in school and community activities, and a 300-word essay on how the job requirements of aviation technicians will change with advancements in technology. Selection is based on merit.

**Financial data:** The stipend is $1,000.

**Duration:** 1 year.

**Number awarded:** 1 each year.

**Deadline:** February of each year.

### 2043 DAVID HOODS MEMORIAL SCHOLARSHIP

Electronic Document Systems Foundation, Attn: EDSF Scholarship Awards
24238 Hawthorne Boulevard
Torrance, CA 90505-6505
Phone: (310) 541-1481; Fax: (310) 541-4803
Web: www.edsf.org/scholarships.cfm

**Summary:** To provide financial assistance to upper-division and graduate students interested in working with electronic documents as a career.

**Eligibility:** Open to full-time juniors, seniors, and graduate students who demonstrate a strong interest in working with electronic documents as a career (including graphic communications, document management, document content, and/or document distribution). Special consideration is given to students interested in marketing and public relations. Applicants must submit a statement of their career goals in the field of document communications, an essay on a topic related to their view of the future of the document management and production industry, a list of current professional and college extracurricular activities and achievements, college transcripts (GPA of 3.0 or higher), samples of their creative work, and 2 letters of recommendation. Financial need is not considered.

**Financial data:** The stipend is $2,000.

**Duration:** 1 year.

**Number awarded:** 1 each year.

**Deadline:** May of each year.

### 2044 DAVID MANN SCHOLARSHIP

American Mensa Education and Research Foundation
1229 Corporate Drive West
Arlington, TX 76006-6103
Phone: (817) 607-0060; (800) 66-MENSA; Fax: (817) 649-5232;
Email: Scholarships@merf.us.mensa.org
Web: merf.us.mensa.org/scholarships/index.php

**Summary:** To provide financial assistance for undergraduate or graduate study in aeronautical engineering or an aerospace field.

**Eligibility:** Open to students who are enrolled or planning to enroll in a degree program at an accredited American institution of postsecondary education with a major or career plans in aeronautical engineering or an aerospace field. Membership in Mensa is not required, but applicants must be U.S. citizens or permanent residents. There are no restrictions as to age, race, gender, level of postsecondary education, GPA, or financial need. Selection is based on a 550-word essay that describes the applicant's career, vocational, or academic goals.

**Financial data:** The stipend is $1,000.

**Duration:** 1 year; nonrenewable.

**Number awarded:** 1 each year.

**Deadline:** January of each year.

### 2045 DAVID SARNOFF RESEARCH CENTER SCHOLARSHIP

Society of Women Engineers
230 East Ohio Street, Suite 400
Chicago, IL 60611-3265
Phone: (312) 596-5223; Fax: (312) 644-8557; Email: hq@swe.org
Web: www.societyofwomenengineers.org/scholarships

**Summary:** To provide financial assistance to upper-division women majoring in engineering or computer science.
**Eligibility:** Open to women who are entering their junior year at an ABET-accredited college or university. Applicants must be majoring in computer science or engineering and have a GPA of 3.5 or higher. Along with their application, they must submit a 1-page essay on why they want to be an engineer or computer scientist, how they believe they will make a difference as an engineer or computer scientist, and what influenced them to study engineering or computer science. Selection is based on merit.
**Financial data:** The stipend is $1,500.
**Duration:** 1 year.
**Number awarded:** 1 each year.
**Deadline:** January of each year.

### 2046 DEAN WARNSTAFF FOUNDATION SCHOLARSHIPS

Missouri Ag Industries Council, Inc.
410 Madison Street
P.O. Box 1728
Jefferson City, MO 65104
Phone: (573) 636-6130; Fax: (573) 636-3299; Email: amber@mo-ag.com
Web: www.mo-ag.com/education.htm
**Summary:** To provide financial assistance to Missouri students working on an undergraduate degree in agriculture.
**Eligibility:** Open to Missouri undergraduate students working on a degree in a field related to agriculture. Selection is based on the applicant's agricultural background and activities, community service, extracurricular activities, work experience, and college course of study.
**Financial data:** The stipend is $1,000.
**Duration:** 1 year.
**Number awarded:** 3 each year.
**Deadline:** October of each year.

### 2047 DECOMMISSIONING, DECONTAMINATION AND REUTILIZATION SCHOLARSHIP

American Nuclear Society, Attn: Scholarship Coordinator
555 North Kensington Avenue
La Grange Park, IL 60526-5592
Phone: (708) 352-6611; Fax: (708) 352-0499; Email: outreach@ans.org
Web: www.ans.org/honors/scholarships
**Summary:** To provide financial assistance to undergraduate students who are working on a degree in engineering or science that is associated with decommissioning, decontamination, or environmental restoration aspects of nuclear power.
**Eligibility:** Open to students entering their junior or senior year in an engineering or science program at an accredited institution in the United States. The program must be associated with 1) decommissioning or decontamination of nuclear facilities; 2) management or characterization of nuclear waste; or 3) restoration of the environment. Applicants must be U.S. citizens and able to demonstrate academic achievement. Along with their application, they must submit a brief essay discussing the importance of an aspect of decommissioning, decontamination, and reutilization to the future of the nuclear field.
**Financial data:** The stipend is $2,000.
**Duration:** 1 year; nonrenewable
**Number awarded:** 1 each year.
**Deadline:** January of each year.

### 2048 DEED TECHNICAL DESIGN PROJECT

American Public Power Association, Attn: DEED Administrator
2301 M Street, N.W.
Washington, DC 20037-1484
Phone: (202) 467-2960; Fax: (202) 467-2910; Email: deed@appanet.org
Web: www.appanet.org
**Summary:** To recognize and reward undergraduate and graduate students who develop and demonstrate outstanding projects related to energy innovation.
**Eligibility:** Open to undergraduate and graduate students in energy-related disciplines at accredited colleges and universities in the United States and Canada. Applicants must complete a technical design project and submit a final report on the project, describing activities, cost, sources used, achievements, problems, results, and recommendations. The project must relate to energy innovation, improving efficiencies, and lowering the cost of providing energy services to the customers of publicly owned electric utilities. Selection is based on the applicability of benefits to public power systems, the applicant's major

in an academic field related to the electric power or energy service industries, academic performance, generalizable methodologies, and promotion of energy efficiency.
**Financial data:** The grant is $5,000. An additional $3,000 is available to pay for travel expenses to attend the engineering and operations technical conference of the American Public Power Association (APPA) and present their project. If more than 1 student is involved in a project, the award funds are split among all participants.
**Duration:** This competition is held annually.
**Number awarded:** 1 each year.
**Deadline:** October of each year.

### 2049 DELAYED EDUCATION SCHOLARSHIP FOR WOMEN

American Nuclear Society, Attn: Scholarship Coordinator
555 North Kensington Avenue
La Grange Park, IL 60526-5592
Phone: (708) 352-6611; Fax: (708) 352-0499; Email: outreach@ans.org
Web: www.ans.org/honors/scholarships
**Summary:** To encourage mature women whose formal studies in nuclear science or nuclear engineering have been delayed or interrupted.
**Eligibility:** Open to mature women who have experienced at least a 1-year delay or interruption of their undergraduate studies and are returning to school to work on an undergraduate or graduate degree in nuclear science or nuclear engineering. They must be U.S. citizens or permanent residents, have proven academic ability, and be able to demonstrate financial need.
**Financial data:** The stipend is $4,000. Funds may be used by the student to cover any bona fide education costs, including tuition, books, room, and board.
**Duration:** 1 year; nonrenewable.
**Number awarded:** 1 each year.
**Deadline:** January of each year.

### 2050 DELL COMPUTER CORPORATION SCHOLARSHIPS

Society of Women Engineers
230 East Ohio Street, Suite 400
Chicago, IL 60611-3265
Phone: (312) 596-5223; Fax: (312) 644-8557; Email: hq@swe.org
Web: www.societyofwomenengineers.org/scholarships
**Summary:** To provide financial assistance to upper-division women majoring in computer science or designated engineering specialties.
**Eligibility:** Open to women who are entering their junior or senior year at an ABET-accredited college or university. Applicants must be majoring in computer science or electrical, computer, or mechanical engineering and have a GPA of 3.0 or higher. Along with their application, they must submit a 1-page essay on why they want to be an engineer or computer scientist, how they believe they will make a difference, and what influenced them to study engineering or computer science. Financial need is considered.
**Financial data:** The stipend is $2,250.
**Duration:** 1 year.
**Number awarded:** 2 each year.
**Deadline:** January of each year.

### 2051 DELL/UNCF CORPORATE SCHOLARS PROGRAM

United Negro College Fund, Attn: Corporate Scholars Program
P.O. Box 1435
Alexandria, VA 22313-9998
Phone: (866) 671-7237; Email: internship@uncf.org
Web: www.uncf.org/internships/index.asp
**Summary:** To provide financial assistance and work experience to undergraduate and graduate students, especially minorities, majoring in designated fields and interested in an internship at Dell Computer Corporation's corporate head quarters near Austin, Texas.
**Eligibility:** Open to rising juniors and graduate students who are enrolled full time at institutions that are members of the United Negro College Fund (UNCF) or at any other 4-year college or university. Applicants must be majoring in business administration, computer science, engineering (computer, electrical, or mechanical), finance, human resources, management information systems, marketing, or supply chain management with a GPA of 3.0 or higher. Along with their application, they must submit a 1-page essay about themselves and their career goals, including information about their personal background and any particular challenges they have faced. Finalists are interviewed by a team of representatives from Dell, the program's sponsor.

**Financial data:** The program provides a paid summer internship, housing accommodations in Austin, round-trip transportation to and from Austin, and (based on financial need and successful internship performance) a $10,000 scholarship.
**Duration:** 10 to 12 weeks for the internship; 1 year for the scholarship.
**Number awarded:** Varies each year.
**Deadline:** January of each year.

## 2052 DELPHI SCHOLARSHIPS

Society of Women Engineers
230 East Ohio Street, Suite 400
Chicago, IL 60611-3265
Phone: (312) 596-5223; Fax: (312) 644-8557; Email: hq@swe.org
Web: www.societyofwomenengineers.org/scholarships
**Summary:** To provide financial assistance to undergraduate women majoring in computer science or engineering.
**Eligibility:** Open to women who are entering their sophomore or junior year at a designated 4-year ABET-accredited college or university. Applicants must be majoring in computer science or engineering and have a GPA of 3.0 or higher. Along with their application, they must submit a 1-page essay on why they want to be an engineer or computer scientist, how they believe they will make a difference as an engineer or computer scientist, and what influenced them to study engineering or computer science. Selection is based on merit.
**Financial data:** The stipend is $2,500.
**Duration:** 1 year.
**Number awarded:** 2 each year.
**Deadline:** January of each year.

## 2053 DELTA AIR LINES AIRCRAFT MAINTENANCE TECHNOLOGY SCHOLARSHIPS

Women in Aviation, International, Attn: Scholarships
101 Corsair Drive, Suite 101
P.O. Box 11287
Daytona Beach, FL 32120-1287
Phone: (386) 226-7996; Fax: (386) 226-7998; Email: scholarships@wai.org
Web: www.wai.org/education/scholarships.cfm
**Summary:** To provide financial assistance to members of Women in Aviation, International (WAI) who are interested in a career in aviation maintenance.
**Eligibility:** Open to WAI members who are full-time students with at least 2 semesters of study remaining. Applicants must be preparing for an aviation maintenance technician license (A&P) or a degree in aviation maintenance technology with a cumulative GPA of 3.0 or higher. U.S. citizenship or permanent resident status is required. As part of the selection process, applicants must submit an essay of 500 to 1,000 words that addresses such topics as who or what influenced them to prepare for a career in aviation maintenance technology, their greatest life challenge, their greatest strength and strongest characteristic, their most memorable academic experience, and why they are the best candidate for this scholarship. In addition to the essay, selection is based on achievements, attitude toward self and others, commitment to success, dedication to career, financial need, motivation, reliability, responsibility, and teamwork.
**Financial data:** The stipend is $5,000.
**Duration:** 1 year.
**Number awarded:** 1 each year.
**Deadline:** December of each year.

## 2054 DELTA AIR LINES ENGINEERING SCHOLARSHIPS

Women in Aviation, International, Attn: Scholarships
101 Corsair Drive, Suite 101
P.O. Box 11287
Daytona Beach, FL 32120-1287
Phone: (386) 226-7996; Fax: (386) 226-7998; Email: scholarships@wai.org
Web: www.wai.org/education/scholarships.cfm
**Summary:** To provide financial assistance to members of Women in Aviation, International (WAI) who are studying engineering in college.
**Eligibility:** Open to WAI members who are full-time juniors or seniors with at least 2 semesters of study remaining. Applicants must be working on a baccalaureate degree in aerospace, aeronautical, electrical, or mechanical engineering with a cumulative GPA of 3.0 or higher. U.S. citizenship is required. As part of the selection process, applicants must submit an essay of 500 to 1,000 words that addresses such questions as who or what influenced them to prepare for a career in engineering, their greatest strength and strongest characteristic, their most memorable academic experience, their greatest life challenge and how has it enriched their life, and why are they the best candidate for this scholarship.

In addition to the essay, selection is based on achievements, attitude toward self and others, commitment to success, dedication to career, financial need, motivation, reliability, responsibility, and teamwork.
**Financial data:** The stipend is $5,000.
**Duration:** 1 year.
**Number awarded:** 1 each year.
**Deadline:** December of each year.

## 2055 DELTA GAMMA FOUNDATION FLORENCE MARGARET HARVEY MEMORIAL SCHOLARSHIP

American Foundation for the Blind, Attn: Scholarship Committee
11 Penn Plaza, Suite 300
New York, NY 10001
Phone: (212) 502-7661; (800) AFB-LINE; Fax: (212) 502-7771;
TDD: (212) 502-7662; Email: afbinfo@afb.net
Web: www.afb.org/scholarships.asp
**Summary:** To provide financial assistance to blind undergraduate and graduate students who wish to study in the field of rehabilitation and/or education of the blind.
**Eligibility:** Open to legally blind juniors, seniors, or graduate students. U.S. citizenship is required. Applicants must be studying in the field of rehabilitation and/or education of visually impaired and blind persons. Along with their application, they must submit an essay that includes the field of study they are pursuing and why they have chosen it; their educational and personal goals; their work experience; any extracurricular activities with which they have been involved, including those in school, religious organizations, and the community; and how they intend to use scholarship monies that may be awarded.
**Financial data:** The stipend is $1,000.
**Duration:** 1 year.
**Number awarded:** 1 each year.
**Deadline:** April of each year.

## 2056 DENISE SCHOLARSHIP FUND

New York State Grange
100 Grange Place
Cortland, NY 13045
Phone: (607) 756-7553; Fax: (607) 756-7757;
Email: nysgrange@nysgrange.com
Web: www.nysgrange.com/education.html
**Summary:** To provide financial assistance to undergraduate students in New York interested in majoring in agriculture.
**Eligibility:** Open to undergraduate students at a 2-year or 4-year college or university anywhere in the country. Applicants must be residents of New York and interested in majoring in the field of agriculture. They must be able to demonstrate financial need.
**Financial data:** A stipend is awarded (amount not specified).
**Duration:** 1 year.
**Number awarded:** 1 or more each year.
**Deadline:** April of each year.

## 2057 DENNY'S SCHOLARSHIP PROGRAM

Hispanic College Fund, Attn: National Director
1717 Pennsylvania Avenue, N.W., Suite 460
Washington, D.C. 20006
Phone: (202) 296-5400; (800) 644-4223; Fax: (202) 296-3774;
Email: hispaniccollegefund@earthlink.net
Web: www.hispanicfund.org
**Summary:** To provide financial assistance to Hispanic American undergraduate students who are interested in preparing for a career in business, computer science, or engineering.
**Eligibility:** Open to U.S. citizens of Hispanic background (at least one grandparent must be 100% Hispanic) who are entering their freshman, sophomore, junior, or senior year of college. Applicants must be working on a bachelor's degree in business, computer science, engineering, or a business-related major and have a cumulative GPA of 3.0 or higher. They must be applying to or enrolled in a college or university in the 50 states or Puerto Rico as a full-time student. Financial need is considered in the selection process.
**Financial data:** Stipends range from $500 to $5,000, depending on the need of the recipient, and average approximately $3,000. Funds are paid directly to the recipient's college or university to help cover tuition and fees.
**Duration:** 1 year; recipients may reapply.
**Number awarded:** Varies each year.
**Deadline:** April of each year.

## 2058 DENVER GEOPHYSICAL SOCIETY SCHOLARSHIPS

Society of Exploration Geophysicists, Attn: SEG Foundation
8801 South Yale, Suite 500
P.O. Box 702740
Tulsa, OK 74170-2740
Phone: (918) 497-5513; Fax: (918) 497-5557; Email: scholarships@seg.org
Web: seg.org/business/foundation/scholarships/index.shtml

**Summary:** To provide financial assistance to undergraduate and graduate students who are interested in studying applied geophysics in Colorado.

**Eligibility:** Open to 1) high school students planning to enter college in the fall, and 2) undergraduate or graduate students whose grades are above average. Preference is given to students at Colorado School of Mines; if no qualified students from that school apply, students at other colleges and universities in Colorado are considered. Applicants must intend to work on a degree directed toward a career in applied geophysics or a closely-related field. Along with their application, they must submit a 150-word essay on how they plan to use geophysics in their future. Financial need is not considered in the selection process.

**Financial data:** The stipend ranges from $1,000 to $3,000 per year.

**Duration:** 1 academic year; may be renewable, based on scholastic standing, availability of funds, and continuance of a course of study leading to a career in applied geophysics.

**Number awarded:** 1 or more each year.

**Deadline:** January of each year.

## 2059 DERIVATIVE DUO SCHOLARSHIP

Pride Foundation, Attn: Scholarships Manager
1122 East Pike, Suite 1001
Seattle, WA 98122-3934
Phone: (206) 323-3318; (800) 735-7287; Fax: (206) 323-1017;
Email: scholarships@pridefoundation.org
Web: www.pridefoundation.org

**Summary:** To provide financial assistance to Washington residents engaged in undergraduate study of mental health or human services.

**Eligibility:** Open to undergraduate students majoring in mental health or human services who are Washington residents. Applicants must demonstrate a connection between their studies and involvement in the community around issues of social justice. Selection is based on financial need, community involvement, and commitment to civil rights for all people.

**Financial data:** Stipends range from $1,000 to $5,000.

**Duration:** 1 year; recipients may reapply.

**Number awarded:** 1 each year. Since it began offering scholarships in 1992, the foundation has awarded more than $500,000 to more than 325 recipients.

**Deadline:** January of each year.

## 2060 DERMIK LABORATORIES CAREER MOBILITY SCHOLARSHIPS

Dermatology Nurses' Association
East Holly Avenue, Box 56
Pitman, NJ 08071-0056
Phone: (856) 256-2330; (800) 454-4DNA; Fax: (856) 589-7463;
Email: dna@ajj.com
Web: www.dnanurse.org

**Summary:** To provide financial assistance to members of the Dermatology Nurses' Association (DNA) who are working on an undergraduate or graduate degree.

**Eligibility:** Open to applicants who 1) have been members of the association for at least 2 years, 2) are employed in the specialty of dermatology, and 3) are working on a degree or advanced degree in nursing. Selection is based on a letter in which applicants describe their professional goals, proposed course of study, time frame for completion of study, funds necessary to meet their educational needs, and financial need.

**Financial data:** The stipend is $2,500.

**Duration:** 1 year.

**Number awarded:** 2 each year.

**Deadline:** October of each year.

## 2061 DES STATE SOCIETY SCHOLARSHIPS

Delaware Engineering Society
c/o Stacy Ziegler
Duffield Associates, Inc.
5400 Limestone Road
Wilmington, DE 19808
Phone: (302) 239-6634; Fax: (302) 239-8485; Email: sziegler@duffnet.com
Web: www.udel.edu/DES

**Summary:** To provide financial assistance to high school seniors in Delaware who are interested in majoring in engineering in college.

**Eligibility:** Open to graduating high school seniors in Delaware who are residents of the state and interested in majoring in engineering at an ABET-accredited college or university. Applicants must have ACT scores of 29 or higher in math and 25 or higher in English (or the equivalent SAT scores). They must submit an essay (up to 500 words) on their interest in engineering, their major area of study and area of specialization, the occupation they propose to pursue after graduation, their long-term goals, and how they hope to achieve them. Selection is based on the essay, academic record, honors and scholarships, volunteer activities, work experience, and letters of recommendation. Financial need is not required.

**Financial data:** The stipend is $1,000 per year.

**Duration:** 1 year; nonrenewable.

**Number awarded:** Varies each year; recently, 3 of these scholarships were awarded.

**Deadline:** November of each year.

## 2062 DEVELOPMENT DISABILITIES SCHOLASTIC EXCELLENCE AWARD FOR LUTHERAN COLLEGE STUDENTS

Bethesda Lutheran Homes and Services, Inc.
Attn: National Christian Resource Center
600 Hoffmann Drive
Watertown, WI 53094
Phone: (920) 261-3050; (800) 369-4636, ext. 3418; Fax: (920) 262-6513;
Email: ncrc@blhs.org
Web: www.blhs.org/youth/scholarships

**Summary:** To provide financial assistance to college students who are Lutherans and interested in preparing for a career in the field of developmental disabilities.

**Eligibility:** Open to active communicant members of a Lutheran congregation who have at least sophomore status at a college or university or are classified as a full-time junior or senior; have an overall GPA of 3.0 or higher; and are interested in preparing for a career in the field of developmental disabilities. Along with their application, they must submit 1) an essay of 250 to 500 words on the career they are planning, why they chose that particular career goal, how they are preparing for that career, and why they would like to receive this scholarship; 2) 4 letters of recommendation; 3) an official college transcript; 4) a 1-page autobiographical narrative, detailing their academic and community honors, awards, and activities; and 5) documentation that they have completed at least 100 hours of volunteer and/or paid work to benefit people who are developmentally disabled. Financial need is not considered in the selection process.

**Financial data:** The stipend is $1,500.

**Duration:** 1 year.

**Number awarded:** Up to 3 each year.

**Deadline:** March of each year.

## 2063 DEVELOPMENT DISABILITIES SCHOLASTIC EXCELLENCE AWARD FOR LUTHERAN NURSING STUDENTS

Bethesda Lutheran Homes and Services, Inc.
Attn: National Christian Resource Center
600 Hoffmann Drive
Watertown, WI 53094
Phone: (920) 261-3050; (800) 369-4636, ext. 3418; Fax: (920) 262-6513;
Email: ncrc@blhs.org
Web: www.blhs.org/youth/scholarships

**Summary:** To provide financial assistance to nursing students who are Lutherans and interested in preparing for a career in the field of developmental disabilities.

**Eligibility:** Open to active communicant members of a Lutheran congregation who have at least sophomore status at an accredited school of nursing or are classified as a full-time junior or senior; have an overall GPA of 3.0 or higher; and are interested in preparing for a career as a nurse in the field of developmental disabilities. Along with their application, they must submit 1) an essay of 250 to 500 words on the career they are planning in the field of nursing, why they chose that particular career goal, how they are preparing for that career, and why they would like to receive this scholarship; 2) 4 letters of recommendation; 3) an official college transcript; 4) a 1-page autobiographical narrative, detailing their academic and community honors, awards, and activities; and 5) documentation that they have completed at least 100 hours of volunteer and/or paid work to benefit people who are developmentally disabled. Financial need is not considered in the selection process.

**Financial data:** The stipend is $1,500.

**Duration:** 1 year.

**Number awarded:** Up to 2 each year.

**Deadline:** March of each year.

## 2064 THE DEVELOPMENT FUND FOR BLACK STUDENTS IN SCIENCE AND TECHNOLOGY SCHOLARSHIPS

The Development Fund for Black Students in Science and Technology
2705 Bladensburg Road, N.E.
Washington, DC 20018
Phone: (202) 635-3604; Email: hattie.carwell@oak.doe.gov
Web: ourworld.compuserve.com/homepages/dlhinson/dfb_sch.htm

**Summary:** To provide scholarships to African American students who enroll in scientific or technical fields of study at Historically Black Colleges and Universities (HBCUs).

**Eligibility:** Open to individuals nominated by deans and faculty members of engineering and science departments at predominantly Black colleges and universities. To be eligible, nominated students must intend to enroll at a predominantly Black college or university or already be enrolled at such a college or university. They must intend to major in a technical field and be U.S. citizens or permanent residents who intend to remain in the United States after graduation. Selection is based on academic achievement (grades and SAT scores, especially in science and mathematics), a personal essay describing career goals and relevant extracurricular activities, recommendations, and financial need.

**Financial data:** The amount of the scholarship is based on merit and financial need. Awards up to $2,000 per year are available.

**Duration:** 1 year; may be renewed for up to 4 years, as long as the recipient remains in good academic standing and enrolled full time in a science or engineering curriculum.

**Number awarded:** Several each year.

**Deadline:** June of each year.

## 2065 DIETETIC TECHNICIAN SCHOLARSHIP

Florida Dietetic Association
Attn: Scholarship Chair, Florida Dietetic Association Foundation
P.O. Box 12608
Tallahassee, FL 32317-2608
Phone: (850) 386-8850; Fax: (850) 386-7918; Email: DIETNUTR@aol.com
Web: www.eatrightflorida.org/general/scholarships.html

**Summary:** To provide financial assistance to students enrolled in a dietetic technician program at an approved program in Florida.

**Eligibility:** Open to Florida residents enrolled full time in a technician program that will prepare them to practice in the field of dietetics. Applicants must be members of the Florida Dietetic Association or attending school in Florida. They must have a GPA of 2.5 or higher and be members of the American Dietetic Association or enrolled in a program leading to eligibility for membership. U.S. citizenship or permanent resident status is required.

**Financial data:** The stipend is $1,000.

**Duration:** 1 year.

**Number awarded:** 1 each year.

**Deadline:** April of each year.

## 2066 DIVISION OF ENGINEERING SERVICES ENGINEERING/ ARCHITECTURAL SCHOLARSHIP

**Summary:** To provide financial assistance to high school seniors in California who plan to study engineering or architecture at a college or university in the state.

*See Listing #1359.*

## 2067 DONALD AND SHIRLEY HASTINGS NATIONAL SCHOLARSHIP

American Welding Society, Attn: AWS Foundation, Inc.
550 N.W. LeJeune Road
Miami, FL 33126
Phone: (305) 445-6628; (800) 443-9353, ext. 461; Fax: (305) 443-7559;
Email: found@aws.org
Web: www.aws.org/foundation/national_scholarships.html

**Summary:** To provide financial assistance to college students majoring in welding engineering.

**Eligibility:** Open to undergraduate students who are working on a 4-year bachelor's degree in welding engineering or welding engineering technology; preference is given to welding engineering students. Applicants must have an overall GPA of 2.5 or higher and be able to demonstrate financial need. U.S. citizenship is required.

**Financial data:** The stipend is $2,500.

**Duration:** 1 year; recipients may reapply.

**Number awarded:** 1 each year.

**Deadline:** January of each year.

## 2068 DONALD F. & MILDRED TOPP OTHMER NATIONAL SCHOLARSHIP AWARDS

American Institute of Chemical Engineers, Attn: Awards Administrator
Three Park Avenue
New York, NY 10016-5991
Phone: (212) 591-7107; Fax: (212) 591-8890; Email: awards@aiche.org
Web: www.aiche.org/awards

**Summary:** To provide financial assistance to student members of the American Institute of Chemical Engineers (AIChE).

**Eligibility:** Open to AIChE student members who are undergraduates in chemical engineering. Each student chapter advisor may nominate 1 student member. Nominees must have completed approximately half of their degree requirements at the start of the academic year (i.e., junior standing in a 4-year program or equivalent for a 5-year co-op program). They must submit a 300-word statement outlining their career plans and objectives in chemical engineering. Selection is based on that statement, academic record, support of the nominee by the student chapter advisor, and involvement in student chapter and other professional activities.

**Financial data:** The stipend is $1,000.

**Duration:** 1 year.

**Number awarded:** 15 each year.

**Deadline:** May of each year.

## 2069 DONALD G. WILLEMS SCHOLARSHIP

American Water Works Association-Montana Section
Attn: Executive Secretary
1029 Washington Avenue
Havre, MT 59501
Phone: (406) 265-9753; Fax: (406) 265-2277; Email: bcoffman@hi-line.net
Web: www.montana-awwa.org/Scholarship.htm

**Summary:** To provide financial assistance to students at colleges and universities in Montana who are working on undergraduate or graduate degrees in water-related fields.

**Eligibility:** Open to students currently enrolled at colleges and universities in Montana who have completed at least 1 academic year with a GPA of 2.0 or higher. Applicants must be working on an associate, bachelor's, or graduate degree in a field that will lead to employment in the water and wastewater fields, including water treatment and distribution, wastewater treatment and collection, water resources, watershed protection, groundwater remediation, and related subdisciplines. Along with their application, they must submit 3 references, a resume, and a 750-word statement of their professional goals. Financial need is not considered.

**Financial data:** The stipend is $1,000.

**Duration:** 1 year.

**Number awarded:** 2 each year.

**Deadline:** February of each year.

## 2070 DONNIE ARTHUR MEMORIAL TURFGRASS SCHOLARSHIP

Alabama Golf Course Superintendents Association
Attn: Scholarship Committee
P.O. Box 661214
Birmingham, AL 35266-1214
Phone: (205) 967-0397; Fax: (205) 967-1466; Email: agcsa@charter.net
Web: www.agcsa.org/scholarshipprogram.htm

**Summary:** To provide financial assistance to students from Alabama who are majoring in turfgrass management in college.

**Eligibility:** Open to residents of Alabama who are currently enrolled full time in an agricultural program emphasizing turfgrass management. Applicants must have a GPA of 2.0 or higher. Along with their application, they must submit a description of themselves that covers their academic ability, dependability, work habits, potential for leadership, and thoughts on what a superintendent needs in the 21st century to be successful.

**Financial data:** The stipend is $1,000. Funds are paid directly to the recipient.

**Duration:** 1 year.

**Number awarded:** 2 each year.

**Deadline:** October of each year.

## 2071 DOROTHY DANN BULLOCK MUSIC THERAPY AWARD

**Summary:** To provide financial assistance to members of the National Federation of Music Clubs (NFMC) who are majoring in music therapy. *See Listing #1363.*

## 2072 DOROTHY LEMKE HOWARTH SCHOLARSHIPS

Society of Women Engineers
230 East Ohio Street, Suite 400
Chicago, IL 60611-3265
Phone: (312) 596-5223; Fax: (312) 644-8557; Email: hq@swe.org
Web: www.societyofwomenengineers.org/scholarships

**Summary:** To provide financial assistance to lower-division women majoring in computer science or engineering.

**Eligibility:** Open to women who are entering their sophomore year at a 4-year ABET-accredited college or university. Applicants must be U.S. citizens majoring in computer science or engineering and have a GPA of 3.0 or higher. Along with their application, they must submit a 1-page essay on why they want to be an engineer or computer scientist, how they believe they will make a difference as an engineer or computer scientist, and what influenced them to study engineering or computer science. Selection is based on merit.

**Financial data:** The stipend is $2,000.

**Duration:** 1 year.

**Number awarded:** 5 each year.

**Deadline:** January of each year.

## 2073 DOROTHY M. & EARL S. HOFFMAN SCHOLARSHIPS

Society of Women Engineers
230 East Ohio Street, Suite 400
Chicago, IL 60611-3265
Phone: (312) 596-5223; Fax: (312) 644-8557; Email: hq@swe.org
Web: www.swe.org
Web: www.societyofwomenengineers.org/scholarships

**Summary:** To provide financial assistance to women who will be entering college as freshmen and are interested in studying engineering or computer science.

**Eligibility:** Open to women who are entering college as freshmen with a GPA of 3.5 or higher. Applicants must be planning to enroll full time at an ABET-accredited 4-year college or university and major in computer science or engineering. Along with their application, they must submit a 1-page essay on why they want to be an engineer or computer scientist, how they believe they will make a difference as an engineer or computer scientist, and what influenced them to study engineering or computer science. Selection is based on merit. Preference is given to students at Bucknell University and Rensselaer Polytechnic Institute.

**Financial data:** The stipend is $3,000 per year.

**Duration:** 1 year; may be renewed for up to 3 additional years.

**Number awarded:** 5 each year.

**Deadline:** May of each year.

## 2074 DOROTHY MORRIS SCHOLARSHIP

Society of Women Engineers
230 East Ohio Street, Suite 400
Chicago, IL 60611-3265
Phone: (312) 596-5223; Fax: (312) 644-8557; Email: hq@swe.org
Web: www.societyofwomenengineers.org/scholarships

**Summary:** To provide financial assistance to undergraduate women from New Jersey majoring in computer science or engineering.

**Eligibility:** Open to women who are graduates of high schools in New Jersey and are now entering their sophomore, junior, or senior year at a 4-year ABET-accredited college or university. Applicants must be U.S. citizens majoring in computer science or engineering and have a GPA of 3.0 or higher. Along with their application, they must submit a 1-page essay on why they want to be an engineer or computer scientist, how they believe they will make a difference as

an engineer or computer scientist, and what influenced them to study engineering or computer science. Selection is based on merit.

**Financial data:** The stipend is $1,000.

**Duration:** 1 year.

**Number awarded:** 1 each year.

**Deadline:** January of each year.

## 2075 DOROTHY MORRISON UNDERGRADUATE SCHOLARSHIP

Alpha Mu Tau Fraternity
c/o American Society for Clinical Laboratory Science
6701 Democracy Boulevard, Suite 300
Bethesda, MD 20817
Phone: (301) 657-2768; Fax: (301) 657-2909; Email: ascls@ascls.org
Web: www.ascls.org/leadership/awards/amt.asp

**Summary:** To provide financial assistance for undergraduate studies to members of Alpha Mu Tau, a national fraternity for professionals in the clinical laboratory sciences.

**Eligibility:** Open to U.S. citizens or permanent residents who are members of Alpha Mu Tau and accepted into or currently enrolled in a program in clinical laboratory science, including clinical laboratory science/medical technology and clinical laboratory technician/medical laboratory technician for undergraduates. They must be entering their last year of study. Along with their application, they must submit a 500-word statement describing their interest and reasons for preparing for a career in clinical laboratory science. Financial need is also considered in the selection process.

**Financial data:** The stipend is $2,000.

**Duration:** 1 year.

**Number awarded:** 1 each year.

**Deadline:** March of each year.

## 2076 DOSATRON INTERNATIONAL SCHOLARSHIP

Floriculture Industry Research and Scholarship Trust
Attn: Scholarship Program
P.O. Box 280
East Lansing, MI 48826-0280
Phone: (517) 333-4617; Fax: (517) 333-4494;
Email: scholarships@firstinfloriculture.org
Web: www.firstinfloriculture.org

**Summary:** To provide financial assistance to upper-division and graduate students in horticulture.

**Eligibility:** Open to juniors, seniors, and graduate students at 4-year colleges and universities who are majoring in horticulture. Applicants must be interested in floriculture production with a career goal of working in a greenhouse environment. They must be U.S. or Canadian citizens or permanent residents with a GPA of 3.0 or higher. Selection is based on academic record, recommendations, career goals, extracurricular activities, and financial need.

**Financial data:** The stipend depends on the availability of funds. Recently, it was $1,000.

**Duration:** 1 year.

**Number awarded:** 1 each year.

**Deadline:** April of each year.

## 2077 DOWNRIVER DETROIT SCHOLARSHIP

Society of Manufacturing Engineers, Attn: SME Education Foundation
One SME Drive
P.O. Box 930
Dearborn, MI 48121-0930
Phone: (313) 425-3304; (800) 733-4763, ext. 3304; Fax: (313) 425-3411;
Email: foundation@sme.org
Web: www.sme.org

**Summary:** To provide financial assistance to students working on an undergraduate or graduate degree in engineering in Michigan.

**Eligibility:** Open to students working on an associate's, bachelor's, or graduate degree in manufacturing engineering, mechanical engineering, industrial engineering, industrial technology, or engineering technology at a college or university in Michigan. Applicants must have a GPA of 2.5 or higher. Preference is given in the following order: first, children and grandchildren of current members of Downriver Detroit Chapter 198 of the Society of Manufacturing Engineers (SME); second, student members of chapters sponsored by SME Chapter 198; third, applicants who reside within Michigan; and fourth, applicants planning to attend a college or university in Michigan.

**Financial data:** The stipend is $1,200.
**Duration:** 1 year; may be renewed.
**Number awarded:** 1 each year.
**Deadline:** January of each year.

### 2078 DR. ALFRED C. FONES SCHOLARSHIP

American Dental Hygienists' Association, Attn: Institute for Oral Health
444 North Michigan Avenue, Suite 3400
Chicago, IL 60611
Phone: (312) 440-8918; (800) 735-4916; Fax: (312) 440-8929;
Email: institute@adha.net
Web: www.adha.org/institute/Scholarship/index.htm
**Summary:** To provide financial assistance to dental hygiene students who are in a bachelor's or graduate degree program and intend to become teachers or educators.
**Eligibility:** Open to dental hygiene students at the baccalaureate, master's, and doctoral level who have completed at least one year of study with a GPA of at least 3.0. Applicants must intend to prepare for a career as a dental hygiene teacher or educator. They must be active members of the Student American Dental Hygienists' Association (SADHA) or the American Dental Hygienists' Association (ADHA) and be able to document financial need of at least $1,500. Along year in an accredited dental hygiene program in the United States. Along with their application, they must submit a statement that covers their long-term career goals, their intended contribution to the dental hygiene profession, their professional interests, and the manner in which their degree will enhance their professional capacity. Graduate applicants must also include a description of the research in which they are involved or would like to become involved and a list of past and/or present involvement in professional and/or community activities.
**Financial data:** Stipends range from $1,000 to $2,000.
**Duration:** 1 year.
**Number awarded:** 1 each year.
**Deadline:** April of each year.

### 2079 DR. ALVIN AND MONICA SAAKE FOUNDATION SCHOLARSHIPS

Hawai'i Community Foundation, Attn: Scholarship Department
1164 Bishop Street, Suite 800
Honolulu, HI 96813
Phone: (808) 566-5570; (888) 731-3863; Fax: (808) 521-6286;
Email: scholarships@hcf-hawaii.org
Web: www.hawaiicommunityfoundation.org/scholar/scholar.php
**Summary:** To provide financial assistance to Hawaii residents who are interested in preparing for a career in designated health fields.
**Eligibility:** Open to Hawaii residents who are enrolled as full-time juniors, seniors, or graduate students. Applicants must be majoring in kinesiology, leisure science, physical education, athletic training, exercise science, sports medicine, physical therapy, or occupational therapy. They must be able to demonstrate academic achievement (GPA of 2.7 or higher), good moral character, and financial need. In addition to filling out the standard application form, applicants must write a short statement indicating their reasons for attending college, their planned course of study, and their career goals.
**Financial data:** The amounts of the awards depend on the availability of funds and the need of the recipient; recently, stipends averaged $2,895.
**Duration:** 1 year.
**Number awarded:** Varies each year; recently, 19 of these scholarships were awarded.
**Deadline:** February of each year.

### 2080 DR. AND MRS. H.H. NININGER METEORITE AWARD

Arizona State University, Attn: Center for Meteorite Studies
P.O. Box 871404
Tempe, AZ 85287-1404
Phone: (602) 965-6511; Email: meteorites@asu.edu
Web: meteorites.asu.edu/nininger
**Summary:** To recognize and reward outstanding student papers dealing with aspects of meteoritic investigation.
**Eligibility:** Open to both undergraduate and graduate students. They are invited to submit a paper (under 10,000 words) reflecting an aspect of meteoritic investigation. Research topics may include (but are not limited to) physical and chemical properties of meteorites, origin of meteoritic material, and cratering. Observational, experimental, statistical, or theoretical investigations are allowed. Students must be the first author of the paper, but they do not have to

be the sole author. Papers must have been written, submitted, or published during the first 10 and a half months of the calendar year. They must cover original research conducted by the student.
**Financial data:** The prize is $2,500.
**Duration:** The competition is held annually.
**Number awarded:** 1 each year.
**Deadline:** November of each year.

### 2081 DR. BERTHA BEAZLEY MEMORIAL ENDOWED SCHOLARSHIP

Indiana Business and Professional Women's Foundation, Inc.
P.O. Box 33
Knightstown, IN 46148-0033
Email: bpwin@msn.com
Web: www.indianabpwfoundation.org
**Summary:** To provide financial assistance to women in Indiana who are enrolled as upper-division undergraduates in a medical field.
**Eligibility:** Open to women who have been an Indiana resident for at least one year. Applicants must be entering their junior or senior year of a 4-year undergraduate program in a medical field. Along with their application, they must submit 1) a statement (up to 200 words) on their career goals and how their education relates to those goals, and 2) documentation of financial need. Preference is given to students attending an Indiana college or university.
**Financial data:** A stipend is awarded (amount not specified). Funds are paid directly to the recipient's school.
**Duration:** 1 year; recipients may reapply.
**Number awarded:** 1 each year.
**Deadline:** February of each year.

### 2082 DR. H. HAROLD HUME HORTICULTURE SCHOLARSHIP

Florida Federation of Garden Clubs, Inc., Attn: Office Manager
1400 South Denning Drive
Winter Park, FL 32789-5662
Phone: (407) 647-7016; Fax: (407) 647-5479; Email: ffgc@earthlink.net
Web: www.ffgc.org/scholarships/index.html
**Summary:** To provide financial aid to Florida college seniors and graduate students majoring in horticulture.
**Eligibility:** Open to Florida residents who are enrolled as full-time seniors or graduate students in a Florida college. They must have a GPA of 3.0 or higher, be in financial need, and be majoring in horticulture. U.S. citizenship is required. Selection is based on academic record, commitment to career, character, and financial need.
**Financial data:** The stipend is $3,000. The funds are sent directly to the recipient's school and distributed semiannually.
**Duration:** 1 year.
**Number awarded:** 1 or more each year.
**Deadline:** April of each year.

### 2083 DR. HANS AND CLARA ZIMMERMAN FOUNDATION HEALTH SCHOLARSHIPS

Hawai'i Community Foundation, Attn: Scholarship Department
1164 Bishop Street, Suite 800
Honolulu, HI 96813
Phone: (808) 566-5570; (888) 731-3863; Fax: (808) 521-6286;
Email: scholarships@hcf-hawaii.org
Web: www.hawaiicommunityfoundation.org/scholar/scholar.php
**Summary:** To provide financial assistance to Hawaii residents who are interested in preparing for a career in the health field.
**Eligibility:** Open to Hawaii residents who are interested in majoring in a health-related field as full-time students at a college or university in the United States (as juniors, seniors or graduate students). Students planning to major in sports medicine, psychology (unless clinical), and social work are not eligible. Applicants must be able to demonstrate academic achievement (GPA of 3.0 or higher), good moral character, and financial need. In addition to filling out the standard application form, they must write a short statement indicating their reasons for attending college, their planned course of study, and their career goals.
**Financial data:** The amounts of the awards depend on the availability of funds and the need of the recipients; recently, stipends averaged $3,065.
**Duration:** 1 year.
**Number awarded:** Varies each year; recently, 195 of these scholarships were awarded.
**Deadline:** February of each year.

**2084** **DR. HAROLD HILLENBRAND SCHOLARSHIP**

American Dental Hygienists' Association, Attn: Institute for Oral Health
444 North Michigan Avenue, Suite 3400
Chicago, IL 60611
Phone: (312) 440-8918; (800) 735-4916; Fax: (312) 440-8929;
Email: institute@adha.net
Web: www.adha.org/institute/Scholarship/index.htm

**Summary:** To provide financial assistance to students enrolled in a baccalaureate dental hygiene program who can demonstrate exceptional academic and clinical performance.

**Eligibility:** Open to full-time undergraduate students who are active members of the Student American Dental Hygienists' Association (SADHA) or the American Dental Hygienists' Association (ADHA). Applicants must have a GPA of 3.5 or higher, be able to document financial need of at least $1,500, be able to demonstrate academic excellence and outstanding clinical performance, and have completed at least one year in an accredited dental hygiene program in the United States. Along with their application, they must submit a statement that covers their long-term career goals, their intended contribution to the dental hygiene profession, their professional interests, and the manner in which their degree will enhance their professional capacity.

**Financial data:** Stipends range from $1,000 to $2,000.

**Duration:** 1 year.

**Number awarded:** 1 each year.

**Deadline:** April of each year.

**2085** **DR. HILDA RICHARDS SCHOLARSHIP**

National Black Nurses Association, Inc., Attn: Scholarship Committee
8630 Fenton Street, Suite 330
Silver Spring, MD 20910
Phone: (301) 589-3200; (800) 575-6298; Fax: (301) 589-3223

**Summary:** To provide financial assistance for nursing education to members of the National Black Nurses Association (NBNA).

**Eligibility:** Open to members of the association who have a diploma or associate degree and are working on a B.S.N. degree with at least one full year of school remaining. Selection is based on participation in student nurse activities, involvement in the African American community, and involvement in community health services activities.

**Financial data:** The stipend ranges from $500 to $2,000 per year.

**Duration:** 1 year; may be renewed.

**Number awarded:** 1 or more each year.

**Deadline:** April of each year.

**2086** **DR. HILDEGARD E. PEPLAU SCHOLARSHIP**

American Psychiatric Nurses Association, Attn: APN Foundation
1555 Wilson Boulevard, Suite 515
Arlington, VA 22209
Phone: (703) 243-2443; Fax: (703) 243-3390; Email: inform@apna.org
Web: www.apna.org/foundation/scholarships.html

**Summary:** To provide financial assistance to students and registered nurses working on a degree in nursing.

**Eligibility:** Open to students and registered nurses enrolled in an NLN-accredited program in nursing. Applicants must submit 3 essays (each up to 500 words) on the following topics: 1) their career goals, how education will enhance those goals, and their contribution to the profession; 2) their professional activities, involvement, continuing education, and scholarly contributions; and 3) their voluntary community activities. Financial need is not considered in the selection process. Minorities are especially encouraged to apply.

**Financial data:** The stipend is $1,000.

**Duration:** 1 year.

**Number awarded:** 1 or more each year.

**Deadline:** January of each year.

**2087** **DR. JESSE BEMLEY SCHOLARSHIP**

BDPA Education Technology Foundation, Attn: Scholarship Committee
4423 Lehigh Road, Number 277
College Park, MD 20740
Phone: (202) 258-3252; Fax: (202) 318-2194; Email: betfscholarship@aol.com
Web: www.betf.org/GrantsFunding/02_scholarships.htm

**Summary:** To provide financial assistance for college to high school students who participate in the annual national computer competition of the Black Data Processing Associates (BDPA).

**Eligibility:** Open to students who are members of a team that participates in the annual high school BDPA computer competition. At the end of the competition, the sponsor sends award letters to all of the eligible team members who have graduated from high school, have been accepted to a 4-year degree program, and plan to major in an information technology field. Letter recipients are invited to apply for this scholarship. Selection is based on performance at the computer competition.

**Financial data:** Awards are $2,500 for first place, $1,500 for second place, and $500 for third place.

**Duration:** The competition is held annually.

**Number awarded:** 15 each year: 5 first-place winners, 5 second-place winners, and 5 third-place winners.

**2088** **DR. JON L. BOYES, VICE ADMIRAL, USN (RET.) MEMORIAL SCHOLARSHIP**

Armed Forces Communications and Electronics Association
Attn: AFCEA Educational Foundation
4400 Fair Lakes Court
Fairfax, VA 22033-3899
Phone: (703) 631-6149; (800) 336-4583, ext. 6149; Fax: (703) 631-4693;
Email: scholarship@afcea.org
Web: www.afcea.org/education/scholarships/rotc/Boyes.asp

**Summary:** To provide financial assistance to Navy ROTC cadets who are majoring in electrical engineering.

**Eligibility:** Open to Navy ROTC cadets enrolled full time at an accredited degree-granting 4-year college or university in the United States. Applicants must be sophomores or juniors at the time of application and have a GPA of 3.0 or higher with a major in electrical engineering. Their application must be endorsed by the professor of Naval Science at their institution. Selection is based on demonstrated dedication, superior performance, and potential to serve as an officer in the United States Navy.

**Financial data:** The stipend is $3,000.

**Duration:** 1 year.

**Number awarded:** 1 each year.

**Deadline:** March of each year.

**2089** **DR. LAURANNE SAMS SCHOLARSHIP**

National Black Nurses Association, Inc., Attn: Scholarship Committee
8630 Fenton Street, Suite 330
Silver Spring, MD 20910
Phone: (301) 589-3200; (800) 575-6298; Fax: (301) 589-3223;
Email: nbna@erols.com
Web: www.nbna.org/memb_scholar.html

**Summary:** To provide financial assistance for undergraduate nursing education to members of the National Black Nurses Association.

**Eligibility:** Open to members of the association who are currently enrolled in a B.S.N., A.D., diploma, or L.P.N./L.V.N. program with at least one full year of school remaining. Selection is based on participation in student nurse activities, involvement in the African American community, and involvement in community health services-related activities.

**Financial data:** The stipend ranges from $500 to $2,000 per year.

**Duration:** 1 year; may be renewed.

**Number awarded:** 1 or more each year.

**Deadline:** April of each year.

**2090** **DR. S. BRADLEY BURSON MEMORIAL SCHOLARSHIP**

American Council of the Blind, Attn: Coordinator, Scholarship Program
1155 15th Street, N.W., Suite 1004
Washington, DC 20005
Phone: (202) 467-5081; (800) 424-8666; Fax: (202) 467-5085;
Email: info@acb.org
Web: www.acb.org

**Summary:** To provide financial assistance to blind students who are working on an undergraduate or graduate degree in science at an accredited college or university.

**Eligibility:** Open to legally blind undergraduate or graduate students majoring in the "hard" sciences (i.e., biology, chemistry, physics, and engineering, but not computer science) in college. They must be U.S. citizens. In addition to letters of recommendation and copies of academic transcripts, applications must include an autobiographical sketch. A cumulative GPA of 3.3 or higher is generally required. Selection is based on demonstrated academic record, involvement in extracurricular and civic activities, and academic objectives. The severity of the applicant's visual impairment and his/her study methods are also taken into account.

**Financial data:** The stipend is $1,000. In addition, the winner receives a Kurzweil-1000 Reading System.

**Duration:** 1 year.

**Number awarded:** 1 each year.

**Deadline:** February of each year.

## 2091 DR. TAYLOR ALEXANDER ECOLOGY SCHOLARSHIP

Florida Federation of Garden Clubs, Inc., Attn: Office Manager
1400 South Denning Drive
Winter Park, FL 32789-5662
Phone: (407) 647-7016; Fax: (407) 647-5479; Email: ffgc@earthlink.net
Web: www.ffgc.org/scholarships/index.html

**Summary:** To provide financial aid to Florida undergraduates and graduate students majoring in ecology.

**Eligibility:** Open to Florida residents who are enrolled as full-time juniors, seniors, or graduate students in a Florida college. They must have a GPA of 3.0 or higher, be in financial need, and be majoring in ecology. U.S. citizenship is required. Selection is based on academic record, commitment to career, character, and financial need.

**Financial data:** The stipend is $2,500. The funds are sent directly to the recipient's school and distributed semiannually.

**Duration:** 1 year.

**Number awarded:** 1 each year.

**Deadline:** April of each year.

## 2092 DR. W. WESLEY ECKENFELDER SCHOLARSHIP

Brown and Caldwell, Attn: Scholarship Program
201 North Civic Drive, Suite 115
P.O. Box 8045
Walnut Creek, CA 94596
Phone: (925) 937-9010; Fax: (925) 937-9026;
Email: scholarships@brwncald.com
Web: www.brownandcaldwell.com

**Summary:** To provide financial assistance to undergraduate students working on an degree in an environmental or engineering field.

**Eligibility:** Open to U.S. citizens and permanent residents enrolled as full-time students in their junior year at an accredited 4-year college or university. Applicants must have a GPA of 3.0 or higher with a declared major in civil, chemical, or environmental engineering or an environmental science (e.g., biology, ecology, geology, hydrogeology, industrial hygiene, toxicology). Along with their application, they must submit an essay (up to 250 words) on why they chose to major in an environmental discipline. Financial need is not considered in the selection process.

**Financial data:** The stipend is $3,000.

**Duration:** 1 year.

**Number awarded:** 1 each year.

**Deadline:** February of each year.

## 2093 DUKE ENERGY MINORITY PROFESSIONAL ASSOCIATION SCHOLARSHIP FUND

Foundation for the Carolinas, Attn: Senior Vice President, Scholarships
217 South Tryon Street
P.O. Box 34769
Charlotte, NC 28234-4769
Phone: (704) 973-4535; (800) 973-7244; Fax: (704) 973-4935;
Email: jseymour@fftc.org
Web: www.fftc.org/scholarships

**Summary:** To provide financial assistance to high school seniors from North and South Carolina who are interested in studying designed fields in college.

**Eligibility:** Open to seniors graduating from high schools in North and South Carolina. Applicants must be planning to attend a 4-year college or university in those states to major in accounting, business administration, computer science, engineering, finance, or the sciences. Selection is based on merit.

**Financial data:** A stipend is awarded (amount not specified).

**Duration:** 1 year.

**Number awarded:** 1 or more each year.

**Deadline:** February of each year.

## 2094 DUPONT CHALLENGE

General Learning Communications, Attn: The DuPont Challenge
900 Skokie Boulevard, Suite 200
Northbrook, IL 60062-4028
Phone: (847) 205-3000; Fax: (847) 564-8197
Web: www.glcomm.com/dupont

**Summary:** To recognize and reward outstanding essays written by junior and senior high school students on scientific subjects.

**Eligibility:** Open to students currently enrolled in grades 7-12 at a public or nonpublic school in the United States, its territories, or Canada. They may submit entries. Essays should be between 700 and 1,000 words and deal with a scientific or technological development, event, or theory. Students compete in 2 divisions: senior, for grades 10 through 12, and junior, for grades 7 through 9. Winning essays generally demonstrate creativity, originality, and a readable style; an appropriate choice of subject matter; careful consideration of how the subject matter affects the student and humankind; and clear, well-organized writing that has been proofread for spelling and grammatical errors.

**Financial data:** In each division, the first-place winner receives $1,500, other finalists receive $500, and honorable mention awardees receive $50. The first place winners are flown to Space Center Houston, along with a parent and sponsoring science and English teachers, as guests of the sponsor. The sponsoring English and science teachers of the winners receive $500 educational grants and teachers of the other finalists receive $250 educational grants.

**Number awarded:** In each division, there is 1 winner, 4 other finalists, and 30 honorable mentions.

**Deadline:** January of each year.

## 2095 DUPONT COMPANY SCHOLARSHIPS

Society of Women Engineers
230 East Ohio Street, Suite 400
Chicago, IL 60611-3265
Phone: (312) 596-5223; Fax: (312) 644-8557; Email: hq@swe.org
Web: www.societyofwomenengineers.org/scholarships

**Summary:** To provide financial assistance to women interested in studying chemical or mechanical engineering at a college or university in the East.

**Eligibility:** Open to women who are enrolled or planning to enroll full time at an ABET-accredited 4-year college or university in an eastern state. Applicants must have a GPA of 3.0 or higher and be planning to major in chemical or mechanical engineering. Along with their application, they must submit a 1-page essay on why they want to be an engineer, how they believe they will make a difference as an engineer, and what influenced them to study engineering. Selection is based on merit.

**Financial data:** The stipend is $2,000 per year.

**Duration:** 1 year.

**Number awarded:** 9 each year: 2 to women entering college for the first time and 7 to women already enrolled in college.

**Deadline:** May of each year for incoming freshmen; January of each year for students already in college.

## 2096 DUTCH AND GINGER ARVER SCHOLARSHIP

Aircraft Electronics Association, Attn: AEA Educational Foundation
4217 South Hocker Drive
Independence, MO 64055-4723
Phone: (816) 373-6565; Fax: (816) 478-3100; Email: info@aea.net
Web: www.aea.net

**Summary:** To provide financial assistance to students preparing for a career in avionics.

**Eligibility:** Open to high school seniors and currently-enrolled college students who are attending (or planning to attend) an accredited postsecondary institution in an avionics program. Applicants must submit an official transcript (cumulative GPA of 2.5 or higher), a statement about their career plans, a description of their involvement in school and community activities, and a 300-word essay on how the job requirements of aviation technicians will change with advancements in technology. Selection is based on merit.

**Financial data:** The stipend is $1,000.

**Duration:** 1 year.

**Number awarded:** 1 each year.

**Deadline:** February of each year.

## 2097 DWIGHT D. GARDNER SCHOLARSHIP

Institute of Industrial Engineers, Attn: Chapter Operations Department
3577 Parkway Lane, Suite 200
Norcross, GA 30092

Phone: (770) 449-0461, ext. 118; (800) 494-0460; Fax: (770) 263-8532;
Email: srichards@iienet.org
Web: www.iienet.org

**Summary:** To provide financial assistance to undergraduate members of the Institute of Industrial Engineers (IIE) who are studying at a school in the United States, Canada, or Mexico.

**Eligibility:** Open to undergraduate students enrolled in any school in the United States and its territories, Canada, or Mexico, provided the school's engineering program is accredited by an agency recognized by the IIE and the student is pursuing a full-time course of study in industrial engineering with a GPA of 3.4 and at least 5 full quarters or 3 full semesters remaining until graduation. Students may not apply directly for these awards; they must be nominated by the head of their industrial engineering department. Nominees must be IIE members. Selection is based on scholastic ability, character, leadership, potential service to the industrial engineering profession, and need for financial assistance.

**Financial data:** The stipend is $1,500.
**Duration:** 1 year.
**Number awarded:** 2 each year.
**Deadline:** November of each year.

## 2098 E. TED SIMS, JR. MEMORIAL SCHOLARSHIP

American Society for Horticultural Science
113 South West Street, Suite 200
Alexandria, VA 22314-2851
Phone: (703) 836-4606; Fax: (703) 836-2024; Email: ashs@ashs.org
Web: www.ashs.org/awards/student.html

**Summary:** To provide financial assistance to undergraduate students majoring in horticulture.

**Eligibility:** Open to full-time juniors and seniors majoring in horticulture at a 4-year institution of higher education. Applicants must be able to demonstrate excellent academic performance in the major, participation in extracurricular activities related to horticulture, and commitment to the horticulture profession. They must be nominated by the chair or head of their department; only one applicant may be nominated per department. Nominees must complete an application form, write an essay of 250 to 500 words on their reasons for interest in horticulture and for selecting their intended field of work after graduating from college, and provide 3 letters of reference. Financial need is not considered in the selection process.

**Financial data:** The stipend is $1,000.
**Duration:** 1 year.
**Number awarded:** 1 each year.
**Deadline:** February of each year.

## 2099 E. WAYNE KAY CO-OP SCHOLARSHIP

Society of Manufacturing Engineers, Attn: SME Education Foundation
One SME Drive
P.O. Box 930
Dearborn, MI 48121-0930
Phone: (313) 425-3304; (800) 733-4763, ext. 3304; Fax: (313) 425-3411;
Email: foundation@sme.org
Web: www.sme.org

**Summary:** To provide financial assistance to undergraduate students enrolled in a co-op degree program in manufacturing engineering or manufacturing engineering technology.

**Eligibility:** Open to full-time undergraduate students enrolled in a manufacturing engineering or technology degree program in North America and working in a co-op program in a manufacturing-related environment. Applicants must have completed at least 30 units in a manufacturing engineering or manufacturing engineering technology curriculum with a GPA of 3.0 or higher. Need is not considered in awarding scholarships (unless 2 or more applicants have equal qualifications).

**Financial data:** The stipend is $2,500.
**Duration:** 1 year; may be renewed.
**Number awarded:** 2 each year.
**Deadline:** January of each year.

## 2100 E. WAYNE KAY COMMUNITY COLLEGE SCHOLARSHIPS

Society of Manufacturing Engineers, Attn: SME Education Foundation
One SME Drive
P.O. Box 930
Dearborn, MI 48121-0930
Phone: (313) 425-3304; (800) 733-4763, ext. 3304; Fax: (313) 425-3411;

Email: foundation@sme.org
Web: www.sme.org

**Summary:** To provide financial assistance to students enrolled or planning to enroll in a community college program in manufacturing engineering or manufacturing engineering technology.

**Eligibility:** Open to entering freshmen and sophomores with less than 60 college credit hours at a community college, trade school, or other 2-year degree-granting institution in the United States or Canada. Applicants must be full-time students interested in preparing for a career in manufacturing engineering or technology and have a GPA of 3.0 or higher. Need is not considered in awarding scholarships (unless 2 or more applicants have equal qualifications).

**Financial data:** The stipend is $1,000.
**Duration:** 1 year.
**Number awarded:** 2 each year.
**Deadline:** January of each year.

## 2101 E. WAYNE KAY HIGH SCHOOL SCHOLARSHIPS

Society of Manufacturing Engineers, Attn: SME Education Foundation
One SME Drive
P.O. Box 930
Dearborn, MI 48121-0930
Phone: (313) 425-3304; (800) 733-4763, ext. 3304; Fax: (313) 425-3411;
Email: foundation@sme.org
Web: www.sme.org

**Summary:** To provide financial assistance to high school seniors planning to enroll in a degree program in manufacturing engineering or manufacturing engineering technology.

**Eligibility:** Open to graduating high seniors who plan to enroll full time in a manufacturing engineering or technology certificate or degree program at a North American institution. Applicants must have a GPA of 3.0 or higher for their senior year in high school. Need is not considered in awarding scholarships (unless 2 or more applicants have equal qualifications).

**Financial data:** The stipend is $1,000 for the first year and $1,500 for the second year.
**Duration:** 2 years.
**Number awarded:** 2 each year.
**Deadline:** January of each year.

## 2102 E. WAYNE KAY SCHOLARSHIPS

Society of Manufacturing Engineers, Attn: SME Education Foundation
One SME Drive
P.O. Box 930
Dearborn, MI 48121-0930
Phone: (313) 425-3304; (800) 733-4763, ext. 3304; Fax: (313) 425-3411;
Email: foundation@sme.org
Web: www.sme.org

**Summary:** To provide financial assistance to undergraduate students enrolled in a degree program in manufacturing engineering or manufacturing engineering technology.

**Eligibility:** Open to full-time undergraduate students enrolled in a manufacturing engineering or technology degree program at a college or university in North America. Applicants must have completed at least 30 units in a manufacturing engineering or manufacturing engineering technology curriculum with a GPA of 3.0 or higher. Need is not considered in awarding scholarships (unless 2 or more applicants have equal qualifications).

**Financial data:** The stipend is $2,500.
**Duration:** 1 year; may be renewed.
**Number awarded:** 10 each year.
**Deadline:** January of each year.

## 2103 EAST MICHIGAN CHAPTER SCHOLARSHIPS

Air & Waste Management Association-East Michigan Chapter
c/o Sol P. Baltimore, Scholarship Committee Chair
28742 Blackstone Drive
Lathrup Village, MI 48076-2616
Phone: (248) 569-3633
Web: www.emawma.org/scholar.html

**Summary:** To provide financial assistance to undergraduate and graduate students in Michigan who are interested in preparing for a career in air and waste management.

**Eligibility:** Open to students enrolled in or entering their senior undergraduate year or any year of graduate or professional school at a college or university in Michigan. They must be full-time students preparing for a career in air pollution control, toxic and/or hazardous waste management, or another environmental area. Preferred courses of study include engineering, physical or natural sciences, public health, law, and natural resources. Selection is based on academic achievement (at least a 3.0 GPA), a paper (between 500 and 600 words) on career interests and objectives, extracurricular activities, and financial need.

**Financial data:** The stipend is $1,500. Winners also receive a 1-year student membership in the Air & Waste Management Association (A&WMA).

**Duration:** 1 year; may be renewed.

**Number awarded:** 5 each year.

**Deadline:** February of each year.

## 2104 EATON MULTICULTURAL SCHOLARS PROGRAM

Eaton Corporation, Attn: EMSP
1111 Superior Avenue
Cleveland, OH 44114-2584
Phone: (216) 523-4354; Email: mildredneumann@eaton.com
Web: www.eatonjobs.com/career/career_choices.asp

**Summary:** To provide financial assistance and work experience to minority college students interested in a career as an engineer.

**Eligibility:** Open to full-time minority students who are U.S. citizens or permanent residents. Applicants must have completed 1 year in an accredited program and have 3 remaining years of course work before completing a bachelor's degree. They must be majoring in computer science/data processing, electrical engineering, or mechanical engineering. Selection is based on academic performance, the student's school recommendation, and an expressed interest in pursuing challenging and rewarding internship assignments.

**Financial data:** Stipends range from $500 to $3,000 per year. Funds are paid directly to the recipient's university to cover the cost of tuition, books, supplies, equipment, and fees.

**Duration:** 3 years.

**Number awarded:** Varies each year.

**Deadline:** December of each year.

## 2105 ECKE FAMILY SCHOLARSHIP

Floriculture Industry Research and Scholarship Trust
Attn: Scholarship Program
P.O. Box 280
East Lansing, MI 48826-0280
Phone: (517) 333-4617; Fax: (517) 333-4494;
Email: scholarships@firstinfloriculture.org
Web: www.firstinfloriculture.org

**Summary:** To provide financial assistance to college students in horticulture.

**Eligibility:** Open to undergraduate students at 4-year colleges and universities who are majoring in horticulture. Applicants must be interested in preparing for a career in production floriculture. They must be U.S. or Canadian citizens or permanent residents with a GPA of 3.0 or higher. Selection is based on academic record, recommendations, career goals, extracurricular activities, and financial need.

**Financial data:** The stipend depends on the availability of funds. Recently, it was $1,000.

**Duration:** 1 year.

**Number awarded:** 1 each year.

**Deadline:** April of each year.

## 2106 ED AND CHARLOTTE RODGERS SCHOLARSHIPS

Alabama Road Builders Association, Attn: Scholarship Committee
630 Adams Avenue
Montgomery, AL 36104-4336
Phone: (334) 832-4331; (800) 239-5828; Fax: (334) 265-4931
Web: www.arba.org/site/ed.html

**Summary:** To provide financial assistance to undergraduate and graduate students from Alabama working on a degree in civil engineering.

**Eligibility:** Open to full-time undergraduate and graduate students in civil engineering in Alabama. Applicants must have completed their freshman year, have a satisfactory GPA, be in good academic standing, and be able to demonstrate financial need. Selection is based on accomplishments in student, community, honorary, or service organizations; excellence in academics; and demonstrated leadership qualities.

**Financial data:** A stipend is awarded (amount not specified).

**Duration:** 1 year.

**Number awarded:** 3 to 5 each year.

**Deadline:** March of each year.

## 2107 EDDIE G. COLE MEMORIAL SCHOLARSHIPS

California State Fair, Attn: Friends of the Fair Scholarship Program
1600 Exposition Boulevard
P.O. Box 15649
Sacramento, CA 95852
Phone: (916) 274-5969; Email: wross@calexpo.com
Web: www.bigfun.org

**Summary:** To provide financial assistance for college to residents of California who are interested in majoring in designated fields or preparing for a career in the Fair industry.

**Eligibility:** Open to residents of California currently working on an undergraduate degree at a college or university in the state. Applicants be 1) majoring in physical education, agriculture, or equine studies; or 2) preparing for a career in the Fair industry. They must have a GPA of 3.0 or higher. Along with their application, they must submit a 2-page essay on why they are pursuing their desired career and life goals. Selection is based on personal commitment, goals established for their chosen field, leadership potential, and civic accomplishments.

**Financial data:** Stipends are $1,000 or $500.

**Duration:** 1 year.

**Number awarded:** 2 each year: 1 at $1,000 and 1 at $500.

**Deadline:** March of each year.

## 2108 EDITH M. ALLEN SCHOLARSHIPS

United Methodist Church
Attn: General Board of Higher Education and Ministry
Office of Loans and Scholarships
1001 19th Avenue South
P.O. Box 340007
Nashville, TN 37203-0007
Phone: (615) 340-7344; Fax: (615) 340-7367; Email: umscholar@gbhem.org
Web: www.gbhem.org

**Summary:** To provide financial assistance to Methodist students who are African American and working on an undergraduate or graduate degree in specified fields

**Eligibility:** Open to full-time undergraduate and graduate students at Methodist colleges and universities (preferably Historically Black United Methodist colleges) who have been active, full members of a United Methodist Church for at least 3 years prior to applying. Applicants must be African Americans working on a degree in education, social work, medicine, and/or other health professions. They must have at least a B+ average and be recognized as a person whose academic and vocational contributions will help improve the quality of life for others.

**Financial data:** A stipend is awarded (amount not specified).

**Duration:** 1 year; recipients may reapply.

**Number awarded:** Varies each year.

**Deadline:** May of each year.

## 2109 EDNA AND JAMES CROWL BOTANY SCHOLARSHIP

Florida Federation of Garden Clubs, Inc., Attn: Office Manager
1400 South Denning Drive
Winter Park, FL 32789-5662
Phone: (407) 647-7016; Fax: (407) 647-5479; Email: ffgc@earthlink.net
Web: www.ffgc.org/scholarships/index.html

**Summary:** To provide financial aid to Florida undergraduates and graduate students majoring in botany.

**Eligibility:** Open to Florida residents who are enrolled as full-time juniors, seniors, or graduate students in a Florida college. They must have a GPA of 3.0 or higher, be in financial need, and be majoring in botany, with an emphasis on research in and study of wildflowers and native plants. U.S. citizenship is required. Selection is based on academic record, commitment to career, character, and financial need.

**Financial data:** The stipend is $2,500. The funds are sent directly to the recipient's school and distributed semiannually.

**Duration:** 1 year.

**Number awarded:** 1 each year.

**Deadline:** April of each year.

## 2110 EDSF BOARD OF DIRECTORS SCHOLARSHIPS

Electronic Document Systems Foundation, Attn: EDSF Scholarship Awards
24238 Hawthorne Boulevard
Torrance, CA 90505-6505
Phone: (310) 541-1481; Fax: (310) 541-4803
Web: www.edsf.org/scholarships.cfm
**Summary:** To provide financial assistance to college juniors, seniors, and graduate students interested in working with electronic documents as a career.
**Eligibility:** Open to juniors, seniors, and graduate students who are working full time on a degree in the field of document communication, including marketing, graphic communication and arts, e-commerce, imaging science, printing, web authoring, electronic publishing, computer science, or telecommunications. Applicants must submit a statement of their career goals in the field of document communications, an essay on a topic related to their view of the future of the document management and production industry, a list of current professional and college extracurricular activities and achievements, college transcripts (GPA of 3.0 or higher), samples of their creative work, and 2 letters of recommendation. Financial need is not considered.
**Financial data:** The stipend is $2,000.
**Duration:** 1 year.
**Number awarded:** 20 each year.
**Deadline:** May of each year.

## 2111 EDSF BOARD OF DIRECTORS TECHNICAL AND COMMUNITY COLLEGE SCHOLARSHIP

Electronic Document Systems Foundation, Attn: EDSF Scholarship Awards
24238 Hawthorne Boulevard
Torrance, CA 90505-6505
Phone: (310) 541-1481; Fax: (310) 541-4803
Web: www.edsf.org/scholarships.cfm
**Summary:** To provide financial assistance to students in technical schools and community colleges who are interested in working with electronic documents as a career.
**Eligibility:** Open to first- and second-year students at technical and trade schools and community colleges. Applicants must be working on a degree in the field of electronic document communication, including marketing, graphic communication and arts, e-commerce, imaging science, printing, web authoring, electronic publishing, computer science, or telecommunications. They must submit a 1-page essay on 1 of the following topics: 1) a definition of their career goals in the field of document management and communications; 2) a recent technological change and how it has or will affect the document communication industry; or 3) a definition of the document communication industry. Selection is based on the essay, extracurricular activities and achievements, high school transcripts (GPA of 3.0 or higher), samples of creative work, and 2 letters of recommendation. Financial need is not considered.
**Financial data:** The stipend is $1,000.
**Duration:** 1 year.
**Number awarded:** 5 each year.
**Deadline:** May of each year.

## 2112 EDUCATIONAL ADVANCEMENT BSN SCHOLARSHIPS

American Association of Critical-Care Nurses
Attn: Educational Advancement Scholarships
101 Columbia
Aliso Viejo, CA 92656-4109
Phone: (949) 362-2000, ext. 338; (800) 899-AACN, ext. 338;
Fax: (949) 362-2020; Email: info@aacn.org
Web: www.aacn.org
**Summary:** To provide financial assistance to members of the American Association of Critical-Care Nurses (AACN) who are working on a B.S.N. degree in nursing.
**Eligibility:** Open to registered nurses who are current members of the association and enrolled in an accredited B.S.N. degree program. Applicants must be nurses who hold an active R.N. license and are currently working in critical care or have one year's experience in the last 3 years. They must have a cumulative GPA of 3.0 or higher and plan to hold junior or upper-division status in the fall semester. Along with their application, they must submit narratives on 1) how they see their nursing practice changing as a result of their baccalaureate degree; and 2) their contributions to critical care nursing, including work, community, and profession-related activities. Financial need is not considered in the selection process. Qualified ethnic minority candidates receive at least 20% of these awards.
**Financial data:** The stipend is $1,500 per year. The funds are sent directly to the recipient's college or university and may be used only for tuition, fees, books, and supplies.
**Duration:** 1 year; recipients may reapply.
**Number awarded:** Varies each year; recently, 5 of these scholarships were awarded.
**Deadline:** March of each year.

## 2113 EDWARD DAVIS SCHOLARSHIP FUND

Edward Davis Education Foundation
585 East Larned Street, Suite 100
Detroit, MI 48226
Phone: (313) 963-2209; (877) 847-9060
Web: www.automag.com/EDEFoundation/default.asp
**Summary:** To provide financial assistance to minority students interested in preparing for a career in an automotive-related profession.
**Eligibility:** Open to minority high school seniors or currently-enrolled college students who are interested in preparing for a career in the automotive industry. Applicants must have a GPA of 2.7 or higher. Along with their application, they must submit a 250-word essay on what diversity in the automotive industry means to them. They should be able to demonstrate leadership qualities as defined by a record of involvement and participation in extracurricular and community activities. U.S. citizenship is required.
**Financial data:** Stipends range from $1,000 to $2,500.
**Duration:** 1 year.
**Deadline:** November of each year.

## 2114 EDWARD J. BRADY SCHOLARSHIP

American Welding Society, Attn: AWS Foundation, Inc.
550 N.W. LeJeune Road
Miami, FL 33126
Phone: (305) 445-6628; (800) 443-9353, ext. 461; Fax: (305) 443-7559;
Email: found@aws.org
Web: www.aws.org/foundation/scholarships/brady.html
**Summary:** To provide financial assistance to college students majoring in welding engineering or welding engineering technology.
**Eligibility:** Open to undergraduate students who are working on a 4-year bachelor's degree in welding engineering or welding engineering technology; preference is given to students in welding engineering. Applicants must have a minimum GPA of 2.5, provide a letter of reference indicating previous hands-on welding experience, be U.S. citizens, submit an essay on "Why I Want to Pursue a Career in Welding," and be able to demonstrate financial need.
**Financial data:** The stipend is $2,500.
**Duration:** 1 year; recipients may reapply.
**Number awarded:** 1 each year.
**Deadline:** January of each year.

## 2115 EDWARD J. DULIS SCHOLARSHIP

ASM International, Attn: ASM Materials Education Foundation
Scholarship Program
9639 Kinsman Road
Materials Park, OH 44073-0002
Phone: (440) 338-5151; (800) 336-5152; Fax: (440) 338-4634;
Email: asmif@asminternational.org
Web: www.asminternational.org
**Summary:** To provide financial assistance to college sophomores and above who are members of ASM International.
**Eligibility:** Open to student members of the association who have an intended or declared major in metallurgy or materials science engineering. Applicants must have completed at least one year of college. Students majoring in related science or engineering disciplines are considered if they demonstrate a strong academic interest in materials science. International students are also eligible. Selection is based on academic achievement; interest in the field; and personal qualities. Financial need is not considered.
**Financial data:** The stipend is $1,500 per year.
**Duration:** 1 year; may be renewed for up to 1 additional year.
**Number awarded:** 1 each year.
**Deadline:** April of each year.

## 2116 EDWARD S. ROTH MANUFACTURING ENGINEERING SCHOLARSHIP

Society of Manufacturing Engineers, Attn: SME Education Foundation
One SME Drive
P.O. Box 930
Dearborn, MI 48121-0930
Phone: (313) 425-3304; (800) 733-4763, ext. 3304; Fax: (313) 425-3411;
Email: foundation@sme.org
Web: www.sme.org
**Summary:** To provide financial assistance to students enrolled or planning to enroll in a degree program in manufacturing engineering at selected universities.
**Eligibility:** Open to U.S. citizens who are graduating high school seniors or currently-enrolled undergraduate or graduate students. Applicants must be enrolled or planning to enroll as a full-time student at 1 of 13 selected 4-year universities to work on a bachelor's or master's degree in manufacturing engineering. They must have a GPA of 3.0 or higher. Preference is given to 1) students demonstrating financial need, 2) minority students, and 3) students participating in a co-op program. Some preference may also be given to graduating high school seniors and graduate students.
**Financial data:** The stipend is $2,500.
**Duration:** 1 year; may be renewed.
**Number awarded:** 1 each year.
**Deadline:** January of each year.

## 2117 EISENHOWER HISPANIC-SERVING INSTITUTIONS FELLOWSHIPS

**Summary:** To provide financial assistance for undergraduate study in transportation-related fields to students at Hispanic Serving Institutions.
*See Listing #1371.*

## 2118 EISENHOWER HISTORICALLY BLACK COLLEGES AND UNIVERSITIES FELLOWSHIPS

**Summary:** To provide financial assistance for undergraduate study in transportation-related fields to students at Historically Black Colleges and Universities.
*See Listing #1372.*

## 2119 EL NUEVO CONSTRUCTOR SCHOLARSHIP PROGRAM

Hispanic College Fund, Attn: National Director
1717 Pennsylvania Avenue, N.W., Suite 460
Washington, D.C. 20006
Phone: (202) 296-5400; (800) 644-4223; Fax: (202) 296-3774;
Email: hispaniccollegefund@earthlink.net
Web: www.hispanicfund.org
**Summary:** To provide financial assistance to Hispanic American undergraduate students who are interested in preparing for a career in the construction industry.
**Eligibility:** Open to U.S. citizens of Hispanic background (at least one grandparent must be 100% Hispanic) who are entering their freshman, sophomore, junior, or senior year of college. Applicants must be working on a bachelor's or associate degree in a field related to construction and have a cumulative GPA of 3.0 or higher. They must be applying to or enrolled in a college or university in the 50 states or Puerto Rico as a full-time student. Financial need is considered in the selection process.
**Financial data:** Stipends range from $500 to $5,000, depending on the need of the recipient, and average approximately $3,000. Funds are paid directly to the recipient's college or university to help cover tuition and fees.
**Duration:** 1 year; recipients may reapply.
**Number awarded:** Varies each year.
**Deadline:** April of each year.

## 2120 ELDON ROESLER SCHOLARSHIP

Wisconsin Agri-Service Association, Inc., Attn: Scholarship Committee
6000 Gisholt Drive, Suite 208
Madison, WI 53713-4816
Phone: (608) 223-1111; Fax: (608) 223-1147; Email: info@wasa.org
Web: www.wasa.org
**Summary:** To provide financial assistance to undergraduates working on a degree in agriculture at colleges and universities in Wisconsin.
**Eligibility:** Open to Wisconsin residents who have completed at least one year of study at a university, college, or vocational technical school in the state. Applicants must be majoring in an agricultural discipline or another field with the stated intent of preparing for a career in agriculture. They must have a GPA of 2.75 or higher. Preference is given to children of members and associates of the Wisconsin Agri-Service Association (WASA) and employees of WASA companies. Selection is based on qualities of leadership, academic ability, and financial need.
**Financial data:** The stipend is $1,000 per year.
**Duration:** 1 year.
**Number awarded:** 1 or more each year.
**Deadline:** April of each year.

## 2121 ELECTRONICS FOR IMAGING SCHOLARSHIPS

Society of Women Engineers
230 East Ohio Street, Suite 400
Chicago, IL 60611-3265
Phone: (312) 596-5223; Fax: (312) 644-8557; Email: hq@swe.org
Web: www.societyofwomenengineers.org/scholarships
**Summary:** To provide financial assistance to women working on an undergraduate or graduate degree in engineering or computer science.
**Eligibility:** Open to women who will be sophomores, juniors, seniors, or graduate students at ABET-accredited colleges and universities. Applicants must be majoring in computer science or engineering and have a GPA of 3.0 or higher. Along with their application, they must submit a 1-page essay on why they want to be an engineer or computer scientist, how they believe they will make a difference as an engineer or computer scientist, and what influenced them to study engineering or computer science. Selection is based on merit. Preference is given to students at designated colleges and universities; for a list, contact the sponsor.
**Financial data:** The stipend is $4,000.
**Duration:** 1 year.
**Number awarded:** 4 each year.
**Deadline:** January of each year.

## 2122 ELIZA D. WATT SCHOLARSHIPS

Royal Neighbors of America, Attn: Fraternal Services
230 16th Street
Rock Island, IL 61201-8645
Phone: (309) 788-4561; (800) 627-4762; Email: contact@royalneighbors.org
Web: www.royalneighbors.org/MemberBenefits/scholarships.cfm
**Summary:** To provide financial assistance for college to women members of the Royal Neighbors of America who plan to enter nontraditional fields.
**Eligibility:** Open to women members of the society who are graduating high school seniors. Applicants must be planning to enter a field considered nontraditional for women, including computer science, engineering, physical sciences, teaching of nontraditional women's fields, business writing, or mathematics.
**Financial data:** The stipend is $2,000 per year.
**Duration:** 4 years.
**Number awarded:** 5 each year.
**Deadline:** December of each year.

## 2123 ELIZABETH J. DAVIS SCHOLARSHIP

Vermont Student Assistance Corporation
Champlain Mill, Attn: Scholarship Programs
P.O. Box 2000
Winooski, VT 05404-2601
Phone: (802) 654-3798; (888) 253-4819; Fax: (802) 654-3765; TDD: (802) 654-3766; TDD: (800) 281-3341 (within VT); Email: info@vsac.org
Web: www.vsac.org
**Summary:** To provide financial assistance to residents of Vermont interested in obtaining an undergraduate degree, graduate degree, or certificate in a field related to home health care.
**Eligibility:** Open to residents of Vermont who are high school seniors, current undergraduate students, and home health care professionals. Applicants must be interested in obtaining a bachelor's degree in a health profession, certification as a home health aide, or (for home health care professionals) an advanced degree. They must be able to demonstrate interest in a career in the home health care field and an intent to work in Vermont for at least 2 years. Selection is based on financial need, required essays, a letter of recommendation, and a personal interview (if necessary).
**Financial data:** Stipends range from $1,000 to $3,000 per year.
**Duration:** 1 year; may be renewed up to 3 additional years.
**Number awarded:** Varies each year; recently, 7 of these scholarships were awarded.
**Deadline:** June of each year.

## 2124 ELIZABETH MCCULLAGH SCHOLARSHIP

**Summary:** To provide financial aid to Florida high school seniors who are interested in majoring in a field related to horticulture in college.
*See Listing #1375.*

## 2125 ELLIS F. HILLNER AWARD

Vasa Order of America, Attn: Vice Grand Master
3236 Berkeley Avenue
Cleveland Heights, OH 44118-2055
Phone: (216) 371-5141; Email: rolf.bergman@sbcglobal.net
Web: www.vasaorder.com
**Summary:** To provide financial assistance for education in a medical field to members of the Vasa Order of America.
**Eligibility:** Open to applicants who have belonged to the organization for at least one year and are attending or planning to attend an accredited institution on a full-time basis for studies in the medical field. Selection is based on a transcript, letters of recommendation from school and local Vasa lodge officials, and an essay of up to 1,000 words on a topic related to Vasa.
**Financial data:** The stipend is $2,000.
**Duration:** 1 year.
**Number awarded:** 1 each year.
**Deadline:** February of each year.

## 2126 ELLISON ONIZUKA MEMORIAL SCHOLARSHIP

Hawai'i Community Foundation, Attn: Scholarship Department
1164 Bishop Street, Suite 800
Honolulu, HI 96813
Phone: (808) 566-5570; (888) 731-3863; Fax: (808) 521-6286;
Email: scholarships@hcf hawaii.org
Web: www.hawaiicommunityfoundation.org/scholar/scholar.php
**Summary:** To provide financial assistance to Hawaii residents who are interested in preparing for a career in aerospace.
**Eligibility:** Open to high school seniors in Hawaii who are interested in preparing for an aerospace career. No direct applications are accepted; candidates must be nominated by their high school principal. Nominees must be residents of the state of Hawaii; able to demonstrate financial need; interested in attending an accredited 2- or 4-year college or university; and able to demonstrate academic achievement (GPA of 2.7 or higher).
**Financial data:** The amounts of the awards depend on the availability of funds and the need of the recipient.
**Duration:** 1 year.
**Number awarded:** Varies each year.
**Deadline:** April of each year.

## 2127 ELSIE BORCK HEALTH CARE SCHOLARSHIP

Kansas Federation of Business & Professional Women's Clubs, Inc.
Attn: Kansas BPW Educational Foundation
c/o Diane Smith, Executive Secretary
10418 Haskins
Lenexa, KS 66215-2162
Email: desmith@fcbankonline.com
Web: www.bpwkansas.org/bpw_foundation.htm
**Summary:** To provide financial assistance to residents of Kansas who are preparing for a career in a health profession in the state.
**Eligibility:** Open to Kansas residents (men and women) who are at least a college junior and preparing to practice in a health profession in the state. Applicants must submit a 3-page personal biography in which they express their career goals, the direction they want to take in the future, their proposed field of study, their reason for selecting that field, the institutions they plan to attend and why, their circumstances for reentering school (if a factor), and what makes them uniquely qualified for this scholarship. They must also be able to document financial need. Applications must be submitted through a local organization of the sponsor.
**Financial data:** A stipend is awarded (amount not specified).
**Duration:** 1 year.
**Number awarded:** 1 or more each year.
**Deadline:** December of each year.

## 2128 ELSON T. KILLAM MEMORIAL SCHOLARSHIP

New England Water Works Association
125 Hopping Brook
Holliston, MA 01746
Phone: (508) 893-7979; Fax: (508) 893-9898
Web: www.newwa.org
**Summary:** To provide financial assistance to undergraduate or graduate students from New England interested in working on a degree in civil or environmental engineering.
**Eligibility:** Open to members and student members of the New England section of the American Water Works Association or the New England Water Works Association. Applicants must be high school seniors, currently-enrolled college students, or graduate students. They must be majoring or planning to major in civil or environmental engineering. Along with their application, they must submit a 100-word essay on why they have chosen their field of study and if it will improve the environment, public health, or the water industry. Financial need is also considered in the selection process.
**Financial data:** The stipend is $1,500.
**Duration:** 1 year.
**Deadline:** July of each year.

## 2129 EMIL VON BEHRING MEDICAL TECHNOLOGIST STUDENT SCHOLARSHIPS

American Society for Clinical Pathology
Attn: Dale Behring Student Scholarships
2100 West Harrison Street
Chicago, IL 60612-3798
Phone: (312) 738-1336; (800) 621-4142; Fax: (312) 738-1619;
Email: info@ascp.org
Web: www.ascp.org
**Summary:** To provide funding to upper-division students enrolled in a medical technologist program.
**Eligibility:** Open to students enrolled in the third or fourth year of an NAACLS-accredited medical technologist program. Applicants must be U.S. citizens with a GPA of 2.5 or higher. Along with their application, they must submit a 500-word essay on their professional goals and what makes them among the best students in the nation. Financial need is not considered in the selection process.
**Financial data:** The stipend is $2,500.
**Duration:** 1 year.
**Number awarded:** 34 each year.
**Deadline:** October of each year.

## 2130 EMPIRE STATE CHAPTER SCHOLARSHIP

Soil and Water Conservation Society-Empire State Chapter
c/o Ellen Luchsinger
USDA-NRCS
Leo O'Brien Federal Building, Room 333
Albany, NY 12207
Phone: (518) 431-4110, ext. 104
Web: www.swcsnewyork.org
**Summary:** To provide financial assistance to currently-enrolled college students in New York who are majoring in conservation and related fields.
**Eligibility:** Open to students in their sophomore junior, or senior year at a college or university in New York. Applicants must be majoring in agriculture, environmental sciences, natural resources, conservation, or related fields of study. They must submit a college transcript and a short essay on their interest in a career in the conservation of natural resources and previous volunteer or work experience in the conservation of natural resources. Selection is based on the essay and academic accomplishment. Preference is given to members of the Soil and Water Conservation Society. Students with demonstrated accomplishments and/or interests in the field of soil and water conservation are encouraged to apply.
**Financial data:** The stipend is $1,000.
**Duration:** 1 year.
**Number awarded:** 2 each year.
**Deadline:** October of each year.

## 2131 EMPMD GILBERT CHIN SCHOLARSHIP

The Minerals, Metals & Materials Society, Attn: TMS Student Awards Program
184 Thorn Hill Road
Warrendale, PA 15086-7514
Phone: (724) 776-9000, ext. 220; Fax: (724) 776-3770;
Email: students@tms.org
Web: www.tms.org/Students/AwardsPrograms/Scholarships.html

**Summary:** To provide financial assistance for college to student members of The Minerals, Metals & Materials Society (TMS).

**Eligibility:** Open to undergraduate members of the society who are studying subjects in relation to synthesis and processing, structure, properties, and performance of electronic, magnetic, photonic, and superconducting materials. Applicants may be from any country. Selection is based on academic achievement, school and community activities, work experience, leadership, a personal profile statement, and letters of recommendation. Preference is given to students in their junior or senior year who are enrolled full time in a program that includes the study of electronic materials.

**Financial data:** The stipend is $2,000 plus a travel stipend of $500 (so the recipient can attend the annual meeting of the society to accept the award).

**Duration:** 1 year.

**Number awarded:** 1 each year.

**Deadline:** April of each year.

## 2132 ENA FOUNDATION UNDERGRADUATE SCHOLARSHIPS

Emergency Nurses Association, Attn: ENA Foundation
915 Lee Street
Des Plaines, IL 60016-6569
Phone: (847) 460-4100; (800) 900-9659, ext. 4100; Fax: (847) 460-4004;
Email: foundation@ena.org
Web: www.ena.org/foundation/grants

**Summary:** To provide financial assistance for baccalaureate study to nurses who are members of the Emergency Nurses Association (ENA).

**Eligibility:** Open to nurses (R.N., L.P.N., L.V.N.) who are working on a bachelor's degree. Applicants must have been members of the association for at least 12 months. They must submit a 1-page statement on their professional and educational goals and how this scholarship will help them attain those goals. Selection is based on content and clarity of the goal statement (45%), professional association involvement (45%), and GPA (10%).

**Financial data:** Stipends are $5,000 or $3,000.

**Duration:** 1 year; nonrenewable.

**Number awarded:** 8 each year: 7 at $3,000 and 1 at $5,000.

**Deadline:** May of each year.

## 2133 ENCOURAGE MINORITY PARTICIPATION IN OCCUPATIONS WITH EMPHASIS ON REHABILITATION

Courage Center, Attn: EMPOWER Scholarship Program
3915 Golden Valley Road
Minneapolis, MN 55422
Phone: (763) 520-0214; (888) 8-INTAKE; Fax: (763) 520-0392;
TTY: (763) 520-0245; Email: suep@courage.org
Web: www.courage.org

**Summary:** To provide financial assistance to students of color interested in preparing for a career in the medical rehabilitation field.

**Eligibility:** Open to ethnically diverse students accepted at or enrolled in an institution of higher learning. Applicants must demonstrate a career interest in the medical rehabilitation field by completing at least 200 hours of career-related volunteer service. They must have a GPA of 2.0 or higher. Selection is based on career intentions and achievements, not academic rank.

**Financial data:** The stipend is $1,500.

**Duration:** 1 year.

**Number awarded:** 2 each year.

**Deadline:** April of each year.

## 2134 ENGINEERING DIVISION SCHOLARSHIPS

Technical Association of the Pulp and Paper Industry, Attn: TAPPI Foundation
15 Technology Parkway South
Norcross, GA 30092
Phone: (770) 209-7536; (800) 332-8686; Fax: (770) 446-6947;
Email: vedmondson@tappi.org
Web: www.tappi.org

**Summary:** To provide financial assistance to student members of the Technical Association of the Pulp and Paper Industry (TAPPI) who are studying engineering or science to prepare for a career in the paper industry.

**Eligibility:** Open to TAPPI student members who are entering their junior or senior year of college as full-time students with a GPA of 3.0 or higher. Applicants must be able to demonstrate a significant interest in the pulp and paper industry. They must be majoring in science or engineering with a focus on the application of engineering principles to the design, construction, operation, and maintenance of facilities for the manufacture of pulp, paper, and

related products. Selection is based on potential career contributions to engineering in the pulp and paper industry; financial need is not considered.

**Financial data:** The stipend is $1,500.

**Duration:** 1 year.

**Number awarded:** Up to 2 each year.

**Deadline:** January of each year.

## 2135 ENGINEERING IN MEDICINE AND BIOLOGY SOCIETY STUDENT DESIGN COMPETITION AWARDS

Institute of Electrical and Electronics Engineers
Engineering in Medicine and Biology Society, Attn: Executive Office
445 Hoes Lane
P.O. Box 1331
Piscataway, NJ 08855-1331
Phone: (732) 981-3433; Fax: (732) 465-6435; Email: emb-exec@ieee.org
Web: embs.gsbme.unsw.edu.au/students.html

**Summary:** To recognize and reward outstanding devices or products in biomedical engineering designed by student members of the Engineering in Medicine and Biology Society (EMBS) of the Institute of Electrical and Electronics Engineers (IEEE).

**Eligibility:** Open to teams of up to 5 undergraduate and graduate student members of the society. Applicants must design and build an original device or product not currently offered on the market that applies engineering principles and technology to problems in medicine and biology. Other acceptable designs include a modification of an existing product, which may consist of hardware, software, or a combination of both. Selection is based on technical merit, structure (abstract, introduction, methods, analysis, results, conclusion, and references), clarity of composition, and originality. Based on the papers describing the designs, 3 finalists are selected to describe their work at the international conference either as an oral or poster presentation.

**Financial data:** First place is $1,000, second $500, and third $250. In addition, each finalist receives complimentary registration at the society's annual international conference, a social function ticket, and up to $250 per person for reimbursement of travel expenses, hotel accommodations, and meals.

**Duration:** The competition is held annually.

**Number awarded:** 3 cash prizes are awarded each year.

**Deadline:** April of each year.

## 2136 ENGINEERS FOUNDATION OF OHIO GENERAL FUND SCHOLARSHIP

Ohio Society of Professional Engineers, Attn: Engineers Foundation of Ohio
4795 Evanswood Drive, Suite 201
Columbus, OH 43229-7216
Phone: (614) 846-1144; (800) 654-9481; Fax: (614) 846-1131;
Email: ospe@iwaynet.net
Web: www.ohioengineer.com/programs/Scholarships.htm

**Summary:** To provide financial assistance to engineering students entering their junior or senior year at a college or university in Ohio.

**Eligibility:** Open to entering juniors and seniors at ABET-accredited colleges and universities in Ohio who are majoring in engineering. Applicants must have a GPA of 3.0 or higher, be U.S. citizens, and be Ohio residents. Along with their application, they must submit a 350-word essay on their interest in engineering, including why they became interested in the field, what specialty interests them most, and why they want to become a practicing engineer. Financial need is also considered in the selection process.

**Financial data:** The stipend is $1,000 per year.

**Duration:** 1 year; nonrenewable.

**Number awarded:** 1 each year.

**Deadline:** December of each year.

## 2137 ENGINEER'S FOUNDATION OF WISCONSIN–BEHLING COLLEGE FRESHMAN SCHOLARSHIP

Wisconsin Society of Professional Engineers
Attn: Engineers Foundation of Wisconsin
7044 South 13th Street
Oak Creek, WI 53154
Phone: (414) 768-8000, ext. 103; Fax: (414) 768-8001; Email: wspe@wspe.org
Web: www.wspe.org/efw.html

**Summary:** To provide financial assistance to high school seniors in Wisconsin who are interested in majoring in engineering in college.

**Eligibility:** Open to seniors graduating from high schools in Wisconsin who intend to enroll in an accredited engineering undergraduate program, earn a degree in engineering, and enter the practice of engineering after graduation. Applicants must have a GPA of 3.0 or higher and an ACT composite score of 24 or higher. As part of the selection process, they must submit a 250-word essay on how they became interested in engineering, the field of engineering that is most interesting to them and why, and why they want to become a practicing engineer. U.S. citizenship is required. Selection is based on academic achievement, community involvement, extracurricular activities, and need.

**Financial data:** The stipend is $1,000.

**Duration:** 1 year.

**Number awarded:** 1 each year.

**Deadline:** December of each year.

### 2138 ENTOMOLOGICAL FOUNDATION UNDERGRADUATE SCHOLARSHIPS

Entomological Society of America, Attn: Entomological Foundation
9332 Annapolis Road, Suite 210
Lanham, MD 20706-3150
Phone: (301) 459-9082; Fax: (301) 459-9084; Email: melodie@entfdn.org
Web: www.entfdn.org/Undergrad.html

**Summary:** To provide financial assistance to undergraduates interested in studying entomology.

**Eligibility:** Open to undergraduate students majoring in entomology, biology, zoology, or a related science at a recognized university or college in the United States, Canada, or Mexico. They must have accumulated a minimum of 30 semester hours at the time the award is presented. Selection is based on academic record, demonstrated enthusiasm, interest, and achievement in biology. Preference is given to students with demonstrated financial need.

**Financial data:** The stipend is $1,500.

**Duration:** 1 year.

**Number awarded:** 3 each year.

**Deadline:** May of each year.

### 2139 ENVIRONMENTAL DIVISION SCHOLARSHIPS

Technical Association of the Pulp and Paper Industry, Attn: TAPPI Foundation
15 Technology Parkway South
Norcross, GA 30092
Phone: (770) 209-7536; (800) 332-8686; Fax: (770) 446-6947;
Email: vedmondson@tappi.org
Web: www.tappi.org

**Summary:** To provide financial assistance to students who are interested in preparing for a career in the paper industry, with a focus on environmental control as it relates to the pulp, paper, and allied industries.

**Eligibility:** Open to students who are attending college full time, are at least sophomores, are enrolled at an ABET-accredited or equivalent college, have a GPA of 3.0 or higher, and are able to demonstrate a strong desire to prepare for a career in environmental control as it relates to the pulp, paper, and allied industries. Applicants may be interviewed.

**Financial data:** The stipend is $2,500.

**Duration:** 1 year.

**Number awarded:** At least 1 each year.

**Deadline:** January of each year.

### 2140 ENVIRONMENTAL EDUCATIONAL SCHOLARSHIP PROGRAM

Missouri Department of Natural Resources
Attn: Environmental Educational Scholarship Program
P.O. Box 176
Jefferson City, MO 65102
Phone: (573) 526-8411; (800) 334-6946; TDD: (800) 379-2419;
Email: daspec@dnr.state.mo.us
Web: www.dnr.state.mo.us/eesp

**Summary:** To provide financial assistance to underrepresented and minority students from Missouri who are or will be working on a bachelor's or master's degree in an environmental field.

**Eligibility:** Open to minority and underrepresented residents of Missouri who have graduated from an accredited high school with a GPA of 3.0 or higher. Students who are already enrolled in college must have a GPA of 2.5 or higher and must be full-time undergraduate or graduate students. Applicants may be 1) engineering students in civil, chemical, environmental, mechanical, or agricultural engineering; 2) environmental students in geology, biology, wildlife management, planning, natural resources, or a closely-related course of study; 3) chemistry students in the field of environmental chemistry; or 4) law

enforcement students in environmental law enforcement. They must submit a 1-page essay on their environmental education career goals. Selection is based on the essay, GPA and test scores, school and community activities, leadership, and character.

**Financial data:** A stipend is $2,000 per year.

**Duration:** 1 year; may be renewed if the recipient maintains a GPA of 2.5 or higher and full-time enrollment.

**Number awarded:** Varies each year.

**Deadline:** June of each year.

### 2141 ENVIRONMENTAL MANAGEMENT SCHOLARSHIP

Hispanic Scholarship Fund Institute
1001 Connecticut Avenue, N.W., Suite 632
Washington, DC 20036
Phone: (202) 296-0009; Fax: (202) 296-3633; Email: info@hsfi.org
Web: www.hsfi.org/scholarships/energy.asp

**Summary:** To provide financial assistance to Hispanic undergraduate students majoring in designated business, engineering, and science fields related to the U.S. Department of Energy (DOE) goals of environmental restoration and waste management.

**Eligibility:** Open to U.S. citizens and permanent residents of Hispanic background who have completed at least 12 undergraduate credits with a GPA of 3.0 or higher. Applicants must be interested in preparing for a career supportive of the DOE goals of environmental restoration and waste management. Eligible academic majors are in the fields of business (management and system analysis), engineering (agricultural, chemical, civil, electrical, environmental, industrial, mechanical, metallurgical, nuclear, and petroleum), and science (applied math/physics, chemistry, computer science, ecology, environmental, epidemiology, geology, health physics, hydrology, radiochemistry, radio-ecology, and toxicology). Along with their application, they must submit a 2-page essay on 1) how their academic major, interests, and career goals correspond to environmental restoration and waste management issues; and 2) how their Hispanic background and family upbringing have influenced their academic and personal goals. Selection is based on the essay, academic record, academic plans and career goals, financial need, commitment to DOE's goal of environmental restoration and waste management, and a letter of recommendation.

**Financial data:** The stipend is $3,000 per year for 4-year university students or $2,000 per year for community college students.

**Duration:** 1 year.

**Number awarded:** Varies each year.

**Deadline:** March of each year.

### 2142 EPA TRIBAL LANDS ENVIRONMENTAL SCIENCE SCHOLARSHIP

American Indian Science and Engineering Society
Attn: Scholarship Coordinator
2305 Renard, S.E., Suite 200
P.O. Box 9828
Albuquerque, NM 87119-9828
Phone: (505) 765-1052, ext. 106; Fax: (505) 765-5608; Email: shirley@aises.org
Web: www.aises.org/highered/scholarships

**Summary:** To provide financial assistance and summer work experience to members of the American Indian Science and Engineering Society (AISES) interested in studying environmental or related sciences at the undergraduate or graduate level.

**Eligibility:** Open to AISES members who are full-time juniors, seniors, or graduate students at 4-year colleges and universities and majoring in environmental, science, or engineering fields leading to an environmental-related career. Applicants must have a GPA of 2.7 or higher and be U.S. citizens or permanent residents. Non-Indians may apply, but all applicants must submit an essay on their knowledge and living experience with American Indian tribal culture, their interest in environmental studies, how that interest relates to environmental issues and needs on tribal lands, and how they will contribute their professional knowledge to a Native community.

**Financial data:** The stipend is $4,000 per year.

**Duration:** 1 year; nonrenewable.

**Deadline:** June of each year.

### 2143 ERBY YOUNG SCHOLARSHIP

Missouri League for Nursing, Inc., Attn: Executive Director
604 Dix Road
P.O. Box 104476
Jefferson City, MO 65110-4476

Phone: (573) 635-5355; Fax: (573) 635-7908; Email: mln@monursing.org

Web: www.monursing.org/programservices/prog_scholarships_erby.htm

**Summary:** To provide financial assistance to L.P.N.s who are working on an R.N. degree or diploma at an accredited school of nursing in Missouri.

**Eligibility:** Open to residents of Missouri enrolled in an accredited school of nursing in the state. Applicants must be L.P.N.s who have an active license in Missouri and are enrolled in an R.N. program above the freshman level in an associate's degree or diploma program or above the sophomore level in a baccalaureate degree program. They must be able to demonstrate financial need, have a GPA of 3.0 or higher, and be nominated by the dean or director of their school. U.S. citizenship is required.

**Financial data:** The stipend depends on the availability of funds.

**Duration:** 1 year.

**Number awarded:** 1 each year.

**Deadline:** Nominations must be submitted by October of each year.

---

## 2144 ERNEST F. HOLLINGS SCHOLARSHIP PROGRAM

Oak Ridge Institute for Science and Education

Attn: Science and Engineering Education

P.O. Box 117

Oak Ridge, TN 37831-0117

Phone: (865) 241-8240; Fax: (865) 241-5219;

Email: hollingsscholarship@orau.gov

Web: www.orau.gov/orise.htm

**Summary:** To provide financial assistance and summer research experience to upper-division students who are working on a degree in a field of interest to the National Oceanic and Atmospheric Administration (NOAA).

**Eligibility:** Open to full-time students entering their junior year at an accredited college or university in the United States or its territories. Applicants must be majoring in a discipline related to oceanic and atmospheric science, research, technology, and education, and supportive of the purposes of NOAA's programs and mission (e.g., biological, life, and agricultural sciences; computer and information sciences; engineering; mathematics; physical sciences; social and behavioral sciences; or teacher education). They must have a GPA of 3.0 or higher. As part of their program, they must be interested in participating in summer research and development activities at NOAA headquarters (Silver Spring, Maryland) or field centers. U.S. citizenship is required.

**Financial data:** This program provides a stipend of $8,000 per academic year and $650 per week during the internship, a housing subsidy and limited travel reimbursement for round-trip transportation to the internship site, and travel expenses to the scholarship program conference at the completion of the internship.

**Duration:** 2 academic years plus 10 weeks during the intervening summer.

**Number awarded:** Approximately 100 each year.

**Deadline:** May of each year.

---

## 2145 ESTHER WILKINS/LIPPINCOTT WILLIAMS & WILKINS SCHOLARSHIP

American Dental Hygienists' Association, Attn: Institute for Oral Health

444 North Michigan Avenue, Suite 3400

Chicago, IL 60611

Phone: (312) 440-8918; (800) 735-4916; Fax: (312) 440-8929;

Email: institute@adha.net

Web: www.adha.org/institute/Scholarship/index.htm

**Summary:** To provide financial assistance to undergraduate students preparing for careers in dental hygiene.

**Eligibility:** Open to full-time undergraduate students who are active members of the Student American Dental Hygienists' Association (SADHA) or the American Dental Hygienists' Association (ADHA). Applicants must have a GPA of 3.5 or higher, be able to document financial need of at least $1,500, and have completed at least one year in an accredited dental hygiene program in the United States. Along with their application, they must submit a statement that covers their long-term career goals, their intended contribution to the dental hygiene profession, their professional interests, and the manner in which their degree will enhance their professional capacity.

**Financial data:** Stipends range from $1,000 to $2,000.

**Duration:** 1 year.

**Number awarded:** 1 each year.

**Deadline:** April of each year.

---

## 2146 ETHAN AND ALLAN MURPHY ENDOWED MEMORIAL SCHOLARSHIP

American Meteorological Society, Attn: Fellowship/Scholarship Program

45 Beacon Street

Boston, MA 02108-3693

Phone: (617) 227-2426, ext. 246; Fax: (617) 742-8718;

Email: scholar@ametsoc.org

Web: www.ametsoc.org/amsstudentinfo/scholfeldocs/scholfel.html

**Summary:** To provide financial assistance to undergraduates majoring in meteorology or an aspect of atmospheric sciences with an interest in weather forecasting.

**Eligibility:** Open to full-time students entering their final year of undergraduate study and majoring in meteorology or an aspect of the atmospheric or related oceanic and hydrologic sciences. Applicants must intend to make atmospheric or related sciences their career and be able to demonstrate, through curricular or extracurricular activities, an interest in weather forecasting or in the value and utilization of forecasts. They must be U.S. citizens or permanent residents enrolled at a U.S. institution and have a cumulative GPA of 3.25 or higher. Along with their application, they must submit 200-word essays on 1) their most important achievements that qualify them for this scholarship, and 2) their career goals in the atmospheric or related oceanic or hydrologic fields. Selection is based on academic excellence and achievement; financial need is not considered. The sponsor specifically encourages applications from women, minorities, and students with disabilities who are traditionally underrepresented in the atmospheric and related oceanic sciences.

**Financial data:** The stipend is $2,000 per year.

**Duration:** 1 year.

**Number awarded:** 1 each year.

**Deadline:** February of each year.

---

## 2147 ETHNIC MINORITY BACHELOR'S SCHOLARSHIPS IN ONCOLOGY NURSING

Oncology Nursing Society, Attn: ONS Foundation

125 Enterprise Drive

Pittsburgh, PA 15275-1214

Phone: (412) 859-6100, ext. 8503; (866) 257-4ONS; Fax: (412) 859-6160;

Email: foundation@ons.org

Web: www.ons.org

**Summary:** To provide financial assistance to ethnic minorities interested in working on undergraduate studies in oncology nursing.

**Eligibility:** Open to candidates who 1) demonstrate an interest in and commitment to cancer nursing; 2) are enrolled in an undergraduate nursing degree program at an NLN- or CCNE-accredited school of nursing (the program must have application to oncology nursing); 3) have a current license to practice as a registered nurse or a practical (vocational) nurse; 4) have not previously received a bachelor's scholarship from this sponsor; and 5) are a member of an ethnic minority group. Applicants must submit an essay of 250 words or less on their role in caring for persons with cancer and a statement of their professional goals and their relationship to the advancement of oncology nursing. Financial need is not considered in the selection process.

**Financial data:** The stipend is $2,000.

**Duration:** 1 year.

**Number awarded:** 3 each year.

**Deadline:** January of each year.

---

## 2148 EUGENE P. PFLEIDER MEMORIAL SCHOLARSHIP

Society for Mining, Metallurgy, and Exploration, Inc., Attn: Student Center

8307 Shaffer Parkway

P.O. Box 277002

Littleton, CO 80127-7002

Phone: (303) 948-4203; (800) 763-3132; Fax: (303) 973-3845;

Email: sme@smenet.org

Web: www.smenet.org/education/students/sme_scholarships.crm

**Summary:** To provide financial assistance to student members of the Society for Mining, Metallurgy, and Exploration (SME) who are majoring in mining engineering.

**Eligibility:** Open to student members who have completed their sophomore year in college and are majoring in mining engineering. Applicants must be U.S. citizens, be able to demonstrate financial need, have a strong academic record, and be committed to a career in mining engineering. Only one candidate from each eligible department may be nominated each academic year.

**Financial data:** The stipend is $1,000.

**Duration:** 1 year.

**Number awarded:** 1 each year.

**Deadline:** November of each year.

## 2149 EUGENE S. KROPF SCHOLARSHIP

University Aviation Association
3410 Skyway Drive
Auburn, AL 36830-6444
Phone: (334) 844-2434; Email: uaa@auburn.edu
Web: www.uaa.aero
**Summary:** To provide financial assistance for college to students enrolled in an aviation-related curriculum at a college or university affiliated with the University Aviation Association (UAA).
**Eligibility:** Open to U.S. citizens who are enrolled in a 2-year or 4-year degree in the field of aviation at a UAA-member college or university and have earned at least a 3.0 GPA. They must submit a 250-word essay on "How Can I Improve Aviation Education."
**Financial data:** The stipend is $1,000.
**Duration:** 1 year.
**Number awarded:** 1 each year.
**Deadline:** April of each year.

## 2150 EXCEL GEOPHYSICS SCHOLARSHIP

Society of Exploration Geophysicists, Attn: SEG Foundation
8801 South Yale, Suite 500
P.O. Box 702740
Tulsa, OK 74170-2740
Phone: (918) 497-5513; Fax: (918) 497-5557; Email: scholarships@seg.org
Web: seg.org/business/foundation/scholarships/index.shtml
**Summary:** To provide financial assistance to undergraduate and graduate students at universities in the United States and Canada who are interested in studying applied geophysics.
**Eligibility:** Open to 1) high school students planning to enter college in the fall, and 2) undergraduate or graduate students whose grades are above average. Applicants must intend to work on a degree directed toward a career in applied geophysics or a closely-related field at a university in the United States or Canada. Along with their application, they must submit a 150-word essay on how they plan to use geophysics in their future. Financial need is not considered in the selection process.
**Financial data:** Stipends range from $1,000 to $3,000 per year.
**Duration:** 1 academic year; may be renewable, based on scholastic standing, availability of funds, and continuance of a course of study leading to a career in applied geophysics.
**Number awarded:** 1 each year.
**Deadline:** January of each year.

## 2151 EXCELLENCE IN EQUINE/AGRICULTURAL INVOLVEMENT SCHOLARSHIP

American Quarter Horse Foundation, Attn: Scholarship Coordinator
2601 I-40 East
Amarillo, TX 79104
Phone: (806) 376-5181; (888) 209-8322; Fax: (806) 376-1005;
Email: lowens@aqha.org
Web: www.aqha.com/foundation/scholarships/index.html
**Summary:** To provide financial assistance for college to members of the American Quarter Horse Association (AQHA) or the American Quarter Horse Youth Association (AQHYA) who are planning a career in an equine field.
**Eligibility:** Open to members of either organization (for at least one year) who are graduating high school seniors or already enrolled in college. They must have a GPA of 3.5 or higher and be planning to prepare for a career that promotes equine involvement. Financial need is considered in the selection process.
**Financial data:** The maximum stipend is $6,250 per year.
**Duration:** Up to 4 years, provided the recipient maintains a GPA of 3.5 or higher and full-time enrollment.
**Number awarded:** 1 each year.
**Deadline:** January of each year.

## 2152 EXECUTIVE BOARD SCHOLARSHIP

Instrumentation, Systems, and Automation Society
Attn: ISA Educational Foundation
67 Alexander Drive
Research Triangle Park, NC 27709
Phone: (919) 549-8411; Fax: (919) 549-8288; Email: info@isa.org
Web: www.isa.org
**Summary:** To provide financial assistance to undergraduate and graduate students majoring in fields related to instrumentation, systems, and automation.
**Eligibility:** Open to full-time undergraduate and graduate students enrolled in a program in instrumentation, systems, automation, or a closely-related field. Applicants must have a GPA of 3.0 or higher. They may be from any country but must be attending an institution in their own country. Applicants in a 2-year program must have completed at least one academic semester of 12 hours or its equivalent. Applicants in a 4-year program must be in their sophomore year or higher. Along with their application, they must submit an essay (up to 400 words) on their ambitions and qualifications as an innovator or future leader in a career in instrumentation, systems, or automation; they should describe their career objectives, how the award of this scholarship will help them attain their objectives, why they want to enter this particular field of engineering, what they have achieved and learned through their studies and activities, and what this indicates about their character and determination. Preference is given to applicants with demonstrated leadership capabilities. Financial need is not considered in the selection process.
**Financial data:** The stipend is $1,800.
**Duration:** 1 year; may be renewed.
**Number awarded:** 1 each year.
**Deadline:** February of each year.

## 2153 EXELON SCHOLARSHIP

Society of Women Engineers
230 East Ohio Street, Suite 400
Chicago, IL 60611-3265
Phone: (312) 596-5223; Fax: (312) 644-8557; Email: hq@swe.org
Web: www.societyofwomenengineers.org/scholarships
**Summary:** To provide financial assistance to women who will be entering college as freshmen and are interested in studying engineering or computer science.
**Eligibility:** Open to women who are entering college as freshmen with a GPA of 3.5 or higher. Applicants must be planning to enroll full time at an ABET-accredited 4-year college or university and major in computer science or engineering. Along with their application, they must submit a 1-page essay on why they want to be an engineer or computer scientist, how they believe they will make a difference as an engineer or computer scientist, and what influenced them to study engineering or computer science. Selection is based on merit.
**Financial data:** The stipend is $1,000.
**Duration:** 1 year.
**Number awarded:** 1 each year.
**Deadline:** May of each year.

## 2154 EXTRACTION AND PROCESSING DIVISION SCHOLARSHIPS

The Minerals, Metals & Materials Society, Attn: TMS Student Awards Program
184 Thorn Hill Road
Warrendale, PA 15086-7514
Phone: (724) 776-9000, ext. 220; Fax: (724) 776-3770;
Email: students@tms.org
Web: www.tms.org/Students/AwardsPrograms/Scholarships.html
**Summary:** To provide financial assistance for college to student members of The Minerals, Metals & Materials Society (TMS).
**Eligibility:** Open to undergraduate members of the society who are majoring in the extraction and processing of minerals, metals, and materials. Applicants may be from any country. Selection is based on academic achievement, school and community activities, work experience, leadership, a personal profile statement, and letters of recommendation. Preference is given to students in their senior year who are enrolled full time.
**Financial data:** The stipend is $2,000 plus a travel stipend of $500 (so the recipient can attend the annual meeting of the society to accept the award).
**Duration:** 1 year.
**Number awarded:** 4 each year.
**Deadline:** April of each year.

## 2155 FAIRFIELD COUNTY SCHOLARSHIP

Society of Manufacturing Engineers, Attn: SME Education Foundation
One SME Drive
P.O. Box 930
Dearborn, MI 48121-0930
Phone: (313) 425-3304; (800) 733-4763, ext. 3304; Fax: (313) 425-3411;
Email: foundation@sme.org
Web: www.sme.org

**Summary:** To provide financial assistance to students, especially those from New Jersey, working on an undergraduate degree in engineering.

**Eligibility:** Open to students working full time on an undergraduate degree in manufacturing engineering, technology, or a closely-related field at a college or university in the United States or Canada. Applicants must have a GPA of 3.0 or higher. Preference is given to residents of New Jersey and students attending school in the state.

**Financial data:** The stipend is $1,500.

**Duration:** 1 year.

**Number awarded:** 1 each year.

**Deadline:** January of each year.

## 2156 FEDERATED GARDEN CLUBS OF CONNECTICUT SCHOLARSHIP

**Summary:** To provide financial assistance to Connecticut residents who are interested in majoring in horticulture-related fields at a Connecticut college or university.

*See Listing #1386.*

## 2157 FLEMING/BLASZCAK SCHOLARSHIP

Society of Plastics Engineers, Attn: SPE Foundation
14 Fairfield Drive
Brookfield, CT 06804-0403
Phone: (203) 740-5447; Fax: (203) 775-1157; Email: foundation@4spe.org
Web: www.4spe.org/foundation/scholarships.php

**Summary:** To provide financial assistance to Mexican American undergraduate and graduate students who have a career interest in the plastics industry.

**Eligibility:** Open to full-time undergraduate and graduate students of Mexican descent who are enrolled in a 4-year college or university. Applicants must be U.S. citizens or legal residents. They must 1) have a demonstrated or expressed interest in the plastics industry; 2) be majoring in or taking courses that would be beneficial to a career in the plastics or polymer industry (e.g., plastics engineering, polymer sciences, chemistry, physics, chemical engineering, mechanical engineering, or industrial engineering); 3) be in good academic standing at their school; and 4) be able to document financial need. Along with their application, they must submit 3 letters of recommendation; a high school and/or college transcript; a 1- to 2-page statement telling why they are interested in the scholarship, their qualifications, and their educational and career goals in the plastics industry; and documentation of their Mexican heritage.

**Financial data:** The stipend is $2,000 per year. Funds are paid directly to the recipient's school.

**Duration:** 1 year.

**Number awarded:** 1 each year.

**Deadline:** January of each year.

## 2158 FLORIDA AWMA SCHOLARSHIPS

Air & Waste Management Association-Florida Section
c/o C. David Cooper
University of Central Florida
Civil and Environmental Engineering Department
Orlando, FL 32816-2450
Email: cooper@mail.ucf.edu
Web: www.flawma.com/scholarship.html

**Summary:** To provide financial assistance to upper-division and graduate students at colleges and universities in Florida who are preparing for a career in the air pollution or waste management fields.

**Eligibility:** Open to juniors, seniors, and graduate students enrolled full time at 4-year colleges and universities in Florida. Applicants must submit a 1-page essay on their interest in the air environment or the waste management field. Selection is based on the essay, academic transcripts, and a letter of reference.

**Financial data:** Stipends are $1,000, $500, or $250.

**Duration:** 1 year.

**Number awarded:** 4 to 6 each year: 1 at $1,000 (the Axel Hendrickson Scholarship), 1 or 2 at $500, and 2 or 3 at $250.

**Deadline:** January of each year.

## 2159 FLORIDA CHAPTER OF THE WILDLIFE SOCIETY SCHOLARSHIP

Wildlife Society-Florida Chapter
c/o Maria Zondervan, Scholarship Committee Chair
St. Johns River Water Management District

975 Keller Road
Altamonte Springs, FL 32714-1618
Phone: (407) 659-4872; Email: mzondervan@sjrwmd.com
Web: fltws.org

**Summary:** To provide financial assistance to upper-division students working on a degree in wildlife ecology and/or management at a Florida college.

**Eligibility:** Open to students entering their junior or senior year at a 4-year college or university in Florida. Applicants must be interested in preparing for a career in wildlife ecology and/or management. They must have a GPA of 2.5 or higher. Along with their application, they must submit a letter describing their professional goals and financial need. Selection is based on goals as expressed in the letter, extracurricular activities, demonstrated leadership, professional potential, and financial need.

**Financial data:** The stipend is $1,000.

**Duration:** 1 year.

**Number awarded:** 1 each year.

**Deadline:** November of each year.

## 2160 FLORIDA CHAPTER UNDERGRADUATE SCHOLARSHIPS

American Public Works Association-Florida Chapter
c/o Gary M. Fitzpatrick, Scholarship Committee Chair
Florida Department of Transportation
605 Suwannee Street MS 25
Tallahassee, FL 32399
Phone: (850) 414-4541; Fax: (850) 414-4508;
Email: Gary.Fitzpatrick@dot.state.fl.us
Web: florida.apwa.net

**Summary:** To provide financial assistance to undergraduate students in Florida who are working on a degree in civil engineering.

**Eligibility:** Open to students who have earned at least 60 units at an ABET-accredited school in Florida. Applicants must be working on a bachelor's degree in civil engineering or a related field. They must submit transcripts and information on their financial situation.

**Financial data:** A stipend is awarded (amount not specified).

**Duration:** 1 year.

**Number awarded:** 1 or more each year.

**Deadline:** January of each year.

## 2161 FLORIDA ENGINEERING FOUNDATION SCHOLARSHIPS

Florida Engineering Society, Attn: Scholarship Coordinator
125 South Gadsden Street
P.O. Box 750
Tallahassee, FL 32302
Phone: (850) 224-7121; Email: fes@fleng.org
Web: www.fleng.org/scholarship.htm

**Summary:** To provide financial assistance to engineering students at colleges and universities in Florida.

**Eligibility:** Open to residents of Florida entering their junior or senior year of an engineering program at a college or university in the state. Applicants must be U.S. citizens with a GPA of 3.0 or higher and be recommended by a faculty member at their institution. Selection is based on academic performance, work experience, activities, honors, and letters of recommendation. Semifinalists are interviewed. Financial need is not considered in the selection process.

**Financial data:** The stipend is $1,000.

**Duration:** 1 year.

**Number awarded:** 2 each year.

**Deadline:** January of each year.

## 2162 FLORIDA ENGINEERING SOCIETY JUNIOR COLLEGE SCHOLARSHIPS

Florida Engineering Society, Attn: Scholarship Coordinator
125 South Gadsden Street
P.O. Box 750
Tallahassee, FL 32302
Phone: (850) 224-7121; Email: fes@fleng.org
Web: www.fleng.org/scholarship.htm

**Summary:** To provide financial assistance to junior college students in Florida who are interested in transferring to a 4-year university to major in engineering.

**Eligibility:** Open to students at Florida junior or community colleges who are in the final year of a pre-engineering program. Applicants must have a GPA of 3.0 or higher and be recommended by an official of the college they are attending. They must be planning to transfer to a designated university in Florida to study engineering. Selection is based on academic performance, work experience, activities, honors, and letters of recommendation, along with evidence of leadership, motivation, character, and self-reliance. Financial need is not considered in the selection process.

**Financial data:** The stipend ranges from $1,000 to $2,000, depending on the university attended.

**Duration:** 1 year; may be renewed.

**Number awarded:** Varies each year.

**Deadline:** January of each year.

## 2163 FLORIDA NURSES FOUNDATION SCHOLARSHIPS

Florida Nurses Association, Attn: Florida Nurses Foundation
P.O. Box 536985
Orlando, FL 32853-6985
Phone: (407) 896-3261; Fax: (407) 896-9042;
Email: foundation@floridanurse.org
Web: www.floridanurse.org/grants.asp

**Summary:** To provide financial assistance to Florida residents who are interested in working on an undergraduate or graduate degree in nursing.

**Eligibility:** Open to Florida residents (for at least one year) who are currently enrolled in an accredited nursing program in the state. They may be working on an associate's, baccalaureate, master's, or doctoral degree. Students who are pursuing initial nursing education (associate or baccalaureate degree and not yet licensed as an R.N.) must have completed at least one semester of the nursing program. Undergraduates must have a GPA of 2.5 or higher and graduate students a GPA of 3.0 or higher. Selection is based on academic record, financial need, and potential for contribution to the nursing profession and society.

**Financial data:** A stipend is awarded (amount not specified).

**Duration:** 1 semester or year.

**Number awarded:** Varies each year.

**Deadline:** May of each year.

## 2164 FLORIDA ROCK INDUSTRIES INTERNSHIP PROGRAM

Florida Independent College Fund
929 North Spring Garden Avenue, Suite 165
DeLand, FL 32720-0981
Phone: (386) 734-2745; Fax: (386) 734-0839; Email: Scholarships@ficf.org
Web: www.ficf.org

**Summary:** To provide financial assistance and work experience to business and engineering students at designated private colleges and universities in Florida who are interested in a career in the construction materials business.

**Eligibility:** Open to students majoring in business or engineering at 24 designated independent colleges or universities in Florida. Applicants must be entering their junior year and have a GPA of 3.0 or higher. They must be able to demonstrate an interest in the construction materials business.

**Financial data:** The stipend is $7,000 per year. A paid internship is also provided.

**Duration:** The stipend is provided for the junior and senior years of college. The internship is provided for the summer between the junior and senior years.

**Number awarded:** 1 each year.

**Deadline:** April of each year.

## 2165 FLORIDA SCHOLARSHIP PROGRAM AWARDS

Florida Institute of Consulting Engineers, Attn: Scholarship Coordinator
P.O. Box 750
Tallahassee, FL 32302-0750
Phone: (850) 224-7121; Email: fes@fleng.org
Web: www.fleng.org/fice/ficeawards.cfm

**Summary:** To provide financial assistance to students in Florida currently working on a bachelor's degree in engineering or land surveying.

**Eligibility:** Open to Florida students who are working on a bachelor's degree in an ABET-approved engineering program or in an accredited land surveying program. Applicants must be U.S. citizens entering their junior, senior, or fifth year. Along with their application, they must submit a 500-word essay on "What is the role or responsibility of the consulting engineer or land surveyor to shaping and protecting the natural environment?" Selection is based on the essay (25 points), cumulative GPA (28 points), work experience (20 points), a letter of recommendation (17 points), and college activities (10 points).

**Financial data:** The stipend is $1,000

**Duration:** 1 year.

**Number awarded:** 1 each year.

**Deadline:** October of each year.

## 2166 FLORIDA SURVEYING AND MAPPING SOCIETY SCHOLARSHIPS

Florida Surveying and Mapping Society
Attn: Florida Surveying and Mapping Society Scholarship Foundation, Inc.
1689-A Mahan Center Boulevard
Tallahassee, FL 32308-5454
Phone: (850) 942-1900; (800) 237-4384; Fax: (850) 877-4852;
Email: fsms@fsms.org
Web: www.fsms.org

**Summary:** To provide financial assistance to Florida residents interested in studying surveying in college.

**Eligibility:** Open to residents of Florida who are working on or planning to work on a degree in surveying. Applicants must submit an essay on their educational and career goals and documentation of financial need. U.S. citizenship or permanent resident status is required.

**Financial data:** A stipend is awarded (amount not specified).

**Duration:** 1 year.

**Number awarded:** 1 or more each year.

## 2167 FNGLA ACTION CHAPTER SCHOLARSHIP

Florida Nurserymen, Growers and Landscape Association-Action Chapter
Attn: Gina Mazzie-Forbrick, Scholarship Committee Chair
ForemostCo, Inc.
1751 Williams Road
Winter Garden, FL 34787-9162
Phone: (407) 877-8876; Fax: (407) 877-8684; Email: gina@foremostco.com

**Summary:** To provide financial assistance to students in Florida interested in preparing for a career in horticulture.

**Eligibility:** Open to students who have been accepted by or be currently enrolled in a Florida junior college, college, or university. They may be attending school full or part time, but they must be majoring in one of the following subjects: environmental horticulture, landscaping, landscape architecture, turf management, or a related field. All applicants must have at least a 2.75 GPA. Selection is based on academic record, work experience, awards received, letters of recommendation, and an essay (300 words) on the applicant's career plans.

**Financial data:** Stipends range from $500 to $1,500.

**Duration:** 1 year.

**Number awarded:** 1 or more each year. A total of $4,000 is available through this program each year.

**Deadline:** June of each year.

## 2168 FORD MOTOR COMPANY SCHOLARSHIP

Society of Women Engineers
230 East Ohio Street, Suite 400
Chicago, IL 60611-3265
Phone: (312) 596-5223; Fax: (312) 644-8557; Email: hq@swe.org
Web: www.societyofwomenengineers.org/scholarships

**Summary:** To provide financial assistance to lower-division women majoring in designated engineering specialties.

**Eligibility:** Open to women who are entering their sophomore year at a 4-year ABET-accredited college or university. Applicants must be majoring in automotive, electrical, industrial, manufacturing, or mechanical engineering and have a GPA of 3.5 or higher. Along with their application, they must submit a 1-page essay on why they want to be an engineer, how they believe they will make a difference as an engineer, and what influenced them to study engineering. Selection is based on merit and leadership potential.

**Financial data:** The stipend is $1,000.

**Duration:** 1 year; may be renewed for 1 additional year.

**Number awarded:** 1 each year.

**Deadline:** January of each year.

## 2169 FORD MOTOR COMPANY/AMERICAN INDIAN COLLEGE FUND CORPORATE SCHOLARS PROGRAM

American Indian College Fund, Attn: Scholarship Department
8333 Greenwood Boulevard
Denver, CO 80221
Phone: (303) 426-8900; (800) 776-FUND; Fax: (303) 426-1200;
Email: info@collegefund.org
Web: www.collegefund.org/scholarships/scholarships.html

**Summary:** To provide financial assistance to Native American college students who are majoring in designated fields at specified colleges and universities.

**Eligibility:** Open to American Indians, Alaska Natives, and Hawaii Natives who have proof of enrollment or descendancy and have achieved at least sophomore status at 1 of 102 designated college and universities. Applicants must have a GPA of 3.0 or higher and be able to demonstrate financial need. They must have declared a major in accounting, computer engineering, electrical engineering, finance, information systems, marketing, mechanical engineering, or operations management. Along with their application, they must submit a 1-page personal essay on how they can become a role model and make a difference in their chosen field. Leadership and commitment to the American Indian community are also considered in the selection process.

**Financial data:** The stipend is $8,000 per year.

**Duration:** 1 year; may be renewed.

**Number awarded:** Varies each year.

**Deadline:** November of each year.

### 2170 FORD/HENAAC SCHOLARS PROGRAM

Hispanic Engineer National Achievement Awards Conference
3900 Whiteside Street
Los Angeles, CA 90063
Phone: (323) 262-0997; Fax: (323) 262-0946; Email: info@henaac.org
Web: www.henaac.org/scholarships.htm

**Summary:** To provide financial assistance to Hispanic undergraduate students majoring in engineering and related fields.

**Eligibility:** Open to Hispanic undergraduate students who are enrolled full time in computer science or the following engineering fields: aeronautical, electrical, industrial, and, mechanical. Applicants must have a GPA of 3.0 or higher. U.S. citizenship is required. Academic achievement and campus community activities are considered in the selection process.

**Financial data:** The stipend is $5,000.

**Duration:** 1 year; recipients may reapply.

**Number awarded:** 5 each year.

**Deadline:** April of each year.

### 2171 FORE UNDERGRADUATE MERIT SCHOLARSHIPS

American Health Information Management Association
Attn: Foundation of Research and Education
233 North Michigan Avenue, Suite 2150
Chicago, IL 60601-5806
Phone: (312) 233-1168; Fax: (312) 233-1090; Email: fore@ahima.org
Web: www.ahima.org/fore/programs.cfm

**Summary:** To provide financial assistance to members of the American Health Information Management Association (AHIMA) who are interested in working on an undergraduate degree in health information administration or technology.

**Eligibility:** Open to AHIMA members who are enrolled in a health information administration or health information technology program accredited by the Commission on Accreditation of Allied Health Education Programs. Applicants must be working on a degree on at least a half-time basis and have a GPA of 3.0 or higher. U.S. citizenship is required. Selection is based (in order of importance) on GPA and academic achievement, volunteer and work experience, commitment to the health information management profession, suitability to the health information management profession, quality and suitability of references provided, and clarity of application.

**Financial data:** Stipends range from $1,000 to $5,000.

**Duration:** 1 year; nonrenewable.

**Number awarded:** Varies each year; recently, 41 of these scholarships were awarded.

**Deadline:** May of each year.

### 2172 FORREST BASSFORD STUDENT AWARD

**Summary:** To provide financial assistance to students majoring in agricultural communications or related fields.

*See Listing #1395.*

### 2173 FORT WAYNE SCHOLARSHIPS

Society of Manufacturing Engineers, Attn: SME Education Foundation
One SME Drive
P.O. Box 930
Dearborn, MI 48121-0930
Phone: (313) 425-3304; (800) 733-4763, ext. 3304; Fax: (313) 425-3411;
Email: foundation@sme.org
Web: www.sme.org

**Summary:** To provide financial assistance to students working on an undergraduate or graduate degree in engineering in Indiana.

**Eligibility:** Open to students working on an associate's, bachelor's, or graduate degree in manufacturing, mechanical, or industrial engineering at a college or university in Indiana. Applicants must have a GPA of 2.5 or higher. Preference is given in the following order: first, children and grandchildren of current members of Fort Wayne Chapter 56 of the Society of Manufacturing Engineers (SME); second, student members of chapters sponsored by SME Chapter 56; third, applicants who reside within Indiana; and fourth, applicants planning to attend a college or university in Indiana.

**Financial data:** The stipend is $2,000.

**Duration:** 1 year; may be renewed.

**Number awarded:** 3 each year.

**Deadline:** January of each year.

### 2174 FORUM FOR CONCERNS OF MINORITIES SCHOLARSHIPS

American Society for Clinical Laboratory Science
Attn: Forum for Concerns of Minorities
6701 Democracy Boulevard, Suite 300
Bethesda, MD 20817
Phone: (301) 657-2768; Fax: (301) 657-2909; Email: ascls@ascls.org
Web: www.ascls.org/leadership/awards/fcm.asp

**Summary:** To provide financial assistance to minority students in clinical laboratory scientist and clinical laboratory technician programs.

**Eligibility:** Open to minority students who are enrolled in a program in clinical laboratory science, including clinical laboratory science/medical technology (CLS/MT) and clinical laboratory technician/medical laboratory technician (CLT/MLT). Applicants must be able to demonstrate financial need. Membership in the American Society for Clinical Laboratory Science is encouraged but not required.

**Financial data:** Stipends depend on the need of the recipients and the availability of funds.

**Duration:** 1 year.

**Number awarded:** 2 each year: 1 to a CLS/MT student and 1 to a CLT/MLT student.

**Deadline:** March of each year.

### 2175 FOUNDATION FOR NEONATAL RESEARCH AND EDUCATION SCHOLARSHIPS

Academy of Neonatal Nursing
Attn: Foundation for Neonatal Research and Education
East Holly Avenue, Box 56
Pitman, NJ 08071-0056
Phone: (856) 256-2343; Fax: (856) 589-7463; Email: FNRE@ajj.com
Web: www.inurse.com/fnre/scholarship.htm

**Summary:** To provide financial assistance to neonatal nurses interested in working on a degree.

**Eligibility:** Open to professionally active neonatal nurses engaged in a service, research, or educational role that contributes directly to the health care of neonates or to the neonatal nursing profession. They must be an active member of a professional association dedicated to enhancing neonatal nursing and the care of neonates. Participation in ongoing professional education in neonatal nursing must be demonstrated by at least 10 contact hours in neonatal content over the past 24 months. Qualified nurses must have been admitted to a college or school of higher education for 1 of the following: bachelor of science in nursing, master of science in nursing for advanced practice in neonatal nursing, doctoral degree in nursing, master's or postmaster's degree in nursing administration or business management. They must have a GPA of 3.0 or higher. Along with their application, they must submit a 250-word statement on how they plan to make a significant difference in neonatal nursing practice. Financial need is not considered in the selection process.

**Financial data:** The stipends are $1,500 or $1,000.

**Duration:** 1 year.

**Number awarded:** The Matthew Hester Scholarship of $1,500 and several scholarships at $1,000 (the exact number depending on the availability of funds) are awarded each year.

**Deadline:** April of each year.

### 2176 FRANCES A. MAYS SCHOLARSHIP AWARD

**Summary:** To provide financial assistance to college seniors majoring in health, physical education, recreation, or dance in Virginia.

*See Listing #1398.*

## 2177 FRANCES SYLVIA ZVERINA SCHOLARSHIPS

Herb Society of America-Western Reserve Unit
c/o Priscilla Jones, Committee Chair
2640 Exeter Road
Cleveland Heights, OH 44118
Phone: (216) 932-6090; Email: cillers@hotmail.com
Web: www.herbsociety.org/scholar.htm
**Summary:** To provide financial assistance to college students interested in preparing for a career in a field related to horticulture.
**Eligibility:** Open to students who have completed their sophomore or junior year of college (or the senior year of a 5-year undergraduate program). Applicants may be residents of any state attending an accredited college or university anywhere in the United States. They must be planning a career in horticulture or a related field, including horticultural therapy. U.S. citizenship is required. Preference is given to applicants whose horticultural career goals involve teaching or research or work in the public or nonprofit sector (such as public gardens, botanical gardens, parks, arboreta, city planning, or public education and awareness). Selection is based on an essay that includes a description of their interests, activities, and achievements; an account of their employment record on or off campus; a description of their career goals; and a discussion of their need for financial aid.
**Financial data:** The stipend is $2,000.
**Duration:** 1 year.
**Number awarded:** Up to 3 each year.
**Deadline:** March of each year.

## 2178 FRANCIS X. CROWLEY SCHOLARSHIP

New England Water Works Association
125 Hopping Brook
Holliston, MA 01746
Phone: (508) 893-7979; Fax: (508) 893-9898
Web: www.newwa.org
**Summary:** To provide financial assistance to undergraduate or graduate students from New England interested in working on a degree in civil or environmental engineering or in business management.
**Eligibility:** Open to members and student members of the New England section of the American Water Works Association or the New England Water Works Association. Applicants must be high school seniors, currently-enrolled college students, or graduate students. They must be majoring or planning to major in civil or environmental engineering or in business management. Along with their application, they must submit a 100-word essay on why they have chosen their field of study and if it will improve the environment, public health, or the water industry. Financial need is also considered in the selection process.
**Financial data:** The stipend is $3,000.
**Duration:** 1 year.
**Deadline:** July of each year.

## 2179 FRANK WILLIAM AND DOROTHY GIVEN MILLER ASME AUXILIARY SCHOLARSHIPS

ASME International, Attn: Coordinator, Educational Operations
Three Park Avenue
New York, NY 10016-5990
Phone: (212) 591-8131; (800) THE-ASME; Fax: (212) 591-7143;
Email: oluwanifiset@asme.org
Web: www.asme.org/education/enged/aid/scholar.htm
**Summary:** To provide financial assistance to undergraduate students who are members of the American Society of Mechanical Engineers (ASME).
**Eligibility:** Open to student members in good standing who are enrolled in an ABET-accredited mechanical engineering baccalaureate program. They must be U.S. citizens entering their sophomore, junior, or senior year. Interested students should submit an application form, a nomination from the applicant's department head, a recommendation from a faculty member, and an official transcript. Only one nomination may be submitted per department. Selection is based on character, integrity, leadership, scholastic ability, and potential contribution to the mechanical engineering profession.
**Financial data:** The stipend is $1,500.
**Duration:** 1 year.
**Number awarded:** 2 each year.
**Deadline:** March of each year.

## 2180 FRED R. HAVENS FELLOWSHIP

American Institute of Steel Construction, Attn: Director of University Relations
One East Wacker Drive, Suite 3100
Chicago, IL 60601-2001
Phone: (312) 670-5408; Fax: (312) 670-5403; Email: rosenberg@aisc.com
Web: www.aisc.org
**Summary:** To provide financial assistance to undergraduate and graduate engineering students at universities in Missouri or Kansas, or at Massachusetts Institute of Technology (MIT), who are interested in the structural field, especially structural steel.
**Eligibility:** Open to full-time civil or architectural engineering students at MIT or at universities in Kansas or Missouri. Applicants may be undergraduates who have completed at least one steel design course or graduate students. Along with their application, they must submit a 2-page essay on their interest in steel structures and an original sample structural steel analysis/design solution, with calculations. Selection is based on those submissions, academic performance, and a faculty recommendation. U.S. citizenship is required.
**Financial data:** The stipend is $5,000.
**Duration:** 1 year.
**Number awarded:** 1 each year.
**Deadline:** April of each year.

## 2181 FREEMAN NURSE SCHOLARSHIPS

Freeman Nurse Scholars Program
c/o University of Vermont
Rowell 216
Burlington, VT 05405
Phone: (802) 656-5496; Email: Toni.Kaeding@uvm.edu
Web: choosenursingvermont.org/enter/freeman.html
**Summary:** To provide financial assistance to students at nursing schools in Vermont who are willing to practice in the state following graduation.
**Eligibility:** Open to students currently enrolled full time in an accredited Vermont associate or bachelor's degree program in nursing. Applicants must have a GPA of 3.0 or higher. They must apply through their school. Students who are already licensed R.N.s are not eligible. Selection is based on academic excellence and promise, commitment to Vermont, leadership, community service, and financial need.
**Financial data:** The stipend is $7,500 per year.
**Duration:** 1 year; may be renewed 1 additional year by associate's degree students or 3 additional years by bachelor's degree students.
**Number awarded:** Varies each year.
**Deadline:** March of each year for new applications; May of each year for renewal applications.

## 2182 FREESCALE/HENAAC SCHOLARS PROGRAM

Hispanic Engineer National Achievement Awards Conference
3900 Whiteside Street
Los Angeles, CA 90063
Phone: (323) 262-0997; Fax: (323) 262-0946; Email: info@henaac.org
Web: www.henaac.org/scholarships.htm
**Summary:** To provide financial assistance to Hispanic undergraduate students majoring in computer science or designated fields of engineering.
**Eligibility:** Open to Hispanic undergraduate students who are enrolled full time in computer science or electrical or computer engineering. Applicants must be entering their sophomore, junior, or senior year and have a GPA of 3.0 or higher. Academic achievement and campus community activities are considered in the selection process.
**Financial data:** The stipend is $5,000.
**Duration:** 1 year; recipients may reapply.
**Number awarded:** 1 or more each year.
**Deadline:** April of each year.

## 2183 FRIENDS OF OREGON STUDENTS PROGRAM

Oregon Student Assistance Commission
Attn: Grants and Scholarships Division
1500 Valley River Drive, Suite 100
Eugene, OR 97401-2146
Phone: (541) 687-7395; (800) 452-8807, ext. 7395; Fax: (541) 687-7419;
Email: awardinfo@mercury.osac.state.or.us
Web: www.osac.state.or.us
**Summary:** To provide financial assistance to students in Oregon who are employed while working on an undergraduate or graduate degree in teaching or nursing.
**Eligibility:** Open to students in Oregon who are working and will continue to work at least 20 hours per week while attending college or graduate school at

least 3/4 of the time. Applicants must be interested in preparing for a career in teaching or nursing. They must be able to demonstrate a cumulative GPA of 2.5 or higher and volunteer or work experience relevant to their chosen profession. Preference is given to applicants who 1) are nontraditional students (e.g., older, returning, single parents), 2) have overcome significant personal obstacles, or 3) graduated from an alternative high school, obtained a GED, or are transferring from an Oregon community college to a 4-year college. Along with their application, they must submit essays and letters of reference on how they balance school, work, and personal life as well as their experiences in overcoming obstacles. Selection is based on work experience, community service and volunteer activities, responses to essay questions, letters of reference, and financial need; academic promise (as indicated by GPA and SAT/ACT scores) is also considered.

**Financial data:** Stipends range from $3,000 to $5,000 per year.

**Duration:** 1 year; may be renewed.

**Number awarded:** Varies each year; recently, 28 of these scholarships were awarded.

**Deadline:** February of each year.

## 2184 FTE UNDERGRADUATE MAJOR IN TECHNOLOGY EDUCATION SCHOLARSHIP

International Technology Education Association
Attn: Foundation for Technology Education
1914 Association Drive, Suite 201
Reston, VA 20191-1539
Phone: (703) 860-2100; Fax: (703) 860-0353; Email: iteaordr@iris.org
Web: www.iteawww.org

**Summary:** To provide financial support to undergraduate members of the International Technology Education Association (ITEA) who are majoring in technology education teacher preparation.

**Eligibility:** Open to members of the association (membership may be enclosed with the scholarship application) who are in college but not yet seniors, majoring in technology education teacher preparation with a GPA of 2.5 or higher, and enrolled full time. Selection is based on interest in teaching, academic ability, and faculty recommendations.

**Financial data:** The stipend is $1,000. Funds are provided directly to the recipient.

**Duration:** 1 year.

**Number awarded:** 1 or more each year.

**Deadline:** November of each year.

## 2185 FUELS AND COMBUSTION TECHNOLOGIES DIVISION SCHOLARSHIPS

ASME International, Attn: Fuels and Combustion Technologies Division
Three Park Avenue
New York, NY 10016-5990
Phone: (212) 591-7055; (800) THE-ASME; Fax: (212) 591-7671;
Email: bendoj@asme.org
Web: www.asme.org/divisions/fact/studentprograms.htm

**Summary:** To provide financial assistance to undergraduate engineering students working on a degree in an area of interest to the Fuels and Combustion Technologies (FACT) division of ASME International (the professional society of mechanical engineers).

**Eligibility:** Open to undergraduate students in engineering disciplines (e.g., mechanical, aerospace, chemical) relevant to FACT division area interests. Preference is given to juniors and seniors. Selection is based on student GPA and academic merit, leadership activities, energy and power-related courses taken, institutional geographical location, course offerings and research activities for undergraduates at the student's university, and a letter of recommendation.

**Financial data:** Stipends are $1,500 or $1,000.

**Duration:** 1 year.

**Number awarded:** 4 each year: 2 at $1,500 and 2 at $1,000.

**Deadline:** February of each year.

## 2186 FUELS AND COMBUSTION TECHNOLOGIES DIVISION STUDENT BEST PAPER AWARD

ASME International, Attn: Fuels and Combustion Technologies Division
Three Park Avenue
New York, NY 10016-5990
Phone: (212) 591-7055; (800) THE-ASME; Fax: (212) 591-7671;
Email: bendoj@asme.org
Web: www.asme.org/divisions/fact/awards.htm

**Summary:** To recognize and reward outstanding student papers on fuel technology.

**Eligibility:** Open to both undergraduate and graduate students; graduate students may not have completed their thesis. Applicants must prepare a paper on an aspect of fuel, combustion, and combustion technology. Review and survey papers and papers in the area of internal combustion engines are not acceptable. Applicants first submit a 200-word abstract; based on those abstracts, finalists are invited to submit full papers. Selection of the best paper is based on originality of the technical work described, significance of the technical work and paper, thoroughness of approach and presentation, organization of the paper, logic of approach, clarity of expression, and other pertinent factors.

**Financial data:** The author of the best paper receives a $1,000 honorarium, a certificate of merit, and a 1-year membership in ASME International.

**Duration:** The competition is held annually.

**Number awarded:** 1 each year.

**Deadline:** Abstracts must be submitted by mid-October of each year. Full papers are due in early January.

## 2187 FUTURE ELECTRONICS/HENAAC SCHOLARS PROGRAM

Hispanic Engineer National Achievement Awards Conference
3900 Whiteside Street
Los Angeles, CA 90063
Phone: (323) 262-0997; Fax: (323) 262-0946; Email: info@henaac.org
Web: www.henaac.org/scholarships.htm

**Summary:** To provide financial assistance to Hispanic undergraduate students majoring in engineering and related fields.

**Eligibility:** Open to Hispanic undergraduate students who are enrolled full time in computer science, engineering, material science, mathematics, or applied science. Applicants must have a GPA of 3.0 or higher. There is no citizenship requirement. Academic achievement and campus community activities are considered in the selection process.

**Financial data:** Stipends range from $1,000 to $5,000.

**Duration:** 1 year; recipients may reapply.

**Number awarded:** 1 or more each year.

**Deadline:** April of each year.

## 2188 FUTURE LEADERS OF MANUFACTURING SCHOLARSHIP

Society of Manufacturing Engineers, Attn: SME Education Foundation
One SME Drive
P.O. Box 930
Dearborn, MI 48121-0930
Phone: (313) 425-3304; (800) 733-4763, ext. 3304; Fax: (313) 425-3411;
Email: foundation@sme.org
Web: www.sme.org

**Summary:** To provide financial assistance to student members of the Society of Manufacturing Engineers (SME) who are working on an undergraduate or graduate degree in manufacturing engineering or a related field.

**Eligibility:** Open to undergraduate and graduate student members of SME who are working full time on a degree in manufacturing engineering, industrial technology, engineering technology, or a related field. They must be nominated by their SME faculty advisor; each advisor may nominate only one student. Letters of nomination must explain why the student should be selected, including participation in the student chapter, accomplishments, awards and honors, work experience, reasons for choosing a career in manufacturing, and how the scholarship will increase the student's leadership skills and career.

**Financial data:** The stipend is $1,000 per year.

**Duration:** 1 year.

**Number awarded:** 10 each year.

**Deadline:** January of each year.

## 2189 F.W. "BEICH" BEICHLEY SCHOLARSHIP

ASME International, Attn: Coordinator, Educational Operations
Three Park Avenue
New York, NY 10016-5990
Phone: (212) 591-8131; (800) THE-ASME; Fax: (212) 591-7143;
Email: oluwanifiset@asme.org
Web: www.asme.org/education/enged/aid/scholar.htm

**Summary:** To provide financial assistance to undergraduate students who are members of the American Society of Mechanical Engineers (ASME).

**Eligibility:** Open to student members in good standing who are enrolled in an ABET-accredited mechanical engineering or mechanical engineering technology baccalaureate program. They must be entering their junior or senior year when they apply. Interested students should submit an application form, a nomination from the applicant's department head, a recommendation from a faculty member, and an official transcript. Only one nomination may be submitted per department. Selection is based on character, integrity, leadership, scholastic ability, potential contribution to the mechanical engineering profession, and financial need.

**Financial data:** The stipend is $2,000.
**Duration:** 1 year.
**Number awarded:** 1 each year.
**Deadline:** March of each year.

### 2190 GABRIEL A. HARTL SCHOLARSHIP

Air Traffic Control Association, Attn: Scholarship Fund
1101 King Street, Suite 300
Alexandria, VA 22314
Phone: (703) 299-2430; Fax: (703) 299-2437; Email: info@atca.org
Web: www.atca.org/activities/scholarships.asp
**Summary:** To provide financial assistance to students enrolled in an air traffic control program.
**Eligibility:** Open to half- or full-time students who are U.S. citizens, enrolled in a 2- or 4-year air traffic control program at an institution approved and/or listed by the Federal Aviation Administration (FAA) as directly supporting its college and training initiative. Applicants must be registered for at least 6 hours and be at least 30 semester or 45 quarter hours away from graduation. They must submit an essay on "How My Educational Efforts Will Enhance My Potential Contribution to Aviation." The essay should address their financial need.
**Financial data:** The amount of the award depends on the availability of funds and the number, qualifications, and need of the applicants.
**Duration:** 1 year; may be renewed.
**Number awarded:** 1 or more each year.
**Deadline:** April of each year.

### 2191 GAIL RICHARDSON SCHOLARSHIP

Vermont Student Assistance Corporation
Champlain Mill, Attn: Scholarship Programs
P.O. Box 2000
Winooski, VT 05404-2601
Phone: (802) 654-3798; (888) 253-4819; Fax: (802) 654-3765; TDD: (802) 654-3766; TDD: (800) 281-3341 (within VT); Email: info@vsac.org
Web: www.vsac.org
**Summary:** To provide financial assistance to residents of Vermont who are interested in majoring in a veterinary field in college or graduate school.
**Eligibility:** Open to residents of Vermont who are graduating high school seniors, high school graduates, or GED recipients. Applicants must be interested in attending an accredited postsecondary institution to work on a degree in veterinary medicine, veterinary technology, animal science, or a related field. Selection is based on academic achievement (GPA of 2.5 or higher), required essays, letters of recommendation, and financial need.
**Financial data:** The stipend is $1,000.
**Duration:** 1 year.
**Number awarded:** 1 each year.
**Deadline:** April of each year.

### 2192 GALDERMA LABORATORIES CAREER MOBILITY SCHOLARSHIPS

Dermatology Nurses' Association
East Holly Avenue, Box 56
Pitman, NJ 08071-0056
Phone: (856) 256-2330; (800) 454-4DNA; Fax: (856) 589-7463;
Email: dna@ajj.com
Web: www.dnanurse.org
**Summary:** To provide financial assistance to members of the Dermatology Nurses' Association (DNA) who are working on an undergraduate or graduate degree.
**Eligibility:** Open to applicants who 1) have been members of the association for at least 2 years, 2) are employed in the specialty of dermatology, and 3) are working on a degree or advanced degree in nursing. Selection is based on a letter in which applicants describe their professional goals, proposed course of study, time frame for completion of study, funds necessary to meet their educational goals, and financial need.
**Financial data:** The stipend is $2,500.
**Duration:** 1 year.
**Number awarded:** 1 each year.
**Deadline:** October of each year.

### 2193 GARDEN CLUB FEDERATION OF MAINE SCHOLARSHIP

**Summary:** To provide financial assistance to Maine residents who are upper-division or graduate students working on a garden-related degree.
*See Listing #1406.*

### 2194 GARDEN CLUB OF OHIO SCHOLARSHIPS

Garden Club of Ohio, Inc.
c/o Margaret C. Bertin, Scholarship Committee Chair
530 Mapleview Drive
Seven Hills, OH 44131-3814
Phone: (216) 524-2453; Email: pudgebert@aol.com
Web: gardencluboohio.com/stateprojects.htm
**Summary:** To provide financial assistance to Ohio residents who are working on an undergraduate or graduate degree in horticulture or related fields.
**Eligibility:** Open to residents of Ohio who are 1) first-year students at a 2-year institution or 2) college juniors, college seniors, or graduate students. Applicants must have a GPA of 3.0 or higher and be working on a degree in one of the following: agricultural education, horticulture, floriculture, landscape architecture, botany, biology, agronomy, forestry, environmental conservation (including engineering and law), plant pathology, environmental concerns, city planning, wildlife science, habitat or forest systems ecology, land management, or an allied subject. They must submit a completed application form, a transcript, a completed financial aid form, a personal statement of financial need and career goals, a list of extracurricular activities, 3 letters of recommendation, and a recent photograph.
**Financial data:** Stipends are generally $1,000 or more per year.
**Duration:** 1 year.
**Number awarded:** Varies each year; recently, 17 of these scholarships, worth $21,300, were awarded.
**Deadline:** January of each year.

### 2195 GARDNER FOUNDATION INS EDUCATION SCHOLARSHIP

Infusion Nursing Society, Attn: Gardner Foundation
220 Norwood Park South
Norwood, MA 02062
Phone: (781) 440-9408, ext. 317; Email: chris.hunt@ins1.org
Web: www.ins1.org/gardner/scholarship_ins_edu.html
**Summary:** To provide financial assistance to members of the Infusion Nursing Society (INS) who are interested in continuing education.
**Eligibility:** Open to INS members interested in a program of continuing education, including working on a college or graduate degree or attending a professional meeting or seminar. Applicants must demonstrate how the continuing education activity will enhance their infusion career, describe their professional goals, and explain how the scholarship will be used.
**Financial data:** The stipend is $1,000.
**Duration:** This is a 1-time award.
**Number awarded:** 1 or more each year.

### 2196 GARLAND DUNCAN SCHOLARSHIPS

ASME International, Attn: Coordinator, Educational Operations
Three Park Avenue
New York, NY 10016-5990
Phone: (212) 591-8131; (800) THE-ASME; Fax: (212) 591-7143;
Email: oluwanifiset@asme.org
Web: www.asme.org/education/enged/aid/scholar.htm
**Summary:** To provide financial assistance to undergraduate students who are members of the American Society of Mechanical Engineers (ASME).
**Eligibility:** Open to student members in good standing who are enrolled in an ABET-accredited mechanical engineering, mechanical engineering technology, or related baccalaureate program. They must be entering their junior or senior year when they apply. There are no geographic or citizenship requirements. Interested students should submit an application form, a nomination from the applicant's department head, a recommendation from a faculty member, and an official transcript. Only one nomination may be submitted per department. Selection is based on leadership, scholastic ability, potential contribution to the mechanical engineering profession, and financial need.
**Financial data:** The stipend is $3,500.
**Duration:** 1 year.
**Number awarded:** 2 each year.
**Deadline:** March of each year.

## 2197 GARMIN INTERNATIONAL SCHOLARSHIP

Aircraft Electronics Association, Attn: AEA Educational Foundation
4217 South Hocker Drive
Independence, MO 64055-4723
Phone: (816) 373-6565; Fax: (816) 478-3100; Email: info@aea.net
Web: www.aea.net
**Summary:** To provide financial assistance to students preparing for a career in avionics or aircraft repair.
**Eligibility:** Open to high school seniors and currently-enrolled college students who are attending (or planning to attend) an accredited postsecondary institution in an avionics or aircraft repair program. Applicants must submit an official transcript (cumulative GPA of 2.5 or higher), a statement about their career plans, a description of their involvement in school and community activities, and a 300-word essay on how the job requirements of aviation technicians will change with advancements in technology. Selection is based on merit.
**Financial data:** The stipend is $2,000.
**Duration:** 1 year.
**Number awarded:** 1 each year.
**Deadline:** February of each year.

## 2198 GAT WINGS TO THE FUTURE MANAGEMENT SCHOLARSHIP

Women in Aviation, International, Attn: Scholarships
101 Corsair Drive, Suite 101
P.O. Box 11287
Daytona Beach, FL 32120-1287
Phone: (386) 226-7996; Fax: (386) 226-7998; Email: scholarships@wai.org
Web: www.wai.org/education/scholarships.cfm
**Summary:** To provide financial assistance to members of Women in Aviation, International (WAI) who are interested in a career in aviation management.
**Eligibility:** Open to WAI members who are enrolled in an aviation management or aviation business program at an accredited college or university. Applicants must be full-time students with a GPA of 3.0 or higher and interested in preparing for an aviation management career. Selection is based on achievements, attitude toward self and others, commitment to success, dedication to career, financial need, motivation, reliability, responsibility, and teamwork.
**Financial data:** The stipend is $2,500.
**Duration:** 1 year.
**Number awarded:** 1 each year.
**Deadline:** December of each year.

## 2199 G.B. GUNLOGSON STUDENT ENVIRONMENTAL DESIGN COMPETITION

American Society of Agricultural and Biological Engineers
Attn: Awards Coordinator
2950 Niles Road
St. Joseph, MI 49085-9659
Phone: (269) 429-0300; Fax: (269) 429-3852; Email: hq@asabe.org
Web: www.asabe.org/membership/students/index.html
**Summary:** To recognize and reward student members of the American Society of Agricultural and Biological Engineers (ASABE) who participate in the basic design of an environmental or biological application in engineering.
**Eligibility:** Open to biological and agricultural engineering students who are student members of the society. Applicants must submit an engineering design that involves an environmental or biological application. Designs should reflect a wide spectrum of approaches, including management practices development, equipment design, or bioreactor or ecological system design. Sociological, economic, aesthetic, legal, and ethical considerations can (and often must) be included as part of the design process. The report must include drawings and/or specifications that describe the design, as well as extensive or substantial test or performance data obtained from a 1) prototype or physical model of the machine or critical component, or 2) computer simulated test of the system or process.
**Financial data:** First prize is $1,000, second $700, and third $300. Teams decide among themselves how to divide the money. The academic department of the first-place entry receives a wall plaque.
**Duration:** The competition is held annually.
**Number awarded:** 3 each year.
**Deadline:** May of each year.

## 2200 GCSAA SCHOLARS COMPETITION

Golf Course Superintendents Association of America
Attn: Scholarship and Student Programs Manager

1421 Research Park Drive
Lawrence, KS 66049-3859
Phone: (785) 832-3678; (800) 472-7878, ext. 3678; Email: psmith@gcsaa.org
Web: www.gcsaa.org/students/scholarships/default.asp
**Summary:** To provide financial assistance to undergraduate student members of the Golf Course Superintendents Association of America (GCSAA) who are preparing for a career in golf course management.
**Eligibility:** Open to members of the association who are planning careers as golf course superintendents. Applicants must have completed at least one year of full-time study in a recognized undergraduate program with a major related to golf/turf management. Selection is based on academic skill, potential to become a leading professional, employment history, extracurricular activities, and letters of recommendation. Financial need is not considered. The highest ranked applicant receives the Mendenhall Award and the second-highest ranked applicant receives the Allan MacCurrach Scholarship.
**Financial data:** Stipends range from $500 to $6,000.
**Duration:** 1 year.
**Number awarded:** Varies each year. Recently, 17 of these scholarships were awarded; including 1 Mendenhall Award (at $6,000), 1 Allan MacCurrach Scholarship (at $5,000), 7 at $2,500, 6 at $1,250, and 2 at $500.
**Deadline:** May of each year.

## 2201 GCSAA STUDENT ESSAY CONTEST

Golf Course Superintendents Association of America
Attn: Scholarship and Student Programs Manager
1421 Research Park Drive
Lawrence, KS 66049-3859
Phone: (785) 832-3678; (800) 472-7878, ext. 3678; Email: psmith@gcsaa.org
Web: www.gcsaa.org/students/scholarships/default.asp
**Summary:** To recognize and reward outstanding undergraduate and graduate essays written on golf course management by members of the Golf Course Superintendents Association of America (GCSAA).
**Eligibility:** Open to undergraduate and graduate students working on a degree in turfgrass science, agronomy, or another field related to golf course management. The essay should focus on golf course management and be from 7 to 12 pages in length. References and/or a bibliography must be included. Essays should be original, compelling, well organized, readable, persuasive, and creative. Technical accuracy, composition skills (spelling, grammar, etc.), and the student's adherence to the contest rules are considered in the selection process.
**Financial data:** First prize is $2,000, second prize is $1,500, and third prize is $1,000.
**Duration:** The competition is held annually.
**Number awarded:** 3 each year.
**Deadline:** March of each year.

## 2202 GENERAL ELECTRIC FUND SCHOLARSHIPS

Society of Women Engineers
230 East Ohio Street, Suite 400
Chicago, IL 60611-3265
Phone: (312) 596-5223; Fax: (312) 644-8557; Email: hq@swe.org
Web: www.societyofwomenengineers.org/scholarships
**Summary:** To provide financial assistance to women who will be entering college as freshmen and are interested in studying engineering or computer science.
**Eligibility:** Open to women who are entering college as freshmen with a GPA of 3.5 or higher. Applicants must be U.S. citizens planning to enroll full time at an ABET-accredited 4-year college or university and major in computer science or engineering. Along with their application, they must submit a 1-page essay on why they want to be an engineer or computer scientist, how they believe they will make a difference as an engineer or computer scientist, and what influenced them to study engineering or computer science. Selection is based on merit.
**Financial data:** The stipend is $1,000 per year. Also provided is $500 for the recipient to attend the sponsor's annual convention.
**Duration:** 1 year; may be renewed up to 3 additional years.
**Number awarded:** 3 each year.
**Deadline:** May of each year.

## 2203 GENERAL ELECTRIC WOMEN'S NETWORK SCHOLARSHIPS

Society of Women Engineers
230 East Ohio Street, Suite 400
Chicago, IL 60611-3265

Phone: (312) 596-5223; Fax: (312) 644-8557; Email: hq@swe.org
Web: www.societyofwomenengineers.org/scholarships
**Summary:** To provide financial assistance to undergraduate women majoring in computer science or engineering.
**Eligibility:** Open to women who are entering their sophomore, junior, or senior year at a 4-year ABET-accredited college or university. Applicants must be U.S. citizens majoring in computer science or engineering and have a GPA of 3.0 or higher. Along with their application, they must submit a 1-page essay on why they want to be an engineer or computer scientist, how they believe they will make a difference as an engineer or computer scientist, and what influenced them to study engineering or computer science. Selection is based on merit. Preference is given to students attending selected schools; for a list, contact the sponsor.
**Financial data:** The stipend is $2,425.
**Duration:** 1 year.
**Number awarded:** 13 each year.
**Deadline:** January of each year.

## 2204 GENERAL EMMETT PAIGE SCHOLARSHIPS

Armed Forces Communications and Electronics Association
Attn: AFCEA Educational Foundation
4400 Fair Lakes Court
Fairfax, VA 22033-3899
Phone: (703) 631-6149; (800) 336-4583, ext. 6149; Fax: (703) 631-4693;
Email: scholarship@afcea.org
Web: www.afcea.org/education/scholarships/undergraduate/genemm.asp
**Summary:** To provide funding to veterans, military personnel, and their family members who are majoring in specified scientific fields in college.
**Eligibility:** Open to veterans, persons on active duty in the uniformed military services, and their spouses or dependents who are currently enrolled full time in an accredited 4-year college or university in the United States. Graduating high school seniors are not eligible, but veterans entering college as freshmen may apply. Spouses or dependents must be sophomores or juniors. Applicants must be U.S. citizens, be of good moral character, have demonstrated academic excellence, be motivated to complete a college education, and be working toward a degree in engineering (aerospace, chemical, computer, or electrical), mathematics, physics, or computer science with a GPA of 3.4 or higher. They must provide a copy of Discharge Form DD214, Certificate of Service, or facsimile of their current Department of Defense or Coast Guard Identification Card.
**Financial data:** The stipend is $2,000.
**Duration:** 1 year; may be renewed.
**Number awarded:** Varies each year; recently, 11 of these scholarships were awarded.
**Deadline:** February of each year.

## 2205 GENERAL JAMES H. DOOLITTLE SCHOLARSHIP

Communities Foundation of Texas, Attn: Scholarship Department
5500 Caruth Haven Lane
Dallas, TX 75225-8146
Phone: (214) 750-4222; Fax: (214) 750-4210; Email: grants@cftexas.org
Web: www.cftexas.org
**Summary:** To provide financial assistance to upper-division and graduate students who are working on a degree in aerospace science or aeronautical engineering.
**Eligibility:** Open to college juniors, seniors, and graduate students who are working on a baccalaureate or advanced degree in aerospace science or aeronautical engineering. Applicants must have completed at least 52 hours of college course work with a GPA of 2.75 or higher. They must be able to demonstrate financial need. Along with their application, they must submit an essay (up to 3 pages) describing their interest in the field of aerospace science or aeronautical engineering, how that interest began, the course of studies pursued as a result of the interest, any special projects or jobs they have held that are related to the field, and their career goals. U.S. citizenship is required.
**Financial data:** The stipend is $5,000 per year.
**Duration:** 1 year; nonrenewable.
**Number awarded:** 1 each year.
**Deadline:** February of each year.

## 2206 GENERAL JOHN A. WICKHAM SCHOLARSHIPS

Armed Forces Communications and Electronics Association
Attn: AFCEA Educational Foundation
4400 Fair Lakes Court

Fairfax, VA 22033-3899
Phone: (703) 631-6149; (800) 336-4583, ext. 6149; Fax: (703) 631-4693;
Email: scholarship@afcea.org
Web: www.afcea.org/education/scholarships/undergraduate/pub2.asp
**Summary:** To provide financial assistance to undergraduate students who are working full time on a degree in engineering or the sciences.
**Eligibility:** Open to full-time students entering their junior or senior year at an accredited degree-granting 4-year college or university in the United States. Applicants must be U.S. citizens working toward a degree in engineering (aerospace, chemical, computer, electrical, or systems), mathematics, physics, or computer science with a GPA of 3.5 or higher. They must be able to demonstrate academic achievement, patriotism, and potential to contribute to the American work force.
**Financial data:** The stipend is $2,000.
**Duration:** 1 year; may be renewed.
**Number awarded:** Varies each year; recently, 11 of these scholarships were awarded.
**Deadline:** April of each year.

## 2207 GENERAL MOTORS ENGINEERING EXCELLENCE AWARD

Hispanic Association of Colleges and Universities
Attn: National Scholarship Program
One Dupont Circle, N.W. Suite 605
Washington, DC 20036
Phone: (202) 467-0893; Fax: (202) 496-9177; TTY: (800) 855-2880;
Email: scholarships@hacu.net
Web: scholarships.hacu.net/applications/applicants
**Summary:** To provide financial assistance to undergraduate and graduate engineering students at institutions that are members of the Hispanic Association of Colleges and Universities (HACU).
**Eligibility:** Open to full-time undergraduate and graduate students at 4-year HACU member and partner colleges and universities who are working on an engineering degree. Applicants must submit an essay of 200 to 250 words that describes their academic and/or career goals, where they expect to be and what they expect to be doing 10 years from now, and what skills they can bring to an employer. They must be able to demonstrate financial need and a GPA of 3.2 or higher.
**Financial data:** The stipend is $2,000 per year.
**Duration:** 1 year; may be renewed.
**Number awarded:** 1 or more each year.
**Deadline:** May of each year.

## 2208 GENERAL MOTORS ENGINEERING SCHOLARSHIP

American Indian Science and Engineering Society
Attn: Scholarship Coordinator
2305 Renard, S.E., Suite 200
P.O. Box 9828
Albuquerque, NM 87119-9828
Phone: (505) 765-1052, ext. 106; Fax: (505) 765-5608; Email: shirley@aises.org
Web: www.aises.org/highered/scholarships
**Summary:** To provide financial assistance to members of the American Indian Science and Engineering Society (AISES) who are working on an undergraduate or graduate degree in engineering.
**Eligibility:** Open to AISES members who are full-time undergraduate or graduate students in engineering, with a preference for electrical, industrial, or mechanical engineering majors. Applicants must have a GPA of 3.0 or higher and be members of an American Indian tribe or Alaskan Native group or otherwise considered to be an American Indian or Alaskan Native by the tribe or group with which affiliation is claimed. They must submit an essay that explains their knowledge of and experiences with American Indian tribal culture, discusses their specific interests in engineering, and states how they will contribute their knowledge or professional experience to a Native American community.
**Financial data:** The stipend is $3,000 per year.
**Duration:** 1 year; nonrenewable.
**Deadline:** June of each year.

## 2209 GENERAL MOTORS FOUNDATION UNDERGRADUATE SCHOLARSHIPS

Society of Women Engineers
230 East Ohio Street, Suite 400
Chicago, IL 60611-3265

Phone: (312) 596-5223; Fax: (312) 644-8557; Email: hq@swe.org

Web: www.societyofwomenengineers.org/scholarships

**Summary:** To provide financial assistance to upper-division women majoring in designated engineering specialties.

**Eligibility:** Open to women who are entering their junior year at a designated ABET-accredited college or university. Applicants must be majoring in automotive, chemical, electrical, industrial, manufacturing, materials, or mechanical engineering and have a GPA of 3.5 or higher. Along with their application, they must submit a 1-page essay on why they want to be an engineer, how they believe they will make a difference as an engineer, and what influenced them to study engineering. Selection is based on merit.

**Financial data:** The stipend is $1,225 per year. Also provided is a $500 travel grant for the recipient to attend the society's national convention and student conference.

**Duration:** 1 year; may be renewed for 1 additional year.

**Number awarded:** 2 each year.

**Deadline:** January of each year.

---

## 2210 GENERAL MOTORS MINORITY ENGINEERING AND SCIENCE SCHOLARSHIP PROGRAM

General Motors Corporation, Attn: GM Scholarship Administration Center

700 West Fifth Avenue

Naperville, IL 60563

Phone: (888) 377-5233; Fax: (630) 428-2695;

Email: scholarshipinfo@gmsac.com

Web: www.gm.com/company/careers/student/stu_scholar.html

**Summary:** To provide financial assistance to underrepresented minority college students interested in majoring in an engineering or science program of interest to General Motors.

**Eligibility:** Open to minority (African American, Hispanic, or Native American) students currently enrolled or planning to enroll full time at a 4-year college or university with sufficient credits to be classified as a sophomore or junior. Applicants must have a GPA of 3.0 or higher and plans to enroll in engineering or science; preference is given to students in chemical, electrical, industrial, manufacturing, or mechanical engineering or other closely related fields of science or engineering. They must be U.S. citizens or have eligibility to work permanently in the United States. Along with their application, they must include a letter of recommendation from a college instructor or other representative, official transcripts from their college, and a personal statement (500 to 750 words) about how their college experiences are shaping their educational and career goals. Selection is based on that statement, academic performance, proficiencies, and demonstrated skills in areas of interest to General Motors. Financial need is not considered.

**Financial data:** The stipend is $5,000 per year.

**Duration:** 1 year.

**Number awarded:** A limited number are awarded each year.

**Deadline:** May of each year.

---

## 2211 GENERAL MOTORS SCHOLARSHIP PROGRAM OF THE HISPANIC SCHOLARSHIP FUND

Hispanic Scholarship Fund, Attn: Selection Committee

55 Second Street, Suite 1500

San Francisco, CA 94105

Phone: (415) 808-2350; (877) HSF-INFO; Fax: (415) 808-2302;

Email: highschool@hsf.net

Web: www.hsf.net/scholarship/programs/gm.php

**Summary:** To provide financial assistance to Hispanic Americans who are interested in attending college to major in engineering or business.

**Eligibility:** Open to U.S. citizens, permanent residents, and visitors with a passport stamped I-551 who are of Hispanic heritage. Applicants must have a GPA of 3.0 or higher and be enrolled or planning to enroll full time at an accredited 4-year college or university in the United States, Puerto Rico, or the U.S. Virgin Islands to major in business or engineering. Along with their application, they must submit 600-word essays on 1) how their Hispanic heritage, family upbringing, and/or role models have influenced their personal long-term goals; 2) how they contribute to their community and what they have learned from their experiences; and 3) an academic challenge they have faced and how they have overcome it. Selection is based on academic achievement, personal strengths, leadership, and financial need.

**Financial data:** The stipend is $2,500 per year.

**Duration:** 1 year.

**Number awarded:** 1 or more each year.

**Deadline:** June of each year.

---

## 2212 GEOPHYSICAL SOCIETY OF ALASKA SCHOLARSHIP

Society of Exploration Geophysicists, Attn: SEG Foundation

8801 South Yale, Suite 500

P.O. Box 702740

Tulsa, OK 74170-2740

Phone: (918) 497-5513; Fax: (918) 497-5557; Email: scholarships@seg.org

Web: seg.org/business/foundation/scholarships/index.shtml

**Summary:** To provide financial assistance to undergraduate and graduate students from Alaska who are interested in studying applied geophysics.

**Eligibility:** Open to 1) high school students planning to enter college in the fall, and 2) undergraduate or graduate students whose grades are above average. Applicants must intend to work on a degree directed toward a career in applied geophysics or a closely-related field. They must be residents of Alaska or a student at a college or university in the state. Along with their application, they must submit a 150-word essay on how they plan to use geophysics in their future. Financial need is not considered in the selection process.

**Financial data:** The stipend ranges from $1,000 to $3,000 per year.

**Duration:** 1 academic year; may be renewable, based on scholastic standing, availability of funds, and continuance of a course of study leading to a career in applied geophysics.

**Number awarded:** 1 each year.

**Deadline:** January of each year.

---

## 2213 GEOPHYSICAL SOCIETY OF HOUSTON SCHOLARSHIPS

Society of Exploration Geophysicists, Attn: SEG Foundation

8801 South Yale, Suite 500

P.O. Box 702740

Tulsa, OK 74170-2740

Phone: (918) 497-5513; Fax: (918) 497-5557; Email: scholarships@seg.org

Web: seg.org/business/foundation/scholarships/index.shtml

**Summary:** To provide financial assistance to undergraduate and graduate students who are interested in studying applied geophysics in Texas.

**Eligibility:** Open to 1) high school students planning to enter college in the fall, and 2) undergraduate or graduate students whose grades are above average. Preference is given to students at schools in Houston, Texas; if no qualified students from that area apply, students at other colleges and universities in Texas are considered. Applicants must intend to work on a degree directed toward a career in applied geophysics or a closely-related field. Along with their application, they must submit a 150-word essay on how they plan to use geophysics in their future. Financial need is not considered in the selection process.

**Financial data:** The stipend ranges from $1,000 to $3,000 per year.

**Duration:** 1 academic year; may be renewable, based on scholastic standing, availability of funds, and continuance of a course of study leading to a career in applied geophysics.

**Number awarded:** 1 or more each year.

**Deadline:** January of each year.

---

## 2214 GEOPHYSICAL SOCIETY OF OKLAHOMA CITY SCHOLARSHIP

Society of Exploration Geophysicists, Attn: SEG Foundation

8801 South Yale, Suite 500

P.O. Box 702740

Tulsa, OK 74170-2740

Phone: (918) 497-5513; Fax: (918) 497-5557; Email: scholarships@seg.org

Web: seg.org/business/foundation/scholarships/index.shtml

**Summary:** To provide financial assistance to undergraduate and graduate students who are interested in studying applied geophysics in Oklahoma.

**Eligibility:** Open to 1) high school students planning to enter college in the fall, and 2) undergraduate or graduate students whose grades are above average. Applicants must intend to attend a college or university in Oklahoma to work on a degree directed toward a career in applied geophysics or a closely-related field. Along with their application, they must submit a 150-word essay on how they plan to use geophysics in their future. Financial need is not considered in the selection process.

**Financial data:** Stipends range from $1,000 to $3,000 per year.

**Duration:** 1 academic year; may be renewable, based on scholastic standing, availability of funds, and continuance of a course of study leading to a career in applied geophysics.

**Number awarded:** 1 each year.

**Deadline:** January of each year.

---

## 2215 GEOPHYSICAL SOCIETY OF TULSA SCHOLARSHIPS

Society of Exploration Geophysicists, Attn: SEG Foundation

8801 South Yale, Suite 500

P.O. Box 702740
Tulsa, OK 74170-2740

Phone: (918) 497-5513; Fax: (918) 497-5557; Email: scholarships@seg.org

Web: seg.org/business/foundation/scholarships/index.shtml

**Summary:** To provide financial assistance to undergraduate and graduate students from Oklahoma who are interested in studying applied geophysics.

**Eligibility:** Open to 1) high school students planning to enter college in the fall, and 2) undergraduate or graduate students whose grades are above average. Applicants must intend to work on a degree directed toward a career in applied geophysics or a closely-related field. They must be residents of Oklahoma or students at a college or university in the state. Along with their application, they must submit a 150-word essay on how they plan to use geophysics in their future. Financial need is not considered in the selection process.

**Financial data:** Stipends range from $1,000 to $3,000 per year.

**Duration:** 1 academic year; may be renewable, based on scholastic standing, availability of funds, and continuance of a course of study leading to a career in applied geophysics.

**Number awarded:** 1 or more each year.

**Deadline:** January of each year.

## 2216 GEORGE A. ROBERTS SCHOLARSHIPS

ASM International, Attn: ASM Materials Education Foundation
Scholarship Program
9639 Kinsman Road
Materials Park, OH 44073-0002

Phone: (440) 338-5151; (800) 336-5152; Fax: (440) 338-4634;

Email: asmif@asminternational.org

Web: www.asminternational.org

**Summary:** To provide financial assistance to upper-division student members of the American Society for Metals (ASM) who are interested in majoring in metallurgy and materials.

**Eligibility:** Open to citizens of the United States, Canada, or Mexico who are enrolled at a college or university in those countries; are members of the society; have an intended or declared major in metallurgy or materials science and engineering (related science or engineering majors may be considered if the applicant demonstrates a strong academic emphasis and interest in materials science and engineering); and are entering their junior or senior year in college. Selection is based on academic achievement; interest in metallurgy/materials (including knowledge of the field, activities, jobs, and potential for a related career); personal qualities (such as social values, maturity, motivation, and goals); and financial need.

**Financial data:** The stipend is $6,000.

**Duration:** 1 year; recipients may reapply for 1 additional year.

**Number awarded:** 7 each year.

**Deadline:** April of each year.

## 2217 GEORGE B. BOLAND NURSES TRAINING TRUST FUND

National Forty and Eight, Attn: Voiture Nationale
777 North Meridian Street
Indianapolis, IN 46204-1170

Phone: (317) 634-1804; Fax: (317) 632-9365;

Email: voiturenationale@msn.com

Web: fortyandeight.org/40_8programs.htm

**Summary:** To provide financial assistance to students working on an undergraduate degree in nursing

**Eligibility:** Open to students working full time on an associate or bachelor's degree in nursing. Applications must be submitted to the local Voiture of the Forty and Eight in the county of student's permanent residence; if the county organization has exhausted all of its nurses training funds, it will provide the student with an application for this scholarship. Students who are receiving assistance from the Eight and Forty Lung and Respiratory Disease Nursing Scholarship Program of the American Legion are not eligible. Financial need must be demonstrated.

**Financial data:** Grants may be used to cover tuition, required fees, room and board or similar living expenses, and other school-related expenses.

**Number awarded:** Varies each year.

## 2218 GEORGE COMSTOCK SCHOLARSHIP FUND

Connecticut Association of Optometrists
342 North Main Street
West Hartford, CT 06117

Phone: (860) 586-7508; Fax: (860) 586-7550; Email: info@cao.org

Web: www.cao.org

**Summary:** To provide financial assistance to undergraduate students from Connecticut who are enrolled in accredited colleges of optometry.

**Eligibility:** Open to Connecticut residents enrolled in accredited colleges of optometry in the United States. Selection is based on scholarship, character, and financial need.

**Financial data:** The stipend ranges from $400 to $1,000 per year. The exact amount depends upon the recipient's scholastic performance and financial need.

**Duration:** 1 year; may be renewed.

**Number awarded:** 6 to 8 each year.

**Deadline:** June of each year.

## 2219 GEORGE D. MILLER SCHOLARSHIP

National Fire Protection Association
Attn: Fire Safety Educational Memorial Fund Committee
1 Batterymarch Park
Quincy, MA 02169-7471

Phone: (617) 984-7244; Fax: (617) 984-7222; Email: cellis@nfpa.org

Web: www.nfpa.org

**Summary:** To provide financial assistance to undergraduate and graduate students enrolled in fire service or public administration programs.

**Eligibility:** Open to students in a fire service or public administration program who are nominated by their college or university (schools must be in the United States or Canada and may nominate up to 2 undergraduate or graduate students). Nominees must exhibit scholastic achievement, leadership qualities, concern for others (volunteerism), and intent to prepare for a career in fire service or public administration

**Financial data:** The stipend is at least $5,000.

**Duration:** 1 year.

**Number awarded:** 1 each year.

**Deadline:** March of each year.

## 2220 GEORGE E. WATTERS MEMORIAL SCHOLARSHIP

New England Water Works Association
125 Hopping Brook
Holliston, MA 01746

Phone: (508) 893-7979; Fax: (508) 893-9898

Web: www.newwa.org

**Summary:** To provide financial assistance to undergraduate or graduate students from New England interested in working on a degree in civil engineering.

**Eligibility:** Open to members and student members of the New England section of the American Water Works Association or the New England Water Works Association. Applicants must be high school seniors, currently-enrolled college students, or graduate students. They must be majoring or planning to major in civil engineering. Along with their application, they must submit a 100-word essay on why they have chosen their field of study and if it will improve the environment, public health, or the water industry. Financial need is also considered in the selection process.

**Financial data:** The stipend is $5,000.

**Duration:** 1 year.

**Deadline:** July of each year.

## 2221 GEORGE F. WALKER MEMORIAL SCHOLARSHIPS

George F. Walker Memorial Scholarship Fund
P.O. Box 58143
Seattle, WA 98168

Phone: (206) 244-2300; Email: jkenner@walkermap.com

Web: www.gfwscholarship.org

**Summary:** To provide financial assistance to residents of Washington who are working on an undergraduate degree in surveying at a college or university in the Pacific Northwest.

**Eligibility:** Open to Washington residents who are working full time on an undergraduate degree at a college or university in the Pacific Northwest. The course of study must be preparing the student for a career in the surveying or mapping sciences. Applicants must submit official transcripts of all course work completed to date, 3 letters of recommendation, and a brief statement of their career-related experience and goals.

**Financial data:** Stipends are $1,500 or $750.

**Duration:** 1 year.

**Number awarded:** Varies each year. Recently, 6 of these scholarships were awarded: 2 at $1,500 and 4 at $750.

**Deadline:** January of each year.

## 2222 GEORGE W. NEIGHBOR, JR. MEMORIAL SCHOLARSHIP

Northeastern Association of Forensic Scientists
c/o Peter Diaczuk, Executive Secretary
John Jay College of Criminal Justice
445 West 59th Street
New York, NY 10019
Phone: (212) 237-8896; Email: pdiaczuk@jjay.cuny.edu
Web: www.neafs.org/scholarship.htm

**Summary:** To provide financial assistance to upper-division and graduate students working on a degree in forensic science at colleges and universities in designated northeastern states.

**Eligibility:** Open to full-time college juniors and seniors and full- or part-time graduate students enrolled in a forensic science or related science program. Applicants must be attending a college or university in Connecticut, Maine, Massachusetts, New Hampshire, New Jersey, New York, Pennsylvania, Rhode Island, or Vermont. Along with their application, they must submit a letter describing their personal goals, achievements, and reasons why they should be considered for this award.

**Financial data:** A stipend is awarded (amount not specified).

**Duration:** 1 year.

**Number awarded:** 1 or more each year.

**Deadline:** April of each year.

## 2223 GEORGIA AEE CHAPTER SCHOLARSHIPS

Association of Energy Engineers-Georgia Chapter
c/o Joseph Clements, Scholarship Chair
Fulton County Schools
Coordinator, Utilities Services
5270 Northfield Boulevard
College Park, GA 30349-3179
Phone: (404) 669-8991; Fax: (404) 765-7155;
Email: clementsj@fulton.k12.ga.us
Web: www.aeegeorgia.org/scholarship.htm

**Summary:** To provide financial assistance to undergraduate and graduate students in Georgia interested in taking courses directly related to energy engineering or energy management.

**Eligibility:** Open to undergraduate and graduate students who are enrolled in engineering or management programs at accredited colleges and universities in Georgia. Applicants must be interested in taking courses directly related to energy engineering or energy management (preferably within a curriculum leading to a major or minor in energy engineering). Selection is based on scholarship, character, and need. In awarding scholarships, preference is given to candidates needing aid their final year; second, to candidates needing aid for the last 2 years; third, to candidates needing aid for 3 years; and finally, to first-year students.

**Financial data:** If a Georgia nominee wins an Association of Energy Engineers (AEE) national scholarship for $500, the Georgia chapter will match that award. If no Georgia nominee wins a national scholarship, the Georgia chapter will award a $1,000 scholarship.

**Duration:** 1 year.

**Number awarded:** Up to 2 each year.

**Deadline:** April of each year.

## 2224 GEORGIA BEEF INDUSTRY INTERNSHIP

**Summary:** To provide financial assistance and work experience to Georgia residents interested in the beef industry.

*See Listing #1411.*

## 2225 GEORGIA DIETETIC FOUNDATION SCHOLARSHIPS

Georgia Dietetic Association, Inc., Attn: Georgia Dietetic Foundation
1260 Winchester Parkway, Suite 205
Smyrna, GA 30080
Phone: (770) 433-9044; Fax: (770) 433-2907; Email: gdaexec@bellsouth.net
Web: www.gda-online.org

**Summary:** To provide financial assistance to members of the American Dietetic Association who are enrolled in an undergraduate, graduate, or supervised practice program in Georgia.

**Eligibility:** Open to association members who are enrolled in or accepted at a program in Georgia. Applicants must be 1) enrolled in an accredited DPD program as an undergraduate; 2) accepted into a CADE-accredited program and either entering a supervised practice program or have at least 5 months remaining in the program; or 3) accepted into a graduate program or have at least 5

months remaining in the program. They must have a GPA of 2.8 or higher and be enrolled or planning to enroll full time. Along with their application, they must submit 1) financial forms; 2) a 300-word letter of intent on how they became interested in dietetics, their short- and long-range professional goals, their plans for the next academic year of study, their leadership activities and organization memberships, their honors and awards, how this program will benefit them as a practitioner, and why they need the scholarship; 3) a 300-word essay on what they consider to be the characteristics of a professionally successful person; 4) scholarship references from faculty members and work supervisors and 5) official transcripts.

**Financial data:** A stipend is awarded (amount not specified).

**Duration:** 1 year.

**Number awarded:** Varies each year.

**Deadline:** May of each year.

## 2226 GEORGIA ENGINEERING FOUNDATION SCHOLARSHIPS

Georgia Engineering Foundation, Inc., Attn: Scholarship and Loan Committee
100 Peachtree Street, Suite 2150
Atlanta, GA 30303
Phone: (404) 521-2324; Fax: (404) 521-0283; Email: info@GEFinc.org
Web: www.GEFinc.org/Scholarships/Guidelines.htm

**Summary:** To provide financial assistance to undergraduate and graduate students from Georgia who are entering an approved engineering program.

**Eligibility:** Open to residents of Georgia who are attending or accepted at an ABET-accredited engineering or engineering technology program in any state. Applications from incoming freshmen must include a high school transcript with final senior grades, SAT scores, 2 letters of recommendation, and a small photograph. Applications from college and graduate students must include a transcript of all college grades, 2 letters of recommendation, and a small photograph. U.S. citizenship is required. Selection is based on demonstrated competence in mathematics, science, and communications skills; interest in a career in engineering or engineering technology; and financial need.

**Financial data:** Stipends range from $500 to $5,000 per year.

**Duration:** 1 year.

**Number awarded:** Approximately 45 each year.

**Deadline:** August of each year.

## 2227 GEORGIA LEGION AUXILIARY PAST PRESIDENT PARLEY NURSING SCHOLARSHIP

American Legion Auxiliary, Attn: Department of Georgia
3035 Mt. Zion Road
Stockbridge, GA 30281-4101
Phone: (678) 289-8446; Email: amlegaux@bellsouth.net

**Summary:** To provide financial assistance to daughters of veterans in Georgia who are interested in preparing for a career in nursing.

**Eligibility:** Open to George residents who are 1) interested in nursing education and 2) the daughters of veterans. Applicants must be sponsored by a local unit of the American Legion Auxiliary. Selection is based on a statement explaining why they want to become a nurse and why they need a scholarship, a transcript of all high school or college grades, and 4 letters of recommendation (1 from a high school principal or superintendent, 1 from the sponsoring American Legion Auxiliary local unit, and 2 from other responsible people).

**Financial data:** The amount of the award depends on the availability of funds.

**Number awarded:** Varies, depending upon funds available.

**Deadline:** May of each year.

## 2228 GERALD V. HENDERSON INDUSTRIAL MINERALS MEMORIAL SCHOLARSHIP

Society for Mining, Metallurgy, and Exploration, Inc., Attn: Student Center
8307 Shaffer Parkway
P.O. Box 277002
Littleton, CO 80127-7002
Phone: (303) 948-4203; (800) 763-3132; Fax: (303) 973-3845;
Email: sme@smenet.org
Web: www.smenet.org/education/students/sme_scholarships.crm

**Summary:** To provide financial assistance to upper-division and graduate student members of the Society for Mining, Metallurgy, and Exploration (SME) who are majoring in fields that will prepare them for a career in industrial minerals.

**Eligibility:** Open to students who 1) are majoring in geology, minerals engineering, mining engineering, or mineral economics at a 4-year college or university, 2) have completed at least their sophomore year in college, 3) are a U.S. citizen, and 4) are a student member of the society. They must be of good character, be of sound health, have demonstrated scholastic aptitude (GPA of 3.0 or higher), and be able to demonstrate financial need. An interview may be required.

**Financial data:** A total of $2,000 is awarded each year.

**Duration:** 1 year.

**Number awarded:** 1 or more each year.

**Deadline:** October of each year.

## 2229 GIBSON–LAEMEL SCHOLARSHIP

**Summary:** To provide financial assistance to college juniors and seniors from Connecticut who are interested in preparing for a career in health, physical education, recreation, or dance.

*See Listing #1414.*

## 2230 GIVAUDAN FLAVOR CORPORATION SCHOLARSHIP

Institute of Food Technologists, Attn: Scholarship Department
525 West Van Buren, Suite 1000
Chicago, IL 60607
Phone: (312) 782-8424; Fax: (312) 782-8348; Email: info@ift.org
Web: www.ift.org

**Summary:** To provide financial assistance to undergraduates interested in studying food science or food technology.

**Eligibility:** Open to sophomores, juniors, and seniors in a food science or food technology program at an educational institution in the United States or Canada. Applicants must have an outstanding scholastic record and a well-rounded personality. Along with their application, they must submit an essay on their career aspirations; a list of awards, honors, and scholarships they have received; a list of extracurricular activities and/or hobbies; and a summary of their work experience. Financial need is not considered in the selection process.

**Financial data:** The stipend is $1,000.

**Duration:** 1 year; recipients may reapply if they are members of the Institute of Food Technologists.

**Number awarded:** 3 each year.

**Deadline:** January of each year.

## 2231 GLADYS ANDERSON EMERSON SCHOLARSHIP

Iota Sigma Pi
c/o National Director for Student Awards
Vicki H. Grassian
University of Iowa
Department of Chemistry
Iowa City, IA 52242
Phone: (319) 335-1392; Fax: (319) 335-1270; Email: vicki-grassian@uiowa.edu
Web: www.iotasigmapi.info/EmersonAward.htm

**Summary:** To provide financial assistance to women undergraduates who have achieved excellence in the study of chemistry or biochemistry.

**Eligibility:** Open to female chemistry or biochemistry students who have attained at least junior standing but have at least 1 semester of work to complete. Both the nominator and the nominee must be members of Iota Sigma Pi, although students who are not members but wish to apply for the scholarship may be made members by National Council action. Selection is based on transcripts; a list of all academic honors and professional memberships; a short essay by the nominee describing herself, her goals in chemistry, any hobbies or talents, and her financial need; and letters of recommendation.

**Financial data:** The stipend is $2,000.

**Duration:** 1 year.

**Number awarded:** 1 each year.

**Deadline:** February of each year.

## 2232 GOLDEN EAGLE AWARD

Tuskegee Airmen, Inc.
1501 Lee Highway, Suite 130
Arlington, VA 22209-1109
Phone: (703) 522-8590; Fax: (703) 522-8542;
Email: hqtai@tuskegeeairmen.org
Web: www.tuskegeeairmen.org/scholarships.htm

**Summary:** To provide financial assistance for college to high school seniors and graduates who are interested in a career in aviation and submit an essay on

the history of Tuskegee Airmen, a group of African Americans who served as pilots in World War II.

**Eligibility:** Open to students who have graduated or will graduate from high school in the current year with a GPA of 3.0 or higher and plan to prepare for a career in aviation, aerospace technology, and research. Applicants must submit a 1-page essay entitled "The Tuskegee Airmen" that reflects an overview of their history. They must also submit documentation of financial need and a 2-page essay that includes a brief autobiographical sketch, educational aspirations, career goals, and an explanation of why financial assistance is essential. Applications must be submitted to individual chapters of Tuskegee Airmen, Inc. which verify them as appropriate, evaluate them, and forward those considered worthy of further consideration to the national competition. Selection is based on academic achievement, extracurricular and community activities, financial need, recommendations, and both essays.

**Financial data:** The stipend is $5,000 per year.

**Duration:** 4 years, provided the recipient maintains a GPA of 2.0 or higher and continues in an aerospace or aviation career path.

**Number awarded:** 1 each year.

**Deadline:** February of each year.

## 2233 GOLDEN KEY ENGINEERING ACHIEVEMENT AWARDS

Golden Key International Honour Society
621 North Avenue N.E., Suite C-100
Atlanta, GA 30308
Phone: (404) 377-2400; (800) 377-2401; Fax: (678) 420-6757;
Email: scholarships@goldenkey.org
Web: www.goldenkey.org/GKweb/ScholarshipsandAwards

**Summary:** To recognize and reward undergraduate and graduate members of the Golden Key International Honour Society who submit outstanding papers on topics related to the field of engineering.

**Eligibility:** Open to undergraduate, graduate, and postgraduate members of the society who submit a paper or report, up to 10 pages in length, on a topic related to engineering. Applicants must also submit 1) an essay, up to 2 pages in length, describing the assignment for writing the paper, the greatest challenge in writing the paper, the lessons learned from completing the assignment, and what they would change if they could redo the paper; 2) a letter of recommendation; and 3) academic transcripts. Selection of the winners is based on academic achievement and the quality of the paper.

**Financial data:** The winner receives a $1,000 scholarship, second place a $750 scholarship, and third place a $500 scholarship.

**Duration:** These awards are presented annually.

**Number awarded:** 3 each year.

**Deadline:** February of each year.

## 2234 GOLDEN KEY INFORMATION SYSTEMS ACHIEVEMENT AWARDS

Golden Key International Honour Society
621 North Avenue N.E., Suite C-100
Atlanta, GA 30308
Phone: (404) 377-2400; (800) 377-2401; Fax: (678) 420-6757;
Email: scholarships@goldenkey.org
Web: www.goldenkey.org/GKweb/ScholarshipsandAwards

**Summary:** To recognize and reward undergraduate members of the Golden Key International Honour Society who submit outstanding papers on topics related to the fields of computer science and information systems.

**Eligibility:** Open to undergraduate, graduate, and postgraduate members of the society who submit a paper or report, up to 10 pages in length, on a topic related to computer science and information systems. Applicants must also submit 1) an essay, up to 2 pages in length, describing the assignment for writing the paper, the greatest challenge in writing the paper, the lessons learned from completing the assignment, and what they would change if they could redo the paper; 2) a letter of recommendation; and 3) academic transcripts. Selection of the winners is based on academic achievement and the quality of the paper.

**Financial data:** The winner receives a $1,000 scholarship, second place a $750 scholarship, and third place a $500 scholarship.

**Duration:** These awards are presented annually.

**Number awarded:** 3 each year.

**Deadline:** February of each year.

## 2235 GRACE BYRNE UNDERGRADUATE SCHOLARSHIP

Women's Transportation Seminar-Puget Sound Chapter
c/o Lorelei Mesic, Scholarship Co-Chair
W&H Pacific

3350 Monte Villa Parkway
Bothell, WA 98021-8972
Phone: (425) 951-4872; Fax: (425) 951-4808; Email: lmesic@whpacific.com
Web: www.wtspugetsound.org/nscholarships.html
**Summary:** To provide financial assistance to women undergraduate students from Washington working on a degree related to transportation.
**Eligibility:** Open to women who are residents of Washington, studying at a college in the state, or working as an intern in the state. Applicants must be currently enrolled in an undergraduate degree program in a transportation-related field, such as engineering, planning, finance, or logistics. They must have a GPA of 3.0 or higher and plans to prepare for a career in a transportation-related field. Minority candidates are encouraged to apply. Along with their application, they must submit a 500-word statement about their career goals after graduation and why they think they should receive this scholarship award. Selection is based on that statement, academic record, and transportation-related activities or job skills. Financial need is not considered.
**Financial data:** The stipend is $1,500.
**Duration:** 1 year.
**Number awarded:** 1 each year.
**Deadline:** October of each year.

## 2236 GRANITE STATE CHAPTER NAWIC SCHOLARSHIPS

National Association of Women in Construction-Granite State Chapter 218
c/o Bayview Construction Corporation
170 West Road, Suite 10
Portsmouth, NH 03801
Web: www.geocities.com/nawicnh/scholarship.htm
**Summary:** To provide financial assistance to New Hampshire residents who are majoring in a construction-related field.
**Eligibility:** Open to New Hampshire residents (male or female) who are entering 1) the final year of a 2-year school or 2) the junior or senior year of a 4-year school. Applicants be majoring in a construction-related field (e.g., engineering, electrical, plumbing, carpentry, or general construction) and have a GPA of 2.0 or higher. Along with their application, they must submit a 150-word essay on why they have chosen the construction industry for their career.
**Financial data:** The stipend is $1,000.
**Duration:** 1 year.
**Number awarded:** 1 each year.
**Deadline:** March of each year.

## 2237 THE GREAT 100 SCHOLARSHIP PROGRAM

The Great 100, Inc.
P.O. Box 4875
Greensboro, NC 27404-4875
Phone: (800) 729-1975; Email: mperdue@hprhs.com
Web: www.great100.org/Scholarship/index.htm
**Summary:** To provide financial assistance to undergraduate and graduate students in North Carolina who are interested in working on a degree in nursing.
**Eligibility:** Open to students working on an associate's degree in nursing, a diploma in nursing, a bachelor's degree in nursing, or a master's degree in nursing. Each year, the sponsor selects 2 North Carolina community colleges that award diplomas and associate degrees, a college or university in the state that awards B.S.N. degrees, and a university in the state that awards M.S.N. degree. The schools selected for that year then nominate students for these awards. The letters of nomination must indicate how the student promotes and advances the profession of nursing in a positive way in the practice setting and/or in the community, and actively seeks ways to support nurses and other health care providers; demonstrates integrity, honesty, and accountability, and functions within scope of practice; displays commitment to patients, families, and colleagues; demonstrates caring and assists others to grow and develop; and radiates energy and enthusiasm, and contributes/makes a difference to overall outcomes in the practice setting. Schools make the final selection of recipients.
**Financial data:** The stipend is $1,000.
**Duration:** 1 year.
**Number awarded:** 4 each year: 1 at each of the participating institutions.

## 2238 GREATER KANAWHA VALLEY MATH AND SCIENCE SCHOLARSHIP

Greater Kanawha Valley Foundation, Attn: Scholarship Coordinator
1600 Huntington Square
900 Lee Street, East
P.O. Box 3041

Charleston, WV 25331-3041
Phone: (304) 346-3620; Fax: (304) 346-3640; Email: tgkvf@tgkvf.com
Web: www.tgkvf.com/scholar.html
**Summary:** To provide financial assistance to residents of West Virginia who are working on a degree in a mathematics or science field.
**Eligibility:** Open to residents of West Virginia who are working full time on a degree in mathematics, science (chemistry, physics, or biology), or engineering at a college or university anywhere in the country. Applicants must have an ACT score of 20 or higher, be able to demonstrate good moral character, and have a GPA of 2.5 or higher.
**Financial data:** The stipend is $1,000 per year.
**Duration:** 1 year; may be renewed.
**Number awarded:** 1 each year.
**Deadline:** February of each year.

## 2239 GREATER MICHIGAN CHAPTER ACI CONCRETE SCHOLARSHIP

American Concrete Institute-Greater Michigan Chapter
c/o Ruben Ramos, President
Testing Engineers and Consultants
1343 Rochester Road
P.O. Box 249
Troy, MI 48099-0249
Phone: (248) 588-6514, ext. 130; Fax: (248) 588-6232;
Email: rramos@tectest.com
Web: www.acigmc.org/Scholarship.html
**Summary:** To provide financial assistance to upper-division students from Michigan and Ontario who are working on a degree related to concrete.
**Eligibility:** Open to residents of Michigan and Essex County, Ontario. Applicants must be enrolled full time at a designated university in the area and studying an engineering or technical field emphasizing concrete or masonry design, construction, or materials.
**Financial data:** The stipend is $2,000.
**Duration:** 1 year.
**Number awarded:** 1 each year.
**Deadline:** March of each year.

## 2240 GREATER OMAHA CHAPTER NAWIC SCHOLARSHIP

**Summary:** To provide financial assistance to students in Nebraska who are preparing for a career in construction.
*See Listing #1426.*

## 2241 GROTTO OF NORTH AMERICA SCHOLARSHIP

DeMolay International, Attn: DeMolay Foundation, Inc.
10200 N.W. Ambassador Drive
Kansas City, MO 64153
Phone: (816) 891-8333; (800) DEMOLAY; Fax: (816) 891-9062;
Email: demolay@demolay.org
Web: www.demolay.org/resources/scholarships/index.shtm
**Summary:** To provide financial assistance to members of the Order of DeMolay who are preparing for a career in dentistry or medicine.
**Eligibility:** Open to active and senior DeMolays who are enrolled in an undergraduate or graduate program to prepare for a career in dentistry or medicine. Selection is based on financial need, scholastic ability, and personal qualifications.
**Financial data:** The stipend is $1,500.
**Duration:** Awards are normally made for one year only.
**Number awarded:** 4 each year.
**Deadline:** March of each year.

## 2242 GROTTO/JOB'S DAUGHTERS SCHOLARSHIP

International Order of Job's Daughters
Supreme Guardian Council Headquarters, Attn: Executive Manager
233 West Sixth Street
Papillion, NE 68046-2177
Phone: (402) 592-7987; Fax: (402) 592-2177; Email: sgc@iojd.org
Web: www.iojd.org
**Summary:** To provide financial assistance to members of Job's Daughters who are working on an undergraduate or graduate degree in a dental field.

**Eligibility:** Open to high school seniors and graduates; junior college, technical, and vocational students; college and university students; and graduate students. Applicants must be Job's Daughters in good standing in their Bethels; unmarried majority members under 30 years of age are also eligible. They must be working on a degree in a dental field, preferably with some training in the field of disabilities. Selection is based on scholastic standing, Job's Daughters activities, the applicant's self-help plan, recommendation by the Executive Bethel Guardian Council, faculty recommendations, achievements outside Job's Daughters, and financial need.

**Financial data:** The stipend is $1,500.

**Duration:** 1 year.

**Number awarded:** 1 or more each year.

**Deadline:** April of each year.

---

### 2243 GSH/CARLTON-FARREN SCHOLARSHIP

Society of Exploration Geophysicists, Attn: SEG Foundation
8801 South Yale, Suite 500
P.O. Box 702740
Tulsa, OK 74170-2740
Phone: (918) 497-5513; Fax: (918) 497-5557; Email: scholarships@seg.org
Web: seg.org/business/foundation/scholarships/index.shtml

**Summary:** To provide financial assistance to undergraduate and graduate students who are interested in studying applied geophysics in Texas.

**Eligibility:** Open to 1) high school students planning to enter college in the fall, and 2) undergraduate or graduate students whose grades are above average. Preference is given to students at schools in Houston, Texas; if no qualified students from that area apply, students at other colleges and universities in Texas are considered. Applicants must intend to work on a degree directed toward a career in applied geophysics or a closely-related field. Along with their application, they must submit a 150-word essay on how they plan to use geophysics in their future. Financial need is not considered in the selection process.

**Financial data:** The stipend ranges from $5,000 to $6,000 per year.

**Duration:** 1 academic year; may be renewable, based on scholastic standing, availability of funds, and continuance of a course of study leading to a career in applied geophysics.

**Number awarded:** 1 each year.

**Deadline:** January of each year.

---

### 2244 GUIDANT CORPORATION SCHOLARSHIPS

Society of Women Engineers
230 East Ohio Street, Suite 400
Chicago, IL 60611-3265
Phone: (312) 596-5223; Fax: (312) 644-8557; Email: hq@swe.org
Web: www.societyofwomenengineers.org/scholarships

**Summary:** To provide financial assistance to upper-division women majoring in computer science or designated engineering specialties.

**Eligibility:** Open to women who are entering their senior year at an ABET-accredited college or university. Applicants must be majoring in computer science or chemical, computer, electrical, industrial, manufacturing, materials, or mechanical engineering and have a GPA of 3.0 or higher. Along with their application, they must submit a 1-page essay on why they want to be an engineer or computer scientist, how they believe they will make a difference as an engineer or computer scientist, and what influenced them to study engineering or computer science. Selection is based on merit.

**Financial data:** The stipend is $5,000.

**Duration:** 1 year.

**Number awarded:** 2 each year.

**Deadline:** January of each year.

---

### 2245 GUILIANO MAZZETTI SCHOLARSHIPS

Society of Manufacturing Engineers, Attn: SME Education Foundation
One SME Drive
P.O. Box 930
Dearborn, MI 48121-0930
Phone: (313) 425-3304; (800) 733-4763, ext. 3304; Fax: (313) 425-3411;
Email: foundation@sme.org
Web: www.sme.org

**Summary:** To provide financial assistance to undergraduate students enrolled in a degree program in manufacturing engineering or manufacturing engineering technology.

**Eligibility:** Open to full-time undergraduate students enrolled in a manufacturing engineering or technology degree program at a college or university in

North America. Applicants must have completed a minimum of 30 units in a manufacturing engineering or manufacturing engineering technology curriculum with a GPA of 3.0 or higher. Need is not considered in awarding scholarships (unless 2 or more applicants have equal qualifications).

**Financial data:** The stipend is $2,000.

**Duration:** 1 year.

**Number awarded:** 3 each year.

**Deadline:** January of each year.

---

### 2246 GULF COAST PAST PRESIDENTS SCHOLARSHIP

American Society of Safety Engineers, Attn: ASSE Foundation
1800 East Oakton Street
Des Plaines, IL 60018
Phone: (847) 768-3441; Fax: (847) 296-9220; Email: mrosario@asse.org
Web: www.asse.org

**Summary:** To provide financial assistance to undergraduate students majoring in fields related to occupational safety and health.

**Eligibility:** Open to undergraduate students who are majoring in occupational safety and health or a closely-related field. Although the program is sponsored by the Gulf Coast (Texas) chapter of the American Society of Safety Engineers (ASSE), there are no geographical restrictions on eligibility. Applicants must be full- or part-time students who have completed at least 60 semester hours with a GPA of 3.0 or higher. Part-time students must be ASSE members. As part of the selection process, all applicants must submit 2 essays of 300 words or less: 1) why they are seeking a degree in safety, a brief description of their current activities, and how those relate to their career goals and objectives; and 2) why they should be awarded this scholarship (including career goals and financial need).

**Financial data:** The stipend is $1,000 per year.

**Duration:** 1 year; nonrenewable.

**Number awarded:** 1 each year.

**Deadline:** November of each year.

---

### 2247 G.W. HOHMANN SCHOLARSHIPS

Society of Exploration Geophysicists, Attn: SEG Foundation
8801 South Yale, Suite 500
P.O. Box 702740
Tulsa, OK 74170-2740
Phone: (918) 497-5513; Fax: (918) 497-5557; Email: scholarships@seg.org
Web: seg.org/business/foundation/scholarships/index.shtml

**Summary:** To provide financial assistance to undergraduate and graduate students who are interested in the field of applied geophysics related to mining or electrical methods.

**Eligibility:** Open to 1) high school students planning to enter college in the fall, and 2) undergraduate or graduate students whose grades are above average. Applicants must intend to work on a degree directed toward a career in applied geophysics with an emphasis on mining or electrical methods. Along with their application, they must submit a 150-word essay on how they plan to use geophysics in their future. Financial need is not considered in the selection process.

**Financial data:** The stipend is $3,000 per year for graduate students or $1,000 per year for undergraduates.

**Duration:** 1 academic year; may be renewable, based on scholastic standing, availability of funds, and continuance of a course of study leading to a career in applied geophysics.

**Number awarded:** 2 each year: 1 for an undergraduate and 1 for a graduate student.

**Deadline:** January of each year.

---

### 2248 HANSEN SCHOLARSHIP

Experimental Aviation Association, Attn: Scholarship Office
EAA Aviation Center
P.O. Box 3086
Oshkosh, WI 54903-3086
Phone: (920) 426-6884; Fax: (920) 426-6865; Email: scholarships@eaa.org
Web: www.eaa.org/education/scholarships/index.html

**Summary:** To provide financial assistance to college students who are majoring in aerospace or aeronautical engineering.

**Eligibility:** Open to students enrolled at an accredited college, university, or technical school and working on a degree in aerospace or aeronautical engineering. Applicants must submit a personal statement that covers their career aspirations, educational plan, why they want to receive this scholarship, what they learned from their work and volunteer experiences, how their education will be financed, and any unusual family circumstances.

**Financial data:** The stipend is $1,000.
**Duration:** 1 year; may be renewed.
**Number awarded:** 1 each year.
**Deadline:** March of each year.

## 2249 HAROLD B. & DOROTHY A. SNYDER SCHOLARSHIPS

**Summary:** To provide financial assistance to undergraduate and graduate students preparing for a career in the areas of Presbyterian ministry, nursing, building construction, or engineering.
*See Listing #1430.*

## 2250 HAROLD BETTINGER MEMORIAL SCHOLARSHIP

Floriculture Industry Research and Scholarship Trust
Attn: Scholarship Program
P.O. Box 280
East Lansing, MI 48826-0280
Phone: (517) 333-4617; Fax: (517) 333-4494;
Email: scholarships@firstinfloriculture.org
Web: www.firstinfloriculture.org
**Summary:** To provide financial assistance to graduate or undergraduate students interested in the business of horticulture.
**Eligibility:** Open to graduate and undergraduate students majoring in horticulture with a business and/or marketing emphasis or majoring in business/marketing with the intent to apply it to a horticulture-related business. Applicants must be U.S. or Canadian citizens or permanent residents with a GPA of 3.0 or higher. Selection is based on academic record, recommendations, career goals, extracurricular activities, and financial need.
**Financial data:** The stipend depends on the availability of funds. Recently, it was $1,000.
**Duration:** 1 year.
**Number awarded:** 1 each year.
**Deadline:** April of each year.

## 2251 HARRY F. GAEKE MEMORIAL SCHOLARSHIP

Associated General Contractors of Ohio
Attn: AGC of Ohio Education Foundation
1755 Northwest Boulevard
Columbus, OH 43212
Phone: (614) 486-6446; (800) 557-OHIO; Fax: (614) 486-6498;
Email: agc@agcohio.com
Web: www.agcohio.com/benefits/Scholarships.htm
**Summary:** To provide financial assistance to students from Indiana, Kentucky, or Ohio who are working on an undergraduate degree in a field related to construction.
**Eligibility:** Open to undergraduates who live or attend school in Indiana, Kentucky, or Ohio and are in at least the second year at a 2-year or 4-year college or university. Applicants must be enrolled in a construction degree program, including architectural engineering, civil engineering, structural engineering, or construction management. They must be U.S. citizens with a GPA of 2.5 or higher. Along with their application, they must submit transcripts, a list of extracurricular activities, a list of awards and achievements, information on their financial situation, and a 500-word essay on their interest in a career in construction.
**Financial data:** The stipend is $1,000.
**Duration:** 1 year.
**Number awarded:** 1 each year.
**Deadline:** March of each year.

## 2252 HARRY J. HARWICK SCHOLARSHIPS

American College of Medical Practice Executives
Attn: ACMPE Scholarship Fund Inc.
104 Inverness Terrace East
Englewood, CO 80112-5306
Phone: (303) 799-1111, ext. 232; (877) ASK-MGMA; Fax: (303) 643-4439;
Email: acmpe@mgma.com
Web: www.mgma.com/academics/scholar.cfm
**Summary:** To provide financial assistance to undergraduate or graduate students who are interested in preparing for a career in medical group management.
**Eligibility:** Open to 1) graduate students enrolled in a program accredited by the Accrediting Commission on Education for Health Services Administration and 2) undergraduate students enrolled in a program that is a member of the Association of University Programs in Health Administration. Applicants must be working on a degree in a program relevant to medical practice management. Students working on a degree in medicine, physical therapy, nursing, or other clinically-related professions are not eligible. Along with their application, they must submit a letter describing their career goals; a resume; 3 reference letters commenting on their performance, character, potential to succeed, and need for scholarship support; and either documentation indicating acceptance into an undergraduate or graduate college or university or academic transcripts indicating undergraduate or graduate work completed to date.
**Financial data:** The stipend is $5,000. Funds are paid directly to the recipient's college or university.
**Duration:** 1 year.
**Number awarded:** 2 each year.
**Deadline:** April of each year.

## 2253 HARRY R. BALL, P.E. GRANT

Michigan Society of Professional Engineers, Attn: Scholarship Coordinator
215 North Walnut Street
P.O. Box 15276
Lansing, MI 48901-5276
Phone: (517) 487-9388; Fax: (517) 487-0635; Email: mspe@voyager.net
Web: www.michiganspe.org/scholarship.htm
**Summary:** To provide financial assistance to high school seniors in Michigan who are interested in working on a college degree in engineering.
**Eligibility:** Open to graduating seniors at high schools in Michigan who have a GPA of 3.0 or higher and a composite ACT score of 26 or higher. U.S. citizenship is required. Applicants must have been accepted at a Michigan college or university accredited by ABET. They must be planning to enroll in an engineering program and enter the practice of engineering after graduation, and they must submit a 250-word essay on "How I Was Influenced to Pursue an Engineering Career." Selection is based on the essay; high school academic record; participation in extracurricular activities; evidence of leadership, character, and self-reliance; and comments from teachers and administrators. Financial need is not considered. Semifinalists are interviewed.
**Financial data:** The stipend is $2,000.
**Duration:** 1 year; nonrenewable.
**Number awarded:** 1 each year.
**Deadline:** January of each year.

## 2254 HARTFORD CHAPTER AWARD OF EXCELLENCE

ASM International-Hartford Chapter
c/o Arnie Grot
Grot Enterprises
87 Chapman Drive
Glastonbury, CT 06033-2729
Email: chair12@asm-hartford.org
Web: www.asm-hartford.org/sch_app.htm
**Summary:** To provide financial aid to engineering and science students who live or go to school in Connecticut.
**Eligibility:** Open to students who are: 1) registered full time or accepted for full-time enrollment at a college or university; 2) preparing for a career in a field of engineering or science that may contribute to the future development of metallurgy and materials; 3) residents of Connecticut or attending a college or university in the state; and 4) able to demonstrate an effort to maintain their GPA. Selection is based on educational background, employment experience, honors and recognition, a 250-word essay on how their chosen major can directly or indirectly contribute to the field of metallurgy and material science, and 2 letters of recommendation; financial need is not considered.
**Financial data:** The stipend is $1,000.
**Duration:** 1 year.
**Number awarded:** 1 or more each year.
**Deadline:** March of each year.

## 2255 HARVEST SCHOLARSHIPS

HARVEST Education Foundation
P.O. Box 100
Romeo, MI 48065-0100
Phone: (586) 752-6066
Web: www.marvac.org/harvestapp.html
**Summary:** To provide financial assistance for college to Michigan residents

interested in preparing for a career in the manufactured homes, recreational vehicles, or campground industries.

**Eligibility:** Open to Michigan students enrolled or planning to enroll at an accredited college or university to prepare for a career in the manufactured homes, recreational vehicles, or campground industries. Fields of study may include engineering, marketing, management, service, design, human resources, or any other discipline that will serve the needs of the industries. Applicants must submit an essay of 200 to 300 words on their career goals and why they feel they deserve this scholarship. Selection is based on merit and/or financial need.

**Financial data:** A stipend is awarded (amount not specified).

**Duration:** 1 year; may be renewed.

**Number awarded:** 1 or more each year.

**Deadline:** March of each year.

## 2256 HAWAII STUDENT NURSES' ASSOCIATION SCHOLARSHIP

Hawai'i Community Foundation, Attn: Scholarship Department
1164 Bishop Street, Suite 800
Honolulu, HI 96813
Phone: (808) 566-5570; (888) 731-3863; Fax: (808) 521-6286;
Email: scholarships@hcf-hawaii.org
Web: www.hawaiicommunityfoundation.org/scholar/scholar.php

**Summary:** To provide financial assistance to Hawaii residents who are interested in preparing for a career in nursing.

**Eligibility:** Open to students enrolled in an undergraduate nursing program in Hawaii. Applicants must be residents of the state of Hawaii; be able to demonstrate financial need; be interested in attending an accredited 2- or 4-year college or university as full-time students; and be able to demonstrate academic achievement (3.0 GPA or above). Current and former officers of the Hawaii Student Nurses' Association and the National Student Nurses' Association are ineligible.

**Financial data:** The amounts of the awards depend on the availability of funds and the need of the recipient.

**Duration:** 1 year.

**Number awarded:** Varies each year.

**Deadline:** February of each year.

## 2257 HAZEL SIMMONS HODGES GARDEN CLUB OBJECTIVES SCHOLARSHIP

**Summary:** To provide financial aid to Florida students majoring or planning to major in designated areas related to gardening.

*See Listing #1440.*

## 2258 HEALTH PROFESSIONS PREGRADUATE SCHOLARSHIP PROGRAM

Indian Health Service, Attn: Scholarship Program
801 Thompson Avenue, Suite 120
Rockville, MD 20852
Phone: (301) 443-6197; Fax: (301) 443-6048; Email: bmiller@na.ihs.gov
Web: www.ihs.gov

**Summary:** To provide financial support to American Indian students interested in majoring in pre-medicine or pre-dentistry in college.

**Eligibility:** Open to American Indians or Alaska Natives who are high school graduates or the equivalent; have the capacity to complete a health professions course of study; and are enrolled or accepted for enrollment in a baccalaureate degree program to prepare for entry into a school of medicine, osteopathy, or dentistry. Priority is given to students entering their junior or senior year; support is provided to freshmen and sophomores only if remaining funds are available. Selection is based on academic performance, work experience and community background, faculty/employer recommendations, and applicant's reasons for seeking the scholarship. Recipients must intend to serve Indian people upon completion of their professional health care education.

**Financial data:** Awards provide a payment directly to the school for tuition and required fees; a stipend for living expenses of approximately $1,160 per month for 10 months; a lump sum to cover the costs of books, travel, and other necessary educational expenses; and up to $400 for approved tutorial costs.

**Duration:** Up to 4 years of full-time study or up to 8 years of part-time study.

**Number awarded:** Varies each year.

**Deadline:** February of each year.

## 2259 HEALTH PROFESSIONS PREPARATORY SCHOLARSHIP PROGRAM

Indian Health Service, Attn: Scholarship Program

801 Thompson Avenue, Suite 120
Rockville, MD 20852
Phone: (301) 443-6197; Fax: (301) 443-6048; Email: bmiller@na.ihs.gov
Web: www.ihs.gov

**Summary:** To provide financial assistance to Native American students who need compensatory or preprofessional education to qualify for enrollment in a health professions school.

**Eligibility:** Open to American Indians or Alaska Natives who are high school graduates or the equivalent; have the capacity to complete a health professions course of study; and are enrolled or accepted for enrollment in a compensatory or preprofessional general education course or curriculum. The qualifying fields of study include pre-medical technology, pre-dietetics, pre-nursing, pre-pharmacy, pre-physical therapy, pre-social work, and pre engineering. Recipients must intend to serve Indian people upon completion of professional health care education as a health care provider in the discipline for which they are enrolled at the pregraduate level.

**Financial data:** Awards provide a payment directly to the school for tuition and required fees; a stipend for living expenses of approximately $1,160 per month for 10 months; a lump sum to cover the costs of books, travel, and other necessary educational expenses; and up to $400 for approved tutorial costs.

**Duration:** Up to 2 years of full-time study or up to 4 years of part-time study.

**Number awarded:** Varies each year.

**Deadline:** February of each year.

## 2260 HEALTH PROFESSIONS SCHOLARSHIPS FOR ELCA SERVICE ABROAD

Women of the Evangelical Lutheran Church in America, Attn: Scholarships
8765 West Higgins Road
Chicago, IL 60631-4189
Phone: (773) 380 2730; (800) 638-3522, ext. 2730; Fax: (773) 380-2419;
Email: womenelca@elca.org
Web: www.womenoftheelca.org/whatwedo/scholarships.html

**Summary:** To provide financial assistance to lay women who are members of Evangelical Lutheran Church of America (ELCA) congregations and who wish to pursue postsecondary education for service abroad in nursing or other health professions.

**Eligibility:** Open to ELCA lay women who are at least 21 years of age and have experienced an interruption of at least 2 years in their education since high school. Applicants must have been admitted to an academic institution to prepare for a career other than a church-certified profession. This program is available only to U.S. citizens studying for service in the health professions associated with ELCA projects abroad.

**Financial data:** The amount of the award depends on the availability of funds.

**Duration:** Up to 2 years.

**Number awarded:** Varies each year, depending upon the funds available.

**Deadline:** February of each year.

## 2261 HELEN N. & HAROLD B. SHAPIRA UNDERGRADUATE SCHOLARSHIP

American Heart Association-Northland Affiliate
Attn: Administrative Assistant
4701 West 77th Street
Minneapolis, MN 55435
Phone: (952) 835-3300; (800) 331-6889 (within MN); Fax: (952) 835-5828;
Email: northland@heart.org
Web: www.americanheart.org

**Summary:** To provide financial assistance to undergraduate students in Minnesota interested in the study of heart and blood vessel diseases.

**Eligibility:** Open to undergraduate students currently enrolled in a 4-year college or university in Minnesota and working in a medically-related curriculum with potential application to patients with diseases of the heart and blood vessel system. Selection is based on merit.

**Financial data:** The stipend is $1,000.

**Duration:** 1 year; may be renewed for 1 additional year.

**Number awarded:** 1 each year.

**Deadline:** March of each year.

## 2262 HENAAC STUDENT LEADERSHIP AWARDS

Hispanic Engineer National Achievement Awards Conference
3900 Whiteside Street
Los Angeles, CA 90063

Phone: (323) 262-0997; Fax: (323) 262-0946; Email: info@henaac.org
Web: www.henaac.org/scholarships.htm
**Summary:** To provide financial assistance to Hispanic undergraduate and graduate students majoring in engineering and related fields.
**Eligibility:** Open to Hispanic undergraduate and graduate students who are enrolled full time in computer science, engineering, material science, mathematics, or applied science. Applicants must have a GPA of 3.0 or higher. There is no citizenship requirement. Academic achievement and campus community activities are considered in the selection process.
**Financial data:** The stipend is $5,000.
**Duration:** 1 year.
**Number awarded:** 2 each year: 1 undergraduate and 1 graduate student.
**Deadline:** April of each year.

### 2263 HENRY RODRIGUEZ RECLAMATION SCHOLARSHIP

American Indian Science and Engineering Society
Attn: Scholarship Coordinator
2305 Renard, S.E., Suite 200
P.O. Box 9828
Albuquerque, NM 87119-9828
Phone: (505) 765-1052, ext. 106; Fax: (505) 765-5608; Email: shirley@aises.org
Web: www.aises.org/highered/scholarships
**Summary:** To provide financial assistance and summer work experience to members of the American Indian Science and Engineering Society (AISES) who are working on an undergraduate degree in engineering or science related to water resources or environmental fields.
**Eligibility:** Open to AISES members who are full-time undergraduate students in engineering or science related to water resources or environmental fields. Applicants must have a GPA of 2.5 or higher and be U.S. citizens or permanent residents. Non-Indians may apply, but all applicants must submit an essay on their first-hand knowledge of Indian tribal culture, their interest in engineering or environmental studies, how that interest relates to water resource issues and needs and concerns of Indian tribes, and how they will contribute their knowledge or professional experience to a Native American community.
**Financial data:** The stipend is $5,000 per year.
**Duration:** 1 year; may be renewed up to 3 additional years.
**Deadline:** June of each year.

### 2264 HILL-ROM MANAGEMENT ESSAY COMPETITION IN HEALTHCARE ADMINISTRATION

American College of Healthcare Executives
Attn: Associate Director, Division of Research and Development
One North Franklin Street, Suite 1700
Chicago, IL 60606-3529
Phone: (312) 424-9444; Fax: (312) 424-0023; Email: ache@ache.org
Web: www.ache.org/Faculty_Students/hillrom.cfm
**Summary:** To recognize and reward undergraduate or graduate student members of the American College of Healthcare Executives (ACHE) who submit outstanding essays on health care administration.
**Eligibility:** Open to ACHE student associates or affiliates who are enrolled in an undergraduate or graduate program in health care management at an accredited college or university in the United States or Canada. Applicants must submit an essay, up to 15 pages in length, on a topic with a focus on such health management topics as strategic planning and policy; accountability of and/or relationships among board, medical staff, and executive management; financial management; human resources management; systems management; plant and facility management; comprehensive systems of services; quality assessment and assurance; professional, public, community, or interorganization relations; government relations or regulation; marketing; education; research; or law and ethics. Selection is based on significance of the subject to health care management, innovativeness in approach to the topic, thoroughness and precision in developing the subject, practical usefulness for guiding management action, and clarity and conciseness of expression.
**Financial data:** The first-place winners in each division (undergraduate and graduate) receive $3,000 and their programs receive $1,000. The second-place winner receives $2,000 and third $1,000.
**Duration:** The competition is held annually.
**Number awarded:** 6 each year: 3 undergraduate and 3 graduate students.
**Deadline:** December of each year.

### 2265 HIMSS FOUNDATION SCHOLARSHIPS

Healthcare Information and Management Systems Society
Attn: HIMSS Foundation Scholarship Program Coordinator
230 East Ohio Street, Suite 500

Chicago, IL 60611-3269
Phone: (312) 664-4467; Fax: (312) 664-6143
Web: www.himss.org/asp/scholarships.asp
**Summary:** To provide financial assistance to upper-division and graduate student members of the Healthcare Information and Management Systems Society (HIMSS) who are interested in the field of health care information and management systems.
**Eligibility:** Open to student members of the society, although an application for membership, including dues, may accompany the scholarship application. Applicants must be upper-division or graduate students enrolled in an accredited program designed to prepare them for a career in health care information or management systems, which may include industrial engineering, health care informatics, operations research, computer science and information systems, mathematics, and quantitative programs in business administration and hospital administration. Selection is based on academic achievement and demonstration of leadership potential, including communication skills and participation in society activity.
**Financial data:** The stipend is $5,000. The award also includes an all-expense paid trip to the annual HIMSS conference and exhibition.
**Duration:** 1 year.
**Number awarded:** 3 each year: 1 to an undergraduate student, 1 to a master's degree student, and 1 to a Ph.D. candidate.
**Deadline:** October of each year.

### 2266 H.I.S. PROGRAM

Hispanic College Fund, Attn: National Director
1717 Pennsylvania Avenue, N.W., Suite 460
Washington, D.C. 20006
Phone: (202) 296-5400; (800) 644-4223; Fax: (202) 296-3774;
Email: hispaniccollegefund@earthlink.net
Web: www.hispanicfund.org
**Summary:** To provide financial assistance and summer work experience to Hispanic American undergraduate students who are interested in preparing for a career in telecommunications.
**Eligibility:** Open to U.S. citizens of Hispanic background (at least one grandparent must be 100% Hispanic) who are entering their freshman, sophomore, junior, or senior year of college. Applicants must be working on a bachelor's degree in accounting, business administration, computer science, economics, engineering specialties, finance, information systems, management, or other relevant technology or business fields. They must have an interest in telecommunications, have a cumulative GPA of 3.0 or higher, and be available to complete at least 2 consecutive summer internships before graduating from college. Financial need is considered in the selection process.
**Financial data:** Stipends range from $500 to $5,000, depending on need and academic achievement. Funds are paid directly to the recipient's college or university to help cover tuition and fees.
**Duration:** 1 year; recipients may reapply.
**Number awarded:** Varies each year.
**Deadline:** April of each year.

### 2267 HOLLIS HANINGTON SCHOLARSHIP

Professional Logging Contractors of Maine
P.O. Box 400
Fort Kent, ME 04743
Phone: (207) 834-3835; (888) 300-6614; Fax: (207) 834-3845;
Email: brawders@aol.com
Web: www.maineloggers.org
**Summary:** To provide financial assistance to high school seniors in Maine who are interested in preparing for a career in the forest products industry.
**Eligibility:** Open to seniors in high school (and home-schooled students) who are residents of Maine. Applicants must be planning to enter college to prepare for a career in the forest products industry.
**Financial data:** The stipend is $1,000. Funds are paid after successful completion of the first semester of college.
**Duration:** 1 year; nonrenewable.
**Number awarded:** 1 each year.
**Deadline:** April of each year.

### 2268 HOME BUILDERS ASSOCIATION OF ILLINOIS STUDENT OF THE YEAR SCHOLARSHIPS

**Summary:** To recognize and reward, with funds for continuing education, students in Illinois who are preparing for a career in the building industry.
*See Listing #1457.*

## 2269 HOMER T. BORTON, P.E., MEMORIAL SCHOLARSHIP

Ohio Society of Professional Engineers, Attn: Engineers Foundation of Ohio
4795 Evanswood Drive, Suite 201
Columbus, OH 43229-7216
Phone: (614) 846-1144; (800) 654-9481; Fax: (614) 846-1131;
Email: ospe@iwaynet.net
Web: www.ohioengineer.com/programs/Scholarships.htm
**Summary:** To provide financial assistance to high school seniors in Ohio who are interested in majoring in engineering in college.
**Eligibility:** Open to high school seniors in Ohio who will be attending a college or university in the state that is approved by the Accreditation Board of Engineering and Technology (ABET) and who plan to major in engineering. Applicants must have a GPA of 3.0 or higher, be U.S. citizens, and have ACT scores of at least 29 in mathematics and 25 in English (or the equivalent on the SAT). Along with their application, they must submit a 350-word essay on their interest in engineering, including why they became interested in the field, what specialty interests them most, and why they want to become a practicing engineer. Financial need is also considered in the selection process.
**Financial data:** The stipend is $1,000 per year.
**Duration:** 1 year; may be renewed up to 3 additional years.
**Number awarded:** 1 every 4 years (2005, 2009, etc.).
**Deadline:** December of the year of the award.

## 2270 HONEYWELL AVIONICS SCHOLARSHIP

Aircraft Electronics Association, Attn: AEA Educational Foundation
4217 South Hocker Drive
Independence, MO 64055-4723
Phone: (816) 373-6565; Fax: (816) 478-3100; Email: info@aea.net
Web: www.aea.net
**Summary:** To provide financial assistance for college to students who are interested in preparing for a career in avionics or aircraft repair.
**Eligibility:** Open to high school seniors and college students who are attending (or planning to attend) an accredited school in an avionics or aircraft repair program. Applicants must submit an official transcript (cumulative GPA of 2.5 or higher), a statement about their career plans, a description of their involvement in school and community activities, and a 300-word essay on how the job requirements of aviation technicians will change with advancements in technology. Selection is based on merit.
**Financial data:** The stipend is $1,000.
**Duration:** 1 year.
**Number awarded:** 1 each year.
**Deadline:** February of each year.

## 2271 "HONOR" AND CARLA CARROL MEMORIAL SCHOLARSHIP

Ninety-Nines, Inc.-Eastern New England Chapter
c/o Katharine Barr
278 Elm Street
North Reading, MA 01864
Email: KayBarr@Primushost.com
**Summary:** To provide financial assistance to residents of New England who are interested in preparing for a career in aviation.
**Eligibility:** Open to high school seniors and current college students who are residents of or studying in Maine, New Hampshire, Rhode Island, Vermont, Massachusetts, or Connecticut. Applicants must be planning a career in aviation and need financial assistance to pursue appropriate education or flight training. Selection is based on aviation activities, science fair projects, aviation employment, recommendations, academic record, aviation goals, and financial need.
**Financial data:** The stipend is $1,000. Funds may be applied to academic tuition, technical school, or flight training.
**Duration:** 1 year.
**Number awarded:** 1 each year.
**Deadline:** January of each year.

## 2272 HOOPER MEMORIAL SCHOLARSHIP

Transportation Clubs International, Attn: Gay Fielding
7031 Manchester Street
New Orleans, LA 70126
Email: GayFielding@bellsouth.net
Web: www.transportationclubsinternational.com
**Summary:** To provide financial assistance to college students interested in preparing for a career in fields related to transportation.
**Eligibility:** Open to students enrolled in an academic institution that offers courses in transportation, logistics, traffic management, or related fields. Applicants must intend to prepare for a career in those fields. Selection is based on scholastic ability, character, potential, professional interest, and financial need.
**Financial data:** The stipend is $1,500.
**Duration:** 1 year.
**Number awarded:** 1 or more each year.
**Deadline:** April of each year.

## 2273 HORIZONS FOUNDATION SCHOLARSHIP PROGRAM

Women in Defense
c/o National Defense Industrial Association
2111 Wilson Boulevard, Suite 400
Arlington, VA 22201-3061
Phone: (703) 247-2552; Fax: (703) 527-6945; Email: jcasey@ndia.org
Web: www.ndia.org/horizon/Scholar.htm
**Summary:** To provide financial assistance to women who are upper-division or graduate students engaged in or planning careers related to the national security interests of the United States.
**Eligibility:** Open to women who are already working in national security fields as well as women planning such careers. Applicants must 1) be currently enrolled at an accredited college or university, either full time or part time, as graduate students or upper-division undergraduates; 2) demonstrate financial need; 3) be U.S. citizens; 4) have a GPA of 3.25 or higher; and 5) demonstrate interest in preparing for a career related to national security. The preferred fields of study include business, computer science, economics, engineering, government relations, international relations, law, mathematics, military history, political science, physics, and security studies; others are considered if the applicant can demonstrate relevance to a career in national security or defense. Selection is based on academic achievement, participation in defense and national security activities, field of study, work experience, statements of objectives, recommendations, and financial need.
**Financial data:** Stipends range up to $1,000.
**Duration:** 1 year; renewable.
**Number awarded:** Varies each year. Recently, 8 of these scholarships were awarded. Since the program was established, 75 women have received nearly $49,000 in support.
**Deadline:** June of each year for fall semester; October of each year for spring semester.

## 2274 HOSA SCHOLARSHIPS

Health Occupations Students of America
6021 Morriss Road, Suite 111
Flower Mound, TX 75028
Phone: (972) 874-0062; (800) 321-HOSA; Fax: (972) 874-0063;
Email: info@hosa.org
Web: www.hosa.org/member/scholar.html
**Summary:** To provide financial assistance for college to members of the Health Occupations Students of America (HOSA).
**Eligibility:** Open to high school seniors and current college students who are members of the association and planning to continue their education in the health care field (including nursing). Applicants must submit a 1-page essay on the contributions they expect to make to the health profession and why they should be selected as the recipient of this scholarship. Selection is based on the essay (26 points), transcripts (20 points), leadership activities and recognition (30 points), community involvement (15 points), and letters of reference (9 points).
**Financial data:** Stipends range from $1,000 to $7,000.
**Duration:** 1 year.
**Number awarded:** Varies each year. Recently, 9 of these scholarships were available: 1 at $7,000, 1 at $4,000, 2 at $2,000, and 5 at $1,000.
**Deadline:** May of each year.

## 2275 HOUSTON AREA SECTION SCHOLARSHIPS

Society of Women Engineers-Houston Area Section, Attn: Scholarship Chair
P.O. Box 3461
Houston, TX 77253-3461
Email: swe-ha@swe.org
Web: www.swe-houston.org

**Summary:** To provide financial assistance to high school women, especially those in Texas, interested in studying engineering in college.

**Eligibility:** Open to female high school seniors planning to attend an ABET-accredited 4-year college or university to major in engineering. Preference is given to students attending high school in Texas, but applicants may be planning to enroll at a college in any state. They must have completed at least 1 regional FIRST (For Inspiration and Recognition of Science and Technology) competition. Along with their application, they must submit transcripts; a 1-page essay on why they would like to be an engineer, and/or how they believe they will make a difference as an engineer, and/or what influenced them to study engineering; a letter of reference regarding their scholastic ability, general character, attitude, ambition, motivation, and leadership characteristics; and a resume. Information on financial situation is purely voluntary and is not used in the selection process.

**Financial data:** The stipend is $1,000.

**Duration:** 1 year; nonrenewable.

**Number awarded:** 1 each year.

**Deadline:** March of each year.

## 2276 HOWARD BROWN RICKARD SCHOLARSHIPS

**Summary:** To provide financial assistance for college or graduate school to blind students studying or planning to study law, medicine, engineering, architecture, or the natural sciences.

*See Listing #1460.*

## 2277 HOWARD E. ADKINS MEMORIAL SCHOLARSHIP

American Welding Society, Attn: AWS Foundation, Inc.
550 N.W. LeJeune Road
Miami, FL 33126
Phone: (305) 445-6628; (800) 443-9353, ext. 461; Fax: (305) 443-7559;
Email: found@aws.org
Web: www.aws.org/foundation/scholarships/adkins.html

**Summary:** To provide financial assistance to college students interested in preparing for a career related to welding.

**Eligibility:** Open to full-time college juniors and seniors who are working on a 4-year bachelor's degree in welding engineering or welding engineering technology; preference is given to students in welding engineering. Applicants must have a GPA of 3.2 or higher in engineering, science, and technical subjects and 2.8 overall. Priority is given to applicants residing or attending school in Wisconsin or Kentucky. U.S. citizenship is required. Financial need is not considered in the selection process.

**Financial data:** The stipend is $2,500.

**Duration:** 1 year; recipients may reapply.

**Number awarded:** 1 each year.

**Deadline:** January of each year.

## 2278 H.P. "BUD" MILLIGAN AVIATION SCHOLARSHIP

Experimental Aviation Association, Attn: Scholarship Office
EAA Aviation Center
P.O. Box 3086
Oshkosh, WI 54903-3086
Phone: (920) 426-6884; Fax: (920) 426-6865; Email: scholarships@eaa.org
Web: www.eaa.org/education/scholarships/index.html

**Summary:** To provide financial assistance to college students majoring in aviation.

**Eligibility:** Open to students enrolled in an accredited aviation program at a college, technical school, or aviation academy. Applicants must submit a personal statement that covers their career aspirations, educational plan, why they want to receive this scholarship, and what they learned from their work and volunteer experiences. Financial need is not considered in the selection process.

**Financial data:** The stipend is $1,000.

**Duration:** 1 year; may be renewed.

**Number awarded:** 1 each year.

**Deadline:** March of each year.

## 2279 HUBERTUS W.V. WILLEMS SCHOLARSHIP FOR MALE STUDENTS

National Association for the Advancement of Colored People
Attn: Education Department
4805 Mt. Hope Drive
Baltimore, MD 21215-3297

Phone: (410) 580-5760; (877) NAACP-98; Email: youth@naacpnet.org
Web: www.naacp.org/work/education/eduscholarship.shtml

**Summary:** To provide funding to males, particularly male members of the National Association for the Advancement of Colored People (NAACP), who are interested in undergraduate or graduate education in selected scientific fields.

**Eligibility:** Open to males who are high school seniors, college students, or graduate students. Applicants must be majoring (or planning to major) in one of the following fields: engineering, chemistry, physics, or mathematics. Membership and participation in the NAACP is highly desirable. The required minimum GPA is 2.5 for graduating high school seniors and undergraduate students or 3.0 for graduate students. Applicants must be able to demonstrate financial need, defined as a family income of less than $13,470 for a family of 1 ranging to less than $46,440 for a family of 8. Along with their application, they must submit a 1-page essay on their interest in their major and a career, their life's ambition, what they hope to accomplish in their lifetime, and what they consider their most significant contribution to their community. Full-time enrollment is required for undergraduate students, although graduate students may be enrolled full or part time. U.S. citizenship is required.

**Financial data:** The stipend is $2,000 per year for undergraduate students or $3,000 per year for graduate students.

**Duration:** 1 year; may be renewed.

**Number awarded:** Varies each year; recently, 8 of these scholarships were awarded.

**Deadline:** April of each year.

## 2280 HYDRO POWER CONTEST

HANDS-ON! Projects
9 Mayflower Road
Northborough, MA 01532
Phone: (508) 351-6023; Fax: (508) 351-6023; Email: hands-on@rcn.com
Web: users.rcn.com/hands-on/hydro/contest/mainpage.html

**Summary:** To recognize and reward students and other interested people who have ideas for turning water into power.

**Eligibility:** Open to individuals or teams interested in constructing a device that converts the gravity potential of water into mechanical power and submitting the device for testing under competition conditions. During the contest, the mechanical power produced by each device and its efficiency is measured. The devices in each of the 6 classes of competition that lift a weight through a fixed distance in the shortest period of time or with the least amount of water win the competition. The 6 competition classes are: student division, power class; student division, efficiency class; open division, power class; open division, efficiency class; pro division, power class; and walk-on class.

**Financial data:** In each of the 6 classes, the following awards are presented (depending on the number of entries): first prize, from $300 to $900; second prize, up to $600; third prize, up to $300; and fourth prize, up to $200. In addition to these prizes, the judges at their discretion may make additional awards for the "most innovative" entry and for the entry showing the "best workmanship." If awarded, these cash prizes are $250 each. The Hydro Research Foundation distributes cash prizes of $700 to some student winners. Students who participate may also be awarded scholarships. For example, recently the Canada Centre for Mines and Energy Technology/Natural Resources Canada (CANMET) awarded a $C1,500 scholarship to a Canadian student or student team that won one of the student division competition classes.

**Duration:** The competition is held annually.

**Number awarded:** Up to 4 winners in each of the 6 competition classes receive cash prizes. The number of other scholarships varies each year.

## 2281 IAHPERD SCHOLARSHIPS

**Summary:** To provide financial assistance to upper-division students in Illinois who are majoring in health, physical education, recreation, or dance.

*See Listing #1463.*

## 2282 ICI EDUCATIONAL FOUNDATION SCHOLARSHIP PROGRAM

Hispanic College Fund, Attn: National Director
1717 Pennsylvania Avenue, N.W., Suite 460
Washington, D.C. 20006
Phone: (202) 296-5400; (800) 644-4223; Fax: (202) 296-3774;
Email: hispaniccollegefund@earthlink.net
Web: www.hispanicfund.org

**Summary:** To provide financial assistance to Hispanic American undergraduate students who are interested in preparing for a career in business, computer science, or engineering.

**Eligibility:** Open to U.S. citizens of Hispanic background (at least one grandparent must be 100% Hispanic) who are entering their freshman, sophomore, junior, or senior year of college. Applicants must be working on a bachelor's or associate's degree in business, computer science, engineering or a business-related major and have a cumulative GPA of 3.0 or higher. They must be applying to or enrolled in a college or university in the 50 states or Puerto Rico as a full-time student. Financial need is considered in the selection process.

**Financial data:** Stipends range from $500 to $5,000, depending on the need of the recipient, and average approximately $3,000. Funds are paid directly to the recipient's college or university to help cover tuition and fees.

**Duration:** 1 year; recipients may reapply.

**Number awarded:** Varies each year.

**Deadline:** April of each year.

---

## 2283 IDAHO STATE BROADCASTERS ASSOCIATION SCHOLARSHIPS

**Summary:** To provide financial assistance to students at Idaho colleges and universities who are preparing for a career in the broadcasting field.

*See Listing #1464.*

---

## 2284 IDSA UNDERGRADUATE SCHOLARSHIPS

**Summary:** To provide financial assistance to upper-division students working on an undergraduate degree in industrial design.

*See Listing #1465.*

---

## 2285 IFEC SCHOLARSHIPS

**Summary:** To provide financial assistance to undergraduate or graduate students who are interested in preparing for a career in communications in the food service industry.

*See Listing #1467.*

---

## 2286 IFFAA SCHOLARSHIPS

Iowa Foundation for Agricultural Advancement
Attn: Department IFFAA/Iowa State Fair
P.O. Box 57130
Des Moines, IA 50317-0003
Phone: (800) 545-FAIR; Email: saleofchampions@yahoo.com
Web: www.iowastatefair.org/saleofchamps

**Summary:** To provide financial assistance for college to Iowa high school seniors interested in majoring in animal science or livestock-related fields.

**Eligibility:** Open to students who will be entering an Iowa 2- or 4-year postsecondary institution in the following fall. Applicants must be residents of Iowa, active in 4-H or FFA livestock projects, and planning to major in animal science or a field in agriculture or home economics that is related to the animal industry. Selection is based on level of 4-H or FFA involvement in livestock project work, livestock exhibition, and/or judging (50%); scholarship (15%); leadership and activities (25%); and curriculum and career plans (10%). The program also includes performance and carcass awards in which animals are selected on the basis of visual appraisal and then evaluated in a carcass contest for economically important traits, such as loin eye or rib eye area, tenth rib fat, and average daily gain.

**Financial data:** Stipends range from $500 to $2,500.

**Duration:** 1 year; nonrenewable.

**Number awarded:** Varies each year. Recently, 74 scholarships (with a value of $77,00) and 64 performance and carcass awards (with a value of $11,500) were presented.

**Deadline:** May of each year.

---

## 2287 IFT 50TH ANNIVERSARY–INSPIRATION FOR TOMORROW SCHOLARSHIP

Institute of Food Technologists, Attn: Scholarship Department
525 West Van Buren, Suite 1000
Chicago, IL 60607
Phone: (312) 782-8424; Fax: (312) 782-8348; Email: info@ift.org
Web: www.ift.org

**Summary:** To provide financial assistance to undergraduates interested in studying food science or food technology.

**Eligibility:** Open to sophomores, juniors, and seniors in a food science or food technology program at an educational institution in the United States or Canada. Applicants must have an outstanding scholastic record and a well-rounded personality. Along with their application, they must submit an essay on their career aspirations; a list of awards, honors, and scholarships they have received; a list of extracurricular activities and/or hobbies; and a summary of their work experience. Financial need is not considered in the selection process.

**Financial data:** The stipend is $2,000.

**Duration:** 1 year; recipients may reapply if they are members of the Institute of Food Technologists.

**Number awarded:** 1 each year.

**Deadline:** January of each year.

---

## 2288 IHC FOUNDATION SCHOLARSHIP

Indiana Health Care Foundation, Inc., Attn: Scholarship Committee
One North Capitol Avenue, Suite 1115
Indianapolis, IN 46204
Phone: (317) 636-6406; (887) 561-3757; Fax: (317) 638-3749
Web: www.ihca.org/foundation.php

**Summary:** To provide financial assistance to students in Indiana who are interested in working on a nursing degree.

**Eligibility:** Open to residents of Indiana who have at least a high school degree or GED, have been accepted by a nursing degree program (R.N. or L.P.N.) in Indiana or a bordering state, and have a GPA of 2.5 or higher. Applicants must submit an essay (up to 750 words) on their reasons for applying for this scholarship, their interest in nursing, and their future professional plans and commitment to long-term care. Finalists are interviewed. Special consideration is given to applicants who show a dedication and commitment to working with the elderly in a long-term care environment. Financial need is not considered in the selection process.

**Financial data:** Stipends range from $750 to $1,500 per year. Funds are paid directly to the recipient's school and must be used for tuition, fees, or campus housing.

**Duration:** 1 year; recipients may reapply.

**Deadline:** April of each year.

---

## 2289 ILLINOIS ACI CHAPTER SCHOLARSHIP AWARD

American Concrete Institute-Illinois Chapter
c/o Mike Morrison, Scholarship Committee
Construction Technology Laboratories
5400 Old Orchard Road
Skokie, IL 60077
Phone: (847) 972-3314; Fax: (847) 965-6541; Email: mmorrison@ctlgroup.com
Web: www.concrete.org/CHAPTERS/Chapter_Scholarships.asp?cid=C034

**Summary:** To provide financial assistance to upper-division students from Illinois working on a degree related to the concrete industry.

**Eligibility:** Open to students who are residents of Illinois or enrolled at a university in the states. Applicants must have completed at least 2 years of undergraduate study in a field related to concrete design, materials, construction, or any combination of those. They must submit a statement on why they should receive the scholarship (financial need is not an important consideration); a statement on their interest in concrete; undergraduate records of academic performance; and their plan for continuing education.

**Financial data:** The stipend is $2,500.

**Duration:** 1 year.

**Number awarded:** 1 each year.

**Deadline:** April of each year.

---

## 2290 ILLINOIS CONSERVATION YOUTH ACHIEVEMENT SCHOLARSHIPS

Illinois Conservation Foundation, Attn: Executive Secretary
One Natural Resources Way
Springfield, IL 62702-1270
Phone: (217) 785-2003; Fax: (217) 785-9236; TTY: (217) 788-9175;
Email: kwheeler@dnrmail.state.il.us
Web: www.ilcf.org

**Summary:** To provide financial assistance for college to high school juniors and seniors in Illinois who have participated in natural resource activities.

**Eligibility:** Open to juniors and seniors at high schools in Illinois who are nominated by a natural resource constituency group, community leader, school administrator, or teacher. Nominees must submit a 500-word essay on why they believe they are qualified to receive this scholarship based on their contributions to natural resource conservation activities, including brief but specific examples of each achievement or contribution. Selection is based on that essay, a letter of support from their school administrator indicating good academic and discipline standing, 2 additional letters of support, media documentation of their natural resource activities, and verification of academic achievement. Female and male candidates are judged separately.

**Financial data:** The stipend is $1,000.

**Duration:** 1 year.

**Number awarded:** 10 each year: 1 female and 1 male in each of the 5 Illinois Department of Natural Resources (DNR) regions.

**Deadline:** May of each year.

## 2291 ILLINOIS HOSPITAL RESEARCH AND EDUCATION FOUNDATION SCHOLARSHIPS

Illinois Hospital Association
Attn: Illinois Hospital Research and Educational Foundation
1151 East Warrenville Road
P.O. Box 3015
Naperville, IL 60566
Phone: (630) 505-7777
Web: www.ihatoday.org/public/volunteers/appinstruct.htm

**Summary:** To provide financial assistance to Illinois residents accepted into or enrolled in a hospital-related health care professional curriculum.

**Eligibility:** Open to Illinois residents who have been accepted into or are currently enrolled in a hospital-related health care professional curriculum. Applicants enrolled in an associate degree or hospital-based program will be considered in their first year only. Students must have been accepted in a health care professional sequence; that is, when courses are open only to student candidates for the degree or certification; pre-nursing, pre-medicine, and pre-pharmacy applicants are not eligible until they are accepted into nursing clinicals, medical school, etc. Applicants who have less than one academic year remaining until graduation are not eligible for consideration. Selection is based on academic record (GPA of 3.5 or higher) and financial need.

**Financial data:** The stipend is $1,000. Funds must be used for tuition, fees, or books.

**Duration:** 1 year.

**Number awarded:** Varies each year; recently, 36 of these scholarships were awarded.

**Deadline:** April of each year.

## 2292 ILMDA ACADEMIC SCHOLARSHIPS

**Summary:** To provide financial assistance to residents of Illinois who are preparing for a career in the lumber and building materials industry.

*See Listing #1469.*

## 2293 INDIAN NURSE SCHOLARSHIP AWARDS

National Society of the Colonial Dames of America
National Patriotic Service Committee
c/o Virginia Van Antwerp
1520 Lake Cove
Atlanta, GA 30338-3429

**Summary:** To provide financial assistance to American Indians interested in preparing for a career in nursing.

**Eligibility:** Open to American Indians who are high school graduates (or the equivalent), are enrolled full time in an accredited school, are in a nursing program, are within 2 years of completing the course for which the scholarship is being given, have maintained the scholastic average required by their school, are recommended by their counselor or school officer, are not receiving an Indian Health Service Scholarship, have a career goal directly related to the needs of the Indian people, and are in financial need.

**Financial data:** Stipends range from $500 to $1,500 per year. Funds are to be used for tuition or fees. The money is sent directly to the recipient's school.

**Duration:** 1 year; those students who continue to meet the eligibility requirements and have been recommended for continuation are given priority consideration for additional periods of support.

**Number awarded:** Varies each year; recently, 17 of these scholarships were awarded.

## 2294 INDIANA AGRIBUSINESS FOUNDATION SCHOLARSHIPS

Agribusiness Council of Indiana, Attn: Indiana Agribusiness Foundation
2350 First Indiana Plaza
135 North Pennsylvania Street
Indianapolis, IN 46204
Phone: (317) 684-5438; (866) 222-6943; Fax: (317) 684-5423;
Email: jmelnyk@inagribiz.org

Web: www.inagribiz.org/iaf.asp

**Summary:** To provide financial assistance to Indiana residents interested in working on an undergraduate degree in a field related to agriculture.

**Eligibility:** Open to Indiana residents who are high school seniors or current undergraduate students. Applicants must be majoring in or planning to major in a field related to agriculture. They must submit 2 letters of recommendation, a recent transcript, and an essay on their course of study and its impact.

**Financial data:** Stipends are normally $1,000.

**Duration:** 1 year.

**Number awarded:** Varies each year; recently, 3 of these scholarships were awarded.

## 2295 INDIANA CHAPTER ACI SCHOLARSHIPS

American Concrete Institute-Indiana Chapter
c/o Brian Stater
Bowen Engineering Corporation, Inc.
10315 Allisonville Road
Fishers, IN 46038
Phone: (317) 842-2616; Fax: (317) 841-4257;
Email: brian@bowenengineering.com
Web: www.concrete.org/CHAPTERS/Chapter_Scholarships.asp?cid=C048

**Summary:** To provide financial assistance to students in Indiana working on a degree in a field related to the concrete industry.

**Eligibility:** Open to sophomores and juniors at colleges and universities in Indiana who are preparing for a career in concrete design or construction. Applicants must submit information on their work experience, career objectives, reasons for seeking this scholarship, and financial need.

**Financial data:** Stipends are $3,000, $2,000, or $1,000.

**Duration:** 1 year

**Number awarded:** 3 each year: 1 each at $3,000, $2,000, and $1,000.

**Deadline:** March of each year.

## 2296 INDIANA SCHOLARSHIP PROGRAM AWARDS

American Council of Engineering Companies of Indiana
Attn: Scholarship Coordinator
One Virginia Avenue, Suite 250
Indianapolis, IN 46204
Phone: (317) 637-3563; (317) 637-9968; Email: staff@acecindiana.org
Web: www.acecindiana.org/content/education.htm

**Summary:** To provide financial assistance to residents of Indiana currently working on a bachelor's degree in engineering or land surveying at a college or university in the state.

**Eligibility:** Open to Indiana residents who are working on a bachelor's degree in an ABET-approved engineering program or in an accredited land surveying program. Applicants must be U.S. citizens entering their junior, senior, or fifth year at a college or university in Indiana. Along with their application, they must submit a 500-word essay on "What is the role or responsibility of the consulting engineer or land surveyor to shaping and protecting the natural environment." Selection is based on the essay (25 points), cumulative GPA (28 points), work experience (20 points), a letter of recommendation (17 points), and college activities (10 points).

**Financial data:** Recently, a total of $18,000 in scholarships was awarded by this program.

**Duration:** 1 year.

**Number awarded:** Varies each year; recently, 6 of these scholarships were awarded.

**Deadline:** November of each year.

## 2297 INDUSTRY MINORITY SCHOLARSHIPS

American Meteorological Society, Attn: Fellowship/Scholarship Program
45 Beacon Street
Boston, MA 02108-3693
Phone: (617) 227-2426, ext. 246; Fax: (617) 742-8718;
Email: scholar@ametsoc.org
Web: www.ametsoc.org/amsstudentinfo/scholfeldocs/scholfel.html

**Summary:** To provide financial assistance to underrepresented minority students entering college and planning to major in meteorology or an aspect of atmospheric sciences.

**Eligibility:** Open to members of minority groups traditionally underrepresented in the sciences (Hispanics, Native Americans, and Black/African Americans) who are entering their freshman year at a college or university and planning to work on a degree in the atmospheric or related oceanic and hydrologic sciences. Applicants must submit an official high school transcript showing grades from the past 3 years, a letter of recommendation from a high school teacher or guidance counselor, a copy of scores from an SAT or similar national entrance exam, and a 500-word essay on how they would use their college education in atmospheric sciences (or a closely-related field) to make their community a better place in which to live. Selection is based on the essay and academic performance in high school.

**Financial data:** The stipend is $3,000 per year.

**Duration:** 1 year; may be renewed for the second year of college study.

**Number awarded:** Varies each year; recently, 10 of these scholarships were awarded.

**Deadline:** February of each year.

## 2298 INDUSTRY UNDERGRADUATE SCHOLARSHIPS

American Meteorological Society, Attn: Fellowship/Scholarship Coordinator
45 Beacon Street
Boston, MA 02108-3693
Phone: (617) 227-2426, ext. 246; Fax: (617) 742-8718;
Email: scholar@ametsoc.org
Web: www.ametsoc.org/amsstudentinfo/scholfeldocs/scholfel.html

**Summary:** To provide financial assistance to undergraduate students preparing for a career in the atmospheric and related oceanic and hydrologic sciences.

**Eligibility:** Open to full-time students entering their junior year who are either 1) enrolled or planning to enroll in a course of study leading to a bachelor's degree in the atmospheric or related oceanic or hydrologic sciences, or 2) enrolled in a program leading to a bachelor's degree in science or engineering who have demonstrated a clear intent to prepare for a career in the atmospheric or related oceanic or hydrologic sciences following completion of appropriate specialized education at the graduate level. Applicants must have a GPA of 3.25 or higher and be U.S. citizens or permanent residents. Along with their application, they must submit 200-word essays on 1) their most important achievements, and 2) their career goals. Selection is based on academic performance and recommendations. The sponsor specifically encourages applications from women, minorities, and students with disabilities who are traditionally underrepresented in the atmospheric and related oceanic sciences.

**Financial data:** The stipend is $2,000 per academic year.

**Duration:** 1 year; may be renewed for the final year of college study.

**Number awarded:** Varies each year; recently, 12 of these scholarships were awarded.

**Deadline:** February of each year.

## 2299 INSTITUTE OF FOOD TECHNOLOGISTS COLLEGE SCHOLARSHIPS

Institute of Food Technologists, Attn: Scholarship Department
525 West Van Buren, Suite 1000
Chicago, IL 60607
Phone: (312) 782-8424; Fax: (312) 782-8348; Email: info@ift.org
Web: www.ift.org

**Summary:** To provide financial assistance to undergraduates interested in studying food science or food technology.

**Eligibility:** Open to sophomores, juniors, and seniors in a food science or food technology program at an educational institution in the United States or Canada. Applicants must have an outstanding scholastic record and a well-rounded personality. Along with their application, they must submit an essay on their career aspirations; a list of awards, honors, and scholarships they have received; a list of extracurricular activities and/or hobbies; and a summary of their work experience. Financial need is not considered in the selection process.

**Financial data:** Stipends are $2,000, $1,500, or $1,000.

**Duration:** 1 year; recipients may reapply if they are members of the Institute of Food Technologists.

**Number awarded:** Varies each year; recently, 50 of these scholarships were awarded: 5 at $2,000, 2 at $1,500, and 43 at $1,000.

**Deadline:** January of each year.

## 2300 INSTITUTE OF FOOD TECHNOLOGISTS HIGH SCHOOL SCHOLARSHIPS

Institute of Food Technologists, Attn: Scholarship Department
525 West Van Buren, Suite 1000
Chicago, IL 60607
Phone: (312) 782-8424; Fax: (312) 782-8348; Email: info@ift.org
Web: www.ift.org

**Summary:** To provide financial assistance to high school seniors interested in studying food science or food technology in college.

**Eligibility:** Open to high school seniors planning to enroll in a food science or food technology program at an educational institution in the United States or Canada. Applicants must have an outstanding scholastic record and a well-rounded personality. Along with their application, they must submit a brief biographical sketch and a statement on why they would like to become a food technologist. Financial need is not considered in the selection process.

**Financial data:** Stipends are either $1,500 or $1,000.

**Duration:** 1 year; recipients may reapply if they are members of the Institute of Food Technologists.

**Number awarded:** Varies each year; recently, 23 of these scholarships were awarded: 1 at $1,500 and 22 at $1,000.

**Deadline:** February of each year.

## 2301 INSTITUTE OF FOOD TECHNOLOGISTS SOPHOMORE SCHOLARSHIPS

Institute of Food Technologists, Attn: Scholarship Department
525 West Van Buren, Suite 1000
Chicago, IL 60607
Phone: (312) 782-8424; Fax: (312) 782-8348; Email: info@ift.org
Web: www.ift.org

**Summary:** To provide financial assistance to lower-division students interested in majoring in food science or food technology.

**Eligibility:** Open to college freshmen entering their sophomore year in a food science or food technology program at an educational institution in the United States or Canada. Applicants must have an outstanding scholastic record (GPA of 2.5 or higher) and a well-rounded personality. Food science majors must submit an essay on why they want to continue in food technology; other majors and transfer students must submit a brief biographical sketch and an essay on why they would like to become a food technologist. Financial need is not considered in the selection process.

**Financial data:** The stipend is $1,000.

**Duration:** 1 year; recipients may reapply if they are members of the Institute of Food Technologists.

**Number awarded:** Varies each year; recently, 22 of these scholarships were awarded.

**Deadline:** February of each year.

## 2302 INTEL INTERNATIONAL SCIENCE AND ENGINEERING FAIR

Science Service, Attn: Director of Youth Programs
1719 N Street, N.W.
Washington, DC 20036
Phone: (202) 785-2255; Fax: (202) 785-1243; Email: sciedu@sciserv.org
Web: www.sciserv.org/isef

**Summary:** To recognize and reward outstanding high school students who enter a science and engineering competition.

**Eligibility:** Open to students from grades 9-12 who compete in one of approximately 500 affiliated Intel International Science and Engineering Fairs around the world. Each fair then sends 2 individuals and 1 team (up to 3 members) to compete in the ISEF in 1 of 15 categories: behavioral and social sciences, biochemistry, botany, chemistry, computer science, earth and space sciences, engineering, environmental science, gerontology, mathematics, medicine and health, microbiology, physics, team projects, and zoology. Each entry consists of a science project and a 250-word abstract that summarizes the project. Judging of individual projects is based on creative ability (30%), scientific thought or engineering goals (30%), thoroughness (15%), skill (15%), and clarity (10%).

**Financial data:** The Intel Foundation Young Scientist Awards, granted to the presenters of the most outstanding research, are $50,000. In each of the categories, the first-place winner receives a $3,000 cash award, second place $1,500, third place $1,000, and fourth place $500. The Intel Best of Category Awards, for the project that exemplifies the best in each scientific category that has also won a first-place in the category, are a $5,000 scholarship and a high-performance computer to the students, $1,000 to their schools, and $1,000 to their science fair. The Intel Achievement Awards are $5,000 each for outstanding work in any field. Other prizes, worth more than $1.5 million, include scholarships from individual colleges and universities, all-expense paid trips to scientific and engineering installations or national conventions, summer jobs at research institutes, and laboratory equipment provided by Intel. Many professional organizations award prizes for projects that meet specified criteria.

**Duration:** The fair is held annually. The Intel Foundation Young Scientist Awards are paid in 8 equal installments. Most other awards are for one year.

**Number awarded:** 3 Intel Foundation Young Scientist Awards are presented each year. In addition, 60 other cash awards are awarded: 4 in each of the 15 categories. Other awards include 14 Intel Best of Category Awards and 14 Intel

Achievement Awards. Many other special awards, regional awards, and scholarships from individual colleges are also presented.

**Deadline:** The fair is always held in May.

## 2303 INTEL SCIENCE TALENT SEARCH SCHOLARSHIPS

Science Service, Attn: Director of Youth Programs
1719 N Street, N.W.
Washington, DC 20036
Phone: (202) 785-2255; Fax: (202) 785-1243; Email: sciedu@sciserv.org
Web: www.sciserv.org/sts

**Summary:** To recognize and reward outstanding high school seniors who are interested in attending college to prepare for a career in mathematics, engineering, or any of the sciences.

**Eligibility:** Open to high school seniors in the United States and its territories, as well as those attending Department of Defense dependents schools and accredited overseas American and international schools. Applicants must complete an independent research project and submit a written report of up to 20 pages. The project may be in the following fields: behavioral and social sciences, biochemistry, botany, chemistry, computer science, earth and space sciences, engineering, environmental science, mathematics, medicine and health, microbiology, physics, and zoology. Based on those reports, 300 students are designated as semifinalists, and from those 40 are chosen as finalists. Selection is based on individual research ability, scientific originality, and creative thinking.

**Financial data:** Semifinalists and their schools each receive $1,000 awards. Among the finalists, first place is a $100,000 scholarship, second place a $75,000 scholarship, third place a $50,000 scholarship, fourth through sixth places $25,000 scholarships, and seventh through tenth places $20,000 scholarships. In addition, 30 other finalists receive $5,000 scholarships. The first 10 awards are paid in 8 equal installments.

**Duration:** The competition is held annually. Scholarships of the first 10 prize winners are for 4 years. The scholarships of the other 30 finalists are for one year.

**Number awarded:** Each year, 300 semifinalists are selected, and from those 40 are designated as finalists. Scholarships for finalists include 1 at $100,000, 1 at $75,000, 1 at $50,000, 3 at $25,000, 4 at $20,000, and 30 at $5,000.

**Deadline:** November of each year.

## 2304 INTERNATIONAL COMMUNICATIONS INDUSTRIES ASSOCIATION COLLEGE SCHOLARSHIPS

**Summary:** To provide financial assistance to college students in their final year of study who are interested in preparing for a career in the audiovisual industry. *See Listing #1474.*

## 2305 INTERNATIONAL FUTURE ENERGY CHALLENGE STUDENT COMPETITION

Institute of Electrical and Electronics Engineers
Industry Applications Society, Attn: Administrative Secretary
799 North Beverly Glen
Los Angeles, CA 90077
Phone: (310) 446-8360; Fax: (310) 446-8390; Email: bob.myers@ieee.org
Web: www.energychallenge.org

**Summary:** To recognize and reward undergraduate engineering students who design and build prototype equipment to support fuel cell power systems.

**Eligibility:** Open to teams of undergraduate students enrolled in an engineering program at a college or university that is ABET-accredited or equivalent. Applicants must have a faculty advisor and the support of the school's administration to design and build a prototype of a low-cost, manufacturable equipment that would accelerate deployment of distributed generation systems. They may submit an entry for one of the following topics: a single-phase adjustable speed motor drive, or a utility interactive inverter system for small distributed generation. Selection is based on cost effectiveness, performance, quality of the prototype and other results, engineering reports, adherence to rules and deadlines, innovation, future, and other criteria related to the specific topic.

**Financial data:** Prizes vary each year, depending on the funding available from sponsors. Recently, they ranged up to $10,000.

**Duration:** The competition is held biennially, extending from mid-May of each even-numbered year to mid-August of the following odd-numbered year.

**Number awarded:** Varies each year. Recently, prizes for the motor topic included first place at $10,000, outstanding design innovation at $6,500, outstanding educational impact at $2,000, outstanding presentation at $2,000, and outstanding technical report at $2,500. For the inverter topic, prizes included first place at $10,000, second place at $8,000, third place at $5,000, outstanding presentation at $2,000, outstanding technical report at $2,000, outstanding

educational impact at $1,500, innovative design at $1,500, innovative packaging at $1,000, and outstanding teamwork at $1,000.

**Deadline:** Initial proposals must be submitted by April of each even-numbered year.

## 2306 INTERNATIONAL STUDENT TECHNICAL COMMUNICATION COMPETITION

Society for Technical Communication
901 North Stuart Street, Suite 904
Arlington, VA 22203-1822
Phone: (703) 522-4114; Fax: (703) 522-2075; Email: stc@stc.org
Web: www.stc.org/studentCompetitions_ISTC.asp

**Summary:** To recognize and reward outstanding technical writing by high school students.

**Eligibility:** Open to students in grades 10 through 12 in any country. Applicants must submit a technical article to a local chapter of the Society for Technical Communication (STC). Entries must not have been entered in any other local or national STC competition. They may be co-authored by up to 4 students and up to 30 pages in length. Selection is based on the quality of writing, clarity of the thesis, significance of the topic, effectiveness of organization, soundness of the conclusions, use and documentation of reference materials, and use of visual and graphic aids.

**Financial data:** Awards are offered in 3 levels: Distinguished ($1,000), Excellence ($500), and Merit ($300).

**Duration:** The competition is held annually.

**Number awarded:** 3 each year.

**Deadline:** Local chapters must submit their winning entries to the international competition by January of each year.

## 2307 INTERNATIONAL SYMPOSIUM ON SUPERALLOYS SCHOLARSHIPS

The Minerals, Metals & Materials Society, Attn: TMS Student Awards Program
184 Thorn Hill Road
Warrendale, PA 15086-7514
Phone: (724) 776-9000, ext. 220; Fax: (724) 776-3770; Email: students@tms.org
Web: www.tms.org/Students/AwardsPrograms/Scholarships.html

**Summary:** To provide financial assistance to undergraduate and graduate student members of The Minerals, Metals & Materials Society (TMS).

**Eligibility:** Open to undergraduate and graduate members of the society who are full-time students majoring in metallurgical and/or materials science and engineering with an emphasis on aspects of the high-temperature, high-performance materials used in the gas turbine industry. Applicants may be from any country. Selection is based on academic achievement, school and community activities, work experience, leadership, a personal profile statement, and letters of recommendation.

**Financial data:** The stipend is $2,000.

**Duration:** 1 year.

**Number awarded:** 2 each year.

**Deadline:** April of each year.

## 2308 IOWA LEGION AUXILIARY PAST PRESIDENTS SCHOLARSHIP

American Legion Auxiliary
Department of Iowa, Attn: Education Committee
720 Lyon Street
Des Moines, IA 50309-5457
Phone: (515) 282-7987; Fax: (515) 282-7583; Email: alasectreas@ialegion.org

**Summary:** To provide financial assistance for nursing education to dependents of Iowa veterans and to veterans who are members of the American Legion.

**Eligibility:** Open to members of the American Legion and the American Legion Auxiliary and the children or grandchildren of veterans of World War I, World War II, Korea, Vietnam, Grenada, Lebanon, Panama, or the Persian Gulf. Applicants must reside in Iowa and be enrolled or planning to enroll in a nursing program in that state. Selection is based on character, Americanism, activities, and financial need.

**Financial data:** The amount of this scholarship depends on the contributions received from past unit, county, district, department, or national presidents.

**Duration:** 1 year.

**Number awarded:** 1 each year.

**Deadline:** May of each year.

## 2309 IOWA MOTOR CARRIERS FOUNDATION SCHOLARSHIPS

**Summary:** To provide financial assistance for college or the study of diesel technology to residents of Iowa.

*See Listing #489.*

## 2310 IOWA READY MIXED CONCRETE ASSOCIATION SCHOLARSHIP PROGRAM

Iowa Ready Mixed Concrete Association, Attn: Scholarship Committee
380 S.E. Delaware Avenue
Ankeny, IA 50021
Phone: (515) 965-4575; Fax: (515) 963-4010
Web: www.iowareadymix.org

**Summary:** To provide financial assistance to undergraduates at colleges and universities in Iowa who are preparing for a career in the concrete, construction, or engineering industries.

**Eligibility:** Open to students who have achieved at least sophomore status at a 4-year college or university in Iowa. Applicants must be working on a degree in an area that will prepare them for a career in the ready mixed concrete or construction and engineering industries. Preference is given to applicants who are residents of Iowa, related to an employee of a member company of the Iowa Ready Mixed Concrete Association, and experienced in the ready mixed concrete industry. Along with their application, they must submit a 1-page essay explaining their career goals, why they are applying for a scholarship, and why they might consider employment in the ready mixed concrete, construction, or engineering fields.

**Financial data:** Stipends are $1,000 or $500.

**Duration:** 1 year.

**Number awarded:** At least 3 scholarships at $1,000 and 4 at $500 are awarded each year.

**Deadline:** December of each year.

## 2311 IRENE E. NEWMAN SCHOLARSHIP

American Dental Hygienists' Association, Attn: Institute for Oral Health
444 North Michigan Avenue, Suite 3400
Chicago, IL 60611
Phone: (312) 440-8918; (800) 735-4916; Fax: (312) 440-8929;
Email: institute@adha.net
Web: www.adha.org/institute/Scholarship/index.htm

**Summary:** To provide financial assistance to students in a baccalaureate or graduate degree program in dental hygiene who demonstrate strong potential in public health or community dental health.

**Eligibility:** Open to students who have completed at least one year in a dental hygiene program at the baccalaureate, master's, or doctoral level with a GPA of at least 3.0. Applicants must demonstrate strong potential in public health or community dental health. They must be active members of the Student American Dental Hygienists' Association (SADHA) or the American Dental Hygienists' Association (ADHA) and be able to document financial need of at least $1,500. Along with their application, they must submit a statement that covers their long-term career goals, their intended contribution to the dental hygiene profession, their professional interests, and the manner in which their degree will enhance their professional capacity. Graduate applicants must also include a description of the research in which they are involved or would like to become involved and a list of past and/or present involvement in professional and/or community activities. and full-time enrollment. Selection is based on their potential in public health or community dental health.

**Financial data:** Stipends range from $1,000 to $2,000.

**Duration:** 1 year.

**Number awarded:** 1 each year.

**Deadline:** April of each year.

## 2312 ISA EDUCATIONAL FOUNDATION SCHOLARSHIPS

Instrumentation, Systems, and Automation Society
Attn: ISA Educational Foundation
67 Alexander Drive
Research Triangle Park, NC 27709
Phone: (919) 549-8411; Fax: (919) 549-8288; Email: info@isa.org
Web: www.isa.org

**Summary:** To provide financial assistance to undergraduate and graduate students majoring in fields related to instrumentation, systems, and automation.

**Eligibility:** Open to full-time undergraduate and graduate students enrolled in a program in instrumentation, systems, automation, or a closely-related field. Applicants must have a GPA of 3.0 or higher. They may be from any country but must be attending an institution in their own country. Applicants in a 2-year program must have completed at least 1 academic semester of 12 hours or its equivalent. Applicants in a 4-year program must be in their sophomore year or higher. Along with their application, they must submit an essay (up to 400 words) on their ambitions and qualifications as an innovator or future leader in a career in instrumentation, systems, or automation; they should describe their career objectives, how the award of this scholarship will help them attain their objectives, why they want to enter this particular field of engineering, what they have achieved and learned through their studies and activities, and what this indicates about their character and determination. Financial need is not considered in the selection process.

**Financial data:** Stipends have ranged from $700 to $3,500.

**Duration:** 1 year; may be renewed.

**Number awarded:** Varies each year. Recently, 5 of these scholarships were awarded: 4 to undergraduates (at $700, $1,000, $3,000, and $3,500) and 1 to a graduate student (at $3,000).

**Deadline:** February of each year.

## 2313 ISADORE N. STERN SCHOLARSHIPS

American Society of Radiologic Technologists
Attn: ASRT Education and Research Foundation
15000 Central Avenue, S.E.
Albuquerque, NM 87123-3917
Phone: (505) 298-4500; (800) 444-2778, ext. 2541; Fax: (505) 298-5063;
Email: foundation@asrt.org
Web: www.asrt.org

**Summary:** To provide financial assistance to members of the American Society of Radiologic Technologists (ASRT) who are interested in continuing their education.

**Eligibility:** Open to licensed radiologic technologists who are current members of ASRT and have worked in the radiologic sciences profession for at least 1 year during the past 5 years in a clinical or didactic setting. Applicants must have applied to 1) an accredited certificate program related to the radiologic sciences, or 2) a course of study at the associate's, baccalaureate, master's, or doctoral level intended to further their career. Along with their application, they must submit an essay of 750 words or less that covers their professional, educational, and career goals and how this scholarship will help them achieve those goals. Financial need is considered in the selection process.

**Financial data:** The stipend is $1,000.

**Duration:** 1 year; may be renewed for 1 additional year.

**Number awarded:** Varies each year; recently, 9 of these scholarships were awarded.

**Deadline:** January of each year.

## 2314 ISPE FOUNDATION SCHOLARSHIP

Illinois Society of Professional Engineers, Attn: ISPE Foundation, Inc.
600 South Second Street, Suite 403
Springfield, IL 62704
Phone: (217) 544-7424; Fax: (217) 528-6545;
Email: info@IllinoisEngineer.com
Web: www.ilspe.com/StudentsAndYouth.asp

**Summary:** To provide financial assistance to college juniors and seniors in Illinois who are working on an engineering degree.

**Eligibility:** Open to Illinois residents who are juniors or seniors enrolled in an ABET-accredited engineering program (not engineering technology) program in the state. Applicants must have at least a 3.0 GPA in those courses that count toward their engineering degree. Selection is based on financial need, scholastic achievement, activities, interest in engineering, and a 200-word essay on "Why I would like to become a professional engineer."

**Financial data:** The stipend is $1,200 per year.

**Duration:** 1 year.

**Number awarded:** 1 each year.

**Deadline:** January of each year.

## 2315 ISTMA SCHOLARSHIPS

Iowa Sports Turf Manager's Association
c/o Iowa Turf Office
17017 U.S. Highway 69
Ames, IA 50010-9294
Phone: (515) 232-8222; (800) 605-0420; Fax: (515) 232-8228
Web: www.iowaturfgrass.org/istma/istmascholarships.htm

**Summary:** To provide financial assistance to students enrolled or planning to enroll in a turfgrass management program at a college or university in Iowa.

**Eligibility:** Open to 1) seniors at high schools in Iowa planning to enroll in turfgrass management or a related program at a university, college, area technical school, or community college in Iowa; and 2) students already enrolled in such a program. Applicants must submit answers to essay questions on what stimulated their initial interest in the sports turf management profession, what they expect from a career as a sports turf manager, and their goals in the next 10 years. Selection is based on their answers to those essay questions, academic excellence and GPA, appropriateness of career preparation, potential to make an outstanding professional contribution, class rank, and reports from academic advisors and employers. Financial need is also considered.

**Financial data:** A stipend is awarded (amount not specified).

**Duration:** 1 year.

**Number awarded:** 1 or more each year.

**Deadline:** October of each year.

## 2316 ITEA UNDERGRADUATE SCHOLARSHIP IN TECHNOLOGY EDUCATION

International Technology Education Association
1914 Association Drive, Suite 201
Reston, VA 20191-1539
Phone: (703) 860-2100; Fax: (703) 860-0353; Email: iteaordr@iris.org
Web: www.iteawww.org

**Summary:** To provide financial support to undergraduate members of the International Technology Education Association (ITEA) who are majoring in technology education teacher preparation.

**Eligibility:** Open to members of the association (membership may be enclosed with the scholarship application), in college but not yet seniors, majoring in technology education teacher preparation with a GPA of 2.5 or higher, and enrolled full time. Applicants must submit a statement on their personal interest in teaching technology, their resume or vitae, a copy of their college transcript, and 3 faculty recommendations.

**Financial data:** The stipend is $1,000. Funds are provided directly to the recipient.

**Duration:** 1 year.

**Number awarded:** 1 or more each year.

**Deadline:** November of each year.

## 2317 ITW WELDING COMPANIES SCHOLARSHIP

American Welding Society, Attn: AWS Foundation, Inc.
550 N.W. LeJeune Road
Miami, FL 33126
Phone: (305) 445-6628; (800) 443-9353, ext. 461; Fax: (305) 443-7559;
Email: found@aws.org
Web: www.aws.org/foundation/scholarships/itw.html

**Summary:** To provide financial assistance to college seniors majoring in welding engineering.

**Eligibility:** Open to entering college seniors who are working full time on a 4-year bachelor's degree in welding engineering or welding engineering technology; preference is given to welding engineering technology students. Applicants must have an overall GPA of 3.0 or higher. Financial need is not required. Priority is given to applicants who exhibit a strong interest in welding equipment and have prior work experience in the welding equipment field. Priority is also given to applicants who attend Ferris State University. U.S. citizenship is required.

**Financial data:** The stipend is $3,000.

**Duration:** 1 year; nonrenewable.

**Number awarded:** 2 each year.

**Deadline:** January of each year.

## 2318 IVY PARKER MEMORIAL SCHOLARSHIP

Society of Women Engineers
230 East Ohio Street, Suite 400
Chicago, IL 60611-3265
Phone: (312) 596-5223; Fax: (312) 644-8557; Email: hq@swe.org
Web: www.societyofwomenengineers.org/scholarships

**Summary:** To provide financial assistance to upper-division women majoring in computer science or engineering.

**Eligibility:** Open to women who are entering their junior or senior year at an ABET-accredited college or university. Applicants must be majoring in computer science or engineering and have a GPA of 3.0 or higher. Along with their application, they must submit a 1-page essay on why they want to be an engineer or computer scientist, how they believe they will make a difference as an engineer or computer scientist, and what influenced them to study engineering or computer science. Financial need is considered in the selection process.

**Financial data:** The stipend is $2,500.

**Duration:** 1 year.

**Number awarded:** 1 each year.

**Deadline:** January of each year.

## 2319 J. FIELDING REED SCHOLARSHIP

American Society of Agronomy, Attn: Scholarship Committee
677 South Segoe Road
Madison, WI 53711
Phone: (608) 273-8008; Fax: (608) 273-2021; Email: awards@agronomy.org
Web: www.asa-cssa-sssa.org/awards

**Summary:** To provide financial assistance to upper-division students preparing for a career in soil or plant sciences.

**Eligibility:** Open to undergraduates with at least junior standing who are preparing for a career in the plant or soil sciences. Applicants must be graduating in the year in which the scholarship is presented. They must have a GPA of 3.0 or higher and be able to document a history of community and campus leadership activities, particularly in agriculture.

**Financial data:** The stipend is $2,000.

**Duration:** 1 year.

**Number awarded:** 1 each year.

**Deadline:** March of each year.

## 2320 J. KEITH BRIMACOMBE PRESIDENTIAL SCHOLARSHIP

The Minerals, Metals & Materials Society, Attn: TMS Student Awards Program
184 Thorn Hill Road
Warrendale, PA 15086-7514
Phone: (724) 776-9000, ext. 220; Fax: (724) 776-3770;
Email: students@tms.org
Web: www.tms.org/Students/AwardsPrograms/Scholarships.html

**Summary:** To provide financial assistance to student members of The Minerals, Metals & Materials Society (TMS).

**Eligibility:** Open to undergraduate members of the society who are full-time students majoring in metallurgical engineering, materials science and engineering, or minerals processing and extraction. Applicants may be from any country. Selection is based on academic achievement, school and community activities, work experience, leadership, a personal profile statement, and letters of recommendation.

**Financial data:** The stipend is $5,000 plus a travel stipend of $1,000 (so the recipient can attend the annual meeting of the society to accept the award).

**Duration:** 1 year.

**Number awarded:** 1 each year.

**Deadline:** April of each year.

## 2321 JACK BRUCE MEMORIAL SCHOLARSHIP

American Council of Engineering Companies of Colorado
Attn: Scholarship Coordinator
899 Logan Street, Suite 109
Denver, CO 80203
Phone: (303) 832-2200; (303) 832-0400; Email: aced@acec-co.org
Web: www.acec-co.org/education/qualifications.html

**Summary:** To provide financial assistance to students in Colorado currently working on a bachelor's degree in engineering.

**Eligibility:** Open to students working on a bachelor's degree in an ABET-approved engineering program in Colorado. Applicants must be U.S. citizens entering their junior, senior, or fifth year. Along with their application, they must submit a 500-word essay on "What is the role or responsibility of the consulting engineer or land surveyor in shaping and protecting the natural environment?" Selection is based on the essay (25 points), cumulative GPA (28 points), work experience (20 points), a letter of recommendation (17 points), and college activities (10 points).

**Financial data:** The stipend is $2,000.

**Duration:** 1 year.

**Number awarded:** 1 each year.

**Deadline:** January of each year.

## 2322 JACK E. BARGER, SR. MEMORIAL NURSING SCHOLARSHIPS

Nursing Foundation of Pennsylvania, Attn: Awards Committee
2578 Interstate Drive, Suite 101
Harrisburg, PA 17110
Phone: (717) 657-1222; (888) 707-PSNA, ext. 205; Fax: (717) 657-3796;
Email: panurses@panurses.org
Web: www.psna.org
**Summary:** To provide financial assistance to veterans, military personnel, and their dependents who are studying nursing in Pennsylvania.
**Eligibility:** Open to veterans, active-duty military personnel, and the children and spouses of veterans and active-duty military personnel. Applicants must be residents of Pennsylvania and currently enrolled in an undergraduate professional school of nursing in the state. Recipients are selected by lottery from among the qualified applicants.
**Financial data:** The stipend is $1,000.
**Duration:** 1 year.
**Number awarded:** 6 each year.
**Deadline:** April of each year.

## 2323 JACOB VAN NAMEN SCHOLARSHIP

Floriculture Industry Research and Scholarship Trust
Attn: Scholarship Program
P.O. Box 280
East Lansing, MI 48826-0280
Phone: (517) 333-4617; Fax: (517) 333-4494;
Email: scholarships@firstinfloriculture.org
Web: www.firstinfloriculture.org
**Summary:** To provide financial assistance to college students preparing for a career in the business of horticulture.
**Eligibility:** Open to undergraduate students at 4-year colleges and universities who are horticulture majors involved in agribusiness marketing and distribution of floral products. Applicants must be U.S. or Canadian citizens or permanent residents with a GPA of 3.0 or higher. Selection is based on academic record, recommendations, career goals, extracurricular activities, and financial need.
**Financial data:** The stipend depends on the availability of funds. Recently, it was $1,000.
**Duration:** 1 year.
**Number awarded:** 1 each year.
**Deadline:** April of each year.

## 2324 JAMES A. HOLEKAMP MEMORIAL SCHOLARSHIP IN FOREST RESOURCES

Technical Association of the Pulp and Paper Industry
Attn: TAPPI Foundation
15 Technology Parkway South
Norcross, GA 30092
Phone: (770) 209-7536; (800) 332-8686; Fax: (770) 446-6947;
Email: vedmondson@tappi.org
Web: www.tappi.org
**Summary:** To provide financial assistance to college students enrolled in a school of forest resources in the South.
**Eligibility:** Open to rising sophomores who are enrolled in a school of forest resources located in one of the southern states. Applicants must include a summary of their goals after graduation. Financial need is considered in the selection process.
**Financial data:** The stipend is $2,000.
**Duration:** 1 year.
**Number awarded:** 1 each year.
**Deadline:** May of each year.

## 2325 JAMES E. ADAMS MEMORIAL SCHOLARSHIP

California Land Surveyors Association, Attn: CLSA Education Foundation
P.O. Box 9098
Santa Rosa, CA 95405-9990
Phone: (707) 578-6016; Fax: (707) 578-4406;
Email: clsa@californiasurveyors.org
Web: californiasurveyors.org/files/scholarsh.html
**Summary:** To provide financial assistance to residents of California studying fields related to surveying in college.

**Eligibility:** Open to California residents currently enrolled in 1) an accredited baccalaureate program in surveying, or 2) an associate's degree program in surveying or survey engineering with the intent to attend an accredited baccalaureate program in surveying or prepare for a career in the land surveying profession. Applicants must have a GPA of 2.5 or higher in college and 3.0 or higher in their major and must be able to demonstrate leadership roles and activity in surveying associations and in educating others. Along with their application, they must submit an essay on their educational objectives, future plans for study or research, professional activities, or need. Selection is based on the essay (30%), academic record (30%), letters of recommendation (20%), and professional activities (20%). Financial need may be considered if other criteria result in a tie.
**Financial data:** The stipend is $1,000.
**Duration:** 1 year.
**Number awarded:** 1 each year.
**Deadline:** December of each year.

## 2326 JAMES E. ROBERTS ENGINEERING SCHOLARSHIP

California Department of Transportation
Attn: Division of Engineering Services
MS 9 5/2J
P.O. Box 168041
Sacramento, CA 95816-8041
Phone: (916) 227-8126; Email: karen_bailey@dot.ca.gov
Web: www.dot.ca.gov/hq/esc/scholarships
**Summary:** To provide financial assistance to high school seniors in California who plan to study civil engineering at a college or university in the state in order to prepare for a career in transportation.
**Eligibility:** Open to seniors graduating from high schools in California and planning to enroll in a civil engineering program at a community college, state college, or university in the state. Applicants must be planning to prepare for a career in transportation. Along with their application, they must submit a 100-word personal statement on their college and career plans and how they believe they can make a contribution to Caltrans as a civil engineer in the transportation field. Selection is based on that statement, community and school activities, work and/or volunteer experience, letters of recommendation, and financial need.
**Financial data:** The stipend is $1,000.
**Duration:** 1 year.
**Number awarded:** 2 each year.
**Deadline:** March

## 2327 JAMES F. REVILLE SCHOLARSHIP

NYSARC, Inc.
393 Delaware Avenue
Delmar, NY 12054
Phone: (518) 439-8311; Fax: (518) 439-1893; Email: info@nysarc.org
Web: www.nysarc.org/family/nysarc-family-scholarships-list.asp
**Summary:** To provide financial assistance to currently-enrolled college students in New York majoring in a field related to mental retardation.
**Eligibility:** Open to high school graduates enrolled full time in any year of college training in a field related to mental retardation. Applications are available through local chapters of NYSARC.
**Financial data:** The stipend is $1,500 per year.
**Duration:** 2 years.
**Number awarded:** 1 each year.
**Deadline:** February of each year.

## 2328 JAMES H. DAVIS MEMORIAL SCHOLARSHIP

National Foliage Foundation
c/o Florida Nursery, Growers and Landscape Association
1533 Park Center Drive
Orlando, FL 32835-5705
Phone: (407) 295-7994; (800) 375-3642; Fax: (407) 295-1619;
Email: lreindl@fngla.org
Web: www.fngla.org/resear-scholar/scholarships.asp
**Summary:** To provide financial assistance to undergraduate and graduate students in Florida who are interested in a career in the horticulture industry.
**Eligibility:** Open to incoming freshmen, sophomores, juniors, seniors, and graduate students planning to attend a college, university, community college, or other postsecondary program in Florida. Applicants must enroll full time in a horticulture program or related field with the intent to graduate in that field.

They must have a GPA of 2.0 or higher. Along with their application, they must submit a short essay about themselves that includes their work and classroom experience with horticulture or related field, the area of horticulture or related field that they are interested in pursuing, what they plan to do after graduation, and why they are qualified to receive the scholarship. Selection is based on the essay, 2 letters of recommendation, transcripts, and financial need.

**Financial data:** A stipend is awarded (amount not specified).

**Duration:** 1 year.

**Number awarded:** Varies each year; recently, 21 of these scholarships were awarded.

**Deadline:** January of each year.

## 2329 JAMES L. ALLHANDS ESSAY COMPETITION

Associated General Contractors of America
Attn: AGC Education and Research Foundation
333 John Carlyle Street, Suite 200
Alexandria, VA 22314
Phone: (703) 548-3118; Fax: (703) 548-3119; Email: agcf@agc.org
Web: www.agc.org/EducationTraining/program_desc.asp

**Summary:** To recognize and reward outstanding student essays on a topic related to construction or civil engineering.

**Eligibility:** Open to college seniors who are enrolled in a 4-year construction or construction-related civil engineering degree program. Applicants must submit an essay, up to 10 pages in length, on a topic that changes annually; recently, it was "The importance of certifying professional constructors." Selection is based on clear expression of thought, completeness of subject coverage, use of specific examples to support opinions, grammar, neatness, creativity, originality and uniqueness of ideas, and adherence to competition guidelines for essay length.

**Financial data:** The first-prize winner receives $1,000 and a trip to the annual convention of the Associated General Contractors (AGC) of America; the second-prize winner receives $500; the third-prize winner receives $300. In addition, the faculty sponsor of the first-prize winner receives $500 and a trip to the AGC convention.

**Duration:** The competition is held annually.

**Deadline:** October of each year.

## 2330 JAMES L. GOODWIN MEMORIAL SCHOLARSHIPS

Connecticut Forest and Park Association
16 Meriden Road
Rockfall, CT 06481-2961
Phone: (860) 346-2372; Fax: (860) 347-7463; Email: info@ctwoodlands.org
Web: www.ctwoodlands.org

**Summary:** To provide financial assistance to residents of Connecticut interested in studying forestry or forest management at the undergraduate or graduate level.

**Eligibility:** Open to Connecticut residents who are graduating high school seniors, currently enrolled in college, or graduate students. Applicants must be attending or planning to attend the University of Connecticut or another school accredited in forest management. Selection is based on financial need, academic record, and a personal statement on why the applicant in interested in forestry or forest management.

**Financial data:** Stipends range from $1,000 to $3,000 per year. Funds may be used for tuition or living costs. Payment is made only to the institution.

**Duration:** 1 year; may be renewed.

**Number awarded:** 5 to 10 each year.

**Deadline:** March of each year.

## 2331 JAMES R. VOGT RADIOCHEMISTRY SCHOLARSHIP

American Nuclear Society, Attn: Scholarship Coordinator
555 North Kensington Avenue
La Grange Park, IL 60526-5592
Phone: (708) 352-6611; Fax: (708) 352-0499; Email: outreach@ans.org
Web: www.ans.org/honors/scholarships

**Summary:** To provide financial assistance to undergraduate and graduate students who are interested in preparing for a career in nuclear science.

**Eligibility:** Open to juniors, seniors, and first-year graduate students who are enrolled in or proposing to undertake research in radio-analytical chemistry, analytical chemistry, or analytical applications of nuclear science. Applicants must be U.S. citizens or permanent residents and able to demonstrate academic achievement.

**Financial data:** The stipend is $2,000 for undergraduate students or $3,000 for graduate students.

**Duration:** 1 year; nonrenewable.

**Number awarded:** 1 each year.

**Deadline:** January of each year.

## 2332 JEAN LEE/JEFF MARVIN COLLEGIATE SCHOLARSHIPS

**Summary:** To provide financial assistance to upper-division students in Indiana who are majoring in health, physical education, recreation, or dance. *See Listing #1487.*

## 2333 JEANNE M. CROWLEY SCHOLARSHIP

AGC of Massachusetts, Attn: Scholarship Selection Panel
888 Worcester Street, Suite 40
Wellesley, MA 02482-3708
Phone: (781) 235-2680; Fax: (781) 235-6020; Email: info@agcmass.org
Web: www.agcmass.org

**Summary:** To provide financial assistance to women residents of Massachusetts who are attending college to prepare for a career in construction.

**Eligibility:** Open to women who are currently enrolled as a college sophomore or junior. Applicants must be residents of Massachusetts, although they may be attending college in any state. They must be full-time students working on a bachelor's degree in construction, civil engineering, construction management, or other field to prepare for a career in construction. Along with their application, they must submit essays on their most important extracurricular activities, their interest in a construction industry career, and any special circumstances concerning their financial need.

**Financial data:** A stipend is awarded (amount not specified).

**Duration:** 1 year; recipients may reapply.

**Number awarded:** 1 or more each year.

**Deadline:** September of each year.

## 2334 JEMS/ELSEVIER NURSING SCHOLARSHIP

Emergency Nurses Association, Attn: ENA Foundation
915 Lee Street
Des Plaines, IL 60016-6569
Phone: (847) 460-4100; (800) 900-9659, ext. 4100; Fax: (847) 460-4004;
Email: foundation@ena.org
Web: www.ena.org/foundation/grants

**Summary:** To provide financial assistance to pre-hospital personnel working on an undergraduate degree in nursing.

**Eligibility:** Open to pre-hospital personnel (emergency medical technician or EMT-paramedic) who are going to school to work on an undergraduate nursing degree. Applicants must submit proof of acceptance into an undergraduate nursing program and proof of at least one year of pre-hospital work experience. Along with their application, they must submit a 1-page statement on their professional and educational goals and how this scholarship will help them attain those goals. Selection is based on content and clarity of the goal statement (45%), professional involvement (45%), and GPA (10%).

**Financial data:** The stipend is $5,000.

**Duration:** 1 year.

**Number awarded:** 1 each year.

**Deadline:** May of each year.

## 2335 JENNET COLLIFLOWER KEYS NURSING SCHOLARSHIP

Dade Community Foundation
Attn: Director of Development and Communications
200 South Biscayne Boulevard, Suite 505
Miami, FL 33131-2343
Phone: (305) 371-2711; Fax: (305) 371-5342;
Email: joe.pena@dadecommunityfoundation.org
Web: www.dadecommunityfoundation.org/Site/programs/scholarships.jsp

**Summary:** To provide financial assistance to upper-division students in Florida who are working on a degree in nursing.

**Eligibility:** Open to students entering their junior or senior year of an undergraduate nursing program. Applicants must be Florida residents enrolled full time in a public or private university in the state. Selection is based on financial need, academic achievement, personal aspirations, career goals and relationship with nursing, volunteer experience, work experience, and school activities.

**Financial data:** The stipend is $1,000.

**Duration:** 1 year.

**Number awarded:** 2 each year.

**Deadline:** May of each year.

## 2336 JERE W. THOMPSON, JR. SCHOLARSHIP

Dallas Foundation, Attn: Scholarship Administrator
900 Jackson Street, Suite 150
Dallas, TX 75202
Phone: (214) 741-9898; Fax: (214) 741-9848;
Email: cmcnally@dallasfoundation.org
Web: www.dallasfoundation.org/gs_schFundProfiles.cfm

**Summary:** To provide financial assistance and work experience to disadvantaged students majoring in civil engineering at public universities in Texas.

**Eligibility:** Open to disadvantaged students in civil engineering or construction engineering at public colleges and universities in Texas; special consideration is given to residents of counties in the service area of the North Texas Tollway Authority: Collin, Dallas, Denton, or Tarrant. At the time of application, students must be full-time sophomores. Finalists may be interviewed. Financial need is considered in the selection process.

**Financial data:** Stipends range up to $2,000 per semester, beginning in the recipient's junior year. The maximum award is $8,000 over 4 semesters.

**Duration:** 1 semester; may be renewed for up to 3 additional semesters, provided the recipient remains a full-time student, maintains at least a 2.5 GPA, and submits a grade report within 45 days after the end of each semester.

**Number awarded:** 1 each year.

**Deadline:** March of each year.

## 2337 JERMAN-CAHOON STUDENT SCHOLARSHIP

American Society of Radiologic Technologists
Attn: ASRT Education and Research Foundation
15000 Central Avenue, S.E.
Albuquerque, NM 87123-3917
Phone: (505) 298-4500; (800) 444-2778, ext. 2541; Fax: (505) 298-5063;
Email: foundation@asrt.org
Web: www.asrt.org

**Summary:** To provide financial assistance to students enrolled in entry-level radiologic sciences programs.

**Eligibility:** Open to U.S. citizens, nationals, and permanent residents who are enrolled in an entry-level radiologic sciences program. Applicants must have a GPA in radiologic sciences core courses of 3.0 or higher and be able to demonstrate financial need. They may not have a previous degree or certificate in the radiologic sciences. Along with their application, they must submit an essay of 450 to 500 words on their reason for entering the radiologic sciences, career goals, and financial need.

**Financial data:** The stipend is $2,500.

**Duration:** 1 year; may be renewed for 1 additional year.

**Number awarded:** Varies each year; recently, 5 of these scholarships were awarded.

**Deadline:** January of each year.

## 2338 JEROME AND JEANETTE COHEN SCHOLARSHIP

Missouri Society of Professional Engineers
Attn: MSPE Educational Foundation
200 East McCarty Street, Suite 200
Jefferson City, MO 65101-3113
Phone: (573) 636-4861; (888) 666-4861; Fax: (573) 636-5475;
Email: jillryan@mspe.org
Web: www.mspe.org

**Summary:** To provide financial assistance to high school seniors in Missouri who are interested in studying engineering at selected universities in the state.

**Eligibility:** Open to high school seniors who are residents of Missouri planning to enroll in an engineering program at one of the following institutions in the state: University of Missouri, College of Engineering, Columbia; University of Missouri, School of Engineering, Kansas City; University of Missouri, School of Engineering, Rolla; University of Missouri, School of Mines and Metallurgy, Rolla; St. Louis University, Parks College of Engineering and Aviation, St. Louis; Southeast Missouri State University, SEMO Physics Program, Cape Girardeau; and Washington University, School of Engineering and Applied Sciences, St. Louis. Applicants must have a GPA of 3.0 or higher and minimum ACT scores of 29 in mathematics and 25 in English. Along with their application, they must submit a 300-word essay on their career plans. Selection is based on the essay (20 points); GPA (20 points); ACT scores (20 points); volunteer activities, work experience, honors, and scholarships (20 points); recommendations from at least 2 teachers (10 points); class ranking (5 points); and completeness of the application (5 points).

**Financial data:** The stipend is $1,500.

**Duration:** 1 year.

**Number awarded:** 1 each year.

**Deadline:** January of each year.

## 2339 JERRY ROBINSON–INWELD CORPORATION SCHOLARSHIP

American Welding Society, Attn: AWS Foundation, Inc.
550 N.W. LeJeune Road
Miami, FL 33126
Phone: (305) 445-6628; (800) 443-9353, ext. 461; Fax: (305) 443-7559;
Email: found@aws.org
Web: www.aws.org/foundation/scholarships/robinson.html

**Summary:** To provide financial assistance to needy high school seniors and graduates interested in preparing for a career in welding.

**Eligibility:** Open to students with significant financial need interested in preparing for a career in welding. By the beginning of the academic year the scholarship is awarded, applicants must 1) be at least 18 years of age, 2) have a high school diploma or GED, 3) have a GPA of 2.5 or higher, 4) have been accepted at a 4-year college or university, and 5) plan to attend full time. They must submit an essay on why the funds are needed, how the scholarship would change their life, and how it would allow them to further the joining sciences. U.S. citizenship is required.

**Financial data:** The stipend is $2,500 per year.

**Duration:** Up to 4 years, provided the recipient maintains full-time status, an acceptable GPA, and enrollment in a welding program.

**Number awarded:** 1 each year.

**Deadline:** January of each year.

## 2340 JIM MURRAY SCHOLARSHIPS

American Public Works Association-Colorado Chapter
c/o Paul A. Hindman
Urban Drainage and Flood Control District
2480 West 26th Avenue, Suite 156-B
Denver, CO 80211
Phone: (303) 455-6277; Fax: (303) 455-7880; Email: coloapwa@eazy.net
Web: www.coloapwa.org/scholarships/scholar.html

**Summary:** To provide financial assistance to civil engineering undergraduate and master's degree students in Colorado.

**Eligibility:** Open to juniors, seniors, and fifth-year undergraduates at colleges and universities in Colorado that have an accredited program in civil engineering. Students entering a master's degree program in civil engineering with an emphasis on a public works field are also eligible. Applicants must have a GPA of 2.5 or higher. Along with their application, they must submit a 300-word essay on an engineering problem over which a local, state, or federal government has jurisdiction, and how they would solve it. Financial need is not considered in the selection process.

**Financial data:** Stipends are $2,500, $2,250, $2,000, or $1,500.

**Duration:** 1 year.

**Number awarded:** At each accredited university in Colorado with a civil engineering program, 1 scholarship at $2,500, 1 at $2,250, 2 at $2,000, and 1 at $1,500 are awarded each year.

**Deadline:** March of each year.

## 2341 JIMMY A. YOUNG MEMORIAL EDUCATION RECOGNITION AWARD

American Association for Respiratory Care
Attn: American Respiratory Care Foundation
9425 North MacArthur Boulevard, Suite 100
Irving, TX 75063-4706
Phone: (972) 243-2272; Fax: (972) 484-2720; Email: info@aarc.org
Web: www.aarc.org/awards/young.html

**Summary:** To provide financial assistance to college students, especially minorities, interested in becoming respiratory therapists.

**Eligibility:** Open to students enrolled in an accredited respiratory therapy program who have completed at least one semester/quarter of the program and have a GPA of 3.0 or higher. Preference is given to nominees of minority origin. Applications must include 6 copies of an original referenced paper on some aspect of respiratory care and letters of recommendation. The foundation prefers that the candidates be nominated by a school or program, but any student may initiate a request for sponsorship by a school (in order that a deserving candidate is not denied the opportunity to compete simply because the school does not initiate the application).

**Financial data:** The stipend is $1,000. The award also provides airfare, one night's lodging, and registration for the association's international congress.

**Duration:** 1 year.

**Number awarded:** 1 each year.

**Deadline:** June of each year.

## 2342 JOE D. SIMMONS MEMORIAL SCHOLARSHIP

American Society for Quality, Attn: Measurement Quality Division
600 North Plankinton Avenue
P.O. Box 3005
Milwaukee, WI 53201-3005
Phone: (414) 272-8575; (800) 248-1946; Fax: (414) 272-1734;
Email: cs@asqu.org
Web: www.asq.org/measure/scholarship/index.html

**Summary:** To provide financial assistance to undergraduate and graduate students working on a degree in a field related to metrology and quality.

**Eligibility:** Open to undergraduate and graduate students who are working on a degree in a field of study related to measurement science and quality. Applicants must submit a 1,000-word essay describing the metrology and quality concepts they have learned and applied in academic or work settings and their career aspirations. Financial need is also considered in the selection process.

**Financial data:** The stipend is $1,500 per year.

**Duration:** 1 year.

**Number awarded:** 1 or more each year.

**Deadline:** April of each year.

## 2343 JOE RODRIGUEZ JR. SCHOLARSHIP

Portuguese Heritage Scholarship Foundation, Attn: Academic Secretary
P.O. Box 30246
Bethesda, MD 20824-0246
Phone: (301) 652-2775; Email: phsf@vivaportugal.com
Web: www.vivaportugal.com/phsf/apply.htm

**Summary:** To provide financial assistance for college to students of Portuguese American heritage interested in studying health sciences.

**Eligibility:** Open to high school seniors or currently-enrolled college students who are of Portuguese American ancestry. Applicants must be U.S. residents and attending or planning to attend an accredited 4-year college or university. They must have a demonstrated interest in the study of health sciences.

**Financial data:** The stipend is $2,000 per year.

**Duration:** 4 years, provided the recipient maintains a GPA of 3.0 or higher.

**Number awarded:** 1 each year.

**Deadline:** January of each year.

## 2344 JOHN A. LOPIANO SCHOLARSHIP

Electronic Document Systems Foundation, Attn: EDSF Scholarship Awards
24238 Hawthorne Boulevard
Torrance, CA 90505-6505
Phone: (310) 541-1481; Fax: (310) 541-4803
Web: www.edsf.org/scholarships.cfm

**Summary:** To provide financial assistance to college juniors, seniors, and graduate students interested in working with electronic documents as a career.

**Eligibility:** Open to juniors, seniors, and graduate students who are working full time on a degree in the field of document communication, including marketing, graphic communication and arts, e-commerce, imaging science, printing, web authoring, electronic publishing, computer science, or telecommunications. Priority consideration is given to students who work in or whose family member has worked or currently works in a segment of the high volume transaction output (HVTO) industry. Applicants must submit a statement of their career goals in the field of document communications, an essay on a topic related to their view of the future of the document management and production industry, a list of current professional and college extracurricular activities and achievements, college transcripts (GPA of 3.0 or higher), samples of their creative work, and 2 letters of recommendation. Financial need is not considered.

**Financial data:** The stipend is $2,000.

**Duration:** 1 year.

**Number awarded:** 1 each year.

**Deadline:** May of each year.

## 2345 JOHN AND ALICE EGAN MULTI-YEAR MENTORING SCHOLARSHIP PROGRAM

Daedalian Foundation, Attn: Scholarship Committee
55 Main Circle (Building 676)
P.O. Box 249
Randolph AFB, TX 78148-0249
Phone: (210) 945-2113; Fax: (210) 945-2112; Email: daedalus@daedalians.org
Web: www.daedalians.org

**Summary:** To provide financial assistance to college students who are participating in a ROTC program and wish to become military pilots.

**Eligibility:** Open to students who have completed at least the freshman year at an accredited 4-year college or university and have a GPA of 3.0 or higher. Applicants must be participating in an ROTC program and be medically qualified for flight training. They must plan to apply for and be awarded a military pilot training allocation at the appropriate juncture in their ROTC program. Selection is based on intention to prepare for a career as a military pilot, demonstrated moral character and patriotism, scholastic and military standing and aptitude, and physical condition and aptitude for flight.

**Financial data:** The stipend is $2,500 per year.

**Duration:** 1 year; may be renewed up to 2 or 3 additional years provided the recipient maintains a GPA of 3.0 or higher and is enrolled in an undergraduate program.

**Number awarded:** Up to 11 each year.

**Deadline:** July of each year.

## 2346 JOHN AND ELSA GRACIK SCHOLARSHIPS

ASME International, Attn: Coordinator, Educational Operations
Three Park Avenue
New York, NY 10016-5990
Phone: (212) 591-8131; (800) THE-ASME; Fax: (212) 591-7143;
Email: oluwanifiset@asme.org
Web: www.asme.org/education/enged/aid/scholar.htm

**Summary:** To provide financial assistance to undergraduate students who are members of the American Society of Mechanical Engineers (ASME).

**Eligibility:** Open to student members in good standing who are enrolled in an ABET-accredited mechanical engineering baccalaureate, mechanical engineering technology, or related program. Applicants must be U.S. citizens entering their sophomore, junior, or senior year. Selection is based on character, leadership, scholastic ability, potential contribution to the mechanical engineering profession, and financial need.

**Financial data:** The stipend is $1,500.

**Duration:** 1 year.

**Number awarded:** 18 each year.

**Deadline:** March of each year.

## 2347 JOHN AND MURIEL LANDIS SCHOLARSHIPS

American Nuclear Society, Attn: Scholarship Coordinator
555 North Kensington Avenue
La Grange Park, IL 60526-5592
Phone: (708) 352-6611; Fax: (708) 352-0499; Email: outreach@ans.org
Web: www.ans.org/honors/scholarships

**Summary:** To provide financial assistance to undergraduate or graduate students who are interested in preparing for a career in nuclear-related fields.

**Eligibility:** Open to undergraduate and graduate students at colleges or universities located in the United States who are preparing for, or planning to prepare for, a career in nuclear science, nuclear engineering, or a nuclear-related field. Qualified high school seniors are also eligible. Applicants must have greater than average financial need and have experienced circumstances that render them disadvantaged. U.S. citizenship or permanent resident status is required. Selection is primarily based on financial need and potential for academic and professional success.

**Financial data:** The stipend is $4,000, to be used to cover tuition, books, fees, and room and board.

**Duration:** 1 year; nonrenewable.

**Number awarded:** Up to 8 each year.

**Deadline:** January of each year.

## 2348 JOHN C. LINCOLN MEMORIAL SCHOLARSHIP

American Welding Society, Attn: AWS Foundation, Inc.
550 N.W. LeJeune Road
Miami, FL 33126
Phone: (305) 445-6628; (800) 443-9353, ext. 461; Fax: (305) 443-7559;
Email: found@aws.org
Web: www.aws.org/foundation/scholarships/lincoln.html

**Summary:** To provide financial assistance to college students majoring in welding engineering.

**Eligibility:** Open to undergraduate students who are working on a 4-year bachelor's degree in welding engineering or welding engineering technology; preference is given to welding engineering students. Applicants must have an overall GPA of 2.5 or higher and be able to demonstrate financial need. U.S. citizenship is required. Priority is given to applicants who reside or attend school in Arizona or Ohio.

**Financial data:** The stipend is $2,500.

**Duration:** 1 year; recipients may reapply.

**Number awarded:** 1 each year.

**Deadline:** January of each year.

## 2349 JOHN DAWE DENTAL EDUCATION SCHOLARSHIP

Hawai'i Community Foundation, Attn: Scholarship Department
1164 Bishop Street, Suite 800
Honolulu, HI 96813
Phone: (808) 566-5570; (888) 731-3863; Fax: (808) 521-6286;
Email: scholarships@hcf-hawaii.org
Web: www.hawaiicommunityfoundation.org/scholar/scholar.php

**Summary:** To provide financial assistance to Hawaii residents who are interested in preparing for a career in the dental field.

**Eligibility:** Open to Hawaii residents who are interested in full-time study in dentistry, dental hygiene, or dental assisting. They must be able to demonstrate academic achievement (GPA of 2.7 or higher), good moral character, and financial need. In addition to filling out the standard application form, applicants must write a short statement indicating their reasons for attending college, their planned course of study, and their career goals.

**Financial data:** The amounts of the awards depend on the availability of funds and the need of the recipient; recently, stipends averaged $1,000.

**Duration:** 1 year.

**Number awarded:** Varies each year; recently, 8 of these scholarships were awarded.

**Deadline:** February of each year.

## 2350 JOHN E. O'CONNOR, JR. SCHOLARSHIPS

Actuarial Foundation, Attn: John E. O'Connor, Jr. Scholarship
475 North Martingale Road, Suite 800
Schaumburg, IL 60173-2226
Phone: (847) 706-3500; Fax: (847) 706-3599
Web: www.actuarialfoundation.org/grant/othergrants/oconnor.htm

**Summary:** To provide financial assistance to high school seniors interested in majoring in mathematics in college.

**Eligibility:** Open to graduating high school seniors who are citizens of the United States or Canada. Applicants must be planning to enroll at a 4-year college or university to prepare for a career in a field related to mathematics. They must have a GPA of 3.5 or higher. Along with their application, they must submit a 500-word essay on an incident in their life that convinced them to pursue a mathematics-based career, and why and which career they are considering. Selection is based on the essay, GPA, letters of recommendation, ACT or SAT scores in mathematics, extracurricular activities, volunteer community service, and work experience.

**Financial data:** The stipend is $2,500. Funds are paid directly to the university.

**Duration:** 1 year.

**Number awarded:** Varies each year; recently, 4 of these scholarships were awarded.

**Deadline:** April of each year.

## 2351 JOHN J. AND IRENE T. POWERS SCHOLARSHIP

Institute of Food Technologists, Attn: Scholarship Department
525 West Van Buren, Suite 1000
Chicago, IL 60607
Phone: (312) 782-8424; Fax: (312) 782-8348; Email: info@ift.org
Web: www.ift.org

**Summary:** To provide financial assistance to undergraduates interested in studying food science or food technology.

**Eligibility:** Open to sophomores, juniors, and seniors in a food science or food technology program at an educational institution in the United States or Canada. Applicants must have an outstanding scholastic record and a well-rounded personality. Along with their application, they must submit an essay on their career aspirations; a list of awards, honors, and scholarships they have received; a list of extracurricular activities and/or hobbies; and a summary of their work experience. Financial need is not considered in the selection process.

**Financial data:** The stipend is $1,500.

**Duration:** 1 year; recipients may reapply if they are members of the Institute of Food Technologists (IFT).

**Number awarded:** 1 each year.

**Deadline:** January of each year.

## 2352 JOHN J. MCKETTA UNDERGRADUATE SCHOLARSHIP

American Institute of Chemical Engineers, Attn: Awards Administrator
Three Park Avenue
New York, NY 10016-5991
Phone: (212) 591-7107; Fax: (212) 591-8890; Email: awards@aiche.org
Web: www.aiche.org/awards

**Summary:** To provide financial assistance to upper-division students majoring in chemical engineering.

**Eligibility:** Open to students entering their junior or senior year of a 4-year program in chemical engineering (or equivalent for a 5-year co-op program). Applicants must be attending an ABET-accredited school in the United States, Canada, or Mexico, and have a GPA of 3.0 or higher. Along with their application, they must submit a 2-page essay outlining their career goals in the chemical engineering process industries. Preference is given to student members of the American Institute of Chemical Engineers (AIChE) and to applicants who can show leadership or activity in either their school's AIChE student chapter or other university-sponsored campus activity. Financial need is not considered in the selection process.

**Financial data:** The stipend is $5,000.

**Duration:** 1 year.

**Number awarded:** 1 each year.

**Deadline:** April of each year.

## 2353 JOHN L. AND SARAH G. MERRIAM SCHOLARSHIP

American Society of Agricultural and Biological Engineers
Attn: ASABE Foundation
2950 Niles Road
St. Joseph, MI 49085-9659
Phone: (269) 429-0300; Fax: (269) 429-3852; Email: hq@asabe.org
Web: www.asabe.org/membership/merriam.html

**Summary:** To provide financial assistance to undergraduate student members of the American Society of Agricultural Engineers (ASAE) interested in soil and water issues.

**Eligibility:** Open to undergraduate students who have a declared major in biological or agricultural engineering (must be accredited by ABET or CEAB), are student members of the society, are in at least the second year of college, have a GPA of 2.5 or higher, have at least one year of undergraduate study remaining, and have a special interest in soil and water issues. Interested applicants should submit a personal letter (up to 2 pages long) explaining why they have selected the soil and water discipline as the focus of their degree. Financial need is not considered in the selection process.

**Financial data:** The stipend is $1,000.

**Duration:** 1 year.

**Number awarded:** 1 each year.

**Deadline:** March of each year.

## 2354 JOHN L. TOMASOVIC SCHOLARSHIP

Floriculture Industry Research and Scholarship Trust
Attn: Scholarship Program
P.O. Box 280
East Lansing, MI 48826-0280
Phone: (517) 333-4617; Fax: (517) 333-4494;
Email: scholarships@firstinfloriculture.org
Web: www.firstinfloriculture.org

**Summary:** To provide financial assistance to undergraduate and graduate students in horticulture.

**Eligibility:** Open to undergraduate students at 4-year colleges and universities and to graduate students. Applicants must be horticulture majors who are U.S. or Canadian citizens or permanent residents with a GPA between 3.0 and 3.5. Selection is based on academic record, recommendations, career goals, extracurricular activities, and (especially) financial need.

**Financial data:** The stipend depends on the availability of funds. Recently, it was $1,000.

**Duration:** 1 year.

**Number awarded:** 1 each year.

**Deadline:** April of each year.

## 2355 JOHN M. CHAMBERS STATISTICAL SOFTWARE AWARD

American Statistical Association, Attn: Statistical Computing Section
1429 Duke Street, Suite 200
Alexandria, VA 22314-3415
Phone: (703) 684-1221; (888) 231-3473; Fax: (703) 684-6456

Web: www.statcomputing.org/awards/jmc/index.html

**Summary:** To recognize and reward undergraduate and graduate students who have written outstanding statistical software.

**Eligibility:** Open to undergraduate or graduate students who have designed and implemented a piece of statistical software. Applicants must have begun the development while a student, and must either currently be a student or have completed all requirements for their last degree within the past 3 years. They must submit a current curriculum vitae; a letter from a faculty mentor at their academic institution confirming that the software is the work of the student; and a brief description of the software, summarizing what it does, how it does it, and why it is an important contribution. They must also provide the award committee members with access to the software for their use on inputs of their choosing.

**Financial data:** The award includes an honorarium of $1,000, payment of registration fees at the next JSM meeting, and reimbursement of up to $1,000 for travel and housing at the meeting.

**Duration:** The award is presented annually.

**Number awarded:** 1 each year.

**Deadline:** February of each year.

### 2356 JOHN M. HANIAK SCHOLARSHIP

ASM International, Attn: ASM Materials Education Foundation
Scholarship Program
9639 Kinsman Road
Materials Park, OH 44073-0002
Phone: (440) 338-5151; (800) 336-5152; Fax: (440) 338-4634;
Email: asmif@asminternational.org
Web: www.asminternational.org

**Summary:** To provide financial assistance to upper-division student members of the American Society for Metals who are interested in majoring in metallurgy and materials.

**Eligibility:** Open to citizens of the United States, Canada, or Mexico who are enrolled at a college or university in those countries; are members of the society; have an intended or declared major in metallurgy or materials science and engineering (related science or engineering majors may be considered if the applicant demonstrates a strong academic emphasis and interest in materials science and engineering); and are entering their junior or senior year in college. Selection is based on academic achievement; interest in metallurgy/materials (including knowledge of the field, activities, jobs, and potential for a related career); personal qualities (such as social values, maturity, motivation, goals, and citizenship); and financial need.

**Financial data:** The stipend is $1,500 per year.

**Duration:** 1 year; recipients may reapply for 1 additional year.

**Number awarded:** 1 each year.

**Deadline:** April of each year.

### 2357 JOHN MABRY FORESTRY SCHOLARSHIP

Railway Tie Association, Attn: Education and Information Committee
115 Commerce Drive, Suite C
Fayetteville, GA 30214
Phone: (770) 460-5553; Fax: (770) 460-5573; Email: ties@rta.org
Web: www.rta.org

**Summary:** To provide financial aid to upper-division college students who are enrolled in accredited forestry schools.

**Eligibility:** Open to juniors and seniors at accredited forestry schools. Selection is based on leadership qualities, career objectives, scholastic achievement, and financial need.

**Financial data:** The stipend is $1,250 per year.

**Duration:** 1 year.

**Number awarded:** 2 each year.

**Deadline:** June of each year.

### 2358 JOHN P. "PAT" HEALY SCHOLARSHIP

Delaware Higher Education Commission
Carvel State Office Building
820 North French Street
Wilmington, DE 19801
Phone: (302) 577-3240; (800) 292-7935; Fax: (302) 577-6765;
Email: dhec@doe.k12.de.us
Web: www.doe.state.de.us/high-ed/healy.pat.htm

**Summary:** To provide financial assistance to high school seniors and college students in Delaware who are interested in majoring in engineering or environmental sciences at a college in the state.

**Eligibility:** Open to high school seniors and full-time college students in their freshman or sophomore years who are Delaware residents and majoring in either environmental engineering or environmental sciences at a Delaware college. Applicants must submit a 500-word essay on "What would you do to protect the environment?" Selection is based on financial need, academic performance, community or school involvement, and leadership ability.

**Financial data:** The stipend is $2,000.

**Duration:** 1 year; automatically renewed for 3 additional years if a GPA of 3.0 or higher is maintained.

**Number awarded:** 1 or more each year.

**Deadline:** March of each year.

### 2359 JOHN R. LILLARD VAOC SCHOLARSHIP

Virginia Airport Operators Council
c/o Betty Wilson
Virginia Aviation and Space Education Forum
5702 Gulfstream Road
Richmond, VA 23250-2422
Phone: (800) 292-1034 (within VA)

**Summary:** To provide financial assistance to high school seniors in Virginia who are interested in preparing for a career in aviation.

**Eligibility:** Open to seniors graduating from high schools in Virginia who have a GPA of 3.75 or higher and are planning a career in the field of aviation. Applicants must have been accepted to an aviation-related program at an accredited college. They must submit an essay of 350 to 500 words on why they wish to prepare for a career in aviation. Selection is based on the essay (30%), academic achievement (35%), accomplishment and leadership (20%), and financial need (15%).

**Financial data:** The stipend is $1,500.

**Duration:** 1 year.

**Number awarded:** 1 each year.

**Deadline:** February of each year.

### 2360 JOHNNY DAVIS MEMORIAL SCHOLARSHIP

Aircraft Electronics Association, Attn: AEA Educational Foundation
4217 South Hocker Drive
Independence, MO 64055-4723
Phone: (816) 373-6565; Fax: (816) 478-3100; Email: info@aea.net
Web: www.aea.net

**Summary:** To provide financial assistance to students preparing for a career in avionics or aircraft repair.

**Eligibility:** Open to high school seniors and currently-enrolled college students who are attending (or planning to attend) an accredited postsecondary institution in an avionics or aircraft repair program. Applicants must submit an official transcript (cumulative GPA of 2.5 or higher), a statement about their career plans, a description of their involvement in school and community activities, and a 300-word essay on how the job requirements of aviation technicians will change with advancements in technology. Selection is based on merit.

**Financial data:** The stipend is $1,000.

**Duration:** 1 year.

**Number awarded:** 1 each year.

**Deadline:** February of each year.

### 2361 JOSEPH FRASCA EXCELLENCE IN AVIATION SCHOLARSHIP

University Aviation Association
3410 Skyway Drive
Auburn, AL 36830-6444
Phone: (334) 844-2434; Email: uaa@auburn.edu
Web: www.uaa.aero

**Summary:** To provide financial assistance to upper-division college students majoring in aviation.

**Eligibility:** Open to juniors or seniors who are currently enrolled at a school affiliated with the University Aviation Association (UAA). Applicants must have earned a GPA of 3.0 or higher in their college courses; have Federal Aviation Administration certification/qualifications in either aviation maintenance or flight; be a member of at least one aviation organization; and have a record of aviation activities, projects, or events that demonstrates an interest and an enthusiasm for aviation. Preference is given to applicants who can document interest or experience in aviation simulation, work experience in aviation, interest or experience in aircraft restoration, work experience while in school, interest or experience in aerobatics, or financial need. They may also submit an optional 250-word essay on their personal philosophy of excellence in aviation.

**Financial data:** The stipend is $1,000.

**Duration:** 1 year.

**Number awarded:** 2 each year.

**Deadline:** April of each year.

## 2362 JOSEPH L. ROSENBAUM, SR. MEMORIAL SCHOLARSHIP PROGRAM

Associated General Contractors of Virginia, Attn: Kelly Ragsdale
11950 Nuckols Road
Glen Allen, VA 23059
Phone: (804) 364-5504; (800) 581-4652; Fax: (804) 364-5511
Web: www.agcva.org/Brochure/scholarships.htm

**Summary:** To provide financial assistance to students in Virginia who are preparing for a career in the construction industry.

**Eligibility:** Open to students at Virginia colleges and universities who are preparing for a career in construction.

**Financial data:** The stipend is $1,250 per year.

**Duration:** 2 years.

**Number awarded:** 1 each year.

## 2363 JOSEPH MURPHY SCHOLARSHIP

New England Water Works Association
125 Hopping Brook
Holliston, MA 01746
Phone: (508) 893-7979; Fax: (508) 893-9898
Web: www.newwa.org

**Summary:** To provide financial assistance to undergraduate or graduate students from New England interested in working on a degree in civil or environmental engineering, business, or a related science field.

**Eligibility:** Open to members and student members of the New England section of the American Water Works Association or the New England Water Works Association. Applicants must be high school seniors, currently-enrolled college students, or graduate students. They must be majoring or planning to major in civil or environmental engineering, business, or a related science field. Along with their application, they must submit a 100-word essay on why they have chosen their field of study and if it will improve the environment, public health, or the water industry. Financial need is also considered in the selection process.

**Financial data:** The stipend is $1,500.

**Duration:** 1 year.

**Deadline:** July of each year.

## 2364 JOSEPH P. AND HELEN T. CRIBBINS SCHOLARSHIP

Association of the United States Army, Attn: National Secretary
2425 Wilson Boulevard
Arlington, VA 22201
Phone: (703) 841-4300, ext. 655; (800) 336-4570, ext. 655;
Email: ausa-info@ausa.org
Web: www.ausa.org

**Summary:** To provide financial assistance to active-duty and honorably-discharged soldiers interested in studying engineering in college.

**Eligibility:** Open to 1) soldiers currently serving in the active Army, Army Reserve, or Army National Guard of any rank; and 2) honorably-discharged soldiers from any component of the total Army. Applicants must have been accepted at an accredited college or university to work on a degree in engineering or a related field. Along with their application, they must submit a 1-page autobiography, 3 letters of recommendation, and a transcript of high school or college grades (depending on which they are currently attending). Selection is based on academic merit and personal achievement. Financial need is not normally a selection criterion, but in some cases of extreme need it may be used as a factor; the lack of financial need is never a cause for non-selection.

**Financial data:** The stipend is $2,000.

**Duration:** 1 year.

**Number awarded:** 1 or more each year.

**Deadline:** June of each year.

## 2365 JOSEPH SHINODA MEMORIAL SCHOLARSHIP

Joseph Shinoda Memorial Scholarship Foundation Inc.
Attn: Executive Secretary
234 Via La Paz
San Luis Obispo, CA 93401
Phone: (805) 544-0717; Email: info@shinodascholarship.org
Web: www.shinodascholarship.org

**Summary:** To provide financial assistance to undergraduates working on a degree in floriculture.

**Eligibility:** Open to undergraduates entering their sophomore, junior, or senior year at an accredited college or university in the United States. Applicants must be majoring in a degree program related to floriculture (production, distribution, research, or retail) and be planning to work in a phase of commercial floriculture after graduation. Financial need is considered in the selection process.

**Financial data:** Stipends range from $1,500 to $3,500.

**Duration:** 1 year.

**Number awarded:** Approximately 6 each year. Since the foundation was established, it has awarded more than $644,000 to 579 floriculture students.

**Deadline:** March of each year.

## 2366 J.R. HAINES MEMORIAL SCHOLARSHIP

Cumberland Valley Volunteer Firemen's Association
Attn: Home Office Manager
11018 Clinton Street
Hagerstown, MD 21740-7701
Phone: (301) 582-2345; Email: info@respondersafety.com
Web: cvvfa.org/scholarship.html

**Summary:** To provide financial assistance to residents of designated eastern states who are interested in working on a degree in fire science.

**Eligibility:** Open to residents of Delaware, Maryland, New Jersey, New York, North Carolina, Pennsylvania, Virginia, and West Virginia. Applicants must be enrolled or planning to enroll at a 2- or 4-year accredited college or university to work on a degree in fire science, including fire, fire investigation, and related subjects. Along with their application, they must submit a 250-word essay on why they are interested in a fire science-related career.

**Financial data:** The stipend is $1,000 per year.

**Duration:** 1 year.

**Number awarded:** 1 each year.

**Deadline:** February of each year.

## 2367 JSHS SCHOLARSHIPS

Academy of Applied Science, Attn: JSHS National Office
24 Warren Street
Concord, NH 03301
Phone: (603) 228-4520; Fax: (603) 228-4730; Email: phampton@jshs.org
Web: www.jshs.org

**Summary:** To recognize and reward outstanding participants in the Army, Navy, and Air Force Junior Science and Humanities Symposia (JSHS).

**Eligibility:** Open to students in grades 9-12, enrolled in public, private, or home schools, who have completed an original research investigation in the sciences, engineering, or mathematics. Investigations reporting on experimental, field, observational, or applied research are eligible. Students present their findings at a regional symposium, held on a university campus in their area. At each regional symposium, selected paper presenters are chosen to receive scholarships. From each of the 48 regional symposia, 5 students are selected to attend the national JSHS, where one of them presents his or her research paper in competition for further awards.

**Financial data:** At each regional symposium, 5 finalists receive all-expense paid trips to the national symposium, the first and second place winners are invited to present their research investigation at the national symposium, and scholarships of $1,500, $1,000, and $500, are awarded. In the national competition, first-place finalists receive $16,000 scholarships, second-place finalists receive $6,000 scholarships, and third-place finalists receive $2,000 scholarships (all national scholarships are in addition to the regional scholarships). Top finalists are also awarded an all-expense paid trip to the International Youth Science Forum, held in London. The outstanding teacher in each region receives a $500 award.

**Duration:** This competition is held annually. National scholarships are paid over a period of 4 years provided the recipients enroll full time and maintain a GPA of at least 3.0.

**Number awarded:** Scholarships are awarded to 3 regional winners in each of the 48 regional symposia, to 6 first-place finalists in the national symposium, to 6 second-place national finalists, and to 6 third-place national finalists. Teacher awards are presented to 48 teachers, 1 in each of the regions.

## 2368 JUDITH RESNIK MEMORIAL SCHOLARSHIP

Society of Women Engineers
230 East Ohio Street, Suite 400
Chicago, IL 60611-3265
Phone: (312) 596-5223; Fax: (312) 644-8557; Email: hq@swe.org
Web: www.societyofwomenengineers.org/scholarships
**Summary:** To provide financial assistance to undergraduate women who are members of the Society of Women Engineers and majoring in designated engineering specialties.
**Eligibility:** Open to women who are entering their sophomore, junior, or senior year at an ABET-accredited 4-year college or university. Applicants must be studying aerospace, aeronautical, or astronautical engineering with a GPA of 3.0 or higher. Along with their application, they must submit a one-page essay on why they want to be an engineer, how they believe they will make a difference as an engineer, and what influenced them to study engineering. Only members of the society are considered for this award. Selection is based on merit.
**Financial data:** The stipend is $2,500.
**Duration:** 1 year.
**Number awarded:** 1 each year.
**Deadline:** January of each year.

## 2369 JULIE VANDE VELDE LEADERSHIP SCHOLARSHIP

Institute of Food Technologists, Attn: Scholarship Department
525 West Van Buren, Suite 1000
Chicago, IL 60607
Phone: (312) 782-8424; Fax: (312) 782-8348; Email: info@ift.org
Web: www.ift.org
**Summary:** To provide financial assistance to undergraduates interested in studying food science or food technology.
**Eligibility:** Open to sophomores, juniors, and seniors in a food science or food technology program at an educational institution in the United States or Canada. Applicants must have an outstanding scholastic record and a well-rounded personality. Along with their application, they must submit an essay on their career aspirations; a list of awards, honors, and scholarships they have received; a list of extracurricular activities and/or hobbies; and a summary of their work experience. Financial need is not considered in the selection process.
**Financial data:** The stipend is $1,000.
**Duration:** 1 year; recipients may reapply if they are members of the Institute of Food Technologists.
**Number awarded:** 1 each year.
**Deadline:** January of each year.

## 2370 JUSTINE E. GRANNER MEMORIAL SCHOLARSHIP

Iowa United Methodist Foundation, Attn: Executive Director
500 East Court Avenue, Suite C
Des Moines, IA 50309
Phone: (515) 283-1991; Fax: (515) 288-1906; Email: david.harmer@iaumc.org
Web: www.iumf.org/scholarships.asp
**Summary:** To provide financial assistance to ethnic minorities in Iowa interested in majoring in a health-related field.
**Eligibility:** Open to American Indian and other ethnic minority students preparing for a career in nursing, public health, or a related field at a college or school of nursing within Iowa. Applicants must have a GPA of 3.0 or higher. Preference is given to graduates of Iowa high schools. Financial need is considered in the selection process.
**Financial data:** The stipend is $1,000.
**Duration:** 1 year.
**Number awarded:** 1 each year.
**Deadline:** February of each year.

## 2371 KAISER PERMANENTE DENTAL ASSISTANT SCHOLARSHIP

Oregon Student Assistance Commission
Attn: Grants and Scholarships Division
1500 Valley River Drive, Suite 100
Eugene, OR 97401-2146
Phone: (541) 687-7395; (800) 452-8807, ext. 7395; Fax: (541) 687-7419;
Email: awardinfo@mercury.osac.state.or.us
Web: www.osac.state.or.us
**Summary:** To provide financial assistance to residents of Oregon or Washington who are enrolled or planning to enroll in a dental assistant program at a designated college.
**Eligibility:** Open to residents of Oregon or Washington who are enrolled or planning to enroll at Blue Mountain Community College (Pendleton), Chemeketa Community College (Salem), Lane Community College (Eugene), Linn-Benton Community College (Albany), Portland Community College (Portland), or Concorde Career Institute (Portland). Applicants must be majoring or planning to major in dental assisting.
**Financial data:** A stipend is awarded (amount not specified).
**Duration:** 1 year; nonrenewable.
**Number awarded:** 1 or more each year.
**Deadline:** February of each year.

## 2372 KATHARINE M. GROSSCUP SCHOLARSHIP

Garden Club of America, Attn: Scholarship Committee
14 East 60th Street
New York, NY 10022-1006
Phone: (212) 753-8287; Fax: (212) 753-0134;
Email: scholarship@gcamerica.org
Web: www.gcamerica.org/scholarship/grosscup.html
**Summary:** To provide financial aid for the study of horticulture and related subjects to upper-division and graduate students.
**Eligibility:** Open to college juniors, seniors, and graduate students interested in studying horticulture or related subjects in the field of gardening. Preference is given to students from Ohio, Pennsylvania, West Virginia, Michigan, Kentucky, and Indiana.
**Financial data:** The stipend is $3,000.
**Duration:** 1 year.
**Number awarded:** Several each year.
**Deadline:** January of each year.

## 2373 KATHRYN D. SULLIVAN SCIENCE AND ENGINEERING FELLOWSHIP

South Carolina Space Grant Consortium
c/o College of Charleston
Department of Geology and Environmental Sciences
66 George Street
Charleston, SC 29424
Phone: (843) 953-5463; Fax: (843) 953-5446; Email: scozzarot@cofc.edu
Web: www.cofc.edu/~scsgrant/scholar/overview.html
**Summary:** To provide financial assistance to outstanding science students in South Carolina.
**Eligibility:** Open to students entering their senior year at a college or university in South Carolina or at the University of the Virgin Islands. Applicants must be studying natural science or engineering. Selection is based on academic qualifications of the applicant; 2 letters of recommendation; a description of past activities, current interests, and future plans concerning natural science-related and engineering-related studies; and faculty sponsorship. U.S. citizenship is required.
**Financial data:** The stipend is $7,000 per year.
**Duration:** 1 year.
**Number awarded:** 1 each year.
**Deadline:** January of each year.

## 2374 KELLIE CANNON MEMORIAL SCHOLARSHIP

American Council of the Blind, Attn: Coordinator, Scholarship Program
1155 15th Street, N.W., Suite 1004
Washington, DC 20005
Phone: (202) 467-5081; (800) 424-8666; Fax: (202) 467-5085;
Email: info@acb.org
Web: www.acb.org
**Summary:** To provide financial assistance to students who are blind and interested in preparing for a career in the computer field.
**Eligibility:** Open to high school seniors, high school graduates, and college students who are blind and are interested in majoring in college in computer information systems or data processing. In addition to letters of recommendation and copies of academic transcripts, applications must include an autobiographical sketch. A cumulative GPA of 3.3 or higher is generally required. Selection is based on demonstrated academic record, involvement in extracurricular and civic activities, and academic objectives. The severity of the applicant's visual impairment and his/her study methods are also taken into account.

**Financial data:** The stipend is $2,000. In addition, the winner receives a Kurzweil-1000 Reading System.
**Duration:** 1 year.
**Number awarded:** 1 each year.
**Deadline:** February of each year.

## 2375 KENNETH ANDREW ROE SCHOLARSHIP

ASME International, Attn: Coordinator, Educational Operations
Three Park Avenue
New York, NY 10016-5990
Phone: (212) 591-8131; (800) THE-ASME; Fax: (212) 591-7143;
Email: oluwanifiset@asme.org
Web: www.asme.org/education/enged/aid/scholar.htm
**Summary:** To provide financial assistance to upper-division students who are members of the American Society of Mechanical Engineers (ASME).
**Eligibility:** Open to student members in good standing who are enrolled in an ABET-accredited mechanical engineering baccalaureate program. They must be U.S. citizens and entering their junior or senior year when they apply. Interested students should submit an application form, a nomination from the applicant's department head, a recommendation from a faculty member, and an official transcript. Only one nomination may be submitted per department. Selection is based on character, integrity, leadership, scholastic ability, and potential contribution to the mechanical engineering profession.
**Financial data:** The stipend is $10,000.
**Duration:** 1 year.
**Number awarded:** 1 each year.
**Deadline:** March of each year.

## 2376 KENNETH B. FISHBECK, P.E. MEMORIAL GRANT

Michigan Society of Professional Engineers, Attn: Scholarship Coordinator
215 North Walnut Street
P.O. Box 15276
Lansing, MI 48901-5276
Phone: (517) 487-9388; Fax: (517) 487-0635; Email: mspe@voyager.net
Web: www.michiganspe.org/scholarship.htm
**Summary:** To provide financial assistance to high school seniors in Michigan who are interested in working on a college degree in engineering.
**Eligibility:** Open to graduating seniors at high schools in Michigan who have a GPA of 3.0 or higher and a composite ACT score of 26 or higher. U.S. citizenship and a demonstration of professional ethics are required. Applicants must have been accepted at a Michigan college or university accredited by ABET. They must be planning to enroll in an engineering program and enter the practice of engineering after graduation. They must submit a 250-word essay on "How I Was Influenced to Pursue an Engineering Career." Selection is based on the essay; high school academic record; participation in extracurricular activities; evidence of leadership, character, and self-reliance; and comments from teachers and administrators. Financial need is not considered. Semifinalists are interviewed.
**Financial data:** The stipend is $1,000.
**Duration:** 1 year; nonrenewable.
**Number awarded:** 1 each year.
**Deadline:** January of each year.

## 2377 KENTUCKY NURSES FOUNDATION SCHOLARSHIPS

Kentucky Nurses Association, Attn: Kentucky Nurses Foundation
1400 South First Street
P.O. Box 2616
Louisville, KY 40201-2616
Phone: (502) 637-2546; (800) 348-5411; Fax: (502) 637-8236
Web: www.kentucky-nurses.org/knf.htm
**Summary:** To provide financial assistance to residents of Kentucky who are interested in working on a prelicensure or advanced degree in nursing.
**Eligibility:** Open to residents of Kentucky who are interested in enrolling in a prelicensure (including associate's and baccalaureate degree) program in nursing or are pursuing a graduate's degree. Along with their application, they must submit a statement on why they are applying and what receiving the scholarship would mean to them.
**Financial data:** A stipend is awarded (amount not specified).
**Duration:** 1 year.
**Number awarded:** Varies each year.
**Deadline:** Applications may be submitted at any time.

## 2378 KENTUCKY TURFGRASS COUNCIL COLLEGE SCHOLARSHIPS

Kentucky Turfgrass Council
c/o David Williams, Executive Secretary
University of Kentucky
Plant and Soil Science Department
N-222 Agriculture Science Center North
Lexington, KY 40546-0091
Phone: (859) 257-2715; Fax: (859) 323-1952; Email: dwilliam@uky.edu
Web: www.uky.edu/Agriculture/ukturf/KTC2002/scholarships.htm
**Summary:** To provide financial assistance to students majoring in turfgrass science at colleges and universities in Kentucky.
**Eligibility:** Open to students who are enrolled full time at Kentucky universities and majoring in turfgrass science or horticulture. Applicants must submit 2 letters of recommendation, an official copy of their university transcripts, a copy of their resume, and 2 paragraphs on 1) their plans after graduation and 2) why they believe they deserve this scholarship. All qualified candidates are interviewed.
**Financial data:** A stipend is awarded (amount not specified).
**Duration:** 1 year.
**Number awarded:** 1 or more each year.
**Deadline:** October of each year.

## 2379 KEY CLUB INTERNATIONAL AG-BAG SCHOLARSHIP

Key Club International, Attn: Manager of Youth Funds
3636 Woodview Trace
Indianapolis, IN 46268-3196
Phone: (317) 875-8755, ext. 244; (800) KIWANIS, ext. 244;
Fax: (317) 879-0204; Email: youthfunds@kiwanis.org
Web: www.keyclub.org
**Summary:** To provide financial assistance for college to high school seniors who are Key Club International members and have been involved in agriculture.
**Eligibility:** Open to college-bound graduating high school members who have completed at least 100 service hours during their Key Club career and have held an elected officer position on the club, district, or international level. Applicants must have a GPA of 3.5 or higher. Along with their application, they must submit 1) a 500-word essay describing the Key Club service project on which they have participated and that has had the greatest impact on them; and 2) a list of the titles, dates, positions, and names of agriculture-related organizations to which they belong. Financial need is not considered in the selection process.
**Financial data:** The stipend is $1,000.
**Duration:** 1 year.
**Number awarded:** 1 each year.
**Deadline:** February of each year.

## 2380 KILBOURN-SAWYER MEMORIAL SCHOLARSHIP

Vermont Student Assistance Corporation
Champlain Mill, Attn: Scholarship Programs
P.O. Box 2000
Winooski, VT 05404-2601
Phone: (802) 654-3798; (888) 253-4819; Fax: (802) 654-3765; TDD: (802) 654-3766; TDD: (800) 281-3341 (within VT); Email: info@vsac.org
Web: www.vsac.org
**Summary:** To provide financial assistance to high school seniors in Vermont who are interested in working on a college degree in construction or engineering.
**Eligibility:** Open to residents of Vermont who are seniors in high school. Applicants must be planning to enroll in a 2-year or 4-year postsecondary degree program in engineering or construction. Selection is based on letters of recommendation, required essays, academic achievement, and financial need.
**Financial data:** The stipend is $1,000.
**Duration:** 1 year; nonrenewable.
**Number awarded:** 1 each year.
**Deadline:** April of each year.

## 2381 KIRSTEN R. LORENTZEN AWARD

Association for Women in Science, Attn: AWIS Educational Foundation
1200 New York Avenue, N.W., Suite 650
Washington, DC 20005
Phone: (202) 326-8940; (866) 657-AWIS; Fax: (202) 326-8960;
Email: awisedfd@awis.org

Web: www.awis.org/resource/edfoundation.html

**Summary:** To provide financial assistance to women undergraduates majoring in physics or geoscience.

**Eligibility:** Open to women who are sophomores or juniors in college and U.S. citizens. Applicants must be studying physics (including space physics and geophysics) or geoscience. They must demonstrate excellence in their studies as well as outdoor activities, service, sports, music, or other non-academic pursuits, or a record of overcoming significant obstacles. Along with their application, they must submit a 2- to 3-page essay on 1) their academic interests and plans, including class work and any relevant research, teaching, or outreach activities; 2) their career goals; 3) the non-academic pursuits that are most important to them; and 4) any significant barriers they have faced and how they overcame them. Financial need is not considered.

**Financial data:** The stipend is $1,000.

**Duration:** 1 year.

**Number awarded:** 1 each year.

**Deadline:** January of each year.

## 2382 KLF SCHOLARSHIP

Kansas Livestock Association, Attn: Kansas Livestock Foundation
6031 S.W. 37th Street
Topeka, KS 66614-5129
Phone: (785) 273-5115; Fax: (785) 273-3399; Email: kla@kla.org
Web: www.kla.org/scholarapp.htm

**Summary:** To provide financial assistance to Kansas residents who are or will be majoring in a field related to agriculture.

**Eligibility:** Open to Kansas residents who are entering or returning to a junior or senior college in the state. Applicants must be majoring or planning to major in a field related to agriculture (e.g., agricultural economics, agronomy, animal science). Selection is based on academic achievement (20 points), personal livestock enterprises (25 points), 4H/FFA/KJLA activities and leadership (30 points), school activities and honors (30 points), other activities and leadership (25 points), work experience (25 points), significant honors or recognition (25 points), and career plans (20 points). Preference is given to students planning to be involved full time in production agriculture after graduation.

**Financial data:** The stipend is $1,000. Funds are paid directly to the recipient in 2 equal installments at the beginning of each semester, upon proof of enrollment.

**Duration:** 1 year.

**Number awarded:** 1 each year.

**Deadline:** April of each year.

## 2383 KSEA SCHOLARSHIPS

Korean-American Scientists and Engineers Association
1952 Gallows Drive, Suite 300
Vienna, VA 22182
Phone: (703) 748-1221; Fax: (703) 748-1331; Email: sejong@ksea.org
Web: www.ksea.org

**Summary:** To provide financial assistance to undergraduate and graduate student members of the Korean-American Scientists and Engineers Association (KSEA).

**Eligibility:** Open to Korean American undergraduate and graduate students who graduated from a high school in the United States, are KSEA members, and are majoring in science, engineering, or a related field. Along with their application, they must submit a 500-word essay on either of the following topics: 1) their career goals and intended contributions to society, or 2) the meaning of Korean heritage in their life. Selection is based on the essay (20%), work experience and extracurricular activities (20%), recommendation letters (30%), and academic performance (30%).

**Financial data:** The stipend is $1,000.

**Duration:** 1 year.

**Number awarded:** Varies each year.

**Deadline:** February of each year.

## 2384 KSPMA SCHOLARSHIPS

Kentucky School Plant Managers Association, Attn: Scholarship Chair
P.O. Box 4559
Lexington, KY 40544-4559
Email: mluscher@scott.k12.ky.us
Web: www.kspma.org/scholarship.htm

**Summary:** To provide financial assistance to high school seniors in Kentucky who are interested in attending college to prepare for a career in school plant operations.

**Eligibility:** Open to Kentucky high school seniors who are planning to attend a postsecondary program with a major in a trade area related to school plant operations (e.g., heating and air conditioning, industrial electronics, mechanical engineering). Applicants must submit a 250-word essay on why they want to receive this scholarship, the course of study and major they plan to follow, their proposed occupation or profession, and what they want to accomplish upon completion of their studies. Selection is based on that essay, ACT and/or SAT scores, GPA, curriculum, attendance, honors, extracurricular and work activities, and financial need.

**Financial data:** The stipend is $500 per semester ($1,000 per year).

**Duration:** 2 years.

**Number awarded:** Varies each year; recently, 5 of these scholarships were awarded.

**Deadline:** March of each year.

## 2385 KYUTARO AND YASUO ABIKO MEMORIAL SCHOLARSHIP

**Summary:** To provide financial assistance for college to student members of the Japanese American Citizens League (JACL), especially those majoring in journalism or agriculture.

*See Listing #1513.*

## 2386 L. PHIL WICKER SCHOLARSHIP

**Summary:** To provide financial assistance to licensed radio amateurs from designated states who are interested in working on an undergraduate or graduate degree, particularly in electronics or communications.

*See Listing #1514.*

## 2387 L-3 AVIONICS SYSTEMS SCHOLARSHIP

Aircraft Electronics Association, Attn: AEA Educational Foundation
4217 South Hocker Drive
Independence, MO 64055-4723
Phone: (816) 373-6565; Fax: (816) 478-3100; Email: info@aea.net
Web: www.aea.net

**Summary:** To provide financial assistance to students who are interested in studying avionics or aircraft repair in college.

**Eligibility:** Open to high school seniors and currently-enrolled college students who are attending (or planning to attend) an accredited school in an avionics or aircraft repair program. Applicants must submit an official transcript (cumulative GPA of 2.5 or higher), a statement about their career plans, a description of their involvement in school and community activities, and a 300-word essay on how the job requirements of aviation technicians will change with advancements in technology. Selection is based on merit.

**Financial data:** The stipend is $2,500.

**Duration:** 1 year.

**Number awarded:** 1 each year.

**Deadline:** February of each year.

## 2388 LADIES OF THE ABBA SCHOLARSHIPS

American Brahman Breeders Association, Attn: Youth Activities Director
3003 South Loop West, Suite 140
Houston, TX 77054
Phone: (713) 349-0854; Fax: (713) 349-9795; Email: abba@brahman.org
Web: www.brahman.org

**Summary:** To provide financial assistance to members of the American Junior Brahman Association (AJBA) interested in attending college to prepare for an agriculture-oriented career.

**Eligibility:** Open to active members of the AJBA, the youth division of the American Brahman Breeders Association (ABBA), who are graduating high school seniors and planning to prepare for an agriculture-oriented career. Applications must be accompanied by a record of 4-H, FFA, and FHA involvement; a record of AJBA involvement; a list of leadership roles and citizenship activities; a summary of other interests and activities (music, athletics, church, work, hobbies, etc.); and a brief essay on why the applicant selected agriculture as a field of study.

**Financial data:** Scholarships range from $500 to $1,000.

**Number awarded:** Varies each year; recently, 6 of these scholarships were awarded

**Deadline:** April of each year.

## 2389 LAURA N. DOWSETT FUND SCHOLARSHIPS

Hawai'i Community Foundation, Attn: Scholarship Department
1164 Bishop Street, Suite 800
Honolulu, HI 96813
Phone: (808) 566-5570; (888) 731-3863; Fax: (808) 521-6286;
Email: scholarships@hcf-hawaii.org
Web: www.hawaiicommunityfoundation.org/scholar/scholar.php
**Summary:** To provide financial assistance to Hawaii residents who are interested in preparing for a career in occupational therapy.
**Eligibility:** Open to Hawaii residents who are studying occupational therapy as full-time juniors, seniors, or graduate students. They must be able to demonstrate academic achievement (GPA of 2.7 or higher), good moral character, and financial need. In addition to filling out the standard application form, applicants must write a short statement indicating their reasons for attending college, their planned course of study, and their career goals.
**Financial data:** The amounts of the awards depend on the availability of funds and the need of the recipient; recently, stipends averaged $1,500.
**Duration:** 1 year.
**Number awarded:** Varies each year; recently, 2 of these scholarships were awarded.
**Deadline:** February of each year.

## 2390 LAWRENCE GINOCCHIO AVIATION SCHOLARSHIPS

National Business Aviation Association, Inc., Attn: Director of Operations
1200 18th Street, N.W., Suite 400
Washington, DC 20036-2527
Phone: (202) 783-9353; Fax: (202) 331-8364; Email: jevans@nbaa.org
Web: www.nbaa.org/public/education.scholarships/ginocchio
**Summary:** To provide financial assistance to undergraduates majoring in aviation at participating colleges and universities.
**Eligibility:** Open to U.S. citizens at the sophomore, junior, or senior level in an aviation related program of study at an institution belonging to the National Business Aviation Association (NBAA) and the University Aviation Association (UAA). Applicants must have at least a 3.0 GPA. Along with their application they must submit an official transcript, an essay of 500 to 1,000 words on their interest in and goals for a career in the business aviation industry, 2 letters of recommendation, and a resume.
**Financial data:** The stipend is $5,000. Checks are made payable to the recipient's institution.
**Duration:** 1 year.
**Number awarded:** 5 each year.
**Deadline:** August of each year.

## 2391 LAWRENCE "LARRY" FRAZIER MEMORIAL SCHOLARSHIP

Lincoln Community Foundation
215 Centennial Mall South, Suite 200
Lincoln, NE 68508
Phone: (402) 474-2345; Fax: (402) 476-8532; Email: lcf@lcf.org
Web: www.lcf.org
**Summary:** To provide financial assistance to residents of Nebraska who are interested in studying designated fields in college.
**Eligibility:** Open to residents of Nebraska who are graduating or have graduated from a high school in the state. Preference is given to applicants who intend to prepare for a career in the field of aviation, insurance, or law. They must attend a 2- or 4-year college or university in Nebraska as a full-time student. Preference is also given to applicants who have experience in debate and who participated in Boy Scouts or Girl Scouts as youth. Selection is based on academic achievement in high school, potential to excel in college, and financial need.
**Financial data:** A stipend is awarded (amount not specified).
**Duration:** 1 year.
**Number awarded:** 1 each year.
**Deadline:** April of each year.

## 2392 LAWRENCE R. FOSTER MEMORIAL SCHOLARSHIP

Oregon Student Assistance Commission
Attn: Grants and Scholarships Division
1500 Valley River Drive, Suite 100
Eugene, OR 97401-2146
Phone: (541) 687-7395; (800) 452-8807, ext. 7395; Fax: (541) 687-7419;
Email: awardinfo@mercury.osac.state.or.us
Web: www.osac.state.or.us
**Summary:** To provide financial assistance for college or graduate school to residents of Oregon who are interested in preparing for a public health career.
**Eligibility:** Open to residents of Oregon who are attending a 4-year college or university in any state to prepare for a career in public health (not private practice). First preference is given to applicants who are either working in public health or enrolled as graduate students in that field. Second preference is given to undergraduates entering the junior or senior year of a health program, including nursing, medical technology, and physician assistant. A general preference is given to applicants from diverse cultures. Along with their application, they must submit a 1- to 2-page essay on their interest, experience, and future plans for a public health career
**Financial data:** Stipend amounts vary; recently, they were at least $4,167.
**Duration:** 1 year.
**Number awarded:** Varies each year; recently, 6 of these scholarships were awarded.
**Deadline:** February of each year.

## 2393 LEADING EDGE STUDENT DESIGN COMPETITION

**Summary:** To recognize and reward undergraduate and graduate students who submit outstanding energy-efficient entries in a design competition.
*See Listing #1520.*

## 2394 LEAF SCHOLARSHIPS

California Landscape Contractors Association
Attn: Landscape Educational Advancement Foundation
1491 River Park Drive, Suite 100
Sacramento, CA 95815
Phone: (916) 830-2780
Web: www.clca.us/leaf/leafSch.html
**Summary:** To provide financial assistance to undergraduate and graduate students in California who are majoring in ornamental horticulture.
**Eligibility:** Open to undergraduate and graduate students attending an accredited California community college or state university and majoring in ornamental horticulture. Applications must submit brief essays on their educational objectives, occupational goals as they relate to the landscape industry, reasons for choosing that field, and reasons for requesting financial assistance. Selection is based on those essays; educational background; awards and honors; high school, college, and community activities related to landscaping; and work experience. Financial need is not considered.
**Financial data:** A stipend is awarded (amount not specified).
**Duration:** 1 year.
**Number awarded:** 1 or more each year.
**Deadline:** February of each year.

## 2395 LEE TARBOX MEMORIAL SCHOLARSHIP

Aircraft Electronics Association, Attn: AEA Educational Foundation
4217 South Hocker Drive
Independence, MO 64055-4723
Phone: (816) 373-6565; Fax: (816) 478-3100; Email: info@aea.net
Web: www.aea.net
**Summary:** To provide financial assistance to students who are interested in studying avionics or aircraft repair in college.
**Eligibility:** Open to high school seniors and currently-enrolled college students who are attending (or planning to attend) an accredited school in an avionics or aircraft repair program. Applicants must submit an official transcript (cumulative GPA of 2.5 or higher), a statement about their career plans, a description of their involvement in school and community activities, and a 300-word essay on how the job requirements of aviation technicians will change with advancements in technology. Selection is based on merit.
**Financial data:** The stipend is $2,500.
**Duration:** 1 year.
**Number awarded:** 1 each year.
**Deadline:** February of each year.

## 2396 LEGACY SCHOLARSHIPS

Legacy, Inc.
P.O. Box 3813
Montgomery, AL 36109
Phone: (334) 270-5921; (800) 240-5115 (within AL); Fax: (334) 270-5527
Web: www.legacyenved.org/fund/fund_college.htm

**Summary:** To provide financial assistance to upper-division and graduate students in Alabama who are interested in preparing for an environmentally-related career.
**Eligibility:** Open to upper-division (juniors and seniors) and graduate students who reside in Alabama, are enrolled in a college or university in the state, and are planning to prepare for an environmentally-related career. Given the inter-disciplinary nature of environmental education, it is not a requirement that all applicants have an environmental title attached to their major; some examples of career fields that have been funded in the past include: business, education, government, law, medicine, public relations, and geography. Finalists are interviewed.
**Financial data:** Undergraduates receive up to $1,500; graduate students receive up to $2,000.
**Duration:** 1 year.
**Number awarded:** 20 each year: 10 to undergraduates, 4 to master's degree students, and 6 to doctoral students.
**Deadline:** May of each year.

## 2397 LEROY APKER AWARD

American Physical Society, Attn: Apker Award Committee
One Physics Ellipse
College Park, MD 20740-3844
Phone: (301) 209-3233; Fax: (301) 209-0865; Email: chodos@aps.org
Web: www.aps.org/praw/apker/index.cfm
**Summary:** To recognize and reward undergraduate students for outstanding work in physics.
**Eligibility:** Open to undergraduate students at colleges and universities in the United States. Nominees should have completed or be completing the requirements for an undergraduate degree with an excellent academic record and should have demonstrated exceptional potential for scientific research by making an original contribution to physics. Each department of physics in the United States may nominate only one student. Each nomination packet should include the student's academic transcript, a description of the original contribution written by the student (such as a manuscript or reprint of a research publication or senior thesis), a 1,000-word summary, and 2 letters of recommendation.
**Financial data:** The award consists of a $5,000 honorarium for the student, a certificate citing the work and school of the recipient, and an allowance for travel expenses to the meeting of the American Physical Society (APS) at which the prize is presented. Each of the finalists receives an honorarium of $2,000 and a certificate. Each of the physics departments whose nominees are selected as recipients and finalists receives a certificate and an award; the departmental award is $5,000 for recipients and $1,000 for finalists.
**Duration:** The award is presented annually.
**Number awarded:** 2 recipients each year: 1 to a student at a Ph.D. granting institution and 1 at a non-Ph.D. granting institution.
**Deadline:** June of each year.

## 2398 LIBERTY MUTUAL SCHOLARSHIP

American Society of Safety Engineers, Attn: ASSE Foundation
1800 East Oakton Street
Des Plaines, IL 60018
Phone: (847) 768-3441; Fax: (847) 296-9220; Email: mrosario@asse.org
Web: www.asse.org
**Summary:** To provide financial assistance to upper-division student members of the American Society of Safety Engineers (ASSE).
**Eligibility:** Open to ASSE student members who are majoring in occupational safety and health or a closely-related field (e.g., safety engineering, safety management, systems safety, environmental science, industrial hygiene, ergonomics, fire science). Applicants must be full-time students who have completed at least 60 semester hours with a GPA of 3.0 or higher. As part of the selection process, they must submit 2 essays of 300 words or less: 1) why they are seeking a degree in safety, a brief description of their current activities, and how those relate to their career goals and objectives; and 2) why they should be awarded this scholarship (including career goals and financial need).
**Financial data:** The stipend is $3,000 per year.
**Duration:** 1 year; nonrenewable.
**Number awarded:** 1 each year.
**Deadline:** November of each year.

## 2399 LIEUTENANT GENERAL CHUBB AWARD

Hanscom Officers' Wives' Club, Attn: Scholarship Chair
P.O. Box 557
Bedford, MA 01730
Phone: (781) 275-1251; Email: scholarship@hanscomowd.org
Web: www.hanscomowc.org
**Summary:** To provide financial assistance to children of military personnel and veterans in New England who are interested in studying engineering or computer science in college.
**Eligibility:** Open to college-bound high school seniors living in New England who are dependents of active-duty, retired, or deceased military members of any branch of service. Also eligible are dependents of military recruiters working in the New York area and students living elsewhere but whose military sponsor is stationed at Hanscom Air Force Base. Applicants must demonstrate qualities of responsibility, leadership, scholastics, citizenship, and diversity of interest. They must have a valid military identification card and be planning to work on a college degree in engineering or computer science. Along with their application, they must submit a 2-page essay on their educational goals, how their educational experience will help prepare them to pursue future goals, and how they intend to apply their education to better their community.
**Financial data:** A stipend is awarded (amount not specified).
**Duration:** 1 year; nonrenewable.
**Number awarded:** 1 each year.
**Deadline:** March of each year.

## 2400 LIGHT METALS DIVISION SCHOLARSHIP

The Minerals, Metals & Materials Society, Attn: TMS Student Awards Program
184 Thorn Hill Road
Warrendale, PA 15086-7514
Phone: (724) 776-9000, ext. 220; Fax: (724) 776-3770;
Email: students@tms.org
Web: www.tms.org/Students/AwardsPrograms/Scholarships.html
**Summary:** To provide financial assistance to student members of The Minerals, Metals & Materials Society (TMS), particularly those interested in both traditional and emerging light metals.
**Eligibility:** Open to undergraduate members of the society majoring in metallurgical and/or materials science and engineering with an emphasis on both traditional and emerging light metals. Applicants may be from any country. Selection is based on academic achievement, school and community activities, work experience, leadership, a personal profile statement, and letters of recommendation. Preference is given to students in their junior or senior year who are enrolled full time and to applicants who have participated in a relevant industrial co-op program.
**Financial data:** The stipend is $4,000 plus a travel stipend of up to $600 (so the recipient can attend the annual meeting of the society to accept the award). In addition, recipients are given the opportunity of selecting up to $300 in LMD-sponsored conference proceedings or textbooks to be donated to their college or university library in their name and up to $400 in books for themselves.
**Duration:** 1 year.
**Number awarded:** 3 each year.
**Deadline:** April of each year.

## 2401 LILLIAN MOLLER GILBRETH SCHOLARSHIP

Society of Women Engineers
230 East Ohio Street, Suite 400
Chicago, IL 60611-3265
Phone: (312) 596-5223; Fax: (312) 644-8557; Email: hq@swe.org
Web: www.societyofwomenengineers.org/scholarships
**Summary:** To provide financial assistance to upper-division women majoring in computer science or engineering.
**Eligibility:** Open to women who are entering their junior or senior year at an ABET-accredited college or university. Applicants must be majoring in computer science or engineering and have a GPA of 3.0 or higher. Along with their application, they must submit a one-page essay on why they want to be an engineer or computer scientist, how they believe they will make a difference as an engineer or computer scientist, and what influenced them to study engineering or computer science. Selection is based on merit.
**Financial data:** The stipend is $6,000 per year.
**Duration:** 1 year; may be renewed.
**Number awarded:** 1 each year.
**Deadline:** January of each year.

## 2402 LISA ZAKEN AWARD FOR EXCELLENCE

Institute of Industrial Engineers, Attn: Chapter Operations Department
3577 Parkway Lane, Suite 200

Norcross, GA 30092
Phone: (770) 449-0461, ext. 118; (800) 494-0460; Fax: (770) 263-8532;
Email: srichards@iienet.org
Web: www.iienet.org
**Summary:** To provide financial assistance to undergraduate and graduate students in industrial engineering.
**Eligibility:** Open to undergraduate and graduate students enrolled full time in industrial engineering at ABET-accredited universities in the United States, Canada, or Mexico. Only student members of the Institute of Industrial Engineers (IIE) are eligible. Direct applications are not accepted; candidates must be nominated by the academic department head at their university. They must have an overall GPA of 3.0 or higher and at least one full year of school remaining. Selection is based on excellence in scholarly activities and leadership and involvement in IIE activities on campus.
**Financial data:** A stipend is awarded (amount not specified).
**Duration:** 1 year.
**Number awarded:** 1 each year.
**Deadline:** November of each year.

## 2403 LITHERLAND/FTE SCHOLARSHIP

International Technology Education Association
Attn: Foundation for Technology Education
1914 Association Drive, Suite 201
Reston, VA 20191-1539
Phone: (703) 860-2100; Fax: (703) 860-0353; Email: ideaordr@iris.org
Web: www.iteawww.org
**Summary:** To provide financial support to undergraduate members of the International Technology Education Association (ITEA) who are majoring in technology education teacher preparation.
**Eligibility:** Open to members of the association (membership may be enclosed with the scholarship application) who are in college but not yet seniors, majoring in technology education teacher preparation with a GPA of 2.5 or higher, and enrolled full time. Selection is based on interest in teaching, academic ability, financial need, and faculty recommendations.
**Financial data:** The stipend is $1,000. Funds are provided directly to the recipient.
**Duration:** 1 year.
**Number awarded:** 1 or more each year.
**Deadline:** November of each year.

## 2404 LOCKHEED AERONAUTICS COMPANY SCHOLARSHIPS

Society of Women Engineers
230 East Ohio Street, Suite 400
Chicago, IL 60611-3265
Phone: (312) 596-5223; Fax: (312) 644-8557; Email: hq@swe.org
Web: www.societyofwomenengineers.org/scholarships
**Summary:** To provide financial assistance to upper-division women majoring in designated engineering specialties.
**Eligibility:** Open to women who are entering their junior year at an ABET-accredited 4-year college or university. Applicants must be majoring in electrical or mechanical engineering and have a GPA of 3.5 or higher. Along with their application, they must submit a 1-page essay on why they want to be an engineer, how they believe they will make a difference as an engineer, and what influenced them to study engineering. Selection is based on merit.
**Financial data:** The stipend is $1,000.
**Duration:** 1 year.
**Number awarded:** 2 each year: 1 to a student in electrical engineering and 1 to a student in mechanical engineering.
**Deadline:** January of each year.

## 2405 LOCKHEED MARTIN CORPORATION SCHOLARSHIPS

Society of Women Engineers
230 East Ohio Street, Suite 400
Chicago, IL 60611-3265
Phone: (312) 596-5223; Fax: (312) 644-8557; Email: hq@swe.org
Web: www.societyofwomenengineers.org/scholarships
**Summary:** To provide financial assistance to women who will be entering college as freshmen and are interested in studying engineering or computer science.
**Eligibility:** Open to women who are entering college as freshmen with a GPA of 3.5 or higher. Applicants must be planning to enroll full time at an ABET-accredited 4-year college or university and major in computer science or engi-

neering. Along with their application, they must submit a 1-page essay on why they want to be an engineer or computer scientist, how they believe they will make a difference as an engineer or computer scientist, and what influenced them to study engineering or computer science. Selection is based on merit.
**Financial data:** The stipend is $3,000. Also provided is $500 for the recipient to attend the sponsor's annual convention.
**Duration:** 1 year.
**Number awarded:** 2 each year.
**Deadline:** May of each year.

## 2406 LOCKHEED MARTIN SCHOLARSHIP PROGRAM

Hispanic College Fund, Attn: National Director
1717 Pennsylvania Avenue, N.W., Suite 460
Washington, D.C. 20006
Phone: (202) 296-5400; (800) 644-4223; Fax: (202) 296-3774;
Email: hispaniccollegefund@earthlink.net
Web: www.hispanicfund.org
**Summary:** To provide financial assistance to Hispanic American undergraduate students who are interested in preparing for a career in computer science or engineering.
**Eligibility:** Open to U.S. citizens of Hispanic background (at least one grandparent must be 100% Hispanic) who are entering their freshman, sophomore, junior, or senior year of college. Applicants must be working on a bachelor's degree in engineering computer science, or on a related major, and have a cumulative GPA of 3.0 or higher. They must be applying to or enrolled in a college or university in the 50 states or Puerto Rico as a full-time student. Financial need is considered in the selection process.
**Financial data:** Stipends range from $500 to $5,000, depending on the need of the recipient, and average approximately $3,000. Funds are paid directly to the recipient's college or university to help cover tuition and fees.
**Duration:** 1 year; recipients may reapply.
**Number awarded:** Varies each year.
**Deadline:** April of each year.

## 2407 LOREN W. CROW MEMORIAL SCHOLARSHIP

American Meteorological Society, Attn: Fellowship/Scholarship Program
45 Beacon Street
Boston, MA 02108-3693
Phone: (617) 227-2426, ext. 246; Fax: (617) 742-8718;
Email: scholar@ametsoc.org
Web: www.ametsoc.org/amsstudentinfo/scholfeldocs/scholfel.html
**Summary:** To provide financial assistance to undergraduates majoring in meteorology or an aspect of atmospheric sciences with an interest in applied meteorology.
**Eligibility:** Open to full-time students entering their final year of undergraduate study and majoring in meteorology or an aspect of the atmospheric or related oceanic and hydrologic sciences. Applicants must intend to make atmospheric or related sciences their career, with preference for students who have demonstrated a strong interest in applied meteorology. They must be U.S. citizens or permanent residents enrolled at a U.S. institution and have a cumulative GPA of 3.25 or higher. Along with their application, they must submit 200-word essays on 1) their most important achievements that qualify them for this scholarship, and 2) their career goals in the atmospheric or related oceanic or hydrologic fields. Selection is based on academic excellence and achievement; financial need is not considered. The sponsor specifically encourages applications from women, minorities, and students with disabilities who are traditionally underrepresented in the atmospheric and related oceanic sciences.
**Financial data:** The stipend is $2,000 per year.
**Duration:** 1 year.
**Number awarded:** 1 each year.
**Deadline:** February of each year.

## 2408 LOUIS STOKES SCIENCE AND TECHNOLOGY AWARD

National Association for the Advancement of Colored People
Attn: Education Department
4805 Mt. Hope Drive
Baltimore, MD 21215-3297
Phone: (410) 580-5760; (877) NAACP-98; Email: youth@naacpnet.org
Web: www.naacp.org/work/education/eduscholarship.shtml
**Summary:** To provide financial assistance to incoming freshmen at Historically

Black Colleges and Universities (HBCUs) interested in majoring in selected scientific fields.

**Eligibility:** Open to students entering an HBCU and planning to be full-time students with a major in one of the following fields: computer science, engineering, biology, chemistry, or physics. Membership and participation in the NAACP is highly desirable. Applicants must have a GPA of 2.5 of higher and be able to demonstrate financial need, defined as a family income of less than $13,470 for a family of one ranging to $46,440 for a family of 8. Along with their application, they must submit a one-page essay on their interest in their major and a career, their life's ambition, what they hope to accomplish in their lifetime, and what they consider their most significant contribution to their community. U.S. citizenship is required.

**Financial data:** The stipend is $2,000.

**Duration:** 1 year; nonrenewable.

**Number awarded:** Varies each year; recently, 6 of these scholarships were awarded.

**Deadline:** April of each year.

### 2409 LOUISE MORITZ MOLITORIS LEADERSHIP AWARD

Women's Transportation Seminar, Attn: National Headquarters
1666 K Street, N.W., Suite 1100
Washington, DC 20006
Phone: (202) 496-4340; Fax: (202) 496-4349; Email: wts@wtsnational.org
Web: www.wtsnational.org

**Summary:** To provide financial assistance to undergraduate women interested in a career in transportation.

**Eligibility:** Open to women who are working on an undergraduate degree in transportation or a transportation-related field (e.g., transportation engineering, planning, finance, or logistics). Applicants must have a GPA of 3.0 or higher. They must submit a 500-word statement about their career goals after graduation and why they think they should receive the scholarship award; their statement should specifically address the issue of leadership. Applications must be submitted first to a local chapter; the chapters forward selected applications for consideration on the national level. Minority candidates are encouraged to apply. Selection is based on transportation involvement and goals, job skills, academic record, and leadership potential; financial need is not considered.

**Financial data:** The stipend is $3,000.

**Duration:** 1 year.

**Number awarded:** 1 each year.

**Deadline:** Applications must be submitted by November to a local WTS chapter.

### 2410 LOWELL GAYLOR MEMORIAL SCHOLARSHIP

Aircraft Electronics Association, Attn: AEA Educational Foundation
4217 South Hocker Drive
Independence, MO 64055-4723
Phone: (816) 373-6565; Fax: (816) 478-3100; Email: info@aea.net
Web: www.aea.net

**Summary:** To provide financial assistance to students who are interested in studying avionics or aircraft repair in college.

**Eligibility:** Open to high school seniors and currently-enrolled college students who are attending (or planning to attend) an accredited school in an avionics or aircraft repair program. Applicants must submit an official transcript (cumulative GPA of 2.5 or higher), a statement about their career plans, a description of their involvement in school and community activities, and a 300-word essay on how the job requirements of aviation technicians will change with advancements in technology. Selection is based on merit.

**Financial data:** The stipend is $1,000.

**Duration:** 1 year.

**Number awarded:** 1 each year.

**Deadline:** February of each year.

### 2411 LOWE'S EDUCATIONAL SCHOLARSHIP PROGRAM

Lowe's Companies, Inc., Attn: Scholarship Program
P.O. Box 1111
North Wilkesboro, NC 28656
Phone: (336) 658-4104; (800) 44-LOWES
Web: www.lowes.com/scholarships

**Summary:** To provide financial assistance to students at selected community and technical colleges who are preparing for a career in a business or technical field related to Lowe's stores.

**Eligibility:** Open to students who are at least 18 years of age and currently enrolled in a community or technical college that is cooperating with Lowe's stores. Applicants must intend to prepare for a career in an approved discipline within the business division (business management, business administration) or vocational/technical division (air conditioning, heating and refrigeration, construction, electrical or electronics, industrial maintenance, machining, mechanical drafting and design, plumbing, carpentry, or horticulture) of Lowe's. They must have completed at least one semester with a GPA of 2.0 or higher. Applications are accepted from current Lowe's employees, but students working for another major retailer are not eligible.

**Financial data:** Stipends are $2,000 for full-time students, $1,000 for three-quarter time students, or $800 for half-time students.

**Duration:** 1 year; may be renewed if the recipient qualifies for employment at Lowe's.

**Number awarded:** Varies each year; since the program was established, more than 150 of these scholarships have been awarded.

### 2412 LSAW AUXILIARY SCHOLARSHIP

Land Surveyors' Association of Washington
424 205th Avenue N.E.
Sammamish, WA 98074-6942
Phone: (425) 868-0200; Fax: (425) 868-1771
Web: www.lsaw.org

**Summary:** To provide financial assistance to undergraduate students who are preparing for a career as a professional land surveyor in the state of Washington.

**Eligibility:** Open to students who are working on 1) a 4-year degree in land surveying with the intent of becoming a professional land surveyor, or 2) a 1-year survey technician certificate. Applicants must demonstrate an interest in practicing in Washington after graduation. Along with their application, they must submit transcripts from any college or university they have attended and 4 letters of reference, including one from an instructor and another from an employer or member of the Land Surveyors' Association of Washington (LSAW).

**Financial data:** A stipend is awarded (amount not specified).

**Duration:** 1 year.

**Number awarded:** Varies each year.

**Deadline:** December of each year.

### 2413 LUCENT GLOBAL SCIENCE SCHOLARS PROGRAM

Institute of International Education
Attn: Lucent Global Science Scholars Program
809 United Nations Plaza
New York, NY 10017-3580
Phone: (212) 984-5419; Fax: (212) 984-5452; Email: sciencescholars@iie.org
Web: www.iie.org/programs/lucent

**Summary:** To provide financial assistance for college to high school students in the United States and university students in other designated countries who are interested in preparing for careers in information technology.

**Eligibility:** Open to high school seniors in the United States and first-year university students in Brazil, Canada, China, France, Germany, Hong Kong, India, Korea, Mexico, the Netherlands, Philippines, Poland, Russia, Spain, and the United Kingdom. Students from the United States must have a GPA of 3.6 or higher. Eligible majors include applied physics, chemistry, computer science, engineering, information science and technology, mathematics and applied mathematics, and physics. Selection is based on a demonstrated record of distinction in science and mathematics and a desire to prepare for a career in information technology.

**Financial data:** The stipend is $5,000 per year.

**Duration:** 1 year; nonrenewable.

**Number awarded:** Varies each year. Recently, 32 students from foreign countries (5 from China, 1 from Hong Kong, and 2 from each of the other countries) and 28 from the United States received these scholarships.

**Deadline:** February of each year for students from the United States; March of each year for students from other countries.

### 2414 LUCILE B. KAUFMAN WOMEN'S SCHOLARSHIPS

Society of Manufacturing Engineers, Attn: SME Education Foundation
One SME Drive
P.O. Box 930
Dearborn, MI 48121-0930
Phone: (313) 425-3304; (800) 733-4763, ext. 3304; Fax: (313) 425-3411;
Email: foundation@sme.org
Web: www.sme.org

**Summary:** To provide financial assistance to undergraduate women enrolled in a degree program in manufacturing engineering or manufacturing engineering technology.

**Eligibility:** Open to female students attending a degree-granting institution in North America on a full-time basis and preparing for a career in manufacturing engineering. They must have completed at least 30 units in a manufacturing engineering or manufacturing engineering technology curriculum with a GPA of 3.0 or higher. Need is not considered in awarding scholarships (unless 2 or more applicants have equal qualifications).

**Financial data:** The stipend is $1,500.

**Duration:** 1 year; may be renewed.

**Number awarded:** 2 each year.

**Deadline:** January of each year.

### 2415 LYDIA J. PICKUP MEMORIAL SCHOLARSHIP

Society of Women Engineers
230 East Ohio Street, Suite 400
Chicago, IL 60611-3265
Phone: (312) 596-5223; Fax: (312) 644-8557; Email: hq@swe.org
Web: www.societyofwomenengineers.org/scholarships

**Summary:** To provide financial assistance to women working on an undergraduate or graduate degree in engineering or computer science.

**Eligibility:** Open to women who will be sophomores, juniors, seniors, or graduate students at ABET-accredited colleges and universities. Applicants must be majoring in computer science or engineering and have a GPA of 3.0 or higher. Along with their application, they must submit a one-page essay on why they want to be an engineer or computer scientist, how they believe they will make a difference as an engineer or computer scientist, and what influenced them to study engineering or computer science. Selection is based on merit.

**Financial data:** The stipend is $2,000.

**Duration:** 1 year.

**Number awarded:** 1 each year.

**Deadline:** January of each year.

### 2416 LYDIA PICKUP MEMORIAL SCHOLARSHIPS

Society of Women Engineers-Pacific Northwest Section
Attn: Scholarship Committee
P.O. Box 31910
Seattle, WA 98103-0010
Email: pnw-swe@engineer.com
Web: www.swe-pnw.org/scholarships.html

**Summary:** To provide financial assistance to women studying engineering at a university in Montana or western Washington.

**Eligibility:** Open to women who have, at the time of application, completed at least 50% of the requirements toward college graduation in an engineering field. Applicants must be attending an ABET-accredited engineering school in western Washington or Montana. U.S. citizenship is required. They must submit an essay in which they describe their reasons for choosing their particular field of engineering; the person, event, or job experience influencing their decision to work on an engineering degree; and the most and least favorite courses they have taken and which course they are most looking forward to and why. Selection is based on the essay, academic achievement, educational goals, extracurricular activities, community service, and financial need.

**Financial data:** Stipends range from $1,000 to $2,000 per year.

**Duration:** 1 year.

**Number awarded:** 2 to 3 each year.

**Deadline:** April of each year.

### 2417 LYDIA'S PROFESSIONAL UNIFORMS/AACN EXCELLENCE IN ACADEMICS NURSING SCHOLARSHIP

American Association of Colleges of Nursing
One Dupont Circle, N.W., Suite 530
Washington, DC 20036
Phone: (202) 887-6791; Fax: (202) 785-8320; Email: rrosseter@aacn.nche.edu
Web: www.aacn.nche.edu

**Summary:** To provide financial assistance to students enrolled in the junior year of a bachelor's degree in nursing program.

**Eligibility:** Open to students entering the junior year of a bachelor of science in nursing (B.S.N.) degree program. Applicants must be enrolled full time, have a GPA of 3.5 or higher, and be able to demonstrate financial need. Along with their application, they must submit a 250-word essay describing their career aspirations and financial need.

**Financial data:** The stipend is $2,500.

**Duration:** 1 year.

**Number awarded:** 2 each year.

**Deadline:** June or October of each year.

### 2418 MACKINAC SCHOLARSHIP

American Society of Civil Engineers-Michigan Section
c/o Laurie Kendal, Scholarship Coordinator
43311 Joy Road
Canton, MI 48187-2075
Phone: (313) 271-2223; Fax: (313) 271-3076; Email: lak@msg-dearborn.com
Web: sections.asce.org/michigan/Resources/scholarships.htm

**Summary:** To provide financial assistance to Michigan residents who are entering the junior year of a civil engineering program.

**Eligibility:** Open to Michigan residents who are enrolled full time in an ABET-accredited civil and/or environmental engineering program. Applicants must be entering their junior year with a GPA of 2.5 or higher. U.S. citizenship is required. Selection is based on academic record, participation in American Society of Civil Engineers (ASCE) and other extracurricular activities, leadership, character, self-reliance, comments from employers and university officials, and financial need. Semifinalists may be contacted for an interview.

**Financial data:** The stipend is $2,500 per year.

**Duration:** 2 years.

**Number awarded:** 1 each year.

**Deadline:** August of each year.

### 2419 MAINE CHAPTER CLMA UNDERGRADUATE SCHOLARSHIPS

Clinical Laboratory Management Association-Maine Chapter
c/o Sonia E. Russell, Scholarship Chair
DCPA
337 State Street
Bangor, ME 04401
Phone: (207) 942-6759; Fax: (207) 942-2613; Email: srussell@mint.net
Web: www.melabs.org/clma/scholarship.htm

**Summary:** To provide financial assistance to residents of Maine working on a degree in laboratory medicine.

**Eligibility:** Open to Maine residents who are preparing for a career as a medical technologist, medical laboratory technician, histotechnologist, cytologist, or clinical laboratory scientist. Applicants must submit a brief essay describing why they have chosen their field of study and why they are applying for this scholarship. Selection is based on academic performance, character, commitment to laboratory medicine, and financial need.

**Financial data:** The stipend is $1,000.

**Duration:** 1 year.

**Number awarded:** 3 each year.

**Deadline:** May of each year.

### 2420 MAINE CHAPTER 276 SCHOLARSHIPS

National Association of Women in Construction-Maine Chapter 276
P.O. Box 366
Hallowell, ME 04347
Phone: (207) 623-4683; Email: nawicmaine@aol.com
Web: www.nawicmaine.org

**Summary:** To provide financial assistance to Maine residents who are working on a college degree in a field related to construction.

**Eligibility:** Open to residents of Maine who are enrolled in a postsecondary educational program. Applicants must be preparing for a career in construction, including carpentry, civil engineering, architecture, welding, electrical, plumbing, or construction management. Along with their application, they must submit a 50-word statement on why they have chosen a career in construction. Selection is based on academic achievement and financial need.

**Financial data:** Stipends range from $500 to $1,000.

**Duration:** 1 year.

**Number awarded:** Varies each year; recently, 7 of these scholarships were awarded.

**Deadline:** April of each year.

### 2421 MAINE METAL PRODUCTS ASSOCIATION SCHOLARSHIP

Maine Education Services, Attn: MES Foundation
One City Center, 11th Floor

Portland, ME 04101
Phone: (207) 791-3600; (800) 922-6352; Fax: (207) 791-3616;
Email: info@mesfoundation.com
Web: www.mesfoundation.com/college/scholarships_mes_metal_products.asp
**Summary:** To provide financial assistance to students in Maine who are interested in furthering their education in the machine or related metal working trades.
**Eligibility:** Open to students who have been accepted into a metal trades program at a college in Maine. The field of specialization may be mechanical engineering, machine tool technology, sheet metal fabrication, welding, or CADCAM for metals industry. Applicants must submit an essay on their goals, aspirations, and accomplishments; why and how they decided on a career in metal working; and why they think they should receive this scholarship. They will be interviewed by a member of the association. Selection is based on aptitude or demonstrated ability in the metal working trades, high school scholastic and extracurricular records, and personal qualifications of attitude, initiative, seriousness of intent, and overall impression.
**Financial data:** A stipend is awarded (amount not specified); funds may be applied toward the costs of tuition, textbooks, lab fees, supplies, and room and board.
**Duration:** 1 year.
**Number awarded:** Varies each year; recently, 9 of these scholarships were awarded.
**Deadline:** April of each year.

### 2422 MAINE RURAL REHABILITATION FUND SCHOLARSHIP

Maine Department of Agriculture, Food and Rural Resources
Attn: Scholarship Program Coordinator
28 State House Station
Augusta, ME 04333-0028
Phone: (207) 287-7628; Fax: (207) 287-7548;
Email: rod.mcCormick@maine.gov
Web: www.state.me.us/agriculture
**Summary:** To provide financial assistance to Maine residents interested in working on a degree in a field related to agriculture in college.
**Eligibility:** Open to residents of Maine who are enrolled or accepted for enrollment at a college or university that offers an agricultural program. Applicants must enroll full time in a program leading to a 2-year, 4-year, or advanced degree in agriculture, including agricultural business, sustainable agriculture, agricultural engineering, animal science, plant science, or soil science. They must have earned a cumulative GPA of 2.7 or higher or a GPA for the most recent semester of 3.0 or higher. They must also be able to demonstrate an unmet financial need.
**Financial data:** Awards are either $1,000 or $800 per year.
**Duration:** 1 year; may be renewed up to 3 additional years.
**Number awarded:** Varies each year; recently, 24 of these scholarships were awarded.
**Deadline:** June of each year.

### 2423 MAINE SOCIETY OF LAND SURVEYORS MERIT SCHOLARSHIPS

Maine Society of Land Surveyors, Attn: Executive Director
126 Western Avenue
PMB 211
Augusta, ME 04330
Phone: (207) 882-5200
Web: www.msls.org/ScholarshipsAvailable.htm
**Summary:** To provide financial assistance for college to Maine residents interested in preparing for a career as a surveyor.
**Eligibility:** Open to residents of Maine who are graduating high school seniors or students currently enrolled in college. Applicants must be interested in preparing for a career as a surveyor. Along with their application, they must submit an essay on their professional aspirations, their goals during and after college, the kind of work they want to do after graduation, and where they want to work. Financial need is considered in the selection process.
**Financial data:** The stipend is $1,000.
**Duration:** 1 year.
**Number awarded:** Varies each year; recently, 4 of these scholarships were awarded.

### 2424 MAINE SOCIETY OF PROFESSIONAL ENGINEERS SCHOLARSHIPS

Maine Society of Professional Engineers, Attn: Secretary

---

142 Mills Road
Kennebunkport, ME 04046-5705
Phone: (207) 967-3741; Fax: (207) 967-3741; Email: kencam@cybertours.com
**Summary:** To provide financial assistance to high school seniors in Maine who are interested in majoring in engineering in college.
**Eligibility:** Open to high school seniors in Maine. They must be interested in preparing for a career in engineering. Selection is based on GPA (20 points), SAT/ACT scores (20 points), activities (15 points), financial need (15 points), and composite application (10 points).
**Financial data:** The stipend is $1,500 per year.
**Duration:** 1 year.
**Number awarded:** 2 each year.
**Deadline:** February of each year.

### 2425 MAINE STATE CHAMBER OF COMMERCE SCHOLARSHIPS

**Summary:** To provide financial assistance for a college-level technical, education, or business program to residents of Maine.
*See Listing #610.*

### 2426 MALCOLM BALDRIGE SCHOLARSHIPS

Connecticut Community Foundation
81 West Main Street, Fourth Floor
Waterbury, CT 06702-1216
Phone: (203) 753-1315; Fax: (203) 756-3054; Email: info@conncf.org
Web: www.conncf.org
**Summary:** To provide financial assistance for college to residents of Connecticut interested in a career in foreign trade or manufacturing.
**Eligibility:** Open to residents of Connecticut who are attending or entering their freshmen year at a college or university in the state. Applicants must be interested in majoring in international business or manufacturing. U.S. citizenship is required. Selection is based on academic achievement, financial need, and (for students studying international business) accomplishment in foreign language study.
**Financial data:** Stipends range from $1,000 to $4,000 per year.
**Duration:** 1 year; renewable.
**Number awarded:** 1 to 3 each year.
**Deadline:** February of each year.

### 2427 MALSCE SCHOLARSHIPS

Massachusetts Association of Land Surveyors and Civil Engineers, Inc.
c/o The Engineering Center
One Walnut Street
Boston, MA 02108-3616
Phone: (617) 227-5551; Fax: (617) 227-6783; Email: malsce@engineers.org
Web: www.engineers.org/malsce/malsce_scholarship.html
**Summary:** To provide financial assistance to Massachusetts residents who are studying surveying, civil engineering, or environmental engineering in college.
**Eligibility:** Open to Massachusetts residents enrolled full time in a college, university, junior college, technical institute, or community college. Applicants must be majoring in surveying, civil engineering, or environmental engineering.
**Financial data:** A stipend is awarded (amount not specified).
**Duration:** 1 year.
**Number awarded:** Varies each year.
**Deadline:** July of each year.

### 2428 MARCELLA THOMPSON DISTINGUISHED SERVICE AWARD SCHOLARSHIP

American Society of Safety Engineers, Attn: ASSE Foundation
1800 East Oakton Street
Des Plaines, IL 60018
Phone: (847) 768-3441; Fax: (847) 296-9220; Email: mrosario@asse.org
Web: www.asse.org
**Summary:** To provide financial assistance to undergraduate student members of the American Society of Safety Engineers (ASSE).
**Eligibility:** Open to ASSE student members who are majoring in occupational safety and health or a closely-related field (e.g., safety engineering, safety management, systems safety, environmental science, industrial hygiene, ergonomics, fire science). Applicants must be full-time students who have completed

at least 60 semester hours with a GPA of 3.0 or higher. As part of the selection process, they must submit 2 essays of 300 words or less: 1) why they are seeking a degree in safety, a brief description of their current activities, and how those relate to their career goals and objectives; and 2) why they should be awarded this scholarship (including career goals and financial need).

**Financial data:** The stipend is $2,000 per year.
**Duration:** 1 year; nonrenewable.
**Number awarded:** 1 each year.
**Deadline:** November of each year.

## 2429 MARCIA PAGE SCHOLARSHIP FOR MATHEMATICS AND SCIENCE EDUCATION

Council of the Great City Schools
1301 Pennsylvania Avenue, N.W., Suite 702
Washington, DC 20004
Phone: (202) 393-2427; Fax: (202) 393-2400
Web: www.cgcs.org
**Summary:** To provide financial assistance to African American women interested in studying engineering, mathematics, science, or technology in college.
**Eligibility:** Open to African American women who are graduating from high school and have been accepted at a 4- or 5-year college or university as a full-time student. Applicants must be able to demonstrate academic achievement in high school, success in overcoming obstacles or achieving goals, and a commitment to a career in science, mathematics, engineering, or technology. They must be enrolled in a school district that is a member of the Council of the Great City Schools, a coalition of 64 of the nation's largest urban public school systems.
**Financial data:** The stipend is $5,000.
**Duration:** 1 year; nonrenewable.
**Number awarded:** 2 each year.
**Deadline:** April of each year.

## 2430 MARGARET A. STAFFORD NURSING SCHOLARSHIP

Delaware Community Foundation, Attn: Executive Vice President
100 West 10th Street, Suite 115
P.O. Box 1636
Wilmington, DE 19899
Phone: (302) 504-5222; Fax: (302) 571-1553; Email: rgentsch@delcf.org
Web: www.delcf.org
**Summary:** To provide financial assistance to residents of Delaware who are interested in preparing for a career in nursing.
**Eligibility:** Open to Delaware residents who have been accepted into the nursing program at an accredited college or university, in Delaware or any other state. Applicants must be beginning or furthering their nursing training. They should be seeking to improve the quality of health care in our society through nursing practices that ensure that patients' needs are a priority. Along with their application, they must submit a 1-page essay on why they desire to undertake a career in nursing. Selection is based on all facets of the applicant's education and activities that point to a successful college experience and nursing career. Preference is given to those students most in need of financial support.
**Financial data:** The stipend is $1,000.
**Duration:** 1 year; nonrenewable.
**Number awarded:** 1 each year.
**Deadline:** March of each year.

## 2431 MARGARET E. SWANSON SCHOLARSHIP

American Dental Hygienists' Association, Attn: Institute for Oral Health
444 North Michigan Avenue, Suite 3400
Chicago, IL 60611
Phone: (312) 440-8918; (800) 735-4916; Fax: (312) 440-8929;
Email: institute@adha.net
Web: www.adha.org/institute/Scholarship/index.htm
**Summary:** To provide financial assistance to students enrolled in a dental hygiene program who demonstrate exceptional organizational leadership potential.
**Eligibility:** Open to students who have completed at least one year in a certificate/associate's, baccalaureate, master's, or doctoral program in dental hygiene with at least a 3.0 GPA. Applicants must be able to demonstrate exceptional organizational leadership potential. They must be active members of the Student American Dental Hygienists' Association (SADHA) or the American Dental Hygienists' Association (ADHA) and be able to document financial need of at least $1,500. Along with their application, they must submit a state-

ment that covers their long-term career goals, their intended contribution to the dental hygiene profession, their professional interests, and the manner in which their degree will enhance their professional capacity. Graduate applicants must also include a description of the research in which they are involved or would like to become involved and a list of past and/or present involvement in professional and/or community activities. and full-time enrollment. Selection is based on their potential in public health or community dental health.
**Financial data:** Stipends range from $1,000 to $2,000.
**Duration:** 1 year.
**Number awarded:** 1 each year.
**Deadline:** April of each year.

## 2432 MARGARET JEROME SAMPSON SCHOLARSHIPS

Phi Upsilon Omicron, Attn: Educational Foundation
P.O. Box 329
Fairmont, WV 26555-0329
Phone: (304) 368-0612; Email: rickards@access.mountain.net
Web: www.phiu.unl.edu
**Summary:** To provide financial assistance to undergraduate student members of Phi Upsilon Omicron, a national honor society in family and consumer sciences, particularly those preparing for a career related to nutrition.
**Eligibility:** Open to members of the society who are working on a bachelor's degree in family and consumer sciences. Preference is given to majors in dietetics or food and nutrition who provide evidence of financial need. Selection is based on scholastic record, participation in society and other collegiate activities, a statement of professional aims and goals, professional services, and recommendations.
**Financial data:** The stipend is $3,000.
**Duration:** 1 year.
**Number awarded:** 4 each year.
**Deadline:** January of each year.

## 2433 MARGARET L. HAGEMAN SCHOLARSHIP

Wyoming Nurses Association, Attn: Finance Committee
Majestic Building, Suite 305
1603 Capitol Avenue
Cheyenne, WY 82001
Phone: (307) 635-3955; Fax: (307) 635-2173; Email: wyonurse@aol.com
**Summary:** To provide financial assistance to students in Wyoming who are working on a degree in nursing.
**Eligibility:** Open to Wyoming residents who are preparing for a career as a registered nurse or registered nurses who are pursuing advanced education in nursing. Applicants must have completed at least one semester in a Wyoming accredited nursing program. An interview may be required. Financial need is considered in the selection process. Preference is given to "nontraditional" students.
**Financial data:** The stipend is $1,200, paid in 2 equal installments.
**Duration:** 1 year.
**Number awarded:** 1 each year.
**Deadline:** July of each year.

## 2434 MARGARET MILLER MEMORIAL UNDERGRADUATE SCHOLARSHIP

Emergency Nurses Association, Attn: ENA Foundation
915 Lee Street
Des Plaines, IL 60016-6569
Phone: (847) 460-4100; (800) 900-9659, ext. 4100; Fax: (847) 460-4004;
Email: foundation@ena.org
Web: www.ena.org/foundation/grants
**Summary:** To provide financial assistance for baccalaureate study to nurses who are members of the Emergency Nurses Association (ENA).
**Eligibility:** Open to nurses (R.N., L.P.N., L.V.N.) who are working on a bachelor's degree. Applicants must have been members of the association for at least 12 months. They must submit a 1-page statement on their professional and educational goals and how this scholarship will help them attain those goals. Selection is based on content and clarity of the goal statement (45%), professional association involvement (45%), and GPA (10%).
**Financial data:** The stipend is $2,000.
**Duration:** 1 year; nonrenewable.
**Number awarded:** 1 each year.
**Deadline:** May of each year.

## 2435 MARGO BALLARD AND VIVIAN MEINECKE MEMORIAL SCHOLARSHIPS

Missouri League for Nursing, Inc., Attn: Executive Director
604 Dix Road
P.O. Box 104476
Jefferson City, MO 65110-4476
Phone: (573) 635-5355; Fax: (573) 635-7908; Email: mln@monursing.org
Web: www.monursing.org/programservices/prog_scholarships_memorial.htm
**Summary:** To provide financial assistance to students in Missouri who are enrolled in an accredited school of nursing.
**Eligibility:** Open to residents of Missouri enrolled in an accredited school of nursing in the state. Applicants may be L.P.N. students, R.N. students above the freshman level in associate's degree or diploma programs, R.N. students above the sophomore level in baccalaureate nursing programs, or M.S.N. candidates who have completed at least 15 hours of courses required for the advanced degree and have an active license in Missouri. They must be able to demonstrate financial need, have a GPA of 3.0 or higher, and be nominated by the dean or director of their school. U.S. citizenship is required.
**Financial data:** A stipend is awarded (amount not specified).
**Duration:** 1 year.
**Number awarded:** Varies each year.
**Deadline:** Nominations must be submitted by October of each year.

## 2436 MARINE SGT. JEANNETTE L. WINTERS MEMORIAL SCHOLARSHIP

Armed Forces Communications and Electronics Association
Attn: AFCEA Educational Foundation
4400 Fair Lakes Court
Fairfax, VA 22033-3899
Phone: (703) 631-6149; (800) 336-4583, ext. 6149; Fax: (703) 631-4693;
Email: scholarship@afcea.org
Web: www.afcea.org/education/scholarships/undergraduate/sgtjean.asp
**Summary:** To provide funding to members and veterans of the U.S. Marine Corps (USMC) who are majoring in specified fields in college.
**Eligibility:** Open to USMC personnel currently on active duty, in the Reserves, or honorably-discharged veterans who are enrolled full or part time in an accredited college or university in the United States. Applicants must be U.S. citizens, be of good moral character, have demonstrated academic excellence, be motivated to complete a college education, and be working on a degree in engineering (aerospace, computer, electrical, or systems), mathematics, physics, or computer science with a GPA of 3.0 or higher. They must provide a copy of Discharge Form DD214, Certificate of Service, or facsimile of their current Department of Defense Identification Card.
**Financial data:** The stipend is $2,000.
**Duration:** 1 year.
**Number awarded:** 1 each year.
**Deadline:** September of each year.

## 2437 MARK J. SCHROEDER ENDOWED SCHOLARSHIP IN METEOROLOGY

American Meteorological Society, Attn: Fellowship/Scholarship Program
45 Beacon Street
Boston, MA 02108-3693
Phone: (617) 227-2426, ext. 246; Fax: (617) 742-8718;
Email: scholar@amet oc.org
Web: www.ametsoc.org/amsstudentinfo/scholfeldocs/scholfel.html
**Summary:** To provide financial assistance to students majoring in meteorology or some aspect of atmospheric sciences who demonstrate financial need.
**Eligibility:** Open to full-time students entering their final year of undergraduate study and majoring in meteorology or an aspect of the atmospheric or related oceanic and hydrologic sciences. Applicants must intend to make atmospheric or related sciences their career. They must be U.S. citizens or permanent residents enrolled at a U.S. institution and have a cumulative GPA of 3.25 or higher. Along with their application, they must submit 200-word essays on 1) their most important achievements that qualify them for this scholarship, and 2) their career goals in the atmospheric or related oceanic or hydrologic fields. Selection is based on academic excellence and achievement and financial need. The sponsor specifically encourages applications from women, minorities, and students with disabilities who are traditionally underrepresented in the atmospheric and related oceanic sciences.
**Financial data:** The stipend is $5,000.
**Duration:** 1 year.
**Number awarded:** 1 each year.
**Deadline:** February of each year.

## 2438 MARSH AFFINITY GROUP SERVICES SCHOLARSHIP

American Dental Hygienists' Association, Attn: Institute for Oral Health
444 North Michigan Avenue, Suite 3400
Chicago, IL 60611
Phone: (312) 440-8918; (800) 735-4916; Fax: (312) 440-8929;
Email: institute@adha.net
Web: www.adha.org/institute/Scholarship/index.htm
**Summary:** To provide financial assistance to undergraduate students preparing for careers in dental hygiene.
**Eligibility:** Open to full-time undergraduate students who are active members of the Student American Dental Hygienists' Association (SADHA) or the American Dental Hygienists' Association (ADHA). Applicants must have a GPA between 3.0 and 3.5, be able to document financial need of at least $1,500, and have completed at least one year in an accredited dental hygiene program in the United States. Along with their application, they must submit a statement that covers their long-term career goals, their intended contribution to the dental hygiene profession, their professional interests, and the manner in which their degree will enhance their professional capacity.
**Financial data:** Stipends range from $1,000 to $2,000.
**Duration:** 1 year.
**Number awarded:** 1 each year.
**Deadline:** April of each year.

## 2439 MARSH RISK CONSULTING SCHOLARSHIP

American Society of Safety Engineers, Attn: ASSE Foundation
1800 East Oakton Street
Des Plaines, IL 60018
Phone: (847) 768-3441; Fax: (847) 296-9220; Email: mrosario@asse.org
Web: www.asse.org
**Summary:** To provide financial assistance to upper-division student members of the American Society of Safety Engineers (ASSE).
**Eligibility:** Open to ASSE student members who are majoring in occupational safety and health or a closely-related field (e.g., safety engineering, safety management, systems safety, environmental science, industrial hygiene, ergonomics, fire science). Applicants must be full-time students who have completed at least 60 semester hours with a GPA of 3.0 or higher. As part of the selection process, they must submit 2 essays of 300 words or less: 1) why they are seeking a degree in safety, a brief description of their current activities, and how those relate to their career goals and objectives; and 2) why they should be awarded this scholarship (including career goals and financial need).
**Financial data:** The stipend is $5,000 per year.
**Duration:** 1 year; nonrenewable.
**Number awarded:** 1 each year.
**Deadline:** November of each year.

## 2440 MARTIN SMILO UNDERGRADUATE SCHOLARSHIP

California Environmental Health Association
110 South Fairfax, A11-175
Los Angeles, CA 90036
Phone: (323) 634-7698; Fax: (323) 571-1889; Email: support@ceha.org
Web: www.ceha.org/awards.html
**Summary:** To provide financial assistance to undergraduates in California interested in preparing for a career in the sciences, especially environmental health.
**Eligibility:** Open to California students who have completed at least 48 semester units of undergraduate study, including at least 12 semester units in science, with a GPA of 3.0 or higher. Applicants must be enrolled full time at an accredited 4-year college or university with an intention to work on a degree and prepare for a career in science. Preference is given to students in environmental health. Along with their application, they must submit a 3-page essay on one of 3 assigned topics related to public health and the role of professional organizations. Financial need is not considered in the selection process.
**Financial data:** The stipend is $2,500.
**Duration:** 1 year.
**Number awarded:** 1 each year.
**Deadline:** February of each year.

## 2441 MARVIN L. ZUIDEMA SCHOLARSHIP AWARD

American Society of Civil Engineers-Michigan Section
c/o Laurie Kendal, Scholarship Coordinator
43311 Joy Road
Canton, MI 48187-2075

Phone: (313) 271-2223; Fax: (313) 271-3076; Email: lak@msg-dearborn.com

Web: sections.asce.org/michigan/Resources/scholarships.htm

**Summary:** To provide financial assistance to Michigan residents who are entering the junior or senior year of a civil engineering program.

**Eligibility:** Open to Michigan residents who are enrolled full time in an ABET-accredited civil and/or environmental engineering program. Applicants must be entering their junior or senior year with a GPA of 2.5 or higher. U.S. citizenship and student membership in the American Society of Civil Engineers (ASCE) are required. Selection is based on academic record, participation in extracurricular activities, leadership, character, self-reliance, comments from employers and university officials, and financial need. Semifinalists may be contacted for an interview.

**Financial data:** The stipend is $1,000.

**Duration:** 1 year.

**Number awarded:** 1 each year.

**Deadline:** August of each year.

### 2442 MARY ANNE WILLIAMS SCHOLARSHIP

United Daughters of the Confederacy-Virginia Division

c/o Suzie Snyder, Education Committee Chair

8440 Bradshaw Road

Salem, VA 24153-2246

Phone: (540) 384-6884; Email: Suzienotes@aol.com

Web: users.erols.com/va-udc/scholarships.html

**Summary:** To provide financial assistance for undergraduate or graduate study in medicine or engineering to Confederate descendants from Virginia.

**Eligibility:** Open to residents of Virginia who are 1) lineal descendants of Confederates, or 2) collateral descendants and also members of the Children of the Confederacy or the United Daughters of the Confederacy. Applicants must be interested in working on an undergraduate or graduate degree in medicine or engineering. They must submit proof of the Confederate military record of at least one ancestor, with the company and regiment in which he served. They must also submit a personal letter pledging to make the best possible use of the scholarship; describing their health, social, family, religious, and fraternal connections within the community; and reflecting on what a Southern heritage means to them (using the term "War Between the States" in lieu of "Civil War"). They must have a GPA of 3.0 or higher and be able to demonstrate financial need.

**Financial data:** The amount of the stipend depends on the availability of funds. Payment is made directly to the college or university the recipient attends.

**Duration:** 1 year; may be renewed up to 3 additional years if the recipient maintains a GPA of 3.0 or higher.

**Number awarded:** This scholarship is offered whenever a prior recipient graduates or is no longer eligible.

**Deadline:** By May of the years in which the scholarship is available.

### 2443 MARY BENEVENTO SCHOLARSHIP

**Summary:** To provide financial assistance to high school seniors in Connecticut who are interested in studying health, physical education, recreation, or dance in college.

*See Listing #1549.*

### 2444 MARY JO CLAYTON SANDERS ENVIRONMENTAL ISSUES SCHOLARSHIP

Florida Federation of Garden Clubs, Inc., Attn: Office Manager

1400 South Denning Drive

Winter Park, FL 32789-5662

Phone: (407) 647-7016; Fax: (407) 647-5479; Email: ffgc@earthlink.net

Web: www.ffgc.org/scholarships/index.html

**Summary:** To provide financial aid to Florida undergraduates and graduate students majoring in environmental issues.

**Eligibility:** Open to Florida residents who are enrolled as full-time juniors, seniors, or graduate students in a Florida college. They must have a GPA of 3.0 or higher, be in financial need, and be majoring in environmental issues (including city planning, land management, environmental control, and allied subjects). U.S. citizenship is required. Selection is based on academic record, commitment to career, character, and financial need.

**Financial data:** The stipend is $3,500. The funds are sent directly to the recipient's school and distributed semiannually.

**Duration:** 1 year.

**Number awarded:** 1 each year.

**Deadline:** April of each year.

### 2445 MARY MCMILLAN SCHOLARSHIP AWARDS

American Physical Therapy Association, Attn: Honors and Awards Program

1111 North Fairfax Street

Alexandria, VA 22314-1488

Phone: (703) 684-APTA; (800) 999-APTA; Fax: (703) 684-7343;

TDD: (703) 683-6748; Email: Governce@apta.org

Web: www.apta.org

**Summary:** To provide financial assistance to students in physical therapist assistant, professional physical therapy education, and post-professional master's degree programs.

**Eligibility:** Open to 1) physical therapist assistant education program students in the final year of study; 2) physical therapist professional education program students (including entry-level doctor of physical therapy degree students) who have completed at least one full year of entry-level education; and 3) post-professional master's degree students who have completed at least one term in the program and are enrolled at the time. Students must be nominated by the school they are attending. Selection is based on scholastic performance, past productivity, evidence of potential contribution to physical therapy, and service to the American Physical Therapy Association.

**Financial data:** The stipend is $3,000 for physical therapist assistant students or $5,000 for physical therapist professional education students (including entry-level doctor of physical therapy degree students) and post-professional master's degree students.

**Duration:** 1 year.

**Number awarded:** Varies each year.

**Deadline:** November of each year.

### 2446 MARY OPAL WOLANIN UNDERGRADUATE SCHOLARSHIP

National Gerontological Nurses Association

7794 Grow Drive

Pensacola, FL 32514-7072

Phone: (850) 473-1174; (800) 723-0560; Fax: (850) 484-8762;

Email: ngna@puctzamc.com

Web: www.ngna.org/html/awards.htm

**Summary:** To provide financial assistance for undergraduate education to members of the National Gerontological Nurses Association (NGNA).

**Eligibility:** Open to members of the association who are full- or part-time nursing students in the junior year of a baccalaureate program or sophomore year of an associate's program at a school accredited by the NLN. Applicants must submit 3 letters of recommendation, a current school catalog describing courses with gerontological nursing content, all academic transcripts (at least a 3.0 GPA is required), a statement of purpose for requesting the scholarship, a statement of future professional and educational goals, and a statement of financial need. They must intend to work in a gerontology/geriatric setting after graduation. U.S. citizenship is required.

**Financial data:** The stipend is $1,500.

**Duration:** 1 year.

**Number awarded:** 1 or more each year.

**Deadline:** July of each year.

### 2447 MARYLAND FIRE FIGHTER, AMBULANCE, AND RESCUE SQUAD MEMBER TUITION REIMBURSEMENT PROGRAM

Maryland Higher Education Commission

Attn: Office of Student Financial Assistance

839 Bestgate Road, Suite 400

Annapolis, MD 21401-3013

Phone: (410) 260-4574; (800) 974-1024, ext. 4574; Fax: (410) 974-5376;

TTY: (800) 735-2258; Email: osfamail@mhec.state.md.us

Web: www.mhec.state.md.us/financialAid/ProgramDescriptions/prog_fire.asp

**Summary:** To provide financial assistance for college and graduate school to fire fighters, ambulance, and rescue squad members in Maryland.

**Eligibility:** Open to fire fighters, ambulance, and rescue squad members who are enrolled as full-time or part-time undergraduate or graduate students at an accredited institution of higher education in Maryland in a degree or certificate program for fire service technology or emergency medical technology. Applicants must have received at least a grade of C in any course required for completion of their program. They must be serving a Maryland community while they are taking college courses.

**Financial data:** Awards provide full reimbursement of tuition charges the student has paid.

**Duration:** 1 year; may be renewed if the recipient maintains satisfactory academic progress and remains enrolled in an eligible program.

**Number awarded:** Varies each year.

**Deadline:** June of each year.

## 2448 MARYLAND LEGION AUXILIARY CHILDREN AND YOUTH FUND SCHOLARSHIP

**Summary:** To provide financial assistance for college to the daughters of veterans who are Maryland residents and wish to study arts, sciences, business, public administration, education, or a medical field.

*See Listing #1552.*

## 2449 MARYLAND LEGION AUXILIARY PAST PRESIDENTS' PARLEY NURSING SCHOLARSHIP

American Legion Auxiliary, Attn: Department of Maryland
1589 Sulphur Spring Road, Suite 105
Baltimore, MD 21227
Phone: (410) 242-9519; Fax: (410) 242-9553; Email: anna@alamd.org
**Summary:** To provide financial assistance for nursing education to the female descendants of Maryland veterans.
**Eligibility:** Open to Maryland residents who are the daughters, granddaughters, great-granddaughters, step-daughters, step-granddaughters, or step-great-granddaughters of ex-servicewomen (or of ex-servicemen, if there are no qualified descendants of ex-servicewomen). Applicants must be interested in becoming a registered nurse and be able to show financial need. They must submit a 300-word essay on the topic "What a Nursing Career Means to Me."
**Financial data:** The stipend is $2,000. Funds are sent directly to the recipient's school.
**Duration:** 1 year; may be renewed for up to 3 additional years if the recipient remains enrolled full time.
**Number awarded:** 1 each year.
**Deadline:** April of each year.

## 2450 MARYLAND SOCIETY OF SURVEYORS SCHOLARSHIPS

Maryland Society of Surveyors, Attn: Educational Trust
P.O. Box 686
College Park, MD 20741-0686
Web: www.marylandsurveyor.org
**Summary:** To provide financial assistance for college to Maryland residents interested in preparing for a career as a surveyor.
**Eligibility:** Open to Maryland residents who are attending or planning to attend a college or university to prepare for a career as a surveyor. Applicants must submit an essay on their educational and career goals and the factors that make them particularly deserving of support. Selection is based on the essay, high school and/or college transcripts, employment experience, and letters of recommendation.
**Financial data:** A stipend is awarded (amount not specified). Funds may be used only for tuition.
**Duration:** 1 year.
**Number awarded:** 1 or more each year.
**Deadline:** July of each year.

## 2451 MASSACHUSETTS HIGH TECHNOLOGY SCHOLAR/INTERN TUITION WAIVER PROGRAM

Massachusetts Office of Student Financial Assistance
454 Broadway, Suite 200
Revere, MA 02151
Phone: (617) 727-9420; Fax: (617) 727-0667; Email: osfa@osfa.mass.edu
Web: www.osfa.mass.edu
**Summary:** To provide financial assistance to students at Massachusetts public institutions of higher education who are participating in a high technology scholar/intern program.
**Eligibility:** Open to students at Massachusetts public institutions who are participating as interns in a computer information science/technology and engineering program approved by the Massachusetts Board of Higher Education. Applicants must be U.S. citizens or permanent residents who are residents of Massachusetts. Their institution must have obtained scholarship funding from business and industry.
**Financial data:** The awards match industry scholarships up to the resident undergraduate tuition rate at the participating institution.
**Duration:** Up to 4 academic years.
**Number awarded:** Varies each year.

## 2452 MASTER BREWERS ASSOCIATION OF THE AMERICAS ACADEMIC SCHOLARSHIP FUND

Master Brewers Association of the Americas, Attn: Chair, Scholarship Committee
3340 Pilot Knob Road
St. Paul, MN 55121-2097
Phone: (651) 454-7250; Fax: (651) 454-0766; Email: mbaa@mbaa.com
Web: www.mbaa.com/scholarship/scholartx.html
**Summary:** To provide financial assistance for college to 1) children of members of the Master Brewers Association of the Americas or 2) persons employed for at least 5 years in the brewing industry, particularly those interested in food science.
**Eligibility:** Open to children of members of the association or individuals who have been employed for at least 5 years in the brewing industry (which is defined to include malt houses, consulting laboratories, or similar services specializing in technical assistance to the brewing industry). Applicants must be entering their third year of full-time study in college. They must be majoring in an area related to malting or brewing, including production, research, quality assurance, engineering, and beer packaging. Preference is given to students in food science programs, particularly in which fermentation science courses are offered. Every application should be endorsed by 2 members of the association. Financial need is not considered in the selection process.
**Financial data:** The annual stipend is $4,000.
**Duration:** 2 years (4 semesters).
**Number awarded:** Several each year.
**Deadline:** February of each year.

## 2453 MASTERFOODS USA UNDERGRADUATE MENTORED SCHOLARSHIPS FOR COLLEGE STUDENTS

Institute of Food Technologists, Attn: Scholarship Department
525 West Van Buren, Suite 1000
Chicago, IL 60607
Phone: (312) 782-8424; Fax: (312) 782-8348; Email: info@ift.org
Web: www.ift.org
**Summary:** To provide financial assistance to minority undergraduates interested in studying food science or food technology.
**Eligibility:** Open to members of minority groups (African Americans, Native Indians, Hispanic Americans, and Asian Americans) who are entering the junior year of a food science or food technology program at an educational institution in the United States. Applicants may be transferring from another program in a 4-year college or from a 2-year junior college. Along with their application, they must submit an essay on their career aspirations; a list of awards, honors, and scholarships they have received; a list of extracurricular activities and/or hobbies; and a summary of their work experience. Financial need is not considered in the selection process.
**Financial data:** The stipend is $4,000 per year. Recipients are also invited to attend the annual meeting of the Institute of Food Technologists (IFT); travel expenses up to $550 are reimbursed.
**Duration:** 1 year; may be renewed if the recipient maintains a GPA of 3.0 or higher and participates in a mentoring program.
**Number awarded:** 5 each year.
**Deadline:** January of each year.

## 2454 MASTERFOODS USA UNDERGRADUATE MENTORED SCHOLARSHIPS FOR HIGH SCHOOL SENIORS

Institute of Food Technologists, Attn: Scholarship Department
525 West Van Buren, Suite 1000
Chicago, IL 60607
Phone: (312) 782-8424; Fax: (312) 782-8348; Email: info@ift.org
Web: www.ift.org
**Summary:** To provide financial assistance to minority high school seniors interested in studying food science or food technology in college.
**Eligibility:** Open to high school seniors planning to enroll in a food science or food technology program at an educational institution in the United States. Applicants must be members of minority groups (African American, Native Indian, Hispanic American, or Asian American) with a GPA of 3.0 or higher and scores of at least 25 on the ACT or the equivalent on the SAT. Along with their application, they must submit a brief biographical sketch and a statement on why they would like to become a food technologist. Financial need is not considered in the selection process.
**Financial data:** The stipend is $4,000 per year. Recipients are also invited to attend the annual meeting of the Institute of Food Technologists (IFT); travel expenses up to $550 are reimbursed.
**Duration:** 1 year; may be renewed if the recipient maintains a GPA of 3.0 or higher and participates in a mentoring program.
**Number awarded:** 2 each year.
**Deadline:** May of each year.

## 2455 MASWE SCHOLARSHIP

Society of Women Engineers
230 East Ohio Street, Suite 400
Chicago, IL 60611-3265
Phone: (312) 596-5223; Fax: (312) 644-8557; Email: hq@swe.org
Web: www.societyofwomenengineers.org/scholarships
**Summary:** To provide financial assistance to undergraduate women majoring in computer science or engineering.
**Eligibility:** Open to women who are entering their sophomore, junior, or senior year at a 4-year ABET-accredited college or university. Applicants must be majoring in computer science or engineering and have a GPA of 3.0 or higher. Along with their application, they must submit a one-page essay on why they want to be an engineer or computer scientist, how they believe they will make a difference as an engineer or computer scientist, and what influenced them to study engineering or computer science. Financial need is considered in the selection process.
**Financial data:** The stipend is $2,000.
**Duration:** 1 year.
**Number awarded:** 1 each year.
**Deadline:** January of each year.

## 2456 MAUREEN L. AND HOWARD N. BLITMAN, P.E. SCHOLARSHIP TO PROMOTE DIVERSITY IN ENGINEERING

National Society of Professional Engineers, Attn: Education Services
1420 King Street
Alexandria, VA 22314-2794
Phone: (703) 684-2833; Fax: (703) 836-4875; Email: jiglesias@nspe.org
Web: www.nspe.org/scholarships/sc1-hs.asp
**Summary:** To provide financial assistance for college to members of underrepresented ethnic minority groups interested in preparing for a career in engineering.
**Eligibility:** Open to members of underrepresented ethnic minorities (African Americans, Hispanics, or Native Americans) who are high school seniors accepted into an ABET-accredited engineering program at a 4-year college or university. Applicants must have a GPA of 3.5 or higher and above average SAT or ACT scores (for example, English ACT score of 29 or higher and math ACT score of 29 or higher). They must submit brief essays on an experience they consider significant to their interest in engineering, how their study of engineering will contribute to their long-term career plans, how their ethnic background has influenced their personal development and perceptions, and anything special about them that they would like the selection committee to know. Financial need is not considered in the selection process. U.S. citizenship is required.
**Financial data:** The stipend is $5,000 per year; funds are paid directly to the recipient's institution.
**Duration:** 1 year; nonrenewable.
**Number awarded:** 1 each year.
**Deadline:** February of each year.

## 2457 MAX ZAR SCHOLARSHIP

Structural Engineers Association of Illinois
Attn: Structural Engineers Foundation
203 North Wabash Avenue, Suite 2010
Chicago, IL 60601
Phone: (312) 372-4198; Fax: (312) 372-5673
Web: www.seaoi.org/html/body_sef.html
**Summary:** To provide financial assistance to upper-division and graduate students at universities in Illinois who are interested in a career in structural engineering.
**Eligibility:** Open to students 1) entering their third or higher year of an undergraduate program, or 2) entering or continuing a graduate program. Applicants must be enrolled in a civil or architectural engineering program at a university in Illinois and planning to continue with a structural engineering specialization. Students enrolled in structural engineering technology programs are also eligible if they are qualified to take the Fundamentals of Engineering and Principles and Practice licensure examinations in their home state upon graduation. U.S. citizenship or permanent resident status is required. Selection is based on a statement giving reasons why the applicant should receive the award (including plans for continued formal education), transcripts, 3 letters of recommendation, and potential for development and leadership. Financial need is not considered.
**Financial data:** The stipend is $1,500.
**Duration:** 1 year; nonrenewable.
**Number awarded:** 1 or more each year.
**Deadline:** March of each year.

## 2458 MCCORMICK AND COMPANY ENDOWMENT SCHOLARSHIP

Institute of Food Technologists, Attn: Scholarship Department
525 West Van Buren, Suite 1000
Chicago, IL 60607
Phone: (312) 782-8424; Fax: (312) 782-8348; Email: info@ift.org
Web: www.ift.org
**Summary:** To provide financial assistance to undergraduates interested in studying food science or food technology.
**Eligibility:** Open to sophomores, juniors, and seniors in a food science or food technology program at an educational institution in the United States or Canada. Applicants must have an outstanding scholastic record and a well-rounded personality. Along with their application, they must submit an essay on their career aspirations; a list of awards, honors, and scholarships they have received; a list of extracurricular activities and/or hobbies; and a summary of their work experience. Financial need is not considered in the selection process.
**Financial data:** The stipend is $1,500.
**Duration:** 1 year; recipients may reapply if they are members of the Institute of Food Technologists (IFT).
**Number awarded:** 1 each year.
**Deadline:** January of each year.

## 2459 MCLEAN SCHOLARSHIP FOR NURSING AND PHYSICIAN ASSISTANT MAJORS

Association of Independent Colleges and Universities of Pennsylvania
101 North Front Street
Harrisburg, PA 17101-1405
Phone: (717) 232-8649; Fax: (717) 233-8574; Email: info@aicup.org
Web: www.aicup.org
**Summary:** To provide financial assistance to students at member institutions of the Association of Independent Colleges and Universities of Pennsylvania (AICUP) who are enrolled in a nursing or physician assistant program.
**Eligibility:** Open to full-time undergraduate students at AICUP colleges and universities. Applicants must be enrolled in a nursing or physician assistant program and have a GPA of 3.0 or higher. Along with their application, they must submit an essay on how they chose their major, the steps they are taking to ensure that they succeed in their major, what they plan to do after graduation, the volunteer and extracurricular activities in which they participate, and how those activities relate to their major. Selection is based on their GPA (30%), steps taken to ensure success in their major (10%), career goals (10%), volunteer work (25%), relationship of volunteer and extracurricular activities to major (10%), and extent of their leadership activities (15%). Applications must be submitted to the financial aid office at the AICUP college or university that the student attends.
**Financial data:** The stipend is $2,500.
**Duration:** 1 year.
**Number awarded:** Varies each year; recently, 7 of these scholarships were awarded.
**Deadline:** April of each year.

## 2460 MCNAUGHTON OCEANOGRAPHIC SCHOLARSHIP

Woman's National Farm and Garden Association, Inc.
P.O. Box 1175
Midland, MI 48641-1175
Web: www.wnfga.org/code/scholarships.htm
**Summary:** To provide financial assistance to undergraduate and graduate students working on a degree in oceanography.
**Eligibility:** Open to undergraduate and graduate students in oceanography and related fields. There is no formal application. Interested students must submit a letter with a statement of their objectives and interests, a resume with references, 2 letters of recommendation, academic transcripts, and a description of their planned program at an educational institution.
**Financial data:** The stipend ranges from $1,000 to $1,500.
**Duration:** 1 year.
**Number awarded:** 1 each year.
**Deadline:** May of each year.

## 2461 M.E. AMSTUTZ MEMORIAL AWARD

Illinois Society of Professional Engineers, Attn: ISPE Foundation, Inc.
600 South Second Street, Suite 403
Springfield, IL 62704
Phone: (217) 544-7424; Fax: (217) 528-6545;

Email: info@IllinoisEngineer.com
410
Web: www.ilspe.com/StudentsAndYouth.asp

**Summary:** To provide financial assistance to college juniors and seniors in Illinois who are working on an engineering degree.

**Eligibility:** Open to Illinois residents who are juniors or seniors in college in the state and enrolled in an engineering program (not engineering technology) accredited by the Accreditation Board of Engineering and Technology (ABET). They must have at least a 3.0 GPA in those courses that count toward their engineering degree. Selection is based on financial need, scholastic achievement, activities, interest in engineering, and a 200-word essay on "Why I would like to become a professional engineer."

**Financial data:** The stipend is $1,500 per year.

**Duration:** 1 year.

**Number awarded:** 1 each year.

**Deadline:** January of each year.

## 2462 MEDTRONIC PHYSIO-CONTROL ACADEMIC SCHOLARSHIP

American Association of Occupational Health Nurses, Inc.
Attn: AAOHN Foundation
2920 Brandywine Road, Suite 100
Atlanta, GA 30341-4146
Phone: (770) 455-7757; Fax: (770) 455-7271; Email: foundation@aaohn.org
Web: www.aaohn.org/foundation/scholarships/academic_study.cfm

**Summary:** To provide financial assistance to registered nurses who are working on a bachelor's or graduate degree to prepare for a career in occupational and environmental health.

**Eligibility:** Open to registered nurses who are enrolled in a baccalaureate or graduate degree program. Applicants must demonstrate an interest in, and commitment to, occupational and environmental health. Selection is based on 2 letters of recommendation and a 500-word essay on the applicant's professional goals as they relate to the academic activity and the field of occupational and environmental health.

**Financial data:** The stipend is $3,000.

**Duration:** 1 year; may be renewed up to 2 additional years.

**Number awarded:** 1 each year.

**Deadline:** November of each year.

## 2463 MELVIN R. GREEN SCHOLARSHIPS

ASME International, Attn: Coordinator, Educational Operations
Three Park Avenue
New York, NY 10016-5990
Phone: (212) 591-8131; (800) THE-ASME; Fax: (212) 591-7143;
Email: oluwanifiset@asme.org
Web: www.asme.org/education/enged/aid/scholar.htm

**Summary:** To provide financial assistance to undergraduate students who are members of the American Society of Mechanical Engineers (ASME).

**Eligibility:** Open to student members in good standing who are enrolled in an ABET-accredited mechanical engineering, mechanical engineering technology, or related baccalaureate program. They must be entering their junior or senior year when they apply. There are no citizenship or geographic requirements. Interested students should submit an application form, a nomination from the applicant's department head, a recommendation from a faculty member, and an official transcript. Only one nomination may be submitted per department. Selection is based on leadership, scholastic ability, potential contribution to the mechanical engineering profession, and financial need.

**Financial data:** The stipend is $3,500.

**Duration:** 1 year.

**Number awarded:** 2 each year.

**Deadline:** March of each year.

## 2464 MENTOR GRAPHICS SCHOLARSHIPS

Oregon Student Assistance Commission
Attn: Grants and Scholarships Division
1500 Valley River Drive, Suite 100
Eugene, OR 97401-2146
Phone: (541) 687-7395; (800) 452-8807, ext. 7395; Fax: (541) 687-7419;
Email: awardinfo@mercury.osac.state.or.us
Web: www.osac.state.or.us

**Summary:** To provide financial assistance to Oregon residents who are working on a college degree in computer science or engineering.

**Eligibility:** Open to residents of Oregon who are U.S. citizens or permanent

residents. Applicants must be full-time students in their junior or senior year of college and majoring in electrical engineering or computer science/engineering. Preference is given to female, African American, Native American, or Hispanic applicants. Financial need must be demonstrated.

**Financial data:** The stipend is at least $2,000.

**Duration:** 1 year.

**Number awarded:** Varies each year; recently, 4 of these scholarships were awarded.

**Deadline:** February of each year.

## 2465 MERIDITH THOMS MEMORIAL SCHOLARSHIPS

Society of Women Engineers
230 East Ohio Street, Suite 400
Chicago, IL 60611-3265
Phone: (312) 596-5223; Fax: (312) 644-8557; Email: hq@swe.org
Web: www.societyofwomenengineers.org/scholarships

**Summary:** To provide financial assistance to undergraduate women majoring in computer science or engineering.

**Eligibility:** Open to women who are entering their sophomore, junior, or senior year at a 4-year ABET-accredited college or university. Applicants must be majoring in computer science or engineering and have a GPA of 3.0 or higher. Along with their application, they must submit a one-page essay on why they want to be an engineer or computer scientist, how they believe they will make a difference as an engineer or computer scientist, and what influenced them to study engineering or computer science. Selection is based on merit.

**Financial data:** The stipend is $2,000.

**Duration:** 1 year.

**Number awarded:** 6 each year.

**Deadline:** January of each year.

## 2466 MESBEC PROGRAM

Catching the Dream
8200 Mountain Road, N.E., Suite 203
Albuquerque, NM 87110-7835
Phone: (505) 262-2351; Fax: (505) 262-0534; Email: NScholarsh@aol.com
Web: www.catchingthedream.org

**Summary:** To provide financial assistance to American Indian students who are interested in working on an undergraduate or graduate degree in selected fields.

**Eligibility:** Open to American Indians who can provide proof that they are at least one-quarter Indian blood and a member of a U.S. tribe that is federally-recognized, state-recognized, or terminated. Applicants must be enrolled or planning to enroll full time and major in the one of the following fields: mathematics, engineering, science, business administration, education, or computer science. They may be entering freshmen, undergraduate students, graduate students, or Ph.D. candidates. Along with their application, they must submit documentation of financial need, 3 letters of recommendation, copies of applications and responses for at least 15 other sources of funding, official transcripts, standardized test scores (ACT, SAT, GRE, MCAT, LSAT, etc.), and an essay explaining their goals in life, college plans, and career plans (especially how those plans include working with and benefiting Indians). Selection is based on merit and potential for improving the lives of Indian people.

**Financial data:** Stipends range from $500 to $5,000.

**Duration:** 1 year; may be renewed.

**Number awarded:** Varies; generally, 30 to 35 each year.

**Deadline:** April of each year for fall term; September of each year for spring and winter terms; March of each year for summer school.

## 2467 MEXICAN AMERICAN ENGINEERS AND SCIENTISTS SCHOLARSHIP PROGRAM

Society of Mexican American Engineers and Scientists
Attn: Scholarship Committee
711 West Bay Area Boulevard, Suite 206
Webster, TX 77598-4051
Phone: (281) 557-3677; Fax: (281) 557-3757;
Email: maesscholars@maes-natl.org
Web: www.maes-natl.org

**Summary:** To provide financial assistance to undergraduate and graduate student members of the Society of Mexican American Engineers and Scientists (MAES).

**Eligibility:** Open to MAES student members who are full-time undergraduate or graduate students at a college or university in the United States. Community college students must be enrolled in majors that can transfer to a 4-year institution offering a baccalaureate degree. All applicants must be majoring in a field of science or engineering. U.S. citizenship or permanent resident status is required. Selection is based on financial need; academic achievement; personal qualities, strengths, and leadership abilities; and timeliness and completeness of the application.

**Financial data:** Stipends are $3,000, $2,000, or $1,000.

**Duration:** 1 year.

**Number awarded:** Varies each year. Recently, 32 of these scholarships were awarded: 3 Padrino/Madrina Scholarships at $4,000, 1 graduate scholarship at $3,000, 2 (the Founder's Scholarship and the President's Scholarship) at $2,500, 1 (the Pipeline Scholarship) at $2,000, 12 general scholarships at $2,000 each, and 13 general scholarships at $1,000 each.

**Deadline:** October of each year.

## 2468 MHEFI SCHOLARSHIP PROGRAM

Material Handling Industry of America
Attn: Material Handling Education Foundation, Inc.
8720 Red Oak Boulevard, Suite 201
Charlotte, NC 28217-3992
Phone: (704) 676-1190; (800) 722-6832; Fax: (704) 676-1199;
Email: vwheeler@mhia.org
Web: www.mhia.org

**Summary:** To provide financial assistance to undergraduate or graduate students who are studying material handling.

**Eligibility:** Open to 1) students at 4-year colleges and universities who have completed at least 2 years of undergraduate study; and 2) graduate students enrolled in a program leading to a master's or doctoral degree. Students from junior or community colleges are eligible if they have been accepted as a transfer student into a 4-year program. Applicants must be U.S. citizens; be attending an academic institution that has been prequalified for foundation funding; have earned a GPA of 3.0 or higher in college; and be enrolled in a course of study relevant to the material handling industry, including engineering (civil, computer, industrial, electrical, or mechanical), engineering technology, computer science, or business administration with an emphasis on production management, industrial distribution, and/or logistics. Along with their application, they must submit 3 letters of recommendation, official transcripts, documentation of financial need, and a 600-word essay on how their course of study, work experience, and career goals make them an appropriate candidate for this scholarship.

**Financial data:** Awards range from $1,500 to $6,000.

**Duration:** 1 year.

**Number awarded:** Varies each year; recently, 28 of these scholarships (with a total value of $73,500) were awarded.

**Deadline:** February of each year.

## 2469 MICHAEL BAKER CORPORATION SCHOLARSHIP PROGRAM FOR DIVERSITY IN ENGINEERING

Association of Independent Colleges and Universities of Pennsylvania
101 North Front Street
Harrisburg, PA 17101-1405
Phone: (717) 232-8649; Fax: (717) 233-8574; Email: info@aicup.org
Web: www.aicup.org

**Summary:** To provide financial assistance to women and minority students at member institutions of the Association of Independent Colleges and Universities of Pennsylvania (AICUP) who are majoring in designated fields of engineering.

**Eligibility:** Open to full-time undergraduate students at designated AICUP colleges and universities who are women and/or members of the following minority groups: American Indians, Alaska Natives, Asians, Blacks/African Americans, Hispanics/Latinos, Native Hawaiians, or Pacific Islanders. Applicants must be juniors majoring in architectural, civil, or environmental engineering with a GPA of 3.0 or higher. Along with their application, they must submit an essay on what they believe will be the greatest challenge facing the engineering profession over the next decade, and why.

**Financial data:** The stipend is $1,000 per year.

**Duration:** 1 year; may be renewed 1 additional year if the recipient maintains appropriate academic standards.

**Number awarded:** 1 each year.

**Deadline:** April of each year.

## 2470 MICHAEL DUNAWAY SCHOLARSHIP

American Society of Extra-Corporeal Technology, Inc.
Attn: AmSECT Foundation
2209 Dickens Road
P.O. Box 11086
Richmond, VA 23230-1086
Phone: (804) 565-6363; Fax: (804) 282-0090; Email: AmSECT@amsect.org
Web: www.amsect.org/scholarships/scholarships_grants.html

**Summary:** To provide financial assistance to student members of the American Society of Extra-Corporeal Technology (AmSECT) who are enrolled in a perfusion training program.

**Eligibility:** Open to student members of the society who are enrolled in (or accepted at) an accredited perfusion training program. Applicants must have completed at least one quarter of the required course work and have at least a 2.75 GPA. They must submit 250-word essays on how they would improve AmSECT, and on how they could improve the perfusion profession. Financial need is not considered in the selection process.

**Financial data:** The stipend is $1,000 per year.

**Duration:** 1 year.

**Number awarded:** 1 each year.

**Deadline:** November of each year.

## 2471 MICHAEL KIDGER MEMORIAL SCHOLARSHIP

SPIE-The International Society for Optical Engineering
Attn: Michael Kidger Memorial Scholarship
1000 20th Street
P.O. Box 10
Bellingham, WA 98227-0010
Phone: (360) 676-3290; Fax: (360) 647-1445; Email: education@spie.org
Web: www.kidger.com/mkms_home.html

**Summary:** To provide financial assistance to undergraduate and graduate students who are preparing for a career in optical design.

**Eligibility:** Open to students of optical design from any country at the undergraduate and graduate level. Applicants must have at least one more year, after the award, to complete their current course of study. They must submit 2 letters of recommendation and a 5-page essay explaining how the scholarship will help them contribute to long-term development in the field of optical design. Financial need is not considered in the selection process.

**Financial data:** A stipend is awarded (amount not specified).

**Duration:** 1 year.

**Number awarded:** 1 or more each year.

**Deadline:** February of each year.

## 2472 MICROSOFT CORPORATION SCHOLARSHIPS

Society of Women Engineers
230 East Ohio Street, Suite 400
Chicago, IL 60611-3265
Phone: (312) 596-5223; Fax: (312) 644-8557; Email: hq@swe.org
Web: www.societyofwomenengineers.org/scholarships

**Summary:** To provide financial assistance to women working on an undergraduate or graduate degree in computer engineering or computer science.

**Eligibility:** Open to women who will be sophomores, juniors, seniors, or graduate students at ABET-accredited colleges and universities. Applicants must be majoring in computer science or computer engineering and have a GPA of 3.5 or higher. Along with their application, they must submit a 1-page essay on why they want to be an engineer or computer scientist, how they believe they will make a difference as an engineer or computer scientist, and what influenced them to study engineering or computer science. Selection is based on merit.

**Financial data:** The stipend is $2,500.

**Duration:** 1 year.

**Number awarded:** 2 each year.

**Deadline:** January of each year.

## 2473 MID-CONTINENT INSTRUMENT SCHOLARSHIP

Aircraft Electronics Association, Attn: AEA Educational Foundation
4217 South Hocker Drive
Independence, MO 64055-4723
Phone: (816) 373-6565; Fax: (816) 478-3100; Email: info@aea.net
Web: www.aea.net

**Summary:** To provide financial assistance to students who are interested in studying avionics in college.

**Eligibility:** Open to high school seniors and currently-enrolled college students who are attending (or planning to attend) an accredited school in an avionics program. Applicants must submit an official transcript (cumulative GPA of 2.5 or higher), a statement about their career plans, a description of their involvement in school and community activities, and a 300-word essay on how the job requirements of aviation technicians will change with advancements in technology. Selection is based on merit.
**Financial data:** The stipend is $1,000.
**Duration:** 1 year.
**Number awarded:** 1 each year.
**Deadline:** February of each year.

## 2474 MIDWEST ALLIANCE FOR NURSING INFORMATICS SCHOLARSHIP

Healthcare Information and Management Systems Society
Attn: HIMSS Foundation Scholarship Program Coordinator
230 East Ohio Street, Suite 500
Chicago, IL 60611-3269
Phone: (312) 664-4467; Fax: (312) 664-6143
Web: www.himss.org/asp/scholarships.asp
**Summary:** To provide financial assistance to student members of the Healthcare Information and Management Systems Society (HIMSS) who are working on an undergraduate or graduate degree in health care informatics or nursing.
**Eligibility:** Open to student members of the society, although an application for membership, including dues, may accompany the scholarship application. Applicants must be graduate students working on an undergraduate or graduate degree in health care informatics. They must submit a 1-page narrative that describes the integration of informatics in their professional practice, with emphasis on actual work responsibilities and how they would utilize the scholarship. Selection is based on that narrative; student, community, or professional activities in the workplace related to nursing and/or health care informatics; and involvement and participation in health care informatics professional organizations.
**Financial data:** The stipend is $2,500. The award includes an all-expense paid trip to the annual HIMSS conference and exhibition.
**Duration:** 1 year; nonrenewable.
**Number awarded:** 1 each year.
**Deadline:** October of each year.

## 2475 MIDWEST CONCRETE INDUSTRY BOARD EDUCATIONAL FUND

Greater Kansas City Community Foundation, Attn: Scholarship Coordinator
1055 Broadway, Suite 130
Kansas City, MO 64105-1595
Phone: (816) 842-0944; Fax: (816) 842-8079; Email: scholars@gkccf.org
Web: www.gkccf.org
**Summary:** To provide financial assistance to undergraduate and graduate engineering students from Missouri and Kansas interested in concrete and concrete design courses.
**Eligibility:** Open to undergraduate and graduate engineering students at accredited colleges and universities who are Missouri or Kansas residents. Applicants must be interested in working on a bachelor's or higher degree that includes concrete and concrete design courses.
**Financial data:** The amounts of the awards vary.
**Duration:** 1 year.
**Number awarded:** 1 or more each year.
**Deadline:** April of each year.

## 2476 MIKKELSON FOUNDATION STUDENT SCHOLARSHIP PROGRAM

Mikkelson Foundation
P.O. Box 768
Monument, CO 80132-9077
Web: www.mikkelson.com
**Summary:** To provide financial assistance to high school seniors in Colorado who plan to study science, engineering, or mathematics in college.
**Eligibility:** Open to seniors graduating from high schools in Colorado. Applicants must be planning to attend an accredited college or university to major in science, engineering, or mathematics. Along with their application, they must submit a 2-page description of their strengths, accomplishments, and interests; their projected course of study in college; their plans following college

graduation; how they plan to finance their education; and how this scholarship will help them achieve their goals.
**Financial data:** The stipend is $3,000 per year.
**Duration:** 1 year; may be renewed up to 3 additional years.
**Number awarded:** 2 each year.
**Deadline:** April of each year.

## 2477 MILLER ELECTRIC INTERNATIONAL YOUTH SKILLS COMPETITION SCHOLARSHIP

American Welding Society, Attn: AWS Foundation, Inc.
550 N.W. LeJeune Road
Miami, FL 33126
Phone: (305) 445-6628; (800) 443-9353, ext. 461; Fax: (305) 443-7559;
Email: found@aws.org
Web: www.aws.org/foundation/national_scholarships.html
**Summary:** To recognize and reward (with college scholarships) winning students who compete in the SkillsUSA competition for welding.
**Eligibility:** Open to high school seniors who compete in the national SkillsUSA (formerly VICA) competition for welding and advance to the American Welding Society (AWS) Weld Trail Competition at the biennial AWS International Welding and Fabricating Exposition and Convention. Applicants must be enrolling in a postsecondary program related to the field of welding or similar joining technologies, including a certificate program, 2-year program, 4-year program, seminar, workshop, or certification course.
**Financial data:** The winner receives a scholarship of up to $10,000 per year, up to $1,000 in AWS publications, a 4-year complimentary full AWS membership, and an AWS certification. Runners-up receive a $1,000 scholarship, a 1-year complimentary full AWS membership, and an AWS certification.
**Duration:** The winner's scholarship is for 4 years. Runners-up scholarships are for 1 year, to be used within 2 years of the Weld Trail Competition.
**Number awarded:** 1 winner and several runners-up every other year.

## 2478 MINERAL AND METALLURGICAL PROCESSING DIVISION SCHOLARSHIP

Society for Mining, Metallurgy, and Exploration, Inc., Attn: Student Center
8307 Shaffer Parkway
P.O. Box 277002
Littleton, CO 80127-7002
Phone: (303) 948-4203; (800) 763-3132; Fax: (303) 973-3845;
Email: sme@smenet.org
Web: www.smenet.org/education/students/sme_scholarships.crm
**Summary:** To provide financial assistance to student members of the Society for Mining, Metallurgy, and Exploration (SME) who are preparing for a career in minerals processing.
**Eligibility:** Open to student members of the society who have completed their sophomore year in college; are enrolled full time in an undergraduate degree program that has required course work in minerals processing, hydrometallurgy, and/or metallurgical engineering; are U.S. citizens; and have a GPA of 2.5 or higher. Only one candidate from each eligible department may be nominated each academic year. Applicants must demonstrate an interest in preparing for a career in mineral processing or metallurgical engineering in the mining industry.
**Financial data:** The first-place recipient is given $2,000 (plus travel to the society's annual meeting). The other winners each receive a $1,000 scholarship.
**Duration:** 1 year.
**Number awarded:** Up to 6 each year.
**Deadline:** October of each year.

## 2479 MINING AND EXPLORATION DIVISION SCHOLARSHIPS

Society for Mining, Metallurgy, and Exploration, Inc., Attn: Student Center
8307 Shaffer Parkway
P.O. Box 277002
Littleton, CO 80127-7002
Phone: (303) 948-4203; (800) 763-3132; Fax: (303) 973-3845;
Email: sme@smenet.org
Web: www.smenet.org/education/students/sme_scholarships.crm
**Summary:** To provide financial assistance to student members of the Society for Mining, Metallurgy, and Exploration (SME) who are preparing for a career in the minerals industry.
**Eligibility:** Open to students who have completed their sophomore year in college and are majoring in mining, geology, or a related field of specialization at an ABET-accredited college or university. They must be U.S. citizens or permanent

residents, be able to demonstrate financial need, have a strong academic record, and be a student member of the society. Only one candidate from each eligible department may be nominated each academic year.

**Financial data:** The stipend is $1,500.
**Duration:** 1 year.
**Number awarded:** Up to 4 each year.
**Deadline:** November of each year.

## 2480 MINNESOTA DIVISION SCHOLARSHIP

Izaak Walton League of America-Minnesota Division
Attn: Scholarship Committee
555 Park Street, Suite 140
St. Paul, MN 55103-2110
Phone: (651) 221-0215; Email: ikes@minnesotaikes.org
Web: www.minnesotaikes.org

**Summary:** To provide financial assistance to Minnesota residents who are studying an environmental field in college.
**Eligibility:** Open to residents of Minnesota who are in at least their second year of college. Applicants must be majoring in environmental education, environmental law, wildlife management, or some other conservation-oriented program. They must be U.S. citizens and able to demonstrate financial need. Along with their application, they must submit a 1-page essay on their belief in conservation and what the future holds for them (including their educational plans and career goals), a transcript, a description of their program of study, and 2 letters of recommendation. An interview may be requested.
**Financial data:** The stipend is $1,000 per year.
**Duration:** 1 year; may be renewed.
**Number awarded:** 1 or more each year.
**Deadline:** May of each year.

## 2481 MINNESOTA PORK INDUSTRY AMBASSADOR SCHOLARSHIPS

Minnesota Pork Board, Attn: Director of Education
360 Pierce Avenue, Suite 106
North Mankato, MN 56003
Phone: (507) 345-8814; Fax: (507) 345-8681; Email: porkmn@hickorytech.net
Web: www.mnpork.com

**Summary:** To recognize and reward, with college scholarships, residents of Minnesota who prepare outstanding essays and speeches on the pork industry.
**Eligibility:** Open to Minnesota residents between 17 and 21 years of age. Participants (or their families) should be 1) actively engaged in pork production or 2) preparing for a career in a related field or business. They must first prepare an essay of 600 to 1,000 words on one of the following topics as related to the pork industry: environment, education, promotion, management, production, economics, or food safety. Then they appear before judges at a county pork congress where they are interviewed and also present a 5-minute speech on the same topic. From each county, a winner and a runner-up advance to the state competition.
**Financial data:** The first-place winner receives a $1,500 scholarship, the first runner-up a $500 scholarship, and the second runner-up a $250 scholarship. The author of the best essay receives an additional $100.
**Duration:** The competition is held annually.
**Number awarded:** 3 state winners are selected each year.
**Deadline:** County boards must submit the names of their winners by April of each year.

## 2482 MINNESOTA SOCIETY OF PROFESSIONAL SURVEYORS SCHOLARSHIP PROGRAM

Minnesota Society of Professional Surveyors
Attn: Minnesota Land Surveyors Foundation
5301 South Park Drive
Savage, MN 55378
Phone: (952) 226-6991; (800) 890-LAND; Fax: (952) 226-3738; Email: sharon@themanagementco.com
Web: www.mnsurveyor.com

**Summary:** To provide financial assistance to Minnesota residents interested in studying surveying at educational institutions in the state.
**Eligibility:** Open to residents of Minnesota who are enrolled, or planning to enroll, full time in 1) an associate's or baccalaureate college degree program; 2) a vocational or technical school program that has signed an articulation agreement with St. Cloud State University; or 3) a vocational or technical school program that has been approved by the sponsor's education committee. The

school must be located in Minnesota and must offer a surveying and mapping program that has been approved by the education committee. Applicants must submit a letter of recommendation, high school and (if applicable) college transcripts, evidence of financial need, and a 2-page essay on their interest in surveying and mapping as a career choice.
**Financial data:** A stipend is awarded (amount not specified).
**Duration:** 1 year.
**Number awarded:** Varies each year.
**Deadline:** October of each year.

## 2483 MINORITY AFFAIRS COMMITTEE AWARD FOR OUTSTANDING SCHOLASTIC ACHIEVEMENT

American Institute of Chemical Engineers, Attn: Awards Administrator
Three Park Avenue
New York, NY 10016-5991
Phone: (212) 591-7107; Fax: (212) 591-8890; Email: awards@aiche.org
Web: www.aiche.org/awards

**Summary:** To recognize and reward underrepresented minority students majoring in chemical engineering who serve as role models for other minority students.
**Eligibility:** Open to any chemical engineering student who serves as a role model for minority students in that field. Students must be nominated by members of the American Institute of Chemical Engineers (AIChE). Nominees must be members of a minority group that is underrepresented in chemical engineering (i.e., African American, Hispanic, Native American, Alaskan Native). Selection is based on the nominee's academic and scholarship achievements, including a GPA of 3.0 or higher, scholastic awards, research contributions, and technical presentations; the nominee's exemplary outreach activities that directly benefit or encourage minority youth in their academic pursuits; a letter from the nominee describing his or her outreach activities; and extraordinary circumstances, such as job or family matters, that impose additional responsibility.
**Financial data:** The award consists of a plaque and a $1,500 honorarium.
**Duration:** The award is presented annually.
**Number awarded:** 1 each year.
**Deadline:** Nominations must be submitted by May of each year.

## 2484 MINORITY GEOSCIENCE STUDENT SCHOLARSHIPS

American Geological Institute, Attn: Minority Participation Program
4220 King Street
Alexandria, VA 22302-1502
Phone: (703) 379-2480, ext. 227; Fax: (703) 379-7563;
Email: cmm@agiweb.org
Web: www.agiweb.org/mpp/index.html

**Summary:** To provide financial assistance to underrepresented minority undergraduate and graduate students interested in working on a degree in the geosciences.
**Eligibility:** Open to members of ethnic minority groups underrepresented in the geosciences (Blacks, Hispanics, American Indians, Eskimos, Hawaiians, and Samoans). U.S. citizenship or permanent resident status is required. Applicants must be full-time students enrolled in an accredited institution working on an undergraduate or graduate degree in the geosciences, including geology, geophysics, hydrology, meteorology, physical oceanography, planetary geology, and earth science education; students in other natural sciences, mathematics, or engineering are not eligible. Selection is based on a 250-word essay on career goals and why the applicant has chosen a geoscience as a major, work experience, recommendations, honors and awards, extracurricular activities, and financial need.
**Financial data:** Stipends range from $500 to $3,000 per year.
**Duration:** 1 academic year; renewable if the recipient maintains satisfactory performance.
**Number awarded:** Varies each year; recently, 19 of these scholarships were awarded.
**Deadline:** March of each year.

## 2485 MINORITY NURSE MAGAZINE SCHOLARSHIP PROGRAM

Minority Nurse Magazine, Attn: Career Recruitment Media
211 West Wacker Drive, Suite 900
Chicago, IL 60606
Phone: (312) 525-3095; Fax: (312) 429-3336;
Email: pam.chwedyk@careermedia.com
Web: www.minoritynurse.com

**Summary:** To provide financial assistance to members of minority groups who are working on a bachelor's degree in nursing.

**Eligibility:** Open to third- and fourth-year minority nursing students currently enrolled in 1) the third or fourth year of an accredited B.S.N. program; 2) an accelerated program leading to a B.S.N. degree (e.g., R.N. to B.S.N., B.A. to B.S.N.); or 3) an accelerated master's entry nursing program (e.g., R.N. to M.S.N., B.S. to M.S.N.) Selection is based on academic excellence (GPA of 3.0 or higher), demonstrated commitment of service to the student's minority community, and financial need. U.S. citizenship of permanent resident status is required.

**Financial data:** The stipends are $1,000 or $500.

**Duration:** 1 year.

**Number awarded:** 4 each year: 2 at $1,000 and 2 at $500.

**Deadline:** June of each year.

### 2486 MINORITY SCHOLARSHIP AWARD IN PHYSICAL THERAPY

American Physical Therapy Association
Attn: Department of Minority/International Affairs
1111 North Fairfax Street
Alexandria, VA 22314-1488
Phone: (703) 706-3144; (800) 999-APTA, ext. 3144; Fax: (703) 706-8519;
TDD: (703) 683-6748; Email: min-intl@apta.org
Web: www.apta.org

**Summary:** To provide financial assistance to minority students who are interested in becoming a physical therapist or physical therapy assistant.

**Eligibility:** Open to U.S. citizens and permanent residents who are members of the following minority groups: African American or Black, Asian, Native Hawaiian or other Pacific Islander, American Indian or Alaska Native, or Hispanic/Latino. Applicants must be in the final year of a professional physical therapy or physical therapy assistant education program. They must submit a personal essay outlining their professional goals and minority service. U.S. citizenship or permanent resident status is required. Selection is based on 1) demonstrated evidence of contributions in the area of minority affairs and services with an emphasis on contributions made while enrolled in a physical therapy program; 2) potential to contribute to the profession of physical therapy; and 3) scholastic achievement.

**Financial data:** The stipend varies; recently, minimum awards were $6,000 for physical therapy students or $3,000 for physical therapy assistant students.

**Duration:** 1 year.

**Number awarded:** Varies each year; recently, 8 of these awards were granted to physical therapy students and 1 to a physical therapy assistant student.

**Deadline:** November of each year.

### 2487 MINORITY SCHOLARSHIP AWARDS FOR COLLEGE STUDENTS IN CHEMICAL ENGINEERING

American Institute of Chemical Engineers, Attn: Awards Administrator
Three Park Avenue
New York, NY 10016-5991
Phone: (212) 591-7107; Fax: (212) 591-8890; Email: awards@aiche.org
Web: www.aiche.org/awards

**Summary:** To provide financial assistance for study in chemical engineering to underrepresented minority college student members of the American Institute of Chemical Engineers (AIChE).

**Eligibility:** Open to undergraduate student AIChE members who are also members of a minority group that is underrepresented in chemical engineering (African Americans, Hispanics, Native Americans, and Alaskan Natives). Each AIChE chapter may nominate one member. Selection is based on academic record (including a GPA of 3.0 or higher), participation in AIChE student and professional activities, a 300-word letter on career objectives and plans, and financial need.

**Financial data:** The stipend is $1,000.

**Duration:** 1 year; nonrenewable.

**Number awarded:** Approximately 10 each year.

**Deadline:** Nominations must be submitted by May of each year.

### 2488 MINORITY SCHOLARSHIP AWARDS FOR INCOMING COLLEGE FRESHMEN IN CHEMICAL ENGINEERING

American Institute of Chemical Engineers, Attn: Awards Administrator
Three Park Avenue
New York, NY 10016-5991
Phone: (212) 591-7107; Fax: (212) 591-8890; Email: awards@aiche.org

Web: www.aiche.org/awards

**Summary:** To provide financial assistance for study in science or engineering to incoming minority freshmen.

**Eligibility:** Open to members of a minority group that is underrepresented in chemical engineering (African Americans, Hispanics, Native Americans, and Alaskan Natives). Applicants must be graduating high school seniors planning to enroll in a 4-year university with a major in science or engineering. They must be nominated by an American Institute of Chemical Engineers (AIChE) local section. Selection is based on academic record (including a GPA of 3.0 or higher), participation in school and work activities, a 300-word letter outlining the reasons for choosing science or engineering, and financial need.

**Financial data:** The stipend is $1,000.

**Duration:** 1 year; nonrenewable.

**Number awarded:** Approximately 10 each year.

**Deadline:** Nominations must be submitted by May of each year.

### 2489 MIRIAM FAY FURLONG GRANT

Alpha Tau Delta, Attn: Central Office
11252 Camarillo Street
Toluca Lake, CA 91602
Email: info@atdnursing.org
Web: www.atdnursing.org/awards.html

**Summary:** To provide financial assistance for undergraduate education in nursing to members of Alpha Tau Delta (a national fraternity for nurses).

**Eligibility:** Open to members in good standing of the fraternity who are entering their junior or senior year of study and can demonstrate financial need.

**Financial data:** Stipends range from $100 to $1,000.

**Duration:** 1 year.

**Number awarded:** 1 each year.

**Deadline:** April of each year.

### 2490 MIRIAM SCHAEFER SCHOLARSHIP

Michigan Council of Teachers of Mathematics, Attn: Scholarship Committee
3300 Washtenaw Avenue, Suite 220
Ann Arbor, MI 48104-4200
Phone: (734) 477-0421; Fax: (734) 677-2270; Email: cfarmer@ucia2.com
Web: www.mictm.org/schols_awards.html

**Summary:** To provide financial assistance to upper-division students who are enrolled in a teacher education program in Michigan with a mathematics specialty.

**Eligibility:** Open to Michigan residents who are currently enrolled as a junior or senior at a college or university in the state. Applicants must be majoring in elementary or secondary education with a mathematics specialty. They must have a GPA of 3.0 or higher. Secondary education majors must have successfully completed the required calculus sequence and elementary education majors must have at least a mathematics minor. Along with their application, they must submit a one-page essay on their personal goals related to the teaching of mathematics, a list of extracurricular and/or community activities and interests, transcripts, evidence of junior or senior standing, and 3 letters of recommendation.

**Financial data:** The stipend of $1,500 is paid to the recipients, with their school as the second payee. The award is to be used for tuition, books, and fees.

**Duration:** 1 year; nonrenewable.

**Number awarded:** Varies each year; recently, 6 of these scholarships were awarded. Since the program began, a total of 82 scholarships, worth $88,500, have been presented.

**Deadline:** June of each year.

### 2491 MLN SCHOLARSHIPS

Missouri League for Nursing, Inc., Attn: Executive Director
604 Dix Road
P.O. Box 104476
Jefferson City, MO 65110-4476
Phone: (573) 635-5355; Fax: (573) 635-7908; Email: mln@monursing.org
Web: www.monursing.org/programservices/prog_scholarships_mln.htm

**Summary:** To provide financial assistance to students in Missouri who are enrolled in an accredited school of nursing.

**Eligibility:** Open to residents of Missouri enrolled in an accredited school of nursing in the state. Applicants may be L.P.N. students, R.N. students above the freshman level in associate's degree or diploma programs, R.N. students above the sophomore level in baccalaureate nursing programs, or M.S.N. candidates who have completed at least 15 hours of courses required for the advanced degree and have an active license in Missouri. They must be able to demonstrate financial need, have a GPA of 3.0 or higher, and be nominated by the dean or director of their school. U.S. citizenship is required.

**Financial data:** The maximum stipend is $2,000.

**Duration:** 1 year.

**Number awarded:** Varies each year.

**Deadline:** Nominations must be submitted by October of each year.

### 2492 MONTANA ACADEMY OF PHYSICIAN ASSISTANTS SCHOLARSHIP

Montana Academy of Physician Assistants
c/o Penny Denning
Scholarship/Awards Committee
107 Dilworth
Glendive, MT 59330-2053
Email: montanapas@aapa.org
Web: www.aapa.org/mapa/sudents.htm

**Summary:** To provide financial assistance to students interested in practicing as physician assistants in Montana.

**Eligibility:** Open to students enrolled in an approved physician assistant program. Preference is given to applicants who are residents of Montana, but residents of all states are encouraged to apply. Selection is based on completeness of the application, professionalism (as demonstrated by application materials), supporting recommendation from program director, academic achievement, financial need, and interest in primary care medicine in Montana.

**Financial data:** A stipend is awarded (amount not specified).

**Duration:** 1 year; may be renewed.

**Number awarded:** 1 or more each year.

**Deadline:** April of each year.

### 2493 MORTON B. DUGGAN, JR. MEMORIAL EDUCATION RECOGNITION AWARD

American Association for Respiratory Care
Attn: American Respiratory Care Foundation
9425 North MacArthur Boulevard, Suite 100
Irving, TX 75063-4706
Phone: (972) 243-2272; Fax: (972) 484-2720; Email: info@aarc.org
Web: www.aarc.org/awards/duggan.html

**Summary:** To provide financial assistance to college students interested in becoming respiratory therapists.

**Eligibility:** Open to U.S. citizens who are enrolled in an accredited respiratory care program and have a GPA of 3.0 or higher. Candidates must submit an original referenced paper on an aspect of respiratory care, an official transcript, and letters of recommendation. Nominations are accepted from all states, but preference is given to applicants from Georgia and South Carolina. Financial need is not considered in the selection process.

**Financial data:** The stipend is $1,000. The award also provides airfare, one night's lodging, and registration for the international congress of the association.

**Duration:** 1 year.

**Number awarded:** 1 each year.

**Deadline:** June of each year.

### 2494 MOTOROLA/HENAAC SCHOLARS PROGRAM

Hispanic Engineer National Achievement Awards Conference
3900 Whiteside Street
Los Angeles, CA 90063
Phone: (323) 262-0997; Fax: (323) 262-0946; Email: info@henaac.org
Web: www.henaac.org/scholarships.htm

**Summary:** To provide financial assistance to Hispanic undergraduate students majoring in electrical engineering.

**Eligibility:** Open to Hispanic undergraduate students who are enrolled full time in electrical engineering. Academic achievement and campus community activities are considered in the selection process.

**Financial data:** Stipends range from $1,000 to $5,000.

**Duration:** 1 year; recipients may reapply.

**Number awarded:** 1 or more each year.

**Deadline:** April of each year.

### 2495 MSPE SCHOLARSHIP TRUST GRANT

Michigan Society of Professional Engineers, Attn: Scholarship Coordinator
215 North Walnut Street
P.O. Box 15276
Lansing, MI 48901-5276
Phone: (517) 487-9388; Fax: (517) 487-0635; Email: mspe@voyager.net
Web: www.michiganspe.org/scholarship.htm

**Summary:** To provide financial assistance to high school seniors in Michigan who are interested in working on a college degree in engineering.

**Eligibility:** Open to graduating seniors at high schools in Michigan who have a GPA of 3.0 or higher and a composite ACT score of 26 or higher. U.S. citizenship is required. Applicants must have been accepted at a Michigan college or university accredited by ABET. They must be planning to enroll in an engineering program and enter the practice of engineering after graduation. They must submit a 250-word essay on "How I Was Influenced to Pursue an Engineering Career." Selection is based on the essay; high school academic record; participation in extracurricular activities; evidence of leadership, character, and self-reliance; and comments from teachers and administrators. Financial need is not considered. Semifinalists are interviewed.

**Financial data:** The stipend is $2,000.

**Duration:** 1 year; nonrenewable.

**Number awarded:** 1 each year.

**Deadline:** January of each year.

### 2496 MSPE 1980 NSPE ANNUAL MEETING COMMITTEE GRANT

Michigan Society of Professional Engineers, Attn: Scholarship Coordinator
215 North Walnut Street
P.O. Box 15276
Lansing, MI 48901-5276
Phone: (517) 487-9388; Fax: (517) 487-0635; Email: mspe@voyager.net
Web: www.michiganspe.org/scholarship.htm

**Summary:** To provide financial assistance to high school seniors in Michigan who are interested in working on a college degree in engineering.

**Eligibility:** Open to graduating seniors at high schools in Michigan who have a GPA of 3.0 or higher and a composite ACT score of 26 or higher. U.S. citizenship is required. Applicants must have been accepted at a Michigan college or university accredited by ABET. They must be planning to enroll in an engineering program and enter the practice of engineering after graduation. They must submit a 250-word essay on "How I Was Influenced to Pursue an Engineering Career." Selection is based on the essay; high school academic record; participation in extracurricular activities; evidence of leadership, character, and self-reliance; and comments from teachers and administrators. Financial need is not considered. Semifinalists are interviewed.

**Financial data:** The stipend is $2,000.

**Duration:** 1 year; nonrenewable.

**Number awarded:** 1 each year.

**Deadline:** January of each year.

### 2497 MUSIC THERAPY SCHOLARSHIP

**Summary:** To provide financial assistance to members of Sigma Alpha Iota (an organization of women musicians) who are interested in working on an undergraduate or graduate degree in music therapy.

*See Listing #1570.*

### 2498 MYRTLE AND EARL WALKER SCHOLARSHIPS

Society of Manufacturing Engineers, Attn: SME Education Foundation
One SME Drive
P.O. Box 930
Dearborn, MI 48121-0930
Phone: (313) 425-3304; (800) 733-4763, ext. 3304; Fax: (313) 425-3411; Email: foundation@sme.org
Web: www.sme.org

**Summary:** To provide financial assistance to undergraduate students enrolled in a degree program in manufacturing engineering or manufacturing engineering technology.

**Eligibility:** Open to full-time students attending a North American degree-granting institution or accredited trade school to prepare for a career in manufacturing engineering. They must have completed at least 15 units in a manufacturing engineering or manufacturing engineering technology curriculum with a GPA of 3.0 or higher. Need is not considered (unless 2 or more applicants have equal qualifications).

**Financial data:** The scholarship is $2,000 per year.
**Duration:** 1 year; may be renewed.
**Number awarded:** 20 each year.
**Deadline:** January of each year.

## 2499 NABTP COLLEGIAN SCHOLARSHIP

National Association of Black Telecommunications Professionals, Inc.
c/o Cynthia L. Newman
2020 Pennsylvania Avenue, N.W.
Box 735
Washington, DC 20006
Phone: (800) 946-6228; Email: office@nabtp.org
Web: www.nabtp.org/about/scholarships.shtml
**Summary:** To provide financial assistance to students who are working on a degree in telecommunications or a related field and are interested in participating in the activities of the National Association of Black Telecommunications Professionals (NABTP).
**Eligibility:** Open to students majoring in telecommunications or a related field (e.g., computer science, business, engineering, mass communications) at an accredited college or university. Applicants must submit an essay on their educational and career goals, the skill sets and values they are able to bring to NABTP as a possible intern, and how they see active involvement in NABTP supportive to their career path and educational goals. As an option, they may also submit an essay in which they provide a profile of a majority-owned African American telecommunications company, including CEO name, number of employees, percentage of minority ownership, annual revenue, address, phone number, web site address, company product and/or services, and company successes. Selection is based on the essays, GPA, notable achievements, and financial need.
**Financial data:** The stipend is $2,000 per year.
**Duration:** 1 year; may be renewed for 2 or 3 additional years if the recipient maintains a GPA of 3.0 or higher and active involvement in NABTP.
**Number awarded:** 1 each year.
**Deadline:** July of each year.

## 2500 NANCY GOODHUE LYNCH SCHOLARSHIP

Datatel Scholars Foundation
4375 Fair Lakes Court
Fairfax, VA 22033
Phone: (703) 968-9000, ext. 4549; (800) 486-4332; Fax: (703) 968-4573;
Email: scholars@datatel.com
Web: www.datatel.com
**Summary:** To provide financial assistance to graduating high school seniors, continuing college students, or graduate students who will be majoring in a field related to information technology at a Datatel client school.
**Eligibility:** Open to students who will attend a Datatel client college or university during the upcoming school year. Applicants must be majoring or planning to major in a program related to information technology. They first apply to their institution, which selects one semifinalist and forwards the application to the sponsor. Along with their application, they must include a personal statement that explains why they chose to study in a technology-related field, the impact of technology and their future, and the importance of receiving this scholarship. Selection is based on the quality of the personal statement (40%), academic merit (30%), achievements and civic involvement (20%), and 2 letters of recommendation (10%).
**Financial data:** The stipend is $2,500. Funds are paid directly to the institution.
**Duration:** 1 year.
**Number awarded:** 2 each year.
**Deadline:** Students must submit online applications to their institution or organization by January of each year.

## 2501 NANCY LORRAINE JENSEN MEMORIAL SCHOLARSHIP FUND

Sons of Norway Foundation
c/o Sons of Norway
1455 West Lake Street
Minneapolis, MN 55408-2666
Phone: (612) 827-3611; (800) 945-8851; Fax: (612) 827-0658;
Email: fraternal@sofn.com
Web: www.sofn.com/foundation/GrantsScholarships.html
**Summary:** To provide financial assistance to women who have a connection to the Sons of Norway and are interested in studying chemistry, physics, or engineering in college.
**Eligibility:** Open to women who are U.S. citizens between 17 and 35 years of age and members (or daughters or granddaughters of members) of the Sons of Norway; they must have been a member for at least 3 years. Female employees of the NASA Goddard Space Flight Center in Greenbelt, Maryland and the daughters and granddaughters of employees are also eligible. Students must have an ACT score of 26 or higher (or the equivalent on the SAT). They must be full-time undergraduate students and have completed at least one quarter or semester of study in chemistry, physics, or chemical, electrical, or mechanical engineering. Selection is based on long-term career goals, clarity of study plan, academic potential, evidence of ability to succeed, and letters of recommendation attesting to good character, eagerness, earnestness, and ambition in the field of science or engineering.
**Financial data:** Stipends range from 50% of tuition for 1 quarter or semester to 100% for 1 year. Grants are issued jointly to the recipient and her institution.
**Duration:** Awards are made for either 1 term (quarter or semester) or 1 year; a student may receive up to 3 awards as an undergraduate.
**Number awarded:** 1 each year.
**Deadline:** February of each year.

## 2502 NAPA RESEARCH AND EDUCATION FOUNDATION SCHOLARSHIP PROGRAM

National Asphalt Pavement Association
Attn: NAPA Research and Education Foundation
5100 Forbes Boulevard
Lanham, MD 20706-4413
Phone: (301) 731-4748, ext. 127; (888) HOT-MIXX; Fax: (301) 731-4621;
Email: cwilson@hotmix.org
Web: www.hotmix.org
**Summary:** To provide financial assistance to undergraduate and graduate engineering students interested in preparing for a career in the asphalt industry.
**Eligibility:** Open to undergraduate and graduate students interested in preparing for a career in the asphalt industry, especially the hot mix asphalt (HMA) industry. Applicants must be U.S. citizens and enrolled full time in a civil engineering, construction management, or construction engineering program at an accredited 4-year college or university or at a 2-year technical institution. The applicant's institution must offer at least one course in HMA technology. Financial need is not considered in the selection process; awards are based on academic performance, future potential, leadership and participation in school and community activities, work experience, career and educational aspirations, goals, unusual personal or family circumstances, and an outside appraisal.
**Financial data:** Stipends range from $1,000 to $5,000 per year.
**Duration:** 1 year; may be renewed for up to 2 years or graduation, whichever occurs first.
**Number awarded:** Varies each year; recently, more than 150 students received assistance through this program.

## 2503 NASA HISPANIC EXPLORERS SCHOLARSHIP PROGRAM

Hispanic College Fund, Attn: National Director
1717 Pennsylvania Avenue, N.W., Suite 460
Washington, D.C. 20006
Phone: (202) 296-5400; (800) 644-4223; Fax: (202) 296-3774;
Email: hispaniccollegefund@earthlink.net
Web: www.hispanicfund.org
**Summary:** To provide financial assistance to Hispanic American undergraduate students who are interested in preparing for a career in a field of interest to the U.S. National Aeronautics and Space Administration (NASA).
**Eligibility:** Open to U.S. citizens of Hispanic background (at least one grandparent must be 100% Hispanic) who are entering their freshman, sophomore, junior, or senior year of college. Applicants must be working on a bachelor's degree in science, computer science, engineering, or a NASA-related major and have a cumulative GPA of 3.0 or higher. They must be applying to or enrolled in a college or university in the 50 states or Puerto Rico as a full-time student. Financial need is considered in the selection process.
**Financial data:** Stipends range from $500 to $5,000, depending on the need of the recipient, and average approximately $3,000. Funds are paid directly to the recipient's college or university to help cover tuition and fees.
**Duration:** 1 year; recipients may reapply.
**Number awarded:** Varies each year.
**Deadline:** April of each year.

## 2504 NATA UNDERGRADUATE SCHOLARSHIPS

National Athletic Trainers' Association
Attn: Research and Education Foundation
2952 Stemmons Freeway, Suite 200
Dallas, TX 75247-6103
Phone: (214) 637-6282; (800) TRY-NATA, ext. 121; Fax: (214) 637-2206;
Email: barbaran@nata.org
Web: www.natafoundation.org/scholarship.html

**Summary:** To provide financial aid to undergraduate student members of the National Athletic Trainers' Association (NATA).

**Eligibility:** Open to members of the association who are sponsored by an NATA certified athletic trainer, have a GPA of 3.2 or higher, and intend to pursue athletic training as a profession. Applicants must apply during their junior year or immediately prior to their final undergraduate year. They must submit a statement on their athletic training background, experience, philosophy, and goals. Selection is based on that essay; participation in their school's athletic training program, academic major, institution, intercollegiate athletics, and American higher education; and participation in campus activities other than academic and athletic training. Financial need is not considered.

**Financial data:** The stipend is $2,000 per year.

**Duration:** 1 year.

**Number awarded:** Varies each year; recently, 30 of these scholarships were awarded.

**Deadline:** February of each year.

## 2505 NATHAN TAYLOR DODSON SCHOLARSHIP

**Summary:** To provide financial assistance for college to members of the North Carolina Alliance for Athletics, Health, Physical Education, Recreation and Dance (NCAAHPERD).

*See Listing #1573.*

## 2506 NATIONAL ACADEMY FOR NUCLEAR TRAINING EDUCATIONAL ASSISTANCE PROGRAM

National Academy for Nuclear Training,
Attn: Educational Assistance Program
301 ACT Drive
P.O. Box 4030
Iowa City, IA 52243-4030
Phone: (800) 294-7492; Email: nant@act.org
Web: www.nei.org

**Summary:** To provide financial assistance for college to students interested in careers in the nuclear power industry.

**Eligibility:** Open to U.S. citizens who are full-time students at accredited 4-year institutions and majoring in nuclear-fission or electric power-related fields, including 1) nuclear, mechanical, or electrical engineering, 2) power generation health physics, or 3) chemical engineering with a nuclear or power option. Applicants must have at least a 3.0 GPA and between 1 and 3 years remaining before graduation. Preference is given to applicants who indicate specific interest in and preparation for careers in the U.S. nuclear power industry. Students with commitments that prevent availability for nuclear utility industry employment immediately after graduation (such as military service) are not eligible. Selection is based on academic performance, motivation and ability to complete a rigorous course of study, and expressed interest and desire to work in the nuclear power industry.

**Financial data:** The stipend is $2,500 per year. Funds are paid directly to the college or university.

**Duration:** 1 year; may be renewed for up to 2 additional years.

**Number awarded:** Approximately 140 new and renewal scholarships are awarded each year.

**Deadline:** February of each year.

## 2507 NATIONAL ASSOCIATION OF HEALTH SERVICES EXECUTIVES SCHOLARSHIP PROGRAM

National Association of Health Services Executives
Attn: Educational Assistance Program
8630 Fenton Street, Suite 126
Silver Spring, MD 20910
Phone: (202) 628-3953; Fax: (301) 588-0011; Email: NationalHQ@nahse.org
Web: www.nahse.org

**Summary:** To provide financial assistance to African Americans who are members of the National Association of Health Services Executives (NAHSE) and interested in preparing for a career in health care administration.

**Eligibility:** Open to African Americans who are either enrolled or accepted in an accredited college or university program, working on a bachelor's, master's, or doctoral degree in health care administration. Applicants must have at least a 2.5 GPA (3.0 if graduate students), be members of NAHSE, and be able to demonstrate financial need. To apply, students must submit a completed application, 3 letters of recommendation, a recent resume, a 3-page essay on "the impact of the team concept approach to organizational improvement when restructuring into an urban integrated healthcare network," a copy of their most recent federal income tax return, transcripts from all colleges attended, and 2 photographs.

**Financial data:** The stipends are $2,500 per year. Funds are sent to the recipient's institution.

**Duration:** 1 year.

**Deadline:** January of each year.

## 2508 NATIONAL ASSOCIATION OF HISPANIC NURSES SCHOLARSHIPS

National Association of Hispanic Nurses
Attn: National Awards and Scholarship Committee Chair
1501 16th Street, N.W.
Washington, DC 20036
Phone: (202) 387-2477; Fax: (202) 483-7183; Email:
thehispanicnurses@earthlink.net
Web: www.thehispanicnurses.org

**Summary:** To provide financial assistance for nursing education to members of the National Association of Hispanic Nurses (NAHN).

**Eligibility:** Open to members of the association enrolled in associate, diploma, baccalaureate, graduate, or practical/vocational nursing programs at NLN-accredited schools of nursing. Applicants must submit a 1-page essay that reflects their qualifications and potential for leadership in nursing for the Hispanic community. U.S. citizenship or permanent resident status is required. Selection is based on academic excellence (preferably a GPA of 3.0 or higher), potential for leadership in nursing, and financial need.

**Financial data:** The stipend is $1,000.

**Duration:** 1 year.

**Number awarded:** Varies each year, depending on the availability of funds.

**Deadline:** April of each year.

## 2509 NATIONAL ASSOCIATION OF WOMEN IN CONSTRUCTION UNDERGRADUATE SCHOLARSHIPS

National Association of Women in Construction
Attn: NAWIC Founders' Scholarship Foundation
327 South Adams
Fort Worth, TX 76104-1081
Phone: (817) 877-5551; (800) 552-3506; Fax: (817) 877-0324;
Email: nawic@nawic.org
Web: www.nawic.org/nfsf.htm

**Summary:** To provide financial assistance for college to students in construction-related degree programs.

**Eligibility:** Open to full-time students who have completed at least one full year of course work and have a minimum of 1 year remaining in a course of study leading to a baccalaureate or associate's degree in a construction-related degree program and a career in construction. Applicants must have a cumulative GPA of 3.0 or higher and be attending school in the United States or Canada. Along with their application, they must submit brief essays on 1) their ultimate goal in the construction industry; 2) their most important extracurricular activity, their most important contribution to it, and what their participation has meant to them as an individual; and 3) why they are interested in a construction industry career and what event or series of events has led them to this decision. Selection is based on GPA, interest in construction, extracurricular activities, employment experience, academic advisor evaluation, and financial need.

**Financial data:** Stipends range from $1,000 to $2,000 per year.

**Duration:** 1 year; recipients may reapply.

**Number awarded:** Varies; a total of $25,000 is available in scholarships each year.

**Deadline:** March of each year.

## 2510 NATIONAL AYRSHIRE YOUTH SCHOLARSHIP

Ayrshire Breeders' Association
1224 Alton Darby Creek Road, Suite B
Columbus, OH 43228
Phone: (614) 335-0020; Fax: (614) 335-0023; Email: info@usayrshire.com

Web: www.usayrshire.com

**Summary:** To provide financial assistance to members of the Ayrshire Breeders' Association who are interested in studying agriculture in college.
**Eligibility:** Open to high school seniors and students currently enrolled in a 2-year or 4-year college or university. Applicants must have been a junior member in good standing with the association for at least the past 5 years. They must be majoring or planning to major in a field related to agriculture. Along with their application, they must submit a description of their involvement in Ayrshire activities on the local, state, and/or national level; a description of their involvement in 4-H and/or FFA activities on the local, state, and/or national level; a description of their involvement in school, church, and community activities; a summary of their career goals and aspirations related to their major area of study; a copy of their high school transcript; a copy of their acceptance into a postsecondary program; and 3 letters of recommendation.
**Financial data:** Stipends are $2,500 or $1,000.
**Duration:** 1 year; nonrenewable.
**Number awarded:** 2 each year: 1 at $2,500 and 1 at $1,000.
**Deadline:** February of each year.

### 2511 NATIONAL CANDY TECHNOLOGISTS SCHOLARSHIP PROGRAM

American Association of Candy Technologists
175 Rock Road
Glen Rock, NJ 07452
Phone: (201) 652-2655; Fax: (201) 652-3419; Email: aact@gomc.com
Web: www.aactcandy.org/natlscholarship.htm
**Summary:** To provide financial assistance to college students interested in preparing for a career in confectionery technology.
**Eligibility:** Open to students who are entering their sophomore, junior, or senior year of college and have demonstrated an interest in confectionary technology (through research projects, work experience, or formal study). Applicants must be attending an accredited 4-year college or university in North America; be majoring in a food science, chemical science, biological science, or related area; and have a GPA of 3.0 or higher. Selection is based on academic activities (including those relating to confectionary technology; experience (e.g., work, internships, volunteer activities); other activities; honors and awards; and a short statement of personal and professional goals.
**Financial data:** The stipend is $5,000.
**Duration:** 1 year; nonrenewable.
**Number awarded:** 1 or more each year.
**Deadline:** January of each year.

### 2512 NATIONAL DENTAL ASSOCIATION FOUNDATION UNDERGRADUATE GRANT PROGRAM

National Dental Association
Attn: National Dental Association Foundation, Inc.
3517 16th Street, N.W.
Washington, DC 20010
Phone: (202) 588-1697; Fax: (202) 588-1242; Email: admin@ndaonline.org
Web: www.nadonline.org/ndaf.htm
**Summary:** To provide financial assistance to underrepresented minority dental and dental hygiene students.
**Eligibility:** Open to members of underrepresented minority groups who are entering their second, third, or fourth year of dental or dental hygiene school. Applicants must be members of the Student National Dental Association (SNDA) and U.S. citizens or permanent residents. Along with their application, they must submit a letter explaining why they should be considered for this scholarship, 2 letters of recommendation, and documentation of financial need. Selection is based on academic performance and service to community and/or country.
**Financial data:** The stipend is $1,000 per year.
**Duration:** 1 year. Recipients may reapply.
**Number awarded:** Varies each year.
**Deadline:** May of each year.

### 2513 NATIONAL FEDERATION OF THE BLIND COMPUTER SCIENCE SCHOLARSHIP

National Federation of the Blind
c/o Peggy Elliott, Scholarship Committee Chair
805 Fifth Avenue
Grinnell, IA 50112
Phone: (641) 236-3366

Web: www.nfb.org/sch_intro.htm
**Summary:** To provide financial assistance to legally blind undergraduate and graduate students working on a degree in computer science.
**Eligibility:** Open to legally blind students who are working on or planning to work full time on an undergraduate or graduate degree in computer science. Selection is based on academic excellence, service to the community, and financial need.
**Financial data:** The stipend is $3,000.
**Duration:** 1 year; recipients may resubmit applications up to 2 additional years.
**Number awarded:** 1 each year.
**Deadline:** March of each year.

### 2514 NATIONAL FFA SCHOLARSHIPS FOR UNDERGRADUATES IN THE SCIENCES

National FFA Organization, Attn: Scholarship Office
6060 FFA Drive
P.O. Box 68960
Indianapolis, IN 46268-0960
Phone: (317) 802-4321; Fax: (317) 802-5321; Email: scholarships@ffa.org
Web: www.ffa.org
**Summary:** To provide financial assistance to FFA members who wish to study agriculture and related fields in college.
**Eligibility:** Open to current and former members of the organization who are working or planning to work full time on a degree in fields related to agriculture; this includes: agricultural mechanics and engineering, agricultural technology, animal science, conservation, dairy science, equine science, floriculture, food science, horticulture, irrigation, lawn and landscaping, and natural resources. For most of the scholarships, applicants must be high school seniors; others are open to students currently enrolled in college. The program includes a large number of designated scholarships that specify the locations where the members must live, the schools they must attend, the fields of study they must pursue, or other requirements. Some consider family income in the selection process, but most do not. Selection is based on academic achievement (10 points for GPA, 10 points for SAT or ACT score, 10 points for class rank), leadership in FFA activities (30 points), leadership in community activities (10 points), and participation in the Supervised Agricultural Experience (SAE) program (30 points). U.S. citizenship is required.
**Financial data:** Stipends vary, but most are at least $1,000.
**Duration:** 1 year or more.
**Number awarded:** Varies; generally, a total of approximately 1,000 scholarships are awarded annually by the association.
**Deadline:** February of each year.

### 2515 NATIONAL GREENHOUSE MANUFACTURERS ASSOCIATION SCHOLARSHIP

Floriculture Industry Research and Scholarship Trust
Attn: Scholarship Program
P.O. Box 280
East Lansing, MI 48826-0280
Phone: (517) 333-4617; Fax: (517) 333-4494;
Email: scholarships@firstinfloriculture.org
Web: www.firstinfloriculture.org
**Summary:** To provide financial assistance to college students majoring in horticulture or bioengineering.
**Eligibility:** Open to undergraduate students at 4-year colleges and universities who are entering their junior, senior, or fifth undergraduate year. Applicants must be majoring in horticulture or bioengineering. They must be U.S. or Canadian citizens or permanent residents with a GPA of 3.0 or higher. Selection is based on academic record, recommendations, career goals, extracurricular activities, and financial need.
**Financial data:** The stipend depends on the availability of funds. Recently, it was $1,000.
**Duration:** 1 year.
**Number awarded:** 1 each year.
**Deadline:** April of each year.

### 2516 NATIONAL HARDWOOD LUMBER ASSOCIATION SCHOLARSHIP

National Hardwood Lumber Association
P.O. Box 34518
Memphis, TN 38184-0518
Phone: (901) 377-1818; Fax: (901) 382-6419; Email: info@natlhardwood.org

Web: www.natlhardwood.org

**Summary:** To provide financial assistance to undergraduate and graduate students working on a degree in forestry or a related field.

**Eligibility:** Open to full-time undergraduate or graduate students working on a degree in wood science, forestry, or a related field at a technical college, junior college, or university. Applicants must have completed 12 credit hours in their chosen major and have at least a 2.5 GPA. Along with their application, they must submit a personal letter of intent, 3 letters of recommendation, a complete resume, and an official transcript. Selection is based on academic achievement and career goals.

**Financial data:** The stipend is either $1,500 or $500.

**Duration:** 1 year.

**Number awarded:** 4 each year: 3 at $1,500 and 1 at $500.

**Deadline:** March of each year.

## 2517 NATIONAL JUNIOR MERIT AWARDS

American Hereford Association, Attn: Department of Youth Activities
P.O. Box 014059
Kansas City, MO 64101
Phone: (816) 842-3757; Fax: (816) 842-6931; Email: aha@hereford.org
Web: www.hereford.org

**Summary:** To recognize and reward members of the National Junior Hereford Association (NJHA) who demonstrate outstanding enthusiasm, leadership, and achievement in the Hereford industry.

**Eligibility:** Open to NJHA members who are high school seniors or already in college and under 22 years of age. Before they can receive an award, they must have completed at least one semester of college with a GPA of 2.0 or higher. Selection is based on Hereford activities (15%), agriculturally-related activities (10%), community and civic activities (10%), employment experience (5%), management practices (10%), goals (15%), productivity and management measures (5%), marketing (10%), summary comments (10%), and overall application presentation and letters of recommendation (10%).

**Financial data:** The top national winner is awarded a $1,000 scholarship and a trip to any polled Hereford ranch in the continental United States. Second- and third-place winners receive $750 and $500, respectively.

**Duration:** The competition is held annually.

**Number awarded:** 3 each year

**Deadline:** September of each year.

## 2518 NATIONAL JUNIOR RED ANGUS ASSOCIATION ESSAY CONTEST

Red Angus Association of America
4201 North Interstate 35
Denton, TX 76207-3415
Phone: (940) 387-3502; Fax: (940) 383-4036
Web: www.redangus1.org

**Summary:** To recognize and reward outstanding essays on the beef industry written by members of the National Junior Red Angus Association (NJRAA).

**Eligibility:** Open to students; they may enter one of the following divisions: junior division: grades K-6; intermediate division: grades 7-9; senior division: grades 10-12; and college division: high school graduates through 21 year olds. Participants in the junior division must write a 250-word essay and cite at least 1 reference; intermediate division participants must write a 500-word essay and cite at least 2 references; senior division participants must write a 750-word essay and cite at least 4 references; college division participants must write a 750-word essay and cite at least 5 references. Individual topics are assigned each year for each division; they relate to the future of the beef industry. Participants must be current, active members of NJRAA. Selection is based on clarity of expression, spelling, and grammar (20%); persuasiveness (10%); originality of thought and topic (35% or 40%); accuracy of information (30%); and references cited, if applicable, (5%).

**Financial data:** Savings bonds and/or cash prizes are awarded in each of the 4 age divisions.

**Duration:** The competition is held annually.

**Deadline:** April of each year.

## 2519 NATIONAL OCEANIC AND ATMOSPHERIC ADMINISTRATION EDUCATIONAL PARTNERSHIP PROGRAM WITH MINORITY SERVING INSTITUTIONS UNDERGRADUATE SCHOLARSHIPS

Oak Ridge Institute for Science and Education
Attn: Science and Engineering Education
P.O. Box 117
Oak Ridge, TN 37831-0117
Phone: (865) 576-9279; Fax: (865) 241-5220; Email: coxre@orau.gov
Web: www.orau.gov/orise.htm

**Summary:** To provide financial assistance and research experience to undergraduate students at minority serving institutions who are majoring in scientific fields of interest to the National Oceanic and Atmospheric Administration (NOAA).

**Eligibility:** Open to juniors and seniors at minority serving institutions, including Hispanic Serving Institutions (HSIs), Historically Black Colleges and Universities (HBCUs), and Tribal Colleges and Universities (TCUs). Applicants must be majoring in atmospheric science, biology, cartography, chemistry, computer science, engineering, environmental science, geodesy, geography, marine science, mathematics, meteorology, photogrammetry, physical science, physics, or remote sensing. They must also be interested in participating in a research internship at a NOAA site. U.S. citizenship is required.

**Financial data:** This program provides payment of tuition and fees (to a maximum of $4,000 per year) and a stipend during the internship of $650 per week.

**Duration:** 1 academic year and 2 summers.

**Number awarded:** 10 each year.

**Deadline:** January of each year.

## 2520 NATIONAL SOCIETY OF BLACK ENGINEERS SCHOLARSHIP PROGRAM

National Society of Black Engineers, Attn: Programs Department
1454 Duke Street
Alexandria, VA 22314
Phone: (703) 549-2207, ext. 305; Fax: (703) 683-5312;
Email: scholarships@nsbe.org
Web: www.nsbe.org/programs/nbescholarships.php

**Summary:** To provide financial assistance to members of the National Society of Black Engineers (NSBE) who are working on an undergraduate or graduate degree in engineering or related subjects.

**Eligibility:** Open to members of the society who are undergraduate or graduate students of engineering or closely-related subjects. The program includes many designated awards with varying GPA and other requirements. Selection is based on an essay; academic achievement; service to the society at the chapter, regional, and/or national level; and other professional, campus, and community activities. The Mike Shinn Distinguished Member of the Year Awards are presented to the highest-ranked female and male applicants

**Financial data:** Stipends range up to $7,500.

**Duration:** 1 year.

**Number awarded:** Varies each year.

**Deadline:** January of each year.

## 2521 NATIONAL SPACE GRANT COLLEGE AND FELLOWSHIP PROGRAM

National Aeronautics and Space Administration, Attn: Program Manager
NASA Headquarters
Washington, DC 20546-0001
Phone: (202) 358-1523; Fax: (202) 358-3048; Email: jdasch@hq.nasa.gov
Web: www.nasa.gov/audience/forstudents/postsecondary/learning/Space_Grant.html

**Summary:** To provide financial assistance to undergraduate and graduate students interested in preparing for a career in a space-related field.

**Eligibility:** Open to undergraduate and graduate students at colleges and universities that participate in the National Space Grant program of the U.S. National Aeronautics and Space Administration (NASA) through their state consortium. Applicants must be interested in a program of study and/or research in a field of science, mathematics, engineering, or technology (SMET) related to space. A specific goal of the program is to increase preparation by members of underrepresented groups (minorities, women, and persons with disabilities) for SMET space-related careers.

**Financial data:** Each consortium establishes the terms of the fellowship program in its state.

**Number awarded:** Varies each year.

**Deadline:** Each consortium sets its own deadlines.

## 2522 NAVY COLLEGE ASSISTANCE/STUDENT HEADSTART (NAVY-CASH) PROGRAM

U.S. Navy, Attn: Navy Personnel Command
5722 Integrity Drive

Millington, TN 38054-5057
Phone: (901) 874-3070; (888) 633-9674; Fax: (901) 874-2651;
Email: nukeprograms@cnrc.navy.mil
Web: www.cnrc.navy.mil/nucfield/college/enlisted_options.htm
**Summary:** To provide financial assistance to high school seniors and current college students interested in attending college for a year and then entering the Navy's nuclear program.
**Eligibility:** Open to students who are able to meet the specific requirements of the Navy's Enlisted Nuclear Field Program. They must be enrolled or accepted for enrollment at an accredited 2-year community or junior college or 4-year college or university.
**Financial data:** While they attend school, participants are paid a regular Navy salary at a pay grade up to E-3 (starting at $1,303.50 per month). They are also eligible for all of the Navy's enlistment incentives, including the Navy College Fund, the Loan Repayment Program, and an enlistment bonus up to $12,000.
**Duration:** 12 months.
**Number awarded:** Varies each year.

## 2523 NAVY NURSE CANDIDATE PROGRAM

U.S. Navy, Attn: Naval Medical Education and Training Command
Code OH
8901 Wisconsin Avenue
Bethesda, MD 20889-5611
Phone: (301) 295-2373; (800) USA-NAVY; Fax: (301) 295-6014;
Email: OH@nmetc.med.navy.mil
Web: nshs.med.navy.mil/hpsp/Pages/Programs.htm
**Summary:** To provide financial assistance for nursing education to students interested in serving in the Navy.
**Eligibility:** Open to full-time students in a bachelor of science in nursing program. Prior to or during their junior year of college, applicants must enlist in the U.S. Navy Nurse Corps Reserve. Following receipt of their degree, they must be willing to serve as a nurse in the Navy.
**Financial data:** This program pays a $10,000 accession bonus upon enlistment and a stipend of $1,000 per month. Students are responsible for paying all school expenses.
**Duration:** Up to 24 months.
**Number awarded:** Varies each year.

## 2524 NAVY NURSE CORPS NROTC SCHOLARSHIP PROGRAM

U.S. Navy, Attn: Chief of Naval Education and Training
Code N79A2
250 Dallas Street
Pensacola, FL 32508-5220
Phone: (850) 452-4941, ext. 29388; (800) NAV-ROTC, ext. 29388; Fax: (850) 452-2486; Email: PNSC_NROTC.scholarship@navy.mil
Web: www.nrotc.navy.mil/nursingoption.cfm
**Summary:** To provide financial assistance to graduating high school seniors who are interested in joining Navy ROTC and majoring in nursing in college.
**Eligibility:** Open to graduating high school seniors who have been accepted at a college with a Navy ROTC unit on campus or a college with a cross-enrollment agreement with such a college. Applicants must be U.S. citizens between the ages of 17 and 23 who plan to study nursing in college and are willing to serve for 4 years as active-duty Navy officers in the Navy Nurse Corps following graduation from college. They must not have reached their 27th birthday by the time of college graduation and commissioning; applicants who have prior active-duty military service may be eligible for age adjustments for the amount of time equal to their prior service, up to a maximum of 36 months. They must have minimum ACT scores of 22 in both English and mathematics (or the equivalent on the SAT).
**Financial data:** This scholarship provides payment of full tuition and required educational fees, as well as $250 per semester for textbooks, supplies, and equipment. The program also provides a stipend for 10 months of the year that is $250 per month as a freshman, $300 per month as a sophomore, $350 per month as a junior, and $400 per month as a senior.
**Duration:** 4 years.
**Number awarded:** Varies each year.
**Deadline:** January of each year.

## 2525 NBNA BOARD OF DIRECTORS SCHOLARSHIP

National Black Nurses Association, Inc., Attn: Scholarship Committee
8630 Fenton Street, Suite 330

Silver Spring, MD 20910
Phone: (301) 589-3200; (800) 575-6298; Fax: (301) 589-3223
**Summary:** To provide financial assistance for nursing education to members of the National Black Nurses Association (NBNA).
**Eligibility:** Open to members of the association who have a nursing license. Applicants must be currently enrolled in a B.S.N. or advanced degree program with at least one full year of school remaining. Selection is based on participation in student nurse activities, involvement in the African American community, and involvement in community health services activities.
**Financial data:** The stipend ranges from $500 to $2,000 per year.
**Duration:** 1 year; may be renewed.
**Number awarded:** 1 or more each year.
**Deadline:** April of each year.

## 2526 NDPRB UNDERGRADUATE SCHOLARSHIP PROGRAM

National Dairy Promotion and Research Board
c/o Dairy Management Inc.
10255 West Higgins Road, Suite 900
Rosemont, IL 60018-5616
Phone: (847) 803-2000; Fax: (847) 803-2077; Email: marykateg@rosedmi.com
Web: www.dairycheckoff.com/DairyCheckoff/about/scholarship.htm
**Summary:** To provide financial assistance to undergraduate students in fields related to the dairy industry.
**Eligibility:** Open to sophomores, juniors, and seniors enrolled in college and university programs that emphasize dairy. Eligible majors include agricultural education, business, communications and/or public relations, economics, food science, journalism, marketing, and nutrition. Fields related to production (e.g., animal science) are not eligible. Selection is based on academic performance; interest in a career in dairy; involvement in extracurricular activities, especially those relating to dairy; and evidence of leadership ability, initiative, character, and integrity. The applicant who is judged most outstanding is awarded the James H. Loper Jr. Memorial Scholarship.
**Financial data:** Stipends are $2,500 or $1,500.
**Duration:** 1 year; may be renewed.
**Number awarded:** 20 each year: the James H. Loper Jr. Memorial Scholarship at $2,500 and 19 other scholarships at $1,500.
**Deadline:** May of each year.

## 2527 NEBRASKA ACTUARIES CLUB SCHOLARSHIPS

Nebraska Actuaries Club
c/o Bob Jurgensmeier
Lincoln Beneficial Life
2940 South 84th Street, Suite 1A3
Lincoln, NE 68506
Fax: (402) 328-6116; Email: bjurg@allstate.com
Web: www.n-a-c.org/Scholarships/Scholarships.php
**Summary:** To provide financial assistance to students in Nebraska who are preparing for an actuarial career.
**Eligibility:** Open to 1) seniors graduating from high schools in Nebraska and planning to attend a campus of the University of Nebraska; and 2) seniors graduating from high schools anywhere in the United States and planning to attend a college or university in Nebraska. Applicants must intend to major in actuarial science, mathematics, statistics, or economics and prepare for a career as an actuary. They must be able to demonstrate mathematical ability. Along with their application, they must submit an essay on their interest in actuarial science and why they would like to be an actuary. Financial need is not considered in the selection process.
**Financial data:** The stipend is $1,000.
**Duration:** 1 year.
**Number awarded:** 3 each year: 2 to Nebraska high school graduates attending the University of Nebraska system (designated Madden Scholarships and supported by the Nebraska Insurance Federation) and one to graduates from other states attending a college or university in Nebraska (supported by the Nebraska Actuaries Club).
**Deadline:** March of each year.

## 2528 NEBRASKA CHAPTER ACI UNDERGRADUATE STUDENT AWARD

American Concrete Institute-Nebraska Chapter, Attn: Scholarships
6901 Vine Street
Lincoln, NE 68505
Phone: (402) 466-4233; Email: rdelorm@msn.com

Web: www.acinebraska.org/students/StudentsUGScholar2.html

**Summary:** To provide financial assistance to students entering their senior year at a college or university in Nebraska and majoring in a field related to the concrete industry.

**Eligibility:** Open to students entering their senior year at a 4-year college or university in Nebraska. Applicants must be majoring in a field of engineering, construction, or technology to prepare for a career in concrete construction. Along with their application, they must submit a 500-word essay explaining their interest, experience, ability, and career objectives as they relate to concrete construction.

**Financial data:** The stipend is $1,000.

**Duration:** 1 year.

**Number awarded:** 1 each year.

**Deadline:** December of each year.

---

## 2529 NELL BRYANT ROBINSON SCHOLARSHIP

Phi Upsilon Omicron, Attn: Educational Foundation
P.O. Box 329
Fairmont, WV 26555-0329
Phone: (304) 368-0612; Email: rickards@access.mountain.net
Web: www.phiu.unl.edu

**Summary:** To provide financial assistance to undergraduate student members of Phi Upsilon Omicron, a national honor society in family and consumer sciences.

**Eligibility:** Open to members of the society who are working on a bachelor's degree in family and consumer sciences or a related area. Preference is given to majors in dietetics or food and nutrition. Selection is based on scholastic record, participation in society and other collegiate activities, a statement of professional aims and goals, professional services, and recommendations.

**Financial data:** The stipend is $1,000.

**Duration:** 1 year.

**Number awarded:** 1 each year.

**Deadline:** January of each year.

---

## 2530 NEUROSCIENCE NURSING FOUNDATION REGULAR SCHOLARSHIPS

American Association of Neuroscience Nurses
Attn: Neuroscience Nursing Foundation
4700 West Lake Avenue
Glenview, IL 60025-1485
Phone: (847) 375-4733; (888) 557-2266; Fax: (877) 734-8677;
Email: aann@aann.org
Web: www.aann.org/nnf

**Summary:** To provide financial assistance to nurses interested in further study in neuroscience nursing.

**Eligibility:** Open to nurses who are working on a bachelor's, master's, or doctoral degree in neuroscience nursing. Applicants must submit their resume and a personal statement on their anticipated contribution to neuroscience nursing practice, research, and/or education.

**Financial data:** The stipend is $1,500.

**Duration:** 1 year.

**Number awarded:** The award is presented when a suitable candidate applies.

**Deadline:** January of each year.

---

## 2531 NEUROSCIENCE RESEARCH PRIZE FOR HIGH SCHOOL STUDENTS

American Academy of Neurology, Attn: Neuroscience Prize Office
1080 Montreal Avenue
St. Paul, MN 55116-2325
Phone: (651) 695-2724; (800) 879-1960; Fax: (651) 695-2791;
Email: hlewis@aan.com
Web: www.aan.com

**Summary:** To recognize and reward high school students for outstanding laboratory reports in neuroscience.

**Eligibility:** Open to students enrolled in grades 9-12 in the United States. Applicants submit an original laboratory research report, up to 10 pages in length, that represents their own written work. The report should be written in the style of a scientific paper, describing actual laboratory or field research experiments or observations performed, the results obtained, and the interpretation of those results. Selection criteria include the paper's relevance to neuroscience, creativity, scientific method, and interpretation of data.

**Financial data:** Winners receive a $1,000 prize and an all-expense paid trip

to a professional neuroscience conference where they present their projects. Teachers are also invited to the conferences, with all their expenses paid.

**Duration:** The prizes are awarded annually.

**Number awarded:** 4 each year; 3 winners receive trips to the AAN meeting and 1 to the CNS meeting.

**Deadline:** October of each year.

---

## 2532 NEVADA CATTLEMEN'S ASSOCIATION SCHOLARSHIP

Nevada Cattlemen's Association, Attn: Research and Education Committee
285 Tenth Street
P.O. Box 310
Elko, NV 89803
Phone: (775) 738-9214; Fax: (775) 738-5208; Email: nca@elko.net
Web: www.nevadacattlemen.org

**Summary:** To provide financial assistance to high school seniors in Nevada who are interested in studying agriculture in college.

**Eligibility:** Open to seniors graduating from high schools in Nevada who plan to attend a 2-year or 4-year college or university and major in a field related to agriculture. Applicants must have a GPA of 2.5 or higher. Along with their application, they must submit 3 letters of recommendation and an essay (from 1,000 to 1,500 words in length) on a current issue involving the beef industry.

**Financial data:** The stipend is $1,000.

**Duration:** 1 year.

**Number awarded:** 1 each year.

**Deadline:** April of each year.

---

## 2533 NEW ENGLAND AEE ACADEMIC SCHOLARSHIPS

Association of Energy Engineers-New England Chapter
c/o Dan Wheatley, Scholarship Chair
Environmental Systems Corporation
750 Main Street
Winchester, MA 01890
Phone: (781) 729-3760; Fax: (781) 729-3778; Email: danw@esccontrols.com
Web: www.aeenewengland.org/Scholarships.html

**Summary:** To provide financial assistance to undergraduate and graduate students in New England interested in taking courses directly related to energy engineering or energy management.

**Eligibility:** Open to undergraduate and graduate students who are enrolled in engineering or management programs at accredited colleges and universities in New England. Applicants must be interested in taking courses directly related to energy engineering or energy management (preferably within a curriculum leading to a major or minor in energy engineering). Selection is based on scholarship, character, and need. In awarding scholarships, preference is given to candidates needing aid their final year; second, to candidates needing aid for the last 2 years; third, to candidates needing aid for 3 years; and finally, to first-year students.

**Financial data:** The stipend is $1,000.

**Duration:** 1 year.

**Number awarded:** Varies each year; recently, 5 of these scholarships were awarded.

**Deadline:** February of each year.

---

## 2534 NEW JERSEY LAND SURVEYING SCHOLARSHIPS

New Jersey Society of Professional Land Surveyors
Attn: Scholarship Foundation
310 West State Street
Trenton, NJ 08618
Phone: (609) 393-1186; (800) 853-LAND; Fax: (609) 394-0637;
Email: rgoldberg@njspls.org
Web: www.njspls.org

**Summary:** To provide financial assistance to New Jersey residents working on an undergraduate or graduate degree in a field related to surveying.

**Eligibility:** Open to residents of New Jersey who are enrolled in an accredited college (in any state) that has been approved by the sponsor's selection committee. Applicants must be working on an undergraduate or graduate degree in surveying or a related field (e.g., cartography, geodesy). Preference is given to full-time students. Along with their application, they must submit an essay explaining what has prompted them to prepare for a career in land surveying or a related field. Selection is based on the essay, academic ability, personal interests, references, and financial need.

**Financial data:** A stipend is awarded (amount not specified).

**Duration:** 1 year (recipients may reapply).

**Number awarded:** Varies each year.

**Deadline:** February of each year.

**2535 NEW JERSEY LEGION AUXILIARY PAST PRESIDENTS' PARLEY NURSES SCHOLARSHIPS**

American Legion Auxiliary, Attn: Department of New Jersey
c/o Lucille M. Miller, Secretary, Treasurer
1540 Kuser Road, Suite A-8
Hamilton, NJ 08619
Phone: (609) 581-9580; Fax: (609) 581-8429

**Summary:** To provide financial assistance for nursing education to New Jersey residents who are the children or grandchildren of veterans.

**Eligibility:** Open to the children and grandchildren of living, deceased, or divorced veterans. Applicants must have been residents of New Jersey for at least 2 years and be graduating high school seniors or the equivalent who plan to study nursing.

**Financial data:** The amount awarded varies, depending upon the needs of the recipient and the money available.

**Duration:** 1 year.

**Number awarded:** Varies each year.

**Deadline:** March of each year.

**2536 NEW JERSEY POST SAME SCHOLARSHIP**

**Summary:** To provide financial assistance to students in New Jersey working on an undergraduate degree in architecture, engineering, or a related field.
*See Listing #1592.*

**2537 NEW JERSEY UTILITIES ASSOCIATION SCHOLARSHIPS**

New Jersey Utilities Association
50 West State Street, Suite 1117
Trenton, NJ 08608
Phone: (609) 392-1000; Fax: (609) 396-4231
Web: www.njua.org

**Summary:** To provide financial assistance to minority, female, and disabled high school seniors in New Jersey interested in majoring in selected subjects in college.

**Eligibility:** Open to women, minorities (Black, Hispanic, American Indian/Alaska Native, or Asian American/Pacific Islander), and persons with disabilities who are high school seniors in New Jersey. They must be able to demonstrate financial need, be planning to enroll on a full-time basis at an institute of higher education, and be planning to work on a bachelor's degree in engineering, environmental science, chemistry, biology, business administration, or accounting. Children of employees of any New Jersey Utilities Association-member company are ineligible. Selection is based on overall academic excellence and demonstrated financial need.

**Financial data:** The stipend is $1,500 per year.

**Duration:** 4 years.

**Number awarded:** 2 each year.

**Deadline:** March of each year.

**2538 NEW MEXICO BROADCASTERS ASSOCIATION SCHOLARSHIPS**

**Summary:** To provide financial assistance to undergraduate students in New Mexico who are preparing for a career in the broadcast industry.
*See Listing #1593.*

**2539 NEW YORK BEEF PRODUCERS' ASSOCIATION SCHOLARSHIP**

**Summary:** To provide financial assistance to college students from New York who are preparing for a career in the cattle industry.
*See Listing #1594.*

**2540 NEW YORK LEGION AUXILIARY PAST PRESIDENTS PARLEY STUDENT SCHOLARSHIP IN MEDICAL FIELD**

American Legion Auxiliary, Attn: Department of New York
112 State Street, Suite 1310
Albany, NY 12207
Phone: (518) 463-1162; (800) 421-6348; Fax: (518) 449-5406;
Email: alanyhdqtrs@worldnet.att.net
Web: www.deptny.org/scholarships.htm

**Summary:** To provide financial assistance to descendants of wartime veterans in New York who are interested in preparing for a career in the medical field.

**Eligibility:** Open to residents of New York who are the children, grandchildren, or great grandchildren of veterans (living or deceased) of World War I, World War II, the Korean Conflict, the Vietnam War, Grenada/Lebanon, Panama, or the Persian Gulf. Applicants must be high school seniors or graduates younger than 20 years of age. They must be interested in attending an accredited college or university to prepare for a career in a medical field. Along with their application, they must submit a 500-word essay on "Why I Selected the Medical Field." Selection is based on character (30%), Americanism (20%), leadership (10%), scholarship (20%), and financial need (20%).

**Financial data:** The stipend is $1,000.

**Duration:** 1 year.

**Number awarded:** 1 each year.

**Deadline:** March of each year.

**2541 NEW YORK SCHOLARSHIP PROGRAM**

American Council of Engineering Companies of New York
Attn: Executive Director
6 Airline Drive
Albany, NY 12205-1022
Phone: (518) 452-8611; Fax: (518) 452-1710; Email: acecny@acecny.org
Web: www.acecny.org/scholarship.htm

**Summary:** To provide financial assistance to upper-division students in specified fields of engineering at colleges and universities in New York.

**Eligibility:** Open to students who have completed their junior year (or the fourth year of a 5-year program) at an approved college or university in New York. Applicants must intend to become a consulting engineer and must be majoring in an engineering field that makes up the primary practices of member firms of the American Council of Engineering Companies of New York (ACEC New York): chemical, civil, electrical, environmental, mechanical, or structural. They must be U.S. citizens who intend to make New York their home and/or career area. Selection is based on work experience (25 points), college activities and recommendations (15 points), a 500-word essay on why they want to prepare for a career in consulting engineering (30 points), and cumulative GPA (30 points).

**Financial data:** Stipends are $5,000 or $2,500.

**Duration:** 1 year.

**Number awarded:** Varies each year. Recently, 6 of these scholarships were available: 1 at $5,000 and 5 at $2,500.

**Deadline:** January of each year.

**2542 NEW YORK SECTION SCHOLARSHIPS**

Institute of Food Technologists, Attn: Scholarship Department
525 West Van Buren, Suite 1000
Chicago, IL 60607
Phone: (312) 782-8424; Fax: (312) 782-8348; Email: info@ift.org
Web: www.ift.org

**Summary:** To provide financial assistance to undergraduates interested in studying food science or food technology.

**Eligibility:** Open to sophomores, juniors, and seniors in a food science or food technology program at an educational institution in the United States or Canada. Applicants must have an outstanding scholastic record and a well-rounded personality. Along with their application, they must submit an essay on their career aspirations; a list of awards, honors, and scholarships they have received; a list of extracurricular activities and/or hobbies; and a summary of their work experience. Financial need is not considered during selection.

**Financial data:** The stipend is $1,000.

**Duration:** 1 year; recipients may reapply if they are members of the Institute of Food Technologists.

**Additional information:** Correspondence and completed applications must be submitted to the department head of the educational institution the applicant is attending.

**Number awarded:** 2 each year.

**Deadline:** January of each year.

**2543 NEW YORK STATE CHAPTER SCHOLARSHIP PROGRAM**

Associated General Contractors of America
New York State Chapter, Inc., Attn: AGC Scholarship Fund
10 Airline Drive, Suite 203
Albany, NY 12205
Phone: (518) 456-1134; Fax: (518) 456-1198; Email: lelvin@agcnys.org
Web: www.agcnys.org/scholarship_program.cfm

**Summary:** To provide financial assistance to students from New York who are majoring in construction or civil engineering.

**Eligibility:** Open to residents of New York who are entering the second, third, or fourth year in a 2-year or 4-year school or the first year of graduate school. Applicants must be intent on a career in the highway construction industry, be working on a degree in construction or civil engineering, be enrolled full time, be a U.S. citizen or documented permanent resident, and have a GPA of 2.5 or higher. Selection is based on academic achievement, extracurricular activities, employment experience, and financial need.

**Financial data:** The stipend is $2,500 per year, payable in 2 equal installments.

**Duration:** 1 year; undergraduates (but not graduate students) may reapply. A student may receive up to 4 awards: 3 as an undergraduate and 1 as a graduate student.

**Number awarded:** At least 12 each year. Since the program was reestablished in 1988, more than 200 students have received scholarships.

**Deadline:** May of each year.

## 2544 NEW YORK STATE ENA SEPTEMBER 11 SCHOLARSHIP FUND

Emergency Nurses Association, Attn: ENA Foundation
915 Lee Street
Des Plaines, IL 60016-6569
Phone: (847) 460-4100; (800) 900-9659, ext. 4100; Fax: (847) 460-4004;
Email: foundation@ena.org
Web: www.ena.org/foundation/grants

**Summary:** To provide financial assistance to rescue workers working on an undergraduate degree in nursing.

**Eligibility:** Open to pre-hospital care providers, fire fighters, and police officers who are going to school to obtain an undergraduate nursing degree. Rescue workers from all states are eligible. Applicants must submit a 1-page statement on their professional and educational goals and how this scholarship will help them attain those goals. Selection is based on content and clarity of the goal statement (45%), professional involvement (45%), and GPA (10%).

**Financial data:** The stipend is $2,000.

**Duration:** 1 year.

**Number awarded:** 1 each year.

**Deadline:** May of each year.

## 2545 NEXT GENERATION OF PUBLIC SERVANTS SCHOLARSHIP

Hispanic Scholarship Fund Institute
1001 Connecticut Avenue, N.W., Suite 632
Washington, DC 20036
Phone: (202) 296-0009; Fax: (202) 296-3633; Email: info@hsfi.org
Web: www.hsfi.org/scholarships/generation.asp

**Summary:** To provide financial assistance to Hispanic and other students majoring in designated business, engineering, social science, and science fields who are interested in employment with the U.S. Department of Energy (DOE).

**Eligibility:** Open to U.S. citizens enrolled full time as sophomores with a GPA of 2.8 or higher. Applicants must be interested in preparing for a career with the DOE in an energy-related field. Eligible academic majors are in the fields of business, engineering, social science, and science. They must be willing to participate in co-ops with the DOE. Along with their application, they must submit a 2-page essay on why a career in public service interests them, how their academic major connects with their stated DOE career goal, why the DOE should invest in them through this program, and how they believe the DOE will benefit from this investment. Selection is based on academic achievement, financial need, demonstrated commitment to public service, and interest in federal employment with the DOE.

**Financial data:** The stipend is $3,000 per year.

**Duration:** 1 year; may be renewed up to 2 additional years if the recipient maintains full-time enrollment and a GPA of 2.8 or higher.

**Number awarded:** Varies each year.

**Deadline:** February of each year.

## 2546 NGPA EDUCATION FUND

National Gay Pilots Association, Attn: NGPA Education Fund
P.O. Box 7271
Dallas, TX 75209-0271
Phone: (214) 336-0873; Fax: (214) 350-0447; Email: info@ngpa.org

Web: www.ngpa.org/education.html

**Summary:** To provide financial assistance to those affiliated with the gay and lesbian community who have expressed an interest in an aviation career as a professional pilot.

**Eligibility:** Open to students preparing for a career as a professional pilot. They must be 1) accepted at or currently enrolled in an accredited college or university with an aviation-related curriculum (aerospace, aerodynamics, engineering, airport management, etc.) or 2) accepted to or currently undergoing a course of study in a recognized professional pilot aviation training program in an institution of higher learning, aviation technical school, or school that provides advanced pilot training under FAR Part 141. They must have at least a Private Pilot Certificate. While scholarships are not awarded on the basis of an individual's sexual orientation, applicants must provide evidence of their contribution to the gay and lesbian community. Selection is based on demonstrated personal excellence, aviation accomplishments, potential to become a successful professional pilot, and financial need.

**Financial data:** The stipend is $2,000 per year. Funds are paid directly to the educational institution and cannot be used to pay for the basic Private Certificate; they must be applied toward advanced flight training at a facility certified under FAR Part 141 or to college tuition if enrolled in an accredited aviation degree program.

**Duration:** 1 year.

**Number awarded:** 1 or more each year.

**Deadline:** November of each year.

## 2547 NHSPE STATE SCHOLARSHIP PROGRAM

New Hampshire Society of Professional Engineers
P.O. Box 1343
Concord, NH 03302-1343
Web: www.nhspe.org/pages/scholarship.htm

**Summary:** To provide financial assistance to New Hampshire residents interested in studying specified fields of engineering in college.

**Eligibility:** Open to residents of New Hampshire who are high school seniors or college undergraduates enrolled in or planning to enroll in an ABET-accredited program of general, civil, structural, mechanical, or electrical engineering. Applicants may be attending college in any state, but preference is given to students at New Hampshire colleges and universities. Along with their application, they must submit a 200-word statement on their interest in engineering and the occupation they plan to pursue after graduation. Selection is based on that statement (10 points), GPA (15 points), activities and work experience during school and summer break (15 points), SAT/ACT scores (10 points), completeness of the application (10 points), attendance at a New Hampshire college or university (20 points), and financial need (20 points).

**Financial data:** The stipend is $1,000.

**Duration:** 1 year.

**Number awarded:** Varies each year; recently, 2 of these scholarships were awarded.

**Deadline:** March of each year.

## 2548 NICHOLAS AND MARY TRIVILLIAN MEMORIAL SCHOLARSHIPS

Greater Kanawha Valley Foundation, Attn: Scholarship Coordinator
1600 Huntington Square
900 Lee Street, East
P.O. Box 3041
Charleston, WV 25331-3041
Phone: (304) 346-3620; Fax: (304) 346-3640; Email: tgkvf@tgkvf.com
Web: www.tgkvf.com/scholar.html

**Summary:** To provide financial assistance to residents of West Virginia who are working on a degree in medicine or pharmacy.

**Eligibility:** Open to residents of West Virginia who are working full time on a degree in the field of medicine or pharmacy at a college or university in the state. Applicants must have an ACT score of 20 or higher, be able to demonstrate good moral character and financial need, and have a GPA of 2.5 or higher.

**Financial data:** The stipend is $1,000 per year.

**Duration:** 1 year; may be renewed.

**Number awarded:** Varies each year; recently, 34 of these scholarships were awarded.

**Deadline:** February of each year.

## 2549 NICHOLAS J. GRANT SCHOLARSHIP

ASM International, Attn: ASM Materials Education Foundation
Scholarship Program

9639 Kinsman Road
Materials Park, OH 44073-0002
Phone: (440) 338-5151; (800) 336-5152; Fax: (440) 338-4634;
Email: asmif@asminternational.org
Web: www.asminternational.org

**Summary:** To provide financial assistance to upper-division student members of the American Society for Metals who are interested in majoring in metallurgy and materials.

**Eligibility:** Open to citizens of the United States, Canada, or Mexico who are enrolled at a college or university in those countries; are members of the society; have an intended or declared major in metallurgy or materials science and engineering (related science or engineering majors may be considered if the applicant demonstrates a strong academic emphasis and interest in materials science and engineering); and are entering their junior or senior year in college. Selection is based on academic achievement; interest in metallurgy/materials (including knowledge of the field, activities, jobs, and potential for a related career); personal qualities (such as social values, maturity, motivation, goals, and citizenship); and financial need.

**Financial data:** The scholarship provides payment of full tuition.

**Duration:** 1 year; recipients may reapply for 1 additional year.

**Number awarded:** 1 each year.

**Deadline:** April of each year.

## 2550 NIGHTINGALE AWARDS OF PENNSYLVANIA SCHOLARSHIP

Nightingale Awards of Pennsylvania
2090 Linglestown Road, Suite 107
Harrisburg, PA 17110
Phone: (717) 909-0350; Email: nightingale@pronursingresources.com
Web: www.nightingaleawards.org/schola.htm

**Summary:** To provide financial assistance to residents of Pennsylvania who are interested in working on an undergraduate or graduate degree in nursing at an institution in the state.

**Eligibility:** Open to Pennsylvania residents who are enrolled in a program of basic (diploma, A.D., B.S.N., L.P.N.) or advanced (master's, doctoral) nursing at an educational institution in the state. Applicants must have a GPA of 3.0 or higher and have completed at least one course designated as "nursing." Along with their application, they must submit an essay on their reasons for preparing for a career in nursing. Students who have already completed a diploma or A.D. nursing program are not eligible. Selection is based on academic achievement, leadership potential, community service, and personal commitment.

**Financial data:** A stipend is awarded (amount not specified).

**Duration:** 1 year.

**Number awarded:** 1 or more each year.

**Deadline:** January of each year.

## 2551 NJSCLS CLINICAL LABORATORY SCIENCE SCHOLARSHIP

New Jersey Society for Clinical Laboratory Science
c/o Lisa Shearn, Scholarship Committee Chair
1038 Kilkormic Street
Toms River, NJ 08753
Phone: (732) 270-5379; Email: Mlt3527@aol.com
Web: www.nj.ascls.org

**Summary:** To provide financial assistance to New Jersey clinical laboratory science students.

**Eligibility:** Open to students enrolled in their final year of a clinical laboratory science program at a New Jersey institution accredited by the National Accrediting Agency for Clinical Laboratory Sciences. Applicants must be accepted into a clinical practicum. Selection is based on financial need, academic record, and letters of recommendation.

**Financial data:** The stipend is $1,000.

**Duration:** 1 year.

**Number awarded:** 1 each year.

**Deadline:** June of each year.

## 2552 NMA UNDERGRADUATE SCHOLARSHIPS

National Meat Association, Attn: NMA Scholarship Foundation
1970 Broadway, Suite 825
Oakland, CA 94612
Phone: (510) 763-1533; Fax: (510) 763-6186; Email: staff@nmaonline.org
Web: www.nmascholars.org

**Summary:** To provide financial assistance to undergraduates working on a degree in the animal, meat, and food sciences.

**Eligibility:** Open to students entering their sophomore, junior, or senior year in an approved program in animal science, meat science, food science, or a related discipline. Applicants must be attending a 4-year college or university and have a GPA of 3.0 or higher. Along with their application, they must submit an essay of 200 to 250 words on their career goals and future endeavors, focusing on how those relate to post harvest and production of meat food products. Financial need, age, gender, race, religion, or national origin are not conditions for eligibility; essays that cite those as reasons for applying are marked down. Selection is based on the essay (25%), work experience (25%), awards and honors (5%), extracurricular activities (5%), a faculty letter of recommendation (10%), official transcript (20%), a list of completed and current courses (5%), and a list of pending courses (5%).

**Financial data:** Stipends are $2,500 or $2,000. Awardees who attend the annual convention of the National Meat Association (NMA) receive a $500 travel award and plaque.

**Duration:** 1 year; nonrenewable.

**Number awarded:** Varies each year: the 3 named scholarships plus several others at $2,000.

**Deadline:** April of each year.

## 2553 NMAHPERD COLLEGE SCHOLARSHIP

**Summary:** To provide financial assistance to residents of New Mexico who are planning to work on an undergraduate degree in health, physical education, recreation, or dance at a college or university in the state.

*See Listing #1600.*

## 2554 NONWOVENS DIVISION SCHOLARSHIP

Technical Association of the Pulp and Paper Industry
Attn: TAPPI Foundation
15 Technology Parkway South
Norcross, GA 30092
Phone: (770) 209-7536; (800) 332-8686; Fax: (770) 446-6947;
Email: vedmondson@tappi.org
Web: www.tappi.org

**Summary:** To provide financial assistance to undergraduate students who are interested in preparing for a career in the paper industry.

**Eligibility:** Open to students who are attending a state-accredited college full time, have earned a GPA of 3.0 or higher, are enrolled in a program preparatory to a career in the nonwovens industry, or can demonstrate an interest in the areas covered by the Nonwovens Division of the Technical Association of the Pulp and Paper Industry, and are recommended and endorsed by an instructor or faculty member. Applicants must be interested in preparing for a career in the paper industry with a focus on the materials, equipment, and processes for the manufacture and use of nonwovens. Selection is based on the candidates' potential career contributions to the pulp and paper industry as it relates to nonwovens; financial need is not considered.

**Financial data:** The stipend is $1,000.

**Duration:** 1 year.

**Number awarded:** 1 each year.

**Deadline:** January of each year.

## 2555 NORMAN E. HUSTON SCHOLARSHIP

Instrumentation, Systems, and Automation Society
Attn: ISA Educational Foundation
67 Alexander Drive
Research Triangle Park, NC 27709
Phone: (919) 549-8411; Fax: (919) 549-8288; Email: info@isa.org
Web: www.isa.org

**Summary:** To provide financial assistance to undergraduate and graduate students majoring in fields related to instrumentation, systems, and automation.

**Eligibility:** Open to full-time undergraduate and graduate students enrolled in a program in instrumentation, systems, automation, or a closely-related field. Applicants must have a GPA of 3.0 or higher. They may be from any country but must be attending an institution in their own country. Applicants in a 2-year program must have completed at least one academic semester of 12 hours or its equivalent. Applicants in a 4-year program must be in their sophomore year or higher. Along with their application, they must submit an essay (up to 400 words) on their ambitions and qualifications as an innovator or future leader in a career in instrumentation, systems, or automation. Financial need is not considered in the selection process.

**Financial data:** The stipend is $4,000.

**Duration:** 1 year; may be renewed.

**Number awarded:** 1 each year.

**Deadline:** February of each year.

## 2556 NORTH AMERICAN SURVEYING HISTORY SCHOLARSHIP

**Summary:** To provide financial assistance to upper-division surveying students in North America who have demonstrated an interest in history.
*See Listing #1602.*

## 2557 NORTH CAROLINA TRAFFIC LEAGUE SCHOLARSHIP

North Carolina Traffic League
P.O. Box 241203
Charlotte, NC 28224-1203
Phone: (704) 357-8800; Fax: (704) 357-8804; Email: nctl@clickcom.com
Web: www.nctl.hypermart.net
**Summary:** To provide financial assistance to upper-division and graduate students from North Carolina who are working on a degree in transportation.
**Eligibility:** Open to residents of North Carolina who are either 1) full-time juniors or seniors or 2) part-time or full-time graduate students. Applicants must be working on a degree in an approved field of transportation studies. They must have a GPA of 3.0 or higher. Along with their application, they must submit an essay on their interest in traffic and transportation, including an outline of their future objectives in the field.
**Financial data:** The stipend is $1,000.
**Duration:** 1 year.
**Number awarded:** 1 each year.

## 2558 NORTH CENTRAL REGION SCHOLARSHIP

Society of Manufacturing Engineers, Attn: SME Education Foundation
One SME Drive
P.O. Box 930
Dearborn, MI 48121-0930
Phone: (313) 425-3304; (800) 733-4763, ext. 3304; Fax: (313) 425-3411;
Email: foundation@sme.org
Web: www.sme.org
**Summary:** To provide financial assistance to students working on an undergraduate degree in engineering in North Central states.
**Eligibility:** Open to students working on an associate's or bachelor's degree in manufacturing engineering, mechanical engineering, industrial engineering, or industrial technology at a 2-year or 4-year college or university in Iowa, Minnesota, Nebraska, North Dakota, South Dakota, Wisconsin, or the upper peninsula of Michigan. Applicants must have a GPA of 3.0 or higher. Preference is given in the following order: first, applicants who are members of Region 9 of the Society of Manufacturing Engineers (SME), their spouses, children, or grandchildren; and second, residents of Iowa, Minnesota, Nebraska, North Dakota, South Dakota, Wisconsin, or the upper peninsula of Michigan.
**Financial data:** The stipend is $1,500.
**Duration:** 1 year; may be renewed.
**Number awarded:** 1 each year.
**Deadline:** January of each year.

## 2559 NORTHROP GRUMMAN SCHOLARSHIPS

Society of Women Engineers
230 East Ohio Street, Suite 400
Chicago, IL 60611-3265
Phone: (312) 596-5223; Fax: (312) 644-8557; Email: hq@swe.org
Web: www.societyofwomenengineers.org/scholarships
**Summary:** To provide financial assistance to women interested in studying specified fields of engineering in college.
**Eligibility:** Open to women who are enrolled or planning to enroll full time at an ABET-accredited 4-year college or university. Applicants must have a GPA of 3.0 or higher and be planning to major in computer science or aerospace, chemical, computer, electrical, industrial, manufacturing, or mechanical engineering. Along with their application, they must submit a 1-page essay on why they want to be an engineer or computer scientist, how they believe they will make a difference as an engineer or computer scientist, and what influenced them to study engineering or computer science. Selection is based on merit.
**Financial data:** The stipend is $5,000.
**Duration:** 1 year.
**Number awarded:** 5 each year: 3 to women entering their freshmen year and 2 to women entering their sophomore, junior, or senior year.
**Deadline:** May of each year for entering freshmen; January of each year for entering sophomores, juniors, and seniors.

## 2560 NORTHROP GRUMMAN/HENAAC SCHOLARS PROGRAM

Hispanic Engineer National Achievement Awards Conference
3900 Whiteside Street
Los Angeles, CA 90063
Phone: (323) 262-0997; Fax: (323) 262-0946; Email: info@henaac.org
Web: www.henaac.org/scholarships.htm
**Summary:** To provide financial assistance to Hispanic undergraduate students majoring in engineering and related fields.
**Eligibility:** Open to Hispanic undergraduate students who are enrolled full time in the following engineering fields: aerospace, chemical, civil, computer, electrical, industrial, manufacturing, marine, mechanical, ocean, or structural. Students majoring in computer science, information science, mathematics, naval architecture, and physics are also eligible. Applicants must be U.S. citizens and have a GPA of 3.0 or higher. Academic achievement and campus community activities are considered in the selection process.
**Financial data:** The stipend is $5,000.
**Duration:** 1 year; recipients may reapply.
**Number awarded:** 5 each year.
**Deadline:** April of each year.

## 2561 NPCA EDUCATIONAL FOUNDATION SCHOLARSHIPS

National Precast Concrete Association, Attn: NPCA Educational Foundation
10333 North Meridian Street, Suite 272
Indianapolis, IN 46290
Phone: (317) 571-9500; (800) 366-7731; Fax: (317) 571-0041;
Email: npca@precast.org
Web: www.precast.org/foundation/scholarship.html
**Summary:** To provide financial assistance for college to students interested in preparing for a career in fields related to the precast concrete industry.
**Eligibility:** Open to high school seniors, high school graduates, and undergraduate students who plan to enroll full time in a college, university, or community college. Applicants must be interested in majoring in architecture, civil engineering, or another field related to the building, construction, or precast concrete industry. They must submit a transcript of high school and/or college grades (including ACT/SAT scores), a letter of recommendation from a faculty member, and a letter of sponsorship from a firm that is a member of the National Precast Concrete Association (NPCA). Financial need is not considered in the selection process.
**Financial data:** The stipend is $1,000 per year.
**Duration:** 1 year; may be renewed up to 3 additional years.
**Number awarded:** Varies each year; recently, 5 of these scholarships were awarded.
**Deadline:** December of each year.

## 2562 NPFDA SCHOLARSHIPS

National Poultry and Food Distributors Association
Attn: NPFDA Scholarship Foundation
958 McEver Road Extension, Unit B-8
Gainesville, GA 30504
Phone: (770) 535-9901; (877) 845-1545; Fax: (770) 535-7385;
Email: info@npfda.org
Web: www.npfda.org
**Summary:** To provide financial assistance to students enrolled in fields related to the poultry and food industries.
**Eligibility:** Open to full-time students entering their junior or senior year of college. Applicants must be studying poultry science, food science, agricultural economics or marketing, nutrition, or another area related to the poultry industry. Along with their application, they must submit a 1-page narrative on their goals and ambitions and their transcripts. Selection is based on academic excellence, past and current involvement in poultry and food-related activities, and professional objectives.
**Financial data:** Stipends range from $1,500 to $2,000.
**Duration:** 1 year.
**Number awarded:** 4 each year.
**Deadline:** May of each year.

## 2563 NSBE/SHPE/SWE MEMBERS SCHOLARSHIP

Morgan Stanley
c/o Joyce Arencibia, IT College Recruiting
750 Seventh Avenue, 30th Floor

New York, NY 10019
Phone: (212) 762-4000; Email: diversityrecruiting@morganstanley.com
Web: www.morganstanley.com/about/diversityrecruit_programs.html
**Summary:** To provide financial assistance and work experience to members of the National Society of Black Engineers (NSBE), Society of Hispanic Professional Engineers (SHPE), and Society of Women Engineers (SWE) who are working on an undergraduate degree in computer science or engineering.
**Eligibility:** Open to active members of NSBE, SHPE, and SWE who are enrolled in their sophomore or junior year of college (or the third or fourth year of a 5-year program). Applicants must be enrolled full time and have a GPA of 3.0 or higher. They must be willing to commit to a paid summer internship in the Morgan Stanley Information Technology Division. All majors and disciplines are eligible, but preference is given to students preparing for a career in computer science or engineering. Along with their application, they must submit 1-page essays on 1) why they are applying for this scholarship and why they should be selected as a recipient; 2) a technical project on which they worked, either through a university course or previous work experience, their role in the project, and how they contributed to the end result; and 3) a software, hardware, or new innovative application of existing technology that they would create if they could and the impact it would have. Financial need is not considered in the selection process.
**Financial data:** Students who receive a scholarship as juniors (or fourth-year students in a 5-year program) receive $10,000 for their final year of college. Students who receive a scholarship as sophomores (or third-year students in a 5-year program) receive $5,000 for their junior year (or fourth year of a 5-year program).
**Duration:** 1 year; may be renewed for the final year for students who receive a scholarship as sophomores (or third-year students in a 5-year program).
**Number awarded:** 1 or more each year.
**Deadline:** February of each year.

## 2564 NSCA CHALLENGE SCHOLARSHIPS

National Strength and Conditioning Association, Attn: Foundation
1955 North Union Boulevard
P.O. Box 9908
Colorado Springs, CO 80932-0908
Phone: (719) 632-6722; (800) 815-6826; Fax: (719) 632-6367;
Email: foundation@nsca-lift.org
Web: www.nsca-lift.org/foundation/challenge.shtml
**Summary:** To provide financial assistance for undergraduate or graduate study in strength training and conditioning to members of the National Strength and Conditioning Association (NSCA).
**Eligibility:** Open to applicants who have been members of the association for at least one year prior to the application deadline. They must be working on an undergraduate or graduate degree in a strength and conditioning-related field. In addition to transcripts and letters of recommendation, applicants must submit an essay of no more than 500 words explaining their need for the scholarship, proposed course of study, and professional goals. Selection is based on scholarship (25 points), strength and conditioning experience (15 points), the essay (15 points), recommendations (5 points), honors and awards (10 points), community involvement (10 points), and NSCA involvement (20 points).
**Financial data:** Awards are $1,000, to be applied toward tuition.
**Duration:** 1 year.
**Number awarded:** 1 or more each year.
**Deadline:** March of each year.

## 2565 NSCA HIGH SCHOOL SCHOLARSHIP

National Strength and Conditioning Association, Attn: Foundation
1955 North Union Boulevard
P.O. Box 9908
Colorado Springs, CO 80932-0908
Phone: (719) 632-6722; (800) 815-6826; Fax: (719) 632-6367;
Email: foundation@nsca-lift.org
Web: www.nsca-lift.org/foundation
**Summary:** To provide financial assistance for undergraduate study in strength training and conditioning to high school seniors.
**Eligibility:** Open to high school students preparing to enter college. Applicants must have a GPA of 3.0 or higher and be planning to major in a strength and conditioning field. Along with their application, they must submit a 500-word essay on their life ambitions, future in the strength and conditioning area, and financial need.
**Financial data:** The stipend is $1,000.
**Duration:** 1 year; nonrenewable.
**Number awarded:** 2 each year.
**Deadline:** March of each year.

## 2566 NSSGA ENGINEERING SCHOLARSHIPS

National Stone, Sand and Gravel Association
Attn: Human Resources Committee
1605 King Street
Arlington, VA 22314
Phone: (703) 525-8788; (800) 342-1415; Fax: (703) 525-7782;
Email: info@nssga.org
Web: www.nssga.org/careers/scholarships.htm
**Summary:** To provide financial assistance to university students intending to pursue a career in the aggregates industry.
**Eligibility:** Open to university students who intend to prepare for a career in the crushed stone industry. Applications must be accompanied by a letter of recommendation and a 300- to 500-word statement describing those career plans. Financial need is not considered in the selection process.
**Financial data:** Each scholarship is $2,500.
**Duration:** 1 year.
**Number awarded:** 10 each year.
**Deadline:** April of each year.

## 2567 NUCLEAR PROPULSION OFFICER CANDIDATE (NUPOC) PROGRAM

U.S. Navy, Attn: Navy Personnel Command
5722 Integrity Drive
Millington, TN 38054-5057
Phone: (901) 874-3070; (888) 633-9674; Fax: (901) 874-2651;
Email: nukeprograms@cnrc.navy.mil
Web: www.cnrc.navy.mil/nucfield/college/officer_options.htm
**Summary:** To provide financial assistance to college juniors and seniors who wish to serve in the Navy's nuclear propulsion training program following graduation.
**Eligibility:** Open to U.S. citizens who are entering their junior or senior year of college as a full-time student. Strong technical majors (mathematics, physics, chemistry, or an engineering field) are encouraged but not required. Applicants must have completed at least one year of calculus and one year of physics and must have earned a grade of C or better in all mathematics, science, and technical courses. Normally, they must be 26 years of age or younger at the expected date of commissioning, although applicants for the design and research specialty may be 29 years old.
**Financial data:** Participants become Active Reserve enlisted Navy personnel and receive a salary of up to $2,500 per month; the exact amount depends on the local cost of living and other factors. A bonus of $10,000 is also paid at the time of enlistment and another $2,000 upon completion of nuclear power training.
**Duration:** Up to 30 months, until completion of a bachelor's degree.
**Number awarded:** Varies each year.

## 2568 NVIDIA CORPORATION/HENAAC SCHOLARS PROGRAM

Hispanic Engineer National Achievement Awards Conference
3900 Whiteside Street
Los Angeles, CA 90063
Phone: (323) 262-0997; Fax: (323) 262-0946; Email: info@henaac.org
Web: www.henaac.org/scholarships.htm
**Summary:** To provide financial assistance to Hispanic undergraduate students majoring in engineering and related fields.
**Eligibility:** Open to Hispanic undergraduate students who are enrolled full time in computer science, engineering, material science, mathematics, or applied science. Applicants must have a GPA of 3.0 or higher. There is no citizenship requirement. Academic achievement and campus community activities are considered in the selection process.
**Financial data:** Stipends range from $1,000 to $5,000.
**Duration:** 1 year; recipients may reapply.
**Number awarded:** 1 or more each year.
**Deadline:** April of each year.

## 2569 NWTF CONSERVATION EDUCATION SCHOLARSHIP PROGRAM

National Wild Turkey Federation
Attn: Juniors Acquiring Knowledge, Ethics, and Sportsmanship (JAKES) Program
770 Augusta Road
P.O. Box 530
Edgefield, SC 29824-1510

Phone: (803) 637-3106; (800) THE-NWTF; Email: mharling@nwtf.net
Web: www.nwtf.org/jakes/scholarship.html

**Summary:** To provide financial assistance for college to high school students who are interested in conservation and hunting.

**Eligibility:** Open to students graduating from high school with a GPA of 3.0 or higher and planning to work on a degree at an accredited college, university, community college, or technical college. Applicants must support the preservation of the hunting tradition and actively participate in hunting sports, be involved in school activities, demonstrate ability as a leader among their peers, and demonstrate community involvement. Along with their application, they must submit 1) a 3-page autobiography including any experience or background that demonstrates their dedication to conservation, and 2) a 3-page essay on why hunting is important to them and/or their family. Financial need is not considered in the selection process. Students first apply to their local chapter of the National Wild Turkey Federation (NWTF). Chapter winners are entered in their state/provincial competition, and those winners are considered for selection as the national scholarship winner.

**Financial data:** Chapter scholarships are at least $250; state/provincial scholarships are at least $1,000; the national scholarship winner receives $10,000. All funds are paid directly to the recipient's institution to be used for tuition, books, fees, and housing.

**Duration:** 1 year; nonrenewable.

**Number awarded:** The number of local and state/provincial scholarships varies each year; 1 national scholarship winner is selected annually.

**Deadline:** Applications must be submitted to local chapters by January of each year.

## 2570 NYSAAF/NYSSA SCHOLARSHIPS

New York State Association of Agricultural Fairs
c/o Norma Hamilton, Executive Secretary
67 Verbeck Avenue
Schaghticoke, NY 12154
Phone: (518) 753-4956
Web: www.nyfairs.org/scholarship.htm

**Summary:** To provide financial assistance to New York residents interested in majoring in agriculture in college.

**Eligibility:** Open to seniors at high schools in New York and New York residents already enrolled in college. Applicants must be working on or planning to work on a degree in agriculture or an agriculture-related field. Their application must be endorsed by a fair that is a member of the New York State Association of Agricultural Fairs (NYSAAF). Selection is based on scholastic standing (25%), citizenship and leadership (25%), fair participation (20%), relationship of field of study to agriculture (15%), financial need (10%), and presentation of application (5%).

**Financial data:** The stipend is $1,000.

**Duration:** 1 year.

**Number awarded:** At least 5 each year.

**Deadline:** Students must submit their application to a member fair by April of each year.

## 2571 OFFICE OF CIVILIAN RADIOACTIVE WASTE MANAGEMENT HISTORICALLY BLACK COLLEGES AND UNIVERSITIES UNDERGRADUATE SCHOLARSHIP PROGRAM

Oak Ridge Institute for Science and Education
Attn: Science and Engineering Education
P.O. Box 117
Oak Ridge, TN 37831-0117
Phone: (865) 576-9279; Fax: (865) 241-5219; Email: coxre@orau.gov
Web: www.orau.gov/orise.htm

**Summary:** To provide scholarships and internship experience to students at Historically Black Colleges and Universities (HBCUs) working on undergraduate degrees in areas related to the Office of Civilian Radioactive Waste Management (OCRWM).

**Eligibility:** Open to juniors and seniors at HBCUs who are working on a degree in science, mathematics, engineering, engineering technology, or social sciences. As part of their program, they must be willing to participate in an internship at a U.S. Department of Energy (DOE) site conducting activities for the OCRWM.

**Financial data:** The program provides for payment of tuition and fees (to a maximum of $8,000) plus a monthly stipend of $600.

**Duration:** 2 years.

**Number awarded:** 10 each year.

**Deadline:** January of each year.

## 2572 OKLAHOMA SOCIETY OF LAND SURVEYORS SCHOLARSHIPS

Oklahoma Society of Land Surveyors, Attn: Scholarship Fund
13905 Twin Ridge Road
Edmonds, OK 73034
Phone: (405) 721-7222; Fax: (405) 330-3432; Email: osls@osls.org
Web: www.osls.org/Scholarship.htm

**Summary:** To provide financial assistance to Oklahoma high school seniors who are interested in studying surveying in college.

**Eligibility:** Open to seniors graduating from high schools in Oklahoma. Applicants must be interested in preparing for a career as a Registered Professional Land Surveyor. They must have a GPA of 2.5 or higher and an ACT score of 19 or higher with a strong emphasis on mathematics. As part of their application, they must submit short essays on how they became interested in land surveying, their long-term goals in the field of land surveying, what they can contribute to the Oklahoma Society of Land Surveyors, and how they will take a leadership role in the future of surveying.

**Financial data:** A stipend is awarded (amount not specified).

**Duration:** 1 year.

**Number awarded:** Varies each year.

## 2573 OLD GUARD ORAL PRESENTATION COMPETITION

ASME International, Attn: Student Center
Three Park Avenue
New York, NY 10016-5990
Phone: (212) 591-7722; (800) THE-ASME; Fax: (212) 591-7674;
Email: students@asme.org
Web: www.asme.org/cma/og/oralprescontest.html

**Summary:** To recognize and reward student members of ASME International (the professional society of mechanical engineers) who deliver outstanding oral presentations on engineering subjects.

**Eligibility:** Open to student members who make 15-minute oral presentations, followed by 5-minute question-and-answer sessions, on subjects related to mechanical engineering. Entrants must be dues-paid student members who have not yet received an engineering degree, have been selected by their student sections to participate, and have been certified by their regional office as a student member in good standing. Selection is based on content, organization, delivery, effectiveness, and discussion. Students first compete on the regional level, from which the winners advance to the national competition.

**Financial data:** At the regional level, the first-place winner receives $300 plus reimbursement of expenses to participate in the national competition, second place $150, third place $100, fourth place $50, and fifth place $25. At the national level, first prize is $2,000, second $1,500, third $1,000, and fourth $500.

**Duration:** The prizes are presented annually.

**Number awarded:** Each year, there are 5 winners in each region and 4 in the national competition.

## 2574 OLIVE LYNN SALEMBIER SCHOLARSHIP

Society of Women Engineers
230 East Ohio Street, Suite 400
Chicago, IL 60611-3265
Phone: (312) 596-5223; Fax: (312) 644-8557; Email: hq@swe.org
Web: www.societyofwomenengineers.org/scholarships

**Summary:** To provide financial assistance to women interested in returning to college or graduate school to study engineering or computer science.

**Eligibility:** Open to women who are planning to enroll at an ABET-accredited 4-year college or university. Applicants must have been out of the engineering workforce and school for at least 2 years and must be planning to return as an undergraduate or graduate student to major in computer science or engineering. Along with their application, they must submit a 1-page essay on why they want to be an engineer or computer scientist, how they believe they will make a difference as an engineer or computer scientist, and what influenced them to study engineering or computer science. Selection is based on merit.

**Financial data:** The award is $2,000.

**Duration:** 1 year.

**Number awarded:** 1 each year.

**Deadline:** May of each year.

## 2575 ONCOLOGY NURSING CERTIFICATION CORPORATION BACHELOR'S SCHOLARSHIPS

Oncology Nursing Society, Attn: ONS Foundation
125 Enterprise Drive

Pittsburgh, PA 15275-1214

Phone: (412) 859-6100, ext. 8503; (866) 257-4ONS; Fax: (412) 859-6160; Email: foundation@ons.org

Web: www.ons.org

**Summary:** To provide financial assistance to nurses who are interested in working on a bachelor's degree in oncology nursing.

**Eligibility:** Open to registered nurses and licensed practical (vocational) nurses with a demonstrated interest in and commitment to oncology nursing. They must be currently enrolled in an undergraduate degree program at an NLN- or CCNE-accredited school of nursing. They may not have previously received a bachelor's level scholarship from this sponsor. Applicants must submit an essay of 250 words or less on their role in caring for persons with cancer and a statement of their professional goals and their relationship to the advancement of oncology nursing. Financial need is not considered in the selection process.

**Financial data:** The stipend is $2,000.

**Duration:** 1 year.

**Number awarded:** Varies each year; recently, 4 of these scholarships were awarded, including 1 for an LPN/LVN.

**Deadline:** January of each year.

### 2576 ONCOLOGY PRACTICE ALLIANCE SCHOLARSHIP

American College of Medical Practice Executives

Attn: ACMPE Scholarship Fund Inc.

104 Inverness Terrace East

Englewood, CO 80112-5306

Phone: (303) 799-1111, ext. 232; (877) ASK-MGMA; Fax: (303) 643-4439; Email: acmpe@mgma.com

Web: www.mgma.com/academics/scholar.cfm

**Summary:** To provide financial assistance to residents of Ohio and West Virginia who are working on an undergraduate or graduate degree in health care management related to hematology or oncology.

**Eligibility:** Open to full-time students working on an undergraduate or graduate degree in a program relevant to medical practice management (e.g., public health, business administration, health care administration) with a specialty in oncology or hematology. Students working on a degree in medicine, physical therapy, nursing, or other clinically-related professions are not eligible. Applicants must have been residents of Ohio or West Virginia for at least 12 months prior to applying. They must submit a letter describing their career goals and objectives relevant to medical practice management; a resume; 3 reference letters commenting on their performance, character, potential to succeed, and need for scholarship support; and either documentation indicating acceptance into an undergraduate or graduate program or academic transcripts indicating undergraduate or graduate work completed to date.

**Financial data:** The stipend is at least $1,000. Funds are paid directly to the recipient's college or university.

**Duration:** 1 year.

**Number awarded:** 1 each year.

**Deadline:** April of each year.

### 2577 OPERATIONS AND POWER DIVISION WALTER A. SIMON SCHOLARSHIP

American Nuclear Society, Attn: Scholarship Coordinator

555 North Kensington Avenue

La Grange Park, IL 60526-5592

Phone: (708) 352-6611; Fax: (708) 352-0499; Email: outreach@ans.org

Web: www.ans.org/honors/scholarships

**Summary:** To provide financial assistance to undergraduate students who are interested in preparing for a career dealing with operations and power aspects of nuclear science or nuclear engineering.

**Eligibility:** Open to students entering their junior or senior year in nuclear science, nuclear engineering, or a nuclear-related field at an accredited institution in the United States. Applicants must be interested in preparing for a career dealing with operations and power aspects of nuclear science or nuclear engineering. They must be U.S. citizens or permanent residents and able to demonstrate academic achievement.

**Financial data:** The stipend is $2,500.

**Duration:** 1 year; nonrenewable.

**Number awarded:** 1 each year.

**Deadline:** January of each year.

### 2578 ORAL-B LABORATORIES DENTAL HYGIENE SCHOLARSHIPS

American Dental Hygienists' Association, Attn: Institute for Oral Health

444 North Michigan Avenue, Suite 3400

Chicago, IL 60611

Phone: (312) 440-8918; (800) 735-4916; Fax: (312) 440-8929; Email: institute@adha.net

Web: www.adha.org/institute/Scholarship/index.htm

**Summary:** To provide financial assistance to baccalaureate students in dental hygiene.

**Eligibility:** Open to full-time undergraduate students who are active members of the Student American Dental Hygienists' Association (SADHA) or the American Dental Hygienists' Association (ADHA). Applicants must have a GPA of 3.5 or higher, be able to document financial need of at least $1,500, be able to demonstrate academic excellence and outstanding clinical performance, and have completed at least one year in an accredited dental hygiene program in the United States. They must be able to demonstrate an intent to encourage professional excellence and scholarship, quality research, and dental hygiene through public and private education. Along with their application, they must submit a statement that covers their long-term career goals, their intended contribution to the dental hygiene profession, their professional interests, and the manner in which their degree will enhance their professional capacity.

**Financial data:** Stipends range from $1,000 to $2,000.

**Duration:** 1 year.

**Number awarded:** 2 each year.

**Deadline:** April of each year.

### 2579 ORAL-B SCHOLARSHIPS FOR DENTAL HYGIENE STUDENTS PURSUING ACADEMIC CAREERS

American Dental Education Association, Attn: Awards Selection Committee

1400 K Street, N.W., Suite 1100

Washington, DC 20005

Phone: (202) 289-7201; Fax: (202) 289-7204; Email: MorganM@ada.org

Web: www.adea.org

**Summary:** To provide financial assistance to dental hygiene students who are interested in an academic career.

**Eligibility:** Open to students who have graduated from an accredited dental hygiene program with an associate's degree or certificate to practice dental hygiene and are currently enrolled in a degree completion program for a bachelor's or graduate degree at an institution that is a member of the American Dental Education Association (ADEA). Applicants must show a commitment to pursuing an academic degree in dental hygiene and be individual ADEA members. Along with their application, they must submit a personal statement that details their experiences, influences, and decision-making that demonstrate a firm commitment to become an allied dental faculty member. Priority is given to qualified candidates enrolled in bachelor's degree completion programs.

**Financial data:** The stipend is $2,500. Funds are applied to tuition and fees.

**Duration:** 1 year; nonrenewable.

**Number awarded:** 2 each year.

**Deadline:** December of each year.

### 2580 OREGON LEGION AUXILIARY DEPARTMENT NURSES SCHOLARSHIP

American Legion Auxiliary, Attn: Department of Oregon

30450 S.W. Parkway Avenue

P.O. Box 1730

Wilsonville, OR 97070-1730

Phone: (503) 682-3162; Fax: (503) 685-5008; Email: pcalhoun@pcez.com

**Summary:** To provide financial assistance for nursing education to the wives, widows, and children of Oregon veterans.

**Eligibility:** Open to the wives of veterans with disabilities, the widows of deceased veterans, and the sons and daughters of veterans who are Oregon residents. Applicants must have been accepted by an accredited hospital or university school of nursing in Oregon. Selection is based on ability, aptitude, character, determination, seriousness of purpose, and financial need.

**Financial data:** The stipend is $1,500.

**Duration:** 1 year; may be renewed.

**Number awarded:** 1 each year.

**Deadline:** May of each year.

### 2581 OREGON SHEEP GROWERS ASSOCIATION SCHOLARSHIP

Oregon Sheep Growers Association, Inc.

1270 Chemeketa Street, N.E.

Salem, OR 97301-4145

Phone: (503) 364-5462; Fax: (503) 585-1921

**Summary:** To provide financial assistance to Oregon residents who are preparing for a career in the sheep industry.

**Eligibility:** Open to Oregon residents who are currently enrolled in a college or university in any state as an undergraduate sophomore or above or as a graduate student. Applicants must be majoring in an agricultural science or veterinary medicine and be interested in a career in the sheep industry.

**Financial data:** Stipends range up to $1,000 per year. Funds are to be used to pay for tuition, books, or related fees. Checks are made payable jointly to the recipient and the recipient's institution.

**Duration:** 1 year.

**Number awarded:** Up to 2 each year.

**Deadline:** June of each year.

### 2582 OSFA NURSE'S SCHOLARSHIP

Ohio State Firefighters' Association

3275 Crestview S.E.

Warren, OH 44484-3206

Phone: (800) 825-OSFA

Web: www.ohiofirefighters.org

**Summary:** To provide financial assistance to high school seniors in Ohio who are interested in preparing for a nursing career.

**Eligibility:** Open to financially disadvantaged high school seniors in Ohio who are interested in working on a nursing degree in college. Applicants must have been Ohio residents for at least 5 years. Selection is based on financial need, academic record, special achievements, leadership qualities, and personality.

**Financial data:** The stipend is $1,600.

**Duration:** 1 year.

**Number awarded:** 3 each year.

**Deadline:** February of each year.

### 2583 OUTSTANDING PULSED POWER STUDENT AWARD

Institute of Electrical and Electronics Engineers

Nuclear and Plasma Sciences Society

c/o Igor Alexeff, NPSS Awards Committee

University of Tennessee

Department of Electrical and Computer Engineering

Ferris 315, Middle Drive

Knoxville, TN 37996-2100

Phone: (865) 974-5467; Fax: (865) 974-5467; Email: alexeff@utk.edu

Web: ewh.ieee.org/soc/nps/awards.htm

**Summary:** To recognize and reward outstanding student contributions to pulsed power engineering, science, and technology.

**Eligibility:** Open to full-time undergraduate and graduate students in pulsed power engineering or science. Nominees must be a student when nominated. Selection is based on quality of research contributions (40 points), quality of educational accomplishments (30 points), and quality and significance of publications and patents (20 points).

**Financial data:** The award consists of $1,000 and a certificate.

**Duration:** The award is presented biennially.

**Number awarded:** 1 each odd-numbered year.

**Deadline:** January of each odd-numbered year.

### 2584 PACIFICARE LATINO HEALTH SCHOLARS PROGRAM

PacifiCare Foundation

3100 Lake Center Drive

P.O. Box 25186

Santa Ana, CA 92799

Phone: (714) 825-5233

Web: www.pacificare.com

**Summary:** To provide financial assistance to Latino high school seniors in designated states planning to major in a health care field in college.

**Eligibility:** Open to seniors graduating from high schools in Arizona, California, Colorado, Nevada, Oklahoma, Oregon, Texas, and Washington. Applicants must have a GPA of 3.0 or higher, be fluent in Spanish, and have been accepted as a full-time student at a university, community college, or accredited technical college. Their proposed field of study must relate to health care, including (but not limited to) nursing, medical interpretation, health claims examiner, health information technology programs, pharmacy technician, public health, psychology, or pre-medical studies. Along with their application, they must submit a 2-page essay (in both English and Spanish) on their

personal and academic accomplishments, community involvement, volunteer and leadership activities, academic plans, and the reason they want a career in the health care field.

**Financial data:** The stipend is $2,000.

**Duration:** 1 year.

**Number awarded:** Approximately 50 each year.

**Deadline:** June of each year.

### 2585 PALH SCHOLARSHIPS

American Academy of Physician Assistants

Attn: Physician Assistants for Latino Health

950 North Washington Street

Alexandria, VA 22314-1552

Phone: (800) 596-7494; Fax: (703) 684-1924; Email: palh@aapa.org

Web: www.palh.org/PALH_Scholarship.html

**Summary:** To provide financial assistance to student members of the Physician Assistants for Latino Health (PALH) within the American Academy of Physician Assistants (AAPA).

**Eligibility:** Open to students who are members of both the AAPA and its PALH caucus enrolled in a physician assistant program. Applicants need not be of Latino descent, but they must be able to demonstrate leadership in the Latino community or an interest in Latino health issues. They must have a GPA of 3.0 or higher. Along with their application, they must submit a statement on their personal background, pertinent experiences working with underserved Latino communities, future goals and expectations upon completing their physician assistant program, and why they should be considered for a PALH scholarship. Financial need is not considered in the selection process.

**Financial data:** A stipend is awarded; amount not specified.

**Duration:** 1 year.

**Number awarded:** 2 each year.

**Deadline:** March of each year.

### 2586 PAPER AND BOARD DIVISION SCHOLARSHIPS

Technical Association of the Pulp and Paper Industry

Attn: TAPPI Foundation

15 Technology Parkway South

Norcross, GA 30092

Phone: (770) 209-7536; (800) 332-8686; Fax: (770) 446-6947;

Email: vedmondson@tappi.org

Web: www.tappi.org

**Summary:** To provide financial assistance to student members of the Technical Association of the Pulp and Paper Industry (TAPPI) who are majoring in a scientific or technical discipline related to the manufacture of paper and paperboard.

**Eligibility:** Open to students who are members of the association, are attending college full time or participating full time in a cooperative work-study program recognized and supported by their college, are at least sophomores on the undergraduate level, are enrolled in an engineering or science program, and are able to demonstrate a significant interest in the paper industry. Selection is based on the candidates' seriousness of purpose in pursuing a course of study related to the science and technology of the paper industry and an intent to make a career in the industry; financial need is not considered.

**Financial data:** The stipend is $1,000.

**Duration:** 1 year.

**Number awarded:** Varies each year; recently, 1 of these scholarships was awarded.

**Deadline:** January of each year.

### 2587 PARIS FRACASSO PRODUCTION FLORICULTURE SCHOLARSHIP

Floriculture Industry Research and Scholarship Trust

Attn: Scholarship Program

P.O. Box 280

East Lansing, MI 48826-0280

Phone: (517) 333-4617; Fax: (517) 333-4494;

Email: scholarships@firstinfloriculture.org

Web: www.firstinfloriculture.org

**Summary:** To provide financial assistance to college students in horticulture.

**Eligibility:** Open to undergraduate students at 4-year colleges and universities who are entering their junior, senior, or fifth undergraduate year. Applicants must be horticulture majors who intend to prepare for a career in floriculture production. They must be U.S. or Canadian citizens or permanent residents with a GPA of 3.0 or higher. Selection is based on academic record, recommendations, career goals, extracurricular activities, and financial need.

**Financial data:** The stipend depends on the availability of funds. Recently, it was $1,000.

**Duration:** 1 year.

**Number awarded:** 2 each year.

**Deadline:** April of each year.

## 2588 PARTNERSHIP IN NURSING EDUCATION PROGRAM

U.S. Army
ROTC Cadet Command, Attn: ATCC-OP-I-S
55 Patch Road, Building 56
Fort Monroe, VA 23651-1052
Phone: (757) 727-4558; (800) USA-ROTC; Email: atccps@usaac.army.mil
Web: www.rotc.usaac.army.mil/scholarship_HPD2/index.asp

**Summary:** To provide financial assistance to high school seniors or graduates who are interested in enrolling in Army ROTC and majoring in nursing in college.

**Eligibility:** Open to applicants who 1) are U.S. citizens; 2) are at least 17 years of age by October of the year in which they are seeking a scholarship; 3) are no more than 27 years of age when they graduate from college after 4 years; 4) score at least 19 on the ACT (or equivalent on the SAT); 5) have a high school GPA of 2.4 or higher; and 6) meet medical and other regulatory requirements. This program is open to ROTC scholarship applicants who wish to enroll in a nursing program at one of approximately 100 designated partner colleges and universities and become Army nurses after graduation.

**Financial data:** This scholarship provides financial assistance toward college tuition and educational fees up to an annual amount of $17,000. In addition, a flat rate of $1,000 is provided for the purchase of textbooks, classroom supplies, and equipment. Recipients are also awarded a stipend for up to 10 months of each year that is $250 per month during their freshman year, $300 per month during their sophomore year, $350 per month during their junior year, and $400 per month during their senior year.

**Duration:** 4 years, until completion of a baccalaureate degree. A limited number of 2-year and 3-year scholarships are also available to students who are already attending an accredited B.S.N. program on a campus affiliated with ROTC.

**Number awarded:** A limited number each year.

**Deadline:** November of each year.

## 2589 PAST PRESIDENTS SCHOLARSHIP

Institute of Food Technologists, Attn: Scholarship Department
525 West Van Buren, Suite 1000
Chicago, IL 60607
Phone: (312) 782-8424; Fax: (312) 782-8348; Email: info@ift.org
Web: www.ift.org

**Summary:** To provide financial assistance to undergraduates interested in studying food science or food technology.

**Eligibility:** Open to sophomores, juniors, and seniors in a food science or food technology program at an educational institution in the United States or Canada. Applicants must have an outstanding scholastic record and a well-rounded personality. Along with their application, they must submit an essay on their career aspirations; a list of awards, honors, and scholarships they have received; a list of extracurricular activities and/or hobbies; and a summary of their work experience. Financial need is not considered in the selection process.

**Financial data:** The stipend is $1,000.

**Duration:** 1 year; recipients may reapply if they are members of the Institute of Food Technologists.

**Number awarded:** 1 each year.

**Deadline:** January of each year.

## 2590 PAUL A. WHELAN AVIATION SCHOLARSHIP

University Aviation Association
3410 Skyway Drive
Auburn, AL 36830-6444
Phone: (334) 844-2434; Email: uaa@auburn.edu
Web: www.uaa.aero

**Summary:** To provide financial assistance to students working on an undergraduate or graduate degree in aviation or a space-related field.

**Eligibility:** Open to sophomore, juniors, seniors, and graduate students who are currently enrolled at a college, university, or community college affiliated with the University Aviation Association (UAA). Applicants must be majoring in aviation or a space-related field and have a GPA of 2.5 or higher overall and 3.0 in their aviation courses. They must be able to demonstrate a love of aviation, extracurricular and community involvement, and leadership. Preference is given to applicants who have Federal Aviation Administration certification as a pilot or mechanic; former or current military service through active duty, ROTC, Air National Guard, or Reserves while in school; or membership in an aviation-related association or professional group.

**Financial data:** The stipend is $2,000.

**Duration:** 1 year.

**Number awarded:** 1 each year.

**Deadline:** August of each year.

## 2591 PAUL AND ELLEN RUCKES SCHOLARSHIP

American Foundation for the Blind, Attn: Scholarship Committee
11 Penn Plaza, Suite 300
New York, NY 10001
Phone: (212) 502-7661; (800) AFB-LINE; Fax: (212) 502-7771; TDD: (212) 502-7662; Email: afbinfo@afb.net
Web: www.afb.org/scholarships.asp

**Summary:** To provide financial assistance to visually impaired students who wish to work on a graduate or undergraduate degree in engineering or computer, physical, or life sciences.

**Eligibility:** Open to visually impaired undergraduate or graduate students who are U.S. citizens working on a degree in engineering or the computer, physical, or life sciences. Legal blindness is not required. Along with their application, they must submit an essay that includes the field of study they are pursuing and why they have chosen it; their educational and personal goals; their work experience; any extracurricular activities with which they have been involved, including those in school, religious organizations, and the community; and how they intend to use scholarship monies that may be awarded.

**Financial data:** The stipend is $1,000.

**Duration:** 1 year.

**Number awarded:** 1 each year.

**Deadline:** April of each year.

## 2592 PAUL AND HELEN L. GRAUER SCHOLARSHIP

**Summary:** To provide financial assistance to licensed radio amateurs who are interested in working on an undergraduate or graduate degree, particularly in electronics or communications.

*See Listing #1620.*

## 2593 PAUL COLE SCHOLARSHIP AWARD

Society of Nuclear Medicine, Attn: Committee on Awards
1850 Samuel Morse Drive
Reston, VA 20190-5316
Phone: (703) 708-9000, ext. 1255; Fax: (703) 708-9020;
Email: grantinfo@snm.org
Web: www.snm.org

**Summary:** To provide financial support to students seeking training in nuclear medicine technology.

**Eligibility:** Open to students in baccalaureate, associate, or certificate programs in nuclear medicine technology. Applicants must have a cumulative GPA of 2.5 or higher. Selection is based on financial need and academic achievement.

**Financial data:** The stipend is $1,000.

**Duration:** 1 year.

**Number awarded:** Varies each year; recently, 30 scholarships were awarded.

**Deadline:** October of each year.

## 2594 PAUL H. ROBBINS SCHOLARSHIP

National Society of Professional Engineers, Attn: Educational Foundation
1420 King Street
Alexandria, VA 22314-2794
Phone: (703) 684-2833; Fax: (703) 836-4875; Email: jiglesias@nspe.org
Web: www.nspe.org/edfoundation/edf1-robbins.asp

**Summary:** To provide financial assistance for college to high school seniors interested in preparing for a career in engineering.

**Eligibility:** Open to high school seniors planning to study engineering in an EAC-ABET accredited college program. Applicants must have earned a GPA of 3.0 or higher and above average SAT or ACT scores. They must submit an essay (up to 500 words) on their interest in engineering, their major area of study and area of specialization, and the occupation they propose to pursue after graduation. Selection is based on GPA (20 points), the essay (20 points), extracurricular activities, including work experience and volunteer activities (25 points), financial need (5 points), SAT/ACT scores (20 points), and the composite application (10 points). U.S. citizenship is required.

**Financial data:** The stipend is $1,000 per year; funds are paid directly to the recipient's institution.

**Duration:** 2 years.

**Number awarded:** 1 each year.

**Deadline:** February of each year.

## 2595 PAUL SMITH SCHOLARSHIP AWARD

Technical Association of the Pulp and Paper Industry
Attn: TAPPI Foundation
15 Technology Parkway South
Norcross, GA 30092
Phone: (770) 209-7536; (800) 332-8686; Fax: (770) 446-6947;
Email: vedmondson@tappi.org
Web: www.tappi.org

**Summary:** To provide financial assistance to undergraduate or graduate students who are interested in preparing for a career in the paper industry, with a focus on science and engineering as it relates to the pulp, paper, and allied industries.

**Eligibility:** Open to students who are attending college full time, are at least sophomores or graduate students, have a GPA of 2.5 or higher, and are enrolled in a program preparatory to a career in the pulp and paper industry. Applicants must include letters of recommendation from persons familiar with their character, interest in the pulp and paper industry, educational accomplishments, school activities, and leadership roles. Selection is based on the candidates' potential career contributions to the pulp and paper industry; financial need is not considered.

**Financial data:** The stipend is $1,000.

**Duration:** 1 year; nonrenewable.

**Number awarded:** 1 each year.

**Deadline:** January of each year.

## 2596 PAULINA L. SORG SCHOLARSHIPS

Hawai'i Community Foundation, Attn: Scholarship Department
1164 Bishop Street, Suite 800
Honolulu, HI 96813
Phone: (808) 566-5570; (888) 731-3863; Fax: (808) 521-6286;
Email: scholarships@hcf-hawaii.org
Web: www.hawaiicommunityfoundation.org/scholar/scholar.php

**Summary:** To provide financial assistance to Hawaii residents who are interested in preparing for a career in physical therapy.

**Eligibility:** Open to Hawaii residents who are studying physical therapy as full-time juniors, seniors, or graduate students. They must be able to demonstrate academic achievement (GPA of 2.7 or higher), good moral character, and financial need. In addition to filling out the standard application form, applicants must write a short statement indicating their reasons for attending college, their planned course of study, and their career goals.

**Financial data:** The amounts of the awards depend on the availability of funds and the need of the recipient; recently, stipends averaged $1,000.

**Duration:** 1 year.

**Number awarded:** Varies each year; recently, 5 of these scholarships were awarded.

**Deadline:** February of each year.

## 2597 PAULINE THOMPSON NURSING EDUCATION SCHOLARSHIP

Nursing Foundation of Pennsylvania, Attn: Awards Committee
2578 Interstate Drive, Suite 101
Harrisburg, PA 17110
Phone: (717) 657-1222; (888) 707-PSNA, ext. 205; Fax: (717) 657-3796;
Email: panurses@panurses.org
Web: www.psna.org

**Summary:** To provide financial assistance to undergraduate nursing students in Pennsylvania.

**Eligibility:** Open to students enrolled in a baccalaureate or associate's degree, or R.N. to B.S.N. competition nursing program located in Pennsylvania that is accredited by the National League for Nursing. Baccalaureate students must be in their junior or senior year (application may be made at the end of the sophomore year). Associate's degree students must be in their final year (application may be made at the end of the first year). Registered nurses must have been accepted into a baccalaureate program. All applicants must be Pennsylvania residents. They must be in good academic standing (GPA of 3.0 or higher) and able to show both leadership qualities and involvement in community service. Applicants must be members of the Student Nurses Association of Pennsylvania, unless there is no school chapter (applicants who are R.N.s must be members of the Pennsylvania State Nurses Association).

**Financial data:** The stipend is $1,000.

**Duration:** 1 year.

**Number awarded:** 5 each year.

**Deadline:** May of each year.

## 2598 PAYZER SCHOLARSHIP

Experimental Aviation Association, Attn: Scholarship Office
EAA Aviation Center
P.O. Box 3086
Oshkosh, WI 54903-3086
Phone: (920) 426-6884; Fax: (920) 426-6865; Email: scholarships@eaa.org
Web: www.eaa.org/education/scholarships/index.html

**Summary:** To provide financial assistance to college students who are studying or planning to study an area that emphasizes technical information.

**Eligibility:** Open to students accepted or enrolled at an accredited college, university, or other postsecondary school with an emphasis on technical information. Applicants must be interested in majoring in (and preparing for a professional career in) engineering, mathematics, or the physical or biological sciences. They must submit a personal statement that covers their career aspirations, educational plan, why they want to receive this scholarship, what they learned from their work and volunteer experiences, how their education will be financed, and any unusual family circumstances.

**Financial data:** The stipend is $5,000.

**Duration:** 1 year.

**Number awarded:** 1 each year.

**Deadline:** March of each year.

## 2599 PDEF MICKEY WILLIAMS MINORITY STUDENT SCHOLARSHIP

Society of Nuclear Medicine, Attn: Committee on Awards
1850 Samuel Morse Drive
Reston, VA 20190-5316
Phone: (703) 708-9000, ext. 1255; Fax: (703) 708-9020;
Email: grantinfo@snm.org
Web: www.snm.org

**Summary:** To provide financial support to minority students working on an associate's or bachelor's degree in nuclear medicine technology.

**Eligibility:** Open to students accepted or enrolled in a baccalaureate or associate's degree program in nuclear medicine technology. Applicants must be members of a minority group: African American, Native American (including American Indian, Eskimo, Hawaiian, and Samoan), Hispanic American, Asian American, or Pacific Islander. They must have a cumulative GPA of 2.5 or higher and be able to demonstrate financial need. U.S. citizenship or permanent resident status is required.

**Financial data:** The stipend is $5,000.

**Duration:** 1 year; may be renewed for 1 additional year.

**Number awarded:** 1 each year.

**Deadline:** October of each year.

## 2600 PEF GRANT

Pennsylvania Society of Professional Engineers
Attn: Pennsylvania Engineering Foundation
908 North Second Street
Harrisburg, PA 17102
Phone: (717) 441-6051; Fax: (717) 236-2046; Email: pspeinfo@pspe.org
Web: www.pspe.org/scholarships.shtml

**Summary:** To provide financial assistance to Pennsylvania high school seniors who are interested in studying engineering at a college or university in the state.

**Eligibility:** Open to graduating seniors at high schools in Pennsylvania. Applicants must be planning to enroll in an engineering program at an ABET-accredited college or university in the state. They must have a GPA of 3.6 or higher and above average SAT scores. U.S. citizenship in required. Interviews are included in the selection process.

**Financial data:** The stipend is $1,000.

**Duration:** 1 year; nonrenewable.

**Number awarded:** 1 each year.

**Deadline:** Each local chapter sets its own deadline. Students who submit their application to the state PEF office must do so by April of each year.

## 2601 PEI SCHOLARSHIP

National Society of Professional Engineers, Attn: Practice Division Manager
1420 King Street
Alexandria, VA 22314-2794
Phone: (703) 684-2884; Fax: (703) 836-4875; Email: egarcia@nspe.org
Web: www.nspe.org/scholarships/sc1-pei.asp

**Summary:** To provide financial assistance to engineering students sponsored by a member of the Professional Engineers in Industry (PEI) division of the National Society of Professional Engineers (NSPE).

**Eligibility:** Open to students who 1) have completed at least 2 semesters or 3 quarters of undergraduate engineering studies, or 2) are enrolled in graduate engineering study. Applicants must be sponsored by a PEI member. Their program must be accredited by the Accreditation Board for Engineering and Technology (ABET). Preference is given to the children and grandchildren of PEI members. Students attending a community or junior college must have applied as an undergraduate engineering student at an ABET-accredited program. Along with their application, they must submit a 500-word essay discussing their interest in engineering, the specific field of engineering that is being pursued, and the occupation they propose to follow after graduation. Selection is based on work experience (25 points), professional and technical society membership and activities (25 points), the essay (25 points), and activities and honors (25 points).

**Financial data:** The stipend is $2,500.
**Duration:** 1 year.
**Number awarded:** 1 or more each year.
**Deadline:** May of each year.

## 2602 PENCON FOUNDATION SCHOLARSHIP

Pennsylvania Energy Consortium, Attn: PENCON Foundation
90 Lawton Lane
Milton, PA 17847-9756
Phone: (570) 542-5602; Email: mwirth@csiu.org
Web: www.pencon.org

**Summary:** To recognize and reward, with college scholarships, seniors at high schools in Pennsylvania who submit outstanding science or environmental projects.

**Eligibility:** Open to seniors graduating from high schools that are members of the Pennsylvania Energy Consortium (PENCON). Applicants must have a GPA of 2.0 or higher and be planning to attend an institution of postsecondary education or training. They must submit an abstract of a scientific or environmental project they have conducted, including its goals and objectives, the activities it entailed, what they learned from it, and its significance for them and for others. Selection is based on the merit and quality of the project, the content and quality of an autobiographical essay, initiative and commitment to school and community service activities, academic achievement, recommendations, and financial need.

**Financial data:** Stipends range from $500 to $1,500 per year.
**Duration:** 1 year; may be renewed up to 3 additional years.
**Number awarded:** Varies each year. Recently, 9 of these scholarships were awarded: 1 at $1,500 per year, 2 at $1,000 per year, 4 at $750 per year, and 2 at $500 per year.
**Deadline:** Letters of intent must be submitted by November of each year. Completed projects are due in February.

## 2603 PENNSYLVANIA STATE COUNCIL OF AUXILIARIES GRANT

Pennsylvania Society of Professional Engineers
Attn: Pennsylvania Engineering Foundation
908 North Second Street
Harrisburg, PA 17102
Phone: (717) 441-6051; Fax: (717) 236-2046; Email: pspeinfo@pspe.org
Web: www.pspe.org/scholarships.shtml

**Summary:** To provide financial assistance to female Pennsylvania high school seniors who are interested in studying engineering at a college or university in the state.

**Eligibility:** Open to females graduating from high schools in Pennsylvania. Applicants must be planning to enroll in an engineering program at a college or university in the state accredited by the Accreditation Board for Engineering and Technology (ABET). They must have a GPA of 3.6 or higher and above average SAT scores. U.S. citizenship in required. Interviews are included in the selection process.

**Financial data:** The stipend is $1,000.
**Duration:** 1 year; nonrenewable.
**Number awarded:** 1 each year.
**Deadline:** Each local chapter sets its own deadline. Students who submit their application to the state PEF office must do so by April of each year.

## 2604 PERENNIAL PLANT ASSOCIATION SCHOLARSHIP

Perennial Plant Association
3383 Schirtzinger Road
Hilliar, OH 43026
Phone: (614) 771-8431; Fax: (614) 876-5238; Email: ppa@perennialplant.org
Web: www.perennialplant.org/education/ppascholar.html

**Summary:** To provide financial assistance to college students majoring in horticulture or a related subject.

**Eligibility:** Open to college students in a 2-year or 4-year program majoring in horticulture or a related subject. Applicants should have at least one quarter or semester remaining, should have at least a 3.0 GPA, and must submit a statement of purpose, college transcript, and recommendation letters.

**Financial data:** The stipend is $1,000 per year. Funds are sent directly to the recipient's school.
**Duration:** 1 year.
**Number awarded:** 6 each year.
**Deadline:** March of each year.

## 2605 PETER D. COURTOIS CONCRETE CONSTRUCTION SCHOLARSHIPS

American Concrete Institute
Attn: Concrete Research and Education Foundation
38800 Country Club Drive
P.O. Box 9094
Farmington Hills, MI 48333-9094
Phone: (248) 848-3700; Fax: (248) 848-3701; TDD: (248) 848-3823;
Email: scholarships@concrete.org
Web: www.concrete.org/STUDENTS/STU_SCHOLAR.HTM

**Summary:** To provide funding to undergraduate students preparing for a career in the field of concrete construction.

**Eligibility:** Open to undergraduate students in the United States or Canada who have achieved senior status in a 4-year or longer program in engineering, construction, or technology. Selection is based on demonstrated interest and ability to work in the field of concrete construction.

**Financial data:** The stipend is $1,000.
**Duration:** 1 year.
**Number awarded:** 1 each year.
**Deadline:** November of each year.

## 2606 PETROLEUM DIVISION COLLEGE SCHOLARSHIPS

International Petroleum Technology Institute
Attn: Student Scholarship Program
11757 Katy Freeway, Suite 865
Houston, TX 77079
Phone: (281) 493-3491; Fax: (281) 493-3493; Email: monesm@asme.org
Web: www.asme-petroleumdiv.org/students/scholarshipsbody.htm

**Summary:** To provide financial assistance to college students majoring in engineering fields related to the petroleum industry.

**Eligibility:** Open to students at an ABET-accredited college or university (or international equivalent) who have completed at least one semester in an engineering program but still have at least 1 semester of undergraduate work remaining before graduation. Applicants must be ASME International (the professional society of mechanical engineers) student members with a GPA of 2.5 or higher. Along with their application, they must submit a 1-page essay that indicates their interest in the petroleum industry, including drilling, completions, facilities, pipelines, rigs, operations, materials, equipment manufacturing, plant design and operation, maintenance, environmental protection, and innovations. Financial need is not considered in the selection process.

**Financial data:** The stipend is $2,000.
**Duration:** 1 year.
**Number awarded:** 5 each year.
**Deadline:** March of each year.

## 2607 PETROLEUM DIVISION HIGH SCHOOL SCHOLARSHIPS

International Petroleum Technology Institute
Attn: Student Scholarship Program
11757 Katy Freeway, Suite 865
Houston, TX 77079
Phone: (281) 493-3491; Fax: (281) 493-3493; Email: monesm@asme.org
Web: www.asme-petroleumdiv.org/students/scholarshipsbody.htm

**Summary:** To provide financial assistance to high school seniors planning to major in mechanical engineering in college.
**Eligibility:** Open to high school seniors who have indicated a pre-declared major in the mechanical engineering field on their application to college. Applicants must have a GPA of 3.0 or higher. They must be approved by their high school guidance counselor and principal and have a letter of recommendation from a teacher in engineering, mathematics, and/or science. Along with their application, they must submit a 1-page essay on their interest in a phase of mechanical engineering. Financial need is not considered in the selection process.

**Financial data:** The stipend is $1,000.

**Duration:** 1 year.

**Number awarded:** 2 each year.

**Deadline:** March of each year.

---

## 2608 PFIZER INC. SCHOLARSHIPS

American Dental Hygienists' Association, Attn: Institute for Oral Health
444 North Michigan Avenue, Suite 3400
Chicago, IL 60611
Phone: (312) 440-8918; (800) 735-4916; Fax: (312) 440-8929;
Email: institute@adha.net
Web: www.adha.org/institute/Scholarship/index.htm

**Summary:** To provide financial assistance to undergraduate students preparing for careers in dental hygiene.

**Eligibility:** Open to full-time undergraduate students who are active members of the Student American Dental Hygienists' Association (SADHA) or the American Dental Hygienists' Association (ADHA). Applicants must have a GPA of 3.5 or higher, be able to document financial need of at least $1,500, and have completed at least one year in an accredited dental hygiene program in the United States. Along with their application, they must submit a statement that covers their long-term career goals, their intended contribution to the dental hygiene profession, their professional interests, and the manner in which their degree will enhance their professional capacity.

**Financial data:** Stipends range from $1,000 to $2,000.

**Duration:** 1 year.

**Number awarded:** 5 each year.

**Deadline:** April of each year.

---

## 2609 PFIZER/UNCF CORPORATE SCHOLARS PROGRAM

United Negro College Fund, Attn: Corporate Scholars Program
P.O. Box 1435
Alexandria, VA 22313-9998
Phone: (866) 671-7237; Email: internship@uncf.org
Web: www.uncf.org/internships/index.asp

**Summary:** To provide financial assistance and work experience to minority undergraduate and graduate students majoring in designated fields and interested in an internship at a Pfizer facility.

**Eligibility:** Open to sophomores, juniors, graduate students, and first-year law students who are African American, Hispanic American, Asian/Pacific Islander American, or American Indian/Alaskan Native. Applicants must have a GPA of 3.0 or higher and be enrolled at an institution that is a member of the United Negro College Fund (UNCF) or at another targeted college or university. They must be working on 1) a bachelor's degree in animal science, business, chemistry (organic or analytical), human resources, logistics, microbiology, organizational development, operations management, pre-veterinary medicine, or supply chain management; 2) a master's degree in chemistry (organic or analytical), finance, human resources, or organizational development; or 3) a law degree. Eligibility is limited to U.S. citizens, permanent residents, asylees, refugees, and lawful temporary residents. Along with their application, they must submit a 1-page essay about themselves and their career goals, including information about their interest in Pfizer (the program's sponsor), their personal background, and any particular challenges they have faced.

**Financial data:** The program provides an internship stipend of up to $5,000, housing accommodations near Pfizer Corporate facilities, and (based on successful internship performance) a $15,000 scholarship.

**Duration:** 8 to 10 weeks for the internship; 1 year for the scholarship.

**Number awarded:** Varies each year.

**Deadline:** January of each year.

---

## 2610 PFLAG SCHOLARSHIPS FOR SCIENCE, ENGINEERING, BUSINESS OR FINANCE

Parents, Families and Friends of Lesbians and Gays

Attn: National Scholarships Program
1726 M Street, N.W., Suite 400
Washington, DC 20036
Phone: (202) 467-8180, ext. 219; Fax: (202) 467-8194;
Email: schools@pflag.org
Web: www.pflag.org

**Summary:** To provide financial assistance for college studies in selected fields to high school seniors and recent graduates who have a connection to Parents, Families and Friends of Lesbians and Gays (PFLAG).

**Eligibility:** Open to high school seniors and prior-year graduates who have not attended college. Applicants must have applied to an accredited high education institution to work on 1) an associate's degree leading to transfer to complete a bachelor's degree in science, engineering, business, or finance, or 2) a bachelor's degree in science, engineering, business, or finance at a 4-year college or university. They must self-identify either as a gay, lesbian, bisexual, or transgender (GLBT) person or as a supporter of GLBT people. Along with their application, they must submit a high school transcript showing a GPA of 3.0 or higher, 2 letters of recommendation, and a 2-page essay discussing either their life as an LGBT student or how they have been involved with and supported the LGBT community. Financial need is also considered in the selection process.

**Financial data:** The stipend is $1,000.

**Duration:** 1 year; nonrenewable.

**Number awarded:** 13 each year.

**Deadline:** February of each year.

---

## 2611 PHILIP R. PATTON SCHOLARSHIPS

Health Occupations Students of America
6021 Morriss Road, Suite 111
Flower Mound, TX 75028
Phone: (972) 874-0062; (800) 321-HOSA; Fax: (972) 874-0063;
Email: info@hosa.org
Web: www.hosa.org/member/scholar.html

**Summary:** To provide financial assistance for college to members of the Health Occupations Students of America (HOSA).

**Eligibility:** Open to high school seniors and current college students who are members of the association and planning to continue their education in the health care field. Applicants must submit a 1- to 2-page essay on why they have chosen to prepare for a nursing or hospital-related career, their financial need, and their career goals. Selection is based on the essay (36 points), transcripts (20 points), leadership activities and recognition (20 points), community involvement (15 points), and letters of reference (9 points).

**Financial data:** The stipend is $1,000.

**Duration:** 1 year.

**Number awarded:** 6 each year.

**Deadline:** May of each year.

---

## 2612 PHOEBE PEMBER MEMORIAL SCHOLARSHIP

United Daughters of the Confederacy, Attn: Education Director
328 North Boulevard
Richmond, VA 23220-4057
Phone: (804) 355-1636; Fax: (804) 353-1396; Email: hqudc@rcn.com
Web: www.hqudc.org/scholarships/scholarships.html

**Summary:** To provide financial assistance for nursing education to lineal descendants of Confederate veterans.

**Eligibility:** Open to lineal descendants of worthy Confederates or collateral descendants who are members of the Children of the Confederacy or the United Daughters of the Confederacy. Applicants must intend to study nursing and must submit a family financial report and certified proof of the Confederate record of one ancestor, with the company and regiment in which he served. They must be at least a 3.0 GPA in high school.

**Financial data:** The amount of this scholarship depends on the availability of funds.

**Duration:** 1 year; may be renewed for up to 3 additional years.

**Number awarded:** 1 each year.

**Deadline:** March of each year.

---

## 2613 PHOENIX SCHOLARSHIPS

Society of Manufacturing Engineers, Attn: SME Education Foundation
One SME Drive
P.O. Box 930
Dearborn, MI 48121-0930

Phone: (313) 425-3304; (800) 733-4763, ext. 3304; Fax: (313) 425-3411; Email: foundation@sme.org

Web: www.sme.org

**Summary:** To provide financial assistance to students enrolled or planning to enroll in a degree program in manufacturing or industrial technology in Arizona.

**Eligibility:** Open to graduating high school seniors and current full-time undergraduate students enrolled or planning to enrolled at an accredited college or university in Arizona. Applicants must be majoring in manufacturing engineering technology, manufacturing technology, industrial technology, or a closely-related field. They must have a GPA of 2.5 or higher.

**Financial data:** The stipend is $2,000.

**Duration:** 1 year; may be renewed if the recipient maintains a GPA of 2.5 or higher.

**Number awarded:** 2 each year.

**Deadline:** January of each year.

---

### 2614 PHYSICIAN ASSISTANT FOUNDATION SCHOLARSHIPS

American Academy of Physician Assistants

Attn: Physician Assistant Foundation

950 North Washington Street

Alexandria, VA 22314-1552

Phone: (703) 519-5686; Fax: (703) 684-1924; Email: aapa@aapa.org

Web: www.aapa.org/paf/pafprog.html

**Summary:** To provide financial assistance to student members of the American Academy of Physician Assistants (AAPA).

**Eligibility:** Open to AAPA student members attending a physician assistant program accredited by the Commission on Accreditation of Allied Health Education Programs. Applicants must have entered the professional phase of the program. Selection is based on financial need, academic achievement, extracurricular activities, and future goals.

**Financial data:** Stipends are $5,000, $3,000, or $2,000.

**Duration:** 1 year; nonrenewable.

**Number awarded:** Varies each year; recently, 35 of these scholarships were awarded.

**Deadline:** January of each year.

---

### 2615 PIONEERS OF FLIGHT SCHOLARSHIP PROGRAM

National Air Transportation Foundation

Attn: Manager, Education and Training

4226 King Street

Alexandria, VA 22302

Phone: (703) 845-9000, ext. 125; (800) 808-6282; Fax: (703) 845-8176;

Email: dhighsmith@nata.aero

Web: www.nata.aero/about/sch_pioneersofflight.jsp

**Summary:** To provide financial assistance for college to students planning careers in general aviation.

**Eligibility:** Open to students intending to enroll full time at an accredited 4-year college or university as juniors or seniors. Applicants must demonstrate an interest in a career in general aviation (not the major commercial airlines) and have a GPA of 3.0 or higher. Along with their application, they must submit a 250-word essay on their goals in general aviation. Selection is based on that essay, academic record, and letter of recommendation.

**Financial data:** The stipend is $1,000.

**Duration:** 1 year; may be renewed 1 additional year if the recipient maintains a 3.0 GPA and full-time enrollment.

**Number awarded:** 2 each year.

**Deadline:** December of each year.

---

### 2616 PLANE AND PILOT MAGAZINE/GARMIN SCHOLARSHIP

Aircraft Electronics Association, Attn: AEA Educational Foundation

4217 South Hocker Drive

Independence, MO 64055-4723

Phone: (816) 373-6565; Fax: (816) 478-3100; Email: info@aea.net

Web: www.aea.net

**Summary:** To provide financial assistance for college to students who are interested in preparing for a career in avionics or aircraft repair.

**Eligibility:** Open to high school, college, or vocational/technical students who are attending (or planning to attend) an accredited vocational/technical school in an avionics or aircraft repair program. Applicants must submit an official transcript (cumulative GPA of 2.5 or higher), a statement about their career plans, a description of their involvement in school and community activities,

and a 300-word essay on how the job requirements of aviation technicians will change with advancements in technology. Selection is based on merit.

**Financial data:** The stipend is $2,000.

**Duration:** 1 year.

**Number awarded:** 1 each year.

**Deadline:** February of each year.

---

### 2617 PLANNING SYSTEMS INCORPORATED SCIENCE AND ENGINEERING SCHOLARSHIP

Navy League of the United States, Attn: Scholarships

2300 Wilson Boulevard

Arlington, VA 22201-3308

Phone: (703) 528-1775; (800) 356-5760; Fax: (703) 528-2333;

Email: cjarvis@navyleague.org

Web: www.navyleague.org/scholarship

**Summary:** To provide financial assistance to dependent children of sea service personnel or veterans who are interested in majoring in science or engineering in college.

**Eligibility:** Open to U.S. citizens who are dependent children of active or honorably discharged members of the U.S. sea service (including the Navy, Marine Corps, or Coast Guard). Applicants must be entering their freshman year of college and planning to major in science or engineering. Along with their application, they must submit transcripts, 2 letters of recommendation, SAT/ACT scores, documentation of financial need, proof of qualifying sea service duty, and a one-page personal statement on why they should be considered for this scholarship.

**Financial data:** The stipend is $2,500 per year.

**Duration:** 4 years, provided the recipient maintains a GPA of 3.0 or higher.

**Number awarded:** 1 each year.

**Deadline:** February of each year.

---

### 2618 PNWIS ENVIRONMENTAL CHALLENGE

Air & Waste Management Association-Pacific Northwest International Section

c/o David J. Dornbush, Environmental Challenge Committee Chair

4449 South Brandon Street

Seattle, WA 98118

Phone: (206) 544-0399; Email: david.j.dornbush@boeing.com

Web: www.pnwis.org

**Summary:** To recognize and reward undergraduate and graduate students at universities in the geographic area of the Pacific Northwest International Section (PNWIS) of the Air & Waste Management Association (AWMA) who present outstanding solutions to environmental problems.

**Eligibility:** Open to undergraduate and graduate students at universities with a program in environmental engineering, technology, or natural sciences in the PNWIS region (the states of Alaska, Idaho, Montana, and Oregon and the provinces of British Columbia and Yukon). Teams of 3 to 5 students receive an environmental problem for which they must develop a solution. They must attend the PNWIS annual conference, at which clues are available in selected technical sessions. They submit papers presenting their solution to the problem and also make oral presentations.

**Financial data:** Prizes are $1,500 for the first-place team, $1,000 for second, $500 for third, and $100 for fourth through eighth.

**Duration:** The competition is held annually.

**Number awarded:** 8 teams win prizes.

**Deadline:** Teams must register by October of each year.

---

### 2619 P.O. PISTILLI SCHOLARSHIPS

Design Automation Conference

c/o Cherrice Traver

Union College

ECE Department

Schenectady, NY 12308

Phone: (518) 388-6326; Fax: (518) 388-6789; Email: traverc@union.edu

Web: doc.union.edu/acsee.html

**Summary:** To provide financial assistance to female, minority, or disabled high school seniors who are interested in preparing for a career in computer science or electrical engineering.

**Eligibility:** Open to "underrepresented" high school seniors: women, African Americans, Hispanic Americans, Native Americans, and persons with disabilities. Applicants must be interested in preparing for a career in electrical engineering, computer engineering, or computer science. They must have at least a 3.0 GPA, have demonstrated high achievements in math and science courses, and be able to demonstrate significant financial need. U.S. citizenship is not required, but applicants must be U.S. residents when they apply and must plan to attend an accredited U.S. college or university. They must submit a completed application form, 3 letters of recommendation, official transcripts, ACT/SAT and/or PSAT scores, a personal statement outlining future goals, a copy of their latest income tax return, and a copy of the FAFSA form they submitted.

**Financial data:** Stipends are $4,000 per year. Awards are paid each year in 2 equal installments.

**Duration:** 1 year; renewable for up to 4 additional years.

**Number awarded:** 2 to 7 each year.

**Deadline:** January of each year.

## 2620 POLYMER MODIFIERS AND ADDITIVES DIVISION SCHOLARSHIPS

Society of Plastics Engineers, Attn: SPE Foundation
14 Fairfield Drive
Brookfield, CT 06804-0403
Phone: (203) 740-5447; Fax: (203) 775-1157; Email: foundation@4spe.org
Web: www.4spe.org/foundation/scholarships.php

**Summary:** To provide financial assistance to undergraduate students who have a career interest in the plastics industry.

**Eligibility:** Open to full-time undergraduate students at 4-year colleges or in 2-year technical programs. Applicants must 1) have a demonstrated or expressed interest in the plastics industry; 2) be majoring in or taking courses that would be beneficial to a career in the plastics or polymer industry (e.g., plastics engineering, polymer sciences, chemistry, physics, chemical engineering, mechanical engineering, or industrial engineering); 3) be in good academic standing at their school; and 4) be able to document financial need. Along with their application, they must submit 3 letters of recommendation; a high school and/or college transcript; and a 1- to 2-page statement telling why they are interested in the scholarship, their qualifications, and their educational and career goals in the plastics industry.

**Financial data:** The stipend is $4,000 per year. Funds are paid directly to the recipient's school.

**Duration:** 1 year.

**Number awarded:** 4 each year.

**Deadline:** January of each year.

## 2621 POST SCHOLARSHIP

American Association of Airport Executives-Northeast Chapter
Attn: Executive Secretary
P.O. Box 8
West Milford, NJ 07480-0008
Phone: (973) 728-6760; Fax: (973) 728-6760
Web: www.necaaae.org/postnec.htm

**Summary:** To provide financial assistance to upper-division students majoring in airport management.

**Eligibility:** Open to juniors and seniors in colleges and universities who are majoring in airport management. Preference is given to those with a permanent residence in the northeast region. Students preparing for a career as commercial pilots are not eligible. Applicants must indicate how they will benefit from the grant and provide documentation of financial need.

**Financial data:** The stipend is $1,000.

**Duration:** 1 year.

**Number awarded:** 4 each year.

**Deadline:** February of each year.

## 2622 POWDER RIVER BASIN SECTION ANNUAL SCHOLARSHIP AWARDS

**Summary:** To provide financial assistance to Wyoming students interested in preparing for a career in the oil and gas industry.
*See Listing #952.*

## 2623 POWER ENGINEERING SOCIETY STUDENT PRIZE PAPER AWARD IN HONOR OF T. BURKE HAYES

Institute of Electrical and Electronics Engineers
Attn: Power Engineering Society
445 Hoes Lane
P.O. Box 1331
Piscataway, NJ 08855-1331

Phone: (732) 562-3883; Fax: (732) 562-3881; Email: pes@ieee.org
Web: www.ieee.org/organizations/society/power

**Summary:** To recognize and reward outstanding papers on power engineering by student members of the Institute of Electrical and Electronics Engineers (IEEE).

**Eligibility:** Open to student members in a program leading to a bachelor's or master's degree in electrical engineering, or the equivalent if the student is from an institution outside the United States. Applicants must submit a paper of approximately 5,000 words on a topic related to the electric power industry. Faculty sponsorship is encouraged, but papers co-authored by faculty are not eligible. Along with the paper, students must submit a supporting letter from their faculty sponsor, a short autobiographical sketch, and a permanent address and telephone number.

**Financial data:** The award is $1,500, a plaque, and a travel subsidy up to $1,000 for the recipient to attend the winter meeting of the Power Engineering Society.

**Duration:** The competition is held annually.

**Number awarded:** 1 each year.

**Deadline:** September of each year.

## 2624 POWER SYSTEMS PROFESSIONAL SCHOLARSHIP

National Strength and Conditioning Association, Attn: Foundation
1955 North Union Boulevard
P.O. Box 9908
Colorado Springs, CO 80932-0908
Phone: (719) 632-6722; (800) 815-6826; Fax: (719) 632-6367;
Email: foundation@nsca-lift.org
Web: www.nsca-lift.org/foundation/prof.shtml

**Summary:** To provide financial assistance for undergraduate or graduate study in strength training and conditioning to members of the National Strength and Conditioning Association (NSCA).

**Eligibility:** Open to applicants who have been members of the association for at least one year prior to the application deadline. They must be undergraduate or graduate students working as a strength and conditioning coach (student assistant, volunteer, or graduate assistant) in their school's athletic department, and they must be nominated by the head strength coach at their school. In addition to transcripts and a resume, nominees must submit an essay of no more than 500 words explaining their career goals and objectives. Selection is based on scholarship (25 points), strength and conditioning experience (15 points), the essay (15 points), recommendations (5 points), honors and awards (10 points), community involvement (10 points), and NSCA involvement (20 points).

**Financial data:** The stipend is $1,000, to be applied toward tuition.

**Number awarded:** 1 each year.

**Deadline:** March of each year.

## 2625 PPQ WILLIAM F. HELMS STUDENT SCHOLARSHIP PROGRAM

Department of Agriculture
Animal and Plant Health Inspection Service
Attn: Marketing and Regulatory Programs Business Services
4700 River Road, Unit 22
Riverdale, MD 20737-1230
Phone: (800) 762-2738
Web: www.aphis.usda.gov/ppq

**Summary:** To provide financial assistance and work experience to college students majoring in the agricultural or biological sciences.

**Eligibility:** Open to college sophomores and juniors who are attending an accredited college or university, are majoring in an agricultural or biological science (such as biology, plant pathology, entomology, virology, bacteriology, mycology, or ecology), are interested in a career in plant protection and quarantine, and are U.S. citizens. To apply, interested students must submit a completed application form, a personal letter describing their career goals and interest in plant protection and quarantine, transcripts, and 3 letters of recommendation.

**Financial data:** The stipend is $5,000 per year.

**Duration:** 1 year; may be renewed if the recipient maintains a GPA of 2.5 or higher.

**Number awarded:** Several each year.

**Deadline:** February of each year.

## 2626 PRAXAIR INTERNATIONAL SCHOLARSHIP

American Welding Society, Attn: AWS Foundation, Inc.
550 N.W. LeJeune Road

Miami, FL 33126
Phone: (305) 445-6628; (800) 443-9353, ext. 461; Fax: (305) 443-7559;
Email: found@aws.org
Web: www.aws.org/foundation/scholarships/praxair.html
**Summary:** To provide financial assistance to college students majoring in welding engineering.
**Eligibility:** Open to undergraduate students who are working on a 4-year bachelor's degree in welding engineering or welding engineering technology; preference is given to welding engineering students. Applicants must be full-time students with an overall GPA of 2.5 or higher. They must be U.S. or Canadian citizens attending an academic institution within the United States or Canada. Selection is based on demonstrated leadership abilities in clubs and organizations, extracurricular and academic activities, and community involvement; financial need is not required.
**Financial data:** The stipend is $2,500.
**Duration:** 1 year; recipients may reapply.
**Number awarded:** 1 each year.
**Deadline:** January of each year.

### 2627 PRESSURE VESSEL AND PIPING DIVISION STUDENT PAPER COMPETITION

ASME International, Attn: Pressure Vessel and Piping Division
Three Park Avenue
New York, NY 10016-5990
Phone: (212) 591-7863; (800) THE-ASME; Fax: (212) 591-7671;
Email: uvilar@asme.org
Web: www.asme.org
**Summary:** To recognize and reward outstanding student papers on pressure vessels and piping.
**Eligibility:** Open to senior undergraduate and graduate students in an engineering or scientific curriculum. Applicants submit previously unpublished papers that present new knowledge or experience in a field related to pressure vessels and piping. The paper must be technically correct and should be of interest to a reasonable number of people working in the field. It may be theoretical or may present the results of laboratory studies, and it may state or analyze a problem. The paper may also be a review-type paper, but it must be of significant value to the technical field. Applicants first submit abstracts; based on those abstracts, finalists are invited to present papers at the annual Pressure Vessels and Piping Conference, where the winning papers are selected on the basis of written technical content (70%) and presentation effectiveness (30%).
**Financial data:** Each finalist receives $600 and a certificate. The authors of the winning papers receive an additional $500.
**Duration:** The competition is held annually.
**Number awarded:** 10 finalists are selected each year. Of those, 2 (1 undergraduate and 1 graduate student) are chosen as the winners.
**Deadline:** Abstracts must be submitted by the end of September of each year.

### 2628 PROCTER & GAMBLE ORAL CARE–HDA FOUNDATION SCHOLARSHIPS

Hispanic Dental Association, Attn: HDA Foundation
188 West Randolph Street, Suite 415
Chicago, IL 60601
Phone: (312) 577-4013; (800) 852-7921; Fax: (312) 577-0052;
Email: HispanicDental@hdassoc.org
Web: www.hdassoc.org
**Summary:** To provide financial assistance to Hispanic students interested in preparing for a career in a dental profession.
**Eligibility:** Open to Hispanics who are entering as first-year students into an accredited dental, dental hygiene, dental assisting, or dental technician program. Applicants must have a GPA of 3.0 or higher. Along with their application, they must submit an essay on their career goals. Selection is based on scholastic achievement, community service, leadership skill, and commitment to improving health in the Hispanic community.
**Financial data:** Stipends are $1,000 or $500.
**Duration:** 1 year.
**Number awarded:** Numerous scholarships are awarded each year.
**Deadline:** June of each year for dental students; July of each year for hygiene, assisting, and laboratory technician students.

### 2629 PROFESSIONAL AVIATION MAINTENANCE ASSOCIATION STUDENT SCHOLARSHIP PROGRAM

Professional Aviation Maintenance Association

Attn: PAMA Scholarship Foundation
717 Princess Street
Alexandria, VA 22314
Phone: (703) 683-3171; (866) 865-PAMA; Fax: (703) 683-0018;
Email: hq@pama.org
Web: www.pama.org
**Summary:** To provide financial assistance to students interested in studying aviation maintenance on the undergraduate level.
**Eligibility:** Open to students currently enrolled in an institution to obtain an airframe and powerplant (A&P) or avionics license. Applicants must have completed 25% of the required curriculum; have at least a 3.0 GPA; and need financial assistance. Selection is based on educational performance, work experience, participation in school and community activities, career commitment and future potential, financial need, and a recommendation by a counselor, advisor, aviation maintenance instructor, or current employer.
**Financial data:** The award is $1,000. Funds may be used for tuition, fees, books, or supplies.
**Duration:** 1 year; recipients may reapply.
**Number awarded:** Varies each year; recently, 15 of these scholarships were awarded.
**Deadline:** November of each year.

### 2630 PROFESSIONAL ENGINEERS IN PRIVATE PRACTICE GRANT

Pennsylvania Society of Professional Engineers
Attn: Pennsylvania Engineering Foundation
908 North Second Street
Harrisburg, PA 17102
Phone: (717) 441-6051; Fax: (717) 236-2046; Email: pspeinfo@pspe.org
Web: www.pspe.org/scholarships.shtml
**Summary:** To provide financial assistance to Pennsylvania high school seniors who are interested in studying engineering at a college or university in the state.
**Eligibility:** Open to graduating seniors at high schools in Pennsylvania. Applicants must be planning to enroll in an engineering program at an ABET-accredited college or university in the state. They must have a GPA of 3.6 or higher and above average SAT scores. U.S. citizenship in required. Interviews are included in the selection process.
**Financial data:** The stipend is $1,000.
**Duration:** 1 year; nonrenewable.
**Number awarded:** 1 each year.
**Deadline:** Each local chapter sets its own deadline. Students who submit their application to the state PEF office must do so by April of each year.

### 2631 PROFESSIONAL LAND SURVEYORS OF OREGON SCHOLARSHIP

Oregon Student Assistance Commission
Attn: Grants and Scholarships Division
1500 Valley River Drive, Suite 100
Eugene, OR 97401-2146
Phone: (541) 687-7395; (800) 452-8807, ext. 7395; Fax: (541) 687-7419;
Email: awardinfo@mercury.osac.state.or.us
Web: www.osac.state.or.us
**Summary:** To provide financial assistance to students in Oregon interested in a career in land surveying.
**Eligibility:** Open to students at colleges and universities in Oregon. Applicants must be enrolled in a program leading to a career as a land surveyor, including community college applicants who intend to transfer to eligible 4-year schools or complete a degree in land surveying at the community college level. They must intend to take the Fundamentals of Land Surveying (FLS) examination. Along with their application, they must submit a brief essay on what led them to prepare for a land surveying career and what surveying means to them.
**Financial data:** The stipend is at least $1,600 per year.
**Duration:** 1 year.
**Number awarded:** Varies each year; recently, 5 of these scholarships were awarded.
**Deadline:** February of each year.

### 2632 QUALITY ASSURANCE DIVISION SCHOLARSHIPS

Institute of Food Technologists, Attn: Scholarship Department
525 West Van Buren, Suite 1000
Chicago, IL 60607

Phone: (312) 782-8424; Fax: (312) 782-8348; Email: info@ift.org
Web: www.ift.org

**Summary:** To provide financial assistance to undergraduates interested in studying food science or food technology.

**Eligibility:** Open to sophomores, juniors, and seniors in a food science or food technology program at an educational institution in the United States or Canada. Applicants must have an outstanding scholastic record and a well-rounded personality. Along with their application, they must submit an essay on their career aspirations; a list of awards, honors, and scholarships they have received; a list of extracurricular activities and/or hobbies; and a summary of their work experience. Preference is given to students who are taking or have taken at least one course in quality assurance and who demonstrate a definite interest in the quality assurance area. Financial need is not considered in the selection process.

**Financial data:** The stipend is $2,000.

**Duration:** 1 year; recipients may reapply if they are members of the Institute of Food Technologists (IFT).

**Number awarded:** 2 each year.

**Deadline:** January of each year.

## 2633 R. FLAKE SHAW SCHOLARSHIP PROGRAM

North Carolina Farm Bureau
5301 Glenwood Avenue
P.O. Box 27766
Raleigh, NC 27611
Phone: (919) 782-1705; Fax: (919) 783-3593; Email: ncfbfed@ncfb.com
Web: www.ncfb.com

**Summary:** To provide financial assistance to North Carolina high school seniors interested in studying agriculture or home economics in college.

**Eligibility:** Open to seniors at high schools in North Carolina who are interested in preparing for a career in agriculture, home economics, or an agriculturally-related field. Applicants must demonstrate satisfactory grades, good character, leadership potential, and financial need. They must obtain an application from their county Farm Bureau office, which conducts an initial screening and submits one application per county to the state office. Preference is given to North Carolina Farm Bureau members.

**Financial data:** The stipend is $1,750 per year.

**Duration:** 4 years, provided the recipient maintains a GPA of 2.0 or higher.

**Number awarded:** 6 each year.

## 2634 RAIL TRANSPORTATION DIVISION UNDERGRADUATE SCHOLARSHIP PROGRAM

ASME International, Attn: Rail Transportation Division
Three Park Avenue
New York, NY 10016-5990
Phone: (212) 591-7797; (800) THE-ASME; Fax: (212) 591-7671;
Email: manese@asme.org
Web: www.asme.org

**Summary:** To provide financial assistance to undergraduate mechanical engineering students who intend to enter the railway industry.

**Eligibility:** Open to undergraduate students in mechanical engineering who are interested in a career in the railway industry and have a family connection to the industry. Applicants must submit 1) a statement of intent to pursue mechanical engineering in the railway industry as a career; 2) a statement of perception of the importance of rail transportation in the overall field of transporting freight and passengers; 3) information on experiences in the railroad realm (i.e., work, model railroading, photography); 4) an abstract of any papers written related to the railroad industry; 5) a list of courses proposed for the upcoming term; 6) a transcript of previous college years; and 7) a letter of recommendation from a faculty advisor or department head. They must plan to attend a college or university in North America (including Alaska, Canada, Hawaii, Mexico, and Puerto Rico). Financial need is not considered.

**Financial data:** The award is $2,000 per year.

**Duration:** 1 year.

**Number awarded:** Varies each year; recently, 2 of these scholarships were awarded.

**Deadline:** September of each year.

## 2635 RALPH A. KLUCKEN SCHOLARSHIP

Technical Association of the Pulp and Paper Industry
Attn: TAPPI Foundation
15 Technology Parkway South
Norcross, GA 30092

Phone: (770) 209-7536; (800) 332-8686; Fax: (770) 446-6947;
Email: vedmondson@tappi.org
Web: www.tappi.org

**Summary:** To provide financial assistance for college or graduate school to students who are interested in preparing for a career in the pulp and paper industry.

**Eligibility:** Open to undergraduate and graduate students who are either enrolled full time or working full time and attending night school as a part-time student. Applicants must be able to demonstrate responsibility and maturity through a history of part-time and summer employment; an interest in the technological areas covered by the Polymers, Laminations, Adhesives, Coatings and Extrusions (PLACE) Division of the Technical Association of the Pulp and Paper Industry (TAPPI); and a GPA of 3.0 or higher. Selection is based on the candidates' potential career contributions to the pulp and paper industry; financial need is not considered.

**Financial data:** The stipend is $1,000.

**Duration:** 1 year. A student may apply for the scholarship each year, but the award will not be given to the same person twice consecutively.

**Number awarded:** 1 each year.

**Deadline:** May of each year.

## 2636 RALPH W. BAIRD SCHOLARSHIP

Society of Exploration Geophysicists, Attn: SEG Foundation
8801 South Yale, Suite 500
P.O. Box 702740
Tulsa, OK 74170-2740
Phone: (918) 497-5513; Fax: (918) 497-5557; Email: scholarships@seg.org
Web: seg.org/business/foundation/scholarships/index.shtml

**Summary:** To provide financial assistance to upper-division students working on a degree in geophysical engineering.

**Eligibility:** Open to juniors and seniors working on a degree in geophysical engineering. Along with their application, they must submit a 150-word essay on how they plan to use geophysics in their future. Financial need is not considered in the selection process.

**Financial data:** Stipends range from $1,000 to $3,000 per year.

**Duration:** 1 academic year.

**Number awarded:** 1 each year.

**Deadline:** January of each year.

## 2637 RAYMOND DAVIS SCHOLARSHIP

Society for Imaging Science and Technology, Attn: Membership Office
7003 Kilworth Lane
Springfield, VA 22151
Phone: (703) 642-9090; Fax: (703) 642-9094; Email: info@imaging.org
Web: www.imaging.org

**Summary:** To provide financial assistance to undergraduate and graduate students interested in studying photographic or imaging science or technology.

**Eligibility:** Open to full-time undergraduate or graduate students who have completed or will complete 2 academic years at an accredited institution before the term of the scholarship begins. Grants are made for academic study or research in photographic or imaging science or engineering. Graduate students must provide an abstract of their plan for advanced study, research, and thesis. All applicants must outline their career objectives and indicate how the academic work they propose to undertake will further their objectives. Financial need is not considered.

**Financial data:** Grants are $1,000 or more.

**Number awarded:** 1 or more each year.

**Deadline:** December of each year.

## 2638 RAYMOND H. FULLER, P.E., MEMORIAL SCHOLARSHIPS

Ohio Society of Professional Engineers, Attn: Engineers Foundation of Ohio
4795 Evanswood Drive, Suite 201
Columbus, OH 43229-7216
Phone: (614) 846-1144; (800) 654-9481; Fax: (614) 846-1131;
Email: ospe@iwaynet.net
Web: www.ohioengineer.com/programs/Scholarships.htm

**Summary:** To provide financial assistance to high school seniors in Ohio who are interested in majoring in engineering in college.

**Eligibility:** Open to high school seniors in Ohio who will be attending an ABET-approved college or university in the state and who plan to major in engineering. Applicants must have a GPA of 3.0 or higher, be U.S. citizens, and have ACT scores of at least 29 in mathematics and 25 in English (or the equivalent on the SAT). Along with their application, they must submit a 350-word essay on their interest in engineering, including why they became interested in the field, what specialty interests them most, and why they want to become a practicing engineer. Financial need is also considered in the selection process.

**Financial data:** The stipend is $1,000 per year.

**Duration:** 1 year; nonrenewable.

**Number awarded:** 2 each year.

**Deadline:** December of each year.

## 2639 RAYMOND R. MOONEY SCHOLARSHIP

Vermont Student Assistance Corporation
Champlain Mill, Attn: Scholarship Programs
P.O. Box 2000
Winooski, VT 05404-2601
Phone: (802) 654-3798; (888) 253-4819; Fax: (802) 654-3765; TDD: (802) 654-3766; TDD: (800) 281-3341 (within VT); Email: info@vsac.org
Web: www.vsac.org

**Summary:** To provide financial assistance to high school seniors in Vermont who plan to study a field related to emergency services in college.

**Eligibility:** Open to high school seniors in Vermont who are enrolled or planning to enroll in an academic, vocational, or technical program in a field related to emergency services. Selection is based on financial need and required essays.

**Financial data:** The stipend is $1,000.

**Duration:** 1 year; may be renewed for 1 additional year.

**Number awarded:** 1 each year.

**Deadline:** April of each year.

## 2640 RAYTHEON/FIRST ROBOTICS SCHOLARSHIP PROGRAM

Raytheon Corporation, Attn: Corporate Contributions
870 Winter Street
Waltham, MA 02451-1449
Phone: (781) 522-5802; Email: corporatecontributions@raytheon.com
Web: www.raytheon.com/community/robotics.html

**Summary:** To provide financial assistance to competitors in the FIRST (For Inspiration and Recognition of Science and Technology) Robotics competition who plan to major in mathematics, science, or technology in college.

**Eligibility:** Open to high school students who participate in the FIRST Robotics competition on teams that include both the students and engineers, technicians, teachers, parents, industry representatives, and (occasionally) college students and faculty. Although the composition of teams varies, most are industry-high school partnerships, university-high school partnerships, industry-university-high school partnerships, or coalitions that involve multiple companies, universities, and/or high schools competing as a single team. Each team starts with the same standard kit of parts and uses their creativity to design and build a robotic vehicle capable of performing a demanding task better than 2 opponents. Teams may enter regional competitions or go directly to the national competition. Participants in the competition are eligible to apply for this scholarship, either while they are still in high school or after they have entered college. Applicants must be majoring or planning to major in mathematics, science, or technology. Selection is based on academic record, field of study, demonstrated leadership and participation in school and community activities, honors, work experience, a statement of goals and aspirations, unusual personal or family circumstances, and a recommendation. Financial need is not considered.

**Financial data:** The stipend is $1,000 per year.

**Duration:** 1 year; may be renewed up to 3 additional years.

**Number awarded:** 1 or more each year.

**Deadline:** April of each year.

## 2641 REBECCA FISK SCHOLARSHIP

American Dental Hygienists' Association, Attn: Institute for Oral Health
444 North Michigan Avenue, Suite 3400
Chicago, IL 60611
Phone: (312) 440-8918; (800) 735-4916; Fax: (312) 440-8929;
Email: institute@adha.net
Web: www.adha.org/institute/Scholarship/index.htm

**Summary:** To provide financial assistance to undergraduate students preparing for careers in dental hygiene.

**Eligibility:** Open to full-time undergraduate students who are active members of the Student American Dental Hygienists' Association (SADHA) or the American Dental Hygienists' Association (ADHA). Applicants must have a

GPA of 3.0 or higher, be able to document financial need of at least $1,500, and have completed at least one year in an accredited dental hygiene program in the United States. Along with their application, they must submit a statement that covers their long-term career goals, their intended contribution to the dental hygiene profession, their professional interests, and the manner in which their degree will enhance their professional capacity.

**Financial data:** Stipends range from $1,000 to $2,000.

**Duration:** 1 year.

**Number awarded:** 1 each year.

**Deadline:** April of each year.

## 2642 REDI-TAG CORPORATION SCHOLARSHIP

American Health Information Management Association
Attn: Foundation of Research and Education
233 North Michigan Avenue, Suite 2150
Chicago, IL 60601-5806
Phone: (312) 233-1168; Fax: (312) 233-1090; Email: fore@ahima.org
Web: www.ahima.org/fore/programs.cfm

**Summary:** To provide financial assistance to members of the American Health Information Management Association (AHIMA) who are single parents interested in working on an undergraduate or graduate degree in health information administration or technology.

**Eligibility:** Open to AHIMA members who are single parents enrolled in a health information administration or health information technology program accredited by the Commission on Accreditation of Allied Health Education Programs. Applicants must be working on an undergraduate or graduate degree on at least a half-time basis and have a GPA of 3.0 or higher. U.S. citizenship is required. Selection is based on (in order of importance) GPA and academic achievement, volunteer and work experience, commitment to the health information management profession, suitability to the health information management profession, quality and suitability of references provided, and clarity of application.

**Financial data:** The stipend ranges from $1,000 to $5,000.

**Duration:** 1 year; nonrenewable.

**Number awarded:** 1 each year.

**Deadline:** May of each year.

## 2643 RHODE ISLAND PILOTS ASSOCIATION SCHOLARSHIP

Rhode Island Pilots Association, Attn: Scholarship Chair
644 Airport Road, Hangar One
Warwick, RI 02886
Phone: (401) 568-3497; Fax: (401) 568-5392; Email: ripaemail@aol.com
Web: www.ripilots.com/Scholarships.htm

**Summary:** To provide financial assistance to Rhode Island residents interested in obtaining pilot flight training or a college degree in an aviation-related field.

**Eligibility:** Open to residents of Rhode Island who are at least 16 years of age. Applicants must be interested in a program of pilot flight training or a college degree program in a field that is related to aviation and approved by the sponsoring organization. Flight training candidates must be able to pass the FAA Class III physical. Along with their application, they must submit a 2-page personal letter describing how scholarship funds would be used to pursue goals in aviation or related areas; a list of extracurricular activities, hobbies, and personal interests; 2 letters of recommendation; details of school record; and documentation of financial need.

**Financial data:** The stipend is $1,000.

**Duration:** 1 year.

**Number awarded:** 2 each year.

**Deadline:** February of each year.

## 2644 RIAHPERD SCHOLARSHIPS

**Summary:** To provide financial assistance for college to Rhode Island residents who are interested in preparing for a career in health education, physical education, recreation, or dance.

*See Listing #1647.*

## 2645 RICHARD A. HERBERT MEMORIAL UNDERGRADUATE SCHOLARSHIP

American Water Resources Association, Attn: Scholarship Coordinator
4 West Federal Street
P.O. Box 1626
Middleburg, VA 20118-1626

Phone: (540) 687-8390; Fax: (540) 687-8395; Email: info@awra.org

Web: www.awra.org/student/herbert.html

**Summary:** To provide financial assistance to undergraduate students enrolled in a program related to water resources.

**Eligibility:** Open to full-time undergraduate students enrolled in a program related to water resources. Applicants must submit a 2-page summary of their academic interests and achievements, extracurricular activities, and career goals. Selection is based on that statement, cumulative GPA, relevance of the student's curriculum to water resources, and leadership in extracurricular activities related to water resources.

**Financial data:** The stipend is $2,000.

**Duration:** 1 year.

**Number awarded:** 1 each year.

**Deadline:** April of each year.

## 2646 RICHARD B. FISHER SCHOLARSHIP

Morgan Stanley

c/o Joyce Arencibia, IT College Recruiting

750 Seventh Avenue, 30th Floor

New York, NY 10019

Phone: (212) 762-4000; Email: diversityrecruiting@morganstanley.com

Web: www.morganstanley.com/about/diversityrecruit_programs.html

**Summary:** To provide financial assistance and work experience to members of minority groups who are preparing for a career in technology within the financial services industry.

**Eligibility:** Open to members of minority groups who are enrolled in their sophomore or junior year of college (or the third or fourth year of a 5-year program). Applicants must be enrolled full time and have a GPA of 3.0 or higher. They must be willing to commit to a paid summer internship in the Morgan Stanley Information Technology Division. All majors and disciplines are eligible, but preference is given to students preparing for a career in technology within the financial services industry. Along with their application, they must submit 1-page essays on 1) why they are applying for this scholarship and why they should be selected as a recipient; 2) a technical project on which they worked, either through a university course or previous work experience, their role in the project, and how they contributed to the end result; and 3) a software, hardware, or new innovative application of existing technology that they would create if they could and the impact it would have. Financial need is not considered in the selection process.

**Financial data:** The stipend is $5,000.

**Duration:** 1 year.

**Number awarded:** 1 or more each year.

**Deadline:** February of each year.

## 2647 RICHARD E. LOMAX NATIONAL TRIG-STAR SCHOLARSHIPS

National Society of Professional Surveyors, Attn: Trig-Star Program

6 Montgomery Village Avenue, Suite 403

Gaithersburg, MD 20879

Phone: (240) 632-9716, ext. 103; Fax: (240) 632-1321; Email: sfrank@acsm.net

Web: www.acsm.net/trigstar/index.html

**Summary:** To recognize and reward (with college scholarships) high school students who participate in a trigonometry contest.

**Eligibility:** Open to high school students who participate at their school in a timed exercise in solving trigonometry problems that incorporate the use of right triangle formulas and the laws of sines and cosines. Contestants have up to one hour to complete the test, and the student who achieves the highest score in the shortest amount of time is the winner. School winners then compete in a state test, and state winners compete in the national test.

**Financial data:** At the national level, the first-place winner receives a $1,000 scholarship, the second-place winner receives a $500 scholarship, and the third-place winner receives a $250 scholarship. The teachers of the 3 winners receive awards of equal amounts. Local and state awards may also be provided by the local chapter or sponsor.

**Duration:** The competition is held annually.

**Number awarded:** 3 students win national awards each year.

## 2648 RICHARD GOOLSBY SCHOLARSHIP

Foundation for the Carolinas, Attn: Senior Vice President, Scholarships

217 South Tryon Street

P.O. Box 34769

Charlotte, NC 28234-4769

Phone: (704) 973-4535; (800) 973-7244; Fax: (704) 973-4935;

Email: jseymour@fftc.org

Web: www.fftc.org/scholarships

**Summary:** To provide financial assistance to college students in North and South Carolina who are preparing for a career in the plastics industry.

**Eligibility:** Open to residents of South Carolina, central North Carolina, or western North Carolina. Applicants must be entering their sophomore, junior, or senior year at a college or university in North or South Carolina and be majoring in a subject that will prepare them for a career in the plastics industry (e.g., chemistry, physics, chemical engineering, mechanical engineering, industrial engineering, business administration). They must be enrolled full time. Along with their application, they must submit a 1- to 2-page statement explaining why they are applying for the scholarship, their qualifications, and their educational and career goals in the plastics industry. Selection is based on academic performance, demonstrated interest in the plastics industry, financial need, school and community involvement, and personal achievements.

**Financial data:** Stipends range up to $4,000 per year; funds are paid directly to the recipient's school to be used for tuition, required fees, books, and supplies.

**Duration:** 1 year; may be renewed.

**Number awarded:** 1 or more each year.

**Deadline:** February of each year.

## 2649 RICHARD J. COPPLE MEMORIAL SCHOLARSHIPS

Kansas Golf Association, Attn: Kansas Golf Foundation

3301 Clinton Parkway Court, Suite 4

Lawrence, KS 66047

Phone: (785) 842-4833, ext. 205; Fax: (785) 842-3831;

Email: foundation@kansasgolf.org

Web: www.kansasgolf.org/KGF/Scholarships.htm

**Summary:** To provide financial assistance to college students from Kansas who are working on a degree in turfgrass management or preparing to become a golf course superintendent.

**Eligibility:** Open to residents of Kansas who are working on a degree in turfgrass management or studying to become a golf course superintendent. Applicants must provide information on their high school and college experiences (including GPA, extracurricular activities, awards, and honors), career plans after graduation, and past involvement with golf (either as a player or work experience).

**Financial data:** A stipend is awarded (amount not specified).

**Duration:** 1 year.

**Number awarded:** 2 each year.

**Deadline:** September of each year.

## 2650 RICHARD L. DAVIS MANAGERS SCHOLARSHIP

American College of Medical Practice Executives

Attn: ACMPE Scholarship Fund Inc.

104 Inverness Terrace East

Englewood, CO 80112-5306

Phone: (303) 799-1111, ext. 232; (877) ASK-MGMA; Fax: (303) 643-4439;

Email: acmpe@mgma.com

Web: www.mgma.com/academics/scholar.cfm

**Summary:** To provide financial assistance to individuals currently employed in medical group management who wish to pursue professional development on the undergraduate or graduate level.

**Eligibility:** Open to medical group management professionals who want to pursue professional development through undergraduate or graduate education in a program relevant to medical practice management, including public health, business administration, health care administration, or other related areas. Professionals interested in studying medicine, physical therapy, nursing, or other clinically-related professions are not eligible. Applicants must submit a letter describing their career goals and objectives relevant to medical practice management; a resume; 3 reference letters commenting on their performance, character, potential to succeed, and need for scholarship support; and either documentation indicating acceptance into an undergraduate or graduate college or university or academic transcripts indicating undergraduate or graduate work completed to date.

**Financial data:** The stipend is $1,500. Funds are paid directly to the recipient's college or university.

**Duration:** 1 year.

**Number awarded:** 1 each year.

**Deadline:** April of each year.

## 2651 RICHARD L. DAVIS/BARBARA B. WATSON NATIONAL SCHOLARSHIP

American College of Medical Practice Executives
Attn: ACMPE Scholarship Fund Inc.
104 Inverness Terrace East
Englewood, CO 80112-5306
Phone: (303) 799-1111, ext. 232; (877) ASK-MGMA; Fax: (303) 643-4439;
Email: acmpe@mgma.com
Web: www.mgma.com/academics/scholar.cfm
**Summary:** To provide financial assistance to undergraduate and graduate students who are interested in preparing for a career in medical group management.
**Eligibility:** Open to full-time students working on an undergraduate or graduate degree in a program relevant to medical practice management, including public health, business administration, health care administration, or other related areas. Students working on a degree in medicine, physical therapy, nursing, or other clinically-related professions are not eligible. Applicants must submit a letter describing their career goals and objectives relevant to medical practice management; a resume; 3 reference letters commenting on their performance, character, potential to succeed, and need for scholarship support; and either documentation indicating acceptance into an undergraduate or graduate college or university or academic transcripts indicating undergraduate or graduate work completed to date.
**Financial data:** The stipend is $1,500. Funds are paid directly to the recipient's college or university.
**Duration:** 1 year.
**Number awarded:** 1 each year.
**Deadline:** April of each year.

## 2652 RICHARD P. COVERT, PH.D., FHIMSS SCHOLARSHIP

Healthcare Information and Management Systems Society
Attn: HIMSS Foundation Scholarship Program Coordinator
230 East Ohio Street, Suite 500
Chicago, IL 60611-3269
Phone: (312) 664-4467; Fax: (312) 664-6143
Web: www.himss.org/asp/scholarships.asp
**Summary:** To provide financial assistance to student members of the Healthcare Information and Management Systems Society (HIMSS) who are working on an undergraduate or graduate degree in management engineering.
**Eligibility:** Open to student members of the society, although an application for membership, including dues, may accompany the scholarship application. Applicants must be upper-division or graduate students working on a degree in management engineering. Selection is based on academic achievement and demonstration of leadership potential, including communication skills and participation in society activity.
**Financial data:** The stipend is $5,000. The award includes an all-expense paid trip to the annual HIMSS conference and exhibition.
**Duration:** 1 year.
**Number awarded:** 1 each year.
**Deadline:** October of each year.

## 2653 RICK PANKOW FOUNDATION SCHOLARSHIP

Rick Pankow Foundation, Attn: Scholarship Program
P.O. Box 226
Issaquah, WA 98027
Phone: (425) 392-6164; Email: chuck@pacificpolants.com
**Summary:** To provide financial assistance to high school seniors in Washington who are interested in majoring in horticulture in college.
**Eligibility:** Open to seniors graduating from high schools in Washington who are planning to enter a 2-year or 4-year program in horticulture or landscape architecture. Selection is based on academic achievement, community and school involvement, leadership, recommendations, and financial need.
**Financial data:** The stipend is $1,000.
**Duration:** 1 year.
**Number awarded:** 1 each year.
**Deadline:** April of each year.

## 2654 RITA LOWE COLLEGE SCHOLARSHIPS

Washington State Mathematics Council
c/o Pat Reistroffer, Scholarship Chair
146 Scenic View Drive
Longview, WA 98632
Phone: (360) 636-5125; Email: preistrof@aol.com
Web: www.wsmc.net
**Summary:** To provide financial assistance to students majoring in mathematics education at colleges and universities in Washington.
**Eligibility:** Open to students currently attending a college or university in Washington and majoring in mathematics education. Applicants must be preparing for teaching certification in order to become a professional educator teaching mathematics at the elementary or secondary level. They must submit a transcript (from the ninth grade to the date of application), a 300-word statement on their experience with and interest in mathematics, and 2 letters of recommendation. Selection is based on academic achievement, demonstrated intent to become a mathematics educator, character, academic potential, and leadership potential.
**Financial data:** The stipend is $1,000 per year.
**Duration:** 1 year.
**Number awarded:** 2 each year.
**Deadline:** March of each year.

## 2655 RITA LOWE HIGH SCHOOL SCHOLARSHIP

Washington State Mathematics Council
c/o Pat Reistroffer, Scholarship Chair
146 Scenic View Drive
Longview, WA 98632
Phone: (360) 636-5125; Email: preistrof@aol.com
Web: www.wsmc.net
**Summary:** To provide financial assistance to high school seniors in Washington planning to major in mathematics education at a college or university in the state.
**Eligibility:** Open to seniors graduating from high schools in Washington and planning to attend a college or university in the state to major in mathematics education. Applicants must be preparing for teaching certification in order to become a professional educator teaching mathematics at the elementary or secondary level. They must submit a transcript (from the ninth grade to the date of application), a 300-word statement on their experience with and interest in mathematics, and 2 letters of recommendation. Selection is based on academic achievement, demonstrated intent to become a mathematics educator, character, academic potential, and leadership potential.
**Financial data:** The stipend is $1,000 per year.
**Duration:** 1 year.
**Number awarded:** 1 each year.
**Deadline:** March of each year.

## 2656 RMEL FOUNDATION SCHOLARSHIPS

Rocky Mountain Electrical League, Attn: RMEL Foundation
2170 South Parker Road, Suite 225
Denver, CO 80231
Phone: (303) 695-0089; Fax: (303) 695-0704; Email: edblum@rmel.org
Web: www.rmel.org/Foundation/scholarships.htm
**Summary:** To provide financial assistance for college to students who are preparing for a career in the electric energy industry and are sponsored by a member company of the Rocky Mountain Electrical League (RMEL).
**Eligibility:** Open to high school seniors and current college undergraduates who are studying or planning to study engineering or other field related to the electric energy industry. Applicants must be sponsored by an RMEL member company. As part of their application, they must submit information on their work experience, activities and honors, and goals and aspirations. Students who are receiving financial assistance from another source are not eligible. U.S. citizenship is required. Selection is based on academic ability, service to community and school, motivation to succeed, and goals and aspirations in the electric energy industry.
**Financial data:** The stipend is $1,000. Funds are paid directly to an institution of higher education for payment of tuition and fees.
**Duration:** 1 year.
**Number awarded:** Varies each year; recently, 4 of these scholarships were awarded.
**Deadline:** March of each year.

## 2657 RMEL FOUNDATION SCHOLARSHIPS

**Summary:** To provide financial assistance to students sponsored by a member of the Rocky Mountain Electrical League (RMEL) who wish to study selected fields in college in order to prepare for a career in the electric energy industry.
*See Listing #2656.*

## 2658 ROBANNA FUND SCHOLARSHIPS

Hawai'i Community Foundation, Attn: Scholarship Department
1164 Bishop Street, Suite 800
Honolulu, HI 96813
Phone: (808) 566-5570; (888) 731-3863; Fax: (808) 521-6286;
Email: scholarships@hcf-hawaii.org
Web: www.hawaiicommunityfoundation.org/scholar/scholar.php
**Summary:** To provide financial assistance to Hawaii residents who are interested in preparing for a career in designated health fields.
**Eligibility:** Open to Hawaii residents who are enrolled as full-time undergraduate students in a health-related field. They must be able to demonstrate academic achievement (GPA of 2.7 or higher), good moral character, and financial need. In addition to filling out the standard application form, applicants must write a short statement indicating their reasons for attending college, their planned course of study, and their career goals.
**Financial data:** The amounts of the awards depend on the availability of funds and the need of the recipient; recently, stipends averaged $1,000.
**Duration:** 1 year.
**Number awarded:** Varies each year; recently, 10 of these scholarships were awarded.
**Deadline:** February of each year.

## 2659 ROBERT B. OLIVER ASNT SCHOLARSHIPS

American Society for Nondestructive Testing, Inc., Attn: Executive Assistant
1711 Arlingate Lane
P.O. Box 28518
Columbus, OH 43228-0518
Phone: (614) 274-6003; (800) 222-2768, ext. 223; Fax: (614) 274-6899;
Email: sthomas@asnt.org
Web: www.asnt.org
**Summary:** To recognize and reward undergraduate students who submit outstanding papers in the field of nondestructive testing.
**Eligibility:** Open to students who are enrolled in a program related to nondestructive testing that leads to an undergraduate degree, associate's degree, or postsecondary certificate. The award is offered to students submitting the best original manuscript (up to 5,000 words) on the topic. The manuscript should develop an original concept and may be based on practical experience, laboratory work, or library research. Papers may be classroom assignments in courses outside the area of nondestructive testing, such as an English class. Applicants must be currently enrolled in school and should submit 4 copies of their paper, their curriculum, a transcript of grades, and a letter from a school official verifying the student's enrollment. Selection is based on creativity (10 points), content (50 points), format and readability (25 points), and the student's hands-on involvement in the project (15 points).
**Financial data:** The award is $2,500.
**Duration:** The award is presented annually.
**Number awarded:** Up to 3 each year.
**Deadline:** February of each year.

## 2660 ROBERT E. ALTENHOFEN MEMORIAL SCHOLARSHIP

American Society for Photogrammetry and Remote Sensing
Attn: Scholarship Administrator
5410 Grosvenor Lane, Suite 210
Bethesda, MD 20814-2160
Phone: (301) 493-0290, ext. 101; Fax: (301) 493-0208;
Email: scholarships@asprs.org
Web: www.asprs.org/membership/scholar.html
**Summary:** To provide financial assistance for undergraduate or graduate education to members of the American Society for Photogrammetry and Remote Sensing (ASPRS).
**Eligibility:** Open to both undergraduate and graduate students enrolled at accredited colleges or universities in the United States. Applicants must be either a student member or active member of the society. Selection is based on academic record, letters of recommendation, samples of the applicant's papers or research reports, and a 2-page statement about the applicant's plans for continuing studies in theoretical photogrammetry.
**Financial data:** The stipend is $2,000.
**Duration:** 1 year.
**Number awarded:** 1 each year.
**Deadline:** September of each year.

## 2661 ROBERT E. CRAMER/PRODUCT DESIGN AND DEVELOPMENT DIVISION/MID-MICHIGAN SECTION SCHOLARSHIP

Society of Plastics Engineers, Attn: SPE Foundation
14 Fairfield Drive
Brookfield, CT 06804-0403
Phone: (203) 740-5447; Fax: (203) 775-1157; Email: foundation@4spe.org
Web: www.4spe.org/foundation/scholarships.php
**Summary:** To provide financial assistance to undergraduate students who have a career interest in the plastics industry.
**Eligibility:** Open to full-time undergraduate students at 4-year colleges or in 2-year technical programs. Applicants must 1) have a demonstrated or expressed interest in the plastics industry; 2) be majoring in or taking courses that would be beneficial to a career in the plastics or polymer industry (e.g., plastics engineering, polymer sciences, chemistry, physics, chemical engineering, mechanical engineering, or industrial engineering); 3) be in good academic standing at their school; and 4) be able to document financial need. Along with their application, they must submit 3 letters of recommendation; a high school and/or college transcript; and a 1- to 2-page statement telling why they are interested in the scholarship, their qualifications, and their educational and career goals in the plastics industry.
**Financial data:** The stipend is $1,000 per year. Funds are paid directly to the recipient's school.
**Duration:** 1 year.
**Number awarded:** 1 each year.
**Deadline:** January of each year.

## 2662 ROBERT E. PEARSON SCHOLARSHIP

American Society of Highway Engineers-Carolina Triangle Section
Attn: Scholarship Committee
5800 Farington Place, Suite 105
Raleigh, NC 27609
Phone: (919) 878-9560; Email: gsboyles@stantec.com
Web: www.carolinatriangle.org/scholar.htm
**Summary:** To provide financial assistance to currently-enrolled college students from North Carolina who are majoring in a transportation-related field.
**Eligibility:** Open to residents of North Carolina who are U.S. citizens currently enrolled full time in a 4-year college or university in any state (must have completed at least one semester) working on a bachelor's degree in a transportation-related field, preferably civil engineering. A copy of the applicant's college transcript is required; high school transcripts, SAT scores, and resumes may also be submitted but are not required. Along with their application, students must submit a paragraph on their career goals, including a description of the value they place on civil engineering or other transportation-related field. Selection is based on that essay (25 points), academic performance (40 points), activities, honors, work experience, leadership, and distinguishing qualifications (25 points), and enrollment in a civil engineering curriculum (10 points). A personal interview may be requested. Financial need is not considered.
**Financial data:** The stipend is $2,500.
**Duration:** 1 year; nonrenewable.
**Number awarded:** 1 each year.
**Deadline:** March of each year.

## 2663 ROBERT F. SAMMATARO PRESSURE VESSEL PIPING DIVISION SCHOLARSHIP

ASME International, Attn: Coordinator, Educational Operations
Three Park Avenue
New York, NY 10016-5990
Phone: (212) 591-8131; (800) THE-ASME; Fax: (212) 591-7143;
Email: oluwanifiset@asme.org
Web: www.asme.org/education/enged/aid/scholar.htm
**Summary:** To provide financial assistance to undergraduate students who are members of the American Society of Mechanical Engineers (ASME).
**Eligibility:** Open to student members in good standing who are enrolled in an ABET-accredited mechanical engineering baccalaureate, mechanical engineering technology, or related program. Applicants must be entering their sophomore, junior, or senior year. Interested students should submit an application form, a nomination from the applicant's department head, a recommendation from a faculty member, and an official transcript. Only one nomination may be submitted per department. Selection is based on scholastic ability and demonstrated special interest in pressure vessels and piping.
**Financial data:** The stipend is $1,000.
**Duration:** 1 year.
**Number awarded:** 1 each year.
**Deadline:** March of each year.

## 2664 ROBERT FELIX MEMORIAL SCHOLARSHIP

Tree Research and Education Endowment Fund, Attn: Executive Director
711 East Roosevelt Road
Wheaton, IL 60187
Phone: (630) 221-8127; Fax: (630) 690-0702; Email: treefund@treefund.org
Web: www.treefund.org/grants/Grants.aspx

**Summary:** To provide financial assistance to undergraduate and technical school students preparing for a career in commercial arboriculture.

**Eligibility:** Open to student members of the International Society of Arboriculture who are entering the second year of a 2-year program or the third or fourth year of a 4-year program. Applicants must be preparing for a career in commercial arboriculture. They must have a GPA of 3.0 or higher. Along with their application, they must submit a 1,000-word essay describing their reasons for pursuing their chosen career, their goals and objectives, and why they should be chosen for this scholarship. Financial need is not considered in the selection process.

**Financial data:** The stipend is $3,000.

**Duration:** 1 year.

**Number awarded:** 4 each year.

**Deadline:** April of each year.

## 2665 ROBERT G. DAILEY/DETROIT SECTION SCHOLARSHIP

Society of Plastics Engineers, Attn: SPE Foundation
14 Fairfield Drive
Brookfield, CT 06804-0403
Phone: (203) 740-5447; Fax: (203) 775-1157; Email: foundation@4spe.org
Web: www.4spe.org/foundation/scholarships.php

**Summary:** To provide financial assistance to undergraduate students who have a career interest in the plastics industry.

**Eligibility:** Open to full-time undergraduate students at 4-year colleges or in 2-year technical programs. Applicants must 1) have a demonstrated or expressed interest in the plastics industry; 2) be majoring in or taking courses that would be beneficial to a career in the plastics or polymer industry (e.g., plastics engineering, polymer sciences, chemistry, physics, chemical engineering, mechanical engineering, or industrial engineering); 3) be in good academic standing at their school; and 4) be able to document financial need. Along with their application, they must submit 3 letters of recommendation; a high school and/or college transcript; and a 1- to 2-page statement telling why they are interested in the scholarship, their qualifications, and their educational and career goals in the plastics industry.

**Financial data:** The stipend is $4,000 per year. Funds are paid directly to the recipient's school.

**Duration:** 1 year.

**Number awarded:** 1 each year.

**Deadline:** January of each year.

## 2666 ROBERT H. WEITBRECHT SCHOLARSHIP

Alexander Graham Bell Association for the Deaf
Attn: Financial Aid Coordinator
3417 Volta Place, N.W.
Washington, DC 20007-2778
Phone: (202) 337-5220; Fax: (202) 337-8314; TTY: (202) 337-5221;
Email: financialaid@agbell.org
Web: www.agbell.org

**Summary:** To provide financial assistance to undergraduate and graduate students with moderate to profound hearing loss.

**Eligibility:** Open to undergraduate and graduate students who have been diagnosed with a moderate to profound hearing loss prior to acquiring spoken language (hearing loss averages 60dB or greater in the better ear in the speech frequencies of 500, 1000, and 2000 Hz). Applicants must be able to demonstrate leadership potential and be committed to using spoken language as their primary mode of communication. They must be accepted or enrolled at a mainstream college or university as a full-time student. Along with their application, they must submit a 1-page essay discussing their career goals and how spoken communication is helping them to reach those goals as a person with a hearing loss. Financial need is considered in the selection process. Priority for this scholarship is given to applicants studying engineering or science.

**Financial data:** The stipend is $2,500 per year.

**Duration:** 1 year; may be renewed 1 additional year.

**Number awarded:** 1 each year.

**Deadline:** April of each year.

## 2667 ROBERT M. LAWRENCE, MD EDUCATION RECOGNITION AWARD

American Association for Respiratory Care
Attn: American Respiratory Care Foundation
9425 North MacArthur Boulevard, Suite 100
Irving, TX 75063-4706
Phone: (972) 243-2272; Fax: (972) 484-2720; Email: info@aarc.org
Web: www.aarc.org/awards/lawrence.html

**Summary:** To provide financial assistance to upper-division students interested in becoming respiratory therapists.

**Eligibility:** Open to students who have completed at least 2 years in an accredited respiratory care bachelor's degree program. Applicants must be U.S. citizens with a GPA of 3.0 or higher. They must submit an original referenced paper on an aspect of respiratory care and a paper of at least 1,200 words describing how the award will assist them in reaching their objective of a baccalaureate degree and their ultimate goal of leadership in health care. Selection is based on academic performance.

**Financial data:** The stipend is $2,500. The award also provides airfare, one night's lodging, and registration for the international congress of the association.

**Duration:** 1 year.

**Number awarded:** 1 each year.

**Deadline:** June of each year.

## 2668 ROBERTA PIERCE SCOFIELD BACHELOR'S SCHOLARSHIPS

Oncology Nursing Society, Attn: ONS Foundation
125 Enterprise Drive
Pittsburgh, PA 15275-1214
Phone: (412) 859-6100, ext. 8503; (866) 257-4ONS; Fax: (412) 859-6160;
Email: foundation@ons.org
Web: www.ons.org

**Summary:** To provide financial assistance to registered nurses who are interested in working on a bachelor's degree in oncology nursing.

**Eligibility:** Open to registered nurses with a demonstrated interest in and commitment to oncology nursing. Applicants must be currently enrolled in an undergraduate degree program at an NLN- or CCNE-accredited school of nursing. They may not have previously received a bachelor's level scholarship from this sponsor. Applicants must submit an essay of 250 words or less on their role in caring for persons with cancer and a statement of their professional goals and their relationship to the advancement of oncology nursing. Financial need is not considered in the selection process.

**Financial data:** The stipend is $2,000.

**Duration:** 1 year.

**Number awarded:** 3 each year.

**Deadline:** January of each year.

## 2669 ROCKEFELLER STATE WILDLIFE SCHOLARSHIP

Louisiana Office of Student Financial Assistance
1885 Wooddale Boulevard
P.O. Box 91202
Baton Rouge, LA 70821-9202
Phone: (225) 922-3258; (800) 259-LOAN, ext. 1012; Fax: (225) 922-0790;
Email: custserv@osfa.state.la.us
Web: www.osfa.state.la.us

**Summary:** To offer competitive scholarships to high school seniors, college undergraduates, and graduate students in Louisiana who are interested in working on a degree in forestry, wildlife, or marine science.

**Eligibility:** Open to residents of Louisiana who are U.S. citizens or eligible non-citizens, are not in default on an educational loan, have applied for state student aid, are or will enroll as a full-time student in a course of study leading to an undergraduate or graduate degree in forestry, wildlife, or marine science from a Louisiana public college or university, and have earned at least a 2.5 GPA in high school or college (if appropriate). This is a merit-based award; financial need is not considered.

**Financial data:** The stipend is $1,000 per year.

**Duration:** Up to 5 years of undergraduate and 2 years of graduate study.

**Number awarded:** Varies; generally, 60 students (30 new and 30 continuing) receive awards each year.

**Deadline:** July of each year.

## 2670 ROCKWELL AUTOMATION SCHOLARSHIPS

Society of Women Engineers
230 East Ohio Street, Suite 400
Chicago, IL 60611-3265
Phone: (312) 596-5223; Fax: (312) 644-8557; Email: hq@swe.org
Web: www.societyofwomenengineers.org/scholarships

**Summary:** To provide financial assistance to upper-division women majoring in computer science or designated engineering specialties.

**Eligibility:** Open to women who are entering their junior year at an ABET-accredited college or university. Applicants must be majoring in computer science or computer, electrical, industrial, mechanical, or software engineering and have at GPA of 3.5 or higher. Along with their application, they must submit a 1-page essay on why they want to be an engineer, how they believe they will make a difference as an engineer, and what influenced them to study engineering. Selection is based on merit and leadership potential. Preference is given to members of underrepresented minority groups.

**Financial data:** The stipend is $3,000.
**Duration:** 1 year.
**Number awarded:** 2 each year.
**Deadline:** January of each year.

## 2671 ROCKY MOUNTAIN SECTION COLLEGE SCHOLARSHIPS

Society of Women Engineers-Rocky Mountain Section
Attn: Scholarship Committee Chair
P.O. Box 260692
Lakewood, CO 80226-0692
Phone: (303) 893-0822
Web: www.swe.org/SWE/RegionI/Sections/RockyMtn/Scholarships.htm

**Summary:** To provide financial assistance to women who are working on an undergraduate or graduate degree in engineering at colleges and universities in Colorado and Wyoming.

**Eligibility:** Open to women who are enrolled as an undergraduate or graduate engineering student in an ABET-accredited engineering or computer science program in Colorado or Wyoming (excluding zip codes 80800-81599). Applicants must have a GPA of 3.0 or higher. They must include with their application an essay on why they have chosen an engineering major, what they will accomplish or how they believe they will make a difference as an engineer, and who or what influenced them to study engineering. Selection is based on merit.

**Financial data:** The stipend is $1,000.
**Duration:** 1 year.
**Number awarded:** 3 each year.
**Deadline:** January of each year.

## 2672 ROYAL SIX SCHOLARSHIP PROGRAM

American Royal Association
1701 American Royal Court
Kansas City, MO 64102
Phone: (816) 221-9800; Fax: (816) 221-889;
Email: nancyp@americanroyal.com
Web: www.americanroyal.com/s/static/education/royal_six.htm

**Summary:** To provide financial assistance to students at colleges in designated midwestern states who demonstrate an interest in agriculture or other areas.

**Eligibility:** Open to incoming sophomores and juniors at 4-year colleges and universities in Missouri, Kansas, Iowa, Nebraska, Oklahoma, Illinois, Colorado, Arkansas, Kentucky, South Dakota, or Tennessee. Special consideration is given to students working on a degree in a field related to agriculture. Applicants must have a GPA of 2.5 or higher and be younger than 24 years of age. Along with their application, they must submit a 300-word essay on how they have served their community within the last 2 years. Financial need is not considered in the selection process.

**Financial data:** The stipend is $3,500.
**Duration:** 1 year; nonrenewable.
**Number awarded:** 6 each year.
**Deadline:** May of each year.

## 2673 ROYCE OSBORN MINORITY STUDENT SCHOLARSHIPS

American Society of Radiologic Technologists
Attn: ASRT Education and Research Foundation
15000 Central Avenue, S.E.
Albuquerque, NM 87123-3917
Phone: (505) 298-4500; (800) 444-2778, ext. 2541; Fax: (505) 298-5063;

Email: foundation@asrt.org
Web: www.asrt.org

**Summary:** To provide financial assistance to minority students enrolled in entry-level radiologic sciences programs.

**Eligibility:** Open to African Americans, Native Americans, Hispanic Americans, Asian Americans, and Pacific Islanders who are enrolled in an entry-level radiologic sciences program. Applicants must have a GPA in radiologic sciences core courses of 3.0 or higher and be able to demonstrate financial need. They may not have a previous degree or certificate in the radiologic sciences. Along with their application, they must submit an essay of 450 to 500 words on their reason for entering the radiologic sciences, career goals, and financial need. Only U.S. citizens, nationals, and permanent residents are eligible.

**Financial data:** The stipend is $4,000.
**Duration:** 1 year; may be renewed for 1 additional year.
**Number awarded:** 5 each year.
**Deadline:** January of each year.

## 2674 ROYCE R. WATTS SR. SCHOLARSHIP

Watts Charity Association, Inc.
6245 Bristol Parkway, Suite 224
Culver City, CA 90230
Phone: (323) 671-0394; Fax: (323) 778-2613; Email: wattscharity@yahoo.com
Web: www.wattscharity.org

**Summary:** To provide financial assistance to upper-division college students interested in health, civil rights, or administration.

**Eligibility:** Open to U.S. citizens of African American descent who are enrolled full time as a college or university junior. Applicants must have an interest in health and pre-medicine, community activities and civil rights, or administration. They must have a GPA of 3.0 or higher, be between 17 and 24 years of age, and be able to demonstrate that they intend to continue their education for at least 2 years. Along with their application, they must submit 1) a 1-paragraph statement on why they should be awarded a Watts Foundation scholarship, and 2) a 1- to 2-page essay on a specific type of cancer, based either on how it has impacted their life or on researched information.

**Financial data:** A stipend is awarded (amount not specified).
**Duration:** 1 year.
**Number awarded:** 1 each year.
**Deadline:** May of each year.

## 2675 RUBBER DIVISION UNDERGRADUATE SCHOLARSHIP PROGRAM

American Chemical Society
Rubber Division, Attn: Chair, Scholarship Committee
250 South Forge Street, Fourth Floor
P.O. Box 499
Akron, OH 44309-0499
Phone: (330) 972-7814; Fax: (330) 972-5269; Email: education@rubber.org
Web: www.rubber.org/awards/scholarships.htm

**Summary:** To provide financial assistance to undergraduate students in fields of interest to the rubber industry.

**Eligibility:** Open to incoming college juniors and seniors at colleges and universities in the United States, Canada, Mexico, or Colombia. Applicants must have a GPA of 3.0 or higher for all of their undergraduate work. Their major must be chemistry, physics, chemical engineering, mechanical engineering, polymer science, or any other technical discipline of relevance to the rubber industry. They must have a serious interest in full-time professional employment in the rubber industry. Financial need is considered in the selection process.

**Financial data:** The stipend is $5,000 per year. Funds may be used to help cover the costs of tuition, fees, and other expenses billed by the college or university.
**Duration:** 1 year.
**Number awarded:** Varies each year; recently, 3 of these scholarships were awarded.
**Deadline:** March of each year.

## 2676 RUDOLPH DILLMAN MEMORIAL SCHOLARSHIP

American Foundation for the Blind, Attn: Scholarship Committee
11 Penn Plaza, Suite 300
New York, NY 10001
Phone: (212) 502-7661; (800) AFB-LINE; Fax: (212) 502-7771;
TDD: (212) 502-7662; Email: afbinfo@afb.net

Web: www.afb.org/scholarships.asp

**Summary:** To provide financial assistance to legally blind undergraduate or graduate students studying in the field of rehabilitation and/or education of visually impaired and blind persons.

**Eligibility:** Open to applicants who are able to submit evidence of legal blindness, U.S. citizenship, and acceptance in an accredited undergraduate or graduate training program within the broad field of rehabilitation and/or education of blind and visually impaired persons. Along with their application, they must submit an essay that includes their educational and personal goals; their work experience; any extracurricular activities with which they have been involved, including those in school, religious organizations, and the community; and how they intend to use scholarship monies that may be awarded. They may also include documentation of financial need.

**Financial data:** The stipend is $2,500 per year.

**Duration:** 1 academic year; previous recipients may not reapply.

**Number awarded:** 4 each year: 3 without consideration of financial need and 1 to an applicant who can submit evidence of financial need.

**Deadline:** April of each year.

---

## 2677 RUSSELL W. MYERS SCHOLARSHIP

**Summary:** To provide financial assistance to undergraduate and graduate students from New Jersey who are working on a degree in an environmental field. *See Listing #1653.*

---

## 2678 RUTH M. FRENCH GRADUATE OR UNDERGRADUATE SCHOLARSHIP

Alpha Mu Tau Fraternity
c/o American Society for Clinical Laboratory Science
6701 Democracy Boulevard, Suite 300
Bethesda, MD 20817
Phone: (301) 657-2768; Fax: (301) 657-2909; Email: ascls@ascls.org
Web: www.ascls.org/leadership/awards/amt.asp

**Summary:** To provide financial assistance for undergraduate or graduate studies to members of Alpha Mu Tau, a national fraternity for professionals in the clinical laboratory sciences.

**Eligibility:** Open to U.S. citizens or permanent residents who are members of Alpha Mu Tau and accepted into or currently enrolled in a program in clinical laboratory science, including clinical laboratory education or management programs for graduate students and clinical laboratory science/medical technology and clinical laboratory technician/medical laboratory technician for undergraduates. Undergraduate applicants must be entering their last year of study. Along with their application, they must submit a 500-word statement describing their interest and reasons for preparing for a career in clinical laboratory science. Financial need is also considered in the selection process.

**Financial data:** The stipend is $3,000.

**Duration:** 1 year.

**Number awarded:** 1 each year.

**Deadline:** March of each year.

---

## 2679 R.V. "GADABOUT" GADDIS CHARITABLE FUND

**Summary:** To provide financial assistance to Maine students interested in the study of outdoor/nature writing. *See Listing #1657.*

---

## 2680 SAFE FOUNDATION SCHOLARSHIPS

Sports Turf Managers Association, Attn: SAFE Foundation
805 New Hampshire, Suite E
Lawrence, KS 66044
Phone: (800) 323-3875; Fax: (800)366-0391;
Email: stmainfo@sportsturfman ager.com
Web: www.sportsturfmanager.org

**Summary:** To provide financial assistance to student members of the Sports Turf Managers Association (STMA) who are interested in preparing for a career in the turf management industry.

**Eligibility:** Open to STMA student members who are preparing for a career in the sports turf industry (excluding golf course management). Applicants must submit lists of 1) awards, honors, or scholarships that they have received; 2) activities in which they have participated related to their school, department, or community; and 3) professional associations and university organizations to which they belong. Selection is based on academic preparation, cumulative

GPA, experience in sports turf management, and references. Financial need is not considered.

**Financial data:** The stipend is $1,000. Winners also receive $500 for travel or lodging expenses to attend the annual conference of the STMA.

**Duration:** 1 year.

**Number awarded:** 1 or more each year.

**Deadline:** September of each year.

---

## 2681 SALLIE MAE FUND FIRST IN MY FAMILY SCHOLARSHIP PROGRAM

Hispanic College Fund, Attn: National Director
1717 Pennsylvania Avenue, N.W., Suite 460
Washington, D.C. 20006
Phone: (202) 296-5400; (800) 644-4223; Fax: (202) 296-3774; Email: hispanic
collegefund@earthlink.net
Web: www.hispanicfund.org

**Summary:** To provide financial assistance to Hispanic American undergraduate students who are the first in their family to attend college and are majoring in business, computer science, or engineering.

**Eligibility:** Open to U.S. citizens of Hispanic background (at least one grandparent must be 100% Hispanic) who are entering their freshman, sophomore, junior, or senior year of college and are the first member of their family to attend college. Applicants must be working on a bachelor's degree in business, computer science, engineering, or a business-related major and have a cumulative GPA of 3.0 or higher. They must be applying to or enrolled in a college or university in the 50 states or Puerto Rico as a full-time student. Financial need is considered in the selection process.

**Financial data:** Stipends range from $1,000 to $5,000, depending on the need of the recipient. Funds are paid directly to the recipient's college or university to help cover tuition and fees.

**Duration:** 1 year; recipients may reapply.

**Number awarded:** Varies each year; recently, 155 of these scholarships were awarded.

**Deadline:** April of each year.

---

## 2682 SALLY TOMPKINS NURSING AND APPLIED HEALTH SCIENCES SCHOLARSHIP

United Daughters of the Confederacy-Virginia Division
c/o Suzie Snyder, Education Committee Chair
8440 Bradshaw Road
Salem, VA 24153-2246
Phone: (540) 384-6884; Email: Suzienotes@aol.com
Web: users.erols.com/va-udc/scholarships.html

**Summary:** To provide financial assistance for college to women who are Confederate descendants from Virginia and working on a degree in nursing.

**Eligibility:** Open to women residents of Virginia interested in working on a degree in nursing. Applicants must be 1) lineal descendants of Confederates, or 2) collateral descendants and also members of the Children of the Confederacy or the United Daughters of the Confederacy. They must submit proof of the Confederate military record of at least one ancestor, with the company and regiment in which he served. They must also submit a personal letter pledging to make the best possible use of the scholarship; describing their health, social, family, religious, and fraternal connections within the community; and reflecting on what a Southern heritage means to them (using the term "War Between the States" in lieu of "Civil War"). They must have a GPA of 3.0 or higher and be able to demonstrate financial need.

**Financial data:** The amount of the stipend depends on the availability of funds. Payment is made directly to the college or university the recipient attends.

**Duration:** 1 year; may be renewed up to 3 additional years if the recipient maintains a GPA of 3.0 or higher.

**Number awarded:** This scholarship is offered whenever a prior recipient graduates or is no longer eligible.

**Deadline:** May of the years in which a scholarship is available.

---

## 2683 SAM S. KUWAHARA MEMORIAL SCHOLARSHIP

Japanese American Citizens League, Attn: National Scholarship Awards
1765 Sutter Street
San Francisco, CA 94115
Phone: (415) 921-5225; Fax: (415) 931-4671; Email: jacl@jacl.org
Web: www.jacl.org/scholarships.html

**Summary:** To provide financial assistance to student members of the Japanese

American Citizens League (JACL) who are working on or planning to work on an undergraduate degree, particularly in agriculture.

**Eligibility:** Open to JACL members who are either high school seniors or current undergraduates. Applicants must be enrolled or planning to enter or reenter a college, university, trade school, business college, or other institution of higher learning. They must submit a statement describing their current level of involvement in the Japanese American community or Asian Pacific community and how they will continue their involvement in future years. Selection is based on academic record, extracurricular activities, financial need, and community involvement. Preference is given to students who wish to study agriculture or a related field.

**Financial data:** The stipend depends on the availability of funds but usually ranges from $1,000 to $5,000.

**Duration:** 1 year; nonrenewable.

**Number awarded:** 2 each year: 1 for a graduating high school senior and 1 for a continuing undergraduate.

**Deadline:** February of each year for graduating high school seniors; March of each year for current college students.

---

## 2684 SAMPE UNDERGRADUATE AWARDS PROGRAM

Society for the Advancement of Material and Process Engineering
Attn: International Business Office
1161 Parkview Drive
P.O. Box 2459
Covina, CA 91722-8459
Phone: (626) 331-0616; (800) 562-7360; Fax: (626) 332-8929;
Email: sampeibo@sampe.org
Web: www.sampe.org/studentp.html

**Summary:** To provide financial assistance for college to undergraduate student members of the Society for the Advancement of Material and Process Engineering (SAMPE).

**Eligibility:** Open to freshmen, sophomores, and juniors who are members of a SAMPE student chapter. Applicants must be recommended by the student chapter faculty advisor; each chapter advisor may nominate only 2 students. Candidates must be studying in either 1) engineering, materials, or process-oriented science programs, or 2) engineering technology programs.

**Financial data:** For engineering and science students, first place is $2,000 and second place is $1,000. For engineering technology students, first place is $1,200 and second place is $750.

**Duration:** The awards are presented annually.

**Number awarded:** 12 each year: for engineering and science students, 1 first place and 8 second places; for engineering technology students, 1 first place and 2 second places.

**Deadline:** January of each year.

---

## 2685 SAMUEL FLETCHER TAPMAN MEMORIAL ASCE STUDENT CHAPTER SCHOLARSHIPS

American Society of Civil Engineers, Attn: Student Services
1801 Alexander Bell Drive
Reston, VA 20191-4400
Phone: (703) 295-6120; (800) 548-ASCE; Fax: (703) 295-6132;
Email: student@asce.org
Web: www.asce.org

**Summary:** To provide financial assistance to members of the American Society of Civil Engineers (ASCE) for undergraduate study in civil engineering.

**Eligibility:** Open to ASCE members who are freshmen, sophomores, juniors, or first-year seniors enrolled in a program of civil engineering. Applicants must submit an essay (up to 500 words) in which they discuss why they chose to become a civil engineer, their specific ASCE student chapter involvement, any special financial needs, and long-term goals and plans. Selection is based on their justification for the award, educational plan, academic performance and standing, potential for development, leadership capacity, ASCE activities, and demonstrated financial need.

**Financial data:** The stipend is $2,000 per year.

**Duration:** 1 year; may be renewed.

**Number awarded:** Approximately 12 each year.

**Deadline:** February of each year.

---

## 2686 SAN ANTONIO CHAPTER NAWIC SCHOLARSHIP

**Summary:** To provide financial assistance to students in Texas working on an undergraduate degree in a construction-related field.
*See Listing #1661.*

---

## 2687 SCHOLARSHIPS IN MATHEMATICS EDUCATION

Illinois Council of Teachers of Mathematics
c/o Beverly Rich, ICTM Scholarship
Illinois State University
Mathematics Department
Campus Box 4520
Normal, IL 61761-4520
Email: bsrich@ilstu.edu
Web: www.ictm.org/scholarship.html

**Summary:** To provide financial assistance to undergraduate students in Illinois who are interested in preparing for a career as a mathematics teacher.

**Eligibility:** Open to juniors and seniors at accredited colleges and universities in Illinois. Applicants must have a GPA of 3.0 or higher and a mathematics education major, a mathematics major with an education minor, or an education major with an official mathematics concentration. Selection is based on transcripts from all colleges attended, letters of recommendation from 2 mathematics teachers (high school or college), and a 200- to 300-word essay on why the students wish to teach mathematics and what they see as their contribution to the profession.

**Financial data:** The stipend is $1,500.

**Duration:** 1 year.

**Number awarded:** 2 to 5 each year.

**Deadline:** March of each year.

---

## 2688 SCHOLARSHIPS IN TECHNICAL COMMUNICATION

**Summary:** To provide financial assistance to undergraduate and graduate students who are preparing for a career in some area of technical communications.
*See Listing #1663.*

---

## 2689 SCIENCE TEACHER PREPARATION PROGRAM

Alabama Alliance for Science, Engineering, Mathematics, and Science Education, Attn: Project Director
University of Alabama at Birmingham
Campbell Hall, Room 401
1300 University Boulevard
Birmingham, AL 35294-1170
Phone: (205) 934-8762; Fax: (205) 934-1650; Email: LDale@uab.edu
Web: www.uab.edu/istp/alabama.html

**Summary:** To provide financial assistance to underrepresented minority students at designated institutions in Alabama who are interested in preparing for a career as a science teacher.

**Eligibility:** Open to members of underrepresented minority groups who have been unconditionally admitted to a participating Alabama college or university. Applicants may 1) be entering freshmen or junior college transfer students who intend to major in science education and become certified to teach in elementary, middle, or high school; 2) have earned a degree in mathematics, science, or education and are seeking to become certified to teach; or 3) have earned a degree in mathematics, science, or education and are enrolled in a fifth-year education program leading to a master's degree and certification.

**Financial data:** The stipend is $1,000 per year.

**Duration:** 1 year; may be renewed.

**Number awarded:** Varies each year.

---

## 2690 SCOTT TARBELL SCHOLARSHIPS

Hemophilia Health Services, Attn: Scholarship Committee
6820 Charlotte Pike, Suite 100
Nashville, TN 37209-4234
Phone: (615) 850-5175; (800) 800-6606, ext. 5175; Fax: (615) 352-2588;
Email: Scholarship@HemophiliaHealth.com
Web: www.hemophiliahealth.com/consumers/products_services/scholarship.htm

**Summary:** To provide financial assistance to high school seniors and current college students who have hemophilia and are interested in working on a degree or certification in computer science and/or mathematics.

**Eligibility:** Open to high school seniors and college freshmen, sophomores, and juniors who have hemophilia A or B severe. Applicants must be enrolled or planning to enroll at an accredited nonprofit college, university, or vocational/technical school in the United States or Puerto Rico. They must be interested in working on a degree or certification in computer science and/or mathematics. Along with their application, they must submit an essay, up to 250 words, on the following topic: "Upon receiving your education in math and/or computer science, how will you use the new technologies (i.e., computer, internet, etc.) to better mankind and what ethical issues will you need to address?" U.S. citizenship is required. Selection is based on academic achievement in relation to tested ability and dedication to the field of computer science or mathematics. Financial need is not considered.

**Financial data:** The stipend is $1,500. Funds are issued payable to the recipient's school.

**Duration:** 1 year; recipients may reapply.

**Number awarded:** Varies each year, depending on the availability of funds.

**Deadline:** April of each year.

## 2691 SCOTTS COMPANY SCHOLARS PROGRAM

Golf Course Superintendents Association of America
Attn: Scholarship and Student Programs Manager
1421 Research Park Drive
Lawrence, KS 66049-3859
Phone: (785) 832-3678; (800) 472-7878, ext. 3678; Email: psmith@gcsaa.org
Web: www.gcsaa.org/students/scholarships/default.asp

**Summary:** To provide financial assistance and summer work experience to high school seniors and college students, particularly those from diverse backgrounds, who are preparing for a career in golf management.

**Eligibility:** Open to high school seniors and college students (freshmen, sophomores, and juniors) who are interested in preparing for a career in golf management (the "green industry"). Applicants should come from diverse ethnic, cultural, and socioeconomic backgrounds, defined to include women, minorities, and people with disabilities. Selection is based on cultural diversity, academic achievement, extracurricular activities, leadership, employment potential, essay responses, and letters of recommendation. Financial need is not considered. Finalists are selected for summer internships and then compete for scholarships.

**Financial data:** Each intern receives a $500 award. Scholarship stipends are $2,500.

**Duration:** 1 year.

**Number awarded:** 5 interns and 2 scholarship winners are selected each year.

**Deadline:** February of each year.

## 2692 SCSPE SCHOLARSHIPS

South Carolina Society of Professional Engineers
Attn: SCSPE Educational Foundation
P.O. Box 11937
Columbia, SC 29211-1937
Phone: (803) 771-4271; Fax: (803) 771-4272;
Email: joe@jma-associations.com
Web: www.scspe.org/scholrshp.htm

**Summary:** To provide financial assistance to high school seniors in South Carolina who are interested in majoring in engineering in college.

**Eligibility:** Open to South Carolina residents who will be entering freshmen at a school in the state with an ABET-accredited engineering program. Applicants must have a GPA of 2.70 or higher and an above average SAT score. Financial need is not considered in the selection process.

**Financial data:** The stipend is $1,000.

**Duration:** 1 year.

**Number awarded:** 2 each year.

**Deadline:** March of each year.

## 2693 SCUDDER ASSOCIATION EDUCATIONAL GRANTS

**Summary:** To assist undergraduate and graduate students preparing for "careers as servants of God in various forms of ministry to men and women around the world."

*See Listing #1667.*

## 2694 SDAPHCC EDUCATIONAL FOUNDATION SCHOLARSHIPS

South Dakota Association of Plumbing, Heating, & Cooling Contractors
Attn: Educational Foundation
P.O. Box 336
Pierre, SC 57501
Phone: (605) 224-2528; (800) 640-PHCC; Fax: (605) 224-1543; Email: PHCC@midco.net
Web: sdaphcc.tripod.com

**Summary:** To provide financial assistance for college to high school seniors and college freshmen in South Dakota who are preparing for a career in plumbing, heating and cooling, construction, or business management.

**Eligibility:** Open to high school seniors and college freshmen in South Dakota who are preparing for a career in plumbing, heating and cooling, construction, or business management. Applicants must be sponsored by a member of the South Dakota Association of Plumbing, Heating & Cooling Contractors (SDAPHCC).

**Financial data:** Stipends are $1,000 or $500.

**Duration:** 1 year.

**Number awarded:** 2 each year: 1 at $1,000 and 1 at $500.

**Deadline:** December of each year.

## 2695 SECRETARY'S AWARD FOR INNOVATIONS IN HEALTH PROMOTION AND DISEASE PREVENTION

American Association of Colleges of Nursing
One Dupont Circle, N.W., Suite 530
Washington, DC 20036
Phone: (202) 463-6930; Fax: (202) 785-8320
Web: www.aacn.nche.edu/SecretarysAward

**Summary:** To recognize and reward undergraduate and graduate students who submit outstanding papers describing projects for health promotion or disease prevention.

**Eligibility:** Open to students enrolled full or part time in a baccalaureate or higher degree health professions education program in a school that is affiliated, through a participating professional association, with the Federation of Associations of Schools of the Health Professions (FASHP). Applicants must submit a proposal, up to 2,500 words, for 1) an innovative health promotion project focusing on a special population group, or 2) a disease prevention project for a targeted community. They must be citizens, nationals, or permanent residents of the United States and attending a U.S. college or university. Papers may be entered in the single discipline category (for 1 or more authors in the same discipline) or the interprofessional category (for students from 2 or more different health profession disciplines collaborate on a single project). Proposals for new projects, as well as completed or currently implemented projects, are acceptable. They may have been developed to meet course requirements or as part of service learning or other academic experiences. Basic or clinical research proposals are not eligible. Students first submit their papers to a faculty sponsor or representative at their school; each school, college, or program selects 1 single discipline paper and one interprofessional paper and submits those to the appropriate professional association. Each association then selects up to 10 of its best papers to be forwarded to the program administrator, and a selection committee chooses 10 top entries for the single discipline category and 10 top entries for the interprofessional category. Selection is based on 1) clarity of problem statement, objectives, implementation plan, project significance, soundness of evaluation plan, and reasonableness of budget; 2) innovation in approach to health promotion or disease prevention; 3) feasibility of approach in regard to implementation of the project; and 4) potential impact on a community or target population. Final selection of winners is then made by senior staff of the U.S. Department of Health and Human Services (DHHS).

**Financial data:** Single discipline awards are $3,500 for first place, $2,500 for second place, and $1,500 for third place. Interprofessional awards are $7,500 for first place, $5,000 for second place, and $3,000 for third place.

**Duration:** This competition is held annually.

**Number awarded:** 6 each year.

**Deadline:** Students must submit entries to their school by mid-February of each year; schools must forward winners to the respective professional associations by mid-March; associations forward their top entries to the program administrator in early April; semifinalist entries must be received by DHHS by the end of April.

## 2696 SEED COMPANIES SCHOLARSHIP

Floriculture Industry Research and Scholarship Trust
Attn: Scholarship Program
P.O. Box 280
East Lansing, MI 48826-0280
Phone: (517) 333-4617; Fax: (517) 333-4494;
Email: scholarships@firstinfloriculture.org
Web: www.firstinfloriculture.org

**Summary:** To provide financial assistance to upper-division and graduate students in horticulture.

**Eligibility:** Open to undergraduate students entering their junior, senior, or fifth year at a 4-year college or university and to graduate students. Applicants must be horticulture majors who intend to prepare for a career in the seed industry, including research, breeding, sales, and marketing. They must be U.S. or Canadian citizens or permanent residents with a GPA of 3.0 or higher. Selection is based on academic record, recommendations, career goals, extracurricular activities, and financial need.

**Financial data:** The stipend depends on the availability of funds. Recently, it was $1,000.
**Duration:** 1 year.
**Number awarded:** 3 each year.
**Deadline:** April of each year.

## 2697 SEG SCHOLARSHIP PROGRAM

Society of Exploration Geophysicists, Attn: SEG Foundation
8801 South Yale, Suite 500
P.O. Box 702740
Tulsa, OK 74170-2740
Phone: (918) 497-5513; Fax: (918) 497-5557; Email: scholarships@seg.org
Web: seg.org/business/foundation/scholarships/index.shtml
**Summary:** To provide financial assistance to undergraduate and graduate students who are interested in the field of applied geophysics.
**Eligibility:** Open to 1) high school students planning to enter college in the fall, and 2) undergraduate or graduate students whose grades are above average. Applicants must intend to work on a degree directed toward a career in applied geophysics or a closely-related field. Along with their application, they must submit a 150-word essay on how they plan to use geophysics in their future. Financial need is not considered in the selection process. Some of the scholarships are set aside for students at recognized colleges or universities in countries outside of the United States.
**Financial data:** The stipends generally range from $500 to $14,000 per year and average $1,500 per year.
**Duration:** 1 academic year; may be renewable, based on scholastic standing, availability of funds, and continuance of a course of study leading to a career in applied geophysics.
**Number awarded:** Varies each year; recently, 70 renewals and 66 new scholarships were awarded. The total value of the scholarships was $268,100.
**Deadline:** January of each year.

## 2698 SENTRY INSURANCE FOUNDATION SCHOLARSHIPS

**Summary:** To provide financial assistance to students majoring in selected fields at member institutions of the Wisconsin Foundation for Independent Colleges (WFIC).
*See Listing #1671.*

## 2699 SERVICE LEAGUE NURSING SCHOLARSHIP

Akron General Medical Center
Attn: Human Resources Department, Nurse Recruitment
400 Wabash Avenue
Akron, OH 44307
Phone: (330) 344-6867; Email: rkovalchik@agmc.org
Web: www.agmc.org/scholar.asp
**Summary:** To provide financial assistance to nursing students from Ohio who are working on a baccalaureate degree.
**Eligibility:** Open to graduates of high schools in Ohio who have been accepted by an accredited baccalaureate nursing program in the state. Employees of Akron General Medical Center and their children and spouses are also eligible. Applicants must have a GPA of 2.8 or higher. They must submit a short essay on the reason they chose nursing as a career and why they believe they have the qualities and skills necessary to be a successful nurse. Selection is based on academic achievement and financial need.
**Financial data:** A stipend is awarded (amount not specified).
**Duration:** 1 year.
**Number awarded:** 1 or more each year.
**Deadline:** February of each year.

## 2700 SGNA RN GENERAL EDUCATION SCHOLARSHIP

Society of Gastroenterology Nurses and Associates, Inc.
Attn: Awards Committee
401 North Michigan Avenue
Chicago, IL 60611-4267
Phone: (312) 321-5165; (800) 245-SGNA; Fax: (312) 527-6658
Web: www.sgna.org/resources/awards.cfm
**Summary:** To provide financial assistance to full-time students working toward licensure as a registered nurse (R.N.).
**Eligibility:** Open to students currently enrolled full time in an accredited nursing program with a GPA of 3.0 or higher. Applicants must be studying to

become an R.N. Along with their application, they must submit a 2-page essay on a challenging situation they see in the health care environment today and how they, as an R.N., would best address and meet that challenge. Financial need is not considered in the selection process.
**Financial data:** The stipend is $2,500. Funds are issued as reimbursement after the recipient has completed the proposed course work with a GPA of 3.0 or higher.
**Duration:** 1 year.
**Number awarded:** 1 or more each year.
**Deadline:** July of each year.

## 2701 SHARON D. BANKS MEMORIAL UNDERGRADUATE SCHOLARSHIP

Women's Transportation Seminar, Attn: National Headquarters
1666 K Street, N.W., Suite 1100
Washington, DC 20006
Phone: (202) 496-4340; Fax: (202) 496-4349; Email: wts@wtsnational.org
Web: www.wtsnational.org
**Summary:** To provide financial assistance to undergraduate women interested in a career in transportation.
**Eligibility:** Open to women who are working on an undergraduate degree in transportation or a transportation-related field (e.g., transportation engineering, planning, finance, or logistics). Applicants must have at least a 3.0 GPA and be interested in a career in transportation. They must submit a 500-word statement about their career goals after graduation and why they think they should receive the scholarship award. Applications must be submitted first to a local chapter; the chapters forward selected applications for consideration on the national level. Minority candidates are encouraged to apply. Selection is based on transportation involvement and goals, job skills, and academic record; financial need is not considered.
**Financial data:** The stipend is $3,000.
**Duration:** 1 year.
**Number awarded:** 1 each year.
**Deadline:** Applications must be submitted by November to a local WTS chapter.

## 2702 SHAW INDUSTRIES/HENAAC SCHOLARS PROGRAM

Hispanic Engineer National Achievement Awards Conference
3900 Whiteside Street
Los Angeles, CA 90063
Phone: (323) 262-0997; Fax: (323) 262-0946; Email: info@henaac.org
Web: www.henaac.org/scholarships.htm
**Summary:** To provide financial assistance to Hispanic undergraduate students majoring in designated fields of engineering at universities in the Southeast.
**Eligibility:** Open to Hispanic undergraduate students who are enrolled full time in chemical, electrical, industrial, mechanical, or textile engineering. Applicants must be entering their junior or senior year at a university in the southeastern United States and have a GPA of 3.0 or higher. Academic achievement and campus community activities are considered in the selection process.
**Financial data:** Stipends range from $1,000 to $5,000.
**Duration:** 1 year; recipients may reapply.
**Number awarded:** 1 or more each year.
**Deadline:** April of each year.

## 2703 SHAW-WORTH SCHOLARSHIP AWARD

Humane Society of the United States, Attn: New England Regional Office
Route 112
P.O. Box 619
Jacksonville, VT 05342-0619
Phone: (802) 368-2790; Fax: (802) 368-2756; Email: htwining@hsus.org
**Summary:** To provide financial assistance for college to New England high school seniors who have contributed to animal protection.
**Eligibility:** Open to seniors graduating from public, parochial, and independent high schools in New England. Applicants must have made a meaningful contribution to animal protection over a significant period of time. The contribution may have taken the form of long-term direct work on behalf of animals; inspiring leadership in animal protection organizations; papers, speeches, or presentations on humane topics; or heroic rescues of animals in danger. A humane attitude, understanding of humane ethics, and past academic performance on behalf of animals are essential. A passive liking for animals or a desire to enter an animal care field is not adequate justification

for the award. High scholastic standing is not required and financial need is not considered.

**Financial data:** The stipend is $1,500. Funds are paid directly to the college of the recipient's choice.

**Duration:** 1 year.

**Number awarded:** 1 each year.

**Deadline:** March of each year.

## 2704 SHELL OIL INTERNATIONAL SCHOLARSHIPS

Society of Exploration Geophysicists, Attn: SEG Foundation
8801 South Yale, Suite 500
P.O. Box 702740
Tulsa, OK 74170-2740
Phone: (918) 497-5513; Fax: (918) 497-5557; Email: scholarships@seg.org
Web: seg.org/business/foundation/scholarships/index.shtml

**Summary:** To provide financial assistance to undergraduate and graduate students who are interested in studying applied geophysics.

**Eligibility:** Open to 1) high school students planning to enter college in the fall, and 2) undergraduate or graduate students whose grades are above average. Applicants must intend to work on a degree directed toward a career in applied geophysics or a closely-related field; preference is given to undergraduates. Along with their application, they must submit a 150-word essay on how they plan to use geophysics in their future. Financial need is not considered in the selection process.

**Financial data:** Stipends range from $1,000 to $3,000 per year.

**Duration:** 1 academic year; may be renewable, based on scholastic standing, availability of funds, and continuance of a course of study leading to a career in applied geophysics.

**Number awarded:** 1 or more each year.

**Deadline:** January of each year.

## 2705 SHUICHI, KATSU AND ITSUYO SUGA SCHOLARSHIP

Hawai'i Community Foundation, Attn: Scholarship Department
1164 Bishop Street, Suite 800
Honolulu, HI 96813
Phone: (808) 566-5570; (888) 731-3863; Fax: (808) 521-6286;
Email: scholarships@hcf-hawaii.org
Web: www.hawaiicommunityfoundation.org/scholar/scholar.php

**Summary:** To provide financial assistance for college to Hawaii residents who are interested in majoring in a scientific field.

**Eligibility:** Open to Hawaii residents who plan to attend an accredited 2- or 4-year college or university as a full-time undergraduate or graduate student. Applicants must be planning to study mathematics, physics, science, or technology. They must be able to demonstrate academic achievement (GPA of 3.0 or higher), good moral character, and financial need. Along with their application, they must submit a short statement indicating their reasons for attending college, planned course of study, and career goals.

**Financial data:** The amounts of the awards depend on the availability of funds and the need of the recipient; recently, stipends averaged $1,000.

**Duration:** 1 year.

**Number awarded:** Varies each year; recently, 9 of these scholarships were awarded.

**Deadline:** February of each year.

## 2706 SIDNEY B. MEADOWS SCHOLARSHIPS

Southern Nursery Association
Attn: Sidney B. Meadows Scholarship Endowment Fund
1827 Powers Ferry Road, Suite 4-100
Atlanta, GA 30339-8433
Phone: (770) 953-3311; Fax: (770) 953-4411; Email: mail@mail.sna.org
Web: www.sna.org/education/sbmsefinfo.shtml

**Summary:** To provide financial assistance to upper-division and graduate students from designated southern states who are interested in preparing for a career in horticulture.

**Eligibility:** Open to residents of Alabama, Arkansas, Florida, Georgia, Kentucky, Louisiana, Maryland, Mississippi, Missouri, North Carolina, Oklahoma, South Carolina, Tennessee, Texas, Virginia, and West Virginia. Applicants must be college juniors, seniors, or graduate students enrolled full time in an accredited ornamental horticulture program or related discipline and have a GPA of 2.25 or higher (for undergraduates) or 3.0 or higher (for graduate students). Preference is given to applicants who plan to work in an aspect of the industry

(including owning their own business) and those in financial need. U.S. citizenship is required.

**Financial data:** The stipend is $2,500 per year.

**Duration:** 1 year; may be renewed up to 1 additional year.

**Number awarded:** 14 each year.

**Deadline:** May of each year.

## 2707 SIEMENS AWARDS FOR ADVANCED PLACEMENT

Siemens Foundation
170 Wood Avenue South
Iselin, NJ 08830
Phone: (877) 822-5233; Fax: (732) 603-5890;
Email: foundation@sc.siemens.com
Web: www.siemens-foundation.org/awards

**Summary:** To recognize and reward high school students with exceptional scores on the Advanced Placement (AP) examinations in mathematics and the sciences.

**Eligibility:** Open to all students in U.S. high schools (including home-schooled students and those in U.S. territories). Each fall, the College Board identifies the male and female seniors in each of its regions who have earned the highest number of scores on 7 AP exams: biology, calculus BC, chemistry, computer science AB, environmental science, physics C (physics C: mechanics and physics C: electricity each count as half), and statistics. Males and females are considered separately. Regional winners receive all-expense paid trips to Washington, D.C., where national winners are announced. The program also recognizes and rewards monetarily 1) schools that have shown the greatest improvement in the number and percentage of students taking AP examinations in biology, calculus, chemistry, computer science, environmental science, physics, and statistics in the past year; and 2) non-magnet urban schools that provide access to AP mathematics and science to a significant number of underrepresented minority students. In addition, teachers are rewarded for their commitment to students and the AP program. Additional teachers are recognized because they have successfully taught AP mathematics and/or science to underrepresented minority students in non-magnet urban schools.

**Financial data:** Regional scholarships are $3,000; national winners receive additional $5,000 scholarships. Awards to teachers and to schools are $1,000.

**Duration:** The awards are presented annually.

**Number awarded:** 24 regional scholarships (2 females and 2 males in each of the 6 regions), 2 national scholarships (1 female and 1 male), 12 high school awards (in each region, one to a school for improvement in the number and percentage of students taking AP examinations, 1 to an urban school for providing access to AP mathematics and science to minorities), and 18 teacher awards (in each region, 2 for commitment to students and the AP program, 1 for teaching minorities) are awarded each year.

**Deadline:** There is no application or nomination process for these awards. The College Board identifies the students, teachers, and high schools for the Siemens Foundation.

## 2708 SIEMENS SCHOLAR AWARD PROGRAM

American Society of Radiologic Technologists
Attn: ASRT Education and Research Foundation
15000 Central Avenue, S.E.
Albuquerque, NM 87123-3917
Phone: (505) 298-4500; (800) 444-2778, ext. 2541; Fax: (505) 298-5063;
Email: foundation@asrt.org
Web: www.asrt.org

**Summary:** To provide financial assistance to members of the American Society of Radiologic Technologists (ASRT) who are interested in continuing their education.

**Eligibility:** Open to licensed radiologic technologists who are current members of ASRT and have worked in the radiologic sciences profession for at least 1 year during the past 5 years in a clinical or didactic setting. Applicants must have applied to 1) an accredited certificate program related to the radiologic sciences, or 2) a course of study at the associate, baccalaureate, master's, or doctoral level intended to further their career. Along with their application, they must submit an essay of 750 words or less that covers their professional, educational, and career goals and how this scholarship will help them achieve those goals. Financial need is considered in the selection process.

**Financial data:** The stipend is $3,000.

**Duration:** 1 year; may be renewed for 1 additional year.

**Number awarded:** Varies each year; recently, 1 of these scholarships was awarded.

**Deadline:** January of each year.

## 2709 SIEMENS WESTINGHOUSE COMPETITION AWARDS

Siemens Foundation
170 Wood Avenue South
Iselin, NJ 08830
Phone: (877) 822-5233; Fax: (732) 603-5890;
Email: foundation@sc.siemens.com
Web: www.siemens-foundation.org/scholarship

**Summary:** To recognize and reward outstanding high school seniors who have undertaken individual or team research projects in science, mathematics, and technology (or in combinations of those disciplines).

**Eligibility:** Open to high school seniors who are legal or permanent U.S. residents. They must be enrolled in a high school in the United States, Puerto Rico, Guam, Virgin Islands, American Samoa, Wake and Midway Islands, or the Marianas. U.S. high school students enrolled in a Department of Defense dependents school, an accredited overseas American or international school, a foreign school as an exchange student, or a foreign school because their parent(s) live and work abroad are also eligible. Students being home-schooled qualify if they obtain the endorsement of the school district official responsible for such programs. Research projects may be submitted in mathematics and the biological and physical sciences, or involve combinations of disciplines, such as astrophysics, biochemistry, bioengineering, biology, biophysics, botany, chemistry, computer science, civil engineering, earth and atmospheric science engineering, electrical engineering, environmental sciences, fluid dynamics, genetics, geology, materials science, mathematics, mechanical engineering, nutritional science, physics, toxicology, and virology. Both individual and team projects (2 or 3 members) may be entered. All team members must meet the eligibility requirements. Team projects may include seniors, but that is not a requirement. Competition entrants must submit a detailed report on their research project, including a description of the purpose of the research, rationale for the research, pertinent scientific literature, methodology, results, discussion, and conclusion. All projects must be endorsed by a sponsoring high school (except home-schooled students, who obtain their endorsement from the district or state home-school official). Each project must have a project advisor or mentor who is a member of the instructional staff or a person approved by the endorsing high school. There are 3 judging phases to the competition. An initial review panel selects outstanding research projects from 6 different regions of the country. The students submitting these projects are identified as regional semifinalists. Out of those, the highest-rated projects from each region are selected and the students who submitted them are recognized as regional finalists. For the next phase, the regional finalists are offered all-expense paid trips to the regional competition on the campus of a regional university partner, where their projects are reviewed by a panel of judges appointed by the host institution. Regional finalists are required to prepare a poster display of their research project, make an oral presentation about the research and research findings, and respond to questions from the judges. The top-rated individual and the top-rated team project in each region are selected as regional winners to represent the region in the national competition as national finalists. At that competition, the national finalists again display their projects, make oral presentations, and respond to judges' questions. At each phase, selection is based on clarity of expression, comprehensiveness, creativity, field knowledge, future work, interpretation, literature review, presentation, scientific importance, and validity.

**Financial data:** At the regional level, finalists receive $1,000 scholarships, both as individuals and members of teams. Individual regional winners receive $3,000 scholarships. Winning regional teams receive $6,000 scholarships to be divided among the team members. Those regional winners then receive additional scholarships as national finalists. In the national competition. first-place winners receive an additional $100,000 scholarship, second place an additional $50,000 scholarship, third place an additional $40,000 scholarship, fourth place an additional $30,000 scholarship, fifth place an additional $20,000 scholarship, and sixth place an additional $10,000 scholarship. Those national awards are provided both to individuals and to teams to be divided equally among team members. Scholarship money is sent directly to the recipient's college or university to cover undergraduate and/or graduate educational expenses. Schools with regional finalists receive a $2,000 award to be used to support science, mathematics, and technology programs in their schools.

**Duration:** The competition is held annually.

**Number awarded:** In the initial round of judging, up to 300 regional semifinalists (up to 50 in each region) are selected. Of those, 60 are chosen as regional finalists (5 individuals and 5 teams in each of the 6 regions). Then 12 regional winners (1 individual and 1 team) are selected in the regional competitions, and they become the national finalists.

**Deadline:** September of each year.

## 2710 SIGMA PHI ALPHA UNDERGRADUATE SCHOLARSHIP PROGRAM

American Dental Hygienists' Association, Attn: Institute for Oral Health
444 North Michigan Avenue, Suite 3400
Chicago, IL 60611
Phone: (312) 440-8918; (800) 735-4916; Fax: (312) 440-8929;
Email: institute@adha.net
Web: www.adha.org/institute/Scholarship/index.htm

**Summary:** To provide financial assistance to full-time students enrolled in undergraduate programs in dental hygiene who are members of Sigma Phi Alpha.

**Eligibility:** Open to full-time undergraduate students who are active members of Sigma Phi Alpha. Applicants must have a GPA of 3.5 or higher, be able to document financial need of at least $1,500, and have completed at least one year in an accredited dental hygiene program in the United States. Along with their application, they must submit a statement that covers their long-term career goals, their intended contribution to the dental hygiene profession, their professional interests, and the manner in which their degree will enhance their professional capacity.

**Financial data:** Stipends range from $1,000 to $2,000.

**Duration:** 1 year.

**Number awarded:** 1 each year.

**Deadline:** April of each year.

## 2711 SISTER HELEN MARIE SCHOLARSHIP

Florida Dietetic Association
Attn: Scholarship Chair, Florida Dietetic Association Foundation
P.O. Box 12608
Tallahassee, FL 32317-2608
Phone: (850) 386-8850; Fax: (850) 386-7918; Email: DIETNUTR@aol.com
Web: www.eatrightflorida.org/general/scholarships.html

**Summary:** To provide financial assistance to upper-division students in Florida preparing for a career in the field of dietetics.

**Eligibility:** Open to Florida residents enrolled full time as upper-division students in a program that will prepare them to practice in the field of dietetics. Applicants must be members of the Florida Dietetic Association or attending school in Florida. They must have a GPA of 2.5 or higher and be members of the American Dietetic Association or enrolled in a program leading to eligibility for membership. U.S. citizenship or permanent resident status is required.

**Financial data:** The stipend is $1,500.

**Duration:** 1 year.

**Number awarded:** 1 each year.

**Deadline:** April of each year.

## 2712 SOCIETY OF COMMERCIAL ARBORICULTURE SCHOLARSHIPS

Society of Commercial Arboriculture
P.O. Box 3129
Champaign, IL 61826-3129
Email: slillg@isa-arbor.com
Web: www.aces.uiuc.edu/~isa.sca

**Summary:** To provide financial assistance to college students majoring in arboriculture, urban forestry, or horticulture.

**Eligibility:** Open to students who are enrolled full time in college, have at least 3 months of work experience with a tree service firm, and are majoring in arboriculture, urban forestry, or horticulture. Along with their application, they must submit a 1-page statement describing goals and aspirations, a letter of recommendation from a faculty member, a transcript, and a letter of reference from the tree service employer. Selection is not based on need or grades but on career goals and work experience.

**Financial data:** A stipend is awarded (amount not specified); funds are sent to the student upon receipt of proof of enrollment.

**Duration:** 1 year.

**Number awarded:** 1 or more each year.

**Deadline:** May of each year.

## 2713 SOCIETY OF HISPANIC PROFESSIONAL ENGINEERS SCHOLARSHIP PROGRAM

Hispanic Scholarship Fund, Attn: Selection Committee
55 Second Street, Suite 1500
San Francisco, CA 94105
Phone: (415) 808-2350; (877) HSF-INFO; Fax: (415) 808-2302;
Email: highschool@hsf.net
Web: www.hsf.net/scholarship/programs/shpe.php

**Summary:** To provide financial assistance for college to Hispanic Americans who are interested in majoring in designated fields of science.

**Eligibility:** Open to U.S. citizens, permanent residents, and visitors with a passport stamped I-551 who are of Hispanic heritage. Applicants may be graduating high school seniors, community college students transferring to a 4-year institution, or continuing college students as long as they have a GPA of 3.0 or higher. They must be enrolled or planning to enroll full time at an accredited college or university in the United States to major in computer science, physical science, applied science, mathematics, or engineering. Along with their application, they must submit 600-word essays on 1) how their Hispanic heritage, family upbringing, and/or role models have influenced their personal long-term goals; 2) how they contribute to their community and what they have learned from their experiences; and 3) an academic challenge they have faced and how they have overcome it. Selection is based on academic achievement, personal strengths, leadership, and financial need.

**Financial data:** Stipends range from $1,250 to $2,500 per year.

**Duration:** 1 year.

**Number awarded:** Varies each year; recently, 69 of these scholarships were awarded: 7 at $1,250, 2 at $1,307, and 60 at $2,500.

**Deadline:** June of each year.

## 2714 SOCIETY OF MANUFACTURING ENGINEERS CORPORATE SCHOLARSHIPS

Society of Manufacturing Engineers, Attn: SME Education Foundation
One SME Drive
P.O. Box 930
Dearborn, MI 48121-0930
Phone: (313) 425-3304; (800) 733-4763, ext. 3304; Fax: (313) 425-3411;
Email: foundation@sme.org
Web: www.sme.org

**Summary:** To provide financial assistance to undergraduate students enrolled in a degree program in manufacturing engineering or manufacturing engineering technology.

**Eligibility:** Open to full-time undergraduate students enrolled in a manufacturing engineering or technology degree program at a college or university in North America. Applicants must have a GPA of 3.0 or higher.

**Financial data:** The stipend is $5,000.

**Duration:** 1 year.

**Number awarded:** Varies each year.

**Deadline:** January of each year.

## 2715 SOCIETY OF MANUFACTURING ENGINEERS DIRECTORS' SCHOLARSHIPS

Society of Manufacturing Engineers, Attn: SME Education Foundation
One SME Drive
P.O. Box 930
Dearborn, MI 48121-0930
Phone: (313) 425-3304; (800) 733-4763, ext. 3304; Fax: (313) 425-3411;
Email: foundation@sme.org
Web: www.sme.org

**Summary:** To provide financial assistance to undergraduate students enrolled in a degree program in manufacturing.

**Eligibility:** Open to full-time undergraduate students enrolled in a manufacturing degree program at a college or university in North America. Applicants must have completed at least 30 units with a GPA of 3.5 or higher and be interested in preparing for a career in manufacturing. Preference is given to students who demonstrate leadership skills in a community, academic, or professional environment. Need is not considered in awarding scholarships (unless 2 or more applicants have equal qualifications).

**Financial data:** The stipend is $5,000.

**Duration:** 1 year; may be renewed.

**Number awarded:** 2 each year.

**Deadline:** January of each year.

## 2716 SOCIETY OF PLASTICS ENGINEERS FOUNDATION SCHOLARSHIPS

Society of Plastics Engineers, Attn: SPE Foundation
14 Fairfield Drive
Brookfield, CT 06804-0403
Phone: (203) 740-5447; Fax: (203) 775-1157; Email: foundation@4spe.org
Web: www.4spe.org/foundation/scholarships.php

**Summary:** To provide financial assistance to undergraduate and graduate students who have a career interest in the plastics industry.

**Eligibility:** Open to full-time undergraduate and graduate students at 4-year colleges or in 2-year technical programs. Applicants must 1) have a demonstrated or expressed interest in the plastics industry; 2) be majoring in or taking courses that would be beneficial to a career in the plastics or polymer industry (e.g., plastics engineering, polymer sciences, chemistry, physics, chemical engineering, mechanical engineering, or industrial engineering); 3) be in good academic standing at their school; and 4) be able to document financial need. Along with their application, they must submit 3 letters of recommendation; a high school and/or college transcript; and a 1- to 2-page statement telling why they are interested in the scholarship, their qualifications, and their educational and career goals in the plastics industry.

**Financial data:** Stipends range up to $4,000 per year. Funds are paid directly to the recipient's school.

**Duration:** 1 year; may be renewed for up to 3 additional years.

**Number awarded:** 10 to 12 each year.

**Deadline:** January of each year.

## 2717 SOCIETY OF WOMEN ENGINEERS-DELMAR SECTION SCHOLARSHIP AWARD

Delaware Engineering Society
c/o Stacy Ziegler
Duffield Associates, Inc.
5400 Limestone Road
Wilmington, DE 19808
Phone: (302) 239-6634; Fax: (302) 239-8485; Email: sziegler@duffnet.com
Web: www.udel.edu/DES

**Summary:** To provide financial assistance to female high school seniors in the DelMar area who are interested in majoring in engineering in college.

**Eligibility:** Open to female high school seniors in Delaware and Maryland who will be enrolling in an engineering program at an ABET-accredited college or university. Applicants must have ACT scores of 29 or higher in math and 25 or higher in English (or the equivalent on the SAT). They must submit an essay (up to 500 words) on their interest in engineering, their major area of study and area of specialization, the occupation they propose to pursue after graduation, their long-term goals, and how they hope to achieve them. Selection is based on the essay, academic record, honors and scholarships, volunteer activities, work experience, and letters of recommendation. Financial need is not required.

**Financial data:** Stipends are $1,000 or $500.

**Duration:** 1 year (freshman year); nonrenewable.

**Number awarded:** Varies each year. Recently, 5 of these scholarships were awarded: 2 at $1,000 and 3 at $500.

**Deadline:** November of each year.

## 2718 SOLE SCHOLARSHIP

SOLE-The International Society of Logistics
Attn: Logistics Education Foundation
8100 Professional Place, Suite 211
Hyattsville, MD 20785
Phone: (301) 459-8446; Fax: (301) 459-1522; Email: solehq@sole.org
Web: www.sole.org/lef.asp

**Summary:** To provide financial assistance to students working on an undergraduate or graduate degree in logistics.

**Eligibility:** Open to students working full time on a bachelor's or master's degree in logistics or a related major. Applicants must submit brief essays on their career interests and objectives, their scholastic and/or extracurricular activities related to logistics, and the topic of a student paper they will submit if they receive a scholarship. Financial need is not considered in the selection process.

**Financial data:** The stipend is $1,000.

**Duration:** 1 year.

**Number awarded:** 1 or more each year.

**Deadline:** May of each year.

## 2719 SOLID WASTE PROGRAM MANAGEMENT UNDERGRADUATE SCHOLARSHIP PROGRAM

ASME International, Attn: Solid Waste Processing Division
Three Park Avenue
New York, NY 10016-5990
Phone: (212) 591-7797; (800) THE-ASME; Fax: (212) 591-7674;
Email: manese@asme.org
Web: www.asme.org/divisions/swpd/studentprograms/index.html

**Summary:** To provide financial assistance to undergraduate students working on a degree in solid waste management.

**Eligibility:** Open to undergraduate students in any branch of engineering who are currently enrolled full time in a solid waste management program. They must attend or plan to attend a college or university in North America (including Alaska, Canada, Hawaii, Mexico, and Puerto Rico). Applications must be submitted jointly by an appropriate faculty member and the student. Required from the faculty member are a description of the school's solid waste management program, an identification of undergraduate and graduate courses offered in the program, an indication of the number of students in the program, a summary of future plans for the solid waste management program, and a proposal for use of the school's portion of the award money. Students must submit a statement of intent to pursue a branch of engineering as a career, a statement of interest in solid waste management, information on any prior experience in the solid waste management field, copies of any papers written on solid waste management, information on proposed studies, a list of current courses, transcripts for previous college years, and a letter of recommendation from the faculty advisor or department head. Financial need is not considered.

**Financial data:** The award is $2,000 per year. One half is given to the student and the other half is given to the recipient's school for support of its solid waste management program.

**Duration:** 1 year.

**Number awarded:** 1 each year.

**Deadline:** June of each year.

### 2720 SOUTH CAROLINA FARM BUREAU FOUNDATION SCHOLARSHIPS

South Carolina Farm Bureau, Attn: Foundation
P.O. Box 754
Columbia, SC 29202-0754
Phone: (803) 936-4210; Email: sanderson@scfb.com
Web: www.scfb.org/scfb_foundation.asp

**Summary:** To provide financial assistance to South Carolina residents working on an undergraduate degree in agriculture or a related field.

**Eligibility:** Open to residents of South Carolina enrolled in their sophomore, junior, or senior year of college. Applicants must be majoring in agriculture or a related field. Selection is based on character, demonstrated leadership abilities, and dedication to agriculture or related fields.

**Financial data:** Stipends are $1,000 or $500.

**Duration:** 1 year.

**Number awarded:** Varies each year. Recently, 6 of these scholarships were awarded: 5 at $1,000 and 1 at $500.

**Deadline:** April of each year.

### 2721 SOUTH CAROLINA SWCS CHAPTER SCHOLARSHIP

Soil and Water Conservation Society-South Carolina Chapter
c/o Hugh Caldwell, Secretary/Treasurer
400 Mill Creek Road
Lexington, SC 29072
Phone: (803) 576-2082; Email: hughcaldwell@richlandonline.com
Web: www.scswcs.org/scholarship.htm

**Summary:** To provide financial assistance to South Carolina residents working on an undergraduate degree in a field related to natural resources.

**Eligibility:** Open to residents of South Carolina who are enrolled or planning to enroll in a college or university. Applicants must be interested in an undergraduate degree in a field of conservation or natural resources. They must submit a 300-word essay on "The Value of This Scholarship to Me." Selection is based on that essay, GPA, community involvement, career goals, and financial need.

**Financial data:** The stipend is $1,000.

**Duration:** 1 year; recipients may not receive the scholarship for any 2 consecutive years.

**Number awarded:** 1 each year.

**Deadline:** March of each year.

### 2722 SOUTH TEXAS UNIT SCHOLARSHIPS

Herb Society of America-South Texas Unit, Attn: Education Committee Chair
P.O. Box 6515
Houston, TX 77265-6515
Phone: (713) 513-7808
Web: www.herbsociety-stu.org/Scholarship.htm

**Summary:** To provide financial assistance to Texas students majoring in agronomy, horticulture, botany, or a related field.

**Eligibility:** Open to students who are studying agronomy, horticulture, botany, or a closely-related discipline at an accredited 4-year college or university. Applicants must be either a permanent resident of Texas or attending an accredited college or university in Texas. They must have completed at least 2 full years of college and be entering their junior or senior year. Selection is based on academic achievement, letters of recommendation, and a 2- to 3-paragraph statement on their short- and long-term career goals, including examples of special interests or projects in plants, herbs, gardening, etc.

**Financial data:** The stipend is $1,000.

**Duration:** 1 year.

**Number awarded:** 2 each year.

**Deadline:** March of each year.

### 2723 SOUTHERN ASSOCIATION OF STEEL FABRICATORS SCHOLARSHIP

American Institute of Steel Construction
Attn: Director of University Relations
One East Wacker Drive, Suite 3100
Chicago, IL 60601-2001
Phone: (312) 670-5408; Fax: (312) 670-5403; Email: rosenberg@aisc.com
Web: www.aisc.org

**Summary:** To provide financial assistance to undergraduate engineering students from southern states who are interested in the structural field, especially structural steel.

**Eligibility:** Open to full-time civil or architectural engineering students entering their fourth year at universities in Alabama, Arkansas, Florida, Georgia, Kentucky, Louisiana, Mississippi, and Tennessee. Preference is given to students who have selected a concentration in the structural field, with particular emphasis on structural steel. Along with their application, they must submit a 2-page essay on their overall career objective and an original sample structural steel analysis/design solution, with calculations. Selection is based on those submissions, academic performance, and a faculty recommendation. U.S. citizenship is required.

**Financial data:** The stipend is $2,500.

**Duration:** 1 year.

**Number awarded:** 1 each year.

**Deadline:** April of each year.

### 2724 SOUTHWEST CHAPTER ACADEMIC SCHOLARSHIPS

American Association of Airport Executives-Southwest Chapter
P.O. Box 4228
Sparks, NV 89432
Phone: (775) 353-2080; Email: swaaae@sbcglobal.net
Web: www.swaaae.org/scholarships.html

**Summary:** To provide financial assistance to students working on an undergraduate or graduate degree in airport management at a college or university in the Southwest.

**Eligibility:** Open to students working on an undergraduate or graduate degree in airport management at colleges and universities in Arizona, California, Hawaii, Nevada, or Utah. Applicants must submit an autobiography (not to exceed 1 page) and a statement of their interest in aviation and airport management (not to exceed one page). Selection is based on academic record, extracurricular activities, and financial need.

**Financial data:** The stipend is $1,000 plus a $500 travel allowance for recipients to attend the award ceremony.

**Duration:** 1 year.

**Number awarded:** 2 each year.

**Deadline:** October of each year.

### 2725 SPENCE REESE SCHOLARSHIPS

Boys & Girls Clubs of Greater San Diego, Attn: Scholarships
4635 Clairemont Mesa Boulevard
San Diego, CA 92117
Phone: (619) 298-3520; (866) SD-YOUTH; Fax: (619) 298-3615
Web: www.sdyouth.org/scholarships.htm

**Summary:** To provide financial assistance to graduating male high school seniors who plan to study designated fields in college.

**Eligibility:** Open to graduating male high school seniors planning to study law, medicine, engineering, or political science in college. They may live anywhere in the United States, but must attend an interview in San Diego, California. Selection is based on academic standing, potential for good citizenship, academic ability, and financial need.

**Financial data:** The stipend is $2,000 per year.

**Duration:** 4 years.

**Number awarded:** 4 each year: 1 in each of the designated fields.

**Deadline:** April of each year.

## 2726 SPIE SCHOLARSHIP PROGRAM

SPIE-The International Society for Optical Engineering
Attn: Scholarship Committee
1000 20th Street
P.O. Box 10
Bellingham, WA 98227-0010
Phone: (360) 676-3290; Fax: (360) 647-1445; Email: scholarships@spie.org
Web: www.spie.org

**Summary:** To provide financial assistance to undergraduate and graduate student members of SPIE-The International Society for Optical Engineering who are preparing for a career in optical science or engineering.

**Eligibility:** Open to high school seniors planning to attend college, current undergraduate students, and current graduate students. Applicants must be society members majoring or planning to enroll full time and major in optical engineering, optical science, or optics at a college or university anywhere in the world. They must submit a 450-word essay that describes 1) their proposed research and/or course of study related to optics, photonics, imaging, or optoelectronics; 2) their career objectives; 3) how this scholarship would help them attain their objectives; and 4) what they have achieved and learned through their studies and activities. Financial need is not considered in the selection process. The International Society for Optical Engineering was founded in 1955 as the Society of Photo-Optical Instrumentation Engineers (SPIE). This program includes the following special named scholarships: the D.J. Lovell Scholarship, sponsored by SPIE with contributions from Labsphere, Inc. and Laser Focus World; the Nakajima Scholarship, sponsored by NAC, Inc.; the William H. Price Scholarship in Optical Engineering, established in 1985 for a full-time graduate or undergraduate student in the field of optical design and engineering; the F-MADE Scholarship, sponsored by the Forum for Military Applications of Directed Energy (F-MADE) in recognition of a student's scholarly achievement in laser technology, engineering, or applications; and the BACUS Scholarship, awarded to a full-time undergraduate or graduate student in the field of microlithography with an emphasis on optical tooling and/or semiconductor manufacturing technologies, sponsored by BACUS (SPIE's photomask international technical group).

**Financial data:** Stipends typically provide support for tuition and related expenses, travel to technical meetings, and supplemental funding for research and teaching assistantships.

**Duration:** 1 year.

**Number awarded:** Varies each year. Recently, this program awarded 68 scholarships: the 5 named awards plus 63 others.

**Deadline:** January of each year.

## 2727 SPORTY'S PILOT SHOP AVIATION EXPLORER SCHOLARSHIPS

Boy Scouts of America
Attn: Learning for Life Division, S210
1325 West Walnut Hill Lane
P.O. Box 152079
Irving, TX 75015-2079
Phone: (972) 580-2418; Fax: (972) 580-2137
Web: www.learning-for-life.org/exploring/scholarships/index.html

**Summary:** To provide financial assistance to Explorer Scouts who are interested in studying aviation in college.

**Eligibility:** Open to Aviation Explorer Scouts who are interested in studying aviation at a college or university. Applicants must submit at least 3 letters of recommendation and a 500-word essay detailing their plans for a career in aviation.

**Financial data:** The stipend is $1,000.

**Duration:** 1 year; nonrenewable.

**Number awarded:** 2 each year.

**Deadline:** March of each year.

## 2728 SPORTY'S/CINCINNATI AVIONICS SCHOLARSHIP

Aircraft Electronics Association
Attn: AEA Educational Foundation
4217 South Hocker Drive
Independence, MO 64055-4723
Phone: (816) 373-6565; Fax: (816) 478-3100; Email: info@aea.net
Web: www.aea.net

**Summary:** To provide financial assistance to students who are interested in majoring in avionics in college.

**Eligibility:** Open to high school seniors and currently-enrolled college students who are attending (or planning to attend) an accredited school in an avionics

program. Applicants must submit an official transcript (cumulative GPA of 2.5 or higher), a statement about their career plans, a description of their involvement in school and community activities, and a 300-word essay on how the job requirements of aviation technicians will change with advancements in technology. Selection is based on merit.

**Financial data:** The stipend is $2,000.

**Duration:** 1 year.

**Number awarded:** 1 each year.

**Deadline:** February of each year.

## 2729 STAN BECK FELLOWSHIP

Entomological Society of America
Attn: Entomological Foundation
9332 Annapolis Road, Suite 210
Lanham, MD 20706-3150
Phone: (301) 459-9082; Fax: (301) 459-9084; Email: melodie@entfdn.org
Web: www.entfdn.org/beck.html

**Summary:** To assist "needy" students working on an undergraduate or graduate degree in science who are nominated by members of the Entomological Society of America (ESA).

**Eligibility:** Open to students working on an undergraduate or graduate degree in entomology at a college or university in Canada, Mexico, or the United States. Candidates must be nominated by members of the society. They must be "needy" students; for the purposes of this program, need may be based on physical limitations, or economic, minority, or environmental conditions.

**Financial data:** The stipend is $2,000 per year.

**Duration:** 1 year; may be renewed up to 3 additional years. Recipients are expected to be present at the society's annual meeting, where the award will be presented.

**Number awarded:** 1 or more each year.

**Deadline:** June of each year.

## 2730 STATE OF DELAWARE NURSING EXPANSION SCHOLARSHIP PROGRAM

Delaware Healthcare Association
1280 South Governors Avenue
Dover, DE 19904-4802
Phone: (302) 674-2853; Fax: (302) 734-2731
Web: www.deha.org

**Summary:** To provide financial assistance to Delaware residents who are studying nursing at a school in the state.

**Eligibility:** Open to residents of Delaware who are currently enrolled in a nursing program in the state (either in a 2-year program or the final 2 years of a 4-year program). Applicants must currently be employed, full or part time, at a Delaware acute care hospital or long-term care facility affiliated with a hospital. They must first apply to the hospital or facility that will conduct a follow-up interview to determine their eligibility, career plans, and potential employment opportunity as a nurse with the hospital or facility. If selected by the hospital or facility, their application is forwarded to the sponsor. Financial need is not required, but students must apply for financial aid as part of the application process.

**Financial data:** Funding provides support for tuition, fees, books, and supplies as well as transportation, child care, medical insurance, and other living expenses.

**Duration:** 1 year.

**Number awarded:** Varies each year.

## 2731 STELLA GRIFFIN MEMORIAL SCHOLARSHIP

American Society for Clinical Laboratory Science-Ohio
c/o Sondra Sutherland, Scholarship Chair
Jefferson Community College
4000 Sunset Boulevard
Steubenville, OH 43952
Phone: (740) 264-5591, ext. 165; Fax: (740) 264-9504;
Email: ssutherlan@jcc.edu
Web: www.oscls.org

**Summary:** To provide financial assistance to college students in Ohio who are interested in preparing for a career in clinical laboratory science.

**Eligibility:** Open to Ohio residents who are enrolled in the clinical laboratory science curriculum of an Ohio college or school of medical technology. They must have at least a 2.5 GPA, be in need of financial assistance, and have the following personal characteristics: an inquiring mind, an aptitude for science, initiative, adaptability to people and situations, patience, consideration for and an interest in others, a sense of responsibility, honesty, and integrity.

**Financial data:** The stipend is $1,000. Funds are paid directly to the recipient.

**Duration:** 1 year; recipients may reapply.

**Additional information:** The sponsor was formerly the Ohio Society for Clinical Laboratory Science.

**Number awarded:** 1 each year.

**Deadline:** March of each year.

---

## 2732 STEVE DEARDUFF SCHOLARSHIP

Community Foundation for Greater Atlanta, Inc.
50 Hurt Plaza, Suite 449
Atlanta, GA 30303
Phone: (404) 688-5525; Fax: (404) 688-3060; Email: vweekes@atlcf.org
Web: www.atlcf.org/GrantsScholarships/Scholarships/SteveDearduff.aspx

**Summary:** To provide financial assistance to Georgia residents who are working on an undergraduate or graduate degree, especially in medicine or social work.

**Eligibility:** Open to legal residents of Georgia who are enrolled in or accepted at an accredited institution of higher learning on the undergraduate or graduate school level. Applicants must be able to demonstrate a history of outstanding community service and potential for success in their chosen field. They must have a GPA of 2.0 or higher. Preference is given to candidates entering the fields of medicine (research or clinical practice) or social work.

**Financial data:** Stipends range up to $2,500 per year.

**Duration:** 1 year; recipients may reapply.

**Number awarded:** Varies each year; recently, 7 of these scholarships were awarded.

**Deadline:** March of each year.

---

## 2733 STEVE HARPER MEMORIAL SCHOLARSHIP

**Summary:** To provide financial assistance to high school seniors in Kansas who plan to attend a college or university in the state to major in natural resources or photography.

*See Listing #1687.*

---

## 2734 STEVE WAGNER SCHOLARSHIP

Saginaw Community Foundation
100 South Jefferson, Suite 201
Saginaw, MI 48607
Phone: (989) 755-0545; Fax: (989) 755-6524;
Email: info@saginawfoundation.org
Web: www.saginawfoundation.org

**Summary:** To provide financial assistance to Michigan residents working on an undergraduate or graduate degree in civil engineering or land surveying.

**Eligibility:** Open to residents of Michigan working on an undergraduate or graduate degree at an ABET-accredited program in civil engineering or land surveying. Applicants must be enrolled full time with a GPA of 2.5 or higher. They must have worked for a firm that is a member of the American Council of Engineering Companies (ACEC) in the last 24 months. Selection is based on academic record (10 points), community service (40 points), recommendations (20 points), and overall involvement in community, school, and work activities (30 points).

**Financial data:** A stipend is awarded (amount not specified).

**Duration:** 1 year.

**Number awarded:** 1 or more each year.

**Deadline:** February of each year.

---

## 2735 STRUCTURAL ENGINEERS FOUNDATION SCHOLARSHIPS

Structural Engineers Association of Illinois
Attn: Structural Engineers Foundation
203 North Wabash Avenue, Suite 2010
Chicago, IL 60601
Phone: (312) 372-4198; Fax: (312) 372-5673
Web: www.seaoi.org/html/body_sef.html

**Summary:** To provide financial assistance to upper-division and graduate students interested in a career in structural engineering.

**Eligibility:** Open to students 1) entering their third or higher year of an under-

graduate program, or 2) entering or continuing a graduate program. Applicants must be enrolled in a civil or architectural engineering program and planning to continue with a structural engineering specialization. Students enrolled in structural engineering technology programs are also eligible if they are qualified to take the Fundamentals of Engineering and Principles and Practice licensure examinations in their home state upon graduation. U.S. citizenship or permanent resident status is required. Students enrolled in military academies or ROTC programs are not eligible. Selection is based on a statement giving reasons why the applicant should receive the award (including plans for continued formal education), transcripts, 3 letters of recommendation, and potential for development and leadership. Financial need is not considered.

**Financial data:** The stipend is $1,500.

**Duration:** 1 year; nonrenewable.

**Number awarded:** 1 or more each year.

**Deadline:** March of each year.

---

## 2736 STRUCTURAL METALS DIVISION SCHOLARSHIP

The Minerals, Metals & Materials Society
Attn: TMS Student Awards Program
184 Thorn Hill Road
Warrendale, PA 15086-7514
Phone: (724) 776-9000, ext. 220; Fax: (724) 776-3770;
Email: students@tms.org
Web: www.tms.org/Students/AwardsPrograms/Scholarships.html

**Summary:** To provide financial assistance to student members of The Minerals, Metals & Materials Society (TMS).

**Eligibility:** Open to undergraduate members of the society who are majoring in metallurgical and/or materials science and engineering with an emphasis on the society and engineering of load-bearing materials. Applicants may be from any country. Selection is based on academic achievement, school and community activities, work experience, leadership, a personal profile statement, and letters of recommendation. Preference is given to students in their senior year who are enrolled full time in an engineering program relating to the structure, properties, and processing of materials.

**Financial data:** The stipend is $2,500 plus a travel stipend of $500 (so the recipient can attend the annual meeting of the society to accept the award).

**Duration:** 1 year.

**Number awarded:** 2 each year.

**Deadline:** April of each year.

---

## 2737 STUDENT ASSOCIATION GEORGE R. FOSTER MEMORIAL SCHOLARSHIP

Institute of Food Technologists
Attn: Scholarship Department
525 West Van Buren, Suite 1000
Chicago, IL 60607
Phone: (312) 782-8424; Fax: (312) 782-8348; Email: info@ift.org
Web: www.ift.org

**Summary:** To provide financial assistance to high school seniors interested in studying food science or food technology in college.

**Eligibility:** Open to high school seniors planning to enroll in a food science or food technology program at an educational institution in the United States or Canada. Applicants must have an outstanding scholastic record and a well-rounded personality. Along with their application, they must submit a brief biographical sketch and a statement on why they would like to become a food technologist. Financial need is not considered in the selection process.

**Financial data:** The stipend is $1,000.

**Duration:** 1 year; recipients may reapply if they are members of the Institute of Food Technologists.

**Number awarded:** 1 each year.

**Deadline:** February of each year.

---

## 2738 STUDENT COMPETITION IN LANDSCAPE ARCHITECTURE FOR AGGREGATE OPERATIONS

**Summary:** To recognize and reward students who submit outstanding designs for site beautification at quarry sites.

*See Listing #1690.*

## 2739 STUDENT DESIGN COMPETITION IN ACOUSTICS

**Summary:** To recognize and reward undergraduate and graduate students who submit outstanding entries in an acoustics design competition.
*See Listing #1691.*

## 2740 STUDENT MANUFACTURING ENGINEERING DESIGN COMPETITION

ASME International
Attn: Manufacturing Engineering Division
Three Park Avenue
New York, NY 10016-5990
Phone: (212) 591-7787; (800) THE-ASME; Fax: (212) 591-7671;
Email: elghobashyn@asme.org
Web: www.asme.org/divisions/med/studentprograms/index.html
**Summary:** To recognize and reward outstanding manufacturing engineering designs by student members of the American Society of Mechanical Engineers (ASME).
**Eligibility:** Open to undergraduate and graduate student members of the society who submit projects that promote the art, science, and practice of manufacturing engineering. Technical areas include, but are not limited to, computer integrated manufacturing and robotics; machine tools, sensors, and controllers; manufacturing systems management and optimization; materials processing; new areas of manufacturing engineering; evolution of new materials and processes; and software and hardware contributing to improvements in manufacturing productivity. Applicants must submit a report, from 1,500 to 3,000 words, that describes 1) the project's concept, idea, model, or system; 2) its design features and manufacturing engineering content; 3) the tools, equipment, and/or computer aided design procedures used and how they enhanced the design process; and 4) the concept's practicality and how it improves upon existing designs that do the same or similar tasks.
**Financial data:** First prize is $1,000, second prize is $750, and third prize is $500.
**Duration:** The competition is held annually.
**Number awarded:** 3 each year.
**Deadline:** May of each year.

## 2741 STUDENT SAFETY ENGINEERING DESIGN CONTEST

ASME International
Attn: Safety Engineering and Risk Analysis Division
Three Park Avenue
New York, NY 10016-5990
Phone: (212) 591-7863; (800) THE-ASME; Fax: (212) 591-7671;
Email: ulvilar@asme.org
Web: www.asme.org/divisions/serad/studentprograms
**Summary:** To recognize and reward outstanding safety engineering design papers by undergraduate and graduate students.
**Eligibility:** Open to undergraduate and graduate students enrolled in an ABET-accredited mechanical engineering curriculum. Applicants must submit a senior design or other in-class project that describes an analysis, design, or engineering study that will prevent occupational injuries, illnesses, and deaths. Selection is based on background (20%), methodology (30%), feasibility (30%), and system safety (20%). Applications and further information are also available from Brian C. Brady, c/o Roger Harvey, 25 Kinkel Street, Westbury, NY 11590, (516) 333-2520, E-mail: bgbrady@cs.com. This program is jointly sponsored by the Safety Engineering and Risk Analysis Division of ASME (the professional organization for mechanical engineering) and the National Institute for Occupational Safety and Health (NIOSH). Additional funding is provided by Westinghouse Electric Company, FM Global, American Hazard Control Consultants, Inc., and several individuals.
**Financial data:** First prize is $2,000 plus a travel allowance of $400 to present the winning paper; the faculty advisor receives $500. Second prize is $500; the faculty advisor receives $200.
**Duration:** The competition is held annually.
**Number awarded:** 2 each year.
**Deadline:** May of each year.

## 2742 SUSAN MISZKOWITZ MEMORIAL SCHOLARSHIP

Society of Women Engineers
230 East Ohio Street, Suite 400
Chicago, IL 60611-3265
Phone: (312) 596-5223; Fax: (312) 644-8557; Email: hq@swe.org
Web: www.societyofwomenengineers.org/scholarships
**Summary:** To provide financial assistance to undergraduate women majoring in computer science or engineering.
**Eligibility:** Open to women who are entering their sophomore, junior, or senior year at a 4-year ABET-accredited college or university. Applicants must be majoring in computer science or engineering and have a GPA of 3.0 or higher. Along with their application, they must submit a 1-page essay on why they want to be an engineer or computer scientist, how they believe they will make a difference as an engineer or computer scientist, and what influenced them to study engineering or computer science. Selection is based on merit. This program was established in 2002 to honor a member of the Society of Women Engineers who was killed in the New York World Trade Center on September 11, 2001.
**Financial data:** The stipend is $1,000.
**Duration:** 1 year.
**Number awarded:** 1 each year.
**Deadline:** January of each year.

## 2743 SWE ARIZONA SECTION SCHOLARSHIP

Society of Women Engineers
230 East Ohio Street, Suite 400
Chicago, IL 60611-3265
Phone: (312) 596-5223; Fax: (312) 644-8557; Email: hq@swe.org
Web: www.swe.org
Web: www.societyofwomenengineers.org/scholarships
**Summary:** To provide financial assistance to women from Arizona who will be entering college as freshmen and interested in studying engineering or computer science.
**Eligibility:** Open to women who are entering college as freshmen with a GPA of 3.5 or higher. Applicants must be residents of Arizona or attending school in the state and planning to enroll full time at an ABET-accredited 4-year college or university and major in computer science or engineering. Along with their application, they must submit a 1-page essay on why they want to be an engineer or computer scientist, how they believe they will make a difference as an engineer or computer scientist, and what influenced them to study engineering or computer science. Selection is based on merit.
**Financial data:** The stipend is $1,000.
**Duration:** 1 year.
**Additional information:** This program was established in 2001.
**Number awarded:** 2 each year.
**Deadline:** May of each year.

## 2744 SWE NEW JERSEY SCHOLARSHIP

Society of Women Engineers
230 East Ohio Street, Suite 400
Chicago, IL 60611-3265
Phone: (312) 596-5223; Fax: (312) 644-8557; Email: hq@swe.org
Web: www.swe.org
Web: www.societyofwomenengineers.org/scholarships
**Summary:** To provide financial assistance to women from New Jersey who will be entering college as freshmen and interested in studying engineering or computer science.
**Eligibility:** Open to women who are entering college as freshmen with a GPA of 3.5 or higher. Applicants must be residents of New Jersey planning to enroll full time at an ABET-accredited 4-year college or university and major in computer science or engineering. Along with their application, they must submit a 1-page essay on why they want to be an engineer or computer scientist, how they believe they will make a difference as an engineer or computer scientist, and what influenced them to study engineering or computer science. Selection is based on merit.
**Financial data:** The stipend is $1,500.
**Duration:** 1 year.
**Number awarded:** 1 each year.
**Deadline:** May of each year.

## 2745 SWE PAST PRESIDENTS SCHOLARSHIPS

Society of Women Engineers
230 East Ohio Street, Suite 400
Chicago, IL 60611-3265
Phone: (312) 596-5223; Fax: (312) 644-8557; Email: hq@swe.org
Web: www.societyofwomenengineers.org/scholarships

**Summary:** To provide financial assistance to women working on an undergraduate or graduate degree in engineering or computer science.
**Eligibility:** Open to women who will be sophomores, juniors, seniors, or graduate students at ABET-accredited colleges and universities. Applicants must be U.S. citizens majoring in computer science or engineering and have a GPA of 3.0 or higher. Along with their application, they must submit a 1-page essay on why they want to be an engineer or computer scientist, how they believe they will make a difference as an engineer or computer scientist, and what influenced them to study engineering or computer science. Selection is based on merit.
**Financial data:** The stipend is $1,500 per year.
**Duration:** 1 year.
**Number awarded:** 2 each year.
**Deadline:** January of each year.

### 2746 SYLVIA W. FARNY SCHOLARSHIP

ASME International
Attn: American Society of Mechanical Engineers Auxiliary, Inc.
Three Park Avenue
New York, NY 10016-5990
Phone: (212) 591-7733; (800) THE-ASME; Fax: (212) 591-7674;
Email: horvathb@asme.org
Web: www.asme.org/auxiliary/scholarshiploans
**Summary:** To provide financial support for the study of mechanical engineering to students in their final year of undergraduate study.
**Eligibility:** Open to students completing the junior year of a 4-year program or the fourth year of a 5-year program in mechanical engineering. Applicants must be U.S. citizens enrolled in colleges and universities with accredited departments of mechanical engineering. If the school has a chapter of the Student Section of the American Society of Mechanical Engineers (ASME), the applicant must be a member. Selection is based on academic performance, financial need, character, and participation in ASME activities. This scholarship was established in 1952 to honor the 11th president and honorary member of the ASME auxiliary. Further information and an application are available by sending a self-addressed stamped envelope to Mrs. Alverta Cover, 5425 Caldwell Mill Road, Birmingham, AL 35242, (205) 991-6109, Email: undergradauxsch@asme.org.
**Financial data:** The grant is $2,000.
**Duration:** 1 year.
**Number awarded:** 6 to 12 each year.
**Deadline:** March of each year.

### 2747 TED NEWARD SCHOLARSHIPS

Society of Plastics Engineers
Attn: SPE Foundation
14 Fairfield Drive
Brookfield, CT 06804-0403
Phone: (203) 740-5447; Fax: (203) 775-1157; Email: foundation@4spe.org
Web: www.4spe.org/foundation/scholarships.php
**Summary:** To provide financial assistance to undergraduate and graduate students who have a career interest in the plastics industry.
**Eligibility:** Open to full-time undergraduate and graduate students at 4-year colleges or in 2-year technical programs. Applicants must 1) have a demonstrated or expressed interest in the plastics industry; 2) be majoring in or taking courses that would be beneficial to a career in the plastics or polymer industry (e.g., plastics engineering, polymer sciences, chemistry, physics, chemical engineering, mechanical engineering, or industrial engineering); 3) be in good academic standing at their school; and 4) be able to document financial need. U.S. citizenship is required. Along with their application, they must submit 3 letters of recommendation; a high school and/or college transcript; and a 1- to 2-page statement telling why they are interested in the scholarship, their qualifications, and their educational and career goals in the plastics industry.
**Financial data:** The stipend is $3,000 per year. Funds are paid directly to the recipient's school.
**Duration:** 1 year.
**Number awarded:** 3 each year.
**Deadline:** January of each year.

### 2748 TENNESSEE SECTION INSTITUTE OF TRANSPORTATION ENGINEERS TRANSPORTATION ENGINEERING SCHOLARSHIP

Institute of Transportation Engineers-Tennessee Section
c/o Jeff Hammond
Neel-Schaffer, Inc.

210 25th Avenue North, Suite 800
Nashville, TN 37203
Phone: (615) 383-8420; Fax: (615) 383-9984
Web: www.tsite.org/scholarship/sscholarship.asp
**Summary:** To provide financial assistance to undergraduate and graduate students majoring in transportation engineering at colleges and universities in Tennessee.
**Eligibility:** Open to undergraduate and graduate students enrolled in a transportation engineering program at colleges and universities in Tennessee. Applicants must submit a 1-page statement on their transportation engineering career objectives and commitment. Selection is based on that statement, academic record, leadership activities, and employment history. Financial need is not considered.
**Financial data:** The stipend is $1,500.
**Duration:** 1 year.
**Number awarded:** 2 each year.
**Deadline:** January of each year.

### 2749 TERRY L. MCKANNA SCHOLARSHIP

American Water Works Association-Kansas Section
c/o Frank Yau, Scholarship Committee Chair
4301 Brenner Road
Kansas City, KS 66104-5531
Phone: (913) 573-9347; Fax: (913) 573-9361; Email: fyau@bpu.com
Web: www.ksawwa.org
**Summary:** To provide financial assistance to undergraduate and graduate students in Kansas who are preparing for a career in the water works industry.
**Eligibility:** Open to undergraduate and graduate students enrolled full time at a 2-year or 4-year college or university in Kansas. Applicants must be interested in preparing for a career in a field associated with the water works industry. Their program must include courses related to civil or environmental engineering or environmental science. U.S. citizenship is required.
**Financial data:** The stipend is $1,000.
**Duration:** 1 year.
**Number awarded:** 1 each year.
**Deadline:** June of each year.

### 2750 TEXAS ASPHALT PAVEMENT ASSOCIATION SCHOLARSHIPS

Texas Asphalt Pavement Association
Attn: Scholarships
149 Commercial Drive
Buda, TX 78610
Phone: (512) 312-2099; Email: info@txhotmix.org
Web: www.txhotmix.org
**Summary:** To provide financial assistance to undergraduate and graduate students in Texas who are preparing for a career in the hot mix asphalt (HMA) field.
**Eligibility:** Open to residents of Texas who are enrolled as sophomores, juniors, seniors, and graduate students at a college or university. Applicants must be working full time on a baccalaureate or graduate degree in civil engineering or construction science, management, or technology with a strong interest in the HMA filed. Preference is given to students who have demonstrated their interest in HMA through summer or part-time employment. Selection is based on academic record and demonstrated interest in the HMA field.
**Financial data:** The stipend is $1,500.
**Duration:** 1 year; sophomores and juniors may reapply.
**Number awarded:** 8 each year.
**Deadline:** May of each year.

### 2751 TEXAS BUSINESS AND TECHNOLOGY EDUCATORS ASSOCIATION SCHOLARSHIPS

Texas Business and Technology Educators Association
c/o Mona Fannon, Scholarship Committee Chair
Route 2 Box 8-14
Fritch, TX 79036
Phone: (806) 857-9320; Email: mona.fannon@borgerisd.net
Web: www.tbtea.org
**Summary:** To provide financial assistance for college to members of Business Professionals of America (BPA) or Future Business Leaders of America (FBLA) in Texas.

**Eligibility:** Open to seniors graduating from high schools in Texas who are members of BPA or FBLA (or were members during their junior year). Applicants must have a GPA of 2.75 or higher and be nominated by a teacher who is a member of the Texas Business and Technology Educators Association. They must be planning to attend college to prepare for a career in business, business education, computer science, computer information systems, or a related field. Along with their application, they must submit a 1-page letter describing why they deserve this scholarship, defining their career goals, and including any information regarding financial need.

**Financial data:** The stipend is $1,000.

**Duration:** 1 year.

**Number awarded:** 4 each year.

**Deadline:** February of each year.

---

## 2752 TEXAS CATTLEWOMEN SCHOLARSHIP

Texas CattleWomen, Inc.
Attn: Sandra Christner, Scholarship Chairperson
P.O. Box 522
Wheeler, TX 79096
Phone: (806) 826-3572; Fax: (806) 826-0052
Web: www.texascattlewomen.org/TCWscholarships.htm

**Summary:** To provide financial assistance to residents of Texas who are majoring in foods and nutrition, agricultural communications, or hotel and restaurant management in college.

**Eligibility:** Open to graduates of a Texas high school who are currently enrolled at the sophomore through senior level in a 4-year college or university in Texas. They must have a GPA of 3.0 or higher and be majoring in foods and nutrition, agricultural communications, or hotel and restaurant management. Selection is based on evidence of potential for continuing education, participation in student activities, evidence of leadership qualities, ability to relate well with others, financial need, and interest in and willingness to support the production and consumption of beef.

**Financial data:** The stipend is $1,000 per year. Funds may be used for any educational expense.

**Duration:** 1 year; recipients may reapply.

**Number awarded:** 3 each year.

**Deadline:** October of each year.

---

## 2753 TEXAS COUNCIL OF CHAPTERS SCHOLARSHIPS

Soil and Water Conservation Society-Texas Council of Chapters
c/o Robert Knight, Scholarship Committee Chair
Texas A&M University
Department of Rangeland Ecology and Management
College Station, TX 77843-2126
Fax: (979) 845-6430; Email: rknight@rlem.tamu.edu
Web: rangeweb.tamu.edu/students/swcs/scholarshipinfo.html

**Summary:** To provide financial assistance to upper-division students working in conservation-related fields at colleges and universities in Texas.

**Eligibility:** Open to students who have completed at least 2 years of undergraduate work at a Texas college or university. Applicants must plan to continue their education by working on a degree in conservation or related field. They must submit a 1-page letter describing their study plans (including subject matter area), attitude toward conservation, career plans, and financial need.

**Financial data:** Stipends are $1,000 or $500. The top-ranked applicant receives the Erwin A. Pavlik Memorial Scholarship.

**Duration:** 1 year; nonrenewable.

**Number awarded:** 3 each year: 1 at $1,000 and 2 at $500.

**Deadline:** April of each year.

---

## 2754 TEXAS PROFESSIONAL NURSING SCHOLARSHIPS

Texas Higher Education Coordinating Board
Attn: Grants and Special Programs
1200 East Anderson Lane
P.O. Box 12788, Capitol Station
Austin, TX 78711-2788
Phone: (512) 427-6340; (800) 242-3062, ext. 6340; Fax: (512) 427-6127;
Email: grantinfo@thecb.state.tx.us
Web: www.collegefortexans.com

**Summary:** To provide financial assistance to Texas students who are interested in preparing for a career as a professional nurse.

**Eligibility:** Open to undergraduate or graduate students who are residents of Texas and enrolled at least half time in a program leading to licensure as a professional nurse at a college or university in the state. Applicants must be able to demonstrate financial need.

**Financial data:** The stipend depends on the need of the recipient, to a maximum of $3,000.

**Duration:** 1 academic year.

**Number awarded:** Varies each year; recently, 131 of these scholarships were awarded.

**Deadline:** Applicants should contact the financial aid director at the professional nursing school in which they plan to enroll for appropriate deadline dates.

---

## 2755 TEXAS RURAL EMERGENCY MEDICAL SERVICES SCHOLARSHIP INCENTIVE PROGRAM

Texas Higher Education Coordinating Board
Attn: Grants and Special Programs
1200 East Anderson Lane
P.O. Box 12788, Capitol Station
Austin, TX 78711-2788
Phone: (512) 427-6367; (800) 242-3062, ext. 6367; Fax: (512) 427-6127;
Email: grantinfo@thecb.state.tx.us
Web: www.collegefortexans.com

**Summary:** To provide financial assistance to residents of Texas who are interested in training as an emergency medical technician (EMT) and working in a rural community in the state.

**Eligibility:** Open to Texas residents who are at least 18 years of age and have a high school diploma or GED certificate. Applicants must be interested in obtaining training as an EMT, EMT-I (must already have a license as an EMT), or EMT-P (must already have a license as an EMT-I). Applicants must enter into a contract with a community in a rural country in Texas to provide emergency medical services upon completion of their training for at least one year. The community must commit to raising funds to match the amount provided by this program. This program is offered in cooperation with the Office of Rural Community Affairs (ORCA), Attn: Texas Health Service Corps, 1700 North Congress, Suite 220, P.O. Box 12877, Austin, TX 78711, (512) 936-6701, (800) 544-2042, Fax: (512) 936-6776, E-mail: orca@orca.state.tx.us.

**Financial data:** This program provides up to $2,000 in matching funds towards the costs of tuition and other expenses associated with EMT, EMT-I, and EMT-P training.

**Duration:** 1 year.

**Number awarded:** Varies each year.

---

## 2756 TEXAS SURVEYORS FOUNDATION SCHOLARSHIPS

Texas Surveyors Foundation, Inc.
2525 Wallingwood Drive, Suite 300
Austin, TX 78746
Phone: (512) 327-7871; Fax: (512) 327-7872; Email: DougL@tsps.org
Web: www.tsps.org

**Summary:** To provide financial assistance to Texas residents interested in working on an undergraduate degree in surveying.

**Eligibility:** Open to residents of Texas who are enrolled, or accepted for enrollment, in a college or university surveying program or surveying-related course of study. Applicants must submit a 2-page essay that includes a brief autobiography, career plans, reason for applying for this scholarship, and reason for choosing land surveying as a career. Selection is based on academic achievement and financial need.

**Financial data:** A stipend is awarded (amount not specified).

**Duration:** 1 year; may be renewed.

**Number awarded:** Varies each year.

**Deadline:** January of each year for spring semester; April of each year for summer semester; September of each year for fall semester.

---

## 2757 TEXAS TRANSPORTATION SCHOLARSHIP

Transportation Clubs International
Attn: Gay Fielding
7031 Manchester Street
New Orleans, LA 70126
Email: GayFielding@bellsouth.net
Web: www.transportationclubinternational.com

**Summary:** To provide financial assistance to college students interested in preparing for a career in fields related to transportation.

**Eligibility:** Open to students enrolled in an academic institution that offers courses in transportation, logistics, traffic management, or related fields. Applicants must intend to prepare for a career in those fields. They must have been enrolled in a school in Texas during some phase of their education (elementary or secondary). Selection is based on scholastic ability, potential, character, professional interest, and financial need. Requests for applications must be accompanied by a stamped self-addressed envelope.

**Financial data:** The stipend is $1,000.

**Duration:** 1 year.

**Number awarded:** 1 each year.

**Deadline:** April of each year.

## 2758 TEXAS VOCATIONAL NURSING SCHOLARSHIPS

Texas Higher Education Coordinating Board
Attn: Grants and Special Programs
1200 East Anderson Lane
P.O. Box 12788, Capitol Station
Austin, TX 78711-2788
Phone: (512) 427-6340; (800) 242-3062, ext. 6340; Fax: (512) 427-6127;
Email: grantinfo@thecb.state.tx.us
Web: www.collegefortexans.com

**Summary:** To provide financial assistance to Texas students who are interested in preparing for a career as a vocational nurse.

**Eligibility:** Open to undergraduate or graduate students who are residents of Texas and enrolled at least half time in a program leading to licensure as a vocational nurse at a college or university in the state. Applicants must be able to demonstrate financial need. Some of these funds are targeted to students from rural communities.

**Financial data:** The stipend depends on the need of the recipient, to a maximum of $1,500.

**Duration:** 1 academic year.

**Number awarded:** Varies each year; recently, 36 of these scholarships were awarded.

**Deadline:** Applicants should contact the financial aid director at the vocational nursing school in which they plan to enroll for appropriate deadline dates.

## 2759 THEODORE M. BRICKLEY/BERNICE SHICKORA SCHOLARSHIP

American Society of Safety Engineers-New Jersey Chapter
c/o New Jersey State Safety Council
6 Commerce Drive
Cranford, NJ 07016
Phone: (732) 269-7683
Web: www.njasse.org

**Summary:** To provide financial assistance to undergraduate and graduate students in safety engineering or other safety-related majors in New Jersey.

**Eligibility:** Open to upper-division and graduate students who are residents of New Jersey enrolled at a college or university in the state. Applicants must be majoring in occupational safety, industrial hygiene, environmental science, or a related field; have completed at least 6 credit hours in occupational safety and health (OSH) and at least 12 credit hours in OSH or related courses; have completed at least 18 credit hours in departmental-related courses (physical sciences, mathematics, engineering); and have a GPA of 2.5 or higher overall and 3.0 or higher in OSH courses. Selection is based on GPA; leadership skills as demonstrated by participation in extracurricular activities; involvement in occupational safety, hygiene, and related activities; involvement with professional occupational safety, hygiene, or related organizations; communication skills; awards and honors; and financial need.

**Financial data:** The stipend is $1,000.

**Number awarded:** 1 or more each year.

**Deadline:** April of each year.

## 2760 THERMOFORMING DIVISION MEMORIAL SCHOLARSHIPS

Society of Plastics Engineers
Attn: SPE Foundation
14 Fairfield Drive
Brookfield, CT 06804-0403
Phone: (203) 740-5447; Fax: (203) 775-1157; Email: foundation@4spe.org
Web: www.4spe.org/foundation/scholarships.php

**Summary:** To provide college scholarships to students who have a career interest in the plastics industry and experience in the thermoforming industry.

**Eligibility:** Open to full-time undergraduate and graduate students at either a 4-year college or in a 2-year technical program. Applicants must have experience in the thermoforming industry, such as courses taken, research conducted, or jobs held. They must 1) have a demonstrated or expressed interest in the plastics industry; 2) be majoring in or taking courses that would be beneficial to a career in the plastics or polymer industry (e.g., plastics engineering, polymer sciences, chemistry, physics, chemical engineering, mechanical engineering, or industrial engineering); 3) be in good academic standing at their school; and 4) be able to document financial need. Along with their application, they must submit 3 letters of recommendation; a high school and/or college transcript; a 1- to 2-page statement telling why they are interested in the scholarship, their qualifications, and their educational and career goals in the plastics industry; and a statement detailing their exposure to the thermoforming industry.

**Financial data:** The stipend is $5,000 per year. Funds are paid directly to the recipient's school.

**Duration:** 1 year.

**Number awarded:** 2 each year.

**Deadline:** January of each year.

## 2761 THERMOPLASTIC MATERIALS AND FOAMS DIVISION SCHOLARSHIP

Society of Plastics Engineers
Attn: SPE Foundation
14 Fairfield Drive
Brookfield, CT 06804-0403
Phone: (203) 740-5447; Fax: (203) 775-1157; Email: foundation@4spe.org
Web: www.4spe.org/foundation/scholarships.php

**Summary:** To provide financial assistance to undergraduate students who have a career interest in the plastics industry.

**Eligibility:** Open to full-time undergraduate students at 4-year colleges or in 2-year technical programs. Applicants must 1) have a demonstrated or expressed interest in the plastics industry; 2) be majoring in a science or engineering program; 3) be in good academic standing at their school; and 4) be able to document financial need. Along with their application, they must submit 3 letters of recommendation; a high school and/or college transcript; and a 1- to 2-page statement telling why they are interested in the scholarship, their qualifications, and their educational and career goals in the plastics industry.

**Financial data:** The stipend is $1,000 per year. Funds are paid directly to the recipient's school.

**Duration:** 1 year.

**Number awarded:** 1 each year.

**Deadline:** January of each year.

## 2762 THERMOSET DIVISION/JAMES I. MACKENZIE SCHOLARSHIP

Society of Plastics Engineers
Attn: SPE Foundation
14 Fairfield Drive
Brookfield, CT 06804-0403
Phone: (203) 740-5447; Fax: (203) 775-1157; Email: foundation@4spe.org
Web: www.4spe.org/foundation/scholarships.php

**Summary:** To provide financial assistance to undergraduate and graduate students who have a career interest in the plastics industry and experience in the thermoset industry.

**Eligibility:** Open to full-time undergraduate and graduate students at either a 4-year college or in a 2-year technical program. Applicants must have experience in the thermoset industry, such as courses taken, research conducted, or jobs held. They must 1) have a demonstrated or expressed interest in the plastics industry; 2) be majoring in or taking courses that would be beneficial to a career in the plastics or polymer industry (e.g., plastics engineering, polymer sciences, chemistry, physics, chemical engineering, mechanical engineering, or industrial engineering); 3) be in good academic standing at their school; and 4) be able to document financial need. Along with their application, they must submit 3 letters of recommendation; a high school and/or college transcript; a 1- to 2-page statement telling why they are interested in the scholarship, their qualifications, and their educational and career goals in the plastics industry; and a statement detailing their exposure to the thermoset industry.

**Financial data:** The stipend is $1,000 per year. Funds are paid directly to the recipient's school.

**Duration:** 1 year.

**Number awarded:** 2 each year: 1 to an undergraduate and 1 to a graduate student.

**Deadline:** January of each year.

### 2763 THOMAS E. DESJARDINS MEMORIAL SCHOLARSHIP

Institute of Transportation Engineers-New England Section
c/o Rod Emery, Scholarship Committee
Edwards and Kelcey Engineers
529 Main Street, Suite 203
Charlestown, MA 02129-1114
Phone: (617) 242-9222; Fax: (617) 242-9824; Email: remery@ekmail.com
Web: www.neite.org/scholar.shtml

**Summary:** To provide financial assistance to engineering undergraduate and graduate students at colleges and universities in New England.

**Eligibility:** Open to undergraduate and graduate students in engineering, especially those who demonstrate a strong commitment to transportation engineering in the course work and outside activities. Applicants may be residents of any state, but they must be attending an accredited engineering school in a New England state. Selection is based on moral character, academic achievement, participation in extracurricular activities, and financial need.

**Financial data:** A stipend is awarded (amount not specified).

**Duration:** 1 year; nonrenewable.

**Number awarded:** 2 each year: 1 to an undergraduate and 1 to a graduate student.

**Deadline:** July of each year.

### 2764 THOMAS PRATTE MEMORIAL SCHOLARSHIPS

Surfrider Foundation
Attn: Pratte Scholarship
P.O. Box 6010
San Clemente, CA 92674-6010
Phone: (949) 492-8170; Fax: (949) 492-8142;
Email: prattescholarship@surfrider.org
Web: www.surfrider.org

**Summary:** To provide financial assistance to members of the Surfrider Foundation working on an undergraduate or graduate degree in an environmental field.

**Eligibility:** Open to members of the foundation working on an undergraduate, master's, or doctoral degree in a field consistent with the foundation's mission, including (but not limited to) oceanography, marine affairs, environmental sciences, public policy, community planning, or natural resources. Applicants must be enrolled at an accredited college or university in the United States or Puerto Rico as an upper-division or graduate student. Undergraduates must have a GPA of 3.4 or higher and graduate students 3.6 or higher. Along with their application, they must submit 1) a personal statement describing their career goals, volunteer activities, work, or summer plans as they pertain to the coastal environmental issues relevant to the foundation and its mission; and 2) a description of their current research and how it relates to the foundation's stated mission and environmental programs. Financial need is not considered in the selection process.

**Financial data:** The stipend is $2,000 for an undergraduate, $3,000 for a master's degree student, and $5,000 for a doctoral student.

**Duration:** 1 year.

**Number awarded:** 3 each year: 1 for a student at each academic level.

**Deadline:** March of each year.

### 2765 THOMSON DELMAR LEARNING SURGICAL TECHNOLOGY SCHOLARSHIP

Association of Surgical Technologists
Attn: Education Department
7108-C South Alton Way
Englewood, CO 80112-2106
Phone: (303) 694-9130; Fax: (303) 694-9169; Email: ast@ast.org
Web: www.ast.org

**Summary:** To provide financial assistance to students enrolled in a surgical technology program.

**Eligibility:** Open to students enrolled or accepted in a surgical technology program accredited by the Commission on Accreditation of Allied Health Education Programs (CAAHEP). Applicants must have a GPA of 2.5 or higher. Along with their application, they must submit a 500-word statement on their professional goals, strengths as a student, and reasons for wanting to enter the surgical technology profession. Selection is based on academic achievement and progress and on the ability to communicate clearly and effectively through writing skills. This program is sponsored by Thomson Delmar Learning.

**Financial data:** The stipend is $1,000.

**Duration:** 1 year.

**Number awarded:** 1 each year.

**Deadline:** March of each year.

### 2766 THRUST EQUINE INDUSTRY/JOURNALISM/ COMMUNICATIONS SCHOLARSHIP

**Summary:** To provide financial assistance to residents of Washington who are studying a field related to the equine industry, journalism, or communications in college.

*See Listing #1703.*

### 2767 TIMOTHY BIGELOW AND PALMER W. BIGELOW, JR. SCHOLARSHIPS

**Summary:** To provide financial support to residents of New England interested in working on an undergraduate or graduate degree in landscape architecture or horticulture.

*See Listing #1705.*

### 2768 TIMOTHY J. O'LEARY SCHOLARSHIPS

American Public Works Association-New England Chapter
Attn: Secretary-Treasurer
404 Woodland Road
Storrs, CT 06268
Phone: (860) 429-3332; Fax: (860) 429-6863;
Email: NECAPWA@MansfieldCT.org
Web: newengland.apwa.net

**Summary:** To provide financial assistance to undergraduate and graduate students from New England interested in preparing for a career in the public works profession.

**Eligibility:** Open to students working on or planning to work on an undergraduate or graduate degree in a public works or related field of study. Applicants are not required to be members of the American Public Works Association (APWA), but they must be sponsored by a member of the New England APWA chapter and committed to a career in the public works profession. U.S. citizenship is required.

**Financial data:** The stipend for full-time students is $1,100 per semester ($2,200 per year). Stipends for part-time students are pro-rated appropriately.

**Duration:** 1 year.

**Number awarded:** 2 each year.

**Deadline:** April of each year.

### 2769 TMS MATERIALS SCIENCE AND ENGINEERING UNDERGRADUATE STUDENT DESIGN COMPETITION

The Minerals, Metals & Materials Society
Attn: TMS Student Awards Program
184 Thorn Hill Road
Warrendale, PA 15086-7514
Phone: (724) 776-9000, ext. 220; Fax: (724) 776-3770;
Email: students@tms.org
Web: www.tms.org/Students/AwardsPrograms/OtherContests.html

**Summary:** To recognize and reward outstanding senior design projects in the fields of materials science and engineering.

**Eligibility:** Open to undergraduate students who prepare senior design projects at their university. Entries may be submitted from departments of materials science and engineering, metallurgy, metallurgical engineering, ceramic engineering, or polymer engineering, or from related departments or programs, including, but not limited to, mechanical engineering, chemical engineering, electrical engineering, physics, or chemistry. Applicants may be from any country. Student project leaders must be members of The Minerals, Metals & Materials Society (TMS) and all design project participants are encouraged to be members. Each institution may submit only 1 entry. Selection is based on demonstration and application of materials science knowledge (20 points); adequate research, experimentation, and simulation (25 points); design decision (25 points); communication (20 points); and consideration of broader issues (10 points).

**Financial data:** The award is $1,000 in cash plus $500 in travel expenses to attend the award ceremony.

**Duration:** The competition is held annually.

**Number awarded:** 1 each year.

**Deadline:** June of each year.

## 2770 TNLA SCHOLARSHIP PROGRAM

Texas Nursery and Landscape Association
Attn: Education and Research Foundation
7730 South IH-35
Austin, TX 78745-6698
Phone: (512) 280-5182; (800) 880-0343; Fax: (512) 280-3012;
Email: info@txnla.org
Web: www.txnla.org

**Summary:** To provide financial assistance to high school seniors and returning college students in Texas who are majoring in horticulture.

**Eligibility:** Open to Texas residents. They may be either high school seniors or returning college students, but they must be majoring or planning to major in horticulture at an approved college in Texas; currently, these include: Collin County Community College, Central Texas College, Houston Community College, Northeast Texas Community College, Palo Alto College, Richland College, Sam Houston State, Southwest Texas State University, Stephen F. Austin State University, Tarleton University, Tarrant County College, Texas A&M University, Texas State Technical College, Texas Tech University, Trinity Valley College, Tyler Junior College, Wharton County Junior College, and Western Texas College. Applicants must complete an application form and submit an official transcript, 2 letters of recommendation, a recent photograph, and a statement on why they are applying for the scholarships and their career objectives as they relate to the field of horticulture and the nursery and landscape industry.

**Financial data:** The standard award is $1,000, divided into a $500 payment per semester. Other scholarships, ranging from $500 to $2,000, are also available.

**Duration:** The standard award is for 1 year.

**Number awarded:** Varies each year.

**Deadline:** May of each year.

## 2771 TOBIN SORENSON PHYSICAL EDUCATION SCHOLARSHIP

Pi Lambda Theta
Attn: Scholarships Committee
4101 East Third Street
P.O. Box 6626
Bloomington, IN 47407-6626
Phone: (812) 339-3411; (800) 487-3411; Fax: (812) 339-3462;
Email: office@pilambda.org
Web: www.pilambda.org/benefits/awards/Scholarships/AwardsHtml.html

**Summary:** To provide financial assistance to students preparing for careers as a teacher of physical education or a related field.

**Eligibility:** Open to students preparing for careers at the K-12 level. Applicants must be interested in becoming a physical education teacher, adaptive physical education teacher, coach, recreational therapist, dance therapist, or similar professional teaching the knowledge and use of the human body. They must be sophomores or above and have a GPA of 3.5 or higher. Selection is based on academic achievement, potential for leadership, and extracurricular involvement in physical/sports education, recreation therapy, or similar activities (e.g., coaching, tutoring, volunteer work for appropriate organizations on or off campus). This program was established in 1999. If the recipient is not already a member of Pi Lambda Theta (an international honor and professional association in education), a complimentary 1 year honorary membership is also awarded.

**Financial data:** The stipend is $1,000.

**Duration:** 1 year.

**Number awarded:** 1 every other year.

**Deadline:** February of each odd-numbered year.

## 2772 TOWNSEND SCHOLARSHIP

Connecticut Nurses' Foundation
Attn: Scholarship Committee
377 Research Parkway, Suite 2D

---

Meriden, CT 06450-7160
Phone: (203) 238-1207; Fax: (203) 238-3437; Email: Amy@ctnurses.org
Web: www.ctnurses.org

**Summary:** To provide financial assistance to Connecticut residents interested in working on an undergraduate or graduate degree in nursing.

**Eligibility:** Open to residents of Connecticut who are entering or enrolled at an accredited school of nursing to work on an associate, bachelor's, master's, or doctoral degree. Selection is based on employment experience; professional, community, and student activities, a statement of professional goals, and financial need.

**Financial data:** The stipend depends on the qualifications of the recipient and the availability of funds.

**Duration:** 1 year.

**Number awarded:** 1 or more each year.

**Deadline:** June of each year.

## 2773 TRANSIT HALL OF FAME SCHOLARSHIP AWARDS

American Public Transportation Association
Attn: American Public Transportation Foundation
1666 K Street, N.W., Suite 1100
Washington, DC 20006
Phone: (202) 496-4803; Fax: (202) 496-4321; Email: pboswell@apta.com
Web: www.apta.com/services/human_resources/program_guidelines.cfm

**Summary:** To provide financial assistance to undergraduate and graduate students who are preparing for a career in transportation.

**Eligibility:** Open to college sophomores, juniors, seniors, and graduate students who are preparing for a career in the transit industry. Any member organization of the American Public Transportation Association (APTA) can nominate and sponsor candidates for this scholarship. Nominees must be enrolled in a fully-accredited institution, have and maintain at least a 3.0 GPA, and be either employed by or demonstrate a strong interest in entering the public transportation industry. They must submit a 1,000-word essay on "In what segment of the public transportation industry will you make a career and why?" Selection is based on demonstrated interest in the transit field as a career, need for financial assistance, academic achievement, essay content and quality, and involvement in extracurricular citizenship and leadership activities. This program was established in 1987. There is an internship component, which is designed to provide substantive training and professional development opportunities. Each year, there are 4 named scholarships offered: the Jack R. Gilstrap Scholarship for the applicant who receives the highest overall score; the Parsons Brickerhoff-Jim Lammie Scholarship for an applicant dedicated to a public transportation engineering career; the Louis T. Klauder Scholarship for an applicant dedicated to a career in the rail transit industry as an electrical or mechanical engineer; and the Dan M. Reichard, Jr. Scholarship for an applicant dedicated to a career in the business administration/management area of the transit industry. In addition, the Donald C. Hyde Memorial Essay Award is presented to the applicant who submits the best response to the required essay component of the program.

**Financial data:** The stipend is at least $2,500. The winner of the Donald C. Hyde Memorial Essay Award receives an additional $500.

**Duration:** 1 year; may be renewed.

**Number awarded:** At least 6 each year.

**Deadline:** June of each year.

## 2774 TRANSPORTATION ENGINEERING SCHOLARSHIP PROGRAM

Virginia Transportation Construction Alliance
Attn: Stephanie Rusnak
620 Moorefield Park Drive, Suite 120
Richmond, VA 23236-3692
Phone: (804) 330-3312; Fax: (804) 330-3850; Email: stephanie@vtca.org
Web: www.vtca.org

**Summary:** To provide financial assistance to students majoring in transportation engineering in Virginia.

**Eligibility:** Open to students enrolled as freshmen, sophomores, or juniors at 4-year colleges and universities in Virginia. Applicants must be working on a degree in transportation engineering and have a GPA of 2.0 or higher. Preference is given to dependents of employees of the Virginia Department of Transportation and member firms of the Virginia Transportation Construction Alliance (VTCA). U.S. citizenship is required. Selection is based on academic performance, employment experience, extracurricular and leadership activities, and interest in the transportation industries. Financial need is not considered.

**Financial data:** The stipend is $1,500.
**Duration:** 1 year; recipients may reapply.
**Number awarded:** 1 each year.
**Deadline:** May of each year.

## 2775 TRANSPORTATION FELLOWSHIP PROGRAM

North Central Texas Council of Governments
Attn: Transportation Department
616 Six Flags Drive, Centerpoint Two
P.O. Box 5888
Arlington, TX 76005-5888
Phone: (817) 695-9242; Fax: (817) 640-7806
Web: www.nctcog.org/trans/admin/fellowship
**Summary:** To provide financial assistance to ethnic minorities, women, and economically disadvantaged persons who are interested in obtaining an undergraduate or graduate degree and work experience in a transportation-related field in Texas.
**Eligibility:** Open to ethnic minorities (African Americans, Hispanics, American Indians, Alaskan Natives, Asians, and Pacific Islanders), women, and those who are economically disadvantaged. Only U.S. citizens or permanent residents may apply. They must attend or be willing to attend a college or university within the 16-county North Central Texas region as an undergraduate or graduate student. Applicants must have a GPA of 2.5 or higher. They may be enrolled full or part time, but they must be majoring in a designated transportation-related field: transportation planning, transportation or civil engineering, urban and regional planning, transportation/environmental sciences, transportation law, urban or spatial geography, logistics, geographic information systems, or transportation management. Selection is based on financial need, interest in a professional career in transportation, and the ability to complete the program.
**Financial data:** The stipend is $2,000.
**Duration:** 1 year; may be renewed if the recipient maintains a GPA of 3.0 or higher.
**Deadline:** March of each year.

## 2776 TRIDENT–HDA FOUNDATION SCHOLARSHIPS

Hispanic Dental Association
Attn: HDA Foundation
188 West Randolph Street, Suite 415
Chicago, IL 60601
Phone: (312) 577-4013; (800) 852-7921; Fax: (312) 577-0052;
Email: HispanicDental@hdassoc.org
Web: www.hdassoc.org
**Summary:** To provide financial assistance to Hispanic students interested in preparing for a career in a dental profession.
**Eligibility:** Open to Hispanics who are entering or enrolled in an accredited dental or dental hygiene program. Applicants must have a GPA of 3.0 or higher. Along with their application, they must submit an essay on their career goals. Selection is based on scholastic achievement, community service, leadership skill, and commitment to improving health in the Hispanic community.
**Financial data:** The stipend is $1,500.
**Duration:** 1 year.
**Number awarded:** 1 or more each year.
**Deadline:** June of each year for dental students; July of each year for dental hygiene students.

## 2777 TRUMAN D. PICARD SCHOLARSHIP PROGRAM

Intertribal Timber Council
Attn: Education Committee
1112 N.E. 21st Avenue
Portland, OR 97232-2114
Phone: (503) 282-4296; Fax: (503) 282-1274; Email: itc1@teleport.com
Web: www.itcnet.org/picard.html
**Summary:** To provide financial assistance to American Indians or Alaskan Natives who are interested in studying natural resources in college.
**Eligibility:** Open to 1) graduating high school seniors or 2) currently-enrolled college students. They must be enrolled in a federally-recognized tribe or Native Alaska corporation. All applicants must be either majoring or planning to major in natural resources. They must provide documentation of their interest in natural resources; commitment to education, community, and culture; academic merit; and financial need.

**Financial data:** The stipend is $1,200 for high school seniors entering college or $1,800 for students already enrolled in college.
**Duration:** 1 year.
**Number awarded:** Varies each year. Recently, 14 of these scholarships were awarded: 4 for high school seniors and 10 for college students.
**Deadline:** March of each year.

## 2778 TTA FOUNDATION SCHOLARSHIP

Texas Telephone Association Foundation
Attn: Scholarship Committee
502 East 11th Street, Suite 400
Austin, TX 78701
Phone: (512) 472-1183; (512) 472-1293; Email: xinao@aams-texas.com
Web: www.tta.org
**Summary:** To provide financial assistance to high school seniors in Texas who are interested in majoring in fields of study related to telecommunications.
**Eligibility:** Open to high school seniors in Texas who are U.S. citizens, have at least a 3.0 GPA, and will be attending a community college or university in the state. Special consideration is given to students who are planning to major in a field of particular interest to the telecommunications industry: mathematics, business, engineering, or computer sciences. Semifinalists are selected on the basis of career interests, extracurricular activities, demonstrated leadership, and financial need. They are asked to submit an essay; finalists are selected from that group.
**Financial data:** The stipend is $1,000.
**Duration:** 1 year.
**Number awarded:** 10 each year.
**Deadline:** March of each year.

## 2779 TWEEDALE SCHOLARSHIPS

U.S. Navy
Attn: Chief of Naval Education and Training
Code N79A2
250 Dallas Street
Pensacola, FL 32508-5220
Phone: (850) 452-4941, ext. 29381; (800) NAV-ROTC, ext. 29381; Fax: (850) 452-2486; Email: PNSC_NROTC.scholarship@navy.mil
Web: www.nrotc.navy.mil/scholarships.cfm
**Summary:** To provide financial assistance to currently-enrolled college students who are interested in joining Navy ROTC and majoring in a technical field in college.
**Eligibility:** Open to students who have completed at least one but not more than 4 academic terms with a cumulative GPA that places them above their peer mean or 3.0, whichever is higher, and a grade of C or better in all classes attempted. They must have a strong mathematics and science background in high school (with a grade of B or higher in calculus, if taken) and completed at least one academic term of college-level mathematics or science. They must be majoring in specified technical fields. Students must be interviewed by the Professor of Naval Science (PNS) at their college or university and must comply with standards of leadership potential and military/physical fitness. They must submit a plan indicating that they will complete the introductory naval science course as soon as possible and be able to complete all naval science requirements and graduate on time with their class.
**Financial data:** These scholarships provide payment of full tuition and required educational fees, as well as a specified amount for textbooks, supplies, and equipment. The program also provides a stipend for 10 months of the year that is $300 per month as a sophomore, $350 per month as a junior, and $400 per month as a senior.
**Duration:** 2 or 3 years, until the recipient completes the bachelor's degree.
**Number awarded:** Approximately 140 each year: 2 at each college and university with a Navy ROTC unit.
**Deadline:** March of each year.

## 2780 TWEET COLEMAN AVIATION SCHOLARSHIP

American Association of University Women-Honolulu Branch
Attn: Scholarship Committee
1802 Keeaumoku Street
Honolulu, HI 96822
Phone: (808) 537-4702; Fax: (808) 537-4702*51; Email: aauwhnb@att.net
**Summary:** To provide financial assistance to women in Hawaii who are interested in a career in aviation.
**Eligibility:** Open to women who are residents of Hawaii and either college

graduates or attending an accredited college in the state. Applicants must be able to pass a First Class FAA medical examination. As part of their application, they must include a 2-page statement on "Why I Want to be a Pilot." Selection is based on the merit of the applicant and a personal interview.

**Financial data:** The amount awarded varies.

**Duration:** 1 year.

**Number awarded:** Varies; at least 1 each year.

**Deadline:** September of each year.

### 2781 TYLENOL SCHOLARSHIPS

McNeil Consumer and Specialty Pharmaceuticals
c/o Scholarship America
Attn: Scholarship Management Services
One Scholarship Way
P.O. Box 297
St. Peter, MN 56082
Phone: (507) 931-0479; (800) 537-4180; Fax: (507) 931-9168;
Email: margjohnson@csfa.org
Web: www.tylenolscholarship.com

**Summary:** To provide financial assistance for college to students intending to prepare for a career in a health-related field.

**Eligibility:** Open to students who will be enrolled in an undergraduate or graduate course of study at an accredited 2-year or 4-year college, university, or vocational/technical school and have 1 or more years of school remaining. Applicants must intend to major in an area that will lead to a career in a health-related field. Selection is based on the number, length of commitment, and quality of leadership responsibilities in community activities and school activities, awards, and honors (40%), a clear statement of education and career goals (10%), and academic record (50%).

**Financial data:** Stipends are $10,000 or $1,000.

**Duration:** 1 year.

**Number awarded:** 160 each year: 10 at $10,000 and 150 at $1,000.

**Deadline:** April of each year

### 2782 UAA JANICE K. BARDEN AVIATION SCHOLARSHIPS

National Business Aviation Association, Inc.
Attn: Director of Operations
1200 18th Street, N.W., Suite 400
Washington, DC 20036-2527
Phone: (202) 783-9353; Fax: (202) 331-8364; Email: jevans@nbaa.org
Web: www.nbaa.org/public/education.scholarships/barden

**Summary:** To provide financial assistance to undergraduates majoring in aviation.

**Eligibility:** Open to U.S. citizens at the sophomore, junior, or senior level in an aviation-related program of study at an institution belonging to the National Business Aviation Association (NBAA) and the University Aviation Association (UAA). Applicants must have at least a 3.0 GPA. Along with their application they must submit an official transcript, a 250-word essay on their interest in and goals for a career in the business aviation industry, a letter of recommendation from a member of the aviation department faculty, and a resume.

**Financial data:** The stipend is $1,000. Checks are made payable to the recipient's institution.

**Duration:** 1 year.

**Number awarded:** 5 each year.

**Deadline:** November of each year.

### 2783 UNCF/MERCK UNDERGRADUATE SCIENCE RESEARCH SCHOLARSHIPS

United Negro College Fund
Attn: Merck Science Initiative
8260 Willow Oaks Corporate Drive, Suite 110
P.O. Box 10444
Fairfax, VA 22031-4511
Phone: (703) 205-3503; Fax: (703) 205-3574; Email: uncfmerck@uncf.org
Web: www.uncf.org/merck

**Summary:** To provide financial assistance and summer work experience to African American undergraduates who are interested in preparing for a career in biomedical research.

**Eligibility:** Open to African American students currently enrolled as full-time juniors and planning to graduate in the coming year. Applicants must be majoring in a life or physical science, have completed 2 semesters of organic

chemistry, be interested in biomedical research, and have a GPA of 3.3 or higher. They must be interested in working at Merck as a summer intern. Candidates for professional (Pharm.D., D.V.M., D.D.S., etc.) and engineering degrees are ineligible. U.S. citizenship or permanent resident status is required. Selection is based on GPA, demonstrated interest in a scientific education and a career in scientific research, and ability to perform in a laboratory environment.

**Financial data:** The total award is $35,000, including up to $25,000 for tuition, fees, room, and board, and at least $10,000 for 2 summer internship stipends. In addition, the department of the award recipient may receive a grant of up to $10,000.

**Duration:** 1 academic year plus internships of 10 to 12 weeks during the preceding and following summers.

**Number awarded:** At least 15 each year.

**Deadline:** December of each year.

### 2784 UNITED AGRIBUSINESS LEAGUE SCHOLARSHIP PROGRAM

United Agribusiness League
Attn: Member Services
54 Corporate Park
Irvine, CA 92606-5105
Phone: (949) 975-1424; (800) 223-4590; Fax: (949) 975-1671;
Email: info@ual.org
Web: www.ual.org

**Summary:** To provide financial assistance to students working on an undergraduate degree in agriculture or agribusiness.

**Eligibility:** Open to students presently enrolled or accepted for enrollment at an accredited college or university offering a degree in agriculture. Applicants must be residents of the United States, Canada, or Mexico. They must submit a 2-page essay on a topic that varies annually but relates to agriculture and 3 letters of recommendation (1 each from a teacher, an employer, and a volunteer organization with which they have been associated). A minimum 2.5 GPA is required. Financial need is considered only if the applicant requests it.

**Financial data:** Stipends range from $1,000 to $5,000.

**Duration:** 1 year; may be renewed.

**Number awarded:** Varies each year. Recently, 12 of these scholarships were awarded: 1 at $5,000, 2 at $4,000, 3 at $3,000, 2 at $2,000, and 4 at $1,000.

**Deadline:** March of each year.

### 2785 UNITED PARCEL SERVICE SCHOLARSHIP FOR FEMALE STUDENTS

Institute of Industrial Engineers
Attn: Chapter Operations Department
3577 Parkway Lane, Suite 200
Norcross, GA 30092
Phone: (770) 449-0461, ext. 118; (800) 494-0460; Fax: (770) 263-8532;
Email: srichards@iienet.org
Web: www.iienet.org

**Summary:** To provide financial assistance to female undergraduates who are studying industrial engineering at a school in the U.S., Canada, or Mexico.

**Eligibility:** Open to female undergraduate students enrolled at any school in the United States and its territories, Canada, or Mexico, provided the school's engineering program is accredited by an agency recognized by the Institute of Industrial Engineers (IIE) and the student is pursuing a full-time course of study in industrial engineering with a GPA of at least 3.4. Students must be nominated. Nominees must have at least 5 full quarters or 3 full semesters remaining until graduation. Students may not apply directly for these awards; they must be nominated by the head of their industrial engineering department. Nominees must be IIE members. Selection is based on scholastic ability, character, leadership, potential service to the industrial engineering profession, and need for financial assistance. Funding for this program is provided by the UPS Foundation.

**Financial data:** The stipend is $4,000.

**Duration:** 1 year.

**Number awarded:** 1 each year.

**Deadline:** November of each year.

### 2786 UNITED PARCEL SERVICE SCHOLARSHIP FOR MINORITY STUDENTS

Institute of Industrial Engineers

Attn: Chapter Operations Department
3577 Parkway Lane, Suite 200
Norcross, GA 30092
Phone: (770) 449-0461, ext. 118; (800) 494-0460; Fax: (770) 263-8532;
Email: srichards@iienet.org
Web: www.iienet.org

**Summary:** To provide financial assistance to minority undergraduates who are studying industrial engineering at a school in the U.S., Canada, or Mexico.

**Eligibility:** Open to minority undergraduate students enrolled at any school in the United States and its territories, Canada, or Mexico, provided the school's engineering program is accredited by an agency recognized by the Institute of Industrial Engineers (IIE) and the student is pursuing a full-time course of study in industrial engineering with a GPA of at least 3.4. Students must be nominated. Nominees must have at least 5 full quarters or 3 full semesters remaining until graduation. Students may not apply directly for these awards; they must be nominated by the head of their industrial engineering department. Nominees must be IIE members. Selection is based on scholastic ability, character, leadership, potential service to the industrial engineering profession, and need for financial assistance.

**Financial data:** The stipend is $4,000.

**Duration:** 1 year.

**Number awarded:** 1 each year.

**Deadline:** November of each year.

## 2787 UPS SCHOLARSHIPS

American Society of Safety Engineers
Attn: ASSE Foundation
1800 East Oakton Street
Des Plaines, IL 60018
Phone: (847) 768-3441; Fax: (847) 296-9220; Email: mrosario@asse.org
Web: www.asse.org

**Summary:** To provide financial assistance to undergraduate student members of the American Society of Safety Engineers (ASSE).

**Eligibility:** Open to ASSE student members who are enrolled in a 4-year degree program in occupational safety and health or a closely-related field (e.g., safety engineering, safety management, systems safety, environmental science, industrial hygiene, ergonomics, fire science). Applicants must be full-time students who have completed at least 60 semester hours with a GPA of 3.0 or higher. As part of the selection process, they must submit 2 essays of 300 words or less: 1) why they are seeking a degree in safety, a brief description of their current activities, and how those relate to their career goals and objectives; and 2) why they should be awarded this scholarship (including career goals and financial need).

**Financial data:** Stipends range from $4,000 to $6,000 per year. Funding for this program is provided by the UPS Foundation.

**Duration:** 1 year; nonrenewable.

**Number awarded:** Varies each year; recently, 4 of these scholarships at $5,250 each were awarded.

**Deadline:** November of each year.

## 2788 USDA/1890 NATIONAL SCHOLARS PROGRAM

Department of Agriculture
Recruitment and Employment Division
Attn: 1890 National Scholars Program Manager
Jamie L. Whitten Federal Building, Room 301-W
14th and Independence Avenue, S.W.
Washington, DC 20250-9600
Phone: (202) 720-6905; Email: Carl.Butler@usda.gov
Web: 1890scholars.program.usda.gov

**Summary:** To provide financial assistance to high school seniors and graduates interested in majoring in a field related to agriculture or agribusiness at 1 of the 18 Historically Black 1890 Land Grant Institutions.

**Eligibility:** Open to U.S. citizens who have or will have a high school diploma or GED certificate with a GPA of 3.0 or higher and a combined verbal/math/written score of at least 1500 on the SAT or a composite score of at least 21 on the ACT. They must be planning to attend 1 of the 18 Historically Black 1890 Land Grant Institutions and study such fields as agriculture, agricultural business/management, agricultural economics, agricultural engineering/mechanics, agricultural production and technology, agronomy or crop science, animal sciences, botany, farm and range management, fish and game management, food sciences/technology, forestry and related services, home economics, horticulture, natural resources management, nutrition, soil conservation/soil science, wildlife management, or other related disciplines. Currently-enrolled undergraduate students attending an

1890 institution are not eligible. The Historically Black Land Grant institutions are: Alabama A&M University, Alcorn State University, University of Arkansas at Pine Bluff, Delaware State University, Florida A&M University, Fort Valley State University, Kentucky State University, Lincoln University of Missouri, Langston University, University of Maryland-Eastern Shore, North Carolina A&T State University, Prairie View A&M University, South Carolina State University, Southern University and A&M College, Tennessee State University, Tuskegee University, Virginia State University, and West Virginia State University. Applications must be submitted to the Liaison Officer of the U.S. Department of Agriculture at a participating 1890 institution.

**Financial data:** Each award provides annual tuition, employment, employee benefits, use of a personal computer and software while receiving the scholarship, fees, books, and room and board. Following graduation, scholars are required to perform 1 year of service to the U.S. Department of Agriculture for each year of support received.

**Duration:** 4 years, provided the scholar maintains normal progress toward the bachelor's degree and satisfactory performance.

**Number awarded:** 36 or more each year: 2 at each of the participating universities.

**Deadline:** January of each year.

## 2789 USREY FAMILY SCHOLARSHIP

**Summary:** To provide financial support to residents of California interested in working on an undergraduate or graduate degree in landscape architecture or horticulture.

*See Listing #1714.*

## 2790 UTAH NURSES FOUNDATION GRANT-IN-AID SCHOLARSHIPS

Utah Nurses Association
Attn: Utah Nurses Foundation
4505 South Wasatch Boulevard, Suite 290
Salt Lake City, UT 84124
Phone: (801) 272-4510; (800) 236-1617; Fax: (801) 293-8458;
Email: una@xmission.com
Web: www.utahnurses.org/groups/UNF/application.htm

**Summary:** To provide financial assistance to Utah residents who are interested in working on a nursing degree.

**Eligibility:** Open to Utah residents (must be U.S. citizens) who have been accepted into an accredited registered nursing program (undergraduate or graduate). Applicants must submit 3 letters of recommendation, demonstration of their financial need, current official transcripts (with a GPA of 3.0 or higher), a letter from the school verifying their acceptance in the nursing program, and a narrative statement describing their anticipated role in nursing in Utah upon completion of the nursing program. Preference is given to applicants engaged in full-time study. Selection is based on the following priorities: 1) R.N.s pursuing a B.S.N.; 2) graduate and postgraduate nursing students; 3) students in formal nursing programs (advanced practice nurses); and 4) undergraduate nursing students. Recipients must agree to work for a Utah health care facility or Utah educational institution as a full-time employee for at least 1 year (2 years if part time). They must also agree to join the Utah Nurses Association within 6 months of graduation.

**Financial data:** A stipend is awarded (amount not specified). Funds may be used only for tuition and books.

**Duration:** 1 year; recipients may reapply.

**Deadline:** March of each year.

## 2791 UTAH SOCIETY OF PROFESSIONAL ENGINEERS SCHOLARSHIP

Utah Society of Professional Engineers
Attn: Dan Church, Scholarship Chair
488 East Winchester Street, Suite 400
Murray, UT 84107
Phone: (801) 288-3224; Email: churchd@pbworld.com
Web: www.uspeonline.com

**Summary:** To provide financial assistance to high school seniors in Utah interested in studying engineering at a college or university in the state.

**Eligibility:** Open to seniors at high schools in Utah who have a cumulative GPA of 3.5 or higher and ACT scores of at least 30 in mathematics and 26 in English. Applicants must be U.S. citizens interested in attending a college or university in Utah that has been accredited by the Engineering Accreditation Commission of the Accreditation Board for Engineering and Technology (ABET-EAC).

Along with their application they must submit an essay of 850 to 1,000 words on their interest in engineering. Selection is based on the essay (20 points), GPA (20 points), recommendations from at least 2 teachers (10 points), a resume (20 points), composite application (10 points), and ACT scores (20 points).

**Financial data:** The stipend is $1,000.

**Duration:** 1 year.

**Number awarded:** 1 or more each year.

**Deadline:** March of each year.

## 2792 VARIAN RADIATION THERAPY SCHOLARSHIPS

American Society of Radiologic Technologists
Attn: ASRT Education and Research Foundation
15000 Central Avenue, S.E.
Albuquerque, NM 87123-3917
Phone: (505) 298-4500; (800) 444-2778, ext. 2541; Fax: (505) 298-5063;
Email: foundation@asrt.org
Web: www.asrt.org

**Summary:** To provide financial assistance to students enrolled in entry-level radiation therapy programs.

**Eligibility:** Open to U.S. citizens, nationals, and permanent residents who are enrolled in an entry-level radiation therapy program. Applicants must have a GPA in radiologic sciences core courses of 3.0 or higher and be able to demonstrate financial need. They may not have a previous degree or certificate in radiation therapy. Along with their application, they must submit an essay of 450 to 500 words on their reason for entering the radiologic sciences, career goals, and financial need.

**Financial data:** The stipend is $5,000.

**Duration:** 1 year; may be renewed for 1 additional year.

**Number awarded:** Varies each year; recently, 11 of these scholarships were awarded.

**Deadline:** January of each year.

## 2793 VELMA BERNECKER GWINN GARDEN CLUB OBJECTIVES SCHOLARSHIP

**Summary:** To provide financial aid to Florida undergraduates and graduate students majoring in designated areas related to gardening.

*See Listing #1715.*

## 2794 VERITAS DGC SCHOLARSHIP

Society of Exploration Geophysicists
Attn: SEG Foundation
8801 South Yale, Suite 500
P.O. Box 702740
Tulsa, OK 74170-2740
Phone: (918) 497-5513; Fax: (918) 497-5557; Email: scholarships@seg.org
Web: seg.org/business/foundation/scholarships/index.shtml

**Summary:** To provide financial assistance to undergraduate and graduate students who are interested in the field of applied geophysics.

**Eligibility:** Open to 1) high school students planning to enter college in the fall, and 2) undergraduate or graduate students whose grades are above average. Applicants must intend to work on a degree directed toward a career in applied geophysics. Along with their application, they must submit a 150-word essay on how they plan to use geophysics in their future. Financial need is not considered in the selection process.

**Financial data:** The stipend ranges from $1,000 to $3,000 per year.

**Duration:** 1 academic year; may be renewable, based on scholastic standing, availability of funds, and continuance of a course of study leading to a career in applied geophysics.

**Number awarded:** 1 each year.

**Deadline:** January of each year.

## 2795 VERIZON WORKFORCE RESPONSE SCHOLARSHIPS

Independent Colleges of Washington
600 Stewart Street, Suite 600
Seattle, WA 98101
Phone: (206) 623-4494; Fax: (206) 625-9621; Email: info@icwashington.org
Web: www.icwashington.org/parents_students/financial_aid/index.htm

**Summary:** To provide financial assistance to minority students preparing for a career in teaching or nursing at colleges and universities that are members of Independent Colleges of Washington (ICW). The ICW-member institutions

are Gonzaga University, Heritage College, Pacific Lutheran University, Saint Martin's College, Seattle Pacific University, Seattle University, University of Puget Sound, Walla Walla College, Whitman College, and Whitworth College.

**Number awarded:** 4 each year.

**Eligibility:** Open to students completing their junior year at ICW-member colleges and universities. Applicants must be members of underserved or minority populations. They must be majoring in education or nursing. Along with their application, they must submit a 1-page essay on why they chose to prepare for a career in teaching and/or nursing. Preference is given to community college graduates. Financial need is considered in the selection process.

**Financial data:** The stipend is $2,500.

**Duration:** 1 year; nonrenewable.

**Deadline:** October of each year.

## 2796 VERMONT DENTAL HYGIENE SCHOLARSHIP

Vermont Student Assistance Corporation
Champlain Mill
Attn: Scholarship Programs
P.O. Box 2000
Winooski, VT 05404-2601
Phone: (802) 654-3798; (888) 253-4819; Fax: (802) 654-3765; TDD: (802) 654-3766; TDD: (800) 281-3341 (within VT); Email: info@vsac.org
Web: www.vsac.org

**Summary:** To provide financial assistance to Vermont residents who are studying dental hygiene.

**Eligibility:** Open to residents of Vermont who are currently enrolled in the second year of a dental hygiene program. Selection is based on academic achievement (GPA of 3.0 or higher), letters of recommendation, required essays, and financial need.

**Financial data:** The maximum stipend is $1,000.

**Duration:** 1 year; nonrenewable.

**Number awarded:** 1 or more each year.

**Deadline:** May of each year.

## 2797 VERMONT FEED DEALERS AND MANUFACTURERS ASSOCIATION SCHOLARSHIP

Vermont Student Assistance Corporation
Champlain Mill
Attn: Scholarship Programs
P.O. Box 2000
Winooski, VT 05404-2601
Phone: (802) 654-3798; (888) 253-4819; Fax: (802) 654-3765; TDD: (802) 654-3766; TDD: (800) 281-3341 (within VT); Email: info@vsac.org
Web: www.vsac.org

**Summary:** To provide financial assistance to residents of Vermont who are interested in majoring in an agriculture-related field in college.

**Eligibility:** Open to high school seniors, high school graduates, and currently-enrolled college students in Vermont who are enrolled or planning to enroll in a postsecondary degree program in agriculture, including but not limited to animal sciences, equine studies, agribusiness, plant and soil science, forestry, horticulture, and veterinary medicine or technology. Selection is based on a letter of recommendation and required essays.

**Financial data:** The maximum stipend is $3,000.

**Duration:** 1 year; recipients may reapply.

**Number awarded:** Varies each year; recently, 6 of these were awarded.

**Deadline:** June of each year.

## 2798 VERMONT HEALTHCARE HUMAN RESOURCES ASSOCIATION SCHOLARSHIP

Vermont Student Assistance Corporation
Champlain Mill
Attn: Scholarship Programs
P.O. Box 2000
Winooski, VT 05404-2601
Phone: (802) 654-3798; (888) 253-4819; Fax: (802) 654-3765; TDD: (802) 654-3766; TDD: (800) 281-3341 (within VT); Email: info@vsac.org
Web: www.vsac.org

**Summary:** To provide financial assistance to adults in Vermont who are interested in majoring in a health-related field or human resources in college.

**Eligibility:** Open to nontraditional-aged students who reside in Vermont and have been accepted to attend an accredited postsecondary school to work on a degree in a health care field and/or human resources. Applicants must intend to work in Vermont for at least one year. Selection is based on commitment to employment in Vermont, financial need, a letter of recommendation, an essay, and a resume. Applications are reviewed and selection is made by the Vermont Healthcare Human Resources Association (formerly the Vermont Hospital Personnel Association) in association with the Vermont Student Assistance Corporation.

**Financial data:** The stipend is $1,000.

**Duration:** 1 year.

**Number awarded:** 1 or 2 each year.

**Deadline:** April of each year.

## 2799 VERTICAL FLIGHT FOUNDATION ENGINEERING SCHOLARSHIPS

Vertical Flight Foundation
Attn: Scholarship Coordinator
217 North Washington Street
Alexandria, VA 22314-2538
Phone: (703) 684-6777; Fax: (703) 739-9279; Email: Staff@vtol.org
Web: www.vtol.org/vff.html

**Summary:** To provide financial assistance to undergraduate and graduate students interested in preparing for a career in rotorcraft and vertical-takeoff-and-landing (VTOL) aircraft engineering.

**Eligibility:** Open to full-time students in the final 2 years of undergraduate study or the first year of graduate study at an accredited school of engineering. They need not be a member or relative of a member of the American Helicopter Society. Along with their application, they must submit a narrative that covers their past and future academic interests, future career interest in the rotorcraft or VTOL engineering field, past work or research experience related to rotorcraft or VTOL aircraft, and other reasons for consideration. Selection is based on academic record, letters of recommendation, and career plans.

**Financial data:** Stipends range from $2,000 to $4,000 per year, depending on the availability of funds.

**Duration:** 1 year; undergraduates may apply for renewal as a graduate student.

**Number awarded:** 5 to 8 each year.

**Deadline:** January of each year.

## 2800 VETERANS OF ENDURING FREEDOM-AFGHANISTAN AND IRAQI FREEDOM COMBAT OPERATIONS SCHOLARSHIP

Armed Forces Communications and Electronics Association
Attn: AFCEA Educational Foundation
4400 Fair Lakes Court
Fairfax, VA 22033-3899
Phone: (703) 631-6149; (800) 336-4583, ext. 6149; Fax: (703) 631-4693;
Email: scholarship@afcea.org
Web: www.afcea.org/education/scholarships/undergraduate/veteran.asp

**Summary:** To provide financial assistance to veterans and military personnel who served in Afghanistan or Iraq and are working on an undergraduate degree in fields related to the support of U.S. intelligence enterprises.

**Eligibility:** Open to active-duty and honorably discharged U.S. military veterans, Reservists, and National Guard personnel who served in combat operations of Enduring Freedom-Afghanistan or Iraqi Freedom. Applicants must be enrolled at a 2- or 4-year institution in the United States and working on an undergraduate degree in computer engineering technology, computer information systems, electronics engineering technology, engineering (aerospace, computer, electrical, or systems), mathematics, physics, or computer science. Along with their application, they must submit an essay that includes a brief synopsis of relevant work experience (including military assignments), a brief statement of career goals after graduation, and a explanation of how their academic and career goals will contribute to the areas related to communications, intelligence and/or information systems, and the mission of the Armed Forces Communications and Electronics Association (AFCEA). Financial need is also considered in the selection process.

**Financial data:** The stipend is $2,000.

**Duration:** 1 year.

**Number awarded:** 1 or more each year.

**Deadline:** October of each year.

## 2801 VINYL PLASTICS DIVISION SCHOLARSHIP

Society of Plastics Engineers
Attn: SPE Foundation
14 Fairfield Drive
Brookfield, CT 06804-0403
Phone: (203) 740-5447; Fax: (203) 775-1157; Email: foundation@4spe.org
Web: www.4spe.org/foundation/scholarships.php

**Summary:** To provide financial assistance to undergraduate students who have a career interest in the plastics industry.

**Eligibility:** Open to full-time undergraduate students at 4-year colleges or in 2-year technical programs. Applicants must 1) have a demonstrated or expressed interest in the plastics industry; 2) be majoring in or taking courses that would be beneficial to a career in the plastics or polymer industry (e.g., plastics engineering, polymer sciences, chemistry, physics, chemical engineering, mechanical engineering, or industrial engineering); 3) be in good academic standing at their school; and 4) be able to document financial need. Along with their application, they must submit 3 letters of recommendation; a high school and/or college transcript; and a 1- to 2-page statement telling why they are interested in the scholarship, their qualifications, and their educational and career goals in the plastics industry. Preference is given to applicants with experience in the vinyl industry, such as courses taken, research conducted, or jobs held.

**Financial data:** The stipend is $1,000 per year. Funds are paid directly to the recipient's school.

**Duration:** 1 year.

**Number awarded:** 1 each year.

**Deadline:** January of each year.

## 2802 VIOLA M. GRIFFIN MEMORIAL SCHOLARSHIP

American Health Information Management Association
Attn: Foundation of Research and Education
233 North Michigan Avenue, Suite 2150
Chicago, IL 60601-5806
Phone: (312) 233-1168; Fax: (312) 233-1090; Email: fore@ahima.org
Web: www.ahima.org/fore/programs.cfm

**Summary:** To provide financial assistance to members of the American Health Information Management Association (AHIMA) from Colorado who are interested in working on an undergraduate or graduate degree in health information administration or technology.

**Eligibility:** Open to AHIMA members who are residents of Colorado and enrolled in a health information administration or health information technology program accredited by the Commission on Accreditation of Allied Health Education Programs. Applicants must be working on an undergraduate or graduate degree on at least a half-time basis and have a GPA of 3.0 or higher. U.S. citizenship is required. Selection is based on (in order of importance) GPA and academic achievement, volunteer and work experience, commitment to the health information management profession, suitability to the health information management profession, quality and suitability of references provided, and clarity of application.

**Financial data:** The stipend ranges from $1,000 to $5,000.

**Duration:** 1 year; nonrenewable.

**Number awarded:** 1 each year.

**Deadline:** May of each year.

## 2803 VIRGINIA ATHLETIC TRAINERS ASSOCIATION SCHOLARSHIP AWARD

Virginia Athletic Trainers Association
c/o Terry Zablocki, Scholarship Committee Chair
Maury High School
322 Shirley Avenue
Norfolk, VA 23517
Phone: (757) 628-9189d2; Email: tzablocki@nps.k12.va.us
Web: www.vata.org/scholarship/index.htm

**Summary:** To provide financial assistance to high school seniors in Virginia who are interested in preparing for a career as an athletic trainer.

**Eligibility:** Open to seniors graduating from high schools in Virginia who intend to study athletic training in college. Applicants must provide evidence of interest in athletic training through experience as a high school student athletic trainer and/or attendance at an athletic training seminar or workshop. Along with their application, they must submit an essay of 250 to 500 words on their interest in a career in the allied health profession of athletic training. Selection is based on academic ability, leadership ability, responsible citizenship, and dedication and interest in athletic training.

**Financial data:** Stipends are $1,000 or $500.
**Duration:** 1 year.
**Number awarded:** 2 each year: 1 at $1,000 and 1 at $500.
**Deadline:** March of each year.

### 2804 VIRGINIA D. HENRY SCHOLARSHIP

National Society of Professional Engineers
Attn: Education Services
1420 King Street
Alexandria, VA 22314-2794
Phone: (703) 684-2833; Fax: (703) 836-4875; Email: jiglesias@nspc.org
Web: www.nspe.org/scholarships/sc1-hs.asp
**Summary:** To provide financial assistance for college to women who are high school seniors and interested in preparing for a career in engineering.
**Eligibility:** Open to women who are high school seniors planning to study engineering in an EAC-ABET accredited college program. Applicants must have earned a GPA of 3.5 or higher and an English ACT score of 29 or higher and math ACT score of 29 or higher (or the equivalent on the SAT). They must submit an essay (up to 500 words) on their interest in engineering, their major area of study and area of specialization, and the occupation they propose to pursue after graduation. Selection is based on GPA (20 points), the essay (20 points), extracurricular activities, including work experience and volunteer activities (25 points), financial need (5 points), SAT/ACT scores (20 points), and the composite application (10 points). U.S. citizenship is required.
**Financial data:** The stipend is $1,000 per year; funds are paid directly to the institution.
**Duration:** 1 year.
**Number awarded:** 1 each year.
**Deadline:** November of each year.

### 2805 VIRGINIA DAR SCHOLARSHIPS

**Summary:** To provide financial assistance to high school seniors in Virginia who wish to study designated fields in college.
*See Listing #1724.*

### 2806 VIRGINIA LEYDA ROBERTS NURSING SCHOLARSHIP

Daughters of the American Revolution-Colorado State Society
c/o Marilyn Fishburn, State Scholarship Chair
1546 West 28th Street
Loveland, CO 80538
Email: admin@coloradodar.org
Web: www.coloradodar.org/scholarships.htm
**Summary:** To provide financial assistance to high school seniors in Colorado who are interested in studying nursing in the state.
**Eligibility:** Open to graduating high school seniors in Colorado who are 1) American citizens, 2) in the top third of their graduating class, and 3) accepted at one of the Colorado colleges offering a B.S.N.: Beth-El College of Nursing, Regis University, Colorado University at Denver, Colorado Health Sciences Center, Metro State University, University of Phoenix, University of Northern Colorado, University of Southern Colorado, or Mesa State College. Applications must include a statement of career interest and goals (up to 500 words), 2 character references, college transcripts, a letter of sponsorship from the Daughters of the American Revolution's Colorado chapter, and a list of scholastic achievements, extracurricular activities, honors, and other significant accomplishments. Selection is based on financial need and academic record.
**Financial data:** The stipend is $1,000. Funds are paid directly to the student's school.
**Duration:** 1 year; nonrenewable.
**Number awarded:** 1 each year.
**Deadline:** January of each year.

### 2807 VIRGINIA NURSING SCHOLARSHIPS

Virginia Daughters of the American Revolution
c/o Catherine Rafferty, Scholarship Chair
10101 Sanders Court
Great Falls, VA 22066-2526
Web: www.vadar.org/history.html
**Summary:** To provide financial assistance to high school seniors in Virginia who wish to study nursing in college.
**Eligibility:** Open to seniors graduating from high schools in Virginia who plan to attend a Virginia school of nursing. Along with their application, they must submit a 500-word letter giving their reasons for interest in preparing for a career in nursing, a transcript of grades, a letter of recommendation from a teacher or guidance counselor, and documentation of financial need.
**Financial data:** Stipends are $1,000 or $500.
**Duration:** 1 year.
**Number awarded:** 2 each year: 1 at $1,000 and 1 at $500.
**Deadline:** January of each year.

### 2808 VONA J. WAGNER MEMORIAL SCHOLARSHIP

National Association of Women in Construction-Metropolitan Denver Chapter 112
c/o Laruie Mullane
P.O. Box 40208
Denver, CO 80204-0204
Phone: (303) 571-5377, ext. 1319
**Summary:** To provide financial assistance to high school seniors in Colorado who are interested in preparing for a career in construction.
**Eligibility:** Open to high school seniors who have applied to or been admitted to a college, university, or trade school in Colorado. Applicants must be interested in studying field related to construction (e.g., architecture, engineering, construction management) in college and planning to work on a bachelor's degree or certificate of completion. They must have a GPA of 2.5 or higher. Financial need is considered but it not an absolute requirement.
**Financial data:** The stipend is $1,000. Money is not paid at the time of the award but only on a reimbursement basis after the recipient submits proof of enrollment at a Colorado institution and receipts for tuition, books, laboratory fees, and other school expenses; living expenses are not reimbursable.
**Duration:** 1 year; nonrenewable.
**Number awarded:** Varies; generally, 3 to 4 each year.
**Deadline:** March of each year.

### 2809 W. DAVID SMITH, JR. GRADUATE STUDENT PAPER AWARD

American Institute of Chemical Engineers
Attn: Awards Administrator
Three Park Avenue
New York, NY 10016-5991
Phone: (212) 591-7107; Fax: (212) 591-8890; Email: awards@aiche.org
Web: www.aiche.org/awards
**Summary:** To recognize and reward outstanding student papers in chemical engineering computing and systems technology.
**Eligibility:** Open to individuals who published works on the application of computing and systems technology to chemical engineering while they were working on a graduate or undergraduate degree in chemical engineering.
**Financial data:** The award consists of a plaque and $1,500.
**Duration:** This award is presented annually.
**Number awarded:** 1 each year.
**Deadline:** April of each year.

### 2810 W. REESE HARRIS AGRICULTURAL SCHOLARSHIP

Florida Federation of Garden Clubs, Inc.
Attn: Office Manager
1400 South Denning Drive
Winter Park, FL 32789-5662
Phone: (407) 647-7016; Fax: (407) 647-5479; Email: ffgc@earthlink.net
Web: www.ffgc.org/scholarships/index.html
**Summary:** To provide financial aid to Florida undergraduates and graduate students working on a degree in a field related to agriculture.
**Eligibility:** Open to Florida residents who are enrolled as full-time juniors, seniors, or graduate students in a Florida college. They must have a GPA of 3.0 or higher, be in financial need, and be enrolled in a college of agriculture to major in agronomy, horticulture, environmental science, or a related field. U.S. citizenship is required. Selection is based on academic record, commitment to career, character, and financial need.
**Financial data:** The stipend is $2,500. The funds are sent directly to the recipient's school and distributed semiannually.
**Duration:** 1 year.
**Number awarded:** 1 each year.
**Deadline:** April of each year.

## 2811 WAHPERD STUDENT SCHOLARSHIP AWARDS

**Summary:** To provide financial assistance to members of the Wisconsin Association for Health, Physical Education, Recreation and Dance (WAHPERD) who are working on a college degree.
*See Listing #1728.*

## 2812 WALMAN OPTICAL COMPANY SCHOLARSHIP

Walman Optical Company
c/o Scholarship America
Attn: Scholarship Management Services
One Scholarship Way
P.O. Box 297
St. Peter, MN 56082
Phone: (507) 931-1682; (800) 537-4180; Fax: (507) 931-9168; Email: smsinfo@csfa.org
Web: www.walman.com/scholarship.html
**Summary:** To provide financial assistance to students enrolled at designated schools and colleges of optometry.
**Eligibility:** Open to students currently enrolled in the second or third year of a full-time 4-year program leading to a Doctor of Optometry degree at a school selected by Walman Optical Company. Selection is based on academic record, demonstrated leadership and participation in school and community activities, honors, work experience, a statement of goals and aspirations, unusual personal or family circumstances, and an outside appraisal. The designated schools are University of Alabama at Birmingham, School of Optometry (Birmingham, Alabama); University of California at Berkeley, School of Optometry (Berkeley, California); Southern California College of Optometry (Fullerton, California); Nova Southeastern University, Health Professions Division, College of Optometry (Ft. Lauderdale, Florida); Illinois College of Optometry (Chicago, Illinois); Indiana University, School of Optometry (Bloomington, Indiana); New England College of Optometry (Boston, Massachusetts); Michigan College of Optometry, Ferris State University (Big Rapids, Michigan); University of Missouri at St. Louis, School of Optometry (St. Louis, Missouri); State University of New York, State College of Optometry (New York, New York); Ohio State University, College of Optometry (Columbus, Ohio); Northeastern State University, College of Optometry (Tahlequah, Oklahoma); Pacific University, College of Optometry (Forest Grove, Oregon); Pennsylvania College of Optometry (Elkins Park, Pennsylvania); Inter American University of Puerto Rico, School of Optometry (San Juan, Puerto Rico); Southern College of Optometry (Memphis, Tennessee); and University of Houston, College of Optometry (Houston, Texas).
**Financial data:** The stipend ranges from $500 to $3,000 per year, depending on the need of the recipient.
**Duration:** 1 year; nonrenewable, although recipients may reapply.
**Number awarded:** Varies each year.
**Deadline:** April of each year.

## 2813 WALT BARTRAM MEMORIAL EDUCATION AWARD

Society of Manufacturing Engineers
Attn: SME Education Foundation
One SME Drive
P.O. Box 930
Dearborn, MI 48121-0930
Phone: (313) 425-3304; (800) 733-4763, ext. 3304; Fax: (313) 425-3411;
Email: foundation@sme.org
Web: www.sme.org
**Summary:** To provide financial assistance to students from Arizona, New Mexico, and southern California who are working on a degree in manufacturing engineering or a closely-related field.
**Eligibility:** Open to graduating high seniors and currently-enrolled college and university students in Desert Pacific Region 12 (Arizona, New Mexico, and southern California) of the Society of Manufacturing Engineers (SME). Applicants must be interested in working on a degree in manufacturing engineering or a closely-related field as a full-time student. College and university applicants must be SME members. All applicants must have a GPA of 3.5 or higher for their senior year of high school.
**Financial data:** The stipend is $1,500 per year. Funds are paid to the recipient's institution.
**Duration:** 1 year.
**Number awarded:** 1 each year.
**Deadline:** January of each year.

## 2814 WALTER G. THORSELL MEMORIAL SCHOLARSHIP

American Society of Safety Engineers-Columbia-Willamette Chapter
c/o Melissa Diede, Scholarship Committee Chair
SAIF Corporation Service Center
15333 S.W. Sequoia Parkway
P.O. Box 4777
Portland, OR 97208-4777
Phone: (503) 598-5808; (800) 848-2372; Fax: (503) 968-5353;
Email: meldie@saif.com
Web: www.assecwc.org/scholarships.html
**Summary:** To provide financial assistance for college to members of the American Society of Safety Engineers (ASSE) from Washington and Oregon.
**Eligibility:** Open to residents of Washington and Oregon who have completed at least 1 term of study toward a bachelor's degree in occupational safety, health, or environmental studies. Applicants must be ASSE student members who are able to demonstrate interest and participation in ASSE and other safety activities. U.S. citizenship and a GPA of 2.75 or higher are required. Selection is based on demonstrated interested in preparing for a career in the field of occupational safety, health, and/or environmental science; a statement of interest in the field; contribution to an ASSE student section or professional chapter; and financial need (considered only if all other qualifications are equal).
**Financial data:** The stipend is $1,500.
**Duration:** 1 year.
**Number awarded:** 1 each year.
**Deadline:** April of each year.

## 2815 WALTER PORKY WHITE SCHOLARSHIP FUND

MIGIZI Communications, Inc.
3123 East Lake Street
Minneapolis, MN 55406
Phone: (612) 721-6631; Fax: (612) 721-3936
Web: migizi.org/mig/organizational/scholarships/default.html
**Summary:** To provide financial assistance to Native American students working on an undergraduate degree in natural resources or an environmental field.
**Eligibility:** Open to Native American undergraduate students enrolled at an accredited 4-year college or university. Applicants must have a GPA of 3.0 or higher and be working on a degree in environmental science, natural resource management, biology, marine biology, or a related discipline. They must also have applied to the Minnesota Indian Scholarship Program sponsored by the Minnesota State Department of Education. Along with their application, they must submit proof of tribal enrollment and/or blood quantum, transcripts, 2 letters of reference, a 250-word essay describing their involvement in the Indian community, and documentation of financial need. Special consideration is given to applicants with prior work experience in a tribal forestry or fisheries program.
**Financial data:** The stipend is $1,000.
**Duration:** 1 year; nonrenewable.
**Number awarded:** 1 each year.
**Deadline:** January of each year.

## 2816 WALTER REED SMITH SCHOLARSHIP PROGRAM

United Daughters of the Confederacy
Attn: Education Director
328 North Boulevard
Richmond, VA 23220-4057
Phone: (804) 355-1636; Fax: (804) 353-1396; Email: hqudc@rcn.com
Web: www.hqudc.org/scholarships/scholarships.html
**Summary:** To provide financial assistance to mature women who are lineal descendants of Confederate veterans and plan to major in selected fields in college.
**Eligibility:** Open to women over the age of 30 who are lineal descendants of worthy Confederates or collateral descendants and members of the Children of the Confederacy or the United Daughters of the Confederacy. Applicants must intend to study business administration, computer science, home economics, nutrition, or nursing. They must submit certified proof of the Confederate record of 1 ancestor, with the company and regiment in which he served, and must have had at least a 3.0 GPA in high school.
**Financial data:** The amount of this scholarship depends on the availability of funds.
**Duration:** 1 year; may be renewed.
**Number awarded:** 1 each year.
**Deadline:** March of each year.

## 2817 WASHINGTON DENTAL SERVICE FOUNDATION SCHOLARSHIPS

Washington Dental Service Foundation
Attn: Grant Administrator
P.O. Box 75688
Seattle, WA 98125
Phone: (206) 528-2337; (800) 572-7835, ext. 2337; Fax: (206) 528-7373;
Email: Foundation@DeltaDentalWA.com
Web: www.DeltaDentalWA.com

**Summary:** To provide financial assistance to members of underrepresented minority groups in Washington who are interested in preparing for a career as a dental hygienist, dental assistant, or laboratory technician.

**Eligibility:** Open to residents of Washington who are African or Black Americans, Native Americans, Alaskan Natives, Hispanics/Latinos, or Pacific Islanders. Applicants must be planning to enroll in an eligible program in dental hygiene, dental assisting, or laboratory technology at a community or technical college in the state. They must be able to demonstrate financial need. Along with their application, they must submit essays of 100 to 300 words on 1) why they are interested in becoming a dental professional; 2) their career goals, how they decided upon those goals, and how completion of their proposed program will help them reach those goals; 3) how they have prepared themselves academically for those chosen program of study; 4) a leadership experience they have had in school, work, athletics, family, church, community, or other area of their life; and 5) how they help or serve others in their family and/or community.

**Financial data:** Stipends range from $1,000 to $4,000 per year, depending on the need of the recipient.

**Duration:** 1 year.

**Number awarded:** 1 or more each year.

**Deadline:** September of each year.

## 2818 WASHINGTON SOCIETY OF PROFESSIONAL ENGINEERS SCHOLARSHIPS

Washington Society of Professional Engineers
P.O. Box 1206
Sumas, WA 98295-1390
Phone: (866) 296-4324; Fax: (866) 296-4324;
Email: wspe@washingtonengineer.org
Web: www.washingtonengineer.org/service_to_students.shtml

**Summary:** To provide financial assistance to high school seniors in Washington who plan to major in engineering in college.

**Eligibility:** Open to seniors graduating from high schools in Washington and planning to attend a college with an ABET-accredited engineering program. Applicants must have achieved minimum ACT scores of 29 on the mathematics and 25 on the English, or Prueba de Aptidud Academica (PAA) of 750 on the quantitative and 640 on the verbal, or equivalent SAT scores. Along with their application, they must submit an essay of 250 to 500 words on the field of engineering they plan to study in college, why that field of engineering is of interest to them, and the specific occupation they propose to enter after graduating from college. Selection is based on the essay (20%); an evaluation of the course work they have completed, especially mathematics, computer science, natural sciences, and mechanical drawing courses (40%); work experience (10%); technical activities (10%); letters of recommendation (10%); leadership (5%); and other activities (5%). U.S. citizenship is required.

**Financial data:** A stipend is awarded (amount not specified).

**Duration:** 1 year.

**Number awarded:** 1 or more each year.

**Deadline:** January of each year.

## 2819 WASHINGTON STATE NURSES FOUNDATION SCHOLARSHIPS

Washington State Nurses Association
Attn: Washington State Nurses Foundation
575 Andover Park West, Suite 101
Seattle, WA 98188-9961
Phone: (206) 575-7979; Fax: (206) 575-1908; Email: wsna@wsna.org
Web: www.wsna.org/snas/wa/wsnf/index.htm

**Summary:** To provide financial assistance to students in Washington preparing for a career as a registered nurse in the state.

**Eligibility:** Open to students who have completed at least 12 nursing credits at a college or university in Washington. Applicants must have a GPA of 3.0 or higher in a program leading to a nursing, generic, RNB, or higher degree. They must submit essays on the following topics: 1) their participation in school and volunteer activities, including offices and positions of leadership; 2) honors and awards they have received and the relevance of those to nursing; 3) special or unusual life experiences or activities that have made an impact on their nursing career or that assisted them to decide on nursing as a profession; 4) their long- and short-term goals for their nursing career; 5) what they anticipate their role in the Washington State Nurses Association will be, what it is important to them, and (if they are already an R.N.) their involvement in the organization and reasons for participation; and 6) their past work experience (both paid and volunteer) and why this may or may not impact their career in nursing. Financial need is not considered in the selection process.

**Financial data:** The stipend is $1,000.

**Duration:** 1 year.

**Number awarded:** 4 each year.

**Deadline:** February of each year.

## 2820 WASTE MANAGEMENT SCHOLARSHIPS

Big 33 Scholarship Foundation
Attn: Scholarship Committee
511 Bridge Street
P.O. Box 213
New Cumberland, PA 17070
Phone: (717) 774-3303; (877) PABIG-33; Fax: (717) 774-1749;
Email: info@big33.org
Web: www.big33.org/scholarships/default.ashx

**Summary:** To provide financial assistance to graduating high school seniors in Ohio and Pennsylvania who plan to study environmental sciences in college.

**Eligibility:** Open to seniors graduating from public and accredited private high schools in Ohio and Pennsylvania who are planning to study an environmental field in college. Applications are available from high school guidance counselors. Selection is based on special talents, leadership, obstacles overcome, academic achievement (at least a 2.0 GPA), community service, unique endeavors, financial need, and a 1-page essay on why they deserve the scholarship and their involvement with preserving the environment. Funds for this program are provided by Waste Management, Inc.

**Financial data:** The stipend is $1,000.

**Duration:** 1 year; nonrenewable.

**Number awarded:** 100 each year.

**Deadline:** February of each year.

## 2821 WAYNE ALEXANDER MEMORIAL SCHOLARSHIP

Electronic Document Systems Foundation
Attn: EDSF Scholarship Awards
24238 Hawthorne Boulevard
Torrance, CA 90505-6505
Phone: (310) 541-1481; Fax: (310) 541-4803
Web: www.edsf.org/scholarships.cfm

**Summary:** To provide financial assistance to college juniors, seniors, and graduate students interested in working with electronic documents as a career.

**Eligibility:** Open to juniors, seniors, and graduate students who are working full time on a degree in the field of document communication, including marketing, graphic communication and arts, e-commerce, imaging science, printing, web authoring, electronic publishing, computer science, or telecommunications. Priority consideration is given to students at the University of Central Florida. Applicants must submit a statement of their career goals in the field of document communications, an essay on a topic related to their view of the future of the document management and production industry, a list of current professional and college extracurricular activities and achievements, college transcripts (GPA of 3.0 or higher), samples of their creative work, and 2 letters of recommendation. Financial need is not considered.

**Financial data:** The stipend is $2,000.

**Duration:** 1 year.

**Number awarded:** 1 each year.

**Deadline:** May of each year.

## 2822 WELCH FOUNDATION SCHOLARSHIPS

University Interscholastic League
Attn: Texas Interscholastic League Foundation
1701 Manor Road
P.O. Box 8028
Austin, TX 78713
Phone: (512) 232-4938; Fax: (512) 471-5908;
Email: carolyn.scott@mail.utexas.edu
Web: www.uil.texas.edu/tilf/scholar.html

**Summary:** To provide financial assistance to students who participate in programs of the Texas Interscholastic League Foundation (TILF) and plan to major in chemistry, biochemistry, or chemical engineering.

**Eligibility:** Open to students who meet the 5 basic requirements of the TILF: 1) graduate from high school during the current year and begin college or university in Texas by the following fall; 2) enroll full time at an approved institution and maintain a GPA of 2.5 or higher during the first semester; 3) compete in a University Interscholastic League (UIL) academic state meet contest in accounting, calculator applications, computer applications, computer science, current issues and events, debate (cross-examination and Lincoln-Douglas), journalism (editorial writing, feature writing, headline writing, and news writing), literary criticism, mathematics, number sense, 1-act play, ready writing, science, social studies, speech (prose interpretation, poetry interpretation, informative speaking, and persuasive speaking), or spelling and vocabulary; 4) submit high school transcripts that include SAT and/or ACT scores; and 5) submit parents' latest income tax returns. Applicants for this scholarship must major in chemistry, biochemistry, or chemical engineering and be interested in engaging in chemical research at the graduate level. Along with their application, they must submit a 50-word essay on why they desire to major in chemistry, biochemistry, or chemical engineering.

**Financial data:** The stipend is $3,500 per year.

**Duration:** 4 years.

**Number awarded:** 20 each year.

**Deadline:** May of each year.

### 2823 WESLEY SCHOOL OF NURSING ALUMNI ASSOCIATION ENDOWED SCHOLARSHIP

Kansas State Nurses Association
Attn: Kansas Nurses Foundation
1208 S.W. Tyler
Topeka, KS 66612-1735
Phone: (785) 233-8638; Fax: (785) 233-5222; Email: ksna@ksna.net
Web: www.nursingworld.org/snas/ks/knf.htm

**Summary:** To provide financial assistance to students in Kansas who are working on a nursing degree on the undergraduate, master's, or doctoral level.

**Eligibility:** Open to students who are working on a nursing degree on the undergraduate or graduate level. Applicants must have a GPA of 3.0 or higher, submit a personal narrative describing their anticipated role in nursing in the state of Kansas, submit 3 original letters of recommendation, and enroll in at least 6 credit hours per semester (preference is given to full-time students). First priority is given to graduates of Wesley School of Nursing, their children, grandchildren, nieces, and nephews. If no applicants qualify for that priority, the program is opened to graduate and postgraduate nursing students, students in formal nursing programs (advanced registered nurse practitioner, etc.), and students enrolled in undergraduate nursing programs.

**Financial data:** The stipend is $1,000.

**Duration:** 1 year.

**Number awarded:** 3 each year.

**Deadline:** June of each year.

### 2824 WESTERN FEDERATION OF PROFESSIONAL SURVEYORS SCHOLARSHIPS

Western Federation of Professional Surveyors
P.O. Box 2722
Santa Rosa, CA 95405
Phone: (707) 578-1130; Fax: (707) 578-4406; Email: admin@wfps.org
Web: www.wfps.org/files/scholarsh.html

**Summary:** To provide financial assistance to upper-division students majoring in surveying at colleges and universities in 13 designated western states.

**Eligibility:** Open to students attending accredited private and public colleges that 1) offer a program leading to a 4-year bachelor's degree with a land surveying major, and 2) that are in the states of Alaska, Arizona, California, Colorado, Hawaii, Idaho, Montana, Nevada, New Mexico, Oregon, Utah, Washington, or Wyoming. Applicants must have completed at least 2 years of study. Community college students must be planning to transfer to an eligible 4-year school. Candidates must submit a 1-page essay on their educational goals, career goals, and why their qualifications justify their receiving this scholarship. Selection is based on the quality and neatness of the essay, academic achievement, professional qualifications, college activities, community activities, work experience, and letters of recommendation.

**Financial data:** The stipend is $1,200.

**Duration:** 1 year; recipients may reapply.

**Number awarded:** At least 2 each year.

**Deadline:** February of each year.

### 2825 WESTERN MICHIGAN GREENHOUSE ASSOCIATION SCHOLARSHIP

Floriculture Industry Research and Scholarship Trust
Attn: Scholarship Program
P.O. Box 280
East Lansing, MI 48826-0280
Phone: (517) 333-4617; Fax: (517) 333-4494;
Email: scholarships@firstinfloriculture.org
Web: www.firstinfloriculture.org

**Summary:** To provide financial assistance to college students from Michigan who are majoring in horticulture.

**Eligibility:** Open to undergraduate students from Michigan who are studying commercial horticulture at a 4-year college or university. Applicants must be U.S. citizens or permanent residents with a GPA of 3.0 or higher. Selection is based on academic record, recommendations, career goals, extracurricular activities, and financial need. Funding for this program, established in 2003, is provided by the Western Michigan Greenhouse Association (WMGA). The sponsoring organization was formed in 2002 as the result of a merger between the Bedding Plants Foundation, Inc., and the Ohio Floriculture Foundation.

**Number awarded:** 1 each year.

**Financial data:** The stipend depends on the availability of funds. Recently, it was $1,000.

**Duration:** 1 year.

**Deadline:** April of each year.

### 2826 WESTERN RESERVE HERB SOCIETY SCHOLARSHIPS

Herb Society of America-Western Reserve Unit
c/o Priscilla Jones, Committee Chair
2640 Exeter Road
Cleveland Heights, OH 44118
Phone: (216) 932-6090; Email: cillers@hotmail.com
Web: www.herbsociety.org/scholar.htm

**Summary:** To provide financial assistance to college students from Ohio interested in preparing for a career in a field related to horticulture.

**Eligibility:** Open to residents of Ohio who have completed at least 1 year of college. Applicants may be attending an accredited college or university anywhere in the United States. They must be planning a career in horticulture or a related field, including horticultural therapy. U.S. citizenship is required. Preference is given to applicants whose horticultural career goals involve teaching or research or work in the public or nonprofit sector (such as public gardens, botanical gardens, parks, arboreta, city planning, or public education and awareness). Selection is based on an essay that includes a description of their interests, activities, and achievements; an account of their employment record on or off campus; a description of their career goals; and a discussion of their need for financial aid.

**Financial data:** The stipend is $1,000.

**Duration:** 1 year.

**Number awarded:** Up to 3 each year.

**Deadline:** March of each year.

### 2827 WICHITA SCHOLARSHIP

Society of Manufacturing Engineers
Attn: SME Education Foundation
One SME Drive
P.O. Box 930
Dearborn, MI 48121-0930
Phone: (313) 425-3304; (800) 733-4763, ext. 3304; Fax: (313) 425-3411;
Email: foundation@sme.org
Web: www.sme.org

**Summary:** To provide financial assistance to undergraduate and graduate students enrolled in a degree program in engineering in Kansas.

**Eligibility:** Open to students working on an associate, bachelor's, or graduate degree at an accredited college or university in Kansas. Applicants must be majoring in manufacturing engineering, mechanical engineering, industrial engineering, industrial technology, or mechanical technology. They must have a GPA of 2.5 or higher. Preference is given in the following order: first, children, grandchildren, and relatives of current members of Wichita Chapter 52 of the Society of Manufacturing Engineers (SME); second, residents of Kansas; and third, students attending a college or university in Kansas.

**Financial data:** The stipend is $2,000.

**Duration:** 1 year; may be renewed.

**Number awarded:** 1 each year.

**Deadline:** January of each year.

## 2828 WILDLIFE LEADERSHIP AWARDS

Rocky Mountain Elk Foundation
Attn: Maggie Engler
2291 West Broadway
P.O. Box 8249
Missoula, MT 59807-8249
Phone: (406) 523-4500; (800) CALL ELK, ext. 496; Fax: (406) 523-4550;
Email: mengler@rmef.org
Web: www.rmef.org/pages/scholar.html
**Summary:** To provide financial assistance to upper-division students who are majoring in wildlife studies.
**Eligibility:** Open to students enrolled in a recognized wildlife program at a 4-year college or university in the United States or Canada. Applicants must be juniors or seniors, have at least 1 semester or 2 quarters remaining in their degree program, and be scheduled to enroll as full-time students the following fall semester/quarter. Previous recipients of this award are ineligible. Selection is based on hobbies and leisure activities (5 points), leadership activities (25 points), employment experience (5 points), a 300-word essay on how wildlife fits into specified federal laws (15 points), a 300-word essay on what they believe to be the most important conservation issues facing North American during the next 10 years (20 points), a 250-word essay on the role of hunting in conservation (15 points), and a 100-word statement on their career goals and objectives (5 points).
**Financial data:** The stipend is $2,000. In addition, recipients are given an engraved plaque and a 1-year membership in the foundation.
**Duration:** 1 year; nonrenewable.
**Number awarded:** 10 each year.
**Deadline:** February of each year.

## 2829 WILLIAM A. AND ANN M. BROTHERS SCHOLARSHIP

American Welding Society
Attn: AWS Foundation, Inc.
550 N.W. LeJeune Road
Miami, FL 33126
Phone: (305) 445-6628; (800) 443-9353, ext. 461; Fax: (305) 443-7559,
Email: found@aws.org
Web: www.aws.org/foundation/scholarships/brothers.html
**Summary:** To provide financial assistance to college students working on a degree in welding.
**Eligibility:** Open to full-time undergraduate students who are working on a 4-year bachelor's degree in welding or a related program at an accredited university. Applicants must have an overall GPA of 2.5 or higher and be able to demonstrate financial need. U.S. citizenship is required. Preference is given to applicants residing or attending school in Ohio.
**Financial data:** The stipend is $2,500.
**Duration:** 1 year; recipients may reapply.
**Number awarded:** 1 each year.
**Deadline:** January of each year.

## 2830 WILLIAM B. HOWELL MEMORIAL SCHOLARSHIP

American Welding Society
Attn: AWS Foundation, Inc.
550 N.W. LeJeune Road
Miami, FL 33126
Phone: (305) 445-6628; (800) 443-9353, ext. 461; Fax: (305) 443-7559;
Email: found@aws.org
Web: www.aws.org/foundation/scholarships/howell.html
**Summary:** To provide financial assistance to college students majoring in welding.
**Eligibility:** Open to full-time undergraduate students who are working on a 4-year bachelor's degree in a welding program at an accredited university. Applicants must have an overall GPA of 2.5 or higher and be able to demonstrate financial need. U.S. citizenship is required. Priority is given to applicants residing or attending school in Florida, Michigan, or Ohio.
**Financial data:** The stipend is $2,500.
**Duration:** 1 year; recipients may reapply.
**Number awarded:** 1 each year.
**Deadline:** January of each year.

## 2831 WILLIAM E. COOPER SCHOLARSHIPS

ASME International
Attn: Coordinator, Educational Operations
Three Park Avenue
New York, NY 10016-5990
Phone: (212) 591-8131; (800) THE-ASME; Fax: (212) 591-7143;
Email: oluwanifiset@asme.org
Web: www.asme.org/education/enged/aid/scholar.htm
**Summary:** To provide financial assistance to undergraduate students who are members of the American Society of Mechanical Engineers (ASME).
**Eligibility:** Open to student members in good standing who are enrolled in an ABET-accredited mechanical engineering, mechanical engineering technology, or related baccalaureate program. They must be entering their junior or senior year when they apply. There are no geographic or citizenship requirements. Interested students should submit an application form, a nomination from the applicant's department head, a recommendation from a faculty member, and an official transcript. Only one nomination may be submitted per department. Selection is based on leadership, scholastic ability, potential contribution to the mechanical engineering profession, and financial need.
**Financial data:** The stipend is $2,500.
**Duration:** 1 year.
**Number awarded:** 2 each year.
**Deadline:** March of each year.

## 2832 WILLIAM E. WEISEL SCHOLARSHIP AWARD

Society of Manufacturing Engineers
Attn: SME Education Foundation
One SME Drive
P.O. Box 930
Dearborn, MI 48121-0930
Phone: (313) 425-3304; (800) 733-4763, ext. 3304; Fax: (313) 425-3411;
Email: foundation@sme.org
Web: www.sme.org
**Summary:** To provide financial assistance to students preparing for a career in robotics or automated systems.
**Eligibility:** Open to U.S. or Canadian citizens who are full-time students attending a regionally accredited school in engineering or technology and preparing for a career in robotics or automated systems used in manufacturing or robotics used in the medical field. They must have completed at least 30 units with a GPA of 3.5 or higher. Need is not considered in awarding scholarships (unless 2 or more applicants have identical qualifications).
**Financial data:** This stipend is $2,000 per year; funds are paid directly to the recipient.
**Duration:** 1 year; may be renewed.
**Number awarded:** 1 each year.
**Deadline:** January of each year.

## 2833 WILLIAM FOSTER TICHENOR TUITION SCHOLARSHIPS

Kentucky Community and Technical College System
Attn: Financial Aid
300 North Main Street
Versailles, KY 40383
Phone: (859) 256-3100; (877) 528-2748 (within KY)
Web: www.kctcs.edu/student/financialaidscholarships/index.htm
**Summary:** To provide financial assistance to sophomores working on a degree in nursing at an institution within the Kentucky Community and Technical College System (KCTCS).
**Eligibility:** Open to KCTCS students entering their sophomore year with a GPA of 2.5 or higher. Applicants must have completed at least 30 hours of a nursing program and be able to demonstrate financial need. Along with their application, they must submit a 1-page essay on their career choice and personal values.
**Financial data:** Stipends vary at each participating college but are intended to provide full payment of tuition and required fees.
**Duration:** 1 year.
**Number awarded:** Varies each year.
**Deadline:** September of each year.

## 2834 WILLIAM J. AND MARIJANE E. ADAMS, JR. AGRICULTURAL ENGINEERING SCHOLARSHIP

American Society of Agricultural and Biological Engineers
Attn: ASABE Foundation
2950 Niles Road
St. Joseph, MI 49085-9659
Phone: (269) 429-0300; Fax: (269) 429-3852; Email: hq@asabe.org
Web: www.asabe.org/membership/students/grant1.html

**Summary:** To provide financial assistance to undergraduate student members of the American Society of Agricultural and Biological Engineers (ASABE).

**Eligibility:** Open to undergraduate students who have a declared major in biological or agricultural engineering (must be accredited by ABET or CEAB), are student members of the society, are in at least the second year of college, have at least one year of undergraduate study remaining, have a GPA of 2.5 or higher, can demonstrate financial need, and have a special interest in agricultural machinery product design and development. Interested applicants should submit a personal letter (up to 2 pages long) stating how the money will be used, outlining their financial need, and describing their interest in the design and development of new agricultural machinery products.

**Financial data:** The stipend is $1,000. Funds must be used for tuition, fees, books, and on-campus room and board.

**Duration:** 1 year.

**Number awarded:** 1 each year.

**Deadline:** March of each year.

## 2835 WILLIAM J. AND MARIJANE E. ADAMS, JR. MECHANICAL ENGINEERING SCHOLARSHIP

ASME International
Attn: Coordinator, Educational Operations
Three Park Avenue
New York, NY 10016-5990
Phone: (212) 591-8131; (800) THE-ASME; Fax: (212) 591-7143;
Email: oluwanifiset@asme.org
Web: www.asme.org/education/enged/aid/scholar.htm

**Summary:** To provide financial support for college to student members of the American Society of Mechanical Engineers (ASME) in California, Hawaii, or Nevada.

**Eligibility:** Open to student members of the society in Region IX (California, Hawaii, and Nevada) who have a declared major in mechanical engineering with a special interest in product development and design. Applicants must be entering their sophomore, junior, or senior year at an ABET-accredited college or university with a GPA of 2.5 or higher. Selection is based on scholastic ability, demonstrated interest in product development and design, and financial need.

**Financial data:** The stipend is $2,000.

**Duration:** 1 year.

**Number awarded:** 1 each year.

**Deadline:** March of each year.

## 2836 WILLIAM J. FEINGOLD SCHOLARSHIP

American Society for Quality
Attn: Biomedical Division
600 North Plankinton Avenue
P.O. Box 3005
Milwaukee, WI 53201-3005
Phone: (414) 272-8575; (800) 248-1946; Fax: (414) 272-1734;
Email: cs@asqu.org
Web: www.asq.org/biomed/scholarship/index.html

**Summary:** To provide financial assistance to undergraduate and graduate students working on a degree in a field related to quality in the biomedical community.

**Eligibility:** Open to students who have completed at least 2 years of study in a program that involves the use of quality principles, concepts, and technologies in the biomedical community. Applicants must have a GPA of 3.0 or higher. Along with their application, they must submit essays on 1) their career objectives and how they relate to quality issues within the biomedical community; and 2) why quality systems are important in the biomedical community. Graduate students are eligible, but preference is given to undergraduates. Priority is given to students who 1) are enrolled in a technical or scientific course of study; 2) have a demonstrated contribution or participation in activities related to quality in the biomedical community; and 3) have a higher GPA or more compelling essay.

**Financial data:** The stipend is $5,000 per year.

**Duration:** 1 year; may be renewed 1 additional year.

**Number awarded:** 1 or more each year.

**Deadline:** April of each year.

## 2837 WILLIAM JAMES AND DOROTHY BADING LANQUIST FUND SCHOLARSHIPS

Hawai'i Community Foundation
Attn: Scholarship Department
1164 Bishop Street, Suite 800
Honolulu, HI 96813
Phone: (808) 566-5570; (888) 731-3863; Fax: (808) 521-6286;
Email: scholarships@hcf-hawaii.org
Web: www.hawaiicommunityfoundation.org/scholar/scholar.php

**Summary:** To provide financial assistance to Hawaii residents who are interested in preparing for a career in the physical sciences.

**Eligibility:** Open to Hawaii residents who are interested in majoring in the physical sciences or related fields (but not the biological or social sciences) on the undergraduate or graduate school level. They must be able to demonstrate academic achievement (GPA of 2.7 or higher), good moral character, and financial need. In addition to filling out the standard application form, applicants must write a short statement indicating their reasons for attending college, their planned course of study, and their career goals.

**Financial data:** The amounts of the awards depend on the availability of funds and the need of the recipient; recently, stipends averaged $1,000.

**Duration:** 1 year.

**Number awarded:** Varies each year; recently, 7 of these scholarships were awarded.

**Deadline:** February of each year.

## 2838 WILLIAM L. CULLISON SCHOLARSHIP

Technical Association of the Pulp and Paper Industry
Attn: TAPPI Foundation
15 Technology Parkway South
Norcross, GA 30092
Phone: (770) 209-7536; (800) 332-8686; Fax: (770) 446-6947;
Email: vedmondson@tappi.org
Web: www.tappi.org

**Summary:** To provide financial assistance to college students who are interested in preparing for a career in the pulp and paper industry.

**Eligibility:** Open to full-time students who have completed the first 2 years at a designated university with a pulp and paper program and have a GPA of 3.5 or better. Applicants must demonstrate outstanding leadership abilities and a significant interest in the pulp and paper industry. They must submit 50-word essays on the persons who have influenced them most deeply and why, what attracts them to a career in the pulp and paper industry, the extent to which they have participated in activities related to the pulp and paper industry, and why they think they are more likely to make a major contribution to the pulp and paper industry than other engineers or scientists. Financial need is not considered in the selection process. This program was established in 1999. In the United States, the participating universities are Auburn University, Georgia Institute of Technology, Miami University of Ohio, Mississippi State University, North Carolina State University, Oregon State University, Rutgers University, San Jose State University, the State University of New York, the University of Idaho, the University of Maine, the University of Minnesota, the University of New Hampshire, the University of Washington, the University of Wisconsin at Stevens Point, and Western Michigan University. Other participating universities are located in several foreign countries.

**Financial data:** The stipend is $4,000 per year.

**Duration:** 1 year (the junior year); may be renewed for the senior year if the recipient maintains at least a 3.0 GPA and pursues courses in the pulp and paper curriculum.

**Number awarded:** 1 each year.

**Deadline:** April of each year.

## 2839 WILLIAM M. FANNING MAINTENANCE SCHOLARSHIP

National Business Aviation Association, Inc.
Attn: Director of Operations
1200 18th Street, N.W., Suite 400
Washington, DC 20036-2527
Phone: (202) 783-9353; Fax: (202) 331-8364; Email: jevans@nbaa.org
Web: www.nbaa.org/public/education.scholarships/fanning

**Summary:** To provide financial assistance to students who are preparing for a career as an aviation maintenance technician.

**Eligibility:** Open to either 1) a student who is currently enrolled in an accredited airframe and powerplant (A&P) program at an approved FAR Part 147 school, or 2) an individual who is not currently enrolled but who has been accepted for enrollment in an A&P program. Applicants must be U.S. citizens. Along with their application, they must submit 1) an official transcript from their program or school or a letter of acceptance, 2) a 250-word essay on their career goals, 3) a letter of recommendation from either a faculty member or other individual familiar with the applicant's abilities, and 4) a resume.

**Financial data:** The stipend is $2,500.

**Duration:** 1 year.

**Number awarded:** 2 each year: 1 for a student who is already enrolled and 1 for a student who has been accepted for enrollment.

**Deadline:** August of each year.

### 2840 WILLIAM P. MURPHY–VISION SCHOLARSHIP

Small Parts, Inc.
Attn: James Edgar
13980 N.W. 58th Court
P.O. Box 4650
Miami Lakes, FL 33014-0650
Phone: (305) 558-1038; Fax: (305) 558-0509; Email: parts@smallparts.com
Web: www.smallparts.com

**Summary:** To recognize and reward high school students who participate in the FIRST (For Inspiration and Recognition of Science and Technology) Robotics competition.

**Eligibility:** Open to high school students who compete on teams that include the students supported by engineers, technicians, teachers, parents, industry representatives, and (occasionally) college students and faculty. Although the composition of teams varies, most are industry-high school partnerships, university-high school partnerships, industry-university-high school partnerships, or coalitions that involve multiple companies, universities, and/or high schools competing as a single team. Each team starts with the same standard kit of parts and uses their creativity to design and build a robotic vehicle capable of performing a demanding task better than 2 opponents. Teams may enter regional competitions or go directly to the national competition. High school seniors who participate in the competition are eligible to apply for this scholarship. Along with their application, they must submit a letter of recommendation from a high school teacher or administrator, a letter of recommendation from an engineer/advisor of their FIRST team, a resume with their GPA (must be 3.5 or higher) and high school transcript, and an essay explaining how they hope to impact the world through their studies in the field of science and/or technology. The award is presented to the student who most clearly possesses a vision of how she or he, as an individual, hopes to impact society through her or his pursuit of science and/or technology. The entry fee is $5,000 for a single competition and $4,000 for each subsequent and the national competition. Other expenses, including travel by team members to a kick-off workshop and the competition, building materials, administrative costs, shipping, and uniforms, bring the total cost for each team to approximately $15,000. Teams must secure financing from local business sponsors and other fund raising activities.

**Financial data:** The stipend is $1,500 per year.

**Duration:** Up to 4 years.

**Number awarded:** 1 each year.

**Deadline:** February of each year.

### 2841 WILLIAM PARK WOODSIDE FOUNDER'S SCHOLARSHIP

ASM International
Attn: ASM Materials Education Foundation
Scholarship Program
9639 Kinsman Road
Materials Park, OH 44073-0002
Phone: (440) 338-5151; (800) 336-5152; Fax: (440) 338-4634;
Email: asmif@asminternational.org
Web: www.asminternational.org

**Summary:** To provide financial assistance to upper-division student members of the American Society for Metals who are interested in majoring in metallurgy and materials.

**Eligibility:** Open to citizens of the United States, Canada, or Mexico who are enrolled at a college or university in those countries; are members of the society; have an intended or declared major in metallurgy or materials science and engineering (related science or engineering majors may be considered if the applicant demonstrates a strong academic emphasis and inter-

est in materials science and engineering); and are entering their junior or senior year in college. Selection is based on academic achievement; interest in metallurgy/materials (including knowledge of the field, activities, jobs, and potential for a related career); personal qualities (such as social values, maturity, motivation, goals, and citizenship); and financial need.

**Financial data:** The scholarship provides payment of full tuition, up to $10,000 per year.

**Duration:** 1 year; recipients may reapply for 1 additional year.

**Number awarded:** 1 each year.

**Deadline:** April of each year.

### 2842 WILLIAM R. AND MILA KIMEL SCHOLARSHIP

American Nuclear Society
Attn: Scholarship Coordinator
555 North Kensington Avenue
La Grange Park, IL 60526-5592
Phone: (708) 352-6611; Fax: (708) 352-0499; Email: outreach@ans.org
Web: www.ans.org/honors/scholarships

**Summary:** To provide financial assistance to undergraduate students who are interested in preparing for a career in nuclear engineering.

**Eligibility:** Open to students entering their junior or senior year in nuclear engineering at an accredited institution in the United States. Applicants must be U.S. citizens or permanent residents and able to demonstrate academic achievement.

**Financial data:** The stipend is $2,000.

**Duration:** 1 year; nonrenewable.

**Number awarded:** 1 each year.

**Deadline:** January of each year.

### 2843 WILLIAM R. KIMEL, P.E. ENGINEERING SCHOLARSHIP

National Society of Professional Engineers
Attn: Practice Division Manager
1420 King Street
Alexandria, VA 22314-2794
Phone: (703) 684-2884; Fax: (703) 836-4875; Email: egarcia@nspe.org
Web: www.nspe.org/scholarships/sc1-pei.asp

**Summary:** To provide financial assistance to undergraduate engineering students in Kansas and Missouri.

**Eligibility:** Open to residents of Kansas and Missouri who are enrolled as juniors in an ABET-accredited engineering program at a college or university in either of those states. Applicants must submit a 500-word essay on "My Engineering Career Goals and Aspirations to Achieve Them." Selection is based on that essay, GPA, internship and co-op experience, involvement in other activities, 2 faculty recommendations, and honors and awards.

**Financial data:** The stipend is $2,500.

**Duration:** 1 year.

**Number awarded:** 1 each year.

### 2844 WILLIAM RUCKER GREENWOOD SCHOLARSHIP

Association for Women Geoscientists
Attn: AWG Foundation
P.O. Box 30645
Lincoln, NE 68503-0645
Email: awgscholarship@yahoo.com
Web: www.awg.org/members/po_scholarships.html

**Summary:** To provide financial assistance to minority women working on an undergraduate or graduate degree in the geosciences in the Potomac Bay region.

**Eligibility:** Open to minority women who are currently enrolled as full-time undergraduate or graduate geoscience majors in an accredited, degree-granting college or university in Delaware, the District of Columbia, Maryland, Virginia, or West Virginia. Selection is based on the applicant's 1) participation in geoscience or earth science educational activities, and 2) potential for leadership as a future geoscience professional.

**Financial data:** The stipend is $1,000. The recipient also is granted a 1-year membership in the Association for Women Geoscientists (AWG).

**Duration:** 1 year.

**Number awarded:** 1 each year.

**Deadline:** April of each year.

## 2845 WILLIAM W. BURGIN, JR. MD EDUCATION RECOGNITION AWARD

American Association for Respiratory Care
Attn: American Respiratory Care Foundation
9425 North MacArthur Boulevard, Suite 100
Irving, TX 75063-4706
Phone: (972) 243-2272; Fax: (972) 484-2720; Email: info@aarc.org
Web: www.aarc.org/awards/burgin.html
**Summary:** To provide financial assistance to second-year college students interested in becoming respiratory therapists.
**Eligibility:** Open to students who have completed 2 semesters in an accredited respiratory care bachelor's degree program. Applicants must be U.S. citizens with a GPA of 3.0 or higher. They must submit an original referenced paper on an aspect of respiratory care and a paper of at least 1,200 words describing how the award will assist them in reaching their objective of a baccalaureate degree and their ultimate goal of leadership in health care. Selection is based on academic performance.
**Financial data:** The stipend is $2,500. The award also provides 1 night's lodging and registration for the international congress of the association.
**Duration:** 1 year.
**Number awarded:** 1 each year.
**Deadline:** June of each year.

## 2846 WILMA E. MOTLEY SCHOLARSHIP

American Dental Hygienists' Association
Attn: Institute for Oral Health
444 North Michigan Avenue, Suite 3400
Chicago, IL 60611
Phone: (312) 440-8918; (800) 735-4916; Fax: (312) 440-8929;
Email: institute@adha.net
Web: www.adha.org/institute/Scholarship/index.htm
**Summary:** To provide financial assistance to undergraduate students who are preparing for careers in dental hygiene and have a 4.0 GPA.
**Eligibility:** Open to full-time undergraduate students who are active members of the Student American Dental Hygienists' Association (SADHA) or the American Dental Hygienists' Association (ADHA). Applicants must have a GPA of 4.0, be able to document financial need of at least $1,500, and have completed at least 1 year in an accredited dental hygiene program in the United States. Along with their application, they must submit a statement that covers their long-term career goals, their intended contribution to the dental hygiene profession, their professional interests, and the manner in which their degree will enhance their professional capacity.
**Financial data:** Stipends range from $1,000 to $2,000.
**Duration:** 1 year.
**Number awarded:** 1 each year.
**Deadline:** April of each year.

## 2847 WILMA MOTLEY CALIFORNIA MERIT SCHOLARSHIP

American Dental Hygienists' Association
Attn: Institute for Oral Health
444 North Michigan Avenue, Suite 3400
Chicago, IL 60611
Phone: (312) 440-8918; (800) 735-4916; Fax: (312) 440-8929;
Email: institute@adha.net
Web: www.adha.org/institute/Scholarship/index.htm
**Summary:** To provide financial assistance to undergraduate students in California preparing for careers in dental hygiene.
**Eligibility:** Open to full-time undergraduate students who are active members of the Student American Dental Hygienists' Association (SADHA) or the American Dental Hygienists' Association (ADHA). Applicants must have a GPA of 3.5 or higher, be able to demonstrate exceptional academic merit, and have completed at least one year in an accredited dental hygiene program in California. Financial need is not considered in the selection process.
**Financial data:** Stipends range from $1,000 to $2,000.
**Duration:** 1 year.
**Number awarded:** 1 each year.
**Deadline:** April of each year.

## 2848 WISCONSIN DIETETIC ASSOCIATION SCHOLARSHIPS

Wisconsin Dietetic Association
Attn: Executive Coordinator
1411 West Montgomery Street
Sparta, WI 54656-1003
Phone: (608) 269-0042; (888) 232-8631; Fax: (608) 269-0043;
Email: wda@centurytel.net
Web: www.eatrightwisc.org
**Summary:** To provide financial assistance to undergraduate and graduate students in dietetics programs at colleges and universities in Wisconsin.
**Eligibility:** Open to students at colleges, universities, and technical schools in Wisconsin who are working on an undergraduate or graduate degree in dietetics or a certificate as a dietetic technician. Applicants must a brief summary of their professional and career goals and what they hope to the profession of dietetics, 3 letters of reference, official transcripts, and a financial statement.
**Financial data:** Stipends are $1,000 for undergraduates and full-time graduate students or $500 for part-time graduate students and dietetic technician students.
**Duration:** 1 year.
**Number awarded:** Generally 5 each year: 2 for undergraduates, 1 for a full-time graduate student, 1 for a part-time graduate students, and 1 for a dietetic technician student.
**Deadline:** February of each year.

## 2849 WISCONSIN GARDEN CLUB FEDERATION SCHOLARSHIP

Community Foundation for the Fox Valley Region, Inc.
Attn: Scholarships
4455 West Lawrence Street
P.O. Box 563
Appleton, WI 54912-0563
Phone: (920) 830-1290; Fax: (920) 830-1293; Email: cffvr@cffoxvalley.org
Web: www.cffoxvalley.org/scholarship_fundslist.html
**Summary:** To provide financial assistance to upper-division and graduate students in Wisconsin who are working on a degree related to gardening.
**Eligibility:** Open to college juniors, seniors, and graduate students at colleges and universities in Wisconsin. Applicants must be majoring in horticulture, floriculture, landscape design/architecture, botany, forestry, agronomy, plant pathology, environmental studies, city planning, land management, or a related field. They must have a 3.0 GPA or higher. This program is sponsored by the Wisconsin Garden Club Federation. Information is also available from Carolyn A. Craig, WGCF Scholarship Chair, 900 North Shore Drive, New Richmond, WI 54017-9466, (715) 246-6242, E-mail: cacraig@frontiernet.net.
**Financial data:** The stipend is $1,000.
**Duration:** 1 year.
**Number awarded:** Varies each year; recently, 4 of these scholarships were awarded.
**Deadline:** February of each year.

## 2850 WISCONSIN LEAGUE FOR NURSING SCHOLARSHIPS

Wisconsin League for Nursing
2121 East Newport Avenue
Milwaukee, WI 53211-2952
Phone: (414) 332-6271
Web: www.cuw.edu/wln/scholarship.htm
**Summary:** To provide financial assistance to residents of Wisconsin attending a school of nursing in the state.
**Eligibility:** Open to residents of Wisconsin who working on an undergraduate or graduate degree at an accredited school of nursing in the state. Applicants must have completed at least half the credits needed for graduation. They may obtain applications only from their school of nursing; no applications are sent from the sponsor's office. Selection is based on scholastic ability, professional abilities and/or community service, understanding of the nursing profession, goals upon graduation, and financial need. Information is also available from Mary Ann Tanner, P.O. Box 107, Long Lake, WI 53542-0107. This program includes the following named scholarships: the Gregory Olson Memorial Award (for graduate students), the Will Ross Memorial Foundation Awards, the Jeannette McKelvey Memorial Scholarships, the Val Prock Memorial Award, and the Suzanne Coyle Memorial Award.
**Financial data:** Stipends range from $500 to $1,000.
**Duration:** 1 year.
**Number awarded:** Varies each year. Recently, 10 of these scholarships were awarded: 9 to undergraduate nursing students and 1 to a graduate student.
**Deadline:** July of each year.

## 2851 WISCONSIN MEDICAL SOCIETY GENERAL MEDICAL EDUCATION SCHOLARSHIPS

Wisconsin Medical Society
Attn: Executive Director, Wisconsin Medical Society Foundation
330 East Lakeside Street
P.O. Box 1109
Madison, WI 53701-1109
Phone: (608) 442-3722; (866) 442-3800, ext. 3722; Fax: (608) 442-3802;
Email: eileenw@wismed.org
Web: www.wisconsinmedicalsociety.org

**Summary:** To provide financial assistance to Wisconsin residents working on a degree in medicine, nursing, or a related field.

**Eligibility:** Open to Wisconsin residents who are enrolled in medical school or in a nursing, physician assistant, or other allied health career program. Preference is given to students at educational institutions in Wisconsin, those close to completing their degree, and those who show a strong interest in practicing in Wisconsin. U.S. citizenship is required. Selection is based on financial need, academic achievement, personal qualities and strengths, and letters of recommendation.

**Financial data:** The stipend is $1,500 for medical students or $750 for registered nurses, physician assistants, and other allied health care careers.

**Duration:** 1 year.

**Number awarded:** 1 or more each year.

**Deadline:** March of each year.

## 2852 WISCONSIN READY MIXED CONCRETE ASSOCIATION SCHOLARSHIPS

Wisconsin Ready Mixed Concrete Association
Attn: Scholarship Committee
16 North Carroll Street, Suite 925
Madison, WI 53703
Phone: (608) 250-6304; Fax: (608) 250-6306; Email: info@wrmca.com
Web: www.wrmca.com

**Summary:** To provide financial assistance to residents of Wisconsin and the upper peninsula of Michigan who are interested in preparing for a career in the ready mixed concrete industry.

**Eligibility:** Open to graduating high school seniors, graduates, and current college students from Wisconsin and the upper peninsula of Michigan. Applicants must be attending or planning to attend Middle Tennessee State University, Alpena Community College in Michigan, or Rhodes State College in Ohio to enroll in their concrete industry management programs. Along with their application, they must submit an essay of 250 to 500 words on why they want to obtain an advanced degree in a concrete-related program.

**Financial data:** Stipends are $5,000 at Middle Tennessee State University or $2,500 at Alpena Community College or Rhodes State College.

**Duration:** 1 year; nonrenewable.

**Number awarded:** 1 or more each year.

**Deadline:** February of each year.

## 2853 WISCONSIN SOCIETY FOR CLINICAL LABORATORY SCIENCE HIGH SCHOOL SCHOLARSHIP

Wisconsin Society for Clinical Laboratory Science
c/o Mary Ann Nelson, Scholarship Fund Secretary
302 Park Avenue
Wausau, WI 54403
Phone: (715) 845-3662; Email: manelson@dwave.net
Web: www.wiscls.org/scholarship.htm

**Summary:** To provide financial assistance to high school seniors in Wisconsin planning to enroll in a laboratory medicine program.

**Eligibility:** Open to seniors graduating from high schools in Wisconsin. Applicants must be planning to attend college to major in medical technology/clinical laboratory science.

**Financial data:** The stipend is $500 per semester ($1,000 per year). Funds are paid directly to the university.

**Duration:** 1 semester; may be renewed up to 7 additional semesters provided the recipient continues to display satisfactory academic progress.

**Number awarded:** 1 or more each year.

## 2854 WOCN SOCIETY ACCREDITED NURSING EDUCATION SCHOLARSHIP PROGRAM

Wound, Ostomy and Continence Nurses Society
Attn: Chair, WOCN Scholarship Committee
4700 West Lake Avenue
Glenview, IL 60025-1485
Phone: (866) 615-8560; (888) 224-WOCN; Fax: (866) 615-8560;
Email: info@wocn.org
Web: www.wocn.org/education/scholarship

**Summary:** To provide financial assistance to individuals interested in preparing for a career in enterostomal therapy (ET) nursing (including wound, ostomy, and continence).

**Eligibility:** Open to applicants able to provide evidence of one of the following: 1) acceptance in a wound, ostomy, and continence education program accredited by the Wound, Ostomy and Continence Nurses (WOCN) Society; 2) current enrollment in a WOCN-accredited wound, ostomy, and continence education program; or 3) certificate of completion from a WOCN-accredited wound, ostomy, and continence education program within 3 months of completion. Selection is based on motivation to be an ET nurse and financial need.

**Financial data:** A stipend is awarded (amount not specified).

**Number awarded:** Varies each year.

**Deadline:** April or October of each year.

## 2855 WOCN SOCIETY ADVANCED EDUCATION SCHOLARSHIP PROGRAM

Wound, Ostomy and Continence Nurses Society
Attn: Chair, WOCN Scholarship Committee
4700 West Lake Avenue
Glenview, IL 60025-1485
Phone: (866) 615-8560; (888) 224-WOCN; Fax: (866) 615-8560;
Email: info@wocn.org
Web: www.wocn.org/education/scholarship

**Summary:** To provide financial assistance to members of the Would, Ostomy and Continence Nurses (WOCN) Society interested in working on an undergraduate or graduate degree.

**Eligibility:** Open to active members of the society who have a current, unrestricted R.N. license and are working on a baccalaureate, master's, or doctoral degree or N.P. certificate. Applicants must provide evidence of current or previous employment as a wound, ostomy, and/or continence nurse during the last 3 years, proof of WOCNCB certification, and proof of current enrollment or acceptance into an accredited nursing program or other accredited college or university program for non-nursing degrees. Selection is based on merit, compliance with the eligibility requirements, and financial need.

**Financial data:** A stipend is awarded (amount not specified).

**Duration:** 1 year.

**Number awarded:** 1 or more each year.

**Deadline:** April of each year.

## 2856 WOMEN IN SCIENCE AND TECHNOLOGY SCHOLARSHIP

Business and Professional Women of Virginia
Attn: Virginia BPW Foundation
P.O. Box 4842
McLean, VA 22103-4842
Web: www.bpwva.org/Foundation.shtml

**Summary:** To provide financial assistance to women in Virginia who are interested in working on a bachelor's or advanced degree in science or technology.

**Eligibility:** Open to women who are at least 18 years of age, U.S. citizens, Virginia residents, accepted at or currently studying at a Virginia college or university, and working on a bachelor's, master's, or doctoral degree in one of the following fields: actuarial science, biology, bioengineering, chemistry, computer science, dentistry, engineering, mathematics, medicine, physics, or a similar scientific or technical field. Applicants must have a definite plan to use their education in a scientific or technical profession. They must be able to demonstrate financial need.

**Financial data:** Stipends range from $500 to $1,000 per year, depending on the need of the recipient; funds may be used for tuition, fees, books, transportation, living expenses, and dependent care.

**Duration:** 1 year; recipients may reapply (but prior recipients are not given priority).

**Additional information:** Recipients must complete their studies within 2 years.

**Number awarded:** At least 1 each year.

**Deadline:** March of each year.

## 2857 WOMEN IN TECHNOLOGY SCHOLARSHIP

Morgan Stanley
c/o Joyce Arencibia, IT College Recruiting
750 Seventh Avenue, 30th Floor
New York, NY 10019
Phone: (212) 762-4000; Email: diversityrecruiting@morganstanley.com
Web: www.morganstanley.com/about/diversityrecruit_programs.html

**Summary:** To provide financial assistance and work experience to women who are working on an undergraduate degree in computer science or engineering.

**Eligibility:** Open to women who are enrolled in their sophomore or junior year of college (or the third or fourth year of a 5-year program). Applicants must be enrolled full time and have a GPA of 3.0 or higher. They must be willing to commit to a paid summer internship in the Morgan Stanley Information Technology Division. All majors and disciplines are eligible, but preference is given to students preparing for a career in computer science or engineering. Along with their application, they must submit 1-page essays on 1) why they are applying for this scholarship and why they should be selected as a recipient; 2) a technical project on which they worked, either through a university course or previous work experience, their role in the project, and how they contributed to the end result; and 3) a software, hardware, or new innovative application of existing technology that they would create if they could and the impact it would have. Financial need is not considered in the selection process.

**Financial data:** Students who receive a scholarship as juniors (or fourth-year students in a 5-year program) receive $10,000 for their final year of college. Students who receive a scholarship as sophomores (or third-year students in a 5-year program) receive $5,000 for their junior year (or fourth year of a 5-year program). The program includes a paid summer internship in the Morgan Stanley Information Technology Division in the summer following the time of application.

**Duration:** 1 year; may be renewed for the final year for students who receive a scholarship as sophomores (or third-year students in a 5-year program).

**Number awarded:** 1 or more each year.

**Deadline:** February of each year.

## 2858 WOMEN'S NATIONAL AGRICULTURAL AVIATION ASSOCIATION SCHOLARSHIP ESSAY CONTEST

National Agricultural Aviation Association
Attn: Women of the NAAA
1005 E Street, S.E.
Washington, DC 20003-2947
Phone: (202) 546-5722; Fax: (202) 546-5726;
Email: information@agaviation.org
Web: www.agaviation.org/scholarship.htm

**Summary:** To recognize and reward outstanding student essays on agricultural aviation.

**Eligibility:** Open to the children, grandchildren, sons-in-law, daughters-in-law, or spouses of any National Agricultural Aviation Association operator, pilot member, retired operator, or pilot who maintains an active membership in the association. The contest is also open to the children, grandchildren, sons-in-law, daughters-in-law, or spouses of an allied industry member. Entrants must be high school seniors, high school graduates, or college students. They may be of any age pursuing any area of education beyond high school. They are invited to submit an essay, up to 1,500 words, on a theme related to agricultural aviation that changes annually; recently, the topic was "Agricultural Aviation's Contribution to the World's Food Supply." A photograph of the entrant and a short biography should accompany the submission. Essays are judged on theme, development, clarity, and originality.

**Financial data:** First prize is $2,000; second prize is $1,000.

**Duration:** The competition is held annually.

**Number awarded:** 2 each year.

**Deadline:** August of each year.

## 2859 WTS MINNESOTA CHAPTER SCHOLARSHIPS

Women's Transportation Seminar-Minnesota Chapter
c/o Jessica Overmohle, Director
URS Corporation
700 Third Street South
Minneapolis, MN 55415-1199

Phone: (612) 373-6404; Fax: (612) 370-1378;
Email: Jessica_Overmohle@URSCorp.com
Web: www.wtsnational.org

**Summary:** To provide financial assistance to women working on an undergraduate or graduate degree in a transportation-related field at colleges and universities in Minnesota.

**Eligibility:** Open to women currently enrolled in a undergraduate or graduate degree program at a college or university in Minnesota. Applicants must be preparing for a career in transportation or a transportation-related field and be majoring in such fields as transportation engineering, planning, finance, or logistics. They must have a GPA of 3.0 or higher. Along with their application, they must submit a 750-word statement on their career goals after graduation and why they think they should receive this award. Selection is based on transportation goals, academic record, and transportation-related activities or job skills.

**Financial data:** The stipend is $1,000.

**Duration:** 1 year.

**Number awarded:** 2 each year: 1 undergraduate and 1 graduate student.

**Deadline:** November of each year.

## 2860 WTS PUGET SOUND CHAPTER SCHOLARSHIP

Women's Transportation Seminar-Puget Sound Chapter
c/o Lorelei Mesic, Scholarship Co-Chair
W&H Pacific
3350 Monte Villa Parkway
Bothell, WA 98021-8972
Phone: (425) 951-4872; Fax: (425) 951-4808; Email: lmesic@whpacific.com
Web: www.wtspugetsound.org/nscholarships.html

**Summary:** To provide financial assistance to women undergraduate and graduate students from Washington who are working on a degree related to transportation and have financial need.

**Eligibility:** Open to women who are residents of Washington, studying at a college in the state, or working as an intern in the state. Applicants must be currently enrolled in an undergraduate or graduate degree program in a transportation-related field, such as engineering, planning, finance, or logistics. They must have a GPA of 3.0 or higher and plans to prepare for a career in a transportation-related field. Minority candidates are encouraged to apply. Along with their application, they must submit a 500-word statement about their career goals after graduation, their financial need, and why they think they should receive this scholarship award. Selection is based on transportation goals, academic record, transportation-related activities or job skills, and financial need. The winner is also nominated for scholarships offered by the national organization of the Women's Transportation Seminar.

**Number awarded:** 1 each year.

**Financial data:** The stipend is $1,500.

**Duration:** 1 year.

**Deadline:** October of each year.

## 2861 WTS/ITS WASHINGTON INTELLIGENT TRANSPORTATION SYSTEMS SCHOLARSHIP

Women's Transportation Seminar-Puget Sound Chapter
c/o Lorelei Mesic, Scholarship Co-Chair
W&H Pacific
3350 Monte Villa Parkway
Bothell, WA 98021-8972
Phone: (425) 951-4872; Fax: (425) 951-4808; Email: lmesic@whpacific.com
Web: www.wtspugetsound.org/nscholarships.html

**Summary:** To provide financial assistance to undergraduate and graduate students from Washington working on a degree related to intelligent transportation systems (ITS).

**Eligibility:** Open to students who are residents of Washington, studying at a college in the state, or working as an intern in the state. Applicants must be currently enrolled in an undergraduate or graduate degree program related to the design, implementation, operation, and maintenance of ITS technologies. They must be majoring in transportation or a related field, including transportation engineering, systems engineering, electrical engineering, planning, finance, or logistics, and be taking courses in such ITS-related fields of study as computer science, electronics, and digital communications. In addition, they must have a GPA of 3.0 or higher and plans to prepare for a career in a transportation-related field. Minority candidates are encouraged to apply. Along with their application, they must submit a 500-word statement about their career goals after graduation, how those relate to ITS, and why they think they should receive this scholarship award. Selection is based on that statement, academic record, and transportation-related activities or job skills. Financial need is not considered.

**Financial data:** The stipend is $1,500.
**Duration:** 1 year.
**Number awarded:** 1 each year.
**Deadline:** October of each year.

## 2862 WYOMING TRUCKING ASSOCIATION SCHOLARSHIPS

Wyoming Trucking Association, Inc.
Attn: WTA Scholarship Trust Fund
555 North Poplar
P.O. Box 1909
Casper, WY 82602
Phone: (307) 234-1579; Fax: (307) 234-7082; Email: wytruck@aol.com
**Summary:** To provide financial assistance to high school seniors and currently-enrolled college students in Wyoming who are interested in preparing for a career in the highway transportation industry.
**Eligibility:** Open to high school seniors and graduates in Wyoming who are enrolled or planning to enroll in a community college in Wyoming, a trade school in the state, or the University of Wyoming. Applicants must be majoring or planning to major in a course of study that could lead to a career in the transportation industry, including (but not limited to) business management, computer skills, accounting, office procedures and management, safety, diesel mechanics, and truck driving. Along with their application, they must submit a 1-page essay on "How is the trucking industry important to you and the State of Wyoming." Financial need is considered in the selection process.
**Financial data:** Stipends range from $500 to $1,000.
**Duration:** 1 year.
**Number awarded:** 1 to 10 each year.
**Deadline:** March of each year.

## 2863 XEROX TECHNICAL MINORITY SCHOLARSHIP PROGRAM

Xerox Corporation
Attn: Technical Minority Scholarship Program
150 State Street, Fourth Floor
Rochester, NY 14614
Phone: (585) 422-7689; Email: xtmsp@imcouncil.com
Web: www.xerox.com
**Summary:** To provide financial assistance to minorities interested in undergraduate or graduate education in the sciences and/or engineering.
**Eligibility:** Open to minorities (people of African American, Asian, Pacific Islander, Native American, Native Alaskan, or Hispanic descent) working full time on an undergraduate or graduate degree in chemistry, computing and software systems, engineering (chemical, computer, electrical, imaging, manufacturing, mechanical, optical, or software), information management, laser optics, material science, physics, or printing management science. Applicants must be U.S. citizens or permanent residents with a GPA of 3.0 or higher and attending, or planning to attend, a 4-year college or university.
**Financial data:** The maximum stipend is $1,000 per year.
**Duration:** 1 year.
**Number awarded:** Approximately 150 each year.
**Deadline:** September of each year.

## 2864 YOUNG NATURALIST AWARDS

American Museum of Natural History
Attn: National Center for Science Literacy, Education, and Technology
Central Park West at 79th Street
New York, NY 10024-5192
Phone: (212) 496-3498; Email: yna@amnh.org
Web: www.amnh.org/nationalcenter/youngnaturalistawards
**Summary:** To recognize and reward high school students who develop outstanding science projects.
**Eligibility:** Open to students in grades 7-12 currently enrolled in a public, private, parochial, or home school in the United States, Canada, the U.S. territories, or U.S.-sponsored schools abroad. Applicants are invited to submit reports of observation-based projects on a scientific theme that is the same every year: "Scientific Discovery Begins with Expeditions." Entries must be between 500 and 2,000 words for grades 7 and 8, between 750 and 2,500 words for grades 9 and 10, or between 1,000 and 3,000 words for grades 11 and 12. Students may include original drawings, photographs, timelines, maps, or graphs to support their writing. Entries are judged by grade level. Selection is based on focus of investigation (15 points), procedure (20 points), analysis and interpretation (20

points), documentation of research materials (15 points), personal voice (10 points), clarity and style (10 points), and use of visuals (10 points).
**Financial data:** This program provides scholarships of $2,500 for grade 12, $2,000 for grade 11, $1,500 for grade 10, $1,000 for grade 9, $750 for grade 8, or $500 for grade 7
**Duration:** Awards are presented annually.
**Number awarded:** 12 awards are presented each year: 2 for each grade level.
**Deadline:** January of each year.

# Social Sciences

## 2865 AACE INTERNATIONAL COMPETITIVE SCHOLARSHIPS

**Summary:** To provide financial assistance to undergraduate and graduate students in the United States or Canada working on a degree related to total cost management (the effective application of professional and technical expertise to plan and control resources, costs, profitability, and risk).

*See Listing #1763.*

## 2866 AAHE UNDERGRADUATE SCHOLARSHIP

**Summary:** To provide financial assistance to undergraduates who are currently enrolled in a health education program.

*See Listing #1764.*

## 2867 AAMI YOUNG INVESTIGATOR COMPETITION

**Summary:** To recognize and reward student authors of outstanding research papers on medical instrumentation and technology.

*See Listing #1766.*

## 2868 ACADEMY OF HOSPITALITY AND TOURISM SCHOLARSHIP

Tourism Cares for Tomorrow
Attn: Program Manager
585 Washington Street
Canton, MA 02021
Phone: (781) 821-5990; Fax: (781) 821-8949; Email: info@tourismcares.org
Web: www.tourismcares.org

**Summary:** To provide financial assistance to high school seniors planning to major in tourism in college.

**Eligibility:** Open to seniors at high schools with an Academy of Hospitality and Tourism program affiliated with the National Academy Foundation (NAF). Applicants must have a GPA of 3.0 or higher and be interested in majoring in a travel or tourism-related field (e.g., hotel management, restaurant management, tourism) in college. Along with their application, they must submit a 2-page essay on the following question: "In your future career in tourism, what responsibility will you have for preservation and conservation of tourism sites around the globe? How will you meet those challenges?" This program was established in 1995 as a partnership between NAF and National Tourism Foundation (now a part of Tourism Cares for Tomorrow).

**Financial data:** The stipend is $1,000.
**Duration:** 1 year.
**Number awarded:** 1 each year.
**Deadline:** March of each year.

## 2869 ACCOUNTANCY BOARD OF OHIO EDUCATION ASSISTANCE PROGRAM

Accountancy Board of Ohio
77 South High Street, 18th Floor
Columbus, OH 43215-6128
Phone: (614) 466-4135; Fax: (614) 466-2628
Web: acc.ohio.gov/edrule.html

**Summary:** To provide financial assistance to minority and financially disadvantaged students enrolled in an accounting education program at Ohio academic institutions approved by the Accountancy Board of Ohio.

**Eligibility:** Open to minority and financially disadvantaged Ohio residents enrolled full time as sophomores, juniors, or seniors in an accounting program at an accredited college or university in the state. Students who remain in good standing at their institutions and who enter a qualified fifth-year program are also eligible, if funds are available. Minority is defined as people with significant ancestry from Africa (excluding the Middle East), Asia (excluding the Middle East), Central America and the Caribbean islands, South America, and the islands of the Pacific Ocean. Financial disadvantage is defined according to information provided on the Free Application for Federal Student Aid (FAFSA). U.S. citizenship or permanent resident status is required.

**Financial data:** The amount of the stipend is determined annually but does not exceed the in-state tuition at Ohio public universities.
**Duration:** 1 year; nonrenewable.
**Number awarded:** Several each year.
**Deadline:** May or November of each year.

## 2870 ACCOUNTEMPS/AICPA STUDENT SCHOLARSHIP

American Institute of Certified Public Accountants
Attn: Academic and Career Development Division
1211 Avenue of the Americas
New York, NY 10036-8775
Phone: (212) 596-6224; Fax: (212) 596-6292; Email: educat@aicpa.org
Web: www.aicpa.org/nolimits/become/ships/AICPA.htm

**Summary:** To provide financial assistance to student affiliate members of the American Institute of Certified Public Accountants (AICPA) who are working on an undergraduate or graduate degree in finance, information systems, or accounting.

**Eligibility:** Open to full-time undergraduate and graduate students who are AICPA student affiliate members with a declared major in accounting, finance, or information systems. Applicants must have completed at least 30 semester hours, including at least 6 semesters in accounting, with a GPA of 3.0 or higher and be a U.S. citizen. Students who will be transferring to a 4-year school must include an acceptance letter from that school. Selection is based on outstanding academic achievement, leadership, and future career interests.

**Financial data:** The stipend is $2,500.
**Duration:** 1 year.
**Number awarded:** 2 each year.
**Deadline:** March of each year.

## 2871 ACCOUNTING CAREERS UIL SCHOLARSHIPS

Texas Society of Certified Public Accountants
Attn: Accounting Education Foundation
14860 Montfort Drive, Suite 150
Dallas, TX 75240-6705
Phone: (972) 687-8500; (800) 428-0272, ext. 233; Fax: (972) 687-8646;
Email: Sking@tscpa.net
Web: www.tscpa.org

**Summary:** To provide financial assistance to high school students in Texas who plan to attend a university in the state and major in accounting.

**Eligibility:** Open to high school seniors in Texas who participate in the state University Interscholastic League (UIL) competition in accounting. Applicants must plan to major in accounting at 1 of 52 Texas colleges and universities, have an ACT score of at least 24 or the equivalent on the SAT, have a GPA of 3.0 or higher, and rank in the top 10% of their high school graduating class.

**Financial data:** The stipend is $1,000 per year.
**Duration:** Up to 5 years.
**Number awarded:** 5 each year: 1 in each of the 5 UIL competition divisions in the state.

## 2872 ACI-NA COMMISSIONERS COMMITTEE SCHOLARSHIP

Airports Council International-North America
1775 K Street, N.W., Suite 500
Washington, DC 20006
Phone: (202) 293-8500; Fax: (202) 331-1362
Web: www.aci-na.org

**Summary:** To provide financial support for college or graduate school to students preparing for a career in airport management or airport administration.

**Eligibility:** Open to students enrolled in a program that focuses on airport management or airport administration at an accredited college or university that is a member of the University Aviation Association (UAA). Students interested in a flight-related major are not eligible. Applicants must have earned at least a 3.0 GPA in college, and they must reside and attend school in the United States, Canada, Saipan (Northern Marianas), the U.S. Virgin Islands, or Guam. Along with their application, they must submit a personal statement (from 250 to 300 words) on their interest in airport management or airport operations. Undergraduates may be majoring in other fields if their goal of a career in airport management can be demonstrated through work experience or the personal essay. Students planning graduate work must provide proof of acceptance to a graduate school and intention to study courses related to airport management and/or operations. Financial need must be demonstrated. Preference is given to students in their junior or senior year of undergraduate study.

**Financial data:** The stipend is $3,000.
**Duration:** 1 year; recipients may reapply.
**Deadline:** December of each year.

## 2873 ACMPE LEADERS SCHOLARSHIPS

**Summary:** To provide financial assistance to practitioners in medical practice management interested in pursuing professional development through undergraduate or graduate education.
*See Listing #1774.*

## 2874 AERO PERSONNEL PREPARATION SCHOLARSHIPS

Association for Education and Rehabilitation of the Blind and Visually Impaired of Ohio
c/o Marjorie E. Ward
1568 Lafayette Drive
Columbus, OH 43220
Email: ward5@osu.edu
Web: www.aerohio.org/schgrts/schol-grant.htm
**Summary:** To provide financial assistance to Ohio residents who are working on an undergraduate or graduate degree in a field related to rehabilitation of the blind.
**Eligibility:** Open to undergraduate and graduate students in rehabilitation counseling, rehabilitation teaching, orientation and mobility, or education of students with visual disabilities. Applicants must be residents of Ohio, although they may be studying in any state. Undergraduates must have at least junior standing. All applicants must have a GPA of 3.0 or higher. Along with their application, they must submit 1) a short essay explaining why they have chosen their specific field as their profession and what they would like to contribute to the field; 2) a short description of volunteer or paid involvement with individuals with visual disabilities or any other disability; 3) transcripts; and 4) 3 letters of recommendation.
**Financial data:** The stipend is $1,000.
**Duration:** 1 year; nonrenewable.
**Number awarded:** 1 each year.
**Deadline:** April of each year.

## 2875 AFDO SCHOLARSHIP AWARDS

**Summary:** To provide financial assistance to currently-enrolled upper-division students who are preparing for a career in an aspect of food, drug, or consumer product safety.
*See Listing #1793.*

## 2876 AGC OF OHIO SCHOLARSHIPS

Associated General Contractors of Ohio
Attn: AGC of Ohio Education Foundation
1755 Northwest Boulevard
Columbus, OH 43212
Phone: (614) 486-6446; (800) 557-OHIO; Fax: (614) 486-6498;
Email: agc@agcohio.com
Web: www.agcohio.com/benefits/Scholarships.htm
**Summary:** To provide financial assistance to residents of Ohio who are working on an undergraduate degree in a field related to the construction industry.
**Eligibility:** Open to residents of Ohio who are undergraduates in at least the second year of a 2-year or 4-year college or university. Applicants must be enrolled in a construction degree program and be preparing for a career in construction. They must be U.S. citizens with a GPA of 2.5 or higher. Along with their application, they must submit transcripts, a list of extracurricular activities, a list of awards and achievements, and a 500-word essay on their interest in a career in construction. Financial need is not a high priority in the selection process, but it is considered.
**Financial data:** The stipend is $1,000.
**Duration:** 1 year.
**Number awarded:** 3 each year.
**Deadline:** March of each year.

## 2877 AGC/I CONSTRUCTION INDUSTRY SCHOLARSHIPS

Associated General Contractors of Indiana
Attn: Scholarship Committee
10 West Market Street, Suite 1050
Indianapolis, IN 46204
Phone: (317) 656-8899; (800) 899-8823; Fax: (317) 656-8889;
Email: kfavory@agcin.org
Web: www.agcin.org/scholarship.wws

**Summary:** To provide financial to residents of Indiana who are working on a degree in construction at a college or university in the state.
**Eligibility:** Open to Indiana residents who have completed at least 60 credit hours in an ACCE or ABET-accredited construction-related program at a 4-year college or university in the state. Applicants must have a GPA of 2.8 or higher. Preference is given to those who intend to work in Indiana and have been active in a campus chapter of the Associated General Contractors of America. Along with their application, they must submit an essay of 250 to 500 words on their previous construction work experience, leadership skills, how and where those were demonstrated, and future construction industry career plans. Financial need is not considered.
**Financial data:** The stipend is $3,000.
**Duration:** 1 year.
**Number awarded:** 4 each year.
**Deadline:** September of each year.

## 2878 A.J. (ANDY) SPIELMAN SCHOLARSHIPS

American Society of Travel Agents
Attn: ASTA Foundation
1101 King Street, Suite 200
Alexandria, VA 22314-2944
Phone: (703) 739-2782; Fax: (703) 684-8319; Email: scholarship@astahq.com
Web: www.astanet.com/education/scholarshipf.asp
**Summary:** To provide financial assistance to reentry students who are interested in preparing for a career in the travel/tourism industry.
**Eligibility:** Open to students who are enrolled or preparing to enroll at a recognized proprietary travel school as reentry students. Applicants must have a GPA of 2.5 or higher, be citizens or permanent residents of the United States or Canada, and write a 500-word essay on "Why I Have Chosen the Travel Profession for My Re-Entry into the Work Force." This scholarship was established in 1988 by the Central Atlantic Chapter of the American Society of Travel Agents (ASTA).
**Number awarded:** 2 each year.
**Financial data:** The stipend is $2,500.
**Duration:** 1 year.
**Deadline:** July of each year.

## 2879 ALABAMA FUNERAL DIRECTORS ASSOCIATION SCHOLARSHIP

Alabama Funeral Directors Association
Attn: Executive Director
P.O. Box 241281
Montgomery, AL 36124-1281
Phone: (334) 277-9565; Fax: (334) 277-8028
Web: www.alabamafda.org
**Summary:** To provide financial assistance to residents of Alabama who are attending an accredited mortuary science school.
**Eligibility:** Open to residents of Alabama who have completed at least 30 credit hours in an accredited mortuary science school in any state with a grade of at least "C" in all required mortuary science classes and have an overall GPA of 2.5 or higher. Applicants must be sponsored by an active member of the Alabama Funeral Directors Association (AFDA) and must submit a 500-word essay on "A Career in Funeral Service." They must be planning to return to Alabama to serve the public in their chosen profession. Selection is based on academic record and evaluation of the required essay; financial need is not considered.
**Financial data:** The stipend is $1,000. Funds are paid directly to the school the recipient attends.
**Duration:** 1 year.
**Number awarded:** 2 each year.
**Deadline:** April of each year.

## 2880 ALABAMA YOUNG BANKERS ESSAY SCHOLARSHIP

Alabama Bankers Association
Attn: Scholarship Applications
534 Adams Avenue
Montgomery, AL 36104
Phone: (334) 834-1890; (800) 239-5521; Fax: (334) 834-4443; Email: info@alabamabankers.org
Web: www.alabamabankers.org
**Summary:** To recognize and reward, with college scholarships, high school seniors in Alabama who submit outstanding essays on personal finance.
**Eligibility:** Open to seniors graduating from high schools in Alabama who can

demonstrate knowledge of good money management skills. Applicants must submit a 3-page essay on a topic that changes annually but relates to personal finance; a recent topic was, "Three Things Every High School Graduate Should Know About Personal Finance." Selection is based on comprehension (20%), organization (20%), conclusions (20%), creativity (20%), and writing (20%).

**Financial data:** The award is a $1,000 college scholarship.
**Duration:** The award is presented annually.
**Number awarded:** 1 each year.
**Deadline:** February of each year.

## 2881 ALASKA AIRLINES SCHOLARSHIP

American Society of Travel Agents
Attn: ASTA Foundation
1101 King Street, Suite 200
Alexandria, VA 22314-2944
Phone: (703) 739-2782; Fax: (703) 684-8319; Email: scholarship@astahq.com
Web: www.astanet.com/education/scholarshipe.asp
**Summary:** To provide financial assistance to undergraduate students working on a degree in travel and tourism or closely-related fields.
**Eligibility:** Open to college sophomores, juniors, or seniors enrolled at a 4-year college or university. Applicants must have a grade GPA of 2.5 or higher, be residents of the United States or Canada, and write a 500-word essay on why they are preparing for a career in the travel and tourism industry, including at least 2 career goals.
**Financial data:** The stipend is $2,000.
**Duration:** 1 year; may be renewed.
**Number awarded:** 1 each year.
**Deadline:** July of each year.

## 2882 ALASKADVANTAGE EDUCATIONAL GRANTS

**Summary:** To provide financial assistance to Alaska residents who attend college in the state to prepare for a career in designated fields with a workforce shortage.
*See Listing #1817.*

## 2883 ALEX POSTLETHWAITE SCHOLARSHIP

Society of Louisiana Certified Public Accountants
Attn: LCPA Education Foundation
2400 Veterans Boulevard, Suite 500
Kenner, LA 70062-4739
Phone: (504) 464-1040; (800) 288-5272; Fax: (504) 469-7930
Web: www.lcpa.org/LCPAScholarships.html
**Summary:** To provide financial assistance to currently-enrolled college students in Louisiana who are interested in becoming certified public accountants.
**Eligibility:** Open to Louisiana residents who are currently enrolled full time in an accounting program at a 4-year college or university in Louisiana. Applicants must have completed at least 4 semesters by the fall of the academic year in which the application is filed and have a GPA of 2.5 or higher. Along with their application, they must submit a 2-page essay on their perception of the C.P.A.'s role on the job and in the community, including how they plan to contribute to the profession and to the community.
**Financial data:** The stipend is $1,000.
**Duration:** 1 year.
**Number awarded:** 1 each year.

## 2884 ALICE GLAISYER WARFIELD MEMORIAL SCHOLARSHIP

**Summary:** To provide financial assistance to college students interested in preparing for a career in fields related to transportation.
*See Listing #1822.*

## 2885 ALICE M. YARNOLD AND SAMUEL YARNOLD SCHOLARSHIP

**Summary:** To provide financial assistance to currently-enrolled college students in New Hampshire who are majoring in nursing, medicine, social work, or other areas.
*See Listing #1823.*

## 2886 ALICE YURIKO ENDO MEMORIAL SCHOLARSHIP

Japanese American Citizens League
Attn: National Scholarship Awards
1765 Sutter Street
San Francisco, CA 94115
Phone: (415) 921-5225; Fax: (415) 931-4671; Email: jacl@jacl.org
Web: www.jacl.org/scholarships.html
**Summary:** To provide financial assistance to student members of the Japanese American Citizens League (JACL) who are working on an undergraduate degree, particularly in public or social service.
**Eligibility:** Open to JACL members who are currently enrolled or planning to reenter a college, university, trade school, business college, or other institution of higher learning. Applicants must submit a statement describing their current level of involvement in the Japanese American community or Asian Pacific community and how they will continue their involvement in future years. Selection is based on academic record, extracurricular activities, financial need, and community involvement. Preference is given to students planning a future in public or social service and/or residing in the Eastern District Council area.
**Financial data:** The stipend depends on the availability of funds but usually ranges from $1,000 to $5,000.
**Duration:** 1 year; nonrenewable.
**Number awarded:** 1 each year.
**Deadline:** March of each year.

## 2887 ALLYN & BACON PSYCHOLOGY AWARDS

Psi Chi
825 Vine Street
P.O. Box 709
Chattanooga, TN 37401-0709
Phone: (423) 756-2044; Fax: (877) 774-2443; Email: awards@psichi.org
Web: www.psichi.org
**Summary:** To recognize and reward outstanding research conducted by undergraduate members of Psi Chi (an honor society in psychology). This program is sponsored by Allyn & Bacon Publishers.
**Eligibility:** Open to all undergraduate students who are members of the society and submit a completed research papers (up to 12 pages long). The awards are presented to the best overall empirical studies.
**Financial data:** First place is $1,000, second $650, and third $350.
**Duration:** The prizes are awarded annually.
**Number awarded:** 3 each year.
**Deadline:** April of each year.

## 2888 ALMA WHITE–DELTA KAPPA GAMMA SCHOLARSHIP

Hawai'i Community Foundation
Attn: Scholarship Department
1164 Bishop Street, Suite 800
Honolulu, HI 96813
Phone: (808) 566-5570; (888) 731-3863; Fax: (808) 521-6286;
Email: scholarships@hcf-hawaii.org
Web: www.hawaiicommunityfoundation.org/scholar/scholar.php
**Summary:** To provide financial assistance to Hawaii residents who are working on an undergraduate or graduate degree in education.
**Eligibility:** Open to Hawaii residents who are enrolled in an education program (as a junior, senior, or graduate student). They must be able to demonstrate academic achievement (GPA of 2.7 or higher), good moral character, and financial need. Applications must be accompanied by a short statement indicating reasons for attending college, planned course of study, and career goals. Recipients must attend college on a full-time basis.
**Financial data:** The amounts of the awards depend on the availability of funds and the need of the recipient; recently, stipends averaged $1,000.
**Duration:** 1 year.
**Number awarded:** Varies each year; recently, 4 of these were awarded.
**Deadline:** February of each year.

## 2889 AMERICAN ENTERPRISE SPEECH CONTEST

National Management Association
Attn: American Enterprise Speech Contest
2210 Arbor Boulevard
Dayton, OH 45439-1580
Phone: (937) 294-0421; Fax: (937) 294-2374; Email: nma@nma1.org
Web: nma1.org/aespeech/index.htm

**Summary:** To recognize and reward outstanding high school speeches on the American competitive enterprise system.

**Eligibility:** Open to students in grades 9-12 in a high school within an area of a sponsoring chapter of the National Management Association (NMA). Contestants prepare speeches of 4 to 6 minutes on a topic related to the economic system of the United States. Non-economic issues (social, medical, environmental, political, etc.) may be utilized, but only if focused on business/entrepreneurial issues or approaches. No audio/visual aids are allowed with the presentations, and speeches may not be read verbatim, although notes are allowed. Winners of the chapter contests advance to council competition, from which winners proceed to compete in 1 of the 6 areas of the NMA. The 6 area winners then compete in the national contest. Speeches are judged on the basis of content (50%), delivery (30%), and language (20%).

**Financial data:** Chapter awards are determined by each chapter, up to a maximum of $500 for the first-place winner; each council also determines its own awards, to a maximum of $750 for the first-place winner. In each of the area contests, first prize is $2,000, second $1,500, and third $1,000. In the national contest, first prize is $10,000, second $5,000, third $3,000, and fourth through sixth $500. All prizes are in the form of savings bonds. All costs for prizes and transportation at chapter and council levels are paid by the individual chapters and councils. The national level of NMA supplies the area prizes, national prizes, and transportation reimbursements for area winners to compete in the national contest.

**Number awarded:** 18 area and 6 national winners are selected each year; the number of chapter and council prizes awarded varies.

**Deadline:** Chapter contests are held in January or early February of each year, council contests in February or March, area contests in April and May, and the national contest in September or October.

## 2890 AMERICAN EXPRESS ACADEMIC SCHOLARSHIPS

American Hotel & Lodging Educational Foundation
Attn: Manager of Foundation Programs
1201 New York Avenue, N.W., Suite 600
Washington, DC 20005-3931
Phone: (202) 289-3188; Fax: (202) 289-3199; Email: ahlef@ahlef.org
Web: www.ahlef.org/scholarships_american_express.asp

**Summary:** To provide financial assistance to undergraduate students interested in majoring in hospitality management in college.

**Eligibility:** Open to applicants who 1) are actively employed (at least 20 hours per week) at a hotel or motel that is a member of the American Hotel & Lodging Association (AH&LA) and have been employed at least 12 months by a hotel or 2) are the dependent of an employee who meets the requirements above and has been employed in the hospitality industry in some capacity in the past. In addition, applicants must be enrolled or planning to enroll as an undergraduate student in a hospitality management program offered by a university or college. Along with their application, they must submit a 500-word essay on their personal background, including when and why they became interested in the hospitality field, what characteristics will allow them to succeed, and how their education will help them to achieve their career objectives and future goals. Selection is based on financial need, industry-related work experience, academic record, extracurricular activities, career goals, the essay, and neatness and completeness of the application.

**Financial data:** Full-time students at 4-year institutions receive $2,000; part-time students at 4-year institutions receive $1,000; full- or part-time students at 2-year institutions receive $500. Funds are paid in 2 equal installments. Checks are made out jointly to the recipient and the academic institution and must be endorsed by both. Funds may be used only for tuition, fees, and books.

**Duration:** 1 year.

**Number awarded:** Varies each year; recently, this program awarded 7 Academic Scholarships.

**Deadline:** April of each year.

## 2891 AMERICAN EXPRESS FOUNDATION OF HOSPITALITY AND TOURISM ACADEMY SCHOLARSHIPS

DECA
1908 Association Drive
Reston, VA 20191-1594
Phone: (703) 860-5000; Fax: (703) 860-4013; Email: decainc@aol.com
Web: www.deca.org/scholarships/index.html

**Summary:** To provide financial assistance for college to DECA members who are also members of an academy of hospitality and tourism affiliated with the National Academy Foundation. This program is sponsored by American Express.

**Eligibility:** Open to DECA members who are high school seniors and also members of an academy of hospitality and tourism affiliated with the National Academy Foundation. Applicants must be interested in enrolling in a 2-year or 4-year course of study in marketing, merchandising, or management at an accredited institution or university. Selection based on DECA involvement, leadership, and grades. Applicants may also include a statement in support of financial need and it will be reviewed.

**Financial data:** The stipend is $1,000.

**Duration:** 1 year.

**Number awarded:** 2 each year.

**Deadline:** February of each year.

## 2892 AMERICAN EXPRESS TRAVEL SCHOLARSHIP

American Society of Travel Agents
Attn: ASTA Foundation
1101 King Street, Suite 200
Alexandria, VA 22314-2944
Phone: (703) 739-2782; Fax: (703) 684-8319; Email: scholarship@astahq.com
Web: www.astanet.com/education/scholarshipf.asp

**Summary:** To provide financial assistance to students preparing for a career in the travel industry at a 2-year college, 4-year college or university, or proprietary travel school.

**Eligibility:** Open to students who are enrolled or able to provide proof of acceptance at a proprietary travel school or a 2- or 4-year college in the United States or Canada that offers a travel and tourism program. Applicants must have a GPA of 2.5 or higher, be residents of the United States or Canada, and write a 500-word essay on their view of the travel industry's future. Selection is based on academic record, work performance, potential, and plans for a career in the travel/tourism industry.

**Financial data:** A stipend is awarded (amount not specified).

**Duration:** 1 year.

**Number awarded:** 1 each year.

**Deadline:** July of each year.

## 2893 AMERICAN FOREIGN SERVICE ASSOCIATION FINANCIAL AID SCHOLARSHIPS

**Summary:** To provide financial assistance to undergraduate students who are dependents of U.S. government employees involved in foreign service activities.

*See Listing #52.*

## 2894 AMERICAN FOREIGN SERVICE ASSOCIATION NATIONAL HIGH SCHOOL ESSAY CONTEST

American Foreign Service Association
Attn: National High School Essay Contest
2101 E Street, N.W.
Washington, DC 20037
Phone: (202) 338-4045; (800) 704-AFSA; Fax: (202) 338-6820;
Email: perrigreen@aol.com
Web: www.afsa.org/essaycontest/essaycontest1.cfm

**Summary:** To recognize and reward high school students who submit essays on a topic related to U.S. foreign relations.

**Eligibility:** Open to students in grades 9-12 attending a public, private, parochial, or home school or participating in a high school correspondence program in any of the 50 states, the District of Columbia, or the U.S. territories. U.S. citizens attending schools overseas are also eligible. Students whose parents are members of the U.S. Foreign Service or have served on the Advisory Committees are not eligible. Applicants must submit an essay of 750 to 1,000 words on a topic that changes annually. Recently, participants were invited to analyze and explain how the members of the Foreign Service promote U.S. national interests by participating in the resolution of today's major international problems. Essays are judged primarily on the basis of originality of analysis and quality of research. They should demonstrate thorough understanding of the major issue of foreign affairs selected and knowledge of the role of members of the Foreign Service in conducting the foreign relations of the United States.

**Financial data:** The first-place winner receives $2,500 and an all-expense paid trip to Washington, D.C. for the awards ceremony. The winner's school or sponsoring organization receives $500. Second place is $1,250 and third place is $750.

**Duration:** The competition is held annually.
**Number awarded:** 3 each year.
**Deadline:** February of each year.

## 2895 AMERICAN HOTEL & LODGING EDUCATIONAL FOUNDATION ANNUAL SCHOLARSHIP GRANT PROGRAM

American Hotel & Lodging Educational Foundation
Attn: Manager of Foundation Programs
1201 New York Avenue, N.W., Suite 600
Washington, DC 20005-3931
Phone: (202) 289-3181; Fax: (202) 289-3199; Email: ahlef@ahlef.org
Web: www.ahlef.org/scholarships_annual_grant.asp
**Summary:** To provide financial assistance to students working on an undergraduate degree in hospitality management at participating schools.
**Eligibility:** Open to applicants who are attending a 2-year or 4-year college in the United States or Canada that is preapproved and participating in the foundation's scholarship program (for a list of schools, write to the foundation). They must be majoring in hospitality management (including hotel and restaurant management) as full-time students with a GPA of 3.0 or higher. Individual schools select the final recipients. Nearly 80 schools are preapproved to participate in this program. This program includes the following named scholarships: the American Hotel and Lodging Association Allied Member Scholarships, the American Hotel and Lodging Foundation Annual Giving Campaign Scholarships, the American Hotel and Lodging Foundation General Scholarships, the Bill Fisher Scholarships, the Cecil B. Day Memorial Scholarships, the Steven Belmonte Scholarships, the Conrad N. Hilton Memorial Scholarships, the J. Willard Marriott Memorial Scholarships, the John Clifford Memorial Scholarships, the Karl Mehlmann Memorial Scholarships, the Richard Kessler Scholarships, the Curtis C. Nelson Scholarships, and the Handlery Scholarships.
**Financial data:** The amount awarded varies by school.
**Duration:** 1 year.
**Number awarded:** Varies each year; recently, 212 students received support from this program.
**Deadline:** Schools must submit their nominations by April of each year.

## 2896 AMERICAN INDIAN FELLOWSHIP IN BUSINESS SCHOLARSHIP

National Center for American Indian Enterprise Development
Attn: Scholarship Committee
953 East Juanita Avenue
Mesa, AZ 85204
Phone: (480) 545-1298, ext. 243; Fax: (480) 545-4208; Email: events@ncaied.org
Web: www.ncaied.org/fundraising
**Summary:** To provide financial assistance to American Indian upper-division and graduate students working on a business degree.
**Eligibility:** Open to American Indians who are currently enrolled full time in college at the upper-division or graduate school level and working on a business degree. Applicants must submit a letter on their reasons for pursuing higher education and their plans following completing of their degree. Selection is based on grades (30%), an essay on their community involvement (30%), an essay on personal challenges they have faced (25%), an essay on their paid or volunteer business experience (10%), and the quality of those essays (10%).
**Financial data:** A stipend is awarded (amount not specified).
**Duration:** 1 year.
**Number awarded:** Up to 5 each year.
**Deadline:** August of each year.

## 2897 AMERICAN LEGION NATIONAL HIGH SCHOOL ORATORICAL CONTEST

American Legion
Attn: Americanism and Children & Youth Division
P.O. Box 1055
Indianapolis, IN 46206-1055
Phone: (317) 630-1249; Fax: (317) 630-1223; Email: acy@legion.org
Web: www.legion.org
**Summary:** To recognize and reward high school students who participate in an oratorical contest on a theme related to the U.S. constitution.
**Eligibility:** Open to U.S. citizens under the age of 20 who are currently enrolled in junior high or high school (grades 9-12). Students enter the contest through their Department (state) American Legion. Each department chooses one contestant to enter the regional contest. Regional winners compete in sectional contests; sectional winners compete on the national level. In all competitions, participants are evaluated on both the content and presentation of their prepared and extemporaneous speeches, which must deal with some aspect of the American Constitution or principles of government under the Constitution.
**Financial data:** Scholarship awards are presented to the 3 finalists in the national contest: $18,000 to the first-place winner; $16,000 to the second-place winner; and $14,000 to the third-place winner. Each Department (state) winner who participates in the first round of the national contest receives a $1,500 scholarship; each first-round winner who advances to and participates in the second round, but does not advance to the final round, receives an additional $1,500 scholarship. The National Organization of the American Legion pays the travel costs of Department winners and their chaperones as they progress in national competition. Scholarships may be used to attend any accredited college or university in the United States. All contestants must be accompanied by a chaperone.
**Duration:** The competition is held annually.
**Number awarded:** 3 national winners; hundreds of sectional, regional, and departmental winners.
**Deadline:** The dates of departmental competitions vary; check with your local American Legion post. The national competition is generally held in April.

## 2898 AMERICAN SOCIETY OF WOMEN ACCOUNTANTS SCHOLARSHIPS

American Society of Women Accountants
Attn: Administrative Director
8405 Greensboro Drive, Suite 800
McLean, VA 22102
Phone: (703) 506-3265; (800) 326-2163; Fax: (703) 506-3266;
Email: aswa@aswa.org
Web: www.aswa.org/scholarship.html
**Summary:** To provide financial assistance to undergraduate and graduate women interested in preparing for a career in accounting. Founded in 1938 to assist women C.P.A.s, the organization has nearly 5,000 members in 30 chapters. Some chapters offer scholarships on the local/regional level. Funding for this program is provided by the Educational Foundation for Women in Accounting.
**Eligibility:** Open to women who are enrolled in a college, university, or professional school as either part-time or full-time students working on a bachelor's or master's degree in accounting. Applicants must have completed at least 60 semester hours with a declared accounting major. Selection is based on career goals, communication skills, GPA, personal circumstances, and financial need. Membership in the American Society of Women Accountants (ASWA) is not required. Applications must be submitted to a local ASWA chapter.
**Financial data:** The stipends range from $1,500 to $4,500 each.
**Duration:** 1 year; recipients may reapply.
**Number awarded:** Varies each year; recently, 8 of these scholarships were available, with a total value of $14,000.
**Deadline:** Local chapters must submit their candidates to the national office by February of each year.

## 2899 ANNIS IRENE FOWLER/KADEN SCHOLARSHIP

South Dakota Board of Regents
Attn: Scholarship Committee
306 East Capitol Avenue, Suite 200
Pierre, SD 57501-2545
Phone: (605) 773-3455; Fax: (605) 773-2422; Email: info@ris.sdbor.edu
Web: www.sdbor.edu/administration/academics/Scholarships.htm
**Summary:** To provide financial assistance to high school seniors planning to attend a public university in South Dakota and major in elementary education.
**Eligibility:** Open to first-time entering freshmen at public universities in South Dakota. Applicants must have a GPA of 3.0 or higher and an intent to major in elementary education. They must submit an essay (from 1,000 to 1,500 words) on a topic that changes annually; recently, the topic related to advantages and disadvantages of No Child Left Behind laws. Special consideration is given to students who demonstrate motivational ability, who have a disability, or who are self-supporting.
**Financial data:** The stipend is $1,000; funds are allocated to the institution for distribution to the student.
**Duration:** 1 year; nonrenewable.
**Number awarded:** 1 each year.
**Deadline:** February of each year.

## 2900 APF/APA TOPSS EXCELLENCE IN HIGH SCHOOL STUDENT RESEARCH AWARDS

American Psychological Association
Attn: Education Directorate
750 First Street, N.E.
Washington, DC 20002-4242
Phone: (202) 572-3013; Fax: (202) 336-5962; Email: eleary@apa.org
Web: www.apa.org/ed/topss/excelhsawards.html

**Summary:** To recognize and reward high school students who conduct outstanding research projects in psychology. This program is cosponsored by the American Psychological Foundation (APF).

**Eligibility:** Open to high school students who have conducted an original psychology research project. Candidates must be sponsored by a current member of the American Psychological Association (APA) Teachers of Psychology in Secondary Schools (TOPSS). They must submit a paper, up to 20 pages in length, describing the project. Selection is based on the literature review (30 points), hypothesis and method (30 points), results (20 points), and discussion (20 points).

**Financial data:** First prize is $1,500, second $1,000, third $500, and fourth $250.

**Duration:** The competition is held annually.

**Number awarded:** 4 each year.

**Deadline:** March of each year.

## 2901 APPLEGATE/JACKSON/PARKS FUTURE TEACHER SCHOLARSHIP

National Institute for Labor Relations Research
Attn: Future Teacher Scholarships
5211 Port Royal Road, Suite 510
Springfield, VA 22151
Phone: (703) 321-9606; Fax: (703) 321-7342; Email: research@nilrr.org
Web: www.nilrr.org/teachers.htm

**Summary:** To provide financial assistance to students majoring in education who oppose compulsory unionism in the education community. This program was established in 1989 to honor Carol Applegate, Kay Jackson, and Dr. Anne Parks, 3 Michigan public school teachers who lost their jobs because they refused to pay union dues.

**Eligibility:** Open to undergraduate students majoring in education in institutions of higher learning in the United States. They must write an essay of approximately 500 words demonstrating an interest in and a knowledge of the right to work principle as it applies to educators. Selection is based on scholastic ability and financial need. Applicants must also demonstrate 1) the potential to complete a degree program in education and receive a teaching license, and 2) an understanding of the principles of voluntary unionism and the problems of compulsory unionism in relation to education.

**Financial data:** The stipend is $1,000.

**Duration:** 1 year.

**Number awarded:** 1 each year.

**Deadline:** December of each year.

## 2902 APPRAISAL INSTITUTE EDUCATION TRUST SCHOLARSHIP

Appraisal Institute
Attn: Appraisal Institute Education Trust
550 West Van Buren Street, Suite 1000
Chicago, IL 60607
Phone: (312) 335-4100; Fax: (312) 335-4400;
Email: ocarreon@appraisalinstitute.org
Web: www.appraisalinstitute.org/education/scolarshp.asp

**Summary:** To provide financial assistance to graduate and undergraduate students majoring in real estate or allied fields.

**Eligibility:** Open to U.S. citizens who are graduate or undergraduate students majoring in real estate appraisal, land economics, real estate, or related fields. Applicants must submit a statement regarding their general activities and intellectual interests in college; college training; activities and employment outside of college; contemplated line of study for a degree; and career they expect to follow after graduation. Selection is based on academic excellence.

**Financial data:** The stipend is $3,000 for graduate students or $2,000 for undergraduate students.

**Duration:** 1 year.

**Number awarded:** At least 1 each year.

**Deadline:** March of each year.

## 2903 APWA HORIZONS FRONT RANGE SCHOLARSHIP

**Summary:** To provide financial assistance to high school seniors in Colorado who plan to attend a college or university in the state to prepare for a career in public works.

*See Listing #1273.*

## 2904 AQHF EDUCATION OR NURSING SCHOLARSHIP

**Summary:** To provide financial assistance for college to members of the American Quarter Horse Association (AQHA) or the American Quarter Horse Youth Association (AQHYA) who are planning a career in education or nursing.

*See Listing #1864.*

## 2905 ARIZONA CHAPTER GOLD SCHOLARSHIP

American Society of Travel Agents
Attn: ASTA Foundation
1101 King Street, Suite 200
Alexandria, VA 22314-2944
Phone: (703) 739-2782; Fax: (703) 684-8319; Email: scholarship@astahq.com
Web: www.astanet.com/education/scholarshipe.asp

**Summary:** To provide financial assistance to college students in Arizona interested in preparing for a career in the travel industry.

**Eligibility:** Open to sophomores, juniors, or seniors at a 4-year college or university in Arizona. Applicants must provide a letter of recommendation, have a GPA of 2.5 or higher, be a U.S. citizen or permanent resident, and write a 500-word essay on their career plans in the travel industry and their interest in the business of travel and tourism.

**Financial data:** The stipend is $3,000.

**Duration:** 1 year.

**Number awarded:** 1 each year.

**Deadline:** July of each year.

## 2906 ARIZONA PRIVATE SCHOOL ASSOCIATION SCHOLARSHIP

**Summary:** To provide financial assistance to high school seniors in Arizona who are interested in attending a career college to prepare for jobs in selected fields.

*See Listing #1870.*

## 2907 ARKANSAS APWA SCHOLARSHIPS

**Summary:** To provide financial assistance to high school seniors in Arkansas who are interested in attending college to prepare for a career related to the public works profession.

*See Listing #1871.*

## 2908 ARNOLD SADLER MEMORIAL SCHOLARSHIP

**Summary:** To provide financial assistance to undergraduate or graduate students who are blind and are interested in studying in a field of service to persons with disabilities.

*See Listing #1874.*

## 2909 ART PFAFF SCHOLARSHIP PROGRAM

Missouri Middle School Association
c/o Jane Haskell, Executive Director
P.O. Box 487
Rolla, MO 65402-0847
Phone: (573) 364-9307; Fax: (573) 364-9307; Email: hasmmsa@fidnet.com
Web: www.mmsa-mo.org/pfaff_scholarship.html

**Summary:** To provide financial assistance to students in Missouri who are working on a degree to receive entry level certification to teach at the middle level school.

**Eligibility:** Open to students currently enrolled in an education program that will qualify them for entry level middle school certification in Missouri. Applicants must be classified as a sophomore or higher by their college or university and have a cumulative GPA of 2.5 or higher. They must have made a commitment to be trained as a middle level teacher and to teach at that level after completing their degree. Along with their application, they must submit a brief autobiographical sketch and essays on why they have chosen to become a middle school teacher, how they think they can make a difference as a middle school teacher, the activities during high school and/or college in which they have been involved with middle school age children, what someone would expect to see if they came into their middle school classroom, why a middle school should be different from a typical junior high school, and how this scholarship will help them attain their career goals. Financial need is not considered.

**Financial data:** The stipend is $1,000.

**Duration:** 1 year.

**Number awarded:** 1 or more each year.

**Deadline:** February of each year.

## 2910 ARTHUR J. PACKARD MEMORIAL SCHOLARSHIP COMPETITION

American Hotel & Lodging Educational Foundation
Attn: Manager of Foundation Programs
1201 New York Avenue, N.W., Suite 600
Washington, DC 20005-3931
Phone: (202) 289-3181; Fax: (202) 289-3199; Email: ahlef@ahlef.org
Web: www.ahlef.org/scholarships_packard_memorial.asp

**Summary:** To recognize and reward outstanding students working on an undergraduate degree in lodging management at participating universities.

**Eligibility:** Open to applicants who are attending a 4-year college or university that is preapproved and participating in the foundation's scholarship program (for a list of schools, write to the foundation). They must be enrolled full time in a hospitality-related degree-granting program, be a sophomore or junior at the time of application, have a GPA of 3.5 or higher, be a U.S. citizen or permanent resident, and be nominated by their school. Selection is based on academic performance, hospitality work experience, financial need, extracurricular involvement (activities and honors), and personal attributes.

**Financial data:** The national winner receives $5,000, the second-place runner-up receives $3,000, and the third-place runner-up receives $2,000.

**Duration:** The competition is held annually.

**Number awarded:** 1 winner and 2 runners-up each year.

**Deadline:** March of each year.

## 2911 ASMC NATIONAL SCHOLARSHIP PROGRAM

American Society of Military Comptrollers
Attn: National Awards Committee
415 North Alfred Street
Alexandria, VA 22314
Phone: (703) 549-0360; (800) 462-5637; (703) 549-3181;
Email: asmchq@aol.com
Web: www.asmconline.org/national/nationalawards.shtml

**Summary:** To provide financial assistance to high school seniors and recent graduates interested in preparing for a career in financial management.

**Eligibility:** Open to high school seniors and to people who graduated from high school during the preceding 6 months. Applicants must be planning to enter college in a field of study directly related to financial resource management, including business administration, economics, public administration, computer science, or operations research related to financial management, accounting, and finance. They must be endorsed by a chapter of the American Society of Military Comptrollers (ASMC). Selection is based on scholastic achievement, leadership ability, extracurricular activities, career and academic goals, and financial need. The ASMC is open to all financial management professionals employed by the U.S. Department of Defense and Coast Guard, both civilian and military.

**Financial data:** Stipends are $2,000 or $1,000 per year.

**Duration:** 1 year.

**Number awarded:** 10 each year: 5 at $2,000 and 5 at $1,000.

**Deadline:** March of each year.

## 2912 ASPARAGUS CLUB SCHOLARSHIPS

Baton Rouge Area Foundation
Attn: Scholarship Programs
402 North Fourth Street
Baton Rouge, LA 70802
Phone: (225) 387-6126; (877) 387-6126; Fax: (225) 387-6153;
Email: rsayes@braf.org
Web: www.braf.org

**Summary:** To provide financial assistance to college students interested in preparing for a career in the grocery industry. The Asparagus Club was founded in 1909 to generate a spirit of cooperation and unity among all segments of the grocery industry. Its scholarship fund has been administered by the Baton Rouge Area Foundation since 2002.

**Eligibility:** Open to college sophomores and juniors who are working on a degree in an academic discipline relevant to the grocery industry. Their field of study may relate to retailing (including supermarket management, convenience store management, produce management, advertising, accounts management, marketing, public relations), processing and manufacturing (including food plant management, personnel management, purchasing management, sales management, packaging, new product development), or wholesaling (including merchandising, marketing, accounting, store construction and remodeling, computer applications). Applicants must submit a letter of recommendation from a professor in the food management and/or business school, transcripts, ACT and/or SAT scores, and documentation of financial need.

**Financial data:** Stipends range up to $1,500 per year. Funds are sent directly to the student with a check payable to him or her and the university to be used for tuition and fees.

**Duration:** 1 year; may be renewed if the recipient maintains a GPA of 2.5 or higher.

**Number awarded:** Varies each year.

**Deadline:** May of each year.

## 2913 ASSOCIATED GENERAL CONTRACTORS OF VERMONT SCHOLARSHIPS

**Summary:** To provide financial assistance to Vermont residents who are interested in studying a field related to construction.
*See Listing #1897.*

## 2914 ASSOCIATED GENERAL CONTRACTORS OF VIRGINIA SCHOLARSHIPS

Associated General Contractors of Virginia
Attn: Kelly Ragsdale
11950 Nuckols Road
Glen Allen, VA 23059
Phone: (804) 364-5504; (800) 581-4652; Fax: (804) 364-5511
Web: www.agcva.org/Brochure/scholarships.htm

**Summary:** To provide financial assistance to students in Virginia who are preparing for a career in the construction industry.

**Eligibility:** Open to students at Virginia colleges and universities who are preparing for a career in construction.

**Financial data:** The stipend is $2,000.

**Duration:** 1 year.

**Number awarded:** 3 each year.

## 2915 ASSOCIATION OF CALIFORNIA WATER AGENCIES SCHOLARSHIPS

**Summary:** To provide financial assistance to upper-division students in California who are majoring in water resources-related fields of study.
*See Listing #1902.*

## 2916 ASSOCIATION OF ENERGY ENGINEERS SCHOLARSHIPS

**Summary:** To provide financial assistance to undergraduate and graduate students interested in taking courses directly related to energy engineering or energy management.
*See Listing #1904.*

## 2917 ASSOCIATION OF GOLF MERCHANDISERS SCHOLARSHIPS

Association of Golf Merchandisers
P.O. Box 7247
Phoenix, AZ 85011-7247
Phone: (602) 604-8250; Fax: (602) 604-8251; Email: info@agmgolf.org
Web: www.agmgolf.org

**Summary:** To provide financial assistance to college students interested in a career in golf merchandising.

**Eligibility:** Open to students who are currently enrolled at a college, university, or technical institute and are actively preparing for a golf merchandising career. Applicants must have completed at least their sophomore year with a GPA of 2.5 or higher.

**Financial data:** The stipend is $1,000.
**Duration:** 1 year.
**Number awarded:** Several each year.

## 2918 ASSOCIATION OF LATINO PROFESSIONALS IN FINANCE AND ACCOUNTING SCHOLARSHIPS

Association of Latino Professionals in Finance and Accounting
Attn: Scholarships
510 West Sixth Street, Suite 400
Los Angeles, CA 90017
Phone: (213) 243-0004; Fax: (213) 243-0006;
Email: scholarships@national.alpfa.org
Web: www.alpfa.org
**Summary:** To provide financial assistance to undergraduate and graduate students of Hispanic descent who are preparing for a career in a field related to finance or accounting.
**Eligibility:** Open to full-time undergraduate and graduate students who have completed at least 15 undergraduate units at a college or university in the United States or Puerto Rico with a GPA of 3.0 or higher. Applicants must be of Hispanic heritage, defined as having 1 parent fully Hispanic or both parents half Hispanic. They must be working on a degree in accounting, finance, information technology, or a related field. Along with their application, they must submit a 2-page personal statement that addresses their Hispanic heritage and family background, personal and academic achievements, academic plans and career goals, efforts and plans for making a difference in their community, and financial need. U.S. citizenship or permanent resident status is required. The sponsoring organization was formerly named the American Association of Hispanic Certified Public Accountants. This program is administered by the Hispanic College Fund, 1717 Pennsylvania Avenue, Suite 460, Washington, DC 20006, (202) 296-5400, (800) 644-4223, Fax: (202) 296-3774, Email: hcf-info@hispanic-fund.org.
**Financial data:** Stipends range from $1,000 to $5,000.
**Duration:** 1 year.
**Number awarded:** Varies each year; recently, 78 of these scholarships, worth $195,000, were awarded.
**Deadline:** April of each year.

## 2919 ATFRA SCHOLARSHIP

Boy Scouts of America
Attn: Learning for Life Division, S210
1325 West Walnut Hill Lane
P.O. Box 152079
Irving, TX 75015-2079
Phone: (972) 580-2418; Fax: (972) 580-2137
Web: www.learning-for-life.org/exploring/scholarships/index.html
**Summary:** To provide financial assistance for college to Explorer Scouts who plan a career as law enforcement executives.
**Eligibility:** Open to Explorer Scouts who are at least seniors in high school and active members of a Law Enforcement Explorer post registered with Boy Scouts of America. Applicants must be interested in a career in law enforcement. Selection is based on academic record, letters of recommendation, and a personal essay describing at least 3 personal attributes or skills that they believe are the most important for a law enforcement professional to develop and how their undergraduate studies will help them develop those attributes and skills. This program is sponsored by the Bureau of Alcohol, Tobacco, Firearms and Explosives Retiree's Association (ATFRA). Information is also available from the Bureau's Office of Law Enforcement, 650 Massachusetts Avenue, N.W., Room 8290, Washington, DC 20226.
**Financial data:** The stipend is $1,000.
**Duration:** 1 year; nonrenewable.
**Number awarded:** 1 or more every other year, depending on the availability of funds.
**Deadline:** March of even-numbered years.

## 2920 AVIATION COUNCIL OF PENNSYLVANIA SCHOLARSHIP

**Summary:** To provide financial assistance for college to students from Pennsylvania preparing for a career in aviation or aviation management.
*See Listing #1910.*

## 2921 AVIATION DISTRIBUTORS AND MANUFACTURERS ASSOCIATION SCHOLARSHIP PROGRAM

**Summary:** To provide financial assistance to students who are preparing for a career in the aviation field.
*See Listing #1911.*

## 2922 AVIS SCHOLARSHIP

American Society of Travel Agents
Attn: ASTA Foundation
1101 King Street, Suite 200
Alexandria, VA 22314-2944
Phone: (703) 739-2782; Fax: (703) 684-8319; Email: scholarship@astahq.com
Web: www.astanet.com/education/scholarshiph.asp
**Summary:** To provide financial assistance to travel industry professionals who have returned to college or graduate school.
**Eligibility:** Open to travel industry professionals who have at least 2 years of full-time experience in the travel industry (e.g., tour operator, travel agency, hotel, airlines, car rental) or an undergraduate degree in travel and tourism. Applicants must be currently employed in the travel industry and enrolled in at least 2 courses per semester in an accredited undergraduate or graduate program in business or equivalent degree program at an accredited 4-year college or university. They must have a GPA of 3.0 or higher during their previous academic term. Selection is based on an essay of 500 to 750 words on how their degree program relates to their future career in the travel industry.
**Financial data:** The stipend is $2,000.
**Duration:** 1 year; may be renewed up to 2 additional years.
**Number awarded:** 1 each year.
**Deadline:** July of each year.

## 2923 BANK OF AMERICA ACHIEVEMENT AWARDS

**Summary:** To recognize and reward high school seniors in California who excel in specific subject areas.
*See Listing #1283.*

## 2924 BARBARA JORDAN MEMORIAL SCHOLARSHIP

Association of Texas Professional Educators
Attn: Scholarships
305 East Huntland Drive, Suite 300
Austin, TX 78752-3792
Phone: (512) 467-0071; (800) 777-ATPE; Fax: (512) 467-2203;
Email: atpe@atpe.org
Web: www.atpe.org/Awards/bjordaninfo.htm
**Summary:** To provide financial assistance to undergraduate and graduate students enrolled in educator preparation programs at predominantly ethnic minority institutions in Texas. The qualifying institutions are Huston-Tillotson College, Jarvis Christian College, Our Lady of the Lake University, Paul Quinn College, Prairie View A&M University, St. Mary's University of San Antonio, Sul Ross State University, Sul Ross State University Rio Grande College, Texas A&M International University, Texas A&M University at Kingsville, Texas Southern University, University of Houston, University of Houston-Downtown, University of Texas at Brownsville and Texas Southmost College, University of Texas at El Paso, University of Texas at San Antonio, University of Texas-Pan American, University of the Incarnate Word, and Wiley College.
**Eligibility:** Open to juniors, seniors, and graduate students enrolled in educator preparation programs at predominantly ethnic minority institutions in Texas. Applicants must submit a 2-page essay on their personal philosophy toward education, why they want to become an educator, who influenced them the most in making their career decision, and why they are applying for the scholarship. Financial need is not considered in the selection process.
**Financial data:** The stipend is $1,500 per year.
**Duration:** 1 year.
**Number awarded:** Up to 6 each year.
**Deadline:** May of each year.

## 2925 BERNARD GRYSEN MEMORIAL CRIMINAL JUSTICE SCHOLARSHIPS

Michigan Sheriffs' Association
Attn: Educational Services
515 North Capitol Avenue
Lansing, MI 48933
Phone: (517) 485-3135; Fax: (517) 485-1013

Web: www.michigansheriff.com

**Summary:** To provide financial assistance to high school seniors in Michigan who are interested in attending college to prepare for a career in criminal justice.

**Eligibility:** Open to seniors graduating from high schools in Michigan who are planning to attend a college or university in the state to prepare for a career in criminal justice. Applicants must be able to demonstrate high academic standing, high moral character, and a high degree of activity in civic and governmental affairs relating to law enforcement. They must be nominated by a member of the Michigan Sheriffs' Association. Along with their application, they must submit a 300-word essay on why they are preparing for a career in criminal justice." Financial need is not considered in he selection process.

**Financial data:** The stipend is $1,000.

**Duration:** 1 year.

**Number awarded:** 10 each year: 2 in each of the association's districts.

**Deadline:** April of each year.

---

### 2926 BETTY BROEMMELSIEK MEMORIAL CONSERVATION SCHOLARSHIPS

**Summary:** To provide financial assistance to undergraduate students at Missouri colleges and universities interested in preparing for a career in natural resources conservation.

*See Listing #1931.*

---

### 2927 BETTY STEVENS-FRECKNALL SCHOLARSHIPS

Association of Information Technology Professionals
Attn: Foundation for Information Technology Education
401 North Michigan Avenue, Suite 2400
Chicago, Il 60611-4267
Phone: (312) 245-1070; (800) 224-9371; Fax: (312) 527-6636;
Email: larry_schmitz@aitp.org
Web: www.edfoundation.org

**Summary:** To provide financial assistance to students working on a degree (at any level) in information technology.

**Eligibility:** Open to full-time students who are working on an associate, bachelor's, master's, or doctoral degree in information technology in the United States. Applicants must be members of the Association of Information Technology Professionals. Selection is based on scholastic ability, leadership potential, and financial need.

**Financial data:** The stipend is $2,000.

**Duration:** 1 year.

**Number awarded:** Varies each year; recently, 2 of these scholarships were awarded.

**Deadline:** May of each year.

---

### 2928 BEV AND WES STOCK SCHOLARSHIP

Seattle Mariners Women's Club
P.O. Box 4100
Seattle, WA 98104
Phone: (206) 628-3555

**Summary:** To provide financial assistance to high school athletes in Washington state who are interested in preparing for an athletic-related career.

**Eligibility:** Open to athletes who display good character both on and off the playing field. They must be graduating high school seniors in Washington state who are planning to prepare for an athletic-related career and will be attending a college or university in the coming academic year. There is no application form. Applicants must submit a typewritten essay outlining why they are applying for the scholarship, their extracurricular activities, their goals, and how receiving the scholarship will be an advantage to them. Also required are a transcript and 3 letters of recommendation. Selection is based on merit.

**Financial data:** The stipend is $1,000.

**Duration:** 1 year; nonrenewable.

**Additional information:** No telephone inquiries are permitted.

**Number awarded:** 1 each year.

**Deadline:** May of each year.

---

### 2929 BICK BICKSON SCHOLARSHIP FUND

Hawai'i Community Foundation
Attn: Scholarship Department
1164 Bishop Street, Suite 800
Honolulu, HI 96813

Phone: (808) 566-5570; (888) 731-3863; Fax: (808) 521-6286;
Email: scholarships@hcf-hawaii.org
Web: www.hawaiicommunityfoundation.org/scholar/scholar.php

**Summary:** To provide financial assistance to Hawaii residents who are interested in studying marketing, law, or travel industry management in college or graduate school.

**Eligibility:** Open to Hawaii residents who are interested in majoring in marketing, law, or travel industry management on the undergraduate or graduate school level. They must be able to demonstrate academic achievement (GPA of 2.7 or higher), good moral character, and financial need. In addition to filling out the standard application form, applicants must write a short statement indicating their reasons for attending college, their planned course of study, and their career goals. Recipients may attend college in Hawaii or on the mainland. Recipients must be full-time students.

**Financial data:** The amounts of the awards depend on the availability of funds and the need of the recipient; recently, stipends averaged $1,250.

**Duration:** 1 year.

**Number awarded:** Varies each year; recently, 2 of these scholarships were awarded.

**Deadline:** February of each year.

---

### 2930 BIRCH TELECOM COMPETITION ROCKS! SCHOLARSHIP PROGRAM & ESSAY CONTEST

Birch Telecom
Attn: Scholarship Committee
2114 Central, Suite 300
Kansas City, MO 64108
Phone: (816) 300-5716; Email: eblackwell@birch.com
Web: www.birch.com/scholarship

**Summary:** To recognize and reward outstanding essays written by high school seniors in selected states on the value of competition.

**Eligibility:** Open to high school seniors who are U.S. citizens or permanent residents and living in 1 of the following states: Alabama, Florida, Georgia, Kansas, Louisiana, Missouri, Mississippi, North Carolina, Oklahoma, South Carolina, Tennessee, or Texas. Interested students must submit an essay on the value of competition: lower prices, better service, more innovative products, etc. Entrants also need to have taken the ACT or SAT and be scheduled to enroll at a college or university in the fall following the competition.

**Financial data:** Awards range from $500 to $2,500; in total, $25,000 is distributed annually.

**Duration:** These are 1-time awards; nonrenewable.

**Number awarded:** 24 each year: 4 at $2,500; 10 at $1,000; and 10 at $500.

**Deadline:** March of each year.

---

### 2931 BNSF SCHOLARSHIP PROGRAM

**Summary:** To provide financial assistance to Hispanic American undergraduate students from designated states who are interested in preparing for a career in a business-related field.

*See Listing #1941.*

---

### 2932 BOEING CAREER ENHANCEMENT SCHOLARSHIP

**Summary:** To provide financial assistance to members of Women in Aviation, International (WAI) who are active in aerospace and need financial support to advance their career.

*See Listing #1943.*

---

### 2933 BOSTON AFFILIATE SCHOLARSHIP

American Woman's Society of Certified Public Accountants-Boston Affiliate
c/o Julie Mead
Ziner, Kennedy & Lehan
2300 Crown Colony Drive
Quincy, MA 02169
Email: julie.m.mead@aexp.com
Web: www.awscpa.org/affiliate_scholarships/boston.html

**Summary:** To provide financial assistance to women who are working on an undergraduate or graduate degree in accounting at a college or university in New England.

**Eligibility:** Open to women who are attending a college in New England and majoring in accounting. Applicants must have completed at least 12 semester hours of accounting or tax courses and have a cumulative GPA of 3.0 or higher. They must be planning to graduate between May of next year and May of the following year or, for the 15-month graduate program, before September of the current year.

**Financial data:** A stipend is awarded (amount not specified).

**Duration:** 1 year.

**Number awarded:** 1 or more each year.

**Deadline:** April of each year.

## 2934 BPA "WHO'S WHO AMONG AMERICAN HIGH SCHOOL STUDENTS" SCHOLARSHIP

Business Professionals of America
5454 Cleveland Avenue
Columbus, OH 43231-4021
Phone: (614) 895-7277; (800) 334-2007; Fax: (614) 895-1165
Web: www.bpa.org

**Summary:** To provide financial assistance for college to members of the Business Professionals of America (BPA).

**Eligibility:** Open to high school seniors who are BPA members with a GPA of 3.0 or higher. Applicants must have held a chapter, state, or national BPA office and received the Ambassador Torch Award. Along with their application, they must submit 1) a 1-page resume of activities involving both BPA and other school and community activities; 2) letters of recommendation from their chapter advisor and 2 other individuals; 3) a high school transcript; and 4) a 1-page essay on where they see themselves professionally in 10 years. Selection is based on academic success and involvement within BPA. These awards are funded by the ECI Scholarship Foundation of Educational Communications, Inc., publisher of *Who's Who Among American High School Students*.

**Financial data:** The stipend is $2,000.

**Duration:** 1 year.

**Number awarded:** 1 each year.

**Deadline:** March of each year.

## 2935 BRIAN CUMMINS MEMORIAL SCHOLARSHIP

National Federation of the Blind of Connecticut
580 Burnside Avenue, Suite 1
East Hartford, CT 06108
Phone: (860) 289-1971; Email: info@nfbct.org
Web: www.nfbct.org/html/bcmsch.htm

**Summary:** To provide financial assistance for college or graduate school to students in Connecticut who plan to become a teacher of the blind and visually impaired. This program was established to honor Brian Cummins, who lost his life in the World Trade Center on September 11, 2001.

**Number awarded:** 1 each year.

**Eligibility:** Open to graduate and undergraduate students enrolled full time at colleges and universities in Connecticut who are preparing for a career as a certified teacher of the blind and visually impaired. Applicants must be planning to reside in Connecticut and work as a teacher of the blind and visually impaired. Along with their application, they must submit a letter on their career goals and how the scholarship might help them achieve those. Applicants do not need to be blind or members of the National Federation of the Blind of Connecticut. Selection is based on academic quality, service to the community, and financial need.

**Financial data:** The stipend is $5,000.

**Duration:** 1 year.

**Deadline:** September of each year.

## 2936 BROADCAST CABLE FINANCIAL MANAGEMENT ASSOCIATION SCHOLARSHIP

**Summary:** To provide financial assistance to members of the Broadcast Cable Financial Management Association who are interested in working on an undergraduate or graduate degree.
*See Listing #1301.*

## 2937 BUDWEISER CONSERVATION SCHOLARSHIP

**Summary:** To provide financial assistance to undergraduate and graduate students who are interested in studying or conducting research related to the field of conservation.
*See Listing #1947.*

## 2938 BUENA M. CHESSHIR MEMORIAL WOMEN'S EDUCATIONAL SCHOLARSHIP

**Summary:** To provide financial assistance to mature women in Virginia who are interested in upgrading their skills or education at a college, law school, or medical school in the state.
*See Listing #143.*

## 2939 BUFFALO CHAPTER NAWIC SCHOLARSHIP

**Summary:** To provide financial assistance to residents of New York attending college in the state to prepare for a career in construction.
*See Listing #1303.*

## 2940 BURLINGTON NORTHERN SANTA FE FOUNDATION SCHOLARSHIP

**Summary:** To provide financial assistance for college to outstanding American Indian high school seniors from designated states who are members of American Indian Science and Engineering Society (AISES).
*See Listing #1952.*

## 2941 CALIFORNIA ASSOCIATION OF REALTORS SCHOLARSHIPS

California Association of Realtors
Attn: Scholarship Foundation
525 South Virgil Avenue
Los Angeles, CA 90020
Phone: (213) 739-8200; Fax: (213) 739-7202; Email: scholarship@car.org
Web: www.car.org

**Summary:** To provide financial assistance to students in California who are interested in a career in real estate.

**Eligibility:** Open to undergraduate and graduate students enrolled at California colleges and universities who are interested in studying real estate brokerage, real estate finance, real estate management, real estate development, real estate appraisal, real estate planning, real estate law, or other related areas of study. Applicants must have completed at least 12 units prior to applying, be currently enrolled for at least 6 units per semester or term, have a cumulative GPA of 2.6 or higher, and have been legal residents of California for at least 1 year. Real estate licensees who wish to pursue advanced real estate designations, degrees, or credentials are also eligible.

**Financial data:** The stipend is $2,000 for students at 4-year colleges or universities or $1,000 for students at 2-year colleges.

**Duration:** 1 year; may be renewed 1 additional year.

**Number awarded:** Varies each year.

**Deadline:** May of each year.

## 2942 CALIFORNIA FOUNDATION FOR PARKS AND RECREATION SCHOLARSHIPS

California Parks and Recreation Society
Attn: California Foundation for Parks and Recreation
7971 Freeport Boulevard
Sacramento, CA 95832-9701
Phone: (916) 665-2777; Fax: (916) 665-9149
Web: www.cprs.org/about-student.htm

**Summary:** To provide financial assistance to upper-division and graduate students majoring in fields related to recreation, parks, and leisure studies at colleges and universities in California.

**Eligibility:** Open to juniors, seniors, and graduate students majoring in aspects of recreation, parks, and leisure studies, including parks operations, natural resource management, therapeutic recreation, commercial recreation, tourism, community recreation, recreation management, recreational sports management, and recreation leadership. Applicants must be enrolled in a 4-year college or university in California with a GPA of 2.5 or higher. Along with their application, they must submit 2 essays of 200 words or less: 1) their career goals as they relate to the recreation, parks, and leisure services profession and how this scholarship will help them achieve their goals; and 2) their financial need. Selection is based on those essays, academic achievement, paid and/or volunteer experience in recreation and park agencies, involvement in campus organizations and leadership activities, community and professional organization membership activity, and 2 letters of recommendation.

**Financial data:** Stipends range from $500 to $2,000. This program includes the following named fellowships: Arvid Pauly Award ($400, sponsored by District II), Edwin L. Berg Memorial Award ($250, sponsored by District

II), and Anthony Shanks Memorial Scholarship (sponsored by District II). Other districts also award scholarships, including the $500 District I scholarship, the $750 District II scholarship, and the $1,000 District XIV scholarship. Information is also available from Curtis Brown, Chair CFPR Scholarship Board, City of Menlo Park, Community Services Department, 701 Laurel Street, Menlo Park, CA 94025.

**Duration:** 1 year.

**Number awarded:** Approximately 30 each year.

**Deadline:** October of each year.

## 2943 CALIFORNIA FUNERAL DIRECTORS ASSOCIATION SCHOLARSHIP

California Funeral Directors Association
Attn: Scholarship Director
One Capitol Mall
Sacramento, CA 95814
Phone: (916) 325-2361; (800) 255-2332; Fax: (916) 444-7462;
Email: cfda@amgroup.us
Web: www.cafda.org

**Summary:** To provide financial assistance to California residents who are interested in attending a mortuary college in the state.

**Eligibility:** Open to students attending or planning to attend a mortuary college in California. Selection is based on academic record, work experience, a 500-word essay on why the applicant is interested in a career in funeral service in California, and financial need.

**Financial data:** The stipend is $1,000. Funds are paid to the recipient's school.

**Duration:** 1 year.

**Number awarded:** 2 each year: 1 for a student in southern California and 1 for a student in northern California.

**Deadline:** April of each year.

## 2944 CALIFORNIA LABOR FEDERATION SCHOLARSHIPS

California Labor Federation, AFL-CIO
Attn: Education Committee
600 Grand Avenue, Suite 410
Oakland, CA 94610-3561
Phone: (510) 663-4024; Fax: (510) 663-4099;
Email: scholarships@calaborfed.org
Web: www.calaborfed.org/Scholarship.htm

**Summary:** To recognize and reward, with college scholarships, graduating high school seniors in California who submit outstanding essays on topics related to labor unions.

**Eligibility:** Open to graduating high school students in public, private, or parochial schools in California who plan to enroll in an accredited college or technical school. Applicants must write an essay of up to 1,000 words on topics that change annually; recently, students were invited to write on an important event in the history of California's unions, why it was important when it happened, and what impact it has on working people in California today. Essays are submitted to high school principals who forward them for judging. This program is administered by the University of California's Center for Labor Research and Education, 2521 Channing Way, Berkeley, CA 94720-5555, (510) 642-0323, Fax: (510) 642-6432, Email: osmer@uclink4.berkeley.edu.

**Financial data:** The award is a $2,000 scholarship.

**Duration:** The competition is held annually.

**Number awarded:** Varies each year; recently, 22 of these awards were presented.

**Deadline:** April of each year.

## 2945 CALIFORNIA PLANNING FOUNDATION OUTSTANDING STUDENT SCHOLARSHIPS

American Planning Association-California Chapter
Attn: California Planning Foundation
c/o Paul Wack
P.O. Box 886
San Luis Obispo, CA 93406
Phone: (805) 544-8282; Fax: (805) 544-8286; Email: pwack@calpoly.edu
Web: www.californiaplanningfoundation.org/scholarships.html

**Summary:** To provide financial assistance to undergraduate and graduate students in accredited planning programs at California universities. The accredited planning programs are at 3 campuses of the California State University system (California State Polytechnic University at Pomona, California

Polytechnic State University at San Luis Obispo, and San Jose State University), 3 campuses of the University of California (Berkeley, Irvine, and Los Angeles), and the University of Southern California.

**Eligibility:** Open to students entering their final year for an undergraduate or master's degree in an accredited planning program at a university in California. Selection is based on academic performance, professional promise, financial need, and increasing diversity in the planning profession.

**Financial data:** Stipends are $4,000 or $2,000.

**Duration:** 1 year.

**Number awarded:** 4 each year: 1 at $4,000 and 3 at $2,000.

**Deadline:** April of each year.

## 2946 CALIFORNIA STATE FAIR INTERNATIONAL STUDIES SCHOLARSHIPS

California State Fair
Attn: Friends of the Fair Scholarship Program
1600 Exposition Boulevard
P.O. Box 15649
Sacramento, CA 95852
Phone: (916) 274-5969; Email: wross@calexpo.com
Web: www.bigfun.org

**Summary:** To provide financial assistance to residents of California working on an undergraduate or graduate degree in international studies at a college or university in the state.

**Eligibility:** Open to residents of California who are enrolled as undergraduate or graduate students at a college or university in the state. Applicants must be studying or majoring in international studies. They must have a GPA of 3.0 or higher. Along with their application, they must submit a 500-word essay on global trade and economic development as it relates to California. Selection is based on personal commitment, goals established for their chosen field, leadership potential, and civic accomplishments.

**Financial data:** Stipends are $2,500 or $1,000.

**Duration:** 1 year.

**Number awarded:** 2 each year: 1 at $2,500 and 1 at $1,000.

**Deadline:** March of each year.

## 2947 CALIFORNIA STATE FAIR TEACHER CREDENTIAL SCHOLARSHIPS

California State Fair
Attn: Friends of the Fair Scholarship Program
1600 Exposition Boulevard
P.O. Box 15649
Sacramento, CA 95852
Phone: (916) 274-5969; Email: wross@calexpo.com
Web: www.bigfun.org

**Summary:** To provide financial assistance to residents of California who are working on a teacher credential.

**Eligibility:** Open to residents of California currently working on a teacher credential at a college or university in the state. Reentry professionals are also eligible. Applicants must have a GPA of 3.0 or higher. Along with their application, they must submit a 2-page essay on why they are pursuing their desired career and life goals. Selection is based on personal commitment, goals established for their chosen field, leadership potential, and civic accomplishments.

**Financial data:** Stipends are $1,500 or $500.

**Duration:** 1 year.

**Number awarded:** 2 each year: 1 at $1,500 and 1 at $500.

**Deadline:** March of each year.

## 2948 CANE CERTIFICATION SCHOLARSHIP

Classical Association of New England
c/o Allen M. Ware
University of Connecticut
Department of History
Box U-103
Storrs, CT 06269-2103
Phone: (860) 486-3722; Fax: (860) 486-0641;
Email: ward@uconnvm.uconn.edu
Web: www.caneweb.org

**Summary:** To provide financial assistance to upper-division and graduate students in New England who are working on certification as a teacher of Latin or Greek.

**Eligibility:** Open to junior and senior undergraduates at colleges and universities in New England and to holders of a master's degree. Applicants must be preparing for secondary school certification as a teacher of Latin or Greek or both in a New England state. Full-time, part-time, and summer programs qualify. Along with their application, they must submit 2 letters of recommendation from college classicists, a letter attesting to their ability to communicate and work with young people and inspire them to high levels of achievement, a 1,000-word personal statement explaining why they are preparing for a career as a secondary school classicist, high school and college transcripts, and a description of their program and the expenses involved.

**Financial data:** The stipend is $1,500. Funds are intended to cover tuition and fees.

**Duration:** 1 year or summer session.

**Number awarded:** 1 each year.

**Deadline:** February of each year.

### 2949 CAREER ADVANCEMENT SCHOLARSHIPS

**Summary:** To provide financial assistance for college or graduate school to mature women who are employed or seeking employment in selected fields.

*See Listing #1311.*

### 2950 CAREERS THAT WORK! SCHOLARSHIP

**Summary:** To provide financial assistance to high school seniors in Washington who are interested in attending a career college and majoring in selected fields.

*See Listing #1973.*

### 2951 CARPE DIEM SCHOLARSHIPS

**Summary:** To provide financial assistance to entering or continuing undergraduate students majoring or planning to major in specified fields.

*See Listing #1313.*

### 2952 CAS TRUST SCHOLARSHIP PROGRAM

Casualty Actuarial Society
Attn: CAS Trust Scholarship Coordinator
1100 North Glebe Road, Suite 600
Arlington, VA 22201-4798
Phone: (703) 276-3100; Fax: (703) 276-3108; Email: office@casact.org
Web: www.casact.org/academ/scholarship.htm

**Summary:** To provide financial assistance to U.S. and Canadian students who are preparing for a career in the property and casualty actuarial profession.

**Eligibility:** Open to U.S. and Canadian citizens who are enrolled full time at a college or university in the United States or Canada. Applicants must be preparing for a career in the property and casualty actuarial profession and pursuit of the Casualty Actuarial Society (CAS) designations. They must have demonstrated high scholastic achievement and strong interest in mathematics or a mathematics-related field. Preference is given to students who have passed an actuarial examination and who have not yet won this or another scholarship from this sponsor or the Society of Actuaries. Selection is based on individual merit.

**Financial data:** The stipend is $1,500.

**Duration:** 1 year.

**Number awarded:** Up to 3 each year.

**Deadline:** April of each year.

### 2953 CASE SCHOLARSHIPS

National Court Reporters Association
Attn: Council on Approved Student Education
8224 Old Courthouse Road
Vienna, VA 22182-3808
Phone: (703) 556-NCRA; (800) 272-NCRA; Fax: (703) 556-6291; TTY: (703) 556-6289; Email: dgaede@ncrahq.org
Web: www.NCRAonline.org/education/students/index.shtml

**Summary:** To provide financial assistance to student members of the National Court Reporters Association (NCRA).

**Eligibility:** Open to students at a court reporting school. Students must be nominated (each school may nominate 2 students). Nominees must be writing 140 to 180 words per minute at the time of application, have an exemplary

academic record, hold student membership in the association, have a proven interest in the field of verbatim reporting of proceedings, and submit an essay of up to 2 pages (a recent topic was "A Marketing Strategy for Recruiting Students into the Reporting Profession"). Selection is based on the essay and academic record.

**Financial data:** The first-place winner receives $1,500, second place $1,000, and third place $500. Scholarships are given directly to the students.

**Duration:** These are 1-time awards.

**Number awarded:** 3 each year.

**Deadline:** March of each year.

### 2954 CASH SCHOLARSHIPS TO ACCOUNTING COMMUNITY COLLEGE STUDENTS

Connecticut Society of Certified Public Accountants
Attn: Educational Trust Fund
845 Brook Street, Building 2
Rocky Hill, CT 06067-3405
Phone: (860) 258-4800; (800) 232-2232 (within CT); Fax: (860) 258-4859; Email: cscpa@cs-cpa.org
Web: www.cs-cpa.org/public/about/trust_fund/scholarships.asp

**Summary:** To provide financial assistance to college students majoring in accounting at community colleges in Connecticut.

**Eligibility:** Open to community college students in Connecticut who are majoring in accounting. Applicants must be committed to majoring in accounting at a 4-year school recognized by the Connecticut State Board of Accountancy.

**Financial data:** Modest stipends are awarded.

**Duration:** 1 year.

**Number awarded:** Up to 5 each year.

### 2955 CENIE JOMO WILLIAMS TUITION SCHOLARSHIP

National Association of Black Social Workers
Attn: National Student Coordinator
1220 11th Street, N.W., Suite 2
Washington, DC 20001
Phone: (202) 589-1850; Fax: (202) 589-1853;
Email: nabsw.harambee@verizon.net
Web: www.nabsw.org

**Summary:** To provide financial assistance for college or graduate school to members of the National Association of Black Social Workers (NABSW).

**Eligibility:** Open to African American members of NABSW enrolled full time at an accredited U.S. social work or social welfare program with a GPA of 2.5 or higher. Applicants must be able to demonstrate community service and a research interest in the Black community. Along with their application, they must submit an essay of 2 to 3 pages on their professional interests, future social work aspirations, previous social work experiences (volunteer and professional), honors and achievements (academic and community service), and research interests within the Black community (for master's and doctoral students). Recommendations are required. Financial need is considered in the selection process.

**Financial data:** The stipend is $2,000. Funds are sent directly to the recipient's school.

**Duration:** 1 year.

**Number awarded:** 1 or more each year.

**Deadline:** December of each year.

### 2956 CFA INSTITUTE 11 SEPTEMBER MEMORIAL SCHOLARSHIP

CFA Institute
Attn: 11 September Memorial Scholarship Fund
560 Ray C. Hunt Drive
P.O. Box 3668
Charlottesville, VA 22903-0668
Phone: (434) 951-5499; (800) 237-8132; Fax: (434) 951-5262;
Email: 11septemberfund@cfainstitute.org
Web: www.cfainstitute.org/research/products/About_September_Scholarship.html

**Summary:** To provide financial assistance to people and their families who were disabled or killed in the September 11 terrorist attacks and who wish to major in designated fields in college.

**Eligibility:** Open to students who meet the following 2 criteria: 1) they were permanently disabled in the attacks, or were the spouses, domestic partners, or children of anyone killed or permanently disabled in the attacks, and 2) they will be working on a college-level education in finance, economics, accounting, or business ethics. Applicants may be residents of any state or country. Selection is based on demonstrated commitment to high levels of professional ethics, academic record, and financial need. The CFA (Chartered Financial Analyst) Institute was formerly the Association for Investment Management and Research (AIMR). It lost at least 60 of its members and CFA candidates in the terrorist attacks of 11 September. This program is managed by Scholarship America, One Scholarship Way, P.O. Box 297, St. Peter, MN 56082, (507) 931-1682, (800) 537-4180, Fax: (507) 931-9168, Email: smsinfo@csfa.org.

**Financial data:** Stipends range from $2,000 to $13,000 per year, depending on the need of the recipient.

**Duration:** 1 year; renewable up to 4 additional years.

**Number awarded:** Varies each year; recently, 12 of these scholarships were awarded.

**Deadline:** May of each year.

## 2957 CHARLES MCDANIEL TEACHER SCHOLARSHIPS

Georgia Student Finance Commission
Attn: Scholarships and Grants Division
2082 East Exchange Place, Suite 200
Tucker, GA 30084-5305
Phone: (770) 724-9000; (800) 505-GSFC; Fax: (770) 724-9089;
Email: info@mail.gsfc.state.ga.us
Web: www.gsfc.org/gsfc/grants/dsp_gcmts.cfm

**Summary:** To provide financial assistance to Georgia residents who wish to prepare for a career as a teacher.

**Eligibility:** Open to residents of Georgia who graduated from a public high school in the state and are currently enrolled as full-time juniors or seniors in a college or department of education within an approved Georgia public institution. Each of the public colleges in Georgia that offers a teaching degree may nominate one student for these scholarships. Nominees must be working toward an initial baccalaureate degree, have a GPA of 3.25 or higher, and indicate a strong desire to prepare for a career as an elementary or secondary school teacher. They must submit an essay discussing their professional goals, reasons for pursuing a teaching career at the elementary or secondary level, and accomplishments, experiences, and honors that relate to teaching.

**Financial data:** The stipend is $1,000 per year.

**Duration:** 1 year.

**Number awarded:** Varies each year; recently, 4 of these scholarships were awarded.

## 2958 CHRISTA MCAULIFFE MEMORIAL SCHOLARSHIP

American Legion
Attn: Department of New Hampshire
State House Annex
25 Capitol Street, Room 431
Concord, NH 03301-6312
Phone: (603) 271-2211; Fax: (603) 271-5352

**Summary:** To provide financial assistance to students in New Hampshire who are interested in becoming a teacher.

**Eligibility:** Open to students who are or will be graduates of a New Hampshire high school and have been New Hampshire residents for at least 3 years. Applicants must be entering their first year of college to study education.

**Financial data:** The stipend is $1,000.

**Duration:** 1 year.

**Number awarded:** 1 each year.

**Deadline:** April of each year.

## 2959 CHRISTOPHER "KIT" SMITH SCHOLARSHIP

Society of Louisiana Certified Public Accountants
Attn: LCPA Education Foundation
2400 Veterans Boulevard, Suite 500
Kenner, LA 70062-4739
Phone: (504) 464-1040; (800) 288-5272; Fax: (504) 469-7930
Web: www.lcpa.org/LCPAScholarships.html

**Summary:** To provide financial assistance to currently-enrolled college students in Louisiana who are interested in becoming certified public accountants.

**Eligibility:** Open to Louisiana residents who are currently enrolled full time in an accounting program at a 4-year college or university in Louisiana.

Applicants must have completed at least 4 semesters by the fall of the academic year in which the application is filed and have a GPA of 2.5 or higher. Along with their application, they must submit a 2-page essay on their perception of the C.P.A.'s role on the job and in the community, including how they plan to contribute to the profession and to the community.

**Financial data:** The stipend is $2,500.

**Duration:** 1 year.

**Number awarded:** 1 each year.

## 2960 CHUCK PEACOCK MEMORIAL SCHOLARSHIP

**Summary:** To provide financial assistance to students preparing for a career in aviation management.

*See Listing #1997.*

## 2961 CLAIR A. HILL SCHOLARSHIP

**Summary:** To provide financial assistance to upper-division students in California who are majoring in water resources-related fields of study.

*See Listing #2000.*

## 2962 CLAN MACBEAN FOUNDATION GRANTS

**Summary:** To provide financial assistance to college students interested in studying subjects or conducting research relating to 1) Scottish culture or 2) the "Human Family."

*See Listing #1327.*

## 2963 CLARK E. DEHAVEN SCHOLARSHIPS

National Association of Colleges and University Food Services
c/o Michigan State University
Manly Miles Building
1405 South Harrison Road, Suite 305
East Lansing, MI 48824-5242
Phone: (517) 332-2494; Fax: (517) 332-8144
Web: www.nacufs.org

**Summary:** To provide financial assistance to college students preparing for a career in the food service industry.

**Eligibility:** Open to U.S. or Canadian citizens currently enrolled full time as sophomores, juniors, or seniors in an accredited program that will lead to an undergraduate degree in food service or a related field. Applicants must be enrolled at institutions that are members of the National Association of Colleges and University Food Services. They must have a GPA of 2.75 or higher. Along with their application, they must submit an official transcript, 2 letters of recommendation, a letter of personal evaluation, and a resume. Selection is based on academic record, financial need, commitment to a career in food service professions, character, campus citizenship, volunteer activities, and campus involvement.

**Financial data:** The stipend is $4,000.

**Duration:** 1 year.

**Number awarded:** 4 each year.

**Deadline:** February of each year.

## 2964 CLEM JUDD, JR. MEMORIAL SCHOLARSHIP

Hawai'i Hotel & Lodging Association
Attn: Hawaii Hotel Industry Foundation
2250 Kalakaua Avenue, Suite 404-4
Honolulu, HI 96815-2564
Phone: (808) 923-0407; Fax: (808) 924-3843; Email: hhla@hawaiihotels.org
Web: www.hawaiihotels.org

**Summary:** To provide financial assistance to Native Hawaiians who are upper-division students working on a degree in hotel management.

**Eligibility:** Open to Hawaii residents who can provide proof of their Hawaiian ancestry through birth certificates of their parents or grandparents. Applicants must be a junior, senior, or fifth-year undergraduate at an accredited college or university (in any state) and majoring in hotel management. They must have a GPA of 2.8 or higher. Financial need is considered in the selection process.

**Financial data:** The stipend ranges from $2,000 to $2,500.

**Duration:** 1 year.

**Number awarded:** 1 each year.

**Deadline:** June of each year.

## 2965 CLOSS/PARNITZKE/CLARKE SCHOLARSHIP

Phi Upsilon Omicron
Attn: Educational Foundation
P.O. Box 329
Fairmont, WV 26555-0329
Phone: (304) 368-0612; Email: rickards@access.mountain.net
Web: www.phiu.unl.edu
**Summary:** To provide financial assistance to undergraduate student members of Phi Upsilon Omicron, a national honor society in family and consumer sciences.
**Eligibility:** Open to members of the society who are working on a bachelor's degree in family and consumer sciences or a related area. Selection is based on scholastic record, participation in society and other collegiate activities, a statement of professional aims and goals, professional services, and recommendations.
**Financial data:** The stipend is $1,500.
**Duration:** 1 year.
**Number awarded:** 1 each year.
**Deadline:** January of each year.

## 2966 COCA-COLA DECA SCHOLARSHIPS

DECA
1908 Association Drive
Reston, VA 20191-1594
Phone: (703) 860-5000; Fax: (703) 860-4013; Email: decainc@aol.com
Web: www.deca.org/scholarships/index.html
**Summary:** To provide financial assistance to DECA members interested in studying business or marketing education in college. This program, established in 2002, is sponsored by the Coca-Cola Company.
**Eligibility:** Open to DECA members who are interested in working full time on a 2-year or 4-year degree in marketing, business, or marketing education. Applicants must be able to demonstrate evidence of DECA activities, academic achievement, leadership ability, and community service involvement. Selection is based on merit, not financial need.
**Financial data:** The stipend is $1,000.
**Duration:** 1 year.
**Number awarded:** Up to 5 each year.
**Deadline:** February of each year.

## 2967 COLORADO SOCIETY OF CPAS ETHNIC DIVERSITY SCHOLARSHIPS FOR COLLEGE STUDENTS

Colorado Society of Certified Public Accountants
Attn: CSCPA Educational Foundation
7979 East Tufts Avenue, Suite 500
Denver, CO 80237-2845
Phone: (303) 741-8613; (800) 523-9082 (within CO); Fax: (303) 773-6344; Email: gmantz@cocpa.org
Web: www.cocpa.org/student_faculty/scholarships.asp
**Summary:** To provide financial assistance to minority undergraduate or graduate students in Colorado who are studying accounting.
**Eligibility:** Open to African Americans, Hispanics, Asian Americans, American Indians, and Pacific Islanders studying at a college or university in Colorado at the associate, baccalaureate, or graduate level. Applicants must have completed at least one intermediate accounting class, be declared accounting majors, have completed at least 8 semester hours of accounting classes, and have a GPA of at least 3.0. Selection is based first on scholastic achievement and second on financial need.
**Financial data:** The stipend is $1,000. Funds are paid directly to the recipient's school to be used for books, tuition, room, board, fees, and expenses.
**Duration:** 1 year; recipients may reapply.
**Number awarded:** 2 each year.
**Deadline:** June of each year.

## 2968 COLORADO SOCIETY OF CPAS ETHNIC DIVERSITY SCHOLARSHIPS FOR HIGH SCHOOL STUDENTS

Colorado Society of Certified Public Accountants
Attn: CSCPA Educational Foundation
7979 East Tufts Avenue, Suite 500
Denver, CO 80237-2845
Phone: (303) 741-8613; (800) 523-9082 (within CO); Fax: (303) 773-6344; Email: gmantz@cocpa.org

Web: www.cocpa.org/student_faculty/scholarships.asp
**Summary:** To provide financial assistance to minority high school seniors in Colorado who plan to study accounting in college.
**Eligibility:** Open to African American, Hispanic, Asian American, American Indian, and Pacific Islander high school seniors in Colorado planning to major in accounting at a college or university in the state. Applicants must have a GPA of 3.0 or higher. Selection is based primarily on scholastic achievement.
**Financial data:** The stipend is $1,000.
**Duration:** 1 year; nonrenewable.
**Number awarded:** 3 each year.
**Deadline:** February of each year.

## 2969 COLORADO SUPPLEMENTAL LEVERAGING EDUCATIONAL ASSISTANCE PARTNERSHIP (SLEAP)

Colorado Commission on Higher Education
1380 Lawrence Street, Suite 1200
Denver, CO 80204
Phone: (303) 866-2723; Fax: (303) 866-4266; Email: cche@state.co.us
Web: www.state.co.us/cche/finaid/students/stateaid/types.html
**Summary:** To provide funding to Colorado undergraduate education students who need assistance while they are working as student teachers.
**Eligibility:** Open to residents of Colorado who are enrolled in an undergraduate or postbaccalaureate teacher education program in the states. Applicants must be engaged full time in a student teaching assignment as preparation for teacher education licensure. They must be able to demonstrate financial need. U.S. citizenship or permanent resident status is required. Applications are available either from the Colorado Commission on Higher Education or from the financial aid office of eligible Colorado institutions.
**Financial data:** The amount of assistance varies, to a maximum of $5,000 per year.
**Duration:** 1 year.
**Number awarded:** Varies each year.
**Deadline:** Each participating institution sets its own deadlines.

## 2970 COLORADO YOUNG FARMER SCHOLARSHIPS

Colorado Young Farmer Educational Association
Northeastern Junior College
100 College Drive
Sterling, CO 80751
Phone: (970) 521-6690; Fax: (970) 521-6801;
Email: info@coloradoyoungfarmer.com
Web: www.coloradoyoungfarmer.com/cyfschol.htm
**Summary:** To provide financial assistance to undergraduate students in Colorado interested in preparing for a career teaching agricultural education.
**Eligibility:** Open to students working on a degree in agriculture at a Colorado state college. Applicants must be interested in teaching agricultural education.
**Financial data:** Stipends are $500 for freshmen and sophomores, $750 for juniors, or $1,250 for seniors.
**Duration:** 1 year.
**Number awarded:** Varies each year; recently, 5 of these scholarships were awarded (2 to entering freshmen and 1 each to a sophomore, junior, and senior).
**Deadline:** March of each year.

## 2971 COLVIN SCHOLARSHIP PROGRAM

**Summary:** To provide financial assistance to upper-division students working on a degree related to the beef industry.
*See Listing #1335.*

## 2972 COMMUNITY SERVICE SCHOLARSHIPS

Association of Government Accountants
Attn: National Awards Committee
2208 Mount Vernon Avenue
Alexandria, VA 22301-1314
Phone: (703) 684-6931; (800) AGA-7211, ext. 131; Fax: (703) 548-9367;
Email: rortiz@agacgfm.org
Web: www.agacgfm.org/membership/awards
**Summary:** To provide financial assistance to undergraduate and graduate students majoring in financial management who are involved in community service.
**Eligibility:** Open to graduating high school seniors, high school graduates, col-

lege and university undergraduates, and graduate students. Applicants must be working on or planning to work on a degree in a financial management discipline, including accounting, auditing, budgeting, economics, finance, information technology, or public administration. They must have a GPA of 2.5 or higher and be actively involved in community service projects. As part of the selection process, they must submit a 2-page essay on "My community service accomplishments," high school or college transcripts, and a reference letter from a community service organization. Selection is based on community service involvement and accomplishments; financial need is not considered.

**Financial data:** The annual stipend is $1,000.

**Duration:** 1 year; renewable.

**Number awarded:** 2 each year: 1 to a high school senior or graduate and 1 to an undergraduate or graduate student.

**Deadline:** March of each year.

## 2973 CONNECTICUT ASSOCIATION OF WOMEN POLICE SCHOLARSHIPS

Connecticut Association of Women Police
P.O. Box 1653
Hartford, CT 06144-1653
Email: admin@cawp.net
Web: www.cawp.net

**Summary:** To provide financial assistance to high school seniors in Connecticut who are interested in studying criminal justice in college.

**Eligibility:** Open to seniors graduating from high schools in Connecticut who are interested in attending a 4-year college or university to prepare for a career in criminal justice. Applicants must submit a personal essay of 200 to 250 words on their personal goals and why they should be selected for this scholarship. Selection is based on the essay and financial need.

**Financial data:** A stipend is awarded (amount not specified).

**Duration:** 1 year.

**Number awarded:** Varies each year; recently, 5 of these scholarships were awarded.

**Deadline:** April of each year.

## 2974 CONNECTICUT BROADCASTERS ASSOCIATION SCHOLARSHIPS

**Summary:** To provide financial assistance to Connecticut residents who are studying a field related to broadcasting in college.
*See Listing #1338.*

## 2975 CONNECTICUT BUILDING CONGRESS SCHOLARSHIPS

**Summary:** To provide financial assistance to high school seniors in Connecticut who are interested in studying a field related to the construction industry in college.
*See Listing #1339.*

## 2976 CONNECTICUT CHAPTER HFMA UNDERGRADUATE SCHOLARSHIP

**Summary:** To recognize and reward, with college scholarships, undergraduate students in fields related to health care financial management at colleges and universities in Connecticut who submit outstanding essays on topics in the field.
*See Listing #2021.*

## 2977 CONNECTICUT FUNERAL DIRECTORS ASSOCIATION MORTUARY SCIENCE SCHOLARSHIP

Connecticut Funeral Directors Association
350 Silas Deane Highway, Suite 202
Wethersfield, CT 06109
Phone: (860) 721-0234; (800) 919-CFDA; Fax: (860) 257-3617;
Email: connfda@aol.com
Web: www.ctfda.org

**Summary:** To provide financial assistance to residents of Connecticut who are working on a degree in mortuary science.

**Eligibility:** Open to residents of Connecticut who are enrolled in an accredited mortuary science school. Applicants must be planning to complete their education and serve the public in their chosen profession in Connecticut. Along with their application, they must submit an essay describing the process they used and the experiences they underwent in their decision to enter the funeral ser-

vice profession. Selection is based on the essay and academic record; financial need is not considered.

**Financial data:** The stipend is $1,000.

**Duration:** 1 year.

**Number awarded:** Up to 2 each year.

**Deadline:** October of each year.

## 2978 CONNECTICUT MINORITY TEACHER INCENTIVE PROGRAM

Connecticut Department of Higher Education
Attn: Office of Student Financial Aid
61 Woodland Street
Hartford, CT 06105-2326
Phone: (860) 947-1855; Fax: (860) 947-1838; Email: mtip@ctdhe.org
Web: www.ctdhe.org/SFA/sfa.htm

**Summary:** To provide financial assistance and loan repayment to minority upper-division college students in Connecticut who are interested in teaching at public schools in the state.

**Eligibility:** Open to minority juniors and seniors enrolled full time in Connecticut college and university teacher preparation programs. Students must be nominated by the education dean at their institution.

**Financial data:** The maximum stipend is $5,000 per year. In addition, if recipients complete a credential and teach at a public school in Connecticut, they may receive up to $2,500 per year, for up to 4 years, to help pay off college loans.

**Duration:** Up to 2 years.

**Number awarded:** Varies each year.

**Deadline:** September of each year.

## 2979 CONNECTICUT PTA CHRISTA MCAULIFFE SCHOLARSHIPS

Parent Teacher Association of Connecticut
60 Connolly Parkway, Building 12
Hamden, CT 06514
Phone: (203) 281-6617; Fax: (203) 281-6749; Email: connecticut.pta@snet.net
Web: www.ctpta.org/programs/scholarship.html

**Summary:** To provide financial assistance to seniors at high schools in Connecticut with a PTA unit who are planning to become a teacher.

**Eligibility:** Open to seniors graduating from Connecticut high schools that have a PTA unit in good standing. Applicants must be planning to attend a 4-year college or university to prepare for a career in teaching. Along with their application, they must submit a 250-word essay giving their reason for entering the teaching profession. Financial need is not considered in the selection process. Each school may submit only one application.

**Financial data:** The stipend is $1,000.

**Duration:** 1 year.

**Number awarded:** 2 each year.

**Deadline:** February of each year.

## 2980 CONNECTICUT SPECIAL EDUCATION TEACHER INCENTIVE GRANT

Connecticut Department of Higher Education
Attn: Education and Employment Information Center
61 Woodland Street
Hartford, CT 06105-2326
Phone: (860) 947-1846; (800) 842-0229 (within CT); Fax: (860) 947-1311; Email: setig@ctdhe.org
Web: www.ctdhe.org/SFA/sfa.htm

**Summary:** To provide financial assistance to undergraduate and graduate students in Connecticut who are preparing for a career as a special education teacher.

**Eligibility:** Open to full-time juniors and seniors and full- or part-time graduate students who are residents of Connecticut. Applicants must be enrolled in 1) special education teacher preparation programs at selected universities in Connecticut; or 2) out-of-state teacher preparation programs seeking cross-endorsement for teaching "low-incidence student" areas. They must be nominated by the dean of education at their school and have a stated intent to teach in a Connecticut public school, an approved private special education facility, or a Regional Educational Service Center. Priority is given to minority (African American, Hispanic/Latino, Asian American, and Native American) and bilingual students and to Connecticut residents enrolled in an approved out-of-state program. The approved in-state programs are at Central Connecticut State University, Fairfield University,

Saint Joseph College, Southern Connecticut State University, University of Connecticut, and University of Hartford. The programs for students seeking cross-endorsement certification for teaching students who are blind and partially-sighted or visually impaired are at Hunter College of CUNY (New York, New York), Dominican College (Orangeburg, New York), Teachers College of Columbia University (New York, New York), and University of Northern Colorado (Greeley, Colorado). The programs for students seeking cross-endorsement certification for teaching students who are deaf or hearing-impaired are at Hunter College, Teachers College, Clarke School for the Deaf at Smith College (Northampton, Massachusetts), and Boston University (Boston, Massachusetts).

**Financial data:** The stipend is $5,000 per year for full-time study or $2,000 per year for part-time graduate study.

**Duration:** 1 year.

**Number awarded:** Varies each year.

**Deadline:** August of each year.

## 2981 CONSTANCE L. LLOYD SCHOLARSHIP

**Summary:** To provide financial assistance to undergraduate or graduate women in Georgia who are working on a degree in health care or health care administration.

*See Listing #2025.*

## 2982 CONSTRUCTMYFUTURE.COM SCHOLARSHIPS

ConstructMyFuture.com
111 East Wisconsin Avenue, Suite 1000
Milwaukee, WI 53202
Phone: (414) 272-0943; (866) AEM-0442; Fax: (414) 272-1170;
Email: nhallada@aem.org
Web: www.constructmyfuture.com/stu-scholar.htm

**Summary:** To provide financial assistance for college to students who are interested in preparing for a career in the construction industry.

**Eligibility:** Open to 1) graduating high school seniors; 2) students currently enrolled in a postsecondary educational institution; and 3) workers currently employed in the construction industry. Applicants must be interested in 1) entering or continuing in a college program to prepare for a career in the construction industry; or 2) purchasing tools for use in a construction industry job. Along with their application, they must submit a 1,000-word essay on their interest in the construction industry, their educational goals, and any other information such as specialized hobbies, skills, rewards, or achievements they wish to share. Selection is based on current and past involvement in the construction field; financial need is not considered.

**Financial data:** The stipend is $1,000.

**Duration:** 1 year; nonrenewable.

**Number awarded:** 3 each year.

**Deadline:** February of each year.

## 2983 CONTINENTAL SOCIETY, DAUGHTERS OF INDIAN WARS SCHOLARSHIP

Continental Society, Daughters of Indian Wars
c/o Mrs. Donald C. Trolinger, Scholarship Chair
61300 East 110 Road
Miami, OK 74354-4726
Email: ottawahillpt@neok.com

**Summary:** To provide financial assistance to Native American college students who are interested in preparing for a career in education.

**Eligibility:** Open to certified tribal members of a federally-recognized tribe who plan to prepare for a career in education or social service, plan to work on a reservation, are a junior at an accredited college, have earned at least a 3.0 GPA, and carry at least 10 quarter hours or 8 semester hours. Selection is based primarily on academic achievement and commitment to the field of study; financial need is not necessary but is considered.

**Financial data:** The stipend is $1,000.

**Duration:** 1 year; may be renewed.

**Number awarded:** 1 each year.

**Deadline:** June of each year.

## 2984 CORDIE HUGHES SCHOLARSHIP

**Summary:** To provide financial assistance to residents of Tennessee working on an undergraduate degree in a construction-related field.

*See Listing #1341.*

## 2985 COUNSELOR, ADVOCATE AND SUPPORT STAFF SCHOLARSHIP

Sunshine Lady Foundation, Inc., Attn: CASS Program
4900 Randall Parkway, Suite H
Wilmington, NC 28403
Phone: (910) 397-7742; (866) 255-7742; Fax: (910) 397-0023;
Email: mitty@sunshineladyfdn.org
Web: www.sunshineladyfdn.org/cass.htm

**Summary:** To provide financial assistance for college or graduate study in related fields to workers at domestic violence service centers.

**Eligibility:** Open to women and men who have been employed for at least one year by a nonprofit domestic violence victim services provider that is willing to provide support for their study. Applicants must be interested in enrolling in a community college, 4-year degree, graduate degree, or certificate program as a full or part time student. Their program should be related to their employment, including social work, counseling, psychology, accounting, nonprofit management, or business management. Financial need is considered in the selection process.

**Financial data:** Funding, paid directly to the educational institution, is provided for tuition, fees, required books, and supplies. A maximum of 3 courses per academic term may be supported.

**Duration:** 1 academic term; may be renewed if the recipient maintains a GPA of 2.5 or higher.

**Number awarded:** Varies each year.

**Deadline:** February of each year for spring quarter; April of each year for summer term; July of each year for fall quarter or semester; November of each year for winter quarter or spring semester.

## 2986 D. ANITA SMALL SCIENCE AND BUSINESS SCHOLARSHIP

**Summary:** To provide financial assistance to women in Maryland who are interested in working on an undergraduate or graduate degree in a science or business-related field.

*See Listing #2033.*

## 2987 DALE E. SIEFKES SCHOLARSHIP

Lincoln Community Foundation
215 Centennial Mall South, Suite 200
Lincoln, NE 68508
Phone: (402) 474-2345; Fax: (402) 476-8532; Email: lcf@lcf.org
Web: www.lcf.org

**Summary:** To provide financial assistance to upper-division students majoring in education in Nebraska.

**Eligibility:** Open to juniors or seniors attending a college or university in Nebraska and majoring in education. Applicants must have a GPA of 3.8 or higher and be able to demonstrate financial need. Along with their application, they must submit an essay on the topic: "If you could change one thing about your hometown, what would it be and why?"

**Financial data:** A stipend is awarded (amount not specified).

**Duration:** 1 year.

**Number awarded:** 1 each year.

**Deadline:** April of each year.

## 2988 DAMON P. MOORE SCHOLARSHIP

Indiana State Teachers Association, Attn: Scholarships
150 West Market Street, Suite 900
Indianapolis, IN 46204
Phone: (317) 263-3400; (800) 382-4037; Fax: (317) 655-3700;
Email: kmcallen@ista-in.org
Web: www.ista-in.org

**Summary:** To provide financial assistance to ethnic minority high school seniors in Indiana who are interested in studying education in college.

**Eligibility:** Open to ethnic minority public high school seniors in Indiana who are interested in studying education in college. Selection is based on academic achievement, leadership ability as expressed through co-curricular activities and community involvement, recommendations, and a 300-word essay on their educational goals and how they plan to use this scholarship.

**Financial data:** The stipend is $1,000.

**Duration:** 1 year; may be renewed for 2 additional years if the recipient maintains at least a C+ GPA.

**Number awarded:** 1 each year.

**Deadline:** February of each year.

**2989 DANIEL T. MULHERAN MEMORIAL SCHOLARSHIP**

Maryland State Funeral Directors Association
Attn: Memorial Scholarship
311 Crain Highway, S.E.
P.O. Box 10
Glen Burnie, MD 21061
Phone: (410) 553-9106; (888) 459-9693; Fax: (410) 553-9107;
Email: msfda@msfda.net
Web: www.msfda.net/scholarship.php

**Summary:** To provide financial assistance to Maryland residents who are interested in preparing for a career in funeral service.

**Eligibility:** Open to Maryland residents who have completed at least two-thirds of their educational requirements in an accredited mortuary science program or have graduated within the past 6 months. Applicants must have an overall GPA of 2.5 or higher and may not have earned a grade of D in any mortuary science class. They must be eligible for licensure in Maryland. Along with their application, they must submit 2 essays of approximately 500 words on 1) the process they used and the experiences they underwent in their decision to enter the funeral service profession, and 2) themselves. Selection is based on academic record and the essays; financial need is not considered.

**Financial data:** The stipend is $1,000.

**Duration:** 1 year.

**Number awarded:** 1 each year.

**Deadline:** September of each year.

---

**2990 DAVID BRODSKY, RUSSELL SCHOFIELD AND MSI SCHOLARSHIP PROGRAM**

American Moving and Storage Association
Attn: Moving and Storage Institute Scholarship Fund
1611 Duke Street
Alexandria, VA 22314
Phone: (703) 683-7410; Fax: (703) 683-8208; Email: csimpson@moving.org
Web: www.promover.org/scholarships/msi.htm

**Summary:** To provide financial assistance to employees of van lines and moving and storage companies who are working on a college degree in a field related to the moving and storage industry.

**Eligibility:** Open to 1) employees affiliated with a van line or moving and storage company; 2) children, grandchildren, and spouses of such an employee; 3) an independent contractor affiliated with a van line or moving and storage company; and 4) children, grandchildren, and spouses of such independent contractors. Applicants must be working full time on a degree in business administration, accounting, or another field related to the moving and storage industry at an accredited college, university, community college, professional school, or technical school. Along with their application they must submit an essay of 500 to 700 words on the importance and role of the moving and storage industry in today's economy or another topic related to the industry. Selection is based on academic achievement, character, integrity, and financial need.

**Financial data:** Stipends range from $1,000 to $2,000 per year. Funds are sent directly to the recipient's institution to be used for tuition only.

**Duration:** 1 year; may be renewed up to 1 additional year provided the recipient maintains full-time enrollment and good academic standing.

**Number awarded:** 1 or more each year.

**Deadline:** January of each year.

---

**2991 DAVID HOODS MEMORIAL SCHOLARSHIP**

**Summary:** To provide financial assistance to upper-division and graduate students interested in working with electronic documents as a career.

*See Listing #2043.*

---

**2992 DELAWARE ASSOCIATION OF SCHOOL ADMINISTRATORS SCHOLARSHIPS**

Delaware Association of School Administrators
860 Silver Lake Boulevard, Suite 150
Dover, DE 19904-2402
Phone: (302) 674-0630; Fax: (302) 674-8305
Web: www.edasa.org

**Summary:** To provide financial assistance to high school seniors in Delaware who plan to major in education in college.

**Eligibility:** Open to seniors who are at high schools in Delaware where at least 1 administrator is a member of the Delaware Association of School Administrators. Applicants must be planning to major in education in college.

---

They are invited to submit an essay (from 300 to 500 words) on "Why I Chose Education as My Career Field." Selection is based primarily on the essay.

**Financial data:** The stipend is $1,000; funds are paid directly to the recipient's college.

**Duration:** 1 year.

**Number awarded:** 2 each year.

**Deadline:** March of each year.

---

**2993 DELAWARE SHRM SCHOLARSHIPS**

Delaware Society for Human Resource Management
c/o Noelle C. Robertson, Student Chapter Liaison
630 Martin Luther King Jr. Boulevard
P.O. Box 231
Wilmington, DE 19899-0231
Phone: (302) 429-3486; Fax: (302) 429-3816;
Email: Noelle.Robertson@Connectiv.com
Web: www.shrmde.org

**Summary:** To provide financial assistance to students working on a bachelor's or master's degree in human resources at colleges and universities in Delaware. The sponsor is the Delaware affiliate of the Society for Human Resource Management (SHRM).

**Eligibility:** Open to 1) undergraduate students enrolled in a human resources program or related programs at a Delaware college, and 2) graduate students currently enrolled in a master's degree program at a Delaware college and clearly pursuing an emphasis area in human resources or related programs. Applicants must have a GPA of 3.0 or higher. Along with their application, they must submit a 2-page essay on their future objectives in the human resources field and why they chose this profession. Selection is based on total achievements and need.

**Financial data:** The stipend is $2,500.

**Duration:** 1 year.

**Number awarded:** 4 each year.

**Deadline:** September of each year.

---

**2994 DELL/UNCF CORPORATE SCHOLARS PROGRAM**

**Summary:** To provide financial assistance and work experience to undergraduate and graduate students, especially minorities, majoring in designated fields and interested in an internship at Dell Computer Corporation's corporate headquarters near Austin, Texas.

*See Listing #2051.*

---

**2995 DELTA AIR LINES AVIATION MAINTENANCE MANAGEMENT/AVIATION BUSINESS MANAGEMENT SCHOLARSHIPS**

Women in Aviation, International
Attn: Scholarships
101 Corsair Drive, Suite 101
P.O. Box 11287
Daytona Beach, FL 32120-1287
Phone: (386) 226-7996; Fax: (386) 226-7998; Email: scholarships@wai.org
Web: www.wai.org/education/scholarships.cfm

**Summary:** To provide financial assistance to members of Women in Aviation, International (WAI) who are interested in a career in aviation management. WAI is a nonprofit professional organization dedicated to encouraging women to consider an aviation career, providing educational outreach activities, and networking resources to women active in the industry. This program is sponsored by Delta Air Lines. In addition to the scholarship, recipients are reimbursed for up to $1,000 in travel and accommodations expenses to attend the WAI annual conference.

**Eligibility:** Open to WAI members who are full-time students with at least 2 semesters of study remaining. Applicants must be working on an associate or baccalaureate degree in aviation maintenance management or aviation business management with a cumulative GPA of 3.0 or higher. U.S. citizenship or permanent resident status is required. As part of the selection process, applicants must submit an essay of 500 to 1,000 words that addresses such topics as who or what influenced them to prepare for a career in aviation maintenance management or aviation business management, their greatest strength and strongest characteristic, their most memorable academic experience, their greatest life challenge and how has it enriched their life, and why are they the best candidate for this scholarship. In addition to the essay, selection is based on achievements, attitude toward self and others, commitment to success, dedication to career, financial need, motivation, reliability, responsibility, and teamwork.

**Financial data:** The stipend is $5,000.
**Duration:** 1 year.
**Number awarded:** 1 each year.
**Deadline:** December of each year.

### 2996 DELTA GAMMA FOUNDATION FLORENCE MARGARET HARVEY MEMORIAL SCHOLARSHIP

**Summary:** To provide financial assistance to blind undergraduate and graduate students who wish to study in the field of rehabilitation and/or education of the blind.
*See Listing #2055.*

### 2997 DELTA MU DELTA SCHOLARSHIP AWARDS

Delta Mu Delta
Attn: Scholarship Chair
2 Salt Creek Lane LL6
Hinsdale, IL 60521
Phone: (630) 321-9522; Fax: (630) 214-6080; Email: dmd@dmd-ntl.org
Web: www.deltamudelta.org/scholarships.html
**Summary:** To provide financial assistance to undergraduate or graduate students majoring in business administration.
**Eligibility:** Open to undergraduate and graduate students who are in at least the final term of their sophomore year and working on a degree in business administration. Although membership in Delta Mu Delta (a national honor society in business administration) is not required, applicants must be attending a school with a chapter of the society. Selection is based on scholarship, leadership, character, motivation, potential, and need.
**Financial data:** Stipends are $2,000, $1,500, $1,000, $750, or $500.
**Duration:** 1 year.
**Number awarded:** Varies each year; recently, 39 of these scholarship were awarded: 1 at $2,000 (the Mildred R. Marion Award), 2 at $1,500 (the Albert J. Escher Award and the A.J. Foranoce Award), 4 at $1,000, 11 at $750 (including the Helen D. Snow Award, the Balwant Singh Award, and the Abderrahman Robana Award), and 21 at $500 (including the Eta Chapter Award).
**Deadline:** February of each year.

### 2998 DENA NIGUS MEMORIAL SCHOLARSHIP

Kansas Federation of Business & Professional Women's Clubs, Inc.
Attn: Kansas BPW Educational Foundation
c/o Diane Smith, Executive Secretary
10418 Haskins
Lenexa, KS 66215-2162
Email: desmith@fcbankonline.com
Web: www.bpwkansas.org/bpw_foundation.htm
**Summary:** To provide financial assistance to residents of Kansas who are preparing for a career in special education in the state.
**Eligibility:** Open to Kansas residents (men and women) who are college juniors, seniors, or graduate students and preparing to teach special education in the state. Applicants must submit a 3-page personal biography in which they express their career goals, the direction they want to take in the future, their proposed field of study, their reason for selecting that field, the institutions they plan to attend and why, their circumstances for reentering school (if a factor), and what makes them uniquely qualified for this scholarship. They must also be able to document financial need. Applications must be submitted through a local organization of the sponsor.
**Financial data:** A stipend is awarded (amount not specified).
**Duration:** 1 year; may be renewed for a total of 4 semesters or 2 summers if the recipient maintains a GPA of 3.0 or higher.
**Number awarded:** 1 or more each year.
**Deadline:** December of each year.

### 2999 DENNY'S SCHOLARSHIP PROGRAM

**Summary:** To provide financial assistance to Hispanic American undergraduate students who are interested in preparing for a career in business, computer science, or engineering.
*See Listing #2057.*

### 3000 DENVER CHAPTER SCHOLARSHIPS

American Society of Women Accountants-Denver Chapter
c/o Nicolette Rounds, Scholarship Trustee
3773 Cherry Creek Drive North, Suite 575
Denver, CO 80209
Phone: (303) 377-4282; Email: roundscpa@qwest.net
Web: www.aswadenver.org
**Summary:** To provide financial assistance to women working on a degree in accounting at a college or university in Colorado.
**Eligibility:** Open to women who have completed at least 60 semester hours toward a degree in accounting with a GPA of 3.0 or higher. Applicants must be attending a college or university in Colorado. Selection is based on academic achievement, extracurricular activities, honors, a statement of career goals and objectives, 3 letters of recommendation, and financial need.
**Financial data:** A total of $7,000 in scholarships is awarded each year.
**Duration:** 1 year.
**Number awarded:** Several each year.
**Deadline:** June of each year.

### 3001 DERIVATIVE DUO SCHOLARSHIP

**Summary:** To provide financial assistance to Washington residents engaged in undergraduate study of mental health or human services.
*See Listing #2059.*

### 3002 DICK LARSEN SCHOLARSHIP

**Summary:** To provide financial assistance to Washington college students who are majoring in a communication-related field at an academic institution in the state.
*See Listing #1357.*

### 3003 DIRECT MARKETING SCHOLARSHIP

**Summary:** To provide financial assistance and work experience to upper-division students in New England preparing for a career in direct marketing.
*See Listing #1358.*

### 3004 DISTRICT OF COLUMBIA AREA CHAPTER SCHOLARSHIPS

American Society of Women Accountants-District of Columbia Area Chapter
c/o Marlane Perry, President
6307 Long Meadow Road
McLean, VA 22101
Email: mperry@keipearson.com
Web: www.aswa-dc.org
**Summary:** To provide financial assistance to students majoring in accounting at colleges and universities in the Washington, D.C. area.
**Eligibility:** Open to students working on a degree in accounting at a college, university, or professional school of accounting in the Washington area (including suburbs in nearby Maryland and northern Virginia). Applicants must have completed sufficient courses in accounting to demonstrate their aptitude and intention to continue in a career in the field. Selection is based primarily on personal interviews and financial need.
**Financial data:** The stipend is $1,000. The highest-ranked applicant receives the Past President's Award and is entered into the national competition for scholarships that range from $1,500 to $4,500. The second-ranked applicant receives the Board of Trustee's Award and the third-ranked applicant (if awarded) receives the June P. Blair Memorial Award.
**Duration:** 1 year.
**Number awarded:** Varies each year; recently, 2 of these scholarships were awarded.

### 3005 DONALD RIEBHOFF MEMORIAL SCHOLARSHIP

American Radio Relay League
Attn: ARRL Foundation
225 Main Street
Newington, CT 06111
Phone: (860) 594-0397; Fax: (860) 594-0259; Email: foundation@arrl.org
Web: www.arrl.org/arrlf
**Summary:** To provide financial assistance to licensed radio amateurs who are members of the American Radio Relay League (ARRL) and interested in working on an undergraduate or graduate degree in international studies.
**Eligibility:** Open to undergraduate or graduate students who are licensed radio

amateurs of technician class. Applicants must be ARRL members majoring in international studies at an accredited postsecondary institution. They must submit an essay on the role amateur radio has played in their lives and provide documentation of financial need.

**Financial data:** The stipend is $1,000.
**Duration:** 1 year.
**Number awarded:** 1 each year.
**Deadline:** January of each year.

## [3006] DONALD W. FOGARTY INTERNATIONAL STUDENT PAPER COMPETITION

American Production & Inventory Control Society
Attn: Educational & Research Foundation
5301 Shawnee Road
Alexandria, VA 22312-2317
Phone: (703) 354-8851, ext. 2202; (800) 444-2742, ext. 2202; Fax: (703) 354-8794; Email: foundation@apicshq.org
Web: www.apics.org/Education/ERFoundation/Competitions/dwf.htm
**Summary:** To recognize and reward outstanding undergraduate and graduate student papers on resource management.
**Eligibility:** Open to undergraduate and graduate students who submit papers on a topic related to resource management, including inventory management, logistics, manufacturing processes, master planning, just-in-time, material and capacity requirements planning, production activity control, systems and technologies, and supply chain management. Papers must be the original work of one or more authors and normally between 10 and 20 pages; they may have been developed as part of a regular class assignments, but theses and dissertations are not acceptable. Papers are first submitted to local chapters, then forwarded to regional competitions, from which the winning entries are submitted to an international level. Selection is based on relevance of the topic to resource management, timeliness, understanding of topic and depth of coverage, accuracy of material, organization and clarity of the presentation, and originality of treatment.
**Financial data:** At the regional level, first prize is $250 and second prize is $150. At the international level, first prize is $1,000 and second prize is $500.
**Number awarded:** 4 prizes are awarded at the international level each year.
**Deadline:** May for the chapter competitions, June for the regional level, and July for the international contest.

## [3007] DOROTHY COOKE WHINERY MUSIC BUSINESS/ TECHNOLOGY SCHOLARSHIP

Sigma Alpha Iota Philanthropies, Inc.
One Tunnel Road
Asheville, NC 28805
Phone: (828) 251-0606; Fax: (828) 251-0644;
Email: philonline@sai-national.org
Web: www.sai-national.org/phil/philmustech.html
**Summary:** To provide financial assistance for college to members of Sigma Alpha Iota (an organization of women musicians).
**Eligibility:** Open to members of the organization entering their junior or senior year of college. Applicants must be working on a degree in the field of music business or music technology, including music marketing, music business administration, entertainment industry, commercial music, recording and production, music management, or other related fields. They must have a GPA of 3.0 or higher. Along with their application, they must submit a statement of purpose that includes their career goals. There is a $25 nonrefundable application fee.
**Financial data:** The stipend is $2,000.
**Duration:** 1 year.
**Number awarded:** 1 each year.
**Deadline:** March of each year.

## [3008] DOROTHY E. SCHOELZEL MEMORIAL SCHOLARSHIP

General Federation of Women's Clubs of Connecticut
c/o Hamden Women's Club
Antoinette Antonucci, Co-President
26 Country Way
Wallingford, CT 06492
Phone: (203) 265-9407; Email: gfwcct@yahoo.com
Web: www.gfwcct.org
**Summary:** To provide financial assistance to women in Connecticut who are working on an undergraduate or graduate degree in education.

**Eligibility:** Open to female residents of Connecticut who have completed at least 3 years of college. Applicants must have a GPA of 3.0 or higher and be working on a bachelor's or master's degree in education.
**Financial data:** The stipend is $1,000.
**Duration:** 1 year.
**Number awarded:** 1 each year.
**Deadline:** February of each year.

## [3009] DR. B.J. STAMPS MEMORIAL ENDOWMENT SCHOLARSHIP

University Interscholastic League
Attn: Texas Interscholastic League Foundation
1701 Manor Road
P.O. Box 8028
Austin, TX 78713
Phone: (512) 232-4938; Fax: (512) 471-5908;
Email: carolyn.scott@mail.utexas.edu
Web: www.uil.texas.edu/tilf/scholar.html
**Summary:** To provide financial assistance to students who participate in programs of the Texas Interscholastic League Foundation (TILF) and plan to enter the teaching profession.
**Eligibility:** Open to students who meet the 5 basic requirements of the TILF: 1) graduate from high school during the current year and begin college or university in Texas by the following fall; 2) enroll full time and maintain a GPA of 2.5 or higher during the first semester; 3) compete in a University Interscholastic League (UIL) academic state meet contest in accounting, calculator applications, computer applications, computer science, current issues and events, debate (cross-examination and Lincoln-Douglas), journalism (editorial writing, feature writing, headline writing, and news writing), literary criticism, mathematics, number sense, 1-act play, ready writing, science, social studies, speech (prose interpretation, poetry interpretation, informative speaking, and persuasive speaking), or spelling and vocabulary; 4) submit high school transcripts that include SAT and/or ACT scores; and 5) submit parents' latest income tax returns. Applicants for this scholarship must have declared their intention to enter the teaching profession.
**Financial data:** Stipends are $1,000 or $500 per year.
**Duration:** 1 year; nonrenewable.
**Number awarded:** 2 each year (1 at $1,000 and 1 at $500).
**Deadline:** May of each year.

## [3010] DR. FELIX H. REYLER MEMORIAL SCHOLARSHIP

Dade Community Foundation
Attn: Director of Development and Communications
200 South Biscayne Boulevard, Suite 505
Miami, FL 33131-2343
Phone: (305) 371-2711; Fax: (305) 371-5342;
Email: joe.pena@dadecommunityfoundation.org
Web: www.dadecommunityfoundation.org/Site/programs/scholarships.jsp
**Summary:** To provide financial assistance to upper-division students who are Florida residents and working on a degree in international business.
**Eligibility:** Open to juniors and seniors who are enrolled full time in a 4-year college or university in Florida and have a GPA of 3.0 or higher. Applicants must be Florida residents (this includes individuals who have resided in Florida long enough to be granted resident status in the state university system), be U.S. citizens or permanent residents, and be working on an undergraduate degree in international business or finance. Selection is based on financial need, academic achievement, personal aspirations, career goals and interests in international business and finance, volunteer experience, work experience, and school activities.
**Financial data:** The stipend is $2,500.
**Duration:** 1 year; juniors may reapply.
**Number awarded:** At least 2 each year.
**Deadline:** May of each year.

## [3011] DR. HANS AND CLARA ZIMMERMAN FOUNDATION EDUCATION SCHOLARSHIPS

Hawai'i Community Foundation
Attn: Scholarship Department
1164 Bishop Street, Suite 800
Honolulu, HI 96813
Phone: (808) 566-5570; (888) 731-3863; Fax: (808) 521-6286;
Email: scholarships@hcf-hawaii.org

Web: www.hawaiicommunityfoundation.org/scholar/scholar.php

**Summary:** To provide financial assistance to Hawaii residents who are nontraditional students planning to major in education.

**Eligibility:** Open to Hawaii residents who have worked for at least 2 years and are returning to school as full-time students majoring in education. Applicants must be able to demonstrate academic achievement (GPA of 2.8 or higher), good moral character, and financial need. In addition to filling out the standard application form, they must write a short statement describing their community service and how their college education will help them achieve their career goals. Preference is given to students of Hawaiian ancestry, students from the neighboring islands who plan to teach in Hawaii, and students with some teaching experience.

**Financial data:** The amount of the award depends on the availability of funds and the need of the recipient; recently, stipends averaged $1,620.

**Duration:** 1 year.

**Number awarded:** Varies each year; recently, 61 of these scholarships were awarded.

**Deadline:** February of each year.

## 3012 DR. JOSEPH C. BASILE, II MEMORIAL SCHOLARSHIP

Greater Kanawha Valley Foundation
Attn: Scholarship Coordinator
1600 Huntington Square
900 Lee Street, East
P.O. Box 3041
Charleston, WV 25331-3041
Phone: (304) 346-3620; Fax: (304) 346-3640; Email: tgkvf@tgkvf.com
Web: www.tgkvf.com/scholar.html

**Summary:** To provide financial assistance to residents of West Virginia who are working on a degree in education.

**Eligibility:** Open to residents of West Virginia who are working or planning to work full time on a degree in the field of education at a college or university in the state. Applicants must have an ACT score of 20 or higher, be able to demonstrate good moral character and financial need, and have a GPA of 2.5 or higher.

**Financial data:** The stipend is $1,000 per year.

**Duration:** 1 year; nonrenewable.

**Number awarded:** 1 each year.

**Deadline:** February of each year.

## 3013 DR. JULIANNE MALVEAUX SCHOLARSHIP

**Summary:** To provide financial assistance to African American women studying journalism, economics, or a related field in college.
*See Listing #1365.*

## 3014 DR. LISA BURKE SCHOLARSHIP

Society for Human Resource Management
Attn: Student Program Manager
1800 Duke Street
Alexandria, VA 22314-3499
Phone: (703) 535-6084; (800) 283-SHRM; Fax: (703) 739-0399; TDD: (703) 548-6999; Email: SHRMStudent@shrm.org
Web: www.shrm.org/students/ags_published

**Summary:** To provide financial assistance to undergraduate student members of the Society for Human Resource Management (SHRM) who are paying their own way through college.

**Eligibility:** Open to undergraduate students who have completed their sophomore year, have maintained a GPA of 2.0 or higher, are majoring in human resources or a related subject, are national student members of the society, and are paying more than 50% of their college expenses. Selection is based on "true passion for the HR profession," scholastic average and standing, campus and charitable activities, leadership positions held, and financial need.

**Financial data:** The winner receives a $1,000 honorarium, a commemorative plaque, and complimentary registration to the society's annual conference and exposition.

**Duration:** 1 year.

**Number awarded:** 1 each year.

**Deadline:** February of each year.

## 3015 DUKE ENERGY MINORITY PROFESSIONAL ASSOCIATION SCHOLARSHIP FUND

**Summary:** To provide financial assistance to high school seniors from North and South Carolina who are interested in studying designed fields in college.
*See Listing #2093.*

## 3016 D.W. SIMPSON & COMPANY ACTUARIAL SCIENCE SCHOLARSHIP

D.W. Simpson & Company
1800 West Larchmont Avenue
Chicago, IL 60613
Phone: (312) 867-2300; (800) 837-8338; Fax: (312) 951-8386;
Email: actuaries@dwsimpson.com
Web: www.actuaryjobs.com/scholar.html

**Summary:** To provide financial assistance to college seniors majoring in actuarial science.

**Eligibility:** Open to students who are entering their senior year of undergraduate study in actuarial science. Applicants must have a GPA of 3.0 or higher, have passed at least one actuarial examination, and be eligible to work in the United States. Financial need is not considered in the selection process.

**Financial data:** The stipend is $1,000 per semester.

**Duration:** 1 semester; nonrenewable.

**Number awarded:** 2 each year (1 per semester).

**Deadline:** April of each year for the fall scholarship; October of each year for the spring scholarship.

## 3017 DYZCO ESSAY CONTEST

Dyzco Technologies, Inc.
720 West Colonial Drive, Suite 204
Orlando, FL 32804
Phone: (800) 303-3352; Fax: (407) 841-1612
Web: www.dyzco.com/campaign/scholarship.asp

**Summary:** To recognize and reward college students who submit outstanding essays on distance learning.

**Eligibility:** Open to students enrolled in an accredited institution of higher education who are 18 years of age or older. Applicants must submit an essay, up to 1,000 words in English, on the question, "What Is the Future of Distance Learning?" Entries must be submitted online, and participants are required to register on the sponsor's web site.

**Financial data:** The award is $10,000. Funds are paid directly to the winner's institution to be used to pay tuition.

**Duration:** The competition is held annually.

**Number awarded:** 1 each year.

**Deadline:** June of each year.

## 3018 E. URNER GOODMAN SCHOLARSHIP FUND

Boy Scouts of America
Attn: Order of the Arrow, S214
1325 West Walnut Hill Lane
P.O. Box 152079
Irving, TX 75015-2079
Phone: (972) 580-2000
Web: www.oa-bsa.org

**Summary:** To provide financial assistance for college to members of the Boy Scouts of America's Order of the Arrow who are interested in preparing for a professional Scouting career.

**Eligibility:** Open to members of the Order of the Arrow who are high school seniors or current college students and planning a Scouting career. Selection is based on a 250- to 500-word essay expressing their reasons for preparing for a professional career with the Boy Scouts of America, results of all aptitude and placement tests taken in high school and college, a high school and (if applicable) college transcript, a copy of their college or university acceptance, an employment record, and letters of recommendations. Applicants with at least one year of college experience receive preference over high school seniors.

**Financial data:** Stipends vary each year, to a maximum of $4,000.

**Duration:** 1 year.

**Number awarded:** Varies each year; a total of $20,000 is available for these awards each year.

**Deadline:** January of each year.

## 3019 EARL G. GRAVES NAACP SCHOLARSHIP

National Association for the Advancement of Colored People
Attn: Education Department
4805 Mt. Hope Drive
Baltimore, MD 21215-3297
Phone: (410) 580-5760; (877) NAACP-98; Email: youth@naacpnet.org
Web: www.naacp.org/work/education/eduscholarship.shtml

**Summary:** To provide financial assistance to upper-division and graduate students majoring in business.

**Eligibility:** Open to full-time juniors, seniors, and graduate students majoring in business. Applicants must be currently in good academic standing, making satisfactory progress toward an undergraduate or graduate degree, and in the top 20% of their class. Along with their application, they must submit a 1-page essay on their interest in their major and a career, their life's ambition, what they hope to accomplish in their lifetime, and what they consider their most significant contribution to their community. Financial need is not considered in the selection process.

**Financial data:** The stipend is $5,000 per year.

**Duration:** 1 year.

**Number awarded:** Varies each year; recently, 20 of these scholarships were awarded.

**Deadline:** April of each year.

## 3020 EAST MICHIGAN CHAPTER SCHOLARSHIPS

**Summary:** To provide financial assistance to undergraduate and graduate students in Michigan who are interested in preparing for a career in air and waste management.

*See Listing #2103.*

## 3021 ECOLAB ACADEMIC SCHOLARSHIP PROGRAM

American Hotel & Lodging Educational Foundation
Attn: Manager of Foundation Programs
1201 New York Avenue, N.W., Suite 600
Washington, DC 20005-3931
Phone: (202) 289-3181; Fax: (202) 289-3199; Email: ahlef@ahlef.org
Web: www.ahlef.org/scholarships_ecolab.asp

**Summary:** To provide financial assistance to students working on a college degree in hospitality management.

**Eligibility:** Open to students working on an associate or baccalaureate degree in hospitality management. They must be enrolled or intending to enroll full time. Along with their application, they must submit a 500-word personal essay on when and why they became interested in the hospitality field, the characteristics or qualifications that will allow them to succeed, and how their education will help them to achieve their career objectives and future goals. Selection is based on industry-related work experience; financial need; academic record and educational qualifications; professional, community, and extracurricular activities; personal attributes, including career goals; the essay; and neatness and completeness of the application. In addition to these academic scholarships, the program also provides support to hospitality professionals seeking certification in the following operational areas: certified hotel administrator, certified lodging manager, certified engineering operations executive, and certified hospitality housekeeping executive. This program is known as EI Certification Scholarship Program. Funds are available to cover the cost of the certification study guide, examination fee, and certification fee. Information on that program is available from the EI at 2113 North High Street, Lansing, MI 48906, (517) 372-8800, (800) 752-4567, Fax: (517) 372-5141, Email: academics@ei-ahla.org. Both academic and certification programs are supported by Ecolab.

**Financial data:** The stipend is $2,000 for students in 4-year baccalaureate programs or $1,000 for students in 2-year associate programs. Funds are distributed in 2 equal installments (in August and December). Checks are made out jointly to the recipient and the recipient's academic institution. Funds may be used only for tuition, fees, and books.

**Duration:** 1 year.

**Number awarded:** Varies each year; recently, 22 of these scholarships were awarded.

**Deadline:** May of each year.

## 3022 EDDIE G. COLE MEMORIAL SCHOLARSHIPS

**Summary:** To provide financial assistance for college to residents of California who are interested in majoring in designated fields or preparing for a career in the Fair industry.

*See Listing #2107.*

## 3023 EDITH M. ALLEN SCHOLARSHIPS

**Summary:** To provide financial assistance to Methodist students who are African American and working on an undergraduate or graduate degree in specified fields

*See Listing #2108.*

## 3024 EDSF BOARD OF DIRECTORS SCHOLARSHIPS

**Summary:** To provide financial assistance to college juniors, seniors, and graduate students interested in working with electronic documents as a career.

*See Listing #2110.*

## 3025 EDSF BOARD OF DIRECTORS TECHNICAL AND COMMUNITY COLLEGE SCHOLARSHIP

**Summary:** To provide financial assistance to students in technical schools and community colleges who are interested in working with electronic documents as a career.

*See Listing #2111.*

## 3026 EDUCATIONAL FOUNDATION COLLEGE/UNIVERSITY SCHOLARSHIPS

Colorado Society of Certified Public Accountants
Attn: CSCPA Educational Foundation
7979 East Tufts Avenue, Suite 500
Denver, CO 80237-2845
Phone: (303) 741-8613; (800) 523-9082 (within CO); Fax: (303) 773-6344; Email: gmantz@cocpa.org
Web: www.cocpa.org/student_faculty/scholarships.asp

**Summary:** To provide financial assistance to undergraduate and graduate students in Colorado who are studying accounting.

**Eligibility:** Open to undergraduate and graduate students at colleges and universities in Colorado who have completed at least 8 semester hours of accounting courses (including at least one intermediate accounting class) and have a GPA, both overall and in accounting, of at least 3.0. Selection is based first on scholastic achievement and second on financial need.

**Financial data:** The stipend is $1,000. Funds are paid directly to the recipient's school to be used for books, tuition, room, board, fees, and expenses.

**Duration:** 1 year; recipients may reapply.

**Number awarded:** 20 each year.

**Deadline:** June of each year for fall semester or quarter; November of each year for winter quarter or spring semester.

## 3027 EDUCATIONAL FOUNDATION HIGH SCHOOL SCHOLARSHIPS

Colorado Society of Certified Public Accountants
Attn: CSCPA Educational Foundation
7979 East Tufts Avenue, Suite 500
Denver, CO 80237-2845
Phone: (303) 741-8613; (800) 523-9082 (within CO); Fax: (303) 773-6344; Email: gmantz@cocpa.org
Web: www.cocpa.org/student_faculty/scholarships.asp

**Summary:** To provide financial assistance to high school seniors in Colorado who plan to study accounting in college.

**Eligibility:** Open to seniors graduating from Colorado high schools who have a GPA of at least 3.0. Applicants must be planning to attend a college in Colorado with an accredited program in accounting. Selection is based on scholastic achievement.

**Financial data:** The stipend is $1,000.

**Duration:** 1 year; nonrenewable.

**Number awarded:** 8 to 10 each year.

**Deadline:** February of each year.

## 3028 EDUCATOR OF TOMORROW AWARD

National Federation of the Blind
c/o Peggy Elliott, Scholarship Committee Chair
805 Fifth Avenue
Grinnell, IA 50112
Phone: (641) 236-3366
Web: www.nfb.org/sch_intro.htm

**Summary:** To provide financial assistance to blind undergraduate or graduate students who wish to prepare for a career as a teacher.

**Eligibility:** Open to legally blind students who are working on or planning to work full time on an undergraduate or graduate degree. Applicants must be preparing for a career in elementary, secondary, or postsecondary teaching. Selection is based on academic excellence, service to the community, and financial need.

**Financial data:** The stipend is $3,000.

**Duration:** 1 year; recipients may resubmit applications up to 2 additional years. Scholarships are awarded at the federation convention in July. Recipients attend the convention at federation expense; that funding is in addition to the scholarship grant.

**Number awarded:** 1 each year.

**Deadline:** March of each year.

## 3029 EDWARD DAVIS SCHOLARSHIP FUND

**Summary:** To provide financial assistance to minority students interested in preparing for a career in an automotive-related profession.

*See Listing #2113.*

## 3030 EDWARD J. DOTY SCHOLARSHIP

Hawai'i Community Foundation
Attn: Scholarship Department
1164 Bishop Street, Suite 800
Honolulu, HI 96813
Phone: (808) 566-5570; (888) 731-3863; Fax: (808) 521-6286;
Email: scholarships@hcf-hawaii.org
Web: www.hawaiicommunityfoundation.org/scholar/scholar.php

**Summary:** To provide financial assistance to Hawaii residents who are interested in studying gerontology on the undergraduate or graduate school level.

**Eligibility:** Open to college juniors, seniors, and graduate students from Hawaii who are studying gerontology on a full-time basis. Applicants must be able to demonstrate academic achievement (GPA of 2.7 or higher), good moral character, and financial need. In addition to filling out the standard application form, applicants must write a short statement indicating their reasons for attending college, their planned course of study, and their career goals. Also eligible for this program are 1) dependents of current or former employees of Doty Equities with 1 year of service, and 2) dependents of former employees of Eagle Distributors, Inc. who were in its employ in 1996 and had at least 1 year of service with the company. Recipients may attend college in Hawaii or on the mainland.

**Financial data:** The amounts of the awards depend on the availability of funds and the need of the recipient; recently, stipends averaged $1,000.

**Duration:** 1 year.

**Number awarded:** Varies each year; recently, 2 of these scholarships were awarded.

**Deadline:** February of each year.

## 3031 EILEEN J. GARRETT SCHOLARSHIP FOR PARAPSYCHOLOGICAL RESEARCH

Parapsychology Foundation, Inc.
Attn: Executive Director
P.O. Box 1562
New York, NY 10021-0043
Phone: (212) 628-1550; Fax: (212) 628-1559; Email: info@parapsychology.org
Web: www.parapsychology.org

**Summary:** To provide financial assistance to undergraduate or graduate students interested in studying or conducting research in parapsychology.

**Eligibility:** Open to undergraduate and graduate students attending accredited colleges and universities who plan to pursue parapsychological studies or research. Funding is restricted to study, research, and experimentation in the field of parapsychology; it is not for general study, nor is it for those with merely a general interest in the subject matter. Applicants must demonstrate a previous academic interest in parapsychology by including, with the application form, a sample of writings on the subject. Letters of reference are also required from 3 individuals who are familiar with the applicant's work and/or studies in parapsychology.

**Financial data:** The stipend is $3,000.

**Duration:** 1 year.

**Number awarded:** 1 each year.

**Deadline:** July of each year.

## 3032 EISENHOWER HISPANIC-SERVING INSTITUTIONS FELLOWSHIPS

**Summary:** To provide financial assistance for undergraduate study in transportation-related fields to students at Hispanic Serving Institutions.

*See Listing #1371.*

## 3033 EISENHOWER HISTORICALLY BLACK COLLEGES AND UNIVERSITIES FELLOWSHIPS

**Summary:** To provide financial assistance for undergraduate study in transportation-related fields to students at Historically Black Colleges and Universities.

*See Listing #1372.*

## 3034 EMILIE HESEMEYER MEMORIAL SCHOLARSHIP

**Summary:** To provide financial assistance for college to Native American students, especially those interested in majoring in education.

*See Listing #317.*

## 3035 ENID HALL GRISWOLD MEMORIAL SCHOLARSHIP

National Society Daughters of the American Revolution
Attn: Scholarship Committee
1776 D Street, N.W.
Washington, DC 20006-5303
Phone: (202) 628-1776
Web: www.dar.org/natsociety/edout_scholar.cfm

**Summary:** To provide financial assistance to upper-division college students majoring in selected social science fields.

**Eligibility:** Open to undergraduate students entering their junior or senior year with a major in political science, history, government, or economics. Applicants must be sponsored by a local chapter of the Daughters of the American Revolution (DAR). Selection is based on academic excellence, commitment to the field of study, and financial need. U.S. citizenship is required.

**Financial data:** The stipend is $1,000.

**Duration:** 1 year; nonrenewable.

**Number awarded:** Varies each year.

**Deadline:** February of each year.

## 3036 ENVIRONMENTAL EDUCATIONAL SCHOLARSHIP PROGRAM

**Summary:** To provide financial assistance to underrepresented and minority students from Missouri who are or will be working on a bachelor's or master's degree in an environmental field.

*See Listing #2140.*

## 3037 ENVIRONMENTAL MANAGEMENT SCHOLARSHIP

**Summary:** To provide financial assistance to Hispanic undergraduate students majoring in designated business, engineering, and science fields related to the U.S. Department of Energy (DOE) goals of environmental restoration and waste management.

*See Listing #2141.*

## 3038 ERNEST F. HOLLINGS SCHOLARSHIP PROGRAM

**Summary:** To provide financial assistance and summer research experience to upper-division students who are working on a degree in a field of interest to the National Oceanic and Atmospheric Administration (NOAA).

*See Listing #2144.*

## 3039 ERNST & YOUNG LLP MINORITY LEADERSHIP AWARDS

New Jersey Society of Certified Public Accountants
Attn: Student Programs Coordinator
425 Eagle Rock Avenue, Suite 100
Roseland, NJ 07068-1723
Phone: (973) 226-4494, ext. 209; Fax: (973) 226-7425;
Email: njscpa@njscpa.org
Web: www.njscpa.org

**Summary:** To provide financial assistance to minority undergraduates in New

Jersey who are preparing for a career as a certified public accountant. This program is sponsored by Ernst & Young.

**Eligibility:** Open to African American, Asian, Hispanic, and Native American residents of New Jersey who are attending a college or university in the state. Applicants must be sophomores who are majoring or concentrating in accounting and have completed at least 3 credits in accounting courses. Along with their application, they must submit a letter of recommendation from an accounting professor, an official transcript indicating a GPA of 3.2 or higher, a resume, and an essay of 250 to 500 words on what motivated them to choose accounting as a career choice.

**Financial data:** The stipend is $5,000.

**Duration:** 1 year.

**Number awarded:** 2 each year.

**Deadline:** January of each year.

## 3040 ERNST & YOUNG SCHOLARSHIP PROGRAM

Hispanic College Fund
Attn: National Director
1717 Pennsylvania Avenue, N.W., Suite 460
Washington, D.C. 20006
Phone: (202) 296-5400; (800) 644-4223; Fax: (202) 296-3774;
Email: hispaniccollegefund@earthlink.net
Web: www.hispanicfund.org

**Summary:** To provide financial assistance to Hispanic American undergraduate students who are interested in preparing for a career in accounting.

**Eligibility:** Open to U.S. citizens of Hispanic background (at least one grandparent must be 100% Hispanic) who are entering their sophomore or junior year of college. Applicants must be working on a bachelor's degree in accounting or a related field and have a cumulative GPA of 3.0 or higher. They must be enrolled in a college or university in the 50 states or Puerto Rico as a full-time student. Financial need is considered in the selection process. This program is sponsored by Ernst & Young. All applications must be submitted online; no paper applications are available.

**Financial data:** Stipends range from $500 to $5,000, depending on the need of the recipient, and average approximately $3,000. Funds are paid directly to the recipient's college or university to help cover tuition and fees.

**Duration:** 1 year; recipients may reapply.

**Number awarded:** Varies each year.

**Deadline:** April of each year.

## 3041 ERWIN BUGBEE MEMORIAL SCHOLARSHIP

Vermont Student Assistance Corporation
Champlain Mill
Attn: Scholarship Programs
P.O. Box 2000
Winooski, VT 05404-2601
Phone: (802) 654-3798; (888) 253-4819; Fax: (802) 654-3765; TDD: (802) 654-3766; TDD: (800) 281-3341 (within VT); Email: info@vsac.org
Web: www.vsac.org

**Summary:** To provide financial assistance to high school seniors in Vermont who are interested in majoring in law enforcement in college. This program was established by the Vermont Police Association, which is responsible for selecting the recipients.

**Eligibility:** Open to high school seniors in Vermont who are interested in working on a degree in law enforcement in college. Selection is based on required essays and financial need.

**Financial data:** The stipend is $1,000.

**Duration:** 1 year.

**Number awarded:** 1 each year.

**Deadline:** April of each year.

## 3042 EXECUTIVE WOMEN INTERNATIONAL SCHOLARSHIP PROGRAM

Executive Women International
Attn: Scholarship Coordinator
515 South 700 East, Suite 2A
Salt Lake City, UT 84102
Phone: (801) 355-2800; (888) EWI-1229; Fax: (801) 355-2852;
Email: ewi@executivewomen.org
Web: www.executivewomen.org

**Summary:** To recognize and reward high school juniors with outstanding business and leadership potential.

**Eligibility:** Open to high school juniors attending public, private, and parochial schools located in Executive Women International (EWI) chapter cities. Applicants must be interested in majoring in business at a 4-year college or university. Because this program targets business students, those planning careers in medicine, law, art, social welfare, political science, or related fields are not eligible to compete. Each high school within the territorial boundaries of a participating EWI chapter may submit the name of one junior class student for the local competition. Students are required to submit a notebook (which includes a student application, autobiographical essay, and list of honors and awards) to their EWI chapter. A sponsoring teacher is also required to submit an endorsement, a transcript of the student's grades, and 1 personal reference. Competing students are interviewed by local judges. Winners then submit their notebooks for competition on the district level. Notebooks and videotaped interviews of the 15 district winners are reviewed by the semifinals' judges and 3 winners (plus 2 alternates) are selected as winners. The winners and their sponsoring teachers receive an all-expense paid trip to the EWI annual meeting, where they compete for first-, second-, and third-place awards. Selection is based on scholastic achievement, honors and awards, ability to work well with others, citizenship, leadership qualities, proven dependability and responsibility, communication skills, and extracurricular activities.

**Financial data:** Stipends are $10,000 for the first-place winner, $6,000 for the second-place winner, $4,000 for the third-place winner, and $2,000 for finalists. These funds are paid to the winners' colleges. Local and district winners also receive scholarships (generally under $2,000). A total of $150,000 is distributed through this program each year.

**Duration:** The scholarship funds are disbursed over a period of no more than 5 years.

**Number awarded:** 6 national winners are selected each year.

**Deadline:** Applications must be received by local chapters by the end of March so they can select their winners by mid-April. Districts complete their judging by mid-May. The final judging is completed by mid-July.

## 3043 F. GRANT WAITE, CPA, MEMORIAL SCHOLARSHIP

Massachusetts Society of Certified Public Accountants
Attn: MSCPA Educational Foundation
105 Chauncy Street, Tenth Floor
Boston, MA 02111
Phone: (617) 556-4000; (800) 392-6145; Fax: (617) 556-4126;
Email: biannoni@MSCPAonline.org
Web: www.cpatrack.com/financial_aid/scholarship.php

**Summary:** To provide financial assistance to college juniors majoring in accounting at a Massachusetts college or university. This program is supported, in part, by the firm of Vitale Caturano & Company CPAs PC

**Eligibility:** Open to Massachusetts residents who have completed their sophomore year and are majoring in accounting at a college or university in the state. Applicants must be enrolled in school on a full-time basis. They must demonstrate superior academic standing, financial need, and an intention to seek a career in a public accounting firm in Massachusetts. Special consideration is given to married students with children.

**Financial data:** The stipend is $1,000.

**Duration:** 1 year.

**Number awarded:** 1 each year.

## 3044 FBLA/PBL FOUNDATION SCHOLARSHIPS

FBLA/PBL Foundation
Attn: Scholarships
P.O. Box 3021010
Montgomery, AL 36130-2101
Phone: (334) 242-9109

**Summary:** To provide financial assistance for college to members of Future Business Leaders of America (FBLA) and Phi Beta Lambda (PBL).

**Eligibility:** Open to high school seniors who are members of FBLA and college students who are members of PBL. Applicants must be enrolled or planning to enroll in a business education program at a college or university. Along with their application, they must submit an essay on a topic administered to them by their adviser at their home site. Selection is based on that essay (20%), FBLA/PBL involvement and leadership (25%), community involvement (20%), honors and awards other than FBLA/PBL (15%), GPA (10%), and financial need (10%).

**Financial data:** The stipend is $1,000.

**Duration:** 1 year.

**Number awarded:** 1 in each FBLA/PBL district.

**Deadline:** September of each year.

## 3045 FEDERAL PLANNING DIVISION ANNUAL STUDENT SCHOLARSHIP

American Planning Association
Attn: Federal Planning Division
122 South Michigan Avenue, Suite 1600
Chicago, IL 60603-6107
Phone: (312) 431-9100; Fax: (312) 431-9985; Email: fpd-info@list.planning.org
Web: www.FedPlan.org
**Summary:** To provide financial assistance to undergraduate and graduate students preparing for a career in planning, especially as it relates to activities of the federal government.
**Eligibility:** Open to juniors, seniors, and graduate students at U.S. and Canadian accredited colleges and universities. Applicants must be preparing for a career in public service, especially at the federal level, as a planner. They must have a GPA of 3.0 or higher. Along with their application, they must submit an essay that addresses the federal government's role in managing its lands and resources in the best interests of the United States. Selection is based primarily on the essay, which is judged on clarity of message, freshness of idea, and potential for implementation. This program began in 2004. Information is also available from Justin Hollander, U.S. General Services Administration, 26 Federal Plaza, Room 1609, New York, NY 10278, (212) 264-1622, Email: Justin.Hollander@gsa.gov.
**Financial data:** Stipends range from $500 to $2,500.
**Duration:** 1 year.
**Number awarded:** 1 or more each year.
**Deadline:** November of each year.

## 3046 FISHER BROADCASTING SCHOLARSHIPS FOR MINORITIES

**Summary:** To provide financial assistance to minority college students in selected states who are interested in preparing for a career in broadcasting, marketing, or journalism.
*See Listing #1392.*

## 3047 FLORENCE TURNER KARLIN SCHOLARSHIP

Lincoln Community Foundation
215 Centennial Mall South, Suite 200
Lincoln, NE 68508
Phone: (402) 474-2345; Fax: (402) 476-8532; Email: lcf@lcf.org
Web: www.lcf.org
**Summary:** To provide financial assistance to upper-division and graduate students majoring in education in Nebraska.
**Eligibility:** Open to graduates of Nebraska high schools working on a degree in education at a college or university in the state. Teachers attending graduate school are encouraged to apply. Applicants must have completed at least their sophomore year and have a GPA of 3.0 or higher. Along with their application, they must submit essays on their plans for teaching after college and where they plan to teach and why.
**Financial data:** A stipend is awarded (amount not specified). Funds may be used only for college credit courses, not for workshops, seminars, or similar types of training opportunities.
**Duration:** 1 year; recipients may reapply.
**Number awarded:** 1 each year.
**Deadline:** March of each year.

## 3048 FLORIDA BANKERS EDUCATIONAL FOUNDATION GRANTS

Florida Bankers Association
Attn: Florida Bankers Educational Foundation
1001 Thomasville Road, Suite 201
P.O. Box 1360
Tallahassee, FL 32302-1360
Phone: (850) 224-2265, ext. 139; Fax: (850) 224-2423;
Email: lnewton@flbankers.net
Web: www.floridabankers.com/scholarship_fbef_grant.cfm
**Summary:** To provide financial assistance to undergraduate and graduate students who are interested in preparing for a career in Florida banking.
**Eligibility:** Open to undergraduate and graduate students who have at least 5 years of full-time experience working in Florida banking. Applicants must be Florida residents, registered at 1 of 27 participating colleges or universities in the state, and taking banking-related classes. They must have a GPA

of 2.5 or higher. Along with their application, they must submit 2 letters of recommendation from their place of employment: 1 from the bank president or other high-level employee and one from an immediate supervisor. Selection is based on interest in Florida banking, scholastic achievement, aptitude, ability, leadership, personality, and character.
**Financial data:** The amount of assistance is based on the number of semester hours the student has remaining until graduation. The maximum award is $1,500 per year for the freshman and sophomore years, $2,000 per year for the junior and senior years, and $5,000 as a graduate student.
**Duration:** Up to 4 years as an undergraduate and another 2 years as a graduate student.
**Additional information:** Recipients must maintain a 2.5 GPA and take at least 12 credit hours per calendar year.
**Number awarded:** Several each year.
**Deadline:** February, May, August, or November of each year.

## 3049 FLORIDA EDUCATIONAL FACILITIES PLANNERS' ASSOCIATION ASSISTANCESHIP

Florida Educational Facilities Planners' Association, Inc.
c/o Bob Griffith, Selection Committee Chair
Florida International University
University Park, CSC 236
Miami, FL 33199
Phone: (305) 348-4000; Fax: (305) 348-4010; Email: griffith@fiu.edu
Web: www.fefpa.org/assist.htm
**Summary:** To provide financial assistance to undergraduate and graduate students in Florida who are preparing for a career in educational facilities management. The sponsor is a statewide organization of facilities planners and associate members involved in the planning of educational facilities in K-12 schools, community colleges, and universities.
**Eligibility:** Open to full-time sophomores, juniors, seniors, and graduate students who are enrolled in a degree program at an accredited public community college or university in Florida. Applicants must be Florida residents and majoring in facilities planning or in a field related to facilities planning with a GPA of 3.0 or higher. Part-time students with full-time employment will also be considered if they are working on a degree in a field related to facilities planning. Along with their application, they must submit transcripts, SAT scores, a 1-page essay on why they deserve this scholarship, and a completed appraisal form from their issuing professor, supervisor, or department head. Selection is based on financial need, academic excellence, community involvement, references, employment, the appraisal form, and the essay.
**Financial data:** The stipend is $3,000 per year, paid in 2 equal installments ($1,500 per semester). Funds are sent directly to the recipients.
**Duration:** 1 year.
**Number awarded:** 2 each year.
**Deadline:** May of each year.

## 3050 FLORIDA ETHICS IN BUSINESS MATCHING SCHOLARSHIPS

Florida Independent College Fund
929 North Spring Garden Avenue, Suite 165
DeLand, FL 32720-0981
Phone: (386) 734-2745; Fax: (386) 734-0839; Email: Scholarships@ficf.org
Web: www.ficf.org
**Summary:** To provide financial assistance to students working on a degree in business at designated private colleges and universities in Florida. The Florida Independent College Fund (FICF) was established in 1956 and merged with the ICUF in 1996. It provides financial assistance to students at the 27 independent colleges and universities that are members of the ICUF.
**Eligibility:** Open to residents of Florida who are attending a private college or university in the state that is a member of the Independent Colleges and Universities of Florida (ICUF). Preference is given to students majoring in business.
**Financial data:** The maximum stipend is $2,600. Funds may be matched on a 1:1 basis by ICUF institutions.
**Duration:** 1 year.
**Number awarded:** Each of the 27 institutions receives one of these scholarships, which it may award as a lump sum to one student or distribute to several students.
**Deadline:** November of each year.

## 3051 FLORIDA HOTEL & MOTEL ASSOCIATION SCHOLARSHIPS

Florida Hotel & Motel Association, Inc.
Attn: Director of Education and Research
Hospitality Square
P.O. Box 1529
Tallahassee, FL 32302-1529
Phone: (850) 224-2888; (800) 476-FHMA; Fax: (850) 222-FHMA;
Email: parker@fhma.net
Web: www.flahotel.com/education
**Summary:** To provide financial assistance to students in Florida interested in preparing for a career in the lodging industry.
**Eligibility:** Open to residents of Florida who are graduating high school seniors or current 2-year and 4-year college students in the state. Applicants must be interested in preparing for a career in the lodging industry. They must have a GPA of 2.5 or higher.
**Financial data:** The stipend is $2,000.
**Duration:** 1 year.
**Number awarded:** 5 each year.
**Deadline:** April of each year.

## 3052 FLORIDA INSTITUTE OF CPAS SCHOLARSHIPS

Florida Institute of CPAs Educational Foundation, Inc.
Attn: FICPA Educational Foundation
325 West College Avenue
P.O. Box 5437
Tallahassee, FL 32314
Phone: (850) 224-2727, ext. 200; (800) 342-3197, ext. 200; Fax: (850) 222-8190
Web: www.ficpa.org
**Summary:** To provide financial assistance to upper division students in Florida who are majoring in accounting.
**Eligibility:** Open to Florida residents who are fourth- or fifth-year accounting students enrolled full time in an accounting program at a Florida college or university. A faculty member in the accounting department of their college must nominate them. Applicants should be planning to sit for the C.P.A. exam and indicate a desire to work in Florida. Selection is based on financial need, educational achievement, and demonstrated professional, social, and charitable activities.
**Financial data:** Stipends range from $1,000 to $1,250.
**Duration:** 1 year; recipients may reapply for 1 additional year of support.
**Number awarded:** Varies each year; recently, a total of 114 scholarships were awarded, including 52 worth $65,000 by the Educational Foundation, 58 worth $60,500 by various chapters of the association, 3 Walter Friedly Memorial Scholarships worth $3,426, and 1 Paychex Entrepreneur Scholarship worth $1,000.

## 3053 FLORIDA ROCK INDUSTRIES INTERNSHIP PROGRAM

**Summary:** To provide financial assistance and work experience to business and engineering students at designated private colleges and universities in Florida who are interested in a career in the construction materials business.
*See Listing #2164.*

## 3054 FLOYD BORING AWARD

Boy Scouts of America
Attn: Learning for Life Division, S210
1325 West Walnut Hill Lane
P.O. Box 152079
Irving, TX 75015-2079
Phone: (972) 580-2418; Fax: (972) 580-2137
Web: www.learning-for-life.org/exploring/scholarships/index.html
**Summary:** To recognize and reward Explorer Scouts who have made an exceptional contribution to law enforcement agencies.
**Eligibility:** Open to Explorer Scouts who assist law enforcement agencies with meaningful and exceptional service. Candidates must be active members of a Law Enforcement Explorer post currently registered with the Boy Scouts of America. They must submit a statement from their post advisor that describes the act for which they are being nominated, 3 letters of recommendation, and their own 1,000-word statement that describes the act for which they are being nominated.

**Financial data:** The award consists of a plaque and a $2,000 scholarship to the college of the awardee's choice.
**Duration:** 1 year; nonrenewable.
**Number awarded:** 2 each year.
**Deadline:** March of each year.

## 3055 FORD MOTOR COMPANY/AMERICAN INDIAN COLLEGE FUND CORPORATE SCHOLARS PROGRAM

**Summary:** To provide financial assistance to Native American college students who are majoring in designated fields at specified colleges and universities.
*See Listing #2169.*

## 3056 FORE UNDERGRADUATE MERIT SCHOLARSHIPS

**Summary:** To provide financial assistance to members of the American Health Information Management Association (AHIMA) who are interested in working on an undergraduate degree in health information administration or technology.
*See Listing #2171.*

## 3057 FORTUNE BRANDS SCHOLARS PROGRAM

United Negro College Fund
Attn: Corporate Scholars Program
P.O. Box 1435
Alexandria, VA 22313-9998
Phone: (866) 671-7237; Email: internship@uncf.org
Web: www.uncf.org/internships/index.asp
**Summary:** To provide financial assistance and work experience to minorities who are either juniors majoring in fields related to business or law students interested in an internship at corporate headquarters of Fortune Brands.
**Eligibility:** Open to juniors and first- and second-year law students who are members of minority groups. Applicants must have a GPA of 3.0 or higher and an undergraduate major in accounting, finance, human resources, information systems, information technology, or marketing. They must be attending a designated college, university, or law school and be interested in an internship at Fortune Brands corporate headquarters in Lincolnshire, Illinois. Along with their application, they must submit a resume, 2 letters of recommendation, and official transcripts. Eligible undergraduate institutions are Florida A&M University, Florida State University, Hampton University, Howard University, Morehouse College, North Carolina A&T State University, Northwestern University, Spelman College, University of Chicago, and University of Wisconsin. Participating law schools are those at Howard University, Northwestern University, University of Chicago, and University of Wisconsin.
**Financial data:** The program provides a paid internship and (based on successful internship performance) a $7,500 scholarship.
**Duration:** 8 to 10 weeks for the internship; 1 year for the scholarship.
**Number awarded:** Varies each year.
**Deadline:** February of each year.

## 3058 FRANCES A. MAYS SCHOLARSHIP AWARD

**Summary:** To provide financial assistance to college seniors majoring in health, physical education, recreation, or dance in Virginia.
*See Listing #1398.*

## 3059 FRANCIS X. CROWLEY SCHOLARSHIP

**Summary:** To provide financial assistance to undergraduate or graduate students from New England interested in working on a degree in civil or environmental engineering or in business management.
*See Listing #2178.*

## 3060 FRANK KAZMIERCZAK MEMORIAL MIGRANT SCHOLARSHIP

Geneseo Migrant Center
27 Lackawanna Avenue
Mount Morris, NY 14510-1096
Phone: (585) 658-7960; (800) 245-5681; Fax: (585) 658-7969;
Email: info@migrant.net
Web: www.migrant.net/sch_kazmierczak.htm

**Summary:** To provide financial assistance for college to migrant farmworker youth interested in preparing for a career in teaching.
**Eligibility:** Open to migrant farmworkers and their children who are interested in preparing for a career as a teacher. Priority is given to applicants who have experienced mobility within the past 3 years. They must submit a personal essay of 300 to 500 words on their reasons for wanting to become a teacher, 2 letters of recommendation, and an official school transcript. Selection is based on financial need, academic achievement, and history of migration for agricultural employment.
**Financial data:** The stipend is $1,000.
**Duration:** 1 year.
**Number awarded:** 1 each year.
**Deadline:** January of each year.

### 3061 FRANK L. GREATHOUSE GOVERNMENT ACCOUNTING SCHOLARSHIP

Government Finance Officers Association
Attn: Scholarship Committee
203 North LaSalle Street, Suite 2700
Chicago, IL 60601-1210
Phone: (312) 977-9700; Fax: (312) 977-4806
Web: www.gfoa.org/services/scholarships.shtml
**Summary:** To provide financial assistance to undergraduate students who are preparing for a career in public accounting.
**Eligibility:** Open to seniors in college who are enrolled full time in an accounting program and preparing for a career in state and local government finance. Applicants must be citizens or permanent residents of the United States or Canada and able to provide a letter of recommendation from their academic advisor or the chair of their accounting program. Selection is based on career plans, academic record, plan of study, letters of recommendation, and GPA. Financial need is not considered.
**Financial data:** The stipend is $3,500.
**Duration:** 1 year.
**Number awarded:** 1 each year.
**Deadline:** February of each year.

### 3062 FRED WIESNER EDUCATIONAL EXCELLENCE SCHOLARSHIP

Association of Texas Professional Educators
Attn: Scholarships
305 East Huntland Drive, Suite 300
Austin, TX 78752-3792
Phone: (512) 467-0071; (800) 777-ATPE; Fax: (512) 467-2203;
Email: atpe@atpe.org
Web: www.atpe.org/Awards/fwiesnerinfo.htm
**Summary:** To provide financial assistance to undergraduate and graduate students enrolled in educator preparation programs at institutions in Texas.
**Eligibility:** Open to juniors, seniors, and graduate students enrolled in educator preparation programs at colleges and universities in Texas. Applicants must submit a 2-page essay on their personal philosophy toward education, why they want to become an educator, who influenced them the most in making their career decision, and why they are applying for the scholarship. Financial need is not considered in the selection process.
**Financial data:** The stipend is $1,500 per year.
**Duration:** 1 year.
**Number awarded:** 4 each year: 3 to undergraduates and 1 to a graduate student.
**Deadline:** May of each year.

### 3063 FRIENDS OF OREGON STUDENTS PROGRAM

**Summary:** To provide financial assistance to students in Oregon who are employed while working on an undergraduate or graduate degree in teaching or nursing.
*See Listing #2183.*

### 3064 FTA SCHOLARSHIPS

North Carolina Association of Educators, Inc.
Attn: Future Teacher Association
700 South Salisbury Street
P.O. Box 27347

Raleigh, NC 27611-7347
Phone: (919) 832-3000; (800) 662-7924; Fax: (919) 839-8229
Web: www.ncae.org
**Summary:** To provide financial assistance to high school seniors in North Carolina who plan to attend college to prepare for a career as an educator.
**Eligibility:** Open to high school seniors who are members of the Future Teacher Association (FTA), an affiliate of the North Carolina Association of Educators. Applicants are interviewed. Selection is based on GPA, school activities, philosophy concerning education, and desire to become an educator.
**Financial data:** Stipends are $1,000 or $500.
**Duration:** 1 year.
**Number awarded:** 3 each year: 1 at $1,000 and 2 at $500.
**Deadline:** January of each year.

### 3065 FTE UNDERGRADUATE MAJOR IN TECHNOLOGY EDUCATION SCHOLARSHIP

**Summary:** To provide financial support to undergraduate members of the International Technology Education Association (ITEA) who are majoring in technology education teacher preparation.
*See Listing #2184.*

### 3066 FUKUNAGA SCHOLARSHIP

Fukunaga Scholarship Foundation
Attn: Scholarship Administrator
900 Fort Street Mall, Suite 600
P.O. Box 2788
Honolulu, HI 96803-2788
Phone: (808) 521-6511, ext. 286; Fax: (808) 523-3937;
Email: sandyw@servco.com
Web: www.servco.com/scholarship
**Summary:** To provide financial assistance to Hawaii residents who are interested in majoring in business in college.
**Eligibility:** Open to Hawaii residents who are graduating from high school or already enrolled in a 4-year college or university. Applicants must be majoring or planning to major in business administration. They should have at least a 3.0 GPA and plan to return to or remain in Hawaii or the Pacific Islands region. Selection is based on academic achievement; interest in business; participation, leadership, and responsibility in school activities and community service; and financial need. To maintain eligibility, recipients must enroll in school full time and maintain at least a 3.0 GPA.
**Financial data:** The stipend is $2,500 per year.
**Duration:** Up to 4 years for high school seniors; up to the remainder of the approved undergraduate program for recipients currently in college.
**Number awarded:** 12 to 16 each year.
**Deadline:** February of each year.

### 3067 FUTURE ENTREPRENEUR OF THE YEAR AWARD

National Association for the Self-Employed
P.O. Box 612067
DFW Airport
Dallas, TX 75261-2067
Phone: (800) 232-NASE; Fax: (800) 551-4446
Web: www.nase.org
**Summary:** To provide financial assistance to high school seniors interested in studying entrepreneurship in college.
**Eligibility:** Open to high school seniors who demonstrate leadership, academic excellence, ingenuity, and entrepreneurial spirit. Applicants must be interested in a college program that stresses the philosophy of entrepreneurship rather than a specific field of study.
**Financial data:** The stipend is $12,000 for the first year and $4,000 for each subsequent year.
**Duration:** 1 year; may be renewed up to 3 additional years.
**Number awarded:** 1 each year.
**Deadline:** April of each year.

### 3068 G.A. MAVON MEMORIAL SCHOLARSHIP

Professional Independent Insurance Agents of Illinois
Attn: College Scholarship Program
4360 Wabash Avenue
Springfield, IL 62707

Phone: (217) 793-6660; (800) 628-6436; Fax: (217) 793-6744;
Email: admin@piiai.org
Web: www.piiai.org/youngagents/scholarship.htm
**Summary:** To provide financial assistance to upper-division students from Illinois who are majoring in business and have an interest in insurance.
**Eligibility:** Open to residents of Illinois who are full-time juniors or seniors in college. Applicants must be enrolled in a business degree program with an interest in insurance. They must have a letter of recommendation from a current or retired member of the Professional Independent Insurance Agents of Illinois. Along with their application, they must submit an essay (500 words or less) on the contribution the insurance industry makes to society. Financial need is not considered in the selection process.
**Financial data:** The stipend is $2,000, payable in 2 equal installments. Funds are paid directly to the recipient's school.
**Duration:** 1 year.
**Number awarded:** 1 each year.
**Deadline:** June of each year.

## 3069 GAE FOUNDATION SCHOLARSHIPS FOR ASPIRING TEACHERS

Georgia Association of Educators
Attn: Professional Development Services
100 Crescent Centre Parkway, Suite 500
Tucker, GA 30084-7049
Phone: (678) 837-1103; (800) 282-7142, ext. 1103
Web: www.gae.org
**Summary:** To provide financial assistance to residents of Georgia who are interested in attending college to prepare for a career as a teacher.
**Eligibility:** Open to 1) seniors graduating from high schools in Georgia who plan to attend an accredited college or university in the state within the next 6 months, and 2) juniors and seniors who have already been admitted to a teacher education program at an accredited Georgia college or university. Applicants must submit a 2-page essay on why they want to become a teacher, their most rewarding educational experience, and how they see the role of the Georgia Association of Educators (GAE) in their professional development. Selection is based on depth of thought and clarity of expression in the essay, academic achievement, 2 letters of recommendation, and financial need.
**Financial data:** The stipend is $1,000. Funds are paid directly to the recipient's college or university.
**Duration:** 1 year.
**Number awarded:** Up to 20 each year: 10 graduating high school seniors and 10 students already enrolled in college.
**Deadline:** March of each year.

## 3070 GAT WINGS TO THE FUTURE MANAGEMENT SCHOLARSHIP

**Summary:** To provide financial assistance to members of Women in Aviation, International (WAI) who are interested in a career in aviation management.
*See Listing #2198.*

## 3071 GENERAL MOTORS SCHOLARSHIP PROGRAM OF THE HISPANIC SCHOLARSHIP FUND

**Summary:** To provide financial assistance to Hispanic Americans who are interested in attending college to major in engineering or business.
*See Listing #2211.*

## 3072 GENERATIONS FOR PEACE ESSAY CONTEST

Generations for Peace
c/o St. James Lutheran Church
1315 S.W. Park Avenue
Portland, OR 97201
Phone: (503) 222-2194
**Summary:** To recognize and reward outstanding essays on the general subject of peace written by high school students.
**Eligibility:** Open to all 11th and 12th grade students who are citizens and residents of the United States. Each year, the exact subject of the essay changes, but it always deals with the theme of peace. Essays may not be more than 750 words.

**Financial data:** The first-place essay receives $1,500; the second-place essay receives $750. Funds are paid directly to the winner's school.
**Duration:** The competition is held annually.
**Number awarded:** 2 each year.
**Deadline:** April of each year.

## 3073 GEORGE A. NIELSEN PUBLIC INVESTOR SCHOLARSHIP

Government Finance Officers Association
Attn: Scholarship Committee
203 North LaSalle Street, Suite 2700
Chicago, IL 60601-1210
Phone: (312) 977-9700; Fax: (312) 977-4806
Web: www.gfoa.org/services/scholarships.shtml
**Summary:** To provide financial assistance to public employees who are undergraduate or graduate students and have research or career interests in the investment of public funds.
**Eligibility:** Open to employees (for at least one year) of a local government or other public entity who are enrolled or planning to enroll in an undergraduate or graduate program in public administration, finance, business administration, or a related field. Applicants must be citizens or permanent residents of the United States or Canada and able to provide a letter of recommendation from their employer. They must have a research or career interest in the efficient and productive investment of public funds. Financial need is not considered in the selection process. Funds for this program are provided by George A. Nielsen LLP.
**Financial data:** The stipend is $5,000 or $2,500.
**Duration:** 1 year.
**Number awarded:** Each year, either 1 scholarship at $5,000 or 2 at $2,500 are awarded.
**Deadline:** February of each year.

## 3074 GEORGE AND DONNA NIGH PUBLIC SERVICE SCHOLARSHIP

Oklahoma State Regents for Higher Education
Attn: Director of Scholarship and Grant Programs
655 Research Parkway, Suite 200
P.O. Box 108850
Oklahoma City, OK 73101-8850
Phone: (405) 225-9239; (800) 858-1840; Fax: (405) 225-9230;
Email: studentinfo@osrhe.edu
Web: www.okhighered.org/student-center/financial-aid/nigh.shtml
**Summary:** To provide financial assistance for college to residents in Oklahoma who are interested in a career in public service.
**Eligibility:** Open to residents of Oklahoma who are enrolled full time in an undergraduate program at a public or private college or university in the state. Applicants must be enrolled in a degree program leading to a career in public service (as determined by the institution). Selection is based on academic achievement, including GPA, class rank, national awards, scholastic achievement, honors, teachers' recommendations, and participation in extracurricular activities. Each participating college or university may nominate one student each year.
**Financial data:** The stipend is $1,000 per year.
**Duration:** 1 year; nonrenewable.
**Number awarded:** Varies each year.

## 3075 GEORGE D. MILLER SCHOLARSHIP

**Summary:** To provide financial assistance to undergraduate and graduate students enrolled in fire service or public administration programs.
*See Listing #2219.*

## 3076 GEORGE M. BROOKER COLLEGIATE SCHOLARSHIP FOR MINORITIES

Institute of Real Estate Management Foundation
Attn: Foundation Coordinator
430 North Michigan Avenue
Chicago, IL 60611-4090
Phone: (312) 329-6008; (800) 837-0706, ext. 6008; Fax: (312) 410-7908;
Email: kholmes@irem.org
Web: www.irem.org
**Summary:** To provide financial assistance to minorities interested in prepar-

ing (on the undergraduate or graduate school level) for a career in the real estate management industry.

**Eligibility:** Open to junior, senior, and graduate minority (non-Caucasian) students majoring in real estate, preferably with an emphasis on management, asset management, or related fields. Applicants must be interested in beginning a career in real estate management upon graduation. They must have earned a GPA of 3.0 or higher in their major, have completed at least 2 college courses in real estate, and write an essay (up to 500 words) on why they want to follow a career in real estate management. U.S. citizenship is required. Selection is based on academic success and a demonstrated commitment to a career in real estate management.

**Financial data:** Stipends are $1,000 for undergraduates or $2,500 for graduate students. Funds are disbursed to the institution the student attends to be used only for tuition expenses.

**Duration:** 1 year; nonrenewable.

**Number awarded:** 3 each year: 2 undergraduate awards and 1 graduate award.

**Deadline:** March of each year.

## 3077 GEORGE MASON BUSINESS SCHOLARSHIP FUND

Hawai'i Community Foundation
Attn: Scholarship Department
1164 Bishop Street, Suite 800
Honolulu, HI 96813
Phone: (808) 566-5570; (888) 731-3863; Fax: (808) 521-6286;
Email: scholarships@hcf-hawaii.org
Web: www.hawaiicommunityfoundation.org/scholar/scholar.php

**Summary:** To provide financial assistance to residents of Hawaii who are interested in preparing for a career in business administration.

**Eligibility:** Open to residents of Hawaii who are entering their senior year at a 4-year college or university in the state. Applicants must be majoring in business administration. They must be able to demonstrate academic achievement (GPA of 3.0 or higher), good moral character, and financial need. In addition to filling out the standard application form, they must write a short statement indicating why they have chosen business as an intended career and how they expect to make a difference in the business world.

**Financial data:** The amount of the award depends on the availability of funds and the need of the recipient; recently, stipends averaged $1,000.

**Duration:** 1 year.

**Number awarded:** Varies each year; recently, 1 of these scholarships was awarded.

**Deadline:** February of each year.

## 3078 GEORGE PULAKOS SCHOLARSHIP

New Mexico Society of Certified Public Accountants
Attn: Scholarships in Accounting
1650 University N.E., Suite 450
Albuquerque, NM 87102-1733
Phone: (505) 246-1699; (800) 926-2522; Fax: (505) 246-1686;
Email: nmcpa@nmcpa.org
Web: www.nmcpa.org

**Summary:** To provide financial assistance to accounting students at New Mexico universities and colleges.

**Eligibility:** Open to full-time students at New Mexico colleges and universities who have completed 12 semester hours in accounting, are currently enrolled in 6 or more accounting hours, have completed 75 hours overall, and have a cumulative GPA of 3.0 or higher. Selection is based on academic achievement, extracurricular activities, career objectives and goals in accounting, and financial need.

**Financial data:** A stipend is awarded (amount not specified).

**Duration:** 1 year; may be renewed 1 additional year.

**Number awarded:** 1 each year.

**Deadline:** September of each year.

## 3079 GEORGE REINKE SCHOLARSHIPS

American Society of Travel Agents
Attn: ASTA Foundation
1101 King Street, Suite 200
Alexandria, VA 22314-2944
Phone: (703) 739-2782; Fax: (703) 684-8319; Email: scholarship@astahq.com
Web: www.astanet.com/education/scholarshipg.asp

**Summary:** To provide financial assistance to vocational or junior college students who are interested in preparing for a career in the travel/tourism industry.

**Eligibility:** Open to students who are registered at a recognized proprietary travel school or 2-year junior college that specializes in travel or tourism studies. Applicants must have a GPA of 2.5 or higher, write a 500-word essay on "My Objectives in the Travel Agency Industry," and explain why they need the scholarship. They must be U.S. citizens studying in the United States.

**Financial data:** The award is $2,000. A copy of the tuition bill is required.

**Duration:** 1 year.

**Number awarded:** Up to 6 each year.

**Deadline:** August or December of each year.

## 3080 GEORGIA AEE CHAPTER SCHOLARSHIPS

**Summary:** To provide financial assistance to undergraduate and graduate students in Georgia interested in taking courses directly related to energy engineering or energy management.

*See Listing #2223.*

## 3081 GEORGIA AFFILIATE SCHOLARSHIP

American Woman's Society of Certified Public Accountants-Georgia Affiliate
c/o Amy Knowles-Jones, President
Internal Audit Department
222 Piedmont Avenue, N.E.
Atlanta, GA 30308-3306
Phone: (404) 653-1242; Fax: (404) 653-1575;
Email: aknowles-jones@oxfordinc.com
Web: www.awscpa.org/affiliate_scholarships/georgia.html

**Summary:** To provide financial assistance to women who are working on an undergraduate degree in accounting at a college or university in Georgia.

**Eligibility:** Open to women who are enrolled in a Georgia college or university. Applicants must have completed or be currently enrolled in a course in intermediate accounting II.

**Financial data:** The stipend is $1,000.

**Duration:** 1 year.

**Number awarded:** 1 each year.

## 3082 GEORGIA PTA EDUCATIONAL SCHOLARSHIPS

Georgia PTA
Attn: Scholarship Committee
114 Baker Street, N.E.
Atlanta, GA 30308-3366
Phone: (404) 659-0214; Fax: (404) 525-0210; Email: gapta@bellsouth.net
Web: www.georgiapta.org

**Summary:** To provide financial assistance for college to students in Georgia who are interested in preparing for a career in a youth-related field.

**Eligibility:** Open to seniors graduating from a Georgia high school with a PTA/PTSA chapter that is in good standing with the Georgia PTA. Applicants must be interested in attending a college or university in the state to prepare to work in a youth-related field. Selection is based on character, academic record, and financial need.

**Financial data:** Stipends range from $1,000 to $1,500.

**Duration:** 1 year; nonrenewable.

**Number awarded:** Varies each year.

**Deadline:** January of each year.

## 3083 GEORGIA SOCIETY OF CPAS SCHOLARSHIP PROGRAM

Georgia Society of CPAs
Attn: Educational Foundation
3353 Peachtree Road, N.E., Suite 400
Atlanta, GA 30326-1414
Phone: (404) 231-8676; (800) 330-8889, ext. 2943; Fax: (404) 237-1291;
Email: gscpaweb@gscpa.org
Web: www.gscpa.org/EducationalFoundation/Scholarships.asp

**Summary:** To provide financial assistance to upper-division and graduate students who are majoring in accounting in Georgia.

**Eligibility:** Open to residents of Georgia who have demonstrated a commitment to a career in accounting. Applicants must be 1) rising junior or senior undergraduate accounting majors, or 2) graduate students enrolled in a master's degree in accounting or a business administration program. They must be enrolled in an accredited public or private college or university in Georgia with a GPA of 3.0 or higher either overall or in their accounting courses. Along with their application, they must submit documentation of financial need, transcripts, a resume, and a 250-word essay on their personal career goals and how this scholarship will help them attain those goals.

**Financial data:** A stipend is awarded (amount not specified). This program includes the following named scholarships: the Time + Plus Scholarship, the Robert H. Lange Memorial Scholarship, the Julius M. Johnson Memorial Scholarship, and the Paychex Entrepreneur Scholarship.

**Duration:** 1 year.

**Number awarded:** Varies each year; recently, 36 of these scholarships were awarded.

**Deadline:** April of each year.

## 3084 GERALDINE CLEWELL SCHOLARSHIP

Phi Upsilon Omicron
Attn: Educational Foundation
P.O. Box 329
Fairmont, WV 26555-0329
Phone: (304) 368-0612; Email: rickards@access.mountain.net
Web: www.phiu.unl.edu

**Summary:** To provide financial assistance to undergraduate student members of Phi Upsilon Omicron, a national honor society in family and consumer sciences.

**Eligibility:** Open to members of the society who are working on a bachelor's degree in family and consumer sciences or a related area. Selection is based on scholastic record, participation in society and other collegiate activities, a statement of professional aims and goals, professional services, and recommendations.

**Financial data:** The stipend is $1,500.

**Duration:** 1 year.

**Number awarded:** 1 each year.

**Deadline:** January of each year.

## 3085 GIBSON–LAEMEL SCHOLARSHIP

**Summary:** To provide financial assistance to college juniors and seniors from Connecticut who are interested in preparing for a career in health, physical education, recreation, or dance.

*See Listing #1414.*

## 3086 GLENN MOON SCHOLARSHIPS

Association of Retired Teachers of Connecticut
240 Pomeroy Avenue, Suite 201
Meriden, CT 06450-7170
Phone: (203) 639-9628; (866) 343-ARTC; Email: artc@artcinc.org
Web: www.artcinc.org/Appl.htm

**Summary:** To provide financial assistance to high school seniors in Connecticut who are interested in majoring in education in college.

**Eligibility:** Open to Connecticut high school seniors who intend to become teachers. Applicants must submit an autobiographical essay that includes their reasons for wishing to teach, history of teaching and/or tutoring experience, desired teaching level and/or subject area, and experiences that influenced their selection of teaching as a career. Selection is based on the essay, academic record, financial need, character and personality, interests, and educational activities.

**Financial data:** Stipends are $1,500 or $1,000.

**Duration:** 1 year; the $1,500 award may be renewed up to 3 additional years; the $1,000 awards are nonrenewable.

**Number awarded:** 4 each year: 1 at $1,500 and 3 at $1,000.

**Deadline:** March of each year.

## 3087 GOLDEN KEY BUSINESS ACHIEVEMENT AWARDS

Golden Key International Honour Society
621 North Avenue N.E., Suite C-100
Atlanta, GA 30308
Phone: (404) 377-2400; (800) 377-2401; Fax: (678) 420-6757;
Email: scholarships@goldenkey.org
Web: www.goldenkey.org/GKweb/ScholarshipsandAwards

**Summary:** To recognize and reward members of the Golden Key International Honour Society who submit outstanding papers on topics related to the field of business.

**Eligibility:** Open to undergraduate, graduate, and postgraduate members of the society who submit a paper or report, up to 10 pages in length, on a topic related to business. Applicants must also submit 1) an essay, up to 2 pages in length, describing the assignment for writing the paper, the greatest challenge in writing the paper, the lessons learned from completing the assignment, and what they would change if they could redo the paper; 2) a letter of recommendation; and 3) academic transcripts. Selection of the winners is based on academic achievement and the quality of the paper.

**Financial data:** The winner receives a $1,000 scholarship, second place a $750 scholarship, and third place a $500 scholarship.

**Duration:** These awards are presented annually.

**Number awarded:** 3 each year.

**Deadline:** February of each year.

## 3088 GOLDEN KEY EDUCATION ACHIEVEMENT AWARDS

Golden Key International Honour Society
621 North Avenue N.E., Suite C-100
Atlanta, GA 30308
Phone: (404) 377-2400; (800) 377-2401; Fax: (678) 420-6757;
Email: scholarships@goldenkey.org
Web: www.goldenkey.org/GKweb/ScholarshipsandAwards

**Summary:** To recognize and reward undergraduate and graduate members of the Golden Key International Honour Society who submit outstanding papers on topics related to the field of education.

**Eligibility:** Open to undergraduate, graduate, and postgraduate members of the society who submit a paper or report, up to 10 pages in length, on a topic related to education. Applicants must also submit 1) an essay, up to 2 pages in length, describing the assignment for writing the paper, the greatest challenge in writing the paper, the lessons learned from completing the assignment, and what they would change if they could redo the paper; 2) a letter of recommendation; and 3) academic transcripts. Selection of the winners is based on academic achievement and the quality of the paper.

**Financial data:** The winner receives a $1,000 scholarship, second place a $750 scholarship, and third place a $500 scholarship.

**Duration:** These awards are presented annually.

**Number awarded:** 3 each year.

**Deadline:** February of each year.

## 3089 GOLDEN KEY INFORMATION SYSTEMS ACHIEVEMENT AWARDS

**Summary:** To recognize and reward undergraduate members of the Golden Key International Honour Society who submit outstanding papers on topics related to the fields of computer science and information systems.

*See Listing #2234.*

## 3090 GORDON SCHEER SCHOLARSHIP

Colorado Society of Certified Public Accountants
Attn: CSCPA Educational Foundation
7979 East Tufts Avenue, Suite 500
Denver, CO 80237-2845
Phone: (303) 741-8613; (800) 523-9082 (within CO); Fax: (303) 773-6344;
Email: gmantz@cocpa.org
Web: www.cocpa.org/student_faculty/scholarships.asp

**Summary:** To provide financial assistance to undergraduate and graduate students in Colorado who are studying accounting.

**Eligibility:** Open to undergraduate and graduate students at colleges and universities in Colorado who have completed at least one intermediate accounting class and have a GPA, both overall and in accounting, of at least 3.5. Selection is based on scholastic achievement.

**Financial data:** The stipend is $1,250. Funds are paid directly to the recipient's school to be used for books, tuition, room, board, fees, and expenses.

**Duration:** 1 year; recipients may reapply.

**Number awarded:** 1 each year.

**Deadline:** June of each year.

## 3091 GRACE BYRNE UNDERGRADUATE SCHOLARSHIP

**Summary:** To provide financial assistance to women undergraduate students from Washington working on a degree related to transportation.

*See Listing #2235.*

### 3092 GREAT FALLS ADVERTISING FEDERATION COMMUNICATION/MARKETING SCHOLARSHIP

**Summary:** To provide financial assistance to high school seniors in Montana interested in preparing for a career related to advertising.
*See Listing #1425.*

### 3093 GREATER OMAHA CHAPTER NAWIC SCHOLARSHIP

**Summary:** To provide financial assistance to students in Nebraska who are preparing for a career in construction.
*See Listing #1426.*

### 3094 GRETCHEN E. VAN ROY MUSIC EDUCATION SCHOLARSHIP

**Summary:** To provide financial assistance to college student members of the National Federation of Music Clubs (NFMC) who are majoring in music education.
*See Listing #1427.*

### 3095 HAINES MEMORIAL SCHOLARSHIP

South Dakota Board of Regents
Attn: Scholarship Committee
306 East Capitol Avenue, Suite 200
Pierre, SD 57501-2545
Phone: (605) 773-3455; Fax: (605) 773-2422; Email: info@ris.sdbor.edu
Web: www.sdbor.edu/administration/academics/Scholarships.htm
**Summary:** To provide financial assistance to students at public universities in South Dakota who are enrolled in a teacher education program.
**Eligibility:** Open to sophomores, juniors, and seniors at public universities in South Dakota. Applicants must have a GPA of 2.5 or higher and a declared major in a teacher education program. They must submit a statement that describes their personal philosophy and their philosophy of education.
**Financial data:** The stipend is $2,150; funds are allocated to the institution for distribution to the student.
**Duration:** 1 year; nonrenewable.
**Number awarded:** 1 each year.
**Deadline:** February of each year.

### 3096 HAROLD AND MARIA RANSBURG AMERICAN PATRIOT SCHOLARSHIPS

Association of Former Intelligence Officers
Attn: Scholarships Committee
6723 Whittier Avenue, Suite 303A
McLean, VA 22101-4533
Phone: (703) 790-0320; Fax: (703) 991-1278; Email: afio@afio.com
Web: www.afio.com/sections/academic/scholarship.html
**Summary:** To provide financial assistance to undergraduate and graduate students who have a career interest in intelligence and national security.
**Eligibility:** Open to undergraduates who have completed their first or second year of study and graduate students who apply in their senior undergraduate year or first graduate year. Applicants must share the sponsor's educational mission on behalf of "national security, patriotism, and loyalty to the constitution." Along with their application, undergraduates must submit a 1-page book review on the subject of intelligence and national security. Graduate students must submit a dissertation or thesis proposal. Selection is based on merit, character, estimated future potential, background, and relevance of their studies to the full spectrum of national security interests and career ambitions.
**Financial data:** Stipends range from $1,500 to $3,000.
**Duration:** 1 year.
**Number awarded:** Several each year.
**Deadline:** August of each year.

### 3097 HAROLD BETTINGER MEMORIAL SCHOLARSHIP

**Summary:** To provide financial assistance to graduate or undergraduate students interested in the business of horticulture.
*See Listing #2250.*

### 3098 HAROLD D. DRUMMOND SCHOLARSHIPS IN ELEMENTARY EDUCATION

Kappa Delta Pi, Attn: Educational Foundation
3707 Woodview Trace
Indianapolis, IN 46268-1158
Phone: (317) 871-4900; (800) 284-3167; Fax: (317) 704-2323;
Email: foundation@kdp.org
Web: www.kdp.org/scholarships/list.php
**Summary:** To provide financial assistance for undergraduate or graduate studies in elementary education to members of Kappa Delta Pi (an international honor society in education).
**Eligibility:** Open to members of the society who are currently enrolled in college or graduate school. Applicants must submit a 500-word essay on a topic that changes annually; recently, the topic was "What I Can Contribute as an Elementary Teacher." The application form must be signed by the chapter counselor and the chapter president; each form must include the applicant's society membership number and the reasons for the needed financial support. No more than one application may be submitted per chapter.
**Financial data:** Stipends range from $500 to $1,000.
**Duration:** 1 year.
**Number awarded:** 4 each year.
**Deadline:** May of each year.

### 3099 HARRY A. APPLEGATE SCHOLARSHIP AWARD

DECA
1908 Association Drive
Reston, VA 20191-1594
Phone: (703) 860-5000; Fax: (703) 860-4013; Email: decainc@aol.com
Web: www.deca.org/scholarships/index.html
**Summary:** To provide financial assistance to DECA members interested in working on a college degree in marketing, entrepreneurship, or management.
**Eligibility:** Open to DECA members in either the high school or Delta Epsilon Chi (collegiate) division. Applicants must intend to work full time on a 2- or 4-year degree in marketing, entrepreneurship, or management. Complete applications are to be submitted to the state advisor. Each state is told the number of applications it may forward to the national organization. Selection is based on DECA involvement, leadership ability, community service, and grades. The program is merit based, but applicants may include a statement in support of financial need and it will be reviewed.
**Financial data:** The stipend is $1,000. Funds are paid directly to the recipient's college or university.
**Duration:** 1 year.
**Number awarded:** Varies each year; recently, 20 of these scholarships were awarded.
**Deadline:** Each state sets its own deadline, usually in January.

### 3100 HARRY F. GAEKE MEMORIAL SCHOLARSHIP

**Summary:** To provide financial assistance to students from Indiana, Kentucky, or Ohio who are working on an undergraduate degree in a field related to construction.
*See Listing #2251.*

### 3101 HARRY J. HARWICK SCHOLARSHIPS

**Summary:** To provide financial assistance to undergraduate or graduate students who are interested in preparing for a career in medical group management.
*See Listing #2252.*

### 3102 HARVEST SCHOLARSHIPS

**Summary:** To provide financial assistance for college to Michigan residents interested in preparing for a career in the manufactured homes, recreational vehicles, or campground industries.
*See Listing #2255.*

### 3103 HAWAI'I COMMUNITY FOUNDATION COMMUNITY SCHOLARSHIP FUND

**Summary:** To provide financial assistance to Hawaii residents who are interested in preparing for a career that will fill gaps in the local job market.
*See Listing #1439.*

## 3104 HBCU MINORITY STUDENT SCHOLARSHIPS

**Summary:** To provide financial assistance to underrepresented minority students attending or planning to attend an Historically Black College or University (HBCU).

*See Listing #1442.*

## 3105 HEALY SCHOLARSHIP

American Society of Travel Agents
Attn: ASTA Foundation
1101 King Street, Suite 200
Alexandria, VA 22314-2944
Phone: (703) 739-2782; Fax: (703) 684-8319; Email: scholarship@astahq.com
Web: www.astanet.com/education/scholarshipe.asp

**Summary:** To provide financial assistance to undergraduate students interested in preparing for a career in the travel/tourism industry.

**Eligibility:** Open to sophomores, juniors, and seniors who are enrolled in travel and tourism courses at a 4-year academic institution in the United States or Canada. Applicants must have a GPA of 2.5 or higher, be residents of the United States or Canada, and write a 500-word essay suggesting improvements in the travel industry.

**Financial data:** The stipend is $2,000.

**Duration:** 1 year; may be renewed.

**Number awarded:** 1 each year.

**Deadline:** July of each year.

## 3106 HEBREW LADIES SHELTERING HOME SCHOLARSHIPS

**Summary:** To provide financial assistance for college to students in Connecticut interested in Jewish education.

*See Listing #1447.*

## 3107 HELEN HOPPER SCHOLARSHIP

Virginia Association of Teachers of Family and Consumer Sciences
c/o Nancy J. Rowe
Graham Park Middle School
3613 Graham Park Road
Triangle, VA 22172
Phone: (703) 221-2118, ext. 285; Fax: (703) 221-1079; Email: njrowe@pscs.edu
Web: www.vatfacs.org

**Summary:** To provide financial assistance to undergraduate and graduate students in Virginia who are interested in studying family and consumer sciences.

**Eligibility:** Open to 1) Virginia high school seniors who plan to attend college and major in family life education or family and consumer sciences education; 2) college students enrolled in a family life education or family and consumer sciences education program; and 3) students working on a master's degree in a family life or family and consumer sciences program who plan to teach the subject.

**Financial data:** The stipend is $1,000.

**Duration:** 1 year.

**Number awarded:** 1 or more each year.

**Deadline:** April of each year.

## 3108 HENRY AND DOROTHY CASTLE MEMORIAL FUND SCHOLARSHIP

Hawai'i Community Foundation
Attn: Scholarship Department
1164 Bishop Street, Suite 800
Honolulu, HI 96813
Phone: (808) 566-5570; (888) 731-3863; Fax: (808) 521-6286;
Email: scholarships@hcf-hawaii.org
Web: www.hawaiicommunityfoundation.org/scholar/scholar.php

**Summary:** To provide financial assistance to Hawaii residents who are interested in preparing for a career in early childhood education.

**Eligibility:** Open to Hawaii residents who are interested in pursuing full-time undergraduate or graduate studies in the field of early childhood education (birth through third grade), including child care and preschool. They must be able to demonstrate academic achievement (GPA of 2.7 or higher), good moral character, and financial need. In addition to filling out the standard application form, applicants must 1) write a short statement indicating their reasons for attending college, their planned course of study, and their career goals, and

2) write an essay that states their interests and goals in studying early childhood education and how they plan to contribute to the field. Recipients may attend college in Hawaii or on the mainland. This scholarship is funded by the Samuel N. and Mary Castle Foundation.

**Financial data:** The amounts of the awards depend on the availability of funds and the need of the recipient; recently, stipends averaged $2,000.

**Duration:** 1 year.

**Number awarded:** Varies each year; recently, 10 of these scholarships were awarded.

**Deadline:** February of each year.

## 3109 HENRY SALVATORI SCHOLARSHIP

Order Sons of Italy in America
Attn: Sons of Italy Foundation
219 E Street, N.E.
Washington, DC 20002
Phone: (202) 547-5106; Fax: (202) 546-8168; Email: scholarships@osia.org
Web: www.osia.org/public/scholarships/grants.asp

**Summary:** To provide financial assistance for college to high school seniors of Italian descent who write about the principles of liberty, freedom, and equality in the United States.

**Eligibility:** Open to U.S. citizens of Italian descent who are high school seniors planning to enroll as full-time students in an undergraduate program at an accredited 4-year college or university. Applications must be accompanied by essays, from 750 to 1,000 words, on the relevance to the United States today of the Declaration of Independence, the Constitution, or the Bill of Rights and the meaning of those documents to the principles of liberty, freedom, and equality in the 21st century. The scholarship is presented to a student who has demonstrated exceptional leadership, distinguished scholarship, and an understanding of the principles for which the country was founded.

**Financial data:** The stipend is $25,000.

**Duration:** 1 year; nonrenewable.

**Number awarded:** 1 each year.

**Deadline:** February of each year.

## 3110 HERB ROBINSON SCHOLARSHIP

**Summary:** To provide financial assistance to Washington high school seniors who are interested in majoring in a communication-related field at an academic institution in the state.

*See Listing #1452.*

## 3111 HERMAN LERDAL SCHOLARSHIP

South Dakota Bankers Association
Attn: Foundation
109 West Missouri Avenue
P.O. Box 1081
Pierre, SD 57501-1081
Phone: (605) 224-1653; Fax: (605) 224-7835
Web: www.sdba.com/SDBA/Foundation/scholarships.htm

**Summary:** To provide financial assistance to students at South Dakota colleges or universities who are preparing for a career in banking or finance.

**Eligibility:** Open to juniors at colleges or universities in South Dakota who are working on a business-related degree in preparation for a career in banking or finance. Applicants must have at least a 3.0 GPA. Along with their application, they must submit a statement on their career interests, a description of their special talents and leadership abilities, a statement on obstacles they have overcome, and 3 letters of recommendation. Financial need is not considered in the selection process.

**Financial data:** The stipend is $1,000.

**Duration:** 1 year.

**Number awarded:** 1 each year.

**Deadline:** March of each year.

## 3112 HERMINE DALKOWITZ TOBOLOWSKY SCHOLARSHIP

**Summary:** To provide financial assistance to women in Texas who are preparing to enter selected professions.

*See Listing #1455.*

### 3113 HILL-ROM MANAGEMENT ESSAY COMPETITION IN HEALTHCARE ADMINISTRATION

**Summary:** To recognize and reward undergraduate or graduate student members of the American College of Healthcare Executives (ACHE) who submit outstanding essays on health care administration.

*See Listing #2264.*

### 3114 HIMSS FOUNDATION SCHOLARSHIPS

**Summary:** To provide financial assistance to upper-division and graduate student members of the Healthcare Information and Management Systems Society (HIMSS) who are interested in the field of health care information and management systems.

*See Listing #2265.*

### 3115 H.I.S. PROGRAM

**Summary:** To provide financial assistance and summer work experience to Hispanic American undergraduate students who are interested in preparing for a career in telecommunications.

*See Listing #2266.*

### 3116 HOLLAND AMERICA LINE–WESTOURS, INC. SCHOLARSHIPS

American Society of Travel Agents
Attn: ASTA Foundation
1101 King Street, Suite 200
Alexandria, VA 22314-2944
Phone: (703) 739-2782; Fax: (703) 684-8319; Email: scholarship@astahq.com
Web: www.astanet.com/education/scholarshipf.asp

**Summary:** To provide financial assistance to undergraduate students interested in preparing for a career in the travel/tourism industry.

**Eligibility:** Open to undergraduates who are enrolled in travel and tourism courses at 2- or 4-year colleges or universities or recognized proprietary travel schools in the United States or Canada. Applicants must have a GPA of 2.5 or higher, be residents of the United States or Canada, and write a 500-word essay on the future of the cruise industry.

**Financial data:** The stipend is $3,000.

**Duration:** 1 year; may be renewed.

**Number awarded:** 2 each year.

**Deadline:** July of each year.

### 3117 HOOPER MEMORIAL SCHOLARSHIP

**Summary:** To provide financial assistance to college students interested in preparing for a career in fields related to transportation.

*See Listing #2272.*

### 3118 HORIZONS FOUNDATION SCHOLARSHIP PROGRAM

**Summary:** To provide financial assistance to women who are upper-division or graduate students engaged in or planning careers related to the national security interests of the United States.

*See Listing #2273.*

### 3119 HOWARD BROWN RICKARD SCHOLARSHIPS

**Summary:** To provide financial assistance for college or graduate school to blind students studying or planning to study law, medicine, engineering, architecture, or the natural sciences.

*See Listing #1460.*

### 3120 HOWARD F. GREENE MEMORIAL SCHOLARSHIP OF MASSACHUSETTS

Massachusetts Society of Certified Public Accountants
Attn: MSCPA Educational Foundation
105 Chauncy Street, Tenth Floor
Boston, MA 02111
Phone: (617) 556-4000; (800) 392-6145; Fax: (617) 556-4126;
Email: biannoni@MSCPAonline.org
Web: www.cpatrack.com/financial_aid/scholarship.php

**Summary:** To provide financial assistance to undergraduate students majoring in accounting at a Massachusetts college or university. This program was established in 1984 by the New England Graduate Accounting Study Conference (NEGASC). Each New England college and university is invited to nominate 1 candidate. The application is submitted to the state C.P.A. society in which the college or university is located. The state society then submits the name of the recipient to NEGASC.

**Eligibility:** Open to undergraduate students at Massachusetts colleges and universities who have earned a cumulative GPA of 3.5 or higher in accounting subjects and 3.2 or higher overall. Applicants must be able to demonstrate writing skills, self-help, involvement in extracurricular activities on and off campus, and financial need.

**Financial data:** The stipend is $1,000.

**Duration:** 1 year.

**Number awarded:** 1 each year.

### 3121 HOWARD F. GREENE MEMORIAL SCHOLARSHIP OF NEW HAMPSHIRE

New Hampshire Society of Certified Public Accountants
Attn: Financial Careers Committee
1750 Elm Street, Suite 403
Manchester, NH 03104
Phone: (603) 622-1999; Fax: (603) 626-0204; Email: info@nhscpa.org
Web: nhscpa.org/student.htm

**Summary:** To provide financial assistance to undergraduates in New Hampshire who are preparing for a career as a certified public accountant.

**Eligibility:** Open to full-time students entering their senior year in an accounting program at an accredited 4-year college or university in New Hampshire. Applicants must have a GPA of 3.5 or higher in accounting subjects and 3.2 or higher overall. They must be able to demonstrate writing skills, self-help, extracurricular activities on and off campus, and financial need.

**Financial data:** The stipend is $1,000.

**Duration:** 1 year.

**Additional information:** This program was established in 1984 by the New England Graduate Accounting Study Conference (NEGASC). Each New England college and university is invited to nominate 1 candidate. The application is submitted to the state C.P.A. society in which the college or university is located. The state society then submits the name of the recipient to NEGASC.

**Number awarded:** 1 each year.

**Deadline:** April of each year.

### 3122 HRA-NCA ACADEMIC SCHOLARSHIPS

Human Resource Association of the National Capital Area
Attn: Chair, College Relations
P.O. Box 7503
Arlington, VA 22207
Phone: (703) 241-0229; Fax: (703) 532-9473; Email: info@hra-nca.org
Web: hra-nca.org/studentservices.asp

**Summary:** To provide financial assistance to students working on an undergraduate or graduate degree in human resources at colleges and universities in the Washington, D.C. metropolitan area.

**Eligibility:** Open to undergraduate and graduate students working on a degree in human resources or a related field at a college or university in the Washington, D.C. metropolitan area. Applicants must have completed at least half of their degree program and have at least a full semester remaining. Selection is based on academic performance and commitment to human resources as demonstrated by participation in a student chapter of the Society for Human Resource Management (SHRM), an internship, or relevant work experience or community service.

**Financial data:** The stipend is $1,500.

**Duration:** 1 year.

**Number awarded:** 2 each year.

**Deadline:** Applications are generally due in spring of each year.

### 3123 HSCPA SCHOLARSHIPS

Hawaii Society of Certified Public Accountants
900 Fort Street Mall, Suite 850
P.O. Box 1754
Honolulu, HI 98606
Phone: (808) 537-9475; Fax: (808) 537-3520; Email: info@hscpa.org

Web: www.hscpa.org

**Summary:** To provide financial assistance to accounting students in Hawaii.

**Eligibility:** Open to residents of Hawaii currently enrolled at a college or university in the state. Applicants must be majoring or concentrating in accounting and be planning to take the C.P.A. examination. They must have completed intermediate accounting and have a GPA of 3.0 or higher.

**Financial data:** Stipends range from $300 to $1,500.

**Duration:** 1 year.

**Number awarded:** Varies each year; recently, 4 of these scholarships were awarded.

---

## 3124 HSMAI SCHOLARSHIPS

Hospitality Sales and Marketing Association International
Attn: HSMAI Foundation
8201 Greensboro Drive, Suite 300
McLean, VA 22102
Phone: (703) 610-9024; Fax: (703) 610-9005
Web: www.hsmai.org/events/scholarship.cfm

**Summary:** To provide financial assistance to undergraduate and graduate students in accredited schools of hospitality management.

**Eligibility:** Open to full-time students who are currently enrolled in hospitality management or a related field, have hospitality work experience, are interested in a career in hospitality sales and marketing, and have good academic standing. Applications are accepted from 2 categories of students: 1) baccalaureate and graduate degree candidates, and 2) associate degree candidates. Along with their application, they must submit 3 essays: their interest in the hospitality industry and their career goals, the personal characteristics that will enable them to succeed in reaching those goals, and a situation in which they faced a challenge or were in a leadership role and how they dealt with the situation. Selection is based on the essays, industry-related work experience, GPA, extracurricular involvement, 2 letters of recommendation, and presentation of the application.

**Financial data:** The stipend is $2,000 for baccalaureate/graduate degree students or $500 for associate degree students.

**Duration:** 1 year.

**Number awarded:** 4 each year: 2 at $2,000 and 2 at $500.

**Deadline:** April of each year.

---

## 3125 HUMANE STUDIES FELLOWSHIPS

**Summary:** To provide financial assistance to undergraduate and graduate students in the United States or abroad who intend to pursue "intellectual careers" and have demonstrated an interest in classical liberal principles.

*See Listing #1461.*

---

## 3126 HYATT HOTELS FUND FOR MINORITY LODGING MANAGEMENT STUDENTS

American Hotel & Lodging Educational Foundation
Attn: Manager of Foundation Programs
1201 New York Avenue, N.W., Suite 600
Washington, DC 20005-3931
Phone: (202) 289-3181; Fax: (202) 289-3199; Email: ahlef@ahlef.org
Web: www.ahlef.org/scholarships_hyatt_hotel.asp

**Summary:** To provide financial assistance to minority college students working on a degree in hotel management.

**Eligibility:** Open to students attending a 4-year college or university that is a member of the Council on Hotel, Restaurant and Institutional Education. They must be minorities and majoring in hotel management. Each member university may nominate 1 student. The most outstanding students receive this scholarship.

**Financial data:** The stipend is $2,000.

**Duration:** 1 year.

**Number awarded:** Varies each year; recently, 18 of these scholarships were awarded.

**Deadline:** March of each year.

---

## 3127 IAHPERD SCHOLARSHIPS

**Summary:** To provide financial assistance to upper-division students in Illinois who are majoring in health, physical education, recreation, or dance.

*See Listing #1463.*

---

## 3128 ICI EDUCATIONAL FOUNDATION SCHOLARSHIP PROGRAM

**Summary:** To provide financial assistance to Hispanic American undergraduate students who are interested in preparing for a career in business, computer science, or engineering.

*See Listing #2282.*

---

## 3129 IDAHO STATE BROADCASTERS ASSOCIATION SCHOLARSHIPS

**Summary:** To provide financial assistance to students at Idaho colleges and universities who are preparing for a career in the broadcasting field.

*See Listing #1464.*

---

## 3130 IFEC SCHOLARSHIPS

**Summary:** To provide financial assistance to undergraduate or graduate students who are interested in preparing for a career in communications in the food service industry.

*See Listing #1467.*

---

## 3131 IFMA FOUNDATION SCHOLARSHIPS

International Facility Management Association
Attn: IFMA Foundation
1 East Greenway Plaza, Suite 1100
Houston, TX 77046
Phone: (713) 623-4362; Fax: (713) 623-6124;
Email: foundation@ifmafoundation.org
Web: www.ifmafoundation.org

**Summary:** To provide financial assistance to undergraduate and graduate students working on a degree in facility management.

**Eligibility:** Open to students enrolled full time at an accredited 4-year college or university in an undergraduate or graduate program in facility management or a related field. Undergraduates must have completed at least 2 years of study and have a GPA of 3.0 or higher. Graduate students must have a GPA of 3.5 or higher. Applicants may not be currently employed full time in facility management. Selection is based on a letter of intent, resume, achievement, accomplishments, involvement, and faculty appraisals; financial need is not considered.

**Financial data:** Stipends range from $1,000 to $5,000.

**Duration:** 1 year.

**Number awarded:** Varies each year. Recently, 15 of these scholarships were awarded: 1 at $5,000, 4 at $3,000, 1 at $2,500, 1 at $1,500, and 8 at $1,000. Since the foundation was established, it has awarded 123 scholarships worth $230,000.

---

## 3132 ILLINOIS REAL ESTATE EDUCATIONAL FOUNDATION ACADEMIC SCHOLARSHIPS

Illinois Association of Realtors
Attn: Illinois Real Estate Educational Foundation
3180 Adloff Lane, Suite 400
P.O. Box 19451
Springfield, IL 62794-9451
Phone: (217) 529-2600; Email: IARaccess@iar.org
Web: www.illinoisrealtor.org/iar/about/scholarships.htm

**Summary:** To provide financial assistance to Illinois residents who are preparing for a career in real estate.

**Eligibility:** Open to U.S. citizens who are Illinois residents, attending a college or university in the state on a full-time basis, and working on a degree with an emphasis in real estate. They must have completed at least 30 credits. As part of the application process, students must submit copies of their transcripts and letters of recommendation and reference. Selection is based on academic record, economic need, references and recommendations, and career plans in the field of real estate or an allied field (e.g., construction, land use planning, mortgage banking, property management, real estate appraising, real estate assessing, real estate brokerage, real estate development, real estate investment counseling, real estate law, and real estate syndication). Finalists are interviewed.

**Financial data:** The stipend is $1,000.

**Duration:** 1 year.

**Number awarded:** 1 or more each year.

**Deadline:** March of each year.

## 3133 ILLINOIS RESTAURANT ASSOCIATION GENERAL SCHOLARSHIPS

Illinois Restaurant Association
Attn: Educational Foundation
200 North LaSalle, Suite 880
Chicago, IL 60601-1014
Phone: (312) 787-4000, ext. 146; (800) 572-1086, ext. 146 (within IL); Fax: (312) 845-1956; Email: edfound@illinoisrestaurants.org
Web: www.illinoisrestaurants.org
**Summary:** To provide financial assistance to Illinois residents interested in preparing for a career in the food service industry. The Illinois ProStart program enables high school juniors and seniors to attend class but learn about the food service industry through 4 semesters of operator-paid internships under the supervision of an industry mentor trained by the Illinois Restaurant Association. Recently, 1,500 students participated in the program at 43 sites throughout the state.
**Eligibility:** Open to permanent residents of Illinois who are high school seniors or college students enrolled or planning to enroll full time in an accredited program in the food service and hospitality industry; the program may be outside Illinois. Individuals who are enrolled in at least 6 credit hours per semester and are employed at least 26 hours per week in the food service industry are also eligible. Preference is given to students who have earned an Illinois ProStart Certificate of Achievement with a passing grade of 70% each year they have been in the program. Applicants must have a GPA of 2.5 or higher. Along with their application, they must submit 3 essays: 1) their career goals; 2) the experience or person that most influenced them to select the restaurant and food service industry as their industry of choice; and 3) how receiving this scholarship will affect their ability to further their education and career in the restaurant and food service industry. Selection is based on the essays, presentation of the application (spelling, grammar, etc.), industry-related work experience (both paid and volunteer), honors and achievements, transcripts, and letters of recommendation.
**Financial data:** Stipends are $2,000 or $1,500.
**Duration:** 1 year; may be renewed upon reapplication.
**Number awarded:** Varies each year; recently, 16 of these scholarships were awarded, including 5 designated as Alvin D. Rose-Tastee Freez Scholarships, 1 designated at the Atwood Cafe Scholarship, 1 designated as the Blue Plate Catering Scholarship, 5 designated as Charlie Trotter's Scholarships, 3 designated as Gary Wales Memorial Scholarships, and 1 designated as the Superior Coffee, a Sara Lee Company Scholarship.
**Deadline:** May of each year.

## 3134 IMA MEMORIAL EDUCATION FUND SCHOLARSHIPS

Institute of Management Accountants
Attn: Committee on Students
10 Paragon Drive
Montvale, NJ 07645-1718
Phone: (201) 573-9000; (800) 638-4427, ext. 1543; Fax: (201) 474-1600; Email: students@imanet.org
Web: www.imanet.org
**Summary:** To provide financial assistance to student members of the Institute of Management Accountants (IMA) who are interested in preparing for a career in a field related to management accounting.
**Eligibility:** Open to undergraduate and graduate student IMA members who have a GPA of 2.8 or higher. Applicants must be preparing for a career in management accounting, financial management, or information technology. They must submit a 2-page statement on their reasons for applying for the scholarship, reasons that they deserve the award, specific contributions to the IMA, ideas on how they will promote awareness and increase membership and certification within IMA, and their career goals and objectives. Selection is based on that statement, academic merit, IMA participation, the quality of the presentation, a resume, and letters of recommendation.
**Financial data:** Stipends range from $1,000 to $2,500 per year.
**Duration:** 1 year.
**Number awarded:** Varies each year; recently, 10 of these scholarships were awarded. Up to 30 finalists in each category (including the scholarship winners) receive a scholarship to take 5 parts of the Certified Management Accountant (CMA) and/or Certified in Financial Management (CFM) examination within a year of graduation.
**Deadline:** February of each year.

## 3135 INDEPENDENCE ESSAY COMPETITION

Cascade Policy Institute
Attn: Program Director
813 S.W. Alder, Suite 450
Portland, OR 97205
Phone: (503) 242-0900; Fax: (503) 242-3822; Email: essay@cascadepolicy.org
Web: www.cascadepolicy.org/essay.html
**Summary:** To recognize and reward high school students in Oregon who write essays on liberty.
**Eligibility:** Open to private, public, and home-schooled students of high school age in Oregon. Applicants must submit an essay of up to 2,000 words on a topic that changes annually but relates to the meaning of liberty and the proper role of government in a free society. A recent topic was "Exploring the Foundations of Freedom." Selection is based on originality, proper grammar, and adherence to the competition topic.
**Financial data:** Awards are $1,000.
**Duration:** The competition is held annually.
**Number awarded:** Up to 5 each year.
**Deadline:** April of each year.

## 3136 INDEPENDENT COLLEGE SCHOLARSHIP

Kansas Society of Certified Public Accountants
Attn: Educational Foundation
1080 S.W. Wanamaker Road, Suite 200
P.O. Box 4291
Topeka, KS 66604-0291
Phone: (785) 272-4366; (800) 222-0452 (within KS); Fax: (785) 262-4468; Email: kscpa@kscpa.org
Web: www.kscpa.org/scholarship.cfm
**Summary:** To provide financial assistance to students in Kansas who are majoring in accounting at independent colleges.
**Eligibility:** Open to juniors who are majoring in accounting at independent colleges in Kansas. Each college may nominate one candidate.
**Financial data:** The stipend is $1,250.
**Duration:** 1 year.
**Number awarded:** 1 each year.
**Deadline:** April of each year.

## 3137 INTEL INTERNATIONAL SCIENCE AND ENGINEERING FAIR

**Summary:** To recognize and reward outstanding high school students who enter a science and engineering competition.
*See Listing #2302.*

## 3138 INTEL SCIENCE TALENT SEARCH SCHOLARSHIPS

**Summary:** To recognize and reward outstanding high school seniors who are interested in attending college to prepare for a career in mathematics, engineering, or any of the sciences.
*See Listing #2303.*

## 3139 IOWA FEDERATION OF LABOR SCHOLARSHIPS

Iowa Federation of Labor, AFL-CIO
Attn: Scholarship Program
2000 Walker Street, Suite A
Des Moines, IA 50317-5290
Phone: (515) 262-9571; (800) 372-4817; Fax: (515) 262-9573; Email: ifl@iowaaflcio.org
Web: www.iowaaflcio.org
**Summary:** To recognize and reward outstanding essays on a labor-related topic written by high school seniors in Iowa.
**Eligibility:** Open to all seniors in accredited high schools in Iowa (public, private, and parochial). Students must write an essay (from 500 to 750 words) on the history of the labor movement in the United States. It is recommended that competitors read *A History of the Labor Movement in the United States* before writing the essay.
**Financial data:** First prize is $1,500, second prize is $1,000, and third prize is $500. Funds may be used as a scholarship at the college or university of the recipient's choice.
**Duration:** The competition is held annually.
**Number awarded:** 3 each year.
**Deadline:** March of each year.

## 3140 ITEA UNDERGRADUATE SCHOLARSHIP IN TECHNOLOGY EDUCATION

**Summary:** To provide financial support to undergraduate members of the International Technology Education Association (ITEA) who are majoring in technology education teacher preparation.
*See Listing #2316.*

## 3141 J. PAUL NORWOOD MEMORIAL SCHOLARSHIP

Oklahoma Funeral Directors Association
Attn: Scholarship Committee
6801 North Broadway, Suite 106
Oklahoma City, OK 73116
Phone: (405) 843-0730; Fax: (405) 843-5404
**Summary:** To provide financial assistance to Oklahoma residents who are interested in attending a mortuary college.
**Eligibility:** Open to high school seniors in Oklahoma who have a GPS of 2.0 or higher. Applicants must be recommended by a member of the sponsoring organization, meet the educational requirements of the Oklahoma State Board of Embalmers and Funeral Directors, and possess the following personal characteristics: an acute mind, a pleasing personality, good character, ambition, and leadership abilities. They must "have abstained from participation in activities which created behavior incidents." Financial need is also considered in the selection process. Recipients must work at a funeral home in Oklahoma for 2 years following graduation. If they fail to complete that obligation, they must repay all funds received plus 10% interest.
**Financial data:** The maximum stipend is $1,500. Funds are sent to the recipient's school and must be used only for tuition and books.
**Duration:** 1 year; may be renewed if the recipient continues to do satisfactory work.

## 3142 JACK J. ISGUR SCHOLARSHIPS

**Summary:** To provide financial assistance to Missouri residents majoring in education and planning to teach humanities in elementary and middle schools in the state after graduation.
*See Listing #1479.*

## 3143 JACOB VAN NAMEN SCHOLARSHIP

**Summary:** To provide financial assistance to college students preparing for a career in the business of horticulture.
*See Listing #2323.*

## 3144 JAMES A. TURNER, JR. MEMORIAL SCHOLARSHIP

American Welding Society
Attn: AWS Foundation, Inc.
550 N.W. LeJeune Road
Miami, FL 33126
Phone: (305) 445-6628; (800) 443-9353, ext. 461; Fax: (305) 443-7559;
Email: found@aws.org
Web: www.aws.org/foundation/turner.html
**Summary:** To provide financial assistance to college students interested in a management career related to welding.
**Eligibility:** Open to full-time undergraduate students who are working on a 4-year bachelor's degree in business that will lead to a management career in welding store operations or a welding distributorship. Applicants must be U.S. citizens who are currently employed for at least 10 hours a week at a welding distributorship. Financial need is not required.
**Financial data:** The stipend is $3,000.
**Duration:** 1 year; recipients may reapply.
**Number awarded:** 1 each year.
**Deadline:** January of each year.

## 3145 JAMES CARLSON MEMORIAL SCHOLARSHIP

Oregon Student Assistance Commission
Attn: Grants and Scholarships Division
1500 Valley River Drive, Suite 100
Eugene, OR 97401-2146
Phone: (541) 687-7395; (800) 452-8807, ext. 7395; Fax: (541) 687-7419;
Email: awardinfo@mercury.osac.state.or.us
Web: www.osac.state.or.us
**Summary:** To provide financial assistance to Oregon residents majoring in education on the undergraduate or graduate school level.
**Eligibility:** Open to residents of Oregon who are U.S. citizens or permanent residents. Applicants must be either 1) college seniors or fifth-year students majoring in elementary or secondary education or 2) graduate students working on an elementary or secondary certificate. Full-time enrollment and financial need are required. Priority is given to 1) members of African American, Asian American, Hispanic, or Native American ethnic groups; 2) dependents of members of the Oregon Education Association; and 3) applicants committed to teaching autistic children.
**Financial data:** Stipend amounts vary; recently, they were at least $1,300.
**Duration:** 1 year.
**Number awarded:** Varies each year; recently, 3 of these scholarships were awarded.
**Deadline:** February of each year.

## 3146 JAMES M. AND VIRGINIA M. SMYTH SCHOLARSHIP FUND

**Summary:** To provide financial assistance for college to high school seniors, especially those from designated states.
*See Listing #1483.*

## 3147 JEAN C. OSAJDA FUND

Polish Roman Catholic Union of America
Attn: Education Fund Scholarship Program
984 North Milwaukee Avenue
Chicago, IL 60622-4101
Phone: (773) 782-2600; (800) 772-8632; Fax: (773) 278-4595;
Email: info@prcua.org
Web: www.prcua.org/benefits/educationfundscholarship.htm
**Summary:** To provide financial assistance to undergraduate and graduate education students of Polish heritage.
**Eligibility:** Open to students enrolled full time as sophomores, juniors, and seniors in an undergraduate program or full or part time as a graduate or professional school student. Applicants must be majoring in education. Selection is based on academic achievement, Polonia involvement, and community service.
**Financial data:** A stipend is awarded (amount not specified). Funds are paid directly to the institution.
**Duration:** 1 year.
**Number awarded:** 1 or more each year.
**Deadline:** May of each year.

## 3148 JEAN LEE/JEFF MARVIN COLLEGIATE SCHOLARSHIPS

**Summary:** To provide financial assistance to upper-division students in Indiana who are majoring in health, physical education, recreation, or dance.
*See Listing #1487.*

## 3149 JEANNE M. CROWLEY SCHOLARSHIP

**Summary:** To provide financial assistance to women residents of Massachusetts who are attending college to prepare for a career in construction.
*See Listing #2333.*

## 3150 JEDIDIAH ZABROSKY SCHOLARSHIP

Vermont Student Assistance Corporation
Champlain Mill
Attn: Scholarship Programs
P.O. Box 2000
Winooski, VT 05404-2601
Phone: (802) 654-3798; (888) 253-4819; Fax: (802) 654-3765; TDD: (802) 654-3766; TDD: (800) 281-3341 (within VT); Email: info@vsac.org
Web: www.vsac.org
**Summary:** To provide financial assistance to Vermont residents who are studying business or education at a college in the state.
**Eligibility:** Open to residents of Vermont who currently attend a public college in the state. Applicants must be working on a 2-year or 4-year degree in business or education and be employed at least 10 hours per week. Selection is based on academic achievement (GPA of 2.5 or higher), school and community involvement, letters of recommendation, required essays, and financial need.
**Financial data:** The stipend is $2,000.

**Duration:** 1 year.
**Number awarded:** 1 each year.
**Deadline:** April of each year.

## 3151 JENNIFER CURTIS BYLER SCHOLARSHIP IN PUBLIC AFFAIRS

National Stone, Sand and Gravel Association
Attn: Human Resources Committee
1605 King Street
Arlington, VA 22314
Phone: (703) 525-8788; (800) 342-1415; Fax: (703) 525-7782;
Email: info@nssga.org
Web: www.nssga.org/careers/scholarships.htm
**Summary:** To provide financial assistance to children of aggregates company employees who are interested in studying public affairs in college.
**Eligibility:** Open to graduating high school seniors and students already enrolled in a public affairs major in college who are sons or daughters of an aggregates company employee. Applicants must demonstrate their commitment to a career in public affairs. Along with their application, they must submit a letter of recommendation and a 300- to 500-word statement describing their plans for a career in public affairs. Financial need is not considered in the selection process.
**Financial data:** The amount of the award depends on the availability of funds.
**Duration:** 1 year; nonrenewable.
**Number awarded:** 1 each year.
**Deadline:** December of each year.

## 3152 J.O. WEBB MEMORIAL SCHOLARSHIP

University Interscholastic League
Attn: Texas Interscholastic League Foundation
1701 Manor Road
P.O. Box 8028
Austin, TX 78713
Phone: (512) 232-4938; Fax: (512) 471-5908;
Email: carolyn.scott@mail.utexas.edu
Web: www.uil.texas.edu/tilf/scholar.html
**Summary:** To provide financial assistance to students who participate in programs of the Texas Interscholastic League Foundation (TILF) and plan to enter the teaching profession after graduating from college.
**Eligibility:** Open to students who meet the 5 basic requirements of the TILF: 1) graduate from high school during the current year and enroll at a designated university in Texas by the following fall; 2) enroll full time and maintain a GPA of 2.5 or higher during the first semester; 3) compete in a University Interscholastic League (UIL) academic state meet contest in accounting, calculator applications, computer applications, computer science, current issues and events, debate, journalism (editorial writing, feature writing, headline writing, and news writing), literary criticism, mathematics, number sense, 1-act play, ready writing, science, social studies, speech (prose interpretation, poetry interpretation, informative speaking, and persuasive speaking), or spelling and vocabulary; 4) submit high school transcripts that include SAT and/or ACT scores; and 5) submit parents' latest income tax returns. Preference for this scholarship is given to students planning to enter the teaching profession. The designated universities are University of North Texas, Sam Houston State University, West Texas A&M University, Texas Women's University, and Southwest Texas State University.
**Financial data:** The stipend is $1,000.
**Duration:** 1 year; nonrenewable.
**Number awarded:** 1 each year.
**Deadline:** May of each year.

## 3153 JOE PERDUE SCHOLARSHIPS

Club Foundation, Attn: Scholarship Coordinator
1733 King Street
Alexandria, VA 22314-2720
Phone: (703) 739-9500; Fax: (703) 739-0124;
Email: schaverr@clubfoundation.org
Web: www.clubfoundation.org/stuscholar.html
**Summary:** To provide financial assistance for college to students planning a career in private club management.
**Eligibility:** Open to students who are currently attending an accredited 4-year college or university and are actively preparing for a managerial career in the private club industry. Applicants must have completed their freshman year with a GPA of 2.5 or higher. Along with their application, they must submit an essay of 500 to 1,000 words on their career objectives and goals, the characteristics they possess that will allow them to succeed as a club manager, how their experiences with the Club Management Association of American (CMAA) shaped their perception of the association and the private club management industry, their specified interests within the private club management field, and why they feel the Club Foundation should select them as a scholarship recipient. Selection is based on academic record (20 points), extracurricular activities (15 points), the essay (20 points), and employment record (15 points).
**Financial data:** The stipend is $2,500 per year. Funds are paid directly to the recipient's college or university.
**Duration:** 1 year.
**Number awarded:** Varies each year; recently, 7 of these scholarships were awarded.
**Deadline:** April of each year.

## 3154 JOHN A. LOPIANO SCHOLARSHIP

**Summary:** To provide financial assistance to college juniors, seniors, and graduate students interested in working with electronic documents as a career.
*See Listing #2344.*

## 3155 JOHN BLANCHARD MEMORIAL SCHOLARSHIP

California School Library Association
717 K Street, Suite 515
Sacramento, CA 95814-3477
Phone: (916) 447-2684; Fax: (916) 447-2695; Email: csla@pacbell.net
Web: www.schoollibrary.org
**Summary:** To provide financial assistance to members of the California School Library Association (CSLA) who are library paraprofessionals interested in preparing for a career as a school library media teacher.
**Eligibility:** Open to members of the association who are working or have worked within the last 3 years in a classified position in the library media field either in a school or at a district or county office. Applicants must be enrolled in a college or university working on a bachelor's or advanced degree to become a school library media teacher. They must be California residents planning to work as a library media teacher in the state upon completion of their credential program.
**Financial data:** The stipend is $1,000 per year, paid in 2 annual installments upon submission by the recipient of documentation showing proof of continuous enrollment at a California college or university in classes leading to an appropriate degree.
**Duration:** 2 years.
**Number awarded:** This award is presented as often as funding is available.
**Deadline:** June of each year.

## 3156 JOHN CULVER WOODDY SCHOLARSHIPS

Actuarial Foundation
Attn: Actuarial Education and Research Fund Committee
475 North Martingale Road, Suite 800
Schaumburg, IL 60173-2226
Phone: (847) 706-3565; Fax: (847) 706-3599; Email: scholarships@actfnd.org
Web: www.aerf.org/research_edu/prize_award.htm
**Summary:** To provide financial assistance to undergraduate students who are preparing for a career in actuarial science.
**Eligibility:** Open to undergraduate students who will have senior standing in the semester after receiving the scholarship. Applicants must rank in the top quartile of their class and have successfully completed one actuarial examination. Each university may nominate only 1 student. Preference is given to candidates who have demonstrated leadership potential by participating in extracurricular activities. Financial need is not considered in the selection process.
**Financial data:** The stipend is $2,000 per academic year.
**Duration:** 1 year.
**Number awarded:** Varies each year; recently, 8 of these scholarships were awarded.
**Deadline:** June of each year.

## 3157 JOHN F. KENNEDY SCHOLARSHIP

**Summary:** To provide financial assistance for college to Massachusetts residents, with preference given to registered Democrats.
*See Listing #1493.*

### 3158 JOHN M. BUNCH STUDENT SCHOLARSHIP

North Carolina Business Education Association
c/o Betsy Tobin, Past President
700 East Stonewal Street, Suite 400
Charlotte, NC 28202
Phone: (980) 343-2384; Email: betsy.tobin@cms.k12.nc.us
Web: www.ncbea.org/bunch.htm
**Summary:** To provide financial assistance to high school seniors in North Carolina who plan to study business or business education in college.
**Eligibility:** Open to seniors graduating from high schools in North Carolina who have taken one or more business education subjects. Applicants must be planning to attend a technical school, community college, college, or university in North Carolina to prepare for a career in business and/or business education. Along with their application, they must submit a 500-word essay on their future goals or aspirations and how college can help them achieve those goals. Financial need is not considered in the selection process.
**Financial data:** Stipends are $1,000 or $500. Funds are disbursed through the financial aid office at the recipient's college.
**Duration:** 1 year.
**Number awarded:** 1 or more each year.
**Deadline:** August of each year.

### 3159 JOSEPH AND MARION GREENBAUM SCHOLARSHIP FUND

**Summary:** To provide financial assistance to Jewish undergraduates from Delaware studying in Israel or Jewish studies in the United States and to Jewish students from outside the United States studying in Delaware.
*See Listing #529.*

### 3160 JOSEPH E. HAGAN MEMORIAL SCHOLARSHIP

Funeral Service Foundation
Attn: Executive Director
13625 Bishop's Drive
Brookfield, WI 53005
Phone: (262) 789-1880; (877) 402-5900
Web: www.funeralservicefoundation.org/scholarships/index.htm
**Summary:** To provide financial assistance to mortuary science students.
**Eligibility:** Open to full-time students who are currently enrolled or accepted for enrolment in a program of mortuary science accredited by the American Board of Funeral Service Education. Selection is based primarily on an essay of 400 to 500 words on the importance of the funeral ceremony and its effect on those who are grieving.
**Financial data:** The stipend is $1,000.
**Duration:** 1 year; nonrenewable
**Number awarded:** 1 each year.
**Deadline:** April of each year.

### 3161 JOSEPH MURPHY SCHOLARSHIP

**Summary:** To provide financial assistance to undergraduate or graduate students from New England interested in working on a degree in civil or environmental engineering, business, or a related science field.
*See Listing #2363.*

### 3162 JOSEPH R. STONE SCHOLARSHIPS

American Society of Travel Agents
Attn: ASTA Foundation
1101 King Street, Suite 200
Alexandria, VA 22314-2944
Phone: (703) 739-2782; Fax: (703) 684-8319; Email: scholarship@astahq.com
Web: www.astanet.com/education/scholarandph.asp
**Summary:** To provide financial assistance to undergraduate students interested in preparing for a career in the travel/tourism industry.
**Eligibility:** Open to undergraduates who are enrolled in travel and tourism courses at a 4-year postsecondary institution in the United States or Canada. At least one parent must be employed in the travel industry (hotel, car rental, airlines, travel agency, etc.). In addition, applicants must have a GPA of 2.5 or higher, be residents of the United States or Canada, and write a 500-word essay on their goals in the travel industry.
**Financial data:** The stipend is $2,400.

**Duration:** 1 year; may be renewed.
**Number awarded:** 3 each year.
**Deadline:** July of each year.

### 3163 JOSEPH T. WEINGOLD SCHOLARSHIP

NYSARC, Inc.
393 Delaware Avenue
Delmar, NY 12054
Phone: (518) 439-8311; Fax: (518) 439-1893; Email: info@nysarc.org
Web: www.nysarc.org/family/nysarc-family-scholarships-list.asp
**Summary:** To provide financial assistance to currently-enrolled college students in New York majoring in special education. NYSARC, Inc., was formerly the New York State Association for Retarded Children.
**Eligibility:** Open to students working on a degree program leading to a special education certification. They must be at least at the sophomore level.
**Financial data:** The stipend is $1,500 per year.
**Duration:** 2 years.
**Number awarded:** 1 each year.
**Deadline:** January of each year.

### 3164 JOYCE C. HALL COLLEGE SCHOLARSHIPS

People to People International
501 East Armour Boulevard
Kansas City, MO 64109-2200
Phone: (816) 531-4701; Fax: (816) 561-7502; Email: ptpi@ptpi.org
Web: www.ptpi.org
**Summary:** To provide financial assistance to members of People to People International (PTPI) who wish to study international relations.
**Eligibility:** Open to full-time students at a college or university who have a GPA of 3.0 or higher and a proposed major in an area of international relations. They must be current members of the organization and have participated within the past 4 years in one of its programs, such as the Student Ambassador Program of summer study overseas for high school students. Applications must include an essay on "Why I believe international friendships are important and how my experiences have increased my understanding of people who have grown up in other countries/cultures." People to People International is a nonprofit, private sector 501(c)(3) organization founded in 1956 by President Dwight D. Eisenhower to promote international understanding through direct people-to-people contacts. Funding for this program is provided through a bequest to PTPI from the estate of Mr. Joyce C. Hall, founder of Hallmark Cards, Inc.
**Financial data:** The stipend is $2,000. Funds are paid directly to the university and cover tuition first, then books and supplies; a special application is required to use the scholarship funds for other educational expenses, such as dormitory fees, off-campus study, or special projects.
**Duration:** 1 year.
**Number awarded:** Up to 5 each year.
**Deadline:** March of each year.

### 3165 JOYCE WASHINGTON SCHOLARSHIP

Watts Charity Association, Inc.
6245 Bristol Parkway, Suite 224
Culver City, CA 90230
Phone: (323) 671-0394; Fax: (323) 778-2613; Email: wattscharity@yahoo.com
Web: http://4watts.tripod.com/wattscharity/
**Summary:** To provide financial assistance to upper-division college students majoring in child development, teaching, or social services.
**Eligibility:** Open to U.S. citizens of African American descent who are enrolled full time as a college or university junior. Applicants must be majoring in child development, teaching, or the study of social services. They must have a GPA of 3.0 or higher, be between 17 and 24 years of age, and be able to demonstrate that they intend to continue their education for at least 2 years. Along with their application, they must submit 1) a 1-paragraph statement on why they should be awarded a Watts Foundation scholarship, and 2) a 1- to 2-page essay on a specific type of cancer, based either on how it has impacted their life or on researched information.
**Financial data:** A stipend is awarded (amount not specified).
**Duration:** 1 year.
**Number awarded:** 1 each year.
**Deadline:** May of each year.

### 3166 J.P. GUILFORD UNDERGRADUATE RESEARCH AWARDS

Psi Chi
825 Vine Street
P.O. Box 709
Chattanooga, TN 37401-0709
Phone: (423) 756-2044; Fax: (877) 774-2443; Email: awards@psichi.org
Web: www.psichi.org

**Summary:** To recognize and reward outstanding research papers written by undergraduate members of Psi Chi (an honor society in psychology).

**Eligibility:** Open to undergraduate students who are members of the honor society; they are invited to submit completed research papers (up to 12 pages long). For the purpose of this award, "research" is broadly defined to be based on any methodology relevant to psychology, including experiments, correlational studies, historical studies, case histories, and evaluation studies.

**Financial data:** First place is $1,000, second $650, and third $350.

**Duration:** The prizes are awarded annually.

**Number awarded:** 3 each year.

**Deadline:** April of each year.

### 3167 JP MORGAN CHASE SCHOLARSHIP PROGRAM OF THE HISPANIC SCHOLARSHIP FUND

Hispanic Scholarship Fund
Attn: Selection Committee
55 Second Street, Suite 1500
San Francisco, CA 94105
Phone: (415) 808-2350; (877) HSF-INFO; Fax: (415) 808-2302;
Email: college1@hsf.net
Web: www.hsf.net/scholarship/programs/jpmorgan.php

**Summary:** To provide financial assistance to Hispanic upper-division students working on a degree in a field related to business.

**Eligibility:** Open to U.S. citizens, permanent residents, and visitors with a passport stamped I-551 who are of Hispanic heritage. Applicants must be currently enrolled full time as a sophomore or junior at an accredited 4-year college or university in the United States, Puerto Rico, or the U.S. Virgin Islands. They must be majoring in business administration, finance, or economics with a GPA of 3.0 or higher. Along with their application, they must submit 600-word essays on 1) how their Hispanic heritage, family upbringing, and/or role models have influenced their personal long-term goals; 2) how they contribute to their community and what they have learned from their experiences; and 3) an academic challenge they have faced and how they have overcome it. Selection is based on academic achievement, personal strengths, leadership, and financial need.

**Financial data:** The stipend is $2,500.

**Duration:** 1 year.

**Number awarded:** 1 or more each year.

**Deadline:** November of each year.

### 3168 JUDITH CARY MEMORIAL SCHOLARSHIP

P. Buckley Moss Society
20 Stoneridge Drive, Suite 102
Waynesboro, VA 22980
Phone: (540) 943-5678; Fax: (540) 949-8408; Email: society@mosssociety.org
Web: www.mosssociety.org

**Summary:** To provide financial assistance to students working on a bachelor's or master's degree in special education.

**Eligibility:** Open to students who have completed at least 2 years of undergraduate study and are working on a bachelor's or master's degree in special education. Nominations may be submitted by society members only. The nomination packet must include proof of acceptance into a specific program to teach special needs students, 2 letters of recommendation, a short essay on school and community work activities and achievements, and an essay of 250 to 500 words on their career goals, teaching philosophies, reasons for choosing this career, and ways in which they plan to make a difference in the lives of special needs students. Financial need is not considered in the selection process.

**Financial data:** The stipend is $1,000. Funds are paid to the recipient's college or university.

**Duration:** 1 year.

**Number awarded:** 2 each year.

**Deadline:** March of each year.

### 3169 JUDITH MCMANUS PRICE SCHOLARSHIPS

American Planning Association
Attn: Leadership Affairs Associate
122 South Michigan Avenue, Suite 1600
Chicago, IL 60603-6107
Phone: (312) 431-9100; Fax: (312) 431-9985; Email: fellowship@planning.org
Web: www.planning.org/institutions/scholarship.htm

**Summary:** To provide financial assistance to women and underrepresented minority students enrolled in undergraduate or graduate degree programs at recognized planning schools.

**Eligibility:** Open to undergraduate and graduate students in urban and regional planning who are women or members of the following minority groups: African American, Hispanic American, or Native American. Applicants must be citizens of the United States and able to document financial need. They must intend to work as practicing planners in the public sector. Along with their application, they must submit a 2- to 5-page personal statement describing how their education will be applied to career goals and why they chose planning as a career path. Selection is based (in order of importance) on 1) commitment to planning as reflected in the personal statement and resume; 2) academic achievement and/or improvement during the past 2 years; 3) letters of recommendation; 4) financial need; and 5) professional presentation.

**Financial data:** Stipends range from $2,000 to $4,000 per year. The money may be applied to tuition and living expenses only. Payment is made to the recipient's university and divided by terms in the school year.

**Duration:** 1 year; recipients may reapply.

**Number awarded:** Varies each year; recently, 3 of these scholarships were awarded.

**Deadline:** April of each year.

### 3170 JULIAN AND JAN HESTER MEMORIAL SCHOLARSHIPS

Community Bankers Association of Georgia
1900 The Exchange, Suite 600
Atlanta, GA 30339-2022
Phone: (770) 541-4490; Fax: (770) 541-4496; Email: info@cbaofga.com
Web: www.cbaofga.com/programs.htm

**Summary:** To provide financial assistance to high school seniors in Georgia who are interested in preparing for a career in banking.

**Eligibility:** Open to high school seniors in Georgia who are planning to attend a college, university, or trade school in the state. They must be interested in preparing for a career in community banking. Selection is based solely on merit; family financial need is not considered.

**Financial data:** The stipend is $1,000.

**Duration:** 1 year; nonrenewable.

**Number awarded:** At least 4 each year.

**Deadline:** March of each year.

### 3171 JUNE NELSON MEMORIAL SCHOLARSHIP

Association of Alaska School Boards
1111 West Ninth Street
Juneau, AK 99801
Phone: (907) 586-1083; Fax: (907) 586-2995; Email: aasb@aasb.org
Web: www.aasb.org/JNMS.html

**Summary:** To provide financial assistance for college to high school seniors in Alaska.

**Eligibility:** Open to seniors graduating from high schools in Alaska who have been accepted as a full-time student by a business, trade, or collegiate institution. Applicants must submit an essay, up to 750 words, on a topic that changes annually but relates to education; recently, the topic was, "Describe the ways specific Developmental Assets have contributed to your personal growth as a member of your community." Selection is based on the essay, high school transcripts, SAT or ACT scores, and 2 letters of recommendation; financial need is not considered.

**Financial data:** The stipend is $1,000, including $500 paid at high school graduation and $500 paid after the recipient completes 1 semester of college with a GPA of 2.5 or higher.

**Duration:** 1 year; nonrenewable.

**Number awarded:** 8 each year.

**Deadline:** March of each year.

## 3172 KANSAS FUNERAL DIRECTORS ASSOCIATION FOUNDATION SCHOLARSHIP

Kansas Funeral Directors and Embalmers Association
Attn: KFDA Foundation
1200 South Kansas Avenue
P.O. Box 1904
Topeka, KS 66601-1904
Phone: (913) 232-7789; Fax: (913) 232-7791; Email: kfda@inlandnet.net
Web: www.ksfda.org/educareer.htm

**Summary:** To provide financial assistance to Kansas residents who are currently enrolled in a school of mortuary science.

**Eligibility:** Open to Kansas residents who are currently attending a mortuary school. They must have at least 1 but not more than 2 semesters of schooling left and be registered with the Kansas State Board of Mortuary Arts. Selection is based on academic achievement, leadership qualities, financial need, and special abilities. Preference is given to applicants who intend to practice in Kansas.

**Financial data:** Stipends range from $250 to $1,500.
**Duration:** 1 year.
**Number awarded:** 2 to 4 each year.
**Deadline:** September of each year.

## 3173 KANSAS RESTAURANT & HOSPITALITY ASSOCIATION EDUCATION FOUNDATION SCHOLARSHIPS

Kansas Restaurant & Hospitality Association
Attn: Education Foundation
359 South Hydraulic
Wichita, KS 67211
Phone: (316) 267-8383; (800) 369-6787 (within KS); Fax: (316) 267-8400;
Email: ncarlson@krha.org
Web: www.krha.org/education.htm

**Summary:** To provide financial assistance to Kansas residents interested in preparing for a career in the restaurant and food service industry.

**Eligibility:** Open to 1) high school seniors in Kansas who have been accepted at an accredited college as a full-time student; and 2) undergraduate full-time students at colleges in Kansas who have completed at least 1 academic term. Applicants must be interested in preparing for a career in the restaurant and food service industry. They must be able to demonstrate a GPA of 2.75 or higher, previous or current employment in the restaurant or hospitality industry, and financial need. Along with their application, they must submit 2 essays of 150 to 200 words each: 1) how their education will help them achieve their career objectives and future goals; and 2) the career path they see themselves pursuing in the food service and/or hospitality industry in the next 5 years. U.S. citizenship or permanent resident status is required.

**Financial data:** A stipend is awarded (amount not specified). Funds are sent directly to the school to be used for tuition, room and board, or any other school-related expenses.

**Duration:** 1 year.
**Number awarded:** 1 or more each year.
**Deadline:** April of each year.

## 3174 KARL CHRISTMAN MEMORIAL SCHOLARSHIPS

New Mexico Society of Certified Public Accountants
Attn: Scholarships in Accounting
1650 University N.E., Suite 450
Albuquerque, NM 87102-1733
Phone: (505) 246-1699; (800) 926-2522; Fax: (505) 246-1686;
Email: nmcpa@nmcpa.org
Web: www.nmcpa.org

**Summary:** To provide financial assistance to accounting students at New Mexico universities and colleges.

**Eligibility:** Open to full-time students at New Mexico colleges and universities who have completed 12 semester hours in accounting, are currently enrolled in 6 or more accounting hours, have completed 75 hours overall, and have a cumulative GPA of 3.0 or higher. Selection is based on academic achievement, extracurricular activities, career objectives and goals in accounting, and financial need.

**Financial data:** The stipend is $1,000.
**Duration:** 1 year; may be renewed 1 additional year.
**Number awarded:** 3 each year.
**Deadline:** September of each year.

## 3175 KATHLEEN M. PEABODY, CPA, MEMORIAL SCHOLARSHIP

Massachusetts Society of Certified Public Accountants
Attn: MSCPA Educational Foundation
105 Chauncy Street, Tenth Floor
Boston, MA 02111
Phone: (617) 556-4000; (800) 392-6145; Fax: (617) 556-4126;
Email: biannoni@MSCPAonline.org
Web: www.cpatrack.com/financial_aid/scholarship.php

**Summary:** To provide financial assistance to college juniors majoring in accounting at a Massachusetts college or university. This program is sponsored by Wolf & Company, PC.

**Eligibility:** Open to Massachusetts residents who have completed their sophomore year and are majoring in accounting at a college or university in the state. Applicants must be enrolled in school on a full-time basis. They must demonstrate superior academic standing, financial need, and an intention to seek a career in a public accounting firm.

**Financial data:** The stipend is $1,000.
**Duration:** 1 year.
**Number awarded:** 1 each year.

## 3176 KEITH PAYNE MEMORIAL SCHOLARSHIP

Professional Independent Insurance Agents of Illinois
Attn: College Scholarship Program
4360 Wabash Avenue
Springfield, IL 62707
Phone: (217) 793-6660; (800) 628-6436; Fax: (217) 793-6744;
Email: admin@piiai.org
Web: www.piiai.org/youngagents/scholarship.htm

**Summary:** To provide financial assistance to upper-division students from Illinois who are majoring in business and have an interest in insurance.

**Eligibility:** Open to residents of Illinois who are full-time juniors or seniors in college. Applicants must be enrolled in a business degree program with an interest in insurance. They must have a letter of recommendation from a current or retired member of the Professional Independent Insurance Agents of Illinois. Along with their application, they must submit an essay (500 words or less) on the contribution the insurance industry makes to society. Financial need is not considered in the selection process.

**Financial data:** The stipend is $1,000, payable in 2 equal installments. Funds are paid directly to the recipient's school.

**Duration:** 1 year.
**Number awarded:** 1 each year.
**Deadline:** June of each year.

## 3177 KEMPER SCHOLARS GRANT PROGRAM

James S. Kemper Foundation
One Kemper Drive
Long Grove, IL 60049-0001
Phone: (312) 332-3114
Web: www.jskemper.org/kemper_scholar_pgm.htm

**Summary:** To provide financial assistance and work experience to freshmen at selected colleges and universities who are interested in preparing for a career in business.

**Eligibility:** Open to students enrolled as freshmen at 1 of 19 participating colleges and universities. Applicants must be interested in preparing for a career in business and must demonstrate enough "maturity, imagination and intelligence" to learn from the program, which includes participation in a full-time summer work program with Kemper Insurance Companies. The 19 participating schools are Beloit College (Beloit, Wisconsin), Brigham Young University (Provo, Utah), Drake University (Des Moines, Iowa), Howard University (Washington, D.C.), Illinois State University (Normal, Illinois), Knox College (Galesburg, Illinois), Lake Forest College (Lake Forest, Illinois), LaSalle University (Philadelphia, Pennsylvania), Loyola University (Chicago, Illinois), Millikin University (Decatur, Illinois), Northern Illinois University (DeKalb, Illinois), Rochester Institute of Technology (Rochester, New York), University of North Florida (Jacksonville, Florida), University of the Pacific (Stockton, California), University of Wisconsin at Whitewater, Valparaiso University (Valparaiso, Indiana), Washington University (St. Louis, Missouri), Washington and Lee University (Lexington, Virginia), and Wake Forest University (Winston-Salem, North Carolina). Summer assignments are within Kemper companies throughout the United States. For at least one of the summers, usually after the junior year, the assignment is at the home office in Long Grove, Illinois.

**Financial data:** All scholars receive a stipend of at least $3,000 per year (regardless of financial need). Scholars who demonstrate financial need may receive up to $8,000 per year. During the summer work experience, scholars receive standard compensation.

**Duration:** 3 years, as long as the scholar maintains a GPA of 3.0 or higher each academic term.

**Number awarded:** 60 to 70 each year.

**Deadline:** Deadlines vary at each institution.

---

### 3178 KEN MILAM SCHOLARSHIP

American Planning Association-California Chapter
Attn: California Planning Foundation
c/o Paul Wack
P.O. Box 886
San Luis Obispo, CA 93406
Phone: (805) 544-8282; Fax: (805) 544-8286; Email: pwack@calpoly.edu
Web: www.californiaplanningfoundation.org/scholarships.html

**Summary:** To provide financial assistance to undergraduate and graduate students in accredited planning programs at California universities.

**Eligibility:** Open to students entering their final year for an undergraduate or master's degree in an accredited planning program at a university in California. Applicants must be interested in preparing for a career in public planning in California. Selection is based on academic excellence, financial need, and commitment to serve the planning profession in California. This program is sponsored by the County Planning Director's Association. The accredited planning programs are at 3 campuses of the California State University system (California State Polytechnic University at Pomona, California Polytechnic State University at San Luis Obispo, and San Jose State University), 3 campuses of the University of California (Berkeley, Irvine, and Los Angeles), and the University of Southern California.

**Financial data:** The stipend is $1,000.

**Duration:** 1 year.

**Number awarded:** 1 each year.

**Deadline:** April of each year.

---

### 3179 KENNETH R. MCCARTHA SCHOLARSHIP

Alabama Bankers Association
Attn: Scholarship Applications
534 Adams Avenue
Montgomery, AL 36104
Phone: (334) 834-1890; (800) 239-5521; Fax: (334) 834-4443;
Email: info@alabamabankers.org
Web: www.alabamabankers.org

**Summary:** To provide financial assistance to seniors at colleges and universities in Alabama who are interested in a career in banking.

**Eligibility:** Open to residents of Alabama entering their senior year at 4-year colleges and universities in the state. Applicants must be majoring in banking, finance, or business and have plans to enter the banking profession. They must be enrolled full time and have a GPA of 2.0 or higher. Selection is based on academic record, probability of entering banking or a bank-related field of employment after graduation, character, leadership, potential for development, and financial need.

**Financial data:** The stipend is $1,500.

**Duration:** 1 year.

**Number awarded:** 1 or more each year.

**Deadline:** February of each year.

---

### 3180 KENTUCKY EARLY CHILDHOOD DEVELOPMENT SCHOLARSHIPS

Kentucky Higher Education Assistance Authority
Attn: Student Aid Branch
100 Airport Road
P.O. Box 798
Frankfort, KY 40602-0798
Phone: (502) 696-7392; (800) 928-8926, ext. 7392; Fax: (502) 696-7373;
TTY: (800) 855-2880; Email: ppolly@kheaa.com
Web: www.kheaa.com/prog_ecds.hmtl

**Summary:** To provide financial assistance to Kentucky residents who are working on a degree or certificate in early childhood education on a part-time basis while they are employed in the field.

**Eligibility:** Open to Kentucky residents who are U.S. citizens, nationals, or permanent residents enrolled at a participating institution in the state for less than

9 credit hours per academic term. Applicants must be working on 1) an associate degree in early childhood education or a bachelor's degree in interdisciplinary early childhood education or an approved related program; 2) a Kentucky Early Childhood Development Director's Certificate; or 3) a child development associate credential. They must be employed at least 20 hours per week in a participating early childhood facility or provide training in early childhood development for an approved organization. They may have no unpaid financial obligation and may not be eligible to receive state or federal training funds through Head Start, a public preschool program, or First Steps.

**Financial data:** Stipends are the lesser of the tuition actually charged by the institution or $1,400 per year. Funds are either credited to the student's account or, if the student has already paid the tuition, disbursed to the student at the beginning of each school term by the institution.

**Duration:** 1 year; may be renewed if funds permit.

**Number awarded:** Varies each year; recently, 990 students received these scholarships.

---

### 3181 KENTUCKY RESTAURANT ASSOCIATION ACADEMIC SCHOLARSHIPS

Kentucky Restaurant Association
Attn: Educational Foundation
133 Evergreen Road, suite 201
Louisville, KY 40243
Phone: (502) 896-0464; (800) 896-0414; Fax: (502) 896-0465; Email: info@kyra.org
Web: www.kyra.org

**Summary:** To provide financial assistance to students in Kentucky who are preparing for a career in the food service industry.

**Eligibility:** Open to Kentucky residents (or residing within 25 miles of Kentucky's borders) for the past 18 months. They must be enrolled or planning to enroll at an accredited college to work on an associate, bachelor's, or master's degree in food service. Work experience in food service is required. Financial need is considered in the selection process.

**Financial data:** Stipend amounts vary, depending on tuition and fees at the school the recipient attends.

**Duration:** 1 year; may be renewed.

**Number awarded:** Varies; generally, up to 25 each year.

**Deadline:** June or December of each year.

---

### 3182 KENTUCKY SOCIETY OF CERTIFIED PUBLIC ACCOUNTANTS COLLEGE SCHOLARSHIPS

Kentucky Society of Certified Public Accountants
Attn: Educational Foundation
1735 Alliant Avenue
Louisville, KY 40299-6326
Phone: (502) 266-5272; (800) 292-1754 (within KY); Fax: (502) 261-9512;
Email: kycpa@kycpa.org
Web: www.kycpa.org

**Summary:** To provide financial assistance to students in Kentucky who are interested in majoring in accounting in college.

**Eligibility:** Open to students who are currently enrolled as a sophomore or above in a Kentucky college or university. Applicants must have an overall GPA of at least 2.75 and an accounting GPA of at least 3.0. They must have completed the "principles of accounting" course and must be currently enrolled in or have completed intermediate accounting. Along with their application, they must submit a 500-word essay on their career goals, reasons for choosing accounting, and financial need. Selection is based on the essay, scholastic achievement, and leadership qualities. At least one scholarship is reserved for a student member of the Kentucky Society of Certified Public Accountants.

**Financial data:** The stipend is $1,000.

**Duration:** 1 year.

**Number awarded:** Varies each year.

**Deadline:** January of each year.

---

### 3183 KEVIN JETTON SERVICE SCHOLARSHIP

Association of Information Technology Professionals
Attn: Foundation for Information Technology Education
401 North Michigan Avenue, Suite 2400
Chicago, Il 60611-4267
Phone: (312) 245-1070; (800) 224-9371; Fax: (312) 527-6636;
Email: larry_schmitz@aitp.org
Web: www.edfoundation.org

**Summary:** To provide financial assistance to students working on a degree (at any level) in information technology.

**Eligibility:** Open to full-time students who are working on an associate, bachelor's, master's, or doctoral degree in information technology in the United States. Applicants must be members of the Association of Information Technology Professionals. Selection is based on scholastic ability, demonstrated record of service to fellow information technology students and professionals, leadership potential, and financial need.

**Financial data:** A stipend is awarded (amount not specified).

**Duration:** 1 year.

**Number awarded:** 1 each year.

**Deadline:** May of each year.

## 3184 KEY MEMORIES SCHOLARSHIPS

Funeral Service Foundation
Attn: Executive Director
13625 Bishop's Drive
Brookfield, WI 53005
Phone: (262) 789-1880; (877) 402-5900
Web: www.funeralservicefoundation.org/scholarships/index.htm

**Summary:** To provide financial assistance to mortuary science students.

**Eligibility:** Open to students who are currently enrolled or accepted for enrollment in an accredited program of mortuary science. Selection is based primarily on an essay of 500 words or more on the following topic: "With the trend in funeral preferences moving from traditional burial, describe how you, as a funeral director, would provide personalized service, regardless of the family's choice of final disposition."

**Financial data:** The stipend is $1,000.

**Duration:** 1 year.

**Number awarded:** 5 each year.

**Deadline:** May of each year.

## 3185 KSCPA COLLEGE SCHOLARSHIPS

Kansas Society of Certified Public Accountants
Attn: Educational Foundation
1080 S.W. Wanamaker Road, Suite 200
P.O. Box 4291
Topeka, KS 66604-0291
Phone: (785) 272-4366; (800) 222-0452 (within KS); Fax: (785) 262-4468; Email: kscpa@kscpa.org
Web: www.kscpa.org/scholarship.cfm

**Summary:** To provide financial assistance to college students in Kansas who are majoring in accounting.

**Eligibility:** Open to upper-division students at each of the 6 regent institutions in Kansas and at Washburn University. Applicants must be studying accounting.

**Financial data:** The stipend is $1,250.

**Duration:** 1 year.

**Number awarded:** 7 each year: 1 at each of the participating institutions.

**Deadline:** June of each year.

## 3186 KSCPA HIGH SCHOOL SCHOLARSHIPS

Kansas Society of Certified Public Accountants
Attn: Educational Foundation
1080 S.W. Wanamaker Road, Suite 200
P.O. Box 4291
Topeka, KS 66604-0291
Phone: (785) 272-4366; (800) 222-0452 (within KS); Fax: (785) 262-4468; Email: kscpa@kscpa.org
Web: www.kscpa.org/scholarship.cfm

**Summary:** To provide financial assistance for college to high school seniors in Kansas who plan to major in accounting.

**Eligibility:** Open to high school seniors who will be entering a Kansas college or university the following academic year. Applicants must be planning to study accounting. Selection is based on ACT or SAT scores.

**Financial data:** Stipends are $1,000, $600, $500, $400, or $200.

**Duration:** 1 year.

**Number awarded:** 9 each year: 1 each at $1,000, $600, $500, and $400, plus 5 at $200.

**Deadline:** Test scores must be submitted by March of each year; applications are due in April.

## 3187 LAGRANT FOUNDATION SCHOLARSHIPS

LAGRANT FOUNDATION
555 South Flower Street, Suite 700
Los Angeles, CA 90071-2423
Phone: (323) 469-8680; Fax: (323) 469-8683
Web: www.lagrantfoundation.org

**Summary:** To provide financial assistance to minority high school seniors or college students who are interested in majoring in advertising, public relations, or marketing.

**Eligibility:** Open to African Americans, Asian Pacific Americans, Hispanics, or Native Americans who are full-time students at a 4-year accredited institution or high school seniors planning to attend a 4-year accredited institution on a full-time basis. Applicants must have a GPA of 2.5 or higher and be majoring or planning to major in advertising, marketing, or public relations. They must submit 1) a 1- to 2-page essay outlining their career goals; what steps they will take to increase ethnic representation in the fields of advertising, marketing, and public relations; and the role of an advertising, marketing, or public relations practitioner; 2) a paragraph explaining how they are financing or planning to finance their education and why they need financial assistance; 3) a paragraph explaining the high school, college, and/or community activities in which they are involved; 4) a brief paragraph describing any honors and awards they have received; 5) if they are currently employed, a paragraph indicating the hours worked each week, responsibilities, and if the job will be kept while attending school; 6) a resume; and 7) an official transcript. Applicants majoring in public relations must write an essay on the importance and relevance of the Arthur W. Page Society Principles.

**Financial data:** The stipend is $5,000 per year.

**Duration:** 1 year.

**Number awarded:** 10 each year.

**Deadline:** March of each year.

## 3188 LAMACCHIA FAMILY SCHOLARSHIP

Tourism Cares for Tomorrow
Attn: Program Manager
585 Washington Street
Canton, MA 02021
Phone: (781) 821-5990; Fax: (781) 821-8949; Email: info@tourismcares.org
Web: www.tourismcares.org

**Summary:** To provide financial assistance to college students in Wisconsin who are majoring in tourism.

**Eligibility:** Open to full-time students enrolled at a 4-year college or university in Wisconsin. Applicants must be entering their junior or senior year, have at least a 3.0 GPA, and be majoring in a travel or tourism-related field (e.g., hotel management, restaurant management, tourism).

**Financial data:** The stipend is $1,000 per year.

**Duration:** 1 year.

**Number awarded:** 1 each year.

**Deadline:** March of each year.

## 3189 LAMAR DANIELSON SCHOLARSHIP

Association of Independent Funeral Directors of Florida
Attn: Scholarship Committee
217 South Adams Street
Tallahassee, FL 32301
Phone: (850) 222-0198; Fax: (850) 425-5268
Web: www.ifdf.org

**Summary:** To provide financial assistance to mortuary science students who are interested in entering the funeral service profession in Florida.

**Eligibility:** Open to full-time students at accredited colleges and departments of mortuary science who have expressed the intent to enter funeral service with an independently-owned firm in Florida after graduation. Applicants must be in the third quarter of study and have an overall scholastic average of 85% or higher for the first 2 quarters of study. They must be recommended and endorsed by the owner/manager of a funeral home that is a member of the Independent Funeral Directors of Florida. Preference is given to applicants who have funeral home employment experience. Financial need is considered in the selection process.

**Financial data:** A stipend is awarded (amount not specified). Funds are to be applied to tuition.

**Duration:** Support is provided for the fourth and fifth quarter of study.

**Number awarded:** 1 or more each year.

**Deadline:** March or September of each year.

## 3190 LAMBDA ALPHA NATIONAL DEAN'S LIST SCHOLARSHIP

Lambda Alpha
c/o National Executive Secretary
Ball State University
Department of Anthropology
Muncie, IN 47306-1099
Phone: (765) 285-1575; Email: 01bkswartz@bsu.edu

**Summary:** To provide financial assistance for further education to members of Lambda Alpha, the national anthropology honor society.

**Eligibility:** Open to anthropology majors with junior standing at a college or university with a chapter of the society. Candidates must be members of the society and nominated by their chapters (each chapter may nominate only one candidate). Selection is based on undergraduate grades and letters of recommendation.

**Financial data:** The stipend is $1,000.

**Duration:** 1 year.

**Number awarded:** 1 each year.

**Deadline:** February of each year.

## 3191 LAURA E. SETTLE SCHOLARSHIPS

California Retired Teachers Association
Attn: Executive Director
800 Howe Avenue, Suite 370
Sacramento, CA 95825
Phone: (916) 923-2200; Fax: (916) 923-1910; Email: admin@calrta.org
Web: www.calrta.org/scholar.htm

**Summary:** To provide financial assistance to undergraduate and graduate students majoring in education in California.

**Eligibility:** Open to senior undergraduates and graduate students majoring in education at a campus of the University of California (UC) or the California State University (CSU) system. Students interested in applying must contact the department of teacher education at their campus.

**Financial data:** The stipend is $2,000.

**Duration:** 1 year.

**Number awarded:** 1 scholarship is offered at each UC and CSU campus.

## 3192 LAWRENCE "LARRY" FRAZIER MEMORIAL SCHOLARSHIP

**Summary:** To provide financial assistance to residents of Nebraska who are interested in studying designated fields in college.

*See Listing #2391.*

## 3193 LCPA EDUCATIONAL FOUNDATION SCHOLARSHIPS

Society of Louisiana Certified Public Accountants
Attn: LCPA Education Foundation
2400 Veterans Boulevard, Suite 500
Kenner, LA 70062-4739
Phone: (504) 464-1040; (800) 288-5272; Fax: (504) 469-7930
Web: www.lcpa.org/LCPAScholarships.html

**Summary:** To provide financial assistance to currently-enrolled college students in Louisiana who are interested in becoming certified public accountants.

**Eligibility:** Open to Louisiana residents who are currently enrolled full time in an accounting program at a 4-year college or university in Louisiana. Applicants must have completed at least 4 semesters by the fall of the academic year in which the application is filed and have a GPA of 2.5 or higher. Along with their application, they must submit a 2-page essay on their perception of the C.P.A.'s role on the job and in the community, including how they plan to contribute to the profession and to the community.

**Financial data:** Stipends range from $500 to $1,000. Individual chapters of the society also offer scholarships. The Baton Rouge Chapter awards $1,000 scholarships to students at in-town colleges and universities. Central Louisiana Chapter awards approximately $500 to students at Louisiana College, Northwestern State University, and Louisiana State University at Alexandria. Lafayette Chapter gives $1,000 to a student at the University of Southwestern Louisiana. Lake Charles Chapter contributes $1,000 to student scholarships at McNeese State. Northeast Chapter grants scholarships between $250 and $1,000 to students at Northeastern Louisiana University, Louisiana Tech, and Grambling State. Shreveport Chapter offers 2 or 3 scholarships (approximately $1,500) to local students. South Central Chapter awards a $250 scholarship to a student at Nicholls State University.

**Duration:** 1 year.

**Number awarded:** Varies each year; recently, 13 of these scholarships were awarded: 1 at $1,000, 2 at $800, and 10 at $500.

## 3194 LEADERSHIP FOUNDATION UNDERGRADUATE SCHOLARSHIPS

Delta Sigma Pi
Attn: Leadership Foundation
330 South Campus Avenue
P.O. Box 230
Oxford, OH 45056-0230
Phone: (513) 523-1907, ext. 230; Fax: (513) 523-7292;
Email: foundation@dspnet.org
Web: www.dspnet.org

**Summary:** To provide financial assistance for college to undergraduate brothers of Delta Sigma Pi, a business education honor society.

**Eligibility:** Open to currently-enrolled undergraduate students who are majoring in business and are members in good standing of the fraternity. Applicants must have at least one full semester or quarter of undergraduate studies remaining. Selection is based on academic achievement, financial need, fraternal service, letters of recommendation, service activities, and overall presentation of the required materials.

**Financial data:** The stipend is either $1,250 or $500.

**Duration:** 1 year; recipients may reapply.

**Number awarded:** 10 each year: 2 at $1,250 and 8 at $500.

**Deadline:** June of each year.

## 3195 LEAP SCHOLARSHIPS

Missouri Society of Certified Public Accountants
Attn: LEAP Program
275 North Lindbergh Boulevard, Suite 10
P.O. Box 419042
St. Louis, MO 63141-9042
Phone: (314) 997-7966; (800) 264-7966 (within MO); Fax: (314) 997-2592;
Email: scholarships@mocpa.org
Web: www.mocpa.org/leap/index.html

**Summary:** To provide financial assistance to residents of Missouri who are majoring or planning to major in accounting at colleges and universities in the state.

**Eligibility:** Open to residents of Missouri who are high school seniors or college students majoring or planning to major in accounting as a full-time student at a college or university in the state. Applicants must submit a 500-word essay on what inspired them to become a C.P.A. Selection is based on the essay, academic achievement, and demonstrated leadership potential. Financial need is not considered.

**Financial data:** The stipend is $1,000 per year.

**Duration:** 1 year.

**Number awarded:** 20 each year: 10 for high school seniors and 10 for current college students.

**Deadline:** January of each year.

## 3196 LEEP DREAM SCHOLARSHIP

Michigan Law Enforcement Education Program
c/o Scholarship Committee
667 East Big Beaver Road, Suite 205
Troy, MI 48083
Phone: (800) 451-1220

**Summary:** To provide financial assistance for college to high school students in Michigan who are interested in preparing for a career in a field related to public safety.

**Eligibility:** Open to seniors graduating from high schools in Michigan who are interested in preparing for a career as a law enforcement officer, police-fire dispatcher, corrections officer, fire fighter, or emergency medical technician. Applicants must be planning to attend a Michigan 4-year university, community college, or vocational training institution that grants a degree, certificate, or license in public safety or related field.

**Financial data:** The stipend is $1,000.

**Duration:** 1 year.

**Number awarded:** Several each year.

**Deadline:** May of each year.

## 3197 LEGACY SCHOLARSHIPS

**Summary:** To provide financial assistance to upper-division and graduate students in Alabama who are interested in preparing for an environmentally-related career.

*See Listing #2396.*

## 3198 LILLIAN AND SAMUEL SUTTON EDUCATION SCHOLARSHIPS

National Association for the Advancement of Colored People
Attn: Education Department
4805 Mt. Hope Drive
Baltimore, MD 21215-3297
Phone: (410) 580-5760; (877) NAACP-98; Email: youth@naacpnet.org
Web: www.naacp.org/work/education/eduscholarship.shtml

**Summary:** To provide financial assistance to members of the National Association for the Advancement of Colored People (NAACP) and others who are working on a degree in education on the undergraduate or graduate level.

**Eligibility:** Open to full-time undergraduates and full- and part-time graduate students majoring in the field of education. The required minimum GPA is 2.5 for graduating high school seniors and current undergraduates or 3.0 for graduate students. Membership and participation in the association is highly desirable. All applicants must be able to demonstrate financial need and be U.S. citizens. Along with their application, they must submit a 1-page essay on their interest in their major and a career, their life's ambition, what they hope to accomplish in their lifetime, and what they consider their most significant contribution to their community.

**Financial data:** The stipend is $1,000 per year for undergraduate students or $2,000 per year for graduate students.

**Duration:** 1 year; may be renewed as long as the recipient maintains a GPA of 2.5 or higher as an undergraduate or 3.0 or higher as a graduate student.

**Number awarded:** Varies each year; recently, 7 of these scholarships were awarded.

**Deadline:** April of each year.

## 3199 LILLIAN E. GLOVER SCHOLARSHIPS

Illinois PTA
901 South Spring Street
Springfield, IL 62704
Phone: (217) 528-9617; (800) 877-9617; Fax: (217) 528-9490;
Email: 2ptaers@ameritech.net
Web: www.illinoispta.org/Scholarship.html

**Summary:** To provide financial assistance to graduating high school seniors in Illinois who plan to major in education or a related field in college.

**Eligibility:** Open to public high school seniors in Illinois who are graduating in the top 25% of their class. Applicants must be interested in preparing for a career in education or in an educationally-related field (school librarian, instructional media specialist, school nurse, school psychologist, or social worker, provided the position requires certification from a state board of education). Along with their application, they must submit a statement giving their ideas on why they want to enter the field of education, what they perceive as the most important aspects of education and why, and how parent involvement enhances educational growth. Selection is based on that statement, academic ability, leadership qualities, school activities, and out-of-school activities. Financial need is not considered.

**Financial data:** Stipends are $1,000 or $500.

**Duration:** 1 year; nonrenewable.

**Number awarded:** 44 each year: 2 in each Illinois PTA district (1 at $1,000 and 1 at $500).

**Deadline:** February of each year.

## 3200 LILLIAN P. SCHOEPHOERSTER SCHOLARSHIP

Phi Upsilon Omicron
Attn: Educational Foundation
P.O. Box 329
Fairmont, WV 26555-0329
Phone: (304) 368-0612; Email: rickards@access.mountain.net
Web: www.phiu.unl.edu

**Summary:** To provide financial assistance to undergraduate student members of Phi Upsilon Omicron, a national honor society in family and consumer sciences.

**Eligibility:** Open to members of the society who are working on a bachelor's degree in family and consumer sciences or a related area. Preference is given to

nontraditional students. Selection is based on scholastic record, participation in society and other collegiate activities, a statement of professional aims and goals, professional services, and recommendations.

**Financial data:** The stipend is $1,500.

**Duration:** 1 year.

**Number awarded:** 1 each year.

**Deadline:** January of each year.

## 3201 LITHERLAND/FTE SCHOLARSHIP

**Summary:** To provide financial support to undergraduate members of the International Technology Education Association (ITEA) who are majoring in technology education teacher preparation.

*See Listing #2403.*

## 3202 LOMA SOCIETY OF NEBRASKA SCHOLARSHIPS

LOMA Society of Nebraska
c/o Jon Boomgaarden, Scholarship Chair
Mutual of Omaha
2 - I/S Micro Server Services Team
Mutual of Omaha Plaza
Omaha, NE 68175
Phone: (402) 351-8579; Fax: (402) 351-5197; Email: jon.boomgaarden@mutualofomaha.com
Web: loma-ne.org

**Summary:** To provide financial assistance to upper-division and graduate students in Nebraska who are preparing for a career in business, especially in the insurance industry.

**Eligibility:** Open to students enrolled full time as juniors, seniors, or graduate students at colleges and universities in Nebraska. Applicants must be preparing for a career in business; preference is given to students who have an interest in a career in an aspect of the insurance industry. They should have a record of academic success, but interest in a chosen field and the ability to express career ambitions are more important factors than high grades. Financial need is also considered in the selection process. Special consideration is given to children and relatives of people holding the LOMA (Life Office Management Association) designation.

**Financial data:** A total of $4,000 is available for this program each year. Individual stipends depend on the number of recipients selected.

**Duration:** 1 year.

**Number awarded:** Varies each year.

**Deadline:** June of each year.

## 3203 LOTUS YEE CHEIGH SCHOLARSHIP

American Society of Women Accountants-Honolulu Chapter
c/o Grace Morioka
1600 Kapiolani Boulevard, Suite 1010
Honolulu, HI 96814
Phone: (808) 949-3522; Fax: (808) 949-4522
Web: community.hei.com/aswa/scholarship.html

**Summary:** To provide financial assistance to accounting students from Hawaii.

**Eligibility:** Open to part- and full-time students from Hawaii working on a bachelor's degree in accounting. Applicants must have completed at least 60 semester hours with a GPA of 2.7 or higher. They are not required to be a member of the American Society of Women Accountants. Selection is based on a statement of career goals, communication skills, GPA, and financial need and circumstances.

**Financial data:** The stipend is $1,000.

**Duration:** 1 year.

**Number awarded:** 1 each year.

**Deadline:** March of each year.

## 3204 LOUISE MORITZ MOLITORIS LEADERSHIP AWARD

**Summary:** To provide financial assistance to undergraduate women interested in a career in transportation.

*See Listing #2409.*

## 3205 LOWE'S EDUCATIONAL SCHOLARSHIP PROGRAM

**Summary:** To provide financial assistance to students at selected community

and technical colleges who are preparing for a career in a business or technical field related to Lowe's stores.
*See Listing #2411.*

### 3206 LUCILE RUST SCHOLARSHIP

Phi Upsilon Omicron,
Attn: Educational Foundation
P.O. Box 329
Fairmont, WV 26555-0329
Phone: (304) 368-0612; Email: rickards@access.mountain.net
Web: www.phiu.unl.edu
**Summary:** To provide financial assistance to undergraduate student members of Phi Upsilon Omicron, a national honor society in family and consumer sciences.
**Eligibility:** Open to members of the society who are working on a bachelor's degree in family and consumer sciences or a related area. Selection is based on scholastic record, participation in society and other collegiate activities, a statement of professional aims and goals, professional services, and recommendations.
**Financial data:** The stipend is $1,000.
**Duration:** 1 year.
**Number awarded:** 1 each year.
**Deadline:** January of each year.

### 3207 MAINE CHAPTER 276 SCHOLARSHIPS

**Summary:** To provide financial assistance to Maine residents who are working on a college degree in a field related to construction.
*See Listing #2420.*

### 3208 MAINE HIGHER EDUCATION ASSISTANCE FOUNDATION SCHOLARSHIPS

Maine Bankers Association
Attn: Maine Higher Education Assistance Foundation
132 State Street
P.O. Box 735
Augusta, ME 04332-0735
Phone: (207) 622-6131; Fax: (207) 622-0314
Web: www.mainebankers.com/index.pl/heaf
**Summary:** To provide financial assistance to college students in Maine who are majoring in a field related to business.
**Eligibility:** Open to students enrolled in the second, third, or fourth year at a designated college or university in Maine. Applicants have graduated from a high school in Maine, be majoring in a business-related subject, have good academic standing, and be able to demonstrate financial need.
**Financial data:** Stipends average $1,000.
**Duration:** 1 year.
**Number awarded:** 13 each year.

### 3209 MAINE INNKEEPERS ASSOCIATION HOSPITALITY SCHOLARSHIPS

**Summary:** To provide financial assistance to Maine residents who wish to prepare for a career in the hospitality industry.
*See Listing #1539.*

### 3210 MAINE QUALITY CHILD CARE EDUCATION SCHOLARSHIP PROGRAM

Finance Authority of Maine
Attn: Education Finance Programs
5 Community Drive
P.O. Box 949
Augusta, ME 04332-0949
Phone: (207) 623-3263; (800) 228-3734; Fax: (207) 623-0095; TTY: (207) 626-2717; Email: info@famemaine.com
Web: www.famemaine.com/html/education/fameprogs.html
**Summary:** To provide financial assistance to Maine residents interested in improving their skills in the child development field.
**Eligibility:** Open to residents of Maine who either currently work as a child care provider or express an interest in becoming a child care provider. Applicants

must be enrolled or planning to enroll in an accredited college or university in Maine, another state, or a foreign country. They must be able to demonstrate financial need (total household adjusted gross income cannot exceed 300% of the federal poverty guidelines).
**Financial data:** The stipend is $500 per course or $2,000 per year.
**Duration:** 1 semester or 1 year.
**Number awarded:** Varies each year; scholarships are awarded on a first-come, first-served basis.
**Deadline:** Applications may be submitted at any time.

### 3211 MAINE ROADS DEGREE SCHOLARSHIP

Maine Roads Scholarship Fund
c/o University of Southern Maine, Muskie School
400 Congress Street
P.O. Box 15010
Portland, ME 04112
Phone: (888) 900-0055; Fax: (207) 780-5817; Email: sturner@usm.maine.edu
Web: muskie.usm.maine.edu/maineroads/scholarship.html
**Summary:** To provide financial assistance to child care providers in Maine who are working on an undergraduate or graduate degree at an institution in the state.
**Eligibility:** Open to child care providers who are residents of Maine working on a bachelor's, master's, or doctoral degree at an institution of higher education in the state. Applicants must have a family income that does not exceed 300% of the federal poverty level (currently, that means an income of $26,940 for a family of 1, rising to $92,880 for a family of 8). They must have experience within the past 2 years working in the child care and early education field in licensed or certified child care facilities or resource development centers. Courses of study may include early childhood education, child development, recreation and leisure services with a special needs focus, social work with an emphasis on early childhood, or child care administration. Along with their application, they must submit brief statements on their plans to work directly with children after completing their degree and how earning their degree will impact their work in child care.
**Financial data:** Stipends range up to $1,800 for undergraduate students or up to $2,400 for graduate students.
**Duration:** 1 year.
**Number awarded:** Varies each year.
**Deadline:** June or October of each year.

### 3212 MAINE RURAL REHABILITATION FUND SCHOLARSHIP

**Summary:** To provide financial assistance to Maine residents interested in working on a degree in a field related to agriculture in college.
*See Listing #2422.*

### 3213 MAINE STATE CHAMBER OF COMMERCE SCHOLARSHIPS

**Summary:** To provide financial assistance for a college-level technical, education, or business program to residents of Maine.
*See Listing #610.*

### 3214 MAJOR JAMES W. LOVELL SCHOLARSHIPS

100th Infantry Battalion Veterans Club
Attn: Scholarship Committee
520 Kamoku Street
Honolulu, HI 96826
Phone: (808) 732-5216; Email: daisyy@hgea.net
Web: emedia.leeward.hawaii.edu/mnakano
**Summary:** To provide financial assistance to high school seniors and college students who major in education and exemplify the sponsor's motto of "Continuing Service."
**Eligibility:** Open to high school seniors planning to attend an institution of higher learning and full-time undergraduate students at community colleges, vocational/trade schools, 4-year colleges, and universities. Applicants must have a GPA of 2.5 or higher and be able to demonstrate civic responsibility and community service. They must be majoring or planning to major in education. Along with their application, they must submit a 4-page essay that explains how lifelong learning (including academic success, experiential learning, intellectual growth, social and economic growth, leadership skills, and civic responsibility) is important for citizens and their state and country. Selection is based on that essay and the applicant's demonstra-

tion that he or she can effectively promote the legacy of the 100th Infantry Battalion and its motto of "Continuing Service." Financial need is not considered.

**Financial data:** The stipend is $1,000.
**Duration:** 1 year; nonrenewable.
**Number awarded:** 2 each year.
**Deadline:** April of each year.

## 3215 MALCOLM BALDRIGE SCHOLARSHIPS

**Summary:** To provide financial assistance for college to residents of Connecticut interested in a career in foreign trade or manufacturing.
*See Listing #2426.*

## 3216 MARION MACCARRELL SCOTT SCHOLARSHIP

**Summary:** To provide financial assistance to residents of Hawaii for undergraduate or graduate studies in fields related to achieving world cooperation and international understanding.
*See Listing #1544.*

## 3217 MARION T. BURR SCHOLARSHIP

American Baptist Churches USA
Attn: National Ministries
P.O. Box 851
Valley Forge, PA 19482-0851
Phone: (610) 768-2067; (800) ABC-3USA, ext. 2067; Fax: (610) 768-2453; Email: karen.drummond@abc-usa.org
Web: www.nationalministries.org/financial-aid/student_info.cfm
**Summary:** To provide financial assistance to Native American Baptists who are interested in preparing for a career in human services.
**Eligibility:** Open to Native Americans who are enrolled full time in a college or seminary and interested in preparing for a career in human services. Applicants must be U.S. citizens who have been a member of a church affiliated with American Baptist Churches USA for at least one year.
**Financial data:** Partial tuition scholarships are offered.
**Duration:** 1 year.
**Number awarded:** Varies each year.
**Deadline:** May of each year.

## 3218 MARION T. WOOD NATIONAL SCHOLARSHIPS

National Association of Educational Office Professionals
Attn: NAEOP Foundation
P.O. Box 12619
Wichita, KS 67277-2619
Phone: (316) 942-4822; Fax: (316) 942-7100; Email: naeop@naeop.org
Web: www.naeop.org/foundation.htm
**Summary:** To provide financial assistance to students interested in preparing for an office-related career.
**Eligibility:** Open to business education students preparing for an office-related career, preferably in the field of education.
**Financial data:** The stipend is $1,000.
**Duration:** 1 year.
**Number awarded:** Varies each year.
**Deadline:** February of each year.

## 3219 MARK MILLER AWARD

National Association of Black Accountants
Attn: Director, Center for Advancement of Minority Accountants
7249-A Hanover Parkway
Greenbelt, MD 20770
Phone: (301) 474-NABA, ext. 114; Fax: (301) 474-3114;
Email: cquinn@nabainc.org
Web: www.nabainc.org/pages/Student_ScholarshipProgram.jsp
**Summary:** To provide financial assistance to student members of the National Association of Black Accountants (NABA) who are working on an undergraduate or graduate degree in a field related to accounting.
**Eligibility:** Open to NABA members who are members of ethnic minority groups enrolled full time as 1) an undergraduate freshman, sophomore, junior, or first-semester senior majoring in accounting, business, or

finance; or 2) a graduate student working on a master's degree in accounting. Applicants must have a GPA of 2.0 or higher in their major and 2.5 or higher overall. Selection is based on grades, financial need, and a 500-word autobiography that discusses career objectives, leadership abilities, community activities, and involvement in NABA.
**Financial data:** The stipend is $1,000 per year.
**Duration:** 1 year.
**Number awarded:** 1 each year.
**Deadline:** December of each year.

## 3220 MARRIOTT INTERNATIONAL SCHOLARSHIPS

DECA
1908 Association Drive
Reston, VA 20191-1594
Phone: (703) 860-5000; Fax: (703) 860-4013; Email: decainc@aol.com
Web: www.deca.org/scholarships/index.html
**Summary:** To provide financial assistance for college to DECA members interested in the hospitality industry.
**Eligibility:** Open to DECA members who are interested in working full time on a 2-year or 4-year degree in business or marketing to prepare for a career in the hospitality industry. Applicants must be able to demonstrate evidence of DECA activities, academic achievement, leadership ability, and interest or experience in the hospitality industry. Selection is based on merit, not financial need.
**Financial data:** The stipend is $1,000.
**Duration:** 1 year.
**Number awarded:** Up to 6 each year.
**Deadline:** February of each year.

## 3221 MARVIN DODSON-CARL PERKINS SCHOLARSHIP

Kentucky Education Association
Attn: Student Program
401 Capital Avenue
Frankfort, KY 40601
Phone: (800) 231-4532, ext. 315; Fax: (502) 227-8062; Email: cmain@kea.org
Web: www.kea.org/studentProgram/scholarships/dodsonInfo.cfm
**Summary:** To provide financial assistance to upper-division and master's degree students in Kentucky who plan to become teachers in the state.
**Eligibility:** Open to juniors, seniors, post-baccalaureate, and M.A.T. students at Kentucky colleges and universities. Applicants must be participating in the Kentucky Education Association's student program and planning to teach in the state. They must have a GPA of 3.0 or higher and be able to demonstrate financial need. Along with their application, they must submit a 650-word essay on why they are applying for this scholarship, why they want to be a teacher, and any special circumstances or obstacles they have overcome.
**Financial data:** Up to $6,000 is available for this program each year.
**Duration:** 1 year.
**Number awarded:** 1 or more each year.
**Deadline:** January of each year.

## 3222 MARY BENEVENTO SCHOLARSHIP

**Summary:** To provide financial assistance to high school seniors in Connecticut who are interested in studying health, physical education, recreation, or dance in college.
*See Listing #1549.*

## 3223 MARY CRAIG SCHOLARSHIP FUND

American Society of Women Accountants-Billings Big Sky Chapter
820 Division Street
Billings, MT 59101
Web: www.imt.net/~aswa
**Summary:** To provide financial assistance to students working on a bachelor's or master's degree in accounting at a college or university in Montana. Information is also available from Jane Crowder, (406) 248-2990, E-mail: jane_bowl@yahoo.com.
**Eligibility:** Open to students working on a bachelor's or master's degree in accounting at an accredited Montana college or university. Applicants must have completed at least 60 semester hours. Selection is based on career goals, communication skills, GPA, personal circumstances, and financial need. Membership in the American Society of Women Accountants is not required.
**Financial data:** The stipend is $1,500.

**Duration:** 1 year.
**Number awarded:** 1 each year.
**Deadline:** March of each year.

### 3224 MARY JO CLAYTON SANDERS ENVIRONMENTAL ISSUES SCHOLARSHIP

**Summary:** To provide financial aid to Florida undergraduates and graduate students majoring in environmental issues.
*See Listing #2444.*

### 3225 MARY MORROW-EDNA RICHARDS SCHOLARSHIP

North Carolina Association of Educators, Inc.
700 South Salisbury Street
P.O. Box 27347
Raleigh, NC 27611-7347
Phone: (919) 832-3000, ext. 216; (800) 662-7924, ext. 216; Fax: (919) 839-8229;
Email: Jackie.Vaughn@ncea.org
Web: www.ncae.org
**Summary:** To provide financial assistance to upper-division college students in North Carolina who are enrolled in a teacher education program.
**Eligibility:** Open to North Carolina residents enrolled in a teacher education program. They must be in their junior year in college and willing to teach in North Carolina public schools for at least 2 years following graduation. Preference is given to children of members of the North Carolina Association of Educators (NCAE) and to members of Student NCAE. Other selection criteria include: character, personality, scholastic achievement, promise as a teacher, and financial need.
**Financial data:** A stipend is awarded (amount not specified).
**Duration:** 1 year (the senior year of college).
**Number awarded:** 1 or more each year.
**Deadline:** January of each year.

### 3226 MARYLAND ASSOCIATION FOR HEALTH, PHYSICAL EDUCATION, RECREATION AND DANCE HIGH SCHOOL SCHOLARSHIPS

Maryland Association for Health, Physical Education, Recreation and Dance
Attn: Office Coordinator
828 Dulaney Valley Road, Suite 8
Towson, MD 21204
Phone: (410) 583-1370; Fax: (410) 583-1374; Email: mewilliams@mahperd.org
Web: www.mahperd.org/hs_scholarships.htm
**Summary:** To provide financial assistance to high school seniors in Maryland who plan to attend college to prepare for a career as a teacher of health, physical education, recreation or dance.
**Eligibility:** Open to seniors graduating from high schools in Maryland who plan to enroll full time at a collegiate institution in a teacher preparation program in dance, health, physical education, or recreation. Applicants must rank in the top half of their class and have a GPA of 2.5 or higher. They should be able to demonstrate leadership qualities in the community and extracurricular participation, especially those that may have an impact on the future career in teaching. Along with their application, they must submit a letter describing their plans for a career, community activities, awards, and other recognitions. Financial need is not considered in the selection process.
**Financial data:** The stipend is $1,000.
**Duration:** 1 year.
**Number awarded:** 1 or more each year.
**Deadline:** April of each year.

### 3227 MARYLAND ASSOCIATION FOR HEALTH, PHYSICAL EDUCATION, RECREATION AND DANCE UNDERGRADUATE SCHOLARSHIPS

Maryland Association for Health, Physical Education, Recreation and Dance
Attn: Office Coordinator
828 Dulaney Valley Road, Suite 8
Towson, MD 21204
Phone: (410) 583-1370; Fax: (410) 583-1374; Email: mewilliams@mahperd.org
Web: www.mahperd.org/hs_scholarships.htm
**Summary:** To provide financial assistance to upper-division students in Maryland who are preparing for a career as a teacher of health, physical education, recreation or dance.

**Eligibility:** Open to students completing their sophomore or junior year at a college or university in Maryland and enrolled full time in a teacher preparation program in dance, health, physical education, or recreation. Applicants must have a GPA of 3.0 or higher in their major and 2.5 or higher overall. They should be able to demonstrate leadership qualities in the community and extracurricular participation, especially those that may have an impact on the future career in teaching. Along with their application, they must submit a letter describing their plans for a career, community activities, awards, and other recognitions. Financial need is not considered in the selection process.
**Financial data:** The stipend is $1,000.
**Duration:** 1 year.
**Number awarded:** 1 or more each year.
**Deadline:** August of each year.

### 3228 MARYLAND ASSOCIATION OF CERTIFIED PUBLIC ACCOUNTANTS SCHOLARSHIP PROGRAM

Maryland Association of Certified Public Accountants
Attn: MACPA Educational Foundation
901 Dulaney Valley Road, Suite 710
Towson, MD 21204-2683
Phone: (410) 296-6250; (800) 782-2036; Fax: (410) 296-8713;
Email: info@macpa.org
Web: www.macpa.org
**Summary:** To provide financial assistance to residents of Maryland working on an undergraduate or graduate degree in accounting.
**Eligibility:** Open to Maryland residents attending a college or university in the state and taking enough undergraduate or graduate courses to qualify as a full-time student at their school. Applicants must have completed at least 60 total credit hours at the time of the award, including at least 6 hours in accounting courses. They must have a GPA of 3.0 or higher and be able to demonstrate financial need. U.S. citizenship is required.
**Financial data:** Stipends are at least $1,000. The exact amount of the award depends upon the recipient's financial need.
**Duration:** 1 year; may be renewed until completion of the 150-hour requirement and eligibility for sitting for the C.P.A. examination in Maryland. Renewal requires continued full-time enrollment and a GPA of 3.0 or higher.
**Number awarded:** Several each year.
**Deadline:** April of each year.

### 3229 MARYLAND BANKERS ASSOCIATION ESSAY CONTEST

Maryland Bankers Association
186 Duke of Gloucester Street
Annapolis, MD 21401
Phone: (410) 269-5977; (800) 327-5977; Fax: (410) 269-1874
Web: www.mdbankers.com
**Summary:** To recognize and reward, with college scholarships, high school seniors in Maryland who submit outstanding essays on a topic related to banking.
**Eligibility:** Open to seniors graduating from high schools in Maryland. Applicants must submit a 2-page essay on a topic that changes annually but relates to banking. Recently, students were asked how they would improve their community's money management skills if they were a bank president.
**Financial data:** Prizes are a $1,000 scholarship for first place, a $500 scholarship for second, and a $250 scholarship for third.
**Duration:** The competition is held annually.
**Number awarded:** 3 each year.
**Deadline:** January of each year.

### 3230 MARYLAND LEGION AUXILIARY CHILDREN AND YOUTH FUND SCHOLARSHIP

**Summary:** To provide financial assistance for college to the daughters of veterans who are Maryland residents and wish to study arts, sciences, business, public administration, education, or a medical field.
*See Listing #1552.*

### 3231 MARYLAND STATE GRANGE DEAF SCHOLARSHIP

**Summary:** To provide financial assistance for college or graduate school to Maryland residents who are either deaf or preparing to work with hearing-impaired people.
*See Listing #646.*

## 3232 MASSACHUSETTS AFL-CIO SCHOLARSHIP AWARDS

**Summary:** To recognize and reward the high school seniors in Massachusetts receiving the highest scores on a statewide labor history written examination.
*See Listing #1554.*

## 3233 MASSACHUSETTS RESTAURANT ASSOCIATION HOSPITALITY INSTITUTE SCHOLARSHIPS

Massachusetts Restaurant Association
Attn: Hospitality Institute
333 Turnpike Road, Suite 102
Southborough, MA 01772-1775
Phone: (508) 303-9905; (800) 852-3042; Fax: (508) 303-9985;
Email: pchristie@massrestaurantassoc.org
Web: www.marestaurantassoc.org/educationscholarships.htm
**Summary:** To provide financial assistance to Massachusetts residents interested in preparing for a career in the restaurant and food service industry.
**Eligibility:** Open to graduating high school seniors, high school graduates, and undergraduate college students who are residents of Massachusetts. Applicants must have been accepted as full-time or substantial part-time students in a restaurant or food service-related postsecondary program. They must have a GPA of 2.75 or higher. High school seniors must have at least 250 hours of restaurant or food service work experience; high school graduates and college students must have at least 750 hours of such experience.
**Financial data:** The stipend is $2,000. Several cooperating colleges and culinary institutes provide matching funds.
**Duration:** 1 year.
**Number awarded:** Varies each year; recently, 32 of these scholarships were awarded.

## 3234 MASSACHUSETTS SOCIETY OF CERTIFIED PUBLIC ACCOUNTANTS STUDENT MANUSCRIPT CONTEST

Massachusetts Society of Certified Public Accountants
Attn: MSCPA Educational Foundation
105 Chauncy Street, Tenth Floor
Boston, MA 02111
Phone: (617) 556-4000; (800) 392-6145; Fax: (617) 556-4126;
Email: biannoni@MSCPAonline.org
Web: www.cpatrack.com/financial_aid/scholarship.php
**Summary:** To recognize and reward undergraduate students in Massachusetts who submit outstanding papers on accounting.
**Eligibility:** Open to undergraduate accounting students at colleges and universities in Massachusetts. Applicants must submit a 2,000-word paper covering financial reporting, accounting principles, socio-economic accounting, interface with computers, auditing, taxation accounting systems, managerial accounting, or management services. Papers may be innovative, descriptive, or evaluative.
**Financial data:** Prizes are $1,500 for first place (the William Holmes Award), $1,000 for second, and $500 for third.
**Duration:** The competition is held annually.
**Number awarded:** 3 each year.
**Deadline:** May of each year.

## 3235 MESBEC PROGRAM

**Summary:** To provide financial assistance to American Indian students who are interested in working on an undergraduate or graduate degree in selected fields.
*See Listing #2466.*

## 3236 MHEFI SCHOLARSHIP PROGRAM

**Summary:** To provide financial assistance to undergraduate or graduate students who are studying material handling.
*See Listing #2468.*

## 3237 MICHAEL B. KRUSE SCHOLARSHIP

Community Foundation of Middle Tennessee
Attn: Scholarship Committee
3833 Cleghorn Avenue, Suite 400
Nashville, TN 37215-2519
Phone: (615) 321-4939; (888) 540-5200; Fax: (615) 327-2746;

Email: mail@cfmt.org
Web: www.cfmt.org/scholarship_info.htm
**Summary:** To provide financial assistance to residents of Tennessee preparing for a career as a certified public accountant.
**Eligibility:** Open to rising juniors, seniors, and graduate students majoring in accounting with a goal of becoming a certified public accountant. Applicants must be residents of Tennessee attending an accredited college or university in the state with a GPA of 3.2 or higher. Special consideration is given to married students. Interested students must submit a completed application, their high school and/or college transcript, and 2 letters of recommendation. Selection is based on academic record, standardized test scores, extracurricular activities, work experience, community involvement, recommendations, and financial need.
**Financial data:** Stipends range from $500 to $2,500 per year. Funds are paid to the recipient's school and must be used for tuition, fees, books, supplies, room, board, or miscellaneous expenses.
**Duration:** 1 year; recipients may reapply.
**Number awarded:** 1 or more each year.
**Deadline:** March of each year.

## 3238 MICHAEL BENDIX SUTTON SCHOLARSHIPS

Michael Bendix Sutton Foundation
c/o Marion B. Sutton
300 Martine Avenue
White Plains, NY 10601
**Summary:** To provide financial assistance to people with hemophilia who are pre-law students.
**Eligibility:** Open to pre-law students who have hemophilia.
**Financial data:** The stipend is $2,000.
**Duration:** 1 year.
**Number awarded:** 2 each year.
**Deadline:** March of each year.

## 3239 MICHIGAN ACCOUNTANCY FOUNDATION FIFTH/ GRADUATE YEAR STUDENT SCHOLARSHIPS

Michigan Association of Certified Public Accountants
Attn: Michigan Accountancy Foundation
5480 Corporate Drive, Suite 200
P.O. Box 5068
Troy, MI 48007-5068
Phone: (248) 267-3700; (888) 877-4CPE; Fax: (248) 267-3737;
Email: maf@michcpa.org
Web: www.michcpa.org/maf/scholarships.asp
**Summary:** To provide financial assistance to students at Michigan colleges and universities who are working on a degree in accounting.
**Eligibility:** Open to U.S. citizens enrolled full time at accredited Michigan colleges and universities with a declared concentration in accounting. Applicants must have completed at least 50% of their school's requirements toward completion of their junior year. They must intend to or have successfully passed the Michigan C.P.A. examination and intend to practice public accounting in the state. Along with their application, they must submit a statement about their educational and career aspirations, including on- and off-campus activities, professional goals, current professional accomplishments, and a summary of personal and professional activities (including community involvement). Documentation of financial need may also be included.
**Financial data:** The stipend is $4,000 per year.
**Duration:** 1 year; may be renewed for the fifth or graduate year of study, provided that all requirements continue to be met and that funding is available.
**Number awarded:** Varies each year; recently, 15 of these scholarships were awarded.
**Deadline:** January of each year.

## 3240 MICHIGAN MORTUARY SCIENCE FOUNDATION SCHOLARSHIP

Michigan Funeral Directors Association
Attn: Michigan Mortuary Science Foundation
2420 Science Parkway
Okemos, MI 48864
Phone: (517) 349-9565; (800) 937-6332; Fax: (517) 349-9819;
Email: info@mfda.org
Web: www.mfda.org

**Summary:** To provide financial assistance to Michigan residents who are interested in preparing for a career in mortuary science.

**Eligibility:** Open to either Michigan residents or full-time mortuary science students at Wayne State University (in Detroit, Michigan). They must be attending school on a full-time basis and must submit the following material as part of the application process: a cover letter, an essay (between 1,000 and 2,500 words) on a topic that changes annually, and a letter of recommendation from the mortuary science school the applicant is attending. Selection is based on the essay, the recommendation of the mortuary college, and financial need.

**Financial data:** The stipends are $2,500, $1,500, or $750. Funds may be used to pay for tuition, books, supplies, room and board, and other educational expenses.

**Duration:** 1 year.

**Number awarded:** 3 each year.

---

### 3241 MIDWEST ALLIANCE FOR NURSING INFORMATICS SCHOLARSHIP

**Summary:** To provide financial assistance to student members of the Healthcare Information and Management Systems Society (HIMSS) who are working on an undergraduate or graduate degree in health care informatics or nursing.

*See Listing #2474.*

---

### 3242 MINNESOTA DIVISION SCHOLARSHIP

**Summary:** To provide financial assistance to Minnesota residents who are studying an environmental field in college.

*See Listing #2480.*

---

### 3243 MINORITIES AND WOMEN EDUCATIONAL SCHOLARSHIP PROGRAM

Appraisal Institute
Attn: Minorities and Women Scholarship Fund
550 West Van Buren Street, Suite 1000
Chicago, IL 60607
Phone: (312) 335-4121; Fax: (312) 335-4118;
Email: sbarnes@appraisalinstitute.org
Web: www.appraisalinstitute.org/education/scolarshp.asp

**Summary:** To provide financial assistance to women and minority undergraduate students majoring in real estate or allied fields.

**Eligibility:** Open to members of groups underrepresented in the real estate appraisal profession. Those groups include women, American Indians, Alaska Natives, Asians, Black or African Americans, Hispanics or Latinos, and Native Hawaiians or other Pacific Islanders. Applicants must be full- or part-time students enrolled in real estate courses within a degree-granting college, university, or junior college. They must submit evidence of demonstrated financial need and a GPA of 2.5 or higher. U.S. citizenship is required.

**Financial data:** The stipend is $1,000 per year. Funds are paid directly to the recipient's institution to be used for tuition and fees.

**Duration:** 1 year.

**Number awarded:** At least 1 each year.

**Deadline:** April of each year.

---

### 3244 MINORITIES IN GOVERNMENT FINANCE SCHOLARSHIP

Government Finance Officers Association
Attn: Scholarship Committee
203 North LaSalle Street, Suite 2700
Chicago, IL 60601-1210
Phone: (312) 977-9700; Fax: (312) 977-4806
Web: www.gfoa.org/services/scholarships.shtml

**Summary:** To provide financial assistance to minority upper-division and graduate students who are preparing for a career in state and local government finance.

**Eligibility:** Open to upper-division and graduate students who are preparing for a career in public finance with a major in public administration, accounting, finance, political science, economics, or business administration (with a specific focus on government or nonprofit management). Applicants must be members of a minority group, citizens or permanent residents of the United States or Canada, and able to provide a letter of recommendation from a representative of their school. Selection is based on career plans, academic record, plan of study, letters of recommendation, and GPA. Financial need is not considered.

**Financial data:** The stipend is $5,000.

**Duration:** 1 year.

**Number awarded:** 1 or more each year.

**Deadline:** February of each year.

---

### 3245 MIRIAM SCHAEFER SCHOLARSHIP

**Summary:** To provide financial assistance to upper-division students who are enrolled in a teacher education program in Michigan with a mathematics specialty.

*See Listing #2490.*

---

### 3246 MISSISSIPPI SOCIETY OF CERTIFIED PUBLIC ACCOUNTANTS UNDERGRADUATE SCHOLARSHIP

Mississippi Society of Certified Public Accountants
Attn: MSCPA Awards, Education and Scholarships Committee
Highland Village, Suite 246
P.O. Box 16630
Jackson, MS 39236
Phone: (601) 366-3473; (800) 772-1099 (within MS); Fax: (601) 856-8255;
Email: mail@ms-cpa.org
Web: www.ms-cpa.org

**Summary:** To provide financial assistance to upper-division students majoring in accounting at designated 4-year institutions in Mississippi.

**Eligibility:** Open to residents of Mississippi who have completed or are completing their junior year of college, are majoring in accounting, have completed at least 6 hours of accounting courses above the principles or introductory level, and are attending one of the following schools in Mississippi: Alcorn State University, Belhaven College, Delta State University, Jackson State University, Millsaps College, Mississippi College, Mississippi State University, Mississippi University for Women, Mississippi Valley State University, University of Mississippi, University of Southern Mississippi, or William Carey College. They must be nominated by their academic institution. Nominees must submit a completed application form, transcripts (GPA of 3.0 or higher both overall and in accounting classes), and a 1-page essay explaining why they plan a career in public accounting. Selection is based on the essay, academic excellence, recommendations, financial need, and campus involvement.

**Financial data:** The stipend is $1,000. Checks are made payable to the recipient's school.

**Duration:** 1 year.

**Number awarded:** 1 each year.

**Deadline:** June of each year.

---

### 3247 MISSOURI INSURANCE EDUCATION FOUNDATION COLLEGE SCHOLARSHIPS

Missouri Insurance Education Foundation
Attn: Scholarship Administrator
P.O. Box 1654
Jefferson City, MO 65102
Phone: (573) 893-4234; Email: miis@midamerica.net
Web: www.mief.org/collegeapp.htm

**Summary:** To provide financial assistance to upper-division students from Missouri who are working on a degree in insurance at a college or university in the state.

**Eligibility:** Open to juniors and seniors majoring in insurance or a related area at a Missouri college or university. Applicants must be enrolled full time, have a GPA of 2.5 or higher, and be residents of Missouri. Preference is given to students who can demonstrate financial need. Finalists may be interviewed. The top-ranked applicant receives the C. Lawrence Leggett Scholarship.

**Financial data:** Stipends are $2,000 or $1,500.

**Duration:** 1 year.

**Number awarded:** 6 each year: 1 at $2,000 (the C. Lawrence Leggett Scholarship) and 5 at $1,500.

**Deadline:** March of each year.

---

### 3248 MISSOURI INSURANCE EDUCATION FOUNDATION HIGH SCHOOL SCHOLARSHIPS

Missouri Insurance Education Foundation
Attn: Scholarship Administrator
P.O. Box 1654
Jefferson City, MO 65102
Phone: (573) 893-4234; Email: miis@midamerica.net

Web: www.mief.org/collegeapp.htm

**Summary:** To provide financial assistance to high school seniors from Missouri who plan to major in insurance or a related field at a college or university in the state.

**Eligibility:** Open to seniors graduating from high schools in Missouri who plan to attend a college or university in the state. Applicants must be planning to major in insurance, risk management, or actuarial science as a full-time student. Selection is based on academic achievement, participation in school and outside activities and organizations, honors and awards, and work experience; financial need is not considered.

**Financial data:** The stipend is $1,000.

**Duration:** 1 year.

**Number awarded:** 4 each year.

**Deadline:** March of each year.

## 3249 MISSOURI TRAVEL COUNCIL SCHOLARSHIP

Missouri Travel Council
204 East High Street
Jefferson City, MO 65101-3287
Phone: (573) 636-2814; Fax: (573) 636-5783; Email: info@missouritravel.com
Web: www.missouritravel.com/scholarship.htm

**Summary:** To provide financial assistance to Missouri residents preparing for a hospitality-related career at a college or university in the state.

**Eligibility:** Open to residents of Missouri currently enrolled as a sophomore or junior at an accredited college or university in the state. Applicants must be working on a degree related to hospitality, including hotel and restaurant management, parks and recreation, etc. They must have a GPA of 3.0 or higher and submit an essay of up to 500 words on the value of Missouri's tourism industry. The essay is judged on originality, clarity, style, and proper English usage. Scholarship winners are selected on the basis of the essay (50%), GPA (20%), community involvement (10%), academic activities and achievement (10%), and hospitality-related experience (10%).

**Financial data:** The stipend is $1,000. Funds are paid directly to the recipient's institution.

**Duration:** 1 year.

**Number awarded:** 2 each year.

**Deadline:** February of each year.

## 3250 MONEY MATTERS SCHOLARSHIPS

Chela Financial USA, Inc.
388 Market Street, 12th Floor
San Francisco, CA 94111
Phone: (415) 283-2800; (866) 34-CHELA; Fax: (415) 283-2888;
Email: scholarships@chelafin.org
Web: www.chelastudentloans.org

**Summary:** To recognize and reward (with scholarships) undergraduate and graduate students who submit outstanding essays on borrowing and money management.

**Eligibility:** Open to undergraduate and graduate students who have a GPA of 2.0 or higher. Applicants must complete an essay, up to 300 words, on "How I Am Financing My College Education." They do not need to have a student loan to qualify, but their essays should focus on how responsible borrowing and money management are helping them pay for college and meet their life goals. Essays are evaluated on the basis of appropriateness to overall theme (30%), persuasiveness (30%), quality of writing (20%), and creativity (20%). U.S. citizenship or permanent resident status is required.

**Financial data:** The award is a $5,000 scholarship.

**Duration:** Awards are presented annually.

**Number awarded:** 15 each year.

**Deadline:** October of each year.

## 3251 MONTANA FUNERAL DIRECTORS ASSOCIATION SCHOLARSHIPS

Montana Funeral Directors Association
P.O. Box 4267
Helena, MT 59604-4267
Phone: (406) 449-7244; Fax: (406) 443-0979; Email: mfda@sy-key.com

**Summary:** To provide financial assistance to Montana residents who are interested in studying mortuary science.

**Eligibility:** Open to Montana residents who are beginning or working on a degree in mortuary science. The sole requirement is that the applicant be willing to return to Montana and work in the funeral service profession. In addition, the following information will strengthen an application (but is not required): a GPA of 3.0 or higher, support of a funeral home that belongs to the sponsoring association, submission of a transcript of mortuary school grades, and 2 letters of recommendation. Financial need is not considered in the selection process.

**Financial data:** The stipend is $1,000.

**Duration:** 1 year.

**Number awarded:** Up to 2 each year.

**Deadline:** May of each year.

## 3252 MONTANA WOMEN IN TRANSITION SCHOLARSHIP

American Society of Women Accountants-Billings Big Sky Chapter
820 Division Street
Billings, MT 59101
Web: www.imt.net/~aswa

**Summary:** To provide financial assistance to women in Montana who are returning to school to work on an undergraduate degree in accounting. Information is also available from Jane Crowder, (406) 248-2990, E-mail: jane_bowl@yahoo.com.

**Eligibility:** Open to women in Montana who are incoming freshmen, currently enrolled, or returning to school with sufficient credits to qualify for freshman status. Applicants must be women who, either through divorce or death of a spouse, have become the sole source of support for themselves and their family and wish to work on a degree in accounting as a means to gainful employment. Selection is based on commitment to the goal of working on a degree in accounting, including evidence of continued commitment after receiving this award; aptitude for accounting and business; clear evidence that the candidate has established goals and a plan for achieving those goals, both personal and professional; and financial need.

**Financial data:** The stipend is $1,500.

**Duration:** 1 year.

**Number awarded:** 1 each year.

**Deadline:** March of each year.

## 3253 MORGAN STANLEY TRIBAL COLLEGE SCHOLARS PROGRAM

American Indian College Fund
Attn: Scholarship Department
8333 Greenwood Boulevard
Denver, CO 80221
Phone: (303) 426-8900; (800) 776-FUND; Fax: (303) 426-1200;
Email: info@collegefund.org
Web: www.collegefund.org/scholarships/morganstanley.html

**Summary:** To provide financial assistance to American Indian students currently enrolled full time at a tribal college or university to prepare for a career in business and the financial services industry. This scholarship is sponsored by Morgan Stanley, in partnership with the American Indian College Fund.

**Eligibility:** Open to American Indians or Alaska Natives who are enrolled full time in either an associate's or bachelor's degree program at an accredited tribal college or university. Applicants must be able to demonstrate exceptional academic achievement (GPA of 3.0 or higher), as well as leadership, service, and commitment to the American Indian community. They must be interested in a career in business and the financial services industry (e.g., information technology, investment banking, marketing, financial accounting). Along with their application, they must submit official college transcripts; personal essays (500 words or less) on their personal and academic background, a role model who has motivated them, and an experience or risk they have taken and its impact on them; 2 letters of recommendation; tribal enrollment information; a statement regarding any financial hardship they have; and a color photograph.

**Financial data:** The stipend is $2,500.

**Duration:** 1 year.

**Number awarded:** 10 each year.

**Deadline:** April of each year.

## 3254 MORGAN STANLEY/AMERICAN INDIAN COLLEGE FUND SCHOLARSHIP AND CAREER DEVELOPMENT PROGRAM

American Indian College Fund
Attn: Scholarship Department
8333 Greenwood Boulevard
Denver, CO 80221
Phone: (303) 426-8900; (800) 776-FUND; Fax: (303) 426-1200;

Email: info@collegefund.org

Web: www.collegefund.org/scholarships/morganstanley.html

**Summary:** To provide financial assistance to American Indian students at 4-year institutions who are preparing for a career in the financial services field. This scholarship is sponsored by Morgan Stanley, in partnership with the American Indian College Fund. The program is augmented by the Fund's student-support program that includes ongoing communications between its staff and selected scholars as well as advice and support as they consider their career options.

**Eligibility:** Open to American Indians or Alaska Natives who are currently enrolled in a 4-year degree program at an accredited college or university in the United States and are interested in exploring career options in the financial services industry (e.g., information technology, investment banking, marketing, financial accounting). Applicants must be able to demonstrate exceptional academic achievement (at least a 3.0 GPA), as well as leadership, service, and commitment to the American Indian community. Along with their application, they must submit official college transcripts; personal essays (500 words or less) on their personal and academic background, a role model who has motivated them, and an experience or risk they have taken and its impact on them; 2 letters of recommendation; tribal enrollment information; a statement regarding any financial hardship they have; and a color photograph.

**Financial data:** The stipend is $10,000 per year.

**Duration:** 1 year.

**Number awarded:** 5 each year.

**Deadline:** April of each year.

## 3255 MOSMILLER SCHOLAR PROGRAM

**Summary:** To provide financial assistance and work experience to students working on an undergraduate degree in floriculture or business.

*See Listing #1566.*

## 3256 MOUNT VERNON CHAPTER SCHOLARSHIPS

American Society of Military Comptrollers-Mount Vernon Chapter

Attn: Awards and Scholarships Director

P.O. Box 99

Fort Belvoir, VA 22060-0099

**Summary:** To provide financial assistance to high school seniors in the Washington, D.C. area who plan to work on an undergraduate degree related to financial management.

**Eligibility:** Open to seniors graduating from high schools in Maryland, Virginia, and Washington, D.C. and to recent (within the past 6 months) graduates of those high schools. Applicants must be entering a field of study directly related to financial management (business administration, economics, public administration, computer science, operations research related to financial management, accounting, and finance). Along with their application, they must submit a 250-word essay on their career and academic goals and their financial need. Selection is based on academic achievement, leadership ability, extracurricular activities, career and academic goals, and financial need.

**Financial data:** The stipend is $1,000.

**Duration:** 1 year.

**Number awarded:** Several each year.

**Deadline:** March of each year.

## 3257 NABA CORPORATE SCHOLARSHIPS

National Association of Black Accountants

Attn: Director, Center for Advancement of Minority Accountants

7249-A Hanover Parkway

Greenbelt, MD 20770

Phone: (301) 474-NABA, ext. 114; Fax: (301) 474-3114;

Email: cquinn@nabainc.org

Web: www.nabainc.org/pages/Student_ScholarshipProgram.jsp

**Summary:** To provide financial assistance to student members of the National Association of Black Accountants (NABA) who are working on an undergraduate or graduate degree in a field related to accounting.

**Eligibility:** Open to NABA members who are members of ethnic minority groups enrolled full time as 1) an undergraduate freshman, sophomore, junior, or first-semester senior majoring in accounting, business, or finance; or 2) a graduate student working on a master's degree in accounting. Applicants must have a GPA of 3.5 or higher in their major and 3.3 or higher overall. Selection is based on grades, financial need, and a 500-word autobiography that discusses

career objectives, leadership abilities, community activities, and involvement in NABA.

**Financial data:** Stipends range from $1,000 to $5,000 per year.

**Duration:** 1 year.

**Number awarded:** Varies each year.

**Deadline:** December of each year.

## 3258 NABTP COLLEGIAN SCHOLARSHIP

**Summary:** To provide financial assistance to students who are working on a degree in telecommunications or a related field and are interested in participating in the activities of the National Association of Black Telecommunications Professionals (NABTP).

*See Listing #2499.*

## 3259 NATHAN TAYLOR DODSON SCHOLARSHIP

**Summary:** To provide financial assistance for college to members of the North Carolina Alliance for Athletics, Health, Physical Education, Recreation and Dance (NCAAHPERD).

*See Listing #1573.*

## 3260 NATIONAL AMERICANISM ESSAY CONTEST

AMVETS National Headquarters

Attn: Programs Department

4647 Forbes Boulevard

Lanham, MD 20706-4380

Phone: (301) 459-9600; (877) 7-AMVETS; Fax: (301) 459-7924;

Email: amvets@amvets.org

Web: www.amvets.org

**Summary:** To recognize and reward the best patriotic essays written by elementary and high school students.

**Eligibility:** Open to students in grades 6-12 at public or private (including parochial) schools in the United States. Applicants are required to write an essay on a topic that changes on a 4-year cycle. Essays by students in grade 6 should be less than 200 words, grades 7-8 less than 300 words, grades 9-10 less than 400 words, and grades 11-12 less than 500 words. The best entries are submitted by the applicants' teachers to department (state) competitions; first-place winners from each department are entered in the national competition. Selection is based on originality, adherence to theme, and literary composition.

**Financial data:** All prizes are in savings bonds. For students in grade 6, first is $250, second $200, third $150; for grades 7-8, first is $300, second $250, third $200; for grade 10, first is $750, second $500, third $300; for grades 11-12, first is $1,000, second $750, and third $500. All winners from grade 9 receive an all-expense paid trip to the Freedoms Foundation at Valley Forge, Pennsylvania for a weekend of youth-oriented activities.

**Duration:** The competition is held annually.

**Number awarded:** Bond prizes are awarded to 18 students: 3 each in grades 6, 7, 8, 10, 11, and 12.

**Deadline:** June of each year.

## 3261 NATIONAL ASSOCIATION OF BLACK ACCOUNTANTS NATIONAL SCHOLARSHIP

National Association of Black Accountants

Attn: Director, Center for Advancement of Minority Accountants

7249-A Hanover Parkway

Greenbelt, MD 20770

Phone: (301) 474-NABA, ext. 114; Fax: (301) 474-3114;

Email: cquinn@nabainc.org

Web: www.nabainc.org/pages/Student_ScholarshipProgram.jsp

**Summary:** To provide financial assistance to student members of the National Association of Black Accountants (NABA) who are working on an undergraduate or graduate degree in a field related to accounting.

**Eligibility:** Open to NABA members who are members of ethnic minority groups enrolled full time as 1) an undergraduate freshman, sophomore, junior, or first-semester senior majoring in accounting, business, or finance; or 2) a graduate student working on a master's degree in accounting. Applicants must have a GPA of 3.5 or higher in their major and 3.3 or higher overall. Selection is based on grades, financial need, and a 500-word autobiography that discusses career objectives, leadership abilities, community activities, and involvement in NABA.

**Financial data:** The stipend ranges from $3,000 to $6,000 per year.

**Duration:** 1 year.

**Number awarded:** 1 each year.

**Deadline:** December of each year.

---

## 3262 NATIONAL ASSOCIATION OF WOMEN IN CONSTRUCTION UNDERGRADUATE SCHOLARSHIPS

**Summary:** To provide financial assistance for college to students in construction-related degree programs.

*See Listing #2509.*

---

## 3263 NATIONAL BLACK MBA ASSOCIATION UNDERGRADUATE SCHOLARSHIP PROGRAM

National Black MBA Association

180 North Michigan Avenue, Suite 1400

Chicago, IL 60601

Phone: (312) 236-2622, ext. 8086; Fax: (312) 236-4131;

Email: scholarship@nbmbaa.org

Web: www.nbmbaa.org

**Summary:** To provide financial assistance to African American students interested in working on an undergraduate business degree.

**Eligibility:** Open to African American students who wish to work on an undergraduate degree in a field related to business. Applicants must submit a completed application, high school or undergraduate transcripts, and an essay on a topic that changes annually. Selection is based on GPA, extracurricular activities, and quality of the essay. This program is funded by the national office of the National Black MBA Association (NBMBAA), which develops the application and selects the essay topics. It is administered by local chapters, which select the winners. Applications must be submitted to local chapters; for the name and address of a contact person at each chapter, write to the association. Recipients must attend college on a full-time basis.

**Financial data:** The stipend is $1,000.

**Duration:** 1 year.

**Number awarded:** Each year, each NBMBAA chapter selects one recipient. Currently, there are 31 chapters in the United States.

**Deadline:** Each chapter determines its deadline date; most are in the spring.

---

## 3264 NATIONAL FFA SCHOLARSHIPS FOR UNDERGRADUATES IN THE SOCIAL SCIENCES

National FFA Organization

Attn: Scholarship Office

6060 FFA Drive

P.O. Box 68960

Indianapolis, IN 46268-0960

Phone: (317) 802-4321; Fax: (317) 802-5321; Email: scholarships@ffa.org

Web: www.ffa.org

**Summary:** To provide financial assistance to FFA members who wish to study agribusiness and related fields in college.

**Eligibility:** Open to current and former members of the organization who are working or planning to work full time on a degree in fields related to business and the social sciences; this includes: agribusiness, agricultural economics, agricultural education, agricultural finance, and agricultural marketing. For most of the scholarships, applicants must be high school seniors; others are open to students currently enrolled in college. The program includes a large number of designated scholarships that specify the locations where the members must live, the schools they must attend, the fields of study they must pursue, or other requirements. Some consider family income in the selection process, but most do not. Selection is based on academic achievement (10 points for GPA, 10 points for SAT or ACT score, 10 points for class rank), leadership in FFA activities (30 points), leadership in community activities (10 points), and participation in the Supervised Agricultural Experience (SAE) program (30 points). U.S. citizenship is required.

**Financial data:** Stipends vary, but most are at least $1,000.

**Duration:** 1 year or more.

**Number awarded:** Varies; generally, a total of approximately 1,000 scholarships are awarded annually by the association.

**Deadline:** February of each year.

---

## 3265 NATIONAL PEACE ESSAY CONTEST

United States Institute of Peace

Attn: National Peace Essay Contest Project Officer

1200 17th Street, N.W., Suite 200

Washington, DC 20036-3011

Phone: (202) 429-3854; Fax: (202) 429-6063; TDD: (202) 457-1719;

Email: essay_contest@usip.org

Web: www.usip.org/ed.html

**Summary:** To recognize and reward winners of the National Peace Essay Contest.

**Eligibility:** Open to students working toward a high school degree in a public, private, or parochial high school in grades 9-12 in the United States or its territories. U.S. citizens studying in other countries are also eligible. Contestants must prepare a 1,500-word essay on a topic that changes each year; recently, the topic was "Rebuilding Societies After Conflict." Judging of the essays is based on quality of the research (one third), quality of the analysis (one third), and style and mechanics (one third).

**Financial data:** Each state-level winner receives a $1,000 scholarship. National-level scholarships are $10,000 for first place, $5,000 for second place, and $2,500 for third place.

**Duration:** The competition is held annually. First-place winners in each state advance to the national competition and also receive an all-expense paid trip to Washington, D.C. that includes visits with various government officials.

**Number awarded:** Each year, 1 winner in each state and 3 national winners receive scholarships.

**Deadline:** January of each year.

---

## 3266 NATIONAL RESTAURANT ASSOCIATION ACADEMIC SCHOLARSHIPS FOR HIGH SCHOOL STUDENTS

National Restaurant Association Educational Foundation

Attn: Scholarships and Mentoring Initiative

175 West Jackson Boulevard, Suite 1500

Chicago, IL 60604-2702

Phone: (312) 715-1010, ext. 733; (800) 765-2122, ext. 733; Fax: (312) 566-9733;

Email: scholars@foodtrain.org

Web: www.nraef.org

**Summary:** To provide financial assistance to high school seniors who are interested in preparing for a career in the hospitality industry.

**Eligibility:** Open to high school seniors who have been accepted to a hospitality-related postsecondary program, either full time or substantial part time. Applicants must have a GPA of 2.75 or better in high school and at least 250 hours of restaurant and hospitality work experience. Along with their application, they must submit essays on 1) why they think they should receive this scholarship, and 2) the experience or person that most influenced them in selecting restaurant and food service as their career. Selection is based on the essays, presentation of the application, GPA, industry-related work experience, and letters of recommendation.

**Financial data:** The stipend is $2,000 per year.

**Duration:** 1 year.

**Number awarded:** Approximately 150 each year.

**Deadline:** April of each year.

---

## 3267 NATIONAL RESTAURANT ASSOCIATION ACADEMIC SCHOLARSHIPS FOR UNDERGRADUATE STUDENTS

National Restaurant Association Educational Foundation

Attn: Scholarships and Mentoring Initiative

175 West Jackson Boulevard, Suite 1500

Chicago, IL 60604-2702

Phone: (312) 715-1010, ext. 733; (800) 765-2122, ext. 733; Fax: (312) 566-9733;

Email: scholars@foodtrain.org

Web: www.nraef.org

**Summary:** To provide financial assistance to undergraduate students who are interested in preparing for a career in the hospitality industry.

**Eligibility:** Open to full-time college students who have completed at least 1 term of a certificate, associate, or bachelor's degree program in food service or hospitality with a GPA of 2.75 or higher. Applicants must have 750 hours of work experience in the restaurant and hospitality industry. Along with their application, they must submit essays on 1) how their education will help them achieve their career objectives and future goals, and 2) a challenging situation or experience related to the restaurant and food service industry that demonstrates their ability to overcome adversity. Selection is based on the essays, presentation of the application, GPA, industry-related work experience, and letters of recommendation.

**Financial data:** The stipend is $2,000 per year.

**Duration:** 1 year.

**Number awarded:** Approximately 200 each year.

**Deadline:** April or November of each year.

## 3268 NATIONAL TOUR ASSOCIATION SCHOLARSHIP

Tourism Cares for Tomorrow
Attn: Program Manager
585 Washington Street
Canton, MA 02021
Phone: (781) 821-5990; Fax: (781) 821-8949; Email: info@tourismcares.org
Web: www.tourismcares.org

**Summary:** To provide financial assistance to upper-division students who are majoring in tourism.

**Eligibility:** Open to students entering their junior or senior year at an accredited 4-year college or university in the United States or Canada. Applicants must be working on a degree in a travel and tourism-related program and have a GPA of 3.0 or higher. Along with their application, they must submit a 2-page essay on why they have chosen to prepare for a career in the hospitality and tourism industry. Financial need is not considered in the selection process.

**Financial data:** The stipend is $2,500.

**Duration:** 1 year.

**Number awarded:** 1 each year.

**Deadline:** March of each year.

## 3269 NATIVE AMERICAN LEADERSHIP IN EDUCATION (NALE) PROGRAM

Catching the Dream
8200 Mountain Road, N.E., Suite 203
Albuquerque, NM 87110-7835
Phone: (505) 262-2351; Fax: (505) 262-0534; Email: NScholarsh@aol.com
Web: www.catchingthedream.org

**Summary:** To provide financial assistance to American Indian paraprofessionals in the education field who wish to return to college or graduate school.

**Eligibility:** Open to paraprofessionals who are working in Indian schools and who plan to return to school to complete their degree in education, counseling, or school administration. Applicants must be able to provide proof that they are at least one-quarter Indian blood and a member of a U.S. tribe that is federally-recognized, state-recognized, or terminated. Along with their application, they must submit documentation of financial need, 3 letters of recommendation, copies of applications and responses for at least 15 other sources of funding, official transcripts, standardized test scores (ACT, SAT, GRE, MCAT, LSAT, etc.), and an essay explaining their goals in life, college plans, and career plans (especially how those plans include working with and benefiting Indians). Selection is based on merit and potential for improving the lives of Indian people. The sponsor was formerly known as the Native American Scholarship Fund.

**Financial data:** Stipends range from $500 to $5,000.

**Duration:** 1 year; may be renewed.

**Number awarded:** Varies; generally, 15 or more each year.

**Deadline:** April of each year for fall term; September of each year for spring and winter terms; March of each year for summer school.

## 3270 NCCPAP SCHOLARSHIPS FOR GRADUATING HIGH SCHOOL SENIORS

National Conference of CPA Practitioners, Inc.
Attn: Scholarship Committee
50 Jericho Turnpike, Suite 106
Jericho, NY 11753
Phone: (516) 333-8282; (888) 488-5400; Fax: (516) 333-4099;
Email: office@nccpap.org
Web: www.nccpap.org

**Summary:** To provide financial assistance to high school seniors planning to attend college to prepare for a career as a certified public accountant (C.P.A.). This program, established in 2003, is offered jointly by the National Conference for CPA Practitioners (NCCPAP) and the American Institute of Certified Public Accountants (AICPA).

**Eligibility:** Open to seniors graduating from high school with a GPA of 3.3 or higher. Applicants must be planning to attend a 2-year or 4-year college or university as a full-time student to prepare for a career as a C.P.A. Along with their application, they must submit a 200-word essay that explains why they desire to prepare for a career as a C.P.A. Financial need is not considered in the selection process.

**Financial data:** The stipend is $1,000.

**Duration:** 1 year.

**Number awarded:** Varies each year; recently, 16 of these scholarships were awarded.

**Deadline:** April of each year.

## 3271 NDPRB UNDERGRADUATE SCHOLARSHIP PROGRAM

**Summary:** To provide financial assistance to undergraduate students in fields related to the dairy industry.
*See Listing #2526.*

## 3272 NEBRASKA ACTUARIES CLUB SCHOLARSHIPS

**Summary:** To provide financial assistance to students in Nebraska who are preparing for an actuarial career.
*See Listing #2527.*

## 3273 NEBRASKA BANKERS EDUCATIONAL FOUNDATION SCHOLARSHIPS

Nebraska Bankers Association
Attn: Educational Foundation
233 South 13th Street, Suite 700
P.O. Box 80008
Lincoln, NE 68501-0008
Phone: (402) 474-1555; Fax: (402) 474-2148;
Email: karen.miller@nebankers.org
Web: www.nebankers.org/public/consumer.html

**Summary:** To provide financial assistance to Nebraska residents working on a degree in business at a college or university in the state.

**Eligibility:** Open to residents of Nebraska who are enrolled as juniors or seniors at a college or university in the state (except for the University of Nebraska). Applicants must be working on a bachelor of science in business administration with an emphasis on finance, accounting, or economics and have a GPA of 3.0 or higher. Along with their application, they must submit an essay of 100 to 200 words on how the banking industry has impacted their community or the role they expect the banking industry to play in their future. Financial need is not considered in the selection process.

**Financial data:** The stipend is $1,000.

**Duration:** 1 year.

**Number awarded:** 8 each year (including 4 designated as William B. Brandt Memorial Scholarships).

**Deadline:** January of each year.

## 3274 NEBRASKA EDUCATIONAL OFFICE PROFESSIONALS ASSOCIATION STUDENT SCHOLARSHIP

Nebraska Educational Office Professionals Association
P.O. Box 83872
Lincoln, NE 68501-3872
Web: neopa.unl.edu/awards.html

**Summary:** To provide financial assistance to residents of Nebraska who are interested in preparing for an office-related career. Information is also available from Edie Schleiger, Scholarship Director, University of Nebraska at Lincoln, Office of Admissions, 1410 Q Street, Lincoln, NE 68588-0417.

**Eligibility:** Open to residents of Nebraska who are graduating high school seniors or students currently enrolled in a postsecondary educational institution. Applicants must have completed 2 or more business education courses (in high school, college, or a combination) from among the following: computer classes, keyboarding/typing, marketing, accounting, office practices and procedures, bookkeeping, business communication, desktop publishing, and/or business law. They must submit a 1-page essay on why they are choosing an office-related career or vocation, 3 letters of recommendation, and high school or college transcripts. Selection is based on academic achievement, initiative of the student, and financial need.

**Financial data:** The stipend is $1,000.

**Duration:** 1 year.

**Number awarded:** 1 each year.

**Deadline:** December of each year.

## 3275 NEBRASKA LEGAL PROFESSIONALS SCHOLARSHIP

Nebraska Legal Professionals Association
c/o Diane Horak, Scholarship Chair
7111 Cedar Creek Circle
Lincoln, NE 68516-3056
Phone: (402) 423-5077; Fax: (402) 466-2288

**Summary:** To provide financial assistance to residents of Nebraska enrolled in a law-related program.

**Eligibility:** Open to residents of Nebraska enrolled full time in a pre-law, paralegal, legal secretary, or other law-related program. Applicants must submit a certified copy of their latest transcript; a resume covering their educational history, school and community activities, and work history for the last 5 years; a 1-page personal statement on why they wish to become a legal secretary/paralegal or why they wish to continue their formal legal secretarial/paralegal education; and a copy of their acceptance to the school of their choice.

**Financial data:** The stipend is $1,000 for first place and $500 for second.

**Duration:** 1 year.

**Number awarded:** 2 each year.

**Deadline:** March of each year.

## 3276 NEBRASKA SOCIETY OF CERTIFIED PUBLIC ACCOUNTANTS SCHOLARSHIPS

Nebraska Society of Certified Public Accountants
Attn: Foundation
635 South 14th Street, Suite 330
Lincoln, NE 68508
Phone: (402) 476-8482; (800) 642-6178; Fax: (402) 476-8731;
Email: nebrscpa@inetnebr.com
Web: www.nescpa.com

**Summary:** To provide financial assistance to upper-division accounting students at colleges and universities in Nebraska.

**Eligibility:** Open to students who are majoring in accounting and have completed their junior year at a Nebraska college or university. Applicants must have the interest and capabilities of becoming a successful C.P.A., be planning to pursue their career in Nebraska, and be planning to take the C.P.A. examination. They must be nominated by accounting faculty members. Institutions having fifth-year accounting (150-hour) programs may also nominate up to 2 students for scholarships specifically designated for such students. Selection is based on scholarship, leadership, and character; the highest scholastic average is not necessarily required.

**Financial data:** Stipends range from $750 to $2,500. Scholarships for fifth-year students are at least $1,500. This program includes the following named awards: the Arnold L. Magnuson Scholarship, the James R. Greisch Scholarship, the Delmar A. Lienemann, Sr. Scholarship, the Nancy J. Stara Scholarship, and the Irving R. Dana III Scholarship. Scholarships for fifth-year students include the Aureus Financial Scholarship (funded by Aureus Financial of Lincoln and Omaha) and the J. Edmunds Miller Scholarship.

**Duration:** March of each year.

**Number awarded:** Varies each year; recently, 50 of these scholarships (including 16 fifth-year scholarships) were awarded.

**Deadline:** March of each year.

## 3277 NEEBC SCHOLARSHIP PROGRAM

New England Employee Benefits Council
440 Totten Pond Road
Waltham, MA 02451
Phone: (781) 684-8700; Fax: (781) 684-9200; Email: info@neebc.org
Web: www.neebc.org/scholar/scholar.html

**Summary:** To provide financial assistance to residents and students in the New England states who are working on an undergraduate or graduate degree in a field related to employee benefits.

**Eligibility:** Open to full-time undergraduate and graduate students who are residents of New England or enrolled in a college in the region. Applicants must be interested in preparing for a career in such areas as health care program design; pension fund design, implementation, or administration; retirement strategies; ERISA and legal aspects of employee benefits; health risk management; multiemployer plans; workers compensation; employee benefits communications; actuarial and underwriting analysis; work/life programs; or institutional investing of retirement savings. Along with their application, they must submit an essay (up to 500 words) describing why they are interested in entering the employee benefits field and what careers within the field are of interest to them and why. Selection is based on 1) study, activities, and goals related to employee benefits; 2) school and community activities; 3) work experience; and 4) academic performance and potential.

**Financial data:** The stipend is $5,000 per year.

**Duration:** 1 year; may be renewed up to 3 additional years or until completion of a degree.

**Number awarded:** 1 or more each year.

**Deadline:** March of each year.

## 3278 NEHRA FUTURE STARS IN HR SCHOLARSHIPS

Northeast Human Resources Association
Attn: Scholarship Awards
One Washington Street, Suite 101
Wellesley, MA 02481
Phone: (781) 235-2900; Fax: (781) 237-8745; Email: info@nehra.com
Web: www.nehra.com/scholarships.php

**Summary:** To provide financial assistance to undergraduate and graduate students at colleges and universities in New England who are preparing for a career in human resources.

**Eligibility:** Open to full-time undergraduate and graduate students at accredited colleges and universities in New England. Applicants must have completed at least one course related to human resources and have a GPA of 3.0 or higher. Along with their application, they must submit 2 essays: 1) why they are interested in becoming a human resources professional; and 2) what qualities they believe are critical to the success of a human resources professional, which of those they currently possess, and how they intend to acquire the others. Selection is based on interest in becoming a human resources professional, academic success, leadership skills, and participation in non-academic activities. The applicant who is judged most outstanding receives the John D. Erdlen Scholarship Award.

**Financial data:** Stipends are $3,000 or $2,500 per year.

**Duration:** 1 year; may be renewed.

**Number awarded:** 4 each year: 1 at $3,000 (the John D. Erdlen Scholarship Award) and 3 at $2,500.

**Deadline:** March of each year.

## 3279 NEW ENGLAND AEE ACADEMIC SCHOLARSHIPS

**Summary:** To provide financial assistance to undergraduate and graduate students in New England interested in taking courses directly related to energy engineering or energy management.
*See Listing #2533.*

## 3280 NEW HAMPSHIRE EDUCATIONAL MEDIA ASSOCIATION SCHOLARSHIP

New Hampshire Educational Media Association
P.O. Box 418
Concord, NH 03302-0418
Web: www.nhema.net/education.htm

**Summary:** To provide financial assistance to residents of New Hampshire who are interested in taking courses related to school librarianship. Information is also available from Ruth Stuart, Scholarship and Awards Committee, Laconia High School, 345 Union Avenue, Laconia, NH 03246, (603) 524-3350, E-mail: rstuart@laconia.k12.nh.us.

**Eligibility:** Open to New Hampshire residents who are interested in taking undergraduate, graduate, post-graduate, continuing education, or techniques courses related to school librarianship. Applicants must submit a statement outlining their professional and educational goals.

**Financial data:** A stipend is awarded (amount not specified).

**Duration:** 1 year.

**Number awarded:** 1 each year.

**Deadline:** March of each year.

## 3281 NEW HAMPSHIRE SOCIETY OF CERTIFIED PUBLIC ACCOUNTANTS SCHOLARSHIP PROGRAM

New Hampshire Society of Certified Public Accountants
Attn: Financial Careers Committee
1750 Elm Street, Suite 403
Manchester, NH 03104
Phone: (603) 622-1999; Fax: (603) 626-0204; Email: info@nhscpa.org
Web: nhscpa.org/student.htm

**Summary:** To provide financial assistance to undergraduate and graduate students in New Hampshire who are preparing for a career as a certified public accountant.

**Eligibility:** Open to residents of New Hampshire who are 1) entering their junior or senior year in an accounting or business program at an accredited 4-year college or university or 2) full-time graduate students in an accredited master's degree program in accounting or business. A recommendation or appraisal from the person in charge of the applicant's accounting program must be included in the application package. Selection is based on academic record, not financial need, although if academic measures between 2 or more students are the same, financial need may be considered secondarily.

**Financial data:** A stipend is awarded (amount not specified).

**Duration:** 1 year.

**Number awarded:** 2 or more each year.

**Deadline:** October of each year.

---

**3282 NEW HORIZONS KATHY LETARTE SCHOLARSHIP**

Tourism Cares for Tomorrow
Attn: Program Manager
585 Washington Street
Canton, MA 02021
Phone: (781) 821-5990; Fax: (781) 821-8949; Email: info@tourismcares.org
Web: www.tourismcares.org

**Summary:** To provide financial assistance to upper-division students from Michigan who are majoring in tourism.

**Eligibility:** Open to residents of Michigan entering their junior year at an accredited 4-year college or university in the United States or Canada. Applicants must be working on a degree in a travel and tourism-related program and have a GPA of 3.0 or higher. Along with their application, they must submit a 2-page essay on niche markets with an emphasis of student markets. Financial need is not considered in the selection process.

**Financial data:** The stipend is $1,000.

**Duration:** 1 year.

**Number awarded:** 1 each year.

**Deadline:** March of each year.

---

**3283 NEW JERSEY FUNERAL SERVICE EDUCATION CORPORATION SCHOLARSHIPS**

New Jersey Funeral Directors Association
Attn: New Jersey Funeral Service Education Corporation
P.O. Box L
Manasquan, NJ 08736
Phone: (732) 974-9444; Fax: (732) 974-8144; Email: njsfda@njsfda.org
Web: www.njsfda.org/education/edu_3scholar.shtml

**Summary:** To provide financial assistance to New Jersey residents who are currently enrolled in a mortuary science program.

**Eligibility:** Open to New Jersey residents who are currently enrolled in a mortuary science program and planning to enter the field of funeral service in the state after graduation. Applicants must have a college GPA of 2.5 or higher. They must submit an essay on either 1) why they have chosen funeral service as a career, or 2) what they feel they can contribute to funeral service. A personal interview is required. Selection is based on the essay, academic record, commitment to funeral service as a career, and (to a lesser extent) financial need.

**Financial data:** The stipend is $2,000.

**Duration:** 1 year.

**Number awarded:** 4 each year.

**Deadline:** June of each year.

---

**3284 NEW JERSEY SCHOOLWOMEN'S CLUB SCHOLARSHIPS**

New Jersey Schoolwomen's Club
c/o Judy Jordan
67 Spray Way
Lavallette, NJ 08735

**Summary:** To provide financial assistance for college to female high school seniors in New Jersey who intend to prepare for a career in education.

**Eligibility:** Open to women graduating from high schools in New Jersey. Applicants must be planning to attend a 4-year college or university to prepare for a career in the field of education. They must have an academic average of C+ or higher. Selection is based on academic achievement, community involvement, and extracurricular activities. This program includes the Patricia Barber Scholarship and the Jeanette Hodge Scholarship.

**Financial data:** The stipend is $1,000.

**Duration:** 1 year.

**Number awarded:** 2 each year.

**Deadline:** February of each year.

---

**3285 NEW JERSEY SOCIETY OF CERTIFIED PUBLIC ACCOUNTANTS ACCOUNTING MANUSCRIPT CONTEST**

New Jersey Society of Certified Public Accountants
Attn: Student Programs Coordinator
425 Eagle Rock Avenue, Suite 100
Roseland, NJ 07068-1723

Phone: (973) 226-4494, ext. 209; Fax: (973) 226-7425;
Email: njscpa@njscpa.org
Web: www.njscpa.org

**Summary:** To recognize and reward outstanding manuscripts on accounting written by college students in New Jersey.

**Eligibility:** Open to sophomores and juniors who are attending 2-year or 4-year colleges or universities in New Jersey and majoring in accounting. They are invited to submit a manuscript on accounting (up to 1,000 words). All submissions must be original work that has not been previously published. Students must select a faculty member to serve as a mentor in the development of the article. No co-authored manuscripts are accepted. Manuscripts are judged on the basis of content, creativity, clarity, ability to communicate effectively the relevance of accountancy to the topic, and ability to communicate information that is relevant to New Jersey businesses.

**Financial data:** First place is a $3,000 scholarship; honorable mentions are $1,000.

**Duration:** The competition is held annually. The winning manuscript is published in *New Jersey Business* magazine, which is also the co-sponsor of this award. The topic changes annually; recently it was "What is the importance of corporate ethics in financial reporting?"

**Number awarded:** Up to 4 each year: 1 first prize and up to 3 honorable mentions.

**Deadline:** January of each year.

---

**3286 NEW JERSEY SOCIETY OF CERTIFIED PUBLIC ACCOUNTANTS COLLEGE SCHOLARSHIP PROGRAM**

New Jersey Society of Certified Public Accountants
Attn: Student Programs Coordinator
425 Eagle Rock Avenue, Suite 100
Roseland, NJ 07068-1723
Phone: (973) 226-4494, ext. 209; Fax: (973) 226-7425;
Email: njscpa@njscpa.org
Web: www.njscpa.org

**Summary:** To provide financial assistance to upper-division and graduate students in New Jersey who are preparing for a career as a certified public accountant.

**Eligibility:** Open to residents of New Jersey who are attending a college or university in the state. Applicants must be 1) juniors who are majoring or concentrating in accounting; or 2) graduate students entering an accounting-related program. Students may apply directly or be nominated by the accounting department chair at their college. Selection is based on academic achievement (GPA of 3.0 or higher).

**Financial data:** Stipends range from $500 to $4,000.

**Duration:** 1 year. Each student may receive only 1 undergraduate and 1 graduate scholarship during their academic career.

**Number awarded:** Varies each year. Recently, 46 of these scholarships were awarded: 1 at $4,000, 35 at $3,000, 3 at $2,000, 2 at $1,000, 3 at $750, and 2 at $500.

**Deadline:** January of each year.

---

**3287 NEW JERSEY SOCIETY OF CERTIFIED PUBLIC ACCOUNTANTS HIGH SCHOOL SCHOLARSHIP PROGRAM**

New Jersey Society of Certified Public Accountants
Attn: Student Programs Coordinator
425 Eagle Rock Avenue, Suite 100
Roseland, NJ 07068-1723
Phone: (973) 226-4494, ext. 209; Fax: (973) 226-7425;
Email: njscpa@njscpa.org
Web: www.njscpa.org

**Summary:** To recognize and reward seniors in New Jersey high schools who are interested in preparing for a career as a certified public accountant and take a statewide accounting examination.

**Eligibility:** Open to all New Jersey high school seniors who are planning to major in accounting in college. Applications for a 1-hour accounting aptitude exam are mailed to New Jersey high school guidance and business departments each September. The exam is given in November and the highest scorers receive accounting scholarships to the college of their choice.

**Financial data:** The stipend ranges up to $1,700 per year.

**Duration:** Up to 5 years.

**Number awarded:** Varies each year; recently, 18 scholarships were awarded

**Deadline:** October of each year.

## 3288 NEW JERSEY UTILITIES ASSOCIATION SCHOLARSHIPS

**Summary:** To provide financial assistance to minority, female, and disabled high school seniors in New Jersey interested in majoring in selected subjects in college.

*See Listing #2537.*

## 3289 NEW MEXICO BROADCASTERS ASSOCIATION SCHOLARSHIPS

**Summary:** To provide financial assistance to undergraduate students in New Mexico who are preparing for a career in the broadcast industry.

*See Listing #1593.*

## 3290 NEW YORK BEEF PRODUCERS' ASSOCIATION SCHOLARSHIP

**Summary:** To provide financial assistance to college students from New York who are preparing for a career in the cattle industry.

*See Listing #1594.*

## 3291 NEW YORK EXCELLENCE IN ACCOUNTING SCHOLARSHIP

New York State Society of Certified Public Accountants
Attn: Foundation for Accounting Education
530 Fifth Avenue, Fifth Floor
New York, NY 10036-5101
Phone: (212) 719-8379; (800) 633-6320; Fax: (212) 719-3364;
Email: jlewis@nysscpa.org
Web: www.nysscpa.org/scholarship/scholarship.htm

**Summary:** To provide financial assistance to residents of New York who are majoring in accounting at a college or university in the state.

**Eligibility:** Open to residents of New York who are either U.S. citizens or permanent residents. They must be entering the third or fourth year of a 4-year or 5-year degree program in accounting at a New York college or university and have a GPA of 3.0 or higher. Students who already have a bachelor's degree and are working on a master's degree in accounting are not eligible. Applications, on behalf of students, are accepted only when forwarded from the applicant's institution. Financial need is considered in the selection process.

**Financial data:** The stipend is $1,500 for full-time students and $750 for part-time students. Payment is made co-payable to the student and the school.

**Duration:** 1 year; may be renewed for 1 additional year for students working on a 4-year bachelor's degree or 2 additional years for students in a "150-hour" 5-year program.

**Number awarded:** Varies each year; recently, the society awarded more than $111,000 in new scholarships and renewals.

**Deadline:** March of each year.

## 3292 NEXT GENERATION OF PUBLIC SERVANTS SCHOLARSHIP

**Summary:** To provide financial assistance to Hispanic and other students majoring in designated business, engineering, social science, and science fields who are interested in employment with the U.S. Department of Energy (DOE).

*See Listing #2545.*

## 3293 NFIB FREE ENTERPRISE SCHOLARS PROGRAM

National Federation of Independent Business
Attn: NFIB Education Foundation
1020 F Street, N.W., Suite 200
Washington, DC 20004
Phone: (202) 554-9000; (800) NFIB-NOW; Email: aaron.taylor@nfib.org
Web: www.nfib.com/page/educationFoundation

**Summary:** To provide financial assistance for college to high school seniors who are interested in private enterprise and entrepreneurship.

**Eligibility:** Open to graduating high school seniors who plan to enter their freshman year at an accredited 2-year college, 4-year college or university, or vocational/technical institute. Students must be nominated by a member of the National Federation of Independent Business (NFIB). Nominees must meet or exceed academic standards, using standardized test scores (ACT/SAT), class rank, and GPA as indicators. They must answer a short, personal question defining their entrepreneurial efforts and compose another essay of 500 words

or less about the importance of free enterprise. Selection is based on those essays, involvement in extracurricular and/or community activities, and special recognition or honors.

**Financial data:** The highest-ranked applicant receives $10,000 and 4 other finalists receive $5,000. Other stipends are $1,000.

**Duration:** 1 year; nonrenewable.

**Number awarded:** Varies each year; recently, a total of 221 of these scholarships were awarded.

**Deadline:** March of each year.

## 3294 NFWL/NRA BILL OF RIGHTS ESSAY CONTEST

National Foundation for Women Legislators, Inc.
910 16th Street, N.W., Suite 100
Washington, DC 20006
Phone: (202) 293-3040; Fax: (202) 293-5430; Email: nfwl@erols.com
Web: www.womenlegistors.org

**Summary:** To recognize and reward the best essays written by female high school juniors or seniors on a topic related to the Bill of Rights. This essay competition is sponsored jointly by the National Foundation of Women Legislators (NFWL) and the National Rifle Association (NRA).

**Eligibility:** Open to female high school juniors or seniors. Applicants are invited to write an essay on a topic (changes annually) related to the Bill of Rights; recently, the topic was how the Bill of Rights relates to women's acts of courage, valor, and heroism. In addition to the essay, candidates must submit 2 personal reference letters.

**Financial data:** Each winner receives a $3,000 unrestricted scholarship to use toward college tuition at any U.S. college or university and an all-expense paid trip to the foundation's annual conference.

**Duration:** The competition is held annually.

**Number awarded:** 7 each year.

**Deadline:** June of each year.

## 3295 NIB GRANT M. MACK MEMORIAL SCHOLARSHIP

American Council of the Blind
Attn: Coordinator, Scholarship Program
1155 15th Street, N.W., Suite 1004
Washington, DC 20005
Phone: (202) 467-5081; (800) 424-8666; Fax: (202) 467-5085;
Email: info@acb.org
Web: www.acb.org

**Summary:** To provide financial assistance to students who are blind and working on an undergraduate or graduate degree in business or management. This scholarship is sponsored by National Industries for the Blind (NIB) in honor of a dedicated leader of the American Council of the Blind. Scholarship winners are expected to be present at the council's annual conference; the council will cover all reasonable expenses connected with convention attendance.

**Eligibility:** Open to all legally blind persons who are majoring in business or management (undergraduate or graduate) and are U.S. citizens or resident aliens. In addition to letters of recommendation and copies of academic transcripts, applications must include an autobiographical sketch. A cumulative GPA of 3.3 or higher is generally required. Selection is based on demonstrated academic record, involvement in extracurricular and civic activities, and academic objectives. The severity of the applicant's visual impairment and his/her study methods are also taken into account.

**Financial data:** The stipend is $2,000. In addition, the winner receives a Kurzweil-1000 Reading System.

**Duration:** 1 year.

**Number awarded:** 1 each year.

**Deadline:** February of each year.

## 3296 NMAHPERD COLLEGE SCHOLARSHIP

**Summary:** To provide financial assistance to residents of New Mexico who are planning to work on an undergraduate degree in health, physical education, recreation, or dance at a college or university in the state.

*See Listing #1600.*

## 3297 NMASBO SCHOLARSHIPS

New Mexico Association of School Business Officials
Attn: Executive Director
P.O. Box 7535
Albuquerque, NM 87194-7535

Phone: (505) 821-1887; Email: jmontano110@comcast.net

Web: www.nmasbo.org

**Summary:** To provide financial assistance to high school seniors in New Mexico who plan to study education in college.

**Eligibility:** Open to seniors graduating from high schools in New Mexico with a GPA of 3.0 or higher. Applicants must be planning to attend a college or university in the state to work full time on a degree related to education.

**Financial data:** The stipend is $1,000.

**Duration:** 1 year.

**Number awarded:** 6 each year.

**Deadline:** April of each year.

---

## 3298 NORA WEBB-MCKINNEY SCHOLARSHIP

American Council of the Blind of Ohio

Attn: Executive Director

2678 Edgevale Road

P.O. Box 21488

Columbus, OH 43221-0488

Phone: (614) 221-6688; (800) 835-2226 (within OH); Fax: (614) 451-0539; Email: kmorlock@gcfn.org

Web: www.acbogcc.org

**Summary:** To provide financial assistance to Ohio students who are interested in working on an undergraduate or graduate degree involving service to blind people.

**Eligibility:** Open to 1) residents of Ohio who are high school seniors or current undergraduate or graduate students, and 2) undergraduate and graduate students at colleges and universities in Ohio. Applicants must be interested in working on or planning to work on a degree in a field related to blindness (e.g., special education, rehabilitation teaching or counseling, orientation and mobility, or a concentration on programs serving people who are blind). They may be blind or sighted. Along with their application, they must submit transcripts (must have a GPA of 3.0 or higher) and an essay of 250 to 500 words on their career objectives, future plans, personal goals, other academic or personal qualities, and why they believe they are qualified to receive this scholarship.

**Financial data:** The stipend is $2,000 per year.

**Duration:** 1 year; recipients may reapply.

**Number awarded:** 1 each year.

**Deadline:** July of each year.

---

## 3299 NORTH CAROLINA CPA FOUNDATION SCHOLARSHIPS

North Carolina Association of Certified Public Accountants

Attn: North Carolina CPA Foundation, Inc.

3100 Gateway Centre Boulevard

P.O. Box 80188

Raleigh, NC 27623-0188

Phone: (919) 469-1040, ext. 133; (800) 722-2836; Fax: (919) 469-3959; Email: vpironio@ncacpa.org

Web: www.ncacpa.org

**Summary:** To provide financial assistance to students majoring in accounting at colleges and universities in North Carolina.

**Eligibility:** Open to North Carolina residents. Applicants must have completed at least 1 upper-division accounting program, must have completed at least 4 semesters, and must be majoring in accounting at a North Carolina college or university. They must be sponsored by 2 accounting faculty members and they must submit an essay on what they believe the C.P.A. of the 21st century will be like. Selection is based equally on GPA (3.0 or higher), extracurricular activities, awards or honors received, essay content, and essay grammar.

**Financial data:** Stipends range from $1,000 to $5,000.

**Duration:** 1 year.

**Number awarded:** Varies each year. Recently, 29 of these scholarships were awarded.

**Deadline:** January of each year.

---

## 3300 NORTH CAROLINA MILLENNIUM TEACHER SCHOLARSHIP PROGRAM

North Carolina State Education Assistance Authority

Attn: Teacher Assistant Scholarship Fund

P.O. Box 13663

Research Triangle Park, NC 27708-3663

Phone: (919) 248-8614, ext. 313; (800) 700-1775, ext. 313; Fax: (919) 248-6632; Email: eew@ncseaa.edu

Web: www.ncseaa.edu

**Summary:** To provide financial assistance to high school seniors in North Carolina who are interested in attending designated public universities in the state to work on a degree in education.

**Eligibility:** Open to seniors graduating from high schools in North Carolina who have been accepted at Elizabeth City State University, Fayetteville State University, or Winston-Salem State University. Applicants must have at least average SAT scores, have a GPA of at least 2.5, and be able to demonstrate at least $3,000 worth of financial aid need. They must be interested in teaching at a North Carolina public school after graduation; priority is given to applicants planning to teach in designated critical shortage licensure areas.

**Financial data:** The stipend is $6,500 per year.

**Duration:** 1 year; may be renewed up to 3 additional years.

**Number awarded:** 6 each year: 2 at each of the participating universities.

**Deadline:** March of each year.

---

## 3301 NORTH CAROLINA SHERIFFS' ASSOCIATION UNDERGRADUATE CRIMINAL JUSTICE SCHOLARSHIPS

North Carolina State Education Assistance Authority

Attn: Scholarship and Grant Services

10 T.W. Alexander Drive

P.O. Box 14103

Research Triangle Park, NC 27709-4103

Phone: (919) 549-8614; (800) 700-1775; Fax: (919) 549-8481; Email: information@ncseaa.edu

Web: www.ncseaa.edu

**Summary:** To provide financial assistance to children of deceased or disabled North Carolina law enforcement officers who are majoring in criminal justice in college.

**Eligibility:** Open to North Carolina residents studying criminal justice at any of the 10 state institutions offering that major: Appalachian State University, East Carolina University, Elizabeth City State University, Fayetteville State University, North Carolina Central University, North Carolina State University, the University of North Carolina at Pembroke, the University of North Carolina at Charlotte, the University of North Carolina at Wilmington, and Western Carolina University. First priority in selection is given to children of law enforcement officers killed in the line of duty; second priority is given to children of sheriffs or deputy sheriffs who are deceased, retired (regular or disability), or currently active in law enforcement in North Carolina; third priority is given to other resident criminal justice students meeting their institution's academic and financial need criteria. Funding for this program is provided by the North Carolina Sheriffs' Association. Recipients are selected by the financial aid office at the university they plan to attend or are currently attending; after selection, students obtain a letter of endorsement from the sheriff of the county in North Carolina where they reside.

**Financial data:** The stipend is $2,000 per year.

**Duration:** 1 year; nonrenewable.

**Number awarded:** Up to 10 each year: 1 at each participating university.

---

## 3302 NORTH CAROLINA TEACHER ASSISTANT SCHOLARSHIP FUND

North Carolina State Education Assistance Authority

Attn: Teacher Assistant Scholarship Fund

P.O. Box 13663

Research Triangle Park, NC 27708-3663

Phone: (919) 248-8614, ext. 313; (800) 700-1775, ext. 313; Fax: (919) 248-6632; Email: eew@ncseaa.edu

Web: www.ncseaa.edu/TAS.htm

**Summary:** To provide financial assistance to public school teacher assistants in North Carolina who are interested in working on a teaching degree.

**Eligibility:** Open to teacher assistants employed full time in North Carolina public schools. Applicants must be enrolled in at least 6 semester hours pursuing teacher licensure at an accredited 4-year college in North Carolina with a teacher education program. They must have a GPA of 2.8 or higher and remain employed as a teacher assistant while attending college part time.

**Financial data:** The stipend is $1,600 per semester (including summer sessions). A student can receive up to $4,800 per year or $28,000 per lifetime.

**Duration:** 1 year; may be renewed if the recipient completes at least 12 semester hours with a GPA of 2.8 or higher.

**Number awarded:** Varies each year. Recently, a total of 239 students were receiving $957,100 in support through this program.

**Deadline:** February of each year.

## 3303 NORTH CAROLINA TRAFFIC LEAGUE SCHOLARSHIP

**Summary:** To provide financial assistance to upper-division and graduate students from North Carolina who are working on a degree in transportation.
*See Listing #2557.*

## 3304 NSA ANNUAL SCHOLARSHIP AWARDS

National Society of Accountants
Attn: NSA Scholarship Foundation
1010 North Fairfax Street
Alexandria, VA 22314-1574
Phone: (703) 549-6400, ext. 1312; (800) 966-6679, ext. 1312; Fax: (703) 549-2512; Email: snoell@nsacct.org
Web: www.nsacct.org
**Summary:** To provide financial assistance to undergraduate students majoring in accounting.
**Eligibility:** Open to undergraduate students enrolled on a full-time basis in an accounting degree program at an accredited 2-year or 4-year college or university with a GPA of 3.0 or better. Students in 2-year colleges may apply during their first year or during their second year if transferring to a 4-year institution, provided they have committed themselves to a major in accounting throughout the remainder of their college career; students in 4-year colleges may apply for a scholarship for their second, third, or fourth year of studies, provided they have committed themselves to a major in accounting through the remainder of their college career. Only U.S. or Canadian citizens attending a U.S. accredited business school, college, or university may apply. Selection is based on academic attainment, demonstrated leadership ability, and financial need.
**Financial data:** The stipend is approximately $500 per year for students entering their second year of studies or approximately $1,000 per year for students entering the third or fourth year. The outstanding student in this competition, designated the Charles H. Earp Memorial Scholar, receives an additional stipend of $200 and an appropriate plaque.
**Duration:** 1 year.
**Number awarded:** Approximately 40 each year.
**Deadline:** March of each year.

## 3305 NTA STATE AND PROVINCIAL SCHOLARSHIP

Tourism Cares for Tomorrow
Attn: Program Manager
585 Washington Street
Canton, MA 02021
Phone: (781) 821-5990; Fax: (781) 821-8949; Email: info@tourismcares.org
Web: www.tourismcares.org
**Summary:** To provide financial assistance to upper-division students who are majoring in tourism.
**Eligibility:** Open to students entering their junior or senior year at an accredited 4-year college or university in the United States or Canada. Applicants must be working on a degree in a travel and tourism-related program and have a GPA of 3.0 or higher. Along with their application, they must submit a 2-page essay on why they have chosen to prepare for a career in the hospitality and tourism industry. Financial need is not considered in the selection process.
**Financial data:** The stipend is $1,000.
**Duration:** 1 year.
**Number awarded:** 1 each year.
**Deadline:** March of each year.

## 3306 NUTMEG STATEWIDE PTA SCHOLARSHIP

Parent Teacher Association of Connecticut
60 Connolly Parkway, Building 12
Hamden, CT 06514
Phone: (203) 281-6617; Fax: (203) 281-6749; Email: connecticut.pta@snet.net
Web: www.ctpta.org/membershi/nspta/scholarship.html
**Summary:** To provide financial assistance to seniors at high schools in Connecticut with a PTA unit who are preparing for a career working with children.
**Eligibility:** Open to seniors graduating from Connecticut high schools that have a PTA unit in good standing. Applicants must be planning to attend a 4-year college or university to prepare for a career in service to children. Along with their application, they must submit a 1-page essay on how they expect to be serving children 10 years after college graduation. Selection is based on the essay (5 points), class rank (3 points), and school and community involvement (2 points). Each school may submit only 1 application.
**Financial data:** The stipend is $1,500.

**Duration:** 1 year.
**Number awarded:** 1 each year.
**Deadline:** February of each year.

## 3307 OELMA SCHOLARSHIPS

Ohio Educational Library Media Association
17 South High Street, Suite 200
Columbus, OH 43215
Phone: (614) 221-1900; Fax: (614) 221-1989; Email: info@oelma.org
Web: www.oelma.org
**Summary:** To provide financial assistance to residents of Ohio who are preparing for a career as a school library media specialist.
**Eligibility:** Open to Ohio residents who are currently enrolled as a college junior, senior, or graduate student. Applicants must be interested in preparing for a career as a school library media specialist at the K-12 or higher education level. They must be able to demonstrate financial need. Membership in the Ohio Educational Library Media Association (OELMA) is preferred but not required.
**Financial data:** Stipends are $1,000 or $500. This program includes the J. Allen Oakum Award for $500, established in 1985.
**Duration:** 1 year.
**Number awarded:** 2 each year: 1 at $1,000 and 1 at $500.
**Deadline:** January of each year.

## 3308 OFFICE OF CIVILIAN RADIOACTIVE WASTE MANAGEMENT HISTORICALLY BLACK COLLEGES AND UNIVERSITIES UNDERGRADUATE SCHOLARSHIP PROGRAM

**Summary:** To provide scholarships and internship experience to students at Historically Black Colleges and Universities (HBCUs) working on undergraduate degrees in areas related to the Office of Civilian Radioactive Waste Management (OCRWM).
*See Listing #2571.*

## 3309 OGR AWARDS OF EXCELLENCE SCHOLARSHIPS

International Order of the Golden Rule
Attn: Education Department
P.O. Box 28689
St. Louis, MO 63146-1189
Phone: (314) 209-7412; (800) 637-8030; Fax: (314) 209-1289;
Email: education@ogr.org
Web: www.ogr.org/scholarships.php
**Summary:** To provide financial assistance to students majoring in mortuary science.
**Eligibility:** Open to students majoring in mortuary science in their final semester of study. Applicants must have a GPA of 3.0 or higher and be able to demonstrate financial need. They must submit an essay of 150 words or less on what they hope to achieve during their funeral service career.
**Financial data:** Stipends are $2,500, $1,500, or $500.
**Duration:** 1 year.
**Number awarded:** 3 each year.
**Deadline:** September of each year.

## 3310 OHIO BUSINESS TEACHERS ASSOCIATION SCHOLARSHIPS

Ohio Business Teachers Association
c/o Victoria Hammer, President
University of Cincinnati
Raymond Walters College
9555 Plainfield Road
Cincinnati, OH 45236
Phone: (513) 745-5791; Fax: (513) 745-5771; Email: victoria.hammer@uc.edu
Web: www.rwc.uc.edu/obta
**Summary:** To provide financial assistance to undergraduate and graduate students and professionals in Ohio who are interested in business education.
**Eligibility:** Open to 1) undergraduate students enrolled full time in a 4-year bachelor's degree program in the field of business education at an accredited Ohio institution; 2) graduate students at Ohio institutions who are members of the Ohio Business Teachers Association (OBTA) and/or the business education division of the Ohio Vocational Association (OVA) and are enrolled in course work for regular academic credit in business, business education, or a

directly-related field; and 3) professional educators who are currently employed as a teacher and/or administrator in business education in Ohio, are current members of OBTA and/or the business education division of OVA, and have the equivalent of 3 academic years of teaching in business education. Applicants must have a GPA of 3.0 or higher.

**Financial data:** The stipend is $1,000.

**Duration:** 1 year.

**Number awarded:** 1 each year.

**Deadline:** August of each year.

## 3311 OHIO CLASSICAL CONFERENCE SCHOLARSHIP FOR PROSPECTIVE LATIN TEACHERS

Ohio Classical Conference
c/o Amy J. Sawan, Scholarship Committee
Medina Senior High School
777 East Union Street
Medina, OH 44256
Phone: (330) 636-3200, ext. 3380; Email: LIAMOT@aol.com
Web: dept.kent.edu/mcls/classics/occ/scholarships.htm

**Summary:** To provide financial assistance to Ohio residents preparing for a career as a Latin teacher.

**Eligibility:** Open to residents of Ohio enrolled at least at the sophomore level at a college or university in the United States. Applicants must be taking courses leading to a career in the teaching of Latin at the K-12 level in a public, private, or parochial school. They must submit college transcripts, 2 letters of recommendation (including one from a member of their classics department), a prospectus of courses completed and to be taken as part of the program, and a 1-page statement of their academic goals and reasons for applying for the scholarship.

**Financial data:** The stipend is $1,500.

**Duration:** 1 year; nonrenewable.

**Number awarded:** 1 each year.

**Deadline:** March of each year.

## 3312 OHIO SOCIETY OF CPAS CHAPTER SCHOLARSHIPS

Ohio Society of Certified Public Accountants
535 Metro Place
P.O. Box 1810
Dublin, OH 43017
Phone: (614) 764-2727; (800) 686-2727; Email: oscpa@ohio-cpa.com
Web: www.ohioscpa.com

**Summary:** To provide financial assistance to students at Ohio colleges and universities who are majoring in accounting.

**Eligibility:** Open to students majoring in accounting at Ohio colleges and universities who are nominated by their department. Applicants must be attending an institution that is located in a section of the state with a chapter of the sponsoring organization that offers a scholarship. Winners of chapter scholarships are then invited to participate in Scholarship Day at the state organization's offices and take part in an interview process. Based on those interviews, a state grand prize winner is selected.

**Financial data:** Chapters provide each recipient with a stipend of $500, which is matched by the state organization. The state prize is $3,000.

**Duration:** 1 year.

**Number awarded:** Varies each year.

## 3313 OHIO SOCIETY OF CPAS MANUSCRIPT CONTEST

Ohio Society of Certified Public Accountants
535 Metro Place
P.O. Box 1810
Dublin, OH 43017
Phone: (614) 764-2727; (800) 686-2727; Email: oscpa@ohio-cpa.com
Web: www.ohioscpa.com

**Summary:** To recognize and reward students at Ohio colleges and universities who submit outstanding manuscripts on a topic related to accounting.

**Eligibility:** Open to students enrolled at Ohio colleges and universities. Applicants must submit a manuscript, up to 10 pages in length, on a topic that changes annually but relates to accounting. Recently, students were invited to write on the topic: "Has the adoption of the Sarbanes-Oxley legislation increased investor confidence in public companies and financial reporting?" Each manuscript must be reviewed by a sponsoring faculty member who is responsible for ensuring that the manuscript conforms to the technical requirements. Each faculty member may serve as a sponsor on a maximum of 5 papers. Co-authored manuscripts are not eligible, nor are manuscripts that have been published or submitted for publication elsewhere. Selection is based on the manuscript's content (manuscript covers specific topic area, approach to coverage of topic indicates originality of thought, relevant and meaningful issues and problems concerning both sides of the subject are discussed, each subdivision of the paper is clearly segregated and is relevant to the discussion) and presentation (organization of the paper is logical and balanced, a clear and concise summary is provided that integrates the presentation into a coherent whole and gives a definite conclusion, writing style clearly conveys meaning with structurally correct sentences and effective use of words, technical aspects of the paper are in good form).

**Financial data:** The author of the first-place manuscript receives a plaque and a cash award of $1,500. The author of the second-place manuscript receives a cash award of $1,000. The sponsoring faculty members receive cash awards of $1,000 for first place and $750 for second place.

**Duration:** The contest is held annually.

**Number awarded:** 2 each year.

**Deadline:** March of each year.

## 3314 OKLAHOMA SOCIETY OF CERTIFIED PUBLIC ACCOUNTANTS SCHOLARSHIP

Oklahoma Society of Certified Public Accountants
Attn: OSCPA Educational Foundation
1900 N.W. Expressway Street, Suite 910
Oklahoma City, OK 73118-1898
Phone: (405) 841-3800, ext. 3829; (800) 522-8261 (within OK); Fax: (405) 841-3801; Email: dmeyer@oscpa.com
Web: www.oscpa.com

**Summary:** To provide financial assistance to upper-division students working on a bachelor's degree in accounting in Oklahoma.

**Eligibility:** Open to juniors and seniors who are nominated by a 4-year or 5-year accounting program at an Oklahoma college or university. Nominees must have successfully completed at least 12 hours of accounting, including 6 hours of intermediate accounting, and 60 hours of general college credit. As part of the application process, nominees must submit a resume, a transcript, standardized test scores, and 3 letters of reference.

**Financial data:** The stipend ranges from $250 to $1,500.

**Duration:** 1 year.

**Number awarded:** Varies each year; recently, 31 of these scholarships were awarded.

**Deadline:** April of each year.

## 3315 OMAHA CHAPTER SCHOLARSHIPS

American Society of Women Accountants-Omaha Chapter
c/o Beth Byrne, Scholarship Committee
823 Auburn Lane
Papillion, NE 68046
Web: www.geocities.com/aswaomaha/scholarships.htm

**Summary:** To provide financial assistance to accounting students in Nebraska.

**Eligibility:** Open to part- and full-time students working on a bachelor's or master's degree in accounting at a college or university in Nebraska. Applicants must have completed at least 60 semester hours. They are not required to be a member of the American Society of Women Accountants. Selection is based on academic achievement, extracurricular activities and honors, a statement of career goals and objectives, letters of recommendation, and financial need.

**Financial data:** A total of $2,000 is available for this program each year. The highest ranked recipient is entered into the national competition for scholarships that range from $1,500 to $4,500.

**Duration:** 1 year.

**Number awarded:** Varies each year; recently, 3 of these scholarships were awarded.

**Deadline:** January of each year.

## 3316 OMAHA VOLUNTEERS FOR HANDICAPPED CHILDREN SCHOLARSHIPS

**Summary:** To provide financial assistance for college to Nebraska residents who have a physical disability or are preparing for a career related to people with orthopedic impairments or physical disabilities.

*See Listing #887.*

## 3317 ONCOLOGY PRACTICE ALLIANCE SCHOLARSHIP

**Summary:** To provide financial assistance to residents of Ohio and West Virginia who are working on an undergraduate or graduate degree in health care management related to hematology or oncology.

*See Listing #2576.*

## 3318 OREGON AFL-CIO SCHOLARSHIPS

Oregon Student Assistance Commission
Attn: Grants and Scholarships Division
1500 Valley River Drive, Suite 100
Eugene, OR 97401-2146
Phone: (541) 687-7395; (800) 452-8807, ext. 7395; Fax: (541) 687-7419;
Email: awardinfo@mercury.osac.state.or.us
Web: www.osac.state.or.us

**Summary:** To provide financial assistance for college to graduating high school seniors in Oregon who submit an essay on a labor-related topic.

**Eligibility:** Open to seniors graduating from high schools in Oregon who submit an essay of 500 words or less on either 1) their own experience as an employee and why it leads them to believe that workers do (or do not) need a union on the job; or 2) why many people who work full time cannot provide a decent standard of living for their families and what they believe should be done about it. Selection is based on the essay, financial need, GPA, and an interview by a panel of individuals with expertise in labor history and labor affairs. Preference is given to applicants from union families.

**Financial data:** The stipends are $3,000, $1,200, $1,000, or $850. The award can be used at an accredited college or university in the United States, at any public community college in Oregon, or at any established trade school. The $3,000 and $1,000 scholarships are designated the May Darling Scholarships, the $1,200 scholarship is designated the Asa T. Williams Scholarship, and the $850 scholarship is designated the Northwest Labor Press Scholarship. This program is sponsored by the Oregon AFL-CIO, 2110 State Street, Salem, OR 97301, (503) 585-6320, Fax: (503) 585-1668.

**Duration:** 1 year; nonrenewable.

**Number awarded:** 4 each year.

**Deadline:** February of each year.

## 3319 OREGON ASSOCIATION OF INDEPENDENT ACCOUNTANTS SCHOLARSHIPS

Oregon Association of Independent Accountants
Attn: OAIA Scholarship Foundation
1804 N.E. 43rd Avenue
Portland, OR 97231
Phone: (503) 282-7247
Web: www.oaia.net/scholarship.html

**Summary:** To provide financial assistance to Oregon residents interested in majoring in accounting in college.

**Eligibility:** Open to Oregon residents who are enrolled in or accepted by an accredited school in the state for the study of accounting. Applicants must intend to carry a minimum of 12 credit hours. Along with their application, they must submit an essay on why they have chosen to study and prepare for a career in accounting. Selection is based on financial need, scholastic achievement, personal qualifications, and professional promise. The Scholarship Foundation is sponsored by the Oregon Association of Independent Accountants (formerly the Oregon Association of Public Accountants). Recipients may attend a college, university, or community college. They are given an honorary 1-year student membership in the Oregon Association of Independent Accountants.

**Financial data:** Stipends range from $1,000 to $2,000. Checks are made payable to the recipient and the recipient's college. Funds may be used for tuition, fees, books, or other academic expenses during the year.

**Duration:** 1 year; renewable.

**Deadline:** March of each year.

## 3320 OREGON COLLECTORS ASSOCIATION BOB HASSON MEMORIAL SCHOLARSHIP

Oregon Student Assistance Commission
Attn: Grants and Scholarships Division
1500 Valley River Drive, Suite 100
Eugene, OR 97401-2146
Phone: (541) 687-7395; (800) 452-8807, ext. 7395; Fax: (541) 687-7419;
Email: awardinfo@mercury.osac.state.or.us
Web: www.osac.state.or.us

**Summary:** To recognize and reward high school seniors in Oregon who submit essays on the proper use of credit.

**Eligibility:** Open to seniors graduating from high schools in Oregon who submit a 3- to 4-page essay entitled "The Proper Use of Credit in the 21st Century." Children and grandchildren of owners and officers of collection agencies registered in Oregon are not eligible.

**Financial data:** Awards are $3,000 for first place, $2,500 for second place, or $1,500 for third place. Funds must be used for tuition and other educational expenses at a college or vocational school in Oregon.

**Duration:** The award, presented annually, may not be renewed.

**Number awarded:** 3 each year.

**Deadline:** February of each year.

## 3321 OSCPA EDUCATIONAL FOUNDATION COLLEGE SCHOLARSHIPS

Oregon Society of Certified Public Accountants
Attn: OSCPA Educational Foundation
10206 S.W. Laurel Street
Beaverton, OR 97005-3209
Phone: (503) 641-7200; (800) 255-1470, ext. 29; Fax: (503) 626-2942;
Email: oscpa@orcpa.org
Web: www.orcpa.org

**Summary:** To provide financial assistance to currently-enrolled undergraduate and graduate students in Oregon who are working on a degree in accounting.

**Eligibility:** Open to Oregon college and university students who are working full time on an undergraduate or master's degree in accounting. Applicants must have a GPA of 3.2 or higher in accounting/business classes and overall. Along with their application, they must submit 3 letters of recommendation and a recent transcript. Selection is based on scholastic ability and interest in the accounting profession.

**Financial data:** For graduate students and undergraduates enrolled in or transferring to 4-year colleges and universities, stipends range from $1,000 to $3,000. For students enrolled in community colleges, the stipend is $500.

**Duration:** 1 year.

**Number awarded:** Varies each year.

**Deadline:** February of each year.

## 3322 OSCPA EDUCATIONAL FOUNDATION HIGH SCHOOL SCHOLARSHIPS

Oregon Society of Certified Public Accountants
Attn: OSCPA Educational Foundation
10206 S.W. Laurel Street
Beaverton, OR 97005-3209
Phone: (503) 641-7200; (800) 255-1470, ext. 29; Fax: (503) 626-2942;
Email: oscpa@orcpa.org
Web: www.orcpa.org

**Summary:** To provide financial assistance to high school seniors in Oregon who are interested in studying accounting in college.

**Eligibility:** Open to seniors at high schools in Oregon who are interested in studying accounting at a college or university in the state. Applicants must have a GPA of 3.5 or higher and be planning to enroll full time. Along with their application, they must submit 3 letters of recommendation and their high school transcript. Selection is based on scholastic ability and interest in the accounting profession.

**Financial data:** For students planning to attend a 4-year college or university, the stipend is $1,000. For students planning to attend a community college, the stipend is $500.

**Duration:** 1 year.

**Number awarded:** Varies each year.

**Deadline:** February of each year.

## 3323 OTIS SPUNKMEYER STUDENT SCHOLARSHIPS

DECA
1908 Association Drive
Reston, VA 20191-1594
Phone: (703) 860-5000; Fax: (703) 860-4013; Email: decainc@aol.com
Web: www.deca.org/scholarships/index.html

**Summary:** To provide financial assistance to DECA members interested in studying management or marketing education in college.

**Eligibility:** Open to DECA members who are interested in working full time on a 2-year or 4-year degree in marketing, management, or marketing education. Applicants must be able to demonstrate evidence of DECA activities, academic achievement, leadership ability, and community service involvement. Selection is based on merit, not financial need.

**Financial data:** The stipend is $1,000.

**Duration:** 1 year.

**Number awarded:** 15 each year.

**Deadline:** February of each year.

---

### 3324 PARALEGAL SCHOLARSHIPS

National Federation of Paralegal Associations, Inc.

Attn: Scholarships

2517 Eastlake Avenue East, Suite 200

Seattle, WA 98102

Phone: (206) 652-4120; Fax: (206) 652-4122; Email: info@paralegals.org

Web: www.paralegals.org

**Summary:** To provide financial assistance to students enrolled in or accepted to a paralegal studies program.

**Eligibility:** Open to part-time or full-time students enrolled or accepted in a paralegal program or college level program with emphasis on paralegal studies. Applicants must have a GPA of 3.0 or higher. Selection is based on academic excellence, participation in campus and paralegal program leadership activities, community service, and a writing sample. Financial need may also be considered.

**Financial data:** The stipends are $3,500 or $1,500.

**Duration:** 1 year.

**Number awarded:** 2 each year: 1 at $3,500 and 1 at $1,500.

**Deadline:** January of each year.

---

### 3325 PAT AND JIM HOST SCHOLARSHIP

Tourism Cares for Tomorrow

Attn: Program Manager

585 Washington Street

Canton, MA 02021

Phone: (781) 821-5990; Fax: (781) 821-8949; Email: info@tourismcares.org

Web: www.tourismcares.org

**Summary:** To provide financial assistance to college students in Kentucky who are majoring in tourism.

**Eligibility:** Open to full-time students enrolled in a 4-year college or university in Kentucky. Applicants must be Kentucky residents, have at least a 3.0 GPA, and be majoring in a travel or tourism-related field (e.g., hotel management, restaurant management, tourism). Along with their application, they must submit an essay of 2 to 5 pages outlining how they perceive the changing role of the group tour industry.

**Financial data:** The stipend is $2,500 per year.

**Duration:** 1 year.

**Number awarded:** 1 each year.

**Deadline:** March of each year.

---

### 3326 PAUL HAGELBARGER MEMORIAL SCHOLARSHIP

Alaska Society of Certified Public Accountants

341 West Tudor Road, Suite 105

Anchorage, AK 99503

Phone: (907) 562-4334; (800) 478-4334; Fax: (907) 562-4025

Web: www.akcpa.org/scholarships.htm

**Summary:** To provide financial assistance to upper-division and graduate students at colleges and universities in Alaska who are preparing for a career in public accounting.

**Eligibility:** Open to juniors, seniors, and graduate students majoring in accounting at 4-year colleges and universities in Alaska. Applicants must submit brief essays on their educational goals, career goals, and financial need. Selection is based on academic achievement, intent to prepare for a career in public accounting in Alaska, and financial need.

**Financial data:** The stipend is at least $2,000.

**Duration:** 1 year.

**Number awarded:** 1 or more each year.

**Deadline:** November of each year.

---

### 3327 PAYCHEX INC. ENTREPRENEUR SCHOLARSHIP

Massachusetts Society of Certified Public Accountants

Attn: MSCPA Educational Foundation

105 Chauncy Street, Tenth Floor

Boston, MA 02111

Phone: (617) 556-4000; (800) 392-6145; Fax: (617) 556-4126;

Email: biannoni@MSCPAonline.org

Web: www.cpatrack.com/financial_aid/scholarship.php

**Summary:** To provide financial assistance to residents of Massachusetts working on an undergraduate degree in accounting at a college or university in the state.

**Eligibility:** Open to Massachusetts residents enrolled full time at a college or university in the state with a cumulative GPA of 3.0 or higher. Applicants must be entering their junior year and be able to demonstrate both financial need and a commitment to preparing for a career as a certified public accountant.

**Financial data:** The stipend is $1,000.

**Duration:** 1 year.

**Number awarded:** 1 each year.

---

### 3328 PENNSYLVANIA AFL-CIO SCHOLARSHIP ESSAY CONTEST

Pennsylvania AFL-CIO

Attn: Director of Education

231 State Street, Seventh Floor

Harrisburg, PA 17101-1110

Phone: (717) 231-2843; (800) 242-2770; Fax: (717) 238-8541

Web: www.paaflcio.org

**Summary:** To recognize and reward high school and college students in Pennsylvania who submit outstanding essays on a labor topic.

**Eligibility:** Open to 1) graduating high school seniors at high schools in Pennsylvania; 2) students currently enrolled in accredited postsecondary school programs in the state; and 3) affiliated union members attending an accredited institution. Applicants must submit essays on topics that change annually but relate to labor unions. Recently, high school students were to write a descriptive essay on the life of a union member (parent, sibling, grandparent, etc.) and why union membership is important to them. College students were to write on the effects of the global economy on working families. Union members were to write on the recent presidential election and its import on working families. In each competition, all essays must be 1,500 words in length and include 3 references, of which at least one must be a labor organization.

**Financial data:** First prize is $2,000, second $1,000, and third $500.

**Duration:** The competition is held annually.

**Number awarded:** 9 each year: 3 in each of the 3 categories.

**Deadline:** January of each year.

---

### 3329 PENNSYLVANIA LEGION STATE HIGH SCHOOL ESSAY CONTEST

American Legion

Attn: Department of Pennsylvania

Attn: Scholarship Secretary

P.O. Box 2324

Harrisburg, PA 17105-2324

Phone: (717) 730-9100; Fax: (717) 975-2836; Email: hq@pa-legion.com

Web: www.pa-legion.com/essay.shtml

**Summary:** To recognize and reward high school students in Pennsylvania who submit outstanding essays on a patriotic topic.

**Eligibility:** Open to students who are currently enrolled in grades 9-12 in a Pennsylvania public, parochial, private, or home school. Applicants must submit an essay, from 600 to 1,000 words, on a topic that changes annually but relates to a patriotic theme; a recent topic was "America-Sweet Land of Liberty." Competitions are held at the level of local American Legion post, county, district, inter-district, sectional, and then state. Selection is based on proper English structure, accuracy, extent of information, and originality.

**Financial data:** At the state level, the first-place winner receives a $3,500 scholarship, second a $3,000 scholarship, and third a $2,500 scholarship. If winners choose not to attend college, prizes are $300 for first place, $200 for second, and $200 for third. Local posts, counties, districts, and sections also offer awards.

**Duration:** The competition is held annually.

**Number awarded:** 3 state winners are selected each year.

**Deadline:** Applications must be submitted to the local American Legion post by February of each year.

---

### 3330 PENNSYLVANIA PLANNING ASSOCIATION SCHOLARSHIPS

Pennsylvania Planning Association

587 James Drive

Harrisburg, PA 17112-2273

Phone: (717) 671-4510; Fax: (717) 545-9247; Email: info@planningpa.org

Web: www.planningpa.org/education_scholarships.shtml

**Summary:** To provide financial assistance to undergraduate and graduate students from Pennsylvania who are working on a degree in planning.

**Eligibility:** Open to residents of Pennsylvania and students at Pennsylvania institutions. Applicants must be enrolled as juniors, seniors, or graduate students in a planning curriculum that has a demonstrated record of preparing students to become planners. They must have a GPA of 3.0 or higher and be able to demonstrate financial need.

**Financial data:** A stipend is awarded (amount not specified).

**Duration:** 1 year.

**Number awarded:** 1 or more each year.

## 3331 PENNSYLVANIA SOCIETY OF PUBLIC ACCOUNTANTS SCHOLARSHIPS

Pennsylvania Society of Public Accountants

Attn: Executive Office

20 Erford Road, Suite 200A

Lemoyne, PA 17043

Phone: (717) 234-4129; (800) 270-3352; Fax: (717) 234-9556;

Email: info@pspa-state.org

Web: www.pspa-state.org/scholarships.html

**Summary:** To provide financial assistance to accounting majors in Pennsylvania.

**Eligibility:** Open to Pennsylvania residents who have completed at least 3 semesters at a college or university in the state with a major in accounting and a GPA of 3.0 or higher. Selection is based primarily on academic merit. Student activities, leadership positions, and financial need may also be considered in the selection process.

**Financial data:** The stipend is $1,000 per year.

**Duration:** 1 year.

**Number awarded:** 3 each year.

**Deadline:** May of each year.

## 3332 PFIZER/UNCF CORPORATE SCHOLARS PROGRAM

**Summary:** To provide financial assistance and work experience to minority undergraduate and graduate students majoring in designated fields and interested in an internship at a Pfizer facility.

*See Listing #2609.*

## 3333 PFLAG SCHOLARSHIPS FOR SCIENCE, ENGINEERING, BUSINESS OR FINANCE

**Summary:** To provide financial assistance for college studies in selected fields to high school seniors and recent graduates who have a connection to Parents, Families and Friends of Lesbians and Gays (PFLAG).

*See Listing #2610.*

## 3334 PHI UPSILON OMICRON PAST PRESIDENT SCHOLARSHIP

Phi Upsilon Omicron

Attn: Educational Foundation

P.O. Box 329

Fairmont, WV 26555-0329

Phone: (304) 368-0612; Email: rickards@access.mountain.net

Web: www.phiu.unl.edu

**Summary:** To provide financial assistance to undergraduate student members of Phi Upsilon Omicron, a national honor society in family and consumer sciences.

**Eligibility:** Open to members of the society who are working on a bachelor's degree in family and consumer sciences or a related area. Selection is based on scholastic record, participation in society and other collegiate activities, a statement of professional aims and goals, professional services, and recommendations.

**Financial data:** The stipend is $1,000.

**Duration:** 1 year.

**Number awarded:** 1 each year.

**Deadline:** January of each year.

## 3335 PHIPPS MEMORIAL SCHOLARSHIP

General Federation of Women's Clubs of Connecticut

c/o Hamden Women's Club

Antoinette Antonucci, Co-President

26 Country Way

Wallingford, CT 06492

Phone: (203) 265-9407; Email: gfwcct@yahoo.com

Web: www.gfwcct.org

**Summary:** To provide financial assistance to women in Connecticut who are working on an undergraduate or graduate degree in education.

**Eligibility:** Open to female residents of Connecticut who have completed at least 2 years of college. Applicants must have a GPA of 3.0 or higher and be working on a bachelor's or master's degree in education.

**Financial data:** The stipend is $1,000.

**Duration:** 1 year.

**Number awarded:** 1 each year.

**Deadline:** February of each year.

## 3336 PICPA SOPHOMORE SCHOLARSHIPS

Pennsylvania Institute of Certified Public Accountants

Attn: Careers in Accounting Team

1650 Arch Street, 17th Floor

Philadelphia, PA 19103-2099

Phone: (215) 496-9272; (888) CPA-2001 (within PA); Fax: (215) 496-9212;

Email: schools@picpa.org

Web: www.cpazone.org/scholar/sophomor.asp

**Summary:** To provide financial assistance to Pennsylvania sophomores majoring in accounting.

**Eligibility:** Open to full-time sophomores at a 4-year college or university in Pennsylvania. They must be nominated by the accounting department chair at that school. Nominees are evaluated on the basis of academic record, SAT scores, intent to become a C.P.A. and practice in Pennsylvania, need, faculty recommendation, work ethic, reasons for career choice, qualities of leadership, and their resume.

**Financial data:** Stipends are $3,000, $1,500, or $1,000. This program includes the Joseph Taricani Memorial Scholarship, a onetime award of $1,000.

**Duration:** 1 year; most may be renewed for up to 2 additional years.

**Number awarded:** 18 each year: 5 at $3,000, 12 at $1,500, and 1 at $1,000.

**Deadline:** March of each year.

## 3337 PICPA STUDENT WRITING COMPETITION

Pennsylvania Institute of Certified Public Accountants

Attn: Careers in Accounting Team

1650 Arch Street, 17th Floor

Philadelphia, PA 19103-2099

Phone: (215) 496-9272; (888) CPA-2001 (within PA); Fax: (215) 496-9212;

Email: schools@picpa.org

Web: www.cpazone.org/contawrd/studwrit.asp

**Summary:** To recognize and reward outstanding essays written by students in Pennsylvania on an accounting topic that changes annually.

**Eligibility:** Open to 1) accounting and business majors at Pennsylvania colleges and universities, and 2) Pennsylvania residents who attend college out-of-state. Candidates are invited to submit an essay on an issue (changes annually) that affects the accounting profession. Recently, the topic was: "Being the Best in Business." Essays should be approximately 1,500 words and include a 50- to 75-word abstract. Selection is based on content, method of presentation, and writing style.

**Financial data:** First place is $2,000, second $1,200, and third $800. The top 3 schools receive, respectively, $1,000, $600, and $400. The first-place manuscript is published in the fall issue of the *Pennsylvania CPA Journal*.

**Duration:** The competition is held annually.

**Number awarded:** 3 each year.

**Deadline:** April of each year.

## 3338 PLANNING AND THE BLACK COMMUNITY DIVISION SCHOLARSHIP

American Planning Association

Attn: Planning and the Black Community Division

122 South Michigan Avenue, Suite 1600

Chicago, IL 60603-6107

Phone: (312) 431-9100; Fax: (312) 431-9985; Email: info_pbcd@planning.org

Web: www.planning.org/blackcommunity/scholarship.htm

**Summary:** To provide financial assistance to African American undergraduate students interested in majoring in planning or a related field.

**Eligibility:** Open to full-time African American undergraduate students entering their junior or senior year. Applicants must be majoring in planning or a related field (e.g., geography, environmental sciences, public administration, transportation, or urban studies) with a GPA of 3.0 or higher. They must submit a 2-page personal statement on the importance of urban planning to the African American community and how they see themselves making a contribution to the urban planning profession. U.S. citizenship is required.

**Financial data:** The stipend is $2,500.

**Duration:** 1 year.

**Number awarded:** 1 each year.

**Deadline:** October of each year.

## 3339 POST SCHOLARSHIP

**Summary:** To provide financial assistance to upper-division students majoring in airport management.

*See Listing #2621.*

## 3340 PRINCESS CRUISES AND PRINCESS TOURS SCHOLARSHIPS

American Society of Travel Agents
Attn: ASTA Foundation
1101 King Street, Suite 200
Alexandria, VA 22314-2944
Phone: (703) 739-2782; Fax: (703) 684-8319; Email: scholarship@astahq.com
Web: www.astanet.com/education/scholarshipf.asp

**Summary:** To provide financial assistance to college students interested in preparing for a career in the travel industry.

**Eligibility:** Open to students admitted to or enrolled in a travel and tourism program at a 2-year or 4-year college or university or proprietary trade school. They must provide a letter of recommendation, have a GPA of 2.5 or higher, be a U.S. or Canadian citizen or permanent resident, and write a 300-word essay on the 2 features cruise ships will need to offer passengers in the next 10 years.

**Financial data:** The stipend is $2,000.

**Duration:** 1 year.

**Number awarded:** 2 each year.

**Deadline:** July of each year.

## 3341 PROFILES IN COURAGE ESSAY CONTEST

John F. Kennedy Library Foundation
Attn: Profile in Courage Essay Contest
Columbia Point
Boston, MA 02125-3313
Phone: (617) 514-1550; Fax: (617) 436-3395;
Email: kennedy.foundation@nara.gov
Web: www.jfkcontest.org

**Summary:** To recognize and reward high school authors of essays on public officials who have demonstrated political courage.

**Eligibility:** Open to 1) U.S. students in grades 9-12 attending public, private, parochial, or home schools; 2) U.S. students under 20 years of age enrolled in a high school correspondence course in any of the 50 states, the District of Columbia, or the U.S. territories; and 3) U.S. citizens attending schools overseas. Applicants must submit an essay, up to 1,000 words, that identifies an elected public official in the United States, either serving currently or since 1956, who is acting or has acted courageously to address a political issue at the local, state, national, or international level. Selection is based on overall originality of the topic and clear communication of ideas through language.

**Financial data:** The first-place winner receives $3,000, the second-place winner receives $1,000, and the other finalists receive $500.

**Duration:** The awards are presented annually.

**Number awarded:** 7 each year: 1 first place, 1 second place, and 5 other finalists.

**Deadline:** January of each year.

## 3342 PROSTART NATIONAL CERTIFICATE OF ACHIEVEMENT SCHOLARSHIPS

National Restaurant Association Educational Foundation
Attn: Scholarships and Mentoring Initiative
175 West Jackson Boulevard, Suite 1500
Chicago, IL 60604-2702
Phone: (312) 715-5385; (800) 765-2122, ext. 385; Fax: (312) 566-9726;
Email: scholars@foodtrain.org
Web: www.nraef.org

**Summary:** To provide financial assistance for college to high school students who have earned a National Certificate of Achievement by participating in the ProStart program.

**Eligibility:** Open to high school juniors and seniors who have received the ProStart National Certificate of Achievement by participating in the HBA/ProStart School-to-Career Initiative. Applicants must have applied and gained acceptance to a food service related postsecondary program, either full time or substantial part time, and plan to enroll at least 2 terms during the school year. If funds are not available for every certificate holder, overall GPA is the deciding factor.

**Financial data:** The stipend is $2,000.

**Duration:** 1 year.

**Number awarded:** Varies each year.

**Deadline:** August of each year.

## 3343 PWC MINORITY SCHOLARS PROGRAM

PricewaterhouseCoopers LLP
Attn: Office of Diversity & WorkLife Quality
1177 Avenue of the Americas
New York, NY 10036
Phone: (646) 471-4000; Fax: (646) 471-3188
Web: www.pwcglobal.com

**Summary:** To provide financial assistance to underrepresented minority undergraduate students interested in preparing for a career in public accounting.

**Eligibility:** Open to African American, Native American, and Hispanic American students entering their sophomore or junior year of college. Applicants must have a GPA of 3.3 or higher, be able to demonstrate interpersonal skills and leadership ability, and intend to prepare for a career in public accounting (audit, tax, or forensic accounting). They must be attending one of the 31 colleges and universities that are part of the PricewaterhouseCoopers (PwC) Priority School Network and must be legally authorized to work in the United States. Finalists are interviewed in person by a PwC partner, manager or recruiter. Recipients also participate in the annual Minorities in Business Leadership Conference (held in New York City), are considered for an internship position with PwC, and engage in a mentoring program. This program began in 1990.

**Financial data:** The stipend is $3,000 per year.

**Duration:** 1 year; may be renewed if a GPA of 3.3 or higher is maintained.

**Number awarded:** 60 each year.

**Deadline:** January of each year.

## 3344 R. FLAKE SHAW SCHOLARSHIP PROGRAM

**Summary:** To provide financial assistance to North Carolina high school seniors interested in studying agriculture or home economics in college.

*See Listing #2633.*

## 3345 RALPH AND VALERIE THOMAS SCHOLARSHIP

National Association of Black Accountants
Attn: Director, Center for Advancement of Minority Accountants
7249-A Hanover Parkway
Greenbelt, MD 20770
Phone: (301) 474-NABA, ext. 114; Fax: (301) 474-3114;
Email: cquinn@nabainc.org
Web: www.nabainc.org/pages/Student_ScholarshipProgram.jsp

**Summary:** To provide financial assistance to student members of the National Association of Black Accountants (NABA) who are working on an undergraduate or graduate degree in a field related to accounting.

**Eligibility:** Open to NABA members who are members of ethnic minority groups enrolled full time as 1) an undergraduate freshman, sophomore, junior, or first-semester senior majoring in accounting, business, or finance; or 2) a graduate student working on a master's degree in accounting. Applicants must have a GPA of 3.5 or higher in their major and 3.3 or higher overall. Selection is based on grades, financial need, and a 500-word autobiography that discusses career objectives, leadership abilities, community activities, and involvement in NABA.

**Financial data:** The stipend is $1,000 per year.
**Duration:** 1 year.
**Number awarded:** 1 each year.
**Deadline:** December of each year.

## 3346 RAMA SCHOLARSHIP FOR THE AMERICAN DREAM

American Hotel & Lodging Educational Foundation
Attn: Manager of Foundation Programs
1201 New York Avenue, N.W., Suite 600
Washington, DC 20005-3931
Phone: (202) 289-3181; Fax: (202) 289-3199; Email: ahlef@ahlef.org
Web: www.ahlef.org/scholarships_rama.asp
**Summary:** To provide financial assistance to minority college students working on a degree in hotel management at designated schools.
**Eligibility:** Open to students attending one of 15 designated hospitality management schools. The schools select the recipients. Preference is given to students of Asian Indian descent and other minority groups and to JHM Hotel employees. The participating institutions are Bethune-Cookman College, California State Polytechnic University at Pomona, Cornell University, Florida International University, Georgia State University, Greenville Technical College, Howard University, Johnson & Wales University (Charleston, South Carolina), Johnson & Wales University (Providence, Rhode Island), Michigan State University, New York University, University of Central Florida, University of Houston, University of South Carolina, and Virginia Polytechnic Institute and State University. This program is funded by JHM Hotels, Inc.
**Financial data:** The stipend varies at each of the participating schools.
**Duration:** 1 year.
**Number awarded:** Varies each year; recently, 24 of these scholarships were awarded.

## 3347 RAY FOLEY MEMORIAL SCHOLARSHIP PROGRAM

American Wholesale Marketers Association
Attn: Distributors Education Foundation
2750 Prosperity Avenue, Suite 530
Fairfax, VA 22031
Phone: (703) 208-3358; (800) 482-2962; Fax: (703) 573-5738;
Email: info@awmanet.org
Web: www.awmanet.org/edu/edu-schol.html
**Summary:** To provide financial assistance to undergraduate or graduate students who are employed by or related to an employee of a member of the American Wholesale Marketers Association (AWMA) and working on a business-related degree.
**Eligibility:** Open to full-time undergraduate and graduate students working on a degree in a business course of study (accounting or business administration) at an accredited college or university. Applicants must be employed by an AWMA wholesaler distributor member or be an immediate family member (spouse, child, stepchild) of an employee of an AWMA wholesaler distributor member. They must be able to demonstrate interest in a career in distribution of candy, tobacco, and convenience products. Selection is based on academic merit and career interest in the candy/tobacco/convenience-products wholesale industry.
**Financial data:** The scholarships are $5,000 per year. Funds are paid directly to the college or university to cover tuition, on-campus room and board, and other direct costs; any remaining funds are paid to the student for reimbursement of school-related expenses, when appropriate receipts are available.
**Duration:** 1 year; nonrenewable.
**Number awarded:** 2 each year.
**Deadline:** May of each year.

## 3348 RAYMOND H. TROTT SCHOLARSHIP FOR BANKING

Rhode Island Foundation
Attn: Scholarship Coordinator
One Union Station
Providence, RI 02903
Phone: (401) 274-4564; Fax: (401) 751-7983; Email: libbym@rifoundation.org
Web: www.rifoundation.org
**Summary:** To provide financial assistance to Rhode Island undergraduates of color interested in preparing for a career in banking.

**Eligibility:** Open to minority residents of Rhode Island who are entering their senior year in college. Applicants must plan to prepare for a career in banking and be able to demonstrate financial need. Along with their application, they must submit an essay (up to 300 words) on the impact they would like to have on the banking industry.
**Financial data:** The stipend is $1,000.
**Duration:** 1 year; nonrenewable.
**Number awarded:** 1 each year.
**Deadline:** June of each year.

## 3349 RAYMOND ROBERT WHITE MEMORIAL SCHOLARSHIP

**Summary:** To provide financial assistance for college to members of the United Methodist Church who are interested in a church-related career.
*See Listing #1640.*

## 3350 RED OAK FOUNDATION SCHOLARSHIPS

University Interscholastic League
Attn: Texas Interscholastic League Foundation
1701 Manor Road
P.O. Box 8028
Austin, TX 78713
Phone: (512) 232-4938; Fax: (512) 471-5908;
Email: carolyn.scott@mail.utexas.edu
Web: www.uil.texas.edu/tilf/scholar.html
**Summary:** To provide financial assistance to students who participate in programs of the Texas Interscholastic League Foundation (TILF) and plan to teach in the public school system after graduating from college.
**Eligibility:** Open to students who meet the 5 basic requirements of the TILF: 1) graduate from high school during the current year and enroll at a 4-year public college or university in Texas (or Baylor University or Texas Wesleyan University) by the following fall; 2) enroll full time and maintain a GPA of 2.75 or higher during the first semester; 3) compete in a University Interscholastic League (UIL) academic state meet contest in accounting, calculator applications, computer applications, computer science, current issues and events, debate (cross-examination and Lincoln-Douglas), journalism (editorial writing, feature writing, headline writing, and news writing), literary criticism, mathematics, number sense, 1-act play, ready writing, science, social studies, speech (prose interpretation, poetry interpretation, informative speaking, and persuasive speaking), or spelling and vocabulary; 4) submit high school transcripts that include SAT and/or ACT scores; and 5) submit parents' latest income tax returns. Applicants for this scholarship must have declared their intention to teach grades K-12 in the public school system.
**Financial data:** The stipend is $1,200 per year.
**Duration:** 4 years.
**Number awarded:** 3 each year.
**Deadline:** May of each year.

## 3351 REDI-TAG CORPORATION SCHOLARSHIP

**Summary:** To provide financial assistance to members of the American Health Information Management Association (AHIMA) who are single parents interested in working on an undergraduate or graduate degree in health information administration or technology.
*See Listing #2642.*

## 3352 RENE CAMPBELL MEMORIAL SCHOLARSHIP

Tourism Cares for Tomorrow
Attn: Program Manager
585 Washington Street
Canton, MA 02021
Phone: (781) 821-5990; Fax: (781) 821-8949; Email: info@tourismcares.org
Web: www.tourismcares.org
**Summary:** To provide financial assistance to upper-division students from North Carolina who are majoring in tourism.
**Eligibility:** Open to residents of North Carolina entering their junior or senior year at an accredited 4-year college or university in the United States or Canada. Applicants must be working on a degree in a travel and tourism-related program and have a GPA of 3.0 or higher. Along with their application, they must submit a resume, a letter of recommendation, and a copy of their transcript. Financial need is not considered in the selection process.
**Financial data:** The stipend is $1,000.

**Duration:** 1 year.
**Number awarded:** 1 each year.
**Deadline:** March of each year.

### 3353 RIAHPERD SCHOLARSHIPS

**Summary:** To provide financial assistance for college to Rhode Island residents who are interested in preparing for a career in health education, physical education, recreation, or dance.
*See Listing #1647.*

### 3354 RICHARD B. COMBS HOSPITALITY SCHOLARSHIP

Connecticut Commission on Culture and Tourism
Attn: Tourism Division
505 Hudson Street, Second Floor
Hartford, CT 06106
Phone: (860) 270-8089; Fax: (860) 270-8077;
Email: joyce.fredericks@po.state.ct.us
Web: www.tourism.state.ct.us/tourism.asp
**Summary:** To provide financial assistance to undergraduate and graduate students from Connecticut who are preparing for a career in the hospitality industry.
**Eligibility:** Open to residents of Connecticut who are high school seniors, high school graduates who have not yet enrolled in college, or enrolled undergraduate or graduate students at an accredited college or university. Applicants must be preparing for a career in the hospitality industry. Along with their application, they must submit an essay on a topic about hospitality as it relates to Connecticut tourism, 2 letters of recommendation, a current transcript, a personal letter of intent explaining how this scholarship will help them to achieve their academic goals, and a personal resume. Selection is based on personal achievement and demonstrated interest in the hospitality industry.
**Financial data:** The stipend is $1,000.
**Duration:** 1 year.
**Number awarded:** 1 each year.
**Deadline:** September of each year.

### 3355 RICHARD G. MUNSELL/CPR SCHOLARSHIP

American Planning Association-California Chapter
Attn: California Planning Foundation
c/o Paul Wack
P.O. Box 886
San Luis Obispo, CA 93406
Phone: (805) 544-8282; Fax: (805) 544-8286; Email: pwack@calpoly.edu
Web: www.californiaplanningfoundation.org/scholarships.html
**Summary:** To provide financial assistance to undergraduate and graduate students in planning programs at California universities.
**Eligibility:** Open to students entering their final year for an undergraduate or master's degree in an accredited or non-accredited planning program at a university in California. Applicants must be interested in preparing for a career in public planning in California. Selection is based on academic excellence, financial need, and commitment to serve the planning profession in California. This program is sponsored by the California Planning Roundtable (CPR). The accredited planning programs are at 3 campuses of the California State University system (California State Polytechnic University at Pomona, California Polytechnic State University at San Luis Obispo, and San Jose State University), 3 campuses of the University of California (Berkeley, Irvine, and Los Angeles), and the University of Southern California. The non-accredited programs are at 5 campuses of the California State University system (San Francisco, Sonoma, Northridge, Chico, and San Diego) and 3 campuses of the University of California (Davis, Santa Barbara, and San Diego).
**Financial data:** The stipend is $1,000.
**Duration:** 1 year.
**Number awarded:** 3 each year: 1 to an undergraduate at an accredited program, 1 to a graduate student at an accredited program, and 1 to a student at a non-accredited program.
**Deadline:** April of each year.

### 3356 RICHARD L. DAVIS MANAGERS SCHOLARSHIP

**Summary:** To provide financial assistance to individuals currently employed in medical group management who wish to pursue professional development on the undergraduate or graduate level.
*See Listing #2650.*

### 3357 RICHARD L. DAVIS/BARBARA B. WATSON NATIONAL SCHOLARSHIP

**Summary:** To provide financial assistance to undergraduate and graduate students who are interested in preparing for a career in medical group management.
*See Listing #2651.*

### 3358 RICHARD P. COVERT, PH.D., FHIMSS SCHOLARSHIP

**Summary:** To provide financial assistance to student members of the Healthcare Information and Management Systems Society (HIMSS) who are working on an undergraduate or graduate degree in management engineering.
*See Listing #2652.*

### 3359 RITA LOWE COLLEGE SCHOLARSHIPS

**Summary:** To provide financial assistance to students majoring in mathematics education at colleges and universities in Washington.
*See Listing #2654.*

### 3360 RITA LOWE HIGH SCHOOL SCHOLARSHIP

**Summary:** To provide financial assistance to high school seniors in Washington planning to major in mathematics education at a college or university in the state.
*See Listing #2655.*

### 3361 RITCHIE-JENNINGS MEMORIAL SCHOLARSHIPS PROGRAM

Association of Certified Fraud Examiners
Attn: Scholarship Program
The Gregor Building
716 West Avenue
Austin, TX 78701-2727
Phone: (512) 478-9070; (800) 245-3321; Fax: (512) 478-9297;
Email: scholarships@cfenet.com
Web: www.cfenet.com/services/scholarships.asp
**Summary:** To provide financial assistance to undergraduate and graduate students working on an accounting or criminal justice degree.
**Eligibility:** Open to students working full time on an undergraduate or graduate degree in accounting or criminal justice. Applicants must submit a short essay on why they deserve the award and how fraud awareness will affect their professional career development. Selection is based on the essay, academic achievement, and several letters of recommendation (including at least 1 from a certified fraud examiner).
**Financial data:** The stipend is $1,000.
**Duration:** 1 year.
**Number awarded:** 15 each year.
**Deadline:** May of each year.

### 3362 RMEL FOUNDATION SCHOLARSHIPS

**Summary:** To provide financial assistance to students sponsored by a member of the Rocky Mountain Electrical League (RMEL) who wish to study selected fields in college in order to prepare for a career in the electric energy industry.
*See Listing #2656.*

### 3363 ROBERT R. COLY PRIZE

Parapsychology Foundation, Inc.
Attn: Executive Director
P.O. Box 1562
New York, NY 10021-0043
Phone: (212) 628-1550; Fax: (212) 628-1559; Email: info@parapsychology.org
Web: www.parapsychology.org
**Summary:** To recognize and reward undergraduate or graduate students who submit outstanding papers on parapsychology.
**Eligibility:** Open to undergraduate and graduate students who submit an essay of 1,000 to 1,500 words on the topic, "The Challenge of Parapsychology." Applicants may be studying in any field, but they must have sufficient interest in the field of parapsychology to understand its complexities and to demonstrate a desire to help conceptualize its future. They may be attending school

in any country, but the essay, application form, and letters of reference must be written in English.
**Financial data:** The award is $1,000.
**Duration:** 1 year.
**Number awarded:** 1 each year.
**Deadline:** November of each year.

## 3364 ROBERT R. ROBINSON SCHOLARSHIP

Michigan Townships Association
Attn: Robert R. Robinson Memorial Scholarship Fund
512 Westshire Drive
P.O. Box 80078
Lansing, MI 48908-0078
Phone: (517) 321-6467; Fax: (517) 321-8908; Email: debra@michigantownships.org
Web: www.michigantownships.org/scholarship.htm
**Summary:** To provide financial assistance to undergraduate and graduate students majoring in fields related to public administration at a college or university in Michigan.
**Eligibility:** Open to juniors, seniors, and graduate students enrolled in a Michigan college or university and majoring in public administration, public affairs management, or some other field closely related to local government administration. Applicants must be considering a career in local government administration. They must submit a letter of recommendation from a professor or instructor, a copy of a resolution of support from a Michigan township board (resolutions from other types of entities or from individual public officials are not sufficient), and a short essay on an important issue facing local government. Selection is based on academic achievement, community involvement, and commitment to a career in local government administration.
**Financial data:** Stipends range from $500 to $1,000.
**Duration:** 1 year.
**Number awarded:** 1 or more each year.
**Deadline:** May of each year.

## 3365 ROGER BUCHHOLZ MEMORIAL SCHOLARSHIPS

Wisconsin Institute of Certified Public Accountants
Attn: WICPA Educational Foundation
235 North Executive Drive, Suite 200
P.O. Box 1010
Brookfield, WI 53008-1010
Phone: (414) 785-0445; (800) 772-6939 (within WI and MN); Fax: (414) 785-0838; Email: Tammy@wicpa.org
Web: www.wicpa.org/Student_Teacher/scholarships.htm
**Summary:** To provide financial assistance to college juniors in Wisconsin working on a degree in finance.
**Eligibility:** Open to juniors majoring in finance at designated universities in Wisconsin. Applicants must submit an essay describing their career objectives.
**Financial data:** The stipend is $2,500 per year.
**Duration:** 1 year.
**Number awarded:** Varies each year; recently, 2 of these scholarships were awarded.
**Deadline:** February of each year.

## 3366 ROLLIE HOPGOOD FUTURE TEACHERS SCHOLARSHIP

Michigan Federation of Teachers & School Related Personnel
Attn: Scholarship Committee
2661 East Jefferson Avenue
Detroit, MI 48207
Phone: (313) 393-2200; (800) MFT-8868; Fax: (313) 393-2236
Web: www.mftsrp.org/scholarships.html
**Summary:** To provide financial assistance to high school seniors in Michigan who are interested in becoming a teacher.
**Eligibility:** Open to seniors graduating from high schools that are represented by the Michigan Federation of Teachers & School Related Personnel (MFT&SRP). Applicants must submit a 500-word essay in which they explain why they want to become a teacher and why they should be considered for this scholarship. Selection is based on the essay, GPA, extracurricular activities, community-related activities, and financial need. Female and male applicants compete separately. Recipients must enroll as full-time students.
**Financial data:** The stipend is $1,000.

**Duration:** 1 year.
**Number awarded:** 2 each year: 1 female and 1 male.
**Deadline:** April of each year.

## 3367 ROY & HARRIET ROBINSON SCHOLARSHIP

Professional Independent Insurance Agents of Illinois
Attn: College Scholarship Program
4360 Wabash Avenue
Springfield, IL 62707
Phone: (217) 793-6660; (800) 628-6436; Fax: (217) 793-6744; Email: admin@piiai.org
Web: www.piiai.org/youngagents/scholarship.htm
**Summary:** To provide financial assistance to upper-division students from Illinois who are majoring in business and have an interest in insurance.
**Eligibility:** Open to residents of Illinois who are full-time juniors or seniors in college. Applicants must be enrolled in a business degree program with an interest in insurance. They must have a letter of recommendation from a current or retired member of the Professional Independent Insurance Agents of Illinois. Along with their application, they must submit an essay (500 words or less) on the contribution the insurance industry makes to society. Financial need is not considered in the selection process.
**Financial data:** The stipend is $1,000, payable in 2 equal installments. Funds are paid directly to the recipient's school.
**Duration:** 1 year.
**Number awarded:** 1 each year.
**Deadline:** June of each year.

## 3368 ROYCE R. WATTS SR. SCHOLARSHIP

**Summary:** To provide financial assistance to upper-division college students interested in health, civil rights, or administration.
*See Listing #2674.*

## 3369 RUDOLPH DILLMAN MEMORIAL SCHOLARSHIP

**Summary:** To provide financial assistance to legally blind undergraduate or graduate students studying in the field of rehabilitation and/or education of visually impaired and blind persons.
*See Listing #2676.*

## 3370 RUSS CASEY SCHOLARSHIPS

Maine Restaurant Association
Attn: Chair, Scholarship Committee
5 Wade Street
P.O. Box 5060
Augusta, ME 04332-5060
Phone: (207) 623-2178; Fax: (207) 623-8377;
Email: info@mainerestaurant.com
Web: www.mainerestaurant.com/scholarships.html
**Summary:** To provide financial assistance for college to Maine residents who are interested in preparing for a career in the food service industry.
**Eligibility:** Open to residents of Maine who are attending or planning to attend an institution of higher education to study culinary arts or restaurant, hotel, or hospitality management. Preference is given to applicants planning to enter the food service industry and to students at educational institutions in Maine. Selection is based on academic achievement, work experience, career interests, financial need, and relationship to the Maine Restaurant Association.
**Financial data:** The stipend is $1,000.
**Duration:** 1 year; nonrenewable.
**Number awarded:** 3 each year.
**Deadline:** March of each year.

## 3371 SAKAE TAKAHASHI SCHOLARSHIP

100th Infantry Battalion Veterans Club
Attn: Scholarship Committee
520 Kamoku Street
Honolulu, HI 96826
Phone: (808) 732-5216; Email: daisyy@hgea.net
Web: emedia.leeward.hawaii.edu/mnakano
**Summary:** To provide financial assistance to high school seniors and college

students who major in business, political science, or law and exemplify the sponsor's motto of "Continuing Service."

**Eligibility:** Open to high school seniors planning to attend an institution of higher learning and full-time undergraduate students at community colleges, vocational/trade schools, 4-year colleges, and universities. Applicants must have a GPA of 2.5 or higher and be able to demonstrate civic responsibility and community service. They must be majoring or planning to major in business, political science, or law. Along with their application, they must submit a 4-page on the characteristics of positive leaders and the ways in which they are an extraordinary leader. Selection is based on that essay and the applicant's demonstration that he or she can effectively promote the legacy of the 100th Infantry Battalion and its motto of "Continuing Service." Financial need is not considered.

**Financial data:** The stipend is $1,000.

**Duration:** 1 year; nonrenewable.

**Number awarded:** 1 each year.

**Deadline:** April of each year.

## 3372 SALLIE MAE FUND FIRST IN MY FAMILY SCHOLARSHIP PROGRAM

**Summary:** To provide financial assistance to Hispanic American undergraduate students who are the first in their family to attend college and are majoring in business, computer science, or engineering.

*See Listing #2681.*

## 3373 SALLY S. JACOBSEN SCHOLARSHIP

National Federation of the Blind
c/o Peggy Elliott, Scholarship Committee Chair
805 Fifth Avenue
Grinnell, IA 50112
Phone: (641) 236-3366
Web: www.nfb.org/sch_intro.htm

**Summary:** To provide financial assistance to blind undergraduate and graduate students working on a degree in the field of education, especially those planning to major in education of disabled youth.

**Eligibility:** Open to legally blind students who are working on or planning to work full time on an undergraduate or graduate degree in education. Preference is given to applicants planning to specialize in education of disabled youth. Selection is based on academic excellence, service to the community, and financial need.

**Financial data:** The stipend is $5,000. Scholarships are awarded at the federation convention in July. Recipients attend the convention at federation expense; that funding is in addition to the scholarship grant.

**Duration:** 1 year; recipients may resubmit applications up to 2 additional years.

**Number awarded:** 1 each year.

**Deadline:** March of each year.

## 3374 SAM PINE SCHOLARSHIP

**Summary:** To provide financial assistance to undergraduate students in planning or architecture at schools in New England and New York.

*See Listing #1659.*

## 3375 SAN ANTONIO CHAPTER NAWIC SCHOLARSHIP

**Summary:** To provide financial assistance to students in Texas working on an undergraduate degree in a construction-related field.

*See Listing #1661.*

## 3376 SCHOLARSHIPS FOR MINORITY ACCOUNTING STUDENTS

American Institute of Certified Public Accountants
Attn: Academic and Career Development Division
1211 Avenue of the Americas
New York, NY 10036-8775
Phone: (212) 596-6223; Fax: (212) 596-6292; Email: educat@aicpa.org
Web: www.aicpa.org/members/div/career/mini/smas.htm

**Summary:** To provide financial assistance to underrepresented minorities interested in studying accounting at the undergraduate or graduate school level.

**Eligibility:** Open to minority undergraduates who are enrolled full time, have completed at least 30 semester hours of college work (including at least 6 semester hours in accounting), are majoring in accounting with an overall GPA of 3.3 or higher, and are U.S. citizens or permanent residents. Minority students who are interested in a graduate degree must be 1) in the final year of a 5-year accounting program; 2) an undergraduate accounting major currently accepted or enrolled in a master's-level accounting, business administration, finance, or taxation program; or 3) any undergraduate major currently accepted in a master's-level accounting program. Selection is based primarily on merit (academic and personal achievement); financial need is evaluated as a secondary criteria. For purposes of this program, the American Institute of Certified Public Accountants (AICPA) considers minority students to be those of Black, Native American/Alaskan Native, Pacific Island, or Hispanic ethnic origin.

**Financial data:** The maximum stipend is $5,000 per year.

**Duration:** 1 year; may be renewed, if recipients are making satisfactory progress toward graduation.

**Number awarded:** Varies each year; recently, 157 students received funding through this program.

**Deadline:** May of each year.

## 3377 SCHOLARSHIPS IN MATHEMATICS EDUCATION

**Summary:** To provide financial assistance to undergraduate students in Illinois who are interested in preparing for a career as a mathematics teacher.

*See Listing #2687.*

## 3378 SCIENCE TEACHER PREPARATION PROGRAM

**Summary:** To provide financial assistance to underrepresented minority students at designated institutions in Alabama who are interested in preparing for a career as a science teacher.

*See Listing #2689.*

## 3379 SCUDDER ASSOCIATION EDUCATIONAL GRANTS

**Summary:** To assist undergraduate and graduate students preparing for "careers as servants of God in various forms of ministry to men and women around the world."

*See Listing #1667.*

## 3380 SDAPHCC EDUCATIONAL FOUNDATION SCHOLARSHIPS

**Summary:** To provide financial assistance for college to high school seniors and college freshmen in South Dakota who are preparing for a career in plumbing, heating and cooling, construction, or business management.

*See Listing #2694.*

## 3381 SEATTLE CHAPTER SCHOLARSHIPS

American Society of Women Accountants-Seattle Chapter
c/o Anne Macnab
800 Fifth Avenue, Suite 101
Seattle, WA 98104-3191
Email: scholarship@aswaseattle.com
Web: www.aswaseattle.com/scholarships.htm

**Summary:** To provide financial assistance to students working on a bachelor's or master's degree in accounting at a college or university in Washington.

**Eligibility:** Open to part-time and full-time students working on an associate's, bachelor's, or master's degree in accounting at a college or university in Washington. Applicants must have completed at least 30 semester hours and have maintained a GPA of at least 2.5 overall and 3.0 in accounting. Membership in the American Society of Women Accountants is not required. Selection is based on career goals, communication skills, GPA, personal circumstances, and financial need.

**Financial data:** The amounts of the awards vary. Recently, a total of $12,000 was available for this program. Funds are paid directly to the recipient's school.

**Duration:** 1 year.

**Number awarded:** April of each year.

**Deadline:** Varies each year.

## 3382 SENTRY INSURANCE FOUNDATION SCHOLARSHIPS

**Summary:** To provide financial assistance to students majoring in selected fields at member institutions of the Wisconsin Foundation for Independent Colleges (WFIC).
*See Listing #1671.*

## 3383 SHARON D. BANKS MEMORIAL UNDERGRADUATE SCHOLARSHIP

**Summary:** To provide financial assistance to undergraduate women interested in a career in transportation.
*See Listing #2701.*

## 3384 SHERYL A. HORAK LAW ENFORCEMENT EXPLORER MEMORIAL SCHOLARSHIP

Boy Scouts of America
Attn: Learning for Life Division, S210
1325 West Walnut Hill Lane
P.O. Box 152079
Irving, TX 75015-2079
Phone: (972) 580-2418; Fax: (972) 580-2137
Web: www.learning-for-life.org/exploring/scholarships/index.html
**Summary:** To provide financial assistance for college to Explorer Scouts who plan a career as a law enforcement executive.
**Eligibility:** Open to Explorer Scouts who are at least seniors in high school. Selection is based on academic record, leadership ability, extracurricular activities, and a personal statement on "Why I want to pursue a career in law enforcement." Applicants must be active members of a Law Enforcement Explorer post registered with Boy Scouts of America.
**Financial data:** The stipend is $1,000.
**Duration:** 1 year; nonrenewable.
**Number awarded:** Varies each year, depending on the availability of funds.
**Deadline:** March of each year.

## 3385 SHRM FOUNDATION UNDERGRADUATE SCHOLARSHIPS

Society for Human Resource Management
Attn: Foundation Administrator
1800 Duke Street
Alexandria, VA 22314-3499
Phone: (703) 535-6020; (800) 283-SHRM; Fax: (703) 535-6490; TDD: (703) 548-6999; Email: speyton@shrm.org
Web: www.shrm.org/students/ags_published
**Summary:** To provide financial assistance for college to undergraduate student members of the Society for Human Resource Management (SHRM).
**Eligibility:** Open to undergraduate student members of the society. Applicants must have completed at least 55 semester hours of course work in a human relations major or human relations emphasis area (including at least one human relations management course) and have an overall GPA of 3.0 or higher.
**Financial data:** The stipend is $2,500.
**Duration:** 1 year.
**Number awarded:** 2 each year.
**Deadline:** October of each year.

## 3386 SIGMA IOTA EPSILON UNDERGRADUATE SCHOLARSHIPS

Sigma Iota Epsilon
c/o Colorado State University
Management Department
324 Rockwell Hall
Fort Collins, CO 80523-1275
Phone: (970) 491-7200; Fax: (970) 491-3522;
Email: brenda.ogden@colostate.edu
Web: www.sienational.com
**Summary:** To provide financial assistance to undergraduate student members of Sigma Iota Epsilon (SIE), the national honorary and professional management fraternity.
**Eligibility:** Open to active undergraduate student members. Applicants must submit a brief description of their career objectives. Selection is based on scholastic, fraternity, and other extracurricular achievements.

**Financial data:** Stipends are $1,000 or $500.
**Number awarded:** Each year, 5 scholarships for $1,000 are awarded; the number of $500 awards varies each year, but has been 2 in recent years.
**Deadline:** May of each year.

## 3387 SOCIETY OF ACTUARIES SCHOLARSHIPS FOR MINORITY STUDENTS

Society of Actuaries
Attn: Minority Scholarship Coordinator
475 North Martingale Road, Suite 800
Schaumburg, IL 60173-2226
Phone: (847) 706-3509; Fax: (847) 706-3599; Email: cleathe@soa.org
Web: www.beanactuary.org/minority/scholarship.cfm
**Summary:** To provide financial assistance to underrepresented minority undergraduate students who are interested in preparing for an actuarial career.
**Eligibility:** Open to African Americans, Hispanics, and Native North Americans who are Canadian or U.S. citizens or have a permanent resident visa. Before applying for this program, students should have taken either the SAT or the ACT. Applicants must be admitted to a college or university offering either a program in actuarial science or courses that will prepare them for an actuarial career. Selection is based on financial need, academic achievement, demonstrated mathematical ability, and understanding of and interest in an actuarial career.
**Financial data:** The amount of the award depends on the need and merit of the recipient. There is no limit to the size of the scholarship. Recipients are awarded an additional $500 for each actuarial examination they have passed.
**Duration:** 1 year; may be renewed.
**Number awarded:** There is no limit to the number of scholarships awarded.
**Deadline:** April of each year.

## 3388 SOCIETY OF AUTOMOTIVE ANALYSTS SCHOLARSHIP

Society of Automotive Analysts, Attn: Scholarships
3300 Washtenaw Avenue, Suite 220
Ann Arbor, MI 48104-4200
Phone: (734) 677-3518; Fax: (734) 677-2407; Email: cybersaa@cybersaa.org
Web: www.cybersaa.org/scholarship_info.html
**Summary:** To provide financial assistance to undergraduate students preparing for a career in an analytic field related to the automotive industry.
**Eligibility:** Open to full-time undergraduate students who are majoring in business, economics, finance, marketing, or management. Applicants must have at least a 3.0 GPA and demonstrate interest in automotive analysis. Along with their application, they must submit a 1-page essay explaining their interest in the automotive industry and 1 letter of reference.
**Financial data:** The stipend is $1,500. Funds are paid to the recipient's school.
**Duration:** 1 year; nonrenewable.
**Number awarded:** 1 or more each year.
**Deadline:** May of each year.

## 3389 SOUTH CAROLINA ALLIANCE OF BLACK SCHOOL EDUCATORS SCHOLARSHIPS

South Carolina Alliance of Black School Educators
Attn: Executive Director
P.O. Box 11737
Columbia, SC 29211
Phone: (803) 786-6478; Fax: (803) 735-1159; Email: jrobin2000@msn.com
Web: www.scabse.com
**Summary:** To provide financial assistance to residents of South Carolina, especially minorities, interested in preparing for a career as a classroom teacher.
**Eligibility:** Open to residents of South Carolina who are high school seniors or college undergraduates planning to attend or attending a college or university in the state. Applicants must be majoring, or planning to major, in education and become a classroom teacher in the state. They should be able to help meet a goal of the program to increase the number of ethnic minorities in South Carolina classrooms. Along with their application, they must submit 1-page essays on 1) what they hope their colleagues and former students will say about them at the close of their career, and 2) the approaches they will take to honor the diversity of the students in their classes. Selection is based on scholarship (20%); school, community, and employment activities (20%); written expression and commitment (40%); and recommendations (20%). This program parallels the goals of the South Carolina Center for Educator Recruitment, Retention, and Advancement (CERRA), which administers this program. Information is also

available from CERRA, Stewart House at Winthop University, Rock Hill, SC 29733, (803) 323-4032, Fax: (803) 323-4044.

**Financial data:** The stipend is $1,000.

**Duration:** 1 year.

**Number awarded:** 4 each year.

**Deadline:** March of each year.

---

### 3390 SOUTH CAROLINA ASSOCIATION OF CPA'S SCHOLARSHIP PROGRAM

South Carolina Association of Certified Public Accountants
Attn: Educational Fund, Inc.
570 Chris Drive
West Columbia, SC 29169
Phone: (803) 791-4181; (888) 557-4814; Fax: (803) 791-4196
Web: www.scacpa.org

**Summary:** To provide financial assistance to upper-division and graduate students majoring in accounting in South Carolina.

**Eligibility:** Open to South Carolina residents who are majoring in accounting at a college or university in the state. Applicants must be juniors, seniors, or graduate students with a GPA of 3.25 or higher overall and 3.5 or higher in accounting. They must submit their college transcripts, a listing of awards and other scholarships, 2 letters of reference, a resume, a 250-word essay on their personal career goals, and certification of their accounting major. Financial need is not considered in the selection process.

**Financial data:** Stipends range from $500 to $1,500. Funds are paid to the recipient's school.

**Duration:** 1 year.

**Number awarded:** Varies each year.

**Deadline:** June of each year.

---

### 3391 SOUTH DAKOTA CPA SOCIETY SCHOLARSHIPS

South Dakota CPA Society
Attn: Executive Director
1000 North West Avenue, Suite 100
P.O. Box 1798
Sioux Falls, SD 57101-1798
Phone: (605) 334-3848; Fax: (605) 334-8595; Email: lcoome@iw.net
Web: www.sdcpa.org

**Summary:** To provide financial assistance to upper-division students in South Dakota who are majoring in accounting.

**Eligibility:** Open to accounting majors in South Dakota who have completed at least 90 credit hours. Applicants must have an excellent academic record, leadership potential, an interest in the profession of public accountancy, and a record of extracurricular activities. They must submit a completed application form, an official transcript, a brief statement of career goals and objectives, a list of awards and extracurricular activities, and information on work experience. Financial need is not considered in the selection process.

**Financial data:** The amount of the awards depends on the availability of funds and the number of qualified applicants.

**Duration:** 1 year; recipients may reapply.

**Number awarded:** Varies each year; recently, 9 accounting students received $6,250 in these scholarships.

**Deadline:** April of each year.

---

### 3392 SOUTH DAKOTA RETAILERS ASSOCIATION SCHOLARSHIPS

South Dakota Retailers Association
P.O. Box 638
Pierre, SD 57501
Phone: (605) 224-5050; (800) 658-5545; Fax: (605) 224-2059;
Email: dleslie@sdra.org
Web: www.sdra.org

**Summary:** To provide financial assistance to South Dakota residents who are interested in preparing for a career in retailing.

**Eligibility:** Open to residents of South Dakota who are interested in a career in a retail field. Examples of eligible fields include, but are not limited to, agribusiness, apparel merchandising, auto mechanics, automotive technology, business administration, business management, computer science, culinary arts, commercial baking, diesel mechanics, electrical maintenance, heating and ventilation, hotel and restaurant management, landscape design, pharmacy, printing industries, refrigeration, sales and marketing management, and tourism indus-

try management. Applicants must have graduated from a South Dakota high school or be enrolled in a vocational school, college, or university in the state. Full-time enrollment is required. Selection is not based solely on financial need or on outstanding scholarship.

**Financial data:** Stipends range from $500 to $1,000.

**Duration:** 1 year.

**Number awarded:** Varies each year; recently, 6 of these scholarships were awarded.

**Deadline:** March of each year.

---

### 3393 SOUTHERN CALIFORNIA CHAPTER/PLEASANT HAWAIIAN HOLIDAYS SCHOLARSHIP

American Society of Travel Agents
Attn: ASTA Foundation
1101 King Street, Suite 200
Alexandria, VA 22314-2944
Phone: (703) 739-2782; Fax: (703) 684-8319; Email: scholarship@astahq.com
Web: www.astanet.com/education/scholarshipe.asp

**Summary:** To provide financial assistance to college students interested in preparing for a career in the travel industry.

**Eligibility:** Open to U.S. citizens who have a GPA of 2.5 or higher, are attending a 4-year college or university either in southern California (Los Angeles, Kern, Riverside, San Bernardino, San Luis Obispo, Santa Barbara, and Ventura counties) or anywhere in the United States, and are working on a travel and tourism degree. They must submit a 500-word essay on "My goals in the travel industry."

**Financial data:** The stipend is $2,500.

**Duration:** 1 year.

**Number awarded:** 2 each year: 1 for students attending school in the southern California chapter area and 1 for applicants attending school anywhere in the United States.

**Deadline:** July of each year.

---

### 3394 SOUTHWEST CHAPTER ACADEMIC SCHOLARSHIPS

**Summary:** To provide financial assistance to students working on an undergraduate or graduate degree in airport management at a college or university in the Southwest.

*See Listing #2724.*

---

### 3395 SPENCE REESE SCHOLARSHIPS

**Summary:** To provide financial assistance to graduating male high school seniors who plan to study designated fields in college.

*See Listing #2725.*

---

### 3396 SPIRIT OF SOVEREIGNTY SCHOLARSHIPS

National Indian Gaming Association
Attn: Spirit of Sovereignty Foundation
224 Second Street, S.E.
Washington, DC 20003
Phone: (480) 820-2464; Email: info@spiritfund.com
Web: www.spiritfund.com/student.htm

**Summary:** To provide financial assistance to Native American upper-division and graduate students who are working on a degree in a business-related field.

**Eligibility:** Open to college juniors, seniors, and graduate students who are working on a degree in business or a related field (e.g., hotel management, information systems, computer science, economics, human resources). Applicants must submit a copy of their Certificate of Degree of Indian Blood (CDIB), current transcript, 2 letters of recommendation, and a 250-word essay that describes their extracurricular activities related to involvement of American Indian programs at their institution, volunteer and community work related to American Indian communities, potential for future interaction and support to Indian communities, tribal and community involvement, and potential to give strong representation to the American Indian community to non-Native constituents.

**Financial data:** A stipend is awarded (amount not specified).

**Duration:** 1 year.

**Number awarded:** 1 or more each year.

**Deadline:** February of each year.

## 3397 STAN AND LEONE POLLARD SCHOLARSHIPS

American Society of Travel Agents
Attn: ASTA Foundation
1101 King Street, Suite 200
Alexandria, VA 22314-2944
Phone: (703) 739-2782; Fax: (703) 684-8319; Email: scholarship@astahq.com
Web: www.astanet.com/education/scholarshipg.asp
**Summary:** To provide financial assistance to individuals attempting to reenter the job market by enrolling in a travel and tourism program at a junior college or travel school.
**Eligibility:** Open to students who are registered at a recognized proprietary travel school or 2-year junior college that specializes in travel or tourism studies. Applicants must be reentering the job market, have been out of high school for at least 5 years, have a GPA of 2.5 or higher, and write a 500-word essay on their objectives in the travel and tourism industry.
**Financial data:** The stipend is $2,000. A copy of the tuition bill is required.
**Duration:** 1 year.
**Number awarded:** 2 each year: 1 to a summer applicant and 1 to a winter applicant.
**Deadline:** August or December of each year.

## 3398 STEVE DEARDUFF SCHOLARSHIP

**Summary:** To provide financial assistance to Georgia residents who are working on an undergraduate or graduate degree, especially in medicine or social work.
*See Listing #2732.*

## 3399 STUART CAMERON AND MARGARET MCLEOD MEMORIAL SCHOLARSHIP

Institute of Management Accountants
Attn: Committee on Students
10 Paragon Drive
Montvale, NJ 07645-1718
Phone: (201) 573-9000; (800) 638-4427, ext. 1543; Fax: (201) 474-1600;
Email: students@imanet.org
Web: www.imanet.org
**Summary:** To provide financial assistance to undergraduate or graduate student members of the Institute of Management Accountants (IMA) who are interested in preparing for a career in management accounting or financial management.
**Eligibility:** Open to undergraduate and graduate student IMA members who have a GPA of 2.8 or higher. Applicants must be preparing for a career in management accounting, financial management, or information technology. They must submit a 2-page statement on their reasons for applying for the scholarship, reasons that they deserve the award, specific contributions to the IMA, ideas on how they will promote awareness and increase membership and certification within IMA, and their career goals and objectives. Selection is based on that statement, academic merit, IMA participation, the quality of the presentation, a resume, and letters of recommendation.
**Financial data:** The stipend is $5,000.
**Duration:** 1 year. The recipient is required to participate in the parent chapter, at the council level, or at the national level.
**Number awarded:** 1 each year.
**Deadline:** February of each year.

## 3400 SWACKHAMER PEACE ESSAY CONTEST

Nuclear Age Peace Foundation
1187 Coast Village Road, Suite 1
PMB 121
Santa Barbara, CA 93108-2794
Phone: (805) 965-3443; Fax: (805) 568-0466; Email: wagingpeace@napf.org
Web: www.wagingpeace.org
**Summary:** To recognize and reward outstanding essays by high school students on a topic related to war and peace.
**Eligibility:** Open to high school students throughout the world. They may enter this contest by writing an essay, up to 1,500 words, on a topic that changes annually but calls for constructive approaches to the problems of war and peace. Recently, students were invited to write on the following topic: "If you were invited to give a nationally televised speech to the American people, including the President and the Congress, what would you say to convince them that the United States should take a leadership role in the global elimination of nuclear weapons?" Essays are judged on the basis of knowledge and analysis of subject matter, originality of ideas, development of point of view, insight, clarity of expression, organization, and grammar. Essays become the property of the Nuclear Age Peace Foundation. The prizewinning essay is published by the foundation and sent to the Secretary-General of the United Nations, the President of the United States, and other world and national leaders.
**Financial data:** First prize is $1,500, second $1,000, and third $500.
**Duration:** The competition is held annually.
**Number awarded:** 3 prizes are awarded each year.
**Deadline:** May of each year.

## 3401 SYSCO SCHOLARSHIP AWARD

Hispanic Association of Colleges and Universities
Attn: National Scholarship Program
One Dupont Circle, N.W. Suite 605
Washington, DC 20036
Phone: (202) 467-0893; Fax: (202) 496-9177; TTY: (800) 855-2880;
Email: scholarships@hacu.net
Web: scholarships.hacu.net/applications/applicants
**Summary:** To provide financial assistance to undergraduate students at member institutions of the Hispanic Association of Colleges and Universities (HACU) who are majoring in food service or business.
**Eligibility:** Open to undergraduate students at HACU member and partner colleges and universities who have a declared major in either food service and hospitality or business with an emphasis on distribution and sales. Applicants must have a GPA of 3.0 or higher and be able to demonstrate financial need. They must submit an essay of 200 to 250 words that describes their academic and/or career goals, where they expect to be and what they expect to be doing 10 years from now, and what skills they can bring to an employer.
**Financial data:** The stipend is $2,000.
**Duration:** 1 year.
**Number awarded:** 1 or more each year.
**Deadline:** May of each year.

## 3402 TDC SCHOLARSHIP

National Association of Black Accountants
Attn: Director, Center for Advancement of Minority Accountants
7249-A Hanover Parkway
Greenbelt, MD 20770
Phone: (301) 474-NABA, ext. 114; Fax: (301) 474-3114;
Email: cquinn@nabainc.org
Web: www.nabainc.org/pages/Student_ScholarshipProgram.jsp
**Summary:** To provide financial assistance to student members of the National Association of Black Accountants (NABA) who are working on an undergraduate or graduate degree in a field related to accounting.
**Eligibility:** Open to NABA members who are members of ethnic minority groups enrolled full time as 1) an undergraduate freshman, sophomore, junior, or first-semester senior majoring in accounting, business, or finance; or 2) a graduate student working on a master's degree in accounting. Applicants must have a GPA of 2.0 or higher in their major and 2.5 or higher overall. Selection is based on grades, financial need, and a 500-word autobiography that discusses career objectives, leadership abilities, community activities, and involvement in NABA.
**Financial data:** The stipend is $1,000 per year.
**Duration:** 1 year.
**Number awarded:** 1 each year.
**Deadline:** December of each year.

## 3403 TENNESSEE FUNERAL DIRECTORS ASSOCIATION MEMORIAL SCHOLARSHIP PROGRAM

Tennessee Funeral Directors Association
Attn: Scholarship Committee
1616 Church Street
Nashville, TN 37203
Phone: (615) 321-8792; (800) 537-1599 (within TN); Fax: (615) 321-8794;
Email: tnfuneral@xspedius.net
Web: www.tnfda.org
**Summary:** To provide financial assistance to Tennessee residents who are preparing for a career in funeral service.
**Eligibility:** Open to applicants who are U.S. citizens, are Tennessee residents, are enrolled in school on a full-time basis and have finished with 2 semesters or

one half of their course of study at a college accredited by the American Board of Funeral Service Education. They must have expressed the intent to enter funeral service upon graduation. As part of the application process, students must submit a completed application form, the latest family federal income tax return, college transcripts, 2 letters of recommendation, and a 2-page hand-written essay about themselves. Selection is based on financial need, academic record, recommendations, extracurricular and community activities, and the required essay.

**Financial data:** The stipend is $1,000.

**Duration:** 1 year.

**Number awarded:** 2 each year.

### 3404 TERRY L. PRIEST EDUCATIONAL SCHOLARSHIPS

Denver Foundation
Attn: Scholarships and Special Projects
950 South Cherry Street, Suite 200
Denver, CO 80246
Phone: (303) 300-1790, ext. 141; Fax: (303) 300-6547; Email: kbellina@denver foundation.org
Web: www.denverfoundation.org

**Summary:** To provide financial assistance to undergraduate and graduate students working on a degree in a transportation, logistics, or supply chain program.

**Eligibility:** Open to undergraduate and graduate students in transportation, logistics, and supply chain programs at accredited 4-year colleges and universities. Applicants must have a cumulative GPA of 3.0 or higher and be able to demonstrate financial need. They must submit a 2-page personal statement on why they chose to work on a degree in their field, their short- and long-term career goals, and their involvement in the transportation/logistics/supply chain profession or the community in general through clubs, activities, or employment.

**Financial data:** Stipend amounts vary each year.

**Duration:** 1 year.

**Number awarded:** 1 or more each year.

**Deadline:** March of each year.

### 3405 TERRY WALKER SCHOLARSHIP

**Summary:** To provide financial assistance to students from New York who are preparing to teach Latin in school.
*See Listing #1696.*

### 3406 TET '68 SCHOLARSHIP

TET '68, Inc.
Attn: Scholarship Competition
P.O. Box 31885
Richmond, VA 23294
Phone: (804) 550-3692; Email: Tet68Info@tet68.org
Web: www.tet68.org/TET68sch.html

**Summary:** To provide financial assistance for college to high school seniors whose parent served in Vietnam.

**Eligibility:** Open to high school seniors whose parent or step-parent is a Vietnam veteran. Applicants must submit a 500-word essay on "What is Freedom;" a copy of the parent's or step-parent's DD214 showing Vietnam service with Campaign Ribbon Award; a cover sheet that includes their full name and contact information for themselves, a person at their high school, and a person at their chosen college; and a statement verifying that they will graduate from high school in the following spring.

**Financial data:** The stipend is $1,000.

**Duration:** 1 year.

**Number awarded:** 3 or 4 each year.

**Deadline:** March of each year.

### 3407 TEXAS BUSINESS AND TECHNOLOGY EDUCATORS ASSOCIATION SCHOLARSHIPS

**Summary:** To provide financial assistance for college to members of Business Professionals of America (BPA) or Future Business Leaders of America (FBLA) in Texas.
*See Listing #2751.*

### 3408 TEXAS CATTLEWOMEN SCHOLARSHIP

**Summary:** To provide financial assistance to residents of Texas who are majoring in foods and nutrition, agricultural communications, or hotel and restaurant management in college.
*See Listing #2752.*

### 3409 TEXAS FIFTH-YEAR ACCOUNTING STUDENT SCHOLARSHIP PROGRAM

Texas Higher Education Coordinating Board
Attn: Grants and Special Programs
1200 East Anderson Lane
P.O. Box 12788, Capitol Station
Austin, TX 78711-2788
Phone: (512) 427-6101; (800) 242-3062; Fax: (512) 427-6127;
Email: grantinfo@thecb.state.tx.us
Web: www.collegefortexans.com

**Summary:** To provide financial assistance to accounting students attending college in Texas.

**Eligibility:** Open to both residents and nonresidents of Texas. Applicants must be enrolled at least half time and have completed at least 120 hours of college course work, including at least 15 semester credit hours of accounting. They may not have already taken the C.P.A. exam, but they must plan to take it in Texas and be willing to sign a written statement confirming their intent to take the written examination conducted by the Texas State Board of Public Accountancy to become a certified public accountant. Selection is based on financial need and scholastic ability and performance. Information and application forms may be obtained from the director of financial aid at the public college or university in Texas the applicant attends. Information is also available from the Texas State Board of Public Accountancy, 333 Guadalupe, Tower III, Suite 900, Austin, TX 78701-3900, (512) 305-7850, Fax: (512) 305-7875, Email: exam@tsbpa.state.tx.us. This program began in 1996. Study must be conducted in Texas; funds cannot be used to support attendance at an out-of-state institution.

**Financial data:** The maximum stipend is $3,000.

**Duration:** 1 year.

**Number awarded:** Varies each year; recently, 328 of these scholarships were awarded.

### 3410 TEXAS TRANSPORTATION SCHOLARSHIP

**Summary:** To provide financial assistance to college students interested in preparing for a career in fields related to transportation.
*See Listing #2757.*

### 3411 TEXAS YOUTH ENTREPRENEUR OF THE YEAR AWARD

Texas Christian University
Attn: M.J. Neeley School of Business
Ryffel Center for Entrepreneurial Studies
TCU Box 298530
Fort Worth, Texas 76129
Phone: (817) 257-6544; Email: g.laney@tcu.edu
Web: www.rces.tcu.edu/youth/index.org

**Summary:** To recognize and reward outstanding high school entrepreneurs in Texas for success in their own business.

**Eligibility:** Open to high school students in Texas who have started and managed a business that has been in operation for at least 1 year. An application may be submitted by the student entrepreneur, family member, friend, teacher, or mentor. Finalists are interviewed.

**Financial data:** The top winner receives a $5,000 award; the other winners receive $1,000 each. Funds may be used to offset tuition at any school of the student's choice.

**Duration:** The competition is held annually.

**Number awarded:** 6 each year: 1 top winner and 5 other winners.

**Deadline:** December of each year.

### 3412 TFBA SCHOLARSHIPS

Texas Family Business Association
Attn: TFBA Scholarship Foundation
5858 SPID, Sunrise Mall, Suite 63
Corpus Christi, TX 78415
Phone: (361) 882-1686; Fax: (361) 888-6602; Email: texasfb@flash.net

Web: www.texasfamilybusiness.org

**Summary:** To provide financial assistance to Texas students who are interested in studying business in college and whose families own a business.

**Eligibility:** Open to residents of Texas whose families own a business. Applicants must be interested in studying business at a college or university in Texas in order to remain active in the family firm. They may be high school seniors, already attending college, or transferring.

**Financial data:** A stipend is awarded (amount not specified).

**Duration:** 1 year.

**Number awarded:** Varies each year; recently, 5 of these scholarships were awarded.

## 3413 THOMAS F. SEAY SCHOLARSHIP

Illinois Association of Realtors
Attn: Illinois Real Estate Educational Foundation
3180 Adloff Lane, Suite 400
P.O. Box 19451
Springfield, IL 62794-9451
Phone: (217) 529-2600; Email: IARaccess@iar.org
Web: www.illinoisrealtor.org/iar/about/scholarships.htm

**Summary:** To provide financial assistance to Illinois residents who are preparing for a career in real estate.

**Eligibility:** Open to U.S. citizens who are Illinois residents, attending a college or university in any state on a full-time basis, and working on a degree with an emphasis in real estate. They must have completed at least 30 credits with a GPA of at least 3.5 on a 5.0 scale. As part of the application process, students must submit copies of their transcripts and letters of recommendation and reference. Selection is based on academic record, economic need, references and recommendations, and career plans in the field of real estate or an allied field (e.g., construction, land use planning, mortgage banking, property management, real estate appraising, real estate assessing, real estate brokerage, real estate development, real estate investment counselling, real estate law, and real estate syndication). Finalists are interviewed.

**Financial data:** The stipend is $2,000.

**Duration:** 1 year.

**Number awarded:** 1 each year.

**Deadline:** March of each year.

## 3414 THOMAS PRATTE MEMORIAL SCHOLARSHIPS

**Summary:** To provide financial assistance to members of the Surfrider Foundation working on an undergraduate or graduate degree in an environmental field.

*See Listing #2764.*

## 3415 TIA FOUNDATION UNDERGRADUATE SCHOLARSHIPS

Travel Industry Association of America
Attn: TIA Foundation
1100 New York Avenue, N.W., Suite 450
Washington, DC 20005-3934
Phone: (202) 408-8422; Fax: (202) 408-1255
Web: www.tia.org/about/foundation_scholarships.html

**Summary:** To provide financial assistance to undergraduate students majoring in travel and tourism.

**Eligibility:** Open to students who are interested in working on an undergraduate degree in the travel and tourism field. Candidates must first be nominated by a department head at a 4-year college or university that has a travel and tourism program. Nominees are then contacted by the foundation and invited to complete an application that includes an essay on what segment of the tourism industry interests them and why. This program, which began in 1993, includes the National Council of Destination Organizations (NCDO) Undergraduate Scholarship, the Shop America Alliance Scholarship, the Tourism Works for America Legacy Scholarship, and the William S. Norman Scholarship.

**Financial data:** The stipend is $3,000.

**Duration:** 1 year.

**Number awarded:** 6 each year.

## 3416 TOBIN SORENSON PHYSICAL EDUCATION SCHOLARSHIP

**Summary:** To provide financial assistance to students preparing for careers as a teacher of physical education or a related field.

*See Listing #2771.*

## 3417 TOURISM CARES FOR TOMORROW STATE SCHOLARSHIPS

Tourism Cares for Tomorrow
Attn: Program Manager
585 Washington Street
Canton, MA 02021
Phone: (781) 821-5990; Fax: (781) 821-8949; Email: info@tourismcares.org
Web: www.tourismcares.org

**Summary:** To provide financial assistance to upper-division students in selected states who are majoring in tourism.

**Eligibility:** Open to students entering their junior or senior year at a designated 4-year college or university in 20 states. Applicants must be residents of 1 of the following states: Alabama, California, Connecticut, Florida, Hawaii, Illinois, Massachusetts, Michigan, Minnesota, Missouri, Montana, Nebraska, Nevada, New Jersey, New York, North Carolina, Ohio, Texas, Utah, or Virginia. They must be attending the designated institution in their state with a major in a field related to travel and tourism and a GPA of 3.0 or higher. Information is also available from a faculty member at each of the 20 colleges and universities participating in this program. For a list of their names and addresses, contact Tourism Cares for Tomorrow.

**Financial data:** Stipends range from $500 to $1,500.

**Duration:** 1 year.

**Number awarded:** 20 each year: 1 in each of the participating states.

**Deadline:** March of each year.

## 3418 TRANSGENDER SCHOLARSHIP AND EDUCATION LEGACY FUND AWARDS

**Summary:** To provide financial assistance to transgender students who are working on an undergraduate or graduate degree in the caring professions.

*See Listing #1707.*

## 3419 TRANSIT HALL OF FAME SCHOLARSHIP AWARDS

**Summary:** To provide financial assistance to undergraduate and graduate students who are preparing for a career in transportation.

*See Listing #2773.*

## 3420 TRANSPORTATION FELLOWSHIP PROGRAM

**Summary:** To provide financial assistance to ethnic minorities, women, and economically disadvantaged persons who are interested in obtaining an undergraduate or graduate degree and work experience in a transportation-related field in Texas.

*See Listing #2775.*

## 3421 TRAVIS C. TOMLIN SCHOLARSHIP

National Association of Black Accountants
Attn: Director, Center for Advancement of Minority Accountants
7249-A Hanover Parkway
Greenbelt, MD 20770
Phone: (301) 474-NABA, ext. 114; Fax: (301) 474-3114; Email: cquinn@nabainc.org
Web: www.nabainc.org/pages/Student_ScholarshipProgram.jsp

**Summary:** To provide financial assistance to student members of the National Association of Black Accountants (NABA) who are working on an undergraduate or graduate degree in a field related to accounting.

**Eligibility:** Open to NABA members who are members of ethnic minority groups enrolled full time as 1) an undergraduate freshman, sophomore, junior, or first-semester senior majoring in accounting, business, or finance; or 2) a graduate student working on a master's degree in accounting. Applicants must have a GPA of 3.5 or higher in their major and 3.3 or higher overall. Selection is based on grades, financial need, and a 500-word autobiography that discusses career objectives, leadership abilities, community activities, and involvement in NABA.

**Financial data:** The stipend ranges from $1,000 to $1,500 per year.

**Duration:** 1 year.

**Number awarded:** 1 each year.

**Deadline:** December of each year.

### 3422 TREVA C. KINTNER SCHOLARSHIPS

Phi Upsilon Omicron
Attn: Educational Foundation
P.O. Box 329
Fairmont, WV 26555-0329
Phone: (304) 368-0612; Email: rickards@access.mountain.net
Web: www.phiu.unl.edu

**Summary:** To provide financial assistance to undergraduate student members of Phi Upsilon Omicron, a national honor society in family and consumer sciences.

**Eligibility:** Open to members of the society who are working on a bachelor's degree in family and consumer sciences or a related area. Preference is given to nontraditional students who have completed at least half of their academic work. Selection is based on scholastic record, participation in society and other collegiate activities, a statement of professional aims and goals, professional services, and recommendations.

**Financial data:** The stipend is $1,000.

**Duration:** 1 year.

**Number awarded:** 2 each year.

**Deadline:** January of each year.

### 3423 TRIBAL BUSINESS MANAGEMENT (TBM) PROGRAM

Catching the Dream
8200 Mountain Road, N.E., Suite 203
Albuquerque, NM 87110-7835
Phone: (505) 262-2351; Fax: (505) 262-0534; Email: NScholarsh@aol.com
Web: www.catchingthedream.org

**Summary:** To provide financial assistance for college to American Indian students interested in studying a field related to economic development for tribes.

**Eligibility:** Open to American Indians who can provide proof that they are at least one-quarter Indian blood and a member of a U.S. tribe that is federally-recognized, state-recognized, or terminated. Applicants must be enrolled or planning to enroll full time and major in the one of the following fields: business administration, finance, management, economics, banking, hotel management, or other fields related to economic development for tribes. They may be entering freshmen, undergraduate students, graduate students, or Ph.D. candidates. Along with their application, they must submit documentation of financial need, 3 letters of recommendation, copies of applications and responses for at least 15 other sources of funding, official transcripts, standardized test scores (ACT, SAT, GRE, MCAT, LSAT, etc.), and an essay explaining their goals in life, college plans, and career plans (especially how those plans include working with and benefiting Indians). Selection is based on merit and potential for improving the lives of Indian people.

**Financial data:** Stipends range from $500 to $5,000.

**Duration:** 1 year.

**Number awarded:** Varies; generally, 30 to 35 each year.

**Deadline:** April of each year for fall term; September of each year for spring and winter terms; March of each year for summer school.

### 3424 TTA FOUNDATION SCHOLARSHIP

**Summary:** To provide financial assistance to high school seniors in Texas who are interested in majoring in fields of study related to telecommunications.
*See Listing #2778.*

### 3425 UAN NATIONAL LABOR EDUCATION SCHOLARSHIP

United American Nurses
Attn: Labor Relations Specialist
8515 Georgia Avenue, Suite 400
Silver Spring, MD 20910
Phone: (301) 628-5140; Fax: (301) 628-5347; Email: Katrina.Blomdahl@uannurse.org
Web: uannurse.org/scholars.htm

**Summary:** To provide financial assistance to members of United American Nurses (UAN) who are interested in working on an undergraduate or graduate degree in labor studies.

**Eligibility:** Open to registered nurses who have been active members of UAN for at least one year. Applicants must have been accepted into a labor-oriented school or program to work on a certificate, bachelor's degree, or master's degree in labor studies or labor relations.

**Financial data:** The stipend is $1,000.

**Duration:** 1 year; recipients may reapply.

**Number awarded:** 1 or more each year.

**Deadline:** May of each year.

### 3426 UNITED AGRIBUSINESS LEAGUE SCHOLARSHIP PROGRAM

**Summary:** To provide financial assistance to students working on an undergraduate degree in agriculture or agribusiness.
*See Listing #2784.*

### 3427 UNITED STATES SENATE YOUTH PROGRAM SCHOLARSHIPS

**Summary:** To recognize and reward, with a trip to Washington, D.C. and college scholarships, outstanding high school student leaders.
*See Listing #1135.*

### 3428 UNITED STATES TOUR OPERATORS ASSOCIATION SCHOLARSHIP

Tourism Cares for Tomorrow
Attn: Program Manager
585 Washington Street
Canton, MA 02021
Phone: (781) 821-5990; Fax: (781) 821-8949; Email: info@tourismcares.org
Web: www.tourismcares.org

**Summary:** To provide financial assistance to upper-division students who are majoring in tourism.

**Eligibility:** Open to students entering their junior or senior year at an accredited 4-year college or university in the United States or Canada. Applicants must be working on a degree in a travel and tourism-related program and have a GPA of 3.0 or higher. Along with their application, they must submit a 2-page essay on why they have chosen to prepare for a career in the hospitality and tourism industry. Financial need is not considered in the selection process.

**Financial data:** The stipend is $2,500.

**Duration:** 1 year.

**Additional information:** This program is sponsored by the United States Tour Operators Association.

**Number awarded:** 1 each year.

**Deadline:** March of each year.

### 3429 URBAN FINANCIAL SERVICES COALITION OF DELAWARE SCHOLARSHIPS

Urban Financial Services Coalition of Delaware
P.O. Box 580
Wilmington, DE 19899-0580
Phone: (302) 286-2566
Web: www.ufscdel.org/scholarship.htm

**Summary:** To provide financial assistance to high school seniors in Delaware who plan to major in business in college.

**Eligibility:** Open to seniors graduating from high schools in Delaware with a GPA of C or higher. Applicants must be planning to major in a business-related field at an accredited college or university. They must be able to demonstrate financial need.

**Financial data:** The stipend is at least $1,000.

**Duration:** 1 year; nonrenewable.

**Number awarded:** 1 or more each year.

**Deadline:** March of each year.

### 3430 USDA/1890 NATIONAL SCHOLARS PROGRAM

**Summary:** To provide financial assistance to high school seniors and graduates interested in majoring in a field related to agriculture or agribusiness at 1 of the 18 Historically Black 1890 Land Grant Institutions.
*See Listing #2788.*

# Subject Index

Use this index when you want to identify funding programs by subject. To help you pinpoint your search, we've also included hundreds of "see" and "see also" references. In addition to looking for terms that represent your specific subject interests, be sure to check the "General programs" entry; hundred of programs are listed there that can be used to support study in any subject area (although the programs may be restricted in other ways). Remember: the numbers cited in this index refer to book entry numbers, not page numbers in the book.

Accounting: 776, 1273, 1371–1372, 1593, 1863, 1941, 2021, 2033, 2093, 2117–2118, 2169, 2266, 2537–2538, 2545, 2862, 2869–2871, 2883, 2898, 2903, 2911–2912, 2918, 2931, 2933, 2954, 2956, 2959, 2967–2968, 2972, 2976, 2985–2986, 2990, 3000, 3004, 3015, 3026–3027, 3032–3033, 3039–3040, 3043, 3052, 3055, 3057, 3061, 3078, 3081, 3083, 3090, 3115, 3120–3121, 3123, 3134, 3136, 3174–3175, 3182, 3185–3186, 3193, 3195, 3203, 3219, 3223, 3228, 3234, 3237, 3239, 3244, 3246, 3252–3254, 3256–3257, 3261, 3270, 3273–3274, 3276, 3281, 3285–3289, 3291–3292, 3299, 3304, 3312–3315, 3319, 3321–3322, 3326–3327, 3331, 3336–3337, 3343, 3345, 3347, 3361, 3376, 3381, 3390–3391, 3399, 3402, 3409, 3421. *See also* Finance; General programs
Acoustics: 1691, 2739. *See also* General programs; Physics
Acting. *See* Performing arts
Actuarial sciences: 1442, 2391, 2527, 2856, 2952, 3016, 3068, 3104, 3156, 3176, 3192, 3202, 3247–3248, 3272, 3277, 3367, 3387. *See also* General programs; Statistics
Administration. *See* Business administration; Education, administration; Management; Nurses and nursing, administration; Personnel administration; Public administration
Adolescents: 1268, 3082. *See also* Child development; General programs
Advertising: 1253, 1261, 1267, 1329, 1358, 1425, 1436, 1510, 1529, 1571, 1586, 1589, 1607, 1614, 1625, 1642, 1651, 1668, 1679, 1721, 1736, 1740, 1752, 1758, 2912, 3003, 3092, 3187. *See also* Communications; General programs; Marketing; Public relations
Aeronautical engineering. *See* Engineering, aeronautical
Aeronautics: 1802–1803, 1982, 2008, 2033, 2546, 2986. *See also* Aviation; Engineering, aeronautical; General programs; Physical sciences
Aerospace engineering. *See* Engineering, aerospace
Aerospace sciences. *See* Space sciences
African American studies: 1532. *See also* General programs
African studies: 1442, 3104. *See also* General programs; Humanities
Aged and aging: 2302, 3030, 3137. *See also* General programs; Social sciences
Agribusiness: 1594, 2323, 2422, 2539, 2784, 2788, 2797, 3143, 3212, 3264, 3290, 3392, 3426, 3430. *See also* Agriculture and agricultural sciences; Business administration; General programs
Agricultural aviation: 2858. *See also* Agriculture and agricultural sciences; Aviation; General programs
Agricultural communications: 1395, 1411, 1577, 1594, 1957, 2172, 2224, 2539, 2752, 3290, 3408. *See also* Agriculture and agricultural sciences; Communications; General programs
Agricultural economics. *See* Economics, agricultural
Agricultural education. *See* Education, agricultural
Agricultural engineering. *See* Engineering, agricultural
Agricultural technology: 2514. *See also* Agriculture and agricultural sciences; General programs; Technology
Agriculture and agricultural sciences: 278, 1283, 1290, 1375, 1513, 1577, 1594, 1715, 1768–1769, 1801, 1902, 1917, 1928, 1935, 1957, 1959–1960, 1963–1966, 1981, 2000, 2013, 2015, 2046, 2056, 2107, 2120, 2124, 2130, 2144, 2294, 2379, 2382, 2385, 2388, 2422, 2452, 2510, 2514, 2532, 2539, 2570, 2581, 2625, 2633, 2664, 2672, 2683, 2720, 2784, 2788, 2793, 2797, 2810, 2915, 2923, 2961, 2970, 3022, 3038, 3212, 3290, 3344, 3426, 3430. *See also* Biological sciences; General programs
Agrimarketing and sales. *See* Agribusiness
Agronomy: 1290, 1375, 1386, 1406, 1715, 1825, 1928, 1931, 1956, 1972, 2124, 2156, 2193–2194, 2201, 2319, 2382, 2722, 2788, 2793, 2810, 2849, 2926, 3430. *See also* Agriculture and agricultural sciences; General programs
Air conditioning industry. *See* Cooling industry
American history. *See* History, American
American Indian studies. *See* Native American studies
American literature. *See* Literature, American
American studies: 1319. *See also* General programs; Humanities
Animal rights: 2703. *See also* General programs; Veterinary sciences
Animal science: 1335, 1411, 1594, 1957, 2014, 2191, 2224, 2286, 2382, 2422, 2514, 2539, 2552, 2609, 2788, 2797, 2971, 3212, 3290, 3332, 3430. *See also* General programs; Sciences; names of specific animal sciences
Animation: 1679, 1753. *See also* Cartoonists and cartoons; Filmmaking; General programs
Anthropology: 1544, 3190, 3216. *See also* General programs; Social sciences
Applied arts. *See* Arts and crafts
Aquatic sciences. *See* Oceanography
Archaeology: 1281. *See also* General programs; History; Social sciences
Architectural engineering. *See* Engineering, architectural
Architecture: 17–18, 1241–1242, 1244–1245, 1250, 1256, 1273, 1276, 1278, 1281, 1288, 1302–1304, 1312–1313, 1318–1319, 1337, 1339, 1341, 1344, 1359, 1364, 1371–1373, 1421, 1426, 1439, 1457, 1460, 1478, 1520, 1592, 1659, 1661, 1671, 1752, 1794, 1813, 1821, 1863, 1872, 1886, 1949–1950, 1978, 2020, 2029, 2031, 2066, 2117–2118, 2240, 2268, 2276, 2393, 2420, 2536, 2561, 2686, 2698, 2808, 2903, 2939, 2951, 2975, 2984, 3032–3033, 3093, 3103, 3119, 3207, 3374–3375, 3382, 3448. *See also* Fine arts; General programs
Architecture, naval. *See* Naval architecture
Arithmetic. *See* Mathematics
Armament and disarmament: 1399. *See also* General programs; Military affairs; Peace studies
Armed services. *See* Military affairs
Art: 1049, 1242, 1262, 1265, 1275, 1283, 1298, 1313, 1315, 1325, 1377–1378, 1383, 1418, 1422, 1424, 1439, 1451, 1471, 1479, 1512, 1515, 1552, 1574–1575, 1626, 1628, 1642, 1664–1665, 1670, 1684, 1727, 1751–1752, 1755, 1794, 1917, 1978, 2448, 2923, 2951, 3103, 3142, 3230. *See also* General programs; Illustrators and illustrations; names of specific art forms
Art conservation: 1356, 1456. *See also* Art; General programs
Art history. *See* History, art
Arts and crafts: 1049, 1509, 1626, 1716, 1751–1752. *See also* Art; General programs; names of specific crafts
Astronautics: 1802–1803, 1982. *See also* General programs; Space sciences
Astronomy: 1901. *See also* General programs; Physical sciences
Astrophysics: 2709. *See also* Astronomy; General programs
Athletic training: 1728, 2079, 2504, 2564–2565, 2624, 2803, 2811. *See also* Athletics; General programs
Athletics: 2771, 2928, 2942, 3416. *See also* Athletic training; Education, physical; General programs; Sports medicine; names of specific sports
Atmospheric sciences: 1805, 1844, 1942, 2146, 2297–2298, 2407, 2437, 2519, 2709. *See also* General programs; Physical sciences
Attorneys. *See* Law, general
Audio engineering. *See* Engineering, audio
Audiology: 1830. *See also* General programs; Health and health care; Medical sciences
Audiovisual materials and equipment: 1474, 1670, 2304. *See also* General programs; specific types of media
Automation. *See* Computer sciences; Information science; Technology
Automobile industry: 108, 756, 2113, 3029, 3388. *See also* General programs
Automotive engineering. *See* Engineering, automotive
Automotive repair: 638, 1765, 2862, 3392. *See also* General programs
Automotive technology: 489, 1765, 2309, 3392. *See also* Engineering, automotive; General programs; Transportation
A.V. *See* Audiovisual materials and equipment
Aviation: 1408, 1759–1760, 1775, 1808–1810, 1843, 1858–1860, 1910–1912, 1943–1944, 1946, 1990, 1997, 2016, 2035, 2039, 2042, 2053, 2096, 2149, 2190, 2197–2198, 2232, 2270–2271, 2278, 2345, 2359–2361, 2387, 2390–2391, 2395, 2410, 2473, 2546, 2590, 2615–2616, 2621, 2629, 2643, 2724, 2727–2728, 2780, 2782, 2799, 2839, 2920–2921, 2932, 2960, 2995, 3070, 3192, 3339, 3394. *See also* General programs; Space sciences; Transportation
Ballet. *See* Dance
Banking: 3048, 3111, 3132, 3170, 3179, 3229, 3253–3254, 3348, 3413, 3423. *See also* Finance; General programs
Barbering. *See* Hair design
Beef industry: 1335, 1411, 1594, 2014, 2224, 2517–2518, 2532, 2539, 2971, 3290. *See also* General programs; Ranching
Beer and wine industries: 1746, 2452, 3476. *See also* General programs
Behavioral sciences: 2144, 2302–2303, 3038, 3137–3138. *See also* General programs; Social sciences; names of special behavioral sciences
Biochemistry: 1787, 1837, 2302–2303, 2452, 2709, 2822, 3137–3138. *See also* Biological sciences; Chemistry; General programs
Biological sciences: 278, 1242, 1273, 1290, 1311, 1313, 1375, 1715, 1773, 1794, 1797, 1816, 1825, 1863, 1880–1881, 1901, 1907, 1928, 1934, 1936, 1945, 1947, 1954, 1971, 1978, 2002, 2090, 2092, 2124, 2138, 2140, 2144, 2194, 2199, 2238, 2353, 2408, 2452, 2511, 2519, 2537, 2545, 2591, 2598, 2609, 2625, 2707, 2709, 2783, 2793, 2815, 2834, 2856, 2903, 2937, 2949, 2951, 3036, 3038, 3288, 3292, 3332. *See also* General programs; Sciences; names of specific biological sciences
Biomedical engineering. *See* Engineering, biomedical
Biomedical sciences: 2836. *See also* Biological sciences; General programs; Medical sciences
Black American studies. *See* African American studies
Blindness. *See* Visual impairments
Botany: 1243, 1287, 1290, 1375, 1386, 1406, 1440, 1715, 1800, 1825, 1926, 1928, 2013, 2109, 2124, 2156, 2193–2194, 2257, 2302–2303, 2319, 2422, 2625, 2709,

2722, 2788, 2793, 2797, 2849, 3137–3138, 3212, 3430. *See also* Biological sciences; General programs

Brain research. *See* Neuroscience

Brazilian language. *See* Language, Portuguese

Broadcast engineering. *See* Engineering, broadcast

Broadcast journalism. *See* Journalism, broadcast

Broadcasting: 638, 1252, 1255, 1285–1286, 1301, 1333–1334, 1338, 1392, 1431, 1435, 1437, 1448, 1464, 1468, 1472, 1481, 1488, 1504, 1507, 1526, 1529, 1538, 1555, 1562, 1591, 1593, 1607, 1611, 1613, 1625, 1627, 1634, 1698, 1701, 1704, 1712, 1721, 1736, 1745, 2283, 2538, 2936, 2974, 3046, 3129, 3289. *See also* Communications; Radio; Television

Building trades: 1250, 1304, 1457, 1469, 1813, 1950, 2027, 2236, 2268, 2292, 2384, 2411, 2420, 3205, 3207. *See also* General programs

Business administration: 176, 610, 705, 776, 1200, 1273, 1283, 1311, 1335, 1371–1372, 1461, 1464, 1552, 1566, 1671, 1748, 1763, 1774, 1863, 1870, 1917, 1952, 1971, 1973, 2014, 2021, 2025, 2033, 2051, 2057, 2093, 2117–2118, 2141, 2164, 2178, 2198, 2211, 2250, 2252, 2265–2266, 2273, 2282–2283, 2363, 2396, 2406, 2425–2426, 2448, 2466, 2468, 2499, 2526, 2537, 2545, 2576, 2609–2610, 2648, 2650–2651, 2657, 2674, 2681, 2694, 2698, 2751, 2773, 2778, 2816, 2862, 2865, 2873, 2889, 2896, 2903, 2906, 2911, 2922–2923, 2934, 2940, 2949–2950, 2956, 2966, 2971, 2976, 2981, 2985–2986, 2990, 2994–2995, 2997, 2999, 3007, 3010, 3015, 3019, 3032–3033, 3037, 3042, 3044, 3050, 3053, 3059, 3066, 3068, 3070–3071, 3073, 3077, 3087, 3097, 3101, 3111, 3114–3115, 3118, 3125, 3128–3129, 3144, 3150, 3158, 3161, 3167, 3176–3177, 3179, 3194, 3197, 3202, 3208, 3213, 3215, 3219–3220, 3230, 3235–3236, 3244, 3253, 3255–3258, 3261, 3263, 3271, 3273, 3281, 3288, 3292, 3295, 3310, 3317, 3332–3333, 3345, 3347, 3356–3357, 3362, 3367–3368, 3371–3372, 3380, 3382, 3388, 3392, 3396, 3401–3402, 3407, 3412, 3419, 3421, 3423–3424, 3429. *See also* Entrepreneurship; General programs; Management

Business education. *See* Education, business

Business enterprises. *See* Entrepreneurship

Business law: 3274. *See also* General programs; Law, general

Cable TV industry: 1301, 2936. *See also* General programs; Television

Cancer: 2147, 2575–2576, 2668, 3317. *See also* Disabilities; General programs; Health and health care; Medical sciences

Cardiology: 2261. *See also* General programs; Medical sciences

Cars. *See* Automobile industry; Engineering, automotive

Cartography: 1732, 2012, 2221, 2482, 2519, 2534. *See also* General programs; Geography

Cartoonists and cartoons: 1320, 1753. *See also* Art; General programs; Illustrators and illustrations

Cattle ranching. *See* Ranching

Censorship: 1401. *See also* Civil liberties; General programs; Intellectual freedom

Ceramic engineering. *See* Engineering, ceramic

Ceramics: 1377, 1381, 1664. *See also* Arts and crafts; General programs

Chemical engineering. *See* Engineering, chemical

Chemistry: 17–18, 1242, 1273, 1313, 1762, 1773, 1787–1788, 1794, 1837, 1845, 1863, 1900–1901, 1907, 1954, 1978, 2002, 2017, 2090, 2140–2141, 2157, 2231, 2238, 2279, 2302–2303, 2331, 2408, 2413, 2452, 2501, 2511, 2519, 2537, 2567, 2609, 2620, 2648, 2661, 2665, 2675, 2707, 2709, 2716, 2747, 2760, 2762, 2769, 2801, 2822, 2856, 2863, 2903, 2951, 3036–3037, 3137–3138, 3288, 3332. *See also* Engineering, chemical; General programs; Physical sciences

Child care. *See* Day care

Child development: 3082, 3165, 3180, 3210–3211, 3306. *See also* Adolescents; General programs

Chinese language. *See* Language, Chinese

Chinese studies: 1289. *See also* General programs; Humanities

Chiropractic: 1828, 2695. *See also* General programs; Medical sciences

Choruses. *See* Voice

Church music. *See* Music, church

Cinema: 1308. *See also* Filmmaking; General programs; Literature

City and regional planning: 1243, 1281, 1290, 1339, 1375, 1386, 1406, 1440, 1659, 1715, 1752, 1800, 1928, 2020, 2124, 2156, 2193–2194, 2257, 2444, 2764, 2775, 2793, 2849, 2859, 2945, 2975, 3045, 3169, 3178, 3224, 3330, 3338, 3355, 3374, 3414, 3420. *See also* General programs

Civil engineering. *See* Engineering, civil

Civil liberties: 3135. *See also* General programs; Political science and politics

Civil rights: 2674, 3368. *See also* Civil liberties; General programs; Political science and politics

Clairvoyance. *See* Parapsychology

Classical music. *See* Music, classical

Classical studies: 1541, 1579. *See also* General programs; Literature

Clerical skills. *See* Secretarial sciences

Clothing: 1733. *See also* Fashion design; General programs; Home economics

Colleges and universities. *See* Education, higher

Commerce. *See* Business administration

Communications: 278, 575, 1249, 1252–1253, 1269, 1274, 1283, 1296, 1298, 1301, 1329, 1333, 1335, 1338, 1357–1358, 1370, 1382, 1391, 1394, 1409, 1425, 1433, 1452, 1454, 1467, 1501, 1507, 1512, 1514, 1521, 1524, 1526, 1529–1530, 1574, 1585, 1607, 1612, 1616, 1620, 1624, 1633, 1642, 1663, 1668, 1685, 1692, 1698, 1703, 1721, 1730, 1736–1737, 1740, 1744–1745, 1917, 2008, 2014, 2285, 2306, 2386, 2499, 2526, 2592, 2688, 2766, 2923, 2936, 2971, 2974, 3002–3003, 3092, 3110, 3130, 3258, 3271. *See also* General programs; Humanities

Communications, agricultural. *See* Agricultural communications

Community colleges. *See* Education, higher

Community services. *See* Social services

Composers and compositions: 1275, 1277, 1293, 1313, 1324, 1420, 1494, 1536, 1545, 1565, 1568, 1622, 1713, 1718, 1756, 1978, 2951. *See also* General programs; Music; Musicals

Computer engineering. *See* Engineering, computer

Computer sciences: 17–18, 176, 278, 1200, 1242, 1278, 1283, 1311, 1336, 1471, 1763, 1766, 1782–1784, 1787, 1790–1792, 1794, 1832, 1852–1854, 1870, 1883, 1886, 1901, 1907, 1917, 1937–1938, 1971, 1973, 1980, 2002, 2018, 2033, 2043, 2045, 2050–2052, 2057, 2072–2074, 2087, 2093, 2104, 2110–2111, 2121–2122, 2141, 2144, 2153, 2162, 2170, 2182, 2187, 2202–2204, 2206, 2234, 2244, 2262, 2265–2266, 2273, 2282, 2302–2303, 2318, 2344, 2374, 2399, 2401, 2405–2406, 2408, 2413, 2415, 2436, 2451, 2455, 2464–2466, 2468, 2472, 2499, 2503, 2513, 2519, 2545, 2559–2560, 2563, 2568, 2574, 2591, 2619, 2670–2671, 2681, 2690, 2707, 2709, 2713, 2742–2745, 2751, 2778, 2800, 2809, 2816, 2821, 2856–2857, 2862–2863, 2865, 2867, 2906, 2911, 2923, 2949–2950, 2986, 2991, 2994, 2999, 3015, 3024–3025, 3037–3038, 3089, 3114–3115, 3118, 3128, 3137–3138, 3154, 3235–3236, 3256, 3258, 3274, 3292, 3372, 3392, 3396, 3407, 3424. *See also* General programs; Information science; Libraries and librarianship; Mathematics; Technology

Computers. *See* Computer sciences

Concrete industry: 1772, 2031, 2239, 2289, 2295, 2310, 2475, 2528, 2561, 2605, 2852. *See also* Building trades; General programs

Conflict resolution. *See* Peace studies

Conservation. *See* Art conservation; Environmental sciences

Construction. *See* Building trades; Housing

Construction engineering. *See* Engineering, construction

Construction industry: 1273, 1303–1304, 1339, 1341, 1426, 1430, 1469, 1661, 1772, 1796, 1815, 1863, 1895–1897, 1924, 1949–1950, 1977, 2020, 2029, 2031–2032, 2119, 2164, 2236, 2239–2240, 2249, 2251, 2292, 2310, 2329, 2333, 2362, 2380, 2411, 2420, 2509, 2528, 2543, 2561, 2686, 2694, 2750, 2808, 2876–2877, 2903, 2913–2914, 2939, 2975, 2982, 2984, 3049, 3053, 3093, 3100, 3132, 3149, 3205, 3207, 3262, 3375, 3380, 3413, 3448. *See also* Building trades; General programs

Consumer affairs: 1793, 2875. *See also* General programs; Home economics

Consumer and family studies education. *See* Education, family and consumer studies

Continence. *See* Nurses and nursing, wound, ostomy and continence

Cooking. *See* Culinary arts

Cooling industry: 2004, 2384, 2411, 2694, 3205, 3380, 3392. *See also* General programs

Cosmetology. *See* Hair design

Costume: 1701, 1752. *See also* Art; Fashion design; General programs

Counseling: 2874, 2985, 3298. *See also* Behavioral sciences; General programs; Psychology

Counselors and counseling, school: 3199, 3269. *See also* Counseling; General programs

Counter–intelligence service. *See* Intelligence service

Court reporting: 2953. *See also* General programs; Paralegal studies

Crafts. *See* Arts and crafts

Creative writing: 694, 1262, 1275, 1467, 1512, 1656, 2285, 3130. *See also* Fine arts; General programs

Criminal justice: 176, 1870, 1953, 1973, 2140, 2906, 2919, 2925, 2950, 2973, 3036, 3041, 3196, 3300, 3301, 3361, 3384. *See also* General programs; Law, general

Critical care nurses and nursing. *See* Nurses and nursing, critical care

Culinary arts: 1258–1260, 1264, 1291, 1305–1307, 1309–1310, 1348, 1467, 1495, 1539, 1581, 1679, 1746, 2285, 3130, 3209, 3370, 3392. *See also* Food service industry; General programs; Home economics

Dairy science: 2514, 2526, 3271. *See also* Agriculture and agricultural sciences; General programs

Dance: 640, 1242, 1277, 1302, 1308, 1378, 1398, 1414, 1420, 1463, 1476, 1479, 1482, 1487, 1549, 1551, 1573, 1600, 1647, 1700–1702, 1728, 1794, 2176, 2229, 2281, 2332, 2443, 2505, 2553, 2644, 2771, 2811, 3058, 3085, 3127, 3142, 3148, 3222, 3226–3227, 3259, 3296, 3353, 3416. *See also* General programs; Performing arts

Data entry. *See* Computer sciences; Secretarial sciences

Day care: 3108. *See also* Education, preschool; General programs

Deafness. *See* Hearing impairments

Defense. *See* Military affairs

Demography. *See* Population studies

Dental hygiene: 1777, 1779–1781, 1841, 1958, 1974, 2009, 2078, 2084, 2145, 2242, 2311, 2349, 2431, 2438, 2512, 2578–2579, 2608, 2628, 2641, 2710, 2776, 2796, 2817, 2846–2847. *See also* Dentistry; General programs

Dental laboratory technology: 1776, 1778, 2371, 2817. *See also* Dental hygiene; General programs

Dentistry: 1311, 1971, 2241–2242, 2258, 2349, 2512, 2628, 2695, 2776, 2856, 2949. *See also* General programs; Health and health care; Medical sciences

Design: 1049, 1302–1303, 1317, 1377, 1425, 1466, 1469, 1512, 1654, 1671, 1752, 1949, 2255, 2292, 2698, 2939, 3092, 3102, 3382. *See also* Art; General programs

Developmental disabilities. *See* Disabilities, developmental

Dietetics. *See* Nutrition

Disabilities: 887, 1486, 1874, 2242, 2908, 3316. *See also* General programs; Rehabilitation; Therapy; names of specific disabilities

Disabilities, developmental: 2062–2063. *See also* Disabilities; General programs

Disabilities, hearing. *See* Hearing impairments

Disabilities, visual. *See* Visual impairments

Disarmament. *See* Armament and disarmament

Discrimination, racial: 1361. *See also* General programs

Discrimination, religious: 1361. *See also* General programs; Religion and religious activities

Divinity. *See* Religion and religious activities

Documentaries. *See* Filmmaking

Domestic science. *See* Home economics

Drafting: 638, 1303, 1520, 1949, 2393, 2411, 2939, 3205. *See also* General programs

Drama. *See* Plays

Early childhood education. *See* Education, preschool

Earth sciences: 1900–1901, 2302–2303, 2381, 2709, 2844, 3137–3138. *See also* General programs; Natural sciences; names of specific earth sciences

Ecology. *See* Environmental sciences

Economic planning. *See* Economics

Economics: 1365, 1531, 1544, 1671, 1941, 2228, 2266, 2273, 2526–2527, 2698, 2889, 2902, 2911, 2931, 2956, 2972, 3013, 3035, 3115, 3118, 3167, 3216, 3243–3244, 3256, 3271–3273, 3382, 3388, 3396, 3423. *See also* General programs; Social sciences

Economics, agricultural: 1594, 1931, 2382, 2539, 2562, 2788, 2926, 3264, 3290, 3430. *See also* Agriculture and agricultural sciences; Economics; General programs

Editors and editing: 1530, 1692. *See also* General programs; Writers and writing

Education: 317, 383, 610, 959, 1311, 1313, 1439, 1475, 1552, 1667, 1707, 1817, 1864, 1931, 1971, 1978, 2108, 2183, 2396, 2425, 2448, 2466, 2480, 2693, 2795, 2882, 2888, 2901, 2904, 2924, 2926, 2947, 2949, 2951, 2958, 2969, 2978–2979, 2983, 2987–2988, 2992, 3008–3009, 3011–3012, 3023, 3034, 3047, 3060, 3062–3064, 3069, 3082, 3086, 3088, 3095, 3103, 3147, 3150, 3152, 3165, 3191, 3197–3199, 3213–3214, 3221, 3225, 3230, 3235, 3242, 3269, 3284, 3297, 3300, 3302, 3306, 3335, 3366, 3373, 3379, 3389, 3418. *See also* General programs; specific types and levels of education

Education, administration: 776, 3049, 3269. *See also* Education; Management

Education, agricultural: 2194, 2526, 2970, 3264, 3271. *See also* Agriculture and agricultural sciences; Education; General programs

Education, business: 2751, 2966, 3044, 3158, 3218, 3310, 3323, 3407. *See also* Education; General programs

Education, elementary: 1479, 1696, 2654–2655, 2689, 2771, 2899, 2957, 3028, 3098, 3108, 3142, 3145, 3311, 3350, 3359–3360, 3378, 3405, 3416. *See also* Education; General programs

Education, family and consumer studies: 3107. *See also* Education; Family and consumer studies; General programs

Education, foreign languages: 1696, 3405, 3442. *See also* Education; General programs; Language and linguistics

Education, health: 1487, 1647, 1764, 2332, 2644, 2866, 3148, 3353. *See also* Education; General programs; Health and health care

Education, higher: 1132, 1711, 3028, 3049. *See also* Education; General programs

Education, music: 1427, 1560, 3094. *See also* Education; General programs; Music

Education, physical: 1398, 1414, 1463, 1487, 1549, 1573, 1600, 1647, 1728, 2079, 2107, 2176, 2229, 2281, 2332, 2443, 2505, 2553, 2564–2565, 2624, 2644, 2771, 2811, 2928, 3022, 3058, 3085, 3127, 3148, 3222, 3226–3227, 3259, 3296, 3353, 3416. *See also* Athletics; Education; General programs

Education, preschool: 3108, 3180, 3211. *See also* Education; General programs

Education, religious: 1447, 1640, 1645, 1750, 3106, 3349. *See also* Education; General programs; Religion and religious activities

Education, science and mathematics: 1900, 2144, 2396, 2484, 2490, 2654–2655, 2687, 2689, 3038, 3197, 3245, 3359–3360, 3377–3378. *See also* Education; General programs; Sciences

Education, secondary: 1696, 2654–2655, 2689, 2771, 2909, 2948, 2957, 3028, 3145, 3311, 3350, 3359–3360, 3378, 3405, 3416. *See also* Education; General programs

Education, special: 646, 781, 887, 1874, 2055, 2676, 2874, 2908, 2935, 2980, 2996, 2998, 3163, 3168, 3180, 3231, 3298, 3316, 3369, 3373. *See also* Disabilities; Education; General programs

Education, technology: 2184, 2316, 2403, 3065, 3140, 3201. *See also* Education; General programs; Technology

Electrical engineering. *See* Engineering, electrical

Electricity. *See* Utilities

Electronic engineering. *See* Engineering, electronic

Electronic journalism. *See* Journalism, broadcast

Electronics: 1242, 1474, 1514, 1620, 1736, 1791, 1794, 1946, 2042, 2096, 2131, 2197, 2270, 2304, 2360, 2384, 2386–2387, 2395, 2410–2411, 2473, 2592, 2616, 2728, 3205. *See also* Engineering, electronic; General programs; Physics

Elementary education. *See* Education, elementary

Emergency medical technician: 3196. *See also* General programs; Health and health care

Emergency nurses and nursing. *See* Nurses and nursing, emergency

Emotional disabilities. *See* Mental health

Employee benefits: 3277. *See also* Employment; General programs

Employment: 1172, 1739. *See also* Employee benefits; General programs; Occupational therapy

Energy: 1242, 1794, 1904, 2048, 2223, 2305, 2506, 2533, 2571, 2656, 2916, 3080, 3279, 3308. *See also* Environmental sciences; General programs; Natural resources

Engineering: 278, 383, 776, 1200, 1250, 1273, 1276, 1278, 1311, 1359, 1430, 1460, 1520, 1592, 1763, 1771–1773, 1782, 1785, 1813, 1832, 1835, 1838, 1840, 1843, 1846, 1854, 1863, 1865, 1867, 1872, 1883, 1886, 1894, 1901–1904, 1907–1909, 1916, 1932, 1937–1938, 1941, 1952, 1971, 1980, 1985, 1992, 1998, 2000, 2002, 2008, 2011, 2023, 2028, 2033, 2045, 2052, 2057, 2061, 2064, 2066, 2072–2074, 2090, 2093, 2121–2122, 2134, 2136–2137, 2142, 2144, 2152–2153, 2161, 2164–2165, 2187, 2202–2203, 2207–2208, 2210–2211, 2223, 2226, 2233, 2238, 2249, 2253, 2255, 2259, 2262–2263, 2266, 2269, 2273, 2275–2276, 2279, 2282, 2296, 2298, 2302–2303, 2305, 2310, 2312, 2314, 2318, 2321, 2338, 2342, 2364, 2367, 2373, 2376, 2380, 2383, 2393, 2399, 2401, 2405–2406, 2408, 2413, 2415–2416, 2424, 2429, 2442, 2455–2456, 2461, 2465–2467, 2475–2476, 2488, 2495–2496, 2499, 2503, 2519–2520, 2528, 2533, 2536–2537, 2546–2547, 2554–2555, 2563, 2567–2568, 2571, 2574, 2586, 2591, 2594–2595, 2598, 2600–2601, 2603, 2605, 2610, 2617, 2630, 2635–2638, 2652, 2656–2657, 2659, 2666, 2671, 2681, 2684, 2692, 2713, 2717, 2719, 2725, 2742–2745, 2761, 2763, 2778, 2791, 2799, 2804, 2818, 2838, 2843, 2856–2857, 2865, 2903, 2915–2916, 2931, 2940, 2949, 2961, 2986, 2999, 3015, 3038, 3053, 3071, 3080, 3102, 3115, 3118–3119, 3128, 3137–3138, 3235, 3258, 3279, 3288, 3308, 3333, 3358, 3362, 3372, 3395, 3424. *See also* General programs; Physical sciences; names of specific types of engineering

Engineering, aeronautical: 17–18, 1805, 1848, 1944, 2002, 2041, 2044, 2054, 2170, 2205, 2248, 2368. *See also* Aeronautics; Engineering; General programs

Engineering, aerospace: 17–18, 1791–1792, 1805, 1943, 2041, 2054, 2162, 2185, 2204, 2206, 2248, 2436, 2521, 2559–2560, 2590, 2800, 2932. *See also* Engineering; General programs; Space sciences

Engineering, agricultural: 1594, 1797, 1825, 1880–1881, 1931, 2140–2141, 2199, 2353, 2422, 2452, 2514, 2539, 2788, 2834, 2926, 3036–3037, 3212, 3290, 3430. *See also* Agriculture and agricultural sciences; Engineering; General programs

Engineering, architectural: 17–18, 1256, 1821, 1923, 1975, 2032, 2162, 2180, 2251, 2457, 2469, 2723, 2735, 3100. *See also* Architecture; Engineering; General programs

Engineering, audio: 2162. *See also* Engineering; General programs

Engineering, automotive: 2168, 2209. *See also* Engineering; General programs

Engineering, biomedical: 1313, 1766, 1798, 1978, 2135, 2162, 2515, 2545, 2836, 2856, 2867, 2951, 3292. *See also* Engineering; General programs

Engineering, broadcast: 1464, 1533, 1593, 1721, 2283, 2538, 3129, 3289. *See also* Engineering; General programs; Radio; Television

Engineering, ceramic: 2769. *See also* Engineering; General programs

Engineering, chemical: 1787–1788, 1790–1792, 1807, 1837, 1845, 1945, 1991–1992, 1994, 2017, 2068, 2092, 2095, 2140–2141, 2157, 2162, 2185, 2204, 2206, 2209–2210, 2244, 2352, 2452, 2483, 2487, 2501, 2506, 2541, 2545, 2559–2560, 2620, 2648, 2661, 2665, 2675, 2702, 2716, 2747, 2760, 2762, 2769, 2801, 2809, 2822, 2863, 3036–3037, 3292. *See also* Chemistry; Engineering; General programs

Engineering, civil: 17–18, 776, 1796, 1805, 1839, 1848, 1871, 1875, 1882, 1896, 1906, 1914, 1923, 1944–1945, 1975–1976, 1994–1995, 2002, 2032, 2092, 2106, 2128, 2140–2141, 2160, 2162, 2178, 2180, 2220, 2251, 2326, 2329, 2333, 2336, 2340, 2363, 2418, 2420, 2427, 2441, 2457, 2468–2469, 2502, 2541, 2543, 2545, 2547, 2560–2561, 2662, 2685, 2709, 2723, 2734–2735, 2749–2750, 2768, 2775, 2907, 3036–3037, 3059, 3100, 3149, 3161, 3207, 3236, 3292, 3420. *See also* Engineering; General programs

Engineering, computer: 17–18, 1782, 1787, 1790–1791, 1798, 1805, 1831, 1852, 1994, 2018, 2050–2051, 2162, 2169, 2182, 2204, 2206, 2244, 2436, 2451, 2464, 2468, 2472, 2545, 2559–2560, 2619, 2670, 2800, 2863, 2994, 3055, 3236, 3292. *See also* Computer sciences; Engineering; General programs

Engineering, construction: 1303, 1339, 1341, 1426, 1661, 1796, 1949, 2020, 2026, 2029, 2031, 2119, 2236, 2240, 2329, 2336, 2502, 2509, 2543, 2686, 2808, 2939, 2975, 2984, 3093, 3262, 3375, 3448. *See also* Engineering; General programs

Engineering, electrical: 17–18, 776, 1787, 1790–1792, 1798, 1805, 1831, 1839, 1848, 1923, 1929, 2002, 2036–2037, 2050–2051, 2054, 2088, 2104, 2141, 2162, 2168–2170, 2182, 2204, 2206, 2208–2210, 2236, 2244, 2404, 2436, 2452, 2464, 2468, 2494, 2501, 2506, 2541, 2545, 2547, 2559–2560, 2583, 2619, 2623, 2670, 2702, 2709, 2769, 2773, 2800, 2861, 2863, 2994, 3037, 3055, 3236, 3292, 3419. *See also* Engineering; General programs

Engineering, electronic: 1787, 1848. *See also* Electronics; Engineering; General programs

Engineering, environmental: 17–18, 1788, 1805, 1825–1826, 1923, 1934, 1944–1945, 2092, 2103, 2128, 2140–2141, 2162, 2178, 2194, 2358, 2363, 2418, 2427, 2441, 2469, 2541, 2545, 2618, 2749, 3020, 3036–3037, 3059, 3161, 3292. *See also* Engineering; Environmental sciences; General programs

Engineering, fire protection: 1812, 1833, 1924, 2246, 2398, 2428, 2439, 2787. *See also* Engineering; Fire science; General programs

Engineering, forestry: 1898. *See also* Engineering; General programs

Engineering, hydraulic: 1906. *See also* Engineering; General programs

Engineering, industrial: 1787, 1845, 1984, 2003, 2017, 2077, 2097, 2141, 2157, 2162, 2168, 2170, 2173, 2208–2210, 2244, 2265, 2402, 2452, 2468, 2545, 2558–2560, 2613, 2620, 2648, 2661, 2665, 2670, 2702, 2716, 2747, 2760, 2762, 2785–2786, 2801, 2827, 3037, 3114, 3236, 3292. *See also* Engineering; General programs

Engineering, manufacturing: 1876, 1979, 1984, 2003, 2077, 2099–2102, 2116, 2155, 2162, 2168, 2173, 2188, 2209–2210, 2244–2245, 2414, 2498, 2558–2560, 2613, 2714–2715, 2740, 2813, 2827, 2832, 2863. *See also* Engineering; General programs

Engineering, materials: 1890, 2031, 2115, 2131, 2154, 2209, 2216, 2239, 2244, 2254, 2307, 2320, 2356, 2400, 2545, 2549, 2736, 2769, 2841, 3292. *See also* Engineering; General programs; Materials sciences

Engineering, mechanical: 17–18, 1787, 1798–1799, 1805, 1807, 1827, 1839, 1842, 1845, 1848, 1865, 1877, 1891–1893, 1923, 1927, 1984, 1994, 2002–2003, 2017, 2036–2037, 2050–2051, 2054, 2077, 2095, 2104, 2140–2141, 2157, 2162, 2168–2170, 2173, 2179, 2185–2186, 2189, 2196, 2208–2210, 2244, 2280, 2346, 2375, 2384, 2404, 2421, 2452, 2463, 2468, 2501, 2506, 2541, 2545, 2547, 2558–2560, 2573, 2607, 2620, 2627, 2634, 2648, 2661, 2663, 2665, 2670, 2675, 2702, 2709, 2716, 2741, 2746–2747, 2760, 2762, 2769, 2773, 2801, 2827, 2831, 2835, 2863, 2994, 3036–3037, 3055, 3236, 3292, 3419. *See also* Engineering; General programs

Engineering, metallurgical: 1890, 1899, 2115, 2141, 2216, 2254, 2307, 2320, 2356, 2400, 2545, 2549, 2769, 2841, 3037, 3292. *See also* Engineering; General programs; Metallurgy

Engineering, mining: 2006, 2148, 2154, 2228, 2320, 2478–2479. *See also* Engineering; General programs; Mining industry

Engineering, naval: 1848. *See also* Engineering; General programs

Engineering, nuclear: 1856–1857, 1989, 2002, 2047, 2049, 2141, 2347, 2506, 2522, 2545, 2577, 2842, 3037, 3292. *See also* Engineering; General programs; Nuclear science

Engineering, ocean: 1848, 2560. *See also* Engineering; General programs; Oceanography

Engineering, optical: 2471, 2726, 2863. *See also* Engineering; General programs

Engineering, packaging: 2452. *See also* Engineering; General programs

Engineering, petroleum: 952, 1992, 1994, 2141, 2545, 2606, 2622, 3037, 3292. *See also* Engineering; General programs

Engineering, plastics: 382, 1845, 1939, 2017, 2157, 2620, 2661, 2665, 2716, 2747, 2760, 2762, 2801. *See also* Engineering; General programs

Engineering, structural: 1875, 1975, 2180, 2251, 2457, 2541, 2547, 2560, 2723, 2735, 3100. *See also* Engineering; General programs

Engineering, surveying: 1786, 2325. *See also* Engineering; General programs; Surveying

Engineering, systems: 776, 1790–1792, 2162, 2206, 2436, 2800, 2861. *See also* Engineering; General programs

Engineering technology: 776, 1787, 1811, 1849, 1867, 1876, 1891, 1893, 1979, 2067, 2077, 2099–2102, 2114, 2116, 2155, 2162, 2188–2189, 2196, 2226, 2245, 2277, 2317, 2346, 2348, 2414, 2457, 2463, 2468, 2498, 2558, 2571, 2613, 2626, 2663, 2684, 2714, 2735, 2800, 2827, 2831–2832, 3236, 3308. *See also* Engineering; General programs

Engineering, textile: 2702. *See also* Engineering; General programs

Engineering, transportation: 1371–1372, 2038, 2117–2118, 2235, 2409, 2701, 2748, 2763, 2774–2775, 2859–2861, 3032–3033, 3091, 3204, 3383, 3420. *See also* Engineering; General programs; Transportation

Engineering, welding: 1811, 1849, 2067, 2114, 2277, 2317, 2339, 2348, 2626. *See also* Engineering; General programs; Welding

English as a second language: 1283, 1917, 2923. *See also* General programs; Language and linguistics

English language. *See* Language, English

English literature. *See* Literature, English

Enology and viticulture: 1847, 1967. *See also* Agriculture and agricultural sciences; Beer and wine industries; General programs

Enterostomal therapy nurses and nursing. *See* Nurses and nursing, wound, ostomy and continence

Entertainment industry: 1704, 3007. *See also* General programs; Performing arts

Entomology: 1290, 1375, 1715, 1928, 1936, 2124, 2138, 2625, 2664, 2793. *See also* General programs; Zoology

Entrepreneurship: 1242, 1794, 2889, 2930, 3067, 3099, 3293, 3411. *See also* Business administration; General programs

Environmental engineering. *See* Engineering, environmental

Environmental law: 1826, 2103, 2396, 2480, 3020, 3197, 3242. *See also* General programs; Law, general

Environmental sciences: 1049, 1243, 1290, 1371–1372, 1375, 1386, 1406, 1440, 1653, 1657, 1669, 1715, 1724, 1749, 1773, 1800, 1825–1826, 1833, 1837, 1851, 1902, 1920, 1924, 1928, 1931, 1934, 1945, 1947, 1953, 1988–1989, 1999–2001, 2047, 2069, 2091–2092, 2103, 2117–2118, 2124, 2130, 2139–2142, 2156, 2158–2159, 2193–2194, 2199, 2246, 2257, 2263, 2302–2303, 2324, 2358, 2396, 2398, 2428, 2439–2440, 2444, 2480, 2514, 2519, 2537, 2569, 2602, 2618, 2625, 2669, 2677, 2679, 2707, 2709, 2721, 2749, 2753, 2759, 2764, 2775, 2787, 2793, 2805, 2810, 2814–2815, 2820, 2828, 2849, 2915, 2926, 2937, 2961, 3020, 3032–3033, 3036–3037, 3137–3138, 3197, 3224, 3242, 3288, 3338, 3414, 3420. *See also* General programs; Sciences

Epidemiology: 2141, 3037. *See also* General programs; Medical sciences

Equine science: 1703, 1866, 2107, 2151, 2514, 2766, 2797, 3022. *See also* Agriculture and agricultural sciences; Animal science; General programs

Equipment: 427, 890. *See also* General programs

Ethics: 1374, 2703. *See also* General programs; Humanities

Exercise science. *See* Athletic training

Extrasensory perception. *See* Parapsychology

Eye doctors. *See* Optometry

Eye problems. *See* Visual impairments

Fabric. *See* Clothing

Family and consumer studies: 1411, 2224, 2432, 2529, 2965, 3084, 3107, 3200, 3206, 3334, 3422. *See also* General programs; Social sciences

Family and consumer studies education. *See* Education, family and consumer studies

Farming. *See* Agriculture and agricultural sciences

Fashion design: 1384, 1733, 1752. *See also* Costume; Design; General programs; Home economics

Feminist movement. *See* Women's studies and programs

Fermentation industries. *See* Beer and wine industries

Fiber. *See* Textiles

Fiction: 93, 1275, 1277, 1279, 1397, 1419, 1462, 1666. *See also* General programs; Writers and writing

Film as a literary art. *See* Cinema

Filmmaking: 1239, 1242, 1277, 1298, 1308, 1316, 1361, 1367, 1401, 1420, 1540, 1625, 1642, 1664, 1668, 1673, 1689, 1701, 1719, 1736, 1749, 1752, 1794. *See also* Audiovisual materials and equipment; General programs; Television

Finance: 776, 1273, 1301, 1748, 1863, 1941, 2021, 2033, 2051, 2093, 2169, 2235, 2266, 2409, 2545, 2609–2610, 2701, 2859–2861, 2870, 2880, 2903, 2911, 2918, 2931, 2936, 2941, 2956, 2972, 2976, 2986, 2994, 3010, 3015, 3055, 3057, 3061, 3073, 3091, 3111, 3115, 3132, 3134, 3167, 3179, 3204, 3219, 3244, 3250, 3253–3254, 3256–3257, 3261, 3264, 3273, 3292, 3332–3333, 3345, 3365, 3383, 3388, 3399, 3402, 3413, 3421, 3423. *See also* Accounting; Banking; Economics; General programs

Fine arts: 360, 694, 1256, 1262, 1344, 1393, 1479, 1626, 1752, 1821, 3142. *See also* General programs; Humanities; names of specific fine arts

Fire protection engineering. *See* Engineering, fire protection

Fire science: 1833, 1924, 2219, 2246, 2366, 2398, 2428, 2439, 2447, 2787, 3075, 3196. *See also* General programs; Sciences

Fishing industry: 1931, 2926. *See also* General programs

Flight science. *See* Aviation

Floriculture. *See* Horticulture

Flying. *See* Aviation

Folklore: 1509. *See also* General programs; Literature

Food. *See* Culinary arts; Nutrition

Food science: 1335, 1467, 1762, 1793, 1878, 1957, 2005, 2014, 2230, 2285, 2287, 2299–2301, 2351, 2369, 2452–2454, 2458, 2511, 2514, 2526, 2542, 2552, 2562, 2589, 2632, 2737, 2752, 2788, 2875, 2971, 3130, 3271, 3408, 3430. *See also* Food service industry; General programs; Nutrition

Food service industry: 1264, 1306–1307, 1309, 1467, 1746, 2005, 2285, 2752, 2868, 2890–2891, 2895, 2910, 2963, 3021, 3130, 3133, 3153, 3173, 3181, 3188, 3220, 3233, 3249, 3266–3268, 3282, 3305, 3325, 3342, 3352, 3354, 3370, 3392, 3401, 3408, 3417, 3428. *See also* General programs

Food technology. *See* Food science

Foreign affairs. *See* International affairs

Foreign language. *See* Language and linguistics

Foreign language education. *See* Education, foreign languages

Forensic science: 2222. *See also* Criminal justice; General programs

Forestry engineering. *See* Engineering, forestry

Forestry management: 1243, 1290, 1375, 1386, 1406, 1440, 1715, 1724, 1800, 1825, 1898, 1928, 1931, 1953, 1988, 2024, 2124, 2156, 2193–2194, 2257, 2267, 2324, 2330, 2357, 2516, 2669, 2712, 2788, 2793, 2797, 2805, 2849, 2926, 3430. *See also* General programs; Management; Wood industry

Funerals. *See* Mortuary science

Gardening. *See* Horticulture

Gender. *See* Women's studies and programs

Genealogy: 1724, 2805. *See also* General programs; History

General programs: 1–69, 71–77, 79–175, 177–277, 279–381, 383–637, 639–693, 695–775, 777–951, 953–958, 960–1236, 1266, 1300, 1314, 1322, 1325–1327, 1352, 1355, 1393, 1397, 1403–1405, 1428, 1442, 1483, 1497, 1500, 1513–1514, 1518, 1521, 1523, 1551, 1554, 1564, 1620, 1632, 1641, 1660, 1670, 1673, 1709–1711, 1719, 1747, 1754, 1757, 1769, 1795, 1801, 1834, 1866, 1948, 2290, 2309, 2385–2386, 2391, 2425, 2481, 2517, 2567, 2569, 2592, 2672, 2683, 2732, 2779, 2858, 2886, 2889, 2893, 2897, 2930, 2938, 2944, 2962, 3017–3018, 3034, 3054, 3096, 3104, 3109, 3146, 3159, 3171, 3192, 3213, 3231–3232, 3260, 3265, 3293, 3316, 3318, 3320, 3328–3329, 3398, 3400, 3406, 3427. *See also* United States

Genetics: 2709. *See also* General programs; Medical sciences

Geography: 1544, 1947, 2012, 2396, 2519, 2775, 2937, 3197, 3216, 3338, 3420. *See also* General programs; Social sciences

Geology: 1773, 1825, 1900, 1906, 1945, 1954, 2092, 2140–2141, 2228, 2381, 2479, 2484, 2545, 2709, 2844, 3036–3037, 3292. *See also* Earth sciences; General programs; Physical sciences

Geophysics: 1900, 1918, 2058, 2150, 2212–2215, 2243, 2247, 2381, 2484, 2636, 2697, 2704, 2794

Geosciences. *See* Earth sciences

Geriatric nurses and nursing. *See* Nurses and nursing, geriatric

Geriatrics. *See* Aged and aging

Gerontology. *See* Aged and aging

Golf: 2917. *See also* Athletics; General programs

Golf course management. *See* Turfgrass science

Government. *See* Political science and politics; Public administration

Grade school. *See* Education, elementary

Graphic arts: 1256, 1275, 1330, 1336, 1390, 1418, 1425, 1434, 1467, 1511, 1527, 1630, 1642, 1663–1664, 1670, 1695, 1727, 1734, 1752, 1821, 2007, 2043, 2110–2111, 2285, 2344, 2688, 2821, 2991, 3024–3025, 3092, 3130, 3154, 3463. *See also* Art; Arts and crafts; General programs

Graphic design: 1263, 1265, 1297, 1343, 1418, 1510, 1517, 1530, 1596, 1668, 1679, 1692, 1740. *See also* Design; General programs; Graphic arts

Greek language. *See* Language, Greek

Grocery industry: 2912. *See also* General programs

Guidance. *See* Counseling

Hair design: 176, 638, 1870, 1973, 2906, 2950. *See also* General programs

Handicapped. *See* Disabilities

Health and health care: 176, 638, 1398, 1414, 1463, 1549, 1573, 1600, 1647, 1707, 1728, 1774, 1817, 1820, 1836, 1870, 1887, 1973, 1999, 2021, 2025, 2083, 2108, 2123, 2127, 2141, 2171, 2176, 2229, 2252, 2259–2260, 2264–2265, 2274, 2281, 2291, 2302–2303, 2343, 2443, 2462, 2474, 2505–2507, 2553, 2576, 2584, 2611, 2642, 2644, 2650–2651, 2658, 2674, 2695, 2781, 2798, 2802, 2811, 2851, 2873, 2882, 2906, 2950, 2976, 2981, 3023, 3037, 3056, 3058, 3085, 3101, 3113–3114, 3127, 3137–3138, 3222, 3226 3227, 3241, 3259, 3296, 3317, 3351, 3353, 3356–3357, 3368, 3418. *See also* General programs; Medical sciences

Health education. *See* Education, health

Hearing impairments: 646, 2980, 3231. *See also* Disabilities; General programs; Rehabilitation

Heart disease. *See* Cardiology

Heating industry: 2004, 2384, 2411, 2694, 3205, 3380, 3392. *See also* Building trades; General programs

High schools. *See* Education, secondary

Higher education. *See* Education, higher

Historical preservation: 1281, 1319, 1344, 1478. *See also* General programs; History

History: 1281, 1283, 1356, 1455–1456, 1493, 1544, 1578, 1602, 1638, 1706, 1732, 1742, 1917, 2273, 2556, 2923, 3035, 3112, 3118, 3157, 3216, 3458. *See also* General programs; Humanities; Social sciences; specific types of history

History, American: 1319, 1349, 1351, 1415, 1449, 1458, 1523, 1528, 1548, 1662, 1723–1724, 2805, 3139. *See also* General programs; History

History, art: 1364, 1684. *See also* Art; General programs; History

History, Norwegian: 1509. *See also* General programs; History

History, Polish: 1693. *See also* General programs

Home economics: 1283, 1724, 1769, 1917, 2633, 2788, 2805, 2816, 2923, 3344, 3430. *See also* Family and consumer studies; General programs

Homeland security. *See* Security, national

Horses. *See* Equine science

Horticulture: 1243, 1254, 1287, 1290, 1375, 1386, 1406, 1440, 1566, 1577, 1653, 1705, 1714–1715, 1717, 1800, 1819, 1868, 1889, 1915, 1926, 1928, 1960, 1969–1970, 2076, 2082, 2098, 2105, 2124, 2156, 2167, 2177, 2193–2194, 2250, 2257, 2323, 2328, 2354, 2365, 2372, 2378, 2394, 2411, 2514–2515, 2587, 2604, 2653, 2664, 2677, 2696, 2706, 2712, 2722, 2767, 2770, 2788–2789, 2793, 2797, 2810, 2825–2826, 2849, 3097, 3143, 3205, 3255, 3430. *See also* Agriculture and agricultural sciences; General programs; Landscape architecture; Sciences

Hospitality industry. *See* Hotel and motel industry

Hospitals. *See* Health and health care

Hotel and motel industry: 1264, 1309, 1467, 1539, 2285, 2868, 2890–2891, 2895, 2910, 2964, 3021, 3051, 3124, 3126, 3130, 3153, 3173, 3188, 3209, 3220, 3249, 3268, 3282, 3305, 3325, 3346, 3352, 3354, 3370, 3392, 3396, 3417, 3423, 3428. *See also* General programs

Housing: 427. *See also* General programs

Human resources. *See* Personnel administration

Human rights. *See* Civil rights

Human services. *See* Social services

Humanities: 531, 1242, 1311, 1326, 1439, 1461, 1479, 1500, 1579, 1794, 1971, 2949, 3103, 3125, 3142. *See also* General programs; names of specific humanities

Hydraulic engineering. *See* Engineering, hydraulic

Hydrology: 1271, 1844, 1855, 1900, 1906, 1942, 1945, 2092, 2141, 2146, 2280, 2297–2298, 2407, 2437, 2484, 3037. *See also* Earth sciences; General programs

Illustrators and illustrations: 1378, 1418, 1753. *See also* Art; General programs; Graphic arts

Industrial design: 1465, 2284. *See also* Design; General programs

Industrial engineering. *See* Engineering, industrial

Industrial hygiene: 1833, 1924, 1945, 2092, 2246, 2398, 2428, 2439, 2759, 2787, 2814. *See also* General programs; Health and health care; Safety studies

Industrial relations: 3385. *See also* General programs; Labor unions and members

Information science: 176, 278, 776, 1474, 1510, 1671, 1870, 1941, 1973, 2021, 2033, 2051, 2087, 2144, 2162, 2169, 2171, 2234, 2265–2266, 2304, 2413, 2451, 2474, 2500, 2545, 2560, 2642, 2657, 2698, 2751, 2802, 2863, 2870, 2906, 2927, 2931, 2950, 2972, 2976, 2986, 2994, 3038, 3055–3057, 3089, 3114–3115, 3134, 3183, 3241, 3253–3254, 3292, 3351, 3362, 3382, 3396, 3399, 3407. *See also* Computer sciences; General programs; Libraries and librarianship

Insurance. *See* Actuarial sciences

Intellectual freedom: 1342. *See also* Censorship; Civil liberties; General programs

Intelligence service: 3096. *See also* General programs; International affairs; Military affairs

Interior design: 1256, 1312, 1317, 1319, 1364, 1466, 1671, 1733, 1752, 1821, 2698, 3382. *See also* Architecture; Design; General programs; Home economics

International affairs: 48, 52, 1544, 1615, 1754, 2273, 2426, 2893–2894, 2946, 3005, 3118, 3164, 3215–3216. *See also* General programs; Political science and politics

International relations. *See* International affairs

Internet design and development: 1336, 1695, 1758, 2043, 2110–2111, 2344, 2821, 2991, 3024–3025, 3154. *See also* General programs; Graphic arts; Technology

Internet journalism. *See* Journalism, online

Iron and steel industry: 1899. *See also* General programs; Metallurgy

Italian language. *See* Language, Italian

Japanese language. *See* Language, Japanese

Japanese studies: 1754. *See also* General programs; Humanities

Jazz. *See* Music, jazz

Jewelry: 1563, 1664, 1748. *See also* Arts and crafts; General programs

Jewish studies: 529, 1447, 1475, 1497, 1564, 3106, 3159. *See also* General programs; Religion and religious activities

Jobs. *See* Employment

Journalism: 1248–1249, 1252–1253, 1274, 1280, 1284, 1295–1298, 1300, 1320, 1335, 1340, 1342–1343, 1345–1347, 1352–1353, 1357, 1364–1365, 1370, 1376, 1379, 1382, 1387, 1391–1392, 1394–1395, 1402, 1405, 1408, 1412–1413, 1419, 1429, 1433, 1445–1446, 1450, 1452, 1454, 1461, 1467, 1470, 1474, 1480, 1501, 1510, 1513, 1517, 1524, 1529, 1547, 1550, 1553, 1556–1558, 1571–1572, 1574, 1589–1590, 1595–1597, 1603, 1606–1607, 1609–1610, 1612, 1615, 1623–1625, 1629, 1633, 1650–1652, 1668–1669, 1674, 1683, 1685, 1703–1704, 1725, 1729–1730, 1733, 1736–1737, 1739, 1744, 2014, 2172, 2285, 2304, 2385, 2526, 2766, 2971, 3002, 3013, 3046, 3110, 3125, 3130, 3271. *See also* Broadcasting; Communications; General programs; Writers and writing; names of specific types of journalism

Journalism, agriculture. *See* Agricultural communications

Journalism, broadcast: 1248, 1253, 1257, 1280, 1285, 1328, 1333, 1343, 1408, 1429, 1443, 1446, 1450, 1464, 1467, 1472, 1489, 1506, 1524, 1543, 1547, 1557, 1559, 1571–1572, 1593, 1597, 1603, 1605, 1613, 1625, 1629, 1634, 1636, 1668–1669, 1712, 1721, 1725, 1736, 1744, 2283, 2285, 2558, 3129–3130, 3289. *See also* Communications; General programs; Radio; Television

Journalism, medical. *See* Science reporting

Journalism, online: 1345–1346, 1429, 1524, 1571–1572, 1669, 1725. *See also* General programs; Journalism

Journalism, religion. *See* Religious reporting

Journalism, science. *See* Science reporting

Journalism, sports. *See* Sports reporting

Junior colleges. *See* Education, higher

Jurisprudence. *See* Law, general

Kinesiology: 2079

Labor unions and members: 1554, 2944, 3139, 3232, 3328, 3425. *See also* General programs; Industrial relations

Landscape architecture: 78, 1243, 1254, 1271, 1287, 1290, 1364, 1368–1369, 1375, 1386, 1406, 1410, 1434, 1438, 1440, 1577, 1637, 1639, 1690, 1705, 1714–1715, 1743, 1752, 1800, 1819, 1825, 1855, 1926, 1928, 2124, 2156, 2167, 2193–2194, 2257, 2394, 2653, 2664, 2738, 2767, 2789, 2793, 2849, 3392. *See also* Botany; General programs; Horticulture

Language and linguistics: 694, 1283, 1917, 2923. *See also* General programs; Humanities; names of specific languages

Language, Brazilian. *See* Language, Portuguese

Language, Chinese: 1289. *See also* General programs; Language and linguistics

Language, English: 694, 1249, 1283, 1296, 1449, 1467, 1601, 1656, 1686, 1917, 2285, 2923, 3130. *See also* General programs; Language and linguistics

Language, Greek: 1240, 1541, 1579, 1708, 2948. *See also* General programs; Language and linguistics

Language, Italian: 1681. *See also* General programs; Language and linguistics

Language, Japanese: 1754. *See also* General programs; Language and linguistics

Language, Latin: 1541, 1579–1580, 1608, 1696, 1708, 2948, 3311, 3405. *See also* General programs; Language and linguistics

Language, Polish: 1693. *See also* General programs; Language and linguistics

Language, Portuguese: 1389, 1453, 1496. *See also* General programs; Language and linguistics
Language, Spanish: 1496. *See also* General programs; Language and linguistics
Language, Swedish: 1049. *See also* General programs; Language and linguistics
Latin. *See* Language, Latin
Law enforcement. *See* Criminal justice
Law, general: 143, 743, 1162, 1311, 1455, 1460–1461, 1544, 1707, 1874, 1948, 1971, 2194, 2273, 2276, 2391, 2609, 2725, 2775, 2908, 2929, 2938, 2941, 2949, 3057, 3112, 3118–3119, 3125, 3192, 3216, 3238, 3275, 3332, 3371, 3395, 3418, 3420. *See also* Criminal justice; General programs; Paralegal studies; Social sciences; names of legal specialties
Lawyers. *See* Law, general
Leadership: 752, 776, 1135, 3427. *See also* General programs; Management
Legal assistants. *See* Paralegal studies
Legal studies and services. *See* Law, general
Leisure studies: 2079, 2942, 3211. *See also* General programs; Recreation
Librarians. *See* Libraries and librarianship
Libraries and librarianship: 1732. *See also* General programs; Information science; Social sciences
Libraries and librarianship, school: 3155, 3199, 3280, 3307. *See also* General programs; Libraries and librarianship
Life insurance. *See* Actuarial sciences
Life sciences. *See* Biological sciences
Lighting: 1256, 1473, 1743, 1821. *See also* Architecture; General programs
Linguistics. *See* Language and linguistics
Literature: 1476, 1479, 1516, 1601, 1649, 1678, 3142. *See also* General programs; Humanities; Writers and writing; specific types of literature
Literature, American: 1279, 1397, 1449. *See also* American studies; General programs; Literature
Literature, English: 1283, 1656, 1917, 2923. *See also* General programs; Literature
Literature, Norwegian: 1509. *See also* General programs; Literature
Literature, Swedish: 1049. *See also* General programs; Literature
Logistics: 2235, 2409, 2468, 2609, 2701, 2718, 2859–2861, 3006, 3091, 3204, 3236, 3332, 3383, 3404. *See also* General programs; Transportation
Long–term care nurses and nursing. *See* Nurses and nursing, long–term care
Machine trades: 2421. *See also* General programs
Magazines. *See* Journalism; Literature
Management: 776, 1262, 1273, 1301, 1339, 1467, 1593, 1728, 1746, 1766, 1774, 1863, 1904, 1910–1911, 1943, 1997, 2020, 2025, 2051, 2141, 2171, 2178, 2198, 2223, 2252, 2255, 2264, 2266, 2285, 2468, 2507, 2533, 2538, 2545, 2609, 2621, 2642, 2650–2652, 2724, 2773, 2775, 2802, 2811, 2862, 2867, 2872–2873, 2891, 2903, 2912, 2916, 2920–2921, 2932, 2936, 2960, 2972, 2975, 2981, 2994–2995, 3006–3007, 3037, 3056, 3059, 3070, 3080, 3099, 3101–3102, 3113, 3115, 3130–3131, 3134, 3144, 3153, 3236, 3263, 3279, 3289, 3292, 3295, 3317, 3323, 3332, 3339, 3351, 3356–3358, 3386, 3388, 3392, 3394, 3399, 3419–3420, 3423. *See also* General programs; Social sciences
Management, nurses and nursing. *See* Nurses and nursing, administration
Manufacturing engineering. *See* Engineering, manufacturing
Maps and mapmaking. *See* Cartography
Marine sciences: 1243, 1290, 1375, 1440, 1715, 1800, 1928, 2124, 2257, 2669, 2764, 2793, 2815, 3414. *See also* General programs; Sciences; names of specific marine sciences
Marketing: 705, 1329, 1335, 1338, 1358, 1392, 1425, 1467, 1510, 1574, 1607, 1668, 1740, 1748, 1758, 1941, 2014, 2043, 2051, 2110–2111, 2169, 2250, 2255, 2285, 2323, 2344, 2526, 2821, 2891, 2912, 2929, 2931, 2966, 2971, 2974, 2991, 2994, 3003, 3007, 3024–3025, 3046, 3055, 3057, 3092, 3097, 3099, 3102, 3130, 3143, 3154, 3187, 3220, 3253–3254, 3264, 3271, 3274, 3323, 3388, 3392. *See also* Advertising; General programs; Public relations; Sales
Marketing education. *See* Education, business
Mass communications. *See* Communications
Massage therapy: 176, 638, 1870, 1973, 2906, 2950. *See also* General programs; Therapy
Materials engineering. *See* Engineering, materials
Materials sciences: 1788, 1832, 1837, 1890, 1894, 1899, 2031, 2115, 2131, 2154, 2187, 2216, 2239, 2254, 2262, 2307, 2320, 2356, 2400, 2549, 2568, 2659, 2684, 2709, 2736, 2769, 2841, 2863. *See also* General programs; Physical sciences
Mathematics: 17–18, 278, 383, 694, 1242, 1283, 1311, 1671, 1785, 1787, 1790–1792, 1794, 1814, 1824, 1832, 1835, 1883, 1901, 1907–1908, 1917, 1952, 1971, 1987, 2002, 2033, 2064, 2122, 2141, 2144, 2187, 2204, 2206, 2238, 2262, 2265, 2273, 2279, 2302–2303, 2350, 2367, 2413, 2429, 2436, 2466, 2476, 2490, 2519, 2521, 2527, 2545, 2560, 2567–2568, 2571, 2598, 2640, 2647, 2654–2655, 2687, 2690, 2698, 2705, 2707, 2709, 2713, 2778, 2800, 2856, 2923, 2940, 2949, 2952, 2986, 3037–3038, 3114, 3118, 3137–3138, 3235, 3245, 3272, 3292, 3308, 3359–3360, 3377, 3382, 3424. *See also* Computer sciences; General programs; Physical sciences; Statistics
Measurement. *See* Testing
Mechanical engineering. *See* Engineering, mechanical
Media. *See* Broadcasting; Communications; names of specific media
Media specialists. *See* Libraries and librarianship; Libraries and librarianship, school

Medical journalism. *See* Science reporting
Medical sciences: 143, 781, 1200, 1311, 1313, 1460, 1552, 1667, 1724, 1761, 1766, 1823, 1908, 1948, 1952, 1971, 1978, 2033, 2081, 2108, 2125, 2241, 2258, 2260, 2276, 2291, 2302–2303, 2396, 2442, 2448, 2540, 2548, 2564–2565, 2584, 2624, 2639, 2674, 2693, 2695, 2725, 2732, 2755, 2805, 2851, 2856, 2867, 2885, 2938, 2940, 2949, 2951, 2986, 3023, 3119, 3137–3138, 3197, 3230, 3368, 3379, 3395, 3398. *See also* General programs; Health and health care; Sciences; names of specific diseases; names of medical specialties
Medical technology: 1766, 1829, 1850, 1884–1885, 1925, 2033–2034, 2075, 2129, 2174, 2259, 2392, 2419, 2447, 2470, 2551, 2584, 2593, 2599, 2678, 2731, 2765, 2817, 2853, 2867, 2986. *See also* General programs; Medical sciences; Technology
Mental health: 2059, 3001. *See also* General programs; Health and health care
Mental retardation: 2327. *See also* Disabilities, developmental; General programs; Medical sciences
Merchandising. *See* Sales
Metal trades. *See* Machine trades
Metallurgical engineering. *See* Engineering, metallurgical
Metallurgy: 1748, 1788, 1890, 1899, 2115, 2216, 2228, 2254, 2307, 2356, 2400, 2478–2479, 2549, 2736, 2769, 2841. *See also* Engineering, metallurgical; General programs; Sciences
Meteorology: 17–18, 1805, 1844, 1900, 1942, 1944, 2002, 2008, 2146, 2297, 2407, 2437, 2484, 2519. *See also* Atmospheric sciences; General programs
Microcomputers. *See* Computer sciences
Microscopy. *See* Medical technology
Military affairs: 2273, 3118, 3260. *See also* General programs
Mineral law. *See* Environmental law
Mining engineering. *See* Engineering, mining
Mining industry: 2154, 2247, 2320. *See also* General programs
Missionary work. *See* Religion and religious activities
Mortuary science: 2879, 2943, 2977, 2989, 3141, 3160, 3172, 3184, 3189, 3240, 3251, 3283, 3309, 3403, 3453. *See also* General programs
Motel industry. *See* Hotel and motel industry
Music: 640, 1049, 1214, 1242, 1247, 1270, 1272, 1277, 1282–1283, 1293, 1302, 1308, 1313, 1360, 1362, 1378, 1396, 1417, 1420, 1423, 1476, 1479, 1483, 1502, 1505, 1509, 1522, 1535, 1551, 1560, 1567, 1569, 1588, 1598, 1618–1619, 1649, 1676–1677, 1680, 1688, 1699, 1701, 1718, 1720, 1726, 1747, 1794, 1917, 1978, 2923, 2951, 3007, 3142, 3146. *See also* Education, music; Fine arts; General programs; Humanities; Performing arts
Music, church: 1282, 1321, 1324, 1388, 1416, 1537, 1560, 1576, 1582, 1655, 1699. *See also* General programs; Music; Performing arts; Religion and religious activities
Music, classical: 1242, 1331, 1362, 1416, 1525, 1726, 1794. *See also* General programs; Music
Music education. *See* Education, music
Music, jazz: 1277, 1484–1485, 1726. *See also* General programs; Music
Music, piano: 1282, 1323, 1396, 1567, 1569. *See also* General programs; Music
Music, strings: 1331, 1490, 1567, 1569. *See also* General programs; Music
Music therapy: 1363, 1570, 2071, 2497. *See also* General programs; Music; Therapy
Music, viola: 1735. *See also* General programs; Music, strings
Music, violin: 1672, 1738. *See also* General programs; Music, strings
Musicals: 1360. *See also* Composers and compositions; General programs; Music
National security. *See* Security, national
Native American studies: 1751. *See also* General programs
Natural resources: 1290, 1375, 1653, 1687, 1715, 1749, 1816, 1825, 1908, 1928, 1931, 1947, 1951–1952, 1981, 2013, 2103, 2124, 2130, 2140, 2290, 2514, 2677, 2721, 2733, 2753, 2764, 2777, 2788, 2793, 2815, 2926, 2937, 2940, 3020, 3036, 3414, 3430. *See also* General programs; names of specific resources
Natural resources law. *See* Environmental law
Natural sciences: 1460, 1932, 2103, 2276, 2373, 3020, 3119. *See also* General programs; Sciences; names of specific sciences
Naval architecture: 1848, 2560. *See also* Architecture; General programs; Naval science
Naval engineering. *See* Engineering, naval
Naval science: 782–784, 2779. *See also* General programs
Neonatal and perinatal nurses and nursing. *See* Nurses and nursing, neonatal and perinatal
Neuroscience: 2531. *See also* General programs; Medical sciences
Neuroscience nurses and nursing. *See* Nurses and nursing, neuroscience
New Jersey: 344
Newspapers. *See* Journalism
Nonfiction: 70, 78, 93, 174, 291, 384, 407, 410, 541, 870, 892, 922, 1113, 1153, 1266, 1275, 1353, 1374, 1387, 1405, 1419, 1428, 1523, 1528, 1531, 1638, 1660, 1666, 1670, 1686, 1732, 1757, 1795, 1801, 1877, 2094, 2201, 2233–2234, 2481, 2518, 2623, 2627, 2659, 2709, 2741, 2864, 2880, 2887, 2894, 2930, 3006, 3017, 3087–3089, 3135, 3229, 3234, 3250, 3265, 3285, 3294, 3313. *See also* General programs; Writers and writing
Nonprofit sector: 2985. *See also* General programs; Public administration
Norwegian history. *See* History, Norwegian

Norwegian literature. *See* Literature, Norwegian
Norwegian studies: 1509. *See also* Humanities
Novels: 1462, 1666. *See also* Fiction; General programs; Writers and writing
Nuclear engineering. *See* Engineering, nuclear
Nuclear science: 1856–1857, 1989, 2047, 2049, 2331, 2347, 2571, 2577, 3308. *See also* General programs; Physical sciences
Nurses and nursing, administration: 2175. *See also* General programs; Management; Nurses and nursing, general
Nurses and nursing, critical care: 2112. *See also* General programs; Nurses and nursing, general
Nurses and nursing, dermatology: 2060, 2192. *See also* General programs; Nurses and nursing, general
Nurses and nursing, emergency: 1986, 2132, 2334, 2434, 2544, 2639. *See also* General programs; Nurses and nursing, general
Nurses and nursing, general: 776, 1200, 1430, 1667, 1770, 1789, 1806, 1818, 1823, 1864, 1869, 1919, 1921, 1930, 1933, 1940, 1961–1962, 1968, 1996, 2010, 2021–2022, 2033, 2063, 2085–2086, 2089, 2143, 2163, 2181, 2183, 2195, 2217, 2227, 2237, 2249, 2256, 2259–2260, 2274, 2288, 2291, 2293, 2308, 2322, 2335, 2370, 2377, 2392, 2417, 2430, 2433, 2435, 2449, 2459, 2474, 2485, 2489, 2491, 2508, 2523–2525, 2535, 2550, 2580, 2582, 2584, 2588, 2597, 2611–2612, 2682, 2693, 2695, 2699–2700, 2730, 2754, 2758, 2772, 2790, 2795, 2806–2807, 2816, 2819, 2823, 2833, 2850–2851, 2885, 2904, 2976, 2986, 3063, 3241, 3379. *See also* General programs; Health and health care; Medical sciences; names of specific nursing specialties
Nurses and nursing, geriatrics: 2446. *See also* Aged and aging; General programs; Nurses and nursing, general
Nurses and nursing, long–term care: 2288. *See also* General programs; Nurses and nursing, general
Nurses and nursing, neonatal and perinatal: 2175. *See also* General programs; Nurses and nursing, general
Nurses and nursing, neuroscience: 2530. *See also* General programs; Neuroscience; Nurses and nursing, general
Nurses and nursing, occupational health: 1820, 1836, 2462. *See also* General programs; Nurses and nursing, general
Nurses and nursing, oncology: 2147, 2575, 2668. *See also* Cancer; General programs; Nurses and nursing, general
Nurses and nursing, operating room: 1861, 1905. *See also* General programs; Nurses and nursing, general; Surgery
Nurses and nursing, rehabilitation: 1873. *See also* General programs; Nurses and nursing, general; Rehabilitation
Nurses and nursing, school health: 3199, 3462. *See also* General programs; Nurses and nursing, general
Nurses and nursing, wound, ostomy and continence: 2854–2855. *See also* General programs; Nurses and nursing, general
Nutrition: 1467, 2005, 2065, 2225, 2259, 2285, 2432, 2526, 2529, 2562, 2709, 2711, 2752, 2788, 2816, 2848, 3130, 3271, 3408, 3430. *See also* General programs; Home economics; Medical sciences
Occupational health nurses and nursing. *See* Nurses and nursing, occupational health
Occupational safety: 1833, 1924, 2246, 2398, 2428, 2439, 2787, 2814. *See also* General programs; Employment; Health and health care
Occupational therapy: 1830, 1879, 2079, 2389. *See also* Counseling; Employment; General programs
Ocean engineering. *See* Engineering, ocean
Oceanography: 1844, 1900, 1942, 2033, 2146, 2297–2298, 2407, 2437, 2460, 2484, 2764, 2986, 3414. *See also* General programs; Marine sciences
Office skills. *See* Secretarial sciences
Oil industry. *See* Petroleum industry
Oncology. *See* Cancer
Oncology nurses and nursing. *See* Nurses and nursing, oncology
Online journalism. *See* Journalism, online
Opera. *See* Music; Voice
Operations research: 17–18, 2169, 2265, 2911, 3055, 3114, 3256. *See also* General programs; Mathematics; Sciences
Optical engineering. *See* Engineering, optical
Optics: 2726, 2863. *See also* General programs; Physics
Optometry: 1804, 2218, 2695, 2812, 3454. *See also* General programs; Medical sciences
Oratory: 409, 891, 893, 1242, 1266, 1314, 1701, 1794, 2481, 2573, 2889, 2897. *See also* General programs
Osteopathy: 2258, 2695. *See also* General programs; Medical sciences
Ostomy. *See* Nurses and nursing, wound, ostomy and continence
Packaging engineering. *See* Engineering, packaging
Packaging industry: 2030. *See also* General programs
Painting: 1242, 1275, 1378, 1381, 1385, 1418, 1664, 1684, 1727, 1794. *See also* Art; General programs
Paper industry: 1330, 1988, 2007, 2030, 2134, 2139, 2324, 2554, 2586, 2595, 2635, 2838. *See also* General programs
Paralegal studies: 1311, 1971, 2949, 3275, 3324. *See also* General programs; Social sciences
Parapsychology: 3031, 3363. *See also* General programs; Psychology

Patriotism: 1755, 2897, 3109, 3260, 3329, 3443, 3447. *See also* General programs
Peace studies: 1162, 1399, 1544, 3072, 3216, 3265, 3400. *See also* General programs; Political science and politics
Performing arts: 705, 1242, 1246, 1251, 1262, 1277, 1302, 1308, 1360, 1378, 1476–1477, 1499, 1628, 1701–1702, 1794. *See also* General programs; Humanities; names of specific performing arts
Perinatal nurses and nursing. *See* Nurses and nursing, neonatal and perinatal
Personnel administration: 776, 1651, 2051, 2255, 2609, 2798, 2912, 2993–2994, 3014, 3057, 3102, 3122, 3277–3278, 3332, 3385. *See also* General programs; Management
Pest management: 1960. *See also* Biological sciences; General programs
Petroleum engineering. *See* Engineering, petroleum
Petroleum industry: 952, 2622. *See also* General programs
Pharmaceutical sciences: 1804, 1887–1888, 2259, 2291, 2548, 2584, 2695, 3392. *See also* General programs; Medical sciences
Philology. *See* Language and linguistics
Philosophy: 1399, 1531, 1544, 3216. *See also* General programs; Humanities
Photogrammetry: 2012, 2519, 2660. *See also* Cartography; General programs; Photography
Photography: 1242, 1277, 1298, 1381, 1418, 1467, 1512, 1664, 1679, 1684, 1687, 1727, 1733, 1752, 1794, 2285, 2637, 2733, 3130. *See also* Fine arts; General programs
Photojournalism: 1280, 1294, 1297–1298, 1332, 1343, 1346–1347, 1444, 1446, 1467, 1498, 1510, 1512, 1517, 1534, 1557, 1572, 1589, 1596–1597, 1603–1605, 1625, 1644, 1652, 2285, 3130. *See also* General programs; Journalism; Photography
Physical education. *See* Education, physical
Physical sciences: 278, 1311, 1766, 1835, 1848, 1907–1908, 1952, 1971, 2033, 2080, 2103, 2122, 2144, 2519, 2591, 2598, 2713, 2783, 2837, 2867, 2940, 2949, 2986, 3020, 3038. *See also* General programs; Sciences; names of specific physical sciences
Physical therapy: 1804, 1830, 1879, 2033, 2079, 2259, 2445, 2486, 2564–2565, 2596, 2624, 2986. *See also* Disabilities; General programs; Health and health care; Rehabilitation
Physician assistant: 1767, 1983, 2392, 2459, 2492, 2585, 2614, 2851. *See also* General programs; Health and health care; Medical sciences
Physics: 17–18, 1242, 1773, 1787, 1790–1792, 1794, 1845, 1862, 1901, 1907, 1954, 2002, 2017, 2090, 2141, 2157, 2204, 2206, 2238, 2273, 2279, 2302–2303, 2381, 2397, 2408, 2413, 2436, 2501, 2506, 2519, 2545, 2560, 2567, 2620, 2648, 2661, 2665, 2675, 2705, 2707, 2709, 2716, 2726, 2747, 2760, 2762, 2769, 2800–2801, 2856, 2863, 3037, 3118, 3137–3138, 3292. *See also* General programs; Mathematics; Physical sciences
Piano. *See* Music, piano
Plastics engineering. *See* Engineering, plastics
Plays: 1242, 1268, 1275, 1277, 1283, 1378, 1486, 1492, 1499, 1508, 1532, 1546, 1587, 1621, 1666, 1675, 1701–1702, 1794, 1917, 2923. *See also* General programs; Literature; Performing arts; Writers and writing
Plumbing industry: 2236, 2411, 2420, 2694, 3205, 3207, 3380. *See also* Building trades; General programs
Podiatry: 2695. *See also* General programs; Medical sciences
Poetry: 93, 1242, 1275, 1277, 1419, 1479, 1656, 1666, 1794, 3142. *See also* General programs; Literature; Writers and writing
Poisons. *See* Toxicology
Police science. *See* Criminal justice
Polish history. *See* History, Polish
Polish language. *See* Language, Polish
Polish studies: 1693. *See also* General programs; Humanities
Political science and politics: 1135, 1313, 1357, 1452, 1455, 1493, 1531, 1544, 1742, 1947, 1978, 2273, 2545, 2725, 2937, 2951, 3002, 3035, 3110, 3112, 3118, 3135, 3157, 3216, 3244, 3292, 3294, 3341, 3371, 3395, 3427. *See also* General programs; Public administration; Social sciences
Pollution: 2103, 3020. *See also* Environmental sciences; General programs
Polymer science: 1845, 2017, 2157, 2620, 2661, 2665, 2675, 2716, 2747, 2760, 2762, 2801. *See also* Chemistry; General programs
Population studies: 1749. *See also* General programs; Social sciences
Pork industry: 2481. *See also* Agriculture and agricultural sciences; General programs
Portuguese language. *See* Language, Portuguese
Portuguese studies: 1389, 1453. *See also* General programs; Humanities
Posters. *See* Graphic arts
Poultry science: 2562. *See also* Agriculture and agricultural sciences; Animal science; General programs
Preschool education. *See* Education, preschool
Preservation, historical. *See* Historical preservation
Presidents, U.S. *See* History, American
Press. *See* Journalism
Print journalism. *See* Journalism
Printing industry: 1390, 1630, 2043, 2110–2111, 2344, 2821, 2991, 3024–3025, 3154, 3392. *See also* General programs
Prints. *See* Art; Graphic arts
Psychology: 278, 1544, 1901, 2545, 2584, 2887, 2900, 2985, 3166, 3199, 3216, 3292. *See also* Behavioral sciences; Counseling; General programs; Social sciences

Public administration: 278, 1455, 1461, 1552, 1871, 1902, 1947, 2000, 2219, 2396, 2448, 2674, 2764, 2768, 2907, 2911, 2915, 2937, 2961, 2972, 3045, 3061, 3073–3075, 3112, 3125, 3151, 3197, 3230, 3244, 3256, 3338, 3341, 3364, 3368, 3414. *See also* General programs; Management; Political science and politics; Social sciences

Public affairs. *See* Public administration

Public health: 1766, 1774, 2025, 2103, 2252, 2311, 2370, 2392, 2440, 2576, 2584, 2650–2651, 2695, 2867, 2873, 2981, 3020, 3101, 3317, 3356–3357. *See also* General programs; Health and health care

Public policy. *See* Public administration

Public relations: 1249, 1253, 1292, 1296, 1350, 1357, 1395, 1407, 1433, 1452, 1459, 1467, 1519, 1529, 1574, 1607, 1625, 1631, 1633, 1658, 1668, 1685, 2043, 2172, 2285, 2396, 2526, 2912, 2991, 3002, 3110, 3130, 3187, 3197, 3271. *See also* General programs; Marketing

Public sector. *See* Public administration

Public service: 1018, 1220, 2886. *See also* General programs; Public administration; Social services

Public speaking. *See* Oratory

Public utilities. *See* Utilities

Publicity. *See* Public relations

Publishers and publishing: 1512, 1530, 1692, 3274. *See also* General programs

Pulp and paper industry. *See* Paper industry

Race relations: 1361. *See also* General programs

Racial discrimination. *See* Discrimination, racial

Racism. *See* Discrimination, racial

Radio: 1238, 1253, 1269, 1298, 1491, 1529, 1616, 1625, 1668, 1701, 1704, 1731, 1745. *See also* Communications; General programs

Radiology: 2141, 2313, 2337, 2673, 2708, 2792, 3037. *See also* General programs; Medical sciences

Ranching: 1957, 1972, 2013, 2286, 2388, 2518. *See also* Agriculture and agricultural sciences; General programs

Real estate: 2902, 2941, 3076, 3132, 3243, 3413. *See also* General programs

Recreation: 1398, 1414, 1463, 1487, 1527, 1549, 1573, 1600, 1647, 1653, 1657, 1728, 2176, 2229, 2281, 2332, 2443, 2505, 2553, 2644, 2677, 2679, 2771, 2811, 2942, 3058, 3085, 3127, 3148, 3211, 3222, 3226–3227, 3249, 3259, 3296, 3353, 3416. *See also* General programs; Leisure studies; names of specific recreational activities

Reentry programs: 47, 59, 107, 114, 121, 137, 143, 160, 233, 413, 479, 507, 623, 663, 767, 799, 820, 847, 934, 993, 1023, 1035, 1084, 1215, 1219, 1311, 1513, 1754, 1916, 1938, 1943, 1948, 1971, 2049, 2260, 2385, 2574, 2671, 2683, 2878, 2886, 2932, 2938, 2949, 3252, 3397, 3422. *See also* General programs

Refrigeration industry. *See* Cooling industry

Regional planning. *See* City and regional planning

Rehabilitation: 1873–1874, 2055, 2133, 2676, 2874, 2908, 2996, 3298, 3369. *See also* General programs; Health and health care; specific types of therapy

Religion and religious activities: 278, 293, 1068, 1130, 1132, 1237, 1266, 1283, 1314, 1325, 1354, 1366, 1380, 1400, 1403–1404, 1430, 1432, 1441, 1475, 1483, 1531, 1561, 1617, 1635, 1640, 1643, 1645–1646, 1648, 1660, 1667, 1682, 1694, 1697, 1702, 1707, 1710–1711, 1719, 1722, 1741, 1750, 1917, 2249, 2260, 2693, 2923, 3146, 3349, 3379, 3418. *See also* General programs; Humanities; Philosophy

Religious education. *See* Education, religious

Religious reporting: 1361, 1382, 1524. *See also* Broadcasting; General programs; Journalism; Religion and religious activities

Resource management: 1825, 1951, 2815. *See also* Environmental sciences; General programs; Management

Respiratory therapy: 2341, 2493, 2667, 2845. *See also* General programs; Health and health care; Therapy

Restaurants. *See* Food service industry

Retailing. *See* Sales

Retardation. *See* Mental retardation

Risk management: 3248. *See also* Actuarial sciences; Business administration; Finance; General programs

Robotics: 2740, 2832. *See also* General programs; Technology

Rubber industry: 2675. *See also* General programs

Safety studies: 1793, 1833, 1924, 1944, 2246, 2398, 2428, 2439, 2741, 2759, 2787, 2814, 2875. *See also* Engineering; General programs

Sales: 1464, 1593, 1733, 2283, 2538, 2891, 2912, 2917, 3129, 3289, 3392, 3401, 3451. *See also* General programs; Marketing

School counselors. *See* Counselors and counseling, school

School health nurses and nursing. *See* Nurses and nursing, school health

School libraries and librarians. *See* Libraries and librarianship, school

Schools. *See* Education

Science education. *See* Education, science and mathematics

Science reporting: 1298. *See also* Broadcasting; General programs; Journalism; Sciences; Writers and writing

Sciences: 383, 694, 1200, 1242, 1283, 1313, 1552, 1724, 1785, 1794, 1832, 1883, 1885, 1908, 1917, 1936, 1952, 1978, 1993, 1998, 2064, 2093–2094, 2134, 2138, 2142, 2187, 2210, 2262–2263, 2298, 2363, 2367, 2383, 2429, 2440, 2448, 2466–2467, 2476, 2488, 2503, 2568, 2571, 2586, 2595, 2602, 2610, 2617, 2635, 2640, 2666, 2705, 2729, 2761, 2805, 2838, 2840, 2856, 2864, 2923, 2940, 2951, 3015, 3161, 3230, 3235, 3308, 3333. *See also* General programs; names of specific sciences

Scottish studies: 1327, 2962. *See also* General programs; Humanities

Sculpture: 1242, 1377–1378, 1381, 1418, 1583–1584, 1664, 1684, 1794. *See also* Fine arts; General programs

Secondary education. *See* Education, secondary

Secret service. *See* Intelligence service

Secretarial sciences: 638, 2862, 3218, 3274–3275. *See also* General programs

Security, national: 2273, 3118. *See also* General programs; Military affairs

Short stories: 93, 1462, 1599, 1666. *See also* Fiction; General programs; Literature; Writers and writing

Sight impairments. *See* Visual impairments

Singing. *See* Voice

Smoking. *See* Tobacco consumption

Social sciences: 278, 694, 1283, 1288, 1311, 1439, 1461, 1917, 1971, 2144, 2302–2303, 2571, 2923, 2949, 3038, 3103, 3125, 3137–3138, 3308. *See also* General programs; names of specific social sciences

Social services: 187, 1483, 1667, 1707, 1817, 2059, 2693, 2882, 2886, 2983, 3001, 3146, 3165, 3217, 3379, 3418. *See also* General programs; Public service; Social work

Social work: 1475, 1823, 2108, 2259, 2732, 2885, 2955, 3023, 3199, 3211, 3398. *See also* General programs; Social sciences

Sociology: 1544, 1931, 2545, 2926, 3216, 3292. *See also* General programs; Social sciences

Soils science: 1825, 1931, 1956, 2130, 2319, 2353, 2422, 2664, 2797, 2926, 3212. *See also* Agriculture and agricultural sciences; General programs; Horticulture

Songs. *See* Music

Space sciences: 19, 1803, 1883, 1943, 2008, 2044, 2126, 2205, 2232, 2302–2303, 2381, 2503, 2521, 2546, 2590, 2932, 3137–3138. *See also* General programs; Physical sciences

Spanish language. *See* Language, Spanish

Special education. *See* Education, special

Speech pathology: 1830. *See also* General programs; Medical sciences

Speeches. *See* Oratory

Sports. *See* Athletics

Sports medicine: 2079. *See also* General programs; Medical sciences

Sports reporting: 1299, 1402, 1517. *See also* Broadcasting; General programs; Journalism; Writers and writing

Spying. *See* Intelligence service

Stage design. *See* Performing arts

Statistics: 1942, 2355, 2527, 2707, 3272. *See also* General programs; Mathematics

Steel industry. *See* Iron and steel industry

Stone industry: 1690, 1922, 2566, 2738. *See also* Building trades; General programs

Structural engineering. *See* Engineering, structural

Surgery: 2765. *See also* General programs; Medical sciences

Surveying: 1339, 1602, 1771, 1786, 1838, 2012, 2019–2020, 2028, 2165–2166, 2221, 2296, 2325, 2412, 2423, 2427, 2450, 2482, 2534, 2556, 2572, 2631, 2734, 2756, 2824, 2975. *See also* General programs

Surveying engineering. *See* Engineering, surveying

Swedish language. *See* Language, Swedish

Swedish literature. *See* Literature, Swedish

Swedish studies: 1049. *See also* General programs

Swine industry. *See* Pork industry

Systems analysis: 2141, 3037. *See also* Computer sciences; General programs

Systems engineering. *See* Engineering, systems

Teaching. *See* Education

Technology: 776, 1313, 1409, 1530, 1663, 1692, 1763, 1785, 1853, 1943, 1952, 1955, 1978, 2171, 2266, 2306, 2429, 2451, 2521, 2528, 2605, 2637, 2640, 2642, 2646, 2688, 2705, 2802, 2840, 2856, 2865, 2932, 2940, 2951, 3007, 3056, 3115, 3351. *See also* Computer sciences; General programs; Sciences

Teenagers. *See* Adolescents

Telecommunications: 1333, 1435, 1472, 1474, 1704, 2043, 2110–2111, 2266, 2304, 2344, 2499, 2778, 2821, 2991, 3024–3025, 3115, 3154, 3258, 3424, 3463. *See also* Communications; General programs; Radio; Television

Telepathy. *See* Parapsychology

Television: 1239, 1253, 1298, 1316, 1361, 1512, 1529, 1533, 1540, 1616, 1668, 1679, 1701, 1704, 1712, 1745. *See also* Communications; Filmmaking; General programs

Testing: 2342. *See also* General programs; Psychology

Textile engineering. *See* Engineering, textile

Textiles: 1356, 1456, 1733. *See also* Arts and crafts; General programs; Home economics

Theater. *See* Entertainment industry; Performing arts; Plays

Theology. *See* Religion and religious activities

Therapy: 1830. *See also* General programs; Health and health care; names of specific types of therapy

Tobacco consumption: 410. *See also* General programs; Medical sciences

Tourism: 2868, 2878, 2881, 2891–2892, 2905, 2922, 2929, 2942, 3079, 3105, 3116, 3162, 3188, 3268, 3282, 3305, 3325, 3340, 3352, 3392–3393, 3397, 3415, 3417, 3428, 3457. *See also* General programs

Toxicology: 1837, 1945, 2092, 2141, 2709, 3037. *See also* General programs;

Medical sciences

Trade unions. *See* Labor unions and members

Translators and translations: 1503. *See also* General programs; Language and linguistics; Writers and writing

Transportation: 1371–1372, 1822, 1976, 2117–2118, 2235, 2272, 2326, 2409, 2557, 2634, 2662, 2701, 2757, 2773, 2775, 2859–2862, 2872, 2884, 3032–3033, 3091, 3117, 3204, 3303, 3338, 3383, 3404, 3410, 3419–3420. *See also* Automobile industry; Aviation; Engineering, transportation; General programs; Space sciences

Transportation engineering. *See* Engineering, transportation

Travel and tourism. *See* Tourism

Turfgrass science: 78, 1271, 1855, 2070, 2167, 2200–2201, 2315, 2378, 2649, 2680, 2691. *See also* Biological sciences; General programs; Management

TV. *See* Television

Typing. *See* Secretarial sciences

Unions and unionization. *See* Industrial relations; Labor unions and members

Universities. *See* Education, higher

Unrestricted programs. *See* General programs

Urban affairs: 3338. *See also* City and regional planning; General programs

Urban planning. *See* City and regional planning

Urban studies: 1288, 1364. *See also* General programs; Urban affairs

Utilities: 2048, 2656–2657, 3362. *See also* Energy; General programs

Veterans. *See* Military affairs

Veterinary sciences: 1866, 2191, 2581, 2609, 2695, 2797, 3332. *See also* Animal science; General programs; Sciences

Veterinary technology: 2191. *See also* Animal science; General programs; Sciences

Video. *See* Filmmaking; Television

Viola. *See* Music, viola

Virology: 2625, 2709. *See also* General programs; Medical sciences

Visual arts: 640, 1242, 1262, 1275, 1277, 1302, 1308, 1378, 1476, 1551, 1716, 1794. *See also* General programs; Humanities; names of specific visual arts

Visual impairments: 441, 2055, 2676, 2874, 2935, 2980, 2996, 3298, 3369. *See also* Disabilities; General programs; Health and health care

Viticulture. *See* Enology and viticulture

Voice: 640, 1247, 1277, 1360, 1417, 1420, 1502, 1525, 1542, 1551, 1567, 1569, 1598, 1676, 1699, 1726. *See also* General programs; Music; Performing arts

Water resources: 78, 1290, 1375, 1715, 1851, 1902, 1920, 1928, 1931, 1934, 2000, 2040, 2069, 2124, 2130, 2263, 2353, 2645, 2749, 2793, 2915, 2926, 2961. *See also* Environmental sciences; General programs; Natural resources

Web design. *See* Internet design and development

Web journalism. *See* Journalism, online

Welding: 176, 1875, 1913, 2114, 2277, 2339, 2420–2421, 2477, 2829–2830, 3144, 3207. *See also* Building trades; General programs

Welding engineering. *See* Engineering, welding

Welfare. *See* Social services

Wildlife management: 1816, 1825, 1947, 1953, 2140, 2159, 2194, 2480, 2669, 2788, 2828, 2937, 3036, 3242, 3430. *See also* Environmental sciences; General programs

Wine industry. *See* Beer and wine industries

Wine making. *See* Enology and viticulture

Women's studies and programs: 1455, 1757, 3112. *See also* General programs

Wood industry: 2267, 2516. *See also* Forestry management; General programs

Work. *See* Employment

World literature. *See* Literature

Wound, ostomy and continence nurses and nursing. *See* Nurses and nursing, wound, ostomy and continence

Writers and writing: 70, 78, 93, 150, 174, 186, 278, 291, 384, 407, 410, 541, 814, 870, 892, 922, 959, 1113, 1153, 1242, 1266, 1268, 1272, 1277, 1279, 1288, 1298, 1353, 1355, 1364, 1374, 1379, 1387, 1397, 1399, 1403–1405, 1415, 1419, 1428, 1462, 1476, 1486, 1492, 1508, 1519, 1523, 1528, 1531–1532, 1546, 1564, 1578, 1587, 1599, 1621, 1631, 1636, 1638, 1650, 1657, 1660, 1663, 1666, 1670, 1675, 1678, 1683, 1686, 1701, 1713, 1732, 1757, 1761, 1766, 1794–1795, 1801, 1877, 1887, 2021, 2080, 2094, 2186, 2201, 2233–2234, 2264, 2306, 2329, 2367, 2481, 2518, 2531, 2623, 2627, 2659, 2679, 2688, 2709, 2741, 2809, 2858, 2864, 2867, 2880, 2887, 2894, 2930, 2944, 2976, 3006, 3017, 3072, 3087–3089, 3109, 3113, 3135, 3139, 3166, 3229, 3234, 3250, 3260, 3265, 3285, 3294, 3313, 3320, 3328–3329, 3337, 3341, 3400. *See also* General programs; Literature; specific types of writing

Youth. *See* Adolescents; Child development

Zoology: 2302–2303, 3137–3138. *See also* General programs; Sciences; names of specific zoological subfields

# Residency Index

Some programs listed in this book are restricted to residents of a particular city, county, state, or region. Others are open to students wherever they live. The Residency Index will help you pinpoint programs available only to residents in your area as well as programs that have no residency restrictions (these are listed under the term "United States"). To use this index, look up the geographic areas that apply to you (always check the listings under "United States"), jot down the entry numbers listed after the subject areas that interest you, and use those numbers to find the program descriptions in the directory. To help you in your search, we've provided some "see also" references in each index entry. Remember: the numbers cited here refer to program entry numbers, not to page numbers in the book.

Adair County, Iowa: **Unrestricted by Subject Area** 22. *See also* Iowa

Adams County, Iowa: **Unrestricted by Subject Area** 22. *See also* Iowa

Alabama: **Unrestricted by Subject Area** 24–30, 128–129, 285–287, 294, 333, 452, 586, 589, 973, **Humanities** 1250–1252, 1449, **Sciences** 1811, 1813–1815, 1980, 2070, 2106, 2396, 2706, **Social Sciences** 2879–2880, 2930, 3179, 3197, 3417. *See also* Southern states; United States; names of specific cities and counties

Alaska: **Unrestricted by Subject Area** 31–33, 386, 452, 1193, **Humanities** 1253, 1529, **Sciences** 1816–1817, 1932, 2212, 2618, **Social Sciences** 2882, 3171, 3326. *See also* Northwestern states; United States; names of specific cities

American Samoa: **Unrestricted by Subject Area** 102, **Humanities** 1616. *See also* United States

Argentina: **Unrestricted by Subject Area** 1219. *See also* Foreign countries; South America

Arizona: **Unrestricted by Subject Area** 51, 81–84, 109, 270, 452, 565, 973, 1072, 1193, **Humanities** 1530, 1548, 1581, **Sciences** 1868–1870, 1941, 1952, 1959, 2348, 2584, 2613, 2656–2657, 2743, 2813, **Social Sciences** 2905–2906, 2931, 2940, 3362. *See also* United States; Western states; names of specific cities and counties

Arkansas: **Unrestricted by Subject Area** 57, 85–92, 270, 285–287, 452, 961, 1002, **Humanities** 1276, 1432, 1530, **Sciences** 1842, 1871–1872, 1980, 2706, **Social Sciences** 2907. *See also* Southern states; United States; names of specific cities and counties

Audubon County, Iowa: **Unrestricted by Subject Area** 22. *See also* Iowa

Avondale, Pennsylvania: **Unrestricted by Subject Area** 529, **Humanities** 1497, **Social Sciences** 3159. *See also* Pennsylvania

Belmont County, Ohio: **Unrestricted by Subject Area** 963. *See also* Ohio

Bolivia: **Unrestricted by Subject Area** 1219. *See also* Foreign countries; South America

Brazil: **Unrestricted by Subject Area** 1219, **Sciences** 2413. *See also* Foreign countries; South America

Bristol County, Massachusetts: **Unrestricted by Subject Area** 300. *See also* Massachusetts

Britain. *See* United Kingdom

Bronx County, New York. *See* New York, New York

Bronx, New York. *See* New York, New York

Brooklyn, New York. *See* New York, New York

Buena Vista County, Iowa: **Unrestricted by Subject Area** 22. *See also* Iowa

Calhoun County, Iowa: **Unrestricted by Subject Area** 22. *See also* Iowa

California: **Unrestricted by Subject Area** 46, 48, 109, 123, 146–149, 151–168, 171, 213–214, 216, 270, 304, 388, 421, 508, 565, 602, 973, 987, 1016, 1020, 1067, 1193, 1199, 1202, **Humanities** 1283, 1306–1310, 1359, 1378, 1453, 1581, 1714, **Sciences** 1786, 1902, 1917, 1941, 1952, 1956, 1959–1967, 1969–1970, 1996, 2000, 2066, 2107, 2325–2326, 2440, 2584, 2725, 2789, 2813, 2835, 2847, **Social Sciences** 2915, 2923, 2931, 2940–2947, 2961, 3022, 3155, 3178, 3191, 3355, 3395, 3417. *See also* United States; Western states; names of specific cities and counties

California, northern: **Humanities** 1377

Canada: **Unrestricted by Subject Area** 263–264, 406, 418, 436, 525, 573, 588, 749, 891–893, 902, 907, 934, 936, 944, 1026, 1219, **Humanities** 1245, 1265, 1268, 1293–1294, 1356, 1367, 1382–1383, 1456, 1477, 1486, 1492, 1498, 1508–1509, 1511, 1532, 1546, 1575, 1587–1588, 1602, 1604–1605, 1617, 1621, 1644, 1664–1666, 1670, 1679, 1686, 1695, 1707, 1756, **Sciences** 1763, 1772, 1811, 1847, 1867, 1878, 1880–1881, 1892, 1915, 1936, 1979, 1987, 2027, 2048, 2076, 2094, 2097, 2099–2102, 2105, 2138, 2147, 2150, 2155, 2188, 2216, 2219, 2230, 2239, 2245, 2250, 2264, 2280, 2287, 2299–2301, 2323, 2350–2354, 2356, 2369, 2402, 2413–2414, 2458, 2498, 2500, 2509, 2511, 2515, 2542, 2549, 2556, 2569, 2575,

2587, 2589, 2605, 2618, 2621, 2626, 2632, 2634, 2668, 2675, 2696, 2714–2715, 2719, 2729, 2737, 2784–2786, 2828, 2832, 2834, 2841, 2864, **Social Sciences** 2865, 2872, 2878, 2881, 2892, 2895, 2910, 2952, 2963, 3045, 3061, 3073, 3075, 3097, 3105, 3113, 3116, 3143, 3162, 3244, 3262, 3268, 3304–3305, 3339–3340, 3387, 3418, 3426, 3428. *See also* Foreign countries

Caribbean: **Unrestricted by Subject Area** 891–893, **Humanities** 1293. *See also* Foreign countries; names of specific countries

Carroll County, Iowa: **Unrestricted by Subject Area** 22. *See also* Iowa

Cass County, Iowa: **Unrestricted by Subject Area** 22. *See also* Iowa

Central America: **Humanities** 1293. *See also* Foreign countries; names of specific countries

Chadds Ford, Pennsylvania: **Unrestricted by Subject Area** 529, **Humanities** 1497, **Social Sciences** 3159. *See also* Pennsylvania

Cherokee County, Iowa: **Unrestricted by Subject Area** 22. *See also* Iowa

Chile: **Unrestricted by Subject Area** 1219. *See also* Foreign countries; South America

China. *See* Hong Kong; People's Republic of China; Taiwan

Clay County, Iowa: **Unrestricted by Subject Area** 22. *See also* Iowa

Collin County, Texas: **Sciences** 2336. *See also* Texas

Colombia: **Sciences** 2675. *See also* Foreign countries; South America

Colorado: **Unrestricted by Subject Area** 51, 132, 194, 233–240, 270, 344, 401, 452, 945, 966, 973, 987, 1020, 1193, **Humanities** 1273, 1333–1334, 1409, 1450, 1458, 1581, 1625, **Sciences** 1863, 1934, 1941, 1952, 1980, 2010–2011, 2013, 2031, 2321, 2340, 2476, 2584, 2656–2657, 2802, 2806, 2808, **Social Sciences** 2903, 2931, 2940, 2967–2970, 3026–3027, 3362. *See also* United States; Western states; names of specific cities and counties

Columbiana County, Ohio: **Unrestricted by Subject Area** 963. *See also* Ohio

Connecticut: **Unrestricted by Subject Area** 172, 247–251, 253, 405, 411, 452, 693, 916, 924, 949, 954, 973, 1017, 1029, 1063, 1070, **Humanities** 1264, 1295, 1299, 1302, 1318, 1337–1339, 1386, 1389, 1414, 1447, 1549, 1607, 1693, **Sciences** 1812, 1896, 2019–2024, 2156, 2218, 2229, 2254, 2271, 2330, 2426, 2443, 2621, 2772, **Social Sciences** 2935, 2954, 2973–2977, 2979–2980, 3008, 3085–3086, 3106, 3215, 3222, 3306, 3335, 3339, 3354, 3417. *See also* New England states; United States; names of specific cities and counties

Costa Rica: **Unrestricted by Subject Area** 1219. *See also* Central America; Foreign countries

Crawford County, Iowa: **Unrestricted by Subject Area** 22, **Humanities** 1360. *See also* Iowa

Dallas County, Texas: **Sciences** 2336. *See also* Texas

Dallas, Texas: **Humanities** 1326. *See also* Texas

Dane County, Wisconsin: **Unrestricted by Subject Area** 1081. *See also* Wisconsin

Delaware: **Unrestricted by Subject Area** 9, 216, 271–274, 280, 347, 378, 434, 497, 522, 529, 665, 924, 973, 1029, 1063, 1070, **Humanities** 1355, 1482, 1497, 1517, 1744, **Sciences** 2061, 2358, 2366, 2430, 2621, 2717, 2730, **Social Sciences** 2992–2993, 3159, 3339, 3429. *See also* Southern states; United States; names of specific cities and counties

Denton County, Texas: **Sciences** 2336. *See also* Texas

Dickinson County, Iowa: **Unrestricted by Subject Area** 22. *See also* Iowa

District of Columbia. *See* Washington, D.C.

East Germany. *See* Germany

Ecuador: **Unrestricted by Subject Area** 1219. *See also* Foreign countries; South America

Elkton, Maryland: **Unrestricted by Subject Area** 529, **Humanities** 1497, **Social Sciences** 3159. *See also* Maryland

Fairfax County, Virginia: **Unrestricted by Subject Area** 139. *See also* Virginia

Federal Republic of Germany. *See* Germany

Florida: **Unrestricted by Subject Area** 128, 216, 285–287, 333, 341–342, 344, 352–355, 357–362, 959, 973, 987, 1049, 1114, 1198, **Humanities** 1243, 1261, 1284–1285, 1290, 1375, 1393–1394, 1410, 1423, 1440, 1449, 1526, 1581, 1715, 1740, **Sciences** 1800, 1811, 1928, 1980, 2001, 2065, 2082, 2091, 2109, 2124, 2158–2167, 2257, 2335, 2444, 2706, 2711, 2793, 2810, 2830, **Social Sciences** 2930, 3010, 3048–3053, 3189, 3224, 3417. *See also* Southern states; United States; names of specific cities and counties

Foreign countries: **Unrestricted by Subject Area** 255, 356, 529, 531, 976, 1006, 1108, 1113, **Humanities** 1288, 1296, 1323, 1348, 1353, 1461, 1475, 1497, 1500, 1531, 1533, 1542, 1565, 1638, 1738, 1749, 1752–1753, **Sciences** 1803, 1890–1892, 1992, 2115, 2131, 2135, 2152, 2154, 2196, 2302, 2305–2307, 2312, 2320, 2400, 2471, 2555, 2606, 2623, 2697, 2726, 2736, 2769, 2838, **Social Sciences** 2956, 3006, 3125, 3137, 3159, 3265, 3363, 3400. *See also* names of specific continents; names of specific countries

France: **Sciences** 2413. *See also* Foreign countries

Fremont County, Iowa: **Unrestricted by Subject Area** 22. *See also* Iowa

Georgia: **Unrestricted by Subject Area** 4, 128, 183, 285–287, 333, 392–396, 448–449, 452, 504, 558, 590, 755, 973, **Humanities** 1281, 1411–1412, 1449, 1478, 1488, 1581, 1651, **Sciences** 1811, 1980, 2025, 2224–2227, 2493, 2706, 2732, **Social Sciences** 2930, 2957, 2981, 3069, 3082–3083, 3170, 3398. *See also* Southern states; United States; names of specific cities and counties

German Democratic Republic. *See* Germany

Germany: **Sciences** 2413. *See also* Foreign countries

Grant County, Wisconsin: **Unrestricted by Subject Area** 1081. *See also* Wisconsin

Great Britain. *See* United Kingdom

Green County, Wisconsin: **Unrestricted by Subject Area** 1081. *See also* Wisconsin

Greene County, Iowa: **Unrestricted by Subject Area** 22. *See also* Iowa

Guam: **Unrestricted by Subject Area** 102, 1140, 1219, **Humanities** 1616, **Social Sciences** 2872. *See also* United States

Guthrie County, Iowa: **Unrestricted by Subject Area** 22. *See also* Iowa

Harrison County, Iowa: **Unrestricted by Subject Area** 22. *See also* Iowa

Harrison County, Ohio: **Unrestricted by Subject Area** 963. *See also* Ohio

Hawaii: **Unrestricted by Subject Area** 45, 136–137, 166–167, 182, 429, 447, 452, 618, 744, 990, 1122, 1124, 1160, 1193, **Humanities** 1263, 1362, 1370, 1381, 1436–1439, 1515, 1544, 1616, 1626, **Sciences** 2079, 2083, 2126, 2256, 2349, 2389, 2596, 2658, 2705, 2780, 2835, 2837, **Social Sciences** 2888, 2929, 2964, 3011, 3030, 3066, 3077, 3103, 3108, 3123, 3203, 3216, 3417. *See also* United States; Western states; names of specific cities and counties

Holland. *See* Netherlands

Hong Kong: **Sciences** 2413. *See also* Foreign countries

Ida County, Iowa: **Unrestricted by Subject Area** 22. *See also* Iowa

Idaho: **Unrestricted by Subject Area** 51, 459–461, 463–464, 977, 1020, 1193, **Humanities** 1392, 1464, **Sciences** 2283, 2618, 2657, **Social Sciences** 3046, 3129, 3362. *See also* Northwestern states; United States; Western states; names of specific cities and counties

Illinois: **Unrestricted by Subject Area** 5, 51, 270, 277, 452, 465–476, 516, 687, 947, 973, 987, 1020, 1070, 1081, **Humanities** 1457, 1463, 1468–1469, 1581, **Sciences** 1941, 1980, 2268, 2281, 2289–2292, 2314, 2461, **Social Sciences** 2931, 3068, 3127, 3132–3133, 3176, 3199, 3367, 3413, 3417. *See also* Midwestern states; United States; names of specific cities and counties

India: **Sciences** 2413. *See also* Foreign countries

Indiana: **Unrestricted by Subject Area** 51, 216, 270, 373, 479–483, 591, 906, 973, 987, 1070, **Humanities** 1472, 1487, 1547, 1581, **Sciences** 1842, 1980, 2003, 2081, 2173, 2251, 2288, 2294–2296, 2332, 2372, **Social Sciences** 2877, 2988, 3100, 3148. *See also* Midwestern states; United States; names of specific cities and counties

Iowa: **Unrestricted by Subject Area** 23, 51, 180, 270, 301, 414, 486–491, 743, 973, 978, 987, 1020, 1162, **Humanities** 1360, 1476, 1581, 1620, 1634, **Sciences** 1980–1981, 2286, 2308–2310, 2315, 2370, 2558, 2592, 2657, **Social Sciences** 3139, 3362. *See also* Midwestern states; United States; names of specific cities and counties

Iowa County, Wisconsin: **Unrestricted by Subject Area** 1081. *See also* Wisconsin

Israel: **Unrestricted by Subject Area** 529, **Humanities** 1497, **Social Sciences** 3159. *See also* Foreign countries

Japan: **Unrestricted by Subject Area** 1219. *See also* Foreign countries

Jefferson County, Ohio: **Unrestricted by Subject Area** 963. *See also* Ohio

Jefferson County, Wisconsin: **Unrestricted by Subject Area** 1081. *See also* Wisconsin

Kansas: **Unrestricted by Subject Area** 51, 178, 259, 452, 532–535, 537–540, 621, 682, 973, 987, **Humanities** 1446, 1504–1505, 1557, 1581, 1597, 1620, 1687, **Sciences** 1941, 1952, 1980, 2127, 2382, 2475, 2592, 2649, 2656–2657, 2733, 2823, 2827, 2843, **Social Sciences** 2930–2931, 2940, 2998, 3136, 3172–3173, 3185–3186, 3362. *See also* Midwestern states; United States; names of specific cities and counties

Kennett Square, Pennsylvania: **Unrestricted by Subject Area** 529, **Humanities** 1497, **Social Sciences** 3159. *See also* Pennsylvania

Kenosha County, Wisconsin: **Unrestricted by Subject Area** 1081. *See also* Wisconsin

Kentucky: **Unrestricted by Subject Area** 3, 36, 128, 140, 243, 330, 410, 412, 544, 547–554, 570, 632, 760, 1056, 1070, 1126, 1229, **Humanities** 1435, **Sciences** 1768, 1842, 2251, 2277, 2372, 2377, 2384, 2706, 2833, **Social Sciences** 3100, 3180–3182, 3221, 3325. *See also* Southern states; United States; names of specific cities and counties

Kings County, New York. *See* New York, New York

Korea. *See* South Korea

Lafayette County, Wisconsin: **Unrestricted by Subject Area** 1081. *See also* Wisconsin

Lake George, New York: **Humanities** 1542. *See also* New York

Landenberg, Pennsylvania: **Unrestricted by Subject Area** 529, **Humanities** 1497, **Social Sciences** 3159. *See also* Pennsylvania

Latin America. *See* Caribbean; Central America; Mexico; South America

Lincoln University, Pennsylvania: **Unrestricted by Subject Area** 529, **Humanities** 1497, **Social Sciences** 3159. *See also* Pennsylvania

Louisiana: **Unrestricted by Subject Area** 285–287, 380, 397, 592–598, **Humanities** 1530, 1581, 1629, 1645, **Sciences** 1842, 1980, 2669, 2706, **Social Sciences** 2883, 2930, 2959, 3193. *See also* Southern states; United States; names of specific cities and parishes

Lyon County, Iowa: **Unrestricted by Subject Area** 22. *See also* Iowa

Maine: **Unrestricted by Subject Area** 115, 218, 379, 452, 454, 493, 505, 520, 581, 605–617, 839–840, 935, 962, 1012, 1063, **Humanities** 1406, 1429, 1518, 1527, 1539, 1657, **Sciences** 1812, 1882, 1895, 1953, 2193, 2267, 2271, 2419–2425, 2621, 2679, **Social Sciences** 3207–3213, 3339, 3370. *See also* New England states;

United States; names of specific cities and counties

Manhattan, New York. *See* New York, New York

Maryland: **Unrestricted by Subject Area** 13, 145, 216, 262, 266, 311, 344, 364, 522, 638–647, 1063, 1070, **Humanities** 1517, 1551–1553, 1733, **Sciences** 1916, 2033, 2366, 2447–2450, 2621, 2706, 2717, **Social Sciences** 2986, 2989, 3122, 3226–3231, 3256, 3339, 3459. *See also* Southern states; United States; names of specific cities and counties

Maryland, regional: **Unrestricted by Subject Area** 173, 322, 603, 785

Massachusetts: **Unrestricted by Subject Area** 11, 135, 244, 371, 402, 405, 452, 521, 651–662, 923, 973, 1061, 1063, **Humanities** 1493, 1554–1555, **Sciences** 1812, 2271, 2333, 2427, 2451, 2621, **Social Sciences** 3043, 3120, 3149, 3157, 3175, 3232–3234, 3327, 3339, 3417. *See also* New England states; United States; names of specific cities and counties

Mexico: **Unrestricted by Subject Area** 1219, **Humanities** 1268, 1293, 1477, 1486, 1492, 1508, 1532, 1546, 1587, 1621, **Sciences** 1847, 1867, 1892, 1936, 2097, 2138, 2216, 2352, 2356, 2402, 2413, 2549, 2634, 2675, 2719, 2729, 2784–2786, 2841, **Social Sciences** 3426. *See also* Foreign countries

Michigan: **Unrestricted by Subject Area** 270, 452, 671–680, 682, 764, 987, 1020, 1025, 1070, **Humanities** 1558, 1581, **Sciences** 1842, 1849, 1980, 2005, 2077, 2103, 2239, 2253, 2255, 2372, 2376, 2418, 2441, 2490, 2495–2496, 2558, 2734, 2825, 2830, **Social Sciences** 2925, 3020, 3102, 3196, 3239–3240, 3245, 3282, 3364, 3366, 3417. *See also* Midwestern states; United States; names of specific cities and counties

Michigan, regional: **Sciences** 2852

Midwestern states: **Humanities** 1599. *See also* United States; names of specific states

Mills County, Iowa: **Unrestricted by Subject Area** 22. *See also* Iowa

Milwaukee County, Wisconsin: **Unrestricted by Subject Area** 1081, **Sciences** 1984. *See also* Wisconsin

Minnesota: **Unrestricted by Subject Area** 51, 254, 270, 388, 682, 694–703, 908, 973, 987, 1020, 1119, 1162, 1186, **Humanities** 1304, 1481, 1630, 1712, **Sciences** 1950, 1952, 1974, 1980, 2480–2482, 2558, 2657, 2859, **Social Sciences** 2940, 3242, 3362, 3417. *See also* Midwestern states; United States; names of specific cities and counties

Mississippi: **Unrestricted by Subject Area** 128, 285–287, 333, 397, 452, 712–717, 843, **Humanities** 1538, 1561, **Sciences** 1980, 2706, **Social Sciences** 2930, 3246. *See also* Southern states; United States; names of specific cities and counties

Missouri: **Unrestricted by Subject Area** 51, 190, 270, 622, 682, 718–726, 748, 987, **Humanities** 1479, 1562, 1620, **Sciences** 1931, 1941, 1980, 2046, 2140, 2143, 2338, 2435, 2475, 2491, 2592, 2656–2657, 2706, 2843, **Social Sciences** 2909, 2926, 2930–2931, 3036, 3142, 3195, 3247–3249, 3362, 3417. *See also* Midwestern states; United States; names of specific cities and counties

Monona County, Iowa: **Unrestricted by Subject Area** 22. *See also* Iowa

Monroe County, Ohio: **Unrestricted by Subject Area** 963. *See also* Ohio

Montana: **Unrestricted by Subject Area** 270, 730–739, 973, 987, 1001, 1020, 1074–1075, 1193, **Humanities** 1392, 1424–1425, **Sciences** 1952, 2416, 2492, 2618, 2657, **Social Sciences** 2940, 3046, 3092, 3251, 3362, 3417. *See also* United States; Western states; names of specific cities and counties

Montgomery County, Iowa: **Unrestricted by Subject Area** 22. *See also* Iowa

Montgomery County, Maryland: **Unrestricted by Subject Area** 139. *See also* Maryland

Nebraska: **Unrestricted by Subject Area** 22–23, 51, 189, 270, 510, 682, 747, 789–796, 848, 887, 901, 903–904, 938, 973, 987, 1020, 1078, **Humanities** 1426, 1581, 1589, 1601, 1620, **Sciences** 1954, 1980, 2240, 2391, 2527–2528, 2558, 2592, 2656–2657, **Social Sciences** 2987, 3047, 3093, 3192, 3202, 3272–3276, 3316, 3362, 3417. *See also* United States; Midwestern states; names of specific cities and counties

Netherlands: **Sciences** 2413. *See also* Foreign countries

Nevada: **Unrestricted by Subject Area** 51, 452, 565, 973, 1020, 1193, **Humanities** 1581, 1632, **Sciences** 2532, 2584, 2657, 2835, **Social Sciences** 3362, 3417. *See also* Western states; names of specific cities

New England states: **Unrestricted by Subject Area** 216, 425, 798, **Humanities** 1247, 1358, 1590, 1659, 1705, **Sciences** 1775, 1944, 2008, 2128, 2178, 2220, 2363, 2399, 2703, 2767–2768, **Social Sciences** 2933, 2948, 3003, 3059, 3161, 3277–3278, 3374. *See also* United States; names of specific states

New Hampshire: **Unrestricted by Subject Area** 113, 175, 427, 452, 619, 630, 799–805, 1063, **Humanities** 1591, **Sciences** 1769, 1812, 1823, 2236, 2271, 2547, 2621, **Social Sciences** 2885, 2958, 3121, 3280–3281, 3339. *See also* New England states; United States; names of specific cities and counties

New Jersey: **Unrestricted by Subject Area** 215–217, 261, 290, 310, 328, 415, 452, 522, 709, 806–815, 924, 973, 1029, 1063, 1070, **Humanities** 1287, 1297, 1430, 1592, 1607, 1653, **Sciences** 1838, 1926, 1935, 2074, 2155, 2249, 2366, 2534–2537, 2551, 2621, 2677, 2744, 2759, **Social Sciences** 3039, 3283–3288, 3339, 3417. *See also* United States; names of specific cities and counties

New Mexico: **Unrestricted by Subject Area** 208, 388, 452, 565, 816–817, 819–826, 973, 1080, 1120, 1193, **Humanities** 1347, 1530, 1581, 1593, 1600, 1694, **Sciences** 1934, 1941, 1952, 2538, 2553, 2656–2657, 2813, **Social Sciences** 2931, 2940, 3289, 3296–3297, 3362. *See also* United States; Western states; names of specific cities and counties

New York: **Unrestricted by Subject Area** 206, 216, 344–345, 433, 452, 637, 827–

838, 924, 965, 973, 1019, 1029, 1063, 1070, **Humanities** 1303, 1322, 1349, 1594, 1607, 1628, 1635, 1659, 1696, **Sciences** 1801, 1879, 1949, 2056, 2130, 2327, 2366, 2539–2541, 2543, 2570, 2621, **Social Sciences** 2939, 3163, 3290–3291, 3339, 3374, 3405, 3417. *See also* United States; names of specific cities and counties

New York County, New York. *See* New York, New York

New York, New York: **Humanities** 1373. *See also* New York

North Carolina: **Unrestricted by Subject Area** 128, 131, 285–287, 452, 502–503, 590, 633, 787–788, 849–856, 973, 1136–1137, **Humanities** 1514, 1517, 1573, 1741, **Sciences** 1976–1977, 1980, 2093, 2237, 2366, 2386, 2505, 2557, 2633, 2662, 2706, **Social Sciences** 2930, 3015, 3064, 3158, 3225, 3259, 3299–3303, 3344, 3352, 3417. *See also* Southern states; United States; names of specific cities and counties

North Carolina, central: **Sciences** 2648

North Carolina, western: **Sciences** 2648

North Dakota: **Unrestricted by Subject Area** 51, 270, 329, 416, 428, 452, 682, 857–861, 973, 987, 1119, 1162, 1193, **Humanities** 1712, **Sciences** 1952, 1974, 1980, 2558, 2656–2657, **Social Sciences** 2940, 3362. *See also* Midwestern states; United States; names of specific cities

Northern Marianas: **Unrestricted by Subject Area** 102, **Humanities** 1616, **Social Sciences** 2872. *See also* United States

Northwestern states: **Unrestricted by Subject Area** 847. *See also* United States; Western states; names of specific states

O'Brien County, Iowa: **Unrestricted by Subject Area** 22. *See also* Iowa

Ohio: **Unrestricted by Subject Area** 51, 124, 270, 452, 873–878, 1070, 1197, **Humanities** 1329, 1581, 1608–1609, 1692, 1734, **Sciences** 1825, 1842, 1933, 2136, 2194, 2251, 2269, 2348, 2372, 2576, 2582, 2638, 2699, 2731, 2820, 2826, 2829–2830, **Social Sciences** 2869, 2874, 2876, 3100, 3298, 3307, 3310–3313, 3317, 3417. *See also* Midwestern states; United States; names of specific cities and counties

Oklahoma: **Unrestricted by Subject Area** 270, 452, 879–886, 969, 973, 987, **Humanities** 1530, 1581, 1611–1612, **Sciences** 1842, 1952, 1980, 2215, 2572, 2584, 2656–2657, 2706, **Social Sciences** 2930, 2940, 3074, 3141, 3314, 3362. *See also* Southern states; United States; names of specific cities and counties

Oregon: **Unrestricted by Subject Area** 51, 116–117, 204, 270, 365–366, 452, 894–899, 937, 948, 987, 1020, 1193, **Humanities** 1377, 1384, 1392, 1480, 1507, 1581, 1613, 1646, **Sciences** 1787, 1898, 1930, 1952, 2183, 2371, 2392, 2464, 2580–2581, 2584, 2618, 2631, 2814, **Social Sciences** 2940, 3046, 3063, 3135, 3145, 3318–3322. *See also* Northwestern states; United States; Western states; names of specific cities and counties

Osceola County, Iowa: **Unrestricted by Subject Area** 22. *See also* Iowa

Ozaukee County, Wisconsin: **Unrestricted by Subject Area** 1081, **Sciences** 1984. *See also* Wisconsin

Pacific Islands: **Humanities** 1616. *See also* Foreign countries; names of specific islands

Pacific Northwest. *See* Northwestern states

Page County, Iowa: **Unrestricted by Subject Area** 22. *See also* Iowa

Panama: **Unrestricted by Subject Area** 1219. *See also* Central America; Foreign countries

Paraguay: **Unrestricted by Subject Area** 1219. *See also* Foreign countries; South America

Pennsylvania: **Unrestricted by Subject Area** 124, 216, 270, 522, 924–932, 941, 963, 973, 987, 1029, 1063, 1070, 1086, **Humanities** 1607, 1623, 1734, **Sciences** 1826, 1910, 1933, 2322, 2366, 2372, 2550, 2597, 2600, 2602–2603, 2621, 2630, 2820, **Social Sciences** 2920, 3328–3331, 3336–3337, 3339. *See also* United States; names of specific cities and counties

People's Republic of China: **Sciences** 2413. *See also* Foreign countries

Peru: **Unrestricted by Subject Area** 1219. *See also* Foreign countries; South America

Philippines: **Unrestricted by Subject Area** 1219, **Sciences** 2413. *See also* Foreign countries

Plymouth County, Iowa: **Unrestricted by Subject Area** 22. *See also* Iowa

Poland: **Sciences** 2413. *See also* Foreign countries

Portland, Maine: **Humanities** 1499. *See also* Maine

Pottawattamie County, Iowa: **Unrestricted by Subject Area** 22. *See also* Iowa

Prince George's County, Maryland: **Unrestricted by Subject Area** 139. *See also* Maryland

Prince William County, Virginia: **Unrestricted by Subject Area** 139. *See also* Virginia

Puerto Rico: **Unrestricted by Subject Area** 49, 60, 111, 227, 344, 439, 442, 445, 453, 620, 936, 960, 1073, 1140, 1219, **Humanities** 1311, **Sciences** 1903, 1971, 1980, 2057, 2119, 2211, 2266, 2282, 2406, 2503, 2634, 2681, 2690, 2719, 2764, **Social Sciences** 2918, 2949, 2999, 3040, 3071, 3115, 3128, 3167, 3372, 3414. *See also* Caribbean; United States

Queens County, New York. *See* New York, New York

Queens, New York. *See* New York, New York

Racine County, Wisconsin: **Unrestricted by Subject Area** 1081. *See also* Wisconsin

Republic of China. *See* Taiwan

Rhode Island: **Unrestricted by Subject Area** 230, 300, 405, 452, 920–921, 970–972, 1063, **Humanities** 1282, 1642, 1647, **Sciences** 1812, 1818, 2271, 2621, 2643–2644, **Social Sciences** 3339, 3348, 3353. *See also* New England states; United States; names of specific cities

Richmond County, New York. *See* New York, New York

Ringgold County, Iowa: **Unrestricted by Subject Area** 22. *See also* Iowa

Rock County, Wisconsin: **Unrestricted by Subject Area** 1081. *See also* Wisconsin

Russia: **Sciences** 2413. *See also* Foreign countries

Sac County, Iowa: **Unrestricted by Subject Area** 22. *See also* Iowa

Samoa. *See* American Samoa

San Diego, California: **Sciences** 2725, **Social Sciences** 3395. *See also* California

Shelby County, Iowa: **Unrestricted by Subject Area** 22. *See also* Iowa

Sioux County, Iowa: **Unrestricted by Subject Area** 22. *See also* Iowa

Siskiyou County, California: **Unrestricted by Subject Area** 366. *See also* California

South America: **Humanities** 1293. *See also* Foreign countries; names of specific countries

South Carolina: **Unrestricted by Subject Area** 128, 285–287, 333, 452, 515, 578, 590, 911, 973, 1035–1043, **Humanities** 1275, 1449, 1514, 1517, 1682–1683, **Sciences** 1977, 1980, 2093, 2373, 2386, 2493, 2648, 2692, 2706, 2720–2721, **Social Sciences** 2930, 3015, 3389–3390. *See also* Southern states; United States; names of specific cities and counties

South Dakota: **Unrestricted by Subject Area** 42, 51, 270, 374, 376, 452, 519, 631, 973, 987, 1008, 1020, 1044–1048, 1119, 1121, 1162, 1193, **Humanities** 1712, **Sciences** 1839, 1952, 1974, 1980, 2558, 2656–2657, 2694, **Social Sciences** 2899, 2940, 3095, 3362, 3380, 3391–3392. *See also* Midwestern states; United States; names of specific cities and counties

South Korea: **Unrestricted by Subject Area** 1219, **Sciences** 2413. *See also* Foreign countries

Southern states: **Unrestricted by Subject Area** 1058. *See also* United States; names of specific states

Spain: **Sciences** 2413. *See also* Foreign countries

Staten Island, New York. *See* New York, New York

Sweden: **Unrestricted by Subject Area** 902. *See also* Foreign countries

Taiwan: **Unrestricted by Subject Area** 1219. *See also* Foreign countries

Tarrant County, Texas: **Sciences** 2336. *See also* Texas

Taylor County, Iowa: **Unrestricted by Subject Area** 22. *See also* Iowa

Tennessee: **Unrestricted by Subject Area** 128, 270, 285–287, 333, 452, 797, 973, 1070, 1089–1094, 1196, **Humanities** 1341, 1449, **Sciences** 1842, 1980, 2029, 2706, 2748, **Social Sciences** 2930, 2984, 3237, 3403. *See also* Southern states; United States; names of specific cities and counties

Texas: **Unrestricted by Subject Area** 130, 176, 192–193, 216, 270, 285–287, 292, 344, 349, 397, 430–431, 495, 565, 690, 973, 987, 1095–1096, 1098–1112, 1117, 1176–1177, **Humanities** 1326, 1331, 1454–1455, 1470, 1501, 1530, 1661, 1673, 1697–1699, 1708, 1730, **Sciences** 1770, 1842, 1941, 1980, 2275, 2336, 2584, 2656–2657, 2686, 2706, 2722, 2750–2758, 2770, 2778, 2822, **Social Sciences** 2871, 2924, 2930–2931, 3009, 3062, 3112, 3152, 3350, 3362, 3375, 3407–3412, 3417, 3424. *See also* Southern states; Western states; United States; names of specific cities and counties

Union County, Iowa: **Unrestricted by Subject Area** 22. *See also* Iowa

United Kingdom: **Unrestricted by Subject Area** 1007, **Sciences** 2413. *See also* Foreign countries; names of specific countries

United States: **Unrestricted by Subject Area** 1–2, 6–8, 10, 12, 14–21, 30, 34–35, 37–41, 43–44, 47, 49–50, 52–56, 58–80, 90, 93–108, 110–112, 118–120, 122, 125–127, 133–134, 138, 141–142, 144, 150, 159, 169–170, 174, 177, 179, 181, 184–188, 191, 195–203, 205, 207, 210–212, 220–229, 231–232, 240–242, 245–246, 252, 255–258, 260, 263–265, 267–269, 275, 278–279, 281, 283–284, 288–289, 291, 293, 295–299, 302–303, 305–309, 312–321, 323, 325–327, 331–332, 334, 336–340, 343–344, 346, 348, 350–351, 356, 363, 367, 369–370, 372, 375, 377, 381–385, 387, 389–391, 398–400, 403–404, 406–409, 413, 417–420, 422–426, 432, 435–439, 441–446, 450–451, 453, 457–458, 462, 477–478, 484–485, 492, 494, 496, 498–501, 506–507, 509, 511–514, 517–518, 522–528, 530–531, 536, 541, 543, 545–546, 555–557, 559–564, 566–569, 571–576, 579–580, 582–585, 588, 599–601, 604, 620, 623–629, 634–636, 648–649, 663–664, 666–670, 681, 683–686, 688–689, 691–692, 704–708, 710–711, 727–729, 740–742, 745–746, 749–754, 756–759, 761–763, 765–784, 786, 816, 818, 836, 841–842, 844–847, 862–872, 882, 888–893, 900, 902, 905, 907, 909–910, 912–915, 917–919, 922, 933–934, 936–937, 939–940, 942–944, 946, 950–951, 953, 955–958, 964, 968, 970, 974–976, 979–986, 988, 991–1000, 1003–1007, 1009–1011, 1013–1015, 1018, 1021–1022, 1024, 1026–1028, 1030–1034, 1050–1055, 1057, 1059–1060, 1062, 1064–1065, 1068–1069, 1071, 1073, 1076–1077, 1079, 1082, 1084–1085, 1087–1088, 1097, 1108, 1111, 1113, 1115–1116, 1118, 1123, 1125, 1127–1133, 1135, 1138–1144, 1152, 1154, 1157–1159, 1161, 1172–1174, 1179–1180, 1189, 1192, 1194–1195, 1200–1201, 1203–1204, 1214–1220, 1227–1228, 1230–1236, **Humanities** 1237–1242, 1244–1249, 1254–1255, 1257–1260, 1262, 1265, 1267–1272, 1274, 1277–1280, 1282, 1284, 1286, 1288–1289, 1291–1296, 1298, 1300–1301, 1311–1325, 1327–1328, 1330, 1332, 1335–1336, 1340, 1342–1346, 1348, 1350–1354, 1356, 1360–1361, 1363–1369, 1371–1372, 1374, 1376, 1379–1380, 1382–1383, 1385, 1387–1388, 1390–1391, 1395–1397, 1399–1405, 1407–1408, 1413, 1415–1422, 1427–1428, 1430–1431, 1433–1434, 1441–1445, 1448, 1451, 1456, 1460–1462, 1465–1467, 1471, 1473–1475, 1477, 1482–1486, 1489–1492, 1494, 1496, 1498, 1500, 1502–1503, 1506–1514, 1516–1517, 1519–1521, 1524–1525, 1528, 1531–1537, 1540–1543, 1545–1546, 1550, 1556,

1559–1560, 1563–1572, 1574–1580, 1582–1588, 1595–1596, 1598, 1602, 1604–1606, 1610, 1614–1615, 1617–1622, 1624, 1627, 1631, 1633, 1636–1640, 1643–1644, 1648–1650, 1652, 1654–1656, 1660, 1663–1667, 1669–1670, 1672–1681, 1684–1686, 1688–1691, 1695, 1700–1702, 1704, 1709–1711, 1713, 1717–1721, 1725–1727, 1729, 1731–1732, 1735, 1738–1739, 1742–1743, 1746–1758, **Sciences** 1759–1767, 1771–1774, 1776–1785, 1788–1799, 1802–1811, 1819–1820, 1822, 1824, 1827–1837, 1840–1841, 1843–1848, 1850–1862, 1864–1867, 1873–1878, 1880–1881, 1883–1894, 1899–1901, 1904–1909, 1911–1916, 1918–1925, 1927, 1929, 1936–1939, 1942–1947, 1951, 1955, 1957–1958, 1968, 1971–1972, 1975, 1978–1979, 1982–1984, 1986–1992, 1994–1995, 1997–1998, 2002, 2004, 2006–2009, 2012, 2014–2018, 2026–2028, 2030, 2032, 2034–2045, 2047–2055, 2057–2058, 2060, 2062–2064, 2067–2069, 2071–2073, 2075–2076, 2078, 2080, 2084–2090, 2092, 2094–2102, 2104–2105, 2108, 2110–2119, 2121–2122, 2125, 2129, 2131–2135, 2138–2139, 2141–2142, 2144–2155, 2157, 2168–2172, 2174–2175, 2177, 2179–2180, 2182, 2184–2190, 2192, 2195–2211, 2213–2214, 2216–2217, 2219, 2222–2223, 2228, 2230–2234, 2241–2250, 2252, 2254, 2258–2266, 2270, 2272–2274, 2276–2280, 2282, 2284–2285, 2287, 2293, 2297–2307, 2311–2313, 2316–2320, 2323–2324, 2328–2329, 2331, 2334, 2336–2337, 2339, 2341–2348, 2350–2357, 2360–2362, 2364–2365, 2367–2370, 2372, 2374–2375, 2378–2379, 2381, 2383, 2385–2388, 2390, 2393–2395, 2397–2411, 2413–2415, 2417, 2428–2429, 2431–2432, 2434, 2436–2439, 2445–2446, 2452–2460, 2462–2463, 2465–2474, 2477–2479, 2483–2489, 2492–2494, 2497–2504, 2506–2527, 2529–2531, 2533, 2542, 2544–2546, 2549, 2552, 2554–2556, 2559–2569, 2571, 2573–2575, 2577–2579, 2583, 2585–2595, 2598–2599, 2601, 2604–2612, 2614–2617, 2619–2621, 2623–2629, 2632, 2634–2637, 2640–2642, 2645–2647, 2650–2652, 2659–2661, 2663–2668, 2670–2676, 2678, 2680–2681, 2683–2685, 2687–2691, 2693, 2695–2697, 2700–2702, 2704, 2707–2710, 2712–2716, 2718–2719, 2722–2729, 2735–2742, 2745–2747, 2749, 2757, 2760–2765, 2769, 2771, 2773, 2775–2777, 2779, 2781–2788, 2792, 2794–2795, 2799–2801, 2804, 2809, 2812, 2815–2816, 2821, 2824, 2828–2832, 2834, 2836, 2838–2842, 2844–2846, 2854–2855, 2857–2858, 2863–2864, **Social Sciences** 2865–2868, 2870, 2872–2873, 2875, 2878, 2881, 2884, 2886–2887, 2889–2898, 2900–2902, 2904, 2908, 2910–2912, 2914, 2916–2919, 2921–2922, 2927, 2932, 2934–2937, 2949, 2951–2953, 2955–2956, 2960, 2962–2963, 2965–2966, 2971–2972, 2978, 2982–2983, 2985, 2990–2991, 2994, 2997, 2999–3000, 3004–3007, 3013–3014, 3016–3019, 3021, 3023–3025, 3028–3029, 3031–3035, 3037–3038, 3040, 3042, 3044–3045, 3054–3057, 3060–3061, 3065, 3067, 3070–3073, 3075–3076, 3078–3081, 3084, 3087–3090, 3094, 3096–3099, 3101, 3104–3105, 3109, 3111, 3113–3119, 3124–3126, 3128, 3130–3131, 3134, 3137–3138, 3140, 3143–3144, 3146–3147, 3151, 3153–3154, 3156, 3160, 3162, 3164–3169, 3174, 3177, 3183–3184, 3187, 3190, 3194, 3198, 3200–3201, 3204–3206, 3214, 3217, 3220, 3223, 3235–3236, 3238, 3241, 3243–3244, 3250, 3252–3255, 3257–3258, 3260–3272, 3279, 3292–3295, 3298, 3305, 3308–3309, 3315, 3323–3324, 3332–3334, 3337–3343, 3345–3347, 3349, 3351, 3356–3358, 3361, 3363, 3368–3369, 3371–3373, 3376–3379, 3381, 3383–3388, 3393–3397, 3399–3402, 3404, 3406, 3409–3410, 3414–3416, 3419–3423, 3425–3428, 3430. *See also* names of specific cities, counties, states, and regions

Utah: **Unrestricted by Subject Area** 51, 452, 577, 650, 967, 973, 1020, 1066, 1145–1151, 1193, **Humanities** 1530, 1581, 1641, **Sciences** 2656–2657, 2790–2791, **Social Sciences** 3362, 3417. *See also* United States; Western states; names of specific cities and counties

Venezuela: **Unrestricted by Subject Area** 1219. *See also* Foreign countries; South America

Vermont. **Unrestricted by Subject Area** 114, 121, 209, 440, 452, 1023, 1063, 1155–1156, **Humanities** 1256, 1305, 1522, 1706, 1716, **Sciences** 1812, 1821, 1897, 2123, 2181, 2191, 2271, 2380, 2621, 2639, 2796–2798, **Social Sciences** 2913, 3041, 3150, 3339. *See also* New England states; United States; names of specific cities and counties

Virgin Islands: **Unrestricted by Subject Area** 227, 442, 620, 1073, 1140, **Humanities** 1311, **Sciences** 1971, 1980, 2211, 2373, **Social Sciences** 2872, 2949, 3071, 3167. *See also* Caribbean; United States

Virginia: **Unrestricted by Subject Area** 128, 143, 216, 219, 262, 285–287, 335, 364, 455, 542, 587, 973, 1063, 1070, 1153, 1163–1171, 1175, **Humanities** 1266, 1398, 1449, 1514, 1517, 1523, 1581, 1721–1724, 1733, **Sciences** 1842, 1916, 1948, 2176, 2359, 2366, 2386, 2442, 2682, 2706, 2774, 2803, 2805, 2807, 2856, **Social Sciences** 2938, 3058, 3107, 3122, 3256, 3417. *See also* Southern states; United States; names of specific cities and counties

Virginia, regional: **Unrestricted by Subject Area** 173, 322, 603, 785

Walworth County, Wisconsin: **Unrestricted by Subject Area** 1081. *See also* Wisconsin

Washington: **Unrestricted by Subject Area** 270, 324, 452, 973, 987, 1020, 1083, 1178, 1182–1185, 1193, **Humanities** 1357, 1392, 1452, 1459, 1495, 1507, 1581, 1603, 1646, 1658, 1662, 1668, 1703, 1737, **Sciences** 1952, 1973, 1999, 2059, 2221, 2235, 2371, 2412, 2416, 2584, 2653–2655, 2766, 2814, 2817–2819, 2860–2861, **Social Sciences** 2928, 2940, 2950, 3001–3002, 3046, 3091, 3110, 3359–3360. *See also* Northwestern states; United States; Western states; names of specific cities and counties

Washington County, Wisconsin: **Unrestricted by Subject Area** 1081, **Sciences** 1984. *See also* Wisconsin

Washington, D.C.: **Unrestricted by Subject Area** 139, 173, 216, 262, 282, 322, 364, 603, 785, 1063, 1070, 1181, **Humanities** 1733, **Sciences** 1916, 1993, 2621,

**Social Sciences** 3122, 3256, 3339. *See also* Southern states; United States

Waukesha County, Wisconsin: **Unrestricted by Subject Area** 1081, **Sciences** 1984. *See also* Wisconsin

West Germany. *See* Germany

West Virginia: **Unrestricted by Subject Area** 216, 270, 368, 452, 963, 973, 989, 1063, 1070, 1187–1191, 1221, **Humanities** 1514, 1581, 1736, **Sciences** 1826, 1842, 2238, 2366, 2372, 2386, 2548, 2576, 2706, **Social Sciences** 3012, 3317. *See also* Southern states; United States; names of specific cities

Westchester, Pennsylvania: **Unrestricted by Subject Area** 529, **Humanities** 1497, **Social Sciences** 3159. *See also* Pennsylvania

Western states: **Humanities** 1422. *See also* United States; names of specific states

Wisconsin: **Unrestricted by Subject Area** 51, 270, 276, 452, 456, 964, 973, 987, 1020, 1070, 1134, 1162, 1205–1213, 1222, **Humanities** 1581, 1671, 1728, 1745, **Sciences** 1940, 1974, 1980, 1984–1985, 2120, 2137, 2277, 2558, 2698, 2811, 2848–2853, **Social Sciences** 3188, 3365, 3382. *See also* Midwestern states; United States; names of specific cities and counties

Wood County, West Virginia: **Unrestricted by Subject Area** 368. *See also* West Virginia

Woodbury County, Iowa: **Unrestricted by Subject Area** 22. *See also* Iowa

Wyoming: **Unrestricted by Subject Area** 452, 952, 973, 987, 1193, 1223–1226, **Humanities** 1581, **Sciences** 1934, 1980, 2433, 2622, 2656–2657, 2862, **Social Sciences** 3362. *See also* United States; Western states; names of specific cities and counties

# Tenability Index

Some programs listed in this book can be used only in specific cities, counties, states, or regions. Others may be used anywhere in the United States (or even abroad). The Tenability Index will help you locate funding that is restricted to a specific area as well as funding that has no tenability restrictions (these are listed under the term "United States"). To use this index, look up the geographic areas where you'd like to go (always check the listings under "United States"), jot down the entry numbers listed under the subject areas that interest you, and use those numbers to find the program descriptions in the directory. To help you in your search, we've provided some "see also" references in each index entry. Remember: the numbers cited here refer to program entry numbers, not to page numbers in the book.

Adair County, Iowa: **Unrestricted by Subject Area** 22. *See also* Iowa

Adams County, Iowa: **Unrestricted by Subject Area** 22. *See also* Iowa

Alabama: **Unrestricted by Subject Area** 24–30, 129, 586, 1051, **Humanities** 1250–1252, 1341, **Sciences** 1811, 1813–1815, 1975, 2029, 2106, 2396, 2689, 2723, **Social Sciences** 2984, 3179, 3197, 3378, 3417. *See also* Southern states; United States; names of specific cities and counties

Alaska: **Unrestricted by Subject Area** 31–32, 1192–1193, **Humanities** 1253, **Sciences** 1932, 2212, 2618, 2824, **Social Sciences** 3326. *See also* Northwestern states; United States; names of specific cities

Albany, Oregon: **Sciences** 2371. *See also* Oregon

Albuquerque, New Mexico: **Humanities** 1345–1346. *See also* New Mexico

Alexandria, Virginia: **Unrestricted by Subject Area** 282. *See also* Virginia

Alpena, Michigan: **Sciences** 2852

American Samoa: **Unrestricted by Subject Area** 102. *See also* United States

Amherst, Massachusetts: **Sciences** 2116. *See also* Massachusetts

Ann Arbor, Michigan: **Sciences** 2104. *See also* Michigan

Argentina: **Unrestricted by Subject Area** 1219. *See also* Foreign countries; South America

Arizona: **Unrestricted by Subject Area** 83–84, 1192–1193, **Humanities** 1530, **Sciences** 1869–1870, 2348, 2613, 2724, 2813, 2824, **Social Sciences** 2905–2906, 3394. *See also* United States; names of specific cities and counties

Arkansas: **Unrestricted by Subject Area** 57, 85–87, 89–92, 169, 961, 1002, 1051, **Humanities** 1530, **Sciences** 1842, 2672, 2723. *See also* Southern states; United States; names of specific cities and counties

Arlington County, Virginia: **Unrestricted by Subject Area** 282. *See also* Virginia

Arlington, Virginia: **Humanities** 1265, 1291, 1383, 1575, 1581, 1665, 1679, 1695, **Sciences** 2002. *See also* Virginia

Asheville, North Carolina: **Unrestricted by Subject Area** 133. *See also* North Carolina

Athens, West Virginia: **Unrestricted by Subject Area** 133. *See also* West Virginia

Atlanta, Georgia: **Unrestricted by Subject Area** 133, **Humanities** 1265, 1291, 1318, 1383, 1575, 1581, 1665, 1679, 1695, **Sciences** 1907, 2064, 2104, 2838, **Social Sciences** 3057, 3346. *See also* Georgia

Auburn, Alabama: **Sciences** 2838. *See also* Alabama

Audubon County, Iowa: **Unrestricted by Subject Area** 22. *See also* Iowa

Austin, Texas: **Sciences** 2051, **Social Sciences** 2994. *See also* Texas

Australia: **Humanities** 1348. *See also* Foreign countries

Baltimore, Maryland: **Sciences** 2064. *See also* Maryland

Barbourville, Kentucky: **Unrestricted by Subject Area** 133. *See also* Kentucky

Baton Rouge, Louisiana: **Sciences** 2064, 2104, 2788, **Social Sciences** 3430. *See also* Louisiana

Beloit, Wisconsin: **Social Sciences** 3177. *See also* Wisconsin

Berea, Kentucky: **Unrestricted by Subject Area** 133. *See also* Kentucky

Berkeley, California: **Sciences** 1956. *See also* California

Big Rapids, Michigan: **Sciences** 2317. *See also* Michigan

Blacksburg, Virginia: **Social Sciences** 3346. *See also* Virginia

Bloomington, Indiana: **Humanities** 1652. *See also* Indiana

Bolivia: **Unrestricted by Subject Area** 1219. *See also* Foreign countries; South America

Boston, Massachusetts: **Sciences** 2002, 2116, **Social Sciences** 2980. *See also* Massachusetts

Boulder, Colorado: **Sciences** 1907. *See also* Colorado

Brazil: **Unrestricted by Subject Area** 1219, **Sciences** 2413. *See also* Foreign countries; South America

Britain. *See* United Kingdom

Bronx County, New York. *See* New York, New York

Bronx, New York. *See* New York, New York

Brookline, Massachusetts: **Humanities** 1265, 1383, 1575, 1665, 1679, 1695. *See also* Massachusetts

Brooklyn, New York. *See* New York, New York

Buckhannon, West Virginia: **Unrestricted by Subject Area** 133. *See also* West Virginia

Buena Vista County, Iowa: **Unrestricted by Subject Area** 22. *See also* Iowa

Calhoun County, Iowa: **Unrestricted by Subject Area** 22. *See also* Iowa

California: **Unrestricted by Subject Area** 46, 48, 147–149, 152–160, 163–165, 168–169, 171, 214, 304, 366, 388, 421, 602, 1067, 1192–1193, 1199, 1202, **Humanities** 1308–1310, 1328, 1359, 1384, 1477, 1506, 1622, 1714, **Sciences** 1783, 1902, 1960–1967, 1969–1970, 1996, 2000, 2028, 2066, 2107, 2326, 2394, 2440, 2724, 2789, 2813, 2824, 2835, 2847, **Social Sciences** 2915, 2941–2943, 2945–2947, 2961, 3022, 3155, 3178, 3191, 3355, 3394, 3417. *See also* United States; names of specific cities and counties

California, northern: **Humanities** 1377

Cambridge, Massachusetts: **Humanities** 1556, **Sciences** 2104, 2180. *See also* Massachusetts

Canada: **Unrestricted by Subject Area** 263–264, 406, 418, 436, 525, 573, 588, 749, 891–893, 907, 934, 936, 944, 972, 1026, 1178, 1219, **Humanities** 1245, 1265, 1293–1294, 1348, 1356, 1367, 1382–1383, 1456, 1477, 1486, 1498, 1508–1509, 1511, 1532, 1546, 1575, 1587–1588, 1602, 1604–1605, 1617, 1621, 1644, 1664–1666, 1670, 1679, 1686, 1695, 1707, 1756, **Sciences** 1763, 1772, 1811, 1847, 1867, 1878, 1880–1881, 1892, 1915, 1936, 1979, 1987, 2027, 2048, 2076, 2094, 2097, 2099–2102, 2105, 2138, 2147, 2150, 2155, 2188, 2216, 2219, 2230, 2239, 2245, 2250, 2264, 2280, 2287, 2299–2301, 2323, 2350–2354, 2356, 2369, 2402, 2413–2414, 2458, 2498, 2500, 2509, 2511, 2515, 2542, 2549, 2556, 2569, 2575, 2587, 2589, 2605, 2618, 2621, 2626, 2632, 2634, 2668, 2675, 2696, 2714–2715, 2719, 2729, 2737, 2784–2786, 2828, 2832, 2834, 2841, 2864, **Social Sciences** 2865, 2872, 2878, 2881, 2892, 2895, 2910, 2952, 2963, 3045, 3061, 3073, 3075, 3097, 3105, 3113, 3116, 3143, 3162, 3244, 3262, 3268, 3282, 3305, 3339–3340, 3352, 3387, 3418, 3426, 3428. *See also* Foreign countries

Cape Girardeau, Missouri: **Sciences** 2338. *See also* Missouri

Caribbean: **Unrestricted by Subject Area** 891–893, **Humanities** 1293. *See also* Foreign countries; names of specific countries

Carroll County, Iowa: **Unrestricted by Subject Area** 22. *See also* Iowa

Cass County, Iowa: **Unrestricted by Subject Area** 22. *See also* Iowa

Central America: **Humanities** 1293. *See also* Foreign countries; names of specific countries

Champaign, Illinois: **Sciences** 2104. *See also* Illinois

Charleston, South Carolina: **Social Sciences** 3346. *See also* South Carolina

Charlotte, North Carolina: **Humanities** 1265, 1291, 1383, 1575, 1581, 1665, 1679, 1695. *See also* North Carolina

Cherokee County, Iowa: **Unrestricted by Subject Area** 22. *See also* Iowa

Chesterfield, Missouri: **Sciences** 1828. *See also* Missouri

Chicago, Illinois: **Humanities** 1265, 1291, 1383, 1575, 1581, 1665, 1679, 1695, 1746, **Sciences** 2104, **Social Sciences** 3057, 3177. *See also* Illinois

Chico, California: **Sciences** 1956. *See also* California

Chile: **Unrestricted by Subject Area** 1219. *See also* Foreign countries; South America

China. *See* Hong Kong; People's Republic of China; Taiwan

Claremont, California: **Sciences** 1907. *See also* California

Clay County, Iowa: **Unrestricted by Subject Area** 22. *See also* Iowa

Cleveland, Ohio: **Sciences** 2104. *See also* Ohio

College Station, Texas: **Sciences** 1907. *See also* Texas

Colombia: **Sciences** 2675. *See also* Foreign countries; South America

Colorado: **Unrestricted by Subject Area** 132, 169, 233–240, 401, 1192–1193, **Humanities** 1273, 1333–1334, 1409, 1450, 1625, **Sciences** 1863, 1934, 2010–2013, 2031, 2058, 2321, 2340, 2671–2672, 2806, 2808, 2824, **Social Sciences** 2903, 2967–2970, 3000, 3026–3027, 3090. *See also* United States; names of specific cities and counties

Columbia, Missouri: **Sciences** 2338. *See also* Missouri

Columbia, South Carolina: **Social Sciences** 3346. *See also* South Carolina

Columbus, Ohio: **Sciences** 2104. *See also* Ohio

Connecticut: **Unrestricted by Subject Area** 172, 247, 249, 252–253, 411, 611, 662, 693, 839–840, 862, 916, **Humanities** 1264, 1295, 1386, **Sciences** 1812, 1896, 2021–2022, 2156, 2222, 2254, 2271, **Social Sciences** 2935, 2954, 2976, 2978, 2980, 3008, 3086, 3335, 3417. *See also* New England states; Northeastern states; United States; names of specific cities and counties

Corvallis, Oregon: **Sciences** 2838. *See also* Oregon

Costa Rica: **Unrestricted by Subject Area** 1219. *See also* Central America; Foreign countries

Crawford County, Iowa: **Unrestricted by Subject Area** 22. *See also* Iowa

Dallas, Texas: **Humanities** 1265, 1291, 1383, 1575, 1581, 1665, 1673, 1679, 1695. *See also* Texas

Danville, Kentucky: **Unrestricted by Subject Area** 133. *See also* Kentucky

Davenport, Iowa: **Sciences** 1828. *See also* Iowa

Davidson, North Carolina: **Unrestricted by Subject Area** 133. *See also* North Carolina

Davis, California: **Sciences** 1956. *See also* California

Daytona Beach, Florida: **Social Sciences** 3346. *See also* Florida

Dearborn, Michigan: **Sciences** 2104. *See also* Michigan

Decatur, Illinois: **Social Sciences** 3177. *See also* Illinois

DeKalb, Illinois: **Sciences** 2104, **Social Sciences** 3177. *See also* Illinois

Delaware: **Unrestricted by Subject Area** 9, 271–273, 303, 378, 434, 522, 529, 665, 839, **Humanities** 1482, 1497, **Sciences** 2358, 2430, 2730, 2844, **Social Sciences** 2993, 3159. *See also* Northeastern states; Southeastern states; Southern states; United States; names of specific cities and counties

Denver, Colorado: **Humanities** 1265, 1291, 1383, 1575, 1581, 1665, 1679, 1695. *See also* Colorado

Des Moines, Iowa: **Social Sciences** 3177. *See also* Iowa

Detroit, Michigan: **Sciences** 2104, **Social Sciences** 3240. *See also* Michigan

Dickinson County, Iowa: **Unrestricted by Subject Area** 22. *See also* Iowa

District of Columbia. *See* Washington, D.C.

Dover, Delaware: **Sciences** 2788, **Social Sciences** 3430. *See also* Delaware

Durham, New Hampshire: **Sciences** 2838. *See also* New Hampshire

East Germany. *See* Germany

East Lansing, Michigan: **Sciences** 2104, **Social Sciences** 3346. *See also* Michigan

Ecuador: **Unrestricted by Subject Area** 1219. *See also* Foreign countries; South America

Edinburg, Texas: **Sciences** 2116. *See also* Texas

El Paso, Texas: **Humanities** 1346. *See also* Texas

Elizabeth City, North Carolina: **Sciences** 2064, **Social Sciences** 3300. *See also* North Carolina

Emory, Virginia: **Unrestricted by Subject Area** 133. *See also* Virginia

England: **Humanities** 1348, **Sciences** 2367. *See also* Foreign countries; United Kingdom

Eugene, Oregon: **Sciences** 2371. *See also* Oregon

Europe: **Unrestricted by Subject Area** 1178, **Sciences** 2302, **Social Sciences** 3137. *See also* Foreign countries; names of specific countries

Evanston, Illinois: **Sciences** 2104, **Social Sciences** 3057. *See also* Illinois

Fairfax County, Virginia: **Unrestricted by Subject Area** 282. *See also* Virginia

Fairfax, Virginia: **Unrestricted by Subject Area** 282. *See also* Virginia

Falls Church, Virginia: **Unrestricted by Subject Area** 282. *See also* Virginia

Fargo, North Dakota: **Sciences** 1907. *See also* North Dakota

Fayetteville, North Carolina: **Social Sciences** 3300. *See also* North Carolina

Federal Republic of Germany. *See* Germany

Ferrum, Virginia: **Unrestricted by Subject Area** 133. *See also* Virginia

Flagstaff, Arizona: **Humanities** 1346. *See also* Arizona

Florida: **Unrestricted by Subject Area** 169, 342, 352–354, 356–362, 959, 1051, 1114, 1133, 1198, **Humanities** 1243, 1284–1285, 1290, 1375, 1393–1394, 1410, 1440, 1526, 1622, 1715, 1740, **Sciences** 1800, 1811, 1876, 1928, 2001, 2065, 2082, 2091, 2109, 2124, 2158–2165, 2167, 2257, 2328, 2335, 2444, 2711, 2723, 2793, 2810, 2830, **Social Sciences** 3010, 3048–3053, 3224, 3417. *See also* Southeastern states; Southern states; United States; names of specific cities and counties

Foreign countries: **Unrestricted by Subject Area** 132, 499, 976, 1006, 1076, 1157, **Humanities** 1288, 1353, 1461, 1475, 1478, 1531, 1533, 1638, 1749, **Sciences** 1890–1892, 1992, 2115, 2131, 2135, 2152, 2154, 2196, 2305–2307, 2312, 2320, 2400, 2471, 2555, 2606, 2623, 2697, 2726, 2769, 2838, **Social Sciences** 2956, 3006, 3125, 3265, 3363, 3400. *See also* names of specific continents; names of specific countries

Fort Lauderdale, Florida: **Humanities** 1265, 1291, 1383, 1575, 1581, 1665, 1679, 1695. *See also* Florida

Fort Valley, Georgia: **Sciences** 2064, 2788, **Social Sciences** 3430. *See also* Georgia

France: **Humanities** 1348, **Sciences** 2413. *See also* Europe; Foreign countries

Frankfort, Kentucky: **Sciences** 2788, **Social Sciences** 3430. *See also* Kentucky

Frederick, Maryland: **Unrestricted by Subject Area** 133. *See also* Maryland

Fremont County, Iowa: **Unrestricted by Subject Area** 22. *See also* Iowa

Fresno, California: **Sciences** 1956. *See also* California

Gaithersburg, Maryland: **Humanities** 1348. *See also* Maryland

Galesburg, Illinois: **Social Sciences** 3177. *See also* Illinois

Georgia: **Unrestricted by Subject Area** 4, 169, 392–396, 448–449, 504, 1051, **Humanities** 1281, 1341, 1412, 1478, 1488, **Sciences** 1811, 2025, 2029, 2223, 2225, 2227, 2493, 2723, **Social Sciences** 2957, 2981, 2984, 3069, 3080–3083, 3170. *See also* Southeastern states; Southern states; United States; names of specific cities and counties

German Democratic Republic. *See* Germany

Germany: **Sciences** 2413. *See also* Europe; Foreign countries

Golden, Colorado: **Sciences** 2058. *See also* Colorado

Great Britain. *See* United Kingdom

Greeley, Colorado: **Social Sciences** 2980. *See also* Colorado

Greencastle, Indiana: **Unrestricted by Subject Area** 133. *See also* Indiana

Greene County, Iowa: **Unrestricted by Subject Area** 22. *See also* Iowa

Greensboro, North Carolina: **Unrestricted by Subject Area** 133, **Humanities** 1517, **Sciences** 1907, 2064, 2104, 2788, **Social Sciences** 3057, 3430. *See also* North Carolina

Greenville, South Carolina: **Social Sciences** 3346. *See also* South Carolina

Guam: **Unrestricted by Subject Area** 102, 1140, 1219, **Social Sciences** 2872.

*See also* United States

Guthrie County, Iowa: **Unrestricted by Subject Area** 22. *See also* Iowa

Hampton, Virginia: **Sciences** 2064, **Social Sciences** 3057. *See also* Virginia

Harbor City, California. *See* Los Angeles, California

Harrison County, Iowa: **Unrestricted by Subject Area** 22. *See also* Iowa

Hawaii: **Unrestricted by Subject Area** 137, 182, 429, 447, 990, 1122, 1124, 1160, 1192–1193, **Humanities** 1263, 1362, 1370, 1381, 1439, 1515, 1626, **Sciences** 2079, 2126, 2256, 2349, 2389, 2596, 2658, 2705, 2724, 2780, 2824, 2835, 2837, **Social Sciences** 2929, 3030, 3066, 3077, 3103, 3108, 3123, 3203, 3394, 3417. *See also* United States; names of specific cities and counties

Hayward, California: **Sciences** 1828

Holland. *See* Netherlands

Hollywood, California. *See* Los Angeles, California

Hong Kong: **Sciences** 2413. *See also* Foreign countries

Houston, Texas: **Humanities** 1265, 1291, 1383, 1575, 1581, 1665, 1679, 1695, **Sciences** 2213, 2243, **Social Sciences** 3346. *See also* Texas

Hyde Park, New York: **Humanities** 1746. *See also* New York

Ida County, Iowa: **Unrestricted by Subject Area** 22. *See also* Iowa

Idaho: **Unrestricted by Subject Area** 169, 459–464, 977, 1192–1193, **Humanities** 1384, 1392, 1464, **Sciences** 2283, 2618, 2824, **Social Sciences** 3046, 3129. *See also* Northwestern states; United States; names of specific cities and counties

Illinois: **Unrestricted by Subject Area** 5, 105, 277, 465–474, 476, 683, 687, **Humanities** 1457, 1463, 1468–1469, 1622, **Sciences** 2042, 2268, 2281, 2288–2289, 2292, 2314, 2457, 2461, 2672, 2687, **Social Sciences** 3127, 3132, 3377, 3417. *See also* Midwestern states; United States; names of specific cities and counties

India: **Sciences** 2413. *See also* Foreign countries

Indiana: **Unrestricted by Subject Area** 373, 479–481, 483, 681, **Humanities** 1472, 1487, 1547, **Sciences** 1842, 2003, 2042, 2081, 2173, 2251, 2288, 2294–2296, 2332, **Social Sciences** 2877, 3100, 3148. *See also* Midwestern states; United States; names of specific cities and counties

Indianapolis, Indiana: **Humanities** 1268. *See also* Indiana

Institute, West Virginia: **Sciences** 2788, **Social Sciences** 3430. *See also* West Virginia

Iowa: **Unrestricted by Subject Area** 23, 180, 301, 487, 489–491, 683, 743, 978, 1162, **Humanities** 1476, 1620, 1634, **Sciences** 2042, 2286, 2308–2310, 2315, 2370, 2558, 2592, 2672. *See also* Midwestern states; United States; names of specific cities and counties

Israel: **Unrestricted by Subject Area** 529, **Humanities** 1497, **Social Sciences** 3159. *See also* Foreign countries

Ithaca, New York: **Sciences** 2104, **Social Sciences** 3346. *See also* New York

Jacksonville, Florida: **Social Sciences** 3177. *See also* Florida

Japan: **Unrestricted by Subject Area** 1219. *See also* Foreign countries

Jefferson City, Missouri: **Sciences** 2788, **Social Sciences** 3430. *See also* Missouri

Johnson City, Tennessee: **Unrestricted by Subject Area** 133. *See also* Tennessee

Kalamazoo, Michigan: **Sciences** 2104, 2838. *See also* Michigan

Kansas: **Unrestricted by Subject Area** 169, 178, 259, 535–540, 621, 682–683, **Humanities** 1446, 1504–1505, 1557, 1597, 1620, 1687, **Sciences** 2042, 2127, 2180, 2382, 2592, 2649, 2672, 2733, 2749, 2823, 2827, 2843, **Social Sciences** 2998, 3136, 3173, 3185–3186. *See also* Midwestern states; United States; names of specific cities and counties

Kansas City, Missouri: **Sciences** 1828, 2338. *See also* Missouri

Kentucky: **Unrestricted by Subject Area** 3, 36, 140, 243, 303, 330, 410, 412, 544, 547–550, 553–554, 632, 1056, 1126, 1229, **Humanities** 1435, **Sciences** 1842, 2251, 2277, 2288, 2378, 2672, 2723, 2833, **Social Sciences** 3100, 3180–3182, 3221, 3325. *See also* Southern states; United States; names of specific cities and counties

Kern County, California: **Social Sciences** 3393. *See also* California

Kings County, New York. *See* New York, New York

Knoxville, Tennessee: **Sciences** 2104. *See also* Tennessee

Korea. *See* South Korea

Lake Forest, Illinois: **Social Sciences** 3177. *See also* Illinois

Langston, Oklahoma: **Sciences** 2064, 2788, **Social Sciences** 3430. *See also* Oklahoma

Las Cruces, New Mexico: **Humanities** 1346. *See also* New Mexico

Las Vegas, Nevada: **Humanities** 1265, 1291, 1383, 1575, 1581, 1665, 1679, 1695. *See also* Nevada

Las Vegas, New Mexico: **Humanities** 1346. *See also* New Mexico

Latin America. *See* Caribbean; Central America; Mexico; South America

Lewisburg, Pennsylvania: **Sciences** 2073. *See also* Pennsylvania

Lexington, Kentucky: **Sciences** 1907. *See also* Kentucky

Lexington, Virginia: **Social Sciences** 3177. *See also* Virginia

Lima, Ohio: **Sciences** 2852. *See also* Ohio

Lincoln, Pennsylvania: **Sciences** 2064. *See also* Pennsylvania

Lincolnshire, Illinois: **Social Sciences** 3057. *See also* Illinois

Logan, Utah: **Sciences** 2116. *See also* Utah

Long Grove, Illinois: **Social Sciences** 3177. *See also* Illinois

Los Angeles, California: **Humanities** 1265, 1316, 1383, 1556, 1575, 1665, 1679, 1695, **Sciences** 1828. *See also* California

Los Angeles County, California: **Social Sciences** 3393. *See also* California

Louisiana: **Unrestricted by Subject Area** 380, 397, 592–598, 1051, **Humani-**

ties 1530, **Sciences** 1842, 2669, 2723, **Social Sciences** 2883, 2959, 3193. *See also* Southern states; United States; names of specific cities and parishes

Lyon County, Iowa: **Unrestricted by Subject Area** 22. *See also* Iowa

Macon, Georgia: **Humanities** 1411, **Sciences** 2224. *See also* Georgia

Madison, Wisconsin: **Sciences** 2104, **Social Sciences** 3057. *See also* Wisconsin

Maine: **Unrestricted by Subject Area** 172, 218, 379, 607–608, 610–615, 662, 839–840, 862, 935, 1012, **Humanities** 1512, 1539, 1657, **Sciences** 1812, 1882, 1895, 2222, 2271, 2419, 2421, 2425, 2679, **Social Sciences** 3208–3211, 3213, 3370. *See also* New England states; Northeastern states; United States; names of specific cities and counties

Manchester, New Hampshire: **Humanities** 1746. *See also* New Hampshire

Manhattan, New York. *See* New York, New York

Marietta, Georgia: **Sciences** 1828. *See also* Georgia

Mars Hill, North Carolina: **Unrestricted by Subject Area** 133. *See also* North Carolina

Maryland: **Unrestricted by Subject Area** 145, 303, 311, 364, 638–642, 644–647, **Humanities** 1551–1553, **Sciences** 1916, 2033, 2447–2448, 2844, **Social Sciences** 2986, 3122, 3227–3228, 3230–3231. *See also* Northeastern states; Southeastern states; Southern states; United States; names of specific cities and counties

Maryland, southern: **Social Sciences** 3004

Maryville, Tennessee: **Unrestricted by Subject Area** 133. *See also* Tennessee

Massachusetts: **Unrestricted by Subject Area** 11, 172, 244, 402, 521, 611, 651–654, 656–662, 839–840, 862, 923, 1061, **Humanities** 1477, 1622, **Sciences** 1812, 2222, 2271, 2451, **Social Sciences** 3043, 3120, 3175, 3234, 3327, 3417. *See also* New England states; Northeastern states; United States; names of specific cities and counties

Meadville, Pennsylvania: **Unrestricted by Subject Area** 133. *See also* Pennsylvania

Mechanicsburg, Pennsylvania: **Humanities** 1734. *See also* Pennsylvania

Medford, Massachusetts: **Sciences** 1907. *See also* Massachusetts

Memphis, Tennessee: **Unrestricted by Subject Area** 133. *See also* Tennessee

Mexico: **Unrestricted by Subject Area** 972, 1219, **Humanities** 1293, 1348, 1477, 1486, 1508, 1532, 1546, 1587, 1621, **Sciences** 1847, 1867, 1892, 1936, 2097, 2138, 2216, 2352, 2356, 2402, 2413, 2549, 2634, 2675, 2719, 2729, 2784–2786, 2841, **Social Sciences** 3426. *See also* Foreign countries

Miami, Florida: **Humanities** 1265, 1383, 1575, 1665, 1679, 1695, **Sciences** 2116. *See also* Florida

Michigan: **Unrestricted by Subject Area** 169, 671–672, 674–676, 678–682, 764, **Humanities** 1558, **Sciences** 1842, 1849, 1853, 2005, 2042, 2077, 2103, 2239, 2253, 2288, 2376, 2490, 2495–2496, 2558, 2830, **Social Sciences** 2925, 3020, 3196, 3239, 3245, 3364, 3417. *See also* Midwestern states; United States; names of specific cities and counties

Midwestern states: **Humanities** 1541, 1599. *See also* United States; names of specific states

Mills County, Iowa: **Unrestricted by Subject Area** 22. *See also* Iowa

Milwaukee, Wisconsin: **Sciences** 2104. *See also* Wisconsin

Minneapolis, Minnesota: **Humanities** 1265, 1291, 1383, 1477, 1575, 1581, 1665, 1679, 1695, **Sciences** 1907, 2104, 2838. *See also* Minnesota

Minnesota: **Unrestricted by Subject Area** 388, 682–683, 694, 697–701, 703, 908, 1162, 1186, 1213, **Humanities** 1304, **Sciences** 1950, 1974, 2042, 2261, 2481–2482, 2558, 2859, **Social Sciences** 3417. *See also* Midwestern states; United States; names of specific cities and counties

Mississippi: **Unrestricted by Subject Area** 169, 397, 712–717, 843, 1051, **Humanities** 1538, 1561, **Sciences** 2723. **Social Sciences** 3246. *See also* Southern states; United States; names of specific cities and counties

Mississippi State, Mississippi: **Sciences** 2838. *See also* Mississippi

Missouri: **Unrestricted by Subject Area** 169, 190, 622, 682–683, 718–719, 721, 723, 725–726, 748, **Humanities** 1479, 1562, 1620, **Sciences** 1931, 2042, 2046, 2143, 2180, 2435, 2491, 2592, 2672, 2843, **Social Sciences** 2909, 2926, 3142, 3195, 3247–3249, 3417. *See also* Midwestern states; United States; names of specific cities and counties

Monona County, Iowa: **Unrestricted by Subject Area** 22. *See also* Iowa

Montana: **Unrestricted by Subject Area** 730–739, 1001, 1074–1075, 1192–1193, **Humanities** 1392, **Sciences** 2069, 2416, 2618, 2824, **Social Sciences** 3046, 3223, 3252, 3417. *See also* United States; names of specific cities and counties

Montgomery County, Iowa: **Unrestricted by Subject Area** 22. *See also* Iowa

Montgomery County, Maryland: **Unrestricted by Subject Area** 282. *See also* Maryland

Montpelier, Vermont: **Humanities** 1348, 1746. *See also* Vermont

Moscow, Idaho: **Sciences** 2838. *See also* Idaho

Murfreesboro, Tennessee: **Sciences** 2852. *See also* Tennessee

Nashville, Tennessee: **Sciences** 2064, 2788, **Social Sciences** 3430. *See also* Tennessee

Nebraska: **Unrestricted by Subject Area** 22–23, 510, 682–683, 790–795, 848, 903–904, 938, 1078, **Humanities** 1426, 1589, 1620, **Sciences** 1954, 2042, 2240, 2391, 2527–2528, 2558, 2592, 2672, **Social Sciences** 2987, 3047, 3093, 3192, 3202, 3272–3273, 3276, 3315, 3417, 3453. *See also* United States; Midwestern states; names of specific cities and counties

Netherlands: **Sciences** 2413. *See also* Europe; Foreign countries

Nevada: **Unrestricted by Subject Area** 1192–1193, **Humanities** 1328, 1506, 1632, **Sciences** 2724, 2824, 2835, **Social Sciences** 3394, 3417. *See also* United States; names of specific cities

New Brunswick, New Jersey: **Sciences** 2838. *See also* New Jersey

New England states: **Unrestricted by Subject Area** 798, 801, **Humanities** 1358, 1590, 1659, **Sciences** 1775, 2128, 2178, 2220, 2363, 2533, 2763, **Social Sciences** 2933, 2948, 3003, 3059, 3161, 3277–3279, 3374. *See also* Northeastern states; United States; names of specific states

New Hampshire: **Unrestricted by Subject Area** 172, 175, 427, 611, 619, 630, 662, 799–800, 802–805, 839–840, 862, **Sciences** 1812, 2222, 2236, 2271, 2547, **Social Sciences** 2958, 3121. *See also* New England states; Northeastern states; United States; names of specific cities and counties

New Jersey: **Unrestricted by Subject Area** 217, 310, 709, 806–809, 812–813, 862, **Humanities** 1592, 1653, **Sciences** 1838, 2155, 2222, 2535–2536, 2551, 2677, 2759, **Social Sciences** 3039, 3285–3287, 3417. *See also* Northeastern states; United States; names of specific cities and counties

New Mexico: **Unrestricted by Subject Area** 169, 208, 388, 816–818, 820–826, 1080, 1120, 1192–1193, **Humanities** 1345, 1530, 1593, 1600, **Sciences** 1934, 2538, 2553, 2813, 2824, **Social Sciences** 3078, 3174, 3289, 3296–3297. *See also* United States; names of specific cities and counties

New Orleans, Louisiana: **Sciences** 2064. *See also* Louisiana

New York: **Unrestricted by Subject Area** 169, 827, 830–838, 862, 1019, **Humanities** 1303, 1349, 1373, 1622, 1659, 1696, **Sciences** 1879, 1949, 2130, 2222, 2327, 2541, 2838, **Social Sciences** 2939, 3163, 3291, 3374, 3405, 3417. *See also* Northeastern states; United States; names of specific cities and counties

New York County, New York. *See* New York, New York

New York, New York: **Humanities** 1265, 1291, 1316, 1348, 1383, 1556, 1575, 1581, 1665, 1679, 1695, 1746, **Sciences** 2002, 2864, **Social Sciences** 2980, 3346. *See also* New York

Norfolk, Virginia: **Humanities** 1517. *See also* Virginia

Normal, Alabama: **Sciences** 2788, **Social Sciences** 3430. *See also* Alabama

Normal, Illinois: **Social Sciences** 3177. *See also* Illinois

North Carolina: **Unrestricted by Subject Area** 131, 303, 502–503, 787, 849–851, 853, 855–856, 1136–1137, **Humanities** 1514, 1573, **Sciences** 1975, 1977, 2093, 2237, 2386, 2505, 2648, **Social Sciences** 3015, 3064, 3158, 3225, 3259, 3299, 3301–3302, 3417. *See also* Southeastern states; Southern states; United States; names of specific cities and counties

North Dakota: **Unrestricted by Subject Area** 682–683, 857–861, 1162, 1193, **Sciences** 1974, 2042, 2558. *See also* Midwestern states; United States; names of specific cities

North Miami, Florida: **Social Sciences** 3346. *See also* Florida

Northampton, Massachusetts: **Social Sciences** 2980. *See also* Massachusetts

Northeastern states: **Sciences** 2095. *See also* United States; names of specific states

Northern Marianas: **Unrestricted by Subject Area** 102, **Social Sciences** 2872. *See also* United States

Northwestern states: **Sciences** 2221. *See also* United States; names of specific states

Norway: **Humanities** 1509. *See also* Europe; Foreign countries

Notre Dame, Indiana: **Sciences** 2002, 2104. *See also* Indiana

Oberlin, Ohio: **Unrestricted by Subject Area** 133. *See also* Ohio

O'Brien County, Iowa: **Unrestricted by Subject Area** 22. *See also* Iowa

Ohio: **Unrestricted by Subject Area** 169, 681, 873–874, 876–878, **Humanities** 1329, 1610, 1692, **Sciences** 1825, 1842, 2136, 2251, 2269, 2288, 2348, 2582, 2638, 2699, 2731, 2829–2830, **Social Sciences** 2869, 3100, 3298, 3310, 3312–3313, 3417. *See also* Midwestern states; United States; names of specific cities and counties

Oklahoma: **Unrestricted by Subject Area** 879–886, 969, 1051, **Humanities** 1530, 1611–1612, **Sciences** 1842, 2214–2215, 2672, **Social Sciences** 3074, 3314. *See also* Southern states; United States; names of specific cities and counties

Omaha, Nebraska: **Sciences** 2002. *See also* Nebraska

Orange County, California: **Humanities** 1265, 1291, 1383, 1575, 1581, 1665, 1679, 1695. *See also* California

Orangeburg, New York: **Social Sciences** 2980. *See also* New York

Orangeburg, South Carolina: **Sciences** 2788, **Social Sciences** 3430. *See also* South Carolina

Oregon: **Unrestricted by Subject Area** 116–117, 169, 204, 365–366, 895–896, 898–899, 1192–1193, **Humanities** 1377, 1384, 1392, 1480, 1507, 1613, **Sciences** 1787, 1930, 2183, 2464, 2580, 2618, 2631, 2824, **Social Sciences** 3046, 3063, 3135, 3145, 3319–3322. *See also* Northwestern states; United States; names of specific cities and counties

Orlando, Florida: **Sciences** 1907, 2821, **Social Sciences** 3346. *See also* Florida

Orono, Maine: **Sciences** 2838. *See also* Maine

Osceola County, Iowa: **Unrestricted by Subject Area** 22. *See also* Iowa

Oxford, Ohio: **Sciences** 1907, 2116, 2838. *See also* Ohio

Pacific Northwest. *See* Northwestern states

Page County, Iowa: **Unrestricted by Subject Area** 22. *See also* Iowa

Panama: **Unrestricted by Subject Area** 1219. *See also* Central America; Foreign countries

Paraguay: **Unrestricted by Subject Area** 1219. *See also* Foreign countries; South America

Pendleton, Oregon: **Sciences** 2371. *See also* Oregon

Pennsylvania: **Unrestricted by Subject Area** 169, 172, 242, 273, 303, 611, 662, 839–840, 874, 925–928, 931–932, 941, 1086, 1188, **Humanities** 1553, 1623,

Sciences 1807, 1826, 1910, 2040, 2222, 2322, 2459, 2469, 2550, 2597, 2600, 2603, 2630, **Social Sciences** 2920, 3329–3331, 3336–3337. *See also* Northeastern states; United States; names of specific cities and counties

People's Republic of China: **Humanities** 1289, **Sciences** 2413. *See also* Foreign countries

Peoria, Illinois: **Sciences** 2116. *See also* Illinois

Peru: **Unrestricted by Subject Area** 1219. *See also* Foreign countries; South America

Petersburg, Virginia: **Sciences** 2788, **Social Sciences** 3430. *See also* Virginia

Philadelphia, Pennsylvania: **Humanities** 1265, 1291, 1318, 1383, 1575, 1581, 1665, 1679, 1695, **Social Sciences** 3177. *See also* Pennsylvania

Philippines: **Unrestricted by Subject Area** 1219, **Sciences** 2413. *See also* Foreign countries

Phoenix, Arizona: **Humanities** 1265, 1291, 1383, 1575, 1581, 1665, 1679, 1695. *See also* Arizona

Pine Bluff, Arkansas: **Sciences** 2788, **Social Sciences** 3430. *See also* Arkansas

Pittsburgh, Pennsylvania: **Humanities** 1265, 1291, 1383, 1575, 1581, 1665, 1679, 1695. *See also* Pennsylvania

Plymouth County, Iowa: **Unrestricted by Subject Area** 22. *See also* Iowa

Point Lookout, Missouri: **Unrestricted by Subject Area** 133. *See also* Missouri

Poland: **Humanities** 1323, 1542, 1693, **Sciences** 2413. *See also* Europe; Foreign countries

Polk City, Florida: **Unrestricted by Subject Area** 754. *See also* Florida

Pomona, California: **Sciences** 1956, 2116, **Social Sciences** 3346. *See also* California

Port Gibson, Mississippi: **Sciences** 2788, **Social Sciences** 3430. *See also* Mississippi

Port Orange, Florida: **Sciences** 1828. *See also* Florida

Portales, New Mexico: **Humanities** 1346. *See also* New Mexico

Portland, Oregon: **Humanities** 1265, 1383, 1507, 1575, 1665, 1679, 1695, **Sciences** 2371. *See also* Oregon

Pottawattamie County, Iowa: **Unrestricted by Subject Area** 22. *See also* Iowa

Prairie View, Texas: **Sciences** 2064, 2788, **Social Sciences** 3430. *See also* Texas

Prince George's County, Maryland: **Unrestricted by Subject Area** 282. *See also* Maryland

Princess Anne, Maryland: **Sciences** 2788, **Social Sciences** 3430. *See also* Maryland

Providence, Rhode Island: **Social Sciences** 3346. *See also* Rhode Island

Provo, Utah: **Sciences** 2116, **Social Sciences** 3177. *See also* Utah

Puerto Rico: **Unrestricted by Subject Area** 49, 60, 111, 169, 227, 344, 439, 442, 445, 453, 620, 936, 960, 1073, 1140, 1219, **Humanities** 1311, 1622, **Sciences** 1941, 1971, 2057, 2119, 2211, 2266, 2282, 2406, 2503, 2634, 2681, 2690, 2719, 2764, **Social Sciences** 2918, 2931, 2949, 2999, 3040, 3071, 3115, 3128, 3167, 3372, 3414. *See also* Caribbean; United States

Queens County, New York. *See* New York, New York

Queens, New York. *See* New York, New York

Rahway, New Jersey: **Sciences** 2783. *See also* New Jersey

Raleigh, North Carolina: **Sciences** 1907, 2104, 2838. *See also* North Carolina

Republic of China. *See* Taiwan

Rhode Island: **Unrestricted by Subject Area** 172, 611, 662, 839, 862, 970–971, **Humanities** 1282, **Sciences** 1812, 1818, 2222, 2271. *See also* New England states; Northeastern states; United States; names of specific cities

Richmond County, New York. *See* New York, New York

Richmond, Indiana: **Unrestricted by Subject Area** 133. *See also* Indiana

Richmond, Virginia: **Unrestricted by Subject Area** 133. *See also* Virginia

Ringgold County, Iowa: **Unrestricted by Subject Area** 22. *See also* Iowa

Riverside, California: **Sciences** 1956. *See also* California

Riverside County, California: **Social Sciences** 3393. *See also* California

Roanoke, Virginia: **Humanities** 1517. *See also* Virginia

Rochester, New York: **Social Sciences** 3177. *See also* New York

Rolla, Missouri: **Sciences** 2338. *See also* Missouri

Rome, Georgia: **Unrestricted by Subject Area** 133. *See also* Georgia

Russia: **Sciences** 2413. *See also* Europe; Foreign countries

Sac County, Iowa: **Unrestricted by Subject Area** 22. *See also* Iowa

Salem, Oregon: **Sciences** 2371. *See also* Oregon

Samoa. *See* American Samoa

San Bernardino County, California: **Social Sciences** 3393. *See also* California

San Diego, California: **Humanities** 1265, 1291, 1383, 1575, 1581, 1665, 1679, 1695, **Sciences** 2783. *See also* California

San Francisco, California: **Humanities** 1265, 1383, 1575, 1665, 1679, 1695. *See also* California

San Jose, California: **Sciences** 1828, 2838. *See also* California

San Luis Obispo, California: **Sciences** 1956, 2116. *See also* California

San Luis Obispo County, California: **Social Sciences** 3393. *See also* California

San Pedro, California. *See* Los Angeles, California

Santa Barbara County, California: **Social Sciences** 3393. *See also* California

Santa Clara, California: **Sciences** 2002. *See also* California

Santa Cruz, California: **Sciences** 1956. *See also* California

Santa Fe, New Mexico: **Humanities** 1346. *See also* New Mexico

Santa Monica, California: **Humanities** 1265, 1291, 1383, 1575, 1581, 1665, 1679, 1695. *See also* California

Schaumburg, Illinois: **Humanities** 1265, 1383, 1575, 1665, 1679, 1695. *See also* Illinois

Seattle, Washington: **Humanities** 1265, 1291, 1383, 1575, 1581, 1665, 1679, 1695, **Sciences** 1907, 2838. *See also* Washington

Seneca Falls, New York: **Sciences** 1828. *See also* New York

Shelby County, Iowa: **Unrestricted by Subject Area** 22. *See also* Iowa

Silver City, New Mexico: **Humanities** 1346

Silver Spring, Maryland: **Sciences** 2144, **Social Sciences** 3038. *See also* Maryland

Singapore: **Humanities** 1348. *See also* Foreign countries

Sioux County, Iowa: **Unrestricted by Subject Area** 22. *See also* Iowa

South America: **Humanities** 1293. *See also* Foreign countries; names of specific countries

South Carolina: **Unrestricted by Subject Area** 515, 578, 911, 1035–1043, 1051, **Humanities** 1275, 1514, 1682–1683, **Sciences** 1975, 1977, 2093, 2373, 2386, 2493, 2648, 2692, **Social Sciences** 3015, 3389–3390. *See also* Southeastern states; Southern states; United States; names of specific cities and counties

South Dakota: **Unrestricted by Subject Area** 42, 374, 376, 631, 683, 1008, 1044–1048, 1162, 1193, **Sciences** 1839, 1974, 2042, 2558, 2672, 2694, **Social Sciences** 2899, 3095, 3111, 3380, 3391–3392. *See also* Midwestern states; United States; names of specific cities and counties

South Hadley, Massachusetts: **Sciences** 2002. *See also* Massachusetts

South Korea: **Unrestricted by Subject Area** 1219, **Sciences** 2413. *See also* Foreign countries

South Orange, New Jersey: **Sciences** 2002. *See also* New Jersey

Southeastern states: **Sciences** 2095, 2702. *See also* Southern states; United States; names of specific states

Southern states: **Unrestricted by Subject Area** 1058, **Humanities** 1541, **Sciences** 1988, 2324. *See also* United States; names of specific states

Spain: **Sciences** 2413. *See also* Europe; Foreign countries

Spartanburg, South Carolina: **Unrestricted by Subject Area** 133. *See also* South Carolina

St. Cloud, Minnesota: **Sciences** 2116. *See also* Minnesota

St. Helena, California: **Humanities** 1348, 1746. *See also* California

St. Louis, Missouri: **Sciences** 1907, 2338, **Social Sciences** 3177. *See also* Missouri

Staten Island, New York. *See* New York, New York

Stevens Point, Wisconsin: **Sciences** 2838. *See also* Wisconsin

Stockton, California: **Social Sciences** 3177. *See also* California

Sundance, Utah: **Humanities** 1477, 1546, 1587. *See also* Utah

Sweden: **Unrestricted by Subject Area** 1049, **Sciences** 2302, **Social Sciences** 3137. *See also* Europe; Foreign countries

Syracuse, New York: **Sciences** 1907. *See also* New York

Taiwan: **Unrestricted by Subject Area** 1219. *See also* Foreign countries

Tallahassee, Florida: **Sciences** 2064, 2104, 2788, **Social Sciences** 3057, 3430. *See also* Florida

Tampa, Florida: **Humanities** 1265, 1383, 1575, 1665, 1679, 1695. *See also* Florida

Taylor County, Iowa: **Unrestricted by Subject Area** 22. *See also* Iowa

Tennessee: **Unrestricted by Subject Area** 797, 1051, 1089–1094, 1196, **Humanities** 1341, **Sciences** 1842, 2029, 2672, 2723, 2748, **Social Sciences** 2984, 3237, 3403. *See also* Southern states; United States; names of specific cities and counties

Texas: **Unrestricted by Subject Area** 169, 176, 292, 397, 430–431, 495, 690, 1051, 1095–1106, 1108–1112, 1117, 1176–1177, **Humanities** 1280, 1331, 1455, 1530, 1622, 1661, 1697–1699, **Sciences** 1770, 1842, 2213, 2243, 2336, 2686, 2722, 2752, 2755, 2758, 2770, 2775, 2778, 2822, **Social Sciences** 2871, 2924, 3009, 3062, 3112, 3152, 3350, 3375, 3408–3409, 3411–3412, 3417, 3420, 3424. *See also* Southern states; United States; names of specific cities and counties

Troy, New York: **Sciences** 2073. *See also* New York

Tucson, Arizona: **Humanities** 1346. *See also* Arizona

Tuskegee, Alabama: **Sciences** 2064, 2788, **Social Sciences** 3430. *See also* Alabama

Union County, Iowa: **Unrestricted by Subject Area** 22. *See also* Iowa

United Kingdom: **Unrestricted by Subject Area** 1007, **Sciences** 2413. *See also* Europe; Foreign countries; names of specific countries

United States: **Unrestricted by Subject Area** 1–6, 8, 10, 12–21, 33–35, 37–41, 43–45, 47, 49–50, 52–56, 58–82, 88, 93–104, 106–113, 115–116, 118–128, 130, 134–136, 138–139, 141–142, 144, 146, 150–151, 161–162, 166–167, 170, 173–175, 177, 179, 181–189, 191–203, 205–207, 209–213, 215–216, 218–232, 241, 245–246, 248, 250–251, 254–258, 260–267, 269–271, 273–275, 278–291, 293–300, 302, 304–309, 312–315, 317–323, 325–329, 331–341, 343–351, 355, 363, 367–372, 375, 377, 381–387, 389–391, 398–400, 403–409, 411, 413–420, 422–426, 428–429, 432–433, 435–447, 450–458, 475, 477–478, 482, 484–486, 488, 492–494, 496–501, 505–509, 511–520, 522–534, 541, 543, 545–546, 551–552, 555–577, 579–585, 587–591, 599–601, 603–606, 609–610, 615–620, 623–629, 633–637, 639, 643, 645, 648–650, 655, 663–664, 666–670, 673, 675, 677, 684–686, 688–689, 691–693, 695–696, 702, 704–708, 710–711, 720, 722, 724, 727–729, 740–747, 749–763, 765–786, 788–789, 796, 799–800, 810–811, 814–815, 819, 828–829, 841–842, 844–847, 852, 854, 863–872, 875, 887–894, 897, 900–902, 905–907, 909–910, 912–915, 917–922, 924, 927–930, 932–934, 936–937, 939–940, 942–951, 953–958, 961–963, 965–966, 968, 972–976, 979–989, 991–1000, 1003–1007, 1009–1018, 1020–1034, 1049–1050, 1052–1055, 1057, 1060, 1062–1066, 1068–1073, 1076–1077, 1079–1082, 1084–1085, 1087–1088, 1107, 1113, 1115–1116,

1118–1119, 1121, 1123, 1125, 1127–1132, 1135, 1138–1144, 1147–1148, 1152–1155, 1157–1161, 1165, 1169, 1172–1175, 1178–1182, 1185, 1189, 1194–1195, 1197, 1200–1201, 1203–1204, 1209, 1214–1223, 1227–1228, 1230–1236, **Humanities** 1237–1242, 1244–1249, 1252, 1254–1265, 1267, 1269–1272, 1274, 1276–1279, 1282–1284, 1286–1289, 1292–1302, 1305–1307, 1311–1327, 1330–1332, 1335–1340, 1342–1344, 1347–1348, 1350–1356, 1360–1372, 1374, 1376, 1378–1383, 1385, 1387–1391, 1395–1397, 1399–1408, 1413–1425, 1427–1434, 1436–1439, 1441–1445, 1447–1449, 1451, 1453–1454, 1456, 1458–1462, 1465–1467, 1470–1471, 1473–1474, 1477–1478, 1481–1486, 1489–1491, 1493–1494, 1496–1503, 1507–1511, 1513–1525, 1527–1529, 1531–1537, 1540, 1542–1546, 1548–1550, 1554–1556, 1559–1560, 1563–1572, 1574–1580, 1582–1588, 1591, 1594–1596, 1598, 1601–1609, 1614–1621, 1624, 1626–1633, 1635–1652, 1654–1656, 1660–1661, 1663–1667, 1669–1670, 1672–1681, 1684–1686, 1688–1691, 1693–1695, 1700–1705, 1707–1713, 1716–1723, 1725–1727, 1729–1736, 1738–1739, 1741, 1743–1744, 1747–1758, **Sciences** 1759–1769, 1771–1774, 1776–1786, 1788–1799, 1801–1806, 1808–1811, 1816–1817, 1819–1824, 1827–1837, 1840–1841, 1843–1852, 1854–1862, 1864–1868, 1871–1878, 1880–1894, 1896–1901, 1903–1906, 1908–1927, 1929–1930, 1932–1933, 1935–1939, 1941–1947, 1951–1953, 1955, 1957–1960, 1968, 1971–1972, 1976, 1978–1983, 1985–1987, 1989–1995, 1997–1998, 2002, 2004, 2006–2009, 2014–2020, 2023–2024, 2026–2027, 2030, 2032, 2034–2039, 2041, 2043–2045, 2047–2057, 2059–2063, 2067–2068, 2070–2076, 2078–2080, 2083–2090, 2092, 2094, 2096–2102, 2105, 2108, 2110–2115, 2117–2119, 2121–2123, 2125–2126, 2129, 2131–2135, 2137–2142, 2144–2155, 2157, 2166, 2168–2172, 2174–2175, 2177, 2179, 2182, 2184–2212, 2215–2219, 2226, 2228–2234, 2238, 2241–2242, 2244–2250, 2252, 2254–2255, 2258–2260, 2262–2267, 2270–2280, 2282, 2284–2285, 2287, 2289–2291, 2293, 2297–2307, 2311–2313, 2316–2320, 2323, 2325, 2329–2331, 2333–2334, 2337, 2339, 2341–2357, 2359–2361, 2364–2369, 2372, 2374–2375, 2377, 2379–2381, 2383–2390, 2392–2393, 2395, 2397–2411, 2413–2415, 2417–2418, 2420, 2422–2432, 2434, 2436–2439, 2441–2443, 2445–2446, 2449–2450, 2452–2456, 2458, 2460, 2462–2463, 2465–2468, 2470–2480, 2483–2489, 2492–2494, 2497–2504, 2506–2526, 2529–2532, 2534, 2537, 2539–2540, 2542–2547, 2549, 2552, 2554–2557, 2559–2579, 2581–2596, 2598–2599, 2601–2602, 2604–2612, 2614–2617, 2619–2621, 2623–2629, 2632–2637, 2639–2647, 2650–2653, 2656–2668, 2670, 2673–2676, 2678, 2680–2686, 2688, 2690–2691, 2693, 2695–2697, 2700–2701, 2703–2710, 2712–2722, 2725–2729, 2732, 2734–2747, 2750–2751, 2756–2757, 2760–2762, 2764–2769, 2771–2773, 2776–2779, 2781–2787, 2790, 2792, 2794, 2796–2804, 2809, 2812, 2814–2816, 2818, 2820–2821, 2825–2826, 2828–2832, 2834, 2836–2837, 2839–2842, 2845–2846, 2851, 2853–2855, 2857–2858, 2863–2864, **Social Sciences** 2865–2868, 2870, 2872–2876, 2878–2882, 2884–2898, 2900–2902, 2904, 2907–2908, 2910–2913, 2916–2923, 2927–2932, 2934, 2936–2937, 2940, 2944, 2949, 2951–2953, 2955–2956, 2960, 2962–2966, 2971–2975, 2977, 2979, 2982–2983, 2985, 2988–2992, 2994–2997, 2999, 3001, 3005–3007, 3011, 3013–3014, 3016–3019, 3021, 3023–3025, 3028–3038, 3040–3042, 3044–3045, 3054–3056, 3060–3061, 3065–3068, 3070–3073, 3075–3076, 3079, 3084–3089, 3092, 3094, 3096–3099, 3101–3106, 3108–3109, 3113–3119, 3124–3126, 3128, 3130–3131, 3133–3134, 3137–3141, 3143–3144, 3146–3147, 3149, 3151, 3153–3154, 3156–3157, 3159–3160, 3162, 3164–3169, 3171–3172, 3176–3177, 3183–3184, 3187, 3189–3190, 3194, 3198–3201, 3204–3207, 3212–3220, 3222, 3226, 3229, 3232–3233, 3235–3236, 3238, 3240–3244, 3250–3251, 3253–3258, 3260–3271, 3274–3275, 3277, 3280–3285, 3287–3288, 3290, 3292–3295, 3298, 3303–3309, 3311, 3316–3318, 3323–3324, 3328, 3330, 3332–3334, 3337–3345, 3347–3349, 3351–3354, 3356–3358, 3361–3363, 3366–3373, 3375–3376, 3379, 3383–3388, 3393, 3395–3404, 3406–3407, 3410, 3413–3416, 3418–3419, 3421–3429. *See also* names of specific cities, counties, states, and regions

University Park, Pennsylvania: **Sciences** 1907. *See also* Pennsylvania

Urbana, Illinois. *See* Champaign, Illinois

Utah: **Unrestricted by Subject Area** 967, 1066, 1145–1146, 1149–1151, 1192–1193, **Humanities** 1530, **Sciences** 2724, 2791, 2824, **Social Sciences** 3394, 3417. *See also* United States; names of specific cities and counties

Valparaiso, Indiana: **Social Sciences** 3177. *See also* Indiana

Venezuela: **Unrestricted by Subject Area** 1219. *See also* Foreign countries; South America

Ventura County, California: **Social Sciences** 3393. *See also* California

Vermont: **Unrestricted by Subject Area** 114, 172, 611, 662, 839–840, 862, 1156, **Humanities** 1706, **Sciences** 1812, 2181, 2222, 2271, **Social Sciences** 3150. *See also* New England states; Northeastern states; United States; names of specific cities and counties

Virgin Islands: **Unrestricted by Subject Area** 227, 442, 620, 1073, 1140, **Humanities** 1311, **Sciences** 1971, 2211, 2373, **Social Sciences** 2872, 2949, 3071, 3167. *See also* Caribbean; United States

Virginia: **Unrestricted by Subject Area** 143, 303, 364, 542, 1163–1164, 1166–1168, 1170–1171, **Humanities** 1266, 1398, 1514, 1553, 1721, 1724, **Sciences** 1842, 1916, 1948, 1975, 2176, 2362, 2386, 2774, 2805, 2807, 2844, 2856, **Social Sciences** 2914, 2938, 3058, 3107, 3122, 3417. *See also* Southeastern states; Southern states; United States; names of specific cities and counties

Virginia, northern: **Social Sciences** 3004

Washington: **Unrestricted by Subject Area** 169, 268, 324, 1059, 1083, 1183–1184, 1192–1193, **Humanities** 1357, 1384, 1392, 1452, 1459, 1495, 1507, 1658, 1662, 1668, 1737, 1742, **Sciences** 1973, 1999, 2235, 2412, 2416, 2654–2655, 2795, 2817, 2819, 2824, 2860–2861, **Social Sciences** 2950, 3002, 3046, 3091,

3110, 3359–3360, 3381. *See also* Northwestern states; United States; names of specific cities and counties

Washington, D.C.: **Unrestricted by Subject Area** 172, 282, 303, 316, 364, 611, 662, 839–840, **Humanities** 1268, 1490, 1492, 1532, 1546, 1553, 1556, 1587, **Sciences** 1916, 2002, 2064, 2844, **Social Sciences** 3004, 3057, 3122, 3177, 3346. *See also* Northeastern states; Southeastern states; Southern states; United States

Waterville, Maine: **Sciences** 2002. *See also* Maine

Waynesburg, Pennsylvania: **Unrestricted by Subject Area** 133. *See also* Pennsylvania

West Germany. *See* Germany

West Lafayette, Indiana: **Sciences** 1907, 2104. *See also* Indiana

West Point, Pennsylvania: **Sciences** 2783. *See also* Pennsylvania

West Virginia: **Unrestricted by Subject Area** 303, 1187–1188, 1190–1191, **Humanities** 1514, **Sciences** 1826, 1842, 2386, 2548, 2844, **Social Sciences** 3012, 3468. *See also* Southern states; United States; names of specific cities

Whitewater, Wisconsin: **Social Sciences** 3177. *See also* Wisconsin

Wilberforce, Ohio: **Sciences** 2064, 2116. *See also* Ohio

Wilmington, California. *See* Los Angeles, California

Winston–Salem, North Carolina: **Social Sciences** 3177, 3300. *See also* North Carolina

Wisconsin: **Unrestricted by Subject Area** 51, 169, 276, 683, 964, 1134, 1162, 1205–1208, 1210–1213, **Humanities** 1671, 1728, 1745, **Sciences** 1940, 1974, 1984, 2042, 2120, 2277, 2558, 2698, 2811, 2848–2851, **Social Sciences** 3188, 3365, 3382. *See also* Midwestern states; United States; names of specific cities and counties

Woodbury County, Iowa: **Unrestricted by Subject Area** 22. *See also* Iowa

Worcester, Massachusetts: **Sciences** 2116. *See also* Massachusetts

Wyoming: **Unrestricted by Subject Area** 952, 1192–1193, 1224–1226, **Sciences** 1934, 2433, 2622, 2671, 2824, 2862, **Social Sciences**. *See also* United States; names of specific cities and counties

Yellow Springs, Ohio: **Unrestricted by Subject Area** 133. *See also* Ohio

# Sponsoring Organization Index

The Sponsoring Organization Index makes it easy to identify agencies that offer college funding. In this index, sponsoring organizations are listed alphabetically, word by word. In addition, we've used a code (within parentheses) to help you identify which programs sponsored by these organizations fall within your scope of interest: U = Unrestricted by Subject Area; H = Humanities; S = Sciences; SS = Social Sciences. Here's how the codes work: if an organization's name is followed by (U) 41, the program sponsored by that organization is described in entry 41, in the Unrestricted by Subject Area section. If that sponsoring organization's name is followed by another entry number—for example, (SS) 2649—the same or a different program is described in entry 2649, in the Social Sciences section. Remember: the numbers cited here refer to program entry numbers, not to page numbers in the book.

AABB, (S) 1761
A.B. "Happy" Chandler Foundation, (U) 3
Abbie Sargent Memorial Scholarship, (S) 1769
ABC News, (H) 1489
Academy of Applied Science, (S) 2367
Academy of Model Aeronautics, (U) 191, 1022
Academy of Motion Picture Arts and Sciences, (H) 1689
Academy of Neonatal Nursing, (S) 2175
Academy of Television Arts & Sciences Foundation, (H) 1239
ACCEL/Exchange Network, (U) 308
Accountancy Board of Ohio, (SS) 2869
Accountemps, (SS) 2870
Acoustical Society of America, (H) 1691, (S) 2739
ACT Recognition Program Services, (U) 275, 557
Acton Institute for the Study of Religion and Liberty, (H) 1531
Actuarial Foundation, (S) 2350, (SS) 3156
Adelante! U.S. Education Leadership Fund, (U) 6
Adirondack Spintacular, (U) 571
Adobe Systems Incorporated, (S) 1783–1784, 2520
Advanced Micro Devices, Inc., (S) 1831
AeA Oregon Council, (S) 1787
Aero Club of New England, (S) 1775
Aerospace Education Foundation, (U) 7
Aetna Foundation, Inc., (S) 1789
AFL–CIO, (U) 8
Ag–Bag International Limited, (S) 2379
AGC of Massachusetts, (S) 2333, (SS) 3149
AgriBusiness Association of Kentucky, (S) 1768
Agribusiness Council of Indiana, (S) 2294
Agriliance, LLC, (S) 1972
Agronomic Science Foundation, (S) 2319
AHF, Inc., (U) 120
Air Force Aid Society, (U) 387
Air Force Association. Paul Revere Chapter, (U) 425, (S) 1944, 2008
Air Force Sergeants Association, (U) 20–21, 202, 425
Air Products and Chemicals, Inc., (S) 1807
Air Traffic Control Association, (U) 142, (S) 1808, 2190
Air & Waste Management Association. Allegheny Mountain Section, (S) 1826
Air & Waste Management Association. Florida Section, (S) 2001, 2158
Air & Waste Management Association. Pacific Northwest International Section, (S) 2618
Air & Waste Management Association–East Michigan Chapter, (S) 2103, (SS) 3020
Aircraft Electronics Association, (S) 1810, 1946, 1997, 2042, 2096, 2197, 2270, 2360, 2387, 2395, 2410, 2473, 2616, 2728, (SS) 2960
Airgas, Inc., (S) 1811
Airmen Memorial Foundation, (U) 21, 202
Airports Council International–North America, (SS) 2872
Akademos, Inc., (U) 1113
Akron General Medical Center, (S) 2699
Alabama Alliance for Science, Engineering, Mathematics, and Science Education, (S) 2689, (SS) 3378
Alabama Bankers Association, (U) 294, (SS) 2880, 3179
Alabama Commission on Higher Education, (U) 26–30, (H) 1251
Alabama Concrete Industries Association, (H) 1250, (S) 1813

Alabama Council of Teachers of Mathematics, (S) 1814
Alabama Department of Veterans Affairs, (U) 25
Alabama Funeral Directors Association, (SS) 2879
Alabama Golf Course Superintendents Association, (S) 2070
Alabama Media Professionals, (H) 1252
Alabama Road Builders Association, (S) 2106
Alaska Broadcasters Association, (H) 1529
Alaska Commission on Postsecondary Education, (U) 386, (S) 1817, (SS) 2882
Alaska Department of Education and Early Development, (U) 386
Alaska. Office of Veterans Affairs, (U) 31
Alaska Press Women, (H) 1253
Alaska Society of Certified Public Accountants, (SS) 3326
Albuquerque Community Foundation, (U) 822, 1080
Albuquerque Journal, (H) 1345–1347
Alcoa Foundation, (S) 1820
Alexander Graham Bell Association for the Deaf, (U) 43, 118, 279, 316, 339, 569, 601, 996, 1173, 1179, (S) 2666
Alice M. Yarnold and Samuel Yarnold Scholarship Trust, (S) 1823, (SS) 2885
All–Ink.com, (U) 37
Allianz Global Investors Distributors LLC, (U) 42
Allyn & Bacon Publishers, (SS) 2887
Alpha Chi, (U) 35
Alpha Mu Tau Fraternity, (S) 1829, 1884, 2075, 2678
Alpha Omega Council, (H) 1624
Alpha Tau Delta, (S) 2489
Amateur Athletic Union, (U) 1230
Amerada Hess Foundation, (S) 1832
American Academy of Allergy, Asthma & Immunology, (U) 110
American Academy of Chefs, (H) 1258–1260
American Academy of Neurology, (S) 2531
American Academy of Physician Assistants, (S) 2585
American Academy of Physician Assistants–Veterans Caucus, (S) 1767, 1983
American Action Fund for Blind Children and Adults, (U) 546
American Advertising Federation, (H) 1574, 1586
American Advertising Federation. Fourth District, (H) 1261
American Airlines, (U) 710, 711
American Angus Association, (U) 72, (S) 1957
American Angus Auxiliary, (S) 1834
American Architectural Foundation, (H) 1244–1245
American Association for Health Education, (S) 1764, (SS) 2866
American Association for Respiratory Care, (S) 2341, 2493, 2667, 2845
American Association of Advertising Agencies, (H) 1267, 1614
American Association of Airport Executives Foundation, (S) 1759–1760
American Association of Airport Executives. Northeast Chapter, (S) 2621, (SS) 3339
American Association of Airport Executives. Southwest Chapter, (S) 2724, (SS) 3394
American Association of Blacks in Energy, (S) 1835
American Association of Candy Technologists, (S) 2511
American Association of Cereal Chemists, (S) 1762
American Association of Colleges for Teacher Education, (U) 39
American Association of Colleges of Nursing, (S) 1968, 2417, 2695
American Association of Colleges of Osteopathic Medicine, (S) 2695
American Association of Colleges of Pharmacy, (S) 2695
American Association of Colleges of Podiatric Medicine, (S) 2695
American Association of Community Colleges, (U) 38
American Association of Critical–Care Nurses, (S) 2112
American Association of Japanese University Women, (U) 48
American Association of Neuroscience Nurses, (S) 2530
American Association of Occupational Health Nurses, Inc., (S) 1820, 1836, 2462
American Association of School Administrators, (U) 281
American Association of State Colleges and Universities, (U) 1116
American Association of Teachers of Spanish and Portuguese, (H) 1496
American Association of University Women. Honolulu Branch, (U) 990, (S) 2780
American Atheists, (U) 297, 584
American Automobile Association, (H) 1670
American Baptist Churches USA, (U) 49, (H) 1237, (SS) 3217
American Brahman Breeders Association, (U) 55, (S) 2388
American Chemical Society, (S) 1837
American Chemical Society. Rubber Division, (S) 2675
American Classical League, (H) 1240, 1580
American Coed Pageants, (U) 707
American College of Healthcare Executives, (S) 2264, (SS) 3113
American College of Medical Practice Executives, (S) 1774, 2025, 2252, 2576, 2650–2651, (SS) 2873, 2981, 3101, 3317, 3356–3357
American Composites Manufacturers Association, (U) 382
American Concrete Institute, (S) 1772, 2605
American Concrete Institute. Greater Michigan Chapter, (S) 2239
American Concrete Institute. Illinois Chapter, (S) 2289

American Concrete Institute. Indiana Chapter, (S) 2295

American Concrete Institute. Nebraska Chapter, (S) 2528

American Congress on Surveying and Mapping. Colorado Section, (S) 2012

American Congress on Surveying and Mapping. Washington State Section, (S) 2221

American Consulting Engineers Council, (S) 1838

American Copy Editors Society, (H) 1340

American Council of Engineering Companies, (S) 1840

American Council of Engineering Companies of Colorado, (S) 2011, 2321

American Council of Engineering Companies of Indiana, (S) 2296

American Council of Engineering Companies of Michigan, Inc., (S) 1771, 2734

American Council of Engineering Companies of New York, (S) 2541

American Council of Engineering Companies of South Dakota, (S) 1839

American Council of Independent Laboratories, (S) 1773

American Council of the Blind, (U) 295–296, 299, 326, 363, 984, (S) 1874, 2090, 2374, (SS) 2908, 3295

American Council of the Blind of Ohio, (SS) 3298

American Council on Education, (U) 39

American Culinary Federation, Inc., (H) 1258–1260

American Darts Organization, (U) 50

American Dental Association, (S) 1776–1778

American Dental Education Association, (S) 2579, 2695

American Dental Hygienists' Association, (S) 1779–1781, 1841, 1958, 1974, 2009, 2078, 2084, 2145, 2311, 2431, 2438, 2578, 2608, 2641, 2710, 2846–2847

American Diabetes Association, (U) 863

American Electric Power, (S) 1842

American Electroplaters and Surface Finishers Society, (S) 1788

American Ex–prisoners of War, Inc. Columbia River Chapter, (U) 937

American Express, (SS) 2890–2891

American Family Insurance, (U) 51, 1119

American Federation of Television and Radio Artists, (U) 179

American Fire Sprinkler Association, (S) 1795

American Floral Endowment, (H) 1566, 1717, (SS) 3255

American Foreign Service Association, (U) 52, (SS) 2893–2894

American Foundation for the Blind, (H) 1416, 1649, (S) 2055, 2591, 2676, (SS) 2996, 3369

American Foundation for Translation and Interpretation, (H) 1503

American Geological Institute, (S) 2484

American Ground Water Trust, (S) 1851, 1920

American Guild of Musical Artists, (U) 179

American Guild of Organists. Greater Bridgeport Chapter, (H) 1537

American Guild of Variety Artists, (U) 179

American Hazard Control Consultants, Inc., (S) 2741

American Health Information Management Association, (S) 2171, 2642, 2802, (SS) 3056, 3351

American Heart Association. Northland Affiliate, (S) 2261

American Helicopter Society, (S) 1843, 2799

American Helicopter Society. Federal City Chapter, (U) 262

American Hellenic Educational Progressive Association, (U) 905, 1032, 1065

American Hellenic Educational Progressive Association. District 1, (U) 333

American Hereford Association, (S) 2517

American Hotel & Lodging Educational Foundation, (SS) 2890, 2895, 2910, 3021, 3126, 3346

American Hotel & Lodging Educational Institute, (SS) 2890, 3021

American Indian Arts Council, Inc., (H) 1262

American Indian College fund, (U) 388, 844, (S) 2169, (SS) 3055, 3253–3254

American Indian Education Foundation, (U) 53

American Indian Graduate Center, (U) 383

American Indian Science and Engineering Society, (S) 1908, 1952, 2142, 2208, 2263, (SS) 2940

American Indian Services, (U) 54

American Institute of Aeronautics and Astronautics, (S) 1802–1803, 1982

American Institute of Architects, (H) 1244–1245, 1319

American Institute of Architects. New York Chapter, (H) 1364, 1373

American Institute of Certified Public Accountants, (SS) 2870, 3270, 3376

American Institute of Chemical Engineers, (S) 1991, 2068, 2352, 2483, 2487–2488, 2809

American Institute of Food and Wine. Connecticut Chapter, (H) 1348

American Institute of Polish Culture, Inc., (H) 1433

American Institute of Steel Construction, (H) 1241, (S) 1975, 2180, 2723

American Institute of Wine & Food. Connecticut Chapter, (H) 1264

American Institute of Wine & Food. Pacific Northwest Chapter, (H) 1495

American Legion, (U) 277

American Legion. Alaska Auxiliary, (U) 32

American Legion. Americanism and Children & Youth Division, (U) 56, 61, 1000, (SS) 2897

American Legion. Arkansas Auxiliary, (U) 57

American Legion Auxiliary, (U) 58–59, 403, 1000, 1053

American Legion Baseball, (U) 60, 306, 385

American Legion. California Auxiliary, (U) 158–160, (S) 1962

American Legion. Colorado Auxiliary, (S) 2010

American Legion. Florida Auxiliary, (U) 358

American Legion. Florida Department, (U) 355

American Legion. Georgia Auxiliary, (U) 395, (S) 2227

American Legion. Illinois Auxiliary, (U) 5, 687

American Legion. Illinois Department, (U) 471

American Legion. Iowa Auxiliary, (S) 2308

American Legion. Kansas Department, (H) 1505

American Legion. Kentucky Auxiliary, (U) 570

American Legion. Maryland Auxiliary, (H) 1552, (S) 2448–2449, (SS) 3230

American Legion. Michigan Auxiliary, (U) 674

American Legion. New Hampshire Auxiliary, (U) 630

American Legion. New Hampshire Department, (U) 802–803, (SS) 2958

American Legion. New Jersey Auxiliary, (U) 217, 807, (S) 2535

American Legion. New York Auxiliary, (U) 345, 433, 637, 828–829, 965, (S) 2540

American Legion. North Dakota Department, (U) 428

American Legion. Ohio Auxiliary, (U) 875

American Legion. Oregon Auxiliary, (U) 896–897, (S) 2580

American Legion. Pennsylvania Department, (SS) 3329

American Legion. Utah Auxiliary, (U) 1149

American Legion. Wisconsin Auxiliary, (U) 456, 1209

American Mathematical Association of Two Year Colleges, (S) 1987

American Mensa Education and Research Foundation, (U) 514, (S) 2044

American Meteorological Society, (S) 1844, 1942, 2146, 2297–2298, 2407, 2437

American Military Spouse Education Foundation, (U) 62

American Moving and Storage Association, (SS) 2990

American Museum of Natural History, (S) 2864

American Nuclear Society, (S) 1856–1857, 1989, 2047, 2049, 2331, 2347, 2577, 2842

American Nursery and Landscape Association, (H) 1705, 1714, (S) 2767, 2789

American Paint Horse Association, (U) 76

American Philosophical Association, (H) 1399

American Physical Society, (S) 1862, 2397

American Physical Therapy Association, (S) 2445, 2486

American Planning Association, (SS) 3045, 3169, 3338

American Planning Association. California Chapter, (SS) 2945, 3178, 3355

American Polish Engineering Association, (S) 1846

American Production & Inventory Control Society, (SS) 3006

American Psychiatric Nurses Association, (S) 2086

American Psychological Association, (SS) 2900

American Psychological Foundation, (SS) 2900

American Public Power Association, (S) 2048

American Public Transportation Association, (S) 2773, (SS) 3419

American Public Works Association. Arkansas Chapter, (S) 1871, (SS) 2907

American Public Works Association. Colorado Chapter, (H) 1273, (S) 1863, 2321, 2340, (SS) 2903

American Public Works Association. Florida Chapter, (S) 2160

American Public Works Association. New England Chapter, (S) 2768

American Quarter Horse Foundation, (U) 64, 77, 334, (H) 1274, (S) 1864–1866, 2151, (SS) 2904

American Radio Relay League, (U) 65, 564, 1004, 1200, (H) 1514, 1620, (S) 2386, 2592, (SS) 3005

American Railway Engineering and Maintenance of Way Association, (S) 1867

American Red Cross, (U) 437

American Road and Transportation Builders Association, (U) 443

American Royal Association, (S) 2672

American Society for Clinical Laboratory Science, (S) 1884, 2034, 2174

American Society for Clinical Laboratory Science. Ohio, (S) 2731

American Society for Clinical Pathology, (S) 1885, 2129

American Society for Enology and Viticulture, (S) 1847

American Society for Horticultural Science, (S) 1889, 2098

American Society for Nondestructive Testing, Inc., (S) 1894, 2659

American Society for Photogrammetry and Remote Sensing, (S) 2660

American Society for Photogrammetry and Remote Sensing. Puget Sound Region, (S) 2221

American Society for Quality, (S) 2342, 2836

American Society of Agricultural and Biological Engineers, (S) 1797, 1880–1881, 2199, 2353, 2834

American Society of Agronomy, (S) 2319

American Society of Agronomy. California Chapter, (S) 1956

American Society of Civil Engineers, (S) 1914, 2026, 2685

American Society of Civil Engineers. Maine Section, (S) 1882

American Society of Civil Engineers. Michigan Section, (S) 2418, 2441

American Society of Composers, Authors and Publishers, (H) 1565

American Society of Engineers of Indian Origin, (H) 1278, (S) 1886

American Society of Extra–Corporeal Technology, Inc., (S) 1850, 1925, 2470

American Society of Health–System Pharmacists, (S) 1887–1888

American Society of Highway Engineers. Carolina Triangle Section, (S) 1976, 2662

American Society of Landscape Architecture, (H) 1690, (S) 2738

American Society of Mechanical Engineers, (S) 2280

American Society of Military Comptrollers, (SS) 2911
American Society of Military Comptrollers. Mount Vernon Chapter, (SS) 3256
American Society of Naval Engineers, (S) 1848
American Society of Radiologic Technologists, (S) 2313, 2337, 2673, 2708, 2792
American Society of Safety Engineers, (S) 1833, 1924, 2246, 2398, 2428, 2439, 2787
American Society of Safety Engineers. Columbia–Willamette Chapter, (S) 2814
American Society of Safety Engineers. New Jersey Chapter, (S) 2759
American Society of Travel Agents, (SS) 2878, 2881, 2892, 2905, 2922, 3079, 3105, 3116, 3162, 3340, 3393, 3397
American Society of Women Accountants, (SS) 2898
American Society of Women Accountants. Billings Big Sky Chapter, (SS) 3223, 3252
American Society of Women Accountants. Denver Chapter, (SS) 3000
American Society of Women Accountants. District of Columbia Area Chapter, (SS) 3004
American Society of Women Accountants. Honolulu Chapter, (SS) 3203
American Society of Women Accountants. Omaha Chapter, (SS) 3315
American Society of Women Accountants. Seattle Chapter, (SS) 3381
American Statistical Association, (S) 2355
American Traffic Safety Services Foundation, (U) 974
American Translators Association, (H) 1503
American Water Resources Association, (S) 2645
American Water Ski Educational Foundation, (U) 66, 754
American Water Works Association. Kansas Section, (S) 2749
American Water Works Association. Montana Section, (S) 2069
American Water Works Association. Pennsylvania Section, (S) 2040
American Welding Society, (S) 1811, 1849, 1875, 1913, 2067, 2114, 2277, 2317, 2339, 2348, 2477, 2626, 2829–2830, (SS) 3144
American Wholesale Marketers Association, (SS) 3347
American Woman's Society of Certified Public Accountants. Boston Affiliate, (SS) 2933
American Woman's Society of Certified Public Accountants. Georgia Affiliate, (SS) 3081
American Woman's Society of Certified Public Accountants. Utah Affiliate, (SS) 3431
Americans for the Arts, (H) 1265
AMTROL Inc., (S) 1851
AMVETS. Department of Illinois, (U) 465–467
AMVETS National Headquarters, (U) 67–68, (SS) 3260
Anchor Scholarship Foundation, (U) 69
Ancient and Accepted Scottish Rite of Freemasonry, Southern Jurisdiction, (U) 922, 1018
Andre Sobel River of Life Foundation, (U) 70
Angus Foundation, (U) 72
Anheuser–Busch Companies, Inc., (U) 309, 846, (S) 1947, (SS) 2937
Anti–Defamation League, (H) 1361
AOPA Air Safety Foundation, (S) 1858–1860
Apple Computer, Inc., (H) 1332
Applied Measurement Professionals, Inc., (S) 2667, 2845
Appraisal Institute, (SS) 2902, 3243
Aquatrols Corporation, (U) 78
Arab American Institute Foundation, (U) 432, (H) 1248
Arabian Horse Association, (U) 485
Arabian Horse Foundation, (U) 79, 289, 528, 1052
Arabian Horse Trust, (U) 1201
Arby's Foundation, (U) 80
Arizona Commission for Postsecondary Education, (U) 83–84
Arizona Nursery Association, (S) 1868
Arizona Nurses Association, (S) 1869
Arizona Private School Association, (S) 1870, (SS) 2906
Arizona Society Daughters of the American Revolution, (H) 1548
Arizona State University. Center for Meteorite Studies, (S) 2080
Arkansas Baptist State Convention, (H) 1432
Arkansas Community Foundation, (U) 92, 1002
Arkansas Department of Higher Education, (U) 85–87, 89–91
Arkansas Student Loan Authority, (U) 961
Armed Forces Communications and Electronics Association, (U) 425, 666, (H) 1336, (S) 1790–1792, 2088, 2204, 2206, 2436, 2800
Armed Services YMCA, (U) 93
Army Emergency Relief, (U) 668
The Art Institutes International, Inc., (H) 1265, 1291, 1383, 1575, 1581, 1665, 1679, 1695
Asian American Journalists Association, (H) 1343, 1550, 1559, 1674
Asian American Journalists Association. Seattle Chapter, (H) 1603
Asian McDonald's Owners/Operators Association, (U) 102
Asian & Pacific Islander American Scholarship Fund, (U) 102
ASM International, (S) 1890, 2115, 2216, 2356, 2549, 2841
ASM International. Hartford Chapter, (S) 2254
ASME International, (S) 1799, 1827, 1842, 1877, 1891–1893, 1927, 2179, 2185–2186, 2189, 2196, 2346, 2375, 2463, 2573, 2627, 2634, 2663, 2719, 2740–2741,

2746, 2831, 2835
Aspen Systems Corporation, (S) 2171, (SS) 3056
Associated Colleges of Illinois, (U) 105
Associated Colleges of the Midwest, (H) 1599
Associated General Constructors of Maine, Inc., (S) 1895
Associated General Contractors of America, (S) 1796, 2329
Associated General Contractors of America. New York State Chapter, (S) 2543
Associated General Contractors of Connecticut, Inc., (S) 1896
Associated General Contractors of Indiana, (SS) 2877
Associated General Contractors of Ohio, (S) 2251, (SS) 2876, 3100
Associated General Contractors of Vermont, (S) 1897, (SS) 2913
Associated General Contractors of Virginia, (S) 2362, (SS) 2914
Associated Oregon Loggers, Inc., (S) 1898
Associated Press Television/Radio Association of California and Nevada, (H) 1328, 1506
Associates of Vietnam Veterans of America, (U) 122
Association for Computing Machinery, (S) 2619
Association for Education and Rehabilitation of the Blind and Visually Impaired of Ohio, (SS) 2874
Association for Education in Journalism and Mass Communication, (H) 1636
Association for Iron & Steel Technology, (S) 1899
Association for the Advancement of Cost Engineering, (S) 1763, (SS) 2865
Association for the Advancement of Medical Instrumentation, (S) 1766, (SS) 2867
Association for Theatre in Higher Education, (H) 1587
Association for Women Geoscientists, (S) 1900, 2844
Association for Women in Communications. Oklahoma City Chapter, (H) 1612
Association for Women in Communications. Seattle Professional Chapter, (H) 1668
Association for Women in Computing. Ann Arbor Chapter, (S) 1853
Association for Women in Mathematics, (S) 1824
Association for Women in Science, (S) 1901, 2381
Association for Women Journalists, (U) 1280
Association of Academic Health Centers, (S) 2695
Association of Alaska School Boards, (SS) 3171
Association of American Medical Colleges, (S) 2695
Association of American Veterinary Medical Colleges, (S) 2695
Association of Blind Citizens, (U) 106
Association of California Water Agencies, (S) 1902, 2000, (SS) 2915, 2961
Association of Certified Fraud Examiners, (SS) 3361
Association of Chiropractic Colleges, (S) 2695
Association of Collegiate Schools of Architecture, (H) 1241, 1312
Association of Cuban Engineers, (S) 1903
Association of Energy Engineers, (S) 1904, (SS) 2916
Association of Energy Engineers. Georgia Chapter, (S) 2223, (SS) 3080
Association of Energy Engineers. New England Chapter, (S) 2533, (SS) 3279
Association of Food and Drug Officials, (S) 1793, (SS) 2875
Association of Former Agents of the United States Secret Service, Inc., (SS) 3054
Association of Former Intelligence Officers, (SS) 3096
Association of Golf Merchandisers, (SS) 2917
Association of Government Accountants, (SS) 2972
Association of Government Accountants. Boston Chapter, (SS) 3455
Association of Independent Colleges and Universities of Pennsylvania, (U) 242, (S) 1807, 2459, 2469
Association of Independent Funeral Directors of Florida, (SS) 3189
Association of Information Technology Professionals, (SS) 2927, 3183
Association of Latino Professionals in Finance and Accounting, (SS) 2918
Association of National Advertisers, (H) 1267
Association of Old Crows, (U) 425
Association of periOperative Registered Nurses, (S) 1861, 1905
Association of Rehabilitation Nurses, (S) 1873
Association of Retired Teachers of Connecticut, (SS) 3086
Association of Schools and Colleges of Optometry, (S) 2695
Association of Schools of Allied Health Professions, (S) 2695
Association of Schools of Journalism and Mass Communication, (H) 1443–1445
Association of Schools of Public Health, (S) 2695
Association of State Dam Safety Officials, (S) 1906
Association of Surgical Technologists, (S) 2765
Association of Texas Professional Educators, (SS) 2924, 3062
Association of the United States Army, (S) 2364
Association of University Programs in Health Administration, (S) 2695
Association on American Indian Affairs, Inc., (U) 44, 317, (SS) 3034
AstraZeneca Pharmaceuticals, L.P., (S) 2614
Astronaut Scholarship Foundation, (S) 1907
Athenaeum of Philadelphia, (H) 1319
Athletes of Good News, (U) 1054–1055
AT&T Foundation, (U) 102
Autism Society of America, (U) 307
Automotive Aftermarket Industry Association, (S) 1765
Automotive Hall of Fame, (U) 108

Aviation Council of Pennsylvania, (S) 1910, (SS) 2920
Aviation Distributors and Manufacturers Association, (S) 1911, (SS) 2921
Aviation Insurance Association, (S) 1912
Avon Foundation, (U) 868
AXA Foundation, (U) 111, 869
AXIS Inc., (S) 2821, (SS) 3463
Ayn Rand Institute, (H) 1279, 1397
Ayrshire Breeders' Association, (S) 2510
Baker Family Foundation, (U) 112
Ball Horticultural Company, (S) 1915, 2696
Bank of America Foundation, (U) 1116, (H) 1283, (S) 1917, (SS) 2923
Bank of New Hampshire, (U) 113
Baptist Communicators Association, (H) 1249, 1296
Baptist Convention of New York, (H) 1635
Baptist General Convention of Texas, (H) 1697
Barking Foundation, (U) 115
Baroid, (S) 1920
The Barron Prize, (U) 406
Baton Rouge Area Foundation, (SS) 2912
Baxter Health Care Corporation, (U) 477, (S) 1761
Bay Area Black Journalists Association, (H) 1534
Bay Area Media Network, (H) 1285
BDPA Education Technology Foundation, (S) 2087
Bechtel Corporation, (S) 1923
Bechtel Foundation, (S) 1924
Bell Helicopter Textron, Inc., (S) 1843
Best Buy Children's Foundation, (U) 119
Bethesda Lutheran Homes and Services, Inc., (S) 2062–2063
Big Brothers Big Sisters of America, (U) 80
Big 33 Scholarship Foundation, (U) 124, (H) 1734, (S) 1933, 2820
Bill and Melinda Gates Foundation, (U) 383
Billie Jean King WTT Charities, Inc., (U) 863
Billy Barty Foundation, (U) 327
Billy Consalo Memorial Agricultural Scholarship Fund, (S) 1935
BioQuip Products, (S) 1936
Birch Telecom, (SS) 2930
Black Women in Sisterhood for Action, (U) 127
Blanche Naugher Fowler Charitable Scholarship Trust, (U) 129
Blind Information Technology Specialist, Inc., (S) 2374
Blinded Veterans Association, (U) 543
Blue Cross Blue Shield of Wisconsin, (S) 1940
Bob Hoffman Foundation, (S) 2564
Bobst Group, (S) 2030
Boeing Company, (U) 425, (S) 1843
Boettcher Foundation, (U) 132
Boomer Esiason Foundation, (U) 134
Boy Scouts of America. Learning for Life Division, (U) 8, 1228, (S) 2727, (SS) 2919, 3054, 3384
Boy Scouts of America. National Jewish Committee on Scouting, (U) 195, 351, 372, 398
Boy Scouts of America. Order of the Arrow, (SS) 3018
Boys & Girls Clubs of America, (U) 138
Boys & Girls Clubs of Greater San Diego, (S) 2725, (SS) 3395
BP Products North America, (U) 139
Broadcast Cable Financial Management Association, (H) 1301, (SS) 2936
Broadcast Education Association, (H) 1238, 1255, 1269, 1286, 1431, 1448, 1627, 1731
Broadcast Music Inc., (H) 1293, 1494, 1622
Broussard, Bush & Hurst, (U) 551
Brown and Caldwell, (S) 1945, 2092
Brown and Root Services, (S) 2336
Builders Association of Minnesota, (H) 1304, (S) 1950
Bureau of Alcohol, Tobacco, Firearms and Explosives Retiree's Association, (SS) 2919
Burlington Northern Santa Fe Foundation, (S) 1867, 1941, 1952, (SS) 2931, 2940
Business and Professional Women of Virginia, (U) 143, 542, (S) 1948, 2856, (SS) 2938
Business and Professional Women's Foundation, (H) 1311, (S) 1971, (SS) 2949
Business Professionals of America, (SS) 2934
C I Host, (S) 1955
Cadbury Adams, (S) 1958, 2776
Cal Mold Inc., (S) 2157
Calcot–Seitz Foundation, (S) 1959
California Alarm Association, (U) 146
California Alliance for Arts Education, (H) 1378
California Association for Postsecondary Education and Disability, (U) 171, 214, 602, 1067, 1199
California Association of Nurseries and Garden Center, (S) 1969–1970
California Association of Pest Control Advisers, (S) 1960
California Association of Realtors, (SS) 2941
California Association of Winegrape Growers, (U) 165

California Department of Transportation, (H) 1359, (S) 2066, 2326
California Department of Veterans Affairs, (U) 152–155
California Environmental Health Association, (S) 2440
California Funeral Directors Association, (SS) 2943
California Governor's Committee on Employment of People with Disabilities, (U) 421
California Interscholastic Federation, (U) 213
California Labor Federation, AFL–CIO, (SS) 2944
California Land Surveyors Association, (S) 1786, 2325
California Landscape Contractors Association, (S) 2394
California League for Nursing, (S) 1961
California Masonic Foundation, (U) 46, 161, 1202
California Parks and Recreation Society, (SS) 2942
California Restaurant Association, (H) 1306–1307
California Retired Teachers Association, (SS) 3191
California Scholarship Federation, (U) 1016
California School Library Association, (SS) 3155
California Scottish Rite Foundation, (U) 162
California State Fair, (U) 163, (H) 1308–1310, (S) 1963–1967, 2107, (SS) 2946–2947, 3022
California Student Aid Commission, (U) 147–149, 151, 157
California Table Grape Commission, (U) 164
California Transportation Foundation, (H) 1359, (S) 2066
California–Hawaii Elks Association, (U) 166–167
Californians for Disability Rights, (U) 168
CampusRN, (S) 1968
Canada Centre for Mines and Energy Technology/Natural Resources Canada, (S) 2280
CAP Charitable Foundation, (U) 981
Capital Press Club of Florida, (H) 1284
Capstone Corporation, (U) 173
Care Communications, Inc., (S) 2171, (SS) 3056
Career Colleges & Schools of Texas, (U) 176
Career Transition for Dancers, (U) 179
Caremark Rx, Inc., (U) 319
Cargill, Inc., (U) 177
Carl's Jr., (U) 565
Carolina Steel Corporation, (S) 1975
Carolinas AGC, (S) 1977
Carpe Diem Foundation of Illinois, (H) 1313, (S) 1978, (SS) 2951
Carter & Burgess, Inc., (S) 2336
Cascade Policy Institute, (SS) 3135
Case IH, (SS) 2970
Casey Family Programs, (U) 181, 900
Casualty Actuarial Society, (SS) 2952, 3387
Catching the Dream, (S) 2466, (SS) 3235, 3269, 3423
Caterpillar, Inc., (S) 1979–1980
Center for Education Solutions, (U) 1
The Center for Reintegration, Inc., (U) 585
The Center for Scholarship Administration, Inc., (U) 1037, (H) 1741
Certified Angus Beef LLC, (H) 1335, (S) 1957, 2014, (SS) 2971
Cessna Aircraft Company, (S) 1982
CFA Institute, (SS) 2956
ChairScholars Foundation, Inc., (U) 185
Chapel of Four Chaplains, (U) 186–187, (H) 1315
Charles and Lucille King Family Foundation, Inc., (H) 1316
Charles B. Wang Foundation, (U) 334, (S) 2151
Charles, Lela and Mary Slough Foundation, (U) 192–193
Charlie Wells Memorial Scholarship Fund, (S) 1990
The Charter Fund, (U) 194
Chartered Property Casualty Underwriters Society. Nebraska Chapter, (S) 2391, (SS) 3192
Chartered Property Casualty Underwriters Society.
Chela Financial USA, Inc., (U) 156, 229, 384, 407, (SS) 3250
ChevronTexaco Corporation, (S) 1994, 2484
Chi Epsilon, (S) 1995
Chicago Mercantile Exchange, (H) 1395, (S) 2172
Child Neurology Society, (S) 2531
Children of Breast Cancer Foundation, (U) 205
Children of Deaf Adults, (U) 691
Children of Injured Workers, Inc., (U) 206
Children of Lesbians and Gays Everywhere, (U) 576
Children's Theatre Foundation of America, (H) 1268
chooseNursing.com, (S) 1996
Choristers Guild, (H) 1655
Christermon Foundation, (U) 123
Christian Church (Disciples of Christ), (U) 436
Christian Connector, Inc., (U) 210
Christian Fellowship of Art Music Composers, (H) 1324
Christian Science Monitor, (U) 211
The Christophers, (H) 1325, 1719

Chronicle of Higher Education, (H) 1353
Church & Dwight Company, Inc., (U) 100
CH2M Hill, (S) 2000, 2623, (SS) 2961
CIT Group Inc., (U) 215
Clan MacBean Foundation, (H) 1327, (SS) 2962
Clare Boothe Luce Fund, (S) 2002
Classical Association of New England, (SS) 2948
Classical Association of the Empire State, (H) 1696, (SS) 3405
Classical Association of the Middle West and South, (H) 1541
Clayfolk, (H) 1377
Cleveland Advertising Association, (H) 1329
Clifford H. "Ted" Rees, Jr. Scholarship Foundation, (S) 2004
Clinical Laboratory Management Association–Maine Chapter, (S) 2419
Club Foundation, (SS) 3153
Clyde Russell Scholarship Fund, (U) 218
CoaguLife, (U) 220
Coalition for Nursing Careers in California, (S) 1996
Coalition of Higher Education Assistance Organizations, (U) 224
Coast Guard Foundation, (U) 99, 221
Coca–Cola Company, (U) 102, (S) 2966
Coca–Cola Scholars Foundation, Inc., (U) 222–223
Cochlear Americas, (U) 413
CODA International, (U) 691
Colburn–Pledge Music Scholarship Foundation, (H) 1331
Colgate–Palmolive Company, (S) 2009, 2512
Colin Higgins Foundation, (U) 225
College Assistance Migrant Program, (U) 169
College Board, (S) 2707, 2709
College Foundation of North Carolina, (U) 850–851
College Planning Network, (U) 1178
College Student of the Year, Inc., (U) 356
CollegeBound Network, (U) 229
CollegeNET, (U) 231
Colorado Broadcasters Association, (H) 1333–1334
Colorado Commission on Higher Education, (U) 234, 236–240, (SS) 2969
Colorado Council on High School/College Relations, (U) 235
Colorado Educational Services and Development Association, (U) 401
Colorado Federation of Business and Professional Women, (U) 233
Colorado Ready Mixed Concrete Association/Colorado Rock Products Association, (S) 2031
Colorado Society of Certified Public Accountants, (SS) 2967–2968, 3026–3027, 3090
Colorado Weed Management Association, (S) 2013
Colorado Young Farmer Educational Association, (SS) 2970
Comedy Central, Inc., (H) 1477, 1546
Commander William S. Stuhr Scholarship Fund, (U) 241
Communities Foundation of Texas, (H) 1408, (S) 2205
Community Bankers Association of Georgia, (SS) 3170
Community Foundation for Greater Atlanta, Inc., (U) 755, (H) 1483, 1651, (S) 2732, (SS) 3146, 3398
Community Foundation for Greater New Haven, (U) 693
Community Foundation for the Fox Valley Region, Inc., (S) 2849
Community Foundation of Middle Tennessee, (SS) 3237
Company Grade Officer's Council, (U) 425
Concord Review, (H) 1638
Concrete Reinforcing Steel Institute, (S) 2032
Congressional Hispanic Caucus Institute, Inc., (U) 245
Congressional Medal of Honor Foundation, (U) 666
Congressional Medal of Honor Society, (U) 246
Connecticut Architecture Foundation, (H) 1318, 1337
Connecticut Association for Health, Physical Education, Recreation and Dance, (H) 1414, 1549, (S) 2229, 2443, (SS) 3085, 3222
Connecticut Association of Land Surveyors, Inc., (S) 2019
Connecticut Association of Optometrists, (S) 2218
Connecticut Association of Schools, (U) 248, (H) 1302
Connecticut Association of Women Police, (SS) 2973
Connecticut Broadcasters Association, (H) 1338, (SS) 2974
Connecticut Building Congress, (H) 1339, (S) 2020, (SS) 2975
Connecticut Chapter of the American Planning Association, (H) 1659, (SS) 3374
Connecticut Commission on Culture and Tourism, (SS) 3354
Connecticut Community Foundation, (H) 1693, (S) 2426, (SS) 3215
Connecticut Daughters of the American Revolution, (U) 251
Connecticut Department of Higher Education, (U) 172, 247, 249, 252–253, (SS) 2978, 2980
Connecticut Forest and Park Association, Inc., (S) 2330
Connecticut Funeral Directors Association, (SS) 2977
Connecticut League for Nursing, (S) 2022
Connecticut National Guard Foundation, Inc., (U) 250, 1017
Connecticut Nurses' Foundation, (S) 2772
Connecticut Society of Certified Public Accountants, (SS) 2954
Connecticut Society of Professional Engineers, (S) 2023

Connecticut Society of Professional Journalists, (H) 1295
Connecticut Sports Writers Alliance, (H) 1299
Connecticut Tree Protective Association, Inc., (S) 2024
Connecticut Women's Golf Association, (U) 916, 954
ConocoPhillips, (S) 2484
Conservation Districts of Iowa, (S) 1981
Consortium of Information and Telecommunications Executives, Inc., (U) 216
ConstructMyFuture.com, (SS) 2982
Consulting Engineers and Land Surveyors of California, (S) 2028
Consulting Engineers Council of New Jersey, (S) 1838
Continental Society, Daughters of Indian Wars, (SS) 2983
ConvaTec, (U) 478
COPI/OutputLinks, (S) 2344, (SS) 3154
Corella and Bertram F. Bonner Foundation, (U) 133
Coty US LLC, (U) 150
Council for Advancement and Support of Education, (U) 39
Council for America's First Freedom, (H) 1266
Council of Citizens with Low Vision International, (U) 375
Council of the Great City Schools, (S) 2429
Courage Center, (U) 254, (S) 2133
Cox Foundation, (H) 1343
Craig Hospital, (S) 2802, (SS) 3440
Crohn's and Colitis Foundation of America, (U) 478
Croplan Genetics, (S) 1972
Cumberland Valley Volunteer Firemen's Association, (S) 2366
Cystic Fibrosis Scholarship Foundation, (U) 260
Czech Cultural Center, (U) 634
Dade Behring Inc., (S) 2034, 2129
Dade Community Foundation, (S) 2335, (SS) 3010
Daedalian Foundation, (S) 2035, 2345
DaimlerChrysler Corporation, (S) 2036–2037
Dairy Management Inc., (U) 999, (S) 2526, (SS) 3271
Dairy Queen, (U) 292
Dallas Foundation, (H) 1326, (S) 2336
Dallas Stars Foundation, (U) 130
Dassault Falcon Jet Corporation, (S) 2039
Datatel Scholars Foundation, (U) 71, 263–264, (S) 2500
Datatrac Information Systems, Inc., (U) 364
Daughters of the American Revolution. Colorado State Society, (H) 1458, (S) 2806
Daughters of the American Revolution. New York State Organization, (H) 1349
Daughters of the American Revolution. Washington State Society, (H) 1662
Daughters of the Cincinnati, (U) 265
Davis–Putter Scholarship Fund, (U) 269
Dawn Ramos Productions, (U) 746, 1087
DECA, (U) 770, (H) 1758, (SS) 2891, 2966, 3099, 3220, 3323
Degree of Honor Foundation, (U) 270
Dekker Foundation, (S) 2352
Delaware Association of School Administrators, (SS) 2992
Delaware Child Placement Review Board, (U) 497
Delaware Community Foundation, (U) 434, (H) 1482, 1744, (S) 2430
Delaware Engineering Society, (S) 2061, 2717
Delaware Healthcare Association, (S) 2730
Delaware Higher Education Commission, (U) 9, 271–273, 280, 347, (H) 1355, (S) 2358
Delaware Society for Human Resource Management, (SS) 2993
Delaware Solid Waste Authority, (S) 2358
Delaware State Federation of Women's Clubs, (U) 274
Dell Computer Corporation, (S) 2050–2051, (SS) 2994
Dell'Arte Mad River Festival, (H) 1477
Delmar Learning, (S) 2274, 2765
Deloitte Foundation, (SS) 3287
Delphi, Inc., (S) 2052
Delta Air Lines, (S) 2053–2054, 2520, (SS) 2995
Delta Gamma Foundation, (S) 2055, (SS) 2996
Delta Mu Delta, (SS) 2997
Delta Sigma Pi, (SS) 3194
Delta Sigma Theta Sorority, Inc. Boston Alumnae Chapter, (U) 135
Delta Sigma Theta Sorority, Inc. Washington DC Alumnae Chapter, (U) 1181
DeMolay International, (S) 2241
Denny's, (S) 2057, (SS) 2999
Denver Foundation, (U) 966, (SS) 3404
Denver Geophysical Society, (S) 2058
Dermatology Nurses' Association, (S) 2060, 2192
Dermik Laboratories, (S) 2060
Deseret News, (U) 1066
Design Automation Conference, (S) 2619
The Development Fund for Black Students in Science and Technology, (S) 2064
Disabled American Veterans, (U) 511
Discover Card, (U) 281
Dixie Boys Baseball, Inc., (U) 285

Dixie Softball, Inc., (U) 286
Dixie Youth Baseball, Inc., (U) 287
Dolphin Scholarship Foundation, (U) 288
Donald and Shelley Rubin Foundation, (H) 1401
Donald F. & Mildred Topp Othmer Foundation, (S) 2068
Donna Reed Foundation for the Performing Arts, (H) 1360
Don't Mess with Texas Scholarship Program, (U) 292
Dosatron International, Inc., (S) 2076
Doug Banks Foundation, (U) 1116
Dow Chemical Company, (U) 1116
D.P. Associates Inc., (U) 773
Dr Pepper/Seven Up, Inc., (H) 1758
Dramatic Publishing Company, (H) 1532
Dramatists Guild, Inc., (H) 1486, 1587
DuBose Associates, Inc., (H) 1318
Dunkin' Donuts, (U) 248, 300
DuPont Center for Collaborative Research & Education, (S) 2094
D.W. Simpson & Company, (SS) 3016
Dyzco Technologies, Inc., (SS) 3017
E–Publishing Group, LLC, (S) 2016
E–Z–EM Inc., (S) 2313
EAR Foundation, (U) 704
Earl G. Graves Ltd., (U) 226
Earth Force, (U) 406
Easter Seals South Carolina, (U) 515
Eastern Star. Grand Chapter of California, (U) 304
Eastman Kodak Company, (H) 1367
Eaton Corporation, (S) 2104
ECI Scholarship Foundation, (U) 305–306, 761, 1194, (H) 1729, (S) 2274, (SS) 2934
Ecolab, (SS) 3021
Edelman Worldwide, Inc., (H) 1350
Education is Freedom Foundation, (U) 309
Educational Communications Scholarship Foundation, (S) 2274
Educational Foundation for Women in Accounting, (SS) 2898
Educational Research Center of America, Inc., (U) 318
Educational Theatre Association, (H) 1701
Edward Davis Education Foundation, (S) 2113, (SS) 3029
E.I. duPont de Nemours and Company, Inc., (S) 2095, 2809
Electronic Document Systems Foundation, (S) 2043, 2110–2111, 2344, 2821, (SS) 2991, 3024–3025, 3154
Electronics for Imaging, Inc., (S) 2121
Eli Lilly and Company, (U) 585, (S) 2520, 2614
Elie Wiesel Foundation for Humanity, (H) 1374
Elizabeth Nash Foundation, (U) 313
Elks National Foundation, (U) 314–315
Elsevier Science Ltd., (U) 1007, (S) 2334
Emergency Nurses Association, (S) 1986, 2132, 2334, 2434, 2544
Endless Sun Apparel, (U) 711
Entomological Society of America, (S) 1936, 2138, 2729
EqualityMaine, (U) 520
Ernst & Young Foundation, (SS) 3039–3040, 3287
Ethel and Emery Fast Scholarship Foundation, Inc., (U) 323
European Power Electronics Association, (S) 2305
Evangelical Press Association, (H) 1382
Evelyn Lindblad Folland Endowment Fund, (H) 1567
Everly Scholarship Fund, Inc., (U) 328
Excel Geophysics, (S) 2150
Executive Women International, (SS) 3042
Exelon Corporation, (S) 2153
Experimental Aviation Association, (S) 2041, 2248, 2278, 2598
Explosive Ordnance Disposal Memorial, (U) 331
ExxonMobil Corporation, (S) 2484, 2520
ExxonMobil Foundation, (S) 1900
Factor Support Network Pharmacy, (U) 685, 692
Family Circle Cup, (U) 590
Farm Bureau Insurance, (U) 335
Fashion Group International of Portland, (H) 1384
Fashion Group International of Washington, (H) 1733
FBLA/PBL Foundation, (SS) 3044
Federal Employee Education and Assistance Fund, (U) 336, 340
Federated Garden Clubs of Connecticut, Inc., (H) 1386, (S) 2156
Federation of Associations of Schools of the Health Professions, (S) 2695
The Fellowship of United Methodists in Music and Worship Arts, (H) 1388, 1702
The Fellowship of United Methodists in Music and Worship Arts. Florida Chapter, (H) 1423
Fidelity Investments Tax–Exempt Services Company, (SS) 3244
Financial Executives International. Milwaukee Chapter, (SS) 3365
Financial Service Centers of America, Inc., (U) 348
Financial Service Centers of Florida, (U) 342
First Church of Christ, (H) 1321

First Command Educational Foundation, (U) 425
First Command Financial Planning, (U) 343
First Corbin Financial Corporation, (U) 1056
First Data Western Union Foundation, (U) 344
First Marine Division Association, (U) 346
Fisher Communications, (H) 1392, (SS) 3046
Fisher House Foundation, (U) 1006
Fleetwood Memorial Foundation, (U) 349
Flexographic Technical Association, (H) 1390
Flicker of Hope Foundation, (U) 350
Floriculture Industry Research and Scholarship Trust, (S) 1915, 2076, 2105, 2250, 2323, 2354, 2515, 2587, 2696, 2825, (SS) 3097, 3143
Florida Association of Broadcasters, (H) 1526
Florida Bankers Association, (SS) 3048
Florida Department of Education, (U) 352–354, 357, 359, 361–362, 1198
Florida Dietetic Association, (S) 2065, 2711
Florida Educational Facilities Planners' Association, Inc., (SS) 3049
Florida Engineering Society, (S) 2161–2162
Florida Federation of Garden Clubs, Inc., (H) 1243, 1290, 1375, 1410, 1440, 1715, (S) 1800, 1928, 2082, 2091, 2109, 2124, 2257, 2444, 2793, 2810, (SS) 3224
Florida High School Athletic Association, (U) 341
Florida Hotel & Motel Association, Inc., (SS) 3051
Florida Independent College Fund, (U) 1133, (H) 1526, (S) 2164, (SS) 3050, 3053
Florida Institute of Consulting Engineers, (S) 2165
Florida Institute of CPAs Educational Foundation, Inc., (SS) 3052
Florida International Bankers Association, (SS) 3010
Florida Leader Magazine, (U) 356
Florida Nurserymen, Growers and Landscape Association. Action Chapter, (S) 2167
Florida Nurses Association, (S) 2163
Florida PTA, (U) 360, (H) 1393
Florida Rock Industries, Inc., (S) 2164, (SS) 3053
Florida Society of Newspaper Editors, (H) 1394
Florida Surveying and Mapping Society, (S) 2166
Florida Wildlife Federation, (S) 2159
FM Global, (S) 2741
Ford Family Foundation, (U) 365–366
Ford Motor Company, (U) 367, (S) 2168–2170, (SS) 3055
Formula Plastics, (S) 2157
Fort Collins Symphony Orchestra, (H) 1396
Fortune Brands, (SS) 3057
Forum for Military Applications of Directed Energy, (S) 2726
Foundation for Rural Service, (U) 369
Foundation for the Carolinas, (S) 2093, 2648, (SS) 3015
Francis Ouimet Scholarship Fund, (U) 371
Freedom Alliance, (U) 377
Freedom Forum, (H) 1402
Freedom from Religion Foundation, (H) 1403–1404
Freeman Foundation, (S) 2181
Freescale Semiconductor, (S) 2182, 2520
Friday Morning Music Club, Inc., (H) 1490
Friends of the Frelinghuysen Arboretum, (H) 1287, (S) 1926
Fujifilm Corporation, (H) 1332
Fukunaga Scholarship Foundation, (SS) 3066
The Fund for Theological Education, Inc., (H) 1617
Funeral Service Foundation, (SS) 3160, 3184
Future Electronics, (S) 2187
Galderma Laboratories, (S) 2192
Garden Club Federation of Maine, (H) 1406, (S) 2193
Garden Club of America, (S) 2372
Garden Club of Ohio, Inc., (S) 2194
Garden State Scholastic Press Association, (H) 1297
GAT Airline Ground Support, (S) 2198, (SS) 3070
GE Fund, (S) 2202, 2520
General Dynamics, (U) 518
General Electric Company. Women's Network, (S) 2203
General Federation of Women's Clubs of Connecticut, (SS) 3008, 3335
General Federation of Women's Clubs of Vermont, (U) 114
General Learning Communications, (S) 2094
General Mills Foundation, (U) 102, 388
General Mills, Inc., (S) 1991
General Motors Corporation, (S) 2207–2208, 2210–2211, (SS) 3071
General Motors Corporation. Chevrolet Motor Division, (U) 196–199
General Motors Foundation, (S) 2209
General Motors Minority Dealers Association, (U) 389
Generations for Peace, (SS) 3072
Geneseo Migrant Center, (U) 684, (SS) 3060
Geoffrey Foundation, (U) 390
Geophysical Society of Alaska, (S) 2212
Geophysical Society of Houston, (S) 2213, 2243

Geophysical Society of Oklahoma City, (S) 2214
Geophysical Society of Tulsa, (S) 2215
George A. Nielsen LLP, (SS) 3073
George and Donna Nigh Institute, (SS) 3074
George Bartol Memorial Scholarship Fund, (U) 391
George F. Walker Memorial Scholarship Fund, (S) 2221
George Mason University. Department of Music, (H) 1588
Georgia Association of Broadcasters, Inc., (H) 1488
Georgia Association of Educators, (SS) 3069
Georgia Association of Homes and Services for Children, (U) 183
Georgia Beef Board, (H) 1411, (S) 2224
Georgia Cattlemen's Association, (H) 1411, (S) 2224
Georgia CattleWomen's Association, (H) 1411, (S) 2224
Georgia Dietetic Association, Inc., (S) 2225
Georgia Engineering Foundation, Inc., (S) 2226
Georgia Press Educational Foundation, Inc., (H) 1412
Georgia PTA, (U) 504, (SS) 3082
Georgia Society of CPAs, (SS) 3083
Georgia Student Finance Commission, (U) 4, 392–394, 396, 448–449, (SS) 2957
Georgia Trust, (H) 1281, 1478
Gibson Musical Instruments, (H) 1569
Gilder Lehrman Institute of American History, (H) 1415
Girl Scouts of the USA, (U) 314, 406
Girls Incorporated, (U) 404
Givaudan Flavor Corporation, (S) 2230
GlaxoSmithKline, (S) 2614
Glenn Miller Birthplace Society, (H) 1417
Glenside/Abington United Methodist Church, (H) 1640, (SS) 3349
Golden Key International Honour Society, (U) 409, (H) 1418–1420, (S) 2233–2234, (SS) 3087–3089
Golf Course Superintendents Association of America, (S) 2200–2201, 2691
Good Samaritan Foundation, Inc., (U) 410
Google Inc., (S) 1852
Government Finance Officers Association, (SS) 3061, 3073, 3244
Government of the District of Columbia, (U) 282
Governor's Coalition for Youth with Disabilities, (U) 411
GR Technologies Family, (H) 1588
Grand Lodge A F & A.M. of Wyoming, (U) 1223
Grand Lodge of Florida Masons, (U) 959
Grand Lodge of Iowa, A.F. & A.M., (U) 414
Great Comebacks Award Program, (U) 478
Great Falls Advertising Federation, (H) 1424–1425, (SS) 3092
The Great 100, Inc., (S) 2237
Greater Kanawha Valley Foundation, (U) 989, 1189, 1221, (H) 1736, (S) 2238, 2548, (SS) 3012
Greater Kansas City Community Foundation, (S) 2475
Grifols, (U) 477
Grotto Humanitarian Foundation, (S) 2241
Guidant Corporation, (S) 2244
Guideposts, (H) 1428
Guy and Gloria Muto Memorial Scholarship Foundation, Inc., (U) 419
Handler Manufacturing, Inc., (S) 1778
HANDS–ON! Projects, (S) 2280
Handweavers Guild of America, Inc., (H) 1356, 1456
Hanley Wood LLC, (S) 2119
Hanscom Officers' Wives' Club, (U) 425, (H) 1247, (S) 1944, 2008, 2399
Harding & Harding Insurance, (S) 2517
Harness Horse Youth Foundation, (U) 258
Harness Tracks of America, (U) 426
Harold B. & Dorothy A. Snyder Scholarship Fund, (H) 1430, (S) 2249
Harry Alan Gregg Foundation, (U) 427
Hartford Foundation for Public Giving, (S) 2330
HARVEST Education Foundation, (S) 2255, (SS) 3102
Hawaii Advertising Federation, (H) 1436
Hawaii Association of Broadcasters, Inc., (H) 1437
Hawai'i Community Foundation, (U) 182, 447, 1122, 1124, 1160, (H) 1263, 1362, 1370, 1381, 1439, 1515, 1544, 1626, (S) 2079, 2083, 2126, 2256, 2349, 2389, 2596, 2658, 2705, 2837, (SS) 2888, 2929, 3011, 3030, 3077, 3103, 3108, 3216
Hawai'i Hotel & Lodging Association, (SS) 2964
Hawaii Society of Certified Public Accountants, (SS) 3123
Hawaiian Civic Club of Honolulu, (U) 429
HBCUConnect.com, LLC., (H) 1442, (SS) 3104
Health Occupations Students of America, (S) 2274, 2611
Healthcare Contract Resources, (S) 2171, (SS) 3056
Healthcare Financial Management Association. Connecticut Chapter, (S) 2021, (SS) 2976
Healthcare Information and Management Systems Society, (S) 2265, 2474, 2652, (SS) 3114, 3241, 3358
Hellenic Times Scholarship Fund, (U) 435
Hemophilia Federation of America, (U) 438, 914, 1021
Hemophilia Foundation of Michigan, (U) 125

Hemophilia Health Services, (U) 439, (S) 2690
Herb Society of America. South Texas Unit, (S) 2722
Herb Society of America. Western Reserve Unit, (S) 2177, 2826
Herff Jones, Inc., (U) 765, 953, (H) 1454
Hewlett–Packard Company, (S) 1787
Hewlett–Packard Company. Agilent Technologies, (S) 1798
HF Fund, (S) 2183, (SS) 3063
Hispanic Alliance for Career Enhancement, (U) 420
Hispanic Association of Colleges and Universities, (U) 756, (H) 1704, (S) 1951, 2207, (SS) 3401, 3451
Hispanic College Fund, (U) 445, (S) 1941, 2057, 2119, 2266, 2282, 2406, 2503, 2681, (SS) 2931, 2999, 3040, 3115, 3128, 3372
Hispanic Dental Association, (S) 2628, 2776
Hispanic Engineer National Achievement Awards Conference, (S) 1784, 1831–1832, 2037, 2170, 2182, 2187, 2262, 2494, 2560, 2568, 2702
Hispanic Scholarship Fund, (U) 227, 383, 442, (S) 2211, 2713, (SS) 2918, 3071, 3167
Hispanic Scholarship Fund Institute, (S) 2141, 2545, (SS) 3037, 3292
History Channel, (H) 1578
Hitachi Foundation, (U) 1227
HNTB Companies, (S) 2336
Hobsons, (S) 2274
Holocaust Human Rights Center of Maine, (H) 1518
Home Builders Association of Alabama, (S) 1815
Home Builders Association of Illinois, (H) 1457, (S) 2268
Horace Mann Companies, (U) 450
Horatio Alger Association of Distinguished Americans, Inc., (U) 451–453
Hospital Corporation of America, (S) 2611
Hospitality Sales and Marketing Association International, (SS) 3124
Huguenot Society of America, (U) 625
Human Resource Association of the National Capital Area, (SS) 3122
Humane Society of the United States, (S) 2703
Hyatt Hotels & Resorts, (SS) 3126
Hydro Research Foundation, (S) 2280
Ice Skating Institute of America, (U) 496
ICI Educational Foundation, (S) 2282, (SS) 3128
Idaho State Board of Education, (U) 459–464, 977
Idaho State Broadcasters Association, (H) 1464, (S) 2283, (SS) 3129
IEEE Computer Society, (S) 2018
Illinois Association for Health, Physical Education, Recreation and Dance, (H) 1463, (S) 2281, (SS) 3127
Illinois Association of Realtors, (U) 516, (SS) 3132, 3413
Illinois Broadcasters Association, (H) 1468
Illinois Conservation Foundation, (S) 2290
Illinois Council of Teachers of Mathematics, (S) 2687, (SS) 3377
Illinois Department of Children and Family Services, (U) 277
Illinois Department of Veterans' Affairs, (U) 473
Illinois Hospital Association, (S) 2291
Illinois Lumber and Material Dealers Association, (H) 1469, (S) 2292
Illinois PTA, (SS) 3199
Illinois Restaurant Association, (SS) 3133
Illinois Society of Professional Engineers, (S) 2314, 2461
Illinois State Board of Education, (U) 468
Illinois Student Assistance Commission, (U) 469–470, 472, 474, 476
Illinois Tool Works Welding Companies, (S) 2317
Imation Corporation, (H) 1471
Immune Deficiency Foundation, (U) 477
Incight Company, (U) 408
Independent Colleges of Washington, (U) 268, 1059, (H) 1742, (S) 2795, (SS) 3435
Independent Order of Odd Fellows. Grand Lodge of Illinois, (U) 475
Indiana Association for Health, Physical Education, Recreation, and Dance, (H) 1487, (S) 2332, (SS) 3148
Indiana Broadcasters Association, (H) 1472
Indiana Business and Professional Women's Foundation, Inc., (U) 479–480, (S) 2081
Indiana Health Care Foundation, Inc., (S) 2288
Indiana State Teachers Association, (U) 591, (SS) 2988
Indiana University. School of Journalism, (H) 1652
Indianapolis Press Club Foundation Inc., (H) 1547
Industrial Designers Society of America, (H) 1465, (S) 2284
Infusion Nursing Society, (S) 2195
INROADS, Inc., (S) 2266, (SS) 3115
Institute for Humane Studies at George Mason University, (H) 1387, 1461, (SS) 3125
Institute of Electrical and Electronics Engineers. Circuits and Systems Society, (S) 2619
Institute of Electrical and Electronics Engineers. Engineering in Medicine and Biology Society, (S) 2135
Institute of Electrical and Electronics Engineers. Industrial Electronics Society, (S) 2305

Institute of Electrical and Electronics Engineers. Industry Applications Society, (S) 2305

Institute of Electrical and Electronics Engineers. Nuclear and Plasma Physics Society, (S) 2583

Institute of Electrical and Electronics Engineers. Power Electronics Society, (S) 2305

Institute of Electrical and Electronics Engineers. Power Engineering Society, (S) 2305, 2623

Institute of Food Technologists, (S) 1878, 2230, 2287, 2299–2301, 2351, 2369, 2453–2454, 2458, 2542, 2589, 2632, 2737

Institute of Food Technologists. Great Lakes Section, (S) 2005

Institute of Industrial Engineers, (S) 2097, 2402, 2785–2786

Institute of International Education, (S) 2413

Institute of Management Accountants, (SS) 3134, 3399

Institute of Nuclear Power Operations, (S) 2506

Institute of Real Estate Management Foundation, (SS) 3076

Institute of Transportation Engineers, (S) 2038

Institute of Transportation Engineers. New England Section, (S) 2763

Institute of Transportation Engineers. Tennessee Section, (S) 2748

Instrumentation, Systems, and Automation Society, (S) 1992, 2152, 2312, 2555

Intel Corporation, (S) 1787, 2302–2303, (SS) 3137–3138

Interlochen Arts Camp, (H) 1588

International Arabian Breeders Sweepstakes Commission, (U) 485

International Association of Culinary Professionals Foundation, (H) 1348

International Association of Lighting Designers, (H) 1473

International Chiropractors Association, (S) 1828

International Communications Industries Association, Inc., (H) 1474, (S) 2304

International Facility Management Association, (SS) 3131

International Foodservice Editorial Council, (H) 1467, (S) 2285, (SS) 3130

International Foundation for Gender Education, (H) 1707, (SS) 3418

International Furnishings and Design Association, (H) 1317, 1466, 1654

International Geographic Information Foundation, (S) 2660

International Order of Job's Daughters, (U) 1079, (S) 2242

International Order of the Golden Rule, (SS) 3309

International Petroleum Technology Institute, (S) 2606–2607

International Symposium on Superalloys, (S) 2307

International Technology Education Association, (S) 2184, 2316, 2403, (SS) 3065, 3140, 3201

International Trumpet Guild, (H) 1588

Intertribal Timber Council, (S) 2777

Inweld Corporation, (S) 2339

Iota Sigma Pi, (S) 2231

Iowa Arts Council, (H) 1476

Iowa Broadcasters Association, (H) 1634

Iowa College Student Aid Commission, (U) 487, 490–491

Iowa Federation of Labor, AFL–CIO, (SS) 3139

Iowa Foundation for Agricultural Advancement, (S) 2286

Iowa Girls' High School Athletic Union, (U) 301, 978

Iowa Motor Truck Association, (U) 489, (S) 2309

Iowa Ready Mixed Concrete Association, (S) 2310

Iowa Sports Turf Manager's Association, (S) 2315

Iowa United Methodist Foundation, (S) 2370

Irene Ryan Foundation, (H) 1477

ITS Washington, (S) 2861

Izaak Walton League of America. Minnesota Division, (S) 2480, (SS) 3242

J. Craig and Page T. Smith Scholarship Foundation, (U) 24

Jack J. Isgur Foundation, (H) 1479, (SS) 3142

Jack Kent Cooke Foundation, (U) 498–499

Jackie Robinson Foundation, (U) 501, 846

Jamatex, (U) 710

James S. Kemper Foundation, (SS) 3177

Japanese American Citizens League, (U) 545, 623, 648–649, 727, 745, 847, 915, 993, 1050, 1232, (H) 1246, 1451, 1513, 1754, (S) 2385, 2683, (SS) 2886

Jay Ramsdell Foundation, (U) 505

Jaycees of Wisconsin Foundation, Inc., (U) 276

Jeannette Rankin Foundation, Inc., (U) 507

Jeff Krosnoff Scholarship Fund, (U) 508

Jefferson United Methodist Church, (H) 1645

Jewish Federation of Delaware, (U) 529, (H) 1497, (SS) 3159

Jewish Federation of Greater Hartford, Inc., (H) 1447, (SS) 3106

Jewish Guild for the Blind, (U) 417

Jews for Jesus, (H) 1441

JHM Hotels, Inc., (SS) 3346

Jimmy Rane Foundation, (U) 517

John B. Lynch Scholarship Foundation, (U) 522

John Bayliss Broadcast Foundation, (H) 1491

John D. O'Bryant National Think Tank for Black Professionals in Higher Education on Predominantly White Campuses, (U) 524

John F. Kennedy Center for the Performing Arts. American College Theater Festival, (H) 1268, 1477, 1486, 1492, 1508, 1532, 1546, 1587, 1621, 1675

John F. Kennedy Library Foundation, (SS) 3341

John Gyles Education Fund, (U) 525

Johnson & Johnson Medical, Inc., (S) 2520

Jolly Green Association, (U) 526

Jon C. Ladda Memorial Foundation, (U) 527

Joseph B. Whitehead Foundation, (U) 223

Joseph Shinoda Memorial Scholarship Foundation Inc., (S) 2365

Josephine de Karman Fellowship Trust, (U) 531, (H) 1500

Jostens Publishing Company, (H) 1501

JPMorgan Chase Foundation, (S) 2864

JPMorganChase, (SS) 3167

JTG, Inc., (H) 1503

Kaiser Permanente, (S) 2274

Kaiser Permanente African American Professional Association, (U) 561

Kansas Association of Broadcasters, (H) 1504

Kansas Board of Regents, (U) 535, 537–540

Kansas City Star, (H) 1379

Kansas Commission on Veterans' Affairs, (U) 536

Kansas Federation of Business & Professional Women's Clubs, Inc., (U) 178, 532–534, 621, (S) 2127, (SS) 2998

Kansas Funeral Directors and Embalmers Association, (SS) 3172

Kansas Golf Association, (S) 2649

Kansas Livestock Association, (S) 2382

Kansas Masonic Foundation, Inc., (U) 259

Kansas Restaurant & Hospitality Association, (SS) 3173

Kansas Society of Certified Public Accountants, (SS) 3136, 3185–3186

Kansas State Nurses Association, (S) 2823

Kansas Wildscape Foundation, Inc., (H) 1687, (S) 2733

Kaplan, Inc., (U) 541

Kappa Delta Pi, (SS) 3098, 3439

KATU–TV, (H) 1507

KCNC–TV News 4, (H) 1625

Ke Ali'i Pauahi Foundation, (U) 429

Kentucky Broadcasters Association, (H) 1435

Kentucky Community and Technical College System, (U) 243, 412, 544, 548, 632, (S) 2833

Kentucky Department of Veterans Affairs, (U) 330, 554, 1126

Kentucky Education Association, (SS) 3221

Kentucky Federation of Business and Professional Women, (U) 140

Kentucky Fire Commission, (U) 549

Kentucky High School Athletic Association, (U) 760, 1056

Kentucky Higher Education Assistance Authority, (U) 547, 550, 553, (SS) 3180

Kentucky Housing Association, (U) 551

Kentucky Nurses Association, (S) 2377

Kentucky Restaurant Association, (SS) 3181

Kentucky School Plant Managers Association, (S) 2384

Kentucky Society of Certified Public Accountants, (SS) 3182

Kentucky Turfgrass Council, (S) 2378

Ketchum, Inc., (U) 1116

Key Club International, (U) 257, 267, 559, 979, 1064, 1231, (S) 2379

Keystone Group Holdings, Inc., (SS) 3184

KFC, (U) 870

KFC Corporation, (U) 557

Kidger Optics Associates, (S) 2471

Kids' Chance, Inc., (U) 558

Kids' Chance Inc. of Missouri, (U) 722

Kids' Chance of Arizona, (U) 82

Kids' Chance of Arkansas, Inc., (U) 88

Kids' Chance of Indiana, Inc., (U) 482

Kids' Chance of Iowa, (U) 488

Kids' Chance of Kentucky, (U) 552

Kids' Chance of Louisiana, (U) 592

Kids' Chance of Maryland, Inc., (U) 643

Kids' Chance of North Carolina, Inc., (U) 852

Kids' Chance of Pennsylvania, (U) 929

Kids' Chance of Washington, (U) 1182

Kids' Chance of West Virginia, Inc., (U) 1189

KING/5 Television, (H) 1603

Kiwanis International Foundation, (U) 267, 559, 1064, 1231

Knight Ridder, Inc., (H) 1510

Knights of Ak–Sar–Ben, (U) 22–23

Knights of Lithuania, (U) 560

Knights of Pythias, (H) 1511

Koch Corporation, (S) 1859

Korean American Scholarship Foundation. Eastern Region, (U) 303

Korean American Scholarship Foundation. Mideastern Region, (U) 681

Korean American Scholarship Foundation. Midwestern Region, (U) 683

Korean American Scholarship Foundation. NorthEastern Region, (U) 862

Korean American Scholarship Foundation. Southern Region, (U) 1051

Korean American Scholarship Foundation. Western Region, (U) 1192

Korean–American Scientists and Engineers Association, (S) 1998, 2383

Kosciuszko Foundation, (H) 1323, 1542, 1738

KPMG Foundation, (SS) 3287
Kruse and Associates, (SS) 3237
KSL–TV, (U) 1066
Kurzweil Foundation, (U) 295–296, 299, 326, 363, 984, (S) 1874, 2090, 2374, (SS) 2908, 3295
Kyle Lee Foundation, Inc., (U) 563
La Unidad Latina Foundation, Inc., (U) 568
Labsphere, Inc., (S) 2726
Ladies Auxiliary of the Fleet Reserve Association, (U) 566–567, 997
LAGRANT FOUNDATION, (SS) 3187
Lambda Alpha, (SS) 3190
Lambda Iota Tau, College Literature Honor Society, (H) 1516
Land O'Lakes, Inc., (S) 1972
Land Surveyors' Association of Washington, (S) 2221, 2412
Landmark Publishing Group, (H) 1517
Landscape Architecture Foundation, (H) 1368–1369, 1434, 1438, 1637, 1639, 1743
Laser Focus World, (S) 2726
Latino Media Association. Seattle Chapter, (H) 1603
LCF Memorial Foundation, Inc., (U) 588
Lebanese American Heritage Club, (U) 575, (H) 1521
Lee Berwick Foundation, (U) 77
Lee–Jackson Foundation, (H) 1523
Legacy, Inc., (S) 2396, (SS) 3197
Leica Camera, (H) 1332
Leopold Schepp Foundation, (U) 580
Lesbian, Bisexual, Gay and Transgendered United Employees (LEAGUE) at AT&T Foundation, (U) 574
Liberty Graphics, Inc., (H) 1527
Liberty Mutual, (S) 2398
Lincoln Community Foundation, (U) 510, 792, 848, (S) 2391, (SS) 2987, 3047, 3192
Lincoln Forum, (H) 1528
Linly Heflin Unit, (U) 586
Lippincott Williams & Wilkins, (S) 2145
Lisa Sechrist Memorial Foundation, (U) 587
Livestock Publications Council, (H) 1395, (S) 2172
Lockheed Martin Corporation, (U) 93, (S) 1883, 2404–2406, 2520
LOMA Society of Nebraska, (SS) 3202
Los Angeles Times, (H) 1300
Louisiana Bar Foundation, (U) 592
Louisiana Department of Veterans Affairs, (U) 598
Louisiana High School Athletic Association, (U) 380
Louisiana Office of Student Financial Assistance, (U) 593–597, (S) 2669
Lowe's Companies, Inc., (S) 2411, (SS) 3205
Lowrider Magazine, (U) 599
Lucent Technologies, (S) 2413
Luso–American Education Foundation, (H) 1453
Lydia's Professional Uniforms, (S) 2417
Lyme Academy College of Fine Arts, (H) 1583
L3 Communications, (U) 773
Maddenmedia, (U) 150
Maids of Athena, (U) 604
Maine Bankers Association, (SS) 3208
Maine. Bureau of Maine Veterans' Services, (U) 615
Maine Community Foundation, (U) 581, 609, 616, (H) 1429, 1657, (S) 2679
Maine DeMolay and Pine Tree Youth Foundation, (U) 606
Maine Department of Agriculture, Food and Rural Resources, (S) 2422, (SS) 3212
Maine Education Services, (U) 607–608, 610, 935, (S) 2421, 2425, (SS) 3213
Maine Employers' Mutual Insurance Company, (U) 454
Maine Federation of Business and Professional Women, (U) 379, 605, 962
Maine. Finance Authority, (U) 493, 611, 613–614, 617, 839–840, (SS) 3210
Maine Innkeepers Association, (H) 1539, (SS) 3209
Maine. Legislative Information Office, (U) 607
Maine Media Women, (H) 1512
Maine Metal Products Association, (S) 2421
Maine Restaurant Association, (SS) 3370
Maine Roads Scholarship Fund, (SS) 3211
Maine Society of Land Surveyors, (S) 2423
Maine Society of Professional Engineers, (S) 2424
Maine State Society of Washington, D.C., (U) 612
Maller Baroque Brass Instruments, (H) 1588
Mamoru and Aiko Takitani Foundation, (U) 618
Marathon Corporation, (S) 2484
Margolis Brown Theater Company, (H) 1477
Marine Corps League, (U) 627
Marine Corps Scholarship Foundation, Inc., (U) 628
Marriott International, Inc., (SS) 3220
Marsh Risk Consulting, (S) 2439
Maryland Association for Health, Physical Education, Recreation and Dance, (SS) 3226–3227
Maryland Association of Certified Public Accountants, (SS) 3228
Maryland Association of Private Colleges and Career Schools, (U) 638
Maryland Bankers Association, (SS) 3229
Maryland Federation of Business and Professional Women's Clubs, Inc., (U) 145, (S) 2033, (SS) 2986
Maryland Higher Education Commission, (U) 311, 639–642, 644–645, 647, (H) 1551, (S) 2447
Maryland Society of Surveyors, (S) 2450
Maryland State Department of Education, (U) 13
Maryland State Funeral Directors Association, (SS) 2989
Maryland State Grange, (U) 646, (SS) 3231
Masonic Foundation of Utah, (U) 650
Massachusetts AFL–CIO, (H) 1554, (SS) 3232
Massachusetts Association of Land Surveyors and Civil Engineers, Inc., (S) 2427
Massachusetts Broadcasters Association, (H) 1555
Massachusetts Community Colleges, (U) 652
Massachusetts Democratic Party, (H) 1493, (SS) 3157
Massachusetts Office of Student Financial Assistance, (U) 11, 244, 402, 521, 651, 653–662, 923, 1061, (S) 2451
Massachusetts Restaurant Association, (SS) 3233
Massachusetts Society of Certified Public Accountants, (SS) 3043, 3120, 3175, 3234, 3327
Master Brewers Association of the Americas, (S) 2452
MasterGuard Corporation, (U) 663
Material Handling Industry of America, (S) 2468, (SS) 3236
MBNA Education Foundation, (U) 665
MC Strategies, Inc., (S) 2171, (SS) 3056
McNeil Consumer and Specialty Pharmaceuticals, (S) 2614, 2781
Media Action Network for Asian Americans, (H) 1540
MedQuist Inc., (S) 2171, (SS) 3056
Medtronic Physio–Control Corporation, (S) 2462
Memorial Foundation for Jewish Culture, (H) 1475
Mennonite Church USA, (U) 1068
Merck Company Foundation, (S) 2783
Michael Baker Corporation, (S) 2469
Michael Bendix Sutton Foundation, (SS) 3238
Michael & Susan Dell Foundation, (U) 275
Michigan Association of Certified Public Accountants, (SS) 3239
Michigan Association of Recreation Vehicles and Campgrounds, (S) 2255, (SS) 3102
Michigan Commission on Law Enforcement Standards, (U) 676
Michigan Council of Teachers of Mathematics, (S) 2490, (SS) 3245
Michigan. Department of Military and Veterans Affairs, (U) 680
Michigan Department of Treasury, (U) 671–672, 675, 678–679
Michigan Elks Association, (U) 673
Michigan Federation of Teachers & School Related Personnel, (SS) 3366
Michigan Funeral Directors Association, (SS) 3240
Michigan Law Enforcement Education Program, (SS) 3196
Michigan Manufactured Housing Association, (S) 2255, (SS) 3102
Michigan Press Association, (H) 1558
Michigan Sheriffs' Association, (SS) 2925
Michigan Society of Professional Engineers, (S) 2253, 2376, 2495–2496
Michigan State Troopers Assistance Fund, (U) 677
Michigan Townships Association, (SS) 3364
Microsoft Corporation, (S) 2018, 2472, 2520
Midwest Concrete Industry Board, (S) 2475
Midwest Dairy Association. Iowa Division, (U) 486
Midwestern Higher Education Commission, (U) 682
MIGIZI Communications, Inc., (H) 1391, (S) 2815
Mike Gallagher Show Charitable Foundation, (U) 381
Mikimoto, (U) 710–711
Mikkelson Foundation, (S) 2476
Military Officers Association of America, (U) 63, 728–729
Military Officers Association of America. Aloha Chapter, (U) 45
Military Officers Association of America. Arizona Chapter, (U) 81
Military Officers' Benevolent Corporation, (U) 688
Military Order of the Purple Heart, (U) 689
Miller Brewing Company, (U) 1116
Miller Electric Manufacturing Company, (S) 2477
The Minerals, Metals & Materials Society, (S) 2131, 2154, 2307, 2320, 2400, 2736, 2769
Minnesota Association of Townships, (U) 695
Minnesota Benefit Association, (U) 696
Minnesota Broadcasters Association, (H) 1481
Minnesota Department of Human Services, (U) 698
Minnesota Department of Veterans Affairs, (U) 699
Minnesota Higher Education Services Office, (U) 694, 697, 700–701, 703
Minnesota Pork Board, (S) 2481
Minnesota Society of Professional Surveyors, (S) 2482

Minnesota State High School League, (U) 702
Minnesota Timberwolves, (U) 1119
Minority Nurse Magazine, (S) 2485
Miss America Pageant, (U) 705–706
Miss Cheerleader of America, (U) 708
Miss Universe Organization, (U) 710–711
Mississippi Association of Broadcasters, (H) 1538
Mississippi Baptist Convention Board, (H) 1561
Mississippi Office of Student Financial Aid, (U) 713–717, 843
Mississippi Society of Certified Public Accountants, (SS) 3246
Mississippi State Veterans Affairs Board, (U) 712
Missouri Ag Industries Council, Inc., (S) 2046
Missouri Association of Fairs & Festivals, (U) 724
Missouri Broadcasters Association, (H) 1562
Missouri Business and Professional Women's Foundation, Inc., (U) 720
Missouri Department of Elementary and Secondary Education, (U) 726
Missouri Department of Higher Education, (U) 190, 622, 718–719, 721, 723, 725
Missouri Department of Natural Resources, (S) 2140, (SS) 3036
Missouri Insurance Education Foundation, (SS) 3247–3248
Missouri League for Nursing, Inc., (S) 2143, 2435, 2491
Missouri Middle School Association, (SS) 2909
Missouri Photo Workshop, (H) 1332
Missouri School of Journalism, (H) 1332
Missouri Society of Certified Public Accountants, (SS) 3195
Missouri Society of Professional Engineers, (S) 2338
Missouri Travel Council, (SS) 3249
Missouri Vocational Special Need Association, (U) 748
The Mitchell Institute, (U) 1012
Mitsubishi Heavy Industries, (S) 2030
Monsanto Company, (S) 2015
Montana Academy of Physician Assistants, (S) 2492
Montana Funeral Directors Association, (SS) 3251
Montana Guaranteed Student Loan Program, (U) 730–739, 1074–1075
Montana State Elks Association, (U) 1001
Montana Water Environment Association, (S) 2069
Monumental Rifle and Pistol Club, Inc., (U) 266
Morgan Stanley, (S) 2563, 2646, 2857, (SS) 3253–3254
Morris J. and Betty Kaplun Foundation, (H) 1564
Morris Land Conservancy, (H) 1653, (S) 2677
Morris Scholarship Fund, (U) 743
Motorola, Inc., (S) 2494
MTNA Foundation, (H) 1567, 1569
Museum of Surveying, (H) 1602, (S) 2556
Music Teachers National Association, (H) 1567–1569
Mystic Tan, (U) 710
NAC, Inc., (S) 2726
NASCAR, (U) 756
National Academy for Nuclear Training, (S) 2506
National Academy of American Scholars, (U) 750–751
National Academy of Television Arts and Sciences. Upper Midwest Chapter, (H) 1712
National Ad 2, (H) 1574
National Agricultural Aviation Association, (S) 2858
National Air Transportation Foundation, (S) 2615
National Alliance for Scholastic Achievement, (U) 757
National AMBUCS, Inc., (S) 1830
National Asphalt Pavement Association, (S) 2502
National Association for Asian and Pacific American Education, (U) 749
National Association for Campus Activities, (U) 752
National Association for Gifted Children, (U) 842
National Association for the Advancement of Colored People, (U) 10, 985, (H) 1242, (S) 1794, 2279, 2408, (SS) 3019, 3198
National Association for the Education of Homeless Children and Youth, (U) 582
National Association for the Self–Employed, (SS) 3067
National Association of Black Accountants, (SS) 3219, 3257, 3261, 3345, 3402, 3421
National Association of Black Journalists, (H) 1257, 1413, 1571, 1595, 1725
National Association of Black Journalists. Seattle Chapter, (H) 1603
National Association of Black Social Workers, (SS) 2955
National Association of Black Telecommunications Professionals, Inc., (S) 2499, (SS) 3258
National Association of Broadcasters, (H) 1431, 1731
National Association of Colleges and University Food Services, (SS) 2963
National Association of Colored Women's Clubs, (U) 422
National Association of Educational Office Professionals, (SS) 3218
National Association of Farm Broadcasters, (S) 2015
National Association of Health Services Executives, (S) 2507
National Association of Hispanic Journalists, (H) 1489, 1543, 1572, 1596
National Association of Hispanic Nurses, (S) 2508
National Association of Independent Colleges and Universities, (U) 39

National Association of Negro Business and Professional Women's Clubs, (U) 753, (H) 1365, (SS) 3013
National Association of Pastoral Musicians, (H) 1576
National Association of Secondary School Principals, (U) 40, 765, 953, 958
National Association of State Universities and Land–Grant Colleges, (U) 39, 1116
National Association of Tobacco Distributors, (SS) 3347
National Association of Vocational Education Special Needs Personnel, (U) 775
National Association of Women in Construction, (S) 2027, 2509, (SS) 3262
National Association of Women in Construction. Buffalo Chapter 172, (H) 1303, (S) 1949, (SS) 2939
National Association of Women in Construction. Granite State Chapter 218, (S) 2236
National Association of Women in Construction. Greater Omaha Chapter 116, (H) 1426, (S) 2240, (SS) 3093
National Association of Women in Construction. Maine Chapter 276, (S) 2420, (SS) 3207
National Association of Women in Construction. Metropolitan Denver Chapter 112, (S) 2808, (SS) 3448
National Association of Women in Construction. Nashville Chapter 16, (H) 1341, (S) 2029, (SS) 2984
National Association of Women in Construction. San Antonio Chapter 11, (H) 1661, (S) 2686, (SS) 3375
National Athletic Trainers' Association, (S) 2504
National Beta Clubs, (U) 758
National Black MBA Association, (SS) 3263
National Black Nurses Association, Inc., (S) 2085, 2089, 2525
National Board for Respiratory Care, (S) 2667, 2845
National Business Aviation Association, Inc., (S) 2390, 2782, 2839
National Candy Wholesalers Association, (SS) 3347
National Center for American Indian Enterprise Development, (SS) 2896
National Center for Learning Disabilities, (U) 74
National City Bank, (U) 760
National Coalition of Ethnic Minority Nurse Associations, (S) 1789
National Collegiate Athletic Association, (U) 283–284, (H) 1402
National Conference of CPA Practitioners, Inc., (SS) 3270
National Council of Acoustical Consultants, (H) 1691, (S) 2739
National Court Reporters Association, (SS) 2953
National Dairy Promotion and Research Board, (S) 2526, (SS) 3271
National Dental Association, (S) 2512
National Education Association, (U) 40
National Farmers Union, (U) 457
National Federation of Independent Business, (SS) 3293
National Federation of Music Clubs, (H) 1270, 1363, 1427, 1502, 1535–1536, 1545, 1598, 1672, 1688, 1700, 1718, 1720, 1735, (S) 2071, (SS) 3094
National Federation of Paralegal Associations, Inc., (SS) 3324
National Federation of the Blind, (U) 188, 325, 424, 441, 509, 546, 562, 762, (H) 1460, (S) 2276, 2513, (SS) 3028, 3119, 3373
National Federation of the Blind of Connecticut, (SS) 2935
National FFA Organization, (U) 177, 198, 367, (H) 1577, (S) 2015, 2514, (SS) 3264
National Fire Protection Association, (S) 2219, (SS) 3075
National Fish and Wildlife Foundation, (S) 1947, (SS) 2937
National Fluid Milk Processor Promotion Board, (U) 999
National Foliage Foundation, (S) 2328
National Forty and Eight, (S) 2217
National Foundation for Advancement in the Arts, (H) 1277
National Foundation for Women Legislators, (U) 211, (SS) 3294
National Fraternal Society of the Deaf, (U) 763
National Gay and Lesbian Task Force, (H) 1556
National Gay Pilots Association, (S) 2546
National Geographic Society Education Foundation, (U) 406
National Gerontological Nurses Association, (S) 2446
National Greenhouse Manufacturers Association, (S) 2515
National Guard Association of Michigan, (U) 764
National Guild of Community Schools of the Arts, (H) 1756
National Hardwood Lumber Association, (S) 2516
National Hemophilia Foundation, (U) 556, 957
National History Day, (H) 1578
National Hook–Up of Black Women, Inc., (U) 98
National Huguenot Society, (U) 766
National Indian Education Association, (U) 523
National Indian Gaming Association, (SS) 3396
National Industries for the Blind, (SS) 3295
National Institute for Labor Relations Research, (H) 1739, (SS) 2901
National Institute for the Blind, (U) 779
National Institutes of Health Black Scientists Association, (S) 1993
National Junior Angus Association, (U) 72, (S) 1834, 1957
National Junior Classical League, (H) 1240, 1579–1580
National Junior Hereford Association, (S) 2517
National Latina Alliance, (U) 767

National League for Nursing, (S) 2695
National Management Association, (SS) 2889
National Meat Association, (S) 2552
National Military Family Association, Inc., (U) 518
National Minority Junior Golf Scholarship Association, (U) 846
National Multiple Sclerosis Society, (U) 768
National Naval Officers Association. Washington, D.C. Chapter, (U) 173, 322, 603, 785
National Organization for Women–New York State, Inc., (U) 1019
National Panhellenic Conference, (U) 864
National PKU News, (U) 976
National Poultry and Food Distributors Association, (S) 2562
National Precast Concrete Association, (S) 2561
National Press Club, (H) 1376
National Press Photographers Foundation, (H) 1294, 1332, 1498, 1604–1605, 1644
National Religious Music Week Alliance, (H) 1582
National Restaurant Association Educational Foundation, (H) 1581, (SS) 3266–3267, 3342
National Rifle Association, (SS) 3294
National Scholastic Press Association, (H) 1300, 1342, 1606, 1729
National School Boards Association, (U) 759
National Science Foundation, (S) 2689, (SS) 3378
National Sculpture Society, (H) 1583–1584
National Society Daughters of the American Revolution, (H) 1351, (SS) 3035
National Society of Accountants, (SS) 3304
National Society of Black Engineers, (S) 2520
National Society of Professional Engineers, (S) 1909, 2456, 2594, 2601, 2804, 2843
National Society of Professional Surveyors, (S) 2647
National Society of the Colonial Dames of America, (S) 2293
National Speakers Association, (H) 1585
National Stone, Sand and Gravel Association, (H) 1690, (S) 1922, 2566, 2738, (SS) 3151
National Strength and Conditioning Association, (S) 2564–2565, 2624
National Technical Honor Society, (U) 770, (S) 2274
National Telecommunications Cooperative Association, (U) 369
National Tongan American Society, (U) 1125
National Tour Association, (SS) 3268, 3305
National Trumpet Competition, (H) 1588
National Water Research Institute, (S) 2263
National Wild Turkey Federation, (S) 2569
National Wild Turkey Federation. Florida Chapter, (S) 2159
National Youth Leadership Council, (U) 406
Native American Journalists Association. Seattle Chapter, (H) 1603
Naval Enlisted Reserve Association, (U) 772
Naval Helicopter Association, (U) 773
Naval Sea Cadet Corps, (U) 583, 865–867
Naval Special Warfare Foundation, (U) 12, 774
Navy League of the United States, (U) 33, 513, 778, 845, 1071, (S) 2617
Navy Supply Corps Foundation, (U) 203, 779–780
Navy Wives Club of America, (U) 636, 781, 786
Navy–Marine Corps Relief Society, (U) 103–104, 933, 1159
Nebraska Academy of Sciences, (S) 1954
Nebraska Actuaries Club, (S) 2527, (SS) 3272
Nebraska Bankers Association, (SS) 3273
Nebraska Cattlemen Association, (U) 789
Nebraska. Coordinating Commission for Postsecondary Education, (U) 791, 793–794
Nebraska. Department of Veterans' Affairs, (U) 795
Nebraska Educational Office Professionals Association, (SS) 3274
Nebraska Elks Association, (U) 790
Nebraska Funeral Directors Association, (SS) 3453
Nebraska Insurance Federation, (S) 2527, (SS) 3272
Nebraska Legal Professionals Association, (SS) 3275
Nebraska Press Association Foundation, (H) 1589
Nebraska Society of Certified Public Accountants, (SS) 3276
Nebraska State Historical Society Foundation, (U) 796
Nevada Cattlemen's Association, (S) 2532
Nevada Council on Problem Gambling, (H) 1632
New Buildings Institute, (H) 1520, (S) 2393
New England Board of Higher Education, (U) 798
New England Direct Marketing Association, (H) 1358, (SS) 3003
New England Employee Benefits Council, (SS) 3277
New England Graduate Accounting Study Conference, (SS) 3120–3121
New England Press Association, (H) 1590
New England Water Works Association, (S) 2128, 2178, 2220, 2363, (SS) 3059, 3161
New Hampshire Association of Broadcasters, (H) 1591
New Hampshire Charitable Foundation, (U) 113, 175, 619, 799–800
New Hampshire Educational Media Association, (SS) 3280

New Hampshire Postsecondary Education Commission, (U) 801, 804–805
New Hampshire Society of Certified Public Accountants, (SS) 3121, 3281
New Hampshire Society of Professional Engineers, (S) 2547
New Jersey Business Magazine, (SS) 3285
New Jersey Commission on Higher Education, (U) 806
New Jersey Department of Military and Veterans Affairs, (U) 809
New Jersey Funeral Directors Association, (SS) 3283
New Jersey Higher Education Student Assistance Authority, (U) 261, 310, 709, 808, 812–813, 815
New Jersey Press Foundation, (H) 1297
New Jersey School Counselor Association, Inc., (U) 810
New Jersey Schoolwomen's Club, (SS) 3284
New Jersey Society for Clinical Laboratory Science, (S) 2551
New Jersey Society of Certified Public Accountants, (SS) 3039, 3285–3287
New Jersey Society of Professional Engineers, (S) 2534
New Jersey Society of Professional Land Surveyors, (S) 2534
New Jersey State Elks, (U) 811
New Jersey Utilities Association, (S) 2537, (SS) 3288
New Jersey Vietnam Veterans' Memorial, (U) 814
New Mexico Association for Health, Physical Education, Recreation, and Dance, (H) 1600, (S) 2553, (SS) 3296
New Mexico Association of School Business Officials, (SS) 3297
New Mexico Baptist Foundation, (H) 1694
New Mexico Broadcasters Association, (H) 1593, (S) 2538, (SS) 3289
New Mexico Commission on Higher Education, (U) 816, 818, 820–821, 823–824, 826
New Mexico Department of Veterans' Services, (U) 817, 825
New Mexico Elks Association, (U) 819
New Mexico Land Title Association, (U) 208
New Mexico Society of Certified Public Accountants, (SS) 3078, 3174
New York Beef Producers' Association, (H) 1594, (S) 2539, (SS) 3290
New York Farm Bureau, (S) 1801
New York Lottery, (U) 831
New York State Association of Agricultural Fairs, (S) 2570
New York State Education Department, (U) 833
New York State Grange, (S) 2056
New York State Higher Education Services Corporation, (U) 827, 830, 832, 834–838
New York State Showpeople's Association, (S) 2570
New York State Society of Certified Public Accountants, (SS) 3291
New York Women in Communications, Inc., (H) 1607
Newhouse Foundation, (H) 1595–1596
Newhouse News Service, (H) 1674
The Newseum, (H) 1342
Newspaper Guild–CWA, (H) 1352
Newsweek Magazine, (U) 541
NextGen Network, Inc., (U) 291
Nightingale Awards of Pennsylvania, (S) 2550
Nina Footwear, (U) 710
Ninety–Nines, Inc. Eastern New England Chapter, (S) 2271
NISH, (U) 779
Nissan North America, Inc., (U) 843–844
North Carolina Alliance for Athletics, Health, Physical Education, Recreation and Dance, (U) 787, (H) 1573, (S) 2505, (SS) 3259
North Carolina Association of Certified Public Accountants, (SS) 3299
North Carolina Association of Educators, Inc., (U) 633, (SS) 3064, 3225
North Carolina Bar Association, (U) 849
North Carolina Business Education Association, (SS) 3158
North Carolina Child Support Council, (U) 131
North Carolina Community College System, (U) 850–851
North Carolina. Division of Veterans Affairs, (U) 855
North Carolina Farm Bureau, (S) 2633, (SS) 3344
North Carolina Fraternal Order of Police, (U) 788
North Carolina PTA, (U) 854
North Carolina Sheriffs' Association, (SS) 3301
North Carolina State Education Assistance Authority, (U) 502–503, 850–851, 853, 856, 1136–1137, (SS) 3300–3302
North Carolina Traffic League, (S) 2557, (SS) 3303
North Central Texas Council of Governments, (S) 2775, (SS) 3420
North Dakota Council on Abused Women's Services, (U) 861
North Dakota. Department of Veterans Affairs, (U) 857
North Dakota University System, (U) 858–860
North Suburban Chamber of Commerce, (S) 2399
North Texas Tollway Authority, (S) 2336
Northeast Human Resources Association, (SS) 3278
Northeastern Association of Forensic Scientists, (S) 2222
Northrop Grumman Corporation, (S) 2520, 2559–2560
Northwest Baptist Convention, (H) 1646
Northwest Education Loan Association, (U) 1083
Northwest Journalists of Color, (H) 1603
Northwestern Mutual Foundation, (U) 1116

Novartis Seed Company, (S) 2696
Novo Nordisk Pharmaceuticals, Inc., (U) 863
Nuclear Age Peace Foundation, (SS) 3400
NuFACTOR, (U) 320, 477
NurseWeek magazine, (S) 1996
Nursing Foundation of Pennsylvania, (S) 2322, 2597
Nursing Spectrum, (S) 2274
NVIDIA Corporation, (S) 2568
NYSARC, Inc., (S) 1879, 2327, (SS) 3163
Oak Ridge Institute for Science and Education, (U) 278, (S) 2144, 2519, 2571, (SS) 3038, 3308
Octapharma, (U) 477
Office Depot, (U) 356
Ohio Board of Regents, (U) 873–874, 876–878
Ohio Business Teachers Association, (SS) 3310
Ohio Classical Conference, (H) 1608, (SS) 3311
Ohio Educational Library Media Association, (SS) 3307
Ohio Newspapers Foundation, (H) 1609–1610
Ohio Society of Certified Public Accountants, (SS) 3312–3313
Ohio Society of Professional Engineers, (S) 2136, 2269, 2638
Ohio State Firefighters' Association, (S) 2582
Oklahoma Association of Broadcasters, (H) 1611
Oklahoma Business and Professional Women, (U) 879
Oklahoma Funeral Directors Association, (SS) 3141
Oklahoma Society of Certified Public Accountants, (SS) 3314
Oklahoma Society of Land Surveyors, (S) 2572
Oklahoma State Regents for Higher Education, (U) 880–886, 969, (SS) 3074
Omaha Public Power District, (U) 747
Omaha Volunteers for Handicapped Children, (U) 887, (SS) 3316
Oncology Nursing Certification Corporation, (S) 2575
Oncology Nursing Society, (S) 2147, 2575, 2668
Open Society Institute, (H) 1401
Opportunities for the Blind, Inc., (U) 890
Optimist International, (U) 891–893
Oral–B Laboratories, (S) 2578–2579
Orange County Community Foundation, (U) 670
Order of the Eastern Star, (H) 1366
Order Sons of Italy in America, (U) 1031, (H) 1681, (SS) 3109
Oregon AFL–CIO, (SS) 3318
Oregon Association of Broadcasters, (H) 1613
Oregon Association of Independent Accountants, (SS) 3319
Oregon. Children, Adult, and Family Services, (U) 204
Oregon Community Foundation, (U) 117, 894, 937, (H) 1480, (S) 2392, 2631, (SS) 3145
Oregon Sheep Growers Association, Inc., (S) 2581
Oregon Society of Certified Public Accountants, (SS) 3321–3322
Oregon Student Assistance Commission, (U) 116–117, 204, 365–366, 894–895, 898–899, 937, 948, (H) 1384, 1480, (S) 1930, 2183, 2371, 2392, 2464, 2631, (SS) 3063, 3145, 3318, 3320
Oregon University System, (S) 1787
Organization of Chinese Americans, Inc., (U) 383, 868–872, 1138
Orphan Foundation of America, (U) 181, 184, 444, 900
Oscar P. Stone Research Trust Fund, (S) 2024
Oticon, Inc., (U) 1015
Otis Spunkmeyer, Inc., (SS) 3323
Outdoor Writers Association of America, (H) 1298
Overseas Press Club, (H) 1615
P. Buckley Moss Society, (U) 73, (SS) 3168
Pacers Foundation, Inc., (U) 906
Pacific Fleet Submarine Memorial Association, (U) 136–137
Pacific Islanders in Communications, (H) 1616
Pacific Southwest Instruments, (S) 2395
PacifiCare Foundation, (S) 2584
Padgett Business Services Foundation, (U) 907
Page Education Foundation, (U) 908
Palomino Horse Breeders of America, (U) 912
Pancretan Association of America, (U) 1154
Papa John's International, Inc., (U) 913
Paper, Allied–Industrial, Chemical and Energy Workers International Union, (U) 841
Parapsychology Foundation, Inc., (SS) 3031, 3363
Parent Teacher Association of Connecticut, (SS) 2979, 3306
Parents, Families and Friends of Lesbians and Gays, (U) 321, 506, 909–910, 940, 994, (S) 2610, (SS) 3333
Parkersburg Area Community Foundation, (U) 368
Patrick Kerr Skateboard Scholarship Fund, (U) 918
Patriot Senior Noncommissioned Officer's Council, (U) 425
Patsy Takemoto Mink Education Foundation for Low–Income Women and Children, (U) 919
Paul F. Ronci Memorial Trust, (U) 921
Pauline S. Young Scholarship Foundation, (U) 1229

peermusic Companies, (H) 1622
Penguin Putnam Inc., (H) 1678
Pennsylvania Academy of the Fine Arts, (H) 1583
Pennsylvania AFL–CIO, (SS) 3328
Pennsylvania. Bureau for Veterans Affairs, (U) 926
Pennsylvania Council of the Blind, (U) 295
Pennsylvania Department of Public Welfare, (U) 925
Pennsylvania Energy Consortium, (S) 2602
Pennsylvania Higher Education Assistance Agency, (U) 925, 927–928, 931–932, 941
Pennsylvania Institute of Certified Public Accountants, (SS) 3336–3337
Pennsylvania Planning Association, (SS) 3330
Pennsylvania Society of Professional Engineers, (S) 2600, 2603, 2630
Pennsylvania Society of Public Accountants, (SS) 3331
Pennsylvania Women's Press Association, (H) 1623
Pennsylvania Youth Foundation, (U) 930
Pentax, (H) 1641
P.E.O. Sisterhood, (U) 934
People to People International, (SS) 3164
Pepsi–Cola Company, (U) 936
Percussive Arts Society, (H) 1618–1619, 1680
Perennial Plant Association, (S) 2604
Peter Kiewit Foundation, (U) 938
Pfizer Inc., (U) 939, (S) 2608–2609, 2614, (SS) 3332
PGA of America, (U) 846
Phi Eta Sigma, (U) 942–943
Phi Theta Kappa, (U) 38, 418, 573, 944
Phi Upsilon Omicron, (S) 2432, 2529, (SS) 2965, 3084, 3200, 3206, 3334, 3422
Philip Morris Companies, (U) 759, 1116
Phillips Foundation, (U) 982
Phoenix Suns Charities, (U) 1072
Pi Lambda Theta, (S) 2771, (SS) 3416
Piney Mountain Press, (U) 775
Pink Sands Swim, (U) 710
Pinnacol Foundation, (U) 945
Pizzagalli Construction Company, (S) 2380
Poetry Magazine, (H) 1656
Point Foundation, (U) 946
Polish Arts Club of Buffalo Inc., (H) 1628
Polish Roman Catholic Union of America, (U) 1060, (SS) 3147
Polish Women's Civic Club, (U) 947
Portland Players, (H) 1499
Portuguese Foundation of Connecticut, (U) 949, (H) 1389
Portuguese Heritage Scholarship Foundation, (U) 492, 530, 579, 624, 950, (H) 1344, (S) 2343
Possible Woman Enterprises, (U) 951
Power Systems, Inc., (S) 2624
Poynter Institute for Media Studies, (H) 1332
Praxair, Inc., (S) 2520, 2626
Preciosa, (U) 710–711
Presbyterian Church (USA), (U) 207, 769, 771, 1069, (H) 1660
Presbyterian Church (USA). Synod of the Trinity, (U) 963
Press Club of New Orleans, (H) 1629
PricewaterhouseCoopers LLP, (S) 2171, (SS) 3056, 3287, 3343
Pride Foundation, (S) 2059, (SS) 3001
Printing Industry of Minnesota, (H) 1630
Private Colleges & Universities, Inc., (U) 956
Procter & Gamble Company, (S) 2628
Procter & Gamble Pharmaceuticals, (S) 2614
Professional Aviation Maintenance Association, (S) 2629
Professional Bowlers Association, (U) 126
Professional Grounds Management Society, (H) 1271, (S) 1855
Professional Independent Insurance Agents of Illinois, (SS) 3068, 3176, 3367
Professional Landcare Network, (H) 1254, (S) 1819
Professional Logging Contractors of Maine, (S) 2267
Prudential Insurance Company of America, (U) 958
Psi Chi, (SS) 2887, 3166
Public Relations Society of America. Puget Sound Chapter, (H) 1459, 1658
Public Relations Student Society of America, (H) 1292, 1350, 1407, 1519, 1631, 1633, 1685
Puerto Rico National Guard, (U) 960
Purdue Pharma L.P., (S) 2614
Railway Tie Association, (S) 2357
Rain Bird Sprinkler Manufacturing Corporation, (H) 1637
Rath Foundation, (U) 964
Rayburn Musical Instrument Company, (H) 1588
Raytheon Corporation, (S) 2640
RBC Dain Rauscher, (U) 966
R.C. Willey Home Furnishings, (H) 1641
RCS Charitable Foundation, (H) 1269
RDW Group, Inc., (H) 1642

Reaching Common Ground, (H) 1643

Reader's Digest Association, Inc., (U) 138

Rebekah Assembly of Texas, (U) 495

Recording for the Blind and Dyslexic, (U) 629, 635

Red Angus Association of America, (S) 2518

Red River Valley Association Foundation, (U) 968

Redi–Tag Corporation, (S) 2642, (SS) 3351

Renee B. Fisher Foundation, (U) 693

Rhode Island Association for Health, Physical Education, Recreation and Dance, (H) 1647, (S) 2644, (SS) 3353

Rhode Island. Division of Veterans' Affairs, (U) 971

Rhode Island Foundation, (U) 920, 970, (H) 1282, 1563, 1642, (S) 1818, (SS) 3348

Rhode Island Higher Education Assistance Authority, (U) 230, 972

Rhode Island Pilots Association, (S) 2643

Rick Pankow Foundation, (S) 2653

Robert Bradford Newman Student Award Fund, (H) 1691, (S) 2739

Robin Romano Memorial Fund, (U) 980

Roche Pharmaceuticals, (S) 2614

Rockwell Automation, Inc., (S) 2670

Rocky Mountain Electrical League, (S) 2656–2657, (SS) 3362

Rocky Mountain Elk Foundation, (S) 2828

Rocky Mountain Water Environment Association, (S) 1934

Rolling Stone, (H) 1650

Ronald McDonald House Charities, (U) 973

Roothbert Fund, Inc., (U) 983

Ropage Group LLC, (U) 917

Roy J. Carver Charitable Trust, (U) 180

Royal Neighbors of America, (U) 986–988, 1174, (S) 2122

Ruffed Grouse Society. Burton L. Spiller Chapter, (S) 1953

Ruth M. Batson Educational Foundation, (U) 991

Safari Club International. Alaska Chapter, (S) 1816

Saginaw Community Foundation, (S) 2734

Sallie Mae Community Foundation for the National Capital Region, (S) 2681, (SS) 3372

Sallie Mae Fund, (S) 2681, (SS) 3372

Sallie Mae 911 Education Fund, (U) 995

Samuel French, Inc., (H) 1587

Samuel N. and Mary Castle Foundation, (SS) 3108

Sanofi–Aventis, (U) 110

Sanofi–Synthelabo, Inc., (S) 1887

SBC Foundation, (U) 1002

Schering/Key Asthma Athlete Scholarship Program, (U) 1003

Scholarly Pursuits, Inc., (U) 913

Scholarship America, (U) 111, 119, 150, 300, 332, 437, 565, 665, 768, 800, 998, 1084–1085, 1121, 1140, 1236, (S) 1921, 2640, 2781, 2812, (SS) 2956, 3454

Scholarship Program Administrators, Inc., (U) 439, (S) 1774, 2025, 2252, 2576, 2650–2651, 2690, (SS) 2873, 2981, 3101, 3317, 3356–3357

Scholastic, Inc., (H) 1664–1666

School Band and Orchestra Magazine, (H) 1272

Science Service, (S) 2302–2303, (SS) 3137–3138

Scottish Rite Foundation of Wyoming, (U) 1224

Scotts Company, (S) 2691

Screen Actors Guild, (U) 179

Scripps Howard Foundation, (H) 1320, 1652

Scudder Association, Inc., (H) 1667, (S) 2693, (SS) 3379

Seabee Memorial Scholarship Association, (U) 1009

Seabury and Smith, Inc., (S) 2274, 2438

Seafarers International Union, (U) 1010

Seattle Mariners Women's Club, (SS) 2928

Seattle Post–Intelligencer, (H) 1603

Seattle Times, (H) 1603

Second (Indianhead) Division Association, (U) 484

Second Marine Division Association, (U) 1011

Seismological Society of America, (S) 2484

Senior Enlisted Academy Alumni Association, (U) 255

Sentry Insurance Foundation, (H) 1671, (S) 2698, (SS) 3382

Sertoma International, (U) 1013–1015

Shaw Industries, (S) 2702

Shell Oil International, (S) 2704

Shook Construction, (S) 2251, (SS) 3100

ShopKo Stores Inc., (U) 1020

Si TV, (H) 1675

Sickle Cell Disease Association of America, (U) 555

Siemens Foundation, (S) 2707, 2709

Siemens Medical Solutions USA, Inc., (S) 2171, 2708, (SS) 3056

Sigma Alpha Iota Philanthropies, Inc., (H) 1484–1485, 1570, 1676–1677, (S) 2497, (SS) 3007

Sigma Iota Epsilon, (SS) 3386

Sikorsky Aircraft Corporation, (U) 773, (S) 1843

Sioux Falls Area Community Foundation, (U) 374, 519

The Sisters of Perpetual Indulgence, Inc., (U) 1024

Skandalaris Family Foundation, (U) 1025

SkillsUSA, (H) 1679, (S) 1765, 2477

Slingerland Drum Company, (H) 1569

Small Parts, Inc., (S) 2840

Smart Corporation, (S) 2171, (SS) 3056

Sociedad Honoraria Hispanica, (H) 1496

Society for Human Resource Management, (SS) 3014, 3385

Society for Imaging Science and Technology, (S) 2637

Society for Mining, Metallurgy, and Exploration, Inc., (S) 2006, 2148, 2228, 2478–2479

Society for Technical Communication, (H) 1663, (S) 2306, 2688

Society for Technical Communication. Central Ohio Chapter, (H) 1692

Society for Technical Communication. Lone Star Chapter, (H) 1530

Society for Technical Communication. Rocky Mountain Chapter, (H) 1409

Society for the Advancement of Material and Process Engineering, (S) 2684

Society for the Preservation of English Language and Literature, (H) 1686

Society of Actuaries, (SS) 3387

Society of American Fight Directors, (H) 1477

Society of American Military Engineers. Anchorage Post, (S) 1932

Society of American Military Engineers. Arkansas Post, (H) 1276, (S) 1872

Society of American Military Engineers. New Jersey Post, (H) 1592, (S) 2536

Society of Automotive Analysts, (SS) 3388

Society of Commercial Arboriculture, (S) 2712

Society of Daughters of the United States Army, (U) 1027

Society of Environmental Journalists, (H) 1669

Society of Exploration Geophysicists, (S) 1918, 2058, 2150, 2212–2215, 2243, 2247, 2636, 2697, 2704, 2794

Society of Fire Protection Engineers. New England Chapter, (S) 1812

Society of Gastroenterology Nurses and Associates, Inc., (S) 2700

Society of Hispanic Professional Engineers, (S) 1785, 2713

Society of Louisiana Certified Public Accountants, (SS) 2883, 2959, 3193

Society of Manufacturing Engineers, (S) 1876, 1979, 1984, 2003, 2077, 2099–2102, 2116, 2155, 2173, 2188, 2245, 2414, 2498, 2558, 2613, 2714–2715, 2813, 2827, 2832

Society of Mexican American Engineers and Scientists, (S) 2467

Society of Motion Picture and Television Engineers, (H) 1533

Society of Nuclear Medicine, (S) 2593, 2599

Society of Petroleum Engineers. Powder River Basin Section, (U) 952, (S) 2622

Society of Plastics Engineers, (S) 1845, 1939, 2017, 2157, 2620, 2661, 2665, 2716, 2747, 2760–2762, 2801

Society of Professional Journalists, (H) 1405

Society of Professional Journalists. Colorado Professional Chapter, (H) 1450

Society of Professional Journalists. Kansas Professional Chapter, (H) 1446, 1557, 1597

Society of Professional Journalists. Maryland Professional Chapter, (H) 1553

Society of Professional Journalists. Western Washington Chapter, (H) 1603, 1737

Society of the First Infantry Division, (U) 458, 669

Society of Women Engineers, (S) 1782–1783, 1798, 1854, 1923, 1929, 1937–1938, 1980, 1994, 2036, 2045, 2050, 2052, 2072–2074, 2095, 2121, 2153, 2168, 2202–2203, 2209, 2211, 2310, 2368, 2401, 2404–2405, 2415, 2455, 2465, 2472, 2559, 2574, 2670, 2742–2745

Society of Women Engineers. Baltimore–Washington Section, (S) 1916

Society of Women Engineers. DelMar Section, (S) 2717

Society of Women Engineers. Houston Section, (S) 2275

Society of Women Engineers. Pacific Northwest Section, (S) 2416

Society of Women Engineers. Rocky Mountain Section, (S) 2671

Sodexho USA, (U) 1028

Soil and Water Conservation Society. All Ohio Chapter, (S) 1825

Soil and Water Conservation Society. Empire State Chapter, (S) 2130

Soil and Water Conservation Society. Missouri Show–Me Chapter, (S) 1931, (SS) 2926

Soil and Water Conservation Society. South Carolina Chapter, (S) 2721

Soil and Water Conservation Society. Texas Council of Chapters, (S) 2753

SOLE–The International Society of Logistics, (S) 2718

Solvay Pharmaceuticals, Inc., (U) 256

Sonlight Curriculum, Ltd., (U) 1030

Sons of Norway Foundation, (H) 1509, (S) 2501

Sons of Union Veterans of the Civil War, (U) 1033

Sopris Foundation, (H) 1749

Soroptimist International of the Americas, (U) 1219

South Carolina Alliance of Black School Educators, (SS) 3389

South Carolina Association of Certified Public Accountants, (SS) 3390

South Carolina Baptist Convention, (H) 1682

South Carolina Center for Educator Recruitment, Retention, and Advancement, (SS) 3389

South Carolina Commission on Higher Education, (U) 578, 911, 1035–1036, 1038–1039

South Carolina Farm Bureau, (S) 2720

South Carolina Governor's Committee on Employment of People with Disabilities, (H) 1683

South Carolina Higher Education Tuition Grants Commission, (U) 1042

South Carolina Junior Golf Foundation, (U) 1037

South Carolina Office of Veterans Affairs, (U) 1043

South Carolina Sea Grant Consortium, (S) 2373

South Carolina Sheriffs' Association, (U) 1040

South Carolina Society of Professional Engineers, (S) 2692

South Carolina Space Grant Consortium, (S) 2373

South Carolina State Department of Education, (H) 1275

South Carolina State Fair, (U) 1041

South Carolina Vocational Rehabilitation Department, (H) 1683

South Dakota Association of Plumbing, Heating, & Cooling Contractors, (S) 2694, (SS) 3380

South Dakota Association of Towns and Townships, (U) 1008

South Dakota Bankers Association, (SS) 3111

South Dakota Board of Regents, (U) 376, 631, 1044–1048, (SS) 2899, 3095

South Dakota CPA Society, (SS) 3391

South Dakota Retailers Association, (SS) 3392

Southern Association of Steel Fabricators, (S) 2723

Southern Baptist Convention. North American Mission Board, (H) 1314

Southern Nursery Association, (S) 2706

Southern Ohio Music Company, (H) 1588

Southern Regional Education Board, (U) 1058

Space Foundation, (S) 1883

SPIE–The International Society for Optical Engineering, (S) 2471, 2726

Spina Bifida Association of America, (U) 370, 572, 889

Spinsters Ink, (H) 1757

Sports Turf Managers Association, (S) 2680

SportsToSchool, (U) 1057

Sprint, (S) 2266, (SS) 3115

St. Anthony Publishing/Medicode, Ingenix Companies, (S) 2171, (SS) 3056

STAATS Custom Awards, (U) 724

Stafford King Wiese Architects, (H) 1421

State Student Assistance Commission of Indiana, (U) 373, 481, 483

State University System of Florida, (U) 1114

Steinway & Sons, (H) 1569

Stephen Phillips Memorial Scholarship Fund, (U) 1063

Steve Madden Footwear, (U) 711

Stokely–Van Camp, (U) 385

Structural Engineers Association of Illinois, (S) 2457, 2735

Student Insights, (U) 1070

Student Loan Finance Corporation, (U) 1121

Student Press Law Center, (H) 1342

Stu's Music Shop, (H) 1588

Stuttgart Chamber of Commerce, (U) 200

Sunkist Growers, (U) 109

Sunshine Lady Foundation, Inc., (U) 1218, (SS) 2985

SunTrust Bank, (U) 356

SuperSibs!, (U) 620, 1073

Surfrider Foundation, (S) 2764, (SS) 3414

Susan G. Komen Breast Cancer Foundation, (U) 1077

Susan Thompson Buffett Foundation, (U) 1078

Swedish Women's Education Association International. South Florida Chapter, (U) 1049

Swiss Benevolent Society of Chicago, (U) 1081

Swiss Benevolent Society of New York, (U) 924, 1029

SYSCO, (SS) 3401

SYSCO Corporation, (U) 871

Tadashi Fashions, (U) 711

Tailhook Educational Foundation, (U) 1082

Talbots, (U) 1084

Talecris Biotherapeutics, (U) 477

Target Stores, (U) 1085

Taylor J. Ertel Foster Children Foundation, (U) 1086

TCF Bank, (U) 1222

Technical Association of the Pulp and Paper Industry, (H) 1330, (S) 1988, 2007, 2030, 2134, 2139, 2324, 2554, 2586, 2595, 2635, 2838

Technology Student Association, (U) 305

Tennessee Funeral Directors Association, (SS) 3403

Tennessee Student Assistance Corporation, (U) 797, 1089–1094, 1196

TET '68, Inc., (SS) 3406

Texaco, (U) 1116

Texas Asphalt Pavement Association, (S) 2750

Texas Association of Broadcasters, (H) 1698

Texas Business and Technology Educators Association, (S) 2751, (SS) 3407

Texas CattleWomen, Inc., (S) 2752, (SS) 3408

Texas Choral Directors Association, (H) 1699

Texas Christian University. Neeley School of Business, (SS) 3411

Texas Classical Association, (H) 1708

Texas Department of Transportation, (S) 2775, (SS) 3420

Texas Family Business Association, (SS) 3412

Texas Federation of Business and Professional Women's Foundation, Inc., (H) 1455, (SS) 3112

Texas Higher Education Coordinating Board, (U) 430–431, 690, 1095–1096, 1098–1106, 1108–1112, 1176–1177, (S) 2754–2755, 2758, (SS) 3409

Texas Instruments, Inc., (S) 2429

Texas Mutual Insurance Company, (U) 1107

Texas Nursery and Landscape Association, (S) 2770

Texas. Office of Rural Community Affairs, (S) 2755

Texas Society of Certified Public Accountants, (SS) 2871

Texas Surveyors Foundation, Inc., (S) 2756

Texas Telephone Association Foundation, (S) 2778, (SS) 3424

Theodore R. and Vivian M. Johnson Foundation, (U) 1114

Third Wave Foundation, (U) 1005, 1115

Thornton Sisters Foundation, (U) 290

Thurgood Marshall Scholarship Fund, (U) 1116

Tiger Woods Foundation, (U) 846

Tim & Tom Gullikson Foundation, (U) 1118

Time Warner, (H) 1704

Tom Joyner Foundation, (U) 1116

Touchstone Energy All "A" Classic, (U) 36

Tourism Cares for Tomorrow, (SS) 2868, 3188, 3268, 3282, 3305, 3325, 3352, 3417, 3428

Town of Williston Historical Society, (H) 1706

Toyota Motor Sales, U.S.A., Inc., (U) 628

Toyota USA Foundation, (U) 1123

Transportation Clubs International, (S) 1822, 2272, 2757, (SS) 2884, 3117, 3410

Travel Industry Association of America, (SS) 3415

Travelers Express, (U) 348

Tree Research and Education Endowment Fund, (S) 2664

Tuskegee Airmen, Inc., (H) 1709, (S) 2232

Two/Ten International Footwear Foundation, (U) 1127

Ulman Cancer Fund for Young Adults, (U) 170, 626, 664, (S) 1919

Unitarian Universalist Association, (H) 1684

United Agribusiness League, (S) 2784, (SS) 3426

United American Nurses, (SS) 3425

United Daughters of the Confederacy, (U) 312, 397, 589, 1128, 1204, (H) 1322, 1449, (S) 2612, 2816, (SS) 3456

United Daughters of the Confederacy. Texas Division, (U) 1097

United Daughters of the Confederacy. Virginia Division, (U) 455, 1165, (S) 2442, 2682

United Methodist Church. Division on Ministries with Young People, (H) 1354, 1648

United Methodist Church. General Board of Higher Education and Ministry, (U) 41, 128, 400, 423, 955, 1129, 1132, (H) 1380, 1560, 1711, (S) 2108, (SS) 3023, 3434

United Methodist Church. Greater New Jersey Conference, (U) 415

United Methodist Communications, (H) 1524

United Methodist Higher Education Foundation, (U) 293, 667, 1130–1131, (H) 1710

United Negro College Fund, (U) 383, (S) 2051, 2609, 2783, (SS) 2994, 3057, 3332

United States Bowling Congress, (U) 34, 75, 212, 302, 399, 1026, 1141–1142, 1195

United States Chess Federation, (U) 1143

United States Institute of Peace, (SS) 3265

United States Naval Sea Cadet Corps, (U) 845

United States Tour Operators Association, (SS) 3428

University Aviation Association, (S) 1858–1860, 2149, 2361, 2590, 2615

University Film and Video Foundation, (H) 1367

University Interscholastic League, (U) 1117, (H) 1454, 1470, 1501, 1730, (S) 1770, 2822, (SS) 3009, 3152, 3350

University of California at Berkeley. Center for Labor Research and Education, (SS) 2944

University of California at Berkeley. Department of Architecture, (H) 1288

University of Hartford. Hartt School, (H) 1756

University of Vermont. Freeman Nurse Scholars Program, (S) 2181

University of Wyoming, (U) 1225–1226

Univision Network, (H) 1543

UPS Foundation, (U) 1133–1134, 1138, (S) 2785–2787

Urban Financial Services Coalition of Delaware, (SS) 3429

Urban League of Nebraska, Inc., (U) 189, 747, 901

U.S. Air Force. Office of Scientific Research, (S) 2367

U.S. Air Force. Reserve Officers' Training Corps, (U) 14–19, (S) 1804–1806

U.S. Army. Human Resources Command, (U) 94

U.S. Army Ordnance Corps Association, (U) 600

U.S. Army. Research Office, (S) 2367

U.S. Army. Reserve Officers' Training Corps, (U) 95–97, 446, (S) 2588

U.S. Bancorp, (U) 1139

U.S. Bureau of Indian Affairs, (U) 144

U.S. Bureau of Land Management, (S) 1951

U.S. Bureau of Reclamation, (S) 2263

U.S. Centers for Disease Control and Prevention. National Institute for Occupational Safety and Health, (S) 2741

U.S. Coast Guard, (U) 228

U.S. Coast Guard Chief Petty Officers Association, (U) 174

U.S. Defense Commissary Agency, (U) 1006

U.S. Department of Agriculture, (S) 2788, (SS) 3430

U.S. Department of Agriculture. Animal and Plant Health Inspection Service, (S) 2625

U.S. Department of Commerce. National Oceanic and Atmospheric Administration, (S) 2144, 2373, 2519, (SS) 3038

U.S. Department of Education, (U) 386

U.S. Department of Education. Office of Postsecondary Education, (U) 337–338, 975

U.S. Department of Education. Office of Special Education and Rehabilitative Services, (U) 1062

U.S. Department of Energy, (S) 2280, 2519

U.S. Department of Energy. National Renewable Energy Laboratory, (S) 2305

U.S. Department of Energy. Office of Civilian Radioactive Waste Management, (S) 2571, (SS) 3308

U.S. Department of Energy. Office of Economic Impact and Diversity, (S) 2545, (SS) 3292

U.S. Department of Energy. Office of Environmental Management, (S) 2141, (SS) 3037

U.S. Department of Health and Human Services, (U) 184, (S) 2695

U.S. Department of Homeland Security, (U) 278

U.S. Department of Transportation. Federal Highway Administration, (H) 1371–1372, (S) 2117–2118, 2775, (SS) 3032–3033, 3420

U.S. Department of Transportation. Federal Transit Administration, (S) 2775, (SS) 3420

U.S. Department of Veterans Affairs, (U) 740–742, 1076, 1157, 1172

U.S. Environmental Protection Agency, (S) 2142

U.S. Fish and Wildlife Service, (H) 1385

U.S. Indian Health Service, (S) 2258–2259

U.S. National Aeronautics and Space Administration, (S) 2373, 2503, 2521

U.S. National Park Service. Historic American Buildings Survey, (H) 1319

U.S. Navy. Naval Education and Training Professional Development and Technology Center, (U) 776

U.S. Navy. Naval Medical Education and Training Command, (S) 2523

U.S. Navy. Naval Personnel Command, (U) 777, (S) 2522, 2567

U.S. Navy. Navy Exchange Service Command, (U) 2

U.S. Navy. Office of Naval Research, (U) 1982, 2367

U.S. Navy. Reserve Officers' Training Corps, (U) 782–784, (S) 2524, 2779

U.S. News and World Report, (U) 111

US Pan Asian American Chamber of Commerce, (U) 101, 141, 298, 500, 992, 1028, 1088, (H) 1289

U.S. Submarine Veterans of World War II, (U) 288

USA Film Festival, (H) 1673

USA Funds, (U) 1140

USA Today, (U) 38–40, 999

USA Weekend, (H) 1713

USAA Insurance Corporation, (U) 772

USS Little Rock Association, (U) 1144

Utah Association of Independent Insurance Agents, (SS) 3432

Utah Education Association, (H) 1641

Utah Elks Association, (U) 1147–1148

Utah Higher Education Assistance Authority, (U) 1145–1146, 1150–1151

Utah Nurses Association, (S) 2790

Utah Society of Professional Engineers, (S) 2791

Utah Sports Hall of Fame Foundation, (U) 967

Varian Medical Systems, (S) 2792

Vasa Order of America, (U) 405, 494, 902, 1152, (S) 2125

Verizon Foundation, (U) 872

Vermont Healthcare Human Resources Association, (S) 2798

Vermont Police Association, (U) 440, (S) 2639, (SS) 3041

Vermont Student Assistance Corporation, (U) 121, 209, 440, 1023, 1155–1156, (H) 1256, 1305, 1522, 1706, 1716, (S) 1821, 2123, 2191, 2380, 2639, 2796–2798, (SS) 3041, 3150

Vermont/New Hampshire Direct Marketing Group

Vertical Flight Foundation, (U) 262, (S) 2799

Very Special Arts, (H) 1486, 1727

Veterans of Foreign Wars. Ladies Auxiliary, (H) 1755

Veterans of Foreign Wars of the United States, (U) 1158, (SS) 3447

Veterans of Foreign Wars of the United States. Pennsylvania Department, (S) 2322

Vietnam Veterans of America, (U) 686

VietNow National Headquarters, (U) 1161

Vincent Bach, (H) 1588

Vincent L. Hawkinson Foundation for Peace & Justice, (U) 1162

Virginia Airport Operators Council, (S) 2359

Virginia Association for Health, Physical Education, Recreation, and Dance, (H) 1398, (S) 2176, (SS) 3058

Virginia Association for Pupil Transportation, (U) 219

Virginia Association of Broadcasters, (H) 1721

Virginia Association of Teachers of English, (SS) 3433

Virginia Association of Teachers of Family and Consumer Sciences, (SS) 3107

Virginia Athletic Trainers Association, (S) 2803

Virginia Baptist Mission Board, (H) 1722

Virginia Coalition of Policy and Deputy Sheriffs, (U) 1153

Virginia Congress of Parents and Teachers, (SS) 3443–3444

Virginia Daughters of the American Revolution, (H) 1723–1724, (S) 2805, 2807

Virginia Department of Social Services, (SS) 3441

Virginia Department of Veterans' Affairs, (U) 1171

Virginia High School League, (U) 335, 1175

Virginia Public Safety Foundation, Inc., (U) 1169

Virginia Sheriffs' Institute, (SS) 3449

Virginia Society for Healthcare Human Resources Administration, (SS) 3445

Virginia Society of Certified Public Accountants Education Foundation, (SS) 3446

Virginia. State Council of Higher Education, (U) 1163–1164, 1166–1168, 1170, (SS) 3442

Virginia Transportation Construction Alliance, (S) 2774

VistaCare Hospice Foundation, (S) 1921

Vitale Caturano & Company CPAs PC, (SS) 3043

Vocational Foundation of Nebraska, (U) 903–904

Volkswagen of America, Inc., (H) 1727

VSA arts, (H) 1726

Wachovia Bank, (U) 1175

Wal–Mart, (SS) 3451

Wal–Mart Foundation, (U) 998

Wal–Mart Stores, Inc., (U) 102

Walgreens, (SS) 3452

Walman Optical Company, (S) 2812, (SS) 3454

Walsworth Publishing Company, (H) 1730

Warner Bros. Publications, Inc., (H) 1568

Washington Dental Service Foundation, (S) 2817

Washington Education Foundation, (U) 1083

Washington Federation of Private Career Schools & Colleges, (S) 1973, (SS) 2950

Washington Financial Aid Association, (U) 324

Washington Higher Education Coordinating Board, (U) 1183–1184

Washington Map Society, (H) 1732, (SS) 3458

Washington Mutual Bank, (U) 759

Washington News Council, (H) 1357, 1452, (SS) 3002, 3110

Washington Society of Certified Public Accountants, (SS) 3460–3461

Washington Society of Professional Engineers, (S) 2818

Washington State Environmental Health Association, (S) 1999

Washington State Mathematics Council, (S) 2654–2655, (SS) 3359–3360

Washington State Nurses Association, (S) 2819

Washington State PTA, (U) 1185

Washington State School Retirees' Association, (SS) 3462

Washington Thoroughbred Breeders Association, (H) 1703, (S) 2766

Wasie Foundation, (U) 1186

Waste Management, Inc., (S) 2820

Watts Charity Association, Inc., (H) 1400, 1525, (S) 2674, (SS) 3165, 3368

Waveline Direct, Inc., (H) 1734

Wells Fargo Bank, (U) 102

Wells Fargo Education Financial Services, (U) 232

West Virginia Broadcasters Association, (H) 1736

West Virginia Division of Veterans' Affairs, (U) 1191

West Virginia Higher Education Policy Commission, (U) 1187–1188, 1190

Western Art Association, (H) 1422

Western Federation of Professional Surveyors, (S) 2824

Western Golf Association, (U) 201

Western Interstate Commission for Higher Education, (U) 1193

Western Michigan Greenhouse Association, (S) 2825

Western Union, (U) 309

Western Union Financial Services, (U) 348

Westfield Corporation, (H) 1302

Westinghouse Electric Company, (S) 2741

Wildlife Society. Florida Chapter, (S) 2159

Willa Cather Pioneer Memorial and Educational Foundation, (H) 1601

William D. Squires Educational Foundation, Inc., (U) 1197

William Morris Agency, (H) 1587

William Randolph Hearst Foundation, (U) 1135, (H) 1443–1445, (SS) 3427

Wilmington Women in Business, (U) 378

Wings Over America Scholarship Foundation, (U) 1203

Wisconsin Agri–Service Association, Inc., (S) 2120

Wisconsin Association for Health, Physical Education, Recreation, and Dance, (H) 1728, (S) 2811, (SS) 3450

Wisconsin Broadcasters Association, (H) 1745

Wisconsin Department of Veterans Affairs, (U) 1206, 1208, 1213

Wisconsin Dietetic Association, (S) 2848

Wisconsin Foundation for Independent Colleges, Inc., (U) 51, 964, 1134, (H) 1671, (S) 2698, (SS) 3382

Wisconsin Garden Club Federation, (S) 2849, (SS)

Wisconsin Higher Educational Aids Board, (U) 1205, 1207, 1210–1212

Wisconsin Institute of Certified Public Accountants, (SS) 3365, 3438

Wisconsin League for Nursing, (S) 1940, 2850

Wisconsin Medical Society, (S) 2851

Wisconsin Ready Mixed Concrete Association, (S) 2852

Wisconsin School Counselor Association, (U) 1222

Wisconsin Society for Clinical Laboratory Science, (S) 2853

Wisconsin Society of Professional Engineers, (S) 1985, 2137

W.K. Kellogg Foundation, (H) 1753

Wolf & Company, PC, (SS) 3175

Woman's Missionary Union, (U) 512

Woman's National Farm and Garden Association, Inc., (S) 2460

Women in Aviation, International, (S) 1809–1810, 1943, 2039, 2053–2054, 2198, (SS) 2932, 2995, 3070

Women in Defense, (S) 2273, (SS) 3118

Women Marines Association, (U) 1214, (H) 1747

Women of the Evangelical Lutheran Church in America, (U) 47, 1215, (S) 2260

Women's Army Corps Veterans' Association, (U) 1216

Women's Basketball Coaches Association, (U) 1217

Women's Jewelry Association, (H) 1748

Women's Overseas Service League, (U) 1220

Women's Transportation Seminar, (S) 2409, 2701, (SS) 3204, 3383

Women's Transportation Seminar. Minnesota Chapter, (S) 2859, (SS)

Women's Transportation Seminar. Puget Sound Chapter, (S) 2235, 2860–2861, (SS) 3091

Wood Products Council, (H) 1312

Worker's Compensation Association of New Mexico, (U) 1120

Workers Compensation Fund, (U) 577

Workforce Safety & Insurance, (U) 329, 416

World Team Tennis, Inc., (U) 863

Worldstudio Foundation, (H) 1751–1753

Wound, Ostomy and Continence Nurses Society, (S) 2854–2855

Wyeth Pharmaceuticals, (U) 1034, (S) 2614

Wyoming Nurses Association, (S) 2433

Wyoming Trucking Association, Inc., (S) 2862

Xerox Corporation, (S) 1787, 2863

Yamaha Corporation of America, (H) 1567, 1588

Young American Bowling Alliance, (U) 936

Youth Free Expression Network, (H) 1401

ZAMI, Inc., (U) 107

ZLB Behring, (U) 477

Zora Neale Hurston/Richard Wright Foundation, (H) 1462

10th Mountain Division Descendants, Inc., (U) 1233

100 Black Men of America, Inc., (U) 1234

100th Infantry Battalion Veterans Club, (U) 744, 888, 1180, (SS) 3214, 3371

11th Armored Cavalry Veterans of Vietnam and Cambodia, (U) 1235

3M Health Information Systems, (S) 2171, (SS) 3056

7–Eleven, Inc., (U) 309

7th Generation Community Service Corporation, (U) 1236

# Calendar Index

Since most financial aid programs have specific deadline dates, some may have already closed by the time you begin to look for funding. You can use the Calendar Index to identify which programs are still open. To do that, look at the subject categories that interest you, think about when you'll be able to complete your application forms, go to the appropriate months, jot down the entry numbers listed there, and use those numbers to find the program descriptions in the directory. Keep in mind that the numbers cited here refer to program entry numbers, not to page numbers in the book. Note: not all sponsoring organizations supplied deadline information to us, so not all programs are listed in this index.

## Unrestricted by Subject Area

*January*: 7, 18, 24, 41, 54, 64–65, 71, 77, 79, 86–87, 123, 168, 179, 218, 251, 263–264, 275, 278, 281, 289, 297, 309, 315, 334, 356, 383, 411, 414, 421, 435, 492, 499, 504, 508, 514, 528, 530–531, 564–565, 579–580, 584–586, 624, 633, 673, 696, 702, 711, 720, 743, 749, 754, 765, 769, 784, 790, 796, 854, 864, 912, 922, 938, 950, 973–974, 978, 981–983, 998, 1004, 1049, 1052, 1066, 1084, 1121, 1125, 1127, 1142, 1147–1148, 1190, 1200–1201, 1236

*February*: 23, 33, 35, 40, 46–47, 52, 54, 57, 63, 76, 78, 98, 101–104, 115–117, 119, 124, 127, 136–137, 141, 147–150, 161, 169, 172, 174, 177, 182, 185, 198, 204–205, 213, 228, 230, 235, 241, 267, 286–287, 293–296, 298–299, 307, 320–321, 326, 331, 355, 360, 363, 365–367, 369–370, 401, 403, 405, 420, 433, 437, 447, 450, 457, 465–467, 479–480, 486, 494, 496, 500, 502–503, 506–507, 511, 513, 517, 541, 545, 563, 568, 572, 590–592, 617–618, 629, 631, 634–635, 639–642, 644–645, 647–649, 668, 671, 688, 704, 727–729, 745, 753, 768, 778, 797, 809, 812–813, 815, 828, 842–843, 873, 875, 889–890, 892, 894, 898, 902, 906–907, 909–910, 915, 936–937, 939–940, 942–943, 946, 948, 959, 972, 979, 984, 989–990, 992, 994, 1006, 1016, 1027–1028, 1031, 1037, 1040, 1050, 1057, 1061, 1071–1072, 1088, 1097, 1119, 1122, 1124, 1139–1140, 1143, 1149, 1152, 1159–1160, 1169, 1178, 1185, 1188–1189, 1192, 1202, 1215, 1220–1221, 1231–1232, 1234

*March*: 1, 3, 5, 12, 21–22, 32, 42, 45, 58–59, 66, 69, 73, 75, 80, 93, 99, 113–114, 129–130, 143, 146, 158, 160, 162–165, 167, 170, 179–180, 188–190, 192–193, 199, 202, 217, 221, 224–225, 233, 255, 259–260, 265, 269–270, 274, 277, 280, 285, 288, 291, 304, 308, 312, 325, 335–336, 344–345, 347, 352–353, 357, 359, 361, 368, 373–374, 379, 390, 397, 399, 409, 415, 419, 423–425, 432, 436, 438, 441, 443–444, 456, 477, 489, 497, 501, 509, 516, 518–519, 522, 524, 527, 535, 542, 546–547, 553, 557, 562, 570, 587, 589, 605–606, 612, 620, 622–623, 626, 637–638, 663–664, 666, 670, 674, 677, 681, 687, 689, 714, 718–719, 747, 757, 759–760, 762, 767, 770, 774, 776, 782–783, 789, 807, 819, 822, 829, 831, 841, 847, 849, 896–897, 900–901, 903–905, 914, 921, 924, 930–931, 945, 949, 951–952, 961–962, 965–967, 975, 993, 999, 1002, 1005, 1008, 1011–1014, 1018, 1021, 1029, 1032–1033, 1041, 1053, 1056, 1065, 1073, 1081–1082, 1115, 1118, 1128, 1161–1162, 1175, 1181, 1186, 1195, 1204, 1209, 1214, 1227

*April*: 8–10, 43, 46, 53, 56, 67–68, 89–90, 92, 100, 106, 109, 118, 120, 128, 131, 135, 139–140, 142, 144, 159, 161, 173, 183, 191, 196–197, 203, 209, 219, 242, 245, 248, 250, 257–258, 268, 273, 279, 284, 292, 300, 302, 314, 316, 322, 328, 339, 364, 375, 380, 384, 387–388, 400, 407–408, 422, 434, 439–440, 445, 454, 471, 487, 493, 520, 526, 539–540, 543, 551–552, 566–567, 569, 573–576, 581, 588, 594–597, 601, 603, 607–611, 616, 628, 630, 640, 659, 662, 676, 685, 692–693, 695, 722, 744, 748, 750–752, 755, 772, 779–780, 785, 800–803, 810–811, 814, 830, 832, 834, 836–840, 844, 846, 848, 855, 863, 868–869, 871–872, 888, 908, 916, 918, 925, 927–929, 932, 935, 941, 954, 963, 985, 996–997, 1003, 1009–1010, 1015, 1017, 1022, 1025, 1034, 1059, 1063, 1069, 1078–1080, 1090–1094, 1113, 1129–1130, 1138, 1153, 1173, 1179–1180, 1196–1197, 1202, 1216, 1223, 1229

*May*: 49, 55, 72, 85, 88, 107–108, 122, 125–126, 138, 145, 179, 194, 210, 216, 223, 229, 232, 254, 262, 276, 283, 290, 303, 305, 348, 378, 386, 395, 406, 429, 455, 458, 484, 525, 583, 599, 636, 646, 691, 698, 756, 761, 771, 781, 786, 799, 813, 815, 845, 865–867, 870, 890, 920, 955, 957, 968, 970, 995, 1060, 1114, 1117, 1141, 1144, 1165, 1194, 1224, 1233, 1235

*June*: 70, 89–90, 144, 156, 175, 207, 211, 256, 266, 282, 318–319, 324, 337, 342, 377, 413, 426, 472, 485, 490–491, 498, 510, 515, 555–556, 560, 571, 594–597, 600, 627, 650, 683–684, 686, 701, 710, 763–764, 787, 861–862, 878, 880, 883, 893, 911, 919, 947, 991, 1023, 1042, 1051, 1080

*July*: 13, 44, 60, 89–90, 121, 179, 220, 311, 317, 393, 396, 434, 529, 678, 709, 721, 792, 835, 887, 927–928, 932, 1089, 1170, 1191

*August*: 54, 147–148, 171, 214, 231, 246, 323, 451, 602, 799, 890, 1048, 1067–1068, 1131, 1199

*September*: 34, 48, 179, 201, 233, 310, 313, 391, 452–453, 478, 512, 523, 582, 706, 713, 717, 806, 809, 812–813, 815, 874, 882, 891, 1005, 1115, 1135

*October*: 132, 140, 144, 222, 227, 261, 327, 410, 434, 452–453, 552, 568, 722, 775, 890, 958, 976, 1085, 1113, 1184

*November*: 17, 39, 54, 89–90, 97, 179, 186, 200, 212, 371, 389, 446, 475, 525, 529, 764, 773, 1020, 1024, 1054–1055, 1077, 1170, 1191, 1222

*December*: 36–38, 74, 96, 110–111, 178, 187, 195, 220, 246, 301, 323, 333, 351, 358, 372, 398, 418, 434, 442, 460–461, 495, 532–534, 561, 621, 665, 724, 758, 799, 833, 911, 917, 953, 956, 977, 986–988, 1007, 1030, 1123, 1133, 1154, 1158, 1174, 1219, 1228, 1230

*Any time*: 14–15, 20, 25, 62, 83–84, 94, 112, 157, 166, 271–272, 332, 349, 427, 476, 619, 667, 715, 723, 741, 777, 933–934, 1019, 1076, 1107, 1157, 1172, 1187, 1206, 1208, 1213, 1218, 1225–1226

## Humanities

*January*: 1240, 1245, 1249, 1254, 1274, 1283, 1296, 1299, 1320, 1325, 1330, 1344, 1349, 1351–1352, 1378–1379, 1391, 1396, 1407, 1412, 1444–1445, 1458, 1473, 1487–1489, 1494, 1500, 1502, 1514, 1543, 1548, 1554, 1572, 1580, 1596, 1598, 1601, 1607, 1620, 1622, 1661–1662, 1666, 1670, 1683, 1688, 1703, 1707, 1723–1724, 1735

*February*: 1241, 1248, 1261, 1263, 1265, 1270, 1275, 1281, 1289, 1291, 1293–1294, 1297–1298, 1312, 1323, 1333–1334, 1339, 1346–1347, 1358, 1360, 1362–1363, 1365, 1370–1372, 1376, 1381, 1384, 1388, 1393, 1395, 1406, 1420, 1424–1425, 1427, 1439, 1443, 1445, 1450, 1453, 1470, 1478, 1480, 1496, 1498, 1505, 1509, 1515, 1535–1537, 1541, 1544–1545, 1551, 1556, 1565–1566, 1575–1577, 1589, 1604–1606, 1613, 1617, 1624, 1626, 1630, 1635, 1640, 1644, 1663–1664, 1668, 1673, 1681, 1684, 1686, 1693, 1702, 1709, 1712–1713, 1717–1718, 1720–1721, 1729, 1734, 1736, 1744, 1758

*March*: 1246–1247, 1252–1253, 1258, 1262, 1273, 1280, 1301–1302, 1305, 1308–1310, 1317, 1322, 1326, 1356, 1359, 1382, 1385, 1389–1390, 1394, 1399, 1405, 1408, 1411, 1417–1419, 1422, 1426, 1430, 1433, 1445–1446, 1449, 1451, 1454, 1456, 1459–1460, 1464, 1466–1467, 1472, 1483–1485, 1501, 1512–1513, 1518, 1524, 1529, 1534, 1549, 1557, 1562, 1564, 1570, 1574, 1582, 1586, 1592, 1597, 1599, 1608–1610, 1612, 1616, 1618–1619, 1625, 1632, 1634, 1636, 1651, 1653–1654, 1657–1658, 1660, 1669, 1672, 1676–1677, 1682, 1689, 1691, 1696, 1705, 1714, 1728, 1730, 1737–1738, 1746–1747, 1750–1753

*April*: 1243, 1257, 1287, 1290, 1295, 1304, 1306–1307, 1311, 1316, 1318, 1327, 1331, 1337, 1343, 1364, 1368–1369, 1373, 1375, 1383, 1392, 1397, 1410, 1413, 1416, 1429, 1434–1435, 1437–1438, 1440, 1444, 1447, 1455, 1465, 1469, 1474, 1479, 1491, 1493, 1504, 1507, 1511, 1521, 1527, 1538–1539, 1547, 1550–1552, 1555, 1559, 1571, 1579, 1583–1584, 1591, 1593, 1595, 1600, 1603, 1623, 1629, 1631, 1633, 1637, 1639, 1647, 1645, 1649, 1652, 1656, 1674, 1678, 1680, 1687, 1690, 1692, 1694, 1710, 1715, 1725, 1733, 1742–1743, 1748, 1756

*May*: 1237, 1256, 1277, 1313, 1319, 1354, 1357, 1361, 1367, 1380, 1400, 1404, 1414, 1423, 1452, 1463, 1481, 1499, 1503, 1522, 1525, 1533, 1540, 1553, 1560, 1563, 1585, 1628, 1641, 1646, 1648, 1698–1699, 1701, 1704, 1706, 1722, 1732, 1741

*June*: 1260, 1271, 1278, 1282, 1284, 1292, 1303, 1342, 1353, 1377, 1386, 1403, 1421, 1516, 1519–1520, 1573, 1614, 1647, 1685, 1708, 1716, 1719, 1749

*July*: 1242, 1436, 1442, 1497, 1528, 1643, 1727

*August*: 1300

*September*: 1238, 1255, 1262, 1269, 1277, 1279, 1286, 1398, 1401, 1431, 1448, 1526, 1567–1569, 1627, 1700, 1731

*October*: 1266, 1324, 1329, 1332, 1336, 1340, 1445, 1482, 1530, 1566, 1602, 1646, 1650, 1717, 1726, 1745

*November*: 1259, 1268, 1335, 1355, 1387, 1428, 1443, 1445, 1475–1476, 1486, 1492, 1497, 1508, 1517, 1531–1532, 1546, 1587, 1615, 1621, 1675, 1740, 1758

*December*: 1239, 1244, 1264, 1272, 1288, 1315, 1321, 1328, 1345, 1348, 1350, 1374, 1402, 1442, 1445, 1461–1462, 1471, 1490, 1506, 1523, 1542, 1558, 1588, 1594, 1611, 1665, 1722, 1739, 1757

## Sciences

*January*: 1771, 1783, 1793, 1795, 1798, 1803, 1811–1812, 1819, 1838, 1845, 1849, 1852, 1857, 1862, 1864–1866, 1875–1876, 1878–1879, 1882, 1901, 1917–1918, 1923, 1939, 1947, 1954, 1979–1980, 1984, 1989, 1994, 2001, 2003, 2007, 2017, 2028, 2036, 2040, 2044–2045, 2047, 2049–2052, 2058–2059, 2067, 2072, 2074, 2077, 2086, 2094–2095, 2099–2102, 2114, 2116, 2121, 2134, 2139, 2147, 2150–2151, 2155, 2157–2158, 2160–2162, 2168, 2173, 2188, 2194, 2203, 2209, 2212–2221, 2230, 2243–2245, 2247, 2253, 2271, 2277, 2287, 2299, 2306, 2313–2314, 2317–2318, 2328, 2331–2332, 2337–2339, 2343, 2347–2348, 2351, 2368–2369, 2372–2373, 2376, 2381, 2386, 2401, 2404, 2414–2415, 2432, 2453, 2455, 2458, 2461, 2465, 2472, 2495–2496, 2498, 2500, 2507, 2511, 2519–2520, 2524, 2529–2530, 2541–2542, 2550, 2554, 2558–2559, 2569, 2571, 2575, 2577, 2583, 2586, 2589, 2592, 2595, 2609, 2613–2614, 2619–2620, 2626, 2632, 2636, 2661, 2665, 2668, 2670–2671, 2673, 2684, 2686, 2697, 2704, 2708, 2714–2716, 2726, 2742, 2745, 2747–2748, 2756, 2760–2762, 2766, 2788, 2792, 2794, 2799, 2801, 2805–2807, 2813, 2815, 2818, 2827, 2829–2830, 2832, 2842, 2864

*February*: 1762, 1767, 1835, 1837, 1844, 1847–1848, 1874, 1877, 1889, 1893, 1912–1914, 1916, 1930, 1933, 1942, 1945–1946, 1968, 1972, 1981, 1983, 1992, 1997–1998, 2015, 2020, 2030, 2042, 2069, 2071, 2079, 2081, 2083, 2090, 2092–2093, 2096, 2098, 2103, 2117–2118, 2125, 2146, 2152, 2172, 2183, 2185, 2193, 2197, 2204–2205, 2231–2234, 2238, 2256, 2258–2260, 2270, 2297–2298, 2300–2301, 2312, 2327, 2349, 2355, 2359–2360, 2366, 2370–2371, 2374, 2379, 2383, 2387, 2389, 2392, 2394–2395, 2407, 2410, 2413, 2424, 2426, 2437, 2440, 2452, 2456, 2464, 2468, 2471, 2473, 2501, 2504, 2506, 2510, 2514, 2533–2534, 2545, 2548, 2555, 2563, 2582, 2594, 2596, 2610, 2616–2617, 2621, 2625, 2631,

2643, 2646, 2648, 2658–2659, 2683, 2685, 2688, 2691, 2695, 2699, 2705, 2728, 2734, 2737, 2751, 2771, 2819–2820, 2824, 2828, 2837, 2840, 2848–2849, 2852, 2857

*March*: 1769, 1775, 1785, 1787, 1791, 1799, 1802, 1815–1816, 1818, 1826–1827, 1829, 1842, 1846, 1853, 1856, 1858, 1860, 1863, 1867, 1880–1881, 1884, 1891, 1895, 1898, 1902, 1906, 1911, 1919, 1927, 1944, 1948, 1953, 1963–1967, 1969–1970, 1976, 1990, 1999–2000, 2008, 2013, 2026–2027, 2038, 2041, 2062–2063, 2066, 2075, 2088, 2106–2107, 2112, 2141, 2174, 2177, 2179, 2181, 2189, 2196, 2201, 2219, 2224, 2236, 2239–2241, 2248–2249, 2251, 2254–2255, 2261, 2275–2276, 2278, 2283, 2285, 2295, 2309, 2319, 2326, 2330, 2336, 2340, 2346, 2353, 2358, 2365, 2375, 2384–2385, 2399, 2430, 2443, 2457, 2463, 2466, 2484, 2497, 2509, 2513, 2516, 2527, 2535–2537, 2540, 2547, 2564–2565, 2585, 2598, 2604, 2606–2607, 2612, 2622, 2624, 2654–2657, 2662–2663, 2675, 2677–2679, 2683, 2687, 2692, 2703, 2721–2722, 2727, 2731–2732, 2735, 2739, 2746, 2764–2765, 2767, 2775, 2777–2779, 2784, 2789–2791, 2803, 2808, 2811, 2816, 2826, 2831, 2834–2835, 2851, 2856, 2862

*April*: 1773–1774, 1779–1781, 1784, 1788, 1800, 1807–1808, 1817, 1822–1823, 1828, 1830–1832, 1841, 1843, 1861, 1868, 1890, 1897, 1899, 1904–1905, 1915, 1921–1922, 1926, 1928, 1934–1935, 1941, 1950, 1952, 1958, 1961–1962, 1968, 1971, 1974–1975, 1996, 2009–2010, 2021, 2025, 2037, 2055–2057, 2065, 2076, 2078, 2082, 2084–2085, 2089, 2091, 2105, 2109, 2115, 2119–2120, 2124, 2126, 2131, 2133, 2135, 2145, 2149, 2154, 2164, 2170, 2175, 2180, 2182, 2187, 2190–2191, 2206, 2216, 2222–2223, 2242, 2250, 2252, 2257, 2262, 2266–2267, 2272, 2279, 2282, 2284, 2288–2289, 2291–2292, 2304–2305, 2307, 2311, 2320, 2322–2323, 2342, 2350, 2352, 2354, 2356, 2361, 2380, 2382, 2388, 2391, 2400, 2406, 2408, 2416, 2420–2421, 2425, 2429, 2431, 2438, 2444, 2448–2449, 2459, 2466, 2469, 2475–2476, 2481, 2489, 2492, 2494, 2503, 2508, 2515, 2518, 2525, 2532, 2538, 2549, 2552–2553, 2560, 2566, 2568, 2570, 2576, 2578, 2587, 2591, 2600, 2603, 2608, 2630, 2639–2641, 2645, 2650–2651, 2653, 2664, 2666, 2676, 2681, 2690, 2696, 2702, 2710–2711, 2720, 2723, 2725, 2733, 2736, 2738, 2753, 2756–2757, 2759, 2768, 2781, 2793, 2798, 2809–2810, 2812, 2814, 2825, 2836, 2838, 2841, 2844, 2846–2847, 2854–2855

*May*: 1759–1760, 1768, 1770, 1782, 1797, 1821, 1825, 1834, 1851, 1854, 1869, 1873, 1887, 1900, 1920, 1929, 1936–1938, 1951, 1957, 1960, 1978, 1980, 1986, 1988, 1993, 2012, 2019, 2033, 2043, 2068, 2073, 2095, 2108, 2110–2111, 2132, 2138, 2144, 2153, 2163, 2171, 2181, 2199–2200, 2202, 2207, 2210, 2225, 2227, 2229, 2274, 2281, 2286, 2290, 2302, 2308, 2324, 2334–2335, 2344, 2396, 2405, 2419, 2434, 2442, 2454, 2460, 2480, 2483, 2487–2488, 2512, 2526, 2543–2544, 2559, 2562, 2574, 2580, 2597, 2601, 2611, 2635, 2642, 2672, 2674, 2682, 2706, 2712, 2718, 2740–2741, 2743–2744, 2750, 2770, 2774, 2796, 2802, 2821–2822

*June*: 1761, 1804, 1806, 1855, 1886, 1908, 1949, 1968, 1991, 2032, 2064, 2123, 2140, 2142, 2156, 2167, 2208, 2211, 2218, 2263, 2273, 2341, 2357, 2364, 2393, 2397, 2417, 2422, 2447, 2485, 2490, 2493, 2505, 2551, 2581, 2584, 2628, 2644, 2667, 2713, 2719, 2729, 2749, 2769, 2772–2773, 2776, 2797, 2823, 2845

*July*: 1790, 1794, 1859, 1910, 1940, 2030–2031, 2034, 2128, 2178, 2220, 2345, 2363, 2427, 2433, 2446, 2450, 2499, 2628, 2669, 2700, 2763, 2776, 2850

*August*: 1777–1778, 1968, 2226, 2390, 2418, 2441, 2590, 2839, 2858

*September*: 1776, 1792, 1824, 1987, 2016, 2176, 2333, 2436, 2466, 2517, 2623, 2627, 2634, 2649, 2660, 2680, 2709, 2756, 2780, 2817, 2833, 2863

*October*: 1763, 1766, 1796, 1896, 1968, 1982, 2004, 2006, 2022–2023, 2046, 2048, 2060, 2070, 2129–2130, 2143, 2165, 2186, 2192, 2228, 2235, 2265, 2273, 2315, 2329, 2378, 2417, 2435, 2467, 2474, 2478, 2482, 2491, 2531, 2556, 2593, 2599, 2618, 2652, 2752, 2795, 2800, 2854, 2860–2861

*November*: 1764, 1772, 1801, 1820, 1833, 1836, 1850, 1885, 1888, 1903, 1909, 1924–1925, 1931–1932, 1995, 2011–2012, 2014, 2018, 2024, 2061, 2080, 2097, 2113, 2148, 2159, 2169, 2184, 2246, 2296, 2303, 2316, 2321, 2398, 2402–2403, 2409, 2428, 2439, 2445, 2462, 2470, 2479, 2486, 2546, 2588, 2602, 2605, 2629, 2701, 2717, 2782, 2785–2787, 2804, 2859

*December*: 1786, 1809–1810, 1839–1840, 1894, 1943, 1956, 1968, 1985, 2005, 2039, 2053–2054, 2104, 2122, 2127, 2136–2137, 2198, 2264, 2269, 2310, 2325, 2412, 2528, 2539, 2561, 2579, 2615, 2637–2638, 2694, 2724, 2783

*Any time*: 2035, 2377

**Social Sciences**

*January*: 2875, 2889, 2904, 2923, 2937, 2965, 2990, 2994, 3001, 3005, 3018, 3039, 3060, 3064, 3082, 3084, 3099, 3144, 3148, 3163, 3182, 3195, 3200, 3206, 3221, 3225, 3229, 3232, 3239, 3265, 3273, 3285–3286, 3299, 3307–3308, 3315, 3324, 3328, 3332, 3334, 3341, 3343, 3375, 3418, 3422, 3430

*February*: 2880, 2888, 2891, 2893–2894, 2898, 2908–2909, 2929, 2948, 2960, 2963, 2966, 2968, 2975, 2979, 2982, 2985, 2988, 2997, 3003, 3008, 3011–3015, 3020, 3027, 3030, 3032–3033, 3035, 3048, 3057, 3061, 3063, 3066, 3073, 3077, 3087–3089, 3092, 3094–3095, 3103, 3108–3109, 3134, 3145, 3179, 3190, 3199, 3215–3216, 3218, 3220, 3236, 3244, 3249, 3255, 3264, 3279, 3284, 3292, 3295, 3302, 3306, 3318, 3320–3323, 3329, 3333, 3335, 3339, 3349, 3365, 3396, 3399, 3407, 3416

*March*: 2868, 2870, 2876, 2886, 2900, 2902–2903, 2910–2911, 2915, 2919, 2921, 2930, 2934, 2936, 2938, 2946–2947, 2953, 2961, 2970, 2972, 2992, 3007, 3022, 3028, 3037, 3042, 3047, 3054, 3069, 3075–3076, 3086, 3093, 3100, 3102, 3111, 3119, 3126, 3129–3130, 3132, 3139, 3146, 3164, 3168, 3170–3171, 3186–3189, 3203, 3222–3223, 3235, 3237–3238, 3247–3248, 3252, 3256, 3262, 3268–3269, 3272, 3275–3278, 3280, 3282, 3288, 3291, 3293, 3300, 3304–3305, 3311, 3313, 3319, 3325, 3336, 3352, 3359–3360, 3362, 3370, 3373, 3377, 3384, 3389, 3392,

3398, 3404–3406, 3413–3414, 3417, 3420, 3423–3424, 3426, 3428–3429

*April*: 2873–2874, 2879, 2882, 2884–2885, 2887, 2890, 2895, 2913, 2916, 2918, 2925, 2931, 2933, 2940, 2943–2945, 2949, 2952, 2958, 2962, 2973, 2976, 2981, 2985, 2987, 2996, 2999, 3016, 3019, 3040–3041, 3046, 3051, 3053, 3067, 3072, 3080, 3083, 3097, 3101, 3106–3107, 3112, 3115, 3117, 3121, 3124, 3128, 3135–3136, 3142–3143, 3150, 3153, 3157, 3160, 3166, 3169, 3173, 3178, 3192, 3198, 3207, 3209, 3213–3214, 3224, 3226, 3228, 3230, 3235, 3243, 3253–3254, 3266–3267, 3269–3270, 3289, 3296–3297, 3314, 3317, 3337, 3355–3357, 3366, 3369, 3371–3372, 3381, 3387, 3391, 3395, 3410, 3423

*May*: 2869, 2912, 2924, 2927–2928, 2941, 2951, 2956, 2986, 2991, 3002, 3006, 3009–3010, 3021, 3023–3025, 3038, 3048–3049, 3056, 3062, 3085, 3098, 3110, 3127, 3133, 3137, 3147, 3152, 3154, 3165, 3183–3184, 3196–3197, 3217, 3231, 3234, 3242, 3251, 3271, 3331, 3347, 3350–3351, 3361, 3364, 3368, 3376, 3386, 3388, 3400–3401, 3425

*June*: 2939, 2964, 2967, 2983, 3000, 3017, 3026, 3036, 3068, 3071, 3090, 3118, 3155–3156, 3176, 3181, 3185, 3194, 3202, 3211–3212, 3245–3246, 3259–3260, 3283, 3294, 3348, 3353, 3367, 3390, 3419

*July*: 2878, 2881, 2892, 2905, 2920, 2922, 2985, 3031, 3034, 3059, 3104–3105, 3116, 3159, 3161–3162, 3258, 3298, 3316, 3340, 3393

*August*: 2896, 2980, 3048, 3079, 3096, 3158, 3227, 3310, 3342, 3397

*September*: 2877, 2935, 2978, 2989, 2993, 3044, 3058, 3078, 3149, 3172, 3174, 3189, 3235, 3269, 3309, 3354, 3423, 3427

*October*: 2865, 2867, 2942, 2977, 3016, 3091, 3114, 3118, 3211, 3241, 3250, 3255, 3281, 3287, 3338, 3358, 3385, 3408

*November*: 2866, 2869, 2926, 2971, 2985, 3026, 3029, 3045, 3048, 3050, 3055, 3065, 3138, 3140, 3159, 3167, 3201, 3204, 3267, 3326, 3363, 3383

*December*: 2872, 2901, 2932, 2955, 2995, 2998, 3070, 3079, 3104, 3113, 3125, 3151, 3181, 3219, 3257, 3261, 3274, 3290, 3345, 3380, 3394, 3397, 3402, 3411, 3421

*Any time*: 3210